Proceedings of the Conference on

Differential & Difference Equations and Applications

Proceedings of the Conference on

Differential & Difference Equations and Applications

Edited By
Ravi P. Agarwal
and Kanishka Perera

Hindawi Publishing Corporation
410 Park Avenue, 15th Floor, #287 pmb, New York, NY 10022, USA
Nasr City Free Zone, Cairo 11816, Egypt
Fax: +1-866-HINDAWI (USA toll-free)

ISBN 977-5945-380

CONTENTS

PREFACE

For the five days August 1–5, 2005, about 240 mathematicians from almost 40 countries attended the *Conference on Differential and Difference Equations and Applications* at the *Florida Institute of Technology (FIT), Melbourne, Florida*. The organizing committee was composed of Ravi Agarwal, Tariel Kiguradze, Kanishka Perera, and Gnana Bhaskar Tenali. Tathagata Samanta served cheerfully and efficiently as secretary of the conference. The main objective of the conference was to promote, encourage, cooperate, and bring together various disciplines of differential and difference equations. This volume contains selected 123 original papers which are based on the research lectures given at the conference.

Many people gave generously their time to help make this conference a success. We would particularly like to thank V. Lakshmikantham who made the original proposal for a conference on Differential and Difference Equations and provided guidance right from the first announcement. The opening remarks for the conference were made by our Provost Dwayne McCay and Dean Gordon Nelson. They also provided all necessary facilities, constant encouragement, and advice which made FIT a unique environment for the conference.

We are also grateful to Lokenath Debnath, Robert Finn, Carlos Kenig, Irena Lasiecka, Gary Lieberman, Mikhail Safonov, Martin Schechter, Roger Temam, and Roberto Triggiani for accepting our invitation and giving state-of-the-art lectures.

Ravi Agarwal
Kanishka Perera

A UNIFIED APPROACH TO MONOTONE METHODS FOR NONLINEAR HYPERBOLIC PROBLEMS

J. O. ADEYEYE, D. H. DEZERN, AND S. G. PANDIT

Hyperbolic partial differential inequalities are developed and applied to derive monotone iterative techniques for nonlinear hyperbolic partial differential equations in a unified setting. Results are illustrated by examples.

1. Introduction

The nonlinear telegraph equation

$$u_{xy} = f(x,y,u), \quad u = u(x,y) \tag{1.1}$$

is the two-dimensional analogue of the ordinary differential equation

$$u' = f(t,u), \quad u = u(t). \tag{1.2}$$

The close relationship between the two, which can be traced in almost the entire theory, however, breaks down while dealing with the monotonicity theorems. It is therefore not surprising that (1.1), in contrast to (1.2), admits extremal (maximal and minimal) solutions only if f is monotonic in the last variable. Indeed, a counter example in [10] shows that the continuity of f alone is not sufficient to assert the existence of extremal solutions of (1.1).

In this paper, we consider the nonlinear hyperbolic initial-boundary value problem (IBVP for short) in a general setting

$$u_{xy} = f(x,y,u,u_x,u_y) + g(x,y,u,u_x,u_y). \tag{1.3}$$

After considering some preliminaries in Section 2, we develop in Section 3 a monotone iterative technique [3–5, 9] which yields monotone sequences converging uniformly to the extremal solutions or to the unique solution of (1.3). The results are illustrated by examples.

Hindawi Publishing Corporation
Proceedings of the Conference on Differential & Difference Equations and Applications, pp. 1–9

2. Preliminaries

For $a,b \in \mathbb{R}$, $a > 0$, $b > 0$, let I, J, and R denote the intervals $[0,a]$, $[0,b]$, and the rectangle $[0,a] \times [0,b]$, respectively. By $z \in C^2[R,\mathbb{R}]$, we mean that z is a continuous function on R, and its partial derivatives z_x, z_y, and z_{xy} exist and are continuous on R. For $z \in C^2[R,\mathbb{R}]$, the triple (z,z_x,z_y) is denoted by $\langle z\rangle$. For a sufficiently smooth function $f = f(x,y,u,v,w) \in C[R\times\mathbb{R}^3,\mathbb{R}]$, f_i, for $3 \le i \le 5$, respectively, denote the first-order partial derivatives of f with respect to u, v, and w. Under this notation, $f_4(x,y,\langle z\rangle)$ means the partial derivative $\partial f(x,y,z,z_x,z_y)/\partial z_x$. The triple (f_3,f_4,f_5) is denoted by $\{f\}$. The expression $f_3z+f_4z_x+f_5z_y$ denotes the usual inner product $\{f\}\cdot\langle z\rangle$. For $v,w \in C^2[R,\mathbb{R}]$, the inequality $\langle v\rangle \le \langle w\rangle$ means that $v(x,y) \le w(x,y)$, $v_x(x,y) \le w_x(x,y)$, and $v_y(x,y) \le w_y(x,y)$ for $(x,y)\in R$. For $v^0,w^0 \in C^2[R,\mathbb{R}]$, such that $\langle v^0\rangle \le \langle w^0\rangle$ on R, the closed set Ω is defined by

$$\Omega = \{(x,y,\langle z\rangle) : \langle v^0\rangle \le \langle z\rangle \le \langle w^0\rangle \text{ on } R\}. \tag{2.1}$$

Under these notations, consider the initial-boundary value problem

$$\begin{gathered} u_{xy} = f(x,y,\langle u\rangle) + g(x,y,\langle u\rangle), \quad (x,y)\in R; \\ u(x,0) = \sigma(x) \quad \text{for } x \in I, \\ u(0,y) = \tau(y) \quad \text{for } y \in J, \\ \sigma(0) = u_0 = \tau(0), \end{gathered} \tag{2.2}$$

where $f,g \in C[R\times\mathbb{R}^3,\mathbb{R}]$, $\sigma \in C^1[I,\mathbb{R}]$, and $\tau \in C^1[J,\mathbb{R}]$.

In the development of the monotone iterative technique, there are four different ways of employing the lower-upper solutions which we define below.

Definition 2.1. Relative to the IBVP (2.2), the functions $v,w \in C^2[\Omega,\mathbb{R}]$, $\langle v\rangle \le \langle w\rangle$ on R, are said to be

(a) *natural* upper-lower solutions if

$$\begin{gathered} v_{xy} \le f(x,y,\langle v\rangle) + g(x,y,\langle v\rangle) \quad \text{for } (x,y)\in R, \\ v_x(x,0) \le \sigma'(x) \quad \text{for } x \in I, \\ v_y(0,y) \le \tau'(y) \quad \text{for } y \in J, \\ v(0,0) \le u_0; \\ w_{xy} \ge f(x,y,\langle w\rangle) + g(x,y,\langle w\rangle) \quad \text{for } (x,y)\in R, \\ w_x(x,0) \ge \sigma'(x) \quad \text{for } x \in I, \\ w_y(0,y) \ge \tau'(y) \quad \text{for } y \in J, \\ w(0,0) \ge u_0, \end{gathered} \tag{2.3}$$

(b) *coupled* lower-upper solutions of Type I if

$$
\begin{aligned}
v_{xy} &\le f(x,y,\langle v\rangle)+g(x,y,\langle w\rangle) \quad \text{for } (x,y)\in R,\\
v_x(x,0) &\le \sigma'(x) \quad \text{for } x\in I,\\
v_y(0,y) &\le \tau'(y) \quad \text{for } y\in J,\\
v(0,0) &\le u_0;\\
w_{xy} &\ge f(x,y,\langle w\rangle)+g(x,y,\langle v\rangle) \quad \text{for } (x,y)\in R,\\
w_x(x,0) &\ge \sigma'(x) \quad \text{for } x\in I,\\
w_y(0,y) &\ge \tau'(y) \quad \text{for } y\in J,\\
w(0,0) &\ge u_0,
\end{aligned}
\tag{2.4}
$$

(c) *coupled* lower-upper solutions of Type II if

$$
\begin{aligned}
v_{xy} &\le f(x,y,\langle w\rangle)+g(x,y,\langle v\rangle) \quad \text{for } (x,y)\in R,\\
v_x(x,0) &\le \sigma'(x) \quad \text{for } x\in I,\\
v_y(0,y) &\le \tau'(y) \quad \text{for } y\in J,\\
v(0,0) &\le u_0;\\
w_{xy} &\ge f(x,y,\langle v\rangle)+g(x,y,\langle w\rangle) \quad \text{for } (x,y)\in R,\\
w_x(x,0) &\ge \sigma'(x) \quad \text{for } x\in I,\\
w_y(0,y) &\ge \tau'(y) \quad \text{for } y\in J,\\
w(0,0) &\ge u_0,
\end{aligned}
\tag{2.5}
$$

(d) *coupled* lower-upper solutions of Type III if

$$
\begin{aligned}
v_{xy} &\le f(x,y,\langle w\rangle)+g(x,y,\langle w\rangle) \quad \text{for } (x,y)\in R,\\
v_x(x,0) &\le \sigma'(x) \quad \text{for } x\in I,\\
v_y(0,y) &\le \tau'(y) \quad \text{for } y\in J,\\
v(0,0) &\le u_0;\\
w_{xy} &\ge f(x,y,\langle v\rangle)+g(x,y,\langle v\rangle) \quad \text{for } (x,y)\in R,\\
w_x(x,0) &\ge \sigma'(x) \quad \text{for } x\in I,\\
w_y(0,y) &\ge \tau'(y) \quad \text{for } y\in J,\\
w(0,0) &\ge u_0.
\end{aligned}
\tag{2.6}
$$

It is apt to note that when f is nondecreasing and g is nonincreasing in the last three variables, inequalities in (a) and (d) in the above definition imply those in (c).

It is well known [8] that there are no general comparison results (max-min principles) for hyperbolic equations, unlike in the case of elliptic or parabolic equations. We need the following comparison result. For an interesting proof of this using the Laplace invariants [1] and Piconne canonical form [2], see [7].

THEOREM 2.2. *Suppose that* $u_{xy}(x,y)+[M]\cdot\langle u\rangle \geq 0$ *in R, and that the Laplace invariant* $M_2M_3 - M_1 \geq 0$*, where* $[M]=(M_1,M_2,M_3)$ *denotes the triple of constants. If*

(i) $u(x,0)\geq 0$*, and* $u_x(x,0)+M_3u(x,0)\geq 0$ *for* $x\in I$*;*

(ii) $u(0,y)\geq 0$*, and* $u_y(0,y)+M_2u(0,y)\geq 0$ *for* $y\in J$*,*

then $u(x,y)$*,* $u_x(x,y)+M_3u(x,y)$*, and* $u_y(x,y)+M_2u(x,y)$ *are all nonnegative everywhere in R. In addition, if* $M_2\leq 0$ *and* $M_3\leq 0$*, then* $\langle u\rangle \geq \langle 0\rangle$ *everywhere in R.*

The following comparison principle, which establishes the nonnegativity of u only under mild conditions, is a consequence of Theorem 2.2.

COROLLARY 2.3. *Suppose that* $u_{xy}(x,y)+[M]\cdot\langle u\rangle \geq 0$ *in R, and that the Laplace invariant* $M_2M_3-M_1\geq 0$*. If*

$$u(x,0)\geq 0 \quad \text{for } x\in I, \qquad u(0,y)\geq 0 \quad \text{for } y\in J, \qquad u(0,0)=0, \tag{2.7}$$

then $u(x,y)\geq 0$ *for all* $(x,y)\in R$*.*

If the Laplace invariant is equal to zero, we obtain the following comparison principle, which is a mild but useful extension of [5, Lemma 4.2], the first such result that appeared in the literature. See also [4, 6] for other related results.

COROLLARY 2.4. *Suppose that* $u_{xy}(x,y)+[M]\cdot\langle u\rangle \geq 0$ *in R, the Laplace invariant* $M_2M_3-M_1=0$*, and* $M_2\leq 0$*,* $M_3\leq 0$*. If*

$$u(0,0)=0, \qquad u_x(x,0)\geq 0 \quad \text{for } x\in I, \qquad u_y(0,y)\geq 0 \quad \text{for } y\in J, \tag{2.8}$$

then $\langle u\rangle\geq\langle 0\rangle$ *everywhere in R.*

We provide three examples to illustrate the sharpness of the above comparison principles. The first shows that the nonnegativity of the Laplace invariants may not be dispensed with in Theorem 2.2 and the two corollaries that follow it; the second shows that the condition $u(0,0)=0$ is essential in Corollary 2.3 even if the Laplace invariant is nonnegative; and the third shows that the "expected" comparison results do not hold for the gradient terms u_x and u_y.

Example 2.5. In the square $[0,1]\times[0,1]$, the function $u(x,y)=\sin(\pi(x+y))$ satisfies the inequality $u_{xy}+[M]\cdot\langle u\rangle\geq 0$ with $[M]=(\pi^2,1,-1)$. Also, $u(x,0)\geq 0$ for $x\in[0,1]$, $u(0,y)\geq 0$ for $y\in[0,1]$, and $u(0,0)=0$. However, u is not nonnegative everywhere in the square. Notice that the Laplace invariant is equal to $-\pi^2-1$.

Example 2.6. In the rectangle $[0,\pi/2]\times[0,\pi/4]$, the function $u(x,y)=\cos(x+y)$ satisfies the inequality $u_{xy}+[M]\cdot\langle u\rangle\geq 0$ with $[M]=(1,-1,-1)$, and the Laplace invariant equal to 0. Also, we have $u(x,0)\geq 0$ for $x\in(0,\pi/2]$, and $u(0,y)\geq 0$ for $y\in(0,\pi/4]$. However, u is not nonnegative everywhere in the rectangle. Note that $u(0,0)=1$.

Example 2.7. In the rectangle $[0,\pi/4] \times [0,\pi/2]$, the function $u(x,y) = 1 - \cos(x+y)$ satisfies the inequality $u_{xy} + [M] \cdot \langle u \rangle \geq 0$ with $[M] = (2,1,3)$, and the Laplace invariant equal to 1. Also, we have $u(x,0) \geq 0$ for $x \in (0,1]$, $u(0,y) \geq 0$ for $y \in (0,1]$ and $u(0,0) = 0$. But u is not nonnegative everywhere in the rectangle. However, since $u_x(x,0) + M_3 u(x,0) \geq 0$ for $x \in [0,\pi/4]$, and $u_y(0,y) + M_2 u(0,y) \geq 0$ for $y \in [0,\pi/2]$, we do have, as required by Theorem 2.2, $u_x(x,y) + M_3 u(x,y) \geq 0$ and $u_y(x,y) + M_2 u(x,y) \geq 0$ everywhere in the rectangle.

3. Main results

We begin by proving the following fundamental result on hyperbolic partial differential inequalities in a general set up, which includes earlier known results [3–5].

THEOREM 3.1. *Let $v,w \in C^2[R,\mathbb{R}]$, and $H(x,y,z,p,q,\bar{z},\bar{p},\bar{q}) \in C[D \times \mathbb{R}^6, \mathbb{R}]$ be nondecreasing in z, p, q and nonincreasing in $\bar{z}$, $\bar{p}$, $\bar{q}$. Suppose that any one of the following conditions holds.*

(H₁) $v_{xy} \leq H(x,y,\langle v \rangle,\langle v \rangle)$, $w_{xy} \geq H(x,y,\langle w \rangle,\langle w \rangle)$; $H(x,y,z_1,p_1,q_1,\bar{z}_1,\bar{p}_1,\bar{q}_1) - H(x,y,z_2,p_2,q_2,\bar{z}_2,\bar{p}_2,\bar{q}_2) \leq L[(z_1 - z_2) + (p_1 - p_2) + (q_1 - q_2) + (\bar{z}_1 - \bar{z}_2) + (\bar{p}_1 - \bar{p}_2) + (\bar{q}_1 - \bar{q}_2)]$, *whenever* $z_1 \geq z_2$, $p_1 \geq p_2$, $q_1 \geq q_2$, $\bar{z}_1 \geq \bar{z}_2$, $\bar{p}_1 \geq \bar{p}_2$, $\bar{q}_1 \geq \bar{q}_2$, *for some* $L > 0$.

(H₂) $v_{xy} \leq H(x,y,\langle v \rangle,\langle w \rangle)$, $w_{xy} \geq H(x,y,\langle w \rangle,\langle v \rangle)$; $H(x,y,z_1,p_1,q_1,\bar{z},\bar{p},\bar{q}) - H(x,y,z_2,p_2,q_2,\bar{z},\bar{p},\bar{q}) \leq L[(z_1 - z_2) + (p_1 - p_2) + (q_1 - q_2)]$, *whenever* $z_1 \geq z_2$, $p_1 \geq p_2$, $q_1 \geq q_2$, *and* $H(x,y,z,p,q,\bar{z}_1,\bar{p}_1,\bar{q}_1) - H(x,y,z,p,q,\bar{z}_2,\bar{p}_2,\bar{q}_2) \geq -L[(\bar{z}_1 - \bar{z}_2) + (\bar{p}_1 - \bar{p}_2) + (\bar{q}_1 - \bar{q}_2)]$, *whenever* $\bar{z}_1 \geq \bar{z}_2$, $\bar{p}_1 \geq \bar{p}_2$, $\bar{q}_1 \geq \bar{q}_2$, *for some* $L > 0$.

(H₃) $v_{xy} \leq H(x,y,\langle w \rangle,\langle v \rangle)$, $w_{xy} \geq H(x,y,\langle v \rangle,\langle w \rangle)$; $H(x,y,z,p,q,\bar{z}_1,\bar{p}_1,\bar{q}_1) - H(x,y,z,p,q,\bar{z}_2,\bar{p}_2,\bar{q}_2) \leq L[(\bar{z}_1 - \bar{z}_2) + (\bar{p}_1 - \bar{p}_2) + (\bar{q}_1 - \bar{q}_2)]$, *whenever* $\bar{z}_1 \geq \bar{z}_2$, $\bar{p}_1 \geq \bar{p}_2$, $\bar{q}_1 \geq \bar{q}_2$, *and* $H(x,y,z_1,p_1,q_1,\bar{z},\bar{p},\bar{q}) - H(x,y,z_2,p_2,q_2,\bar{z},\bar{p},\bar{q}) \geq -L[(z_1 - z_2) + (p_1 - p_2) + (q_1 - q_2)]$, *whenever* $z_1 \geq z_2$, $p_1 \geq p_2$, $q_1 \geq q_2$, *for some* $L > 0$.

(H₄) $v_{xy} \leq H(x,y,\langle w \rangle,\langle w \rangle)$, $w_{xy} \geq H(x,y,\langle v \rangle,\langle v \rangle)$; $H(x,y,z_1,p_1,q_1,\bar{z}_1,\bar{p}_1,\bar{q}_1) - H(x,y,z_2,p_2,q_2,\bar{z}_2,\bar{p}_2,\bar{q}_2) \geq -L[(z_1 - z_2) + (p_1 - p_2) + (q_1 - q_2) + (\bar{z}_1 - \bar{z}_2) + (\bar{p}_1 - \bar{p}_2) + (\bar{q}_1 - \bar{q}_2)]$, *whenever* $z_1 \geq z_2$, $p_1 \geq p_2$, $q_1 \geq q_2$, $\bar{z}_1 \geq \bar{z}_2$, $\bar{p}_1 \geq \bar{p}_2$, $\bar{q}_1 \geq \bar{q}_2$, *for some* $L > 0$.

If $v(0,0) \leq w(0,0)$, $v_x(x,0) \leq w_x(x,0)$, and $v_y(0,y) \leq w_y(0,y)$ for $x \in I$ and $y \in J$, then

$$\langle v \rangle \leq \langle w \rangle \quad \text{everywhere in } R. \tag{3.1}$$

Proof. The conclusion relative to **(H₁)** is known [3, 5]. We will prove the result relative to **(H₂)**. Conclusions relative to **(H₃)** and **(H₄)** can be proved using similar arguments. For $\lambda > 2L + \sqrt{4L^2 + 2L}$, and sufficiently small $\epsilon > 0$, set $\bar{v}(x,y) = v(x,y) - \epsilon e^{\lambda(x+y)}$, and $\bar{w}(x,y) = w(x,y) + \epsilon e^{\lambda(x+y)}$. Then, $\langle \bar{v} \rangle < \langle v \rangle$, $\langle \bar{w} \rangle > \langle w \rangle$, and we have

$$\begin{aligned}
\bar{v}_{xy} &= v_{xy} - \lambda^2 \epsilon e^{\lambda(x+y)} \\
&\leq H(x,y,\langle v \rangle,\langle w \rangle) - \lambda^2 \epsilon e^{\lambda(x+y)} \\
&\leq H(x,y,\langle v \rangle,\langle \bar{w} \rangle) - \epsilon e^{\lambda(x+y)}[\lambda^2 - 2L\lambda - L]
\end{aligned}$$

$$\begin{aligned} &\le H(x,y,\langle\overline{v}\rangle,\langle\overline{w}\rangle) - \epsilon e^{\lambda(x+y)}[\lambda^2 - 4L\lambda - 2L] \\ &< H(x,y,\langle\overline{v}\rangle,\langle\overline{w}\rangle). \end{aligned} \tag{3.2}$$

We assert that $\langle\overline{v}\rangle < \langle\overline{w}\rangle$ everywhere in R. To this end, it suffices to prove that

$$(\overline{v}_x,\overline{v}_y) < (\overline{w}_x,\overline{w}_y) \quad \text{in } R. \tag{3.3}$$

Suppose (3.3) is false. Let t_0 be the greatest lower bound of numbers $t > x + y$ such that (3.3) holds for $x+y<t_0$. Then, there is a point $(x_0,y_0) \in R$, with $x_0 + y_0 = t_0$, and (say) $\overline{v}_x(x_0,y_0) = \overline{w}_x(x_0,y_0)$. Clearly, $y_0 > 0$ since $\overline{v}_x(x_0,0) < \overline{w}_x(x_0,0)$. Also, since $(\overline{v}(x_0,y_0), \overline{v}_y(x_0,y_0)) \le (\overline{w}(x_0,y_0),\overline{w}_y(x_0,y_0))$, using the monotonicity of H, we obtain the following contradiction:

$$\begin{aligned} \overline{v}_x(x_0,y_0) &\le \overline{v}_x(x_0,0) + \int_0^{y_0} H(x_0,s,\langle\overline{v}(x_0,s)\rangle,\langle\overline{w}(x_0,s)\rangle)\,ds \\ &< \overline{w}_x(x_0,0) + \int_0^{y_0} H(x_0,s,\langle w(x_0,s)\rangle,\langle\overline{v}(x_0,s)\rangle)\,ds \\ &\le \overline{w}_x(x_0,y_0). \end{aligned} \tag{3.4}$$

A similar contradiction can be arrived at if we assume $\overline{v}_y(x_0,y_0) = \overline{w}_y(x_0,y_0)$. The inequalities in (3.3) are therefore established. Letting $\epsilon \to 0$, the desired conclusion in (3.1) is obtained, and the proof is complete. □

It is apt to note that the one-sided Lipschitz conditions in Theorem 3.1, which assure uniqueness of solutions, are required in the proof for *nonstrict* inequalities only. In the absence of such a uniqueness condition, conclusion (3.1) may not be true, as can be seen from the following.

Example 3.2. Consider $u_{xy} = f(u) = \sqrt{u}$, $u \ge 0$, $(x,y) \in [0,1]\times[0,1]$; $u(x,0) \equiv u(0,y) \equiv 0$. Then, $v^0(x,y) = x^2y^2/16$, $w^0(x,y) \equiv 0$ satisfy $v^0_{xy} = f(\langle v^0\rangle)$, $w^0_{xy} = f(\langle w^0\rangle)$, $v^0(x,0) = u(x,0) = w^0(x,0)$. However, (3.1) is false.

As noted earlier, it is sufficient to employ coupled lower-upper solutions of Types I and II in the monotone iterative technique when f and g are, respectively, monotonically nondecreasing and nonincreasing in the last three variables. Coupled lower-upper solutions of Type I have been effectively employed in [4] to construct two monotone sequences converging uniformly to the coupled minimal and maximal solutions of (2.2). In our Theorem 3.4 below, we employ coupled lower-upper solutions of Type II with a different outcome. Interestingly enough, their existence is always guaranteed, as the following lemma shows.

Lemma 3.3. *Assume that $f,g \in C[R\times\mathbb{R}^3,\mathbb{R}]$, f is nondecreasing and g is nonincreasing in the last three variables. Then, there exist coupled lower-upper solutions v^0, w^0 of Type II for (2.2) such that $\langle v^0\rangle \le \langle w^0\rangle$ on R.*

Proof. Let $v^0(x,y) = -M(x+y)+z(x,y)$, $w^0(x,y) = M(x+y)+z(x,y)$, where M is a constant and $z(x,y)$ is the (unique) solution of $z_{xy} = f(x,y,\langle 0\rangle)+g(x,y,\langle 0\rangle)$, with the same initial-boundary conditions as in (2.2). Select $M>0$ sufficiently large so that $\langle v^0\rangle \le \langle 0\rangle \le \langle w^0\rangle$ on R. Then, by the monotonicity of f and g in the last three variables, it is easy to see that v^0, w^0 form a pair of coupled lower-upper solutions of Type II for (2.2) on R. □

THEOREM 3.4. *Under the conditions of Lemma 3.3, the iterates* $\{v^n(x,y)\}$, $\{w^n(x,y)\}$ *satisfy*

$$\langle v^0\rangle \le \langle v^2\rangle \le \cdots \le \langle v^{2n}\rangle \le \langle u\rangle \le \langle v^{2n-1}\rangle \le \cdots \le \langle v^3\rangle \le \langle v^1\rangle \quad \text{in } \Omega, \tag{3.5}$$

$$\langle w^1\rangle \le \langle w^3\rangle \le \cdots \le \langle w^{2n-1}\rangle \le \langle u\rangle \le \langle w^{2n}\rangle \le \cdots \le \langle w^2\rangle \le \langle w^0\rangle \quad \text{in } \Omega, \tag{3.6}$$

provided $v^0 \le v^2$, $w^2 \le w^0$ *in* Ω, *where* u *is any solution of (2.2) with* $v^0 \le u \le w^0$ *in* Ω. *The iteration schemes are given by*

$$\begin{gathered}
v^n_{xy} = f(x,y,\langle w^{n-1}\rangle)+g(x,y,\langle v^{n-1}\rangle), \quad (x,y)\in R;\\
v^n_x(x,0) = \sigma'(x), \quad x\in I; \qquad v^n_y(0,y) = \tau'(y), \quad y\in J; \qquad v^n(0,0) = u_0,\\
w^n_{xy} = f(x,y,\langle v^{n-1}\rangle)+g(x,y,\langle w^{n-1}\rangle), \quad (x,y)\in R;\\
w^n_x(x,0) = \sigma'(x), \quad x\in I; \qquad w^n_y(0,y) = \tau'(y), \quad y\in J; \qquad w^n(0,0) = u_0.
\end{gathered} \tag{3.7}$$

Moreover, the monotone sequences $\{v^{2n}\}$, $\{v^{2n-1}\}$, $\{w^{2n}\}$, $\{w^{2n-1}\} \in C^2[\Omega,\mathbb{R}]$ *converge uniformly to* ρ, r, ρ^*, r^* *in* $C^2[\Omega,\mathbb{R}]$, *respectively, and satisfy*

$$\begin{aligned}
r_{xy} &= f(x,y,\langle \rho^*\rangle)+g(x,y,\langle \rho\rangle),\\
\rho_{xy} &= f(x,y,\langle r^*\rangle)+g(x,y,\langle r\rangle),\\
r^*_{xy} &= f(x,y,\langle \rho\rangle)+g(x,y,\langle \rho^*\rangle),\\
\rho^*_{xy} &= f(x,y,\langle r\rangle)+g(x,y,\langle r^*\rangle)
\end{aligned} \tag{3.8}$$

in Ω. *Also,* $\langle \rho\rangle \le \langle u\rangle \le \langle r\rangle$, *and* $\langle r^*\rangle \le \langle u\rangle \le \langle \rho^*\rangle$ *in* Ω.

Proof. We shall only indicate the proof of inequalities (3.5). The proof of (3.6) is similar. Setting $p = v^1 - v^0$, we see that $p_{xy} = v^1_{xy} - v^0_{xy} \ge f(x,y,\langle w^0\rangle)+g(x,y,\langle v^0\rangle) - f(x,y,\langle w^0\rangle) - g(x,y,\langle v^0\rangle) = 0$, $p_x(x,0)\ge 0$, $p_y(0,y)\ge 0$, and $p(0,0)\ge 0$. Therefore, Theorem 2.2 yields $\langle v^0\rangle \le \langle v^1\rangle$ on R. Using similar arguments, we can successively show that $\langle u\rangle \le \langle v^1\rangle$, $\langle v^2\rangle \le \langle u\rangle$, $\langle v^3\rangle \le \langle v^1\rangle$, and $\langle u\rangle \le \langle v^3\rangle$ on R. Consequently, we have $\langle v^0\rangle \le \langle v^2\rangle \le \langle u\rangle \le \langle v^3\rangle \le \langle v^1\rangle$ on R. Inequalities in (3.5) now follow by induction. The remaining conclusions in the theorem can be proved by using standard arguments [3], completing the proof. □

The following corollary is a consequence of Theorem 3.1.

Corollary 3.5. *In addition to conditions of Theorem 3.4, if f and g also satisfy the one-sided Lipschitz conditions in* ($\mathbf{H}_3$) *of Theorem 3.1, then* $\langle\rho\rangle \equiv \langle r\rangle \equiv \langle\rho^*\rangle \equiv \langle r^*\rangle \equiv \langle u\rangle$.

Proof. Since $\langle\rho\rangle \le \langle r\rangle$, and $\langle r^*\rangle \le \langle\rho^*\rangle$ in Ω by Theorem 3.4, it is enough to prove that

$$\langle\rho\rangle \ge \langle r\rangle, \qquad \langle r^*\rangle \ge \langle\rho^*\rangle \text{ in } \Omega. \tag{3.9}$$

To this end, set $v = r - \rho$, $w = \rho^* - r^*$, so that we have $v \ge 0$ and $w \ge 0$ on Ω. Then, utilizing Theorem 3.1 ($\mathbf{H}_3$) and the monotone character of f and g, it follows that $v_{xy} \le [L]\cdot(\langle v\rangle + \langle w\rangle)$, $w_{xy} \le [L]\cdot(\langle v\rangle + \langle w\rangle)$, and $p_{xy} \le 2[L]\cdot\langle p\rangle$, where $[L] = (L,L,L)$ and $p = v + w$. Also, $p_x(x,0) = 0$, $x \in I$, $p_y(0,y) = 0$, $x \in J$, and $p(0,0) = 0$. By Theorem 3.1, we have $\langle p\rangle \le \langle 0\rangle$, which implies $\langle v\rangle \le \langle 0\rangle$ and $\langle w\rangle \le \langle 0\rangle$. This completes the proof. □

Example 3.6. For $(x,y) \in R = [0,1]\times[0,1]$, consider

$$\begin{gathered} u_{xy} = g(x,y,\langle u\rangle), \\ u(x,0) \equiv 0, \qquad u(0,y) \equiv 0, \end{gathered} \tag{3.10}$$

where

$$g(x,y,\langle u\rangle) = \begin{cases} \exp(-2u) & \text{if } u \ge 0, \\ 1 & \text{if } u < 0. \end{cases} \tag{3.11}$$

It is easy to see that the functions $v^0 \equiv 0$ and $w^0(x,y) = xy$ form a pair of coupled lower-upper solutions of Type II for (3.10). For $n = 1,2,3,\ldots$, define the iterates v_n to be the (unique) solutions of

$$v^n_{xy} = g(x,y,\langle v^{n-1}\rangle), \quad v^n(x,0) \equiv 0,\ v^n(0,y) \equiv 0. \tag{3.12}$$

It is not hard to see that $\langle v^0\rangle \le \langle v^2\rangle$ on R. Also, g is monotonically nonincreasing in the last three variables and satisfies the Lipschitz condition of ($\mathbf{H}_3$) in Theorem 3.1. Therefore, by Theorem 3.4 and Corollary 3.5, the sequences $\{v^{2n}\}$ and $\{v^{2n-1}\}$ both converge to the unique solution u of (3.10). We note in passing that the solution u of (3.10) is $u(x,y) = \ln(xy+1)$.

References

[1] S. Agmon, L. Nirenberg, and M. H. Protter, *A maximum principle for a class of hyperbolic equations and applications to equations of mixed elliptic-hyperbolic type*, Communications on Pure and Applied Mathematics **6** (1953), 455–470.

[2] T. Kiguradze, *Some boundary value problems for systems of linear partial differential equations of hyperbolic type*, Memoirs on Differential Equations and Mathematical Physics **1** (1994), 144.

[3] G. S. Ladde, V. Lakshmikantham, and A. S. Vatsala, *Monotone Iterative Techniques for Nonlinear Differential Equations*, Monographs, Advanced Texts and Surveys in Pure and Applied Mathematics, vol. 27, Pitman, Massachusetts, 1985.

[4] V. Lakshmikantham and S. Köksal, *Monotone Flows and Rapid Convergence for Nonlinear Partial Differential Equations*, Series in Mathematical Analysis and Applications, vol. 7, Taylor & Francis, London, 2003.

[5] V. Lakshmikantham and S. G. Pandit, *The method of upper, lower solutions and hyperbolic partial differential equations*, Journal of Mathematical Analysis and Applications **105** (1985), no. 2, 466–477.

[6] S. G. Pandit, *Variation of parameters formulas and maximum principles for linear hyperbolic problems in two independent variables*, Dynamics of Continuous, Discrete and Impulsive Systems **4** (1998), no. 2, 295–312.

[7] ———, *Hyperbolic partial differential equations and Volterra integral equations with nonincreasing nonlinearities*, Bulletin of the Marathwada Mathematical Society **6** (2005), no. 1, 24–38.

[8] M. H. Protter and H. F. Weinberger, *Maximum Principles in Differential Equations*, Springer, New York, 1984.

[9] D. H. Sattinger, *Monotone methods in nonlinear elliptic and parabolic boundary value problems*, Indiana University Mathematics Journal **21** (1972), 979–1000.

[10] W. Walter, *On the non-existence of maximal solutions for hyperbolic differential equations*, Annales Polonici Mathematici **19** (1967), 307–311.

J. O. Adeyeye: Department of Mathematics, Winston-Salem State University, Winston-Salem, NC 27110, USA
E-mail address: adeyeyej@wssu.edu

D. H. Dezern: Department of Mathematics, Winston-Salem State University, Winston-Salem, NC 27110, USA
E-mail address: dezernd@wssu.edu

S. G. Pandit: Department of Mathematics, Winston-Salem State University, Winston-Salem, NC 27110, USA
E-mail address: pandits@wssu.edu

ON THE INTEGRAL MANIFOLDS OF THE DIFFERENTIAL EQUATION WITH PIECEWISE CONSTANT ARGUMENT OF GENERALIZED TYPE

MARAT AKHMET

We introduce a general type of differential equations with piecewise constant argument (EPCAG). The existence of global integral manifolds of the quasilinear EPCAG established when the associated linear homogeneous system has an exponential dichotomy. A new technique of investigation of equations with piecewise argument, based on an integral representation formula, is proposed. An appropriate illustrating example is given.

1. Introduction

Let $\mathbb{Z}$, $\mathbb{N}$, and $\mathbb{R}$ be the sets of all integers, natural, and real numbers, respectively. Denote by $\|\cdot\|$ the Euclidean norm in $\mathbb{R}^n$, $n \in \mathbb{N}$.

In this paper, we are concerned with the quasilinear system

$$y' = A(t)y + f(t, y(t), y(\beta(t))), \tag{1.1}$$

where $y \in \mathbb{R}^n$, $t \in \mathbb{R}$, $\beta(t) = \theta_i$ if $\theta_i \le t < \theta_{i+1}$, $i = Z$, is an identification function, θ_i, $i \in \mathbb{Z}$, is a strictly ordered sequence of real numbers, $|\theta_i| \to \infty$ as $|i| \to \infty$, and there exists a number $\theta > 0$ such that $\theta_{i+1} - \theta_i \le \theta$, $i \in \mathbb{Z}$. The theory of differential equations with piecewise constant argument (EPCA) of the type

$$\frac{dx(t)}{dt} = f(t, x(t), x([t])), \tag{1.2}$$

where $[\cdot]$ signifies the greatest integer function, was initiated in [3] and developed by many authors [1, 2, 6, 7, 9–12]. The novel idea of this paper is that system (1.1) is a general case (EPCAG) of equation (1.2). Indeed, if we take $\theta_i = i$, $i \in \mathbb{Z}$, then (1.1) takes the form of (1.2).

The existing method of investigation of EPCA, as proposed by its founders, is based on the reduction of EPCA to discrete equations. We propose another approach to the problem. In fact, this approach consists of the construction of the equivalent integral

Hindawi Publishing Corporation
Proceedings of the Conference on Differential & Difference Equations and Applications, pp. 11–20

equation. Consequently, for every result of our paper, we prove a corresponding equivalence lemma. Thus, while investigating EPCAG, we need not impose any conditions on the reduced discrete equations, and hence, we require more easily verifiable conditions, similar to those for ordinary differential equations.

In what follows, we use the uniform norm $\|T\| = \sup\{\|Tx\| \|x\| = 1\}$ for matrices. The following assumptions will be needed throughout the paper.

(C1) $A(t)$ is a continuous $n \times n$ matrix and $\sup_R \|A(t)\| = \mu < \infty$.

(C2) $f(t,x,z)$ is continuous in the first argument, $f(t,0,0) = 0$, $t \in \mathbb{R}$, and f is Lipschitzian such that $\|f(t,y_1,w_1) - f(t,y_2,w_2)\| \leq l(\|y_1 - y_2\| + \|w_1 - w_2\|)$.

(C3) There exist a projection P and positive constants K and σ such that

$$\begin{aligned} \|X(t)PX^{-1}(s)\| &\leq K\exp(-\sigma(t-s)), \quad t \geq s, \\ \|X(t)(I-P)X^{-1}(s)\| &\leq K\exp(\sigma(s-t)), \quad t \leq s, \end{aligned} \tag{1.3}$$

where $X(t)$ is a fundamental matrix of the associated linear homogeneous system.

2. The solutions of the EPCAG

The problem of the definition of solutions for functional differential equations in general, and for differential equations with deviating argument in particular, is one of the most difficult and important problems. EPCAG is not an exception in that sense. An especially complex task is to formulate initial value problem (IVP) for these equations. In [3, 10], the problem was reduced to the case when the initial moment is an integer, and global solutions have been considered. The approach is reasonable since it is a consequence of the method of reduction to the discrete equations.

We combine the approach of EPCA [3, 7, 10, 11] with a more careful analysis of the initial data. The analysis of the general problem of IVP for EPCAG is the subject of discussion for another paper.

In our paper, it is assumed that all solutions are continuous functions.

Solutions which start at points θ_i, $i \in \mathbb{Z}$, and exist to the right.

Definition 2.1. A solution $y(t) = y(t,\theta_i,y_0)$, $y(\theta_i) = y_0$, $i \in \mathbb{Z}$, of (1.1) on $[\theta_i,\infty)$ is a continuous function such that

(i) the derivative $y'(t)$ exists at each point $t \in [\theta_i,\infty)$, with the possible exception of the points θ_j, $j \geq i$, where one-sided derivatives exist;

(ii) equation (1.1) is satisfied by $y(t)$ at each interval $[\theta_j,\theta_{j+1})$, $j \geq i$.

Definition 2.1 is a version of [10, Definition 1.1] adapted to our general case.

THEOREM 2.2. *Suppose conditions* (C1)–(C3) *are fulfilled. Then for every $y_0 \in \mathbb{R}^n$ and $i \in \mathbb{Z}$, there exists a unique solution $y(t)$ of (1.1) in the sense of Definition 2.1.*

Proof. If $\theta_i \leq t \leq \theta_{i+1}$, then $y(t)$ coincides with a solution of the following IVP:

$$\begin{aligned} \frac{d\xi}{dt} &= A(t)\xi + f(t,\xi,y_0), \\ \xi(\theta_i) &= y_0. \end{aligned} \tag{2.1}$$

Equation (2.1) is an ordinary differential equation, where function $f(t,\xi,y_0)$ is Lipschitzian in ξ, and consequently $y(t)$ exists and is unique on $[\theta_i,\theta_{i+1}]$.

Assume, now, that $y(t)$ is defined uniquely on an interval $[\theta_i,\theta_k]$, $k \geq i+1$. Then for $[\theta_k,\theta_{k+1}]$, it is a solution of the IVP

$$\frac{d\xi}{dt} = A(t)\xi + f(t,\xi,y(\theta_k)), \qquad \xi(\theta_k) = y(\theta_k). \tag{2.2}$$

It is obvious that $y(t)$ exists and is unique on the interval.

By induction, we can conclude that for every $y_0 \in \mathbb{R}^n$ and $i \in \mathbb{Z}$, there exists a unique solution $y(t)$ of (1.1) on $[\theta_i,\infty)$, satisfying $y(\theta_i) = y_0$. The theorem is proved. □

The existence and the uniqueness of solutions on $\mathbb{R}$.

It can be easily shown that there exist constants m, M, $0 < m < M$, such that $\|X(t,s)\| \leq M$, $\|X(t,s)\| \geq m$, if $|t-s| \leq \theta$.

From now on, we make the following assumptions:

(C4) $2Ml\theta < 1$;

(C5) $Ml\theta[1+M(1+l\theta)\exp(Ml\theta)] < m$.

THEOREM 2.3. *Assume that conditions* (C1)–(C5) *are fulfilled. Then for every* $y_0 \in \mathbb{R}^n$, $t_0 \in \mathbb{R}$, $\theta_i < t_0 \leq \theta_{i+1}$, $i \in \mathbb{Z}$, *there exists a unique solution* $\bar{y}(t) = y(t,\theta_i,\bar{y}_0)$ *of (1.1) in sense of Definition 2.1 such that* $\bar{y}(t_0) = y_0$.

Proof

Existence. Consider a solution $\xi(t) = y(t,t_0,y_0)$ of the equation

$$\frac{dy}{dt} = A(t)y + f(t,y,\eta) \tag{2.3}$$

on $[\theta_i,t_0]$.

We have that

$$\xi(t) = X(t,t_0)y_0 + \int_{t_0}^{t} X(t,s)f(s,\xi(s),\eta)\,ds, \tag{2.4}$$

and should prove that there exists a vector $\eta \in \mathbb{R}^n$ such that the solution $\xi(t)$ of (2.4) satisfies $\xi(\theta_i) = \eta$.

Take $\xi_0(t) = X(t,t_0)y_0$ and construct

$$\xi_{m+1}(t) = X(t,t_0)y_0 + \int_{t_0}^{t} X(t,s)f(s,\xi_m(s),\xi_m(\theta_i))\,ds, \quad m \geq 0. \tag{2.5}$$

One can easily check that

$$\max_{[\theta_i,t_0]} \|\xi_{m+1}(t) - \xi_m(t)\|_0 \leq [2Ml\theta]^m M\|y_0\|. \tag{2.6}$$

It is obvious that the limit of the sequence $\xi_m(t)$ is request $\xi(t)$ with $\eta = \xi(\theta_i)$. The existence is proved.

Uniqueness. It is sufficient to check that for each $t \in (\theta_i, \theta_{i+1}]$, and $y_2, y_1 \in \mathbb{R}^n$, $y_2 \neq y_1$, the condition $y(t,\theta_i,y_1) \neq y(t,\theta_i,y_2)$ is valid.

Denote by $y_1(t) = y(t,\theta_i,y_1)$, $y_2(t) = y(t,\theta_i,y_2)$, $y_1 \neq y_2$, solutions of (1.1). Assume, on the contrary, that there exists $t^* \in (\theta_i, \theta_{i+1}]$ such that $y_1(t^*) = y_2(t^*)$. Then

$$X(t^*,\theta_i)(y_2 - y_1) = \int_{\theta_i}^{t^*} X(t^*,s)[f(s,y_1(s),y_1) - f(s,y_2(s),y_2)]ds. \tag{2.7}$$

We have that

$$||X(t^*,\theta_i)(y_2 - y_1)|| \geq m||y_2 - y_1||. \tag{2.8}$$

Moreover, for $t \in (\theta_i, \theta_{i+1}]$, the following inequality is valid:

$$||y_1(t) - y_2(t)|| \leq M||y_2 - y_1|| + \int_{\theta_i}^{t} Ml[||y_1(s) - y_2(s)|| + ||y_2 - y_1||]ds. \tag{2.9}$$

Hence, using Gronwall-Bellman inequality, we can write that

$$||y_1(t) - y_2(t)|| \leq M(1 + l\theta)\exp(Ml\theta)||y_2 - y_1||. \tag{2.10}$$

Consequently,

$$\begin{aligned} &\left|\left| \int_{\theta_i}^{t^*} X(t^*,s)[f(s,y_1(s),y_1) - f(s,y_2(s),y_2)]ds \right|\right| \\ &\quad \leq lM\theta[1 + M(1 + l\theta)\exp(Ml\theta)]||y_2 - y_1||. \end{aligned} \tag{2.11}$$

Finally, one can see that (C5), (2.8), and (2.11) contradict (2.7). The theorem is proved. □

Example 2.4. Consider the following EPCAG:

$$x'(t) = 3x(t) - x(t)x(\beta(t)), \tag{2.12}$$

where $\beta(t) = \theta_i$ if $\theta_i \leq t < \theta_{i+1}$, $i \in \mathbb{Z}$, $\theta_{2j-1} = j - 1/5$, $\theta_{2j} = j + 1/5$, $j \in \mathbb{Z}$. The distance $\theta_{i+1} - \theta_i$, $i \in \mathbb{Z}$, is equal either to $\theta = 3/5$ or to $\bar{\theta} = 2/5$.

Let us find conditions when a solution $x(t)$ of (2.12) can be continued to the left from $t = \theta_{i+1}$. If $t \in [\theta_i, \theta_{i+1}]$ for a fixed $i \in \mathbb{Z}$, then $x(t)$ satisfies the following equation:

$$x'(t) = 3x(t) - x(t)x(\theta_i). \tag{2.13}$$

Hence,

$$x(t) = x(\theta_i)\,e^{(3 - x(\theta_i))(t - \theta_i)}. \tag{2.14}$$

From the last equality, it is implied that every nontrivial solution of (2.12) is either positive or negative. That is why, without loss of generality, we consider only positive solutions. For a fixed $H > 0$, denote $G_H = \{x : 0 < x < H\}$.

If $x_1, x_2, y_1, y_2 \in G_H$, then $|x_1 y_1 - x_2 y_2| \leq H(|x_1 - x_2| + |y_1 - y_2|)$. Moreover, we have that

$$m = \min_{|t-s| \leq \theta} e^{2(t-s)} = e^{-9/5}, \qquad M = \max_{|t-s| \leq \theta} e^{2(t-s)} = e^{9/5}. \tag{2.15}$$

Hence, condition (C4) for continuation of solutions of (2.12) to the left in G_H has the form

$$H < \frac{5}{6} e^{-9/5}. \tag{2.16}$$

Let us consider another way to define values $x(\theta_i)$ such that the solution $x(t)$ can be continued to the left from $t = \theta_{i+1}$.

Using (2.14), we find that

$$x(\theta_{i+1}) = x(\theta_i) e^{(3-x(\theta_i))(\theta_{i+1}-\theta_i)}. \tag{2.17}$$

Consider (2.17) as an equation with respect to $x = x(\theta_i)$. Introduce the functions $F_1(x) = x e^{(3-x)\bar{\theta}}$ and $F_2(x) = x e^{(3-x)\theta}$. The critical values of x for the functions are $x_{\max}^{(1)} = \bar{\theta}^{-1} = 5/2 < 3$ and $x_{\max}^{(2)} = \theta^{-1} = 5/3 < 3$, respectively, and maximal values of these functions are

$$F_{\max}^{(1)} = F_1(x_{\max}^{(1)}) = \frac{5}{2} e^{1/5}, \qquad F_{\max}^{(2)} = F_2(x_{\max}^{(2)}) = \frac{5}{3} e^{4/5}. \tag{2.18}$$

Denote $F_{\max} = \min(F_{\max}^{(1)}, F_{\max}^{(2)})$.

If $x(\theta_{i+1}) \leq F_{\max}$, then the solution can be continued to $t = \theta_i$.

Comparing (2.16) and (2.18), we see that $H < F_{\max}$. That is, the evaluation of H by (C4) is reliable for equation (2.12).

We will use the following definition, which is a version of a definition from [7], adapted for our general case.

Definition 2.5. A function $y(t)$ is a solution of (1.1) on $\mathbb{R}$ if

(i) $y(t)$ is continuous on $\mathbb{R}$;

(ii) the derivative $y'(t)$ exists at each point $t \in \mathbb{R}$ with the possible exception of the points θ_i, $i \in \mathbb{Z}$, where one-sided derivatives exist;

(iii) equation (1.1) is satisfied on each interval $[\theta_i, \theta_{i+1})$, $i \in \mathbb{Z}$.

Theorem 2.6. *Suppose that conditions* (C1)–(C5) *are fulfilled. Then for every* $(t_0, y_0) \in \mathbb{R} \times \mathbb{R}^n$, *there exists a unique solution* $y(t) = y(t, t_0, y_0)$ *of (1.1) in sense of Definition 2.5 such that* $y(t_0) = y_0$.

Proof. Assume that $\theta_i < t_0 \leq \theta_{i+1}$ for a fixed $i \in \mathbb{Z}$. By Theorem 2.2, there exists a unique solution $y(t, \theta_i, y^i)$ of (1.1) with some vector $y^i \in \mathbb{R}^n$ such that $y(t_0, \theta_i, y^i) = y_0$. Applying the theorem again, we can find a unique solution $y(t, \theta_{i-1}, y^{i-1})$ of (1.1) such that $y(\theta_i, \theta_{i-1}, y^{i-1}) = y^i$, and hence, $y(t_0, \theta_{i-1}, y^{i-1}) = y_0$. We can complete the proof using induction. The theorem is proved. □

The last theorem is of major importance for our paper. It arranges the correspondence between points $(t_0, y_0) \in \mathbb{R} \times \mathbb{R}^n$ and all solutions of (1.1), and there is not a solution of the equation out of the correspondence. Using the assertion, we can say that definition of the IVP for the EPCAG is similar to the problem for an ordinary differential equation, although the EPCAG is an equation with delay argument. In the rest of the paper, we will use the correspondence to prove main theorems.

Using Gram-Schmidt orthogonalization of the columns of $X(t)$ [4], one can obtain that by the transformation $y = U(t)z$, where $U(t)$ is a Lyapunov matrix, (1.1) can be reduced to the following system:

$$\begin{aligned} \frac{du}{dt} &= B_+(t)u + g_+(t, z(t), z(\beta(t))), \\ \frac{dv}{dt} &= B_-(t)v + g_-(t, z(t), z(\beta(t))), \end{aligned} \tag{2.19}$$

where

$$\begin{gathered} z = (u, v), \quad u \in \mathbb{R}^k, \quad v \in \mathbb{R}^{n-k}, \quad \operatorname{diag}\{B_+(t), B_-(t)\} = U^{-1}(t)A(t)U(t), \\ (g_+(t, z(t), z(\beta(t))), g_-(t, z(t), z(\beta(t)))) = f((t, U(t)z(t)), U(\beta(t))z(\beta(t))). \end{gathered} \tag{2.20}$$

One can check that the Lipschitz condition is valid,

$$\begin{aligned} &||g_+(t, z_1, w_1) - g_+(t, z_2, w_2)|| + ||g_-(t, z_1, w_1) - g_-(t, z_2, w_2)|| \\ &\quad \leq L(||z_1 - z_2|| + ||w_1 - w_2||) \end{aligned} \tag{2.21}$$

for all $t \in \mathbb{R}$, $z_1, z_2 \in \mathbb{R}^k$, $w_1, w_2 \in \mathbb{R}^{(n-k)}$, and $L = 2\sup_R \|U(t)\| l$.

The normed fundamental matrices $U(t,s)$, $V(t,s)$ of the systems

$$\frac{du}{dt} = B_+(t)u, \qquad \frac{dv}{dt} = B_-(t)v, \tag{2.22}$$

respectively, satisfy the following inequalities:

$$||U(t,s)|| \leq K\exp(-\sigma(t-s)), \quad t \geq s, \qquad ||V(t,s)|| \leq K\exp(\sigma(s-t)), \quad t \leq s. \tag{2.23}$$

3. The integral surfaces

The following two lemmas are of major importance for our paper.

Lemma 3.1. *Fix $N \in \mathbb{R}$, $N > 0$, $\alpha \in (0, \sigma)$, and assume that conditions* (C1)–(C3) *are valid. A function $z(t) = (u, v)$, $\|z(t)\| \leq N\exp(-\alpha(t - t_0))$, $t \geq t_0$, where t_0 is a real fixed number, is a solution of (2.19) on $\mathbb{R}$ if and only if it is a solution on $\mathbb{R}$ of the following system of integral equations:*

$$\begin{aligned} u(t) &= U(t, t_0)u(t_0) + \int_{t_0}^{t} U(t,s)g_+(s, z(s), z(\beta(s)))\,ds, \\ v(t) &= -\int_t^\infty V(t,s)g_-(s, z(s), z(\beta(s)))\,ds. \end{aligned} \tag{3.1}$$

Proof

Necessity. Assume that $z(t) = (u, v)$, $\|z(t)\| \le N\exp(-\alpha(t - t_0))$, $t \ge t_0$, is a solution of (2.19). Denote

$$\begin{aligned} \phi(t) &= U(t,t_0)u(t_0) + \int_{t_0}^{t} U(t,s)g_+(s,z(s),z(\beta(s)))ds, \\ \psi(t) &= -\int_{t}^{\infty} V(t,s)g_-(s,z(s),z(\beta(s)))ds. \end{aligned} \tag{3.2}$$

By straightforward evaluation, we can see that the integrals converge and are bounded if $t \in [t_0, \infty)$.

Assume that $t \ne \theta_i$, $i \in \mathbb{Z}$. Then,

$$\begin{aligned} \phi'(t) &= B_+(t)\phi(t) + g_+(t,z(t),z(\beta(t))), \\ \psi'(t) &= B_-(t)\psi(t) + g_-(t,z(t),z(\beta(t))), \\ u'(t) &= B_+(t)u(t) + g_+(t,z(t),z(\beta(t))), \\ v'(t) &= B_-(t)v(t) + g_-(t,z(t),z(\beta(t))). \end{aligned} \tag{3.3}$$

Hence,

$$\begin{aligned} [\phi(t) - u(t)]' &= B_+(t)[\phi(t) - u(t)], \\ [\psi(t) - v(t)]' &= B_-(t)[\psi(t) - v(t)]. \end{aligned} \tag{3.4}$$

Calculating the limit values at $\theta_j \in \mathbb{Z}$, we can find that

$$\begin{aligned} \phi'(\theta_j \pm 0) &= B_+(\theta_j \pm 0)\phi(\theta_j \pm 0) + g_+(\theta_j \pm 0, z(\theta_j \pm 0), z(\beta(\theta_j \pm 0))), \\ u'(\theta_j \pm 0) &= B_+(\theta_j \pm 0)u(\theta_j \pm 0) + g_+(\theta_j \pm 0, z(\theta_j \pm 0), z(\beta(\theta_j \pm 0))), \\ \psi'(\theta_j \pm 0) &= B_+(\theta_j \pm 0)\psi(\theta_j \pm 0) + g_-(\theta_j \pm 0, z(\theta_j \pm 0), z(\beta(\theta_j \pm 0))), \\ v'(\theta_j \pm 0) &= B_+(\theta_j \pm 0)v(\theta_j \pm 0) + g_-(\theta_j \pm 0, z(\theta_j \pm 0), z(\beta(\theta_j \pm 0))). \end{aligned} \tag{3.5}$$

Consequently,

$$\begin{aligned} [\phi(t) - u(t)]' \,|_{t=\theta_j+0} &= [\phi(t) - u(t)]' \,|_{t=\theta_j-0}, \\ [\psi(t) - v(t)]' \,|_{t=\theta_j+0} &= [\psi(t) - v(t)]' \,|_{t=\theta_j-0}. \end{aligned} \tag{3.6}$$

Thus, $(\phi(t) - u(t), \psi(t) - v(t))$ is a continuously differentiable function on $\mathbb{R}$ satisfying (2.22) with the initial condition $\phi(t_0) - u(t_0) = 0$. Assume that $\psi(t_0) - v(t_0) \ne 0$. Then $\psi(t) - v(t)$ is unbounded on $[t_0, \infty)$. This contradiction proves that $\phi(t) - u(t) = 0$ and $\psi(t) - v(t) = 0$ on $\mathbb{R}$.

Sufficiency. Suppose that $z(t)$ is a solution of (3.1). Fix $i \in \mathbb{Z}$ and consider the interval $[\theta_i, \theta_{i+1})$. If $t \in (\theta_i, \theta_{i+1})$, then differentiating one can see that $z(t)$ satisfies (2.19). Moreover, considering $t \to \theta_i+$, and taking into account that $z(\beta(t))$ is a right-continuous function, we find that $z(t)$ satisfies (2.19) on $[\theta_i, \theta_{i+1})$. The lemma is proved. □

Similarly to the last lemma, one can prove that the following assertion is valid.

LEMMA 3.2. *Fix $N \in \mathbb{R}$, $N > 0$, $\alpha \in (0, \sigma)$, and assume that conditions* (C1)–(C3) *are valid. A function $z(t) = (u, v)$, $\|z(t)\| \le N\exp(\alpha(t - t_0))$, $t \le t_0$, where t_0 is a real fixed number, is a solution of (2.19) on $\mathbb{R}$ if and only if it is a solution of the following system of integral equations:*

$$u(t) = \int_{-\infty}^{t} U(t,s)g_+(s, z(s), z(\beta(s)))\,ds,$$
$$v(t) = V(t,t_0)v(t_0) + \int_{t_0}^{t} V(t,s)g_-(s, z(s), z(\beta(s)))\,ds. \tag{3.7}$$

The proof of the next theorems is very similar to that of the classic assertions about integral manifolds [5, 8], and can be done by using previous assertions. We will prove the first of them.

THEOREM 3.3. *Suppose that conditions* (C1)–(C5) *are satisfied. Then for arbitrary $\epsilon > 0$, $\alpha \in (0, \sigma)$, and a sufficiently small Lipschitz constant L, there exists a continuous function $F(t, u)$ satisfying*

$$F(t,0) = 0, \qquad \|F(t,u_1) - F(t,u_2)\| \le \frac{2K^2L(1 + \exp(\sigma\theta))}{\sigma + \alpha}\|u_1 - u_2\|, \tag{3.8}$$

for all t, u_1, u_2, such that $v_0 = F(t_0, u_0)$ determines a solution $z(t)$ of (2.19) on $\mathbb{R}$ and

$$\|z(t)\| \le (K + \epsilon)\|u_0\|\exp(-\alpha(t - t_0)), \quad t \ge t_0. \tag{3.9}$$

Proof. Let us consider system (3.1) and apply the method of successive approximations to it. Denote $z_0 = (0,0)^T$, $z_m = (u_m, v_m)^T$, $m \in \mathbb{N}$, where for $m \ge 0$,

$$u_{m+1}(t) = U(t,t_0)u(t_0) + \int_{t_0}^{t} U(t,s)g_+(s, z_m(s), z_m(\beta(s)))\,ds,$$
$$v_{m+1}(t) = -\int_{t}^{\infty} V(t,s)g_-(s, z_m(s), z_m(\beta(s)))\,ds. \tag{3.10}$$

One can show by induction that

$$\|z_m(t,c)\| \le (K + \epsilon)\|c\|\exp(-\alpha(t - t_0)), \quad t \ge t_0, \tag{3.11}$$

provided that

$$K(K + \epsilon)\frac{2\sigma}{\sigma^2 - \alpha^2}(1 + \exp(\sigma\theta))L < \epsilon. \tag{3.12}$$

One can find that if $4\sigma KL(1+\exp(\sigma\theta)) < \sigma^2 - \alpha^2$, then

$$\|z_m(t,c) - z_{m-1}(t,c)\| \leq K\|c\| \left(\frac{2KL(1+\exp(\sigma\theta))}{\sigma - \alpha}\right)^{m-1} \exp\left(-\alpha(t-t_0)\right). \tag{3.13}$$

The last inequality and the assumption

$$L < \frac{\sigma - \alpha}{2K(1+\exp(\sigma\theta))} \tag{3.14}$$

imply that the sequence z_m converges uniformly for all c and $t \geq t_0$. Define the limit function $z(t,t_0,c) = (u(t,t_0,c), v(t,t_0,c))$. It can be easily seen that this function is a solution of (3.1). By Lemma 3.1, $z(t,t_0,c)$ is also a solution of (2.19). Taking $t = t_0$ in (3.1), we have that

$$u(t_0,t_0,c) = c, \qquad v(t_0,t_0,c) = -\int_{t_0}^{\infty} V(t,s)g_-\left(s, z(s,t_0,c), z(\beta(s),t_0,c)\right)ds. \tag{3.15}$$

Denote $F(t_0,c) = v(t_0,t_0,c)$. One can see that it satisfies all the conditions which should be verified. The theorem is proved. □

Theorem 3.4. *For every fixed $(t_0, u(t_0))$, system (3.1) admits only one solution bounded on $[t_0,\infty)$.*

Let us denote by S^+ the set of all points from the (t,z)-space such that $v = F(t,u)$.

Theorem 3.5. *If $(t_0,z_0) \notin S^+$, then the solution $z(t,t_0,z_0)$ of (2.19) is unbounded on $[t_0,\infty)$.*

It is not difficult to see that applying Lemma 3.2, one can formulate and prove for the case $(-\infty,t_0]$ the theorems concerning the surface S^- similar to the assertions for S^+.

On the basis of Theorems 3.3–3.5 and their analogues for $t \to -\infty$, one can conclude that there exist two integral surfaces Σ^+, Σ^- of equation (1.1) such that every solution which starts at Σ^+ tends to zero as $t \to \infty$, and every solution which starts at Σ^- tends to zero as $t \to -\infty$. If a solution starts outside of Σ^+, then it is unbounded on $[t_0,\infty)$, and if a solution starts outside of Σ^-, then it is unbounded on $(-\infty,t_0]$.

Remark 3.6. The extended version of the paper has been submitted to Nonlinear Analysis: Theory, Methods, and Applications.

References

[1] A. R. Aftabizadeh, J. Wiener, and J.-M. Xu, *Oscillatory and periodic solutions of delay differential equations with piecewise constant argument*, Proceedings of the American Mathematical Society **99** (1987), no. 4, 673–679.

[2] A. I. Alonso, J. Hong, and R. Obaya, *Almost periodic type solutions of differential equations with piecewise constant argument via almost periodic type sequences*, Applied Mathematics Letters **13** (2000), no. 2, 131–137.

[3] K. L. Cooke and J. Wiener, *Retarded differential equations with piecewise constant delays*, Journal of Mathematical Analysis and Applications **99** (1984), no. 1, 265–297.

[4] W. A. Coppel, *Dichotomies in Stability Theory*, Lecture Notes in Mathematics, vol. 629, Springer, Berlin, 1978.

[5] P. Hartman, *Ordinary Differential Equations*, John Wiley & Sons, New York, 1964.
[6] Y. Muroya, *Persistence, contractivity and global stability in logistic equations with piecewise constant delays*, Journal of Mathematical Analysis and Applications **270** (2002), no. 2, 602–635.
[7] G. Papaschinopoulos, *Linearization near the integral manifold for a system of differential equations with piecewise constant argument*, Journal of Mathematical Analysis and Applications **215** (1997), no. 2, 317–333.
[8] V. A. Pliss, *Integral Sets of Periodic Systems of Differential Equations*, Nauka, Moscow, 1977.
[9] G. Seifert, *Almost periodic solutions of certain differential equations with piecewise constant delays and almost periodic time dependence*, Journal of Differential Equations **164** (2000), no. 2, 451–458.
[10] J. Wiener, *Generalized Solutions of Functional-Differential Equations*, World Scientific, New Jersey, 1993.
[11] J. Wiener and V. Lakshmikantham, *A damped oscillator with piecewise constant time delay*, Nonlinear Studies **7** (2000), no. 1, 78–84.
[12] R. Yuan, *The existence of almost periodic solutions of retarded differential equations with piecewise constant argument*, Nonlinear Analysis. Theory, Methods & Applications **48** (2002), no. 7, 1013–1032.

Marat Akhmet: Department of Mathematics and Institute of Applied Mathematics, Middle East Technical University, 06531 Ankara, Turkey
E-mail address: marat@metu.edu.tr

IMPULSIVE CONTROL OF THE POPULATION DYNAMICS

M. U. AKHMET, D. ARUĞASLAN, AND M. BEKLIOĞLU

We investigate the dynamics of the *Lotka-Volterra* system with variable time of impulses. Sufficient conditions are obtained for the existence of focus in the noncritical case. The focus-center problem in the critical case and the Hopf bifurcation are considered.

1. Introduction

The *Lotka-Volterra* system describes the interaction of two species in an ecosystem, a prey and a predator. Since there are two species, this system involves two equations,

$$\begin{aligned} \frac{dx}{dt} &= x' = ax - bxy, \\ \frac{dy}{dt} &= y' = -cy + dxy, \end{aligned} \tag{1.1}$$

where x and y denote the prey and predator population densities, respectively, a (the growth rate of prey), b (the rate at which predators consume prey), c (the death rate of predator), and d (the rate at which predators increase by consuming prey) are positive constants. This system has only one positive equilibrium that is $(c/d, a/b)$ as a center. However, having the equilibrium as a center, this system is ecologically undesirable. In other words, the hypothesis of (1.1) does not seem to be in accordance with the observations [8].

The system (1.1) describes populations whose members can respond immediately to any change in the environment. But, in real populations, both prey and predator require reaction time lags. By introducing a time lag into system (1.1), instead of a center, the point of equilibrium may be either a stable focus or a stable node. Moreover, this point may be an unstable focus surrounded by a stable limit cycle [10].

The *Lotka-Volterra* population growth model does not assume human activities at all. We introduce human intervention by impulsive perturbation. In general, the appearence

Hindawi Publishing Corporation
Proceedings of the Conference on Differential & Difference Equations and Applications, pp. 21–29

of the discontinuities can be explained by the fact that a development of a biological system may have sudden changes. It is natural that the obtained systems can be written in the form of impulsive differential equations [5, 9]. In this paper, our idea is to perturb system (1.1) by impulses at nonfixed moments of time. These impulses, in particular, may include man-made controls which are introduced when the state of species satisfies certain criteria. That is, we consider introducing or removing some members from the population as impulsive control. The approach of impulsive control was also proposed by Liu in [7, 6] and in the paper [3].

We mainly use the results which were obtained in [1, 2]. One can verify that our sytems satisfy the properties of discontinuous dynamical systems described in [1], that is, the continuation of solutions on R, group property, continuous dependence of solutions on initial data, and differentiability of solutions in initial data.

In Section 2, we formulate two problems: Problem (D) and Problem (U). In the next section, we investigate these problems. Lastly, the Hopf bifurcation for two systems which are associated with Problems (D) and (U) is considered in Section 4.

2. Formulation of the problems

In order to be more convenient, we first translate the equilibrium $(c/d, a/b)$ to the origin by the linear transformation

$$\begin{bmatrix} x - \dfrac{c}{d} \\ y - \dfrac{a}{b} \end{bmatrix} = \begin{bmatrix} 2 & 0 \\ 0 & \dfrac{2d\sqrt{ac}}{bc} \end{bmatrix} \begin{bmatrix} x_1 \\ x_2 \end{bmatrix}. \tag{2.1}$$

This transformation takes system (1.1) into the form

$$\begin{aligned} x_1' &= -\sqrt{ac}x_2 - \frac{2d\sqrt{ac}}{c}x_1x_2, \\ x_2' &= \sqrt{ac}x_1 + 2dx_1x_2. \end{aligned} \tag{2.2}$$

We have new variables x_1 and x_2 possibly with negative values. But, the positiveness of the issue variables x and y in a neighborhood of the equilibrium $(c/d, a/b)$ is certainly saved.

Clearly, systems (1.1) and (2.2) are qualitatively equivalent. Since $(c/d, a/b)$ is a center of (1.1), the origin is a center of (2.2).

In what follows, we will consider how an impulsive perturbation may change the behaviour of the system (2.2) around the origin.

We introduce impulses into the system (2.2) with a more careful assumption that they are considered as impulsive control and we are sure that the more adequate explanation of the discontinuous population dynamics is a deal of future and is a deal of a closer collaboration of mathematicians and biologists. For that reason, we consider the impulsive control as the ability to instantly introduce or remove some members from the environment. It is acceptable and easily realizable as an ecological project. From this point of view, we formulate two problems to investigate.

Problem (D). Our objective is to bioregulate the *Lotka-Volterra* system by impulsive perturbation. Ecologically, it seems reasonable to control only the predator density. On the basis of this idea, we consider the impulsive action by means of removing some members of predators from the system. For example, if we have fish as predator (and daphnia as prey) in a lake, the decrease in its density can be expressed by harvesting for commercial fishery. This type of dynamics can be modelled as follows:

$$\begin{aligned} x_1' &= -\sqrt{ac}x_2 - \frac{2d\sqrt{ac}}{c}x_1x_2, \\ x_2' &= \sqrt{ac}x_1 + 2dx_1x_2, \quad (x_1,x_2) \notin \Gamma_1, \\ \Delta x_1|_{(x_1,x_2)\in\Gamma_1} &= 0, \\ \Delta x_2|_{(x_1,x_2)\in\Gamma_1} &= \kappa x_2, \end{aligned} \tag{2.3}$$

where $\kappa < 0$ and Γ_1 is a half straight line in the second quadrant defined by the equation $x_2 = -\sqrt{3}x_1$ for $x_1 < 0$. When the solution meets the set Γ_1 at the time t_1, there exists a vertical jump $\Delta x_2|_{t_1} = \kappa x_2(t_1) := x_2(t_1+) - x_2(t_1)$ going *down*.

We define determining the behaviour of solutions of system (2.3) around the origin as Problem (D). Furthermore, in Section 4, we will introduce a system with a small parameter μ associated with (2.3) and the Hopf bifurcation for that system is considered as Problem (DH).

Remark 2.1. Writing (2.3) in x, y coordinates, we obtain the following system:

$$\begin{aligned} x' &= ax - bxy, \\ y' &= -cy + dxy, \quad (x,y) \notin \tilde{\Gamma}_1, \\ \Delta x|_{(x,y)\in\tilde{\Gamma}_1} &= 0, \\ \Delta y|_{(x,y)\in\tilde{\Gamma}_1} &= \kappa\left(y - \frac{a}{b}\right), \end{aligned} \tag{2.4}$$

where $\tilde{\Gamma}_1$ is a half-line defined by the equation $y - a/b = -(\sqrt{3}d\sqrt{ac}/bc)(x - c/d)$ with $x < c/d$. So, we see that the corresponding impulsive control is only applied to the predator density.

Problem (U). Similar to Problem (D), we can formulate Problem (U) for the system

$$\begin{aligned} x_1' &= -\sqrt{ac}x_2 - \frac{2d\sqrt{ac}}{c}x_1x_2, \\ x_2' &= \sqrt{ac}x_1 + 2dx_1x_2, \quad (x_1,x_2) \notin \Gamma_2, \\ \Delta x_1|_{(x_1,x_2)\in\Gamma_2} &= 0, \\ \Delta x_2|_{(x_1,x_2)\in\Gamma_2} &= \kappa x_2, \end{aligned} \tag{2.5}$$

where $\kappa < 0$ and $\Gamma_2\colon x_2 = -\sqrt{3}x_1, x_1 > 0$ is a straight line in the fourth quadrant. In this system, we control the predator density by introducing new members into the environment and thus we have a vertical jump going *up*. For the Hopf bifurcation, we will define Problem (UH) in a manner similar to the Problem (DH).

3. Existence of foci and centers

3.1. Investigation of Problem (D). Let $x_1 = r\cos\phi$, $x_2 = r\sin\phi$. In system (2.3), we have discontinuity when $(x_1,x_2) \in \Gamma_1$. In polar coordinates r and ϕ, we have a jump when the angle is equal to $2\pi/3 + 2\pi n$, $n \in \mathbb{Z}$. Using polar transformation, we can write (2.3) in the following form:

$$\begin{gathered} \frac{dr}{d\phi} = P(r,\phi), \quad \phi \neq \frac{2\pi}{3} (\mathrm{mod}\ 2\pi), \\ \Delta r|_{\phi=(2\pi/3)(\mathrm{mod}\ 2\pi)} = \lambda r, \\ \Delta\phi|_{\phi=(2\pi/3)(\mathrm{mod}\ 2\pi)} = \theta(\kappa), \end{gathered} \tag{3.1}$$

where $P(r,\phi) = (-(2d/c)\cos\phi + (2d/\sqrt{ac})\sin\phi)\cos\phi\sin\phi r^2/(1 + ((2d/\sqrt{ac})\cos\phi + (2d/c)\sin\phi)\cos\phi\sin\phi r)$, $\lambda = (1/2)\sqrt{1+3(1+\kappa)^2} - 1$, $\theta(\kappa) = \tan^{-1}(-\sqrt{3}\kappa/(4+3\kappa))$, and ϕ is ranged over the time-scale $\cup_{i=-\infty}^{\infty}(2\pi i + 2\pi/3 + \theta(\kappa), 2\pi(i+1) + 2\pi/3]$. Clearly, the function P is 2π-periodic in ϕ and $P = o(r)$. Since (3.1) is a 2π-periodic system, we will consider it only for $\phi \in [0,2\pi] \setminus (2\pi/3, 2\pi/3 + \theta(\kappa)]$, that is, the system

$$\begin{gathered} \frac{dr}{d\phi} = P(r,\phi), \quad \phi \neq \frac{2\pi}{3}, \\ \Delta r|_{\phi=2\pi/3} = \lambda r, \\ \Delta\phi|_{\phi=2\pi/3} = \theta(\kappa). \end{gathered} \tag{3.2}$$

System (3.2) is a time-scale differential equation. In order to obtain an impulsive differential equation, we use the ψ-substitution method which is defined in [2]. The development of this method is given in [4]. Then one can obtain that the solution $r(\phi, r_0)$ of (3.2) starting at the point $(0, r_0)$ has the form

$$r(\phi, r_0) = \begin{cases} r_0 + \displaystyle\int_0^{\phi} P\,du & \text{if } 0 \le \phi \le \dfrac{2\pi}{3}, \\ (1+\lambda)\left(r_0 + \displaystyle\int_0^{2\pi/3} P\,du\right) + \displaystyle\int_{2\pi/3+\theta(\kappa)}^{\phi} P\,du & \text{if } \dfrac{2\pi}{3} + \theta(\kappa) < \phi \le 2\pi. \end{cases} \tag{3.3}$$

Now, let us construct the Poincaré return map $r(2\pi, r_0)$:

$$r(2\pi, r_0) = (1+\lambda)r_0 + (1+\lambda)\int_0^{2\pi/3} P\,du + \int_{2\pi/3+\theta(\kappa)}^{2\pi} P\,du. \tag{3.4}$$

From (3.4), we conclude that the origin of (2.3) is a stable focus if $1 + \lambda = (1/2)\sqrt{1+3(1+\kappa)^2} < 1$ and it is an unstable focus if $1 + \lambda > 1$. Then for the noncritical case, the following theorem is valid.

THEOREM 3.1. *If*
(a) $-2 < \kappa < 0$, *then the origin is a stable focus;*
(b) $\kappa < -2$, *then the origin is an unstable focus of system (2.3).*

However, if $1+\lambda = 1$, (i.e., if $\kappa = -2$), then we have the critical case and the origin is either a focus or a center. In what follows, we solve this problem of distinguishing between the focus and the center.

We can easily see that the angle $\theta(\kappa)$ is equal to $2\pi/3$ for $\kappa = -2$.

The solution $r(\phi, r_0)$ of (3.2), $r(0, r_0) = r_0$, for sufficiently small r, has the expansion [4]

$$r(\phi, r_0) = \sum_{j=0}^{\infty} r_j(\phi) r_0^j, \tag{3.5}$$

with $\phi \in [0, 2\pi] \setminus (2\pi/3, 4\pi/3]$, $r_o(\phi) = 0$, and $r_1(\phi) = 1$. Then, we have $r(2\pi, r_0) = \sum_{j=1}^{\infty} a_j r_0^j$, where $a_j = r_j(2\pi)$ and $a_1 = 1$. The function P also has the following expansion [4]:

$$P(r, \phi) = \sum_{j=2}^{\infty} P_j(\phi) r^j, \tag{3.6}$$

where

$$\begin{aligned} P_2(\phi) &= \left(-\frac{2d}{c} \cos\phi + \frac{2d}{\sqrt{ac}} \sin\phi \right) \cos\phi \sin\phi, \\ P_3(\phi) &= \left(\frac{\cos^2\phi - \sin^2\phi}{c\sqrt{ac}} + \frac{\cos\phi \sin\phi}{c^2} - \frac{\cos\phi \sin\phi}{ac} \right) 4d^2 \cos^2\phi \sin^2\phi. \end{aligned} \tag{3.7}$$

From the differential part of (3.2) and the expansion (3.6), one can find that

$$\begin{aligned} \frac{dr_2(\phi)}{d\phi} &= P_2(\phi) := \widetilde{P}_2(\phi), \\ \frac{dr_3(\phi)}{d\phi} &= 2P_2(\phi) r_2(\phi) + P_3(\phi) := \widetilde{P}_3(\phi), \end{aligned} \tag{3.8}$$

and similarly we define $dr_j(\phi)/d\phi := \widetilde{P}_j(\phi)$ for $j = 4, 5, \ldots$.

From the second equation of (3.2), we obtain that $r_j(4\pi/3) - r_j(2\pi/3) = 0$ for $j = 2, 3, \ldots$. Hence, the coefficients $r_j(\phi)$, $j = 2, 3, \ldots$, with $r_j(0) = 0$ are solutions of the system

$$\begin{aligned} \frac{dr}{d\phi} &= \widetilde{P}_j(\phi), \quad \phi \neq \frac{2\pi}{3}, \\ \Delta r|_{\phi = 2\pi/3} &= 0, \\ \Delta\phi|_{\phi = 2\pi/3} &= \frac{2\pi}{3}. \end{aligned} \tag{3.9}$$

As $a_j = r_j(2\pi)$, we can now evaluate a_j's in the expansion of $r(2\pi, r_0)$:

$$a_j = \int_0^{2\pi/3} \widetilde{P}_j(\phi)d\phi + \int_{4\pi/3}^{2\pi} \widetilde{P}_j(\phi)d\phi \tag{3.10}$$

for $j = 2,3,\ldots$.

For the critical case, the sign of the first nonzero element of the sequence a_j determines what type of a singular point the origin is. The origin is a stable (unstable) focus if the first nonzero element is negative (positive). If all $a_j = 0$, $j = 2,3,\ldots$, then the origin is a center [2]. That is why we first need a_2 to solve this focus-center problem:

$$a_2 = \int_0^{2\pi/3} P_2(\phi)d\phi + \int_{4\pi/3}^{2\pi} P_2(\phi)d\phi = \frac{d\sqrt{3}}{2\sqrt{ac}}. \tag{3.11}$$

Since a_2 is positive, we have the following theorem.

THEOREM 3.2. *If $\kappa = -2$, then the origin of system (2.3) is an unstable focus.*

3.2. Investigation of Problem (U). Introducing polar coordinates, the system (2.5) can be written as follows:

$$\begin{gathered} \frac{dr}{d\phi} = P(r,\phi), \quad \phi \neq \frac{5\pi}{3}, \\ \Delta r|_{\phi=5\pi/3} = \lambda r, \\ \Delta\phi|_{\phi=5\pi/3} = \theta(\kappa), \end{gathered} \tag{3.12}$$

where P, λ, and $\theta(\kappa)$ are the same as for system (3.2). For a solution $r(\phi, r_0)$, $r(0, r_0) = r_0$ of (3.12), the Poincaré return map is given by

$$r(2\pi, r_0) = (1+\lambda)r_0 + (1+\lambda)\int_0^{5\pi/3} P\,du + \int_{\varphi(\kappa)}^{2\pi} P\,du \tag{3.13}$$

where $5\pi/3 + \theta(\kappa) \equiv \varphi(\kappa) (\mathrm{mod}\ 2\pi)$.

Clearly, the noncritical case, that is, $1+\lambda < 1$ or $1+\lambda > 1$, is treated similarly as in the investigation of Problem (D). But, the critical case, $1+\lambda = 1$, gives us a different result since the first element a_2 of the sequence a_j is negative:

$$a_2 = \int_0^{5\pi/3} P_2(\phi)d\phi + \int_{\pi/3}^{2\pi} P_2(\phi)d\varphi = -\frac{d\sqrt{3}}{2\sqrt{ac}}. \tag{3.14}$$

Combining the results for noncritical and critical cases, we obtain the following assertion.

THEOREM 3.3. *If*

(a) $-2 \le \kappa < 0$, *then the origin is a stable focus;*

(b) $\kappa < -2$, *then the origin is an unstable focus of (2.5).*

4. Hopf bifurcation

Since the origin is a center, and not a focus, it is not possible to apply Hopf bifurcation theorem for system (2.2) which is the transformed *Lotka-Volterra* population growth model into x_1, x_2 coordinates [8]. But, with the impulsive control, one can obtain the origin as a stable or an unstable focus, and hence Hopf bifurcation can be investigated.

4.1. Problem (DH). We introduce the following discontinuous dynamical system:

$$\begin{aligned} x_1' &= \mu x_1 - \sqrt{ac}x_2 - \frac{2d\sqrt{ac}}{c}x_1x_2, \\ x_2' &= \sqrt{ac}x_1 + \mu x_2 + 2dx_1x_2, \quad (x_1,x_2) \notin \Gamma_1(\mu), \\ \Delta x_1|_{(x_1,x_2)\in\Gamma_1(\mu)} &= 0, \\ \Delta x_2|_{(x_1,x_2)\in\Gamma_1(\mu)} &= \kappa x_2, \end{aligned} \tag{4.1}$$

where $\Gamma_1(\mu)$ is not a linear set and it is defined by the equation $x_2 = -\sqrt{3}x_1 + \mu x_1x_2$ for $x_1 < 0$. System (2.3) is associated with (4.1). In other words, (4.1) for $\mu = 0$ is the system (2.3) described in Section 2. In this system, μ appears to be an internal control parameter of the populations.

We will also need the following system:

$$\begin{aligned} x_1' &= \mu x_1 - \sqrt{ac}x_2, \\ x_2' &= \sqrt{ac}x_1 + \mu x_2, \quad (x_1,x_2) \notin \Gamma_1, \\ \Delta x_1|_{(x_1,x_2)\in\Gamma_1} &= 0, \\ \Delta x_2|_{(x_1,x_2)\in\Gamma_1} &= \kappa x_2. \end{aligned} \tag{4.2}$$

Using polar coordinates, (4.1) and (4.2) can be written as follows:

$$\begin{aligned} \frac{dr}{d\phi} &= \frac{\mu}{\sqrt{ac}}r + P(r,\phi,\mu), \quad (r,\phi) \notin \Gamma_1(\mu), \\ \Delta r|_{(r,\phi)\in\Gamma_1(\mu)} &= \lambda r, \\ \Delta \phi|_{(r,\phi)\in\Gamma_1(\mu)} &= \theta(\kappa), \end{aligned} \tag{4.3}$$

$$\begin{aligned} \frac{dr}{d\phi} &= \frac{\mu}{\sqrt{ac}}r, \quad \phi \neq \frac{2\pi}{3}, \\ \Delta r|_{\phi=2\pi/3} &= \lambda r, \\ \Delta \phi|_{\phi=2\pi/3} &= \theta(\kappa), \end{aligned} \tag{4.4}$$

respectively.

Now, the solution $r(\phi,r_0,\mu)$, $r(0,r_0,\mu)=r_0$ of (4.4) given by

$$r(\phi,r_0,\mu)=\begin{cases}\exp\left(\dfrac{\mu}{\sqrt{ac}}\phi\right)r_0 & \text{if } 0\le\phi\le\dfrac{2\pi}{3},\\[2ex] (1+\lambda)\exp\left(\dfrac{\mu}{\sqrt{ac}}(\phi-\theta(\kappa))\right)r_0 & \text{if } \dfrac{2\pi}{3}+\theta(\kappa)<\phi\le 2\pi,\end{cases} \tag{4.5}$$

implies that $r(2\pi,r_0,\mu)=(1+\lambda)\exp((\mu/\sqrt{ac})(2\pi-\theta(\kappa)))r_0$.

Denote

$$q(\mu)=(1+\lambda)\exp\left(\frac{\mu}{\sqrt{ac}}(2\pi-\theta(\kappa))\right). \tag{4.6}$$

Then we get $r(2\pi,r_0,\mu)=q(\mu)r_0$. $q(0)=1$ and $q'(0)\neq 0$ are the necessary conditions [2] for the existence of periodical processes in system (4.3). It is easy to see that if $\lambda=0$ (i.e., $\kappa=-2$), then $q(0)=1$ and $q'(0)=4\pi/3\sqrt{ac}\neq 0$.

Applying the technique which is used in the paper [2], we can prove the following theorem.

Theorem 4.1. *If $\kappa=-2$, then for sufficiently small r_0, there exists a function $\mu=\delta(r_0)$ such that the solution $r(\phi,r_0,\delta(r_0))$ of (4.3) is periodic with period $T=4\pi/3\sqrt{ac}+o(|\mu|)$. Moreover, the closed trajectory is an unstable limit cycle.*

4.2. Problem (UH). We consider the system

$$\begin{gathered} x_1'=\mu x_1-\sqrt{ac}x_2-\frac{2d\sqrt{ac}}{c}x_1x_2,\\ x_2'=\sqrt{ac}x_1+\mu x_2+2dx_1x_2,\quad (x_1,x_2)\notin\Gamma_2(\mu),\\ \Delta x_1|_{(x_1,x_2)\in\Gamma_2(\mu)}=0,\\ \Delta x_2|_{(x_1,x_2)\in\Gamma_2(\mu)}=\kappa x_2,\end{gathered} \tag{4.7}$$

where $\Gamma_2(\mu)$ is a curve given by $x_2=-\sqrt{3}x_1+\mu x_1x_2$ with $x_1>0$. Clearly, system (2.5) is associated with (4.7). This system, in polar coordinates, is as follows:

$$\begin{gathered} \frac{dr}{d\phi}=\frac{\mu}{\sqrt{ac}}r+P(r,\phi,\mu),\quad (r,\phi)\notin\Gamma_2(\mu),\\ \Delta r|_{(r,\phi)\in\Gamma_2(\mu)}=\lambda r,\\ \Delta\phi|_{(r,\phi)\in\Gamma_2(\mu)}=\theta(\kappa).\end{gathered} \tag{4.8}$$

Using the similar discussions made in Problem (DH) and using the paper [2], we can conclude the following result.

Theorem 4.2. *If $\kappa=-2$, then for sufficiently small r_0, there exists a function $\mu=\delta(r_0)$ such that the solution $r(\phi,r_0,\delta(r_0))$ of (4.8) is periodic with period $T=4\pi/3\sqrt{ac}+o(|\mu|)$. Moreover, the closed trajectory is a stable limit cycle.*

5. Conclusion

Under the assumption that the coefficients a, b, c, and d of the *Lotka-Volterra* system are positive, we may conclude that the complex behaviour of solutions entirely depends on the values of the coefficient κ which appears in the impulsive part of systems (2.3), (2.5), (4.1), and (4.7). That is, the problem of controllability of the *Lotka-Volterra* system by the proposed impulsive control is constructive.

References

[1] E. Akalin and M. U. Akhmet, *The principles of B-smooth discontinuous flows*, Nonlinear Analysis **49** (2005), 981–995.

[2] M. U. Akhmet, *Perturbations and Hopf bifurcation of the planar discontinuous dynamical system*, Nonlinear Analysis **60** (2005), no. 1, 163–178.

[3] M. U. Akhmet, M. Beklioğlu, T. Ergenç, and V. I. Tkachenko, *On impulsive ratio-dependent predator-prey system with diffusion*, to appear in Nonlinear Analysis: Real World Applications.

[4] M. U. Akhmet and N. A. Perestyuk, *Asymptotic representation of solutions of regularly perturbed systems of differential equations with a nonclassical right-hand side*, Ukrainian Mathematical Journal **43** (1991), no. 10, 1209–1214 (1992).

[5] V. Lakshmikantham, D. D. Baĭnov, and P. S. Simeonov, *Theory of Impulsive Differential Equations*, Series in Modern Applied Mathematics, vol. 6, World Scientific, New Jersey, 1989.

[6] X. Z. Liu, *Impulsive stabilization and control of chaotic system*, Nonlinear Analysis **47** (2001), no. 2, 1081–1092.

[7] X. Z. Liu and K. Rohlf, *Impulsive control of a Lotka-Volterra system*, IMA Journal of Mathematical Control and Information **15** (1998), no. 3, 269–284.

[8] N. Minorsky, *Nonlinear Oscillations*, D. Van Nostrand, New Jersey, 1962.

[9] A. M. Samoĭlenko and N. A. Perestyuk, *Impulsive Differential Equations*, World Scientific Series on Nonlinear Science. Series A: Monographs and Treatises, vol. 14, World Scientific, New Jersey, 1995.

[10] P. J. Wangersky and W. J. Cunningham, *Time lag in prey-predator population models*, Ecology **38** (1957), 136–139.

M. U. Akhmet: Department of Mathematics and Institute of Applied Mathematics,
Middle East Technical University (METU), 06531 Ankara, Turkey
E-mail address: marat@metu.edu.tr

D. Aruğaslan: Department of Mathematics, Middle East Technical University (METU),
06531 Ankara, Turkey
E-mail address: aduygu@metu.edu.tr

M. Beklioğlu: Department of Biology, Middle East Technical University (METU),
06531 Ankara, Turkey
E-mail address: meryem@metu.edu.tr

L_p CONVERGENCE WITH RATES OF SMOOTH PICARD SINGULAR OPERATORS

GEORGE A. ANASTASSIOU

We continue with the study of smooth Picard singular integral operators on the line regarding their convergence to the unit operator with rates in the L_p norm, $p \geq 1$. The related established inequalities involve the higher-order L_p modulus of smoothness of the engaged function or its higher-order derivative.

1. Introduction

The rate of convergence of singular integrals has been studied in [3–7, 9–11] and these articles motivate this work. Here we study the L_p, $p \geq 1$, convergence of smooth Picard singular integral operators over $\mathbb{R}$ to the unit operator with rates over smooth functions in $L_p(\mathbb{R})$. These operators were introduced and studied in [5] with respect to $\|\cdot\|_\infty$. We establish related Jackson-type inequalities involving the higher L_p modulus of smoothness of the engaged function or its higher-order derivative. The discussed operators are not in general positive. Other motivation derives from [1, 2].

2. Results

Next we deal with the *smooth Picard singular integral operators* $P_{r,\xi}(f;x)$ defined as follows.

For $r \in \mathbb{N}$ and $n \in \mathbb{Z}_+$, we set

$$\alpha_j = \begin{cases} (-1)^{r-j}\binom{r}{j} j^{-n}, & j = 1,\ldots,r, \\ 1 - \sum_{j=1}^{r} (-1)^{r-j}\binom{r}{j} j^{-n}, & j = 0, \end{cases} \tag{2.1}$$

that is $\sum_{j=0}^{r} \alpha_j = 1$.

Hindawi Publishing Corporation
Proceedings of the Conference on Differential & Difference Equations and Applications, pp. 31–45

Let $f \in L_p(\mathbb{R}) \cap C^n(\mathbb{R})$, $1 \le p < \infty$, we define for $x \in \mathbb{R}$, $\xi > 0$ the Lebesgue integral

$$P_{r,\xi}(f;x) = \frac{1}{2\xi}\int_{-\infty}^{\infty}\left(\sum_{j=0}^{r}\alpha_j f(x+jt)\right)e^{-|t|/\xi}dt. \tag{2.2}$$

$P_{r,\xi}$ operators are not positive operators, see [5].

We notice by $(1/2\xi)\int_{-\infty}^{\infty} e^{-|t|/\xi}dt = 1$, that $P_{r,\xi}(c,x) = c$, c constant, and

$$P_{r,\xi}(f;x) - f(x) = \frac{1}{2\xi}\left(\sum_{j=0}^{r}\alpha_j\int_{-\infty}^{\infty}(f(x+jt)-f(x))e^{-|t|/\xi}dt\right). \tag{2.3}$$

We use also that

$$\int_{-\infty}^{\infty} t^k e^{-|t|/\xi}dt = \begin{cases} 0, & k \text{ odd}, \\ 2k!\xi^{k+1}, & k \text{ even}. \end{cases} \tag{2.4}$$

We need the rth L_p-modulus of smoothness

$$\omega_r(f^{(n)},h)_p := \sup_{|t|\le h}\|\Delta_t^r f^{(n)}(x)\|_{p,x}, \quad h > 0, \tag{2.5}$$

where

$$\Delta_t^r f^{(n)}(x) := \sum_{j=0}^{r}(-1)^{r-j}\binom{r}{j}f^{(n)}(x+jt), \tag{2.6}$$

see [8, page 44]. Here we have $\omega_r(f^{(n)},h)_p < \infty$, $h > 0$.

We need to introduce

$$\delta_k := \sum_{j=1}^{r}\alpha_j j^k, \quad k = 1,\dots,n \in \mathbb{N}, \tag{2.7}$$

and denote by $\lfloor\cdot\rfloor$ the integral part. Call

$$\tau(w,x) := \sum_{j=0}^{r}\alpha_j j^n f^{(n)}(x+jw) - \delta_n f^{(n)}(x). \tag{2.8}$$

Notice also that

$$-\sum_{j=1}^{r}(-1)^{r-j}\binom{r}{j} = (-1)^r\binom{r}{0}. \tag{2.9}$$

According to [3, page 306] and [1], we get

$$\tau(w,x) = \Delta_w^r f^{(n)}(x). \tag{2.10}$$

Thus

$$\|\tau(w,x)\|_{p,x} \le \omega_r\left(f^{(n)}, |w|\right)_p, \quad w \in \mathbb{R}. \tag{2.11}$$

Using Taylor's formula, one has

$$\sum_{j=0}^{r} \alpha_j [f(x+jt) - f(x)] = \sum_{k=1}^{n} \frac{f^{(k)}(x)}{k!} \delta_k t^k + \mathcal{R}_n(0,t,x), \tag{2.12}$$

where

$$\mathcal{R}_n(0,t,x) := \int_0^t \frac{(t-w)^{n-1}}{(n-1)!} \tau(w,x)\,dw, \quad n \in \mathbb{N}. \tag{2.13}$$

Using the above terminology, we obtain

$$\Delta(x) := P_{r,\xi}(f;x) - f(x) - \sum_{m=1}^{\lfloor n/2 \rfloor} f^{(2m)}(x) \delta_{2m} \xi^{2m} = \mathcal{R}_n^*(x), \tag{2.14}$$

where

$$\mathcal{R}_n^*(x) := \frac{1}{2\xi} \int_{-\infty}^{\infty} \mathcal{R}_n(0,t,x) e^{-|t|/\xi}\,dt, \quad n \in \mathbb{N}. \tag{2.15}$$

In $\Delta(x)$, see (2.14), the sum collapses when $n = 1$.

We present our first result.

Theorem 2.1. *Let $p, q > 1$ such that $1/p + 1/q = 1$, $n \in \mathbb{N}$, and the rest as above. Then*

$$\|\Delta(x)\|_p \le \frac{2^{1/q} \tau^{1/p} \xi^n}{(rp+1)^{1/p} \left(q^2(n-1)+q\right)^{1/q} (n-1)!} w_r\left(f^{(n)}, \xi\right)_p, \tag{2.16}$$

where

$$\tau := \left[\int_0^{\infty} (1+u)^{rp+1} u^{np-1} e^{-(p/2)u}\,du - \left(\frac{2}{p}\right)^{np} \Gamma(np)\right] < \infty. \tag{2.17}$$

Hence, as $\xi \to 0$, $\|\Delta(x)\|_p \to 0$.

Proof. We observe that

$$\begin{aligned} |\Delta(x)|^p &= \frac{1}{(2\xi)^p} \left| \int_{-\infty}^{\infty} \mathcal{R}_n(0,t,x) e^{-|t|/\xi}\,dt \right|^p \\ &\le \frac{1}{(2\xi)^p} \left(\int_{-\infty}^{\infty} \left(\int_0^{|t|} \frac{(|t|-w)^{n-1}}{(n-1)!} |\tau(w,x)|\,dw \right) e^{-|t|/\xi}\,dt \right)^p. \end{aligned} \tag{2.18}$$

Hence we have

$$I := \int_{-\infty}^{\infty} |\Delta(x)|^p dx \leq \frac{1}{(2\xi)^p}\left(\int_{-\infty}^{\infty}\left(\int_{-\infty}^{\infty} \gamma(t,x)e^{-|t|/\xi}dt\right)^p dx\right), \tag{2.19}$$

where

$$\gamma(t,x) := \int_0^{|t|} \frac{(|t|-w)^{n-1}}{(n-1)!} |\tau(w,x)| dw \geq 0. \tag{2.20}$$

Therefore by using Hölder's inequality, suitably we obtain

$$\text{R.H.S. (2.19)} \leq \frac{2^{p-2}\xi^{-1}}{q^{p-1}}\left(\int_{-\infty}^{\infty}\left(\int_{-\infty}^{\infty} \gamma^p(t,x)e^{-|pt|/2\xi}dt\right)dx\right). \tag{2.21}$$

Again by Hölder's inequality, we have

$$\gamma^p(t,x) \leq \frac{\left(\int_0^{|t|} |\tau(w,x)|^p dw\right)}{((n-1)!)^p} \frac{|t|^{np-1}}{(q(n-1)+1)^{p/q}}. \tag{2.22}$$

Consequently, we have

$$\text{R.H.S. (2.21)} \leq \frac{2^{p-2}\xi^{-1}}{q^{p-1}}\left(\int_{-\infty}^{\infty}\left(\int_{-\infty}^{\infty} \frac{\left(\int_0^{|t|} |\tau(w,x)|^p dw\right)|t|^{np-1}}{((n-1)!)^p(q(n-1)+1)^{p/q}} \times e^{-|pt|/2\xi}dt\right)dx\right) =: (*), \tag{2.23}$$

calling

$$c_1 := \frac{2^{p-2}}{\xi q^{p-1}((n-1)!)^p(q(n-1)+1)^{p/q}}, \tag{2.24}$$

and

$$\begin{aligned}
(*) &= c_1\left(\int_{-\infty}^{\infty}\left(\left(\int_{-\infty}^{\infty}\left(\int_0^{|t|} |\tau(w,x)|^p dw\right)|t|^{np-1}e^{-|pt|/2\xi}\right)dx\right)dt\right) \\
&= c_1\left(\int_{-\infty}^{\infty}\left(\left(\int_0^{|t|}\left(\int_{-\infty}^{\infty} |\Delta_w^r f^{(n)}(x)|^p dx\right)dw\right)|t|^{np-1}e^{-|pt|/2\xi}\right)dt\right) \\
&\leq c_1\left(\int_{-\infty}^{\infty}\left(\left(\int_0^{|t|} \omega_r(f^{(n)},w)_p^p dw\right)|t|^{np-1}e^{-|pt|/2\xi}\right)dt\right).
\end{aligned} \tag{2.25}$$

So far we have proved

$$I \leq c_1\left(\int_{-\infty}^{\infty}\left(\left(\int_0^{|t|}\omega_r\left(f^{(n)},w\right)_p^p dw\right)|t|^{np-1}e^{-|pt|/2\xi}\right)dt\right). \tag{2.26}$$

By [8, page 45], we have

$$\begin{aligned}\text{R.H.S. (2.26)} \leq\ & c_1\left(\omega_r\left(f^{(n)},\xi\right)_p\right)^p \\ & \times\left(\int_{-\infty}^{\infty}\left(\left(\int_0^{|t|}\left(1+\frac{w}{\xi}\right)^{rp}dw\right)\cdot|t|^{np-1}e^{-|pt|/2\xi}\right)dt\right) =: (**).\end{aligned} \tag{2.27}$$

But we see that

$$(**) = \left(\frac{\xi c_1}{rp+1}\right)\left(\omega_r\left(f^{(n)},\xi\right)_p\right)^p \mathcal{J}, \tag{2.28}$$

where

$$\mathcal{J} = 2\int_0^{\infty}\left(\left(1+\frac{t}{\xi}\right)^{rp+1}-1\right)t^{np-1}e^{-pt/2\xi}dt. \tag{2.29}$$

Here we find

$$\mathcal{J} = 2\xi^{np}\left[\int_0^{\infty}(1+u)^{rp+1}u^{np-1}e^{-(p/2)u}du-\left(\frac{2}{p}\right)^{np}\Gamma(np)\right]. \tag{2.30}$$

Thus by (2.17) and (2.30), we obtain

$$\mathcal{J} = 2\xi^{np}\tau. \tag{2.31}$$

Using (2.28) and (2.31), we get

$$\begin{aligned}(**) &= \left(\frac{\xi c_1}{rp+1}\right)\left(\omega_r\left(f^{(n)},\xi\right)_p\right)^p 2\xi^{np}\tau \\ &= \frac{2^{p/q}\tau\xi^{np}}{(rp+1)\left(q^2(n-1)+q\right)^{p/q}((n-1)!)^p}\left(\omega_r\left(f^{(n)},\xi\right)_p\right)^p.\end{aligned} \tag{2.32}$$

This means that we have established that

$$I \leq \frac{2^{p/q}\tau\xi^{np}\omega_r\left(f^{(n)},\xi\right)_p^p}{(rp+1)\left(q^2(n-1)+q\right)^{p/q}((n-1)!)^p}. \tag{2.33}$$

That finishes the proof of the theorem. □

The counterpart of Theorem 2.1 follows, case of $p = 1$.

THEOREM 2.2. *Let* $f \in L_1(\mathbb{R}) \cap C^n(\mathbb{R})$, $n \in \mathbb{N}$. *Then*

$$\|\Delta(x)\|_1 \le r! \left(\sum_{k=1}^{r+1} \left(\frac{\left(\prod_{j=1}^{k}(n-1+j)\right)}{k!(r+1-k)!} \right) \right) \xi^n \omega_r\left(f^{(n)}, \xi\right)_1. \tag{2.34}$$

Hence, as $\xi \to 0$, $\|\Delta(x)\|_1 \to 0$.

Proof. It follows that

$$\begin{aligned} |\Delta(x)| &= \frac{1}{2\xi} \left| \int_{-\infty}^{\infty} \mathcal{R}_n(0,t,x) e^{-|t|/\xi} dt \right| \\ &\le \frac{1}{2\xi} \int_{-\infty}^{\infty} \left(\int_0^{|t|} \frac{(|t|-w)^{n-1}}{(n-1)!} |\tau(w,x)| \, dw \right) e^{-|t|/\xi} dt. \end{aligned} \tag{2.35}$$

Thus

$$\begin{aligned} \|\Delta(x)\|_1 &= \int_{-\infty}^{\infty} |\Delta(x)| \, dx \\ &\le \frac{1}{2\xi} \int_{-\infty}^{\infty} \left(\int_{-\infty}^{\infty} \left(\int_0^{|t|} \frac{(|t|-w)^{n-1}}{(n-1)!} |\tau(w,x)| \, dw \right) e^{-|t|/\xi} dt \right) dx =: (*). \end{aligned} \tag{2.36}$$

But we see that

$$\int_0^{|t|} \frac{(|t|-w)^{n-1}}{(n-1)!} |\tau(w,x)| \, dw \le \frac{|t|^{n-1}}{(n-1)!} \int_0^{|t|} |\tau(w,x)| \, dw. \tag{2.37}$$

Therefore it holds that

$$\begin{aligned} (*) &\le \frac{1}{2\xi} \int_{-\infty}^{\infty} \left(\int_{-\infty}^{\infty} \left(\frac{|t|^{n-1}}{(n-1)!} \int_0^{|t|} |\tau(w,x)| \, dw \right) e^{-|t|/\xi} dt \right) dx \\ &= \frac{1}{2\xi(n-1)!} \left(\int_{-\infty}^{\infty} \left(\left(\int_0^{|t|} \left(\int_{-\infty}^{\infty} |\tau(w,x)| \, dx \right) dw \right) |t|^{n-1} e^{-|t|/\xi} \right) dt \right) \\ &\le \frac{1}{2\xi(n-1)!} \left(\int_{-\infty}^{\infty} \left(\left(\int_0^{|t|} \omega_r\left(f^{(n)}, w\right)_1 dw \right) |t|^{n-1} e^{-|t|/\xi} \right) dt \right). \end{aligned} \tag{2.38}$$

That is we get

$$\|\Delta(x)\|_1 \le \frac{1}{2\xi(n-1)!} \left(\int_{-\infty}^{\infty} \left(\left(\int_0^{|t|} \omega_r\left(f^{(n)}, w\right)_1 dw \right) |t|^{n-1} e^{-|t|/\xi} \right) dt \right). \tag{2.39}$$

Consequently, we have

$$\begin{aligned}\|\Delta(x)\|_1 &\le \frac{1}{2\xi(n-1)!}\omega_r(f^{(n)},\xi)_1\left(\int_{-\infty}^{\infty}\left(\left(\int_0^{|t|}\left(1+\frac{w}{\xi}\right)^r dw\right)|t|^{n-1}e^{-|t|/\xi}\right)dt\right)\\ &= \frac{\omega_r(f^{(n)},\xi)_1\xi^n}{(n-1)!(r+1)}\left(\int_0^{\infty}((1+t)^{r+1}-1)t^{n-1}e^{-t}dt\right).\end{aligned} \tag{2.40}$$

We have gotten so far

$$\|\Delta(x)\|_1 \le \frac{\omega_r(f^{(n)},\xi)_1\xi^n\cdot\lambda}{(n-1)!(r+1)}, \tag{2.41}$$

where

$$\lambda := \int_0^{\infty}((1+t)^{r+1}-1)t^{n-1}e^{-t}dt. \tag{2.42}$$

One easily finds that

$$\lambda = \sum_{k=0}^{r+1}\binom{r+1}{k}(n+k-1)!-(n-1)!. \tag{2.43}$$

But then one observes that

$$\frac{\lambda}{(n-1)!} = \sum_{k=1}^{r+1}\binom{r+1}{k}\frac{(n+k-1)!}{(n-1)!}. \tag{2.44}$$

We have proved (2.34). □

The case $n=0$ is met next.

Proposition 2.3. *Let $p,q>1$ such that $1/p+1/q=1$ and the rest as above. Then*

$$\|P_{r,\xi}(f)-f\|_p \le \left(\frac{2}{q}\right)^{1/q}\theta^{1/p}\omega_r(f,\xi)_p, \tag{2.45}$$

where

$$\theta := \int_0^{\infty}(1+x)^{rp}e^{-(p/2)x}dx < \infty. \tag{2.46}$$

Hence, as $\xi \to 0$, $P_{r\xi} \to$ unit operator I in the L_p norm, $p>1$.

Proof. With some work, we notice that, see also [5],

$$P_{r,\xi}(f;x)-f(x)=\frac{1}{2\xi}\left(\int_{-\infty}^{\infty}((\Delta_t^r f)(x))e^{-|t|/\xi}dt\right). \tag{2.47}$$

And then

$$|P_{r,\xi}(f;x)-f(x)|\leq\frac{1}{2\xi}\int_{-\infty}^{\infty}|\Delta_t^r f(x)|e^{-|t|/\xi}dt. \tag{2.48}$$

We next estimate

$$\begin{aligned}
&\int_{-\infty}^{\infty}|P_{r,\xi}(f;x)-f(x)|^p dx\\
&\quad\leq\frac{1}{2^p\xi^p}\left(\int_{-\infty}^{\infty}\left(\int_{-\infty}^{\infty}|\Delta_t^r f(x)|^p e^{-|pt|/2\xi}dt\right)\left(\int_{-\infty}^{\infty}e^{-|qt|/2\xi}dt\right)^{p/q}dx\right)\\
&\quad=\frac{1}{2^p\xi^p}\left(\frac{4\xi}{q}\right)^{p/q}\left(\int_{-\infty}^{\infty}\left(\int_{-\infty}^{\infty}|\Delta_t^r f(x)|^p dx\right)e^{-|pt|/2\xi}dt\right)\\
&\quad\leq\frac{1}{2^p\xi^p}\left(\frac{4\xi}{q}\right)^{p/q}\left(\int_{-\infty}^{\infty}\omega_r(f,|t|)_p^p e^{-|pt|/2\xi}dt\right)\\
&\quad\leq\frac{1}{2^{p-1}\xi^p}\left(\frac{4\xi}{q}\right)^{p/q}\omega_r(f,\xi)_p^p\left(\int_0^{\infty}\left(1+\frac{t}{\xi}\right)^{rp}e^{-pt/2\xi}dt\right)\\
&\quad=\left(\frac{2}{q}\right)^{p/q}\omega_r(f,\xi)_p^p\left(\int_0^{\infty}(1+x)^{rp}e^{-(p/2)x}dx\right).
\end{aligned} \tag{2.49}$$

Clearly we have established (2.45). □

We also give the following.

PROPOSITION 2.4. *It holds that*

$$\|P_{r,\xi}f-f\|_1\leq\lfloor er!\rfloor\omega_r(f,\xi)_1. \tag{2.50}$$

Hence, as $\xi\to 0$, $P_{r,\xi}\to I$ in the L_1 norm.

Proof. We do have again

$$|P_{r,\xi}(f;x)-f(x)|\leq\frac{1}{2\xi}\int_{-\infty}^{\infty}|\Delta_t^r f(x)|e^{-|t|/\xi}dt. \tag{2.51}$$

We estimate

$$\begin{aligned}\int_{-\infty}^{\infty} |P_{r,\xi}(f;x) - f(x)|\, dx &\le \frac{1}{2\xi}\int_{-\infty}^{\infty}\left(\int_{-\infty}^{\infty} |\Delta_t^r f(x)|\, e^{-|t|/\xi} dt\right) dx \\ &\le \frac{1}{2\xi}\int_{-\infty}^{\infty} \omega_r(f,|t|)_1 e^{-|t|/\xi} dt \le \frac{\omega_r(f,\xi)_1}{\xi}\int_0^{\infty}\left(1+\frac{t}{\xi}\right)^r e^{-t/\xi} dt \\ &= \omega_r(f,\xi)_1 \int_0^{\infty} (1+x)^r e^{-x} dx = \omega_r(f,\xi)_1 \left(\sum_{k=0}^{r}\binom{r}{k} k!\right) \\ &= \omega_r(f,\xi)_1 \left(r! \sum_{k=0}^{r} \frac{1}{k!}\right) = \omega_r(f,\xi)_1 \lfloor er! \rfloor.\end{aligned} \tag{2.52}$$

We have proved (2.50). □

Next we consider $f \in C^n(\mathbb{R}) \cap L_p(\mathbb{R})$, $n = 0$ or $n \ge 2$ even, $1 \le p < \infty$, and the similar *smooth singular operator of symmetric convolution type*

$$P_\xi(f;x) = \frac{1}{2\xi}\int_{-\infty}^{\infty} f(x+y) e^{-|y|/\xi} dy \quad \forall x \in \mathbb{R},\ \xi > 0. \tag{2.53}$$

That is

$$P_\xi(f;x) = \frac{1}{2\xi}\int_0^{\infty} (f(x+y) + f(x-y)) e^{-y/\xi} dy \tag{2.53*}$$

for all $x \in \mathbb{R}$, $\xi > 0$. Notice that $P_{1,\xi} = P_\xi$. Let the central second-order difference

$$(\widetilde{\Delta}_y^2 f)(x) := f(x+y) + f(x-y) - 2f(x). \tag{2.54}$$

Notice that $(\widetilde{\Delta}_{-y}^2 f)(x) = (\widetilde{\Delta}_y^2 f)(x)$. When $n \ge 2$ even using Taylor's formula with Cauchy remainder we eventually find

$$(\widetilde{\Delta}_y^2 f)(x) = 2\sum_{\rho=1}^{n/2} \frac{f^{(2\rho)}(x)}{(2\rho)!} y^{2\rho} + \mathcal{R}_1(x), \tag{2.55}$$

where

$$\mathcal{R}_1(x) := \int_0^y (\widetilde{\Delta}_t^2 f^{(n)})(x) \frac{(y-t)^{n-1}}{(n-1)!} dt. \tag{2.56}$$

Notice that

$$P_\xi(f;x) - f(x) = \frac{1}{2\xi}\int_0^{\infty} (\widetilde{\Delta}_y^2 f(x)) e^{-y/\xi} dy. \tag{2.57}$$

Furthermore by (2.4), (2.55), and (2.57) we easily see that

$$\begin{aligned} K(x) :=& P_\xi(f;x) - f(x) - \sum_{\rho=1}^{n/2} f^{(2\rho)}(x)\xi^{2\rho} \\ =& \frac{1}{2\xi}\int_0^\infty \left(\int_0^y (\widetilde{\Delta}_t^2 f^{(n)})(x)\frac{(y-t)^{n-1}}{(n-1)!}dt\right)e^{-y/\xi}dy. \end{aligned} \tag{2.58}$$

Therefore we have

$$|K(x)| \le \frac{1}{2\xi}\int_0^\infty \left(\int_0^y |\widetilde{\Delta}_t^2 f^{(n)}(x)| \frac{(y-t)^{n-1}}{(n-1)!}dt\right)e^{-y/\xi}dy. \tag{2.59}$$

Here we estimate in L_p norm, $p \ge 1$, the error function $K(x)$. Notice that we have $\omega_2(f^{(n)}, h)_p < \infty$, $h > 0$, $n = 0$, or $n \ge 2$ even. Operators P_ξ are positive operators.

The related main L_p result here comes next.

THEOREM 2.5. *Let $p,q > 1$ such that $1/p + 1/q = 1$, $n \ge 2$ even, and the rest as above. Then*

$$\|K(x)\|_p \le \left(\frac{\widetilde{\tau}^{1/p}}{(4p+2)^{1/p}(q^2(n-1)+q)^{1/q}(n-1)!}\right)\xi^n\omega_2(f^{(n)},\xi)_p, \tag{2.60}$$

where

$$\widetilde{\tau} := \left(\int_0^\infty (1+x)^{2p+1}x^{np-1}e^{-(p/2)x}dx - \left(\frac{2}{p}\right)^{np}\Gamma(np)\right) < \infty. \tag{2.61}$$

Hence, as $\xi \to 0$, $\|K(x)\|_p \to 0$.

Proof. We observe that

$$|K(x)|^p \le \frac{1}{2^p\xi^p}\left(\int_0^\infty \left(\int_0^y |\widetilde{\Delta}_t^2 f^{(n)}(x)| \frac{(y-t)^{n-1}}{(n-1)!}dt\right)e^{-y/\xi}dy\right)^p. \tag{2.62}$$

Call

$$\widetilde{\gamma}(y,x) := \int_0^y |\widetilde{\Delta}_t^2 f^{(n)}(x)| \frac{(y-t)^{n-1}}{(n-1)!}dt \ge 0, \tag{2.63}$$

then we have

$$|K(x)|^p \le \frac{1}{2^p\xi^p}\left(\int_0^\infty \widetilde{\gamma}(y,x)e^{-y/\xi}dy\right)^p. \tag{2.64}$$

And hence

$$\begin{aligned}\Lambda &:= \int_{-\infty}^{\infty} |K(x)|^p dx \leq \frac{1}{2^p\xi^p}\int_{-\infty}^{\infty}\left(\int_0^{\infty}\widetilde{\gamma}(y,x)e^{-y/\xi}dy\right)^p dx \quad \text{(by Hölder's inequality)}\\ &\leq \frac{1}{2^p\xi^p}\left(\int_{-\infty}^{\infty}\left(\int_0^{\infty}(\widetilde{\gamma}(y,x))^p e^{-py/2\xi}dy\right)\left(\int_0^{\infty}e^{-qy/2\xi}dy\right)^{p/q}dx\right)\\ &= \frac{1}{2\xi q^{p/q}}\left(\int_{-\infty}^{\infty}\left(\int_0^{\infty}(\widetilde{\gamma}(y,x))^p e^{-py/2\xi}dy\right)dx\right) =: (*).\end{aligned} \tag{2.65}$$

By applying again Hölder's inequality, we see that

$$\widetilde{\gamma}(y,x) \leq \frac{\left(\int_0^y |\widetilde{\Delta}_t^2 f^{(n)}(x)|^p dt\right)^{1/p}}{(n-1)!}\frac{y^{(n-1+1/q)}}{(q(n-1)+1)^{1/q}}. \tag{2.66}$$

Therefore it holds that

$$\begin{aligned}(*) \leq \frac{1}{(q(n-1)+1)^{p/q}((n-1)!)^p 2\xi q^{p/q}}&\left(\int_0^{\infty}\left(\left(\int_{-\infty}^{\infty}\left(\int_0^y |\widetilde{\Delta}_t^2 f^{(n)}(x)|^p dt\right)\right.\right.\right.\\ &\left.\left.\left.\cdot\, y^{pn-1}e^{-py/2\xi}\right)dx\right)dy\right) =: (**).\end{aligned} \tag{2.67}$$

We call

$$c_2 := \frac{1}{2\xi q^{p/q}((n-1)!)^p(q(n-1)+1)^{p/q}}. \tag{2.68}$$

And hence

$$\begin{aligned}(**) &= c_2\left(\int_0^{\infty}\left(\left(\int_{-\infty}^{\infty}\left(\int_0^y |\widetilde{\Delta}_t^2 f^{(n)}(x)|^p dt\right)dx\right)y^{pn-1}e^{-py/2\xi}\right)dy\right)\\ &= c_2\left(\int_0^{\infty}\left(\left(\int_0^y\left(\int_{-\infty}^{\infty} |\widetilde{\Delta}_t^2 f^{(n)}(x)|^p dx\right)dt\right)y^{pn-1}e^{-py/2\xi}\right)dy\right)\\ &= c_2\left(\int_0^{\infty}\left(\left(\int_0^y\left(\int_{-\infty}^{\infty} |\Delta_t^2 f^{(n)}(x-t)|^p dx\right)dt\right)y^{pn-1}e^{-py/2\xi}\right)dy\right)\\ &\leq c_2\left(\int_0^{\infty}\left(\left(\int_0^y \omega_2(f^{(n)},t)_p^p dt\right)y^{pn-1}e^{-py/2\xi}\right)dy\right)\\ &\leq c_2\omega_2(f^{(n)},\xi)_p^p\left(\int_0^{\infty}\left(\left(\int_0^y\left(1+\frac{t}{\xi}\right)^{2p}dt\right)y^{pn-1}e^{-py/2\xi}\right)dy\right).\end{aligned} \tag{2.69}$$

That is so far we proved that

$$\Lambda \leq c_2\omega_2(f^{(n)},\xi)_p^p\left(\int_0^\infty\left(\left(\int_0^y\left(1+\frac{t}{\xi}\right)^{2p}dt\right)y^{pn-1}e^{-py/2\xi}\right)dy\right). \tag{2.70}$$

But

$$\text{R.H.S. (2.70)} = \frac{c_2\xi}{(2p+1)}\omega_2(f^{(n)},\xi)_p^p\left(\int_0^\infty\left(\left(1+\frac{y}{\xi}\right)^{2p+1}-1\right)y^{pn-1}e^{-py/2\xi}dy\right). \tag{2.71}$$

Call

$$M := \int_0^\infty\left(\left(1+\frac{y}{\xi}\right)^{2p+1}-1\right)y^{pn-1}e^{-py/2\xi}dy. \tag{2.72}$$

Thus

$$M = \xi^{pn}\left(\int_0^\infty(1+x)^{2p+1}x^{pn-1}e^{-(p/2)x}dx - \left(\frac{2}{p}\right)^{np}\Gamma(np)\right). \tag{2.73}$$

That is we get

$$M = \xi^{pn}\widetilde{\tau}. \tag{2.74}$$

Therefore it holds that

$$\Lambda \leq \frac{\widetilde{\tau}\xi^{pn}\omega_2(f^{(n)},\xi)_p^p}{2(2p+1)((n-1)!)^p(q^2(n-1)+q)^{p/q}}. \tag{2.75}$$

We have established (2.60). □

The counterpart of Theorem 2.5 follows, $p = 1$ case.

Theorem 2.6. *Let $f \in L_1(\mathbb{R}) \cap C^n(\mathbb{R})$, $n \geq 2$ even. Then*

$$\|K(x)\|_1 \leq n\left(\frac{(n+1)(n+2)}{6}+\frac{(n+1)}{2}+\frac{1}{2}\right)\xi^n\omega_2(f^{(n)},\xi)_1. \tag{2.76}$$

Hence, as $\xi \to 0$, $\|K(x)\|_1 \to 0$.

Proof. Notice that

$$\widetilde{\Delta}_t^2 f^{(n)}(x) = \Delta_t^2 f^{(n)}(x-t), \tag{2.77}$$

all $x, t \in \mathbb{R}$. Also it holds that

$$\int_{-\infty}^{\infty}|\Delta_t^2 f^{(n)}(x-t)|\,dx = \int_{-\infty}^{\infty}|\Delta_t^2 f^{(n)}(w)|\,dw \leq \omega_2(f^{(n)},t)_1, \quad \text{all } t \in \mathbb{R}_+. \tag{2.78}$$

Here we obtain

$$
\begin{aligned}
\|K(x)\|_1 &= \int_{-\infty}^{\infty} |K(x)|dx \overset{(2.59)}{\leq} \frac{1}{2\xi}\int_{-\infty}^{\infty}\left(\int_0^{\infty}\left(\int_0^y |\widetilde{\Delta}_t^2 f^{(n)}(x)| \frac{(y-t)^{n-1}}{(n-1)!}dt\right)e^{-y/\xi}dy\right)dx \\
&\leq \frac{1}{2\xi}\int_{-\infty}^{\infty}\left(\int_0^{\infty}\left(\frac{y^{n-1}}{(n-1)!}\left(\int_0^y |\widetilde{\Delta}_t^2 f^{(n)}(x)|dt\right)e^{-y/\xi}\right)dy\right)dx \\
&= \frac{1}{2\xi}\left(\int_0^{\infty}\left(\left(\int_{-\infty}^{\infty}\left(\int_0^y |\widetilde{\Delta}_t^2 f^{(n)}(x)|dt\right)dx\right)\frac{y^{n-1}}{(n-1)!}e^{-y/\xi}\right)dy\right) \\
&\overset{(2.77)}{=} \frac{1}{2\xi}\left(\int_0^{\infty}\left(\left(\int_0^y\left(\int_{-\infty}^{\infty} |\Delta_t^2 f^{(n)}(x-t)|dx\right)dt\right)\frac{y^{n-1}}{(n-1)!}e^{-y/\xi}\right)dy\right) \\
&\overset{(2.78)}{\leq} \frac{1}{2\xi}\left(\int_0^{\infty}\left(\left(\int_0^y \omega_2(f^{(n)},t)_1 dt\right)\frac{y^{n-1}}{(n-1)!}e^{-y/\xi}\right)dy\right) \\
&\leq \frac{\omega_2(f^{(n)},\xi)_1}{2\xi}\left(\int_0^{\infty}\left(\left(\int_0^y\left(1+\frac{t}{\xi}\right)^2 dt\right)\frac{y^{n-1}}{(n-1)!}e^{-y/\xi}\right)dy\right) \\
&= \frac{\xi^n\omega_2(f^{(n)},\xi)_1}{6(n-1)!}\left(\int_0^{\infty}((1+x)^3-1)x^{n-1}e^{-x}dx\right) \\
&= n\left(\frac{(n+1)(n+2)}{6}+\frac{(n+1)}{2}+\frac{1}{2}\right)\xi^n\omega_2(f^{(n)},\xi)_1.
\end{aligned}
\tag{2.79}
$$

We have proved (2.76). □

The related case here of $n = 0$ comes next.

PROPOSITION 2.7. *Let $p, q > 1$ such that $1/p + 1/q = 1$ and the rest as above. Then*

$$
\|P_\xi(f) - f\|_p \leq \frac{\rho^{1/p}}{2^{1/p}q^{1/q}}\omega_2(f,\xi)_p, \tag{2.80}
$$

where

$$
\rho := \int_0^{\infty}(1+x)^{2p}e^{-(p/2)x}dx < \infty. \tag{2.81}
$$

Hence, as $\xi \to 0$, $P_\xi \to I$ in the L_p norm, $p > 1$.

Proof. From (2.57), we get

$$
|P_\xi(f;x) - f(x)|^p \leq \frac{1}{2^p\xi^p}\left(\int_0^{\infty}|\widetilde{\Delta}_y^2 f(x)|e^{-y/\xi}dy\right)^p. \tag{2.82}
$$

We then estimate

$$
\begin{aligned}
&\int_{-\infty}^{\infty} |P_\xi(f;x) - f(x)|^p dx \\
&\le \frac{1}{2^p \xi^p}\left(\int_{-\infty}^{\infty}\left(\int_0^\infty |\widetilde{\Delta}_y^2 f(x)|^p e^{-py/2\xi} dy\right)\left(\int_0^\infty e^{-qy/2\xi} dy\right)^{p/q} dx\right) \\
&= \frac{1}{2\xi q^{p/q}}\left(\int_0^\infty\left(\int_{-\infty}^{\infty} |\Delta_y^2 f(x-y)|^p dx\right) e^{-py/2\xi} dy\right) \\
&= \frac{1}{2\xi q^{p/q}}\left(\int_0^\infty\left(\int_{-\infty}^{\infty} |\Delta_y^2 f(x)|^p dx\right) e^{-py/2\xi} dy\right) \\
&\le \frac{1}{2\xi q^{p/q}}\left(\int_0^\infty \omega_2(f,y)_p^p e^{-py/2\xi} dy\right) \\
&\le \frac{\omega_2(f,\xi)_p^p}{2q^{p/q}}\left(\int_0^\infty (1+x)^{2p} e^{-(p/2)x} dx\right).
\end{aligned}
\tag{2.83}
$$

The proof of (2.80) is now evident. □

Also we give the following.

PROPOSITION 2.8. *It holds that*

$$
\|P_\xi f - f\|_1 \le \frac{5}{2}\omega_2(f,\xi)_1. \tag{2.84}
$$

Hence, as $\xi \to 0$, $P_\xi \to I$ in the L_1 norm.

Proof. From (2.57), we have

$$
|P_\xi(f;x) - f(x)| \le \frac{1}{2\xi}\int_0^\infty |\widetilde{\Delta}_y^2 f(x)| e^{-y/\xi} dy. \tag{2.85}
$$

Hence we get

$$
\begin{aligned}
\int_{-\infty}^{\infty} |P_\xi(f;x) - f(x)| dx &\le \frac{1}{2\xi}\int_0^\infty\left(\int_{-\infty}^{\infty} |\Delta_y^2 f(x-y)| dx\right) e^{-y/\xi} dy \\
&= \frac{1}{2\xi}\int_0^\infty\left(\int_{-\infty}^{\infty} |\Delta_y^2 f(x)| dx\right) e^{-y/\xi} dy \\
&\le \frac{1}{2\xi}\int_0^\infty \omega_2(f,y)_1 e^{-y/\xi} dy \\
&\le \frac{\omega_2(f,\xi)_1}{2}\int_0^\infty (1+x)^2 e^{-x} dx = \frac{5}{2}\omega_2(f,\xi)_1.
\end{aligned}
\tag{2.86}
$$

We have established (2.84). □

References

[1] G. A. Anastassiou, *Rate of convergence of nonpositive generalized convolution type operators*, Journal of Mathematical Analysis and Applications **142** (1989), no. 2, 441–451.
[2] ———, *Sharp inequalities for convolution-type operators*, Journal of Approximation Theory **58** (1989), no. 3, 259–266.
[3] ———, *Moments in Probability and Approximation Theory*, Pitman Research Notes in Mathematics Series, vol. 287, Longman Scientific & Technical, Harlow, 1993.
[4] ———, *Quantitative Approximations*, Chapman & Hall/CRC, Florida, 2001.
[5] ———, *Basic convergence with rates of smooth Picard singular integral operators*, Journal of Computational Analysis and Applications **8** (2006), no. 4, 313–334.
[6] G. A. Anastassiou and S. G. Gal, *Convergence of generalized singular integrals to the unit, multivariate case*, Applied Mathematics Reviews, Vol. 1, World Scientific, New Jersey, 2000, pp. 1–8.
[7] ———, *Convergence of generalized singular integrals to the unit, univariate case*, Mathematical Inequalities & Applications **3** (2000), no. 4, 511–518.
[8] R. A. DeVore and G. G. Lorentz, *Constructive Approximation*, Fundamental Principles of Mathematical Sciences, vol. 303, Springer, Berlin, 1993.
[9] S. G. Gal, *Remark on the degree of approximation of continuous functions by singular integrals*, Mathematische Nachrichten **164** (1993), 197–199.
[10] ———, *Degree of approximation of continuous functions by some singular integrals*, Revue d'Analyse Numérique et de Théorie de l'Approximation **27** (1998), no. 2, 251–261.
[11] R. N. Mohapatra and R. S. Rodriguez, *On the rate of convergence of singular integrals for Hölder continuous functions*, Mathematische Nachrichten **149** (1990), 117–124.

George A. Anastassiou: Department of Mathematical Sciences, The University of Memphis, Memphis, TN 38152, USA
E-mail address: ganastss@memphis.edu

BOUNDARY ESTIMATES FOR BLOW-UP SOLUTIONS OF ELLIPTIC EQUATIONS WITH EXPONENTIAL GROWTH

C. ANEDDA, A. BUTTU, AND G. PORRU

We investigate blow-up solutions of the equation $\Delta u = e^u + g(u)$ in a bounded smooth domain Ω. If $g(t)$ satisfies a suitable growth condition (compared with the growth of e^t) as t goes to infinity, we find second-order asymptotic estimates of the solution $u(x)$ in terms of the distance of x from the boundary $\partial\Omega$.

1. Introduction

Let $\Omega \subset R^N$ be a bounded smooth domain. It is known since 1916 [10] that the problem

$$\Delta u = e^u \quad \text{in } \Omega, \qquad u(x) \longrightarrow \infty \quad \text{as } x \longrightarrow \partial\Omega, \tag{1.1}$$

has a classical solution called a boundary blow-up (explosive, large) solution. Moreover, if $\delta = \delta(x)$ denotes the distance from x to $\partial\Omega$, we have [10]

$$u(x) - \log\frac{2}{\delta^2(x)} \longrightarrow 0 \quad \text{as } x \longrightarrow \partial\Omega. \tag{1.2}$$

Recently, Bandle [3] has improved the previous estimate, finding the expansion

$$u(x) = \log\frac{2}{\delta^2(x)} + (N-1)K(\overline{x})\delta(x) + o(\delta(x)), \tag{1.3}$$

where $K(\overline{x})$ denotes the mean curvature of $\partial\Omega$ at the point $\overline{x}$ nearest to x, and $o(\delta)$ has the usual meaning. Boundary estimates for more general nonlinearities have been discussed in several papers, see [4–6, 8, 12, 14–17].

In Section 2 of the present paper we investigate the problem

$$\Delta u = e^u + g(u) \quad \text{in } \Omega, \qquad u(x) \longrightarrow \infty \quad \text{as } x \longrightarrow \partial\Omega, \tag{1.4}$$

Hindawi Publishing Corporation
Proceedings of the Conference on Differential & Difference Equations and Applications, pp. 47–55

where $g(t)$ is a smooth function which satisfies $|g(t)| \leq Ae^{\theta t}$. Here A and θ are constants with $A > 0$ and $0 < \theta < 1$.

If $0 < \theta < 1/2$, we prove the asymptotic boundary estimate

$$u(x) = \log \frac{2}{\delta^2(x)} + (N-1)K(x)\delta(x) + O(1)(\delta(x))^{2(1-\theta)}, \tag{1.5}$$

where $K(x)$ is the mean curvature of the surface $\{x \in \Omega : \delta(x) = \text{constant}\}$ and $O(1)$ is a bounded quantity. Observe that $1 < 2(1-\theta) < 2$.

If $\theta \geq 1/2$, then we find the estimate

$$u(x) = \log \frac{2}{\delta^2(x)} + O(1)(\delta(x))^{2(1-\theta)}. \tag{1.6}$$

Now we have $0 < 2(1-\theta) \leq 1$.

The effect of the geometry of the domain in the boundary behaviour of blow-up solutions for special elliptic equations has been observed in various papers, see for example, [1, 7, 9, 11].

2. Main results

Let $g(t)$ be a smooth function such that

$$0 < e^t + g(t), \quad 0 < e^t + g'(t), \quad \forall t \in R. \tag{2.1}$$

In addition to (2.1) we assume the condition

$$\exists \theta \in (0,1) : g(t) = O(1)e^{\theta t}, \tag{2.2}$$

where $O(1)$ is a bounded quantity, holds. Observe that, since $0 < \theta$, we have $\int_{-\infty}^{t}(e^\tau + g(\tau))d\tau < \infty$. Define $\Phi = \Phi(s)$ such that

$$\int_{\Phi(s)}^{\infty} \frac{dt}{\sqrt{2F(t)}} = s, \quad F(t) = \int_{-\infty}^{t} (e^\tau + g(\tau))d\tau. \tag{2.3}$$

We have $\Phi(s) \to \infty$ as $s \to 0$.

LEMMA 2.1. *Let $g(t)$ satisfy (2.1) and (2.2). If $u(x)$ is a boundary blow-up solution of the equation $\Delta u = e^u + g(u)$ in Ω, then*

$$u(x) = \log \frac{2}{\delta^2} + O(1)\delta^{2(1-\theta)} + O(1)\delta \log \frac{2}{\delta^2}, \tag{2.4}$$

where $\delta = \delta(x)$ is the distance from x to $\partial\Omega$, and $O(1)$ denotes a bounded quantity.

Proof. By (2.3) we find

$$\Phi'(s) = -(2F(\Phi))^{1/2}. \tag{2.5}$$

Using condition (2.2) we obtain

$$F(t) = \int_{-\infty}^{t} e^{\tau}\,d\tau + \int_{-\infty}^{t} g(\tau)\,d\tau = e^{t} + O(1)e^{\theta t}. \tag{2.6}$$

Hence,

$$\Phi'(s) = -\sqrt{2}\left(e^{\Phi} + O(1)e^{\theta\Phi}\right)^{1/2}. \tag{2.7}$$

Putting $\rho(s) = e^{-\Phi/2}$, we have

$$\rho'(s) = -e^{-\Phi/2}\frac{\Phi'}{2}. \tag{2.8}$$

Insertion of (2.7) into the last equation yields

$$\rho'(s) = \frac{1}{\sqrt{2}}\left(1 + O(1)e^{(\theta-1)\Phi}\right)^{1/2}. \tag{2.9}$$

It follows that

$$\rho'(0) = \frac{1}{\sqrt{2}}, \qquad \rho(s) = O(1)s, \qquad e^{(\theta-1)\Phi(s)} = O(1)s^{2(1-\theta)}. \tag{2.10}$$

Hence, by (2.9) we find

$$\rho'(s) = \frac{1}{\sqrt{2}}\left(1 + O(1)s^{2(1-\theta)}\right). \tag{2.11}$$

Integration over $(0, s)$ yields

$$\rho(s) = \frac{s}{\sqrt{2}}\left(1 + O(1)s^{2(1-\theta)}\right). \tag{2.12}$$

Recalling that $\rho(s) = e^{-\Phi/2}$, we have

$$e^{\Phi} = \rho^{-2} = \frac{2}{s^2}\left(1 + O(1)s^{2(1-\theta)}\right), \tag{2.13}$$

$$\Phi(s) = \log\frac{2}{s^2} + O(1)s^{2(1-\theta)}. \tag{2.14}$$

By (2.14) and (2.7) we also find

$$\Phi'(s) = s^{-1}\left[-2 + O(1)s^{2(1-\theta)}\right]. \tag{2.15}$$

Under our assumptions, the function $e^t + g(t)$ is increasing for all t and the function $t^{-2}F(t)$, with $F(t) = \int_{-\infty}^{t}(e^\tau + g(\tau))d\tau$, is increasing for large t. Moreover, using (2.15) we find

$$\limsup_{\vartheta\to 1,\delta\to 0} \frac{\Phi'(\vartheta\delta)}{\Phi'(\delta)} < \infty. \tag{2.16}$$

Hence, we can use [7, Theorem 4(i)] to find

$$u(x) = \Phi(\delta) + O(1)\delta\Phi(\delta). \tag{2.17}$$

Insertion of (2.14) with $s = \delta$ into the last equation proves the assertion of the lemma. □

Recall that $\delta = \delta(x)$ denotes the distance of x from $\partial\Omega$. If Ω is smooth, then also $\delta(x)$ is smooth for x near to $\partial\Omega$. We have [13]

$$\sum_{i=1}^{N} \delta_{x_i}\delta_{x_i} = 1, \qquad \sum_{i=1}^{N} \delta_{x_ix_i} = -(N-1)K = -H, \tag{2.18}$$

where K is the mean curvature of the surface $\{x \in \Omega : \delta(x) = \text{constant}\}$.

Theorem 2.2. *Let Ω be a bounded smooth domain in R^N, $N \geq 2$, and let $g(t)$ be a smooth function which satisfies (2.1) and (2.2). If $u(x)$ is a boundary blow-up solution of $\Delta u = e^u + g(u)$ in Ω, then*

$$u(x) = \log\frac{2}{\delta^2} + H\delta + O(1)\delta^{2(1-\theta)}, \tag{2.19}$$

where H is defined in (2.18) and $O(1)$ is a bounded quantity.

Proof. We look for a supersolution of the form

$$w(x) = \log\frac{2}{\delta^2} + H\delta + \alpha\delta^\sigma, \tag{2.20}$$

where $\sigma = 2(1-\theta)$ and α is a positive constant to be determined. We have

$$w_{x_i} = -\frac{2}{\delta}\delta_{x_i} + H_{x_i}\delta + H\delta_{x_i} + \alpha\sigma\delta^{\sigma-1}\delta_{x_i}. \tag{2.21}$$

Recalling (2.18), we find

$$\Delta w = \frac{2}{\delta^2} + \frac{2}{\delta}H + 2\nabla H\cdot\nabla\delta + \Delta H\delta - H^2 + \alpha\sigma(\sigma-1)\delta^{\sigma-2} - \alpha\sigma H\delta^{\sigma-1}. \tag{2.22}$$

Denoting by M_i, $i = 1,2,\ldots$, nonnegative constants independent of α, we find

$$\Delta w < \frac{2}{\delta^2}\left[1 + H\delta + M_1\delta^2 + \alpha\delta^\sigma\left(\frac{\sigma(\sigma-1)}{2} + M_2\delta\right)\right]. \tag{2.23}$$

On the other side, using Taylor's expansion, we have

$$e^w = \frac{2}{\delta^2}e^{H\delta+\alpha\delta^\sigma} > \frac{2}{\delta^2}(1 + H\delta + \alpha\delta^\sigma). \tag{2.24}$$

We take α and δ_0 so that, for $\{x \in \Omega : \delta(x) < \delta_0\}$,

$$H\delta + \alpha\delta^{\sigma} < 1. \tag{2.25}$$

Then, by condition (2.2) we find $g(w) = O(1)e^{\theta w} \geq -M_3(2/\delta^2)^{\theta}$. Note that in case of $g(t) \geq 0$ we can take $M_3 = 0$. Using this estimate and inequality (2.24), we find

$$e^w + g(w) > \frac{2}{\delta^2}\left[1 + H\delta + \alpha\delta^{\sigma} - M_3\left(\frac{2}{\delta^2}\right)^{\theta-1}\right]. \tag{2.26}$$

By (2.23) and (2.26) we find that

$$\Delta w < e^w + g(w) \tag{2.27}$$

when

$$1 + H\delta + M_1\delta^2 + \alpha\delta^{\sigma}\left(\frac{\sigma(\sigma-1)}{2} + M_2\delta\right) < 1 + H\delta + \alpha\delta^{\sigma} - M_3\left(\frac{2}{\delta^2}\right)^{\theta-1}. \tag{2.28}$$

Rearranging, we get

$$M_1\delta^2 + M_3\left(\frac{\delta^2}{2}\right)^{1-\theta} < \alpha\delta^{\sigma}\left[\frac{(1+\sigma)(2-\sigma)}{2} - M_2\delta\right]. \tag{2.29}$$

Since $\sigma = 2(1-\theta)$, (2.29) yields

$$M_1\delta^{2\theta} + M_3 2^{\theta-1} < \alpha[(1 + 2(1-\theta))\theta - M_2\delta]. \tag{2.30}$$

Since $0 < \theta < 1$, we can take δ_0 small and α large so that (2.30) and (2.25) hold for $\delta(x) < \delta_0$.

By Lemma 2.1 we have

$$u(x) - w(x) = O(1)\delta^{2(1-\theta)} + O(1)\delta\log\frac{2}{\delta^2} - H\delta - \alpha\delta^{2(1-\theta)}. \tag{2.31}$$

It follows that, for α fixed, $u(x) - w(x) \to 0$ as $x \to \partial\Omega$. We show now that we can choose α and δ_0 so that $u(x) < w(x)$ for $\{x \in \Omega : \delta(x) = \delta_0\}$. Let $\alpha\delta_0^{2(1-\theta)} = q$, with α and δ_0 as above. Decrease δ_0 and increase α so that $\alpha\delta_0^{2(1-\theta)} = q$ and

$$O(1)\delta^{2(1-\theta)} + O(1)\delta\log\frac{2}{\delta^2} - H\delta - q < 0 \tag{2.32}$$

for $\{x \in \Omega : \delta(x) = \delta_0\}$. By (2.27) and the comparison principle [13], it follows that $u(x) \leq w(x)$ on $\{x \in \Omega : \delta(x) < \delta_0\}$.

Now we look for a subsolution of the kind

$$v(x) = \log\frac{2}{\delta^2} + H\delta - \alpha\delta^{\sigma}, \tag{2.33}$$

where, as in the previous case, $\sigma = 2(1-\theta)$ and α is a positive constant to be determined. We find

$$\Delta v = \frac{2}{\delta^2} + \frac{2}{\delta}H + 2\nabla H \cdot \nabla\delta + \Delta H\delta - H^2 - \alpha\sigma(\sigma-1)\delta^{\sigma-2} + \alpha\sigma H\delta^{\sigma-1}, \tag{2.34}$$

$$\Delta v > \frac{2}{\delta^2}\left[1 + H\delta - M_4\delta^2 - \alpha\delta^\sigma\left(\frac{\sigma(\sigma-1)}{2} + M_5\delta\right)\right]. \tag{2.35}$$

We take α and δ_0 so that, for $\{x \in \Omega : \delta(x) < \delta_0\}$,

$$H\delta - \alpha\delta^\sigma < 1. \tag{2.36}$$

Then, using Taylor's expansion, we have

$$e^v = \frac{2}{\delta^2}e^{H\delta - \alpha\delta^\sigma} < \frac{2}{\delta^2}\left(1 + H\delta - \alpha\delta^\sigma + M_6\left(\delta^2 + (\alpha\delta^\sigma)^2\right)\right). \tag{2.37}$$

Using condition (2.2) and (2.36) we find $g(v) = O(1)e^{\theta v} \le M_7(2/\delta^2)^\theta$. Note that in case of $g(t) \le 0$ we can take $M_7 = 0$. Using this estimate and inequality (2.37) we find

$$e^v + g(v) < \frac{2}{\delta^2}\left[1 + H\delta - \alpha\delta^\sigma + M_6\left(\delta^2 + (\alpha\delta^\sigma)^2\right) + M_7\left(\frac{2}{\delta^2}\right)^{\theta-1}\right]. \tag{2.38}$$

By (2.35) and (2.38) we find that

$$\Delta v > e^v + g(v) \tag{2.39}$$

when

$$\begin{aligned} &H\delta - M_4\delta^2 - \alpha\delta^\sigma\left(\frac{\sigma(\sigma-1)}{2} + M_5\delta\right) \\ &\quad > H\delta - \alpha\delta^\sigma + M_6\delta^2 + M_6(\alpha\delta^\sigma)^2 + M_7\left(\frac{2}{\delta^2}\right)^{\theta-1}. \end{aligned} \tag{2.40}$$

Rearranging, we find

$$(M_4 + M_6)\delta^2 + M_7\left(\frac{\delta^2}{2}\right)^{1-\theta} < \alpha\delta^\sigma\left[\frac{(1+\sigma)(2-\sigma)}{2} - M_5\delta - M_6\alpha\delta^\sigma\right]. \tag{2.41}$$

Since $\sigma = 2(1-\theta)$, (2.41) yields

$$(M_4 + M_6)\delta^{2\theta} + M_7 2^{\theta-1} < \alpha\left[(1 + 2(1-\theta))\theta - M_5\delta - M_6\alpha\delta^{2(1-\theta)}\right]. \tag{2.42}$$

We can take δ_0 small and α large so that (2.42) and (2.36) hold for $\delta(x) < \delta_0$.

By using Lemma 2.1, we have

$$u(x) - v(x) = O(1)\delta^{2(1-\theta)} + O(1)\delta\log\frac{2}{\delta^2} - H\delta + \alpha\delta^{2(1-\theta)}. \tag{2.43}$$

It follows that, for α fixed, $u(x) - v(x) \to 0$ as $x \to \partial\Omega$. Let $\alpha\delta_0^{2(1-\theta)} = q$, with α and δ_0 as above. Decrease δ_0 and increase α so that $\alpha\delta_0^{2(1-\theta)} = q$ and

$$O(1)\delta^{2(1-\theta)} + O(1)\delta\log\frac{2}{\delta^2} - H\delta + q > 0 \tag{2.44}$$

for $\{x \in \Omega : \delta(x) = \delta_0\}$. By (2.39), it follows that $v(x) \le u(x)$ on $\{x \in \Omega : \delta(x) < \delta_0\}$.

Therefore, near $\partial\Omega$ we have

$$\log\frac{2}{\delta^2} + H\delta - \alpha\delta^{2(1-\theta)} \le u(x) \le \log\frac{2}{\delta^2} + H\delta + \alpha\delta^{2(1-\theta)}. \tag{2.45}$$

The theorem is proved. □

COROLLARY 2.3. *Let Ω be a bounded smooth domain in R^N, $N \ge 2$, and let $g(t)$ be a smooth function which satisfies (2.1) and the estimate $g(t) = O(1)t^p$, where p is a real number. If $u(x)$ is a boundary blow-up solution of $\Delta u = e^u + g(u)$ in Ω, then*

$$u(x) = \log\frac{2}{\delta^2} + H\delta + O(1)\delta^\sigma, \tag{2.46}$$

where σ is any real number with $\sigma < 2$.

Proof. Given $\sigma < 2$, take $\theta = 1 - \sigma/2$. Since $g(t) = O(1)t^p$, we have $g(t) = O(1)e^{\theta t}$. The result follows by Theorem 2.2. □

Remark 2.4. If $\theta < 1/2$, the perturbation $g(t)$ makes effects at the third level only. When $\theta \ge 1/2$, $2(1-\theta) \le 1$, and the statement of Theorem 2.2 can be written as

$$u(x) = \log\frac{2}{\delta^2} + O(1)\delta^{2(1-\theta)}. \tag{2.47}$$

Hence, in this case the perturbation $g(t)$ produces its effects at the second level.

3. Conclusion

The results of the present paper are close to those of [2], where the problem

$$\Delta u = u^p + g(u) \quad \text{in } \Omega, \qquad u(x) \longrightarrow \infty \quad \text{as } x \longrightarrow \partial\Omega, \tag{3.1}$$

is discussed. Here $p > 1$ and $g(t)$ is a function which satisfies $|g(t)| \le Mt^q$, $q < p$. The following results follow from [2].

With $p > 5$, $0 < q < p$, let

$$\Delta u = u^p + u^q \quad \text{in } \Omega, \qquad u(x) \longrightarrow \infty \quad \text{as } x \longrightarrow \partial\Omega. \tag{3.2}$$

(i) If $0 < q < 1$, then

$$u(x) = (a_p\delta)^{2/(1-p)}\left[1 + A_1\delta + A_2\delta^2 + O(1)\delta^\beta\right], \tag{3.3}$$

where

$$a_p = \frac{p-1}{\sqrt{2(1+p)}}, \qquad \beta = \frac{2(p-q)}{p-1},$$
$$A_1 = \frac{H}{p+3}, \quad A_2 = \frac{9-p-2p^2}{12(p+3)^2}H^2 + \frac{p-3}{6(p+3)}\nabla H \cdot \nabla \delta, \quad H = (N-1)K. \tag{3.4}$$

(ii) If $1 \le q < (p+1)/2$, then

$$u(x) = (a_p\delta)^{2/(1-p)}[1 + A_1\delta + O(1)\delta^\beta]. \tag{3.5}$$

(iii) If $(p+1)/2 \le q < p$, then

$$u(x) = (a_p\delta)^{2/(1-p)}[1 + O(1)\delta^\beta]. \tag{3.6}$$

Two questions arise: *what is the second-order effect in the asymptotic expansion of the blow-up solution in case of more general nonlinearities? How is the geometry of the boundary* $\partial\Omega$ *involved?* We have the following result relative to the problem

$$\Delta u = e^{u|u|^{\beta-1}} \quad \text{in } \Omega, \qquad u(x) \longrightarrow \infty \quad \text{as } x \longrightarrow \partial\Omega, \tag{3.7}$$

with $0 < \beta \neq 1$. We have found the following asymptotic expansion:

$$u(x) = \Phi(\delta) + \beta^{-1}H\delta(\Phi(\delta))^{1-\beta} + O(1)\delta(\Phi(\delta))^{1-2\beta}, \tag{3.8}$$

where $H = (N-1)K$ and $\Phi(\delta)$ is defined as

$$\int_{\Phi(\delta)}^{\infty} (2F(t))^{-1/2}dt = \delta, \quad F(t) = \int_{-\infty}^{t} f(\tau)d\tau, \; f(\tau) = e^{\tau|\tau|^{\beta-1}}. \tag{3.9}$$

The proof of the above result will appear in a forthcoming paper.

References

[1] L. Andersson and P. T. Chruściel, *Solutions of the constraint equations in general relativity satisfying "hyperboloidal boundary conditions"*, Dissertationes Mathematicae **355** (1996), 1–100.

[2] C. Anedda and G. Porru, *Higher order boundary estimates for blow-up solutions of elliptic equations*, Differential and Integral Equations **19** (2006), no. 3, 345–360.

[3] C. Bandle, *Asymptotic behaviour of large solutions of quasilinear elliptic problems*, Zeitschrift für Angewandte Mathematik und Physik **54** (2003), no. 5, 731–738.

[4] C. Bandle, Y. Cheng, and G. Porru, *Boundary blow-up in semilinear elliptic problems with singular weights at the boundary*, Applicable Mathematics (J. C. Misra, ed.), Narosa, New Delhi, 2001, pp. 68–81.

[5] C. Bandle and E. Giarrusso, *Boundary blow up for semilinear elliptic equations with nonlinear gradient terms*, Advances in Differential Equations **1** (1996), no. 1, 133–150.

[6] C. Bandle and M. Marcus, *"Large" solutions of semilinear elliptic equations: existence, uniqueness and asymptotic behaviour*, Journal d'Analyse Mathématique **58** (1992), 9–24.

[7] ———, *On second-order effects in the boundary behaviour of large solutions of semilinear elliptic problems*, Differential and Integral Equations **11** (1998), no. 1, 23–34.

[8] ———, *Dependence of blowup rate of large solutions of semilinear elliptic equations, on the curvature of the boundary*, Complex Variables. Theory and Application **49** (2004), no. 7–9, 555–570.
[9] S. Berhanu and G. Porru, *Qualitative and quantitative estimates for large solutions to semilinear equations*, Communications in Applied Analysis **4** (2000), no. 1, 121–131.
[10] L. Bieberbach, $\Delta u = e^u$ *und die automorphen Funktionen*, Mathematische Annalen **77** (1916), no. 2, 173–212.
[11] M. del Pino and R. Letelier, *The influence of domain geometry in boundary blow-up elliptic problems*, Nonlinear Analysis. Theory, Methods & Applications **48** (2002), no. 6, 897–904.
[12] E. Giarrusso, *Asymptotic behaviour of large solutions of an elliptic quasilinear equation in a borderline case*, Comptes Rendus de l'Académie des Sciences. Série I. Mathématique **331** (2000), no. 10, 777–782.
[13] D. Gilbarg and N. S. Trudinger, *Elliptic Partial Differential Equations of Second Order*, Springer, Berlin, 1977.
[14] A. Greco and G. Porru, *Asymptotic estimates and convexity of large solutions to semilinear elliptic equations*, Differential and Integral Equations **10** (1997), no. 2, 219–229.
[15] J. B. Keller, *On solutions of* $\Delta u = f(u)$, Communications on Pure and Applied Mathematics **10** (1957), 503–510.
[16] A. C. Lazer and P. J. McKenna, *Asymptotic behavior of solutions of boundary blowup problems*, Differential and Integral Equations **7** (1994), no. 3-4, 1001–1019.
[17] R. Osserman, *On the inequality* $\Delta u \geq f(u)$, Pacific Journal of Mathematics **7** (1957), 1641–1647.

C. Anedda: Department of Mathematics, University of Cagliari, Via Ospedale 72,
09124 Cagliari, Italy
E-mail address: canedda@unica.it

A. Buttu: Department of Mathematics, University of Cagliari, Via Ospedale 72,
09124 Cagliari, Italy
E-mail address: buttu@unica.it

G. Porru: Department of Mathematics, University of Cagliari, Via Ospedale 72,
09124 Cagliari, Italy
E-mail address: porru@unica.it

BACKWARD STOCHASTIC VOLTERRA INTEGRAL EQUATIONS IN HILBERT SPACES

VO ANH AND JIONGMIN YONG

We establish the well-posedness of backward stochastic Volterra integral equations in Hilbert spaces.

1. Introduction

Throughout this paper, we let H and $\bar{H}$ be two separable Hilbert spaces, and let $(\Omega, \mathcal{F}, \mathbb{F}, \mathbb{P})$ be a complete filtered probability space on which an $\bar{H}$-valued standard Brownian motion $W(\cdot)$ is defined with $\mathbb{F} \equiv \{\mathcal{F}_t\}_{t\geq 0}$ being its natural filtration augmented by all the $\mathbb{P}$-null sets in $\mathcal{F}$. Let $A : \mathcal{D}(A) \subseteq H \to H$ be the generator of a C_0-semigroup, denoted by e^{At}, on the space H. Note that operator A could be a differential operator or a pseudo-differential operator which generates a diffusion process. Consider the following forward stochastic partial differential equation (FSPDE, for short):

$$\begin{gathered} dX(t) = [AX(t) + b(t,X(t))]dt + \sigma(t,X(t))dW(t), \quad t \in [0,T], \\ X(0) = X_0, \end{gathered} \tag{1.1}$$

where $b : [0,T] \times H \to H$ and $\sigma : [0,T] \times H \to \mathcal{L}_2(\bar{H};H)$ (the space of all Hilbert-Schmidt operators from $\bar{H}$ to H, endowed with Hilbert-Schmidt norm; see next section for details). The mild or integral form of the above equation reads [1]

$$X(t) = e^{At}X_0 + \int_0^t e^{A(t-s)}b(s,X(s))ds + \int_0^t e^{A(t-s)}\sigma(s,X(s))dW(s), \quad t \in [0,T]. \tag{1.2}$$

Inspired by the above, we may more generally consider the following equation:

$$X(t) = \varphi(t) + \int_0^t b(t,s,X(s))ds + \int_0^t \sigma(t,s,X(s))dW(s), \quad t \in [0,T], \tag{1.3}$$

where $b : [0,T]\times[0,T]\times H \to H$, and $\sigma : [0,T]\times[0,T]\times H \to \mathcal{L}_2(\bar{H},H)$. We call the above a forward stochastic Volterra integral equation (FSIE, for short). The well-posedness

Hindawi Publishing Corporation
Proceedings of the Conference on Differential & Difference Equations and Applications, pp. 57–66

of such an equation in a suitable space and a suitable sense can be established and lead to many related problems. Among them, one can consider optimal control problems related to the above equation. More precisely, instead of (1.3) we may consider the following controlled FSIE:

$$X(t) = \varphi(t) + \int_0^t b(t,s,X(s),u(s))\,ds + \int_0^t \sigma(t,s,X(s),u(s))\,dW(s), \quad t \in [0,T], \tag{1.4}$$

where $X(\cdot)$ is the state and $u(\cdot)$ is the control. If we introduce the following cost functional:

$$J(u(\cdot)) = E\left[\int_0^T f(t,X(t),u(t))\,dt + h(X(T))\right], \tag{1.5}$$

for some maps $f : [0,T] \times H \times U \times \Omega \to \mathbb{R}$ and $h : H \times \Omega \to \mathbb{R}$, then one can pose an optimal control problem: minimize (1.5) subject to the state equation (1.4). One expected result related to this optimal control problem is the Pontryagin-type maximum principle (as a necessary condition for optimal controls). In the statement of such a maximum principle, one will have an adjoint equation associated with the linearized state equation. This adjoint equation will be a terminal value problem for a stochastic integral equation. Therefore, inspired by [7, 8] (see also [3]), one should study the following type integral equation:

$$Y(t) = \psi(t) - \int_t^T g(t,s,Y(s),Z(t,s),Z(s,t))\,ds - \int_t^T Z(t,s)\,dW(s), \quad t \in [0,T], \tag{1.6}$$

where $g : [0,T] \times [0,T] \times H \times \mathcal{L}_2(\bar{H},H) \times \mathcal{L}_2(\bar{H},H) \times \Omega \to H$ is a given map, called the *generator*, and $\psi : [0,T] \times \Omega \to H$ is a given *free term*. Equation (1.6) is called a *backward stochastic Volterra integral equation* (BSIE, for short). An adapted solution to (1.6) is a pair of processes $(Y(\cdot),Z(\cdot,\cdot))$ for which $t \mapsto Y(t)$ is $\mathbb{F}$-adapted, and for almost all $t \in [0,T]$, $s \mapsto Z(t,s)$ is $\mathbb{F}$-adapted, such that (1.6) is satisfied in the usual Itô sense (see the next section).

The purpose of this paper is to establish the well-posedness of BSIE (1.6) under proper conditions. Our results extend those found in [7, 8]. For relevant results for stochastic differential equations and stochastic integral equations, see [2, 4–6], and so forth.

2. Preliminaries

In what follows, for any Hilbert space K, we will denote its norm by $|\cdot|$ (or $|\cdot|_K$ if K needs to be emphasized). Since $\bar{H}$ is a separable Hilbert space, we may let $\{\bar{e}_i\}_{i\geq 1}$ be an orthonormal basis of $\bar{H}$. Then we define $\mathcal{L}_2(\bar{H},H)$ to be the set of all linear bounded operators $B : \bar{H} \to H$ such that

$$|B| = \left(\sum_{i\geq 1} |B\bar{e}_i|^2\right)^{1/2} < \infty. \tag{2.1}$$

Clearly, $\mathcal{L}_2(\bar{H},H)$ is a Hilbert space with an obvious inner product induced by the above norm. Any $B \in \mathscr{L}_2(\bar{H}, H)$ is called a Hilbert-Schmidt operator. Next, for any Hilbert space K, we introduce the following spaces:

$$
\begin{aligned}
L^2(\Omega) &= \{\xi : \Omega \longrightarrow K \mid \xi \text{ is } \mathscr{F}_T\text{-measurable}, \; E|\xi|^2 < \infty\}, \\
L^2((0,T)\times\Omega) &= \Big\{\varphi : (0,T)\times\Omega \longrightarrow K \mid \varphi(\cdot) \text{ is } \mathscr{B}([0,T]) \\
&\qquad \otimes \mathscr{F}_T\text{-measurable}, E\int_0^T |\varphi(t)|^2 dt < \infty\Big\}, \\
L^2_{\mathscr{F}}(0,T) &= \{\varphi(\cdot) \in L^2((0,T)\times\Omega) \mid \varphi(\cdot) \text{ is } \mathbb{F}\text{-adapted}\}.
\end{aligned}
\tag{2.2}
$$

In the above, we have suppressed the range space K in the notations. In case that the range space K needs to be emphasized, we use the notations $L^2(\Omega;K)$, $L^2((0,T)\times\Omega;K)$, and so on.

The above are the spaces for the processes $\psi(\cdot)$ (see (1.6), which does not have to be $\mathbb{F}$-adapted) and $Y(\cdot)$ (which is required to be $\mathbb{F}$-adapted). Now for the process $Z(\cdot,\cdot)$, we need to introduce the space $L^2(0,T;L^2_{\mathscr{F}}(0,T)) \equiv L^2(0,T;L^2_{\mathscr{F}}(0,T;\mathscr{L}_2(\bar{H},H)))$. By definition, any $Z : [0,T]\times[0,T]\times\Omega \to \mathscr{L}_2(\bar{H},H)$ belongs to this space if for almost all $t \in [0,T]$, $s \mapsto Z(t,s)$ is $\mathbb{F}$-adapted and

$$
E\int_0^T\int_0^T |Z(t,s)|^2 ds\,dt < \infty. \tag{2.3}
$$

Next, we assume that $W(\cdot)$ is given by the following expansion:

$$
W(t) = \sum_{i\geq 1} W_i(t)\bar{e}_i, \quad t \geq 0, \tag{2.4}
$$

where for each $n \geq 1$, $(W_1(\cdot),\ldots,W_n(\cdot))$ is an n-dimensional standard Brownian motion. Then for any process $\sigma(\cdot) \in L^2_{\mathscr{F}}(0,T;\mathscr{L}_2(\bar{H},H))$, the Itô integral

$$
\int_0^t \sigma(s)dW(s) = \sum_{i\geq 1}\int_0^t \sigma(s)\bar{e}_i dW_i(s), \quad t \in [0,T], \tag{2.5}
$$

is well defined, and

$$
E\left|\int_0^t \sigma(t)dW(s)\right|^2 = \int_0^T \sum_{i\geq 1} E|\sigma(t)\bar{e}_i|^2 dt = \int_0^T E|\sigma(t)|^2 dt < \infty. \tag{2.6}
$$

3. Well-posedness of BSIEs

We denote

$$
\begin{aligned}
\Delta &= \{(t,s) \in [0,T]^2 \mid 0 \leq s \leq t \leq T\}, \\
\Delta^c &= \{(t,s) \in [0,T]^2 \mid 0 \leq t \leq s \leq T\}.
\end{aligned}
\tag{3.1}
$$

Let us introducc thc following definition (see [8]).

Definition 3.1. A pair $(Y(\cdot),Z(\cdot,\cdot)) \in L^2_{\mathcal{F}}(0,T) \times L^2(0,T;L^2_{\mathcal{F}}(0,T))$ is called an *adapted M-solution* of (1.6) if (1.6) is satisfied in the Itô sense and the following holds:

$$Y(t) = EY(t) + \int_0^t Z(t,s)dW(s), \quad t \in [0,T]. \tag{3.2}$$

In the above, "M" in "M-solution" stands for "martingale representation" (for $Y(t)$). The following standing assumption will be used below.

(H1) Let $g : \Delta^c \times H \times \mathcal{L}_2(\bar{H},H) \times \mathcal{L}_2(\bar{H},H) \times \Omega \to H$ be $\mathcal{B}(\Delta^c \times H \times \mathcal{L}_2(\bar{H},H) \times \mathcal{L}_2(\bar{H},H)) \otimes \mathcal{F}_T$-measurable, such that

$$E\int_0^T \left(\int_t^T |g(t,s,0,0,0)|\,ds\right)^2 dt < \infty. \tag{3.3}$$

Moreover, for some deterministic functions L_y, L_z, L_ζ: $\Delta^c \to \mathbb{R}$ satisfying

$$\begin{aligned} &\sup_{t\in[0,T]} \int_t^T [L_y(t,s)^2 + L_\zeta(t,s)^2]ds < \infty, \\ &\sup_{t\in[0,T]} \int_t^T L_z(t,s)^2 ds < 1, \end{aligned} \tag{3.4}$$

it holds that

$$\begin{aligned} |g(t,s,y,z,\zeta) - g(t,s,\bar{y},\bar{z},\bar{\zeta})| &\le L_y(t,s)|y-\bar{y}| + L_z(t,s)|z-\bar{z}| + L_\zeta(t,s)|\zeta-\bar{\zeta}|, \\ &\forall (t,s) \in \Delta^c,\ y,\bar{y} \in H,\ z,\bar{z},\zeta,\bar{\zeta} \in \mathcal{L}_2(\bar{H},H), \text{ a.s.} \end{aligned} \tag{3.5}$$

Note that if L_y and L_ζ are uniformly bounded, the first condition in (3.4) is automatically true. The second condition in (3.4) is very crucial below.

Our main result of this section is the following well-posedness result for BSIE (1.6).

THEOREM 3.2. *Let* (H1) *hold. Then for any* $\psi(\cdot) \in L^2((0,T)\times\Omega)$*, BSIE (1.6) admits a unique adapted M-solution* $(Y(\cdot),Z(\cdot,\cdot)) \in L^2_{\mathcal{F}}(0,T) \times L^2(0,T;L^2_{\mathcal{F}}(0,T))$*. Moreover, the following estimate holds:*

$$\begin{aligned} &E\int_r^T |Y(t)|^2 dt + E\int_r^T\int_r^T |Z(t,s)|^2 ds\,dt \\ &\le CE\left[\int_r^T |\psi(t)|^2 dt + \int_r^T \left(\int_t^T |g(t,s,0,0,0)|\,ds\right)^2 dt\right], \quad \forall r \in [0,T]. \end{aligned} \tag{3.6}$$

Let $\bar{g} : \Delta^c \times H \times \mathcal{L}_2(\bar{H},H) \times \mathcal{L}_2(\bar{H},H) \times \Omega \to \mathbb{R}^m$ *also satisfy* (H1)*. Let* $\bar{\psi}(\cdot) \in L^2((0,T)\times\Omega)$ *and* $(\bar{Y}(\cdot),\bar{Z}(\cdot,\cdot)) \in L^2_{\mathcal{F}}(0,T) \times L^2(0,T;L^2_{\mathcal{F}}(0,T))$ *be the adapted M-solution of (1.6)* *with g replaced by $\bar{g}$, corresponding to $\bar{\psi}(\cdot)$, then the following stability condition holds:*

$$
\begin{aligned}
&E\int_r^T |Y(t)-\bar{Y}(t)|^2 dt + E\int_r^T\int_r^T |Z(t,s)-\bar{Z}(t,s)|^2 ds\,dt \\
&\quad \le CE\Big[\int_r^T |\psi(t)-\bar{\psi}(t)|^2 dt + \int_r^T\Big(\int_r^T |g(t,s,Y(s),Z(t,s),Z(s,t)) \\
&\qquad\qquad - \bar{g}(t,s,Y(s),Z(t,s),Z(s,t))|\,ds\Big)^2 dt\Big], \\
&\qquad\qquad\qquad \forall r\in[0,T].
\end{aligned}
\tag{3.7}
$$

Sketch of the proof. First of all, by (3.4), we can find a finite sequence $0 = T_0 < T_1 < \cdots < T_{k-1} < T_k = T$ and a $\delta\in(0,1)$ such that

$$
\sup_{t\in[T_{i-1},T_i]}\int_t^{T_i} [L_z(t,s)^2 + L_\zeta(t,s)^2]ds \le 1-\delta, \quad 1\le i\le k. \tag{3.8}
$$

The proof is split into several steps.

Proof

Step 1. BSIE (1.6) is solvable on $[T_{k-1},T]$.

Let $\mathcal{M}^2[T_{k-1},T]$ be the (nontrivial closed) subspace of all $(y(\cdot),z(\cdot,\cdot))\in L^2_{\mathcal{F}}(T_{k-1},T)\times L^2(T_{k-1},T;L^2_{\mathcal{F}}(0,T))$ such that

$$
y(t) = Ey(t) + \int_0^t z(t,s)dW(s), \quad t\in[T_{k-1},T]. \tag{3.9}
$$

Clearly, for any $(y(\cdot),z(\cdot,\cdot))\in\mathcal{M}^2[T_{k-1},T]$, we have

$$
\begin{aligned}
&E\int_r^t |z(t,s)|^2 ds \le E\int_0^t |z(t,s)|^2 ds = E|y(t)|^2 - |Ey(t)|^2 \le E|y(t)|^2, \\
&\qquad (t,r)\in\Delta, \quad t\in[T_{k-1},T].
\end{aligned}
\tag{3.10}
$$

Next, for any $(y(\cdot),z(\cdot,\cdot))\in\mathcal{M}^2[T_{k-1},T]$, denote

$$
\widetilde{\psi}(t) = \psi(t) + \int_t^T g(t,s,y(s),z(t,s),z(s,t))ds, \quad t\in[T_{k-1},T]. \tag{3.11}
$$

Then by (H1), using the Cauchy-Schwartz inequality, with some careful calculations, for any $t\in[T_{k-1},T]$,

$$
\begin{aligned}
|\widetilde{\psi}(t)|^2 &\le C\Big[|\psi(t)|^2 + \Big(\int_t^T g_0(t,s)ds\Big)^2 + \int_t^T |y(s)|^2 ds\Big] \\
&\quad + (1-\delta^2)\Big[\int_t^T |z(t,s)|^2 ds + \int_t^T |z(s,t)|^2 ds\Big].
\end{aligned}
\tag{3.12}
$$

In the above, $g_0(t,s) = |g(t,s,0,0,0)|$. Thus, for any $r \in [T_{k-1}, T]$, noting (3.10), we obtain

$$E\int_r^T |\widetilde{\psi}(t)|^2 dt \leq CE\left[\int_r^T |\psi(t)|^2 dt + \int_r^T \left(\int_t^T g_0(t,s)ds\right)^2 dt + \int_r^T \int_t^T |y(s)|^2 ds\,dt\right] + (1-\delta^2)E\left[\int_r^T |y(t)|^2 dt + \int_r^T \int_t^T |z(t,s)|^2 ds\,dt\right], \tag{3.13}$$

which implies that $\widetilde{\psi}(\cdot) \in L^2((T_{k-1}, T) \times \Omega)$. We now consider the following BSIE:

$$Y(t) = \widetilde{\psi}(t) - \int_t^T Z(t,s)dW(s), \quad t \in [T_{k-1}, T]. \tag{3.14}$$

Using the martingale presentation theorem, together with some approximation arguments, we obtain a unique adapted M-solution $(Y(\cdot), Z(\cdot,\cdot)) \in \mathcal{M}^2[T_{k-1}, T]$ to (3.14), that is,

$$Y(t) = \psi(t) - \int_t^T g(t,s,y(s),z(t,s),z(s,t))ds - \int_t^T Z(t,s)dW(s), \quad t \in [T_{k-1}, T]. \tag{3.15}$$

Now, if $(Y(\cdot), Z(\cdot,\cdot)) \in \mathcal{M}^2[T_{k-1}, T]$ is an adapted M-solution to (1.6), then by taking $(y(\cdot), z(\cdot,\cdot))$ to be $(Y(\cdot), Z(\cdot,\cdot))$ in the above, we obtain that for any $r \in [T_{k-1}, T]$,

$$\begin{aligned} &E\int_r^T |Y(t)|^2 dt + E\int_r^T \int_t^T |Z(t,s)|^2 ds\,dt \\ &\leq CE\left[\int_r^T |\psi(t)|^2 dt + \int_r^T \left(\int_t^T g_0(t,s)ds\right)^2 dt + \int_r^T \int_t^T |Y(s)|^2 ds\,dt\right] \\ &\quad + (1-\delta^2)E\left[\int_r^T |Y(t)|^2 dt + \int_r^T \int_t^T |Z(t,s)|^2 ds\,dt\right]. \end{aligned} \tag{3.16}$$

Hence, first absorbing the last term on the right-hand side into the left-hand side, then using Gronwall's inequality, we obtain that for all $t \in [T_{k-1}, T]$,

$$\begin{aligned} &E\int_r^T |Y(t)|^2 dt + E\int_r^T \int_t^T |Z(t,s)|^2 ds\,dt \\ &\leq CE\left[\int_r^T |\psi(t)|^2 dt + \int_r^T \left(\int_t^T g_0(t,s)ds\right)^2 dt\right]. \end{aligned} \tag{3.17}$$

Further, by (3.2) and (3.10), we obtain that for all $r \in [T_{k-1}, T]$,

$$
\begin{aligned}
&E\int_r^T |Y(t)|^2 dt + E\int_r^T\int_r^T |Z(t,s)|^2 ds\,dt \\
&\quad \le CE\left[\int_r^T |\psi(t)|^2 dt + \int_r^T \left(\int_t^T g_0(t,s)ds\right)^2 dt\right].
\end{aligned}
\tag{3.18}
$$

This gives estimate (3.6) for any adapted M-solution $(Y(\cdot), Z(\cdot,\cdot))$ of (1.6) on $[T_{k-1}, T]$.

Now, let $(y(\cdot), z(\cdot,\cdot)), (\bar{y}(\cdot)), \bar{z}(\cdot,\cdot)) \in \mathcal{M}^2[T_{k-1}, T]$, and let $(Y(\cdot), Z(\cdot,\cdot))$ and $(\bar{Y}(\cdot), \bar{Z}(\cdot,\cdot))$ be the corresponding adapted M-solutions of (3.15). Then

$$
\begin{aligned}
&E|Y(t) - \bar{Y}(t)|^2 + \int_t^T E|Z(t,s) - \bar{Z}(t,s)|^2 ds \\
&\quad \le C\int_t^T E|y(s) - \bar{y}(s)|^2 ds + (1-\delta^2)\int_t^T E|z(t,s) - \bar{z}(t,s)|^2 ds \\
&\qquad + (1-\delta^2)\int_t^T E|z(s,t) - \bar{z}(s,t)|^2 ds.
\end{aligned}
\tag{3.19}
$$

Similar to (3.10), we have

$$
E\int_r^t |z(t,s) - \bar{z}(t,s)|^2 ds \le E|y(t) - \bar{y}(t)|^2, \quad (t,r) \in \Delta.
\tag{3.20}
$$

Consequently, for $r \in [T_{k-1}, T)$, by some direct computations,

$$
\begin{aligned}
&E\int_r^T |Y(t) - \bar{Y}(t)|^2 dt + \int_r^T\int_t^T E|Z(t,s) - \bar{Z}(t,s)|^2 ds\,dt \\
&\quad \le (1-\delta^2)\left[\int_r^T E|y(t) - \bar{y}(t)|^2 dt + \int_r^T\int_t^T E|z(t,s) - \bar{z}(t,s)|^2 ds\,dt\right] \\
&\qquad + C\int_r^T\left[\int_t^T E|y(s) - \bar{y}(s)|^2 ds + \int_t^T\int_s^T E|z(s,\tau) - \bar{z}(s,\tau)|^2 d\tau\,ds\right]dt.
\end{aligned}
\tag{3.21}
$$

The above actually implies that adapted M-solution to BSIE (1.1) is unique on $[T_{k-1}, T]$. In fact, if $(Y(\cdot), Z(\cdot,\cdot))$ and $(\bar{Y}(\cdot), \bar{Z}(\cdot,\cdot))$ are two adapted M-solutions to (1.6) on $[T_{k-1}, T]$, then the above leads to the following:

$$
\begin{aligned}
&E\int_r^T |Y(t) - \bar{Y}(t)|^2 dt + \int_r^T\int_t^T E|Z(t,s) - \bar{Z}(t,s)|^2 ds\,dt \\
&\quad \le (1-\delta^2)\left[\int_r^T E|Y(t) - \bar{Y}(t)|^2 dt + \int_r^T\int_t^T E|Z(t,s) - \bar{Z}(t,s)|^2 ds\,dt\right] \\
&\qquad + C\int_r^T\left[\int_t^T E|Y(s) - \bar{Y}(s)|^2 ds + \int_t^T\int_s^T E|Z(s,\tau) - \bar{Z}(s,\tau)|^2 d\tau\,ds\right]dt.
\end{aligned}
\tag{3.22}
$$

Thus, absorbing the first term on the right-hand side, then using Gronwall's inequality, we obtain

$$E\int_r^T |Y(t)-\bar{Y}(t)|^2 dt + \int_r^T\int_t^T E|Z(t,s)-\bar{Z}(t,s)|^2 ds\,dt = 0, \quad r\in[T_{k-1},T], \tag{3.23}$$

proving the uniqueness.

To obtain the existence, we define the Picard iteration sequence as follows. Let

$$(Y_0(\cdot),Z_0(\cdot,\cdot)) = (0,0)\in\mathcal{M}^2[T_{k-1},T], \tag{3.24}$$

and inductively, we let $(Y_{k+1}(\cdot),Z_{k+1}(\cdot,\cdot))\in\mathcal{M}^2[T_{k-1},T]$ be the unique M-solution of the following BSIE:

$$\begin{aligned} Y_{k+1}(t) &= \psi(t) - \int_t^T g(t,s,Y_k(s),Z_k(t,s),Z_k(s,t))ds \\ &\quad - \int_t^T Z_{k+1}(t,s)dW(s), \quad t\in[0,T]. \end{aligned} \tag{3.25}$$

Then with some lengthy calculations and estimations, we can obtain

$$\lim_{k\to\infty}\left[\int_r^T E|Y_k(s)-Y(s)|^2 ds + \int_r^T\int_t^T E|Z_k(t,s)-Z(t,s)|^2 ds\,dt\right] = 0, \tag{3.26}$$

for some $(Y(\cdot),Z(\cdot,\cdot))$. Also, due to

$$Y_k(t) = EY_k(t) + \int_0^t Z_k(t,s)dW(s), \quad t\in[T_{k-1},T], \text{ a.s.}, \tag{3.27}$$

we have

$$\int_{T_{k-1}}^T\int_0^t E|Z_k(t,s)-Z(t,s)|^2 ds\,dt \le \int_{T_{k-1}}^T |Y_k(t)-Y(t)|^2 dt \longrightarrow 0, \quad k\longrightarrow\infty. \tag{3.28}$$

Hence, we obtain an M-solution $(Y(\cdot),Z(\cdot,\cdot))$ to BSIE (1.1) over $[T_{k-1},T]$.

Step 2. A stochastic Fredholm integral equation is solvable over $[T_{k-1},T]$.

For $(t,s)\in[T_{k-2},T_{k-1}]\times[T_{k-1},T]$, from Step 1, we know that the values $Y(s)$ and $Z(s,t)$ are all already determined. Hence, we can define

$$g^{k-1}(t,s,z) = g(t,s,Y(s),z,Z(s,t)), \quad (t,s,z)\in[T_{k-2},T_{k-1}]\times[T_{k-1},T]\times\mathbb{R}^{m\times d}. \tag{3.29}$$

Now, consider the following stochastic Fredholm integral equation:

$$\begin{aligned} \psi^{k-1}(t) &= \psi(t) - \int_{T_{k-1}}^T g^{k-1}(t,s,Z(t,s))ds \\ &\quad - \int_{T_{k-1}}^T Z(t,s)dW(s), \quad t\in[T_{k-2},T_{k-1}]. \end{aligned} \tag{3.30}$$

Making use of the second condition in (3.4) (which is crucial here), the above admits a unique adapted solution $(\psi^{k-1}(\cdot),Z(\cdot,\cdot))$ (with $\psi^{k-1}(t)$ being $\mathscr{F}_{T_{k-1}}$-adapted). This uniquely determines the values $Z(t,s)$ for $(t,s)\in[T_{k-2},T_{k-1}]\times[T_{k-1},T]$.

Step 3. Complete the proof by induction.

By Steps 1 and 2, we see that the values $Y(t)$ for $t\in[T_{k-1},T]$ and the values $Z(t,s)$ for $(t,s)\in([T_{k-1},T]\times[0,T])\bigcup([T_{k-2},T_{k-1}]\times[T_{k-1},T])$ have been determined. By the definition of $g^{k-1}(t,s,z)$, we see that $(\psi^{k-1}(\cdot),Z(\cdot,\cdot))$ satisfies

$$\begin{aligned}\psi^{k-1}(t)=\psi(t)&-\int_{T_{k-1}}^{T}g(t,s,Y(s),Z(t,s),Z(s,t))\,ds\\&-\int_{T_{k-1}}^{T}Z(t,s)\,dW(s),\quad t\in[T_{k-2},T_{k-1}].\end{aligned}\tag{3.31}$$

Now, we consider

$$\begin{aligned}Y(t)=\psi^{k-1}(t)&-\int_{t}^{T_{k-1}}g(t,s,Y(s),Z(t,s),Z(s,t))\,ds\\&-\int_{t}^{T_{k-1}}Z(t,s)\,dW(s),\quad t\in[0,T_{k-1}].\end{aligned}\tag{3.32}$$

Since $\psi^{k-1}(t)$ is $\mathscr{F}_{T_{k-1}}$-adapted, (3.32) is a BSIE over $[0,T_{k-1}]$. Hence, by Step 1, we may prove that (3.32) is solvable on $[T_{k-2},T_{k-1}]$. This solvability determines the values $Y(t)$ for $t\in[T_{k-2},T_{k-1}]$ and the values $Z(t,s)$ for $(t,s)\in[T_{k-2},T_{k-1}]\times[0,T_{k-1}]$, which is disjoint with the set $([T_{k-1},T]\times[0,T])\bigcup([T_{k-2},T_{k-1}]\times[T_{k-1},T])$. Therefore, we obtain the values $Y(t)$ for $t\in[T_{k-2},T]$ and the values $Z(t,s)$ for $(t,s)\in[T_{k-2},T]\times[0,T]$. Further, we note that for $t\in[T_{k-2},T_{k-1}]$,

$$\begin{aligned}Y(t)&=\psi^{k-1}(t)-\int_{t}^{T_{k-1}}g(t,s,Y(s),Z(t,s),Z(s,t))\,ds-\int_{t}^{T_{k-1}}Z(t,s)\,dW(s)\\&=\psi(t)-\int_{t}^{T}g(t,s,Y(s),Z(t,s),Z(s,t))\,ds-\int_{t}^{T}Z(t,s)\,dW(s).\end{aligned}\tag{3.33}$$

Hence, we obtain the solvability of BSIE (1.1) on $[T_{k-2},T]$. Then we can use induction to obtain the solvability of (1.6) over $[0,T]$.

Finally, we can similarly prove the stability estimate. □

References

[1] M. Fuhrman and G. Tessitore, *Nonlinear Kolmogorov equations in infinite dimensional spaces: the backward stochastic differential equations approach and applications to optimal control*, The Annals of Probability **30** (2002), no. 3, 1397–1465.

[2] N. Ikeda and S. Watanabe, *Stochastic Differential Equations and Diffusion Processes*, 2nd ed., North-Holland Mathematical Library, vol. 24, North-Holland, Amsterdam, 1989.

[3] J. Lin, *Adapted solution of a backward stochastic nonlinear Volterra integral equation*, Stochastic Analysis and Applications **20** (2002), no. 1, 165–183.

[4] J. Ma and J. Yong, *Forward-Backward Stochastic Differential Equations and Their Applications*, Lecture Notes in Mathematics, vol. 1702, Springer, Berlin, 1999.

[5] É. Pardoux and P. Protter, *Stochastic Volterra equations with anticipating coefficients*, The Annals of Probability **18** (1990), no. 4, 1635–1655.

[6] P. Protter, *Volterra equations driven by semimartingales*, The Annals of Probability **13** (1985), no. 2, 519–530.

[7] J. Yong, *Backward stochastic Volterra integral equations and some related problems*, Stochastic Processes and Their Applications **116** (2006), no. 5, 779–795.

[8] ———, *Well-posedness and regularity of backward stochastic Volterra integral equations*, preprint, 2006.

Vo Anh: Florida Space Institute, University of Central Florida, Orlando, FL 32816, USA
E-mail address: vanh@mail.ucf.edu

Jiongmin Yong: Department of Mathematics, University of Central Florida, Orlando, FL 32816, USA
E-mail address: jyong@mail.ucf.edu

SECOND-ORDER DIFFERENTIAL GRADIENT METHODS FOR SOLVING TWO-PERSON GAMES WITH COUPLED VARIABLES

ANATOLY ANTIPIN

A two-person nonzero-sum game is considered both the classical statement and the form of a coupled-variables game. Second-order gradient method for solving coupled-variables game is offered and justified. The convergent analysis is given.

1. Statement of introduction

Let us consider the problem of computing a fixed point of a two-person nonzero-sum game: find $x_1^* \in X_1$, $x_2^* \in X_2$ such that

$$\begin{aligned} x_1^* &\in \operatorname{Argmin}\{f_1(z_1,x_2^*)+\varphi_1(z_1) \mid z_1 \in X_1\},\\ x_2^* &\in \operatorname{Argmin}\{f_2(x_1^*,z_2)+\varphi_2(z_2) \mid z_2 \in X_2\}, \end{aligned} \tag{1.1}$$

where $X_1 \in R_1^{n_1}$, $X_2 \in R_2^{n_2}$ are convex closed sets in finite-dimensional Euclidean spaces with various dimensionality in general. Objective functions $f_1(x_1,x_2)+\varphi_1(x_1)$, $f_2(x_1,x_2)+\varphi_2(x_2)$ are defined on the product spaces $R_1^{n_1}$, $R_2^{n_2}$. If the functions $f_1(z_1,x_2)+\varphi(z_1)$, $f_2(x_1,z_2)+\varphi(z_2)$ are continuous and convex in their own variables, that is, the first function is convex in z_1 and second one is convex in z_2 for any values of x_1 and x_2, where X_i, $i=1,2$, are convex compact sets, then there exists a solution $x^*=(x_1^*,x_2^*)$ of (1.1) [10].

Any solution of (1.1) or Nash equilibrium describes some compromise with a summarized gain $f_1(x_1^*,x_2^*)+\varphi_1(x_1^*)+f_2(x_1^*,x_2^*)+\varphi_2(x_2^*)$. If the sum $f_1(x_1,x_2)+\varphi_1(x_1)+f_2(x_1,x_2)+\varphi_2(x_2)$ $\forall x_1 \in X_1$, $x_2 \in X_2$ is equal to zero, then a problem is called as zero-sum two-person game. Following conceptions accepted in decision making, we suppose that functions $\varphi_i(x_i)$, $i=1,2$, describe the preferences of every player in choosing their alternatives over their own subsets X_i, $i=1,2$. In turn, the functions $f_i(x_1,x_2)$, $i=1,2$, describe a dependence or an effect of one player on the other player, if one of them is taking his choice.

Hindawi Publishing Corporation
Proceedings of the Conference on Differential & Difference Equations and Applications, pp. 67–79

Problem (1.1) always can be scalarized [11] and presented as problem of finding a fixed point of an extreme mapping [2]. To this end, we introduce the normalized function

$$\Phi(v,w)+\varphi(w)=f_1(z_1,x_2)+\varphi_1(z_1)+f_2(x_1,z_2)+\varphi_2(z_2), \quad (1.2)$$

where $w=(z_1,z_2)$, $v=(x_1,x_2)$, $v,w\in\Omega=X_1\times X_2$. In the terms of new macrovariables, the problem (1.1) can be presented in the form

$$v^*\in \operatorname{Argmin}\{\Phi(v^*,w)+\varphi(w)\mid w\in\Omega\}. \quad (1.3)$$

It is easy to make sure that both problems (1.1) and (1.3) are equivalent.

Note that the scalarized game (1.3) can be reformulated in the equivalent form of operator equation

$$v^*=\pi_\Omega(v^*-\alpha(\nabla_2\Phi(v^*,v^*)+\nabla\varphi(v^*))), \quad (1.4)$$

where $\nabla_2\Phi(v,w)$, $\nabla\varphi(w)$ are the gradients in w for any $v,\pi_\Omega(\cdots)$ is a projection operator of some vector onto Ω, $\alpha>0$ is a parameter like the step length.

The discrepancy, that is, the difference between the left- and right-hand sides of (1.4), which vanishes at the point v^* and does not vanish at an arbitrary point v, is a transformation of the space $R^n\times R^n$ into itself. This transformation generates a vector field [1], whose fixed point is v^*. Consider the problem of drawing a trajectory such that linear combination of velocity and acceleration on this trajectory coincides with the field vector at each point. Formally, the problem is described by the system of differential equation

$$\mu\frac{d^2v}{dt^2}+\beta\frac{dv}{dt}+v=\pi_\Omega\{v-\alpha(\nabla_2\Phi(v,v)+\nabla\varphi(v))\}. \quad (1.5)$$

Here $\mu>0$ and $\beta>0$ are parameters. If $\mu=0$ and $\beta=1$, then we have [2, 7, 8]. Other cases can be seen in [1, 9].

To ensure the convergence of the trajectory for differential system (1.5) to a fixed point of problem (1.3), we introduce an additive feedback control. The choice of various feedback types results in various controlled differential systems [4]. In the present paper, we consider the process (1.5) with control in the form of prediction [2]. In this case, the differential second-order controlled gradient system for solving (1.3) takes the form

$$\mu\frac{d^2v}{dt^2}+\beta\frac{dv}{dt}+v=\pi_\Omega\{v-\alpha(\nabla_2\Phi(\bar v,\bar v)+\nabla\varphi(\bar v))\}, \quad (1.6)$$

where the feedback control is as follows:

$$\bar v=\pi_\Omega(v-\alpha(\nabla_2\Phi(v,v)+\nabla\varphi(v))),\quad v(t_0)=v^0,\quad \dot v(t_0)=\dot v^0. \quad (1.7)$$

To justify the convergence of the process (1.6)-(1.7), we need to use the property of positive semidefiniteness introduced by [3]

$$\Phi(w,w)-\Phi(w,v)-\Phi(v,w)+\Phi(v,v)\ge 0\quad \forall v,w\in\Omega\times\Omega. \quad (1.8)$$

This condition can be considered as nonlinear generalization of conception for positive semidefiniteness for matrices. If a function has a bilinear structure $\Phi(v,w) = \langle \Phi v, w\rangle$ where Φ is a square matrix, then (1.8) takes the form $\langle \Phi(v-w), v-w\rangle \geq 0$, $\forall v,w \in \Omega\times\Omega$.

The condition of positive semidefiniteness of (1.8) is sufficient to guarantee the monotonicity of gradient restriction $\nabla_2\Phi(v,w)|_{v=w}$, if the function $\Phi(v,w)$ is convex in w for any v. Indeed, using the system of inequalities

$$\langle \nabla f(x), y-x\rangle \leq f(y)-f(x) \leq \langle f(y), y-x\rangle \quad \forall x,y \in X, \tag{1.9}$$

we get the property of monotonicity [5] for gradient restriction from (1.8)

$$\langle \nabla_2\Phi(w,w) - \nabla_2\Phi(v,v), w-v\rangle \geq 0 \quad \forall v,w \in \Omega. \tag{1.10}$$

Additionally, it is supposed that the gradient restriction satisfy the Lipschitz condition

$$|\nabla_2\Phi(v+h,v+h)+\nabla\varphi(v+h)-\nabla_2\Phi(v,v)-\nabla\varphi(v)| \leq C|h| \quad \forall v,w \in \Omega\times\Omega. \tag{1.11}$$

Using the introduced property, one can prove the following theorem [4].

THEOREM 1.1. *Suppose that a solution set of scalarized game problem (1.3) is nonempty, function* $\Phi(v,w)$ *is positive semidefinite and convex in* w *for any* v*, the Lipschitz condition (1.11) holds,* $\Omega \subseteq R^n$ *is convex closed set. Then, the trajectory* $v(t)$ *generated by method (1.6)-(1.7) with the parameters* $0<\alpha<1/(\sqrt{2}C)$, $0<\mu<\beta^2/2$ *converges monotonically under the norm to one of the equilibrium solutions, that is,* $v(t)\to v^*$ *as* $t\to\infty$.

2. Second-order discrepancy-controlled gradient process with coupled variables

Consider the extension of (1.1) as the game with coupled variables

$$\begin{aligned} x_1^* &\in \text{Argmin}\{f_1(z_1,x_2^*)+\varphi_1(z_1) \mid g(z_1,x_2^*) \leq 0,\ z_1\in X_1\},\\ x_2^* &\in \text{Argmin}\{f_2(x_1^*,z_2)+\varphi_2(z_2) \mid g(x_1^*,z_2) \leq 0,\ z_2\in X_2\}, \end{aligned} \tag{2.1}$$

where constrained function $g(x_1,x_2)$ is convex in x_1 for any fixed x_2 and convex in x_2 for any fixed x_1 but not convex in both variables jointly generally speaking. Each of the players in this problem has the same functional constraint but with respect to own variables. The level of independence behaviour of players in this situation is not high since variables of players are coupled both in the objective functions and in the constraints. Therefore, it is natural to consider the problem in scalarized form, that is, as the equilibrium programming problem in space of macrovariables $v,w\in\Omega\times\Omega$. To this end, we enter two normalized functions of the kind

$$\begin{aligned} \Phi(v,w)+\varphi(w) &= f_1(z_1,x_2)+\varphi_1(z_1)+f_2(x_1,z_2)+\varphi_2(z_2),\\ G(v,w) &= g(z_1,x_2)+g(x_1,z_2), \end{aligned} \tag{2.2}$$

where $w = (z_1, z_2)$, $v = (x_1, x_2)$, $v, w \in \Omega = X_1 \times X_2 \in R_1^{n_1} \times R_2^{n_2}$. In terms of new variables, problem (2.1) can be presented as follows:

$$v^* \in \operatorname{Argmin}\{\Phi(v^*, w) + \varphi(w) \mid G(v^*, w) \le 0,\ w \in \Omega\}, \tag{2.3}$$

or that is the same as

$$\Phi(v^*, v^*) + \varphi(v^*) \le \Phi(v^*, w) + \varphi(w), \quad G(v^*, w) \le 0 \quad \forall w \in \Omega. \tag{2.4}$$

Easy to be convinced of equivalence of problems (2.1) and (2.3) [7].

To solve the game (2.1), it is enough to solve the equilibrium problem (2.3). With this purpose, we introduce the Lagrange function for problem

$$\mathcal{L}(v, w, \lambda) = \Phi(v, w) + \varphi(w) + \langle \lambda, G(v, w) \rangle, \tag{2.5}$$

where $v \in \Omega$, $w \in \Omega$, $\lambda \ge 0$. Assuming that this function has gotten a saddle point v^*, λ^* in the state of equilibrium $v = v^*$ for problem (2.3), then we can write the system of inequalities

$$\mathcal{L}(v^*, v^*, \lambda) \le \mathcal{L}(v^*, v^*, \lambda^*) \le \mathcal{L}(v^*, w, \lambda^*) \quad \forall w \in \Omega,\ \lambda \ge 0. \tag{2.6}$$

This system of inequalities can be rewritten in the equivalent forms as follows: variational inequalities

$$\begin{gathered} \langle \nabla_2 \Phi(v^*, v^*) + \nabla \varphi(v^*) + \nabla_2 G^T(v^*, v^*) \lambda^*, w - v^* \rangle \ge 0 \quad \forall w \in \Omega, \\ -\langle G(v^*, v^*), \lambda - \lambda^* \rangle \ge 0 \quad \forall \lambda \ge 0, \end{gathered} \tag{2.7}$$

where $\nabla_2 \Phi(v, w) = (\partial/\partial w)\Phi(v, w)$, $\nabla \varphi(w)$, are gradients in w for any v for functions $\Phi(v, w)$, $\varphi(w)$, respectively, $\nabla_2 G(v, w)$ is a matrix, where $\nabla_2 G_i(v, w)$, $i = 1, 2, \ldots, n_1 + n_2$, is vector-row of gradient for $G_i(v, w)$ in w, $\nabla_2 G^T(\cdot, \cdot)$ is a transposed matrix and operator equations

$$\begin{gathered} v^* = \pi_\Omega\big(v^* - \alpha(\nabla_2 \Phi(v^*, v^*) + \nabla \varphi(v^*) + \nabla_2 G^T(v^*, v^*) \lambda^*)\big), \\ \lambda^* = \pi_+\left(\lambda^* + \left(\frac{\alpha}{2}\right) G(v^*, v^*)\right), \end{gathered} \tag{2.8}$$

where $\pi_\Omega(\cdots)$, $\pi_+(\cdots)$, are projection operators of some vector onto Ω and the positive orthant R_+^n, respectively, $\alpha > 0$ is a parameter like step length.

Before passing to discuss the solution methods of the system of equations (2.8), we consider properties of function $G(v, w)$ in more details. First of all, we mark properties of symmetry for this function. Indeed, from $G(v, w) = g(z_1, x_2) + g(x_1, z_2) = g(x_1, z_2) + g(z_1, x_2) = G(w, v)$, it follows that

$$G(v, w) = G(w, v) \quad \forall v \in \Omega,\ w \in \Omega. \tag{2.9}$$

Differentiating this identity in w, we receive

$$\nabla_2 G(v,w) = \nabla_1 G(w,v) \quad \forall v \in \Omega,\ w \in \Omega, \tag{2.10}$$

where $\nabla_1 G(\cdot,\cdot)$, $\nabla_2 G(\cdot,\cdot)$ are partial gradients (derivatives) in first and second variables.

Using the assertion obtained, it is very easy to prove [5] the key property of symmetrical function $G(v,w)$, namely, private in w gradient restriction of function $G(v,w)$ on the diagonal of square $\Omega \times \Omega$ is equal to a half of gradient of restricted function $G(v,w)$ onto this diagonal of square

$$2\nabla_2 G(v,w)\big|_{v=w} = \nabla G(v,v) \quad \forall v \in \Omega. \tag{2.11}$$

We suppose also that functions $\Phi(v,w), G(v,w)$ are subject to property of positive semidefiniteness (1.8). Using statements (1.8)–(1.10), we transform the first variational inequality from (2.7). To this end, we consider separately third term in this inequality. Taking into account the key property of symmetric (2.11) and convexity of vector function $G(v,v)$ componently (1.9), we have

$$\begin{aligned} \langle \nabla_2 G^T(v^*,v^*)\lambda^*, w - v^*\rangle &= \frac{1}{2}\langle \lambda^*, \nabla G(v^*,v^*)(w - v^*)\rangle \\ &\le \frac{1}{2}\langle \lambda^*, G(w,w) - G(v^*,v^*)\rangle \ge 0. \end{aligned} \tag{2.12}$$

In view of an obtained evaluation, we rewrite the first inequality from (2.7) as

$$\langle \nabla_2 \Phi(v^*,v^*) + \nabla\varphi(v^*), w - v^*\rangle + \left(\frac{1}{2}\right)\langle \lambda^*, G(w,w) - G(v^*,v^*)\rangle \ge 0 \tag{2.13}$$

for all $w \in \Omega$. According to (1.10), the operator $\nabla_2\Phi(v,v) + \varphi(v)$ is monotone, then we get from (2.13) that

$$\langle \nabla_2 \Phi(w,w) + \nabla\varphi(w), w - v^*\rangle + \left(\frac{1}{2}\right)\langle \lambda^*, G(w,w) - G(v^*,v^*)\rangle \ge 0 \tag{2.14}$$

for all $w \in \Omega$. These estimates are underlying in the convergence analysis of controlled gradient methods for computing of equilibrium solutions [6].

Repeating the reasoning (1.5)–(1.7) in new situation, we obtain the system of differential equations

$$\begin{aligned} \mu\frac{d^2\lambda}{dt^2} + \beta\frac{d\lambda}{dt} + \lambda &= \pi_+\left(\lambda + \left(\frac{\alpha}{2}\right)G(\bar v,\bar v)\right), \\ \mu\frac{d^2 v}{dt^2} + \beta\frac{dv}{dt} + v &= \pi_\Omega(v - \alpha\nabla_2\mathcal{L}(\bar v,\bar v,\bar\lambda)), \end{aligned} \tag{2.15}$$

where the feedbacks are as follows:

$$\begin{aligned} \bar\lambda &= \pi_+\left(\lambda + \left(\frac{\alpha}{2}\right)G(v,v)\right), \\ \bar v &= \pi_\Omega(v - \alpha\nabla_2\mathcal{L}(v,v,\bar\lambda)). \end{aligned} \tag{2.16}$$

The value of parameter α in (2.15) is chosen from certain interval

$$0 < \varepsilon \leq \alpha < \alpha_0, \quad \varepsilon > 0, \tag{2.17}$$

and $\nabla_2\mathcal{L}(\bar{v},\bar{v},\bar{\lambda}) = \nabla_2\Phi(\bar{v},\bar{v}) + \nabla\varphi(\bar{v}) + \nabla_2 G^T(\bar{v},\bar{v})\bar{\lambda}$, $\nabla_2\mathcal{L}(v,v,\bar{\lambda}) = \nabla_2\Phi(v,v) + \nabla\varphi(v) + \nabla_2 G^T(v,v)\bar{\lambda}$.

The iterative analog of this process has the kind [4]

$$\begin{aligned}
\bar{\lambda}^n &= \pi_+\left(\lambda^n + \left(\frac{\alpha}{2}\right)G(v^n,v^n)\right),\\
\bar{v}^n &= \pi_\Omega\left(v^n - \alpha\nabla_2\mathcal{L}(v^n,v^n,\bar{\lambda}^n)\right),\\
\lambda^{n+1} &= \pi_+\left(\lambda^n + \left(\frac{\alpha}{2}\right)G(\bar{v}^n,\bar{v}^n)\right) + \beta(\lambda^n - \lambda^{n-1}),\\
v^{n+1} &= \pi_\Omega\left(v^n - \alpha\nabla_2\mathcal{L}(\bar{v}^n,\bar{v}^n,\bar{\lambda}^n)\right) + \beta(v^n - v^{n-1}).
\end{aligned} \tag{2.18}$$

The particular cases of (2.15), (2.17) for solving the game problem (1.3) have the forms, respectively, (1.6), (1.7).

For the justification of correctness of selecting out parameter α, we receive evaluations of deviations for vectors $\mu\ddot{\lambda} + \beta\dot{\lambda} + \lambda$ and $\bar{\lambda}$, $\mu\ddot{v} + \beta\dot{v} + v$ and $\bar{v}$ in (2.15)

$$|\mu\ddot{\lambda} + \beta\dot{\lambda} + \lambda - \bar{\lambda}| \leq \left(\frac{\alpha}{2}\right)|G(\bar{v},\bar{v}) - G(v,v)| \leq \left(\frac{\alpha}{2}\right)C_3|v - \bar{v}|, \tag{2.19}$$

$$\begin{aligned}
|\mu\ddot{v} + \beta\dot{v} + v - \bar{v}| &\leq \alpha|\nabla_2\mathcal{L}(\bar{v},\bar{v},\bar{\lambda}) - \nabla_2\mathcal{L}(v,v,\bar{\lambda})|\\
&\leq \big(|\nabla_2\Phi(\bar{v},\bar{v}) + \nabla\varphi(\bar{v}) - \nabla_2\Phi(v,v) - \nabla\varphi(v)|\\
&\qquad + |\nabla_2 G^T(\bar{v},\bar{v}) - \nabla_2 G^T(v,v)|\,|\bar{\lambda}|\big) \leq \alpha(C_1 + C_2|\bar{\lambda}|)|\bar{v} - v|\\
&\leq \alpha(C_1 + C_2 C)|\bar{v} - v|,
\end{aligned} \tag{2.20}$$

where

$$\begin{aligned}
\big(|\nabla_2\Phi(v,v) + \nabla\varphi(v) - \nabla_2\Phi(\bar{v},\bar{v}) - \nabla\varphi(\bar{v})|\big) &\leq C_1|\bar{v} - v|,\\
|\nabla_2 G^T(v,v) - \nabla_2 G^T(\bar{v},\bar{v})| &\leq C_2|\bar{v} - v|,\\
|G(v,v) - G(\bar{v},\bar{v})| \leq C_3|v - \bar{v}|, &\qquad |\bar{\lambda}| \leq C.
\end{aligned} \tag{2.21}$$

We rewrite process (2.15) in the form of variational inequalities

$$\begin{aligned}
&\left\langle \mu\ddot{\lambda} + \beta\dot{\lambda} - \left(\frac{\alpha}{2}\right)G(\bar{v},\bar{v}), y - \mu\ddot{\lambda} - \beta\dot{\lambda} - \lambda\right\rangle \geq 0,\\
&\langle \mu\ddot{v} + \beta\dot{v} + \alpha\nabla_2\mathcal{L}(\bar{v},\bar{v},\bar{\lambda}), z - \mu\ddot{v} - \beta\dot{v} - v\rangle \geq 0,
\end{aligned} \tag{2.22}$$

$$\begin{aligned}
&\left\langle \bar{\lambda} - \lambda - \left(\frac{\alpha}{2}\right)G(v,v), y - \bar{\lambda}\right\rangle \geq 0,\\
&\langle \bar{v} - v + \alpha\nabla_2\mathcal{L}(v,v,\bar{\lambda}), z - \bar{v}\rangle \geq 0,
\end{aligned} \tag{2.23}$$

for all $z \in \Omega$, $y \geq 0$.

3. Proof of convergence

We show that the process (2.15)-(2.17) converges monotonically under the norm to one of equilibrium solutions.

THEOREM 3.1. *Suppose that a solution set of scalarized game problem (2.3) is nonempty, functions $\Phi(v,w)$, $G(v,w)$ are positive semidefinite and convex in w for any v, the Lipschitz conditions hold in (2.21), dual trajectory $|\bar{\lambda}(t)| \le C$ is bounded for all $t \ge t_0$, $\Omega \subseteq R^n$ is convex closed set. Then, the trajectories $v(t)$, $\lambda(t)$ generated by method (2.15)-(2.17) with the parameters*

$$0 < \varepsilon \le \alpha < \frac{1}{\sqrt{2(C_1 + C_2 C)^2 + (1/4)C_3^2}}, \quad 0 < \mu < \frac{\beta^2}{2}, \ \varepsilon > 0, \tag{3.1}$$

converge monotonically under the norm to one of the equilibrium solutions, that is, $v(t)$, $\lambda(t) \to v^*, \lambda^* \in \Omega^* \times R^n_+$ as $t \to \infty$.

Proof. By putting $z = v^*$ in (2.22), we get

$$\begin{aligned} &-|\mu\ddot{v} + \beta\dot{v}|^2 + \langle \mu\ddot{v} + \beta\dot{v}, v^* - v\rangle + \alpha\langle \nabla_2 \mathcal{L}(\bar{v},\bar{v},\bar{\lambda}), v^* - \bar{v}\rangle \\ &\quad + \alpha\langle \nabla_2 \mathcal{L}(\bar{v},\bar{v},\bar{\lambda}), \bar{v} - \mu\ddot{v} - \beta\dot{v} - v\rangle \ge 0. \end{aligned} \tag{3.2}$$

Using the condition (2.11) and the convexity condition (1.9), we transform the third term occurring in (3.2)

$$\begin{aligned} &\langle \nabla_2 \mathcal{L}(\bar{v},\bar{v},\bar{\lambda}), v^* - \bar{v}\rangle \\ &\quad = \langle \nabla_2 \Phi(\bar{v},\bar{v}) + \nabla\varphi(\bar{v}) + \nabla_2 G^T(\bar{v},\bar{v})\bar{\lambda}, v^* - \bar{v}\rangle \\ &\quad = \langle \nabla_2 \Phi(\bar{v},\bar{v}) + \nabla\varphi(\bar{v}), v^* - \bar{v}\rangle + \left(\frac{1}{2}\right)\langle \bar{\lambda}, \nabla G(\bar{v},\bar{v})(v^* - \bar{v})\rangle \\ &\quad \le \langle \nabla_2 \Phi(\bar{v},\bar{v}) + \nabla\varphi(\bar{v}), v^* - \bar{v}\rangle + \left(\frac{1}{2}\right)\langle \bar{\lambda}, G(v^*,v^*) - G(\bar{v},\bar{v})\rangle. \end{aligned} \tag{3.3}$$

Using (2.20), we estimate the fourth term

$$\begin{aligned} &\langle \nabla_2 \mathcal{L}(\bar{v},\bar{v},\bar{\lambda}), \bar{v} - \mu\ddot{v} - \beta\dot{v} - v\rangle \\ &\quad = \langle \nabla_2 \mathcal{L}(\bar{v},\bar{v},\bar{\lambda}) - \nabla_2 \mathcal{L}(v,v,\bar{\lambda}), \bar{v} - \mu\ddot{v} - \beta\dot{v} - v\rangle \\ &\qquad + \langle \nabla_2 \mathcal{L}(v,v,\bar{\lambda}), \bar{v} - \mu\ddot{v} - \beta\dot{v} - v\rangle \\ &\quad \le \alpha(C_1 + C_2 C)^2 |\bar{v} - v|^2 + \langle \nabla_2 \mathcal{L}(v,v,\bar{\lambda}), \bar{v} - \mu\ddot{v} - \beta\dot{v} - v\rangle. \end{aligned} \tag{3.4}$$

Using the obtained estimations, we present (3.2) as

$$
\begin{aligned}
&-|\mu\ddot{v}+\beta\dot{v}|^2+\langle\mu\ddot{v}+\beta\dot{v},v^*-v\rangle\\
&\quad+\alpha\langle\nabla_2\Phi(\bar{v},\bar{v})+\nabla\varphi(\bar{v}),v^*-\bar{v}\rangle+\left(\frac{\alpha}{2}\right)\langle\bar{\lambda},G(v^*,v^*)-G(\bar{v},\bar{v})\rangle\\
&\quad+\alpha^2(C_1+C_2C)^2|\bar{v}-v|^2+\alpha\langle\nabla_2\mathcal{L}(v,v,\bar{\lambda}),\bar{v}-\mu\ddot{v}-\beta\dot{v}-v\rangle.
\end{aligned}
\tag{3.5}
$$

We put $z=v+\beta\dot{v}+\mu\ddot{v}$ at (2.23), then

$$
\langle\bar{v}-v+\alpha\nabla_2\mathcal{L}(v,v,\bar{\lambda}),v+\beta\dot{v}+\mu\ddot{v}-\bar{v}\rangle\geq 0.
\tag{3.6}
$$

Add inequality obtained to (3.5),

$$
\begin{aligned}
&-|\mu\ddot{v}+\beta\dot{v}|^2+\langle\mu\ddot{v}+\beta\dot{v},v^*-v\rangle\\
&\quad+\alpha\langle\nabla_2\Phi(\bar{v},\bar{v})+\nabla\varphi(\bar{v}),v^*-\bar{v}\rangle+\left(\frac{\alpha}{2}\right)\langle\bar{\lambda},G(v^*,v^*)-G(\bar{v},\bar{v})\rangle\\
&\quad+\alpha^2(C_1+C_2C)^2|\bar{v}-v|^2+\langle\bar{v}-v,v+\beta\dot{v}+\mu\ddot{v}-\bar{v}\rangle\geq 0.
\end{aligned}
\tag{3.7}
$$

Putting $w=\bar{v}$ at (2.14), we add the inequality obtained to (3.7), and we have

$$
\begin{aligned}
&-|\mu\ddot{v}+\beta\dot{v}|^2+\langle\mu\ddot{v}+\beta\dot{v},v^*-v\rangle+\left(\frac{\alpha}{2}\right)\langle\bar{\lambda}-\lambda^*,G(v^*,v^*)-G(\bar{v},\bar{v})\rangle\\
&\quad+\alpha^2(C_1+C_2C)^2|\bar{v}-v|^2+\langle\bar{v}-v,v+\beta\dot{v}+\mu\ddot{v}-\bar{v}\rangle\geq 0.
\end{aligned}
\tag{3.8}
$$

Let us perform a similar sequence of manipulation for the first inequalities (2.22), (2.23). Setting $y=\lambda+\beta\dot{\lambda}+\mu\ddot{\lambda}$ in (2.23), then

$$
\begin{aligned}
&\langle\bar{\lambda}-\lambda,\lambda+\beta\dot{\lambda}+\mu\ddot{\lambda}-\bar{\lambda}\rangle+\left(\frac{\alpha}{2}\right)\langle G(\bar{v},\bar{v})-G(v,v),\lambda+\beta\dot{\lambda}+\mu\ddot{\lambda}-\bar{\lambda}\rangle\\
&\quad-\left(\frac{\alpha}{2}\right)\langle G(\bar{v},\bar{v}),\lambda+\beta\dot{\lambda}+\mu\ddot{\lambda}-\bar{\lambda}\rangle\geq 0.
\end{aligned}
\tag{3.9}
$$

We estimate the second term of the inequality with the help of (2.19), (2.21) and add it to the inequality obtained from the first inequality (2.22) by the substitution $y=\lambda^*$, then

$$
\begin{aligned}
&\langle\bar{\lambda}-\lambda,\lambda+\beta\dot{\lambda}+\mu\ddot{\lambda}-\bar{\lambda}\rangle+\left(\left(\frac{\alpha}{2}\right)C_3\right)^2|v-\bar{v}|^2\\
&\quad+\langle\mu\ddot{\lambda}+\beta\dot{\lambda},\lambda^*-\mu\ddot{\lambda}-\beta\dot{\lambda}-\lambda\rangle-\left(\frac{\alpha}{2}\right)\langle G(\bar{v},\bar{v}),\lambda^*-\bar{\lambda}\rangle\geq 0.
\end{aligned}
\tag{3.10}
$$

Taking into account the relations $\langle\bar{\lambda}, G(v^*,v^*)\rangle \leq 0$ and $\langle\bar{\lambda}^*, G(v^*,v^*)\rangle = 0$, we rewrite the last inequality in the form

$$\begin{aligned}&\langle\bar{\lambda}-\lambda,\lambda+\beta\dot{\lambda}+\mu\ddot{\lambda}-\bar{\lambda}\rangle+\left(\left(\frac{\alpha}{2}\right)C_3\right)^2|v-\bar{v}|^2\\&-|\mu\ddot{\lambda}+\beta\dot{\lambda}|^2+\langle\mu\ddot{\lambda}+\beta\dot{\lambda},\lambda^*-\lambda\rangle\\&-\left(\frac{\alpha}{2}\right)\langle\bar{\lambda}-\lambda^*,G(v^*,v^*)-G(\bar{v},\bar{v})\rangle\geq 0.\end{aligned}\tag{3.11}$$

Next, we add inequalities (3.8) and (3.11),

$$\begin{aligned}&-|\mu\ddot{v}+\beta\dot{v}|^2-|\mu\ddot{\lambda}+\beta\dot{\lambda}|^2+\langle\mu\ddot{v}+\beta\dot{v},v^*-v\rangle\\&+\langle\mu\ddot{\lambda}+\beta\dot{\lambda},\lambda^*-\lambda\rangle+\alpha^2\left((C_1+C_2C)^2+\left(\frac{1}{4}\right)C_3^2\right)|\bar{v}-v|^2\\&+\langle\bar{v}-v,v+\beta\dot{v}+\mu\ddot{v}-\bar{v}\rangle+\langle\bar{\lambda}-\lambda,\lambda+\beta\dot{\lambda}+\mu\ddot{\lambda}-\bar{\lambda}\rangle\geq 0.\end{aligned}\tag{3.12}$$

We denote $s=(v,\lambda)^T$, $\dot{s}=(\dot{v},\dot{\lambda})^T$, $\bar{s}=(\bar{v},\bar{\lambda})^T$, $s^*=(v^*,\lambda^*)^T$, and $\ddot{s}=(\ddot{v},\ddot{\lambda})^T$, and rewrite the last inequality as

$$\begin{aligned}&-|\mu\ddot{s}+\beta\dot{s}|^2+\langle\mu\ddot{s}+\beta\dot{s},s^*-s\rangle\\&+\alpha^2\left((C_1+C_2C)^2+\left(\frac{1}{4}\right)C_3^2\right)|\bar{v}-v|^2+\langle\bar{s}-s,s+\beta\dot{s}+\mu\ddot{s}-\bar{s}\rangle\geq 0.\end{aligned}\tag{3.13}$$

By virtue of the identity

$$|x_1-x_2|^2=|x_1-x_3|^2+2\langle x_1-x_3,x_3-x_2\rangle+|x_3-x_2|^2,\tag{3.14}$$

we have the expansion

$$2\langle s+\beta\dot{s}+\mu\ddot{s}-\bar{s},\bar{s}-s\rangle=|\beta\dot{s}+\mu\ddot{s}|^2-|\bar{s}-s|^2-|s+\beta\dot{s}+\mu\ddot{s}-\bar{s}|^2,\tag{3.15}$$

which allows us to represent inequality (3.13) in the form

$$\begin{aligned}&-|\mu\ddot{s}+\beta\dot{s}|^2-2\langle\mu\ddot{s}+\beta\dot{s},s-s^*\rangle-\left(1-2\alpha^2\left((C_1+C_2C)^2+\left(\frac{1}{4}\right)C_3^2\right)\right)|v-\bar{v}|^2\\&+|\lambda-\bar{\lambda}|^2-|s+\beta\dot{s}+\mu\ddot{s}-\bar{s}|^2\geq 0.\end{aligned}\tag{3.16}$$

Next, using the identity

$$\frac{d}{dt}\langle\mu\dot{s}+\beta(s-s^*),s-s^*\rangle=\langle\mu\ddot{s}+\beta\dot{s},s-s^*\rangle+\langle\mu\dot{s}+\beta(s-s^*),\dot{s}\rangle,\tag{3.17}$$

we rewrite (3.16) as

$$\begin{aligned}&|\mu\ddot{s}+\beta\dot{s}|^2-2\langle\mu\dot{s}+\beta(s-s^*),\dot{s}\rangle+2\frac{d}{dt}\langle\mu\dot{s}+\beta(s-s^*),s-s^*\rangle\\&+d_1|s-\bar{s}|^2+|s+\beta\dot{s}+\mu\ddot{s}-\bar{s}|^2\leq 0,\end{aligned}\tag{3.18}$$

where $d_1 = 1 - 2\alpha^2((C_1 + C_2C)^2 + (1/4)C_3^2) > 0$ by the assumption of the theorem, and consequently we have

$$0 < \varepsilon \le \alpha < \frac{1}{\sqrt{2(C_1 + C_2C)^2 + (1/4)C_3^2}}, \qquad \varepsilon > 0. \tag{3.19}$$

Let us consider the first and third terms at (3.18) separately,

$$\begin{aligned} |\mu\ddot{s} + \beta\dot{s}|^2 &= \mu^2|\ddot{s}|^2 + \mu\beta\frac{d}{dt}|\dot{s}|^2 + \beta^2|\dot{s}|^2, \\ \frac{d}{dt}\langle\mu\dot{s} + \beta(s - s^*), s - s^*\rangle &= \frac{\mu}{2}\frac{d^2}{dt^2}|s - s^*|^2 + \beta\frac{d}{dt}|s - s^*|^2. \end{aligned} \tag{3.20}$$

Taking into account the resultant expansions, we rewrite inequality (3.18) as

$$\begin{aligned} &\mu\frac{d^2}{dt^2}|s - s^*|^2 + \beta\frac{d}{dt}|s - s^*|^2 + \mu\beta\frac{d}{dt}|\dot{s}|^2 + \mu^2|\ddot{s}|^2 \\ &\quad + (\beta^2 - 2\mu)|\dot{s}|^2 + d_1|s - \bar{s}|^2 + |s + \beta\dot{s} + \mu\ddot{s} - \bar{s}|^2 \le 0, \end{aligned} \tag{3.21}$$

where $d_2 = \beta^2 - 2\mu > 0$ by the theorem conditions.

Integrating inequality (3.21) from t_0 to t, we obtain

$$\begin{aligned} &\mu\frac{d}{dt}|s - s^*|^2 + \beta|s - s^*|^2 + \mu\beta|\dot{s}|^2 + \mu^2\int_{t_0}^{t}|\ddot{s}|^2 d\tau + d_2\int_{t_0}^{t}|\dot{s}|^2 d\tau \\ &\quad + d_1\int_{t_0}^{t}|s - \bar{s}|^2 d\tau + \int_{t_0}^{t}|\bar{s} - s - \beta\dot{s} - \mu\ddot{s}|^2 d\tau \le C. \end{aligned} \tag{3.22}$$

Let us show that the trajectory $s(t)$ is bounded. By virtue of the assumptions of the theorem, the last five terms are nonnegative; therefore, from (3.22) we obtain

$$\mu\frac{d}{dt}|s - s^*|^2 + \beta|s - s^*|^2 \le C. \tag{3.23}$$

Hence

$$\mu\exp\left(-\left(\frac{\beta}{\mu}\right)t\right)\frac{d}{dt}\left(\exp\left(\left(\frac{\beta}{\mu}\right)t\right)|s - s^*|^2\right) \le C. \tag{3.24}$$

Let us integrate the resultant inequality:

$$\exp\left(\left(\frac{\beta}{\mu}\right)t\right)|s - s^*|^2 \le C_1\exp\left(\left(\frac{\beta}{\mu}\right)t\right) + C_2, \tag{3.25}$$

whence

$$|s - s^*|^2 \le C_1 + C_2\exp\left(-\left(\frac{\beta}{\mu}\right)t\right) \le C_0. \tag{3.26}$$

The boundedness of the trajectory $s(t)$ for all $t \ge t_0$ is thereby justified.

Let us show that the first term occurring in (3.23) is bounded below. First, we show that $|\dot{s}(t)|^2$ is bounded for all $t \geq t_0$. Obviously, integrating inequality (3.21), we obtain

$$2\langle s - s^*, \dot{s}\rangle + \beta|\dot{s}|^2 \leq C. \tag{3.27}$$

Extracting a complete square, we have

$$\left|\left(\frac{1}{\sqrt{\beta}}\right)(s - s^*) + \sqrt{\beta}\dot{s}\right|^2 - \left(\frac{1}{\beta}\right)|s - s^*|^2 \leq C. \tag{3.28}$$

Since $|s - s^*|^2 \leq C_0$, it follows from the last inequality that $|\dot{s}|^2 \leq C_1$.

Now we can estimate the first term in (3.18). By virtue of the obvious estimate $0 \leq |s - s^* + \dot{s}|^2 = |s - s^*|^2 + 2\langle s - s^*, \dot{s}\rangle + |\dot{s}|^2$, we have $\langle s - s^*, \dot{s}\rangle \geq -(1/2)(C_0 + C_1)$.

Taking into account the above estimates, we can represent inequality (3.22) as

$$\begin{aligned}\mu^2 \int_{t_0}^{t} |\ddot{s}|^2 d\tau + d_2 \int_{t_0}^{t} |\dot{s}|^2 d\tau + d_1 \int_{t_0}^{t} |s - \bar{s}|^2 d\tau \\ + \int_{t_0}^{t} |\bar{s} - s - \beta\dot{s} - \mu\ddot{s}|^2 d\tau \leq C + \left(\frac{\mu}{2}\right)(C_0 + C_1)\end{aligned} \tag{3.29}$$

Hence, the integrals

$$\begin{aligned}\int_{t_0}^{t} |\ddot{s}|^2 d\tau < \infty, \qquad \int_{t_0}^{t} |\dot{s}|^2 d\tau < \infty, \\ \int_{t_0}^{t} |s - \bar{s}|^2 d\tau < \infty, \qquad \int_{t_0}^{t} |\bar{s} - s - \beta\dot{s} - \mu\ddot{s}|^2 d\tau < \infty\end{aligned} \tag{3.30}$$

are convergent as $t \to \infty$.

Let us prove the convergence of the trajectory $s(t)$ to the equilibrium solution of the problem. Supposing that there exists an $\varepsilon > 0$ such that $|\ddot{s}(t)| \geq \varepsilon$, $|\dot{s}(t)| \geq \varepsilon$, $|s - \bar{s}|^2 \geq \varepsilon$ for all $t \geq t_0$, we arrive at a contradiction with the convergence of the integrals.

Consequently, there exists a subsequence $t_i \to \infty$ of time instants such that $|\ddot{s}(t_i)| \to 0$, $|\dot{s}(t_i)| \to 0$, $|s(t_i) - \bar{s}(t_i)| \to 0$. Since $s(t)$ is bounded, it follows that we choose once more a subsequence of time instant (denote by t_i again) such that $|s(t_i)| \to s'$, $|s(t_i) - \bar{s}(t_i)| \to 0$, $|\dot{s}(t_i)| \to 0$, $|\ddot{s}(t_i)| \to 0$.

Let us consider equations (2.15), (2.17) for all time instants $t_i \to \infty$, passing to the limit, we write out the limit relation

$$\begin{aligned}v' &= \pi_\Omega(v' - \alpha(\nabla_2\Phi(v', v') + \nabla\varphi(v') + \nabla_2 G^T(v', v')\lambda')), \\ \lambda' &= \pi_+\left(\lambda' + \left(\frac{\alpha}{2}\right)G(v', v')\right).\end{aligned} \tag{3.31}$$

The system of equations coincides with (2.8); consequently, we have $s' = (v', \lambda') = s^* = (v^*, \lambda^*) \in \Omega^*$. Therefore, any limit point of the trajectory $s(t) = (v(t), \lambda(t))$ is a solution of problem (2.1). Let us show that trajectory $s(t)$ has only one limit point.

Of i indices of the above-defined subsequence, we chose i_0 such that $|s(t_{i_0}) - s'| \le \varepsilon$, $|\dot{s}(t_{i_0})| \le \varepsilon$, where $\varepsilon > 0$ is an arbitrarily small number. Then we omit positive terms in (3.21) and integrate the resultant inequality from t_{i_0} to t:

$$\begin{aligned} &\mu\frac{d}{dt}|s(t) - s'|^2 + \beta|s(t) - s'|^2 + \mu\beta|\dot{s}(t)|^2 \\ &\quad \le \mu\frac{d}{dt}|s(t_{i_0}) - s'|^2 + \beta|s(t_{i_0}) - s'|^2 + \mu\beta|\dot{s}(t_{i_0})|^2. \end{aligned} \tag{3.32}$$

Taking into account the identity $(d/dt)|s(t) - s'|^2 = 2\langle s(t) - s', \dot{v}\rangle$, we estimate the right-hand side of the last inequality as

$$\mu\frac{d}{dt}|s(t) - s'|^2 + \beta|s(t) - s'|^2 + \mu\beta|\dot{s}|^2 \le 2\mu\varepsilon^2 + \beta\varepsilon^2 + \mu\beta\varepsilon^2 \le C\varepsilon^2. \tag{3.33}$$

In particular, from the resultant estimate and (3.32), we have

$$\mu\frac{d}{dt}|s(t) - s'|^2 + \beta|s(t) - s'|^2 \le C\varepsilon^2, \tag{3.34}$$

which is an exact analog of (3.23). Repeating once more the arguments used below (3.23), we obtain the estimate

$$|s - s'|^2 \le C_1\varepsilon^2, \tag{3.35}$$

for all $t \le t_{i_0}$. Therefore, starting with some time t_{i_0}, the entire trajectory $s(t)$ lies in the ball with center s' and radius $C_1\varepsilon^2$. The last assertion means that the trajectory $s(t)$ cannot have other limit points, since $\varepsilon > 0$ is arbitrary. We have thereby proved the convergence of the trajectory $s(t)$ to the solution of the problem, that is, $s(t) = (v(t), \lambda(t)) \to s^* = (v^*, \lambda^*)$ as $t \to \infty$ for any initial condition s_0, $\dot{s}_0$. □

References

[1] A. Antipin, *Minimization of convex functions on convex sets by means of differential equations*, Differential Equations **30** (1994), no. 9, 1365–1375 (1995).

[2] ———, *On differential gradient methods of predictive type for computing fixed points of extremal mappings*, Differential Equations **31** (1995), no. 11, 1754–1763 (1996).

[3] ———, *The convergence of proximal methods to fixed points of extremal mappings and estimates of their rate of convergence*, Computational Mathematics and Mathematical Physics **35** (1995), no. 5, 539–551.

[4] ———, *Second-order controlled differential gradient methods for solving equilibrium problems*, Differential Equations **35** (1999), no. 5, 592–601.

[5] ———, *Gradient approach of computing fixed points of equilibrium problems*, Journal of Global Optimization **24** (2002), no. 3, 285–309.

[6] ———, *Extragradient approach to the solution of two person non-zero sum games*, Optimization and Optimal Control (Ulaanbaatar, 2002), Ser. Comput. Oper. Res., vol. 1, World Scientific, New Jersey, 2003, pp. 1–28.

[7] ———, *Solution of two-person nonzero-sum games by means of differential equations*, Differential Equations **39** (2003), no. 1, 11–22.

[8] ———, *Controlled differential equations for solving two-person nonzero-sum games with coupled constraints*, Dynamic Systems and Applications. Vol. 4, Dynamic, California, 2004, pp. 39–45.

[9] H. Attouch and F. Alvarez, *The heavy ball with friction dynamical system for convex constrained minimization problems*, Optimization (Namur, 1998), Lecture Notes in Economics and Mathematical Systems, vol. 481, Springer, Berlin, 2000, pp. 25–35.

[10] J.-P. Aubin and H. Frankowska, *Set-Valued Analysis*, Systems & Control: Foundations & Applications, vol. 2, Birkhäuser Boston, Massachusetts, 1990.

[11] H. Nikaidô and K. Isoda, *Note on non-cooperative convex games*, Pacific Journal of Mathematics **5** (1955), 807–815.

Anatoly Antipin: Computing Center of Russian Academy of Sciences, 40 Vavilov Street,
119991 Moscow, Russia
E-mail address: antipin@ccas.ru

ON THE EIGENVALUE OF INFINITE MATRICES WITH NONNEGATIVE OFF-DIAGONAL ELEMENTS

N. APREUTESEI AND V. VOLPERT

The paper is devoted to infinite-dimensional difference operators. Some spectral properties of such operators are studied. Under some assumptions on the essential spectrum, it is shown that a real eigenvalue with a positive eigenvector is simple and that the real parts of all other eigenvalues are less than for this one. It is a generalization of the Perron-Frobenius theorem for infinite matrices.

1. Introduction

Consider the Banach spaces E of infinite sequences $u = (\dots, u_{-1}, u_0, u_1, \dots)$ with the norm

$$||u|| = \sup_j |u_j| \tag{1.1}$$

and the operator L acting in E,

$$(Lu)_j = a_{-m}^j u_{j-m} + \cdots + a_0^j u_j + \cdots + a_m^j u_{j+m}, \quad j = 0, \pm 1, \pm 2, \dots, \tag{1.2}$$

where m is a positive integer and $a_k^j \in \mathbb{R}$, $-m \leq k \leq m$ are given coefficients. We assume that there exist the limits

$$a_k^{\pm} = \lim_{j \to \pm\infty} a_k^j, \quad k = 0, \pm 1, \dots, \pm m. \tag{1.3}$$

Consider the limiting operators $L^{\pm}$,

$$(L^{\pm}u)_j = a_{-m}^{\pm} u_{j-m} + \cdots + a_0^{\pm} u_j + \cdots + a_m^{\pm} u_{j+m}, \quad j = 0, \pm 1, \pm 2, \dots. \tag{1.4}$$

Hindawi Publishing Corporation
Proceedings of the Conference on Differential & Difference Equations and Applications, pp. 81–89

Let

$$a_{-m}^{\pm} \neq 0, \qquad a_m^{\pm} \neq 0, \tag{1.5}$$

and suppose that the equations

$$L^{\pm}u - \lambda u = 0 \tag{1.6}$$

do not have nonzero bounded solutions for any real $\lambda \geq 0$. We will call it Condition NS(λ).

Recall that a linear operator $L : E \to E$ is *normally solvable* if its image ImL is closed. If L is normally solvable with a finite-dimensional kernel and the codimension of its image is also finite, then L is called *Fredholm operator*. Denoting by $\alpha(L)$ and $\beta(L)$ the dimension of ker$L$ and the codimension of ImL, respectively, we can define *the index* $\kappa(L)$ of the operator L as $\kappa(L) = \alpha(L) - \beta(L)$.

In [1], the following result is proved (Theorem 4.10).

Theorem 1.1. *If Condition* NS(λ) *is satisfied, then L is a Fredholm operator with the zero index.*

Consider the polynomials

$$P_{\lambda}^{\pm}(\sigma) = a_m^{\pm}\sigma^{2m} + \cdots + a_1^{\pm}\sigma^{m+1} + (a_0^{\pm} - \lambda)\sigma^m + a_{-1}^{\pm}\sigma^{m-1} + \cdots + a_{-m}^{\pm}. \tag{1.7}$$

Lemma 2.1 in [2] for $L - \lambda I$ leads to the following conclusion.

Theorem 1.2. *Condition* NS(λ) *is satisfied if and only if the polynomials $P_{\lambda}^{\pm}(\sigma)$ do not have roots σ with $|\sigma| = 1$.*

As a consequence, we can obtain the following corollary.

Corollary 1.3. *If Condition* NS(λ) *is satisfied, then*

$$a_{-m}^{\pm} + \cdots + a_m^{\pm} < 0, \tag{1.8}$$

that is, $L^{\pm}q < 0$, where q is a sequence with all elements equal 1.

Proof. Suppose that the assertion of the corollary does not hold. Then $P_0^{\pm}(1) \geq 0$. On the other hand, for λ sufficiently large, $P_{\lambda}^{\pm}(1) < 0$. Therefore for some λ, $P_{\lambda}^{\pm}(1) = 0$. We obtain a contradiction with Theorem 1.2, so the conclusion is proved. □

We recall that the formally adjoint operator L^* is defined by the equality

$$(Lu, v) = (u, L^*v). \tag{1.9}$$

If we consider L as an infinite matrix, then L^* is the adjoint matrix. Let $\alpha(L^*)$ be the dimension of kerL^* and let $f = \{f_j\}_{j=-\infty}^{\infty} \in E$ be fixed. The below solvability conditions are established in [2].

THEOREM 1.4. *The equation $Lu = f$ is solvable if and only if*

$$\sum_{j=-\infty}^{\infty} f_j v_j^l = 0, \quad l = 1,\dots,\alpha(L^*), \tag{1.10}$$

where $v^l = \{v_j^l\}_{j=-\infty}^{\infty}$ are linearly independent solutions of the equation $L^* v = 0$.

In what follows, we say that u is positive (nonnegative) if all elements of this sequence are positive (nonnegative).

From now on, we suppose that

$$a_k^j > 0, \quad k = \pm 1, \pm 2, \dots, \pm m, \ j = 0, \pm 1, \pm 2, \dots, \tag{1.11}$$

and that there exists a positive solution w of the equation

$$Lu = 0. \tag{1.12}$$

This means that L has a zero eigenvalue. The goal of this paper is to show that it is simple and all other eigenvalues lie in the left half-plane. Moreover, the adjoint operator L^* has a positive solution, which is unique up to a constant factor. It is a generalization of the Perron-Frobenius theorem for infinite matrices. The method of the proof follows the method developed for elliptic problems, in unbounded domains [3, 4]. Similarly to elliptic problems, it is assumed that the essential spectrum lies to the left of the eigenvalue with a positive eigenvector.

We note that the operator L can be considered as infinite-dimensional $(2m+1)$-diagonal matrix with positive elements in all nonzero diagonals except for the main diagonal where the signs of the elements are not prescribed.

In Section 2, we present some auxiliary results. The main result is proved in Section 3.

2. Auxiliary results

Suppose that conditions (1.3), (1.5), (1.11) are satisfied. In order to prove our main result, we first present some auxiliary results. We begin with the positiveness of the solution of equation $Lu = f$ for $f \le 0$. We will use the notations

$$U_-(N) = (u_{N-m}, \dots, u_{N-1}), \qquad U_+(N) = (u_{N+1}, \dots, u_{N+m}). \tag{2.1}$$

LEMMA 2.1. *Let $Lu = f$, where $f \le 0$, $u \ge 0$, $u \not\equiv 0$. Then $u > 0$.*

Proof. Suppose that $u_j = 0$ for some j. Since $u \not\equiv 0$, there exists i such that $u_i = 0$, and either $u_{i+1} \neq 0$ or $u_{i-1} \neq 0$. The equation $(Lu)_i = f_i$ gives a contradiction in signs. The lemma is proved. □

LEMMA 2.2. *If the initial condition u^0 of the problem*

$$\frac{du}{dt} = Lu, \qquad u(0) = u^0 \tag{2.2}$$

is nonnegative, then the solution $u(t)$ is also nonnegative for all $t \in (0, \infty)$.

Proof. Consider the approximate problem

$$\begin{aligned} &\frac{du_i}{dt} = (Lu)_i, \quad -N \leq i \leq N,\ t \geq 0, \\ &U_-(-N) = 0, \quad U_+(N) = 0, \quad t \geq 0, \\ &u(0) = u^0, \end{aligned} \tag{2.3}$$

where the unknown function is $u = (u_{-N}, u_{-N+1}, \dots u_0, \dots, u_{N-1}, u_N)$.

Since $u^0 \geq 0$ and Lu has nonnegative off-diagonal coefficients, it follows that the solution $u^N = (u^N_{-N}, u^N_{-N+1}, \dots u^N_0, \dots, u^N_{N-1}, u^N_N)$ of the above problem is nonnegative.

If we compare the solution u^N at the interval $[-N, N]$ and the solution u^{N+1} at the interval $[-N-1, N+1]$, we find $u^{N+1} \geq u^N$. Indeed, the difference $u^{N+1} - u^N$ verifies a problem similar to the above one, but with a nonnegative initial condition and with zero boundary conditions. The solution of this problem is nonnegative, that is, $u^{N+1} \geq u^N$. So the sequence is monotonically increasing with respect to N. The sequence is also bounded with respect to N: $||u^N(t)|| \leq M$, for all N and $t \in [0, T]$, where T is any positive number, $M > 0$ depends on u^0 and on the coefficients a^i_k of L, which are bounded. Being bounded and monotone, it follows that u^N is convergent as $N \to \infty$ in $C([0, T]; E)$, say $u^N \to u$. By the equations, we have also $u^N \to u$ in $C^1([0, T]; E)$. Then u verifies the problem (2.2) and $u \geq 0$ (because $u^N \geq 0$), as claimed. □

Corollary 2.3 (comparison theorem). *Let $u^1(t)$ and $u^2(t)$ be solutions of the equation*

$$\frac{du}{dt} = Lu, \tag{2.4}$$

with the initial conditions $u^1(0)$ and $u^2(0)$, respectively. If $u^1(0) \leq u^2(0)$, then $u^1(t) \leq u^2(t)$ for $t \geq 0$.

Lemma 2.4. *If the initial condition u^0 of the problem*

$$\frac{du}{dt} = L^+ u, \qquad u(0) = u^0 \tag{2.5}$$

is constant (independent of j), then the solution $u(t)$ is also constant. For any bounded initial condition, the solution of problem (2.5) converges to the trivial solution $u = 0$.

The proof of this lemma follows from Corollaries 1.3 and 2.3.

Lemma 2.5. *If u is a solution of the problem*

$$Lu = f, \quad j \geq N,\ U_-(N) \geq 0, \tag{2.6}$$

where $f \leq 0$, $u_j \to 0$ as $j \to \infty$, and N is sufficiently large, then $u_j \geq 0$ for $j \geq N$.

Proof. By virtue of Corollary 1.3, there exists a constant $\epsilon > 0$ such that $L^+ q < -\epsilon$. Let us take N large enough such that

$$\left| ((L - L^+)q)_j \right| \leq \frac{\epsilon}{2}, \quad j \geq N. \tag{2.7}$$

Suppose that $u_j < 0$ for some $j > N$. By the assumption $u_j \to 0$ as $j \to \infty$, we can choose $\tau > 0$ such that $v_j = u_j + \tau q_j \geq 0$ for all $j \geq N$, and there exists $i > N$ such that $v_i = 0$. Since $V_-(N) > 0$ and $v_j > 0$ for all j sufficiently large, there exists $k > N$ such that $v_k = 0$ and either $v_{k+1} \neq 0$ or $v_{k-1} \neq 0$ (i.e., $v_{k+1} > 0$ or $v_{k-1} > 0$).

We have

$$Lv = Lu + \tau L^+ q + \tau(L - L^+)q = f + \tau L^+ q + \tau(L - L^+)q. \tag{2.8}$$

In view of (2.7), $L^+ q < -\epsilon$ and $f \leq 0$, the right-hand side of this equality is less than or equal to 0 for $j \geq N$. As in the proof of Lemma 2.1, we obtain a contradiction in signs in the equation corresponding to k. The lemma is proved. □

Remark 2.6. The assertion of the lemma remains true if we replace (2.6) by

$$Lu \leq \alpha u, \quad j \geq N, \quad U_-(N) \geq 0, \tag{2.9}$$

for some positive α. Indeed, one obtains $Lv \leq \alpha u + \tau L^+ q + \tau(L - L^+)q$ instead of (2.8), where $(Lv)_k > 0$ and $\alpha u_k + \tau L^+ q_k + \tau(L - L^+)q_k < \alpha u_k - \epsilon\tau/2 = -\tau(\alpha + \epsilon/2) < 0$, because $v_k = 0$.

3. The main result

In this section, we present the main result of this work and study some spectral properties of infinite-dimensional matrices with nonnegative off-diagonal elements.

THEOREM 3.1. *Let (1.12) have a positive bounded solution w. Then, the following hold.*

(i) *The equation*

$$Lu = \lambda u \tag{3.1}$$

does not have nonzero bounded solutions for $\operatorname{Re}\lambda \geq 0$, $\lambda \neq 0$.

(ii) *Each solution of (1.12) has the form $u = kw$, where k is a constant.*

(iii) *The equation*

$$L^* u = 0 \tag{3.2}$$

has a positive solution unique up to a constant factor.

Proof. (1) In order to prove the first assertion, we analyze two cases.

Case 1. We consider first the case where in (3.1) $\lambda = \alpha + i\beta$, $\alpha \geq 0$, $\beta \neq 0$. Suppose by contradiction that there exists a bounded nonzero solution $u = u^1 + iu^2$ of this equation. Then $Lu^1 = \alpha u^1 - \beta u^2$ and $Lu^2 = \beta u^1 + \alpha u^2$. Consider the equation

$$\frac{dv}{dt} = Lv - \alpha v, \qquad v(0) = u^1. \tag{3.3}$$

Its solution is

$$v(t) = u^1 \cos\beta t - u^2 \sin\beta t. \tag{3.4}$$

For the sequence $u = \{u_j\} = \{u_j^1 + iu_j^2\}$, we denote $\hat{u} = \{|u_j|\}$. Let us take the value of N as in Lemma 2.5 and choose $\tau > 0$ such that

$$\hat{u}_j \le \tau w_j, \quad |j| \le N, \tag{3.5}$$

where at least for one j_0 with $|j_0| \le N$, we have the equality

$$\hat{u}_{j_0} = \tau w_{j_0}. \tag{3.6}$$

For $j \ge N$, consider the problem

$$\frac{dy}{dt} = Ly - \alpha y,$$
$$y_{N-k}(t) = \hat{u}_{N-k}, \quad k = 1,\dots,m, \quad y_\infty(t) = 0, \tag{3.7}$$

$$y(0) = \hat{u}, \tag{3.8}$$

and the corresponding stationary problem

$$L\bar{y} - \alpha\bar{y} = 0, \quad \bar{y}_{N-k} = \hat{u}_{N-k}, \quad k = 1,\dots,m, \ \bar{y}_\infty = 0. \tag{3.9}$$

The operator corresponding to problem (3.9) satisfies the Fredholm property (see [2]). The corresponding homogeneous problem has only the zero solution. (For L^+ instead of L, it follows from the explicit form of the solution, see [1]; for N big enough, L and L^+ are close.) Therefore, problem (3.9) is uniquely solvable.

We show that the solution $y(t)$ of problem (3.7)-(3.8) converges to $\bar{y}$ as $t \to \infty$. For this, we consider the solution $y^*(t)$ of problem (3.7) with the initial condition $y^*(0) = \rho q$, where ρ is such that

$$\rho q_j \ge \hat{u}_j, \quad j \ge N. \tag{3.10}$$

By Corollary 1.3, we have $L^\pm q < 0$. Since L^+ is close to L for $j \ge N$, with N large enough, it follows that $(Lq)_j < 0$, $j \ge N$. Then $y^*(t)$ monotonically decreases in t for each $j \ge N$ fixed. From the positiveness and the decreasing monotonicity of y^*, we deduce that $y^*(t)$ converges as $t \to \infty$ to some $x = \lim_{t\to\infty} y^*(t) \ge 0$. It satisfies the equation $Lx - \alpha x = 0$. Taking the limit also in the boundary conditions, one obtains that $x_{N+k} = \hat{u}_{N+k}$, for $k = 1,\dots,m$ and $x_\infty = 0$, so x is a solution of problem (3.9). By the uniqueness, we get $x = \bar{y}$, that is, there exists the limit $\lim_{t\to\infty} y^*(t) = \bar{y}$.

On the other hand, let y_* be the solution of (3.7) with the initial condition $y_*(0) = 0$. It can be shown that y_* increases in time and it has an upper bound. As above, we can deduce that y_* converges to $\bar{y}$. Therefore,

$$\lim_{t\to\infty} y_*(t) = \lim_{t\to\infty} y^*(t) = \bar{y}. \tag{3.11}$$

By virtue of the comparison theorem applicable in this case (because $0 \le \hat{u}_j \le \rho q_j$, $j \ge N$), we have

$$y_*(t) \le y(t) \le y^*(t), \quad j \ge N. \tag{3.12}$$

Hence

$$\lim_{t\to\infty} y_j(t) = \bar{y}_j, \quad j \geq N. \tag{3.13}$$

One can easily verify that

$$v_j(t) \leq \hat{u}_j \quad \forall j \in \mathbb{Z}. \tag{3.14}$$

Then it follows from the comparison theorem that

$$v_j(t) \leq y_j(t), \quad j \geq N,\ t \geq 0. \tag{3.15}$$

From this, we have

$$v_j(t) = v_j\left(t + \frac{2\pi n}{\beta}\right) \leq y_j\left(t + \frac{2\pi n}{\beta}\right). \tag{3.16}$$

Passing to the limit as $n \to \infty$, we obtain

$$v_j(t) \leq \bar{y}_j, \quad j \geq N,\ t \geq 0. \tag{3.17}$$

Observe that $L(\tau w - \overline{y}) \leq \alpha(\tau w - \overline{y})$, $j \geq N$, and $\tau w_N - \overline{y}_N \geq 0$. We can apply Remark 2.6 to $\tau w - \bar{y}$. Therefore,

$$\bar{y}_j \leq \tau w_j, \quad j \geq N. \tag{3.18}$$

Hence,

$$v_j(t) \leq \tau w_j \tag{3.19}$$

for $j \geq N, t \geq 0$. The similar estimate can be obtained for $j \leq -N$. Together with (3.5), these prove (3.19) for all $j \in \mathbb{Z}$.

The sequence $z(t) = \tau w - v(t)$ is a solution of the equation

$$\frac{dz}{dt} = Lz - \alpha z + \alpha \tau w. \tag{3.20}$$

Since $z(t) \geq 0$ (via (3.19) for all $j \in \mathbb{Z}$), z is not identically zero, and is periodic in t, it follows that $z_j(t) > 0$ for all j and $t \geq 0$. Indeed, suppose that for some $t = t_1$ and $j = j_1$, $z_{j_1}(t_1) = 0$. Consider first the case where $\alpha > 0$. Since $(dz_{j_1}/dt)(t_1) \leq 0$ and $w_{j_1} > 0$, we obtain a contradiction in signs in the equation for z_{j_1}. If $\alpha = 0$, then the equation becomes

$$\frac{dz}{dt} = Lz. \tag{3.21}$$

Assuming that $z(t)$ is not strictly positive, we easily obtain that it is identically zero for all j. We have $(dz_{j_1}/dt)(t_1) \leq 0$ and $(Lz)_{j_1}(t_1) \geq 0$. Then $(Lz)_{j_1}(t_1) = 0$, so all $z_j(t_1) = 0$. Since z_{j_1} verifies $dz_{j_1}/dt = (Lz)_{j_1}$, $z_{j_1}(t_1) = 0$, by the uniqueness we find $z_{j_1}(t) = 0$, $t \geq t_1$. Combining this with $z_j(t_1) = 0$, $(\forall) j \in \mathbb{Z}$, we get $z_j(t) = 0$, $(\forall) j \in \mathbb{Z}$, $(\forall) t \in (0, \infty)$.

Thus in both cases, $z_j(t)$ is positive for all j and t. We take $t \geq 0$ such that

$$e^{-i\beta t} = \frac{u_{j_0}}{|u_{j_0}|}, \tag{3.22}$$

with j_0 from (3.6), that is, $\cos\beta t = u_{j_0}^1/|u_{j_0}|$ and $\sin\beta t = -u_{j_0}^2/|u_{j_0}|$. Then, $v_{j_0}(t) = u_{j_0}^1 \cos\beta t - u_{j_0}^2 \sin\beta t = |u_{j_0}|$, hence with the aid of (3.6) we obtain the contradiction

$$z_{j_0}(t) = \tau w_{j_0} - |u_{j_0}| = 0. \tag{3.23}$$

The first assertion of the theorem is proved for nonreal λ.

Case 2. Assume now that $\lambda \geq 0$ is real and that u is a nonzero bounded solution of (3.1). We suppose that at least one of the elements of the sequence $\{u_j\}$ is negative. Otherwise, we could change the sign of u. We consider the sequence $v = u + \tau w$, where $\tau > 0$ is chosen such that $v \geq 0$ for $|j| \leq N$, but $v_{j_0} = 0$ for some j_0, $|j_0| \leq N$. We have

$$Lv = \lambda v - \lambda \tau w, \tag{3.24}$$

and therefore $v_j \geq 0$ for all j by virtue of Lemma 2.5. Indeed, for $|j| \leq N$, the inequality holds because of the way we have chosen τ. For $j \geq N$, one applies Lemma 2.5 for (3.24) written in the form $(L - \lambda I)v = -\lambda \tau w$, $j \geq N$, with $v_N \geq 0$. If $j \leq -N$, the reasoning is similar.

If $\lambda > 0$, then the equation for v_{j_0} leads to a contradiction in signs. Thus, (3.1) cannot have different-from-zero solutions for real positive λ.

(2) If $\lambda = 0$, then we define $v = u + \tau w$ as in Case 2 above. Here u is the solution of (3.1) with $\lambda = 0$, that is, $Lu = 0$. Using the above reasoning for $\lambda \geq 0$, we have $v_j \geq 0$, $(\forall) j \in \mathbb{Z}$, but it is not strictly positive (at least $v_{j_0} = 0$). In addition, v satisfies the equation $Lv = 0$. It follows from Lemma 2.1 that $v \equiv 0$. This implies that $u_j = -\tau w_j$, $(\forall) j \in \mathbb{Z}$.

(3) The limiting operators $L^{\pm}$ are operators with constant coefficients. The corresponding matrices are $(2m+1)$-diagonal matrices with constant elements along each diagonal. The matrices associated to the limiting operators L_*^+, L_*^- of L^* are the transposed matrices, which are composed by the same diagonals reflected symmetrically with respect to the main diagonal. Therefore, the polynomials $(P_\lambda^*)^{\pm}(\sigma)$ for the operator L^* will be the same as for the operator L. By virtue of Theorem 1.2, the operator L^* satisfies the Fredholm property and it has the zero index.

We note first of all that (3.2) has a nonzero bounded solution v. Indeed, if such solution does not exist, then by virtue of the solvability conditions, the equation

$$Lu = f \tag{3.25}$$

is solvable for any f. This implies that $\operatorname{Im} L = E$, and hence $\operatorname{codim}(\operatorname{Im} L) = 0$. Since the index of L is zero, it follows that $\dim(\ker L) = 0$. But by part two of the theorem, we get $\dim(\ker L) = 1$. This contradiction shows that a nonzero bounded solution v of (3.2) exists and it is exponentially decreasing at infinity (see [2, Theorem 3.2]).

We recall next (see Theorem 1.4) that (3.25) is solvable if and only if

$$(f, v) = 0. \tag{3.26}$$

Case 1. If $v \geq 0$, then from Lemma 2.1 for equation $L^*v = 0$, it follows that v is strictly positive, as claimed.

Case 2. If we assume that a nonnegative solution of (3.2) does not exist, then it has an alternating sign. Then we can find a bounded sequence $f < 0$ such that (3.26) is satisfied.

Let u be the corresponding solution of (3.25). There exists a τ (not necessarily positive), such that $\widetilde{u} = u + \tau w \geq 0$ for $|j| \leq N$, but not strictly positive. Since $L\widetilde{u} = f$ and $f < 0$, $\widetilde{u}_N \geq 0$, and $\widetilde{u}_j \to 0$ as $j \to \infty$, by virtue of Lemma 2.5, one finds $\widetilde{u} \geq 0$ for all j. But for those j where $\widetilde{u}$ vanish, this leads to a contradiction in signs in the equation. Therefore $\widetilde{u} > 0$. The theorem is proved. □

References

[1] N. Apreutesei and V. Volpert, *Some properties of infinite dimensional discrete operators*, Topological Methods in Nonlinear Analysis **24** (2004), no. 1, 159–181.

[2] ———, *Solvability conditions for some difference operators*, Advances in Difference Equations **2005** (2005), no. 1, 1–13.

[3] A. I. Volpert and V. Volpert, *Spectrum of elliptic operators and stability of travelling waves*, Asymptotic Analysis **23** (2000), no. 2, 111–134.

[4] A. I. Volpert, V. Volpert, and V. Volpert, *Traveling Wave Solutions of Parabolic Systems*, Translations of Mathematical Monographs, vol. 140, American Mathematical Society, Rhode Island, 1994.

N. Apreutesei: Department of Mathematics, "Gh. Asachi" Technical University of Iaşi, 700506 Iaşi, Romania
E-mail address: napreut@math.tuiasi.ro

V. Volpert: Camille Jordan Institute of Mathematics, UMR 5208 CNRS, University Lyon 1, 69622 Villeurbanne, France
E-mail address: volpert@math.univ-lyon1.fr

ON STRUCTURE OF FRACTIONAL SPACES GENERATED BY THE POSITIVE OPERATORS WITH THE NONLOCAL BOUNDARY CONDITIONS

ALLABEREN ASHYRALYEV AND NERGIZ YAZ

In the present paper, a structure of fractional spaces $E_\alpha = E_\alpha(C[0,1], A^x)$ generated by the differential operator A^x defined by the formula $A^x u = -a(x)(d^2u/dx^2) + \delta u$ with domain $\mathcal{D}(A^x) = \{u \in C^{(2)}[0,1] : u(0) = u(\mu),\ u'(0) = u'(1),\ 1/2 \leq \mu \leq 1\}$ is investigated. Here $a(x)$ is a smooth function defined on the segment $[0,1]$ and $a(x) \geq a > 0$, $\delta > 0$. It is established that for any $0 < \alpha < 1/2$, the norms in the spaces $E_\alpha(C[0,1], A^x)$ and $C^{2\alpha}[0,1]$ are equivalent. The positivity of the differential operator A^x in $C^{2\alpha}[0,1] (0 \leq \alpha < 1/2)$ is established. In applications, the coercive inequalities for the solution of the nonlocal boundary value problem for two-dimensional elliptic equation are obtained.

1. Introduction

Let us consider a differential operator A^x defined by the formula

$$A^x u = -a(x)\frac{d^2u}{dx^2} + \delta u, \tag{1.1}$$

with domain $D(A^x) = \{u \in C^{(2)}[0,1] : u(0) = u(\mu),\ u'(0) = u'(1), 1/2 \leq \mu \leq 1\}$. Here $a(x)$ is a smooth function defined on the segment $[0,1]$ and $a(x) \geq a > 0$, $\delta > 0$.

For positive operator A in Banach space E, we will define the fractional spaces $E_\alpha = E_\alpha(E, A)(0 < \alpha < 1)$ consisting of those $v \in E$ for which the norm (see [9])

$$\|v\|_{E_\alpha} = \sup_{\lambda>0} \lambda^\alpha \|A(\lambda + A)^{-1}v\|_E + \|v\|_E \tag{1.2}$$

is finite.

We introduce the Banach space $C^\beta[0,1](0 < \beta < 1)$ of all continuous functions $\varphi(x)$ defined on $[0,1]$ and satisfying a Hölder condition for which the following norms are

Hindawi Publishing Corporation
Proceedings of the Conference on Differential & Difference Equations and Applications, pp. 91–101

finite:

$$\|\varphi\|_{C^{\beta}[0,1]} = \|\varphi\|_{C[0,1]} + \sup_{0\le x<x+\tau\le 1} \frac{|\varphi(x+\tau)-\varphi(x)|}{\tau^{\beta}}, \tag{1.3}$$

where $C[0,1]$ is the space of all continuous functions $\varphi(x)$ defined on $[0,1]$ with the usual norm

$$\|\varphi\|_{C[0,1]} = \max_{0\le x\le 1} |\varphi(x)|. \tag{1.4}$$

In the present paper, we will investigate the resolvent of the operator $-A^x$, that is, in solving the equation

$$A^x u + \lambda u = f \tag{1.5}$$

or

$$\begin{gathered} -a(x)\frac{d^2u(x)}{dx^2} + \delta u(x) + \lambda u(x) = f(x), \\ u(0) = u(\mu), \qquad u'(0) = u'(1), \quad \frac{1}{2} \le \mu \le 1. \end{gathered} \tag{1.6}$$

The positivity of the differential operator A^x in $C[0,1]$ is established. A structure of fractional spaces $E_\alpha(C[0,1],A^x)$ is investigated. It is established that for any $0<\alpha<1/2$, the norms in the spaces $E_\alpha(C[0,1],A^x)$ and $C^{2\alpha}[0,1]$ are equivalent. This result permits us to prove the positivity of A^x in $C^{2\alpha}[0,1](0<\alpha<1/2)$. In applications, the coercive inequalities for the solution of nonlocal boundary value problem for two-dimensional elliptic equation are obtained.

Theory and applications of positive operators in Banach spaces have been studied extensively by many researchers (see [1–3, 5–9, 11–24], and the references therein).

2. Green's function and positivity of A^x in $C[0,1]$

In this section, we will study the positivity in $C[0,1]$ of the operator A^x defined by formula (1.1).

First, we will consider the operator A^x for $a(x)\equiv 1$.

Lemma 2.1. *Let $\lambda \ge 0$. Then the equation*

$$A^x u + \lambda u = f \tag{2.1}$$

is uniquely solvable, and the following formula holds:

$$u(x) = (A^x+\lambda)^{-1} f(x) = \int_0^1 J(x,s;\lambda+\delta) f(s)\,ds, \tag{2.2}$$

where

$$
\begin{aligned}
J(x,s;\lambda+\delta) = {} & T\Big\{\Big(e^{-\sqrt{\delta+\lambda}x} - e^{-\sqrt{\delta+\lambda}(2-x)}\Big) \\
& \times \widetilde{T}\Big\{T\Big(e^{-\sqrt{\delta+\lambda}(1-\mu)} - e^{-\sqrt{\delta+\lambda}(1+\mu)}\Big)\frac{1}{\sqrt{\delta+\lambda}}\Big(e^{-\sqrt{\delta+\lambda}s} - e^{-\sqrt{\delta+\lambda}(1-s)}\Big) \\
& - \Big(1+e^{-\sqrt{\delta+\lambda}}\Big)^{-1}\Big(e^{-\sqrt{\delta+\lambda}(1-\mu)} - e^{-\sqrt{\delta+\lambda}(1+\mu)}\Big)\frac{1}{2\sqrt{\delta+\lambda}} \\
& \times \Big(e^{-\sqrt{\delta+\lambda}(1-s)} - e^{-\sqrt{\delta+\lambda}(1+s)}\Big) + \Big(1-e^{-\sqrt{\delta+\lambda}}\Big)\frac{1}{2\sqrt{\delta+\lambda}} \\
& \times \Big(e^{-\sqrt{\delta+\lambda}|\mu-s|} - e^{-\sqrt{\delta+\lambda}(\mu+s)}\Big)\Big\} + \Big(e^{-\sqrt{\delta+\lambda}(1-x)} - e^{-\sqrt{\delta+\lambda}(1+x)}\Big) \\
& \times \widetilde{T}\Big\{\Big(1 - T\Big(e^{-\sqrt{\delta+\lambda}\mu} - e^{-\sqrt{\delta+\lambda}(2-\mu)}\Big)\Big)\frac{1}{\sqrt{\delta+\lambda}}\Big(e^{-\sqrt{\delta+\lambda}s} - e^{-\sqrt{\delta+\lambda}(1-s)}\Big) \\
& - \Big(1+e^{-\sqrt{\delta+\lambda}}\Big)^{-1}\Big(e^{-\sqrt{\delta+\lambda}(1-\mu)} - e^{-\sqrt{\delta+\lambda}(1+\mu)}\Big)\frac{1}{2\sqrt{\delta+\lambda}} \\
& \times \Big(e^{-\sqrt{\delta+\lambda}(1-s)} - e^{-\sqrt{\delta+\lambda}(1+s)}\Big) - \Big(1-e^{-\sqrt{\delta+\lambda}}\Big)\frac{1}{2\sqrt{\delta+\lambda}} \\
& \times \Big(e^{-\sqrt{\delta+\lambda}|\mu-s|} - e^{-\sqrt{\delta+\lambda}(\mu+s)}\Big)\Big\} - \Big(e^{-\sqrt{\delta+\lambda}(1-x)} - e^{-\sqrt{\delta+\lambda}(1+x)}\Big) \\
& \times \frac{1}{2\sqrt{\delta+\lambda}}\Big(e^{-\sqrt{\delta+\lambda}(1-s)} - e^{-\sqrt{\delta+\lambda}(1+s)}\Big)\Big\} \\
& + \frac{1}{2\sqrt{\delta+\lambda}}\Big(e^{-\sqrt{\delta+\lambda}(x-s)} - e^{-\sqrt{\delta+\lambda}(x+s)}\Big)
\end{aligned}
\tag{2.3}
$$

for $0 \le s \le x \le 1$, *and*

$$
\begin{aligned}
J(x,s;\lambda+\delta) = {} & T\Big\{\Big(e^{-\sqrt{\delta+\lambda}x} - e^{-\sqrt{\delta+\lambda}(2-x)}\Big) \\
& \times \widetilde{T}\Big\{T\Big(e^{-\sqrt{\delta+\lambda}(1-\mu)} - e^{-\sqrt{\delta+\lambda}(1+\mu)}\Big)\frac{1}{\sqrt{\delta+\lambda}}\Big(e^{-\sqrt{\delta+\lambda}s} - e^{-\sqrt{\delta+\lambda}(1-s)}\Big) \\
& - \Big(1+e^{-\sqrt{\delta+\lambda}}\Big)^{-1}\Big(e^{-\sqrt{\delta+\lambda}(1-\mu)} - e^{-\sqrt{\delta+\lambda}(1+\mu)}\Big)\frac{1}{2\sqrt{\delta+\lambda}} \\
& \times \Big(e^{-\sqrt{\delta+\lambda}(1-s)} - e^{-\sqrt{\delta+\lambda}(1+s)}\Big) + \Big(1-e^{-\sqrt{\delta+\lambda}}\Big)\frac{1}{2\sqrt{\delta+\lambda}} \\
& \times \Big(e^{-\sqrt{\delta+\lambda}|\mu-s|} - e^{-\sqrt{\delta+\lambda}(\mu+s)}\Big)\Big\} + \Big(e^{-\sqrt{\delta+\lambda}(1-x)} - e^{-\sqrt{\delta+\lambda}(1+x)}\Big)
\end{aligned}
$$

$$
\begin{aligned}
&\times \tilde{T}\Big\{\Big(1-T\big(e^{-\sqrt{\delta+\lambda}\mu}-e^{-\sqrt{\delta+\lambda}(2-\mu)}\big)\Big)\frac{1}{\sqrt{\delta+\lambda}}\big(e^{-\sqrt{\delta+\lambda}s}-e^{-\sqrt{\delta+\lambda}(1-s)}\big)\\
&\quad-\big(1+e^{-\sqrt{\delta+\lambda}}\big)^{-1}\big(e^{-\sqrt{\delta+\lambda}(1-\mu)}-e^{-\sqrt{\delta+\lambda}(1+\mu)}\big)\frac{1}{2\sqrt{\delta+\lambda}}\\
&\quad\times\big(e^{-\sqrt{\delta+\lambda}(1-s)}-e^{-\sqrt{\delta+\lambda}(1+s)}\big)-\big(1-e^{-\sqrt{\delta+\lambda}}\big)\frac{1}{2\sqrt{\delta+\lambda}}\\
&\quad\times\big(e^{-\sqrt{\delta+\lambda}|\mu-s|}-e^{-\sqrt{\delta+\lambda}(\mu+s)}\big)\Big\}-\big(e^{-\sqrt{\delta+\lambda}(1-x)}-e^{-\sqrt{\delta+\lambda}(1+x)}\big)\\
&\times\frac{1}{2\sqrt{\delta+\lambda}}\big(e^{-\sqrt{\delta+\lambda}(1-s)}-e^{-\sqrt{\delta+\lambda}(1+s)}\big)\Big\}\\
&+\frac{1}{2\sqrt{\delta+\lambda}}\big(e^{-\sqrt{\delta+\lambda}(s-x)}-e^{-\sqrt{\delta+\lambda}(x+s)}\big)
\end{aligned}
\tag{2.4}
$$

for $0\le x\le s\le 1$. *Here*

$$
T=\big(1-e^{-2\sqrt{\delta+\lambda}}\big)^{-1},\qquad \tilde{T}=\big(1-e^{-\sqrt{\delta+\lambda}}+e^{-\sqrt{\delta+\lambda}(1-\mu)}-e^{-\sqrt{\delta+\lambda}\mu}\big)^{-1}. \tag{2.5}
$$

Proof. We see that the problem (2.1) can be obviously rewritten as the equivalent nonlocal boundary value problem for second-order linear differential equations

$$
-\frac{d^2u}{dx^2}+(\delta+\lambda)u=f(x),\quad 0<x<1,\ u(0)=\alpha u(\mu),\ u'(0)=u'(1). \tag{2.6}
$$

We have the following formula:

$$
\begin{aligned}
u(x)=T\Big\{&\big(e^{-\sqrt{\delta+\lambda}x}-e^{-\sqrt{\delta+\lambda}(2-x)}\big)\varphi+\big(e^{-\sqrt{\delta+\lambda}(1-x)}-e^{-\sqrt{\delta+\lambda}(1+x)}\big)\psi\\
&-\big(e^{-\sqrt{\delta+\lambda}(1-x)}-e^{-\sqrt{\delta+\lambda}(1+x)}\big)\frac{1}{2\sqrt{\delta+\lambda}}\\
&\times\int_0^1\big(e^{-\sqrt{\delta+\lambda}(1-s)}-e^{-\sqrt{\delta+\lambda}(1+s)}\big)f(s)ds\Big\}+\frac{1}{2\sqrt{\delta+\lambda}}\\
&\times\int_0^1\big(e^{-\sqrt{\delta+\lambda}|x-s|}-e^{-\sqrt{\delta+\lambda}(x+s)}\big)f(s)ds
\end{aligned}
\tag{2.7}
$$

for the solution of the boundary value problem

$$
-\frac{d^2u}{dx^2}+(\delta+\lambda)u=f(x),\quad 0<x<1,\ u(0)=\varphi,\ u(1)=\psi, \tag{2.8}
$$

for second-order linear differential equations. Applying formula (2.7) and nonlocal boundary conditions $u(0) = u(\mu)$, $u'(0) = u'(1)$, we get

$$\begin{aligned}
\varphi &= T\Big\{\Big(e^{-\sqrt{\delta+\lambda}\mu} - e^{-\sqrt{\delta+\lambda}(2-\mu)}\Big)\varphi + \Big(e^{-\sqrt{\delta+\lambda}(1-\mu)} - e^{-\sqrt{\delta+\lambda}(1+\mu)}\Big)\psi \\
&\quad - \Big(e^{-\sqrt{\delta+\lambda}(1-\mu)} - e^{-\sqrt{\delta+\lambda}(1+\mu)}\Big)\frac{1}{2\sqrt{\delta+\lambda}}\int_0^1 \Big(e^{-\sqrt{\delta+\lambda}(1-s)} - e^{-\sqrt{\delta+\lambda}(1+s)}\Big)f(s)ds\Big\} \\
&\quad + \frac{1}{2\sqrt{\delta+\lambda}}\int_0^1 \Big(e^{-\sqrt{\delta+\lambda}|\mu-s|} - e^{-\sqrt{\delta+\lambda}(\mu+s)}\Big)f(s)ds, \\
&T\Big\{\sqrt{\delta+\lambda}\Big(-1 - e^{-\sqrt{\delta+\lambda}2}\Big)\varphi + \sqrt{\delta+\lambda}2e^{-\sqrt{\delta+\lambda}}\psi \\
&\qquad - e^{-\sqrt{\delta+\lambda}}\int_0^1 \Big(e^{-\sqrt{\delta+\lambda}(1-s)} - e^{-\sqrt{\delta+\lambda}(1+s)}\Big)f(s)ds\Big\} \\
&\qquad + \frac{1}{2}\int_0^1 e^{-\sqrt{\delta+\lambda}s}f(s)ds + \frac{1}{2}\int_0^1 e^{-\sqrt{\delta+\lambda}s}f(s)ds \\
&\quad = T\Big\{\sqrt{\delta+\lambda}(-2)e^{-\sqrt{\delta+\lambda}}\varphi + \sqrt{\delta+\lambda}\Big(1 + e^{-\sqrt{\delta+\lambda}2}\Big)\psi \\
&\qquad - \Big(1 + e^{-\sqrt{\delta+\lambda}2}\Big)\frac{1}{2}\int_0^1 \Big(e^{-\sqrt{\delta+\lambda}(1-s)} - e^{-\sqrt{\delta+\lambda}(1+s)}\Big)f(s)ds\Big\} \\
&\qquad + \frac{1}{2}\int_0^1 e^{-\sqrt{\delta+\lambda}(1+s)}f(s)ds - \frac{1}{2}\int_0^1 e^{-\sqrt{\delta+\lambda}(1-s)}f(s)ds.
\end{aligned} \tag{2.9}$$

Solving the last system of equations, we obtain

$$\begin{aligned}
\varphi &= \tilde{T}\Big\{T\Big(e^{-\sqrt{\delta+\lambda}(1-\mu)} - e^{-\sqrt{\delta+\lambda}(1+\mu)}\Big)\frac{1}{\sqrt{\delta+\lambda}}\int_0^1 \Big(e^{-\sqrt{\delta+\lambda}s} - e^{-\sqrt{\delta+\lambda}(1-s)}\Big)f(s)ds \\
&\quad - \Big(1 + e^{-\sqrt{\delta+\lambda}}\Big)^{-1}\Big(e^{-\sqrt{\delta+\lambda}(1-\mu)} - e^{-\sqrt{\delta+\lambda}(1+\mu)}\Big)\frac{1}{2\sqrt{\delta+\lambda}} \\
&\quad \times \int_0^1 \Big(e^{-\sqrt{\delta+\lambda}(1-s)} - e^{-\sqrt{\delta+\lambda}(1+s)}\Big)f(s)ds + \Big(1 - e^{-\sqrt{\delta+\lambda}}\Big)\frac{1}{2\sqrt{\delta+\lambda}} \\
&\quad \times \int_0^1 \Big(e^{-\sqrt{\delta+\lambda}|\mu-s|} - e^{-\sqrt{\delta+\lambda}(\mu+s)}\Big)f(s)ds\Big\},
\end{aligned} \tag{2.10}$$

$$\begin{aligned}
\psi &= \tilde{T}\Big\{\Big(1 - T\Big(e^{-\sqrt{\delta+\lambda}\mu} - e^{-\sqrt{\delta+\lambda}(2-\mu)}\Big)\Big)\frac{1}{\sqrt{\delta+\lambda}}\int_0^1 \Big(e^{-\sqrt{\delta+\lambda}s} - e^{-\sqrt{\delta+\lambda}(1-s)}\Big)f(s)ds \\
&\quad - \Big(1 + e^{-\sqrt{\delta+\lambda}}\Big)^{-1}\alpha\Big(e^{-\sqrt{\delta+\lambda}(1-\mu)} - e^{-\sqrt{\delta+\lambda}(1+\mu)}\Big)\frac{1}{2\sqrt{\delta+\lambda}} \\
&\quad \times \int_0^1 \Big(e^{-\sqrt{\delta+\lambda}(1-s)} - e^{-\sqrt{\delta+\lambda}(1+s)}\Big)f(s)ds - \Big(1 - e^{-\sqrt{\delta+\lambda}}\Big)\frac{1}{2\sqrt{\delta+\lambda}} \\
&\quad \times \int_0^1 \Big(e^{-\sqrt{\delta+\lambda}|\mu-s|} - e^{-\sqrt{\delta+\lambda}(\mu+s)}\Big)f(s)ds\Big\}.
\end{aligned} \tag{2.11}$$

Finally, applying formulas (2.7), (2.10), and (2.11), we obtain (2.2). Lemma 2.1 is proved. □

The function $J(x,s;\lambda+\delta)$ is called Green's function of the resolvent equation (2.1). Notice that

$$J(x,s;\lambda+\delta)=J(s,x;\lambda+\delta)\geq 0,$$
$$\int_0^1 J(x,s;\lambda+\delta)ds=\frac{1}{\lambda+\delta},\quad 0\leq x\leq 1. \tag{2.12}$$

Thus, we obtain the formula for the resolvent $(\lambda I+A^x)^{-1}$ in the case $\lambda\geq 0$. In the same way, we can obtain a formula as (2.2) for the resolvent $(\lambda I+A^x)^{-1}$ in the case of complex λ. But we need to obtain that $1\pm e^{-\sqrt{\delta+\lambda}}$ and $1-e^{-\sqrt{\delta+\lambda}}+e^{-\sqrt{\delta+\lambda}(1-\mu)}-e^{-\sqrt{\delta+\lambda}\mu}$ are not equal to zero. Applying (2.2), we can establish the positivity of A^x in the case $a(x)\equiv 1$ in $C[0,1]$ as follows.

Theorem 2.2. *For all λ, $\lambda\in R_\varphi=\{\lambda:|\arg\lambda|\leq\varphi,\ \varphi<\pi/2\}$, the resolvent $(\lambda I+A^x)^{-1}$ defined by the formula (2.2) is subject to the bound*

$$\|(\lambda I+A^x)^{-1}\|_{C[0,1]\to C[0,1]}\leq M(\varphi,\delta)(1+|\lambda|)^{-1}, \tag{2.13}$$

where $M(\varphi,\delta)$ does not depend on λ.

Second, we will investigate the positivity of A^x in $C[0,1]$. In the sequel, we will need the Nirenberg's inequality

$$\|v'\|_{C[0,1]}\leq K[\alpha\|v''\|_{C[0,1]}+\alpha^{-1}\|v\|_{C[0,1]}], \tag{2.14}$$

where K is a constant, $\alpha>0$ is a small number.

If $a_k=a=\text{const}$, then using the substitution $\lambda+\delta=a\lambda_1$, we can obtain the estimate

$$\left\|(\lambda I+A^x)^{-1}\right\|_{C[0,1]\to C[0,1]}\leq M(\varphi,\delta)(1+|\lambda|)^{-1} \tag{2.15}$$

or

$$\|u\|_{C[0,1]}\leq M(\delta,\varphi)\frac{1}{1+|\lambda|}\|f\|_{C[0,1]} \tag{2.16}$$

and the coercive estimate

$$\|u''\|_{C[0,1]}\leq M(\varphi,\delta)\|f\|_{C[0,1]} \tag{2.17}$$

for the solutions of problem (1.5) with constant coefficients. Here $M(\varphi,\delta)$ does not depend on λ.

Now, let $a(x)$ be a continuous function on $[0,1]=\Omega$. Similarly to [1], using the method of frozen coefficients and the coercive estimate (2.17) for the solutions of the differential equation with constant coefficients, we obtain the following theorem.

Theorem 2.3. *For all $\lambda \in R_\varphi$ and $|\lambda| \geq K_0 > 0$, the resolvent $(\lambda I + A^x)^{-1}$ is subject to the bound*

$$\|(\lambda I + A^x)^{-1}\|_{C[0,1]\to C[0,1]} \leq M(\varphi,\delta)(1+|\lambda|)^{-1}, \tag{2.18}$$

where $M(\varphi,\delta)$ does not depend on λ.

Proof. Given $\varepsilon > 0$, there exists a system $\{Q_j\}$, $j = 1,\dots,r$, of intervals and two half-intervals (containing 0 and 1, resp.) that covers the segment $[0,1]$ and such that $|a(x_1) - a(x_2)| < \varepsilon$, $x_1, x_2 \in Q_j$ because of the compactness of $[0,1]$. For this system, we construct a partition of unity, that is, a system of smooth nonnegative functions $\xi_j(x)(i = 1,\dots,r)$ with $\operatorname{supp}\xi_j(x) \subset Q_j$, $\xi_j(0) = \xi_j(1) = \xi_j(\mu)$, $\xi_j'(0) = \xi_j'(1) = 0$, and $\xi_1(x) + \cdots + \xi_r(x) = 1$ in $\bar{\Omega} = [0,1]$.

It is clear that for positivity of A^x in $C[0,1]$, it suffices to establish the estimate

$$\|u\|_{C[0,1]} \leq M(\delta,\varphi)\frac{1}{1+|\lambda|}\|f\|_{C[0,1]} \tag{2.19}$$

for the solutions of (2.1).

Using $w(x) = \xi_j(x)u(x)$, we obtain $w(0) = w(\mu) + \zeta$, $w'(0) = w'(1) + \eta$, where

$$\begin{gathered} \zeta = \xi_j(0)u(0) - \xi_j(\mu)u(\mu) = (\xi_j(0) - \xi_j(\mu))u(0) = 0, \\ \eta = \xi_j'(0)u(0) + \xi_j(0)u'(0) - \xi_j'(1)u(1) - \xi_j(1)u'(1) = (\xi_j(0) - \xi_j(1))u'(0) = 0, \\ (\delta+\lambda)w(x) - a(x)w''(x) = \xi_j(x)f(x) - a(x)(2\xi_j'(x)u'(x) + \xi_j''(x)u(x)). \end{gathered} \tag{2.20}$$

Then we have the following nonlocal boundary value problem:

$$\begin{gathered} (\delta+\lambda)w(x) - a^j w''(x) = F^j(x), \quad 0 < x < 1, \\ w(0) = w(\mu), \qquad w'(0) = w'(1), \end{gathered} \tag{2.21}$$

where $a^j = a(x^j)$ and

$$F^j(x) = \xi_j(x)f(x) - a(x)(2\xi_j'(x)u'(x) + \xi_j''(x)u(x)) - (a^j - a(x))w''(x). \tag{2.22}$$

Since (2.21) is an equation with constant coefficients, we have the estimates

$$(1+|\lambda|)\|w\|_{C[0,1]} \leq K(\varphi,\delta)\|F^j\|_{C[0,1]}, \quad \lambda \in R_\varphi, \tag{2.23}$$

$$\|w''\|_{C[0,1]} \leq M(\varphi,\delta)\|F^j\|_{C[0,1]}. \tag{2.24}$$

Using the definition of Q_j and the continuity of $a(x)$, as well as the smoothness of $\xi_i(x)$, we obtain

$$\|F^j\|_{C[0,1]} \leq M(\varphi,\delta)\left[\|f\|_{C[0,1]} + \|u\|_{C[0,1]} + \|u'\|_{C[0,1]}\right] + \varepsilon\|w''\|_{C[0,1]}. \tag{2.25}$$

Assume that $0 < \varepsilon < 1/M(\varphi,\delta)$, then from the last estimate, it follows that

$$\begin{aligned} \|w''\|_{C[0,1]} &\leq \frac{M(\varphi,\delta)}{1-\varepsilon M(\varphi,\delta)}\left[\|f\|_{C[0,1]} + \|u'\|_{C[0,1]} + \|u\|_{C[0,1]}\right], \\ \|F^j\|_{C[0,1]} &\leq \frac{M(\varphi,\delta)}{1-\varepsilon M(\varphi,\delta)}\left[\|f\|_{C[0,1]} + \|u'\|_{C[0,1]} + \|u\|_{C[0,1]}\right]. \end{aligned} \tag{2.26}$$

From this and estimate (2.23), it follows that

$$\begin{aligned} &(1+|\lambda|)\|w\|_{C[0,1]} \\ &\quad \leq K(\varphi,\delta)\frac{M(\varphi,\delta)}{1-\varepsilon M(\varphi,\delta)}\left[\|f\|_{C[0,1]} + \|u'\|_{C[0,1]} + \|u\|_{C[0,1]}\right]. \end{aligned} \tag{2.27}$$

Using the triangle inequality, we obtain

$$\|u''\|_{C[0,1]} \leq K_1(\varphi,\delta)\left[\|f\|_{C[0,1]} + \|u'\|_{C[0,1]} + \|u\|_{C[0,1]}\right], \tag{2.28}$$

$$(1+|\lambda|)\|u\|_{C[0,1]} \leq M_1(\varphi,\delta)\left[\|f\|_{C[0,1]} + \|u'\|_{C[0,1]} + \|u\|_{C[0,1]}\right]. \tag{2.29}$$

Now using the inequality (2.14), we can write

$$\begin{aligned} F &= \|f\|_{C[0,1]} + \|u\|_{C[0,1]} + \|u'\|_{C[0,1]} \\ &\leq M_2(\varphi,\delta)\left[\|f\|_{C[0,1]} + \alpha^{-1}\|u\|_{C[0,1]} + \alpha\|u''\|_{C[0,1]}\right]. \end{aligned} \tag{2.30}$$

Hence for small α from the last inequality and the inequality (2.28), it follows that

$$F \leq M_3(\varphi,\delta)\left[\alpha^{-1}\|u\|_{C[0,1]} + \|f\|_{C[0,1]}\right]. \tag{2.31}$$

Therefore from (2.29), it follows that

$$(1+|\lambda|)\|u\|_{C[0,1]} \leq M_3(\varphi,\delta)\left[\alpha^{-1}\|u\|_{C[0,1]} + \|f\|_{C[0,1]}\right]. \tag{2.32}$$

Hence for all λ,

$$|\lambda| > \frac{M_3(\varphi,\delta)}{\alpha} = K_0, \tag{2.33}$$

we have the estimate (2.19). Theorem 2.3 is proved. □

3. The structure of fractional spaces and positivity of A^x in $C^\alpha[0,1]$

The operator A^x commutes with its resolvent $(\lambda+A^x)^{-1}$. Then using the definition of the norm in the space $E_\alpha(C[0,1],A^x)$, we obtain

$$\|(\lambda+A^x)^{-1}\|_{E_\alpha(C[0,1],A^x)\to E_\alpha(C[0,1],A^x)} \leq \|(\lambda+A^x)^{-1}\|_{C[0,1]\to C[0,1]}. \tag{3.1}$$

Therefore, by Theorem 2.3 we have the positivity of the operator A^x in fractional spaces $E_\alpha(C[0,1],A^x)$. Furthermore, we have the following theorem.

Theorem 3.1. *For $0<\alpha<1/2$, the norms of the spaces $E_\alpha(C[0,1],A^x)$ and $C^{2\alpha}[0,1]$ are equivalent.*

The proof of this theorem follows the scheme of the proof of the theorem in [7] and it is based on the formulas

$$\begin{aligned} A^x(\lambda+A^x)^{-1}f(x) &= \frac{\delta}{\lambda+\delta}f(x) - \left(\frac{1}{\lambda+\delta} - (\lambda+A^x)^{-1}\right)f(x) \\ &= \frac{\delta}{\lambda+\delta}f(x) + \int_0^1 J(x,s;\lambda+\delta)(f(x)-f(s))ds, \end{aligned} \tag{3.2}$$

$$f(x) = \int_0^1\int_0^\infty J(x,s;\lambda+t+\delta)A^x(\lambda+t+A^x)^{-1}f(s)dt\,ds$$

for the positive operator A^x and on the estimates for Green's function of the resolvent equation (2.1).

The results of Theorems 2.3 and 3.1 permit us to obtain the positivity of the operator A^x in $C^{2\alpha}[0,1]$.

Theorem 3.2. *For all $\lambda\in R_\varphi$, $|\lambda|\geq K_0>0$, and $0<\alpha<1/2$, the resolvent $(\lambda+A^x)^{-1}$ is subject to the bound*

$$\|(\lambda+A^x)^{-1}\|_{C^{2\alpha}[0,1]\to C^{2\alpha}[0,1]} \leq \frac{M(\varphi,\delta)}{\alpha(1-2\alpha)}(1+|\lambda|)^{-1}, \tag{3.3}$$

where $M(\varphi,\delta)$ does not depend on λ and α.

4. Applications

We consider the nonlocal boundary value problem for two-dimensional elliptic equation

$$\begin{aligned} &-\frac{\partial^2 u}{\partial y^2} - a(x)\frac{\partial^2 u}{\partial x^2} + \delta u = f(y,x), \quad 0<y<T,\ 0<x<1, \\ &u(0,x)=\varphi(x), \quad u(T,x)=\psi(x), \quad 0\leq x\leq 1, \\ &u(y,0)=u(y,\mu), \quad \frac{1}{2}\leq\mu\leq 1, \quad u_x(y,0)=u_x(y,1), \quad 0\leq y\leq T, \end{aligned} \tag{4.1}$$

where $a(x)$, $\varphi(x)$, $\psi(x)$, and $f(y,x)$ are sufficiently given smooth functions and $a(x)\geq a>0$, $\delta>0$, is a sufficiently large number.

THEOREM 4.1. *For the solution of the boundary value problem (4.1), the following coercive inequalities are valid:*

$$\|u\|_{C_{0T}^{2+\beta,\gamma}(C^{\nu}[0,1])}+\|u\|_{C_{0T}^{\beta,\gamma}(C^{2+\nu}[0,1])}\le\frac{M(\nu)}{(\beta-\gamma)(1-\beta)}\|f\|_{C_{0T}^{\beta,\gamma}(C^{\nu}[0,1])}$$
$$+M(\nu)\big(\|\varphi\|_{C^{2+\nu}[0,1]}+\|\psi\|_{C^{2+\nu}[0,1]}\big),\quad 0\le\gamma<\beta<1,\ 0\le\nu\le1,$$
$$\|u\|_{C_{0T}^{2+\beta,\gamma}(C^{2(\alpha-\beta)}[0,1])}+\|u\|_{C_{0T}^{\beta,\gamma}(C^{2+2(\alpha-\beta)}[0,1])}\tag{4.2}$$
$$\le M(\alpha,\beta)\big[\|f\|_{C_{0T}^{\beta,\gamma}(C^{2(\alpha-\beta)}[0,1])}+\|\varphi\|_{C^{2+2(\alpha-\beta)}[0,1]}+\|\psi\|_{C^{2+2(\alpha-\beta)}[0,1]}\big],$$
$$0\le\gamma\le\beta\le\alpha,\quad 0<\alpha-\beta<\frac{1}{2}.$$

Here $M(\nu)$ and $M(\alpha,\beta)$ are independent of γ, $f(y,x)$, $\varphi(x)$, $\psi(x)$.

The proof of Theorem 4.1 is based on Theorem 3.1 on the structure of the fractional spaces $E_\alpha(C[0,1],A^x)$ and Theorem 3.2 on the positivity of the operator A^x in $C^\nu(R^n)$, and the theorems on coercivity inequalities for the solution of the abstract boundary value problem for differential equation

$$-v''(t)+Av(t)=f(t),\quad (0\le t\le T)v(0)=v_0,\quad v(T)=v_T,\tag{4.3}$$

in an arbitrary Banach space E with the linear positive operator A in $C_{0T}^{\beta,\gamma}(E)(0\le\gamma\le\beta,\ 0<\beta<1)$ and $C_{0T}^{\beta,\gamma}(E_{\alpha-\gamma})$ $(0\le\gamma\le\beta\le\alpha,\ 0<\alpha<1)$ (see [4, 10]). Here $C_{0T}^{\beta,\gamma}(E)$, $(0\le\gamma\le\beta,\ 0<\beta<1)$, denotes the Banach space obtained by completion of the set of smooth E-valued functions $\varphi(t)$ on $[0,T]$ in the norm

$$\|\varphi\|_{C_{0T}^{\beta,\gamma}(E)}=\|\varphi\|_{C(E)}+\sup_{0\le t<t+\tau\le T}\frac{\|\varphi(t+\tau)-\varphi(t)\|_E}{\tau^\beta}(T-t)^\gamma(t+\tau)^\gamma.\tag{4.4}$$

Acknowledgment

The second author is supported by The Scientific and Technological Research Council of Turkey (TÜBİTAK).

References

[1] Kh. A. Alibekov, *Investigations in C and L_p of difference schemes of high order accuracy for approximate solution of multidimensional parabolic boundary value problems*, Ph.D. thesis, Voronezh State University, Voronezh, 1978, 134 p.

[2] Kh. A. Alibekov and P. E. Sobolevskiĭ, *The stability of difference schemes for parabolic equations*, Doklady Akademii Nauk SSSR **232** (1977), no. 4, 737–740 (Russian).

[3] ———, *Stability and convergence of high-order difference schemes of approximation for parabolic equations*, Ukrainskiĭ Matematicheskiĭ Zhurnal **31** (1979), no. 6, 627–634, 765 (Russian).

[4] A. Ashyralyev, *Coercive solvability of elliptic equations in spaces of smooth functions*, Boundary Value Problems for Nonclassical Equations in Mathematical Physics (Novosibirsk, 1989), Akad. Nauk SSSR Sibirsk. Otdel. Inst. Mat., Novosibirsk, 1989, pp. 82–86.

[5] ———, *Method of positive operators of investigations of the high order of accuracy difference schemes for parabolic and elliptic equations*, Doctor Sciences thesis, Institute of Mathematics, Academic Sciences, Kiev, 1992.

[6] A. Ashyralyev and B. Kendirli, *Positivity in C_h of one dimensional difference operators with nonlocal boundary conditions*, Some Problems of Applied Mathematics, Fatih University, Istanbul, 2000, pp. 45–60.

[7] ———, *Positivity in Hölder norms of one-dimensional difference operators with nonlocal boundary conditions*, Applications of Mathematics in Engineering and Economics (Sozopol, 2000), Heron Press, Sofia, 2001, pp. 134–137.

[8] A. Ashyralyev and P. E. Sobolevskiĭ, *The theory of interpolation of linear operators and the stability of difference schemes*, Doklady Akademii Nauk SSSR **275** (1984), no. 6, 1289–1291 (Russian).

[9] ———, *Well-Posedness of Parabolic Difference Equations*, Operator Theory: Advances and Applications, vol. 69, Birkhäuser, Basel, 1994.

[10] ———, *New Difference Schemes for Partial Differential Equations*, Operator Theory: Advances and Applications, vol. 148, Birkhäuser, Basel, 2004.

[11] A. Ashyralyev and N. Yenial, *Positivity of difference operators generated by the nonlocal boundary conditions*, Proceedings of Turkey-Dynamical Systems and Applications, Antalya, July 2004, pp. 113–135.

[12] S. I. Danelich, *Positive difference operators in R_{h1}*, Voronezh. Gosud. Univ. 1987, 13p. Deposited VINITI 3. 18. 1987, no. 1936-B87. (Russian).

[13] ———, *Positive difference operators with constant coefficients in half-space*, Voronezh. Gosud. Univ. 1987, 56p. Deposited VINITI 11. 5. 1987, no. 7747-B87. (Russian).

[14] ———, *Positive difference operators with variable coefficients on the half-line*, Voronezh. Gosud. Univ. 1987, 16p. Deposited VINITI 11. 9. 1987, no. 7713-B87. (Russian).

[15] A. M. Krasnoselʹskiĭ, P. P. Zabreĭko, E. I. Pustyl'nik, and P. E. Sobolevskiĭ, *Integral Operators in Spaces of Summable Functions*, Noordhoff International, Leiden, 1976.

[16] Yu. A. Smirnitskiĭ and P. E. Sobolevskiĭ, *Positivity of multidimensional difference operators in the C-norm*, Uspekhi Matematicheskikh Nauk **36** (1981), no. 4, 202–203 (Russian).

[17] ———, *Pointwise estimates of the Green function of the resolvent of a difference elliptic operator*, Vychislitel'nyĭ Tsentr. Chislennye Metody Mekhaniki Sploshnoĭ Sredy **13** (1982), no. 4, 129–142 (Russian).

[18] ———, *Pointwise estimates of the Green function of the resolvent of a difference elliptic operator with variable coefficients in R^n*, Voronezh. Gosud. Uni. 1982, 32p., Deposited VINITI 5.2.1982, no. 1519.(Russian).

[19] P. E. Sobolevskiĭ, *The coercive solvability of difference equations*, Doklady Akademii Nauk SSSR **201** (1971), no. 5, 1063–1066 (Russian).

[20] P. E. Sobolevskiĭ and Yu. A. Smirnitskiĭ, *Positivity of difference operators*, in: Spline Methods, Novosibirsk (1981) (Russian).

[21] M. Z. Solomyak, *Analytic semigroups generated by elliptic operator in space L_p*, Doklady Akademii Nauk SSSR **127** (1959), no. 1, 37–39 (Russian).

[22] ———, *Evaluation of norm of the resolvent of elliptic operators in L_p-spaces*, Uspekhi Matematicheskikh Nauk **15** (1960), no. 6 (96), 141–148 (Russian).

[23] H. B. Stewart, *Generation of analytic semigroups by strongly elliptic operators*, Transactions of the American Mathematical Society **199** (1974), 141–162.

[24] ———, *Generation of analytic semigroups by strongly elliptic operators under general boundary conditions*, Transactions of the American Mathematical Society **259** (1980), no. 1, 299–310.

Allaberen Ashyralyev: Department of Mathematics, Faculty of Arts & Sciences, Fatih University, 34500 Büyükçekmece, Istanbul, Turkey
E-mail address: aashyr@fatih.edu.tr

Nergiz Yaz: Department of Mathematics, Faculty of Sciences, Ankara University, 06100 Tandogan, Ankara, Turkey
E-mail address: nergizyaz@yahoo.com

WELL-POSEDNESS OF THE NONLOCAL BOUNDARY VALUE PROBLEM FOR ELLIPTIC EQUATIONS

ALLABEREN ASHYRALYEV

In the present paper, the well-posedness of the nonlocal boundary value problem for elliptic difference equation is investigated. The almost coercive inequality and coercive inequalities for the solution of this problem are obtained.

1. Introduction. The nonlocal boundary value problem

The role played by coercive inequalities in the study of local boundary value problems for elliptic and parabolic differential equations is well known (see, e.g., [20, 21, 29]). We consider the nonlocal boundary value problem

$$\begin{gathered} -v''(t)+Av(t)=f(t) \quad (0\le t\le 1),\\ v(0)=v(1), \quad v'(0)=v'(1) \end{gathered} \tag{1.1}$$

in an arbitrary Banach space with positive operator A. It is known (see, e.g., [2, 14, 17–19, 23]) that various nonlocal boundary value problems for the elliptic equations can be reduced to the boundary value problem (1.1).

A function $v(t)$ is called a solution of the problem (1.1) if the following conditions are satisfied:

(i) $v(t)$ is twice continuously differentiable function on the segment $[0,1]$;

(ii) the element $v(t)$ belongs to $D(A)$ for all $t\in[0,1]$, and the function $Av(t)$ is continuous on the segment $[0,1]$;

(iii) $v(t)$ satisfies the equation and boundary conditions (1.1).

A solution of problem (1.1) defined in this manner will from now on be referred to as a solution of problem (1.1) in the space $C(E)=C([0,1],E)$. Here $C(E)$ stands for the Banach space of all continuous functions $\varphi(t)$ defined on $[0,1]$ with values in E equipped with the norm

$$\|\varphi\|_{C(E)}=\max_{0\le t\le 1}\|\varphi(t)\|_E. \tag{1.2}$$

Hindawi Publishing Corporation
Proceedings of the Conference on Differential & Difference Equations and Applications, pp. 103–116

The well-posedness in $C(E)$ of the boundary value problem (1.1) means that coercive inequality

$$\|v''\|_{C(E)} + \|Av\|_{C(E)} \leq M\|f\|_{C(E)} \tag{1.3}$$

is true for its solution $v(t) \in C(E)$ with some M, not depending on $f(t) \in C(E)$.

It is known that from the coercive inequality (1.3) the positivity of the operator A in the Banach space E follows under the assumption that the operator $I\lambda + A$ has bounded in E inverse $(I\lambda + A)^{-1}$ for any $\lambda \geq 0$, and estimate

$$||(\lambda I + A)^{-1}||_{E\to E} \leq \frac{M}{1+\lambda} \tag{1.4}$$

holds for some $1 \leq M < \infty$. It turns out that this positivity property of the operator A in E is necessary condition of well-posedness of the boundary value problem (1.1) in $C(E)$. Is the positivity of the operator A in E a sufficient condition for the well-posedness of the nonlocal boundary value problem (1.1)? The problem (1.1) is not well posed for the general positive operators. The corresponding counterexample is given in [8].

It is known (see, e.g., [25]) that the operator $A^{1/2}$ has better spectral properties than the positive operator A. In particular, the operator $\lambda I + A^{1/2}$ has a bounded inverse for any complex number λ with $\operatorname{Re}\lambda \geq 0$, and the estimate

$$\left\|(\lambda I + A^{1/2})^{-1}\right\|_{E\to E} \leq M(|\lambda| + 1)^{-1} \tag{1.5}$$

is true for some $M \geq 1$. This means that $B = A^{1/2}$ is a strongly positive operator in a Banach space E. Therefore, the operator $-B$ is a generator of an analytic semigroup $\exp\{-tB\}$ $(t \geq 0)$ with exponentially decreasing norm, when $t \to +\infty$, that is, the estimates

$$||\exp(-tB)||_{E\to E}, \quad ||tB\exp(-tB)||_{E\to E} \leq M(B)e^{-\alpha(B)t} \quad (t > 0) \tag{1.6}$$

hold for some $M(B) \in [1,+\infty)$, $a(B) \in (0,+\infty)$. From that it follows that the operator $I - e^{-B}$ has the bounded inverse $(I - e^{-B})^{-1}$ and the following estimate holds:

$$\left\|(I - e^{-B})^{-1}\right\|_{E\to E} \leq M(B)(1 - e^{-\alpha(B)})^{-1}. \tag{1.7}$$

Sufficient condition for the well-posedness of the boundary value problem (1.1) can be established if one considers this problem in certain spaces $F(E)$ of smooth E-valued functions on $[0,T]$.

A function $v(t)$ is said to be a solution of problem (1.1) in $F(E)$ if it is a solution of this problem in $C(E)$ and the functions $v''(t)$ and $Av(t)$ belong to $F(E)$.

As in the case of the space $C(E)$, we say that the problem (1.1) is well posed in $F(E)$, if the following coercive inequality:

$$\|v''\|_{F(E)} + \|Av\|_{F(E)} \leq M\|f\|_{F(E)} \tag{1.8}$$

is true for its solution $v(t) \in F(E)$ with some M, not depending on $f(t) \in F(E)$.

First, we set $F(E)$ equal to $C_{01}^{\beta,\gamma}(E)$ $(0 \le \gamma \le \beta,\ 0 < \beta < 1)$ the Banach space obtained by completion of the set of smooth E-valued functions $\varphi(t)$ on $[0,1]$ in the norm

$$\|\varphi\|_{C_{01}^{\beta,\gamma}(E)} = \max_{0\le t\le 1}\|\varphi(t)\|_E + \sup_{0\le t<t+\tau\le 1}\frac{(t+\tau)^{\gamma}(1-t)^{\gamma}\|\varphi(t+\tau)-\varphi(t)\|_E}{\tau^{\beta}}. \tag{1.9}$$

Note that the Banach space $E_\alpha = E_\alpha(B,E)$, $0<\alpha<1$, consists of those $v \in E$ for which the following norm:

$$\|v\|_{E_\alpha} = \sup_{\lambda>0}\lambda^{1-\alpha}\|B\exp(-\lambda B)v\|_E \tag{1.10}$$

is finite.

Theorem 1.1 [8]. *Let A be the positive operator in a Banach space E. Suppose $f(0)-f(1)\in E_{\beta-\gamma}$ and $f(t)\in C_{01}^{\beta,\gamma}(E)$ $(0\le\gamma\le\beta,\ 0<\beta<1)$. Then for the solution $v(t)$ in $C_{01}^{\beta,\gamma}(E)$ of the boundary value problem (1.1), the stability inequalities*

$$\|v''\|_{C(E_{\beta-\gamma})} \le M\left[\|f(0)-f(1)\|_{E_{\beta-\gamma}} + \beta^{-1}(1-\beta)^{-1}\|f\|_{C_{01}^{\beta,\gamma}(E)}\right] \tag{1.11}$$

hold, where M does not depend on β, γ, and $f(t)$.

Theorem 1.2 [8]. *Let A be the positive operator in a Banach space E. Suppose $f(0)-f(1)\in E_0^{\beta,\gamma}$ and $f(t)\in C_{01}^{\beta,\gamma}(E)$ $(0\le\gamma\le\beta,\ 0<\beta<1)$. Then for the solution $v(t)$ in $C_{01}^{\beta,\gamma}(E)$ of the boundary value problem (1.1), the coercive inequalities*

$$\|v''\|_{C_{01}^{\beta,\gamma}(E)} + \|Av\|_{C_{01}^{\beta,\gamma}(E)} \le M\left[|f(0)-f(1)|_0^{\beta,\gamma} + \beta^{-1}(1-\beta)^{-1}\|f\|_{C_{01}^{\beta,\gamma}(E)}\right] \tag{1.12}$$

hold, where M does not depend on β, γ, and $f(t)$. Here, $|w|_0^{\beta,\gamma}$ denotes norm of the Banach space $E_0^{\beta,\gamma}$ consisting of those $w\in E$ for which the norm

$$|w|_0^{\beta,\gamma} = \max_{0\le z\le 1}\|e^{-zB}w\|_E + \sup_{0\le z<z+\tau\le 1}\tau^{-\beta}(z+\tau)^{\gamma}(1-z)^{\gamma}\|(e^{-(z+\tau)B}-e^{-zB})w\|_E \tag{1.13}$$

is finite.

Note that the parameter γ can be chosen freely in $[0,\beta)$, which increases the number of function spaces in which problem (1.1) is well posed. In particular, it is important that the problem (1.1) is well posed in the Holder space without a weight $(\gamma = 0)$.

Second, let us study now the boundary value problem (1.1) in the spaces $C_{01}^{\beta,\gamma}(E_{\alpha-\beta})$ $(0\le\gamma\le\beta\le\alpha,\ 0<\alpha<1)$. To these there correspond the spaces of traces $E_{\alpha-\beta}^{\beta,\gamma}$, which consist of elements $w\in E$ for which the norm

$$\begin{aligned}|w|_{\alpha-\beta}^{\beta,\gamma} &= \max_{0\le z\le 1}\|e^{-zB}w\|_{E_{\alpha-\beta}}\\ &\quad + \sup_{0\le z<z+\tau\le 1}\tau^{-\beta}(z+\tau)^{\gamma}(1-z)^{\gamma}\|(e^{-(z+\tau)B}-e^{-zB})w\|_{E_{\alpha-\beta}}\end{aligned} \tag{1.14}$$

is finite.

Theorem 1.3 [8]. *Let A be the positive operator in a Banach space E and $f(0)-f(1)\in E_{\alpha-\gamma}$ and $f(t)\in C_{01}^{\beta,\gamma}(E_{\alpha-\beta})$ $(0\le\gamma\le\beta\le\alpha,\ 0<\alpha<1)$. Then for the solution $v(t)$ in $C_{01}^{\beta,\gamma}(E_{\alpha-\beta})$ of the boundary value problem (1.1), the coercive inequality*

$$\|v''\|_{C(E_{\alpha-\gamma})}\le M\alpha^{-1}(1-\alpha)^{-1}\Big[\|f(0)-f(1)\|_{E_{\alpha-\gamma}}+\|f\|_{C_{01}^{\beta,\gamma}(E_{\alpha-\beta})}\Big] \tag{1.15}$$

holds, where M does not depend on α, β, γ, and $f(t)$.

Theorem 1.4 [8]. *Let A be the positive operator in a Banach space E, $f(0)-f(1)\in E_{\alpha-\beta}^{\beta,\gamma}$ and $f(t)\in C_{01}^{\beta,\gamma}(E_{\alpha-\beta})$ $(0\le\gamma\le\beta\le\alpha,\ 0<\alpha<1)$. Then for the solution $v(t)$ in $C_{01}^{\beta,\gamma}(E_{\alpha-\beta})$ of the boundary value problem (1.1), the coercive inequality*

$$\begin{aligned}&\|v''\|_{C_{01}^{\beta,\gamma}(E_{\alpha-\beta})}+\|Av\|_{C_{01}^{\beta,\gamma}(E_{\alpha-\beta})}\\&\quad\le M\Big[\,|f(0)-f(1)|_{\alpha-\beta}^{\beta,\gamma}+\alpha^{-1}(1-\alpha)^{-1}\|f\|_{C_{01}^{\beta,\gamma}(E_{\alpha-\beta})}\Big]\end{aligned} \tag{1.16}$$

holds, where M does not depend on α, β, γ, and $f(t)$.

Note that the spaces of smooth functions $C_{01}^{\beta,\gamma}(E_{\alpha-\beta})$, in which coercive solvability has been established, depend on the parameters α, β, and γ. However, the constants in the coercive inequalities depend only on α. Hence, we can choose the parameters β and γ freely, which increases the number of function spaces in which problem (1.1) is well posed. In particular, Theorem 1.4 implies the well-posedness Theorem 1.2 in $C(E_\alpha)$.

Third, let us study now the boundary value problem in the spaces $L_p(E)=L_p([0,1],E)$ $(1\le p<\infty)$ of all strongly measurable E-valued functions $v(t)$ on $[0,1]$ for which the norm

$$\|v\|_{L_p(E)}=\left(\int_0^1\|v(t)\|_E^p dt\right)^{1/p} \tag{1.17}$$

is finite.

A function $v(t)$ is said to be a solution of the problem (1.1) in $L_p(E)$ if it is absolutely continuous, the functions $v''(t)$ and $Av(t)$ belong to $L_p(E)$, (1.1) is satisfied for almost every t, and $v(0)=v(1)$, $v'(0)=v'(1)$. From this definition, it follows that a necessary condition for the solvability of problem (1.1) in $L_p(E)$ is that $f(t)\in L_p(E)$. It will be shown that in certain cases that this condition is also sufficient for the solvability of problem (1.1).

From the unique solvability of (1.1), it follows that the operator $v(t;f(t))$ is bounded in $L_p(E)$ and one has coercive inequality

$$\|v''\|_{L_p(E)}+\|Av\|_{L_p(E)}\le M_C\|f\|_{L_p(E)}, \tag{1.18}$$

where M_C $(1\le M_C<+\infty)$ does not depend on $f(t)$. From that, we can obtain the positivity of A under the stronger assumption that the operator A^{-1} is compact in E.

Theorem 1.5 [9]. *Let A be the positive operator in a Banach space E. Suppose the problem*

$$-v''(t) + Av(t) = f(t) \quad (0 \le t \le 1),$$
$$v(0) = v_0, \qquad v(1) = v_1 \tag{1.19}$$

is well posed in $L_{p_0}(E)$ for some p_0, $1 < p_0 < \infty$. Then problem (1.1) is well posed in $L_p(E)$ for any p, $1 < p < \infty$, and the coercivity inequality holds:

$$\|v''\|_{L_p(E)} + \|Av\|_{L_p(E)} + \|v\|_{C(E_{1-1/p,p})} \le \frac{M(p_0)p^2}{p-1}\|f\|_{L_p(E)}, \tag{1.20}$$

where $M(p_0)$ does not depend on p and $f(t)$.

Here, the Banach space $E_{1-1/p,p} = E_{1-1/p,p}(E, A^{1/2})$ $(0 < \alpha < 1)$ consists of those $v \in E$ for which the norm

$$\|v\|_{E_{1-1/p,p}} = \left(\int_0^1 \|A^{1/2}\exp\{-zA^{1/2}\}v\|_E^p\,dz\right)^{1/p}, \quad 1 \le p < \infty, \tag{1.21}$$

is finite.

Theorem 1.6 [9]. *Let $1 \le p \le \infty$ and $0 < \alpha < 1$. Suppose that A is the positive operator in a Banach space E. Then problem (1.1) is well posed in $L_p(E_{\alpha,p})$ and the coercivity inequality holds:*

$$\|v''\|_{L_p(E_{\alpha,p})} + \|Av\|_{L_p(E_{\alpha,p})} \le \frac{M}{\alpha(1-\alpha)}\|f\|_{L_p(E_{\alpha,p})}, \tag{1.22}$$

where M does not depend on α, p, and $f(t)$.

From Theorems 1.5 and 1.6, we have Theorem 1.7.

Theorem 1.7. *Let $1 < p, q < \infty$, and $0 < \alpha < 1$. Suppose that A is the positive operator in a Banach space E. Then problem (1.1) is well posed in $L_p(E_{\alpha,q})$ and the coercivity inequality holds:*

$$\|v''\|_{L_p(E_{\alpha,q})} + \|Av\|_{L_p(E_{\alpha,q})} \le \frac{M(q)}{\alpha(1-\alpha)}\|f\|_{L_p(E_{\alpha,q})}, \tag{1.23}$$

where $M(q)$ does not depend on α, p, and $f(t)$.

Here, the Banach space $E_{\alpha,q} = E_{\alpha,q}(E, A^{1/2})$ $(0 < \alpha < 1,\ 1 < q < \infty)$ consists of those $v \in E$ for which the norm

$$\|v\|_{E_{\alpha,q}} = \left(\int_0^\infty \lambda^{1-\alpha}\|A^{1/2}\exp\{-\lambda A^{1/2}\}v\|_E^q\frac{d\lambda}{\lambda}\right)^{1/q} \tag{1.24}$$

is finite.

Methods of the solutions of the elliptic differential equations have been studied extensively by many researches (see [1, 3–8, 11, 13–18, 22–24, 26–28], and the references therein).

In the present paper, we study the well-posedness of the nonlocal boundary value problem for elliptic difference equation generated by problem (1.1). The almost coercive inequality and coercive inequalities for the solution of this problem are established. In applications, the almost coercive inequality and coercive inequalities for the solution of the difference schemes are obtained.

2. Well-posedness of the nonlocal problem for difference equations of elliptic type

Let us associate to the boundary value problem (1.1) the corresponding difference problem

$$\begin{gathered}-\frac{1}{\tau^2}\left[u_{k+1}-2u_k+u_{k-1}\right]+Au_k=\varphi_k,\quad 1\le k\le N-1,\\ u_0=u_N,\qquad -u_2+4u_1-3u_0=u_{N-2}-4u_{N-1}+3u_N,\qquad N\tau=1.\end{gathered}\tag{2.1}$$

It is known (see [26]) that for a positive operator A it follows that $B=(1/2)(\tau A+\sqrt{4A+\tau^2A^2})$ is strongly positive and $R=(I+\tau B)^{-1}$ which is defined on the whole space E is a bounded operator. Furthermore, we have that

$$\|R^k\|_{E\to E}\le M(1+\delta\tau)^{-k},\qquad k\tau\|BR^k\|_{E\to E}\le M,\quad k\ge 1,\ \delta>0,\tag{2.2}$$

$$\|B^\beta(R^{k+r}-R^k)\|_{E\to E}\le M\frac{(r\tau)^\alpha}{(k\tau)^{\alpha+\beta}},\quad 1\le k<k+r\le N,\ 0\le\alpha,\ \beta\le 1.\tag{2.3}$$

From (2.2), it follows that

$$\left\|(I-R^N)^{-1}\right\|_{E\to E}\le M,\qquad \left\|\left(I-(2I-\tau B)(2I+3\tau B)^{-1}R^{N-2}\right)^{-1}\right\|_{E\to E}\le M.\tag{2.4}$$

For any φ_k, $1\le k\le N-1$, the solution of the problem (2.1) exists and the following formula holds:

$$u_k=\sum_{j=1}^{N-1}G(k,j)\varphi_j\tau,\quad 0\le k\le N,\tag{2.5}$$

where

$$G(k,1)=G(k,N-1)=C(R^{N-3}+1)(4R-1)(2B)^{-1}(I-DR^{N-2})^{-1}\tag{2.6}$$

for $k=0$ and $k=N$;

$$G(k,j)=-C(R^2-4R+1)(R^{j-2}+R^{N-j-2})(2B)^{-1}(I-DR^{N-2})^{-1}\tag{2.7}$$

for $2 \le j \le N-2$ and $k=0$, $k=N$;

$$\begin{aligned}
G(k,1) = {} & CC_1(2B)^{-1}\{R^{k-1}(2(R+3)+R^2(R-3))+R^{N-k}(4-R)(1+R) \\
& +R^{N+k-3}(1-4R)(1+R) \\
& +R^{2N-k-3}(3R-1-2R^2(3R+1))\} \\
& \times (1-R^N)^{-1}(I-DR^{N-2})^{-1}, \\
G(k,N-1) = {} & -CC_1(2B)^{-1}\{R^k(R-4)(R+1)+R^{N-k-1}(-2(R+3)+R^2(3-R)) \\
& +R^{N+k-3}(1-3R+2R^2(3R+1)) \\
& +R^{2N-k-3}(4R-1)(R+1)\} \\
& \times (1-R^N)^{-1}(I-DR^{N-2})^{-1}, \\
G(k,j) = {} & CC_1(2B)^{-1}\{(R-1)^3(R^{j+k-2}+R^{2N-2-j-k}) \\
& +(-1+3R+R^2(3-R))(R^{N-k+j-2}+R^{N+k-j-2}) \\
& +2(1-3R)(R^{2N-2+j-k}+R^{2N-2-j+k}) \\
& +2R^{|j-k|}(R^N-1)(R-3+R^{N-2}(-1+3R))\} \\
& \times (1-R^N)^{-1}(I-DR^{N-2})^{-1}
\end{aligned} \tag{2.8}$$

for $2 \le j \le N-2$ and $1 \le k \le N-1$. Here

$$\begin{aligned}
C = (I+\tau B)(2I+3\tau B)^{-1}, \quad & C_1 = (I+\tau B)(2I+\tau B)^{-1}, \\
D = (2I-\tau B)&(2I+3\tau B)^{-1},
\end{aligned} \tag{2.9}$$

where I is the unit operator.

Let $F_\tau(E)$ be the linear space of mesh functions $\varphi^\tau = \{\varphi_k\}_1^{N-1}$ with values in the Banach space E. Next on $F_\tau(E)$, we introduce the Banach spaces $C_\tau(E) = C([0,1]_\tau, E)$, $C_\tau^{\beta,\gamma}(E) = C^{\beta,\gamma}([0,1]_\tau, E)$ $(0 \le \gamma \le \beta < 1)$, and $L_{p,\tau}(E) = L_p([0,1]_\tau, E)$, $1 \le p < \infty$, with the norms

$$\begin{aligned}
||\varphi^\tau||_{C_\tau(E)} &= \max_{1\le k\le N} ||\varphi_k||_E, \\
||\varphi^\tau||_{C_\tau^{\beta,\gamma}(E)} &= ||\varphi^\tau||_{C_\tau(E)} + \sup_{1\le k<k+r\le N-1} ||\varphi_{k+r}-\varphi_k||_E \frac{((k+r)\tau)^\gamma(1-k\tau)^\gamma}{(r\tau)^\beta}, \\
||\varphi^\tau||_{L_{p,\tau}(E)} &= \left(\sum_{k=1}^{N-1} ||\varphi_k||_E^p \tau\right)^{1/p}.
\end{aligned} \tag{2.10}$$

With the help of $B = A^{1/2}$, we introduce the Banach space $E'_{\alpha,q} = E'_{\alpha,q}(E,B)$ $(0 < \alpha < 1)$ consisting of all $v \in E$ for which the following norms are finite:

$$\|v\|_{E'_{\alpha,q}} = \left(\int_0^\infty [z^\alpha \|B(z+B)^{-1}v\|_E]^q \frac{dz}{z} \right)^{1/q}, \quad 1 \le q < \infty,$$
$$\|v\|_{E'_\alpha} = \|v\|_{E'_{\alpha,\infty}} = \sup_{\lambda>0} \lambda^\alpha \|B(\lambda+B)^{-1}v\|_E. \tag{2.11}$$

The nonlocal boundary value problem (2.1) is said to be coercively stable (well posed) in $F_\tau(E)$ if we have the coercive inequality

$$\left\| \{\tau^{-2}(u_{k+1} - 2u_k + u_{k-1})\}_1^{N-1} \right\|_{F_\tau(E)} \le M \|\varphi^\tau\|_{F_\tau(E)}, \tag{2.12}$$

where M is independent not only of φ^τ but also of τ.

In [10], the coercive stability (well-posedness) of the difference problem (2.1) in the spaces $C_\tau^{\alpha,0}(E), C_\tau(E_\alpha)$ $(0 < \alpha < 1)$ and the almost coercive stability (with multiplier $\min\{\ln(1/\tau), 1 + |\ln \|B\|_{E\to E}|\}$) of the difference problem (2.1) in the spaces $C_\tau(E)$ were established.

Now let us consider the difference problem (2.1) in the spaces $L_{p,\tau}(E)$, $1 \le p < \infty$, of all grid functions. We have not been able to obtain the coercivity inequality

$$\left\| \{\tau^{-2}(u_{k+1} - 2u_k + u_{k-1})\}_1^{N-1} \right\|_{L_{p,\tau}(E)} \le M \|\varphi^\tau\|_{L_{p,\tau}(E)} \tag{2.13}$$

in the arbitrary Banach space E and for the general positive operator A. Nevertheless, we can establish the following almost coercivity inequality.

Theorem 2.1. *The solutions of the difference problem (2.1) in $L_{p,\tau}(E)$ obey the almost coercive inequality*

$$\left\| \{\tau^{-2}(u_{k+1} - 2u_k + u_{k-1})\}_1^{N-1} \right\|_{L_{p,\tau}(E)}$$
$$\le M_1 \min\left\{ \ln\frac{1}{\tau}, 1 + |\ln \|B\|_{E\to E}| \right\} \|\varphi^\tau\|_{L_{p,\tau}(E)}, \tag{2.14}$$

where M_1 does not depend on φ^τ, p, and τ.

Proof. By [12],

$$\left\| \{\tau^{-2}(u_{k+1} - 2u_k + u_{k-1})\}_1^{N-1} \right\|_{L_{p,\tau}(E)}$$
$$\le M\Big[\|u_0\|_{E'_{1-(1/p)}(D(B),B)} + \|u_N\|_{E'_{1-(1/p)}(D(B),B)} \tag{2.15}$$
$$+ \min\left\{ \ln\frac{1}{\tau}, 1 + |\ln \|B\|_{E\to E}| \right\} \|\varphi^\tau\|_{L_{p,\tau}(E)} \Big]$$

for the solutions of the boundary value problem

$$-\frac{1}{\tau^2}[u_{k+1}-2u_k+u_{k-1}]+Au_k=\varphi_k, \quad 1\le k\le N-1,$$
$$u_0=\varphi, \qquad u_N=\psi, \qquad N\tau=1. \tag{2.16}$$

Here the Banach space $E'_{1-(1/p)}=E'_{1-(1/p)}(E,B)$ consists of those $v\in E$ for which the norm

$$\|v\|_{E'_{1-(1/p)}}=\sup_{0<\tau\le\tau_0}\left(\sum_{k=1}^{N-1}\|BR^k v\|_E^{pq}\tau\right)^{1/p}+\|v\|_E \tag{2.17}$$

is finite.

Using the estimates (2.2), (2.3), (2.4), and the formula (2.5), we obtain

$$\|u_0\|_{E'_{1-(1/p)}(D(B),B)}\le M_1\min\left\{\ln\frac{1}{\tau},1+|\ln\|B\|_{E\to E}|\right\}\|\varphi^\tau\|_{L_{p,\tau}(E)} \tag{2.18}$$

for the solutions of the boundary value problem (2.1). Hence, from the last two estimates, (2.14) follows. Theorem 2.1 is proved. □

Finally, let us give the following results about well-posedness of the difference problem (2.1) in the spaces $L_{p,\tau}(E)$, $1\le p<\infty$.

Theorem 2.2. *Suppose that the difference problem (2.16) is well posed in $L_{p_0,\tau}(E)$ for some p_0, $1<p_0<\infty$. Then problem (2.1) is well posed in $L_{p,\tau}(E)$ for all p, $1<p<\infty$, and the following coercivity inequality holds:*

$$\left\|\{\tau^{-2}(u_{k+1}-2u_k+u_{k-1})\}_1^{N-1}\right\|_{L_{p,\tau}(E)}\le M(p_0)\frac{p^2}{p-1}\|\varphi^\tau\|_{L_{p,\tau}(E)}, \tag{2.19}$$

where $M(p_0)$ does not depend on φ^τ, p, and τ.

Proof. By [12],

$$\begin{aligned}&\left\|\{\tau^{-2}(u_{k+1}-2u_k+u_{k-1})\}_1^{N-1}\right\|_{L_{p,\tau}(E)}\\&\quad\le M\left[\|u_0\|_{E'_{1-(1/p)}(D(B),B)}\|+\|u_N\|_{E'_{1-(1/p)}(D(B),B)}\right]+M(p_0)\frac{p^2}{p-1}\|\varphi^\tau\|_{L_{p,\tau}(E)}\end{aligned} \tag{2.20}$$

for the solutions of the boundary value problem (2.16). Using the estimates (2.2), (2.3), (2.4), and the formula (2.5), we obtain

$$\|u_0\|_{E'_{1-(1/p)}(D(B),B)}\le M_1\frac{p^2}{p-1}\|\varphi^\tau\|_{L_{p,\tau}(E)} \tag{2.21}$$

for the solutions of the boundary value problem (2.1). Hence, from the last two estimates, (2.19) follows. Theorem 2.2 is proved. □

THEOREM 2.3. *Let $1 \leq p \leq \infty$ and $0 < \alpha < 1$. The difference problem (2.1) is well posed in $L_{p,\tau}(E'_{\alpha,p})$ and the following coercivity inequality holds:*

$$\left\|\{\tau^{-2}(u_{k+1} - 2u_k + u_{k-1})\}_1^{N-1}\right\|_{L_{p,\tau}(E'_{\alpha,p})} \leq M\frac{1}{\alpha(1-\alpha)}\|\varphi^\tau\|_{L_{p,\tau}(E'_{\alpha,p})}, \tag{2.22}$$

where M does not depend on φ^τ, p, α, and τ.

Proof. By [6],

$$\begin{aligned}&\left\|\{\tau^{-2}(u_{k+1} - 2u_k + u_{k-1})\}_1^{N-1}\right\|_{L_{p,\tau}(E'_{\alpha,p})}\\ &\quad\leq M\left[\|Au_0\|_{E'_{\alpha,p}} + \|Au_N\|_{E'_{\alpha,p}}\right] + \frac{1}{\alpha(1-\alpha)}\|\varphi^\tau\|_{L_{p,\tau}(E'_{\alpha,p})}\end{aligned} \tag{2.23}$$

for the solutions of the boundary value problem (2.16). Using the estimates (2.2), (2.3), (2.4), and the formula (2.5), we obtain

$$\|Au_0\|_{E'_{\alpha,p}} \leq M_1\frac{1}{\alpha(1-\alpha)}\|\varphi^\tau\|_{L_{p,\tau}(E)} \tag{2.24}$$

for the solutions of the boundary value problem (2.1). Hence, from the last two estimates, (2.22) follows. Theorem 2.3 is proved. □

From Theorems 2.2 and 2.3, we have Theorem 2.4.

THEOREM 2.4. *Let $1 < p, q < \infty$, and $0 < \alpha < 1$. The difference problem (2.1) is well posed in $L_{p,\tau}(E'_{\alpha,q})$ and the following coercivity inequality holds:*

$$\left\|\{\tau^{-2}(u_{k+1} - 2u_k + u_{k-1})\}_1^{N-1}\right\|_{L_{p,\tau}(E'_{\alpha,q})} \leq M(q)\frac{p^2}{p-1}\frac{1}{\alpha(1-\alpha)}\|\varphi^\tau\|_{L_{p,\tau}(E'_{\alpha,q})}, \tag{2.25}$$

where $M(q)$ does not depend on φ^τ, p, α, and τ.

Note that by passing to the limit for $\tau \to 0$, one can recover Theorems 1.5–1.7.

Now we consider the applications of Theorems 2.1–2.4. We consider the boundary value problem on the range $\{0 \leq y \leq 1,\ x \in \mathcal{R}^n\}$ for elliptic equation

$$\begin{gathered}-\frac{\partial^2 u}{\partial y^2} + \sum_{|r|=2m} a_r(x)\frac{\partial^{|\tau|}u}{\partial x_1^{r_1}\cdots\partial x_n^{r_n}} + \delta u(y,x) = f(y,x),\\ f(0,x) = f(1,x), \quad 0 < y < 1,\ x, r \in \mathcal{R}^n,\ |r| = r_1 + \cdots + r_n,\\ u(0,x) = u(1,x), \qquad u_y(0,x) = u_y(1,x), \quad x \in \mathcal{R}^n,\end{gathered} \tag{2.26}$$

where $a_r(x)$ and $f(y,x)$ are given sufficiently smooth functions and $\delta > 0$ is the sufficiently large number.

We will assume that the symbol

$$B^x(\xi) = \sum_{|r|=2m} a_r(x)(i\xi_1)^{r_1}\cdots(i\xi_n)^{r_n}, \quad \xi = (\xi_1,\ldots,\xi_n) \in R^n, \tag{2.27}$$

of the differential operator of the form

$$B^x = \sum_{|r|=2m} a_r(x)\frac{\partial^{|r|}}{\partial x_1^{r_1}\cdots\partial x_n^{r_n}} \tag{2.28}$$

acting on functions defined on the space $\mathcal{R}^n$ satisfies the inequalities

$$0 < M_1|\xi|^{2m} \le (-1)^m B^x(\xi) \le M_2|\xi|^{2m} < \infty \tag{2.29}$$

for $\xi \neq 0$.

The discretization of problem (2.26) is carried out in two steps. In the first step, let us give the difference operator A_h^x by the formula

$$A_h^x u_x^h = \sum_{2m\le|r|\le S} b_r^x D_h^r u_x^h + \delta u_x^h. \tag{2.30}$$

The coefficients are chosen in such a way that the operator A_h^x approximates in a specified way the operator

$$\sum_{|r|=2m} a_r(x)\frac{\partial^{|r|}}{\partial x_1^{r_1}\cdots\partial x_n^{r_n}} + \delta. \tag{2.31}$$

We will assume that for $|\xi_k h| \le \pi$ and the symbol $A(\xi h, h)$ of the operator $A_h^x - \delta$ satisfies the inequalities

$$(-1)^m A^x(\xi h,h) \ge M_1|\xi|^{2m}, \qquad |\arg A^x(\xi h,h)| \le \phi < \phi_0 < \frac{\pi}{2}. \tag{2.32}$$

With the help of A_h^x, we arrive at the boundary value problem

$$\begin{gathered} -\frac{d^2 v^h(y,x)}{dy^2} + A_h^x v^h(y,x) = \varphi^h(y,x), \quad 0 < y < 1, \\ v^h(0,x) = v^h(1,x), \qquad v_y^h(0,x) = v_y^h(1,x), \quad x \in \mathbb{R}_h^n, \end{gathered} \tag{2.33}$$

for an infinite system of ordinary differential equations.

In the second step, we replace problem (2.33) by the difference scheme

$$\begin{gathered} -\frac{1}{\tau^2}[u_{k+1}^h - 2u_k^h + u_{k-1}^h] + A_h^x u_k^h = \varphi_k^h, \quad 1 \le k \le N-1, \\ u_0^h = u_N^h, -u_2^h + 4u_1^h - 3u_0^h = u_{N-2}^h - 4u_{N-1}^h + 3u_N^h, \quad N\tau = 1. \end{gathered} \tag{2.34}$$

To formulate our result, we need to introduce the space $C_h = C(R_h^n)$ of all bounded grid functions $u^h(x)$ defined on R_h^n, equipped with the norm

$$||u^h||_{C_h} = \sup_{x\varepsilon R_h^n} |u^h(x)|. \tag{2.35}$$

THEOREM 2.5. *The solutions of the difference scheme (2.34) satisfy the following almost coercive stability estimates:*

$$\left\|\{\tau^{-2}(u_{k+1}^h - 2u_k^h + u_{k-1}^h)\}_1^{N-1}\right\|_{L_{p,\tau}(C_h)} \le M \ln\frac{1}{\tau+h}\|\varphi^{\tau,h}\|_{L_{p,\tau}(C_h)}, \quad 1 \le p \le \infty, \tag{2.36}$$

where M does not depend on $\varphi^{\tau,h}$, p, h, and τ.

The proof of Theorem 2.5 is based on the abstract, Theorem 2.1, on the positivity of the operator A_h^x in C_h, on the almost coercivity inequality for an elliptic operator A_h^x in C_h [14], and on estimate

$$\min\left\{\ln\frac{1}{\tau}, 1 + |\ln\|B_h^x\|_{C_h \to C_h}|\right\} \le M \ln\frac{1}{\tau+h}. \tag{2.37}$$

Next, to formulate our result, we need to introduce the space $W_{p,h}^{\beta} = W_p^{\beta}(R_h^n)$, $0 \le \beta \le 1$, $1 \le p < \infty$, of all bounded grid functions $u^h(x)$ defined on R_h^n, equipped with the norm

$$\|u^h\|_{W_{p,h}^{\beta}} = \left[\sum_{x\varepsilon R_h^n}\sum_{y\varepsilon R_h^n, y\neq 0}\frac{|u^h(x) - u^h(x+y)|^p}{|y|^{n+\beta p}}h^{2n} + \|u^h\|_{L_{p,h}}^p\right]^{1/p}. \tag{2.38}$$

Here $L_{p,h} = L_p(R_h^n)$ denotes the Banach space of bounded grid functions $u^h(x)$ defined on R_h^n, equipped with the norm

$$\|u^h\|_{L_{p,h}} = \left[\sum_{x\varepsilon R_h^n}|u^h(x)|^p h^n\right]^{1/p}. \tag{2.39}$$

THEOREM 2.6. *The solutions of the difference scheme (2.34) satisfy the following coercive stability estimates:*

$$\left\|\{\tau^{-2}(u_{k+1}^h - 2u_k^h + u_{k-1}^h)\}_1^{N-1}\right\|_{L_{p,\tau}(W_{q,h}^{m\alpha})} \le M(\alpha,p,q)\|\varphi^{\tau,h}\|_{L_{p,\tau}(W_{q,h}^{m\alpha})}, \quad 1 < p,q < \infty,\ 0 < \alpha < \frac{1}{m}, \tag{2.40}$$

where $M(\alpha,p,q)$ does not depend on $\varphi^{\tau,h}$, h, and τ.

The proof of Theorem 2.6 is based on the abstract, Theorem 2.4, and the positivity of the operator A_h^x in $L_{p,h}$ in [14], on the coercivity inequality for an elliptic operator A_h^x in $W_{p,h}^{\beta}$ in [13], and on the following theorem.

THEOREM 2.7 [14]. *For any $0 < \beta < 1/m$, the norms in the spaces $E'_{\beta,q}(L_{q,h},(A_h^x)^{1/2})$ and $W_{q,h}^{m\beta}$ are equivalent uniformly in h.*

References

[1] R. P. Agarwal, M. Bohner, and V. B. Shakhmurov, *Maximal regular boundary value problems in Banach-valued weighted space*, Boundary Value Problems **2005** (2005), no. 1, 9–42.

[2] S. Agmon, *Lectures on Elliptic Boundary Value Problems*, Van Nostrand Mathematical Studies, no. 2, D. Van Nostrand, New Jersey, 1965.

[3] S. Agmon, A. Douglis, and L. Nirenberg, *Estimates near the boundary for solutions of elliptic partial differential equations satisfying general boundary conditions. II*, Communications on Pure and Applied Mathematics **17** (1964), 35–92.

[4] A. Aibeche and A. Favini, *Coerciveness estimate for Ventcel boundary value problem for a differential equation*, Semigroup Forum **70** (2005), no. 2, 269–277.

[5] A. Ashyralyev, *Coercive solvability of elliptic equations in spaces of smooth functions*, Boundary Value Problems for Nonclassical Equations in Mathematical Physics (Novosibirsk, 1989), Akad. Nauk SSSR Sibirsk. Otdel. Inst. Mat., Novosibirsk, 1989, pp. 82–86.

[6] ———, *Method of positive operators of investigations of the high order of accuracy difference schemes for parabolic and elliptic equations*, Doctor Sciences thesis, Institute of Mathematics, Academic Sciences, Kiev, 1992.

[7] ———, *Well-posed solvability of the boundary value problem for difference equations of elliptic type*, Nonlinear Analysis. Theory, Methods & Applications **24** (1995), no. 2, 251–256.

[8] ———, *On well-posedness of the nonlocal boundary value problems for elliptic equations*, Numerical Functional Analysis and Optimization **24** (2003), no. 1-2, 1–15.

[9] ———, *Nonlocal boundary value problems for partial differential equations: well-posedness*, AIP Conference Proceedings Global Analysis and Applied Mathematics: International Workshop on Global Analysis, vol. 729, 2004, pp. 325–331.

[10] A. Ashyralyev and N. Altay, *A note on the well-posedness of the nonlocal boundary value problem for elliptic difference equations*, Applied Mathematics and Computation **175** (2006), 49–60.

[11] A. Ashyralyev and K. Amanov, *On coercive estimates in Hölder norms*, Izvestiya Akademii Nauk Turkmenskoĭ SSR. Seriya Fiziko-Tekhnicheskikh, Khimicheskikh i Geologicheskikh Nauk (1996), no. 1, 3–10 (Russian).

[12] A. Ashyralyev and S. Piskarev, *On well-posedness of the difference schemes for abstract elliptic equations in $L^p([0,T],E)$ spaces*, SFB 701: preprints, University of Bielefeld (Germany), 2005, 17p.

[13] A. Ashyralyev and P. E. Sobolevskiĭ, *Well-Posedness of Parabolic Difference Equations*, Operator Theory: Advances and Applications, vol. 69, Birkhäuser, Basel, 1994.

[14] ———, *New Difference Schemes for Partial Differential Equations*, Operator Theory: Advances and Applications, vol. 148, Birkhäuser, Basel, 2004.

[15] Ph. Clément and S. Guerre-Delabrière, *On the regularity of abstract Cauchy problems and boundary value problems*, Atti della Accademia Nazionale dei Lincei. Classe di Scienze Fisiche, Matematiche e Naturali. Rendiconti Lincei. Serie IX. Matematica e Applicazioni **9** (1998), no. 4, 245–266 (1999).

[16] L. M. Gershteyn and P. E. Sobolevskiĭ, *Well-posedness of the a Banach space*, Differentsial'nye Uravneniya **10** (1974), no. 11, 2059–2061 (Russian).

[17] V. L. Gorbachuk and M. L. Gorbachuk, *Boundary Value Problems for Differential-Operator Equations*, Naukova Dumka, Kiev, 1984.

[18] P. Grisvard, *Elliptic Problems in Nonsmooth Domains*, Monographs and Studies in Mathematics, vol. 24, Pitman (Advanced Publishing Program), Massachusetts, 1985.

[19] S. G. Krein, *Linear Differential Equations in Banach Space*, Nauka, Moscow, 1966.

[20] O. A. Ladyzhenskaya, V. A. Solonnikov, and N. N. Ural'tseva, *Linear and Quasilinear Equations of Parabolic Type*, "Nauka", Moscow, 1967.

[21] O. A. Ladyzhenskaya and N. N. Ural'tseva, *Linear and Quasilinear Equations of Elliptic Type*, Izdat. "Nauka", Moscow, 1973.

[22] V. B. Shakhmurov, *Coercive boundary value problems for regular degenerate differential-operator equations*, Journal of Mathematical Analysis and Applications **292** (2004), no. 2, 605–620.
[23] A. L. Skubachevskii, *Elliptic Functional-Differential Equations and Applications*, Operator Theory: Advances and Applications, vol. 91, Birkhäuser, Basel, 1997.
[24] Yu. A. Smirnitskiĭ and P. E. Sobolevskiĭ, *Positivity of multidimensional difference operators in the C-norm*, Uspekhi Matematicheskikh Nauk **36** (1981), no. 4, 202–203 (Russian).
[25] P. E. Sobolevskiĭ, *Elliptic equations in a Banach space*, Differentsial'nye Uravneniya **4** (1968), no. 7, 1346–1348 (Russian).
[26] ______, *The theory of semigroups and the stability of difference schemes*, Operator Theory in Function Spaces (Proc. School, Novosibirsk, 1975), Izdat. "Nauka" Sibirsk. Otdel., Novosibirsk, 1977, pp. 304–337, 344.
[27] ______, *Well-posedness of difference elliptic equation*, Discrete Dynamics in Nature and Society **1** (1997), 219–231.
[28] P. E. Sobolevskiĭ and M. E. Tiunchik, *On the well-posedness of the second boundary value problem for difference equations in weighted Hölder norms*, Qualitative Methods of the Theory of Dynamical Systems, Dal'nevost. Gos. University, Vladivostok, 1982, pp. 27–37.
[29] M. L. Vishik, A. D. Myshkis, and O. A. Oleinik, *Partial differential equations*, Mathematics in USSR in the Last 40 Years, 1917–1957, vol. 1, Fizmatgiz, Moscow, 1959, pp. 563–599.

Allaberen Ashyralyev: Department of Mathematics, Fatih University, 34500 Buyukcekmece, Istanbul, Turkey
E-mail address: aashyr@fatih.edu.tr

ON THE STABILITY OF THE DIFFERENCE SCHEMES FOR HYPERBOLIC EQUATIONS

ALLABEREN ASHYRALYEV AND MEHMET EMIR KOKSAL

The second order of accuracy unconditional stable difference schemes approximately solving the initial value problem $d^2u(t)/(dt^2) + A(t)u(t) = f(t)$ $(0 \leq t \leq T)$, $u(0) = \varphi$, $u'(0) = \psi$, for differential equation in a Hilbert space H with the selfadjoint positive definite operators $A(t)$ is considered. The stability estimates for the solution of these difference schemes and first- and second-order difference derivatives are presented. The numerical analysis is given. The theoretical statements for the solution of these difference schemes are supported by the results of numerical experiments.

1. Introduction

It is known (see, e.g., [3, 4]) that various initial boundary value problems for the hyperbolic equations can be reduced to the initial value problem

$$\frac{d^2u(t)}{dt^2} + A(t)u(t) = f(t) \quad (0 \leq t \leq T),$$
$$u(0) = \varphi, \qquad u'(0) = \psi, \tag{1.1}$$

for differential equation in a Hilbert space H. Here $A(t)$ are the selfadjoint positive definite operators in H with a t-independent domain $D = D(A(t))$.

A large cycle of works on difference schemes for hyperbolic partial differential equations (see, e.g., [1, 5–7] and the references given therein) in which stability was established under the assumption that the magnitudes of the grid steps τ and h with respect to the time and space variables are connected. In abstract terms this means, in particular, that the condition $\tau \|A_{\tau,h}\| \to 0$ when $\tau \to 0$ is satisfied.

Of great interest is the study of absolute stable difference schemes of a high order of accuracy for hyperbolic partial differential equations, in which stability was established without any assumptions to respect of the grid steps τ and h. Such type stability

Hindawi Publishing Corporation
Proceedings of the Conference on Differential & Difference Equations and Applications, pp. 117–130

inequalities for the solutions of the first order of accuracy difference scheme

$$\tau^{-2}(u_{k+1}-2u_k+u_{k-1})+A_k u_{k+1}=f_k,$$
$$A_k=A(t_k),\quad f_k=f(t_k),\quad t_k=k\tau,\ 1\le k\le N-1,\ N\tau=T, \tag{1.2}$$
$$\tau^{-1}(u_1-u_0)+iA_1^{1/2}u_1=iA_0^{1/2}u_0+\psi,\quad u_0=\varphi,$$

for approximately solving problem (1.1) were established for the first time in [8].

We are interested in studying the high order of accuracy two-step difference schemes for the approximate solutions of the problem (1.1) in a Hilbert space H with selfadjoint positive definite operators $A(t)$. In the paper [2] one new difference scheme of a second order of accuracy for the approximately solving this initial value problem

$$\begin{aligned}
&\tau^{-2}(u_{k+1}-2u_k+u_{k-1})+A_{k+1/2}4^{-1}(u_{k+1}+u_k)+A_{k+1/2}^{1/2}A_{k-1/2}^{1/2}4^{-1}(u_k+u_{k-1})\\
&\quad+\tau^{-1}(A_{k-1/2}^{1/2}-A_{k+1/2}^{1/2})A_{k-1/2}^{-1/2}\tau^{-1}(u_k-u_{k-1})\\
&\quad+2^{-1}\tau^{-1}(A_{k+1}^{1/2}-A_k^{1/2})A_{k+1/2}^{-1/2}\tau^{-1}(u_{k+1}-u_k)\\
&\quad+A_{k+1/2}^{1/2}A_{k-1/2}^{-1/2}2^{-1}\tau^{-1}(A_k^{1/2}-A_{k-1}^{1/2})A_{k-1/2}^{-1/2}\tau^{-1}(u_k-u_{k-1})\\
&\quad=2^{-1}(f_{k-1/2}+f_{k+1/2})+(A_{k+1/2}^{1/2}-A_{k-1/2}^{1/2})A_{k-1/2}^{-1/2}2^{-1}f_{k-1/2},\quad 1\le k\le N-1,\ u_0=u(0),\\
&\tau^{-1}(u_1-u_0)+\frac{\tau}{2}A_{1/2}2^{-1}(u_1+u_0)+\frac{\tau}{2}(A_{1/2}^{1/2})'A_{1/2}^{-1/2}\tau^{-1}(u_1-u_0)=\frac{\tau}{2}f_{1/2}+A_{1/2}^{1/2}A_{1/2}^{-1/2}u_0'
\end{aligned} \tag{1.3}$$

is presented. Let the operator-function $A^{\rho}(t)A^{-\rho}(z)$, $\rho\in[0,1]$, satisfy the condition

$$\|[A^{\rho}(t)-A^{\rho}(s)]A^{-\rho}(z)\|\le M_{\rho}|t-s|, \tag{1.4}$$

where M_ρ is a positive constant independent of t, s, z for $t,s,z\in[0,T]$. Furthermore, let the operator-function $A^{1/2}(p)A^{1/2}(t)A^{-1}(z)$ satisfy the condition

$$\|A^{1/2}(p)[A^{1/2}(t)-A^{1/2}(s)]A^{-1}(z)\|\le M_{1/2}|t-s|, \tag{1.5}$$

where $M_{1/2}$ is a positive constant independent of t, s, z, p for $t,s,z,p\in[0,T]$. Then the following theorems on the stability of this difference scheme are established.

Theorem 1.1. *Let $u(0)\in D(A^{1/2}(0))$. Then for the solution of the difference scheme (1.3) the stability estimate*

$$\left\|\left\{\frac{u_k-u_{k-1}}{\tau}\right\}_1^{N-1}\right\|_{C_\tau}+\|u^\tau\|_{C_\tau}\le C_1\left[\|A^{1/2}(0)u_0\|_H+\|u_0'\|_H+\sum_{s=0}^{N-1}\|f_{s+1/2}\|_H\tau\right] \tag{1.6}$$

holds, where C_1 does not depend on u_0, u_0', $f_{s+1/2}$ $(0\le s\le N-1)$ and τ. Here C_τ is the norm space of the mesh functions $u^\tau=\{u_k\}_1^{N-1}$ with the norm

$$\|u^\tau\|_{C_\tau}=\max_{1\le k\le N-1}\|u_k\|_H. \tag{1.7}$$

THEOREM 1.2. *Let $u(0) \in D(A(0))$, $u'(0) \in D(A^{1/2}(0))$. Then for the solution of the difference scheme (1.3) the stability estimate*

$$\begin{aligned}
&\left\|\left\{A^{1/2}(0)\frac{u_k - u_{k-1}}{\tau}\right\}_1^{N-1}\right\|_{C_\tau} \\
&\quad + \|A_{k+1/2}4^{-1}(u_{k+1}+u_k) + A_{k+1/2}^{1/2}A_{k-1/2}^{1/2}4^{-1}(u_k+u_{k-1}) \\
&\quad + \tau^{-1}(A_{k-1/2}^{1/2} - A_{k+1/2}^{1/2})A_{k-1/2}^{-1/2}\tau^{-1}(u_k - u_{k-1}) \\
&\quad + 2^{-1}\tau^{-1}(A_{k+1}^{1/2} - A_k^{1/2})A_{k+1/2}^{-1/2}\tau^{-1}(u_{k+1} - u_k) \\
&\quad + A_{k+1/2}^{1/2}A_{k-1/2}^{-1/2}2^{-1}\tau^{-1}(A_k^{1/2} - A_{k-1}^{1/2})A_{k-1/2}^{-1/2}\tau^{-1}(u_k - u_{k-1})\|_H \\
&\quad + \left\|\{\tau^{-2}(u_{k+1} - 2u_k + u_{k-1})\}_1^{N-1}\right\|_{C_\tau} \\
&\le C_2\left[\|A(0)u_0\|_H + \|A^{1/2}(0)u_0'\|_H + \max_{0\le s\le k}\|f_{s+1/2}\|_H + \sum_{s=0}^{N-2}\|f_{s+1/2} - f_{s-1/2}\|_H\right]
\end{aligned} \tag{1.8}$$

holds, where C_2 does not depend on u_0, u_0', $f_{s+1/2}$ $(0 \le s \le N-1)$ and τ.

Furthermore, using the approach of the paper [2] the second new difference scheme of a second order of accuracy for the approximately solving the initial value problem (1.1)

$$\begin{aligned}
&\tau^{-2}(u_{k+1} - 2u_k + u_{k-1}) \\
&\quad + \Big\{\frac{i}{\tau}A_{k+1/2}^{1/2}\Big[I - \frac{\tau^2}{2}A_{k+1/2} + \tau A_{k+1/2}^{-1/2}(A_{k+1/2}^{1/2})' \\
&\qquad + \frac{\tau^2}{2}A_{k+1/2}^{-1}(A_{k+1/2}^{1/2})'(A_{k+1}^{1/2})'\Big]\Big[i\tau A_{k+1/2}^{1/2} + i\frac{\tau^2}{2}(A_{k+1}^{1/2})'\Big]^{-1}\Big(I - \frac{\tau^2}{2}A_{k+1/2}\Big) \\
&\qquad - \frac{i}{\tau}A_{k+1/2}^{1/2}\Big[i\tau A_{k+1/2}^{1/2} + i\frac{\tau^2}{2}(A_{k+1/2}^{1/2})'\Big] - \frac{1}{\tau^2}\Big\}u_{k+1} \\
&\quad + \Big\{\frac{i}{\tau}A_{k+1/2}^{1/2}\Big[I - \frac{\tau^2}{2}A_{k+1/2} - \tau A_{k+1/2}^{-1/2}(A_{k+1/2}^{1/2})' + \frac{\tau^2}{2}A_{k+1/2}^{-1}(A_{k+1/2}^{1/2})'(A_{k+1}^{1/2})'\Big] \\
&\qquad \times \Big[i\tau A_{k+1/2} + i\frac{\tau^2}{2}(A_{k+1}^{1/2})'\Big]^{-1} - \frac{i}{\tau}A_{k+1/2}^{1/2}\Big[i\tau A_{k-1/2}^{1/2} + i\frac{\tau^2}{2}(A_k^{1/2})'\Big]^{-1} \\
&\qquad \times \Big(I - \frac{\tau^2}{2}A_{k-1/2}\Big) + \frac{2}{\tau^2}\Big\}u_k + \Big\{\frac{i}{\tau}A_{k+1/2}^{1/2}\Big[i\tau A_{k-1/2}^{1/2} + i\frac{\tau^2}{2}(A_k^{1/2})'\Big]^{-1} - \frac{1}{\tau^2}\Big\}u_{k-1} \\
&= \Big\{-\frac{i\tau}{2}A_{k+1/2}^{1/2}\Big[I - \frac{\tau^2}{2}A_{k+1/2} + \tau A_{k+1/2}^{-1/2}(A_{k+1/2}^{1/2})' + \frac{\tau^2}{2}A_{k+1/2}^{-1}(A_{k+1/2}^{1/2})'(A_{k+1}^{1/2})'\Big] \\
&\qquad \times \Big[i\tau A_{k+1/2}^{1/2} + i\frac{\tau^2}{2}(A_{k+1}^{1/2})'\Big]^{-1} + I + \frac{\tau}{2}A_{k+1/2}^{-1/2}(A_{k+1/2}^{1/2})'\Big\}f_{k+1/2} \\
&\quad + \Big\{\frac{i\tau}{2}A_{k+1/2}^{1/2}\Big[i\tau A_{k-1/2}^{1/2} + i\frac{\tau^2}{2}(A_k^{1/2})'\Big]^{-1}\Big\}f_{k-1/2}, \quad 1 \le k \le N-1,\ u_0 = u(0),
\end{aligned}$$

$$\begin{aligned}
&\Big\{I-\Big[\frac{\tau^2}{2}A_{1/2}-\tau A_{1/2}^{-1/2}(A_{1/2}^{1/2})'-\frac{\tau^2}{2}A_{1/2}^{-1}(A_{1/2}^{1/2})'(A_1^{1/2})'\Big]\Big\}\Big[iA_{1/2}^{1/2}+i\frac{\tau}{2}(A_{1/2}^{1/2})'\Big]^{-1}\tau^{-1}(u_1-u_0)\\
&\quad+\Big[-\frac{\tau}{2}A_{1/2}-i\tau A_{1/2}^{1/2}-i\frac{\tau^2}{2}(A_{1/2}^{1/2})'\Big]u_1+(iA_0^{-1/2})u_0'\\
&\quad=\Big\{-\frac{\tau}{2}\Big\{I-\Big[\frac{\tau^2}{2}A_{1/2}-\tau A_{1/2}^{-1/2}(A_{1/2}^{1/2})'-\frac{\tau^2}{2}A_{1/2}^{-1}(A_{1/2}^{1/2})'(A_1^{1/2})'\Big]\Big\}\\
&\qquad\times\Big[iA_{1/2}^{1/2}+i\frac{\tau}{2}(A_{1/2}^{1/2})'\Big]^{-1}-i\tau A_{1/2}^{-1/2}-i\frac{\tau^2}{2}A_{1/2}^{-1}(A_{1/2}^{1/2})'\Big\}f_{1/2}
\end{aligned} \tag{1.9}$$

is presented. Applying this approach we can obtain the stability estimates for solutions of the difference scheme (1.9).

2. Numerical analysis

We have not been able to obtain a sharp estimate for the constants figuring in the stability inequality. Therefore we will give the following results of numerical experiments of the initial boundary value problem

$$\begin{gathered}
\frac{\partial^2 u(t,x)}{\partial t^2}-\frac{\partial^2 u(t,x)}{\partial x^2}=2\exp(-t)\cos x,\quad 0<t<1,\ 0<x<\pi,\\
u(0,x)=\cos x,\quad u_t(0,x)=-\cos x,\quad 0\le x\le\pi,\\
u_x(t,0)=u_x(t,\pi)=0,\quad 0\le t\le 1,
\end{gathered} \tag{2.1}$$

for hyperbolic equation. The exact solution of this problem is

$$u(t,x)=\exp(-t)\cos x. \tag{2.2}$$

First, applying the first order of accuracy difference scheme (1.2), we present the following first order of accuracy difference scheme for the approximate solutions of the problem (2.1):

$$\begin{gathered}
\frac{u_n^{k+1}-2u_n^k+u_n^{k-1}}{\tau^2}-\frac{u_{n+1}^{k+1}-2u_n^{k+1}+u_{n-1}^{k+1}}{h^2}=f(t_k,x_n),\\
t_k=k\tau,\quad x_n=nh,\quad 1\le k\le N-1,\quad 1\le n\le M-1,\\
u_n^0=\varphi(x_n),\quad 1\le n\le M-1,\\
\frac{u_n^1-u_n^0}{\tau}=-\varphi(x_n),\quad 1\le n\le M-1,\quad u_0^k=u_1^k,\quad u_{M-1}^k=u_M^k,\quad 0\le k\le N,\\
f(t,x)=2\exp(-t)\cos x,\qquad \varphi(x)=\cos(x).
\end{gathered} \tag{2.3}$$

We have $(N+1)\times(N+1)$ system of linear equations in (2.3) and we will write them in the matrix form

$$\begin{gathered} AU_{n+1}+BU_n+CU_{n-1}=D\varphi_n, \quad 0\le n\le M, \\ U_0=U_1, \qquad U_{M-1}=U_M, \end{gathered} \tag{2.4}$$

where

$$A=\begin{bmatrix} 0 & 0 & 0 & 0 & \dots & 0 & 0 & 0 \\ 0 & 0 & a & 0 & \dots & 0 & 0 & 0 \\ 0 & 0 & 0 & a & \dots & 0 & 0 & 0 \\ \dots & \dots & \dots & \dots & \dots & \dots & \dots & \dots \\ 0 & 0 & 0 & 0 & \dots & a & 0 & 0 \\ 0 & 0 & 0 & 0 & \dots & 0 & a & 0 \\ 0 & 0 & 0 & 0 & \dots & 0 & 0 & a \\ 0 & 0 & 0 & 0 & \dots & 0 & 0 & 0 \end{bmatrix}_{(N+1)\times(N+1)},$$

$$B=\begin{bmatrix} 1 & 0 & 0 & 0 & 0 & \dots & 0 & 0 & 0 \\ d & c & b & 0 & 0 & \dots & 0 & 0 & 0 \\ 0 & d & c & b & 0 & \dots & 0 & 0 & 0 \\ \dots & \dots & \dots & \dots & \dots & \dots & \dots & \dots & \dots \\ 0 & 0 & 0 & 0 & 0 & \dots & b & 0 & 0 \\ 0 & 0 & 0 & 0 & 0 & \dots & c & b & 0 \\ 0 & 0 & 0 & 0 & 0 & \dots & d & c & b \\ e & -e & 0 & 0 & 0 & \dots & 0 & 0 & 0 \end{bmatrix}_{(N+1)\times(N+1)}, \tag{2.5}$$

$$C=A, \qquad D=\begin{bmatrix} 1 & 0 & \dots & 0 \\ 0 & 1 & \dots & 0 \\ \dots & \dots & \dots & \dots \\ 0 & 0 & \dots & 1 \end{bmatrix}_{(N+1)\times(N+1)},$$

$$U_s=\begin{bmatrix} U_s^0 \\ U_s^1 \\ \dots \\ U_s^N \end{bmatrix}_{(N+1)\times(1)}, \quad \text{where } s=n\pm 1, n.$$

Here

$$a=-\frac{1}{h^2}, \qquad b=\frac{1}{\tau^2}+\frac{2}{h^2}, \qquad c=-\frac{2}{\tau^2}, \qquad d=\frac{1}{\tau^2}, \qquad e=\frac{1}{\tau},$$

$$\varphi_n^k=\begin{cases} \cos(x_n), & k=0, \\ f(t_k,x_n), & 1\le k\le N-1, \\ \cos(x_n), & k=N, \end{cases} \qquad \varphi_n=\begin{bmatrix} \varphi_n^0 \\ \varphi_n^1 \\ \dots \\ \varphi_n^N \end{bmatrix}_{(N+1)\times 1}. \tag{2.6}$$

So, we have the second-order difference equation with respect to n with matrix coefficients. To solve this difference equation we have applied a procedure of modified Gauss elimination method for difference equation with respect to n with matrix coefficients. Hence, we seek a solution of the matrix equation in the following form:

$$U_n = \alpha_{n+1} U_{n+1} + \beta_{n+1}, \quad n = M-1, \ldots, 2, 1, 0, \tag{2.7}$$

where α_j $(j = 1, \ldots, M)$ are $(N+1) \times (N+1)$ square matrices and β_j $(j = 1, \ldots, M)$ are $(N+1) \times 1$ column matrices defined by

$$\alpha_{n+1} = -(B + C\alpha_n)^{-1} A, \quad \beta_{n+1} = (B + C\alpha_n)^{-1} (D\varphi_n - C\beta_n), \quad n = 1, 2, 3, \ldots, M-1. \tag{2.8}$$

Here

$$\alpha_1 = \begin{bmatrix} 1 & 0 & \cdots & 0 \\ 0 & 1 & \cdots & 0 \\ \cdots & \cdots & \cdots & \cdots \\ 0 & 0 & \cdots & 1 \end{bmatrix}_{(N+1)\times(N+1)},$$

$$\beta_1 = \begin{bmatrix} 0 \\ 0 \\ \cdots \\ 0 \end{bmatrix}_{(N+1)\times 1}, \tag{2.9}$$

$$u_M = (I - \alpha_M)^{-1} \beta_M.$$

Second, applying the second order of accuracy difference scheme (1.3) and using simple formulas

$$\begin{aligned} &\frac{2u(0) - 5u(\tau) + 4u(2\tau) - u(3\tau)}{\tau^2} - u''(0) = O(\tau^2), \\ &\frac{2u(1) - 5u(1-\tau) + 4u(1-2\tau) - u(1-3\tau)}{\tau^2} - u''(1) = O(\tau^2), \end{aligned} \tag{2.10}$$

we present the following second order of accuracy difference scheme for the approximate solutions of the problem (2.1):

$$\begin{aligned} &\frac{u_n^{k+1} - 2u_n^k + u_n^{k-1}}{\tau^2} - \frac{u_{n+1}^k - 2u_n^k + u_{n-1}^k}{2h^2} - \frac{u_{n+1}^{k+1} - 2u_n^{k+1} + u_{n-1}^{k+1}}{4h^2} - \frac{u_{n+1}^{k-1} - 2u_n^{k-1} + u_{n-1}^{k-1}}{4h^2} \\ &\quad = f(t_k, x_n), \quad x_n = nh, \ t_k = k\tau, \ 1 \le k \le N-1, \ 1 \le n \le M-1, \\ &u_n^0 = \varphi(x_n), \quad x_n = nh, \ 1 \le n \le M-1, \end{aligned}$$

$$\frac{u_n^1 - u_n^0}{\tau} = \frac{\tau}{2}\left(\frac{u_{n+1}^1 - 2u_n^1 + u_{n-1}^1}{h^2} + f(0,x_n)\right) - \varphi(x_n), \quad x_n = nh,\ 1 \le n \le M-1,$$
$$\frac{u_1^k - u_1^k}{h} = \lambda_k(u_1^{k+1} - 2u_1^k + u_1^{k-1}) + \lambda_k \tau^2 f(t_k,h), \quad 1 \le k \le N-1,$$
$$\frac{u_1^0 - u_0^0}{h} = \lambda_0(2u_0^0 - 5u_0^1 + 4u_0^2 - u_0^3) + \lambda_0 \tau^2 f(0,h),$$
$$\frac{u_1^N - u_0^N}{h} = \lambda_N(2u_0^N - 5u_0^{N-1} + 4u_0^{N-2} - u_0^{N-3}) + \lambda_N \tau^2 f(1,h),$$
$$3u_M^k = 4u_{M-1}^k - u_{M-2}^k, \quad 0 \le k \le N,$$
$$f(t,x) = 2\exp(-t)\cos x, \qquad \lambda_k = \frac{h}{2g(t_k)\tau^2}, \quad 0 \le k \le N. \tag{2.11}$$

We have again $(N+1)\times(N+1)$ system of linear equations and we will write them in the matrix form

$$\begin{aligned} &AU_{n+1} + BU_n + CU_{n-1} = D\varphi_n, \quad 1 \le n \le M-1, \\ &3U_M = 4U_{M-1} - U_{M-2}, \qquad \gamma_0 U_0 = \theta_1 U_1 + T_1, \end{aligned} \tag{2.12}$$

where

$$A = \begin{bmatrix} 0 & 0 & 0 & 0 & \dots & 0 & 0 & 0 & 0 \\ c & b & a & 0 & \dots & 0 & 0 & 0 & 0 \\ 0 & c & b & a & \dots & 0 & 0 & 0 & 0 \\ 0 & 0 & c & b & \dots & 0 & 0 & 0 & 0 \\ \dots & \dots & \dots & \dots & \dots & \dots & \dots & \dots & \dots \\ 0 & 0 & 0 & 0 & \dots & b & a & 0 & 0 \\ 0 & 0 & 0 & 0 & \dots & c & b & a & 0 \\ 0 & 0 & 0 & 0 & \dots & 0 & c & b & a \\ 0 & r & 0 & 0 & \dots & 0 & 0 & 0 & 0 \end{bmatrix}_{(N+1)\times(N+1}, $$

$$B = \begin{bmatrix} 1 & 0 & 0 & 0 & \dots & 0 & 0 & 0 & 0 \\ f & e & d & 0 & \dots & 0 & 0 & 0 & 0 \\ 0 & f & e & d & \dots & 0 & 0 & 0 & 0 \\ 0 & 0 & f & e & \dots & 0 & 0 & 0 & 0 \\ \dots & \dots & \dots & \dots & \dots & \dots & \dots & \dots & \dots \\ 0 & 0 & 0 & 0 & \dots & f & e & d & 0 \\ 0 & 0 & 0 & 0 & \dots & 0 & f & e & d \\ g & p & 0 & 0 & \dots & 0 & 0 & 0 & 0 \end{bmatrix}_{(N+1)\times(N+1)}, $$

$$C = A, \qquad D = \begin{bmatrix} 1 & 0 & \dots & 0 \\ 0 & 1 & \dots & 0 \\ \dots & \dots & \dots & \dots \\ 0 & 0 & \dots & 1 \end{bmatrix}_{(N+1)\times(N+1)},$$

$$y_0 = \begin{bmatrix} 1+2\lambda_0 & -5\lambda_0 & 4\lambda_0 & -\lambda_0 & 0 & \dots & 0 & 0 & 0 & 0 \\ 0 & 1 & 0 & 0 & 0 & \dots & 0 & 0 & 0 & 0 \\ 0 & 0 & 1 & 0 & 0 & \dots & 0 & 0 & 0 & 0 \\ 0 & 0 & 0 & 1 & 0 & \dots & 0 & 0 & 0 & 0 \\ \dots & \dots & \dots & \dots & \dots & \dots & \dots & \dots & \dots & \dots \\ 0 & 0 & 0 & 0 & 0 & \dots & 1 & 0 & 0 & 0 \\ 0 & 0 & 0 & 0 & 0 & \dots & 0 & 1 & 0 & 0 \\ 0 & 0 & 0 & 0 & 0 & \dots & 0 & 0 & 1 & 0 \\ 0 & 0 & 0 & 0 & 0 & \dots & -\lambda_N & 4\lambda_N & -5\lambda_N & 1+2\lambda_N \end{bmatrix}_{(N+1)\times(N+1)},$$

$$\theta_0 = \begin{bmatrix} 1 & 0 & 0 & 0 & \dots & 0 & 0 & 0 \\ l & s & l & 0 & \dots & 0 & 0 & 0 \\ 0 & l & s & l & \dots & 0 & 0 & 0 \\ 0 & 0 & l & s & \dots & 0 & 0 & 0 \\ \dots & \dots & \dots & \dots & \dots & \dots & \dots & \dots \\ 0 & 0 & 0 & 0 & \dots & s & l & 0 \\ 0 & 0 & 0 & 0 & \dots & l & s & l \\ 0 & 0 & 0 & 0 & \dots & 0 & 0 & 1 \end{bmatrix}_{(N+1)\times(N+1)}, \quad \text{where } l = \frac{h^2}{2\tau^2},\ s = \frac{h^2}{\tau^2},$$

$$T_1 = \begin{bmatrix} F_0^0 \\ F_1^1 \\ \dots \\ F_0^N \end{bmatrix}_{(N+1)\times(1)}, \qquad U_s = \begin{bmatrix} U_s^0 \\ U_s^1 \\ \dots \\ U_s^N \end{bmatrix}_{(N+1)\times(1)}, \quad \text{where } s = n \pm 1, n,$$

$$F_0^0 = \tau^2 h^2, \qquad F_0^N = \frac{3}{4}\tau^2 \exp(-1), \qquad F_1^k = \tau^2 \lambda_k f(t_k, h), \quad 1 \le k \le N-1. \tag{2.13}$$

Here

$$\begin{gathered} a = -\frac{1}{4h^2}, \qquad b = -\frac{1}{2h^2}, \qquad c = -\frac{1}{4h^2}, \\ d = \frac{1}{\tau^2} + \frac{1}{2h^2}, \qquad e = -\frac{2}{\tau^2} + \frac{1}{h^2}, \qquad f = \frac{1}{\tau^2} + \frac{1}{2h^2}, \\ r = -\frac{\tau}{2h^2}, \qquad g = -\frac{1}{\tau}, \qquad p = \frac{1}{\tau^2} + \frac{\tau}{h^2}, \\ \varphi_n^k = \begin{cases} \cos(x_n), & k = 0, \\ f(t_k, x_n), & 1 \le k \le N-1, \\ \cos(x_n), & k = N, \end{cases} \qquad \varphi_n = \begin{bmatrix} \varphi_n^0 \\ \varphi_n^1 \\ \dots \\ \varphi_n^N \end{bmatrix}_{(N+1)\times 1} \end{gathered} \tag{2.14}$$

So, we obtain the second-order difference equation (2.12) with respect to n with matrix coefficients. To solve this difference equation we have applied the same modified

Gauss elimination method for the difference equation (2.12) with respect to n with matrix coefficients. Hence, we seek a solution U_n, $n = M-1,\dots,2,1,0$ of the matrix equation (2.12), where $\alpha_{n+1}, \beta_{n+1}$, $n = 1,\dots,M-1$, are obtained. Note that for obtaining $\alpha_{n+1}, \beta_{n+1}$, $n = 1,\dots,M-1$, we need to find α_1 and β_1. We can find them from $U_0 = \alpha_1 U_1 + \beta_1$. Using the formula $\gamma_0 U_0 = \theta_1 U_1 + T_1$, we obtain

$$U_0 = \operatorname{inv}(\gamma_0)\theta_1 U_1 + \operatorname{inv}(\gamma_0) T_1, \tag{2.15}$$

where

$$\begin{aligned} \alpha_1 &= \operatorname{inv}(\gamma_0)\theta_1, \\ \beta_1 &= \operatorname{inv}(\gamma_0) T_1. \end{aligned} \tag{2.16}$$

Now, we will find u_n, $0 \le n \le M$, by the formula (2), but for this we need to find u_M. We can find u_M from $3U_M = 4U_{M-1} - U_{M-2}$ and $u_{M-1} = \alpha_M u_M + \beta_M$, $u_{M-2} = \alpha_{M-1} u_{M-1} + \beta_{M-1}$. Namely,

$$u_M = \left[3I - 4\alpha_M + \alpha_{M-1}\alpha_M\right]^{-1}\left[4\beta_M - \alpha_{M-1}\beta_M - \beta_{M-1}\right]. \tag{2.17}$$

Third, applying the second order of accuracy difference scheme (1.9) and using simple formulas

$$\begin{aligned} &\frac{u(x_{n+2}) - 4u(x_{n+1}) + 6u(x_n) - 4u(x_{n-1}) + u(x_{n-2})}{h^4} - u^{\text{iv}}(x_n) = O(h^2), \\ &\frac{10u(0) - 15u(h) + 6u(2h) - u(3h)}{h^3} - u'''(0) = O(h^2), \\ &\frac{-10u(\pi) + 15u(\pi-h) - 6u(\pi-2h) + u(\pi-3h)}{h^3} - u'''(\pi) = O(h^2), \end{aligned} \tag{2.18}$$

we present the following second order of accuracy difference scheme for the approximate solutions of the problem (2.1):

$$\begin{gathered} \frac{u_n^{k+1} - 2u_n^k + u_n^{k-1}}{\tau^2} - \frac{u_{n+1}^k - 2u_n^k + u_{n-1}^k}{h^2} + \tau^2\left(\frac{u_{n+2}^{k+1} - 4u_{n+1}^{k+1} + 6u_n^{k+1} - 4u_{n-1}^{k+1} + u_{n-2}^{k+1}}{4h^4}\right) \\ = f(t_k, x_n), \quad x_n = nh,\ t_k = k\tau,\ 1 \le k \le N-1,\ 2 \le n \le M-2, \\ u_n^0 = \varphi(x_n), \quad x_n = nh,\ 0 \le n \le M, \\ \frac{u_n^1 - u_n^0}{\tau} - \frac{\tau}{2}\left(\frac{u_{n+1}^1 - 2u_n^1 + u_{n-1}^1}{h^2} + f(0, x_n)\right) g - \varphi(x_n), \quad x_n = nh,\ 1 \le n \le M-1, \\ 3u_M^k = 4u_{M-1}^k - u_{M-2}^k, \qquad 10u_M^k = 15u_{M-1}^k - 6u_{M-2}^k + u_{M-3}^k, \quad 0 \le k \le N, \\ 10u_0^k = 15u_1^k - 6u_2^k + u_3^k, \quad 0 \le k \le N. \end{gathered} \tag{2.19}$$

We have again $(N+1)\times(N+1)$ system of linear equations and we will write them in the matrix form

$$\begin{gathered} AU_{n+2}+BU_{n+1}+CU_n+DU_{n-1}+EU_{n-2}=R\varphi_n, \quad 2\le n\le M-2, \\ 10U_0=15U_1-6U_2+U_3, \qquad \gamma_0U_0=\theta_1U_1+T_1, \\ 3U_M=4U_{M-1}-U_{M-2}, \qquad 10U_M=15U_{M-1}-6U_{M-2}+U_{M-3}, \end{gathered} \tag{2.20}$$

where

$$A=\begin{bmatrix} 0&0&0&0&\dots&0&0&0&0\\ 0&0&a&0&\dots&0&0&0&0\\ 0&0&0&a&\dots&0&0&0&0\\ 0&0&0&0&\dots&0&0&0&0\\ \dots&\dots&\dots&\dots&\dots&\dots&\dots&\dots&\dots\\ 0&0&0&0&\dots&0&a&0&0\\ 0&0&0&0&\dots&0&0&a&0\\ 0&0&0&0&\dots&0&0&0&a\\ 0&0&0&0&\dots&0&0&0&0 \end{bmatrix}_{(N+1)\times(N+1)},$$

$$B=\begin{bmatrix} 0&0&0&0&\dots&0&0&0&0\\ 0&c&b&0&\dots&0&0&0&0\\ 0&0&c&b&\dots&0&0&0&0\\ 0&0&0&c&\dots&0&0&0&0\\ \dots&\dots&\dots&\dots&\dots&\dots&\dots&\dots&\dots\\ 0&0&0&0&\dots&c&b&0&0\\ 0&0&0&0&\dots&0&c&b&0\\ 0&0&0&0&\dots&0&0&c&b\\ 0&l&0&0&\dots&0&0&0&0 \end{bmatrix}_{(N+1)\times(N+1)},$$

$$C=\begin{bmatrix} 1&0&0&0&\dots&0&0&0&0\\ f&e&d&0&\dots&0&0&0&0\\ 0&f&e&d&\dots&0&0&0&0\\ 0&0&f&e&\dots&0&0&0&0\\ \dots&\dots&\dots&\dots&\dots&\dots&\dots&\dots&\dots\\ 0&0&0&0&\dots&e&d&0&0\\ 0&0&0&0&\dots&f&e&d&0\\ 0&0&0&0&\dots&0&f&e&d\\ g&p&0&0&\dots&0&0&0&0 \end{bmatrix}_{(N+1)\times(N+1)},$$

$$D=B, \qquad E=A,$$

$$R = \begin{bmatrix} 1 & 0 & \dots & 0 \\ 0 & 1 & \dots & 0 \\ \dots & \dots & \dots & \dots \\ 0 & 0 & \dots & 1 \end{bmatrix}_{(N+1)\times(N+1)},$$

$$U_s = \begin{bmatrix} U_s^0 \\ U_s^1 \\ \cdots \\ U_s^N \end{bmatrix}_{(N+1)\times(1)}, \quad \text{where } s = n \pm 2,\ n \pm 1, n. \tag{2.21}$$

Here

$$\begin{gathered}
a = \frac{\tau^2}{4h^4}, \qquad b = -\frac{\tau^2}{h^4}, \qquad c = -\frac{1}{h^2}, \\
d = \frac{6\tau^2}{4h^4} + \frac{1}{\tau^2}, \qquad e = \frac{2}{h^2} - \frac{2}{\tau^2}, \qquad f = \frac{1}{\tau^2}, \\
l = -\frac{\tau}{2h^2}, \qquad g = -\frac{1}{\tau}, \qquad p = \frac{1}{\tau} + \frac{\tau}{h^2}, \\
\varphi_n^k = \begin{cases} \cos(x_n), & k = 0, \\ f(t_k, x_n), & 1 \le k \le N-1, \\ (-1+\tau)\cos(x_n), & k = N, \end{cases}
\end{gathered} \tag{2.22}$$

$$\varphi_n = \begin{bmatrix} \varphi_n^0 \\ \varphi_n^1 \\ \cdots \\ \varphi_n^N \end{bmatrix}_{(N+1)\times 1}.$$

So, we have the fourth-order difference equation with respect to n with matrix coefficients. To solve this difference equation we have applied the modified Gauss elimination method for difference equation with respect to n with matrix coefficients. Hence, we seek a solution of the matrix equation in the following form:

$$U_n = \alpha_{n+1} U_{n+1} + \beta_{n+1} U_{n+2} + \gamma_{n+1}, \quad n = M-2, \dots, 2, 1, 0, \tag{2.23}$$

where

$$\begin{gathered}
\alpha_{n+1} = -\left(C + D\alpha_n + E\beta_{n-1} + E\alpha_{n-1}\alpha_n\right)^{-1}\left(B + D\beta_n + E\alpha_{n-1}\beta_n\right), \\
\beta_{n+1} = -\left(C + D\alpha_n + E\beta_{n-1} + E\alpha_{n-1}\alpha_n\right)^{-1}(A), \\
\gamma_{n+1} = \left(C + D\alpha_n + E\beta_{n-1} + E\alpha_{n-1}\alpha_n\right)^{-1}\left(R\varphi_n - D\gamma_n - E\alpha_{n-1}\gamma_n - E\gamma_{n-1}\right),
\end{gathered} \tag{2.24}$$

where $n = 2, \dots, M-2$. Note that for obtaining $\alpha_{n+1}, \beta_{n+1}, \gamma_{n+1}$, $n = 1, \dots, M-1$, we need to find $\alpha_1, \beta_1, \gamma_1$ and $\alpha_2, \beta_2, \gamma_2$. We can find them from $U_0 = \alpha_1 U_1 + \beta_1$. Using the formula

$\gamma_0 U_0 = \theta_1 U_1 + T_1$, we obtain

$$U_0 = \text{inv}(\gamma_0)\theta_1 U_1 + \text{inv}(\gamma_0) T_1, \tag{2.25}$$

where

$$\alpha_1 = \text{inv}(\gamma_0)\theta_1, \qquad \beta_1 = \sigma, \qquad \gamma_1 = \text{inv}(\gamma_0) T_1. \tag{2.26}$$

Using the formulas

$$10U_0 = 15U_1 - 6U_2 + U_3, \quad U_0 = \alpha_1 U_1 + \beta_1 U_2 + \gamma_1, \; U_1 = \alpha_2 U_2 + \beta_2 U_3 + \gamma_2, \tag{2.27}$$

we obtain

$$\begin{gathered} \alpha_2 = (10\alpha_1 - 15I)^{-1}(-6I - 10\beta_1), \qquad \beta_2 = (10\alpha_1 - 15I)^{-1}, \\ \gamma_2 = (10\alpha_1 - 15I)^{-1}(-10\gamma_1). \end{gathered} \tag{2.28}$$

Now, we will find u_n, $0 \le n \le M$, by the formula (2.19), but for this we need to find u_M and u_{M-1}. We can find u_M and u_{M-1} from

$$\begin{gathered} 3U_M = 4U_{M-1} - U_{M-2}, \qquad 10U_M = 15U_{M-1} - 6U_{M-2} + U_{M-3}, \\ U_{M-2} = \alpha_{M-1}U_{M-1} + \beta_{M-1}U_M + \gamma_{M-1}, \qquad U_{M-3} = \alpha_{M-2}U_{M-2} + \beta_{M-2}U_{M-1} + \gamma_{M-2}. \end{gathered} \tag{2.29}$$

Solving this system, we obtain

$$\begin{aligned} U_M &= [(4I - \alpha_{M-1})^{-1}(3I + \beta_{M-1}) - (9I - \beta_{M-2} - 4\alpha_{M-2})^{-1}(8I - 3\alpha_{M-2})]^{-1} \\ &\quad \times [-(4I - \alpha_{M-1})^{-1}\gamma_{M-1} + (9I - \beta_{M-2} - 4\alpha_{M-2})^{-1}\gamma_{M-2}], \\ U_{M-1} &= [(3I + \beta_{M-1})^{-1}(-4I + \alpha_{M-1}) + (8I - 3\alpha_{M-2})^{-1}(9I - \beta_{M-2} - 4\alpha_{M-2})]^{-1} \\ &\quad \times [-(3I + \beta_{M-1})^{-1}\gamma_{M-1} + (8I - 3\alpha_{M-2})^{-1}\gamma_{M-2}]. \end{aligned} \tag{2.30}$$

Now, we will give the results of the numerical analysis. For their comparison, the errors computed by

$$E_M^N = \max_{1 \le k \le N-1,\ 1 \le n \le M-1} |u(t_k, x_n) - u_n^k| \tag{2.31}$$

of the numerical solutions and the computer CPU times are recorded for different values of $N = M$, where $u(t_k, x_n)$ represents the exact solution and u_n^k represents the numerical solution at (t_k, x_n). The results are shown in Table 2.1 for $N = M = 20$, 93, 200, and 300, respectively. The simulation results are obtained by a PC Pentium (R) 4CPV, 3.00 6Hz, 2.99 6Hz, 512 Mb of RAM.

Table 2.1. Comparison of the errors and CPU times (E_M^N / N *CPU times*(*s*)) of different difference schemes for $N = M = 20, 93, 200$, and 300. *A* is the first order of accuracy difference scheme (2.3), *B* is the second order of accuracy difference scheme (2), and *C* is the second order of accuracy difference scheme (2.19).

Difference schemes \N = M	20	93	200	300
A	0.0143/0.27	0.0039/0.8	0.0019/14	0.0013/245
B	0.0013/0.23	0.0001/0.8	0.0000/11	0.0000/34
C	0.0039/0.26	0.0017/1.1	0.0005/13	0.0003/62

All recorded CPU times are on the arrange base with an error less than ∓15%, which does not affect the conclusions stated below basically.

Comparison of the results in the table reveal the following factors:

(i) for $N = M = 20$, although the CPU times of all three difference schemes are more or less equal, the second order of accuracy difference schemes produces $0.0143/0.0013 \cong 11$ times smaller error than the first order of accuracy difference scheme. For the second order of accuracy difference scheme generated by 5 points, this ratio reduces to $0.0143/0.0039 \cong 3.6$ times;

(ii) to have the same accuracy of computation (error = 0.0039) of the second order of accuracy difference scheme generated by 5 points and $N = M = 20$, the first order of accuracy difference scheme needs $N = M = 93$ intervals and $0.8/0.26 \cong 3.07$ times larger CPU time;

(iii) to have the same accuracy of computation (error = 0.0013) of the second order of accuracy difference scheme generated by 3 points with $N = M = 20$, the first order of accuracy difference scheme needs $N = M = 300$ intervals and $245/0.23 \cong 1065$ times larger CPU time;

(iv) all CPU times exceed ones after approximately $N = M = 100$;

(v) as it is observed from the last column of Table 2.1, CPU time for the first order of accuracy difference scheme increases drastically for large values of $N = M$ (i.e., for highly accurate numerical results) and is much larger than needed for the second order of accuracy difference schemes.

References

[1] A. Ashyralyev, *Difference schemes of a higher order of accuracy for second-order evolution equations*, Functional-Differential Equations, Perm. Politekh. Inst., Perm, 1989, pp. 145–150.

[2] A. Ashyralyev and M. E. Koksal, *On the second order of accuracy difference scheme for hyperbolic equations in a Hilbert space*, Numerical Functional Analysis and Optimization **26** (2005), no. 7-8, 739–772.

[3] H. O. Fattorini, *Second Order Linear Differential Equations in Banach Spaces*, Notas de Matemática, vol. 99, North-Holland, Amsterdam, 1985.

[4] S. G. Kreĭn, *Linear Differential Equations in a Banach Space*, Izdat. "Nauka", Moscow, 1967.

[5] S. Piskarev, *Approximation of holomorphic semigroups*, Tartu Riikliku Ülikooli Toimetised (1979), no. 492, 3–14.

[6] ______, *Stability of difference schemes in Cauchy problems with almost periodic solutions*, Differentsial'nye Uravneniya **20** (1984), no. 4, 689–695 (Russian).

[7] ———, *Principles of discretization methods III*, Report, Acoustic Institute, Academy of Science USSR, 1986, 87 p.
[8] P. E. Sobolevskiĭ and L. M. Čebotareva, *Approximate solution of the Cauchy problem for an abstract hyperbolic equation by the method of lines*, Izvestija Vysših Učebnyh Zavedeniĭ Matematika (1977), no. 5(180), 103–116 (Russian).

Allaberen Ashyralyev: Department of Mathematics, Fatih University, Buyukcekmece, 34900 Istanbul, Turkey
E-mail address: aashyr@fatih.edu.tr

Mehmet Emir Koksal: Department of Mathematics and computer science, University of Bahcesehir, Ciragan Street, 34100 Besiktas, Istanbul, Turkey; Department of Mathematics, Gebze Institute of Technology, 41400 Gebze, Kocaeli, Turkey
E-mail address: emir_koksal@hotmail.com

AN EXISTENCE RESULT FOR A CLASS OF SINGULAR PROBLEMS WITH CRITICAL EXPONENTS

R. B. ASSUNÇÃO, P. C. CARRIÃO, AND O. H. MIYAGAKI

Combining some arguments used by Brézis and Nirenberg, and by Gazzola and Ruf, together with the generalized mountain pass theorem due to Rabinowitz, we prove a result of existence of a nontrivial solution for a class of degenerate elliptic problems involving the critical Hardy-Sobolev exponent in a bounded smooth domain containing the origin.

1. Introduction

In this paper, we consider the following class of singular quasilinear elliptic problems in a smooth bounded domain $\Omega \subset \mathbb{R}^N$, with $0 \in \Omega$, namely,

$$\begin{aligned} Lu &= \lambda |x|^{-(a+1)p+c}|u|^{p-2}u + |x|^{-bq}|u|^{q-2}u \quad \text{in } \Omega, \\ u &= 0 \quad \text{on } \partial\Omega, \end{aligned} \tag{P}$$

where $Lu = -\operatorname{div}[|x|^{-ap}|\nabla u|^{p-2}\nabla u]$, a, b, c, p are given numbers and $q \equiv Np/[N - p(a+1-b)]$ is the critical Hardy-Sobolev exponent.

Brézis and Nirenberg in [3] proved that problem (P) has a positive solution in the case $p = 2$, $a = b = 0$, $c = 2$, $q = 2^* \equiv 2N/(N-2)$, and $0 < \lambda < \lambda_1$, where λ_1 is the first eigenvalue of the Laplacian operator in a smooth bounded domain $\Omega \subset \mathbb{R}^N$. After this pioneering work, several authors treated generalizations of the problem (P), among which we would like to cite Cappozi, Fortunato, and Palmieri [5], and Cerami, Fortunato, and Struwe [7], who obtained nontrivial solutions for all positive λ. (See also Zhang [14].) These results were extended by Gazzola and Ruf in [10], still in a semilinear problem.

On the other hand, Clément, de Figueiredo, and Mitidieri in [9] studied problem (P) in a ball, getting a similar result as that obtained in [3] for all $\lambda < \lambda_1$ where λ_1 is the first eigenvalue of the operator Lu in a radial form. See Xuan [13] for problem (P) in a general domain Ω.

In 2003, Alves, Carrião, and Miyagaki [1], by combining some arguments used in [5, 10], showed that there exists a constant $\lambda^* > \lambda_1$ such that problem (P), in a ball, possesses at least one nontrivial solution for all $\lambda \in (0, \lambda^*)$.

Hindawi Publishing Corporation
Proceedings of the Conference on Differential & Difference Equations and Applications, pp. 131–140

We recall that by a Pohozaev-type identity, (see, e.g., [8]), problem (P) has no nontrivial solution when $\lambda \le 0$.

The main goal of this paper is to show that the techniques developed in [1] can be generalized for a class of problems studied in [12] in order to show the existence of nontrivial solution for problem (P) when $0 < \lambda < \lambda^*$ for some λ^* defined below and Ω is any smooth domain containing the origin. Among the difficulties related to this problem, we recall that the space involved is no longer a Hilbert space and that the critical Hardy-Sobolev exponent is present in the equation, which brings us to the question of lack of compactness of the embeddings of Sobolev spaces in the weighted L_q^b spaces. To overcome these difficulties we combine an inequality due to Caffarelli, Kohn, and Nirenberg [4] with some techniques used in [3] in order to recover the compactness of Palais-Smale sequences.

To state our result, we need to define the following numbers: $1 < p < N$, $0 \le a < (N-p)/p$, $a \le b < a+1$, $\mu \equiv [N - p(a+1)]/(p-1) \ge c > 0$, and $q \equiv Np/[N - p(a+1-b)] > p$.

Let λ_1 be the first eigenvalue of Lu and $\phi_1 > 0$ the corresponding eigenfunction. Define

$$\lambda^* \equiv \inf\left\{\frac{1}{p}\int_\Omega |x|^{-ap}|\nabla u|^p : \int_\Omega |x|^{-(a+1)p+c}|u|^p = 1,\ u \in E_2\right\}, \tag{1.1}$$

where

$$E_2 \equiv \left\{u \in D_a^{1,p}(\Omega) : \int_\Omega |x|^{-(a+1)p+c}\,|\phi_1|^{p-2}\phi_1 u = 0\right\}. \tag{1.2}$$

We remark that adapting some arguments in [1] (see also [12]), we can prove that $\lambda^* > \lambda_1$.

Hereafter $\int_\Omega f$ denotes $\int_\Omega f(x)dx$.

Now we state our main result.

THEOREM 1.1. *Suppose that constants a, b, c, p, and q are in the previously defined intervals. Then problem (P) has a nontrivial solution, provided that we have one of the following conditions:*

(1) $\eta \equiv c - \mu < 0$ *for all* $0 < \lambda < \lambda^*$;

(2) $\eta = 0$ *for all* $0 < \lambda < \lambda^*$ *with* $\lambda \ne \lambda_1$.

2. Preliminary results

The main tool for the variational approach to these problems is the following weighted Hardy-Sobolev inequality due to Caffarelli, Kohn, and Nirenberg [4] (see also [6]): for $1 < p < N$ and for all $u \in C_0^\infty(\mathbb{R}^N)$, there is a positive constant $C_{a,b}$ such that

$$\left[\int_{\mathbb{R}^N} |x|^{-bq}|u|^q\right]^{p/q} \le C_{a,b}\int_{\mathbb{R}^N} |x|^{-ap}|\nabla u|^p. \tag{2.1}$$

We define the spaces $D_a^{1,p}(\Omega)$ as the completion of $C_0^\infty(\Omega)$ with respect to the norm given by

$$\|u\| \equiv \left[\int_\Omega |x|^{-ap}|\nabla u|^p\right]^{1/p}. \tag{2.2}$$

We also define

$$S(a,b) \equiv \inf_{u\in D_a^{1,p}(\Omega)\setminus\{0\}} E_{a,b}(u), \qquad S_R(a,b) \equiv \inf_{u\in D_{a,R}^{1,p}(\Omega)\setminus\{0\}} E_{a,b}(u), \tag{2.3}$$

where

$$E_{a,b}(u) \equiv \frac{\int_\Omega |x|^{-ap}|\nabla u|^p}{\left[\int_\Omega |x|^{-bq}|u|^q\right]^{p/q}},$$
$$D_{a,R}^{1,p}(\Omega) \equiv \{u \in D_a^{1,p}(\Omega) : u \text{ is radial}\}. \tag{2.4}$$

We recall (see [9]) that $S_R(a,b)$ is attained by the function

$$\begin{aligned}\hat{u}_\varepsilon &= u_{\varepsilon_{a,b}}(r)\\ &= \overline{C}\varepsilon^{(N-p(a+1))/p(p-1)}\left[\varepsilon^{(p(a+1)-bq)/(p-1)} + r^{(p(a+1)-bq)/(p-1)}\right]^{-(N-p(a+1))/(p(a+1)-bq)},\end{aligned} \tag{2.5}$$

where $r = |x|$ and

$$\overline{C} = \left[\mu^{p-1}(N-bq)\right]^{(N-p(a+1))/(p[p(a+1)-bq])}. \tag{2.6}$$

Besides, $S(a,b)$ is attained in the case $p = 2$ (see [11]) and in the case $p \neq 2$ (see [2]).

In the Sobolev space $D_a^{1,p}(\Omega)$, we define the energy functional $I_\lambda : D_a^{1,p}(\Omega) \to \mathbb{R}$ by

$$I_\lambda(u) \equiv \frac{1}{p}\int_\Omega |x|^{-ap}|\nabla u|^p - \frac{1}{q}\int_\Omega |x|^{-bq}|u|^q - \frac{\lambda}{p}\int_\Omega |x|^{-\alpha p}|u|^p, \tag{2.7}$$

where $\alpha \equiv (a+1) - c/p$. From the Caffarelli-Kohn-Nirenberg inequality, it follows that I_λ is well defined in $D_a^{1,p}(\Omega)$; we also have $I_\lambda \in C^1(D_a^{1,p}(\Omega),\mathbb{R})$ and

$$I_\lambda'(u)v = \int_\Omega |x|^{-ap}|\nabla u|^{p-2}\nabla u\nabla v - \int_\Omega |x|^{-bq}|u|^{q-2}uv - \lambda\int_\Omega |x|^{-\alpha p}|u|^{p-2}uv. \tag{2.8}$$

Furthermore, the critical points of I_λ are weak solutions of problem (P).

3. Proof of the theorem

To prove Theorem 1.1 we use some arguments due to Brézis and Nirenberg [3] as well as Capozzi, Fortunato, and Palmieri [5], Gazzola and Ruf [10], and Alves, Carrião, and Miyagaki [1]. Specifically, we apply the following version of the Rabinowitz generalized mountain pass theorem in Banach spaces.

THEOREM 3.1. *Let E be a real Banach space and let $I : E \to \mathbb{R}$ be a differentiable functional verifying the following conditions.*

(1) *$I(-u) = I(u)$ for all $u \in E$ and $I(0) = 0$.*

(2) *There exists $d > 0$ such that I verifies the $(PS)_c$ condition for all $0 < c < d$.*

(3) *There are real constants $\rho > 0$, $e > 0$ (with $e < d$) and a k-dimensional subspace $E_1 \subset E$ with a topological complementar subspace E_2 such that*

  (a) *$I(u) \geq 0$ on $(B_\rho \cap E_2) \setminus \{0\}$;*

  (b) *$I(u) \geq e$ on $\partial B_\rho \cap E_2$.*

(4) *There is a constant $r > 0$ and an m-dimensional subspace $E_3 \subset E$ (with $m > k$) such that $I(u) < r$, for all $u \in E_3$ with $e < r < d$.*

Then I has at least $m - k$ distinct pairs of nonzero critical points. In addition, if $e = 0$, then I has at least $m - k - 1$ distinct pairs of nonzero critical points.

We are going to show that the energy functional I_λ verifies the geometric conditions and the other hypotheses of Theorem 3.1. To do so, we will use the function

$$u_\varepsilon(r) \equiv \psi(r)\hat{u_\varepsilon}(r), \tag{3.1}$$

where $r = |x|$ and ψ is a cutoff function such that $\psi(r) = 1$ for $r \in [0, R_0]$, $\psi(r) = 0$ for $r \in [2R_0, +\infty)$ and $0 \leq \psi \leq 1$ and R_0 is such that $0 < 2R_0 < R < \infty$ with $B_R(0) \subset \Omega$.

Claim 1. There exist $e > 0$ and $\rho > 0$ such that $I(u) \geq e$ for all $u \in E_2$ with $\|u\| = \rho$.

In fact, let $u \in E_2$; then

$$\begin{aligned} I_\lambda(u) &\geq \frac{1}{p}\left(1 - \frac{\lambda}{\lambda^*}\right)\int_\Omega |x|^{-ap}|\nabla u|^p - \frac{1}{q}\int_\Omega |x|^{-bq}|u|^q \\ &\geq \frac{1}{p}\left(1 - \frac{\lambda}{\lambda^*}\right)\|u\|^p - \frac{S(a,b)^{q/p}}{q}\|u\|^{q/p}. \end{aligned} \tag{3.2}$$

Since $q > p$ and $\lambda < \lambda^*$, the claim follows.

Claim 2. The energy functional I_λ verifies the Palais-Smale condition $(PS)_c$ for all values $0 < c < (1/p - 1/q)S_R(a,b)^{q/(q-p)}$.

In other words, for all c in the specified interval, let $\{u_n\}$ be a sequence in E verifying the conditions, as $n \to \infty$,

$$I_\lambda(u_n) \longrightarrow c, \qquad I'_\lambda(u_n) \longrightarrow 0; \tag{3.3}$$

then $\{u_n\}$ contains a strongly convergent subsequence in E.

To prove the claim, let $0 < c < (1/p - 1/q)S_R(a,b)^{q/(q-p)}$. First we will show that the sequence $\{u_n\}$ is bounded in E. In fact,

$$\begin{aligned} C[1+\|u\|] &\geq I_\lambda(u_n) - \frac{1}{p}I'_\lambda(u_n)u_n \\ &= \left(\frac{1}{p} - \frac{1}{q}\right)\int_\Omega |x|^{-bq}\,|u_n|^q \\ &\equiv \left(\frac{1}{p} - \frac{1}{q}\right)\|u\|^q_{L^b_q}, \end{aligned} \tag{3.4}$$

where $L^b_q(\Omega)$ is the weighted space $L_q(\Omega)$ with the above-defined norm.

By (2.7) we have

$$||u_n||^p \leq C + \lambda||u_n||^p_{L^\alpha_p} + \frac{p}{q}||u_n||^q_{L^b_q}. \tag{3.5}$$

Since $c > 0$, it follows by the Hölder inequality that

$$\|u\|_{L^\alpha_p} \leq \|u\|_{L^b_q}. \tag{3.6}$$

Following up, we have

$$\|u\|^p \leq C + \lambda||u_n||^p_{L^b_q} + ||u_n||^p_{L^b_q} \leq C + \lambda C_1(1+||u_n||)^{p/q} + C_2(1+||u_n||). \tag{3.7}$$

This way, we have the boundedness of the sequence $\{u_n\}$ in $D^{1,p}_a(\Omega)$.

Passing to a subsequence, still denoted in the same way, we have $u_n \rightharpoonup u$ weakly in $D^{1,p}_a(\Omega)$; it is standard to prove that $u \in D^{1,p}_a(\Omega)$ is a weak solution of problem (P).

Now we define $w_n \equiv u_n - u$. Since $I'_\lambda(u_n)u_n = o(1)$ and $I'_\lambda(u_n) = 0$, using the Brézis-Lieb lemma, as $n \to \infty$, we have

$$\begin{aligned} o(1) &= ||w_n||^p - ||w_n||^q_{L^b_q} + o(1), \\ &\int_\Omega |x|^{-\alpha p}\,|u_n - u|^p \longrightarrow 0. \end{aligned} \tag{3.8}$$

The last limit follows from the compact immersion $D^{1,p}_a(\Omega) \hookrightarrow L^\alpha_r(\Omega)$ where $1 \leq r < Np/(N-p)$ and $\alpha < (a+1)r + N(1-r/p)/r = a+1$ if $r = p$. (See [12].)

Now we suppose that $\|w_n\|^p \to l$; then $\|w_n\|^q_{L^b_q} \to l$. We also have

$$I_\lambda(u) = I_\lambda(u) - \frac{1}{p}I'_\lambda(u)u = \left(\frac{1}{p} - \frac{1}{q}\right)\|u\|^q_{L^b_q} \geq 0; \tag{3.9}$$

passing to the limit, as $n \to \infty$, in

$$I_\lambda(w_n) = I_\lambda(u_n) - I_\lambda(u) + o(1), \tag{3.10}$$

we have

$$d \equiv \lim_{n\to\infty} I_\lambda(w_n) = c - I(u) \le c, \tag{3.11}$$

that is, $d \le c$.

On the other hand, by the definition of $S_R(a,b)$, we know that $S_R(a,b)^{q/(q-p)} \le l$. Therefore,

$$d \le c < \left(\frac{1}{p} - \frac{1}{q}\right) S_R(a,b)^{q/(q-p)} \le \left(\frac{1}{p} - \frac{1}{q}\right) l = d \tag{3.12}$$

(the last equality follows from $d = I_\lambda(w_n) = (1/p - 1/q)\|w_n\|^q_{L^b_q} = l$) which is a contradiction; hence, we have $l = 0$, that is, $u_n \to u$ strongly in $D^{1,p}_a(\Omega)$ as $n \to \infty$.

Claim 3. $\sup\{I(u) \mid u \in W_\varepsilon\} < (1/p - 1/q)\widetilde{S}_R(a,b)^{q/(q-p)}$ where $\widetilde{S}_R(a,b) \equiv S_R(a,b)^{N/p(a+1-b)}$ and

$$W_\varepsilon \equiv \{u \in D^{1,p}_a(\Omega) : u \equiv u^- + tu_\varepsilon,\ u^- \in \langle \phi_1 \rangle\}. \tag{3.13}$$

To prove this claim, we begin by fixing some $u \in D^{1,p}_a(\Omega)$. Then $\sup\{I_\lambda(tu) : t > 0$ and $u \in D^{1,p}_a(\Omega)$ fixed$\}$ is equal to

$$\left(\frac{1}{p} - \frac{1}{q}\right)\left[\frac{\|u\|^p - \lambda\|u\|^p_{L^a_p}}{\|u\|^p_{L^b_q}}\right]^{q/(q-p)}. \tag{3.14}$$

Affirmative. $\sup\{\|u\|^p - \lambda\|u\|^p_{L^a_p} : \|u\|^p_{L^b_q} = 1,\ u \in W_\varepsilon\} < S_R(a,b)$ for ε small enough.

Due to the cutoff function, at this point of the proof we are working with problem (P) in the radial form. This way the proof of the affirmative follows the ideas of [1, Claim 3.1]. For the sake of completeness we sketch it here.

We remark that

$$\|u_\varepsilon\|^p = \widetilde{S}_R(a,b) + O(\varepsilon^\mu). \tag{3.15}$$

Moreover,

$$\|u_\varepsilon\|^q_{L^b_q} = \widetilde{S}_R(a,b) + O\left(\varepsilon^{N\mu/(N-p(a+1-b))}\right), \tag{3.16}$$

$$\|u_\varepsilon\|^p_{L^a_p} \ge C\varepsilon^c + \begin{cases} C\varepsilon^c & \text{if } \eta < 0, \\ C(\varepsilon^\mu |\log\varepsilon|) & \text{if } \eta = 0. \end{cases} \tag{3.17}$$

From (3.15), (3.16), (3.17), for ε small enough, we have

$$\frac{\|u_\varepsilon\|^p + \lambda\|u_\varepsilon\|^p_{L^a_p}}{\|u_\varepsilon\|^p_{L^a_p}} = \begin{cases} S_R(a,b) - \lambda C\varepsilon^c + \varepsilon^\mu & \text{if } \eta < 0, \\ S_R(a,b) - \lambda C\varepsilon^\mu |\log\varepsilon| + O(\varepsilon^\mu) & \text{if } \eta = 0. \end{cases} \tag{3.18}$$

In the case $\lambda > \lambda_1$ and $\eta \leq 0$, let $u \equiv u^- + tu_\varepsilon$, with $u^- \in \langle \phi_1 \rangle$ and $t > 0$. Then t and $\|u^-\|_{L_p^\alpha}$ are bounded.

Indeed, by the embedding of the weighted spaces, we have

$$\|u^-\|_{L_p^\alpha} \leq C\|u\|_{L_q^b} + C|t|^p\|u_\varepsilon\|_{L_q^b}. \tag{3.19}$$

Supposing that t is bounded, we obtain the boundedness of $\|u^-\|_{L_p^\alpha}$. Now we prove that t is bounded. First we use the inequalities

$$\begin{aligned}
&\Big| \|u^- + tu_\varepsilon\|_{L_q^b}^q - \|u^-\|_{L_q^b}^q - \|tu_\varepsilon\|_{L_q^b}^q \Big| \\
&\quad \leq C\Big\{ |t|^q \|u_\varepsilon\|_{L_{q-1}^b}^{q-1} \|u^-\|_{L_2^b} + \frac{1}{4}\|u^-\|_{L_q^b}^q + C|t|^q\|u_\varepsilon\|_{L_q^b}^q \Big\} \\
&\quad \leq C|t|^q \varepsilon^{(N[N-p(a+1)])/(N(p-1)+p(a+1-b))} + \frac{1}{2}\|u^-\|_{L_q^b}^q,
\end{aligned} \tag{3.20}$$

where we used the fact that the eigenspace generated by ϕ_1 has dimension one and $\|u^-\|_{L_\infty^b}$ is bounded (see [12]), and also we combined the Hölder and the Young inequalities.

Finally, from the last inequality above we get

$$1 = \|u\|_{L_q^b} \leq |t|^q \|u_\varepsilon\|_{L_q^b}^q - C|t|^q \varepsilon^{(N[N-p(a+1)])/(N(p-1)+p(a+1-b))}. \tag{3.21}$$

For ε small enough, from (3.16) we conclude that t is bounded.

We take $u \in W_\varepsilon$ such that $\|u\|_{L_q^b} = 1$. This way we have

$$\|u\|^p - \lambda\|u\|_{L_p^\alpha}^p \leq \Lambda + \frac{\|tu_\varepsilon\|^p - \lambda\|tu_\varepsilon\|_{L_p^\alpha}^p}{\|tu_\varepsilon\|_{L_q^b}^p}\|tu_\varepsilon\|_{L_q^b}^p, \tag{3.22}$$

where

$$\Lambda = \Lambda(\varepsilon, c, u) \equiv (\lambda_1 - \lambda)\|u^-\|_{L_p^\alpha}^p + C\|u^-\|_{L_p^\alpha}\varepsilon^{\mu((p-1)/p)^2}, \tag{3.23}$$

satisfying

$$\Lambda \leq 0 \quad \text{or} \quad \Lambda \leq C\varepsilon^{\mu((p-1)/p)^2}. \tag{3.24}$$

Following up,

$$\begin{aligned}
&\|u\|^p - \lambda\|u\|_{L_p^\alpha}^p \\
&\quad \leq C\varepsilon^{\mu((p-1)/p)^2} + [S_R(a,b) - \lambda C\varepsilon^c + O(\varepsilon^\mu)][1 + C\varepsilon^{(N-p(a+1))/(N(p-1)+p(a+1-b))}]^{p/q} \\
&\quad < S_R(a,b)
\end{aligned} \tag{3.25}$$

for ε small enough.

For the case $\lambda = \lambda_1$ and $\eta < 0$, let $\phi_1 > 0$ be the first eigenvalue of the operator Lu such that $\int_0^R |r|^{-\alpha p+N-1}|\phi|^p = 1$. Denote by Pu the projection of $u \in E$ onto the eigenspace $\langle \phi_1 \rangle$; then

$$Pu = \left[\int_0^R r^{-\alpha p+N-1}\phi_1 u\right]\phi_1. \tag{3.26}$$

Also denote $\hat{u} \equiv u - Pu \in E_2$. It is easy to verify that $\|Pu_\varepsilon\|_{L_q^b}$, $\|Pu_\varepsilon\|_{L_p^\alpha}$, and $\|Pu_\varepsilon\|$ are $O(\varepsilon^\mu)$.

Then, for $\eta < 0$, (3.18) still holds after replacing u_ε by $\hat{u_\varepsilon}$, where

$$\hat{u_\varepsilon} \equiv u_\varepsilon - Pu_\varepsilon. \tag{3.27}$$

Let $u \in \widehat{W_\varepsilon}$ such that $\|u\|_{L_q^b} = 1$, where

$$\widehat{W_\varepsilon} \equiv \{u \in E : u = u^- + t\hat{u_\varepsilon},\ u^- \in \langle \phi_1 \rangle,\ t \in \mathbb{R}\}. \tag{3.28}$$

Then, since $u = \widehat{u^-} + Pu^- + t\hat{u_\varepsilon}$, we have

$$\begin{aligned} \|u\|^p - \lambda_1\|u\|_{L_p^\alpha}^p \le{}& \|\widehat{u^-}\|^p - \lambda_1\|\widehat{u^-}\|_{L_p^\alpha}^p + \|Pu^-\|^p - \lambda_1\|Pu^-\|_{L_p^\alpha}^p \\ &+ \|t\hat{u_\varepsilon}\|^p - \lambda_1\|t\hat{u_\varepsilon}\|_{L_p^\alpha}^p + C\varepsilon^{\mu((p-1)/p)^2}; \end{aligned} \tag{3.29}$$

thus the proof follows by arguing as in the previous case.

4. Final comments

By using the same approach of Gazzola and Ruf [10], our result still holds when the function $\lambda|x|^{-\alpha p}|u|^{p-2}u$ is substituted by a function g verifying the following.

(G0) $g : \Omega \times \mathbb{R} \to \mathbb{R}$ is a Carathéodory function, and for every $\varepsilon > 0$, there exists $a_\varepsilon \in L_{q'}^b(\Omega)$ (where $1/q + 1/q' = 1$) such that

$$|g(x,s)| \le a_\varepsilon(x) + \varepsilon|x|^{-bq}|s|^{q-1} \tag{4.1}$$

for a.e. $x \in \mathbb{R}$ and for all $s \in \mathbb{R}$.

(G1) $G(x,s) \equiv \int_0^s g(x,t) \ge 0$ for a.e. $x \in \Omega$ and for all $s \in \mathbb{R}$.

(G2) There exist $\delta_0 > 0$ and $\mu \in (\lambda_1, \lambda^*)$ such that

$$\frac{1}{p}\lambda_1|x|^{-\alpha p}|s|^p \le G(x,s) \le \frac{\mu}{p}|x|^{-\alpha p}|s|^p \tag{4.2}$$

for a.e. $x \in \Omega$ and $|s| < \delta_0$.

(G3) There exists $\sigma \in (0, 1/q)$ such that

$$G(x,s) \geq \frac{\lambda_1}{p}|x|^{-\alpha p}|s|^p - \left(\frac{1}{q} - \sigma\right)|x|^{-bq}|s|^q \tag{4.3}$$

for a.e. $x \in \Omega$ and $s \in \mathbb{R}$.

(G4) There exist $0 \in \Omega_0 \subset \Omega$ such that

$$\lim_{s\to\infty} \frac{G(x,s)}{|x|^{-\alpha p}|s|^{\alpha_1}} = +\infty, \quad \text{uniformly for } x \in \Omega_0, \tag{4.4}$$

where α_1 is given by

$$\alpha_1 \equiv \left(\frac{N(p-N)[N-p(a+1)]}{k} - [p(a+1)-c-N]\right)\frac{p}{N-p(a+1)} \tag{4.5}$$

and $k = p(a+1-b)[N-p(a+1)] - N(p-N)(p-1)$.

We remark that when $p = c = 2$ and $a = b = \alpha = 0$, $\alpha_1 = 8N/(N^2-4)$ is the Gazzola-Ruf "magic number."

Acknowledgments

The second author is partially supported by CNPq/Brazil. The third author is supported in part by CNPq, Brazil and AGIMB, Millennium Institute MCT, Brazil.

References

[1] C. O. Alves, P. C. Carrião, and O. H. Miyagaki, *Nontrivial solutions of a class of quasilinear elliptic problems involving critical exponents*, Nonlinear Equations: Methods, Models and Applications (Bergamo, 2001), Progress in Nonlinear Differential Equations Appl., vol. 54, Birkhäuser, Basel, 2003, pp. 225–238.

[2] R. B. Assunção, P. C. Carrião, and O. H. Miyagaki, *Critical singular problems via concentration-compactness lemma*, to appear in Journal of Mathematical Analysis and Applications.

[3] H. Brézis and L. Nirenberg, *Positive solutions of nonlinear elliptic equations involving critical Sobolev exponents*, Communications on Pure and Applied Mathematics **36** (1983), no. 4, 437–477.

[4] L. Caffarelli, R. Kohn, and L. Nirenberg, *First order interpolation inequalities with weights*, Compositio Mathematica **53** (1984), no. 3, 259–275.

[5] A. Capozzi, D. Fortunato, and G. Palmieri, *An existence result for nonlinear elliptic problems involving critical Sobolev exponent*, Annales de l'Institut Henri Poincaré **2** (1985), no. 6, 463–470.

[6] F. Catrina and Z.-Q. Wang, *On the Caffarelli-Kohn-Nirenberg inequalities: sharp constants, existence (and nonexistence), and symmetry of extremal functions*, Communications on Pure and Applied Mathematics **54** (2001), no. 2, 229–258.

[7] G. Cerami, D. Fortunato, and M. Struwe, *Bifurcation and multiplicity results for nonlinear elliptic problems involving critical Sobolev exponents*, Annales de l'Institut Henri Poincaré **1** (1984), no. 5, 341–350.

[8] K.-S. Chou and D. Geng, *On the critical dimension of a semilinear degenerate elliptic equation involving critical Sobolev-Hardy exponent*, Nonlinear Analysis **26** (1996), no. 12, 1965–1984.

[9] P. Clément, D. G. de Figueiredo, and E. Mitidieri, *Quasilinear elliptic equations with critical exponents*, Topological Methods in Nonlinear Analysis **7** (1996), no. 1, 133–170.

[10] F. Gazzola and B. Ruf, *Lower-order perturbations of critical growth nonlinearities in semilinear elliptic equations*, Advances in Differential Equations **2** (1997), no. 4, 555–572.

[11] Z.-Q. Wang and M. Willem, *Singular minimization problems*, Journal of Differential Equations **161** (2000), no. 2, 307–320.

[12] B. Xuan, *The eigenvalue problem for a singular quasilinear elliptic equation*, Electronic Journal of Differential Equations **2004** (2004), no. 16, 1–11.

[13] ———, *The solvability of quasilinear Brezis-Nirenberg-type problems with singular weights*, Nonlinear Analysis **62** (2005), no. 4, 703–725.

[14] D. Zhang, *On multiple solutions of* $\Delta u+\lambda u+|u|^{4/(n-2)}u=0$, Nonlinear Analysis **13** (1989), no. 4, 353–372.

R. B. Assunção: Departmento de Matemática, Universidade Federal de Minas Gerais,
31270-010 Belo Horizonte, MG, Brazil
E-mail address: ronaldo@mat.ufmg.br

P. C. Carrião: Departmento de Matemática, Universidade Federal de Minas Gerais,
31270-010 Belo Horizonte, MG, Brazil
E-mail address: carrion@mat.ufmg.br

O. H. Miyagaki: Departmento de Matemática, Universidade Federal Viçosa,
36570-000 Viçosa, MG, Brazil
E-mail address: olimpio@ufv.br

TWO-WEIGHTED POINCARÉ-TYPE INTEGRAL INEQUALITIES

GEJUN BAO

Some new two-weighted integral inequalities for differential forms are obtained, which can be considered as generalizations of the classical Poincaré-type inequality.

1. Introduction

Differential forms are important generalizations of distributions, and the classical Poincaré-type inequality plays a fundamental role in the theory. Many interesting results and applications of differential forms on Poincaré-type inequality have recently been found.

We always suppose that Ω is a connected open subset of $\mathbb{R}^n$ throughout this paper. Balls are denoted by B, and σB is the ball with the same center as B and with $\operatorname{diam}(\sigma B) = \sigma \mathrm{B}$. The n-dimensional Lebesgue measure of a set $E \subseteq \mathbb{R}^n$ is denoted by $|E|$. We call w a weight if $w \in L^1_{\text{loc}}(\mathbb{R}^n)$ and $w > 0$ a.e. We use $D'(\Omega,\Lambda^l)$ to denote the space of all differential l-forms $\omega(x) = \sum_I \omega_I(x)\mathrm{d}x_I = \sum \omega_{i_1\cdots i_l}(x)\mathrm{d}x_{i_1} \wedge \cdots \wedge \mathrm{d}x_{i_l}$, and we write $L^p(\Omega,\Lambda^l)$ for the l-forms with $\omega_I \in L^p(\Omega,\mathbb{R})$ for all ordered l-tuples I. Thus $L^p(\Omega,\Lambda^l)$ is a Banach space with norm

$$\|\omega\|_{p,\Omega} = \left(\int_\Omega |\omega(x)|^p \mathrm{d}x\right)^{1/p} = \left(\int_\Omega \left(\sum_I |\omega_I(x)|^2\right)^{p/2} \mathrm{d}x\right)^{1/p}. \tag{1.1}$$

The following result appears in [2]. Let $Q \subset \mathbb{R}^n$ be a cube or a ball. Then to each $y \in Q$, there corresponds a linear operator $K_y : C^\infty(Q,\Lambda^l) \to C^\infty(Q,\Lambda^{l-1})$ defined by

$$(K_y\omega)(x;\xi_1,\ldots,\xi_l) = \int_0^1 t^{l-1}\omega(tx+y-ty;x-y,\xi_1,\ldots,\xi_{l-1})\mathrm{d}t. \tag{1.2}$$

and the decomposition $\omega = \mathrm{d}(K_y\omega) + K_y(\mathrm{d}\omega)$.

Hindawi Publishing Corporation
Proceedings of the Conference on Differential & Difference Equations and Applications, pp. 141–148

We define another linear operator $T_Q : C^\infty(Q,\Lambda^l) \to C^\infty(Q,\Lambda^{l-1})$ by averaging K_y over all points y in Q:

$$T_Q\omega = \int_Q \varphi(y)K_y\omega\,\mathrm{d}y, \tag{1.3}$$

where $\varphi \in C^\infty(Q)$ is normalized by $\int_Q \varphi(y)\mathrm{d}y = 1$, we define the l-forms $\omega_Q \in D'(Q,\Lambda^l)$ by

$$\omega_Q = |Q|^{-1}\int_Q \omega(y)\mathrm{d}y, \quad l = 0, \quad \omega_Q = \mathrm{d}(T_Q\omega), \quad l = 1,\dots,n, \tag{1.4}$$

for all $\omega \in L^p(Q,\Lambda^l)$, $l < \infty$.

2. Preliminaries

Defintions 2.1 [1]. Let a pair of weights $(w_1(x), w_2(x))$ satisfy the $A_{r,\lambda}$-condition in a set $\Omega \subset \mathbb{R}^n$. Write $(w_1(x), w_2(x)) \in A_{r,\lambda}(\Omega)$, for some $\lambda \geq 1$ and $1 < r < \infty$, with $1/r + 1/r' = 1$ if

$$\sup_{B\subset\Omega}\left(\frac{1}{|B|}\int_B (w_1)^\lambda \mathrm{d}x\right)^{1/\lambda r}\left(\frac{1}{|B|}\int_B \left(\frac{1}{w_2}\right)^{\lambda r'/r}\mathrm{d}x\right)^{1/\lambda r'} < \infty \tag{2.1}$$

for all $B \subset \mathbb{R}^n$.

Defintions 2.2 [4]. Let the weight $w(x) \in L^1_{\mathrm{loc}}(\mathbb{R}^n)$ satisfy the A_r^λ-condition, and write $w \in A_r^\lambda$ if $w(x) > 0$ a.e., and

$$\sup\left(\frac{1}{|B|}\int_B w\,\mathrm{d}x\right)\left(\frac{1}{|B|}\int_B \left(\frac{1}{w}\right)^{1/(r-1)}\mathrm{d}x\right)^{\lambda(r-1)} < \infty. \tag{2.2}$$

LEMMA 2.3. *Let $(w_1, w_2) \in A_{r,\lambda}(\Omega)$ and $p > r$, then $(w_{1,2}) \in A_{p,\lambda}(\Omega)$.*

LEMMA 2.4. *Let $p > 1$, $u(x) \geq v(x) \geq 0$ if*

$$\left(\frac{1}{|I|}\int_I u^p \mathrm{d}x\right)^{1/p} \leq K\frac{1}{|I|}\int_I v\,\mathrm{d}x \tag{2.3}$$

for all subintervals I of some interval I_0, then

$$\left(\frac{1}{|I_0|}\int_{I_0} u^r \mathrm{d}x\right)^{1/r} \leq C(p,K,r)\left(\frac{1}{|I_0|}\int_{I_0} v\,\mathrm{d}x\right) \tag{2.4}$$

for $p \leq r < p + \eta$, where $\eta = \eta(p,K) > 0$.

Lemma 2.5. *Let $(w_1, w_2) \in A_{r,1}(\Omega)$ and $w_2 \le w_1$ a.e., then there are $\beta > 1$ and $C > 0$ such that*

$$||w_1||_{\beta,B} \le C|B|^{(1-\beta)/\beta}||w_2||_{1,B} \tag{2.5}$$

for any cube or any ball $B \subset \mathbb{R}^n$.

The following version of the Poincaré inequality appears in [3].

Lemma 2.6. *Let $u \in D'(Q,\Lambda^l)$ and $\mathrm{d}u \in L^p(Q,\Lambda^{l+1})$. Then $u - u_Q$ is in $W_p^1(Q,\Lambda^l)$ with $1 < p < \infty$ and*

$$||u - u_Q||_{p,Q} \le C(n,p)|Q|^{1/n}\|\mathrm{d}u\|_{p,Q} \tag{2.6}$$

for Q is a cube or a ball in $\mathbb{R}^n$, $l = 0,1,\ldots,n$.

Tadeusz Iwaniec and Adam Lutoborski prove the following local Poincaré-type inequality in [2].

Lemma 2.7. *Let $u \in D'(Q,\Lambda^l)$ and $\mathrm{d}u \in L^p(Q,\Lambda^{l+1})$. Then $u - u_Q$ is in $L^{np/(n-p)}(Q,\Lambda^l)$ and*

$$\left(\int_Q |u - u_Q|^{np/(n-p)}\mathrm{d}x\right)^{(n-p)/np} \le C_p(n)\left(\int_Q |\mathrm{d}u|^p\mathrm{d}x\right)^{1/p} \tag{2.7}$$

for Q a cube or a ball in $\mathbb{R}^n$, $l = 0,1,\ldots,n$ and $1 < p < n$.

3. Local two-weighted integral inequalities

We now give the following version of the local two-weighted Poincaré-type inequality for differential forms.

Theorem 3.1. *Let $u \in D'(B,\Lambda^l)$ and $\mathrm{d}u \in L^p(B,\Lambda^{l+1})$, $l = 0,1,\ldots,n$. Assume that $1 < s < p < \infty$, then there exists a constant $\beta > 1$, such that if $w_2 \le w_1$ a.e., with $(w_1, w_2) \in A_{r,1}$, $w_2 \in A_{p/k}^{s/p}$, for some $r > 1$ and k with $s\beta/(\beta - 1) \le k < p$, then*

$$\left(\frac{1}{|B|}\int_B |u - u_B|^s w_1 \mathrm{d}x\right)^{1/s} \le C|B|^{1/n}\left(\frac{1}{|B|}\int_B |\mathrm{d}u|^p w_2\,\mathrm{d}x\right)^{1/p} \tag{3.1}$$

for all balls $B \subset \mathbb{R}^n$, here C is a constant independent of u and d*u.*

Proof. Since $(w_1, w_2) \in A_{r,1}(\Omega)$ for some $r > 1$ and $w_2 \le w_1$, by Lemma 2.5, there exist constants $\beta > 1$ and $C_1 > 0$, such that

$$||w_1||_{\beta,B} \le C_1|B|^{(1-\beta)/\beta}||w_2||_{1,B} \tag{3.2}$$

for any cube or any ball $B \subset \mathbb{R}^n$. Choose $t = s\beta/(\beta-1)$, then $1 < s < t$ and $\beta = t/(t-s)$, since $1/s = 1/t + (t-s)/st$, by Hölder's inequality, (3.2), and Lemma 2.6, we have

$$\begin{aligned}
\|u-u_B\|_{s,B,w_1} &= \left(\int_B \left(|u-u_B| w_1^{1/s}\right)^s dx\right)^{1/s} \\
&\le \left(\int_B |u-u_B|^t dx\right)^{1/t} \left(\int_B (w_1^{1/s})^{st/(t-s)} dx\right)^{(t-s)/st} \\
&\le C_2 |B|^{(1-\beta)/\beta s} \|w_2\|_{1,B}^{1/s} \|u-u_B\|_{t,B} \\
&\le C_3 |B|^{1/n} |B|^{(1-\beta)/\beta s} \|w_2\|_{1,B}^{1/s} \|du\|_{t,B}.
\end{aligned} \tag{3.3}$$

Now $t = s\beta/(\beta-1) < p$ and $1/t = 1/p + (p-t)/pt$. By Hölder'inequality again, we obtain

$$\begin{aligned}
\|du\|_{t,B} &= \left(\int_B |du|^t dx\right)^{1/t} \\
&= \left(\int_B \left(|du| w_2^{1/p} w_2^{-1/p}\right)^t dx\right)^{1/t} \\
&\le \left(\int_B \left(|du| w_2^{1/p}\right)^p dx\right)^{1/p} \left(\int_B \left(w_2^{-1/p}\right)^{pt/(p-t)} dx\right)^{(p-t)/pt} \\
&= \left\|\frac{1}{w_2}\right\|_{t/(p-t),B}^{1/p} \left(\int_B |du|^p w_2 \, dx\right)^{1/p}.
\end{aligned} \tag{3.4}$$

Note $t = s\beta/(\beta-1) \le k$, then $p/k \le p/t$. By [4, Theorem 2.4], we find that $w_2 \in A_{p/k}^{s/p} \subset A_{p/t}^{s/p}$. Therefore we have

$$\begin{aligned}
&\|w_2\|_{1,B}^{1/s} \left\|\frac{1}{w_2}\right\|_{t/(p-t),B}^{1/p} \\
&= \left(\int_B w_2 \, dx\right)^{1/s} \left(\int_B \left(\frac{1}{w_2}\right)^{t/(p-t)} dx\right)^{(p-t)/pt} \\
&= \left(\left(\int_B w_2 \, dx\right)\left(\int_B \left(\frac{1}{w_2}\right)^{t/(p-t)} dx\right)^{s(p-t)/pt}\right)^{1/s} \\
&= \left(|B|^{1+s(p-t)/pt}\right)^{1/s} \\
&\quad \cdot \left(\left(\frac{1}{|B|}\int_B w_2 \, dx\right)\left(\frac{1}{|B|}\int_B \left(\frac{1}{w_2}\right)^{1/(p/t-1)} dx\right)^{(s/p)(p/t-1)}\right)^{1/s} \\
&\le C_4 |B|^{1/s+1/t-1/p}.
\end{aligned} \tag{3.5}$$

Substituting (3.4) and the above inequality into (3.3) implies

$$||u - u_B||_{s,B,w_1} \le C_5|B|^{1/n+1/s-1/p}\left(\int_B |du|^p dx\right)^{1/p}, \tag{3.6}$$

that is,

$$\left(\frac{1}{|B|}\int_B |u-u_B|^s w_1(x)dx\right)^{1/s} \le C|B|^{1/n}\left(\frac{1}{|B|}\int_B |du|^p w_2\, dx\right)^{1/p}. \tag{3.7}$$

Now we can prove the other version of the local two-weighted Poincaré-type inequality for differential forms. □

THEOREM 3.2. *Let $u \in D'(B,\Lambda^l)$ and $du \in L^p(B,\Lambda^{l+1})$, $l = 0,1,\dots,n$. Then there exists a constant $\beta > 1$ such that if $w_2 \le w_1$ a.e. with $(w_1,w_2) \in A_{r,1}$ and $_2 \in A^{s/n}_{n/s}$, where $s = n/\beta$ and $r > 1$, then*

$$\left(\frac{1}{|B|}\int_B |u-u_B|^s w_1\, dx\right)^{1/s} \le C|B|^{1/n}\left(\frac{1}{|B|}\int_B |du|^n w_2\, dx\right)^{1/n} \tag{3.8}$$

for all balls $B \subset \mathbb{R}^n$. Here C is a constant independent of u and du.

THEOREM 3.3. *Let $u \in D'(B,\Lambda^l)$ and $du \in L^p(B,\Lambda^{l+1})$, $l = 0,1,\dots,n$. If $1 < s < n$ and $(w_1,w_2) \in A_{n/s,1}$, then there exists a constant C, which is independent of u and du, such that*

$$\left(\frac{1}{|B|}\int_B |u-u_B|^s w_1^{s/n} dx\right)^{1/s} \le C|B|^{1/n}\left(\frac{1}{|B|}\int_B |du|^n w_2\, dx\right)^{1/n} \tag{3.9}$$

for any ball or any cube $B \subset \mathbb{R}^n$.

4. Global two-weighted integral inequality

Now we give the following global two-weighted Poincaré-type inequality in $L^s(\mu)$-averaging domains.

THEOREM 4.1. *Let $u \in D'(\Omega,\Lambda^l)$ and $du \in L^p(\Omega,\Lambda^{l+1})$, $l = 0,1,\dots,n$. Assume that $s > 1$ and $p > \max(s,n)$. Then there exists a constant $\beta > 1$, such that if $(w_1,w_2) \in A_{r,1}$ with $w_2 \le w_1$ a.e., $w_2 \in A^{s/p}_{p/k}$, where $r > 1$, $s\beta/(\beta-1) \le k < p$, and $w_2 \ge \eta > 0$, then*

$$\left(\frac{1}{\mu_1(\Omega)}\int_\Omega |u-u_{B_0}|^s w_1\, dx\right)^{1/s} \le C\mu_2(\Omega)^{1/n}\left(\frac{1}{\mu_2(\Omega)}\int_\Omega |du|^p w_2\, dx\right)^{1/p}. \tag{4.1}$$

for any $L^s(\mu)$-averaging domain Ω and some ball B_0 with $2B_0 \subset \Omega$. Here the measure μ_i is defined by $d\mu_i = w_i(x)dx$, $i = 1,2$, and C is a constant independent of u and du.

Proof. Note $\mu_1(B) \geq \mu_2(B) = \int_B w_2\,\mathrm{d}x \geq \int_B \eta\mathrm{d}x = \eta|B|$.
Then

$$|B| \leq C_1\mu_2(B) \leq C_1\mu_1(B), \tag{4.2}$$

where $C_1 = 1/\eta$, since $p > n$, then $1/n - 1/p > 0$, and from (4.2) we have

$$\begin{aligned}\mu_1(B)^{-1/s}|B|^{1/s+1/n-1/p} &\leq \mu_2(B)^{-1/s}|B|^{1/s+1/n-1/p}\\ &= C_2\mu_2(B)^{1/n-1/p} \leq C_2\mu_2(\Omega)^{1/n-1/p}.\end{aligned} \tag{4.3}$$

By Theorem 3.1, the definition of $L^s(\mu)$-averaging domain, and (4.3), we have

$$\begin{aligned}&\left(\frac{1}{\mu_1(\Omega)}\int_\Omega |u-u_{B_0}|^s\mathrm{d}\mu_1\right)^{1/s}\\ &\quad\leq \left(\frac{1}{\mu_1(B_0)}\int_\Omega |u-u_{B_0}|^s\mathrm{d}\mu_1\right)^{1/s}\\ &\quad\leq C_3\sup_{2B\subset\Omega}\left(\frac{1}{\mu_1(B)}\int_B |u-u_B|^s\mathrm{d}\mu_1\right)^{1/s}\\ &\quad= C_3\sup_{2B\subset\Omega}\left(\left(\frac{|B|}{\mu_1(B)}\right)^{1/s}\left(\frac{1}{|B|}\int_B |u-u_B|^s\mathrm{d}\mu_1\right)^{1/s}\right)\\ &\quad\leq C_3\sup_{2B\subset\Omega}\left(\left(\frac{|B|}{\mu_1(B)}\right)^{1/s}C_4|B|^{1/n}\left(\frac{1}{|B|}\int_B |\mathrm{d}u|^p w_2\,\mathrm{d}x\right)^{1/p}\right)\\ &\quad\leq C_5\sup_{2B\subset\Omega}\left(\mu_1(B)^{-1/s}|B|^{1/s+1/n-1/p}\left(\int_B |\mathrm{d}u|^p w_2\,\mathrm{d}x\right)^{1/p}\right)\\ &\quad\leq C_5\sup_{2B\subset\Omega}\left(C_2\mu_2(\Omega)^{1/n-1/p}\left(\int_B |\mathrm{d}u|^p w_2\,\mathrm{d}x\right)^{1/p}\right)\\ &\quad\leq C_6\sup_{2B\subset\Omega}\left(\mu_2(\Omega)^{1/n-1/p}\left(\int_\Omega |\mathrm{d}u|^p w_2\,\mathrm{d}x\right)^{1/p}\right)\\ &\quad= C_6\mu_2(\Omega)^{1/n-1/p}\left(\int_\Omega |\mathrm{d}u|^p w_2\,\mathrm{d}x\right)^{1/p}\\ &\quad= C_6\mu_2(\Omega)^{1/n}\left(\frac{1}{\mu_2(\Omega)}\int_\Omega |\mathrm{d}u|^p w_2\,\mathrm{d}x\right)^{1/p}.\end{aligned} \tag{4.4}$$

Hence we obtain

$$\left(\frac{1}{\mu_1(\Omega)}\int_\Omega |u-u_{B_0}|^s\mathrm{d}\mu_1\right)^{1/s} \leq C\mu_2(\Omega)^{1/n}\left(\frac{1}{\mu_2(\Omega)}\int_\Omega |\mathrm{d}u|^p w_2\,\mathrm{d}x\right)^{1/p}. \tag{4.5}$$

This completes the proof of Theorem 4.1. □

Defintions 4.2. Call Ω, a proper subdomain of $\mathbb{R}^n$, δ-John domain, $\delta > 0$, if there exists a point $x_0 \in \Omega$ which can be joined with any other point $x \in \Omega$ by a continuous curve $\gamma \subset \Omega$ so that

$$d(\xi,\partial\Omega) \geq \delta|x-\xi| \tag{4.6}$$

for each $\xi \in \gamma$. Here $d(\xi,\partial\Omega)$ is the Euclidean distance between ξ and $\partial\Omega$.

As we know that a δ-John domain has the following properties in [3].

LEMMA 4.3. *Let $\Omega \subset \mathbb{R}^n$ be a δ-John domain, then there exists a covering* V *of Ω consisting of open cubes such that*

(1) $\sum_{Q\in V}\chi_{\sigma Q}(x) \leq N\chi_{\Omega}(x)$, $\sigma > 1$ *and* $x \in \mathbb{R}^n$;

(2) *there is a distinguished cube $Q_0 \in V$ (called the central cube) which can be connected with every $Q \in V$ by a chain of cubes $Q_0, Q_1, \dots, Q_k = Q$ from* V *such that for each* $i = 0, 1, \dots, k-1$,

$$Q \subset NQ_i. \tag{4.7}$$

Now we prove the following two-weighted global result in a δ-John domain.

THEOREM 4.4. *Let $u \in D'(\Omega,\Lambda^l)$ and $du \in L^p(\Omega,\Lambda^{l+1})$, $l = 0, 1, \dots, n$. If $1 < s < n$ and $(w_1, w_2) \in A_{n/s,1}$, then there exists a constant C independent of u and du such that*

$$\left(\frac{1}{|\Omega|}\int_{\Omega}|u-u_Q|^s w_1^{s/n}dx\right)^{1/s} \leq C\left(\int_{\Omega}|du|^n w_2\,dx\right)^{1/n} \tag{4.8}$$

for any δ-John domain $\Omega \subset \mathbb{R}^n$. Here Q is any cube in the covering V *of Ω appearing in Lemma 4.3.*

Proof. We can write (3.9) as

$$\int_{Q}|u-u_Q|^s w_1^{s/n}dx \leq C_1|Q|\left(\int_{Q}|du|^n w_2\,dx\right)^{s/n}, \tag{4.9}$$

where $Q \subset \mathbb{R}^n$ is any cube. Suppose $\sigma > 1$, by (4.9) and Lemma 4.3, we have

$$\begin{aligned}
\int_{\Omega}|u-u_Q|^s w_1^{s/n}dx &\leq \sum_{Q\in V}\int_{Q}|u-u_Q|^s w_1^{s/n}dx \\
&\leq C_1\sum_{Q\in V}|Q|\left(\int_{Q}|du|^n w_2\,dx\right)^{s/n} \\
&\leq C_1|\Omega|\sum_{Q\in V}\left(\int_{\sigma Q}|du|^n w_2\,dx\right)^{s/n} \\
&\leq C_1|\Omega|N\left(\int_{\Omega}|du|^n w_2\,dx\right)^{s/n} \\
&= C_2|\Omega|\left(\int_{\Omega}|du|^n w_2\,dx\right)^{s/n}.
\end{aligned} \tag{4.10}$$

Thus we have

$$\left(\frac{1}{|\Omega|}\int_{\Omega}|u-u_Q|^s w_1^{s/n}\mathrm{d}x\right)^{1/s} \le C\left(\int_{\Omega}|\mathrm{d}u|^n w_2\,\mathrm{d}x\right)^{1/n}. \tag{4.11}$$

We have completed the proof of Theorem 4.4. □

Applying Theorem 3.2 and using the same method that used in the proof of Theorem 4.1, we can have the following global result.

THEOREM 4.5. *Let $u \in D'(\Omega,\Lambda^l)$ and $\mathrm{d}u \in L^p(\Omega,\Lambda^{l+1})$, $l=0,1,\dots,n$. Then there exists a constant $\beta>1$, such that if $w_2 \le w_1$ a.e., $(w_1,w_2)\in A_{r,1}$, and $w_2 \in A_{n/s}^{s/n}$, where $s=n/\beta$, $r>1$ and $w_2 \ge \eta > 0$. Then*

$$\left(\frac{1}{\mu_1(\Omega)}\int_{\Omega}|u-u_{B_0}|^s w_1\,\mathrm{d}x\right)^{1/s} \le C\mu_2(\Omega)^{1/n}\left(\frac{1}{\mu_2(\Omega)}\int_{\Omega}|\mathrm{d}u|^n w_2\,\mathrm{d}x\right)^{1/n} \tag{4.12}$$

for any $L^s(\mu)$-averaging domain Ω and some ball B_0 with $2B_0 \subset \Omega$. Here the measure μ_i is defined by $\mathrm{d}\mu_i = w_i(x)\mathrm{d}x$, $i=1,2$, and C is a constant independent of u and $\mathrm{d}u$.

Remark 4.6. Since $L^s(\mu)$-averaging domains reduce to L^s-averaging domains, if $w_1 = w_2 = 1$, then Theorems 4.1 and 4.5 also hold if $\Omega \subset \mathbb{R}^n$ is an L^s-averaging domain.

Remark 4.7. From all of the above, we can find which has given a method of generalization about one-weighted integral inequalities; it plays an important role in generalization of the integral inequality.

References

[1] S. Ding, *Two-weight Caccioppoli inequalities for solutions of nonhomogeneous A-harmonic equations on Riemannian manifolds*, Proceedings of the American Mathematical Society **132** (2004), no. 8, 2367–2375.

[2] T. Iwaniec and A. Lutoborski, *Integral estimates for null Lagrangians*, Archive for Rational Mechanics and Analysis **125** (1993), no. 1, 25–79.

[3] C. A. Nolder, *Hardy-Littlewood theorems for A-harmonic tensors*, Illinois Journal of Mathematics **43** (1999), no. 4, 613–632.

[4] S. G. Staples, *L^p-averaging domains and the Poincaré inequality*, Annales Academiae Scientiarum Fennicae. Series A I. Mathematica **14** (1989), no. 1, 103–127.

Gejun Bao: Department of Mathematics, Harbin Institute of Technology, 150001 Harbin, China
E-mail address: baogj@hit.edu.cn

INVERSE SOURCE PROBLEM FOR THE WAVE EQUATION

MOURAD BELLASSOUED AND MASAHIRO YAMAMOTO

We prove a uniqueness and stability theorem for an inverse source problem for the wave equation.

1. Introduction

The main interest of this paper lies in an inverse problem of identifying an unknown source term of a wave equation from the measurement on a lateral boundary. Physically speaking, we are required to determine an external force from measurements of boundary displacements.

There is a considerable amount of papers dealing with the uniqueness and stability in an inverse problem of identifying unknown coefficients or source terms, see [10, 14], and the references therein. However, the majority of results deal with Dirichlet or Neumann measurements on a sufficiently large part of the boundary (or the whole boundary). Moreover there are no available results for the case where the measurement is done on an arbitrary part of the boundary.

We will address our inverse problem precisely. Let Ω be a bounded open domain with sufficiently smooth boundary $\Gamma = \partial\Omega$ and let ν be the outward unit normal vector to $\partial\Omega$, $\partial_\nu u = \nabla u \cdot \nu$. We consider a Dirichlet mixed problem for a second-order hyperbolic equation:

$$\begin{aligned} \partial_t^2 u(x,t) - \Delta u(x,t) &= f(x)\Phi(x,t) && \text{in } \Omega \times [0,T], \\ u(x,0) = \partial_t u(x,0) &= 0 && \text{in } \Omega, \\ u(x,t) &= 0 && \text{in } \Gamma \times [0,T], \end{aligned} \tag{1.1}$$

where $f \in W^{1,\infty}(\Omega)$ and $\Phi \in \mathscr{C}^1(\overline{\Omega} \times [0,T])$. Although we can consider a general second-order hyperbolic equation, we here discuss the wave equation with constant coefficients.

Hindawi Publishing Corporation
Proceedings of the Conference on Differential & Difference Equations and Applications, pp. 149–158

Under the above assumption, there exists a unique solution $u = u_f$ to (1.1) such that

$$u_f \in \mathscr{C}^1([0,T];H_0^1(\Omega)) \cap \mathscr{C}^2([0,T];L^2(\Omega)), \qquad \partial_\nu u_f \in H^1(0,T;L^2(\Gamma)). \tag{1.2}$$

Let $\Gamma_1 \subset \Gamma$ be a given part of the boundary $\Gamma = \partial\Omega$. A uniqueness question for our inverse problem is, can we conclude that $f(x) = 0, x \in \Omega$, under the observation $\partial_\nu u_f(x,t) = 0$, $(x,t) \in \Sigma_1 = \Gamma_1 \times (0,T)$?

When Γ_1 is the whole boundary Γ, a strong affirmation result is known for the uniqueness in multidimensional inverse problems with a single observation, and Bukhgeim and Klibanov [5] firstly proposed a useful methodology on the basis of Carleman estimates. Further works discussing inverse problems by Carleman estimates include [4, 10, 14].

In the case where Γ_1 is an arbitrary part of Γ, the condition for the unique identification has been an open problem. In recent years several related works (see [8, 11]) have appeared, but are mainly concerned with the uniqueness and stability in determining a source term or a coefficient of the zeroth-order term when the part Γ_1 is given by $\Gamma_1 = \{x \in \Gamma, (x - x_0) \cdot \nu(x) \geq 0\}$, which is related with the geometric optics condition for the observability (see [1]).

In [7], Imanuvilov and Yamamoto give the uniqueness and the global Lipschitz stability by the Neumann data on a sufficiently large part of the boundary Γ over a sufficiently long time interval. See also [2, 3, 8, 9, 12, 13, 20] for inverse problems by Carleman estimates.

Stability estimates are important in the theory of inverse problems of mathematical physics. Those inverse problems are ill-posed in the classical sense [15], so that for stable numerics, we need regularizing techniques. The stability results determine the choice of regularization parameters and the rate at which solutions of regularized problems converge to an exact solution.

In the present paper, we show that even if the geometrical condition is not fulfilled (or the subboundary Γ_1 is small), we have the uniqueness and a logarithmic stability result in determining f, under the assumption that T is sufficiently large and $f(x) = 0$ in a neighborhood ω of the whole boundary Γ. The key ideas are an application of the Carleman estimates proved in [3, 7] and an application of the Fourier-Bros-Iagolnitzer (FBI) transformation used by Robbiano [17]. We use the idea of [17] to apply the Fourier-Bross-Iagolnitzer transformation to change the problem near the boundary into another problem where elliptic estimates can be applied. Throughout this paper, let us set

$$\Lambda(M,\omega) = \{f \in W^{1,\infty}(\Omega); \|f\|_{W^{1,\infty}(\Omega)} \leq M,\ f_{|\omega} = 0\} \tag{1.3}$$

for any fixed $M > 0$. The main result of this paper can be stated as follows.

Theorem 1.1. *Let ω be a neighborhood of the boundary $\Gamma = \partial\Omega$. Assume that $|\Phi(x,0)| \geq \epsilon_0 > 0$, $x \in \overline{\Omega\backslash\omega}$. Then there exist $T > 0$ sufficiently large and a constant $C > 0$ such that*

$$\|f\|_{L^2(\Omega)} \leq C\left[\log\left(2 + \frac{C}{\|\partial_\nu u_f\|_{H^1(0,T;L^2(\Gamma_1))}}\right)\right]^{-1/2} \tag{1.4}$$

for all $f \in \Lambda(M,\omega)$. Here the constant C is dependent on Ω, ω, T, M, and independent of f.

The remainder of the paper is organized as follows. In Section 2, we give some estimates which are used for the proof of the main results. In Section 3, we prove Theorem 1.1.

2. Preliminary estimates

In this section, we derive several estimates. We will begin with a fundamental Carleman estimate. We will use the following notations. Let $\varrho, \varrho_1, \varrho_2 > 0$ such that

$$\begin{aligned} \omega(8\varrho) &= \{x \in \Omega,\ \mathrm{dist}(x,\Gamma) \le 8\varrho\} \subset \omega, \\ \omega(\varrho_1,\varrho_2) &= \{x \in \Omega,\ \varrho_1 \le \mathrm{dist}(x,\Gamma) \le \varrho_2\} \subset \omega, \quad \varrho_1 < \varrho_2 < 8\varrho, \\ \omega_T(\varrho) &= \omega(\varrho) \times [-T,T], \qquad \omega_T(\varrho_1,\varrho_2) = \omega(\varrho_1,\varrho_2) \times [-T,T]. \end{aligned} \tag{2.1}$$

2.1. Carleman estimate. Here we present the Carleman estimate for the wave equation. Although Carleman estimates for a second-order hyperbolic operator with constant coefficients are classical, we would like to recall briefly. As for related Carleman estimates, see [2, 3, 6, 7, 14, 18, 19].

In order to formulate our Carleman estimate, we introduce some notations. Without loss of generality, we may assume that $0 \notin \overline{\Omega}$. Define

$$\psi(x,t) = |x|^2 - \gamma |t|^2, \quad \forall x \in \Omega. \tag{2.2}$$

Put $T_0 = (\max_{x\in\Omega} |x|^2)^{1/2}$. Let $T > T_0$ and let us fix $\delta > 0$ and $\gamma \in (0,1)$ such that

$$\gamma T^2 > \max_{x\in\Omega} |x|^2 + \delta. \tag{2.3}$$

Therefore, by definition (2.2) of $\psi(x,t)$ and (2.3) we have

$$\psi(x,0) = |x|^2 > 0, \quad \psi(x,-T) = \psi(x,T) < -\delta, \quad \forall x \in \Omega. \tag{2.4}$$

We introduce the pseudoconvex function $\varphi : \Omega \times R \to R$ by setting

$$\varphi(x,t) = e^{\beta\psi(x,t)}, \quad \beta > 0, \tag{2.5}$$

where β is a large parameter.

Now we would like to consider the following second-order hyperbolic operator:

$$P(D) = \partial_t^2 - \Delta. \tag{2.6}$$

For α such that $0 < \alpha < T$ we set

$$\begin{aligned} Q_\alpha &= \Omega \times [-T+\alpha, T-\alpha] \subset Q, \\ Q_\alpha(\varrho) &= \Omega(\varrho) \times [-T+\alpha, T-\alpha], \quad \Omega(\varrho) = \Omega \backslash \omega(\varrho). \end{aligned} \tag{2.7}$$

Finally we set $\nabla v(t,x) = (\partial_t v, \nabla_x v)$.

The following Carleman estimate holds.

Proposition 2.1. *Let $T > T_0$. Then there exist a constant $C > 0$, which is independent of τ, and a parameter τ_* such that, for all $\tau \geq \tau_*$, the following Carleman estimate holds:*

$$C\tau \int_{Q_\alpha(3\varrho)} e^{2\tau\varphi}(|\nabla v|^2 + \tau^2|v|^2)\,dx\,dt \leq \int_Q e^{2\tau\varphi}\,|P(x)v|^2 dx\,dt$$
$$+\tau \int_{\omega_T(\varrho,3\varrho)} e^{2\tau\varphi}(|\nabla v|^2 + \tau^2|v|^2)\,dx\,dt \tag{2.8}$$
$$+\tau \int_{Q\setminus Q_\alpha} e^{2\tau\varphi}(|\nabla v|^2 + \tau^2|v|^2)\,dx\,dt,$$

whenever $v \in H^1(Q)$ and the right-hand side is finite.

Proof. Inequality (2.8) can be deduced from a more general theorem [3, Theorem 2]. For the sake of clarity and completeness of the exposition, we will give the proof. We first apply the following standard Carleman estimate which was proved in [3, 19], and so forth:

$$\tau \int_{Q_\alpha} e^{2\tau\varphi}(|\nabla v|^2 + \tau^2|v|^2)\,dx\,dt \leq C\int_Q e^{2\tau\varphi}\,|P(D)v|^2 dx\,dt$$
$$+ C\tau \int_{\Gamma\times[-T,T]} e^{2\tau\varphi}(|\nabla v|^2 + \tau^2|v|^2)\,ds\,dt \tag{2.9}$$
$$+\tau \int_{Q\setminus Q_\alpha} e^{2\tau\varphi}(|\nabla v|^2 + \tau^2|v|^2)\,dx\,dt.$$

We introduce a cutoff function χ satisfying $0 \leq \chi \leq 1, \chi \in C^\infty(R^n)$, and

$$\chi(x) = 0, \quad x \in \omega(\varrho), \quad \chi(x) = 1, \quad x \in \Omega(3\varrho). \tag{2.10}$$

Then we apply (2.9) to $\widetilde{v} = \chi v$ and we obtain

$$\tau \int_{Q_\alpha} e^{2\tau\varphi}(|\nabla \widetilde{v}|^2 + \tau^2|\widetilde{v}|^2)\,dx\,dt \leq C\int_Q e^{2\tau\varphi}\,|P(x)\widetilde{v}|^2 dx\,dt$$
$$+\tau \int_{Q\setminus Q_\alpha} e^{2\tau\varphi}(|\nabla \widetilde{v}|^2 + \tau^2|\widetilde{v}|^2)\,dx\,dt. \tag{2.11}$$

Furthermore $P(D)\widetilde{v} = \chi P(D)v + [P,\chi]v$ where $[A,B]$ stands for the commutator of operators A and B. Since $[P,\chi]$ is a first-order operator and supported in $\omega(\varrho, 3\varrho)$, we obtain (2.8). □

2.2. Weak observation estimate

Proposition 2.2 (see [2]). *Let $f \in \Lambda(M,\omega)$. Let u_f be the solutions of (1.1). Then there exists $T > 0$ sufficiently large such that the following estimate holds:*

$$||\partial_t u_f||^2_{H^1(\omega_T(\varrho,3\varrho))} \leq C\left[\log\left(2 + \frac{C}{||\partial_\nu u_f||_{H^1(0,T;L^2(\Gamma_1))}}\right)\right]^{-1}. \tag{2.12}$$

Here the constant C is dependent on Ω, ω, T, M and independent of f.

To prove Proposition 2.2, we use the idea of Robbiano [17] which is based on the Fourier-Bros-Iagolnitzer transformation, and we refer also to the proof of [2, Proposition 2.2].

3. Proof of the main result

This section is devoted to the proof of Theorem 1.1. The idea of the proof is based on a Carleman estimates method which was initiated by [5], but we apply an argument similar to [8] which is a modification of [5].

3.1. Preliminaries. We need the following preliminaries, which are essentially known and we will present them for completeness. Let $F \in L^2(Q)$ and let $\phi(x,t)$ satisfy

$$\partial_t^2\phi(x,t) - \Delta\phi(x,t) = F(x,t), \quad (x,t) \in Q = \Omega \times [-T,T], \tag{3.1}$$

$$\phi(x,t) = 0, \quad (x,t) \in \Sigma = \Gamma \times [-T,T], \tag{3.2}$$

and $\phi \in \mathscr{C}([-T,T];H^1(\Omega)) \cap \mathscr{C}^1([-T,T];L^2(\Omega))$. Then the following identity holds true for each $t_1,t_2 \in [-T,T]$:

$$\int_\Omega |\nabla\phi(t_1)|^2 dx - \int_\Omega |\nabla\phi(t_2)|^2 dx = \int_{t_1}^{t_2}\int_\Omega F(x,t)\partial_t\phi(x,t)dx\,dt. \tag{3.3}$$

In fact, we multiply both sides of (3.1) by $\partial_t\phi$ and integrate over $[t_1,t_2]\times\Omega$ by the Green formula, so that (3.3) follows.

Furthermore we need the following lemma, which is a simple consequence of (3.3).

Lemma 3.1. *Let $F \in L^2(Q)$ and $\phi_1 \in L^2(\Omega)$. Let ϕ be a given solution of*

$$\begin{aligned} &\partial_t^2\phi - \Delta\phi = F(x,t) && \text{in } Q = \Omega\times[-T,T],\\ &\phi(x,0) = 0, \qquad \partial_t\phi(x,0) = \phi_1 && \text{in } \Omega,\\ &\phi(x,t) = 0 && \text{on } \Sigma = \Gamma\times[-T,T] \end{aligned} \tag{3.4}$$

within the following class:

$$\phi \in \mathscr{C}([-T,T];H^1(\Omega)) \cap \mathscr{C}^1([-T,T];L^2(\Omega)). \tag{3.5}$$

Then the following estimate holds true:

$$\|\phi_1\|^2_{L^2(\Omega(4\varrho))} \le C\left\{\|\phi\|^2_{H^1(Q_\alpha(3\varrho))} + \int_{Q_\alpha(3\varrho)} |F(x,t)\partial_t\phi(x,t)|\,dx\,dt\right\} \tag{3.6}$$

for some positive constant $C > 0$ which is independent of F and ϕ.

Proof. We introduce a cutoff function χ satisfying $0 \le \chi \le 1, \chi \in C^\infty(R^n)$, such that $\chi(x) = 0$ for $x \in \omega(3\varrho)$ and $\chi(x) = 1$ for $x \in \Omega(4\varrho)$. We set

$$\widetilde{\phi}(x,t) = \chi(x)\phi(x,t) \in \mathscr{C}([-T,T];H^1(\Omega)) \cap \mathscr{C}^1([-T,T];L^2(\Omega)). \tag{3.7}$$

By (3.4), the function $\widetilde{\phi}$ satisfies the equation

$$\begin{aligned} &\partial_t^2\widetilde{\phi} - \Delta\widetilde{\phi} = \chi(x)F(x,t) - [\Delta,\chi]\phi && \text{in } Q = \Omega\times[-T,T], \\ &\widetilde{\phi}(x,0) = 0, \qquad \partial_t\widetilde{\phi}(x,0) = \chi(x)\phi_1(x) && \text{in } \Omega, \\ &\widetilde{\phi}(x,t) = 0 && \text{on } \Sigma = \Gamma\times[-T,T]. \end{aligned} \tag{3.8}$$

Apply energy identity (3.3) with $t_1 = 0$ and $t_2 = t$, where $-T+\alpha < t < T-\alpha$ to the solution $\widetilde{\phi}$ of (3.8) and we obtain

$$\begin{aligned} \int_{\Omega(4\varrho)} |\phi_1(x)|^2 dx \le C\int_{\Omega(3\varrho)} |\nabla\phi|^2 dx + C\int_{Q_\alpha(3\varrho)} |\nabla\phi|\,|\partial_t\phi|\,dx\,dt \\ + \int_{Q_\alpha(3\varrho)} |F(x,t)\partial_t\phi|\,dx\,dt, \end{aligned} \tag{3.9}$$

where we have used the fact that $[\Delta,\chi]$ is a first-order operator and supported in $\Omega(3\varrho)$.

Integrating (3.9) over $[-T+\alpha, T-\alpha]$, we obtain (3.6). □

Let u satisfy (1.1). Then by [16], we obtain

$$u \in \bigcap_{j=0}^{2} \mathscr{C}^j([0,T];H^{2-j}(\Omega)), \qquad \|u\|_{H^2(\Omega\times(0,T))} \le C\|f\|_{L^2(\Omega)}. \tag{3.10}$$

We extend the function u in $\Omega\times[0,T]$ by the formula $u(x,t) = u(x,-t)$ to all $(x,t)\in\Omega\times[-T,0]$. By $u(x,0) = \partial_t u(x,0) = 0$, we have

$$u \in \bigcap_{j=0}^{2} \mathscr{C}^j([-T,T];H^{2-j}(\Omega)), \qquad \|u\|_{H^2(\Omega\times(-T,T))} \le C\|f\|_{L^2(\Omega)}. \tag{3.11}$$

We extend Φ_t on $[-T,T]$ as an even function in t and denote the extension by the symbol Φ_t. Then $\Phi_t \in L^2(-T,T;L^2(\Omega))$.

The above preparation now allows us to begin the proof of Theorem 1.1.

3.2. Proof of Theorem 1.1. We proceed to the proof of Theorem 1.1.

Let $\varphi(x,t)$ be the function defined by (2.5). Then

$$\varphi(x,t) = e^{\beta\psi(x,t)} =: \rho(x)\sigma(t), \tag{3.12}$$

where $\rho(x) \ge 1$ and $\sigma(t) \le 1$ are defined by

$$\rho(x) = e^{\beta|x|^2} \ge 1, \quad \forall x\in\Omega, \qquad \sigma(t) = e^{-\beta\gamma t^2} \le 1, \quad \forall t\in[-T,T]. \tag{3.13}$$

Let $v = \partial_t u$, where u is the solution of (1.1). Then we have

$$\begin{aligned} &\partial_t^2 v - \Delta v = f(x)\Phi_t(x,t) && \text{in } Q = \Omega\times[-T,T], \\ &v(x,0) = 0, \qquad \partial_t v(x,0) = f(x)\Phi(x,0) && \text{in } \Omega, \\ &v(x,t) = 0 && \text{on } \Sigma = \Gamma\times[0,T]. \end{aligned} \tag{3.14}$$

We apply Proposition 2.1 to obtain the following estimate:

$$\tau\int_{Q_\alpha(3\varrho)} e^{2\tau\varphi}(|\nabla v|^2+\tau^2|v|^2)\,dx\,dt \le C\int_Q e^{2\tau\varphi}\left|f(x)\Phi_t(t,x)\right|^2 dx\,dt$$
$$+C\tau\int_{\omega_T(\varrho,3\varrho)} e^{2\tau\varphi}(|\nabla v|^2+\tau^2|v|^2)\,dx\,dt \tag{3.15}$$
$$+C\tau\int_{Q\setminus Q_\alpha} e^{2\tau\varphi}(|\nabla v|^2+\tau^2|v|^2)\,dx\,dt,$$

provided $\tau>0$ is large enough.

LEMMA 3.2. *Let v be the solution of (3.14). Then there exist constants $C>0$ and $0<\kappa<1$ such that for all $\tau>0$ large enough, there exists a constant $C_\tau>0$ such that*

$$\tau\int_{Q_\alpha(3\varrho)} e^{2\tau\varphi}(|\nabla v|^2+\tau^2|v|^2)\,dx\,dt$$
$$\le C\left[\int_Q e^{2\tau\varphi}\left|f(x)\Phi_t(t,x)\right|^2 dx\,dt+e^{2\kappa\tau}\|f\|^2_{L^2(\Omega)}\right]+C_\tau\|v\|^2_{H^1(\omega_T(\varrho,3\varrho))}. \tag{3.16}$$

Proof. It follows from (3.11) and condition (2.4) that we can choose $\alpha>0$ sufficiently small such that

$$\tau\int_{Q\setminus Q_\alpha} e^{2\tau\varphi}(|\nabla v|^2+\tau^2|v|^2)\,dx\,dt \le Ce^{2\kappa\tau}\|f\|^2_{L^2(\Omega)}, \tag{3.17}$$

where $\kappa<1$ and $C>0$ are generic constants.

Substituting (3.17) into (3.15), we obtain

$$\tau\int_{Q_\alpha(3\varrho)} e^{2\tau\varphi}(|\nabla v|^2+\tau^2|v|^2)\,dx\,dt \le C\int_Q e^{2\tau\varphi}\left|f(x)\Phi_t(t,x)\right|^2 dx\,dt$$
$$+Ce^{2\tau\kappa}\|f\|^2_{L^2(\Omega)}+C\tau\int_{\omega_T(\varrho,3\varrho)} e^{2\tau\varphi}(|\nabla v|^2+\tau^2|v|^2)\,dx\,dt. \tag{3.18}$$

This completes the proof of (3.16). □

LEMMA 3.3. *Let v be the solution of (3.14). Then there exists a constant $C>0$ such that for all $\tau>0$ large enough, there exists a constant $C_\tau>0$ such that*

$$C\|e^{\tau\rho}f\|^2_{L^2(\Omega)} \le \tau\int_{Q_\alpha(3\varrho)} e^{2\tau\varphi}(\tau^2|v|^2+|\nabla v|^2)\,dx\,dt$$
$$+\int_Q\left|f(x)\Phi_t(x,t)\right|^2 e^{2\tau\varphi}\,dx\,dt. \tag{3.19}$$

Proof. Let $\phi=e^{\tau\varphi}v$. By direct calculations and (3.14), we obtain

$$\begin{aligned}
&\partial_t^2\phi-\Delta\phi=f(x)\Phi_t(x,t)e^{\tau\varphi}+e^{\tau\varphi}K(x,D,\tau)v && \text{in } Q,\\
&\phi(x,0)=0,\qquad \partial_t\phi(x,0)=f(x)\Phi(x,0)e^{\tau\rho(x)} && \text{in } \Omega,\\
&\phi(x,t)=0 && \text{on } \Sigma,
\end{aligned} \tag{3.20}$$

where

$$K(x,D,\tau)v = \left\{\tau^2\left(|\partial_t\varphi|^2 - |\nabla_x\varphi|^2\right) + \tau P(D)\varphi\right\}v \\ + 2\tau\{(\partial_t\varphi)(\partial_t v) - (\nabla_x\varphi\cdot\nabla_x v)\}. \tag{3.21}$$

Next we apply (3.6) with $\phi = e^{\tau\varphi}v$ and, by $|\Phi(x,0)| \ge \epsilon_0$, we obtain that

$$C||e^{\tau\rho} f||^2_{L^2(\Omega)} \le \int_{Q_\alpha(3\varrho)} e^{2\tau\varphi}(\tau^2|v|^2 + |\nabla v|^2)\,dx\,dt \\ + \int_{Q_\alpha} e^{2\tau\varphi}|f(x)\Phi_t(x,t)|^2\,dx\,dt \\ + \int_{Q_\alpha(3\varrho)} e^{\tau\varphi}|K(x,D,\tau)v|\,|\partial_t\phi|\,dx\,dt. \tag{3.22}$$

By (3.21) and the Schwarz inequality, we obtain

$$\int_{Q_\alpha(3\varrho)} e^{\tau\varphi}|K(x,D,\tau)v|\,|\partial_t\phi|\,dx\,dt \le C\tau\int_{Q_\alpha(3\varrho)} e^{2\tau\varphi}(\tau^2|v|^2 + |\nabla v|^2)\,dx\,dt. \tag{3.23}$$

Substituting (3.23) into the right-hand side of (3.22), we obtain (3.19). □

We will now complete the proof of Theorem 1.1. By substituting (3.16) into the right-hand side of (3.19), we have

$$||e^{\tau\rho} f||^2_{L^2(\Omega)} \le C\left\{\int_Q e^{2\tau\varphi}|f(x)\Phi_t(x,t)|^2\,dx\,dt + e^{2\tau\kappa}||f||^2_{L^2(\Omega)}\right\} \\ + C_\tau||v||^2_{H^1(\omega_T(\varrho,3\varrho))}. \tag{3.24}$$

Now we return to the first integral term on the right-hand side term of (3.24). We have

$$\int_Q e^{2\tau\varphi}|f(x)\Phi_t(x,t)|^2\,dx\,dt \\ \le \int_\Omega e^{2\tau\rho(x)}|f(x)|^2\left(\int_0^T e^{-2\tau(\rho-\varphi)}||\Phi_t(t,\cdot)||^2_{L^\infty(\Omega)}dt\right)dx. \tag{3.25}$$

On the other hand, by the Lebesgue theorem, we obtain

$$\int_0^T e^{-2\tau(\rho-\varphi)}||\Phi_t(t,\cdot)||^2_{L^\infty(\Omega)}dt = \int_0^T e^{-2\tau\rho(x)(1-\sigma(t))}||\Phi_t(t,\cdot)||^2_{L^\infty(\Omega)}dt \\ \le \int_0^T e^{-2\tau(1-\sigma(t))}||\Phi_t(t,\cdot)||^2_{L^\infty}dt = o(1) \tag{3.26}$$

as $\tau \to \infty$. By (3.24) and (3.26), we obtain

$$||e^{\tau\rho} f||^2_{L^2(\Omega)} \le o(1)||e^{\tau\rho} f||^2_{L^2(\Omega)} + Ce^{2\tau\kappa}||f||^2_{L^2(\Omega)} \\ + C_\tau||v||^2_{H^1(\omega_T(\varrho,3\varrho))}. \tag{3.27}$$

Here we note that the first term of the right-hand side of (3.27) can be absorbed into the left-hand side if we take large $\tau > 0$. On the other hand, since $\rho(x) \geq 1$ for all $x \in \Omega$ and $\kappa < 1$ for τ sufficiently large, we have

$$\|f\|^2_{L^2(\Omega)} \leq C\|\partial_t u\|^2_{H^1(\omega_T(\varrho,3\varrho))}. \tag{3.28}$$

Hence, in terms of Proposition 2.2, the proof of Theorem 1.1 is complete.

Acknowledgments

The second named author was partly supported by Grant 15340027 from the Japan Society for the Promotion of Science and Grant 17654019 from the Ministry of Education, Culture, Sports, and Technology.

References

[1] C. Bardos, G. Lebeau, and J. Rauch, *Sharp sufficient conditions for the observation, control, and stabilization of waves from the boundary*, SIAM Journal on Control and Optimization **30** (1992), no. 5, 1024–1065.

[2] M. Bellassoued, *Global logarithmic stability in inverse hyperbolic problem by arbitrary boundary observation*, Inverse Problems **20** (2004), no. 4, 1033–1052.

[3] ———, *Uniqueness and stability in determining the speed of propagation of second-order hyperbolic equation with variable coefficients*, Applicable Analysis **83** (2004), no. 10, 983–1014.

[4] A. L. Bukhgeim, *Introduction to the Theory of Inverse Problems*, VSP, Utrecht, 2000.

[5] A. L. Bukhgeim and M. V. Klibanov, *Global uniqueness of class of multidimentional inverse problems*, Soviet Mathematics Doklady **24** (1981), 244–247.

[6] L. Hörmander, *The Analysis of Linear Partial Differential Operators*, vol. 1–4, Springer, Berlin, 1983–1985.

[7] O. Yu. Imanuvilov and M. Yamamoto, *Global Lipschitz stability in an inverse hyperbolic problem by interior observations*, Inverse Problems **17** (2001), no. 4, 717–728.

[8] ———, *Global uniqueness and stability in determining coefficients of wave equations*, Communications in Partial Differential Equations **26** (2001), no. 7-8, 1409–1425.

[9] ———, *Determination of a coefficient in an acoustic equation with a single measurement*, Inverse Problems **19** (2003), no. 1, 157–171.

[10] V. Isakov, *Inverse Problems for Partial Differential Equations*, Applied Mathematical Sciences, vol. 127, Springer, New York, 1998.

[11] V. Isakov and M. Yamamoto, *Carleman estimate with the Neumann boundary condition and its applications to the observability inequality and inverse hyperbolic problems*, Differential Geometric Methods in the Control of Partial Differential Equations (Boulder, CO, 1999), Comptemporary Mathematics, vol. 268, American Mathematical Society, Rhode Island, 2000, pp. 191–225.

[12] A. Khaïdarov, *Estimates for stability in multidimensional inverse problems for differential equations*, Soviet Mathematics Doklady **38** (1989), no. 3, 614–617.

[13] M. V. Klibanov, *Inverse problems and Carleman estimates*, Inverse Problems **8** (1992), no. 4, 575–596.

[14] M. V. Klibanov and A. Timonov, *Carleman Estimates for Coefficient Inverse Problems and Numerical Applications*, Inverse and Ill-Posed Problems Series, VSP, Utrecht, 2004.

[15] M. M. Lavrent'ev, *Some Ill-Posed Problems of Mathematics Physics*, Springer, Berlin, 1967.

[16] J.-L. Lions and E. Magenes, *Non-Homogenous Boundary Value Problems and Applications*, vol. 1-2, Springer, Berlin, 1972.

[17] L. Robbiano, *Fonction de coût et contrôle des solutions des équations hyperboliques*, Asymptotic Analysis **10** (1995), no. 2, 95–115.

[18] D. Tataru, *Carleman estimates and unique continuation for solutions to boundary value problems*, Journal de Mathématiques Pures et Appliquées **75** (1996), no. 4, 367–408.

[19] R. Triggiani and P. F. Yao, *Carleman estimates with no lower-order terms for general Riemann wave equations. Global uniqueness and observability in one shot*, Applied Mathematics and Optimization **46** (2002), no. 2-3, 331–375.

[20] M. Yamamoto, *Uniqueness and stability in multidimensional hyperbolic inverse problems*, Journal de Mathématiques Pures et Appliquées. Neuvième Série **78** (1999), no. 1, 65–98.

Mourad Bellassoued: Département des Mathematiques, Faculté des Sciences de Bizerte, Université du 7 Novembre à Carthage, 7021 Jarzouna, Bizerte, Tunisia
E-mail address: mourad.bellassoued@fsb.rnu.tn

Masahiro Yamamoto: Department of Mathematical Sciences, The University of Tokyo, 3-8-1 Komaba, Meguro, Tokyo 153, Japan
E-mail address: myama@ms.u-tokyo.ac.jp

PRODUCT DIFFERENCE EQUATIONS APPROXIMATING RATIONAL EQUATIONS

KENNETH S. BERENHAUT AND JOHN D. FOLEY

We introduce a family of recursive sequences, involving products which, for certain initial values, approximate some heavily studied rational equations. Some of the structure of solutions which holds for the rational equation but not for the associated linearized equation appear to be satisfied for the product approximation. Convergence of solutions for one particular second-order member of the family is proved.

1. Introduction

Solutions to rational difference equations of the form

$$y_n = A + \frac{y_{n-k}}{y_{n-m}}, \tag{1.1}$$

for $n \geq 1$, with $k, m \in \{1, 2, \ldots\}$, have been studied extensively in recent years (cf. [1–7], and the references therein).

Setting $z_n = y_n - (A+1)$, (1.1) can be rewritten in the form

$$z_n = \frac{z_{n-k} - z_{n-m}}{A+1+z_{n-m}}. \tag{1.2}$$

We then have for $|z_{n-m}| < A+1$,

$$z_n = \frac{z_{n-k} - z_{n-m}}{A+1}\left(1 - \frac{z_{n-m}}{A+1} + \left(\frac{z_{n-m}}{A+1}\right)^2 - \cdots\right). \tag{1.3}$$

A first-order approximation to the equation is the linearized equation (see [6])

$$z_n = \frac{z_{n-k} - z_{n-m}}{A+1}, \tag{1.4}$$

Hindawi Publishing Corporation
Proceedings of the Conference on Differential & Difference Equations and Applications, pp. 159–168

while a second-order approximation is

$$z_n = \frac{z_{n-k} - z_{n-m}}{A+1}\left(1 - \frac{z_{n-m}}{A+1}\right). \tag{1.5}$$

Dividing through by $(A+1)^2$ in (1.5), and setting $a = (A+1)^{-1}$ and $u_n = a^2 z_n$, gives the equation

$$u_n = (u_{n-k} - u_{n-m})(a - u_{n-m}). \tag{1.6}$$

It seems reasonable to believe that when solutions do stabilize, these solutions could tend to share more of the interesting periodicities and so forth of solutions of the rational equation. For some computational aspects and further discussion, see Section 3. One particularly interesting conjecture, suggested by computations, is the following (see Example 3.3 in Section 3).

CONJECTURE 1.1. *If $\{u_i\}$ satisfies (1.6), with $k = 2$, $m = a = 1$, and $(u_{-1}, u_0) \in (0,1) \times (0,1)$, then u_i tends to the period-two solution $\ldots, 0, 1, 0, 1, \ldots$.*

In Section 2, we prove the following result for the case $(k,m,a) = (1,2,1)$ which corresponds to the rational equation

$$y_n = \frac{y_{n-1}}{y_{n-2}}, \tag{1.7}$$

for which it is known that all solutions with positive initial values are periodic with period six (cf. [6]).

THEOREM 1.2. *Suppose that $\{u_i\}$ satisfies (1.6), with $k = a = 1$ and $m = 2$, that is,*

$$u_i = (u_{i-1} - u_{i-2})(1 - u_{i-2}) \tag{1.8}$$

for $i \geq 1$. If

$$(u_{-1}, u_0) \in (0,1) \times (0,1), \tag{1.9}$$

then u_i converges to zero.

The rest of the paper proceeds as follows. In Section 2, we introduce some lemmas concerning the structure of solutions to (1.8), and also we prove Theorem 1.2. Section 3 then concludes the paper with some discussion of further cases of (k,m,a).

2. Preliminary lemmas and results

In this section, we establish some properties of solutions to (1.8) which will be useful in proving Theorem 1.2.

In what follows, we will make use of the following expressions, which are direct consequences of (1.8).

LEMMA 2.1. *If $\{u_i\}$ satisfies (1.8), then*

$$u_i - u_{i-1} = -u_{i-2}(1+u_{i-1}-u_{i-2}), \quad i \geq 1, \tag{2.1}$$

$$u_i = -u_{i-3}(1-u_{i-2})(1+u_{i-2}-u_{i-3}), \quad i \geq 2, \tag{2.2}$$

$$u_i = u_{i-6}(1-u_{i-2})(1-u_{i-5})(1+u_{i-5}-u_{i-6})(1+u_{i-2}-u_{i-3}), \quad i \geq 5. \tag{2.3}$$

Proof. Equation (2.1) follows directly from (1.8). Equation (2.2) is a consequence of (1.8) and (2.1), and (2.3) follows from repeated application of (2.2). □

Next, we have the following result on bounds and semicycle structure for solutions.

LEMMA 2.2. *If $\{u_i\}$ satisfies (1.8) and (1.9), then*
(a) $-0.5 \leq u_i \leq 1$ *for* $i \geq -1$,
(b) $-1 \leq u_i - u_{i-1} \leq 1$ *for* $i \geq 0$,
(c) *if* $0 \leq u_0 \leq u_1 \leq 1$, *then the solution is of the form*

$$u_0 \leq u_1 \geq u_2 \geq 0 \geq u_3 \geq u_4 \leq u_5 \leq 0 \leq u_6 \leq u_7 \ldots. \tag{2.4}$$

Similarly, if $1 \geq u_0 \geq u_1 \geq 0$, *then the solution is of the form*

$$u_0 \geq u_1 \geq 0 \geq u_2 \geq u_3 \leq u_4 \leq 0 \leq u_5 \leq u_6 \geq u_7 \ldots. \tag{2.5}$$

In particular, aside from possibly the first positive semicycle, all semicycles of $\{u_i\}$ are of length three, with the extreme value in each semicycle occurring at the middle term.

Proof. First, assume $1 \geq u_0 \geq u_1 \geq 0$. Then, by (1.8) and (2.1), $u_2 = (u_1 - u_0)(1-u_0) \leq 0$, and $|u_2 - u_1| = u_0(1+u_1-u_0) \leq u_0 \leq 1$. In addition,

$$|u_2| = (u_0 - u_1)(1-u_0) \leq u_0(1-u_0) \leq 0.25. \tag{2.6}$$

Hence, suppose the lemma holds for $i < n$ with $n \geq 3$. Now, note that (1.8) and (2.1) together with (a) and (b) for $i \leq n-1$ give the structure in (c) for $i \leq n$. To see this, note that from (1.8) and (2.1),

$$\begin{aligned} \operatorname{sign}(u_n) &= \operatorname{sign}(u_{n-1} - u_{n-2}), \\ \operatorname{sign}(u_n - u_{n-1}) &= -\operatorname{sign}(u_{n-2}). \end{aligned} \tag{2.7}$$

Thus, given the assumptions on the initial values and the properties of u_2, we have that the sign sequence of $\{u_i\}_{0 \leq i \leq n}$, is $(++---+++---+++\cdots)$ and that for $\{u_i - u_{i-1}\}_{1 \leq i \leq n}$, the sign sequence is $(---+++---+++-\cdots)$, as required.

Now, set $v = |u_{n-3} - u_{n-2}|$, $w = |u_{n-2} - u_{n-1}|$ and $\epsilon - |u_{n-2}|$. To prove (a) and (b), we consider six cases, depending upon the status of the values of u_{n-1} and u_{n-2} relative to zero. The structure implied by (c) for $\{u_i\}_{0\le i\le n}$, is used throughout.

(1) $(1 \ge u_{n-1} \ge u_{n-2} \ge 0)$. Here $0 \le u_n \le u_{n-1} \le 1$ and (a) and (b) are necessarily satisfied.

(2) $(-0.5 \le u_{n-1} \le u_{n-2} \le 0)$. Here $-0.5 \le u_{n-1} \le u_n \le 0$ and (a) and (b) are satisfied.

(3) $(1 \ge u_{n-3} \ge u_{n-2} \ge 0 \ge u_{n-1})$. Then, we have $0 \ge u_{n-1} \ge u_n$ and from (2.2),

$$\begin{aligned} |u_n| &= (\epsilon+v)(1-\epsilon)(1-v) \\ &= \epsilon(1-\epsilon)(1-v)+v(1-\epsilon)(1-v) \\ &\le \epsilon(1-\epsilon)+v(1-v) \le 0.5. \end{aligned} \tag{2.8}$$

(4) $(-0.5 \le u_{n-3} \le u_{n-2} \le 0 \le u_{n-1} \le 1)$. Here $u_n \ge u_{n-1} \ge 0$ and $v+\epsilon \le 0.5$. From (2.2), we then have

$$\begin{aligned} u_n &= (v+\epsilon)(1+\epsilon)(1+v) \\ &= (v+\epsilon)(1+(v\epsilon)+(v+\epsilon)) \\ &\le (0.5)(1+0.25+0.5) \le 1. \end{aligned} \tag{2.9}$$

(5) $(1 \ge u_{n-2} \ge u_{n-1} \ge 0)$. Here $u_n \le 0$, and from (1.6),

$$|u_n| = w(1-w-\epsilon) \le w(1-w) \le 0.5. \tag{2.10}$$

In addition,

$$|u_n - u_{n-1}| = \epsilon(1-w) \le 1. \tag{2.11}$$

(6) $(-0.5 \le u_{n-2} \le u_{n-1} \le 0)$. Here $u_n \ge 0$, and

$$u_n = w(1+\epsilon) \le (0.5)(1.5) < 1, \tag{2.12}$$

$$u_n - u_{n-1} = \epsilon(1+w) \le 1. \tag{2.13}$$

The proof for the case $0 \le u_0 \le u_1 \le 1$ is similar, and will be omitted. □

Next, we show the following, which will be crucial for obtaining stability of solutions.

THEOREM 2.3. *Suppose $n \ge 6$. If $0 \le u_{n-1} \le u_n$ and $u_n > u_{n+1} \ge 0$, that is, u_n is the extreme value in a positive semicycle, then $u_n \le u_{n-6}$.*

Proof. From (2.3), it suffices to show that

$$(1-u_{n-2})(1-u_{n-5})(1+u_{n-5}-u_{n-6})(1+u_{n-2}-u_{n-3}) \le 1 \tag{2.14}$$

as each term on the left-hand side of (2.14) is nonnegative, by Lemma 2.2.

Now, note that by Lemma 2.2, we have $1 \geq u_{n-6} \geq u_{n-5} \geq 0 \geq u_{n-4} \geq u_{n-3} \geq -0.5$ and $1 \geq u_n \geq u_{n-1} \geq 0 \geq u_{n-2} \geq u_{n-3} \geq -0.5$. Since $(1+u_{n-5})(1-u_{n-5})(1+u_{n-5}-u_{n-6})(1+u_{n-6}-u_{n-5}) = (1-u_{n-5}^2)(1-(u_{n-6}-u_{n-5})^2) \leq 1$, the problem of showing (2.14) is reduced to proving that $-u_{n-2} \leq u_{n-5}$ and $u_{n-2}-u_{n-3} \leq u_{n-6}-u_{n-5}$.

Employing (2.2), we have

$$\begin{aligned} -u_{n-2} &= u_{n-5}(1-u_{n-4})(1+u_{n-4}-u_{n-5}) \\ &= u_{n-5}+u_{n-5}(-u_{n-4}^2-u_{n-5}+u_{n-5}u_{n-4}) \leq u_{n-5}. \end{aligned} \tag{2.15}$$

Similarly, we have $-u_{n-3} = u_{n-6}+u_{n-6}(-u_{n-5}^2-u_{n-6}+u_{n-6}u_{n-5})$. This with (2.15) gives

$$\begin{aligned} u_{n-2}-u_{n-3} &= (u_{n-6}-u_{n-5})+(u_{n-5}^2-u_{n-6}^2) \\ &\quad - u_{n-5}u_{n-4}(u_{n-5}-u_{n-4}) \\ &\quad + u_{n-5}u_{n-6}(u_{n-6}-u_{n-5}). \end{aligned} \tag{2.16}$$

Setting $\Delta = (u_{n-2}-u_{n-3})-(u_{n-6}-u_{n-5})$, and noting that (by (1.8)) $u_{n-4} = (u_{n-5}-u_{n-6})(1-u_{n-6})$, equation (2.16) then gives

$$\begin{aligned} \Delta = &(u_{n-5}-u_{n-6})(u_{n-6}(1-u_{n-5})) \\ &+u_{n-5}(1-(u_{n-5}-u_{n-4})(1-u_{n-6})). \end{aligned} \tag{2.17}$$

Finally, noting that $1 \geq u_{n-6} \geq u_{n-5} \geq 0$ and $0 \leq u_{n-5}-u_{n-4} \leq 1$ gives $\Delta \leq 0$, and the result follows. □

We may now proceed to the proof of Theorem 1.2.

Proof of Theorem 1.2. Suppose that n satisfies the requirements of Theorem 2.3. Then, we have $0 \geq u_{n-2} \geq u_{n-3}$, and hence employing (2.2) gives

$$|u_n| = |u_{n-3}|(1-u_{n-2})(1+u_{n-2}-u_{n-3}) \geq |u_{n-3}|, \tag{2.18}$$

that is, the modulus of the largest term in a positive semicycle is at least as large as that of the extreme term in the preceding negative semicycle.

Thus, it suffices to show that u_{n+t6} tends to zero as t tends to infinity. Since by Theorem 2.3, the sequence $\{u_{n+t6}\}$ is nonnegative and monotonically decreasing, it has a limit $D \geq 0$. Assume that $D > 0$. Then,

$$\lim_{t\to\infty} \frac{u_{n+(t+1)6}}{u_{n+t6}} = 1. \tag{2.19}$$

However, as in the proof of Theorem 2.3, we have

$$\frac{u_{n+(t+1)6}}{u_{n+t6}} \leq (1-u_{n+t6-1}^2)\left(1-(u_{n+t6}-u_{n+t6-1})^2\right), \tag{2.20}$$

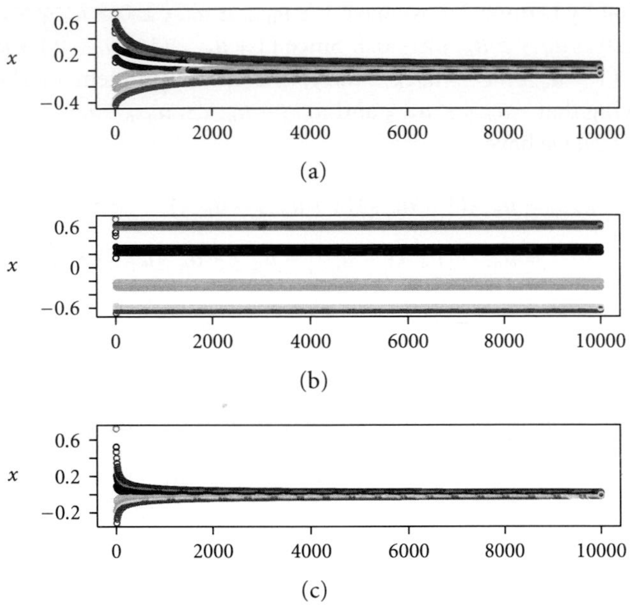

Figure 3.1. Behavior of the (a) rational, (b) linearized, and (c) product equations for $A = \rho$ and $(u_{-2}, u_{-1}, u_0) = (0.52, 0.47, 0.72)$.

and hence $\lim_{t\to\infty} u_{n+t6-1} = 0$ and $\lim_{t\to\infty}(u_{n+t6} - u_{n+t6-1}) = 0$. Thus,

$$\lim_{t\to\infty} u_{n+t6} = 0. \tag{2.21}$$

The limit in (2.21) contradicts the assumption that $D > 0$. Hence $D = 0$, and the theorem is proved. □

We now turn to some preliminary computations regarding stability, periodicity, and boundedness properties of solutions to (1.6).

3. Computations and discussion

In this section, we consider characteristics of solutions to (1.6) for some specific values of k, m, and $a = (A+1)^{-1}$.

Example 3.1 ($(k, m) = (1, 3)$). It is conjectured that all solutions to the rational equation

$$z_n = \frac{z_{n-1} - z_{n-3}}{A + 1 + z_{n-3}}, \tag{3.1}$$

with positive initial values, converge to zero if $A > \sqrt{2} - 1 \stackrel{\text{def}}{=} \rho$ (cf. [1]). It is currently known that convergence holds for $A > (\sqrt{5} - 1)/2$ (see [1, 3]). Figure 3.1 shows a comparison of the behavior of the rational, linearized, and product equations for $A = \rho$, with

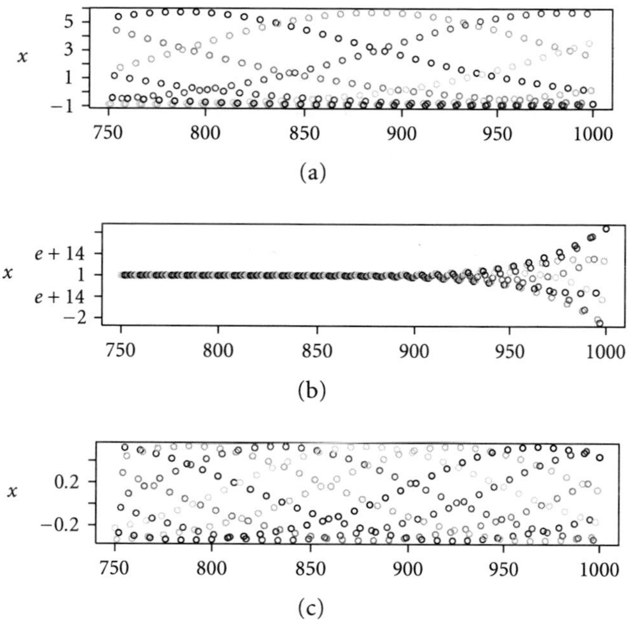

Figure 3.2. Behavior of solutions for $A = 0.3 < \rho$ and $(u_{-2}, u_{-1}, u_0) = (0.14, 0.62, 0.48)$.

random initial values in $(0,1)$ (in particular $(u_{-2}, u_{-1}, u_0) = (0.52, 0.47, 0.72)$). In Figure 3.2, we have a comparison of behavior of solutions for $A = 0.3 < \rho$ and $(u_{-2}, u_{-1}, u_0) = (0.14, 0.62, 0.48)$. Note that in Figure 3.1 the slow convergence for the solution to the rational equation appears to carry over in the product case, while in Figure 3.2, much of the "interwoven" structure is captured.

While for (1.6) there is no need for restrictions on initial values, it seems natural to ask for what values of (u_{-2}, u_{-1}, u_0) will solutions remain bounded. Hence, we pose the following question.

Question 3.2. For given (k, m, a), for what initial values does the solution to (1.6) remain bounded?

Initial computations suggest that, even for small values of (k, m), the region of initial values, leading to bounded solutions, can have quite interesting topological and geometric characteristics.

Example 3.3. As mentioned in Section 1, some interesting asymptotic periodicities appear to hold for some solutions to (1.6). Figure 3.3 displays behavior of solutions to the equation

$$u_i = (u_{i-2} - u_{i-1})(1 - u_{i-1}), \tag{3.2}$$

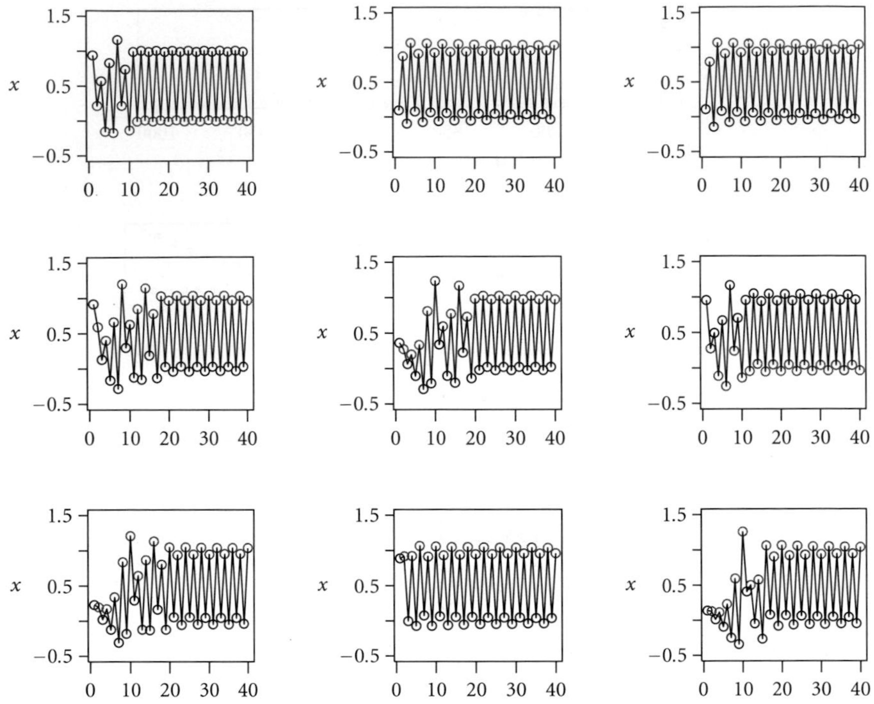

Figure 3.3. Behavior of solutions to the equation in (3.2), for random initial values in (0,1).

for random initial values in (0,1). Solutions appear to converge to the period-two solution

$$\dots,0,1,0,1,0,\dots. \tag{3.3}$$

In fact, despite the fact that $0,0,0,\dots$ and $\dots,2,2,0,2,2,0,\dots$ are solutions to (3.2), even very slight variations in initial values from (2,2), (2,0), (0,0) or (0,2) still lead to quite rapid convergence to the solution in (3.3). Figure 3.4 shows behavior of solutions to (3.2) with initial values close to these values.

Finally, it could be interesting to consider the behavior of solutions to higher-order truncations of (1.3). For instance, we have the following question.

Question 3.4. For what values of $W \geq 0$, do all solutions of the equation

$$u_i = (u_{i-1} - u_{i-2})\left(\sum_{0 \leq p \leq W} (-u_{i-2})^p\right) \tag{3.4}$$

for $i \geq 1$, with $(u_{-1}, u_0) \in (0,1) \times (0,1)$, converge to the zero solution?

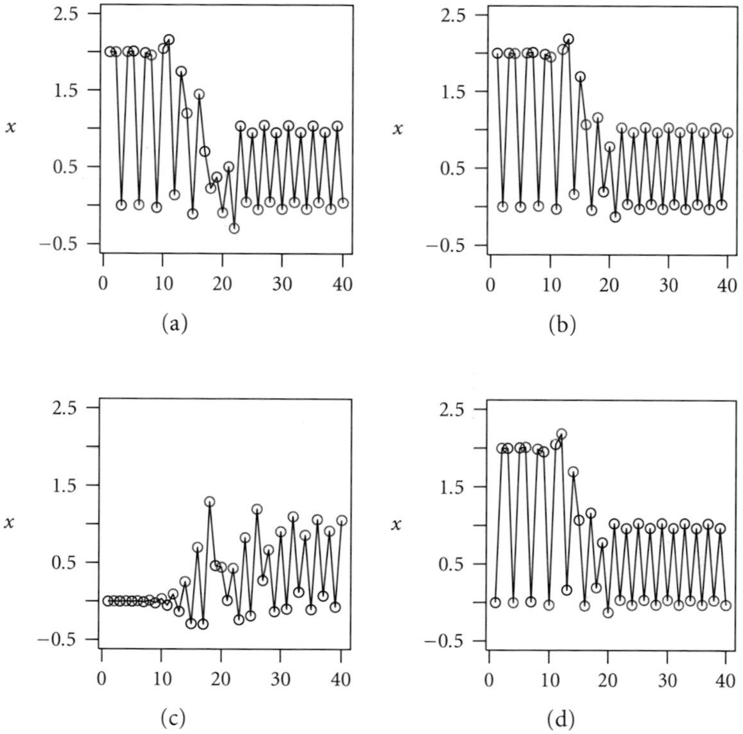

Figure 3.4. Behavior of solutions to the equation in (3.2), for initial values (a) (2.001, 2), (b) (1.999, 0), (c) (0, 0.001), and (d) (0, 1.999).

Acknowledgment

The first author acknowledges financial support from a Sterge Faculty Fellowship.

References

[1] R. M. Abu-Saris and R. DeVault, *Global stability of* $y_{n+1} = A + y_n/y_{n-k}$, Applied Mathematics Letters **16** (2003), no. 2, 173–178.

[2] A. M. Amleh, E. A. Grove, G. Ladas, and D. A. Georgiou, *On the recursive sequence* $x_{n+1} = \alpha + x_{n-1}/x_n$, Journal of Mathematical Analysis and Applications **233** (1999), no. 2, 790–798.

[3] K. S. Berenhaut, J. D. Foley, and S. Stević, *Quantitative bounds for the recursive sequence* $y_n = A + y_{n-1}/y_{n-k}$, to appear in Applied Mathematics Letters.

[4] ———, *The periodic character of the rational difference equation* $y_n = 1 + y_{n-k}/y_{n-m}$, to appear in Proceedings of the American Mathematical Society.

[5] R. DeVault, C. Kent, and W. Kosmala, *On the recursive sequence* $x_{n+1} = p + x_{n-k}/x_n$, Journal of Difference Equations and Applications **9** (2003), no. 8, 721–730.

[6] E. A. Grove and G. Ladas, *Periodicities in Nonlinear Difference Equations*, Advances in Discrete Mathematics and Applications, vol. 4, Chapman & Hall/CRC, Florida, 2005.

[7] W. T. Patula and H. D. Voulov, *On the oscillation and periodic character of a third order rational difference equation*, Proceedings of the American Mathematical Society **131** (2003), no. 3, 905–909.

Kenneth S. Berenhaut: Department of Mathematics, Wake Forest University, Winston-Salem, NC 27109, USA
E-mail address: berenhks@wfu.edu

John D. Foley: Department of Mathematics, Wake Forest University, Winston-Salem, NC 27109, USA
E-mail address: folejd4@wfu.edu

ON EXPONENTIAL DICHOTOMY FOR LINEAR DIFFERENCE EQUATIONS WITH BOUNDED AND UNBOUNDED DELAY

LEONID BEREZANSKY AND ELENA BRAVERMAN

We consider the exponential dichotomy for solutions of a linear delay difference equation in a Banach space. If the delay is bounded, then the equivalence of the dichotomy in the delay and nondelay cases is demonstrated, with further application of some recently obtained results for nondelay difference equations. In the case, when the delay is not bounded, but there is a certain memory decay in coefficients, the exponential dichotomy of solutions is also proved.

1. Introduction

For linear differential equations in a Banach space, the dichotomy result is well known since obtained in 1948 by Krein [4]: if a solution of a linear ordinary differential equation is bounded for any bounded right-hand side, then the equation is exponentially stable. More generally, it can be formulated as follows: what type of stability can be deduced from the fact that a solution belongs to space X for any right-hand side in space Y? The latter property was referred as "admissibility of a pair of spaces" and studied by Halanay [7], Halanay and Wexler [8]. Theorems of this type for difference equations of the first order were recently obtained by Aulbach and Van Minh [1] and Pituk [12] and for high order (with a bounded delay) in [2, 3]. Here we consider equations with unbounded delay, under some restrictions on memory decay. The present paper appeared due to fruitful questions and discussions following the second author's talk in Melbourne, Florida. We are greatful to Professor Alexander Domoshnitsky and Professor Vladimir Răsvan for their valuable questions and suggestions during the conference and to Professor Ravi P. Agarwal who organized this wonderful and stimulating event.

2. Preliminaries

Let $\mathbf{B}$ be a Banach space, we will use $|\cdot|$ for the norm in this space and for the induced norm in the space of bounded linear operators in $\mathbf{B}$, while $\|\cdot\|$ will be used for the

Hindawi Publishing Corporation
Proceedings of the Conference on Differential & Difference Equations and Applications, pp. 169–178

operator norm in some space of sequences (usually it will be indicated in which space the operator is considered). I is an identity operator. We will introduce the following spaces of sequences (everywhere below we assume $x(n) \in \mathbf{B}$ or $x(n) : \mathbf{B} \to \mathbf{B}$ is a linear bounded operator): $\mathbf{l}^\infty$ is a space of bounded sequences $v = \{x(n)\} : \|v\|_{\mathbf{l}^\infty} = \sup_{n\geq 0} |x(n)| < \infty$; $\mathbf{l}^p$ is a space of sequences $v = \{x(n)\} : \|v\|_{\mathbf{l}^p}^p = \sum_{n=1}^{\infty} |x(n)|^p < \infty$, $1 \leq p < \infty$.

We consider the linear difference equation

$$x(n+1) = \sum_{k=0}^{n} A(n,k)x(k) + f(n), \quad n \geq 0, \tag{2.1}$$

where $A(n,k) : \mathbf{B} \to \mathbf{B}$ are linear operators, $f(n) \in \mathbf{B}$.

In addition to (2.1), the equation with some prehistory

$$x(n+1) = \sum_{k=-d}^{n} A(n,k)x(k) + f(n), \quad n \geq 0, \tag{2.2}$$

and with the following initial conditions:

$$x(n) = \varphi(n), \quad n \leq 0, \tag{2.3}$$

will be considered, as well as the homogeneous difference equations

$$x(n+1) = \sum_{k=0}^{n} A(n,k)x(k), \quad n \geq 0, \tag{2.4}$$

$$x(n+1) = \sum_{k=-d}^{n} A(n,k)x(k), \quad n \geq 0. \tag{2.5}$$

We will also consider for any $l \geq 0$ the following homogeneous equation:

$$x(n+1) = \sum_{k=l}^{n} A(n,k)x(k), \quad n \geq l. \tag{2.6}$$

Definition 2.1. The solution $X(n,l)$ of (2.6), with $X(l,l) = I$ (I is the identity operator), is called *the fundamental function* of (2.1).

Assume $X(n,l) = 0$, $n < l$. Let us note that (2.1), (2.2), (2.4), (2.5) have the same fundamental function.

Definition 2.2. Equation (2.2) is said to be *exponentially stable* if there exist positive constants N and λ, such that for any solution of the homogeneous equation (2.5), with the initial conditions (2.3), the following inequality holds:

$$|x(n)| \le Ne^{-\lambda n} \max_{-d\le k\le 0} |\varphi(k)|, \quad n \ge 0. \tag{2.7}$$

Remark 2.3. The linear equation with several variable delays

$$x(n+1) = \sum_{k=1}^{m} A(n,k)x(h_k(n)) + f(n), \quad h_k(n) \le n,\ n \ge 0, \tag{2.8}$$

is an example of (2.2).

We will need the following result for (2.1).

LEMMA 2.4 [5, 6]. *Let $X(n,l)$ be the fundamental function of (2.1). Then the solution of (2.1) can be presented as*

$$x(n) = X(n,0)x(0) + \sum_{k=0}^{n-1} X(n,k+1)f(k), \quad n > 0. \tag{2.9}$$

It is to be noted that the above result was obtained for matrices and (2.1) with a finite delay ($A(n,k) = 0,\ n-k > T$), however, the proof can be immediately extended to the case when the delay is not bounded and A, X are operators in a Banach space.

LEMMA 2.5 [3]. *The solution of (2.2), (2.3) can be presented as*

$$\begin{aligned} x(n) &= X(n,0)x(0) + \sum_{l=0}^{n-1} X(n,l+1)f(l) \\ &\quad + \sum_{l=0}^{n-1} X(n,l+1) \sum_{k=-d}^{-1} A(l,k)\varphi(k), \quad n > 0. \end{aligned} \tag{2.10}$$

3. Reduction of order

In this section, we will assume that the delay is bounded, that is, for some $r > 0$,

$$A(n,k) = 0, \quad n-k > r. \tag{3.1}$$

Under this condition, (2.2) has the form

$$x(n+1) = \sum_{k=0}^{r} \widetilde{A}(n,k)x(n-k) + f(n), \quad n \ge 0, \tag{3.2}$$

where $\widetilde{A}(n,k) = A(n,n-k)$.

Denote by $Y(n)$, Y_0, $F(n)$, and $D(n)$ the following vectors and the operator matrix, respectively:

$$Y(n)=\begin{bmatrix} y_1 \\ y_2 \\ \vdots \\ y_{r+1}\end{bmatrix}=\begin{bmatrix} x(n) \\ x(n-1) \\ \vdots \\ x(n-r)\end{bmatrix},\qquad Y_0=\begin{bmatrix} \varphi(0) \\ \varphi(-1) \\ \vdots \\ \varphi(-r)\end{bmatrix},\qquad F(n)=\begin{bmatrix} rf(n) \\ 0 \\ \vdots \\ 0\end{bmatrix},$$
$$D(n)=\begin{bmatrix} \widetilde{A}(n,0) & \widetilde{A}(n,1) & \cdots & \widetilde{A}(n,r-1) & \widetilde{A}(n,r) \\ I & 0 & \cdots & 0 & 0 \\ 0 & I & \cdots & 0 & 0 \\ 0 & 0 & \cdots & I & 0 \end{bmatrix}. \tag{3.3}$$

Then (2.2) with initial conditions (2.3) becomes

$$Y(n+1)=D(n)Y(n)+F(n),\qquad Y(0)=Y_0. \tag{3.4}$$

Let us introduce some norm in the $r+1$-dimensional space (each component of which is in the Banach space) $\mathbf{B}^{r+1}$, say,

$$|Y|=\max_{1\le k\le r+1}|y_k|, \tag{3.5}$$

and the induced norm in the space of operator matrices D. Let us note the following.

(1) If there exists $M>0$, such that $\sup_{n\ge 0}\sum_{k=\max\{n-r,0\}}^{n}|A(n,k)|\le M$, then in the induced norm $|D(n)|\le M$.

(2) $\{Y(n)\}\in\mathbf{l}^p$ if and only if $\{x(n)\}\in\mathbf{l}^p$, where $\mathbf{l}^p$ is over $\mathbf{B}^{r+1}$ and $\mathbf{B}$, respectively.

(3) Exponential decay of $|x(n)|$ is equivalent to the exponential decay of $|Y(n)|$.

Thus all results known for (3.4) can be applied to the delay equation with a bounded delay. In particular, the following result is an immediate corollary of [12, Theorem 1] and results in [1].

Theorem 3.1. *Suppose $1<p\le\infty$, (3.1) holds and*

$$\sup_{n\ge 0}\sum_{k=\max\{n-r,0\}}^{n}|A(n,k)|\le M. \tag{3.6}$$

Equation (2.1) is exponentially stable if and only if for any sequence $\{f(n)\}\in\mathbf{l}^p$ the solution $\{x(n)\}$ of (2.1) with the zero initial condition is bounded: $\{x(n)\}\in\mathbf{l}^\infty$.

A similar approach was used in [9–11]. However, the scheme is not applicable if we have an unbounded delay.

4. Equations with an unbounded delay

Definition 4.1. Let us define the following operator in $\mathbf{l}^\infty$:

$$\mathscr{C}\left(\{f(n)\}_{n=0}^{\infty}\right) = \{z(n)\}_{n=1}^{\infty} = \left\{\sum_{l=0}^{n-1} X(n,l+1)f(l)\right\}_{n=1}^{\infty}, \tag{4.1}$$

where $z(0) = 0$. Call $\mathscr{C}$ *the Cauchy operator.*

For the zero initial conditions $x(n) = 0$, $n \le 0$, each one of (2.1) and (2.2) describes the linear map $\mathscr{L}$

$$\{g(n)\}_{n=0}^{\infty} = \mathscr{L}\left(\{x(n)\}_{n=1}^{\infty}\right) = \left\{x(n+1) - \sum_{k=1}^{n} A(n,k)x(k)\right\}_{n=1}^{\infty}. \tag{4.2}$$

Lemma 4.2 [3]. *Let $\mathscr{L}, \mathscr{M} : \mathbf{l}^\infty \to \mathbf{l}^\infty$ be linear bounded operators of type (4.2), let $\mathscr{C}_{\mathscr{L}}, \mathscr{C}_{\mathscr{M}}$ be the Cauchy operators of equations $\mathscr{L}(\{x(n)\}) = \{f(n)\}$, and $\mathscr{M}(\{x(n)\}) = \{f(n)\}$, respectively. Suppose the Cauchy operator $\mathscr{C}_{\mathscr{L}}$ is a bounded operator which maps $\mathbf{l}^\infty$ onto $\mathbf{l}^\infty$ and $\mathscr{M}\mathscr{C}_{\mathscr{L}} : \mathbf{l}^\infty \to \mathbf{l}^\infty$ is invertible.*

Then $\mathscr{C}_{\mathscr{M}}$ also maps $\mathbf{l}^\infty$ onto $\mathbf{l}^\infty$ and is bounded.

Lemma 4.3 [2]. *Suppose for (2.1) the following condition holds.*

(a1) *There exists M_0, such that $\sup_{n\ge 0}\sum_{k=-d}^{n}|A(n,k)| \le M_0$.*

Then (4.2) is a bounded operator in $\mathbf{l}^\infty$, with $\|\mathscr{L}\|_{\mathbf{l}^\infty\to\mathbf{l}^\infty} \le 1 + M_0$.

Let us recall that under (a1), if the delay is not bounded, the boundedness of solutions for any bounded f does not necessarily imply exponential stability.

Example 4.4. Consider the equation with an unbounded delay

$$x(n+1) = \frac{1}{3}x(n) + x(0) + f(n). \tag{4.3}$$

Then, for any right-hand side bounded by c ($|f(n)| \le c$), the solution is bounded by $1.5(|x(0)| + c) : |x(1)| = |(4/3)x(0) + f(0)| \le |(4/3)x(0)| + c \le 1.5(|x(0)| + c)$ and assuming $|x(n)| < 1.5(|x(0)| + c)$ we have

$$|x(n+1)| = \left|\frac{1}{3}x(n) + x(0) + f(n)\right| \le \frac{1}{3}\cdot\frac{3}{2}(|x(0)| + c) + |x(0)| + c = 1.5(|x(0)| + c). \tag{4.4}$$

However, solutions of the homogeneous equation $x(n+1) = (1/3)x(n) + x(0)$ do not decay exponentially: for example, the solution with $x(0) = 1$ is increasing and tends to 1.5.

Let us introduce the restriction that the memory of the original operator decays exponentially:

(a2) There exist $M > 0$, $\zeta > 0$, such that $|A(n,k)| \le Me^{-\zeta(n-k)}$.

Below we present examples of (2.1) with an unbounded delay for which (a2) holds.

Example 4.5. The equation $x(n+1) = \sum_{k=0}^{n} a\lambda^k x(n-k)$, $0 < \lambda < 1$, satisfies (a2) with $M = |a|$, $\zeta = -\ln\lambda$.

Example 4.6. The equation $x(n+1) - x(n) = a\exp\{-\beta n\}x([\alpha n])$, $0 < \alpha < 1$, $\beta > 0$, with a "piecewise constant delay" also satisfies (a2). Here $[t]$ is the maximal integer not exceeding t, $M = \max\{1, |a|\}$, $\zeta = \beta$, since $-\beta n \le -\beta(n - [\alpha n])$ for any $n \ge 1$.

THEOREM 4.7. *Suppose (a2) holds and for every bounded sequence $\{f(n)\} \in \mathbf{l}^\infty$, the solution $\{x(n)\}$ of (2.1) with the zero initial condition is also bounded: $\{x(n)\} \in \mathbf{l}^\infty$.*

Then there exist $N > 0$, $\lambda > 0$, such that the fundamental function X of (2.1) satisfies the exponential estimate

$$|X(n,l)| \le Ne^{-\lambda(n-l)}. \tag{4.5}$$

Proof. First, let us establish an exponential estimate for $X(n,0)$. For some positive number λ, define $y(n) = x(n)e^{\lambda n}$, assume $x(0) = y(0) = 0$, and consider the operator

$$\mathcal{L}(\{x(n)\}) = \left\{x(n+1) - \sum_{k=0}^{n} A(n,k)x(k)\right\}. \tag{4.6}$$

After substituting $x(n) = y(n)e^{-\lambda n}$, we have

$$\begin{aligned}
\mathcal{L}(\{x(n)\}) &= \left\{y(n+1)e^{-\lambda(n+1)} - \sum_{k=0}^{n} A(n,k)y(k)e^{-\lambda k}\right\} \\
&= \left\{e^{-\lambda(n+1)}\left[y(n+1) - \sum_{k=0}^{n} A(n,k)y(k)e^{\lambda(n+1-k)}\right]\right\} \\
&= \{e^{-\lambda(n+1)}\mathcal{L}(\{y(n)\})\} + \left\{e^{-\lambda(n+1)}\left[-\sum_{k=0}^{n} A(n,k)y(k)\left(e^{\lambda(n+1-k)} - 1\right)\right]\right\}.
\end{aligned} \tag{4.7}$$

Denote

$$\mathcal{G}(\{y(n)\}) = \left\{-\sum_{k=0}^{n} A(n,k)y(k)\left(e^{\lambda(n+1-k)} - 1\right)\right\}, \qquad \mathcal{M} = \mathcal{L} + \mathcal{G}. \tag{4.8}$$

Then

$$\mathcal{L}(\{x(n)\}) = \{e^{-\lambda(n+1)}\mathcal{M}(\{y(n)\})\}. \tag{4.9}$$

Let us introduce the space of sequences, with $x(0) = 0$,

$$\mathbf{l}_0^\infty = \{\{x(n)\} \in \mathbf{l}^\infty,\ x(0) = 0\}. \tag{4.10}$$

Lemma 4.3 implies that operator $\mathcal{L}$ is bounded and maps $\mathbf{l}_0^\infty$ onto $\mathbf{l}^\infty$. Therefore, by the Banach theorem, the Cauchy operator $\mathcal{C}_{\mathcal{L}}: \mathbf{l}^\infty \to \mathbf{l}_0^\infty$, which is the inverse operator, is bounded. Let $\|\mathcal{C}_{\mathcal{L}}\|_{\mathbf{l}^\infty \to \mathbf{l}^\infty} = P$.

Now let us demonstrate that for any $\varepsilon > 0$ there is such λ, $0 < \lambda < \zeta/2$, that $\|\mathcal{G}\|_{\mathbf{l}^\infty \to \mathbf{l}^\infty} < \varepsilon$. By the definition of $\mathcal{G}$, we have

$$\begin{aligned}
\|\mathcal{G}\|_{\mathbf{l}^\infty \to \mathbf{l}^\infty} &\le \sum_{k=0}^{n} |A(n,k)| \left[e^{\lambda(n+1-k)} - 1\right] \le \sum_{k=0}^{n} M e^{-\zeta(n-k)} \left[e^{\lambda(n+1-k)} - 1\right] \\
&= M \sum_{k=0}^{n} \left[e^{-(\zeta-\lambda)n+\lambda} e^{(\zeta-\lambda)k} - e^{-\zeta n} e^{\zeta k}\right] \\
&= M \left[e^{-(\zeta-\lambda)n+\lambda} \frac{e^{(\zeta-\lambda)(n+1)} - 1}{e^{\zeta-\lambda} - 1} - e^{-\zeta n} \frac{e^{\zeta(n+1)} - 1}{e^{\zeta} - 1}\right] \\
&= M \left[\frac{e^{\zeta} - e^{-(\zeta-\lambda)n+\lambda}}{e^{\zeta-\lambda} - 1} - \frac{e^{\zeta} - e^{-\zeta n}}{e^{\zeta} - 1}\right] \\
&\le M \left[\frac{1}{e^{\zeta-\lambda} - 1} - \frac{1}{e^{\zeta} - 1}\right] \left(e^{\zeta} - e^{-\zeta n}\right) \le M \left[\frac{e^{\zeta}}{e^{\zeta-\lambda} - 1} - \frac{e^{\zeta}}{e^{\zeta} - 1}\right].
\end{aligned} \tag{4.11}$$

Since the right-hand side of the last inequality tends to zero as $\lambda \to 0$, then such ε exists.

Let us fix such a λ. Since $\mathcal{L}: \mathbf{l}^\infty \to \mathbf{l}^\infty$ and $\mathcal{G}: \mathbf{l}^\infty \to \mathbf{l}^\infty$ are continuous, so is $\mathcal{M} = \mathcal{L} + \mathcal{G}$. By Lemma 4.2, the Cauchy operator $\mathcal{C}_{\mathcal{M}}$ of the difference equation $\mathcal{M}(\{y(n)\}) = \{g(n)\}$ maps $\mathbf{l}^\infty$ onto $\mathbf{l}_0^\infty$ and is bounded.

Let $Y(n,l)$ be a fundamental function of the equation $\mathcal{M}(\{y(n)\}) = \{g(n)\}$, this equation can also be written as

$$y(n+1) = \sum_{k=0}^{n} A(n,k) y(k) e^{\lambda(n+1-k)} + g(n). \tag{4.12}$$

Then $Y(n) = Y(n,0)$ is a solution of (4.12), with $Y(0) = I$ and $g(n) \equiv 0$.

Denote $G(n) = e^{-\mu n} I - Y(n,0)$, where μ is an arbitrary number satisfying $\mu > \lambda$. Then we get an equation $\mathcal{M}(G(n)) = F(n)$, $G(0) = 0$, $\{F(n)\} \in \mathbf{l}^\infty$, it has a solution $\{G(n)\} = \{(\mathcal{C}_{\mathcal{M}} F)(n)\}$ which is in $\mathbf{l}^\infty$. Thus $\{G(n)\} \in \mathbf{l}^\infty$ and $|G(n)|$ are uniformly bounded, therefore $|Y(n,0)| = |e^{-\mu n} I - G(n)|$ are also uniformly bounded, that is, for some $N_0 > 0$ we have $|Y(k,0)| \le N_0$ for any k.

The equality $X(n,0) = e^{-\lambda n} Y(n,0)$ implies

$$|X(n,0)| \le N_0 e^{-\lambda n}. \tag{4.13}$$

After making a shift to the initial point k, $k > 0$, denoting

$$Y(n,k) = e^{\lambda(n-k)} X(n,k) \tag{4.14}$$

and repeating this argument for an arbitrary positive integer k, one obtains

$$|X(n,k)| \leq N_k e^{-\lambda_k (n-k)}. \tag{4.15}$$

Finally, we have to prove that N_k and λ_k can be chosen independently of k. To this end we will show that the constants in the previous estimates can be chosen independently of k. Indeed, let $\|\mathcal{C}_{\mathcal{L}}\|_{\mathbf{l}^\infty \to \mathbf{l}^\infty} = P$ as above. Since $\mathbf{l}^\infty$ contains sequences with k first vanishing terms (they form a subspace $\mathbf{l}^\infty(k)$), $\|\mathcal{C}_{\mathcal{L}}\|_{\mathbf{l}^\infty(k) \to \mathbf{l}^\infty(k)} \leq P$ for any positive integer k. Further, if λ is chosen such that $\|\mathcal{G}\|_{\mathbf{l}^\infty \to \mathbf{l}^\infty} < 1/P$, then $\|\mathcal{G}\|_{\mathbf{l}^\infty(k) \to \mathbf{l}^\infty(k)} < 1/P$ and hence

$$r = \left\|\mathcal{G}\mathcal{C}_{\mathcal{L}}\right\|_{\mathbf{l}^\infty(k) \to \mathbf{l}^\infty(k)} \leq \|\mathcal{G}\| \|\mathcal{C}_{\mathcal{L}}\| < \frac{1}{P} P = 1, \tag{4.16}$$

where λ and $r < 1$ do not depend on k. Since the norm of the operator is less than 1, then the inverse $(I + \mathcal{G}\mathcal{C}_{\mathcal{L}})^{-1}$ exists and its norm satisfies $\|(I + \mathcal{G}\mathcal{C}_{\mathcal{L}})^{-1}\|_{\mathbf{l}^\infty \to \mathbf{l}^\infty} \leq 1/(1-r)$. We recall $\mathcal{M} = \mathcal{L} + \mathcal{G}$, $\mathcal{C}_{\mathcal{L}} = \mathcal{L}^{-1}$, so $\mathcal{M}\mathcal{C}_{\mathcal{L}} = I + \mathcal{G}\mathcal{C}_{\mathcal{L}}$ is invertible. Then by Lemma 4.2,

$$\left\|\mathcal{C}_{\mathcal{M}}\right\|_{\mathbf{l}^\infty(k) \to \mathbf{l}^\infty(k)} \leq \left\|\mathcal{C}_{\mathcal{L}}\right\|_{\mathbf{l}^\infty(k) \to \mathbf{l}^\infty(k)} \left\|\left(I + \mathcal{G}\mathcal{C}_{\mathcal{L}}\right)^{-1}\right\|_{\mathbf{l}^\infty(k) \to \mathbf{l}^\infty(k)} \leq \frac{P}{1-r}. \tag{4.17}$$

For any fixed k, the fundamental function $Y(n,k)$ of the equation $\mathcal{M}(\{y_n\}) = 0$ is a solution of this equation with the initial condition $y_0 = \cdots = y_{k-1} = 0$, $y_k = I$.

Denote $G(n,k) = I - Y(n,k)$. Then $\mathcal{M}(\{G(n,k)\}) = \{F(n,k)\}$, where

$$F(n,k) = -\sum_{l=k}^{n} A(n,l) e^{\lambda(n+1-l)}, \quad n \geq k. \tag{4.18}$$

Here

$$|F(n,k)| \leq \sum_{l=k}^{n} e^{-\zeta(n-l)} e^{\lambda(n-l)} e^{\lambda} < \frac{e^\lambda}{1 - e^{\lambda - \zeta}} = P_1, \tag{4.19}$$

so $|\{G(n,k)\}| \leq \|\mathcal{C}_{\mathcal{M}}\|_{\mathbf{l}^\infty(k) \to \mathbf{l}^\infty(k)} |\{F(n,k)\}| \leq P_1 P/(1-r) = N$, where N does not depend on k. Thus $Y(n,k)$ is bounded for all $n,k : |Y(n,k)| \leq N$. $X(n,k) = Y(n,k)e^{-\lambda(n-k)}$ implies $|X(n,k)| \leq N e^{-\lambda(n-k)}$. □

Now let us demonstrate that the exponential estimate of the fundamental function implies the exponential stability of the solution.

THEOREM 4.8. *Suppose (a2) holds. Equation (2.2) is exponentially stable if and only if for every bounded sequence* $\{f(n)\} \in \mathbf{l}^\infty$ *the solution* $\{x(n)\}$ *of (2.1) with the zero initial condition is also bounded.*

Proof. First, let us assume that for every bounded right-hand side the solution is bounded. Then, by Theorem 4.7, the exponential estimate (4.5) is valid for the fundamental function. Without loss of generality, we may assume $\lambda < \zeta$ (otherwise, we can use a weaker estimate (4.5) which is also valid). Since $|X(n,k)| \le Ne^{-\lambda(n-k)}$, then by Lemma 2.5 (see (2.10) and (a2)) the solution of (2.5), (2.3) satisfies

$$\begin{aligned}
|x(n)| &\le |X(n,0)|\,|x(0)| + \sum_{l=0}^{n-1} |X(n,l+1)| \sum_{k=-d}^{-1} |A(l,k)|\,|\varphi(k)| \\
&\le Ne^{-\lambda n}|x(0)| + \sum_{l=0}^{n-1} Ne^{-\lambda(n-l-1)} \sum_{k=-d}^{-1} Me^{-\zeta(l-k)}|\varphi(k)| \\
&\le Ne^{-\lambda n}|x(0)| + NM\sum_{l=0}^{n-1} e^{-\lambda(n-l-1)} \sum_{k=-d}^{-1} e^{-\zeta l}|\varphi(k)| \\
&= Ne^{-\lambda n}|x(0)| + NM\left(\sum_{k=-d}^{-1} |\varphi(k)|\right)\sum_{l=0}^{n-1} e^{-\lambda(n-l-1)-\zeta l} \\
&\le Ne^{-\lambda n}|x(0)| + NMd \max_{-d\le k\le -1} |\varphi(k)|\, e^{-\lambda n}e^{\lambda}\sum_{l=0}^{\infty} e^{-(\zeta-\lambda)l} \\
&= Ne^{-\lambda n}|x(0)| + NMd \max_{-d\le k\le -1} |\varphi(k)|\, e^{-\lambda n}e^{\lambda}\frac{1}{1-e^{\lambda-\zeta}} \\
&\le Ce^{-\lambda n}\max\left\{|x(0)|,\ \max_{-d\le k\le -1}|\varphi(k)|\right\},
\end{aligned} \tag{4.20}$$

where C can be chosen as $C = N(1 + Mde^{\lambda}1/(1-e^{\lambda-\zeta}))$.

If the solution is exponentially stable, then an exponential estimate is valid for the fundamental function, thus the solution representation (2.10) immediately implies the boundedness of a solution for any bounded right-hand side. □

5. Conclusion

We have demonstrated that in the sense of the exponential dichotomy, difference equations with a finite delay can be reduced to a first-order equation. Such reduction is impossible for equations with an unbounded delay and exponentially decaying coefficients with memory, but, as proved above, the exponential dichotomy result is still valid. However, there are still some relevant problems.

(1) If coefficients do not decay with memory, there is no exponential dichotomy (see Example 4.4), unlike the case of an exponential decay of coefficients with memory. What is the minimal requirement to coefficients (type of decay) so that the exponential dichotomy of solutions is still valid?

(2) In order to deduce dichotomy results, we assume the solution with the zero initial conditions is bounded (or belongs to a certain space) for any bounded (or belonging to some space) right-hand side. Let us assume that for any bounded right-hand side there are initial conditions, such that the solution is also bounded. Does this imply exponential

decay of solutions of the homogeneous equation? For a scalar first-order equation, the positive answer is obvious, but not that obvious for equations in Banach spaces.

Acknowledgments

The first author is partially supported by Israeli Ministry of Absorption. The second author is partially supported by the NSERC Research Grant and the AIF Research Grant.

References

[1] B. Aulbach and N. Van Minh, *The concept of spectral dichotomy for linear difference equations. II*, Journal of Difference Equations and Applications **2** (1996), no. 3, 251–262.

[2] L. Berezansky and E. Braverman, *On Bohl-Perron type theorems for linear difference equations*, Functional Differential Equations **11** (2004), no. 1-2, 19–28, dedicated to I. Győri on the occasion of his sixtieth birthday.

[3] ———, *On exponential dichotomy, Bohl-Perron type theorems and stability of difference equations*, Journal of Mathematical Analysis and Applications **304** (2005), no. 2, 511–530.

[4] Ju. L. Dalec'kiĭ and M. G. Kreĭn, *Stability of Solutions of Differential Equations in Banach Space*, American Mathematical Society, Rhode Island, 1974.

[5] S. Elaydi, *Periodicity and stability of linear Volterra difference systems*, Journal of Mathematical Analysis and Applications **181** (1994), no. 2, 483–492.

[6] S. Elaydi and S. Zhang, *Stability and periodicity of difference equations with finite delay*, Funkcialaj Ekvacioj **37** (1994), no. 3, 401–413.

[7] A. Halanay, *Differential Equations: Stability, Oscillations, Time Lags*, Academic Press, New York, 1966.

[8] A. Halanay and D. Wexler, *The Qualitative Theory of Systems with Impulse*, Editura Academiei Republicii Socialiste România, Bucharest, 1968.

[9] U. Krause and M. Pituk, *Boundedness and stability for higher order difference equations*, Journal of Difference Equations and Applications **10** (2004), no. 4, 343–356.

[10] E. Liz and J. B. Ferreiro, *A note on the global stability of generalized difference equations*, Applied Mathematics Letters **15** (2002), no. 6, 655–659.

[11] E. Liz and M. Pituk, *Asymptotic estimates and exponential stability for higher-order monotone difference equations*, Advances in Difference Equations **2005** (2005), no. 1, 41–55.

[12] M. Pituk, *A criterion for the exponential stability of linear difference equations*, Applied Mathematics Letters **17** (2004), no. 7, 779–783.

Leonid Berezansky: Department of Mathematics, Ben-Gurion University of the Negev, Beer-Sheva 84105, Israel
E-mail address: brznsky@cs.bgu.ac.il

Elena Braverman: Department of Mathematics & Statistics, University of Calgary, 2500 University Drive NW, Calgary, AB, Canada T2N 1N4
E-mail address: maelena@math.ucalgary.ca

QUASIDIFFUSION MODEL OF POPULATION COMMUNITY

F. BEREZOVSKAYA

By methods of qualitative theory of ODE and theory bifurcations we analyze the model dynamics of the community consisting of "predator-prey" and "prey" systems affected by prey intermigrations; we suppose that the Allee effect is incorporated in each prey population. We show that the model community persists with parameter values for which any "separate" population system can go to extinction. We investigate the dynamics of coexistence, and in particular show that the model community can either exist in steady state or with oscillations, or realize extinction depending on initial densities.

1. Dynamics of local model with the Allee effect

1.1. Two population models. The Allee effect [1, 10] means that the fertility of a population depends nonmonotonically on the population size and function of population growth has maximum and minimum values. The simplest model describing this effect is

$$u' = \beta f(u) = u(u-l)(1-u), \tag{1.1}$$

where u is a normalized population density, l is a parameter satisfying $0 \le l \le 1$. With $0 < l < 1$, (1.1) has three equilibriums: $u = 0$, $u = l$, $u = 1$; the equilibria $u = 0$, $u = 1$ are sinks, and the domains of their attractions are divided by the source $u = l$.

1.2. "Predator-prey" system. Let us suppose that $f(u)$ gives the dynamics of prey population density u in the absence of a predator (of normalized density v) and predator population is governed by the original second equation of the Volterra model. Then we obtain the model ([4, 5], see also [6])

$$u' = f(u) - uv, \qquad v' = \gamma v(u-m). \tag{1.2}$$

Hindawi Publishing Corporation
Proceedings of the Conference on Differential & Difference Equations and Applications, pp. 179–188

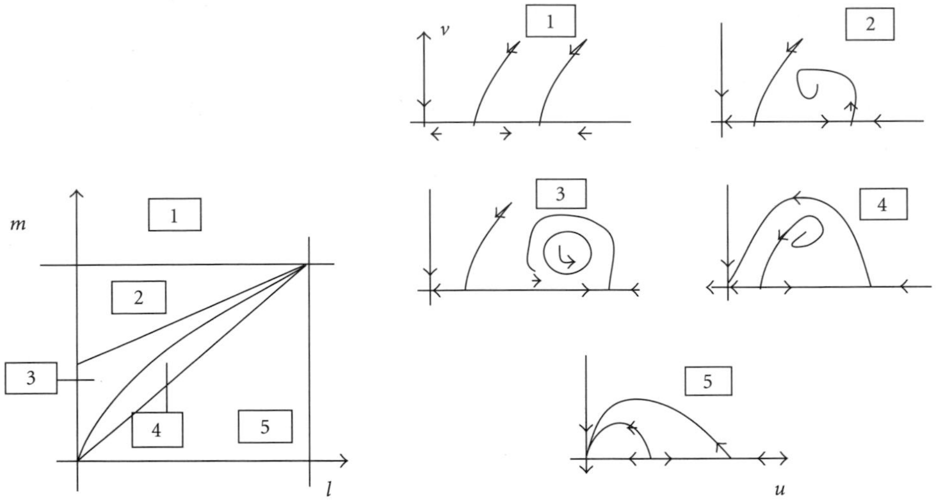

Figure 1.1. Schematically presented: the parameter-phase portrait of model (1.2).

The biological meaning of the parameters in this system are defined as follows: l is the ratio of the lower critical density of the prey population and the density determined by the prey's resources in the absence of a predator; γ is the coefficient of conversion of prey biomass into predator biomass (in scaled variables u and v can be less or bigger than one); m is natural to be regarded as a measure of predator adaptation to the prey.

The model has the nonnegative equilibria, $O(0,0), O_1(1,0), O_l(l,0)$, and also equilibrium $A(m,(m-l)(1-m))$ for $0 \leq l \leq m \leq 1$. The main result of the analysis of system (1.2) is the following.

THEOREM 1.1. *Let $0 \leq l \leq 1$, $m \geq 0$. For arbitrary fixed $\gamma > 0$ the bifurcation diagram of system (1.2) is presented in Figure 1.1. The parameter space of the system for $0 \leq l \leq 1$, $m \geq 0$, is divided into 5 regions of qualitatively different phase portraits. Boundaries between regions correspond to the bifurcations of codimension 1 and are of the form*

(**S**$_1$) $m = 1$ *which corresponds to the appearance/disappearance of points A and O_1;*

(**S**$_l$) $m = l$ *which corresponds to the appearance/disappearance of points A and O_l;*

(**H**$_1$) $m = (l+1)/2$ *which corresponds to the change of stability of point A in the supercritical Andronov-Hopf bifurcation (with appearance/disappearance of a stable limit cycle);*

(**L**) $m = m(l)$ *which corresponds to the appearance/disappearance of the stable limit cycle in a heteroclinic bifurcation where the separatrices connect points O_1 and O_l; this boundary of the nonlocal bifurcation was found numerically.*

Biological interpretations of these results are the following. For any positive value of parameter γ preys and predator can coexist with parameters m and l belonging to the domains 2 and 3 of the parametric portrait in Figure 1.1 in a steady state (domain 2) or in oscillations (domain 3); remark that population system persistence essentially depends on initial densities, that is, for some initial densities populations get to extinction even with mentioned parameter values. If parameters m and l belong to domain 1 ($m > 1$), then predators become extinct for any of their initial densities, whereas preys can exist with steady density $u = l$, or get to extinction with $t \to \infty$ depending on their initial density. At last, domains 4 and 5 correspond to extinction of both populations that happens independently of initial data.

2. Community model

2.1. Description of the model. The model consists of the prey and predator-prey subsystems based on the "local" models (1.1) and (1.2); the model allows migration of the preys from system 1 to system 2 if $u_1 > u_2$ and from system 2 to system 1 if $u_1 < u_2$. The model is of the form

$$\begin{aligned} u_1' &= \beta f(u_1) + \alpha_1(u_2 - u_1), \\ u_2' &= f(u_2) - u_2 v_2 + \alpha_2(u_1 - u_2), \\ v_2' &= \gamma v_2(u_2 - m), \\ f(u) &= u(u - l)(1 - u). \end{aligned} \tag{2.1}$$

Here u_1, u_2, v_2 are the respective normalized densities of populations of preys and predators in the systems 1 and 2; positive parameters γ, m and l_1, l_2 have the same sense as in (1.1) and (1.2), and positive β is ratio of fertilities of prey populations 2 and 1, $\alpha_1, \alpha_2 > 0$ characterize the interconnection between population systems.

In this work we study the symmetric case $l_1 - l_2 = l$ and $\alpha_1 = \alpha_2 = \alpha$, $\beta = 1$. Then model (2.1) takes the form

$$\begin{aligned} u_1' &= u_1(u_1 - l)(1 - u_1) + \alpha(u_2 - u_1) \equiv F_1(u_1, u_2, v_2), \\ u_2' &= u_2(u_2 - l)(1 - u_2) - u_2 v_2 + \alpha(u_1 - u_2) \equiv F_2(u_1, u_2, v_2), \\ v_2' &= \gamma v_2(u_2 - m) \equiv F_3(u_1, u_2, v_2). \end{aligned} \tag{2.2}$$

We consider (2.2) in the biologically relevant parameter domain $\mathbf{M}\{\alpha \geq 0,\ \gamma > 0,\ 0 \leq l \leq m \leq 1\}$.

2.2. Equilibria

2.2.1. Nullclines. We call equilibrium (x, y, z) "*symmetric*" if $x = y$, "*trivial*" if $z = 0$, and "*nontrivial*" otherwise. System (2.2) has the nullclines

$$v_2' = 0, \qquad v_2 - 0, \qquad u_2 = m, \tag{2.3}$$

$$u_2' = 0, \qquad f(u_2) - u_2 v_2 + \alpha(u_1 - u_2) = 0, \tag{2.4}$$

$$u_1' = 0, \qquad f(u_1) + \alpha(u_2 - u_1) = 0. \tag{2.5}$$

For $\alpha = 0$ as well as for $u_1 = u_2$ the model describes two independent subsystems (1.1) and (1.2). For arbitrary positive α system (2.2) has trivial symmetric equilibria

$O_{00}(0,0,0), O_{11}(1,1,0), O_{ll}(l,l,0)$; can have trivial equilibria $C(x_1,x_2,0)$, where (x_1,x_2) are roots of the system (2.4), (2.5) for $v_2 = 0$:

$$F_1(u_1,u_2,0) \equiv f(u_2) + \alpha(u_1 - u_2) = 0,$$
$$F_2(u_1,u_2,0) \equiv f(u_1) + \alpha(u_2 - u_1) = 0; \qquad (2.6)$$

can have nontrivial equilibria $B(X,m,Z)$, where (X,Z) are roots of the system (2.4), (2.5) for $u_2 = m$:

$$f(m) - mv + \alpha(u_1 - m) = 0, \qquad u_1(u_1 - l)(1 - u_1) + \alpha(m - u_1) = 0. \qquad (2.7)$$

2.2.2. Trivial equilibria. Besides the symmetric points of intersections $(u_1,u_2) = (0,0)$, $(l,l), (1,1)$, the nullclines (2.6) can intersect up to three times more. The critical cases of coalescing of points of intersections is defined by system (2.6) with the additional requirement that

$$\left|\frac{\partial(F_1,F_2)}{\partial(u_1,u_2)}\right| = f'_u(u_1)f'_u(u_2) - (f'_u(u_1) + f'_u(u_2))\alpha = 0. \qquad (2.8)$$

Systems (2.6), (2.8) define (in implicit form) the boundaries between these cases.

PROPOSITION 2.1. *System (2.2) has*

(1) *three pair of positive equilibria* $C_1{}^i(u_1{}^i,u_2{}^i,0)$, $C_2{}^i(u_2{}^i,u_1{}^i,0)$, $i = 1,2,3$ *if*

$$\alpha > \frac{((1 - l + l^2) - ((2l - 1)(l - 2)(l + 1))^{2/3}/2)}{9}, \qquad (2.9)$$

(2) *one pair of positive equilibria* $C_1{}^1(u_1{}^1,u_2{}^1,0)$, $C_2{}^1(u_2{}^1,u_1{}^1,0)$ *if* $(l - l^2)/2 < \alpha < ((1 - l + l^2) - ((2l - 1)(l - 2)(l + 1))^{2/3}/2)/9$,

(3) *no equilibria if* $\alpha < (-l^2/2 + l/2)$.

For any fixed m the curve $\mathbf{SC}_{12}$, $\alpha = ((1 - l + l^2) - ((2l - 1)(l - 2)(l + 1))^{2/3}/2)/9$, *is the parameter boundary between cases (1) and (2) and curve* $\mathbf{SC}_{23}$, $\alpha = (-l^2 + l)/2$, *is the parameter boundary between cases (2) and (3).*

2.2.3. Nontrivial equilibria. Consider now system (2.7). It defines from one up to three of real roots $(u_1{}^i, v_2{}^i = (f(m) + \alpha(u_1{}^i - m))/m)$. Three roots exist for small α, they can be ordered such that $u_1{}^1 \to 0$, $u_1{}^2 \to l$, and $u_1{}^3 \to 1$ at $\alpha \to 0$. Denote by $B^i(u_1{}^i,m,v_2{}^i)$ respective *nontrivial* equilibriums.

The root u_1 is *two-multiple* if it satisfies system (2.7) as well as

$$f_u(u_1) - \alpha = 0, \qquad f_{uu}(u_1) \neq 0. \qquad (2.10)$$

u_1 is *three-multiple* if it satisfies (2.7), (2.10) as well as equation

$$f_{uu}(u_1;l) = 0, \qquad f_{uuu}(u_1;l) \neq 0. \tag{2.11}$$

Excluding u_1 from systems (2.7), (2.10) we get the surface **SB** in the (γ,α,m,l)-parameter space:

$$\mathbf{SB}: D = 0, \quad \text{where } D \equiv \left(27\alpha m - 9(\alpha+l)(1+l) + 2(1+l)^3\right)^2 + 4\left(3\alpha - 1 + l - l^2\right)^3, \quad \alpha < \frac{1-l+l^2}{3}. \tag{2.12}$$

System (2.2) has three equilibria, $B^i(u_1{}^i, m, v_2{}^i)$, $i = 1,2,3$, inside the domain bounded by $\mathbf{SB}_{12}$ and $\mathbf{SB}_{23}$ and only one, $B(u_1, m, v_2)$, outside this domain. (u_1, v_2)-coordinates of B are

$$u_1 = \frac{(1+l) + 2^{1/3}V/Z - Z/2^{1/3}}{3}, \tag{2.13}$$

where $V = -1 + l - l^2 + 3\alpha > 0$, $Z = W + \sqrt{(4V^3 + W^2)^{1/3}}$, $W = (1+l)(2-l)(2l-1) + 9\alpha(1+l-3m)$, and $v_2 = (f(m;l) + \alpha(u_1 - m))/m$.

The following proposition summarizes the previous results and gives the asymptotic values (explicitly to $O(\alpha^2)$) of coordinates of the points B^i.

Proposition 2.2. (1) *In the four-parameter space* **M** *there exists the subdomain* $\mathbf{M}_f$; *its boundary* **SB** *defined by (2.12) corresponds to the fold bifurcation in (2.2). The boundary* **SB** *consists of two branches,* $\mathbf{SB}_{12}$ *along which equilibrium pair* B^1, B^2 *coalesces and* $\mathbf{SB}_{23}$ *along which equilibrium pairs* B^2, B^3 *coalesces. At the branch* $\mathbf{SB}_{12}$ *the system has equilibria* $B^{1,2}(u_1{}^{1,2} = ((l+1) - \sqrt{(1-l+l^2-3\alpha)})/3, m, v_2{}^{1,2})$ *and* $B^3(u_1{}^3 = ((l+1) + 2\sqrt{(1-l+l^2-3\alpha)})/3, m, v_2{}^3)$; *at the branch* $\mathbf{SB}_{23}$ *the system has equilibria* $B^{2,3}(u_1{}^{2,3} = ((l+1) + \sqrt{(1-l+l^2-3\alpha)})/3, \mathbf{m}, v_2{}^{2,3})$ *and* $B^1(u_1{}^1 = ((l+1) + 2\sqrt{(1-l+l^2-3\alpha)})/3, m, v_2{}^1)$, *where* $v = (f(m;l) + \alpha(u-m))/m$. *The cusp line* $\alpha = (1-l+l^2)/3$, $m = (l+1)^3/(27\alpha)$ *belonging to the fold surface corresponds to the three-multiple equilibrium* $B_{123}(u^*, m, v^*)$, *where* $u^* = (l+1)/3$, $v^* = (f(m) + \alpha(u^* - m))/m$.

(2) *System (2.2) has only one equilibrium* $B(u_1, m, v_2)$ *outside* $\mathbf{M}_f$ *(i.e., for* $\alpha > (1-l+l^2)/3$*) and three equilibria* $B^i(u_1{}^i, m, v_2{}^i)$ *inside* M_f *(i.e., for* $\alpha < (1-l+l^2)/3$*).* $(u_1{}^i, v_2{}^i)$ *coordinates of* B^i *explicitly to* $O(\alpha^2)$ *are of the form*

$$u_1{}^1 = \frac{m\alpha}{l}, \qquad v_2{}^1 = (m-l)(1-m) - \alpha, \tag{2.14}$$

$$u_1{}^2 = l - \frac{(m-l)\alpha}{l(1-l)}, \qquad v_2{}^2 = (m-l)(1-m) - \frac{(m-l)\alpha}{m}, \tag{2.15}$$

$$u_1{}^3 = 1 - \frac{(1-m)\alpha}{(1-l)}, \qquad v_2{}^3 = (m-l)(1-m) + \frac{(1-m)\alpha}{m}. \tag{2.16}$$

3. Topological and asymptotical characteristics of equilibria

3.1. Linear analysis. The Jacobian of system (2.2), $J(u_1,u_2,v_2)=\partial(F_1,F_2,F_2)/\partial(u_1,u_2,v_2)$, where $F=(F_1,F_2,F_3)$ has the form

$$J(u_1,u_2,v_2)=\begin{pmatrix} \dfrac{df(u_1)}{du}-\alpha & \alpha & 0 \\ \alpha & \dfrac{df(u_2)}{du}-v_2-\alpha & -u_2 \\ 0 & \gamma v_2 & -\gamma(m-u_2) \end{pmatrix}. \tag{3.1}$$

Setting $A\equiv df(u_1)/du-\alpha$, $E\equiv df(u_2)/du-v_2-\alpha$, $H\equiv-\gamma(m-u_2)$, $F\equiv -u_2$, $G\equiv \gamma v_2$ we can write the characteristic polynomial of matrix (3.1) in the form:

$$\Lambda(\lambda)\equiv\lambda^3-(A+E)\lambda^2+(AE-GF-\alpha^2)\lambda+GFA=0. \tag{3.2}$$

Proposition 3.1. (1) *Eigenvalues of the system (2.2) in the symmetric trivial equilibria are*

$$\begin{aligned} &\lambda_1(O_{00})=-\gamma m, && \lambda_2(O_{00})=-l, && \lambda_3(O_{00})=-l-2\alpha;\\ &\lambda_1(O_{ll})=-\gamma(m-l), && \lambda_2(O_{ll})=l(1-l), && \lambda_3(O_{ll})=l(1-l)-2\alpha;\\ &\lambda_1(O_{11})=-\gamma(m-1), && \lambda_2(O_{11})=-(1-l), && \lambda_3(O_{11})=-(1-l)-2\alpha. \end{aligned} \tag{3.3}$$

(2) *Eigenvalues of the equilibrium points $C_1{}^i(u^i{}_{12},u^i{}_{21},0)$, $C_2{}^i(u^i{}_{21},u^i{}_{12},0)$, where $(u^i{}_{12},u^i{}_{21})$ are real roots of the systems in (2.6), are*

$$\lambda_1(C_1{}^i)=-\gamma(m-u^i{}_{21}),\qquad \lambda_1(C_2{}^i)=-\gamma(m-u^i{}_{12}), \tag{3.4}$$

and for both cases, $\lambda_{2,3}$ are roots of equations

$$\lambda^2-(A+E)\lambda+(AE-\alpha^2)=0, \tag{3.5}$$

where A and E are taken with $(u_1,u_2)=(u_{12},u_{21})$ for C_1 and $(u_1,u_2)=(u_{21},u_{12})$ for C_2.

Corollary 3.2. *Trivial equilibrium points of system (2.2) are saddles, nodes, or saddle-nodes.*

3.2. Analysis of nontrivial points. Let us study now the stability characteristics of the equilibria. If $A=0$, then $\lambda_1=0$ is the root of the characteristic polynomial (3.2) in the two-multiple equilibrium B^* with respect to **SB**. Then, eigenvalues $\lambda_2(B^*)$, $\lambda_3(B^*)$ (correct to $O(\alpha^2)$) satisfy equation

$$\lambda^2-\left(\frac{df(m)}{du}-v_2-\alpha\right)\lambda+\gamma m v_2=0. \tag{3.6}$$

Remind, that $B^*\equiv B^{1,2}$ at the branch $\mathbf{SB}_{12}$ and $B^*\equiv B^{2,3}$ at the branch $\mathbf{SB}_{23}$. In the first case the system also has equilibrium B^3, in the second B^1. The point B^* disappears after an intersecting **SB**. Point B "succeeds" to the eigenvalues of B^3 if we cross $\mathbf{SB}_{12}$ and the eigenvalues of B^1 if we cross $\mathbf{SB}_{23}$. In both cases in point B, $\lambda_1=1+l(l-1)-4\alpha$ and

Table 3.1. Coordinates and eigenvalues of equilibria B^i for $(27\alpha m - 9(\alpha + l)(1 + l) + 2(1 + l)^3)^2 + 4(3\alpha - 1 + l - l^2)^3 < 0$, explicitly to $O(\alpha^2)$, $i = 1,2,3$.

$\mathbf{B}^1(u_1{}^1, m, v_2{}^1)$		$\mathbf{B}^2(u_1{}^2, m, v_2{}^2)$		$\mathbf{B}^3(u_1{}^3, m, v_2{}^3)$	
$u_1{}^1 = m\alpha/l$		$u_1{}^2 = l - (m-l)\alpha/(l(1-l))$		$u_1{}^3 = 1 - (1-m)\alpha/(1-l)$	
$v_2{}^1 = (m-l)(1-m) - \alpha$		$v_2{}^2 = (m-l)(1-m) - (m-l)\alpha/m$		$v_2{}^3 = (m-l)(1-m) + (1-m)\alpha/m$	
$\lambda_1{}^1$	$-\gamma m(1-\alpha/l)$	$\lambda_1{}^2$	$-\gamma(m-l)(1+\alpha/(l(1-l))$	$\lambda_1{}^3$	$\gamma(1-m)(1-\alpha/(1-l))$
$\lambda_{2,3}{}^1$	$(Tr_1 \pm \sqrt{\delta_1})/2$, where	$\lambda_{2,3}{}^2$	$(Tr_2 \pm \sqrt{\delta_2})/2$, where	$\lambda_{2,3}{}^3$	$(Tr_3 \pm \sqrt{\delta_3})/2$, where
Tr_1	$(1+l-2m)m$	Tr_2	$(1+l-2m)m - \alpha l/m$	Tr_3	$(1+l-2m)m - \alpha/m$
δ_1	$(Tr_1)^2 - 4\gamma m(m-l)(1-m) + 4\gamma m\alpha$	δ_2	$(Tr_2)^2 - 4\gamma m(m-l)(1-m) + 4\gamma(m-l)\alpha$	δ_3	$(Tr_3)^2 - 4\gamma m(m-l)(1-m) - 4\gamma(1-m)\alpha$

$\lambda_2 + \lambda_3 = m(2m - l - 1) - \alpha(l + 1 - 3m \pm 2\sqrt{(1 - l + l^2 - 3\alpha)})/3m$, where sign "+" is set with respect to $\mathbf{SB}_{12}$, sign "−" is set with respect to $\mathbf{SB}_{23}$.

One can prove that if $A \neq 0$, then the root of (3.2) is $\lambda_1 = A + O(\alpha^2)$ and two other roots at least for small α satisfy the relations $\lambda_2\lambda_3 = \gamma m v_2 + O(\alpha^2)$, $\lambda_1 + \lambda_2 = df(m;l)/du - v_2 - \alpha + O(\alpha^2)$, where u_1,v_2 are roots of system (2.7). Then, the following statement is valid.

Proposition 3.3. *$\lambda_1 = df(u_1{}^i)/du - \alpha$, λ_2,λ_3 satisfying (3.6) are (explicitly to α^2) eigenvalues of points $B^i(u_1{}^i, m, v_2{}^i)$, where $u_1{}^i$ is a root of F_1 and $v_2{}^i = (f(m) + \alpha(u_1{}^i - m))/m$.*

Corollary 3.4. *The necessary conditions for changing stability of points B^i are given (explicitly to α^2) by the next system:*

$$F_1(u_1, m, v_2) \equiv u_1{}^i(u_1 - l)(1 - u_1{}^i) + \alpha(m - u_1{}^i) = 0,$$
$$\frac{df(m;l)}{du} - v_2 - \alpha \equiv m(1 + l - 2m) - \frac{2u_1{}^i}{m} = 0. \tag{3.7}$$

Asymptotic coordinates and eigenvalues of equilibria $B_1{}^i$ $(i = 1,2,3)$ are presented in the Table 3.1.

Now we can define parameter surfaces where the point B changes stability in the Hopf bifurcation: $\mathbf{H} : \{(\gamma,\alpha,m,l) \in \mathbf{M}$, $\mathrm{Re}\lambda_2(B) + \mathrm{Re}\lambda_3(B) = 0$, $\lambda_2(B)\lambda_3(B) > 0$, the first Lyapunov quantity $L_1 \neq 0\}$.

For $(\gamma,\alpha,m,l) \in \mathbf{M}_f$ we have three surfaces $\mathbf{H}^i$ whose asymptotic (on α) presentation is

$$\mathbf{H}^1\left\{\gamma,\alpha,m,l : m = \frac{(1+l)}{2} \text{ for } \alpha < (m-l)(1-m),\ L_1{}^1 \neq 0\right\},$$
$$\mathbf{H}^2\left\{\gamma,\alpha,m,l : \alpha = \frac{m^2(1+l-2m)}{l} \text{ for } \alpha < m(1-m),\ L_1{}^2 \neq 0\right\}, \tag{3.8}$$
$$\mathbf{H}^3\{\gamma,\alpha,m,l : \alpha = m^2(1+l-2m) \text{ for any } \alpha > 0,\ L_1{}^3 \neq 0\},$$

where $L_1{}^i$ $(i = 1,2,3)$ are the first Lyapunov quantities taken in the $\mathbf{H}^i$. Note that $\mathbf{H}^1$ has to coincide with the Hopf surface $\mathbf{H}(B)$ in $\mathbf{M}$ after crossing $\mathbf{SB}_{23}$, as well as $\mathbf{H}^3$ coincides with $\mathbf{H}(B)$ after crossing $\mathbf{SB}_{12}$.

To compute the first Lyapunov quantity and justify our analysis for a reasonable α, we used the packages LOCBIF [7] and TRAX [9]. The results of the computations have confirmed the asymptotical analysis presented above, so that we can formulate the next statement.

PROPOSITION 3.5. *The first Lyapunov quantity*

(i) *is negative:* $L_1{}^1 < 0$, *for positive* γ, α, m, l *belonging to* $\mathbf{H}^1$,

(ii) *is positive:* $L_1{}^1 > 0$, *for positive* γ, α, m, l *belonging to* $\mathbf{H}^2$,

(iii) *vanishes:* $L_1{}^3 = 0$, *at the set* $\mathbf{h}$ *of positive* γ, α, m, l *belonging to* $\mathbf{H}^3$, *that is, for any fixed* $(\gamma, l) \in \mathbf{h}$ *there exists point* (α^L, m^L) *on* $\mathbf{H}^3$ *such that* $L_1{}^3 > 0$ *along curve* $\mathbf{H}^3$ *for* (α, m) *above* (α^L, m^L) *and* $L_1{}^3 < 0$ *for* (α, m) *below* (α^L, m^L).

COROLLARY 3.6. *With parameters belonging to domain* $\mathbf{M}$, *there exists the boundary surface* $\mathbf{C}$ *of multiple limit cycles at the phase space of system (2.2) corresponding to the nonlocal bifurcation of appearance/disappearance of two cycles. Parameter surfaces* $\mathbf{C}$ *and* $\mathbf{H}^3$ *have common set* $\mathbf{h} \cap (\alpha^L, m^L)$ *whose points correspond to bifurcation codimension 2 [2, 8] in system (2.2).*

Parameter surfaces $\mathbf{H}^i$ and $\mathbf{SB}$, generally, can have a common set. If this set exists, it contains points corresponding to bifurcations of codimension 2, as per Bogdanov-Takens [5], and codimension "$1+1$" (or higher codimension, see [3, 8]) in the system. Our computer investigations revealed such points. From the existence of the Bogdanov-Takens bifurcation we have the following.

PROPOSITION 3.7. *With parameters belonging to M, there exist at least three surfaces* $\mathbf{L}_B{}^1$, $\mathbf{L}_B{}^2$, $\mathbf{L}_B{}^3$ *corresponding to homoclinic loops in system (2.2) formed by the separatrices of points* B^1, B^2, B^3, *respectively.*

4. Discussion of bifurcation portrait of system (2.2)

Combining the previous results proves the next statement.

THEOREM 4.1. (1) *In the parameter domain* $\mathbf{M}$, *system (2.2) has the following nonnegative equilibria:*

(a) *trivial symmetric locally asymptotically stable nodes* $O_{00}(0,0,0)$, $O_{11}(1,1,0)$, *and saddle* $O_{ll}(l,l,0)$;

(b) *from zero up to three pairs of trivial equilibria:* $C_1{}^i(u^i{}_{12}, u^i{}_{21}, 0)$, $C_2{}^i(u^i{}_{21}, u^i{}_{12}, 0)$ *where* $(u^i{}_{12}, u^i{}_{21})$ *are roots of the system in (2.6) whose conditions of existence are given in Proposition 2.1. Any equilibrium* $C_1{}^i, C_2{}^i$ *is saddle, node, or saddle-node, if it exists;*

(c) *from one nontrivial equilibrium* $B(u_1, m, v_2)$, *where* (u_1, v_2) *are given in (2.12), up to three nontrivial equilibria* $B^i(u_1{}^i, m, v_2{}^i)$, *where* $(u_1{}^i, v_2{}^i)$ *are roots of system (2.7) whose conditions of existence and asymptotic (on* α*) expansions (2.14)–(2.16) are given in Proposition 2.2. For small enough* α, *each point possesses a manifold containing a spiral.*

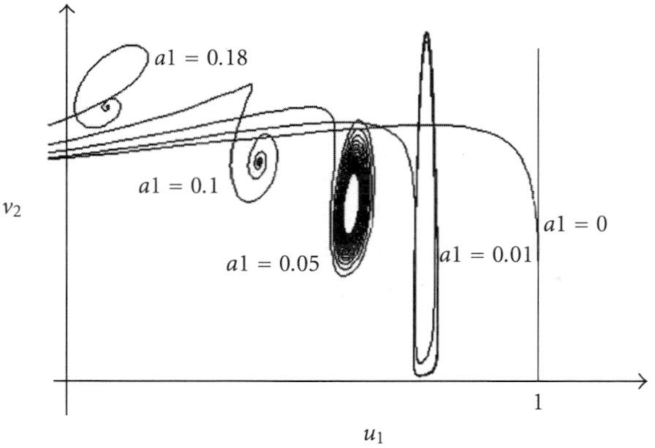

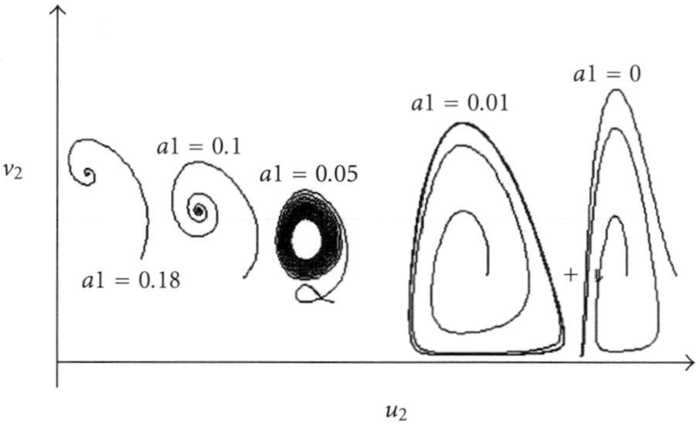

Figure 4.1. (u_1, v_2)- and (u_2, v_2)-cuts of phase portraits of system (2.2) for $\gamma = 1$, $m = 0.4$, $l = 0.1$.

(2) *Parameter portrait of system (2.2)*
  (a) *contains the boundaries corresponding to the codimension* 1 *bifurcations: saddle-node (fold)* $\mathbf{SB}_{12} \cap \mathbf{SB}_{23}$, *three Hopf bifurcations* $\mathbf{H}^1$, $\mathbf{H}^2$, $\mathbf{H}^3$, *multiple limit cycle bifurcation* **C**, *and homoclinic bifurcation* $\mathbf{L}_B{}^1$, $\mathbf{L}_B{}^2$, $\mathbf{L}_B{}^3$ *inside* $\mathbf{M}_f$;
  (b) *contains the boundaries corresponding to the Hopf bifurcation* **H**, *multiple limit cycle bifurcation* **C**, *and homoclinic bifurcation* $\mathbf{L}_B$ *outside* $\mathbf{M}_f$.

The following corollary of Theorem 4.1 supported by computations can be formulated.

Corollary 4.2. *For any parameter values* (γ, m, l) *belonging to the interiors of domains 2,3, and 4 (see Figure 1.1) there exists such a positive value of the parameter* α *that system (2.2) with parameters* (γ, m, l, α) *has at least one nontrivial stable mode: equilibrium or periodic oscillations (see Figure 4.1).*

Let us proceed with the biological interpretation of the obtained result. Firstly, for the suitable migrations between preys, the predator can control numbers of both prey populations in a stable stationary equilibrium or in an oscillatory regime. Secondly, existence of migrations between preys stabilizes the community originating a coexistence of populations with parameter values for which any "separate" population system is doomed to die out for all initial values.

Acknowledgments

I appreciate the assistance provided by Dr. S. Wirkus. This work has been partially supported by NSF Grant 634156 to Howard University.

References

[1] W. C. Allee, A. E. Emerson, and O. Park, *Principals of Animal Ecology*, Saunders, Pennsylvania, 1949.
[2] N. N. Bautin, *Behavior of Dynamic Systems Close to the Boundary of Domain of Stability*, OGIZ Gostehizdat, Moscow, 1948.
[3] A. D. Bazykin, *Nonlinear Dynamics of Interacting Populations*, World Scientific Series on Nonlinear Science, Ser. A, vol. 11, World Scientific, Singapore, 2000.
[4] A. D. Bazykin and F. Berezovskaya, *Allee effect, a low critical value of population and dynamics of system 'predator-prey'*, Ed. by Acad. Izrael. 'Problems of Ecological Monitoring and Modeling of Ecosystems', vol. 2, Gostehizdat, Moscow, 1979, pp. 161–175.
[5] R. I. Bogdanov, *The versal deformation of a singular point of a vector field on the plane in the case of zero eigenvalues*, Trudy Seminara imeni I. G. Petrovskogo (1976), no. Vyp. 2, 37–65.
[6] F. Brauer and A. C. Soudack, *Stability regions in predator-prey systems with constant-rate prey harvesting*, Journal of Mathematical Biology **8** (1979), no. 1, 55–71.
[7] A. I. Khibnik, Yu. A. Kuznetsov, V. V. Levitin, and E. V. Nikolaev, *Continuation techniques and interactive software for bifurcation analysis of ODEs and iterated maps*, Physica D **62** (1993), no. 1–4, 360–371.
[8] Yu. A. Kuznetsov, *Elements of Applied Bifurcation Theory*, Applied Mathematical Sciences, vol. 112, Springer, New York, 1995.
[9] V. V. Levitin, *TRAX: Simulations and Analysis of Dynamical Systems*, Exeter Software, New York, 1989.
[10] E. Odum, *Fundamentals in Ecology*, 3rd ed., Saunders, Pennsylvania, 1971.

F. Berezovskaya: Department of Mathematics, Howard University, Washington, DC 20059, USA
E-mail address: fberezovskaya@howard.edu

ECONOMIC CONTROL OF EPILEPSY IN A GIVEN TIME PERIOD

D. K. BHATTACHARYA AND S. K. DAS

The paper discusses an economically viable way of control of epilepsy in a given span of time under a given budget of expenditure for populations of three consecutive generations. First it considers a discrete mathematical model to express populations of three consecutive generations involving diseased and susceptible ones. The given time is divided into finite number of equal intervals called cohorts. In each cohort a continuous dynamics explains the change in the population for each generation. As a result, the study practically reduces to that of a continuous-discrete mathematical model for each generation. Next an objective function is formed for each generation and for the given span of time. This measures the net indirect profit of curing the individuals less than the cost involved in the process of identifying and treating them individually for the given period of time. Finally the method of optimal control is used to maximize the total net profit.

1. Introduction

In many countries, especially which are underdeveloped, there arises a question of eradicating or minimizing the growth of diseases in a prescribed time period with least possible expenditure involved. In this connection, we made a recent survey on three generations of people who were either epileptic or susceptible to epilepsy [3]. The survey reported different types of prevalence of the disease in the different categories of people, differing in age and social status. From these data, *prevalence* of the disease in the community of diseased and susceptible populations of three generations was calculated. This was purely based on the statistical inferences on the data.

Now the following allied questions may be raised.

(1) As the disease is mostly a vertically transmitted one, can the dynamics of the three generations be expressed in the form of a discrete dynamical system and can the "prevalence" be calculated in terms of the birth rates of the diseased and susceptible ones?

Hindawi Publishing Corporation
Proceedings of the Conference on Differential & Difference Equations and Applications, pp. 189–199

(2) Is it possible to express the dynamics of the population, when the treatment continues successively during different equal intervals of the total span of time, in the form of a continuous-discrete mathematical model and calculate the concentration of the diseased population at the end of the given span of time?
(3) Can the "prevalence" of disease before and after the treatment be compared? Can a definite conclusion be made from the two results out of the given parameters of the model?
(4) How can the mathematical theory of control be applied so as to maximize the net profit coming out of the process?

The present paper attempts to answer all the questions in the affirmative. It develops a continuous-discrete mathematical model for control of epilepsy. It is not out of context to mention that although the use of discrete or continuous-discrete models is completely new for vertically transmitted diseases like epilepsy, but the use of similar models in economics and fishery is well known. To help in properly appreciating the analysis of this paper, the following references may be cited. Samuelson [10, 11] considers economic implications of discrete-time models. General references on discrete models are given by Maynard Smith [6], May [5], Nicholson and Belly [8]. A standard stock recruitment relation F between the recruit R_k and the parent stock P_k at the kth stage is known from Ricker curve [8]. Maynard Smith [7] and Oster [9] studied the dynamic behavior of stock recruitment relation F. Some other standard models of stock recruitment relationships based on hypothesis concerning life history of various fish species are also known [2]. So far as continuous-discrete mathematical models are concerned, there are two types of models. The first type of models is the model for which the allied control problem may be solved without applying the general discrete optimal control technique and that the choice of control sequence normally involves *most rapid* or *bang-bang* approach to equilibrium. Such problems are termed as "separable" by Spence and Starrett and as "myopic" by Heyman and Sobel [4]. Other type of problem is called nonseparable (nonmyopic), where the corresponding control problem can be solved only by the general discrete optimal control technique, and in this case the choice of control sequence involves asymptotic approaches to the equilibrium. Our present problem is of separable *myopic* type, and hence optimization is done by using the "most rapid" approach path.

2. Some of the experimental data and analysis on the prevalence of epilepsy [3]

We first highlight, in brief, some of the recent experimental work and analysis on the disease epilepsy. This helps in the motivation of the corresponding mathematical modeling of the occurrence of the disease epilepsy and its mathematical control.

2.1. Persons with epilepsy. A total 597 persons were found to have seizure disorders. After evaluation by the neurologist, 292 persons (162 men and 130 women) were diagnosed with active epilepsy yielding a crude prevalence rate of 557.5 and an age-adjusted prevalence rate (US 2000) 516.77 per 100 000 populations (Table 2.1). Among the others, 28 had inactive epilepsy, 40 had single seizure, and 207 had febrile convulsion. The highest age-specific prevalence rate of 811 per 100 000 populations was observed between 10–19 years age group. Age and sex-specific prevalence shows the highest prevalence of epilepsy

Table 2.1. Age and sex distribution of our sample population.

Age range	Population of men (%)	Population of women (%)	Total	Cumulative (%)	Indian population (2001) (%)
0–4	1690–6.12	1467–5.93	3157–6.03	3157–6.03	10.77
5–9	1985–7.19	1859–7.51	3844–7.34	7001–13.37	12.51
10–14	25060–9.07	2349–9.49	4855–9.27	11856–22.64	12.17
15–19	2717–9.83	2406–9.72	5123–9.78	16979–2.42	9.77
20–24	2711–9.81	2304–9.31	5015–9.57	21994–41.99	8.75
25–29	2471–8.94	2319–9.37	4790–9.15	26784–51.14	8.13
30–34	2231–8.08	2078–8.40	4309–8.23	31093–59.36	7.24
35–39	2259–8.18	2126–8.59	4385–8.37	35478–67.74	6.88
40–44	1965–7.11	1689–6.82	3654–6.98	39132–74.71	5.43
45–49	2042–7.39	1601–6.47	3643–6.96	42775–81.67	4.62
50–54	1248–4.52	1042–4.21	2290–4.37	45065–86.04	3.57
55–59	1029–3.72	853–3.45	1882–3.59	46947–89.63	2.7
60–64	920–3.33	891–3.60	1811–3.46	48758–93.09	2.68
65–69	662–2.40	664–2.68	1326–2.53	50084–95.62	1.93
70–74	579–2.10	538–2.17	1117–2.13	51201–97.75	1.43
75–79	302–1.09	236–0.95	538–1.03	51709–98.78	0.64
80≥	309–1.12	329–1.33	638–1.22	52377–100.00	0.78
Total	27626	24751	52377		

in the age range between 15 and 29, and males are predominant sufferers except in elderly groups when women are predominantly affected.

2.2. Distribution of sample population. Table 2.1 shows age and sex distribution of sample population.

2.3. Prevalence rates of neurological disease (epilepsy) in the study.

2.3.1. Observation. Prevalence rate of epilepsy is nonuniform amongst different age groups. If we roughly assume that the three generations consist of people of ages over 60, of ages between 30–60, and of ages less than 30, respectively, then we find that the prevalence rates in the three generations do not follow a definite pattern. It is the highest for the third generation consisting of people of both sexes between the ages 15–29. We cannot say definitely whether the prevalence rates decrease or increase from one generation to the next. But we may naturally expect that in any generation, the prevalence rate of the persons should decline if proper medical treatments are offered to them. With this in mind, we formulate a mathematical model that tallies with the realistic data and show how it may be used for control of the disease in a given span of time.

3. Discrete mathematical model of vertically transmitted diseases [1]

Let I_n and S_n denote, respectively, the concentration of diseased and susceptible populations in the nth generation. Under normalization, the total carrying capacity of the environment reduces to one. Hence, $1 - S_{n-1} - I_{n-1}$ represents the logistic control on the oviposition. Let b_I and b_S be, respectively, the birth rates of infected and susceptible populations. They do not depend on n due to their periodicity. Let p and $q = 1 - p$, $0 \leq q \leq 1$, be the portions of a diseased female that become, respectively, susceptible and infected offspring in the next generation. If no maturation period is present, then there is no horizontal transmission of the disease. It is purely a case of vertical transmission. In this case, the discrete dynamics of the populations are given by

$$I_n(n) = (1 - p)b_I I_{n-1}[1 - I_{n-1} - S_{n-1}], \tag{3.1}$$

$$S_n(n) = [b_S S_{n-1} + p b_I I_{n-1}][1 - I_{n-1} - S_{n-1}]. \tag{3.2}$$

The prevalence rate $r_n = I_n(n)/(I_n(n) + S_n(n))$ has the following form:

$$r_n = \frac{(1 - p)b_I I_{n-1}}{b_I I_{n-1} + b_S S_{n-1}}. \tag{3.3}$$

It is noted that in the case of epilepsy, horizontal transmission does not play a major role, and so the above model may serve our purpose.

In our case, if I_1 and S_1 denote, respectively, the concentration of diseased and susceptible classes in the first generation, then the next two generations give rise to populations I_2, S_2 and I_3, S_3, which are related as

$$\begin{aligned} I_2 &= (1 - p)b_I I_1[1 - I_1 - S_1], \\ S_2 &= [b_S S_1 + p b_I I_1][b_I S_1 + p b_I I_1][1 - I_1 - S_1], \end{aligned} \tag{3.4}$$

$$\begin{aligned} I_3 &= (1 - p)b_I I_2[1 - I_2 - S_2], \\ S_3 &= [b_S S_2 + p b_I I_2][b_I S_2 + p b_I I_2][1 - I_2 - S_2]. \end{aligned} \tag{3.5}$$

Expressions (3.4) and (3.5) describe the discrete dynamics for our model involving three generations of diseased and susceptible populations I_1, S_1, I_2, S_2 and I_3, S_3, respectively.

4. Relation between prevalence rates of consecutive generations

From (3.3), it is noted that prevalence rate of disease in the nth generation is given by $r_n = I_n/(I_n + S_n) = q b_I I_{n-1}/(b_I I_{n-1} + b_S S_{n-1})$. So we have $r_{n+1} = I_{n+1}/(I_{n+1} + S_{n+1}) = q b_I I_n/(b_I I_n + b_S S_n)$, and hence

$$\frac{r_n}{r_{n+1}} = \left(\frac{b_I I_n + b_S S_n}{I_n}\right)\left(\frac{I_{n-1}}{b_I I_{n-1} + b_S S_{n-1}}\right) = \frac{b_I + b_S(S_n/I_n)}{b_I + b_S(S_{n-1}/I_{n-1})} < 1 \tag{4.1}$$

if $S_n/I_n < S_{n-1}/I_{n-1}$. So we see that $r_n < r_{n+1}$ if $S_n/I_n < S_{n-1}/I_{n-1}$. Naturally, the changes in the prevalence rates in the successive generations depend on the ratio of the susceptible and the diseased ones. It cannot be said definitely whether the prevalence rate decreases or increases from generation to generation. This relates to our observations in the realistic data.

We now affirm from the following mathematical model that the prevalence rate of epilepsy actually decreases when diseased ones are properly treated.

5. Formation of continuous-discrete mathematical model for treatment of epilepsy

We first consider diseased populations of three consecutive generations related as above separately. In the first generation, let $I_1(0) = I_{10}$ and $S_1(0) = S_{10}$ be the initial values of I_1 and S_1, respectively, when treatment starts. Let $E_{10}(t)$ be the total effort exerted in diagnosing and treating $I_1(t)$ at time t. $E_{10}(t)$ is quantified in terms of total team of workers engaged in the survey work and the total number of medical persons involved in the treatment process, and also in terms of total amount of medicine and medical appliances used in the process. Let the rate of improvement of the affected persons (indicating decay in their growth) be proportional to the αth power of $E_{10}(t)$ and βth power of $I_1(t)$, $0 < \alpha < 1$, $0 < \beta < 1$ (the growth equation is of general type, Cobb-Douglass one. Special type occurs when $\alpha = 1$, $\beta = 1$). Then the continuous dynamics of this process is given by

$$\frac{dI_1}{dt} = -\delta E_{10}^{\alpha}(t) I_1^{\beta}(t), \tag{5.1}$$

δ is the constant of proportionality.

Let t_ϵ be the time for which the process continues and U_{10} be the net improvement at the end of the time t_ϵ. Then solving (5.1), we have

$$(U_{10})^{1-\beta} = \delta(1-\beta)E_{10}^{\alpha} t_\epsilon. \tag{5.2}$$

Hence $R_{10} = I_{10} - U_{10}$ is the total diseased concentration at the end of time t_ϵ in the first cohort of the first generation. Let us assume that the given span of time is divided into m number of cohorts of equal duration P (cohort time). Now R_{10} decays with its own dynamics for the rest of the time $P - t_\epsilon$ of the first cohort. This dynamics is expressed as

$$\frac{d\theta}{dt} = \theta_1 x(t), \quad x(0) = R_{10}, \tag{5.3}$$

θ_1 is the natural death rate of $I_1(t)$. The solution is given by

$$x(t) = R_{10} e^{\theta_1(t)}. \tag{5.4}$$

So the value of $x(t)$ at the end of the time period P becomes $I_{11} = R_{10}e^{-\theta_1(P-t_\epsilon)}$. We write $I_{11} = F(R_{10})$, where $F(R_{10}) = R_{10}e^{-\theta_1(P-t_\epsilon)}$. In fact, I_{11} is the concentration of the diseased one at the end of the first cohort (equivalently at the starting of the second cohort). Now at this stage, second phase of treatment starts and continues for time t_ϵ. There is no necessity that the same t_ϵ is to be taken. But it is better to use the same t_ϵ to avoid complications of calculations. Now the most important point to be noted is that same effort is not needed for the dynamics of the next cohort time P, as some improvement to the diseased population has already been made. In fact, the effort is now of the form $E_{11}(t)$, where $E_{11}(t) < E_{10}(t)$. So replacing E_{10} by E_{11} and writing equation similar to (5.3), we get the net improvement U_{11} at the next phase for time t_ϵ as

$$(U_{11})^{1-\beta} = \delta(1-\beta)E_{11}^{\alpha}t_\epsilon. \tag{5.5}$$

So $R_{11} = I_{11} - U_{11}$ is the total diseased concentration at the end of second improvement. As usual, R_{11} runs out of its own dynamics according to (5.4) for the time period $P - t_\epsilon$ and the whole process continues. In this way, we get R_{1m-1}, the diseased population at the end of the improvement in the mth cohort. Finally, the population at the end of the mth cohort is found to be $I_{1m} = F(R_{1m-1}) = R_{1m-1}e^{-\theta_1(P-t_\epsilon)}$.

The whole process cited above explains the continuous-discrete dynamics for the given span of time. Had there been no updating at the start of each cohort, the whole process would have been governed by a discrete dynamics. The updating at regular intervals of time has made the process governed by a continuous-discrete dynamics.

6. Formation of the objective function for the continuous-discrete model

As our program is to update the diseased population in an economically viable way, so at the end of each kth cohort, when the concentration is I_{1k}, the updating U_{1k} is to be so adjusted that the total profit out of improvement in the diseased population less than the corresponding cost incurred is maximum. If c is the cost per unit effort, then the total cost for the first updating is $\int_0^{t_\epsilon} cE_{10}(t)dt$. We first express this cost in terms of cost per person treated, which is taken as C. We note that $cE_{10}(t)$ amount of cost was needed for $\delta E_{10}^{\alpha} I_1^{\beta}$. So

$$C_1(t) = \frac{cE_{10}}{\delta E_{10}^{\alpha} I_1^{\beta}} = \frac{c}{\delta E_{10}^{\alpha-1} I_1^{\beta}}. \tag{6.1}$$

Assuming solution of (5.1) also gives t as a function of I_1, we write $dt = -(1/\delta E_{10}^{\alpha} I_1^{\beta})dI_1$. So finally, we have $cE_1(t)dt = -C(I_1)dI_1$. Hence the total cost of first updating can be expressed as

$$\int_0^{t_\epsilon} cE_{10}(t)dt = -\int_{I_{10}}^{I_{10}-U_{10}} C(I_1)dI_1 = \int_{I_{10}-U_{10}}^{I_{10}} C(I_1)dt = \int_{R_{10}}^{I_{10}} C(I_1)dt. \tag{6.2}$$

Also p being the projected price out of improvement U_{01} to the diseased population, the total projected price during this time period comes to be $pU_{01} = -\int_{I_{01}}^{I_{01}-U_{01}} pdI_1 = \int_{R_{10}}^{I_{10}} pdI_1$.

Also p being the projected price out of improvement U_{01} to the diseased population, the total projected price during this time period comes to be $pU_{01} = -\int_{I_{01}}^{I_{01}-U_{01}} pdI_1 = \int_{R_{10}}^{I_{10}} pdI_1$. So the net profit for this period is equal to $\int_{R_{01}}^{I_{01}} (p - C(I_1))dI_1$. We denote it by

$\pi(I_{10}, U_{10})$ and call it the total profit of improvement in the first cohort. Thus, the total profit for the whole process is found to be

$$\sum_{k=0}^{m-1} \pi(I_{1k}, U_{1k}) = \sum_{k=0}^{m-1} \int_{R_{1k}}^{I_{1k}} (p - C(I_1))dI_1$$
$$= \sum_{k=0}^{m-1} \int_{R_{1k}}^{X_{1k}} (p - C(I_1))dI_1 + \sum_{k=0}^{m-1} \int_{X_{1k}}^{I_{1k}} (p - C(I_1))dI_1, \tag{6.3}$$

where $R_{1k} < X_{1k} < I_{1k}$ and X_{1k} is that amount of diseased concentration of the kth cohort, for which the projected profit equals the corresponding cost. Such a concentration is called a bionomic equilibrium point. $k = 0, 1, 2, \ldots, m-1$. X_{1k} are different for each cohort, but they have definitely fixed values. If we now write $\int_{X_{1k}}^{I_{1k}} (p - C(I_1))dI_1$, then

$$\sum_{k=0}^{m-1} \pi(I_{1k}, U_{1k}) = \sum_{k=0}^{m-1} [-\phi(R_{1k}) + \phi(I_{1k})]$$
$$= -\sum_{k=0}^{m-1} \phi(R_{1k}) + \phi(I_{10}) + \sum_{k=1}^{m-1} \phi(I_{1k})$$
$$= -\sum_{k-0}^{m-1} \phi(R_{1k}) + \phi(I_{10}) + \sum_{k-1}^{m-1} \phi(F(R_{1k-1}))$$
$$= -\sum_{k=0}^{m-1} \phi(R_{1k}) + \phi(I_{10}) + \sum_{k=0}^{m-1} \phi(F(R_{1k-1}))$$
$$= -\sum_{k=0}^{m-1} \phi(R_{1k}) + \phi(I_{10}) + \sum_{k=0}^{m-2} \phi(F(R_{1k}))$$
$$= -\sum_{k=0}^{m-2} \phi(R_{1k}) - \phi(R_{1m-1}) + \phi(I_{10}) + \sum_{k=0}^{m-2} \phi(F(R_{1k}))$$
$$= \sum_{k=0}^{m-2} W(R_{1k}) + \phi(I_{10}) - \phi(R_{1m-1}), \quad W(R_{1k}) = \phi(F(R_{1k})) - \phi(R_{1k}). \tag{6.4}$$

The objective function is given by

$$\sum_{k=0}^{m-1} \pi(I_{1k}, U_{1k}) = \sum_{k=0}^{m-2} W(R_{1k}) + \phi(I_{10}) - \phi(R_{1m-1}), \tag{6.5}$$

where $W(R_{1k}) = \phi(F(R_{1k})) - \phi(R_{1k})$.

7. Optimal criteria for the continuous-discrete model

We first divide the allotted expenditure for three generations of diseased persons, keeping in mind that more money is needed as we pass on from one generation to the next generation successively, because of the increasing number of diseased ones in the successive generations. Anyway, we first stick to the first generation. We see that $\phi(I_{10})$ depends only on I_10 and depends only on $\phi(R_{1m-1})$, where I_{10} is given and R_{1m-1} is the last improved result due to improvement U_{1m-1}. Now U_{1m-1} being the last improvement, it can be chosen according to the total amount of money left for expenditure. Naturally, R_{1m-1} does not depend on the choice of the other R_{1k}, $k = 0,1,\dots,m-2$. So if the problem is to maximize the total profit of the whole process for the first generation, then practically the maximum value of the profit depends on the choice of R_{1k}, $k = 0,2,\dots,m-2$. Thus the optimal criteria reduces to the following. Find out the optimal sequence $\{R_{1k}^*\}$, and hence $\{U_{1k}^*\}$, $k = 1,2,\dots,m-2$, such that

$$\sum_{k=0}^{m-1} \pi(I_{1k}, U_{1k}) = \sum_{k=0}^{m-2} W(R_{1k}) + \phi(I_{10}) - \phi(R_{1m-1}), \tag{7.1}$$

where $W(R_{1k}) = \phi(F(R_{1k})) - \phi(R_{1k})$.

8. Solution of the problem of control of epilepsy

THEOREM 8.1. *Let the dynamic model for control of epilepsy be given by equations (5.1)–(5.5). Let the objective function and the objective criteria be given by (5.5) and (6.5), respectively. Let $A_{1k} = c/\delta E_{1k}^{\alpha-1}$. Then the profit given by $\sum_{k=0}^{m-1} \pi(I_{1k}, U_{1k})$ is maximum if $\sum_{k=0}^{m-2} [\phi(F(R_{1k})) - \phi(R_{1k})]$ is maximum, the condition for which $\{R_{1k}\}$ should be chosen as $\{R_{1k}^*\}$, $k = 0,1,\dots,m-2$, where in each cohort, R_{1k}^* is related to A_{1k}^* as*

$$R_{1k}^* = \left[\frac{A_{1k}^*(1 - e^{-\theta(1+\beta)(P-t_\epsilon)})}{p(1 - e^{-\theta(P-t_\epsilon)})}\right], \tag{8.1}$$

where $A_{1k}^* = c/\delta(E_{1k}^*)^{\alpha-1}$.

Proof. If $W(R_{1k}) = \phi(F(R_{1k})) - \phi(R_{1k})$ is maximum at $R_{1k} = R_{1k}^*$, then we should have

$$W'(R_{1k}^*) = [p - C(F(R_{1k}^*))]F'(R_{1k}^*) - [p - C(R_{1k}^*)] = 0. \tag{8.2}$$

Again, we have

$$C(I_{1k}) = \frac{cE_{1k}}{\delta(E_{1k})^\alpha x^\beta} = \frac{c}{\delta(E_{1k})^{\alpha-1} x^\beta} = A_{1k}x^{-\beta}, \quad A_{1k} = \frac{c}{\delta(E_{1k})^{\alpha-1}}. \tag{8.3}$$

So from (8.2), we get

$$F'(R_{1k}^*) = \frac{p - C(R_{1k}^*)}{p - C(F(R_{1k}^*))} = \frac{p - A_{1k}^*(R_{1k}^*)^{-\beta}}{p - A_{1k}^*(F(R_{1k}^*))^{-\beta}}. \tag{8.4}$$

Now, $F_{1k} = R_{1k}e^{-\theta(P-t_\epsilon)} \Rightarrow F'(R_{1k}) = e^{-\theta(P-t_\epsilon)}$, so we have

$$\frac{p - A_{1k}^*(R_{1k}^*)^{-\beta}}{p - A_{1k}^*(F(R_{1k}^*))^{-\beta}} = e^{-\theta(P-t_\epsilon)}. \tag{8.5}$$

This gives $(p - A_{1k}^*(R_{1k}^*)^{-\beta})/(p - A_{1k}^*(F(R_{1k}^*))^{-\beta}e^{-\theta\beta(P-t_\epsilon)}) = e^{-\theta(P-t_\epsilon)}$.

So finally, R_{1k}^* is expressed in terms of A_{1k}^* as

$$R_{1k}^* = \left[\frac{A_{1k}^*(1 - e^{-\theta(1+\beta)(P-t_\epsilon)})}{p(1 - e^{-\theta(P-t_\epsilon)})}\right], \tag{8.6}$$

where $A_{1k}^* = c/\delta(E_{1k}^*)^{\alpha-1}$. □

Remark 8.2. Equation (7.1) determines R_{1k}^* in terms of A_{1k}^*. Again $U_{1k}^* = [\delta(1-\beta)(E_{1k}^*)^\alpha t_\epsilon]^{1-\beta}$ is also expressed in terms of A_{1k}^*, as $A_{1k}^* = c/\delta(E_{1k}^*)^{\alpha-1}$. Now we explain that A_{1k}^* can be calculated from the relation $R_{1k}^* = I_{1k} - U_{1k}^*$. Let us start with $R_{10}^* = I_{10} - U_{10}^*$, where I_{10} is known. Naturally, this determines A_{10}^*, as both R_{10}^* and U_{10}^* are expressed in terms of A_{10}^*. This known value of A_{10}^* determines both U_{10}^* and R_{10}^*. Now R_{10}^* being known, $I_{11} = F(R_{10}^*)$ is also known. So proceeding as above, it may be shown that finally $\{U_{1k}^*\}$ and $\{R_{1k}^*\}$ can be determined, where $k = 0, 1, \ldots, m-2$. This explains that the control strategy as stated above is very nicely workable from the practical point of view, provided the parameters of the model can be determined suitably.

9. Optimal control strategy for all the generations

Depending on the money year marked for the three generations, the control strategy for the three generations is carried out separately and the results of updating may be summarized as follows.

THEOREM 9.1. *Let $I_{1k}, U_{1k}, R_{1k}, E_{1k}, A_{1k}, \theta_1$ for the first generation be replaced by $I_{sk}, U_{sk}, R_{sk}, E_{sk}, A_{sk}, \theta_s$; $s = 2, 3$ (i.e., for the second and third generations, resp.), where $\theta_1 > \theta_2 > \theta_3$; $E_{1k} < E_{2k} < E_{3k}$. Then the net profit*

$$\sum_{l=1}^{3}\sum_{k=0}^{m-1} \pi(I_{lk}, U_{lk}) = \sum_{l=1}^{3}\sum_{k=0}^{m-2} W(R_{lk}) + \sum_{l=1}^{3}\phi(I_{l0}) - \sum_{l=1}^{3}\phi(R_{lm-1}), \tag{9.1}$$

where $W(R_{1k}) = \phi(F(R_{1k})) - \phi(R_{1k})$ is maximum if R_{lk}^* are expressed in terms of A_{1k}^* as

$$R_{lk}^* = \left[\frac{A_{lk}^*(1 - e^{-\theta(1+\beta)(P-t_\epsilon)})}{p(1 - e^{-\theta(P-t_\epsilon)})}\right], \tag{9.2}$$

where $A_{lk}^* = c/\delta(E_{lk}^*)^{\alpha-1}$, $l = 1, 2, 3$.

This determines finally the successive improvements in the diseased populations of the three generations, which are given by U_{lk}^*, $l = 1, 2, 3$; $k = 0, 1, 2, \ldots, m-2$.

10. Relation between prevalence rates of consecutive generations and effect on the prevalence rate of the same generation due to measures of control

We have already seen that the changes in the prevalence rates in the successive generations depend on the ratio of the susceptible and the diseased ones. It is expected that it should decrease if measures are taken to control the disease, but nothing could be concluded definitely. Now, we show that due to proper treatment of the diseased ones, the prevalence rate of the disease decreases definitely in any generation.

We note that the prevalence rate of the nth generation depends on the concentration of diseased and susceptible populations of $(n-1)$th generation. Let us assume that uI_{n-1}, $0 < u < 1$, is the net improvement in the diseased population during the given time of treatment. Then, the new prevalence rate r_N of the nth generation is given by $r_N = qb_1(1-u)I_{n-1}/((1-u)I_{n-1} + b_S S_{n-1})$. We like to show that $r_N < r_n$. In fact, we have

$$\begin{aligned} r_N - r_n &= \frac{qb_1(1-u)I_{n-1}}{(1-u)I_{n-1} + b_S S_{n-1}} - \frac{qb_I I_{n-1}}{b_I I_{n-1} + b_S S_{n-1}} \\ &= (qb_1 I_{n-1})\left[\frac{(1-u)}{b_I(1-u)I_{n-1} + b_S S_{n-1}} - \frac{1}{b_I I_{n-1} + b_S S_{s-1}}\right] \qquad (10.1) \\ &= \frac{(-ub_S S_{n-1})(qb_1 I_{n-1})}{(1-u)b_I I_{n-1} I_{n-1} + b_S S_{n-1}[b_I I_{n-1} + b_S S_{n-1}]} < 0. \end{aligned}$$

Thus $r_N < r_n$ for any nth stage.

11. Conclusion

(1) Experimentally, it is observed that the prevalence ratio is universally almost 6 : 1000. This fixed value occurs because it is calculated from the whole populations of different generations exposed during the period of observations. Had it been calculated for population of each generation exposed separately, the ratio might not be the same. Actually, this has been observed mathematically in (9.2).

(2) It is observed mathematically in (10.1) that by treating epileptic persons of a generation, not only the number of diseased persons but also the prevalence rate of the disease, which is a ratio, can also be reduced.

(3) It is shown mathematically that the whole program of treatment can be so carried out that under a given time and under a given budget, it runs in an economically viable way. This is really needed in the budget of any nation to minimize the virulence of a disease. Our model suits the case of vertically transmitted diseases only.

References

[1] S. Busenburg and K. Cooke, *Vertically Transmitted Diseases-Biomathematics*, vol. 23, Springer, New York, 1992.

[2] C. W. Clark, *Mathematical Bioeconomics. The Optimal Management of Renewable Resources*, Pure and Applied Mathematics (New York), John Wiley & Sons, New York, 1990.

[3] S. K. Das, A. Biswas, T. Roy, T. K. Banerjee, C. S. Mukherjee, D. K. Raut, and A. Chowdhuri, *Prevalence of major neurological disorders in the city of Kolkata — random sample survey*, to appear in Indian Journal of Medical Research.

[4] D. P. Heyman and M. J. Sobel, *Stochastic Model in Operation Research*, vol. 2, McGraw-Hill, New York, 1984.

[5] R. M. May, *Stability and Complexity in Model Ecosystems*, Monographs in Population Biology, vol. 6, Princeton University Press, Princeton, 1973.

[6] J. Maynard Smith, *Models in Ecology*, Cambridge University Press, Cambridge, 1971.

[7] ———, *Mathematical Ideas in Biology*, Cambridge University Press, Cambridge, 1974.

[8] A. J. Nicholson and V. A. Belly, *The balance of animal populations*, Proceedings of the Zoological Society of London **3** (1935), 551–598.

[9] G. Oster, *Stochastic behavior of deterministic models*, Ecosystem Analysis and Prediction (Proc. SIAM-SIMS Conf., Alta, Utah, 1974) (S. A. Levin, ed.), SIAM, Pennsylvania, 1974, pp. 24–37.

[10] P. A. Samuelson, *A catenary turnpike theorem involving consumption and the golden rule*, American Economic Review **55** (1965), 486–496.

[11] ———, *Foundations of Economic Analysis*, Harvard University Press, Cambridge, 1965.

D. K. Bhattacharya: Department of Pure Mathematics, University of Calcutta, Kolkata 700 019, India
E-mail address: dkb_math@yahoo.com

S. K. Das: Department of Neuromedicine, Bangur Institute of Neurology, Kolkata 700 025, India
E-mail address: das_sk70@hotmail.com

FIXED-SIGN EIGENFUNCTIONS OF TWO-POINT RIGHT FOCAL BOUNDARY VALUE PROBLEMS ON MEASURE CHAIN

K. L. BOEY AND PATRICIA J. Y. WONG

We consider the boundary value problem $(-1)^{n-1}y^{\Delta^n}(t) = \lambda(-1)^{p+1}F(t,y(\sigma^{n-1}(t)))$, $t \in [a,b] \cap \mathbf{T}$, $y^{\Delta^i}(a) = 0$, $0 \le i \le p-1$, $y^{\Delta^i}(\sigma(b)) = 0$, $p \le i \le n-1$, where $\lambda > 0$, $n \ge 2$, $1 \le p \le n-1$ is fixed, and $\mathbf{T}$ is a measure chain. The values of λ are characterized so that this problem has a fixed-sign solution. In addition, explicit intervals of λ are established.

1. Introduction

Throughout, for any c, d $(> c)$, the interval $[c,d]$ is defined as $[c,d] = \{t \in \mathbf{T} \mid c \le t \le d\}$. We also use the notation $\mathbb{R}[c,d]$ to denote the real interval $\{t \in \mathbb{R} \mid c \le t \le d\}$. Analogous notations for open and half-open intervals will also be used.

In this paper, we present results governing the existence of fixed-sign solutions to the differential equation on measure chains of the form

$$(-1)^{n-1}y^{\Delta^n}(t) = \lambda(-1)^{p+1}F(t,y(\sigma^{n-1}(t))), \quad t \in [a,b], \tag{1.1}$$

subject to the two-point right focal boundary conditions:

$$y^{\Delta^i}(a) = 0, \quad 0 \le i \le p-1, \qquad y^{\Delta^i}(\sigma(b)) = 0, \quad p \le i \le n-1, \tag{1.2}$$

where $\lambda > 0$, p,n are fixed integers satisfying $n \ge 2$, $1 \le p \le n-1$, $a,b \in \mathbf{T}$ with $a < \sigma(b)$ and $\rho(\sigma(b)) = b$ and $F : [a,b] \times \mathbb{R} \to \mathbb{R}$ is continuous.

A solution y of (1.1), (1.2) will be sought in $C[a,\sigma^n(b)]$, the space of continuous functions $\{y : [a,\sigma^n(b)] \to \mathbb{R}\}$. We say that y is a *fixed-sign solution* if $\mu y(t) \ge 0$ for $t \in [a,\sigma^n(b)]$, where $\mu \in \{-1,1\}$ is fixed. Note that positive solution (the usual consideration in the literature) is a special case of fixed-sign solution. If, for a particular λ, the boundary value problem (1.1), (1.2) has a fixed-sign solution y, then λ is called an

Hindawi Publishing Corporation
Proceedings of the Conference on Differential & Difference Equations and Applications, pp. 201–210

eigenvalue and y a corresponding *eigenfunction* of (1.1), (1.2). We let

$$E = \{\lambda > 0 \mid (1.1),\ (1.2) \text{ has a fixed-sign solution}\} \tag{1.3}$$

be the set of eigenvalues of the boundary value problem (1.1), (1.2).

The paper is outlined as follows. In Section 2, we will state Krasnosel'skiĭ fixed point theorem, and also present some properties of certain Green's function which are needed later. In Section 3, we show that the set of eigenvalues E is an interval and establish conditions under which E is a bounded or unbounded interval. The final section is concerned with the derivation of explicit eigenvalue intervals. Our approach and results in this work not only unifies the analysis for the real and the discrete cases in [3, 4], but also leads to *new* results which, when reduced to $\mathbb{R}$ and $\mathbb{Z}$, are also *new* in the literature.

2. Preliminaries

First, we state a fixed point theorem that is due to Krasnosel'skiĭ [2].

Theorem 2.1 [2]. *Let $B = (B, \|\cdot\|)$ be a Banach space, and let C ($\subset B$) be a cone. Assume Ω_1 and Ω_2 are open bounded subsets of B with $0 \in \Omega_1$, $\overline{\Omega}_1 \subset \Omega_2$, and let*

$$S : C \cap (\overline{\Omega}_2 \setminus \Omega_1) \longrightarrow C \tag{2.1}$$

be a continuous and completely continuous operator such that, either
(a) $\|Sy\| \le \|y\|$, $y \in C \cap \partial\Omega_1$, *and* $\|Sy\| \ge \|y\|$, $y \in C \cap \partial\Omega_2$, *or*
(b) $\|Sy\| \ge \|y\|$, $y \in C \cap \partial\Omega_1$, *and* $\|Sy\| \le \|y\|$, $y \in C \cap \partial\Omega_2$.
Then, S has a fixed point in $C \cap (\overline{\Omega}_2 \setminus \Omega_1)$.

To obtain a solution for (1.1), (1.2), we require a mapping whose kernel $G(t,s)$ is the Green's function of the boundary value problem (1.2):

$$(-1)^{n-1} y^{\Delta^n}(t) = 0, \quad t \in [a,b]. \tag{2.2}$$

Lemma 2.2 [1]. *For $(t,s) \in [a,\sigma^n(b)] \times [a,b]$,*

$$0 \le (-1)^{p+1} G(t,s) \le (-1)^{p+1} G(\sigma^n(b),s). \tag{2.3}$$

Throughout this paper, for a fixed number $\delta \in \mathbb{R}(0,1/2)$, we let

$$\begin{aligned} c &= \min\{t \in \mathbf{T} \mid t \ge a + \delta(\sigma^n(b) - a)\}, \\ d &= \max\{t \in \mathbf{T} \mid t \le \sigma^n(b) - \delta(\sigma^n(b) - a)\}, \end{aligned} \tag{2.4}$$

and assume the existence of c and d such that $a < c < \rho^{n-1}(d) < \sigma(b)$.

Lemma 2.3 [1]. *For $(t,s) \in [c,d] \times [a,b]$,*

$$(-1)^{p+1} G(t,s) \ge k(-1)^{p+1} G(\sigma^n(b),s), \tag{2.5}$$

where $0 < k < 1$ is a constant given by $k = \inf_{s \in [a,b]} G(c,s)/G(\sigma^n(b),s)$.

3. Characterization of eigenvalues

In this section, we provide conditions under which the set of eigenvalues E contains/is an interval. We list conditions that are needed later as follows. In these conditions, $\mu \in \{1,-1\}$ is fixed, f, u, v are continuous functions such that $u,v:[a,b]\to\mathbb{R}[0,\infty)$ and $f:\mathbb{R}[0,\infty)_\mu\to\mathbb{R}[0,\infty)$ where

$$\mathbb{R}[0,\infty)_\mu=\begin{cases}\mathbb{R}[0,\infty), & \mu=1,\\ \mathbb{R}(-\infty,0], & \mu=-1.\end{cases} \tag{3.1}$$

(A1) If $|x|\le|y|$, then $f(x)\le f(y)$.
(A2) For $\mu y\ge 0$ and $t\in[a,b]$, $\mu F(t,y)$ is nonnegative.
(A3) For $t\in[a,b]$ and $\mu y\ge 0$,

$$u(t)f(y(\sigma^{n-1}(t)))\le \mu F(t,y(\sigma^{n-1}(t)))\le v(t)f(y(\sigma^{n-1}(t))). \tag{3.2}$$

(A4) $u(t)$ is nonnegative and it is not identically zero on any nondegenerate subinterval of $[a,b]$, and there exists a number $\eta\in\mathbb{R}(0,1]$ such that $u(t)\ge\eta v(t)$ for $t\in[a,b]$.
(A5) If $|x|\le|y|$, then $\mu F(t,x)\le\mu F(t,y)$.
(A6) $\int_a^{\sigma(b)}(-1)^{p+1}G(\sigma^n(b),s)v(s)\Delta s<\infty$.

Further, we define the constant

$$\theta=k\eta, \tag{3.3}$$

where k is given in Lemma 2.3. It is clear that $0<\theta<1$.

We let the Banach space $B=C[a,\sigma^n(b)]$ be equipped with the norm

$$\|y\|=\sup_{t\in[a,\sigma^n(b)]}|y(t)|. \tag{3.4}$$

Let $\delta\in\mathbb{R}(0,1/2)$ be fixed, and define

$$C=\Big\{y\in B\mid \mu y(t)\ge 0,\ t\in[a,\sigma^n(b)];\ \min_{t\in[c,d]}\mu y(t)\ge\theta\|y\|\Big\}. \tag{3.5}$$

We note that C is a cone in B. Let the operator $S:C\to B$ be defined by

$$Sy(t)=\lambda\int_a^{\sigma(b)}(-1)^{p+1}G(t,s)F(s,y(\sigma^{n-1}(s)))\Delta s,\quad t\in[a,\sigma^n(b)]. \tag{3.6}$$

If (A2) and (A3) hold, then we have, for $\mu y\ge 0$ and $t\in[a,\sigma^n(b)]$,

$$\begin{aligned}&\lambda\int_a^{\sigma(b)}(-1)^{p+1}G(t,s)u(s)f(y(\sigma^{n-1}(s)))\Delta s\\ &\quad\le\mu Sy(t)\le\lambda\int_a^{\sigma(b)}(-1)^{p+1}G(t,s)v(s)f(y(\sigma^{n-1}(s)))\Delta s.\end{aligned} \tag{3.7}$$

To obtain a fixed-sign solution of (1.1), (1.2), we seek a fixed point of S in the cone C.

LEMMA 3.1 [1]. *The operator $S : C \to B$ is continuous and completely continuous.*

LEMMA 3.2. *Let (A2)–(A4) hold. Then, the operator S maps C into C.*

Proof. The proof of the result is similar to that in [1]. □

THEOREM 3.3. *Let (A2)–(A4) and (A6) hold. Then, there exists a constant $r > 0$ such that the real interval $\mathbb{R}(0,r] \subseteq E$.*

Proof. Let $L > 0$ be given and $C(L) = \{y \in C \mid \|y\| \le L\}$. Define

$$r = \frac{L}{\sup_{x\in\mathbb{R}[-L,L]} f(x)} \left[\int_a^{\sigma(b)} (-1)^{p+1} G(\sigma^n(b),s)v(s)\Delta s \right]^{-1}. \tag{3.8}$$

Let $\lambda \in \mathbb{R}(0,r]$ and $y \in C(L)$. By Lemma 3.2, S maps C into C. Next, by using (3.7), Lemma 2.2, and (3.8), we get, for $t \in [a,\sigma^n(b)]$,

$$\begin{aligned} |Sy(t)| = \mu Sy(t) &\le \lambda \int_a^{\sigma(b)} (-1)^{p+1} G(\sigma^n(b),s)v(s)f(y(\sigma^{n-1}(s)))\Delta s \\ &\le r\Big(\sup_{x\in\mathbb{R}[-L,L]} f(x)\Big) \int_a^{\sigma(b)} (-1)^{p+1} G(\sigma^n(b),s)v(s)\Delta s = L. \end{aligned} \tag{3.9}$$

Thus, $\|Sy\| \le L$. We have shown that $S(C(L)) \subseteq C(L)$. From Lemma 3.1, S is continuous and completely continuous. By Schauder fixed point theorem, S has a fixed point in $C(L)$. It is clear that this fixed point is a fixed-sign solution of (1.1), (1.2) and hence λ is an eigenvalue of (1.1), (1.2). Since $\lambda \in \mathbb{R}(0,r]$ is arbitrary, it follows that $\mathbb{R}(0,r] \subseteq E$. □

The next result uses the monotonicity and compactness of the operator S on the cone C.

THEOREM 3.4. *Let (A2) and (A5) hold. If $\lambda_0 \in E$, then, for each $0 < \lambda < \lambda_0$, $\lambda \in E$.*

Proof. Let y_0 be the eigenfunction corresponding to the eigenvalue λ_0. Then

$$y_0(t) = \lambda_0 \int_a^{\sigma(b)} (-1)^{p+1} G(t,s)F(s,y_0(\sigma^{n-1}(s)))\Delta s, \quad t \in [a,\sigma^n(b)]. \tag{3.10}$$

For $y \in K$, where $K = \{y \in B \mid 0 \le \mu y(t) \le \mu y_0(t),\ t \in [a,\sigma^n(b)]\}$, $\lambda \in \mathbb{R}(0,\lambda_0)$, and $t \in [a,\sigma^n(b)]$, we have

$$\begin{aligned} |Sy(t)| = \mu Sy(t) &= \mu\lambda \int_a^{\sigma(b)} (-1)^{p+1} G(t,s)F(s,y(\sigma^{n-1}(s)))\Delta s \\ &\le \mu\lambda_0 \int_a^{\sigma(b)} (-1)^{p+1} G(t,s)F(s,y_0(\sigma^{n-1}(s)))\Delta s = \mu y_0(t). \end{aligned} \tag{3.11}$$

Hence, S maps K into K. Moreover, since S is continuous and completely continuous, Schauder fixed point theorem guarantees that S has a fixed point in K, which is a fixed-sign solution of (1.1), (1.2). Thus λ is an eigenvalue of (1.1), (1.2). □

As a result, we arrive at the following corollary.

COROLLARY 3.5. *Let (A2) and (A5) hold. If E is nonempty, then E is an interval.*

We now establish conditions under which E is a bounded or unbounded interval. We will prove the following results.

THEOREM 3.6. *Let (A1)–(A3) and (A6) hold. Let λ be an eigenvalue of (1.1), (1.2) and let $y \in C$ be a corresponding eigenfunction. Further, let $\|y\| = q$. Then*

$$\lambda \geq \frac{q}{f(q)} \left[\int_a^{\sigma(b)} (-1)^{p+1} G(\sigma^n(b), s) v(s) \Delta s \right]^{-1}, \tag{3.12}$$

$$\lambda \leq \frac{q}{f(\theta q)} \left[\int_a^{\rho^{n-1}(d)} k(-1)^{p+1} G(\sigma^n(b), s) u(s) \Delta s \right]^{-1}. \tag{3.13}$$

Proof. Let $t_0 \in [a, \sigma^n(b)]$ be such that $q = \|y\| = \mu y(t_0)$. Applying Lemma 2.2, (3.7), and (A1), we find

$$q = \mu y(t_0) = \mu(Sy)(t_0) \leq \lambda f(q) \int_a^{\sigma(b)} (-1)^{p+1} G(\sigma^n(b), s) v(s) \Delta s, \tag{3.14}$$

which is (3.12).

Next, using $\mu y(s) \geq \theta \|y\| = \theta q$ for $s \in [c, d]$, we have

$$\mu y(\sigma^{n-1}(s)) \geq \theta q, \quad s \in [c, \rho^{n-1}(d)]. \tag{3.15}$$

In view of (3.7), Lemma 2.3, and (A1), it follows that

$$\begin{aligned} q \geq \mu y(c) &\geq \lambda \int_c^{\rho^{n-1}(d)} (-1)^{p+1} G(c, s) u(s) f(y(\sigma^{n-1}(s))) \Delta s \\ &\geq \lambda \int_c^{\rho^{n-1}(d)} k(-1)^{p+1} G(\sigma^n(b), s) u(s) f(\theta q) \Delta s, \end{aligned} \tag{3.16}$$

which is (3.13). □

THEOREM 3.7. *Let (A1)–(A6) hold. Define*

$$\begin{aligned} F_B &= \left\{ f : \mathbb{R}[0, \infty)_\mu \longrightarrow \mathbb{R}[0, \infty) \;\middle|\; \frac{|u|}{f(u)} \text{ is bounded for } u \in \mathbb{R}[0, \infty)_\mu \right\}, \\ F_0 &= \left\{ f : \mathbb{R}[0, \infty)_\mu \longrightarrow \mathbb{R}[0, \infty) \;\middle|\; \lim_{|u| \to \infty} \frac{|u|}{f(u)} = 0 \right\}, \\ F_\infty &= \left\{ f : \mathbb{R}[0, \infty)_\mu \longrightarrow \mathbb{R}[0, \infty) \;\middle|\; \lim_{|u| \to \infty} \frac{|u|}{f(u)} = \infty \right\}. \end{aligned} \tag{3.17}$$

(a) *If $f \in F_B$, then $E = \mathbb{R}(0, r)$ or $\mathbb{R}(0, r]$ for some $r \in \mathbb{R}(0, \infty)$.*
(b) *If $f \in F_0$, then $E = \mathbb{R}(0, r]$ for some $r \in \mathbb{R}(0, \infty)$.*
(c) *If $f \in F_\infty$, then $E = \mathbb{R}(0, \infty)$.*

Proof. (a) This is immediate from (3.13) and Corollary 3.5.

(b) Here, we have $F_0 \subseteq F_B$. By Theorem 3.7(a), $E = \mathbb{R}(0,r)$ or $\mathbb{R}(0,r]$ for some $r \in \mathbb{R}(0,\infty)$. In particular, $r = \sup E$.

Let $\{\lambda_n\}_{n=1}^{\infty}$ be a monotonically increasing sequence in E, with $\lim_{n\to\infty}\lambda_n = r$, and let $\{y_n\}_{n=1}^{\infty}$ in $\tilde{K} = \{y \in B \mid \mu y(t) \geq 0,\ t \in [a,\sigma^n(b)]\}$ be a corresponding sequence of eigenfunctions. We write $q_n = \|y_n\|$. Then, (3.13) together with $f \in F_0$ implies that no subsequence of $\{q_n\}$ can diverge. Thus, there exists $L > 0$ such that $q_n \leq L$ for all n. So $\|y_n\| \leq L$ for every n and $\{y_n\}_{n=1}^{\infty}$ is uniformly bounded. Hence there exists a subsequence of $\{y_n\}_{n=1}^{\infty}$ relabeled as the original sequence such that it converges to $y(\in \tilde{K})$ uniformly. Thus,

$$y_n(t) = \lambda_n \int_a^{\sigma(b)} (-1)^{p+1} G(t,s) F\big(s, y_n(\sigma^{n-1}(s))\big)\Delta s, \quad t \in [a,\sigma^n(b)]. \tag{3.18}$$

Letting $n \to \infty$ in the above inequality gives

$$y(t) = r \int_a^{\sigma(b)} (-1)^{p+1} G(t,s) F\big(s, y(\sigma^{n-1}(s))\big)\Delta s, \quad t \in [a,\sigma^n(b)]. \tag{3.19}$$

This shows that r is an eigenvalue with corresponding eigenfunction y. So $r = \sup E \in E$ and hence $E = \mathbb{R}(0,r]$.

(c) Let $\lambda > 0$ be fixed. Choose $\epsilon > 0$ such that

$$\lambda \int_a^{\sigma(b)} (-1)^{p+1} G(\sigma^n(b),s) v(s)\Delta s \leq \frac{1}{\epsilon}. \tag{3.20}$$

Since $f \in F_\infty$, there exists $M = M(\epsilon) > 0$ such that for $|u| \geq M$,

$$f(u) < \epsilon |u|. \tag{3.21}$$

Let $y \in C(M) = \{y \in C \mid \|y\| \leq M\}$. By Lemma 3.2, we have $Sy \in C$. We use (3.7), Lemma 2.2, (A1), (3.21), and (3.20) to get, for $t \in [a,\sigma^n(b)]$,

$$\begin{aligned} |Sy(t)| = \mu Sy(t) &\leq \lambda \int_a^{\sigma(b)} (-1)^{p+1} G(\sigma^n(b),s) f(M) v(s)\Delta s \\ &\leq \lambda\epsilon M \int_a^{\sigma(b)} (-1)^{p+1} G(\sigma^n(b),s) v(s)\Delta s \leq M. \end{aligned} \tag{3.22}$$

Thus, $\|Sy\| \leq M$ and so $S(C(M)) \subseteq C(M)$. Since S is continuous and completely continuous, Schauder fixed point theorem guarantees that S has a fixed point in $C(M)$. This fixed point is a fixed-sign solution of (1.1), (1.2) and hence λ is an eigenvalue of (1.1), (1.2). Since $\lambda > 0$ is arbitrary, therefore, $E = \mathbb{R}(0,\infty)$. □

Example 3.8. Let $m \in \mathbb{R}^+$ and $\mathbf{T} = m\mathbb{Z}$. Consider the boundary value problem

$$y^{\Delta^3}(t) = \frac{\lambda(9y+2)^r}{\left(9\sigma^2(t)\{3\sigma(b)[\sigma(b)-t]+t\sigma(t)\}+2\right)^r}, \quad t \in [0,b],$$
$$y(0) = y^{\Delta}(\sigma(b)) = y^{\Delta^2}(\sigma(b)) = 0, \tag{3.23}$$

where $\lambda > 0$, $r \geq 0$, and $b \in \mathbf{T}$.

In this example, $n = 3$ and $p = 1$. Fix $\mu = 1$. We take $f(y) = (9y+2)^r$ and choose $u(t) = v(t) = [(9\sigma^2(t)\{3\sigma(b)[\sigma(b)-t]+t\sigma(t)\}+2)^r]^{-1}$. Then, conditions (A1)–(A6) are satisfied, and we have $y/f(y) = y/(9y+2)^r$.

Case 1 ($0 \leq r < 1$). Since $f \in F_\infty$, by Theorem 3.7(c), the set $E = \mathbb{R}(0,\infty)$. Note that when $\lambda = 6$, the boundary value problem has a fixed-sign solution given by $y(t) = t\{3\sigma(b)[\sigma^3(b) - t] + \rho(t)\rho^2(t)\}$. It is easy to obtain $y^{\Delta}(t) = 3\sigma(b)(\sigma^2(b)-2t)+3t\rho(t)$ and $y^{\Delta^2}(t) = 6(t - \sigma(b))$.

Case 2 ($r = 1$). Since $f \in F_B$, by Theorem 3.7(a), the set $E = \mathbb{R}(0,c)$ or $\mathbb{R}(0,c]$ for some real value c. From Case 1 and Theorem 3.4, E contains $\mathbb{R}(0,6]$.

Case 3 ($r > 1$). Since $f \in F_0$, by Theorem 3.7(b), the set $E = \mathbb{R}(0,c]$ for some real c. From Case 1 and Theorem 3.4, $\mathbb{R}(0,6] \subseteq E$.

4. Intervals of eigenvalues

In this section, we will employ Krasnosel'skiĭ fixed point theorem [2] to derive explicit eigenvalue intervals. We introduce the notations

$$\underline{f}_0 = \liminf_{|x|\to 0} \frac{f(x)}{|x|}, \qquad \overline{f}_0 = \limsup_{|x|\to 0} \frac{f(x)}{|x|},$$
$$\underline{f}_\infty = \liminf_{|x|\to \infty} \frac{f(x)}{|x|}, \qquad \overline{f}_\infty = \limsup_{|x|\to \infty} \frac{f(x)}{|x|}. \tag{4.1}$$

Theorem 4.1. *Let (A2)–(A4) and (A6) hold. Then, for each λ satisfying*

$$L < \lambda < R, \tag{4.2}$$

where $L = [\theta\underline{f}_\infty \int_c^{\rho^{n-1}(d)}(-1)^{p+1}G(\sigma^n(b),s)u(s)\Delta s]^{-1}$ and $R = [\overline{f}_0 \int_a^{\sigma(b)}(-1)^{p+1}G(\sigma^n(b), s)v(s)\Delta s]^{-1}$, the boundary value problem (1.1), (1.2) has a fixed-sign solution.

Proof. Let $L < \lambda < R$ and let $\epsilon > 0$ be such that

$$\left[\theta(\underline{f}_\infty - \epsilon)\int_c^{\rho^{n-1}(d)}(-1)^{p+1}G(\sigma^n(b),s)u(s)\Delta s\right]^{-1}$$
$$\leq \lambda \leq \left[(\overline{f}_0 + \epsilon)\int_a^{\sigma(b)}(-1)^{p+1}G(\sigma^n(b),s)v(s)\Delta s\right]^{-1}. \tag{4.3}$$

Next, we choose $w > 0$ so that

$$f(x) \leq (\overline{f}_0 + \epsilon)|x|, \quad 0 < |x| \leq w. \tag{4.4}$$

Let $y \in C$ be such that $\|y\| = w$. Then applying (3.7), Lemma 2.2, (4.4), and (4.3), we find that, for $t \in [a, \sigma^n(b)]$,

$$\begin{aligned} |Sy(t)| &\leq \lambda \int_a^{\sigma(b)} (-1)^{p+1} G(\sigma^n(b), s) v(s) (\overline{f}_0 + \epsilon) |y(\sigma^{n-1}(s))| \Delta s \\ &\leq \lambda (\overline{f}_0 + \epsilon) \|y\| \int_a^{\sigma(b)} (-1)^{p+1} G(\sigma^n(b), s) v(s) \Delta s \leq \|y\|. \end{aligned} \tag{4.5}$$

Hence,

$$\|Sy\| \leq \|y\|. \tag{4.6}$$

If we set $\Omega_1 = \{y \in B \mid \|y\| < w\}$, then (4.6) holds for $y \in C \cap \partial\Omega_1$.

Further, we let $T_1 > w > 0$ be such that

$$f(x) \geq \left(\underline{f}_\infty - \epsilon\right)|x|, \quad |x| \geq T_1. \tag{4.7}$$

Let $y \in C$ be such that $\|y\| = T_1/\theta$. Then, for $t \in [c, d]$,

$$|y(t)| = \mu y(t) \geq \theta \|y\| \geq \theta \cdot \frac{T_1}{\theta} = T_1, \tag{4.8}$$

which, by (4.7), leads to

$$f(y(\sigma^{n-1}(t))) \geq \left(\underline{f}_\infty - \epsilon\right) |y(\sigma^{n-1}(t))|, \quad t \in [c, \rho^{n-1}(d)]. \tag{4.9}$$

Using (3.7), (4.9), and (4.3),

$$\begin{aligned} |Sy(\sigma^n(b))| &= \mu(Sy)(\sigma^n(b)) \\ &\geq \lambda \int_c^{\rho^{n-1}(d)} (-1)^{p+1} G(\sigma^n(b), s) u(s) \left(\underline{f}_\infty - \epsilon\right) |y(\sigma^{n-1}(s))| \Delta s \\ &\geq \lambda \left(\underline{f}_\infty - \epsilon\right) \theta \|y\| \int_c^{\rho^{n-1}(d)} (-1)^{p+1} G(\sigma^n(b), s) u(s) \Delta s \geq \|y\|. \end{aligned} \tag{4.10}$$

Therefore,

$$\|Sy\| \geq \|y\|. \tag{4.11}$$

If we set $\Omega_2 = \{y \in B \mid \|y\| < T_1/\theta\}$, then (4.11) holds for $y \in C \cap \partial\Omega_2$.

With (4.6) and (4.11), it follows from Theorem 2.1 that S has a fixed point $y \in C \cap (\overline{\Omega}_2 \setminus \Omega_1)$ such that $w \leq \|y\| \leq T_1/\theta$. It is obvious that y is a fixed-sign solution of (1.1), (1.2). □

The following result is immediate from Theorem 4.1.

Corollary 4.2. *Let (A2)–(A4) and (A6) hold. Then,*

$$\mathbb{R}(L,R) \subseteq E, \tag{4.12}$$

where L and R are defined in Theorem 4.1.

Theorem 4.3. *Let (A2)–(A4) and (A6) hold. Then, for each λ satisfying*

$$L' < \lambda < R', \tag{4.13}$$

where $L' = [\theta \underline{f}_0 \int_c^{\rho^{n-1}(d)} (-1)^{p+1} G(\sigma^n(b),s)u(s)\Delta s]^{-1}$ *and* $R' = [\overline{f}_\infty \int_a^{\sigma(b)} (-1)^{p+1} G(\sigma^n(b), s)v(s)\Delta s]^{-1}$, *the boundary value problem (1.1), (1.2) has a fixed-sign solution.*

Proof. Let $L' < \lambda < R'$. We let $\epsilon > 0$ be such that

$$\begin{aligned} &\left[\theta\left(\underline{f}_0 - \epsilon\right) \int_c^{\rho^{n-1}(d)} (-1)^{p+1} G(\sigma^n(b),s) u(s)\Delta s\right]^{-1} \\ &\qquad \le \lambda \le \left[\left(\overline{f}_\infty + \epsilon\right) \int_a^{\sigma(b)} (-1)^{p+1} G(\sigma^n(b),s) v(s)\Delta s\right]^{-1}. \end{aligned} \tag{4.14}$$

Let $\overline{w} > 0$ be such that

$$f(x) \ge \left(\underline{f}_0 - \epsilon\right)|x|, \quad 0 < |x| \le \overline{w}. \tag{4.15}$$

Let $y \in C$ be such that $\|y\| = \overline{w}$. Applying (3.7), (4.15), and (4.14), using the same argument as in proving (4.11) in Theorem 4.1, we have

$$\|Sy\| \ge \|y\|. \tag{4.16}$$

If we set $\Omega_1 = \{y \in B \mid \|y\| < \overline{w}\}$, then $\|Sy\| \ge \|y\|$ holds for $y \in C \cap \partial\Omega_1$.

Next, we choose $T_2 > 0$ such that

$$f(x) \le \left(\overline{f}_\infty + \epsilon\right)|x|, \quad |x| \ge T_2. \tag{4.17}$$

We will consider two cases, f is bounded and f is unbounded.

Case 1. Suppose f is bounded, that is, there exists $M^* > 0$ such that

$$f(x) \le M^*, \quad x \in \mathbb{R}. \tag{4.18}$$

We define $T_3 = \max\{2\overline{w}, \lambda M^* \int_a^{\sigma(b)} (-1)^{p+1} G(\sigma^n(b),s)v(s)\Delta s\}$ and let $y \in C$ be such that $\|y\| = T_3$. From Lemma 2.2, (3.7), and (4.18), for $t \in [a,\sigma^n(b)]$,

$$|Sy(t)| = \mu(Sy)(t) \le \lambda M^* \int_a^{\sigma(b)} (-1)^{p+1} G(\sigma^n(b),s) v(s)\Delta s \le T_3 = \|y\|. \tag{4.19}$$

Therefore, $\|Sy\| \le \|y\|$.

Case 2. Suppose f is unbounded. Then there exists $T_3 > \max\{2\overline{w}, T_2\}$ such that

$$f(x) \le f(T_3), \quad 0 < |x| \le T_3. \tag{4.20}$$

Let $y \in C$ be such that $\|y\| = T_3$. Applying Lemma 2.2, (4.20), (4.17), and (4.14), we find, for $t \in [a, \sigma^n(b)]$,

$$\begin{aligned} |Sy(t)| = \mu(Sy)(t) &\le \lambda \int_a^{\sigma(b)} (-1)^{p+1} G(\sigma^n(b), s) v(s) f(T_3) \Delta s \\ &\le \lambda \int_a^{\sigma(b)} (-1)^{p+1} G(\sigma^n(b), s) v(s) (\overline{f}_\infty + \epsilon) T_3 \Delta s \\ &= \lambda (\overline{f}_\infty + \epsilon) \|y\| \int_a^{\sigma(b)} (-1)^{p+1} G(\sigma^n(b), s) v(s) \Delta s \le \|y\|. \end{aligned} \tag{4.21}$$

Once again, we have $\|Sy\| \le \|y\|$.

In both cases, if we set $\Omega_2 = \{y \in B \mid \|y\| < T_3\}$, then $\|Sy\| \le \|y\|$ holds for $y \in C \cap \partial\Omega_2$.

It now follows from Theorem 2.1 that S has a fixed point $y \in C \cap (\overline{\Omega}_2 \setminus \Omega_1)$ such that $\overline{w} \le \|y\| \le T_3$, and y is a fixed-sign solution of (1.1), (1.2). □

From the preceding theorem, we obtain the following corollary.

Corollary 4.4. *Let (A2)–(A4) and (A6) hold. Then,*

$$\mathbb{R}(L', R') \subseteq E, \tag{4.22}$$

where L' and R' are defined in Theorem 4.3.

Remark 4.5. If f is superlinear (i.e., $\overline{f}_0 = 0$ and $\underline{f}_\infty = \infty$) or sublinear (i.e., $\underline{f}_0 = \infty$ and $\overline{f}_\infty = 0$), we conclude from Corollaries 4.2 and 4.4, respectively, that $E = \mathbb{R}(0, \infty)$. Thus the boundary value problem (1.1), (1.2) has a fixed-sign solution for any positive λ.

References

[1] K. L. Boey and P. J. Y. Wong, *Two-point right focal eigenvalue problems on time scales*, Applied Mathematics and Computation **167** (2005), no. 2, 1281–1303.

[2] M. A. Krasnosel'skiĭ, *Positive Solutions of Operator Equations*, P. Noordhoff, Groningen, 1964.

[3] P. J. Y. Wong, *Two-point right focal eigenvalue problems for difference equations*, Dynamic Systems and Applications **7** (1998), no. 3, 345–364.

[4] P. J. Y. Wong and R. P. Agarwal, *On two-point right focal eigenvalue problems*, Zeitschrift für Analysis und ihre Anwendungen **17** (1998), no. 3, 691–713.

K. L. Boey: School of Electrical and Electronic Engineering, Nanyang Technological University, 50 Nanyang Avenue, Singapore 639798
E-mail address: boey_kok_leong@moe.gov.sg

Patricia J. Y. Wong: School of Electrical and Electronic Engineering, Nanyang Technological University, 50 Nanyang Avenue, Singapore 639798
E-mail address: ejywong@ntu.edu.sg

LOWER BOUND FOR THE EIGENVALUES OF QUASILINEAR HILL'S EQUATION

G. BOGNÁR

We consider the eigenvalues of the one-dimensional p-Laplacian with potential $Q(t)$ of the form $y''|y'|^{p-2}+[\lambda+Q(t)]y|y|^{p-2}=0$, $p>1$, with periodic or antiperiodic boundary conditions. The purpose of this paper is to give a lower bound on λ depending only on properties of $Q(t)$ in order to get eigenvalues slightly larger than the pth power of certain integers.

1. Introduction

We consider the quasilinear differential equation of the form

$$y''|y'|^{p-2}+[\lambda+Q(t)]y|y|^{p-2}=0, \quad p>1, \tag{1.1}$$

where $p>1$, λ is a parameter, and $Q(t)$ is a real periodic function of t with period T. In [3], Elbert established the existence and uniqueness of solutions to the initial value problem for this equation.

If $\lambda=1$ and $Q(t)\equiv 0$, then the solution of

$$y''|y'|^{p-2}+y|y|^{p-2}=0 \tag{1.2}$$

with the initial conditions $y(0)=0$, $y'(0)=1$, is called the generalized sine function:

$$y=S_p(t), \quad t\in(-\infty,+\infty) \tag{1.3}$$

introduced by Elbert in [3]. For $t\in[0,\hat{\pi}/2]$, where $\hat{\pi}/2=(\pi/p)/\sin(\pi/p)$, function S_p satisfies

$$t=\int_0^{S_p}\frac{dy}{\sqrt[p]{1-y^p}}. \tag{1.4}$$

Hindawi Publishing Corporation
Proceedings of the Conference on Differential & Difference Equations and Applications, pp. 211–219

We extend S_p to all $\mathbb{R}$ (and still denote this extension by S_p) in the following form:

$$
\begin{aligned}
S_p(t) &= S_p(\hat{\pi} - t) \quad \text{for } t \in \left[\frac{\hat{\pi}}{2}, \hat{\pi}\right], \\
S_p(t) &= -S_p(-t) \quad \text{for } t \in [-\hat{\pi}, 0], \\
S_p(t) &= S_p(t + 2\hat{\pi}) \quad \text{for } t \in \mathbb{R}.
\end{aligned}
\tag{1.5}
$$

From (1.2) we have that

$$|S_p(t)|^p + |S_p'(t)|^p = 1 \quad \forall t \in \mathbb{R}. \tag{1.6}$$

If $p = 2$, then

$$S_2(x) = \sin x, \qquad \hat{\pi} = \pi, \tag{1.7}$$

and (1.6) is equivalent to $\sin^2 t + \cos^2 t = 1$. Moreover differential equation (1.1) has the form

$$y'' + [\lambda + Q(t)]y = 0, \tag{1.8}$$

called Hill's equation. Different approaches to the investigation of (1.8) have been developed in [2, 4, 6].

Let us assume that $Q(t)$ is periodic function with period $\hat{\pi}$. First we consider the periodic solutions of the periodic problem (1.1) with conditions

$$y(\hat{\pi}, \lambda) = y(0, \lambda), \qquad y'(\hat{\pi}, \lambda) = y'(0, \lambda), \tag{1.9}$$

and then the solutions of the antiperiodic problem (1.1) with conditions

$$y(\hat{\pi}, \tilde{\lambda}) = -y(0, \tilde{\lambda}), \qquad y'(\hat{\pi}, \tilde{\lambda}) = -y'(0, \tilde{\lambda}). \tag{1.10}$$

The values λ and $\tilde{\lambda}$ are called eigenvalues corresponding to the periodic or antiperiodic problem. To both problems there exist two monotonically increasing infinite sequences of real numbers:

$$\lambda_0, \lambda_1, \lambda_2, \ldots, \lambda_k, \ldots, \qquad \tilde{\lambda}_1, \tilde{\lambda}_2, \ldots, \tilde{\lambda}_k, \ldots, \tag{1.11}$$

such that (1.1) with (1.9) has the solution of period $\hat{\pi}$ if $\lambda = \lambda_k$, $k = 0, 1, 2, \ldots$, and the solution of period $2\hat{\pi}$ if $\tilde{\lambda} = \tilde{\lambda}_k$, $k = 1, 2, 3, \ldots$. Values λ, called eigenvalues, satisfy the inequalities

$$\lambda_0 \leq \lambda_1 \leq \lambda_2 \leq \cdots \leq \lambda_k \leq \cdots \tag{1.12}$$

accumulating at ∞, and the eigenvalues $\tilde{\lambda}$ of the antiperiodic problem satisfy

$$\tilde{\lambda}_1 \le \tilde{\lambda}_2 \le \cdots \le \tilde{\lambda}_k \le \cdots \tag{1.13}$$

accumulating at ∞ [7].

If we assume that $Q(t)$ is periodic with period $\hat{\pi}$, has mean value 0, and its second derivative exists and continuous, then the asymptotic form of the large characteristic values was obtained in [1]. The asymptotic formula implies that for values λ_k and $\tilde{\lambda}_k$ corresponding to solution (1.1) with conditions (1.9) and (1.10), respectively, for large values of k,

$$\begin{gathered}
\sqrt[p+1]{\lambda_{2k-1}} - 2k = O\left(\frac{1}{k^{\nu}}\right), \\
\sqrt[p+1]{\lambda_{2k}} - 2k = O\left(\frac{1}{k^{\nu}}\right), \\
\sqrt[p+1]{\tilde{\lambda}_{2k-1}} - (2k-1) = O\left(\frac{1}{k^{\nu}}\right), \\
\sqrt[p+1]{\tilde{\lambda}_{2k}} - (2k-1) = O\left(\frac{1}{k^{\nu}}\right),
\end{gathered} \tag{1.14}$$

where

$$\nu = \begin{cases} 2p-1 & \text{if } 1 < p < 2, \\ p+1 & \text{if } p \ge 2. \end{cases} \tag{1.15}$$

The question arises that how large is the "large" eigenvalue has to be. The purpose of this paper is to show that for "large" λ and $\tilde{\lambda}$, the eigenvalues concerning the periodic and antiperiodic conditions are slightly larger than the pth power of certain integers. We intend to generalize the method and results obtained by Hochstadt for Hill's equation [5].

It was showed in [6, Theorem 6.4] if $p = 2$, then for the π periodic solutions of (1.8)

$$\lambda_0 + \sum_{k=1}^{\infty} (\lambda_{2k-1} + \lambda_{2k} - 8k^2) = 0, \tag{1.16}$$

and for the 2π periodic solutions

$$\sum_{k=1}^{\infty} (\tilde{\lambda}_{2k-1} + \tilde{\lambda}_{2k} - 2(2k-1)^2) = 0. \tag{1.17}$$

Therefore for some λ and $\tilde{\lambda}$, the eigenvalues are slightly smaller than the squares of integers.

2. Results

We may write the solution of (1.1) and its derivative such as

$$\begin{aligned} y(t,\lambda) &= A(t)S_p(\varphi(t)),\\ y'(t,\lambda) &= \sqrt[p]{\lambda+Q(t)}A(t,\lambda)S_p'(\varphi(t,\lambda)), \end{aligned} \tag{2.1}$$

where the functions $A(t)$ and $\varphi(t)$ are determined by their initial values and the system of differential equations,

$$\varphi'(t,\lambda) = \sqrt[p]{\lambda+Q(t)} + \frac{1}{p}\frac{Q'(t)}{\lambda+Q(t)}G(\varphi(t,\lambda)), \tag{2.2}$$

$$\frac{A'(t,\lambda)}{A(t,\lambda)} = -\frac{1}{p}\frac{Q'(t)}{\lambda+Q(t)}\left|S_p(\varphi(t,\lambda))\right|^p, \tag{2.3}$$

where $G(\varphi) = S_p(\varphi(t,\lambda))|S_p'(\varphi(t,\lambda))|^{p-2}S_p'(\varphi(t,\lambda))$.

The differential equations (2.2) and (2.3) together with (1.1) imply (2.1), and vice versa.

We consider the eigenvalues λ with respect to the periodic boundary conditions (1.9) with period $\hat{\pi}$, and the eigenvalues $\tilde{\lambda}$ to the antiperiodic boundary condition (1.10).

In the first case, we have from (2.1) that

$$A(\hat{\pi},\lambda) = A(0), \qquad \varphi(\hat{\pi},\lambda) - \varphi(0,\lambda) = 2k\hat{\pi}, \tag{2.4}$$

where k is a nonnegative integer. In the second case, we derive from (1.10) that

$$A(\hat{\pi},\tilde{\lambda}) = A(0,\tilde{\lambda}), \qquad \varphi(\hat{\pi},\tilde{\lambda}) - \varphi(0,\tilde{\lambda}) = (2k-1)\hat{\pi}, \tag{2.5}$$

where k is a positive integer.

Proposition 2.1. *For $G(\tau) = S_p(\tau)|S_p'(\tau)|^{p-2}S_p'(\tau)$, the estimation*

$$\left|G'(\tau)\right| \le \max\left(1,|1-p|\right) \tag{2.6}$$

is valid.

Proof. By differentiation, we obtain

$$G'(\tau) = \left|S_p'(\tau)\right|^p + (p-1)S_p(\tau)\left|S_p'(\tau)\right|^{p-2}S_p''(\tau). \tag{2.7}$$

Applying (1.6) with (1.2), we get that

$$G'(\tau) = 1 - p\left|S_p(\tau)\right|^p \tag{2.8}$$

from which (2.6) can be obtained. □

LEMMA 2.2. *Let M be a uniform bound for $|Q|$, $|Q'|$, and let $\lambda > M + (1 + M/p^2)^p$, then*

$$|\varphi'|_{\min} > \beta(\lambda - M)^{1/p}, \tag{2.9}$$

where $\beta = [1 - (p/(p+1))^{p+1}]$.

Proof. We get an estimate on φ' from (2.2):

$$|\varphi'|_{\min} > (\lambda - M)^{1/p} - \frac{1}{p}\frac{M}{\lambda - M}. \tag{2.10}$$

Since

$$\left(1 + \frac{M}{p^2}\right)^p \geq \left(\frac{p+1}{p}\right)^p \left(\frac{M}{p}\right)^{p/(p+1)} \tag{2.11}$$

for any $p > 1$ and $M > 0$, with equality only if $M = p$, with the assumption on λ and (2.11), we have

$$\lambda > M + \left(1 + \frac{M}{p^2}\right)^p \geq M + \left(\frac{p+1}{p}\right)^p \left(\frac{M}{p}\right)^{p/(p+1)} \tag{2.12}$$

from which inequality (2.9) follows. □

Next we can obtain an upper bound for $|\varphi'|$.

LEMMA 2.3. *Let M be a uniform bound for $|Q|$, $|Q'|$, and let $\lambda > M + (1 + M/p^2)^p$, then for function φ' inequality*

$$|\varphi'| < (\lambda - M)^{1/p} + \frac{M}{p} \tag{2.13}$$

is satisfied.

Proof. From (2.12) it follows that $\lambda - M > 1$, and from (2.2) we obtain the estimate (2.13) on $|\varphi'|$. □

LEMMA 2.4. *Let M be a uniform bound for $|Q|$, $|Q'|$, $|Q''|$, and let $\lambda > M + (1 + M/p^2)^p$, then*

$$|\varphi''| < (\lambda - M)^{-1/p+1}\left[(2+\rho)\frac{M}{p} + (p+\rho)\frac{M^2}{p^2}\right], \tag{2.14}$$

where $\rho = \max(1, |1 - p|)$.

Proof. From (2.2) we get

$$\begin{aligned} \varphi'' &= \frac{1}{p}\frac{Q'(t)}{(\lambda + Q(t))^{-1/p+1}} + \frac{1}{p}\frac{Q''(t)}{\lambda + Q(t)}G(\varphi) \\ &\quad - \frac{1}{p}\frac{Q'^2(t)}{(\lambda + Q(t))^2}G(\varphi) + \frac{1}{p}\frac{Q'(t)}{\lambda + Q(t)}G'(\varphi)\varphi'. \end{aligned} \tag{2.15}$$

Hence with $|G'(\varphi)| \leq \rho$,

$$|\varphi''| < \frac{1}{p}\frac{M}{(\lambda - M)^{-1/p+1}} + \frac{1}{p}\frac{M}{\lambda - M} + \frac{1}{p}\frac{M^2}{(\lambda - M)^2} + \frac{1}{p}\frac{M}{\lambda - M}\rho\left[(\lambda - M)^{1/p} + \frac{M}{p}\right] \tag{2.16}$$

which gives the estimate (2.14). □

Theorem 2.5. *Let $Q(t)$ be periodic with period $\hat{\pi}$ and let M be a uniform bound for $|Q|$, $|Q'|$, $|Q''|$, $|Q'''|$. Then the eigenvalues λ and $\tilde{\lambda}$ belonging to the problem (1.1)–(1.9) and (1.1)–(1.10) when $p \neq 3$ satisfy the inequalities*

$$\sqrt[p+1]{\lambda_{2k-1}} > 2k, \qquad \sqrt[p+1]{\lambda_{2k}} > 2k,$$
$$\sqrt[p+1]{\tilde{\lambda}_{2k-1}} > (2k-1), \qquad \sqrt[p+1]{\tilde{\lambda}_{2k}} > (2k-1), \tag{2.17}$$

provided that they are greater than constant Λ defined by

$$\Lambda = \max\left(M + \left(1 + \frac{M}{p^2}\right)^p, M + \left(\frac{2p}{p-1} \cdot \frac{C_1 + C_2 M + C_3 M^2}{M}\right)^{p/(3-p)}\right), \tag{2.18}$$

where $C_1 = C_1(p)$, $C_2 = C_2(p)$, $C_3 = C_3(p)$.

Proof. From (2.2) with (1.9) or (1.10) we can write

$$\int_0^{\hat{\pi}} \sqrt[p]{\lambda + Q(\tau)}\,d\tau + \frac{1}{p}\int_0^{\hat{\pi}} \frac{Q'(\tau)}{\lambda + Q(\tau)} G(\varphi)\,d\tau = l\hat{\pi}, \tag{2.19}$$

where $l = 2k$ concerning the periodic case (1.9) and $l = 2k - 1$ concerning the antiperiodic case (1.10). Integrating by parts, the second integral has the form

$$\frac{1}{p}\int_0^{\hat{\pi}} \frac{Q'(\tau)}{\lambda + Q(\tau)} G(\varphi)\,d\tau = \frac{1}{p}\left[\frac{1}{\varphi'}\frac{Q'(t)}{\lambda + Q(t)} F(\varphi(t))\right]_0^{\hat{\pi}} - \frac{1}{p}\int_0^{\hat{\pi}} F(\varphi(\tau))\frac{d}{d\tau}\left(\frac{1}{\varphi'}\frac{Q'(\tau)}{\lambda + Q(\tau)}\right)d\tau, \tag{2.20}$$

where $F(\varphi(t)) = \int_0^t \varphi'(\tau) G(\varphi(\tau))\,d\tau$.

Since $-1 \leq G(\varphi) \leq 1$, then $|F(\varphi(t))| \leq \mu$ for $t \in [a, b]$.

On the right side of (2.20), the first term vanishes as Q is a periodic function with period $\hat{\pi}$, and we can write the integral (2.20) in the form

$$\begin{aligned}\frac{1}{p}\int_0^{\hat{\pi}}\frac{Q'(\tau)}{\lambda+Q(\tau)}G(\varphi)d\tau &= \frac{1}{p}\int_0^{\hat{\pi}}F(\varphi(\tau))\frac{\varphi''}{\varphi'^2}\frac{Q'}{\lambda+Q(\tau)}d\tau\\ &\quad+\frac{1}{p}\int_0^{\hat{\pi}}F(\varphi(\tau))\frac{1}{\varphi'}\frac{Q'^2}{(\lambda+Q(\tau))^2}d\tau\\ &\quad-\frac{1}{p}\int_0^{\hat{\pi}}F(\varphi(\tau))\frac{1}{\varphi'}\frac{Q''}{\lambda+Q(\tau)}d\tau\\ &= I_1+I_2+I_3.\end{aligned}\tag{2.21}$$

By (2.13) and (2.14), we get the estimates on integrals I_1 and I_2:

$$\begin{aligned}|I_1| &< \frac{\mu}{p(1-(1/p\beta))^2}\left[(2+\rho)\frac{M^2}{p}+(p+\rho)\frac{M^3}{p^2}\right]\frac{\hat{\pi}}{(\lambda-M)^{2+1/p}},\\ |I_2| &< \frac{\mu}{p(1-(1/p\beta))}M^2\frac{\hat{\pi}}{(\lambda-M)^{2+1/p}}.\end{aligned}\tag{2.22}$$

Using notation $H(\varphi(t))=\int_0^{\hat{\pi}}\varphi'(\tau)F(\varphi(\tau))d\tau$ and applying an integration by parts for I_3, we find

$$\begin{aligned}I_3 &= -\frac{1}{p}\left[H(\varphi(t))\frac{1}{\varphi'^2}\frac{Q''(t)}{\lambda+Q(t)}\right]_0^{\hat{\pi}}+\frac{1}{p}\int_0^{\hat{\pi}}H(\varphi(\tau))\frac{d}{d\tau}\left(\frac{1}{\varphi'^2}\frac{Q''(\tau)}{\lambda+Q(\tau)}\right)d\tau\\ &= -\frac{2}{p}\int_0^{\hat{\pi}}H(\varphi(\tau))\frac{\varphi''}{\varphi'^3}\frac{Q''(\tau)}{\lambda+Q(\tau)}d\tau+\frac{1}{p}\int_0^{\hat{\pi}}H(\varphi(\tau))\frac{1}{\varphi'^2}\frac{Q'''(\tau)}{\lambda+Q(\tau)}d\tau\\ &\quad-\frac{1}{p}\int_0^{\hat{\pi}}H(\varphi(\tau))\frac{1}{\varphi'^2}\frac{Q'(\tau)Q''(\tau)}{(\lambda+Q(\tau))^2}d\tau = I_4+I_5+I_6.\end{aligned}\tag{2.23}$$

The integrated term vanishes and for the three integrals we have the following estimates with $|H(\varphi(t))|\le\nu$ for $t\in[a,b]$:

$$\begin{aligned}|I_4| &< \frac{2\nu}{p\beta^3}\left[(2+\rho)\frac{M^2}{p}+(p+\rho)\frac{M^3}{p^2}\right]\frac{\hat{\pi}}{(\lambda-M)^{2+2/p}},\\ |I_5| &< \frac{\nu}{p\beta^2}M\frac{\hat{\pi}}{(\lambda-M)^{1+2/p}},\\ |I_6| &< \frac{\nu}{p\beta^2}M^2\frac{\hat{\pi}}{(\lambda-M)^{2+2/p}}.\end{aligned}\tag{2.24}$$

From the estimates above, we obtain

$$\frac{1}{p}\int_0^{\hat{\pi}}\frac{Q'(\tau)}{\lambda+Q(\tau)}G(\varphi)d\tau < \left[C_1M+C_2M^2+C_3M^3\right]\frac{\hat{\pi}}{(\lambda-M)^{1+2/p}},\tag{2.25}$$

where

$$C_1 = \frac{\nu}{p\beta^2},$$
$$C_2 = \frac{(2\nu+\mu)(2+\rho)+p(\nu+\mu)-\mu/\beta}{p^2\beta^2}, \tag{2.26}$$
$$C_3 = \frac{p+\rho}{p^3\beta^3}(2\nu+\mu\beta)$$

are obtained from the estimates on $I_1, I_2, \dots, I_6$.

For the integral $\int_0^{\hat{\pi}} \sqrt[p]{\lambda+Q(\tau)}d\tau$ in (2.19), we use the Taylor series with the remainder

$$\begin{aligned}\int_0^{\hat{\pi}} \sqrt[p]{\lambda+Q(\tau)}d\tau &= \sqrt[p]{\lambda}\hat{\pi} + \frac{1}{p}\frac{1}{\sqrt[p]{\lambda^{p-1}}}\int_0^{\hat{\pi}} Q(\tau)d\tau \\ &\quad - \frac{p-1}{2p^2}\frac{1}{\sqrt[p]{\lambda^{2p-1}}}\int_0^{\hat{\pi}} \frac{Q^2(\tau)}{(\lambda+\overline{Q}(\tau))^{(2p-1)/p}}d\tau,\end{aligned} \tag{2.27}$$

where $|\overline{Q}(t)| \le M$.

Since $Q(t)$ has zero-mean value $\int_0^{\hat{\pi}} Q(\tau)d\tau = 0$, then from (2.19) we get

$$\sqrt[p]{\lambda} = l + \frac{p-1}{2\hat{\pi}p^2}\int_0^{\hat{\pi}} \frac{Q^2(\tau)}{(\lambda+\overline{Q}(\tau))^{(2p-1)/p}}d\tau - \frac{1}{p\hat{\pi}}\int_0^{\hat{\pi}} \frac{Q'(\tau)}{\lambda+Q(\tau)}G(\varphi(\tau))d\tau. \tag{2.28}$$

The necessary condition for $\sqrt[p]{\lambda} > l$ is that

$$\frac{p-1}{2\hat{\pi}p^2}\int_0^{\hat{\pi}} \frac{Q^2(\tau)}{(\lambda+\overline{Q}(\tau))^{(2p-1)/p}}d\tau > \frac{1}{p\hat{\pi}}\int_0^{\hat{\pi}} \frac{Q'(\tau)}{\lambda+Q(\tau)}G(\varphi(\tau))d\tau \tag{2.29}$$

which is satisfied if

$$\frac{p-1}{2p}\frac{M^2}{(\lambda-M)^{(2p-1)/p}} > \frac{C_1M+C_2M^2+C_3M^3}{(\lambda-M)^{1+2/p}} \tag{2.30}$$

for $p \neq 3$ and

$$\lambda > M + \left(\frac{2p}{p-1}\cdot\frac{C_1+C_2M+C_3M^2}{M}\right)^{p/(3-p)}. \tag{2.31}$$

If $p = 3$, then $(2p-1)/p = 1+2/p = 5/3$, and we do not get from (2.30) a bound for λ. □

We note that the bound obtained for [4, Hill's equation (1.5)] is better than our bound since in the linear case we are able to use trigonometric formulas but if $p \neq 2$, then these formulas do not exist.

References

[1] G. Bognár, *Asymptotic forms of large eigenvalues for quasilinear Hill's equation*, to appear.
[2] E. A. Coddington and N. Levinson, *Theory of Ordinary Differential Equations*, McGraw-Hill, New York, 1955.
[3] Á. Elbert, *A half-linear second order differential equation*, Qualitative Theory of Differential Equations, Vol. I, II (Szeged, 1979), Colloq. Math. Soc. János Bolyai, vol. 30, North-Holland, Amsterdam, 1981, pp. 153–180.
[4] H. Hochstadt, *Asymptotic estimates for the Sturm-Liouville spectrum*, Communications on Pure and Applied Mathematics **14** (1961), 749–764.
[5] ———, *On the asymptotic spectrum of Hill's equation*, Archiv für Mathematische **14** (1963), 34–38.
[6] W. Magnus and S. Winkler, *Hill's Equation*, Dover, New York, 1979.
[7] M. Zhang, *The rotation number approach to eigenvalues of the one-dimensional p-Laplacian with periodic potentials*, Journal of the London Mathematical Society. Second Series **64** (2001), no. 1, 125–143.

G. Bognár: Institute of Mathematics, University of Miskolc, 3515 Miskolc-Egyetemváros, Hungary
E-mail address: matvbg@uni-miskolc.hu

MULTIPLE POSITIVE SOLUTIONS OF SUPERLINEAR ELLIPTIC PROBLEMS WITH SIGN-CHANGING WEIGHT

DENIS BONHEURE, JOSÉ MARIA GOMES, AND PATRICK HABETS

We prove the existence of multibump solutions to a superlinear elliptic problem where a sign-changing weight is affected by a large parameter μ. Our method relies in variational arguments. A special care is paid to the localization of the deformation along lines of steepest descent of an energy functional constrained to a $C^{1,1}$-manifold in the space $H_0^1(\Omega)$.

1. Introduction

We consider positive solutions of the boundary value problem

$$\begin{gathered} \Delta u+(a_+(x)-\mu a_-(x))|u|^\gamma u=0, \quad x\in\Omega, \\ u(x)=0, \quad x\in\partial\Omega, \end{gathered} \tag{1.1}$$

where $\Omega\subset\mathbb{R}^N$ is a bounded domain of class $\mathscr{C}^1$, a_+ and a_- are continuous functions which are positive on nonoverlapping domains, and μ is a large parameter. Positive solutions u are defined to be such that $u(x)>0$ for almost every $x\in\Omega$.

For the ODE equivalent of (1.1) and for large values of μ, complete results were worked out in [2, 3] concerning, respectively, the cases of the weight $a_+(t)$ being positive in two or three nonoverlapping intervals. In the present note, we summarize the results obtained in [1]. By using a variational approach, we extend the results obtained in [2, 3] to the PDE problem (1.1).

Note first that finding positive solutions of problem (1.1) is equivalent to finding nontrivial solutions of

$$\begin{gathered} \Delta u+(a_+(x)-\mu a_-(x))u_+^{\gamma+1}=0, \quad x\in\Omega, \\ u(x)=0, \quad x\in\partial\Omega, \end{gathered} \tag{1.2}$$

Hindawi Publishing Corporation
Proceedings of the Conference on Differential & Difference Equations and Applications, pp. 221–229

where $u_+ = \max\{u,0\}$, since nontrivial solutions of (1.2) are positive. In the sequel, we also write $u_- = \max\{-u,0\}$.

We suppose that the following assumption holds.

(H) $\gamma > 0$, $\gamma+2 < 2^* = 2N/(N-2)$ if $N \geq 3$, $a_+, a_- : \overline{\Omega} \to \mathbb{R}$ are continuous functions, and there exist n disjoint domains $\omega_i \subset \Omega$, with $i = 1,\dots,n$, which are of class $\mathscr{C}^1$ and such that

(a) for all $x \in \Omega_+ := \bigcup_{i=1}^n \omega_i$, $a_-(x) = 0$, $a_+(x) > 0$,
(b) for all $x \in \Omega_- := \Omega\setminus\overline{\Omega}_+$, $a_-(x) > 0$, $a_+(x) = 0$.

Solutions of (1.1) can be obtained as critical points of the energy functional under a convenient constraint. Namely, we define the constraint functional $V_\mu : H_0^1(\Omega) \to \mathbb{R}$ by

$$V_\mu(u) := \int_\Omega (a_+(x) - \mu a_-(x)) \frac{u_+^{\gamma+2}(x)}{\gamma+2} dx. \tag{1.3}$$

From the continuous imbedding of $H_0^1(\Omega)$ into $L^{\gamma+2}(\Omega)$, it can be seen that $V_\mu(u)$ is of class $\mathscr{C}^{1,1}$. Next, we define the manifold

$$\mathfrak{V}_\mu := \{u \in H_0^1(\Omega) \mid V_\mu(u) = 1\} \tag{1.4}$$

and the energy functional $J : H_0^1(\Omega) \to \mathbb{R}$, $u \mapsto J(u)$, where

$$J(u) := \frac{1}{2}\int_\Omega |\nabla u(x)|^2 dx. \tag{1.5}$$

We consider then the critical points of J under the constraint $u \in \mathfrak{V}_\mu$. It is a standard fact that such critical points satisfy the Euler-Lagrange equation

$$\nabla J(u) = \lambda \nabla V_\mu(u) \tag{1.6}$$

for some *Lagrange multiplier* $\lambda \in \mathbb{R}$. It then follows that u solves the problem

$$\begin{aligned} \Delta u + \lambda(a_+(x) - \mu a_-(x))u_+^{\gamma+1} &= 0, \quad x \in \Omega, \\ u(x) &= 0, \quad x \in \partial\Omega. \end{aligned} \tag{1.7}$$

Standard arguments show that $\lambda > 0$. Hence, any critical point of J on $\mathfrak{V}_\mu$ is such that the rescaled function $v = \lambda^{1/\gamma}u$ is a positive solution of (1.1). Our purpose is to prove the existence of multiple solutions for large values of the parameter μ. These solutions can be distinguished by their contribution of volume on some prescribed family of ω_i's.

We can then state our main theorem.

THEOREM 1.1. *Let assumption (H) be satisfied. Then, for $\mu > 0$ large enough, there exist at least $2^n - 1$ positive solutions of (1.1). Moreover, for each set $\omega = \omega_{i_1} \cup \cdots \cup \omega_{i_p}$, one of those solutions defines a family of positive solutions of (1.1) with limit support in $\overline{\omega}$.*

2. Preliminary results

2.1. Setting of a variational framework. The following lemmas set the background of our variational approach. We refer the reader to [1] for the complete proofs of the results.

LEMMA 2.1. *The set $\mathfrak{V}_\mu$ defined from (1.4) is a nonempty, weakly closed, and an arc-connected manifold in $H_0^1(\Omega)$. Further, the function Q_μ defined on* $\operatorname{dom} Q_\mu = \{u \in H_0^1(\Omega) \mid V_\mu(u) > 0\}$ *by*

$$(Q_\mu u)(x) := [V_\mu(u)]^{-1/(\gamma+2)} u(x). \tag{2.1}$$

is a continuous projector on $\mathfrak{V}_\mu$.

LEMMA 2.2. *If u_1, u_2 are different critical points of J in $\mathfrak{V}_\mu$, then there exist $\lambda_1, \lambda_2 > 0$ such that $v_1 = \lambda_1^{1/\gamma} u_1$ and $v_2 = \lambda_2^{1/\gamma} u_2$ are two distinct positive solutions of (1.1).*

LEMMA 2.3. *The functional J has a nonnegative minimum $\hat{u}_i$ on each of the disjoint manifolds*

$$\widehat{\mathfrak{V}}_i := \{u \in \mathfrak{V}_\mu \mid \operatorname{supp} u \subset \overline{\omega}_i\}, \quad i = 1, \dots, n. \tag{2.2}$$

Remark 2.4. Note that the sets $\widehat{\mathfrak{V}}_i$ and the functions $\hat{u}_i$ are independent of μ since they only involve functions u so that $\operatorname{supp} u \subset \overline{\omega}_i$.

We consider the gradient of J constrained to $\mathfrak{V}_\mu$:

$$\nabla_\mu J(u) := \nabla J(u) - \frac{\langle \nabla J(u), \nabla V_\mu(u) \rangle}{\|\nabla V_\mu(u)\|^2} \nabla V_\mu(u). \tag{2.3}$$

LEMMA 2.5. *Let J and V_μ be defined from (1.5) and (1.3). The gradient of J constrained to $\mathfrak{V}_\mu$ satisfies Palais-Smale condition.*

2.2. Decomposition of $H_0^1(\Omega)$. We introduce the following orthogonal decomposition of $H_0^1(\Omega)$. Let $\overline{H} := \{u \in H_0^1(\Omega) \mid \operatorname{supp} u \subset \overline{\Omega}_+\}$ be the space of the multibumps functions and $\widetilde{H} := (\overline{H})^\perp$ its orthogonal complement. Given $u \in H_0^1(\Omega)$, we define then $\overline{u} \in \overline{H}$ from the following lemma.

LEMMA 2.6. *Let $u \in H_0^1(\Omega)$. Then the problem*

$$\int_{\Omega_+} \nabla \overline{u}(x) \nabla \varphi(x) dx = \int_{\Omega_+} \nabla u(x) \nabla \varphi(x) dx, \quad \forall \varphi \in H_0^1(\Omega_+), \tag{2.4}$$

has a unique solution $\overline{u} \in \overline{H}$. Further, the function

$$\overline{R} : H_0^1(\Omega) \longrightarrow \overline{H} \subset H_0^1(\Omega), \qquad u \longmapsto \overline{R}u = \overline{u} \tag{2.5}$$

is a continuous projector for the weak topologies, that is,

$$u_n \overset{H_0^1}{\rightharpoonup} u \Longrightarrow \overline{R}u_n \overset{H_0^1}{\rightharpoonup} \overline{R}u. \tag{2.6}$$

Also,

$$J(\overline{R}u) \le J(u). \tag{2.7}$$

At last, the function $\widetilde{u} := u - \overline{u}$ *is in* $\widetilde{H}$ *and satisfies*

$$\int_{\Omega_+} \nabla \widetilde{u}(x) \nabla \varphi(x) dx = 0, \quad \forall \varphi \in H_0^1(\Omega_+). \tag{2.8}$$

LEMMA 2.7. *Let* $r > 0$ *and* $\epsilon > 0$ *be given. Then, for all* $\mu > 0$ *large enough and* $u \in \mathfrak{B}_{\mu,r}$,

$$\widehat{V}(\overline{u}) \ge 1 - \epsilon. \tag{2.9}$$

2.3. The nonlinear simplex $\mathfrak{S}$. Let $\hat{u}_i$ be the local minimizers of J in $\widehat{\mathfrak{V}}_i$ defined by Lemma 2.3 and consider the nonlinear simplex

$$\mathfrak{S} := \left\{ u = \sum_{i=1}^{n} s_i^{1/(\gamma+2)} \hat{u}_i \mid (s_1, \dots, s_n) \in \Delta \right\} \subset \mathfrak{V}_\mu, \tag{2.10}$$

where

$$\Delta := \left\{ (s_1, \dots, s_n) \in \mathbb{R}_+^n \mid \sum_{i=1}^{n} s_i = 1 \right\}. \tag{2.11}$$

We can evaluate J along functions of $\mathfrak{S}$ and introduce

$$f(s) := J\left(\sum_{i=1}^{n} s_i^{1/(\gamma+2)} \hat{u}_i \right) = \sum_{i=1}^{n} s_i^{2/(\gamma+2)} J(\hat{u}_i), \quad s \in \Delta. \tag{2.12}$$

Note that the set $\mathfrak{S}$ will be a key ingredient in the minimax characterization of the multi-bumps solutions as the geometry of f on Δ is a good model of the geometry of J on $\mathfrak{V}_\mu$ for large μ. The following lemmas study this geometry.

LEMMA 2.8. *The function* $f : \Delta \to \mathbb{R}$ *defined from (2.12) is such that the apexes* $(1,0,\dots,0)$, $\dots, (0,\dots,0,1)$ *of* Δ *are strict local minima of* f.

LEMMA 2.9. *Let* $E := \{i_1, \dots, i_k\}$, $2 \le k \le n$, *let* $\Delta_k := \{s = (s_1, \dots, s_k) \in \mathbb{R}_+^k \mid \sum_{j=1}^{k} s_j = 1\}$, *and let* $\hat{u}_i$ *be the local minimizers in* $\widehat{\mathfrak{V}}_i$ *defined by Lemma 2.3. Then the function* $f_E : \Delta_k \to \mathbb{R}$ *defined from*

$$f_E(s) := \sum_{j=1}^{k} s_j^{2/(\gamma+2)} J(\hat{u}_{i_j}) \tag{2.13}$$

has a unique global maximum c_E *at some point* $s^* = (s_1^*, \dots, s_k^*) \in \Delta_k$ *such that* $s_j^* > 0$ *for all* $j = 1, \dots, k$. *Further, if* $F \underset{\neq}{\subset} E$, *then* $c_F < c_E$.

2.4. Projection on $\mathfrak{S}$. The following lemmas define a continuous projector on the nonlinear simplex $\mathfrak{S}$ that increases the energy as little as we wish.

LEMMA 2.10. *The mapping $R_\mu : H_0^1(\Omega) \to H_0^1(\Omega)$, defined by*

$$R_\mu u := Q_\mu((\overline{u})_+), \tag{2.14}$$

is continuous. Further if $r > 0$ and $\delta > 0$ are given, then for $\mu > 0$ large enough and $u \in \mathfrak{B}_{\mu,r}$,

$$J(R_\mu u) \leq J(u) + \delta. \tag{2.15}$$

For the next lemma, it is convenient to define the local constraints

$$\widehat{V}_i(u) := \int_{\omega_i} a_+(x) \frac{u_+^{\gamma+2}(x)}{\gamma+2} dx. \tag{2.16}$$

These are such that if $v \in \mathfrak{V}_\mu$ and $\operatorname{supp} v \subset \overline{\Omega}_+$, then

$$V_\mu(v) = \widehat{V}(u) = \sum_{i=1}^{n} \widehat{V}_i(v) = 1. \tag{2.17}$$

LEMMA 2.11. *The mapping $P_\mu : H_0^1(\Omega) \to \mathfrak{S} \subset H_0^1(\Omega)$, defined by*

$$P_\mu u := \sum_{i=1}^{n} [\widehat{V}_i(R_\mu u)]^{1/(\gamma+2)} \widehat{u}_i, \tag{2.18}$$

where $\widehat{u}_i$ are the local minimizers in $\widehat{\mathfrak{V}}_i$, is continuous. Further if $r > 0$ and $\delta > 0$ are given, then for $\mu > 0$ large enough and $u \in \mathfrak{B}_{\mu,r}$,

$$J(P_\mu u) \leq J(u) + \delta. \tag{2.19}$$

3. Multibumps solutions

We prove in this section that for any p with $1 < p < n$, we can find C_n^p families of positive p-bumps solutions of (1.1). For that purpose, we introduce the following notations.

Let us fix p of the functions $\widehat{u}_i$ defined by Lemma 2.3. To simplify the notations, we assume that these functions are numbered in such a way that they correspond to $\widehat{u}_1, \dots, \widehat{u}_p$. We denote by $E = \{1, \dots, p\}$ the set of corresponding indices. Define then the corresponding nonlinear simplex $\mathfrak{S}_E$ constructed on the function $\widehat{u}_1, \dots, \widehat{u}_p$,

$$\mathfrak{S}_E := \left\{ u = \sum_{j=1}^{p} s_j^{1/(\gamma+2)} \widehat{u}_j \mid (s_1, \dots, s_p) \in \Delta_p \right\}, \tag{3.1}$$

where Δ_p is defined in Lemma 2.9. It follows from this lemma that J has a unique global maximum on $\mathfrak{S}_E$ at some interior point $w = (s_1^*)^{1/(\gamma+2)} \widehat{u}_1 + \cdots + (s_p^*)^{1/(\gamma+2)} \widehat{u}_p$.

In the next lemma, we identify disconnected regions where the gradient of J constrained to $\mathfrak{V}_\mu$ is bounded away from zero. As in Lemma 2.9, we write $c_E = J(w)$, where $w = \sum_{j=1}^{p}(s_j^*)^{1/(\gamma+2)}\hat{u}_j$ is the maximizer of J on the corresponding nonlinear simplex $\mathfrak{S}_E$, and we define for $\rho \in]0,1/4[$,

$$\mathfrak{E}_\mu(\rho) := \{u \in \mathfrak{V}_\mu \mid J(u) \leq c_E,\ \forall i = 1,\ldots,p,\ s_i = \hat{V}_i(R_\mu u) \geq \rho,\ |s_i - s_i^*| \geq \rho\}. \tag{3.2}$$

Lemma 3.1. *There exists $\theta > 0$ such that for any $\mu > 0$ large enough and all $u \in \mathfrak{E}_\mu(\rho)$, $\|\nabla_\mu J(u)\| \geq \theta$, where*

$$\nabla_\mu J(u) = \nabla J(u) - \frac{\langle \nabla J(u), \nabla V_\mu(u)\rangle}{\|\nabla V_\mu(u)\|^2}\nabla V_\mu(u). \tag{3.3}$$

Proof. Let us assume by contradiction that there exist $(\mu_j)_j \subset \mathbb{R}$ and $(u_j)_j \subset \mathfrak{E}_{\mu_j}(\rho)$ such that

$$\lim_{j\to\infty}\mu_j = \infty, \qquad \lim_{j\to\infty}\|\nabla_{\mu_j} J(u_j)\| = 0. \tag{3.4}$$

As the sequence $(u_j)_j$ is bounded in $H_0^1(\Omega)$, going to a subsequence if necessary, we can assume that there exists $u \in H_0^1(\Omega)$ such that

$$u_j \overset{H_0^1}{\rightharpoonup} u, \qquad u_j \overset{L^{2+\gamma}}{\longrightarrow} u. \tag{3.5}$$

We introduce now the manifold

$$\hat{\mathfrak{V}} := \{u \in H_0^1(\Omega) \mid \operatorname{supp} u \subset \overline{\Omega}_+,\ \hat{V}(u) = 1\}, \tag{3.6}$$

which is such that $\hat{\mathfrak{V}} \subset \mathfrak{V}_\mu$ for any $\mu > 0$. We denote the tangent space to $\hat{\mathfrak{V}}$ at u by

$$T_u(\hat{\mathfrak{V}}) := \left\{v \in H_0^1(\Omega) \mid \operatorname{supp} v \subset \overline{\Omega}_+,\ \int_\Omega a_+ u_+^{\gamma+1} v\,dx = 0\right\}. \tag{3.7}$$

Claim 3.2 $\langle \nabla J(u), v\rangle = 0$ for all $v \in T_u(\hat{\mathfrak{V}})$. Let $v \in T_u(\hat{\mathfrak{V}})$. We first observe that we can choose λ_j such that $v - \lambda_j u_j \in T_{u_j}(\mathfrak{V}_{\mu_j})$, where

$$T_{u_j}(\mathfrak{V}_{\mu_j}) := \left\{v \in H_0^1(\Omega) \mid \int_\Omega (a_+ - \mu_j a_-)(u_j)_+^{\gamma+1} v\,dx = 0\right\} \tag{3.8}$$

is the tangent space to $\mathfrak{V}_{\mu_j}$ at u_j. Indeed, as v is supported in Ω^+, we just need to take

$$\lambda_j = \frac{1}{\gamma+2}\int_\Omega a_+ (u_j)_+^{\gamma+1} v\,dx. \tag{3.9}$$

We then notice that since $(u_j)_+ \overset{L^{2+\gamma}}{\to} u_+$ and $v \in T_u(\widehat{\mathfrak{V}})$, we have

$$\int_\Omega a_+ (u_j)_+^{\gamma+1} v\,dx \longrightarrow \int_\Omega a_+ u_+^{\gamma+1} v\,dx = 0. \tag{3.10}$$

Hence, we deduce that $\lambda_j \to 0$. Computing

$$\begin{aligned}\langle \nabla J(u), v\rangle &= \int_\Omega \nabla u \nabla v\,dx \\ &= \int_\Omega (\nabla u - \nabla u_j)\nabla v\,dx + \int_\Omega \nabla u_j \nabla (v - \lambda_j u_j)\,dx + \lambda_j \int_\Omega |\nabla u_j|^2 dx\end{aligned} \tag{3.11}$$

and using the fact that

$$u_j \overset{H^1}{\rightharpoonup} u, \quad v - \lambda_j u_j \in T_{u_j}(\mathfrak{V}_{\mu_j}), \quad \nabla_{\mu_j} J(u_j) \longrightarrow 0, \quad \lambda_j \longrightarrow 0, \tag{3.12}$$

the claim follows.

Claim 3.3 $u \in \overline{H}$ so that $u = \overline{u}$. We write $u_j = \overline{u}_j + \widetilde{u}_j$ and $u = \overline{u} + \widetilde{u}$, where $\overline{u}_j, \overline{u} \in \overline{H}$ and $\widetilde{u}_j, \widetilde{u} \in \widetilde{H}$. We first deduce from Lemma 2.6 that

$$\overline{u}_j \overset{H_0^1}{\rightharpoonup} \overline{u}, \qquad \widetilde{u}_j \overset{H_0^1}{\rightharpoonup} \widetilde{u} \tag{3.13}$$

so that

$$\overline{u}_j \overset{L^{2+\gamma}}{\longrightarrow} \overline{u}, \qquad \widetilde{u}_j \overset{L^{2+\gamma}}{\longrightarrow} \widetilde{u}. \tag{3.14}$$

The arguments of Claims 3.2 and 3.3 in the proof of Lemma 2.6 then imply that $\widetilde{u}_+ = 0$. Let us prove that $\widetilde{u}_- = 0$ a.e. in Ω_-. Since

$$\lim_{j\to\infty} ||\nabla_{\mu_j} J(u_j)|| = 0 \tag{3.15}$$

and $(u_j)_- \in T_{u_j}(\mathfrak{V}_{\mu_j})$, we deduce that

$$\int_\Omega |\nabla (u_j)_-|^2 dx = \langle \nabla_{\mu_j} J(u_j), (u_j)_-\rangle \longrightarrow 0. \tag{3.16}$$

This means that $(u_j)_- \to 0$ in $H_0^1(\Omega)$, and therefore $u_- = 0$. This in turn implies that $\widetilde{u}_-(x) = 0$ for a.e. $x \in \Omega_-$. It follows that u is supported in $\overline{\Omega}_+$ which means that $u \in \overline{H}$.

Define $w_i := \chi_i u$, where χ_i is the characteristic function of the set ω_i, and let $F := \{i = 1,\dots,n \mid w_i \neq 0\}$. Observe that $w_i \neq 0$ for all $i = 1,\dots,p$. Indeed, this follows from the convergence of u_j in $L^{2+\gamma}(\Omega)$ and the definition of $\mathfrak{E}_\mu(\rho)$. Changing the order of the indices of the subdomains ω_i's for $i > p$ if necessary, we may assume without loss of generality that $F = \{1,2,\dots,m\}$ for some $p \le m \le n$. Next, we introduce the function

$$\phi(s) := \sum_{i=1}^m s_i^{1/(\gamma+2)} Q_\mu w_i \in \widehat{\mathfrak{V}}, \tag{3.17}$$

where $s \in \Delta_m$ and Δ_m is defined in Lemma 2.9. Observe that $Q_\mu w_i$ is independent of μ since the w_i's are, respectively, supported in $\overline{\omega}_i$. We also define $\overline{s}$ to be such that $\phi(\overline{s}) = Q_\mu u$, that is, $\overline{s}_i = \widehat{V}(w_i)/\widehat{V}(u)$, and we write

$$g(s) := J(\phi(s)) = \sum_{i=1}^{m} s_i^{2/(\gamma+2)} J(Q_\mu w_i). \tag{3.18}$$

Claim 3.4 For all $i \in E = \{1,\dots,p\}$, $\overline{s}_i \geq \rho$ and $|\overline{s}_i - s_i^*| \geq \rho$. This follows from the convergence of u_j in $L^{2+\gamma}(\Omega)$.

Claim 3.5 $\widehat{V}(u) \geq 1$.

Claim 3.6 $g(\overline{s}) = J(Q_\mu u) \leq c_E$. Using the convexity of J and the weak convergence of the sequence $(u_j)_j$, we can write

$$c_E \geq \lim_{j\to\infty} J(u_j) \geq J(u). \tag{3.19}$$

It then follows from Claim 3.5 that

$$J(u) = \widehat{V}^{2/(\gamma+2)}(u) J(Q_\mu u) \geq J(Q_\mu u). \tag{3.20}$$

Claim 3.7 $g(\overline{s}) < \max_{s\in\Delta_m} g(s)$. In case $m > p$, we have

$$g(s) \geq \sum_{i=1}^{m} s_i^{2/(\gamma+2)} J(\widehat{u}_i) = f_F(s) \tag{3.21}$$

and therefore we infer from Lemma 2.9 that

$$\max_{s\in\Delta_m} g(s) \geq c_F > c_E = c \geq g(\overline{s}). \tag{3.22}$$

On the other hand, if $m = p$ and for some $i_0 \in E$, $J(Q_\mu w_{i_0}) \neq J(\widehat{u}_{i_0})$, we have

$$\begin{aligned} g(s) &\geq \sum_{i=1}^{p} s_i^{2/(\gamma+2)} J(\widehat{u}_i) + s_{i_0}^{2/(\gamma+2)} \left(J(Q_\mu w_{i_0}) - J(\widehat{u}_{i_0})\right) \\ &= f_E(s) + s_{i_0}^{2/(\gamma+2)} \left(J(Q_\mu w_{i_0}) - J(\widehat{u}_{i_0})\right), \end{aligned} \tag{3.23}$$

where f_E is defined in Lemma 2.9 and

$$\max_{s\in\Delta_m} g(s) \geq c + \left(s_{i_0}^*\right)^{2/(\gamma+2)} \left(J(Q_\mu w_{i_0}) - J(\widehat{u}_{i_0})\right) > c \geq g(\overline{s}). \tag{3.24}$$

At last, if $m = p$ and for all $i = 1,\dots,m$, $J(Q_\mu w_i) = J(\widehat{u}_i)$, then $g(s) = f_E(s)$ so that the claim follows from Claim 3.4 and Lemma 3.1 as $|\overline{s}_i - s_i^*| \geq \rho$.

Conclusion 3.8. As $\phi(s) \in \widehat{\mathfrak{V}}$, we deduce $\phi'(\bar{s}) \in T_{\phi(s)}(\widehat{\mathfrak{V}})$, and it follows from Claim 3.2 that

$$g'(\bar{s}) = \langle \nabla J(\phi(\bar{s})), \phi'(\bar{s}) \rangle = \langle \nabla J(Q_\mu u), \phi'(\bar{s}) \rangle = 0. \tag{3.25}$$

Since the only stationary point of g is its maximum, this contradicts Claim 3.7. □

The previous result is the basic tool to prove the existence of C_n^p families of positive p-bumps solutions of (1.1) for any p with $2 \le p \le n-1$.

THEOREM 3.9. *Let assumption (H) be satisfied. Let $\omega = \omega_{i_1} \cup \cdots \cup \omega_{i_p}$ with $2 \le p \le n-1$. Then, for μ sufficiently large, there exists a family of positive p-bumps solutions of (1.1) with limit support in $\overline{\omega}$.*

General idea of the proof. We consider a deformation along the lines of steepest descent of J constrained to the manifold. An intersection property allows us to estimate the inf-max level of the deformations of subsimplex consisting of nonlinear combinations of p local minima. The previous lemma, together with Palais-Smale condition, implies the existence of a critical point lying in $\mathfrak{C}_\mu(\rho)$ (see [1] for all the details).

Acknowledgments

The second author is supported by Fundação para a Ciência e a Tecnologia. We are grateful to Luís Sanchez for enlightening discussions and helpful suggestions.

References

[1] D. Bonheure, J. M. Gomes, and P. Habets, *Multiple positive solutions of superlinear elliptic problems with sign-changing weight*, Journal of Differential Equations **214** (2005), no. 1, 36–64.

[2] M. Gaudenzi, P. Habets, and F. Zanolin, *Positive solutions of superlinear boundary value problems with singular indefinite weight*, Communications on Pure and Applied Analysis **2** (2003), no. 3, 411–423.

[3] ———, *A seven-positive-solutions theorem for a superlinear problem*, Advanced Nonlinear Studies **4** (2004), no. 2, 149–164.

Denis Bonheure: Institut de Mathématique Pure et Appliquée, Université Catholique de Louvain, 2 Chemin du Cyclotron, 1348 Louvain-la-Neuve, Belgium
E-mail address: bonheure@anma.ucl.ac.be

José Maria Gomes: Centro de Matemática e Aplicações Fundamentais (CMAF), Faculdade de Ciências, Universidade de Lisboa, 2 Avenida Professor Gama Pinto, 1649-003 Lisboa, Portugal
E-mail address: zemaria@cii.fc.ul.pt

Patrick Habets: Institut de Mathématique Pure et Appliquée, Université Catholique de Louvain, 2 Chemin du Cyclotron, 1348 Louvain-la-Neuve, Belgium

POSITIVE SOLUTIONS OF SECOND-ORDER BOUNDARY VALUE PROBLEMS

ABDELKADER BOUCHERIF

This paper is devoted to the study of the existence of positive solutions of two-point boundary value problems of the form $u''(t) + f(t,u(t)) = h(t)$, $0 < t < 1$, $u(0) = u(1) = 0$. Our approach is based on the notion of points of sign-variations of a continuous function on an interval.

1. Introduction

We are interested in the investigation of the existence of positive solutions of the following two-point boundary value problems:

$$u''(t) + f(t,u(t)) = h(t), \quad 0 < t < 1, \tag{1.1}$$

$$u(0) = u(1) = 0. \tag{1.2}$$

Problems of this type arise naturally in the description of physical phenomena, where only positive solutions, that is, solutions u satisfying $u(t) > 0$ for all $t \in (0,1)$, are meaningful. It is well known that Krasnoselskii's fixed point theorem in a cone has been instrumental in proving existence of positive solutions of problems (1.1), (1.2) when $h(t) = 0$ for all $t \in [0,1]$. Most of the previous works have assumed the following: $f : [0,1] \times [0,+\infty) \to [0,+\infty)$ is continuous and satisfies $\liminf_{u\to 0+}\min_{0\le t\le 1} f(t,u)/u = +\infty$ and $\limsup_{u\to+\infty}\max_{0\le t\le 1} f(t,u)/u = 0$, (sublinear case) or $\limsup_{u\to 0+}\max_{0\le t\le 1} f(t,u)/u = 0$ and $\liminf_{u\to+\infty}\min_{0\le t\le 1} f(t,u)/u = +\infty$ (superlinear case). See, for instance, [1, 6, 8–10] and the references therein. The above conditions have been relaxed in [11, 12], where the author removes the condition f nonnegative, and considers the behavior of f with respect to π^2. Notice that π^2 is the first eigenvalue of the operator $u \to -u''$, subject to the boundary condition (1.2). The arguments in [11, 12] are based on the fixed point index theory in cones. When the nonlinear term depends also on the first derivative of u, we refer the interested reader to [2], where the authors consider, also, the problem of the existence of multiple solutions.

Hindawi Publishing Corporation
Proceedings of the Conference on Differential & Difference Equations and Applications, pp. 231–236

In this paper, we will adopt a totally different approach. We do not require the nonnegativity of the nonlinearity f, and our arguments are based on the simple notion of points of sign-variations of solutions of nonhomogeneous boundary value problems. Also, the sign of the Green's function of the corresponding linear homogeneous problem plays no role in our study.

Let I denote the real interval $[0,1]$, and consider the following linear problem:

$$u''(t)+q(t)u(t)=g(t), \quad 0<t<1. \tag{1.3}$$

Let $u:I\to\mathbb{R}$ be a continuous function, and let $t_0\in I$. We say that t_0 is a point of sign-variations of u if

(i) $u(t_0)=0$,

(ii) for every small $\epsilon>0$, we have $u(t_0-\epsilon)u(t_0+\epsilon)<0$.

Assuming $q(t)\le\pi^2$ and $q(t)\ne\pi^2$ on a subset of I of positive measure, it was shown in [3] that if the forcing term $g(\cdot)$ has n points of sign-variations in I, then the solution u of problems (1.2), (1.3) has at most n points of sign-variations in I. The obvious consequence of this result is that if $g(\cdot)$ has a constant sign on I, then the solution of (1.2), (1.3) has also a constant sign on I. This result was extended later to solutions of nonlinear problems in [4].

Remark 1.1. The condition $q(t)\le\pi^2$ and $q(t)\ne\pi^2$ on a subset of I of positive measure is known in the literature as a nonresonance condition.

2. Topological transversality theory

In this section, we recall the most important notions and results related to the topological transversality theory due to Granas (see [7] for the details of the theory).

Let X be a Banach space, $\mathscr{C}$ a convex subset of X, and U an open set in $\mathscr{C}$.

(i) $g:X\to X$ is compact if $\overline{g(X)}$ is compact.

(ii) $H:[0,1]\times X\to X$ is a compact homotopy if H is a homotopy and, for all $\lambda\in[0,1]$, $H(\lambda,\cdot):X\to X$ is compact.

(iii) $g:\overline{U}\to\mathscr{C}$ is called admissible if g is compact and has no fixed points on $\Gamma=\partial U$. $\mathcal{M}_\Gamma(\overline{U},\mathscr{C})$ will denote the class of all admissible maps from $\overline{U}$ to $\mathscr{C}$.

(iv) A compact homotopy H is admissible if, for each $\lambda\in[0,1]$, $H(\lambda,\cdot)$ is admissible.

(v) Two mappings g and h in $\mathcal{M}_\Gamma(\overline{U},\mathscr{C})$ are homotopic if there is an admissible homotopy $H:[0,1]\times\overline{U}\to\mathscr{C}$ such that $H(0,\cdot)=g$ and $H(1,\cdot)=h$.

(vi) $g\in\mathcal{M}_\Gamma(\overline{U},\mathscr{C})$ is called inessential if there is a fixed point free compact map $h:\overline{U}\to\mathscr{C}$ such that $g\,|_\Gamma=h\,|_\Gamma$. Otherwise, g is called essential.

Lemma 2.1. *Let q be an arbitrary point in U and let $g\in\mathcal{M}_\Gamma(\overline{U},\mathscr{C})$ be the constant map $g(x)\equiv q$. Then g is essential.*

Lemma 2.2. *$g\in\mathcal{M}_\Gamma(\overline{U},\mathscr{C})$ is inessential if and only if g is homotopic to a fixed point free compact map.*

Theorem 2.3. *Let g and h in $\mathcal{M}_\Gamma(\overline{U},\mathscr{C})$ be homotopic maps. Then g is essential if and only if h is essential.*

3. Main results

Elementary arguments from calculus show that positive solutions of (1.1), (1.2) satisfy $u'(0) > 0$, $u'(1) < 0$.

Let $C_0^1(I,\mathbb{R})$ denote the set of all functions $u : I \to \mathbb{R}$ that are continuously differentiable, with $u(0) = u(1) = 0$.

Lemma 3.1. *Let $u \in C_0^1(I,\mathbb{R})$ satisfy $u'(0) > 0$, $u'(1) < 0$. Then the number of points of sign-variations of u in I is even or zero.*

Proof. (i) If u does not vanish in $(0,1)$, then the number of points of sign-variations of u is zero.

(ii) Suppose u has n points of sign-variations, which we label $t_1, t_2, \ldots, t_n$ in $(0,1)$ such that $0 < t_1 < t_2 < \cdots < t_n < 1$. Then we have

$$\begin{aligned} &u(t_j) = 0, \quad u(t_j - \epsilon)u(t_j + \epsilon) < 0, \quad j = 1,2,\ldots,n, \\ &u(t_1 - \epsilon) > 0, \qquad u(t_2 + \epsilon) > 0, \ldots, u(t_n + \epsilon) > 0, \\ &u(t_1 + \epsilon) < 0, \qquad u(t_2 - \epsilon) < 0, \ldots, u(t_n - \epsilon) < 0. \end{aligned} \tag{3.1}$$

It follows that

$$\begin{gathered} u'(0)u(t_1 - \epsilon) > 0, \quad u(t_j + \epsilon)u(t_{j+1} - \epsilon) > 0, \quad j = 1,2,\ldots,n-1, \\ u(t_n + \epsilon)u'(1) < 0. \end{gathered} \tag{3.2}$$

This implies that $u'(0)u'(1)$ and $\prod_{j=1}^{n} u(t_j - \epsilon)u(t_j + \epsilon)$ have opposite sign. Since $u'(0)u'(1) < 0$ and $\operatorname{sign}[\prod_{j=1}^{n} u(t_j - \epsilon)u(t_j + \epsilon)] = (-1)^n$, it follows that $(-1)^n = 1$. This shows that n is even. This completes the proof of the lemma. □

Remark 3.2. The result is also true if we assume $u'(0) < 0$ and $u'(1) > 0$.

Lemma 3.3. *Assume $f : I \times \mathbb{R} \to \mathbb{R}$ is continuous and satisfies the condition:*

(H1) for all $u \in \mathbb{R}$ $f(t,u)u \le \pi^2 u^2$ and $f(t,u)u \ne \pi^2 u^2$ on a subset of I of positive measure.

Then for all $u \in C_0^1(I,\mathbb{R})$ we have $\int_0^1 [u'(t)^2 - f(t,u(t))u(t)]dt > 0$.

Proof. It is clear that $\int_0^1 [u'(t)^2 - f(t,u(t))u(t)]dt > \int_0^1 [u'(t)^2 - \pi^2 u(t)^2]dt$. A classical result in the theory of calculus of variations (see, for instance, [5]) shows that $\int_0^1 [u'(t)^2 - \pi^2 u(t)^2]dt \ge 0$. The proof of the lemma is complete. □

We will assume throughout the remainder of the paper that $h : I \to \mathbb{R}$ is continuous and does not vanish in I.

Lemma 3.4. *Assume (H1) is satisfied. Let u be a solution of (1.1), (1.2) with two consecutive points, $0 \le t_1 < t_2 \le 1$, of sign-variations. Then u and h cannot have the same sign on $[t_1, t_2]$.*

Proof. First, notice that $u(t) \neq 0$ for all $t \in (t_1, t_2)$. Multiply both sides of (1.1) by $u(t)$ and integrate the resulting equation from t_1 to t_2. Taking into account (1.2), we get

$$-\int_{t_1}^{t_2} u'(t)^2 dt + \int_{t_1}^{t_2} f(t, u(t))u(t)dt = \int_{t_1}^{t_2} h(t)u(t)dt. \tag{3.3}$$

Hence

$$\int_{t_1}^{t_2} h(t)u(t)dt = -\int_{t_1}^{t_2} [u'(t)^2 - f(t, u(t))u(t)]dt < 0 \quad \text{(by Lemma 3.3).} \tag{3.4}$$

Therefore u and h cannot have the same sign on $[t_1, t_2]$, and this completes the proof. □

An obvious consequence of this result is the following.

Lemma 3.5. *If (H1) is satisfied, a necessary condition for (1.1), (1.2) to have positive solutions is that $h(t) < 0$ for all $t \in I$.*

We now provide a sufficient condition on the nonlinearity f in order to obtain a priori bounds on solutions of (1.1), (1.2).

Theorem 3.6. *Assume $f : I \times \mathbb{R} \to \mathbb{R}$ is continuous and satisfies the condition:*

(H2) there exists $R > 0$, such that for all $t \in I$, $\operatorname{sgn} u[f(t, u) - h(t)] < 0$ whenever $|u| > R$.

Then all possible solutions of (1.1), (1.2) satisfy $|u(t)| \leq R$ for all $t \in I$.

Proof. Suppose, on the contrary, that there is a $\tau \in I$ such that $|u(\tau)| > R$. Then, we have either $u(\tau) > R$ or $u(\tau) < -R$. We consider the first case. It follows from the continuity of u that there exists τ_0 such that $u(\tau_0) = \max\{u(t); t \in I\}$. Hence $u'(\tau_0) = 0$, $u''(\tau_0) \leq 0$. Also, our assumption implies that $u(\tau_0) > R$. The differential equation (1.1) yields

$$0 \leq -u''(\tau_0) = f(\tau_0, u(\tau_0)) - h(\tau_0) < 0. \tag{3.5}$$

We obtain a contradiction.

Thus $u(t) \leq R$ for all $t \in I$.

Similarly, we can show that $u(t) \geq -R$ for all $t \in I$.

Therefore, we have $-R \leq u(t) \leq R$ for all $t \in I$. □

Theorem 3.7. *If the conditions (H1) and (H2) are satisfied, then problems (1.1), (1.2) have at least one solution.*

Proof. For $\lambda \in [0, 1]$, consider the one-parameter family of problems

$$-u''(t) = \lambda[f(t, u(t)) - h(t)], \quad 0 < t < 1, \quad u(0) = u(1) = 0. \tag{3.6}$$

Notice that for $\lambda = 0$, (3.6) has only the trivial solution, while for $\lambda = 1$, (3.6) is exactly our original problem.

Theorem 3.6 shows that all possible solutions of (3.6) are a priori bounded, independent of λ. It is easily seen that (3.6) is equivalent to

$$u(t) = \lambda \int_0^1 G(t,s)[f(s,u(s)) - h(s)]ds, \tag{2.λ}$$

where $G(t,s)$ is the Green's function corresponding to (3.6) for $\lambda = 0$.

Consider $\Omega := \{u \in C_0(I;\mathbb{R}); \|u\|_0 < R+1\}$, where R is the constant from (H2). This is an open, bounded, and convex subset of $C_0(I;\mathbb{R})$. Define an operator $H : [0,1] \times \overline{\Omega} \to C_0^2(I;\mathbb{R})$ by

$$H(\lambda,u)(t) := \lambda \int_0^1 G(t,s)[f(s,u(s)) - h(s)]ds \tag{3.λ}$$

This defines a compact homotopy without fixed points on $\partial\Omega$. Hence it is an admissible homotopy between the essential map $H(0,\cdot) = 0$ and the map $H(1,\cdot)$. The topological transversality theorem of Granas implies that $H(1,\cdot)$ is essential; that is, it has at least one fixed point, and this fixed point of $H(1,\cdot)$ is a solution of problems (1.1), (1.2). □

THEOREM 3.8. *If (H1) and (H2) are satisfied, then a necessary and sufficient conditon for (1.1), (1.2) to have positive solutions is that $h(t) < 0$ for all $t \in I$.*

Proof. Theorem 3.7 shows that (1.1), (1.2) has at least one solution u_0. Lemma 3.4 shows that u_0 and h cannot have the same sign on $[0,1]$. Hence $u_0(t) > 0$ in $(0,1)$ if and only if $h(t) < 0$ for all $t \in I$. □

Acknowledgment

The author is grateful to KFUPM for its constant support.

References

[1] R. P. Agarwal, D. O'Regan, and P. J. Y. Wong, *Positive Solutions of Differential, Difference and Integral Equations*, Kluwer Academic, Dordrecht, 1999.

[2] Z. Bai and W. Ge, *Existence of three positive solutions for some second-order boundary value problems*, Computers & Mathematics with Applications **48** (2004), no. 5-6, 699–707.

[3] R. Bellman, *On variation-diminishing properties of Green's functions*, Bollettino dell'Unione Matematica Italiana (3) **16** (1961), 164–166.

[4] A. Boucherif and B. A. Slimani, *On the sign-variations of solutions of nonlinear two-point boundary value problems*, Nonlinear Analysis **22** (1994), no. 12, 1567–1577.

[5] R. Courant and D. Hilbert, *Methods of Mathematical Physics*, John Wiley & Sons, New York, 1962.

[6] L. H. Erbe and H. Wang, *On the existence of positive solutions of ordinary differential equations*, Proceedings of the American Mathematical Society **120** (1994), no. 3, 743–748.

[7] A. Granas and J. Dugundji, *Fixed Point Theory*, Springer Monographs in Mathematics, Springer, New York, 2003.

[8] D. J. Guo and V. Lakshmikantham, *Nonlinear Problems in Abstract Cones*, Notes and Reports in Mathematics in Science and Engineering, vol. 5, Academic Press, Massachusetts, 1988.

[9] J. Henderson and H. Wang, *Positive solutions for nonlinear eigenvalue problems*, Journal of Mathematical Analysis and Applications **208** (1997), no. 1, 252–259.

[10] M. A. Krasnosel'skiĭ, *Positive Solutions of Operator Equations*, P. Noordhoff, Groningen, 1964.
[11] Y. Li, *Positive solutions of second-order boundary value problems with sign-changing nonlinear terms*, Journal of Mathematical Analysis and Applications **282** (2003), no. 1, 232–240.
[12] ———, *On the existence and nonexistence of positive solutions for nonlinear Sturm-Liouville boundary value problems*, Journal of Mathematical Analysis and Applications **304** (2005), no. 1, 74–86.

Abdelkader Boucherif: Department of Mathematical Sciences, King Fahd University of Petroleum and Minerals, P. O. Box 5046, Dhahran 31261, Saudi Arabia
E-mail address: aboucher@kfupm.edu.sa

SPECTRAL STABILITY OF ELLIPTIC SELFADJOINT DIFFERENTIAL OPERATORS WITH DIRICHLET AND NEUMANN BOUNDARY CONDITIONS

VICTOR I. BURENKOV AND PIER DOMENICO LAMBERTI

We present a general spectral stability theorem for nonnegative selfadjoint operators with compact resolvents, which is based on the notion of a transition operator, and some applications to the study of the dependence of the eigenvalues of uniformly elliptic operators upon domain perturbation.

1. Introduction

Let Ω be a nonempty open set in $\mathbb{R}^N$. Let H be a nonnegative selfadjoint operator defined on a dense subspace of $L^2(\Omega)$ (briefly, a nonnegative selfadjoint operator on $L^2(\Omega)$) with compact resolvent. It is well known that the spectrum of H is discrete and its eigenvalues $\lambda_n[H]$, arranged in nondecreasing order and repeated according to multiplicity, can be represented by means of the min-max principle. Namely,

$$\lambda_n[H] = \inf_{\substack{L\subset \mathrm{Dom}(H^{1/2})\\ \dim L=n}} \sup_{\substack{u\in L\\ u\neq 0}} \frac{(H^{1/2}u,H^{1/2}u)_{L^2(\Omega)}}{(u,u)_{L^2(\Omega)}} \tag{1.1}$$

for all $n\in\mathbb{N}$, where $H^{1/2}$ denotes the square root of H. (For basic definitions and results, we refer to Davies [7].)

Here we study the variation of $\lambda_n[H]$ upon variation of H, on the understanding that Ω may vary as well. Namely, given two nonnegative selfadjoint operators H_1, H_2 on $L^2(\Omega_1)$, $L^2(\Omega_2)$, respectively, we aim at finding estimates of the type

$$\lambda_n[H_2] \leq \lambda_n[H_1] + c_n\delta(H_1,H_2), \tag{1.2}$$

where $\delta(H_1,H_2)$ is a prescribed measure of vicinity of H_1 and H_2, and $c_n\geq 0$. To do so, we present a general spectral stability result which, roughly speaking, claims that the validity

Hindawi Publishing Corporation
Proceedings of the Conference on Differential & Difference Equations and Applications, pp. 237–245

of inequality (1.2) for all $n \in \mathbb{N}$ is equivalent to the existence of a "transition operator from H_1 to H_2."

Then we present some applications to selfadjoint uniformly elliptic operators of the type

$$Hu = (-1)^m \sum_{|\alpha|=|\beta|=m} \frac{\partial^m}{\partial x^\alpha}\left(A_{\alpha\beta}(x)\frac{\partial^m u}{\partial x^\beta}\right), \quad x \in \Omega, \tag{1.3}$$

with homogeneous Dirichlet or Neumann boundary conditions. We assume that the coefficients $A_{\alpha\beta}$ are fixed, hence the eigenvalues of H depend only on Ω, that is, $\lambda_n[H] = \lambda_n[\Omega]$. Under the sole assumption that Ω belongs to a fixed family of open sets with continuous boundary, we prove that for any order $m \geq 1$, the eigenvalues $\lambda_n[\Omega]$ are stable under perturbations of Ω in such a class.

Moreover, for $m = 1$, we give sufficient conditions on the coefficients and the open sets in order to guarantee that the estimate

$$|\lambda_n[\Omega_1] - \lambda_n[\Omega_2]| \leq c_n |\Omega_1 \vartriangle \Omega_2|^\gamma \tag{1.4}$$

holds for some $\gamma > 0$. Here $\Omega_1 \vartriangle \Omega_2$ denotes the symmetric difference of Ω_1 and Ω_2. It turns out that the exponent γ depends on summability and differentiability properties of eigenfunctions. For open sets of class $C^{1,1}$, $\gamma = 1$ (which is the sharp exponent).

Some of the results in this paper have been presented without proof in [3] and proved in [4].

We mention that the case of Robin boundary conditions for the Laplace operator has been recently investigated by Burenkov and Lanza de Cristoforis [5].

2. A general spectral stability theorem

Let Ω be a nonempty open set in $\mathbb{R}^N$. Let H be a nonnegative selfadjoint operator on $L^2(\Omega)$ with compact resolvent. By $\varphi_n[H]$, $n \in \mathbb{N}$, we denote an orthonormal sequence of eigenfunctions corresponding to the eigenvalues $\lambda_n[H]$. We denote by $L_n[H]$ the linear space generated by $\varphi_1[H], \dots, \varphi_n[H]$ and we set $\mathcal{L}[H] = \bigcup_{n=1}^{\infty} L_n[H]$.

We start with recalling the notion of a transition operator introduced in [3, 4].

Definition 2.1. Let $\mathcal{A}_1$ and $\mathcal{A}_2$ be two nonempty families of nonempty open sets in $\mathbb{R}^N$, for all $\Omega_1 \in \mathcal{A}_1$, $\Omega_2 \in \mathcal{A}_2$, let $H_1 \equiv H_1[\Omega_1]$ and $H_2 \equiv H_2[\Omega_2]$ be nonnegative selfadjoint linear operators on $L^2(\Omega_1)$, $L^2(\Omega_2)$, respectively, with compact resolvents, and let $\mathcal{B}_1 = \{H_1[\Omega_1] : \Omega_1 \in \mathcal{A}_1\}$, $\mathcal{B}_2 = \{H_2[\Omega_2] : \Omega_2 \in \mathcal{A}_2\}$.

Moreover, let $\delta : \mathcal{B}_1 \times \mathcal{B}_2 \to [0,\infty)$ (a *measure of vicinity* of $H_1 \in \mathcal{B}_1$ and $H_2 \in \mathcal{B}_2$), $0 \leq a_{mn}, b_{mn} < \infty$, $0 < \delta'_{mn}, \delta''_{mn} \leq \infty$, for all $m,n \in \mathbb{N}$.

Given $H_1 \in \mathcal{B}_1$ and $H_2 \in \mathcal{B}_2$, we say that a linear operator $T_{12} : \mathcal{L}(H_1) \to \mathrm{Dom}(H_2^{1/2})$ is a *transition operator from H_1 to H_2 with the measure of vicinity δ and parameters a_{mn}*, b_{mn}, δ'_{mn}, and δ''_{mn} (briefly, a *transition operator from* H_1 to H_2), if the following conditions are satisfied:

(i) $(T_{12}\varphi_n[H_1], T_{12}\varphi_n[H_1])_{L^2(\Omega_2)} \geq 1 - a_{nn}\delta(H_1,H_2)$, $n \in \mathbb{N}$, if $\delta(H_1,H_2) < \delta'_{nn}$;

(ii) $|(T_{12}\varphi_m[H_1], T_{12}\varphi_n[H_1])_{L^2(\Omega_2)}| \leq a_{mn}\delta(H_1,H_2)$, $m,n \in \mathbb{N}$, $m \neq n$, if $\delta(H_1,H_2) < \delta'_{mn}$;

(iii) $(H_2^{1/2}T_{12}\varphi_n[H_1], H_2^{1/2}T_{12}\varphi_n[H_1])_{L^2(\Omega_2)} \le \lambda_n[H_1] + b_{nn}\delta(H_1,H_2)$, $n \in \mathbb{N}$, if $\delta(H_1, H_2) < \delta''_{nn}$;

(iv) $|(H_2^{1/2}T_{12}\varphi_m[H_1], H_2^{1/2}T_{12}\varphi_n[H_1])_{L^2(\Omega_2)}| \le b_{mn}\delta(H_1,H_2)$, $m,n \in \mathbb{N}$, $m \ne n$, if $\delta(H_1, H_2) < \delta''_{mn}$.

Then we have the following spectral stability theorem proved in [4].

THEOREM 2.2. *Let $\mathcal{A}_1$, $\mathcal{A}_2$, $\mathcal{B}_1$, $\mathcal{B}_2$, and $\delta : \mathcal{B}_1 \times \mathcal{B}_2 \to [0,\infty)$ be as in Definition 2.1. Then the following statements are equivalent:*

(s_1) for each $H_1 \in \mathcal{B}_1$ and for each $n \in \mathbb{N}$ there exist $c_n = c_n(H_1) \in [0,\infty[$ and $\epsilon_n = \epsilon_n(H_1) \in]0,\infty]$ such that inequality (1.2) holds for all $H_2 \in \mathcal{B}_2$ satisfying $\delta(H_1,H_2) < \epsilon_n$;

(s_2) for each $H_1 \in \mathcal{B}_1$ and for each $m,n \in \mathbb{N}$ there exist $a_{mn} = a_{mn}(H_1)$, $b_{mn} = b_{mn}(H_1) \in [0,\infty[$, $\delta'_{mn} = \delta'_{mn}(H_1)$, $\delta''_{mn} = \delta''_{mn}(H_1) \in]0,\infty]$ such that for each $H_2 \in \mathcal{B}_2$ there exists a transition operator T_{12} from H_1 to H_2 with the measure of vicinity δ and the parameters a_{mn}, b_{mn}, δ'_{mn}, δ''_{mn}.

Moreover, if statement (s_2) holds, then inequality (1.2) holds for all $H_1 \in \mathcal{B}_1$ and $H_2 \in \mathcal{B}_2$ satisfying $\delta(H_1,H_2) < \epsilon_n$ with

$$c_n = 2(a_n\lambda_n[H_1] + b_n), \qquad \epsilon_n = \min\left\{\delta'_n, \delta''_n, (2a_n)^{-1}\right\}, \tag{2.1}$$

where

$$\begin{gathered} a_n = \left(\sum_{k,l=1}^{n} a_{kl}^2\right)^{1/2}, \qquad b_n = \left(\sum_{k,l=1}^{n} b_{kl}^2\right)^{1/2}, \\ \delta'_n = \min_{k,l\le n}\delta'_{kl}, \qquad \delta''_n = \min_{k,l\le n}\delta''_{kl}. \end{gathered} \tag{2.2}$$

3. On a class of uniformly elliptic operators

Let Ω be an open set in $\mathbb{R}^N$. For all $m \in \mathbb{N}$, we denote by $W^{m,2}(\Omega)$ the Sobolev space of all those functions in $L^2(\Omega)$ whose weak derivatives of order m are in $L^2(\Omega)$, endowed with the norm

$$\|u\|_{W^{m,2}(\Omega)} = \|u\|_{L^2(\Omega)} + \sum_{|\alpha|=m}\left\|\frac{\partial^m u}{\partial x^\alpha}\right\|_{L^2(\Omega)}. \tag{3.1}$$

As usual $|\alpha| = \alpha_1 + \cdots + \alpha_N$ for all $\alpha = (\alpha_1,\dots,\alpha_N) \in \mathbb{N}_0^N$. We denote by $W_0^{m,2}(\Omega)$ the closure in $W^{m,2}(\Omega)$ of the space of all infinitely continuously differentiable functions with compact support in Ω.

For all $|\alpha| = |\beta| = m$, let $A_{\alpha\beta}$ be bounded measurable real-valued functions on Ω satisfying $A_{\alpha\beta} = A_{\beta\alpha}$ and the uniform ellipticity condition

$$\sum_{|\alpha|=|\beta|=m} A_{\alpha\beta}(x)\xi_\alpha\xi_\beta \ge \theta|\xi|^2, \tag{3.2}$$

for all $x \in \Omega$ and $\xi = (\xi_\alpha)_{|\alpha|=m}$, where $|\xi|$ denotes the Euclidean modulus of ξ and $\theta > 0$ is independent of x and ξ.

Let $V(\Omega)$ be a closed subspace of $W^{m,2}(\Omega)$ containing $W_0^{m,2}(\Omega)$. Then we consider the following eigenvalue problem:

$$\int_\Omega \sum_{|\alpha|=|\beta|=m} A_{\alpha\beta} \frac{\partial^m u}{\partial x^\alpha} \frac{\partial^m v}{\partial x^\beta} dx = \lambda \int_\Omega uv\, dx, \tag{3.3}$$

for all functions $v \in V(\Omega)$, in the unknowns $u \in V(\Omega)$, $u \not\to 0$ on Ω (the eigenfunctions) and $\lambda \in \mathbb{C}$ (the eigenvalues).

Clearly, problem (3.3) is the weak formulation of an eigenvalue problem for the operator H in (1.3) subject to suitable homogeneous boundary conditions. (The choice of $V(\Omega)$ corresponds to the choice of the boundary conditions.) We recall the following well-known result (cf. Davies [7, Theorem 4.4.2]).

Theorem 3.1. *Let $m \in \mathbb{N}$ and let Ω be an open set in $\mathbb{R}^N$ such that the embedding $V(\Omega) \subset L^2(\Omega)$ is compact. Let $\theta > 0$ and, for all $(\alpha,\beta) \in \mathbb{N}_0^N \times \mathbb{N}_0^N$ such that $|\alpha| = |\beta| = m$, let $A_{\alpha\beta}$ be bounded measurable real-valued functions defined on Ω, satisfying $A_{\alpha\beta} = A_{\beta\alpha}$ and condition (3.2).*

Then there exists a nonnegative selfadjoint linear operator H_V on $L^2(\Omega)$ with compact resolvent such that $\mathrm{Dom}(H_V^{1/2}) = V(\Omega)$ *and*

$$(H_V^{1/2}u, H_V^{1/2}v)_{L^2(\Omega)} = \int_\Omega \sum_{|\alpha|=|\beta|=m} A_{\alpha\beta} \frac{\partial^m u}{\partial x^\alpha} \frac{\partial^m \bar{v}}{\partial x^\beta} dx \tag{3.4}$$

for all $(u,v) \in V(\Omega) \times V(\Omega)$. Moreover, the eigenvalues defined by equation (3.3) coincide with the eigenvalues $\lambda_n[H_V]$ of H_V.

As usual, we speak about Dirichlet boundary conditions when $V(\Omega) = W_0^{m,2}(\Omega)$ and Neumann boundary conditions when $V(\Omega) = W^{m,2}(\Omega)$.

In the sequel we consider bounded open sets in $\mathbb{R}^N$ with continuous boundaries. For all $E \subset \mathbb{R}^N$ and $\rho > 0$, we set $E_\rho = \{x \in E : \mathrm{dist}(x, \partial E) > \rho\}$; then we recall the following definition.

Definition 3.2. Let $\rho > 0$, $s, s' \in \mathbb{N}$, $s' \le s$, and let $\{V_j\}_{j=1}^s$ be a family of bounded open cuboids and let $\{r_j\}_{j=1}^s$ be a family of rotations. We say that a bounded open set Ω in $\mathbb{R}^N$ has a continuous boundary with the parameters ρ, s, s', $\{V_j\}_{j=1}^s$, $\{r_j\}_{j=1}^s$ if

(i) $\Omega \subset \bigcup_{j=1}^s (V_j)_\rho$ and $(V_j)_\rho \cap \Omega \neq \emptyset$ for all $j = 1,\dots,s$;

(ii) $V_j \cap \partial\Omega \neq \emptyset$ for all $j = 1,\dots,s'$, and $V_j \cap \partial\Omega = \emptyset$ for all $s' < j \le s$;

(iii) there exist real numbers a_{jl}, b_{jl} with $a_{jl} < b_{jl}$ for all $j = 1,\dots,s$, $l = 1,\dots,N$ such that

$$r_j(V_j) = \{x \in \mathbb{R}^N : a_{jl} < x_l < b_{jl},\ l = 1,\dots,N\}, \tag{3.5}$$

for all $j = 1,\dots,s$, and

$$r_j(\Omega \cap V_j) = \{x \in \mathbb{R}^N : a_{jN} < x_N < g_j(\bar{x}),\ \bar{x} \in W_j\}, \tag{3.6}$$

for all $j = 1,\dots,s'$, where $x = (\bar{x},x_N)$, $\bar{x} = (x_1,\dots,x_{N-1})$, $W_j = \{\bar{x} \in \mathbb{R}^{N-1} : a_{jl} < x_l < b_{jl}, l = 1,\dots,N-1\}$ and g_j is a continuous function on W_j; moreover,

$$a_{jN} + \rho \le g_j(\bar{x}) \le b_{jN} - \rho, \tag{3.7}$$

for all $j = 1,\dots,s'$, $\bar{x} \in W_j$.

We also say that a bounded open set Ω in $\mathbb{R}^N$ has a continuous boundary if Ω has a continuous boundary with the parameters ρ, s, s', $\{V_j\}_{j=1}^s$, $\{r_j\}_{j=1}^s$ for some parameters ρ, s, s', $\{V_j\}_{j=1}^s$, $\{r_j\}_{j=1}^s$.

We recall that for any open set Ω in $\mathbb{R}^N$ of finite measure the embedding $W_0^{m,2}(\Omega) \subset L^2(\Omega)$ is compact. Moreover, if Ω has a continuous boundary, then the embedding $W^{m,2}(\Omega) \subset L^2(\Omega)$ is also compact (cf. Burenkov [1, Theorem 8, page 169]).

4. Spectral stability for Dirichlet and Neumann boundary conditions

In case of Dirichlet or Neumann boundary conditions and for fixed coefficients $A_{\alpha\beta}$, the eigenvalues $\lambda_n[H_V]$ of (3.3) depend only on Ω; in this case we simply write $H[\Omega]$, $\lambda_n[\Omega]$, $\varphi_n[\Omega]$, $\mathcal{L}[\Omega]$ instead of H_V, $\lambda_n[H_V]$, $\varphi_n[H_V]$, $\mathcal{L}[H_V]$, respectively.

It is well known that if Ω_1 and Ω_2 are open sets of finite measure and $\Omega_2 \subset \Omega_1$, then in the case of Dirichlet boundary conditions for all $n \in \mathbb{N}$

$$\lambda_n[\Omega_1] \le \lambda_n[\Omega_2]. \tag{4.1}$$

The following semicontinuity result in [3, 4] is a kind of a replacement of this property for the case of Neumann boundary conditions.

THEOREM 4.1. *Let $m \in \mathbb{N}$, $0 > 0$ and let Ω_1 be a fixed nonempty open set in $\mathbb{R}^N$ such that the embedding $W^{m,2}(\Omega_1) \subset L^2(\Omega_1)$ is compact. Assume that the coefficients $A_{\alpha\beta}$ are as in Theorem 3.1.*

Then for all $n \in \mathbb{N}$ and for all $\epsilon > 0$ there exists $\sigma > 0$ such that for all nonempty open sets $\Omega_2 \subset \Omega_1$ such that the embedding $W^{m,2}(\Omega_2) \subset L^2(\Omega_2)$ is compact and $|\Omega_1 \setminus \Omega_2| < \sigma$, we have, in case of Neumann boundary conditions,

$$\lambda_n[\Omega_2] \le \lambda_n[\Omega_1] + \epsilon. \tag{4.2}$$

Remark 4.2. If there are no further assumptions on Ω_1 and Ω_2, then no kind of inequalities reverse to (4.1) and (4.2) can hold. In the case of Neumann boundary conditions, there exist bounded open sets Ω_1 and $\Omega_{2,k} \subset \Omega_1$, $k \in \mathbb{N}$, such that

$$\lim_{k\to\infty} \inf_{(\Omega_1)_\epsilon \subset \Omega_{2,k}} \epsilon = 0, \tag{4.3}$$

hence

$$\lim_{k\to\infty} |\Omega_1 \setminus \Omega_{2,k}| = 0, \tag{4.4}$$

$\lambda_2[\Omega_1] > 0$ and $\lim_{k\to\infty}\lambda_2[\Omega_{2,k}] = 0$ (Courant and Hilbert [6, page 420]). In the case of Dirichlet boundary conditions, there exist bounded open sets Ω_1 and $\Omega_{2,k} \subset \Omega_1$, $k \in \mathbb{N}$, satisfying (4.4) and such that $\lim_{k\to\infty}\lambda_n[\Omega_{2,k}] = \infty$ for all $n \in \mathbb{N}$.

However, if Ω_1 and Ω_2 have continuous boundaries and there is some control over the parameters describing Ω_1 and Ω_2, it is possible to prove stability of eigenvalues for all $m, n \in \mathbb{N}$.

Given an open set Ω_1 in $\mathbb{R}^N$ with continuous boundary, we first consider perturbations Ω_2 of Ω_1 satisfying the condition

$$(\Omega_1)_\epsilon \subset \Omega_2 \subset (\Omega_1)^\epsilon, \tag{4.5}$$

for $\epsilon > 0$ sufficiently small, where $(\Omega_1)^\epsilon = \{x \in \mathbb{R}^N : d(x,\Omega_1) < \epsilon\}$.

Let $\omega : [0,\infty[\to [0,\infty[$ be a continuous increasing function such that $\omega(0) = 0$ and such that

$$\inf_{\substack{0\le a\le 1\\ 0<b\le 1}} \frac{\omega(a+b)-\omega(a)}{b} > 0. \tag{4.6}$$

We say that a bounded open set having a continuous boundary with the parameters ρ, s, s', $\{V_j\}_{j=1}^s$, $\{r_j\}_{j=1}^s$ is of class $C^\omega(M,\rho,s,s',\{V_j\}_{j=1}^s,\{r_j\}_{j=1}^s)$ where $M > 0$ if all the functions g_j in Definition 3.2 satisfy the condition

$$|g_j(\bar{x}) - g_j(\bar{y})| \le M\omega(|\bar{x}-\bar{y}|) \tag{4.7}$$

for all $\bar{x}, \bar{y} \in W_j$.

Then we have the following uniform continuity result.

THEOREM 4.3. *Let ρ, s, s', $\{V_j\}_{j=1}^s$, $\{r_j\}_{j=1}^s$ be as in Definition 3.2. Let $M > 0$ and ω be a continuous increasing function of $[0,\infty[$ to itself satisfying $\omega(0) = 0$ and condition (4.6). Let $m \in \mathbb{N}$, $\theta > 0$ and, for all $(\alpha,\beta) \in \mathbb{N}_0^N \times \mathbb{N}_0^N$ such that $|\alpha| = |\beta| = m$, let $A_{\alpha\beta}$ be Lipschitz continuous real-valued functions defined on $\bigcup_{j=1}^s V_j$ satisfying $A_{\alpha\beta} = A_{\beta\alpha}$ and condition (3.2) for all $x \in \bigcup_{j=1}^s V_j$.*

Then there exists a continuous increasing function f of $[0,\infty[$ to itself such that $f(0) = 0$ and for all $n \in \mathbb{N}$ there exist $c_n, \epsilon_n > 0$, such that, for both Dirichlet and Neumann boundary conditions,

$$|\lambda_n[\Omega_1] - \lambda_n[\Omega_2]| \le c_n f(\epsilon), \tag{4.8}$$

for all $\epsilon \in [0,\epsilon_n[$ and all open sets Ω_1, Ω_2 in $\mathbb{R}^N$ of class $C^\omega(M,\rho,s,s',\{V_j\}_{j=1}^s,\{r_j\}_{j=1}^s)$, satisfying (4.5).

In what follows, we focus our attention on second-order operators; thus *in the sequel we consider only the case $m = 1$.*

Let $0 < \gamma \le 1$ and $\omega(a) = a^\gamma$ for all $a \ge 0$. In this case, if Ω is of class $C^\omega(M,\rho,s,s',\{V_j\}_{j=1}^s,\{r_j\}_{j=1}^s)$, then Ω has a Hölder continuous boundary and we say that Ω is of class $C^{0,\gamma}(M,\rho,s,s',\{V_j\}_{j=1}^s,\{r_j\}_{j=1}^s)$.

THEOREM 4.4. *Let ρ, s, s', $\{V_j\}_{j=1}^{s}$, $\{r_j\}_{j=1}^{s}$ be as in Definition 3.2, $M > 0$ and $0 < \gamma \leq 1$. Assume that the coefficients $A_{\alpha\beta}$ are as in Theorem 4.3.*

Then for all $n \in \mathbb{N}$ there exist $c_n, \epsilon_n > 0$ such that for both Dirichlet and Neumann boundary conditions,

$$|\lambda_n[\Omega_1] - \lambda_n[\Omega_2]| \leq c_n \epsilon^\gamma, \tag{4.9}$$

for all $\epsilon \in [0, \epsilon_n[$ and all open sets Ω_1, Ω_2 in $\mathbb{R}^N$ of class $C^{0,\gamma}(M,\rho,s,s',\{V_j\}_{j=1}^{s},\{r_j\}_{j=1}^{s})$ satisfying (4.5).

For Neumann boundary conditions and $\Omega_2 \subset \Omega_1$ this result was proved in Burenkov and Davies [2]. For related results in case of Dirichlet boundary conditions see Davies [8] and Pang [9].

Under stronger assumptions on Ω_1 and Ω_2 it is possible to obtain a better estimate of $|\lambda_n[\Omega_1] - \lambda_n[\Omega_2]|$ via the measure of the difference of Ω_1 and Ω_2 if $\Omega_2 \subset \Omega_1$.

THEOREM 4.5. *Let $\theta > 0$, $2 < p \leq \infty$ and let Ω_1 be a fixed nonempty open set in $\mathbb{R}^N$ such that the embedding $W^{1,2}(\Omega_1) \subset L^2(\Omega_1)$ is compact. Assume that the coefficients $A_{\alpha\beta}$ are as in Theorem 3.1.*

Assume that, for Neumann boundary conditions,

$$\varphi_n[\Omega_1] \in L^p(\Omega_1), \tag{4.10}$$

for all $n \in \mathbb{N}$. Then for all $n \in \mathbb{N}$ there exist $c_n, \epsilon_n > 0$ such that

$$\lambda_n[\Omega_2] \leq \lambda_n[\Omega_1] + c_n |\Omega_1 \setminus \Omega_2|^{1-(2/p)}, \tag{4.11}$$

for all nonempty open sets $\Omega_2 \subset \Omega_1$ such that the embedding $W^{1,2}(\Omega_2) \subset L^2(\Omega_2)$ is compact and $|\Omega_1 \setminus \Omega_2| < \epsilon_n$.

This theorem is proved in [4].

THEOREM 4.6. *Let ρ, s, s', $\{V_j\}_{j=1}^{s}$, $\{r_j\}_{j=1}^{s}$ be as in Definition 3.2, and $M, \theta > 0$, $2 < p \leq \infty$. Let Ω_1 be an open set in $\mathbb{R}^N$ of class $C^{0,1}(M,\rho,s,s',\{V_j\}_{j=1}^{s},\{r_j\}_{j=1}^{s})$.*

Assume that the coefficients $A_{\alpha\beta}$ are as in Theorem 3.1 and that, for Dirichlet boundary conditions,

$$\varphi_n[\Omega_1] \in W^{1,p}(\Omega_1), \tag{4.12}$$

for all $n \in \mathbb{N}$.

Then for all $n \in \mathbb{N}$ there exist $c_n, \epsilon_n > 0$ such that

$$\lambda_n[\Omega_1] \leq \lambda_n[\Omega_2] \leq \lambda_n[\Omega_1] + c_n |\Omega_1 \setminus \Omega_2|^{1-(2/p)}, \tag{4.13}$$

for all open sets $\Omega_2 \subset \Omega_1$ of class $C^{0,1}(M,\rho,s,s',\{V_j\}_{j=1}^{s},\{r_j\}_{j=1}^{s})$ satisfying $|\Omega_1 \setminus \Omega_2| < \epsilon_n$.

We observe that the exponent $1 - 2/p$ depends only on summability and differentiability properties of the eigenfunctions in Ω_1.

Example 4.7. Let $0 < \gamma \le 1$. We say that a bounded open set in $\mathbb{R}^N$ having continuous boundary with parameters ρ, s, s', $\{V_j\}_{j=1}^s$, $\{r_j\}_{j=1}^s$ is of class $C^{1,\gamma}(M,\rho,s,s',\{V_j\}_{j=1}^s, \{r_j\}_{j=1}^s)$ if all the functions g_j in Definition 3.2 are differentiable and satisfy the condition

$$\left|\frac{\partial g_j}{\partial x_i}(\bar{x})\right| \le M, \qquad \left|\frac{\partial g_j}{\partial x_i}(\bar{x}) - \frac{\partial g_j}{\partial x_i}(\bar{y})\right| \le M|\bar{x}-\bar{y}|^{\gamma}, \tag{4.14}$$

for all $\bar{x}, \bar{y} \in W_j$, $i = 1,\ldots,N-1$.

If Ω_1 is of class $C^{1,\gamma}(M,\rho,s,s',\{V_j\}_{j=1}^s,\{r_j\}_{j=1}^s)$ and the coefficients $A_{\alpha\beta}$ are of class $C^{0,\gamma}(\bar{\Omega}_1)$ for some $0 < \gamma \le 1$, then one can choose $p = \infty$ in (4.12), hence the sharp exponent $1 - 2/p = 1$ in (4.13).

Under still stronger assumptions on Ω_1 and Ω_2 we can deal with perturbations Ω_2 of Ω_1 not necessarily contained in Ω_1.

Theorem 4.8. *Let ρ, s, s', $\{V_j\}_{j=1}^s$, $\{r_j\}_{j=1}^s$ be as in Definition 3.2, and $M,\theta > 0$, $2 < p \le \infty$. Assume that the coefficients $A_{\alpha\beta}$ are bounded measurable functions defined on $\bigcup_{j=1}^s V_j$ satisfying $A_{\alpha\beta} = A_{\beta\alpha}$ and condition (3.2) for all $x \in \bigcup_{j=1}^s V_j$.*

Moreover, assume that $\mathcal{A}$ is a nonempty family of open sets of class $C^{0,1}(M,\rho,s,s',\{V_j\}_{j=1}^s,\{r_j\}_{j=1}^s)$ such that for Dirichlet or Neumann boundary conditions

$$\sup_{\Omega\in\mathcal{A}} \|\varphi_n[\Omega]\|_{W^{1,p}(\Omega)} < \infty \tag{4.15}$$

for all $n \in \mathbb{N}$.

Then for all $n \in \mathbb{N}$ there exist $c_n, \epsilon_n > 0$ such that

$$|\lambda_n[\Omega_1] - \lambda_n[\Omega_2]| \le c_n |\Omega_1 \triangle \Omega_2|^{1-(2/p)} \tag{4.16}$$

for all $\Omega_1, \Omega_2 \in \mathcal{A}$ satisfying $|\Omega_1 \triangle \Omega_2| < \epsilon_n$.

Theorem 4.9. *Let ρ, s, s', $\{V_j\}_{j=1}^s$, $\{r_j\}_{j=1}^s$ be as in Definition 3.2, and $M,\theta > 0$. Assume that the coefficients $A_{\alpha\beta}$ are as in Theorem 4.3.*

Then for all $n \in \mathbb{N}$ there exist $c_n, \epsilon_n > 0$ such that, for both Dirichlet and Neumann boundary conditions,

$$|\lambda_n[\Omega_1] - \lambda_n[\Omega_2]| \le c_n |\Omega_1 \triangle \Omega_2|, \tag{4.17}$$

for all open sets Ω_1, Ω_2 in $\mathbb{R}^N$ of class $C^{1,1}(M,\rho,s,s',\{V_j\}_{j=1}^s,\{r_j\}_{j=1}^s)$ satisfying $|\Omega_1 \triangle \Omega_2| < \epsilon_n$.

For Neumann boundary conditions Theorems 4.8 and 4.9 are proved in [4].

The proofs of all above results are based on Theorem 2.2. Given two open sets Ω_1, Ω_2 in $\mathbb{R}^N$, the idea is to find suitable transition operators from the operator $H[\Omega_1]$ to the operator $H[\Omega_2]$ and vice versa. The choice of the measure of vicinity depends on the problem: for instance, in Theorems 4.5 and 4.6 we use the measure of vicinity $\delta(H[\Omega_1],H[\Omega_2]) = |\Omega_1 \setminus \Omega_2|^{1-2/p}$, while in Theorem 4.9 $\delta(H[\Omega_1],H[\Omega_2]) = |\Omega_1 \triangle \Omega_2|$.

The proof of Theorem 4.3 is more complicated and requires several technical steps involving different measures of vicinity which we do not report here.

We find it interesting to describe the main idea used to prove Theorem 4.6. Given two open sets Ω_1, Ω_2 of class $C^{0,1}(M,\rho,s,s',\{V_j\}_{j=1}^s,\{r_j\}_{j=1}^s)$ such that $\Omega_2 \subset \Omega_1$, it is possible to construct a linear operator T_{12} of $L^1_{\mathrm{loc}}(\Omega_1)$ to $L^1_{\mathrm{loc}}(\Omega_2)$ such that the following conditions are satisfied:

(i) for all $1 \le p \le \infty$, T_{12} is bounded from $L^p(\Omega_1)$ to $L^p(\Omega_2)$, from $W^{1,p}(\Omega_1)$ to $W^{1,p}(\Omega_2)$, and from $W_0^{1,p}(\Omega_1)$ to $W_0^{1,p}(\Omega_2)$;

(ii) there exists $c > 0$ depending only on N, M, ρ, s, s', $\{V_j\}_{j=1}^s$, $\{r_j\}_{j=1}^s$, and there exists an open set $\Omega_3 \subset \Omega_2$ such that $|\Omega_2 \setminus \Omega_3| \le c|\Omega_1 \setminus \Omega_2|$, and $T_{12}[u](x) = u(x)$, for all $u \in L^1_{\mathrm{loc}}(\Omega_1)$ and for almost all $x \in \Omega_3$.

Then we set $\mathcal{A}_1 \equiv \{\Omega_1\}$, $\mathcal{A}_2 \equiv \{\Omega_2 \subset \Omega_1 : \Omega_2$ is of class $C^{0,1}(M,\rho,s,s',\{V_j\}_{j=1}^s,\{r_j\}_{j=1}^s)\}$, $\mathcal{B}_1 \equiv \{H[\Omega_1]\}$, $\mathcal{B}_2 \equiv \{H[\Omega_2] : \Omega_2 \in \mathcal{A}_2\}$, and $\delta(H[\Omega_1], H[\Omega_2]) \equiv |\Omega_1 \setminus \Omega_2|^{1-2/p}$. We recall that for Dirichlet boundary conditions and second-order operators $\mathrm{Dom}(H^{1/2}[\Omega]) = W_0^{1,2}(\Omega)$, hence T_{12} maps $\mathcal{L}[\Omega_1]$ to $\mathrm{Dom}(H^{1/2}[\Omega_2])$. Finally, by assumption (4.12), it is possible to prove that T_{12} satisfies conditions (i)–(iv) in Definition 2.1 for some parameters a_{mn}, b_{mn}, δ'_{mn}, δ''_{mn} not depending on Ω_2. Thus T_{12} is a transition operator from $H[\Omega_1]$ to $H[\Omega_2]$ with the measure of vicinity δ and by Theorem 2.2 and (4.1) it follows that there exist $c_n, \epsilon_n > 0$ such that inequality (4.13) holds if $|\Omega_1 \setminus \Omega_2| < \epsilon_n$.

References

[1] V. I. Burenkov, *Sobolev Spaces on Domains*, Teubner Texts in Mathematics, vol. 137, B. G. Teubner, Stuttgart, 1998.

[2] V. I. Burenkov and E. B. Davies, *Spectral stability of the Neumann Laplacian*, Journal of Differential Equations **186** (2002), no. 2, 485–508.

[3] V. I. Burenkov and P. D. Lamberti, *Spectral stability of nonnegative selfadjoint operators*, Rossiĭskaya Akademiya Nauk. Doklady Akademii Nauk **403** (2005), no. 2, 159–164 (Russian), English translation in Doklady Mathematics **72** (2005), 507–511.

[4] ———, *Spectral stability of general nonnegative selfadjoint operators with applications to Neumann-type operators*, preprint, 2005.

[5] V. I. Burenkov and M. Lanza de Cristoforis, *Spectral stability of the Robin Laplacian*, preprint, 2005.

[6] R. Courant and D. Hilbert, *Methods of Mathematical Physics. Vol. I*, Interscience, New York, 1953.

[7] E. B. Davies, *Spectral Theory and Differential Operators*, Cambridge Studies in Advanced Mathematics, vol. 42, Cambridge University Press, Cambridge, 1995.

[8] ———, *Sharp boundary estimates for elliptic operators*, Mathematical Proceedings of the Cambridge Philosophical Society **129** (2000), no. 1, 165–178.

[9] M. M. H. Pang, *Approximation of ground state eigenvalues and eigenfunctions of Dirichlet Laplacians*, The Bulletin of the London Mathematical Society **29** (1997), no. 6, 720–730.

Victor I. Burenkov: Cardiff School of Mathematics, Cardiff University, Cardiff, CF24 4AG, UK
E-mail address: burenkov@cardiff.ac.uk

Pier Domenico Lamberti: Dipartimento di Matematica Pura ed Applicata, Università degli Studi di Padova, 35131 Padova, Italy
E-mail address: lamberti@math.unipd.it

MAXIMUM PRINCIPLES FOR THIRD-ORDER INITIAL AND TERMINAL VALUE PROBLEMS

ALBERTO CABADA

This paper is devoted to the study of positive solutions of third-order linear problems. We give an abstract formula to obtain the expression of the solutions of the nth-order initial value problems. We apply this expression to third-order equations and obtain maximum principles in different spaces. We translate the given results for terminal problems.

1. Introduction

The study of maximum principles is a very well-known tool to deduce the existence of solutions of nonlinear problems. This kind of results are related with the constant sign of solutions of initial or boundary value problems. Such constant sign property is fundamental to ensure the monotonicity of suitable operators (the solutions of the considered equations coincide with their fixed points), such monotonicity character, even in the case of discontinuity [11, 15], remains as a sufficient condition to warrant the existence of fixed points of the treated operator.

One of the most common applications, where such comparison results are used, is the method of upper and lower solutions coupled with iterative methods. In general, the applicability of this kind of technique depends strongly on the sign of Green's function representations for the solutions of certain linear problems associated to the considered initial or boundary value problem. One can find classical results of this theory in the monographs [3, 16], more recent results can be found in [12–14]. Periodic problems for second-, third-, and higher-order ordinary differential equations have been studied in [4–6, 9], impulsive equations have been considered in [7, 8], difference equations can be found in [1, 2, 10]. Multiplicity [17] or stability results [12] are deduced from comparison principles.

In this paper we are interested in the study of third-order initial value problems. We only present the range of the values for which the considered operators satisfy maximum principles in suitable spaces. The applications can be deduced as a direct consequence of the previously mentioned works.

Hindawi Publishing Corporation
Proceedings of the Conference on Differential & Difference Equations and Applications, pp. 247–255

In Section 2 of the present paper, we find an integral representation for the solutions of the following nth-order linear differential equation.

$$L_n u(t) \equiv u^{(n)}(t) + \sum_{i=0}^{n-1} a_i u^{(i)}(t) = \sigma(t) \quad \text{for a.e. } t \in I,$$
$$u^{(i)}(a) = \lambda_i, \quad i = 0,\dots,n-1, \tag{1.1}$$

where $I = [a,b]$, $\sigma \in L^1(I)$, and $a_i, \lambda_i \in \mathbb{R}$, $i = 0,\dots,n-1$.

We are looking for solutions on the space

$$W^{n,1}(I) \equiv \{u \in C^{n-1}(I),\ u^{(n-1)} \text{ is absolutely continuous in } I\}. \tag{1.2}$$

Section 3 is devoted to the study of the parameters of different third-order operators for which they are inverse positive on adequate spaces.

In Section 4, we obtain comparison results for third-order terminal value problems.

2. Expression of the solutions of nth-order initial value problems

In this section we obtain the expression of the unique solution of problem (1.1) as a function of the unique solution of the following problem:

$$z^{(n)}(t) + \sum_{i=0}^{n-1} a_i z^{(i)}(t) = 0 \quad \text{for a.e. } t \in I,$$
$$z^{(i)}(a) = 0, \quad i = 0,\dots,n-2, \tag{2.1}$$
$$z^{(n-1)}(a) = 1.$$

This formula improves the one obtained in [7] for the particular case of $a_1 = \cdots = a_{n-1} = 0$. The result is the following.

Lemma 2.1. *Let r be the unique solution of problem (2.1). Then the unique solution of problem (1.1) is given by the following expression:*

$$u(t) = \int_a^t r(a+t-s)\sigma(s)ds + \sum_{i=0}^{n-1} r_i(t)\lambda_i, \tag{2.2}$$

where

$$r_i(t) = r^{(n-1-i)}(t) + \sum_{j=i+1}^{n-1} a_j r^{(j-i-1)}(t), \quad t \in I,\ i = 0,\dots,n-1. \tag{2.3}$$

Proof. Let

$$v(t) = \int_a^t r(a+t-s)\sigma(s)ds. \tag{2.4}$$

From the definition of r, we obtain

$$v^{(i)}(t) = \int_a^t r^{(i)}(a+t-s)\sigma(s)ds \tag{2.5}$$

for $i = 0, 1, \ldots, n-1$, and

$$v^{(n)}(t) = \int_a^t r^{(n)}(a+t-s)\sigma(s)ds + \sigma(t). \tag{2.6}$$

In consequence,

$$v^{(i)}(a) = 0, \quad \forall i = 0, 1, \ldots, n-1 \tag{2.7}$$

and, for a.e. $t \in I$,

$$\begin{aligned} &v^{(n)}(t) + \sum_{i=0}^{n-1} a_i v^{(i)}(t) \\ &= \int_a^t \left[r^{(n)}(a+t-s) + \sum_{i=0}^{n-1} a_i r^{(i)}(a+t-s) \right] \sigma(s)ds + \sigma(t) = \sigma(t). \end{aligned} \tag{2.8}$$

On the other hand, it is clear that

$$\begin{gathered} r'^{(n)}(t) + \sum_{i=0}^{n-1} a_i r'^{(i)}(t) = 0, \\ r^{(n)}(a) = -a_{n-1}. \end{gathered} \tag{2.9}$$

Thus, the function $r_{n-2} \equiv r' + a_{n-1} r$ is the unique solution of the problem

$$\begin{gathered} z^{(n)}(t) + \sum_{i=0}^{n-1} a_i z^{(i)}(t) = 0, \\ z^{(i)}(a) = 0, \quad i = 0, \ldots, n-1, \ i \neq n-2, \\ z^{(n-2)}(a) = 1. \end{gathered} \tag{2.10}$$

Analogously, we can prove that for all $j \in \{0, 1, \ldots, n-1\}$, function r_{n-1-j} is the unique solution of

$$\begin{gathered} z^{(n)}(t) + \sum_{i=0}^{n-1} a_i z^{(i)}(t) = 0, \\ z^{(i)}(a) = 0, \quad i = 0, \ldots, n-1, \ i \neq n-1-j, \\ z^{(n-1-j)}(a) = 1. \end{gathered} \tag{2.11}$$

Hence, the function

$$u(t) = v(t) + \sum_{i=0}^{n-1} r_i(t)\lambda_i \tag{2.12}$$

is the unique solution of the problem (1.1). □

3. Maximum principles for third-order initial value problems

In this section we study some particular cases of third-order linear operators, obtaining the values for which they satisfy maximum principles in suitable spaces.

First we define the concept of inverse positive operator as follows.

Definition 3.1. The nth-order linear operator L_n defined in a real Banach space Ω, that contains the set $C[a,b]$, is inverse positive on Ω if and only if $Lu \geq 0$ in $[a,b]$ implies $u \geq 0$ in $[a,b]$, for all $u \in \Omega$.

Consider now the set

$$\Omega^n_{a,b} = \{u \in W^{n,1}[a,b],\ u^{(i)}(a) \geq 0,\ i = 0,\dots,n-1\}. \tag{3.1}$$

Following the arguments of [7, Lemmas 2.1 and 3.1 and Corollary 2.1], we can prove the following results.

Lemma 3.2. *The operator L_n is inverse positive on $\Omega^n_{a,b}$ if and only if the operator $u^{(n)} + \sum_{i=0}^{n-1}((b-a)/(d-c))^{n-i}a_i u^{(i)}$ is inverse positive on $\Omega^n_{c,d}$.*

Lemma 3.3. *Assume that L_n is inverse positive on $\Omega^n_{a,b}$ and $0 < d-c \leq b-a$. Then the operator L_n is inverse positive on $\Omega^n_{c,d}$.*

Lemma 3.4. *If the operator L_n is inverse positive on $\Omega^n_{a,b}$, then the operator $u^{(n)}+\sum_{i=0}^{n-1}\mu a_i u^{(i)}$ is inverse positive on $\Omega^n_{a,b}$ for all $\mu \in (0,1]$.*

Define the following sets and operators:

$$\begin{aligned}
\Omega_0 &= \{u \in W^{3,1}[a,b],\ u(a) \geq 0,\ u'(a) \geq 0,\ u''(a) \geq 0\},\\
\Omega_1 &= \{u \in W^{3,1}[a,b],\ u(a) = 0,\ u'(a) \geq 0,\ u''(a) \geq 0\},\\
\Omega_2 &= \{u \in W^{3,1}[a,b],\ u(a) = 0,\ u'(a) = 0,\ u''(a) \geq 0\},\\
\Omega_3 &= \{u \in W^{3,1}[a,b],\ u(a) \geq 0,\ u'(a) = 0,\ u''(a) \geq 0\},\\
L_3^1 u &\equiv u''' + Mu,\\
L_3^2 u &\equiv u''' + Mu',\\
L_3^3 u &\equiv u''' + Mu''.
\end{aligned} \tag{3.2}$$

One can verify that Lemmas 3.2, 3.3, and 3.4 remain valid for spaces Ω_1, Ω_2, and Ω_3. Moreover, as a consequence of Lemma 3.4, it is not difficult to deduce the following result.

Corollary 3.5. *The range of values for which operators L_3^1, L_3^2, and L_3^3 are inverse positive on Ω_i for some $i = 0,1,2,3$ is an interval.*

The following result is a direct consequence of Definition 3.1 and the expression (2.2).

Lemma 3.6. *The following properties hold.*

(1) *Operator L_3 is inverse positive on Ω_0 if and only if $r_0, r_1, r \geq 0$ on $[a,b]$.*
(2) *Operator L_3 is inverse positive on Ω_1 if and only if $r_1, r \geq 0$ on $[a,b]$.*
(3) *Operator L_3 is inverse positive on Ω_2 if and only if $r \geq 0$ on $[a,b]$.*
(4) *Operator L_3 is inverse positive on Ω_3 if and only if $r_0, r \geq 0$ on $[a,b]$.*

In the next result we obtain maximum principles for operator L_3^1.

Lemma 3.7. *The following properties hold.*

(1) *L_3^1 is inverse positive on Ω_0 and Ω_3 if and only if*

$$M \in \left(-\infty, \left(\frac{m_0}{b-a} \right)^3 \right], \tag{3.3}$$

where $m_0 \approx 1.84981$ is the smallest positive solution of the equation

$$e^{-3m/2} = -2\cos\left(\frac{\sqrt{3}m}{2} \right). \tag{3.4}$$

(2) *L_3^1 is inverse positive on Ω_1 if and only if*

$$M \in \left(-\infty, \left(\frac{m_1}{b-a} \right)^3 \right], \tag{3.5}$$

where $m_1 \approx 3.01674$ is the smallest positive solution of the equation

$$e^{-3m/2} = \cos\left(\frac{\sqrt{3}m}{2} \right) + \sqrt{3}\sin\left(\frac{\sqrt{3}m}{2} \right). \tag{3.6}$$

(3) *L_3^1 is inverse positive on Ω_2 if and only if*

$$M \in \left(-\infty, \left(\frac{m_2}{b-a} \right)^3 \right], \tag{3.7}$$

where $m_0 \approx 3.33334$ is the smallest positive solution of the equation

$$e^{-3m/2} = \cos\left(\frac{\sqrt{3}m}{2} \right) - \sqrt{3}\sin\left(\frac{\sqrt{3}m}{2} \right). \tag{3.8}$$

Proof. One can verify that, in this case, function r is given by the following expression in $[0,1]$:

$$r(t)=\begin{cases}\dfrac{e^{-mt/2}\left(e^{3mt/2}-\sqrt{3}\sin(\sqrt{3}mt/2)-\cos(\sqrt{3}mt/2)\right)}{3m^2} & \text{if } M=-m^3<0,\\[2mm] \dfrac{t^2}{2} & \text{if } M=0,\\[2mm] \dfrac{e^{mt/2}\left(e^{-3mt/2}+\sqrt{3}\sin(\sqrt{3}mt/2)-\cos(\sqrt{3}mt/2)\right)}{3m^2} & \text{if } M=m^3>0.\end{cases} \tag{3.9}$$

Moreover $r_1 \equiv r'$ and $r_0 = r''$.

The proof is a direct consequence of Lemma 3.6 and Corollary 3.5. □

Remark 3.8. In [7, Lemma 2.4] it is proved case 1 in Ω_0 for $M \in (0,(m_0/(b-a))^3]$.

Now, we give comparison results for operator L_3^2.

Lemma 3.9. *The following properties are fulfilled.*

(1) *L_3^2 is inverse positive on Ω_0 and Ω_1 if and only if*

$$M \in \left(-\infty, \frac{\pi^2}{(b-a)^3}\right]. \tag{3.10}$$

(2) *L_3^2 is inverse positive on Ω_2 and Ω_3 for all $M \in \mathbb{R}$.*

Proof. Now, function r is given by the following expression in $[0,1]$:

$$r(t)=\begin{cases}\dfrac{e^{mt}+e^{-mt}-2}{2m^2} & \text{if } M=-m^2<0,\\[2mm] \dfrac{t^2}{2} & \text{if } M=0,\\[2mm] \dfrac{1-\cos mt}{m^2} & \text{if } M=m^2>0.\end{cases} \tag{3.11}$$

Moreover $r_1 \equiv r'$ and $r_0 = r'' + Mr \equiv 1$.

The proof follows from Lemma 3.6 and Corollary 3.5. □

Now, we study operator L_3^3.

Lemma 3.10. *The operator L_3^3 is inverse positive on Ω_i, $i = 0,1,2,3$ for all $M \in \mathbb{R}$.*

Proof. The proof follows from the fact that, in $[0,1]$, $r(t) = e^{-Mt}$ and $r_1 \equiv r_0 \equiv 0$. □

4. Maximum principles for third-order terminal value problems

In this section we obtain the values for which operators L_3^1, L_3^2, and L_3^3 satisfy maximum principles in the following sets:

$$\begin{gathered}\Lambda_0 = \{u \in W^{3,1}[a,b],\ u(a) \geq 0,\ u'(a) \leq 0,\ u''(a) \geq 0\},\\ \Lambda_1 = \{u \in W^{3,1}[a,b],\ u(a) = 0,\ u'(a) \leq 0,\ u''(a) \geq 0\},\\ \Lambda_2 = \Omega_2,\\ \Lambda_3 = \Omega_3.\end{gathered} \tag{4.1}$$

First, we present the following result. The proof follows by direct computation.

Lemma 4.1. *u is a solution of (1.1) if and only if $v(t) \equiv u(b+a-t)$ is a solution of the equation*

$$\begin{gathered}v^{(n)}(t) + \sum_{i=0}^{n-1}(-1)^i a_i v^{(i)}(t) = \sigma(b+a-t) \quad \text{for a.e. } t \in I,\\ v^{(i)}(a) = (-1)^i \lambda_i, \quad i = 0,\dots,n-1.\end{gathered} \tag{4.2}$$

So, by using Lemma 4.1, we attain the following results.

Lemma 4.2. *The following properties are satisfied.*

(1) *L_3^1 is inverse positive on Λ_0 and Λ_3 if and only if*

$$M \in \left(-\infty, \left(\frac{m_0}{b-a}\right)^3\right], \tag{4.3}$$

with m_0 given in Lemma 3.7.

(2) *L_3^1 is inverse positive on Λ_1 if and only if*

$$M \in \left(-\infty, \left(\frac{m_1}{b-a}\right)^3\right], \tag{4.4}$$

with m_1 given in Lemma 3.7.

(3) *L_3^1 is inverse positive on Λ_2 if and only if*

$$M \in \left(-\infty, \left(\frac{m_2}{b-a}\right)^3\right], \tag{4.5}$$

with m_2 given in Lemma 3.7.

LEMMA 4.3. *The following properties hold.*

(1) L_3^2 *is inverse positive on* Λ_0 *and* Λ_1 *if and only if*

$$M \in \left[-\frac{\pi^2}{(b-a)^3}, \infty \right). \tag{4.6}$$

(2) L_3^2 *is inverse positive on* Λ_2 *and* Λ_3 *for all* $M \in \mathbb{R}$.

LEMMA 4.4. *The operator* L_3^3 *is inverse positive on* Λ_i, $i = 0,1,2,3$ *for all* $M \in \mathbb{R}$.

References

[1] R. P. Agarwal, A. Cabada, and V. Otero-Espinar, *Existence and uniqueness results for n-th order nonlinear difference equations in presence of lower and upper solutions*, Archives of Inequalities and Applications **1** (2003), no. 3-4, 421–431.

[2] R. P. Agarwal, A. Cabada, V. Otero-Espinar, and S. Dontha, *Existence and uniqueness of solutions for anti-periodic difference equations*, Archives of Inequalities and Applications **2** (2004), no. 4, 397–411.

[3] S. R. Bernfeld and V. Lakshmikantham, *An Introduction to Nonlinear Boundary Value Problems*, Mathematics in Science and Engineering, vol. 109, Academic Press, New York, 1974.

[4] A. Cabada, *The method of lower and upper solutions for nth-order periodic boundary value problems*, Journal of Applied Mathematics and Stochastic Analysis **7** (1994), no. 1, 33–47.

[5] ———, *The method of lower and upper solutions for second, third, fourth, and higher order boundary value problems*, Journal of Mathematical Analysis and Applications **185** (1994), no. 2, 302–320.

[6] ———, *The method of lower and upper solutions for third-order periodic boundary value problems*, Journal of Mathematical Analysis and Applications **195** (1995), no. 2, 568–589.

[7] A. Cabada and E. Liz, *Boundary value problems for higher order ordinary differential equations with impulses*, Nonlinear Analysis **32** (1998), no. 6, 775–786.

[8] A. Cabada, E. Liz, and S. Lois, *Green's function and maximum principle for higher order ordinary differential equations with impulses*, Rocky Mountain Journal of Mathematics **30** (2000), no. 2, 435–446.

[9] A. Cabada and S. Lois, *Maximum principles for fourth and sixth order periodic boundary value problems*, Nonlinear Analysis **29** (1997), no. 10, 1161–1171.

[10] A. Cabada and V. Otero-Espinar, *Optimal existence results for nth order periodic boundary value difference equations*, Journal of Mathematical Analysis and Applications **247** (2000), no. 1, 67–86.

[11] S. Carl and S. Heikkilä, *Nonlinear Differential Equations in Ordered Spaces*, Chapman & Hall/CRC Monographs and Surveys in Pure and Applied Mathematics, vol. 111, Chapman & Hall/CRC, Florida, 2000.

[12] C. De Coster and P. Habets, *Upper and lower solutions in the theory of ODE boundary value problems: classical and recent results*, Non-Linear Analysis and Boundary Value Problems for Ordinary Differential Equations (Udine), CISM Courses and Lectures, vol. 371, Springer, Vienna, 1996, pp. 1–78.

[13] ———, *An overview of the method of lower and upper solutions for ODEs*, Nonlinear Analysis and Its Applications to Differential Equations (Lisbon, 1998), Progr. Nonlinear Differential Equations Appl., vol. 43, Birkhäuser Boston, Massachusetts, 2001, pp. 3–22.

[14] ———, *The lower and upper solutions method for boundary value problems*, Handbook of Differential Equations I (A. Cañada, P. Drábek, and A. Fonda, eds.), chapter 2, Elsevier/North-Holland, Amsterdam, 2004, pp. 69–160.

[15] S. Heikkilä and V. Lakshmikantham, *Monotone Iterative Techniques for Discontinuous Nonlinear Differential Equations*, Monographs and Textbooks in Pure and Applied Mathematics, vol. 181, Marcel Dekker, New York, 1994.

[16] G. S. Ladde, V. Lakshmikantham, and A. S. Vatsala, *Monotone Iterative Techniques for Nonlinear Differential Equations*, Monographs, Advanced Texts and Surveys in Pure and Applied Mathematics, vol. 27, Pitman, Massachusetts, 1985.

[17] P. J. Y. Wong, *Three fixed-sign solutions of system model with Sturm-Liouville type conditions*, Journal of Mathematical Analysis and Applications **298** (2004), no. 1, 120–145.

Alberto Cabada: Departamento de Análise Matemática, Facultade de Matemáticas, Universidade de Santiago de Compostela, 15782 Santiago de Compostela, Galicia, Spain
E-mail address: cabada@usc.es

HO CHARACTERISTIC EQUATIONS SURPASS CONTRADICTIONS OF MODERN MATHEMATICS

L. A. V. CARVALHO

In these notes, we further explain the use of higher-order characteristic equations to detect exponentially oscillatory solutions of difference equations. The method is illustrated for continuous-time linear difference equations with two integral delays, although it can be straightly extended to many other types of evolution equations. An advantage is that it avoids the use of some disputed concepts of modern mathematics.

1. Introduction

Modern mathematics adopts the *classical* scheme for detecting the existence of exponential or periodic solutions of real linear evolution equations, for instance, of the scalar difference equation

$$x(t) = Ax(t-1) + Bx(t-2), \quad t \geq 0, \tag{1.1}$$

where $A, B \in \mathbb{R}$. The scheme relies on the analysis of the *nonzero* roots of its *characteristic equation*

$$\lambda^2 - A\lambda - B = 0. \tag{1.2}$$

These roots λ are usually called *eigenvalues* or *characteristic values* of (1.1). It was shown in [6] that this kind of analysis is far from being complete. Indeed, as the natural initial value problem of (1.1) is of functional nature, an initial map $\psi : [-2,0) \to R$ such that $x(t) = \psi(t)$ for $t \in [-2,0)$ must be given in advance. Then, the unique solution through it exists and is denoted by $x(\cdot,\psi)$. Its shift chunk x_t is defined by $x_t(s) = x(t+s)$, $s \in [-2,0)$. These chunks must belong to a certain function space $\mathcal{F}$ such that $\psi \in \mathcal{F} \Rightarrow x_t(\cdot,\psi) \in \mathcal{F}$, $t \geq 0$, the *phase space*. Several spaces, $L_p([-2,0),\mathbb{R})$, $p \geq 1$, $BV([-2,0),\mathbb{R})$, [10], and so forth, are phase spaces for (1.1). The space $\mathcal{C}([-2,0),\mathbb{R})$ of the continuous maps from $[-2,0)$

Hindawi Publishing Corporation
Proceedings of the Conference on Differential & Difference Equations and Applications, pp. 257–265

into $\mathbb{R}$ equipped with the uniform metric topology is not a phase space. But, its dense subspace

$$\mathcal{A} = \left\{\psi \in \mathcal{C}([-2,0),\mathbb{R}) : \lim_{s\to 0-} \psi(\theta) = A\psi(-1) + B\psi(-2)\right\} \tag{1.3}$$

is a phase space [9]. The *functional* concept of *uniqueness* allows distinct solutions to intercept several times and even coincide inside intervals of length less than 2. This feature indicates that solutions of difference equations are more susceptive to oscillate. Let us restrict attention to the case of (1.1).

2. Periodic and oscillatory solutions

We say a real function $x(t)$ is *oscillatory* when *there are a constant* $c \in \mathbb{R}$ *and sequences* $\{t_n\}_1^\infty$, $\{t'_n\}_1^\infty$, $t_n, t'_n \to \infty$ *such that* $(x(t'_n) - c)(x(t_n - c)) < 0$. Moreover, a map $x : \mathbb{R} \to \mathbb{R}$ is T*-periodic*, $T \neq 0$, when $x(t+T) = x(t)$ for all t. T is a *period* of x. Usually, *the* period T of a map is its *least positive* period. In particular, a nonconstant periodic map is oscillatory since it repeats the value $x(t_o)$ at $t_n = t_o + nT$. Solutions of (1.1) of the form $x(t) = \lambda^t v(t)$, with $\lambda \in \mathbb{R}$ and $v(t)$ being an oscillatory map will be referred to as an *exponential oscillatory* solution. If, besides, v is T-periodic, $x(t) = \lambda^t v(t)$ will be called as (T,λ)-exponential oscillatory function. In particular a $(T,1)$-exponential oscillatory map is just a T-periodic map. Periodic solutions of (1.1) are defined as such for all t.

3. Classical characteristic equation

Classically, the exponential solutions of (1.1) are determined by its eigenvalues. When these eigenvalues are complex conjugate, the corresponding real solutions are exponential oscillatory. As (1.2) has two roots, λ_1, λ_2, this scheme (see [8–13] furnishes that (1) if $A^2 + 4B > 0$, these roots are real and distinct, and there are two families of exponential solutions, $c_1\lambda_1^t$ and $c_2\lambda_2^t$ with c_1, c_2 arbitrary in $\mathbb{R}$; (2) if, say, $0 < \lambda_1 < 1$, then $c_1\lambda^t \to 0$ as $t \to \infty$; if $\lambda_1 > 1$, then $c_1\lambda^t \to \infty$ as $t \to \infty$; if $-1 < \lambda < 0$, then $c_1\lambda^t$ oscillates and $|c_1\lambda_1^t| \to 0$, exponentially as $t \to \infty$. This latter property can be seen as follows. Since $\lambda_1 = |\lambda_1|(\cos\pi + i\sin\pi)$ with $0 < |\lambda_1| < 1$, we have $\lambda_1^t = |\lambda_1|^t(\cos\pi t + i\sin\pi t)$. The linear combinations of the real solutions $|\lambda_1|^t\cos\pi t$ and $|\lambda_1|^t\sin\pi t$ make up a family of oscillatory solutions such that their modules decay to zero as $t \to \infty$; (3) a similar argument shows that if $\lambda_1 < -1$, then the corresponding solutions are oscillatory and their modules grow without bound as $t \to \infty$. (4) if $A^2 + 4B = 0$, then $\lambda_1 = \lambda_2 = A/2$ is real and we obtain the families of solutions $c_1(A/2)^t$ and $c_2t(A/2)^t$, where c_1, c_2 are arbitrary real constants. When $c_2 = 0$, we have the usual exponential solutions which behave as described above, depending on the sign of A and its magnitude. When $c_2 \neq 0$, the corresponding solution is oscillatory if $A < 0$ but it is not classified as an exponentially oscillatory solution, according to our definition. If $-1 < A/2 < 0$ (or $A/2 < -1$), the solution decays to zero in modulus (or grows without bound) as $t \to \infty$; (5) if $A > 0$, the corresponding solutions is not oscillatory, but decays to zero or grows to infinity as $t \to \infty$ according to whether $A/2 < 1$ or $A/2 > 1$, respectively; (6) if $A^2 + 4B < 0$, then λ_1 is complex and $\lambda_2 = \bar{\lambda}_1$. Two complex exponential solutions are $x(t) = c\lambda_1^t$, $\bar{x}(t) = \bar{c}\bar{\lambda}_1^t$, c arbitrary in $\mathcal{C}$. In this case, $\lambda_1 = |\lambda_1|(\cos\theta + i\sin\theta)$, where $\theta = \arg(\lambda_1) = \sqrt{-A^2 - 4B} \neq 0$. Let $c = a + ib$.

Then, $x(t) = |\lambda_1|^t[a\cos\theta t - b\sin\theta t + i(a\sin\theta t + b\cos\theta t)]$ so that the two real solutions stemming from $x(t)$ are its real and imaginary parts, namely, $|\lambda_1|^t(a\cos\theta t - b\sin\theta t)$ and $|\lambda_1|^t(a\sin\theta t + b\cos\theta t)$. These two solutions are $(2\pi/\theta, |\lambda_1|)$-exponentially oscillatory. The above are the types of exponential and exponentially oscillatory solutions of (1.1) that can be detected via (1.2).

Equation (1.2) is obtained when we look for exponential maps $x(t) = \lambda^t c$ as solutions of (1.1). This procedure uses the fact that a constant c is the closed formula of a periodic map of any period. It has no minimum period. One moment of reflection shows that if one has at hand the closed formula for a generic map $v(t)$ of a given period T, then the formula $x(t) = \lambda^t c$ can be used with c replaced by $v(t)$, in order to obtain a refinement of (1.2). This is the basic idea in this work. Firstly, observe that (1.2) may be obtained if, instead of a constant map c, we use a nonconstant 1-periodic map. In fact, if we try a solution of the form $x(t) = \lambda^t a(t)$, where a is a nontrivial 1-periodic map, we see that we must have $\lambda^t a(t) = Aa(t-1)\lambda^{(t-1)} + Ba(t-2)\lambda^{(t-2)}$; then, since $a(t) = a(t-1) = a(t-2)$ is not zero everywhere, we promptly get (1.2) by cancelling out $\lambda^t a(t)$. Moreover, if a is continuous, then $x(t)$ is continuous ($x_t \in \mathcal{A}$ for all $t \in \mathbb{R}$). This result means that we can take any 1-periodic map $a(t)$ in place of the arbitrary constant c in order to obtain a solution $x(t) = \lambda^t a(t)$, as long as λ satisfies (1.2). The oscillatory property of x depends on our choice of a, and the (nonzero) eigenvalue λ.

4. Extended characteristic equations

We now refine the notion of characteristic equation by means of the following result (see [1–7, 13]) introduced in [6]. It is based on the following lemma.

LEMMA 4.1. *If v is an m-periodic scalar map, m is a positive integer, then v satisfies*

$$v(t) = \sum_{j=0}^{[m/2]} \left[a_j(t)\cos\frac{2j\pi}{m}t + b_j(t)\sin\frac{2j\pi}{m}t\right], \tag{4.1}$$

where $a_j = a_j(t)$ and $b_j = b_j(t)$ are 1-periodic maps, with $b_{m/2}(t) \equiv 0$ if m is even.

In other words, any map v of period m must be a linear combination of m-periodic sines and cosines with 1-periodic coefficients. So, the expressions for $v(t-k)$, $k \in \mathbb{Z}$, can be obtained using trigonometric identities:

$$v(t-1) = a_o - a_q\cos\pi t + \sum_{j=1}^{q-1}\left[(c_j a_j - s_j b_j)\cos\frac{2j\pi}{m}t + (s_j a_j + c_j b_j)\sin\frac{2j\pi}{m}t\right], \tag{4.2}$$

where $c_j = \cos(2j\pi/m)$, $s_j = \sin(2j\pi/m)$, $j = 1,\ldots,q-1$, and, if $m = 2q+1$, then

$$v(t-1) = a_o + \sum_{j=1}^{q}\left[(c_j a_j - s_j b_j)\cos\frac{2j\pi}{m}t + (s_j a_j + c_j b_j)\sin\frac{2j\pi}{m}t\right], \tag{4.3}$$

and so on (see also Section 6). The equation obtained from (1.1) upon substitution of $\lambda^t v(t)$ for $x(t)$, where v is an n-periodic map, is its *nth-order characteristic equation*. Thus, when v is 1-periodic, it is a *first-order characteristic equation*, when v is 2-periodic, it is a *second-order characteristic equation*, and so forth. A root λ of an extended characteristic equation is called an *extended eigenvalue*. The first-order characteristic equation is just the classical one (1.2), but yielding now new oscillatory solutions of (1.1), of the form $\lambda^t v(t)$. The second-order characteristic equation of (1.1) is obtained when we try a solution $v(t) = \lambda^t[a + b\cos\pi t]$ with $a = a(t)$ and $b = b(t)$ being 1-periodic maps, not both being identically zero. We get

$$\lambda[a + b\cos\pi t] = A[a - b\cos\pi t] + B\lambda^{-1}[a + b\cos\pi t], \tag{4.4}$$

so that we must have

$$a(\lambda^2 - A\lambda - B) = 0, \tag{4.5}$$

$$b(\lambda^2 + A\lambda - B)\cos\pi t = 0, \tag{4.6}$$

and these two equations are the second-order characteristic equation of (1.1). They are simultaneous with respect to the unknown λ. So, they cannot be solved for this unknown when $a \neq 0$ and $b \neq 0$ unless $A = 0$. In this case, the solution is $\lambda = \sqrt{B}$ and the general $(\lambda, 2)$-exponential solution is $x(t) = \sqrt{B}^t(a + b\cos\pi t)$, where a, b are arbitrary 1-periodic functions. Equation (4.6) is the first-order characteristic equation described in the previous section when $a \neq 0$ and $b = 0$. Equation (5.1) forces the λ's to yield the $(\lambda, 2)$-exponential solution for $b \neq 0$. Thus, if we have $A \neq 0$, then we must have $a = 0$ and $(\lambda, 2)$-exponential solution of (1.1) given by the eigenvalues λ_1, λ_2 of $\lambda^2 + A\lambda - B = 0$. If they are real and distinct, there are two families $\lambda_k^t b\cos\pi t$, $k = 1, 2$ of $(\lambda_k, 2)$-exponential periodic solutions. The choice of the 1-periodic map $b \neq 0$ is arbitrary, subject only to our choice of phase space. We leave, for reasons of space, the analysis of these solutions' behavior in various subcases: $\lambda \in \mathbb{R}$, $\lambda \in \mathscr{C}, b(t)$ continuous, and so forth. It is apparent that depending on A and B, the use of complex eigenvalues may spoil the (integer) value of T of the found (λ, T)-exponential oscillatory solution.

5. Discrete versus continuous

The discrete version of (1.1),

$$x(n) = Ax(n-1) + Bx(n-2), \tag{5.1}$$

is obtained, of course, when we pick $t \in \mathbb{Z}$. Equation (5.1) has fewer oscillatory solutions than (1.1), since to each solution of the discrete equation there correspond infinitely many oscillatory solutions of the continuous-time equation that agree with the discrete solution at $t \in \mathbb{Z}$. The oscillation takes place within intervals of length one, integers excluded. The classical characteristic equation of (5.1) is also (1.2). But while an exponential solution of (5.1) is $x(n) = \lambda^n c$, where c is an arbitrary constant, the similar solution of (1.1) is of the form $x(t) = \lambda^t a(t)$, where $a(t)$ is an arbitrary 1-periodic map in $\mathscr{A}$. Thus, the solution of (1.1) may be oscillatory without its discrete version being so. In particular, consider the following corollary of an important theorem due to Györi and Ladas (see [8]).

THEOREM 5.1. *The discrete k-delay scalar equation* $x(n) = \sum_{i=1}^{k} a_i x(n-i)$ *has no oscillatory solution if all roots of its characteristic equation are distinct and positive.*

6. Characteristic equation of mth-order

The procedure depicted so far may be used in equations with integral delays. It can be applied even to the case of nonlinear equations. In this case, of course, one obtains a nonlinear "extended characteristic equation." The counterparts of the extended characteristic equations in linear multidimensional cases with several delays were studied in [5], the extended characteristic roots being restricted to be real. The vector case of Lemma 4.1 in the more general situation of rational periods was studied in [12]. Applications of Lemma 4.1 to nonlinear problems may be seen, for instance, in [1, 7, 9]. For the sake of completeness, we furnish here the mth-order characteristic equation for the k-delay version of (1.1) (see [6]),

$$x(t) = \sum_{i=1}^{k} A_i x(t-i). \tag{6.1}$$

If we try a solution $x(t) = \lambda^t v(t)$, $\lambda \neq 0$, to (6.1) with v being m-periodic, we get the following set of independent equations, *the mth-order characteristic equation*:

$$\left(\lambda^k - \sum_{i=1}^{k} \lambda^{k-i} A_i\right) \quad a_0 = 0,$$

$$\left(1 + \sum_{i=1}^{k} (-1)^i A_i\right) a_q = 0,$$

$$\left(1 - \sum_{i=2}^{k} \lambda^{k-i} c_i A_i\right) a_1 + \left(\sum_{i=1}^{k} \lambda^{k-i} s_i A_i\right) b_1 = 0,$$

$$-\left(\sum_{i=1}^{k} \lambda^{k-i} s_i A_i\right) a_1 + \left(1 - \sum_{i=1}^{k} \lambda^{k-i} c_i A_i\right) b_1 = 0,$$

$$\left(1 - \sum_{i=2}^{k} \lambda^{k-i} c_{2i} A_i\right) a_2 + \left(\sum_{i=1}^{k} \lambda^{k-i} s_{2i} A_i\right) b_2 = 0,$$

$$-\left(\sum_{i=1}^{k} \lambda^{k-i} s_{2i} A_i\right) a_2 + \left(1 - \sum_{i=1}^{k} \lambda^{k-i} c_{2i} A_i\right) b_2 = 0,$$

$$\vdots$$

$$\left(1-\sum_{i=2}^{k}\lambda^{k-i}c_{([(m-1)/2])^{i}A_i}\right)a_{[(m-1)/2]}+\left(\sum_{i=1}^{k}\lambda^{k-i}s_{([(m-1)/2])^{i}A_i}\right)b_{[(m-1)/2]}=0,$$

$$-\left(\sum_{i=1}^{k}\lambda^{k-1}s_{([(m-1)/2])^{i}A_i}\right)a_{[(m-1)/2]}+\left(1-\sum_{i=0}^{k}\lambda^{k-i}c_{([(m-1)/2])^{i}A_i}\right)b_{[(m-1)/2]}=0. \tag{6.2}$$

7. Related inconsistencies in multidimensional mathematics

The fact that the classical characteristic equation is not capable of detecting all oscillatory solutions of linear autonomous difference arose in 1754, when d'Alembert missused for the first time the idea of *transformation of coordinates* (in $\mathbb{R}^2$) suggested by the recently discovered (1750) Cramer's rule that yields the solution of the (simultaneous) system

$$\begin{aligned} x &= a\xi + b\eta, \\ y &= c\xi + d\eta, \end{aligned} \qquad \left(\text{or } \begin{bmatrix} x \\ y \end{bmatrix} = \begin{bmatrix} a & b \\ c & d \end{bmatrix}\begin{bmatrix} \xi \\ \eta \end{bmatrix}\right), \tag{7.1}$$

when $ad-bc \neq 0$. D'Alembert assumed it to be a valid transformation of the variables x, y to the (new) variables ξ, η in order to change the wave equation $u_{tt}=u_{xx}$ to a simpler equation $v_{\xi\eta}=0$. He chose $a=b=c=-d=1$. Despite strong opposition from prominent mathematicians, d'Alembert's idea was adopted by some, including Euler, and was later telescoped to the foundations of modern mathematics. The development of the concept (*definition*) of a transformation of coordinates in the following decades promoted the idea that n linear independent variables correspond to n independent coordinate axes (*dimensions*). This idea is mathematically false. In fact, taking $n=2$ and (7.1) as a pattern, we see that the original lines corresponding the axes Ox, Oy and $O\xi$, $O\eta$ are on a plane. Yet, the equation of Ox in the system of coordinates xy is simply $y=0$, while Oy's equation is simply $x=0$. Note that $x=0$ and $y=0$ in (7.1) means that $a\xi+b\eta=0$ and $c\xi+d\eta=0$, which denotes just one point in that plane, the common origin $(0,0)$. Thus, the two lines are transformed into one point via d'Alembert's transformation of coordinates, a contradiction. To fix this, we must use correct algebraic equations for these axes, say, $a\xi_1+b\eta_1=0$ and $c\xi_2+d\eta_2=0$, where ξ_1, ξ_2, η_1, η_2 are independent variables. Thus, the equations hold in $\mathbb{R}^4$. We may concede them to be hosted in $\mathbb{R}^3$ instead if we assume (without loss of generality) that, say, $\xi_1=\xi_2=\xi$, in which case we can write $a\xi+b\eta_1=0$ and $c\xi+d\eta_2=0$ for the axes $x=0$ and $y=0$ in terms of the system of coordinates $\xi\eta$. Using modern mathematics' procedure of attaching independent axes to independent variables, we see that the transformation takes the form, according to linear algebra,

$$\begin{aligned} x &= a\xi + b\eta_1, \\ y &= c\xi + d\eta_2, \end{aligned} \qquad \left(\text{or } \begin{bmatrix} x \\ y \end{bmatrix} = \begin{bmatrix} a & b & 0 \\ c & 0 & d \end{bmatrix}\begin{bmatrix} \xi \\ \eta_1 \\ \eta_2 \end{bmatrix}\right), \tag{7.2}$$

representing thus a transformation from $\mathbb{R}^3$ onto $\mathbb{R}^2$. Consequently, the lines (axes) $x=0$, $y=0$, $\xi=0$, and $\eta=0$ are not in the same plane, as assumed in modern mathematics.

In other words, Cramer's system alone cannot produce the transformation of coordinates alleged by modern mathematicians. Moreover if besides $ad - bc \neq 0$ we also assume that $abcd \neq 0$, then (7.2) cannot be reduced to (7.1) unless we take $b = 0$ or $d = 0$, an absurd equivalent to $1 = 0$, the ultimate irrationality in mathematics. Since this irrationality is in fact assumed in all theories that followed d'Alembert's idea, we may expect several contradictions in modern mathematics concepts.

We present below two major contradictions of this kind.

7.1. Rotations. In order to show that modern mathematics' concept of rotation is both arithmetically and geometrically inconsistent, it is enough to show by an example how this happens. A rotation T_θ is of the form (7.1) with $a = d = \cos\theta$ and $-c = b = \sin\theta$, for some $-2\pi \leq \theta \leq 2\pi$. Let us take, for example, $\theta = \pi/4$, so that $a = b = -c = d = \cos\theta = \sin\theta = \sqrt{2}/2$, obtaining

$$\xi = \frac{\sqrt{2}}{2}(x + y), \qquad \eta = \frac{\sqrt{2}}{2}(-x + y). \tag{7.3}$$

Then, we have $\xi\eta = 1/2(y^2 - x^2)$. According to modern mathematics, $1/2(y^2 - x^2) = k$ represents a rectangular hyperbola in the (x, y) system whenever k is a constant, while $\xi\eta = k$ is the equation of the same curve in terms of the coordinates (ξ, η). A rectangular hyperbola has its transversal axis coinciding with one of the coordinate axis, depending on the sign of k. Already, the hyperbola $\xi\eta = k$ is not rectangular. This shows that this rotation will not rotate the curves along with the coordinate axes. It will simply change the coordinates of the plane's points. In (7.3), the axes Ox and Oy "rotate" 45° counter-clockwise. Their new coordinates correspond to those of the axes $O\xi$ and $O\eta$, and $O\xi$ is on the position of the diagonal $y = x$ of (x, y) while O_η is on the position of $y = -x$. This explains the switch from the equation $1/2(y^2 - x^2) = k$ to $\xi\eta = k$ of the nonrotated curve. Thus, the concept of rotation has to explain the following data (1) the fact of $O\xi$'s equation is $\eta = 0$ in its own system; (2) the fact that $O\xi$ is the image under (7.3) of Ox, whose equation is $y = 0$. These data require that we should obtain $\eta = 0$ from (7.3) by making $y = 0$ there. Computations give $y = 0 \Rightarrow \xi = \sqrt{2}/2x = -\eta$. Of course this cannot be the axis $\eta = 0$ unless $ab = 0$ or $\xi = \eta = x = y = 0$, the common origin of the two systems. Since we assume that $ab \neq 0$, it follows that $(x, 0)$ must be "rotated" onto the origin, an absurd that makes $\mathbb{R} = \{0\}$. What is wrong in modern mathematics concept of a rotation? It is the assumption that (7.1) furnishes the axes $O\xi$ and $O\eta$ on the same plane of Ox and Oy. Actually, they are not!

An alternative proof follows. We know from modern mathematics' advanced calculus that $z = x^2 + y^2$ satisfies $dz = z_x dx + z_y dy = 2xdx + 2ydy$. Thus, if y is made constant, then $dy = 0$ and this formula yields $dz/dx = z_x = 2x$. Similarly, if x is made constant, we must have $dz/dy = z_y = 2y$. Therefore, the ratio $z_x/z_y = x/y = dy/dx$ must hold at any point (x, y) such that $y \neq 0$. This ratio is equivalent to the differential equation $ydy = xdx$, which has solutions $y^2 - x^2 = k$, for some k constant. Now, a rotation (7.1) has $a = d$, $c = -b$, $a^2 + b^2 = 1$, and implies that $z = x^2 + y^2 = \xi^2 + \eta^2$ (circle preservation property), so that, we also must have $z_\xi/z_\eta = d\eta/d\xi = \xi/\eta$. This furnishes square hyperbolas $\eta^2 - \xi^2 = h$. Consequently, as $(\xi, \eta) = T_\theta(x, y)$, it follows that any rotation "rotates" square hyperbolas, against its own interpretation. In fact, modern mathematics states that $y^2 - x^2 = k$ is transformed into $(-b^{\xi} + a\eta)^2 - (a\xi + b\eta)^2 = (b^2 - a^2)\xi^2 - (b^2 - a^2)\eta^2 = k + 4ab\xi\eta$, which is not a square hyperbola, unless $ab = 0$ and the inconsistency follows from the assumption that $abcd = a^2b^2 \neq 0$.

7.2. Complex logarithm. To see the second conflict, let us recall [11, pages 119–120] that John Bernoulli, a former professor of Euler, had raised to Leibniz the argument that the inclusion of negative numbers in arithmetics would force the following formal property of the logarithm extension to these numbers: $(-a)^2 = a^2 \Rightarrow \ln(a)^2 = \ln(-a)^2 \Rightarrow 2\ln(a) = 2\ln(-a) \Rightarrow \ln(a) = \ln(-a)$. Nevertheless, this property is obviously contradictory since it implies that $e^{\ln(a)} = e^{\ln(-a)}$ and $a = -a$. This question remained unanswered till after Bernoulli's death. Euler found an extension of the concept of logarithm to complex numbers claimed to be capable of avoiding Bernoulli's remark. He achieved this in 1751. Let us denote by ln the usual real logarithm and Ln Euler's extension to the complex numbers. Using his own formula

$$e^{i\phi} = e^{i(\phi+2k\pi)} = \cos(\phi + 2k\pi) + i\sin(\phi + 2k\pi), \quad k \in \mathbb{Z}, \tag{7.4}$$

and the corresponding polar expression $z = re^{i\phi}$ for a generic complex number, where $r = |z|$ and ϕ is the argument of z, he defined Ln [14, pages 99–100] as the multivalued function

$$\operatorname{Ln}(z) = \ln(r) + i(\phi + 2k\pi), \quad k \in \mathbb{Z} \tag{7.5}$$

for all $z \neq 0$, with the argument ϕ of z measured in radians. $\operatorname{Ln}(z)$ is thus a set of complex values. Its argument is the set $\{\phi + 2k\pi,\ k \in \mathbb{Z}\}$. We readily see that $\operatorname{Ln}(x) = \ln x$ for the real $x > 0$ as it has argument $\{2k\pi,\ k \in \mathbb{Z}\}$. Consequently, $\operatorname{Ln}(a) \neq \operatorname{Ln}(-a)$ for the real $a > 0$ because the argument of $-a$ is $\{(2k+1)\pi,\ k \in \mathbb{Z}\}$, promptly avoiding Bernoulli's contradiction. Consequently, Ln cannot satisfy $\operatorname{Ln}(a)^2 = 2\operatorname{Ln}(a)$ for $a < 0$, which means that $\operatorname{Ln}(z^c) = c\operatorname{Ln}(z)$ *is not always valid for z, c complex, $z \neq 0$*. On the other hand, $z = e^{\operatorname{Ln}(z)}$, $z \neq 0$, is clearly valid. Already, $z^c = e^{c\operatorname{Ln}(z)}$ for all z, c complex, $z \neq 0$, is assumed valid by definition [14, page 100]. Consequently, it is immediate that $\operatorname{Ln}(z^c) = \operatorname{Ln}(e^{c\operatorname{Ln}(z)}) = c\operatorname{Ln}(z)$ holds for all z, c complex, $z \neq 0$. Hence, $\operatorname{Ln}(z^c) = c\operatorname{Ln}(z)$ holds for such z, c and Ln's theory is contradictory and should be promptly abandoned.

Observe now that the higher-order characteristic equation discussed here precludes complex number theory as a necessary tool to detect exponential oscillatory and periodic solutions of (1.1). On the contrary, we have seen in Section 4 that depending on the values of A and B, the use of complex eigenvalues may corrupt the integral period of the searched map v.

References

[1] L. A. V. Carvalho, *On a method to investigate bifurcation of periodic solutions in retarded differential equations*, Journal of Difference Equations and Applications **4** (1998), no. 1, 17–27.

[2] L. A. V. Carvalho, K. L. Cooke, and L. A. C. Ladeira, *On periodic solutions for a class of linear scaled differential equations. I*, Communications in Applied Analysis **3** (1999), no. 3, 399–413.

[3] ———, *On periodic solutions for a class of linear scaled differential equations. II*, Communications in Applied Analysis **3** (1999), no. 3, 415–431.
[4] L. A. V. Carvalho and L. A. C. Ladeira, *On periodic orbits of autonomous differential-difference equations*, Differential Equations and Applications to Biology and to Industry (Claremont, CA, 1994) (and M. Martelli, et al., eds.), World Scientific, New Jersey, 1996, pp. 57–64.
[5] ———, *Extended characteristic equations, oscillations and stability*, Analysis **20** (2000), no. 3, 285–302.
[6] ———, *Difference equations: detecting oscillations via higher order characteristic equations*, Journal of Difference Equations and Applications **8** (2002), no. 3, 277–291.
[7] K. L. Cooke and L. A. C. Ladeira, *Applying Carvalho's method to find periodic solutions of difference equations*, Journal of Difference Equations and Applications **2** (1996), no. 2, 105–115.
[8] S. N. Elaydi, *An Introduction to Difference Equations*, Springer, New York, 2000.
[9] J. K. Hale, *Theory of Functional Differential Equations*, Springer, New York, 1977.
[10] J. Hurt, *Some stability theorems for ordinary difference equations*, SIAM Journal on Numerical Analysis **4** (1967), no. 4, 582–596.
[11] M. Kline, *Mathematics. The Loss of Certainty*, 3rd ed., Oxford University Press, New York, 1980.
[12] L. A. C. Ladeira and S. M. Tanaka, *A method to calculate periodic solutions of functional-differential equations*, Journal of Mathematical Analysis and Applications **209** (1997), no. 1, 1–19.
[13] R. E. Mickens, *Difference Equations. Theory and Applications*, 2nd ed., Van Nostrand Reinhold, New York, 1990.
[14] A. G. Sveshnikov and A. N. Tikhonov, *The Theory of Functions of a Complex Variable*, Mir, Moscow, 1971.

L. A. V. Carvalho: Departamento de Matemática, Universidade Estadual de Maringá, Avenida Colombo 5790, CEP 87020-900, Maringá, Paraná, Brazil
E-mail address: lavcarvalho@uem.br

ON CHEBYSHEV FUNCTIONAL BOUNDS

P. CERONE

Numerous developments in bounding the Chebyshev functional are examined in the current paper. The results have wide applicability in numerical quadrature, integral transforms, probability problems, and the bounding of special functions. A review is presented focusing in particular on the contributions of the author in this area. Some examples are given demonstrating the diverse applications.

1. Introduction and review of some recent results

The weighted Chebyshev functional is defined by

$$T(f,g;p) := \mathcal{M}(fg;p) - \mathcal{M}(f;p)\mathcal{M}(g;p), \tag{1.1}$$

where the weighted integral mean is given by

$$P \cdot \mathcal{M}(f;p) = \int_a^b p(x)f(x)dx, \tag{1.2}$$

with $0 < P = \int_a^b p(x)dx < \infty$ and $f,g : [a,b] \to \mathbb{R}$ are two measurable functions and the integrals in (1.1) are assumed to exist. We note that

$$T(f,g;1) \equiv T(f,g), \qquad \mathcal{M}(f;1) \equiv \mathcal{M}(f), \tag{1.3}$$

where $T(f,g)$ is simply known as the Chebyshev functional.

The Chebyshev functional (1.1) has a long history and an extensive repertoire of applications in many fields including numerical quadrature, transform theory, probability and statistical problems, and special functions. Its basic appeal stems from a desire to approximate, for example, information in the form of a particular measure of the product of functions in terms of the products of the individual function measures. This inherently involves an error which may be bounded. Such problems appear in obtaining perturbed quadrature rules via Peano kernel arguments and the reader is referred to [16] for many applications.

Hindawi Publishing Corporation
Proceedings of the Conference on Differential & Difference Equations and Applications, pp. 267–277

The current section gives the background and a review of, in particular, the author's involvement in the quest to bound the Chebyshev functional and its variants.

Section 2 demonstrates the application of the Chebyshev functional by reference to some examples.

It is worthwhile noting that a number of identities relating to the Chebyshev functional already exist. The reader is referred to [18, Chapters IX and X]. Korkine's identity is well known, see [18], and is given by

$$T(f,g)=\frac{1}{2(b-a)^2}\int_a^b\int_a^b (f(x)-f(y))(g(x)-g(y))\,dx\,dy. \tag{1.4}$$

It is identity (1.4) that is often used to prove an inequality due to Grüss for functions bounded above and below, [18].

For $\phi_f \le f(x) \le \Phi_f$, $x \in [a,b]$, then the Grüss inequality is given by

$$|T(f,g)| \le \frac{1}{4}(\Phi_f-\phi_f)(\Phi_g-\phi_g). \tag{1.5}$$

If we let $S(f)$ be an operator defined by

$$S(f)(x) := f(x) - \mathcal{M}(f), \tag{1.6}$$

which shifts a function by its integral mean, then the following identity:

$$T(f,g)=T(S(f),g)=T(f,S(g))=T(S(f),S(g)) \tag{1.7}$$

holds, and so, since $\mathcal{M}(S(f))=\mathcal{M}(S(g))=0$,

$$T(f,g)=\mathcal{M}(S(f)g)=\mathcal{M}(fS(g))=\mathcal{M}(S(f)S(g)). \tag{1.8}$$

For the last term in (1.7) or (1.8) only one of the functions needs to be shifted by its integral mean. If the other function was to be shifted by any other quantity, the identities would still hold. A weighted version of (1.8) related to

$$T(f,g)=\mathcal{M}((f(x)-\gamma)S(g)) \tag{1.9}$$

for γ arbitrary was given by Sonin [21] (see [18, page 246]).

The interested reader is also referred to Dragomir [15] and Fink [17] for extensive treatments of the Grüss and related inequalities.

The work of Andrica and Badea [4] obtains results from a positive linear functional perspective, while Pečarić et al. [19] attack the problem in terms of isotonic linear functionals, while Anastassiou [3] investigates multivariate Grüss type inequalities.

Identity (1.4) may also be used to prove the Chebyshev inequality which states that for $f(\cdot)$ and $g(\cdot)$ synchronous, namely, $(f(x)-f(y))(g(x)-g(y)) \ge 0$, a.e. $x,y \in [a,b]$, then

$$T(f,g) \ge 0. \tag{1.10}$$

There are many identities involving the Chebyshev functional (1.1). Recently, Cerone [6] obtained, for $f,g:[a,b]\to\mathbb{R}$ where f is of bounded variation and g continuous on $[a,b]$, the identity

$$T(f,g)=\frac{1}{(b-a)^2}\int_a^b \psi(t)df(t), \tag{1.11}$$

where

$$\psi(t)=(t-a)G(t,b)-(b-t)G(a,t) \quad \text{with } G(c,d)=\int_c^d g(x)dx. \tag{1.12}$$

THEOREM 1.1 [6]. *Let $f,g:[a,b]\to\mathbb{R}$, where f is of bounded variation and g is continuous on $[a,b]$. Then*

$$(b-a)^2|T(f,g)|\le\begin{cases}\sup\limits_{t\in[a,b]}|\psi(t)|\bigvee\limits_a^b(f), & \\ L\displaystyle\int_a^b|\psi(t)|dt, & \text{for } f \text{ } L\text{-Lipschitzian},\\ \displaystyle\int_a^b|\psi(t)|df(t), & \text{for } f \text{ monotonic nondecreasing},\end{cases} \tag{1.13}$$

where $\bigvee_a^b(f)$ is the total variation of f on $[a,b]$.

In [14], bounds were obtained for the approximations of moments and moment generating functions, although the work in [6] places less stringent assumptions on the behaviour of the probability density function.

In a subsequent paper to [6], Cerone and Dragomir [13] obtained a refinement of the classical Chebyshev inequality (1.10).

THEOREM 1.2. *Let $f:[a,b]\to\mathbb{R}$ be a monotonic nondecreasing function on $[a,b]$ and $g:[a,b]\to\mathbb{R}$ a continuous function on $[a,b]$ so that $\varphi(t)\ge 0$ for each $t\in(a,b)$. Then one has the inequality*

$$T(f,g)\ge\frac{1}{(b-a)^2}\left|\int_a^b\big[(t-a)|G(t,b)|-(b-t)|G(a,t)|\big]df(t)\right|\ge 0, \tag{1.14}$$

where

$$\varphi(t)=\frac{G(t,b)}{b-t}-\frac{G(a,t)}{t-a} \tag{1.15}$$

and $G(c,d)$ is as defined in (1.12).

Bounds were also found for $|T(f,g)|$ in terms of the Lebesgue norms $\|\phi\|_p$, $p\ge 1$, effectively utilising (1.13) and noting that $\psi(t)=(t-a)(b-t)\varphi(t)$.

It should be mentioned here that the author in [7] demonstrated relationships between the Chebyshev functional $T(f,g;a,b)$, the generalised trapezoidal functional $GT(f;a,x,b)$, and the Ostrowski functional $\Theta(f;a,x,b)$ defined by

$$\begin{aligned} T(f,g;a,b) &:= M(fg;a,b) - M(f;a,b)M(g;a,b), \\ GT(f;a,x,b) &:= \left(\frac{x-a}{b-a}\right)f(a) + \left(\frac{b-x}{b-a}\right)f(b) - M(f;a,b), \end{aligned} \tag{1.16}$$

and $\Theta(f;a,x,b) := f(x) - M(f;a,b)$ where the integral mean is defined by

$$M(f;a,b) := \frac{1}{b-a}\int_a^b f(x)dx. \tag{1.17}$$

This was made possible through the fact that both $GT(f;a,x,b)$ and $\Theta(f;a,x,b)$ satisfy identities like (1.11) involving appropriate Peano kernels, namely,

$$\begin{aligned} GT(f;a,x,b) &= \int_a^b q(x,t)df(t), \quad q(x,t) = \frac{t-x}{b-a};\ x,t \in [a,b], \\ \Theta(f;a,x,b) &= \int_a^b p(x,t)df(t), \quad (b-a)p(x,t) = \begin{cases} t-a, & t \in [a,x], \\ t-b, & t \in (x,b], \end{cases} \end{aligned} \tag{1.18}$$

respectively.

The reader is referred to [16] and the references therein for applications of these functionals to numerical quadrature. For other Grüss type inequalities, see the books [18, 20].

Recently, Cerone and Dragomir [11] pointed out generalisations of the above results for integrals defined on two different intervals $[a,b]$ and $[c,d]$.

Define the functional (generalised Chebyshev functional)

$$\begin{aligned} T(f,g;a,b,c,d) := &\, M(fg;a,b) + M(fg;c,d) \\ &- M(f;a,b)M(g;c,d) - M(f;c,d)M(g;a,b), \end{aligned} \tag{1.19}$$

then Cerone and Dragomir [11] proved a number of results relating to (1.19) utilising the following generalisation of the classical identity due to Korkine, namely,

$$T(f,g;a,b,c,d) = \frac{1}{(b-a)(d-c)}\int_a^b\int_c^d (f(x)-f(y))(g(x)-g(y))dy\,dx. \tag{1.20}$$

In [13], the authors procured bounds for the generalised Chebyshev functional (1.19) in terms of the integral means and bounds of f and g over the two intervals.

Results were procured in [5] for f and g of Hölder type involving the generalised Chebyshev functional (1.19) with (1.17).

Another generalised Chebyshev functional involving the mean of the product of two functions, and the product of the means of each of the functions, where one is over a different interval was examined in [11]. Namely,

$$\mathcal{T}(f,g;a,b,c,d) := M(fg;a,b) - M(f;a,b)M(g;c,d), \tag{1.21}$$

which may be demonstrated to satisfy the Korkine-like identity:

$$\mathcal{T}(f,g;a,b,c,d) = \frac{1}{(b-a)(d-c)} \int_a^b \int_c^d f(x)(g(x)-g(y))\,dy\,dx. \tag{1.22}$$

It may be noticed from (1.21) and (1.1) that $2\mathcal{T}(f,g;a,b;a,b) = T(f,g;a,b)$.

It may further be noticed that (1.13) is related to (1.19) by the identity

$$T(f,g;a,b,c,d) = \mathcal{T}(f,g;a,b,c,d) + \mathcal{T}(g,f;c,d,a,b). \tag{1.23}$$

Cerone [9] analysed the Chebyshev functional defined on a measurable space setting $(\Omega,\mathcal{A},\mu)$ consisting of a set Ω, a σ-algebra $\mathcal{A}$ of parts of Ω, and a countably additive and positive measure μ on $\mathcal{A}$ with values in $\mathbb{R}\cup\{\infty\}$.

For a μ-measurable function $w:\Omega\to\mathbb{R}$, with $w(x)\geq 0$ for μ, a.e. $x\in\Omega$, consider the Lebesgue space $L_w(\Omega,\mathcal{A},\mu) := \{f:\Omega\to\mathbb{R},\ f$ is μ-measurable and $\int_\Omega w(x)|f(x)|d\mu(x) < \infty\}$. Assume $\int_\Omega w(x)d\mu(x) > 0$.

If $f,g:\Omega\to\mathbb{R}$ are μ-measurable functions and $f,g,fg\in L_w(\Omega,\mathcal{A},\mu)$, then we may consider the Chebyshev functional

$$\begin{aligned} T_w(f,g) &= T_w(f,g;\Omega) \\ &:= \frac{1}{\int_\Omega w(x)d\mu(x)} \int_\Omega w(x)f(x)g(x)d\mu(x) \\ &\quad - \frac{1}{\int_\Omega w(x)d\mu(x)} \int_\Omega w(x)f(x)d\mu(x) \frac{1}{\int_\Omega w(x)d\mu(x)} \int_\Omega w(x)g(x)d\mu(x). \end{aligned} \tag{1.24}$$

Grüss-like bounds were obtained from (1.24) in [9, 12] together with generalisations.

2. Applications of the Chebyshev functional bounds

There are a number of results that provide bounds for integrals of products of functions. There have been some developments in the recent past with which the current author has been involved. These have been put to fruitful use in a variety of areas of applied mathematics including quadrature rules, in the approximation of integral transforms, as well as in applied probability problems (see [6, 13, 16]).

It is the intention that in the current section the techniques will be utilised to obtain useful bounds for special functions.

The functional $T(f,g;p)$ from (1.1)-(1.2) is known to satisfy a number of identities, in particular, those attributed to Sonin, namely,

$$P\cdot T(f,g;p) = \int_a^b p(t)[f(t)-\gamma][g(t)-\mathcal{M}(g;p)]dt, \quad \text{for } \gamma\in\mathbb{R} \text{ a constant.} \tag{2.1}$$

Also, an identity attributed to Korkine, namely,

$$P^2 \cdot T(f,g;p) = \frac{1}{2}\int_a^b \int_a^b p(x)p(y)(f(x)-f(y))(g(x)-g(y))\,dx\,dy \tag{2.2}$$

may also easily be shown to hold.

Here we will utilize the following results bounding the Chebyshev functional to determine bounds on the Zeta function. (See [8] for more general applications to special functions.)

From (2.1) we note that

$$P \cdot |T(f,g;p)| = \left| \int_a^b p(x)(f(x)-\gamma)(g(x)-\mathcal{M}(g;p))\,dx \right| \tag{2.3}$$

to give

$$P \cdot |T(f,g;p)| \le \begin{cases} \inf_{\gamma\in\mathbb{R}} \|f(\cdot)-\gamma\| \int_a^b p(x)\,|g(x)-\mathcal{M}(g;p)|\,dx, \\ \left(\int_a^b p(x)(f(x)-\mathcal{M}(f;p))^2 dx \right)^{1/2} \\ \times \left(\int_a^b p(x)(g(x)-\mathcal{M}(g;p))^2 dx \right)^{1/2}, \end{cases} \tag{2.4}$$

where

$$\int_a^b p(x)(h(x)-\mathcal{M}(h;p))^2 dx = \int_a^b p(x)h^2(x)\,dx - P \cdot \mathcal{M}^2(h;p) \tag{2.5}$$

and it may be easily shown by direct calculation that

$$P \cdot \inf_{\gamma\in\mathbb{R}} \left[\int_a^b p(x)(f(x)-\gamma)^2 dx \right] = \int_a^b p(x)(f(x)-\mathcal{M}(f;p))^2 dx. \tag{2.6}$$

2.1. Bounding the beta function. The incomplete beta function is defined by

$$B(x,y;z) = \int_0^z t^{x-1}(1-t)^{y-1}\,dt, \quad 0 < z \le 1. \tag{2.7}$$

We will restrict our attention to $x > 1$ and $y > 1$.

The following pleasing result is valid.

Theorem 2.1. *For $x > 1$ and $y > 1$,*

$$0 \le \frac{1}{xy} - B(x,y) \le \frac{x-1}{x\sqrt{2x-1}} \cdot \frac{y-1}{y\sqrt{2y-1}} \le 0.090169437\ldots, \tag{2.8}$$

where the upper bound is obtained at $x = y = (3+\sqrt{5})/2 = 2.618033988\ldots$.

Proof. We have from (2.1)–(2.5)

$$(b-a)\,|\,T(f,g)\,| \le \left(\int_a^b f^2(t)dt - \mathcal{M}^2(f)\right)^{1/2}\left(\int_a^b g^2(t)dt - \mathcal{M}^2(g)\right)^{1/2}, \tag{2.9}$$

that is, taking $f(t) = t^{x-1}$, $g(t) = (1-t)^{y-1}$, then

$$0 \le \frac{1}{xy} - B(x,y) \le \left(\int_0^1 t^{2x-2}dt - \frac{1}{x^2}\right)^{1/2}\left(\int_0^1 (1-t)^{2y-2}dt - \frac{1}{y^2}\right)^{1/2}. \tag{2.10}$$

Now,

$$\int_0^1 t^{2x-2}dt = \frac{1}{2x-1}, \qquad \int_0^1 (1-t)^{2y-2}dt = \frac{1}{2y-1} \tag{2.11}$$

and so from (2.10) we have the first inequality in (2.8).

Now, consider

$$C(x) = \frac{x-1}{x\sqrt{2x-1}}. \tag{2.12}$$

The maximum occurs when $x = x^* = (3+\sqrt{5})/2$ to give $C(x^*) = 0.3002831\ldots$. Hence, because of the symmetry we have the upper bound as stated in (2.8). □

Remark 2.2. In a recent paper, Alzer [1] shows that

$$0 \le \frac{1}{xy} - B(x,y) \le b_A = \max_{x\ge 1}\left(\frac{1}{x^2} - \frac{\Gamma^2(x)}{\Gamma(2x)}\right) = 0.08731\ldots, \tag{2.13}$$

where 0 and b_A are shown to be the best constants. This uniform bound is only smaller for a small area around $((3+\sqrt{5})/2, (3+\sqrt{5})/2)$ while the first upper bound in (2.8) provides a better bound over a much larger region of the $x-y$ plane (see Figure 2.1).

2.2. Zeta bounds via Chebyshev. The Zeta function

$$\zeta(x) := \sum_{n=1}^{\infty} \frac{1}{n^x} = \frac{1}{\Gamma(x)}\int_0^{\infty} \frac{t^{x-1}}{e^t - 1}dt, \quad x > 1, \tag{2.14}$$

was originally introduced in 1737 by the Swiss mathematician Leonhard Euler (1707–1783) for real x who proved the identity

$$\zeta(x) := \prod_p \left(1 - \frac{1}{p^x}\right)^{-1}, \quad x > 1, \tag{2.15}$$

where p runs through all primes.

Using (2.3)–(2.6), the following theorem was proved in [10].

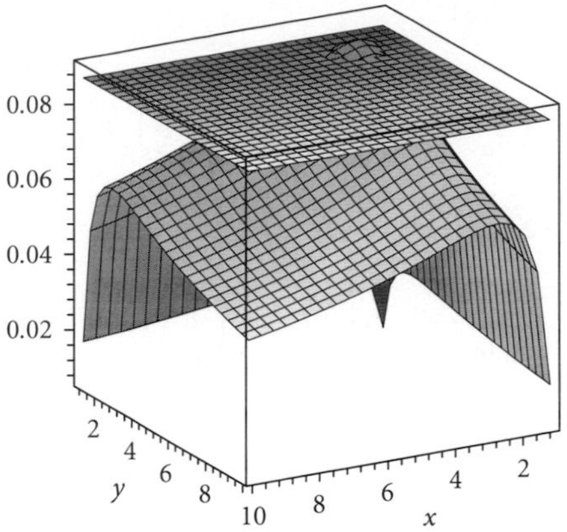

Figure 2.1. Three-dimensional plot of $C(x)C(y)$ and b_A, where $C(x)$ is defined in (2.12) and $b_A = 0.08731\ldots$ from (2.13).

Theorem 2.3. *For $\alpha > 1$ and $m = \lfloor \alpha \rfloor$, the zeta function satisfies the inequality*

$$\begin{aligned} &\left|\Gamma(\alpha+1)\zeta(\alpha+1) - 2^{\alpha-m}\Gamma(m+1)\zeta(m+1)\zeta(\alpha-m+1)\right| \\ &\quad \le 2^{(\alpha-m+1/2)} \cdot E \cdot \left[\Gamma(2\alpha-2m+1) - \Gamma^2(\alpha-m+1)\right]^{1/2}, \end{aligned} \tag{2.16}$$

where

$$E^2 = 2^{2m}\Gamma(2m+1)\left[\lambda(2m) - \lambda(2m+1)\right] - \frac{1}{2}\Gamma^2(m+1)\zeta^2(m+1), \tag{2.17}$$

with $\lambda(x) = \sum_{n=0}^{\infty}(1/(2n+1)^x)$.

The following corollary provides upper bounds for the zeta function at odd integers.

Corollary 2.4. *The inequality*

$$\Gamma(2m+1)\left[2 \cdot (2^{2m}-1)\zeta(2m) - (2^{2m+1}-1)\zeta(2m+1)\right] - \Gamma^2(m+1)\zeta^2(m+1) > 0 \tag{2.18}$$

holds for $m = 1, 2, \ldots$.

Remark 2.5. In (2.18), if m is odd, then $2m$ and $m+1$ are even so that an expression in the form

$$\alpha(m)\zeta(2m) - \beta(m)\zeta(2m+1) - \gamma(m)\zeta^2(m+1) > 0 \tag{2.19}$$

results, where

$$\begin{gathered} \alpha(m) = 2(2^{2m}-1)\Gamma(2m+1), \qquad \beta(m) = (2^{2m+1}-1)\Gamma(2m+1), \\ \gamma(m) = \Gamma^2(m+1). \end{gathered} \tag{2.20}$$

Thus for m odd we have

$$\zeta(2m+1) < \frac{\alpha(m)\zeta(2m) - \gamma(m)\zeta^2(m+1)}{\beta(m)}, \tag{2.21}$$

that is, for $m = 2k - 1$, we have from (2.21)

$$\zeta(4k-1) < \frac{\alpha(2k-1)\zeta(4k-2) - \gamma(2k-1)\zeta^2(2k)}{\beta(2k-1)} \tag{2.22}$$

giving for $k = 1,2,3$, $\zeta(3) < (\pi^2/7)(1 - \pi^2/72) = 1.21667148$, $\zeta(7) < (2\pi^6/1905)(1 - \pi^2/2160) = 1.00887130$, $\zeta(11) < (62\pi^{10}/5803245)(1 - \pi^2/492150) = 1.00050356$, which may be compared with the numerical values $\zeta(3) = 1.202056903$, $\zeta(7) = 1.008349277$, and $\zeta(11) = 1.000494189$.

If m is *even*, then for $m = 2k$ we have from (2.21)

$$\zeta(4k+1) < \frac{\alpha(2k)\zeta(4k) - \gamma(2k)\zeta^2(2k+1)}{\beta(2k)}, \quad k = 1,2,\ldots. \tag{2.23}$$

We notice that in (2.23), or equivalently (2.19) with $m = 2k$, there are two zeta functions with odd arguments. There are a number of possibilities for resolving this, but firstly it should be noticed that $\zeta(x)$ is monotonically decreasing for $x > 1$ so that $\zeta(x_1) > \zeta(x_2)$ for $1 < x_1 < x_2$.

For $b(x) = 1/(2^x - 1)$, Cerone [10] obtained the following two results.

THEOREM 2.6. *The Zeta function satisfies the bounds*

$$L(x) \le \zeta(x+1) \le U(x) \tag{2.24}$$

with

$$L(x) = (1 - b(x))\zeta(x) + \left(\ln 2 - \frac{1}{2}\right)b(x), \qquad U(x) = (1 - b(x))\zeta(x) + \frac{b(x)}{2} \tag{2.25}$$

and the coefficients of $b(x)$ are the best possible (see also Alzer [2]).

COROLLARY 2.7. *The Zeta function satisfies the bounds*

$$L_2(x) \le \zeta(x+1) \le U_2(x), \tag{2.26}$$

where

$$L_2(x) = \frac{\zeta(x+2) - b(x+1)/2}{1 - b(x+1)}, \qquad U_2(x) = \frac{\zeta(x+2) - (\ln 2 - 1/2)b(x+1)}{1 - b(x+1)}. \tag{2.27}$$

Firstly, we may use a lower bound as given by (2.24) or (2.27). But from [10, Table 1], it seems that $L_2(x) > L(x)$ for positive integer x and so we have from (2.23)

$$\zeta_L(4k+1) < \frac{\alpha(2k)\zeta(2k) - \gamma(2k)L_2^2(2k)}{\beta(2k)}, \tag{2.28}$$

where we have used the fact that $L_2(x) < \zeta(x+1)$ and $L_2(x)$ is given by (2.27).

Secondly, since the even argument $\zeta(2k+2) < \zeta(2k+1)$, then from (2.23) we have

$$\zeta_E(4k+1) < \frac{\alpha(2k)\zeta(4k) - \gamma(2k)\zeta^2(2k+2)}{\beta(2k)}. \tag{2.29}$$

Finally, we have that $\zeta(m+1) > \zeta(2m+1)$ so that (2.19) gives, with $m = 2k$ on solving the resulting quadratic equation,

$$\zeta_Q(4k+1) < \frac{-\beta(2k) + \sqrt{\beta^2(2k) + 4\gamma(2k)\alpha(2k)\zeta(4k)}}{2\gamma(2k)}. \tag{2.30}$$

For $k = 1$ we have from (2.28)–(2.30) that $\zeta_L(5) < \pi^4/93 - (1/186)(7\pi^4/540 - 1/12)^2 = 1.039931461$, $\zeta_E(5) < (\pi^4/93)(1 - \pi^4/16200) = 1.041111605$, $\zeta_Q(5) < -93 + \sqrt{8649 + 2\pi^4} = 1.04157688$; and for $k = 2$, $\zeta_L(9) < (17/160965)\pi^8 - (1/35770)((31/28350)\pi^6 - 1/60)^2 = 1.002082506$, $\zeta_E(9) < (17/160965)\pi^8(1 - (\pi^4/337650)) = 1.0020834954$, $\zeta_Q(9) < -17885 + (1/3)\sqrt{2878859025 + 34\pi^8} = 1.00208436$.

These are to be compared with the numerical values $\zeta(5) = 1.036927755$ and $\zeta(9) = 1.002008393$.

Numerical experimentation using Maple seems to indicate that the upper bounds for $\zeta_L(4k+1)$, $\zeta_E(4k+1)$, and $\zeta_Q(4k+1)$ are increasing.

We note that the above upper bounds for the Zeta function at odd integer values are tighter than those resulting from (2.25) and (2.27).

References

[1] H. Alzer, *Some beta-function inequalities*, Proceedings of the Royal Society of Edinburgh. Section A **133** (2003), no. 4, 731–745.

[2] ______, *Remark on a double-inequality for the Riemann zeta function*, Expositiones Mathematicae **23** (2005), no. 4, 349–352.

[3] G. Anastassiou, *On Grüss type multivariate integral inequalities*, Mathematica Balkanica **17** (2003), no. 1-2, 1–13.

[4] D. Andrica and C. Badea, *Grüss' inequality for positive linear functionals*, Periodica Mathematica Hungarica **19** (1988), no. 2, 155–167.

[5] I. Budimir, P. Cerone, and J. E. Pečarić, *Inequalities related to the Chebychev functional involving integrals over different intervals*, Journal of Inequalities in Pure and Applied Mathematics **2** (2001), no. 2, 8, article 22.

[6] P. Cerone, *On an identity for the Chebychev functional and some ramifications*, Journal of Inequalities in Pure and Applied Mathematics **3** (2002), no. 1, 15, article 4.

[7] ______, *On relationships between Ostrowski, trapezoidal and Chebychev identities and inequalities*, Soochow Journal of Mathematics **28** (2002), no. 3, 311–328.

[8] ______, *On applications of the integral of products of functions and its bounds*, RGMIA Research Report Collection **6** (2003), no. 4, article 4.

[9] ______, *On some results involving the Chebychev functional and its generalisations*, Journal of Inequalities in Pure and Applied Mathematics **4** (2003), no. 3, 17, article 55.

[10] ______, *Bounds for zeta and related functions*, Journal of Inequalities in Pure and Applied Mathematics **6** (2005), no. 5, 19 pages, article 134.

[11] P. Cerone and S. S. Dragomir, *Generalisations of the Grüss, Chebychev and Lupaş inequalities for integrals over different intervals*, International Journal of Applied Mathematics **6** (2001), no. 2, 117–128.

[12] ______, *A refinement of the Grüss inequality and applications*, RGMIA Research Report Collection **5** (2002), no. 2, article 14.

[13] ______, *New upper and lower bounds for the Chebychev functional*, Journal of Inequalities in Pure and Applied Mathematics **3** (2002), no. 5, 13, article 77.

[14] ______, *On some inequalities arising from Montgomery's identity (Montgomery's identity)*, Journal of Computational Analysis and Applications **5** (2003), no. 4, 341–367.

[15] S. S. Dragomir, *Some integral inequalities of Grüss type*, Indian Journal of Pure and Applied Mathematics **31** (2000), no. 4, 397–415.

[16] S. S. Dragomir and Th. M. Rassias (eds.), *Ostrowski Type Inequalities and Applications in Numerical Integration*, Kluwer Academic, Dordrecht, 2002.

[17] A. M. Fink, *A treatise on Grüss' inequality*, Analytic and Geometric Inequalities and Applications, Math. Appl., vol. 478, Kluwer Academic, Dordrecht, 1999, pp. 93–113.

[18] D. S. Mitrinović, J. E. Pečarić, and A. M. Fink, *Classical and New Inequalities in Analysis*, Mathematics and Its Applications (East European Series), vol. 61, Kluwer Academic, Dordrecht, 1993.

[19] J. E. Pečarić, S. S. Dragomir, and J. Sándor, *On some Grüss type inequalities for isotonic functionals*, Rad Hrvatske Akademije Znanosti i Umjetnosti **467** (1994), 41–47.

[20] J. E. Pečarić, F. Proschan, and Y. L. Tong, *Convex Functions, Partial Orderings, and Statistical Applications*, Mathematics in Science and Engineering, vol. 187, Academic Press, Massachusetts, 1992.

[21] N. Ja. Sonin, *O nekotoryh neravenstvah otnosjašcihsjak opredelennym integralam*, Zapiski Imperatorskoi Akademii Nauk. Fiziko-Matematicheskoe Otdelenie **6** (1898), 1–54.

P. Cerone: School of Computer Science & Mathematics, Victoria University, P. O. Box 14428, MCMC, Victoria 8001, Australia

E-mail address: pietro.cerone@vu.edu.au

ASYMPTOTIC STABILITY IN DISCRETE MODELS FOR ITEROPAROUS SPECIES

DAVID M. CHAN

Species either reproduce multiple times in their lifetime or they reproduce only once in their lifetime. The former are called *iteroparous* species and the latter are called *semelparous* species. In this paper we examine a general model for a single species with multiple age or stage classes. This model assumes there are limited resources for the species and so it assumes competition for these resources between the age classes. Sufficient conditions for extinction are given, as well as conditions for having a positive stable equilibrium.

1. Introduction

Plant and animal species reproduce at least once in their lifetime. Some species can reproduce multiple times as they age such as humans, carabid beatles, and oak trees. Species that reproduce multiple times are called *iteroparous* species.

Other species, on the other hand, only reproduce once. These include salmon, wheat, and the cecropia moth. These species that only reproduce once are called *semelparouos* species. In general, iteroparous species are more common than semelparous species.

Many species can be divided into one or more age classes or stage classes. In a structured population with multiple age classes, iteroparous species may have more than one particular age class that can reproduce. We consider a model for a single species with multiple age classes where the next age class, the nth age class or stage class, is denoted by x_n and is determined by the previous m age classes. Thus,

$$x_n = f(x_{n-1}, x_{n-2}, \ldots, x_{n-m}). \tag{1.1}$$

So under this structure, x_n is the youngest age class and x_{n-m} is the oldest. Note that at each iteration, each age class "ages" to the next older age class.

We consider f to be of the Kolmorgorov-type form where we take the current population of each reproductive age class and multiply it by a growth function. The growth function that will be considered in this paper is a decreasing exponential that will depend

Hindawi Publishing Corporation
Proceedings of the Conference on Differential & Difference Equations and Applications, pp. 279–286

on the population of each age class. Similiar models using a decreasing exponential have been studied; see May [8], Hofbauer et al. [7], Chan and Franke [2, 3], and Franke and Yakubu [4, 5].

For an iteroparous species, (1.1) becomes

$$x_n = (a_1x_{n-1} + a_2x_{n-2} + \cdots + a_mx_{n-m})e^{-(b_1x_{n-1}^k + b_2x_{n-2}^k + \cdots + b_kx_{n-m}^k)}, \tag{1.2}$$

where the a_i's represent proportionality coefficients that depend on the fucudity of age class i, b_i's are a measure of the consumption of the available resources by age class i, and k is some positive number. We assume each $b_i > 0$ in order to model the competition of resources.

A special case of (1.2) can be used for semelparous species,

$$x_n = ax_{n-j}e^{-(b_1x_{n-1}^k + b_2x_{n-2}^k + \cdots + b_kx_{n-m}^k)}, \tag{1.3}$$

where the x_{n-j} age class is the only age class that contributes to the x_n age class. Here we assume that $1 \le j \le m$, so all but one of the $a_i = 0$ from (1.2).

In the following paper, we apply results from Sedaghat [9], Hautus and Bolis [6], and Sedaghat et al. [1]. Sufficient conditions for extinction of both types of species will be given. We also give conditions for having a positive stable equilibrium.

2. Background

First we define some basic notation. Let $\mathbb{R}_+ = [0, \infty)$, the set of nonnegative real numbers, and $\mathbb{R}_+^n$ is the cartesian product of n $\mathbb{R}_+$. For this model, $f : \mathbb{R}_+^m \to \mathbb{R}_+$. We will use the max norm for a distance function on $\mathbb{R}^n$, so $\|(x_1, x_2, \ldots, x_n)\| = \max_i\{x_i\}$.

In proving the extinction results, we use the following theorem.

Theorem 2.1 (Sedaghat [9]). *Let $\bar{x} \in \mathbb{R}$ be a fixed point of $x_n = f(x_{n-1}, \ldots, x_{n-m})$ and for fixed $\alpha \in (0,1)$, define the closed set:*

$$A_\alpha = \{X \in \mathbb{R}^m : |f(X) - \bar{x}| \le \alpha\|X - \bar{X}\|\}. \tag{2.1}$$

Then $\bar{X}$ is exponentially stable relative to the largest invariant subset of A_α.

We use this result to show that the origin is attracting. This then implies that the species is going to extinct.

For the persistence results, we use the following two theorems. Each gives sufficient conditions for a fixed point to be attractive on some interval. They both utilize the diagonal operator $g(u) = f(u, \ldots, u)$ to analyze the equation. The first theorem examines when the g function is nondecreasing near the fixed point.

Theorem 2.2 (Hautus and Bolis [6]). *In (1.1), assume that $f \in C(I^m, I)$ is nondecreasing in each coordinate, where I is a nontrivial interval in $\mathbb{R}$. If the function $g(u) = f(u, \ldots, u)$ has a fixed point $x^* \in I$ and*

$$g(u) > u \quad \text{if } u < x^*, \qquad g(u) < u \quad \text{if } u > x^*,\ u \in I, \tag{2.2}$$

then x^* attracts all solutions of (1.1) with initial values in I.

The other result involves the following theorem that examines when g is decreasing at the fixed point.

THEOREM 2.3 (Sedaghat et al. [1]). *Assume there exist* $-\infty \le r_0 < s_0 \le \infty$ *such that*

(H1) $f(u_1, u_2, \dots, u_m)$ *is nonincreasing in each* $u_1, u_2, \dots, u_m \in I_0 = (r_0, s_0]$, *if* $s_0 < \infty$, *and* $I_0 = (r_0, s_0)$ *otherwise;*

(H2) $g(u) = f(u, u, \dots, u)$ *is continuous and decreasing for* $u \in I_0$;

(H3) *there is* $r \in [r_0, s_0)$ *such that* $r < g(r) \le s_0$. *If* $r_0 = -\infty$ *or* $\lim_{t \to r_0^+} g(t) = \infty$, *then* $r \in (r_0, s_0)$ *is assumed.*

(H4) *There is* $s \in [r, x^*)$ *such that* $g^2(u) > u$ *for all* $u \in (s, x^*)$.

If the preceding hypotheses hold, then x^* *is stable and attracts all solutions of (1.1) with initial values in* $(s, g(s))$.

3. Extinction results

For the iteroparous species model, we have the following.

THEOREM 3.1. *For system (1.2), if* $0 < a_1 + a_2 + \cdots + a_m < 1$, *then the species will go extinct.*

Proof. Let $0 < a_1 + a_2 + \cdots + a_m < 1$. Let $(x_{n-1}, x_{n-2}, \dots, x_{n-m}) \in \mathbb{R}_+^{n-m}$. Note that

$$\begin{aligned} x_n &= \left(a_1 x_{n-1} + a_2 x_{n-2} + \cdots + a_m x_{n-m}\right) \cdot e^{-(b_1 x_{n-1} + b_2 x_{n-2} + \cdots + b_m x_{n-m})} \\ &\le a_1 x_{n-1} + a_2 x_{n-2} + \cdots + a_m x_{n-m} \\ &< \left(a_1 + a_2 + \cdots + a_m\right) \|x\|. \end{aligned} \tag{3.1}$$

So using the max norm obtains $|f(x_{n-1}, \dots, x_{n-m})| < a\|(x_{n-1}, \dots, x_{n-m})\|$. Thus by Theorem 2.1, the origin is globally asymptotically stable, since A_α in this case is $\mathbb{R}_+^m$. □

Consider the situation when $0 < a < 1$ in system (1.3). In this situation, the fecudity of the single reproductive age class of the species is not strong enough to perpetuate the species.

THEOREM 3.2. *For system (1.3), if* $0 < a < 1$, *then the species will go extinct.*

Proof. For the single species model with a single reproductive age class, we have

$$\begin{aligned} x_n &= x_{n-j} f\left(x_{n-1}, x_{n-2}, \dots, x_{n-m}\right) \\ &= a x_{n-j} e^{-(b_1 x_{n-1} + b_2 x_{n-2} + \cdots + b_k x_{n-m})}. \end{aligned} \tag{3.2}$$

Assuming $0 < a < 1$, we have

$$\left| f\left(x_{n-1}, \dots, x_{n-m}\right) \right| = \left| a \cdot e^{-(b_1 x_{n-1} + \cdots + b_k x_{n-m})} \right| \le a. \tag{3.3}$$

This implies that $|f(x_{n-1}, \dots, x_{n-m})| < a\|(x_{n-1}, \dots, x_{n-m})\|$. By [9, Theorem 2.1], we have the origin in globally asymptotically stable. □

Again for this result the set $A_\alpha = \mathbb{R}_+^m$. So both are global results since only positive populations are considered.

4. Persistence results

The following results give sufficient conditions for an interior stable fixed point to be attracting on some interval. Theorem 2.2 is only applicable to iteroparous species. For convenience, let $a_{\min} = \min_i\{a_i\}$, $a_{\max} = \max_i\{a_i\}$, and $b_{\max} = \max_i\{b_i\}$.

THEOREM 4.1. *In system (1.2), if $a_i > 0$ for $1 \le i \le m$ and*

$$\frac{\ln\left(\sum_{i=1}^{m} a_i\right)}{\sum_{i=1}^{m} b_i} < \frac{a_{\min}}{b_{\max} a_{\max} k m}, \tag{4.1}$$

then $x^* = \sqrt[k]{\ln(\sum_{i=1}^{m} a_i)/\sum_{i=1}^{m} b_i}$ attracts all the solutions with initial conditions in the interval $I = (0, \sqrt[k]{a_{\min}/b_{\max} a_{\max} k m})$.

Proof. Consider the following equation:

$$x_n = (a_1 x_{n-1} + a_2 x_{n-2} + \cdots + a_m x_{n-m}) e^{-(b_1 x_{n-1}^k + b_2 x_{n-2}^k + \cdots + b_k x_{n-m}^k)}. \tag{4.2}$$

Note that

$$\frac{\delta f}{\delta u_i} = e^{-(b_1 x_{n-1}^k + b_2 x_{n-2}^k + \cdots + b_k x_{n-m}^k)} \left[a_i - b_i k \left(\sum_{j=1}^{m} a_j u_j \right) u_i^{k-1} \right]. \tag{4.3}$$

In order for $\delta f/\delta u_i > 0$ for each u_i, we need

$$a_i - b_i k \left(\sum_{j=1}^{m} a_j u_j \right) u_i^{k-1} > 0. \tag{4.4}$$

This implies that a_i must be strictly positive for all i. Note that

$$a_i - b_i k \left(\sum_{j=1}^{m} a_j u_j \right) u_i^{k-1} > a_{\min} - b_{\max} k \left(\sum_{j=1}^{m} a_{\max} u_j \right) u_i^{k-1}. \tag{4.5}$$

Letting $u_i = u$ gives that $u < \sqrt[k]{a_{\min}/b_{\max} a_{\max} k m}$. So let $I = [0, \sqrt[k]{a_{\min}/b_{\max} a_{\max} k m}]$ if $(u_1, u_2, \ldots, u_m) \in I^m$, then f is increasing in each coordinate.

The fixed point for f is $u^* = \sqrt[k]{\ln(\sum_{i=1}^{m} a_i)/\sum_{i=1}^{m} b_i}$. So in order for $u^* \in I$,

$$\frac{\ln\left(\sum_{i=1}^{m} a_i\right)}{\sum_{i=1}^{m} b_i} < \frac{a_{\min}}{b_{\max} a_{\max} k m}, \tag{4.6}$$

which is true by assumption.

Now consider $g(u) - u$. Since $g(u) = (\sum_{i=1}^{m} a_i) u e^{-(\sum_{i=1}^{m} b_i) u^k}$, this gives

$$\begin{aligned} g(u) - u &= \left(\sum_{i=1}^{m} a_i \right) u e^{-(\sum_{i=1}^{m} b_i) u^k} - u \\ &= u \left[\left(\sum_{i=1}^{m} a_i \right) e^{-(\sum_{i=1}^{m} b_i) u^k} - 1 \right]. \end{aligned} \tag{4.7}$$

Note if $u < u^* = \sqrt[k]{\ln(\sum_{i=1}^m a_i)/\sum_{i=1}^m b_i}$, then

$$g(u) - u > u\left[\left(\sum_{i=1}^m a_i\right)e^{-(\sum_{i=1}^m b_i)(\sqrt[k]{\ln(\sum_{i=1}^m a_i)/\sum_{i=1}^m b_i})^k} - 1\right] = 0. \tag{4.8}$$

Thus $g(u) > u$. Similarly if $u > u^* = \sqrt[k]{\ln(\sum_{i=1}^m a_i)/\sum_{i=1}^m b_i}$, then

$$g(u) - u < u\left[\left(\sum_{i=1}^m a_i\right)e^{-(\sum_{i=1}^m b_i)(\sqrt[k]{\ln(\sum_{i=1}^m a_i)/\sum_{i=1}^m b_i})^k} - 1\right] = 0. \tag{4.9}$$

Thus $g(u) < u$. Therefore u^* attracts all solutions with initial values in I. □

Note that Theorem 2.2 is not applicable to system (1.3). This is due to the fact that in all but one coordinate, the equation is decreasing. This is also why it is assumed that $a_i > 0$ for all i in the above theorem. For this next result, we utilize Theorem 2.3.

THEOREM 4.2. *For system (1.2), let* $a = a_1 + a_2 + \cdots + a_m$, $b = b_1 + b_2 + \cdots + b_m$, $\mu = \max_i\{\sqrt[k]{a_i/b_ika}\}$, *and* $e^{b\mu^k} < a < e^{2/k}$, *then* $x^* = \sqrt[k]{\ln(a)/b}$ *is stable and attracts all solutions with initial conditions in the interval* $(\mu, g(\mu))$.

Proof. For (H1), we show that $f(u_1, u_2, \ldots, u_m)$ is nonincreasing for $u_1, u_2, \ldots, u_m \in (\mu, \infty)$. Note that

$$\frac{\delta f}{\delta u_i} = e^{-\sum_{i=1}^m b_i u_i^k}\left[a_i - b_ik\left(\sum_{j=1}^m a_ju_j\right)u_i^{k-1}\right]. \tag{4.10}$$

So $\delta f/\delta u_i \le 0$ if

$$a_i - b_ik\left(\sum_{j=1}^m a_ju_j\right)u_i^{k-1} \le 0. \tag{4.11}$$

For (H1), we need a single interval for each coordinate, so letting $u_i = u$, the left-hand side of (4.11) becomes

$$a_i - b_iku_i^{k-1}\left(\sum_{j=1}^m a_ju\right) = a_i - b_iku^ka. \tag{4.12}$$

Now observe

$$\begin{gathered} a_i - b_iku^ka \le 0, \\ a_i \le b_iku^ka, \\ \sqrt[k]{\frac{a_i}{b_ika}} \le u. \end{gathered} \tag{4.13}$$

And since $\mu = \max_i\{\sqrt[k]{a_i/b_ika}\}$, if $u_i > \mu$, $\delta f/\delta u_i \le 0$. So f is nondecreasing for $u_1, u_2, \ldots, u_m \in (\mu, \infty)$.

For (H2), we want to show that $g(u) = f(u, u, \ldots, u) = aue^{-bu^k}$ is continuous and decreasing for $u \in (\mu, \infty)$. Since g is a product of continuous functions, it is also continuous.

Differentiating g gives

$$g'(u) = ae^{-bu^k}[1 - kbu^k]. \tag{4.14}$$

So g is decreasing if

$$\begin{aligned} 1 - kbu^k &< 0, \\ 1 &< kbu^k, \\ \sqrt[k]{\frac{1}{kb}} &< u. \end{aligned} \tag{4.15}$$

Now note that $\sqrt[k]{1/kb} \le \mu$. So g is nonincreasing on (μ, ∞) as well.

For (H3), we show for $u \in (\mu, \sqrt[k]{\ln(a)/b})$ that $g(u) > u$. This implies that there is a $u^* \in (\mu, \infty)$ with $g(u^*) > u^*$. Note that if $\mu < \sqrt[k]{\ln(a)/b}$, then $a > e^{b\mu^k}$, which is true by assumption. Let $\mu < u < \sqrt[k]{\ln(a)/b}$. Note that

$$g(u) - u = aue^{-bu^k} - u = u[ae^{-bu^k} - 1]. \tag{4.16}$$

Since $u < \sqrt[k]{\ln(a)/b}$,

$$ae^{-bu^k} - 1 > ae^{-b(\sqrt[k]{\ln(a)/b})^k} - 1 = 0. \tag{4.17}$$

Thus $g(u) - u > 0$, which implies that $g(u) > u$.

For (H4), we want to show for $u \in (\mu, \sqrt[k]{\ln(a)/b})$ that $g^2(u) > u$. Let $\mu < u < \sqrt[k]{\ln(a)/b}$. This gives

$$\begin{aligned} g^2(u) &= a(aue^{(-bu^k)})e^{-b(aue^{-(bu^k)})^k)} \\ &= a^2ue^{-bu^k - (ba^ku^ke^{(-kbu^k)})} \\ &= a^2ue^{-bu^k[1+a^ke^{(-kbu^k)}]}. \end{aligned} \tag{4.18}$$

So this gives

$$\begin{aligned} g^2(u) - u &= a^2ue^{-bu^k[1+a^ke^{(-kbu^k)}]} - u \\ &= u[a^2e^{-bu^k[1+a^ke^{(-kbu^k)}]} - 1]. \end{aligned} \tag{4.19}$$

Let $u = \sqrt[k]{x/b}$. Substituting this into (4.19) and simplifying gives

$$\begin{aligned} g^2\left(\sqrt[k]{\frac{x}{b}}\right) - \sqrt[k]{\frac{x}{b}} &= \sqrt[k]{\frac{x}{b}}[a^2e^{(-b(\sqrt[k]{x/b})^k[1+a^ke^{(-kb(\sqrt[k]{x/b})^k)}])} - 1] \\ &= \sqrt[k]{\frac{x}{b}}[a^2e^{(-x[1+a^ke^{-kx}])} - 1]. \end{aligned} \tag{4.20}$$

Consider $h(x) = a^2 e^{(-x[1+a^k e^{-kx}])} - 1$. Differentiating h gives

$$h'(x) = a^2 e^{(-x[1+a^k e^{-kx}])} \cdot [a^k x k e^{-kx} - 1 - a^k e^{-kx}]. \tag{4.21}$$

Let $p(x) = a^k x k e^{-kx} - 1 - a^k e^{-kx}$. Differentiating p obtains

$$\begin{aligned} p'(x) &= a^k k e^{-kx} - a^k k^2 x e^{-kx} + a^k k e^{-kx} \\ &= a^k k e^{-kx}[2 - kx]. \end{aligned} \tag{4.22}$$

Thus for $x < 2/k$, we have $p'(x) > 0$. This implies that p is increasing for $x < 2/k$. Since

$$\begin{aligned} p\left(\frac{2}{k}\right) &= a^k \left(\frac{2}{k}\right) k e^{-k(2/k)} - 1 - a^k e^{-k(2/k)} \\ &= 2a^k e^{-2} - 1 - a^k e^{-2} \\ &= a^k e^{-2} - 1, \end{aligned} \tag{4.23}$$

by assumption $a < e^{2/k}$, so $p(x) < 0$ for $x < 2/k$. This then implies that $h'(x) < 0$ and so h is decreasing for $x < 2/k$.

Since $a < e^{2/k}$ and $u < \sqrt[k]{\ln(a)/b}$, we have that $x < \ln(a) < 2/k$. Observe that $h(\ln(a)) = 0$. This gives that $g^2(u) - u > 0$ for $u < \sqrt[k]{\ln(a)/b}$, which implies $g^2(u) > u$. This completes the proof. □

A similar result for semelparous species is below. The proof of the following theorem is similar to the previous proof and is omitted. The main difference here is that the result depends on the reproductive age class, x_{n-j}.

THEOREM 4.3. *For system (1.3) where x_{n-j} is the only reproductive age class, if $e^{b/(b_j k)} < a < e^{2/k}$, then $x^* = \sqrt[k]{\ln(a)/b}$ is stable and attracts all solutions with initial conditions in the interval $(\sqrt[k]{1/b_j k}, g(\sqrt[k]{1/b_j k}))$.*

5. Summary

This paper deals with a general model for a single species with multiple age or stage classes. This model assumes there is a limited amount of resources available to the species. This limitation restricts the reproduction of the species.

There are two basic types of species: iteroparous and semelparous. Iteroparous species can reproduce multiple times in their lifetime, whereas semelparous species only reproduce once.

In general, this model can produce very complicated and chaotic dynamics in some parameter ranges. We have given sufficient conditions under which the species will go extinct. These are global results for both iteroparous and semelparous species. We also have given sufficient conditions for stable equilibriums. These results are valid on particular intervals, though it is believed that more global results do exist.

References

[1] D. M. Chan, E. R. Chang, M. Dehghan, C. M. Kent, R. Mazrooei-Sebdani, and H. Sedaghat, *Asymptotic stability for difference equations with decreasing arguments*, Journal of Difference Equations and Applications **12** (2006), no. 2, 109–123.

[2] D. M. Chan and J. E. Franke, *Extinction, weak extinction and persistence in a discrete, competitive Lotka-Volterra model*, International Journal of Applied Mathematics and Computer Science **10** (2000), no. 1, 7–36.

[3] ———, *Multiple extinctions in a discrete competitive system*, Nonlinear Analysis. Real World Applications **2** (2001), no. 1, 75–91.

[4] J. E. Franke and A.-A. Yakubu, *Mutual exclusion versus coexistence for discrete competitive systems*, Journal of Mathematical Biology **30** (1991), no. 2, 161–168.

[5] ———, *Geometry of exclusion principles in discrete systems*, Journal of Mathematical Analysis and Applications **168** (1992), no. 2, 385–400.

[6] M. L. J. Hautus, T. S. Bolis, and A. Emerson, *Problems and solutions: solutions of elementary problems: E2721*, The American Mathematical Monthly **86** (1979), no. 10, 865–866.

[7] J. Hofbauer, V. Hutson, and W. Jansen, *Coexistence for systems governed by difference equations of Lotka-Volterra type*, Journal of Mathematical Biology **25** (1987), no. 5, 553–570.

[8] R. M. May, *Biological populations obeying difference equations: stable points, stable cycles, and chaos*, Journal of Thermal Biology **51** (1975), no. 2, 511–524.

[9] H. Sedaghat, *Nonlinear Difference Equations*, Mathematical Modelling: Theory and Applications, vol. 15, Kluwer Academic, Dordrecht, 2003.

David M. Chan: Department of Mathematics, Virginia Commonwealth University, B. O. 842014, 1001 West Main Street, Richmond, VA 23284-2014, USA
E-mail address: dmchan@vcu.edu

MATHEMATICAL ANALYSIS OF FLY FISHING ROD STATIC AND DYNAMIC RESPONSE

DER-CHEN CHANG, GANG WANG, AND NORMAN M. WERELEY

We develop two mathematical models to study the fly fishing rod static and dynamic response. Due to the flexible characteristics of fly fishing rod, the geometric nonlinear models must be used to account for the large static and dynamic fly rod deformations. A static nonlinear beam model is used to calculate the fly rod displacement under a tip force and the solution can be represented as elliptic integrals. A nonlinear finite element model is applied to analyze static and dynamic responses of fly rods.

1. Introduction

The literature of fishing is the richest among all sports and its history dates back to 2000 B.C. The literature of fishing is restrict among any other sports. Even for a subset of fly fishing, much literature is available. However, a significant fraction of fly fishing literature is devoted to its history, rod makers, casting techniques, and so forth. There is a lack of literature about the technology of fly rods in terms of technical rod analysis, rod design, and rod performance evaluation.

In this paper, we will use two different approaches to discuss mathematics for a fly rod based on its geometry and material properties. The first mathematical model is based on the nonlinear equation of a fly rod under a static tip force. The fly rod responses can be solved using an elliptic integrals. The second mathematical model is based on the finite element method, in which a nonlinear finite element model was developed to account for both static and dynamic responses of a fly rod. Typically, a fly rod is considered a long slender tapered beam. The variation of fly rod properties along its length will add complexities to our problem. In this paper, we focus on the presentation of two mathematical models and demonstrate the solution approach. We will continue the follow-up study to provide simplified and accurate solution/formulas for fly rod design and analysis. The paper is based on lectures given by the first author during the International Conference on Differential and Difference Equations which was held at the Florida Institute of Technology, August 1 to 6, 2005. The first author takes great pleasure in expressing his thank

Hindawi Publishing Corporation
Proceedings of the Conference on Differential & Difference Equations and Applications, pp. 287–297

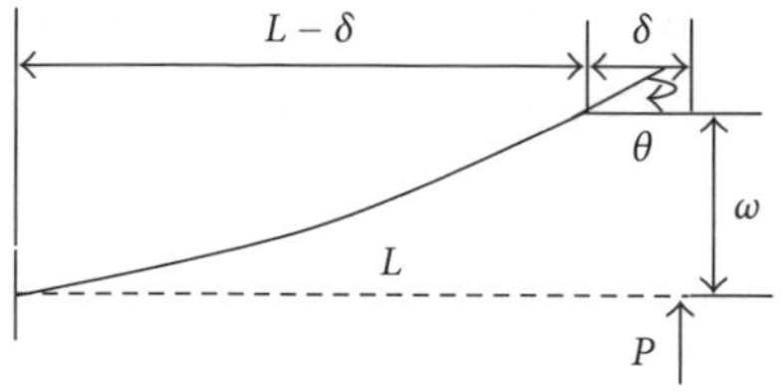

Figure 2.1. Uniform cantilever beam under tip point force.

to Professor Ravi Agarwal for organizing this activity and for the warm hospitality that he received while his visit to Melbourne, Florida.

2. Nonlinear model of fly fishing rod

It was Leonard Euler who first published a result concerning the large deflection of flexible rods in 1744, and it was continued in the Appendix of his book *Des Curvis Elastics.* He stated that for a rod in bending, the slope of the deflection curve cannot be neglected in the expression of the curve unless the deflections are small. Later, this theory was further developed by Jacob Bernoulli, Johann Bernoulli, and L. Euler. The derivation of a mathematical model of a fly rod is based on their fundamental work, which states that the bending moment M is proportional to the change in the curvature produced by the action of the load (see Bisshopp and Drucker [4], also Fertis [6]). Of course, one has to assume that bending does not alter the length of the rod. Now let us consider a long, thin cantilevel leaf spring. Denote L the length of the rod, δ the horizontal component of the displacement of the loaded end of the rod, ω the corresponding vertical displacement, P the concentrated vertical load at the free end, B the flexural stiffness (see Figure 2.1). It is known that

$$B = EI, \tag{2.1}$$

where E is the modulus of elasticity and I is the cross-sectional moment of inertia. If x is the horizontal coordinate measured from the fixed end of the rod, then the product of B and the curvature of the rod equal the bending moment M:

$$B\frac{d\theta}{ds} = P(L - x - \delta) = M \Longleftrightarrow \frac{d^2\theta}{ds^2} = -\frac{P}{B}\frac{dx}{ds} = -\frac{P}{EI}\cos\theta, \tag{2.2}$$

where s is the arc length and θ is the slope angle. It follows that

$$\frac{1}{2}\left(\frac{d\theta}{ds}\right)^2 = -\frac{P}{EI}\sin\theta + C. \tag{2.3}$$

The constant C can be determined by observing that the curvature at the loaded end is zero. If θ_0 is the corresponding slope, then

$$\frac{d\theta}{ds} = \sqrt{\frac{2P}{EI}}\sqrt{\sin\theta_0 - \sin\theta}. \tag{2.4}$$

Since the rod is inextensible, the value of θ_0 can be calculated implicitly as follows:

$$\sqrt{\frac{2PL^2}{EI}} = \sqrt{\frac{2P}{EI}}\int_0^L ds = \int_0^{\theta_0} \frac{d\psi}{\sqrt{\sin\theta_0 - \sin\theta}}. \tag{2.5}$$

Let

$$1 + \sin\theta = 2k^2 \sin^2\psi = (1 + \sin\theta_0)\sin^2\psi. \tag{2.6}$$

Denote

$$\sin\psi_1 = \frac{1}{\sqrt{2}k}, \qquad \gamma^2 = \frac{2PL^2}{EI}. \tag{2.7}$$

Then

$$\begin{aligned}\gamma &= \int_{\psi_1}^{\pi/2} \frac{d\psi}{\sqrt{1-2k^2\sin^2\psi}}\\ &= \int_0^{\pi/2} \frac{d\psi}{\sqrt{1-2k^2\sin^2\psi}} - \int_0^{\psi_1} \frac{d\psi}{\sqrt{1-2k^2\sin^2\psi}}\\ &= K(\sqrt{2}k) - \mathrm{sn}^{-1}(\sin\psi_1, \sqrt{2}k)\\ &= K(\sqrt{2}k) - F(\psi_1, \sqrt{2}k),\end{aligned} \tag{2.8}$$

where

$$K(k) = \frac{\pi}{2}\left[1 + \left(\frac{1}{2}\right)^2 k^2 + \left(\frac{1\cdot 3}{2\cdot 4}\right)^2 k^4 + \left(\frac{1\cdot 3\cdot 5}{2\cdot 4\cdot 6}\right)^2 k^6 + \cdots\right] \tag{2.9}$$

is the *complete elliptic integral of the first kind* and $F(\psi, k)$ is the Legendre's form of the integral sn^{-1}. Next, one needs to represent the deflection ω in terms of γ and an elliptic integral. Since

$$\frac{dy}{d\theta}\frac{d\theta}{ds} = \frac{dy}{ds} = \sin\theta, \tag{2.10}$$

then we have

$$\frac{dy}{d\theta}\frac{2P}{EI}\sqrt{\sin\theta_0 - \sin\theta} = \sin\theta. \tag{2.11}$$

It follows that

$$\omega = \int_0^y dy = \frac{EI}{2P}\int_0^{\theta_0} \frac{\sin\theta\, d\theta}{\sqrt{\sin\theta_0 - \sin\theta}}. \tag{2.12}$$

Plugging (2.6) into the above equation, one has

$$\frac{\omega}{L} = \frac{1}{\sqrt{2}\gamma}\int_0^{\theta_0} \frac{\sin\theta\, d\theta}{\sqrt{\sin\theta_0 - \sin\theta}} = \frac{1}{\gamma}\int_{\psi_1}^{\pi/2} \frac{(2k^2\sin^2\psi - 1)d\psi}{\sqrt{1-k^2\sin^2\psi}}. \tag{2.13}$$

It is known that (see Lawden [7])

$$\int_0^{\pi/2} \frac{\sin^2\psi\, d\psi}{\sqrt{1-k^2\sin^2\psi}} = \frac{1}{k^2}(K-E), \tag{2.14}$$

where

$$E = \frac{\pi}{2}\left[1-\left(\frac{1}{2}\right)^2 k^2 - \frac{1}{3}\left(\frac{1\cdot 3}{2\cdot 4}\right)^2 k^4 - \frac{1}{5}\left(\frac{1\cdot 3\cdot 5}{2\cdot 4\cdot 6}\right)^2 k^6 + \cdots\right] \tag{2.15}$$

is the *complete integral of the second kind*. Hence,

$$\int_0^{\pi/2} \frac{2k^2\sin^2\psi\, d\psi}{\sqrt{1-k^2\sin^2\psi}} = \frac{\pi}{2}\left[k^2+\frac{3}{2}\left(\frac{1}{2}\right)^2 k^4 + \frac{5}{3}\left(\frac{1\cdot 3}{2\cdot 4}\right)^2 k^6 + \frac{7}{4}\left(\frac{1\cdot 3\cdot 5}{2\cdot 4\cdot 6}\right)^2 k^8 + \cdots\right]. \tag{2.16}$$

Now we need to look at the term

$$\int_0^{\psi_1} \frac{\sin^2\psi\, d\psi}{\sqrt{1-k^2\sin^2\psi}}. \tag{2.17}$$

After changing variables, this elliptic integral can be expressed as a Jacobi's epsilon function $E(u,k)$ defined by

$$E(\psi_1,k) = \int_0^{\psi_1} \mathrm{dn}^2 u\, du = \int_0^{\mathrm{sn}\,\psi_1} \sqrt{\frac{1-k^2\,\mathrm{sn}^2 v}{1-\mathrm{sn}^2 v}}\, \mathrm{cn}\, v\, \mathrm{dn}\, v\, dv. \tag{2.18}$$

Therefore,

$$\begin{aligned} \frac{\omega}{L} &= \frac{1}{\gamma}[2K-2E-E(\psi_1,k)+K(\sqrt{2}k)-F(\psi_1,\sqrt{2}k)] \\ &= \frac{1}{\gamma}[1-2J-E(\psi_1,k)], \end{aligned} \tag{2.19}$$

where

$$J = K - E = k^2\int_0^K \mathrm{sn}^2 u\, du. \tag{2.20}$$

Now the horizontal displacement of the loaded end can be calculated with $x=0$ and $\theta=0$. It follows that

$$P(L-\delta) = EI\left(\frac{d\theta}{ds}\right)\bigg|_{\theta=0} = \sqrt{2PEI\sin\theta_0} \tag{2.21}$$

or

$$\frac{L-\delta}{L} = \frac{\sqrt{2}}{\gamma}\sqrt{\sin\theta_0}. \tag{2.22}$$

Then from (2.6), one has $\sin\theta_0 = 2k^2 - 1$. We have presented a detailed mathematical solution of beam responses under a tip force. However, in the above solution, a uniform beam with constant flexural stiffness was assumed. Normally it is not valid for a fly fishing rod because it has a tapered shape and the flexural stiffness varies along the rod length. In order to utilize the above elliptic integral solution, we could smear the tapered rod properties and represent it using an equivalent uniform rod. Also, we can account for the flexural stiffness variation and conduct similar elliptic integrals. We will continue such study in a future paper. The goal is to provide a simple engineering solution to fly rod design and analysis. We need to extract and create such simple solution based on the results from elliptic integrals.

3. Finite element method

The key idea is to express the nonlinear strain of deformed configuration in terms of unknown displacements, which are defined with respect to the initial coordinates (see Wang and Wereley [11]). The Newton-Raphson method must be used to iteratively solve for the displacement in the nonlinear finite element model. In the finite strain beam theory, we included the shearing deformation, which leads to the Timosenko beam theory and rotation angle is an independent variable and not equal the slope of transverse displacement. By doing this, we obtain a simple kinematic relationship between strain and displacements. As discussed in Reissner [9], the nonlinear beam axial strain, ε, shear strain, γ, and bending curvature, κ, can be expressed in terms of axial displacement, $u(x)$, transverse displacement, $w(x)$, and rotational displacement, θ, as follows for a straight beam (see also Antman [1]):

$$\begin{aligned} \varepsilon &= \left(1 + \frac{du}{dx}\right)\cos\theta + \frac{dw}{dx}\sin\theta - 1, \\ \gamma &= \frac{du}{dx}\cos\theta - \left(1 + \frac{du}{dx}\right)\sin\theta, \\ \kappa &= \frac{d\theta}{dx}. \end{aligned} \tag{3.1}$$

The next step is to apply the finite element techniques to discretize the beam system. Figure 3.1 shows the two-node geometrically nonlinear finite element based on the finite strain beam theory.

This has been called a geometrically nonlinear Timosenko beam element. The element is not aligned to the x axis for general consideration, which has an initial angel ϕ_0. The nodal degrees of freedom were defined in the fixed frame except that the rotation angles θ_1 and θ_2 were calculated with respect to the initial element orientation. All displacements were linearly interpolated within an element using nodal degrees of freedom

$$\begin{aligned} u(x) &= N_1(x)U_1 + N_2(x)U_2, \\ w(x) &= N_1(x)W_1 + N_2(x)W_2, \\ \theta(x) &= N_1(x)\theta_1 + N_2(x)\theta_2, \end{aligned} \tag{3.2}$$

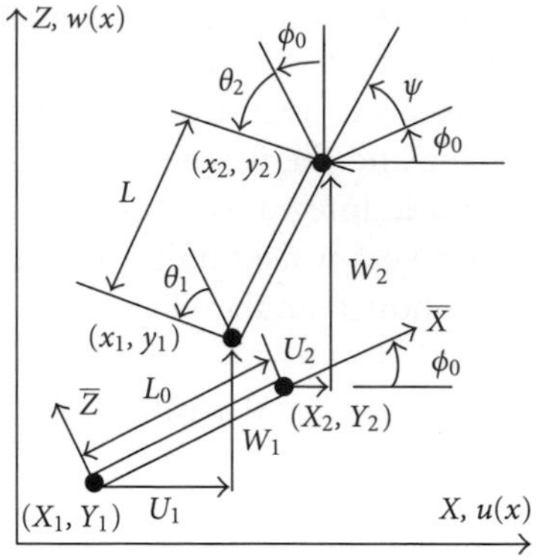

Figure 3.1. Two-node nonlinear finite element based on finite strain beam theory.

where the interpolation functions, $N_1(x)$ and $N_2(x)$, were defined as

$$N_1(x) = 1 - \frac{x}{L}, \qquad N_2(x) = \frac{x}{L}. \tag{3.3}$$

Let us first study the geometric relationships as shown in Figure 2.1. Given the node coordinates at node 1 (X_1, Y_1), and node 2 (X_2, Y_2), the initial reference angle ϕ_0 is determined by

$$\cos\phi_0 = \frac{X_2 - X_1}{L_0}, \qquad \sin\phi_0 = \frac{Y_2 - Y_1}{L_0}, \tag{3.4}$$

where

$$L_0 = \sqrt{(X_2 - X_1)^2 + (Y_2 - Y_1)^2}. \tag{3.5}$$

The angle $\phi_0 + \psi$ can be expressed by

$$\cos(\phi_0 + \psi) = \frac{x_2 - x_1}{L}, \qquad \sin(\phi_0 + \psi) = \frac{y_2 - y_1}{L}, \tag{3.6}$$

where

$$\begin{aligned} x_1 &= X_1 + U_1, \qquad x_2 = X_2 + U_2, \qquad y_1 = Y_1 + W_1, \\ y_2 &= Y_2 + W_2, \qquad L = \sqrt{(x_2 - x_1)^2 + (y_2 - y_1)^2}. \end{aligned} \tag{3.7}$$

Solving for ψ, one has

$$\begin{aligned} \cos\psi &= \frac{(X_2 - X_1)(x_2 - x_1) + (Y_2 - Y_1)(y_2 - y_1)}{LL_0}, \\ \sin\psi &= \frac{(X_2 - X_1)(x_2 - x_1) - (Y_2 - Y_1)(y_2 - y_1)}{LL_0}. \end{aligned} \tag{3.8}$$

In order to derive the basic stiffness matrices, we need to study the strain and displacement variational relationship

$$\delta\vec{\mathcal{H}} = B\delta\vec{\mathcal{Q}}, \tag{3.9}$$

where δ is a variation operator and $\vec{\mathcal{H}}$ is the strain vector. Here $\vec{\mathcal{Q}}$ is the nodal displacement vector:

$$\mathcal{H} = \begin{bmatrix} \varepsilon & \gamma & \kappa \end{bmatrix}^T, \qquad \mathcal{Q} = \begin{bmatrix} U_1 & W_1 & \theta_1 & U_2 & W_2 & \theta_2 \end{bmatrix}^T. \tag{3.10}$$

The matrix B is calculated by taking partial derivatives of strain vector with respect to nodal displacements which can be written as follows:

$$\begin{bmatrix} \cos(\omega N_1') & \sin(\omega N_1') & N_1\gamma & \cos(\omega N_2') & \sin(\omega N_2') & N_2\gamma \\ -\sin(\omega N_1') & \cos(\omega N_1') & -(1+\varepsilon)N_1 & -\sin(\omega N_2') & \cos(\omega N_2') & -(1+\varepsilon)N_2 \\ 0 & 0 & N_1' & 0 & 0 & N_2' \end{bmatrix}, \tag{3.11}$$

where $\omega = \theta + \phi_0$, ε, and γ are evaluated by

$$\begin{aligned} \varepsilon &= \frac{L\cos\psi\cos\theta + L\sin\psi\sin\theta}{L_0} - 1, \\ \gamma &= \frac{L\sin\psi\cos\theta - L\cos\psi\sin\theta}{L_0}. \end{aligned} \tag{3.12}$$

Here ε and γ are defined in (3.1). Finally, the beam element potential energy based on the finite strain beam theory is

$$\begin{aligned} U &= \frac{1}{2}\int_0^{L_0} \left\{ EA(\tilde{x})\varepsilon^2 + GA(\tilde{x})\gamma^2 + EI(\tilde{x})\left(\frac{d\theta}{d\tilde{x}}\right)^2 \right\} d\tilde{x} \\ &= \frac{1}{2}\int_0^{L_0} \mathcal{P}^T \mathcal{H}\, d\tilde{x}, \end{aligned} \tag{3.13}$$

where G is the shear modulus and $\mathcal{P} = [EA(\tilde{x})\varepsilon \quad GA(\tilde{x})\gamma \quad EI(\tilde{x})\theta']^T$ is the stress resultant vector. For isotropic materials, it can be expressed in terms of Young's modulus, E, and material constant Poisson ratio, ν:

$$G = \frac{E}{2(1+\nu)}. \tag{3.14}$$

The internal nodal force vector can be obtained by taking the first variation of potential energy. Hence,

$$\delta U = \int_0^{L_0} \mathcal{P}^T B\, d\tilde{x} \times \delta\mathcal{Q} \tag{3.15}$$

and the nodal internal force vector is

$$f = \int_0^{L_0} B^T \mathcal{P}^T d\tilde{x}. \tag{3.16}$$

It follows that f is a 6×1 vector. The tangent stiffness matrix can be defined by taking the first variation of internal force vector. Therefore,

$$\delta f = \int_0^{L_0} (B^T \delta\mathcal{P}^T + \delta B^T \mathcal{P}^T) d\tilde{x} = (\mathcal{K}_m + \mathcal{K}_g)\delta\mathcal{Q} = \mathcal{K}\delta\mathcal{Q}. \tag{3.17}$$

The tangent stiffness matrix $\mathcal{K}$ is the sum of material stiffness $\mathcal{K}_m$ and geometric stiffness $\mathcal{K}_g$. It is known that the material stiffness matrix is

$$\mathcal{K}_m = \int_0^{L_0} B^T \begin{bmatrix} EA(\tilde{x}) & 0 & 0 \\ 0 & GA(\tilde{x}) & 0 \\ 0 & 0 & EI(\tilde{x}) \end{bmatrix} B^T d\tilde{x}. \tag{3.18}$$

In order to calculate the geometric stiffness matrix $\mathcal{K}_g$, the important step is to calculate the variation of the matrix B with respect to nodal displacement. From (3.11), we know that the matrix B is a function of ε, γ, and θ. Then B is also a matrix-valued function of nodal displacement. The variation of B with respect to nodal displacements can be calculated by

$$\delta B = \frac{\partial B}{\partial q_j}\delta q_j = B_j \delta q_j, \quad j = 1,\ldots,6. \tag{3.19}$$

After some calculation, the geometric stiffness matrix $\mathcal{K}_g$ can be written as follows:

$$\mathcal{K}_g = \int_0^{L_0} (EA(\tilde{x})\varepsilon B_u + GA(\tilde{x})\gamma B_w) d\tilde{x}, \tag{3.20}$$

where B_u and B_w are 6×6 matrices, and they are assembled using the matrices defined in (3.19) where

$$\begin{aligned} B_u &= \begin{bmatrix} B_1(1,\cdot)^T & B_2(1,\cdot)^T & B_3(1,\cdot)^T & B_4(1,\cdot)^T & B_5(1,\cdot)^T & B_6(1,\cdot)^T \end{bmatrix}, \\ B_w &= \begin{bmatrix} B_1(2,\cdot)^T & B_2(2,\cdot)^T & B_3(2,\cdot)^T & B_4(2,\cdot)^T & B_5(2,\cdot)^T & B_6(2,\cdot)^T \end{bmatrix}. \end{aligned} \tag{3.21}$$

In order to take flexibility of a fly rod during a cast into account, we must include the inertia terms in our nonlinear finite element model. The kinetic energy of a fly rod is

$$T = \frac{1}{2}\int_0^{L_0} \left[\rho A(\tilde{x}) \left(\frac{\partial u}{\partial t}\right)^2 + \rho A(\tilde{x}) \left(\frac{\partial w}{\partial t}\right)^2 + \rho I(\tilde{x}) \left(\frac{\partial \theta}{\partial t}\right)^2 \right] d\tilde{x}, \tag{3.22}$$

where ρ is the density of the fly rod material. Using the same interpolation functions for axial displacement, $u(\widetilde{x})$, transverse displacement, $w(\widetilde{x})$, and rotation angular displacement, $\theta(\widetilde{x})$, we finally obtain the element mass matrix M which is a 6×6 matrix with components

$$
\begin{aligned}
M_{11} &= M_{22} = \int_0^{L_0} \rho A(\widetilde{x}) N_1^2 d\widetilde{x}, \\
M_{33} &= \int_0^{L_0} \rho I(\widetilde{x}) N_1^2 d\widetilde{x}, \\
M_{44} &= M_{55} = \int_0^{L_0} \rho A(\widetilde{x}) N_2^2 d\widetilde{x}, \\
M_{66} &= \int_0^{L_0} \rho I(\widetilde{x}) N_2^2 d\widetilde{x}, \\
M_{14} &= M_{41} = M_{25} = M_{52} = \int_0^{L_0} \rho A(\widetilde{x}) N_1 N_2 d\widetilde{x}, \\
M_{36} &= M_{63} = \int_0^{L_0} \rho I(\widetilde{x}) N_1 N_2 d\widetilde{x},
\end{aligned}
\tag{3.23}
$$

and the rest components are zero. Next, we need to solve the nonlinear dynamic response by using nonlinear finite element approach. The Newton-Raphson equilibrium iteration loop can be used to achieve this goal (see Simo and Vu-Quoc [10] and Newmark [8]). The algorithm of this approach used in our work is listed as follows.

Step 1. Initialize i, $i = 0$.

Step 2. Predictor

$$
\begin{gathered}
U^i_{t+\Delta t} = U_t, \qquad \ddot{U}^i_{t+\Delta t} = \frac{-1}{\beta \Delta t}\dot{U}_t + \frac{2\beta - 1}{2\beta}\ddot{U}_t, \\
\dot{U}^i_{t+\Delta t} = \dot{U}_t + \Delta t\left[(1-\gamma)\ddot{U}_t + \gamma \ddot{U}^i_{t+\Delta t}\right].
\end{gathered}
\tag{3.24}
$$

Step 3. Increment i, $i = i + 1$.

Step 4. Calculate effective stiffness, K^i_{eff}, and residual force vector, Y^i,

$$
\begin{aligned}
K^i_{\text{eff}} &= \frac{1}{\beta \Delta t^2} M^{i-1} + \frac{\gamma}{\beta \Delta t} D^{i-1} + K^{i-1}_m + K^{i-1}_g, \\
Y^i &= R^i_{\text{ext}} - M^{i-1} \ddot{U}^{i-1}_{t+\Delta t} - D^{i-1} \dot{U}^{i-1}_{t+\Delta t} - F^{i-1}_{t+\Delta t}.
\end{aligned}
\tag{3.25}
$$

Step 5. Solve for displacement increment, $\Delta U^i = (K^i_{\text{eff}})^{-1} Y^i$.

Table 3.1. Tip vertical displacement results for a tapered cantilevered beam under tip point force.

Taper parameter r	Exact ω [m]	NFEM ω [m]	Error [%]
1.0	18.594	18.586	−0.04
1.2	16.302	16.303	0.00
1.4	13.990	13.995	0.03
1.5	12.881	12.885	0.04
1.6	11.822	11.827	0.05
1.8	9.900	9.905	0.05
2.0	8.264	8.270	0.08
2.2	6.910	6.916	0.09
2.5	5.331	5.337	0.10
3.0	3.580	3.585	0.13

Step 6. Corrector

$$U^i_{t+\Delta t} = U^{i-1}_{t+\Delta t} + \Delta U^i, \qquad \dot{U}^i_{t+\Delta t} = \dot{U}^{i-1}_{t+\Delta t} + \frac{\gamma}{\beta \Delta t}\Delta U^i,$$
$$\ddot{U}^i_{t+\Delta t} = \ddot{U}^{i-1}_{t+\Delta t} + \frac{1}{\beta \Delta t^2}\Delta U^i. \tag{3.26}$$

Step 7. If $\| Y^i \| > 1.0 \times 10^{-5}$, repeat iteration, go to Step 4. Otherwise, $t = t + \Delta t$ and go to Step 1.

The parameter values of $\beta = 0.25$ and $\gamma = 0.5$ were used in our calculation, and D matrix is damping matrix for the fly rod system. We assume that D is the Rayleigh damping matrix and it is expressed as $D = \eta M$ where η is a constant. In order to obtain the convergent and accurate solution, the time step size should be as small as possible. Here we use $\Delta t \le 1.0 \times 10^{-3}$. The convergence of this process has been discussed by Belytschko-Huges [3] and Argyris-Mlejnek [2]. Similar to the discussion in Chang-Wang-Wereley [5], one can give a mathematical proof of the convergence of this algorithm. Our predictions of tip displacements were compared to those obtained by Fertis [6], as shown in Table 3.1. Here we just list the table of the numerical results for tip vertical displacement results. The beam was 25.4 meters (1000 in) long, and bending stiffness, EI, was assumed to be $EI = 516.21\ N - m^2$ (180×10^3 kip- in^2). The variations of beam moment of inertia and cross-section areas were defined as

$$EI(x) = EI_0\left(r + \frac{1-r}{L}x\right)^3,$$
$$A(x) = A_0\left(r + \frac{1-r}{L}x\right), \tag{3.27}$$

where r is a taper parameter, and cross-section area is assumed as $A_0 = 32.258\ \text{cm}^2\ (5\ \text{in}^2)$, where Poisson's ratio is $\nu = 0$. For a fixed tip loading, $P = 4448.22N$ (1 kip), we calculated tip deflection under different taper rates, or a taper parameter r varying from 1.0 to 3.0. We will give a detailed discussion and comparison of elliptic integrals and finite element solution for the fly rod in a forthcoming paper. A simplified engineering solution will be developed based on the elliptic integral results.

Acknowledgment

This work is partially supported by, under Maryland Industrial Partnerships (MIPs), grant from the Maryland Technology Enterprise Institute (MTECH) and Beaverkill Rod Co.

References

[1] S. S. Antman, *Kirchhoff's problem for nonlinearly elastic rods*, Quarterly of Applied Mathematics **32** (1974), 221–240.

[2] J. Argyris and H.-P. Mlejnek, *Dynamics of Structures*, Texts on Computational Mechanics, vol. 5, North-Holland, Amsterdam, 1991.

[3] T. Belytschko, T. J. R. Hughes, and K.-J. Bathe, *Computational Methods for Transient Analysis*, North-Holland, New York, 1983.

[4] K. E. Bisshopp and D. C. Drucker, *Large deflection of cantilever beams*, Quarterly of Applied Mathematics **3** (1945), 272–275.

[5] D.-C. Chang, T. Nguyen, G. Wang, and N. M. Wereley, *Applications of the Poincaré inequality to extended Kantorovich method*, Journal Inequalities and Applications **2006** (2006), 1–21.

[6] D. G. Fertis, *Nonlinear Mechanics*, 2nd ed., CRC Press, New York, 1999.

[7] D. F. Lawden, *Elliptic Functions and Applications*, Applied Mathematical Sciences, vol. 80, Springer, New York, 1989.

[8] N. M. Newmark, *A method of computation for structural dynamics*, ASCE Journal of Engineering Mechanics **85** (1959), 67–94.

[9] E. Reissner, *On a one-dimensional finite strain beam: the plane problem*, Journal of Applied Mathematics and Physics **23** (1972), no. 5, 795–804.

[10] J. C. Simo and L. Vu-Quoc, *On the dynamics of flexible beam under large overall motions-the plane case: part I and II*, ASME Journal of Applied Mechanice **53** (1986), 849–863.

[11] G. Wang and N. M. Wereley, *Analysis of flexible fly fishing rod and casting dynamics*, Proceedings of IMECE '03, Washington, DC, 2003, pp. 1–8.

Der-Chen Chang: Department of Mathematics, Georgetown University, Washington, DC 20057, USA
E-mail address: chang@georgetown.edu

Gang Wang: Department of Aerospace Engineering, University of Maryland, College Park, MD 20742, USA
E-mail address: gwang@eng.umd.edu

Norman M. Wereley: Department of Aerospace Engineering, University of Maryland, College Park, MD 20742, USA
E-mail address: wereley@eng.umd.edu

CONTINUOUS AND DISCRETE NONLINEAR INEQUALITIES AND APPLICATIONS TO BOUNDARY VALUE PROBLEMS

WING-SUM CHEUNG

We give some new nonlinear integral and discrete inequalities of the Gronwall-Bellman-Ou-Iang type in two variables. These on the one hand generalize and on the other hand furnish a handy tool for the study of qualitative as well as quantitative properties of solutions of differential and difference equations. We illustrate this by applying our new results to certain boundary value problems.

1. Introduction

In studying the boundedness behavior of the solutions of certain second-order differential equations, Ou-Iang established the following Gronwall-Bellman-type integral inequality which is now known as Ou-Iang's inequality in the literature.

THEOREM 1.1 (Ou-Iang [17]). *If u and f are nonnegative functions on $[0,\infty)$ satisfying*

$$u^2(x) \le k^2 + 2\int_0^x f(s)u(s)ds \tag{1.1}$$

for all $x \in [0,\infty)$, where $k \ge 0$ is a constant, then

$$u(x) \le k + \int_0^x f(s)ds, \quad \forall x \in [0,\infty). \tag{1.2}$$

An important feature of Ou-Iang-type inequalities or more generally Gronwall-Bellman-Ou-Iang-type inequalities [2, 10] is that they provide explicit bounds on the unknown function in terms of known functions. This makes such inequalities especially important in many practical situations. In fact, over the years, such inequalities and their generalizations to various settings have proven to be very effective in the study of many qualitative as well as quantitative properties of solutions of differential equations. These include, among others, the global existence, boundedness, uniqueness, stability, and continuous dependence on initial data (see, e.g., [3–5, 7, 8, 11, 13–16, 18–22]). For example,

Hindawi Publishing Corporation
Proceedings of the Conference on Differential & Difference Equations and Applications, pp. 299–313

in the process of establishing a connection between stability and the second law of thermodynamics, Dafermos established the following result.

Theorem 1.2 (Dafermos [9]). *If* $u \in \mathscr{L}^{\infty}[0,r]$ *and* $f \in \mathscr{L}^{1}[0,r]$ *are nonnegative functions satisfying*

$$u^2(x) \leq M^2u^2(0) + 2\int_0^x [Nf(s)u(s) + Ku^2(s)]ds \tag{1.3}$$

for all $x \in [0,r]$, *where* M, N, K *are nonnegative constants, then*

$$u(r) \leq \left[Mu(0) + N\int_0^r f(s)ds\right]e^{Kr}. \tag{1.4}$$

More recently, Pachpatte established the following further generalizations of Theorem 1.2.

Theorem 1.3 (Pachpatte [18]). *If* u, f, g *are continuous nonnegative functions on* $[0,\infty)$ *satisfying*

$$u^2(x) \leq k^2 + 2\int_0^x [f(s)u(s) + g(s)u^2(s)]ds \tag{1.5}$$

for all $x \in [0,\infty)$, *where* $k \geq 0$ *is a constant, then*

$$u(x) \leq \left(k + \int_0^x f(s)ds\right)\exp\left(\int_0^x g(s)ds\right), \quad \forall x \in [0,\infty). \tag{1.6}$$

Theorem 1.4 (Pachpatte [18]). *Suppose* u, f, g *are continuous nonnegative functions on* $[0,\infty)$ *and* w *a continuous nondecreasing function on* $[0,\infty)$ *with* $w(r) > 0$ *for* $r > 0$. *If*

$$u^2(x) \leq k^2 + 2\int_0^x \big(f(s)u(s) + g(s)u(s)w(u(s))\big)ds \tag{1.7}$$

for all $x \in [0,\infty)$, *where* $k \geq 0$ *is a constant, then*

$$u(x) \leq \Omega^{-1}\left[\Omega\left(k + \int_0^x f(s)ds\right) + \int_0^x g(s)ds\right] \tag{1.8}$$

for all $x \in [0,x_1]$, *where* $\Omega(r) := \int_1^r (ds/w(s))$, $r > 0$, *and* $x_1 \in [0,\infty)$ *is chosen in such a way that* $\Omega(k + \int_0^x f(s)ds) + \int_0^x g(s)ds \in \mathrm{Dom}(\Omega^{-1})$ *for all* $x \in [0,x_1]$.

On the other hand, Bainov-Simeonov and Lipovan observed the following Gronwall-Bellman-type inequalities which are handy in the study of the global existence of solutions to certain integral equations and functional differential equations.

Theorem 1.5 (Bainov-Simeonov [1]). *Let* $I = [0,a]$, $J = [0,b]$, *where* $a,b \leq \infty$. *Let* $c \geq 0$ *be a constant, let* $\varphi \in C([0,\infty),[0,\infty))$ *be nondecreasing with* $\varphi(r) > 0$ *for* $r > 0$, *and* $b \in C$ $(I \times J,[0,\infty))$. *If* $u \in C(I \times J,[0,\infty))$ *satisfies*

$$u(x,y) \leq c + \int_0^x\int_0^y b(s,t)\varphi(u(s,t))dt\,ds \tag{1.9}$$

for all $(x,y) \in I \times J$, *then*

$$u(x,y) \le \Phi^{-1}\left[\Phi(c) + \int_0^x \int_0^y b(s,t)\,dt\,ds\right] \tag{1.10}$$

for all $(x,y) \in [0,x_1] \times [0,y_1]$, *where* $\Phi(r) := \int_1^r (ds/\varphi(s))$, $r > 0$, *and* $(x_1,y_1) \in I \times J$ *is chosen such that* $\Phi(c) + \int_0^x \int_0^y b(s,t)\,dt\,ds \in \operatorname{Dom}(\Phi^{-1})$ *for all* $(x,y) \in [0,x_1] \times [0,y_1]$.

THEOREM 1.6 (Lipovan [12]). *Suppose* u, f *are continuous nonnegative functions on* $[x_0,X)$, w *a continuous nondecreasing function on* $[0,\infty)$ *with* $w(r) > 0$ *for* $r > 0$, *and* $\alpha : [x_0,X) \to [x_0,X)$ *a continuous nondecreasing function with* $\alpha(x) \le x$ *on* $[x_0,X)$. *If*

$$u(x) \le k + \int_{\alpha(x_0)}^{\alpha(x)} f(s)w(u(s))\,ds \tag{1.11}$$

for all $x \in [x_0,X)$, *where* $k \ge 0$ *is a constant, then*

$$u(x) \le \Omega^{-1}\left[\Omega(k) + \int_{\alpha(x_0)}^{\alpha(x)} f(s)\,ds\right] \tag{1.12}$$

for all $x \in [x_0,x_1)$, *where* Ω *is defined as in Theorem 1.4, and* $x_1 \in [x_0,X)$ *is chosen in such a way that* $\Omega(k) + \int_{\alpha(x_0)}^{\alpha(x)} f(s)\,ds \in \operatorname{Dom}(\Omega^{-1})$ *for all* $x \in [x_0,x_1)$.

The purpose of this paper is to establish some new Gronwall-Bellman-Ou-Iang-type inequalities with explicit bounds on unknown functions along the line of Theorems 1.1–1.6. These results on the one hand generalize the inequalities given in Theorems 1.1–1.6 and on the other hand furnish a handy tool for the study of qualitative as well as quantitative properties of solutions of differential and integral equations. We illustrate this by applying our new inequalities to study the boundedness, uniqueness, and continuous dependence properties of the solutions of a boundary value problem. Finally, we also give discrete analogs of these results and their applications to discrete boundary value problems.

2. Gronwall-Bellman-Ou-Iang-type inequalities

Throughout this paper, $x_0, y_0 \in \mathbb{R}$ are two fixed numbers. Let $\mathbb{R}_+ := [0,\infty)$, $I := [x_0,X) \subset \mathbb{R}$, $J := [y_0,Y) \subset \mathbb{R}$, and $\Delta := I \times J \subset \mathbb{R}^2$. Note that here we allow X or Y to be $+\infty$. As usual, $C^i(U,V)$ will denote the set of all i-times continuously differentiable functions of U into V, and $C^0(U,V) := C(U,V)$. Partial derivatives of a function $z(x,y)$ are denoted by z_x, z_y, z_{xy}, and so forth. The identity function will be denoted as id and, so in particular, id_U is the identity function of U onto itself.

For any φ, $\psi \in C(\mathbb{R}_+,\mathbb{R}_+)$ and any constant $\beta > 0$, define

$$\begin{aligned}
\Phi_\beta(r) &:= \int_1^r \frac{ds}{\varphi(s^{(1/\beta)})}, & \Psi_\beta(r) &:= \int_1^r \frac{ds}{\psi(s^{(1/\beta)})}, \quad r > 0, \\
\Phi_\beta(0) &:= \lim_{r\to 0^+} \Phi_\beta(r), & \Psi_\beta(0) &:= \lim_{r\to 0^+} \Psi_\beta(r).
\end{aligned} \tag{2.1}$$

Note that we allow $\Phi_\beta(0)$ and $\Psi_\beta(0)$ to be $-\infty$ here.

Theorem 2.1. *Let $c \geq 0$ and $p > 0$ be constants. Let $b \in C(\Delta, \mathbb{R}_+)$, $\gamma \in C^1(I,I)$, $\delta \in C^1(J,J)$, and $\varphi \in C(\mathbb{R}_+, \mathbb{R}_+)$ be functions satisfying the following:*

(i) *γ, δ are nondecreasing and $\gamma \leq id_I$, $\delta \leq id_J$;*

(ii) *φ is nondecreasing with $\varphi(r) > 0$ for $r > 0$.*

If $u \in C(\Delta, \mathbb{R}_+)$ satisfies

$$u^p(x,y) \leq c + \int_{\gamma(x_0)}^{\gamma(x)} \int_{\delta(y_0)}^{\delta(y)} b(s,t)\varphi(u(s,t))\,dt\,ds \tag{2.2}$$

for all $(x,y) \in \Delta$, then

$$u(x,y) \leq \left\{\Phi_p^{-1}\left[\Phi_p(c) + B(x,y)\right]\right\}^{1/p} \tag{2.3}$$

for all $(x,y) \in [x_0,x_1] \times [y_0,y_1]$, where

$$B(x,y) := \int_{\gamma(x_0)}^{\gamma(x)} \int_{\delta(y_0)}^{\delta(y)} b(s,t)\,dt\,ds, \tag{2.4}$$

and $(x_1,y_1) \in \Delta$ is such that $\Phi_p(c) + B(x,y) \in \operatorname{Dom}(\Phi_p^{-1})$ for all $(x,y) \in [x_0,x_1] \times [y_0,y_1]$.

Remark 2.2. (i) In many cases the nondecreasng function φ satisfies $\int_1^\infty (ds/\varphi(s^{1/p})) = \infty$. Examples of such functions are $\varphi \equiv 1$, $\varphi(s) = s^p$, $\varphi(s) = s^{p/2}$, and so forth. In such cases, $\Phi_p(\infty) = \infty$ and so we may take $x_1 = X$, $y_1 = Y$. In particular, inequality (2.3) holds for all $(x,y) \in \Delta$.

(ii) Theorem 2.1 reduces to Theorem 2.1 of Cheung [6] when $p = 1$, and reduces further to Theorem 1.5 if we set $\gamma(x) = x$, $\delta(y) = y$.

(iii) Theorem 2.1 is also a generalization of Theorem 1.6 to the case of two independent variables. In fact, if we set $p = 1$ and $\delta(y) = \delta(y_0)$ for all $y \in J$, Theorem 2.1 reduces to Theorem 1.6. If we further require $\gamma(x) = x$ for all $x \in I$, Theorem 2.1 further reduces to the famous Bihari inequality [4].

Theorem 2.3. *Let $k \geq 0$ and $p > 1$ be constants. Let $a, b \in C(\Delta, \mathbb{R}_+)$, $\alpha, \gamma \in C^1(I,I)$, $\beta, \delta \in C^1(J,J)$, and $\varphi \in C(\mathbb{R}_+, \mathbb{R}_+)$ be functions satisfying the following:*

(i) *α, β, γ, δ are nondecreasing with $\alpha, \gamma \leq id_I$ and $\beta, \delta \leq id_J$;*

(ii) *φ is nondecreasing with $\varphi(r) > 0$ for $r > 0$.*

If $u \in C(\Delta, \mathbb{R}_+)$ satisfies

$$\begin{aligned} u^p(x,y) \leq k &+ \frac{p}{p-1} \int_{\alpha(x_0)}^{\alpha(x)} \int_{\beta(y_0)}^{\beta(y)} a(s,t)u(s,t)\,dt\,ds \\ &+ \frac{p}{p-1} \int_{\gamma(x_0)}^{\gamma(x)} \int_{\delta(y_0)}^{\delta(y)} b(s,t)u(s,t)\varphi(u(s,t))\,dt\,ds \end{aligned} \tag{2.5}$$

for all $(x,y) \in \Delta$, then

$$u(x,y) \leq \left\{\Phi_{p-1}^{-1}\left[\Phi_{p-1}\left(k^{1-(1/p)} + A(x,y)\right) + B(x,y)\right]\right\}^{1/(p-1)} \tag{2.6}$$

for all $(x,y) \in [x_0,x_1] \times [y_0,y_1]$, *where*

$$A(x,y) := \int_{\alpha(x_0)}^{\alpha(x)} \int_{\beta(y_0)}^{\beta(y)} a(s,t)\,dt\,ds, \qquad B(x,y) := \int_{\gamma(x_0)}^{\gamma(x)} \int_{\delta(y_0)}^{\delta(y)} b(s,t)\,dt\,ds, \tag{2.7}$$

and $(x_1,y_1) \in \Delta$ *is such that* $\Phi_{p-1}(k^{1-(1/p)} + A(x,y)) + B(x,y) \in \mathrm{Dom}(\Phi_{p-1}^{-1})$ *for all* $(x,y) \in [x_0,x_1] \times [y_0,y_1]$.

Remark 2.4. (i) Similar to (i) of Remark 2.2, if $\Phi_{p-1}(\infty) = \infty$, (2.6) holds for all $(x,y) \in \Delta$.

(ii) Similar to (ii) of Remark 2.2, if we set $\beta(y) = \beta(y_0)$ and $\delta(y) = \delta(y_0)$ for all $y \in J$ in Theorem 2.3, we easily arrive at the following 1-dimensional result.

Corollary 2.5. *Let* $k \geq 0$ *and* $p > 1$ *be constants. Let* $a,b \in C(I,\mathbb{R}_+)$, $\alpha,\gamma \in C^1(I,I)$, *and* $\varphi \in C(\mathbb{R}_+,\mathbb{R}_+)$ *be functions satisfying the following:*

(i) α, γ *are nondecreasing with* $\alpha,\gamma \leq id_I$;

(ii) φ *is nondecreasing with* $\varphi(r) > 0$ *for* $r > 0$.

If $u \in C(I,\mathbb{R}_+)$ *satisfies*

$$u^p(x) \leq k + \frac{p}{p-1} \int_{\alpha(x_0)}^{\alpha(x)} a(s)u(s)\,ds + \frac{p}{p-1} \int_{\gamma(x_0)}^{\gamma(x)} b(s)u(s)\varphi(u(s))\,ds \tag{2.8}$$

for all $x \in I$, *then*

$$u(x) \leq \left\{\Phi_{p-1}^{-1}\left[\Phi_{p-1}(k^{1-(1/p)} + A(x)) + B(x)\right]\right\}^{1/(p-1)} \tag{2.9}$$

for all $x \in [x_0,x_1]$, *where*

$$A(x) := \int_{\alpha(x_0)}^{\alpha(x)} a(s)\,ds, \qquad B(x) := \int_{\gamma(x_0)}^{\gamma(x)} b(s)\,ds, \tag{2.10}$$

and $x_1 \in I$ *is chosen in such a way that* $\Phi_{p-1}(k^{1-(1/p)} + A(x)) + B(x) \in \mathrm{Dom}(\Phi_{p-1}^{-1})$ *for all* $x \in [x_0,x_1]$.

Remark 2.6. (i) Same as before, in case $\Phi_{p-1}(\infty) = \infty$, inequality (2.9) holds for all $x \in I$.

(ii) Corollary 2.5 generalizes a result of Pachpatte in [18] (Theorem 1.4). In fact, if we impose the conditions $p = 2$, $x_0 = 0$, and $\alpha(x) = \gamma(x) = x$ for all $x \in I$, Corollary 2.5 reduces to Theorem 1.4.

Theorem 2.3 can easily be applied to generate other useful nonlinear integral inequalities in more general situations. For example, we have the following.

Theorem 2.7. *Let* $k \geq 0$ *and* $p > q > 0$ *be constants. Let* $a,b \in C(\Delta,\mathbb{R}_+)$, $\alpha,\gamma \in C^1(I,I)$, $\beta,\delta \in C^1(J,J)$, *and* $\varphi \in C(\mathbb{R}_+,\mathbb{R}_+)$ *be functions satisfying the following:*

(i) α, β, γ, δ *are nondecreasing with* $\alpha,\gamma \leq id_I$ *and* $\beta,\delta \leq id_J$;

(ii) φ *is nondecreasing with* $\varphi(r) > 0$ *for* $r > 0$.

If $u \in C(\Delta, \mathbb{R}_+)$ *satisfies*

$$
\begin{aligned}
u^p(x,y) \leq k &+ \frac{p}{p-q}\int_{\alpha(x_0)}^{\alpha(x)}\int_{\beta(y_0)}^{\beta(y)} a(s,t)u^q(s,t)\,dt\,ds \\
&+ \frac{p}{p-q}\int_{\gamma(x_0)}^{\gamma(x)}\int_{\delta(y_0)}^{\delta(y)} b(s,t)u^q(s,t)\varphi(u(s,t))\,dt\,ds
\end{aligned}
\tag{2.11}
$$

for all $(x,y) \in \Delta$, *then*

$$
\begin{aligned}
u(x,y) \leq &\left\{\Phi_{p-q}^{-1}\left[\Phi_{p-q}\left(k^{1-(q/p)} + A(x,y)\right) + B(x,y)\right]\right\}^{1/(p-q)} \\
&\forall (x,y) \in [x_0,x_1]\times[y_0,y_1],
\end{aligned}
\tag{2.12}
$$

where $A(x,y)$ *and* $B(x,y)$ *are defined as in Theorem 2.3, and* $(x_1,y_1) \in \Delta$ *is chosen in such a way that* $\Phi_{p-q}(k^{1-(q/p)} + A(x,y)) + B(x,y) \in \mathrm{Dom}(\Phi_{p-q}^{-1})$ *for all* $(x,y) \in [x_0,x_1]\times[y_0,y_1]$.

An important special case of Theorem 2.7 is the following.

Corollary 2.8. *Let* $k \geq 0$ *and* $p > 1$ *be constants. Let* $a, b \in C(\Delta, \mathbb{R}_+)$, $\alpha, \gamma \in C^1(I,I)$, $\beta, \delta \in C^1(J,J)$, *and* $\varphi \in C(\mathbb{R}_+, \mathbb{R}_+)$ *be functions satisfying the following:*

(i) α, β, γ, δ *are nondecreasing with* $\alpha, \gamma \leq id_I$ *and* $\beta, \delta \leq id_J$;

(ii) φ *is nondecreasing with* $\varphi(r) > 0$ *for* $r > 0$.

If $u \in C(\Delta, \mathbb{R}_+)$ *satisfies*

$$
\begin{aligned}
u^p(x,y) \leq k &+ p\int_{\alpha(x_0)}^{\alpha(x)}\int_{\beta(y_0)}^{\beta(y)} a(s,t)u^{p-1}(s,t)\,dt\,ds \\
&+ p\int_{\gamma(x_0)}^{\gamma(x)}\int_{\delta(y_0)}^{\delta(y)} b(s,t)u^{p-1}(s,t)\varphi(u(s,t))\,dt\,ds
\end{aligned}
\tag{2.13}
$$

for all $(x,y) \in \Delta$, *then*

$$
u(x,y) \leq \Phi_1^{-1}\left[\Phi_1\left(k^{1/p} + A(x,y)\right) + B(x,y)\right], \quad \forall (x,y) \in [x_0,x_1]\times[y_0,y_1], \tag{2.14}
$$

where $A(x,y)$ *and* $B(x,y)$ *are defined as in Theorem 2.3, and* $(x_1,y_1) \in \Delta$ *is chosen in such a way that* $\Phi_1(k^{1/p} + A(x,y)) + B(x,y) \in \mathrm{Dom}(\Phi_1^{-1})$ *for all* $(x,y) \in [x_0,x_1]\times[y_0,y_1]$.

In particular, we have the following useful consequence.

Corollary 2.9. *Let* $k \geq 0$ *and* $p > 1$ *be constants. Let* $a, b \in C(\Delta, \mathbb{R}_+)$, $\alpha, \gamma \in C^1(I,I)$, *and* $\beta, \delta \in C^1(J,J)$ *be functions such that* α, β, γ, δ *are nondecreasing with* $\alpha, \gamma \in id_I$ *and* $\beta, \delta \leq id_J$. *If* $u \in C(\Delta, \mathbb{R}_+)$ *satisfies*

$$
\begin{aligned}
u^p(x,y) \leq k &+ p\int_{\alpha(x_0)}^{\alpha(x)}\int_{\beta(y_0)}^{\beta(y)} a(s,t)u^{p-1}(s,t)\,dt\,ds \\
&+ p\int_{\gamma(x_0)}^{\gamma(x)}\int_{\delta(y_0)}^{\delta(y)} b(s,t)u^{p}(s,t)\,dt\,ds
\end{aligned}
\tag{2.15}
$$

for all $(x,y) \in \Delta$, *then*

$$u(x,y) \le (k^{1/p} + A(x,y)) \exp B(x,y) \tag{2.16}$$

for all $(x,y) \in \Delta$, *where* $A(x,y)$ *and* $B(x,y)$ *are as defined in Theorem 2.3.*

Remark 2.10. Corollary 2.9 generalizes the results of Pachpatte (Theorem 1.3), Dafermos (Theorem 1.2), and Ou-Iang (Theorem 1.1).

Corollary 2.11. *Let* $k \ge 0$ *and* $p > 1$ *be constants. Let* $b \in C(\Delta, \mathbb{R}_+)$, $\gamma \in C^1(I,I)$, *and* $\delta \in C^1(J,J)$ *be functions such that* γ, δ *are nondecreasing with* $\gamma \le id_I$ *and* $\delta \le id_J$. *If* $u \in C(\Delta, \mathbb{R}_+)$ *satisfies*

$$u^p(x,y) \le k + p \int_{\gamma(x_0)}^{\gamma(x)} \int_{\delta(y_0)}^{\delta(y)} b(s,t) u^p(s,t)\,dt\,ds \tag{2.17}$$

for all $(x,y) \in \Delta$, *then*

$$u(x,y) \le k^{1/p} \exp B(x,y) \tag{2.18}$$

for all $(x,y) \in \Delta$, *where* $B(x,y)$ *is as defined in Theorem 2.3.*

Remark 2.12. Corollary 2.11 generalizes Corollary 2 in Lipovan [12] to the case of two independent variables. In fact, if we set $p = 2$ and $\delta(y) = \delta(y_0)$ for all $y \in J$, Corollary 2.11 reduces to the said Corollary 2. In particular, if we further require $\gamma(x) = x$ for all $x \in I$, Corollary 2.11 further reduces to the famous Gronwall-Bellman inequality [3, 8].

Remark 2.13. It is evident that the results above can easily be generalized to obtain explicit bounds for functions satisfying certain integral inequalities involving more retarded arguments. It is also clear that these results can be extended to functions of more than 2 variables in the obvious way. Details of these are rather algorithmic and so will not be given here.

3. Applications to boundary value problems

We will in this section illustrate how the results in Section 2 can be applied to study the boundedness, uniqueness, and continuous dependence of the solutions of certain initial boundary value problems for hyperbolic partial differential equations. Consider the following *boundary value problem* (BVP):

$$z^{p-1} z_{xy} + (p-1) z^{p-2} z_x z_y = F(x,y,z(\rho(x),\lambda(y))) \tag{3.1}$$

satisfying

$$z(x,y_0) = f(x), \qquad z(x_0,y) = g(y), \qquad f(x_0) = g(y_0) = 0, \tag{3.2}$$

where $p \ge 2$, $F \in C(\Delta \times \mathbb{R}, \mathbb{R})$, $f \in C^1(I,\mathbb{R})$, $g \in C^1(J,\mathbb{R})$, $\rho \in C^1(I,I)$, $\lambda \in C^1(J,J)$, $0 < \rho'$, $\lambda' \le 1$, $\rho(x_0) = x_0$, $\lambda(y_0) = y_0$.

Remark 3.1. Setting $\rho(x) = x - h(x)$ and $\lambda(y) = y - k(y)$, (BVP) becomes an initial boundary value problem with delay.

Our first result deals with the boundedness of solutions.

THEOREM 3.2. *Consider (BVP). If*

$$\begin{gathered} |F(x,y,v)| \leq b(x,y)|v|^p, \\ |f^p(x)+g^q(y)| \leq k, \end{gathered} \tag{3.3}$$

where $b \in C(\Delta, \mathbb{R}_+)$ and $k \geq 0$ is a constant, then all solutions $z(x,y)$ of (BVP) satisfy

$$|z(x,y)| \leq k^{1/p} \exp \overline{B}(x,y), \quad (x,y) \in \Delta, \tag{3.4}$$

where

$$\begin{gathered} \overline{B}(x,y) := MN \int_{\rho(x_0)}^{\rho(x)} \int_{\lambda(y_0)}^{\lambda(y)} \overline{b}(\sigma,\tau)d\tau\, d\sigma, \quad \overline{b}(\sigma,\tau) := b(\rho^{-1}(\sigma),\lambda^{-1}(\tau)), \\ M := \max\left\{\frac{1}{\rho'(x)} : x \in I\right\}, \qquad N := \max\left\{\frac{1}{\lambda'(y)} : y \in J\right\}. \end{gathered} \tag{3.5}$$

In particular, if $\overline{B}$ is bounded on Δ, then every solution z of (BVP) is bounded on Δ.

The next result is about uniqueness.

THEOREM 3.3. *Consider (BVP). If*

$$|F(x,y,v_1) - F(x,y,v_2)| \leq b(x,y)\,|v_1^p - v_2^p|, \tag{3.6}$$

where $b \in C(\Delta, \mathbb{R}_+)$, then (BVP) has at most one solution on Δ.

Finally, we will investigate the continuous dependence of the solutions of (BVP) on the function F and the boundary data. For this we consider a variation of (BVP):

($\overline{\text{BVP}}$)

$$z^{p-1}z_{xy} + (p-1)z^{p-2}z_x z_y = \overline{F}(x,y,z(\rho(x),\lambda(y))) \tag{3.7}$$

satisfying

$$z(x,y_0) = \overline{f}(x), \qquad z(x_0,y) = \overline{g}(y), \qquad \overline{f}(x_0) = \overline{g}(y_0) = 0, \tag{3.8}$$

where $p \geq 2, \overline{F} \in C(\Delta \times \mathbb{R}, \mathbb{R}), \overline{f} \in C^1(I,\mathbb{R}), \overline{g} \in C^1(J,\mathbb{R}), \rho \in C^1(I,I), \lambda \in C^1(J,J), 0 < \rho'$, $\lambda' \leq 1$, $\rho(x_0) = x_0$, $\lambda(y_0) = y_0$.

THEOREM 3.4. *Consider (BVP) and ($\overline{BVP}$). If*

(i) $|F(x,y,v_1) - F(x,y,v_2)| \leq b(x,y)|v_1^p - v_2^p|$ *for some $b \in C(\Delta, \mathbb{R}_+)$;*

(ii) $|(f(x) - \overline{f}(x)) + (g(y) - \overline{g}(y))| \leq \varepsilon/2$;

(iii) *for all solutions $\overline{z}(x,y)$ of ($\overline{BVP}$),*

$$\int_{x_0}^{x}\int_{y_0}^{y} |F(s,t,\overline{z}(\rho(s),\lambda(t))) - \overline{F}(s,t,\overline{z}(\rho(s),\lambda(t)))|\,dt\,ds \leq \frac{\varepsilon}{2}, \tag{3.9}$$

then

$$|z^p(x,y) - \overline{z}^p(x,y)| \le \varepsilon \exp(p\overline{B}(x,y)), \tag{3.10}$$

where $\overline{B}(x,y)$ is as defined in Theorem 3.2. Hence $z^p(x,y)$ depends continuously on F, f, and g. In particular, if $z(x,y)$ does not change sign, it depends continuously on F, f, and g.

Remark 3.5. The initial boundary value problem (BVP) considered in this section is clearly not the only problem for which the boundedness, uniqueness, and continuous dependence of its solutions can be studied by using the main results in Section 2. For example, one can arrive at similar results (much more complicated computations are involved though) for the following variation of our (BVP):

$$z^{p-1}z_{xy} + (p-1)z^{p-2}z_x z_y = F(x,y,z(\rho(x),\lambda(y)),z(\mu(x),\nu(y)) \cdot w(\mu(x),\nu(y))) \tag{3.11}$$

satisfying

$$z(x,y_0) = f(x), \qquad z(x_0,y) = g(y), \qquad f(x_0) = g(y_0) = 0, \tag{3.12}$$

where $w \in C(\mathbb{R}_+,\mathbb{R}_+)$ is nondecreasing with $w(r) > 0$ for $r > 0$.

4. Discrete Gronwall-Bellman-Ou-Iang-type inequalities

In what follows, $I := [m_0, M) \cap \mathbb{Z}$ and $J := [n_0, N) \cap \mathbb{Z}$ are two fixed lattices of integral points in $\mathbb{R}$, where $m_0, n_0 \in \mathbb{Z}$, $M, N \in \mathbb{Z} \cup \{\infty\}$. Let $\Omega := I \times J \subset \mathbb{Z}^2$, and for any $(s,t) \in \Omega$, the sublattice $[m_0,s] \times [n_0,t] \cap \Omega$ of Ω will be denoted as $\Omega_{(s,t)}$.

If U is a lattice in $\mathbb{Z}$ (resp. $\mathbb{Z}^2$), the collection of all $\mathbb{R}$-valued functions on U is denoted by $\mathcal{F}(U)$, and that of all $\mathbb{R}_+$-valued functions by $\mathcal{F}_+(U)$. For the sake of convenience, we extend the domain of definition of each function in $\mathcal{F}(U)$ and $\mathcal{F}_+(U)$ trivially to the ambient space $\mathbb{Z}$ (resp., $\mathbb{Z}^2$). So, for example, a function in $\mathcal{F}(U)$ is regarded as a function defined on $\mathbb{Z}$ (resp., $\mathbb{Z}^2$) with support in U.

If U is a lattice in $\mathbb{Z}$, the difference operator Δ on $f \in \mathcal{F}(\mathbb{Z})$ or $\mathcal{F}_+(\mathbb{Z})$ is defined as

$$\Delta f(n) := f(n+1) - f(n), \quad n \in U, \tag{4.1}$$

and if V is a lattice in $\mathbb{Z}^2$, the partial difference operators Δ_1 and Δ_2 on $u \in \mathcal{F}(\mathbb{Z}^2)$ or $\mathcal{F}_+(\mathbb{Z}^2)$ are defined as

$$\begin{aligned} \Delta_1 u(m,n) &:= u(m+1,n) - u(m,n), \quad (m,n) \in V, \\ \Delta_2 u(m,n) &:= u(m,n+1) - u(m,n), \quad (m,n) \in V. \end{aligned} \tag{4.2}$$

THEOREM 4.1. *Suppose $u \in \mathcal{F}_+(\Omega)$. If $c \ge 0$, $\alpha > 0$, $b \in \mathcal{F}_+(\Omega)$, and $\varphi \in C(\mathbb{R}_+,\mathbb{R}_+)$ satisfy the following:*

(i) *φ is nondecreasing with $\varphi(r) > 0$ for $r > 0$;*

(ii) *for any $(m,n) \in \Omega$,*

$$u^\alpha(m,n) \le c + \sum_{s=m_0}^{m-1} \sum_{t=n_0}^{n-1} b(s,t)\varphi(u(s,t)), \tag{4.3}$$

then

$$u(m,n) \leq \left\{\Phi_\alpha^{-1}\left[\Phi_\alpha(c) + B(m,n)\right]\right\}^{1/\alpha} \tag{4.4}$$

for all $(m,n) \in \Omega_{(m_1,n_1)}$, *where*

$$B(m,n) := \sum_{s=m_0}^{m-1} \sum_{t=n_0}^{n-1} b(s,t), \tag{4.5}$$

and $(m_1,n_1) \in \Omega$ *is chosen such that* $\Phi_\alpha(c) + B(m,n) \in \operatorname{Dom}(\Phi_\alpha^{-1})$ *for all* $(m,n) \in \Omega_{(m_1,n_1)}$.

Remark 4.2. (i) When $\alpha = 1$, Theorem 4.1 reduces to [6, Theorem 2.1].

(ii) In case $\Phi_\alpha(\infty) = \infty$, we may take $m_1 = M$, $n_1 = N$. In particular, (4.4) holds for all $(m,n) \in \Omega$.

Theorem 4.3. *Suppose* $u \in \mathcal{F}_+(\Omega)$. *If* $k \geq 0$, $p > 1$, $a, b \in \mathcal{F}_+(\Omega)$, *and* $\varphi \in C(\mathbb{R}_+, \mathbb{R}_+)$ *satisfy the following:*

(i) φ *is nondecreasing with* $\varphi(r) > 0$ *for* $r > 0$;

(ii) *for any* $(m,n) \in \Omega$,

$$u^p(m,n) \leq k + \sum_{s=m_0}^{m-1} \sum_{t=n_0}^{n-1} a(s,t)u(s,t) + \sum_{s=m_0}^{m-1} \sum_{t=n_0}^{n-1} b(s,t)u(s,t)\varphi(u(s,t)), \tag{4.6}$$

then

$$u(m,n) \leq \left\{\Phi_{p-1}^{-1}\left[\Phi_{p-1}\left(k^{1-(1/p)} + A(m,n)\right) + B(m,n)\right]\right\}^{1/(p-1)} \tag{4.7}$$

for all $(m,n) \in \Omega_{(m_1,n_1)}$, *where*

$$A(m,n) := \sum_{s=m_0}^{m-1} \sum_{t=n_0}^{n-1} a(s,t), \qquad B(m,n) := \sum_{s=m_0}^{m-1} \sum_{t=n_0}^{n-1} b(s,t), \tag{4.8}$$

and $(m_1,n_1) \in \Omega$ *is such that* $\Phi_{p-1}(k^{1-(1/p)} + A(m,n)) + B(m,n) \in \operatorname{Dom}\Phi_{p-1}^{-1}$ *for all* $(m,n) \in \Omega_{(m_1,n_1)}$.

Remark 4.4. (i) When $p = 2$, Theorem 4.3 reduces to Theorem 1.6.

(ii) In case $\Phi_{p-1}(\infty) = \infty$, inequality (4.7) holds for all $(m,n) \in \Omega$.

In case Ω degenerates into a 1-dimensional lattice, Theorem 4.3 takes the following simpler form which is a generalization of a result of Pachpatte in [18].

Corollary 4.5. *Suppose* $u \in \mathcal{F}_+(I)$. *If* $k \geq 0$, $p > 1$, $a, b \in \mathcal{F}_+(I)$, *and* $\varphi \in C(\mathbb{R}_+, \mathbb{R}_+)$ *satisfy the following:*

(i) φ *is nondecreasing with* $\varphi(r) > 0$ *for* $r > 0$;

(ii) *for any* $m \in I$,

$$u^p(m) \leq k + \sum_{s=m_0}^{m-1} a(s)u(s) + \sum_{s=m_0}^{m-1} b(s)u(s)\varphi(u(s)), \tag{4.9}$$

then

$$u(m) \leq \left\{\Phi_{p-1}^{-1}\left[\Phi_{p-1}\left(k^{1-(1/p)} + \sum_{s=m_0}^{m-1} a(s)\right) + \sum_{s=m_0}^{m-1} b(s)\right]\right\}^{1/(p-1)}, \quad \forall m \in [m_0, m_1] \cap I, \tag{4.10}$$

where $m_1 \in I$ *is such that* $\Phi_{p-1}(k + \sum_{s=m_0}^{m-1} a(s)) + \sum_{s=m_0}^{m-1} b(s) \in \operatorname{Dom}\Phi_{p-1}^{-1}$ *for all* $m \in [m_0, m_1] \cap I$.

Theorem 4.3 can easily be applied to generate other useful discrete inequalities in more general situations. For example, we have the following.

Theorem 4.6. *Suppose* $u \in \mathcal{F}_+(\Omega)$. *If* $k \geq 0$, $p > q > 0$, $a, b \in \mathcal{F}_+(\Omega)$, *and* $\varphi \in C(\mathbb{R}_+, \mathbb{R}_+)$ *satisfy the following:*

(i) φ *is nondecreasing with* $\varphi(r) > 0$ *for* $r > 0$;

(ii) *for any* $(m,n) \in \Omega$,

$$u^p(m,n) \leq k + \sum_{s=m_0}^{m-1}\sum_{t=n_0}^{n-1} a(s,t)u^q(s,t) + \sum_{s=m_0}^{m-1}\sum_{t=n_0}^{n-1} b(s,t)u^q(s,t)\varphi(u(s,t)), \tag{4.11}$$

then

$$u(m,n) \leq \left\{\Phi_{p-q}^{-1}\left[\Phi_{p-q}(k^{1-(q/p)} + A(m,n)) + B(m,n)\right]\right\}^{1/(p-q)} \tag{4.12}$$

for all $(m,n) \in \Omega_{(m_1,n_1)}$, *where* $A(m,n)$, $B(m,n)$ *are defined as in Theorem 4.3, and* $(m_1, n_1) \in \Omega$ *is chosen such that* $\Phi_{p-q}(k^{1-(q/p)} + A(m,n)) + B(m,n) \in \operatorname{Dom}\Phi_{p-q}^{-1}$ *for all* $(m,n) \in \Omega_{(m_1,n_1)}$.

An important special case of Theorem 4.6 is the following.

Corollary 4.7. *Suppose* $u \in \mathcal{F}_+(\Omega)$. *If* $k \geq 0$, $p > 1$, $a, b \in \mathcal{F}_+(\Omega)$, *and* $\varphi \in C(\mathbb{R}_+, \mathbb{R}_+)$ *satisfy the following:*

(i) φ *is nondecreasing with* $\varphi(r) > 0$ *for* $r > 0$;

(ii) *for any* $(m,n) \in \Omega$,

$$u^p(m,n) \leq k + \sum_{s=m_0}^{m-1}\sum_{t=n_0}^{n-1} a(s,t)u^{p-1}(s,t) + \sum_{s=m_0}^{m-1}\sum_{t=n_0}^{n-1} b(s,t)u^{p-1}(s,t)\varphi(u(s,t)), \tag{4.13}$$

then

$$u(m,n) \leq \Phi_1^{-1}\left[\Phi_1(k^{1/p} + A(m,n)) + B(m,n)\right], \quad \forall (m,n) \in \Omega_{(m_1,n_1)}, \tag{4.14}$$

where $A(m,n)$, $B(m,n)$ *are defined as in Theorem 4.3, and* $(m_1, n_1) \in \Omega$ *is chosen such that* $\Phi_1(k^{1/p} + A(m,n)) + B(m,n) \in \operatorname{Dom}\Phi_1^{-1}$ *for all* $(m,n) \in \Omega_{(m_1,n_1)}$.

In particular, we have the following useful consequence.

Corollary 4.8. *Suppose $u \in \mathcal{F}_+(\Omega)$. If $k \geq 0$, $p > 1$, and $a, b \in \mathcal{F}_+(\Omega)$ satisfy*

$$u^p(m,n) \leq k + \sum_{s=m_0}^{m-1}\sum_{t=n_0}^{n-1} a(s,t)u^{p-1}(s,t) + \sum_{s=m_0}^{m-1}\sum_{t=n_0}^{n-1} b(s,t)u^p(s,t) \quad \text{for any } (m,n) \in \Omega, \tag{4.15}$$

then

$$u(m,n) \leq \left(k^{1/p} + A(m,n)\right)\exp B(m,n), \quad \forall (m,n) \in \Omega, \tag{4.16}$$

where $A(m,n)$, $B(m,n)$ are defined as in Theorem 4.3

In case Ω degenerates into a 1-dimensional lattice, Corollary 4.8 takes the following simpler form which generalizes another result of Pachpatte in [23].

Corollary 4.9. *Suppose $u \in \mathcal{F}_+(I)$. If $k \geq 0$, $p > 1$, and $a, b \in \mathcal{F}_+(I)$ satisfy*

$$u^p(m) \leq k + \sum_{s=m_0}^{m-1} a(s)u^{p-1}(s) + \sum_{s=m_0}^{m-1} b(s)u^p(s) \quad \text{for any } m \in I, \tag{4.17}$$

then

$$u(m) \leq \left[k^{1/p} + \sum_{s=m_0}^{m-1} a(s)\right]\prod_{s=m_0}^{m-1} \exp b(s), \qquad \forall m \in I. \tag{4.18}$$

A special situation of Corollary 4.8 is the following 2-dimensional discrete version of Ou-Iang's inequality.

Corollary 4.10. *Suppose $u \in \mathcal{F}_+(\Omega)$. If $k \geq 0$, $p > 1$, and $b \in \mathcal{F}_+(\Omega)$ satisfy*

$$u^p(m,n) \leq k + \sum_{s=m_0}^{m-1}\sum_{t=n_0}^{n-1} b(s,t)u^p(s,t) \quad \text{for any } (m,n) \in \Omega, \tag{4.19}$$

then

$$u(m,n) \leq k^{1/p}\exp B(m,n), \quad \forall (m,n) \in \Omega, \tag{4.20}$$

where $B(m,n)$ is as defined in Theorem 4.3.

In case Ω degenerates into a 1-dimensional lattice, Corollary 4.10 takes the following simpler form which is a generalized 1-dimensional discrete analogue of Ou-Iang's inequality.

Corollary 4.11. *Suppose $u \in \mathcal{F}_+(I)$. If $k \geq 0$, $p > 1$, and $b \in \mathcal{F}_+(I)$ satisfy*

$$u^p(m) \leq k + \sum_{s=m_0}^{m-1} b(s)u^p(s) \quad \text{for any } m \in I, \tag{4.21}$$

then

$$u(m) \leq k^{1/p} \prod_{s=m_0}^{m-1} \exp b(s), \quad \forall m \in I. \tag{4.22}$$

Remark 4.12. It is evident that the results above can be generalized to obtain explicit bounds for functions satisfying certain discrete sum inequalities involving more retarded arguments. It is also clear that these results can be extended to functions on higher dimensional lattices in the obvious way. As details of these are rather algorithmic, they will not be carried out here.

5. Applications to boundary value problems

In this section, we will illustrate how the results obtained in Section 4 can be applied to study the boundedness, uniqueness, and continuous dependence of the solutions of certain boundary value problems for difference equations involving 2 independent variables.

We consider the following *boundary value problem* (BVP):

$$\Delta_{12} z^p(m,n) = F(m,n,z(m,n)) \tag{5.1}$$

satisfying

$$z(m,n_0) = f(m), \qquad z(m_0,n) = g(n), \qquad f(m_0) = g(n_0) = 0, \tag{5.2}$$

where $p > 1$, $F \in \mathcal{F}(\Omega \times \mathbb{R})$, $f \in \mathcal{F}(I)$, and $g \in \mathcal{F}(J)$ are given.

Our first result deals with the boundedness of solutions.

Theorem 5.1. *Consider (BVP). If*

$$\begin{aligned} |F(m,n,v)| &\leq b(m,n)|v|^p, \\ |f(m)|^p + |g(n)|^p &\leq k^p \end{aligned} \tag{5.3}$$

for some $k \geq 0$, where $b \in \mathcal{F}_+(\Omega)$, then all solutions of (BVP) satisfy

$$|z(m,n)| \leq k \exp B(m,n), \quad (m,n) \in \Omega, \tag{5.4}$$

where $B(m,n)$ is defined as in Theorem 4.1. In particular, if $B(m,n)$ is bounded on Ω, then every solution of (BVP) is bounded on Ω.

The next result is about uniqueness.

Theorem 5.2. *Consider (BVP). If*

$$|F(m,n,v_1) - F(m,n,v_2)| \leq b(m,n)|v_1^p - v_2^p| \tag{5.5}$$

for some $b \in \mathcal{F}_+(\Omega)$, then (BVP) has at most one solution on Ω.

Finally, we investigate the continuous dependence of the solutions of (BVP) on the function F and the boundary data f and g. For this we consider the following variation of (BVP):
$(\overline{\text{BVP}})$

$$\Delta_{12} z^p(m,n) = \overline{F}(m,n,z(m,n)) \tag{5.6}$$

with

$$z(m,n_0) = \overline{f}(m), \qquad z(m_0,n) = \overline{g}(n), \qquad \overline{f}(m_0) = \overline{g}(n_0) = 0, \tag{5.7}$$

where $p > 1$, $\overline{F} \in \mathcal{F}(\Omega \times \mathbb{R})$, $\overline{f} \in \mathcal{F}(I)$, and $\overline{g} \in \mathcal{F}(J)$ are given.

THEOREM 5.3. *Consider (BVP) and $(\overline{\text{BVP}})$. If*
(i) $|F(m,n,v_1) - F(m,n,v_2)| \le b(m,n)|v_1^p - v_2^p|$ *for some* $b \in \mathcal{F}_+(\Omega)$;
(ii) $|(f^p(m) - \overline{f}^p(m)) + (g^p(n) - \overline{g}^p(n))| \le \varepsilon/2$;
(iii) *for all solutions* $\overline{z}(m,n)$ *of* $(\overline{\text{BVP}})$,

$$\sum_{s=m_0}^{m-1}\sum_{t=n_0}^{n-1} \left| F(s,t,\overline{z}(s,t)) - \overline{F}(s,t,\overline{z}(s,t)) \right| \le \frac{\varepsilon}{2}, \quad \forall (m,n) \in \Omega,\ v_1,v_2 \in \mathbb{R}, \tag{5.8}$$

then

$$\left| z^p(m,n) - \overline{z}^p(m,n) \right| \le \varepsilon \exp\left(pB(m,n)\right), \tag{5.9}$$

where $B(m,n)$ is as defined in Theorem 4.1. Hence z^p depends continuously on F, f, and g. In particular, if z does not change sign, it depends continuously on F, f, and g.

Remark 5.4. The boundary value problem (BVP) is clearly not the only problem for which the boundedness, uniqueness, and continuous dependence of its solutions can be studied by using the results in Section 4. For example, one can arrive at similar results (with much more complicated computations) for the following variation of the (BVP):

$$\Delta_{12} z^p(m,n) = F\Big(m,n,z(m,n),z(m,n)\cdot\varphi\big(|z(m,n)|\big)\Big) \tag{5.10}$$

with

$$z(m,n_0) = f(m), \qquad z(m_0,n) = g(n), \qquad f(m_0) = g(n_0) = 0, \tag{5.11}$$

where $p > 1$, $F \in \mathcal{F}(\Omega \times \mathbb{R}^2)$, $f \in \mathcal{F}(I)$, $g \in \mathcal{F}(J)$, and $\varphi \in C(\mathbb{R}_+,\mathbb{R}_+)$ are given.

Acknowledgment

This research is supported in part by the Research Grants Council of the Hong Kong SAR (Project no. HKU7017/05P).

References

[1] D. Baĭnov and P. Simeonov, *Integral Inequalities and Applications*, Mathematics and Its Applications (East European Series), vol. 57, Kluwer Academic, Dordrecht, 1992.

[2] E. F. Beckenbach and R. Bellman, *Inequalities*, Springer, Berlin, 1961.

[3] R. Bellman, *The stability of solutions of linear differential equations*, Duke Mathematical Journal **10** (1943), no. 4, 643–647.

[4] I. Bihari, *A generalization of a lemma of Bellman and its application to uniqueness problems of differential equations*, Acta Mathematica Academiae Scientiarum Hungaricae **7** (1956), 81–94.

[5] W.-S. Cheung, *On some new integrodifferential inequalities of the Gronwall and Wendroff type*, Journal of Mathematical Analysis and Applications **178** (1993), no. 2, 438–449.

[6] ———, *Some discrete nonlinear inequalities and applications to boundary value problems for difference equations*, Journal of Difference Equations and Applications **10** (2004), no. 2, 213–223.

[7] ———, *Some retarded Gronwall-Bellman-Ou-Iang-type inequalities and applications to initial boundary value problems*, preprint, 2006.

[8] W.-S. Cheung and Q. H. Ma, *Nonlinear retarded integral inequalities for functions in two variables*, Journal of Concrete and Applicable Mathematics **2** (2004), no. 2, 119–134.

[9] C. M. Dafermos, *The second law of thermodynamics and stability*, Archive for Rational Mechanics and Analysis **70** (1979), no. 2, 167–179.

[10] T. H. Gronwall, *Note on the derivatives with respect to a parameter of the solutions of a system of differential equations*, Annals of Mathematics. Second Series **20** (1919), no. 4, 292–296.

[11] A. Haraux, *Nonlinear Evolution Equations: Global Behavior of Solutions*, Lecture Notes in Mathematics, vol. 841, Springer, Berlin, 1981.

[12] O. Lipovan, *A retarded Gronwall-like inequality and its applications*, Journal of Mathematical Analysis and Applications **252** (2000), no. 1, 389–401.

[13] Q. H. Ma and E.-H. Yang, *On some new nonlinear delay integral inequalities*, Journal of Mathematical Analysis and Applications **252** (2000), no. 2, 864–878.

[14] ———, *Some new Gronwall-Bellman-Bihari type integral inequalities with delay*, Periodica Mathematica Hungarica **44** (2002), no. 2, 225–238.

[15] D. S. Mitrinović, *Analytic Inequalities*, Springer, New York, 1970.

[16] D. S. Mitrinović, J. E. Pečarić, and A. M. Fink, *Inequalities Involving Functions and Their Integrals and Derivatives*, Mathematics and Its Applications (East European Series), vol. 53, Kluwer Academic, Dordrecht, 1991.

[17] L. Ou-Iang, *The boundedness of solutions of linear differential equations* $y'' + A(t)y = 0$, Shuxue Jinzhan **3** (1957), 409–415.

[18] B. G. Pachpatte, *On some new inequalities related to certain inequalities in the theory of differential equations*, Journal of Mathematical Analysis and Applications **189** (1995), no. 1, 128–144.

[19] ———, *Inequalities for Differential and Integral Equations*, Mathematics in Science and Engineering, vol. 197, Academic Press, California, 1998.

[20] ———, *On some new inequalities related to a certain inequality arising in the theory of differential equations*, Journal of Mathematical Analysis and Applications **251** (2000), no. 2, 736–751.

[21] ———, *Explicit bounds on certain integral inequalities*, Journal of Mathematical Analysis and Applications **267** (2002), no. 1, 48–61.

[22] ———, *On some retarded integral inequalities and applications*, Journal of Inequalities in Pure and Applied Mathematics **3** (2002), no. 2, 7, article 18.

[23] P. Y. H. Pang and R. P. Agarwal, *On an integral inequality and its discrete analogue*, Journal of Mathematical Analysis and Applications **194** (1995), no. 2, 569–577.

Wing-Sum Cheung: Department of Mathematics, University of Hong Kong, Hong Kong
E-mail address: wscheung@hku.hk

OSCILLATION OF HIGHER-ORDER NEUTRAL TYPE FUNCTIONAL DIFFERENTIAL EQUATIONS WITH DISTRIBUTED ARGUMENTS

R. S. DAHIYA AND A. ZAFER

This paper is concerned with the oscillation of the solutions of the nth-order neutral functional differential equation with distributed arguments of the form $[x(t)+\int_a^b p(t,r)x(\tau(t,r))dr]^{(n)}+\delta\int_c^d q(t,r)f(x(\sigma(t,r)))dr=0$, $\delta=\pm 1$. Sufficient conditions are presented for which every solution $x(t)$ is either oscillatory or else $\lim_{t\to\infty}|x(t)|=\infty$ or $\liminf_{t\to\infty}x(t)=0$ depending on $(-1)^n\delta=\pm 1$.

1. Introduction

We consider the nth-order neutral equations of the form

$$\left[x(t)+\int_a^b p(t,r)x(\tau(t,r))dr\right]^{(n)}+\delta\int_c^d q(t,r)f(x(\sigma(t,r)))dr=0, \tag{1.1}$$

where the following conditions are tacitly assumed:

(a) $p\in C([t_0,\infty)\times[a,b],\mathbb{R}_+)$, where $\mathbb{R}_+=[0,\infty)$ and $t_0\geq 0$ is fixed;

(b) $q\in C([t_0,\infty)\times[c,d],\mathbb{R}_+)$, $q(t,u)\neq 0$ for all $(t,u)\in[t_*,\infty)\times[c,d]$ for any $t_*\geq t_0$;

(c) $f\in C(\mathbb{R},\mathbb{R})$, $xf(x)>0$ for all $x\neq 0$;

(d) $\tau\in C([t_0,\infty)\times[a,b],\mathbb{R}_+)$, $\tau(t,u)\leq t$ for each $u\in[a,b]$, $\tau(t,u)\to\infty$ as $t\to\infty$ for each $u\in[a,b]$;

(e) $\sigma\in C([t_0,\infty)\times[c,d],\mathbb{R}_+)$ is nondecreasing in both variables, $\sigma(t,u)>t$ for all $u\in[c,d]$, $\sigma(t,u)\to\infty$ as $t\to\infty$ for each $u\in[c,d]$.

By a solution of (1.1) we mean a real-valued function x which satisfies (1.1) and $\sup\{x(t):t\geq t_*\}\neq 0$ for any $t_*\geq t_0$. A solution $x(t)$ of (1.1) is called oscillatory if the set of its zeros is unbounded from above, otherwise it is said to be nonoscillatory. We make the standing hypothesis that (1.1) possesses such solutions.

The oscillation of solutions of neutral equations has been investigated by many authors, see [1–9, 14–21]. However, all the equations involved in these studies, except the

Hindawi Publishing Corporation
Proceedings of the Conference on Differential & Difference Equations and Applications, pp. 315–323

ones considered in [3, 18, 19], greatly differ from (1.1) in the sense that they do not contain distributed arguments. It is obvious that (1.1) contains a large class of previously studied neutral equations. In particular, if $\tau(t,r) = \tau_0(t)$, $\sigma(t,r) = \sigma_0(t)$, $q(t,r) = q_0(t)$, $p(t,r) = p_0(t)$, $a = c = 0$, and $b = d = 1$, then (1.1) reduces to

$$[x(t) + p_0(t)x(\tau_0(t))]^{(n)} + q_0(t)f(\sigma_0(t)) = 0 \tag{1.2}$$

whose oscillation has been the topic of many studies including the ones mentioned above.

In this work we present oscillation criteria for solutions of (1.1) which are new even for the nonneutral equations ($p(t,r) \equiv 0$) and their special cases, and which reduce to known results obtained previously for (1.2) in [4]. For some related results in the case when $\sigma(t,u)$ is nondecreasing and $\sigma(t,u) \geq t + k$ for some $k > 0$ and for all $u \in [c,d]$ we refer to [3].

2. Main results

In the sequel, we will also assume without further mention that

$$H(t) := 1 - \int_a^b p(t,r)dr \tag{2.1}$$

is eventually nonnegative, bounded, and not identically zero.

THEOREM 2.1. *Suppose that $xf(x) \geq x^2$ for all $x \in \mathbb{R}$ and that*

$$\limsup_{t\to\infty} \int_t^{\sigma(t,c)} (s-t)^{n-1} \int_c^d q(s,r)H(\sigma(s,r))dr\,ds > (n-1)!. \tag{2.2}$$

(i) *If $\delta = +1$, then every solution $x(t)$ of (1.1) is oscillatory when n is even, and is either oscillatory or satisfies $\liminf_{t\to\infty} x(t) = 0$ when n is odd.*

(ii) *If $\delta = -1$, then every solution $x(t)$ of (1.1) is either oscillatory or else satisfies $\lim_{t\to\infty} |x(t)| = \infty$ or $\liminf_{t\to\infty} x(t) = 0$ when n is even, and is either oscillatory or satisfies $\lim_{t\to\infty} |x(t)| = \infty$ when n is odd.*

Proof. Suppose that there exists an eventually positive solution $x(t)$ of (1.1), and let

$$z(t) = x(t) + \int_a^b p(t,r)x(\tau(t,r))dr. \tag{2.3}$$

Clearly, $z(t)$ is eventually positive, and from (1.1), $z^{(n)}(t) \leq 0$ eventually. Applying the well-known lemma of Kiguradze [12], we see that there exist a $T > t_0$ and an integer $l \in \{0,1,\ldots,n\}$ with $(-1)^{n-l-1}\delta = 1$ such that for $t \geq T$,

$$\begin{gathered} z^{(k)}(t) > 0, \quad k = 1,2,\ldots,l; \\ (-1)^{n-k-1}z^{(k)}(t) > 0, \quad k = l,\ldots,n-1. \end{gathered} \tag{2.4}$$

Suppose that $0 \leq l \leq n-1$. By Taylor's formula for $r > t \geq T$ we have

$$z^{(l)}(t) = \sum_{i=0}^{n-l-1} \frac{z^{(l+i)}(r)}{i!}(t-r)^i + \int_t^r \frac{(t-r)^{n-l-1}}{(n-l-1)!}\left(-z^{(n)}(r)\right)dr. \tag{2.5}$$

In view of (2.4), it follows from (2.5) that

$$z^{(l)}(t) \geq \int_t^r \frac{(s-t)^{n-l-1}}{(n-l-1)!}\left(-z^{(n)}(s)\right)ds, \quad T \leq t < r, \tag{2.6}$$

and hence

$$z^{(l)}(t) \geq \int_t^\infty \frac{(s-t)^{n-l-1}}{(n-l-1)!}\int_c^d q(s,r)f\left(x(\sigma(s,r))\right)dr\,ds. \tag{2.7}$$

If $l = 0$, that is, $(-1)^n\delta = -1$, then from (2.7) we have

$$\int_T^\infty (s-T)^{n-1}\int_c^d q(s,r)f\left(x(\sigma(s,r))\right)dr\,ds \leq (n-1)!z(T). \tag{2.8}$$

On the other hand,

$$\int_T^\infty t^{n-1}\int_c^d q(t,r)dr\,dt = \infty. \tag{2.9}$$

Otherwise, in view of (2.1), we would have

$$\int_T^\infty t^{n-1}\int_c^d q(t,r)H\left(\sigma(t,r)\right)dr\,dt < \infty. \tag{2.10}$$

Then by (2.2) we would obtain the contradiction that

$$(n-1)! < \limsup_{t\to\infty}\int_t^\infty s^{n-1}\int_c^d q(s,r)H\left(\sigma(s,r)\right)dr\,ds = 0. \tag{2.11}$$

From (2.8) and (2.9) it follows that

$$\liminf_{t\to\infty} x(t) = 0. \tag{2.12}$$

If $l = n$ $(\delta = -1)$, we see that $\lim_{t\to\infty} z(t) = \infty$ and so $\lim_{t\to\infty} x(t) = \infty$.
Lastly, we need to consider the possibility that $1 \leq l \leq n-1$. In this case we claim that

$$z(\sigma(t,c)) \geq \int_t^{\sigma(t,c)} \frac{(s-t)^{n-1}}{(n-1)!}\int_c^d q(s,r)f\left(x(\sigma(s,r))\right)dr\,ds. \tag{2.13}$$

In case $l = 1$, inequality (2.13) follows easily by integrating (2.7) from t to $\sigma(t,c)$. If $l > 1$, then since $z^{(l-1)}(t) > 0$ for $t \geq T$, integrating (2.7) from T to t leads to

$$z^{(l-1)}(t) \geq \frac{(t-T)}{(n-l)!}\int_t^\infty \int_c^d q(s,r)f(x(\sigma(s,r)))\,dr\,ds. \tag{2.14}$$

In view of (2.4) if we integrate the above inequality from T to t recurrently $(l-2)$ times, we obtain

$$z'(t) \geq \frac{(t-T)^{n-2}}{(n-2)!}\int_t^\infty \int_c^d q(s,r)f(x(\sigma(s,r)))\,dr\,ds. \tag{2.15}$$

Integrating (2.15) from t to $\sigma(t,c)$ we arrive at (2.13). Now, since z is increasing, $\tau(t,u) \leq t$, and $x(t) \leq z(t)$, it follows that

$$z(t) \leq x(t) + z(t)\int_a^b p(t,u)\,du \tag{2.16}$$

or

$$H(t)z(t) \leq x(t). \tag{2.17}$$

Using (2.17) and the fact that $\sigma(t,u)$ is nondecreasing in (2.13), it also follows that

$$(n-1)! \geq \limsup_{t\to\infty}\int_t^{\sigma(t,c)} (s-t)^{n-1}\int_c^d q(s,r)H(\sigma(s,r))\,dr\,ds. \tag{2.18}$$

Clearly, (2.18) contradicts (2.2). □

In the next theorem we will make use of the notation

$$M_f = \max\left\{\limsup_{x\to\infty}\frac{x}{f(x)}, \limsup_{x\to-\infty}\frac{x}{f(x)}\right\} \geq 0. \tag{2.19}$$

Theorem 2.2. *Suppose that $M_f < \infty$ and*

$$\limsup_{t\to\infty}\int_t^{\sigma(t,c)} (s-t)^{n-1}\int_c^d q(s,r)H(\sigma(s,r))\,dr\,ds > (n-1)!M_f. \tag{2.20}$$

(i) *If $\delta = +1$, then every solution $x(t)$ of (1.1) is oscillatory or satisfies* $\liminf_{t\to\infty} x(t) = 0$.

(ii) *If $\delta = -1$, then every solution $x(t)$ of (1.1) is either oscillatory or satisfies* $\lim_{t\to\infty}|x(t)| = \infty$ *or* $\liminf_{t\to\infty} x(t) = 0$.

Proof. Assume that $x(t)$ is a nonoscillatory solution of (1.1), say $x(t) > 0$ eventually. As in the previous theorem, for $0 \le l \le n-1$ with $(-1)^{n-l-1}\delta = 1$,

$$z^{(l)}(t) \ge \int_t^\infty \frac{(s-t)^{n-l-1}}{(n-l-1)!} \int_c^d q(s,r) f(x(\sigma(s,r)))\, dr\, ds. \tag{2.21}$$

We will distinguish the following three possibilities.

Case 1. $l = 0$, $((-1)^n\delta = -1)$. From (2.21), we have

$$\int_t^\infty \frac{(s-t)^{n-l-1}}{(n-l-1)!} \int_c^d q(s,r) f(x(\sigma(s,r)))\, dr\, ds \le z(T). \tag{2.22}$$

On the other hand,

$$\int^\infty t^{n-1} \int_c^d q(t,r) H(\sigma(t,r))\, dr\, dt = \infty, \tag{2.23}$$

since otherwise by (2.20) we would get

$$(n-1)! M_f < \limsup_{t\to\infty} \int_t^\infty s^{n-1} \int_c^d q(s,r) H(\sigma(s,r))\, dr\, ds = 0, \tag{2.24}$$

a contradiction with $M_f \ge 0$. Now it follows from (2.23) that

$$\int^\infty t^{n-1} \int_c^d q(t,r)\, dr\, dt = \infty. \tag{2.25}$$

In view of (2.22) and (2.25), we get

$$\liminf_{t\to\infty} x(t) = 0. \tag{2.26}$$

Case 2. $l = 1$, $(-1)^n\delta = 1$, with $z(t)$ bounded. Integrating (2.21) from T to ∞, we have

$$z(\infty) - z(T) \ge \int_T^\infty \frac{(s-T)^{n-2}}{(n-1)!} \int_c^d q(s,r) f(x(\sigma(s,r)))\, dr\, ds. \tag{2.27}$$

Employing the above argument, one can easily see that

$$\liminf_{t\to\infty} x(t) = 0. \tag{2.28}$$

Case 3. $l > 1$ or $l = 1$ with $z(t)$ unbounded. Note that if $l > 1$ then $x(t)$ is unbounded, and that (2.13) holds if $l \ge 1$ (see the proof of the previous theorem). Thus, from (2.13) we see that

$$\begin{aligned} z(\sigma(t,c)) \ge{}& \frac{1}{(n-1)!} \inf\left\{ \frac{f(x(\sigma(s,r)))}{x(\sigma(t,r))} : (s,r) \in [t,\sigma(t,c)] \times [c,d] \right\} \\ &\times \int_t^{\sigma(t,c)} (s-t)^{n-1} \int_c^d q(s,r) x(\sigma(s,r))\, dr\, ds. \end{aligned} \tag{2.29}$$

In view of (2.17), we obtain from (2.29) that

$$z(\sigma(t,c)) \geq \frac{1}{(n-1)!} \inf\left\{ \frac{f(x(\sigma(s,r)))}{x(\sigma(t,r))} : (s,r) \in [t,\sigma(t,c)] \times [c,d] \right\} \times \int_t^{\sigma(t,c)} (s-t)^{n-1} \int_c^d q(s,r)H(\sigma(s,r))z(\sigma(s,r))\,dr\,ds. \tag{2.30}$$

Using the fact that $z(t)$ is increasing, we obtain

$$(n-1)!\sup\left\{ \frac{x(\sigma(s,r))}{f(x(\sigma(t,r)))} : (s,r) \in [t,\sigma(t,c)] \times [c,d] \right\} \geq \int_t^{\sigma(t,c)} (s-t)^{n-1} \int_c^d q(s,r)H(\sigma(s,r))\,dr\,ds. \tag{2.31}$$

Letting $t \to \infty$ in (2.31) results in a contradiction with (2.20). If $l = n$, as before we obtain $\lim_{t\to\infty} x(t) = \infty$. This completes the proof. □

THEOREM 2.3. *Suppose that*

$$uf(vu) \geq uf_1(v)f_2(u), \quad u \in \mathbb{R},\ v \geq 0, \tag{2.32}$$

for some functions $f_1 \in C(\mathbb{R}_+, \mathbb{R}_+)$ *and* $f_2 \in C(\mathbb{R}, \mathbb{R})$, *where* $uf_2(u) > 0$ *for all* $u \neq 0$. *Let* f_2 *be nondecreasing and superlinear in the sense that*

$$\int^{\infty} \frac{du}{f_2(u)} < \infty, \qquad \int^{-\infty} \frac{du}{f_2(u)} < \infty. \tag{2.33}$$

If

$$\int^{\infty} t^{n-1} \int_c^d q(t,r) f_1(H(\sigma(t,r)))\,dr\,dt = \infty, \tag{2.34}$$

then the conclusion of Theorem 2.1 holds.

Proof. Let $x(t)$ be a nonoscillatory solution of (1.1) which eventually takes on positive values only. As in the proof of Theorem 2.1, for $t \geq T$ and $(-1)^{n-l-1}\delta = 1$, $0 \leq l \leq n-1$, we arrive at

$$z^{(l)}(t) \geq \int_t^{\infty} \frac{(s-t)^{n-l-1}}{(n-l-1)!} \int_c^d q(s,r) f(x(\sigma(s,r)))\,dr\,ds. \tag{2.35}$$

If $l = 0$, then $(-1)^n\delta = -1$, and from (2.35) we have

$$\int_T^{\infty} (s-T)^{n-1} \int_c^d q(s,r) f(x(\sigma(s,r)))\,dr\,ds \leq (n-1)!z(T), \tag{2.36}$$

which, in view of (2.34), leads to $\liminf_{t\to\infty} x(t) = 0$.

Let $l \geq 1$. Clearly, (2.17) holds and hence

$$x(\sigma(s,r)) \geq H(\sigma(s,r))z(t), \quad s \geq t,\ r \in [c,d]. \tag{2.37}$$

Using this inequality in (2.35) we have

$$z^{(l)}(t) \geq \int_t^\infty \frac{(s-t)^{n-l-1}}{(n-l-1)!} \int_c^d q(s,r) f(H(\sigma(s,r))z(t))\, dr\, ds. \tag{2.38}$$

If $l = 1$, integrating (2.38) divided by $f_2(z(t))$ from T to ∞, we get

$$\int_{z(T)}^{z(\infty)} \frac{du}{f_2(u)} \geq \int_T^\infty \frac{(s-T)^{n-1}}{(n-1)!} \int_c^d q(s,r) f_1(H(\sigma(s,r)))\, dr\, ds, \tag{2.39}$$

which contradicts (2.33) and (2.34).

To complete the proof it suffices to show that (2.39) holds also if $1 < l \leq n-1$, since the case $l = n$ leads to $\delta = -1$ and $\lim_{t\to\infty} x(t) = \infty$. Notice that (2.15) is satisfied and therefore

$$\frac{z'(t)}{f_2(z(t))} \geq \frac{(t-T)^{n-2}}{(n-2)!} \int_t^\infty \int_c^d q(s,r) f_1(H(\sigma(s,r)))\, dr\, ds. \tag{2.40}$$

Integrating the last inequality from T to ∞ we see that (2.39) holds. □

We note that condition (2.32) provides quite a large class of functions of interest. In particular, if $f(x) = |x|^{\beta-1}x$ $(\beta > 1)$, then $f_1 = f_2 = f$. One may also take linear combinations of functions $|x|^{\beta-1}x$.

3. Generalizations

The results in the previous section can be easily extended to equations of the form

$$(k(t)z^{(n-1)})' + \delta \int_c^d q(t,r) f(x(\sigma(t,r)))\, dr = h(t), \tag{3.1}$$

where $z(t) = x(t) + \int_a^b p(t,r)x(\tau(t,r))\,dr$, and

(i) $k(t) > 0$, $k'(t) \geq 0$, $\int^\infty (1/k(t))\,dt = \infty$;

(ii) $h(t) = \rho^{(n)}(t)$ for some oscillatory function $\rho(t)$, $\lim_{t\to\infty} \rho(t) = 0$.

Below we state without proof the analogous theorems. For details on the methods we refer to [4] for (i) and to [1, 3, 10] in the case of (ii). We should note that the technique used in [3] to handle forcing terms satisfying (ii) was first introduced by Kartsatos in [10].

Theorem 3.1. *Suppose that $xf(x) \geq x^2$ for all $x \in \mathbb{R}$ and*

$$\limsup_{t\to\infty} \int_t^{\sigma(t,c)} (s-t)^{n-1} \int_c^d \frac{q(s,r)}{k(s)} H(\sigma(s,r))\, dr\, ds > (n-1)!. \tag{3.2}$$

(i) *If $\delta = +1$, then every solution $x(t)$ of (3.1) is oscillatory when n is even, and is either oscillatory or satisfies $\liminf_{t\to\infty} x(t) = 0$ when n is odd.*

(ii) *If $\delta = -1$, then every solution $x(t)$ of (3.1) is either oscillatory or else satisfies $\lim_{t\to\infty} |x(t)| = \infty$ or $\liminf_{t\to\infty} x(t) = 0$ when n is even, and is either oscillatory or satisfies $\lim_{t\to\infty} |x(t)| = \infty$ when n is odd.*

THEOREM 3.2. *Suppose that $M_f < \infty$ and*

$$\limsup_{t\to\infty}\int_t^{\sigma(t,c)}(s-t)^{n-1}\int_c^d \frac{q(s,r)}{k(s)}H(\sigma(s,r))\,dr\,ds > (n-1)!M_f. \tag{3.3}$$

(i) *If $\delta = +1$, then every solution $x(t)$ of (3.1) is oscillatory or satisfies* $\liminf_{t\to\infty} x(t) = 0$.

(ii) *If $\delta = -1$, then every solution $x(t)$ of (3.1) is either oscillatory or satisfies* $\lim_{t\to\infty}|x(t)| = \infty$ *or* $\liminf_{t\to\infty} x(t) = 0$.

THEOREM 3.3. *Suppose that*

$$uf(vu) \geq uf_1(v)f_2(u), \quad u \in \mathbb{R},\ v \geq 0, \tag{3.4}$$

for some functions $f_1 \in C(\mathbb{R}_+,\mathbb{R}_+)$ and $f_2 \in C(\mathbb{R},\mathbb{R})$, where $uf_2(u) > 0$ for all $u \neq 0$. Let f_2 be nondecreasing and superlinear in the sense that

$$\int^{\infty}\frac{du}{f_2(u)} < \infty, \qquad \int^{-\infty}\frac{du}{f_2(u)} < \infty. \tag{3.5}$$

If

$$\int^{\infty} t^{n-1}\int_c^d \frac{q(t,r)}{k(t)}f_1\big(H(\sigma(t,r))\big)\,dr\,dt = \infty, \tag{3.6}$$

then the conclusion of Theorem 3.1 holds.

The problem of finding similar oscillation criteria when $k \in L^1([t_0,\infty))$ or when (ii) fails to hold (e.g., ρ is nonoscillatory and/or not approaching zero as $t \to \infty$) seems to be interesting. In the case when $\rho(t)$ is periodic (not necessarily small) there is a possibility of employing the arguments developed by Kartsatos in [11]. More results on forced differential equations can be found in [1]. Another challenging and more difficult problem in this setup is to allow q to change sign for which there is hardly any result in the literature.

As a last remark the oscillation criteria presented in this paper reduce to some results derived for (1.2) in [4] and thereby extend and improve some results previously given in [13].

References

[1] R. P. Agarwal, S. R. Grace, and D. O'Regan, *Oscillation Theory for Difference and Functional Differential Equations*, Kluwer Academic, Dordrecht, 2000.

[2] D. D. Baĭnov and D. P. Mishev, *Oscillation Theory for Neutral Differential Equations with Delay*, IOP, Bristol, 1992.

[3] T. Candan and R. S. Dahiya, *Oscillation behavior of nth order neutral differential equations with continuous delay*, Journal of Mathematical Analysis and Applications **290** (2004), no. 1, 105–112.

[4] R. S. Dahiya and A. Zafer, *Oscillation theorems of higher order neutral type differential equations. Dynamical systems and differential equations, Vol. I (Springfield, MO, 1996)*, Discrete and Continuous Dynamical Systems **Added Volume I** (1998), 203–219.

[5] P. Das, *Oscillation criteria for odd order neutral equations*, Journal of Mathematical Analysis and Applications **188** (1994), no. 1, 245–257.
[6] L. H. Erbe, Q. Kong, and B. G. Zhang, *Oscillation Theory for Functional-Differential Equations*, Monographs and Textbooks in Pure and Applied Mathematics, vol. 190, Marcel Dekker, New York, 1995.
[7] K. Gopalsamy, B. S. Lalli, and B. G. Zhang, *Oscillation of odd order neutral differential equations*, Czechoslovak Mathematical Journal **42(117)** (1992), no. 2, 313–323.
[8] S. R. Grace, *Oscillation theorems of comparison type for neutral nonlinear functional-differential equations*, Czechoslovak Mathematical Journal **45(120)** (1995), no. 4, 609–626.
[9] M. K. Grammatikopoulos, E. A. Grove, and G. Ladas, *Oscillations of first-order neutral delay differential equations*, Journal of Mathematical Analysis and Applications **120** (1986), no. 2, 510–520.
[10] A. G. Kartsatos, *On the maintenance of oscillations of nth order equations under the effect of a small forcing term*, Journal of Differential Equations **10** (1971), 355–363.
[11] ———, *Maintenance of oscillations under the effect of a periodic forcing term*, Proceedings of the American Mathematical Society **33** (1972), 377–383.
[12] I. T. Kiguradze, *On the oscillatory character of solutions of the equation* $d^m u/dt^m + a(t)u^m \operatorname{sgn} u = 0$, Matematicheskiĭ Sbornik. New Series **65 (107)** (1964), 172–187.
[13] R. Oláh, *On oscillation of solutions of linear deviating differential equation*, Archivum Mathematicum **21** (1985), no. 2, 77–83.
[14] Ch. G. Philos, I. K. Purnaras, and Y. G. Sficas, *Oscillations in higher-order neutral differential equations*, Canadian Journal of Mathematics **45** (1993), no. 1, 132–158.
[15] I. P. Stavroulakis, *Oscillations of mixed neutral equations*, Hiroshima Mathematical Journal **19** (1989), no. 3, 441–456.
[16] S. Tanaka, *Oscillation of solutions of even order neutral differential equations*, Dynamic Systems and Applications **9** (2000), no. 3, 353–360.
[17] Z. Wang, *A necessary and sufficient condition for the oscillation of higher-order neutral equations*, The Tohoku Mathematical Journal. Second Series **41** (1989), no. 4, 575–588.
[18] P. Wang, *Oscillations of nth-order neutral equation with continuous distributed deviating arguments*, Annals of Differential Equations **14** (1998), no. 3, 570–575.
[19] P. Wang and W. Shi, *Oscillatory theorems of a class of even-order neutral equations*, Applied Mathematics Letters **16** (2003), no. 7, 1011–1018.
[20] A. Zafer, *Oscillation criteria for even order neutral differential equations*, Applied Mathematics Letters **11** (1998), no. 3, 21–25.
[21] G. Zhang, *Eventually positive solutions of odd order neutral differential equations*, Applied Mathematics Letters **13** (2000), no. 6, 55–61.

R. S. Dahiya: Department of Mathematics, Iowa State University, Ames, IA 50010, USA
E-mail address: rdahiya@iastate.edu

A. Zafer: Department of Mathematics, Middle East Technical University, 06531 Ankara, Turkey
E-mail address: zafer@metu.edu.tr

ON PARABOLIC SYSTEMS WITH DISCONTINUOUS NONLINEARITIES

H. DEGUCHI

We present existence, uniqueness, and stability results for the initial value problems for parabolic systems with discontinuous nonlinearities.

1. Introduction

In this paper, we will study weak solutions of the initial value problem

$$\begin{aligned} u_t &= u_{xx} + f(u) - f(1)H(v-\beta), \quad 0 < t < T,\ x \in \mathbf{R}, \\ v_t &= v_{xx} + g(v) - g(1)H(u-\alpha), \quad 0 < t < T,\ x \in \mathbf{R}, \\ u\,|_{t=0} &= u_0, \qquad v\,|_{t=0} = v_0, \quad x \in \mathbf{R}, \end{aligned} \tag{1.1}$$

where $0 < \alpha, \beta < 1$ are two constants, H is the function on $\mathbf{R}$ given by

$$H(u) = 0 \quad \text{in } (-\infty, 0), \qquad H(u) = 1 \quad \text{in } (0,\infty), \quad 0 \le H(0) \le 1, \tag{1.2}$$

and f and g satisfy the following condition.

(A1) f and g are two Lipschitz continuous functions on $\mathbf{R}$ such that $f(0) = g(0) = 0$, $f(1) < f(u) < 0$ in $(0,1)$, and $g(1) < g(v) < 0$ in $(0,1)$.

The concept of Nash equilibrium has played a central role as a solution concept in game theory. However, when a game has multiple Nash equilibria, the players face a problem which equilibrium they should play. As an example, let us consider the following game.

(1.3)

		Player 2: A_2	Player 2: B_2
Player 1	A_1	a_1, a_2	$0, 0$
	B_1	$0, 0$	b_1, b_2

Hindawi Publishing Corporation
Proceedings of the Conference on Differential & Difference Equations and Applications, pp. 325–334

with $a_i, b_i > 0$ for $i = 1,2$. This game is a coordination game and has two strict Nash equilibria A and B. Let u and v denote the frequencies of the B_1-strategy for player 1 and the B_2-strategy for player 2, respectively. Then the payoffs for player 1 playing A_1 or B_1, respectively, are given by $a_1(1-v)$ and $b_1 v$. The payoffs for player 2 playing A_2 or B_2, respectively, are given by $a_2(1-u)$ and $b_2 u$. In the coordinates (u,v), we can identify the equilibria $A = (0,0)$ and $B = (1,1)$.

As an important concept of equilibrium selection, there is the concept of risk-dominance by Harsanyi and Selten [5]. For the game (1.3), B is said to *risk-dominate* A if $a_1 a_2 < b_1 b_2$. On the other hand, Hofbauer [7] introduced the concept of spatial dominance by means of a problem like (1.1), and compared it with the concept of risk-dominance for the game (1.3). We now explain his approach and results for the game (1.3). We consider two player populations distributed on $\mathbf{R}$. Then $(u,v) = (u(t,x), v(t,x))$ is a function of time t and space $x \in \mathbf{R}$, and takes values between $(0,0)$ and $(1,1)$. Assume that the local interaction among the players is described by the best response dynamics. This dynamics models the situation that a certain proportion of players at each x switches to locally best responses at any t. Assume further that the random motion of the players can be modeled by diffusion. These assumptions yield the initial value problem

$$\begin{aligned} &u_t = u_{xx} - u + H(v-\beta), \quad 0<t<T,\ x\in\mathbf{R},\\ &v_t = v_{xx} - v + H(u-\alpha), \quad 0<t<T,\ x\in\mathbf{R},\\ &u\,|_{t=0} = u_0, \qquad v\,|_{t=0} = v_0, \quad x\in\mathbf{R}, \end{aligned} \tag{1.4}$$

where $(\alpha,\beta) = (a_2/(a_2+b_2), a_1/(a_1+b_1))$. A Nash equilibrium C is said to be *spatially dominant* if the corresponding constant stationary solution (u_c, v_c) of problem (1.4) is asymptotically stable in the compact-open topology, that is, there exist two constants $r > 0$ and $\varepsilon > 0$ such that, for any initial datum satisfying $|(u_0(x), v_0(x)) - (u_c, v_c)| < \varepsilon$ for $x \in [-r, r]$, the solution $(u(t,x), v(t,x))$ of problem (1.4) converges to (u_c, v_c) as $t \uparrow \infty$, uniformly on any compact subset of $\mathbf{R}$. In other words, if a spatially dominant equilibrium prevails initially on a large enough finite part of the space, then it eventually takes over on the whole space. By definition, at most one equilibrium can be spatially dominant. Hofbauer [7] proved that (i) B is spatially dominant if $0 < \alpha + \beta < 1$, that is, B risk-dominates A, and (ii) A is spatially dominant if $\alpha + \beta > 1$, that is, A risk-dominates B. Also, Hofbauer [6] showed that problem (1.4) has a unique monotone traveling wave solution connecting the two equilibria A and B. Moreover, he proved that its wave speed is zero if $\alpha + \beta = 1$, that is, A and B are equally risky. This explains that (iii) neither A nor B is spatially dominant if A and B are equally risky. It is easy to see that the converses of (i), (ii), and (iii) are true. Thus, for the game (1.3), the concept of spatial dominance is equivalent to the concept of risk-dominance. However, the problem of the existence and uniqueness of solutions of problem (1.4) was not treated. Note that problem (1.4) is a special case of problem (1.1) if we take $f(u) = -u$ and $g(v) = -v$.

The purposes of this paper are to show the existence and uniqueness of solutions of problem (1.1), and to extend the stability results of Hofbauer [6, 7].

The rest of this paper is organized as follows. In Section 2, after giving the definition of a weak solution of problem (1.1), we obtain existence, uniqueness, and stability results for problem (1.1) (Theorems 2.3, 2.6, 2.8, 2.10, 2.11, and 2.12). In Section 3, we discuss solutions of problem (1.1) formulated as differential inclusions (Propositions 3.2 and 3.3). The details and proofs will be given in [2].

2. Existence, uniqueness, and stability theorems

Let us first explain some notation and definitions. Let $C_B(\mathbf{R})$ and $C_B([0,T)\times\mathbf{R})$ denote the space of bounded continuous functions on $\mathbf{R}$ and $[0,T)\times\mathbf{R}$, respectively. Let $C^{0,1}((0,T)\times\mathbf{R})$ be the space of continuous functions on $(0,T)\times\mathbf{R}$ that are continuously differentiable in $x\in\mathbf{R}$. If u, $v\in C_B([0,T)\times\mathbf{R})\cap C^{0,1}((0,T)\times\mathbf{R})$ and $u\le v$ in $[0,T)\times\mathbf{R}$, then $[u,v]$ denotes the order interval $\{w\in C_B([0,T)\times\mathbf{R})\cap C^{0,1}((0,T)\times\mathbf{R}) \mid u\le w\le v\}$.

Definition 2.1. A pair (u,v) of functions u, $v\in C_B([0,T)\times\mathbf{R})\cap C^{0,1}((0,T)\times\mathbf{R})$ is called a *weak solution* of problem (1.1) if it satisfies the following two conditions:

(i) for all $\varphi\in\mathcal{D}((0,T)\times\mathbf{R})$,

$$\int_0^T\int_{\mathbf{R}}\big(u\varphi_t-u_x\varphi_x+\big(f(u)-f(1)H(v-\beta)\big)\varphi\big)\,dx\,dt=0,$$
$$\int_0^T\int_{\mathbf{R}}\big(v\varphi_t-v_x\varphi_x+\big(g(v)-g(1)H(u-\alpha)\big)\varphi\big)\,dx\,dt=0; \tag{2.1}$$

(ii) for all $x_0\in\mathbf{R}$,

$$\lim_{t\downarrow 0,x\to x_0}u(t,x)=u_0(x_0),\qquad \lim_{t\downarrow 0,x\to x_0}v(t,x)=v_0(x_0). \tag{2.2}$$

A similar definition to Definition 2.1 will be used for the case where nonlinearities depend on t and x as well as u and v.

Definition 2.2. A pair (u,v) of functions $u,v\in C_B([0,T)\times\mathbf{R})\cap C^{0,1}((0,T)\times\mathbf{R})$ is said to be a *weak upper solution* of problem (1.1) if it satisfies the following two conditions:

(i′) for all nonnegative functions $\varphi\in\mathcal{D}((0,T)\times\mathbf{R})$,

$$\int_0^T\int_{\mathbf{R}}\big(u\varphi_t-u_x\varphi_x+\big(f(u)-f(1)H(v-\beta)\big)\varphi\big)\,dx\,dt\le 0,$$
$$\int_0^T\int_{\mathbf{R}}\big(v\varphi_t-v_x\varphi_x+\big(g(v)-g(1)H(u-\alpha)\big)\varphi\big)\,dx\,dt\le 0; \tag{2.3}$$

(ii′) for all $x_0\in\mathbf{R}$,

$$\lim_{t\downarrow 0,x\to x_0}u(t,x)\ge u_0(x_0),\qquad \lim_{t\downarrow 0,x\to x_0}v(t,x)\ge v_0(x_0). \tag{2.4}$$

A *weak lower solution* of problem (1.1) is defined by reversing the inequalities in conditions (i′) and (ii′).

To state an existence theorem for problem (1.1), we will impose the following two conditions:

(B1) $(u_0, v_0) \in C_B(\mathbf{R}) \times C_B(\mathbf{R})$, and $(0,0) \leq (u_0(x), v_0(x)) \leq (1,1)$ on $\mathbf{R}$;

(A2) problem (1.1) has a weak upper solution $(\overline{u}, \overline{v})$ and a weak lower solution $(\underline{u}, \underline{v})$ such that $(\underline{u}, \underline{v}) \leq (\overline{u}, \overline{v})$ in $(0,T) \times \mathbf{R}$. Moreover, there exist the two nonpositive functions $W_1, W_2 \in L^\infty((0,T) \times \mathbf{R})$ and the two nonnegative functions $w_1, w_2 \in L^\infty((0,T) \times \mathbf{R})$ such that, for any nonnegative function $\varphi \in \mathcal{D}((0,T) \times \mathbf{R})$,

$$
\begin{aligned}
&\int_0^T \int_{\mathbf{R}} (\overline{u}\varphi_t - \overline{u}_x\varphi_x + (f(\overline{u}) - f(1)\widetilde{H}(\overline{v} - \beta) - W_1)\varphi)\,dx\,dt = 0,\\
&\int_0^T \int_{\mathbf{R}} (\overline{v}\varphi_t - \overline{v}_x\varphi_x + (g(\overline{v}) - g(1)\widetilde{H}(\overline{u} - \alpha) - W_2)\varphi)\,dx\,dt = 0,\\
&\int_0^T \int_{\mathbf{R}} (\underline{u}\varphi_t - \underline{u}_x\varphi_x + (f(\underline{u}) - f(1)\widehat{H}(\underline{v} - \beta) - w_1)\varphi)\,dx\,dt = 0,\\
&\int_0^T \int_{\mathbf{R}} (\underline{v}\varphi_t - \underline{v}_x\varphi_x + (g(\underline{v}) - g(1)\widehat{H}(\underline{u} - \alpha) - w_2)\varphi)\,dx\,dt = 0,
\end{aligned}
\tag{2.5}
$$

where

$$
\widetilde{H}(u) = \begin{cases} 1 & \text{if } u \geq 0, \\ 0 & \text{if } u < 0, \end{cases} \qquad \widehat{H}(u) = \begin{cases} 1 & \text{if } u > 0, \\ 0 & \text{if } u \leq 0. \end{cases} \tag{2.6}
$$

Theorem 2.3. *Let $0 < \alpha$, $\beta < 1$, and assume that conditions (A1), (A2), and (B1) are satisfied. Then problem (1.1) has the global maximal and minimal weak solutions (U,V) and (u,v) in the order interval $[\underline{u}, \overline{u}] \times [\underline{v}, \overline{v}]$.*

Sketch of the proof of Theorem 2.3. We will prove only the existence of maximal weak solution in the order interval $[\underline{u}, \overline{u}] \times [\underline{v}, \overline{v}]$. Fix $T > 0$ arbitrarily and consider the iteration scheme

$$
\begin{aligned}
&U_t^{n+1} - U_{xx}^{n+1} + MU^{n+1} = f(U^n) - f(1)\widetilde{H}(V^n - \beta) + MU^n, \quad 0 < t < T,\ x \in \mathbf{R},\\
&V_t^{n+1} - V_{xx}^{n+1} + MV^{n+1} = g(V^n) - g(1)\widetilde{H}(U^n - \alpha) + MV^n, \quad 0 < t < T,\ x \in \mathbf{R},\\
&U^{n+1}|_{t=0} = u_0, \qquad V^{n+1}|_{t=0} = v_0, \quad x \in \mathbf{R},
\end{aligned}
\tag{2.7}
$$

where $(U^0, V^0) = (\overline{u}, \overline{v})$ and $M > 0$ is a constant such that $u \mapsto f(u) + Mu$ and $v \mapsto g(v) + Mv$ are nondecreasing on $\mathbf{R}$. We see that, for each $n \in \mathbf{N}_0$, problem (2.7) has a unique weak solution (U^{n+1}, V^{n+1}), which satisfies

$$
\begin{aligned}
&\underline{u} \leq U^{n+1} \leq U^n \leq \cdots \leq U^1 \leq U^0 = \overline{u},\\
&\underline{v} \leq V^{n+1} \leq V^n \leq \cdots \leq V^1 \leq V^0 = \overline{v}.
\end{aligned}
\tag{2.8}
$$

Hence, the limit $(U,V) \in [\underline{u},\overline{u}] \times [\underline{v},\overline{v}]$ is a weak solution of the problem

$$U_t - U_{xx} = f(U) - f(1)\widetilde{H}(V-\beta), \quad 0<t<T,\ x \in \mathbf{R},$$
$$V_t - V_{xx} = g(V) - g(1)\widetilde{H}(U-\alpha), \quad 0<t<T,\ x \in \mathbf{R}, \tag{2.9}$$
$$U\,|_{t=0} = u_0, \qquad V\,|_{t=0} = v_0, \quad x \in \mathbf{R}.$$

We can show that the Lebesgue measures of $\{(t,x) \in (0,T)\times\mathbf{R} \mid U(t,x)=\alpha\}$ and $\{(t,x) \in (0,T)\times\mathbf{R} \mid V(t,x)=\beta\}$ are zero. Hence, (U,V) is a weak solution of problem (1.1).

For any weak solution $(u_1,v_1) \in [\underline{u},\overline{u}] \times [\underline{v},\overline{v}]$ of problem (1.1), we find that $(U^n, V^n) \geq (u_1,v_1)$ in $(0,T)\times\mathbf{R}$ for $n \in \mathbf{N}$. Therefore $(U,V) \geq (u_1,v_1)$ in $(0,T)\times\mathbf{R}$. Thus, (U,V) is the maximal weak solution in $[\underline{u},\overline{u}] \times [\underline{v},\overline{v}]$. □

Remark 2.4. Problem (1.1) has the global maximal and minimal weak solutions (U,V) and (u,v) in the order interval $[0,1]\times[0,1]$ if $0<\alpha,\beta<1$ and if conditions (A1) and (B1) are satisfied, since $(\overline{u},\overline{v}) \equiv (1,1)$ and $(\underline{u},\underline{v}) \equiv (0,0)$ are a weak upper solution and a weak lower solution, respectively, of problem (1.1) as in condition (A2).

Concerning the size of weak solutions of problem (1.1), the following proposition holds.

PROPOSITION 2.5. *Let $0<\alpha$, $\beta<1$, and assume that conditions (A1) and (B1) are satisfied. Then any weak solution of problem (1.1) is contained in the order interval $[0,1]\times[0,1]$.*

To state a uniqueness theorem for problem (1.1), we will impose the following two conditions:

(A3) there exists a constant $L>0$ such that $f(u) \geq -Lu$ in $(0,1)$, $g(v) \geq -Lv$ in $(0,1)$ and $f(1)=g(1)=-L$;

(B2) (u_0,v_0) satisfies the following five conditions:

(B2-1) $(u_0,v_0) \in C^1(\mathbf{R})\times C^1(\mathbf{R})$;

(B2-2) (u_0,v_0) is even on $\mathbf{R}$;

(B2-3) $(u_0'(x),v_0'(x)) \leq (0,0)$ in $(0,\infty)$;

(B2-4) $(u_0(x_1),v_0(x_2)) = (\alpha,\beta)$ and $(u_0'(x_1),v_0'(x_2)) < (0,0)$ for some $x_1, x_2 > 0$;

(B2-5) $(u_0(\infty),v_0(\infty)) = (0,0)$.

THEOREM 2.6. *Choose $0<\alpha$, $\beta<1$ so that $0<\alpha+\beta<1$. Assume that conditions (A1), (A3), (B1), and (B2) are satisfied. Then there exist two constants $r>0$ and $\varepsilon>0$ such that, if $|(u_0(x),v_0(x))-(1,1)|<\varepsilon$ for $x \in [-r,r]$, then the weak solution of problem (1.1) is globally unique in time.*

The following proposition is needed in the proof of Theorem 2.6.

PROPOSITION 2.7. *Choose $0<\alpha$, $\beta<1$ so that $0<\alpha+\beta<1$. Assume that conditions (A1), (A3), (B1), and (B2) are satisfied. Then there exist two constants $r>0$ and $\varepsilon>0$ such that, if $|(u_0(x),v_0(x))-(1,1)|<\varepsilon$ for $x\in[-r,r]$, then problem (1.1) has a weak lower solution $(\underline{u},\underline{v}) \in [0,1]\times[0,1]$ with the three properties that*

(i) *$(\underline{u},\underline{v})$ is as in condition (A2);*

(ii) *there exist three constants* $p > 0$, $\theta_1 > 0$, *and* $\theta_2 > 0$ *such that* $\underline{u}(t,x) > \alpha$ *on* $(0,T) \times [-p\sqrt{t} - \theta_2, p\sqrt{t} + \theta_2]$ *and* $\underline{v}(t,x) > \beta$ *on* $(0,T) \times [-p\sqrt{t} - \theta_1, p\sqrt{t} + \theta_1]$ *for each* $T > 0$;

(iii) $(\underline{u}(t,x), \underline{v}(t,x))$ *converges to* $(1,1)$ *as* $t \uparrow \infty$, *uniformly on any compact subset of* $\mathbf{R}$.

Sketch of the proof of Proposition 2.7. A weak lower solution $(\underline{u}, \underline{v})$ as in the statement is obtained as a unique weak solution of the problem

$$\begin{aligned} &\underline{u}_t = \underline{u}_{xx} - L\underline{u} + Lh_1(t,x), \quad 0 < t < T,\ x \in \mathbf{R}, \\ &\underline{v}_t = \underline{v}_{xx} - L\underline{v} + Lh_2(t,x), \quad 0 < t < T,\ x \in \mathbf{R}, \\ &\underline{u}\,|_{t=0} = u_0, \qquad \underline{v}\,|_{t=0} = v_0, \quad x \in \mathbf{R}, \end{aligned} \tag{2.10}$$

where

$$h_i(t,x) := \begin{cases} 1 & \text{if } |x| \le p\sqrt{t} + \theta_i, \\ 0 & \text{otherwise}, \end{cases} \tag{2.11}$$

with suitable positive constants p and θ_i. □

Sketch of the proof of Theorem 2.6. Fix $T > 0$ arbitrarily. By Proposition 2.5, it suffices to show that the maximal weak solution $(U,V) \in [0,1] \times [0,1]$ coincides with the minimal weak solution $(u,v) \in [0,1] \times [0,1]$. Put $T_0 := \sup\{t \in [0,T) \mid (U,V) = (u,v)$ on $[0,t] \times \mathbf{R}\}$. We will prove that $(U,V) = (u,v)$ in $(T_0, T_0 + T_1) \times \mathbf{R}$ for some $0 < T_1 < T - T_0$. To do this, we use an idea of Feireisl [3]. For simplicity, we consider only the case $T_0 = 0$.

Define $E(t) := \|V - v\|_{L^\infty((0,t)\times\mathbf{R})}$ and $J_{s,\beta,t} := \{y \in \mathbf{R} \mid |V(s,y) - \beta| \le E(t)\}$. Let $K(t,x)$ be the heat kernel. Then $U(t,x) - u(t,x)$ satisfies

$$\begin{aligned} U(t,x) - u(t,x) &= \int_0^t \int_{\mathbf{R}} K(t-s,x-y)\big(f(U(s,y)) - f(u(s,y))\big)\,dy\,ds \\ &\quad - f(1)\int_0^t \int_{J_{s,\beta,t}} K(t-s,x-y)\big(H(V(s,y)-\beta) - H(v(s,y)-\beta)\big)\,dy\,ds \\ &=: A(t,x) + B(t,x). \end{aligned} \tag{2.12}$$

(1) Estimate of $A(t,x)$: by the Lipschitz continuity of f, there exists a constant $L_1 > 0$ such that, for $0 < t < T$ and $x \in \mathbf{R}$,

$$|A(t,x)| \le L_1 t \|U - u\|_{L^\infty((0,t)\times\mathbf{R})}. \tag{2.13}$$

(2) Estimate of $B(t,x)$: the general shape of v_0 is inherited by $V \in [0,1]$, and $V(t,0) > \beta$ on $[0,T)$ by Proposition 2.7. Therefore, there exist two constants $\nu_1 > 0$ and $0 < T_2 < T$ such that $|V_x(t,x)| \ge \nu_1 > 0$ on $\{(t,x) \in (0,T_2) \times \mathbf{R} \mid |V(t,x) - \beta| \le E(T_2)\}$. Further, for any $0 < t < T_2$, the cardinal number of $\{x \in \mathbf{R} \mid V(t,x) = \beta\}$ equals 2. Hence, for any

$0 < t < T_2$ and any $0 < s < t$, we get the inequality

$$\mu(J_{s,\beta,t}) = \mu(\{y \in \mathbf{R} \mid |V(s,y) - \beta| \leq E(t)\}) \leq \frac{4E(t)}{\nu_1}, \tag{2.14}$$

so that, for $0 < t < T_2$ and $x \in \mathbf{R}$,

$$|B(t,x)| \leq \frac{8|f(1)|\sqrt{t}}{\sqrt{\pi}\nu_1} \|V - v\|_{L^\infty((0,t)\times\mathbf{R})}. \tag{2.15}$$

By combining (2.12), (2.13), and (2.15), we have, for $0 < t < T_2$,

$$\|U - u\|_{L^\infty((0,t)\times\mathbf{R})} \leq L_1 t \|U - u\|_{L^\infty((0,t)\times\mathbf{R})} + \frac{8|f(1)|\sqrt{t}}{\sqrt{\pi}\nu_1} \|V - v\|_{L^\infty((0,t)\times\mathbf{R})}. \tag{2.16}$$

Similarly, there exist three constants $L_2 > 0$, $\nu_2 > 0$, and $T_3 > 0$ such that, for $0 < t < T_3$,

$$\|V - v\|_{L^\infty((0,t)\times\mathbf{R})} \leq \frac{8|g(1)|\sqrt{t}}{\sqrt{\pi}\nu_2} \|U - u\|_{L^\infty((0,t)\times\mathbf{R})} + L_2 t \|V - v\|_{L^\infty((0,t)\times\mathbf{R})}. \tag{2.17}$$

By combining inequalities (2.16) and (2.17) and choosing suitably $0 < T_1 < \min(T_2, T_3)$, we find that $(U,V) = (u,v)$ in $(0,T_1) \times \mathbf{R}$. □

We consider the following condition on (u_0, v_0):
(B3) (u_0, v_0) satisfies the following four conditions:
- (B3-1) $(u_0, v_0) \in C^1(\mathbf{R}) \times C^1(\mathbf{R})$;
- (B3-2) $(u_0'(x), v_0'(x)) \geq (0,0)$ on $\mathbf{R}$;
- (B3-3) $(u_0(x_1), v_0(x_2)) = (\alpha, \beta)$ and $(u_0'(x_1), v_0'(x_2)) > (0,0)$ for some $x_1, x_2 \in \mathbf{R}$;
- (B3-4) $(u_0(-\infty), v_0(-\infty)) = (0,0)$ and $(u_0(\infty), v_0(\infty)) = (1,1)$.

Then, in a similar way to the proof of Theorem 2.6, we can prove the following theorem.

Theorem 2.8. *Let $0 < \alpha$, $\beta < 1$, and assume that conditions (A1) and (B3) are satisfied. Then the weak solution of problem (1.1) is globally unique in time.*

Remark 2.9. Nonuniqueness results for parabolic equations with discontinuous nonlinearities have been obtained in Feireisl and Norbury [4] and Deguchi [1].

We next describe results on stability of two constant stationary solutions $(0,0)$ and $(1,1)$ of problem (1.1). The following theorem is a consequence of Proposition 2.7.

Theorem 2.10. *Let $0 < \alpha$, $\beta < 1$, and assume that conditions (A1) and (A3) are satisfied. Then the constant stationary solution $(1,1)$ of problem (1.1) is asymptotically stable in the compact-open topology if $0 < \alpha + \beta < 1$.*

Instead of condition (A3), we consider the following condition:
(A4) there exists a constant $L > 0$ such that $f(u) \leq -Lu$ in $(0,1)$, $g(v) \leq -Lv$ in $(0,1)$ and $f(1) = g(1) = -L$.

Then we obtain the following theorem.

Theorem 2.11. *Let $0 < \alpha$, $\beta < 1$, and assume that conditions (A1) and (A4) are satisfied. Then the constant stationary solution $(0,0)$ of problem (1.1) is asymptotically stable in the compact-open topology if $\alpha + \beta > 1$.*

We next discuss the case $\alpha+\beta=1$.

THEOREM 2.12. *Let $0<\alpha,\ \beta<1$, and assume that conditions (A1), (A3), and (A4) are satisfied. Then both the constant stationary solutions $(0,0)$ and $(1,1)$ of problem (1.1) are asymptotically unstable in the compact-open topology if $\alpha+\beta=1$.*

Sketch of the proof of Theorem 2.12. We consider the following condition on (u_0,v_0):

(B4) (u_0,v_0) satisfies the following three conditions:

(B4-1) $(u_0,v_0)\in C^1(\mathbf{R})\times C^1(\mathbf{R})$;

(B4-2) $(u_0'(x),v_0'(x))\geq(0,0)$ on $\mathbf{R}$;

(B4-3) $(u_0(x),v_0(x))$ equals either $(0,0)$ or $(1,1)$ outside a finite interval.

Under this condition, it suffices to construct a weak lower solution $(\underline{u},\underline{v})\in[0,1]\times[0,1]$ and a weak upper solution $(\overline{u},\overline{v})\in[0,1]\times[0,1]$ of problem (1.1) which are as in condition (A2) and converge neither to $(0,0)$ nor $(1,1)$ on $\mathbf{R}$ as $t\uparrow\infty$. Such a weak lower solution $(\underline{u},\underline{v})$ is obtained as a unique weak solution of the problem

$$\begin{aligned}\underline{u}_t&=\underline{u}_{xx}-L\underline{u}+Lh_2(x),\quad 0<t<T,\ x\in\mathbf{R},\\ \underline{v}_t&=\underline{v}_{xx}-L\underline{v}+Lh_1(x),\quad 0<t<T,\ x\in\mathbf{R},\\ \underline{u}\,|_{t=0}&=u_0,\qquad \underline{v}\,|_{t=0}=v_0,\quad x\in\mathbf{R},\end{aligned}\tag{2.18}$$

where $L>0$ is as in condition (A3) and

$$h_i(x):=\begin{cases}1 & \text{if } \theta_i\leq x<\infty,\\ 0 & \text{otherwise},\end{cases}\tag{2.19}$$

with a suitable positive constant θ_i. A weak upper solution $(\overline{u},\overline{v})$ with the above properties can be constructed similarly. □

3. Concluding remarks

We discuss the relationship between weak solutions of problem (1.1) and solutions of problem (1.1) formulated as differential inclusions. To distinguish between these two kinds of solutions, we call the latter "w-solutions." The definition of a w-solution of problem (1.1) is given as follows.

Definition 3.1. A pair (u,v) of functions $u,\ v\in C_B([0,T)\times\mathbf{R})\cap C^{0,1}((0,T)\times\mathbf{R})$ is called a *w-solution* of problem (1.1) if it satisfies the following two conditions:

(i) there exist two bounded measurable functions k and ℓ on $(0,T)\times\mathbf{R}$ such that, for all $\varphi\in\mathcal{D}((0,T)\times\mathbf{R})$,

$$\begin{aligned}&\int_0^T\int_{\mathbf{R}}(u\varphi_t-u_x\varphi_x+(f(u)+k(t,x))\varphi)\,dx\,dt=0,\\ &\int_0^T\int_{\mathbf{R}}(v\varphi_t-v_x\varphi_x+(g(v)+\ell(t,x))\varphi)\,dx\,dt=0,\end{aligned}\tag{3.1}$$

and that

$$
\begin{aligned}
-f(1)\widehat{H}(v(t,x)-\beta) &\le k(t,x) \le -f(1)\widetilde{H}(v(t,x)-\beta),\\
-g(1)\widehat{H}(u(t,x)-\alpha) &\le \ell(t,x) \le -g(1)\widetilde{H}(u(t,x)-\alpha)
\end{aligned}
\tag{3.2}
$$

almost everywhere in $(0,T)\times\mathbf{R}$, where $\widetilde{H}$ and $\widehat{H}$ are as in condition (A2);

(ii) for all $x_0 \in \mathbf{R}$,

$$
\lim_{t\downarrow 0, x\to x_0} u(t,x) = u_0(x_0), \qquad \lim_{t\downarrow 0, x\to x_0} v(t,x) = v_0(x_0). \tag{3.3}
$$

We can easily check that the maximal and minimal weak solutions (U,V), $(u,v) \in [\underline{u},\overline{u}] \times [\underline{v},\overline{v}]$ obtained in Theorem 2.3 of problem (1.1), are w-solutions of problem (1.1). The following proposition shows the relationship between them and other w-solutions.

Proposition 3.2. *Let $0<\alpha$, $\beta<1$, and assume that conditions (A1), (A2), and (B1) are satisfied. Then the maximal and minimal weak solutions (U,V), $(u,v)\in[\underline{u},\overline{u}]\times[\underline{v},\overline{v}]$ obtained in Theorem 2.3 of problem (1.1), are the maximal and minimal w-solutions, respectively, of problem (1.1) in the order interval $[\underline{u},\overline{u}]\times[\underline{v},\overline{v}]$.*

Concerning the size of w-solutions of problem (1.1), the following proposition holds.

Proposition 3.3. *Let $0<\alpha$, $\beta<1$, and assume that conditions (A1) and (B1) are satisfied. Then any w-solution of problem (1.1) is contained in the order interval $[0,1]\times[0,1]$.*

Remark 3.4. By Propositions 3.2 and 3.3, Theorems 2.6, 2.8, 2.10, 2.11, and 2.12 also hold for w-solutions of problem (1.1).

Acknowledgments

The author expresses hearty thanks to Professor R. P. Agarwal for giving him the opportunity to talk in this conference. This work was partially supported by Grant-in-Aid for JSPS Fellows (No. 0500097).

References

[1] H. Deguchi, *Existence, uniqueness and non-uniqueness of weak solutions of parabolic initial-value problems with discontinuous nonlinearities*, Proceedings of the Royal Society of Edinburgh. Section A. Mathematics **135** (2005), no. 6, 1139–1167.

[2] ———, *Existence, uniqueness and stability of weak solutions of parabolic systems with discontinuous nonlinearities*, 2005, submitted.

[3] E. Feireisl, *A note on uniqueness for parabolic problems with discontinuous nonlinearities*, Nonlinear Analysis **16** (1991), no. 11, 1053–1056.

[4] E. Feireisl and J. Norbury, *Some existence, uniqueness and nonuniqueness theorems for solutions of parabolic equations with discontinuous nonlinearities*, Proceedings of the Royal Society of Edinburgh. Section A **119** (1991), no. 1-2, 1–17.

[5] J. C. Harsanyi and R. Selten, *A General Theory of Equilibrium Selection in Games*, MIT Press, Massachusetts, 1988.

[6] J. Hofbauer, *Equilibrium selection via travelling waves*, Game Theory, Experience, Rationality (W. Leinfellner and E. Köhler, eds.), Vienna Circ. Inst. Yearb., vol. 5, Kluwer Academic, Dordrecht, 1998, pp. 245–259.

[7] ———, *The spatially dominant equilibrium of a game*, Annals of Operations Research **89** (1999), 233–251.

H. Deguchi: Department of Mathematics, University of Toyama, Toyama 930-8555, Japan
E-mail address: hdegu@sci.u-toyama.ac.jp

ASYMPTOTIC STABILITY FOR A HIGHER-ORDER RATIONAL DIFFERENCE EQUATION

M. DEHGHAN, C. M. KENT, AND H. SEDAGHAT

For the rational difference equation $x_n = (\alpha + \sum_{i=1}^{m} a_i x_{n-i})/(\beta + \sum_{i=1}^{m} b_i x_{n-i})$, $n = 1, 2, \ldots$, we obtain sufficient conditions for the asymptotic stability of a unique fixed point relative to an invariant interval. We focus on negative values for the coefficients a_i, a range that has not been considered previously.

1. Introduction

Consider the higher-order difference equation

$$x_n = f(x_{n-1}, \ldots, x_{n-m}), \quad n = 1, 2, \ldots, \tag{1.1}$$

where m is a nonnegative integer and $f : \mathbb{R}^m \to \mathbb{R}$ is a given function. In the literature on difference equations, problems involving the asymptotic stability of fixed points of (1.1) in the case in which f is monotonic (nonincreasing or nondecreasing) in each of its arguments or coordinates arise frequently. In particular, the general rational difference equation

$$x_n = \frac{\alpha + \sum_{i=1}^{m} a_i x_{n-i}}{\beta + \sum_{i=1}^{m} b_i x_{n-i}}, \quad n = 1, 2, \ldots, \tag{1.2}$$

and various special cases of it have been studied extensively in the literature; see, for example, [3, 5] for a discussion of (1.2) in its general form and [4] for a discussion of the second-order case. The bibliographies in these books contain numerous references to additional results that discuss asymptotic stability for various special cases.

In this paper we consider (1.2) in its general form above and give conditions for the asymptotic stability of a fixed point relative to an invariant interval that contains the fixed point. Our results concern a range of parameters, including negative coefficients, that extend those previously considered elsewhere.

Hindawi Publishing Corporation
Proceedings of the Conference on Differential & Difference Equations and Applications, pp. 335–339

2. The main results

We first quote a basic result from [1] as a lemma. This result concerns the general equation (1.1) and was inpired by the study of pulse propagation in a ring of excitable media in [7] which involved an equation of type (1.1).

LEMMA 2.1. *Let r_0, s_0 be extended real numbers where $-\infty \le r_0 < s_0 \le \infty$ and consider the following hypotheses:*

(H1) *$f(u_1,\ldots,u_m)$ is nonincreasing in each $u_1,\ldots,u_m \in I_0$, where $I_0 = (r_0,s_0]$ if $s_0 < \infty$ and $I_0 = (r_0,\infty)$ otherwise;*

(H2) *$g(u) = f(u,\ldots,u)$ is continuous and decreasing for $u \in I_0$;*

(H3) *there is $r \in [r_0,s_0)$ such that $r < g(r) \le s_0$. If $r_0 = -\infty$ or $\lim_{t\to r_0^+} g(t) = \infty$, then we assume that $r \in (r_0,s_0)$;*

(H4) *there is $s \in [r,x^*)$ such that $g^2(s) \ge s$, where $g^2(s) = g(g(s))$;*

(H5) *there is $s \in [r,x^*)$ such that $g^2(u) > u$ for all $u \in (s,x^*)$.*

Then the following is true.

(a) *If (H2) and (H3) hold, then (1.1) has a unique fixed point x^* in the open interval $(r,g(r))$.*

(b) *Let $I = [s,g(s)]$. If (H1)–(H4) hold, then I is an invariant interval for (1.1) and $x^* \in I$.*

(c) *If (H1)–(H3) and (H5) hold, then x^* is stable and attracts all solutions of (1.1) with initial values in $(s,g(s))$.*

(d) *If (H1)–(H3) hold, then x^* is an asymptotically stable fixed point of (1.1) if it is an asymptotically stable fixed point of the mapping g; for example, if g is continuously differentiable with $g'(x^*) > -1$.*

Remarks 2.2. (1) If f is continuous on $[s,g(s)]^m$, then the attractivity of x^* in Lemma 2.1(c) also follows from the general [2, Theorem 1.15]; see [1] for additional comments in this regard.

(2) Condition (H5) is equivalent to x^* being an asymptotically stable fixed point of the function g relative to the interval $(s,g(s))$; see [5, Theorem 2.1.2]. Hence Lemma 2.1(d) follows from Lemma 2.1(c).

Now we consider the rational difference equation (1.2) which we rewrite for notational convenience as follows:

$$x_n = \frac{\alpha - \sum_{i=1}^{m} a_i x_{n-i}}{\beta + \sum_{i=1}^{m} b_i x_{n-i}}, \tag{2.1}$$

where

$$\begin{gathered} \alpha > 0, \qquad a_i, b_i \ge 0, \quad i = 1,2,\ldots,m, \\ a = \sum_{i=1}^{m} a_i > 0, \qquad b = \sum_{i=1}^{m} b_i > 0, \qquad \beta > a. \end{gathered} \tag{2.2}$$

We note that the special case where $a_i = 0$ for all i is discussed in [1, 6], so we will not consider that case here. The functions f and g in Lemma 2.1 take the following forms for (2.1):

$$f(u_1,\dots,u_m)=\frac{\alpha-\sum_{i=1}^m a_iu_i}{\beta+\sum_{i=1}^m b_iu_i},\quad g(u)=\frac{\alpha-au}{\beta+bu},\quad u,u_i\in\mathbb{R}. \tag{2.3}$$

THEOREM 2.3. *Assume that f, g are given by (2.3) and that conditions (2.2) hold. If $s=-\alpha(\beta-a)/(a^2+\alpha b)$, then*

(a) *$g(s)=\alpha/a$ and $s>-\beta/b$;*

(b) *$I=[s,g(s)]$ is an invariant interval for (2.1);*

(c) *every solution of (2.1) with initial values in $(s,g(s))$ converges to the fixed point*

$$x^*=\frac{-(a+\beta)+\sqrt{(a+\beta)^2+4\alpha b}}{2b}\in(0,g(s))\subset I. \tag{2.4}$$

Proof. (a) The first assertion is easily verified by substitution, and the second follows from the observation that the value of s is an increasing function of a when $\beta>a$ and the infimum of s is $-\beta/b$.

(b) and (c) In Lemma 2.1, set $r_0=-\beta/b$ and let $s_0=\alpha/a$. For $u\in(r_0,s_0]=I_0$, we have $\alpha-au\geq 0$ and $\beta+bu>0$. Thus, g has a decreasing numerator and an increasing denominator on I_0, so g is decreasing on I_0. Similarly, if $(u_1,\dots,u_m)\in I_0^m$, then

$$\begin{aligned}\alpha-\sum_{i=1}^m a_iu_i&\geq\alpha-a\max\{u_1,\dots,u_m\}\geq\alpha-as_0=0,\\ \beta+\sum_{i=1}^m b_iu_i&\geq\beta+b\min\{u_1,\dots,u_m\}>\beta+br_0=0,\end{aligned} \tag{2.5}$$

so that $f(u_1,\dots,u_m)\geq 0$. Thus, for $(u_1,\dots,u_m)\in I_0^m$, the numerator of f is a decreasing function of u_j and its denominator an increasing function of u_j for each $j=1,\dots,m$ with u_i fixed for $i\neq j$. It follows that f is a decreasing function on I_0^m in each of its coordinates. Therefore, hypotheses (H1) and (H2) are satisfied in Lemma 2.1, and (H3) also holds since for $r=s\in(r_0,0)$ it is true that

$$r=s<0<\frac{\alpha}{a}=s_0=g(s)=g(r). \tag{2.6}$$

Further, the interval I is invariant because g is decreasing with $g(g(s))=0\in I$ so $g(I)\subset I$ and part (b) is established. To complete the proof of part (c), we now establish (H5). First, we may verify by a straightforward calculation that x^* is a solution of the equation $g(u)=u$ so that x^* is a fixed point of (2.1). Also, under conditions (2.2) $x^*>0$ and $x^*<g(s)$ if and only if

$$\begin{aligned}&\frac{-(a+\beta)+\sqrt{(a+\beta)^2+4\alpha b}}{2b}<\frac{\alpha}{a},\\ &\text{iff } a\sqrt{(a+\beta)^2+4\alpha b}<2\alpha b+a(a+\beta),\\ &\text{iff } a^2(a+\beta)^2+4a^2\alpha b<[2\alpha b+a(a+\beta)]^2,\\ &\text{iff } 0<\alpha^2b^2+\alpha\beta ab.\end{aligned} \tag{2.7}$$

The last inequality is true under conditions (2.2), so it follows that $x^* \in (0, g(s)) \subset I$. Since g is decreasing on $I_0 \supset I$, we conclude that x^* is the only fixed point of g in I. Now the inequality $g^2(u) > u$ can be written as

$$\frac{\alpha(\beta - a) + (\alpha b + a^2)u}{(\beta^2 + \alpha b) + b(\beta - a)u} > u \tag{2.8}$$

or equivalently as

$$b(\beta - a)u^2 + (\beta^2 - a^2)u + \alpha(\beta - a) > 0. \tag{2.9}$$

If $\beta > a$, then dividing by $\beta - a$ gives

$$bu^2 + (\beta + a)u - \alpha < 0. \tag{2.10}$$

For this last inequality to hold, we need $u \in (u_-, u_+)$ where u_- and u_+ are the two roots of the equation

$$bu^2 + (\beta + a)u - \alpha = 0. \tag{2.11}$$

But $u_+ = x^*$ and

$$u_- = \frac{-(a+\beta) - \sqrt{(a+\beta)^2 + 4\alpha b}}{2b} < \frac{-(a+\beta) - (a+\beta)}{2b} < -\frac{\beta}{b}. \tag{2.12}$$

Therefore, (2.10) holds for $u \in (-\beta/b, x^*)$ and, in particular, for $u \in (s, x^*)$. Thus (H5) holds and by Lemma 2.1 x^* is a stable attractor of all solutions in $(s, g(s))$. This completes the proof. □

Remarks 2.4. The function g above is in fact decreasing on $(-\beta/b, \infty)$, and iterates of g starting from an initial value $u_0 \in (-\beta/b, \infty)$ converge to x^* if $\beta > a$. This inequality assures that $(-\beta/b, \infty)$ is an invariant interval for g in addition to (H5) holding on $(-\beta/b, x^*)$ as shown in the proof of Theorem 2.3. However, the fixed point x^* above will *not* in general attract solutions of the higher-order equation (2.1) that start from initial values outside the interval $I = [s, g(s)]$. One reason for this is that (H1) does not hold if the numerator of f can be negative, which is possible if some of the coordinates of the point $(u_1, \ldots, u_m)$ are large and positive.

For example, consider the following special case of (2.1):

$$x_n = \frac{1 - ax_{n-2}}{1 + b_1x_{n-1} + b_2x_{n-2}}, \tag{2.13}$$

where $\alpha = \beta = 1$, $b_1, b_2 > 0$, and $a_1 = 0$ so $a = a_2$. The second-order equation (2.13) has a 2-cycle $\{p, q\}$ if

$$p = \frac{1 - ap}{1 + b_1q + b_2p}, \qquad q = \frac{1 - aq}{1 + b_1p + b_2q}. \tag{2.14}$$

If, for example,

$$b_2 < b_1 < 4b_2^2 + b_2, \qquad a > \frac{2b_2}{\sqrt{b_1 - b_2}} - 1, \tag{2.15}$$

then the system of (2.14) has real solutions:

$$p = \frac{c \pm \sqrt{c^2 - 4(b_1 - b_2)}}{2(b_1 - b_2)}, \qquad q = -p - \frac{1+a}{b_2} = \frac{c \mp \sqrt{c^2 - 4(b_1 - b_2)}}{2(b_1 - b_2)}, \tag{2.16}$$

where $c = (1+a)(1 - b_1/b_2)$. In particular, if $b_2 = 1/4$, $b_1 = 1$, and $a = 0.8$, then $c = -5.4$ and from (2.16) we obtain $p \approx -7.01$ and $q \approx -0.19$. Also, here $\alpha/a = 1/0.8 = 1.25$ and the invariant interval is $I \approx [-0.106, 1.25]$. Choosing at least one initial condition greater than 1.25 may cause a trajectory of (2.13) to reach the 2-cycle $\{p, q\}$. With, for example, $x_0 = 0.4$ and $x_{-1} = 5$ as initial values, we obtain $x_1 \approx -1.13$ which is less than $-\beta/b = -0.8$, and after this the solutions oscillate about the point of discontinuity $-\beta/b$. Of course, if both initial conditions are in the interval of Theorem 2.3, then the corresponding solution of (2.13) converges to the fixed point $x^* \approx 0.45$.

References

[1] D. Chan, E. R. Chang, M. Dehghan, C. M. Kent, R. Mazrooei-Sebdani, and H. Sedaghat, *Asymptotic stability for difference equations with decreasing arguments*, Journal of Difference Equations and Applications **12** (2006), no. 2, 109–123.

[2] E. A. Grove and G. Ladas, *Periodicities in Nonlinear Difference Equations*, Chapman & Hall/CRC, Florida, 2005.

[3] V. L. Kocić and G. Ladas, *Global Behavior of Nonlinear Difference Equations of Higher Order with Applications*, Mathematics and Its Applications, vol. 256, Kluwer Academic, Dordrecht, 1993.

[4] M. R. S. Kulenović and G. Ladas, *Dynamics of Second Order Rational Difference Equations. With Open Problems and Conjectures*, Chapman & Hall/CRC, Florida, 2001.

[5] H. Sedaghat, *Nonlinear Difference Equations. Theory with Applications to Social Science Models*, Mathematical Modelling: Theory and Applications, vol. 15, Kluwer Academic, Dordrecht, 2003.

[6] ———, *Stability in a class of monotone nonlinear difference equations*, International Journal of Pure and Applied Mathematics **21** (2005), no. 2, 167–174.

[7] H. Sedaghat, C. M. Kent, and M. A. Wood, *Criteria for the convergence, oscillations and bistability of pulse circulation in ring of excitable media*, SIAM Journal on Applied Mathematics **66** (2005), 573–590.

M. Dehghan: Department of Applied Mathematics, Amirkabir University of Technology, P.O. Box 15875-4413, Tehran, Iran
E-mail address: mdehghan@aut.ac.ir

C. M. Kent: Department of Mathematics, Virginia Commonwealth University, Richmond, VA 23284-2014, USA
E-mail address: cmkent@vcu.edu

H. Sedaghat: Department of Mathematics, Virginia Commonwealth University, Richmond, VA 23284-2014, USA
E-mail address: hsedagha@vcu.edu

INEQUALITIES FOR POSITIVE SOLUTIONS OF THE EQUATION $\dot{y}(t) = -\sum_{i=1}^{n}(a_i + b_i/t)y(t-\tau_i)$

JOSEF DIBLÍK AND MÁRIA KÚDELČÍKOVÁ

The equation $\dot{y}(t) = -\sum_{i=1}^{n}(a_i + b_i/t)y(t-\tau_i)$, where $a_i, \tau_i \in (0,\infty)$, $i = 1,2,\dots,n$, and $b_i \in R$ are constants, is considered when $t \to \infty$ under supposition that the transcendental equation $\lambda = \sum_{i=1}^{n} a_i e^{\lambda\tau_i}$ has two real and different roots. The existence of a positive solution is proved as well as its asymptotic behaviour.

1. Introduction

We consider equation

$$\dot{y}(t) = -\sum_{i-1}^{n}\left(a_i + \frac{b_i}{t}\right)y(t-\tau_i), \tag{1.1}$$

where $a_i, \tau_i \in R^+ := (0,\infty)$, $i = 1,2,\dots,n$, and $b_i \in R$ are constants. The case when there exist positive solutions is studied. In the supposition of existence of two real (positive) different roots λ_j, $j = 1,2$, $\lambda_1 < \lambda_2$, of the transcendental equation

$$\lambda = \sum_{i=1}^{n} a_i e^{\lambda\tau_i}, \tag{1.2}$$

we prove the existence of a positive solution $y = y(t)$ having for $t \to \infty$ asymptotic behaviour

$$y(t) \sim e^{-\lambda_1 t} t^{r_1} \tag{1.3}$$

with an appropriate number r_1. Corresponding below and upper inequalities are given for $y(t)$, too.

Hindawi Publishing Corporation
Proceedings of the Conference on Differential & Difference Equations and Applications, pp. 341–350

2. A nonlinear theorem

Let R^n be equipped with the maximum norm. With $R^n_{\geq 0}$ ($R^n_{>0}$) we denote the set of all componentwise nonnegative (positive) vectors v in R^n, that is, $v = (v^1,\dots,v^n)$ with $v^i \geq 0$ ($v^i > 0$) for $i = 1,\dots,n$. For $u,v \in R^n$, we say $u \leq v$ if $v - u \in R^n_{\geq 0}$, $u \ll v$ if $v - u \in R^n_{>0}$, $u < v$ if $u \leq v$ and $u \neq v$.

Let $C([a,b],R^n)$, where $a,b \in R$, $a < b$, be the Banach space of the continuous mappings from the interval $[a,b]$ into R^n equipped with the supremum norm $\|\psi\| = \sup_{\theta\in[a,b]} |\psi(\theta)|$, $\psi \in C([a,b],R^n)$. We will denote this space as C_r if $a = -r < 0$ and $b = 0$.

Let us consider a system of functional differential equations

$$\dot{y}(t) = f(t, y_t), \tag{2.1}$$

where $f : \Omega \to R^n$ is a continuous quasibounded functional which satisfies a local Lipschitz condition with respect to the second argument and Ω is an open subset in $R \times C_r$. We assume that the derivative in (2.1) is at least right-sided.

If $\sigma \in R^n$, $A \geq 0$, and $y \in C([\sigma - r,\sigma + A],R^n)$, then for each $t \in [\sigma,\sigma + A]$ we define $y_t \in C_r$ by means of relation $y_t(\theta) = y(t+\theta)$, $\theta \in [-r,0]$.

In accordance with [2], a function y is said to be a *solution of the system* (2.1) *on* $[\sigma - r,\sigma + A)$ with $A > 0$ if $y \in C([\sigma - r,\sigma + A),R^n)$, $(t, y_t) \in \Omega$ for $t \in [\sigma,\sigma + A)$ and $y(t)$ satisfies (2.1) for $t \in [\sigma,\sigma + A)$. For given $\sigma \in R$, $\varphi \in C_r$, we say $y(\sigma,\varphi)$ is a solution of (2.1) through $(\sigma,\varphi) \in \Omega$ if there is an $A > 0$ such that $y(\sigma,\varphi)$ is a solution of system (2.1) on $[\sigma - r,\sigma + A)$ and $y_\sigma(\sigma,\varphi) = \varphi$. In view of the above conditions, each element $(\sigma,\varphi) \in \Omega$ determines a unique solution $y(\sigma,\varphi)$ of system (2.1) through $(\sigma,\varphi) \in \Omega$ on its maximal interval of existence which depends continuously on the initial data [2].

For given $k \in R^n_{>0}$, let us consider the integro-functional inequalities

$$\begin{aligned} L_1(t) &\leq -\lambda(t) - (I(k,L_1)(t))^{-1} f(t,I(k,L_1)_t), \\ L_2(t) &\geq -\lambda(t) - (I(k,L_2)(t))^{-1} f(t,I(k,L_2)_t) \end{aligned} \tag{2.2}$$

on $[t_0,\infty)$, $t_0 \in R^n$, for $L_j \in C([t_0 - r,\infty),R^n)$, $j = 1,2$, where

$$I : R^n_{>0} \times C([t_0 - r,\infty),R^n) \longrightarrow C([t_0 - r,\infty),R^n) \tag{2.3}$$

is defined by

$$I^i(k,L)(t) := k^i \exp\left(-\int_{t_0-r}^{t} \lambda^i(s)ds + \int_t^\infty L^i(s)ds\right), \tag{2.4}$$

$i = 1,\dots,n$, $t \in [t_0 - r,\infty)$ with a fixed function $\lambda \in C([t_0 - r,\infty),R^n)$, provided that improper integrals $\int^\infty L^i(s)ds$ exist.

We consider an operator equation

$$L(t) = (TL)(t) := -\lambda(t) - (I(k,L)(t))^{-1} f(t,I(k,L)_t), \tag{2.5}$$

where λ is a fixed function on interval $[t_0 - r, \infty)$. It is easy to verify that system (2.1) is connected with operator equation (2.5) by the substitution

$$y(t) = I(k, L)(t). \tag{2.6}$$

A function L is said to be a solution of operator equation (2.5) on interval $[\sigma - r, \sigma + A)$ with $A > 0$ if $L \in C([\sigma - r, \sigma + A), R^n)$, $(t, L_t) \in \Omega$ for $t \in [\sigma, \sigma + A)$ and $L(t)$ satisfies (2.5) for $t \in [\sigma, \sigma + A)$. The next theorem which is necessary for our investigation and taken from [1] indicates conditions under which there exists solution of system (2.1).

Theorem 2.1. *Let us suppose that*

(i) *for any $M \geq 0$, $\vartheta \geq t_0$, there are K_1, K_2 such that*

$$\begin{aligned} |(TL)(t)| &\leq K_1, \\ |(TL)(t) - (TL)(t')| &\leq K_2 |t - t'| \end{aligned} \tag{2.7}$$

for any $t, t' \in [t_0, \vartheta]$ and any function $L \in C([t_0 - r, \vartheta), R^n)$ with $|L| \leq M$;

(ii) *there are $k \in R^n_{>0}$ and functions $L_j \in C([t_0 - r, \infty), R^n)$, $j = 1, 2$, with convergent integrals $\int^\infty L^i_j(s)ds$, $j = 1, 2; i = 1, \ldots, n$, satisfying $L_1(t) \leq L_2(t)$ on $[t_0 - r, \infty)$ and the inequalities (2.2) on $[t_0, \infty)$, that is, the inequalities:*

$$L_1(t) \leq (TL_1)(t), \qquad L_2(t) \geq (TL_2)(t); \tag{2.8}$$

(iii) *there is a Lipschitz continuous function $\varphi : [t_0 - r, t_0] \to R^n$ satisfying $\varphi(t_0) = 0$ and on $[t_0 - r, t_0]$ inequalities*

$$L_1(t) \leq (TL_1)(t_0) + \varphi(t), \qquad L_2(t) \geq (TL_2)(t_0) + \varphi(t); \tag{2.9}$$

(iv) *for any functions $\Lambda_j(t) \in C([t_0 - r, \vartheta), R^n)$, $j = 1, 2$, with $\Lambda_1(t) \leq \Lambda_2(t)$ for $t \in [t_0 - r, \vartheta)$, $\vartheta \geq t_0$, we have*

$$(T\Lambda_1)(t) \leq (T\Lambda_2)(t), \quad t \in [t_0, \infty). \tag{2.10}$$

Then there exists a solution y of the system (2.1) on $[t_0 - r, \infty)$ satisfying

$$I(k, L_1)(t) \leq y(t) \leq I(k, L_2)(t) \tag{2.11}$$

on $t \in [t_0 - r, \infty)$.

3. Linear corollary of the theorem

Let us apply Theorem 2.1 to the investigation of delayed linear equation of the type (2.1) with $f(t, y_t) := -\sum_{i=1}^n c_i(t) y(t - \tau_i(t))$, that is, to the equation

$$\dot{y}(t) = -\sum_{i=1}^{n} c_i(t) y(t - \tau_i(t)) \tag{3.1}$$

with a positive Lipschitz continuous bounded coefficients c_i on $[t_0,\infty)$ and Lipschitz continuous bounded positive delays $\tau_i(t) \le r$, $r \in R^+$, where we suppose differences $t-\tau_i(t)$ increasing on $[t_0,\infty)$. Let us define $\tau(t) := \max\{\tau_i(t)\}$, $i = 1,2,\dots,n$. Using the substitution (2.6) for linear case we obtain the operator $(TL)(t)$ defined by formula (2.5) in the form

$$(TL)(t) := -\lambda(t) + \sum_{i=1}^{n} c_i(t)\exp\left(\int_{t-\tau_i(t)}^{t}[\lambda(s)+L(s)]ds\right). \tag{3.2}$$

Now we apply Theorem 2.1 to linear equation (3.1). We omit corresponding (technically cumbersome) proof.

Theorem 3.1. *Let us suppose that there are continuous functions $L_j : [t_0-\tau(t_0),\infty) \to R$, $j = 1,2$, and a Lipschitz continuous function $\varphi(t) : [t_0-\tau(t_0),t_0) \to R$ satisfying $\varphi(t_0) = 0$, $L_1(t) \le L_2(t)$ for $t \in [t_0-\tau(t_0),\infty)$ and integrals $\int^{\infty} L_j(s)ds$, $j = 1,2$, exist. Let a Lipschitz continuous bounded function $\lambda : [t_0-\tau(t_0),\infty) \to R$ be given such that also the following inequalities are satisfied:*

$$\lambda(t) + L_1(t) \le \sum_{i=1}^{n} c_i(t)\exp\left(\int_{t-\tau_i(t)}^{t}[\lambda(s)+L_1(s)]ds\right), \tag{3.3}$$

$$\lambda(t) + L_2(t) \ge \sum_{i=1}^{n} c_i(t)\exp\left(\int_{t-\tau_i(t)}^{t}[\lambda(s)+L_2(s)]ds\right) \tag{3.4}$$

on interval $[t_0,\infty)$, and

$$\lambda(t_0) + L_1(t) \le \sum_{i=1}^{n} c_i(t_0)\exp\left(\int_{t_0-\tau_i(t_0)}^{t_0}[\lambda(s)+L_1(s)]ds\right) + \varphi(t), \tag{3.5}$$

$$\lambda(t_0) + L_2(t) \ge \sum_{i=1}^{n} c_i(t_0)\exp\left(\int_{t_0-\tau_i(t_0)}^{t_0}[\lambda(s)+L_2(s)]ds\right) + \varphi(t) \tag{3.6}$$

on interval $[t_0-\tau(t_0),t_0]$.

Then there exists a solution $y = y(t)$ of (3.1) on $[t_0-\tau(t_0),\infty)$, such that

$$\exp\left[\int_t^{\infty} L_1(s)ds\right] \le y(t)\cdot e^{\int_{t_0-\tau(t_0)}^{t}\lambda(s)ds} \le \exp\left[\int_t^{\infty} L_2(s)ds\right]. \tag{3.7}$$

4. Investigation of (1.1)

We consider delayed equation of the type (3.1) with $c_i(t) := (a_i + b_i/t)$, $\tau_i(t) := \tau_i = \text{const}$, where $a_i, \tau_i \in R^+$ and $b_i \in R$, $i = 1,2,\dots,n$, that is, (1.1).

We will try to find so-called approximative solutions corresponding to (1.1) in the form

$$y^{as}(t) \propto e^{-\lambda t} t^r \left(1 + \frac{A}{t}\right), \tag{4.1}$$

where r and A are coefficients (specified below in Theorem 4.3) and λ is one from two real positive different roots $\lambda_1 < \lambda_2$ of the transcendental equation (1.2), the existence of which is supposed. We show that these solutions satisfy formally for $t \to \infty$ (1.1) with the order of accuracy $O(e^{-\lambda t} t^{r-2})$.

We define the auxiliary function $f(\lambda) := \lambda - \sum_{i=1}^{n} a_i e^{\lambda \tau_i}$. Then

$$f'(\lambda) = 1 - \sum_{i=1}^{n} a_i \tau_i e^{\lambda \tau_i}, \qquad f''(\lambda) = -\sum_{i=1}^{n} a_i {\tau_i}^2 e^{\lambda \tau_i}. \tag{4.2}$$

LEMMA 4.1. *Let positive constants a_i, τ_i, $i = 1, 2, \ldots, n$, be given and let just two real different positive roots λ_j, $j = 1, 2$, $\lambda_1 < \lambda_2$ of (1.2) exist. Then $f'(\lambda_1) > 0$ and $f'(\lambda_2) < 0$.*

Proof. The second derivative (4.2) of the function f is on R negative. Therefore the first derivative f' is a decreasing function, $f'(0) = 1$ and $f'(+\infty) = -\infty$. Since (1.2) has just two different positive roots, it means that there exists just one point (extremal point) $\lambda_\epsilon \in (\lambda_1, \lambda_2)$ for which it holds $f'(\lambda_\epsilon) = 0$. At λ_ϵ the auxiliary function $f(\lambda)$ reaches its maximum and $f(\lambda_\epsilon) > 0$. Since that $f'(\lambda_1) > 0$ (function $f(\lambda)$ increases to its maximum) and $f'(\lambda_2) < 0$ (function $f(\lambda)$ decreases from its maximum). □

The following lemma, the proof of which can be made easily using the binomial formula and the method of induction and therefore is omitted, will be used in the proof of next theorem.

LEMMA 4.2. *Let $r \in R$ be given. Then the asymptotic representation*

$$(t - \tau)^r = t^r \left[1 - \frac{r\tau}{t} + \frac{r(r-1)\tau^2}{2t^2} + o\left(\frac{1}{t^2}\right)\right] \tag{4.3}$$

holds for $t \to \infty$.

THEOREM 4.3. *Let positive constants a_i, τ_i, $i = 1, 2, \ldots, n$, be given and (1.2) has just two real different roots λ_j, $j = 1, 2$, $\lambda_1 < \lambda_2$. Then there exist two approximative solutions of (1.1) having the form (4.1):*

$$y_j^{as}(t) \propto e^{-\lambda_j t} t^{r_j} \left(1 + \frac{A_j}{t}\right), \quad j = 1, 2, \tag{4.4}$$

with

$$r_j = \left(-\sum_{i=1}^{n} b_i e^{\lambda_j \tau_i}\right) [f'(\lambda_j)]^{-1}, \tag{4.5}$$

$$A_j = \frac{1}{f'(\lambda_j)} \left[-\frac{r_j(r_j - 1)}{2} f''(\lambda_j) - r_j \sum_{i=1}^{n} b_i \tau_i e^{\lambda_j \tau_i}\right]. \tag{4.6}$$

Proof. At first, note that the coefficients r_j, A_j, $j = 1,2$, are well defined since, due to Lemma 4.1, $f'(\lambda_j) \neq 0$. Now substituting the approximative solution (4.1) into (1.1), we expect that

$$\begin{aligned} &-\lambda e^{-\lambda t}(t^r + At^{r-1}) + e^{-\lambda t}(rt^{r-1} + A(r-1)t^{r-2}) \\ &\quad \propto -\sum_{i=1}^{n}\left(a_i + \frac{b_i}{t}\right)e^{-\lambda(t-\tau_i)}\left((t-\tau_i)^r + A(t-\tau_i)^{r-1}\right). \end{aligned} \tag{4.7}$$

With the aid of Lemma 4.2 and after some necessary computations, we get

$$\begin{aligned} &-\lambda - \frac{\lambda A}{t} + \frac{r}{t} + \frac{A(r-1)}{t^2} \\ &\quad \propto -\sum_{i=1}^{n} e^{\lambda\tau_i}\bigg(a_i + \frac{1}{t}(a_iA - a_ir\tau_i + b_i) \\ &\qquad + \frac{1}{t^2}\left(a_iA\tau_i + A(-a_ir\tau_i + b_i) + \frac{1}{2}a_ir\tau_i^2(r-1) - b_ir\tau_i\right)\bigg). \end{aligned} \tag{4.8}$$

Now comparing the coefficients at the members with the same powers t^0, t^{-1}, and t^{-2} of t, we obtain

$$\begin{aligned} \lambda &= \sum_{i=1}^{n} a_i e^{\lambda\tau_i}, \\ -\lambda A + r &= -\sum_{i=1}^{n} e^{\lambda\tau_i}(a_iA - a_ir\tau_i + b_i), \\ A(r-1) &= -\sum_{i=1}^{n} e^{\lambda\tau_i}\tau_i\left(a_iA - a_iAr + b_iA + \frac{1}{2}a_ir(r-1)\tau_i - b_ir\right). \end{aligned} \tag{4.9}$$

When using the first relation, from the second one, we get

$$r = \frac{1}{f'(\lambda)}\left(-\sum_{i=1}^{n} b_ie^{\lambda\tau_i}\right)\left(1 - \sum_{i=1}^{n} a_i\tau_ie^{\lambda\tau_i}\right)^{-1}\left(-\sum_{i=1}^{n} b_ie^{\lambda\tau_i}\right). \tag{4.10}$$

From the third equation (using above relations) after some simplifications, we have

$$A = \frac{1}{f'(\lambda)}\left[-\frac{r(r-1)}{2}f''(\lambda) - r\sum_{i=1}^{n} b_i\tau_ie^{\lambda\tau_i}\right]. \tag{4.11}$$

Now identifying the corresponding λ, r, A with λ_1, r_1, A_1 or with λ_2, r_2, A_2, we get the pair of approximative solutions $y_1^{as}(t)$ and $y_2^{as}(t)$. Thus the proof is finished. □

Now we define with the aid of coefficients of approximative solutions function $\lambda(t)$ and functions $L_1(t)$ and $L_2(t)$, $L_1(t) \le L_2(t)$, corresponding to the root $\lambda = \lambda_1$ of (1.2) as

$$\begin{aligned} \lambda(t) &:= \lambda_1 - \frac{r_1}{t}, \\ L_1(t) &:= \frac{(A_1 - \varepsilon_1)}{t^2}, \\ L_2(t) &:= \frac{(A_1 + \varepsilon_1)}{t^2}, \end{aligned} \tag{4.12}$$

with a constant $\varepsilon_1 \in (0,1)$.

THEOREM 4.4. *Suppose that (1.2) has just two real different roots λ_j, $j = 1,2$, $\lambda_1 < \lambda_2$. Then for every $\varepsilon_1 \in (0,1)$ there exist a $t_0 \in R$, $t_0 > \tau$, $\tau = \max\{\tau_i\}$, $i = 1,2,\dots,n$, and a positive solution $y^*(t)$ of (1.1) on $[t_0 - \tau, \infty)$ satisfying inequalities*

$$e^{-\lambda_1 t} t^{r_1} \left(1 + \frac{A_1 - \varepsilon_1}{t}\right) \le y^*(t) \le e^{-\lambda_1 t} t^{r_1} \left(1 + \frac{A_1 + \varepsilon_1}{t}\right), \tag{4.13}$$

where coefficients r_1, A_1 are defined by formulas (4.5), (4.6).

Proof. We employ Theorem 3.1. It is supposed that ε_1 is a fixed positive number and t_0 is large enough to indicate the asymptotic relations and inequalities are valid. Let $\lambda(t)$, $L_1(t)$, $L_2(t)$ be defined by formulae (4.12). At first we show that functions $L_1(t)$, $L_2(t)$ really satisfy inequalities (3.3) and (3.4). We have to verify that

$$\lambda_1 - \frac{r_1}{t} + \frac{(A_1 - \varepsilon_1)}{t^2} \le \sum_{i=1}^{n} \left(a_i + \frac{b_i}{t}\right) e^{\int_{t-\tau_i(t)}^{t} (\lambda_1 - r_1/s + (A_1 - \varepsilon_1)/s^2) ds} \tag{4.14}$$

holds. Let us simplify the right-hand side (denote it by $\mathcal{R}$). After integration we obtain

$$\begin{aligned} \mathcal{R} &= \sum_{i=1}^{n} \left(a_i + \frac{b_i}{t}\right) \exp\left[\lambda_1 \tau_i - r_1 \ln \frac{t}{t - \tau_i} - (A_1 - \varepsilon_1)\left(\frac{1}{t} - \frac{1}{t - \tau_i}\right)\right] \\ &= \sum_{i=1}^{n} \left(a_i + \frac{b_i}{t}\right) e^{\lambda_1 \tau_i} \left(\frac{t - \tau_i}{t}\right)^{r_1} \cdot \mathcal{E}(\tau_i) \end{aligned} \tag{4.15}$$

with

$$\mathcal{E}(\tau_i) := \exp\left[\frac{\tau_i (A_1 - \varepsilon_1)}{t(t - \tau_i)}\right]. \tag{4.16}$$

It is easy to see that for sufficiently large t,

$$\mathcal{E}(\tau_i) = \exp\left[\tau_i (A_1 - \varepsilon_1) \frac{1}{t^2} \left(1 + \frac{\tau_i}{t} + o\left(\frac{1}{t}\right)\right)\right] = 1 + \frac{\tau_i (A_1 - \varepsilon_1)}{t^2} + o\left(\frac{1}{t^2}\right). \tag{4.17}$$

With the aid of Lemma 4.2, we get

$$\begin{aligned}
\mathcal{R} &= \sum_{i=1}^{n}\left(a_i + \frac{b_i}{t}\right)e^{\lambda_1\tau_i}\left(1 - \frac{r_1\tau_i}{t} + \frac{r_1(r_1-1)\tau_i^2}{2t^2} + o\left(\frac{1}{t^2}\right)\right)\cdot\mathcal{E}(\tau_i)\\
&= \sum_{i=1}^{n}\left(a_i + \frac{b_i}{t}\right)e^{\lambda_1\tau_i}\left(1 - \frac{r_1\tau_i}{t} + \frac{(A_1-\varepsilon_1)\tau_i}{t^2} + \frac{r_1(r_1-1)\tau_i^2}{2t^2} + o\left(\frac{1}{t^2}\right)\right)\\
&= e^{\lambda_1\tau_i}\cdot\left[a_i + \frac{1}{t}(b_i - a_ir_1\tau_i) + \frac{1}{t^2}\left(a_iA_1\tau_i - a_i\varepsilon_1\tau_i - b_ir_1\tau_i + \frac{a_ir_1(r_1-1)\tau_i^2}{2}\right) + o\left(\frac{1}{t^2}\right)\right]\\
&= \lambda_1 + [-r_1f'(\lambda_1) + r_1(f'(\lambda_1)-1)]\frac{1}{t}\\
&\quad + \frac{1}{t^2}\left[-\frac{1}{2}r_1(r_1-1)f''(\lambda_1) - r_1\sum_{i=1}^{n}b_i\tau_ie^{\lambda_1\tau_i} + (A_1-\varepsilon_1)(1-f'(\lambda_1))\right] + o\left(\frac{1}{t^2}\right).
\end{aligned} \tag{4.18}$$

Now we compare coefficients at the members with the same powers (t^0, t^{-1}, and t^{-2}) of t at left-hand and right-hand sides of the inequality (4.14). Left-hand sides are denoted as $\mathcal{L}$ and right-hand sides as $\mathcal{R}$ with corresponding indices. We obtain

$$\begin{gathered}
\mathcal{L}_0 = \lambda_1, \qquad \mathcal{R}_0 = \lambda_1,\\
\mathcal{L}_{-1} = -r_1, \qquad \mathcal{R}_{-1} = -r_1,\\
\mathcal{L}_{-2} = A_1 - \varepsilon_1,\\
\mathcal{R}_{-2} = -\frac{1}{2}r_1(r_1-1)f''(\lambda_1) - r_1\sum_{i=1}^{n}b_i\tau_ie^{\lambda_1\tau_i} + (A_1-\varepsilon_1)(1-f'(\lambda_1)).
\end{gathered} \tag{4.19}$$

Obviously $\mathcal{L}_0 = \mathcal{R}_0$ and $\mathcal{L}_{-1} = \mathcal{R}_{-1}$ is valid. Since, in view of (4.2), (4.5), and (4.6),

$$\mathcal{R}_{-2} = A_1f'(\lambda_1) + A_1 - A_1f'(\lambda_1) - \varepsilon_1 + \varepsilon_1f'(\lambda_1) = A_1 - \varepsilon_1 + \varepsilon_1f'(\lambda_1), \tag{4.20}$$

then, for the validity of inequality $\mathcal{L}_{-2} < \mathcal{R}_{-2}$, the inequality $f'(\lambda_1) > 0$ is sufficient. This is true (see Lemma 4.1). That means (3.3) is fulfilled. Inequality (3.4) for $L_2(t)$ holds by the same arguments.

Let us show that also inequalities (3.5) and (3.6) hold on $[t_0 - \tau, t_0]$ with Lipschitz continuous function

$$\varphi(t) := L_1(t) - L_1(t_0). \tag{4.21}$$

At first we verify validity of (3.5), that is, validity of

$$\lambda_1 - \frac{r_1}{t_0} + \frac{A_1-\varepsilon_1}{t^2} \le \sum_{i=1}^{n}\left(a_i + \frac{b_i}{t_0}\right)e^{\int_{t_0-\tau_i}^{t_0}(\lambda_1 - r_1/s + (A_1-\varepsilon_1)/s^2)ds} + \frac{A_1-\varepsilon_1}{t^2} - \frac{A_1-\varepsilon_1}{t_0^2}, \tag{4.22}$$

which holds automatically since the inequality

$$\lambda_1 - \frac{r_1}{t_0} + \frac{A_1 - \varepsilon_1}{t_0^2} \le \sum_{i=1}^{n} \left(a_i + \frac{b_i}{t_0}\right) e^{\int_{t_0-\tau_i}^{t_0} (\lambda_1 - r_1/s + (A_1-\varepsilon_1)/s^2) ds} \tag{4.23}$$

is a special case of (3.3) with $t = t_0$. To show (3.6), we have to verify if

$$\lambda_1 - \frac{r_1}{t_0} + \frac{A_1 + \varepsilon_1}{t^2} \ge \sum_{i=1}^{n} \left(a_i + \frac{b_i}{t_0}\right) e^{\int_{t_0-\tau_i}^{t_0} (\lambda_1 - r_1/s + (A_1-\varepsilon_1)/s^2) ds} + \frac{A_1 - \varepsilon_1}{t^2} - \frac{A_1 - \varepsilon_1}{t_0^2} \tag{4.24}$$

holds on $[t_0 - \tau, t_0]$. After integration, some simplifications, using (4.2), (4.6), and above computation for $\mathcal{R}$, we can see that it is necessary to verify the inequality

$$\frac{A_1 - \varepsilon_1}{t_0^2} + \frac{2\varepsilon_1}{t^2} \ge \frac{1}{t_0^2}\left((A_1 - \varepsilon_1)(1 - f'(\lambda_1)) + A_1 f'(\lambda_1)\right), \tag{4.25}$$

which can be simplified to $2t_0^2 \ge f'(\lambda_1)t^2$ or (since $t_0 \ge t$) to the inequality $f'(\lambda_1) \le 2$ which holds obviously. Hence (3.6) is fulfilled on $[t_0 - \tau, t_0]$.

All conditions of Theorem 3.1 are valid. It follows from inequalities (3.7) that there exists a solution $y = y(t)$ such that

$$y_1(t) \le y(t) \le y_2(t) \tag{4.26}$$

with $y_1(t) := I(k, L_1)(t)$ and $y_2(t) := I(k, L_2)(t)$. After some simplifications, we get

$$\begin{aligned}
y_j(t) = I(k, L_j)(t) &= \exp\left(- \int_{t_0-\tau}^{t} \lambda(s) ds + \int_{t}^{\infty} L_j(s) ds \right) \\
&= \exp\left(- \int_{t_0-\tau}^{t} \left[\lambda_1 - \frac{r_1}{s}\right] ds + \int_{t}^{\infty} \frac{A_1 - \varepsilon_1}{s^2} ds \right) \\
&= \exp\left(- [\lambda_1 s - r_1 \ln s]_{t_0-\tau}^{t} + \left[- \frac{A_1 - \varepsilon_1}{s} \right]_t^{\infty} \right) \\
&= \exp\left(- \lambda_1 (t - t_0 + \tau) + r_1 \ln \frac{t}{t_0 - \tau} + \frac{A_1 - \varepsilon_1}{t} \right) \\
&= e^{-\lambda_1 (t - t_0 + \tau)} \left(\frac{t}{t_0 - \tau} \right)^{r_1} \exp\left(\frac{A_1 - \varepsilon_1}{t} \right) \\
&= e^{-\lambda_1 (\tau - t_0)} \frac{1}{(t_0 - \tau)^{r_1}} e^{-\lambda_1 t} t^{r_1} \left(1 + \frac{A_1 - \varepsilon_1}{t} + o\left(\frac{1}{t}\right) \right) \\
&= K_j e^{-\lambda_1 t} t^{r_1} \left(1 + \frac{A_1 - \varepsilon_1}{t} + o\left(\frac{1}{t}\right) \right), \quad j = 1, 2,
\end{aligned} \tag{4.27}$$

with

$$K_j := e^{-\lambda_1 (\tau - t_0)} (t_0 - \tau)^{-r_1}, \quad j = 1, 2. \tag{4.28}$$

Put $y = y^*(t) := y(t)/K_1$. Since $K_1 = K_2$, inequality (4.13) holds due to the linearity of (3.1). □

Acknowledgments

The first author was supported by the Grant A 1163401 of Grant Agency of the AS CR and by the Council of Czech Government MSM 0021630503. The second author was supported by the Grants nos. 1/0026/03 and 1/3238/06 of the Grant Agency of Slovak Republic (VEGA).

References

[1] J. Diblík and M. Kúdelčíková, *Inequalities for positive solutions of the equation* $\dot{y}(t) = -(a_0 + a_1/t)y(t - \tau_1) - (b_0 + b_1/t)y(t - \tau_2)$, Studies of the University of Žilina. Mathematical Series **17** (2003), no. 1, 27–46.

[2] J. K. Hale and S. M. Verduyn Lunel, *Introduction to Functional-Differential Equations*, Applied Mathematical Sciences, vol. 99, Springer, New York, 1993.

Josef Diblík: Department of Mathematics, Faculty of Electrical Engineering and Communication, Brno University of Technology, Technická 8, 61600 Brno, Czech Republic
E-mail address: diblik@feec.vutbr.cz

Mária Kúdelčíková: Department of Mathematical Analysis and Applied Mathematics, Faculty of Science, Žilina University, Hurbanova 15, 01026 Žilina, Slovak Republic
E-mail address: maria.kudelcikova@fpv.utc.sk

LOCAL AND GLOBAL ESTIMATES FOR SOLUTIONS TO THE A-HARMONIC EQUATION AND RELATED OPERATORS

SHUSEN DING

We summarize different versions of the A-harmonic equations for both of differential forms and functions. We also prove the Hardy-Littlewood inequalities with Orlicz norms.

1. Introduction

The A-harmonic equations belong to the nonlinear elliptic equations written in terms of an operator A satisfying certain structural assumptions. The A-harmonic equations are of particular importance because they have wide applications in many fields, including quasiconformal analysis, nonlinear elasticity, and potential theory, see [5–7, 9]. The A-harmonic equations are important extensions of the p-harmonic equation in $\mathbb{R}^n$, $p > 1$. In recent years, there have been remarkable advances made in studying the different versions of the A-harmonic equations for differential forms, see [1–3, 6, 7, 9]. In this paper, we first summarize different versions of the A-harmonic equations. Then, we prove some versions of the Hardy-Littlewood inequalities with $L^s(\log L)^\alpha$-norms.

We first introduce some definitions and notation. We always assume Ω is a connected open subset of $\mathbb{R}^n$. For $0 \le k \le n$, a k-form $\omega(x)$ is defined by

$$\omega(x) = \sum_I \omega_I(x)dx_I = \sum \omega_{i_1 i_2 \dots i_k}(x) dx_{i_1} \wedge dx_{i_2} \wedge \cdots \wedge dx_{i_k}, \tag{1.1}$$

where $\omega_{i_1 i_2 \dots i_k}(x)$ are real functions in $\mathbb{R}^n$, $I = (i_1, i_2, \dots, i_k)$, $i_j \in \{1, 2, \dots, n\}$, and $j = 1, 2, \dots, k$. When $\omega_{i_1 i_2 \dots i_k}(x)$ are differentiable functions, $\omega(x)$ is called a differential k-form. We write $|\omega(x)|^p = (\sum_I |\omega_I(x)|^2)^{p/2}$ and $\|\omega\|_{p,\Omega} = (\int_\Omega |\omega(x)|^p dx)^{1/p}$. We should note that a differential 0-form is a differentiable function $f : \mathbb{R}^n \to \mathbb{R}$. Let $\wedge^l = \wedge^l(\mathbb{R}^n)$ denote all l-forms in $\mathbb{R}^n$, generated by $dx_{i_1} \wedge dx_{i_2} \wedge \cdots \wedge dx_{i_l}$, $l = 1, 2, \dots, n$. We denote the space of differential l-forms by $D'(\Omega, \wedge^l)$. We use $L^p(\Omega, \wedge^l)$ to denote the space of all l-forms with $\omega_I \in L^p(\Omega, \mathbb{R})$.

Hindawi Publishing Corporation
Proceedings of the Conference on Differential & Difference Equations and Applications, pp. 351–361

We define the Hodge star operator $\star : \wedge \to \wedge$ as follows: if $\omega = \alpha_{i_1,i_2,\ldots,i_k}(x_1,x_2,\ldots,x_n)dx_{i_1} \wedge dx_{i_2} \wedge \cdots \wedge dx_{i_k}$, $i_1 < i_2 < \cdots < i_k$, is a differential k-form, then

$$\star\omega = \operatorname{sign}(\pi)\alpha_{i_1,i_2,\ldots,i_k}(x_1,x_2,\ldots,x_n)dx_{j_1} \wedge \cdots \wedge dx_{n-k}, \tag{1.2}$$

where $\pi = (i_1,\ldots,i_k,j_1,\ldots,j_{n-k})$ is a permutation of $(1,\ldots,n)$ and $\operatorname{sign}(\pi)$ is the signature of permutation. The Hodge star operator $\star$ has the properties

$$\star\omega_I(x)dx_I = \star\omega_{i_1 i_2\cdots i_k}dx_{i_1} \wedge dx_{i_2} \wedge \cdots \wedge dx_{i_k} = (-1)^{\sum(I)}\omega_I dx_J, \tag{1.3}$$

where $I = (i_1,i_2,\ldots,i_k)$, $J = \{1,2,\ldots,n\} - I$, $\sum(I) = k(k+1)/2 + \sum_{j=1}^{k} i_j$. We should notice that $\star$ maps k-forms in $\mathbb{R}^n$ to $(n-k)$-forms for $0 \le k \le n$. For example, in $\mathbb{R}^3$, $\star dx_1 = (-1)^2 dx_2 \wedge dx_3 = dx_2 \wedge dx_3$.

2. Different versions of A-harmonic equations

We denote differential operator by $d : D'(\Omega, \wedge^l) \to D'(\Omega, \wedge^{l+1})$, for $l = 0,1,\ldots,n$. The Hodge codifferential operator $d^\star : D'(\Omega, \wedge^{l+1}) \to D'(\Omega, \wedge^l)$ is given by $d^\star = (-1)^{nl+1} \star d \star$ on $D'(\Omega, \wedge^{l+1})$, $l = 0,1,\ldots,n$. The differential equation

$$d^\star A(x, d\omega) = 0 \tag{2.1}$$

is called the A-*harmonic equation* and the nonlinear elliptic equation

$$d^\star A(x, d\omega) = B(x, d\omega) \tag{2.2}$$

is called the *nonhomogeneous* A-*harmonic equation* for differential forms, where $A : \Omega \times \wedge^l(\mathbb{R}^n) \to \wedge^l(\mathbb{R}^n)$ and $B : \Omega \times \wedge^l(\mathbb{R}^n) \to \wedge^{l-1}(\mathbb{R}^n)$ are operators satisfying the following conditions:

$$|A(x,\xi)| \le a|\xi|^{p-1}, \qquad |B(x,\xi)| \le b|\xi|^{p-1}, \qquad \langle A(x,\xi),\xi\rangle \ge |\xi|^p, \tag{2.3}$$

for almost every $x \in \Omega$ and all $\xi \in \wedge^l(\mathbb{R}^n)$. Here $a, b > 0$ are constants and $1 < p < \infty$ is a fixed exponent associated with (2.2). A solution to (2.2) is an element of the Sobolev space $W^{1,p}_{\text{loc}}(\Omega, \Lambda^{\ell-1})$ such that

$$\int_\Omega A(x, d\omega) \cdot d\varphi + B(x, d\omega) \cdot \varphi = 0, \tag{2.4}$$

for all $\varphi \in W^{1,p}_{\text{loc}}(\Omega, \Lambda^{\ell-1})$ with compact support. The solutions of the A-harmonic equation are called A-harmonic tensors.

Let $A : \Omega \times \wedge^l(\mathbb{R}^n) \to \wedge^l(\mathbb{R}^n)$ be defined by $A(x,\xi) = \xi|\xi|^{p-2}$ with $p > 1$. Then A satisfies the required conditions and (2.1) becomes the p-harmonic equation

$$d^\star(d\omega|d\omega|^{p-2}) = 0 \tag{2.5}$$

for differential forms. If we choose $p = 2$ in (2.5), (2.5) reduces to the Laplace equation

$$d^\star(d\omega) = 0. \tag{2.6}$$

If we choose ω to be a function u in (2.1), (2.2), (2.5), and (2.6), respectively, we obtain the following corresponding A-harmonic equation:

$$\operatorname{div} A(x, \nabla u) = 0, \tag{2.7}$$

the nonhomogeneous A-harmonic equation:

$$\operatorname{div} A(x, \nabla u) = B(x, \nabla u), \tag{2.8}$$

the p-Laplace equation or p-harmonic equation:

$$\operatorname{div}\left(\nabla u |\nabla u|^{p-2}\right) = 0, \tag{2.9}$$

and the Laplace equation or harmonic equation:

$$\operatorname{div}(\nabla u) = 0 \quad or \quad \Delta u = 0 \tag{2.10}$$

for functions. By a simple calculation, we know that (2.9) is equivalent to

$$(p-2)\sum_{k=1}^{n}\sum_{i=1}^{n} u_{x_k} u_{x_i} u_{x_k x_i} + |\nabla u|^2 \Delta u = 0. \tag{2.11}$$

In addition to the above harmonic equations for functions and differential forms, another kind of differential equations, the conjugate harmonic equations for differential forms, has also received much investigation in recent years, see [2, 6, 7]. Let u, v, g, and h be differential forms. Then, the equations

$$A(x, g + du) = h + d^\star v, \tag{2.12}$$

$$A(x, du) = d^\star v \tag{2.13}$$

are called the conjugate A-harmonic equations and the equation

$$du|du|^{p-2} = d^\star v \tag{2.14}$$

is called the conjugate p-harmonic equation [6]. Considering the length of the paper, we cannot list the results about these equations here. See [3, 6, 7] for recent results about (2.12) and (2.13). We should notice that (2.12) is also called the nonhomogeneous A-harmonic equation. It should be mentioned that in (2.12), (2.13), and (2.14), u is an $(l-1)$-form and v is an $(l+1)$-form. A pair (u, v) is called the conjugate A-harmonic fields or conjugate A-harmonic tensors.

3. Inequality with Orlicz norms

A continuously increasing function $\varphi : [0, \infty] \to [0, \infty]$ with $\varphi(0) = 0$ and $\varphi(\infty) = \infty$ is called an Orlicz function. The Orlicz space $L^\varphi(\Omega)$ consists of all measurable functions f on Ω such that $\int_\Omega \varphi(|f|/\lambda)dx < \infty$ for some $\lambda = \lambda(f) > 0$. $L^\varphi(\Omega)$ is equipped with the nonlinear Luxemburg functional

$$\|f\|_\varphi = \inf\left\{\lambda > 0 : \int_\Omega \varphi\left(\frac{|f|}{\lambda}\right) dx \le 1\right\}. \tag{3.1}$$

A convex Orlicz function φ is often called a Young function. If φ is a Young function, then $\|\cdot\|_\varphi$ defines a norm in $L^\varphi(\Omega)$, which is called the Luxemburg norm. For $\varphi(t) = t^p \log^\alpha(e+t)$, $0<p<\infty$, and $\alpha \geq 0$ (note that φ is convex for $1 \leq p < \infty$ and any real α with $\alpha \geq 1-p$), we have

$$\|f\|_{L^p \log^\alpha L} = \inf\left\{k : \int_\Omega |f|^p \log^\alpha\left(e + \frac{|f|}{k}\right) dx \leq k^p\right\}. \tag{3.2}$$

Let $0<p<\infty$ and $\alpha \geq 0$ be real numbers and let E be any subset of $\mathbb{R}^n$. We define the functional on a measurable function f over E by

$$[f]_{L^p(\log L)^\alpha(E)} = \left(\int_E |f|^p \log^\alpha\left(e + \frac{|f|}{\|f\|_p}\right) dx\right)^{1/p}, \tag{3.3}$$

where $\|f\|_p = (\int_E |f(x)|^p dx)^{1/p}$.

In 1999, Iwaniec and Verde proved in [8] that the norm $\|f\|_{L^p \log^\alpha L}$ is equivalent to the norm $[f]_{L^p(\log L)^\alpha(\Omega)}$ if $1 \leq p < \infty$ and $\alpha \geq 0$. Recently, we proved the following theorem (Theorem 3.1) in [4] which indicates that the norm $\|f\|_{L^p \log^\alpha L}$ is also equivalent to $[f]_{L^p(\log L)^\alpha(\Omega)}$ for $0<p<1$ and $\alpha \geq 0$.

Theorem 3.1. *For each $f \in L^p(\log L)^\alpha(\Omega)$, $0<p<\infty$, and $\alpha \geq 0$,*

$$\|f\|_p \leq \|f\|_{L^p \log^\alpha L} \leq [f]_{L^p(\log L)^\alpha(\Omega)} \leq C\|f\|_{L^p \log^\alpha L}, \tag{3.4}$$

where $C = 2^{\alpha/p}(1+(\alpha/ep)^\alpha)^{1/p}$ is a constant independent of f.

In 1999, Nolder proved the following local Hardy-Littlewood inequality for solutions to the conjugate A-harmonic equation in [9].

Lemma 3.2. *Let u and v be conjugate A-harmonic tensors in $\Omega \subset \mathbb{R}^n$, $\sigma > 1$, and $0 < s$, $t < \infty$. Then there exists a constant C, independent of u and v, such that*

$$\begin{aligned} \|u - u_Q\|_{s,Q} &\leq C|Q|^\beta \|v - c_1\|_{t,\sigma Q}^{q/p}, \\ \|v - v_Q\|_{t,Q} &\leq C|Q|^{-\beta p/q} \|u - c_2\|_{s,\sigma Q}^{p/q}, \end{aligned} \tag{3.5}$$

for all cubes Q with $\sigma Q \subset \Omega$. Here c_1 is any form in $W^1_{p,\mathrm{loc}}(\Omega,\Lambda)$ with $d^\star c_1 = 0$, c_2 is any form in $W^1_{q,\mathrm{loc}}(\Omega,\Lambda)$ with $dc_2 = 0$, and $\beta = 1/s + 1/n - (1/t+1/n)q/p$.

Using Lemma 3.2 and Theorem 3.1, we prove the following Hardy-Littlewood inequality with $L^p(\log L)^\alpha$-norms.

Theorem 3.3. *Let u and v be solutions to the conjugate A-harmonic equation (2.13) in $\Omega \subset \mathbb{R}^n$, $\sigma > 1$, and $0 < s, t < \infty$. Then there exists a constant C, independent of u and v, such that*

$$\|u - u_B\|_{L^s(\log L)^\alpha(B)} \leq C|B|^\gamma \|v - c\|_{L^t(\log L)^\beta(\sigma B)}^{q/p}, \tag{3.6}$$

for all balls or cubes B with $\sigma B \subset \Omega$ and all α with $0 < \alpha < s$ and $\beta \geq 0$. Here c is any form in $W^1_{p,\mathrm{loc}}(\Omega,\Lambda)$ with $d^\star c = 0$ and $\gamma = 1/s + 1/n - (1/t+1/n)q/p - \alpha/s^2$.

Proof. First, using Hölder inequality with $1/s = 1/(s^2/(s-\alpha)) + 1/(s^2/\alpha)$, we have

$$\begin{aligned}
&\left(\int_B |u-u_B|^s \log^\alpha\left(e+\frac{|u-u_B|}{\|u-u_B\|_s}\right)dx\right)^{1/s}\\
&= \left(\int_B \left(|u-u_B| \log^{\alpha/s}\left(e+\frac{|u-u_B|}{\|u-u_B\|_s}\right)\right)^s dx\right)^{1/s}\\
&\leq \left(\int_B |u-u_B|^{s^2/(s-\alpha)} dx\right)^{(s-\alpha)/s^2} \left(\int_B \log^s\left(e+\frac{|u-u_B|}{\|u-u_B\|_s}\right)dx\right)^{\alpha/s^2}\\
&= \|u-u_B\|_{s^2/(s-\alpha),B}\left(\int_B \log^s\left(e+\frac{|u-u_B|}{\|u-u_B\|_s}\right)dx\right)^{\alpha/s^2}.
\end{aligned} \tag{3.7}$$

Choosing parameter m with $0 < m < t$ and using the Hardy-Littlewood inequality (Lemma 3.2), we have

$$\|u-u_B\|_{s^2/(s-\alpha),B} \leq C_1|B|^{\gamma_1}\|v-c\|_{m,\sigma B}^{q/p}, \tag{3.8}$$

where $\gamma_1 = (s-\alpha)/s^2 + 1/n - (1/m+1/n)q/p$ and c is any coclosed form. Applying Hölder inequality with $1/m = 1/t + (t-m)/mt$, we obtain

$$\begin{aligned}
&\|v-c\|_{m,\sigma B}\\
&= \left(\int_{\sigma B}\left(|v-c|\log^{\beta/t}\left(e+\frac{|v-c|}{\|v-c\|_t}\right)\log^{-\beta/t}\left(e+\frac{|v-c|}{\|v-c\|_t}\right)\right)^m dx\right)^{1/m}\\
&\leq \left(\int_{\sigma B}|v-c|^t\log^\beta\left(e+\frac{|v-c|}{\|v-c\|_t}\right)dx\right)^{1/t}\left(\int_{\sigma B}\log^{-\beta m/(t-m)}\left(e+\frac{|v-c|}{\|v-c\|_t}\right)dx\right)^{(t-m)/mt}\\
&\leq \left(\int_{\sigma B}|v-c|^t\log^\beta\left(e+\frac{|v-c|}{\|v-c\|_t}\right)dx\right)^{1/t}\left(\int_{\sigma B}1dx\right)^{(t-m)/mt}\\
&\leq C_2|B|^{(t-m)/mt}\left(\int_{\sigma B}|v-c|^t\log^\beta\left(e+\frac{|v-c|}{\|v-c\|_t}\right)dx\right)^{1/t}.
\end{aligned} \tag{3.9}$$

Combining (3.7), (3.8), and (3.9) yields

$$\begin{aligned}
&\left(\int_B |u-u_B|^s \log^\alpha\left(e+\frac{|u-u_B|}{\|u-u_B\|_s}\right)dx\right)^{1/s}\\
&\leq C_3|B|^{\gamma_1+q(t-m)/mpt}\left(\int_{\sigma B}|v-c|^t\log^\beta\left(e+\frac{|v-c|}{\|v-c\|_t}\right)dx\right)^{q/pt}\\
&\quad\times\left(\int_B \log^s\left(e+\frac{|u-u_B|}{\|u-u_B\|_s}\right)dx\right)^{\alpha/s^2}.
\end{aligned} \tag{3.10}$$

Note that $x > \log(e+x)$ if $x \geq e$. Then

$$
\begin{aligned}
&\int_B \log^s\left(e+\frac{|u-u_B|}{\|u-u_B\|_s}\right)dx\\
&\quad=\int_{\{B:(|u-u_B|/\|u-u_B\|_s)<e\}} \log^s\left(e+\frac{|u-u_B|}{\|u-u_B\|_s}\right)dx\\
&\qquad+\int_{\{B:(|u-u_B|/\|u-u_B\|_s)\geq e\}} \log^s\left(e+\frac{|u-u_B|}{\|u-u_B\|_s}\right)dx \qquad (3.11)\\
&\quad\leq C_4+\int_B\left(\frac{|u-u_B|}{\|u-u_B\|_s}\right)^s dx\\
&\quad= C_4+\frac{1}{\|u-u_B\|_s^s}\int_B|u-u_B|^s dx\\
&\quad= C_5.
\end{aligned}
$$

Substituting (3.11) into (3.10), we find that

$$
\begin{aligned}
&\left(\int_B|u-u_B|^s\log^\alpha\left(e+\frac{|u-u_B|}{\|u-u_B\|_s}\right)dx\right)^{1/s}\\
&\quad\leq C_6|B|^{\gamma_1+q(t-m)/mpt}\left(\int_{\sigma B}|v-c|^t\log^\beta\left(e+\frac{|v-c|}{\|v-c\|_t}\right)dx\right)^{q/pt}.
\end{aligned}
\tag{3.12}
$$

A simple calculation gives

$$
\gamma_1+\frac{q(t-m)}{mpt}=\frac{1}{s}+\frac{1}{n}-\left(\frac{1}{n}+\frac{1}{t}\right)\frac{q}{p}-\frac{\alpha}{s^2}. \tag{3.13}
$$

Substituting (3.13) into (3.12), we have

$$
\left(\int_B|u-u_B|^s\log^\alpha\left(e+\frac{|u-u_B|}{\|u-u_B\|_s}\right)dx\right)^{1/s} \tag{3.14}
$$

$$
\leq C_6|B|^{\gamma}\left(\int_{\sigma B}|v-c|^t\log^\beta\left(e+\frac{|v-c|}{\|v-c\|_t}\right)dx\right)^{q/pt}, \tag{3.15}
$$

where $\gamma = 1/s+1/n-(1/t+1/n)q/p-\alpha/s^2$. By the equivalence of the norm $\|f\|_{L^p\log^\alpha L}$ and the functional $[f]_{L^p(\log L)^\alpha(\Omega)}$, we know that (3.15) is equivalent to (3.6). The proof of Theorem 3.3 has been completed. □

Iwaniec and Lutoborski proved the following result in [7]. Let $D\subset\mathbb{R}^n$ be a bounded, convex domain. To each $y\in D$ there corresponds a linear operator $K_y : C^\infty(D,\Lambda^l)\to C^\infty(D,\Lambda^{l-1})$ defined by

$$
(K_y\omega)(x;\xi_1,\ldots,\xi_l)=\int_0^1 t^{l-1}\omega(tx+y-ty;x-y,\xi_1,\ldots,\xi_{l-1})\,dt \tag{3.16}
$$

and the decomposition $\omega = d(K_y\omega) + K_y(d\omega)$. A homotopy operator $T : C^\infty(D,\Lambda^l) \to C^\infty(D,\Lambda^{l-1})$ is defined by averaging K_y over all points y in D $T\omega = \int_D \varphi(y)K_y\omega dy$, where $\varphi \in C_0^\infty(D)$ is normalized by $\int_D \varphi(y)dy = 1$. We define the l-form $\omega_D \in D'(D,\wedge^l)$ by

$$\omega_D = |D|^{-1}\int_D \omega(y)dy, \quad l = 0, \qquad \omega_D = d(T\omega), \quad l = 1,2,\dots,n, \tag{3.17}$$

for all $\omega \in L^p(D,\Lambda^l)$, $1 \le p < \infty$, then $T(d\omega) = \omega - \omega_D$. Thus, from Theorem 3.3, we have the following estimate for the composition of the homotopy operator T and the differential operator d:

$$||T(du)||_{L^s(\log L)^\alpha(B)} \le C|B|^\gamma \|v - c\|^{q/p}_{L^t(\log L)^\beta(\sigma B)} \tag{3.18}$$

if the condition in Theorem 3.3 is satisfied.

We will need the following A_r-weights or Muckenhoupt weights, and the weak reverse Hölder inequality for A_r-weights [5].

Muckenhoupt weights. A weight $w(x)$ is called an $A_r(E)$-weight in a set $E \subset \mathbb{R}^n$ for $r > 1$, write $w \in A_r(E)$ if

$$\sup_B \left(\frac{1}{|B|}\int_B w dx\right)\left(\frac{1}{|B|}\int_B \left(\frac{1}{w}\right)^{1/(r-1)} dx\right)^{r-1} < \infty \tag{3.19}$$

for any ball $B \subset E$.

Lemma 3.4. *If $w \in A_r$, $r > 1$, then there exist constants $\lambda > 1$ and C, independent of w, such that*

$$\|w\|_{\lambda,B} \le C|B|^{(1\ \ \lambda)/\lambda}\|w\|_{1,B} \tag{3.20}$$

for all cubes or balls $B \subset \mathbb{R}^n$.

We also prove the $A_r(\Omega)$-weighted Hardy-Littlewood inequality with $L^s(\log L)^\alpha$-norms.

Theorem 3.5. *In addition to the conditions in Theorem 3.3, assume that $w(x) \in A_r(\Omega)$ for some $r > 1$. Then*

$$||u - u_B||_{L^s(\log L)^\alpha(B,w)} \le C|B|^\gamma \|v - c\|^{q/p}_{L^t(\log L)^\beta(\sigma B, w^{pt/qs})} \tag{3.21}$$

for any ball B, where $\gamma = 1/s + 1/n - (1/n + 1/t)q/p - \alpha(\lambda - 1)/\lambda s^2$ and $\lambda > 1$ is the constant appearing in Lemma 3.4.

Proof. By Lemma 3.4, there exist constants $\lambda > 1$ and C_1, independent of w, such that

$$\|w\|_{\lambda,B} \le C_1|B|^{(1-\lambda)/\lambda}\|w\|_{1,B}. \tag{3.22}$$

For any constants $k_i > 0$, $i = 1,2,3$, there are constants $m > 0$ and $M > 0$ such that

$$m\log\left(e + \frac{x}{k_1}\right) \le \log\left(e + \frac{x}{k_2}\right) \le M\log\left(e + \frac{x}{k_3}\right), \tag{3.23}$$

for any $x > 0$. Therefore, we have

$$
\begin{aligned}
m&\left(\int_B |u|^t \log^\alpha\left(e+\frac{|u|}{k_1}\right)dx\right)^{1/t} \\
&\le \left(\int_B |u|^t \log^\alpha\left(e+\frac{|u|}{k_2}\right)dx\right)^{1/t} \le M\left(\int_B |u|^t \log^\alpha\left(e+\frac{|u|}{k_3}\right)dx\right)^{1/t}.
\end{aligned}
\tag{3.24}
$$

By properly selecting constants k_i, we will have different inequalities that we need. Choose $k = \lambda s/(\lambda - 1)$. Applying the Hölder inequality with $1/s = 1/k + (k-s)/ks$ and using (3.22) and (3.24), we find that

$$
\begin{aligned}
&\left(\int_B |u-u_B|^s \log^\alpha\left(e+\frac{|u-u_B|}{\|u-u_B\|_s}\right)w\,dx\right)^{1/s} \\
&\le \left(\int_B |u-u_B|^k \log^{\alpha k/s}\left(e+\frac{|u-u_B|}{\|u-u_B\|_s}\right)dx\right)^{1/k}\left(\int_B w^{k/(k-s)}dx\right)^{(k-s)/ks} \\
&\le \left(\int_B |u-u_B|^k \log^{\alpha k/s}\left(e+\frac{|u-u_B|}{\|u-u_B\|_s}\right)dx\right)^{1/k}\left(\int_B w^{\lambda}dx\right)^{1/\lambda s} \\
&\le C_2|B|^{(1-\lambda)/\lambda s}\left(\int_B |u-u_B|^k \log^{\alpha k/s}\left(e+\frac{|u-u_B|}{\|u-u_B\|_k}\right)dx\right)^{1/k}\|w\|_{1,B}^{1/s}.
\end{aligned}
\tag{3.25}
$$

Next, choose $m = qst/(qs + pt(r-1))$. Then, $0 < m < t$. From Theorem 3.3, we have

$$
\begin{aligned}
&\left(\int_B |u-u_B|^k \log^{\alpha k/s}\left(e+\frac{|u-u_B|}{\|u-u_B\|_k}\right)dx\right)^{1/k} \\
&\qquad \le C_3|B|^{\gamma'}\left(\int_{\sigma B} |v-c|^m \log^{\beta'}\left(e+\frac{|v-c|}{\|v-c\|_m}\right)dx\right)^{q/pm},
\end{aligned}
\tag{3.26}
$$

where $\gamma' = 1/k + 1/n - (1/n + 1/m)q/p - \alpha/ks$ and the parameter β' will be determined later. Using Hölder inequality again with $1/m = 1/t + (t-m)/mt$ and (3.24), we obtain

$$
\begin{aligned}
&\left(\int_{\sigma B} |v-c|^m \log^{\beta'}\left(e+\frac{|v-c|}{\|v-c\|_m}\right)dx\right)^{1/m} \\
&= \left(\int_{\sigma B}\left(|v-c|\log^{\beta'/m}\left(e+\frac{|v-c|}{\|v-c\|_m}\right)w^{p/qs}w^{-p/qs}\right)^m dx\right)^{1/m} \\
&\le \left(\int_{\sigma B} |v-c|^t \log^{\beta' t/m}\left(e+\frac{|v-c|}{\|v-c\|_m}\right)w^{pt/qs}dx\right)^{1/t}\left(\int_{\sigma B}\left(\frac{1}{w}\right)^{mpt/qs(t-m)}dx\right)^{(t-m)/mt} \\
&\le C_3\left(\int_{\sigma B} |v-c|^t \log^{\beta' t/m}\left(e+\frac{|v-c|}{\|v-c\|_t}\right)w^{pt/qs}dx\right)^{1/t}\left(\int_{\sigma B}\left(\frac{1}{w}\right)^{1/(r-1)}dx\right)^{p(r-1)/qs}.
\end{aligned}
\tag{3.27}
$$

Since $w \in A_r$, then

$$\begin{aligned} &\|w\|_{1,B}^{1/s}\left(\int_{\sigma B}\left(\frac{1}{w}\right)^{1/(r-1)}dx\right)^{(r-1)/s} \\ &\leq |\sigma B|^{r/s}\left(\left(\frac{1}{|\sigma B|}\int_{\sigma B} wdx\right)\left(\frac{1}{|\sigma B|}\int_{\sigma B}\left(\frac{1}{w}\right)^{1/(r-1)}dx\right)^{r-1}\right)^{1/s} \\ &\leq C_4|B|^{r/s}. \end{aligned} \tag{3.28}$$

Combining (3.25), (3.26), (3.27), and (3.28), we conclude that

$$\begin{aligned} &\left(\int_B |u-u_B|^s \log^{\alpha}\left(e+\frac{|u-u_B|}{\|u-u_B\|_s}\right)wdx\right)^{1/s} \\ &\leq C_5|B|^{\gamma}\left(\int_{\sigma B}|v-c|^t \log^{\beta' t/m}\left(e+\frac{|v-c|}{\|v-c\|_m}\right)w^{pt/qs}dx\right)^{q/pt}, \end{aligned} \tag{3.29}$$

where $\gamma = \gamma' + (1-\lambda)/\lambda s + r/s = 1/s + 1/n - (1/n + 1/t)q/p - \alpha(\lambda-1)/\lambda s^2$. Selecting $\beta' = \beta m/t$ and using (3.24), we have

$$\begin{aligned} &\left(\int_{\sigma B}|v-c|^t \log^{\beta' t/m}\left(e+\frac{|v-c|}{\|v-c\|_m}\right)w^{pt/qs}dx\right)^{q/pt} \\ &\leq C_6\left(\int_{\sigma B}|v-c|^t \log^{\beta}\left(e+\frac{|v-c|}{\|v-c\|_t}\right)w^{pt/qs}dx\right)^{q/pt}. \end{aligned} \tag{3.30}$$

Substituting (3.30) into (3.29) yields

$$\begin{aligned} &\left(\int_B |u-u_B|^s \log^{\alpha}\left(e+\frac{|u-u_B|}{\|u-u_B\|_s}\right)wdx\right)^{1/s} \\ &\leq C_7|B|^{\gamma}\left(\int_{\sigma B}|v-c|^t \log^{\beta}\left(e+\frac{|v-c|}{\|v-c\|_t}\right)w^{pt/qs}dx\right)^{q/pt}, \end{aligned} \tag{3.31}$$

which is equivalent to

$$\|u-u_B\|_{L^s(\log L)^{\alpha}(B,w)} \leq C|B|^{\gamma}\|v-c\|^{q/p}_{L^t(\log L)^{\beta}(\sigma B, w^{pt/qs})} \tag{3.32}$$

by the equivalence of the norm $\|f\|_{L^p\log^{\alpha}L}$ and the functional $[f]_{L^p(\log L)^{\alpha}(\Omega)}$. The proof of Theorem 3.5 has been completed. □

From [5], we know that if $w \in A_r(E)$ and $0 < \eta \leq 1$, then $w^{\eta} \in A_r(E)$. Therefore, under the same condition of Theorem 3.5, we also have the following local estimate:

$$\|u-u_B\|_{L^s(\log L)^{\alpha}(B,w^{\eta})} \leq C|B|^{\gamma}\|v-c\|^{q/p}_{L^t(\log L)^{\beta}(\sigma B, w^{\eta pt/qs})}. \tag{3.33}$$

In 1999, Nolder also proved the following global Hardy-Littlewood inequality with L^s-norms in John domain Ω [9].

THEOREM 3.6. *Let $u \in D'(\Omega, \Lambda^0)$ and $v \in D'(\Omega, \Lambda^2)$ be conjugate A-harmonic tensors. Let $q \le p$, $v - c \in L^t(\Omega, \Lambda^2)$, and $s > 0$ and $t > 0$ satisfy $1/s + 1/n - (1/t + 1/n)q/p = 0$. Then there exists a constant C, independent of u and v, such that*

$$||u - u_{B_0}||_{s,\Omega} \le C||v - c||_{t,\Omega}^{q/p}, \tag{3.34}$$

for any δ-John domain $\Omega \subset \mathbb{R}^n$. Here c is any form in $W^1_{q,\mathrm{loc}}(\Omega, \Lambda)$ with $d^*c = 0$ and $B_0 \subset \Omega$ is a fixed ball.

Finally, we prove the following global Hardy-Littlewood inequality with $L^s(\log L)^\alpha$-norms in δ-John domains. See [2] or [9] for the definition of the δ-John domains.

THEOREM 3.7. *Let $u \in D'(\Omega, \Lambda^0)$ and $v \in D'(\Omega, \Lambda^2)$ be solutions to the conjugate A-harmonic equation (2.13) in a δ-John domain $\Omega \subset \mathbb{R}^n$. Let $q \le p$, $v - c \in L^t(\log L)^\beta(\Omega, \Lambda^2)$, and $s > 0$ and $t > 0$ satisfy $1/s + 1/n - (1/t + 1/n)q/p - \alpha/s^2 = 0$. Then there exists a constant C, independent of u and v, such that*

$$||u - u_{B_0}||_{L^s(\log L)^\alpha(\Omega)} \le C||v - c||_{L^t(\log L)^\beta(\Omega)}^{q/p}, \tag{3.35}$$

where $0 < \alpha < s$ and $\beta > 0$ are constants, c is any form in $W^1_{q,\mathrm{loc}}(\Omega, \Lambda)$ with $d^*c = 0$, and $B_0 \subset \Omega$ is a fixed ball.

Proof. Applying the Hölder inequality with $1/s = 1/(s^2/(s-\alpha)) + 1/(s^2/\alpha)$, we obtain

$$\begin{aligned}
||u - u_{B_0}||_{L^s(\log L)^\alpha(\Omega)} &= \left(\int_\Omega |u - u_{B_0}|^s \log^\alpha\left(e + \frac{|u - u_{B_0}|}{||u - u_{B_0}||_{s,\Omega}}\right) dx\right)^{1/s} \\
&\le \left(\int_\Omega |u - u_{B_0}|^{s^2/(s-\alpha)} dx\right)^{(s-\alpha)/s^2} \left(\int_\Omega \log^s\left(e + \frac{|u - u_{B_0}|}{||u - u_{B_0}||_{s,\Omega}}\right) dx\right)^{\alpha/s^2} \\
&= ||u - u_{B_0}||_{s^2/(s-\alpha),\Omega} \left(\int_\Omega \log^s\left(e + \frac{|u - u_{B_0}|}{||u - u_{B_0}||_{s,\Omega}}\right) dx\right)^{\alpha/s^2}.
\end{aligned} \tag{3.36}$$

Since $(s-\alpha)/s^2 + 1/n - (1/m + 1/n)q/p = 0$, using Theorem 3.6, we have

$$||u - u_{B_0}||_{s^2/(s-\alpha),\Omega} \le C_1 ||v - c||_{t,\Omega}^{q/p}. \tag{3.37}$$

Combining (3.36) and (3.37) yields

$$||u - u_{B_0}||_{L^s(\log L)^\alpha(\Omega)} \le C_1 ||v - c||_{t,\Omega}^{q/p} \cdot \left(\int_\Omega \log^s\left(e + \frac{|u - u_{B_0}|}{||u - u_{B_0}||_{s,\Omega}}\right) dx\right)^{\alpha/s^2}. \tag{3.38}$$

Similar to (3.11), we can prove that

$$\int_\Omega \log^s\left(e + \frac{|u - u_{B_0}|}{||u - u_{B_0}||_{s,\Omega}}\right) dx \le C_2. \tag{3.39}$$

Substituting (3.39) into (3.38) and using $\log^{\beta}(e+|v-c|/\|v-c\|_{t,\Omega})>1$, we find that

$$\begin{aligned}\|u-u_{B_0}\|_{L^s(\log L)^{\alpha}(\Omega)} &\leq C_3\|v-c\|_{t,\Omega}^{q/p}\\ &\leq C_3\left(\int_{\Omega}|v-c|^t\log^{\beta}\left(e+\frac{|v-c|}{\|v-c\|_{t,\Omega}}\right)dx\right)^{q/pt}\\ &\leq C_3\|v-c\|_{L^t(\log L)^{\beta}(\Omega)}^{q/p}.\end{aligned} \tag{3.40}$$

The proof of Theorem 3.7 has been completed. □

References

[1] R. P. Agarwal and S. Ding, *Advances in differential forms and the A-harmonic equation*, Mathematical and Computer Modelling **37** (2003), no. 12-13, 1393–1426.

[2] S. Ding, *Weighted Hardy-Littlewood inequality for A-harmonic tensors*, Proceedings of the American Mathematical Society **125** (1997), no. 6, 1727–1735.

[3] ———, *Local and global norm comparison theorems for solutions to the nonhomogeneous A-harmonic equation*, preprint.

[4] S. Ding and B. Liu, *Global integrability of the Jacobian of a composite mapping*, to appear in Journal of Inequalities and Applications.

[5] J. Heinonen, T. Kilpeläinen, and O. Martio, *Nonlinear Potential Theory of Degenerate Elliptic Equations*, Oxford Mathematical Monographs, The Clarendon Press, Oxford University Press, New York, 1993.

[6] T. Iwaniec, *p-harmonic tensors and quasiregular mappings*, Annals of Mathematics. Second Series **136** (1992), no. 3, 589–624.

[7] T. Iwaniec and A. Lutoborski, *Integral estimates for null Lagrangians*, Archive for Rational Mechanics and Analysis **125** (1993), no. 1, 25–79.

[8] T. Iwaniec and A. Verde, *On the operator $L(f)=f\log|f|$*, Journal of Functional Analysis **169** (1999), no. 2, 391–420.

[9] C. A. Nolder, *Hardy-Littlewood theorems for A-harmonic tensors*, Illinois Journal of Mathematics **43** (1999), no. 4, 613–632.

Shusen Ding: Department of Mathematics, Seattle University, Seattle, WA 98122, USA
E-mail address: sding@seattleu.edu

NONOSCILLATION OF ONE OF THE COMPONENTS OF THE SOLUTION VECTOR

ALEXANDER DOMOSHNITSKY

Theorem about equivalence on nonoscillation of one of the components of the solution vector, positivity of corresponding elements of the Green matrix, and an assertion about a differential inequality of the de La Vallee Poussin type is presented in this paper. On this basis, several coefficient tests of the component's nonoscillation are obtained. It is demonstrated that each of the tests is best possible in a corresponding sense.

1. Comparison of solutions

Consider the following system:

$$(M_i x)(t) \equiv x_i'(t) + \sum_{j=1}^{n} (B_{ij}x_j)(t) = f_i(t), \quad t \in [0,\omega],\ i = 1,\dots,n, \tag{1.1}$$

where $x = \mathrm{col}(x_1,\dots,x_n)$, $B_{ij} : C_{[0,\omega]} \to L_{[0,\omega]}$, $i,j = 1,\dots,n$, are linear continuous operators, $C_{[0,\omega]}$ and $L_{[0,\omega]}$ are the spaces of continuous and summable functions $y : [0,\omega] \to R^1$, respectively.

Oscillation of two-dimensional linear differential systems with deviating arguments was defined by many authors as oscillation of all components of the solution vector (see the recent paper [9] and bibliography therein). However, the components of the solution vector can have a different oscillation behavior. For example, in the system

$$\begin{aligned} x_1'(t) + p_{11}x_1(t-\tau_{11}) &= 0,\\ x_2'(t) + p_{22}x_2(t-\tau_{22}) &= 0, \end{aligned} \tag{1.2}$$

where $p_{11}\tau_{11} \le 1/e$, $p_{22}\tau_{22} > 1/e$, the first component nonoscillates and the second one oscillates. The different oscillation behavior can be also found in a case of systems with

Hindawi Publishing Corporation
Proceedings of the Conference on Differential & Difference Equations and Applications, pp. 363–371

off-diagonal terms. For instance, the system

$$x_1'(t) - x_1(t) + \cos t\, x_2(t) + \sin t\, x_2\left(t - \frac{\pi}{2}\right) = 0,$$
$$x_2'(t) + a\sin t\, x_1(t) + bx_2\left(t - \frac{\pi}{2}\right) = 0, \tag{1.3}$$

where $a+b=1$, has a solution $x_1 = 1$, $x_2 = \cos t$.

In this paper, we study nonoscillation of one of the components of the solution vector. A relation between nonoscillation of the component x_r and the property D (see Definition 1.1) will be established.

Let $l : C^n_{[0,\omega]} \to \mathbb{R}^n$ be a linear bounded functional. The following boundary value problem:

$$(M_i x)(t) = f_i(t), \quad t \in [0,\omega],\ i = 1,\dots,n,\ lx = \alpha, \tag{1.4}$$

where $\alpha \in R^n$, can be considered. We focus our attention upon the problem of comparison for one of the components of solution vector.

Definition 1.1. Say that boundary value problem (1.4) satisfies the property D for the component x_r if from the conditions

$$(-1)^{k_i}\left[(M_i x)(t) - (M_i y)(t)\right] \geq 0, \quad t \in [0,\omega],\ lx = ly,\ i = 1,\dots,n, \tag{1.5}$$

where k_i $(i = 1,\dots,n)$ is either 1 or 2, the inequality

$$x_r(t) \geq y_r(t), \quad t \in [0,\omega], \tag{1.6}$$

follows.

In the main assertion of this paper, an equivalence of this property for the Cauchy and several other boundary value problems and nonoscillation of the component x_r of the solution vector of system (1.1) on $[0,\omega]$ will be established. Various coefficient tests of nonoscillation of x_r will be proposed. It is demonstrated that these tests are best possible in corresponding cases.

The property D is weakening of the following property, known in the literature [12] as the applicability of Tchaplygin's theorem.

Definition 1.2. Say that Tchaplygin's theorem is applicable to boundary value problem (1.4) if from the conditions

$$(M_i x)(t) \geq (M_i y)(t), \quad t \in [0,\omega],\ i = 1,\dots,n,\ lx = ly, \tag{1.7}$$

it follows that

$$x_i(t) \geq y_i(t), \quad t \in [0,\omega],\ i = 1,\dots,n. \tag{1.8}$$

Let us find up the relation between this property and the positivity of Green's matrices.

If the homogeneous boundary value problem $(M_i x)(t) = 0$, $t \in [0,\omega]$, $i = 1,\dots,n$, $lx = 0$, has only the trivial solution, then the boundary value problem (1.4) has for each $f_i \in L_{[0,\omega]}$, $i = 1,\dots,n$, $\alpha \in \mathbb{R}^n$ a unique solution, which has the following representation [2]:

$$x(t) = \int_0^{\omega} G(t,s)f(s)ds + X(t)\alpha, \quad t \in [0,\omega], \tag{1.9}$$

where the $n\times n$ matrix $G(t,s)$ is called Green's matrix of problem (1.4), $X(t)$ is an $n\times n$ fundamental matrix of the system $(M_i x)(t) = 0$, $i = 1,\dots,n$, such that $lX = E$ (E is the unit $n\times n$ matrix), and $f = \operatorname{col}(f_1,\dots,f_n)$. It is clear from the solution representation (1.9) that the matrices $G(t,s)$ and $X(t)$ determine all properties of solutions. If Green's matrix $G(t,s)$ is positive, for example, then Tchaplygin's theorem is applicable to problem (1.4). From the formula of the solution's representation, it follows that the property D is reduced to sign-constancy of all elements standing only in the rth row of Green's matrix.

The great importance of the property (1.7)-(1.8) in the approximate integration was noted by Tchaplygin [13]. Series of papers, started with the known paper by Luzin [12], were devoted to the various aspects of Tchaplygin's approximate method of integration. Note in this connection the well-known monograph by Lakshmikantham and Leela [10] and the recent monograph by Kiguradze and Puza [8].

As a particular case of system (1.1), let us consider the delay system

$$x_i'(t) + \sum_{j=1}^{n} p_{ij}(t)x_j(h_{ij}(t)) = f_i(t), \quad i = 1,\dots,n,\ t \in [0,\omega], \tag{1.10}$$

$$x(\theta) = 0 \quad \text{for } \theta < 0, \tag{1.11}$$

where p_{ij} are measurable essentially bounded functions, and h_{ij} are measurable functions such that $h_{ij}(t) \le t$ for $i,j = 1,\dots,n$, $t \in [0,\omega]$. Its general solution has the representation

$$x(t) = \int_0^{t} C(t,s)f(s)ds + C(t,0)x(0), \quad t \in [0,\omega], \tag{1.12}$$

where $C(t,s) = \{C_{ij}(t,s)\}_{i,j=1,\dots,n}$ is called the Cauchy matrix of system (1.10). Note that for each fixed s, the matrix $C(t,s)$ is the fundamental matrix of the system

$$\begin{gathered} x_i'(t) + \sum_{j=1}^{n} p_{ij}(t)x_j(h_{ij}(t)) = 0, \quad i = 1,\dots,n,\ t \in [0,\omega], \\ x(\theta) = 0 \quad \text{for } \theta < s, \end{gathered} \tag{1.13}$$

such that $C(s,s)$ is the unit $n\times n$ matrix [2].

The classical Wazewskii's theorem [14] claims that the condition

$$p_{ij} \leq 0 \quad \text{for } j \neq i,\ i,j = 1,\dots,n, \tag{1.14}$$

is necessary and sufficient for nonnegativity of all elements $C_{ij}(t,s)$ of the Cauchy matrix and consequently of the property (1.7)-(1.8) for system of ordinary differential equations:

$$x_i'(t) + \sum_{j=1}^{n} p_{ij}(t)x_j(t) = f_i(t), \quad i = 1,\dots,n,\ t \in [0,\omega]. \tag{1.15}$$

The property D leads to essentially less-hard limitations on the given system.

Our technique in proofs of main assertions of the paper is based on a construction of a corresponding scalar functional differential equation for the nth component of the solution vector and then we use the assertions of [1] about the differential inequalities, nonoscillation, and positivity of Green's functions of corresponding boundary value problems for first-order scalar functional differential equations. In this sense this approach is similar to the idea of the classical Gauss method for solving systems of the linear algebraic equations.

The problem of the asymptotic stability of delay differential systems is one of the most important applications of results on positivity of the Cauchy matrix $C(t,s)$. The corresponding technique in study of the exponential stability was presented in [4] and in other terminologies in [5], where necessary and sufficient conditions of the exponential stability for system possessing positivity of the Cauchy matrix were obtained, (see, also, a development of this approach in [6]).

2. Nonoscillation of the nth component of the solution vector

In this section, we consider the system

$$(M_i x)(t) \equiv x_i'(t) + \sum_{j=1}^{n} (B_{ij}x_j)(t) = f_i(t), \quad t \in [0,\omega],\ i = 1,\dots,n, \tag{2.1}$$

where $B_{ij} : C_{[0,\omega]} \to L_{[0,\omega]}$ are linear bounded Volterra operators for $i,j = 1,\dots,n$.

Together with system (2.1), let us consider the following auxiliary system of the order $n-1$:

$$x_i'(t) + \sum_{j=1}^{n-1} (B_{ij}x_j)(t) = f_i(t), \quad t \in [0,\omega],\ i = 1,\dots,n-1, \tag{2.2}$$

and denote by $K(t,s) = \{K_{ij}(t,s)\}_{i,j=1,\dots,n-1}$ its Cauchy matrix. Denote by $G(t,s) = \{G_{ij}(t,s)\}_{i,j=1,\dots,n}$ and $P(t,s) = \{P_{ij}(t,s)\}_{i,j=1,\dots,n}$ Green's matrices of the problems consisting of (2.1) and one of the boundary conditions

$$x_i(0) = 0, \quad i = 1,\dots,n-1, \qquad x_n(\omega) = 0, \tag{2.3}$$

or

$$x_i(0) = 0, \quad i = 1,\dots,n-1, \qquad x_n(0) = x_n(\omega), \tag{2.4}$$

respectively.

THEOREM 2.1. *Let all elements of the* $(n-1)\times(n-1)$ *Cauchy matrix* $K(t,s)$ *of system (2.2) be nonnegative, let each of the operators* B_{jn} *and* B_{nj} *be positive or negative, while let the product* $-B_{nj}B_{jn}$ *be positive operators for* $j = 1,\dots,n-1$.

If B_{ni} *for* $i = 1,\dots,n-1$ *are negative operators, then the following five assertions are equivalent:*

(1) *there exists an absolutely continuous vector function* v *such that* $v_n(t) > 0$, $v_i(0) \le 0$ *for* $i = 1,\dots,n-1$, $(M_iv)(t) \le 0$ *for* $i = 1,\dots,n$, $t \in [0,\omega]$;

(2) $C_{nn}(t,s) > 0$, $C_{nj}(t,s) \ge 0$ *for* $j = 1,\dots,n-1$, $0 \le s \le t \le \omega$;

(3) *the boundary value problem (2.1), (2.3) is uniquely solvable and its Green's matrix satisfies the inequalities* $G_{nj}(t,s) \le 0$ *for* $j = 1,\dots,n$, $t,s \in [0,\omega]$, *while* $G_{nn}(t,s) < 0$ *for* $0 \le t < s \le \omega$;

(4) *if in addition the operator* B, *determined by equality*

$$(Bx_n)(t) \equiv -\sum_{i=1}^{n-1} B_{ni}\left\{\int_0^t \sum_{j=1}^{n-1} K_{ij}(t,s)(B_{jn}x_n)(s)ds\right\}(t) + (B_{nn}x_n)(t), \quad t \in [0,\omega], \tag{2.5}$$

is nonzero operator, the boundary value problem (2.1), (2.4) is uniquely solvable and its Green's matrix satisfies the inequalities $P_{nj}(t,s) \ge 0$ *for* $j = 1,\dots,n$, *while* $P_{nn}(t,s) > 0$ *for* $t,s \in [0,\omega]$;

(5) *the nth component of the solution vector* x *of the homogeneous system* $M_ix = 0$, $i = 1,\dots,n$, *such that* $x_i(0) \ge 0$, $i = 1,\dots,n-1$, $x_n(0) > 0$, *is positive for* $t \in [0,\omega]$.

If B_{ni} *for* $i = 1,\dots,n-1$ *are positive operators, then the following five assertions are equivalent:*

(1*) *there exists an absolutely continuous vector function* v *such that* $v_n(t) > 0$, $v_i(0) \ge 0$, $(M_iv)(t) \ge 0$ *for* $i = 1,\dots,n-1$, $(M_nv)(t) \le 0$ *for* $t \in [0,\omega]$;

(2*) $C_{nn}(t,s) > 0$, $C_{nj}(t,s) \le 0$ *for* $j = 1,\dots,n-1$, $0 \le s \le t \le \omega$;

(3*) *the boundary value problem (2.1), (2.3) is uniquely solvable and its Green's matrix satisfies the inequalities* $G_{nj}(t,s) \ge 0$ *for* $j = 1,\dots,n-1$, $G_{nn}(t,s) \le 0$ *for* $t,s \in [0,\omega]$ *while* $G_{nn}(t,s) < 0$ *for* $0 \le t < s \le \omega$;

(4*) *if in addition the operator* B, *is nonzero operator, the boundary value problem (2.1), (2.4) is uniquely solvable and its Green's matrix satisfies the inequalities* $P_{nj}(t,s) \le 0$ *for* $j = 1,\dots,n$, $P_{nn}(t,s) > 0$ *for* $t,s \in [0,\omega]$;

(5*) *the nth component of the solution vector* x *of the homogeneous system* $M_ix = 0$, $i = 1,\dots,n$, *such that* $x_i(0) \le 0$, $i = 1,\dots,n-1$, $x_n(0) > 0$, *is positive for* $t \in [0,\omega]$.

Remark 2.2. The assertions (1)–(5) and (1*)–(5*) are analogs for the nth component of the solution vector of nth-order functional differential systems of the classical de La Vallee Poussin theorem about the differential inequality obtained in [3] for ordinary second-order equations. Assertions (2)–(5), (2*)–(5*), (3)–(5), and (3*)–(5*) are analogs of the corresponding assertions connecting nonoscillation and positivity of Green's functions for the nth-order ordinary differential equations [11].

Let us write system (1.10) in the following form:

$$x_i'(t)+\sum_{j=1}^{n} p_{ij}(t)x_j(t-\tau_{ij}(t)) = f_i(t), \quad i=1,\dots,n,\ t\in[0,+\infty), \tag{2.6}$$

where $\tau_{ij}\geq 0$ for $i,j=1,\dots,n$.

Let us introduce the following denotations: $p_{ij}^{*}=\operatorname{ess\,sup} p_{ij}(t)$, $p_{ij*}=\operatorname{ess\,inf} p_{ij}(t)$, $\tau_{ij}^{*}=\operatorname{ess\,sup}\tau_{ij}(t)$, $\tau_{ij*}=\operatorname{ess\,inf}\tau_{ij}(t)$, $p_{ij}^{+}(t)=\max\{0,p_{ij}(t)\}$.

Theorem 2.3. *Let the following conditions be fulfilled:*

(1) $p_{ij}\leq 0$ *for* $i\neq j$, $i,j=1,\dots,n-1$;
(2) $p_{jn}\geq 0$, $p_{nj}\leq 0$ *for* $j=1,\dots,n-1$;
(3) $\tau_{ii}^{*}(p_{ii}^{+})^{*}\leq 1/e$, *for* $i=1,\dots,n-1$;
(4) *there exists a positive* α *such that* $\tau_{ij}^{*}\alpha\leq 1/e$ *for* $i=1,\dots,n$, *and*

$$p_{nn}^{+}(t)e^{\alpha\tau_{nn}(t)}-\sum_{j=1}^{n-1}p_{nj}(t)e^{\alpha\tau_{nj}(t)}\leq\alpha\leq\min_{1\leq i\leq n-1}\Big\{p_{ii}(t)e^{\alpha\tau_{ii}(t)}+\sum_{j=1,i\neq j}^{n}p_{ij}(t)e^{\alpha\tau_{nj}(t)}\Big\}, \tag{2.7}$$

where $t\in[0,+\infty)$.

Then the elements of the nth row of the Cauchy matrix of system (2.6) satisfy the inequalities

$$C_{nj}(t,s)\geq 0,\quad C_{nn}(t,s)>0,\quad j=1,\dots,n-1,\ 0\leq s\leq t<+\infty. \tag{2.8}$$

The idea of the proof is to demonstrate that the vector

$$v_i(t)=-e^{-\alpha t},\quad i=1,\dots,n-1,\qquad v_n(t)=e^{-\alpha t},\quad t\in[0,+\infty), \tag{2.9}$$

satisfies condition (1) of Theorem 2.1.

For the ordinary differential system

$$x_i'(t)+\sum_{j=1}^{n}p_{ij}(t)x_j(t)=f_i(t),\quad i=1,\dots,n,\ t\in[0,+\infty), \tag{2.10}$$

Theorem 2.3 implies the following assertion.

Theorem 2.4. *Let the following conditions be fulfilled:*

(1) $p_{ij}\leq 0$ *for* $i\neq j$, $i,j=1,\dots,n-1$;
(2) $p_{jn}\geq 0$, $p_{nj}\leq 0$ *for* $j=1,\dots,n-1$;
(3) *there exists a positive* α *such that*

$$p_{nn}^{+}(t)-\sum_{j=1}^{n-1}p_{nj}(t)\leq\alpha\leq\min_{1\leq i\leq n-1}\Big\{p_{ii}(t)+\sum_{j=1,i\neq j}^{n}p_{ij}(t)\Big\},\quad t\in[0,+\infty). \tag{2.11}$$

Then the elements of the nth row of the Cauchy matrix of system (2.10) satisfy the inequalities $C_{nn}(t,s) > 0$, $C_{nj}(t,s) \geq 0$ *for* $j = 1,\ldots,n-1$, $0 \leq s \leq t < +\infty$.

Consider now the following ordinary differential system of the second order

$$\begin{aligned} x_1'(t) + p_{11}(t)x_1(t) + p_{12}(t)x_2(t) &= f_1(t), \\ x_2'(t) + p_{21}(t)x_1(t) + p_{22}(t)x_2(t) &= f_2(t), \end{aligned} \quad t \in [0,+\infty). \tag{2.12}$$

THEOREM 2.5. *Let the following conditions be fulfilled:*
(1) $p_{11} \geq 0$, $p_{12} \geq 0$, $p_{21} \leq 0$, $p_{22} \geq 0$;
(2) *there exists a positive* α *such that*

$$p_{22}(t) - p_{21}(t) \leq \alpha \leq p_{11}(t) - p_{12}(t), \quad t \in [0,+\infty). \tag{2.13}$$

Then the elements of the second row of the Cauchy matrix of system (2.12) satisfy the inequalities $C_{21}(t,s) \geq 0$, $C_{22}(t,s) > 0$ *for* $0 \leq s \leq t < +\infty$.

Remark 2.6. If coefficients p_{ij} are constants, the second condition in Theorem 2.5 is as follows:

$$p_{22} - p_{21} \leq p_{11} - p_{12}. \tag{2.14}$$

Remark 2.7. Let us demonstrate that inequality (2.14) (and consequently inequality (2.13)) is best possible in a corresponding case. It is known that for each fixed s the 2×2 matrix $C(t,s)$ is a fundamental matrix $X(t)$ of system (2.15) satisfying the condition $C(s,s) = E$, where E is the unit 2×2 matrix. Theorem 2.5 claims that the elements in the second row of the fundamental matrices are positive. The characteristic equation of the system

$$\begin{aligned} x_1'(t) + p_{11}x_1(t) + p_{12}x_2(t) &= 0, \\ x_2'(t) + p_{21}x_1(t) + p_{22}x_2(t) &= 0, \end{aligned} \quad t \in [0,+\infty), \tag{2.15}$$

with constant coefficients is as follows:

$$\lambda^2 + (p_{11} + p_{22})\lambda + p_{11}p_{22} - p_{12}p_{21} = 0, \tag{2.16}$$

and its roots are real if and only if

$$(p_{11} - p_{22})^2 \geq -4p_{12}p_{21}. \tag{2.17}$$

Let us instead of inequality (2.14) consider

$$p_{22} - p_{21} \leq p_{11} - p_{12} + \varepsilon, \tag{2.18}$$

where ε is any positive constant. We can set $p_{11} = p_{22}$, then the inequality becomes of the following form $p_{12} - p_{21} \leq \varepsilon$. If $p_{12}p_{21} < 0$, then inequality (2.17) is not satisfied and consequently each element of the fundamental and the Cauchy matrices oscillates.

In the following assertion, we propose an efficient test of nonnegativity of elements in the nth row of the Cauchy matrix in case when the coefficients $|p_{nj}|$ are small enough for $j = 1,\dots,n-1$.

THEOREM 2.8. *Let the following conditions be fulfilled:*
(1) $p_{ij} \le 0$ *for* $i \ne j$, $i, j = 1,\dots,n-1$;
(2) $p_{jn} \ge 0$, $p_{nj} \le 0$ *for* $j = 1,\dots,n-1$;
(3) $\tau_{ij} = 0$ *for* $i = 1,\dots,n$, $j = 1,\dots,n-1$, $\tau_{nn} = \text{const}$;
(4) *the following inequalities*

$$p_{nn}^{+}(t)\tau_{nn}\exp\left\{\tau_{nn}\sum_{j=1}^{n-1}|p_{nj}|^{*}\right\} \le \frac{1}{e}, \quad t \in [0,+\infty), \tag{2.19}$$

$$\frac{1}{\tau_{nn}} + \sum_{j=1}^{n-1}|p_{nj}|^{*} \le \min_{1\le i\le n-1}\left\{p_{ii}(t) + \sum_{j=1,i\ne j}^{n} p_{ij}(t)\right\}, \quad t \in [0,+\infty), \tag{2.20}$$

are fulfilled.

Then the elements of the nth row of the Cauchy matrix of system (2.6) satisfy the inequalities $C_{nn}(t,s) > 0$, $C_{nj}(t,s) \ge 0$ *for* $j = 1,\dots,n-1$, $0 \le s \le t < +\infty$.

Remark 2.9. It should be noted that inequality (2.19) is best possible in the following sense. If $p_{nj} = 0$ for $j = 1,\dots,n-1$, $p_{nn} = \text{const} > 0$, then inequality (2.19) becomes as follows:

$$p_{nn}\tau_{nn} \le \frac{1}{e}, \quad t \in [0,+\infty), \tag{2.21}$$

and $C_{nn}(t,s) = c_n(t,s)$, where $c_n(t,s)$ is the Cauchy function of the diagonal equation

$$x_n'(t) + p_{nn}x(t-\tau_{nn}) = 0, \quad t \in [0,+\infty). \tag{2.22}$$

The opposite inequality $p_{nn}\tau_{nn} > 1/e$ implies oscillation of all solutions [7] and by virtue of [1] $c_n(t,s)$ changes its sign. Now it is clear that we cannot substitute

$$p_{nn}^{+}(t)\tau_{nn}\exp\left\{\tau_{nn}\sum_{j=1}^{n-1}|p_{nj}|^{*}\right\} \le \frac{1+\varepsilon}{e}, \quad t \in [0,+\infty), \tag{2.23}$$

where ε is any positive number instead of inequality (2.19).

References

[1] R. P. Agarwal and A. Domoshnitsky, *Non-oscillation of the first-order differential equations with unbounded memory for stabilization by control signal*, Applied Mathematics and Computation **173** (2006), no. 1, 177–195.

[2] N. Azbelev, V. Maksimov, and L. Rakhmatullina, *Introduction to the Theory of Linear Functional-Differential Equations*, Advanced Series in Mathematical Science and Engineering, vol. 3, World Federation Publishers, Georgia, 1995.

[3] Ch. J. de La Vallee Poussin, *Sur l'equation differentielle lineaire du second ordre*, Journal de Mathématiques Pures et Appliquées **8** (1929), no. 9, 125–144.

[4] A. Domoshnitsky and M. V. Sheina, *Nonnegativity of the Cauchy matrix and the stability of a system of linear differential equations with retarded argument*, Differentsial'nye Uravneniya **25** (1989), no. 2, 201–208, 360.

[5] I. Györi, *Interaction between oscillations and global asymptotic stability in delay differential equations*, Differential & Integral Equations **3** (1990), no. 1, 181–200.

[6] I. Györi and F. Hartung, *Fundamental solution and asymptotic stability of linear delay differential equations*, Dynamics of Continuous, Discrete and Impulsive Systems **13** (2006), no. 2, 261–287.

[7] I. Györi and G. Ladas, *Oscillation Theory of Delay Differential Equations*, Oxford Mathematical Monographs, The Clarendon Press, Oxford University Press, New York, 1991.

[8] I. Kiguradze and B. Půža, *Boundary Value Problems for Systems of Linear Functional Differential Equations*, Folia Facultatis Scientiarium Naturalium Universitatis Masarykianae Brunensis. Mathematica, vol. 12, Masaryk University, Brno, 2003.

[9] R. Koplatadze, N. Partsvania, and I. P. Stavroulakis, *Asymptotic behaviour of solutions of two-dimensional linear differential systems with deviating arguments*, Archivum Mathematicum (Brno) **39** (2003), no. 3, 213–232.

[10] V. Lakshmikantham and S. Leela, *Differential and Integral Inequalities: Theory and Applications. Vol. II: Functional, Partial, Abstract, and Complex Differential Equations*, Mathematics in Science and Engineering, vol. 55, Academic Press, New York, 1969.

[11] A. Ju. Levin, *The non-oscillation of solutions of the equation* $x^{(n)} + p_1(t)x^{(n-1)} + \cdots + p_n(t)x = 0$, Uspekhi Matematicheskikh Nauk **24** (1969), no. 2 (146), 43–96.

[12] N. N. Luzin, *On the method of approximate integration of academician S. A. Čaplygin*, Uspekhi Matematicheskikh Nauk **6** (1951), no. 6(46), 3–27.

[13] S. A. Tchaplygin, *New Method of Approximate Integration of Differential Equations*, GTTI, Moscow, 1932.

[14] T. Ważewski, *Systèmes des équations et des inégalités différentielles ordinaires aux deuxièmes membres monotones et leurs applications*, Annales Polonici Mathematici **23** (1950), 112–166.

Alexander Domoshnitsky: Department of Mathematics and Computer Sciences, The Academic College of Judea and Samaria, 44837 Ariel, Israel
E-mail address: adom@yosh.ac.il

MODULATED POISSON MEASURES ON ABSTRACT SPACES

JEWGENI H. DSHALALOW

We introduce a notion of a random measure ξ whose parameters change in accordance with the evolution of a stochastic process η. Such a measure is called an η-modulated random measure. A class of problems like this stems from stochastic control theory, but in the present paper we are more focused on various constructions of modulated random measures on abstract spaces as well as the formation of functionals of a random process η with respect to measurable functions and an η-modulated random measure (so-called potentials), specifically applied to the class of η-modulated marked Poisson random measures.

1. Introduction

This paper deals with a formalism of modulated random measures that stem from core applications in physical sciences, engineering and technology, and applied probability [5, 10, 11]. One of the typical models is a stock market being constantly perturbed by economic news, random cataclysms and disasters, including famine, earthquakes, hurricanes, and political events and wars. This causes the main parameters of stocks or mutual funds, as well as major indexes to alter dependent on these events. We can think of the stock market as a stochastic process (such as Brownian motion) modulated by some other "external" stochastic process that takes values in some space and moving randomly from state to state. The parameters of stock market will remain homogeneous as long as the external process sojourns in a set. Once it moves on to another set, the parameters of the stock market change.

One of the widely accepted forms of modulated processes in the literature is found in Markov-modulated Poisson processes, in which a Poisson process alters its rate in accordance with an external Markov chain with continuous time parameter. It goes back to at least 1977 or even earlier in one of the seminal Neuts' articles (cf. [9]) and it is still a very popular topic in queueing known under batch Markov arrival processes. A main

Hindawi Publishing Corporation
Proceedings of the Conference on Differential & Difference Equations and Applications, pp. 373–381

advantage of this type of processes is the emulation of a more general point-counting process, along with huge computational benefits.

In the present paper, we introduce several simple and more complex constructions of general classes of random processes ξ (random measures) modulated by another process η, whose nature is not restricted to being a Markov or other special process, although some applications do benefit from a special assumption on η to be semi-Markov or semiregenerative [2, 3]. For some related literature, the reader is advised to see [6–8]. Our main goal is to extend earlier efforts we made for some constructions [1] basically from random measures on Euclidean spaces to random measures on topological spaces. Our intention is to generalize a basic formula for the intensity of a random measure and the intensity of a modulated random measure to a functional of the stochastic process η with respect to random measure ξ being modulated by η. This we call the potential of η with respect to ξ. A very compact formula for the class of potentials of random processes with respect to marked Poisson random measure was derived. The results can be found useful in stochastic control.

2. Preliminaries

We will use the following notation throughout. $[X, Y, f]$ denotes a function with X as its domain and Y as its codomain. If Y' is a subset of Y, by $f^*(Y')$ we denote the inverse image of Y'. If $\mathscr{E}(Y)$ is a system of subsets of Y, then the set of all inverse images of $\mathscr{E}(Y)$ under f will be denoted by $f^{**}(\mathscr{E}(Y))$.

Let $(\mathfrak{X}, \tau_{\mathfrak{X}})$ be an LCHS (locally compact Hausdorff space), often abbreviated as $\mathfrak{X}$ and let $\mathscr{B}_{\mathfrak{X}} = \mathscr{B}(\mathfrak{X})$ be the corresponding Borel σ-algebra (generated by $\tau_{\mathfrak{X}}$).

Let $\mathscr{R}_{\mathfrak{X}}$ denote the set of all relatively compact Borel subsets of $\mathfrak{X}$ (which is a ring) and let $\mathscr{K}_{\mathfrak{X}}$ denote the set of all compact subsets. A Borel measure μ on $\mathscr{B}_{\mathfrak{X}}$ is called locally finite if μ is finite on $\mathscr{R}_{\mathfrak{X}}$. Notice that μ is a Borel-Lebesgue-Stieltjes measure on $\mathscr{B}_{\mathbb{R}^d}$ (cf. Dshalalow [4]) if and only if it is locally finite.

Let $\mathfrak{M}_{\mathfrak{X}}$ denote the set of all locally finite (Borel) measures on $\mathscr{B}_{\mathfrak{X}}$. We assume that all measures we will deal with will be positive.

Definition 2.1 (cf. Dshalalow [4]). Let A be a Borel set and $\mu \in \mathfrak{M}_{\mathfrak{X}}$.

μ is *inner regular at* A if

$$\mu(A) = \sup\{\mu(K) : K \subseteq A, A \in \mathscr{K}_{\mathfrak{X}}\}. \tag{2.1}$$

μ is *outer regular at* A if

$$\mu(A) = \inf\{\mu(U) : A \subseteq U, U \in \tau_{\mathfrak{X}}\}. \tag{2.2}$$

Measure μ is *weakly regular* or *Radon* if it is inner regular on $\tau_{\mathfrak{X}}$, that is, at each open set, and it is outer regular on $\mathscr{B}_{\mathfrak{X}}$, that is, at each Borel set.

Measure μ is *regular* if it is inner and outer regular on $\mathscr{B}_{\mathfrak{X}}$.

Regularity of locally finite Borel measures is a special feature and either it is to be assumed or it follows from some assumptions imposed on the topology $\tau_{\mathfrak{X}}$. One of them is as follows.

THEOREM 2.2 (cf. Dshalalow [4]). *If* $(\mathfrak{X},\tau_{\mathfrak{X}})$ *is* σ*-compact, then any locally finite measure on* $\mathcal{B}_{\mathfrak{X}}$ *is regular (in particular, Radon) and* σ*-finite.*

Thus assuming $(\mathfrak{X},\tau_{\mathfrak{X}})$ to be σ-compact (and LCHS as we have previously assumed), $\mathfrak{M}_{\mathfrak{X}}$ turns out to be the set of all regular measures (in particular, Radon).

Remark 2.3. It is very common in the literature to assume that $\mathfrak{X}$ is second countable, which would make it metrizable, separable, and σ-compact. While metrization is a valuable asset, it is not always mandatory, and σ-compactness of $\mathfrak{X}$, while often sufficient, is a relatively weak assumption. The Euclidean space with its natural topology is LCHS, σ-compact, and Lindelöf compact. Thus, any locally finite measure on $\mathcal{B}_{\mathbb{R}^d}$ is Borel-Lebesgue-Stieltjes, Radon, and regular. Of course, Euclidean space is also second countable and complete and, therefore, it is Polish. Notice that not every LCHS $\mathfrak{X}$, which is second countable, is Polish. For instance, if $\mathfrak{X} = (0,1)$ with the relative topology $\tau_e \cap (0,1)$, then it is a second countable LCHS, but not complete.

Thus, under the assumption that $(\mathfrak{X},\tau_{\mathfrak{X}})$ is σ-compact (and LCHS), we have that $\mathfrak{M}_{\mathfrak{X}}$ is the set of all regular (in particular, Radon) measures. We will continue assuming this throughout.

Given a Borel set B, denote the map $\mu \mapsto \mu(B)$ by $\psi_B : \mathfrak{M}_{\mathfrak{X}} \to \overline{\mathbb{R}}_+$. The family $\{\psi_B : B \in \mathcal{B}_{\mathfrak{X}}\}$ of all such maps indexed by elements of $\mathcal{B}_{\mathfrak{X}}$ induces the smallest σ-algebra $\mathcal{M}_{\mathfrak{X}}$ in $\mathfrak{M}_{\mathfrak{X}}$ relative to which every such map ψ_B is measurable, that is,

$$\mathcal{M}_{\mathfrak{X}} = \sigma\left(\bigcup_{B\in\mathcal{B}_{\mathfrak{X}}} \psi_B^{**}\left(\mathcal{B}\left(\overline{\mathbb{R}}_+\right)\right) \right). \tag{2.3}$$

Definition 2.4. Let $(\Omega,\mathfrak{A}(\Omega),P)$ be a probability space. A random measure ξ is any measurable mapping from $(\Omega,\mathfrak{A}(\Omega),P)$ to $(\mathfrak{M}_{\mathfrak{X}},\mathcal{M}_{\mathfrak{X}})$. (It is a parametric family of measures in $\mathfrak{M}_{\mathfrak{X}}$ indexed by $\omega \in \Omega$ such that $\xi^{**}(\mathcal{M}_{\mathfrak{X}}) \subseteq \mathfrak{A}(\Omega)$. It is an r.v. generating a family $P\xi^*$ of distributions on $\mathcal{M}_{\mathfrak{X}}$.) The integral measure

$$E\xi = \int \xi\, dP \tag{2.4}$$

is called the *intensity* of ξ. Observe that while $E\xi$ is a Borel measure on $\mathcal{B}_{\mathfrak{X}}$, in general, $E\xi \notin \mathfrak{M}_{\mathfrak{X}}$.

3. Modulated random measures

Construction 1. We begin with a special construction of a random measure to be used for modulation. Let $\mu \in \mathfrak{M}_{\mathfrak{X}}$ and let G be a measurable subset of the product space $\Omega \times \mathfrak{X}$, that is, $G \in \mathfrak{A}(\Omega) \otimes \mathcal{B}_{\mathfrak{X}}$ and, for any $\omega \in \Omega$, let G_ω denote the ω-section of G. Since μ is σ-finite (due to σ-compactness assumption on $\mathfrak{X}$, see Theorem 2.2), the map $\omega \mapsto \mu(G_\omega)$ is $\mathfrak{A}(\Omega)$-$\mathcal{B}(\overline{\mathbb{R}}_+)$-measurable and thus it can be regarded as a random variable on $(\Omega,\mathfrak{A}(\Omega),P)$. Hence, given a fixed G, the map

$$(\omega,B) \longmapsto \nu_G(\omega,B) := \mu(G_\omega \cap B), \quad B \in \mathcal{B}_{\mathfrak{X}}, \tag{3.1}$$

is a random measure from $(\Omega, \mathfrak{A}(\Omega), P)$ to $(\mathfrak{M}_{\mathfrak{X}}, \mathcal{M}_{\mathfrak{X}})$. The intensity $E\nu_G$, as for any random measure, is a measure itself, but in this case, it is also locally finite and thus regular. Indeed, it is readily seen that

$$E\nu_G \leq E\nu_{\Omega\times\mathfrak{X}} = \mu \tag{3.2}$$

and thus, for every $G \in \mathfrak{A}(\Omega) \otimes \mathcal{B}_{\mathfrak{X}}$, $E\nu_G \in \mathfrak{M}_{\mathfrak{X}}$. In particular, it follows that the measure $E\nu_G$ is absolutely continuous with respect to μ, that is, if $[g]_\mu$ is the corresponding Radon-Nikodym derivative, then

$$E\nu_G\Big(= \int \mu(G_\omega \cap \cdot)P(d\omega)\Big) = \mu[g]_\mu\Big(= \int [g]_\mu d\mu\Big). \tag{3.3}$$

Now modulation is based on the following concept.

Definition 3.1. A sequence of locally finite regular measures $\{\mu_1, \mu_2, \dots\}$ is locally bounded if for any relatively compact Borel set $R \in \mathcal{R}_{\mathfrak{X}}$, there is a locally finite regular Borel measure δ_R such that

$$\mu_i(B) \leq \delta_R(B), \quad \forall B \in R \cap \mathcal{B}_{\mathfrak{X}},\ i = 1, 2, \dots. \tag{3.4}$$

Construction 2. Let $\{\mu_1, \mu_2, \dots\}$ be a locally bounded sequence from $\mathfrak{M}_{\mathfrak{X}}$, let

$$\{G_1, G_2, \dots\} \in \mathfrak{A}(\Omega) \otimes \mathcal{B}_{\mathfrak{X}} \tag{3.5}$$

be a measurable partition of $\Omega \times \mathfrak{X}$, and let $\{a_1, a_2, \dots\}$ be a bounded sequence of non-negative real numbers. Define

$$\xi = \xi(\omega, \cdot) = \sum_{i=1}^{\infty} a_i \mu_i\big((G_i)_\omega \cap \cdot\big). \tag{3.6}$$

Proposition 3.2. *Given a locally bounded sequence of regular measures $\{\mu_1, \mu_2, \dots\}$, a measurable partition $\{G_1, G_2, \dots\}$ of $\Omega \times \mathfrak{X}$, and a bounded sequence $\{a_1, a_2, \dots\}$, ξ is a random measure and its intensity $E\xi$ is a locally finite regular measure.*

Proof. Since each μ_i is σ-finite, $\mu_i((G_i)_\omega \cap B)$ is measurable for each i and for each $B \in \mathcal{B}_{\mathfrak{X}}$, and so is $\xi(\cdot, B)$. Now, the condition of local boundedness of the sequence $\{\mu_1, \mu_2, \dots\}$ is equivalent to the existence of a family $\{\delta_R : R \in \mathcal{R}_{\mathfrak{X}}\} \subseteq \mathfrak{M}_{\mathfrak{X}}$ such that for each relatively compact Borel set R, there is a locally finite Borel measure δ_R such that for each $B \in R \cap \mathcal{B}_{\mathfrak{X}}$,

$$\mu_i(B) \leq \delta_B(B), \quad \forall i = 1, 2, \dots. \tag{3.7}$$

Then, if a is an upper bound for $\{a_i\}$, we have that

$$\xi(\omega, R) \leq a \sum_i \delta_B\big((G_i)_\omega \cap R\big) = a\delta_B\Big(\sum_i (G_i)_\omega \cap R\Big) = a\delta_R(R) < \infty, \tag{3.8}$$

good for all ω. It means that ξ is for every ω locally finite and thus regular and, consequently, a random measure. Finally, $E\xi(R) \leq a\delta_R(R) < \infty$ and hence $E\xi \in \mathfrak{M}_{\mathfrak{X}}$. □

Notice that local boundedness of the sequence $\{\mu_1,\mu_2,\dots\}$ is a relatively weak restriction to the sequence (resembling pointwise boundedness of a sequence of functions) applied to only the ring of relatively compact Borel sets, and that this is obviously a weaker condition than $\mu_i \le \delta$ for all i.

Construction 3. Let η be a stochastic process from probability space $(\Omega,\mathfrak{A}(\Omega),P)$ to $(Y,\mathcal{B}(\tau(Y)))$ parameterized by $t\in\mathfrak{X}$ (which, as before, is LCHS and σ-compact) and let $\{Y_1,Y_2,\dots\}$ be a measurable countable partition of Y. Then, $\{\eta^*(Y_i),\ i=1,2,\dots\}$ is a measurable partition of $\Omega\times\mathfrak{X}$. Under the condition of Construction 2 (as regards μ_i's and a), denote

$$\xi_\eta = \sum_i a_i\mu_i\left(\left(\eta^*(Y_i)\right)_\omega \cap \cdot\right). \tag{3.9}$$

Then, by Proposition 3.2, ξ_η is a random measure. We will call ξ_η the random measure modulated by stochastic process η with respect to the sequence $\{\mu_1,\mu_2,\dots\}$. Obviously, the intensity

$$E\xi_\eta = \sum_i a_i E\mu_i\left(\left(\eta^*(Y_i)\right)_\omega \cap \cdot\right) \tag{3.10}$$

is a locally finite regular measure as per Proposition 3.2.

Construction 4. Under the condition of Construction 3, let us assume that for each i, $\mu_i \ll \sigma \in \mathfrak{M}_{\mathfrak{X}}$ (which would be automatically yielded should $\mu_i \le \sigma$ in place of much weaker local boundedness be assumed) and let λ_i be a Radon-Nikodym density from the class $d\mu_i/d\sigma$. Then,

$$\mu_i\eta^*(Y_i) = \int \mathbf{1}_{Y_i}\circ\eta\, d\mu_i = \int \mathbf{1}_{Y_i}\circ\eta\lambda_i\, d\sigma. \tag{3.11}$$

Now, we have the following proposition.

Proposition 3.3.

$$E\mu_i\eta^*(Y_i) = \int E\left[\mathbf{1}_{Y_i}\circ\eta\right]\lambda_i\, d\sigma = \int_{t\in\mathfrak{X}} P\{\eta(t)\in Y_i\}\lambda_i(t)\,d\sigma(t), \tag{3.12}$$

and thus the intensity $E\xi_\eta$ is

$$E\xi_\eta = \sum_i a_i \int_{t\in\mathfrak{X}} P\{\eta(t)\in Y_i\}\lambda_i(t)\,d\sigma(t). \tag{3.13}$$

4. Modulated Poisson measures

We begin with some basic notions of Poisson random measures due to [6–8].

Definition 4.1 (cf. Kallenberg [6]). Let

$$\xi = \sum_{i=1}^{\nu} X_i\varepsilon_{\tau_i}, \tag{4.1}$$

where $X_1, X_2, \ldots$ are i.i.d. nonnegative r.v.'s, $\tau_1, \tau_2, \ldots$ are i.i.d. r.v.'s valued in $\mathfrak{X}$, and ν is a Poisson r.v. with mean b. Then ξ is a random measure and it is called a *marked Poisson random measure* (MPRM). Assume here position independent marking (i.e., X_i's and τ_i's are independent). Alternatively, ξ is referred to as a compound Poisson process or marked Poisson process, in this case with position independent marking.

The associated random measure $N = \sum_{i=1}^{\nu} \varepsilon_{\tau_i}$ is called the support counting measure of ξ. Random measures ξ and N are known to have the following properties:

(i) for disjoint $B_1, \ldots, B_k \in \mathcal{B}_{\mathfrak{X}}$, the r.v.'s $\xi(B_1), \ldots, \xi(B_k)$ are independent;

(ii) there is a regular locally finite measure $\mu \in \mathfrak{M}_{\mathfrak{X}}$ such that

$$Ee^{\theta\xi(\cdot)} = e^{\mu(\cdot)[m(\theta)-1]}, \tag{4.2}$$

where $m(\theta) = Ee^{\theta X_1}$ and, in particular,

$$Ee^{\theta N(\cdot)} = e^{\mu(\cdot)(e^{\theta}-1)}, \tag{4.3}$$

with μ being called the mean measure of N. ξ is also said to be *directed by measure μ*.

Notice that

$$\mu = bP_{\tau}, \quad b = E\nu, \tag{4.4}$$

where $\tau \sim \tau_1$.

The intensity of ξ is

$$E\xi = a\mu, \tag{4.5}$$

where $a = EX$ and $X \sim X_1$.

Assume that $\xi_1, \xi_2, \ldots$ is a locally bounded sequence of MPRMs such that for a fixed k,

$$\xi_k = \sum_{i=1}^{\nu_k} X_i^{(k)} \varepsilon_{\tau_i^{(k)}} \tag{4.6}$$

directed by mean measure μ_k and $E\xi_k = a_k\mu_k$, where $a_k = EX_k$. Then, under the condition of Construction 3,

$$\Pi_\eta = \sum_i \xi_i(\omega, (\eta^*(Y_i))_\omega \cap \cdot) \tag{4.7}$$

is a random measure modulated by η, which we will call a *marked Poisson random measure modulated by η*.

From formula (4.5), the intensity of Π_η is

$$E\Pi_\eta = \sum_i a_i E\mu_i((\eta^*(Y_i)) \cap \cdot). \tag{4.8}$$

Now, if each respective mean measure μ_i is continuous with respect to some $\sigma \in \mathfrak{M}_{\mathfrak{X}}$ and if $\lambda_i \in d\mu_i/d\sigma$, then by formulas (3.12)-(3.13) and (4.8),

$$E\Pi_\eta = \sum_i a_i \int_{t\in\mathfrak{X}} P\{\eta(t) \in Y_i\}\lambda_i(t)d\sigma(t), \tag{4.9}$$

which is identical to (3.13) having $a_i = EX_i$ in mind and due to original conditions of Construction 2, assuming the sequence $\{a_i\}$ bounded.

5. Potentials of stochastic processes with respect to a modulated Poisson measure

Recall from (4.5) that the intensity of a marked Poisson measure ξ directed by a mean measure μ is $E\xi - a\mu$. We will present an analog of this equation for a class of functionals of stochastic processes with respect to random measures and then extend it to modulated Poisson measures.

Definition 5.1. Let η be a stochastic process from $(\Omega, \mathfrak{A}(\Omega), P)$ to $(Y, \mathfrak{B}(\tau(Y)))$ parameterized by $t \in \mathfrak{X}$ (LCHS and σ-compact), let $[Y, \mathbb{R}, f]$ be Borel measurable function, and let ξ be a random measure. Then, call $E\int f(\eta)d\xi$ the *potential* of η with respect to f and random measure ξ (provided that the integral exists).

THEOREM 5.2. *In the condition of Definition 5.3, the potential of stochastic process η with respect to f and a marked Poisson measure ξ directed by a mean measure μ satisfies the following equation:*

$$E\int f(\eta)d\xi = aE\int f(\eta)d\mu, \tag{5.1}$$

provided that the integrals in (5.1) exist.

Proof. Let Y' be a measurable subset of Y. By (4.5),

$$E\xi\eta^*(Y') = aE\mu\eta^*(Y'). \tag{5.2}$$

On the other hand, the left- and right-hand sides of (5.2) yield

$$E\int \mathbf{1}_{Y'} \circ \eta d\xi = aE\int \mathbf{1}_{Y'} \circ \eta d\mu. \tag{5.3}$$

Thus, for a simple function $h = \sum_{i=1}^k b_i \mathbf{1}_{Y_i}$, (5.3) yields

$$E\int \sum_{i=1}^k b_i \mathbf{1}_{Y_i} d\xi\eta^* = aE\int \sum_{i=1}^k b_i \mathbf{1}_{Y_i} d\mu\eta^*, \tag{5.4}$$

and for any measurable nonnegative $f = \sup h_n$,

$$E\int f d\xi\eta^* = \sup E\int h_n d\xi\eta^* = a \sup E\int h_n d\mu\eta^*. \tag{5.5}$$

Using the change of variables and extending (5.5) to real-valued function, we are done with the proof. □

Definition 5.3. Let η be a stochastic process from $(\Omega, \mathfrak{A}(\Omega), P)$ to $(Y, \mathcal{B}(\tau(Y)))$ parameterized by $t \in \mathfrak{X}$ and let $F = \{f_i\}$ be a sequence of measurable functions. The *potential* of η with respect to F and an η-modulated Poisson measure

$$\Pi_\eta = \sum_i \xi_i(\omega, (\eta^*(Y_i))_\omega \cap \cdot) \tag{5.6}$$

is defined as

$$E\Pi_\eta F(\eta) = E\int \sum_i f_i(\eta) d\xi_i, \tag{5.7}$$

provided that the integral on the right of (5.7) exists.

From Theorem 5.2, we have the following theorem.

Theorem 5.4. *Under the condition of Definition 5.3, the potential of η with respect to F and an η-modulated Poisson measure satisfies the formula*

$$E\Pi_\eta F(\eta) = \sum_i a_i E\int f_i(\eta) d\mu_i. \tag{5.8}$$

The result of Theorem 5.4 can be very useful in stochastic control theory where the right-hand side of (5.8) can be interpreted as a reward function for a Poisson process controlled by a stochastic process.

References

[1] R. Agarwal, J. H. Dshalalow, and D. O'Regan, *Generalized modulated random measures and their potentials*, Stochastic Analysis and Applications **22** (2004), no. 4, 971–988.
[2] J. H. Dshalalow, *Ergodic theorems for modulated stochastic processes*, Proceedings of the 1st Congress of IFNA, W. de Gruyter, Florida, 1996, pp. 1745–1755.
[3] ———, *On intensities of modulated Cox measures*, Journal of Applied Mathematics and Stochastic Analysis **11** (1998), no. 3, 411–423.
[4] ———, *Real Analysis*, Studies in Advanced Mathematics, Chapman & Hall/CRC, Florida, 2001.
[5] W. Fischer and K. Meier-Hellstern, *The Markov-modulated Poisson process (MMPP) cookbook*, Performance Evaluation **18** (1993), no. 2, 149–171.
[6] O. Kallenberg, *Random Measures*, 4th ed., Akademie and Academic Press, Berlin, 1986.
[7] A. F. Karr, *Point Processes and Their Statistical Inference*, 2nd ed., Probability: Pure and Applied, vol. 7, Marcel Dekker, New York, 1991.
[8] J. F. C. Kingman, *Poisson Processes*, Oxford Science Publications, vol. 3, The Clarendon Press, Oxford University Press, New York, 1993.

[9] M. F. Neuts, *Matrix-Geometric Solutions in Stochastic Models. An Algorithmic Approach*, Johns Hopkins Series in the Mathematical Sciences, vol. 2, Johns Hopkins University Press, Maryland, 1981.

[10] N. U. Prabhu and Y. Zhu, *Markov-modulated queueing systems*, Queueing Systems **5** (1989), no. 1–3, 215–245.

[11] I. Stavrakakis, *Queueing analysis of a class of star-interconnected networks under Markov modulated output process modeling*, IEEE Transactions on Communications **40** (1992), no. 8, 1345–1354.

Jewgeni H. Dshalalow: Department of Mathematical Sciences, College of Science, Florida Institute of Technology, Melbourne, FL 32901, USA
E-mail address: eugene@fit.edu

ANNULAR JET AND COAXIAL JET FLOW

JOSHUA DU AND JUN JI

The dispersion relations for supersonic, in-viscid, and compressible jet flow of annular and coaxial jets under vortex sheet model are derived. The dispersion relation in either case, in a form of determinant of a 4×4 matrix, is an implicit function of ω and wave number κ, and provides the foundation to investigate Kelvin-Helmholtz instability and acoustic waves. The dispersion relation of jet flow under more realistic model, like finite thickness model, can also be derived.

1. Introduction

Jet aircrafts were introduced right after the Second World War. Because of the very high speed of the jet, and the large tangential gradient of the velocity of jet flow, the Kelvin-Helmholtz instability waves caused the instability and dramatically reduced life spans of jets. Hence jet noise prediction and reduction became important economical, environmental, and safety issues.

Many researchers, like Tam and Morris [6], Tam and Burton [3, 4], and Tam and Hu [5], found that Kelvin-Helmholtz instability waves in supersonic jets constitute the basic elements of the feedback loop responsible for the generation of multiple-jet resonance tones. They successfully modeled the jet flow and interpreted the characteristics of instability waves and upstream propagated acoustic wave through numerical computation.

At the same time many researchers, like Morris et al. [1], Wlezien [9], Tam and Ahuja [2], Tam and Norum [7], and Tam and Thies [8], also investigated the problems of how jet nozzles of different geometries affect the generation of the instability wave, focusing on rectangular jets.

We are interested in studying annular and coaxial jets. In this paper, we modeled the jet flow and derived dispersion relations for single annular and coaxial jet flow as an introduction to the investigation of multiple annular and coaxial jets flow.

Hindawi Publishing Corporation
Proceedings of the Conference on Differential & Difference Equations and Applications, pp. 383–390

2. Annular jets

Consider an annular jet with radii R_1 and R_2, respectively. The intersection of the jet with yz-plane is shown in Figure 2.1. The x-axis points to down stream direction which is perpendicular to yz-plane.

The cylindrical coordinate system, (r,θ,x), is introduced at the center of the circle. The whole region of the yz-plane can be divided into three regions:

(i) region 1: $r < R_1$;
(ii) region 2: $R_1 < r < R_2$;
(iii) region 3: $r > R_2$.

Here dimensionless variables will be used in the analysis. We define u and $\vec{V}_\perp$ to be the components of velocity in the directions of x and yz-plane, respectively, ρ to be the jet density, p to be the pressure, and $\bar{u}(r)$ and $\bar{\rho}(r)$ to be the mean velocity and the mean density of the jet. The jet Mach number M is the ratio of the jet speed to the sound speed inside the jet. We assume that the mean pressure p_∞ is a constant.

The standard linearized conservation of mass, momentum, and energy equations of a compressible inviscid fluid are

$$\frac{\partial \rho}{\partial t} + \nabla \cdot (\bar{\rho}\vec{V}_\perp + \rho\bar{u}\vec{x}) = 0, \tag{2.1}$$

$$\bar{\rho}\left(\frac{\partial u}{\partial t} + \bar{u}\frac{\partial u}{\partial x} + \vec{V}_\perp \cdot \nabla_\perp \bar{u}\right) = -\frac{\partial p}{\partial x}, \tag{2.2}$$

$$\bar{\rho}\left(\frac{\partial \vec{V}_\perp}{\partial t} + \bar{u}\frac{\partial \vec{V}_\perp}{\partial x}\right) = -\nabla_\perp p, \tag{2.3}$$

$$M^2\left(\frac{\partial p}{\partial t} + \bar{u}\frac{\partial p}{\partial x}\right) + \nabla_\perp \cdot \vec{V}_\perp + \frac{\partial u}{\partial x} = 0, \tag{2.4}$$

where $\vec{x}$ is the unit vector in x-direction. Operator ∇ is the gradient in xyz-space, and $\nabla_\perp$, $\nabla_\perp^2$ are gradient and Laplacian operators in yz-plane, respectively, that is,

$$\nabla = \frac{\partial}{\partial x}\vec{x} + \frac{\partial}{\partial y}\vec{y} + \frac{\partial}{\partial z}\vec{z}, \qquad \nabla_\perp = \frac{\partial}{\partial y}\vec{y} + \frac{\partial}{\partial z}\vec{z}, \qquad \nabla_\perp^2 = \frac{\partial^2}{\partial y^2} + \frac{\partial^2}{\partial z^2}, \tag{2.5}$$

where $\vec{y}$ and $\vec{z}$ are the unit vectors in the directions of y and z, respectively.

Since the pressure and velocity have wave structure, we define

$$u = \hat{u}e^{i(\kappa x - \omega t)}, \qquad \vec{V}_\perp = \hat{\vec{V}}_\perp e^{i(\kappa x - \omega t)}, \qquad p = \hat{p}e^{i(\kappa x - \omega t)}, \tag{2.6}$$

and then (2.2)–(2.4), after separating wave factor $e^{i(\kappa x - \omega t)}$, can be reduced to the following:

$$i\bar{\rho}\hat{\vec{V}}_\perp \cdot \nabla_\perp \bar{u} + \bar{\rho}(\omega - \bar{u}\kappa)\hat{u} = \kappa\hat{p}, \tag{2.7}$$

$$\hat{\vec{V}}_\perp = \frac{\nabla_\perp \hat{p}}{i\bar{\rho}(\omega - \bar{u}\kappa)}, \tag{2.8}$$

$$M^2(\omega - \bar{u}\kappa)\hat{p} - \kappa\hat{u} = -i\nabla_\perp \cdot \hat{\vec{V}}_\perp. \tag{2.9}$$

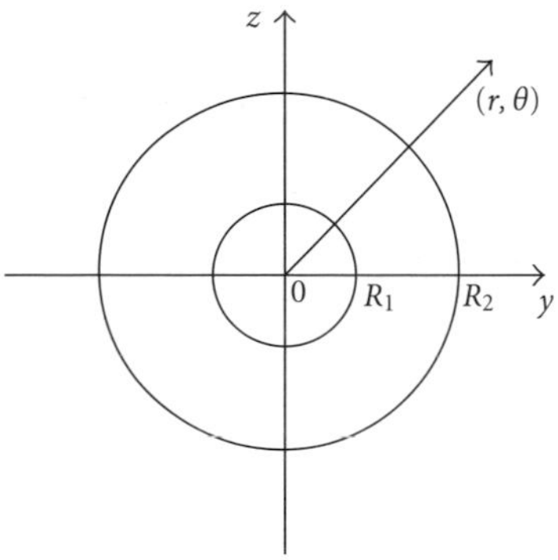

Figure 2.1

From (2.7) and (2.9), eliminating $\widehat{u}$, we have

$$i\bar{\rho}(\omega - \bar{u}\kappa)\nabla_\perp \cdot \widehat{\vec{V}}_\perp + i\kappa\bar{\rho}\widehat{\vec{V}}_\perp \cdot \nabla_\perp \bar{u} + (\bar{\rho}M^2(\omega - \bar{u}\kappa)^2 - \kappa^2)\widehat{p} = 0. \quad (2.10)$$

Substituting (2.8) into (2.10), we have

$$\nabla_\perp^2 \widehat{p} + \left(\frac{2\kappa\nabla_\perp \bar{u}}{\omega - \kappa\bar{u}} - \frac{\nabla_\perp \bar{\rho}}{\bar{\rho}}\right) \cdot \nabla_\perp \widehat{p} + (\bar{\rho}M^2(\omega - \bar{u}\kappa)^2 - \kappa^2)\widehat{p} = 0. \quad (2.11)$$

Thus, the original nonlinear system (2.1)–(2.4) with unknown functions $\rho, u, \vec{V}_\perp$, and p has been reduced to a Bessel type equation (2.11) involving $\widehat{p}$ only. Consequently, $\widehat{\vec{V}}_\perp$ and $\widehat{u}$ can be solved from (2.8) and (2.9) after solving $\widehat{p}$ from (2.11). Finally, u, $\vec{V}_\perp$, and p can be obtained from (2.6) and then ρ from (2.1). The solution of (2.11) in the region α will be denoted by $\widehat{p}_\alpha$ for each α, $\alpha = 1,2,3$.

Upon using polar coordinate (r,θ), with the fact that

$$\nabla_\perp = \frac{\partial}{\partial r}\vec{r} + \frac{1}{r}\frac{\partial}{\partial \theta}\vec{\theta}, \qquad \nabla_\perp^2 = \frac{\partial^2}{\partial r^2} + \frac{1}{r}\frac{\partial}{\partial r} + \frac{1}{r^2}\frac{\partial^2}{\partial \theta^2}, \quad (2.12)$$

where $\vec{r}$ and $\vec{\theta}$ are unit vectors in the directions of r and θ, respectively, (2.11) can be written as

$$\frac{\partial^2 \widehat{p}_2}{\partial r^2} + \left(\frac{1}{r} + \frac{2\kappa\partial\bar{u}/\partial r}{\omega - \bar{u}\kappa} - \frac{1}{\bar{\rho}}\frac{\partial\bar{\rho}}{\partial r}\right)\frac{\partial \widehat{p}_2}{\partial r} + \frac{1}{r^2}\frac{\partial^2 \widehat{p}_2}{\partial \theta^2} + (\bar{\rho}M^2(\omega - \bar{u}\kappa)^2 - \kappa^2)\widehat{p}_2 = 0. \quad (2.13)$$

We use vortex sheet model. The profile of mean velocity of the jet is shown as in Figure 2.2.

For the vortex sheet model, the mean velocity $\bar{u}(r)$ is 1 inside the jet and 0 outside the jet while the mean density $\bar{\rho}$ is 1 inside the jet and $\bar{\rho}_o$ outside the jet:

$$\bar{u}(r) = \begin{cases} 0 & \text{if } r < R_1, \\ 1 & \text{if } R_1 < r < R_2, \\ 0 & \text{if } r > R_2, \end{cases} \qquad \bar{\rho}(r) = \begin{cases} \bar{\rho}_o & \text{if } r < R_1, \\ 1 & \text{if } R_1 < r < R_2, \\ \bar{\rho}_o & \text{if } r > R_2, \end{cases} \quad (2.14)$$

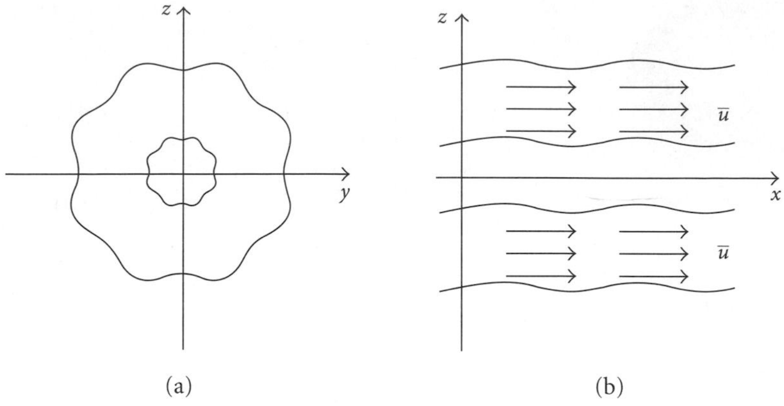

Figure 2.2

where γ is the ratio of the specific heats of gas and

$$\bar{\rho}_o = \frac{1}{1 + ((\gamma - 1)/2)M^2} \tag{2.15}$$

is the density of the gas outside the jet. It is easily seen from (2.13) and (2.14) that the governing equation in the first or third region becomes

$$\frac{\partial^2 \widehat{p}_\alpha}{\partial r^2} + \frac{1}{r}\frac{\partial \widehat{p}_\alpha}{\partial r} + \frac{1}{r^2}\frac{\partial^2 \widehat{p}_\alpha}{\partial \theta^2} + \lambda_o^2 \widehat{p}_\alpha = 0, \quad \alpha = 1 \text{ (with } r < R_1) \text{ or } \alpha = 3 \text{ (with } r > R_2), \tag{2.16}$$

where $\lambda_o = \sqrt{\bar{\rho}_o M^2 \omega^2 - \kappa^2}$, and that the governing equation (2.13) in the second region is reduced to

$$\frac{\partial^2 \widehat{p}_2}{\partial r^2} + \frac{1}{r}\frac{\partial \widehat{p}_2}{\partial r} + \frac{1}{r^2}\frac{\partial^2 \widehat{p}_2}{\partial \theta^2} + \lambda^2 \widehat{p}_2 = 0, \quad R_1 < r < R_2, \tag{2.17}$$

where $\lambda = \sqrt{M^2(\omega - \kappa)^2 - \kappa^2}$. We comment that the branch cuts of λ and λ_o are chosen to have $0 \le \arg\lambda, \arg\lambda_o < \pi$.

The dynamic and kinematic boundary conditions at the vortex sheets ($r = R_1$ or $r = R_2$) are

$$\begin{aligned}
\widehat{p}_1 &= \widehat{p}_2 \quad \text{if } r = R_1, \\
\widehat{p}_2 &= \widehat{p}_3 \quad \text{if } r = R_2, \\
\frac{1}{\bar{\rho}_o \omega^2}\frac{\partial \widehat{p}_1}{\partial r} &= \frac{1}{(\omega - \kappa)^2}\frac{\partial \widehat{p}_2}{\partial r} \quad \text{if } r = R_1, \\
\frac{1}{\bar{\rho}_o \omega^2}\frac{\partial \widehat{p}_3}{\partial r} &= \frac{1}{(\omega - \kappa)^2}\frac{\partial \widehat{p}_2}{\partial r} \quad \text{if } r = R_2.
\end{aligned} \tag{2.18}$$

The general solution of the governing equation in each region can be written in the form of Fourier series of cosine and sine functions, for instance,

$$\hat{p}_1 = \sum_{n=0}^{\infty} A_n J_n(\lambda_o r)\cos(n\theta), \tag{2.19}$$

$$\hat{p}_2 = \sum_{n=0}^{\infty} (B_n J_n(\lambda r)\cos(n\theta) + C_n H_n^{(1)}(\lambda r)\cos(n\theta)), \tag{2.20}$$

$$\hat{p}_3 = \sum_{n=0}^{\infty} D_n H_n^{(1)}(\lambda_o r)\cos(n\theta). \tag{2.21}$$

Applying the boundary conditions (2.18), we have

$$A_n J_n(\lambda_o R_1) = B_n J_n(\lambda R_1) + C_n H_n^{(1)}(\lambda R_1), \tag{2.22}$$

$$B_n J_n(\lambda R_2) + C_n H_n^{(1)}(\lambda R_2) = D_n H_n^{(1)}(\lambda_o R_2), \tag{2.23}$$

$$\frac{\lambda_o}{\bar{\rho}_o \omega^2} A_n J_n'(\lambda_o R_1) = \frac{\lambda}{(\omega-\kappa)^2}(B_n J_n'(\lambda R_1) + C_n (H_n^{(1)})'(\lambda R_1)), \tag{2.24}$$

$$\frac{\lambda_o}{\bar{\rho}_o \omega^2} D_n (H_n^{(1)})'(\lambda_o R_2) = \frac{\lambda}{(\omega-\kappa)^2}(B_n J_n'(\lambda R_2) + C_n (H_n^{(1)})'(\lambda R_2)). \tag{2.25}$$

Let $\beta \equiv (\omega-\kappa)^2\lambda_o/(\bar{\rho}_o\omega^2\lambda)$. Equations (2.22)–(2.25) can be rewritten as a system of linear equations in unknowns A_n, B_n, C_n, and D_n:

$$\begin{aligned}
A_n J_n(\lambda_o R_1) - B_n J_n(\lambda R_1) - C_n H_n^{(1)}(\lambda R_1) &= 0,\\
B_n J_n(\lambda R_2) + C_n H_n^{(1)}(\lambda R_2) - D_n H_n^{(1)}(\lambda_o R_2) &= 0,\\
\beta A_n J_n'(\lambda_o R_1) - B_n J_n'(\lambda R_1) - C_n (H_n^{(1)})'(\lambda R_1) &= 0,\\
B_n J_n'(\lambda R_2) + C_n (H_n^{(1)})'(\lambda R_2) - \beta D_n (H_n^{(1)})'(\lambda_o R_2) &= 0.
\end{aligned} \tag{2.26}$$

For nontrivial solutions of A_n, B_n, C_n, and D_n, we have

$$\det\begin{pmatrix}
J_n(\lambda_o R_1) & -J_n(\lambda R_1) & -H_n^{(1)}(\lambda R_1) & 0\\
0 & J_n(\lambda R_2) & H_n^{(1)}(\lambda R_2) & -H_n^{(1)}(\lambda_o R_2)\\
\beta J_n'(\lambda_o R_1) & -J_n'(\lambda R_1) & -(H_n^{(1)})'(\lambda R_1) & 0\\
0 & J_n'(\lambda R_2) & (H_n^{(1)})'(\lambda R_2) & -\beta(H_n^{(1)})'(\lambda_o R_2)
\end{pmatrix} = 0, \tag{2.27}$$

which is the dispersion relation of annular and coaxial jet flow under the vortex sheet model.

3. Coaxial circular jets

A coaxial circular jet consists of two circular jets with radii R_1 and R_2, respectively. Let $R_1 < R_2$. Obviously, the yz-plane is divided into three regions in this situation: region 1 ($r < R_1$), region 2 ($R_1 < r < R_2$), and region 3 ($r > R_2$). However, in this case, the region 1 is the inside of the jet with radius R_1, the region 3 is the outside of the jet with radius R_2, and the region 2 is the intersection of the inside of the jet with radius R_2 and outside of the jet with radius R_1. Thus, the mean velocity and the mean density of these jets can be defined as follows:

$$\bar{u}(r) = \begin{cases} 1 & \text{if } r < R_1, \\ \bar{u}_2 & \text{if } R_1 < r < R_2, \\ 0 & \text{if } r > R_2, \end{cases} \qquad \bar{\rho}(r) = \begin{cases} 1 & \text{if } r < R_1, \\ \bar{\rho}_2 & \text{if } R_1 < r < R_2, \\ \bar{\rho}_o & \text{if } r > R_2, \end{cases} \tag{3.1}$$

where $\bar{u}_2$ and $\bar{\rho}_2$ are constants ($0 < \bar{u}_2 < 1$, $\bar{\rho}_o < \bar{\rho}_2 < 1$) and $\bar{\rho}_o$ is defined as in (2.15) under the vortex sheet model assumption. We observe the similarity between the coaxial circular engine jet and the annular jet of the previous section. The only difference is the values of the mean velocity and mean density functions on three regions. The governing equations on all these regions can be easily obtained from (2.13) and (3.1). In the first region ($r < R_1$), the governing equation is

$$\frac{\partial^2 \hat{p}_1}{\partial r^2} + \frac{1}{r}\frac{\partial \hat{p}_1}{\partial r} + \frac{1}{r^2}\frac{\partial^2 \hat{p}_2}{\partial \theta^2} + \lambda_1^2 \hat{p}_1 = 0, \quad r < R_1, \tag{3.2}$$

where $\lambda_1 = \sqrt{M^2(\omega - \kappa)^2 - \kappa^2}$ and its general solution in Fourier cosine/sine is

$$\hat{p}_1 = \sum_{n=0}^{\infty} A_n J_n(\lambda_1 r) \cos(n\theta). \tag{3.3}$$

In the second region ($R_1 < r < R_2$), the governing equation is

$$\frac{\partial^2 \hat{p}_2}{\partial r^2} + \frac{1}{r}\frac{\partial \hat{p}_2}{\partial r} + \frac{1}{r^2}\frac{\partial^2 \hat{p}_2}{\partial \theta^2} + \lambda_2^2 \hat{p}_2 = 0, \quad R_1 < r < R_2, \tag{3.4}$$

where $\lambda_2 = \sqrt{\bar{\rho}_2 M^2(\omega - \bar{u}_2\kappa)^2 - \kappa^2}$ and its general solution in Fourier cosine/sine is

$$\hat{p}_2 = \sum_{n=0}^{\infty} (B_n J_n(\lambda_2 r) \cos(n\theta) + C_n H_n^{(1)}(\lambda_2 r) \cos(n\theta)). \tag{3.5}$$

Finally, in the third region ($r > R_2$), the governing equation is

$$\frac{\partial^2 \hat{p}_3}{\partial r^2} + \frac{1}{r}\frac{\partial \hat{p}_3}{\partial r} + \frac{1}{r^2}\frac{\partial^2 \hat{p}_3}{\partial \theta^2} + \lambda_o^2 \hat{p}_3 = 0, \quad r > R_2, \tag{3.6}$$

where $\lambda_o = \sqrt{\bar{\rho}_o M^2 \omega^2 - \kappa^2}$ and its general solution in Fourier cosine/sine is

$$\hat{p}_3 = \sum_{n=0}^{\infty} (D_n H_n^{(1)}(\lambda_o r) \cos(n\theta)). \tag{3.7}$$

The dynamic and kinematic boundary conditions at the vortex sheets on $r = R_1$ and $r = R_2$ are

$$\begin{aligned} \hat{p}_1 &= \hat{p}_2 \quad \text{if } r = R_1, \\ \hat{p}_2 &= \hat{p}_3 \quad \text{if } r = R_2, \\ \frac{1}{(\omega-\kappa)^2}\frac{\partial \hat{p}_1}{\partial r} &= \frac{1}{\bar{\rho}_2(\omega-\bar{u}_2\kappa)^2}\frac{\partial \hat{p}_2}{\partial r} \quad \text{if } r = R_1, \\ \frac{1}{\bar{\rho}_o\omega^2}\frac{\partial \hat{p}_3}{\partial r} &= \frac{1}{\bar{\rho}_2(\omega-\bar{u}_2\kappa)^2}\frac{\partial \hat{p}_2}{\partial r} \quad \text{if } r = R_2. \end{aligned} \tag{3.8}$$

Applying the boundary conditions (3.8), we have

$$\begin{aligned} A_n J_n(\lambda_1 R_1) &= B_n J_n(\lambda_2 R_1) + C_n H_n^{(1)}(\lambda_2 R_1), \\ B_n J_n(\lambda_2 R_2) + C_n H_n^{(1)}(\lambda_2 R_2) &= D_n H_n^{(1)}(\lambda_3 R_2), \\ \frac{\lambda_1}{(\omega-\kappa)^2} A_n J_n'(\lambda_1 R_1) &= \frac{\lambda_2}{\bar{\rho}_2(\omega-\bar{u}_2\kappa)^2}\left(B_n J_n'(\lambda_2 R_1) + C_n (H_n^{(1)})'(\lambda_2 R_1)\right), \\ \frac{\lambda_o}{\bar{\rho}_o\omega^2} D_n (H_n^{(1)})'(\lambda_o R_2) &= \frac{\lambda_2}{\bar{\rho}_2(\omega-\bar{u}_2\kappa)^2}\left(B_n J_n'(\lambda_2 R_2) + C_n (H_n^{(1)})'(\lambda_2 R_2)\right). \end{aligned} \tag{3.9}$$

Define

$$\beta_1 \equiv \frac{\bar{\rho}_2(\omega-\bar{u}_2\kappa)^2\lambda_1}{(\omega-\kappa)^2\lambda_2}, \qquad \beta_2 \equiv \frac{\bar{\rho}_2(\omega-\bar{u}_2\kappa)^2\lambda_o}{\bar{\rho}_o\omega^2\lambda_2}. \tag{3.10}$$

Equations (3.9) can be rewritten as a system of linear equations in unknowns A_n, B_n, C_n, and D_n:

$$\begin{aligned} A_n J_n(\lambda_1 R_1) - B_n J_n(\lambda_2 R_1) - C_n H_n^{(1)}(\lambda_2 R_1) &= 0, \\ B_n J_n(\lambda_2 R_2) + C_n H_n^{(1)}(\lambda_2 R_2) - D_n H_n^{(1)}(\lambda_o R_2) &= 0, \\ \beta_1 A_n J_n'(\lambda_1 R_1) - B_n J_n'(\lambda_2 R_1) - C_n (H_n^{(1)})'(\lambda_2 R_1) &= 0, \\ B_n J_n'(\lambda_2 R_2) + C_n (H_n^{(1)})'(\lambda_2 R_2) - \beta_2 D_n (H_n^{(1)})'(\lambda_o R_2) &= 0. \end{aligned} \tag{3.11}$$

For nontrivial solutions, we have the following dispersion relation:

$$\det\begin{pmatrix} J_n(\lambda_1 R_1) & -J_n(\lambda_2 R_1) & -H_n^{(1)}(\lambda_2 R_1) & 0 \\ 0 & J_n(\lambda_2 R_2) & H_n^{(1)}(\lambda_2 R_2) & -H_n^{(1)}(\lambda_o R_2) \\ \beta_1 J_n'(\lambda_1 R_1) & -J_n'(\lambda_2 R_1) & -(H_n^{(1)})'(\lambda_2 R_1) & 0 \\ 0 & J_n'(\lambda_2 R_2) & (H_n^{(1)})'(\lambda_2 R_2) & -\beta_2 (H_n^{(1)})'(\lambda_o R_2) \end{pmatrix} = 0. \tag{3.12}$$

Acknowledgment

It is with great pleasure that we acknowledge the support from the Mentor-Protege Program, College of Science and Mathematics, Kennesaw State University.

References

[1] P. J. Morris, T. R. S. Bhat, and G. Chen, *Shock structure in jets of arbitrary exit geometry*, AIAA Paper 1987-2697.
[2] C. K. W. Tam and K. K. Ahuja, *Theoretical model of discrete tone generation by impinging jets*, Journal of Fluid Mechanics **214** (1990), 67–87.
[3] C. K. W. Tam and D. E. Burton, *Sound generated by instability waves of supersonic flows. I. Two-dimensional mixing layers*, Journal of Fluid Mechanics **138** (1984), 249–271.
[4] ______, *Sound generated by instability waves of supersonic flows. II. Axisymmetric jets*, Journal of Fluid Mechanics **138** (1984), 273–295.
[5] C. K. W. Tam and F. Q. Hu, *On the three families of instability waves of high-speed jets*, Journal of Fluid Mechanics **201** (1989), 447–483.
[6] C. K. W. Tam and P. J. Morris, *The radiation of sound by the instability waves of a compressible plane turbulent shear layer*, Journal of Fluid Mechanics **98** (1980), no. 2, 349–381.
[7] C. K. W. Tam and T. D. Norum, *Impingement tones generation by impinging jets*, Journal of Fluid Mechanics **30** (1992), 304–311.
[8] C. K. W. Tam and A. T. Thies, *Instability of rectangular jets*, Journal of Fluid Mechanics **248** (1993), 425–448.
[9] R. W. Wlezien, *Nozzle geometry effects on supersonic jet interaction*, AIAA Paper number 1987-2694.

Joshua Du: Department of Mathematics, Kennesaw State University, Kennesaw, GA 30144, USA
E-mail address: jdu@kennesaw.edu

Jun Ji: Department of Mathematics, Kennesaw State University, Kennesaw, GA 30144, USA
E-mail address: jji@kennesaw.edu

ON THE GLOBAL BEHAVIOR OF SOLUTIONS TO NONLINEAR INVERSE SOURCE PROBLEMS

A. EDEN AND V. K. KALANTAROV

We find conditions on data guaranteeing global nonexistence of solutions to inverse source problems for nonlinear parabolic and hyperbolic equations. We also establish stability results on a bounded domain for corresponding problems with the opposite sign on the power-type nonlinearities.

1. Introduction

Inverse problems are most of the time ill-posed. Therefore, the powerful tools and techniques of the dynamical systems theory usually do not apply. However, in the rare and fortunate cases where the given inverse problem is well-posed one can study the long time behavior of solutions. The questions that can be addressed are, but not limited to (i) the global existence or nonexistence of solutions; (ii) the stability of solutions, (iii) the regularity of solutions; (iv) the stability of solutions in a wider sense, that is, the existence of an (exponential) attractor, its finite dimensionality, the structure of the global attractor and so forth.

In [5, 6], we have tried to address some of these questions for a class of semilinear parabolic and hyperbolic inverse source problems with integral constraints. In particular, depending on the sign of the nonlinearity we have established both global nonexistence results as well as stability results. One of the standard tools for establishing the global nonexistence of solutions is the concavity argument that was introduced by Levine [11, 10] and was generalized in [9]. This approach requires the appropriate functional to satisfy the desired differential inequality, with a judicious choice of the initial data. The main trust of the work in [5, 6] was to prove global nonexistence results for parabolic and hyperbolic inverse source problems using the generalized concavity argument given in [9]. In the same works, when the nonlinearities have the opposite sign, it was shown that the solutions converge to zero in H^1-norm when the integral constraint that drives the system tends to 0.

Hindawi Publishing Corporation
Proceedings of the Conference on Differential & Difference Equations and Applications, pp. 391–402

In this note, we start by recalling some of the relevant previous work that address the questions (i)–(iv) raised above. Then we summarize our work in this field without going into all the details.

The papers that address the issues raised above are few in number. This fact might be partially explained by the absence of a variety of well-posed nonlinear inverse problems. We classify these results on the global behavior of solutions under two headings: point source problems, problems with integral constraints.

The works of Riganti and Savateev [13] and Trong and Ang [14] are both point source problems, they are also called coefficient identification problems. In [13] the authors prove the global solvability of the solutions for the problem

$$\begin{aligned} u_t &= u_{xx} + F(t)u^p, \quad x \in (0,l),\ t \in (0,T), \\ u(x,0) &= u_0(x), \quad x \in [0,l], \\ u_x(0,t) &= u_x(l,t) = 0, \quad \forall t \in [0,T]. \end{aligned} \tag{1.1}$$

Here $0 < p < 1$ is a given number, $F(t)$ and $u(x,t)$ are the functions to be determined under the additional condition

$$u(x_0,t) = \phi(t), \quad t \in [0,T],\ x_0 \in (0,l), \tag{1.2}$$

and compatibility conditions

$$u_0'(0) = u_0'(l) = 0, \quad u_0(x_0) = \phi(0). \tag{1.3}$$

This is in fact an interior source problem where $\phi(t)$ is a given function that measures the intensity of the interior source and u and F are unknown functions. They also prove the stability of the stationary solution under some restrictions on the data. In [14] Trong and Ang consider the following boundary source problem:

$$\begin{aligned} u_t &= u_{xx} + b(t)u_x, \quad 0 < x < 1, \\ u(x,0) &= u_0(x), \quad 0 \le x \le 1, \\ u(0,t) = f(t), \quad u_x(1,t) = 0, \quad t > 0, &\qquad u_x(0,t) + b(t)u(0,t) = 0, \quad t > 0, \end{aligned} \tag{1.4}$$

where f, u_0 are given functions, $b(t)$ and $u(x,t)$ are unknown functions. They prove the global nonexistence of solutions. In [1] a stability result has been proven for the solution of the problem

$$\begin{aligned} u_t &= u_{xx} + u^2 - K^2(t), \quad x \in (0,1),\ t > 0, \\ u_x(0,t) &= u_x(1,t) = 0, \quad t > 0, \end{aligned} \tag{1.5}$$

with the integral constraint $\int_0^1 u(x,t)dx = 0$. In fact, the authors proved that for initial data with small L^2-norm the solution converges to zero in H^1-norm.They also established a blowup result by considering some conditions on the first two Fourier coefficients of the initial data u_0. In [15] Vasin and Kamynin established the stability of the zero solution in the L^2-norm for an inverse problem for a second-order linear parabolic equation. Whereas in [7], Guvenilir and Kalantarov showed the asymptotic stability in the H^1-norm for linear parabolic- and hyperbolic-type problems. Last but not the least, Hu and Yin [8] have considered the problem of global nonexistence when $b = 0$ in (2.1), with Neumann boundary condition instead of (2.2) and when $w(x) \equiv 1$. They also treat the problem

$$\begin{aligned} u_t &= \Delta u + k(t)u^p \quad \text{for } x \in \Omega,\ t > 0, \\ \int_\Omega u(x,t)dx &= g(t), \end{aligned} \tag{1.6}$$

and established global existence result as well as a blowup result for radially symmetric solutions.

Let us recall also the basic lemma from [9].

Lemma 1.1. *Let $\alpha > 0$, $C_1, C_2 \geq 0$, and $C_1 + C_2 > 0$. Suppose that $\Psi(t)$ is a twice differentiable positive function satisfying*

$$\Psi''\Psi - (1+\alpha)[\Psi']^2 \geq -2C_1\Psi\Psi' - C_2[\Psi]^2 \tag{1.7}$$

for all $t \geq 0$. If $\Psi(0) > 0$, and $\Psi'(0) + \gamma_2\alpha^{-1}\Psi(0) > 0$, then

$$\Psi(t) \longrightarrow \infty \quad \text{as } t \longrightarrow t_1 \leq t_2 = \frac{1}{2\sqrt{C_1^2 + \alpha C_2}} \ln \frac{\gamma_1\Psi(0) + \alpha\Psi'(0)}{\gamma_2\Psi(0) + \alpha\Psi'(0)}. \tag{1.8}$$

Here $\gamma_1 = -C_1 + \sqrt{C_1^2 + \alpha C_2}$, $\gamma_2 = -C_1 - \sqrt{C_1^2 + \alpha C_2}$.

2. Parabolic equations

In this section we consider the global in time behavior of solutions of inverse source problems for nonlinear second-order parabolic equations. First we consider the following problem:

$$u_t - \Delta u - |u|^p u + b(x,t,u,\nabla u) = F(t)w(x), \quad x \in \Omega,\ t > 0, \tag{2.1}$$

$$u(x,t) = 0, \quad x \in \partial\Omega,\ t > 0, \tag{2.2}$$

$$u(x,0) = u_0(x), \quad x \in \Omega, \tag{2.3}$$

$$\int_\Omega u(x,t)w(x)dx = 1, \quad t > 0. \tag{2.4}$$

Here and in the rest of the paper Ω is a domain of R^n with smooth boundary $\partial\Omega, p$ is a given positive number, $w(x), u_0(x)$, and $b(x,t,u,q)$ are given functions. Assume that

$$w \in H^2(\Omega) \cap H_0^1(\Omega) \cap L^{p+2}(\Omega), \qquad \int_\Omega w^2(x)dx = 1, \tag{2.5}$$

and, for some $M_1, M_2 > 0$,

$$|b(x,t,u,q)| \le M_1|q| + M_2|u|, \quad \forall x \in \Omega,\ t \in R^+,\ u \in R,\ q \in R^n. \tag{2.6}$$

The problem is to find a pair of functions $\{u(x,t), F(t)\}$ satisfying (2.1)–(2.4) when

$$u_0 \in H_0^1(\Omega) \cap L^{p+2}(\Omega), \qquad \int_\Omega u_0(x)w(x)dx = 1. \tag{2.7}$$

THEOREM 2.1. *Let the conditions (2.5)–(2.7) be satisfied and assume that* $\|u_0\| > 0$ *and*

$$\left[||u_0||_{p+2}^{p+2} - \frac{1}{2}||\nabla u_0||^2 - \left(\frac{\lambda_0}{2} + \frac{3M_1^2}{8\epsilon_1} + \frac{\delta(1+\alpha)^2}{\alpha(p+4)} \right) ||u_0||^2 \right] > \widetilde{C}(p, M_1, M_2, w), \tag{2.8}$$

where $\|\cdot\|$ *is the norm and* $\langle\cdot,\cdot\rangle$ *is the inner product of* $L^2(\Omega)$, $\widetilde{C}(p, M_1, M_2, w)$ *is sufficiently large positive number,* $\epsilon_1 = p/8 + 2p, \delta = -\gamma_2/\alpha, \lambda_0 = 3p + 6/p[1 + M_1^2(p+4)/p]$, $\alpha = -1 + (1 + p/8)^{1/2}$.

Then there exists a finite t_1 *such that*

$$||u(t)|| \longrightarrow +\infty \quad as\ t \longrightarrow t_1^-. \tag{2.9}$$

To prove the theorem we consider the following problem that is obtained from (2.1)–(2.4) by substituting $v(x,t) = u(x,t)e^{-\lambda t}$:

$$v_t - \Delta v + \lambda v - e^{\lambda pt}|v|^p v + b(x,t,e^{\lambda t}v, e^{\lambda t}\nabla v)e^{-\lambda t} = Fwe^{-\lambda t}, \quad x \in \Omega,\ t > 0, \tag{2.10}$$

$$v(x,t) = 0, \quad x \in \partial\Omega,\ t > 0, \tag{2.11}$$

$$v(x,0) = u_0(x), \quad x \in \Omega, \tag{2.12}$$

$$\langle v, w \rangle = e^{-\lambda t}, \quad t > 0. \tag{2.13}$$

The value of the parameter λ will be prescribed later. We, multiplying (2.10) by w and using (2.13), obtain

$$F(t) = -e^{\lambda t}\langle v, \Delta w\rangle - e^{\lambda(p+1)t}\langle |v|^p v, w\rangle + \langle b(x,t,e^{\lambda t}v, e^{\lambda t}\nabla v), w\rangle. \tag{2.14}$$

Substituting (2.14) into (2.10) one obtains a problem that is shown to be equivalent to (2.10)–(2.13). (See, e.g. [12], or [2].)

Following [9, 11], we define the functional as

$$\Psi(t) = \int_0^t ||v(\tau)||^2 d\tau + C_3, \tag{2.15}$$

where $C_3 > 0$ is judiciously chosen constant that depends on $M_1, M_2, \lambda_0, p, w(x)$, and $\|u_0\|$. It is clear that

$$\Psi'(t) = ||v(t)||^2 = 2\int_0^t \langle v_\tau, v\rangle d\tau + ||u_0||^2, \qquad \Psi''(t) = \frac{d}{dt}||v(t)||^2. \tag{2.16}$$

In order to obtain a differential inequality of the form (2.10), we need to bound from below $\Psi''(t)$ for solutions of (2.10)–(2.13).

The following notations are introduced to simplify the estimates:

$$\begin{aligned} \hat{b}(t,v) &\equiv b(x,t,e^{\lambda t}v,e^{\lambda t}\nabla v), \qquad & G(t,v) &\equiv e^{\lambda pt}\int_\Omega |v|^{p+2}dx, \\ L(v(t)) &\equiv \|\nabla v(t)\|^2+\lambda\|v(t)\|^2, \qquad & j(t) &\equiv -\frac{1}{2}L(v)+\frac{1}{p+2}G(t,v). \end{aligned} \tag{2.17}$$

To achieve our task first we estimate $d/dt\|v\|^2$ from below in terms of $j(t)$ and $-\|v\|^2$, then estimate $j(t)$ from below by $\int_0^t \|v_\tau\|^2 d\tau$ and $\int_0^t \|v\|^2 d\tau$. And finally combine the previous lower estimates to obtain a lower estimate for $\Psi''\Psi-(1+\alpha)[\Psi']^2$ for a suitably chosen $\alpha>0$.

To get the lower estimate for $d/dt\|v\|^2$, we multiply (2.10) by v, integrate over Ω, using (2.13) and (2.14)

$$\begin{aligned} \frac{1}{2}\Psi''(t) &= \frac{1}{2}\frac{d}{dt}\|v\|^2+L(v)-G(t,v)+\langle\hat{b}(t,v),v\rangle e^{-\lambda t} \\ &= -e^{-\lambda t}\langle v,\Delta w\rangle - e^{\lambda(p-1)t}\langle |v|^p v,w\rangle+\langle\hat{b}(t,v),w\rangle e^{-2\lambda t}. \end{aligned} \tag{2.18}$$

On the other hand, multiplying (2.10) by v_t, integrating over Ω, and using in addition to (2.13) and (2.18) the fact that $\langle w,v_t\rangle=-\lambda e^{-\lambda t}$, we get

$$\begin{aligned} &\|v_t\|^2-\frac{d}{dt}j(t)+\frac{\lambda p}{p+2}G(t,v)+\langle\hat{b}(t,v),v_t\rangle e^{-\lambda t} \\ &\quad=\lambda\Big[e^{-\lambda t}\langle v,\Delta w\rangle+e^{\lambda(p-1)t}\langle |v|^p v,w\rangle-\langle\hat{b}(t,v),w\rangle e^{-2\lambda t}\Big]. \end{aligned} \tag{2.19}$$

Now we are going to estimate various terms on the right-hand side of (2.19) by the appropriate combinations of $G(t,v)$ and $j(t)$. Let us recall that Young's inequality implies that, for $a,b\geq 0$,

$$ab\leq \beta a^q+C(\beta,q)b^{q'} \tag{2.20}$$

for $1/q+1/q'=1$ and where $\beta>0, C(\beta,q)=1/q'(\beta q)^{q'/q}$.

Taking $a=\|v\|, b=\|\Delta w\|e^{-\lambda t}, q=q'=2$, and $\beta=\lambda p/8$, we get

$$|\langle v,\Delta w\rangle e^{-\lambda t}|\leq\frac{\lambda p}{8}\|v\|^2+\frac{2}{p\lambda}\|\Delta w\|^2 e^{-2\lambda t}, \tag{2.21}$$

and taking $q=(p+2)/p+1, q'=p+2, a=e^{(\lambda(p^2+p)/p+2)t}\|v\|_{p+2}^{p+1}, b=\|w\|_{p+2}e^{-2\lambda t/(p+2)}$, and $\beta=p/(2(p+2))$, we get

$$e^{\lambda(p-1)t}\int_\Omega |v|^p v w dx\leq\frac{p}{2(p+2)}G(t,v)+\frac{e^{-2\lambda t}}{(p+2)[p/(2p+2)]^{p+1}}\int_\Omega |w|^{p+2}dx. \tag{2.22}$$

By using the condition (2.6) similarly, we obtain

$$e^{-2\lambda t}\,|\,\langle\hat{b}(t,v),w\rangle\,|\;\le\frac{p}{8}\|\nabla v\|^2+\frac{2}{p}M_1^2\|w\|^2e^{-2\lambda t}+\frac{\lambda p}{4}\|v\|^2+\frac{M_2^2}{\lambda p}\|w\|^2e^{-2\lambda t},\tag{2.23}$$

$$e^{-\lambda t}\,|\,\langle\hat{b}(t,v),v\rangle\,|\;\le M_1\|\nabla v\|\|v\|+M_2\|v\|^2\le\left(M_2+\frac{2M_1^2}{p}\right)\|v\|^2+\frac{p}{8}\|\nabla v\|^2.\tag{2.24}$$

Rewriting (2.18) and using (2.21)–(2.24),

$$\frac{1}{2}\frac{d}{dt}\|v\|^2\ge\left(\frac{p}{2}+2\right)j(t)-\left(M_1+\frac{2}{p}M_2^2\right)\|v\|^2-D_0,\tag{2.25}$$

where $D_0=2\lambda/p\|\Delta w\|^2+(1/(p+2)[p/(2p+2)]^{p+1})\|w\|_{p+2}^{p+2}+((2/p)M_1^2+(M_2^2/\lambda p))\|w\|^2$.

The last inequality gives us a lower bound of $\Psi''(t)$ in terms of $j(t)$ and $-\|v\|^2$. Thus we next set out to estimate $j(t)$ from below using (2.19). We proceed to estimate the terms on the right-hand side of (2.19) similar to (2.21) and (2.22) with $\beta=1/2$ and $b=\lambda\|\Delta w\|e^{-\lambda t}$ in the first case and with $\beta=1$ and $b=\lambda\|w\|_{p+2}e^{-2\lambda t/(p+2)}$ in the second case to get

$$|\,\lambda e^{-\lambda t}\langle v,\Delta w\rangle\,|\;\le\frac{1}{2}\|v\|^2+\frac{\lambda^2}{2}\|\Delta w\|^2e^{-2\lambda t},\tag{2.26}$$

$$|\,\lambda e^{\lambda(p-1)t}\langle|v|^pv,w\rangle\,|\;\le G(t,v)+C(p)\lambda^{p+2}e^{-2\lambda t}\int_\Omega|w|^{p+2}dx.\tag{2.27}$$

From Young's inequality we get the estimates

$$e^{-\lambda t}\,|\,\langle\hat{b}(t,v),v_t\rangle\,|\;\le\epsilon_1\|v_t\|^2+\frac{3M_1^2}{8\epsilon_1}\|\nabla v\|^2+\frac{3M_2^2}{4\epsilon_1}\|v\|^2,\tag{2.28}$$

$$\lambda e^{-2\lambda t}\,|\,\langle\hat{b}(t,v),w\rangle\,|\;\le\frac{1}{2}\|\nabla v\|^2+\frac{1}{2}(M_1^2+M_2^2)\lambda^2e^{-2\lambda t}\|w\|^2+\frac{1}{2}\|v\|^2.\tag{2.29}$$

Rewriting (2.19) and using (2.26)–(2.29),

$$\begin{aligned}\frac{d}{dt}j(t)\ge{}&(1-\epsilon_1)\|v_t\|^2+\left(\frac{\lambda p}{p+2}-1\right)G(t,v)-\left[\frac{3M_1^2}{8\epsilon_1}+\frac{1}{2}\right]\|\nabla v\|^2-\left[\frac{3M_2^2}{4\epsilon_1}+1\right]\|v\|^2\\&-\frac{\lambda^2}{2}\|\Delta w\|^2e^{-2\lambda t}-C(p)\lambda^{p+2}e^{-2\lambda t}\|w\|_{p+2}^{p+2}-\frac{1}{2}(M_1^2+M_2^2)\lambda^2\|w\|^2e^{-2\lambda t}.\end{aligned}\tag{2.30}$$

Integrating the inequality (2.30) from 0 to t and estimating $1-e^{-2\lambda t}$ by 1, we get

$$\begin{aligned}j(t)\ge{}&j(0)+(1-\epsilon_1)\int_0^t\|v_\tau\|^2d\tau+\left(\frac{\lambda p}{p+2}-1\right)\int_0^tG(\tau,v)d\tau\\&-\left[\frac{3M_1^2}{8\epsilon_1}+\frac{1}{2}\right]\int_0^t\|\nabla v\|^2d\tau-\left[\frac{3M_2^2}{4\epsilon_1}+1\right]\int_0^t\|v\|^2d\tau-D_1,\end{aligned}\tag{2.31}$$

where $D_1=\lambda/4\|\Delta w\|^2+(C(p)\lambda^{p+1})/2\|w\|_{p+2}^{p+2}+\lambda/4[M_1^2+M_2^2]\|w\|^2$.

In (2.31), we still need to estimate from above $\int_0^t \|\nabla v\|^2 d\tau$, we will achieve estimating this term from (2.18):

$$\begin{aligned}
&\frac{1}{2}\frac{d}{dt}\|v(t)\|^2 + \|\nabla v(t)\|^2 + \lambda\|v(t)\|^2 \\
&\quad \le 2G(t,v) + C(p)e^{-2\lambda t}\|w\|_{p+2}^{p+2} + \frac{1}{4}\|\nabla v\|^2 + (M_1^2 + M_2)\|v\|^2 + \frac{\lambda}{2}\|v\|^2 \qquad (2.32)\\
&\qquad + \frac{1}{2\lambda}\|\Delta w\|^2 e^{-2\lambda t} + \frac{\lambda}{2}\|v\|^2 + \frac{M_2^2}{2\lambda}\|w\|^2 e^{-2\lambda t} + \frac{1}{4}\|\nabla v\|^2 + M_1^2\|w\|^2 e^{-2\lambda t}.
\end{aligned}$$

Rearranging and integrating (2.32) from 0 to t,

$$\frac{1}{2}\|v(t)\|^2 + \frac{1}{2}\int_0^t \|\nabla v\|^2 d\tau \le \frac{1}{2}\|u_0\|^2 + 2\int_0^t G(\tau, v(\tau))d\tau + (M_1^2 + M_2)\int_0^t \|v\|^2 d\tau + D_2, \qquad (2.33)$$

where $D_2 = C(p)/2\lambda \int_\Omega |w|^{p+2}dx + (M_2^2/4\lambda^2 + M_1^2/2\lambda)\|w\|^2 + 1/4\lambda^2\|\Delta w\|^2$.

Dropping the first term on the left-hand side of (2.33), we get

$$\int_0^t \|\nabla v(\tau)\|^2 d\tau \le 2D_2 + \|u_0\|^2 + 4\int_0^t G(\tau, v(\tau))d\tau + 2(M_1^2 + M_2)\int_0^t \|v\|^2 d\tau. \qquad (2.34)$$

Using this estimate in (2.31),

$$j(t) \ge (1-\epsilon_1)\int_0^t \|v_\tau\|^2 d\tau - M_4\int_0^t \|v\|^2 d\tau + D_3, \qquad (2.35)$$

where $D_3 = j(0) - (3M_1^2/8\epsilon_1 + (1/2))[\|u_0\|^2 + 2D_2] - D_1, M_4 = 3M_2^2/4\epsilon_1 + (1/2) + (3M_1^2/4\epsilon_1 + 2)(M_1^2 + M_2)$.

We are now set for the application of the lemma. Combining (2.25) with (2.35),

$$\begin{aligned}
\Psi''(t) = \frac{d}{dt}\|v\|^2 &\ge (4+p)j(t) - 2\left(M_1 + \frac{2}{p}M_2^2\right)\|v\|^2 - 2D_0 \\
&\ge 4\left(1+\frac{p}{4}\right)(1-\epsilon_1)\int_0^t \|v_\tau\|^2 d\tau - 4\left(1+\frac{p}{4}\right)M_4\int_0^t \|v\|^2 d\tau \qquad (2.36)\\
&\quad - 2\left(M_1 + \frac{2}{p}M_2^2\right)\|v\|^2 + 4\left(1+\frac{p}{4}\right)D_3 - 2D_0.
\end{aligned}$$

We take $\epsilon_1 = (p/8)/(1+(p/4))$ and $\lambda = \lambda_0$ given in Theorem 2.1. Then the last inequality takes the form

$$\Psi''(t) \ge 4\left(1+\frac{p}{8}\right)\int_0^t \|v_\tau\|^2 d\tau - (4+p)M_4\Psi(t) - 2C_1\|v\|^2 + A_0 + (4+p)M_4C_3, \qquad (2.37)$$

where $C_1 = (M_1 + (2/p)M_2^2)$ and $A_0 = (4+p)D_3 - 2D_0$. It is easy to see that

$$\begin{aligned}[\Psi'(t)]^2 &= \left(\|u_0\|^2 + 2\int_0^t \langle v, v_\tau\rangle d\tau\right)^2 \\ &\le \left(1+\frac{1}{\epsilon_4}\right)\|u_0\|^4 + 4(1+\epsilon_4)\left(\int_0^t \|v\|^2 d\tau\right)\left(\int_0^t \|v_\tau\|^2 d\tau\right).\end{aligned} \tag{2.38}$$

Thus

$$\begin{aligned}\Psi''(t)\Psi(t) - (1+\alpha)[\Psi'(t)]^2 &\ge 4\left(1+\frac{p}{8}\right)\int_0^t \|v_\tau\|^2 d\tau\left(\int_0^t \|v\|^2 d\tau + C_3\right) \\ &\quad + [A_0 - (p+4)M_4\Psi(t) + (p+4)M_4C_3 - 2C_1\Psi'(t)]\Psi(t) \\ &\quad - 4(1+\alpha)(1+\epsilon_4)\int_0^t \|v_\tau\|^2 d\tau \\ &\quad \times \int_0^t \|v\|^2 d\tau - (1+\alpha)\left(1+\frac{1}{\epsilon_4}\right)\|u_0\|^4.\end{aligned} \tag{2.39}$$

Let us choose $\alpha = \epsilon_4 > 0$ so that $(1+\alpha)^2 = 1 + (p/8)$, that is, $\alpha = -1 + \sqrt{1+(p/8)}$. So due to the Cauchy-Schwarz inequality, we have $\int_0^t \|v_\tau\|^2 d\tau \int_0^t \|v\|^2 d\tau - (\int_0^t \langle v, v_\tau\rangle d\tau)^2 \ge 0$ and the inequality (2.39) can be simplified to

$$\Psi''(t)\Psi(t) - \left(1+\frac{p}{4}\right)[\Psi'(t)]^2 \ge -2C_1\Psi'(t)\Psi(t) - (p+4)M_4\Psi^2(t) + D_4, \tag{2.40}$$

where $D_4 = A_0C_3 + (p+4)M_4C_3^2 - ((1+\alpha)^2/\alpha)\|u_0\|^4$. So the lemma can be applied if $D_4 \ge 0$ and $\psi'(0) > \delta\Psi(0)$, where $\delta = -\gamma_2/\alpha$. Assume that $\|u_0\| > 0$, $A_0 > (\delta(1+\alpha)^2/\alpha)\|u_0\|^2$ and let us choose $C_3 = ((1+\alpha)^2/\alpha)(\|u_0\|^4/A_0)$. Then $D_4 \ge 0$ and $\delta\Psi(0) = \delta C_3 = ((1+\alpha)^2\delta/\alpha)(\|u_0\|^4/A_0) < \|u_0\|^2 = \Psi'(0)$.

So the function $\Psi(t)$ satisfies all conditions of lemma and therefore there exists $0 < t_1 < \infty$, such that $\|u(t)\|$ tends to infinity as $t \to t_1^-$. Hence the conclusion of Theorem 2.1 is true.

2.1. Stability problem. Here we consider the following inverse source problem:

$$u_t - \Delta u + |u|^p u = F(t)w(x), \quad x \in \Omega,\ t > 0, \tag{2.41}$$

$$u(x,t) = 0, \quad x \in \partial\Omega,\ t > 0, \tag{2.42}$$

$$u(x,0) = u_0(x), \quad x \in \Omega, \tag{2.43}$$

$$\int_\Omega u(x,t)w(x)dx = \phi(t), \quad t > 0, \tag{2.44}$$

where Ω is a bounded domain. We assume that w satisfies the condition (2.5), and u_0 satisfies conditions

$$u_0 \in H_0^1(\Omega) \cap L^{p+2}(\Omega), \quad \int_\Omega u_0(x)w(x)dx = \phi(0). \tag{2.45}$$

THEOREM 2.2. *Assume that the conditions (2.5) and (2.45) are satisfied and suppose that ϕ, ϕ' are continuous functions defined on $[0,\infty)$, which tend to 0 as $t \to \infty$. Then*

$$\lim_{t\to\infty} \left[\|\nabla u(t)\|^2 + \|u(t)\|_{p+2}^{p+2} \right] = 0. \tag{2.46}$$

Proof. Multiplying (2.41) by w, integrating over Ω, and using (2.44), we obtain

$$F(t) = \phi'(t) - \langle \nabla u, \nabla w \rangle + \langle |u|^p u, w \rangle. \tag{2.47}$$

Thus (2.41) takes the form

$$u_t - \Delta u + |u|^p u = [\phi'(t) - \langle \nabla u, \nabla w \rangle + \langle |u|^p u, w \rangle] w(x), \quad x \in \Omega,\ t > 0. \tag{2.48}$$

To show (2.46) we multiply the last equation by $u_t + u$ and integrate over Ω:

$$\begin{aligned} &\frac{d}{dt}\left[\frac{1}{2}\|u\|^2 + \frac{1}{2}\|\nabla u\|^2 + \frac{1}{p+2}\|u\|_{p+2}^{p+2}\right] + \|\nabla u\|^2 + \|u\|_{p+2}^{p+2} \\ &\quad \le \phi'(t)^2 + |\phi'(t)\phi(t)| + \|\nabla u\|\,\|\nabla w\|(|\phi'(t)| + |\phi(t)|) \\ &\quad + |\langle |u|^p u, w\rangle| (|\phi'(t)| + |\phi(t)|). \end{aligned} \tag{2.49}$$

By using the Young inequality with ϵ in the right-hand side of the last inequality, we obtain

$$\frac{d}{dt}E(t) + k_0(1-\epsilon)E(t) \le h(t). \tag{2.50}$$

Here $\epsilon \in (0,1), E(t) \equiv (1/2)\|u\|^2 + (1/2)\|\nabla u\|^2 + (1/p+2)\|u\|_{p+2}^{p+2}$, $h(t) \equiv \phi'(t)^2 + |\phi'(t)\phi(t)| + (1/2\epsilon)\|\nabla w\|^2(|\phi'(t)|^2 + |\phi(t)|^2) + C(\epsilon,p)\|w\|_{p+2}^{p+2}(|\phi'(t)|^{p+2} + |\phi(t)|^{p+2})$. Since $h(t) \to 0$ as $t \to \infty$, the result follows. □

3. Wave equations

The inverse problem we consider first in this section consists of finding a pair of functions $\{u(x,t), F(t)\}$ satisfying

$$u_{tt} - \Delta u - |u|^p u + b(x,t,u,\nabla u) = F(t)w(x), \quad x \in \Omega,\ t > 0, \tag{3.1}$$

$$u(x,t) = 0, \quad x \in \partial\Omega,\ t > 0, \tag{3.2}$$

$$u(x,0) = u_0(x), \quad u_t(x,0) = u_1(x), \quad x \in \Omega, \tag{3.3}$$

$$\int_\Omega u(x,t)w(x)dx = 1, \quad t > 0. \tag{3.4}$$

THEOREM 3.1. *Let the conditions (2.5)–(2.7) be satisfied, $u_1 \in L^2(\Omega), \langle u_1, w\rangle = 0$, and assume that*

$$E(0) = \left[-\frac{1}{2}||u_1||^2 - \frac{1}{2}||\nabla u_0||^2 - \frac{\lambda^2}{2}||u_0||^2 + \frac{1}{p+2}||u_0||_{p+2}^{p+2}\right] > D(p, M_1, M_2, w), \quad (3.5)$$

where $\lambda = \max\{(p+2/p)(M_1 + M_2 + 1); (M_2/2)^{1/3}\}$, and $D(p, M_1, M_2, w)$ is sufficiently large positive number. Then there exists a finite t_1 such that the solution of the problem (3.1)–(3.4) blows up in a finite time, that is,

$$||u(t)|| \longrightarrow +\infty \quad \text{as } t \longrightarrow t_1^-. \quad (3.6)$$

The way of proof of this theorem is similar to the proof of Theorem 2.1. Here we show that $\Psi(t) = \|u(t)\|^2$ blows up in a finite time.

3.1. Stability problem and the exponential attractor. Now we consider the following inverse source problem:

$$u_{tt} - \Delta u + au_t + |u|^p u - bu = F(t)w(x), \quad x \in \Omega,\ t > 0, \quad (3.7)$$

$$u(x,t) = 0, \quad x \in \partial\Omega,\ t > 0, \quad (3.8)$$

$$u(x,0) = u_0(x), \quad u_t(x,0) = u_1(x), \quad x \in \Omega, \quad (3.9)$$

$$\int_\Omega u(x,t)w(x)dx = \phi(t), \quad t > 0. \quad (3.10)$$

THEOREM 3.2. *Assume that the conditions (2.5) and (2.45) are satisfied, the damping coefficient $b \in (0, \lambda_1)$ and suppose that ϕ, ϕ', ϕ'' are continuous functions defined on $[0, \infty)$, such that ϕ'' is a bounded function and ϕ, ϕ' tend to 0 as $t \to \infty$. Then*

$$\lim_{t\to\infty}\left[||u_t||^2 + ||\nabla u(t)||^2 + ||u(t)||_{p+2}^{p+2}\right] = 0. \quad (3.11)$$

Multiplying (3.7) by w, integrating over Ω, and using (3.10), we obtain

$$F(t) = \phi''(t) + \langle \nabla u, \nabla w\rangle + a\phi'(t) + \langle |u|^p u, w\rangle - b\phi(t). \quad (3.12)$$

Substituting (3.12) in (3.7), we get

$$\begin{aligned} &u_{tt} - \Delta u + au_t + |u|^p u - bu \\ &\quad = \left[\phi''(t) + \langle \nabla u, \nabla w\rangle + a\phi'(t) + \langle |u|^p u, w\rangle - b\phi(t)\right]w(x), \quad x \in \Omega,\ t > 0. \end{aligned} \quad (3.13)$$

To get the result we derive the inequality

$$\frac{d}{dt}E_\eta(t) + \delta\frac{d}{dt}E_\eta(t) \le H(t) \quad (3.14)$$

for the Lyapunov-like functional

$$E_\eta(t) \equiv \frac{1}{2}\|u_t\|^2 + \frac{1}{2}\|\nabla u\|^2 + \frac{1}{p+2}\|u\|_{p+2}^{p+2} - \frac{b}{2}\|u\|^2 + \eta\frac{a}{2}\|u\|^2 + \eta\langle u_t, u\rangle, \tag{3.15}$$

where

$$\begin{aligned} H(t) \equiv{}& |\phi''(t)\phi'(t)| + (b+\eta a)|\phi'(t)\phi(t)| \\ &+ \frac{1}{4\epsilon}\|\nabla w\|^2(|\phi'(t)| + \eta|\phi(t)|)^2 \\ &+ C(\epsilon,p)\|w\|_{p+2}^{p+2}(|\phi'(t)| + \eta|\phi(t)|)^{p+2} \end{aligned} \tag{3.16}$$

and δ is some positive number. Since $H(t) \to 0$ as $t \to \infty$ by the conditions imposed on $\phi(t)$, the result of the theorem follows from the estimate

$$\|u_t(t)\|^2 + \|\nabla u(t)\|^2 + \|u(t)\|_{p+2}^{p+2} \le C_0 E_\eta(t), \tag{3.17}$$

which we derived using $0 < b < \lambda_1$, for $\eta < a/2$.

3.2. Strongly damped wave equation. Now we consider the following inverse source problem:

$$\begin{aligned} u_{tt} - \Delta u - \Delta u_t + |u|^p u &= F(t)w(x), \quad x \in \Omega,\ t > 0, \\ u(x,t) &= 0, \quad x \in \partial\Omega,\ t > 0, \\ u(x,0) = u_0(x), \quad u_t(x,0) &= u_1(x), \quad x \in \Omega, \\ \int_\Omega u(x,t)w(x)dx &= \phi(t), \quad t > 0. \end{aligned} \tag{3.18}$$

We assume that w satisfies the condition (2.6), $u_1 \in L^2(\Omega)$, $\langle u_1, w\rangle w = \phi'(0)$ and u_0 satisfy condition (2.45).

Similarly we can show that the energy integral

$$E(t) = \frac{1}{2}\|u_t(t)\|^2 + \frac{1}{2}\|\nabla u(t)\|^2 + \frac{1}{p+2}\|u(t)\|_{p+2}^{p+2} \tag{3.19}$$

is tending to zero with an exponential rate as $t \to +\infty$. When $\phi(t) \equiv 1$, this problem is equivalent to the following initial boundary value problem:

$$\begin{aligned} &u_{tt} - \Delta u - \Delta u_t + |u|^p u \\ &\quad = [\langle \nabla u, \nabla w\rangle + \langle \nabla u_t, \nabla w\rangle + \langle |u|^p u, w\rangle - b\langle u, w\rangle]w, \quad x \in \Omega,\ t > 0, \end{aligned} \tag{3.20}$$

$$u(x,t) = 0, \quad x \in \partial\Omega,\ t > 0, \tag{3.21}$$

$$u(x,0) = u_0(x), \quad u_t(x,0) = u_1(x), \quad x \in \Omega. \tag{3.22}$$

A proper modification of arguments in [3, 4] allows us to show that, if $p < (n+2)/(n-2)$, when $n \geq 3$ and $p > 0$ when $n = 1,2$, this problem generates a continuous semigroup $V_t, t > 0$, in a phase space $X_1 : H_0^1(\Omega) \times L^2(\Omega)$, which has an exponential attractor $A \subset X_1$.

References

[1] C. Budd, B. Dold, and A. Stuart, *Blowup in a partial differential equation with conserved first integral*, SIAM Journal on Applied Mathematics **53** (1993), no. 3, 718–742.

[2] J. R. Cannon, *The One-Dimensional Heat Equation*, Encyclopedia of Mathematics and Its Applications, vol. 23, Addison-Wesley, Massachusetts, 1984.

[3] A. Eden and V. K. Kalantarov, *Finite-dimensional attractors for a class of semilinear wave equations*, Turkish Journal of Mathematics **20** (1996), no. 3, 425–450.

[4] ———, *On the discrete squeezing property for semilinear wave equations*, Turkish Journal of Mathematics **22** (1998), no. 3, 335–341.

[5] ———, *On global behavior of solutions to an inverse problem for semi-linear hyperbolic equations*, Zapiski Nauchnykh Seminarov (POMI) **318** (2004), no. 35, 120–134.

[6] ———, *On global behavior of solutions to an inverse problem for nonlinear parabolic equations*, Journal of Mathematical Analysis and Applications **307** (2005), no. 1, 120–133.

[7] A. F. Güvenilir and V. K. Kalantarov, *The asymptotic behavior of solutions to an inverse problem for differential operator equations*, Mathematical and Computer Modelling **37** (2003), no. 9-10, 907–914.

[8] B. Hu and H.-M. Yin, *Semilinear parabolic equations with prescribed energy*, Rendiconti del Circolo Matematico di Palermo. Serie II **44** (1995), no. 3, 479–505.

[9] V. K. Kalantarov and O. A. Ladyženskaja, *Formation of collapses in quasilinear equations of parabolic and hyperbolic types*, Zapiski Naučnyh Seminarov Leningradskogo Otdelenija Matematičeskogo Instituta (LOMI) **69** (1977), 77–102.

[10] H. A. Levine, *Some nonexistence and instability theorems for solutions of formally parabolic equations of the form $Pu_t = -Au + F(u)$*, Archive for Rational Mechanics and Analysis **51** (1973), 371–386.

[11] ———, *Instability and nonexistence of global solutions to nonlinear wave equations of the form $Pu_{tt} = -Au + F(u)$*, Transactions of the American Mathematical Society **192** (1974), 1–21.

[12] A. I. Prilepko, D. G. Orlovsky, and I. A. Vasin, *Methods for Solving Inverse Problems in Mathematical Physics*, Monographs and Textbooks in Pure and Applied Mathematics, vol. 231, Marcel Dekker, New York, 2000.

[13] R. Riganti and E. Savateev, *Solution of an inverse problem for the nonlinear heat equation*, Communications in Partial Differential Equations **19** (1994), no. 9-10, 1611–1628.

[14] D. D. Trong and D. D. Ang, *Coefficient identification for a parabolic equation*, Inverse Problems **10** (1994), no. 3, 733–752.

[15] I. A. Vasin and V. L. Kamynin, *On the asymptotic behavior of solutions of inverse problems for parabolic equations*, Siberian Mathematical Journal **38** (1997), no. 4, 647–662.

A. Eden: Department of Mathematics, Bogaziçi University, 34342 Istanbul, Turkey
E-mail address: eden@boun.edu.tr

V. K. Kalantarov: Department of Mathematics, Koç University, 34450 Istanbul, Turkey
E-mail address: vkalantarov@ku.edu.tr

JUSTIFICATION OF QUADRATURE-DIFFERENCE METHODS FOR SINGULAR INTEGRODIFFERENTIAL EQUATIONS

A. FEDOTOV

Here we propose and justify quadrature-difference methods for different kinds (linear, nonlinear, and multidimensional) of periodic singular integrodifferential equations.

1. Introduction

In Section 2 we propose and justify quadrature-difference methods for linear and nonlinear singular integrodifferential equations with Hölder-continuous coefficients and right-hand sides. In Section 3 the same method is justified for linear singular integrodifferential equations with discontinuous coefficients and right-hand sides. In Section 4 we propose and justify cubature-difference method for multidimensional singular integrodifferential equations in Sobolev space.

2. Linear and nonlinear singular integrodifferential equations with continuous coefficients

Let us consider the linear singular integrodifferential equation

$$\sum_{\nu=0}^{m}\left(a_\nu(t)x^{(\nu)}(t)+b_\nu(t)(Jx^{(\nu)})(t)+(J^0h_\nu x^{(\nu)})(t)\right)=y(t) \tag{2.1}$$

and the nonlinear singular integrodifferential equation

$$F(t,x^{(m)}(t),\dots,x(t),(Jx^{(m)})(t),\dots,(Jx)(t),(J^0h_mx^{(m)})(t),\dots,(J^0h_0x)(t))=y(t), \tag{2.2}$$

where $x(t)$ is a desired unknown, $a_\nu(t)$, $b_\nu(t), h_\nu(t,\tau), \nu=0,1,\dots,m-1, y(t)$, and $F(t, u_m,\dots,u_0,v_m,\dots,v_0,w_m,\dots,w_0)$ are given continuous 2π-periodic by the variables t,τ

Hindawi Publishing Corporation
Proceedings of the Conference on Differential & Difference Equations and Applications, pp. 403–411

functions, singular integrals

$$(Jx^{(\nu)})(t) = \frac{1}{2\pi}\int_0^{2\pi} x^{(\nu)}(\tau)\cot\frac{\tau - t}{2}d\tau, \quad \nu = 0,1,\ldots,m-1, \tag{2.3}$$

are to be interpreted as the Cauchy-Lebesgue principal value, and

$$(J^0 h_\nu x^{(\nu)})(t) = \frac{1}{2\pi}\int_0^{2\pi} h_\nu(t,\tau)x^{(\nu)}(\tau)d\tau, \quad \nu = 0,1,\ldots,m-1, \tag{2.4}$$

are regular integrals.

Let us fix $n \in \mathbb{N}$ and define on $[0,2\pi]$ the grid

$$t_k = \frac{2\pi k}{n}, \quad k = 0,1,\ldots,n-1. \tag{2.5}$$

An approximate solution of (2.1), (2.2) we seek in the form of the vector

$$\mathbf{x}_n = (x_0, x_1, \ldots, x_{n-1}) \tag{2.6}$$

of values of the unknown function in the nodes (2.5). The components $[\mathbf{x}_n]_k = x_k$, $k = 0,1,\ldots,n-1$, of this vector are a solution of the systems of linear algebraic equations

$$\begin{aligned}\sum_{\nu=0}^{m}\Bigg(a_\nu(t_k)\left[D_n^\nu \mathbf{x}_n\right]_k + \frac{b_\nu(t_k)}{n}\sum_{l=0}^{n-1}\gamma_{k-l}\left[D_n^\nu \mathbf{x}_n\right]_l \\ + \frac{1}{N}\sum_{l=0}^{n-1} h_\nu(t_k,t_l)\left[D_n^\nu \mathbf{x}_n\right]_l\Bigg) = y(t_k), \quad k = 0,1,\ldots,n-1,\end{aligned} \tag{2.7}$$

and the system of nonlinear algebraic equations

$$\begin{aligned}F\Bigg(t_k, \left[D_n^m \mathbf{x}_n\right]_k, \ldots, \left[D_n^0 \mathbf{x}_n\right]_k, \frac{1}{n}\sum_{l=0}^{n-1}\gamma_{k-l}\left[D_n^m \mathbf{x}_n\right]_l, \ldots, \frac{1}{n}\sum_{l=0}^{n-1}\gamma_{k-l}\left[D_n^0 \mathbf{x}_n\right]_l, \\ \frac{1}{n}\sum_{l=0}^{n-1} h_m(t_k,t_l)\left[D_n^m \mathbf{x}_n\right]_l, \ldots, \frac{1}{n}\sum_{l=0}^{n-1} h_0(t_k,t_l)\left[D_n^0 \mathbf{x}_n\right]_l\Bigg) = y(t_k), \quad k = 0,1,\ldots,n-1.\end{aligned} \tag{2.8}$$

Here $D_n^\nu \mathbf{x}_n$, $\nu = 0,1,\ldots,m$, are arbitrary convergent difference formulas defined on the grid (2.5):

$$\begin{aligned}\left[D_n^\nu \mathbf{x}_n\right]_k &= h^{-\nu}\sum_{j=-r_\nu}^{s_\nu} c_{\nu j}x_{k+j}, \quad h = \frac{2\pi}{n}, \ \nu = 0,1,\ldots,m, \\ x_{k+j} &= \begin{cases} x_{k+j+n}, & k+j < 0, \\ x_{k+j-n}, & k+j \geq n, \end{cases} \quad k = 0,1,\ldots,n-1,\end{aligned} \tag{2.9}$$

and $\gamma_{k-l} = \gamma_{k-l}^{(n)}$, $k,l = 0,1,\dots,n-1$,

$$\begin{aligned} \gamma_r^{(n)} &= \left\{ \tan\frac{r\pi}{2n},\ r-\text{even}, -\cot\frac{r\pi}{2n},\ r-\text{odd} \right\}, \quad n-\text{odd}, \\ \gamma_r^{(n)} &= \left\{ 0,\ r-\text{even}, 2\cot\frac{r\pi}{2n},\ r-\text{odd} \right\}, \quad n-\text{even}, \end{aligned} \tag{2.10}$$

are the coefficients of the quadrature formulas.

Let us fix $\beta \in \mathbb{R}$, $0 < \beta \le 1$ and $r \in \mathbb{N}$. By $\mathrm{H}_\beta^{(r)}$ ($\mathrm{H}_\beta^{(0)} = \mathrm{H}_\beta$) and $\mathrm{H}_{\beta,n}^{(r)}(\mathrm{H}_{\beta,n}^{(0)} = \mathrm{H}_{\beta,n})$ we denote the space of 2π-periodic functions with Hölder continuous rth derivative and the space of vectors (2.6) with norms

$$\begin{gathered} \|x\|_{\mathrm{H}_\beta^{(r)}} = \max\left\{ \max_{0\le\nu\le r} \|x^{(\nu)}\|_{\mathrm{C}}, H(x^{(r)};\beta) \right\}, \\ \|x\|_{\mathrm{C}} - \max_{0\le t\le 2\pi} |x(t)|, \qquad H(x;\beta) = \sup_{\substack{t\ne\tau \\ t,\tau\in[0,2\pi]}} \frac{|x(t)-x(\tau)|}{|t-\tau|^\beta}, \\ \|\mathbf{x}_n\|_{\mathrm{H}_{\beta,n}^{(r)}} = \max\left\{ \max_{0\le\nu\le r} \|\bar{D}_n^\nu \mathbf{x}_n\|_{\mathrm{C}_n}, H_n(\bar{D}_n^r \mathbf{x}_n;\beta) \right\}, \\ \|\mathbf{x}_n\|_{\mathrm{C}_n} = \max_{0\le k\le n-1} |[\mathbf{x}_n]_k|, \qquad H_n(\mathbf{x}_n;\beta) = \max_{k\ne l} \frac{|[\mathbf{x}_n]_k - [\mathbf{x}_n]_l|}{|t_k - t_l|^\beta}, \qquad t_k, t_l \in \Delta_n, \\ \bar{D}_n^\nu \mathbf{x}_n = \bar{D}_n(\bar{D}_n^{\nu-1}\mathbf{x}_n), \quad \nu = 1,2,\dots,r, \qquad \bar{D}_n^0 \mathbf{x}_n = \mathbf{x}_n, \\ [\bar{D}_n \mathbf{x}_n]_k = \frac{x_{k+1} - x_k}{h}, \quad k = 0,1,\dots,n-2, \qquad [\bar{D}_n \mathbf{x}_n]_{n-1} = \frac{x_0 - x_{n-1}}{h}, \\ \Delta_n : t_k = \frac{2\pi k}{n}, \quad k = 0,1,\dots,n-1,\ h = \frac{2\pi}{n}, \end{gathered} \tag{2.11}$$

correspondently.

The spaces $\mathrm{H}_\beta^{(m)}, \mathrm{H}_{\beta,n}^{(m)}$ and $\mathrm{H}_\beta, \mathrm{H}_{\beta,n}$ we bind by the operators

$$\begin{aligned} p_n x &= (x(t_0), x(t_1), \dots, x(t_{n-1})), \quad p_n : \mathrm{H}_\beta^{(m)} \longrightarrow \mathrm{H}_{\beta,n}^{(m)}, \\ q_n x &= (x(t_0), x(t_1), \dots, x(t_{n-1})), \quad q_n : \mathrm{H}_\beta \longrightarrow \mathrm{H}_{\beta,n}. \end{aligned} \tag{2.12}$$

Theorem 2.1 [1]. *Assume that (2.1) and the system of equations (2.7) satisfy the following conditions:*

(A1) *functions $a_\nu(t), b_\nu(t), h_\nu(t,\tau)$, $\nu = 0,1,\dots,m$, and $y(t)$ belong to H_α, $0 < \alpha \le 1$;*
(A2) *$a_m^2(t) + b_m^2(t) \ne 0, t \in [0,2\pi]$;*
(A3) *$\kappa = \mathrm{ind}(a_m(t) + ib_m(t)) = 0$;*
(A4) *equation (2.1) has a unique solution $x^*(t) \in \mathrm{H}_\beta^{(m)}$ for any right-hand side $y(t) \in \mathrm{H}_\beta$, $0 < \beta < \alpha$;*
(B1) *the formulas for numerical differentiation $D_n^\nu \mathbf{x}_n$, $\nu = 0,1,\dots,m$, converge;*
(B2) *characteristical values of the formula D_n^m do not lie on the unit circle.*

Then, for sufficiently large n, the system of equations (2.7) is uniquely solvable and the approximate solutions $\mathbf{x}_n^*$ *converge to the exact solution* $x^*(t)$ *of (2.1):*

$$\begin{aligned} ||\mathbf{x}_n^* - p_n x^*||_{\mathrm{H}_{\beta,n}^{(m)}} &\leq C\left(n^{-\alpha+\beta}\ln n + \varepsilon_n\right), \\ \varepsilon_n &= \max_{0\leq\nu\leq m} ||D_n^\nu p_n x^* - q_n x^{*(\nu)}||_{\mathrm{H}_{\beta,n}}. \end{aligned} \tag{2.13}$$

If, moreover, functions $a_\nu(t), b_\nu(t), h_\nu(t,\tau)$, $\nu = 0,1,\ldots,m$, *and* $y(t)$ *belong to* $H_\alpha^{(r)}$, $r \in \mathbb{N}$, *then*

$$||\mathbf{x}_n^* - p_n x^*||_{\mathrm{H}_{\beta,n}^{(m)}} \leq C\left(n^{-r-\alpha+\beta}\ln n + \varepsilon_n\right), \quad r+\alpha > \beta. \tag{2.14}$$

Theorem 2.2 [3]. *Assume that (2.2) and the system of equations (2.8) satisfy the following conditions:*

(A1) *functions* $h_\nu(t,\tau)$, $\nu = 0,1,\ldots,m$, *(by both variables),* $F(t,u_m,\ldots,u_0,v_m,\ldots,v_0,w_m,\ldots,w_0)$, *and* $y(t)$ *(by the variable t) belong to* H_α, $0 < \alpha \leq 1$;

(A2) *equation (2.2) has a unique solution* $x^*(t) \in H_\alpha^{(m)}$ *in some sphere of the space* $\mathrm{H}_\beta^{(m)}$, $0 < \beta < \alpha$;

(A3) *function* $F(t,u_m,\ldots,u_0,v_m,\ldots,v_0,w_m,\ldots,w_0)$ *is continuously differentiable by the variables* u_ν, v_ν, w_ν, $\nu = 0,1,\ldots,m$, *in some neighborhood*

$$\begin{aligned} |t| < \infty, \quad \left|u_\nu - x^{*(\nu)}(t)\right| \leq C, \quad \left|v_\nu - \left(Jx^{*(\nu)}\right)(t)\right| \leq C, \\ \left|w_\nu - \left(J^0 h_\nu x^{*(\nu)}\right)(t)\right| \leq C, \quad \nu = 0,1,\ldots,m, \end{aligned} \tag{2.15}$$

and its partial derivatives $F'_{u_\nu}, F'_{v_\nu}, F'_{w_\nu}$, $\nu = 0,1,\ldots,m$, *belong to* H_α *by t and are Lipschitz-continuous by* u_ν, v_ν, w_ν, $\nu = 0,1,\ldots,m$;

(A4) $F'^2_{u_m}(x^*) + F'^2_{v_m}(x^*) \neq 0, t \in [0,2\pi]$;

(A5) $\kappa = \operatorname{ind}\left(F'_{u_m}(x^*) + iF'_{v_m}(x^*)\right) = 0$;

(A6) *the equation*

$$\sum_{\nu=0}^{m} \left(F'_{u_\nu}(x^*)x^{(\nu)}(t) + F'_{v_\nu}(x^*)\left(Jx^{(\nu)}\right)(t) + F'_{w_\nu}(x^*)\left(J^0 h_\nu x^{(\nu)}\right)(t)\right) = 0, \tag{2.16}$$

has only zero solution in $\mathrm{H}_\beta^{(m)}$;

(B1) *the formulas for numerical differentiation* $D_n^\nu \mathbf{x}_n$, $\nu = 0,1,\ldots,m$, *converge;*

(B2) *characteristical values of the formula* D_n^m *do not lie on the unit circle.*

Then, for sufficiently large n, the system of equations (2.8) is uniquely solvable in some sphere

$$||\mathbf{x}_n - p_n x^*||_{\mathrm{H}_{\beta,n}^{(m)}} \leq C, \tag{2.17}$$

and the approximate solutions $\mathbf{x}_n^*$ *converge to the exact solution* $x^*(t)$ *of (2.2):*

$$\begin{aligned} ||\mathbf{x}_n^* - p_n x^*||_{\mathrm{H}_{\beta,n}^{(m)}} &\leq C\left(n^{-\alpha+\beta}\ln n + \varepsilon_n\right), \\ \varepsilon_n &= \max_{0\leq\nu\leq m} ||D_n^\nu p_n x^* - q_n x^{*(\nu)}||_{\mathrm{H}_{\beta,n}}. \end{aligned} \tag{2.18}$$

If, moreover, functions $h_\nu(t,\tau)$, $\nu = 0,1,\dots,m$, *(by both variables),* $F(t,u_m,\dots,u_0,v_m,\dots,v_0,w_m,\dots,w_0)$, *and* $y(t)$ *(by the variable t) belong to* $\mathrm{H}_\alpha^{(r)}$, $r \in \mathbb{N}$, *then*

$$\|\mathbf{x}_n^* - p_n x^*\|_{\mathrm{H}_{\beta,n}^{(m)}} \leq C(n^{-r-\alpha+\beta}\ln n + \varepsilon_n), \quad r+\alpha > \beta. \tag{2.19}$$

3. Linear singular integrodifferential equations with discontinuous coefficients

Let us consider a linear singular integrodifferential equation

$$\sum_{\nu=0}^{m} (a_\nu(t)x^{(\nu)}(t) + b_\nu(t)(Jx^{(\nu)})(t) + (J^0 h_\nu x^{(\nu)})(t)) = y(t), \tag{3.1}$$

where $x(t)$ is a desired unknown, $a_\nu(t)$, $b_\nu(t)$, $h_\nu(t,\tau)$, $\nu = 0,1,\dots,m-1$, and $y(t)$ are given 2π-periodic by the variables t,τ functions.

Denote by $x(t_k)$ values and by

$$\bar{x}(t_k) = \frac{1}{h}\int_{t_k}^{t_{k+1}} x(\tau)d\tau, \quad k = 0,1,\dots,n-1,\ h = \frac{2\pi}{n}, \tag{3.2}$$

the average values of the function $x(t)$ in the nodes of the grid (2.5).

We seek an approximate solution of (3.1), as in Section 2, in the form of the vector (2.6) of values of the unknown function in the nodes (2.5). The components of this vector are a solution of the system of linear algebraic equations

$$\begin{aligned}
&a_m(t_k)[D_n^m \mathbf{x}_n]_k + \frac{b_m(t_k)}{n}\sum_{l=0}^{n-1}\alpha_{k-l}[D_n^m\mathbf{x}_n]_l + \frac{1}{n}\sum_{l=0}^{n-1}\bar{h}_m(t_k,t_l)[D_n^m\mathbf{x}_n]_l \\
&\quad + \sum_{\nu=0}^{m-1}\left(\bar{a}_\nu(t_k)[D_n^\nu\mathbf{x}_n]_k + \frac{\bar{b}_\nu(t_k)}{n}\sum_{l=0}^{n-1}\alpha_{k-l}[D_n^\nu\mathbf{x}_n]_l + \frac{1}{n}\sum_{l=0}^{n-1}\bar{h}_\nu(t_k,t_l)[D_n^\nu\mathbf{x}_n]_l\right) \\
&= \bar{y}(t_k), \quad k = 0,1,\dots,n-1.
\end{aligned} \tag{3.3}$$

Here formulas D_n^ν and coefficients $\gamma_{k-l} = \gamma_{k-l}^{(n)}$, $k,l = 0,1,\dots,n-1$, are defined in Section 2.

Let us fix $r \in \mathbb{N}$. By $\mathrm{W}_2^{(r)}(\mathrm{W}_2^{(0)} = \mathrm{L}_2)$ and $\mathrm{W}_{2,n}^{(r)}(\mathrm{W}_{2,n}^{(0)} = \mathrm{L}_{2,n})$ we denote the space of 2π-periodic functions with $r-1$ absolutely continuous derivatives and rth derivative from L_2 and the space of vectors (2.6) with norms

$$\begin{aligned}
\|x\|_{\mathrm{W}_2^{(r)}} &= \max_{0\leq\nu\leq r}\|x^{(\nu)}\|_{\mathrm{L}_2}, \quad x \in \mathrm{W}_2^{(r)}, \\
\|x^{(\nu)}\|_{\mathrm{L}_2} &= \left(\frac{1}{2\pi}\int_0^{2\pi}|x^{(\nu)}(\tau)|^2 d\tau\right)^{1/2}, \quad \nu = 0,1,\dots,r, \\
\|\mathbf{x}_n\|_{\mathrm{W}_{2,n}^{(r)}} &= \max_{0\leq\nu\leq r}\|\bar{D}_n^{(\nu)}\mathbf{x}_n\|_{\mathrm{L}_{2,n}}, \quad \mathbf{x}_n \in \mathrm{W}_{2,n}^{(r)}, \\
\|\bar{D}_n^\nu\mathbf{x}_n\|_{\mathrm{L}_{2,n}} &= \left(\frac{1}{n}\sum_{k=0}^{n-1}[\bar{D}_n^\nu\mathbf{x}_n]_k^2\right)^{1/2}, \quad \nu = 0,1,\dots,r,
\end{aligned} \tag{3.4}$$

correspondently.

The spaces $W_2^{(m)}, W_{2,n}^{(m)}$, $m \geq 1$, and $L_2, L_{2,n}$ we bind by the operators

$$\begin{aligned} p_n x &= (x(t_0), x(t_1), \dots, x(t_{n-1})), \quad p_n : W_2^{(m)} \longrightarrow W_{2,n}^{(m)}, \\ q_n x &= (\bar{x}(t_0), \bar{x}(t_1), \dots, \bar{x}(t_{n-1})), \quad q_n : L_2 \longrightarrow L_{2,n}. \end{aligned} \tag{3.5}$$

THEOREM 3.1 [2]. *Assume that (3.1) and the system of equations (3.3) satisfy the following conditions:*

(A1) $a_m(t), b_m(t) \in H_\alpha$, $0 < \alpha \leq 1$, $a_\nu(t), b_\nu(t), h_\nu(t,\tau)$, $\nu = 0,1,\dots,m-1$, $h_m(t,\tau)$ *and* $y(t)$ *belong to* L_2;

(A2) $a_m^2(t) + b_m^2(t) \neq 0, t \in [0,2\pi]$;

(A3) $\kappa = \operatorname{ind}(a_m(t) + ib_m(t)) = 0$;

(A4) *equation (3.1) has a unique solution* $x^*(t) \in W_2^{(m)}$ *for any right-hand side* $y(t) \in L_2$;

(B1) *the formulas for numerical differentiation* $D_n^\nu \mathbf{x}_n$, $\nu = 0,1,\dots,m$, *converge;*

(B2) *characteristical values of the formula* D_n^m *do not lie on the unit circle.*

Then, for sufficiently large n, the system of equations (3.3) is uniquely solvable, and the approximate solutions $\mathbf{x}_n^*$ *converge to the exact solution* $x^*(t)$ *of (3.1):*

$$\|\mathbf{x}_n^* - p_n x^*\|_{W_{2,n}^{(m)}} \leq c\left(n^{-\alpha} + \sum_{\nu=0}^{m}\left(\omega_\tau\left(h_\nu; \frac{1}{n}\right)_2 + \omega\left(x^{*(\nu)}; \frac{1}{n}\right)_2\right) + \varepsilon_n\right),$$

$$\varepsilon_n = \max_{0 \leq \nu \leq m} \|D_n^\nu p_n x^* - q_n x^{*(\nu)}\|_{L_{2,n}},$$

$$\omega(x^{*(\nu)}; \delta)_2 = \sup_{0<\eta\leq\delta}\left\{\int_0^{2\pi} |x^{*(\nu)}(t+\eta) - x^{*(\nu)}(t)|^2 dt\right\}^{1/2}, \tag{3.6}$$

$$\omega_\tau(h_\nu; \delta)_2 = \left\| \sup_{0\leq\eta\leq\delta}\left\{\int_0^{2\pi} |h_\nu(t,\tau+\eta) - h_\nu(t,\tau)|^2 d\tau\right\}^{1/2}\right\|_{L_2},$$

$$\nu = 0,1,\dots,m.$$

4. Multidimensional singular integrodifferential equations

Let us consider multidimensional (here, for the sake of simplicity, we consider only the 2-dimensional case) singular integrodifferential equation

$$(ABu)(\mathbf{t}) + (Tu)(\mathbf{t}) = y(\mathbf{t}), \quad \mathbf{t} = (t^{(1)}, t^{(2)}) \in \mathbf{\Delta} = [-\pi,\pi]^2, \tag{4.1}$$

where $u(\mathbf{t})$ is a desired unknown, coefficients $a_{kl}(\mathbf{t})$, $k,l = 0,1$, and $b_{\boldsymbol{\alpha\beta}}(\mathbf{t})$, $|\boldsymbol{\alpha}| = \alpha_1 + \alpha_2 = m$, $|\boldsymbol{\beta}| = \beta_1 + \beta_2 = m$ of the operators

$$\begin{aligned} Au &\equiv a_{00}(\mathbf{t})u(\mathbf{t}) + a_{01}(\mathbf{t})(J_{01}u)(\mathbf{t}) + a_{10}(\mathbf{t})(J_{10}u)(\mathbf{t}) + a_{11}(\mathbf{t})(J_{11}u)(\mathbf{t}), \\ Bu &\equiv (Bu)(\mathbf{t}) = \sum_{|\boldsymbol{\alpha}|=|\boldsymbol{\beta}|=m} b_{\boldsymbol{\alpha\beta}}(\mathbf{t})(D^{\boldsymbol{\alpha}+\boldsymbol{\beta}}u)(\mathbf{t}), \end{aligned} \tag{4.2}$$

and right-hand side $y(\mathbf{t})$ are given 2π-periodic, by each variable functions, singular integrals

$$
\begin{aligned}
(J_{01}u)(\mathbf{t}) &= \frac{1}{2\pi}\int_{-\pi}^{\pi} u(t^{(1)},\tau^{(2)})\cot\frac{\tau^{(2)}-t^{(2)}}{2}\,d\tau^{(2)},\\
(J_{10}u)(\mathbf{t}) &= \frac{1}{2\pi}\int_{-\pi}^{\pi} u(\tau^{(1)},t^{(2)})\cot\frac{\tau^{(1)}-t^{(1)}}{2}\,d\tau^{(1)},\\
(J_{11}u)(\mathbf{t}) &= \frac{1}{4\pi^2}\int_{-\pi}^{\pi}\int_{-\pi}^{\pi} u(\tau^{(1)},\tau^{(2)})\cot\frac{\tau^{(1)}-t^{(1)}}{2}\cot\frac{\tau^{(2)}-t^{(2)}}{2}\,d\tau^{(2)}d\tau^{(1)},\\
\mathbf{t} &= (t^{(1)},t^{(2)}), \qquad \boldsymbol{\tau} = (\tau^{(1)},\tau^{(2)}) \in \boldsymbol{\Delta} = [-\pi,\pi]^2,
\end{aligned}
\tag{4.3}
$$

are to be interpreted as the Cauchy-Lebesgue principal values, and T is a known linear operator.

Let us fix $\mathbf{n} = (n_1,n_2) \in \mathbf{N} = \mathbb{N}^2$, denote by

$$
\mathbf{I_n} = I_{n_1} \times I_{n_2},\ I_{n_j} = \{k_j \mid k_j \in Z, |k_j| \le n_j\}, \quad j = 1,2, \tag{4.4}
$$

an index set, and define on $\boldsymbol{\Delta}$ the grid

$$
\boldsymbol{\Delta}_\mathbf{n} = \{\mathbf{t_k} = (t_{k_1},t_{k_2}) \mid \mathbf{k} = (k_1,k_2) \in \mathbf{I_n},\ t_{k_j} = k_j h_j,\ h_j = 2\pi/(2n_j+1),\ j = 1,2\}. \tag{4.5}
$$

An approximate solution of (4.1) we seek in the form of the grid function (matrix of values) $u_\mathbf{n} = u_\mathbf{n}(\mathbf{t})$, defined on $\boldsymbol{\Delta}_\mathbf{n}$. The values of this function in the nodes of the grid (4.5) are a solution of the system of linear algebraic equations

$$
\begin{aligned}
&a_{00}(\mathbf{t_k}) \sum_{|\boldsymbol{\alpha}|=|\boldsymbol{\beta}|=m} b_{\boldsymbol{\alpha\beta}}(\mathbf{t_k})(D_\mathbf{n}^{\boldsymbol{\alpha}+\boldsymbol{\beta}}u_\mathbf{n})(\mathbf{t_k})\\
&\quad + a_{01}(\mathbf{t_k})(2n_2+1)^{-1}\sum_{l_2\in I_{n_2}}\gamma_{k_2-l_2}^{(n_2)}\sum_{|\boldsymbol{\alpha}|=|\boldsymbol{\beta}|=m} b_{\boldsymbol{\alpha\beta}}(t_{k_1},t_{l_2})(D_\mathbf{n}^{\boldsymbol{\alpha}+\boldsymbol{\beta}}u_\mathbf{n})(t_{k_1},t_{l_2})\\
&\quad + a_{10}(\mathbf{t_k})(2n_1+1)^{-1}\sum_{l_1\in I_{n_1}}\gamma_{k_1-l_1}^{(n_1)}\sum_{|\boldsymbol{\alpha}|=|\boldsymbol{\beta}|=m} b_{\boldsymbol{\alpha\beta}}(t_{l_1},t_{k_2})(D_\mathbf{n}^{\boldsymbol{\alpha}+\boldsymbol{\beta}}u_\mathbf{n})(t_{l_1},t_{k_2})\\
&\quad + a_{11}(\mathbf{t_k})[2\mathbf{n}+\mathbf{1}]^{-1}\sum_{\mathbf{l}\in I_n}\gamma_{k_1-l_1}^{(n_1)}\gamma_{k_2-l_2}^{(n_2)}\sum_{|\boldsymbol{\alpha}|=|\boldsymbol{\beta}|=m} b_{\boldsymbol{\alpha\beta}}(t_{l_1},t_{l_2})(D_\mathbf{n}^{\boldsymbol{\alpha}+\boldsymbol{\beta}}u_\mathbf{n})(\mathbf{t_l})\\
&\quad + (T_\mathbf{n}u_\mathbf{n})(\mathbf{t_k}) = f(\mathbf{t_k}), \quad \mathbf{t_k} = (t_{k_1},t_{k_2}),\ \mathbf{t_l} = (t_{l_1},t_{l_2}) \in \boldsymbol{\Delta}_\mathbf{n},\ \mathbf{1} = (1,1),
\end{aligned}
\tag{4.6}
$$

of the cubature-difference method.

Here

$$D_{\mathbf{n}}^{\alpha+\beta} u_{\mathbf{n}} = \frac{1}{2}(\partial^{\alpha}\bar{\partial}^{\beta} + \bar{\partial}^{\alpha}\partial^{\beta}) u_{\mathbf{n}}, \tag{4.7}$$

where

$$\begin{gathered} \partial^{\alpha} u_{\mathbf{n}} = \partial_1^{\alpha_1}\partial_2^{\alpha_2} u_{\mathbf{n}}, \qquad \bar{\partial}^{\alpha} u_{\mathbf{n}} = \bar{\partial}_1^{\alpha_1}\bar{\partial}_2^{\alpha_2} u_{\mathbf{n}}, \\ \partial_j u_{\mathbf{n}} = h_j^{-1}(u_{\mathbf{n}}(\mathbf{t}+h_j\boldsymbol{\delta}_j) - u_{\mathbf{n}}(\mathbf{t})), \qquad \bar{\partial}_j u_{\mathbf{n}} = h_j^{-1}(u_{\mathbf{n}}(\mathbf{t}) - u_{\mathbf{n}}(\mathbf{t}-h_j\boldsymbol{\delta}_j)), \\ \boldsymbol{\delta}_j = (\delta_{j1}, \delta_{j2}), \quad j = 1,2, \end{gathered} \tag{4.8}$$

are difference formulas defined on the grid (4.5), $T_{\mathbf{n}}$ is arbitrary convergent to T operator, and $\gamma_{k_j-l_j}^{(n_j)}$, $j = 1,2$,

$$\gamma_r^{(q)} = \left\{\tan\frac{r\pi}{2(2q+1)},\ r-\text{even},\ -\cot\frac{r\pi}{2(2q+1)},\ r-\text{odd}\right\}, \tag{4.9}$$

are coefficients of the quadrature formulas.

Let us fix $s \in \mathbb{R}$, $s > 1$. By H^s and $\mathrm{H}_{\mathbf{n}}^s$ we denote Sobolev space of functions and space of grid functions (matrix of values) with norms

$$\|u\|_{\mathrm{H}^s} = \left(\sum_{\mathbf{k}\in\mathbf{Z}} (1+\mathbf{k}^2)^s \,|\,\hat{u}(\mathbf{k})\,|^2\right)^{1/2}, \quad \mathbf{Z} = \mathbb{Z}^2, \tag{4.10}$$

where

$$\hat{u}(\mathbf{k}) = (2\pi)^{-2}\int_{\Delta} u(\boldsymbol{\tau})\bar{e}_{\mathbf{k}}(\boldsymbol{\tau})d\boldsymbol{\tau} \tag{4.11}$$

are the Fourier coefficients of the function $u(\boldsymbol{\tau})$ by the system of trigonometric monomials

$$e_{\mathbf{k}}(\boldsymbol{\tau}) = \exp(i\mathbf{k}\cdot\boldsymbol{\tau}), \qquad \mathbf{k}\in\mathbf{Z},\ \boldsymbol{\tau}\in\boldsymbol{\Delta}, \tag{4.12}$$

$$\|u_{\mathbf{n}}\|_{\mathrm{H}_{\mathbf{n}}^s} = \left(\sum_{\mathbf{k}\in\mathbf{I_n}} (1+\mathbf{k}^2)^s \,|\,\hat{u}_{\mathbf{n}}(\mathbf{k})^{(\mathbf{n})}\,|^2\right)^{1/2}, \tag{4.13}$$

where

$$\hat{u}_{\mathbf{n}}(\mathbf{k})^{(\mathbf{n})} = [2\mathbf{n}+\mathbf{1}]^{-1}\sum_{\mathbf{l}\in\mathbf{I_n}} u_{\mathbf{n}}(\mathbf{t_l})\bar{e}_{\mathbf{k}}(\mathbf{t_l}), \quad \mathbf{k}\in\mathbf{I_n}, \tag{4.14}$$

are Fourier-Lagrange coefficients of the function $u_{\mathbf{n}}(\mathbf{t})$ with respect to the grid $\boldsymbol{\Delta}_{\mathbf{n}}$.

Spaces H^s and $\mathrm{H}_{\mathbf{n}}^s$ we bind by the operator

$$p_{\mathbf{n}} u = (u(\mathbf{t_k}))_{\mathbf{k}\in\mathbf{I_n}}, \quad p_{\mathbf{n}} : H^s \longrightarrow H_{\mathbf{n}}^s. \tag{4.15}$$

THEOREM 4.1 [4]. *Assume that (4.1) and the system of equations (4.6) satisfy the following conditions:*

(A1) *for any* $\mathbf{n}$ *operator* A *maps the set of all trigonometric polynomials of order not higher than* $\mathbf{n}$ *to itself;*

(A2) B *is elliptic operator; that is, for any point* $\mathbf{t} \in \mathbf{\Delta}$ *and real numbers* τ_α, τ_β, *the following inequality is valid:*

$$\sum_{|\alpha|=|\beta|=m} b_{\alpha\beta}(\mathbf{t})\tau_\alpha\tau_\beta \geq C \sum_{|\alpha|=m} \tau_\alpha^2; \tag{4.16}$$

(A3) *operator* $T : \mathrm{H}^{s+2m} \to \mathrm{H}^{s+\varepsilon}$ *is bounded for some* $\varepsilon \in \mathbb{R}, \varepsilon > 0$;

(A4) *equation (4.1) has a unique solution* $u^*(\mathbf{t}) \in \mathrm{H}^{s+2m}$ *for any right-hand side* $y(\mathbf{t}) \in \mathrm{H}^s$;

(B1) *operator* $T_\mathbf{n}$ *approximates operator* T *with respect to* $p_\mathbf{n}$; *that is, for any function* $u(\mathbf{t}) \in \mathrm{H}^s$,

$$||T_\mathbf{n} p_\mathbf{n} u - p_\mathbf{n} T u||_{\mathrm{H}^s_\mathbf{n}} = \eta_\mathbf{n} \longrightarrow 0 \quad \text{for } \mathbf{n} \longrightarrow \infty. \tag{4.17}$$

Then for all $\mathbf{n}$, *beginning from some* $\mathbf{n}_0$, *the system of equations (4.6) is uniquely solvable and approximate solutions* $u^*_\mathbf{n}$ *converge to the exact solution* $u^*(\mathbf{t})$ *of (4.1):*

$$||u^*_\mathbf{n} - p_\mathbf{n} u^*||_{\mathrm{H}^{s+2m}_\mathbf{n}} \longrightarrow 0, \quad \mathbf{n} \longrightarrow \infty. \tag{4.18}$$

If, in addition, $u^*(\mathbf{t}) \in \mathrm{H}^{s+2m+2}$, *then the error estimation*

$$\begin{gathered} ||u^*_\mathbf{n} - p_\mathbf{n} u^*||_{\mathrm{H}^{s+2m}_\mathbf{n}} \leq C(\mathbf{h}^2 + \eta_\mathbf{n}), \\ \mathbf{h} = (h_1, h_2), \qquad h_j = 2\pi/(2n_j + 1), \quad j = 1, 2, \end{gathered} \tag{4.19}$$

is valid.

References

[1] A. Fedotov, *Convergence of quadrature-difference methods for linear singular integro-differential equations*, Zhurnal Vychislitel' noĭ Matematiki i Matematicheskoĭ Fiziki **29** (1989), no. 9, 1301–1307, 1436.

[2] ———, *Convergence of the quadrature-difference method for linear singular integro-differential equations with discontinuous coefficients*, Zhurnal Vychislitel' noĭ Matematiki i Matematicheskoĭ Fiziki **31** (1991), no. 2, 261–271.

[3] ———, *Convergence of the quadrature-difference method for nonlinear singular integro-differential equations*, Zhurnal Vychislitel' noĭ Matematiki i Matematicheskoĭ Fiziki **31** (1991), no. 5, 781–787.

[4] ———, *Convergence of cubature-differences method for multidimensional singular integro-differential equations*, Archivum Mathematicum **40** (2004), no. 2, 181–191.

A. Fedotov: Chebotarev Research Institute of Mathematics and Mechanics, Kazan State University, Universitetskaya ul. 17, Kazan 420008, Russia
E-mail address: fedotov@mi.ru

EXISTENCE AND MULTIPLICITY RESULTS FOR HEMIVARIATIONAL INEQUALITIES

MICHAEL E. FILIPPAKIS

We prove an existence and a multiplicity result for hemivariational inequalities in which the potential $-j(z,x)$ is only partially coercive. Our approach is variational based on the nonsmooth critical point theory, see Chang, Kourogenis, and Papageorgiou and on an auxiliary result due to Tang and Wu relating uniform coercivity and subadditivity.

1. Introduction

In this paper, we prove an existence theorem and a multiplicity theorem for nonlinear hemivariational variational inequalities driven by the p-Laplacian. Hemivariational inequalities are a new type of variational expressions, which arise in theoretical mechanics and engineering, when one deals with nonsmooth and nonconvex energy functionals. For concrete applications, we refer to the book of Naniewicz and Panagiotopoulos [25]. Hemivariational inequalities have intrinsic mathematical interest as a new form of variational expressions. They include as a particular case problems with discontinuities.

In the last decade, hemivariational inequalities have been studied from a mathematical viewpoint primarily for Dirichlet problems. We refer to the works of Goeleven et al. [13], Motreanu and Panagiotopoulos [24], Radulescu and Panagiotopoulos [27], Radulescu [26], and the references therein. Quasilinear Dirichlet problems were studied recently by Gasiński and Papageorgiou [9–12]. The study of the Neumann problem is lagging behind. In the past, Neumann problems with a C^1 energy functional (i.e., smooth potential) were studied by Mawhin et al. [23], Drabek and Tersian [8] (semilinear problems), and Huang [17], Arcoya and Orsina [2], Hu and Papageorgiou [16]. The semilinear Neumann problem with a discontinuous forcing term was studied by Costa and Goncalves [7] with a forcing term independent of the space variable $z \in Z$, bounded and with zero mean value.

In this paper, we prove an existence and a multiplicity result for hemivariational inequalities where the potential $-j(z,x)$ is only partially coercive. Our present approach is variational based on the nonsmooth critical point theory (see Chang [5] and Kourogenis

Hindawi Publishing Corporation
Proceedings of the Conference on Differential & Difference Equations and Applications, pp. 413–421

and Papageorgiou [21]) and an auxiliary result due to Tang and Wu [28] relating uniform coercivity and subadditivity.

Let $Z \subseteq \mathbb{R}^N$ be a bounded domain with a C^1-boundary Γ. The problem under consideration is the following:

$$\begin{gathered} -\operatorname{div}\left(\|Dx(z)\|^{p-2}Dx(z)\right) \in \partial j(z,x(z)) \quad \text{a.e. on } Z, \\ \frac{\partial x}{\partial n_p} = 0 \quad \text{on } \Gamma,\ 1 < p < \infty. \end{gathered} \tag{1.1}$$

Here $\partial x/\partial n_p = \|Dx(z)\|^{p-2}(Dx(z),n(z))$, $z \in \Gamma$, with $n(z)$ being the outward normal on the boundary and the boundary condition is interpreted in the sense of trace.

2. Mathematical background

The nonsmooth critical point theory is based on the subdifferential calculus for locally Lipschitz functions. So let X be a Banach space. For a locally Lipschitz function $\varphi : X \to \mathbb{R}$, the generalized directional derivative at $x \in X$ in the direction $h \in X$ $\varphi^0(x;h)$, is defined by

$$\varphi^0(x;h) = \limsup_{\substack{x' \to x \\ \lambda \downarrow 0}} \frac{\varphi(x'+\lambda h) - \varphi(x')}{\lambda}. \tag{2.1}$$

We define the nonempty, w^*-compact, and convex set $\partial\varphi(x) \subseteq X^*$:

$$\partial\varphi(x) = \{x^* \in X^* : \langle x^*,h\rangle \le \varphi^0(x;h)\ \forall h \in X\}. \tag{2.2}$$

The multifunction $x \to \partial\varphi(x)$ is called the generalized subdifferential of φ. If $\varphi \in C^1(X)$, then $\partial\varphi(x) = \{\varphi'(x)\}$ for all $x \in X$. Also if $\varphi, \psi : X \to \mathbb{R}$ are locally Lipschitz functions and $\mu \in \mathbb{R}$, then

$$\partial(\varphi+\psi) \subseteq \partial\varphi + \partial\psi, \qquad \partial(\mu\varphi) = \mu\partial\varphi. \tag{2.3}$$

A point $x \in X$ is a critical point of the locally Lipschitz function φ, if $0 \in \partial\varphi(x)$.

In this setting, the well-known Palais-Smale condition has the following form.

> "A locally Lipschitz function $\varphi : X \to \mathbb{R}$ satisfies the nonsmooth Palais-Smale condition (the nonsmooth PS-condition for short), if every sequence $\{x_n\}_{n\ge1}$ such that $\{\varphi(x_n)\}_{n\ge1} \subseteq \mathbb{R}$ is bounded and $m(x_n) = \inf\{\|x^*\| : x^* \in \partial\varphi(x_n)\} \to 0$ as $n \to \infty$ has a strongly convergent subsequence."

The auxiliary result of Tang and Wu that we will need is the following.

Lemma 2.1. *If $j : Z \times \mathbb{R} \to \mathbb{R}$ is a function such that for all $x \in \mathbb{R}$, $z \to j(z,x)$ is measurable, for almost all $z \in Z$, $x \to j(z,x)$ is continuous, for every $M > 0$ there exists $\alpha_M \in L^1(Z)$ such that for almost all $z \in Z$ and all $|x| \le M$, $|j(z,x)| \le \alpha_M(z)$, and $j(z,x) \to -\infty$ as $|x| \to +\infty$ uniformly for almost all $z \in E$ with $|E| > 0$, then there exist $g \in C(\mathbb{R})$ subadditive such that $g(x) \to +\infty$ as $|x| \to +\infty$ and $g(x) \le |x| + 4$ and $\eta \in L^1(Z)$, such that for almost all $z \in E$ and all $x \in \mathbb{R}$, $j(z,x) \le -g(x) + \eta(z)$.*

3. Existence and multiplicity results

Our hypotheses on the nonsmooth potential $j(z,x)$ are the following.

$H(j)_1$: $j : Z \times \mathbb{R} \to \mathbb{R}$ is a function such that $j = j_1 + j_2$ and for $i = 1,2$, we have $j_i(\cdot,0) \in L^\infty(Z)$ and

(i) for all $x \in \mathbb{R}$, $z \to j_i(z,x)$ is measurable;

(ii) for almost all $z \in Z$, $x \to j_i(z,x)$ is locally Lipschitz;

(iii) for almost all $z \in Z$, all $x \in \mathbb{R}$, and all $u \in \partial j_1(z,x)$, we have

$$|u| \leq \alpha(z) + c|x|^{p-1} \quad \text{with } \alpha \in L^\infty(Z), \quad c > 0; \tag{3.1}$$

(iv) $j_1(z,x) \to -\infty$ as $|x| \to \infty$ uniformly for almost all $z \in E$, $|E| > 0$ and there exists $\xi \in L^1(Z)$ such that for almost all $z \in Z$ and all $x \in \mathbb{R}$, $j_1(z,x) \leq \xi(z)$;

(v) there exists $\theta \in L^q(Z)$ such that for almost all $z \in Z$, all $x \in \mathbb{R}$, and all $u \in \partial j_2(z,x)$, we have $|u| \leq \theta(z)$ and for all $x \in \mathbb{R}$ $\int_Z j_2(z,x)dz \leq c_0$ for some $c_0 > 0$.

Our first existence theorem reads as follows.

Theorem 3.1. *If hypotheses $H(j)_1$ hold, then problem (1.1) has a solution.*

Proof. Let $\varphi : W_0^{1,p}(Z) \to \mathbb{R}$ be the energy functional defined by

$$\begin{aligned}\varphi(x) &= \frac{1}{p}\|Dx\|_p^p - \int_Z j(z,x(z))dz \\ &= \frac{1}{p}\|Dx\|_p^p - \int_Z j_1(z,x(z))dz - \int_Z j_2(z,x(z))dz.\end{aligned} \tag{3.2}$$

We know (see, e.g., Chang [5] or Hu and Papageorgiou [15]) that φ is locally Lipschitz. By virtue of Lemma 2.1, for almost all $z \in E$ and all $x \in \mathbb{R}$, we have

$$j_1(z,x) \leq -g(x) + \eta(z), \tag{3.3}$$

where $g \in C(\mathbb{R})$ is subadditive, coercive, and $\eta \in L^1(Z)$. We have

$$\begin{aligned}\int_Z j_1(z,x(z))dz &= \int_E j_1(z,x(z))dz + \int_{Z\setminus E} j_1(z,x(z))dz \\ &\leq -\int_E g(x(z))dz + \int_E \eta(z)dz + \int_{Z\setminus E} \xi(z)dz.\end{aligned} \tag{3.4}$$

Consider the following direct sum decomposition:

$$W^{1,p}(Z)(Z) = \mathbb{R} \oplus V \tag{3.5}$$

with $V = \{v \in W^{1,p}(Z) : \int_Z v(z)dz = 0\}$. So if $x \in W^{1,p}(Z)$, we can write in a unique way that $x = \overline{x} + \hat{x}$, with $\overline{x} \in \mathbb{R}$ and $\hat{x} \in V$. Exploiting the subadditivity of g, we have

$$\begin{aligned}&g(\overline{x}) = g(x(z) - \hat{x}(z)) \leq g(x(z)) + g(-\hat{x}(z)) \quad \forall z \in Z, \\ &\Longrightarrow g(\overline{x}) - g(-\hat{x}(z)) \leq g(x(z)) \quad \forall z \in Z.\end{aligned} \tag{3.6}$$

In addition from Lemma 2.1, we have

$$g(-\widehat{x}(z)) \leq |\widehat{x}(z)| + 4. \tag{3.7}$$

So we can write that

$$\begin{aligned} -\int_E g(x(z))dz &\leq -g(\overline{x})|Z| + \int_E (|\widehat{x}(z)| + 4)dz \\ &\leq -g(\widehat{x})|Z| + b^{1/q}\|\widehat{x}\|_p + 4|Z| \\ &\leq -g(\overline{x})|Z| + c_1\|Dx\|_p + 4|Z| \quad \text{for some } c_1 > 0. \end{aligned} \tag{3.8}$$

Here we have used the Poincare-Wirtinger inequality.

Let $\theta(t) = \{(v,\lambda) \in \mathbb{R} \times (0,1) : v \in \partial j_2(z,\overline{x}+\lambda\widehat{x}(z)),\ j_2(z,\overline{x}+\widehat{x}(z)) - j_2(z,\overline{x}) = v\widehat{x}(z)\}$. From the Lebourg mean value theorem (see, e.g., Clarke [6, page 41]), we know that for almost all $z \in Z$, $\theta(z) \neq \varnothing$. By redefining $\theta(\cdot)$ on an exceptional Lebesgue-null set, we may assume without any loss of generality that $\theta(z) \neq \varnothing$ for all $z \in Z$. We will show that in every direction $h \in \mathbb{R}$, the function $(z,\lambda) \to j_2^0(z,\overline{x}+\lambda\widehat{x}(x);h)$ is measurable. Indeed, from the definition of the generalized directional derivative, we have

$$j_2^0(z,\overline{x}+\lambda\widehat{x}(z);h) = \inf_{m \geq 1} \sup_{\substack{r,s \in Q \cap (-1/m,1/m) \\ \lambda \downarrow 0}} \frac{j_2(z,\overline{x}+\lambda\widehat{x}(z)+r+sh) - j_2(z,\overline{x}+\lambda\widehat{x}(z)+r)}{s}. \tag{3.9}$$

Since j_2 is jointly measurable (see Hu and Papageorgiou [14, page 142]), it follows that $(z,\lambda) \to j_2^0(z,\overline{x}+\lambda\widehat{x}(z);h)$ is measurable. Set $S(z,\lambda) = \partial j_2(z,\overline{x}+\lambda\widehat{x}(z))$ and let $\{h_m\}m \geq 1 \subseteq \mathbb{R}$ be an enumeration of the rational numbers. Because $j_2^0(z,\overline{x}+\lambda\widehat{x}(z);\cdot)$ is a continuous function, we can write that

$$\begin{aligned} \operatorname{Gr} S &= \{(z,\lambda,u) \in Z \times (0,1) \times \mathbb{R} : u \in S(z,\lambda)\} \\ &= \bigcap_{m \geq 1} \{(z,\lambda,u) \in Z \times (0,1) \times \mathbb{R} : uh_m \leq j_2^0(z,\overline{x}+\lambda\widehat{x}(z);h_m)\} \\ &\Longrightarrow \operatorname{Gr} S \in \mathcal{L}(Z) \in B(0,1) \times B(\mathbb{R}) \end{aligned} \tag{3.10}$$

with $\mathcal{L}(Z)$ being the Lebesgue σ-field of Z and $B(0,1)$ (resp., $B(\mathbb{R})$) the Borel σ-field of $(0,1)$ (resp., of $\mathbb{R}$). So we can apply the Yankov-von Neumann-Aumann selection theorem (see Hu and Papageorgiou [14, page 158]) to obtain measurable functions $v : Z \to \mathbb{R}$ and $\lambda : Z \to (0,1)$ such that $(v(z),\lambda(z)) \in \theta(z)$ for all $z \in Z$ and $j_2(z,\overline{x}+\widehat{x}(z)) - j_2(z,\overline{x}) = v(z)\widehat{x}(z)$, $v(z) \in \partial j_2(z,\overline{x}+\lambda(z)\widehat{x}(z))$ a.e. on Z. Using hypothesis $H(j)_1(v)$ and the Poincare-Wirtinger inequality, we obtain

$$\begin{aligned} \int_Z j_2(z,x(z))dz &= \int_Z j_2(z,\overline{x}+\widehat{x}(z))dz \\ &\leq \int_Z j_2(z,\overline{x})dz + c_2\|Dx\|_p\|\theta\|_1 \quad \text{for some } c_2 > 0. \end{aligned} \tag{3.11}$$

Thus finally we have that

$$\begin{aligned}\varphi &= \frac{1}{p}\|Dx\|_p^p - \int_Z j_1(z,x(z))\,dz - \int_Z j_2(z,x(z))\,dz \\ &\geq \frac{1}{p}\|Dx\|_p^p + g(\overline{x})|Z| - c_1\|Dx\|_p - 4|Z| - \|\eta\|_1 - c_2\|\theta\|_1\|Dx\|_p.\end{aligned} \tag{3.12}$$

From this inequality and recalling that $g(\cdot)$ is coercive, we infer that φ is coercive. Because the Sobolev space $W^{1,p}(Z)$ is embedded compactly in $L^p(Z)$, we can easily check that φ is weakly lower semicontinuous. Then by the Weierstrass theorem, we can find that $x \in W^{1,p}(Z)$ such that $\varphi(x) = \inf\varphi$. So we have $0 \in \partial\varphi(x)$. Let $A : W^{1,p}(Z) \to W^{1,p}(Z)^*$ be the nonlinear operator defined by

$$\langle A(x), y\rangle = \int_Z \|Dx(z)\|^{p-2}(Dx(z), Dy(z))_{\mathbb{R}^N}\,dz. \tag{3.13}$$

We have $A(x) = u$ with $u \in S^q_{\partial j(\cdot,x(\cdot))}$. For every $\psi \in C_c^\infty(0,b)$, we have

$$\int_Z \|Dx(z)\|^{p-2}(Dx(z), D\psi(z))_{\mathbb{R}^N}\,dz = \int_Z u(z)\psi(z)\,dz. \tag{3.14}$$

From a well-known representation theorem (see Adams [1, page 50], or Hu and Papageorgiou [14]) and since $\operatorname{div}(\|Dx(\cdot)\|^{p-2}Dx(\cdot)) \in W_0^{1,p}(Z)^* = W^{-1,q}(Z)$, we have

$$\langle -\operatorname{div}(\|Dx\|^{p-2}Dx), \psi\rangle_0 = \int_0^b u(z)\psi(z)\,dz = \langle u, \psi\rangle_0 \tag{3.15}$$

with $\langle\cdot,\cdot\rangle_0$ denoting the duality brackets for the pair $(W_0^{1,p}(Z), W^{-1,q}(Z))$. Since the test functions $C_c^\infty(Z)$ are dense in $W_0^{1,p}(Z)$, it follows that

$$-\operatorname{div}(\|Dx(z)\|^{p-2}Dx(z)) = u(z) \in \partial j(z,x(z)) \quad \text{a.e. on } Z. \tag{3.16}$$

From the quasilinear Green's identity (see Kenmochi [19], or Casas and Fernández [4], or Hu and Papageorgiou [15, page 867]), for every $v \in W^{1,p}(Z)$, we have

$$\int_Z \operatorname{div}(\|Dx\|^{p-2}Dx)v\,dz + \int_Z \|Dx\|^{p-2}(Dx, Dv)_{\mathbb{R}^N}\,dz = \left\langle \frac{\partial x}{\partial n_p}, \gamma(v)\right\rangle_\Gamma \tag{3.17}$$

with $\langle\cdot,\cdot\rangle_\Gamma$ being the duality brackets for the pair $(W^{1/q,p}(\Gamma), W^{-1/q,q}(\Gamma))$ and $\gamma : W^{1,p}(z) \to L^p(Z)$ is the trace operator.

From (3.16) and since $A(x) = u$, we obtain

$$0 = \langle A(x), v\rangle + \int_Z -uv\,dz = \left\langle \frac{\partial x}{\partial n_p}, \gamma(v)\right\rangle_\Gamma. \tag{3.18}$$

But $\gamma(W^{1,p}(Z)) = W^{1/q,p}(\Gamma)$ (see Kufner et al. [22, page 338]). It follows that $\partial x/\partial n_p = 0$. So x is a solution of problem (1.1). □

Next imposing an extra condition about the behavior of $j(z,\cdot)$ near the origin, we can have a multiplicity result for problem (1.1). This result is based on a nonsmooth extension of the local linking theorem of Brezis and Nirenberg [3] established recently by Kandilakis et al. [18].

Theorem 3.2. *If X is a reflexive Banach space such that $X = Y \oplus V$ with* $\dim Y < +\infty$, *$\varphi : X \to \mathbb{R}$ is Lipschitz continuous on bounded sets, satisfies the nonsmooth PS-condition, $\varphi(0) = 0$, and*

(a) *there exists $r > 0$ such that*

$$\varphi(y)\begin{cases} \leq 0 & \text{if } y \in Y,\ \|y\| \leq r, \\ \geq 0 & \text{if } y \in V,\ \|y\| \leq r; \end{cases} \tag{3.19}$$

(b) *φ is bounded below and* $\inf \varphi < 0$,

then φ has at least two nontrivial critical points.

The hypotheses on the nonsmooth potential are the following.

$H(j)_2$: $j : Z \times \mathbb{R} \to \mathbb{R}$ is a function which satisfies hypotheses $H(j)_1$ and

(vi) $\lim_{x\to 0}(pj(z,x)/|x|^p) = 0$ uniformly for almost all $z \in Z$ and there exists $r_0 > 0$ such that for almost all $z \in Z$ and all $|x| \leq r_0$, we have $j(z,x) \geq 0$.

Theorem 3.3. *If hypotheses $H(j)_2$ hold, then problem (1.1) has at least two nontrivial solutions.*

Proof. Let $\varphi : W^{1,p} \to \mathbb{R}$ be the Lipschitz continuous on bounded sets energy functional defined by

$$\varphi(x) = \frac{1}{p}\|Dx\|_p^p - \int_Z j(z,x(z))\,dz. \tag{3.20}$$

From the proof of Theorem 3.1, we know that φ is coercive, hence it satisfies the nonsmooth PS-condition (see Kourogenis and Papageorgiou [20]). As before, we consider the direct sum decomposition

$$W^{1,p}(Z) = \mathbb{R} \oplus V, \tag{3.21}$$

with $V = \{v \in W^{1,p}(Z) : \int_Z v(z) = 0\}$. By virtue of hypothesis $H(j)_2$(vi), given $\varepsilon > 0$, we can find, $\delta > 0$ such that for almost all $z \in Z$ and all $|x| \leq \delta$, we have $j(z,x) \leq (\varepsilon/p)|x|^p$.

Also from the Lebourg mean value theorem, we have that for almost all $z \in Z$ and all $x \in \mathbb{R}$

$$j(z,x) \leq \alpha_1(z)(1+|x|^p) \tag{3.22}$$

with $\alpha_1 \in L^\infty(Z)$. So for almost all $z \in Z$ and all $|x| > \delta$, we have

$$j(z,x) \leq c_3 + c_4|x|^\beta p < \beta < p^* \quad \text{and some } c_3, c_4 > 0. \tag{3.23}$$

So finally we can write that for almost all $z \in Z$ and all $x \in \mathbb{R}$, we have

$$j(z,x) \leq \frac{\varepsilon}{p}|x|^p + c_5|x|^\beta \quad \text{for some } c_5 > 0. \tag{3.24}$$

Then for $v \in V$, we have

$$\varphi(x) \geq \frac{1}{p}\|Dv\|_p^p - \frac{\varepsilon}{p}\|v\|_p^p - c_5\|v\|_\beta^\beta. \tag{3.25}$$

From the Poincare-Wirtinger inequality and since $\beta < p^*$, we obtain for $\varepsilon > 0$ small that

$$\varphi(v) \geq c_6\|Dv\|_p^p - c_7\|Dv\|_p^\beta \quad \text{for some } c_6, c_7 > 0. \tag{3.26}$$

Since $\beta > p$, for $r_1 > 0$ small, if $\|Dv\|_p \leq r_1$, we have

$$\varphi(v) \geq 0. \tag{3.27}$$

Also from hypothesis $H(j)_2$(vi) if $y \in \mathbb{R}$, $\|y\| \leq r_0$, we have

$$\varphi(y) \leq 0. \tag{3.28}$$

Note that φ being coercive is bounded below.

If $\inf \varphi < 0$, then using $r = \min\{r_0, r_1\} > 0$, we can apply Theorem 3.2 and obtain two nontrivial critical points of φ. As in the proof of Theorem 3.1, we can easily check that these are two nontrivial solutions of (1.1).

If $\inf \varphi \geq 0$, then evidently for every $y \in \mathbb{R}^N$ with $\beta^{1/q}|y| \leq r$ (hypothesis $H(j)_2$(vi)), we have that $\varphi(y) = 0$ and so φ has a continuum of nontrivial critical points. □

Consider the nonsmooth locally Lipschitz potential $j(z,x)$ defined by

$$j(z,x) = \begin{cases} |x|^p \ln(1+|x|^p) & \text{if } |x| \leq 1, \\ -\chi_E(z)\ln|x| + \chi_{E^c}(z)\sin|x| & \text{if } |x| > 1, \end{cases} \tag{3.29}$$

with $|E| > 0$. It is easy to see that this $j(z,x)$ satisfies hypotheses $H(j)_2$.

Acknowledgment

The researcher is supported by a grant of the National Scholarship Foundation of Greece (IKY).

References

[1] R. Adams, *Sobolev Spaces*, Pure and Applied Mathematics, vol. 65, Academic Press, New York, 1978.

[2] D. Arcoya and L. Orsina, *Landesman-Lazer conditions and quasilinear elliptic equations*, Nonlinear Analysis **28** (1997), no. 10, 1623–1632.

[3] H. Brezis and L. Nirenberg, *Remarks on finding critical points*, Communications on Pure and Applied Mathematics **44** (1991), no. 8-9, 939–963.

[4] E. Casas and L. A. Fernández, *A Green's formula for quasilinear elliptic operators*, Journal of Mathematical Analysis and Applications **142** (1989), no. 1, 62–73.

[5] K. C. Chang, *Variational methods for nondifferentiable functionals and their applications to partial differential equations*, Journal of Mathematical Analysis and Applications **80** (1981), no. 1, 102–129.

[6] F. H. Clarke, *Optimization and Nonsmooth Analysis*, Canadian Mathematical Society Series of Monographs and Advanced Texts, John Wiley & Sons, New York, 1983.

[7] D. G. Costa and J. V. A. Gonçalves, *Critical point theory for nondifferentiable functionals and applications*, Journal of Mathematical Analysis and Applications **153** (1990), no. 2, 470–485.

[8] P. Drábek and S. A. Tersian, *Characterizations of the range of Neumann problem for semilinear elliptic equations*, Nonlinear Analysis **11** (1987), no. 6, 733–739.

[9] L. Gasiński and N. S. Papageorgiou, *Nonlinear hemivariational inequalities at resonance*, Bulletin of the Australian Mathematical Society **60** (1999), no. 3, 353–364.

[10] ———, *An existence theorem for nonlinear hemivariational inequalities at resonance*, Bulletin of the Australian Mathematical Society **63** (2001), no. 1, 1–14.

[11] ———, *Multiple solutions for semilinear hemivariational inequalities at resonance*, Publicationes Mathematicae Debrecen **59** (2001), no. 1-2, 121–146.

[12] ———, *Solutions and multiple solutions for quasilinear hemivariational inequalities at resonance*, Proceedings of the Royal Society of Edinburgh. Section A. Mathematics **131** (2001), no. 5, 1091–1111.

[13] D. Goeleven, D. Motreanu, and P. D. Panagiotopoulos, *Eigenvalue problems for variational-hemivariational inequalities at resonance*, Nonlinear Analysis **33** (1998), no. 2, 161–180.

[14] S. Hu and N. S. Papageorgiou, *Handbook of Multivalued Analysis. Vol. I. Theory*, Mathematics and Its Applications, vol. 419, Kluwer Academic, Dordrecht, 1997.

[15] ———, *Handbook of Multivalued Analysis. Vol. II. Applications*, Mathematics and Its Applications, vol. 500, Kluwer Academic, Dordrecht, 2000.

[16] ———, *Nonlinear elliptic problems of Neumann-type*, Rendiconti del Circolo Matematico di Palermo. Serie II **50** (2001), no. 1, 47–66.

[17] Y. X. Huang, *On eigenvalue problems of p-Laplacian with Neumann boundary conditions*, Proceedings of the American Mathematical Society **109** (1990), no. 1, 177–184.

[18] D. Kandilakis, N. Kourogenis, and N. S. Papageorgiou, *Two nontrivial critical points for nonsmooth functionals via local linking and applications*, Journal of Global Optimization **34** (2006), no. 2, 219–244.

[19] N. Kenmochi, *Pseudomonotone operators and nonlinear elliptic boundary value problems*, Journal of the Mathematical Society of Japan **27** (1975), 121–149.

[20] N. C. Kourogenis and N. S. Papageorgiou, *A weak nonsmooth Palais-Smale condition and coercivity*, Rendiconti del Circolo Matematico di Palermo. Serie II **49** (2000), no. 3, 521–526.

[21] ———, *Nonsmooth critical point theory and nonlinear elliptic equations at resonance*, Journal of Australian Mathematical Society. Series A **69** (2000), no. 2, 245–271.

[22] A. Kufner, O. John, and S. Fučík, *Function Spaces*, Monographs and Textbooks on Mechanics of Solids and Fluids; Mechanics: Analysis, Noordhoff International, Leyden, 1977.

[23] J. Mawhin, J. R. Ward Jr., and M. Willem, *Variational methods and semilinear elliptic equations*, Archive for Rational Mechanics and Analysis **95** (1986), no. 3, 269–277.

[24] D. Motreanu and P. D. Panagiotopoulos, *A minimax approach to the eigenvalue problem of hemivariational inequalities and applications*, Applicable Analysis **58** (1995), no. 1-2, 53–76.

[25] Z. Naniewicz and P. D. Panagiotopoulos, *Mathematical Theory of Hemivariational Inequalities and Applications*, Monographs and Textbooks in Pure and Applied Mathematics, vol. 188, Marcel Dekker, New York, 1995.

[26] V. Radulescu, *Mountain pass theorems for nondifferentiable functions and applications*, Proceedings of Japan Academy. Series A. Mathematical Sciences **69** (1993), no. 6, 193–198.

[27] V. Radulescu and P. Panagiotopoulos, *Periodic solutions for second order systems with not uniformly coercive potential*, Journal of Mathematical Analysis and Applications **259** (2001), no. 2, 386–397.

[28] C.-L. Tang and X.-P. Wu, *Periodic solutions for second order systems with not uniformly coercive potential*, Journal of Mathematical Analysis and Applications **259** (2001), no. 2, 386–397.

Michael E. Filippakis: Department of Mathematics, National Technical University of Athens, Zografou Campus, 15780 Zografou, Greece
E-mail address: mfilip@math.ntua.gr

VLASOV-ENSKOG EQUATION WITH THERMAL BACKGROUND IN GAS DYNAMICS

WILLIAM GREENBERG AND PENG LEI

In order to describe dense gases, a smooth attractive tail is added to the hard core repulsion of the Enskog equation, along with a velocity diffusion. The existence of global-in-time renormalized solutions to the resulting diffusive Vlasov-Enskog equation is proved for L^1 initial conditions.

1. Introduction

One of the problems of greatest current interest in the kinetic theory of classical systems is the construction and analysis of systems which describe dense gases. The Boltzmann equation, employed for more than a century to give the time evolution of gases, is accurate only in the dilute-gas regime, yielding transport coefficients of an ideal fluid. In 1921, Enskog introduced a Boltzmann-like collision process with hard core interaction, representing molecules with nonzero diameter. The Enskog equation, as revised in the 1970's in order to obtain correct hydrodynamics, describes a nonideal fluid with transport coefficients within 10% of those of realistic numerical models up to one-half close packing density. A limitation, however, in its usefulness is that, unlike the Boltzmann equation, no molecular interaction is modeled beyond the hard sphere collision.

A strategy to rectify this is the addition of a smooth attractive tail to a hard repulsive core of radius a, thereby approximating a van der Waals interaction. The potential must be introduced at the Liouville level. Following the pioneering work of de Sobrino [1], Grmela [5, 6], Karkhech and Stell [7, 8], van Beijeren [11], and van Beijeren and Ernst [12], with a potential satisfying the Poisson equation, one obtains the coupled kinetic equations:

$$\begin{aligned}\left[\frac{\partial}{\partial t}+\vec{v}\cdot\nabla_{\vec{r}}\right]f(\vec{r},\vec{v},t) &= -\vec{E}\cdot\nabla_{\vec{v}}f(\vec{r},\vec{v},t)+C_E(f,f),\\ \operatorname{div}_{\vec{r}}\vec{E}(\vec{r},t) &= -\int d\vec{v}\, f(\vec{r},\vec{v},t)\end{aligned} \tag{1.1}$$

Hindawi Publishing Corporation
Proceedings of the Conference on Differential & Difference Equations and Applications, pp. 423–432

with $C_E(f,f)$ the Enskog collision term

$$\begin{aligned} C_E(f,f)(\vec{r},\vec{v},t) = a^2 \iint_{R^2\times S_+^2} & [Y(\vec{r},\vec{r}-a\vec{\epsilon})f(\vec{r},\vec{v}',t)f(\vec{r}-a\vec{\epsilon},\vec{v}_1',t) \\ & - Y(\vec{r},\vec{r}+a\vec{\epsilon})f(\vec{r},\vec{v},t)f(\vec{r}+a\vec{\epsilon},\vec{v}_1,t)]\langle\vec{\epsilon},\vec{v}-\vec{v}_1\rangle d\vec{\epsilon}\, d\vec{v}_1, \\ \vec{v}' = \vec{v}-\vec{\epsilon}\langle\vec{\epsilon},\vec{v}-\vec{v}_1\rangle, \qquad & \vec{v}_1' = \vec{v}_1+\vec{\epsilon}\langle\vec{\epsilon},\vec{v}-\vec{v}_1\rangle. \end{aligned} \tag{1.2}$$

The geometric factor $Y(\vec{r}_1,\vec{r}_2)$ is a functional of f which, in principle, should be determined by the Mayer cluster expansion [10].

In the derivation of these equations from the BBGKY hierarchy, velocity correlations have been neglected. This is a small angle scatttering effect. We account for this effect by the addition of a velocity diffusion $\lambda\Delta_{\vec{v}}f$. Thus we are led to consider the following *diffusive Vlasov-Enskog* system:

$$\left[\frac{\partial}{\partial t}+\vec{v}\cdot\nabla_{\vec{r}}\right]f(\vec{r},\vec{v},t)-\lambda\Delta_{\vec{v}}f+\vec{E}(\vec{r},t)\cdot\nabla_{\vec{v}}f(\vec{r},\vec{v},t)=C_E(f,f), \tag{1.3}$$

$$\operatorname{div}_{\vec{r}}\vec{E}(\vec{r},t) = -\int d\vec{v} f(\vec{r},\vec{v},t), \tag{1.4}$$

with initial condition

$$f(\vec{r},\vec{v},t)|_{t=0} = f_0(\vec{r},\vec{v}). \tag{1.5}$$

In this paper we will outline an existence proof for (*renormalized*) solutions of the Cauchy problem for the diffusive Vlasov-Enskog system, including initial conditions far from equilibrium.

In Section 2 we give bounds related to mass, energy, and entropy, which imply the weak precompactness of the set of solutions. Then we derive sequential stability results. In Section 3 we construct solutions to some approximate equations. Finally, in Section 4 we construct approximate solutions to the diffusive system, which form a weakly precompact set. Then sequential stability will show that limits provide global-in-time solutions to the Cauchy initial value problem.

2. Bounds and stability

Throughout we will assume the natural symmetry condition of the geometric factor

$$Y(\sigma,\tau) = Y(\tau,\sigma) \tag{2.1}$$

as well as joint continuity, and the cutoff

$$\sup_{\sigma,\tau} \tau Y(\tau,\sigma) \le M_Y < \infty \tag{2.2}$$

with Y a function of the local densities

$$\sigma = n(\vec{r}) = \int_{R^3} f(\vec{r},\vec{v},t)d\vec{v}, \tag{2.3}$$

and so fourth. Since molecules have nonzero diameter, densities should not be expected to exceed close packing, which is represented by the cutoff on Y.

By straightforward calculation one may derive for solutions of (1.3), (1.4) conservation of mass

$$\iint_{R^3\times R^3} f(\vec{r},\vec{v},t)d\vec{v}\,d\vec{r} = \iint_{R^3\times R^3} f(\vec{r},\vec{v},0)d\vec{v}\,d\vec{r} = M_1, \quad \forall t \ge 0, \tag{2.4}$$

as well as the energy bound

$$\iint_{R^3\times R^3} v^2 f(\vec{r},\vec{v},t)d\vec{v}\,d\vec{r} + \int_{R^3} \|\vec{E}(\vec{r},t)\|^2 d\vec{r} = M_2 + 2\lambda M_1 t, \quad \forall t \ge 0, \tag{2.5}$$

where

$$M_2 = \iint_{R^3\times R^3} v^2 f(\vec{r},\vec{v},0)d\vec{v}\,d\vec{r} + \int_{R^3} d\vec{r}\,\|\vec{E}(\vec{r},0)\|^2. \tag{2.6}$$

If, in addition,

$$\iint_{R^3\times R^3} r^2 f(\vec{r},\vec{v},0)d\vec{v}\,d\vec{r} = M_3, \tag{2.7}$$

then

$$\iint_{R^3\times R^3} r^2 f(\vec{r},\vec{v},t)d\vec{v}\,d\vec{r} \le \frac{1}{M_1^2}(M_2 + 2\lambda M_1 t)^3 + 2M_3. \tag{2.8}$$

For this system we may introduce an entropy functional

$$\Gamma(t) = \iint_{R^3\times R^3} f(\vec{r},\vec{v},t)\log f(\vec{r},\vec{v},t)d\vec{v}\,d\vec{r} - \int_0^t I(s)ds + \int_0^t J(s)ds, \tag{2.9}$$

where

$$\begin{aligned} I(t) &= \frac{1}{2}\iint\iint_{R^3\times R^3\times R^3\times S_+^2} d\vec{\epsilon}\,d\vec{v}_1\,d\vec{v}\,d\vec{r} f(\vec{r},\vec{v},t) \\ &\quad \times [f(\vec{r}-a\vec{\epsilon},\vec{v}_1,t)\cdot Y(\vec{r},\vec{r}-a\vec{\epsilon}) - f(\vec{r}+a\vec{\epsilon},\vec{v}_1,t)Y(\vec{r},\vec{r}+a\vec{\epsilon})]\langle\vec{\epsilon},\vec{v}-\vec{v}_1\rangle \\ &= I^+(t) - I^-(t), \\ J(t) &= 4\lambda\iint_{R^3\times R^3} \left\|\nabla_{\vec{v}}\sqrt{f(\vec{r},\vec{v},t)}\right\|^2 d\vec{v}\,d\vec{r}. \end{aligned} \tag{2.10}$$

By convexity arguments one has $(d/dt)\Gamma(t) \le 0$ and the bound

$$\iint_{R^3\times R^3} f(\vec{r},\vec{v},t)\,|\log f(\vec{r},\vec{v},t)|\,d\vec{v}\,d\vec{r} \le M_4 < \infty, \quad 0 \le t \le T, \tag{2.11}$$

for any $T > 0$, if the left-hand side is finite at $t = 0$. In particular, for any $T > 0$, if

$$\iint_{R^3\times R^3} f_0(\vec{r},\vec{v})(1 + r^2 + v^2 + |\log f_0|)d\vec{v}\,d\vec{r} < \infty, \tag{2.12}$$

then

$$\iint_{R^3\times R^3} f(\vec{r},\vec{v},t)(1+r^2+v^2+|\log f|)\,d\vec{v}\,d\vec{r} \le C_T < \infty, \tag{2.13}$$

$$\int_{R^3} \|\vec{E}(\vec{r},t)\|^2 d\vec{r} \le C_T, \quad 0<t<T. \tag{2.14}$$

Now consider a sequence f_n of nonnegative solutions of (1.3), (1.4) with functions $f_n \in W^{2,\infty}(R^3 \times R^3 \times [0,\infty))$, $f_n \to 0$ as $(\vec{r},\vec{v}) \to \infty$ uniformly in $t \in [0,T]$ for all $T < \infty$, $E_n \in W^{2,\infty}(R^3 \times [0,\infty))$, $E^n \to 0$ as $\vec{r} \to \infty$, and

$$\iint_{R^3\times R^3} f_n(\vec{r},\vec{v},t)(1+r^2+v^2+|\log f_n|)\,d\vec{v}\,d\vec{r} \le C_T < \infty, \tag{2.15}$$

$$\int_{R^3} \|\vec{E}(\vec{r},t)\|^2 d\vec{r} \le C_T, \quad 0<t<T, \tag{2.16}$$

with C_T independent of n, as well as

$$\int_0^T \iint_{R^3\times R^3} \left\{\left\|\nabla_{\vec{v}}\sqrt{f_n}\right\|^2 + |\log f_n C_E(f_n,f_n)|\right\} d\vec{v}\,d\vec{r} \le C_T. \tag{2.17}$$

By (2.15), (2.16), we may assume, possibly by passing to a subsequence, that f_n converges weakly in $L^1(R^n \times R^n \times [0,T])$ to f for all T, and $\vec{E}_n$ converges weakly in $L_2(R^n \times [0,T])$ to $\vec{E}$.

In order to deal with initial values far from equilibrium, DiPerna and Lions in their treatment of the Boltzmann equation introduced the renormalization of the dependent variable f by a suitable nonlinear transformation [2–4]. This setting carries over to the Enskog equation, and to the diffusive system we study as well. Suppose f is a smooth nonnegative solution of (1.3), (1.4). Then $g_\delta = (1/\delta)\log(1+\delta f)$ solves the following renormalized version of (1.3):

$$\frac{\partial}{\partial t}g_\delta + \vec{v}\cdot\nabla_{\vec{r}}g_\delta - \lambda\Delta_{\vec{v}}g_\delta = \frac{1}{1+\delta f}C_E(f,f) - \vec{E}\cdot\nabla_{\vec{v}}g_\delta + \lambda\delta\|\nabla_{\vec{v}}g_\delta\|^2, \tag{2.18}$$

which motivates the following definition.

Definition 2.1. A nonnegative element f of $C([0,\infty),L^1(R^3_{\vec{r}}\times R^3_{\vec{v}}))$ is a renormalized solution of the diffusive Vlasov-Enskog system (1.3), (1.4) if the composite function $g_\delta = (1/\delta)\log(1+\delta f)$ satisfies the renormalized equations (1.4)–(2.18) in the sense of distributions.

We may now posit the sequential stability of solutions to the diffusive Vlasov-Enskog system.

Theorem 2.2. *Under the assumptions (2.15), (2.16), (2.17), $1 \le p < \infty$, and $T > 0$, the sequence f_n converges in $L^p([0,T];L^1(R^3_{\vec{r}}\times R^3_{\vec{v}}))$ to a renormalized solution f of the diffusive Vlasov-Enskog system which satisfies the bounds (2.13), (2.14) for almost everywhere $t \in (0,T)$ as well as (2.17). Furthermore, for every $\delta > 0$, the renormalized Enskog interaction* *terms satisfy*

$$\begin{aligned} C_E^+(f,f)(1+\delta f)^{-1}|_{\vec{v}\in B_R} &\in L^1([0,\infty)\times R^3_{\vec{r}}\times B_R), \\ C_E^-(f,f)(1+\delta f)^{-1}|_{\vec{v}\in B_R} &\in C([0,\infty);L^1(R^3_{\vec{r}}\times B_R)), \end{aligned} \tag{2.19}$$

and $g_\delta|_{\vec{v}\in B_R} \in L^2((0,T)\times R^3_{\vec{r}};H^1(B_R))$ *for all* $R, T < \infty$.

Proof. The proof of the theorem is both lengthy and delicate, and details are beyond the scope of this short paper. We will restrict ourselves to an outline of the key steps.

It is necessary first to study properties of the partial diffusive linear transport operator

$$L_\lambda = \frac{\partial}{\partial t} + \vec{v}\cdot\nabla_{\vec{r}} - \lambda\Delta_{\vec{v}}. \tag{2.20}$$

It is known that $(L_\lambda)^{-1}$ maps precompact sequences onto precompact sequences in $L^1([0,T]\times R^3\times R^3)$. However, we need to apply $(L_\lambda)^{-1}$ to sequences in $L^1([0,T]\times R^3\times R^3)\oplus L^1([0,T]\times R^3_{\vec{r}};L^2(R^3_{\vec{v}}))$, that is, to show that L_λ is similar to a hypoelliptic operator from $L^1([0,T]\times R^3\times R^3)$ to $L^1([0,T]\times R^3\times R^3)\oplus L^1([0,T]\times R^3_{\vec{r}};L^2(R^3_{\vec{v}}))$.

Lemma 2.3. *Suppose* $\{h_n\}$ *is a bounded sequence in* $L^1([0,T]\times R^3\times R^3)$ *satisfying*

$$\sup_n \int_0^T \iint_{|(\vec{r},\vec{v})|\geq R} |h^n|\, d\vec{r}\, d\vec{v}\, dt \longrightarrow 0 \quad \text{as } R\longrightarrow\infty. \tag{2.21}$$

Suppose $\{\hat{h}^n\}$ *is a bounded sequence in* $L^1([0,T]\times R^3_{\vec{r}};L^2(R^3_{\vec{v}}))$ *satisfying*

$$\sup_n \int_0^T dt \int_{R^3} d\vec{r}\left(\int_{|\vec{r}|+|\vec{v}|\geq R} |\hat{h}^n|^2(\vec{r},\vec{v},t)\,d\vec{v}\right)^{1/2} \longrightarrow 0 \quad \text{as } R\longrightarrow\infty. \tag{2.22}$$

Suppose $\{g_0^n\}$ *is a bounded sequence in* $L^1(R^3\times R^3)$ *satisfying*

$$\sup_n \iint_{|(\vec{r},\vec{v})|\geq R} |g_0^n|\, d\vec{r}\, d\vec{v} \longrightarrow 0 \quad \text{as } R\longrightarrow\infty. \tag{2.23}$$

Then the set of solutions $\{g^n\}$ *of the equations*

$$\begin{aligned} L_\lambda g^n = h^n + \hat{h}^n \quad &\text{in } (0,T)\times R^3\times R^3, \\ g^n|_{t=0} = g_0^n&, \end{aligned} \tag{2.24}$$

is precompact in $L^1([0,T]\times R^3\times R^3)$.

Now the proof of Theorem 2.2 proceeds in four steps. The first is to show that $\{C_E(f_n, f_n)\}$ forms a bounded set in $L^1([0,T]\times R^3\times R^3)$. In fact, $C_E^-(f_n,f_n)(1+\delta f_n)^{-1}$ is bounded in $L^\infty([0,T];L^1(R^3_{\vec{r}}\times R^3_{\vec{v}}))$. The L^1 bound on $C_E^+(f_n,f_n)$ depends on Enskog gain bounds due to Polewczak. [9]

The second step is to demonstrate the precompactness of $\{g_\delta^n\}$, where $g_\delta^n = (1/\delta)\log(1+\delta f^n)$. Although the lemma cannot be applied directly to $\{g_\delta^n\}$, we introduce cutoff functions $\phi_m(\vec{r},\vec{v})$ in $\mathcal{D}(R^3\times R^3)$ with $\text{supp}(\phi_m)\in\{B_m\times B_m\}$, $0\leq\phi_m\leq 1$, $\phi_m|_{B_{m-1}\times B_{m-1}} = 1$.

Here and subsequently, B_m are balls in R^3 centered about the origin with radius $R_m \to \infty$. Then $L_\lambda(\phi_m g_\delta^n)$ is bounded in $L^1([0,T] \times R^3 \times R^3) \oplus L^1([0,T] \times R^3_{\vec{r}}; L^2(R^3_{\vec{v}}))$ by the assumptions (2.15), (2.16), and the lemma will show that $\{\phi_m g_\delta^n\}$ is precompact for fixed m. Now a diagonal argument and applications of classical measure theory will eventually prove that $\{g_\delta^n\}$ converges in $L^p([0,T]; L^1(R^3 \times R^3))$ to g_δ for all $1 \le p < \infty$ and all $T < \infty$, and that f^n converges to f.

The third step is to demonstrate that $C_E(f^n, f^n)(1+\delta f^n)^{-1}$ converges in L^1 to $C_E(f, f)(1+\delta f)^{-1}$, and that $C_E^{\pm}(f,f)(1+\delta f)^{-1} \in L^1$. This hinges, again, on the Enskog gain bounds.

Finally, one must pass to the limit in the renormalized equation. This is the crucial step in the proof. One starts with the following lemma.

Lemma 2.4. *There exist a bounded nonnegative measure μ^1 and a locally bounded measure μ^2 on $[0,T] \times R^3 \times R^3$ such that*

$$\begin{aligned} \left|\nabla_{\vec{v}} g_\delta^n\right|^2 &\longrightarrow_n \left|\nabla_{\vec{v}} g_\delta\right|^2 + \mu^1 \quad \text{in } \mathcal{D}'([0,T] \times R^3 \times R^3), \\ -\vec{E}^n \cdot \nabla_{\vec{v}} g_\delta^n &\longrightarrow_n -\vec{E} \cdot \nabla_{\vec{v}} g_\delta + \mu^2 \quad \text{in } \mathcal{D}'([0,T] \times R^3 \times R^3). \end{aligned} \tag{2.25}$$

One then can pass to the limit in the renormalized equations in the sense of distributions and deduce

$$\frac{\partial g_\delta}{\partial t} + \vec{v} \cdot \nabla_{\vec{r}} g_\delta - \lambda \Delta_{\vec{v}} g_\delta = \frac{1}{1+\delta f} C_E(f,f) + \lambda\delta \left|\nabla_{\vec{v}} g_\delta\right|^2 - \vec{E} \cdot \nabla_{\vec{v}} g_\delta + \mu \tag{2.26}$$

in $\mathcal{D}'([0,T] \times R^3 \times R^3)$,

$$\operatorname{div}_{\vec{r}} \vec{E} = -n(\vec{r}, t) \tag{2.27}$$

in $D'([0,T] \times R^3)$, where $\mu = \lambda \mu^1 - \mu^2$.

The issue then is to show that the measure μ vanishes. This is accomplished by a lengthy series of estimates using convolution regularization and the weak precompactness of $\{\vec{E}^n(\vec{r},t)\}$ in $L^2([0,T] \times R^3_{\vec{r}})$. It remains still to prove that both μ^1 and μ^2 vanish, which is, however, anticlimactic. □

3. Existence of approximate solutions

Let $X = L^p(R^3 \times R^3)$, $1 \le p < \infty$, and define the diffusive operator $\mathcal{A} f = -\vec{v} \cdot \nabla_{\vec{r}} f + \lambda \Delta_{\vec{v}} f$ on $W^{p,\infty}(R^3 \times R^3)$. It is easy to see that $\mathcal{A}$ generates a positive contraction semigroup on X. Similarly, for $\vec{E}(\vec{r},t)$ bounded continuous on $R^3 \times [0,T]$ and $L(\vec{r},\vec{v},t)$ nonnegative and measurable on $R^3 \times R^3 \times [0,T]$, define the time-dependent Vlasov-Enskog operator $\mathcal{B}(t) f(\vec{r},\vec{v},t) = -\vec{E}(\vec{r},t) \cdot \nabla_{\vec{v}} f(\vec{r},\vec{v},t) - L(\vec{r},\vec{v},t) f(\vec{r},\vec{v},t)$ with domain $\{f \in X : \|\nabla_{\vec{v}} f\| \in X, \lim_{v \to \infty} f(\vec{r},\vec{v},t) = 0\}$, which generates a two-parameter positive contractive evolution operator U_B on X. By virtue of the Trotter product formula we may obtain from U_A and U_B the two-parameter positive evolution operator U.

Consider the initial value problem

$$\frac{\partial}{\partial t} f(\vec{r},\vec{v},t) + \vec{v}\cdot\nabla_{\vec{v}} f - \lambda\Delta_{\vec{v}} f + \vec{E}(\vec{r},t)\cdot\nabla_{\vec{v}} f = \hat{C}_E(f,f), \tag{3.1}$$

$$\vec{E}(\vec{r},t) = \frac{1}{4\pi}\int d\vec{r}'\,\nabla_{\vec{r}}\frac{1}{\|\vec{r}-\vec{r}'\|}\int d\vec{v}\, f(\vec{r}',\vec{v},t), \tag{3.2}$$

$$\lim_{t\to 0^+} f(\vec{r},\vec{v},t) = f_0(\vec{r},\vec{v}), \tag{3.3}$$

where

$$\begin{aligned}
&\hat{C}_E(f,f)(\vec{r},\vec{v},t)\\
&= \iint_{R^3\times S_+^2} [\hat{Y}((\vec{r},\vec{r}-a\vec{\epsilon},t)\eta_B(\vec{v},\vec{v}_1) f(\vec{r},\vec{v}',t) f(\vec{r}-a\vec{\epsilon},\vec{v}_1',t)\\
&\qquad - Y(\vec{r},\vec{r}+a\vec{\epsilon},t)\eta_B(\vec{v},\vec{v}_1) f(\vec{r},\vec{v},t) f(\vec{r}+a\vec{\epsilon},\vec{v}_1,t)]\langle\vec{\epsilon},\vec{v}-\vec{v}_1\rangle d\vec{\epsilon}\,\vec{v}_1\\
&= \hat{C}_E^+ - \hat{C}_E^-.
\end{aligned} \tag{3.4}$$

Writing $B = \{(\vec{v},\vec{v}_1) : v^2 + v_1^2 \le k\}$ for some positive constant k, we will assume

(A1) $f_0 \in C_0^\infty(R^3\times R^3)\cap L_+^1(R^3\times R^3)$,

(A2) for a bounded function Y' satisfying (2.1), (2.2),

$$\hat{Y}(\vec{r}_1,\vec{r}_2) = (1+n(\vec{r}_1))^{-1}(1+n(\vec{r}_2))^{-1} Y'(n(\vec{r}_1),n(\vec{r}_2)), \tag{3.5}$$

(A3) Y' satisfies the Lipschitz condition $|Y'(\sigma_1,\tau_1) - Y'(\sigma_2,\tau_2)| \le C(|\sigma_1-\sigma_2| + |\tau_1 - \tau_2|)$ for a constant C independent of σ and τ,

(A4) $\eta_B(\vec{v},\vec{v}_1) = \eta_B(\vec{v}_1,\vec{v}) = \eta_B(\vec{v}_1',\vec{v}')$ is a smooth nonnegative function, $\eta \le 1$, with support in B.

Theorem 3.1. *Under the assumptions (A1)–(A4), (3.1), (3.2), and (3.3) have a unique nonnegative solution which for $1 \le p \le \infty$ belongs to $C([0,T];L^p(R^3_{\vec{r}};L^1(R^3_{\vec{v}})))$ for each $T \in (0,\infty)$.*

Proof. Let us introduce the spaces $X = C(R^3_{\vec{r}};L^1(R^3_{\vec{v}}))$ with

$$\|f\|_X = \sup_{\vec{r}}\int |f(\vec{r},\vec{v})|\,d\vec{v}, \tag{3.6}$$

the space $M = X\cap L^1(R^3\times R^3)$ with

$$\|f\|_M = \max\{\|f\|_{L^1}, \|f\|_X\}, \tag{3.7}$$

and the space $M_T = C([0,T];M)$ with

$$\|g\|_T = \sup_{0\le t\le T}\|g(t)\|_M. \tag{3.8}$$

We will first prove that the equation has a unique solution in $M_{T'}$ for T' sufficiently small.

We consider the integral equation

$$f(t) = U_A(t)f_0 + \int_0^t U_A(t-s)[\hat{C}_E(f,f)(s) - \vec{E}\cdot\nabla_{\vec{v}}f(s)]ds. \tag{3.9}$$

The right-hand side can be written as the sum of an Enskog term, a Vlasov term, and the boundary term $U_A(t)f_0$. Then (A2) and (A3) may be used to show that $\hat{C}_E$ is globally Lipschitz, and consequently the Enskog term is Lipschitz continuous in M. The second term can be rewritten with some care to show that it is locally Lipschitz continuous in M_t.

Define the sequence of functions:

$$\begin{aligned} f^{(0)} &= 0,\\ L^{(i)}(\vec{r},\vec{v},t) &= \hat{C}_E^-(f^{(i)},f^{(i)}),\\ \vec{E}^{(i)}(\vec{r},t) &= \frac{1}{4\pi}\iint \nabla_{\vec{r}}\frac{1}{|\vec{r}-\vec{r}_1|}f^{(i)}(\vec{r}_1,\vec{v},t)d\vec{r}_1\,d\vec{v},\\ f^{(i+1)} &= U(t,0;\vec{E}^{(i)})f_0 + \int_0^t U(t,s;\vec{E}^{(i)})\hat{C}_E^+(f^{(i)},f^{(i)})(s)ds. \end{aligned} \tag{3.10}$$

It is not difficult to show that the sequence converges to a nonnegative solution f of (3.9) for sufficiently small time t. Indeed, one may estimate

$$||f^{(i+1)}||_M \le ||f_0||_M + tC||f^{(i)}||_M^2. \tag{3.11}$$

Letting $T_1 = 1/4C\|f_0\|_M$, one has inductively $\|f^{(i)}\|_{T_1} \le 2\|f_0\|_M$. By contraction mapping and the previously demonstrated Lipschitz continuity, one concludes that f is a unique positive solution in $M_{T'}$ for some $0 < T' \le T$. From the estimates $\|f(t)\|_{L^1} \le \|f_0\|_{L^1}$ and $\|f(t)\|_X \le \int_{R^3} d\vec{v}\sup_{\vec{r}} f_0(\vec{r},\vec{v}) < \infty$, the local solution can be extended to a global solution.

The solution of the integral equation can be carried from $L^1(R^3_{\vec{r}};L^1(R^3_{\vec{v}})) \cap C(R^3_{\vec{r}};L^1(R^3_{\vec{v}}))$ to $L^p(R^3_{\vec{r}};L^1(R^3_{\vec{v}}))$ for any $1 \le p < \infty$ by interpolation theory. Finally, to show that the solution of the integral equation is the solution of the differential equations (3.1), (3.2) it is sufficient to show that $f(t) \in C([0,T];\mathfrak{D}(\mathcal{A}))$, which follows from estimates on the derivates of f, which we omit. □

4. Global existence

We now state and prove the main result.

THEOREM 4.1. *Assume that $f_0(\vec{r},\vec{v}) \ge 0$ satisfies*

$$\iint_{R^3\times R^3} d\vec{r}d\vec{v}\, f_0(\vec{r},\vec{v})(1 + r^2 + v^2 + |\log f_0|) \le C < \infty, \tag{4.1}$$

and that $\vec{E}_0(\vec{r}) = \nabla_{\vec{r}}(1/|\vec{r}| \star \int_{R^3} f_0(\vec{r},\vec{v})d\vec{v})$ satisfies

$$\int_{R^3} |\vec{E}_0(\vec{r})|^2 d\vec{r} \le C < \infty. \tag{4.2}$$

Then there exists $f \in C([0,\infty); L^1(R^3 \times R^3))$ *which satisfies (1.4), (1.5) and such that, for all* $\delta > 0$, $g_\delta = (1/\delta)\log(1+\delta f)(f)$ *satisfies (2.18) in the sense of distributions, and* $g_\delta|_{(0,T)\times R^3 \times B_R} \in L^2([0,T]\times R^3; H^1(B_R))$, *for all* $R, T < \infty$. *In other words,* f *is a renormalized solution of the diffusive Vlasov-Enskog system satisfying the initial condition.*

Proof. Truncating f_0 and regularizing the truncated function by convolution, one can obtain a sequence $f_0^n \in \mathcal{D}(R^3 \times R^3)$ such that $f_0 \geq 0$ and

$$\begin{gathered} \iint_{R^3\times R^3} d\vec{r}\, d\vec{v}\, |f_0 - f_0^n|\,(1+r^2+v^2) \longrightarrow_n 0, \\ \int_{R^3} d\vec{r}\, \big|\vec{E}_0^n - \vec{E}_0\big|^2 \longrightarrow_n 0, \\ \iint_{R^3\times R^3} d\vec{r}\, d\vec{v}\, f_0^n\, |\log f_0^n| \leq C \end{gathered} \tag{4.3}$$

for some constant $C \geq 0$ independent of n.

Now choose η_n so that $0 \leq \eta_n \leq 1$, $\operatorname{supp}\eta_n \subset B_{n+1}$, and $\eta_n|_{B_n} = 1$. Further, let $Y_n' \in C^\infty(R\times R)$ satisfy (A2) and (A3) with the Lipschitz constant $C = C_n$ depending on n only and such that $\lim_n \sup_{\sigma,\tau} |Y(\sigma,\tau) - Y_n'(\sigma,\tau)| = 0$. Define the approximating geometric factors

$$\hat{Y}_n(\sigma,\tau) = \left(1+\frac{1}{n\sigma}\right)^{-1}\left(1+\frac{1}{n\tau}\right)^{-1} Y_n'(\sigma,\tau)\chi\{\|\vec{r}\| \leq n\} \tag{4.4}$$

and consider the solution of the system

$$\begin{gathered} L_\lambda f_n + \vec{E}_n(\vec{r},t)\cdot\nabla_{\vec{v}} f_n = \hat{C}_E^n(f_n, f_n), \\ \vec{E}_n(\vec{r},t) = \frac{1}{4\pi}\iint \nabla_{\vec{r}}\frac{1}{|\vec{r}-\vec{r}_1|} f_n(\vec{r}_1,\vec{v},t)\, d\vec{r}_1\, d\vec{v}. \end{gathered} \tag{4.5}$$

Then, by Theorem 3.1, for each n there exists a unique nonnegative solution $f_n(t) \in L^1 \cap L_\infty(R^3\times R^3)$. Furthermore, the conditions (2.15), (2.16), and (2.17) are automatically satisfied for f_n and $\hat{C}_E^n(f_n, f_n)$ provided the equalities and inequalities (2.4), (2.5), (2.8), and (2.11) are justified for f_n and $\vec{E}_n$. (2.4), (2.5), and (2.8) can be checked without difficulty by the regularity and decay of f_n and $\vec{E}_n$. In view of the choice of f_0^n, (2.11) may be justified by the lower bound method on Γ. See [2, pages 17-18].

Despite the fact that f_n is not a solution of (1.3), (1.4), we can see from a careful examination of the proof of Theorem 2.2 that the theorem still applies to the sequence of solutions of the approximate equations. Passing to a subsequence if necessary, one obtains convergence in $C([0,T]; L^1(R^3, R^3))$, for all $T > 0$, to a renormalized solution, as given by (2.18), thus completing the proof. □

References

[1] L. de Sobrino, *On the kinetic theory of a van der Waals gas*, Canadian Journal of Physics **45** (1967), 363–385.

[2] R. J. DiPerna and P.-L. Lions, *On the Fokker-Planck-Boltzmann equation*, Communications in Mathematical Physics **120** (1988), no. 1, 1–23.

[3] ———, *Global weak solutions of Vlasov-Maxwell systems*, Communications on Pure and Applied Mathematics **42** (1989), no. 6, 729–757.
[4] ———, *On the Cauchy problem for Boltzmann equations: global existence and weak stability*, Annals of Mathematics **130** (1989), no. 2, 321–366.
[5] M. Grmela, *Kinetic equation approach to phase transitions*, Journal of Statistical Physics **3** (1971), 347–364.
[6] ———, *On the approach to equilibrium in kinetic theory*, Journal of Mathematical Physics **15** (1974), 35–40.
[7] J. Karkhech and G. Stell, *Kinetic mean-field theories*, The Journal of Chemical Physics **75** (1981), 1475–1487.
[8] ———, *Maximization of entropy, kinetic equations, and irreversible thermodynamics*, Physical Review. A **25** (1982), no. 6, 3302–3327.
[9] J. Polewczak, *Global existence in* L^1 *for the modified nonlinear Enskog equation in* R^3, Journal of Statistical Physics **56** (1989), no. 1-2, 159–173.
[10] ———, *Global existence in* L^1 *for the generalized Enskog equation*, Journal of Statistical Physics **59** (1990), no. 1-2, 461–500.
[11] H. van Beijeren, *Kinetic theory of dense gases and liquids*, Fundamental Problems in Statistical Mechanics VII: Proceedings of the 7th International Summer School—Altenberg (H. van Beijeren, ed.), North Holland, Amsterdam, 1990, pp. 357–380.
[12] H. van Beijeren and M. H. Ernst, *The modified Enskog equation*, Physica **68** (1973), 437–456.

William Greenberg: Department of Mathematics, Virginia Polytechnic Institute and State University, Blacksburg, VA 24061, USA
E-mail address: greenberg@vt.edu

Peng Lei: Electronic Data Systems, Falls Church, VA 22041, USA
E-mail address: lei.peng@cox.net

THE RELATIONSHIP BETWEEN KINETIC SOLUTIONS AND RENORMALIZED ENTROPY SOLUTIONS OF SCALAR CONSERVATION LAWS

SATOMI ISHIKAWA AND KAZUO KOBAYASI

We consider L^1 solutions of Cauchy problem for scalar conservation laws. We study two types of unbounded weak solutions: renormalized entropy solutions and kinetic solutions. It is proved that if u is a kinetic solution, then it is indeed a renormalized entropy solution. Conversely, we prove that if u is a renormalized entropy solution which satisfies a certain additional condition, then it becomes a kinetic solution.

1. Introduction

We consider the following Cauchy problem for the scalar conservation law:

$$\partial_t u + \operatorname{div} A(u) = 0, \qquad (t,x) \in Q \equiv (0,T) \times \mathbb{R}^d, \tag{1.1}$$

$$u(0,x) = u_0(x), \quad x \in \mathbb{R}^d, \tag{1.2}$$

where $A : \mathbb{R} \to \mathbb{R}^d$ is locally Lipschitz continuous, $u_0 \in L^1(\mathbb{R}^d)$, $T > 0$, $d \geq 1$. It is well known by Kružkov [7] that if $u_0 \in L^\infty(\mathbb{R}^d)$, then there exists a unique bounded entropy solution u of (1.1)-(1.2). By nonlinear semigroup theory (cf. [3, 4]) a generalized (mild) solution u of (1.1)-(1.2) has been constructed in L^1 spaces for any $u_0 \in L^1(\mathbb{R}^d)$. However, since the mild solution u is, in general, unbounded and the flux A is assumed no growth condition, the function $A(u)$ may fail to be locally integrable. Consequently, $\operatorname{div} A(u)$ cannot be defined even in the sense of distributions, so that it is not clear in which sense the mild solution satisfies (1.1). In connection with this matter, Bénilan et al. [1] introduced the notion of renormalized entropy solutions in order to characterize the mild solutions constructed via nonlinear semigroup theory in the L^1 framework.

On the other hand, Chen and Perthame [2] (also see [8]) introduced the notion of kinetic solutions and established a well-posedness theory for L^1 solutions of (1.1)-(1.2) by developing a kinetic formulation and using the regularization by convolution.

Hindawi Publishing Corporation
Proceedings of the Conference on Differential & Difference Equations and Applications, pp. 433–440

Our purpose of this paper is to clear up the relationship between renormalized entropy solutions and kinetic solutions. An equivalent definition of renormalized entropy solutions is also considered in [6].

2. Statement of the results

We start with some notations. Define

$$\operatorname{sgn}^+(r) = \begin{cases} 1 & \text{if } r > 0, \\ 0 & \text{if } r \leq 0, \end{cases} \qquad \operatorname{sgn}^-(r) = \begin{cases} -1 & \text{if } r < 0, \\ 0 & \text{if } r \geq 0, \end{cases} \tag{2.1}$$

and $r^\pm = \operatorname{sgn}^\pm(r)r$. Let $a \vee b$ denote $\max\{a,b\}$, and let $a \wedge b$ denote $\min\{a,b\}$. Set $Q = (0,T) \times \mathbb{R}^d$ and $\overline{Q} = [0,T) \times \mathbb{R}^d$. For a function $u : Q \to \mathbb{R}$, we define

$$f_\pm(t,x,\xi) = \operatorname{sgn}^\pm\left(u(t,x) - \xi\right), \quad (t,x) \in Q,\ \xi \in \mathbb{R}. \tag{2.2}$$

Similarly, for the initial data u_0 we define

$$f_\pm^0(x,\xi) = \operatorname{sgn}^\pm\left(u_0(x) - \xi\right), \quad x \in \mathbb{R}^d,\ \xi \in \mathbb{R}. \tag{2.3}$$

The entropy fluxes which we use here will be given by

$$\Phi^\pm(u,\kappa) = \operatorname{sgn}^\pm(u-\kappa)\left(A(u) - A(\kappa)\right). \tag{2.4}$$

We now recall the notions of kinetic solutions and renormalized entropy solutions of the Cauchy problem (1.1)-(1.2), which were introduced by Chen and Perthame [2] and by Bénilan et al. [1], respectively.

Definition 2.1. A measurable function $u : Q \to \mathbb{R}$ is said to be a kinetic solution of (1.1)-(1.2) if the following properties hold:

(i) $u \in L^\infty(0,T;L^1(\mathbb{R}^d))$;

(ii) there exist nonnegative measures $m_+(t,x,\xi)$, $m_-(t,x,\xi) \in C(\mathbb{R}_\xi;\text{w-}\mathcal{M}(\overline{Q}))$ such that

$$\lim_{\xi \to \pm\infty} \int_{\overline{Q}} m_\pm(t,x,\xi)\,dt\,dx = 0 \tag{2.5}$$

and such that for any $\phi \in C_0^\infty(\overline{Q} \times \mathbb{R})$, $\phi \geq 0$,

$$\begin{aligned} &\int_{\overline{Q}\times\mathbb{R}} f_\pm\left(\partial_t + A'(\xi)\cdot\nabla_x\right)\phi\,dt\,dx\,d\xi + \int_{\mathbb{R}^{d+1}} f_\pm^0\phi(0,x,\xi)\,dx\,d\xi \\ &\quad = \int_{\overline{Q}\times\mathbb{R}} \partial_\xi\phi\, m_\pm(t,x,\xi)\,dt\,dx\,d\xi. \end{aligned} \tag{2.6}$$

Definition 2.2. A measurable function $u: Q \to \mathbb{R}$ is said to be a renormalized entropy subsolution (resp., supersolution) of (1.1)-(1.2) if the following properties hold:

(i) $u \in L^\infty(0,T;L^1(\mathbb{R}^d))$;

(ii) for every $\ell > 0$ there exists a nonnegative bounded measure μ_ℓ^+ (resp., μ_ℓ^-) on $\overline{Q}$ such that

$$\lim_{\ell \to \infty} \mu_\ell^\pm(\overline{Q}) = 0 \tag{2.7}$$

and such that for every $\ell, \kappa \in \mathbb{R}$ with $|\kappa| \le \ell$ and for every $\varphi \in C_0^\infty(\overline{Q})$, $\varphi \ge 0$,

$$\begin{aligned}\int_Q &\{(u \wedge \ell - \kappa)^+ \varphi_t + \Phi^+(u \wedge \ell, \kappa) \cdot \nabla_x \varphi\} dt\, dx \\ &+ \int_{\mathbb{R}^d} (u_0 \wedge \ell - \kappa)^+ \varphi(0,x) dx \ge - \int_{\overline{Q}} \varphi \mu_\ell^+(t,x) dt\, dx\end{aligned} \tag{2.8}$$

respectively,

$$\begin{aligned}\int_Q &\{(u \vee (-\ell) - \kappa)^- \varphi_t + \Phi^-(u \vee (-\ell), \kappa) \cdot \nabla_x \varphi\} dt\, dx \\ &+ \int_{\mathbb{R}^d} (u_0 \vee (-\ell) - \kappa)^- \varphi(0,x) dx \ge - \int_{\overline{Q}} \varphi \mu_\ell^-(t,x) dt\, dx.\end{aligned} \tag{2.9}$$

Moreover, if u is a renormalized entropy subsolution and a renormalized entropy supersolution of (1.1)-(1.2), then u is said to be a renormalized entropy solution of (1.1)-(1.2).

Then we have the following theorem.

Theorem 2.3. *Let $u \in L^\infty(0,T;L^1(\mathbb{R}^d))$. Then u is a kinetic solution of (1.1)-(1.2) if and only if u is a renormalized entropy solution of (1.1)-(1.2) and the following additional condition holds.*

(A) *For each $\zeta(t,x) \in C_0^\infty(\mathbb{R}^{d+1})$, $\zeta \ge 0$, and each $\xi \in \mathbb{R}$, there exists a constant $C(\zeta,\xi) \ge 0$, such that*

$$\lim_{\xi \to \pm\infty} C(\zeta,\xi) = 0 \tag{2.10}$$

and for any $\ell > 0$,

$$\begin{aligned}\int_Q &\{(T_\ell(u) - \xi)^\pm \partial_t \zeta + \Phi^\pm(T_\ell(u), \xi) \cdot \nabla_x \zeta\} dt\, dx \\ &+ \int_{\mathbb{R}^d} (T_\ell(u_0) - \xi)^\pm \zeta(0,x) dx \le C(\zeta,\xi),\end{aligned} \tag{2.11}$$

where $T_\ell(u) = (u \wedge \ell) \vee (-\ell)$.

3. Proof of Theorem 2.3

In this section, let u be always a function of $L^\infty(0,T;L^1(\mathbb{R}^d))$, and let κ and ℓ be real numbers such that $|\kappa| \le \ell$. First, we assume that u is a kinetic solution of (1.1)-(1.2). Let $\xi \mapsto E_n^\pm(\xi)$ be a smooth approximation of $\xi \mapsto (\xi-\kappa)^\pm$ such that $|(E_n^\pm)'(\xi)| \le 1$ for any positive integer n. Let Φ_n be a smooth approximation of the characteristic function $\chi_{(-\ell,\ell)}$ on $(-\ell,\ell)$ such that $\operatorname{supp}\Phi_n \subset (-\ell,\ell)$ and $0 \le \Phi_n \le 1$. Now, let $\varphi \in C_0^\infty(\mathbb{R}^{d+1})$, $\varphi \ge 0$, and apply (2.6) to the test function $\phi(t,x,\xi) = (E_n^\pm)'(\xi)\Phi_n(\xi)\varphi(t,x)$:

$$\begin{aligned}&\int_Q \Big[\int_{\mathbb{R}} \Phi_n(\xi)(E_n^\pm)'(\xi) f_\pm d\xi\Big]\varphi_t + \Big[\int_{\mathbb{R}} A'(\xi)\Phi_n(\xi)(E_n^\pm)'(\xi) f_\pm d\xi\Big]\cdot \nabla_x \varphi\, dt\, dx\\ &\qquad + \int_{\mathbb{R}^d}\Big[\int_{\mathbb{R}} \Phi_n(\xi)(E_n^\pm)'(\xi) f_\pm^0 d\xi\Big]\varphi(0,x)dx \\ &\quad = \int_{\overline{Q}\times\mathbb{R}} [\Phi_n{}'(E_n^\pm)' + \Phi_n(E_n^\pm)'']\varphi m_\pm\, dt\, dx\, d\xi.\end{aligned} \tag{3.1}$$

Passing n to infinity, we get

$$\begin{aligned}&\int_Q \{(T_\ell(u)-\kappa)^\pm \varphi_t + \Phi^\pm(T_\ell(u),\kappa)\cdot\nabla_x\varphi\}dt\, dx\\ &\qquad + \int_{\mathbb{R}^d} (T_\ell(u_0)-\kappa)^\pm \varphi(0,x)dx\\ &\quad = -\int_{\overline{Q}}\{m_\pm(t,x,\pm\ell) - m_\pm(t,x,\kappa)\}\varphi(t,x)dt\, dx\\ &\quad \ge -\int_{\overline{Q}}\varphi(t,x)m_\pm(t,x,\pm\ell)dt\, dx.\end{aligned} \tag{3.2}$$

By setting $\mu_\ell^\pm(t,x) = m_\pm(t,x,\pm\ell)$ for $(t,x)\in\overline{Q}$, we have (2.7) from (2.5), and both (2.8) and (2.9) follow from (3.2). Therefore, in order to see that u is a renormalized entropy solution it suffices to show that the condition (A) holds. To this end, let $\zeta \in C_0^\infty(\mathbb{R}^{d+1})$, $\zeta \ge 0$, and let η be a function in $C_0^\infty(\mathbb{R}^{d+1})$ such that $0\le\eta\le 1$ and $\eta = 1$ on $\operatorname{supp}\zeta$. Next, applying (2.6) to the test function $\phi(t,x,\xi) = (E_n^\pm)'(\xi)\Phi_n(\xi)\zeta(t,x)\eta(t,x)$ and passing n to infinity, we get

$$\begin{aligned}&\int_Q \{(T_\ell(u)-\kappa)^\pm \partial_t(\zeta\eta) + \Phi^\pm(T_\ell(u),\kappa)\cdot\nabla_x(\zeta\eta)\}dt\, dx\\ &\qquad + \int_{\mathbb{R}^d} (T_\ell(u_0)-\kappa)^\pm \zeta(0,x)dx\\ &\quad = \int_{\overline{Q}}\zeta\eta\{m_\pm(\cdot,\cdot,\kappa) - m_\pm(\cdot,\cdot,\ell)\}dt\, dx\\ &\quad \le \int_{\overline{Q}}\zeta\eta m_\pm(\cdot,\cdot,\kappa)dt\, dx.\end{aligned} \tag{3.3}$$

Note that $(\zeta\eta)_t = \zeta_t\eta$, $\nabla_x(\zeta\eta) = \eta\nabla_x\zeta$ because $\eta = 1$ on suppζ. Therefore, the above inequality comes to

$$\begin{aligned}\int_Q \{(T_\ell(u)-\kappa)^{\pm}\zeta_t + \Phi^{\pm}(T_\ell(u),\kappa)\cdot\nabla_x\zeta\}dt\,dx + \int_{\mathbb{R}^d}(T_\ell(u_0)-\kappa)^{\pm}\zeta(0,x)dx \\ \leq \int_{\overline{Q}} \zeta m_{\pm}(\cdot,\cdot,\kappa)dt\,dx.\end{aligned} \tag{3.4}$$

By setting $C(\zeta,\xi) = \int_{\overline{Q}}\zeta m_{\pm}(\cdot,\cdot,\xi)dt\,dx$, we have (2.10) and (2.11), and hence condition (A) holds.

Conversely, we assume that u is a renormalized entropy solution of (1.1)-(1.2). Define a linear form $m_\ell^{\pm}$ on $C_0^\infty(Q)$ by

$$\begin{aligned}m_\ell^{\pm}(\varphi) = \int_Q \{(T_\ell(u)-\xi)^{\pm}\varphi_t + \Phi^{\pm}(T_\ell(u),\xi)\cdot\nabla_\varphi\}dt\,dx \\ + \int_Q \varphi\mu_\ell^{\pm}\,dt\,dx \quad \text{for } \varphi\in C_0^\infty(Q).\end{aligned} \tag{3.5}$$

By virtue of (2.8) and (2.9) we see that $m_\ell^{\pm}(\varphi)$ are nonnegative for any $\phi \geq 0$. Hence, we conclude that for any ξ there are a nonnegative measure $m_\ell^{+}(t,x,\xi)$ on Q and a nonnegative measure $m_\ell^{-}(t,x,\xi)$ on Q such that for any $\varphi \in C_0^\infty(Q)$,

$$\int_Q \varphi m_\ell^{\pm}(t,x,\xi)dt\,dx = m_\ell^{\pm}(\varphi). \tag{3.6}$$

It is easy to see that $m_\ell^{\pm} \in C(\mathbb{R}_\xi; \text{w-}\mathcal{M}(Q)^+)$ and $m_\ell^{\pm} = \mu_\ell^{\pm}$ for $\pm\xi \geq \ell$. In particular, (2.7) implies (2.5). We have only to prove (2.6). By (3.5) and (3.6) we have

$$(\partial_t + A'(\xi)\cdot\nabla_x)f_{\ell\pm} = \partial_\xi m_\ell^{\pm} \quad \text{in } \mathcal{D}'(Q\times\mathbb{R}_\xi), \tag{3.7}$$

where $f_{\ell\pm}(t,x,\xi) = \text{sgn}^{\pm}(T_\ell(u(t,x))-\xi)$. By the proof of [9, Proposition 3.4], there exists a function $f_{\ell\pm}^{\tau_0} \in L^\infty(\mathbb{R}_x^d\times\mathbb{R}_\xi)$ such that (see [9, (3.10)])

$$\begin{aligned}\int_{Q\times\mathbb{R}} f_{\ell\pm}(\partial_t + A'(\xi)\cdot\nabla_x)\phi\,dt\,dx\,d\xi + \int_{\mathbb{R}^d\times\mathbb{R}} f_{\ell\pm}^{\tau_0}\phi(0,x,\xi)dx\,d\xi \\ = \int_{Q\times\mathbb{R}} \partial_\xi\phi m_\ell^{\pm}\,dt\,dx\,d\xi\end{aligned} \tag{3.8}$$

for any $\phi \in C_0^\infty(\overline{Q}\times\mathbb{R})$. Applying (3.8) to the test function $\phi(t,x,\xi) = \text{sgn}^{\pm}(\xi-\kappa)\varphi(t,x)$ with $\varphi \in C_0^\infty(\mathbb{R}^{d+1})$, $\varphi \geq 0$, we get

$$\begin{aligned}\int_Q \{(T_\ell(u)-\kappa)^{\pm}\partial_t\varphi + \Phi^{\pm}(T_\ell(u),\kappa)\cdot\nabla_x\varphi\}dt\,dx + \int_{\mathbb{R}^d}\left[\int_{\mathbb{R}} f_{\ell\pm}^{\tau_0}\text{sgn}^{\pm}(\xi-\kappa)d\xi\right]\varphi(0,x)dx \\ = \int_Q \varphi m_\ell^{\pm}(\cdot,\cdot,\kappa)dt\,dx.\end{aligned} \tag{3.9}$$

Since u is a renormalized entropy solution, it follows from (2.8), (2.9), and (3.5) that

$$-\int_{\overline{Q}} \varphi \mu_\ell^\mp \,dt\,dx - \int_{\mathbb{R}^d} (T_\ell(u_0)-\kappa)^\pm \varphi(0,x)\,dx + \int_{\mathbb{R}^d}\Big[\int_{\mathbb{R}} f_{\ell\pm}^{\tau_0}\operatorname{sgn}^\pm(\xi-\kappa)\,d\xi\Big]\varphi(0,x)\,dx \le \int_Q \varphi m_\ell^\mp(\cdot,\cdot,\kappa)\,dt\,dx, \tag{3.10}$$

which implies

$$\int_{\mathbb{R}^d}\Big[\int_{\mathbb{R}} f_{\ell\pm}^{\tau_0}\operatorname{sgn}^\pm(\xi-\kappa)\,d\xi\Big]\psi(x)\,dx \le \int_{\mathbb{R}^d} (T_\ell(u_0)-\kappa)^\pm \psi(x)\,dx + \int_{\mathbb{R}^d}\psi(x)\mu_\ell^\mp(0,\cdot)\,dx \tag{3.11}$$

for any $\psi \in C_0^\infty(\mathbb{R}^d)$, $\psi \ge 0$. Now, for any κ, define the measures $m_{\ell+}(\cdot,\kappa)$ and $m_{\ell-}(\cdot,\kappa)$ on $\mathbb{R}^d$ by

$$m_{\ell\pm} = (T_\ell(u_0)-\kappa)^\pm - \int_\kappa^{\pm\infty} f_{\ell\pm}^{\tau_0}\,d\xi + \mu_\ell^\mp(0,\cdot). \tag{3.12}$$

By virtue of (3.11) we easily see that

$$\begin{aligned} f_{\ell\pm}^0 &= \partial_\xi m_{\ell\pm}^0 + f_{\ell\pm}^0 \quad \text{in } \mathcal{D}'(\mathbb{R}_x^d\times\mathbb{R}_\xi),\\ m_{\ell\pm}^0 &\in C([-\ell,\ell];\mathcal{M}(\mathbb{R}^d)^+),\\ m_{\ell\pm}^0 &= \mu_\ell^\mp(0,\cdot) \quad \text{for } \pm\xi>\ell. \end{aligned} \tag{3.13}$$

Hence, by (3.8) we have

$$\begin{aligned} &\int_{Q\times\mathbb{R}} f_{\ell\pm}(\partial_t + A'(\xi)\cdot\nabla_x)\phi\,dt\,dx\,d\xi + \int_{\mathbb{R}^{d+1}} f_{\ell\pm}^0\phi^{(t=0)}\,dx\,d\xi\\ &= \int_{Q\times\mathbb{R}} \partial_\xi\phi m_\ell^\mp\,dt\,dx\,d\xi + \int_{\mathbb{R}^{d+1}}\partial_\xi\phi^{(t=0)} m_{\ell\pm}^0\,dx\,d\xi\\ &= \int_{\overline{Q}\times\mathbb{R}} \partial_\xi\phi\overline{m}_\ell^\mp\,dt\,dx\,d\xi \quad \text{for any } \phi\in C_0^\infty(\overline{Q}\times\mathbb{R}), \end{aligned} \tag{3.14}$$

where the measures $\overline{m}_\ell^\mp$ on $\overline{Q}\times\mathbb{R}$ are defined by

$$\overline{m}_\ell^\mp = m_\ell^\mp \mathbf{1}_{Q\times\mathbb{R}} + m_{\ell\pm}^0 \mathbf{1}_{\{0\}\times\mathbb{R}^d\times\mathbb{R}}. \tag{3.15}$$

Set

$$\omega(\xi_1,\xi_2) = \sup_{\kappa_1,\kappa_2\in[\xi_1\wedge\xi_2,\xi_1\vee\xi_2]} |A(\kappa_1)-A(\kappa_2)|, \quad \xi_1,\xi_2\in\mathbb{R}. \tag{3.16}$$

Then, (3.5), (3.6), and (3.12) give that for any $\phi \in C_0^\infty(\overline{Q})$ and for any $\xi_1, \xi_2 \in \mathbb{R}$ with $\xi_1 \leq \xi_2$, we have

$$\begin{aligned}
&\left| \int_{\overline{Q}} \varphi(t,x)(\overline{m}_\ell^\pm(t,x,\xi_1) - \overline{m}_\ell^\pm(t,x,\xi_2))\,dt\,dx \right| \\
&\quad \leq \int_Q |(T_\ell(u)-\xi_1)^\pm - (T_\ell(u)-\xi_2)^\pm|\,|\varphi_t|\,dt\,dx \\
&\qquad + \int_Q |\Phi^\pm(T_\ell(u),\xi_1) - \Phi^\pm(T_\ell(u)-\xi_2)|\,|\nabla_x\varphi|\,dt\,dx \\
&\qquad + \int_{\mathbb{R}^d} |(T_\ell(u_0)-\xi_1)^\pm - (T_\ell(u_0)-\xi_2)^\pm|\,|\varphi^{(t=0)}|\,dx \\
&\qquad + \int_{\mathbb{R}^d}\int_{\xi_2}^{\xi_2} |f_{\ell\pm}^{\tau_0}|\,d\xi\,|\varphi^{(t=0)}|\,dx \\
&\quad \leq C(\varphi)(\omega(\xi_1,\xi_2) + |\xi_1-\xi_2|),
\end{aligned} \tag{3.17}$$

where $C(\varphi)$ is a positive constant which may depend upon φ.

On the other hand, let $K \subset \overline{Q}$ be a compact set, and take $\zeta \in C_0^\infty(\mathbb{R}^{d+1})$ such that $\zeta \geq 0$ and $\zeta = 1$ on K. By virtue of (3.5), (3.6), (3.9), (3.11), (3.12), (3.15), and condition (A), we get

$$\begin{aligned}
&\int_K \overline{m}_\ell^\pm(t,x,\xi)\,dt\,dx \\
&\quad \leq \int_Q \{(T_\ell(u)-\xi)^\pm\zeta_t\Phi^\pm(T_\ell(u),\xi)\cdot\nabla_x\zeta\}\,dt\,dx \\
&\qquad + 2\int_{\mathbb{R}^d}(T_\ell(u_0)-\xi)^\pm\zeta(0,x)\,dx + 2\int_{\mathbb{R}^d}\zeta(0,x)\mu_\ell^\pm(0,x)\,dx \\
&\quad \leq C(\zeta,\xi) + \mu_\ell^\pm(\overline{Q}).
\end{aligned} \tag{3.18}$$

This estimate and (2.7) imply that $m_\ell^\pm$ is bounded in $L^1_{\mathrm{loc}}(\overline{Q}\times\mathbb{R})$ uniformly with respect to ℓ. By the weak compactness for measures (e.g., see [5]) there exists a subsequence $\{\ell_k\}$ and $m^\pm \in \mathcal{M}(\overline{Q}\times\mathbb{R})^+$ such that $\overline{m}_{\ell_k}^\pm(t,x,\xi) \rightharpoonup m^\pm(t,x,\xi)$, as $k \to \infty$, in the topology w-$\mathcal{M}(\overline{Q}\times\mathbb{R}_\xi)$ as well as in the topology w-$\mathcal{M}(\overline{Q})$ for any rational number ξ. Notice that by (3.17), this convergence in w-$\mathcal{M}(\overline{Q})$ is also valid for any real number ξ. Consequently, we conclude that $\overline{m}^\pm \in C(\mathbb{R}_\xi;\text{w-}\mathcal{M}(\overline{Q}))$ and $\lim_{\xi\to\pm\infty} m^\pm(t,x,\xi) = 0$ in w-$\mathcal{M}(\overline{Q})$. Moreover, passing to the limit with $\ell = \ell_k \to \infty$ in (3.14) yields (2.6). Thus, we see that u is a kinetic solution of (1.1)-(1.2). Thus the proof of Theorem 2.3 is completed.

Acknowledgment

This research was partially supported by Grant-in-Aid for Scientific Research (no. 16540174), the Japan Society for the Promotion of Science.

References

[1] P. Bénilan, J. Carrillo, and P. Wittbold, *Renormalized entropy solutions of scalar conservation laws*, Annali della Scuola Normale Superiore di Pisa. Classe di Scienze. Serie IV **29** (2000), no. 2, 313–327.

[2] G.-Q. Chen and B. Perthame, *Well-posedness for non-isotropic degenerate parabolic-hyperbolic equations*, Annales de l'Institut Henri Poincaré. Analyse Non Linéaire **20** (2003), no. 4, 645–668.

[3] M. G. Crandall, *The semigroup approach to first order quasilinear equations in several space variables*, Israel Journal of Mathematics **12** (1972), 108–132.

[4] M. G. Crandall and T. M. Liggett, *Generation of semi-groups of nonlinear transformations on general Banach spaces*, American Journal of Mathematics **93** (1971), 265–298.

[5] L. C. Evans and R. F. Gariepy, *Measure Theory and Fine Properties of Functions*, Studies in Advanced Mathematics, CRC Press, Florida, 1992.

[6] K. Kobayasi and S. Takagi, *An equivalent definition of renormalized entropy solutions for scalar conservation laws*, Differential Integral Equations **18** (2005), no. 1, 19–33.

[7] S. N. Kružkov, *First order quasilinear equations with several independent variables*, Matematicheskiĭ Sbornik. Novaya Seriya **81(123)** (1970), 228–255.

[8] B. Perthame, *Uniqueness and error estimates in first order quasilinear conservation laws via the kinetic entropy defect measure*, Journal de Mathématiques Pures et Appliquées. Neuvième Série **77** (1998), no. 10, 1055–1064.

[9] A. Porretta and J. Vovelle, *L^1 solutions to first order hyperbolic equations in bounded domains*, Communications in Partial Differential Equations **28** (2003), no. 1-2, 381–408.

Satomi Ishikawa: Department of Mathematical Science, Graduate School of Science and Engineering, Waseda University, Tokyo 165-8555, Japan

Kazuo Kobayasi: Department of Mathematics, School of Education, Waseda University, Tokyo 169-8050, Japan
E-mail address: kzokoba@waseda.jp

SUBDIFFERENTIAL OPERATOR APPROACH TO THE DIRICHLET PROBLEM OF NONLINEAR DEGENERATE PARABOLIC EQUATIONS

A. ITO, M. KUBO, AND Q. LU

We define a convex function on $H^{-1}(\Omega)$ whose subdifferential generates an evolution equation for the Dirichlet problem of a nonlinear parabolic equation associated with an arbitrary maximal monotone graph. Some applications to the Penrose-Fife phase transition model are given.

1. Introduction

This paper is concerned with the following initial-boundary value problem for a nonlinear parabolic partial differential equation.

Problem 1.1.

$$\begin{gathered} u_t - \Delta v = f(t,x), \quad v \in \alpha(u) \text{ in } (0,T)\times\Omega, \\ v = h(x) \quad \text{on } (0,T)\times\partial\Omega, \\ u(0,x) = u_0(x) \quad \text{in } \Omega, \end{gathered} \tag{1.1}$$

where $\Omega \subset \mathbb{R}^N$ $(N \geq 1)$ is a bounded domain, $f(t,x)$ is a given function in $(0,T)\times\Omega$, $h(x)$ is a given boundary value on $\partial\Omega$, u_0 is a given initial value in Ω, and α is a maximal monotone graph in $\mathbb{R}\times\mathbb{R}$.

The present paper aims to formulate Problem 1.1 in a form of the Cauchy problem of an evolution equation as follows.

Problem 1.2.

$$\begin{gathered} u'(t) + \partial\varphi(u(t)) \ni f^*(t), \quad 0 < t < T, \\ u(0) = u_0. \end{gathered} \tag{1.2}$$

Hindawi Publishing Corporation
Proceedings of the Conference on Differential & Difference Equations and Applications, pp. 441–449

Here $\varphi : H^{-1}(\Omega) \to \mathbb{R} \cup \{+\infty\}$ is a proper, l.s.c., and convex function, $\partial\varphi$ is the subdifferential of φ, and

$$f^*(t) := f(t) + \Delta h. \tag{1.3}$$

Our subject is to find φ such that Problem 1.2 is equivalent to Problem 1.1.

In the case where α is coercive (or surjective cf. [3, Proposition 2.14, Remark 2.3]), Brézis [2] and Damlamian [7] succeeded in defining a convex function with which Problems 1.1 and 1.2 are equivalent to each other.

However, in various physical models, one has to study Problem 1.1 with a noncoercive (or nonsurjective) maximal monotone function (or graph) α. For example, the function defined by

$$\alpha(r) = -\frac{1}{r} \quad (r > 0) \tag{1.4}$$

has been used to define the heat flux of a general energy balance law in nonequilibrium thermodynamics (cf. de Groot and Mazur [11]), in the phase transition models proposed by Penrose and Fife [27] and by Alt and Pawlow [1] (cf. [4]), and the related Stefan problem is studied by Colli and Savarè [6]. Another example is

$$\alpha(r) = \log r \quad (r > 0), \tag{1.5}$$

which appears in plasma physics (cf. Longren and Hirose [26]) and in the hydrodynamical limit in gas dynamics (cf. Kurtz [24] and Lions and Toscani [25]). These examples are out of scope of the results in [2, 7].

When one replaces the Dirichlet boundary condition in Problem 1.1 by the third boundary condition ($n_0 > 0$),

$$\frac{\partial v}{\partial n} + n_0 v = h \quad \text{on } (0,T) \times \partial\Omega. \tag{1.6}$$

Damlamian and Kenmochi [10] succeeded in defining a convex function whose subdifferential generates Problem 1.2 which is equivalent to the corresponding initial-boundary value problem for an arbitrary maximal monotone graph.

The results and methods in the above cited paper [2, 7, 10] are not directly applicable to our Problem 1.1 with the Dirichlet boundary conditions and an arbitrary maximal monotone graph.

Let us give here a formal calculation in order to explain the basic idea. Assume that Problem 1.1 has a solution. Then, we have

$$u_t - \Delta(\alpha(u) - h) = f^* (= f + \Delta h). \tag{1.7}$$

Testing this by $(-\Delta_0)^{-1} u_t$ (Δ_0 is the Laplace operator with homogeneous Dirichlet boundary condition), we obtain

$$|u_t|^2_{H^{-1}(\Omega)} + \frac{d}{dt}\left\{\int_\Omega \hat{\alpha}(u)dx - (h,u)\right\} = \left(f^*, (-\Delta_0)^{-1} u_t\right). \tag{1.8}$$

Here $|\cdot|_{H^{-1}(\Omega)}$ is the dual norm in $H^{-1}(\Omega)$ defined by the gradient norm in $H_0^1(\Omega)$ and the duality map

$$-\Delta_0 : H_0^1(\Omega) \longrightarrow H^{-1}(\Omega), \tag{1.9}$$

$(\cdot,\cdot)$ is the inner product in $L^2(\Omega)$, the boundary value h is assumed to be defined in the interior of Ω, and $\hat{\alpha} : \mathbb{R} \to \mathbb{R} \cup \{+\infty\}$ is a proper, l.s.c., and convex function such that

$$\partial\hat{\alpha} = \alpha. \tag{1.10}$$

The energy identity (1.8) suggests the form of the desired convex function. In fact, the desired φ should coincide on $L^2(\Omega)$ with φ_0 defined by

$$\varphi_0(z) := \int_\Omega \hat{\alpha}(z(x))\,dx - (h,z) \tag{1.11}$$

for $z \in L^2(\Omega)$. We have to extend this φ_0 on $H^{-1}(\Omega)$ to justify the above identity (1.8) since we can expect that the time derivative u_t belongs only to $H^{-1}(\Omega)$ if no regularity of α (or its inverse) is assumed.

If $\hat{\alpha}$ (or α) is coercive, then we can define $\varphi = +\infty$ in $H^{-1}(\Omega) \setminus L^2(\Omega)$ (cf. [2, 7]) in order that the evolution equation (1.2) generated by its subdifferential $\partial\varphi$ is equivalent to Problem 1.1. Also in this case, one can take $\Delta h = 0$ in Ω, that is, $f = f^*$.

If $\hat{\alpha}$ is not coercive, this does not work. We have to employ the duality argument of convex functionals (cf. [12, 28]).

In Section 2, we give the main result (Theorem 2.2) and the outline of the proof. In Section 3, we apply Theorem 2.2 to the Penrose-Fife phase transition model. The detailed proofs are given in the papers [16, 17, 23].

2. Main result

Let us first observe that there arises a kind of necessary condition for Problem 1.1 to admit a solution. That is, since we have $v \in \alpha(u)$ and $v = h$, we must have $h \in R(\alpha)$ (the range of α). Hence, we assume hereafter that the following condition holds:

(C) $h \in H^1(\partial\Omega)$ and there exists $\tilde{h} \in H^1(\partial\Omega)$ such that $h \in \alpha(\tilde{h})$ on $\partial\Omega$.

Lemma 2.1 ([23, Proposition 2.2]). *We can extend h, $\tilde{h}$ so that $h, \tilde{h} \in H^1(\Omega)$ and*

$$\int_\Omega \hat{\alpha}^*(h(x))\,dx < +\infty. \tag{2.1}$$

Here $\hat{\alpha}^*$ is the conjugate convex function of $\hat{\alpha}$ (cf. (1.10)):

$$\hat{\alpha}^*(r^*) := \sup_{r\in\mathbb{R}} \{r^* \cdot r - \hat{\alpha}(r)\}. \tag{2.2}$$

Now, we state the main result.

THEOREM 2.2 ([23, Theorem 2.1]). *There exists* $\varphi : H^{-1}(\Omega) \to \mathbb{R} \cup \{+\infty\}$ *a proper, l.s.c., and convex function such that the following hold:*

(i) $\varphi|_{L^2(\Omega)} = \varphi_0$ *on* $L^2(\Omega)$ *(cf. (1.11));*

(ii) *for* $z \in L^2(\Omega)$ *and* $z^* \in H^{-1}(\Omega)$, $z^* \in \partial\varphi(z)$ *if and only if there exists* $\tilde{z} \in L^2(\Omega)$ *such that* $\tilde{z} \in \alpha(z)$ *in* Ω, $\tilde{z} - h \in H_0^1(\Omega)$, *and* $z^* = -\Delta(\tilde{z} - h)$.

From this theorem, we can conclude that for $u \in L^\infty(0,T;L^2(\Omega))$ Problem 1.2 is equivalent to Problem 1.1.

Idea of the proof of Theorem 2.2. Here we give the definition of φ. Let $\psi : H^{-1}(\Omega) \to \mathbb{R} \cup \{+\infty\}$ be defined by

$$\psi(z) := \int_\Omega \hat{\alpha}^*\left((-\Delta_0)^{-1}z + h\right)dx. \tag{2.3}$$

By Lemma 2.1, ψ is proper since

$$\psi(0) = \int_\Omega \hat{\alpha}^*(h(x))\,dx < +\infty. \tag{2.4}$$

Now, we define $\varphi := \psi^* : H^{-1}(\Omega) \to \mathbb{R} \cup \{+\infty\}$ (the conjugate convex function of ψ):

$$\varphi(z) := \sup_{w \in H^{-1}(\Omega)} \{\langle w, (-\Delta_0)^{-1}z\rangle - \psi(w)\}. \tag{2.5}$$

Then, by employing the property of convex functions and their conjugate functions (cf. [12, 28]), we can show that this function φ has the desired properties. We refer to [23, Section 3] for the details. □

By the theory of subdifferential evolution equations (cf. [3]), Problem 1.2 admits a unique solution $u \in W^{1,2}(0,T;H^{-1}(\Omega))$ for any initial value $u_0 \in D(\varphi)$. The next theorem assures that if $u_0 \in L^2(\Omega)$, the solution of (1.2) gives a solution of Problem 1.1.

THEOREM 2.3 ([23, Theorem 2.1]). *If* $u_0 \in D(\varphi) \cap L^2(\Omega)$, *then the solution* u *of (1.2) belongs to* $L^\infty(0,T;L^2(\Omega))$, *hence, by Theorem 2.2, is a solution of (1.1).*

Remark 2.4. The condition (C) (or (2.1) in Lemma 2.1) for the solvability of Problem 1.1 was first noticed in [20], where the case of time-dependent Dirichlet data was studied without using the evolution equation of the form (1.2). By the strong nonlinearity implied by the maximal monotone graph α, each boundary condition has its own difficulty to overcome. We refer to [22] for the Neumann problem, and to [14, 29] for the case $\Omega = \mathbb{R}^N$.

3. Applications to the Penrose-Fife model

3.1. Nonconserved order parameters. Here we consider the following system which was proposed by Penrose and Fife [27] as a nonisothermal phase transition dynamics model consistent with the laws of thermodynamics:

$$\begin{aligned} &e_t - \Delta v = f(t,x), \quad v \in \alpha(u)\ (u := e - \lambda(w)) \text{ in } (0,T)\times\Omega, \\ &w_t - \kappa\Delta w + g(w) + \xi - v\lambda'(w) = 0, \quad \xi \in \beta(w) \text{ in } (0,T)\times\Omega. \end{aligned} \tag{3.1}$$

Here e, u, and w are the specific internal energy, the (absolute) temperature and the order parameter, respectively. The first equation refers to the energy balance law. The second one describes the dynamics of the order parameter, which is here assumed to be nonconserved and subject to the constraint imposed by the maximal monotone graph β. Other given data $f, \lambda, \kappa > 0, g$ will be specified later. The model for a conserved order parameter will be briefly discussed in the next Section 3.2.

A lot of studies have been done for this system. So far, most of the works treated the third boundary condition (cf. [4, 8, 19]) $n_0 > 0$,

$$\frac{\partial v}{\partial n} + n_0 v = h \quad \text{on } (0,T)\times\partial\Omega \tag{3.2}$$

or the Neumann condition (cf. [5, 15, 18, 31, 32])

$$\frac{\partial v}{\partial n} = h \quad \text{on } (0,T)\times\partial\Omega. \tag{3.3}$$

Recently, Gilardi and Marson [13] treated the Dirichlet boundary condition for the temperature

$$v = h(x) \quad \text{on } (0,T)\times\partial\Omega, \tag{3.4}$$

assuming that $\alpha(u)$ behaves asymptotically like $-1/u$ as $u \to 0$ and like a linear function as $u \to \infty$. Notice that in this case one has $R(\alpha) = \mathbb{R}$.

By the strong nonlinearity caused by the maximal monotone graph α, each boundary condition for the temperature demands a different kind of difficulty (cf. [15, Section 1]).

Usually, one considers the Neumann boundary condition for the order parameter

$$\frac{\partial w}{\partial n} = 0 \quad \text{in } (0,T)\times\partial\Omega. \tag{3.5}$$

And one may treat other standard boundary conditions likewise, since the principal part of the equation for the order parameter is linear (cf. [18]).

Here, we study the problems (3.1)–(3.5) with the initial condition

$$e(0,x) = e_0(x), \quad w(0,x) = w_0(x) \quad \text{in } \Omega, \tag{3.6}$$

for an arbitrary maximal monotone graph α by applying Theorem 2.2.

As in Section 2, we assume that α is an arbitrary maximal monotone graph and that the boundary data h is given as in the condition (C) and Lemma 2.1. Other data are given as follows:

(i) $f \in L^2(0,T;H)$;
(ii) $\lambda \in C^{1,1}(\mathbb{R})$;

(iii) $\kappa > 0$ is a constant;
(iv) $g \in C^{0,1}(\mathbb{R})$ with $\hat{g} \in C^{1,1}(\mathbb{R})$ such that $\hat{g}' = g$;
(v) β is a maximal monotone graph with $\beta = \partial\hat{\beta}$. The domain $D(\beta)$ of β is bounded;
(vi) $[e_0, w_0] \in L^2(\Omega) \times H^1(\Omega)$.

We denote by (PF) (the Penrose-Fife model or the phase field model) the system (3.1)–(3.6). The notion of its solution is defined below.

Definition 3.1. We call that a pair of functions $[e,w] : [0,T] \to L^2(\Omega) \times H^1(\Omega)$ is a (weak) solution of (PF) if the following (a)–(e) hold (e' and w' denote, respectively, the time derivatives of e and w):

(a) $e \in L^\infty(0,T;L^2(\Omega)) \cap W^{1,2}(0,T;H^{-1}(\Omega))$;
(b) $w \in L^\infty(0,T;H^1(\Omega)) \cap W^{1,2}(0,T;L^2(\Omega))$;
(c) there exists $v \in L^2(0,T;H^1(\Omega))$ such that $v \in \alpha(u)$, $u := e - \lambda(w)$, in $(0,T) \times \Omega$, and $\tilde{\alpha} = h$ on $(0,T) \times \partial\Omega$. For all $z \in H_0^1(\Omega)$ and almost everywhere $t \in (0,T)$ there holds

$$\langle e', z\rangle + \int_\Omega \nabla v \cdot \nabla z \, dx = (f, z), \tag{3.7}$$

where $\langle \cdot, \cdot \rangle$ denotes the duality pairing between $H^{-1}(\Omega)$ and $H_0^1(\Omega)$;
(d) there exists $\xi \in L^2(0,T;L^2(\Omega))$ such that $\xi \in \beta(w)$ in $\Omega \times (0,T)$, and for all $z \in H^1(\Omega)$ and almost everywhere $t \in (0,T)$ there holds

$$(w', z) - \kappa \int_\Omega \nabla w \cdot \nabla z \, dx + (g(w) + \xi - v\lambda'(w), z) = 0; \tag{3.8}$$

(e) $e(0) = e_0$ and $w(0) = w_0$.

Next, we define the generating functional of the problem.

Definition 3.2. Define a functional $\Phi : L^2(\Omega) \times H^1(\Omega) \to \mathbb{R} \cup \{+\infty\}$ by ($u := e - \lambda(w)$),

$$\Phi(e,w) = \varphi_0(u) + \frac{\kappa}{2}\int_\Omega |\nabla w|^2 dx + \int_\Omega \hat{g}(w)\,dx + \int_\Omega \hat{\beta}(w)\,dx, \tag{3.9}$$

for $[e,w] \in L^2(\Omega) \times H^1(\Omega)$, where φ_0 is defined by (1.11).

Now, applying Theorem 2.2, we will prove the following fundamental energy identity of the problem (PF).

THEOREM 3.3. *Let $[e,w]$ be a solution of (PF). Then, the function $t \mapsto \Phi(t) := \Phi(e(t), w(t))$ is absolutely continuous on $[0,T]$ and the following equality holds for almost everywhere $t \in (0,T)$:*

$$|e'|^2_{H^{-1}(\Omega)} + |w'|^2_{L^2(\Omega)} + \frac{d}{dt}\Phi(t) = \langle f^*, -\Delta_0^{-1} e'\rangle + (h, (\lambda(w))'). \tag{3.10}$$

Proof. First note that $(\lambda(w))' = \lambda'(w)w' \in L^2(0,T;L^2(\Omega))$. Hence, $u' = e' - \lambda'(w)w' \in L^2(0,T;H^{-1}(\Omega))$. Next note that by Theorem 2.2(ii) we have for almost everywhere $t \in (0,T)$:

$$-\Delta(v - h) \in \partial\varphi(u). \tag{3.11}$$

Hence, by the chain rule [3, Lemma 3.3] and Theorem 2.2(i), we obtain

$$\langle v-h,u'\rangle = \frac{d}{dt}\varphi(u) = \frac{d}{dt}\varphi_0(u). \tag{3.12}$$

Therefore, by choosing $z = -\Delta_0^{-1}e'$ in Definition 3.1(c) (with Δh added to the both hand sides), we have

$$\begin{aligned}
&\langle e', -\Delta_0^{-1}e'\rangle + \int_\Omega \nabla(v-h)\cdot\nabla(-\Delta_0^{-1}e') \\
&= |e'|^2_{H^{-1}(\Omega)} + \langle v-h,u'\rangle + \langle v-h,\lambda'(w)w'\rangle \\
&= |e'|^2_{H^{-1}(\Omega)} + \frac{d}{dt}\varphi_0(u) + (v-h,\lambda'(w)w') \\
&= \langle f^*, -\Delta_0^{-1}e'\rangle.
\end{aligned} \tag{3.13}$$

Similarly, choosing $z = w'$ in Definition 3.1(d) and noting that $\widehat{\beta}$ and $\widehat{g}$ are, respectively, primitives of β and g, we have

$$(w',w') + \frac{d}{dt}\left\{\frac{\kappa}{2}\int_\Omega |\nabla w|^2 dx + \int_\Omega \widehat{g}(w)dx + \int_\Omega \widehat{\beta}(w)dx\right\} - \int_\Omega v\lambda'(w)w'dx = 0. \tag{3.14}$$

Adding the above two equalities, we obtain the desired identity. □

The identity in Theorem 3.3 is very important from both physical and mathematical viewpoints.

Physically, the functional Φ refers to the negative of the total entropy of the system, and is introduced by Penrose and Fife [27] so that the system (3.1) is consistent with the entropy law (the second law of thermodynamics). The right-hand side of the identity in Theorem 3.3 refers to the external supply of entropy due to the given data f and h.

Also, the identity in Theorem 3.3 can be used to prove the existence of a solution. In fact, we use this kind of identity to show uniform bounds of solutions of appropriately regularized problems. The detailed analysis is given in [17].

Notice that Theorem 3.3 implies a necessary condition $\Phi(e_0,w_0) < +\infty$ on the initial value, in order for a solution to exist. This means that the total entropy of the initial state must be finite, which is physically reasonable.

3.2. Conserved order parameters. The model with a conserved order parameter is given as follows:

$$\begin{aligned}
&e_t - \Delta v = f(t,x), \quad v\in\alpha(u)\ (u := e-\lambda(w)) \text{ in } (0,T)\times\Omega, \\
&w_t - \Delta\{-\kappa\Delta w + g(w) + \xi - v\lambda'(w)\} = 0, \quad \xi\in\beta(w) \text{ in } (0,T)\times\Omega, \\
&v = h(x) \quad \text{on } (0,T)\times\partial\Omega, \\
&\frac{\partial w}{\partial n} = \frac{\partial}{\partial n}\{-\kappa\Delta w + g(w) + \xi - v\lambda'(w)\} = 0 \quad \text{on } (0,T)\times\partial\Omega, \\
&e(0,x) = e_0(x), \quad w(0,x) = w_0(x) \text{ in } \Omega.
\end{aligned} \tag{3.15}$$

This model has been studied so far with the Neumann boundary condition (cf. [15, 30, 32]) or the third boundary condition (cf. [4, 9, 21]) imposed on the first equation.

We can employ the idea in the previous sections to study the model with the Dirichlet boundary condition as above for an arbitrary maximal monotone graph α. The details will be given in the paper [16].

References

[1] H. W. Alt and I. Pawlow, *On the entropy principle of phase transition models with a conserved order parameter*, Advances in Mathematical Sciences and Applications **6** (1996), no. 1, 291–376.

[2] H. Brézis, *Monotonicity methods in Hilbert spaces and some applications to nonlinear partial differential equations*, Contributions to Nonlinear Functional Analysis (Proceedings of Sympos., Math. Res. Center, University of Wisconsin, Madison, Wis, 1971), Academic Press, New York, 1971, pp. 101–156.

[3] ———, *Opérateurs Maximaux Monotones et Semi-Groupes de Contractions dans les Espaces de Hilbert*, North-Holland, Amsterdam, 1973.

[4] M. Brokate and J. Sprekels, *Hysteresis and Phase Transitions*, Applied Mathematical Sciences, vol. 121, Springer, New York, 1996.

[5] P. Colli, G. Gilardi, E. Rocca, and G. Schimperna, *On a Penrose-Fife phase-field model with nonhomogeneous Neumann boundary conditions for the temperature*, Differential Integral Equations **17** (2004), no. 5-6, 511–534.

[6] P. Colli and G. Savarè, *Time discretization of Stefan problems with singular heat flux*, Free Boundary Problems, Theory and Applications (Zakopane, 1995), Pitman Res. Notes Math. Ser., vol. 363, Longman, Harlow, 1996, pp. 16–28.

[7] A. Damlamian, *Some results on the multi-phase Stefan problem*, Communications in Partial Differential Equations **2** (1977), no. 10, 1017–1044.

[8] A. Damlamian and N. Kenmochi, *Evolution equations associated with non-isothermal phase transitions*, Functional Analysis and Global Analysis (Quezon City, 1996) (T. Sunada and P. W. Sy, eds.), Springer, Singapore, 1997, pp. 62–77.

[9] ———, *Evolution equations associated with non-isothermal phase separation: subdifferential approach*, Annali di Matematica Pura ed Applicata **176** (1999), 167–190.

[10] ———, *Evolution equations generated by subdifferentials in the dual space of $H^1(\Omega)$*, Discrete and Continuous Dynamical Systems **5** (1999), no. 2, 269–278.

[11] S. R. de Groot and P. Mazur, *Nonequilibrium Thermodynamics*, Dover, New York, 1984, reprint of the 1962 original.

[12] I. Ekeland and R. Témam, *Convex Analysis and Variational Problems*, Classics in Applied Mathematics, vol. 28, SIAM, Pennsylvania, 1999.

[13] G. Gilardi and A. Marson, *On a Penrose-Fife type system with Dirichlet boundary conditions for temperature*, Mathematical Methods in the Applied Sciences **26** (2003), no. 15, 1303–1325.

[14] M. A. Herrero, *A limit case in nonlinear diffusion*, Nonlinear Analysis **13** (1989), no. 6, 611–628.

[15] A. Ito, N. Kenmochi, and M. Kubo, *Non-isothermal phase transition models with Neumann boundary conditions*, Nonlinear Analysis **53** (2003), no. 7-8, 977–996.

[16] A. Ito and M. Kubo, *The Penrose-Fife phase separation model with the Dirichlet boundary condition for the temperature*, in preparation.

[17] ———, *Well-posedness of the Penrose-Fife phase field model with the Dirichlet boundary condition for the temperature*, preprint.

[18] A. Ito and T. Suzuki, *Asymptotic behavior of the solution to the non-isothermal phase field equation*, Nonlinear Analysis **64** (2006), no. 11, 2454–2479.

[19] N. Kenmochi and M. Kubo, *Weak solutions of nonlinear systems for non-isothermal phase transitions*, Advances in Mathematical Sciences and Applications **9** (1999), no. 1, 499–521.

[20] M. Kubo, *Well-posedness of initial boundary value problem of degenerate parabolic equations*, Nonlinear Analysis **63** (2005), no. 5–7, e2629–e2637, Proceedings of WCNA 2004.

[21] M. Kubo, A. Ito, and N. Kenmochi, *Non-isothermal phase separation models: weak well-posedness and global estimates*, Free Boundary Problems: Theory and Applications, II (Chiba, 1999) (N. Kenmochi, ed.), GAKUTO Internat. Ser. Math. Sci. Appl., vol. 14, Gakkōtosho, Tokyo, 2000, pp. 311–323.

[22] M. Kubo and Q. Lu, *Nonlinear degenerate parabolic equations with Neumann boundary condition*, Journal of Mathematical Analysis and Applications **307** (2005), no. 1, 232–244.

[23] ______, *Evolution equations for nonlinear degenerate parabolic PDE*, Nonlinear Analysis **64** (2006), no. 8, 1849–1859.

[24] T. G. Kurtz, *Convergence of sequences of semigroups of nonlinear operators with an application to gas kinetics*, Transactions of the American Mathematical Society **186** (1973), 259–272 (1974).

[25] P. L. Lions and G. Toscani, *Diffusive limit for finite velocity Boltzmann kinetic models*, Revista Matemática Iberoamericana **13** (1997), no. 3, 473–513.

[26] K. E. Longren and A. Hirose, *Expansion of an electron cloud*, Physics Letters A **59** (1976), no. 4, 285–286.

[27] O. Penrose and P. C. Fife, *Thermodynamically consistent models of phase-field type for the kinetics of phase transitions*, Physica D **43** (1990), no. 1, 44–62.

[28] R. T. Rockafellar, *Integrals which are convex functionals*, Pacific Journal of Mathematics **24** (1968), 525–539.

[29] S. Sakaguchi and T. Suzuki, *Nonexistence of solutions for a degenerate parabolic equation describing imperfect ignition*, Nonlinear Analysis **31** (1998), no. 5-6, 665–669.

[30] W. X. Shen and S. M. Zheng, *On the coupled Cahn-Hilliard equations*, Communications in Partial Differential Equations **18** (1993), no. 3-4, 701–727.

[31] S. M. Zheng, *Global existence for a thermodynamically consistent model of phase field type*, Differential and Integral Equations **5** (1992), no. 2, 241–253.

[32] ______, *Nonlinear Parabolic Equations and Hyperbolic-Parabolic Coupled Systems*, Pitman Monographs and Surveys in Pure and Applied Mathematics, vol. 76, Longman, Harlow, 1995.

A. Ito: School of Engineering, Kinki University, Higashi-Hiroshima 739-2116, Japan
E-mail address: aito@hiro.kindai.ac.jp

M. Kubo: Department of Mathematics, Nagoya Institute of Technology, Nagoya 466-8555, Japan
E-mail address: kubo.masahiro@nitech.ac.jp

Q. Lu: Jiangxi Medical College, Nanchang Jianxi 330006, China
E-mail address: quqin6@hotmail.com

A DISCRETE-TIME HOST-PARASITOID MODEL

SOPHIA R.-J. JANG AND JUI-LING YU

We study a discrete-time host-parasitoid model proposed by May et al. In this model, the parasitoid attacks the host first then followed by density dependence, where density dependence depends only on those host populations that escaped from being parasitized. Asymptotic dynamics of the resulting system are derived. There exist thresholds for which both populations can coexist indefinitely.

1. Introduction

It is well known that the sequence of density dependence and parasitism in the host life cycle can have a significant effect on the population dynamics of the host-parasitoid interaction. Consequently, the effect can have important implications for biological control. In [10], May et al. proposed and numerically simulated three host-parasitoid models based on the timing of parasitism and density dependence. In this work, we will study a model proposed by May et al. [10] in which parasitism occurs first then followed by density dependence. However, density dependence only depends on the remaining host population that escaped being parasitized.

2. The model

Let N_t be the host population at time t. The parasitoid population at time t is denoted by P_t. An individual parasitoid must find a host to deposit its eggs so that the parasitoid can reproduce. It is assumed that parasitism occurs first then followed by density dependence. Let β be the average number of offsprings that a parasitized host can reproduce for a parasitoid individual. It is assumed that the number of encounters between host and parasitoid populations at any time $t \geq 0$ follows that of simple mass action, bN_tP_t, where the searching efficiency b is a constant. We assume that the number of encounters is distributed randomly with a Poisson distribution. Consequently, the probability that an individual host will escape from being parasitized when the parasitoid population is

Hindawi Publishing Corporation
Proceedings of the Conference on Differential & Difference Equations and Applications, pp. 451–455

of size P is e^{-bp}. For simplicity, the host population in the absence of the parasitoid is modeled by a simple Beverton-Holt equation $\lambda N/(1+kN)$, where parameters λ and k are positive. Since density dependence occurs after parasitism, the interaction between the host and the parasitoid is governed by the following system of difference equations:

$$N_{t+1} = \frac{\lambda N_t}{1+kN_t e^{-bP_t}} e^{-bP_t}, \tag{2.1}$$

$$P_{t+1} = \beta N_t (1-e^{-bP_t}), \quad N_0, P_0 \geq 0. \tag{2.2}$$

Steady state $E_0 = (0,0)$ always exists. The Jacobian matrix can be given by

$$J = \begin{pmatrix} J_{11} & J_{12} \\ \beta(1-e^{-bP}) & \beta b N e^{-bP} \end{pmatrix}, \tag{2.3}$$

where

$$J_{11} = \frac{\lambda e^{-bP}}{(1+kNe^{-bP})^2}, \quad J_{12} = \frac{-\lambda b N e^{-bP}}{(1+kNe^{-bP})^2}. \tag{2.4}$$

Note that

$$J(0,0) = \begin{pmatrix} \lambda & 0 \\ 0 & 0 \end{pmatrix}. \tag{2.5}$$

Thus it can be easily seen that E_0 is the only steady state of system (2.1) if $\lambda < 1$ and it is globally asymptotically stable. Indeed,

$$\begin{aligned} N_{t+1} &= \frac{\lambda N_t}{1+kN_t e^{-bP_t}} e^{-bP_t} = \frac{\lambda N_t}{kN_t + e^{bP_t}} \\ &\leq \frac{\lambda N_t}{1+kN_t} < \lambda N_t, \end{aligned} \tag{2.6}$$

for $t \geq 0$ implies $\lim_{t\to\infty} N_t = 0$ as $\lambda < 1$. As a result, we can show that $\lim_{t\to\infty} P_t = 0$ and hence $E_0 = (0,0)$ is globally asymptotically stable.

Suppose now $\lambda > 1$. Then (2.1) has another boundary steady state $E_1 = ((\lambda-1)/k, 0) = (\bar{N}, 0)$ and the Jacobian matrix of the system associated with E_1 is

$$J(\bar{N},0) = \begin{pmatrix} \frac{1}{\lambda} & J_{12}(E_1) \\ 0 & \beta b \frac{\lambda-1}{k} \end{pmatrix}. \tag{2.7}$$

Thus E_1 is locally asymptotically stable if $\beta b(\lambda-1)/k = \beta b\bar{N} < 1$. We show that (2.1) has no interior steady state if $\beta b\bar{N} < 1$. Notice that the P-component of an interior steady state (N^*, P^*) must satisfy

$$\lambda = e^{bP} + kh(P), \tag{2.8}$$

where $h(P) = P/\beta(1-e^{-bP})$ for $P > 0$. Since $\lim_{P\to 0^+} h(P) = 1/\beta b$, $h'(P) > 0$ for $P > 0$ and $\lim_{t\to\infty} h(\infty) = \infty$, we see that (2.8) has a positive solution P^* if and only if

$$\frac{\beta b + k}{\beta b} < \lambda \quad \text{iff}\ \beta b\bar{N} > 1. \tag{2.9}$$

In this case $P^* > 0$ is unique and there is a unique interior steady state $E_1 = (N^*, P^*)$ if $\beta b\bar{N} > 1$. We conclude that if $\lambda > 1$ and $\beta b\bar{N} < 1$, then E_1 is locally asymptotically stable and there is no interior steady state. We show that solutions of (2.1) with $N_0 > 0$ all converge to E_1.

To this end,

$$N_{t+1} = \frac{\lambda N_t}{e^{bP_t} + kN_t} \leq \frac{\lambda N_t}{1 + kN_t}, \tag{2.10}$$

for $t \geq 0$ implies $\limsup_{t\to\infty} N_t \leq (\lambda - 1)/k$ by a simple comparison argument. Then for any $\epsilon > 0$ there exists $t_0 > 0$ such that $N_t < (\lambda-1)/k + \epsilon$ for $t \geq t_0$. Since $\beta b\bar{N} < 1$, we choose $\epsilon > 0$ such that

$$\beta b(\bar{N} + \epsilon) < 1. \tag{2.11}$$

But then

$$P_{t+1} = \beta N_t(1 - e^{-bP_t}) < \beta(\bar{N} + \epsilon)(1 - e^{-bP_t}) \leq \beta b(\bar{N} + \epsilon)P_t, \tag{2.12}$$

for $t \geq t_0$ implies $\lim_{t\to\infty} P_t = 0$. Consequently, we can prove that $\liminf_{t\to\infty} N_t \geq (\lambda - 1)/k$ if $N_0 > 0$. Therefore, $\lim_{t\to\infty} N_t = \bar{N}$ and E_1 is globally asymptotically stable.

Suppose now $\lambda > 1$ and $\beta b\bar{N} > 1$. Notice E_0 and E_1 are unstable and (2.1) has a unique interior steady state. We prove that the system is uniformly persistent by using a result of Hofbaur and So [6]. Clearly, system (2.1) has a global attractor X. Let $Y = \{(N,P) \in \mathbb{R}^2_+ : N = 0 \text{ or } P = 0\}$, that is, Y is the union of nonnegative coordinate axes, and let M be the maximal invariant set in Y. Then $M = \{E_0, E_1\}$, where $\{E_0\}$ and $\{E_1\}$ are isolated in X. We claim that the stable set $W^+(E_0) = \{(N,P) \in \mathbb{R}^2_+ : N_t \to 0, P_t \to 0 \text{ as } t \to \infty\}$ lies in Y.

For suppose there exists a solution (N_t, P_t) of (2.1) with $N_0 > 0$, $P_0 > 0$ such that $\lim_{t\to\infty}(N_t, P_t) = E_0$, then since $\lambda > 1$, we can choose $\epsilon > 0$ such that $\lambda - e^{b\epsilon} > 0$. For this $\epsilon > 0$ there exists $t_1 > 0$ such that $P_t < \epsilon$ for $t \geq t_1$, and consequently

$$N_{t+1} = \frac{\lambda N_t}{e^{bP_t} + kN_t} > \frac{\lambda N_t}{e^{b\epsilon} + kN_t}, \tag{2.13}$$

for $t \geq t_1$. Hence $\liminf_{t\to\infty} N_t > (\lambda - e^{b\epsilon})/k > 0$ and we obtain a contradiction. Therefore $W^+(E_0)$ lies on Y. Similarly, if there exists a solution (N_t, P_t) of (2.1) with $N_0, P_0 > 0$ such that $\lim_{t\to\infty}(N_t, P_t) = E_1 = ((\lambda - 1)/k, 0)$, then for any $\epsilon > 0$ there exists $t_2 > 0$ such that $N_t > (\lambda - 1)/k - \epsilon$ if $t \geq t_2$. Since $\beta b\bar{N} > 1$, we choose $\epsilon > 0$ such that $\beta b((\lambda - 1)/k - \epsilon) > 1$. But then

$$P_{t+1} > \beta\left(\frac{\lambda - 1}{k} - \epsilon\right)\left(1 - e^{-bP_t}\right), \tag{2.14}$$

for $t \geq t_2$ implies $\liminf_{t\to\infty} P_t > 0$ and we obtain a contradiction. Therefore $W^+(E_1)$ lies on Y and system (2.1) is uniformly persistent by Hofbauer and So [6, Theorem 4.1].

We summarize the above discussion in the following theorem.

THEOREM 2.1. *Dynamics of system (2.1) can be summarized below.*

(a) *If $\lambda < 1$, then solutions of (2.1) all converge to $E_0 = (0,0)$.*

(b) *If $\lambda > 1$, then system (2.1) has another boundary steady state $E_1 = (\bar{N}, 0)$. In addition if $\beta b\bar{N} < 1$, then solutions of (2.1) with $N_0 > 0$ all converge to E_1. If $\beta b\bar{N} > 1$, then system (2.1) has a unique interior steady state $E_2 = (N^*, P^*)$ and (2.1) is uniformly persistent, that is, there exists $M > 0$ such that $\liminf_{t\to\infty} N_t \geq M$ and $\liminf_{t\to\infty} P_t \geq M$ for all solutions (N_t, P_t) of (2.1) with $N_0 > 0$ and $P_0 > 0$.*

3. Discussion

In this short chapter we investigated a model proposed by May et al. [10], where parasitism occurs before density dependence and density dependence depends only on the remaining population that escaped from being parasitized. The model exhibits simple asymptotic dynamics. Both populations go to extinction if the intrinsic growth rate λ of the host is less than 1. When the host intrinsic growth rate is greater than 1, then the host can stabilize in a positive steady state $\bar{N}$ in the absence of the parasitoid. Therefore the parasitoid population becomes extinct if $\beta b\bar{N} < 1$, where $\beta b\bar{N}$ can be interpreted as the growth rate of the parasitoid when the host is stabilized at the level $\bar{N}$. Both populations can coexist indefinitely if $\lambda > 1$ and $\beta b\bar{N} > 1$.

Notice the per capita population growth rate of the host in the absence of the parasitoid population is a decreasing function of the host population. Allee effects occur when the per capita growth rate of a species is initially an increasing function of the population size [1]. Allee effects may due to a variety of causes ranging from mating limitation, predator saturation, and antipredator defense and so forth. Among these is the uncertainty of finding mates to reproduce or lack of cooperative individuals to exploit resources efficiently in spars populations. We refer the reader to [1, 2, 4, 5] for more biological discussion about Allee effects. See also [3, 7–9, 11–14] and references cited therein for models of Alee effects. We will next incorporate Allee effects into the host population and examine the Allee effects upon the dynamics of the host-parasitoid interaction studied in this manuscript.

References

[1] W. C. Allee, *The Social Life of Animals*, William Heinemann, London, 1938.

[2] M. Begon, J. Harper, and C. Townsend, *Ecology: Individuals, Populations and Communities*, Blackwell Science, New York, 1996.

[3] J. M. Cushing, *The Allee effect in age-structured population dynamics*, Mathematical Ecology (Trieste, 1986) (T. Hallam, L. Gross, and S. Levin, eds.), World Scientific, New Jersey, 1988, pp. 479–505.

[4] B. Dennis, *Allee effects: population growth, critical density, and the chance of extinction*, Natural Resource Modeling **3** (1989), no. 4, 481–538.

[5] ———, *Allee effects in stochastic populations*, Oikos **96** (2002), 389–401.

[6] J. Hofbauer and J. W.-H. So, *Uniform persistence and repellors for maps*, Proceedings of the American Mathematical Society **107** (1989), no. 4, 1137–1142.

[7] S. R.-J. Jang, *Allee effects in a discrete-time host-parasitoid model*, Journal of Difference Equations and Applications **12** (2006), no. 2, 165–181.

[8] S. R.-J. Jang and S. L. Diamond, *A host-parasitoid interaction with Allee effects on the host*, submitted to Computers and Mathematics with Applications.

[9] M. R. S. Kulenović and A.-A. Yakubu, *Compensatory versus overcompensatory dynamics in density-dependent Leslie models*, Journal of Difference Equations and Applications **10** (2004), no. 13–15, 1251–1265.

[10] R. M. May, M. P. Hassell, R. M. Anderson, and D. W. Tonkyn, *Density dependence in host-parasitoid models*, Journal of Animal Ecology **50** (1981), no. 3, 855–865.

[11] A. Morozov, S. Petrovskii, and B.-L. Li, *Bifurcations and chaos in a predator-prey system with the Allee effect*, Proceedings of the Royal Society. Series B **271** (2004), 1407–1414.

[12] S. Schreiber, *Allee effects, extinctions, and chaotic transients in simple population models*, Theoretical Population Biology **64** (2003), 201–209.

[13] A.-A. Yakubu, *Multiple attractors in juvenile-adult single species models*, Journal of Difference Equations and Applications **9** (2003), no. 12, 1083–1098.

[14] S. Zhou, Y. Liu, and G. Wang, *The stability of predator-prey systems subject to the Allee effects*, Theoretical Population Biology **67** (2005), 23–31.

Sophia R.-J. Jang: Department of Mathematics, University of Louisiana at Lafayette, Lafayette, LA 70504-1010, USA
E-mail address: jang@louisiana.edu

Jui-Ling Yu: Department of Applied Mathematics, Providence University, Taichung 43301, Taiwan
E-mail address: jlyu@pu.edu.tw

A DISCRETE EIGENFUNCTIONS METHOD FOR NUMERICAL SOLUTION OF RANDOM DIFFUSION MODELS

L. JÓDAR, J. C. CORTÉS, AND L. VILLAFUERTE

This paper deals with the construction of numerical solution of random diffusion models whose coefficients functions and the source term are stochastic processes depending on a common random variable and an initial condition which depends on a different one. After discretization, the random difference scheme is solved using a random discrete eigenfunctions method. Mean-square stability of the numerical solution is studied, and a procedure for computing the expectation and the variance of the discrete approximate stochastic process is given.

1. Introduction

Mathematical models regarding spatial uncertainty are frequent in geostatistic description of natural variables [4] and modeling hydrology problems [5, 6]. Wave propagation in random media has been treated in [2] and fishering problems are modeled in [3] using stochastic processes. In this paper, we consider random diffusion models of the form

$$\begin{gathered} u_t = \left[p(x,\beta)u_x\right]_x - q(x,\beta)u + F(x,t,\beta), \quad 0 < x < 1,\ t > 0, \\ a_1 u(0,t) + a_2 u_x(0,t) = 0, \quad t > 0,\ |a_1| + |a_2| > 0, \\ b_1 u(1,t) + b_2 u_x(1,t) = 0, \quad t > 0,\ |a_1| + |a_2| > 0, \\ u(x,0) = f(x,\gamma), \quad 0 \leq x \leq 1, \end{gathered} \tag{1.1}$$

where the unknown $u(x,t)$ as well as coefficient $p(x,\beta)$, the initial condition $f(x,\gamma)$, and the source term $F(x,t,\beta)$ are second-order stochastic processes depending on mutually independent second-order random variables β, and γ defined on a common probability space $(\Omega,\mathcal{F},P)$.

Model (1.1) assumes that random variations of the internal influences of the system undergoing diffusion are stochastic processes depending on the random variable β and that random external sources to the medium in which the diffusion takes places is also a

Hindawi Publishing Corporation
Proceedings of the Conference on Differential & Difference Equations and Applications, pp. 457–466

stochastic process $F(x,t,\beta)$ which depends on β. The initial condition $f(x,\gamma)$ is a spatial stochastic process depending on the random variable γ. We assume that

$$\begin{gathered}\beta \text{ and } \gamma \text{ are mutually independent random variables}\\ \text{defined on the same probability space } (\Omega,\mathcal{F},P),\end{gathered} \tag{1.2}$$

and there exist positive constants m and M, such that

$$0 \le m \le p(x,\beta(\omega)) \le M, \quad 0 \le x \le 1,\ \omega \in \Omega. \tag{1.3}$$

Problem (1.1) with $F = 0$ and where $f(x)$ is a deterministic function has been recently studied in [9]. A discrete deterministic eigenfunctions method has been recently proposed in [8]. Numerical methods for approximating partial differential equations based on the Itô stochastic calculus have been proposed in [10] and references therein.

This paper is organized as follows. Section 2 deals with some preliminary results about the mean-square calculus. In Section 3, the problem (1.1) is discretized a discrete separation method of variables is proposed. Section 4 deals with the construction of a solution of the discretized problem using a discrete eigenfunctions method. Finally, in Section 5, the stability of the discretized solution and an illustrative example are included.

2. Preliminaries

For the sake of clarity in the presentation, we begin this section by recalling some concepts, notations, and results related to the mean-square stochastic calculus, that may be found in [12]. Let $(\Omega,\mathcal{F},P)$ be a probability space. A real random variable (r.v.) Y is a real function defined on Ω and it is said to be continuous if its distribution function F_Y is continuous and almost everywhere differentiable. In this case, its density function is defined by

$$g_Y(y) = \frac{dF_Y(y)}{dy}. \tag{2.1}$$

If Y satisfies the additional property

$$E[Y^2] = \int_{-\infty}^{\infty} y^2 g_Y(y)\,dy < +\infty, \tag{2.2}$$

then Y is said to be a second-order random variable (2-r.v.) and the above integral is the expectation of Y^2. If $\{p(x)\}_{x\in I}$ is a real stochastic process on the probability space $(\Omega,\mathcal{F},P)$, we say that it is a second-order process (2-s.p.), if $E[p(x)^2] < +\infty$, for all $x \in I$.

Throughout this paper, a random variable will mean a 2-r.v. and a stochastic process will denote a 2-s.p. If Y is a 2-r.v., then $\|Y\| = \sqrt{E[Y^2]}$ is a norm and the set of all 2-r.v.'s endowed with this norm is a Banach space denoted by L_2 [12] but is not a Banach algebra.

A sequence of 2-r.v.'s $\{Y_n\}$ converges in mean-square (m.s.) to a 2-r.v. Y as $n \to \infty$ if

$$\lim_{n\to\infty} \|Y_n - Y\|^2 = \lim_{n\to\infty} E\big[\,|Y_n - Y|^2\big] = 0. \tag{2.3}$$

This type of stochastic convergence is called mean-square convergence. A 2-s.p. $\{p(x)\}_{x\in I}$ is m.s. continuous if, for each $x, x+\tau \in I$, one satisfies

$$\lim_{\tau\to 0} \|p(x+\tau) - p(x)\| = 0. \tag{2.4}$$

This process $\{p(x)\}_{x\in I}$ is m.s. differentiable to the process $\{p'(x)\}_{x\in I}$ at $x = x_0 \in I$ if

$$E\left[\left(\frac{p(x_0+\Delta x) - p(x_0)}{\Delta x} - p'(x_0)\right)^2\right] \longrightarrow 0 \quad \text{as } \Delta x \longrightarrow 0. \tag{2.5}$$

The following result shows under which conditions a 2-s.p. $\{p(x)\}_{x\in I}$, such that for a fixed event $\omega \in \Omega$, satisfies the property that the realization $p(x)(\omega)$ is differentiable in the deterministic sense, and is m.s. differentiable.

Theorem 2.1. *Let $f(x) = f(x,\beta)$ be a 2-s.p. defined on $(\Omega,\mathcal{F},P)$ which depends on the 2-r.v. β. Assume that for each $\omega \in \Omega$ the realization $f(x,\omega)$ is a twice differentiable deterministic function, and assume that its second derivative $f''(x,\omega)$ satisfies the property*

$$|f''(y,\omega)| \leq M < +\infty, \quad \forall (y,\omega) \in [x-\delta, x+\delta] \times \Omega,\ \delta > 0. \tag{2.6}$$

Then the process $f(x,\beta)$ is m.s. differentiable and $f'(x)$ is defined for each $\omega \in \Omega$ by

$$f'(x)(\omega) = f'(x,\omega) = \lim_{\Delta x\to 0} \frac{f(x+\Delta x,\omega) - f(x,\omega)}{\Delta x}. \tag{2.7}$$

Proof. Let $\omega \in \Omega$ be fixed, and considering Taylor's expansion about x of the deterministic differentiable function $f(x,\omega)$, one gets

$$f(x+\Delta x,\omega) = f(x,\omega) + f'(x,\omega)\Delta x + \frac{1}{2} f''(x_\omega,\omega)(\Delta x)^2, \tag{2.8}$$

for some x_ω between x and $x+\Delta x$. Let $f'(x)$ be the s.p. defined by (2.7). As for each Δx, $f(x+\Delta x,\beta)$ is a 2-r.v. that is a function of the r.v. β, then by [7, page 93] it follows that $f'(x)$ is also a function of β, and by (2.8) one gets

$$E\left[\left(\frac{f(x+\Delta x) - f(x)}{\Delta x} - f'(x)\right)^2\right] = \left(\int_{-\infty}^{+\infty} f''(x_\beta,\beta)^2 g_\beta(\beta)\,d\beta\right)\frac{(\Delta x)^2}{4}, \tag{2.9}$$

where g_β is the density function of β. Under hypothesis (2.6), taking limits in (2.9) as $\Delta x \to 0$, one gets

$$\lim_{\Delta x\to 0} E\left[\left(\frac{f(x+\Delta x) - f(x)}{\Delta x} - f'(x)\right)^2\right] = 0. \tag{2.10}$$

Thus the result is established. □

3. Discretization and random Sturm-Liouville problems

Let us subdivide the domain $[0,1] \times [0,\infty[$ into equal rectangles of sides $\Delta x = h$, $\Delta t = k$, and introduce coordinates of a typical mesh point $P(ih, jk)$. Let us denote $u(ih, jk) = U(i,j)$, $F(ih, jk) = F(i,j)$, and $f(ih) = f(i)$. Approximating the mean-square partial derivatives of the stochastic process $u(x,t)$ by the random variables

$$u_t(ih, jk) \approx \frac{U(i,j+1) - U(i,j)}{k},$$

$$[p(ih)u_x(ih, jk)]_x \approx \frac{1}{h^2}\{p(i)U(i+1,j) - (p(i)+p(i-1))U(i,j) + p(i-1)U(i-1,j)\}, \tag{3.1}$$

one gets the random difference scheme

$$\begin{aligned} &-a\{p(i,\beta)U(i+1,j) - [p(i,\beta)+p(i-1,\beta)+h^2q(i,\beta)]U(i,j) + p(i-1,\beta)U(i-1,j)\} \\ &\quad + [U(i,j+1) - U(i,j)] = kF(i,j,\beta), \quad 1 \le i \le K,\ j \ge 0, \end{aligned} \tag{3.2}$$

$$U(0,j) = cU(1,j), \quad j \ge 0, \tag{3.3}$$

$$U(K+1,j) = dU(K,j), \quad j \ge 0, \tag{3.4}$$

$$U(i,0) = f(i,\gamma), \quad 1 \le i \le K, \tag{3.5}$$

where

$$a = \frac{k}{h^2}, \qquad h = \frac{1}{K}, \qquad c = a_2(a_2 - ha_1)^{-1}, \qquad d = (b_2 - hb_1)b_2^{-1}. \tag{3.6}$$

Looking for solutions of the homogeneous problem obtained taking $F = 0$ in (3.2) together with (3.3), (3.4), of the form

$$U(i,j) = H(i)G(j), \quad 1 \le i \le K,\ j \ge 0, \tag{3.7}$$

one gets the random discrete Sturm-Liouville problem; see [8, Section 3]

$$\begin{aligned} &p(i,\beta)H(i+1) - [p(i,\beta)+p(i-1,\beta)+h^2q(i,\beta)-\lambda]H(i) \\ &\quad + p(i-1,\beta)H(i-1) = 0, \quad 1 \le i \le K, \\ &H(0) = cH(1), \qquad H(K+1) = dH(K), \end{aligned} \tag{3.8}$$

together with the random difference equation

$$G(j+1) - (1 - a\lambda)G(j) = 0, \quad j \ge 0. \tag{3.9}$$

For each event $\omega \in \Omega$, taking realizations $p(i,\omega)$, $q(i,\omega)$, problem (3.8) is a deterministic discrete Sturm-Liouville problem, that by [1, page 667] admits a sequence of eigenpairs $(\lambda_m(\omega), \phi_m(i,\omega))$ that can be computed as eigenpairs of the algebraic problem:

$$A(\omega)u = \lambda u, \tag{3.10}$$

where u is a real vector of dimension K and $A(\omega)$ is the matrix

$$A(\omega) = \begin{bmatrix} \bar{s}(1,\omega) & -p(1,\omega) & 0 & \cdots & 0 \\ -p(1,\omega) & s(2,\omega) & -p(2,\omega) & \cdots & 0 \\ \vdots & \ddots & \ddots & \ddots & \vdots \\ 0 & \vdots & \ddots & \ddots & -p(K-1,\omega) \\ 0 & \cdots & \cdots & -p(K-1,\omega) & \bar{s}(K,\omega) \end{bmatrix}, \tag{3.11}$$

where

$$\begin{aligned} s(i,\omega) &= p(i,\omega) + p(i-1,\omega) + h^2 q(i,\omega), \quad 1 \le i \le K, \\ \bar{s}(1,\omega) &= s(1,\omega) - cp(0,\omega), \\ \bar{s}(K,\omega) &= s(K,\omega) - dp(K,\omega). \end{aligned} \tag{3.12}$$

Thus eigenvalues $\lambda_m(\omega)$ and eigenvectors $\phi_m(i,\omega)$ are random variables defined on the probability space $(\Omega, \mathcal{F}, P)$, that can be chosen so that eigenvectors $\phi_m(i,\omega)$ are orthonormal with respect to the weight function $r(i) = 1$, $1 \le i \le K$,

$$\langle \phi_m(i,\omega), \phi_n(i,\omega) \rangle = \sum_{i=1}^{K} \phi_m(i,\omega)\phi_n(i,\omega) = \delta_{mn}, \tag{3.13}$$

where δ_{mn} is the Kronecker symbol. If $\{u(i,\omega),\ 1 \le i \le K\}$ is an arbitrary variable sequence, then for each $\omega \in \Omega$,

$$u(i,\omega) = \sum_{m=1}^{K} c_m(\omega)\phi_m(i,\omega), \quad 1 \le i \le K, \tag{3.14}$$

where the mth Fourier coefficient is the random variable defined by

$$c_m(\omega) = \frac{\sum_{i=1}^{K} u(i,\omega)\phi_m(i,\omega)}{\sum_{i=1}^{K} \phi_m^2(i,\omega)} = \sum_{i=1}^{K} u(i,\omega)\phi_m(i,\omega). \tag{3.15}$$

Expansion (3.14) is called the random discrete Fourier series expansion of $u(i,\cdot)$ with respect to the eigensystem $\{\phi_m(i,\cdot)\}_{m=1}^{K}$, $1 \le i \le K$.

4. Constructive approximate stochastic discrete solution

In this section, we construct a discrete solution process of the random difference scheme (3.2)–(3.5). Let $(\lambda_n(\omega), \phi_n(i,\omega))$ be the random eigenpairs of the random discrete Sturm-Liouville problem (3.8). Let us seek a candidate discrete stochastic solution process of problem (3.2)–(3.5) of the form

$$U(i,j,\omega) = \sum_{n=1}^{K} b_n(j,\omega)\phi_n(i,\omega), \quad \omega \in \Omega, \tag{4.1}$$

where $b_n(j,\omega)$ are r.v.'s to be determined for $1 \le n \le K$, $j \ge 0$.

Consider the Fourier series expansion of $f(1,y),\dots,f(K,y)$ in terms of the eigensystem $\{\phi_n(i,\omega)\}_{n=1}^{K}$, $1 \le i \le K$, $\omega \in \Omega$,

$$U(i,0,\omega) = f(i,y(\omega)) = \sum_{n=1}^{K} b_n(0,\omega)\phi_n(i,\omega), \tag{4.2}$$

$$\alpha_n(\omega) = b_n(0,\omega) = \sum_{i=1}^{K} f(i,y(\omega))\phi_n(i,\omega), \quad 1 \le n \le K. \tag{4.3}$$

For each j fixed, consider the random discrete Fourier series of $F(\cdot, j)$,

$$F(i,j,\omega) = \sum_{n=1}^{K} \gamma_n(j,\omega)\phi_n(i,\omega), \tag{4.4}$$

$$\gamma_m(j,\omega) = \sum_{n=1}^{K} F(n,j,\omega)\phi_m(n,\omega), \quad j \ge 0. \tag{4.5}$$

By imposing to (4.1) that satisfies (3.2) and taking into account (4.4), it follows that

$$\begin{aligned} a\sum_{n=1}^{K} \{&p(i,\omega)\phi_n(i+1,\omega) - [p(i,\omega) + p(i-1,\omega) + h^2 q(i,\omega)]\phi_n(i,\omega) \\ &+ p(i-1,\omega)\phi_n(i-1,\omega)\} b_n(j,\omega) \\ &= \sum_{n=1}^{K} [b_n(j+1,\omega) - b_n(j,\omega)]\phi_n(i,\omega) - k\sum_{n=1}^{K} \gamma_n(j,\omega)\phi_n(i,\omega). \end{aligned} \tag{4.6}$$

Note that as $(\lambda_n(\omega), \phi_n(i,\omega))$ are eigenpairs of (3.8) it follows that

$$\begin{aligned} p(i,\omega)\phi_n(i+1,\omega) &- [p(i,\omega) + p(i-1,\omega) + h^2 q(i,\omega)]\phi_n(i,\omega) \\ &+ p(i-1,\omega)\phi_n(i-1,\omega) = -\lambda_n(\omega)\phi_n(i,\omega), \end{aligned} \tag{4.7}$$

and from (4.6) one gets

$$\begin{aligned} -a\sum_{n=1}^{K} \lambda_n(\omega) b_n(j,\omega)\phi_n(i,\omega) &= \sum_{n=1}^{K} [b_n(j+1,\omega) - b_n(j,\omega)]\phi_n(i,\omega) \\ &\quad - k\sum_{n=1}^{K} \gamma_n(j,\omega)\phi_n(i,\omega). \end{aligned} \tag{4.8}$$

By identifying coefficients of $\phi_n(i,\omega)$ in both sides of (4.8), one gets that

$$b_n(j+1,\omega) - (1 - a\lambda_n(\omega)) b_n(j,\omega) = k\gamma_n(j,\omega), \quad 1 \le n \le K,\ j \ge 0. \tag{4.9}$$

By [1, page 68], for each $\omega \in \Omega$ fixed, the solution of (4.9) takes the form

$$b_n(j,\omega) = (1 - a\lambda_n(\omega))^j b_n(0,\omega) + \sum_{l=0}^{j-1} k(1 - a\lambda_n(\omega))^{j-1-l} \gamma_n(l,\omega), \quad j \geq 1, \tag{4.10}$$

where $b_n(0,\omega)$ is given by (4.3). By (4.1), (4.3), and (4.10), one gets the solution of (3.2)–(3.5).

Note that from (1.2), (3.10)–(3.12), the eigenvalues λ_n and eigenvectors $\phi_n(i)$ are functions of the random variable β, by the independence of the r.v.'s $\phi_n(i)$ and γ and by theorems of [7, page 93] and [7, page 103] it follows that

$$E\left[(1 - a\lambda_n)^h \gamma_n(j)\phi_n(i)\right] = \sum_{n=1}^{K} \int_{-\infty}^{\infty} (1 - a\lambda_n)^h F(n,j)\phi_m(n)\phi_n(i) f_\beta(\beta) d\beta, \tag{4.11}$$

$$E\left[\alpha_n (1 - a\lambda_n)^h \phi_n(i)\right] = \int_{-\infty}^{\infty} \int_{-\infty}^{\infty} \alpha_n(\beta,\gamma)\left[(1 - a\lambda_n)^h \phi_n(i)\right](\beta) f_\beta(\beta) f_\gamma(\gamma) d\beta\, d\gamma, \tag{4.12}$$

where f_β and f_γ are the density functions of β and γ, respectively. The expectation of $U(i,j)$ can be computed from (4.11), (4.12) and hence using the expression

$$V[X] = E[X^2] - E^2[X], \tag{4.13}$$

one computes the variance of $U(i,j)$, denoted by $V[U(i,j)]$.

5. Mean-square stability

In this section, we address the mean-square stability of the discrete approximate stochastic process $U(i,j)$ constructed in Section 4. In order to fix ideas, we introduce the following definition.

Definition 5.1. A solution $U(i,j)$ of the random discrete problem (3.2)–(3.5) is mean-square stable in the fixed station sense with respect to the time, if, for every fixed $T > 0$ and $h_0 > 0$, with $Kh_0 = 1$, $\Delta t = k$, $J = T/k$ integer, one gets

$$\sup_{1 \leq j \leq J, k \to 0} \|U(i,j)\| < +\infty. \tag{5.1}$$

Let us consider the discrete solution process given by (4.1), (4.3), and (4.10). Let us take the eigenpairs $(\lambda_n(\omega), \phi_n(i,\omega))$ of the underlying discrete Sturm-Liouville problem (3.8) so that for each $\omega \in \Omega$, $\{\phi_n(i,\omega)\}$ satisfies the orthonormality condition (3.13). Hence, as $\phi_n = \phi_n(i,\beta)$ is a function of the r.v. β, one gets

$$|\phi_n(i,\omega)| \leq 1, \qquad \|\phi_n^2(i)\|^2 = \int_{-\infty}^{+\infty} \phi_n(i,\beta)^2 f_\beta(\beta) d\beta \leq 1. \tag{5.2}$$

Assume that apart from hypothesis (1.2) the initial process $f(x)$ satisfies

$$|f(x)(\omega)| \le M_f, \quad \forall (x,\omega) \in [0,1] \times \Omega, \tag{5.3}$$

and the source term process satisfies

$$|F(x,t,\omega)| \le M_F(T), \quad \forall (x,t,\omega) \in [0,1] \times [0,T] \times \Omega. \tag{5.4}$$

From (4.3), (4.5), and (5.3), for each realization it follows that

$$|\alpha_n(\omega)| \le KM_f, \quad |\gamma_m(j,\omega)| \le KM_F(T), \quad 1 \le n,m \le K, \; j \ge 0, \; \omega \in \Omega. \tag{5.5}$$

Note that by the first Gerschgorin theorem [11, page 60] and condition (1.3) it follows that there exists a positive constant L such that

$$|\lambda_n(\omega)| \le L, \quad 1 \le n \le K, \; \omega \in \Omega. \tag{5.6}$$

By (5.6) and Bernouilli's inequality, for $1 \le j \le J$, $Jk = T$, $a = kh_0^{-2}$, one gets

$$(|1 - a\lambda_n(\omega)|)^j \le (1 + a|\lambda_n(\omega)|)^j \le e^{Jkh_0^{-2}|\lambda_n(\omega)|} \le e^{TLh_0^{-2}}. \tag{5.7}$$

Using (4.1), (5.2), and (5.5)–(5.7), it is not difficult to obtain that

$$\|U(i,j)\|^2 \le SK^3 e^{2TLh_0^{-2}}, \tag{5.8}$$

where

$$S = (2K+1)M_f^2 + 2TM_F(T)M_f(2K+1) + T^2 M_F(T)^2(2K+3). \tag{5.9}$$

Hence, one gets the stability of the solution of problem (3.2)–(3.5).

Example 5.2. Let us consider the random diffusion problem

$$\begin{gathered} u_t = [p(x,\beta)u_x]_x + 4t\beta^3 \sin\left(\frac{3\pi x}{2}\right), \quad 0 < x < 1, \; t > 0, \\ u(0,t) = 0, \quad t > 0, \\ u_x(1,t) = 0, \quad t > 0, \\ u(x,0) = 2\beta, \quad 0 \le x \le 1, \end{gathered} \tag{5.10}$$

where $p(x,\beta) = \beta + \cos(\beta x)$ and β is a truncated Gaussian r.v. on the interval $[-0.5, 1.5]$ with parameters $\mu = 0.5$, $\sigma^2 = 1/12$, $f_\beta(\beta) = \sqrt{6/\pi}e^{-12(\beta-0.5)^2}$, so that $p(x,\beta) > 0$, for all $0 \le x \le 1$.

Table 5.1. Numerical results for $K = 30$, $a = 1/5$.

(x,t)	$E[U(x,t)]$	$V[U(x,t)]$
$(1/10,1)$	0.0022	0.0084×10^{-3}
$(2/10,1)$	0.0043	0.0327×10^{-3}
$(3/10,1)$	0.0063	0.0709×10^{-3}
$(4/10,1)$	0.0082	0.1195×10^{-3}
$(5/10,1)$	0.0099	0.1742×10^{-3}
$(6/10,1)$	0.0114	0.2299×10^{-3}
$(7/10,1)$	0.0126	0.2815×10^{-3}
$(8/10,1)$	0.0136	0.3240×10^{-3}
$(9/10,1)$	0.0142	0.3529×10^{-3}

Table 5.2. Numerical results for $K = 40$, $a = 1/5$.

(x,t)	$E[U(x,t)]$	$V[U(x,t)]$
$(1/10,1)$	0.0021	0.0080×10^{-3}
$(2/10,1)$	0.0042	0.0312×10^{-3}
$(3/10,1)$	0.0062	0.0676×10^{-3}
$(4/10,1)$	0.0080	0.1139×10^{-3}
$(5/10,1)$	0.0097	0.1659×10^{-3}
$(6/10,1)$	0.0111	0.2189×10^{-3}
$(7/10,1)$	0.0123	0.2677×10^{-3}
$(8/10,1)$	0.0132	0.3077×10^{-3}
$(9/10,1)$	0.0138	0.3347×10^{-3}

In Tables 5.1 and 5.2, we calculate the expectation and the variance of $U(i,j)$ from (4.11)–(4.13). The numerical integration of previous expressions is performed using composite Simpson's rule with 20 points. Note that for different values of K, the expectation $E[U(i,j)]$ remains similar on the same point of the grid.

References

[1] R. P. Agarwal, *Difference Equations and Inequalities*, Monographs and Textbooks in Pure and Applied Mathematics, vol. 155, Marcel Dekker, New York, 1992.

[2] W. E. Boyce, *Random eigenvalue problems*, Probabilistic Methods in Applied Mathematics (A. T. Bharucha-Reid, ed.), vol. 1, Academic Press, New York, 1960, pp. 1–73.

[3] C. A. Braumann, *Variable effort fishing models in random environments*, Mathematical Biosciences **156** (1999), no. 1-2, 1–19.

[4] J.-P. Chilès and P. Delfiner, *Geostatistics. Modeling Spatial Uncertainty*, Wiley Series in Probability and Statistics: Applied Probability and Statistics, John Wiley & Sons, New York, 1999.

[5] R. A. Freeze, *A stochastic conceptual analysis of one dimensional groundwater in nonuniform homogeneous media*, Water Resources Research **11** (1975), no. 5, 725–741.

[6] L. W. Gelhar, A. L. Gutjahr, and R. L. Naff, *Stochastic analysis of macrodispersion in stratified aquifer*, Water Resources Research **15** (1979), no. 6, 1387–1397.

[7] G. R. Grimmett and D. R. Stirzaker, *Probability and Random Processes*, The Clarendon Press, Oxford University Press, New York, 1992.
[8] L. Jódar and L. A. Caudillo-Mata, *A low computational cost numerical method for solving mixed diffusion problems*, Applied Mathematics and Computation **170** (2005), no. 1, 673–685.
[9] L. Jódar, J. C. Cortés, P. Sevilla, and L. Villafuerte, *Approximating processes of stochastic diffusion models under spatial uncertainty*, Proceedings of Int. Symp. on Applied Stochastic Models and Data Analysis, Brest, 2005, pp. 1303–1312.
[10] P. E. Kloeden and E. Platen, *Numerical Solution of Stochastic Differential Equations*, Applications of Mathematics (New York), vol. 23, Springer, Berlin, 1992.
[11] G. D. Smith, *Numerical Solution of Partial Differential Equations: Finite Difference Methods*, 3rd ed., Oxford University Press, Oxford, 1984.
[12] T. T. Soong, *Random Differential Equations in Science and Engineering*, Academic Press, New York, 1973.

L. Jódar: Instituto de Matemática Multidisciplinar, Universidad Politécnica de Valencia, Valencia 46022, Spain
E-mail address: ljodar@imm.upv.es

J. C. Cortés: Instituto de Matemática Multidisciplinar, Universidad Politécnica de Valencia, Valencia 46022, Spain
E-mail address: jccortes@imm.upv.es

L. Villafuerte: Instituto de Matemática Multidisciplinar, Universidad Politécnica de Valencia, Valencia 46022, Spain
E-mail address: lauvilal@doctor.upv.es

THE IMMEDIATE DUALITY AS THE MOST SIMPLE SENSOR FOR SOLVING SMOOTH MULTIDISCIPLINARY ELLIPTIC PROBLEMS (DOMAIN VARIATION)

V. KAMINSKY

The paper deals with numerical methods for multidisciplinary optimization (MDO) problems. Different traditional approaches for MDO problems on the base of Lagrange's multipliers (LM) have troubles with numerical calculation of the LM values in view of nonlinear equations systems on each step of the recursion. The approach proposed in the paper makes it possible to get these values almost "free of charge" on each step of the recursion by more full use of the results of the problem linearization.

1. Introduction

This paper has represented new approach in solving MDO problems which contain (1) some boundary value problem (BVP) (as condition of the connection), (2) a convex object functional, and (3) traditional constraints on all parameters (design variables -(DV)) and variables. Such problems are represented widely in design optimization [1, 2, 9, 14–16], wherein the DV parameters can be present in differential operators, in the right part of differential equations, in boundary conditions, and in description of the domain. A kernel of the methods for MDO problems is usually the sensitivity analysis with respect to the DV for succeeding recursion [2, 11, 16] (the so-called material derivatives). The Main distinction between traditional and proposed approaches lies in the fact that we use the linearization result more fully, applying for this purpose the pair of linear interrelated problems: the primary (P-) problem and dual (D-) problem. Then the proposed technique of improvement of the quality criteria becomes simpler and more precise specifically in two situations: (a) the sensitivity matrix may be obtained semianalytically [10], and (b) the description of DV variation is sufficiently simple (domain variation in BVP or right part of differential equation variation in BVP, see please [1]) for elliptic operators.

2. Problem formulation

In what follows, the names of all the assumed conditions have been designed by the capital character $\Lambda_{\square}^{\square}$ with two indexes: (upper) for a number of the condition and (lower) for

Hindawi Publishing Corporation
Proceedings of the Conference on Differential & Difference Equations and Applications, pp. 467–475

the condition object. Our main target in the paper is to show the essence of the proposed approach, since we resorted to two self-restraints: (a) for all results described here especially, we take very "good" initial characteristics of spaces, sets, functions, operators, and maps, (b) we give an outline of the proofs only.

2.1. The domain and differential operator. Let $P = \{p\} \subset B$ be a convex compact $(\Lambda^{(1)}_{(P)})$ in some Banach space B with a suitable norm $\|\cdot\|_B$, let $\omega^\star \subset \omega, \omega_p, \subset \omega^0 \subset R^{(k)}$, $k = 2,3$, be bounded domains $(\Lambda^{(1)}_{(\omega)})$ with C^2—Jordan boundaries $\gamma^\star$, γ, γ_p, γ^0—of Lipschitz-1 property, that is, $(\Lambda^{(2)}_{(\omega)})$ where ω is a certain fixed domain and the strongly monotone potential one-to-one map $\Pi = \Pi(p) : (p,\omega) \Longleftrightarrow \omega_p$, $p \in P$ which conserves the given BVP. Let Π be a Lipschitz-1 smooth homeomorphism $(\Lambda^{(1)}_{(\Pi)})$. The compact P and the map Π generate three homeomorphic compacts: $\widetilde{\Omega}_p = \{\omega_p\}_{p\in P}$, $\widetilde{\Gamma}_p = \{\gamma_p\}_{p\in P}$ (the variation object in our problem), and its isomorphic image $\widetilde{\Theta} = \{\theta_p \in W^{(1,2)} : \theta_p \Leftrightarrow \gamma_p\}_{p\in P}$ in the space $W^{(1,2)}$.

Now consider an elliptic operator $D = D(x,p)$ and a right part operator $\bar{f} = f(x,p)$, where $u \in H$ defined on ω_p is the so-called state vector or the solution of the corresponding differential equation $D(x,p)u = \bar{f}(x,p)u$, wherein H is some Hilbert space (in our case, the Sobolev space $W^{(1,2)}(\omega^0)$ with $W_0^{(1,2)}$—the closure of $C_0^\infty(\omega^0)$ in $W^{(1,2)}$). From here on, we use the same symbol $W^{(1,2)}$ for all domains $\omega^\star$, ω, ω_p, ω^0. The map $\bar{f} : (R^{(k)} \times B_p) \to R^{(1)}$ is sufficiently smooth with respect to both arguments—$(\Lambda^{(1)}_{(\bar{f})})$ since it is evident that $u = u(x,p)$.

2.2. Boundary conditions of BVP. Boundary conditions are established by the boundary operator $G = G(p) : H \to H'$, where H' is also Hilbert space, that is, $Gu = g(x)$ for $x \in \gamma_p = \gamma'_p \cup \gamma''_p$, where γ'_p and γ''_p are relatively two open disjoint parts of the boundary γ_p. The operator G can be defined on γ'_p and γ''_p by different kinds of boundary conditions.

2.3. Special case. The special case we are interested is as follows: $D\Box = \sum_{i,j=1}^{k}(\partial/\partial_{x_j})(a_{ij}(x,p)(\partial/\partial_{x_i})\Box) + a_i(x,p)\partial_{x_i}\Box + a_0(x,p)$ and $\bar{f}(x,p) = f(x,p)$, where f is a scalar function. Thus we consider the Dirichlet problem

$$D(x,p)u = f(x,p), \tag{2.1}$$

where D is a uniform elliptic operator $(\Lambda^{(1)}_{(D)})$. Besides, suppose that $a_{ij}, a_i, a_0 \in C^\infty(\omega^0 \times P)$, that is, the condition $(\Lambda^{(1)}_{(a)})$ and $\inf_{(x,p)\in(\omega^0\times P)} a_0(x,p) > 0$ and $\{f \in C(\omega^0 \times P \times W^{(1,2)})\}$ is the set of functions defined on ω^0 and uniformly continuous on $p \in P$, that is, the condition $(\Lambda^{(1)}_{(f)})$.

The most interesting boundary conditions (for practical applications) are represented by

$$G(p)u = n\bar{A}(p)\nabla u + \alpha(p)u = g(x,p), \tag{2.2}$$

where $\bar{A} \equiv 0$ and $\alpha(p) \equiv 1$ for $x \in \gamma'_p$ and otherwise for $x \in \gamma''_p$, n is the unit outward normal to γ''_p, and $g \in C(\gamma \times P)$, that is, the condition $(\Lambda^{(1)}_{(g)})$.

In applied optimization problems in parallel with integral constraints

$$E_1(p,u) = \int_{\omega_p} b_1(x,u,p)(dx) \leq e_1, \tag{2.3}$$

where $E_1 : (B \times W^{(1,2)}) \to R^m$, $e_1 \in R^{(m)}$, and $b_1(x,u,p)$ is a convex Lipschitz-1 function $(\Lambda^{(1)}_{(b_1)})$ on ω_0 with respect to all arguments, pointwise state constraints are of frequent occurrence (e.g., stress and displacements in all the points of the given domain):

$$\begin{gathered} E_2(x,u) \leq e_2(x), \quad x \in \omega_p, \text{ or in special case,} \\ c_i(x,u_p) \leq \sigma(x), \quad i = 1;I,\ x \in \omega_p \end{gathered} \tag{2.4}$$

(see, for instance, [3]), where $E_2 : (R^{(k)} \times W^{(1,2)}) \to R^{(s)}$ and $c(x,u)$ is a Lipschitz-1 vector-function defined on ω^0, that is, $(\Lambda^{(1)}_{(c_i)})$ with components $c_i(x,u)\, i = 1;I$—convex functions on ω^0, that is, $(\Lambda^{(2)}_{(c_i)})$. Thus the feasible set Θ for the problem is

$$\Theta = \{\theta_p \in \widetilde{\Theta} \subset W^{(1,2)} : \text{such that (2.2), (2.3), (2.4) are fulfilled}\}. \tag{2.5}$$

Now define the object function in the following way:

$$F(u) = F_1(p) = \int_{\omega^*} b_0(x,u(p))\mu_0(dx) \longrightarrow \min_{\omega(p)\in\Omega} = \min_{p\in P} = \min_{\theta_p\in\Theta}, \tag{2.6}$$

where $b_0(x,u)$ is a convex Lipschitz-1 function $(\Lambda^{(1)}_{(b_0)})$ on ω_0 as well. In what follows, the problems (2.1)-(2.2) and (2.1)–(2.6) are specified by (Ψ) and (Φ) correspondingly.

Proposition 2.1 (existence of solutions in (Ψ) [4, page 9]). *Suppose that the problem (Ψ) has satisfied the following conditions enumerated in Sections 2.1, 2.2, 2.3: $(\Lambda^{(1)}_{(\omega)})$, $(\Lambda^{(2)}_{(\omega)})$, $(\Lambda^{(1)}_{(D)})$, $(\Lambda^{(1)}_{(a)})$, $(\Lambda^{(1)}_{(f)})$, and $(\Lambda^{(1)}_{(g)})$ correspondingly on the domain ω, the operator D and its elements, the right part f, and the boundary condition g. Then the problem (Ψ) has a unique solution $u \in W^{(1,2)} = W^{(1,2)}(\omega)$.*

Remark 2.2. Under conditions enumerated in Theorem 2.3, the statement $\lim_{\nu\to\infty} \|p^{(\nu)} - p^{(\nu+\kappa)}\|_B = 0$ implies (a) $\lim_{\nu\to\infty} r_H(\omega_{p^{(\nu)}}, \omega_{p^{(\nu+\kappa)}}) = 0$, where r_H is Hausdorf's distance, (b) $u^{(\nu)} \rightharpoonup \bar{u}$, and (c) $\lim_{\nu\to\infty} \|u^{(\nu)} - \bar{u}\|_{W^{(1,2)}} = 0$, where κ is any integer positive number and $\bar{u} \in W^{(1,2)}$.

Theorem 2.3 (existence of solutions (Φ)). *Let the suppositions $(\Lambda^{(1)}_{(P)})$, $(\Lambda^{(1)}_{(\Pi)})$, $(\Lambda^{(1)}_{(b_0)})$, $(\Lambda^{(1)}_{(b_1)})$, $(\Lambda^{(1)}_{(c_i)})$, $(\Lambda^{(2)}_{(c_i)})$ be valid under all conditions of Proposition 2.1. Then there exists the solution of the problem (Φ).*

Proof. Without loss of generality, we have restricted ourselves to (1) the simplest case—domain variation only and (2) setting $\omega^{(\nu+1)} \subset \omega^{(\nu)}$ to prevent difficulties connected with the functions definition domains f and g on the sequence $\{\omega^{(\nu)}\}_{\nu=1}^{(\infty)}$. We will study the characteristics of $F_1(p)$, $p \in P$, instead of $F(p,u)$. Let the sequence $\{\omega^{(\nu)} = \omega_{p^{(\nu)}}\}_{\nu=1}^{\infty}$ be such that (a) $\lim_{\nu\to\infty} \omega^{(\nu)} = \ddot{\omega}$ (in sense of r_Ω because of $(\Lambda_{(P)}^{(1)})$, $(\Lambda_{(\Pi)}^{(1)})$), and (b) $\lim_{\nu\to\infty} F_1(p^{(\nu)}) = \inf_{p\in P} F_1(p)$. Then for the corresponding sequence $\{u^{(\nu)} = u(p^{(\nu)})\}_{\nu=1}^{\infty}$, we have $u^{(\nu)} \rightharpoonup \ddot{u}$ by $\nu \to \infty$, where $\ddot{u} \in W^{(1,2)}$ and $p^{(\nu)} \to \ddot{p} \in P$. Then $\lim_{\nu\to\infty} \inf F(u^{(\nu)}, p^{(\nu)}) = \lim_{\nu\to\infty} \inf F_1(p^{(\nu)}) \geq F(\ddot{u},\ddot{p}) = F_1(\ddot{p})$. On the other hand, in view of $\Lambda_{(P)}^{(1)}$, $\Lambda_{(b_0)}^{(1)}$, and Remark 2.2, there exists minimizing sequence $\{p^{(\nu)}\}_{\nu=1}^{\infty}$ such that $\lim_{\nu\to\infty} F_1(p^{(\nu)}) = \inf_{p\in P} F_1(p)$ since $\ddot{u}$ is the solution of the problem (Φ). □

3. Examples

Example 3.1 [6]. (*Control of bar cross-section in elastic torsion conditions to maximize torsional rigidity.*) $D(x,p)\square \equiv -div(h(x)\nabla\square)$, $f(x,p,u) \equiv 1$, $G(x,p)u \equiv u(x)$, $g(x) \equiv 0$, $x \in \gamma$, $F(p,u) = (1/mes(\omega)) \int_\omega u(x)(dx)$, where ω is a ring with the controlled parameter $h(x)$.

Example 3.2 [8]. (*The optimal shape of the cross-section of plasmas in axisymmetric toroids.*) $D(x,p)\square \equiv \Delta\square - (\nu(x) \cdot \nabla\square)$, $f(x,p,u) \equiv f(x,u)$, $G(x,p)u \equiv u(x)$, $g(x) \equiv c = \text{const}$, $x \in \gamma$, $F(u,\omega_p) = \int_{\omega_p} b_0(x,u)(dx) = \int_{\omega_p} b_0(x,u)(d\omega)$ subject to the integral constraint (2.3), where $b_1(x,u,p) \equiv h(x)$, $e_1 = M = \text{const}$, where the vector function $\nu(x)$ and the function $h(x)$ are suitably defined.

Example 3.3 [5, 12]. (*The optimal shape of the magnet poles both in medical MRI tomography for diagnostics and MGD-plasm generators.*) $D(x,p)\square \equiv \Delta\square$, $f(x,p,u) \equiv 0$, $G(x,p)u \equiv u(x)$, $g(x) \equiv 0$, $x \in \gamma_p$, $x \in \gamma_p = \gamma_p' \cup \gamma_p''$, only the part γ_p' of γ_p would be subject to vary, $F(u,\omega_p) = \int_{\omega^*} (u(x) - u^0)^2(dx)$ subject to the pointwise state constraint (2.4) with $E_2(x,u) \equiv u(x)$ for $x \in \omega_p$, and $e_2(x) \equiv \text{constant}$, $x \in \omega_p$, $u^0 \equiv \text{constant}$, $x \in \omega_p$.

Example 3.4 (see [13, page 201]). (*Structural design of an elastic plate defined on the given domain ω to minimize the total weight.*) $D(x,p)\square \equiv \nabla^2\nabla^2\square$, $f(x,p,u) \equiv f(x,p)$, $x \in \omega$ (external normal forces), $G(x,p)u \equiv u(x)$, $g(x) \equiv 0$, $x \in \gamma = \gamma' \cup \gamma''$ under pointwise state constraints both on displacements (the operator $E_2'(x,u) = u(x)$) and stresses (the operator $E_2'' = \sigma(x) = \sigma(u(x))$) for all $x \in \omega$, where $\sigma = Su$ and S is a linear bounded operator; here $e_2'(x)$ and e_2'' are some continuous function and number. The prime interest here is connected with the minimal weight of the plate and hence $F(x,p,u) \equiv F(p) = \int_\omega \rho(x)(dx) = \int_\omega \rho(x)(d\omega)$, where $\rho(\cdot)$ is the density of the plate linearly connected with a thickness $h(x)$ of the plate.

4. Main idea of the approach

In the main, we are interested in the numerical aspect of the procedure since the main idea of the approach has been outlined in finite dimensional spaces.

4.1. Bottleneck of LM-approach for nonlinear problems. As a rule the MDO problems are nonlinear in one form or another. In this situation traditional methods in the MDO problems construct usually so called sensitivity matrices on the base of LM for the given nonlinear problem (on the whole, the admissible set), but just as this takes place, numerical procedure presents a real challenge to solving LM. At the same time, numerical procedure used for linear systems makes it possible to obtain numerical values of LM essentially "without payment".

4.2. The pair of conjugated problems—a linear case. Let R^n and R^m be two finite dimensional spaces, let $\langle\cdot,\cdot\rangle$ be a scalar product, and let $A:\xi\to y=A\xi$, $\xi\in R^{(n)}$, $y\in R^{(m)}$ be a linear operator. Introducing two admissible domains $\omega=\{\xi\in R^{(n)}: A\xi=\le b, \text{ for } \xi\ge 0\}$ and $\tilde{\omega}=\{y\in R^{(m)}: A^\star y\ge p, \text{ for } y\ge 0\}$, we consider two problems situated at duality: $z(\xi)=\langle p\xi\rangle\to\max_\omega$ (the P-problem) and $\tilde{z}(y)=\langle by\rangle\to\min_{\tilde{\omega}}$ (the D-problem), where $\xi,p\in R^{(n)}$, $b,y\in R^{(m)}$ and matrices A and $A^\star$ are conjugated. Denote ξ^*, y^* and $z^*=z(\xi^*)$, $\tilde{z}^*=\tilde{z}(y^*)$, correspondingly, their optimal solutions and their optimal values.

Theorem 4.1 (existence of solutions) (see [17, page 89]). *Two linear problems (primary and dual ones) either coincidentally possess optimal solutions x^* and y^* and then $z(\xi^*)=\tilde{z}(y^*)$ or the P- and D-problems are not solvable at the same time. In the first case, the solving process finished for one of these problems has been finished also for another problem. It is evident that $z^*=z^*(b,p)$ and $\tilde{z}^*=\tilde{z}^*(b,p)$ and then $z^*=\tilde{z}^*$.*

4.3. perturbation of the pair of conjugated dual problems. Suppose that one of two dual problems has the solution, that is, $\omega\ne\varnothing$ and there exists $\xi^0\in\omega$ such that $|z^*|<\infty$ (or $\tilde{\omega}\ne\varnothing$ and $|\tilde{z}^*|<\infty$), then the following theorem holds.

Theorem 4.2 (perturbation of the minimum) (see [7, page 41]). *Under conditions and suppositions enumerated in this section on the primary and dual problems,*

$$\frac{\partial z^*(b)}{\partial b_i}=y_i^*=y_i^*(b),\qquad \frac{\partial\tilde{z}^*(p)}{\partial p_j}=\xi_j^*=\xi_j^*(p), \tag{4.1}$$

correspondingly for $i=1,\dots,m$ and $j=1,\dots,n$.

5. Digitalization of the problem

Note that in what follows, the boundary points only are subjected to variation.

5.1. Approximation of space, its elements, and the BVP. The symbol $\hat{\cdot}$ sets up a correspondence between the same concepts of the initial problem and its digitalized finite dimensional analogies: $B_p\Rightarrow\hat{B}_p=R^{(n_p)}$, $P\Rightarrow\hat{P}\subset R^{(n_p)}$, $f\Rightarrow\hat{f}$, $D\Rightarrow\hat{D}$, $\omega_p\Rightarrow\hat{\omega}_p$, $\Pi(p)\Rightarrow\hat{\Pi}(\hat{p})$, $u\Rightarrow\hat{u}\in\widehat{W}^{(1,2)}=R^{(n_u)}$, $g\Rightarrow\hat{g}$, $\gamma\Rightarrow\hat{g}$, $\mu^0\Rightarrow\hat{\mu}^0$, $\Theta\Rightarrow\hat{\Theta}\subset R^{(n_\theta)}$. Note that all suppositions $\Lambda_\square^\square$ taken in the initial BVP have been conserved or enhanced in the digitalized BVP, that is, $\hat{\Lambda}_\square^\square\succeq\Lambda_\square^\square$, in particular, $\hat{D}$, as a rule, is a positive and bounded operator; since $\hat{D}^{-1}$ exists and it is a completely continuous operator. Let digitalization method taken by us for the problem (Φ) be sufficiently regular, stable, and consistent in some sense—($\Lambda^{(1)}_{(\mathrm{dig})}$)—in other words, conditions on the step of the mesh and approximation of functions. Then we have $\hat{u}(x,\hat{p}^{(\nu)}) \to u(x,p)$ uniformly on x and $F(\hat{u},\hat{p}^{(\nu)}) \to F(u,p)$ by $\nu \to \infty$ and $\hat{p}^{(\nu)} \to p$ uniformly on u, for example, finite element method (FEM) and finite differences method (FDM). In addition, we suppose that the domains ω^0 and ω_p have been partitioned by the same strongly regular mesh depending on the digitalization parameter δ. As a result, we obtain the polygonal sets $\hat{\omega}^0$ and $\hat{\omega}_p \subset \omega_p$.

5.2. The numerical solution of $\hat{D}\hat{u} = \hat{f}$. Here $\hat{D}$ is a nondegenerate operator. Then $\hat{u} = \hat{u}(\xi) = \hat{u}_{\hat{p}}(\xi) = \sum_{i=1}^{n_\theta} \hat{u}^{(i)}(\hat{p})\xi_i$, $\xi \in R^{(n_\theta)}$ (a digital analogy of the PDE solution (2.1)).

5.3. Approximation of the object functional. $\hat{F}(\xi,\hat{p}) = \sum_{i=1}^{n_\theta} \hat{b}_0^{(i)}(\xi_i,\hat{p})\hat{\mu}_i^0$ is approximating the given object functional.

5.4. Approximation of the initial constraints. (a) To simplify consideration, we assume that $m = 1$ in (2.3). Then the integral constraint similar to (2.3) is $\sum_{i=1}^{n_\theta} \hat{b}_1^{(i)}(\xi_i) \le e_1$, where $\hat{b}_1^{(i)}$ is a numerical result of the locally linearized function b_1. (b) Pointwise state constraints similar to (2.4) are $\langle \hat{c}^{(j)}\xi\rangle = \sum_{i=1}^{n_\theta} \hat{c}_{ji}(\xi_i) \le \hat{\pi}_j(\hat{p})$ for $j = 1,K$, where $\hat{c}^{(j)}$ is digitally linearized vector-function $c(\cdot)$ and K is the number of the considered points inside $\hat{\omega}_p$.

5.5. The digital analogy $(\hat{\Phi}) = (\hat{\Phi}_{(\hat{\omega}_p)})$ of the problem $(\Phi) = (\Phi_{\omega_p})$. The set of feasible points in the problem $(\hat{\Phi})$ is denoted as $\hat{\Theta} = \{\xi \in R^{(n_\theta)} : \sum_{i=1}^{n_\theta} a_{ji}(\xi_i,\hat{p}) \le p_j,\ j = 1;M(\delta)\}$ combining [5.4a], [5.4b], and [5.5] to the same form with unified designations. It is evident that $\hat{\Theta} = \hat{\Theta}(\hat{p},\delta)$. Then we obtain the following digital optimization problem: $(\hat{\Phi}) : \xi^* = \arg\min_{\xi\in\hat{\Theta}}\{\hat{F}(\xi) = \hat{F}(\xi,\hat{p},\delta) = \sum_i^{n_\theta} \hat{\beta}_{0i}(\xi_i,\hat{p}) : \xi \in \hat{\Theta}\}$, where the function $\hat{F}(\xi)$ is convex in view of $\Lambda^{(1)}_{(b_0)}$. In this point, essence digitalization of all the initial problem has been completed. In Section 6.1, we define special additional constraints to the problem $(\hat{\Phi})$ motivated by our algorithm. Let $\{\omega^{(\nu)} = \omega(p^{(\nu)},\delta)\}_{\nu=1}^{(\infty)}$ be such that $\lim_{\nu\to\infty} \omega(p^{(\nu)},\delta) = \omega^*(\delta) \in \Omega_p$ and $\hat{\Theta}^{(\nu)}$ and $\hat{\Theta}^*(\delta)$ are digital analogies for $\Theta^{(\nu)}$ and Θ^*. Then the following theorem holds.

THEOREM 5.1 (existence of solutions in $(\hat{\Phi})$). *Let under the conditions of Theorem 2.3 there exist the digital analogies of all suppositions of this theorem and the condition $\Lambda^{(1)}_{(\mathrm{dig})}$ is valid. Then the problem $(\hat{\Phi})$ has the solution.*

The theorem proof is similar to the proof of Theorem 2.3.

6. Algorithm

6.1. Control constraints-sensors. Fundamental role in the recursive process belongs to the procedure of correction of the DV (parameters). The special linearized sensitive constraints-sensors are in the heart of this procedure. These constraints have been introduced into the considered problem with the controlled parameter $\hat{\varepsilon}_1 > 0$, that is, $-\varepsilon_1 < \hat{p}_i - \hat{p}_i^{(\nu)} < \varepsilon_1$ for $i = 1,n_p$, where ν is the recursion number. These constraints have generated some sequence of the new admissible sets-sensors $\hat{\omega}^{(\nu)}$, $\nu = 0;\infty$ such that $\widehat{\omega}^{(\nu)} \cap \widehat{\omega}^{(\nu+1)} \neq \varnothing$ for all ν. Here the set $\widehat{\omega}^{(\nu)}(\delta) = \widehat{\omega}^{(\nu)} = \{\xi \in R^{(n_u)} : |\xi_i - \widetilde{\xi}_i^{(\nu)}| \leq \widehat{\varepsilon}_1,\ i = 1; n_u\}$ is sufficiently little in the Lebesgue's measure L defined on $\widehat{\Theta}(\widehat{p}) \subset R^{(n_u)}$, that is, $L(\widehat{\omega}^{(\nu)}) \ll L(\widehat{\omega}(\delta))$ for little δ. The controlled parameter ε (or ε_1) defines conceptually the real step of recursion process and it can be big enough. Thus in parallel with the macroproblems $(\widehat{\Phi}_{\widehat{\omega}_p})$, that is, $\widehat{F}(\xi) = \sum_{i=1}^{n_u} \widehat{\beta}_{0i}(\xi_i) \to \min_{\xi \in \widehat{\omega}}$, we consider the sequence of auxiliary microproblems connected with ν, that is, $\Phi_{\widehat{\omega}^{(\nu)}}(\delta)$ under constraints [5.4a], [5.4b], [5.5], [6.1] unified to a standard form on the admissible set $\omega^{(\nu)}$ with the new object function (a local linearization of the function $\widehat{\Phi}(\cdot)$ with respect to the current center $\widetilde{\xi}^{(\nu)}$) and a locally linearized constraints on the same center, that is, $\widehat{L}^{(\nu)}(\xi) = \sum_{i=1}^{n_\theta} \widehat{\beta}_{0i}^{(\nu)} \xi_i \to \min_{\xi \in \omega^{(\nu)}}$, where $\omega^{(\nu)} = \widehat{\omega}^{(\nu)} \cap \widehat{\Theta}$, that is, $\omega^{(\nu)} = \{\xi \in R^{(n_\theta)} : \sum_{i=1}^{n_\theta} a_{ji}(\widehat{p})\xi_i \leq p_j,\ j = 1; M(\delta),\ |\xi_i - \widetilde{\xi}_i^{(\nu)}| \leq \widehat{\varepsilon}_1,\ i = 1, n_u\}$, where $\widetilde{\xi}^{(\nu)}$ is a center of $\omega^{(\nu)}$.

6.2. The digital auxiliary problem $(\widehat{\Phi}^{(\nu)}) = (\widehat{\Phi}_{\widehat{\omega}^{(\nu)}})$ for recursion. We obtain the following problem $(\widehat{\Phi}^{(\nu)}) : \xi^* = \arg\min_{\xi \in \omega^{(\nu)}} \{\widehat{L}(\xi; \widehat{p}) = \sum_{i=1}^{n_\theta} \widehat{\beta}_{0i}(\widehat{p})\xi_i : \xi \in \omega^{(\nu)}\}$.

6.3. Construction of the algorithm. The following stages produce one step of the recursion process generating some sequence of points $\{\widetilde{\xi}^{(\nu)}\}_{\nu=0}^{\infty} \subset \widehat{R}^{(n_\theta)}$ (centers of $\omega^{(\nu)}$) improving the object function value $\widetilde{\xi}^{(\nu)} = \xi^{(\nu-1)*}$, where $\xi^{(\nu)*}$ is the solution of the P-problem $(\widehat{\Phi}^{(\nu-1)})$.

(a) *Reconstruction* of special subsidiary constraints-sensors around the point $\{\widetilde{\xi}^{(\nu)}\}$ on every step of the recursive process; in other words, correction of all the constraints-sensors by (4.1), in essence, the change-over from $\omega^{(\nu-1)}$ to $\omega^{(\nu)}$. It is clear from the construction of $\omega^{(\nu)}$ that $\widehat{\omega}^{(\nu-1)} \cap \widehat{\omega}^{(\nu)} \neq \varnothing$.

(b) *Generation* of pair linear programming (LP) P- and D-problems.

(c) *Using special simplex procedure of LP* to solve simultaneously the problem $(\widehat{\Phi}^{(\nu)}) = (\widehat{\Phi}_{\omega^{(\nu)}})$; in essence, two dual problems—the P-problems (in the space $\widehat{R}^{(n_\theta)}$) and the corresponding D-problem (Theorem 4.1).

(d) *Analysis of the LP-solutions* obtained for the P- and D-problems in order to find the location of the next set-sensor $\omega^{(\nu+1)}$ (Theorem 4.2).

(e) *Searching* of the new point $\widehat{p}^{(\nu)} \in R^{(n_p)}$—the new value of the parameter $\widehat{p}$ corresponding to going from the point $\xi^{(\nu-1)}$ to the next one $\xi^{(\nu)}$. This stage is motivated by the following local linearization all functions involved in the solution process.

(f) *Linearization* of the object function, constraints, and inclusions with respect to the current center $\xi^{(\nu)}(\widehat{p}) \in \widehat{R}^{(n_\theta)}$ (the linearization has been corrected on every step of the recursion).

(g) *Checking* of the $(\widehat{\Phi}_{\omega^{(\nu)}})$-solution for the completion of the recursion process.

(h) *Transition* to one of the following stage: whole repetition of all stages of one recursion or completion of the process.

Recall the analogies $\widehat{\Lambda}_{(\square)}^{(\square)}$ of the corresponding initial suppositions $\Lambda_{(\square)}^{(\square)}$ (the assumptions list $\widehat{\Lambda}$): $\widehat{\Lambda}_{(\widehat{P})}^{(1)}$—$\widehat{P}$ is a convex compact, $\widehat{\Lambda}_{(\widehat{\Pi})}^{(1)}$—$\widehat{\Pi}$ is a nondegenerate positive operator, $\widehat{\Lambda}_{(\widehat{f})}^{(1)}$—$\widehat{f}$ is a smooth function, $\widehat{\Lambda}_{(\widehat{b}_0)}^{(1)}$, $\widehat{\Lambda}_{(\widehat{b}_1)}^{(1)}$, $\widehat{\Lambda}_{(c)}^{(1)}$—the functions $\widehat{b}_0, \widehat{b}_1, \widehat{c}$ are smooth and convex, $\widehat{\Lambda}_{(\widehat{D})}^{(1)}$—$\widehat{D}$ is a nondegenerate operator, and $\widehat{\Lambda}_{(\widehat{g})}^{(1)}$—$\widehat{g}$ is a continuous function.

THEOREM 6.1 (convergence). *Suppose that the list of assumptions* $(\widehat{\Lambda})$ *presented above and* $\Lambda^{(1)}_{(\text{dig})}$ *are valid. Let the sequence* $\{\widetilde{\xi}^{(\nu)}\}_{\nu=1}^{\infty}$ *of the centers of sets* $\tilde{\omega}^{(\nu)}$ *be such that* $\widetilde{\xi}^{(\nu)} = \xi^{(\nu-1)*}$, *where* $\xi^{(\nu)*}$ *is the solution of the problem* $\widehat{\Phi}^{(\nu)}$. *Then*

$$\lim_{\nu\to\infty} \widehat{F}(\xi^{(\nu)}, \widehat{p}^{(\nu)}) = \min_{\xi\in\widehat{\Theta}, \widehat{p}\in\widehat{P}} \widehat{F}(\xi, \widehat{p}) = \min_{\xi(\widehat{p})\in\widehat{\Theta}, \widehat{p}\in\widehat{P}} \widehat{F}_1(\widehat{p}). \tag{6.1}$$

Proof. (a) It follows from $\Lambda^{(1)}_{(\Pi)}$ and $\Lambda^{(1)}_{(P)}$ that $\widetilde{\Theta}$ is a convex compact. The characteristics $\Lambda^{(1)}_{(b_1)}$ and $\Lambda^{(1)}_{(c)}$ in the initial problem imply conservation of convexity of the admissible set Θ (see (2.5)). There exists $\widehat{\delta} > 0$ such that additional conditions $\widehat{\Lambda}^{(1)}_{(\widehat{\Pi})}$ and $\widehat{\Lambda}^{(1)}_{(\widehat{P})}$ retain convexity and compactness of $\widehat{\Theta}$. $\widehat{\Lambda}^{(1)}_{(b_0)}$ involves convexity of the object function $\widehat{F}(\cdot)$, besides, $\Theta \neq \varnothing$, whence it follows that $\widehat{\Theta} \neq \varnothing$. Thus there exists $\xi^* = \arg\min_{\xi\in\widehat{\Theta}} \widehat{F}(\xi)$.

(b) Taking $\widehat{\varepsilon}_1 > 0$ sufficiently small, it can easily be shown that in view of the assumptions list $(\widehat{\Lambda})$, there exists the solution $\xi^{(\nu)*}$ of each problem $(\widehat{\Phi}_{\tilde{\omega}^{(\nu)}})$, besides, $|\widehat{F}(\xi) - \widehat{L}(\xi)| = O(\widehat{\varepsilon}_1^2)$ (see $\widehat{\Lambda}^{(1)}_{(\widehat{D})}$). On the sequence $\{\xi^{(\nu)*}\}_{\nu=1}^{\infty}$, the function $(\widehat{\cdot})$ decreases monotonically. Assume that $\lim_{\nu\to\infty} \xi^{(\nu)} = \xi^{**}$ and $\xi^* \neq \xi^{**}$, besides $\widehat{F}(\xi^*) < \widehat{F}(\xi^{**})$. We came to contradiction. In fact, on the one hand, the segment $[\xi^*;\xi^{**}] \subset \widehat{\Theta}$, on the other hand, there exists the point $\dot{\xi} \in [\xi^*;\xi^{**}]$ inside the set $\widehat{\tilde{\omega}}^{(\nu)}$ such that $\widehat{F}(\dot{\xi}) < \widehat{F}(\xi^{**})$. □

References

[1] D. Bucur, *Capacity Extension and two dimensional Shape Optimization*, preprint INLN., **93.24** (1993), October 402–414.

[2] D. Bucur and J.-P. Zolésio, *N-dimensional shape optimization under capacitary constraint*, Journal of Differential Equations **123** (1995), no. 2, 504–522.

[3] E. Casas, *Control of an elliptic problem with pointwise state constraints*, SIAM Journal on Control and Optimization **24** (1986), no. 6, 1309–1318.

[4] J. Chabrowski, *The Dirichlet Problem with L^2-Boundary Data for Elliptic Linear Equations*, Lecture Notes in Mathematics, vol. 1482, Springer, Berlin, 1991.

[5] M. Crouzeix, *Variational approach of a magnetic shaping problem*, European Journal of Mechanics. B Fluids **10** (1991), no. 5, 527–536.

[6] B. de Saint-Venant, *Memoire sur la torsion des prismes*, Mémoires présentés par divers savants à l'Académie des sciences de l'Institut de France **14** (1856), 233–560.

[7] I. Ekeland and R. Temam, *Convex Analysis and Variational Problems*, North-Holland, Amsterdam, 1976.

[8] N. Fujii, *Necessary conditions for a domain optimization problem in elliptic boundary value problems*, SIAM Journal on Control and Optimization **24** (1986), no. 3, 346–360.

[9] E. J. Haug, K. K. Choi, and V. Komkov, *Structural Design Sensitivity*, Academic Press, New York, 1984.

[10] V. Kaminsky, *Local linearization and immediate duality in smooth optimal design problems*, Proceedings of 4th European Congress on Computational Methods in Applied Sciences and Engineering (ECCOMAS '04), Jyvaskyla, Finland, 2004.

[11] V. Komkov, *The optimization of the domain problem. I. Basic concepts*, Journal of Mathematical Analysis and Applications **82** (1981), no. 2, 317–333.

[12] A. Marrocco and O. Pironneau, *Optimum design with Lagrangian finite elements*, Computer Methods in Applied Mechanics and Engineering **15** (1978), no. 3, 277–308.

[13] S. N. Nikiforov, *Elasticity and Plasticity Theory*, GILSA Press, Moscow, 1965.

[14] O. Pironneau, *Optimal Shape Design for Elliptic Systems*, Springer Series in Computational Physics, Springer, New York, 1984.
[15] ———, *Optimal shape design by local boundary variations*, Optimal Shape Design (Tróia, 1998), Lecture Notes in Math., vol. 1740, Springer, Berlin, 2000, pp. 343–384.
[16] J.-P. Zolésio, *The material derivative (or speed) method for shape optimization*, Optimization of Distributed Parameter Structures, Vol. I, II (E. J. Haug and J. Cea, eds.), Sitjthoff-Noordhoff, Maryland, 1980, pp. 1089–1151.
[17] S. I. Zuchovitsky and L. I. Avdeeva, *Linear and Convex Programming*, Nauka Fizmatgiz, Moscow, 1967.

V. Kaminsky: NEASOL Inc, 1245 Cardinal Avenue, Saint-Laurent (Montreal), Quebec, Canada H4L 3E9
E-mail address: vkamin@mail.com

ON NONLINEAR SCHRÖDINGER EQUATIONS INDUCED FROM NEARLY BICHROMATIC WAVES

S. KANAGAWA, B. T. NOHARA, A. ARIMOTO, AND K. TCHIZAWA

We consider a bichromatic wave function $u_b(x,t)$ defined by the Fourier transformation and show that it satisfies a kind of nonlinear Schrödinger equation under some conditions for the spectrum function $S(k)$ and the angular function $\omega(\xi,\eta)$.

1. Introduction

We consider a wave function defined by the following Fourier transformation:

$$u_m(x,t) = \int_{-\infty}^{\infty} S_m(k)e^{i\{kx-\omega(k)t\}}\,dk, \quad x \in \mathbb{R},\ t \geq 0, \tag{1.1}$$

where $i = \sqrt{-1}$, k is a frequency number, $S_m(k)$ is a spectrum function, and $\omega(k)$ is an angular frequency. From the definition, we can see that $u_m(x,t)$ is a mixture of some waves with different frequencies on some bandwidth controlled by the spectrum function $S_m(k)$. When $S_m(k)$ is a delta function $\delta_{k_0}(\cdot)$ concentrated on a frequency k_0, the wave function $u_m(x,t)$ is called the (purely) monochromatic wave $u_1(x,t)$, that is,

$$\begin{aligned} u_1(x,t) &= \int_{-\infty}^{\infty} \delta_{k_0}(k)e^{i\{kx-\omega(k)t\}}\,dk \\ &= \cos\{k_0x - \omega(k)t\} + i\sin\{k_0x - \omega(k)t\}. \end{aligned} \tag{1.2}$$

On the other hand, $u_m(x,t)$ is called a nearly monochromatic wave function if $S_m(k)$ is a unimodal function with a small compact support. As to some application of nearly monochromatic waves, see, for example [6]. In this paper, we focus on the envelope function defined by

$$A_m(x,t) = \frac{u_m(x,t)}{u_1(x,t)}, \tag{1.3}$$

Hindawi Publishing Corporation
Proceedings of the Conference on Differential & Difference Equations and Applications, pp. 477–485

and show that the envelope function $A_m(x,t)$ satisfies Schrödinger equation under some conditions for the spectrum function $S_m(k)$ and the angular function $\omega(k)$. Furthermore, we deal with the cases when the spectrum function is a bimodal function $S_b(k)$ with a compact support which constructs a bichromatic wave function $u_b(x,t)$ and the angular frequency is a two-dimensional function $\omega(k,\cdot)$, respectively. In these cases, we show that the envelope function satisfies a kind of nonlinear Schrödinger equation under some conditions for the spectrum function and the angular function. As for the details of the nearly monochromatic waves, see, for example, [6]. Further, for more applications of nearly monochromatic waves and bichromatic waves, see [1–5].

2. Profile of nearly monochromatic waves

For analyzing the envelope function $A_m(x,t)$, we first introduce a profile of it which approximates $A_m(x,t)$ by the Taylor expansion of $\omega(k)$ or $\omega(k,\cdot)$ in $u_m(x,t)$.

Definition 2.1. Suppose that an angular function $\omega(k) \in C^\infty$ can be represented by

$$\omega(k) = \sum_{j=0}^{\infty} \frac{\omega^{(j)}(k_0)}{j!}(k-k_0)^j \tag{2.1}$$

from the Taylor expansion. The nth-order profile of the envelope function of nearly monochromatic wave is defined by

$$\widetilde{A}_m^n(x,t) = \frac{\int_K S_m(k)\exp\left[i\left\{kx - \sum_{j=0}^{n}\left(\omega^{(j)}(k_0)/j!\right)(k-k_0)^j t\right\}\right]dk}{u_1(x,t)}, \tag{2.2}$$

where K is a compact support of $S_m(k)$.

THEOREM 2.2. *The second-order profile*

$$\widetilde{A}_m^2 = \frac{1}{u_1(x,t)}\int_K (k-k_0)^2 S(k)e^{i\{kx-\sum_{j=0}^{2}(\omega^{(j)}(k_0)/j!)t\}}dk \tag{2.3}$$

satisfies the linear Schrödinger equation

$$i\left\{\frac{\partial \widetilde{A}_m^2(x,t)}{\partial t} + \omega'(k_0)\frac{\partial \widetilde{A}_m^2(x,t)}{\partial x}\right\} + \frac{1}{2!}\omega''(k_0)\frac{\partial^2 \widetilde{A}_m^2(x,t)}{\partial x^2} = 0. \tag{2.4}$$

Before proving the theorem, we show the following lemma. The proof of the lemma can be obtained by a simple calculation and is omitted.

LEMMA 2.3. *Let* $\alpha(x,k,t) = e^{i[(k-k_0)x-\{\omega'(k_0)(k-k_0)+(1/2)\omega''(k_0)(k-k_0)^2\}]}$. *Then* $\alpha(x,k,t)$ *satisfies the equation*

$$i\left\{\frac{\partial}{\partial t}\alpha(x,k,t) + \omega'(k_0)\frac{\partial}{\partial x}\alpha(x,k,t)\right\} + \frac{1}{2!}\omega''(k_0)\frac{\partial^2}{\partial x^2}\alpha(x,k,t) = 0. \tag{2.5}$$

Proof of Theorem 2.2. Since K is a compact support and $S(k)$ and $\alpha(x,k,t)$ are bounded and continuous, we can change the order of differentiation and integration. Hence, by

Lemma 2.3, we have

$$\begin{aligned}
&\int_K S(k)\Big[i\Big\{\frac{\partial}{\partial t}\alpha(x,k,t)+\omega'(k_0)\frac{\partial}{\partial x}\alpha(x,k,t)\Big\}+\frac{1}{2!}\omega''(k_0)\frac{\partial^2}{\partial x^2}\alpha(x,k,t)\Big]dk\\
&=i\Big\{\frac{\partial}{\partial t}\int_K S(k)\alpha(x,k,t)dk+\omega'(k_0)\frac{\partial}{\partial x}\int_K S(k)\alpha(x,k,t)dk\Big\}\\
&\quad+\frac{1}{2!}\omega''(k_0)\frac{\partial^2}{\partial x^2}\int_K S(k)\alpha(x,k,t)dk\\
&=i\Big\{\frac{\partial\widetilde{A}_m^2(x,t)}{\partial t}+\omega'(k_0)\frac{\partial\widetilde{A}_m^2(x,t)}{\partial x}\Big\}+\frac{1}{2!}\omega''(k_0)\frac{\partial^2\widetilde{A}_m^2(x,t)}{\partial x^2}=0.
\end{aligned}\tag{2.6}$$

□

3. Bichromatic waves and nearly bichromatic waves

Put $S_2(k)=(\delta_{k_0}(k)+\delta_{k_1}(k))/2$ for some frequencies k_0 and k_1 with $|k_1-k_0|=O(\Delta)$ for sufficiently small positive constant Δ. Then the (purely) bichromatic wave is defined by

$$u_2(x,t)=\int_{-\infty}^{\infty}S_2(k)e^{i\{kx-\omega(k)t\}}dk=\frac{1}{2}\Big[e^{i\{k_0x-\omega(k_0)t\}}+e^{i\{k_1x-\omega(k_1)t\}}\Big].\tag{3.1}$$

Furthermore, let $S_b(k)$ be a bimodal and continuous spectrum function taking two local maximal values at $k=k_0$ and $k=k_1$, respectively. Suppose that $S_b(k)$ has a compact support K whose length is $|K|=O(\Delta)$. Let $u_b(x,t)$ be a nearly bichromatic wave defined by

$$u_b(x,t)=\int_K S_b(k)e^{i\{kx-\omega(k)t\}}dk\tag{3.2}$$

and let $A_b(x,t)$ be the envelope function of $u_b(x,t)$ defined by

$$A_b(x,t)=\begin{cases}\dfrac{u_b(x,t)}{u_2(x,t)}, & |(k_1-k_0)x|\neq n\pi,\ n=1,2,\dots,\\ 0, & \text{otherwise.}\end{cases}\tag{3.3}$$

Furthermore $\widetilde{A}_b^n(x,t)$ is the nth-order profile of $\widetilde{A}_b(x,t)$ defined by

$$\begin{aligned}
\widetilde{A}_b^n(x,t)&=\frac{\int_K S_b(k)e^{i\{kx-\sum_{j=0}^n(\omega^{(j)}(k_0)/j!)(k-k_0)^j t\}}dk}{\widetilde{u}_n(x,t)}\\
&=\frac{1}{\widetilde{u}_n(x,t)}\int_K S_b(k)e^{i\{kx-\omega_n(k)t\}}dk,
\end{aligned}\tag{3.4}$$

where

$$\begin{aligned}
\widetilde{u}_2(x,t)&=\frac{1}{2}\Big[e^{i\{k_0x-\omega_n(k_0)t\}}+e^{i\{k_1x-\omega_n(k_1)t\}}\Big],\\
\omega_n(k)&=\sum_{j=0}^n\frac{\omega^{(j)}(k_0)}{j!}.
\end{aligned}\tag{3.5}$$

THEOREM 3.1. *The second-order profile of the envelope function of nearly bichromatic waves*

$$\widetilde{A}_b^2 = \frac{1}{\widetilde{u}_2(x,t)} \int_K S_b(k) e^{i\{kx-\omega_2(k)t\}} dk \tag{3.6}$$

satisfies the Ginzburg-Landau-type equation

$$\frac{\partial \widetilde{A}_b^2(x,t)}{\partial t} + \left\{\omega'(k_0) + (k_1 - k_0)\omega''(k_0)\frac{e^{ig(x,t)}}{1+e^{ig(x,t)}}\right\}\frac{\partial \widetilde{A}_b^2(x,t)}{\partial x} = \frac{i}{2!}\omega''(k_0)\frac{\partial^2 \widetilde{A}_b^2(x,t)}{\partial x^2}, \tag{3.7}$$

where

$$g(x,t) = (k_1 - k_0)x - \left\{(k_1 - k_0)\omega'(k_0) + \frac{1}{2!}(k_1 - k_0)^2\omega''(k_0)\right\}t. \tag{3.8}$$

For the proof of the theorem, we show the next lemma.

LEMMA 3.2. *Since S_b is a bounded continuous spectrum function with a compact support K,*

$$\begin{aligned}
&\frac{1}{\widetilde{u}_1}\int_K (k-k_0)S_b(k)e^{i\{kx-\omega_2(k)t\}}dk \\
&\quad = -\frac{i}{2}\frac{\partial \widetilde{A}_b^2}{\partial x}\left(1+e^{i\{(k-k_0)x-(\omega_2(k)-\omega_2(k_0))t\}}\right) + \frac{1}{2}\widetilde{A}_b^2(k-k_0)e^{i\{(k-k_0)x-(\omega_2(k)-\omega(k_0))t\}}, \\
&\frac{1}{\widetilde{u}_1}\int_K (k-k_0)^2 S_b(k)e^{i\{kx-\omega_2(k)t\}}dk \\
&\quad = -\frac{1}{2}\frac{\partial^2 \widetilde{A}_b^2}{\partial x^2}\left(1+e^{i\{(k-k_0)x-(\omega_2(k)-\omega_2(k_0))t\}}\right) - \frac{\partial \widetilde{A}_b^2}{\partial x}(k-k_0)e^{i\{(k-k_0)x-(\omega_2(k)-\omega_2(k_0))t\}} \\
&\qquad + \frac{1}{2}\widetilde{A}_b^2(k-k_0)^2 e^{i\{(k-k_0)x-(\omega_2(k)-\omega_2(k_0))t\}}.
\end{aligned} \tag{3.9}$$

Proof. By changing the order of integration and differentiation, we obtain

$$\begin{aligned}
&\frac{1}{2}\frac{\partial}{\partial x}\left\{\widetilde{A}_b^2\left(1+e^{i\{(k-k_0)x-(\omega_2(k)-\omega_2(k_0))t\}}\right)\right\} \\
&\quad = \frac{1}{2}\frac{\partial \widetilde{A}_b^2}{\partial x}\left(1+e^{i\{(k-k_0)x-(\omega_2(k)-\omega_2(k_0))t\}}\right) + \frac{1}{2}\widetilde{A}_b^2\frac{\partial}{\partial x}\left(1+e^{i\{(k-k_0)x-(\omega_2(k)-\omega_2(k_0))t\}}\right) \\
&\quad = \frac{1}{2}\frac{\partial \widetilde{A}_b^2}{\partial x}\left(1+e^{i\{(k-k_0)x-(\omega_2(k)-\omega_2(k_0))t\}}\right) - \frac{i}{2}\widetilde{A}_b^2(k-k_0)e^{i\{(k-k_0)x-(\omega_2(k)-\omega_2(k_0))t\}}, \\
&\frac{\partial}{\partial x}\left\{\frac{1}{\widetilde{u}_1(x,t)}\int_K S_b(k)e^{i\{kx-\omega_2(k)t\}}dk\right\} \\
&\quad = \int_K S_b(k)\frac{\partial}{\partial x}e^{i\{(k-k_0)x-(\omega_2(k)-\omega_2(k_0))t\}}dk \\
&\quad = \int_K i(k-k_0)S_b(k)e^{i\{(k-k_0)x-(\omega_2(k)-\omega_2(k_0))t\}}dk.
\end{aligned} \tag{3.10}$$

On the other hand, since

$$\begin{aligned}\widetilde{u}_2(x,t) &= \frac{1}{2}\left(e^{i\{k_0x-\omega_2(k_0)t\}}+e^{i\{k_1x-\omega_2(k_1)t\}}\right)\\ &= \frac{1}{2}e^{i\{k_0x-\omega_2(k_0)t\}}\left(1+e^{i\{(k-k_0)x-(\omega_2(k)-\omega_2(k_0))t\}}\right)\\ &= \frac{1}{2}\widetilde{u}_1(x,t)\left(1+e^{i\{(k-k_0)x-(\omega_2(k)-\omega_2(k_0))t\}}\right),\end{aligned}\tag{3.11}$$

we have

$$\frac{1}{\widetilde{u}_1(x,t)}\int_K S_b(k)e^{i\{kx-\omega_2(k)t\}}\,dk = \frac{1}{2}\widetilde{A}_b^2\left(1+e^{i\{(k-k_0)x-(\omega_2(k)-\omega_2(k_0))t\}}\right).\tag{3.12}$$

By differentiation of the both sides of (3.12), we have from (3.10) that

$$\begin{aligned}&\frac{1}{\widetilde{u}_1}\int_K (k-k_0)S_b(k)e^{i\{kx-\omega_2(k)t\}}\,dk\\ &\quad= -\frac{i}{2}\frac{\partial\widetilde{A}_b^2}{\partial x}\left(1+e^{i\{(k-k_0)x-(\omega_2(k)-\omega_2(k_0))t\}}\right)+\frac{1}{2}\widetilde{A}_b^2(k-k_0)e^{i\{(k-k_0)x-(\omega_2(k)-\omega(k_0))t\}}.\end{aligned}\tag{3.13}$$

The rest of the proof is similar to the above and is omitted. □

Proof of Theorem 3.1. Put $\widetilde{u}_1(x,t)=e^{i\{k_0x-\omega_2(k_0)t\}}$. Since

$$\widetilde{u}_2(x,t) = \frac{1}{2}\widetilde{u}_1(x,t)\left(1+e^{i\{(k-k_0)x-(\omega_2(k)-\omega_2(k_0))t\}}\right),\tag{3.14}$$

we have

$$\begin{aligned}&\frac{1}{2}\widetilde{A}_b^2\left(1+e^{i\{(k-k_0)x-(\omega_2(k)-\omega_2(k_0))t\}}\right)\\ &\quad= \frac{1}{2}\frac{\int_K S_b(k)e^{i\{kx-\omega_2(k)t\}}\,dk}{\widetilde{u}_2(x,t)}\left(1+e^{i\{(k-k_0)x-(\omega_2(k)-\omega_2(k_0))t\}}\right)\\ &\quad= \frac{\int_K S_b(k)e^{i\{kx-\omega_2(k)t\}}\,dk}{\widetilde{u}_1(x,t)}.\end{aligned}\tag{3.15}$$

Hence,

$$\begin{aligned}&\frac{1}{2}\frac{\partial}{\partial t}\left\{\widetilde{A}_b^2\left(1+e^{i\{(k-k_0)x-(\omega_2(k)-\omega_2(k_0))t\}}\right)\right\}\\ &\quad= \frac{1}{2}\frac{\partial\widetilde{A}_b^2}{\partial t}\left(1+e^{i\{(k-k_0)x-(\omega_2(k)-\omega_2(k_0))t\}}\right)+\frac{1}{2}\widetilde{A}_b^2\frac{\partial}{\partial t}\left(1+e^{i\{(k-k_0)x-(\omega_2(k)-\omega_2(k_0))t\}}\right)\\ &\quad= \frac{1}{2}\frac{\partial\widetilde{A}_b^2}{\partial t}\left(1+e^{i\{(k-k_0)x-(\omega_2(k)-\omega_2(k_0))t\}}\right)-\frac{i}{2}\widetilde{A}_b^2(\omega(k)-\omega(k_0))e^{i\{(k-k_0)x-(\omega_2(k)-\omega_2(k_0))t\}}.\end{aligned}\tag{3.16}$$

Therefore, combining (3.9), (3.15), and (3.16), we have

$$
\begin{aligned}
&\frac{1}{2}\frac{\partial \widetilde{A}_b^2}{\partial t}\left(1+e^{i\{(k-k_0)x-(\omega_2(k)-\omega_2(k_0))t\}}\right)\\
&\quad=\frac{i}{2}\widetilde{A}_b^2(\omega(k_1)-\omega(k_0))e^{i\{(k-k_0)x-(\omega_2(k)-\omega_2(k_0))t\}}\\
&\qquad-\frac{i}{\widetilde{u}_1}\int_K(\omega_2(k_1)-\omega_2(k_0))S_b(k)e^{i\{kx-\omega_2(k)t\}}dk\\
&\quad=\frac{i}{2}\widetilde{A}_b^2\left\{\omega'(k_0)(k_1-k_0)+\frac{1}{2!}\omega''(k_0)(k_1-k_0)^2\right\}e^{i\{(k-k_0)x-(\omega_2(k)-\omega_2(k_0))t\}}\\
&\qquad-\frac{i}{\widetilde{u}_1}\int_K\left\{\omega'(k_0)(k_1-k_0)+\frac{1}{2!}\omega''(k_0)(k-k_0)^2\right\}S_b(k)e^{i\{kx-\omega_2(k)t\}}dk\\
&\quad=\frac{i}{2}\widetilde{A}_b^2\left\{\omega'(k_0)(k_1-k_0)+\frac{1}{2!}\omega''(k_0)(k_1-k_0)^2\right\}e^{i\{(k-k_0)x-(\omega_2(k)-\omega_2(k_0))t\}}\\
&\qquad-i\omega'(k_0)\int_K(k_1-k_0)S_b(k)e^{i\{(k-k_0)x-(\omega_2(k)-\omega_2(k_0))t\}}dk\\
&\qquad-\frac{i}{2}\omega''(k_0)\int_K(k_1-k_0)^2S_b(k)e^{i\{(k-k_0)x-(\omega_2(k)-\omega_2(k_0))t\}}dk\\
&\quad=\frac{i}{2}\widetilde{A}_b^2\left\{\omega'(k_0)(k_1-k_0)+\frac{1}{2!}\omega''(k_0)(k_1-k_0)^2\right\}e^{i\{(k-k_0)x-(\omega_2(k)-\omega_2(k_0))t\}}\\
&\qquad-i\omega'(k_0)\left[-\frac{i}{2}\frac{\partial\widetilde{A}_b^2}{\partial x}\left(1+e^{i\{(k-k_0)x-(\omega_2(k)-\omega_2(k_0))t\}}\right)\right.\\
&\qquad\qquad\left.+\frac{1}{2}\widetilde{A}_b^2(k_1-k_0)e^{i\{(k-k_0)x-(\omega_2(k)-\omega(k_0))t\}}\right]\\
&\qquad-\frac{i}{2}\omega''(k_0)\left[-\frac{1}{2}\frac{\partial^2\widetilde{A}_b^2}{\partial x^2}\left(1+e^{i\{(k-k_0)x-(\omega_2(k)-\omega_2(k_0))t\}}\right)\right.\\
&\qquad\qquad\left.-\frac{\partial\widetilde{A}_b^2}{\partial x}(k-k_0)e^{i\{(k-k_0)x-(\omega_2(k)-\omega_2(k_0))t\}}\right]\\
&\qquad-\frac{i}{2}\omega''(k_0)\widetilde{A}_b^2(k_1-k_0)^2e^{i\{(k-k_0)x-(\omega_2(k)-\omega_2(k_0))t\}}\\
&\quad=\frac{\partial\widetilde{A}_b^2}{\partial x}\left\{-\frac{1}{2}\omega'(k_0)\left(1+e^{i\{(k-k_0)x-(\omega_2(k)-\omega_2(k_0))t\}}\right)\right.\\
&\qquad\qquad\left.-\frac{1}{2}\omega''(k_0)(k_1-k_0)e^{i\{(k-k_0)x-(\omega_2(k)-\omega_2(k_0))t\}}\right\}\\
&\qquad+\frac{i}{4}\frac{\partial\widetilde{A}_b^2}{\partial x}\omega''(k_0)\left(1+e^{i\{(k-k_0)x-(\omega_2(k)-\omega_2(k_0))t\}}\right).
\end{aligned}
\tag{3.17}
$$

Hence, we obtain

$$\frac{\partial \widetilde{A}_b^2}{\partial t} = \frac{\partial \widetilde{A}_b^2}{\partial x}\{-\omega'(k_0) - \omega''(k_0)(k_1 - k_0)\} + \frac{i}{2}\frac{\partial \widetilde{A}_b^2}{\partial x}\omega''(k_0), \tag{3.18}$$

which implies (3.7) and concludes the proof of the theorem. □

Applying Theorems 2.2 and 3.1, we can show a kind of integral-type wave equation in the following sections.

4. Nearly monochromatic waves with $\omega(\xi,\eta)$

We next consider the wave equation given by

$$\widehat{u}_m(x,t) = \int_K S_m(k) e^{i\{kx - \omega(k,|\widehat{A}_m(x,t)|)t\}} dk, \tag{4.1}$$

where $\omega(\xi,\eta)$ is a two-dimensional angular frequency function and

$$\widehat{A}_m(x,t) = \frac{\widehat{u}_m(x,t)}{u_1(x,t)} \tag{4.2}$$

is the envelope function of $\widehat{u}_m(x,t)$. Since the above equation is a kind of an integral equation and it is difficult to obtain its exact solution, we give a relation between the integral equation and nonlinear Schrödiger equation to investigate the solution.

THEOREM 4.1. *Assume the following conditions hold:*

(1) $\Delta > 0$ *is small enough;*

(2) *all partial derivatives of* $\omega(\xi,\eta)$ *less than third degree are uniformly bounded in a neighborhood of* $(k_0, 0)$*;*

(3) $S_m(k)$ *is bounded and its bound is independent of the following.*

Then for $0 \le t \le \text{Const}\,\Delta$, *as* $\Delta \to 0$,

$$\begin{aligned} &i\left\{\frac{\partial \widehat{A}_m(x,t)}{\partial t} + \omega_\xi(k_0,0)\frac{\partial \widehat{A}_m(x,t)}{\partial x}\right\} + \frac{1}{2!}\omega_{\xi\xi}(k_0)\frac{\partial^2 \widehat{A}_m(x,t)}{\partial x^2} \\ &\quad - \omega_\eta(k_0,0)\,|\widehat{A}_m(x,t)|^2 \widehat{A}_m(x,t) = O(\Delta^4). \end{aligned} \tag{4.3}$$

5. Nearly bichromatic waves with $\omega(\xi,\eta)$

We next consider the wave equation

$$\widehat{u}_b(x,t) = \int_K S_b(k) e^{i\{kx - \omega(k,|\widehat{A}_b(x,t)|)t\}} dk, \tag{5.1}$$

where $\widehat{A}_b(x,t)$ is the envelope function of $\widehat{u}_b(x,t)$ defined by

$$\widehat{A}_b(x,t) = \frac{\widehat{u}_b(x,t)}{u_2(x,t)}. \tag{5.2}$$

Similarly to $\widehat{A}_m(x,t)$, the above wave equation means an integral equation and it is difficult to obtain the exact solution. From the next theorem, we can see the exact equation as the solution of nonlinear Schrödinger equation.

Theorem 5.1. *Suppose all assumptions of Theorem 4.1 hold. If* $|k_1 - k_0| = O(\Delta^2)$, *then* $\widehat{A}_b(x,t)$ *satisfies the same nonlinear Schrödinger equation in Theorem 4.1,*

$$\begin{aligned} & i\left\{\frac{\partial \widehat{A}_b(x,t)}{\partial t} + \omega_\xi(k_0,0)\frac{\partial \widehat{A}_b(x,t)}{\partial x}\right\} + \frac{1}{2!}\omega_{\xi\xi}(k_0)\frac{\partial^2 \widehat{A}_b(x,t)}{\partial x^2} \\ & \quad - \omega_\eta(k_0,0)\left|\widehat{A}_b(x,t)\right|^2 \widehat{A}_b(x,t) = O(\Delta^4), \end{aligned} \tag{5.3}$$

for $0 \le t \le \text{Const}\,\Delta$, *as* $\Delta \to 0$.

Theorem 5.2. *Suppose all assumptions of Theorem 4.1 hold. If* $|k_1 - k_0| = O(\Delta)$, *then* $\widehat{A}_b(x,t)$ *satisfies the following nonlinear Schrödinger equation:*

$$\begin{aligned} & i\left\{\frac{\partial \widehat{A}_b(x,t)}{\partial t} + \left(\omega_\xi(k_0,0) + \frac{1}{2}\omega_{\xi\xi}(k_0,0)\left|k_1 - k_0\right|\right)\frac{\partial \widehat{A}_b(x,t)}{\partial x}\right\} \\ & \quad + \frac{1}{2!}\omega_{\xi\xi}(k_0)\frac{\partial^2 \widehat{A}_b(x,t)}{\partial x^2} - \omega_\eta(k_0,0)\left|\widehat{A}_b(x,t)\right|^2 \widehat{A}_b(x,t) = O(\Delta^4), \end{aligned} \tag{5.4}$$

for $0 \le t \le \text{Const}\,\Delta$, *as* $\Delta \to 0$.

Acknowledgment

This research was supported in part by Grant-in-Aid Scientific Research (no. 16540124) and Ministry of Education, Science, and Culture.

References

[1] G. P. Agrawal, *Fiber-Optic Communication System*, 2nd ed., John Wiley & Sons, New York, 1997.
[2] R. E. Collin, *Field Theory of Guided Waves*, International Series in Pure and Applied Physics, McGraw-Hill, New York, 1960.
[3] H. Hashimoto and H. Ono, *Nonlinear modulation of gravity waves*, Journal of the Physical Society of Japan **33** (1972), no. 3, 805–811.
[4] Y. Kuramoto, *Chemical Oscillations, Waves, and Turbulence*, Springer Series in Synergetics, vol. 19, Springer, Berlin, 1984.
[5] M. S. Longuet-Higgins, *The statistical analysis of a random, moving surface*, Philosophical Transactions of the Royal Society of London. Series A **249** (1957), 321–387.

[6] B. T. Nohara, *Derivation and consideration of governing equations of the envelope surface created by directional, nearly monochromatic waves*, Nonlinear Dynamics. An International Journal of Nonlinear Dynamics and Chaos in Engineering Systems **31** (2003), no. 4, 375–392.

S. Kanagawa: Department of Mathematics, Faculty of Engineering, Musashi Institute of Technology, Tokyo 158-8557, Japan
E-mail address: kanagawa@ma.ns.musashi-tech.ac.jp

B. T. Nohara: Department of Computer Science and Media Engineering, Faculty of Engineering, Musashi Institute of Technology, Tokyo 158-8557, Japan
E-mail address: drben@ac.cs.musashi-tech.ac.jp

A. Arimoto: Department of Mathematics, Faculty of Engineering, Musashi Institute of Technology, Tokyo 158-8557, Japan
E-mail address: arimoto@ma.ns.musashi-tech.ac.jp

K. Tchizawa: Department of Mathematics, Faculty of Engineering, Musashi Institute of Technology, Tokyo 158-8557, Japan
E-mail address: tchizawa@aol.com

VOLTERRA INTEGRAL EQUATION METHOD FOR THE RADIAL SCHRÖDINGER EQUATION

SHEON-YOUNG KANG

A new Volterra-type method extended from an integral equation method by Gonzales et al. for the numerical solution of the radial Schrödinger equation is investigated. The method, carried out in configuration space, is based on the conversion of differential equations into a system of integral equations together with the application of a spectral-type Clenshaw-Curtis quadrature. Through numerical examples, the Volterra-type integral equation method is shown to be superior to finite difference methods.

1. Introduction

This paper extends the integral equation method for solving a single channel one-dimensional Schrödinger equation presented by Gonzales et al. [6] to the Volterra-type method. The advantage of using the Volterra-type rather than non-Volterra type integral equation is the reduced complexity. The usual disadvantage of integral equation method is that the associated matrices are not sparse, making the numerical method computationally "expensive," in contrast to differential techniques, which lead to sparse matrices. In the method presented here the "big" matrix is entirely lower triangular, and hence the solution for the coefficients A and B required to get the solution of (1.1) can be set up as simple recursion, which is more efficient and requires less memory. The Volterra method is thus preferred, especially in the case of large scale systems of coupled equations.

The radial Schrödinger equation is one of the most common equations in mathematical physics. Its solution gives the probability amplitude of finding a particle moving in a force field. In the case of the radial Schrödinger equation which models the quantum mechanical interaction between particles represented by spherical symmetric potentials, the corresponding three-dimensional partial differential equation can be reduced to a family of boundary value problems for ordinary differential equation,

$$\left[-\frac{d^2}{dr^2}+\frac{l(l+1)}{r^2}+\bar{V}(r)\right]R_l(r)=k^2R_l(r), \quad 0<r<\infty, \tag{1.1}$$

$$R_l(0)=0. \tag{1.2}$$

Hindawi Publishing Corporation
Proceedings of the Conference on Differential & Difference Equations and Applications, pp. 487–500

Here l is the angular momentum number, k is the wave number, $\bar{V}(r)$ is the given potential, and $R_l(r)$ is the partial radial wave function to be determined, corresponding to l. Assume here that $\bar{V}$ is continuous on $(0,\infty)$ and has the following behavior at the end points: it tends to zero as fast or faster than $1/r^2$, as $r \to \infty$, and as $r \to 0$ it does not grow faster than $1/r$. Most of the physically meaningful potentials except the Coulomb potential satisfy these conditions. However, the Coulomb potential also can be handled by the method described here. Under these conditions on $\bar{V}(r)$, the initial value problem (1.1) has a unique bounded solution on $(0,\infty)$ (see [4]), satisfying asymptotic condition

$$\lim_{r\to\infty}\left(R_l(r) - \sin\left(kr - \frac{l\pi}{2}\right) - \omega e^{i(kr-l\pi/2)}\right) = 0, \tag{1.3}$$

where ω is an unknown constant uniquely determined by the problem, together with the solution $R_l(r)$. A more detailed description of the Schrödinger equation and its reduction to a family of ordinary differential equation can be found in [12, 14]. The Volterra-type integral equation transformed from (1.1) is as follows:

$$\begin{aligned}\phi_T(r) &+ \frac{1}{k}\cos(kr)\int_0^r \sin(kr')V(r')\phi_T(r')dr' - \frac{1}{k}\sin(kr)\int_0^r \cos(kr')V(r')\phi_T(r')dr'\\ &= \left[1 - \frac{1}{k}\int_0^T \cos(kr')V(r')\phi_T(r')dr'\right]\sin(kr) = \alpha\sin(kr),\end{aligned} \tag{1.4}$$

where $\alpha = 1 - (1/k)\int_0^T \cos(kr')V(r')\phi_T(r')dr'$, and $V(r) = \bar{V}(r) + l(l+1)/r^2$. As is explained in detail later in the text, the solution $\phi_T(r)$ of (1.4) differs from the solution $R_l(r)$ of the boundary value problem (1.1) by constant multiple which can be calculated numerically without any difficulty from the asymptotic condition (1.3) for a sufficiently large T. The kernel of the integral equation is obtained from Green's functions multiplied by the potential $V(r)$. The former is written in terms of simple sine and cosine functions of the wave number k times radial distance r. The method can be described briefly as follows. The interval $[0,T]$ is divided into m subintervals. The restricted integral equation on each subintervals i ($i = 1,2,\ldots,m$) is solved to get two local solutions $y_i(r)$ and $z_i(r)$. It is shown that the global solution $\phi_T(r)$ of (1.4) is a linear combination of the local solutions for the r restricted to any subinterval i, namely,

$$\phi_T(r) = A^{(i)}y_i(r) + B^{(i)}z_i(r), \tag{1.5}$$

where $A^{(i)}$ and $B^{(i)}$ are constants yet to be determined. These unknown coefficients $A^{(i)}$ and $B^{(i)}$ can be found by simple recursion. The local solutions $y_i(r)$ and $z_i(r)$ are calculated at Chebyshev support points in the ith subinterval using Clenshaw-Curtis quadrature. The value of ϕ_T at T or any other point in $[0,T]$ can be found using Chebyshev-Fourier coefficients in any subinterval $[b_{i-1}, b_i]$ and recursion formula of Chebyshev polynomials as described in Section 4.

In this paper the Numerov algorithm is chosen as a generic finite difference method because it is easy to implement, often produces satisfactory solutions, and is a widely used method, although there are more advanced finite difference methods such as the recently developed exponentially fitted methods, see [15, 16] and references therein. The method has its drawback common to all explicit finite difference methods, namely, round-off error accumulations cause to put a limit on acceptable step size. Therefore, if it is required to have high accuracy, this method and other finite difference methods may not be appropriate. The Volterra-type integral equation method described here provides an alternative method for the solution of radial Schrödinger equation which gives high accuracy at a cost comparable to that of the Numerov method. The method is based on the transformation of the boundary value problem (1.1) into Volterra-type integral equation which is then discretized with the Clenshaw-Curtis quadrature [3]. Greengard [8] and Greengard and Rokhlin [9] proposed this integral equation method. Gonzales et al. [6] then improved and adapted the method to the specific features of the Schrödinger equation. The method described in their paper is a superalgebraic-type numerical technique, provided that the function being approximated is indefinitely differentiable. The author and Koltracht [11] then introduced a new spectral-type numerical technique for Fredholm integral equations of the second kind whose kernel is either "discontinuous" or "not smooth" along the main diagonal. This technique is shown to be applicable to the Schrödinger equation with "nonsmooth potential" $V(r,r')$ such as Yukawa and Perey-Buck potentials. It is also shown to be applicable to the case which models the nonlocalities corresponding to a nucleon-nucleon interaction.

In Section 2 the integral equation and normalization constant formulation are presented. It is described in Section 3 that the global solution can be found as a linear combination of local solutions of integral equations restricted to small subintervals of the partition of the whole radial interval. The discretization techniques for local solutions and interpolating technique for the numerical values at any point other than Chebyshev points are presented in Section 4. In Section 5 the results of numerical experiments and comparison with the results obtained via the Numerov method are shown.

2. Integral equation formulation

The radial Schrödinger equation with $E > 0$ to be solved is as follows:

$$\left[-\frac{\hbar^2}{2m}\frac{d^2}{dr^2}+\frac{\hbar^2 l(l+1)}{2mr^2}+v(r)\right]R_l(r)=ER_l(r), \tag{2.1}$$

subject to the conditions (1.2) and (1.3). Here r is the radial distance of the particle of mass m to the scattering center, E is the energy, l is the angular momentum number, v is the potential, and $\hbar$ is Planck's constant divided by 2π. With $k = \sqrt{2mE/\hbar}$, (2.1) can be rewritten as

$$\left[\frac{d^2}{dr^2}+k^2\right]R_l(r)=V(r)R_l(r), \tag{2.2}$$

where $V(r) = l(l+1)/r^2 + \bar{V}(r)$ with $\bar{V}(r) = (2m/\hbar^2)v(r)$. The following proposition shows that the solution of integral equation is a constant multiple of the solution of the differential equation.

PROPOSITION 2.1. *Let $R_l(r)$ be the unique solution of (1.1)–(1.3), and let*

$$\Phi(r) = R_l(r)\sin(kr) + \frac{1}{k}\cos(kr) - \frac{1}{k}\int_0^r \cos(kr')V(r')R_l(r')dr'. \tag{2.3}$$

For a fixed $0 < T < \infty$,

(i) *if $\Phi(T) \neq 0$, then the integral equation*

$$\phi_T(r) + \frac{1}{k}\cos(kr)\int_0^r \sin(kr')V(r')\phi_T(r')dr' - \frac{1}{k}\sin(kr)\int_0^r \cos(kr')\phi_T(r')dr' = \sin(kr) \tag{2.4}$$

has a unique solution

$$\phi_T(r) = \frac{1}{\Phi(T)}R_l(r); \tag{2.5}$$

(ii) *if $\Phi(T) = 0$, then (2.4) has no solution, while the homogeneous equation*

$$\phi_T(r) + \frac{1}{k}\cos(kr)\int_0^r \sin(kr')V(r')\phi_T(r')dr' - \frac{1}{k}\sin(kr)\int_0^r \cos(kr')\phi_T(r')dr' = 0 \tag{2.6}$$

has a nontrivial solution. Each such solution is a constant multiple of $R_l(r)$.

The detailed proof of Proposition 2.1 can be found in [10].

How small T can be taken so that the asymptotic constant ω in (1.3) can be determined to a given accuracy depends on the range of the potential $v(r)$. Since $v(r)$ decays faster than $1/r^2$, there is no need to go to distances where $1/r^2$ is negligible. Indeed, if $v(r)$ is negligible, then $R_L(r)$ satisfies the differential equation

$$\left[\frac{d^2}{dr^2} - \frac{l(l+1)}{r^2} + k^2\right]R_l(r) \approx 0, \tag{2.7}$$

and therefore $R_l(r)$ can be represented as a linear combination of the Riccati-Bessel functions [1] which are two linearly independent solutions of (2.7),

$$F_l(r) = zj_l(z) = \sqrt{\frac{\pi z}{2}}J_{l+1}(z), \qquad G_l(r) = -zy_l(z) = \sqrt{\frac{\pi z}{2}}Y_{l+1}(z), \tag{2.8}$$

where $z = kr$. Since $\phi_T(r)$ is a constant multiple of $R_l(r)$, it can be expressed as a linear combination of F_l and G_l, for T sufficiently large and $r \approx T$. Thus let

$$\phi_T(r) = \alpha F_l(r) + \beta G_l(r). \tag{2.9}$$

The constants α and β can be determined numerically as follows. Set $T_1 = T$ and T_2 near T and get

$$\phi(T_1) = \alpha F_l(T_1) + \beta G_l(T_1), \qquad \phi(T_2) = \alpha F_l(T_2) + \beta G_l(T_2). \tag{2.10}$$

Therefore, α and β can be calculated solving

$$\begin{bmatrix} \alpha \\ \beta \end{bmatrix} = \begin{bmatrix} F_l(T_1) & G_l(T_1) \\ F_l(T_2) & G_l(T_2) \end{bmatrix}^{-1} \begin{bmatrix} \phi_T(T_1) \\ \phi_T(T_2) \end{bmatrix}. \tag{2.11}$$

The values of F_l and G_l are readily available from the recursive relations of the type satisfied by Bessel functions. The value $\phi_T(r)$ for $r = T1$ or $r = T_2$ can also be found using the recursion satisfied by Chebyshev polynomials,

$$T_{k+1}(x) = 2xT_k(x) - T_{k-1}(x), \tag{2.12}$$

because $\phi_T(r)$ is obtained numerically as a linear combination of them. Given α and β, one can find the normalization constant λ for which $\lambda\phi_T(r)$ satisfies the condition (1.3). Asymptotically, the Riccati-Bessel functions $F_l(r)$ and $G_L(r)$ behave like $\sin(kr - l\pi/2)$ and $\cos(kr - l\pi/2)$, respectively. Hence, from

$$\lambda\alpha \sin\left(kr - \frac{l\pi}{2}\right) + \lambda\beta\cos\left(kr - \frac{l\pi}{2}\right) \sim (1 + i\omega)\sin\left(kr - \frac{l\pi}{2}\right) + \omega\cos\left(kr - \frac{l\pi}{2}\right), \tag{2.13}$$

equations for λ and α are obtained: $\lambda\alpha = 1 + i\omega$ and $\lambda\beta = \omega$. Thus, $\lambda = (\alpha + i\beta)/(\alpha^2 + \beta^2)$ and $\omega = \beta(\alpha + i\beta)/(\alpha^2 + \beta^2)$.

3. Local solutions

Because of the structure of the kernel of the integral equation (1.4), the Clenshaw-Curtis quadrature, which gives at no extra cost the whole antiderivative function, is for this reason the most appropriate method for discretizing (1.4). In order to avoid working with high-degree polynomials, the composite Clenshaw-Curtis quadrature is suggested by Greengard and Rokhlin [9] by partitioning the interval $[0, r]$ into sufficiently small subintervals. Each partition will be denoted by the subscript, i, $i = 1, 2, \ldots, m$.

Consider the family of the restricted integral equation in each partition, i,

$$\begin{aligned} y_i(r) + \frac{1}{k}\cos(kr)\int_{b_{i-1}}^{r} \sin(kr')V(r')y_i(r')dr' - \frac{1}{k}\sin(kr)\int_{b_{i-1}}^{r} \cos(kr')V(r')y_i(r')dr' \\ = \sin(kr), \quad b_{i-1} < r < b_i, \end{aligned} \tag{3.1}$$

$$\begin{aligned} z_i(r) + \frac{1}{k}\cos(kr)\int_{b_{i-1}}^{r} \sin(kr')V(r')z_i(r')dr' - \frac{1}{k}\sin(kr)\int_{b_{i-1}}^{r} \cos(kr')V(r')z_i(r')dr' \\ = \cos(kr), \quad b_{i-1} < r < b_i, \end{aligned} \tag{3.2}$$

where $b_0 < b_1 < \cdots < b_{m-1} < b_m = T$ is some partitioning of the interval $[0, T]$. For a sufficiently small interval, these equations have unique solutions y_i and z_i. It is now observed that the solution $\phi_T(r)$ of (2.4) on $[b_{i-1}, b_i]$ is a linear combination of y_i and z_i. Indeed, it follows from (2.4) that for $b_{i-1} \le r \le b_i$,

$$\begin{aligned} \phi_T(r) &+ \frac{1}{k}\cos(kr)\int_{b_{i-1}}^{r} \sin(kr')V(r')\phi_T(r')dr' - \frac{1}{k}\sin(kr)\int_{b_{i-1}}^{r} \cos(kr')V(r')\phi_T(r')dr' \\ &= \left[1 + \frac{1}{k}\int_0^{b_{i-1}} \cos(kr')V(r')\phi_T(r')dr'\right]\sin(kr) \\ &\quad + \left[-\frac{1}{k}\int_0^{b_{i-1}} \sin(kr')V(r')\phi_T(r')dr'\right]\cos(kr) \\ &= A^{(i)}\sin(kr) + B^{(i)}\cos(kr), \end{aligned} \tag{3.3}$$

where

$$A^{(i)} = 1 + \frac{1}{k}\int_0^{b_{i-1}} \cos(kr')V(r')\phi_T(r')dr', \tag{3.4}$$

$$B^{(i)} = -\frac{1}{k}\int_0^{b_{i-1}} \sin(kr')V(r')\phi_T(r')dr'. \tag{3.5}$$

It follows from (3.1) and (3.2) that the global solution, for r in the ith subinterval, is a linear combination of the local solutions,

$$\phi_T(r) = A^{(i)}y_i(r) + B^{(i)}z_i(r). \tag{3.6}$$

Assuming that y_i and z_i are known, the coefficients $A^{(i)}$, $B^{(i)}$ are found from a simple recursion, rather than solving a block-tridiagonal system of equations as in [6]. The procedure to find $A^{(i)}$ and $B^{(i)}$ is as follows. Based on $\phi_T(r) = A^{(j)}y_j(r) + B^{(j)}z_j(r)$, on $[b_{j-1}, b_j]$, $A^{(i)}$ of (3.4) can be rewritten as

$$A^{(i)} = 1 + \frac{1}{k}\sum_{j=1}^{i-1}\int_{b_{j-1}}^{b_j} \cos(kr')V(r')\phi_T(r')dr' = 1 + \sum_{j=1}^{i-1}\left[A^{(j)}(cy)_j + B^{(j)}(cz)_j\right], \tag{3.7}$$

where

$$(cy)_j = \frac{1}{k}\int_{b_{j-1}}^{b_j} \cos(kr')V(r')y_j(r')dr', \qquad (cz)_j = \frac{1}{k}\int_{b_{j-1}}^{b_j} \cos(kr')V(r')z_j(r')dr'. \tag{3.8}$$

Similarly, $B^{(i)} = -\sum_{j=1}^{i-1}[A^{(j)}(sy)_j + B^{(j)}(sz)_j]$ with

$$(sy)_j = \frac{1}{k}\int_{b_{j-1}}^{b_j} \sin(kr')V(r')y_j(r')dr', \qquad (sz)_j = \frac{1}{k}\int_{b_{j-1}}^{b_j} \sin(kr')V(r')z_j(r')dr'. \tag{3.9}$$

Note that $A^{(1)} = 1$ and $B^{(1)} = 0$, and for $k = 2,\dots,m$,

$$A^{(k)} = 1 + \left[\left(A^{(1)}(cy)_1 + B^{(1)}(cz)_1\right) + \cdots + \left(A^{(k-1)}(cy)_{k-1} + B^{(k-1)}(cz)_{k-1}\right) \right], \tag{3.10}$$

$$B^{(k)} = \left[\left(A^{(1)}(sy)_1 + B^{(1)}(sz)_1\right) + \cdots + \left(A^{(k-1)}(sy)_{k-1} + B^{(k-1)}(sz)_{k-1}\right) \right]. \tag{3.11}$$

The integral equation method for the Schrödinger equation proposed in [6] contains a huge block-triangular linear system of equations requiring both time and memory to get the coefficients $A^{(i)}$ and $B^{(i)}$. These difficulties are overcome by replacing the Fredholm integral equation by Volterra integral equation which requires a simple recursion. Apart from making the whole algorithm more efficient and accurate, it also simplifies substantially the corresponding C^{++} code.

4. Discretization of local solutions

In this section the numerical technique to discretize the local equations (3.1) and (3.2) is presented. It is based on the Clenshaw-Curtis quadrature which is well suited for computing antiderivatives and hence for discretizing integrals presented in (3.1) and (3.2). Before getting into discretizing the local equations, consider a more general equation

$$x(r) + \int_a^r f(r,r')x(r')dr' + \int_a^r g(r,r')x(r')dr' = y(r'), \tag{4.1}$$

where $x(r) \in C^p_{[a,b]}$ and $y(r) \in C^q_{[a,b]}$, $p,q > 1$. Without loss of generality, assume that $a = -1$, $b = 1$, and let

$$F(r) = \int_{-1}^r f(r,r')x(r')dr', \qquad \widetilde{F}(r,\lambda) = \int_{-1}^{\lambda} f(r,r')x(r')dr', \tag{4.2}$$

such that $F(r) = \widetilde{F}(r,r)$, and let

$$G(r) = \int_{-1}^r g(r,r')x(r')dr', \qquad \widetilde{G}(r,\lambda) = \int_{-1}^{\lambda} g(r,r')x(r')dr'. \tag{4.3}$$

Further, assume that $f(r_k,r')x(r')$ can be expanded in a finite set of polynomials, that is,

$$f(r_k,r')x(r') = \sum_{i=0}^{n} \alpha_{ki}T_i(r'), \quad T_i(r) = \cos\left(i\arccos(r)\right), \quad i = 0,1,\dots,n \tag{4.4}$$

are the Chebyshev polynomials. Clenshaw and Curtis [3] showed that if

$$\widetilde{F}(r_k,\lambda) = \sum_{j=0}^{n+1} \beta_{kj}T_j(\lambda), \tag{4.5}$$

then

$$[\beta_{k0},\beta_{k1},\ldots,\beta_{kn+1}]^T = \mathbf{S}_L[\alpha_{k0},\alpha_{k1},\ldots,\alpha_{kn}]^T, \tag{4.6}$$

where

$$\mathbf{S}_L = \begin{pmatrix} 1 & 1 & -1 & 1 & \cdots & (-1)^n \\ & 1 & & & & 0 \\ & & 1 & & & \\ & & & \ddots & & \\ 0 & & & & & 1 \end{pmatrix} \begin{pmatrix} 0 & & & & & & 0 \\ 1 & 0 & -\frac{1}{2} & & & & \\ & \frac{1}{4} & 0 & -\frac{1}{4} & & & \\ & & \ddots & & & & \\ & & & \frac{1}{(2n-1)} & & 0 & -\frac{1}{2(n-1)} \\ 0 & & & & & \frac{1}{2n} & 0 \end{pmatrix} \tag{4.7}$$

is the so-called left spectral integration matrix. Here $[\nu]^T$ denotes the transpose of the column vector ν. One can find the Chebyshev-Fourier coefficients, α_{kj}, of $f(r_k,r')x(r')$ as follows. Let τ_k, $k=0,\ldots,n$, denote the zeros of T_{n+1}, viz., $\tau_k = \cos(2k+1)\pi/2(n+1)$ so that

$$T_j(\tau_k) = \cos\frac{(2k+1)j\pi}{2(n+1)}, \quad k,j = 0,\ldots,n. \tag{4.8}$$

Substituting $r' = \tau_k$, $k = 0,\ldots,n$, into (4.5), we obtain that

$$[f(r_k,\tau_0)x(\tau_0),\ldots,f(r_k,\tau_n)x(\tau_n)]^T = \mathbf{C}[\alpha_{k0},\ldots,\alpha_{kn}]^T, \tag{4.9}$$

where $\mathbf{C}$ is a discrete cosine transform matrix whose elements are specified by $\mathbf{C}_{kj} = T_j(\tau_k)$, $k,j=0,\ldots,n$. Note that $\mathbf{C}^T\mathbf{C} = \operatorname{diag}(n,n/2,\ldots,n/2)$, and $\mathbf{C}^{-1} = \operatorname{diag}(1/n,2/n,\ldots,2/n)\mathbf{C}^T$. Moreover, the matrix $\mathbf{C}$ (as well as $\mathbf{C}^T$ and $\mathbf{C}^{-1}$) can be applied to a vector at the cost of $O(n\log n)$ arithmetic operations. These and other properties of discrete cosine transforms can be found in C (Golub and Van Loan [5]). Thus the vector

$$[\alpha_{k0},\alpha_{k1},\ldots,\alpha_{kn}]^T = \mathbf{C}^{-1}\operatorname{diag}(f(r_k,\tau_0),f(r_k,\tau_1),\ldots,f(r_k,\tau_n))[x(\tau_1),\ldots,x(\tau_n)]^T \tag{4.10}$$

can be written in terms of $f(r_k,\tau i)$ and $x(\tau_i)$, $i=0,1,\ldots,n$. Substituting $\lambda = \tau_k$, $k = 0,1,\ldots,n$, into (4.5), we obtain that

$$[\widetilde{F}(r_k,\tau_0),\ldots,\widetilde{F}(r_k,\tau_n)]^T = \mathbf{C}\mathbf{S}_L\mathbf{C}^{-1}\operatorname{diag}(f(r_k,\tau_0),\ldots,f(r_k,\tau_n))[x(\tau_0),\ldots,x(\tau_n)]^T. \tag{4.11}$$

The author wants to remark that in writing the equality sign in (4.6), $\beta_{n+1} = 0$ is assumed. This is an acceptable assumption because in practical approximations the kernel $f(r,r')$ and the right-hand side $y(r')$ are not polynomials and equality (4.4) is only approximate. In fact, following Clenshaw and Curtis [3], we use the size of α_n's and β_n's, as a readily available tool, to control the accuracy of approximation, and choose n large enough such that α_n's and β_n's are less than a prescribed tolerance. Therefore setting β_{n+1} to zero does not affect the overall accuracy. Since $F(\tau_k) = \widetilde{F}(\tau_k, \tau_k)$, we get

$$\begin{aligned} F(\tau_k) &= [0,\dots,1,\dots,0]\mathbf{C}\mathbf{S}_L\mathbf{C}^{-1}\operatorname{diag}(f(\tau_k,\tau_0),\dots,f(\tau_k,\tau_n))[x(\tau_0),\dots,x(\tau_n)]^T \\ &= [w_{k0},w_{k1},\dots,w_{kn}]\operatorname{diag}(x(\tau_0),\dots,x(\tau_n))[f(\tau_k,\tau_0),\dots,f(\tau_k,\tau_n)]^T, \end{aligned} \tag{4.12}$$

where $[w_{k0},\dots,w_{kn}]$ is the $(k+1)$th row of the matrix $\mathbf{W} \overset{\text{def}}{=} \mathbf{C}\mathbf{S}_L\mathbf{C}^{-1}$. We need now the following identity which can be verified by direct calculation.

Lemma 4.1. *Let* $\mathbf{A}$ *and* $\mathbf{B}$ *be* $n \times n$ *matrices and* $\mathbf{c} = [c_1,\dots,c_n]^T$. *Then* $(\mathbf{A} \circ \mathbf{B})\mathbf{c} = \operatorname{diag}(\mathbf{A}\operatorname{diag}(c_1,\dots,c_n)\mathbf{B}^T)$, *where* $\mathbf{A} \circ \mathbf{B}$ *denotes the Schur product of* $\mathbf{A}$ *and* $\mathbf{B}$, $(\mathbf{A} \circ \mathbf{B})_{ij} = a_{ij}b_{ij}$, $i,j = 1,\dots,n$.

Using this lemma one can find that

$$\begin{aligned} [F(\tau_0),\dots,F(\tau_n)]^T &= \operatorname{diag}(\mathbf{W}\operatorname{diag}(x(\tau_0),\dots,x(\tau_n))\mathbf{F}^T) \\ &= (\mathbf{W} \circ \mathbf{F})[x(\tau_0),\dots,x(\tau_n)]^T, \end{aligned} \tag{4.13}$$

where $\mathbf{F} = (f(\tau_i,\tau_j))_{i,j=0}^n$. Similarly,

$$[G(\tau_0),G(\tau_1),\dots,G(\tau_n)]^T = (\mathbf{W} \circ \mathbf{G})[x(\tau_0),\dots,x(\tau_n)]^T, \tag{4.14}$$

where $\mathbf{G} = (g(\tau_i,\tau_j))_{i,j=0}^n$. The formula (4.13) can be generalized for an interval $[a,b]$ other than $[-1,1]$ by the linear change of variables, $h(\tau) = (1/2)(b-a)\tau + (1/2)(a+b)$. Thus if $\eta_j = h(\tau_j)$, $j = 0,1,\dots,n$, and with the notation $F_a(r) = \int_a^r f(r,r')x(r')dr'$, $G_a(r) = \int_a^r g(r,r')x(r')dr'$, we have

$$[F_a(\eta_0),F_a(\eta_1),\dots,F_a(\eta_n)]^T = \frac{b-a}{2}(\mathbf{W} \circ \mathbf{F})[x(\eta_0),x(\eta_1),\dots,x(\eta_n)]^T, \tag{4.15}$$

$$[G_a(\eta_0),G_a(\eta_1),\dots,G_a(\eta_n)]^T = \frac{b-a}{2}(\mathbf{W} \circ \mathbf{G})[x(\eta_0),x(\eta_1),\dots,x(\eta_n)]^T. \tag{4.16}$$

Using (4.15) and (4.16) one can now discretize (4.1) as follows:

$$\left[\mathbf{I} + \frac{b-a}{2}\mathbf{W} \circ (\mathbf{F}+\mathbf{G})\right]\bar{\mathbf{x}} = \bar{\mathbf{y}}, \tag{4.17}$$

where $\mathbf{I}$ is the identity matrix of an appropriate size, $\bar{\mathbf{x}} = [x(\eta_0),\dots,x(\eta_n)]^T$, and $\bar{\mathbf{y}} = [y(\eta_0),\dots,y(\eta_n)]^T$. Using (4.17) one can now discretize the local equation (3.1) as

$$\left[\mathbf{I} + \frac{b_i - b_{i-1}}{2k}\mathbf{W} \circ (\mathbf{F} - \mathbf{G})\right]\bar{\mathbf{y}}_i = \bar{\mathbf{s}}_i, \tag{4.18}$$

where

$$\begin{aligned} \mathbf{W} &= \mathbf{C}\mathbf{S}_L\mathbf{C}^{-1}, \qquad \mathbf{F} = \left(\cos\left(k\tau_j^{(i)}\right)\sin\left(k\tau_k^{(i)}\right)V\left(\tau_k^{(i)}\right)\right)_{j,k=0}^{n}, \\ \bar{\mathbf{s}}_i &= \left[\sin\left(k\tau_0^{(i)}\right),\dots,\sin\left(k\tau_n^{(i)}\right)\right], \qquad \bar{\mathbf{y}}_i = \left[y\left(\tau_0^{(i)}\right),\dots,y\left(\tau_n^{(i)}\right)\right]. \end{aligned} \tag{4.19}$$

In the same way,

$$\left[\mathbf{I} + \frac{b_i - b_{i-1}}{2k}\mathbf{W} \circ (\mathbf{F} - \mathbf{G})\right]\bar{\mathbf{z}}_i = \bar{\mathbf{c}}_i, \tag{4.20}$$

where $\mathbf{G} = (\sin(k\tau_j^{(i)})\cos(k\tau_k^{(i)})V(\tau_k^{(i)}))_{j,k=0}^{n}$. The solution of (4.18) and (4.20) can be done using standard software, for example, Gaussian elimination with partial pivoting at the cost of $O(n^3)$ arithmetic operations. The solutions $\bar{\mathbf{y}}_i$ and $\bar{\mathbf{z}}_i$ give the approximate values to the local solutions $y_i(r)$ and $z_i(r)$ at the Chebyshev nodes in each of the subintervals $[b_{i-1}, b_i]$, $i = 1,\dots,m$. We now estimate the accuracy of approximation of the integral equation (4.1) with the linear system of (4.17). The following property of Chebyshev expansions can be derived along the lines of an argument by Gottlieb and Orszag [7, page 29].

Proposition 4.2. *Let* $f \in C^r[-1,1]$, $r > 1$, *and let*

$$f(t) = \sum_{j=0}^{\infty} \alpha_j T_j(t), \quad -1 \le t \le 1. \tag{4.21}$$

Then

$$\begin{aligned} |\alpha_j| &\le \frac{2}{\pi}\int_0^{\pi}\left|\frac{d^r}{d\theta^r}f(\cos\theta)\right|d\theta\frac{1}{j^r} = \frac{c}{j^r}, \\ \left|f(t) - \sum_{j=0}^{n}\alpha_j T_j(t)\right| &\le \frac{c}{r-1}\frac{1}{n^{r-1}}. \end{aligned} \tag{4.22}$$

It implies that if $f(r)$ is analytic, then the convergence of Chebyshev expansions is superalgebraic. Let now $F_l(x) = \int_{-1}^{x} f(t)dt$. The following result can be found by Greengard and Rokhlin [9].

Proposition 4.3. *Suppose that* $f \in C^r_{[-1,1]}$, $r > 1$, *and that* $\bar{f} = (f(\tau_0),\dots,f(\tau_n))^T$, *is the vector of the function values at the roots of* $T_{n+1}(x)$. *Suppose further that* $\bar{F}_l$ *is defined by*

$$\bar{F}_l = \left(F_l(\tau_0),\dots,F_l(\tau_n)\right)^T. \tag{4.23}$$

Then

$$\|\bar{F}_l - \mathbf{CS}_L\mathbf{C}^{-1}\bar{f}\|_\infty = O\left(\frac{1}{n^{r-1}}\right). \tag{4.24}$$

Furthermore, all elements of the matrix $\mathbf{CS}_L\mathbf{C}^{-1}$ *are strictly positive.*

Let now

$$\bar{F}_a = (F_a(\eta_0),\dots,F_a(\eta_n))^T. \tag{4.25}$$

It follows from Proposition 4.3 that

$$\left\|\bar{F}_a - \frac{b-a}{2}(\mathbf{W}\circ\mathbf{F})\hat{\mathbf{x}}\right\|_\infty = O\left(\frac{1}{n^{r-1}}\right). \tag{4.26}$$

Theorem 4.4. *Let* $\bar{\mathbf{x}}$ *be a solution vector of (4.17), and* $\hat{\mathbf{x}}$ *the vector of values of the solution* $x(t)$ *at* $t = \eta_i$, $i = 0,1,\dots,n$. *Suppose* $y(t) \in C^q_{[a,b]}$ *and that (4.1) defines an invertible operator on* $C^r_{[a,b]}$, *where* $r = \min\{p,q\} > 1$. *Then,*

$$\left\|\left(\mathbf{I}+\frac{b-a}{2}\mathbf{W}\circ(\mathbf{F}+\mathbf{G})\right)(\hat{\mathbf{x}}-\bar{\mathbf{x}})\right\|_\infty = O\left(\frac{1}{n^{r-1}}\right). \tag{4.27}$$

It follows from the collectively compact operator theory, see Anselone [2], that for sufficiently large n the matrices $\mathbf{I}+((b-a)/2)\mathbf{W}\circ(\mathbf{F}-\mathbf{G})$, which depend on n, are invertible and their inverses are uniformly bounded. Therefore Theorem 4.4 implies that, for increasing n, the convergence of $\bar{x}$ to $\hat{x}$ is of order $O(n^{1-r})$. The detailed discretization technique for the inner products (3.8) and (3.9) can be obtained in [10]. The overall cost of the computation is dominated by the $O(n^3m)$ cost of solving local equations (4.18) and (4.20). The cost of solving local equations can be reduced by the use of parallel processors since the calculation of $\bar{\mathbf{y}}_i$ and $\bar{\mathbf{z}}_i$ on each subinterval is independent. Using sparseness of $\mathbf{S}_L$ and the fast implementation of the discrete cosine transformation, one may also try to reduce the cost of solving (4.18) and (4.20) by the use of iterative algorithms.

After coefficients $A^{(i)}$ and $B^{(i)}$ of linear combination of the local solutions are determined by the recursions (3.10) and (3.11), the value of $\phi(t)$ for $t \neq \tau_k$ can be found as follows. Applying $\mathbf{C}^{-1}$, one can find "Chebyshev-Fourier" coefficients of $\phi(t)$, $[\alpha_0,\alpha_1,\dots,\alpha_n]^T = \mathbf{C}^{-1}[\phi(\tau_0),\phi(\tau_1),\dots,\phi(\tau_n)]^T$. Thus, $\phi(t) \cong \sum_{j=0}^n \alpha_j T_j(h(t))$, $b_k \le t \le b_{k+1}$, where $h(t) = (2/(b_{k+1}-b_k))t - (b_k - b_{k+1})/(b_{k+1}-b_k)$. The value of $T_j(t)$ for $t \neq \tau_k$ is found now using the recursion satisfied by Chebyshev polynomials, $T_{j+1}(t) = 2tT_j(t) - T_{j-1}(t)$.

5. Numerical examples

In this section the author reports the numerical properties such as accuracy of the numerical solution and stability of the algorithm of Volterra-type integral equation method. In the examples presented in the section Volterra-type method is compared with a finite difference method, so as to obtain a comparison of accuracy of both methods. The finite difference method used is the Numerov algorithm [17], along with the more sophisticated variable step-size method of Raptis and Cash [13], based on fourth-order Numerov

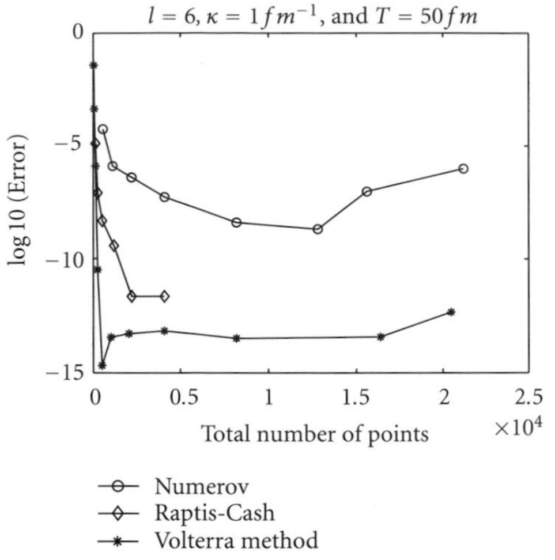

Figure 5.1. Error comparison of the numerical calculation of a Ricatti-Bessel function.

and sixth order of their own for numerical comparisons. The author would like to emphasize once more that the purpose of the numerical experiments in this paper is mainly to illustrate the new features characteristic to Volterra type opposed to Fredholm integral equation method, rather than comparing the accuracy of numerical methods. He chooses here the Numerov method as a generic finite difference method because it is easy to implement, reliable, and widely used method, although he is now aware of more advanced finite difference methods such as the recently developed exponentially fitted methods, see [15, 16] and references therein. In order to compare the Volterra-type method's accuracy with finite difference methods, the author calculated the solution of the corresponding differential equation $(d^2/dr^2 - l(l+1)/r^2 + \kappa^2)R_l(r) = 0$. The comparison of the accuracy of the numerical solution of the first case, $l = 6$, $\kappa = 1fm^{-1}$, and $T = 50fm$ is given in Figure 5.1. The error is obtained by comparison with a Bessel function called through the **IMSL** library. All computations were done on a DELL workstation with operating system RedHat Linux 7.1 in double precision. The accuracy of Numerov's method, which is of $O(h^4)$ (see [17, page 540]), is shown by means of the hexagon in Figure 5.1. It is clearly shown from the figure that the accuracy in Numerov's method increases much less quickly with the number of points than the Volterra-type method. The best accuracy in Numerov's method of 2.3×10^{-9} is reached for 12,800 points, which is 32 times more than the number required by the Volterra-type method to reach its best accuracy of 1.5×10^{-14}. The variable step-size method of Raptis and Cash is also compared with the Volterra-type method. As expected, being a high-order variable step-size method, it achieves better accuracy at fewer mesh points than the Numerov method but still is not able to achieve the accuracy of the Volterra method.

Table 5.1 demonstrates the stability of the algorithm of the Volterra method with respect to the change of T. Adopted number of uniform partitions is $m = 25$, the number of points at each subinterval $n = 16$, angular momentum $l = 6$, and the wave number

Table 5.1

T	48	49	50	51	52
Error	$4.36e-15$	$4.11e-15$	$3.89e-15$	$4.66e-15$	$7.1e-15$

is $\kappa = 1fm^{-1}$. This result supports the insensitivity of the Volterra method to round off errors. The accuracy of each of the local functions can be determined by the size of the coefficients of the highest order Chebyshev polynomials, as recommended by Clenshaw and Curtis [3]. One can use as a measure of the accuracy of the Volterra method the magnitude of the last three Chebyshev expansion coefficients of the solution $\phi(r)$ in each partition which is automatically obtained during the calculation. If the last three coefficients are sufficiently small, then the remaining coefficients may be considered negligible.

Acknowledgment

The work of the author is partially supported by a research grant from Purdue University North Central and the Purdue University Research Foundation.

References

[1] M. Abramovitz and I. Stegun, *Handbook of Mathematical Functions*, Dover, New York, 1972.

[2] P. M. Anselone, *Collectively Compact Operator Approximation Theory and Applications to Integral Equations*, Prentice-Hall Series in Automatic Computation, Prentice-Hall, New Jersey, 1971.

[3] C. W. Clenshaw and A. R. Curtis, *A method for numerical integration on an automatic computer*, Numerische Mathematik **2** (1960), no. 1, 197–205.

[4] L. D. Faddeev, *The inverse problem in the quantum theory of scattering*, Russian Mathematical Surveys **14** (1959), no. 4, 57.

[5] G. H. Golub and C. F. Van Loan, *Matrix Computations*, Johns Hopkins Series in the Mathematical Sciences, vol. 3, Johns Hopkins University Press, Maryland, 1983.

[6] R. A. Gonzales, J. Eisert, I. Koltracht, M. Neumann, and G. Rawitscher, *Integral equation method for the continuous spectrum radial Schrödinger equation*, Journal of Computational Physics **134** (1997), no. 1, 134–149.

[7] D. Gottlieb and S. A. Orszag, *Numerical Analysis of Spectral Methods: Theory and Applications*, CBMS-NSF Regional Conference Series in Applied Mathematics, no. 26, SIAM, Pennsylvania, 1977.

[8] L. Greengard, *Spectral integration and two-point boundary value problems*, SIAM Journal on Numerical Analysis **28** (1991), no. 4, 1071–1080.

[9] L. Greengard and V. Rokhlin, *On the numerical solution of two-point boundary value problems*, Communications on Pure and Applied Mathematics **44** (1991), no. 4, 419–452.

[10] S.-Y. Kang, *Volterra type integral equation method for the radial Schrödinger equation: single channel case*, Computers & Mathematics with Applications **48** (2004), no. 10-11, 1425–1440.

[11] S.-Y. Kang, I. Koltracht, and G. Rawitscher, *Nyström-Clenshaw-Curtis quadrature for integral equations with discontinuous kernels*, Mathematics of Computation **72** (2003), no. 242, 729–756.

[12] R. H. Landau, *Quantum Mechanics. II. A Second Course in Quantum Theory*, John Wiley & Sons, New York, 1990.

[13] A. D. Raptis and J. R. Cash, *A variable step method for the numerical-integration of one dimensional Schrödinger-equation*, Computer Physics Communications **36** (1985), no. 2, 113–119.

[14] L. I. Schiff, *Quantum Mechanics*, 3rd ed., McGraw-Hill, New York, 1968.

[15] T. E. Simos, *Exponential fitted methods for the numerical solution of the Schrödinger equation*, Journal of Computational Mathematics **14** (1996), no. 2, 120–134.
[16] T. E. Simos and P. S. Williams, *Bessel and Neumann-fitted methods for the numerical solution of the radial Schrödinger equation*, Computers & Chemistry **21** (1997), no. 3, 175–179.
[17] J. Stoer and R. Bulirsch, *Introduction to Numerical Analysis*, 2nd ed., Texts in Applied Mathematics, vol. 12, Springer, New York, 1993.

Sheon-Young Kang: Mathematics Department, Purdue University North Central, Westville, IN 46391, USA
E-mail address: skang@pnc.edu

NUMERICAL SOLUTION OF A TRANSMISSION LINE PROBLEM OF ELECTRODYNAMICS IN A CLASS OF DISCONTINUOUS FUNCTIONS

TURHAN KARAGULER AND MAHIR RASULOV

A special numerical method for the solution of first-order partial differential equation which represents the transmission line problem in a class of discontinuous functions is described. For this, first, an auxiliary problem having some advantages over the main problem is introduced. Since the differentiable property of the solution of the auxiliary problem is one order higher than the differentiability of the solution of the main problem, the application of classical methods to the auxiliary problem can easily be performed. Some economical algorithms are proposed for obtaining a numerical solution of the auxiliary problem, from which the numerical solution of the main problem can be obtained. In order to show the effectiveness of the suggested algorithms, some comparisons between the exact solution and the numerical solution are carried out.

1. The Cauchy problem

It is known from the electromagnetic field and the circuit theories that the equations for a current and potential in a transmission line have the following form [1, 3, 4]:

$$L\frac{\partial i(x,t)}{\partial t}+\frac{\partial v(x,t)}{\partial x}+Ri(x,t)=0, \tag{1.1}$$

$$C\frac{\partial v(x,t)}{\partial t}+\frac{\partial i(x,t)}{\partial x}+Gv(x,t)=0. \tag{1.2}$$

Here $v(x,t)$ and $i(x,t)$ are potential and current at any points x and t, R is resistance per unit length, L is inductance per unit length, C is capacitance per unit length, and G is conductance per unit length. These line parameters are taken constant since the medium is assumed as linear and homogeneous.

The initial condition for (1.1), (1.2) are

$$i(x,0)=i_0(x), \tag{1.3}$$

$$v(x,0)=v_0(x), \tag{1.4}$$

where $i_0(x)$ and $v_0(x)$ are given as continuous or piecewise continuous functions.

Hindawi Publishing Corporation
Proceedings of the Conference on Differential & Difference Equations and Applications, pp. 501–508

From the Biot-Savard law of electromagnetic theory, when a wire carrying a current produces a magnetic field around it [1], if this magnetic field changes, the source of it, which is the current, changes too. This results with a wave which travels through the wire. This wave will be examined in the frame of transmission line problem.

Heaviside showed that if $G/C = R/L$ equality exsists between the parameter of the transmission line, then (1.1), (1.2) are reduced to the well-known second-order wave equation such that

$$\frac{\partial^2 u}{\partial t^2} = a^2 \frac{\partial^2 u}{\partial x^2}, \tag{1.5}$$

where $a = 1/\sqrt{LC}$.

Using the general solution of (1.5) which is obtained from D'Alembert's formula for both unknown functions $i(x,t)$ and $v(x,t)$, we have (see, [2, 4])

$$v(x,t) = e^{-(R/L)t}\left[\phi(x-at) + \psi(x+at)\right], \tag{1.6}$$

$$i(x,t) = \sqrt{\frac{C}{L}} e^{-(R/L)t}\left[\phi(x-at) - \psi(x+at)\right]. \tag{1.7}$$

Here, the arbitrary functions $\varphi(\xi)$ and $\psi(\xi)$ are found from the initial conditions such as $v(x,0) = f(x)$ and $i(x,0) = \sqrt{(C/L)}F(x)$.

When the transmission line is too long, which is the common case in practice, then the following problem occurs. The functions $F(x)$ and $f(x)$ are definite in the $(0,l)$ interval, however, the solutions obtained with the formulas of (1.6) and (1.7) require values of $f(x)$ and $F(x)$ functions for arbitrary x values. This will enforce the extension of $f(x)$ and $F(x)$ functions beyond the interval of $(0,l)$.

On the other hand, it is known from the literature that the solution of (1.5) has weak discontinuity on the characteristics. This means that the solution is on the characteristics, and continuously differentiable, but its first-order derivatives are piecewise continously differentiable. This property prevents applying well-known numerical methods in the literature to the equation of type (1.5) such as the system of (1.1) and (1.2). Furthermore, if the initial functions posses the singular points, the numerical methods mentioned above fail even worst. The weak solutions of the problem of (1.1)–(1.4) are defined as follows.

Definition 1.1. The functions $i(x,t)$, $v(x,t)$ satisfying the initial conditions (1.3), (1.4) are called the weak solutions of the problem (1.1)–(1.4) if for any test functions $f(x,t)$ which are equal to zero at the value $t = T$ and at the boundary of the plane $t+ \mid x \mid$, the integral relations

$$\begin{gathered}\int_{D_T} \left(Li(x,t)f_t + v(x,t)f_x - Ri(x,t)\right)dx\,dt + L\int_{-\infty}^{+\infty} i_0(x)f(x,0)dx = 0,\\ \int_{D_T} \left(Cv(x,t)f_t + i(x,t)f_x - Gv(x,t)\right)dx\,dt + C\int_{-\infty}^{+\infty} v_0(x)f(x,0)dx = 0\end{gathered} \tag{1.8}$$

hold.

As seen from (1.8), $i(x,t)$ and $v(x,t)$ are not necessarily to be countinous.

1.1. Auxiliary problem. As it is known, the derivatives of the solutions of (1.1), (1.2) with respect to x and t are discontinuous on the characteristics of the equations. This requires that the applied method to find the numerical solution must have high accuracy. Because of this, in this paper, a new numerical method to obtain the weak solution of the problem (1.1)–(1.4) in a class of discontinuous functions is suggested. For this aim, along with the references [4–7], a special auxiliary problem, as below,

$$L\frac{\partial I(x,t)}{\partial t} + V(x,t) + RI(x,t) = 0, \tag{1.9}$$

$$C\frac{\partial V(x,t)}{\partial t} + I(x,t) + GV(x,t) = 0, \tag{1.10}$$

$$I(x,0) = I_0(x), \tag{1.11}$$

$$V(x,0) = V_0(x) \tag{1.12}$$

is introduced. Here $I_0(x)$ and $V_0(x)$ are any continuously differentiable functions which satisfy the equations of $dI_0(x)/dx = i_0(x)$ and $dV_0(x)/dx = v_0(x)$.

The auxiliary problem has the following advantages.

(1) When to employ the $i(x,t)$ and $v(x,t)$, no need to use their derivatives with respect to x and t.

(2) The differentiability property of $I(x,t)$, $V(x,t)$ functions is one degree higher than differentiability property of $i(x,t)$ and $v(x,t)$ functions.

One of the most significant advantages of the auxiliary problem is that the well-known methods are applicable to it. Even on the basis of auxiliary problem, the higher-order finite-differences scheme are allowed to develop.

THEOREM 1.2. *If $I(x,t)$ and $V(x,t)$ are the solutions of the problem (1.9)–(1.12), then the functions $i(x,t)$ and $v(x,t)$ defined by*

$$i(x,t) = \frac{\partial I(x,t)}{\partial x}, \tag{1.13}$$

$$v(x,t) = \frac{\partial V(x,t)}{\partial x} \tag{1.14}$$

expressions are the weak solutions of the problem (1.1)–(1.4) only in a sense of (1.8).

As it is obvious from (1.9), (1.10) that the equations are freed from the time and space derivative terms of $i(x,t)$ and $v(x,t)$. Therefore the functions $i(x,t)$ and $v(x,t)$ can be discontinuous too. This would make it possible to develop accurate and economical algorithms for obtaining the solution which represent the physical properties of the problem.

2. Initial-boundary value problem for transmission line equation

As usual, we denote $R_+ = \{(x,t),\ x > 0,\ t > 0\}$. In this section, by adding the following boundary conditions, we will investigate the considered initial value problem:

$$i(0,t) = i_1(t), \tag{2.1}$$

$$v(0,t) = v_1(t). \tag{2.2}$$

Here, i_1 and v_1 are known functions. In general, we assume that the functions i_k and v_k $(k = 1,2)$ can be discontinuous too. The weak solution of the problem is specified in the following definition as follows.

Definition 2.1. The functions $i(x,t)$ and $v(x,t)$ satisfy the (1.3)-(1.4) initial, and the (2.1) and (2.2) boundary conditions are called the weak solutions of the initial-boundary value problem if for any test function $f(x,t)$ satisfying $f(x,T) = 0$ and is equal to zero on the boundary of the $t + x$ half-space, the integral relations

$$\begin{aligned}&\int_{R_t} (Li(x,t)f_t(x,t) + v(x,t)f_x(x,t) - Ri(x,t))\,dx\,dt \\ &\qquad + L\int_0^{\infty} i_0(x)f(x,0)\,dx + \int_0^T v_1(t)f(0,t)\,dt = 0, \\ &\int_{R_t} (Cv(x,t)f_t(x,t) + i(x,t)f_x(x,t) - Gv(x,t))\,dx\,dt \\ &\qquad + C\int_0^{\infty} v_0(x)f(x,0)\,dx + \int_0^T i_1(t)f(0,t)\,dt = 0\end{aligned} \tag{2.3}$$

hold.

According to [5, 6], the auxiliary problem for the initial-boundary value problem which is shown above can be written as

$$L\frac{\partial}{\partial t}\int_0^x i(\xi,t)\,d\xi + v(x,t) + R\int_0^x i(\xi,t)\,d\xi = v(0,t), \tag{2.4}$$

$$C\frac{\partial}{\partial t}\int_0^x v(\xi,t)\,d\xi + i(x,t) + G\int_0^x v(\xi,t)\,d\xi = i(0,t). \tag{2.5}$$

The initial conditions for the auxiliary equations (2.4), (2.5) will be the same as the boundary conditions of the main problem (1.3)-(1.4).

3. Finite-differences schema and numerical experiments

In order to obtain the numerical solution of the problem (1.1)–(1.4), at first, we cover the domain of definition of the definition of the solutions by the following grid as

$$\omega_{h,\tau} = \{(x_i,t_k) \mid x_i = ih;\ t_k = k\tau,\ i = 0,\pm 1,\pm 2,\ldots;\ k = 0,1,2,\ldots;\ h > 0,\ \tau > 0\}. \tag{3.1}$$

Here, h and τ are the steps of the grid $\omega_{h,\tau}$ with respect to x and t variables, respectively.

Then the auxiliary problem (1.9)–(1.12) is approximated at any grid point (i,k),

$$I_{i,k+1} = I_{i,k} - \frac{\tau}{L}(v_{i,k} + RI_{i,k}), \tag{3.2}$$

$$V_{i,k+1} = V_{i,k} - \frac{\tau}{C}(i_{i,k} + GV_{i,k}), \tag{3.3}$$

$$I_{i,0} = I_0(x_i), \tag{3.4}$$

$$V_{i,0} = V_0(x_i). \tag{3.5}$$

Here, $I_{i,k}$ and $V_{i,k}$ represent the approximate values of the functions $I(x,t)$ and $V(x,t)$ at the point (i,k) of the $w_{h,\tau}$ grid.

THEOREM 3.1. *If the mesh functions* $I_{i,k}$ *and* $V_{i,k}$ *are the numerical solutions of the auxiliary problem (3.2)–(3.5), then*

$$\begin{aligned} i_{i,k} &= I_{\bar{x}}, \\ v_{i,k} &= V_{\bar{x}} \end{aligned} \tag{3.6}$$

are the numerical solutions of the main problem.

Equations (3.2), (3.3) suggest that the algorithm is very simple and economical. Furthermore, on the basis of auxiliary equations (1.9), (1.10), higher-order finite-difference schemes with respect to t can be developed.

In order to approximate the auxiliary equations (2.4), (2.5) by means of finite-difference method, the quadrature formula is applied to the $\int_0^x \phi(z)dz$ as

$$\int_0^x \phi(z)dz \approx h\Sigma_{j=1}^{i}\phi(z_j). \tag{3.7}$$

Considering (3.7), (2.4), and (2.5) can be approximated by means of finite difference as

$$\begin{aligned} I_{i,k+1} &= \frac{h_t}{L}(V_1(t_k) - RI_{i,k} - V_{i,k}) - \sum_{j=0}^{i-1}(I_{j,k+1} - I_{j,k}) + I_{i,k}, \\ V_{i,k+1} &= \frac{h_t}{C}(I_1(t_k) - I_{i,k} - GV_{i,k}) - \sum_{j=0}^{i-1}(V_{j,k+1} - V_{j,k}) + V_{i,k}. \end{aligned} \tag{3.8}$$

In order to demonstrate the effectiveness of the suggested algorithm, firstly, we investigate (1.5) with the initial conditions (1.3), (1.4). As initial functions, we have a piecewise differentiable functions given as

$$f(x) = \begin{cases} 0, & x < x_1, \\ \dfrac{u_1}{x_3 - x_1}(x - x_1), & x_1 \le x \le x_3, \\ \dfrac{u_1}{x_3 - x_2}(x - x_2), & x_3 \le x \le x_2, \\ 0, & x > x_2, \end{cases} \qquad F(x) = \begin{cases} 0, & x < x_1, \\ c_0, & x_1 \le x \le x_2, \\ 0, & x > x_2. \end{cases} \tag{3.9}$$

The numerical experiments have been carried out for the data $x_1 = -2.0$, $x_2 = 2.0$, $x_3 = 0.0$, $u_1 = 1.0$, $c_0 = 2.0$.

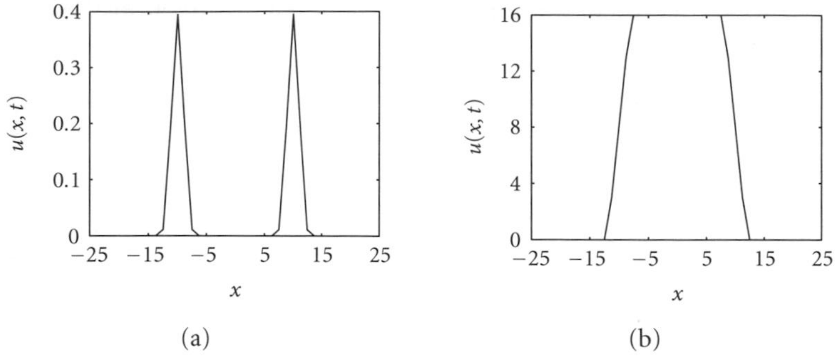

Figure 3.1. The graphs of the exact solution at $T = 40$ for (a) the case $f(x) \neq 0$ and $F(x) = 0$; (b) the case $f(x) = 0$ and $F(x) \neq 0$.

In order to implement the auxiliary problem, at first the functions I_0, V_0 are obtained as follows:

$$I_0(x) = \begin{cases} 0, & x < x_1, \\ A\dfrac{(x-x_1)^3}{6}, & x_1 \leq x \leq x_3, \\ \dfrac{B}{6}(x-x_2)^3 + \dfrac{u_1}{2}(x-x_1)x + E, & x_3 \leq x \leq x_2, \\ \dfrac{u_1}{2}x(x_2-x_1), & x > x_2, \end{cases} \tag{3.10}$$

$$V_1(x) = \begin{cases} 0, & x < x_1, \\ c_0\dfrac{(x-x_1)^2}{2}, & x_1 \leq x \leq x_2, \\ c_0 x(x_2-x_1) + \dfrac{c_0}{2}(x_1^2 - x_2^2), & x > x_2. \end{cases}$$

Here $A = u_1/(x_3 - x_1)$, $B = u_1/(x_3 - x_2)$, $E = (B/6)x_1^2 + x_3(x_2 - x_1) - x_2^2$.

In Figure 3.1, the solution of the Cauchy problem of (1.5) defined by the D'Alembert's formula is illustrated. Figure 3.2 shows the solution of the auxiliary problem having the same initial data as the main problem.

As these graphs, Figures 3.1 and 3.2 illustrate that the solutions of the auxiliary and main problems match very well. This clearly proves the usefulness of the auxiliary problem. The graphics of solutions obtained by the auxiliary problem are given in Figure 3.3. Comparing the results shown in Figures 3.1(a) and 3.3(b), we observe that the numerical solution obtained from the auxiliary problem is very much similar to the solutions obtained from the classical methods.

The graphs of solutions of the problem (1.5) with the data $f(x) = 2\cos x$, $F(x) = 10\cos x$, $R = 0.02$, $L = 2.5 \cdot 10^5$, $C = 10^5$, $G = 0.2$ are demonstrated in Figure 3.4.

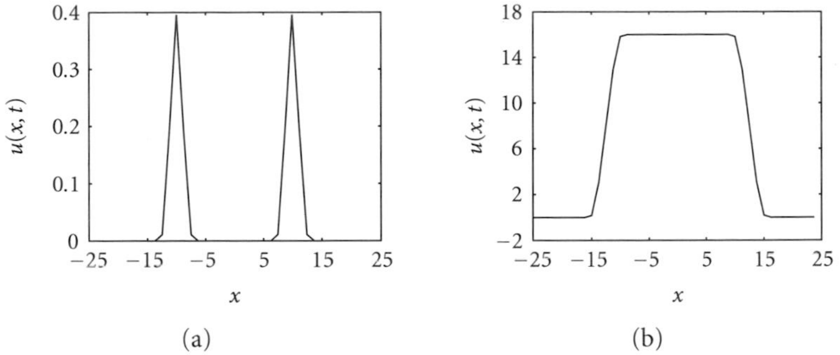

Figure 3.2. (a) The time evolution of the solution of the auxiliary problem; (b) the graph of $u(x,t) = \partial^2 v(x,t)/\partial x^2$, $f(x) \neq 0$, $F(x) = 0$ at $T = 40$.

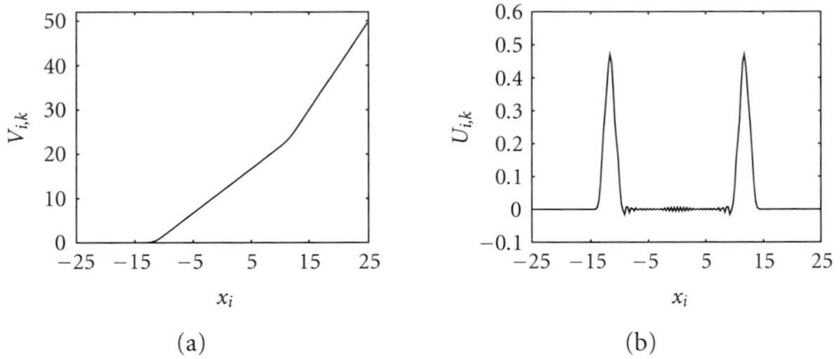

Figure 3.3. The time evolution of the numerical solution obtained by using the auxiliary problem $f(x) \neq 0$, $F(x) = 0$. (a) Solution of the auxiliary problem; (b) the graph of $U_{i,k} = V_{x\bar{x}}$.

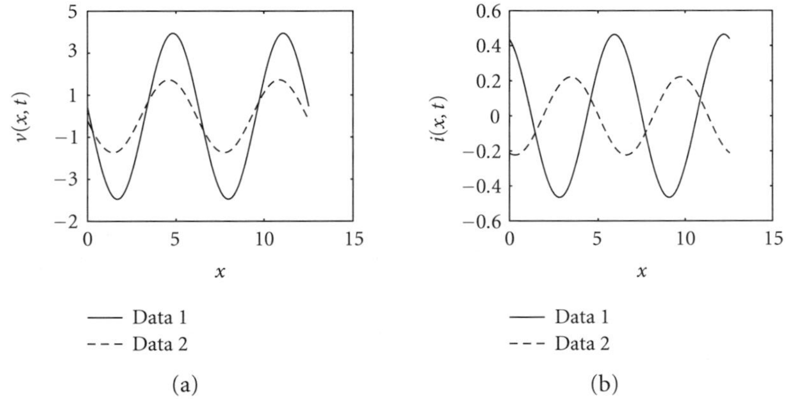

Figure 3.4. The graphs of $v(x,t)$ and $i(x,t)$ solutions.

4. Conclusion

Introduction of the auxiliary problem has several advantages over the main problem. Firstly, the well-known numerical methods can easily be applied to the auxiliary problem. Further, the auxiliary problem lets higher-order finite-differences schemes be used. This leads to developing simple algorithms.

References

[1] D. K. Cheng, *Field and Wave Electromagnetics*, Addison-Wesley, New York, 2001.
[2] S. K. Godunov, *Equations of Mathematical Physics*, Nauka, Moscow, 1979.
[3] W. H. Hayt and J. A. Buck, *Engineering Electromagnetics*, 6th ed., McGraw-Hill, New York, 2001.
[4] N. S. Koshlakov, *Partial Differential Equations of Mathematical Physics*, Bishaya Skola, Moscow, 1970.
[5] M. Rasulov, *On a method of solving the Cauchy problem for a first order nonlinear equation of hyperbolic type with a smooth initial condition*, Soviet Mathematics Doklady **43** (1991), no. 1, 150–153.
[6] ______, *Finite Difference Scheme for Solving of Some Nonlinear Problems of Mathematical Physics in a Class of Discontinuous Functions*, Baku, 1996.
[7] M. Rasulov and T. A. Ragimova, *A numerical method of the solution of the nonlinear equation of a hyperbolic type of the first order differential equations*, Minsk **28** (1992), no. 7, 2056–2063.

Turhan Karaguler: Department of Mathematics and Computing, Faculty of Science and Letters, Beykent University, Beykent 34500, Büyükçekmece-Istanbul, Turkey
E-mail address: turank@beykent.edu.tr

Mahir Rasulov: Department of Mathematics and Computing, Faculty of Science and Letters, Beykent University, Beykent 34500, Büyükçekmece-Istanbul, Turkey
E-mail address: mresulov@beykent.edu.tr

INHOMOGENEOUS MAPS: THE BASIC THEOREMS AND SOME APPLICATIONS

GEORGY P. KAREV

Nonlinear maps can possess various dynamical behaviors varying from stable steady states and cycles to chaotic oscillations. Most models assume that individuals within a given population are identical ignoring the fundamental role of variation. Here we develop a theory of inhomogeneous maps and apply the general approach to modeling heterogeneous populations with discrete evolutionary time step. We show that the behavior of the inhomogeneous maps may possess complex transition regimes, which depends both on the mean and the variance of the initial parameter distribution. The examples of inhomogeneous models are discussed.

1. Statement of the problem and basic theorem

Let us assume that a population consists of individuals, each of those is characterized by its own parameter value $\mathbf{a} = (a_1,\dots,a_k)$. These parameter values can take any particular value from set A. Let $n_t(\mathbf{a})$ be the density of the population at the moment t. Then the number of individuals having parameter values in set $\widetilde{\mathrm{A}} \subseteq \mathrm{A}$ is given by $\widetilde{N}_t = \int_{\widetilde{\mathrm{A}}} n_t(\mathbf{a})d\mathbf{a}$, and the total population size is $N_t = \int_{\mathrm{A}} n_t(\mathbf{a})d\mathbf{a}$.

The theory of inhomogeneous models of populations with continuous time was developed earlier (see, e.g., [2, 3]). Here we study the inhomogeneous model of population dynamics with discrete time of the form

$$n_{t+1}(\mathbf{a}) = W(N_t,\mathbf{a})n_t(\mathbf{a}), \quad N_t = \int_{\mathrm{A}} n_t(\mathbf{a})d\mathbf{a}, \tag{1.1}$$

where $W \geq 0$ is the reproduction rate (fitness); we assume that the reproduction rate depends on the specific parameter value $\mathbf{a}$ and the total size of the population N_t, but does not depend on the particular densities n_t.

Let us denote $p_t(\mathbf{a}) = n_t(\mathbf{a})/N_t$ the current probability density of the vector-parameter $\mathbf{a}$ at the moment t. We have a probability space (A,P_t) where the probability P_t has the

Hindawi Publishing Corporation
Proceedings of the Conference on Differential & Difference Equations and Applications, pp. 509–517

density $p_t(\mathbf{a})$, and model (1.1) defines a transformation of the initial probability density $p_0(\mathbf{a})$ with time. Below we show that problem (1.1) can be reduced to a nonautonomous map on $I \subseteq \mathbf{R}^1$ under supposition that the reproduction rate has the form $W(N,\mathbf{a}) = f(\mathbf{a})g(N)$, so that the model takes the form

$$n_{t+1}(\mathbf{a}) = n_t(\mathbf{a})f(\mathbf{a})g(N_t), \quad N_t = \int_A n_t(\mathbf{a})d\mathbf{a}, \tag{1.2}$$

for the given initial density $n_0(\mathbf{a})$.

Theorem 1.1. *Let $p_0(\mathbf{a})$ be the density of the initial probability distribution of the vector-parameter $\mathbf{a}$ for inhomogeneous map (1.2). Then*

(i) *the population size N_t satisfies the recurrence relation*

$$N_{t+1} = E_t[f]N_t g(N_t); \tag{1.3}$$

(ii) *the current mean of f can be computed by the formula*

$$E_t[f] = \frac{E_0[f^{t+1}]}{E_0[f^t]}; \tag{1.4}$$

(iii) *the density of the current distribution is*

$$p_t(\mathbf{a}) = \frac{p_0(\mathbf{a})f^t(\mathbf{a})}{E_0[f^t]}. \tag{1.5}$$

Proof. Rewriting the first equation in (1.2) as $n_{t+1}(\mathbf{a})/n_t(\mathbf{a}) = f(\mathbf{a})g(N_t)$, we obtain $n_t(\mathbf{a}) = n_0(\mathbf{a})f^t(\mathbf{a})G_{t-1}$, where $G_t = g(N_0)\cdot\cdots\cdot g(N_t)$. Then

$$N_t = \int_A n_t(\mathbf{a})d\mathbf{a} = \int_A n_0(\mathbf{a})f^t(\mathbf{a})G_{t-1}d\mathbf{a} = N_0E_0[f^t]G_{t-1}, \tag{1.6}$$

where $E_0[f^k] = \int_A f^k(\mathbf{a})p_0(\mathbf{a})d\mathbf{a}$. So one has $p_t(\mathbf{a}) = n_t(\mathbf{a})/N_t = p_0(\mathbf{a})(f^t(\mathbf{a})/E_0[f^t])$.

Integrating over $\mathbf{a}$ the equation $n_{t+1}(\mathbf{a}) = f(\mathbf{a})p_t(\mathbf{a})N_tg(N_t)$ implies $N_{t+1} = E_t[f]N_tg(N_t)$ where $E_t[f] = \int_A f(\mathbf{a})p_t(\mathbf{a})d\mathbf{a}$. Next,

$$E_t[f] = \frac{1}{E_0[f^t]}\int_A f^{t+1}(\mathbf{a})p_0(\mathbf{a})d\mathbf{a} = \frac{E_0[f^{t+1}]}{E_0[f^t]}. \tag{1.7}$$

□

2. Dynamics of the parameter distributions

The problem of the evolution of parameter distribution due to inhomogeneous model (1.1) is of special interest. Formally, assertion (iii) of Theorem 1.1 contains complete description of $p_t(\mathbf{a})$. Roughly, the density $p_t(\mathbf{a})$ tends to 0 if $f(\mathbf{a}) < 1$ and tends to ∞ if $f(\mathbf{a}) > 1$ at $t \to \infty$. The following proposition that immediately follows from Theorem 1.1 gives some additional useful relations.

PROPOSITION 2.1.

$$p_{t+1}(\mathbf{a}) = p_t(\mathbf{a})\frac{f(\mathbf{a})}{E_t[f]}; \qquad \frac{p_t(\mathbf{a}_1)}{p_t(\mathbf{a}_2)} = \frac{p_0(\mathbf{a}_1)}{p_0(\mathbf{a}_2)}\left[\frac{f(\mathbf{a}_1)}{f(\mathbf{a}_2)}\right]^t. \tag{2.1}$$

COROLLARY 2.2. *If $f(\mathbf{a}_1) < f(\mathbf{a}_2)$ and $p_0(\mathbf{a}_2) > 0$, then $p_t(\mathbf{a}_1)/p_t(\mathbf{a}_2) \to 0$ at $t \to \infty$.*

The density independent component of the reproduction rate $f(\mathbf{a})$ can be considered as a random variable on the probability space (A, P_t). Let $p_f(t;x)$ be the probability density function (pdf) of this random variable $f(\mathbf{a})$; then $E_t[f] = \int_{-\infty}^{\infty} x p_f(t;x)dx$ and $\mathrm{Var}_t[f] = E_t[f^2] - (E_t[f])^2 = E_0[f^{t+2}]/E_0[f^t] - (E_0[f^{t+1}]/E_0[f^t])^2$ according to Theorem 1.1(ii).

PROPOSITION 2.3. $E_{t+1}[f] = E_t[f^2]/E_t[f]$, $E_{t+1}[f]/E_t[f] = 1 + \mathrm{Var}_t[f]/(E_t[f])^2$.

COROLLARY 2.4. $\Delta E_t[f] = \mathrm{Var}_t[f]/E_t[f]$.

Hence, $E_{t+1}[f] > E_t[f]$ for all t and $E_{t+1}[f] = E_t[f]$ if and only if $\mathrm{Var}_t[f] = 0$, that is, if $f(\mathbf{a}) = \text{const}$ for almost all $\mathbf{a}$ over the probability P_t. Remark that this corollary is a version of the Fisher fundamental theorem of natural selection within a framework of model (1.2).

Next, let us explore the evolution of the distribution of $f(\mathbf{a})$ in detail.

THEOREM 2.5. *Let the initial pdf of $f(\mathbf{a})$ be*

(1) *Gamma-distribution with the parameters (s,k), that is,*

$$p_f(0;x) = \frac{s^k x^{k-1}\exp[-xs]}{\Gamma(k)} \tag{2.2}$$

for $x \geq 0$, where s, k are positive, $\Gamma(k)$ is the Γ-function. Then

$$p_f(t;x) = \frac{s^{t+k} x^{t+k-1}\exp[-xs]}{\Gamma(k+t)} \tag{2.3}$$

is again the Gamma-distribution with the parameters $(s, k+t)$; its mean is $E_t[f] = (k+t)/s$ and variance $\mathrm{Var}_t[f] = (k+t)^2/s^2$;

(2) *exponential, that is, $p_f(0;x) = s\exp[-xs]$, $s \geq 0$ is a parameter. Then*

$$p_f(t;x) = \frac{s\exp[-xs](sx)^t}{t!} \tag{2.4}$$

is the density of Gamma-distribution with the parameters $(s, 1+t)$;

(3) *Beta-distribution with positive parameters (α,β), that is to say, $p_f(0;x) = \Gamma(\alpha+\beta)/(\Gamma(\alpha)\Gamma(\beta))x^{\alpha-1}(1-x)^{\beta-1}$, $0 < x < 1$. Then*

$$p_f(t;x) = \frac{\Gamma(\alpha+t+\beta)}{\Gamma(\alpha+t)\Gamma(\beta)} x^{\alpha+t-1}(1-x)^{\beta-1} \tag{2.5}$$

is again the density of Beta-distribution with parameters $(\alpha+t, \beta)$; its mean is $E_t[f] = (\alpha+t)/(\alpha+t+\beta)$ and variance $\mathrm{Var}_t[f] = (\alpha+t)\beta/[(\alpha+t+\beta)^2(\alpha+t+\beta+1)]$;

(4) *hyper-exponential, that is,* $p_f(0;x) = \sum_{k=1}^{m} \alpha_k s_k \exp[-s_k x]$, $x \geq 0$. *Then*

$$p_f(t;x) = \frac{x^t \sum_{k=1}^{m} \alpha_k s_k \exp[-s_k x]}{\left(t! \sum_{k=1}^{m} \alpha_k / s_k^t\right)}; \tag{2.6}$$

(5) *log-normal, that is,* $p_f(0;x) = 1/(x\sigma\sqrt{2\pi}) \exp\{-(\ln x - m)^2/2\sigma^2\}$, $x > 0$. *Then*

$$p_f(t;x) = \frac{x^{t-1}}{\sigma\sqrt{2\pi}} \exp\left\{-\frac{(\ln x - m)^2}{2\sigma^2} - \frac{t^2\sigma^2}{2} - tm\right\}; \tag{2.7}$$

(6) *Pareto distribution with the parameters* α, x_0, *that is,* $p_f(0;x) = \alpha/x_0 (x/x_0)^{-\alpha-1}$, $x > x_0 > 0$. *Then*

$$p_f(t;x) = \frac{\alpha - t}{x_0}\left(\frac{x}{x_0}\right)^{-\alpha-1+t} \tag{2.8}$$

is again the Pareto distribution for $t < \alpha$ *with the parameters* $\alpha - t$, x_0;

(7) *Veibull distribution with the parameters* (k,s), *that is,* $p_f(0;x) = ksx^{k-1}\exp[-sx^k]$, $x > 0$. *Then*

$$p_f(t;x) = \frac{ks^{1+t/k} x^{t+k-1} \exp[-sx^k]}{\Gamma(t/k+1)}; \tag{2.9}$$

(8) *uniform distribution in the interval* $[0,B]$. *Then*

$$p_f(t;x) = \frac{(t+1)x^t}{B^{t+1}}. \tag{2.10}$$

Proof. (1) If $p_f(0;x) = s^k x^{k-1} \exp[-xs]/\Gamma(k)$, then $E_0[f^t] = \Gamma(k+t)/(s^t\Gamma(k))$. According to formula (1.5), $p_f(t;x) = p_f(0;x)x^t/E_0[f^t] = s^{t+k}x^{t+k-1}\exp[-xs]/\Gamma(k+t)$, and $p_f(t;x)$ is again the Gamma-distribution with the parameters $(s, k+t)$.

(2) If $p_f(0;x) = s\exp[-xs]$, then $E_0[f^t] = t!/s^t$. Hence,

$$p_f(t;x) = \frac{p_f(0;x)x^t}{E_0[f^t]} = \frac{s\exp[-xs](sx)^t}{t!}. \tag{2.11}$$

Remark that under fixed value of x the last formula defines (up to normalized constant $1/s$) the Poissonian distribution over time instants with the parameter sx.

(3) If $p_f(0;x) = \Gamma(\alpha+\beta)/(\Gamma(\alpha)\Gamma(\beta))x^{\alpha-1}(1-x)^{\beta-1}$, then $E_0[f^t] = \Gamma(\alpha+t)\Gamma(\alpha+\beta)/\Gamma(\alpha)\Gamma(\alpha+t+\beta)$. Hence,

$$p_f(t;x) = \frac{p_f(0;x)x^t}{E_0[f^t]} = \frac{\Gamma(\alpha+t+\beta)}{\Gamma(\alpha+t)\Gamma(\beta)} x^{\alpha+t-1}(1-x)^{\beta-1} \tag{2.12}$$

is the Beta-distribution with the parameters $(\alpha+t, \beta)$.

(4) If $p_f(0;x) = \sum_{k=1}^{m} \alpha_k s_k \exp[-s_k x]$, then $E_0[f^t] = t! \sum_{k=1}^{m} \alpha_k/s_k^t$. Hence,

$$p_f(t;x) = \frac{x^t \sum_{k=1}^{m} \alpha_k s_k \exp[-s_k x]}{\left(t! \sum_{k=1}^{m} \alpha_k / s_k^t\right)}. \tag{2.13}$$

(5) If $p_f(0;x) = 1/(x\sigma\sqrt{2\pi})\exp\{-(\ln x - m)^2/2\sigma^2\}$, then $E_0[f^t] = \exp\{(t^2\sigma^2/2) + tm\}$. Hence,

$$p_f(t;x) = \frac{p_f(0;x)x^t}{E_0[f^t]} = \frac{x^{t-1}}{\sigma\sqrt{2\pi}}\exp\left\{-\frac{(\ln x - m)^2}{2\sigma^2} - \frac{t^2\sigma^2}{2} - tm\right\}. \tag{2.14}$$

(6) If $p_f(0;x) = \alpha/x_0(x/x_0)^{-\alpha-1}$, then $E_0[f^t] = \alpha/(\alpha - t)x_0^t$ for $t < \alpha$. Hence,

$$p_f(t;x) = \frac{(\alpha - t)}{x_0(x/x_0)^{-\alpha-1+t}}. \tag{2.15}$$

(7) If $p_f(0;x) = ksx^{k-1}\exp[-sx^k]$, then $E_0[f^t] = s^{-t/k}\Gamma(t/k+1)$, hence

$$p_f(t;x) = \frac{ks^{1+t/k}x^{t+k-1}\exp[-sx^k]}{\Gamma(t/k+1)}. \tag{2.16}$$

(8) If $p_f(0;x) = 1/B$, then $E_0[f^t] = B^t/(t+1)$, hence

$$p_f(t;x) = \frac{(t+1)x^t}{B^{t+1}}. \tag{2.17}$$

□

Evolution of other initial distributions of the fitness can be explored similarly.

3. Examples

Example 3.1 (Malthusian model of the population growth). Inhomogeneous version of the Malthusian model reads $n(t+1,\mathbf{a}) = f(\mathbf{a})n(t,\mathbf{a})$. Even in this simplest case the dynamics of the mean fitness and the evolution of the fitness distribution over the individuals dramatically depend on the initial distribution of the fitness. Let us consider some important examples.

(A1) Let the initial pdf $p_f(0;x)$ of $f(\mathbf{a})$ be the Gamma-distribution with the parameters s, k. Then, according to Theorem 2.5, (1) $p_f(t;x)$ is again the Gamma-distribution with the parameters s, $k+t$; its mean is $E_t[f] = (k+t)/s$, $\text{Var}_t[f] = (k+t)^2/s^2$, and $N_{t+1} = E_t[f]N_t = (k+t)/sN_t$. Hence in this case the mean fitness increases linearly with time, while $N_t = N_0\Gamma(k+t)/(s^t\Gamma(k))$.

(A2) Let $p_f(0;x)$ be the Beta-distribution in interval $[0,B]$. Then $E_t[f] = B(\alpha+t)/(\alpha+t+\beta) \cong B$. Next, $N_{t+1} = E_t[f]N_t = B(\alpha+t)/(\alpha+t+\beta)N_t$, so

$$N_t = N_0B^t\frac{\Gamma(\alpha+t-1)\Gamma(\alpha+\beta)}{\Gamma(\alpha+\beta+t-1)\Gamma(\alpha)} \sim N_0B^t\frac{\Gamma(\alpha+\beta)}{\Gamma(\alpha)}t^{-\beta}. \tag{3.1}$$

Hence, the fate of a population dramatically depends on the value of B: if $B \le 1$, the population goes extinct; if $B > 1$, the size of the population increases indefinitely. In the case $B = 1$ the mean fitness tends to 1 and one could expect that the total population size tends to a stable nonzero value in course of time, but actually the population goes extinct with a power rate.

(A3) Let $p_f(0;x)$ be the uniform distribution in the interval $[0,B]$. Then $E_0[f^t] = B^t/(t+1)$, hence $E_t[f] = B(t+1)/(t+2) \cong B$, and $N_t = N_0B^t/(t+1)$.

Similar to the previous example, the fate of the population depends on the value of B: if $B \leq 1$, the population goes extinct; if $B > 1$, the size of the population increases indefinitely.

(A4) Let $p_f(0;x)$ be the log-normal distribution. Then $E_t[f] = \exp\{(\sigma^2/2)(2t+3) + m\} \sim \exp\{\sigma^2 t\}$ and $\Delta E_t[f] = \exp\{\sigma^2 t + 3/2\sigma^2 + m\}(1-\exp\{-\sigma^2\})$. The mean fitness increases exponentially with time. Next, $N_{t+1} = E_t[f]N_t = \exp\{(\sigma^2/2)(2t+3) + m\}N_t$, so

$$N_t = N_0 \exp\left\{\frac{1}{2}\sigma^2(t^2+2t) + mt\right\} \sim N_0 \exp\left\{\frac{1}{2}\sigma^2 t^2\right\}. \tag{3.2}$$

Example 3.2 (Ricker's model). The Ricker model is the map of the following form $N_{t+1} = N_t\lambda\exp(-\beta N_t)$, $\lambda, \beta > 0$ are parameters.

Consider the inhomogeneous version of this model with distributed parameter λ,

$$n_{t+1}(\mathbf{a}) = n_t(\mathbf{a})F(\mathbf{a}, N_t) = n_t(\mathbf{a})\lambda_0 f(\mathbf{a})\exp(-\beta N_t), \tag{3.3}$$

where λ_0 is the scaling multiplier. Let the initial pdf of $f(\mathbf{a})$, $p_f(0;x)$ be the Gamma-distribution with the parameters (s,k). Then, according to Theorem 1.1, $p_f(t;x)$ is the Gamma-distribution with parameters $(s, k+t)$, and $E_t[F] = \lambda_0(k+t)/s\exp(-\beta N_t)$. So,

$$N_{t+1} = \frac{N_t\lambda_0(k+t)}{s}\exp(-\beta N_t). \tag{3.4}$$

The coefficient $\lambda_0(k+t)/s$, which determines the dynamics of the Ricker model, increases indefinitely with time and hence after some time moment the population size begins to oscillate with increasing amplitude (according to the theory of the plain Ricker's model). If the parameter λ_0 is small and/or s is large, then the sequence $\{\lambda_0(k+t)/s,\ t = 0,1,\ldots\}$ takes the values close to all bifurcation values of the coefficient λ of the plain Ricker's model. A notable phenomenon thus follows: "almost complete" (with the step λ_0/s) sequence of all possible bifurcations of the Ricker model is realized in frameworks of unique inhomogeneous Ricker's model, see Figure 3.1. The trajectory $\{N_t\}_\infty^0$ in some sense mimics the bifurcation diagram of the plain Ricker's model. The model's evolution does go through different stages with the speed depending on λ_0/s.

We can observe the similar phenomenon for any initial distribution of the parameter with unbounded range of values of $f(\mathbf{a})$. For example, if $p_f(0;x)$ is the log-normal distribution, then corresponding version of inhomogeneous model reads $N_{t+1} = N_t\lambda_0\exp\{(\sigma^2/2)(2t+3) + m - \beta N_t\}$.

The model shows another behavior if the range of values of $f(\mathbf{a})$ is bounded. It is clear (see Corollary 2.2) that the final dynamics at $t \to \infty$ of models with any initial distribution and bounded range of values of $f(\mathbf{a})$ is determined by the maximal possible value of $f(\mathbf{a})$.

Let, for example, $p_f(0;x)$ be the uniform distribution in the interval $[0,1]$. Then

$$N_{t+1} = \frac{N_t\lambda_0(t+1)}{(t+2)}\exp(-\beta N_t). \tag{3.5}$$

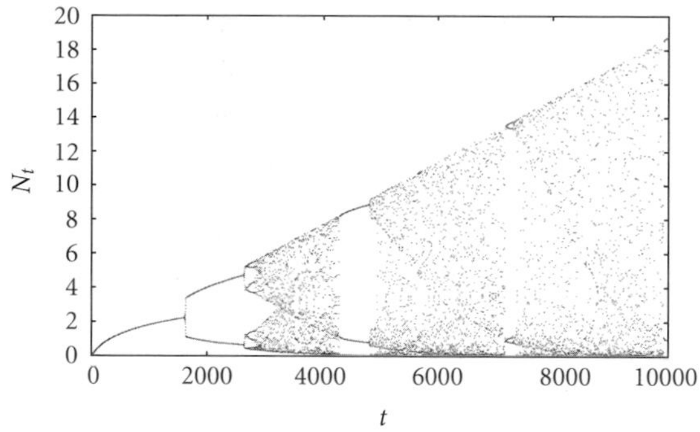

Figure 3.1. The trajectory of the inhomogeneous Ricker's model with Gamma-distributed parameter.

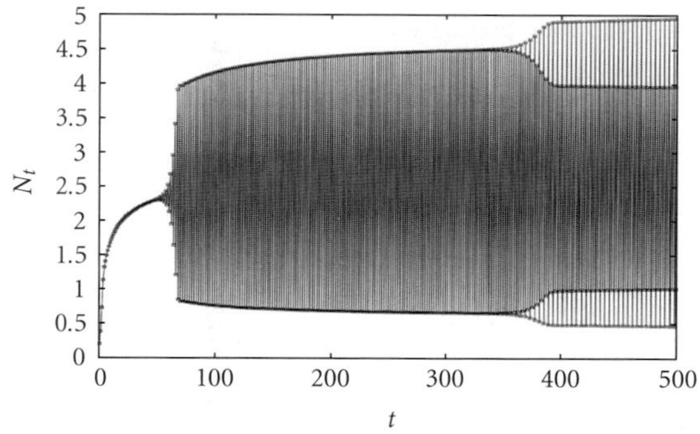

Figure 3.2. The trajectory of the inhomogeneous Ricker's model with Beta-distributed parameter, $\lambda_0 = 14$, $\alpha = 3$, $\beta = 20$. The final dynamics of the model is 4-cycle.

If $p_f(0;x)$ is the Beta-distribution in $[0,1]$ with the parameters (α,β), then, as it was shown above, $p_f(t;x)$ is again the Beta-distribution with parameters $(\alpha+t,\beta)$ and hence

$$N_{t+1} = \frac{N_t\lambda_0(t+\alpha)}{(t+\alpha+\beta)}\exp\left(-\beta N_t\right). \tag{3.6}$$

Choosing appropriate value of λ_0, we will observe as the final dynamics behavior any possible behavior of the model. Figure 3.2 illustrates this assertion.

Inhomogeneous versions of other well-known maps such as logistic, Skellam's model, and so forth can be explored the same way.

Example 3.3 (nonhomogeneous model of natural rotifer population). The mathematical model of zooplankton populations, extracted as deterministic dynamics components from noisy ecological time series and studied systematically in [1], is of the form

$$N_{t+1} = N_t\exp\left\{-a+\frac{1}{N_t}-\frac{\gamma}{N_t^2}\right\}. \tag{3.7}$$

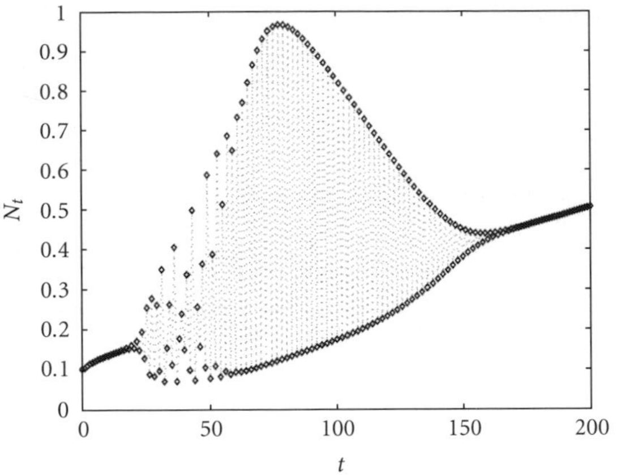

Figure 3.3. The behavior of total population size N_t in model (3.8) with $b = 0$ and $\gamma = 0.046$.

Here a is the parameter characterizing the environment quality, and γ is the species-specific parameter. Assuming that parameter a is distributed, we have the model in the form (1.2) with $f(a) = \exp\{-a\}$, and $g(N) = \exp\{1/N - \gamma/N^2\}$. Let us assume that the initial distribution of a is a Gamma-distribution with parameters b, k, s, $p_0(a) = (s^k/\Gamma(k))(a-b)^{k-1}\exp\{-(a-b)s\}$. Then $E_0[f^t] = \exp\{-bt\}s^k/(s+t)^k$; from Theorem 1.1, the dynamics of the total population size is governed by the recurrence equation

$$N_{t+1} = N_t \exp\{-b\}\left[\frac{s+t}{s+t+1}\right]^k \exp\left\{\frac{1}{N_t} - \frac{\gamma}{N_t^2}\right\}. \tag{3.8}$$

Possible dynamical behavior of the population is shown in Figure 3.3.

Figure 3.3 shows that the total size of the population on its way to a stable state can experience dramatically different behavior with time from apparently chaotic oscillations to oscillatory-like changes and then to smooth changes. The "moving in the opposite direction" from the smooth changes to chaotic oscillations is also possible dependent on the particular parameter distribution and the initial values of the parameter γ and the population size.

The main peculiarity of the inhomogeneous model (3.8) compared to the homogeneous one, (3.7), is that the complex transition behavior can exist. The inhomogeneous versions of model (3.7) are explored in detail in [4].

4. Discussion

We have shown that inhomogeneous maps possess some essential new dynamical behaviors comparing with their homogeneous counterparts. Nonhomogeneity of the population together with the natural selection lead to changing of the structure of population with time. As a result, typical trajectory of an inhomogeneous map mimics in some sense the bifurcation diagram of the corresponding homogeneous map.

It is well known that mathematical models constructed in the framework of nonlinear maps can describe some surprising phenomena in behavior of biological populations (see, e.g., [5]). Most models assume that individuals within a given population are identical; equivalently, these models operate with the mean value of the reproduction rate. We have shown that modeling of inhomogeneous population dynamics on the basis of only the mean value of the reproduction rate without taking into account its distribution or at least variance is likely to be substantially incorrect. Indeed, even the dynamics of simplest inhomogeneous maps of the Malthusian type with the same initial mean value of the Malthusian parameter can be very different depending on the initial distribution of the parameter (see Theorem 2.5 and Example 3.1).

The complex transition behaviors of inhomogeneous maps are the consequence of interplay of two independent factors: heterogeneity of the population and density-dependent regulatory mechanism. Let us emphasize that the evolution of the distribution of the parameter (i.e., the behavior of frequencies of different type individuals) is regular and completely described by Theorem 1.1. In many important cases (see Theorem 2.5) the distribution of parameters is of the same "type" as the initial one (i.e., Gamma- or Beta-distributions), but with changing in time parameters. Let us point out that all real populations are inhomogeneous.

References

[1] F. S. Berezovskaya, G. P. Karev, and T. W. Snell, *Modeling the dynamics of natural rotifer populations: phase-parametric analysis*, Journal of Ecological Complexity **2** (2005), no. 4, 395–409.

[2] G. P. Karev, *Dynamics of a non-uniform population*, International Conference EQUADIFF 99 (P. Maini, ed.), vol. 2, World Scientic, Berlin, 2000, pp. 1217–1220.

[3] ———, *Dynamics of heterogeneous populations and communities and evolution of distributions*, Discrete and Continuous Dynamical Systems. Series A (2005), no. suppl., 487–496.

[4] G. P. Karev, A. S. Novozhilov, and F. S. Berezovskaya, *Modeling the dynamics of inhomogeneous natural rotifer populations under toxicant exposure*, submitted to Journal of Ecological Modelling.

[5] R. M. May, *Biological populations obeying difference equations: stable points, stable cycles, and chaos*, Journal of Theoretical Biology **51** (1975), no. 2, 511–524.

Georgy P. Karev: National Center for Biotechnology Information, National Institutes of Health, Bethesda, MD 20894, USA
E-mail address: karev@ncbi.nlm.nih.gov

THE SEMILINEAR EVOLUTION EQUATION FOR UNIVERSAL CONTINGENT CLAIMS: EXAMPLES AND APPLICATIONS

VALERY A. KHOLODNYI

We present and further develop the concept of a universal contingent claim introduced by the author in 1995. This concept provides a unified framework for the analysis of a wide class of financial derivatives. Those, for example, include Bermudan and American contingent claims. We also show that the value of a universal contingent claim is determined, generally speaking, by an impulsive semilinear evolution equation also introduced by the author in 1995.

1. Introduction

We present and further develop the concept of a universal contingent claim introduced by the author in [4, 5, 8, 9]. This concept provides a unified framework for the analysis of a wide class of financial derivatives in a general market environment. Those, for example, include Bermudan and American contingent claims. We also show that the value of a universal contingent claim is determined, generally speaking, by an impulsive semilinear evolution equation introduced by the author in [4–6, 8, 9].

2. Market environment

In this section we present the framework of a market environment in which contingent claims are being priced that was introduced by the author in [4, 5, 8]. For the sake of financial clarity, but without loss of generality, we only consider the case of a single underlying security throughout the article. Consider an economy without transaction costs in which trading is allowed at any time in a *trading time set* $\mathcal{T}$, an arbitrary subset of the real numbers $\mathbb{R}$. Denote by $s_t > 0$ the unit price of the (only) underlying security at time t in $\mathcal{T}$. Whenever ambiguity is unlikely, we will write s in place of s_t. Denote by Π the vector space of all real-valued functions on the set of positive real numbers $\mathbb{R}_{++}$. Equipped with the partial order generated by the nonnegative cone Π_+ consisting of all nonnegative real-valued functions on $\mathbb{R}_{++}$, Π is a partially ordered vector space. Moreover, equipped with

Hindawi Publishing Corporation
Proceedings of the Conference on Differential & Difference Equations and Applications, pp. 519–528

the lattice operations of supremum $\vee$ and infimum $\wedge$ defined as pointwise maximum and minimum, Π is a vector lattice.

Definition 2.1. A *European contingent claim* with inception time t, expiration time T (t and T in $\mathcal{T}$ with $t \leq T$), and payoff g in Π is a contract that gives the right, but not the obligation, to receive the payoff $g^+(s_T)$ and the obligation to deliver the payoff $g^-(s_T)$ at the expiration time T, where g^+ and g^- in Π_+ are the nonnegative and nonpositive parts of g in Π defined by $g^+ = g \vee 0$ and $-g^- = g \wedge 0$, so that $g = g^+ - g^-$. A European contingent claim with payoff g in Π_+ is called a *European option.*

For each t and T in $\mathcal{T}$ with $t \leq T$, denote by $\mathbf{V}(t,T)$ the operator that maps the payoff g of a European contingent claim with inception time t and expiration time T to its value $\mathfrak{E}(t,T,g) = \mathfrak{E}(t,T,g)(s_t)$ at inception time t as a function in Π of the price s_t of the underlying security at this time t:

$$\mathfrak{E}(t,T,g) = \mathbf{V}(t,T)g. \tag{2.1}$$

Definition 2.2. For each t and T in $\mathcal{T}$ with $t \leq T$, the operator $\mathbf{V}(t,T)$ on Π is called [4, 5, 8] a *valuation* or *evolution operator.*

It can be shown [4, 5, 8] that, by the no-arbitrage argument, $\mathbf{V}(t,T)$ is a linear operator on Π that preserves the nonnegative cone Π_+ in Π, that is, $\mathbf{V}(t,T)$ is a nonnegative linear operator on Π. Moreover, $\mathbf{V}(t,T)$ is the identity operator on Π whenever $t = T$.

Definition 2.3. A *market environment* [4, 5, 8] is the family of evolution operators $\mathbf{V} = \{\mathbf{V}(t,T) : \Pi \to \Pi \mid t,T \in \mathcal{T},\ t \leq T\}$ such that the following *intervention* or *intertemporal no-arbitrage* condition holds $\mathbf{V}(t,T) = \mathbf{V}(t,\tau)\mathbf{V}(\tau,T)$ for each t, τ and T in $\mathcal{T}$ with $t \leq \tau \leq T$.

A market environment $\mathbf{V}$ such that its trading time set $\mathcal{T}$ is an interval, either finite or infinite, of nonnegative real numbers and its evolution operators $\mathbf{V}(t,T)$ are sufficiently smooth functions of time, admits the following characterization introduced by the author in [4, 5, 8].

Definition 2.4. The one-parameter family of linear operators $\boldsymbol{L} = \{\boldsymbol{L}(t) : \Pi \to \Pi \mid t \in \mathcal{T}\}$ is said [4, 5, 8] to *generate* a market environment $\mathbf{V}$ if for each t and T in the trading time set $\mathcal{T}$ with $t \leq T$ and for each admissible payoff v_T in Π the function $\mathbf{V}(t,T)v_T$ of t is a solution, possibly generalized, of the Cauchy problem for the evolution equation:

$$\begin{gathered} \frac{d}{dt}v + \boldsymbol{L}(t)v = 0, \quad t < T, \\ v(T) = v_T. \end{gathered} \tag{2.2}$$

An operator $\boldsymbol{L}(t)$ in the family $\boldsymbol{L}$ is called a *generator at time* t, or simply a *generator.*

It is clear that according to the definition of the evolution operator $\mathbf{V}(t,T)$ in (2.1), the Cauchy problem in (2.2) determines the value of a European contingent claim with inception time t, expiration time T, and payoff v_T.

Following [4, 5, 8] we present an example of one of the major market environments, the Black-Scholes market environment, that corresponds to the Black-Scholes model.

Definition 2.5. A market environment $\mathbf{V}^{BS} = \{\mathbf{V}^{BS}(t,T) : \Pi \to \Pi \mid t,T \in \mathcal{T},\ t \le T\}$ generated by the family $\boldsymbol{L}^{BS} = \{\boldsymbol{L}^{BS}(t) : \Pi \to \Pi \mid t \in \mathcal{T}\}$ with the generator $\boldsymbol{L}^{BS}(t)$ at time t defined by

$$\boldsymbol{L}^{BS}(t) = \frac{1}{2}\sigma^2(s,t)s^2\frac{\partial^2}{\partial s^2} + (r(s,t) - d(s,t))s\frac{\partial}{\partial s} - r(s,t) \tag{2.3}$$

is called a *Black-Scholes* market environment, where $\sigma(s,t)$ is the volatility, $r(s,t)$ is the continuously compounded interest rate, and $d(s,t)$ is the continuously compounded dividend yield in terms of the underlying security being a stock.

Further in the article we will need the values of European call and put options, European cash-or-nothing call and put options, and European asset-or-nothing call and put options in the special case of the Black-Scholes market environment with $\sigma(s,t)$, $r(s,t)$, and $d(s,t)$ being independent of the price s of the underlying security. (For the derivation of these values and related financial terminology see, e.g., [1, 10].)

The values $C^{BS}_{\sigma,d,r}(t,T,s_t,X)$ and $P^{BS}_{\sigma,d,r}(t,T,s_t,X)$ of the European call and put options with inception time t, expiration time T, and strike price X are given by the Black-Scholes formulas:

$$\begin{aligned} C^{BS}_{\sigma,d,r}(t,T,s_t,X) &= s_te^{-d(T-t)}N(d_+) - Xe^{-r(T-t)}N(d_-),\\ P^{BS}_{\sigma,d,r}(t,T,s_t,X) &= Xe^{-r(T-t)}N(-d_-) - s_te^{-d(T-t)}N(-d_+), \end{aligned} \tag{2.4}$$

where

$$\begin{aligned} d_\pm &= \frac{\ln(s_t/X) + (r - d \pm (1/2)\sigma^2)(T-t)}{\sigma\sqrt{T-t}}, \qquad N(x) = \frac{1}{\sqrt{2\pi}}\int_{-\infty}^{x} e^{-y^2/2}dy,\\ \sigma^2 &= \frac{1}{T-t}\int_t^T \sigma^2(\tau)d\tau, \qquad r = \frac{1}{T-t}\int_t^T r(\tau)d\tau, \qquad d = \frac{1}{T-t}\int_t^T d(\tau)d\tau. \end{aligned} \tag{2.5}$$

The values $\mathrm{CONC}^{BS}_{\sigma,d,r}(t,T,s_t,X)$ and $\mathrm{CONP}^{BS}_{\sigma,d,r}(t,T,s_t,X)$ of the European cash-or-nothing call and put options with inception time t, expiration time T, and strike price X are given by

$$\begin{aligned} \mathrm{CONC}^{BS}_{\sigma,d,r}(t,T,s_t,X) &= e^{-r(T-t)}N(d_-),\\ \mathrm{CONP}^{BS}_{\sigma,d,r}(t,T,s_t,X) &= e^{-r(T-t)}N(-d_-). \end{aligned} \tag{2.6}$$

Finally, the values $\mathrm{AONC}^{BS}_{\sigma,d,r}(t,T,s_t,X)$ and $\mathrm{AONP}^{BS}_{\sigma,d,r}(t,T,s_t,X)$ of the European asset-or-nothing call and put options with inception time t, expiration time T, and strike price X are given by

$$\begin{aligned}\text{AONC}^{BS}_{\sigma,d,r}(t,T,s_t,X) &= s_t e^{-d(T-t)} N(d_+),\\ \text{AONP}^{BS}_{\sigma,d,r}(t,T,s_t,X) &= s_t e^{-d(T-t)} N(-d_+).\end{aligned} \tag{2.7}$$

3. Bermudan and American contingent claims

In order to motivate the introduction of the concept of a universal claim, we first consider the following practically important examples of Bermudan and American contingent claims.

Assume that for t and T in the trading time set $\mathcal{T}$ with $t \leq T$, the *exercise time set* $E = \{t_i : i = 0,1,\ldots,n\}$ with $t \leq t_0 < t_1 \cdots < t_{n-1} < t_n = T$ is contained in $\mathcal{T}$.

Definition 3.1. A *Bermudan contingent claim* [4, 5, 8] with inception time t, expiration time T, exercise time set E, and (time-dependent) payoff $g : E \to \Pi$ is a contract that gives the right, but not the obligation, to receive the payoff $g_\tau(s_\tau)$ at any time τ in the exercise time set E except for the expiration time T, and the right, but not the obligation, to receive the payoff $g_T^+(s_T)$ and the obligation to deliver the payoff $g_T^-(s_T)$ at the expiration time T. A Bermudan contingent claim with payoff $g : E \to \Pi_+$ is called a *Bermudan option*.

For a Bermudan contingent claim with inception time t, expiration time T, exercise time set E, and payoff g, denote by $\mathfrak{B}(t,T,E,g) = \mathfrak{B}(t,T,E,g)(s_t)$, its value at the inception time t as a function in Π of the price s_t of the underlying security at this time t. It can be shown [8] that in a market environment $\mathbf{V}$ the value $\mathfrak{B}(t,T,E,g)$ of a Bermudan contingent claim is given by

$$\mathfrak{B}(t,T,E,g) = \mathbf{V}(t,t_0)\mathbf{M}_{g_{t_0}}\mathbf{V}(t_0,t_1)\mathbf{M}_{g_{t_1}}\mathbf{V}(t_1,t_2)\cdots\mathbf{M}_{g_{t_{n-1}}}\mathbf{V}(t_{n-1},T)g_T, \tag{3.1}$$

where the nonlinear operator $\mathbf{M}_h : \Pi \to \Pi$, h in Π, is given by $\mathbf{M}_h f = h \vee f$.

Now assume that for t and T in the trading time set $\mathcal{T}$ with $t \leq T$, the interval $[t,T]$ is contained in $\mathcal{T}$.

Definition 3.2. An *American contingent claim* [4, 5, 8] with inception time t, expiration time T, and (time-dependent) payoff $g : [t,T] \to \Pi$ is a contract that gives the right, but not the obligation, to receive the payoff $g_\tau(s_\tau)$ at any time τ in $[t,T]$ except for the expiration time T, and the right, but not the obligation, to receive the payoff $g_T^+(s_T)$ and the obligation to deliver the payoff $g_T^-(s_T)$ at the expiration time T. An American contingent claim with payoff $g : [t,T] \to \Pi_+$ is called an *American option*.

For an American contingent claim with inception time t, expiration time T, and payoff g, denote by $\mathfrak{A}(t,T,g) = \mathfrak{A}(t,T,g)(s_t)$ its value at the inception time t as a function of the price s_t of the underlying security at this time t. Let the exercise time set $E = \{t_i : i = 0,1,\ldots,n\}$ be a net of the interval $[t,T]$, that is, let $t = t_0 < t_1 \cdots < t_{n-1} < t_n = T$. Then it can be shown [8] that in a market environment $\mathbf{V}$ the value $\mathfrak{A}(t,T,g)$ of the American contingent claim can be viewed as a limit of the values $\mathfrak{B}(t,T,E,g|_E)$ of the Bermudan contingent claims when the norm $\|E\| = \max\{t_i - t_{i-1} : i = 1,\dots,n\}$ of E as a net tends to zero, where $g|_E : E \to \Pi$ is the restriction of $g : [t,T] \to \Pi$ to the exercise time set E.

4. Universal contingent claims

We present the definition of a universal contingent claim introduced by the author in [4, 5, 8, 9] and show that the value of a universal contingent claim is determined, generally speaking, by an impulsive semilinear evolution equation introduced by the author in [4–6, 8, 9].

Assume that for t and T in the trading time set $\mathcal{T}$ with $t \le T$, the *activation time set* $J = \{t_i : i = 0,1,\dots,n\}$ with $t \le t_0 < t_1 \cdots < t_{n-1} < t_n < T$ is contained in $\mathcal{T}$. Let $\mathbf{O} = \mathbf{O}(\Pi)$ be the set of all, not necessarily linear, operators on Π.

Definition 4.1. A *discretely activated universal contingent claim* [8, 9] with inception time t, expiration time T, activation operator $\boldsymbol{A} : J \to \mathbf{O}$, and payoff p in Π is a contract whose value $\mathcal{U}(t,T,\boldsymbol{A},p)$ in Π for a market environment $\mathbf{V}$ is given by

$$\mathcal{U}(t,T,\boldsymbol{A},p) = \mathbf{V}(t,t_0)\boldsymbol{A}(t_0)\mathbf{V}(t_0,t_1)\boldsymbol{A}(t_1)\mathbf{V}(t_1,t_2)\cdots\boldsymbol{A}(t_n)\mathbf{V}(t_n,T)p. \tag{4.1}$$

Assume that for t and T in the trading time set $\mathcal{T}$ with $t \le T$, the interval $[t,T]$ is contained in $\mathcal{T}$. Let $\mathfrak{n} = \{t_i : i = 0,1,\dots,n\}$ with $t = t_0 < t_1 < \cdots < t_{n-1} < t_n = T$ be a net of the interval $[t,T]$ with the norm $\|\mathfrak{n}\| = \max\{t_i - t_{i-1} : i = 1,\dots,n\}$. Denote by $J_\mathfrak{n}$ the activation time set defined by $J_\mathfrak{n} = \mathfrak{n} \setminus T$.

Definition 4.2. A *continously activated universal contingent claim* [8, 9] with inception time t, expiration time T, activation operator $\boldsymbol{A} : [t,T) \to \mathbf{O}$, and payoff p in Π is a contract whose value $\mathcal{U}(t,T,\boldsymbol{A},p)$ in Π for a market environment $\mathbf{V}$ is given by

$$\mathcal{U}(t,T,\boldsymbol{A},p) = \lim_{\|\mathfrak{n}\|\to 0} \mathcal{U}(t,T,\boldsymbol{A}|_{J_\mathfrak{n}},p), \tag{4.2}$$

where $\mathcal{U}(t,T,\boldsymbol{A}|_{J_\mathfrak{n}},p)$ is the value of the discretely activated universal contingent claim with inception time t, expiration time T, activation operator $\boldsymbol{A}|_{J_\mathfrak{n}}$, and payoff p with $\boldsymbol{A}|_{J_\mathfrak{n}}$ being the restriction of $\boldsymbol{A} : [t,T) \to \mathbf{O}$ to the activation time set $J_\mathfrak{n}$.

We comment that Bermudan and American contingent claims presented earlier in the article are examples of a discretely and continously activated universal contingent claim.

It can be shown [4–6, 8, 9] that in a market environment $\mathbf{V}$ generated by the family of linear operators $\boldsymbol{L}$, the value $\mathcal{U}(t,T,\boldsymbol{A},p)$ of a universal contingent claim is a solution, possibly generalized, of the Cauchy problem for the following semilinear evolution equation:

$$\begin{aligned} \frac{d}{dt}v + \boldsymbol{L}(t)v + \boldsymbol{F}(t,v) = 0, \quad t < T, \\ v(T) = p, \end{aligned} \tag{4.3}$$

where the nonlinear term $\boldsymbol{F}(t,v)$ is the Lie derivative

$$\boldsymbol{F}(t,v) = -\mathbf{F}_t(t,v) + \mathbf{F}_v(t,v)(\boldsymbol{L}(t)v), \tag{4.4}$$

of the *payoff operator* $\mathbf{F} : [t,T) \to \mathbf{O}$ defined by

$$\boldsymbol{A}(\tau) = \mathbf{I} + \mathbf{F}(\tau), \quad \tau \in [t,T), \tag{4.5}$$

with $\mathbf{I}$ being the identity operator on Π, and where the subscripts denote suitably interpreted partial derivatives. We note that in the case of a discretely activated universal contingent claim the equation in (4.3) is an impulsive semilinear evolution equation.

It can be shown [4–6, 8, 9] that the semilinear evolution equation for an American contingent claim with inception time t, expiration time T, and payoff g introduced by the author in [2–5, 8] is a special case of the preceeding semilinear evolution equation in (4.3) with $v(T) = g_T$ and the nonlinear term $\boldsymbol{F}(t,v)$ in (4.4) of the form

$$\boldsymbol{F}(t,v)(s) = \left(-\left(\frac{\partial}{\partial t}g_t + \boldsymbol{L}(t)v\right)\right)^+(s)H(g_t(s) - v(s)), \tag{4.6}$$

where g_t is the value in Π at time t of the payoff $g : [t,T] \to \Pi$, and $H(x)$ is the Heaviside function, that is, $H(x) = 1$ for $x \geq 0$ and $H(x) = 0$ for $x < 0$. In the Black-Scholes market environment, since the generators $\boldsymbol{L}^{BS}(t)$ in (2.3) are local operators, the nonlinear term in (4.6) in the semilinear evolution equation for American contingent claims takes the following form [2–5, 8]:

$$\boldsymbol{F}(t,v)(s) = \left(-\left(\frac{\partial}{\partial t}g_t + \boldsymbol{L}^{BS}(t)g_t\right)\right)^+(s)H(g_t(s) - v(s)). \tag{4.7}$$

For example, in the special case of American call and put options with inception time t, expiration time T, and strike price X, the nonlinear term in (4.7) is of the form [2–5, 8]:

$$\begin{aligned} \boldsymbol{F}_{\text{call}}(t,v)(s) &= (d(s,t)s - r(s,t)X)^+ H((s-X)^+ - v(s)), \\ \boldsymbol{F}_{\text{put}}(t,v)(s) &= (r(s,t)X - d(s,t)s)^+ H((X-s)^+ - v(s)), \end{aligned} \tag{4.8}$$

with $v_{\text{call}}(T,s_T) = (s_T - X)^+$ and $v_{\text{put}}(T,s_T) = (X - s_T)^+$, where $x^+ = \max\{x,0\}$. The nonlinear terms in (4.8) can also be represented [2–5, 8] in terms of the optimal exercise boundaries $s_c(t)$ and $s_p(t)$ for American call and put options as follows:

$$\begin{aligned} \boldsymbol{F}_{\text{call}}(t,v)(s) &= (d(s,t)s - r(s,t)X)^+ H(s - s_c(t)), \\ \boldsymbol{F}_{\text{put}}(t,v)(s) &= (r(s,t)X - d(s,t)s)^+ H(s_p(t) - s). \end{aligned} \tag{4.9}$$

We comment that the nonlinear term $F(t,v)$ in the semilinear evolution equation in (4.3) can be financially interpreted [2–6, 8, 9] as a cash flow that should be paid or received during the life of a universal contingent claim. For example, the nonlinear term $F(t,v)$ of the form (4.6) in the semilinear evolution equation in (4.3) in the special case of American contingent claims can be financially interpreted [2–5, 8] as a cash flow that should be received to compensate for the losses due to holding an American contingent claim unexercised in the exercise region.

We also comment that the semilinear evolution equation for universal contingent claims in (4.3) can be represented [4–6, 8, 9] as the following integral equation:

$$v(t) = \mathbf{V}(t,T)p + \int_t^T \mathbf{V}(t,\tau)\boldsymbol{F}(\tau,v(\tau))\,d\tau, \quad t \le T. \tag{4.10}$$

In view of the relationship in (2.1) the proceeding integral equation in (4.10) can be financially interpreted [4–6, 8, 9] as a representation of the value $\mathcal{U}(t,T,\mathbf{A},p)$ of a universal contingent claim with inception time t, expiration time T, activation operator $\mathbf{A}$, and payoff p as the sum of two summands. The first summand is the value $\mathbf{V}(t,T)p$ of the European contingent claim with inception time t, expiration time T, and payoff p, and the second summand is value $\int_t^T \mathbf{V}(t,\tau)\boldsymbol{F}(\tau,v(\tau))d\tau$ at time t of the cash flow $\boldsymbol{F}(\tau,v(\tau))$ with $t \le \tau \le T$. Moreover, in view of the proceeding integral equation in (4.10), a universal contingent claim with the value $\mathcal{U}(t,T,\mathbf{A},p)$ can be financially interpreted as a portfolio that consists of long positions on the European contingent claim with the value $\mathbf{V}(t,T)p$ and the continuous strip of European contingent claims with values $\mathbf{V}(t,\tau)\boldsymbol{F}(\tau,v(\tau))$, $t \le \tau \le T$. This allows for the static replication in a general market environment of universal contingent claims by portfolios of European contingent claims. This also allows for the dynamic replication in a general market environment of universal contingent claims viewed as portfolios of European contingent claims, provided that these European contingent claims can be dynamically replicated.

For example, the proceeding integral equation in (4.10) with $\boldsymbol{F}(t,v)$ of the form (4.6), that is, in the special case of American contingent claims, can be financially interpreted [4, 5, 8] as the *early exercise premium representation* of the value $\mathfrak{A}(t,T,g)$ of an American contingent claim with inception time t, expiration time T, and payoff g as the sum of two summands. The first summand is the value $\mathbf{V}(t,T)g_T$ of the European contingent claim with inception time t, expiration time T, and payoff g_T, and the second summand is the *early exercise premium* $\int_t^T \mathbf{V}(t,\tau)\boldsymbol{F}(\tau,v(\tau))d\tau$. Moreover, in view of the proceeding integral equation in (4.10) with $\boldsymbol{F}(t,v)$ of the form (4.6), an American contingent claim with the value $\mathfrak{A}(t,T,g)$ can be financially interpreted [4, 5, 8] as a portfolio that consists of long positions on the European contingent claim with the value $\mathbf{V}(t,T)g_T$ and the continuous strip of European contingent claims with values $\mathbf{V}(t,\tau)\boldsymbol{F}(\tau,v(\tau))$, $t \le \tau \le T$. This allows [4, 5, 8] for the static replication in a general market environment of American contingent claims by portfolio of European contingent claims. This also allows [4, 5, 8] for the dynamic replication in a general market environment of American contingent claims viewed as portfolios of European contingent claims, provided that these European contingent claims can be dynamically replicated. For example, in the special case of American call and put options in the Black-Scholes market environment with price-independent

$\sigma(s,t)$, $r(s,t)$, and $d(s,t)$, the proceeding integral equation in (4.10) with $\boldsymbol{F}(t,v)$ of the form (4.8) and hence (4.9) can be represented [4, 5, 8] with the help of (2.4)–(2.7) as

$$\begin{aligned}
&\mathscr{C}^{BS}_{\sigma,d,r}(t,T,s_t,X)\\
&\quad = C^{BS}_{\sigma,d,r}(t,T,s_t,X)\\
&\qquad + \int_t^T \Big(d(\tau)\,\mathrm{AONC}^{BS}_{\sigma,d,r}(t,\tau,s_t,s_c(\tau)) - r(\tau)X\,\mathrm{CONC}^{BS}_{\sigma,d,r}(t,\tau,s_t,s_c(\tau))\Big)d\tau,\\
&\mathscr{P}^{BS}_{\sigma,d,r}(t,T,s_t,X)\\
&\quad = P^{BS}_{\sigma,d,r}(t,T,s_t,X)\\
&\qquad + \int_t^T \Big(r(\tau)X\,\mathrm{CONP}^{BS}_{\sigma,d,r}(t,\tau,s_t,s_p(\tau)) - d(\tau)\,\mathrm{AONP}^{BS}_{\sigma,d,r}(t,\tau,s_t,s_p(\tau))\Big)d\tau,
\end{aligned} \tag{4.11}$$

where $\mathscr{C}^{BS}_{\sigma,d,r}(t,T,s_t,X)$ and $\mathscr{P}^{BS}_{\sigma,d,r}(t,T,s_t,X)$ are the values of the American call and put options with inception time t, expiration time T, and strike price X. Therefore, in view of (4.11), the American call (put) option with the value $\mathscr{C}^{BS}_{\sigma,d,r}(t,T,s_t,X)$ ($\mathscr{P}^{BS}_{\sigma,d,r}(t,T,s_t,X)$) can be financially interpreted [4, 5, 8] as a portfolio of a long position on the European call (put) option with the value $C^{BS}_{\sigma,d,r}(t,T,s_t,X)$ ($P^{BS}_{\sigma,d,r}(t,T,s_t,X)$), a long position on the continuous strip of $d(\tau)$ units of the European asset-or-nothing call options with the value $\mathrm{AONC}^{BS}_{\sigma,d,r}(t,\tau,s_t,s_c(\tau))$ ($r(\tau)X$ units of the European cash-or-nothing put options with the value $\mathrm{CONP}^{BS}_{\sigma,d,r}(t,\tau,s_t,s_p(\tau))$), and a short position on the continuous strip of $r(\tau)X$ units of the European cash-or-nothing call options with the value $\mathrm{CONC}^{BS}_{\sigma,d,r}(t,\tau,s_t,s_c(\tau))$ ($d(\tau)$ units of the European asset-or-nothing put options with the value $\mathrm{AONP}^{BS}_{\sigma,d,r}(t,\tau,s_t,s_p(\tau))$), $t \le \tau \le T$. We comment that an American call (put) option can also be financially interpreted [4, 5, 8] as a portfolio of long positions on the European call (put) option and a continuous strip of European gap call (put) options.

We note [4–9] that, in general, the successive approximations

$$v_{n+1}(t) = \mathbf{V}(t,T)p + \int_t^T \mathbf{V}(t,\tau)\boldsymbol{F}(\tau,v_n(\tau))\,d\tau, \quad n = 0,1,2\ldots, \tag{4.12}$$

do not converge to the exact solution $v(t)$ of the integral equation in (4.10). However, for a suitable initial approximation $v_0(t)$ such as the value $\mathbf{V}(t,T)p$ of the European contingent claim with inception time t, expiration time T and payoff p the successive approximations in (4.12) can provide us [4–9] with relatively simple approximations as well as lower and upper bounds for the exact solution $v(t)$ of the integral equation in (4.10).

For example [4–9], in the special case of American call and put options in the Black-Scholes market environment with price-independent $\sigma(s,t)$, $r(s,t)$, and $d(s,t)$, if the initial approximations $c_0(t) = c_0(t,s_t)$ and $p_0(t) = p_0(t,s_t)$ are chosen as admissible subsolutions (supersolutions) of the integral equation in (4.10) with $\boldsymbol{F}(\tau,v)$ of the form (4.8), then the successive approximations $c_n(t) = c_n(t,s_t)$ and $p_n(t) = p_n(t,s_t)$ are subsolutions (supersolutions) for even n and supersolutions (subsolutions) for odd n. Moreover, the corresponding approximations $s_c^{(n)}(t)$ and $s_p^{(n)}(t)$ for the optimal exercise boundaries $s_c(t)$

and $s_p(t)$ obtained as solutions of the following equations:

$$c_n\left(t, s_c^{(n)}(t)\right) = \left(s_c^{(n)}(t) - X\right)^+, \qquad p_n\left(t, s_p^{(n)}(t)\right) = \left(X - s_p^{(n)}(t)\right)^+, \tag{4.13}$$

are such that $s_c^{(n)}(t) \leq s_c(t)$ and $s_p^{(n)}(t) \geq s_p(t)$ ($s_c^{(n)}(t) \geq s_c(t)$ and $s_p^{(n)}(t) \leq s_p(t)$) for even n, and $s_c^{(n)}(t) \geq s_c(t)$ and $s_p^{(n)}(t) \leq s_p(t)$ ($s_c^{(n)}(t) \leq s_c(t)$ and $s_p^{(n)}(t) \geq s_p(t)$) for odd n.

We note [4–9] that, given approximations $s_c^{(n)}(t)$ and $s_p^{(n)}(t)$ for the optimal exercise boundaries, we can find approximations $c_{n+1}(t)$ and $p_{n+1}(t)$ for the values of the American call and put options by replacing $s_c(t)$ and $s_p(t)$ with $\max\{s_c^{(n)}(t), r(t)/d(t)X, X\}$ and $\min\{s_p^{(n)}(t), r(t)/d(t)X, X\}$ in the right-hand sides of relationships (4.11), and find $s_c^{(n+1)}(t)$ and $s_p^{(n+1)}(t)$ by solving (4.13), and so on. In this way, we can directly start with suitable initial approximations $s_c^{(0)}(t)$ and $s_p^{(0)}(t)$ for the optimal exercise boundaries to obtain the approximations $c_n(t)$, $p_n(t)$ and $s_c^{(n)}(t)$, $s_p^{(n)}(t)$ for $n > 0$. For example, if the initial approximations $s_c^{(0)}(t)$ and $s_p^{(0)}(t)$ are such that $s_c^{(0)}(t) \leq s_c(t)$ and $s_p^{(0)}(t) \geq s_p(t)$ ($s_c^{(0)}(t) \geq s_c(t)$ and $s_p^{(0)}(t) \leq s_p(t)$), then the successive approximations $c_n(t)$ and $p_n(t)$ are subsolutions (supersolutions) for even n and supersolutions (subsolutions) for odd n. Moreover, the approximations $s_c^{(n)}(t)$ and $s_p^{(n)}(t)$ are such that $s_c^{(n)}(t) \leq s_c(t)$ and $s_p^{(n)}(t) \geq s_p(t)$ ($s_c^{(n)}(t) \geq s_c(t)$ and $s_p^{(n)}(t) \leq s_p(t)$) for even n, and $s_c^{(n)}(t) \geq s_c(t)$ and $s_p^{(n)}(t) \leq s_p(t)$ ($s_c^{(n)}(t) \leq s_c(t)$ and $s_p^{(n)}(t) \geq s_p(t)$) for odd n.

Finally, we note [4–9] that, in general, the successive approximations

$$s_c^{(n,l+1)}(t) = X + c_n\left(t, s_c^{(n,l)}(t)\right), \qquad s_p^{(n,l+1)}(t) = X - p_n\left(t, s_p^{(n,l)}(t)\right), \tag{4.14}$$

with $l = 0, 1, 2\ldots$, do not converge to the exact solutions $s_c^{(n)}(t)$ and $s_p^{(n)}(t)$ of the equations in (4.13). However, for suitable $c_n(t)$ and $p_n(t)$ and suitable initial approximations $s_c^{(n,0)}(t)$ and $s_p^{(n,0)}(t)$ such as $s_c^{(n-1)}(t)$ and $s_p^{(n-1)}(t)$ for $n > 0$ and X for $n = 0$, the successive approximations in (4.14) can provide us [4–9] with relatively simple approximations as well as lower and upper bounds for the exact solutions $s_c^{(n)}(t)$ and $s_p^{(n)}(t)$ of the equations in (4.13). For example, it can be shown [4–9] that for $c_0(t) = c_0(t, s_t)$ and $p_0(t) = p_0(t, s_t)$ chosen as subsolutions $C^{BS}_{\sigma,d,r}(t, T, s_t, X)$ and $P^{BS}_{\sigma,d,r}(t, T, s_t, X)$, the values of the European call and put options, the successive approximations $s_c^{(0,l)}(t)$ and $s_p^{(0,l)}(t)$ in (4.14) with the initial approximations $s_c^{(0,0)}(t) = X$ and $s_p^{(0,0)}(t) = X$ converge to the exact solutions $s_c^{(0)}(t)$ and $s_p^{(0)}(t)$ of the equations in (4.13) for $n = 0$. Moreover, $s_c^{(0,1)}(t)$ and $s_p^{(0,1)}(t)$ are explicitely given by

$$s_c^{(0,1)}(t) = X + C^{BS}_{\sigma,d,r}(t, T, X, X), \qquad s_p^{(0,1)}(t) = X - P^{BS}_{\sigma,d,r}(t, T, X, X), \tag{4.15}$$

and $s_c^{(0,1)}(t) \leq s_c(t)$ and $s_p^{(0,1)}(t) \geq s_p(t)$.

Acknowledgment

I thank my wife Larisa and my sons Nikita and Ilya for their love, patience, and care.

References

[1] E. G. Haug, *The Complete Guide to Option Pricing Formulas*, McGraw-Hill, New York, 1997.
[2] V. A. Kholodnyi, *A nonlinear partial differential equation for American options in the entire domain of the state variable*, Nonlinear Analysis **30** (1997), no. 8, 5059–5070.
[3] ______, *A semilinear evolution equation for general derivative contracts*, Derivatives and Financial Mathematics (J. F. Price, ed.), Nova Science, New York, 1997, pp. 119–138.
[4] ______, *A nonlinear partial differential equation for American options in the entire domain of the state variable*, IES preprint, 1995.
[5] ______, *A semilinear evolution equation for general derivative contracts*, IES preprint, 1995.
[6] ______, *A semilinear evolution equation for universal contingent claims*, IES preprint, 1995.
[7] ______, *Approximations and bounds for the values of American options based on the semilinear evolution equation*, IES preprint, 1995.
[8] ______, *On the linearity of European, Bermudan and American options with general time-dependent payoffs in partial semimodules*, IES preprint, 1995.
[9] ______, *Universal contingent claims*, IES preprint, 1995.
[10] P. Wilmott, *Derivatives*, John Wiley & Sons, New York, 1998.

Valery A. Kholodnyi: Department of Mathematical Sciences, Middle Tennessee State University, Murfreesboro, Tennessee 37132, USA
E-mail address: kholodnyi@mtsu.edu

ON NONLINEAR BOUNDARY VALUE PROBLEMS FOR HIGHER-ORDER ORDINARY DIFFERENTIAL EQUATIONS

I. KIGURADZE

Sufficient conditions are established for the solvability and unique solvability of nonlinear boundary value problems of the type $u^{(n)} = f(t,u,\dots,u^{(n-1)})$, $\sum_{k=1}^{n}(\alpha_{ik}(u)u^{(k-1)}(a)+\beta_{ik}(u)u^{(k-1)}(b)) = \gamma_i(u)$ $(i = 1,\dots,n)$, where $f : [a,b]\times\mathbb{R}^n \to \mathbb{R}$ is a function from the Carathéodory class, and $\alpha_{ik},\beta_{ik} : \mathbb{C}^{n-1} \to \mathbb{R}$ $(i,k = 1,\dots,n)$ are nonlinear continuous functionals.

1. Statement of the problem and formulation of the main results

We investigate the nonlinear differential equation

$$u^{(n)} = f(t,u,\dots,u^{(n-1)}) \tag{1.1}$$

with the nonlinear boundary conditions

$$\sum_{k=1}^{n}(\alpha_{ik}(u)u^{(k-1)}(a)+\beta_{ik}(u)u^{(k-1)}(b)) = \gamma_i(u) \quad (i = 1,\dots,n). \tag{1.2}$$

Throughout the paper, we assume that $-\infty < a < b < +\infty$, $\mathbb{C}^{n-1}$ is the space of $n-1$ times continuously differentiable functions $u : [a,b] \to \mathbb{R}$ with the norm

$$\|u\|_{\mathbb{C}^{n-1}} = \max\left\{\sum_{k=1}^{n}|u^{(k-1)}(t)| : a \le t \le b\right\}, \tag{1.3}$$

$f : [a,b]\times\mathbb{R}^n \to \mathbb{R}$ is a function, satisfying the local Carathéodory conditions, $\alpha_{ik} : \mathbb{C}^{n-1} \to \mathbb{R}$, $\beta_{ik} : \mathbb{C}^{n-1} \to \mathbb{R}$ $(i,k = 1,\dots,n)$ are functionals, continuous, and bounded on every bounded set of the space $\mathbb{C}^{n-1}$, and $\gamma_i : \mathbb{C}^{n-1} \to \mathbb{R}$ $(i = 1,\dots,n)$ are continuous functionals such that

$$\sup\{|\gamma_i(v)| : v \in \mathbb{C}^{n-1}\} < +\infty \quad (i = 1,\dots,n). \tag{1.4}$$

Hindawi Publishing Corporation
Proceedings of the Conference on Differential & Difference Equations and Applications, pp. 529–540

By a solution of (1.1) we mean the function $u \in \mathbb{C}^{n-1}$ having absolutely continuous $(n-1)$th derivative and almost everywhere on $[a,b]$ satisfying (1.1).

A solution of (1.1) satisfying the conditions (1.2) is called *a solution of the problem* (1.1), (1.2).

Set

$$\nu_n(x_1,\dots,x_n;y_1,\dots,y_n) = \begin{cases} \sum_{k=1}^{m}(-1)^k(x_{n-k+1}x_k - y_{n-k+1}y_k) & \text{for } n = 2m, \\ \sum_{k=1}^{m}(-1)^k(x_{n-k+1}x_k - y_{n-k+1}y_k) - \frac{(-1)^m}{2}(x_{m+1}^2 - y_{m+1}^2) & \text{for } n = 2m+1. \end{cases} \tag{1.5}$$

Below we will consider the case when there exist numbers $j \in \{1,2\}$ and $\mu > 0$ such that for any $x_i \in \mathbb{R}$, $y_i \in \mathbb{R}$ $(i = 1,\dots,n)$ and $v \in \mathbb{C}^{n-1}$ the functionals α_{ik}, β_{ik} $(i,k = 1,\dots,n)$ satisfy the inequalities

$$(-1)^{m+j}\nu_n(x_1,\dots,x_n,y_1,\dots,y_n) \le \mu\sum_{k=1}^{n}(|x_k| + |y_k|)\sum_{i=1}^{n}\left|\sum_{k=1}^{n}(\alpha_{ik}(v)x_k + \beta_{ik}(v)y_k)\right|. \tag{1.6$_j$}$$

As for the function f, on the set $[a,b]\times\mathbb{R}^n$ it satisfies the condition

$$p(t)h(|x_1|) - q(t) \le (-1)^{m+j}f(t,x_1,\dots,x_n)\operatorname{sgn}x_1 \le p^*(t,|x_1|), \tag{1.7$_j$}$$

where p and $q : [a,b] \to [0,+\infty[$ are integrable functions, $h : [0,+\infty[\to [0,+\infty[$ is a nondecreasing function, and $p^* : [a,b]\times[0,+\infty[\to [0,+\infty[$ is an integrable in the first argument and nondecreasing in the second argument function. Moreover,

$$\int_a^b p(t)dt > 0, \qquad \lim_{x\to+\infty} h(x) = +\infty. \tag{1.8}$$

For $n = 2m$, the problems

$$\begin{gathered} \alpha_i(u)u^{(i-1)}(a) + \alpha_{m+i}(u)u^{(n-i)}(a) = \gamma_i(u), \\ \beta_i(u)u^{(i-1)}(b) + \beta_{m+i}(u)u^{(n-i)}(b) = \gamma_{m+i}(u) \quad (i = 1,\dots,m), \end{gathered} \tag{1.9}$$

$$u^{(i-1)}(a) = \eta_i(u)u^{(i-1)}(b) + \gamma_i(u), \quad u^{(n-i)}(a) = \frac{u^{(n-i)}(b)}{\eta_i(u)} + \gamma_{m+i}(u) \quad (i = 1,\dots,m) \tag{1.10}$$

are considered separately.

For $n = 2m+1$, to the boundary conditions (1.9) (to the boundary conditions (1.10)) we add one of the following two conditions:

$$u^{(m)}(a) = \eta(u)u^{(m)}(b) + \gamma_n(u) \tag{1.11$_j$}$$

or

$$u^{(m)}(b) = \eta(u)u^{(m)}(a) + \gamma_n(u). \tag{1.11$_2$}$$

Here, $\alpha_i : \mathbb{C}^{n-1} \to \mathbb{R}$, $\beta_i : \mathbb{C}^{n-1} \to \mathbb{R}$ $(i = 1,\dots,2m)$, $\eta_i : \mathbb{C}^{n-1} \to \mathbb{R}$ $(i = 1,\dots,m)$, and $\eta : \mathbb{C}^{n-1} \to \mathbb{R}$ are continuous and bounded on every bounded set of the space $\mathbb{C}^{n-1}$ functionals such that

$$\begin{gathered}(-1)^{m+i+j}\alpha_i(v)\alpha_{m+i}(v) \geq 0, \qquad (-1)^{m+i+j}\beta_i(v)\beta_{m+i}(v) \leq 0,\\ \inf\{|\alpha_i(v)| + |\alpha_{m+i}(v)| : v \in \mathbb{C}^{n-1}\} > 0,\\ \inf\{|\beta_i(v)| + |\beta_{m+i}(v)| : v \in \mathbb{C}^{n-1}\} > 0 \quad (i = 1,\dots,m);\end{gathered} \tag{1.12$_j$}$$

$$\inf\{|\eta_i(v)| : v \in \mathbb{C}^{n-1}\} > 0 \quad (i = 1,\dots,m), \tag{1.13}$$

$$|\eta(v)| \leq 1 \tag{1.14}$$

for any $v \in \mathbb{C}^{n-1}$.

The class of boundary conditions under consideration involves the well-known boundary conditions

$$u^{(i-1)}(b) = u^{(i-1)}(a) + c_i \quad (i = 1,\dots,n), \tag{1.15}$$

$$u^{(n-i)}(b) = c_{1i} \quad (i = 1,\dots,m+j-1), \qquad u^{(n-i)}(a) = c_{2i} \quad (i = 1,\dots,n-m-j+1), \tag{1.16$_j$}$$

$$u^{(i-1)}(a) = c_{1i} \quad (i = 1,\dots,m+j-1), \qquad u^{(i-1)}(b) = c_{2i} \quad (i = 1,\dots,n-m-j+1), \tag{1.17$_j$}$$

$$u^{(i-1)}(b) = c_{1i} \quad (i = 1,\dots,m+j-1), \qquad u^{(n-i)}(a) = c_{2i} \quad (i = 1,\dots,n-m-j+1), \tag{1.18$_j$}$$

where c_i, c_{1i}, and $c_{2i} \in \mathbb{R}$. A vast literature is devoted to the problems (1.1), (1.15); (1.1), (1.16$_j$); (1.1), (1.17$_j$), and (1.1), (1.18$_j$) (see, e.g., [1–13, 15–20] and the references therein), but the problem (1.1), (1.2) in the general case remains still studied insufficiently. The present paper is devoted to fill this gap.

Theorem 1.1. *Let $n = 2m$, $j = 1$ ($n = 2m+1$, $j \in \{1,2\}$), and let the conditions (1.4), (1.6$_j$), (1.7$_j$), and (1.8) be fulfilled. Then the problem (1.1), (1.2) has at least one solution.*

Corollary 1.2. *Let $n = 2m$, and let the conditions (1.4), (1.7$_j$), (1.8), and (1.12$_j$) (the conditions (1.4), (1.7$_j$), (1.8), and (1.13)) be fulfilled. Then the problem (1.1), (1.9) (the problem (1.1), (1.10)) has at least one solution.*

Corollary 1.3. *Let $n = 2m + 1$, $j \in \{1,2\}$, and let the conditions (1.4), (1.7$_j$), (1.8), (1.12$_j$), and (1.14) (the conditions (1.4), (1.7$_j$), (1.8), (1.13), and (1.14)) be fulfilled. Then the problem (1.1), (1.9), (1.11$_j$) (the problem (1.1), (1.10), (1.11$_j$)) has at least one solution.*

Corollary 1.4. *Let $n = 2m$, $j = 1$ ($n = 2m+1$, $j \in \{1,2\}$) and let the conditions (1.7$_j$) and (1.8) be fulfilled. Then every one of the problems (1.1), (1.15); (1.1), (1.16$_j$); (1.1), (1.17$_j$), and (1.1), (1.18$_j$) has at least one solution.*

We will now proceed to considering the case when the right part of (1.1) does not contain intermediate derivatives, and the functionals α_{ik}, β_{ik}, γ_i, α_i, β_i, η_i, and η are constant, that is, when (1.1) and the above-mentioned boundary conditions have, respectively, the form

$$u^{(n)} = f(t,u), \tag{1.19}$$

$$\sum_{k=1}^{n} \left(\alpha_{ik}u^{(i-1)}(a) + \beta_{ik}u^{(i-1)}(b)\right) = \gamma_i \quad (i = 1,\dots,n); \tag{1.20}$$

$$\alpha_i u^{(i-1)}(a) + \alpha_{m+i}u^{(n-i)}(a) = \gamma_i, \quad \beta_i u^{(i-1)}(b) + \beta_{m+i}u^{(n-i)}(b) = \gamma_{m+i} \quad (i = 1,\dots,m); \tag{1.21}$$

$$u^{(i-1)}(a) = \eta_i u^{(i-1)}(b) + \gamma_i, \quad u^{(n-i)}(a) = \frac{u^{(n-i)}(b)}{\eta_i} + \gamma_{m+i}, \quad (i = 1,\dots,m); \tag{1.22}$$

$$u^{(m)}(a) = \eta u^{(m)}(b) + \gamma_n; \tag{1.23$_j$}$$

$$u^{(m)}(b) = \eta u^{(m)}(a) + \gamma_n. \tag{1.23$_2$}$$

As for the inequalities (1.6$_j$) and (1.12$_j$), they take the form

$$(-1)^{m+j}\nu_n(x_1,\dots,x_n;y_1,\dots,y_n) \le \mu \sum_{k=1}^{n} \left(|x_k| + |y_k|\right) \sum_{i=1}^{n} \left| \sum_{k=1}^{n} \left(\alpha_{ik}x_k + \beta_{ik}y_k\right) \right|; \tag{1.24$_j$}$$

$$\begin{gathered} (-1)^{m+i+j}\alpha_i\alpha_{m+i} \ge 0, \qquad (-1)^{m+i+j}\beta_i\beta_{m+i} \le 0, \\ |\alpha_i| + |\alpha_{m+i}| > 0, \quad |\beta_i| + |\beta_{m+i}| > 0 \quad (i = 1,\dots,m). \end{gathered} \tag{1.25$_j$}$$

Just as above, we assume that $f : [a,b] \times \mathbb{R} \to \mathbb{R}$ is the function from the Carathéodory class, satisfying on $[a,b] \times \mathbb{R}$ the inequality

$$(-1)^{m+j} f(t,x)\operatorname{sgn} x \ge p(t)h(|x|) - q(t), \tag{1.26$_j$}$$

where p and $q : [a,b] \to [0,+\infty[$ are integrable, and $h : [0,+\infty[\to [0,+\infty[$ is a nondecreasing function. Moreover,

$$(-1)^{m+j}\left(f(t,x) - f(t,y)\right) > 0 \quad \text{for } x > y. \tag{1.27$_j$}$$

Theorem 1.5. *Let $n = 2m$, $j = 1$ ($n = 2m+1$, $j \in \{1,2\}$), and let the conditions (1.24$_j$), (1.26$_j$), (1.27$_j$), and (1.8) be fulfilled. Then the problem (1.19), (1.20) has one and only one solution.*

Corollary 1.6. *Let $n = 2m$, and let the conditions (1.26$_j$), (1.27$_j$), and (1.8) be fulfilled. If, moreover, the inequalities (1.25$_j$) (the inequalities $\eta_i \neq 0$ ($i = 1,\dots,m$)) hold, then the problem (1.19), (1.21) (the problem (1.19), (1.22)) has one and only one solution.*

Corollary 1.7. *Let $n = 2m+1$, $j \in \{1,2\}$, and let the conditions (1.26$_j$), (1.27$_j$), and (1.8) be fulfilled. If, moreover, $|\eta| \leq 1$ and the inequalities (1.25$_j$) (the inequalities $\eta_i \neq 0$ ($i = 1,\dots,m$)) hold, then the problem (1.19), (1.21), (1.23$_j$) (the problem (1.19), (1.22), (1.23$_j$)) has one and only one solution.*

Corollary 1.8. *Let $n = 2m$, $j = 1$ ($n = 2m+1$, $j \in \{1,2\}$), and let the conditions (1.26$_j$), (1.27$_j$), and (1.8) be fulfilled. Then every one of the problems ((1.19), (1.15); (1.19), (1.16$_j$); (1.19), (1.17$_j$), and (1.19), (1.18$_j$)) has one and only one solution.*

As an example, let us consider the differential equation

$$u^{(n)} = g_0(t)f_0(u) + g(t), \tag{1.28}$$

where g_0 and $g : [a,b] \to \mathbb{R}$ are integrable and $f_0 : \mathbb{R} \to \mathbb{R}$ is a continuous, increasing function. By Corollary 1.8, if $n = 2m$, $j = 1$ ($n = 2m+1$, $j \in \{1,2\}$),

$$\begin{gathered} (-1)^{m+j} g_0(t) > 0 \quad \text{for } a < t < b, \\ \lim_{x \to -\infty} f_0(x) = -\infty, \qquad \lim_{x \to +\infty} f_0(x) = +\infty, \end{gathered} \tag{1.29}$$

then each of the problems (1.28), (1.15); (1.28), (1.16$_j$); (1.28), (1.17$_j$), and (1.28), (1.18$_j$) has one and only one solution. On the other hand, it is clear that if

$$|f_0(x)| \leq \ell \quad \text{for } x \in \mathbb{R}, \qquad g(t) > \ell |g_0(t)| \quad \text{for } a < t < b, \tag{1.30}$$

then just as the problem (1.28), (1.15), the problem (1.28), (1.16$_j$) has no solution.

The above example shows that the restriction (1.8) in Theorems 1.1, 1.5 and in their corollaries is in some sense optimal and cannot be weakened.

2. Auxiliary propositions

2.1. Lemmas on a priori estimates. Consider the system of differential inequalities:

$$(-1)^{m+j} u^{(n)}(t) \operatorname{sgn} u(t) \geq p(t)h(|u(t)|) - q(t), \tag{2.1$_j$}$$

$$|u^{(n)}(t)| \leq p^*(t, |u(t)|) \tag{2.2}$$

with the boundary condition

$$(-1)^{m+j}\nu_n(u(a),\dots,u^{(n-1)}(a);u(b),\dots,u^{(n-1)}(b)) \le \mu_0\|u\|. \tag{2.3$_j$}$$

Here, $n=2m$, $j=1$ ($n=2m+1$, $j\in\{1,2\}$), $\mu_0\ge 0$, p, and $q:[a,b]\to[0,+\infty[$ are integrable functions, $p^*:[a,b]\times[0,+\infty[\to[0,+\infty[$ is a function, integrable in the first and nondecreasing in the second argument, and ν_n is a function given by the equality (1.5).

By a solution of the problem (2.1$_j$), (2.2), (2.3$_j$), we mean the function $u\in\mathbb{C}^{n-1}$ having absolutely continuous $(n-1)$th derivative and satisfying both the system of differential inequalities (2.1$_j$), (2.2) almost everywhere on $[a,b]$ and the condition (2.3$_j$).

Lemma 2.1. *If the condition (1.8) holds, then there exists a positive constant r such that an arbitrary solution u of the problem (2.1$_j$), (2.2), (2.3$_j$) admits the estimate*

$$\|u\|\le r. \tag{2.4}$$

Proof. By virtue of (1.8), there exist numbers $\delta\in]0,1[$, $a_k\in[a,b[$, $b_k\in]a_k,b]$ ($k=1,\dots,n$), and $r_1>0$ such that

$$a_{k+1}-b_k>\delta \quad (k=1,\dots,n-1), \tag{2.5}$$

$$h(r_1)\int_{a_k}^{b_k}p(t)dt>\varepsilon \quad (k=1,\dots,n), \tag{2.6}$$

where

$$\varepsilon=\delta^{n-1}(1+b-a)^{1-n}\big(2(n+2)!(1+\mu_1)\big)^{-1} \tag{2.7}$$

and $\mu_1=\mu_0+2\int_a^b q(t)dt$. Suppose

$$r_2=\frac{2(1+\mu_1)r_1}{\varepsilon},\qquad r=\frac{2r_1\left(1+\int_a^b p^*(t,r_2)dt\right)}{\varepsilon}. \tag{2.8}$$

Let u be a solution of the problem (2.1$_j$), (2.2), (2.3$_j$). Then almost everywhere on $[a,b]$ the inequality

$$\eta(t)\overset{\text{def}}{=}(-1)^{m+j}u^{(n)}(t)u(t)-p(t)h(|u(t)|)|u(t)|+q(t)|u(t)|\ge 0 \tag{2.9}$$

is satisfied.

On the other hand, according to (1.5), we have

$$\begin{aligned}\int_a^b u^{(n)}(t)u(t)dt&=(-1)^m\sigma_n\int_a^b|u^{(m)}(t)|^2dt\\&\quad+\nu_n(u(a),\dots,u^{(n-1)}(a);u(b),\dots,u^{(n-1)}(b)),\end{aligned} \tag{2.10}$$

where $\sigma_n = 1$ for $n = 2m$, and $\sigma_n = 0$ for $n = 2m+1$. Therefore,

$$\int_a^b |u^{(n)}(t)u(t)|\,dt \le \int_a^b (\eta(t) + p(t)h(|u(t)|)\,|u(t)|)\,dt + \int_a^b q(t)\,|u(t)|\,dt,$$

$$\begin{aligned} \int_a^b p(t)h(|u(t)|)\,|u(t)|\,dt &\le \int_a^b (\eta(t) + p(t)h(|u(t)|)\,|u(t)|)\,dt \\ &= (-1)^{m+j}\int_a^b u^{(n)}(t)u(t)dt + \int_a^b q(t)\,|u(t)|\,dt \\ &\le (-1)^{m+j}\nu(u(a),\dots,u^{(n-1)}(a);u(b),\dots,u^{(n-1)}(b)) + \|u\|\int_a^b q(t)dt. \end{aligned} \tag{2.11}$$

Taking now into account the inequality (2.3_j), we can see that

$$\int_a^b p(t)h(|u(t)|)\,|u(t)|\,dt \le \mu_1\|u\|, \tag{2.12}$$

$$\int_a^b |u^{(n)}(t)u(t)|\,dt \le \mu_1\|u\|. \tag{2.13}$$

For every $k \in \{1,\dots,n\}$, we choose $t_k \in [a_k, b_k]$ so that

$$|u(t_k)| = \min\{|u(t)| : a_k \le t \le b_k\}. \tag{2.14}$$

If $|u(t_k)| \ge r_1$, then by (2.6), we have

$$\int_{a_k}^{b_k} p(t)h(|u(t)|)\,|u(t)|\,dt \ge |u(t_k)|\,h(r_1)\int_{a_k}^{b_k} p(t)dt > \frac{|u(t_k)|}{\varepsilon}. \tag{2.15}$$

Consequently,

$$|u(t_k)| < r_1 + \varepsilon\int_a^b p(t)h(|u(t)|)\,|u(t)|\,dt \quad (k = 1,\dots,n). \tag{2.16}$$

On the other hand, it follows from (2.5) that

$$t_{k+1} - t_k > \delta \quad (k = 1,\dots,n-1). \tag{2.17}$$

Therefore,

$$\begin{aligned}\min\{|u^{(i-1)}|(t)|: a\le t\le b\}&\\ &\le i!\delta^{1-i}\max\{|u(t_k)|: k=1,\dots,n\}\\ &< i!\delta^{1-i}\Big(r_1+\varepsilon\int_a^b p(t)h(|u(t)|)|u(t)|dt\Big)\quad (i=1,\dots,n),\end{aligned}\tag{2.18}$$

$$\begin{aligned}\|u\|&<(n+2)!(1+b-a)^{n-1}\delta^{1-n}\Big(r_1+\varepsilon\int_a^b p(t)h(|u(t)|)|u(t)|dt\Big)\\ &\quad+n(1+b-a)^{n-1}\int_a^b|u^{(n)}(t)|dt.\end{aligned}\tag{2.19}$$

With regard for (2.7) and (2.19), from (2.12), we find

$$\begin{aligned}&\int_a^b p(t)h(|u(t)|)|u(t)|dt\\ &\quad<\frac{r_1}{2\varepsilon}+\frac{1}{2}\int_a^b p(t)h(|u(t)|)|u(t)|dt+\frac{r_1}{2\varepsilon}\int_a^b|u^{(n)}(t)|dt\end{aligned}\tag{2.20}$$

and consequently,

$$\int_a^b p(t)h(|u(t)|)|u(t)|dt<\frac{\big(1+\int_a^b|u^{(n)}(t)|dt\big)r_1}{\varepsilon}.\tag{2.21}$$

By virtue of the above estimate and the equality (2.7), from (2.13) and (2.19), we obtain

$$\|u\|<\frac{\big(1+\int_a^b|u^{(n)}(t)|dt\big)r_1}{\varepsilon},\tag{2.22}$$

$$\int_a^b|u^{(n)}(t)u(t)|dt\le\frac{\big(1+\int_a^b|u^{(n)}(t)|dt\big)\mu_1r_1}{\varepsilon}.\tag{2.23}$$

Let

$$I_1=\{t\in[a,b]:|u(t)|\le r_2\},\qquad I_2=\{t\in[a,b]:|u(t)|>r_2\}.\tag{2.24}$$

Then by means of (2.2) and (2.23), we get

$$\begin{aligned}\int_a^b|u^{(n)}(t)|dt&=\int_{I_1}|u^{(n)}(t)|dt+\int_{I_2}|u^{(n)}(t)|dt\\ &\le\int_{I_1}p^*(t,r_2)dt+\frac{1}{r_2}\int_{I_1}|u^{(n)}(t)u(t)|dt\\ &<\int_a^b p^*(t,r_2)dt+\frac{1}{2}+\frac{1}{2}\int_a^b|u^{(n)}(t)|dt\end{aligned}\tag{2.25}$$

and consequently,

$$\int_a^b |u^{(n)}(t)|\,dt < 1 + 2\int_a^b p^*(t,r_2)\,dt. \tag{2.26}$$

According to the latter inequality, from (2.22) follows the estimate (2.4), where r is the positive, independent of u constant given by the equalities (2.8). □

Let $n = 2m$, $j = 1$ ($n = 2m+1$, $j \in \{1,2\}$), and let $p : [a,b] \to [0,+\infty[$ be an integrable function, different from zero on the set of positive measure. For arbitrary $c_i \in \mathbb{R}$ ($i = 1,\dots,n$), $v \in \mathbb{C}^{n-1}$ and integrable function $g : [a,b] \to \mathbb{R}$, consider the linear boundary value problem

$$u^{(n)} = (-1)^{m+j} p(t)u + g(t), \tag{2.27}$$

$$\sum_{k=1}^{n} \left(\alpha_{ik}(v)u^{(k-1)}(a) + \beta_{ik}(v)u^{(k-1)}(b)\right) = c_i \quad (i = 1,\dots,n). \tag{2.28}$$

Analogously to Lemma 2.1 we can prove the following lemma.

Lemma 2.2. *Let the condition* (1.6_j) *be fulfilled, where* μ *is an independent of* x_k, y_k ($k = 1,\dots,n$), *and* v *constant. Then there exists an independent of* c_i ($i = 1,\dots,n$), v, *and* g *positive constant* r_0 *such that an arbitrary solution* u *of the problem (2.27), (2.28) admits the estimate*

$$\|u\| \le r_0\left(\sum_{i=1}^{n} |c_i| + \int_a^b |g(t)|\,dt\right). \tag{2.29}$$

2.2. Lemma on the solvability of the problem (1.1), (1.2). From [14, Theorem 1] and Lemma 2.2, we have the following lemma.

Lemma 2.3. *Let* $n = 2m$, $j = 1$ ($n = 2m+1$, $j \in \{1,2\}$), *and let* $p : [a,b] \to [0,+\infty[$ *be an integrable function, different from zero on the set of positive measure. Let, moreover, the condition* (1.6_j) *be fulfilled and there exists a positive constant* r *such that for every* $\lambda \in]0,1[$ *an arbitrary solution* u *of the boundary value problem*

$$u^{(n)} = (-1)^{m+j}(1-\lambda)p(t)u + \lambda f(t,u,\dots,u^{(n-1)}), \tag{2.30}$$

$$\sum_{k=1}^{n} \left(\alpha_{ik}(u)u^{(k-1)}(a) + \beta_{ik}(u)u^{(k-1)}(b)\right) = \lambda\gamma_i(u) \quad (i = 1,\dots,n) \tag{2.31}$$

admits the estimate (2.4). Then the problem (1.1), (1.2) has at least one solution.

3. Proof of the main results

Proof of Theorem 1.1. By the condition (1.7_j), without loss of generality, we can assume that on $[a,b] \times \mathbb{R}^n$ the inequalities

$$h(|x_1|) \le |x_1|, \qquad |f(t,x_1,\dots,x_n)| + p(t)|x_1| \le p^*(t,|x_1|) \tag{3.1}$$

are satisfied. On the other hand, by (1.4), we have

$$\mu_0 = 2\mu \sup\left\{ \sum_{i=1}^{n} |\gamma_i(v)| : v \in \mathbb{C}^{n-1} \right\} < +\infty. \tag{3.2}$$

Let $\lambda \in]0,1[$, and let u be an arbitrary solution of the problem (2.30), (2.31). Then by virtue of the conditions (1.6_j), (1.7_j), (3.1), and (3.2), the function u is likewise the solution of the problem (2.1_j), (2.2), (2.3_j). From the above reasoning, by Lemma 2.1 we obtain the estimate (2.4), where r is the positive constant, independent of u and λ. Using now Lemma 2.3, it is not difficult to see that Theorem 1.1 is valid. □

Proof of Theorem 1.5. By Theorem 1.1, the conditions (1.24_j), (1.26_j), and (1.8) guarantee the solvability of the problem (1.19), (1.20). Therefore it remains to prove that this problem does not have more than one solution. Assume the contrary that the problem (1.19), (1.20) has two different solutions u_1 and u_2. Suppose

$$u(t) = u_2(t) - u_1(t), \qquad g(t) = (-1)^{m+j}\big(f(t,u_2(t)) - f(t,u_1(t))\big)u(t). \tag{3.3}$$

Then

$$g(t) = (-1)^{m+j} u^{(n)}(t)u(t), \tag{3.4}$$

$$\sum_{k=1}^{m} \left(\alpha_{ik}u^{(k-1)}(a) + \beta_{ik}u^{(k-1)}(b)\right) = 0 \quad (i = 1,\dots,n). \tag{3.5}$$

Integrating both parts of the identity (3.4) from a to b, by virtue of the conditions (1.24_j), (1.27_j), and (3.5), we find that

$$0 < \int_a^b g(t)dt = (-1)^{m+j}\nu_n\left(u(a),\dots,u^{(n-1)}(a); u(b),\dots,u^{(n-1)}(b)\right) \le 0. \tag{3.6}$$

The obtained contradiction proves the theorem. □

Proof of Corollary 1.2. We choose a number $\delta \in]0,1[$ such that for arbitrary $v \in \mathbb{C}^{n-1}$ and $k \in \{1,\dots,m\}$ the inequalities

$$|\alpha_k(v)| + |\alpha_{m+k}(v)| \ge 2\delta, \qquad |\beta_k(v)| + |\beta_{m+k}(v)| \ge 2\delta \qquad (|\eta_k(v)| \ge \delta) \tag{3.7}$$

are satisfied.

For arbitrarily fixed $x_k \in \mathbb{R}$, $y_k \in \mathbb{R}$ $(k = 1,\dots,n)$, and $v \in \mathbb{C}^{n-1}$, we put

$$\begin{gathered}\alpha_k(v)x_k + \alpha_{m+k}(v)x_{n-k+1} = z_k, \quad \beta_k(v)y_k + \beta_{m+k}(v)y_{n-k+1} = z_{m+k} \quad (k = 1,\dots,m),\\ \left(x_k - \eta_k(v)y_k = z_k,\ x_{n-k+1} - \frac{y_{n-k+1}}{\eta_k(v)} = z_{m+k}\ (k = 1,\dots,m)\right).\end{gathered} \tag{3.8}$$

Then by virtue of the conditions (1.12_j) and (3.7), we have

$$\begin{gathered}(-1)^{m+1+k}(x_{n-k+1}x_k - y_{n-k+1}y_k) \\ \leq \delta^{-1}(|x_k| + |x_{n-k+1}| + |y_k| + |y_{n-k+1}|)(|z_k| + |z_{m+k}|), \\ (|x_{n-k+1}x_k - y_{n-k+1}y_k| \leq (1+\delta^{-1})(|x_k| + |y_{n-k+1}|)(|z_k| + |z_{m+k}|)).\end{gathered} \tag{3.9}$$

Hence with regard for the notation (1.5), we find

$$(-1)^{m+1+k}\nu(x_1,\dots,x_n;y_1,\dots,y_n) \leq \mu\sum_{k=1}^{n}(|x_k| + |y_k|)\sum_{i=1}^{n}|z_i|, \tag{3.10}$$

where $\mu = 1+\delta^{-1}$ is the constant, independent of x_k, y_k $(k = 1,\dots,n)$, and ν.

Applying now Theorem 1.1, the validity of Corollary 1.2 becomes obvious. □

Corollaries 1.3, 1.6, and 1.7 can be proved analogously.

Corollary 1.4 follows directly from Corollaries 1.2 and 1.3, while Corollary 1.8 follows from Corollaries 1.6 and 1.7.

Acknowledgment

This work was supported by INTAS (Grant no. 03-51-5007).

References

[1] R. P. Agarwal, *Focal Boundary Value Problems for Differential and Difference Equations*, Mathematics and Its Applications, vol. 436, Kluwer Academic, Dordrecht, 1998.

[2] R. P. Agarwal and I. Kiguradze, *Two-point boundary value problems for higher order linear differential equations with strong singularities*, Boundary Value Problems **2006** (2006), Article ID 83910, 32 pages.

[3] R. P. Agarwal and D. O'Regan, *Singular Differential and Integral Equations with Applications*, Kluwer Academic, Dordrecht, 2003.

[4] P. W. Bates and J. R. Ward Jr., *Periodic solutions of higher order systems*, Pacific Journal of Mathematics **84** (1979), no. 2, 275–282.

[5] S. R. Bernfeld and V. Lakshmikantham, *An Introduction to Nonlinear Boundary Value Problems*, Academic Press, New York, 1974.

[6] R. E. Gaines and J. L. Mawhin, *Coincidence Degree, and Nonlinear Differential Equations*, Springer, Berlin, 1977.

[7] G. T. Gegelia, *On boundary value problems of periodic type for ordinary odd order differential equations*, Archivum Mathematicum **20** (1984), no. 4, 195–203.

[8] ———, *Boundary value problems of periodic type for ordinary differential equations*, Tbilisskiĭ Gosudarstvennyĭ Universitet. Institut Prikladnoĭ Matematiki. Trudy **17** (1986), 60–93 (Russian).

[9] ———, *On bounded and periodic solutions of even-order nonlinear ordinary differential equations*, Differentsial'nye Uravneniya **22** (1986), no. 3, 390–396, 547 (Russian).

[10] ———, *On periodic solutions of ordinary differential equations*, Qualitative Theory of Differential Equations (Szeged, 1988), Colloq. Math. Soc. János Bolyai, vol. 53, North-Holland, Amsterdam, 1990, pp. 211–217.

[11] I. Kiguradze, *Bounded and periodic solutions of higher-order linear differential equations*, Matematicheskie Zametki **37** (1985), no. 1, 48–62, 138 (Russian), English translation in Mathematical Notes **37** (1985), 28–36.
[12] I. Kiguradze and T. Kusano, *On conditions for the existence and uniqueness of a periodic solution of nonautonomous differential equations*, Differentsial'nye Uravneniya **36** (2000), no. 10, 1301–1306, 1436 (Russian), English translation in Differential Equations **36**(2000), no. 10, 1436–1442.
[13] ———, *On periodic solutions of even-order ordinary differential equations*, Annali di Matematica Pura ed Applicata. Series IV **180** (2001), no. 3, 285–301.
[14] I. Kiguradze and B. Půža, *On boundary value problems for functional-differential equations*, Memoirs on Differential Equations and Mathematical Physics **12** (1997), 106–113.
[15] I. Kiguradze, B. Půža, and I. P. Stavroulakis, *On singular boundary value problems for functional differential equations of higher order*, Georgian Mathematical Journal **8** (2001), no. 4, 791–814.
[16] I. Kiguradze and G. Tskhovrebadze, *On the two-point boundary value problems for systems of higher order ordinary differential equations with singularities*, Georgian Mathematical Journal **1** (1994), no. 1, 31–45.
[17] L. A. Kipnis, *On periodic solution of higher order nonlinear differential equations*, Prikladnaya Matematika i Mekhanika **41** (1977), no. 2, 362–365 (Russian).
[18] A. Lasota and Z. Opial, *Sur les solutions périodiques des équations différentielles ordinaires*, Annales Polonici Mathematici **16** (1964), no. 1, 69–94.
[19] V. E. Maĭorov, *On the existence of solutions of higher-order singular differential equations*, Matematicheskie Zametki **51** (1992), no. 3, 75–84 (Russian).
[20] P. J. Y. Wong and R. P. Agarwal, *Singular differential equations with (n,p) boundary conditions*, Mathematical and Computer Modelling **28** (1998), no. 1, 37–44.

I. Kiguradze: A. Razmadze Mathematical Institute, Georgian Academy of Sciences, M. Aleksidze St. 1, Tbilisi 0193, Georgia
E-mail address: kig@rmi.acnet.ge

ON DOUBLY PERIODIC SOLUTIONS OF QUASILINEAR HYPERBOLIC EQUATIONS OF THE FOURTH ORDER

T. KIGURADZE AND T. SMITH

The problem on doubly periodic solutions is considered for a class of quasilinear hyperbolic equations. Effective sufficient conditions of solvability and unique solvability of this problem are established.

The problem on periodic solutions for second-order partial differential equations of hyperbolic type has been studied rather intensively by various authors [1–9, 11–14]. Analogous problem for higher-order hyperbolic equations is little investigated. In the present paper for the quasilinear hyperbolic equations

$$u^{(2,2)} = f_0(x,y,u) + f_1(y,u)u^{(2,0)} + f_2(x,u)u^{(0,2)} + f\left(x,y,u,u^{(1,0)},u^{(0,1)},u^{(1,1)}\right), \tag{1}$$

$$\begin{aligned} u^{(2,2)} = {} & f_0(x,y,u) + \left(f_1(x,y,u)u^{(1,0)}\right)^{(1,0)} + \left(f_2(x,y,u)u^{(0,1)}\right)^{(0,1)} \\ & + f\left(x,y,u,u^{(1,0)},u^{(0,1)},u^{(1,1)}\right) \end{aligned} \tag{2}$$

we consider the problem on doubly periodic solutions

$$u(x+\omega_1,y) = u(x,y), \quad u(x,y+\omega_2) = u(x,y) \quad \text{for } (x,y) \in \mathbb{R}^2. \tag{3}$$

Here ω_1 and ω_2 are prescribed positive numbers,

$$u^{(j,k)}(x,y) = \frac{\partial^{j+k}u(x,y)}{\partial x^j \partial y^k}, \tag{4}$$

$f_0(x,y,z)$, $f_1(y,z)$, $f_2(x,z)$, $f_1(x,y,z)$, $f_2(x,y,z)$, and $f(x,y,z,z_1,z_2,z_3)$ are continuous functions, ω_1-periodic in x, and ω_2-periodic in y.

Hindawi Publishing Corporation
Proceedings of the Conference on Differential & Difference Equations and Applications, pp. 541–553

This problem was studied thoroughly for the linear equation

$$u^{(2,2)} = p_0(x,y)u + p_1(x,y)u^{(2,0)} + p_2(x,y)u^{(0,2)} + q(x,y) \tag{5}$$

in [10]. The goal of the present paper is on the basis of the methods developed in [10] to obtain effective sufficient conditions of solvability, unique solvability, and well-posedness of problems (1), (3) and (2), (3).

Throughout the paper, we will use the following notation:

$$\operatorname{sgn}(z) = \begin{cases} 1, & z > 1, \\ 0, & z = 0, \\ -1, & z < 0. \end{cases} \tag{6}$$

$C^{m,n}_{\omega_1\omega_2}(\mathbb{R}^2)$ is the space of continuous functions $z : \mathbb{R}^2 \to \mathbb{R}$ ω_1-periodic in the first and ω_2-periodic in the second arguments, having the continuous partial derivatives $u^{(j,k)}$ $j \in \{0,\dots,m\}$, $k \in \{0,\dots,n\}$, with the norm

$$\|z\|_{C^{m,n}_{\omega_1\omega_2}} = \sup\left\{ \sum_{j=0}^{m}\sum_{k=0}^{n} \left| z^{(j,k)}(x,y) \right| : (x,y) \in \mathbb{R}^2 \right\}. \tag{7}$$

$L^2_{\omega_1\omega_2}(\mathbb{R}^2)$ is the space of locally square-integrable functions $z : \mathbb{R}^2 \to \mathbb{R}$, ω_1-periodic in the first and ω_2-periodic in the second arguments, with the norm

$$\|z\|_{L^2_{\omega_1\omega_2}} = \left(\int_0^{\omega_1}\int_0^{\omega_2} |z(s,t)|^2 ds\,dt \right)^{1/2}. \tag{8}$$

$H^{m,n}_{\omega_1\omega_2}(\mathbb{R}^2)$ is the space of functions $z \in L^2_{\omega_1\omega_2}(\mathbb{R}^2)$, having the generalized partial derivatives $u^{(j,k)} \in L^2_{\omega_1\omega_2}(\mathbb{R}^2)$, $j \in \{0,\dots,m\}$, $k \in \{0,\dots,n\}$, with the norm

$$\|z\|_{H^{m,n}_{\omega_1\omega_2}} = \sum_{j=0}^{m}\sum_{k=0}^{n} \left\| u^{(j,k)} \right\|_{L^2_{\omega_1\omega_2}}. \tag{9}$$

By a solution of problem (1), (3) (problem (2), (3)), we understand a classical solution, that is, a function $u \in C^{2,2}_{\omega_1\omega_2}(\mathbb{R}^2)$ satisfying (1) (equation (2)) everywhere in $\mathbb{R}^2$.

Theorem 1. *Let there exists a positive constant δ such that*

$$f_1(y,z) \geq \delta, \quad f_2(x,z) \geq \delta \quad \text{for } (x,y,z) \in \mathbb{R}^3. \tag{10}$$

Moreover let the functions f_1, f_2, f_0, and f satisfy the conditions

$$(f_1(y,z) - f_1(y,\bar{z}))\operatorname{sgn}(z-\bar{z})\operatorname{sgn}(z) \geq 0 \quad \text{for } y \in \mathbb{R},\ z\bar{z} \geq 0, \tag{11}$$

$$(f_2(x,z) - f_2(x,\bar{z}))\operatorname{sgn}(z-\bar{z})\operatorname{sgn}(z) \geq 0 \quad \text{for } x \in \mathbb{R},\ z\bar{z} \geq 0, \tag{12}$$

$$\begin{gathered} f_0(x,y,z)\operatorname{sgn}(z) < 0 \quad \text{for } (x,y) \in \mathbb{R}^2,\ z \neq 0, \\ \lim_{z\to\infty} \operatorname{sgn}(z) \int_0^{\omega_1}\int_0^{\omega_2} f_0(x,y,z)\,dx\,dy = -\infty, \end{gathered} \tag{13}$$

$$\lim_{z\to\infty} \frac{f(x,y,z,z_1,z_2,z_3)}{f_0(x,y,z)} = 0 \quad \text{uniformly on } \mathbb{R}^2 \times \mathbb{R}^4. \tag{14}$$

Then problem (1), (3) is solvable.

THEOREM 2. *Let f_1 and f_2 be continuously differentiable functions such that*

$$f_1(x,y,z) \geq \delta, \quad f_2(x,y,z) \geq \delta \quad \text{for } (x,y,z) \in \mathbb{R}^3 \tag{15}$$

for some positive δ. Moreover, let the functions f_0 and f satisfy the conditions of Theorem 1. Then problem (2), (3) is solvable.

Remark 1. Note that conditions (10) and (15) are optimal in a sense that we cannot take $\delta = 0$. Indeed, consider the problems

$$u^{(2,2)} = -F(u) + \left(F'(u)u^{(1,0)}\right)^{(1,0)} + u^{(0,2)} + \pi \sin x, \tag{16}$$

$$u(x+2\pi,y) = u(x,y), \qquad u(x,y+2\pi) = u(x,y), \tag{17}$$

where $F(z) = z^3$, or $F(z) = \arctan(z)$. Problem (16), (17) satisfies all of the conditions of Theorem 2 except condition (15). Instead of (15), we have that $F'(z)$ is nonnegative and vanishes at 0, or at ∞ only.

Let us show that problem (16), (17) has no solution. Assume the contrary: let u be a solution of (16), (17), and set $v(x,y) = u^{(0,2)}(x,y) - F(u(x,y))$. Then for every $y \in \mathbb{R}$, the function $v(\cdot,y)$ is a solution to the periodic problem

$$v'' = v + \pi \sin x, \qquad v(x+2\pi) = v(x). \tag{18}$$

This problem has a unique solution $v(x) = -\pi/2 \sin x$. Therefore, problem (16), (17) is equivalent to the problem

$$u^{(0,2)} = F_1(u) - \frac{\pi}{2}\sin x, \qquad u(x,y+2\pi) = u(x,y). \tag{19}$$

However, problem (19) has no more than one solution. Indeed, let u_1 and u_2 be arbitrary solutions to problem (19). Then one easily gets the identity

$$\int_0^{\omega_2} \left(\left(u_1^{(0,1)}(x,t) - u_2^{(0,1)}(x,t)\right)^2 + (F(u_1(x,t)) - F(u_2(x,t)))(u_1(x,t) - u_2(x,t))\right)dt \equiv 0, \tag{20}$$

whence it follows that $u_1(x,y) \equiv u_2(x,y)$.

Due to uniqueness, a solution of problem (19) should be independent of y. So finally we arrive to the functional equation

$$F(u) = \frac{\pi}{2}\sin x, \tag{21}$$

whence we get

$$\begin{aligned} u(x,y) &= \sqrt[3]{\frac{\pi}{2}\sin x} \quad \text{for } F(z) = z^3, \\ u(x,y) &= \tan\left(\frac{\pi}{2}\sin x\right) \quad \text{for } F(z) = \arctan(z). \end{aligned} \tag{22}$$

In the first case u is not differentiable at πk, $k \in \mathbb{Z}$, while in the second case u itself is a discontinuous function, because it blows up at points $\pi/2 + \pi k$, $k \in \mathbb{Z}$.

Thus, it is clear that of problem (16), (17) has no solutions in the both cases.

Remark 2. The conditions of Theorem 1 (as well as Theorem 2) do not guarantee the uniqueness of a solution. Indeed, for the equation

$$u^{(2,2)} = -u^n + u^{(2,0)} + u^{(0,2)} - \left(\prod_{k=1}^{n}(u-k) - u^n\right), \tag{23}$$

all of the conditions of Theorem 1 (and Theorem 2) are fulfilled. Nevertheless, it has at least n solutions $u_k(x,y) \equiv k$ $(k = 1,2,\ldots,n)$ satisfying conditions (3).

We will give a uniqueness theorem for the equations

$$u^{(2,2)} = f_0(x,y,u) + \left(f_1(x,y)u^{(1,0)}\right)^{(1,0)} + \left(f_2(x,y)u^{(0,1)}\right)^{(0,1)}, \tag{24}$$

$$\begin{aligned} u^{(2,2)} = {} & f_0(x,y,u) + \left(f_1(x,y)u^{(1,0)}\right)^{(1,0)} + \left(f_2(x,y)u^{(0,1)}\right)^{(0,1)} \\ & + \varepsilon f\left(x,y,u,u^{(1,0)},u^{(0,1)},u^{(1,1)},u^{(2,0)},u^{(0,2)},u^{(2,1)},u^{(1,2)}\right). \end{aligned} \tag{25}$$

Theorem 3. *Let there exists $\delta > 0$ such that*

$$f_1(x,y) \geq \delta, \quad f_2(x,y) \geq \delta \quad \text{for } (x,y) \in \mathbb{R}^2, \tag{26}$$

$$\left(f_0(x,y,z) - f_0(x,y,\bar{z})\right)\operatorname{sgn}(z-\bar{z}) \leq -\delta|z-\bar{z}| \quad \text{for } (x,y) \in \mathbb{R}^2,\ z,\bar{z} \in \mathbb{R}. \tag{27}$$

Then problem (24), (3) is uniquely solvable. Moreover, for every $f(x,y,z_1,z_2,z_3,z_4,z_5,z_6,z_7,z_8)$ that is Lipschitz continuous with respect to the last eight phase variables, there exists a positive ε_0 such that problem (25), (3) is uniquely solvable for every $\varepsilon \in (-\varepsilon_0,\varepsilon_0)$.

To prove Theorems 1–3, we will need the following lemmas.

LEMMA 1. *Let* p_0, p_1, p_2, *and* $q \in C_{\omega_1\omega_2}(\mathbb{R}^2)$, *and let there exist a positive constant* δ *and a nondecreasing continuous function* $\eta : [0,+\infty) \to [0,+\infty)$, $\eta(0) = 0$ *such that*

$$p_1(x,y) \ge \delta, \qquad p_2(x,y) \ge \delta, \tag{28}$$

$$\begin{aligned} &|p_1(x_1,y_1) - p_1(x_2,y_2)| + |p_2(x_1,y_1) - p_2(x_2,y_2)| \\ &\quad \le \eta(|x_1 - x_2| + |y_1 - y_2|) \quad \text{for } (x_i,y_i) \in \mathbb{R}^2 \ (i = 1,2). \end{aligned} \tag{29}$$

Then an arbitrary solution u *of problem (5), (3) admits the estimate*

$$\begin{aligned} &\int_0^{\omega_1}\int_0^{\omega_2}\Big(\big|u^{(2,0)}(x,y)\big|^2 + \big|u^{(0,2)}(x,y)\big|^2 + \big|u^{(2,1)}(x,y)\big|^2 + \big|u^{(1,2)}(x,y)\big|^2\Big)dx\,dy \\ &\quad \le M\int_0^{\omega_1}\int_0^{\omega_2}\Big(|u(x,y)|^2 + \big|u^{(1,0)}(x,y)\big|^2 + \big|u^{(0,1)}(x,y)\big|^2 + q^2(x,y)\Big)dx\,dy, \end{aligned} \tag{30}$$

where the constant $M > 0$ *depends on* δ, $\|p_0\|_{C_{\omega_1\omega_2}}$, *and the function* η.

Proof. Let u be a an arbitrary solution of problem (5), (3). For any $h > 0$, set

$$\begin{aligned} p_{ih}(x,y) &= \frac{1}{h^2}\int_x^{x+h}\int_y^{y+h} p_i(s,t)\,ds\,dt \quad (i = 1,2), \\ Q_h[u](x,y) &= (p_1(x,y) - p_{1h}(x,y))u^{(2,0)}(x,y) + (p_2(x,y) - p_{2h}(x,y))u^{(0,2)}(x,y). \end{aligned} \tag{31}$$

Then u satisfies the equation

$$u^{(2,2)} = p_0(x,y)u + p_{1h}(x,y)u^{(2,0)} + p_{2h}(x,y)u^{(0,2)} + Q_h[u](x,y) + q(x,y). \tag{32}$$

Multiplying successively (32) by $u(x,y)$, $u^{(2,0)}$, and $u^{(0,2)}$, integrating over the rectangle $[0,\omega_1] \times [0,\omega_2]$, and using integration by parts, we observe that

$$\begin{aligned} &\int_0^{\omega_1}\int_0^{\omega_2}\Big(p_{1h}(x,y)\big|u^{(1,0)}(x,y)\big|^2 + p_{2h}(x,y)\big|u^{(0,1)}(x,y)\big|^2 + \big|u^{(1,1)}(x,y)\big|^2\Big)dx\,dy \\ &\quad = \int_0^{\omega_1}\int_0^{\omega_2}\Big(Q_h[u](x,y) - p_{1h}^{(1,0)}(x,y)u^{(1,0)}(x,y) - p_{2h}^{(0,1)}(x,y)u^{(0,1)}(x,y) \\ &\qquad + p_0(x,y)u(x,y) + q(x,y)\Big)u(x,y)\,dx\,dy, \end{aligned} \tag{33}$$

$$\begin{aligned}
&\int_0^{\omega_1}\int_0^{\omega_2}\Big(p_{1h}(x,y)\left|u^{(2,0)}(x,y)\right|^2+p_{2h}(x,y)\left|u^{(1,1)}(x,y)\right|^2+\left|u^{(2,1)}(x,y)\right|^2\Big)dx\,dy\\
&\quad=\int_0^{\omega_1}\int_0^{\omega_2}\Big(p_{2h}^{(0,1)}(x,y)u^{(2,0)}(x,y)u^{(0,1)}(x,y)-p_{2h}^{(1,0)}(x,y)u^{(1,1)}(x,y)u^{(0,1)}(x,y)\Big)dx\,dy\\
&\quad\quad-\int_0^{\omega_1}\int_0^{\omega_2}\big(Q_h[u](x,y)+p_0(x,y)u(x,y)+q(x,y)\big)u^{(2,0)}(x,y)dx\,dy,
\end{aligned}\tag{34}$$

$$\begin{aligned}
&\int_0^{\omega_1}\int_0^{\omega_2}\Big(p_{1h}(x,y)\left|u^{(1,1)}(x,y)\right|^2+p_{2h}(x,y)\left|u^{(0,2)}(x,y)\right|^2+\left|u^{(1,2)}(x,y)\right|^2\Big)dx\,dy\\
&\quad=\int_0^{\omega_1}\int_0^{\omega_2}\Big(p_{1h}^{(1,0)}(x,y)u^{(0,2)}(x,y)u^{(1,0)}(x,y)-p_{1h}^{(0,1)}(x,y)u^{(1,1)}(x,y)u^{(1,0)}(x,y)\Big)dx\,dy\\
&\quad\quad-\int_0^{\omega_1}\int_0^{\omega_2}\big(Q_h[u](x,y)+p_0(x,y)u(x,y)+q(x,y)\big)u^{(0,2)}(x,y)dx\,dy.
\end{aligned}\tag{35}$$

However,

$$\begin{aligned}
&\int_0^{\omega_1}\int_0^{\omega_2}\left|Q_h[u](x,y)\right|\Big(|u(x,y)|+\left|u^{(2,0)}(x,y)\right|+\left|u^{(0,2)}(x,y)\right|\Big)dx\,dy\\
&\quad\le 2\eta(h)\Big(\|u\|^2_{L^2_{\omega_1\omega_2}}+\left\|u^{(2,0)}\right\|^2_{L^2_{\omega_1\omega_2}}+\left\|u^{(0,2)}\right\|^2_{L^2_{\omega_1\omega_2}}\Big),
\end{aligned}\tag{36}$$

$$\begin{aligned}
&\int_0^{\omega_1}\int_0^{\omega_2}\big(|p_0(x,y)|\,|u(x,y)|+|q(x,y)|\big)\Big(|u(x,y)|+\left|u^{(2,0)}(x,y)\right|+\left|u^{(0,2)}(x,y)\right|\Big)dx\,dy\\
&\quad\le\Big(\frac{2}{\varepsilon}\|p_0\|_{C_{\omega_1\omega_2}}+2\varepsilon\Big)\|u\|^2_{L^2_{\omega_1\omega_2}}+\frac{2}{\varepsilon}\|q\|^2_{L^2_{\omega_1\omega_2}}+2\varepsilon\Big(\left\|u^{(2,0)}\right\|^2_{L^2_{\omega_1\omega_2}}+\left\|u^{(0,2)}\right\|^2_{L^2_{\omega_1\omega_2}}\Big),
\end{aligned}\tag{37}$$

$$\begin{aligned}
&\int_0^{\omega_1}\int_0^{\omega_2}\Big(\left|p_{2h}^{(0,1)}(x,y)\right|\left|u^{(2,0)}(x,y)\right|\left|u^{(0,1)}(x,y)\right|\\
&\qquad+\left|p_{2h}^{(1,0)}(x,y)\right|\left|u^{(1,1)}(x,y)\right|\left|u^{(0,1)}(x,y)\right|\Big)dx\,dy\\
&\quad\le\frac{2\eta(h)}{h}\varepsilon\Big(\left\|u^{(2,0)}\right\|^2_{L^2_{\omega_1\omega_2}}+\left\|u^{(1,1)}\right\|^2_{L^2_{\omega_1\omega_2}}\Big)+\frac{2\eta(h)}{h\varepsilon}\left\|u^{(0,1)}\right\|^2_{L^2_{\omega_1\omega_2}},
\end{aligned}\tag{38}$$

$$\begin{aligned}
&\int_0^{\omega_1}\int_0^{\omega_2}\Big(\left|p_{1h}^{(1,0)}(x,y)\right|\left|u^{(0,2)}(x,y)\right|\left|u^{(1,0)}(x,y)\right|\\
&\qquad+\left|p_{1h}^{(0,1)}(x,y)\right|\left|u^{(1,1)}(x,y)\right|\left|u^{(1,0)}(x,y)\right|\Big)dx\,dy\\
&\quad\le\frac{2\eta(h)}{h}\varepsilon\Big(\left\|u^{(0,2)}\right\|^2_{L^2_{\omega_1\omega_2}}+\left\|u^{(1,1)}\right\|^2_{L^2_{\omega_1\omega_2}}\Big)+\frac{2\eta(h)}{h\varepsilon}\left\|u^{(1,0)}\right\|^2_{L^2_{\omega_1\omega_2}}.
\end{aligned}\tag{39}$$

Now taking $h>0$ and $\varepsilon>0$ sufficiently small from (33)–(39), we immediately get estimate (30). □

The following lemma immediately follows from [10, Lemma 2.7].

Lemma 2. *Let p_0, p_1, p_2, and $q \in C_{\omega_1\omega_2}(\mathbb{R}^2)$, and let p_1 and p_2 satisfy conditions (28). Then an arbitrary solution u of problem (5), (3) admits the estimate*

$$\|u\|_{C^{2,2}_{\omega_1\omega_2}} \leq r\left(\int_0^{\omega_1}\int_0^{\omega_2}\left(|u(x,y)| + \left|u^{(2,0)}(x,y)\right| + \left|u^{(0,2)}(x,y)\right|\right)dx\,dy + \|q\|_{C_{\omega_1\omega_2}}\right), \tag{40}$$

where r is a positive constant depending on δ, $\|p_0\|_{C_{\omega_1\omega_2}}$, $\|p_1\|_{C_{\omega_1\omega_2}}$, and $\|p_2\|_{C_{\omega_1\omega_2}}$ only.

Lemma 3. *Let $p_1, p_2 \in C_{\omega_1\omega_2}(\mathbb{R}^2)$ satisfy the conditions of Lemma 1. Then there exist $\lambda > 0$ and $M_\lambda > 0$ depending on δ, $\|p_1\|_{C_{\omega_1\omega_2}}$, $\|p_2\|_{C_{\omega_1\omega_2}}$, and the function η such that for every $q \in C_{\omega_1\omega_2}(\mathbb{R}^2)$, the equation*

$$u^{(2,2)} = -\lambda u + p_1(x,y)u^{(2,0)} + p_2(x,y)u^{(0,2)} + q(x,y) \tag{41}$$

has a unique solution u satisfying conditions (3), and

$$\|u\|_{C^{2,2}_{\omega_1\omega_2}} \leq M_\lambda \|q\|_{C_{\omega_1\omega_2}}. \tag{42}$$

Proof. This lemma easily follows from Lemmas 1 and 2. Indeed, let u be an arbitrary solution of problems (41), (3). Multiplying successively (41) by $u(x,y)$, $u^{(2,0)}$, and $u^{(0,2)}$, integrating over the rectangle $[0,\omega_1] \times [0,\omega_2]$, and using integration by parts, we get

$$\begin{aligned}&\lambda\left(\|u\|^2_{L^2_{\omega_1\omega_2}} + \|u^{(1,0)}\|^2_{L^2_{\omega_1\omega_2}} + \|u^{(0,1)}\|^2_{L^2_{\omega_1\omega_2}}\right)\\ &\quad\leq \left(1 + \|p_1\|^2_{C_{\omega_1\omega_2}} + \|p_2\|^2_{C_{\omega_1\omega_2}}\right)\left(\|u\|^2_{L^2_{\omega_1\omega_2}} + \|u^{(2,0)}\|^2_{L^2_{\omega_1\omega_2}} + \|u^{(0,2)}\|^2_{L^2_{\omega_1\omega_2}}\right) + \|q\|^2_{L^2_{\omega_1\omega_2}}.\end{aligned} \tag{43}$$

Validity of Lemma 3 immediately follows from estimates (30), (40), and (43). □

Consider the linear equation

$$u^{(2,2)} = p_0(x,y)u + \left(p_1(x,y)u^{(1,0)}\right)^{(1,0)} + \left(p_2(x,y)u^{(0,1)}\right)^{(0,1)} + q(x,y). \tag{44}$$

If p_1 and p_2 satisfy (28), then by $g_1(\cdot,\cdot,x) : \mathbb{R}^2 \to \mathbb{R}$ and $g_2(\cdot,\cdot,y) : \mathbb{R}^2 \to \mathbb{R}$, respectively, denote Green's functions of the problems

$$\begin{aligned}\frac{d^2z}{dy^2} &= p_1(x,y)z, \qquad z(y+\omega_2) = z(y),\\ \frac{d^2z}{dx^2} &= p_2(x,y)z, \qquad z(x+\omega_1) = z(x),\end{aligned} \tag{45}$$

(see [10, Lemmas 2.1 and 2.2]).

Lemma 4. *Let u be a solution of problem (44), (3). Then the following representation is valid*

$$
\begin{aligned}
u^{(2,0)}(x,y) &= p_2(x,y)u \\
&\quad + \int_y^{y+\omega_2} g_1(y,t,x)\Big((p_0(x,t)+p_1(x,t)p_2(x,t))u(x,t) \\
&\qquad\qquad + p_1^{(1,0)}(x,t)u^{(1,0)}(x,t)+q(x,t)\Big)dt, \\
u^{(0,2)}(x,y) &= p_1(x,y)u \\
&\quad + \int_x^{x+\omega_1} g_2(x,s,y)\Big((p_0(s,y)+p_1(s,y)p_2(s,y))u(s,y) \\
&\qquad\qquad + p_2^{(0,1)}(s,y)u^{(0,1)}(s,y)+q(s,y)\Big)ds, \\
u(x,y) &= \int_y^{y+\omega_2}\int_x^{x+\omega_1} g_1(y,t,x)g_2(x,s,t)\Big((p_0(s,t)+p_1(s,t)p_2(s,t))u(s,t) \\
&\qquad\qquad + p_2^{(0,1)}(s,t)u^{(0,1)}(s,t)+q(s,t)\Big)ds\,dt.
\end{aligned}
\tag{46}
$$

We omit the proof of Lemma 4, since it is similar to the proof of [10, Lemma 2.7]. Let

$$
\varphi_\rho(z) = \begin{cases} 1 & \text{for } |z| \le \rho, \\ \rho+1-|z| & \text{for } |z| \in [\rho,\rho+1], \\ 0 & \text{for } |z| \ge \rho+2, \end{cases} \qquad \chi_\rho(z) = \int_0^z \varphi_\rho(s)ds, \tag{47}
$$

and let $\Phi_\rho : C^1_{\omega_1\omega_2} \to \mathbb{R}$ be a continuous nonlinear functional defined by the equality

$$
\Phi_\rho(u) = \varphi_\rho\Big(\|u\|_{C^1_{\omega_1\omega_2}}\Big). \tag{48}
$$

Consider the equation

$$
\begin{aligned}
u^{(2,2)} &= f_0(x,y,\chi_\rho(u)) + f_1(y,\Phi_\rho(u)u)u^{(2,0)} + f_2(x,\Phi_\rho(u))u^{(0,2)} \\
&\quad + \Phi_\rho(u)f\Big(x,y,u,u^{(1,0)},u^{(0,1)},u^{(1,1)}\Big) - \lambda u + \lambda\chi_\rho(u).
\end{aligned}
\tag{49}
$$

Lemma 5. *Let $\lambda > 0$ and $\rho > 0$. Then every solution u of problem (49), (3) admits the estimates*

$$
\begin{aligned}
\int_0^{\omega_1}\int_0^{\omega_2} \Big(&|f_0(x,y,\chi_\rho(u(x,y)))|\,|u(x,y)| + \Big|u^{(1,0)}(x,y)\Big|^2 \\
&+ \Big|u^{(0,1)}(x,y)\Big|^2 + \Big|u^{(1,1)}\Big|^2\Big)dx\,dy \le r_0,
\end{aligned}
\tag{50}
$$

where r_0 is a positive constant independent of ρ, λ, and u.

Proof. Let u be a solution of problems (49), (3). Multiplying (49) by $u(x,y)$, integrating over the rectangle $[0,\omega_1]\times[0,\omega_2]$, and using integration by parts, we get

$$\int_0^{\omega_1}\int_0^{\omega_2}\Big(\big(-f_0(x,y,\chi_\rho(u(x,y)))+\lambda u-\lambda\chi_\rho(u)\big)u(x,y)-f_1(y,u(x,y))u^{(2,0)}(x,y)u(x,y)$$
$$-f_2(x,u(x,y))u^{(0,2)}(x,y)u(x,y)+\big|u^{(1,1)}(x,y)\big|^2\Big)dx\,dy$$
$$=\int_0^{\omega_1}\int_0^{\omega_2}\Phi_\rho(u)f\Big(x,y,u(x,y),u^{(1,0)}(x,y),u^{(0,1)}(x,y),u^{(1,1)}(x,y)\Big)u(x,y)dx\,dy. \tag{51}$$

By conditions (13) and (14), we have

$$\begin{aligned}&\big(-f_0(x,y,\chi_\rho(u(x,y)))+\lambda(u(x,y)-\chi_\rho(u(x,y)))\big)u(x,y)\\&\quad\geq|f_0(x,y,\chi_\rho(u(x,y)))u(x,y)|,\end{aligned} \tag{52}$$

$$\begin{aligned}&\Phi_\rho(u)\Big|f\Big(x,y,u(x,y),u^{(1,0)}(x,y),u^{(0,1)}(x,y),u^{(1,1)}(x,y)\Big)\Big|\,|u(x,y)|\\&\quad\leq r_1+\frac{1}{2}|f_0(x,y,\chi_\rho(u(x,y)))|\,|u(x,y)|,\end{aligned} \tag{53}$$

where r_1 is a positive constant independent of ρ, λ, and u.

For $h>0$, set

$$f_{ih}(y,z)=\frac{1}{h}\int_z^{z+h}f_i(y,\xi)d\xi. \tag{54}$$

Then by condition (11), we have

$$\begin{aligned}&-\int_0^{\omega_1}\int_0^{\omega_2}f_{1h}(y,\Phi_\rho(u)u(x,y))u(x,y)u^{(2,0)}(x,y)dx\,dy\\
&\quad=\int_0^{\omega_1}\int_0^{\omega_2}f_{1h}(y,\Phi_\rho(u)u(x,y))\Big|u^{(1,0)}(x,y)\Big|^2dx\,dy\\
&\qquad+\frac{\Phi_\rho(u)}{h}\int_0^{\omega_1}\int_0^{\omega_2}\Big(f_1(y,\Phi_\rho(u)(u(x,y)+h)\\
&\qquad\qquad-f_1(y,\Phi_\rho(u)u(x,y))\Big)u(x,y)\Big|u^{(1,0)}(x,y)\Big|^2dx\,dy\\
&\quad\geq\int_0^{\omega_1}\int_0^{\omega_2}f_{1h}(y,\Phi_\rho(u)u(x,y))\Big|u^{(1,0)}(x,y)\Big|^2dx\,dy\\
&\qquad-\Phi_\rho(u)\iint_{D_h}|f_1(y,\Phi_\rho(u)(u(x,y)+h)-f_1(y,\Phi_\rho(u)u(x,y)|\,\Big|u^{(1,0)}(x,y)\Big|^2dx\,dy,\end{aligned} \tag{55}$$

where $D_h = \{(x,y) \in [0,\omega_1] \times [0,\omega_2] : |u(x,y)| \le h\}$. Hence we immediately get that

$$-\int_0^{\omega_1}\int_0^{\omega_2} f_1(y,\Phi_\rho(u)u(x,y))u(x,y)u^{(2,0)}(x,y)dx\,dy \\ \ge \int_0^{\omega_1}\int_0^{\omega_2} f_1(y,\Phi_\rho(u)u(x,y))\left|u^{(1,0)}(x,y)\right|^2 dx\,dy. \tag{56}$$

In the same way, we show that

$$-\int_0^{\omega_1}\int_0^{\omega_2} f_2(x,\Phi_\rho(u)u(x,y))u(x,y)u^{(0,2)}(x,y)dx\,dy \\ \ge \int_0^{\omega_1}\int_0^{\omega_2} f_2(y,\Phi_\rho(u)u(x,y))\left|u^{(0,1)}(x,y)\right|^2 dx\,dy. \tag{57}$$

Taking into account (52)–(57), from (51), we immediately get (50) with $r_0 = (2+\delta^{-1})r_1$. □

Proof of Theorem 1. Let $v \in C^{1,1}_{\omega_1\omega_2}(\mathbb{R}^2)$ be an arbitrary function. Set

$$\begin{aligned} p_1[v](x,y) &= f_1(y,\Phi_\rho(v)v(x,y)), \qquad p_2[v](x,y) = f_2(x,\Phi_\rho(v)v(x,y)), \\ q[v](x,y) &= f_0(X,y,\chi_\rho(v(x,y))) \\ &\quad + \Phi_\rho(v)f\left(x,y,v(x,y),v^{(1,0)}(x,y),v^{(0,1)}(x,y),v^{(1,1)}(x,y)\right). \end{aligned} \tag{58}$$

Consider the equation

$$u^{(2,2)} = -\lambda u + p_1[v](x,y)u^{(2,0)} + p_2[v](x,y)u^{(0,2)} + \lambda\chi_\rho(v(x,y)) + q[v](x,y). \tag{59}$$

Note that due to definitions of p_1 and p_2 for every $\rho > 0$, there exists a continuous function $\eta_\rho : [0,+\infty) \to [0,+\infty)$, $\eta_\rho(0) = 0$ such that

$$\left| p_1[v](x_1,y_1) - p_2[v](x_2,y_2)\right| + \left| p_2[v](x_1,y_1) - p_2[v](x_2,y_2)\right| \\ \le \eta_\rho(|x_1 - x_2| + |y_1 - y_2|). \tag{60}$$

By Lemma 3, there exist $\lambda > 0$ and $M_\lambda > 0$ depending on ρ, δ, and the function η_ρ only, such that for every $v \in C^{1,1}_{\omega_1\omega_2}(\mathbb{R}^2)$, problem (59), (3) has a unique solution $u[v]$ admitting the estimate

$$||u[v]||_{C^{2,2}_{\omega_1\omega_2}} \le M_\lambda(||q[v]||_{C_{\omega_1\omega_2}} + \lambda\rho). \tag{61}$$

It is easy to see that the operator $\mathcal{A} : v \to u[v]$ is a continuous operator from $C^{1,1}_{\omega_1\omega_2}(\mathbb{R}^2)$ into $C^{2,2}_{\omega_1\omega_2}(\mathbb{R}^2)$, and therefore it is a completely continuous operator from $C^{1,1}_{\omega_1\omega_2}(\mathbb{R}^2)$ into $C^{1,1}_{\omega_1\omega_2}(\mathbb{R}^2)$. Moreover,

$$||\mathcal{A}(v)||_{C^{2,2}_{\omega_1\omega_2}} \le M_\lambda(||q[v]||_{C_{\omega_1\omega_2}} + \lambda\rho) \le M_\lambda c_\rho, \tag{62}$$

where c_ρ is a positive constant independent of v.

By Schauder's fixed point theorem, the operator $\mathscr{A}$ has a fixed point $u \in C^{2,2}_{\omega_1\omega_2}(\mathbb{R}^2)$, which is a solution of the functional differential equation (49).

By Lemma 5, u admits estimate (50). Conditions (13) and (50) imply the estimate

$$\|u\|_{H^{1,1}_{\omega_1\omega_2}} \le r_1, \tag{63}$$

where r_1 is a positive constant independent of ρ, λ, and u. On the other hand, one can easily establish the inequalities

$$\|u\|_{C_{\omega_1\omega_2}} \le \Omega\|u\|_{H^{1,1}_{\omega_1\omega_2}}, \tag{64}$$

$$|u(x_1,y_1) - u(x_2,y_2)| \le \Omega\|u\|_{H^{1,1}_{\omega_1\omega_2}}\left(\sqrt{|x_1 - x_2|} + \sqrt{|y_1 - y_2|}\right), \tag{65}$$

where

$$\Omega = \frac{1}{\sqrt{\omega_1}} + \frac{1}{\sqrt{\omega_2}} + \frac{1}{\sqrt{\omega_1\omega_2}} + \sqrt{\omega_1} + \sqrt{\omega_2}. \tag{66}$$

Choosing $\rho > \Omega r_1$, we observe that u is a solution of the equation

$$\begin{aligned} u^{(2,2)} &= f_0(x,y,u) + f_1(y,\Phi_\rho(u)u)u^{(2,0)} + f_2(x,\Phi_\rho(u))u^{(0,2)} \\ &\quad + \Phi_\rho(u) f\left(x,y,u,u^{(1,0)},u^{(0,1)},u^{(1,1)}\right). \end{aligned} \tag{67}$$

Due to (63) and (65), there exists a nondecreasing continuous function $\eta : [0,+\infty) \to [0,+\infty)$, $\eta(0) = 0$ independent of ρ such that

$$\begin{aligned} &|f_1(y_1,\Phi_\rho(u)u(x_1,y_1)) - f_1(y_2,\Phi_\rho(u)u(x_2,y_2))| \\ &\quad + |f_2(x_1,\Phi_\rho(u)u(x_1,y_1)) - f_2(x_2,\Phi_\rho(u)u(x_2,y_2))| \le \eta(|x_1 - x_2| + |y_1 - y_2|). \end{aligned} \tag{68}$$

By Lemma 1 and inequality (68), there exists a positive constant M independent of ρ such that u admits the estimate (30). Choosing $\rho > \Omega(r_1 + M)$, we get that an arbitrary solution of problems (67), (3) satisfies the inequality

$$\|u\|_{C^1_{\Omega_1\omega_2}} < \rho. \tag{69}$$

Consequently u is a solution of problem (1), (3) too. □

We omit the proof of Theorem 2, since it can be proved in much the same way. The only difference is that instead of Lemmas 1–3 one should use Lemma 4 to get necessary a priori estimates.

Proof of Theorem 3. Let $q \in C_{\omega_1\omega_2}(\mathbb{R}^2)$. Consider the equation

$$u^{(2,2)} = f_0(x,y,u) + \left(f_1(x,y)u^{(1,0)}\right)^{(1,0)} + \left(f_2(x,y)u^{(0,1)}\right)^{(0,1)} + q(x,y). \tag{70}$$

By Theorem 2, problems (70), (3) are solvable. Let u_1 and u_2 be two arbitrary solutions of problems (70), (3), and let $v(x,y) = u_1(x,y) - u_2(x,y)$. Then applying (27), we easily get the inequality

$$\int_0^{\omega_1}\int_0^{\omega_2}\left(\delta v^2(x,y)+f_1(x,y)\left|v^{(1,0)}(x,y)\right|^2+f_2(x,y)\left|v^{(0,1)}(x,y)\right|^2\right)dx\,dy\le 0. \tag{71}$$

Hence it follows that $u_1(x,y)\equiv u_2(x,y)$.

Thus for every $q\in C_{\omega_1\omega_2}(\mathbb{R}^2)$, problem (70), (3) has a unique solution $u[q]$. Applying Lemmas 1 and 2, one can easily show that the operator $\mathcal{A}: q\to u[q]$ is a continuous operator from $C_{\omega_1\omega_2}(\mathbb{R}^2)$ into $C^{2,2}_{\omega_1\omega_2}(\mathbb{R}^2)$ and that

$$\|\mathcal{A}(q_1)-\mathcal{A}(q_2)\|_{C^{2,2}_{\omega_1\omega_2}}\le a\|q_1-q_2\|_{C_{\omega_1\omega_2}}, \tag{72}$$

where a is a positive constant independent of q_1 and q_2. Therefore problem (25), (3) is equivalent to the operator equation

$$u(x,y)=\mathcal{A}\left(\varepsilon f\left(x,y,u,u^{(1,0)},u^{(0,1)},u^{(1,1)},u^{(2,0)},u^{(0,2)},u^{(2,1)},u^{(1,2)}\right)\right)(x,y)=\mathcal{B}_\varepsilon(u)(x,y). \tag{73}$$

Due to Lipschitz continuity of the function f, there exists a positive constant b such that

$$\left|f(x,y,z_1,\dots,z_8)-f(x,y,\overline{z}_1,\dots,\overline{z}_8)\right|\le b\sum_{i=1}^{8}\left|z_i-\overline{z}_i\right|. \tag{74}$$

From (72) and (74), it is clear that for $\varepsilon\in(-1/ab,1/ab)$, the operator $\mathcal{B}_\varepsilon$ is a contractive operator from $C^{2,2}_{\omega_1\omega_2}(\mathbb{R}^2)$ into $C^{2,2}_{\omega_1\omega_2}(\mathbb{R}^2)$. Hence (73), and consequently, problem (25), (3) is uniquely solvable. □

References

[1] A. K. Aziz and S. L. Brodsky, *Periodic solutions of a class of weakly nonlinear hyperbolic partial differential equations*, SIAM Journal on Mathematical Analysis **3** (1972), no. 2, 300–313.

[2] A. K. Aziz and M. G. Horak, *Periodic solutions of hyperbolic partial differential equations in the large*, SIAM Journal on Mathematical Analysis **3** (1972), no. 1, 176–182.

[3] L. Cesari, *Existence in the large of periodic solutions of hyperbolic partial differential equations*, Archive for Rational Mechanics and Analysis **20** (1965), no. 2, 170–190.

[4] ———, *Periodic solutions of nonlinear hyperbolic differential equations*, Colloques Internationaux du Centre National de la Recherche Scientifique **148** (1965), 425–437.

[5] ———, *Smoothness properties of periodic solutions in the large of nonlinear hyperbolic differential systems*, Funkcialaj Ekvacioj. Serio Internacia **9** (1966), 325–338.

[6] T. Kiguradze, *Some boundary value problems for systems of linear partial differential equations of hyperbolic type*, Memoirs on Differential equations and Mathematical Physics **1** (1994), 1–144.

[7] ———, *On periodic in the plane solutions of second order linear hyperbolic systems*, Archivum Mathematicum **33** (1997), no. 4, 253–272.

[8] ———, *Doubly periodic solutions of a class of nonlinear hyperbolic equations*, Differential Equations **34** (1998), no. 2, 242–249, translation from Differentsial'nye Uravneniya **34** (1998), no. 2, 238–245.

[9] ———, *On periodic in the plane solutions of nonlinear hyperbolic equations*, Nonlinear Analysis, Series A: Theory Methods **39** (2000), no. 2, 173–185.

[10] T. Kiguradze and V. Lakshmikantham, *On doubly periodic solutions of fourth-order linear hyperbolic equations*, Nonlinear Analysis, Series A: Theory Methods **49** (2002), no. 1, 87–112.

[11] B. P. Liu, *The integral operator method for finding almost periodic solutions of nonlinear wave equations*, Nonlinear Analysis. Theory, Methods & Applications **11** (1987), no. 5, 553–564.

[12] Yu. O. Mitropol's'kiĭ, G. P. Khoma, and P. V. Tsinaĭko, *A periodic problem for an inhomogeneous equation of string vibration*, Ukraïns'kiĭ Matematichniĭ Zhurnal **49** (1997), no. 4, 558–565 (Ukrainian).

[13] N. A. Perestyuk and A. B. Tkach, *Periodic solutions of a weakly nonlinear system of partial differential equations with impulse action*, Ukraïns'kiĭ Matematichniĭ Zhurnal **49** (1997), no. 4, 601–605 (Russian).

[14] B. I. Ptashnik, *Ill-Posed Boundary Value Problems for Partial Differential Equations*, Naukova Dumka, Kiev, 1984.

T. Kiguradze: Department of Mathematical Sciences, Florida Institute of Technology, Melbourne, FL 32901, USA
E-mail address: tkigurad@fit.edu

T. Smith: Department of Mathematical Sciences, Florida Institute of Technology, Melbourne, FL 32901, USA
E-mail address: smitht@fit.edu

SYMMETRIES OF THE PLANE PLASTICITY SYSTEM WITH A GENERAL YIELD CRITERION

PETR KIRIAKOV AND ALEXANDER YAKHNO

Some classes of invariant solution for the system of two-dimensional plasticity with general yield criterion are considered. In particular, the system with Coulomb law is investigated from the point of view of symmetry analysis. Moreover, the classification of the groups of point transformations admitted by the system with respect to the function of plasticity is realized. The mechanical sense of obtained invariant solutions is discussed.

1. Introduction

In general, the processes of plastic deformations of materials are expressed by the systems of nonlinear differential equations. For such systems, the numerical methods are used widely for resolving of the concrete boundary value problems. But as for the exact solution, there is a lack of them, because of strong nonlinearity of stress-strain relations. In this case, the symmetry (group) analysis of differential equations is a powerful method of the construction of exact solutions. It seems that the first application of these methods to the plasticity theory was made in [2].

The equations of plane plasticity describe stresses of deformed region, when the plastic flow is everywhere parallel to a given plane (usually x_1Ox_2 plane). This system consists of two equilibrium equations [4],

$$\frac{\partial \sigma_{x_1}}{\partial x_1} + \frac{\partial \tau_{x_1x_2}}{\partial x_2} = 0, \qquad \frac{\partial \sigma_{x_2}}{\partial x_2} + \frac{\partial \tau_{x_1x_2}}{\partial x_1} = 0, \tag{1.1}$$

and the law defining the limit of elasticity under some combination of stresses which is called the yield criterion $p(\sigma,\tau) = 0$, where σ_{x_i}, $\tau_{x_1x_2}$ are the components of stress tensor, σ is the hydrostatic pressure, and τ is the shear stress:

$$\sigma = \frac{(\sigma_{x_1} + \sigma_{x_2})}{2}, \qquad \tau^2 = \frac{(\sigma_{x_1} - \sigma_{x_2})^2}{4} + \tau_{x_1x_2}^2. \tag{1.2}$$

Hindawi Publishing Corporation
Proceedings of the Conference on Differential & Difference Equations and Applications, pp. 555–564

Considering the angle $\theta = (1,x_1) - \pi/4$, where $\tan 2(1,x_1) \equiv \tan 2\phi = (2\tau_{x_1x_2})/(\sigma_{x_1} - \sigma_{x_2})$ is a slope of principal axes of stress with respect to the x_1 – axis, and making the change of variables:

$$\begin{aligned}\sigma_{x_1} &= \sigma - \tau(\sigma,\theta)\sin 2\theta,\\ \sigma_{x_2} &= \sigma + \tau(\sigma,\theta)\sin 2\theta,\\ \tau_{x_1x_2} &= \tau(\sigma,\theta)\cos 2\theta,\end{aligned} \tag{1.3}$$

we will obtain that the system (1.1) has the form

$$\begin{aligned}\frac{\partial\sigma}{\partial x_1} - 2\tau\left(\frac{\partial\theta}{\partial x_1}\cos 2\theta + \frac{\partial\theta}{\partial x_2}\sin 2\theta\right) &= \frac{\partial\tau}{\partial x_1}\sin 2\theta - \frac{\partial\tau}{\partial x_2}\cos 2\theta,\\ \frac{\partial\sigma}{\partial x_2} - 2\tau\left(\frac{\partial\theta}{\partial x_1}\sin 2\theta - \frac{\partial\theta}{\partial x_2}\cos 2\theta\right) &= -\frac{\partial\tau}{\partial x_1}\cos 2\theta - \frac{\partial\tau}{\partial x_2}\sin 2\theta.\end{aligned} \tag{1.4}$$

The system (1.4) in the polar coordinates $\{r,\varphi\}$ takes the form

$$\begin{aligned}&r\left(1 - \sin 2\theta\frac{\partial\tau}{\partial\sigma}\right)\frac{\partial\sigma}{\partial r} + \cos 2\theta\frac{\partial\tau}{\partial\sigma}\frac{\partial\sigma}{\partial\varphi} - r\frac{\partial}{\partial\theta}(\tau\sin 2\theta)\frac{\partial\theta}{\partial r} + \frac{\partial}{\partial\theta}(\tau\cos 2\theta)\frac{\partial\theta}{\partial\varphi} = 2\tau\sin 2\theta,\\ &r\cos 2\theta\frac{\partial\tau}{\partial\sigma}\frac{\partial\sigma}{\partial r} + \left(1 + \sin 2\theta\frac{\partial\tau}{\partial\sigma}\right)\frac{\partial\sigma}{\partial\varphi} + \frac{\partial}{\partial\theta}(\tau\cos 2\theta)\frac{\partial\theta}{\partial r} + \frac{\partial}{\partial\theta}(\tau\sin 2\theta)\frac{\partial\theta}{\partial\varphi} = -2\tau\cos 2\theta,\end{aligned} \tag{1.5}$$

and the components of the stress tensor are the following:

$$\begin{aligned}\sigma_r &= \sigma - \tau(\theta+\varphi)\sin 2\theta,\\ \sigma_\varphi &= \sigma + \tau(\theta+\varphi)\sin 2\theta,\\ \tau_{r\varphi} &= \tau(\theta+\varphi)\cos 2\theta,\end{aligned} \tag{1.6}$$

here $\theta = (1,r) - \pi/4 = \psi - \pi/4$, and ψ means the angle between principal axes of stress with respect to the radius-vector r.

The plastic state of concrete material is described by an appropriated form of the function τ:

(i) von Mises' criterion [4]: $\tau^2 = k^2 = \text{const}$ is used for plastic metals. In [8] the complete analysis of groups of symmetries was performed. There were constructed invariant solutions and all conservation laws of this system were described;

(ii) the linear criterion [5]: $\tau = a\sigma + b$ and, in particular, Coulomb's criterion [3]: $\tau^2 = (\sigma\sin\Phi + k\cos\Phi)^2$, $(a,b,k,\Phi = \text{consts})$ are used for the free-flowing (granular) media [9];

(iii) nonlinear generalizations of the function τ [10]: $\tau = \tau(\sigma)$ are used for the soil media and low-plastic metals. The special criterion of Sokolovsky $\tau = k\sin((\sigma - \sigma_0)/k)$ and the "parabolic" one $\tau = (1/2)(ak - \sigma^2/(ak))$ are between them;

(iv) general form: $\tau = \tau(\sigma,\theta)$ can be used to describe a plastic state of anisotropic media. In particular, one can find a plastic anisotropy in some polycrystals and metals after a critical sequence of mechanical and heat treatments, and so forth.

The paper is structured as follows. In Section 2, the complete analysis of point transformations for the plane plasticity with Coulomb's criterion is presented and invariant solutions are constructed. Section 3 is devoted to the symmetry analysis of the system (1.4) when $\tau = \tau(\theta)$. Using the well-known method of [6], the group classification of such a system will be done. The basic group of point transformations (kernel) admitted by this system for any form of τ is calculated, and specifications of τ for which there is an extension of basic group are shown. For every Lie algebra of admitted operators, we performed the classification of nonsimilar subalgebras and determined the corresponding invariant solutions using the method of [7].

2. Plasticity with Coulomb's criterion

2.1. Point transformations. Let us consider the yield criterion of Coulomb [3]: $\tau = \sigma \sin\Phi + k\cos\Phi$, where $\Phi \in (-\pi/2, \pi/2)$ is a constant angle of internal friction, k is a constant of the coupling. For convenience, let us introduce the angle $\alpha = -\Phi/2 + \pi/4$, then $\sin\Phi = \cos 2\alpha$, $\alpha \in (0, \pi/2)$, and now $\tau = \sigma\cos 2\alpha + k\sin 2\alpha$. If $\Phi = 0$, then we have Mises' criterion, for which the complete symmetry analysis was made in [8], so we assume $\alpha \neq \pi/4$. The system (1.4) will have the form

$$\begin{aligned}(\sec 2\alpha + \cos 2\phi)\sigma_{x_1} + \sin 2\phi\sigma_{x_2} &= 2\tau\sec 2\alpha(\sin 2\phi\phi_{x_1} - \cos 2\phi\phi_{x_2}),\\ \sin 2\phi\sigma_{x_1} + (\sec 2\alpha - \cos 2\phi)\sigma_{x_2} &= -2\tau\sec 2\alpha(\cos 2\phi\phi_{x_1} + \sin 2\phi\phi_{x_2}).\end{aligned} \tag{2.1}$$

Hereafter, the indices mean the derivation with respect to corresponding variables. The system (2.1) will be investigated in this section. This system is a hyperbolic one, and by passing to characteristic variables

$$\begin{aligned}\xi &= \frac{1}{2\cos 2\alpha}\ln(\cot 2\alpha\sigma + k) - \frac{\phi}{\sin 2\alpha},\\ \eta &= \frac{1}{2\cos 2\alpha}\ln(\cot 2\alpha\sigma + k) + \frac{\phi}{\sin 2\alpha},\end{aligned} \tag{2.2}$$

the system (2.1) takes the form

$$\xi_{x_1} + \xi_{x_2}\tan(\phi - \alpha) = 0, \qquad \eta_{x_1} + \eta_{x_2}\tan(\phi + \alpha) = 0. \tag{2.3}$$

Moreover, by applying the hodograph transformations $x_1 = x_1(\xi,\eta)$, $x_2 = x_2(\xi,\eta)$ (where the Jacobian $D(\xi,\eta)/D(x_1,x_2) \neq 0$) and by changing variables

$$\begin{aligned}u &= \sqrt{\cot 2\alpha\sigma + k}\,(x_1\sin(\phi+\alpha) - x_2\cos(\phi+\alpha)),\\ v &= \sqrt{\cot 2\alpha\sigma + k}\,(-x_1\sin(\phi-\alpha) + x_2\cos(\phi-\alpha)),\end{aligned} \tag{2.4}$$

the system (2.3) is reduced to the following:

$$u_\xi + \frac{v}{2} = 0, \qquad v_\eta + \frac{u}{2} = 0. \tag{2.5}$$

The Lie algebra of admissible operators for the system (2.5) is known [8] and is formed by

$$Z_1 = \partial_\xi, \qquad Z_2 = \partial_\eta, \qquad Z_3 = \xi\partial_\xi - \eta\partial_\eta + \frac{u}{2}\partial_u - \frac{v}{2}\partial_v,$$
$$Z_4 = u\partial_u + v\partial_v, \qquad Z_\infty = h^1(\xi,\eta)\partial_u + h^2(\xi,\eta)\partial_v, \tag{2.6}$$

where (h^1,h^2) is an arbitrary solution of the system (2.5). Using the known formulas for the transformation of operators under the change of coordinates, we will obtain the Lie algebra $L = \langle X_1,X_2,X_3,X_4\rangle \oplus \langle X_\infty\rangle = L_4 \oplus L_\infty$ of symmetries admitted by the initial system (2.1):

$$X_1 = \omega_1\partial_{x_1} + \omega_2\partial_{x_2} - \sin 2\alpha \tan 2\alpha \ln(\sigma\cot 2\alpha + k)\partial_\phi - 4\tau\phi\partial_\sigma,$$
$$X_2 = x_1\partial_{x_2} - x_2\partial_{x_1} + \partial_\phi, \qquad X_3 = \tau\partial_\sigma, \tag{2.7}$$
$$X_4 = x_1\partial_{x_1} + x_2\partial_{x_2}, \qquad X_\infty = F(\sigma,\phi)\partial_{x_1} + G(\sigma,\phi)\partial_{x_2},$$

where (F,G) is an arbitrary solution of the linear system,

$$(1+\cos 2\alpha\cos 2\phi)G_\phi - \cos 2\alpha \sin 2\phi F_\phi = -2\tau(\sin 2\phi G_\sigma + \cos 2\phi F_\sigma),$$
$$\cos 2\alpha \sin 2\phi G_\phi - (1-\cos 2\alpha \cos 2\phi)F_\phi = 2\tau(\cos 2\phi G_\sigma - \sin 2\phi F_\sigma), \tag{2.8}$$

and the coefficients w_1, w_2 are the following:

$$\omega_1 = x_1\sin 2\phi - 2x_2\cos(\phi-\alpha)\cos(\phi+\alpha) + x_1\phi 2\cos 2\alpha + x_2\sin 2\alpha\tan 2\alpha\ln(\sigma\cot 2\alpha + k),$$
$$\omega_2 = 2x_1\sin(\phi-\alpha)\sin(\phi+\alpha) - x_2\sin 2\phi - x_1\sin 2\alpha\tan 2\alpha\ln(\sigma\cot 2\alpha + k) + x_2\phi 2\cos 2\alpha. \tag{2.9}$$

2.2. Optimal system and invariant solutions. The Lie algebra L_4 constructed in Section 2.1 has the following nonzero commutators: $[X_1,X_2] = 4X_3$, $[X_1,X_3] = \sin^2 2\alpha X_2$; therefore X_4 is a center of this algebra. X_∞ is an infinite-dimensional ideal of L, the finite algebra L_4 is a solvable one.

The optimal system of one-dimensional subalgebras for L_4 consists of four classes: $\langle X_1 + aX_4\rangle$, $\langle X_2 + aX_3 + bX_4\rangle$, $\langle aX_3 + X_4\rangle$, $\langle X_3\rangle$, where a, b are arbitrary constants. The first three classes satisfy to the necessary condition of the existence of invariant solution.

(1) $\langle X_1 + aX_4\rangle$. The calculation of the basis of invariants leads to representation in the form

$$J_1 = \xi\eta, \qquad J_2 = u\eta^{(1/2+a)}, \qquad J_3 = v\xi^{(1/2-a)}, \tag{2.10}$$

where ξ, η, u, v are defined by the formulas (2.2), (2.4). The variables are not separated, but if we take u, v as new dependent variables, and ξ, η as new independent variables, then the system (2.1), is reduced to the system (2.5). With respect to the system (2.5), the variables in (2.10) are separated and the invariant solution has the form $u = \hat{u}(\xi\eta)\eta^{(-1/2-a)}$, $v = \hat{v}(\xi\eta)\xi^{(-1/2+a)}$. Substituting it to (2.5) and resolving obtained factor system, we have the following invariant solution:

$$u = \xi^{1/2+a}\left[C_1 \mathrm{I}_{-a-1/2}\left(\sqrt{\xi\eta}\right) + C_2 \mathrm{K}_{-a-1/2}\left(\sqrt{\xi\eta}\right)\right],$$
$$v = \eta^{1/2-a}\left[C_1 \mathrm{I}_{-a+1/2}\left(\sqrt{\xi\eta}\right) + C_2 \mathrm{K}_{-a+1/2}\left(\sqrt{\xi\eta}\right)\right], \tag{2.11}$$

where $\mathrm{I}_\nu(x)$, $\mathrm{K}_\nu(x)$ are the Bessel functions of the first and the second kind of an imaginary argument, C_1, C_2 are arbitrary constants.

If a is an integer number, then the solution is expressed by the elemental functions. For example, if $a = 0$, then

$$u = \frac{\left(C_1 e^{\sqrt{\xi\eta}} + C_2 e^{-\sqrt{\xi\eta}}\right)}{\sqrt{\eta}}, \qquad v = \frac{\left(-C_1 e^{\sqrt{\xi\eta}} + C_2 e^{-\sqrt{\xi\eta}}\right)}{\sqrt{\xi}}. \tag{2.12}$$

(2) $\langle \partial_{x_1} + aX_3 \rangle$. For convenience, let us make the change of variable $\sigma + k\tan 2\alpha = \tilde{\sigma}$ in the system (2.1). After the deleting of the tilde, the operator X_3 takes the form $X_3 = \sigma\partial_\sigma$.

Let us take $F = 1$, $G = 0$ as the solution of the system (2.8), and let us construct the invariant solution on the subalgebra $\partial_{x_1} + aX_3$. The form of the solution is $\sigma = \exp(ax_1)\chi(x_2)$, $\phi = \phi(x_2)$. Substituting this form to (2.1) and resolving the corresponded factor system, we will obtain the invariant solution

$$x_2 + C_1 = \frac{\cos 2\alpha}{a\sin^2 2\alpha}(2\phi\cos 2\alpha - \sin 2\phi), \qquad \sigma = C_2\exp\left(ax_1 + \cos 2\phi\right). \tag{2.13}$$

This invariant solution is an analog of Prandtl's solution of ideal plane plasticity and can be interpreted as a compression of the thin layer of free-flowing (granular) media by two parallel plates. The corresponding characteristic lines (slip lines on the theory of the plane plasticity) have the form

$$ax_1 = \pm 2\phi\cot 2\alpha + \frac{\cos 2\alpha}{a\sin^2 2\alpha}\cos 2\phi + \text{const},$$
$$x_2 = 2\phi\cot^2 2\alpha - \frac{\cos 2\alpha}{a\sin^2 2\alpha}\sin 2\phi. \tag{2.14}$$

(3) $\langle aX_3 + X_4 \rangle$. The system (1.5) with Coulomb's condition $\tau = \sigma\cos 2\alpha + k\sin 2\alpha$ has the form

$$r(1 + \cos 2\alpha\cos 2\psi)\sigma_r + \cos 2\alpha\sin 2\psi\sigma_\theta$$
$$= 2(\sigma\cos 2\alpha + \sin 2\alpha k)(r\sin 2\psi\psi_r - \cos 2\psi(\psi_\theta + 1)),$$
$$r\cos 2\alpha\sin 2\psi\sigma_r + (1 - \cos 2\alpha\cos 2\psi)\sigma_\theta$$
$$= -2(\sigma\cos 2\alpha + \sin 2\alpha k)(r\cos 2\psi\psi_r + \sin 2\psi(\psi_\theta + 1)). \tag{2.15}$$

The operator X_4 in polar coordinates $\{r, \varphi\}$ looks like $X_4 = r\partial_r$. The form of invariant solution is $\sigma = r^a\chi(\varphi)$, $\psi = \psi(\varphi)$. Resolving the corresponding factor system, taking ψ a new independent variable, and denoting $\nu = (a\sin^2 2\alpha)/(2\cos 2\alpha) - \cos 2\alpha$, we have the invariant solution of (2.15):

$$\begin{aligned}
\varphi - C_1 &= -\psi + \frac{(1+\cos 2\alpha)}{2\tan\psi} \quad (\nu = 1), \\
\varphi - C_1 &= \frac{\cos 2\alpha + \nu}{\sqrt{1-\nu^2}} \operatorname{arccot}\left(\sqrt{\frac{\nu-1}{\nu+1}}\tan\psi\right) - \psi \quad (\nu > 1), \\
\varphi - C_1 &= \frac{\cos 2\alpha + \nu}{\sqrt{1-\nu^2}} \operatorname{arctanh}\left(\sqrt{\frac{1-\nu}{1+\nu}}\tan\psi\right) - \psi \quad (\nu < 1).
\end{aligned} \tag{2.16}$$

The second function looks like $\chi = C_2|\cos 2\psi + \nu|^{a/2}$. These integrals where obtained by Sokolovsky [9].

The corresponding characteristic lines have the form

$$r^a \chi \exp\left(\mp(\varphi+\psi)\cot 2\alpha\right) = \text{const.} \tag{2.17}$$

This solution contains two arbitrary constants and permits to investigate the limit equilibrium of weightless wedge of ideal-granular media, when the stress is distributed by the potential law.

(4) $\langle X_2 + aX_3 + bX_4\rangle$. The operator X_2 in polar coordinates has the form $X_2 = \partial_\varphi$. The form of invariant solutions is $\sigma = \exp(b\varphi)\chi(t)$, $\psi = \psi(t)$, $t = r\exp(-\alpha\varphi)$. From the corresponding factor system, it follows that one can find the functions ψ, χ by quadratures from the system of ODE:

$$\begin{aligned}
t\frac{d\psi}{dt} &= \frac{a\cos 2\psi + \sin 2\psi - a\cos 2\alpha + b/2\sin 2\alpha\tan 2\alpha}{(a^2-1)\cos 2\psi + 2a\sin 2\psi - (a^2+1)\cos 2\alpha}, \\
\frac{d\chi}{d\psi} &= -\frac{\chi(ab(\cos 2\alpha - \cos 2\psi) - b\sin 2\psi - 2\cos 2\alpha)}{a(\cos 2\psi - \cos 2\alpha) + \sin 2\psi + b/2\sin 2\alpha\tan 2\alpha}.
\end{aligned} \tag{2.18}$$

This solution can be used for description of plastic flow in curvilinear channel bounded by logarithmic spirals.

3. Angular anisotropy

In the case when $\tau = \tau(\theta)$ ("angular anisotropy") the system (1.4) has the form

$$\begin{aligned}
\sigma_{x_1} - \theta_{x_1}(\tau\sin 2\theta)'_\theta + \theta_{x_2}(\tau\cos 2\theta)'_\theta &= 0, \\
\sigma_{x_2} + \theta_{x_1}(\tau\cos 2\theta)'_\theta + \theta_{x_2}(\tau\sin 2\theta)'_\theta &= 0,
\end{aligned} \tag{3.1}$$

and is a hyperbolic one for any form of the function τ; such kind of dependence is used widely in the mathematical theory of plasticity [5]. Further we will investigate the system (3.1).

The group analysis of the system (3.1) gives the following results.

3.1. $\tau(\theta)$ is an arbitrary function. In this case Lie algebra has the form $L_k = L_2 \oplus L_\infty$:

$$L_2 = \langle X_3, X_4 \rangle = \langle \partial_\sigma, x_1\partial_{x_1} + x_2\partial_{x_2} \rangle,$$
$$L_\infty = \langle X_\infty \rangle = \langle h^1(\sigma,\theta)\partial_{x_1} + h^2(\sigma,\theta)\partial_{x_2} \rangle, \tag{3.2}$$

where $h^1(\sigma,\theta)$, $h^2(\sigma,\theta)$ is any solution of the system

$$h^1_\theta = h^1_\sigma(\tau\sin 2\theta)' - h^2_\sigma(\tau\cos 2\theta)',$$
$$h^2_\theta = -h^1_\sigma(\tau\cos 2\theta)' - h^2_\sigma(\tau\sin 2\theta)'. \tag{3.3}$$

3.2. $\tau = 1/\sin 2\theta$. After appropriate calculus, we conclude that Lie algebra of symmetries of the system (3.1) with such form of dependence is formed by the following operator:

$$Y_\infty = (f+g)\partial_{x_1} + (f-g)\partial_{x_2} + \frac{(\eta^2+\eta^1)}{2}\partial_\sigma + \frac{\sin^2 2\theta(\eta^2-\eta^1)}{4}\partial_\theta, \tag{3.4}$$

where $f(x_1,x_2,T), g(x_1,x_2,S), \eta^1(x_1,x_2,S), \eta^2(x_1,x_2,T)$ is any solution of the linear system ($S = \sigma + \cot 2\theta$, $T = \sigma - \cot 2\theta$):

$$f_{x_1} - f_{x_2} = 0, \qquad g_{x_2} - g_{x_1} = 0,$$
$$\eta^1_{x_1} + \eta^1_{x_2} = 0, \qquad \eta^2_{x_1} - \eta^2_{x_2} = 0. \tag{3.5}$$

Such kind of dependence of τ has not a mechanic sense because of the presence of singular points; therefore we will not investigate this case.

3.3. If τ is any solution of classification equation $A = w' + \tau'(2w-1)/\tau = \text{const} \neq 0$, then we have two additional operators to the L_2 of the kernel (3.2):

$$X_1 = \left[\frac{x_1(-w(\tau\sin 2\theta)' - A\sigma)}{2} + \left(-\sigma + \frac{w(\tau\cos 2\theta)'}{2}\right)x_2\right]\partial_{x_1}$$
$$+ \left[\left(\sigma + \frac{w(\tau\cos 2\theta)'}{2}\right)x_1 + \frac{x_2(w(\tau\sin 2\theta)' - A\sigma)}{2}\right]\partial_{x_2}$$
$$+ \frac{[A\sigma^2 + w^2(4\tau^2+\tau'^2)/A]}{2}\partial_\sigma + \sigma w\partial_\theta, \tag{3.6}$$
$$X_2 = -x_2\partial_{x_1} + x_1\partial_{x_2} + A\sigma\partial_\sigma + w\partial_\theta, \qquad w(\theta) = \frac{4\tau^2+\tau'^2}{4\tau^2+2\tau'^2-\tau\tau''}.$$

Nonzero commutators of Lie algebra are

$$[X_2,X_1] = AX_1, \qquad [X_4,X_1] = AX_2 - \frac{A^2}{2X_3}, \qquad [X_4,X_2] = AX_4. \tag{3.7}$$

Without loss of generality, let $A = 1$. Using the classic method of classification of non-conjugate subalgebras [7], it is easy to demonstrate that optimal system of one-dimensional subalgebras looks like

$$\Theta_1 : \langle X_1 + \beta X_4 + \alpha X_3 \rangle, \quad \beta = \{0,1\}, \quad \langle X_2 + \alpha X_3 \rangle, \quad \langle X_3 \rangle, \quad \alpha = \text{const}. \tag{3.8}$$

Brief analysis of Θ_2 shows that there are no interesting invariant solutions. From Θ_1, all subalgebras satisfy to the necessary condition of the existence of invariant solution. The specification of an arbitrary element is $\tau = e^{C\theta}$, this form of τ could be taken as a criterion for anisotropic material because it is reduced to von Mises' law when the anisotropy is vanishing small. The corresponding factor system is obtained by substituting this form of τ and the form of invariant solution to (3.1). Let us consider some of them.

(1) Let $\beta = 0$ for the first subalgebra of Θ_1, that is, subalgebra has the form $H_1 = \langle X_1 + \alpha X_3\rangle$. Here we can apply the procedure like the one in Section 2.1. Let $C = 2$, passing to characteristic coordinates $\xi = \sigma - e^{2\theta}\sqrt{2}$, $\eta = \sigma + e^{2\theta}\sqrt{2}$, applying hodograph transformation, and changing of variables

$$\begin{aligned} u &= x_1 \cos\left(\theta - \frac{\pi}{8}\right) + x_2 \sin\left(\theta - \frac{\pi}{8}\right), \\ v &= -x_1 \sin\left(\theta - \frac{\pi}{8}\right) + x_2 \cos\left(\theta - \frac{\pi}{8}\right), \end{aligned} \tag{3.9}$$

the initial system (3.1) is reduced to the following one:

$$u_\xi = \frac{v}{(2(\xi - \eta))}, \qquad v_\eta = \frac{u}{(2(\xi - \eta))}. \tag{3.10}$$

For the system (3.10), the invariant solution looks like

$$u = \frac{e^{-\alpha/\eta}\hat{u}(t)}{\eta}, \qquad v = \frac{e^{-\alpha/\xi}\hat{v}(t)}{\xi}, \qquad t = \frac{(\eta - \xi)}{(\xi\eta)}. \tag{3.11}$$

From the corresponding factor system of ODEs, one can obtain the general form of $\hat{u}$:

$$\hat{u}(t) = C_1 \mathrm{W}_{-1/2,i/2}(\alpha t)t^{-1/2}e^{(\alpha/2)t} + C_2\sqrt{t}e^{-(\alpha/2)t}\left[\mathrm{I}_{(i-1)/2}\left(\frac{\alpha t}{2}\right) + \mathrm{I}_{(1+i)/2}\left(\frac{\alpha t}{2}\right)\right], \tag{3.12}$$

where $\mathrm{W}_{\mu,\nu}(z)$ is the Whittaker function and $\mathrm{I}_\nu(x)$ is the Bessel function of the first kind [1]. The function v is reconstructed from (3.10).

When $\alpha = 0$, the solution takes the simple form

$$\hat{u}(t) = C_1 \cos(\ln\sqrt{t}) + C_2 \sin(\ln\sqrt{t}), \qquad \hat{v}(t) = -C_1 \sin(\ln\sqrt{t}) + C_2\cos(\ln\sqrt{t}). \tag{3.13}$$

(2) Subalgebra $H_2 = \langle X_3\rangle$ in polar coordinates $\{r, \varphi\}$ has the form $\langle r\partial_r\rangle$, and the initial system (3.1) looks like

$$\begin{aligned} r\sigma_r - r\theta_r(\tau\sin 2\theta)' + \theta_\varphi(\tau\cos 2\theta)' &= 2\tau\sin 2\theta, \\ \sigma_\varphi + r\theta_r(\tau\cos 2\theta)' + \theta_\varphi(\tau\sin 2\theta)' &= -2\tau\cos 2\theta. \end{aligned} \tag{3.14}$$

Invariant solution has the form $\sigma = \sigma(\varphi)$, $\theta = \theta(\varphi)$. After substituting this form of solution to the system (3.14), we can determine it by quadratures from the corresponding factor system:

$$\begin{aligned} \theta'(C\cos 2\theta - 2\sin 2\theta) &= 2\sin 2\theta, \\ \sigma' + \theta'\tau(C\sin 2\theta + 2\cos 2\theta) &= -2\tau\cos 2\theta. \end{aligned} \tag{3.15}$$

(3) Let us take solution of the system (3.3) in the form $h^1 = 1, h^2 = 0$. Then $X_\infty = \partial_{x_1}$. Let us consider subalgebra $\langle \partial_{x_1} + \alpha\partial_\sigma \rangle$. The invariant solution has the form $\sigma = \sigma(x_2) + \alpha x_1, \theta = \theta(x_2)$. Resolving correspnding factor system, we obtain that

$$\sigma = -e^{C\theta}\sin 2\theta + \alpha x_1 + C_2, \qquad x_2 = \frac{-e^{C\theta}}{\alpha}\cos 2\theta + C_1, \tag{3.16}$$

which is an analog of the well-known solution of Prandtl for a plastic region in a thin block compressed between perfectly rough plates. Here the constant $2/\alpha$ plays the role of the height of the block.

The corresponding charactcristics are (for $C = 2$)

$$\begin{aligned} x_1 &= \frac{\mp\sqrt{2}\tan^2\theta(\tan\theta + 1) \pm (2 \mp \sqrt{2})(\tan\theta - 1)}{2(\tan^2\theta + 1)(\tan\theta + 1 \pm \sqrt{2})} + K_i, \quad K_i = \text{const}, \\ x_2 &= -\frac{e^{2\theta}}{\alpha}\cos 2\theta. \end{aligned} \tag{3.17}$$

3.4. If $A = 0$, then we need to add two operators to L_2 of the kernel L_k:

$$\begin{aligned} X_1 &= \left[\frac{-x_1 w(\tau\sin 2\theta)'}{2} + x_2\left(-\sigma + \frac{w(\tau\cos 2\theta)'}{2}\right)\right]\partial_{x_1} \\ &\quad + \left[x_1\left(\sigma + \frac{w(\tau\cos 2\theta)'}{2}\right) + \frac{x_2 w(\tau\sin 2\theta)'}{2}\right]\partial_{x_2} + \left[K\int\frac{d\theta}{w}\right]\partial_\sigma + \sigma w\partial_\theta, \\ X_2 &= -x_2\partial_{x_1} + x_1\partial_{x_2} + w\partial_\theta, \qquad K = w^2(4\tau^2 + \tau'^2) = \text{const} > 0. \end{aligned} \tag{3.18}$$

The representative is $\tau = 1/(\cos 2\theta + \sqrt{1 + \cos^2 2\theta})$. Such kind of the function τ could be used for description of some materials because it is not equal to zero for any θ.

In this case, the nonzero commutators are: $[X_2, X_1] = KX_4$, $[X_4, X_1] = X_2$, and Lie algebra is a solvable one. The optimal system of nonsimilar one-dimensional subalgebras looks like

$$\Theta_1 : \langle X_1 + \alpha X_3\rangle, \langle X_4 + \alpha X_3\rangle, \langle X_2 + \beta X_4 + \alpha X_3\rangle, \langle X_3\rangle, \quad \beta^2 = \{K, 0\},\ \alpha = \text{const}. \tag{3.19}$$

(1) To construct the invariant solution for the subalgebra $H_1 = \langle X_1 + \alpha X_3\rangle$ as in a previous case for any form of τ, we have to pass to characteristic variables and make hodograph transformations, because of complicity of operator X_1 in terms of original variables.

(2) In polar coordinates, the subalgebra $H_2 = \langle X_4 + \alpha X_3\rangle$ looks like $\langle \partial_\sigma + \alpha r\partial_r\rangle$. Invariant solution has the form $\sigma = \sigma(\varphi) + \ln r^{1/\alpha}$, $\theta = \theta(\varphi)$, $\alpha \neq 0$. If $\alpha = 0$, there is no invariant solution.

(3) For subalgebra $H_3 = \langle X_2 + \beta X_4 + \alpha X_3 \rangle$ in polar system of coordinates one can find the form of invariant solution from

$$\sigma = \sigma(re^{-\alpha\varphi}) + \beta\varphi, \qquad \int \frac{d\theta}{w} = \theta(re^{-\alpha\varphi}) + \varphi. \tag{3.20}$$

Here it should be noted for the other specification $\tau = 2k\cos 2\theta$ by change of variables $\theta = \bar{\theta}/2$ that the initial system (3.1) is reduced to the system of isotropic plasticity ($\tau = k = \text{const}$). One can construct the analogs of all known invariant solutions.

Acknowledgments

The authors are grateful to Professor Sergey Senashov for useful discussions and interesting comments. This research was partially supported by PROMEP (103.5/03/1140), Mexico.

References

[1] M. Abramowitz and I. Stegun, *Handbook of Mathematical Functions*, 1972.
[2] B. D. Annin, V. O. Bytev, and S. I. Senashov, *Group Properties of Equations of Elasticity and Plasticity*, Nauka, Novosibirsk, 1985.
[3] A. M. Freidental and H. Geiringer, *The Mathematical Theories of the Inelastic Continuum*, Springer, Berlin, 1958.
[4] R. Hill, *The Mathematical Theory of Plasticity*, Clarendon Press, Oxford, 1960.
[5] A. Yu. Ishlinskij and D. D. Ivlev, *Mathematical Theory of Plasticity*, Fizmatlit, Moscow, 2001.
[6] L. V. Ovsyannikov, *Group Analysis of Differential Equations*, Academic Press, New York, 1982.
[7] ———, *Optimal systems of subalgebras*, Russian Academy of Sciences. Doklady. Mathematics **48** (1994), no. 3, 645–649.
[8] S. I. Senashov and A. M. Vinogradov, *Symmetries and conservation laws of 2-dimensional ideal plasticity*, Proceedings of the Edinburgh Mathematical Society. Series II **31** (1988), no. 3, 415–439.
[9] V. V. Sokolovsky, *Statics of Granular Media*, Pergamon Press, Oxford, 1965.
[10] V. V. Sokolovsky, D. H. Jones, and A. N. Schofield, *Statics of Soil Media*, Butterworths Scientific, London, 1960.

Petr Kiriakov: Institute of Computational Modelling, SB of the Russian Academy of Sciences, 660036 Krasnoyarsk, Russia
E-mail address: gm@krasu.ru

Alexander Yakhno: Departamento de Matemáticas, CUCEI, Universidad de Guadalajara, CP 44430, Mexico
E-mail address: alexander.yakhno@cucei.udg.mx

DYNAMICS OF A DISCONTINUOUS PIECEWISE LINEAR MAP

V. L. KOCIC

Our aim in this paper is to investigate the global asymptotic behavior, oscillation, and periodicity of positive solutions of difference equation: $x_{n+1} = (a - bh(x_n - c))x_n$, where a, b, and c are positive constants such that $0 < b < 1 < a < b + 1$, h is Heaviside function and the initial condition is nonnegative. The above equation appears in the discrete model of West Nile epidemics when the spraying against mosquitoes is conducted only when the number of mosquitoes exceeds some predefined threshold level.

1. Introduction and preliminaries

In this paper we study the global asymptotic behavior, oscillation, and periodicity of positive solutions of the following difference equation:

$$x_{n+1} = (a - bh(x_n - c))x_n, \tag{1.1}$$

where $x_0 \geq 0$, a, b, and c are positive constants such that

$$0 < b < 1 < a < b + 1, \tag{1.2}$$

and h is Heaviside function:

$$h(t) = \begin{cases} 0 & \text{if } t < 0, \\ 1 & \text{if } t \geq 0. \end{cases} \tag{1.3}$$

The motivation for studying the dynamics of (1.1) comes from the discrete model of the West Nile-like epidemics [1, 5]. The model consists of a system of twelve nonlinear difference equations and it describes the spread of epidemics among population of mosquitoes, birds, and humans. One of the equations which describes the total number

Hindawi Publishing Corporation
Proceedings of the Conference on Differential & Difference Equations and Applications, pp. 565–574

of mosquitoes is

$$T_M(n+1) = (1 + r_m - d_m - s(n))T_M(n), \tag{1.4}$$

where $T_M(n)$ denotes the number of mosquitoes in the week n, r_m and d_m are mosquito birth rate and death rate, respectively, and $s(n)$ is a spraying function representing the rate of mosquito deaths due to spraying. Assuming that the spraying will occur in the week n if the total population of mosquitoes in the same week exceeds the threshold level T and that the death rate due to spraying is constant S (when spraying is applied) we arrive to the following model:

$$T_M(n+1) = (1 + r_m - d_m - Sh(T_M(n) - T))T_M(n). \tag{1.5}$$

Clearly $1 + r_m - d_m > 1$, $0 < S < 1$, $1 + r_m - d_m - S > 0$. By putting $x_n = T_M(n)$, $a = 1 + r_m - d_m$, $b = S$, and $c = T$, we obtain (1.1).

The map $f(x) = (a - bh(x - c))x$ is a piecewise linear discontinuous map, so standard techniques for studying the dynamics of one-dimensional maps could not be directly applied. Discontinuous maps have applications in neural networks [4, 3, 8, 9] and in flip-flop processes in the Lorenz flow [6, 7].

A sequence $\{x_n\}$ is said to *oscillate about zero* or simply to *oscillate* if the terms x_n are neither eventually all positive nor eventually all negative. Otherwise the sequence is called *nonoscillatory*. A sequence $\{x_n\}$ is said to *oscillate about* $\bar{x}$ if the sequence $\{x_n - \bar{x}\}$ oscillates. A *positive semicycle* of $\{x_n\}$ *with respect to* $\bar{x}$ consists of a "string" of terms $C_+ = \{x_{l+1}, x_{l+2}, \dots, x_m\}$, such that $x_i \geq \bar{x}$ for $i = l+1, \dots, m$ with $l \geq -k$ and $m \leq \infty$ and such that either $l = -k$ or $l \geq 0$ and $x_l < \bar{x}$ and either $m = \infty$ or $m < \infty$ and $x_{m+1} < \bar{x}$. A *negative semicycle* of $\{x_n\}$ *with respect to* $\bar{x}$ consists of a "string" of terms $C_- = \{x_{j+1}, x_{j+2}, \dots, x_l\}$, such that $x_i < \bar{x}$ for $i = j+1, \dots, l$, with $j \geq -k$ and $l \leq \infty$ and such that either $j = -k$ or $j \geq 0$ and $x_j \geq \bar{x}$ and either $l = \infty$ or $l < \infty$ and $x_{l+1} \geq \bar{x}$. The first semicycle of a solution starts with the term x_0 and is positive if $x_0 \geq \bar{x}$ and negative if $x_0 < \bar{x}$. A solution may have a finite number of semicycles or infinitely many.

In recent years, the study of semicycles of oscillatory solutions played an important role in the analysis of asymptotic behavior of solutions of nonlinear difference equations. In particular the analysis of the length and position of extreme terms in semicycles led to a number of results about the global asymptotic stability and attractivity in nonlinear difference equations (see, e.g., [2]). In the context of the West Nile epidemics model, the semicycles of the number of mosquitoes $\{T_M(n)\}$ with respect to the threshold T have a very important practical meaning. Namely, the positive semicycles correspond to weeks when the spraying is applied, while the negative semicycles correspond to weeks when there are no spraying. So, the goal in controlling the epidemics is to maximize the length of negative semicycles and minimize the length of positive semicycles or to minimize spraying.

2. Boundedness and persistence

The following technical lemma will be useful in the sequel.

Lemma 2.1. *Assume (1.2) holds and let*

$$f(x) = (a - bh(x - c))x, \tag{2.1}$$

where h is the Heaviside function. Then the following statements are true.
(i) $\bar{x} = 0$ *is the only nonnegative equilibrium of (1.1).*
(ii) $x_n = 0$, *for all* $n = 0, 1, \ldots$, *if and only if* $x_0 = 0$.
(iii) f *is discontinuous at* $x = c$.
(iv) f *satisfies the negative feedback condition:*

$$(f(x) - x)(x - c) < 0 \quad \text{for } x > 0,\ x \neq c. \tag{2.2}$$

Proof. The proof is omitted. □

The next result establishes the existence of an invariant interval for f.

Theorem 2.2. *Assume (1.2) holds and let* f *be defined by (2.1). Then the following statements are true.*
(i) *The interval*

$$I = [(a - b)c, ac] \tag{2.3}$$

is invariant under f*; that is,* $f([(a - b)c, ac]) \subseteq [(a - b)c, ac]$.
(ii) *Equation (1.1) does not have positive convergent solutions.*
(iii) *All positive solutions of (1.1) become trapped in an interval* I.
(iv) *Equation (1.1) is permanent.*

Proof. (i) From (1.2) it follows that $(a - b)ac \in [(a - b)c, ac]$. If $x \in [(a - b)c, c)$, then $f(x) \in [(a - b)ac, ac) \subseteq [(a - b)c, ac]$. Similarly, if $x \in [c, ac]$, then $f(x) \in [(a - b)c, (a - b)ac) \subseteq [(a - b)c, ac]$ and the proof of part (i) is complete.

(ii) Assume, for the sake of contradiction, that $\{x_n\}$ is a positive convergent solution of (1.1). Then $\lim_{n\to\infty} x_n = x \geq 0$. If $x = 0$, then for sufficiently large n, $0 < x_n < c$, for $n > N_0$. Furthermore, we get $x_{n+1} = ax_n > x_n$, and that is, impossible since $\{x_n\}$ converges to 0. Let $x > 0$. If $0 < x < c$, for sufficiently large n, we have $x_{n+1} = ax_n$, and $x = ax$ which is a contradiction. The case when $x > c$ is similar. So it remains the case when $x = c$. Let $\{x'_k\}$ and $\{x''_k\}$ be subsequences of $\{x_n\}$ such that $x'_k < c$, and $x''_k \geq c$. Clearly $\lim_{k\to\infty} x'_k = \lim_{k\to\infty} x''_k = c$ and at least one of these two subsequences has infinite number of terms. Then at least one of the following two conditions must be satisfied:

$$c = ac \quad \text{or} \quad c = (a - b)b \tag{2.4}$$

and this is impossible.

(iii) Assume, for the sake of contradiction, that $\{x_n\}$ is a positive solution of (1.1) which is not trapped in an invariant interval $I = [(a - b)c, ac]$. Then, for every n, $x_n \notin I$. Let $\{x'_k\}$ and $\{x''_k\}$ be subsequences of $\{x_n\}$ such that $x'_k < (a - b)c$, and $x''_k > ac$. Clearly, at most one of the subsequences $\{x'_k\}$ and $\{x''_k\}$ may have only a finite number of terms or no terms at all. Assume that $\{x''_k\}$ has a finite number of terms. Then, for sufficiently large n, $x_n < (a - b)c$. Then $x_{n+1} = ax_n > x_n$, and the sequence $\{x_n\}$ converges, which is a contradiction. The similar conclusion follows in the case when $\{x'_k\}$ has only a finite number of terms. So the remaining case is when both $\{x'_k\}$ and $\{x''_k\}$ have infinitely many terms. Let $x_m < (a-b)c$ and $x_{m+1} > ac$. Then $x_{m+1} = ax_m < ac(a-b)$ and $ac < ac(a-b)$ or $a > b+1$. This contradicts (1.2) and the proof of part (iii) is complete.

(iv) This part directly follows from (i) and (iii). The proof of the theorem is complete. □

3. Oscillation

In this section we study the oscillation character of solution of (1.1). First, we will consider the sequences $\{\alpha_n\}$ and $\{\beta_n\}$ defined as

$$\alpha_k \text{ is the unique root in } (1, b+1) \text{ of } f_k(x) = x^k(x-b) - 1; \tag{3.1}$$

$$\beta_k \text{ is the unique root in } (b, b+1) \text{ of } g_k(x) = x(x-b)^k - 1. \tag{3.2}$$

Clearly, since $f_k(1) = -b < 0$, $f_k(b+1) = (b+1)^k - 1 > 0$, $g_k(b) = -1 < 0$, $g_k(b+1) = b > 0$, and f_k, g_k are increasing on (b, ∞), it follows that indeed both f_k and g_k have unique roots in (b, ∞). The next lemma establishes some properties of sequences $\{\alpha_n\}$ and $\{\beta_n\}$.

Lemma 3.1. *Assume (1.2) holds and let $\{\alpha_n\}$ and $\{\beta_n\}$ be defined by (3.1) and (3.2), respectively. Then the following statements are true.*

(i) $\alpha_1 = \beta_1 = (b + \sqrt{b^2+4})/2$.

(ii) *$\{\alpha_n\}$ is a decreasing sequence and $\{\beta_n\}$ is an increasing sequence.*

(iii)

$$\lim_{n\to\infty} \alpha_n = 1, \qquad \lim_{n\to\infty} \alpha_n^n = \frac{1}{1-b}, \qquad \lim_{n\to\infty} \beta_n = b+1, \qquad \lim_{n\to\infty} (\beta_n - b)^n = \frac{1}{1+b}. \tag{3.3}$$

Proof. (i) It follows from the fact that $f_1(x) = g_1(x) = x(x-b) - 1$.

(ii) Since $f_{k+1}(x) = x^{k+1}(x-b) - 1 = x(f_k(x)+1) - 1$, we obtain $f_{k+1}(\alpha_k) = \alpha_k(f_k(\alpha_k)+1) - 1 = \alpha_k - 1 > 0$. The function f_{k+1} is increasing and $f_{k+1}(\alpha_{k+1}) = 0$, so we have $\alpha_{k+1} < \alpha_k$. The proof that $\{\beta_n\}$ increases is similar and will be omitted.

(iii) The sequence $\{\alpha_n\}$ is bounded and therefore convergent. Let

$$\lim_{n\to\infty} \alpha_n = \alpha \geq 1. \tag{3.4}$$

Assume $\alpha > 1$. Then, there is $\varepsilon > 0$, such that for sufficiently large n, $\alpha_n > \alpha - \varepsilon > 1$. Hence $\alpha_n^n > (\alpha - \varepsilon)^n$, and $\lim_{n\to\infty} \alpha_n^n = \infty$. On the other hand, $f_n(\alpha_n) = 0$ implies $\alpha_n^n = 1/(\alpha_n - b)$ wherefrom follows $\lim_{n\to\infty} \alpha_n^n = 1/(\alpha - b)$ which is impossible. Therefore, $\alpha = 1$ and $\lim_{n\to\infty} \alpha_n^n = 1/(1-b)$. Similarly one may prove the remaining part of the lemma. □

Lemma 3.2. *Assume (1.2) holds. Then all positive solutions of (1.1) strictly oscillate about c.*

Proof. Otherwise, there exists a nonoscillatory solution $\{x_n\}$. Assume $x_n < c$ for sufficiently large n. Then $x_{n+1} = ax_n > x_n$ and $\{x_n\}$ converges which is impossible. The case when $x_n \geq c$ for sufficiently large n is similar. □

The following theorem represents a "trichotomy" result about the semicycles of length one for (1.1).

THEOREM 3.3. *Assume (1.2) holds and let $\{x_n\}$ be a positive solution of (1.1). Then the following statements are true.*

(i) *If $a > (b+\sqrt{b^2+4})/2$, then every negative semicycle relative to c, except perhaps the first one, has exactly one term.*
(ii) *If $a < (b+\sqrt{b^2+4})/2$, then every positive semicycle relative to c, except perhaps the first one, has exactly one term.*
(iii) *If $a = (b+\sqrt{b^2+4})/2$, then every semicycle relative to c, except perhaps the first one, has exactly one term.*

Proof. We will consider only the case when $a \geq (b+\sqrt{b^2+4})/2$. Clearly (i) and the part of (iii) follow from this case. The proof in the case $a \leq (b+\sqrt{b^2+4})/2$, which implies (ii) and the remaining part of (iii) is similar and will be omitted.

Let x_k be the last term in a positive semicycle such that $x_k \in [c, c/(a-b)) \subset [c, ac]$. Then $x_{k+1} = (a-b)x_k \in [(a-b)c, c) \subset [c/a, c)$ belongs to a negative semicycle. Furthermore, $x_{k+2} = ax_{k+1} \in [c, ac)$ so it belongs to a positive semicycle. To complete the proof it remains to show that the last term of any positive semicycle always belongs to the interval $[c, c/(a-b))$. Assume, for the sake of contradiction, that $x_k \in [c/(a-b), ac]$ be the last term of a positive semicycle. Then $x_{k+1} = (a-b)x_k \in [c, a(a-b)c] \subset [c, ac]$ also belongs to the positive semicycle. This is a contradiction and the proof is complete. □

Next, we will further study the semicycles of solutions of (1.1).

LEMMA 3.4. *Assume (1.2) holds and let*

$$\alpha_{k+1} < a < \alpha_k \quad \text{for some positive integer } k. \tag{3.5}$$

Furthermore, let $\{p_i\}_{i=0}^{k+1}$ and $\{q_i\}_{i=0}^{k+1}$ be finite sequences defined by

$$p_i = c(a-b)a^i, \quad q_i = ca^{-k+i}, \quad i = 0, 1, \ldots, k+1, \tag{3.6}$$

and let

$$P_i = [p_i, q_i), \quad i = 0, \ldots, k+1, \qquad Q_i = [q_i, p_{i+1}), \quad i = 0, \ldots, k. \tag{3.7}$$

Then the following statements are true.

(i) *$p_0 = c(a-b)$, $q_k = c$, $q_{k+1} = ac$, so the invariant interval for (1.1) is $I = [p_0, q_{k+1}]$.*
(ii) *For f_k is defined by (3.1):*

$$f_k(a) = a^k(a-b) - 1 < 0, \qquad f_{k+1}(a) = a^{k+1}(a-b) - 1 > 0. \tag{3.8}$$

(iii) *$p_i < q_i < p_{i+1} < q_{i+1}$ for $i = 0, 1, \ldots, k$.*
(iv) *$P_i \cap Q_j = \varnothing$, $i \neq j$ and $(\bigcup_{i=0}^{k+1} P_i) \cup (\bigcup_{i=0}^{k} Q_i) \cup \{q_{i+1}\} = I$.*

Proof. Part (i) follows directly from (3.6). From (3.1) it follows that $f_k(x) < 0$, for $1 < x < \alpha_k$, and $f_k(x) > 0$, for $\alpha_k < x < b+1$, which implies (ii). Since $p_i < q_i$ is equivalent to $f_k(a) < 0$, and $q_i < p_{i+1}$ is equivalent to $f_{k+1}(a) > 0$, so (iii) follows. Finally, (iv) follows from (i)–(iii) and (3.7). □

LEMMA 3.5. *Assume (1.2), (3.5) hold and let the sequences* $\{p_i\}_{i=0}^{k+1}$ *and* $\{q_i\}_{i=0}^{k+1}$ *and intervals* P_i, Q_i *be defined by (3.6) and (3.7), respectively. Let* $\{x_n\}$ *be a positive solution of (1.1), then the following statements are true.*

(i) *If* $x_n \in P_i$, *then* $x_{n+1} \in P_{i+1}$, $i = 0,1,\dots,k$.

(ii) *If* $x_n \in Q_i$, *then* $x_{n+1} \in Q_{i+1}$, $i = 0,1,\dots,k-1$.

(iii) *If* $x_n \in P_{k+1}$, *then* $x_{n+1} \in P_0 \cup Q_0$.

(iv) *If* $x_n \in Q_k$, *then* $x_{n+1} \in P_0 \cup Q_0$.

(v) *If* $x_n \in P_0$, *then*

$$\begin{gathered} x_{n+i} \in P_i \subset [c(a-b),c), \quad i = 0,1,\dots,k, \\ x_{n+k+1} \in P_{k+1} \subset [c,ac), \\ x_{n+k+2} \in P_0 \cup Q_0 \subset [c(a-b),c), \quad x_{n+k+2} > x_n. \end{gathered} \tag{3.9}$$

(vi) *If* $x_n \in Q_0$, *then*

$$\begin{gathered} x_{n+i} \in Q_i \subset [c(a-b),c), \quad i = 0,1,\dots,k-1, \\ x_{n+k} \in Q_k \subset [c,ac), \\ x_{n+k+1} \in P_0 \cup Q_0 \subset [c(a-b),c), \quad x_{n+k+1} < x_n. \end{gathered} \tag{3.10}$$

(vii) *If* $x_n = q_{k+1}$, *then* $x_{n+i} = p_i$, $i = 1,\dots,k+1$.

Proof. (i) Since $p_i \le x_n < q_i \le c$, then $x_{n+1} = ax_n$ and $p_{i+1} = ap_i \le x_{n+1} < aq_i = q_{i+1}$.

(ii) The proof is similar to (i) and will be omitted.

(iii) Since $c < c(a-b)a^{k+1} = p_{k+1} \le x_n \le q_{k+1} = ac$, then $x_{n+1} = (a-b)x_n$ and from (3.8) it follows that $p_0 = c(a-b) < c(a-b)^2a^{k+1} = (a-b)p_{k+1} \le x_{n+1}$ and $x_{n+1} \le (a-b)q_{k+1} = c(a-b)a = p_1$.

(iv) Similarly as in (iii), $c = q_k \le x_n < p_{k+1} = c(a-b)a^{k+1} < ac$ and (3.8) imply that $x_{n+1} = (a-b)x_n$, $p_0 = c(a-b) = (a-b)q_k \le x_{n+1}$, and $x_{n+1} \le (a-b)p_{k+1} = c(a-b)^2a^{k+1} < c(a-b)a = p_1$.

(v) From (i) it follows that $x_n \in P_0$ implies $x_{n+1} \in P_1$, $x_{n+2} \in P_2,\dots,x_{n+k} \in P_k$, and $x_{n+k+1} \in P_{k+1}$. Furthermore, from (iii) we get $x_{n+k+2} \in P_0 \cup Q_0$. Since $x_n,\dots,x_{n+k} < c$ and $x_{n+k+1} > c$, we get

$$x_{n+k+2} = a^{k+1}(a-b)x_n > x_n. \tag{3.11}$$

The proof of (vi) is similar to (v) and is omitted. Finally, (vii) follows directly from the definition of $\{p_i\}_{i=0}^{k+1}$ and $\{q_i\}_{i=0}^{k+1}$. □

The following two lemmas are analog to Lemmas 3.4 and 3.5 and we formulate them without proof.

Lemma 3.6. *Assume (1.2) holds and let*

$$\beta_k < a < \beta_{k+1} \quad \text{for some positive integer } k. \tag{3.12}$$

Furthermore, let $\{r_i\}_{i=0}^{k+1}$ *and* $\{s_i\}_{i=0}^{k+1}$ *be finite sequences defined by*

$$r_i = c(a-b)^{-k+i}, \quad s_i = ca(a-b)^i, \quad i = 0,1,\ldots,k+1, \tag{3.13}$$

and let $R_i = [r_i, s_i)$, $i = 0,\ldots,k+1$ *and* $S_j = [s_{j+1}, r_j)$, $j = 0,\ldots,k$.

Then the following statements are true.

(i) $r_{k+1} = c(a-b)$, $r_k = c$, $s_0 = ac$, *so the invariant interval for (1.1) is* $I = [r_{k+1}, s_0]$.

(ii) *For* g_k *is defined by (3.2),*

$$\begin{aligned} g_k(a) &= a(a-b)^k - 1 > 0, \\ g_{k+1}(a) &= a(a-b)^{k+1} - 1 < 0. \end{aligned} \tag{3.14}$$

(iii) $r_{i+1} < s_{i+1} < r_i < s_i$ *for* $i = 0,1,\ldots,k$.

(iv) $R_i \cap S_j = \varnothing$, $i \neq j$, *and* $(\bigcup_{i=0}^{k+1} R_i) \cup (\bigcup_{i=0}^{k} S_i) \cup \{s_0\} = I$.

Lemma 3.7. *Assume (1.2), (3.12) hold and let the sequences* $\{r_i\}_{i=0}^{k+1}$ *and* $\{s_i\}_{i=0}^{k+1}$ *be defined by (3.13). Let* $\{x_n\}$ *be a positive solution of (1.1), then the following statements are true.*

(i) *If* $x_n \in R_i$, *then* $x_{n+1} \in R_{i+1}$, $i = 1,\ldots,k+1$.

(ii) *If* $x_n \in S_i$, *then* $x_{n+1} \in S_{i+1}$, $i = 1,\ldots,k$.

(iii) *If* $x_n \in R_{k+1}$, *then* $x_{n+1} \in R_0 \cup S_0$.

(iv) *If* $x_n \in S_k$, *then* $x_{n+1} \in R_0 \cup S_0$.

(v) *If* $x_n \in R_0$, *then*

$$\begin{aligned} x_{n+i} &\in R_i \subset [c, ac), \quad i = 0,1,\ldots,k, \\ x_{n+k+1} &\in R_{k+1} \subset [c(a-b), c), \\ x_{n+k+2} &\in R_0 \cup S_0 \subset [c, ac), \quad x_{n+k+2} < x_n. \end{aligned} \tag{3.15}$$

(vi) *If* $x_n \in S_0$, *then*

$$\begin{aligned} x_{n+i} &\in S_{i+1} \subset [c, ac), \quad i = 0,1,\ldots,k-1, \\ x_{n+k} &\in S_k \subset [c(a-b), c), \\ x_{n+k+1} &\in R_0 \cup S_0 \subset [c, ac), \quad x_{n+k+1} > x_n. \end{aligned} \tag{3.16}$$

(vii) *If* $x_n = s_0$, *then* $x_{n+i} = s_i$, $i = 1,\ldots,k+1$.

The following theorem follows directly from Lemmas 3.5 and 3.7.

Theorem 3.8. *Assume (1.2) holds and let* $\{x_n\}$ *be a positive solution of (1.1). Then the following statements are true.*

(i) *If (3.5) holds, then every positive semicycle, except perhaps the first one, has the length one, and every negative semicycle, except perhaps the first one, has the length equal to either* k *or* $k+1$.

(ii) *If (3.12) holds, then every negative semicycle, except perhaps the first one, has the length one, and every positive semicycle, except perhaps the first one, has the length equal to either* k *or* $k+1$.

Theorem 3.9. *Assume (1.2) holds and let* $\{x_n\}$ *be a positive solution of (1.1). Then the following statements are true.*

(i) *If* $a=\alpha_k$, *then* $\{x_n\}$ *is eventually periodic with period* $k+1$. *Moreover, every positive semicycle, except perhaps the first one, has the length one, and every negative semicycle, except perhaps the first one, has the length* k.

(ii) *If* $a=\beta_k$, *then* $\{x_n\}$ *is eventually periodic with period* $k+1$. *Moreover, every negative semicycle, except perhaps the first one, has the length one, and every positive semicycle, except perhaps the first one, has the length* k.

Proof. We will prove only the part (i). The proof of the part (ii) is similar and will be omitted. Since every solution of (1.1) becomes eventually trapped in an invariant interval I, we need only to show $x_{k+1}=x_0$, for every $x_0\in I$. Since $a=\alpha_k$, then $a^k(a-b)=1$ and we have $I=(\bigcup_{i=0}^{k-1}[ca^i(a-b),ca^{i+1}(a-b)))\cup[c,ca]$. Without loss of generality, we may assume $x_0\in[c(a-b),ca(a-b))$. Then

$$\begin{aligned}
x_1 &= ax_0\in\big[ca(a-b),ca^2(a-b)\big),\\
x_2 &= a^2x_0\in\big[ca^2(a-b),ca^3(a-b)\big),\\
&\vdots\\
x_{k-1} &= a^{k-1}x_0\in\big[ca^{k-1}(a-b),ca^k(a-b)\big)=\big[ca^{k-1}(a-b),c\big),\\
x_k &= a^kx_0\in[c,ca).
\end{aligned}\tag{3.17}$$

Finally, $x_{k+1}=(a-b)x_k=a^k(a-b)x_0=x_0$ and the proof is complete. □

4. Computer simulation

The previous results are illustrated with some computer simulations displayed in Figures 4.1 and 4.2. Table 4.1 contains numerical values for the first ten terms of both sequences $\{\alpha_n\}$ and $\{\beta_n\}$ when $b=0.6$.

Software Phaser 2.1 was used for computer simulations and to generate time series graph representing first 100 terms of the sequence $\{x_n\}$ and corresponding stair case diagrams. Two different values of the parameter a are used: $a=1.1$ and $a=1.4$. In both cases $b=0.6$ and $c=4$. In the case $a=1.1$, from Table 4.1, we find $\alpha_8<a<\alpha_7$, so according to Theorem 3.8(i), every positive semicycle, except perhaps the first one, has length 1, and

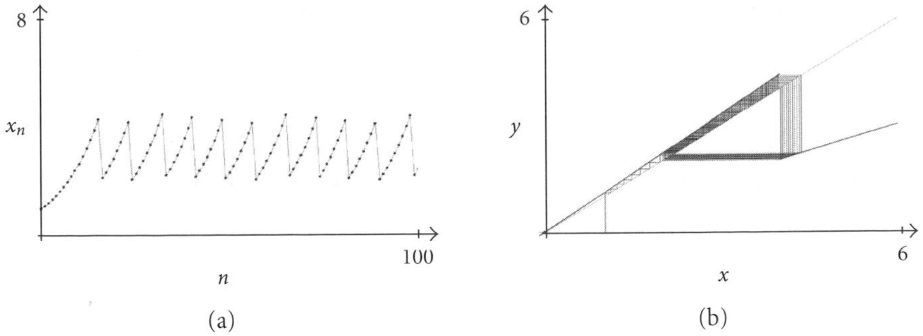

Figure 4.1. (a) Time series graph and (b) the stair case diagram for $a = 1.1$, $b = 0.6$, $c = 4$.

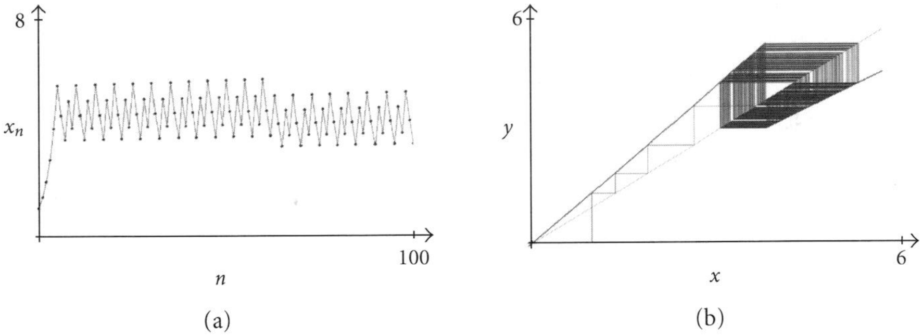

Figure 4.2. (a) Time series graph and (b) the stair case diagram for $a = 1.4$, $b = 0.6$, $c = 4$.

Table 4.1

k	1	2	3	4	5	6	7	8	9	10
α_k	1.344	1.2451	1.1914	1.1574	1.1338	1.1164	1.1031	1.0926	1.0840	1.0769
β_k	1.344	1.4348	1.4779	1.5031	1.5197	1.5314	1.5402	1.5469	1.5523	1.5567

every negative semicycle, except perhaps the first one, has length either 7 or 8. Similarly when $a = 1.4$, we have $\beta_1 < a < \beta_2$. Again, from Theorem 3.8(ii) it follows that every negative semicycle, except perhaps the first one, has length 1, and every positive semicycle, except perhaps the first one, has length either 1 or 2.

Figure 4.3 contains typical bifurcation diagrams in the cases: (i) a and c are constants and b varies; (ii) b and c are constants and a varies.

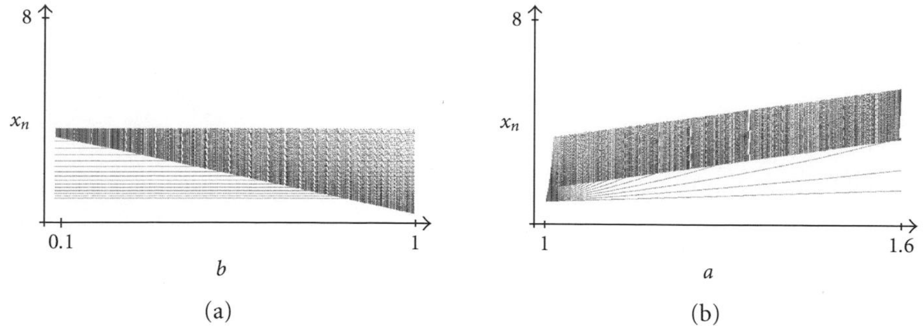

Figure 4.3. Bifurcation diagrams for $a = 1.1$, $b \in (0.1, 1)$, $c = 4$ and $a \in (1, 1.6)$, $b = 0.6$, $c = 4$.

Acknowledgment

The work in this paper was supported by the Louisiana Board of Regents Grant LEQSF(2004-07)-RD-A-40 and by the Howard Hughes Medical Institute through the special sabbatical program.

References

[1] T. Darensburg and V. L. Kocic, *On the discrete model of West Nile-like epidemics*, Dynamic Systems and Applications. Vol. 4, Dynamic, Georgia, 2004, pp. 358–366.

[2] V. L. Kocic and G. Ladas, *Global Behavior of Nonlinear Difference Equations of Higher Order with Applications*, Mathematics and Its Applications, vol. 256, Kluwer Academic, Dordrecht, 1993.

[3] Y. Liu, L. Huang, and Z. Yuan, *Asymptotic behavior and periodicity of solutions for a difference equation with piecewise constant nonlinearity*, Differences and Differential Equations, Fields Institute Communications, vol. 42, American Mathematical Society, Rhode Island, 2004, pp. 241–251.

[4] K. Liu and H. Zhang, *Asymptotic behavior in nonlinear discrete-time neural networks with delayed feedback*, Differences and Differential Equations, Fields Institute Communications, vol. 42, American Mathematical Society, Rhode Island, 2004, pp. 231–240.

[5] D. M. Thomas and B. Urena, *A model describing the evolution of West Nile-like encephalitis in New York City*, Mathematical and Computer Modelling **34** (2001), no. 7-8, 771–781.

[6] R. Wackerbauer, *Noise-induced stabilization of one-dimensional maps*, Physical Review E **58** (1998), no. 3, 3036–3044.

[7] ———, *When noise decreases deterministic difusion*, Physical Review E **59** (1999), no. 3, 2872–2879.

[8] Z. Zhou and Q. Zhang, *Periodic solutions of a class of difference systems*, Differences and Differential Equations, Fields Institute Communications, vol. 42, American Mathematical Society, Rhode Island, 2004, pp. 397–404.

[9] H. Zhu and L. Huang, *Dynamic analysis of a discrete-time network of two neurons with delayed feedback*, Differences and Differential Equations, Fields Institute Communications, vol. 42, American Mathematical Society, Rhode Island, 2004, pp. 405–414.

V. L. Kocic: Department of Mathematics, Xavier University of Louisiana, New Orleans, LA 70125, USA
E-mail address: vkocic@xula.edu

ASYMPTOTIC ANALYSIS OF TWO COUPLED REACTION-DIFFUSION PROBLEMS

DIALLA KONATE

The current paper is a contribution to the attempt to have a systematic and mathematically rigorous method to solve singularly perturbed equations using asymptotic expansions. We are dealing with a system of coupled and singularly perturbed second-order evolution equations. This problem has not collected much efforts in the literature yet. Starting from the classical outer expansion (the current problem exhibits two disjoint boundary layers), using the Hilbert spaces approach, we develop a systematic and rigorous method to construct a higher-order corrector which results in a uniform approximation solution to any prescribed order which is valid throughout the geometric domain of interest, say Ω. To solve the given problem, the literature provides a dedicated numerical method of Shiskin-type (cf. [9]). The system of equations under consideration is related to actual problems arising in physics, chemistry, and engineering where the use of new scientific instruments requires highly accurate approximation solutions which are out of reach of known numerical methods. This makes it necessary and useful to develop analytical solutions which are easy to computerize. The author has developed and successfully applied the strategy used in the current paper to various classes of problems (cf. [5–7]). This strategy works very well on linear problems of all types thanks to the availability of a priori estimates. In this regard the current paper is self-contained. For more on a priori estimates related to some other families of singularly perturbed problems, the reader may refer to Gartland [2, 3], Geel [4]. The reader who is not very familiar with singular perturbation may get some basics from Eckhaus [1], Lions [8], and O'Malley [10].

1. Introduction

Consider the problem

$$\mathcal{L}_\varepsilon U(x) = \begin{pmatrix} -\varepsilon\dfrac{d^2}{dx^2} & 0 \\ 0 & -\varepsilon\dfrac{d^2}{dx^2} \end{pmatrix} U(x) + A(x)U(x) = F,$$

Hindawi Publishing Corporation
Proceedings of the Conference on Differential & Difference Equations and Applications, pp. 575–592

$$U(0) = (u_1(0), u_2(0))^T,$$
$$U(1) = (u_1(1), u_2(1))^T, \tag{1.1}$$

where

$$A(x) = \begin{pmatrix} a_{1,1}(x) & a_{1,2}(x) \\ a_{2,1}(x) & a_{2,2}(x) \end{pmatrix}; \qquad U(x) = \begin{pmatrix} u_1(x) \\ u_2(x) \end{pmatrix};$$
$$F(x) = \begin{pmatrix} f_1(x) \\ f_2(x) \end{pmatrix}. \tag{1.2}$$

We make the following assumptions:

$$a_{i,j}(x) \in \mathbf{C}^0(\Omega), \quad f_i(x) \in \mathbf{L}^2(\Omega), \quad i,j = 1,2;$$
$$0 < \varepsilon \ll 1;$$
$$a_{1,1}(x) > \max[1, |a_{1,2}(x)|], \quad a_{2,2}(x) > \max[1, |a_{2,1}(x)|], \quad x \in \overline{\Omega};$$
$$a_{1,2}(x) \le 0, \quad a_{2,1}(x) \le 0, \quad x \in \overline{\Omega}. \tag{H.1}$$

Throughout this article, we assume that hypotheses $(H.1)$ hold true.

We consider the usual Lebesgue space $\mathbf{L}^2(\Omega)$ equipped with the usual scalar product and its associated norm which are

$$\langle f,g\rangle = \int_\Omega f(x)g(x)dx; \quad |f|_{\mathbf{L}^2} = \left(\int_\Omega (f(x))^2 dx\right)^{1/2}, \tag{1.3}$$

while the space $\mathbf{L}_2 = \mathbf{L}^2(\Omega) \times \mathbf{L}^2(\Omega)$ is equipped with the following scalar product and its associated norm:

$$\langle\langle F,G\rangle\rangle = \langle f_1,g_1\rangle + \langle f_2,g_2\rangle; \qquad |F|_2 = |f_1|_{\mathbf{L}^2} + |f_2|_{\mathbf{L}^2}, \tag{1.4}$$

with $F = (f_1, f_2)^T \in \mathbf{L}_2$ and $G = (g_1, g_2)^T \in \mathbf{L}_2$. The Sobolev space made of functions, which together with their first derivatives (in the sense of distribution) are in $\mathbf{L}^2(\Omega)$, is denoted $\mathbf{H}^1(\Omega)$ while $\mathbf{H}_1 = \mathbf{H}^1(\Omega) \times \mathbf{H}^1(\Omega)$. We also make use of the following notations:

$$\mathbf{H}_0 = \{v \in \mathbf{H}^1(\Omega);\ v(0) = 0;\ v(1) = 0\};$$
$$\mathbf{V}_0 = \{V \in \mathbf{H}_1;\ V(0) = (0,0)^T;\ V(1) = (0,0)^T\};$$
$$\mathbf{W}_0 = \left\{V = (v_1, v_2)^T \in \mathbf{L}_2; \frac{d^2}{dx^2} v_1 \in \mathbf{L}^2(\Omega); \frac{d^2}{dx^2} v_2 \in \mathbf{L}^2(\Omega)\right\}. \tag{1.5}$$

The spaces $\mathbf{H}^1(\Omega)$ and $\mathbf{H}_1$ are, respectively, equipped with the following norms:

$$\|f\|_{\mathbf{H}^1} = \left[(|f|_{\mathbf{L}^2})^2 + \left(\left| \frac{d}{dx} f \right|_{\mathbf{L}^2} \right)^2 \right]^{1/2},$$
$$\|F\|_1 = \left[\left(\|f_1\|_{\mathbf{H}^1} \right)^2 + \left(\|f_2\|_{\mathbf{H}^1} \right)^2 \right]^{1/2}, \tag{1.6}$$

that is,

$$\|F\|_1 = \left[\left(|f_1|_{\mathbf{L}^2} \right)^2 + \left(\left| \frac{d}{dx} f_1 \right|_{\mathbf{L}^2} \right)^2 + \left(|f_2|_{\mathbf{L}^2} \right)^2 + \left(\left| \frac{d}{dx} f_2 \right|_{\mathbf{L}^2} \right)^2 \right]^{1/2}. \tag{1.7}$$

Under hypotheses $(H.1)$, the following problem well posed in $\mathbf{L}_2$ is also of interest and is called the formal limiting problem to (1):

$$AW = F. \tag{1.8}$$

We set

$$\mathcal{M} = \begin{pmatrix} -\dfrac{d^2}{dx^2} & 0 \\ 0 & -\dfrac{d^2}{dx^2} \end{pmatrix}. \tag{1.9}$$

We also define the following bilinear form:

$$\mathcal{B}(Y,V) = \varepsilon \langle \langle \mathcal{M}Y, V \rangle \rangle + \langle \langle AY, V \rangle \rangle; \quad Y \in \mathbf{V}_0,\ V \in \mathbf{V}_0. \tag{1.10}$$

2. Existence of a unique solution U

We state the following theorem.

THEOREM 2.1. *Assume $U(0) = (0,0)^T$ and $U(1) = (0,0)^T$. Then problem (1) has a unique solution $U \in \mathbf{V}_0 \cap \mathbf{W}_0$.*

Proof of Theorem 2.1. Thanks to the classical Lax-Milgram theorem, to prove Theorem 2.1 it suffices to show that the bilinear form $\mathcal{B}$ defined by equation (1.10) is symmetric, continuous, and coercitive.

Consider $Y = (y_1, y_2)^T$ and $V = (v_1, v_2)^T$ are two generic elements in $\mathbf{V}_0 \cap \mathbf{W}_0$. We have

$$\varepsilon \langle \langle \mathcal{M}Y, V \rangle \rangle = -\varepsilon \left\langle \frac{d^2}{dx^2} y_1, v_1 \right\rangle - \varepsilon \left\langle \frac{d^2}{dx^2} y_2, v_2 \right\rangle,$$
$$\varepsilon \langle \langle \mathcal{M}Y, V \rangle \rangle = \varepsilon \left\langle \frac{d}{dx} y_1, \frac{d}{dx} v_1 \right\rangle + \varepsilon \left\langle \frac{d}{dx} y_2, \frac{d}{dx} v_2 \right\rangle, \tag{2.1}$$

which, thanks to the Schwarz inequality and the inequality $|a| \leq [|a|^2 + |b|^2]^{1/2}$, leads to

$$|\varepsilon\langle\langle \mathcal{M}Y, V\rangle\rangle| \leq \varepsilon \|Y\|_1 \|V\|_1. \tag{2.2}$$

Then the same token leads to

$$\langle\langle AY, V\rangle\rangle = \langle a_{1,1}y_1 + a_{1,2}y_2, v_1\rangle + \langle a_{2,1}y_1 + a_{2,2}y_2, v_2\rangle, \tag{2.3}$$

which goes to

$$|\langle\langle AY, V\rangle\rangle| \leq \alpha \|Y\|_1 \|V\|_1, \tag{2.4}$$

where $\alpha = \max[\overline{a}_{1,1}, \overline{a}_{2,2}]$ and $\overline{a} = \max_{x\in\Omega} |a(x)|$. Put together, inequalities (2.2) and (2.4) result in

$$|\mathcal{B}(Y, V)| = |\varepsilon\langle\langle \mathcal{M}Y, V\rangle\rangle + \langle\langle AY, V\rangle\rangle| \leq \alpha \|Y\|_1 \|V\|_1, \tag{2.5}$$

where inequality (2.5) says that the bilinear form $\mathcal{B}$ is continuous.

For a typical element $V = (v_1, v_2)^T$ in $\mathbf{V}_0 \cap \mathbf{W}_0$, we have

$$\varepsilon\langle\langle \mathcal{M}V, V\rangle\rangle = \varepsilon \left| \frac{d}{dx} v_1 \right|^2_{\mathbf{L}^2} + \varepsilon \left| \frac{d}{dx} v_2 \right|^2_{\mathbf{L}^2}, \tag{2.6}$$

$$\langle\langle AV, V\rangle\rangle = \int_\Omega a_{1,1}v_1^2 + (a_{1,2} + a_{2,1})v_1v_2 + av_2^2 dx, \tag{2.7}$$

which implies

$$\langle\langle AV, V\rangle\rangle \geq \beta \int_\Omega (v_1 - v_2)^2 dx \geq 0, \tag{2.8}$$

where $\beta = \mathrm{Min}[\underline{a}_{1,1}, \underline{a}_{2,2}]$ where $\underline{a(x)} = \inf_{x\in\Omega} |a(x)|$. Taking equalities (2.6) and inequality (2.8) into account, we get

$$\varepsilon\langle\langle \mathcal{M}V, V\rangle\rangle + \langle\langle AV, V\rangle\rangle + |V|_2^2 \geq \varepsilon \|V\|_1^2. \tag{2.9}$$

Inequality (2.9) says that the bilinear form $\mathcal{B}$ is coercitive. Therefore problem (1) has a unique solution $U \in \mathbf{V}_0 \cap \mathbf{W}_0$, and Theorem 2.1 is proved true. □

3. Existence of a boundary layer

We state the following theorem.

Theorem 3.1. (i) *The solution $W = (w_1, w_2)^T$ to the formal limiting problem (1.8) is such that*

$$|W|_2 \leq \beta^{-1} |F|_2. \tag{3.1a}$$

(ii) *Assume $U \in \mathbf{V}_0 \cap \mathbf{W}_0$. Then*

$$\begin{aligned} |U|_2 &\leq \beta^{-1} |F|_2, \\ \|U\|_1 &\leq \varepsilon^{-1}\beta^{-1} |F|_2. \end{aligned} \tag{3.1b}$$

(iii) *Assume* $U \in \mathbf{H}_1 \cap \mathbf{W}_0$, *and* $U \notin \mathbf{V}_0$. *Then*

$$|U|_2 \le \beta^{-1}\max[1,3\alpha](|F|_2 + |U(0)| + |U(1)|),$$
$$\|U\|_1 \le \varepsilon^{-1}\beta^{-1}\max[1,3\alpha](|F|_2 + |U(0)| + |U(1)|), \tag{3.1c}$$

where $|U(x)| = \max[|u_1(x)|, |u_2(x)|]$.

Proof of Theorem 3.1. We have

$$\langle\langle AW, W\rangle\rangle = \int_\Omega a_{1,1}w_1^2 + (a_{1,2}+a_{2,1})w_1w_2 + a_{2,2}w_2^2 dx. \tag{3.2}$$

The quadratic integrand in the right-hand side term is such that

$$\begin{aligned} &a_{1,1}w_1^2 + (a_{1,2}+a_{2,1})w_1w_2 + a_{2,2}w_2^2 \\ &\quad = a_{1,1}\left[w_1 + \frac{(a_{1,2}+a_{2,1})w_2}{2a_{1,1}}\right]^2 + \left[a_{2,2} - \frac{(a_{1,2}+a_{2,1})}{2a_{1,1}}\right]w_2^2 \\ &\quad \ge \left[a_{2,2} - \frac{(a_{1,2}+a_{2,1})}{2a_{1,1}}\right]w_2^2. \end{aligned} \tag{3.3}$$

Since the coefficients $a_{1,1}$ and $a_{2,2}$ are playing similar roles in the quadratic form, then, by using the same token, one gets

$$a_{1,1}w_1^2 + (a_{1,2}+a_{2,1})w_1w_2 + a_{2,2}w_2^2 \ge \left[a_{1,1} - \frac{(a_{1,2}+a_{2,1})}{2a_{2,2}}\right]w_1^2. \tag{3.4}$$

Since $-(a_{1,2}+a_{2,1}) \ge 0$, then

$$\begin{aligned} \left[a_{1,1} - \frac{(a_{1,2}+a_{2,1})}{2a_{2,2}}\right] &\ge a_{1,1} \ge \beta, \\ \left[a_{2,2} - \frac{(a_{1,2}+a_{2,1})}{2a_{1,1}}\right] &\ge a_{2,2} \ge \beta. \end{aligned} \tag{3.5}$$

So, putting together equations (3.3), (3.4), and (3.5) leads to

$$2\langle\langle AW, W\rangle\rangle \ge 2\beta\int_\Omega (w_1^2 + w_2^2)dx, \tag{3.6}$$

that is,

$$\langle\langle AW, W\rangle\rangle \ge \beta|W|_2^2. \tag{3.7}$$

Applying the Schwarz inequality to the right-hand side term of the equality

$$\langle\langle AW, W\rangle\rangle = \langle\langle F, W\rangle\rangle \tag{3.8}$$

leads to

$$\langle\langle AW, W\rangle\rangle \le |F|_2|W|_2. \tag{3.9}$$

From equations (3.7) and (3.9), we get

$$\beta|W|_2 \le |F|_2 \tag{3.10}$$

which is inequality (3.1a).

Next, we have to show that points (ii) and (iii) of Theorem 3.1 hold true.

Consider the functions $P(x) = (p_1(x), p_2(x))^T$, where

$$\begin{aligned} p_1(x) &= (u_1(1) - u_1(0))x + u_1(0), \\ p_2(x) &= (u_2(1) - u_2(0))x + u_2(0). \end{aligned} \tag{3.11}$$

The function $Y(x) = U(x) - P(x)$ is such that $Y \in| VAO \cap \mathbf{W}_0$. Y satisfies

$$\varepsilon\mathcal{M}Y + AY = F - (a_{1,1}p_1(x) + a_{1,2}p_2(x),\ a_{2,1}p_1(x) + a_{2,2}p_2(x))^T. \tag{3.12}$$

Multiplying this equality by a generic element $V \in \mathbf{V}_0 \cap \mathbf{W}_0$, we get

$$\varepsilon\langle\langle \mathcal{M}Y, V\rangle\rangle + \langle\langle AY, V\rangle\rangle = \langle\langle G, V\rangle\rangle, \tag{3.13}$$

where

$$G = F - (a_{1,1}p_1(x) + a_{1,2}p_2(x),\ a_{2,1}p_1(x) + a_{2,2}p_2(x))^T. \tag{3.14}$$

This variational equality remains valid when we set $V = Y$ since $Y \in \mathbf{V}_0 \cap \mathbf{W}_0$. Taking into account inequality (3.7), we have

$$\begin{aligned} \langle\langle G, Y\rangle\rangle &= \varepsilon\langle\langle \mathcal{M}Y, Y\rangle\rangle + \langle\langle AY, Y\rangle\rangle, \\ \langle\langle AY, Y\rangle\rangle &\ge \beta|Y|_2^2. \end{aligned} \tag{3.15}$$

Applying the Schwarz inequality to the $\langle\langle AY, Y\rangle\rangle$, this chain of inequalities leads to

$$\beta|Y|_2^2 \le \langle\langle AY, Y\rangle\rangle \le |G|_2|Y|_2, \tag{3.16}$$

which proves the first segment of (3.1b). The chain of inequalities above put together with the coercitivity of $\mathcal{B}$ and an appropriate use of the Schwarz inequality ($Y \in \mathbf{V}_0$ so $|\langle\langle G, Y\rangle\rangle| \le |G|_2\|Y\|_1$) leads to

$$\varepsilon\|Y\|_1^2 \le |\langle\langle G, Y\rangle\rangle| \le |G|_2\|Y\|_1, \tag{3.17}$$

which achieves the proof of point (ii).

According to point (ii), since $Y \in \mathbf{V}_0 \cap \mathbf{W}_0$, we have

$$\begin{aligned} |Y|_2 &\le \beta^{-1}|G|_2, \\ \|Y\|_1 &\le \varepsilon^{-1}\beta^{-1}|G|_2, \end{aligned} \tag{3.18}$$

in which we are going to evaluate $|G|_2$ with

$$G = (g_1, g_2)^T = F - (a_{1,1}p_1(x) + a_{1,2}p_2(x),\ a_{2,1}p_1(x) + a_{2,2}p_2(x))^T. \tag{3.19}$$

We have

$$
\begin{aligned}
|g_i|_{L^2}^2 &\le |f_i|_{L^2}^2 + 2\alpha^2\left(|p_1|_{L^2}^2 + |p_2|_{L^2}^2\right),\\
|p_i|_{L^2}^2 &\le 3\left(|u_i(0)|^2 + |u_i(1)|^2\right).
\end{aligned}
\tag{3.20}
$$

These two inequalities, put together with the fact that the application $x \to \sqrt{x}$ is concave over its domain of definition, lead to

$$
|G|_2 \le \max[3\alpha, 1]\left(|F|_2 + |U(0)| + |U(1)|\right),
\tag{3.21}
$$

where $|U(x)| = \max[|u_1(x)|, |u_2(x)|]$. Then take inequality (3.21) into the system (3.18) to prove point (iii) and achieve the proof of Theorem 3.1. □

We state the following theorem.

THEOREM 3.2. (i) *Assume W the solution to the formal limiting problem (1.8) is such that*

$$
\begin{aligned}
&W \in \mathbf{H}_1,\\
&W \notin \mathbf{V}_0 \cap \mathbf{W}_0,
\end{aligned}
\tag{3.22}
$$

then,

$$
\beta |U - W|_2 \le \left(1 + \alpha\beta^{-1}\right)|F|_2.
\tag{3.23}
$$

(ii) *Assume W the solution to the formal limiting problem (1.8) is such that*

$$
W \in \mathbf{H}_1 \cap \mathbf{W}_0.
\tag{3.24}
$$

Then $(U - W)$ converges strongly to zero in $\mathbf{L}_2$ and more precisely

$$
\begin{aligned}
\beta |U - W|_2 &\le \varepsilon \left|\frac{d^2}{dx^2} W\right|_2,\\
\|U - W\|_1 &\le \left|\frac{d^2}{dx^2} W\right|_2.
\end{aligned}
\tag{3.25}
$$

Remark 3.3. The loss of the boundary conditions on W solution of the formal limiting problem (1.8) causes the loss of its strong convergence to U solution to problem (1) all over Ω. The subregion of the domain Ω, over which the loss of convergence occurs, is called the boundary layer.

Proof of Theorem 3.2. We have

$$
\forall V \in \mathbf{L}_2; \quad \langle\langle AW, V\rangle\rangle = \langle\langle F, V\rangle\rangle.
\tag{3.26}
$$

Since $(W - U) \in \mathbf{L}_2$, equality (3.26) is still valid when we set $V = W - U$ to get

$$
\langle\langle AW, W - U\rangle\rangle = \langle\langle F, W - U\rangle\rangle,
\tag{3.27}
$$

that is,

$$\langle\langle A(W-U), W-U\rangle\rangle = \langle\langle F, W-U\rangle\rangle - \langle\langle AU, W-U\rangle\rangle. \tag{3.28}$$

We make use of inequations (3.7) and the Schwarz inequality to get

$$\beta|U-W|_2^2 \leq [|F|_2+\alpha|U|_2]|U-W|_2, \tag{3.29}$$

which combined with inequality (3.1b) results in inequality (3.23) and achieves the proof of point (i) of Theorem 3.2.

If $W \in \mathbf{H}_1 \cap \mathbf{W}_0$, then for any generic element $V \in \mathbf{H}_1 \cap \mathbf{W}_0$, we have

$$\begin{gathered}\langle\langle \mathcal{M}U, V\rangle\rangle + \langle\langle AU, V\rangle\rangle = \langle\langle F, V\rangle\rangle,\\ \langle\langle AW, V\rangle\rangle = \langle\langle F, V\rangle\rangle\end{gathered} \tag{3.30}$$

in which we set $V = U - W$ before taking the difference between the two equations of (3.30) to get

$$\langle\langle \mathcal{M}U, U-W\rangle\rangle + \langle\langle A(U-W), U-W\rangle\rangle = 0, \tag{3.31}$$

that is,

$$\langle\langle \mathcal{M}(U-W), U-W\rangle\rangle + \langle\langle A(U-W), U-W\rangle\rangle = -\langle\langle \mathcal{M}W, U-W\rangle\rangle. \tag{3.32}$$

Making use of (2.6), inequations (3.7), and the Schwarz inequality, (3.32) leads to

$$\varepsilon\|U-W\|_1^2 \leq \varepsilon\left|\frac{d^2}{dx^2}W\right|_2\|U-W\|_1. \tag{3.33}$$

This proves the second inequalities of the system (3.25).

In equality (3.32), since $\langle\langle \mathcal{M}(U-W),\ U-W\rangle\rangle \geq 0$, then we have

$$\langle\langle A(U-W), U-W\rangle\rangle \leq -\langle\langle \mathcal{M}W, U-W\rangle\rangle. \tag{3.34}$$

Calling again inequalities (3.7) and the Schwarz inequality, we get from (3.34) that

$$\beta|U-W|_2^2 \leq \varepsilon\left|\frac{d^2}{dx^2}W\right|_2|U-W|_2 \tag{3.35}$$

which is the first inequality of system (3.25). The proof of Theorem 3.2 is achieved. □

4. Weak corrector and thickness of the boundary layers

Consider the following regular function $\Theta(x) = (\theta_1(x), \theta_2(x))^T$, such that

$$\begin{aligned}\theta_1(x) &= (u_1(0)-w_1(0))\exp\left(-\frac{x}{\sqrt{\varepsilon}}\right) + (u_1(1)-w_1(1))\exp\left(-\frac{1-x}{\sqrt{\varepsilon}}\right),\\ \theta_2(x) &= (u_2(0)-w_2(0))\exp\left(-\frac{x}{\sqrt{\varepsilon}}\right) + (u_2(1)-w_2(1))\exp\left(-\frac{1-x}{\sqrt{\varepsilon}}\right).\end{aligned} \tag{4.1}$$

We need to define the notion of threshold of acceptance and by the following definition.

Definition 4.1. A real constant η such that $0 < \eta \ll 1$ and $\varepsilon \ln(\eta^{-1}) \ll 1$ is called a threshold of acceptance if

$$\forall x \in \mathbf{R}; \quad |x| \leq \eta \Longrightarrow x = 0. \tag{4.2}$$

Remark 4.2. Set $M = \max[M_1, M_2]$ where $M_1 = \max[|(u_1(0) - w_1(0))|, |(u_2(0) - w_2(0))|]$; $M_2 = \max[|(u_1(1) - w_1(1))|, |(u_2(1) - w_2(1))|]$; and $\Omega_\varepsilon = \Omega_{\varepsilon,0} \cup \Omega_{\varepsilon,1}$; $\Omega_o = \Omega \setminus \Omega_\varepsilon$ where $\Omega_{\varepsilon,0} = \{x \in \Omega;\, x \leq \sqrt{\varepsilon}\ln(M\eta^{-1})\}$ and $\Omega_{\varepsilon,1} = \{x \in \Omega;\, 1 - x \leq \sqrt{\varepsilon}\ln(M\eta^{-1})\}$.

That is,

$$\begin{aligned} \Omega_{\varepsilon,0} &= \{x \in \Omega;\ 0 \leq x \leq \sqrt{\varepsilon}\ln(M\eta^{-1})\}, \\ \Omega_{\varepsilon,1} &= \{x \in \Omega;\ 1 - \sqrt{\varepsilon}\ln(M\eta^{-1}) \leq x \leq 1\}. \end{aligned} \tag{4.3}$$

Set $\overline{x}_\varepsilon = \sqrt{\varepsilon}\ln(M\eta^{-1})$.

With regard to Definition 4.1, we have

$$\begin{aligned} \Theta(x) &= (0,0)^T; \quad x \in \Omega_o, \\ \Theta(0) &= \big(u_1(0) - w_1(0), u_2(0) - w_2(0)\big)^T, \\ \Theta(1) &= \big(u_1(1) - w_1(1), u_2(1) - w_2(1)\big)^T. \end{aligned} \tag{4.4}$$

We state the following theorem.

Theorem 4.3. *In addition to hypotheses (H.1), assume*

$$W \in \mathbf{H}_1 \cap \mathbf{W}_0. \tag{4.5}$$

Then the boundary-layer-type function Θ is such that

$$|U - (W + \Theta)|_2 \leq C\varepsilon^{1/2}, \tag{4.6}$$

where C is a constant which is independent from ε.

Proof of Theorem 4.3. Set $K_{1,1} = u_1(0) - w_1(0)$; $K_{1,2} = u_1(1) - w_1(1)$; $K_{2,1} = u_2(0) - w_2(0)$; $K_{1,2} = u_2(1) - w_2(1)$.

By virtue of Remark 4.2, we have $(U - (W+))(0) = (0,0)^T$. Then,

$$\begin{gathered} \begin{pmatrix} -\varepsilon \dfrac{d^2}{dx^2} & 0 \\ 0 & -\varepsilon \dfrac{d^2}{dx^2} \end{pmatrix} (U - (W+))(x) + A(x)(U - (W+))(x) = G, \\ (U - (W+))(0) = (0,0)^T, \qquad (U - (W+))(1) = (0,0)^T, \end{gathered} \tag{4.7}$$

where $G = -\mathcal{M}W - \mathcal{M}\Theta - A\Theta$.

Multiplying the first equation of system (4.7) by $V \in \mathbf{V}_0 \cap \mathbf{W}_0$, we get the following expressions:

$$\langle\langle \mathcal{M}(U-(W+\Theta)), V\rangle\rangle + \langle\langle A(U-(W+\Theta)), V\rangle\rangle, \tag{4.8}$$

$$-\langle\langle \mathcal{M}W, V\rangle\rangle - \langle\langle \mathcal{M}\Theta, V\rangle\rangle - \langle\langle A\Theta, V\rangle\rangle \tag{4.9}$$

with *expression* (4.8)= *expression* (4.9). Expression (4.9) is equal to $\langle\langle G, V\rangle\rangle$. Use the properties of the bilinear form $\mathcal{B}$ established in Section 2 and the Schwarz inequality to bound above *expression* (4.8) as follows:

$$\begin{aligned} &\left|\langle\langle \mathcal{M}W, V\rangle\rangle + \langle\langle \mathcal{M}\Theta, V\rangle\rangle + \langle\langle A\Theta, V\rangle\rangle\right| \\ &\quad \le \varepsilon\left|\frac{d^2}{dx^2}W\right|_2 |V|_2 + \varepsilon\left|\frac{d^2}{dx^2}\Theta\right|_2 |V|_2 + \alpha|\Theta|_2|V|_2. \end{aligned} \tag{4.10}$$

Both *expression* (4.8) and *expression* (4.10) remain valid when we set $V = (U-(W+\Theta)) \in \mathbf{V}_0 \cap \mathbf{W}_0$. Again, use the properties of the bilinear form $\mathcal{B}$, to bound *expression* (4.8) below to get

$$\beta|V|_2^2 \le \langle\langle \mathcal{M}V, V\rangle\rangle + \langle\langle AV, V\rangle\rangle; \quad V = (U-(W+\Theta)). \tag{4.11}$$

Putting together inequalities (4.10) and (4.11), we get

$$\beta\left|(U-(W+\Theta))\right|_2 \le \varepsilon\left|\frac{d^2}{dx^2}W\right|_2 + \varepsilon\left|\frac{d^2}{dx^2}\Theta\right|_2 + \alpha|\Theta|_2. \tag{4.12}$$

Each expression in the right-hand side of inequality (4.12) may be bounded as follows:

$$\begin{aligned} \left|\frac{d^2}{dx^2}\Theta\right|_2 &\le \left[\int_0^{\overline{x}_\varepsilon} \varepsilon^{-1}M\exp\left(-x\varepsilon^{-1/2}\right) + \int_{1-\overline{x}_\varepsilon}^1 \varepsilon^{-1}M\exp\left(-x\varepsilon^{-1/2}\right)\right]^{1/2} \\ &\le \sqrt{2}\varepsilon^{-1}M\varepsilon^{1/4}\left(\ln\left(M\eta^{-1}\right)\right)^{1/2}, \end{aligned} \tag{4.13}$$

$$\begin{aligned} |\Theta|_2 &\le \left[\int_0^{\overline{x}_\varepsilon} M\exp\left(-x\varepsilon^{-1/2}\right) + \int_{1-\overline{x}_\varepsilon}^1 M\exp\left(-x\varepsilon^{-1/2}\right)\right]^{1/2} \\ &\le M\varepsilon^{1/4}\left(\ln\left(M\eta^{-1}\right)\right)^{1/2}. \end{aligned} \tag{4.14}$$

Putting together inequalities (4.12), (4.13), and (4.14), we get

$$\beta\left|(U-(W+\Theta))\right|_2 \le C_1\varepsilon^{1/4}, \tag{4.15}$$

where $C_1 = 3\max[1,\alpha]M(\ln(M\eta^{-1}))^{1/2}$ is a constant which is independent of ε, and Theorem 4.3 is proved true with constant $C = \beta^{-1}C_1$ independent of ε. □

Definition 4.4. The boundary layer function Θ will be called a zero-order weak corrector for problem (1). The common width of $\Omega_{\varepsilon,0}$ and $\Omega_{\varepsilon,1}$ is called the thickness of the boundary layers $\Omega_{\varepsilon,0}$ and $\Omega_{\varepsilon,1}$, subsets of Ω over which the corrector is needed to secure a weak convergence over Ω to zero of $(U-(W+\Theta))$.

5. Existence of an outer expansion

We need to explore the existence of an outer asymptotic solution to problem (1). Consider a qth-order regular expansion to U, say $\overline{U}$, such that $\overline{U} = (\overline{u}_1, \overline{u}_2)^T = (\sum_{i=0}^{q} \varepsilon^i u_{1,i}, \sum_{i=0}^{q} \varepsilon^i u_{2,i})^T$. Set

$$\begin{aligned}
\mathcal{L}_1 Y &= -\varepsilon \frac{d^2}{dx^2} y_1 + a_{1,1} y_1 + a_{1,2} y_2, \\
\mathcal{L}_2 Y &= -\varepsilon \frac{d^2}{dx^2} y_2 + a_{2,1} y_1 + a_{2,2} y_2, \\
Y &= (y_1, y_2)^T,
\end{aligned} \tag{5.1}$$

and $U_i = (u_{1,i}, u_{2,i})^T$, so $\overline{U} = \sum_{i=0}^{q} \varepsilon^i U_i$. We state the following theorem.

THEOREM 5.1. *For any given and arbitrary natural number q, there exists a qth-order outer expansion $\overline{U} = (\sum_{i=0}^{q} \varepsilon^i u_{1,i}, \sum_{i=0}^{q} \varepsilon^i u_{2,i})^T$ to U such that the coefficient functions $(u_{1,i}, u_{2,i})^T$ satisfy*

$$\begin{aligned}
a_{1,1} u_{1,0} + a_{1,2} u_{2,0} &= f_1, \\
a_{2,1} u_{1,0} + a_{2,2} u_{2,0} &= f_2, \\
a_{1,1} u_{1,i} + a_{1,2} u_{2,i} &= \frac{d^2}{dx^2} u_{1,i-1}, \\
a_{2,1} u_{1,i} + a_{2,2} u_{2,i} &= \frac{d^2}{dx^2} u_{2,i-1}, \\
1 \le i &\le q.
\end{aligned} \tag{5.2}$$

Furthermore,

$$\begin{aligned}
\sum_{i=0}^{q} \varepsilon^i \mathcal{L}_1 U_i &= f_1 - \varepsilon^{q+1} \frac{d^2}{dx^2} u_{1,q}, \\
\sum_{i=0}^{q} \varepsilon^i \mathcal{L}_2 U_i &= f_2 - \varepsilon^{q+1} \frac{d^2}{dx^2} u_{2,q},
\end{aligned} \tag{5.3a}$$

or

$$\mathcal{L}_\varepsilon(\overline{U}) = F - \varepsilon^{q+1} \left(\frac{d^2}{dx^2} u_{1,q}, \frac{d^2}{dx^2} u_{2,q} \right)^T, \tag{5.3b}$$

and, consequently,

$$\mathcal{L}_1(U - \overline{U}) = \varepsilon^{q+1} \frac{d^2}{dx^2} u_{1,q}, \qquad \mathcal{L}_2(U - \overline{U}) = \varepsilon^{q+1} \frac{d^2}{dx^2} u_{2,q}, \tag{5.4a}$$

or

$$\mathcal{L}_\varepsilon(U - \overline{U}) = \varepsilon^{q+1} \left(\frac{d^2}{dx^2} u_{1,q}, \frac{d^2}{dx^2} u_{2,q} \right)^T. \tag{5.4b}$$

Proof of Theorem 5.1. Replace U with $\overline{U}$ in problem (1) and apply the classical WKB principle in matching the alike power terms in the parameter ε. We get system (5.2). Each coefficient function is solution of a two-by-two subsystem whose determinant is $\det(A) = a_{1,1}a_{2,2} - a_{1,2}a_{2,1}$. The fact that A is a strictly diagonal dominant matrix (cf. hypotheses $(H.1)$) secures $\det(A) > 0$. This secures the existence of the coefficient functions $(\overline{u}_1, \overline{u}_2)^T$.

From system (5.2) we get

$$\begin{aligned}
\mathcal{L}_1 U_0 &= -\varepsilon \frac{d^2}{dx^2} u_{1,0} + a_{1,1}u_{1,0} + a_{1,2}u_{2,0} = f_1 - \varepsilon \frac{d^2}{dx^2} u_{1,0},\\
\varepsilon \mathcal{L}_1 U_1 &= \varepsilon\left[-\varepsilon \frac{d^2}{dx^2} u_{1,1} + a_{1,1}u_{1,1} + a_{1,2}u_{2,1}\right] = \varepsilon \frac{d^2}{dx^2} u_{1,0} - \varepsilon^2 \frac{d^2}{dx^2} u_{1,1},\\
\varepsilon^2 \mathcal{L}_1 U_2 &= \varepsilon^2\left[-\varepsilon \frac{d^2}{dx^2} u_{1,2} + a_{1,1}u_{1,2} + a_{1,2}u_{2,2}\right] = \varepsilon^2 \frac{d^2}{dx^2} u_{1,1} - \varepsilon^3 \frac{d^2}{dx^2} u_{1,2},\\
&\ \ \vdots\\
\varepsilon^i \mathcal{L}_1 U_i &= \varepsilon^i\left[-\varepsilon \frac{d^2}{dx^2} u_{1,i} + a_{1,1}u_{1,i} + a_{1,2}u_{2,i}\right] = \varepsilon^i \frac{d^2}{dx^2} u_{1,i-1} - \varepsilon^{i+1} \frac{d^2}{dx^2} u_{1,i},\\
&\ \ \vdots\\
\varepsilon^q \mathcal{L}_1 U_q &= \varepsilon^q\left[-\varepsilon \frac{d^2}{dx^2} u_{1,q} + a_{1,1}u_{1,q} + a_{1,2}u_{2,q}\right] = \varepsilon^q \frac{d^2}{dx^2} u_{1,q-1} - \varepsilon^{q+1} \frac{d^2}{dx^2} u_{1,q},
\end{aligned} \tag{5.5}$$

that is,

$$\begin{aligned}
\mathcal{L}_1 U_0 &= f_1 - \varepsilon \frac{d^2}{dx^2} u_{1,0},\\
\varepsilon \mathcal{L}_1 U_1 &= \varepsilon \frac{d^2}{dx^2} u_{1,0} - \varepsilon^2 \frac{d^2}{dx^2} u_{1,1},\\
\varepsilon^2 \mathcal{L}_1 U_2 &= \varepsilon^2 \frac{d^2}{dx^2} u_{1,1} - \varepsilon^3 \frac{d^2}{dx^2} u_{1,2},\\
&\ \ \vdots\\
\varepsilon^i \mathcal{L}_1 U_i &= \varepsilon^i \frac{d^2}{dx^2} u_{1,i-1} - \varepsilon^{i+1} \frac{d^2}{dx^2} u_{1,i},\\
&\ \ \vdots\\
\varepsilon^q \mathcal{L}_1 U_q &= \varepsilon^q \frac{d^2}{dx^2} u_{1,q-1} - \varepsilon^{q+1} \frac{d^2}{dx^2} u_{1,q}.
\end{aligned} \tag{5.6}$$

Sum up the left-hand side terms and sum up the right-hand side terms of system (5.6) to get

$$\sum_{i=0}^{q} \varepsilon^i \mathcal{L}_{U_i} = f_1 - \varepsilon^{q+1} \frac{d^2}{dx^2} u_{1,q}, \tag{5.7}$$

which is the first equality of system (5.3). Alike reasoning based on $\mathcal{L}_2 U_i$ leads to the second inequality of system (5.3).

In another hand, the string of equalities

$$
\begin{aligned}
\mathcal{L}_1\overline{U} &= \mathcal{L}_1\left(\sum_{i=0}^{q}\varepsilon^i U_i\right) \\
&= -\varepsilon\frac{d^2}{dx^2}\left[\sum_{i=0}^{q}\varepsilon^i u_{1,i}\right] + a_{1,1}\left[\sum_{i=0}^{q}\varepsilon^i u_{1,i}\right] + a_{1,2}\left[\sum_{i=0}^{q}\varepsilon^i u_{2,i}\right] \\
&= -\varepsilon\left[\sum_{i=0}^{q}\varepsilon^i\frac{d^2}{dx^2}u_{1,i}\right] + \left[\sum_{i=0}^{q}\varepsilon^i a_{1,1}u_{1,i}\right] + \left[\sum_{i=0}^{q}\varepsilon^i a_{1,2}u_{2,i}\right] \\
&= \varepsilon^i\left[-\varepsilon\frac{d^2}{dx^2}u_{1,i} + a_{1,1}u_{1,i} + a_{1,2}u_{2,i}\right] = \sum_{i=0}^{q}\varepsilon^i\mathcal{L}_1(U_i)
\end{aligned}
\tag{5.8}
$$

says that

$$
\mathcal{L}_1(\overline{U}) = \sum_{i=0}^{q}\varepsilon^i\mathcal{L}_1(U_i). \tag{5.9}
$$

Also we have another string of equalities

$$
\begin{aligned}
&\mathcal{L}_1(U) - \mathcal{L}_1(\overline{U}) \\
&\quad = -\varepsilon\frac{d^2}{dx^2}u_1 + a_{1,1}u_1 + a_{1,2}u_2 - \left[-\varepsilon\frac{d^2}{dx^2}\overline{u}_1 + a_{1,1}\overline{u}_1 + a_{1,2}\overline{u}_2\right] \\
&\quad = -\varepsilon\frac{d^2}{dx^2}(u_1 - \overline{u}_1) + a_{1,1}(u_1 - \overline{u}_1) + a_{1,2}(u_2 - \overline{u}_2) = \mathcal{L}_1(U - \overline{U})
\end{aligned}
\tag{5.10}
$$

which says

$$
\mathcal{L}_1(U) - \mathcal{L}_1(\overline{U}) = \mathcal{L}_1(U - \overline{U}). \tag{5.11}
$$

Putting together $\mathcal{L}_1(U) = f_1$, system (5.3), and equality (5.11), we get to the first equality of system (5.4). Alike reasoning based on the operator $\mathcal{L}_2$ leads to the second equality of system (5.4) and achieves the proof of Theorem 5.1. □

6. Higher-order strong corrector and approximation

Consider two qth-order regular expansions, say $\overline{\Psi}(\tau)$ and $\overline{\Phi}(\rho)$, such that

$$
\overline{\Psi}(\tau) = \left(\overline{\psi}_1(\tau), \overline{\psi}_2(\tau)\right)^T = \left(\sum_{i=0}^{q}\varepsilon^i\exp(-\tau)\psi_{1,i}(\tau), \sum_{i=0}^{q}\varepsilon^i\exp(-\tau)\psi_{2,i}(\tau)\right)^T, \tag{6.1}
$$

where $\tau = x/\sqrt{\varepsilon}$, and

$$\overline{\Phi}(\rho) = (\overline{\phi}_1(\rho), \overline{\phi}_2(\rho))^T = \left(\sum_{i=0}^{q} \varepsilon^i \exp(-\rho)\phi_{1,i}(\rho), \sum_{i=0}^{q} \varepsilon^i \exp(-\tau)\phi_{2,i}(\rho) \right)^T, \tag{6.2}$$

where $\rho = (1-x)/\sqrt{\varepsilon}$.

Set $\Psi_i = (\psi_{1,i}(\tau), \psi_{2,i}(\tau))^T$ and $\Phi_i = (\phi_{1,i}(\rho), \phi_{2,i}(\rho))^T$, so $\overline{\Psi}(\tau) = \sum_{i=0}^{q} \varepsilon^i \exp(-\tau)\Psi_i(\tau)$ and $\overline{\Phi}(\rho) = \sum_{i=0}^{q} \varepsilon^i \exp(-\rho)\Phi_i(\rho)$. We state the following theorem.

Theorem 6.1. *There exist some coefficient functions*

$$\begin{aligned} (\psi_{1,i}(\tau), \psi_{2,i}(\tau))^T &= \Psi_i, \\ (\phi_{1,i}(\rho), \phi_{2,i}(\rho))^T &= \Phi_i, \end{aligned} \qquad 0 \le i \le q, \tag{6.3}$$

such that

$$\begin{aligned} \mathcal{L}_\varepsilon(\overline{\Psi}) &= 0, \\ \mathcal{L}_\varepsilon(\overline{\Phi}) &= 0. \end{aligned} \tag{6.4}$$

More precisely, these coefficient functions $(\psi_{1,i}(\tau), \psi_{2,i}(\tau))^T$ *and* $(\phi_{1,i}(\rho), \phi_{2,i}(\rho))^T$, $0 \le i \le q$, *satisfy*

$$\mathcal{M}\Psi_i + 2\mathcal{D}\Psi_i + A_-\Psi_i = (0,0)^T, \tag{6.5}$$

$$\mathcal{M}\Phi_i + 2\mathcal{D}\Phi_i + A_-\Phi_i = (0,0)^T, \tag{6.6}$$

where

$$\begin{aligned} \mathcal{D} &= \begin{pmatrix} \dfrac{d}{dx} & 0 \\ 0 & \dfrac{d}{dx} \end{pmatrix}, \\ A_- &= \begin{pmatrix} a_{1,1}(x) - 1 & a_{1,2}(x) \\ a_{2,1}(x) & a_{2,2} - 1(x) \end{pmatrix}. \end{aligned} \tag{6.7}$$

Proof of Theorem 6.1. At first, for $1 \le j \le 2; 0 \le i \le q$, we have

$$\begin{aligned} \frac{d}{dx}\overline{\psi}_j(\tau) &= \varepsilon^{-1/2}\left[-\sum_{i=0}^{q} \varepsilon^i \psi_{j,i}(\tau) + \sum_{i=0}^{q} \varepsilon^i \frac{d}{dx}\psi_{j,i}(\tau) \right] \exp(-\tau), \\ \frac{d^2}{dx^2}\overline{\psi}_j(\tau) &= \varepsilon^{-1}\left[\sum_{i=0}^{q} \varepsilon^i \frac{d^2}{dx^2}\psi_{j,i}(\tau) - 2\sum_{i=0}^{q} \varepsilon^i \frac{d}{dx}\psi_{j,i}(\tau) + \sum_{i=0}^{q} \varepsilon^i \psi_{j,i}(\tau) \right] \exp(-\tau). \end{aligned} \tag{6.8}$$

A straightforward application of the matching principle to the equality

$$\mathcal{L}_\varepsilon \overline{\Psi} = (0,0)^T \tag{6.9}$$

leads to

$$\begin{gathered}
-\frac{d^2}{dx^2}\psi_{1,i}(\tau) + 2\frac{d}{dx}\psi_{1,i}(\tau) + (a_{1,1}-1)\psi_{1,i}(\tau) + a_{1,2}\psi_{2,i}(\tau) = 0,\\
-\frac{d^2}{dx^2}\psi_{2,i}(\tau) + 2\frac{d}{dx}\psi_{2,i}(\tau) + a_{2,1}\psi_{1,i}(\tau) + (a_{1,2}-1)\psi_{2,i}(\tau) = 0,\\
0 \le i \le q.
\end{gathered} \tag{6.10}$$

The system (6.10) is equivalent to equality (6.5) and to equality (6.9) when we rewrite it using the operator matrices.

A reasoning similar to what is above leads to the equivalence between (6.6) and equality

$$\mathcal{L}_\varepsilon \overline{\Phi} = 0, \tag{6.11}$$

$$\begin{gathered}
-\frac{d^2}{dx^2}\phi_{1,i}(\rho) + 2\frac{d}{dx}\phi_{1,i}(\rho) + (a_{1,1}-1)\phi_{1,i}(\rho) + a_{1,2}\phi_{2,i}(\rho) = 0,\\
-\frac{d^2}{dx^2}\phi_{2,i}(\rho) + 2\frac{d}{dx}\phi_{2,i}(\rho) + a_{2,1}\phi_{1,i}(\rho) + (a_{1,2}-1)\phi_{2,i}(\rho) = 0,\\
0 \le i \le q.
\end{gathered} \tag{6.12}$$

We have now to ascertain the existence of the coefficient functions in equalities (6.5) and (6.6). We multiply system (6.10) by $V \in \mathbf{V}_0 \cap \mathbf{W}_0$ to get

$$\langle\langle \mathcal{M}\Psi_i, V\rangle\rangle + 2\langle\langle \mathcal{D}\Psi_i, V\rangle\rangle + \langle\langle A_-\Psi_i, V\rangle\rangle = (0,0)^T. \tag{6.13}$$

We take into account the fact that for $V \in \mathbf{V}_0 \cap \mathbf{W}_0$ we have $v_i(0) = v_i(1) = 0$; $i = 1,2$, and so

$$2\int_0^1 \frac{d}{dx}v_i(x)v_i(x)dx = v_i^2(1) - v_i^2(0) = 0 \tag{6.14}$$

to see that the bilinear form

$$\mathcal{B}_-(Y,V) = \langle\langle \mathcal{M}Y, V\rangle\rangle + \langle\langle \mathcal{D}Y, V\rangle\rangle + \langle\langle AY, V\rangle\rangle, \tag{6.15}$$

which is associated with (6.13) and so with the systems (6.9) and (6.10), is, alike $\mathcal{B}$, continuous and coercitive under hypotheses $(H.1)$ $(a_{1,1} - 1 > 0;\ a_{2,2} - 1 > 0)$. The continuity and the coercitivity of $\mathcal{B}_-$ lead to the existence of coefficient functions $(\Psi_1,\Psi_2)^T$ and $(\Phi_1,\Phi_2)^T$. This ends the proof of Theorem 6.1. □

Next we ascertain the uniqueness of the coefficient functions $\Psi_i = (\psi_{1,i}(\tau), \psi_{2,i}(\tau))^T$ and $\Phi_i = (\phi_{1,i}(\rho), \phi_{2,i}(\rho))^T$ by supplementing systems (6.10) and (6.12) with some boundary conditions at $t = 0$ and $t = 1$:

$$\begin{aligned}
\psi_{1,0}(0) &= u_1(0) - u_{1,0}(0),\\
\psi_{1,i}(0) &= -u_{1,i}(0); \quad 0 \le i \le q,\\
\psi_{2,0}(0) &= u_2(0) - u_{2,0}(0),\\
\psi_{2,i}(0) &= -u_{2,i}(0); \quad 0 \le i \le q,\\
\phi_{1,0}(1) &= u_1(1) - u_{1,0}(1),\\
\phi_{1,i}(1) &= -u_{1,i}(1); \quad 0 \le i \le q,\\
\phi_{2,0}(1) &= u_2(1) - u_{2,0}(1),\\
\phi_{2,i}(1) &= -u_{2,i}(1); \quad 0 \le i \le q.
\end{aligned} \tag{6.16}$$

In fact, we select the components of these coefficient functions which are rapidly decaying. A consequence of this choice is that

$$\begin{aligned}
\Psi_i(1) &= (0,0)^T,\\
\Phi_i(0) &= (0,0)^T.
\end{aligned} \tag{6.17}$$

The boundary conditions set in equalities (6.16) and (6.17) make it

$$\begin{aligned}
\overline{W}(0) &= U(0),\\
\overline{W}(1) &= U(1).
\end{aligned} \tag{6.18}$$

Next, we state as follows the main result of this paper.

THEOREM 6.2. *Set* $\overline{W} = \overline{U} + \overline{\Psi} + \overline{\Phi}$. *Then*

$$\|U - \overline{W}\|_1 \le C\varepsilon^q, \tag{6.19a}$$

which is to say that

$$U(x) = \overline{U}(x) + \overline{\Psi}(\tau) + \overline{\Phi}(\rho) + \mathcal{O}(\varepsilon^q). \tag{6.19b}$$

Proof of Theorem 6.2. Set $Z = U - \overline{W} = (U - \overline{U}) - \overline{\Psi} - \overline{\Phi}$. By construction, we have $\mathcal{L}_\varepsilon\overline{\Psi} = (0,0)^T$ and $\mathcal{L}_\varepsilon\overline{\Phi} = (0,0)^T$. Thus equality (5.4b) leads to

$$\mathcal{L}_\varepsilon Z = \mathcal{L}_\varepsilon(U - \overline{W}) = \varepsilon^{q+1}\left(\frac{d^2}{dx^2}u_{1,q}, \frac{d^2}{dx^2}u_{2,q}\right)^T. \tag{6.20}$$

Thanks to the equalities (6.18), the conditions to apply point (ii) of Theorem 3.1 are satisfied. Inequality (3.1b) says that

$$\|U - \overline{W}\|_1 \le C \cdot \varepsilon^q, \tag{6.21}$$

where the constant C is independent of ε. This achieves the proof of Theorem 6.2. □

Definition 6.3. The regular expansion $\overline{\Theta} = \overline{\Psi} + \overline{\Phi}$ is called the qth-order strong corrector to U.

7. Numerical validation

For a numerical validation purpose, we consider the following problem:

$$\mathcal{L}_\varepsilon U(x) = \begin{pmatrix} -\varepsilon \dfrac{d^2}{dx^2} & 0 \\ 0 & -\varepsilon \dfrac{d^2}{dx^2} \end{pmatrix} U(x) + A(x)U(x) = F(x), \qquad U(0) = (1,2)^T, \quad U(1) = (2,1)^T, \tag{7.1}$$

where

$$A(x) = \begin{pmatrix} 2 & 0 \\ 0 & 2 \end{pmatrix}; \qquad U(x) = \begin{pmatrix} u_1(x) \\ u_2(x) \end{pmatrix}; \qquad F(x) = \begin{pmatrix} \cos(x) \\ \sin(x) \end{pmatrix}. \tag{7.2}$$

The conditions of hypotheses $(H.1)$ are satisfied. Set

$$\mu = \sqrt{\frac{2}{\varepsilon}}; \quad d = \exp(-\mu) - \exp(\mu). \tag{7.3}$$

This problem is very difficult to solve directly. The outer expansion $\overline{U} = (\overline{u}_1, \overline{u}_2)^T = (\sum_{i=0}^{q} \varepsilon^i u_{1,i}, \sum_{i=0}^{q} \varepsilon^i u_{2,i})^T$ is such that

$$u_{1,i} = (-1)^i \frac{1}{2^{i+1}} \cos(t); \qquad u_{2,i} = (-1)^i \frac{1}{2^{i+1}} \sin(t). \tag{7.4}$$

The qth-order strong corrector $\overline{\Theta} = \overline{\Psi} + \overline{\Phi}$ with

$$\overline{\Psi}(\tau) = \left(\overline{\psi}_1(\tau), \overline{\psi}_2(\tau)\right)^T = \left(\sum_{i=0}^{q} \varepsilon^i \exp(-\tau)\psi_{1,i}(\tau), \sum_{i=0}^{q} \varepsilon^i \exp(-\tau)\psi_{2,i}(\tau) \right)^T, \tag{7.5}$$

where $\tau = x/\sqrt{\varepsilon}$ and

$$\overline{\Phi}(\rho) = \left(\overline{\phi}_1(\rho), \overline{\phi}_2(\rho)\right)^T = \left(\sum_{i=0}^{q} \varepsilon^i \exp(-\rho)\phi_{1,i}(\rho), \sum_{i=0}^{q} \varepsilon^i \exp(-\tau)\phi_{2,i}(\rho) \right)^T, \tag{7.6}$$

is such that

$$\begin{gathered}
\exp(-\tau)\psi_{1,i}(\tau) = \alpha_i \exp(-\mu x); \qquad \exp(-\tau)\psi_{2,i}(\tau) = \beta_i \exp(-\mu x), \\
\alpha_0 = u_1(0) - \frac{1}{2} = 1 - \frac{1}{2}; \qquad \alpha_i = (-1)^{i+1}\frac{1}{2^{i+1}}, \\
\beta_0 = u_2(0) = 2; \qquad \beta_i = 0, \\
1 \le i \le q, \\
\exp(-\rho)\phi_{1,i}(\rho) = \gamma_i \exp\big(-\mu(1-x)\big); \qquad \exp(-\rho)\psi_{2,i}(\rho) = \delta_i \exp\big(-\mu(1-x)\big), \\
\gamma_0 = u_1(1) - \frac{1}{2}\cos(1) = 2 - \frac{1}{2}\cos(1); \qquad \gamma_i = (-1)^{i+1}\frac{1}{2^{i+1}}\cos(1), \\
\delta_0 = u_2(1) - \frac{1}{2}\sin(1) = 1 - \frac{1}{2}\sin(1); \qquad \delta_i = (-1)^{i+1}\frac{1}{2^{i+1}}\sin(1), \\
1 \le i \le q.
\end{gathered} \tag{7.7}$$

The thickness of the boundary layers is $\overline{x}_\varepsilon = \sqrt{\varepsilon}\ln(2\eta^{-1})$ for any choice of ε and η. This method provides a very accurate solution.

References

[1] W. Eckhaus, *Asymptotic Analysis of Singular Perturbations*, Studies in Mathematics and Its Applications, vol. 9, North-Holland, Amsterdam, 1979.

[2] E. C. Gartland Jr., *Uniform high-order difference schemes for a singularly perturbed two-point boundary value problem*, Mathematics of Computation **48** (1987), no. 178, 551–564, S5–S9.

[3] ———, *Graded-mesh difference schemes for singularly perturbed two-point boundary value problems*, Mathematics of Computation **51** (1988), no. 184, 631–657.

[4] R. Geel, *Singular Perturbations of Hyperbolic Type*, Mathematical Centre Tracts, vol. 98, Mathematisch Centrum, Amsterdam, 1978.

[5] D. Konate, *Asymptotic solution for the perturbed Stokes problem in a bounded domain in two and three dimensions*, Proceedings of the Royal Society of Edinburgh. Section A **129** (1999), no. 4, 811–824.

[6] ———, *Uniformly convergent schemes for singularly perturbed differential equations based on collocation methods*, International Journal of Mathematics and Mathematical Sciences **24** (2000), no. 5, 305–313.

[7] ———, *Strong uniform approximation for some singularly perturbed differential equations arising in chemical reactor theory*, Portugaliae Mathematica. Nova Série **60** (2003), no. 1, 23–36.

[8] J.-L. Lions, *Perturbations singulières dans les problèmes aux limites et en contrôle optimal*, Lecture Notes in Mathematics, vol. 323, Springer, Berlin, 1973.

[9] S. Matthews, E. O'Riordan, and G. I. Shishkin, *A numerical method for a system of singularly perturbed reaction-diffusion equations*, Journal of Computational and Applied Mathematics **145** (2002), no. 1, 151–166.

[10] R. E. O'Malley Jr., *Singular Perturbation Methods for Ordinary Differential Equations*, Applied Mathematical Sciences, vol. 89, Springer, New York, 1991.

Dialla Konate: Department of Mathematics, Virginia Tech, Blacksburg, VA 24061-0123, USA; Institute for High Performance Computing and its Applications, Winston-Salem State University, Winston-Salem, NC 27110, USA

E-mail address: dkonate@math.vt.edu

PROBABILISTIC SOLUTIONS OF THE DIRICHLET PROBLEM FOR ISAACS EQUATION

JAY KOVATS

In this expository paper, we examine an open question regarding the Dirichlet problem for the fully nonlinear, uniformly elliptic Isaacs equation in a smooth, bounded domain in $\mathbb{R}^d$. Specifically, we examine the possibility of obtaining a probabilistic expression for the continuous viscosity solution of the Dirichlet problem for the nondegenerate Isaacs equation.

1. Question

Let $D \subset \mathbb{R}^d$ be a bounded domain whose boundary satisfies a uniform exterior sphere condition. What is the general form of the continuous viscosity solution of the Dirichlet problem for the uniformly elliptic Isaacs equation

$$\begin{gathered}\min_{z\in Z}\max_{y\in Y}\{L^{y,z}v(x)+f(y,z,x)\}=0 \quad \text{in } D,\\ v=g \quad \text{on } \partial D,\end{gathered} \tag{$*$}$$

where $L^{y,z}u = L^{y,z}(x)u := \operatorname{tr}[a(y,z,x)u_{xx}] + b(y,z,x)\cdot u_x - c(y,z,x)u$? Here, we assume that our coefficients, a, b, c, f, are continuous, uniformly bounded, and Lipschitz continuous in x (uniformly in y, z), $c \geq 0$, and $g(x)$ is Lipschitz continuous in $\bar{D}$. Y, Z are compact sets in $\mathbb{R}^p$, $\mathbb{R}^q$, respectively.

The Isaacs equation, which comes from the theory of differential games, is of the form $F[v](x) := F(v_{xx}, v_x, v, x) = 0$, where $F : \mathcal{S}\times\mathbb{R}^d\times\mathbb{R}\times D \to \mathbb{R}^d$ is given by

$$F(m,p,r,x)=\min_{z\in Z}\max_{y\in Y}\{\operatorname{tr}[a(y,z,x)\cdot m]+b(y,z,x)\cdot p-c(y,z,x)r+f(y,z,x)\}, \tag{1.1}$$

and by the structure of this equation, that is, our conditions on our coefficients as well as the nondegeneracy of a (uniform ellipticity), we know by Ishii and Lions (see [10]) that

Hindawi Publishing Corporation
Proceedings of the Conference on Differential & Difference Equations and Applications, pp. 593–604

there exists a unique viscosity solution $v \in C(\bar{D})$ to this Dirichlet problem. Hence if we find a $C(\bar{D})$ viscosity solution to $(*)$, it must be *the* solution.

2. Definitions, examples

Definition 2.1. $F : \mathcal{S} \times \mathbb{R}^d \times \mathbb{R} \times D \to \mathbb{R}$ is *uniformly elliptic* in D if there exist constants $0 < \lambda \leq \Lambda$ such that for all $m \in \mathcal{S}$, $p \in \mathbb{R}^d$, $r \in \mathbb{R}$, $x \in D$,

$$\lambda \|n\| \leq F(m+n,p,r,x) - F(m,p,r,x) \leq \Lambda \|n\|, \quad \forall n \geq 0, \tag{2.1}$$

where for $a \in \mathcal{S}$, $\|a\| = \sup_{e \in \mathbb{R}^d, |e|=1} |ae|$. Here, $\mathcal{S}$ denotes the space of real symmetric $d \times d$ matrices.

Hence uniformly elliptic equations are generalizations of linear equations in nondivergence form $L(x)u(x) + f(x) = 0$, where

$$L(x)u := \operatorname{tr}\left[a(x) \cdot u_{xx}\right] + b(x) \cdot u_x - c(x)u \tag{2.2}$$

and $a(x) \in \mathcal{S}$ satisfies $\lambda I_d \leq a(x) \leq \Lambda I_d$, for all $x \in D$.

(i) *Bellman equation.* This equation comes from the theory of controlled diffusion processes (see [12]) and is the prototypical convex second-order uniformly elliptic equation

$$F[u](x) := \sup_{\alpha \in A} \left\{ \operatorname{tr}\left[a(\alpha,x)u_{xx}\right] + b(\alpha,x) \cdot u_x - c(\alpha,x)u + f^\alpha(x) \right\} = 0, \tag{2.3}$$

where for all $\alpha \in A$, $x \in D$, $\lambda I_d \leq a(\alpha,x) \leq \Lambda I_d$. From the elementary inequalties

$$\inf_\alpha h_\alpha^1 - \inf_\alpha h_\alpha^2 \leq \inf_\alpha \left(h_\alpha^1 - h_\alpha^2\right) \leq \sup_\alpha h_\alpha^1 - \sup_\alpha h_\alpha^2 \leq \sup_\alpha \left(h_\alpha^1 - h_\alpha^2\right), \tag{2.4}$$

it follows that the Bellman equations are uniformly elliptic with ellipticity constants λ, $d\Lambda$.

(ii) *Isaacs equations.* These equations come from the theory of stochastic differential games (see [5, 7, 9]). The upper Isaacs equation F^+ and the lower Isaacs equation F^- are defined by

$$\begin{aligned} F^+[u](x) &:= \min_{z \in Z} \max_{y \in Y} \left\{ \operatorname{tr}\left[a(y,z,x)u_{xx}\right] + b(y,z,x) \cdot u_x - c(y,z,x)u + f(y,z,x) \right\} = 0, \\ F^-[u](x) &:= \max_{y \in Y} \min_{z \in Z} \left\{ \operatorname{tr}\left[a(y,z,x)u_{xx}\right] + b(y,z,x) \cdot u_x - c(y,z,x)u + f(y,z,x) \right\} = 0, \end{aligned} \tag{2.5}$$

where for all $y \in Y$, $z \in Z$, $x \in D$, $\lambda I_d \leq a(y,z,x) \leq \Lambda I_d$. The Isaacs equations are uniformly elliptic with ellipticity constants λ, $d\Lambda$, yet neither convex nor concave on $\mathcal{S}$.

Equations (2.3) and (2.5) are fully nonlinear (i.e., nonlinear in second-order derivatives) and their corresponding Dirichlet problems do not, in general, have C^2 solutions. Hence we need the notion of weak or *viscosity* solution.

Definition 2.2. We say that $u \in C(D)$ is a *viscosity subsolution* of the equation

$$F(u_{xx}, u_x, u, x) = 0, \quad x \in D, \tag{2.6}$$

if for any $x_0 \in D$, and $\varphi \in C^2(D)$, if $u - \varphi$ has a local maximum at x_0, then

$$F(\varphi_{xx}(x_0), \varphi_x(x_0), u(x_0), x_0) \geq 0. \tag{2.7}$$

Viscosity *supersolutions* are defined similarly. Finally, $u \in C(D)$ is a viscosity *solution* if it is both a viscosity subsolution and supersolution.

Remark 2.3. Wanting to characterize solutions of the Dirichlet problem for the nondegenerate Isaacs equation is justified because (i) *any* uniformly elliptic equation of the form $F(u_{xx}, x) = 0$ can be shown to be of Isaacs type (see [1]) and (ii) the Isaacs equation is an example of a second-order partial differential equation which is, in general, neither convex nor concave in u_{xx}, (i.e., the Isaacs operator $F(m, p, r, x)$ is neither convex nor concave in m). And the $C^{2+\alpha}$ regularity theory has not been extended to solutions of even the simplest such equations $F(u_{xx}) = 0$, that is, $F = F(m)$.

We recall (1982) the Evans-Krylov theorem (see [4, 14]) which states that if $u \in C^2(B)$ satisfies the uniformly elliptic equation $F(u_{xx}) = 0$, where $F = F(m)$ is either convex or concave, then $\exists \alpha \in (0,1)$ for which $u \in C^{2+\alpha}_{\text{loc}}(B)$. In 1989, Caffarelli (see [2, 3]) extended this result to continuous viscosity solutions of $F(u_{xx}) = 0$. That is, if $u \in C(B)$ is a viscosity solution of the uniformly elliptic equation $F(u_{xx}) = 0$, where F is either convex or concave, then u is actually a classical solution and $u \in C^{2+\alpha}_{\text{loc}}(B)$.

But, for example, what can be said about the regularity of viscosity solutions of

$$\begin{aligned} \Delta v + (v_{x^1x^1})_+ - (v_{x^2x^2})_- &= 0 \quad \text{in } B, \\ v &= g \quad \text{on } \partial B, \end{aligned} \tag{2.8}$$

for arbitrary $g \in C(\partial B)$? This equation is of Isaacs type, since it can be written as

$$\max_{1\leq y\leq 2} \min_{1\leq z\leq 2} \operatorname{tr}\left[a(y,z)v_{xx}\right] = 0, \quad \text{where } a(y,z) = \begin{pmatrix} y & & & & \\ & z & & & \\ & & 1 & & \\ & & & \ddots & \\ & & & & 1 \end{pmatrix}. \tag{2.9}$$

Observe that the operator in (2.8) is of the form

$$\min\{\max\{L_1v, L_2v\}, \max\{L_3v, L_4v\}\}, \tag{2.10}$$

where $L_1v = \Delta v = (1,1,1)$, $L_2v = (2,1,1)$, $L_3v = (1,2,1)$, $L_4v = (2,2,1)$ and *not* of the "3-operator" form $\min\{L_1v, \max\{L_2v, L_3v\}\}$, to which recent $C^{2+\alpha}$ regularity results (see [1]) apply. Any viscosity solution of $\Delta v + (v_{x^1x^1})_+ - (v_{x^2x^2})_- = 0$ must be locally $C^{1,\alpha}$ for some $\alpha \in (0,1)$, but do there exist viscosity solutions that are not $C^{1,1}$?

An interesting variation of the above is provided, for $\varepsilon \in [0,1]$, by the uniformly elliptic equation

$$\Delta v + \varepsilon(v_{x^1x^1})_+ - (1-\varepsilon)(v_{x^2x^2})_- = 0, \tag{2.11}$$

which is of Isaacs type, since it can be expressed as

$$\max_{0\le y\le 1}\min_{0\le z\le 1} \operatorname{tr}\left[a^{\varepsilon}(y,z)v_{xx}\right]=0, \quad \text{where } a^{\varepsilon}(y,z)=\begin{pmatrix}1+\varepsilon y & & \\ & 1+(1-\varepsilon)z & \\ & & 1\end{pmatrix}. \tag{2.12}$$

Observe that this is a concave Bellman equation for $\varepsilon=0$, a convex Bellman equation for $\varepsilon=1$, yet neither convex nor concave for $\varepsilon\in(0,1)$. The Dirichlet problems (continuous boundary values) for the two Bellman equations corresponding to the cases $\varepsilon=0$, $\varepsilon=1$ are both locally solvable in $C^{2,\alpha}(B)$. Let us look to "probabilistic" solutions of our problems.

3. Probabilistic solutions

We recall from the theory of linear equations that the probabilistic solution of the Dirichlet problem

$$\begin{aligned} Lv+f&=0 \quad \text{in } D,\\ v&=g \quad \text{on } \partial D, \end{aligned} \tag{3.1}$$

(as usual $L(x)u:=\operatorname{tr}[a(x)u_{xx}]+b(x)\cdot u_x-c(x)u$) is given by the expression

$$v(x)=\mathbf{E}\left[\int_0^{\tau(x)} f(x_r(x))e^{-\varphi_r(x)}dr+g(x_{\tau(x)}(x))e^{-\varphi_{\tau(x)}(x)}\right], \tag{3.2}$$

where for $x\in D$, $\tau(x)=\tau_D(x):=\inf\{t\ge 0: x_t(x)\notin D\}$ and for any $x\in D$ and $t\ge 0$, $x_t(x)$ is the solution of the stochastic integral equation

$$x_t=x+\int_0^t\sigma(x_r)dw_r+\int_0^t b(x_r)dr,$$
$$\text{where } a(x):=\frac{1}{2}\sigma(x)\sigma(x)^*, \quad \varphi_t(x):=\int_0^t c(x_r(x))dr. \tag{3.3}$$

Here, $\sigma(x)$ is a Lipschitz continuous $d\times d_1$ matrix and w_t is a d_1-dimensional Wiener process defined on a probability space $(\Omega,\mathcal{F}_t,\mathbf{P})$. By Itô's theorem and the Lipschitz and boundedness conditions on σ and b, such a solution exists and is unique (up to indistinguishability).

It follows immediately from Itô's formula that if $\exists u\in C^2(D)\cap C(\bar{D})$ solution of (3.1), then $u=v$. (hence the term *probabilistic solution*). Indeed, since $x_{\tau(x)}(x)\in\partial D$ a.s., we have

$$\mathbf{E}_x g(x_\tau)e^{-\varphi_\tau}=\mathbf{E}_x u(x_\tau)e^{-\varphi_\tau}=u(x)+\mathbf{E}_x\int_0^\tau Lu(x_r)e^{-\varphi_r}dr=u(x)-\mathbf{E}_x\int_0^\tau f(x_r)e^{-\varphi_r}dr, \tag{3.4}$$

and transposing gives $v(x)=u(x)$. Hence we have uniqueness in the class $C^2(D)\cap C(\bar{D})$ for the Dirichlet problem (3.1). In particular, if $a(x)$ is nondegenerate and the coefficients are locally Hölder (certainly satisfied by Lipschitz coefficients) in D, where D satisfies an exterior sphere condition, then by the Schauder theory (see [8, Chapter 6.3]), we have that our probabilistic solution v in (3.2) is the unique solution to (3.1) belonging to $C^{2+\alpha}(D) \cap C(\bar{D})$.

Remark 3.1. The exit time $\tau_D(x)$ is, in general, discontinuous in x. Even in the linear case, the probabilistic solution $v(x)$ given by (3.2) will be discontinuous, unless additional restrictions (e.g., nondegeneracy) are imposed. There are examples in which v is discontinuous even for constant coefficients $b \equiv c \equiv f \equiv 0$. In cases where v is continuous, a direct proof of this fact uses the strong Markov property of solutions of (3.3).

The probabilistic solution of the Dirichlet problem for the Bellman equation (see [11, 12, 15–18]),

$$\sup_{\alpha \in A} \{L^\alpha(x)v + f^\alpha(x)\} = 0 \quad \text{in } D, \qquad v = g \quad \text{on } \partial D, \tag{3.5}$$

where $L^\alpha(x)u := \operatorname{tr}[a(\alpha,x)u_{xx}] + b(\alpha,x) \cdot u_x - c(\alpha,x)u$, is given by the payoff function

$$v(x) = \sup_{\alpha \in \mathfrak{U}} \mathbf{E}_x^\alpha \left[\int_0^\tau f^{\alpha_r}(x_r)e^{-\varphi_r}dr + g(x_\tau)e^{-\varphi_\tau} \right], \tag{3.6}$$

where for any strategy $\alpha = \{\alpha_t\} \in \mathfrak{U}$, $x \in D$, $\tau^\alpha(x) := \inf\{t \geq 0 : x_t^{\alpha,x} \notin D\}$ and $x_t^{\alpha,x}$ is the solution of the stochastic integral equation

$$x_t = x + \int_0^t \sigma(\alpha_r, x_r)\,dw_r + \int_0^t b(\alpha_r, x_r)\,dr,$$
$$\text{where } a(\alpha,x) := \frac{1}{2}\sigma(\alpha,x)\sigma(\alpha,x)^*, \quad \varphi_t^{\alpha,x} := \int_0^t c(\alpha_r, x_r^{\alpha,x})\,dr. \tag{3.7}$$

Again, if $\exists u \in C^2(D) \cap C(\bar{D})$ solution of (3.5), we can show $u = v$. Similarly, if we assume a priori $v \in C^2(D)$, we can show v satisfies (3.5). Note that by definition (3.6), $v = g$ on ∂D. But in general, solutions of (3.5) will not be C^2. If we *assume* $v \in C(D)$, we can show that v is a viscosity solution of (3.5). This is done using Bellman's principle, Itô's formula (applied to the test function), and an interior uniform bound (in α, x) on $\mathbf{P}_x^\alpha\{\tau \leq h\}$ by any positive power of h. Bellman's principle (or the dynamic programming principle (DPP)) allows us to rewrite the payoff function v, for any $h > 0$, as

$$v(x) = \sup_{\alpha \in \mathfrak{U}} \mathbf{E}_x^\alpha \left[\int_0^{h\wedge\tau} f^{\alpha_r}(x_r)e^{-\varphi_r}dr + v(x_{h\wedge\tau})e^{-\varphi_{h\wedge\tau}} \right]. \tag{3.8}$$

The difficulty lies in verifying that $v(x)$ is continuous. (From the linear case, we know this will not be true in general.) In cases where smoothness assumptions on coefficients, and so forth, do guarantee continuity of v, one can verify continuity by using a "strong" version of Bellman's principle, which allows us to substitute for h in (3.8) any Markov time (with respect to $\mathcal{F}_t$). In the nondegenerate case, other approaches are available (see [19]). As in the linear case, this strong Markov version of Bellman's principle follows from the strong Markov property of solutions of stochastic equations with bounded, Lipschitz coefficients. The smoothness of the payoff function (3.6) was studied independently by Krylov and Lions in [11–13, 15–18] (see also [19]) and their results even covered the case of degenerate equations. In [15], Krylov exhaustively examined the smoothness of the payoff function, covering all cases of interest.

4. Stochastic differential games and Isaacs equations

For controls y, z (controlled by players I, II, resp.) and $x \in \mathbb{R}^d$, we have a solution $x_t^{y,z,x}$ of the stochastic equation

$$x_t = x + \int_0^t \sigma(y_r, z_r, x_r)\,dw_r + \int_0^t b(y_r, z_r, x_r)\,dr. \tag{4.1}$$

We assume that the coefficients σ and b (as well as c, f below) are continuous, uniformly bounded in (y,z,x), and uniformly Lipschitz in x. For each choice of controls for the diffusion process (4.1) above, we associate a functional

$$\begin{aligned} J(y,z,x) &:= \mathbf{E}\int_0^\infty f\left(y_r, z_r, x_r^{y,z,x}\right)e^{-\lambda r}\,dr \\ &= \mathbf{E}_x^{y,z}\int_0^\infty f(y_r, z_r, x_r)e^{-\lambda r}\,dr. \end{aligned} \tag{4.2}$$

(For convenience, we are assuming $c(y,z,x) \equiv \lambda > 0$.)

The idea is this: a game is played between two players, I and II. Player I chooses controls y for (4.1) in order to maximize J, while player II chooses controls z for (4.1) to minimize J. Players choose strategies based on knowledge of how the other has previously chosen. There are 2 values for this game—an "upper" value (of J) in which player I has the advantage and a "lower" value in which player II has the advantage. The differential game is said to have *value* if the upper and lower values are equal.

Definition 4.1. An admissible control for player I (resp., II) is a process $y_t(\omega)$ (resp., $z_t(\omega)$), progressively measurable with respect to a system of σ-algebras of $\{\mathcal{F}_t\}$, having values in a compact metric space Y (resp., Z). The set of all admissible controls for player I (resp., II) is denoted by $\mathcal{M}$ (resp., $\mathcal{N}$). Controls are identified up to indistinguishability. That is, controls ξ and η are equal on $[0,t]$ if $\mathbf{P}\{\sup_{0\le s\le t}|\xi_s - \eta_s| > 0\} = 0$.

Definition 4.2. An admissible strategy for player I (resp., II) is a mapping $\alpha : \mathcal{N} \to \mathcal{M}$ (resp., $\beta : \mathcal{M} \to \mathcal{N}$) which preserves indistinguishability of controls. That is, if $z^1, z^2 \in \mathcal{N}$, and $z^1 = z^2$ on $[0,t]$, then $\alpha[z^1] = \alpha[z^2]$ on $[0,t]$. The set of all admissible strategies for player I (resp., II) is denoted by Γ (resp., Δ).

Definition 4.3. We define the lower value v^- of the differential game by

$$\begin{aligned} v^-(x) &:= \inf_{\beta \in \Delta} \sup_{y \in \mathcal{M}} J(y, \beta[y], x) \\ &= \inf_{\beta \in \Delta} \sup_{y \in \mathcal{M}} \mathbf{E}_x^{y,\beta[y]} \int_0^\infty f(y_r, \beta[y]_r, x_r) e^{-\lambda r} dr \end{aligned} \tag{4.3}$$

and the upper value v^+ of the differential game by

$$\begin{aligned} v^+(x) &:= \sup_{\alpha \in \Gamma} \inf_{z \in \mathcal{N}} J(\alpha[z], z, x) \\ &= \sup_{\alpha \in \Gamma} \inf_{z \in \mathcal{N}} \mathbf{E}_x^{\alpha[z],z} \int_0^\infty f(\alpha[z]_r, z_r, x_r) e^{-\lambda r} dr. \end{aligned} \tag{4.4}$$

It follows from Fleming and Souganidis (see [6]) that both v^+ and v^- satisfy a dynamic programming principle. From this it can be shown that v^+ is the unique bounded viscosity solution of the upper Isaacs equation $F^+[v] = 0$ in $\mathbb{R}^d$ and v^- is the unique bounded viscosity solution of the lower Isaacs equation $F^-[v] = 0$ in $\mathbb{R}^d$. Hence if the *Isaacs condition* holds, that is, $F^+ = F^-$, we immediately have that $v^+ = v^-$ and the differential game has value (see also Święch [21]). For $\lambda > 0$, the assumption of nondegeneracy is not needed. Actually, in [6], the authors looked at the Cauchy problem for the parabolic Isaacs equation in a strip $H_T := [0, T) \times \mathbb{R}^d$, with terminal data function $g(x)$, where the coefficients depended on t and x (as well as controls y, z). Their results were obtained for this setting, yet the elliptic analogues follow.

In [20], Nisio studied the same Cauchy problem using semigroup methods, hence with coefficients independent of t. Under the Isaacs condition $F^+ = F^-$, she showed that both $v^+(t,x)$ and $v^-(t,x)$ are viscosity solutions of the Isaacs equation $F[v] - v_t = 0$ in the strip H_T. Nondegeneracy was required for a uniqueness result.

Remark 4.4. Note that in the definitions of v^+ and v^-, the upper limit of integration in each of the integrals inside the expectation is $+\infty$. In this situation, verifying continuity is straightforward, by the uniform Lipschitz continuity of f. We will show in Section 4 (Theorem 5.2) that the value functions are actually Lipschitz continuous in $\mathbb{R}^d$ when the discount factor λ in (4.2) is appropriately large.

Let us return to our original Dirichlet problem

$$\begin{aligned} F[v] &= 0 \quad \text{in } D, \\ v &= g \quad \text{on } \partial D, \end{aligned} \tag{4.5}$$

where, say, $F = F^+$ is the upper Isaacs operator and D satisfies an exterior sphere condition. The question is: if $J(y,z,x)$ from (4.2) is defined instead by

$$J(y,z,x) := \mathbf{E}_x^{y,z}\left[\int_0^\tau f(y_r, z_r, x_r) e^{-\varphi_r} dr + g(x_\tau) e^{-\varphi_\tau}\right], \quad \text{where } \varphi_t^{y,z,x} = \int_0^t c(y_s, z_s, x_s^{y,z,x}) ds \tag{4.6}$$

and the process (4.1) is nondegenerate, will

$$\begin{aligned} v^+(x) &:= \sup_{\alpha\in\Gamma}\inf_{z\in\mathcal{N}} J(\alpha[z],z,x) \\ &= \sup_{\alpha\in\Gamma}\inf_{z\in\mathcal{N}} \mathbf{E}_x^{\alpha[z],z}\left[\int_0^\tau f(\alpha[z]_r,z_r,x_r)e^{-\varphi_r}dr + g(x_\tau)e^{-\varphi_\tau}\right] \end{aligned} \tag{4.7}$$

be a $C(\bar{D})$ viscosity solution of (4.4)? If so, then by Ishii's uniqueness result, it will be the only one. The analogous question, of course, holds for v^- and F^-. In (4.6), $\tau^{y,z,x} = \tau_D^{y,z,x} := \inf\{t \geq 0 : x_t^{y,z,x} \notin D\}$, where $x_t^{y,z,x}$ is the solution of our stochastic integral equation (4.1).

A reasonable approach would be to establish a DPP (see (3.8)) for v^+ and then use standard probabilistic techniques to show that under the assumption $v^+ \in C(D)$, it is a viscosity solution of $F^+[v] = 0$. But one must still show that $v^+ \in C(\bar{D})$ and for this, it would be sufficient to prove a strong version of the DPP (see the comments following (3.8)) so that the proof of the continuity of v^+ would proceed like the proof of the continuity of the payoff function (3.6). It is also reasonable to expect that, by using a semigroup approach as in [20], we can circumvent establishing a DPP and directly show that v^+ is a viscosity solution of $F^+[v] = 0$. Nonetheless, the continuity issue seems to be the most profound one.

5. Continuity of the value function in $\mathbb{R}^d$

We close this note by giving a proof of the continuity of the value function(s) in $\mathbb{R}^d$ with an expression for v^+ and v^- slightly more general than in (4.3), (4.4) as seen in [6] or [21]. In those papers, the discount factor $c(y,z,x) \equiv \lambda$ is constant. Here, in our (easier) setting of the whole space, (see Remark 4.4) the assumption of nondegeneracy is not required. We simply require that the lower bound of the discount factor is large compared to the Lipschitz constant for coefficients σ and b, (see assumption (5.5) below). Our Lemma 5.1 below is an easier version of [19, Lemma 2.6]. Under these assumptions, we establish the Lipschitz continuity of the upper value function v^+. The proof for v^- is exactly the same. As in (4.2), we define a functional

$$J(y,z,x) := \mathbf{E}\int_0^\infty f(y_r,z_r,x_r^{y,z,x})e^{-\varphi_r^{y,z,x}}dr = \mathbf{E}_x^{y,z}\int_0^\infty f(y_r,z_r,x_r)e^{-\varphi_r}dr, \tag{5.1}$$

where

$$\varphi_t^{y,z,x} = \int_0^t c(y_s,z_s,x_s^{y,z,x})\,ds. \tag{5.2}$$

We now define the upper value function v^+ by the formula

$$\begin{aligned} v^+(x) &:= \sup_{\alpha\in\Gamma}\inf_{z\in\mathcal{N}} J(\alpha[z],z,x) \\ &= \sup_{\alpha\in\Gamma}\inf_{z\in\mathcal{N}} \mathbf{E}_x^{\alpha[z],z}\int_0^\infty f(\alpha[z]_r,z_r,x_r)e^{-\varphi_r}dr. \end{aligned} \tag{5.3}$$

We assume

$$|h(y,z,x) - h(y,z,x')| \le K_1 |x - x'|, \quad |h(y,z,x)| \le K \quad \text{for } h = f, c, \tag{5.4}$$

$$\inf_{\substack{bx\in\mathbb{R}^d\\(y,z)\in\mathcal{Y}\times\mathcal{Z}}} c(y,z,x) = c_0 > \mu_0,$$

$$\text{where } \mu_0 = \sup_{\substack{x,x'\in\mathbb{R}^d\\(y,z)\in\mathcal{Y}\times\mathcal{Z}}} \left\{ \frac{1}{2} \frac{\operatorname{tr}[(\sigma(y,z,x) - \sigma(y,z,x'))(\sigma(y,z,x) - \sigma(y,z,x'))^*]}{|x - x'|^2} + \frac{(b(y,z,x) - b(y,z,x')) \cdot (x - x')}{|x - x'|^2} \right\}. \tag{5.5}$$

LEMMA 5.1. *For all admissible controls $y \in \mathcal{M}$, $z \in \mathcal{N}$, and any $t \ge 0$,*

$$\mathbf{E}^{y,z}\left[|x_t^x - x_t^{x'}|^2 e^{-2\mu_0 t} \right] \le |x - x'|^2. \tag{5.6}$$

Proof. Observe that the process $z_t^{y,z,x,x'} = x_t^{y,z,x} - x_t^{y,z,x'}$ satisfies a.s.

$$z_t = x - x' + \int_0^t [\sigma(y_r,z_r,x_r^x) - \sigma(y_r,z_r,x_r^{x'})]dw_r + \int_0^t [b(y_r,z_r,x_r^x) - b(y_r,z_r,x_r^{x'})]dr. \tag{5.7}$$

The definition of μ_0 and Itô's formula applied to the function $z \to |z|^2$ and the process $z_t^{y,z,x,x'}$ yields

$$\begin{aligned}
&\mathbf{E}^{y,z}\left[|x_t^x - x_t^{x'}|^2 e^{-2\mu_0 t} \right] \\
&= |x-x'|^2 + \mathbf{E}^{y,z} \int_0^t \Big\{ \operatorname{tr}\left[(\sigma(y_r,z_r,x_r^x) - \sigma(y_r,z_r,x_r^{x'}))(\sigma(y_r,z_r,x_r^x) - \sigma(y_r,z_r,x_r^{x'}))^* \right] \\
&\qquad + 2(b(y_r,z_r,x_r^x) - b(y_r,z_r,x_r^{x'})) \cdot (x_r^x - x_r^{x'}) \\
&\qquad - 2\mu_0 |x_r^x - x_r^{x'}|^2 \Big\} e^{-2\mu_0 r} dr \le |x - x'|^2.
\end{aligned} \tag{5.8}$$

□

THEOREM 5.2. *Under the above assumptions, there is a constant $C = C(K, K_1, c_0, \mu_0)$ such that for any $x, x' \in \mathbb{R}^d$,*

$$|v^+(x) - v^+(x')| \le C|x - x'|. \tag{5.9}$$

Proof. For any $x, x' \in \mathbb{R}^d$,

$$\begin{aligned}
|v^+(x) - v^+(x')| &= \left| \sup_{\alpha\in\Gamma} \inf_{z\in\mathcal{N}} J(\alpha[z],z,x) - \sup_{\alpha\in\Gamma} \inf_{z\in\mathcal{N}} J(\alpha[z],z,x') \right| \\
&\le \sup_{\alpha\in\Gamma} \sup_{z\in\mathcal{N}} |J(\alpha[z],z,x) - J(\alpha[z],z,x')|.
\end{aligned} \tag{5.10}$$

For any $y \in \mathcal{M}$, $z \in \mathcal{N}$,

$$\begin{aligned} J(y,z,x) - J(y,z,x') &= \mathbf{E}^{y,z} \int_0^\infty \left[f(y_t,z_t,x_t^x) e^{-\varphi_t^x} - f(y_t,z_t,x_t^{x'}) e^{-\varphi_t^{x'}} \right] dt \\ &= \mathbf{E}^{y,z} \int_0^\infty f(y_t,z_t,x_t^x) \left[e^{-\varphi_t^x} - e^{-\varphi_t^{x'}} \right] dt \\ &\quad + \mathbf{E}^{y,z} \int_0^\infty e^{-\varphi_t^{x'}} \left[f(y_t,z_t,x_t^x) - f(y_t,z_t,x_t^{x'}) \right] dt. \end{aligned} \tag{5.11}$$

By Fubini's theorem and the fact that f is bounded and Lipschitz, we have

$$|J(y,z,x) - J(y,z,x')| \le K \int_0^\infty \mathbf{E}^{y,z} \left| e^{-\varphi_t^x} - e^{-\varphi_t^{x'}} \right| dt + K_1 \int_0^\infty \mathbf{E}^{y,z} \left[e^{-\varphi_t^{x'}} \left| x_t^x - x_t^{x'} \right| \right] dt. \tag{5.12}$$

By the mean value theorem, $e^{-\varphi_t^{y,z,x}} - e^{-\varphi_t^{y,z,x'}} = e^{-\xi}(\varphi_t^{y,z,x'} - \varphi_t^{y,z,x})$, for some random function $\xi(y,z,t,x,x')$ on the segment between $\varphi_t^{y,z,x'}$, $\varphi_t^{y,z,x}$. More precisely, for some $r \in (0,1)$, $\xi = (1-r)\varphi_t^{y,z,x'} + r\varphi_t^{y,z,x} = \int_0^t [(1-r)c(y_s,z_s,x_s^{y,z,x'}) + rc(y_s,z_s,x_s^{y,z,x})] ds \ge c_0 t$, by (5.5). Moreover, $|\varphi_t^{y,z,x'} - \varphi_t^{y,z,x}| \le \int_0^t |c(y_s,z_s,x_s^{y,z,x'}) - c(y_s,z_s,x_s^{y,z,x})| ds \le K_1 \int_0^t |x_s^{y,z,x} - x_s^{y,z,x'}| ds$. Hence

$$\mathbf{E}^{y,z} \left| e^{-\varphi_t^x} - e^{-\varphi_t^{x'}} \right| \le \mathbf{E}^{y,z} \left[e^{-\xi} \left| \varphi_t^{x'} - \varphi_t^x \right| \right] \le K_1 e^{-c_0 t} \int_0^t \mathbf{E}^{y,z} \left| x_s^x - x_s^{x'} \right| ds. \tag{5.13}$$

By Lemma 5.1, $\mathbf{E}^{y,z}|x_t^x - x_t^{x'}|^2 e^{-2\mu_0 t} \le |x - x'|^2$, and hence by Cauchy's inequality, $\mathbf{E}^{y,z}|x_t^x - x_t^{x'}| \le |x - x'| e^{\mu_0 t}$. This immediately yields, by the above inequality,

$$\mathbf{E}^{y,z} \left| e^{-\varphi_t^x} - e^{-\varphi_t^{x'}} \right| \le \frac{K_1}{\mu_0} |x - x'| e^{(\mu_0 - c_0)t}. \tag{5.14}$$

From this, the fact that $e^{-\varphi_t^{y,z,x'}} \le e^{-c_0 t}$, and our assumption that $c_0 > \mu_0$, we get

$$\begin{aligned} &|J(y,z,x) - J(y,z,x')| \\ &\quad \le K \frac{K_1}{\mu_0} |x - x'| \int_0^\infty e^{(\mu_0 - c_0)t} dt + K_1 |x - x'| \int_0^\infty e^{(\mu_0 - c_0)t} dt = \frac{K_1 |x - x'|}{c_0 - \mu_0} \left\{ \frac{K}{\mu_0} + 1 \right\}. \end{aligned} \tag{5.15}$$

But for $z \in \mathcal{N}$ and $\alpha \in \Gamma$, $\alpha[z] \in \mathcal{M}$. Hence

$$\begin{aligned} |v^+(x) - v^+(x')| &\le \sup_{\alpha \in \Gamma} \sup_{z \in \mathcal{N}} |J(\alpha[z],z,x) - J(\alpha[z],z,x')| \\ &\le \sup_{y \in \mathcal{M}} \sup_{z \in \mathcal{N}} |J(y,z,x) - J(y,z,x')| \le C|x - x'|. \end{aligned} \tag{5.16}$$

□

References

[1] X. Cabré and L. A. Caffarelli, *Interior $C^{2,\alpha}$ regularity theory for a class of nonconvex fully nonlinear elliptic equations*, Journal de Mathématiques Pures et Appliquées. Neuvième Série **82** (2003), no. 5, 573–612.

[2] L. A. Caffarelli, *Interior a priori estimates for solutions of fully nonlinear equations*, Annals of Mathematics. Second Series **130** (1989), no. 1, 189–213.

[3] L. A. Caffarelli and X. Cabré, *Fully Nonlinear Elliptic Equations*, American Mathematical Society Colloquium Publications, vol. 43, American Mathematical Society, Rhode Island, 1995.

[4] L. C. Evans, *Classical solutions of fully nonlinear, convex, second-order elliptic equations*, Communications on Pure and Applied Mathematics **35** (1982), no. 3, 333–363.

[5] L. C. Evans and P. E. Souganidis, *Differential games and representation formulas for solutions of Hamilton-Jacobi-Isaacs equations*, Indiana University Mathematics Journal **33** (1984), no. 5, 773–797.

[6] W. H. Fleming and P. E. Souganidis, *On the existence of value functions of two-player, zero-sum stochastic differential games*, Indiana University Mathematics Journal **38** (1989), no. 2, 293–314.

[7] A. Friedman, *Differential Games*, Pure and Applied Mathematics, vol. 25, John Wiley & Sons, New York, 1971.

[8] D. Gilbarg and N. S. Trudinger, *Elliptic Partial Differential Equations of Second Order*, 2nd ed., Fundamental Principles of Mathematical Sciences, vol. 224, Springer, Berlin, 1983.

[9] R. Isaacs, *Differential Games. A Mathematical Theory with Applications to Warfare and Pursuit, Control and Optimization*, John Wiley & Sons, New York, 1965.

[10] H. Ishii and P.-L. Lions, *Viscosity solutions of fully nonlinear second-order elliptic partial differential equations*, Journal of Differential Equations **83** (1990), no. 1, 26–78.

[11] N. V. Krylov, *Control of a solution of a stochastic integral equation*, Theory of Probability and Its Applications **1** (1972), 114–131.

[12] ———, *Controlled Diffusion Processes*, Nauka, Moscow, 1977, English transl. Springer, New York, 1980.

[13] ———, *On the control of a diffusion process until the moment of the first exit from the domain*, Izvestiya Academii Nauk SSSR. Seriya Matematicheskaya **45** (1981), no. 5, 1029–1048, 1199, English transl. in Mathematics of the USSR Izvestiya **19** (1982), 297–313.

[14] ———, *Boundedly inhomogeneous elliptic and parabolic equations*, Izvestiya Academii Nauk SSSR. Seriya Matematicheskaya **46** (1982), no. 3, 487–523, 670, English transl. in Mathematics of the USSR Izvestiya **20** (1983), 459–492.

[15] ———, *Smoothness of the payoff function for a controllable diffusion process in a domain*, Izvestiya Academii Nauk SSSR. Seriya Matematicheskaya **53** (1989), no. 1, 66–96, English transl. in Mathematics of the USSR Izvestiya **34** (1990), 65–95.

[16] P.-L. Lions, *Optimal control of diffusion processes and Hamilton-Jacobi-Bellman equations. I. The dynamic programming principle and applications*, Communications in Partial Differential Equations **8** (1983), no. 10, 1101–1174.

[17] ———, *Optimal control of diffusion processes and Hamilton-Jacobi-Bellman equations. II. Viscosity solutions and uniqueness*, Communications in Partial Differential Equations **8** (1983), no. 11, 1229–1276.

[18] ———, *Optimal control of diffusion processes and Hamilton-Jacobi-Bellman equations. III. Regularity of the optimal cost function*, Nonlinear Partial Differential Equations and Their Applications. Collège de France Seminar, Vol. V (Paris, 1981/1982), Res. Notes in Math., vol. 93, Pitman, Massachusetts, 1983, pp. 95–205.

[19] P.-L. Lions and J.-L. Menaldi, *Optimal control of stochastic integrals and Hamilton-Jacobi-Bellman equations. I, II*, SIAM Journal on Control and Optimization **20** (1982), no. 1, 58–81, 82–95.

[20] M. Nisio, *Stochastic differential games and viscosity solutions of Isaacs equations*, Nagoya Mathematical Journal **110** (1988), 163–184.

[21] A. Święch, *Another approach to the existence of value functions of stochastic differential games*, Journal of Mathematical Analysis and Applications **204** (1996), no. 3, 884–897.

Jay Kovats: Department of Mathematical Sciences, Florida Institute of Technology, Melbourne, FL 32901, USA
E-mail address: jkovats@fit.edu

ON AN ESTIMATE FOR THE NUMBER OF SOLUTIONS OF THE GENERALIZED RIEMANN BOUNDARY VALUE PROBLEM WITH SHIFT

V. G. KRAVCHENKO, R. C. MARREIROS, AND J. C. RODRIGUEZ

An estimate for the number of linear independent solutions of a generalized Riemann boundary value problem with the shift $\alpha(t) = t+h$, $h \in \mathbb{R}$, on the real line, is obtained.

1. Introduction

In $\widetilde{L}_2(\mathbb{R})$, the real space of all Lebesgue measurable complex valued functions on $\mathbb{R}$ with $p = 2$ power, we consider the generalized Riemann boundary value problem.

Find functions $\varphi_+(z)$ and $\varphi_-(z)$ analytic in $\operatorname{Im} z > 0$ and $\operatorname{Im} z < 0$, respectively, satisfying the condition

$$\varphi_+ = a\varphi_- + b\varphi_-(\alpha) + c\overline{\varphi_-} + d\overline{\varphi_-(\alpha)}, \quad \varphi_-(\infty) = 0, \tag{1.1}$$

imposed on their boundary values on $\mathbb{R}$, where

$$\alpha(t) = t+h, \quad h \in \mathbb{R}, \tag{1.2}$$

is the shift on the real line, and a, b, c, and d are continuous functions on $\overset{\circ}{\mathbb{R}} = \mathbb{R} \cup \{\infty\}$, the one point compactification of $\mathbb{R}$.

This kind of problems was studied during the last fifty years. Specially, during the sixties and seventies of the last century the theory of this type of boundary value problems was intensively developed, and apparently stimulated by Vekua's book [14], in 1959 (1st ed.). In this book, in particular, it was shown that the problem of rigidity of a closed surface which consists of two glued pieces, under additional conditions, leads to the solvability of (1.1) (see [14, pages 363–366]).

In the mentioned decades the Fredholm theory of the boundary value problems with the so-called Carleman shift, that is, a shift whose iterations form a finite group, was constructed. However, more fine (and interesting for applications) questions about solvability of boundary value problems, with shift, were only considered under very restrictive

Hindawi Publishing Corporation
Proceedings of the Conference on Differential & Difference Equations and Applications, pp. 605–614

conditions for the respective coefficients. These results are included in Litvinchuk's book [11].

Recently, successful development in the theory of singular integral operators with linear fractional Carleman shift and conjugation (see, e.g., [3, 6–8]) makes possible the construction of the solvability theory for the related boundary value problems (see [12]). However, the question about the solvability of boundary value problems of the type (1.1) is still open, in the case of non-Carleman shift, that is, shift whose iterations define an infinite group.

In the present paper we construct an estimate for the number of linear independent solutions of a generalized Riemann boundary value problem (1.1).

2. Preliminaries

Let $U:\widetilde{L}_2(\mathbb{R})\to\widetilde{L}_2(\mathbb{R})$ be the shift operator

$$(U\varphi)(t)=\varphi(t+h), \tag{2.1}$$

and $C:\widetilde{L}_2(\mathbb{R})\to\widetilde{L}_2(\mathbb{R})$ the bounded operator of complex conjugation

$$C\varphi=\overline{\varphi}. \tag{2.2}$$

The operators U and C enjoy the properties

$$C^2=I,\qquad CU=UC,\qquad UP_\pm=P_\pm U,\qquad CP_\pm=P_\mp C, \tag{2.3}$$

where $P_\pm:\widetilde{L}_2(\mathbb{R})\to\widetilde{L}_2(\mathbb{R})$ are the complementary projection operators

$$P_\pm=\frac{1}{2}(I\pm S), \tag{2.4}$$

generated by $S:\widetilde{L}_2(\mathbb{R})\to\widetilde{L}_2(\mathbb{R})$, the singular integral operator with Cauchy kernel

$$(S\varphi)(t)=\frac{1}{\pi i}\int_{\mathbb{R}}\frac{\varphi(\tau)}{\tau-t}d\tau. \tag{2.5}$$

We consider the paired operator

$$T_1=-P_++(aI+bU+cC+dUC)P_-; \tag{2.6}$$

it is clear that

$$n=\dim\ker T_1, \tag{2.7}$$

where n is the number of linear independent solutions of the boundary value problem (1.1).

In the sequel, $\widetilde{L}_2^m(\mathbb{R})$ denotes the space $[\widetilde{L}_2(\mathbb{R})]^m$, and by abuse of notation we use the same symbols, $P_\pm:\widetilde{L}_2^m(\mathbb{R})\to\widetilde{L}_2^m(\mathbb{R})$, equivalent to the projection operators $P_\pm E_m:\widetilde{L}_2^m(\mathbb{R})\to\widetilde{L}_2^m(\mathbb{R})$, where E_m is the $m\times m$ identity matrix.

Proposition 2.1. *Let $T_2 : \widetilde{L}_2^2(\mathbb{R}) \to \widetilde{L}_2^2(\mathbb{R})$ be the paired operator with shift*

$$T_2 = (\mathcal{M}_1 I + \mathcal{M}_2 U)P_+ + (\mathcal{M}_3 I + \mathcal{M}_4 U)P_-, \tag{2.8}$$

where $\mathcal{M}_i$, $i = \overline{1,4}$, are the matrix functions

$$\mathcal{M}_1 = \begin{pmatrix} -1 & c \\ 0 & \overline{a} \end{pmatrix}, \qquad \mathcal{M}_2 = \begin{pmatrix} 0 & d \\ 0 & \overline{b} \end{pmatrix},$$
$$\mathcal{M}_3 = \begin{pmatrix} a & 0 \\ \overline{c} & -1 \end{pmatrix}, \qquad \mathcal{M}_4 = \begin{pmatrix} b & 0 \\ \overline{d} & 0 \end{pmatrix}, \tag{2.9}$$

then

$$n = \frac{1}{2} \dim\ker T_2. \tag{2.10}$$

Proof. It is well known (see, e.g., [12]) that using (2.3) holds the following relation:

$$M \operatorname{diag}(T_1, \widetilde{T}_1) M^{-1} = T_2, \tag{2.11}$$

between the operators T_2, T_1 and its companion operator

$$\widetilde{T}_1 = -P_+ + (aI + bU - cC - dUC)P_-, \tag{2.12}$$

where $M : \widetilde{L}_2^2(\mathbb{R}) \to \widetilde{L}_2^2(\mathbb{R})$ is the invertible operator $M = 1/\sqrt{2}\begin{pmatrix} I & I \\ C & -C \end{pmatrix}$. Since T_1 and $\widetilde{T}_1$ are similar operators, we have (2.10). □

3. The case $b \equiv 0$

If the continuous scalar function a enjoys the property

$$a(t) \neq 0, \quad t \in \mathring{\mathbb{R}}, \tag{3.1}$$

the coefficients of the paired operator (2.8) are invertible, that is, the functional operators $\mathcal{M}_1 I + \mathcal{M}_2 U$ and $\mathcal{M}_3 I + \mathcal{M}_4 U$ are invertible and then the operator (2.8) is Fredholm in $\widetilde{L}_2^2(\mathbb{R})$ (see, e.g., [9]).

Let

$$\widetilde{T}_2 = (\mathcal{M}_3 I + \mathcal{M}_4 U)^{-1} T_2, \tag{3.2}$$

then

$$\widetilde{T}_2 = (\mathcal{A}_0 I + \mathcal{A}_1 U + \mathcal{A}_2 U^2)P_+ + P_-, \tag{3.3}$$

where

$$\mathcal{A}_0 = a^{-1}\begin{pmatrix} -1 & c \\ -\bar{c} & |c|^2 - |a|^2 \end{pmatrix}, \tag{3.4}$$

$$\mathcal{A}_1 = \begin{pmatrix} 0 & da^{-1} \\ -\bar{d}a^{-1}(\alpha) & \bar{c}da^{-1} + \bar{d}a^{-1}(\alpha)c(\alpha) \end{pmatrix}, \tag{3.5}$$

$$\mathcal{A}_2 = \begin{pmatrix} 0 & 0 \\ 0 & f \end{pmatrix}, \qquad f = a^{-1}(\alpha)\bar{d}d(\alpha). \tag{3.6}$$

Due to (2.10) and (3.2), we have

$$n = \frac{1}{2}\dim\ker \widetilde{T}_2. \tag{3.7}$$

Proposition 3.1. *Let $T_3 : \widetilde{L}_2^3(\mathbb{R}) \to \widetilde{L}_2^3(\mathbb{R})$ be the paired operator*

$$T_3 = (\mathcal{B}_0 I + \mathcal{B}_1 U)P_+ + P_-, \tag{3.8}$$

where $\mathcal{B}_0$ and $\mathcal{B}_1$ are the matrix functions

$$\mathcal{B}_0 = \begin{pmatrix} \mathcal{A}_0 & \vdots & 0_{1\times 2} \\ \cdots & \cdots & \cdots \\ 0_{2\times 1} & \vdots & 1 \end{pmatrix}, \qquad \mathcal{B}_1 = \begin{pmatrix} \mathcal{A}_1 & \vdots & \begin{matrix} 0 \\ f \end{matrix} \\ \cdots & \cdots & \cdots \\ 0 \quad -1 & \vdots & 0 \end{pmatrix}, \tag{3.9}$$

and $\mathcal{A}_0$, $\mathcal{A}_1$, and f are given, respectively, by (3.4), (3.5), and (3.6), then

$$n = \frac{1}{2}\dim\ker T_3. \tag{3.10}$$

Proof. By $N : \widetilde{L}_2^3(\mathbb{R}) \to \widetilde{L}_2^3(\mathbb{R})$, we denote the invertible operator

$$N = \begin{pmatrix} I & 0 & 0 \\ 0 & I & 0 \\ 0 & UP_+ & I \end{pmatrix}; \tag{3.11}$$

it is easy to see that

$$T_3 N = \begin{pmatrix} \widetilde{T}_2 & \vdots & \begin{matrix} 0 \\ fUP_+ \end{matrix} \\ \cdots & \cdots & \cdots \\ 0_{2\times 1} & \vdots & I \end{pmatrix}, \tag{3.12}$$

where $\widetilde{T}_2$ is the paired operator (3.2). From (3.7), the statement of the proposition is straightforward. □

It is known that (see, e.g., [13]; see also [1, 4, 5]) if $\mathcal{A}_0 \in C^{2\times 2}(\mathring{\mathbb{R}})$ verifies $\det \mathcal{A}_0 \neq 0$, for all $t \in \mathring{\mathbb{R}}$, then the continuous matrix function $\mathcal{A}_0$ admits the (right) factorization in $L_2^{2\times 2}(\mathbb{R})$:

$$\mathcal{A}_0 = \mathcal{A}_- \Lambda \mathcal{A}_+, \tag{3.13}$$

where

$$\begin{gathered} (t-i)^{-1}\mathcal{A}_-^{\pm 1} \in \left[\hat{L}_2^-(\mathbb{R})\right]^{2\times 2}, \qquad (t+i)^{-1}\mathcal{A}_+^{\pm 1} \in \left[\hat{L}_2^+(\mathbb{R})\right]^{2\times 2}, \\ \Lambda = \operatorname{diag}\left(\theta^{\varkappa_1}, \theta^{\varkappa_2}\right), \qquad \theta(t) = \frac{t-i}{t+i}, \end{gathered} \tag{3.14}$$

$\varkappa_j \in \mathbb{Z}$, $j = 1,2$, with $\varkappa_1 \geq \varkappa_2$, $\hat{L}_2^\pm$ are the spaces of the Fourier transforms of the functions of $L_2^\pm$, respectively, and, as usual, $L_2^+ = P_+L_2, L_2^- = P_-L_2 \oplus \mathbb{C}$. Moreover, we assume that $(t-i)^{-1}\mathcal{A}_-^{\pm 1}$, $(t+i)^{-1}\mathcal{A}_+^{\pm 1} \in L_\infty^{2\times 2}(\mathbb{R})$. The numbers $\varkappa_j$, $j = 1,2$, being uniquely determined by the matrix function $\mathcal{A}_0$, are called the partial indices of $\mathcal{A}_0$.

Proposition 3.2. *Let $a \in C(\mathring{\mathbb{R}})$ be a scalar function with the property (3.1) and*

$$a = a_- \theta^{\kappa_a} a_+, \quad \kappa_a = \operatorname*{ind}_{\mathring{\mathbb{R}}} a, \tag{3.15}$$

a factorization of a in $L_2(\mathbb{R})$, then the partial indices of the matrix function (3.4) are

$$\varkappa_1 = -\kappa_a + \kappa, \qquad \varkappa_2 = -\kappa_a - \kappa, \tag{3.16}$$

where κ is a multiplicity of 1 as an eigenvalue of the operator

$$P_+ \overline{u}_- P_- u_- P_+, \tag{3.17}$$

and $u_- = P_- u$, $u = c_-(\overline{a}_- a_+)^{-1}$, $c_- = P_- c$.

Proof. $\mathcal{A}_0$ can be expressed as the following product:

$$\mathcal{A}_0 = \theta^{-\kappa_a} \mathcal{B}_- \mathcal{M} \mathcal{B}_+, \tag{3.18}$$

where

$$\begin{gathered} \mathcal{B}_- = \begin{pmatrix} 1 & 0 \\ \overline{c}_+ & 1 \end{pmatrix} \begin{pmatrix} a_-^{-1} & 0 \\ 0 & \overline{a}_+ \end{pmatrix} \begin{pmatrix} 1 & 0 \\ \overline{u}_+ & 1 \end{pmatrix}, \\ \mathcal{B}_+ = \begin{pmatrix} 1 & u_+ \\ 0 & 1 \end{pmatrix} \begin{pmatrix} a_+^{-1} & 0 \\ 0 & \overline{a}_- \end{pmatrix} \begin{pmatrix} -1 & c_+ \\ 0 & 1 \end{pmatrix}, \\ \mathcal{M} = \begin{pmatrix} 1 & u_- \\ \overline{u}_- & |u_-|^2 - 1 \end{pmatrix}, \end{gathered} \tag{3.19}$$

and $c_\pm = P_\pm c$, $u_\pm = P_\pm u$.

Then, in order to construct the factorization in $L_2^{2\times 2}(\mathbb{R})$ of the matrix function $\mathcal{A}_0$, we need to factorize the central factor $\mathcal{M}$. It is well known (see, e.g., [12]) that the Hermitian matrix function $\mathcal{M}$ admits the following factorization in $L_2^{2\times 2}(\mathbb{R})$:

$$\mathcal{M} = \mathcal{M}_- \operatorname{diag}(\theta^{\kappa}, \theta^{-\kappa})\mathcal{M}_+, \tag{3.20}$$

in which κ is a multiplicity of 1 as an eigenvalue of a selfadjoint operator (3.17). The last equality means that

$$\mathcal{A}_0 = \mathcal{B}_- \mathcal{M}_- \operatorname{diag}(\theta^{-\kappa_a+\kappa}, \theta^{-\kappa_a-\kappa})\mathcal{M}_+\mathcal{B}_+ \tag{3.21}$$

is a factorization in $L_2^{2\times 2}(\mathbb{R})$ of the matrix function $\mathcal{A}_0$ and the integers (3.16) are its partial indices. □

It must be remarked that in the case when the matrix function $\mathcal{M}$ admits a canonical factorization ($\kappa = 0$) in $L_2^{2\times 2}(\mathbb{R})$, the explicit formulas for the external factors $\mathcal{M}_\pm$ can be found in [2].

Next let us introduce some notations:

$$\varkappa_j = \varkappa_j^+ + \varkappa_j^-, \quad j = 1,2, \tag{3.22}$$

where $\varkappa_j^\mp = 1/2(\varkappa_j \pm |\varkappa_j|)$, respectively, then

$$\Lambda = \Lambda_- \Lambda_+, \quad \Lambda_\pm = \operatorname{diag}(\theta^{\varkappa_1^\pm}, \theta^{\varkappa_2^\pm}). \tag{3.23}$$

Lemma 3.3. *If the scalar function $a \in C(\mathring{\mathbb{R}})$ satisfies (3.1), $\mathcal{B}_1$ is the matrix function defined in (3.9), $\mathcal{A}_\pm$ and $\varkappa_{1,2}$ are, respectively, the external factors and the partial indices of the factorization in $L_2^{2\times 2}(\mathbb{R})$ of the matrix function (3.4), then*

$$n \le \frac{1}{2}(\dim\ker T + 2k), \tag{3.24}$$

where $T : \widetilde{L}_2^3(\mathbb{R}) \to \widetilde{L}_2^3(\mathbb{R})$ is the paired operator

$$T = [I + \mathcal{A}U]P_+ + P_-, \tag{3.25}$$

$\mathcal{A}$ is the matrix function

$$\mathcal{A} = \operatorname{diag}(\Lambda_-^{-1}\mathcal{A}_-^{-1}, 1)\mathcal{B}_1 \operatorname{diag}(\mathcal{A}_+^{-1}(\alpha)\Lambda_+^{-1}(\alpha), 1), \tag{3.26}$$

$$k = -\varkappa_1^- - \varkappa_2^-. \tag{3.27}$$

Proof. The operator (3.8) admits the following factorization:

$$T_3 = \operatorname{diag}(\mathcal{A}_-, 1)T_\Lambda[\operatorname{diag}(\mathcal{A}_+, 1)P_+ + \operatorname{diag}(\mathcal{A}_-^{-1}, 1)P_-], \tag{3.28}$$

where

$$T_\Lambda = \left[\operatorname{diag}(\Lambda, 1)I + \widetilde{\mathcal{A}}U\right]P_+ + P_-,$$
$$\widetilde{\mathcal{A}} = \operatorname{diag}\left(\mathcal{A}_-^{-1}, 1\right)\mathcal{B}_1 \operatorname{diag}\left(\mathcal{A}_+^{-1}(\alpha), 1\right). \tag{3.29}$$

The following equalities hold:

$$T_\Lambda T_- = \operatorname{diag}\left(\Lambda_-, 1\right)\widetilde{T}, \tag{3.30}$$
$$\widetilde{T} = TT_+, \tag{3.31}$$

where

$$T_- = P_+ + \operatorname{diag}\left(\Lambda_-, 1\right)P_-, \qquad T_+ = \operatorname{diag}\left(\Lambda_+, 1\right)P_+ + P_-,$$
$$\widetilde{T} = \left[\operatorname{diag}\left(\Lambda_+, 1\right)I + \operatorname{diag}\left(\Lambda_-^{-1}, 1\right)\widetilde{\mathcal{A}}U\right]P_+ + P_-, \tag{3.32}$$

and T is the paired operator (3.25). From (3.30) it is possible to conclude that

$$\dim\ker T_\Lambda \le \dim\ker \widetilde{T} + \dim\operatorname{coker} T_-, \tag{3.33}$$

and using (3.31),

$$\dim\ker \widetilde{T} \le \dim\ker T. \tag{3.34}$$

Since the external factors in the factorization (3.28) are invertible operators, we have

$$n = \frac{1}{2}\dim\ker T_\Lambda \le \frac{1}{2}\left(\dim\ker T + \dim\operatorname{coker} T_-\right). \tag{3.35}$$

Finally, it is well known (see, e.g., [13]) that in $\widetilde{L}_2^3(\mathbb{R})$

$$\dim\operatorname{coker} T_- = -2\left(\varkappa_1^- + \varkappa_2^-\right). \tag{3.36}$$

□

Let $\mathbb{T}_+$ stand for the interior of the unit circle $\mathbb{T}$. The following two propositions can be found in [10].

Proposition 3.4. *For any continuous matrix function $\mathcal{A} \in C^{m\times m}(\mathring{\mathbb{R}})$ such that*

$$\sigma[\mathcal{A}(\infty)] \subset \mathbb{T}_+, \tag{3.37}$$

there exist an induced matrix norm $\|\cdot\|_0$ and a rational matrix $\mathcal{R}$ satisfying the following conditions:

(i) *the entries have the form $r_{ij} = p_{ij}(\theta)$, where p_{ij} is a polynomial;*

(ii) $\max_{t\in\mathring{\mathbb{R}}} \|\mathcal{R}\mathcal{A}\mathcal{R}^{-1}(\alpha)\|_0 < 1$;

(iii) $P_+\mathcal{R}^{\pm 1}P_+ = \mathcal{R}^{\pm 1}P_+$.

Let $R_{\mathcal{A}}$ be the set of all rational matrices $\mathcal{R}$ satisfying the conditions (i), (ii), and (iii).

Proposition 3.5. *If $\mathcal{A} \in \overset{\circ}{C}^{m\times m}(\mathbb{R})$ satisfies the condition (3.37), then the estimate*

$$\dim\ker T \leq l(\mathcal{A}) \tag{3.38}$$

holds, where $T : L_2^m(\mathbb{R}) \to L_2^m(\mathbb{R})$ is the singular integral operator:

$$T = [I + \mathcal{A}U]P_+ + P_-; \tag{3.39}$$

$l(\mathcal{A})$ is the constant:

$$l(\mathcal{A}) = \min_{R_{\mathcal{A}}} \left(\sum_{i=1}^{m} \max_{j=\overline{1,m}} l_{i,j} \right), \tag{3.40}$$

and $l_{i,j}$ is the degree of the polynomial p_{ij}, corresponding to $r_{i,j} = p_{i,j}(\theta)$, the ij-entry of the $m \times m$ rational matrix $\mathcal{R} \in R_{\mathcal{A}}$.

These results can be used to improve the estimate for the number of solutions of the boundary value problem (1.1).

Lemma 3.6. *Let T be the operator (3.25) and $a \in C(\overset{\circ}{\mathbb{R}})$ a scalar function with the property (3.1), then*

$$\dim\ker T \leq 2l(\mathcal{A}). \tag{3.41}$$

Proof. Taking into account the last proposition, for the proof, it is sufficient to show that the matrix function (3.26) enjoys the property (3.37). In fact, if $\mathcal{A}_\pm$ are the external factors of the factorization (3.13) of the matrix function (3.4), then $\mathcal{A}_0(\infty) = \mathcal{A}_-(\infty)\mathcal{A}_+(\infty)$, so

$$\mathcal{A}(\infty) = \operatorname{diag}(\mathcal{A}_-^{-1}(\infty), 1)\mathcal{B}_1(\infty)\operatorname{diag}(\mathcal{A}_0^{-1}(\infty)\mathcal{A}_-(\infty), 1). \tag{3.42}$$

The last equality means that the matrices $\mathcal{A}(\infty)$ and

$$\mathcal{B}_1(\infty)\operatorname{diag}(\mathcal{A}_0^{-1}(\infty), 1) = |a|^{-2} \left.\begin{pmatrix} \bar{c}d & -d & 0 \\ \bar{d}|a|^2 + (\bar{c})^2 d & -\bar{c}d & \bar{a}|d|^2 \\ -a\bar{c} & a & 0 \end{pmatrix}\right|_{\infty} \tag{3.43}$$

are similar, that is, $\mathcal{A}(\infty)$ is nilpotent. □

Using Lemmas 3.3 and 3.6 we can state our main result.

Theorem 3.7. *If the scalar function $a \in C(\overset{\circ}{\mathbb{R}})$ enjoys (3.1), then the number of linear independent solutions in $\widetilde{L}_2(\mathbb{R})$ of the generalized Riemann boundary value problem (1.1) admits the estimate*

$$n \leq l(\mathcal{A}) + \max(\kappa_a + \kappa, 0) + \max(\kappa_a - \kappa, 0), \tag{3.44}$$

where $\mathscr{A}$ *is the matrix function defined by (3.26),* $l(\mathscr{A})$ *is the constant introduced in Proposition 3.5,* $\kappa_a = \operatorname{ind}_{\mathring{\mathbb{R}}} a$*, and* κ *is a multiplicity of* 1 *as an eigenvalue of operator (3.17).*

Remark 3.8. Taking $\widetilde{\alpha}(t) = t - h$ and

$$\psi_+ = \varphi_+(\widetilde{\alpha}), \qquad \psi_- = \varphi_-, \qquad \widetilde{a} = b(\widetilde{\alpha}), \qquad \widetilde{c} = d(\widetilde{\alpha}), \qquad \widetilde{d} = c(\widetilde{\alpha}), \tag{3.45}$$

it is possible to see that the boundary value problem

$$\varphi_+ = b\varphi_-(\alpha) + c\overline{\varphi}_- + d\overline{\varphi_-(\alpha)}, \quad \varphi_-(\infty) = 0, \tag{3.46}$$

is equivalent to the problem (1.1), in case $b \equiv 0$. Then it is easy to obtain the analogue of Theorem 3.7 for the case $a \equiv 0$.

Acknowledgment

This research was supported by Centro de Matemática e Aplicações do Instituto Superior Técnico, which is financed by FCT (Portugal) and by the project POCI/MAT/58452/2004.

References

[1] K. F. Clancey and I. Gohberg, *Factorization of Matrix Functions and Singular Integral Operators*, Operator Theory: Advances and Applications, vol. 3, Birkhäuser, Basel, 1981.

[2] A. I. Conceição, V. G. Kravchenko, and F. S. Teixeira, *Factorization of Some Classes of Matrix Functions and The Resolvent of a Hankel Operator*, Operator Theory: Advances and Applications, vol. 142, Birkhäuser, Basel, 2003.

[3] T. Ehrhardt, *Invertibility theory for Toeplitz plus Hankel operators and singular integral operators with flip*, Journal of Functional Analysis **208** (2004), no. 1, 64–106.

[4] I. Gohberg and N. Krupnik, *One-Dimensional Linear Singular Integral Equations. I*, Operator Theory: Advances and Applications, vol. 53, Birkhäuser, Basel, 1992.

[5] ———, *One-Dimensional Linear Singular Integral Equations. Vol. II*, Operator Theory: Advances and Applications, vol. 54, Birkhäuser, Basel, 1992.

[6] V. G. Kravchenko, A. B. Lebre, and J. S. Rodríguez, *Factorization of singular integral operators with a Carleman shift and spectral problems*, Journal of Integral Equations and Applications **13** (2001), no. 4, 339–383.

[7] ———, *Factorization of singular integral operators with a Carleman shift via factorization of matrix functions*, Singular Integral Operators, Factorization and Applications, Oper. Theory Adv. Appl., vol. 142, Birkhäuser, Basel, 2003, pp. 189–211.

[8] ———, *Factorization of singular integral operators with a Carleman shift via factorization of matrix functions: the anticommutative case*, to appear in Mathematische Nachrichten.

[9] V. G. Kravchenko and G. S. Litvinchuk, *Introduction to the Theory of Singular Integral Operators with Shift*, Mathematics and Its Applications, vol. 289, Kluwer Academic, Dordrecht, 1994.

[10] V. G. Kravchenko and R. C. Marreiros, *On the kernel of some one-dimensional singular integral operators with shift*, to appear in International Workshop on Operator Theory and Applications (IWOTA '04), Operator Theory: Advances and Applications.

[11] G. S. Litvinchuk, *Boundary Value Problems and Singular Integral Equations with Shift*, Nauka, Moscow, 1977.

[12] ———, *Solvability Theory of Boundary Value Problems and Singular Integral Equations with Shift*, Mathematics and Its Applications, vol. 523, Kluwer Academic, Dordrecht, 2000.

[13] G. S. Litvinchuk and I. M. Spitkovskii, *Factorization of Measurable Matrix Functions*, Operator Theory: Advances and Applications, vol. 25, Birkhäuser, Basel, 1987.
[14] I. N. Vekua, *Generalized Analytic Functions*, Nauka, Moscow, 1988.

V. G. Kravchenko: Departamento de Matemática, Faculdade de Ciências e Technologia, Universidade do Algarve, Campus de Gambelas, 8005-139 Faro, Portugal
E-mail address: vkravch@ualg.pt

R. C. Marreiros: Departamento de Matemática, Faculdade de Ciências e Technologia, Universidade do Algarve, Campus de Gambelas, 8005-139 Faro, Portugal
E-mail address: rmarrei@ualg.pt

J. C. Rodriguez: Departamento de Matemática, Faculdade de Ciências e Technologia, Universidade do Algarve, Campus de Gambelas, 8005-139 Faro, Portugal
E-mail address: jsanchez@ualg.pt

MONOTONICITY RESULTS AND INEQUALITIES FOR SOME SPECIAL FUNCTIONS

A. LAFORGIA AND P. NATALINI

By using a generalization of the Schwarz inequality we prove, in the first part of this paper, Turán-type inequalities relevant to some special functions as the psi-function, the Riemann ξ-function, and the modified Bessel functions of the third kind. In the second part, we prove some monotonicity results for the gamma function.

1. Introduction

In the first part of this paper, we prove new inequalities of the following type:

$$f_n(x)f_{n+2}(x) - f_{n+1}^2(x) \leq 0, \tag{1.1}$$

with $n = 0,1,2,\ldots$, which have importance in many fields of mathematics. They are named, by Karlin and Szegö, Turánians because the first type of inequalities was proved by Turán [13]. More precisely, by using the classical recurrence relation [11, page 81]

$$\begin{gathered}(n+1)P_{n+1}(x) = (2n+1)xP_n(x) - nP_{n-1}(x), \quad n = 0,1,\ldots, \\ P_{-1}(x) = 0, \qquad P_0(x) = 1,\end{gathered} \tag{1.2}$$

and the differential relation [11, page 83]

$$(1-x^2)P_n'(x) = nP_{n-1}(x) - nxP_n(x), \tag{1.3}$$

he proved the following inequality:

$$\begin{vmatrix} P_n(x) & P_{n+1}(x) \\ P_{n+1}(x) & P_{n+2}(x) \end{vmatrix} \leq 0, \quad -1 \leq x \leq 1, \tag{1.4}$$

Hindawi Publishing Corporation
Proceedings of the Conference on Differential & Difference Equations and Applications, pp. 615–621

where $P_n(x)$ is the Legendre polynomial of degree n (the equality occurs only if $x = \pm 1$). This classical result has been extended in several directions: ultraspherical polynomials, Laguerre and Hermite polynomials, Bessel functions of first kind, modified Bessel functions, and so forth.

For example, Lorch [9] established Turán-type inequalities for the positive zeros $c_{\nu k}$, $k = 1, 2, \ldots$, of the general Bessel function

$$C_\nu(x) = J_\nu(x)\cos\alpha - Y_\nu(x)\sin\alpha, \quad 0 \le \alpha < \pi, \tag{1.5}$$

where $J_\nu(x)$ and $Y_\nu(x)$ denote the Bessel functions of the first and the second kinds, respectively, while the corresponding results for the positive zeros $c'_{\nu k}$, $\nu \ge 0$, $k = 1, 2, \ldots$, of the derivative $C'_\nu(x) = (d/dx)C_\nu(x)$ and for the zeros of ultraspherical, Laguerre and Hermite polynomials have been established in [2, 3, 7], respectively.

Recently, in [8], we proved Turán-type inequalities for some special functions, as well as the polygamma and the Riemann zeta-functions, by using the following generalization of the Schwarz inequality:

$$\int_a^b g(t)[f(t)]^m dt \cdot \int_a^b g(t)[f(t)]^n dt \ge \left[\int_a^b g(t)[f(t)]^{(m+n)/2} dt\right]^2, \tag{1.6}$$

where f and g are two nonnegative functions of a real variable and m and n belong to a set S of real numbers, such that the integrals in (1.6) exist.

As mentioned in [8], this approach represents an alternative method with respect to the classical ones used by the above cited authors and based, prevalently, on the Sturm theory.

In Section 2 of this paper, by using again (1.6), we will give three results. In the first one, we will use the well-known psi-function defined by

$$\psi(x) = \frac{\Gamma'(x)}{\Gamma(x)}, \quad x > 0, \tag{1.7}$$

with the usual notation for the gamma function.

In the second one, we will use the so-called Riemann ξ-function which can be defined (see [12, page 16], cf. [10, page 285]) by

$$\xi(s) = \frac{1}{2}s(s-1)\pi^{-s/2}\Gamma\frac{s}{2}\zeta(s), \tag{1.8}$$

where ζ is the Riemann ζ-function. This function has the following representation (see [5]):

$$\xi\left(s + \frac{1}{2}\right) = \sum_{k=0}^{\infty} b_k s^{2k}, \tag{1.9}$$

where the coefficients b_k are given by the formula

$$b_k = 8\frac{2^{2k}}{(2k)!}\int_0^{\infty} t^{2k}\Phi(t)dt, \quad k = 0,1,\ldots, \tag{1.10}$$

$$\Phi(t) = \sum_{n=1}^{\infty} (2\pi^2 n^4 e^{9t} - 3\pi n^2 e^{5t})e^{-\pi n^2 e^{4t}}. \tag{1.11}$$

In [1], the following Turán-type inequality was proved:

$$b_k^2 - \frac{k+1}{k} b_{k+1} b_{k-1} \geq 0, \quad k = 0,1,\ldots, \tag{1.12}$$

relevant to the theory of the Riemann ξ-function (see [5]).

In the third one, we will use the modified Bessel functions of the third kind $K_\nu(x)$, $x > 0$, defined as follows:

$$\begin{gathered} K_\nu(x) = \frac{\pi}{2}\frac{I_{-\nu}(x) - I_\nu(x)}{\sin \nu\pi}, \quad \nu \neq 0, \pm 1, \pm 2, \ldots, \\ K_n(x) = \lim_{\nu \to n} K_\nu(x), \quad n = 0, \pm 1, \pm 2, \ldots, \end{gathered} \tag{1.13}$$

where

$$I_\nu(x) = \sum_{k=0}^{\infty} \frac{(x/2)^{\nu+2k}}{k!\Gamma(\nu+k+1)} \tag{1.14}$$

are the modified Bessel functions of the first kind.

The second part of the paper is devoted to the study of monotonicity properties of the function $x^\alpha[\Gamma(1+1/x)]^x$, for real α and positive x, where, as usual, Γ denotes the gamma function defined by

$$\Gamma(a) = \int_0^{\infty} e^{-t} t^{a-1} dt, \quad a > 0. \tag{1.15}$$

Kershaw and Laforgia [6] investigated some monotonicity properties of the above function and, in particular, they proved that for $x > 0$ and $\alpha = 0$ the function $[\Gamma(1+1/x)]^x$ decreases with x, while when $\alpha = 1$ the function $x[\Gamma(1+1/x)]^x$ increases. Moreover they also showed that the values $\alpha = 0$ and $\alpha = 1$, in the properties mentioned above, cannot be improved if $x \in (0, +\infty)$.

In this paper, we continue the investigation on the monotonicity properties for the gamma function proving, in Section 3, the following theorem.

Theorem 1.1. *The functions* $f(x) = \Gamma(x + 1/x)$, $g(x) = [\Gamma(x + 1/x)]^x$, *and* $h(x) = \Gamma'(x + 1/x)$ *decrease for* $0 < x < 1$, *while increase for* $x > 1$.

2. Turán-type inequalities

THEOREM 2.1. *For $n = 1, 2, \ldots$, denote by $h_n = \sum_{k=1}^{n}(1/k)$ the partial sum of the harmonic series. Let*

$$a_n = h_n - \log n, \tag{2.1}$$

then

$$(a_n - \gamma)(a_{n+2} - \gamma) \geq (a_{n+1} - \gamma)^2, \tag{2.2}$$

where γ is the Euler-Mascheroni constant defined by

$$\gamma = -\psi(1) = 0,5772156649\ldots. \tag{2.3}$$

Proof. For the psi-function we use the following expression:

$$\psi(n+1) = \sum_{k=1}^{n} \frac{1}{k} - \gamma, \quad n = 1, 2, \ldots, \tag{2.4}$$

and the following integral representation:

$$\psi(z+1) = \int_0^\infty \left(\frac{e^{-t}}{t} - \frac{e^{-zt}}{e^{-t} - 1} \right) dt, \quad \Re ez > 0. \tag{2.5}$$

By putting $z = n$ in (2.5), for $n = 1, 2, \ldots$, we obtain from (2.4) and (2.5)

$$\begin{aligned} \sum_{k=1}^{n} \frac{1}{k} - \gamma &= \int_0^\infty \left(\frac{e^{-t}}{t} - \frac{e^{-nt}}{e^{-t} - 1} \right) dt \\ &= \int_0^\infty \frac{e^{-t} - e^{-nt}}{t} dt + \int_0^\infty e^{-nt} \frac{e^t - 1 - t}{t(e^t - 1)} dt. \end{aligned} \tag{2.6}$$

Since

$$\int_0^\infty \frac{e^{-t} - e^{-nt}}{t} dt = \log n, \tag{2.7}$$

we have

$$\sum_{k=1}^{n} \frac{1}{k} - \log n - \gamma = \int_0^\infty \frac{e^t - 1 - t}{t(e^t - 1)} e^{-nt} dt. \tag{2.8}$$

By (1.6) with $g(t) = (e^t - 1 - t)/t(e^t - 1)$, $f(t) = e^{-t}$, and $a = 0$, $b = +\infty$, we get

$$\int_0^\infty \frac{e^t - 1 - t}{t(e^t - 1)} e^{-nt} dt \cdot \int_0^\infty \frac{e^t - 1 - t}{t(e^t - 1)} e^{-(n+2)t} dt \geq \left[\int_0^\infty \frac{e^t - 1 - t}{t(e^t - 1)} e^{-(n+1)t} dt \right]^2, \tag{2.9}$$

that is, the inequality (2.2). □

THEOREM 2.2. *For $k = 1, 2, \ldots$, let b_k $(k = 1, 2, \ldots)$ be the coefficients in (1.9), then*

$$b_k^2 - \frac{(2k+1)(k+1)}{k(2k-1)} b_{k+1} b_{k-1} \leq 0, \quad k = 1, 2, \ldots. \tag{2.10}$$

Proof. By (1.10) and (1.6), with $g(t) = 8\Phi(t)$, $f(t) = (2t)^2$ and $a = 0$, $b = +\infty$, we get

$$\int_0^\infty 8\Phi(t)(2t)^{2k+2}dt \cdot \int_0^\infty 8\Phi(t)(2t)^{2k-2}dt \geq \left[\int_0^\infty 8\Phi(t)(2t)^{2k}dt\right]^2. \tag{2.11}$$

Dividing (2.11) by $(2k)!$ this inequality becomes

$$\frac{(2k+2)!}{(2k)!}b_{k+1}\frac{(2k-2)!}{(2k)!}b_{k-1} \geq b_k^2, \quad k = 1,2,\ldots, \tag{2.12}$$

from which, since $((2k+2)!/(2k)!)((2k-2)!/(2k)!) = (2k+1)(k+1)/k(2k-1)$, we obtain the conclusion of Theorem 2.2. □

Remark 2.3. It is important to note that inequalities (2.10) and (1.12) together give

$$\frac{k+1}{k}b_{k+1}b_{k-1} \leq b_k^2 \leq \frac{k+1}{k}\frac{2k+1}{2k-1}b_{k+1}b_{k-1}, \quad k = 1,2,\ldots. \tag{2.13}$$

THEOREM 2.4. *Let $K_\nu(x)$, $x > 0$, be the modified Bessel function of the third kind. Then, for $\nu > -1/2$ and $\mu > -1/2$,*

$$K_\nu(x) \cdot K_\mu(x) \geq K^2_{(\nu+\mu)/2}(x). \tag{2.14}$$

Proof. By (1.6) with $g(t) = e^{-\beta/t-\gamma t}$, $f(t) = t^{-1}$ and $a = 0$, $b = +\infty$, we get

$$\int_0^\infty t^{m-1}e^{-\beta/t-\gamma t}dt \cdot \int_0^\infty t^{n-1}e^{-\beta/t-\gamma t}dt \geq \left[\int_0^\infty t^{(m+n)/2-1}e^{-\beta/t-\gamma t}dt\right]^2. \tag{2.15}$$

Using the following formula (see [4, integral 3.471(9)]):

$$\int_0^\infty t^{\nu-1}e^{-\beta/t-\gamma t}dt = 2\left(\frac{\beta}{\gamma}\right)^{\nu/2}K_\nu\left(2\sqrt{\beta\gamma}\right), \quad \nu > -\frac{1}{2}, \tag{2.16}$$

from (2.15) we have

$$K_\nu\left(2\sqrt{\beta\gamma}\right) \cdot K_\mu\left(2\sqrt{\beta\gamma}\right) \geq K^2_{(\nu+\mu)/2}\left(2\sqrt{\beta\gamma}\right), \tag{2.17}$$

which, putting $x = 2\sqrt{\beta\gamma}$, is equivalent to the conclusion of Theorem 2.4.

In the particular case $\mu = \nu + 2$, we find

$$K_\nu(x) \cdot K_{\nu+2}(x) \geq K^2_{\nu+1}(x), \quad \nu > -\frac{1}{2}. \tag{2.18}$$

□

Remark 2.5. By means of (1.6) we can establish Turán-type inequalities for many other complicated integrals as well as, for example, $s_n = \int_0^{\pi}(\log\sin x)^n dx$ ($n = 0,1,\dots$) for which we have

$$s_n(x)s_{n+2}(x) \geq s_{n+1}^2(x). \tag{2.19}$$

3. Proof of Theorem 1.1

It is easy to note that $\min_{x>0}(x+1/x) = 2$, consequently $\Gamma'(x+1/x) > 0$ for every $x > 0$. We have

$$f'(x) = \left(1 - \frac{1}{x^2}\right)\Gamma'\left(x + \frac{1}{x}\right). \tag{3.1}$$

Since $f'(x) < 0$ for $x \in (0,1)$ and $f'(x) > 0$ for $x > 1$, it follows that $f(x)$ decreases for $0 < x < 1$, while increases for $x > 1$.

Now consider $G(x) = \log[g(x)]$. We have $G(x) = x\log[\Gamma(x+1/x)]$. Then

$$\begin{aligned} G'(x) &= \log\left[\Gamma\left(x + \frac{1}{x}\right)\right] + \left(x - \frac{1}{x}\right)\psi\left(x + \frac{1}{x}\right), \\ G''(x) &= 2\psi\left(x + \frac{1}{x}\right) + \left(x - \frac{1}{x}\right)\left(1 - \frac{1}{x^2}\right)\psi'\left(x + \frac{1}{x}\right). \end{aligned} \tag{3.2}$$

Since $G'(1) = 0$ and $G''(x) > 0$ for $x > 0$, it follows that $G'(x) < 0$ for $x \in (0,1)$ and $G'(x) > 0$ for $x \in (1,+\infty)$. Therefore $G(x)$, and consequently $g(x)$, decreases for $0 < x < 1$, while increases for $x > 1$.

Finally

$$h'(x) = \left(1 - \frac{1}{x^2}\right)\Gamma''\left(x + \frac{1}{x}\right). \tag{3.3}$$

Since $\Gamma''(x+1/x) > 0$, hence $h'(x) < 0$ for $x \in (0,1)$ and $h'(x) > 0$ for $x > 1$. It follows that $h(x)$ decreases on $0 < x < 1$, while increases for $x > 1$.

References

[1] G. Csordas, T. S. Norfolk, and R. S. Varga, *The Riemann hypothesis and the Turán inequalities*, Transactions of the American Mathematical Society **296** (1986), no. 2, 521–541.

[2] Á. Elbert and A. Laforgia, *Some monotonicity properties of the zeros of ultraspherical polynomials*, Acta Mathematica Hungarica **48** (1986), no. 1-2, 155–159.

[3] ———, *Monotonicity results on the zeros of generalized Laguerre polynomials*, Journal of Approximation Theory **51** (1987), no. 2, 168–174.

[4] I. S. Gradshteyn and I. M. Ryzhik, *Table of Integrals, Series, and Products*, 6th ed., Academic Press, California, 2000.

[5] O. M. Katkova, *Multiple positivity and the Riemann zeta-function*, 2005, http://arxiv.org/abs/math.CV/0505174.

[6] D. Kershaw and A. Laforgia, *Monotonicity results for the gamma function*, Atti della Accademia delle Scienze di Torino **119** (1985), no. 3-4, 127–133 (1986).

[7] A. Laforgia, *Sturm theory for certain classes of Sturm-Liouville equations and Turánians and Wronskians for the zeros of derivative of Bessel functions*, Indagationes Mathematicae **44** (1982), no. 3, 295–301.
[8] A. Laforgia and P. Natalini, *Turán-type inequalities for some special functions*, Journal of Inequalities in Pure and Applied Mathematics **7** (2006), no. 1.
[9] L. Lorch, *Turánians and Wronskians for the zeros of Bessel functions*, SIAM Journal on Mathematical Analysis **11** (1980), no. 2, 223–227.
[10] G. Pólya, *Collected Papers. Vol. II: Location of Zeros*, edited by R. P. Boas, MIT Press, Cambridge, 1974.
[11] G. Szegö, *Orthogonal Polynomials*, 4th ed., Colloquium Publications, vol. 23, American Mathematical Society, Rhode Island, 1975.
[12] E. C. Titchmarsh, *The Theory of the Riemann Zeta-Function*, Clarendon Press, Oxford, UK, 1951.
[13] P. Turán, *On the zeros of the polynomials of Legendre*, Časopis Pro Pěstování Matematiky A Fyziky **75** (1950), 113–122.

A. Laforgia: Department of Mathematics, Roma Tre University, Largo San Leonardo Murialdo 1, 00146 Rome, Italy
E-mail address: laforgia@mat.uniroma3.it

P. Natalini: Department of Mathematics, Roma Tre University, Largo San Leonardo Murialdo 1, 00146 Rome, Italy
E-mail address: natalini@mat.uniroma3.it

POSITIVE CHARACTERISTIC VALUES AND OPTIMAL CONSTANTS FOR THREE-POINT BOUNDARY VALUE PROBLEMS

K. Q. LAN

The smallest characteristic value μ_1 of the linear second-order differential equation of the form $u''(t)+\mu_1 g(t)u(t)=0$, a.e. on $[0,1]$, subject to the three-point boundary condition $z(0)=0$, $\alpha z(\eta)=z(1)$, $0<\eta<1$, and $0<\alpha<1/\eta$ is investigated. The upper and lower bounds for μ_1 are provided, namely, $m<\mu_1<M(a,b)$, where m and $M(a,b)$ are computable definite integrals related to the kernels arising from thc abovc boundary valuc problem. When $g\equiv 1$, the minimum values for $M(a,b)$ for some $a,b\in(0,1]$ with $a<b$ are discussed. All of these values obtained here are useful in studying the existence of nonzero positive solutions for some nonlinear three-point boundary value problems.

1. Introduction

We estimate the nonzero positive characteristic value μ_1 with positive eigenfunctions of the second-order linear differential equation of the form

$$u''(t)+\mu_1 g(t)u(t)=0 \quad \text{a.e on } [0,1], \tag{1.1}$$

with the three-point boundary condition

$$z(0)=0, \quad \alpha z(\eta)=z(1), \quad 0<\eta<1,\ 0<\alpha<\frac{1}{\eta}. \tag{1.2}$$

The problems are motivated by the study of the existence of positive solutions for the nonlinear boundary value problem

$$u''(t)+g(t)f(u(t))=0 \quad \text{a.e on } [0,1], \tag{1.3}$$

with (1.2), where $f:\mathbb{R}_+\to\mathbb{R}_+$ is continuous. It is known that if there exists $\rho>0$ such that the following condition holds.

Hindawi Publishing Corporation
Proceedings of the Conference on Differential & Difference Equations and Applications, pp. 623–633

(H) $f(u) < m\rho$ for all $u \in [0,\rho]$ and $M(a,b) < \liminf_{u\to 0+} f(u)/u \le \infty$, then (1.2)-(1.3) has one nonzero positive solution, where m and $M(a,b)$ are definite integrals related to the product of g and Green's function k to $-z'' = 0$ subject to (1.2) (see [11]). The result remains valid if (1.1)-(1.2) has a unique nonzero positive characteristic value μ_1 with positive eigenfunctions and $M(a,b)$ is replaced by μ_1 (see [19]). It is proved in [19] that $m \le \mu_1 \le M(a,b)$ for $a,b \in (0,1]$ with $a < b$. We refer to [2, 4–6, 13, 14, 16, 17] for the study of (1.2)-(1.3).

In this paper, we show that the above inequalities are strict. According to these inequalities and the condition (H) in the results on the existence of positive solutions mentioned above, one expects $M(a,b)$ as small as possible. Therefore, we are interested in finding the minimum values for $M(a,b)$. We will seek the minimum values for $M(a,b)$ when $g \equiv 1$. We refer to [10, 17, 18] for the study of similar optimal values for other boundary value problems.

2. Positive characteristic values

It is known that Green's function $k : [0,1]\times[0,1] \to \mathbb{R}_+$ is defined by

$$k(t,s) = \frac{1}{1-\alpha\eta}\begin{cases} t[1-\alpha\eta-(1-\alpha)s] & \text{if } t \le s \le \eta, \\ s[1-\alpha\eta-(1-\alpha)t] & \text{if } s \le t,\ s \le \eta, \\ t(1-s) & \text{if } t \le s,\ \eta < s, \\ (1-\alpha\eta)s-(s-\alpha\eta)t & \text{if } \eta < s \le t. \end{cases} \tag{2.1}$$

For $0 < \alpha \le 1$, we define

$$\Phi(s) = k(s,s) = \frac{1}{1-\alpha\eta}\begin{cases} s[1-\alpha\eta-(1-\alpha)s] & \text{if } s \le \eta, \\ s(1-s) & \text{if } s > \eta, \end{cases}$$
$$c(t) = \begin{cases} \min\left\{t, 1-\dfrac{1-\alpha}{1-\alpha\eta}t\right\} & \text{if } 0 \le t \le \eta, \\ \min\left\{t, 1-\dfrac{1-\alpha}{1-\alpha\eta}t, \dfrac{\alpha\eta}{t}\right\} & \text{if } \eta \le t \le 1. \end{cases} \tag{2.2}$$

For $1 < \alpha < 1/\eta$, we define

$$\Phi(s) = \frac{1}{1-\alpha\eta}\begin{cases} \alpha(1-\eta)s & \text{if } s \le \eta, \\ \alpha\eta(1-s) & \text{if } \eta < s \le \alpha\eta, \\ s(1-s) & \text{if } s > \alpha\eta, \end{cases}$$
$$c(t) = \begin{cases} t, & \text{if } 0 \le t \le \sqrt{\alpha\eta}, \\ \dfrac{\alpha\eta}{t} & \text{if } \sqrt{\alpha\eta} \le t \le 1. \end{cases} \tag{2.3}$$

The following results which can be found in [11, Theorem 2.1] provide upper and lower bounds of k.

THEOREM 2.1. *The kernel k has the following properties:*

(i) $c(t)\Phi(s) \leq k(t,s) \leq \Phi(s)$ *for* $t,s \in [0,1]$. *Moreover, the inequalities are strict for* $t,s \in (0,1)$;

(ii) $\Phi(s) \geq \xi s(1-s)$ *for* $s \in [0,1]$, *where*

$$\xi = \begin{cases} \dfrac{1-\eta}{1-\alpha\eta} & \text{if } 0 < \alpha \leq 1, \\ \dfrac{\min\{\alpha\eta, \alpha(1-\eta)\}}{1-\alpha\eta} & \text{if } 1 < \alpha < \dfrac{1}{\eta}. \end{cases} \tag{2.4}$$

Let $a,b \in (0,1]$ with $a < b$ and let

$$c(a,b) = \begin{cases} \min\left\{a, \dfrac{1-\alpha\eta-(1-\alpha)b}{1-\alpha\eta}, \dfrac{\alpha\eta}{b}\right\} & \text{if } 0 < \alpha \leq 1, \\ \min\left\{a, \dfrac{\alpha\eta}{b}\right\} & \text{if } 1 < \alpha < \dfrac{1}{\eta}. \end{cases} \tag{2.5}$$

Let $P = \{u \in C[0,1] : u \geq 0\}$ denote the standard cone of nonnegative continuous functions defined on $[0,1]$. Using the constant $c(a,b)$ defined above, we define the following cone:

$$K = \{u \in P : q(u) \geq c(a,b)\|u\|\}, \tag{2.6}$$

where $q(u) = \min\{u(t) : t \in [a,b]\}$ is continuous from P to $\mathbb{R}_+$. This type of cone has been extensively used, for example, in [3, 7–9, 11, 12].

Throughout this paper, we assume that g satisfies the following conditions:

(C_1) $g : [0,1] \to \mathbb{R}_+$ is measurable such that $\int_0^1 s(1-s)g(s)ds < \infty$;

(C_2) there exist $a,b \in (0,1]$ with $a < b$ such that $\int_a^b s(1-s)g(s)ds > 0$.

Recall that $\mu_1 > 0$ is called a positive characteristic value of the following linear compact operator L from P into K:

$$Lu(t) := \int_0^1 k(t,s)g(s)u(s)ds, \tag{2.7}$$

if there exists $u \in K$ with $u \neq 0$ such that $u = \mu_1 Lu$. It is shown in [19] that under (C_1)-(C_2), $\mu_1 = 1/r(L)$ is the smallest positive characteristic value of L, where $r(L) = \lim_{n\to\infty} \|L^n\|^{1/n}$ is the radius of the spectrum of L and is the largest eigenvalue of L (see [15]). If $g \equiv 1$, L satisfies the so-called (UPE), that is, $r(L)$ is the only positive eigenvalue of L with an eigenfunction in the cone P. It is not clear whether L satisfies UPE for a general function $g \not\equiv 1$. The smallest positive characteristic value of L has been widely used to study some boundary value problems, for example, see [1, 19].

Notation 2.2. Let

$$m = \left(\max_{t \in [0,1]} \int_0^1 k(t,s)g(s)ds \right)^{-1}, \qquad M(a,b) = \left(\min_{t \in [a,b]} \int_a^b k(t,s)g(s)ds \right)^{-1}. \tag{2.8}$$

It is well known that the following inequalities hold (see [19]):

$$m \le \mu_1 \le M(a,b). \tag{2.9}$$

By Theorem 2.1(ii) and (C_2), $M(a,b)$ is well defined for $a,b \in (0,1]$ with $a<b$.

The following new result shows that the inequalities in (2.9) are strict.

Theorem 2.3. *Assume that there exist $a_1,b_1 \in [a,b]$ such that $g(s)>0$ a.e on $[a_1,b_1]$. Then $m<\mu_1<M(a,b)$ for $a,b \in [0,1]$.*

Proof. Let $d=\int_0^1 \Phi(s)g(s)(1-\varphi_1(s))ds$, where $\varphi_1 \in K$ with $\|\varphi_1\|=1$ and $\varphi_1=\mu_1 L\varphi_1$. Then $d>0$. In fact, if $d=0$, then $\Phi(s)g(s)(1-\varphi_1(s))=0$ a.e. on $[a_1,b_1]$ and $\varphi_1(s)=1$ a.e. on $[a_1,b_1]$. Since $\varphi_1''(s)=-\mu_1 g(s)\varphi_1(s)$ a.e. on $[a_1,b_1]$, we have $g(s)=0$ a.e on $[a_1,b_1]$, which contradicts our hypothesis. Let $t_0 \in [0,1]$ satisfy $\varphi_1(t_0)=\|\varphi_1\|=1$. Then $t_0>0$ since $\varphi_1(0)=0$, and thus we have $c(t_0)>0$. By Theorem 2.1(i), we have

$$\begin{aligned} \frac{1}{m} &\ge \int_0^1 k(t_0,s)g(s)ds = \left(\frac{1}{\mu_1}\right)\varphi_1(t_0) + \int_0^1 k(t_0,s)g(s)(1-\varphi_1(s))ds \\ &\ge \frac{1}{\mu_1} + c(t_0)\int_0^1 \Phi(s)g(s)(1-\varphi_1(s))ds = \left(\frac{1}{\mu_1}\right)c(t_0)d > \frac{1}{\mu_1}. \end{aligned} \tag{2.10}$$

Let $d(a,b)=c(a,b)\xi\int_a^b s(1-s)g(s)(\varphi_1(s)-q(\varphi_1))ds$. We prove that $d(a,b)>0$. In fact, if $d(a,b)=0$, then $\int_{a_1}^{b_1} s(1-s)g(s)(\varphi_1(s)-q(\varphi_1))ds=0$. This, together with the hypothesis $g(s)>0$ a.e on $[a',b']$ and continuity of φ_1, implies that $\varphi_1(s)=q(\varphi_1)$ for $s \in [a_1,b_1]$. Since $\varphi_1''(s)=-\mu_1 g(s)\varphi_1(s)$ a.e. on $[a_1,b_1]$, $q(\varphi_1)\ge c(a,b)>0$, we have $g(s)=0$ a.e on $[a_1,b_1]$, which contradicts our hypothesis.

By Theorem 2.1(i) and (ii), we have for $t \in [0,1]$,

$$\int_a^b k(t,s)g(s)(\varphi_1(s)-q(\varphi_1))ds \ge c(t)\int_a^b \Phi(s)g(s)(\varphi_1(s)-q(\varphi_1))ds \ge d(a,b)>0. \tag{2.11}$$

This implies that $\int_a^b k(t,s)g(s)\varphi_1(s)ds \ge d(a,b)+\int_a^b k(t,s)g(s)q(\varphi_1)ds$. Therefore,

$$\begin{aligned} \left(\frac{1}{\mu_1}\right)\varphi_1(t) &= \int_0^1 k(t,s)g(s)\varphi_1(s)ds \ge \int_a^b k(t,s)g(s)\varphi_1(s)ds \\ &\ge d(a,b)+q(\varphi_1)\int_a^b k(t,s)g(s)ds \ge d(a,b)+\frac{q(\varphi_1)}{M(a,b)}. \end{aligned} \tag{2.12}$$

Taking minimum over $[a,b]$ gives

$$\left(\frac{1}{\mu_1}\right)q(\varphi_1) \geq d(a,b) + \frac{q(\varphi_1)}{M(a,b)} > \frac{q(\varphi_1)}{M(a,b)}. \tag{2.13}$$

This implies that $\mu_1 < M(a,b)$. □

The following result gives an upper bound of μ_1 which is independent of a, b.

THEOREM 2.4. *If there exist $a_1, b_1 \in [a,b]$ such that $g(s) > 0$ a.e on $[a_1,b_1]$, then*

$$\mu_1 < \left[c(t_1)\int_0^1 \Phi(s)g(s)c(s)ds\right]^{-1}, \tag{2.14}$$

where $c(t_1) = \max\{c(t) : t \in [0,1]\}$.

Proof. Let $d_1 = \int_0^1 [k(t_1,s) - c(t_1)\Phi(s)]g(s)ds$. Then $d_1 > 0$. In fact, if not, then

$$0 = d_1 \geq \int_{a_1}^{b_1} [k(t_1,s) - c(t_1)\Phi(s)]g(s)ds. \tag{2.15}$$

This implies that $[k(t_1,s) - c(t_1)\Phi(s)]g(s) = 0$ a.e on $[a_1,b_1]$. By Theorem 2.1, we have $g(s) = 0$ a.e on $[a_1,b_1]$, a contradiction. It follows from Theorem 2.1 that $\varphi_1(s) \geq c(s)$ for $s \in [0,1]$ and

$$\begin{aligned}\frac{1}{\mu_1} &\geq \left(\frac{1}{\mu_1}\right)\varphi_1(t_1) \geq c(t_1)\int_0^1 \Phi(s)g(s)\varphi_1(s)ds + d_1 \\ &\geq c(t_1)\int_0^1 \Phi(s)g(s)c(s)ds + d_1 > c(t_1)\int_0^1 \Phi(s)g(s)c(s)ds.\end{aligned} \tag{2.16}$$

The result follows. □

3. Optimal constants

As mentioned in the introduction, we want $M(a,b)$ as small as possible. In this section, we consider the minimum values for $M(a,b)$ when $g \equiv 1$. In this case, we have

$$M(a,b) = \left(\min_{t\in[a,b]} \int_a^b k(t,s)ds\right)^{-1}, \tag{3.1}$$

where k is defined in (2.1). It is shown in [11] that

$$M(a,b)=\begin{cases}\dfrac{2(1-\alpha\eta)}{a(b-a)[2(1-\alpha\eta)-(1-\alpha)(a+b)]} & \text{if } a<b\le\eta,\\[2ex] \left(\min\left\{\displaystyle\int_a^b k(a,s)ds,\int_a^b k(b,s)ds\right\}\right)^{-1} & \text{if } a\le\eta\le b,\\[2ex] \dfrac{2(1-\alpha\eta)}{a(b-a)(2-a-b)} & \text{if } \eta\le a<b,\ a+b\le 1+\alpha\eta,\\[2ex] \dfrac{2(1-\alpha\eta)}{(b-1+\alpha\eta)a^2-2ab\alpha\eta+(1+\alpha\eta-b)b^2} & \text{if } \eta\le a<b,\ a+b>1+\alpha\eta.\end{cases} \tag{3.2}$$

Now, we can find the minimum values of $M(a,b)$ for the following three cases: (i) $0<a<b\le\eta$; (ii) $\eta\le a<b$, $a+b\le 1+\alpha\eta$, and (iii) $\eta\le a<b$, $a+b>1+\alpha\eta$.

Theorem 3.1. *Let $0<a<b\le\eta$. Then*

$$M(a,b)\ge\begin{cases}M\left(\dfrac{\eta}{2},\eta\right)=\dfrac{4}{\eta^2} & \text{if } \alpha=1,\\[2ex] M(a_0,\eta)=\dfrac{2(1-\alpha\eta)}{a_0(\eta-a_0)[2-\eta-\alpha\eta-(1-\alpha)a_0]} & \text{if } \alpha<1,\\[2ex] M(a_3,\eta)=\dfrac{2(1-\alpha\eta)}{a_3(\eta-a_3)[2-\eta-\alpha\eta-(1-\alpha)a_3]} & \text{if } \alpha>1,\end{cases} \tag{3.3}$$

where $a_0=(2(1-\alpha\eta)-\sqrt{3(1-\eta)^2+(1-\alpha\eta)^2})/3(1-\alpha)$ *and* $a_3=(-2(1-\alpha\eta)+\sqrt{3(1-\eta)^2+(1-\alpha\eta)^2})/3(\alpha-1)$.

Proof. Let $S^*=\{(a,b):a\in(0,\eta]$ and $b\in(a,1]\}$ and

$$h(a,b)=a(b-a)[2(1-\alpha\eta)-(1-\alpha)(a+b)]\quad\text{for } (a,b)\in S^*. \tag{3.4}$$

Then we have for each $a\in(0,\eta]$,

$$\frac{\partial h}{\partial b}(a,b)=2a[(1-\alpha\eta)-(1-\alpha)b]. \tag{3.5}$$

Note that if $\alpha\le 1$, then $(1-\alpha\eta)-(1-\alpha)b\ge(1-\alpha\eta)-(1-\alpha)\eta\ge 0$ and if $\alpha\ge 1$, $(1-\alpha\eta)-(1-\alpha)b\ge 0$. Hence, $(\partial h/\partial b)(a,b)\ge 0$ and $h(a,b)\le h(a,\eta)$ for $(a,b)\in S^*$. Let $g(a)=h(a,\eta)=(\eta a-a^2)[2-\eta-\alpha\eta-(1-\alpha)a]$ for $a\in(0,\eta]$. We consider the following three cases.

(i) If $\alpha=1$, then $g(a)=2a(\eta-a)(1-\eta)$ and $g'(a)=2(1-\eta)(\eta-2a)$ for $a\in(0,\eta]$. This implies that $g(a)\le g(\eta/2)$ and $h(a,b)\le h(\eta/2,\eta)=\eta^2(1-\eta)/2$ for $(a,b)\in S^*$. Hence, we have $M(a,b)\ge 4/\eta^2$ for $(a,b)\in S^*$. It is easy to verify that if $\alpha\ne 1$,

then

$$g'(a) = 3(1-\alpha)\left[\left(a - \frac{2(1-\alpha\eta)}{3(1-\alpha)}\right)^2 - \frac{3(1-\eta)^2 + (1-\alpha\eta)^2}{9(1-\alpha)^2}\right] \quad \text{for } a \in (0,\eta]. \tag{3.6}$$

(ii) If $\alpha < 1$, then $g'(a) = 0$ has two solutions:

$$\begin{aligned} a_0 &= \frac{2(1-\alpha\eta) - \sqrt{3(1-\eta)^2 + (1-\alpha\eta)^2}}{3(1-\alpha)}, \\ a_1 &= \frac{2(1-\alpha\eta) + \sqrt{3(1-\eta)^2 + (1-\alpha\eta)^2}}{3(1-\alpha)}. \end{aligned} \tag{3.7}$$

It is easy to verify that $a_0 \in (0,\eta]$, $a_1 > \eta$, and g is increasing on $(0,a_0]$ and decreasing on $[a_0,\eta]$. This implies that $g(a) \le g(a_0)$ for $(0,\eta]$ and

$$\begin{aligned} h(a,b) \le h(a_0,\eta) &= a_0(\eta - a_0)\left[2-\eta-\alpha\eta-(1-\alpha)a_0\right] \quad \text{for } (a,b) \in S^*, \\ M(a,b) &\ge \frac{2(1-\alpha\eta)}{h(a_0,\eta)} \quad \text{for } (a,b) \in S^*. \end{aligned} \tag{3.8}$$

(iii) If $\alpha > 1$, then it follows from (3.6) that $g'(a) = 0$ has two solutions:

$$\begin{aligned} a_3 &= \frac{-2(1-\alpha\eta) + \sqrt{3(1-\eta)^2 + (1-\alpha\eta)^2}}{3(\alpha-1)}, \\ a_4 &= \frac{-2(1-\alpha\eta) - \sqrt{3(1-\eta)^2 + (1-\alpha\eta)^2}}{3(\alpha-1)}. \end{aligned} \tag{3.9}$$

Note that $a_3 \in (0,\eta]$, $a_4 < 0$, and $g(a) \le g(a_3)$ for $a \in (0,\eta]$. This implies that $M(a,b) \ge M(a_3,\eta)$ for $(a,b) \in S^*$. □

THEOREM 3.2. *Let $\eta \le a < b$ and $a + b \le 1 + \alpha\eta$.*

(1) *If $\alpha \le 1$, then*

$$M(a,b) \ge \begin{cases} M\left(\dfrac{1+\alpha\eta}{4}, \dfrac{3(1+\alpha\eta)}{4}\right) = \dfrac{16}{(1+\alpha\eta)^2} & \text{if } \eta \le \dfrac{1}{4-\alpha}, \\ M(\eta, 1-(1-\alpha)\eta) = \dfrac{2}{\eta(1-2\eta+\alpha\eta)} & \text{if } \eta \ge \dfrac{1}{4-\alpha}. \end{cases} \tag{3.10}$$

(2) *If* $1 < \alpha < 1/\eta$, *then*

$$M(a,b) \geq \begin{cases} M\left(\frac{1+\alpha\eta}{4}, \frac{3(1+\alpha\eta)}{4}\right) = \frac{16}{(1+\alpha\eta)^2} & \text{if } \alpha\eta \leq \frac{1}{3}, \\ M\left(\frac{1}{3}, 1\right) = \frac{27}{2}(1-\alpha\eta) & \text{if } \eta \leq \frac{1}{3},\ \alpha\eta \geq \frac{1}{3}, \\ M(\eta,1) = \frac{2(1-\alpha\eta)}{\eta(1-\eta)^2} & \text{if } \eta \geq \frac{1}{3}. \end{cases} \tag{3.11}$$

Proof. Let $h(a,b) = a(b-a)(2-a-b)$ for $a,b \in (0,1)$. Then $h(a,\cdot)$ is increasing on $(0,1)$ for each $a \in (0,1)$. Then we have

$$M(a,b) = \frac{2(1-\alpha\eta)}{h(a,b)} \quad \text{for } (a,b) \in S. \tag{3.12}$$

Let $S = \{(a,b) : \eta \leq a < b \text{ and } a+b \leq 1+\alpha\eta\}$.

(1) If $\alpha \leq 1$, then $S = \{(a,b) : \eta \leq a \leq (1+\alpha\eta)/2 \text{ and } a < b \leq 1+\alpha\eta - a\}$ and

$$h(a,b) \leq h(a, 1+\alpha\eta - a) = (1-\alpha\eta)a(1+\alpha\eta - 2a) \quad \text{for } a \in \left[\eta, \frac{1+\alpha\eta}{2}\right]. \tag{3.13}$$

Let $g(a) = (1-\alpha\eta)a(1+\alpha\eta-2a)$ for $a \in [0,1]$. Then $g'(a) = (1-\alpha\eta)(1+\alpha\eta-4a)$ for $a \in [0,1]$. Note that $\eta \leq 1/(4-\alpha)$ if and only if $\eta \leq (1+\alpha\eta)/4$. Then we have for $a \in [\eta, (1+\alpha\eta)/2]$,

$$g(a) \leq \begin{cases} g\left(\frac{1+\alpha\eta}{4}\right) = \frac{(1-\alpha\eta)(1+\alpha\eta)}{8} & \text{if } \eta \leq \frac{1+\alpha\eta}{4}, \\ g(\eta) = (1-\alpha\eta)\eta(1+\alpha\eta-2\eta) & \text{if } \eta > \frac{1+\alpha\eta}{4}. \end{cases} \tag{3.14}$$

The result (1) follows from (3.12), (3.13), and (3.14).

If $1 < \alpha < 1/\eta$, then $S = S_1 \cup S_2$, where $S_1 = \{(a,b) : \eta \leq a < \alpha\eta \text{ and } a < b \leq 1\}$ and $S_2 = \{(a,b) : \alpha\eta \leq a < (1+\alpha\eta)/2 \text{ and } a < b \leq 1+\alpha\eta - a\}$. Since $h(a,\cdot)$ is increasing on $(0,1)$ for each $a \in (0,1)$, we have

$$h(a,b) \leq \begin{cases} h(a,1) & \text{if } (a,b) \in S_1, \\ h(a, 1+\alpha\eta - a) & \text{if } (a,b) \in S_2. \end{cases} \tag{3.15}$$

Let $g(a) = a(1-a)^2$ for $a \in [0,1]$. Then $g(a) = h(a,1)$ for $a \in [\eta, \alpha\eta]$. Note that g is increasing on $[0,1/3]$ and decreasing on $[1/3,1]$. Hence, we have for $a \in [\eta, \alpha\eta]$,

$$g(a) \leq \begin{cases} g(\alpha\eta) = \alpha\eta(1-\alpha\eta)^2 & \text{if } \alpha\eta \leq \frac{1}{3}, \\ g\left(\frac{1}{3}\right) = \frac{4}{27} & \text{if } \eta \leq \frac{1}{3},\ \alpha\eta \geq \frac{1}{3}, \\ g(\eta) = \eta(1-\eta)^2 & \text{if } \eta > \frac{1}{3}. \end{cases} \tag{3.16}$$

Therefore, we have for $(a,b) \in S_1$,

$$M(a,b) \geq \begin{cases} M(\alpha\eta,1) = \dfrac{2}{\alpha\eta(1-\alpha\eta)} & \text{if } \alpha\eta \leq \dfrac{1}{3}, \\ M\left(\dfrac{1}{3},1\right) = \dfrac{27}{2}(1-\alpha\eta) & \text{if } \eta \leq \dfrac{1}{3},\ \alpha\eta \geq \dfrac{1}{3}, \\ M(\eta,1) = \dfrac{2(1-\alpha\eta)}{\eta(1-\eta)^2} & \text{if } \eta \geq \dfrac{1}{3}. \end{cases} \tag{3.17}$$

Let $\omega(a) = (1-\alpha\eta)a(1+\alpha\eta-2a)$ for $a \in [0,1]$. Then $\omega(a) = h(a,1+\alpha\eta-a)$ for $\alpha\eta \leq a \leq (1+\alpha\eta)/2$ and ω is increasing on $[0,(1+\alpha\eta)/4]$ and decreasing on $[(1+\alpha\eta)/4,1]$. Note that $\alpha\eta \leq (1+\alpha\eta)/4$ if and only if $\alpha\eta \leq 1/3$. Hence, we have for $a \in [\alpha\eta,(1+\alpha\eta)/2]$,

$$\omega(a) \leq \begin{cases} \omega\left(\dfrac{1+\alpha\eta}{4}\right) = \dfrac{(1-\alpha\eta)(1+\alpha\eta)^2}{8} & \text{if } \alpha\eta \leq \dfrac{1}{3}, \\ \omega(\alpha\eta) = \alpha\eta(1-\alpha\eta)^2 & \text{if } \alpha\eta \geq \dfrac{1}{3}. \end{cases} \tag{3.18}$$

Therefore, we have for $(a,b) \in S_2$,

$$M(a,b) \geq \begin{cases} M\left(\dfrac{1+\alpha\eta}{4},\dfrac{3(1+\alpha\eta)}{4}\right) = \dfrac{16}{(1+\alpha\eta)^2} & \text{if } \alpha\eta \leq \dfrac{1}{3}, \\ M(\alpha\eta,1) = \dfrac{2}{\alpha\eta(1-\alpha\eta)} & \text{if } \alpha\eta \geq \dfrac{1}{3}. \end{cases} \tag{3.19}$$

Comparing (3.17) and (3.19), we obtain the result (2). □

THEOREM 3.3. *Let $\eta \leq a < b \leq 1$ and $a+b \geq 1+\alpha\eta$. Then*

$$M(a,b) \geq \begin{cases} M\left(\dfrac{(1+\alpha\eta)}{4},\dfrac{3(1+\alpha\eta)}{4}\right) = \dfrac{16}{(1+\alpha\eta)^2} & \textit{if } \alpha\eta \leq \dfrac{1}{3}, \\ M(\alpha\eta,1) = \dfrac{2}{\alpha\eta(1-\alpha\eta)} & \textit{if } \alpha\eta \geq \dfrac{1}{3}. \end{cases} \tag{3.20}$$

Proof. Let $S' = \{(a,b) : \eta \leq a < b \leq 1 \text{ and } a+b \geq 1+\alpha\eta\}$ and let

$$h(a,b) = (b-1+\alpha\eta)a^2 - 2ab\alpha\eta + (1+\alpha\eta-b)b^2 \quad \text{for } (a,b) \in S'. \tag{3.21}$$

Then $M(a,b) = 2(1-\alpha\eta)/h(a,b)$ for $(a,b) \in S'$. It is easy to verify that $S' = \{(a,b) : b \in [(1+\alpha\eta)/2,1] \text{ and } a \in [1+\alpha\eta-b,b)\}$. Let $b \in [(1+\alpha\eta)/2,1]$. Then we have

$$\frac{\partial h}{\partial a}(a,b) = 2(b-1+\alpha\eta)a - 2b\alpha\eta \quad \text{for } a \in [1+\alpha\eta-b,b). \tag{3.22}$$

Note that if $b-1+\alpha\eta>0$, then $(b-1+\alpha\eta)a-b\alpha\eta\le(b-1+\alpha\eta)b-b\alpha\eta\le 0$. Hence, $(\partial h/\partial a)(a,b)\le 0$ for $a\in[1+\alpha\eta-b,b)$ and

$$h(a,b)\le h(1+\alpha\eta-b,b)\quad\text{for } a\in[1+\alpha\eta-b,b). \tag{3.23}$$

Let $g(b)=h(1+\alpha\eta-b,b)=(1+\alpha\eta-b)[(\alpha\eta)^2-1+2(1-\alpha\eta)b]$ for $b\in[(1+\alpha\eta)/2,1]$. Then $g'(b)=(1-\alpha\eta)[3(1+\alpha\eta)-4b]$ for $b\in[(1+\alpha\eta)/2,1]$. This implies that

$$g(b)\le\begin{cases} g\left(\dfrac{3(1+\alpha\eta)}{4}\right) & \text{if } \alpha\eta\le\dfrac{1}{3},\\ g(1) & \text{if } \alpha\eta\ge\dfrac{1}{3}.\end{cases} \tag{3.24}$$

Hence, we have

$$h(a,b)\le\begin{cases} h\left(\dfrac{(1+\alpha\eta)}{4},\dfrac{3(1+\alpha\eta)}{4}\right)=\dfrac{(1-\alpha\eta)(1+\alpha\eta)^2}{8} & \text{if } \alpha\eta\le\dfrac{1}{3},\\ h(\alpha\eta,1)=\alpha\eta(1-\alpha\eta)^2 & \text{if } \alpha\eta\ge\dfrac{1}{3},\end{cases} \tag{3.25}$$

and the result follows. □

Acknowledgment

The author was supported in part by the Natural Sciences and Engineering Research Council of Canada.

References

[1] L. Erbe, *Eigenvalue criteria for existence of positive solutions to nonlinear boundary value problems*, Mathematical and Computer Modelling **32** (2000), no. 5-6, 529–539.

[2] Y. Guo and W. Ge, *Positive solutions for three-point boundary value problems with dependence on the first order derivative*, Journal of Mathematical Analysis and Applications **290** (2004), no. 1, 291–301.

[3] D. J. Guo and V. Lakshmikantham, *Nonlinear Problems in Abstract Cones*, Notes and Reports in Mathematics in Science and Engineering, vol. 5, Academic Press, Massachusetts, 1988.

[4] C. P. Gupta, *Solvability of a three-point nonlinear boundary value problem for a second order ordinary differential equation*, Journal of Mathematical Analysis and Applications **168** (1992), no. 2, 540–551.

[5] X. He and W. Ge, *Triple solutions for second-order three-point boundary value problems*, Journal of Mathematical Analysis and Applications **268** (2002), no. 1, 256–265.

[6] J. Henderson, *Double solutions of three-point boundary-value problems for second-order differential equations*, Electronic Journal of Differential Equations **2004** (2004), no. 115, 1–7.

[7] M. A. Krasnosel'skiĭ and P. P. Zabreĭko, *Geometrical Methods of Nonlinear Analysis*, Fundamental Principles of Mathematical Sciences, vol. 263, Springer, Berlin, 1984.

[8] K. Q. Lan, *Multiple positive solutions of Hammerstein integral equations with singularities*, Differential Equations and Dynamical Systems **8** (2000), no. 2, 175–192.

[9] ———, *Multiple positive solutions of semilinear differential equations with singularities*, Journal of the London Mathematical Society. Second Series **63** (2001), no. 3, 690–704.

[10] ———, *Properties of kernels and eigenvalues for three point boundary value problems*, Discrete and Continuous Dynamical Systems **2005** (2005), 546–555.

[11] ———, *Properties of kernels and multiple positive solutions for three-point boundary value problems*, to appear in Applied Mathematics Letters.

[12] K. Q. Lan and J. R. L. Webb, *Positive solutions of semilinear differential equations with singularities*, Journal of Differential Equations **148** (1998), no. 2, 407–421.

[13] R. Ma, *Positive solutions of a nonlinear three-point boundary-value problem*, Electronic Journal of Differential Equations **1999** (1999), no. 34, 1–8.

[14] ———, *Multiplicity of positive solutions for second-order three-point boundary value problems*, Computers & Mathematics with Applications **40** (2000), no. 2-3, 193–204.

[15] R. D. Nussbaum, *Eigenvectors of nonlinear positive operators and the linear Kreĭn-Rutman theorem*, Fixed Point Theory (Sherbrooke, Que., 1980) (E. Fadell and G. Fournier, eds.), Lecture Notes in Math., vol. 886, Springer, Berlin, 1981, pp. 309–330.

[16] J. R. L. Webb, *Positive solutions of some three point boundary value problems via fixed point index theory*, Nonlinear Analysis **47** (2001), no. 7, 4319–4332.

[17] ———, *Remarks on positive solutions of some three point boundary value problems*, Discrete and Continuous Dynamical Systems **2003** (2003), suppl., 905–915, Dynamical systems and differential equations (Wilmington, NC, 2002).

[18] ———, *Multiple positive solutions of some nonlinear heat flow problems*, Discrete and Continuous Dynamical Systems **2005** (2005), 895–903.

[19] J. R. L. Webb and K. Q. Lan, *Eigenvalue criteria for existence of multiple positive solutions of nonlinear boundary value problems of local and nonlocal type*, Topological Methods in Nonlinear Analysis **27** (2006), no. 1, 91–116.

K. Q. Lan: Department of Mathematics, Ryerson University, Toronto, ON, Canada M5B 2K3
E-mail address: klan@ryerson.ca

WELL-POSEDNESS AND BLOW-UP OF SOLUTIONS TO WAVE EQUATIONS WITH SUPERCRITICAL BOUNDARY SOURCES AND BOUNDARY DAMPING

IRENA LASIECKA AND LORENA BOCIU

We present local and global existence of finite-energy solutions of the wave equation driven by boundary sources with critical and supercritical exponents. The results presented depend on the boundary damping present in the model. In the absence of boundary "overdamping," finite-time blow-up of weak solutions is exhibited.

1. Introduction

Let $\Omega \subset \mathbb{R}^n$ be a bounded domain with sufficiently smooth boundary Γ. We consider the following model of semilinear wave equation with nonlinear boundary/interior monotone dissipation and nonlinear boundary/interior sources

$$\begin{aligned} u_{tt} + g_0(u_t) &= \Delta u + f(u) \quad \text{in } \Omega \times [0,\infty), \\ \partial_\nu u + cu + g(u_t) &= h(u) \quad \text{in } \Gamma \times [0,\infty), \\ u(0) = u_0 \in H^1(\Omega), &\qquad u_t(0) = u_1 \in L_2(\Omega). \end{aligned} \tag{1.1}$$

Our main aim is to discuss the well-posedness of the system given by (1.1), with $c \geq 0$, on a finite-energy space $H = H^1(\Omega) \times L_2(\Omega)$. This includes existence and uniqueness of both local and global solutions and also blow-up of the solutions with nonpositive initial energy. The main difficulty of the problem is related to the presence of the boundary nonlinear term $h(u)$, and it has to do with the fact that Lopatinski condition does not hold for the Neumann $(c = 0)$ or Robin $(c > 0)$ problem, that is, the linear map $h \to U(t) = (u(t), u_t(t))$, where $U(t)$ solves

$$\begin{aligned} u_{tt} &= \Delta u \quad \text{in } \Omega \times [0,\infty), \\ \partial_\nu u + cu &= h \quad \text{in } \Gamma \times [0,\infty), \\ u(0) = u_0 \in H^1(\Omega), &\qquad u_t(0) = u_1 \in L_2(\Omega), \end{aligned} \tag{1.2}$$

Hindawi Publishing Corporation
Proceedings of the Conference on Differential & Difference Equations and Applications, pp. 635–643

is not bounded from $L_2(\Sigma) \to H^1(\Omega) \times L_2(\Omega)$, unless the dimension of Ω is equal to one or initial data are compactly supported [12, 20]. In fact, the maximal amount of regularity that one obtains is in general $H^{2/3}(\Omega) \times H^{-1/3}(\Omega)$ [13, 21]. The above lack of regularity is a major predicament in studying nonlinear problems, within finite-energy framework, with nonlinearity located at the boundary. Indeed, no matter how smooth or regular the nonlinearity $h(u)$ is, the effect of this nonlinear source is not only non-Lipschitz with respect to the phase space but also non-Lipschitz with respect to the weak semigroup formulation of solutions [8] (unlike Dirichlet problem for which Lopatinski condition is satisfied [18]). In fact, the results in the past literature on local existence of finite-energy solutions that are driven by boundary sources assumed that initial data are suitably small. The corresponding theory, developed within the framework of potential well theory [15], provides existence results for undamped equation (1.1) with $g_0 = g = 0$, $f = 0$. In such case, the issue of Lopatinski condition does not enter the picture, since the candidate solutions remain invariant within the well. However, this approach is totally inadequate for studying local or global existence of solutions *without any restrictions on the size of initial data.* For initial data of an arbitrary size, [10] develops theory based on "sharp" regularity $H^{2/3}(\Omega) \times H^{1/3}(\Omega)$ of the Neumann map [12, 13], which gives well-posedness of solutions to the semilinear boundary problem without any dissipation ($g = g_0 = 0$) and within the framework of spaces just above finite-energy level.

Thus the difficulties implied by not having Lopatinski condition satisfied have been recognized a long time ago and have been dealt with (particularly in the context of control theory) by exploiting boundary dissipation as a sort of "regularization" [14]. In fact, even linear dissipation $g(u_t) = \alpha^2 u_t$ changes the problem to the one where Lopatinski condition is satisfied. As a consequence, (1.2) with added linear dissipation on the boundary $(\partial/\partial\nu)u + cu + \alpha^2 u_t = h$ has finite-energy solutions with L_2 boundary input, that is, $h \in L_2(\Sigma)$. This property has been since used in control theory of PDEs, particularly in the context of boundary stabilization and well-posedness of Riccati equations with boundary nonlinearities [14]. In [11], it was shown that finite-energy solutions do exist locally for locally Lipschitz functions f, h of subcritical growth and for any dissipation g that is continuous, monotone, and bounded linearly at infinity. This last condition on linear bound of dissipation $g(s)$ at infinity was dictated by the main goal of [11], which was obtaining uniform decay rates for solutions (for which such a condition is necessary).

Most recently, [23] revisited the problem by proving local existence of finite-energy solutions to (1.1) with $g_0 = 0, f = 0$, boundary damping $g(u_t)$, and source $h(u)$ of polynomial structures. More specifically, $h(u) = |u|^{k-1}u$, $g(u) = |u|^{q-1}u$, under the restrictions

$$2 \le k+1 < \frac{2(n-1)}{n-2}, \qquad k < \frac{2(n-1)q}{(n-2)(q+1)}. \tag{1.3}$$

The proof given in [23] uses Schauder's fixed point theorem, which is based on compactness of Sobolev's embeddings and excludes critical and supercritical exponents in the nonlinear sources considered. By "critical" we mean sources for which potential energy is well defined on $H^1(\Omega)$ solutions. Since the energy function associated with (1.1) and polynomial sources takes the form

$$E(t) = \frac{1}{2}\int_\Omega \left[|\nabla u|^2 + |u_t|^2 \right] dx - \frac{1}{k+1}\int_\Gamma |u|^{k+1} dx \tag{1.4}$$

on the strength of Sobolev embeddings $H^{1/2}(\Gamma) \subset L_{2(n-1)/(n-2)}(\Gamma)$, the value $k+1 = 2(n-1)/(n-2)$ becomes critical. Thus the values for parameter k assumed in (1.3) are *subcritical.* On the other hand, local existence of finite-energy solutions should not depend on criticality of k (though the method might, as it does in [23]). This is particularly true if one considers high powers for the damping operator. Indeed, by taking $q \to \infty$, one should be able to obtain local existence of solutions assuming only $k < 2(n-1)/(n-2)$, that is, k may be "supercritical." Thus, a question becomes whether the "subcriticality" assumption imposed on k in [23] is intrinsic to the problem or rather to the method.

It turns out that techniques developed in [11], and based on a combination of monotonicity-regularization methods, lead to a positive answer to that question. In addition, these methods are considerably simpler and more powerful than compactness methods used in [23]. They handle not only critical and supercritical cases, but they also allow for a much larger range of nonlinear sources/dampings to be considered.

The present paper is a continuation and expansion of some results and techniques developed in [11]. By using monotone operator theory techniques, we will extend the existing results in order to incorporate more general damping terms and more general sources of supercritical nature. The main novel contribution of the present manuscript can be summarized as follows:

(i) local existence theory for critical and supercritical boundary/interior sources;
(ii) global existence theory exploiting boundary/interior overdamping;
(iii) blow-up of finite-energy solutions with boundary/interior damping.

Thus, the results presented in this paper extend those obtained recently in the literature [23], where boundary sources dampings subject to polynomial structure of *subcritical* exponents were considered. In addition, our proofs are considerably simpler. Finally, we demonstrate sharpness of local and global existence theories by exhibiting blow-up phenomenon in the complementary (to global existence) region.

Remark 1.1. We note that the use of the damping as a tool to control local existence is well established in the study of quasilinear hyperbolic equations, see [1, 9]. The use of the interior overdamping as a control mechanism for longevity of solutions (global solutions) is also well known [7]. However, the smoothing effect of the damping in the semilinear-boundary hyperbolic problem has different mechanism as it relates to Lopatinski condition not being satisfied. This aspect of the problem was addressed in [11], where for the first time it was shown that boundary damping is critical for *local existence* of solutions driven by nonlinear subcritical terms on the boundary. One of the aims in this paper is to fully exhibit the role of the boundary damping played in both local and global existence theories. The issue of exploiting the damping as a mechanism for controlling long-time behavior (including stability and attractors) in the presence of the boundary sources involves different technical aspects [5, 6, 11], and will be relegated to another paper.

2. Main results

Our main results are formulated below. Due to space limitations, we provide only brief ideas about the proofs. Complete proofs are given in [3].

2.1. Local existence. Our first result deals with the case where the dissipation is assumed to be strongly monotone. Later on, we will consider the problem without a strong monotonicity assumption.

THEOREM 2.1 (local existence and uniqueness). *With reference to model (1.1), assume that*

(1) *$g(s)$ and $g_0(s)$ are continuous and monotone increasing functions. In addition, the following strong monotonicity condition is imposed on g, that is, there exists $m_0 > 0$ such that $(g(s) - g(v))(s - v) \geq m_0|s - v|^2$;*
(2) *f is locally Lipschitz: $H^1(\Omega) \to L_2(\Omega)$;*
(3) *$\widehat{h}(u) \equiv h(u|_\Gamma)$ is locally Lipschitz: $H^1(\Omega) \to L_2(\Gamma)$.*

Then there exists a local unique solution $U \in C[(0, T_M), H]$, where T_M (maximal time of existence) depends on initial data $|U(0)|_H$, local Lipschitz constants corresponding to h, f, and the constant m_1 such that $g(s)s \geq m_1|s|^2$, $|s| \geq 1$.

The proof of Theorem 2.1 is based on an extended monotonicity method developed in [11]. The boundary value problem is formulated as a locally Lipschitz perturbation of an m-monotone problem. This is accomplished by a suitable use of semigroup theory, allowing the representation of boundary conditions via a singular variation of parameter formula [10, 11, 14]. Maximal monotone operator theory is then extended in order to incorporate locally Lipschitz perturbations (see [6, Theorem 7.1]).

Remark 2.2. Note here that the maximal time of existence T_M depends on the constant m_1 generated by the growth condition imposed on g, but does not depend on m_0, the constant of strong monotonicity. This feature will allow us to eliminate the strong monotonicity assumption.

THEOREM 2.3 (local existence revisited). *With reference to (1.1), assume that*

(1) *g, g_0 are monotone increasing and continuous. In addition, the following growth conditions at infinity are satisfied. There exist positive constants m_q, M_q, l_m, L_m such that for $|s| > 1$, $m_q|s|^{q+1} \leq g(s)s \leq M_q|s|^{q+1}$ and $l_m|s|^{m+1} \leq g_0(s)s \leq L_m|s|^{m+1}$ with $q > 0$, $m \geq 0$ positive;*
(2) *f is locally Lipschitz: $H^1(\Omega) \to L_2(\Omega)$ when $m \leq 1$ and $H^1(\Omega) \to L_r(\Omega)$, $r \leq (m+1)/m$ when $m > 1$;*
(3) *$h(u|_\Gamma)$ is locally Lipschitz from $H^{1-\varepsilon}(\Omega) \to L_{(q+1)/q}(\Gamma)$.*

Then there exists a local in-time weak solution $U \in C[(0, T_M), H]$, where the maximal time of existence T_M depends on initial data $|U(0)|_H$, locally Lipschitz constants, and m_q, l_m when $r > 2$. The solution may not be unique in this case.

THEOREM 2.4 (uniqueness). *Solutions referred to in Theorem 2.3 are unique provided that the first 2 assumptions of Theorem 2.3 are the same and h is assumed locally Lipschitz: $H^{1/2}(\Gamma) \to L_2(\Gamma)$ and also $h \in C^2(\mathbb{R})$.*

Remark 2.5. As evidenced by assumption (3), the local existence result of Theorem 2.3 depends (as in [11]) on the presence of coercive boundary damping $g(s)s \geq m_q|s|^{q+1}$.

A less regular nonlinear term and more damping (overdamping) are necessary to counteract the nonlinearity. The role of interior damping, however, is much less critical. As long as the interior source is bounded in $L_2(\Omega)$, there is no need for any interior damping. The interior damping becomes critical once the interior source is exiting in the $L_2(\Omega)$ space.

The proof of Theorem 2.3 relies on the following idea. We first approximate the original problem by the regularized one which falls into the framework of Theorem 2.1. Limit passage exploiting monotonicity of the damping allows us to construct the sought after solutions as weak limits of the regularized problem. The important feature of the proof is the approximation of the boundary damping, where $g(s)$ is replaced by

$$g_n(s) = \frac{1}{n}s + g(s), \quad n \longrightarrow \infty, \tag{2.1}$$

which, for each n, readily satisfies hypotheses of Theorem 2.1. Two level approximations of h (resp., f) by a sequence $h_{n,K}$ (resp., $f_{n,K}$), $n, K \to \infty$, are introduced next. $h_{n,K}$ (resp., $f_{n,K}$) for each fixed n are locally Lipschitz from $H^1(\Omega) \to L_2(\Gamma)$. The parameter K controls Lipschitz behavior. Since the function g_n satisfies the strong coercivity assumption of Theorem 2.1 and the functions $h_{n,K}$, $f_{n,K}$ satisfy the necessary requirements of Theorem 2.1, existence of local solutions $u_{n,K}(t)$ follows from that theorem. The final solution to the problem is obtained via the limit process. For this, suitable a priori bounds are necessary. An important feature of the proof is to control the time of local existence $T_{n,K}$ uniformly with respect to the parameters. This is accomplished by exploiting the damping parameter q and condition (3) in Theorem 2.3. It is at this stage when the role of the damping is critical for local existence. Similar phenomena have been observed and taken advantage of in [11]. Having established a priori bounds, the ultimate passage with the limit is accomplished by exploiting the monotonicity method along with convergence properties of regularizations.

Remark 2.6. In the particular case when the function $h \in C^1(\mathbb{R})$ is polynomially bounded at infinity with the bound

$$|h(s)| \le C|s|^k, \quad |s| \ge 1,\ 0 \le k < \frac{2(n-1)q}{(n-2)(q+1)}, \tag{2.2}$$

then Sobolev's embeddings along with standard methods of nonlinear analysis show that condition (3) holds, hence Theorem 2.3 applies. Thus, the result of Theorem 2.3 extends those of [23] not only in allowing more general structure of the damping functions and sources h, f, but it allows us to obtain a larger domain of parameters k, q: $0 \le k < 2(n-1)q/(n-2)(q+1)$, while the domain of parameters in [23] is $1 \le k < \min[n/(n-2), 2(n-1)q/(n-2)(q+1)]$.

Remark 2.7. The uniqueness result of Theorem 2.4 is completely *new*. The only available results on uniqueness so far are when the damping g satisfies assumption (1) of Theorem 2.1, that is, the strong monotonicity condition.

2.2. Global existence

THEOREM 2.8 (global existence). *Solutions referred to in Theorem 2.3 are global and defined for all* $0 \leq t \leq T$ *with an arbitrary* $T < \infty$ *provided the following bounds are satisfied for* $|s| \geq 1$.

(1) $f(s)s \leq M|s|^2$, *or* $|f(s)| \leq M|s|^p$, $p+1 \leq 2n/(n-2)$, *and* $p \leq m$, *when* $p > 1$.

(2) $h(s)s \leq Ms^2$ *or* $|h(s)| \leq M|s|^k$, $k+1 \leq 2(n-1)/(n-2)$, *and* $k \leq \max[q, 2q/(q+1)]$.

We note that the conditions for global existence put more stringent assumptions on the source parameter k. Indeed, when $q \to \infty$, Theorem 2.3 allows $k < 2(n-1)/(n-2)$ while Theorem 2.8 demands that $k+1 < 2(n-1)/(n-2)$. This is due to the fact that the arguments in Theorem 2.8 exploit the structure of "potential energy," which must be well defined. In addition, the damping parameter q serves as a barrier to control global behavior of solutions. This particular use of damping at the level of global theory has been introduced earlier in [2, 7, 19] in the context of global solutions with internal sources.

Remark 2.9. It may be interesting to note the dual role of boundary damping as a carrier for both local and global existence. Not only does local solvability depend on boundary damping, but it is also responsible for extending the life span of local solutions. In that sense, the problem with boundary sources is very different from that with interior sources where the role of the damping is mostly at the global level [7]. Local theory depends on interior damping only when the sources are *not* in $L_2(\Omega)$ [2, 17, 19].

Our second global existence result is obtained for initial data confined to a potential well defined below. Let $|u|_{p,\Omega} \equiv |u|_{L_p(\Omega)}$ and $\|u\|_{s,\Omega} \equiv |u|_{H^s(\Omega)}$.

Define $B_\Omega = \sup_{u \in H^1(\Omega), u \neq 0} |u|_{p,\Omega}/\|u\|_{1,\Omega} < \infty$ and $B_\Gamma = \sup_{u \in H^1(\Omega), u \neq 0} |u|_{k,\Gamma}/\|u\|_{1,\Omega} < \infty$. Let $F(\lambda) = (1/2)\lambda^2 - (1/p)B_\Omega^p \lambda^p - (1/k)B_\Gamma^k \lambda^k$ for $\lambda > 0$ and let λ_∞ be the smallest critical point of F, that is, $\lambda_\infty \neq 0$ is the smallest value that satisfies the equation $1 = B_\Omega^p \lambda^{p-2} + B_\Gamma^k \lambda^{k-2}$. Finally, let $d \equiv F(\lambda_\infty)$. Then potential well set W is $W = \{(u_0, u_1) \in H \mid \|u_0\|_{1,\Omega} < \lambda_\infty, E(0) < d\}$.

THEOREM 2.10. *Under the hypotheses of Theorem 2.3 imposed on the damping functions* $g_0(s), g(s)$, *consider the initial value problem (1.1) with*

$$f(u) = |u|^{p-1}u, \quad p > 1,\ p+1 \leq \frac{2n}{n-2},$$
$$h(u) = |u|^{k-1}u, \quad k > 1,\ k+1 \leq \frac{2(n-1)}{n-2}. \tag{2.3}$$

If the initial conditions are confined to the potential well W *(as defined above), then finite-energy solutions for (1) obtained in Theorem 2.3 exist globally, that is, for all* $T < \infty$.

The proof of Theorem 2.10 follows from local existence, Theorem 2.3, and a priori bounds generated by the parameters of the potential well. Potential well solutions, in the context of boundary and internal sources, have been studied by many authors [15–17, 22, 23]. A result close in the spirit to Theorem 2.10 is given in [23] for (1.1) with $g_0 = 0$, $f = 0$. In that case, potential well solutions are established for subcritical values of the parameter k, $k+1 < 2(n-1)/(n-2)$. Thus the result obtained in Theorem 2.10 extends that of [23] to include the *critical value* of k.

Remark 2.11. The restriction $k < 2(n-1)q/(n-2)(q+1)$, assumed (implicitly) in Theorem 2.10, results from the fact that we consider solutions obtained in "local" Theorem 2.3. On the other hand, since the solutions considered are "small," one may conjecture that the presence of damping may not be necessary. And, indeed, this is the case. By having initial data confined to the potential well, one can directly prove (using only Theorem 2.1 applied to regularization (2.1), with $g = 0$) local and global existence of finite-energy solutions with internal/boundary sources up to critical exponents and without any damping. Thus, the statement of Theorem 2.10 is still valid with $g = g_0 = 0$ and p, k satisfying strict inequalities formulated in Theorem 2.10. In the case when $f = 0$ and $g = g_0 = 0$, the corresponding result was proved in [15].

2.3. Blow-up of solutions

THEOREM 2.12. *For the initial boundary value problem (1.1) with $f(u) = u|u|^{p-1}$ and $h(u) = u|u|^{k-1}$, where the parameters k, q, m, and p satisfy*

(1) *$p > 1$ and $k > 1$, along with Sobolev embedding restrictions $p+1 \leq 2n/(n-2)$ and $k+1 \leq (2n-2)/(n-2)$;*
(2) *$k > q$ and $p > m$, all weak solutions (established in Theorem 2.3), whose initial energy is negative (i.e., $E(0) < 0$), blow-up in finite time.*

Remark 2.13. (1) The blow-up result for a potential well solution without damping and with $f = 0$ has been established in [15]. It was also shown in [15] that for $k > 1$, finite energy $E(t)$ tends to minus infinity. However, convexity methods of [15] do not apply to the problems with damping. In addition, the result in [15] is a nonexistence result rather than a blow-up result (it is a blow-up result for potential well solutions only). In light of this, Theorem 2.12 is the first result exhibiting blow-up of solutions applicable to all local weak solutions (not necessarily from a potential well) and with the boundary damping/source combination. In particular, it shows that the presence of the boundary dissipation does extend the life span of local solutions ($k \leq q$), however the value $k = q$ is critical. In other words, $k > q$ with an incremental interior source $p > 1$ causes solutions to blow-up.

(2) One could also consider blow-up of solutions corresponding to positive initial energy taken from the complement of a potential well. Indeed, in the case of internal source and boundary damping, such result was proved in [22]. Extension of that result which incorporates boundary sources as well is given in [4]. However, the blow-up result presented in [5, 22] requires high singularity of the internal sources, rather than of boundary sources, as in Theorem 2.12.

(3) Whether one can obtain the same result with $p \leq 1$ is an open question.

3. Conclusions

For an illustration, we summarize our results in the case where we assume polynomial structures for the boundary damping g, no interior damping $g_0 = 0$, and source h (where q is the exponent for g and k is the exponent for h). The dimension of $\Omega : n = 3$.

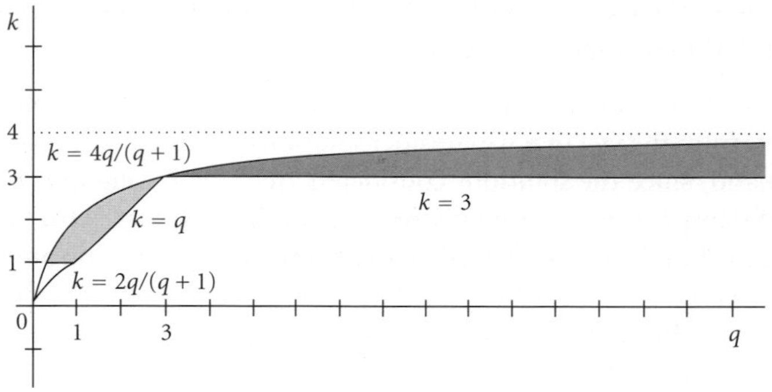

Figure 3.1

Figure 3.1 above illustrates the following phenomena:

(1) local existence when $k < 4q/(q+1)$: note here that this is an improvement to the results obtained in [23], where local existence was obtained under the additional restriction $k < 3$;

(2) global existence when $k \leq 3$, $k \leq 2q/(q+1)$, and $q \leq 1$, $k \leq q$, and $1 \leq q \leq 3$;

(3) blow-up of solutions in finite time when $k > 1$, $k > q$ and $k < 4q/(q+1)$.

Thus, as evidenced above, the existence-nonexistence results are optimal, as they cover the complementary regions $k \leq q$ (global existence) and $k > q$ (blow-up).

References

[1] A. Arosio and S. Spagnolo, *Global existence for abstract evolution equations of weakly hyperbolic type*, Journal de Mathématiques Pures et Appliquées. Neuvième Série **65** (1986), no. 3, 263–305.

[2] V. Barbu, I. Lasiecka, and M. A. Rammaha, *On nonlinear wave equations with degenerate damping and source terms*, Transactions of the American Mathematical Society **357** (2005), no. 7, 2571–2611.

[3] L. Bociu and I. Lasiecka, *Wellposedness and Blow-up of Solutions Generated by Wave Equations with Semilinear Boundary Sources and Nonlinear Boundary Damping*, preprint.

[4] M. Cavalcanti, *Blow up Results for the Wave Equation with Nonlinear Boundary Damping and Boundary Source*, preprint, 2005.

[5] M. M. Cavalcanti, V. N. Domingos Cavalcanti, and P. Martinez, *Existence and decay rate estimates for the wave equation with nonlinear boundary damping and source term*, Journal of Differential Equations **203** (2004), no. 1, 119–158.

[6] I. Chueshov, M. Eller, and I. Lasiecka, *On the attractor for a semilinear wave equation with critical exponent and nonlinear boundary dissipation*, Communications in Partial Differential Equations **27** (2002), no. 9-10, 1901–1951.

[7] V. Georgiev and G. Todorova, *Existence of a solution of the wave equation with nonlinear damping and source terms*, Journal of Differential Equations **109** (1994), no. 2, 295–308.

[8] I. Lasiecka, J.-L. Lions, and R. Triggiani, *Nonhomogeneous boundary value problems for second order hyperbolic operators*, Journal de Mathématiques Pures et Appliquées. Neuvième Série **65** (1986), no. 2, 149–192.

[9] I. Lasiecka and J. Ong, *Global solvability and uniform decays of solutions to quasilinear equation with nonlinear boundary dissipation*, Communications in Partial Differential Equations **24** (1999), no. 11-12, 2069–2107.

[10] I. Lasiecka and A. Stahel, *The wave equation with semilinear Neumann boundary conditions*, Nonlinear Analysis **15** (1990), no. 1, 39–58.

[11] I. Lasiecka and D. Tataru, *Uniform boundary stabilization of semilinear wave equations with nonlinear boundary damping*, Differential and Integral Equations **6** (1993), no. 3, 507–533.

[12] I. Lasiecka and R. Triggiani, *Trace regularity of the solutions of the wave equation with homogeneous Neumann boundary conditions and data supported away from the boundary*, Journal of Mathematical Analysis and Applications **141** (1989), no. 1, 49–71.

[13] ———, *Regularity theory of hyperbolic equations with nonhomogeneous Neumann boundary conditions. II. General boundary data*, Journal of Differential Equations **94** (1991), no. 1, 112–164.

[14] ———, *Control Theory for Partial Differential Equations: Continuous and Approximation Theories*, Cambridge University Press, Cambridge, 2000.

[15] H. A. Levine and R. A. Smith, *A potential well theory for the wave equation with a nonlinear boundary condition*, Journal für die reine und angewandte Mathematik **374** (1987), 1–23.

[16] L. E. Payne and D. H. Sattinger, *Saddle points and instability of nonlinear hyperbolic equations*, Israel Journal of Mathematics **22** (1975), no. 3-4, 273–303.

[17] P. Radu, *Weak solutions to the Cauchy problem of a semilinear wave equation with damping and source terms*, Advances in Differential Equations **10** (2005), no. 11, 1261–1300.

[18] R. Sakamoto, *Mixed problems for hyperbolic equations*, Journal of Mathematics of Kyoto University **10-2** (1970), 243–373.

[19] J. Serrin, G. Todorova, and E. Vitillaro, *Existence for a nonlinear wave equation with damping and source terms*, Differential and Integral Equations **16** (2003), no. 1, 13–50.

[20] W. W. Symes, *A trace theorem for solutions of the wave equation, and the remote determination of acoustic sources*, Mathematical Methods in the Applied Sciences **5** (1983), no. 2, 131–152.

[21] D. Tataru, *On the regularity of boundary traces for the wave equation*, Annali della Scuola Normale Superiore di Pisa. Classe di Scienze. Serie IV **26** (1998), no. 1, 185–206.

[22] E. Vitillaro, *A potential well theory for the wave equation with nonlinear source and boundary damping terms*, Glasgow Mathematical Journal **44** (2002), no. 3, 375–395.

[23] ———, *Global existence for the wave equation with nonlinear boundary damping and source terms*, Journal of Differential Equations **186** (2002), no. 1, 259–298.

Irena Lasiecka: Department of Mathematics, University of Virginia, Charlottesville, VA 22904-4137, USA
E-mail address: il2v@virginia.edu

Lorena Bociu: Department of Mathematics, University of Virginia, Charlottesville, VA 22904-4137, USA
E-mail address: lvb9b@virginia.edu

ON A GENERAL MINIMIZATION PROBLEM WITH CONSTRAINTS

VY K. LE AND DUMITRU MOTREANU

The paper studies the existence of solutions and necessary conditions of optimality for a general minimization problem with constraints. We focus mainly on the case where the cost functional is locally Lipschitz. Applications to an optimal control problem and Lagrange multiplier rule are given.

1. Introduction

The paper deals with the following general minimization problem with constraints:

$$\inf_{v \in S} \Phi(v). \tag{P}$$

Here, $\Phi : X \to \mathbb{R} \cup \{+\infty\}$ is a function on a Banach space X and S is an arbitrary nonempty subset of X. We suppose that $S \cap \operatorname{dom}(\Phi) \neq \varnothing$, where the notation $\operatorname{dom}(\Phi)$ stands for the effective domain of Φ, that is,

$$\operatorname{dom}(\Phi) = \{x \in X : \Phi(x) < +\infty\}. \tag{1.1}$$

First, we discuss the existence of solutions to problem (P). Precisely, we give an existence result making use of a new type of Palais-Smale condition formulated in terms of tangent cone to the set S and of contingent derivative for the function Φ. As a particular case, one recovers the global minimization result for a locally Lipschitz functional satisfying the Palais-Smale condition in the sense of Chang (cf. [7]). Then, by means of the notion of generalized gradient (see Clarke [8]), we obtain necessary conditions of optimality for problem (P) in the case where the cost functional Φ is locally Lipschitz. A specific feature of our optimality conditions consists in the fact that the set of constraints S is basically involved through its tangent cone. In addition, the costate variable provided by the given necessary conditions makes use essentially of the imposed tangency hypothesis. Finally, we present two applications of the necessary conditions of optimality that

Hindawi Publishing Corporation
Proceedings of the Conference on Differential & Difference Equations and Applications, pp. 645–654

demonstrate the generality of our results. The first application concerns the minimization of a locally Lipschitz functional subject to a boundary value problem for semilinear elliptic equations depending on a parameter that runs in a function space. If this parameter is a control variable, the result can be interpreted as a maximum principle for the stated optimal control problem. The second application of the abstract result concerning the necessary conditions of optimality shows that the Lagrange multiplier rule fits into this setting. In particular, the Lagrange multiplier rule for locally Lipschitz functionals is derived.

The approach relies on various methods including Ekeland's variational principle, Palais-Smale condition, tangency, generalized subdifferential calculus, orthogonality relations, Nemytskii operators, and semilinear elliptic equations. In this respect, it is worth to mention that a related work has been developed in [2–4] in the context of nonlinear mathematical programming problems. Here, the basic idea is represented by a kind of linearizing for the set of constraints S which allows to handle S locally by taking advantage of a continuous linear operator related to the tangent cone. This treatment has a unifying effect and can be applied to different problems in the optimization theory.

The rest of the paper is organized as follows. Section 2 is devoted to the existence of solutions to problem (P). Sections 3 presents our necessary conditions of optimality. Section 4 contains an example in solving an optimal control problem subject to a semilinear elliptic equation. Section 5 deals with an application to the Lagrange multiplier rule.

2. Existence of solutions

In the following, we make use of the notion of tangent vector to the set S at a given point $v \in S$. Precisely, the tangent cone T_vS to S at $v \in S$ (T_vS is sometimes called the contingent cone to S at v) is defined as

$$T_vS = \left\{ w \in X : \liminf_{t \downarrow 0} \frac{1}{t} d(v + tw, S) = 0 \right\}, \tag{2.1}$$

where the notation $d(\cdot, S)$ stands for the distance function to the subset S in X. It is well known that T_vS is a closed cone in X. If S is a convex subset of X, then for every $v \in S$ a very convenient description for T_vS holds:

$$T_vS = \operatorname{cl}\left(\bigcup_{t>0} \frac{1}{t}(S - v) \right), \tag{2.2}$$

where cl means the strong closure of a set in X. For further information on the tangent cone, we refer to [5, Chapter 6].

Another useful tool in our approach is the contingent derivative $\Phi^D(u; v)$ of a function $\Phi : X \to \mathbb{R} \cup \{+\infty\}$ at a point $u \in \operatorname{dom}(\Phi)$ in any direction $v \in X$ which is defined by

$$\Phi^D(u; v) = \limsup_{\substack{t \downarrow 0 \\ w \to 0}} \frac{1}{t} (\Phi(u + t(v + w)) - \Phi(u)). \tag{2.3}$$

The following example points out a significant particular case.

Example 2.1. If the function $\Phi : X \to \mathbb{R} \cup \{+\infty\}$ is locally Lipschitz at a point $u \in X$, then one has

$$\Phi^D(u;v) = \Phi^o(u;v), \quad \forall v \in X, \tag{2.4}$$

where Φ^o means the generalized directional derivative in the sense of Clarke (cf. [8]), that is,

$$\Phi^o(u;v) = \limsup_{\substack{t \downarrow 0 \\ x \to u}} \frac{1}{t}(\Phi(x+tv) - \Phi(x)). \tag{2.5}$$

This is clearly seen due to the locally Lipschitz property of Φ near u because then we may write

$$\begin{aligned} &\limsup_{\substack{t \downarrow 0 \\ w \to 0}} \frac{1}{t}(\Phi(u+t(v+w)) - \Phi(u)) \\ &\quad = \limsup_{\substack{t \downarrow 0 \\ w \to 0}} \frac{1}{t}(\Phi(u+tw+tv) - \Phi(u+tw)) + \lim_{\substack{t \downarrow 0 \\ w \to 0}} \frac{1}{t}(\Phi(u+tw) - \Phi(u)) \\ &\quad = \limsup_{\substack{t \downarrow 0 \\ x \to u}} \frac{1}{t}(\Phi(x+tv) - \Phi(x)). \end{aligned} \tag{2.6}$$

We now introduce a new type of Palais-Smale condition for nonsmooth functionals involving the tangent cone and contingent derivative.

Definition 2.2. The functional $\Phi : X \to \mathbb{R} \cup \{+\infty\}$ is said to satisfy the Palais-Smale condition (for short, (PS)) at the level c ($c \in \mathbb{R}$) on the subset S of X if every sequence $(u_n) \subset S$ such that

$$\Phi(u_n) \longrightarrow c, \tag{2.7}$$

$$\Phi^D(u_n;v) \geq -\varepsilon_n \|v\|, \quad \forall v \in T_{u_n}S, \tag{2.8}$$

for a sequence $\varepsilon_n \to 0^+$, contains a strongly convergent subsequence in X.

Note that in our existence result below (Theorem 2.4), we only need the (PS) condition at the level $c = \inf_S \Phi$. The next example establishes that the (PS) condition in Definition 2.2 reduces to the usual Palais-Smale condition in the case of locally Lipschitz functionals.

Example 2.3. If $\Phi : X \to \mathbb{R} \cup \{+\infty\}$ is locally Lipschitz and $S = X$, then Definition 2.2 becomes. Every sequence (u_n) in X such that (2.7) holds and

$$\lambda(u_n) := \inf_{z \in \partial\Phi(u_n)} \|z\| \longrightarrow 0 \quad \text{as } n \longrightarrow \infty \tag{2.9}$$

possesses a strongly convergent subsequence. This equivalence follows readily from Definition 2.2, Example 2.1, and the definition of generalized gradient

$$\partial\Phi(u_n) = \{z \in X^* : \langle z, v \rangle \leq \Phi^o(u_n;v), \ \forall v \in X\}. \tag{2.10}$$

We present our existence result in solving problem (P).

Theorem 2.4. *Let S be a closed subset of X and $\Phi : X \to \mathbb{R} \cup \{+\infty\}$ a function such that $S \cap \operatorname{dom}(\Phi) \neq \emptyset$. Assume that $\Phi|_S$ is lower semicontinuous and bounded from below, and Φ satisfies the* (PS) *condition in Definition 2.2 on S at the level $c = \inf_S \Phi$. Then problem (P) has at least a solution $u \in S$ and it is a critical point of Φ on S in the following sense:*

$$\Phi^D(u;v) \geq 0, \quad \forall v \in T_u S. \tag{2.11}$$

Proof. Applying Ekeland's variational principle (cf. [9]) to the function $\Phi|_S$ yields a sequence $(u_n) \subset S$ such that (2.7) and

$$\Phi(y) \geq \Phi(u_n) - \frac{1}{n}||y - u_n||, \quad \forall y \in S. \tag{2.12}$$

hold. Fix any $v \in T_{u_n} S$. By (2.1) there exist sequences $t_k \to 0^+$ in $\mathbb{R}$ and $w_k \to 0$ in X as $k \to \infty$ such that $u_n + t_k(v + w_k) \in S$ for all k. Plugging in (2.12) gives

$$\frac{1}{t_k}\left(\Phi(u_n + t_k(v + w_k)) - \Phi(u_n)\right) \geq -\frac{1}{n}||v + w_k||. \tag{2.13}$$

Letting $k \to \infty$ shows that

$$\liminf_{k \to \infty} \frac{1}{t_k}\left(\Phi(u_n + t_k(v + w_k)) - \Phi(u_n)\right) \geq -\frac{1}{n}\|v\|, \quad \forall v \in T_{u_n} S. \tag{2.14}$$

It turns out that (2.8) is verified with $\varepsilon_n = 1/n$. Therefore, the (PS) condition as formulated in Definition 2.2 provides a relabelled subsequence satisfying $u_n \to u$ in X. Moreover, we have that $u \in S$ because S is closed. Taking into account that Φ is lower semicontinuous on S, we conclude $\Phi(u) = \inf_S \Phi$.

In order to check (2.11), let $v \in T_u S$. By (2.1) there exist sequences $t_k \to 0^+$ in $\mathbb{R}$ and $w_k \to 0$ in X as $k \to \infty$ such that $u + t_k(v + w_k) \in S$ for all k. Since $\Phi(u + t_k(v + w_k)) \geq \Phi(u)$, we readily obtain (2.11) that completes the proof. □

We illustrate the applicability of Theorem 2.4 by deriving the existence result of Chang [7, Theorem 3.5].

Corollary 2.5. *Assume that $\Phi : X \to \mathbb{R}$ is a locally Lipschitz function on a Banach space X, Φ is bounded from below and satisfies the Palais-Smale condition in the sense of Chang in [7]. Then there exists $u \in X$ such that $\Phi(u) = \inf_X \Phi$ and u is a critical point of Φ, that is, it solves the inclusion problem*

$$0 \in \partial\Phi(u), \tag{2.15}$$

where $\partial\Phi(u)$ stands for the generalized gradient of Φ at u.

Proof. By Example 2.3 we know that the (PS) condition in the sense of Definition 2.2 is fulfilled with $S = X$. Then it is straightforward to deduce the result by applying Theorem 2.4 □

3. Necessary conditions of optimality

From now on we assume that the function $\Phi : X \to \mathbb{R}$ entering problem (P) is locally Lipschitz on a Banach space X and S is an arbitrary nonempty subset of X. We formulate the following condition on the set S.

(H) For every $v \in S$, there exists a (possibly unbounded) linear operator

$$A_v : D(A_v) \subset X \longrightarrow Y_v, \tag{3.1}$$

where Y_v is a Banach space, such that the domain $D(A_v)$ of A_v is dense in X, A_v is a closed operator (i.e., its graph is closed in $X \times Y_v$), and

$$\text{the range } R(A_v) \text{ is closed in } Y_v. \tag{3.2}$$

Moreover, the null space $N(A_v)$ of A_v satisfies

$$N(A_v) \subset T_v S, \tag{3.3}$$

where $T_v S$ stands for the tangent cone to S at v as introduced in (2.1).

Theorem 3.1. *Under hypothesis (H), if $u \in S$ is a solution of problem (P) (at least locally), then the following necessary condition of optimality holds. There exists an element $p \in D(A_u^*)$ such that*

$$A_u^*(p) \in \partial\Phi(u), \tag{3.4}$$

where $A_u^* : D(A_u^*) \subset Y_u^* \to X^*$ is the adjoint operator of A_u and $\partial\Phi(u)$ denotes the generalized gradient of Φ at u.

Proof. Fix any $z \in N(A_u)$. It follows from (3.3) that

$$z \in T_u S. \tag{3.5}$$

Taking into account (2.1), we deduce from (3.5) that there exist sequences $t_n \to 0^+$ in $\mathbb{R}$ and $x_n \to 0$ in X such that

$$u + t_n(z + x_n) \in S, \quad \forall n. \tag{3.6}$$

Using the optimality of $u \in S$, we obtain

$$\Phi(u + t_n(z + x_n)) \geq \Phi(u), \quad \forall n, \tag{3.7}$$

that leads to

$$\liminf_{n\to\infty} \frac{1}{t_n}[\Phi(u + t_n(z + x_n)) - \Phi(u)] \geq 0. \tag{3.8}$$

In particular, according to (2.5), inequality (3.8) implies that

$$\Phi^o(u;z) \geq 0, \quad \forall z \in N(A_u). \tag{3.9}$$

On the basis of (3.9), we may apply the Hahn-Banach theorem to obtain the existence of some $\xi \in X^*$ with the properties

$$\langle \xi, z \rangle_{X^*,X} = 0, \quad \forall z \in N(A_u), \tag{3.10}$$

$$\langle \xi, y \rangle_{X^*,X} \leq \Phi^o(u;y), \quad \forall y \in X. \tag{3.11}$$

We see from (3.11) that

$$\xi \in \partial\Phi(u), \tag{3.12}$$

while (3.10) ensures that

$$\xi \in [N(A_u)]^\perp. \tag{3.13}$$

Because $[N(A_u)]^\perp = \overline{R(A_u^*)}$ (see, e.g., [6]), in view of (3.2), relation (3.13) reads

$$\xi \in \overline{R(A_u^*)} = R(A_u^*) \tag{3.14}$$

(note that because $\overline{R(A_u)} = R(A_u)$, we also have $\overline{R(A_u^*)} = R(A_u^*)$, see again [6]).

Combining relations (3.12), (3.13), and (3.14), we arrive at the desired conclusion. □

Remark 3.2. (a) By Theorem 3.1, we have the system

$$\begin{gathered} u \in S, \\ A_u^*(p) \in \partial\Phi(u) \end{gathered} \tag{3.15}$$

formed by two relations with two unknowns u and p which eventually permit to determine the optimal solution u.

(b) We consider here the problem with the functional Φ being locally Lipschitz, which is a good and convenient model for our calculations. However, it could be possible to study such problem with other types of functionals and subdifferentials (see, e.g., [8, 10, 11, 13]).

4. An example

For an example of the general result in Theorem 3.1, let us consider the problem of minimizing the functional $\Phi(v,w)$ subject to the following conditions expressed as a Dirichlet problem:

$$\begin{gathered} (v,w) \in [H^2(\Omega) \cap H_0^1(\Omega)] \times L^2(\Omega), \\ -\Delta v = f(x,v) + w \quad \text{in } \Omega, \\ v = 0 \quad \text{on } \partial\Omega. \end{gathered} \tag{4.1}$$

Interpreting the parameter w as a control variable, this is in fact an optimal control problem. Here, Φ is a locally Lipschitz functional defined on $X = L^2(\Omega) \times L^2(\Omega)$, $f : \Omega \times \mathbb{R} \to \mathbb{R}$ is a Carathéodory function with $f(\cdot, 0) \in L^2(\Omega)$. Moreover, the partial derivative $(\partial f/\partial v)(x, v)$ exists for a.e. $x \in \Omega$, all $v \in \mathbb{R}$ with $\partial f/\partial v$ being a bounded Carathéodory function, that is,

$$\left|\frac{\partial f}{\partial v}(x,v)\right| \le c \quad \text{for a.e. } x \in \Omega, \text{ all } v \in \mathbb{R}, \tag{4.2}$$

for some constant $c > 0$. Notice that the considered problem is of the general form (P) in Section 1 with

$$S = \{(v,w) \in X : -\Delta v = f(x,v) + w \text{ in } \Omega,\ v = 0 \text{ on } \partial\Omega\}. \tag{4.3}$$

Let us prove that under the above conditions, hypothesis (H) holds. Specifically, for any $(v,w) \in S$, let

$$Y_{(v,w)} = L^2(\Omega) \times L^2(\Omega), \tag{4.4}$$

and let

$$A_{(v,w)} : [H^2(\Omega) \cap H_0^1(\Omega)] \times L^2(\Omega) \longrightarrow L^2(\Omega) \times L^2(\Omega) \tag{4.5}$$

be given by

$$A_{(v,w)}(z,q) = \left(-\Delta z - \frac{\partial f}{\partial v}(\cdot, v) z, q \right) \tag{4.6}$$

whenever $(z,q) \in [H^2(\Omega) \cap H_0^1(\Omega)] \times L^2(\Omega)$. From (4.2) and the classical results of Agmon in [1] on linear elliptic operators , we see that the range of the operator

$$z \longmapsto -\Delta z - \frac{\partial f}{\partial v}(\cdot, v) z (\in L^2(\Omega)) \tag{4.7}$$

is closed in $L^2(\Omega)$ (cf., e.g., [12, Theorem 8.41]). It follows immediately that the range $R(A_{(v,w)})$ of $A_{(v,w)}$ is closed in $L^2(\Omega) \times L^2(\Omega)$. Condition (3.2) is thus verified.

In order to check (3.3), let $(z, 0) \in N(A_{(v,w)})$. Because

$$-\Delta v = f(x,v) + w \quad \text{in } \Omega, \tag{4.8}$$

$$-\Delta z - \frac{\partial f}{\partial v}(\cdot, v) z = 0 \quad \text{in } \Omega, \tag{4.9}$$

by multiplying (4.9) by $t > 0$ and adding with (4.8), we obtain

$$-\Delta(v + tz) = f(x, v + tz) + w + tq(t), \tag{4.10}$$

where

$$q(t) = -\frac{1}{t}\left[f(\cdot,v+tz) - f(\cdot,v) - t\frac{\partial f}{\partial v}(\cdot,v)z\right], \quad \forall t>0. \tag{4.11}$$

Assumption (4.2) guarantees that

$$q(t) \longrightarrow 0 \quad \text{in } L^2(\Omega) \text{ as } t \longrightarrow 0^+. \tag{4.12}$$

Consequently, setting

$$p(t) = (0,q(t)) \in L^2(\Omega)\times L^2(\Omega), \tag{4.13}$$

we see from (4.10) that condition (3.3) is fulfilled since

$$(v,w)+t[(z,0)+p(t)] = (v,w)+t[(z,0)+(0,q(t))] \in S, \quad \forall t>0. \tag{4.14}$$

We have checked all assumptions of Theorem 3.1. According to that theorem, if Φ has a local minimum at (v,w), then there exists a pair $(p_1,p_2)\in L^2(\Omega)\times L^2(\Omega)$ such that

$$\begin{gathered} p_1 \in H^2(\Omega)\cap H_0^1(\Omega), \\ \left(-\Delta p_1 - \frac{\partial f}{\partial v}(\cdot,v)p_1, p_2\right) \in \partial\Phi(v,w) \end{gathered} \tag{4.15}$$

(p_2 is not significant for our purpose).

Remark 4.1. If the constant c in (4.2) is less than the first eigenvalue λ_1 of $-\Delta$ on $H_0^1(\Omega)$, then the range of $A_{(v,w)}$ is in fact the whole space $L^2(\Omega)\times L^2(\Omega)$. In this case, we observe that the auxiliary variable p_1 can be explicitly determined. Consequently, the necessary condition of optimality can be expressed only with the local solution (v,w).

5. Application to Lagrange multiplier rule

Assume now that the subset S in problem (P) is given by

$$S = \bigcup_{j\in J} G_j^{-1}(0). \tag{5.1}$$

Here, for each $j\in J$, $G_j : X \to Y_j$ is a C^1 mapping with Y_j being a Banach space and 0 a regular value of G_j, that is, the differential $G_j'(x) : X \to Y_j$ is surjective and $N[G_j'(x)]$ has a topological complement whenever $G_j(x)=0$. Moreover, assume that the sets $G_j^{-1}(0)$ ($j \in J$) are mutually disjoint, that is,

$$G_i^{-1}(0)\cap G_j^{-1}(0) = \varnothing \quad \text{if } i \neq j. \tag{5.2}$$

We check that hypothesis (H) is satisfied. In fact, for any $v \in S$, there is a unique $j \in J$ such that $v \in G_j^{-1}(0)$. Let $Y_v = Y_j$ and $A_v = G_j'(v)$. Then we have $R(A_v) = Y_v$, so (3.2) is verified. Moreover, we know that

$$N(A_v) = N[G_j'(v)] = T_v[G_j^{-1}(0)] = T_v S, \tag{5.3}$$

because $G_j^{-1}(0)$ is a C^1-submanifold of X, which implies (3.3). Consequently, Theorem 3.1 can be applied, ensuring the existence of $p \in Y_j^*$ with the property that whenever $u \in S$ is a solution of (P) with $u \in G_j^{-1}(0)$, then

$$[G_j'(u)]^*(p) \in \partial\Phi(u). \tag{5.4}$$

In the particular case where J is a singleton, that is,

$$S = G^{-1}(0), \tag{5.5}$$

and G is a mapping from X to $\mathbb{R}$ (also 0 is a regular value of G), then (5.4) becomes

$$\lambda G'(u) \in \partial\Phi(u) \tag{5.6}$$

for some $\lambda \in \mathbb{R}$. This is the classical Lagrange multiplier rule for locally Lipschitz functionals.

References

[1] S. Agmon, *Lectures on Elliptic Boundary Value Problems*, D. Van Nostrand, New Jersey, 1965.

[2] S. Aizicovici, D. Motreanu, and N. H. Pavel, *Nonlinear programming problems associated with closed range operators*, Applied Mathematics and Optimization **40** (1999), no. 2, 211–228.

[3] ———, *Fully nonlinear programming problems with closed range operators*, Differential Equations and Control Theory (Athens, OH, 2000), Lecture Notes in Pure and Appl. Math., vol. 225, Marcel Dekker, New York, 2002, pp. 19–30.

[4] ———, *Nonlinear mathematical programming and optimal control*, Dynamics of Continuous, Discrete & Impulsive Systems. Series A. Mathematical Analysis **11** (2004), no. 4, 503–524.

[5] J.-P. Aubin and H. Frankowska, *Set-Valued Analysis*, Systems & Control: Foundations & Applications, vol. 2, Birkhäuser Boston, Massachusetts, 1990.

[6] H. Brezis, *Analyse Fonctionnelle. Théorie et Applications*, Collection of Applied Mathematics for the Master's Degree, Masson, Paris, 1983.

[7] K. C. Chang, *Variational methods for nondifferentiable functionals and their applications to partial differential equations*, Journal of Mathematical Analysis and Applications **80** (1981), no. 1, 102–129.

[8] F. H. Clarke, *Optimization and Nonsmooth Analysis*, Classics in Applied Mathematics, vol. 5, SIAM, Pennsylvania, 1990.

[9] I. Ekeland, *Nonconvex minimization problems*, American Mathematical Society. Bulletin. New Series **1** (1979), no. 3, 443–474.

[10] B. S. Mordukhovich, *Variational Analysis and Generalized Differentiation, Vol. I, II*, Springer, New York, 2006.

[11] D. Motreanu and P. D. Panagiotopoulos, *Minimax Theorems and Qualitative Properties of the Solutions of Hemivariational Inequalities*, Nonconvex Optimization and Its Applications, vol. 29, Kluwer Academic, Dordrecht, 1999.

[12] M. Renardy and R. C. Rogers, *An Introduction to Partial Differential Equations*, Texts in Applied Mathematics, vol. 13, Springer, New York, 1993.
[13] R. T. Rockafellar and R. J.-B. Wets, *Variational Analysis*, Fundamental Principles of Mathematical Sciences, vol. 317, Springer, Berlin, 1998.

Vy K. Le: Department of Mathematics and Statistics, University of Missouri-Rolla, Rolla, MO 65409, USA
E-mail address: vy@umr.edu

Dumitru Motreanu: Département de Mathématiques, Université de Perpignan, 52 avenue Paul Alduy, 66860 Perpignan, France
E-mail address: motreanu@univ-perp.fr

REARRANGEMENT ON THE UNIT BALL FOR FUNCTIONS WITH MEAN VALUE ZERO WITH APPLICATIONS TO SOBOLEV AND MOSER INEQUALITIES

MARK LECKBAND

A rearrangement and properties are discussed, as well as the application to the proof of the corresponding Sobolev and Moser inequalities.

1. Introduction

Rearranging a function to a more simpler form is a standard tool of analysis. The rearranged function is normally equimeasurable to the original function, hence the L^p norms for $1 \leq p < \infty$ are the same. Another desirable property is that the rearrangement of a function reduces the gradient, usually in the sense of reducing the L^p norm of the gradient.

We are interested in Moser and Sobolev inequalities with sharp constants and whether there are extremals. The two properties of equimeasurability and "gradient reduction" make the rearrangement an indispensible tool. We begin with some standard notation.

Let $B^n = \{y \in \mathbb{R}^n : |y| \leq 1\}$ be the unit ball for $n \geq 2$. The boundary of B^n is the unit sphere, and we set $\omega_{n-1} = |\partial B^n|$. Let $W_0^{1,p}(B^n)$, $1 \leq p \leq n$, be the Sobolev space obtained from the space of C^∞ functions compactly supported in B^n by completion in the norm $\int_{B^n} |\nabla u|^p < \infty$. Let $W^{1,p}(B^n)$ be the Sobolev space obtained from the space of C^∞ functions with $\int_{B^n} u = 0$ by completion using the same norm.

The functions of $W_0^{1,p}(B^n)$ vanish at the boundary and thus are said to have the Dirichlet condition. The mean value zero property of functions of $W^{1,p}(B^n)$ is sometimes called the Neumann condition. Since such functions are allowed to amass at the boundary, the boundary of a domain plays a critical role. We consider the simplest of all bounded domains: the unit ball B^n.

Let us state three important and well-known theorems for Sobolev functions established using the notion of rearrangement. Our objective is to discuss a rearrangement for their analogs on $W^{1,p}(B^n)$.

Hindawi Publishing Corporation
Proceedings of the Conference on Differential & Difference Equations and Applications, pp. 655–660

2. Carleson-Chang, Moser, and Sharp Sobolev inequalities

THEOREM 2.1 (Aubin [1], Talenti [7]). *Let u be sufficiently smooth on $\mathbb{R}^n$, $n \geq 2$, and decaying fast enough at infinity. Then, for $1 \leq p < n$ and $q = np/(n-p)$,*

$$\|u\|_q \leq C(n,p)\|\nabla u\|_p, \quad 1 < p < n, \qquad \|u\|_{n/(n-1)} \leq C(n,1)\|\nabla u\|_1. \tag{2.1}$$

For $1 < p < n$, the extremal functions are translations and dilations of

$$u(x) = c\left(\frac{1}{\mu + |x|^{p/(p-1)}}\right)^{(n-p)/p}, \tag{2.2}$$

where $c, \mu > 0$. For $p = 1$, the extremal functions are the characteristic functions of balls and

$$C(n,1) = \frac{1}{n}\left(\frac{n}{\omega_{n-1}}\right), \tag{2.3}$$

the isoperimetric constant of $\mathbb{R}^n$. The value of $C(n,p)$, $1 < p < n$, can be found in the references.

There are two important observations of this theorem. First, translation and dilation imply the same sharp constants for functions of $W_0^{1,p}(B^n)$, $1 \leq p < n$, or for any other bounded domain, and that there are no extremals. Second, an easy corollary of this theorem is for the upper half space $\mathbb{R}^n_+ = \{x : x_n \geq 0\}$. An analogous theorem holds for constants $2^{1/n}C(n,p)$, $1 \leq p < n$, and the corresponding extremals are "centered" on the boundary $\partial\mathbb{R}^n_+ = \{x : x_n = 0\}$.

THEOREM 2.2 (Moser's inequality [6]). *Let u be sufficiently smooth on a bounded open set $\Omega \subset \mathbb{R}^n$, $n \geq 2$, and vanishing at the boundary $\partial\Omega$. Let $\|\nabla u\|_n \leq 1$. Then,*

$$\int_\Omega e^{\alpha|u|^{n/(n-1)}} \leq A_n \tag{2.4}$$

for $\alpha \leq \alpha_n = n(\omega_{n-1})^{1/(n-1)}$. The constant α_n is sharp in the sense that the above integral can be made arbitrarily large for $\alpha > \alpha_n$.

Observe that Moser's inequality says the supremum of its exponential integral is bounded on the unit ball of $W_0^{1,n}(\Omega)$. The value of A_n is not known at this time. However, the next theorem says this supremum is attained for $\Omega = B^n$.

THEOREM 2.3 (Carleson-Chang [3]). *Moser's inequality on $W_0^{1,p}(B^n)$ has extremals for $n \geq 2$.*

Unfortunately the corresponding variational equation does not allow a simple formula for the extremals.

3. Rearrangement

The classical rearrangement is defined as the essential inverse of the distribution function $\lambda_u(t) = |\{x : |u(x)| > t\}|$, that is, $u^*(t) = \inf\{s : \lambda_u(s) \leq t\}$. The associated spherical rearrangement is $u^{\#}(x) = u^*((\omega_{n-1}/n)|x|^n)$ which is equivalent to (and better and for our purpose)

$$u^{\#}(x) = \inf\{s : \lambda_u(s) \leq |B(x)|\}, \tag{3.1}$$

where $B(x) = \{y : |y| \leq |x|\}$ and $|B(x)| = (\omega_{n-1}/n)|x|^n$.

The spherical rearrangement $u^{\#}$ has a much simpler form than the original function. For example, $u^{\#}(x)$ is radially nonincreasing and $\nabla u^{\#}(x) = (\partial/\partial r)u^{\#}(r)$, $r = |x|$. Moreover, equimeasurability gives

$$\|u\|_p = \|u^*\|_p, \tag{3.2}$$

and we have a gradient reducing property expressed by the following inequality:

$$\|\nabla u^{\#}\|_p \leq \|\nabla u\|_p. \tag{3.3}$$

Standard proofs of the above use the following equation of geometric measure theory. This equation shows how the gradient reducing property is intimately related to the boundary of minimum area for a given volume:

$$\int f|\nabla u| = \int_{-\infty}^{\infty} \int_{u^{-1}(t)} f d^{n-1} y dt. \tag{3.4}$$

Surfaces of minimal area are spheres which give us the inequality $|(u^{\#})^{-1}(t)| \leq |u^{-1}(t)|$ essential for deriving the above gradient reducing property (for more details see Talenti [7]).

3.1. Rearrangement on the unit ball for functions with mean value zero. Our objective is to find a rearrangement that is equimeasurable, preserves mean value of zero, and reduces the p-norm of the gradient. The property of mean value zero results is not including the boundary of B^n in computing $|u^{-1}(t)|$. In other words, we need to know what the minimum surfaces are for the open ball, $B^n \backslash \partial B^n = \{x : |x| < 1\}$.

The minimum boundary for a given volume of $B^n \backslash \partial B^n$ is [2, 4]

an arc of a circle intersecting the boundary of B^n orthogonally, $n = 2$,
a cap of an $n-1$ sphere intersecting the boundary of B^n orthogonally, $n \geq 2$.

These will be the boundaries of the level sets of our new rearrangement.

Recall that circles, or $n-1$ spheres, are the boundaries of the level sets of the spherical rearrangement and they are centered at the origin parametrized by their radius r. To set up the analogous situation for the mean value zero preserving rearrangement, we begin by choosing two axes denoted by the x_1-axis and the x_n-axis. The boundaries of the level sets of the rearrangement will be the circular arcs, or $n-1$ spherical caps, symmetric with respect to the x_1-axis parametrized by θ, $0 \leq \theta \leq \pi$, measured from the positive x_1-axis to the point of intersection in the x_1,x_n-plane. It may be helpful to visualize the $n = 2$ case.

The $n-1$ sphere of radius r encloses a ball of radius r, $B(r)$, where

$$|B(r)| = \frac{\omega_{n-1}}{n} r^n. \tag{3.5}$$

The $n-1$ spherical cap of angle θ encloses a volume $A(\theta)$, where

$$|A(\theta)| = \frac{\omega_{n-1}}{n}\frac{\theta^n}{2} + O(\theta^{n-1}). \tag{3.6}$$

We define the rearrangement for mean value zero functions on the unit ball as

$$v(\theta) = \inf\{s : \lambda_u(s) \le |A(\theta)|\}, \tag{3.7}$$

where $\lambda_u(s) = |\{x \epsilon B^n : u(x) > s\}|$. There are many close analogies and comparisons between this rearrangement and the spherical rearrangement. We now list a few of them.

The spherically symmetric rearrangement has volume element $\omega_{n-1}r^{n-1}dr$, and so

$$\int_\Omega \Phi(u) = \int_0^{\mathbb{R}} \Phi(u^\#(r))\omega_{n-1}r^{n-1}dr. \tag{3.8}$$

The mean value zero rearrangement has volume element $\rho(\theta)d\theta$ and so

$$\int_{B^n} \Phi(u) = \int_0^\pi \Phi(v(\theta))\rho(\theta)d\theta, \tag{3.9}$$

where $0 \le \theta \le \pi/2$ and is symmetric about $\theta = \pi/2$.

For the spherically symmetric rearrangement we have for $1 \le p < \infty$,

$$\|\nabla u^\#\|_p^p = \int_0^{\mathbb{R}} \left|\frac{\partial}{\partial r}u^\#(r)\right|^p \omega_{n-1}r^{n-1}dr \le \int_\Omega |\nabla u|^p. \tag{3.10}$$

For our mean value zero rearrangement we have for $1 \le p < \infty$,

$$\int_0^\pi |v'(\theta)|^p \rho(\theta)d\theta \le \int_{B^n} |\nabla u|^p. \tag{3.11}$$

For more details and information please see Leckband [5].

4. Applications of the mean-value preserving rearrangemnt on B^n

The mean-value preserving rearrangement was used by Leckband [5] in proving the following Moser inequality.

THEOREM 4.1. *Let $n \ge 2$ be an integer. For functions u such that $\|\nabla u\|_n \le 1$ and $\int_{B^n} u = 0$, there is a bound A_n that depends only upon n such that*

$$\int_{B^n} e^{\beta|u|^{n/(n-1)}} \le A_n \tag{4.1}$$

for $\beta \le \beta_n = n(\omega_{n-1}/2)^{1/(n-1)}$. The constant β_n is sharp in the sense that the above integral can be made arbitrarily large for $\beta > \beta_n$.

The mean-value preserving rearrangement can also provide an easy proof of the following Sobolev inequality.

THEOREM 4.2 (Sobolev's inequality). *Let u be sufficiently smooth on $B = \{x \mid \|x\| \le 1\}$ with mean value zero. Then,*

$$\begin{gathered}\|u\|_q \le A(n,p)\|\nabla u\|_p, \quad 1 < p < n, \\ \|u\|_{n/(n-1)} \le A(n,1)\|\nabla u\|_1,\end{gathered} \tag{4.2}$$

The sharp values of the constants $A(n,p)$ and $A(n,1)$ are presently unknown.

Proof. Let u be any sufficiently smooth radial function on $\mathbb{R}^n$. Then, Theorem 2.1 implies

$$\frac{\left(\omega_{n-1}\int_0^r |u(y)-u(r)|^q|y|^{n-1}dy\right)^{1/q}}{\left(\omega_{n-1}\int_0^r |\nabla u(y)|^p|y|^{n-1}dy\right)^{1/p}}, \tag{4.3}$$

is bounded independent of u, and $r > 0$. We need this result below for $r = \pi/2$.

Let $v(\theta)$ be the mean-value preserving rearrangement of $u \in W^{1,p}(B^n)$. Then,

$$\frac{\|u\|_q}{\|\nabla u\|_p} \le \frac{\left[\int_0^\pi |v(\theta)|^q\rho(\theta)d\theta\right]^{1/q}}{\left[\int_0^\pi |v'(\theta)|^p\rho(\theta)d\theta\right]^{1/p}}. \tag{4.4}$$

□

We now show $|v(\pi/2)| \le C[\int_0^\pi |v'(\theta)|^p\rho(\theta)d\theta]^{1/p}$.

$$\begin{aligned}v\left(\frac{\pi}{2}\right) &= \frac{1}{|B^n|}\int_0^\pi \left(v\left(\frac{\pi}{2}\right) - v(s)\right)\rho(s)ds & (4.5)\\ &\le \frac{1}{|B^n|}\int_{\pi/2}^\pi \left(v\left(\frac{\pi}{2}\right) - v(s)\right)\rho(s)ds & (4.6)\\ &= \frac{1}{|B^n|}\int_{\pi/2}^\pi \left(\int_{\pi/2}^s |v'(t)|dt\right)\rho(s)ds & (4.7)\\ &= \frac{1}{|B^n|}\int_{\pi/2}^\pi |v'(t)|\left(\int_t^\pi \rho(s)ds\right)dt\,ds & (4.8)\\ &\le \frac{1}{|B^n|}\|v'\|_{p,\rho}\left(\int_{\pi/2}^\pi \frac{\left(\int_t^\pi \rho(s)ds\right)^{p'}}{\rho(t)^{p'/p}}dt\right)^{1/p'}. & (4.9)\end{aligned}$$

Statement (4.8) and the above give $v(\pi/2) \le C\|v'\|_{p,\rho}$. A similar argument shows $v(\pi/2) \ge -C\|v'\|_{p,\rho}$.

Thus $\|u\|_q/\|\nabla u\|_p \le [\int_0^\pi |v(\theta) - v(\pi/2)|^q\rho(\theta)d\theta]^{1/q}/[\int_0^\pi |v'(\theta)|^p\rho(\theta)d\theta]^{1/p} + C$. We may assume without loss of argument that $\int_0^\pi |v(\theta) - v(\pi/2)|^q\rho(\theta)d\theta \le 2\int_0^{\pi/2} |v(\theta) - v(\pi/2)|^q\rho(\theta)d\theta$.

Then, using the asymptotic estimate for $\rho(\theta)$, we have the above is bounded by

$$\frac{C[\omega_{n-1}\int_0^{\pi/2}|v(\theta)-v(\pi/2)|^q(\theta)^{n-1}d\theta]^{1/q}}{[\omega_{n-1}\int_0^{\pi/2}|v'(\theta)|^p(\theta)^{n-1}d\theta]^{1/p}}+C \tag{4.10}$$

As previously noted, this is bounded independent of v.

References

[1] T. Aubin, *Espaces de Sobolev sur les variétés riemanniennes*, Bulletin des Sciences Mathématiques. 2e Série **100** (1976), no. 2, 149–173.

[2] J. Bokowski and E. Sperner Jr., *Zerlegung konvexer Körper durch minimale Trennflächen*, Journal für die reine und angewandte Mathematik **311/312** (1979), 80–100.

[3] L. Carleson and S.-Y. A. Chang, *On the existence of an extremal function for an inequality of J. Moser*, Bulletin des Sciences Mathématiques. 2e Série **110** (1986), no. 2, 113–127.

[4] M. Hutchings, *The structure of area-minimizing double bubbles*, The Journal of Geometric Analysis **7** (1997), no. 2, 285–304.

[5] M. Leckband, *Moser's inequality on the ball B^n for functions with mean value zero*, Communications on Pure and Applied Mathematics **58** (2005), no. 6, 789–798.

[6] J. Moser, *A sharp form of an inequality by N. Trudinger*, Indiana University Mathematics Journal **20** (1971), 1077–1092.

[7] G. Talenti, *Best constant in Sobolev inequality*, Annali di Matematica Pura ed Applicata. Serie Quarta **110** (1976), 353–372.

Mark Leckband: Department of Mathematical Science, Florida International University, Miami, FL 33199, USA
E-mail address: leckband@fiu.edu

FAST CONVERGENT ITERATIVE METHODS FOR SOME PROBLEMS OF MATHEMATICAL BIOLOGY

HENRYK LESZCZYŃSKI

We investigate how fast some iterative methods converge to the exact solution of a differential-functional von Foerster-type equation which describes a single population dependent on its past time, state densities, and on its total size.

1. Introduction

Von Foerster and Volterra-Lotka equations arise in biology, medicine and chemistry, see [1, 9]. The independent variables x_j and the unknown function u stand for certain features and densities, respectively. It follows from this natural interpretation that $x_j \geq 0$ and $u \geq 0$. We are interested in von Foerster-type models, which are essentially nonlocal, because there are included also the total sizes of population $\int u(t,x)dx$.

Existence results for certain von Foerster-type problems have been established by means of the Banach contraction principle, the Schauder fixed point theorem or iterative method, see [2–5]. These theorems are closely related to direct iterations for a natural integral fixed point operator. Because of nonlocal terms, these methods demand very thorough calculations and a proper choice of subspaces of continuous and integrable functions. Sometimes, it may cost some simplifications of the real model. On the other hand, there is a very consistent theory of first-order partial differential-functional equations in [7], based on properties of bicharacteristics and on fixed point techniques with respect to the uniform norms. Our research group has also obtained some convergence results for the direct iterative method under nonlinear comparison conditions.

In the present paper, we find natural conditions which guarantee $L^\infty \cap L^1$-convergence of iterative methods of Newton type. These conditions are preceded by analogous (slightly weaker) conditions for direct iterations, however, we do not formulate any convergence results for them (this will be stated in another paper).

Let $\tau = (\tau_1,\dots,\tau_n) \in \mathbb{R}^n_+$, $\tau_0 > 0$, where $\mathbb{R}_+ := [0,+\infty)$. Define $B = [-\tau_0,0] \times [-\tau,\tau]$, where $[-\tau,\tau] = [-\tau_1,\tau_1] \times \cdots \times [-\tau_n,\tau_n]$ and $E_0 = [-\tau_0,0] \times \mathbb{R}^n$, $E = [0,a] \times \mathbb{R}^n$, $a > 0$.

Hindawi Publishing Corporation
Proceedings of the Conference on Differential & Difference Equations and Applications, pp. 661–666

For each function w defined on $[-\tau_0,a]$, we have the Hale functional w_t (see [6]), which is the function defined on $[-\tau_0,0]$ by

$$w_t(s) = w(t+s) \quad (s \in [-\tau_0,0]). \tag{1.1}$$

For each function u defined on $E_0 \cup E$, we similarly write a Hale-type functional $u_{(t,x)}$, defined on B by

$$u_{(t,x)}(s,y) = u(t+s,x+y) \quad \text{for } (s,y) \in B. \tag{1.2}$$

(see [7]). Let $\Omega_0 = E \times C([-\tau_0,a],\mathbb{R}_+)$ and $\Omega = E \times C(B,\mathbb{R}_+) \times C([-\tau_0,a],\mathbb{R}_+)$. Take $v : E_0 \to \mathbb{R}_+$ and $c_j : \Omega_0 \to \mathbb{R}$, $\lambda : \Omega \to \mathbb{R}$ $(j = 1,\dots,n)$. Consider the differential-functional equation

$$\frac{\partial u}{\partial t} + \sum_{j=1}^{n} c_j(t,x,z[u]_t)\frac{\partial u}{\partial x_j} = u(t,x)\lambda(t,x,u_{(t,x)},z[u]_t), \tag{1.3}$$

where

$$z[u](t) := \int_{\mathbb{R}^n} u(t,y)dy, \quad t \in [-\tau_0,a], \tag{1.4}$$

with the initial conditions

$$u(t,x) = v(t,x), \quad (t,x) \in E_0, \quad x = (x_1,\dots,x_n) \in \mathbb{R}^n. \tag{1.5}$$

We are looking for Caratheodory's solutions to (1.3)–(1.5), see [2, 3, 8]. The functional dependence includes a possible delayed and integral dependence of the Volterra type. The Hale functional $z[u]_t$ takes into consideration the whole population within the time interval $[t-\tau_0,t]$, whereas the Hale-type functional $u_{(t,x)}$ shows the dependence on the density u locally in a neighborhood of (t,x). The functional dependence demands some initial data on a "thick" initial set E_0, which means that a complicated ecological niche must be observed for some time and (perhaps) in some space in order to determine and predict its further evolution.

2. Bicharacteristics

First, for a given function $z \in C([-\tau_0,a],\mathbb{R}_+)$, consider the bicharacteristic equations for problem (1.3), (1.5):

$$\eta'(s) = c(s,\eta(s),z_s), \quad \eta(t) = x. \tag{2.1}$$

Denote by $\eta = \eta[z](\cdot;t,x)$ the bicharacteristic curve passing through $(t,x) \in E$, that is, the solution to the above problem. Next, we consider the following equation:

$$\frac{d}{ds}u(s,\eta[z](s;t,x)) = u(s,\eta[z](s;t,x))\lambda(s,\eta[z](s;t,x),u_{(s,\eta[z](s;t,x))},z_s), \tag{2.2}$$

with the initial condition $u(0,\eta[z](0;t,x)) = v(0,\eta[z](0;t,x))$. For any given function $z \in C([-\tau_0,a],\mathbb{R}_+)$, a solution of the equation along bicharacteristics is a solution of (1.4). Their initial conditions correspond to each other. Assume that

(V0) $v \in CB(E_0,\mathbb{R}_+)$ (nonnegative, bounded, and continuous function);

(V1) $z[v] \in C([-\tau_0,0],\mathbb{R}_+)$, where

$$z[v](t) = \int_{\mathbb{R}^n} v(t,x)dx; \tag{2.3}$$

(V2) the function v satisfies the Lipschitz condition

$$|v(t,x) - v(t,\bar{x})| \le L_v\|x-\bar{x}\| \quad \text{on } E_0 \tag{2.4}$$

with some constant $L_v > 0$;

(C0) $c_j : \Omega_0 \to \mathbb{R}$ are continuous in (t,x,q) and

$$\|c(t,x,q) - c(t,\bar{x},\bar{q})\| \le L_c\|x-\bar{x}\| + L_c^*\|q-\bar{q}\|. \tag{2.5}$$

For the sake of simplicity, we assume that $L_c^* = 0$, that is, c does not depend on the last variable.

(Λ0) $\lambda : \Omega \to \mathbb{R}$ is continuous in (t,x,w,q) and

$$|\lambda(t,x,w,q) - \lambda(t,\bar{x},\bar{w},\bar{q})| \le M_\lambda(\|x-\bar{x}\| + \|w-\bar{w}\| + \|q-\bar{q}\|). \tag{2.6}$$

(Λ1) There exists a function $L_\lambda \in L^1([0,a],\mathbb{R}_+)$, such that

$$\lambda(t,x,w,q) \le L_\lambda(t) \tag{2.7}$$

for $(t,x) \in E$, $w \in C(B,\mathbb{R}_+^m)$, $q \in C([-\tau_0,a],\mathbb{R}_+^m)$.

Denote $W(t,x,w,q) = \lambda(t,x,w,q) + \operatorname{tr}\partial_x c(t,x,q)$ for $(t,x) \in E$, $w \in C(B,\mathbb{R}_+)$, $q \in C([-\tau_0,a],\mathbb{R}_+)$, where $\operatorname{tr}\partial_x c$ stands for the trace of the matrix $\partial_x c = [\partial_{x_k} c_j]_{j,k=1,\dots,n}$.

(W0) There exists $M_W \in \mathbb{R}_+$, such that

$$|W(t,x,w,q) - W(t,\bar{x},\bar{w},\bar{q})| \le M_W(\|x-\bar{x}\| + \|w-\bar{w}\| + \|q-\bar{q}\|). \tag{2.8}$$

(W1) There exists a function $L_W \in L^1([0,a],\mathbb{R}_+)$, such that

$$W(t,x,w,q) \le L_W(t) \tag{2.9}$$

for $(t,x) \in E$, $w \in C(B,\mathbb{R}_+)$, $q \in C([-\tau_0,a],\mathbb{R}_+)$.

Let $L_\lambda \le L_W$ and $L_W(s) = 0$ for $s \in [-\tau_0,0]$. Define

$$Z(t) = \max_{-\tau_0 \le s \le 0}\{\|v\|_\infty, \|v(s,\cdot)\|_1\}\exp\Big(\int_0^t L_W(s)ds\Big), \tag{2.10}$$

and $\mathcal{Z} = \{z \in CB([-\tau_0,a],\mathbb{R}_+) : z(t) \le Z(t)\}$.

LEMMA 2.1. *If the conditions* (V0), (Λ1) *are satisfied, then any solution u of the equation along bicharacteristics has the estimate*

$$0 \le u(t,x) \le \|v(0,\cdot)\|_\infty \exp\left(\int_0^t L_\lambda(s)ds\right) \quad \text{on } E. \tag{2.11}$$

Consider the operator $\mathcal{T}: \mathcal{X} \to \mathcal{X}$ given by the formula

$$\mathcal{T}[z](t) = \int_{\mathbb{R}^n} u[z](t,x)dx \quad \text{for } t \ge 0, \tag{2.12}$$

where $u = u[z] \in C(E, \mathbb{R}_+)$ is the solution of the equation along bicharacteristics with the initial condition $u[z](t,x) = v(t,x)$ on E_0. The function $u = u[z]$ has on E the following integral representation:

$$u[z](t,x) = v(0,\eta(0)) \exp\left(\int_0^t \lambda(s,\eta(s),u_{(s,\eta(s))},z_s)ds\right), \tag{2.13}$$

where $\eta(s) = \eta[z](s;t,x)$. By the representation of solutions along bicharacteristics, we write the operator in the following way:

$$\mathcal{T}[z](t) = \int_{\mathbb{R}^n} v(0,\eta(0)) \exp\left(\int_0^t \lambda(s,\eta(s),u_{(s,\eta(s))},z_s)ds\right)dx \tag{2.14}$$

for $t \ge 0$. Notice that the bicharacteristics admit the following group property $y = \eta[z](0;t,x) \Leftrightarrow \eta[z](s;t,x) = \eta[z](s;0,y)$, that is, any bicharacteristic curve passing through the points $(0,y)$ and (t,x) has the same value at $s \in [0,a]$.

If we change the variables $y = \eta[z](0;t,x)$, then, by the Liouville theorem, the Jacobian $J = \det[\partial c/\partial x]$ is given by the formula

$$J(0;t,x) = \exp\left(-\int_0^t \operatorname{tr}\partial_x c(s,\eta_i[z](s;0,y),z_s)ds\right). \tag{2.15}$$

Hence the integral operator can be written in the form

$$\mathcal{T}[z](t) = \int_{\mathbb{R}^n} v(0,y) \exp\left(\int_0^t W(s,\eta(s),u_{(s,\eta(s))},z_s)ds\right)dy, \tag{2.16}$$

where $\eta(s) = \eta[z](s;0,y)$.

LEMMA 2.2. *If the conditions* (V0), (V1), *and* (W1) *are satisfied, then*

$$0 \le \mathcal{T}[z](t) \le Z(t) < +\infty \quad \text{for } t \in [0,a]. \tag{2.17}$$

The respective fixed point equation for bicharaceristics $\eta = \eta[z]$ has the form

$$\eta(s;t,x) = x - \int_s^t c(\zeta,\eta(\zeta;t,x),z_\zeta)d\zeta. \tag{2.18}$$

3. Iterative methods

We sketch direct iterative method and some faster iterative methods of the Newton type. Define the iterative method by $z^{(k+1)} = \mathcal{T}[z^{(k)}]$ with an arbitrary function $z^{(0)} \in \mathcal{X}$. This scheme uniformly converges under natural assumptions on the given functions (see Section 2). The algorithm splits into three stages: (1) finding $\eta^{(k)} = \eta[z^{(k)}]$, given by the fixed point equation for bicharacteristics, (2) finding $u^{(k)} = u[z^{(k)}]$ as a solution of the equation along bicharacteristics, (3) calculating $z^{(k+1)} = \mathcal{T}[z^{(k)}]$. In this way, there are given the integral equations

$$\eta^{(k)}(s;t,x) = x - \int_s^t c(\zeta,\eta^{(k)}(\zeta;t,x),z_\zeta^{(k)})d\zeta,$$
$$u^{(k)}(t,x) = v(0,\eta^{(k)}(0;t,x))\exp\Big(\int_0^t \lambda(Q^{(k)}(s))ds\Big), \tag{3.1}$$
$$z^{(k+1)}(t) = \int_{\mathbb{R}^n} v(0,y)\exp\Big(\int_0^t W(Q^{(k)}(s))ds\Big)dy,$$

where $Q^{(k)}(s) = (s,\eta^{(k)}(s;t,x),u^{(k)}_{(s,\eta^{(k)}(s;t,x))},z_s^{(k)})$.

Assume now that $L_c^* = 0$, that is, c does not depend on q, thus we write $c(t,x)$. This simplifies stating and analyzing faster techniques. The Newton-type method is defined in the following way:

$$\begin{aligned}\frac{\partial u^{(k+1)}}{\partial t} &+ \sum_{j=1}^n c_j(t,x)\frac{\partial u^{k+1}}{\partial x_j}\\ &= u^{(k)}(t,x)\lambda(R^{(k)}(t,x)) + \Delta u^{(k)}(t,x)\lambda(R^{(k)}(t,x))\\ &\quad + u^{(k)}(t,x)\Big[\partial_w\lambda(R^{(k)}(t,x))\Delta u^{(k)}_{(t,x)} + \partial_q\lambda(R^{(k)}(t,x))\Delta z_t^{(k)}\Big],\end{aligned} \tag{3.2}$$

where $R^{(k)}(t,x) = (t,x,u_{(t,x)},z[u]_t)$, $\Delta u^{(k)} = u^{(k+1)} - u^{(k)}$,

$$z^{(k)}(t) := \int_{\mathbb{R}^n} u^{(k)}(t,y)dy, \quad t \in [-\tau_0,a], \tag{3.3}$$

with the initial conditions $u^{(k+1)}(t,x) = v(t,x)$ on E_0.

Added to the assumptions of Section 2, we need the following regularity assumption on the Frechet derivatives $\partial_w\lambda$ and $\partial_q\lambda$.

($\partial\Lambda$) There are positive constants γ_0,γ_1 and monotone, positive, integrable functions L_{ww}, L_{ww}^* such that

$$|\partial_w\lambda(t,x,w,q)\bar{w}| \le \gamma_0\{|\bar{w}(0,0)| + L_{ww}(x)\|\bar{w}\|_*\},$$
$$|\Delta_w\partial_w\lambda(t,x,\cdot,q)\bar{w}| \le \gamma_1\{|w(0,0)|\,\|\bar{w}\|_* + \|w\|_*\,|\bar{w}(0,0)| + L_{ww}^*(x)\|w\|_*\|\bar{w}\|_*\}, \tag{3.4}$$

where Δ_w indicates an increment w with respect to the functional variable, and

$$\|w\|_* = \|w\|_\infty + \sup_s \int_{[-\tau,\tau]} | w(s,y)dy. \tag{3.5}$$

Similar inequalities are assumed on $\partial_q \lambda$.

THEOREM 3.1. *Under the assumptions of Section 2 and* $(\partial\Lambda)$ *there is a positive constant C such that*

$$||\Delta u^{(k+1)}(t,\cdot)||_* \leq C \int_0^t \left\{ ||\Delta u^{(k+1)}_{|_s}||_* + ||\Delta u^{(k)}_{|_s}||_*^2 \right\} ds, \tag{3.6}$$

where the norm $\|\cdot\|_*$ *is analogously defined as in Assumption* $(\partial\Lambda)$.

Proof. One writes error equations for $\Delta u^{(k+1)}$ and $\Delta z^{(k+1)}$ similarly as in a convergence proof for the Newton method. □

Remark 3.2. The above theorem implies a local in t convergence, since the kth error can be estimated by $\text{const} \cdot (t \cdot \text{const})^{2^k}$.

Remark 3.3. Theorem 3.1 indicates that the cost of Newton-type speed is quite serious. This is due to the complicated nonlocal nature of the problem on an unbounded domain.

Acknowledgment

The research is supported by the Grant BW UG 5100-5-0384-5.

References

[1] F. Brauer and C. Castillo-Chávez, *Mathematical Models in Population Biology and Epidemiology*, Texts in Applied Mathematics, vol. 40, Springer, New York, 2001.
[2] A. L. Dawidowicz, *Existence and uniqueness of solutions of generalized von Foerster integro-differential equation with multidimensional space of characteristics of maturity*, Bulletin de L'Academie Polonaise des Sciences. Serie des Sciences Mathematiques **38** (1990), 1–12.
[3] A. L. Dawidowicz and K. Łoskot, *Existence and uniqueness of solution of some integro-differential equation*, Annales Polonici Mathematici **47** (1986), no. 1, 79–87.
[4] M. E. Gurtin, *A system of equations for age-dependent population diffusion*, Journal of Theoretical Biology **40** (1973), no. 2, 389–392.
[5] M. E. Gurtin and R. C. MacCamy, *Non-linear age-dependent population dynamics*, Archive for Rational Mechanics and Analysis **54** (1974), no. 3, 281–300.
[6] J. K. Hale and S. M. Verduyn Lunel, *Introduction to Functional-Differential Equations*, Applied Mathematical Sciences, vol. 99, Springer, New York, 1993.
[7] Z. Kamont, *Hyperbolic Functional Differential Inequalities and Applications*, Mathematics and Its Applications, vol. 486, Kluwer Academic, Dordrecht, 1999.
[8] H. Leszczyński and P. Zwierkowski, *Existence of solutions to generalized von Foerster equations with functional dependence*, Annales Polonici Mathematici **83** (2004), no. 3, 201–210.
[9] A. J. Lotka, *Elements of Physical Biology*, Wiliams and Wilkins, Maryland, 1925, republished as *Elements of Mathematical Biology*, Dover, New York, 1956.

Henryk Leszczyński: Institute of Mathematics, University of Gdańsk, Gdańsk 80-952, Poland
E-mail address: hleszcz@math.univ.gda.pl

CONVERGENCE OF SERIES OF TRANSLATIONS BY POWERS OF TWO

GUODONG LI

We will give a necessary and sufficient condition on $c = (c_n)$ such that $\sum c_n f\{2^n x\}$ converges in L_2-norm for all $f \in L_2^0$ or L_2.

1. Introduction

Let $f(x)$ be a real or complex function defined on the interval $[0,1]$. Let $\{x\} = x \mod (1)$. Hence, $f\{x\}$ means $f(\{x\})$. Let L_2 be the space of all square integrable functions on $[0,1]$ and L_2^0 is the space of all zero-mean functions in L_2. Let $L_2(2)$ be the set of all functions in L_2 with Fourier coefficients supported by powers of 2, that is,

$$L_2(2) = \left\{ f(x) = \sum_{k=-\infty}^{\infty} a_k \exp\left(\operatorname{sign}(k) 2\pi i 2^{|k|} x\right) : a = (a_n) \in l_2 \right\}. \tag{1.1}$$

Let $L_2^0(2)$ denote the set of functions in $L_2(2)$ with $a_0 = 0$ and let l_2^0 denote the set of sequences $a = (a_n) \in l_2$ with $a_0 = 0$.

Diophantine approximations have been well studied by many authors. It is well known that $(1/n)\sum_{k=1}^n f\{nx\}$ converges in L_2-norm to $\int_0^1 f(x)dx$. Khinchin conjectured that $(1/n)\sum_{k=1}^n f\{nx\}$ converges almost everywhere to $\int_0^1 f(x)dx$ for all $f \in L_\infty$. But this was disproved by Marstrand (see [4]). Let c_n be a sequence of real or complex numbers. The consideration of a.e. convergence and L_2-norm convergence of series $\sum c_n f\{nx\}$ is another natural problem in Diophantine approximations. Some sufficient conditions for this series to converge are given in [5] and category counterexamples can be found in [2]. There are similar considerations in ergodic theory, too. Several authors have used Rokhlin's lemma and inductive constructions to provide counterexamples to the convergence of this series (see [2, 5, 3, 1]).

The series $\sum c_n f\{2^n x\}$ is a lacunary series, which is clearly closely related to the Diophantine series $\sum c_n f\{nx\}$. Using the techniques in [5], it is easy to give a sufficient

Hindawi Publishing Corporation
Proceedings of the Conference on Differential & Difference Equations and Applications, pp. 667–676

condition that series $\sum c_n f\{2^n x\}$ converges a.e. and in the L_2-norm. If $c_n \geq 0$ and $\sum c_n = \infty$, category counterexamples to these convergences can be constructed (see [2]). We will explore necessary and sufficient conditions of the L_2-norm convergence of series $\sum c_n f\{2^n x\}$. A necessary and sufficient condition on $c = (c_n)$ such that $\sum c_n f\{2^n x\}$ converges in L_2-norm for all $f \in L_2^0$ or L_2 is obtained (see Section 2). Indeed, $\lim_{N\to\infty} \sum_{n=-N}^{N} c_n f\{\text{sign}(n)2^{|n|}x\}$ converges in the L_2-norm for all $f \in L_2^0$ if and only if $\sum_{n=1}^{\infty} c_n f\{2^n x\}$ and $\sum_{n=1}^{\infty} c_{-n} f\{-2^n x\}$ converge in L_2-norm for all $f \in L_2^0$. Moreover, $\sum_{n=1}^{\infty} c_n f\{2^n x\}$ converges in the L_2-norm for all $f \in L_2^0$ if and only if partial sums $\sum_{n=1}^{N} c_n e^{2\pi i n x}$ are uniformly bounded in N and x (see Section 2).

2. Necessary and sufficient conditions on given sequences $c = (c_n)$

The function sign(x) denotes the regular sign function. For a given sequence of complex numbers $c = (c_n)$, the operator $S_{1,N}$ on $L_2^0(2)$ is defined by

$$S_{1,N} f(x) = \sum_{k=-N}^{N} c_k f\{\text{sign}(k)2^{|k|}x\} \tag{2.1}$$

for any $f \in L_2^0(2)$. Then $S_{1,N}$ is a linear bounded operator from $L_2^0(2)$ to $L_2^0(2)$. It is also well defined on L_2 and is a linear bounded operator from L_2 to L_2, which is denoted by S_N or $S_{2,N}$. We will assume that $c_0 = 0$ and $a_0 = 0$.

Assume that $a = (a_n) \in \ell_2$. Then the function $f(x) = \sum_{n=-\infty}^{+\infty} a_n \exp(\text{sign}(n)2\pi i x 2^{|n|})$ is well defined in $L_2(2)$ since it is convergent in L_2-norm. Then

$$\begin{aligned} S_{1,N} f(x) &= \sum_{n=-N}^{+N} \sum_{k=-\infty}^{+\infty} a_k c_n \exp\left(\text{sign}(nk)2\pi i x 2^{|n|+|k|}\right) \\ &= \sum_{k=-\infty}^{+\infty} b_{N,k} \exp\left(\text{sign}(k)2\pi i x 2^{|k|}\right). \end{aligned} \tag{2.2}$$

Since $S_{1,N} f(x)$ is a sum of finite numbers of convergent Fourier series, the above expression is well defined in the sense of the L_2-norm.

LEMMA 2.1. *The coefficients $b_{N,k}$ in the expression above are given by*

$$b_{N,k} = \begin{cases} \displaystyle\sum_{l=0}^{\min(N,k)} \left(c_l a_{k-l} + c_{-l} a_{-(k-l)}\right) & \textit{if } k > 0,\ k \leq N, \\ \displaystyle\sum_{l=0}^{\min(N,|k|)} \left(c_l a_{k+l} + c_{-l} a_{-(k+l)}\right) & \textit{if } k < 0,\ |k| \leq N, \\ \displaystyle\sum_{k=-N}^{N} c_k a_0 & \textit{if } k = 0. \end{cases} \tag{2.3}$$

For a given sequence of complex numbers $c = (c_n)$, define $g_c(x)$ as

$$g_c(x) = \sum_{0<|n|<+\infty} c_n \exp\left(\operatorname{sign}(n) 2\pi i x 2^{|n|}\right). \tag{2.4}$$

Then, clearly, $g_c(x) \in L_2(2) \subset L_2$. Define the operator $\Omega_{1,N}$ on l_2 by

$$(\Omega_{1,N}a)(x) = \sum_{k=-N}^{N} a_k g_c\{\operatorname{sign}(k) 2^{|k|} x\} \tag{2.5}$$

for any $a = (a_n) \in l_2$. Then $\Omega_{1,N}$ is a linear bounded operator from l_2 to $L_2(2)$.

Lemma 2.2. *$\Omega_{1,N}$ can be rewritten as*

$$(\Omega_{1,N}a)(x) = \sum_{k=-\infty}^{+\infty} b'_{N,k} \exp\left(\operatorname{sign}(k) 2\pi i x 2^{|k|}\right), \tag{2.6}$$

where $b_{N,k}$ is defined by

$$b'_{N,k} = \begin{cases} \sum_{l=0}^{\min(N,k)} \left(a_l c_{k-l} + a_{-l} c_{-(k-l)}\right) & \text{if } k > 0,\ k \le N, \\ \sum_{l=0}^{\min(N,|k|)} \left(a_l c_{k+l} + a_{-l} c_{-(k+l)}\right) & \text{if } k < 0,\ |k| \le N, \\ \sum_{k=-N}^{N} a_k c_0 & \text{if } k = 0. \end{cases} \tag{2.7}$$

For a given sequence of complex numbers $c = (c_n)$, the operator $S_{3,N}$ from l_2 to l_2 is defined by

$$(S_{3,N}a)(k) = b_k, \tag{2.8}$$

for any $a = (a_n) \in l_2$, where $b = (b_n)$ is defined by

$$b_k = \begin{cases} \sum_{l=0}^{k} \left(a_l c_{k-l} + a_{-l} c_{-(k-l)}\right) & \text{if } k > 0,\ k \le N, \\ \sum_{l=0}^{|k|} \left(a_l c_{k+l} + a_{-l} c_{-(k+l)}\right) & \text{if } k < 0,\ |k| \le N, \\ a_0 c_0 & \text{if } k = 0, \\ 0 & \text{otherwise.} \end{cases} \tag{2.9}$$

Lemma 2.3. *Assume that $a_0 = 0$ and $c_0 = 0$. With the above notations,*

$$\begin{aligned} \|S_{3,N}\| &\le \|S_{1,N}\| \le \|S_{2,N}\|, \\ \|S_{3,N}\| &\le \|\Omega_{1,N}\|, \end{aligned} \tag{2.10}$$

where $\|\cdot\|$ is the operator norm on the corresponding spaces

Proof. For a given sequence $c=(c_n)$, fix an element $a=(a_n)\in l_2$ with $\|a\|_2=1$. Then we can define a function $f\in L_2(2)$ by

$$f(x)=\sum_{n=-\infty}^{+\infty} a_n \exp\left(\operatorname{sign}(n)2\pi i x 2^{|n|}\right) \tag{2.11}$$

with $\|f\|_2=1$. Thus

$$\begin{aligned}
\|S_{3,N}a\|^2 &= \sum_{k=1}^{N}\left|\sum_{l=0}^{k}\left(a_l c_{k-l}+a_{-l}c_{-(k-l)}\right)\right|^2+\sum_{k=-N}^{-1}\left|\sum_{l=0}^{-k}\left(a_l c_{k+l}+a_{-l}c_{-(k+l)}\right)\right|^2\\
&=\sum_{k=1}^{N}\left|\sum_{l=0}^{\min(N,k)}\left(a_l c_{k-l}+a_{-l}c_{-(k-l)}\right)\right|^2+\sum_{k=-N}^{-1}\left|\sum_{l=0}^{\min(N,-k)}\left(a_l c_{k+l}+a_{-l}c_{-(k+l)}\right)\right|^2\\
&\le\sum_{k=1}^{\infty}\left|\sum_{l=0}^{\min(N,k)}\left(a_l c_{k-l}+a_{-l}c_{-(k-l)}\right)\right|^2+\sum_{k=-\infty}^{-1}\left|\sum_{l=0}^{\min(N,-k)}\left(a_l c_{k+l}+a_{-l}c_{-(k+l)}\right)\right|^2\\
&=\sum_{k=-\infty}^{\infty}\left|b'_{N,k}\right|^2=\|\Omega_{1,N}f\|^2\le\|\Omega_{1,N}\|^2\le\|\Omega_{2,N}\|^2,
\end{aligned} \tag{2.12}$$

which implies that

$$\|S_{3,N}\|\le\|\Omega_{1,N}\|. \tag{2.13}$$

Similarly, we can prove that

$$\|S_{3,N}\|\le\|S_{1,N}\|\le\|S_{2,N}\|. \tag{2.14}$$

□

Lemma 2.4. *If L_2 and $L_2(2)$ are complex spaces, then*

$$\|S_{2,N}\|\ge\|S_{1,N}\|\ge\frac{1}{\sqrt{2}}\sup_x\left(\left|\sum_{k=1}^{N}c_k e^{2\pi i k x}\right|^2+\left|\sum_{k=1}^{N}c_{-k}e^{2\pi i k x}\right|^2\right)^{1/2}. \tag{2.15}$$

Proof. Fix an integer $n>2N$ and set

$$a_k=\begin{cases}\dfrac{1}{\sqrt{2N+1}}e^{-2\pi i k x} & \text{if } n-2N\le k\le n,\\ 0 & \text{otherwise.}\end{cases} \tag{2.16}$$

Clearly, $\|a\|_2 = \|(a_k)\|_2 = 1$. By using this $a = (a_n)$, we can define a function f in L_2 by (2.11). For this function f, we have $\|f\|_2 = 1$ and

$$\begin{aligned}
||S_{2,N}|| &\geq ||S_{1,N}|| \geq ||S_{1,N}f||_2 = \sum_{k=-\infty}^{\infty} |b_{N,k}|^2 \\
&\geq \sum_{k=n-N}^{n} \left| \sum_{l=0}^{N} \left(c_l a_{k-l} + c_{-l} a_{-(k-l)}\right) \right|^2 + \sum_{k=-n}^{-(n-N)} \left| \sum_{l=0}^{N} \left(c_l a_{k+l} + c_{-l} a_{-(k+l)}\right) \right|^2 \\
&\geq \sum_{k=n-N}^{n} \left| \sum_{l=0}^{N} c_l \frac{1}{\sqrt{2N+1}} e^{-2\pi i(k-l)x} \right|^2 + \sum_{k=-n}^{-(n-N)} \left| \sum_{l=0}^{N} c_l \frac{1}{\sqrt{2N+1}} e^{-2\pi i(k+l)x} \right|^2 \qquad (2.17) \\
&= \frac{N+1}{2N+1} \left(\left| \sum_{k=1}^{N} c_k e^{2\pi ikx} \right|^2 + \left| \sum_{k=1}^{N} c_{-k} e^{2\pi ikx} \right|^2 \right) \\
&\geq \frac{1}{2} \left(\left| \sum_{k=1}^{N} c_k e^{2\pi ikx} \right|^2 + \left| \sum_{k=1}^{N} c_{-k} e^{2\pi ikx} \right|^2 \right),
\end{aligned}$$

which gives the lemma. □

Lemma 2.5. *If L_2 and $L_2(2)$ are real spaces, then*

$$||S_{2,N}|| \geq ||S_{1,N}|| \geq \frac{1}{2\sqrt{2}} \sup_x \left(\left| \sum_{k=1}^{N} c_k e^{2\pi ikx} \right|^2 + \left| \sum_{k=1}^{N} c_{-k} e^{2\pi ikx} \right|^2 \right)^{1/2}. \qquad (2.18)$$

Proof. Let $f(x) = f_1(x) + i f_2(x)$ and $\|f\|_2 \leq 1$, where $f_1(x)$ and $f_2(x)$ are real functions. Clearly, $\|f_1\|_2 \leq 1$ and $\|f_2\|_2 \leq 1$. Denote the norm on the corresponding complex space by $\|S_{1,N}\|_C$. Then

$$||S_{1,N}f||_c \leq ||S_{1,N}f_1||_2 + ||S_{1,N}f_2||_2 \leq ||S_{1,N}||\,||f_1||_2 + ||S_{1,N}||\,||f_2||_2 \leq 2||S_{1,N}||. \qquad (2.19)$$

Hence,

$$||S_{1,N}|| \geq \frac{1}{2}||S_{1,N}||_C. \qquad (2.20)$$

By Lemma 2.4, the lemma follows. □

Lemma 2.6.

$$||S_{1,N}|| \leq ||S_{2,N}|| \leq \sup_x \left| \sum_{k=1}^{N} c_k e^{2\pi ikx} \right| + \sup_x \left| \sum_{k=1}^{N} c_{-k} e^{2\pi ikx} \right|. \qquad (2.21)$$

Proof. Let $f \in L_2$ and $\|f\|_2 \le 1$. Then

$$\|S_N f\|_2 = \|S_{2,N} f\|_2 \le \left\| \sum_{k=1}^{N} c_k f\{2^k x\} \right\|_2 + \left\| \sum_{k=1}^{N} c_{-k} f\{-2^k x\} \right\|_2. \tag{2.22}$$

The operator T defined by $T : f(x) \to f\{2x\}$ is a contraction operator. But it is not a unitary operator since T^{-1} does not exist. However, by the dilation theorem (see [7, page 11]), there exist a Hilbert space H, an orthogonal projection $P : H \to L_2$, and a unitary operator $U : H \to H$ such that L_2 is a closed subspace of H and $PU^l f = T^l f$ for all $l \ge 0$ and $f \in L_2$. Hence, by using the spectral representation of a unitary operator, we have

$$\begin{aligned}\left\| \sum_{k=1}^{N} c_k f\{2^k x\} \right\|_2^2 &= \left\| \sum_{k=1}^{N} c_k T^k f \right\|_2^2 = \left\| \sum_{k=1}^{N} c_k P U^k f \right\|_2^2 \\ &\le \|P\| \cdot \left\| \sum_{k=1}^{N} c_k U^k f \right\|_2^2 = \left\| \sum_{k=1}^{N} c_k U^k f \right\|_2^2 \\ &= \int_0^1 \left| \sum_{k=1}^{N} c_k e^{2\pi i k x} \right|^2 d\mu_f \le \sup_x \left| \sum_{k=1}^{N} c_k e^{2\pi i k x} \right|^2.\end{aligned} \tag{2.23}$$

Similarly, we have

$$\left\| \sum_{k=1}^{N} c_{-k} f\{-2^k x\} \right\|_2^2 \le \sup_x \left| \sum_{k=1}^{N} c_{-k} e^{2\pi i k x} \right|^2. \tag{2.24}$$

Combining (2.23) and (2.24) gives the lemma. □

Theorem 2.7. *Suppose that $c = (c_n)$ is a sequence of complex numbers. Then*

$$\lim_{N \to \infty} \sum_{k=-N}^{N} c_k f\{\operatorname{sign}(k) 2^{|k|} x\} \tag{2.25}$$

converges in L_2-norm for all $f \in L_2^0$ if and only if there is a constant M such that

$$\sup_{N,x} \left| \sum_{k=1}^{N} c_k e^{2\pi i k x} \right| \le M, \qquad \sup_{N,x} \left| \sum_{k=1}^{N} c_{-k} e^{2\pi i k x} \right| \le M. \tag{2.26}$$

If either of two suprema in (2.26) is unbounded, then there is a dense G_δ subset G of L_2^0 (or L_2, or $L_2^0(2)$, or $L_2(2)$) such that $\sup_N \|S_N f\|_2 = \infty$ for all $f \in G$.

Proof. Let L_c be the subset of L_2, in which $\lim_{N\to\infty} \sum_{k=-N}^{N} c_k f\{\operatorname{sign}(k) 2^k x\}$ converges in the L_2-norm. Assume that there is a constant M such that

$$\sup_{N,x} \left| \sum_{k=1}^{N} c_k e^{2\pi i k x} \right| \le M, \qquad \sup_{N,x} \left| \sum_{k=1}^{N} c_{-k} e^{2\pi i k x} \right| \le M, \tag{2.27}$$

which imply that $c = (c_n) \in l_2$ and $\|c\|_2 \le 2M$. Hence, the series

$$\sum_{k=1}^{N} c_k \exp(2\pi i m 2^k x) + \sum_{k=1}^{N} c_{-k} \exp(-2\pi i m 2^k x) \tag{2.28}$$

converges in L_2-norm for any integer $m \neq 0$. Thus, $e^{2\pi imx} \in L_c$ for any integer $m \neq 0$. However, $\{e^{2\pi imx} : m \neq 0\}$ is a base generating L_2^0. Hence, $L_c = L_2^0$ since L_c is a closed linear subspace of L_2^0. □

If either of two suprema in (2.12) is unbounded, without loss of generality, we may assume that

$$\sup_{N,x} \left| \sum_{k=1}^{N} c_k e^{2\pi ikx} \right| = \infty. \tag{2.29}$$

By Lemmas 2.4 and 2.5, we have $\sup_N \|S_N\|_2 = \infty$. The rest of Theorem 2.7 follows from the Banach-Steinhaus theorem (see [6, page 98]).

Corollary 2.8. *$\lim_{N\to\infty} \sum_{k=-N}^{N} c_k f\{\text{sign}(k)2^{|k|}x\}$ converges in L_2-norm for all $f \in L_2^0$ if and only if $\sum_{k=1}^{\infty} c_k f\{2^k x\}$ and $\sum_{k=1}^{\infty} c_{-k} f\{-2^k x\}$ converge in L_2-norm for all $f \in L_2^0$.*

An important consequence is that $\sum_{k=1}^{\infty} c_k f\{2^{n_k} x\}$ converges in L_2-norm for all $f \in L_2$ or L_2^0 if and only if there is a constant M such that $\sup_{N,x} |\sum_{k=1}^{N} c_k e^{2\pi i n_k x}| \le M$.

Corollary 2.9. *If $g(x) = \sum_{k=1}^{\infty} c_k e^{2\pi ikx}$ is of bounded variation, then $\sum_{k=1}^{\infty} c_k f\{2^k x\}$ converges in the L_2-norm for all $f \in L_2^0$.*

Proof. For a bounded variation function, partial sums of Fourier series are uniformly bounded, which allow us to apply Theorem 2.7. □

Corollary 2.10. *Assume that $\{n_k\}$ is a lacunary sequence. Then the following statements are equivalent:*

(1) *$\sum_{k=1}^{\infty} c_k f\{2^{n_k} x\}$ converges in L_2-norm for all $f \in L_2$ or L_2^0;*
(2) *$\sum_{k=1}^{\infty} c_k f\{2^{n_k} x\}$ converges almost everywhere for all $f \in L_2$ or L_2^0;*
(3) *$\sum_{k=1}^{\infty} |c_k| < \infty$.*

Proof. By Theorem 2.7, $\sum_{k=1}^{\infty} c_k f\{2^{n_k} x\}$ converges in the L_2-norm for all $f \in L_2^0$ if and only if for some constant M,

$$\sup_{N,x} \left| \sum_{k=1}^{N} c_k e^{2\pi i n_k x} \right| \le M. \tag{2.30}$$

Since $\sum_{k=1}^{\infty} c_k e^{2\pi i n_k x}$ is a lacunary series, partial sums are uniformly bounded if and only if $\sum_{k=1}^{\infty} |c_k| < \infty$, which implies (2). That (2) implies (1) follows from Corollary 2.8, Lemma 2.5, and the proof of Theorem 2.7. □

Corollary 2.11. *$\sum_{k=1}^{\infty} c_k f\{2^k x\}$ converges in L_2-norm for all $f \in L_2^0$ if and only if $\sum_{k=1}^{\infty} c_k \gamma^k f\{2^k x\}$ converges in L_2-norm for all $f \in L_2^0$ and all γ with $|\gamma| = 1$.*

Corollary 2.12. *If* $\sum_{k=1}^{\infty} c_k f\{2^k x\}$ *diverges in* L_2*-norm for some* $f \in L_2^0$, *then for any* γ *with* $|\gamma| = 1$, $\sum_{k=1}^{\infty} c_k \gamma^k f\{2^k x\}$ *diverges in* L_2*-norm for a residual set of functions* $f \in L_2$.

Corollary 2.13. $\sum_{k=1}^{\infty} ((-1)^k/k) f\{2^k x\}$ *diverges in* L_2*-norm for a residual set of functions* $f \in L_2^0$.

Corollary 2.14. *If* $\sum_{k=1}^{\infty} c_k f\{2^k x\}$ *converges in* L_2*-norm for all* $f \in L_2^0$, *then* $\sum_{n=1}^{\infty} | \sum_{k=1}^{n} c_k a_{n-k}|^2$ *converges in* L_2*-norm for all* $a \in l_2$.

Proof. It can be proved similarly as for Theorem 2.7. □

Lemma 2.15. *Assume that one of two suprema in (2.26) is unbounded. Then for any* $\epsilon > 0$ *and* $K > 0$, *there exists a function* $f \in L_2^0$ *with* $\|f\|_2 \le 1$ *such that*

$$m\left(x : \sup_N \left| \sum_{k=-N}^{N} c_k f\{\operatorname{sign}(k) 2^{|k|} x\} \right| \ge K\right) \ge 1 - \epsilon. \tag{2.31}$$

Proof. By Theorem 2.7, there is a function $f \in L_2^0$ such that $\sup_N \|S_N f\|_2 = +\infty$. Let $f(x) = \sum_{n=-\infty}^{+\infty} a_n \exp(\operatorname{sign}(n) 2\pi i x 2^{|n|}) \in L_2(2)$, where $a_0 = 0$. Then by a theorem in [8] (see [8, page 203, volume I]), for any set $E \subset [0,1)$ with $m(E) > 0$, we can find $\lambda_1(E) > 0$ and $\lambda_2(E) > 0$, and $N_0 > 0$ such that

$$\lambda_2(E) \sum_{|k|=N_0}^{\infty} |b_{N,k}|^2 \le \int_E \left| \sum_{|k|=N_0}^{\infty} c_k f\{\operatorname{sign}(k) 2^{|k|} x\} \right|^2 dx \le \lambda_1(E) \sum_{|k|=N_0}^{\infty} |b_{N,k}|^2. \tag{2.32}$$

Since $\sup_N \|S_N f\|_2 = +\infty$, so $\lim_{N\to\infty} \sum_{|k|=N_0}^{\infty} |b_{N,k}|^2 = +\infty$. Hence,

$$\lim_{N\to\infty} \int_E |S_N f(x)|^2 dx = +\infty, \tag{2.33}$$

which gives

$$m\left(x : \sup_N \left| \sum_{k=-N}^{N} c_k f\{\operatorname{sign}(k) 2^{|k|} x\} \right| \ge K\right) \ge 1 - \epsilon \tag{2.34}$$

for any $\epsilon > 0$ and $K > 0$. Suppose not, then let

$$E = \left\{x : \sup_N \|S_N f\| < K\right\} \tag{2.35}$$

and we have $m(E) \ge \epsilon$. Hence,

$$\int_E |S_N f(x)|^2 dx \le K m(E) < +\infty. \tag{2.36}$$

The contradiction proves the lemma. □

Theorem 2.16. *If either of two suprema in (2.26) is unbounded, then there is a dense* G_δ *subset* G *of* L_2^0 *(or* L_2, *or* $L_2^0(2)$, *or* $L_2(2)$*) such that* $\sup_N |S_N f| = \infty$ *almost everywhere for all* $f \in G$.

Proof. It follows from [2, Lemma 2.7 and Theorem 1.1]. □

THEOREM 2.17. *Suppose that $c = (c_n)$ is a sequence of numbers. Then*

$$\lim_{N\to\infty} \sum_{k=-N}^{N} c_k f\{\operatorname{sign}(k)2^{|k|}x\} \tag{2.37}$$

converges in L_2-norm for all $f \in L_2$ if and only if there is a constant M such that

$$\sup_{N,x}\left|\sum_{k=1}^{N} c_k e^{2\pi ikx}\right| \le M, \qquad \sup_{N,x}\left|\sum_{k=1}^{N} c_{-k} e^{2\pi ikx}\right| \le M, \tag{2.38}$$

and $\lim_{n\to\infty}\sum_{k=-N}^{N} c_k$ converges.

The next theorem is an immediate consequence of Theorem 2.7.

THEOREM 2.18. *The series $\sum_{n=1}^{\infty} c_n f\{2^n x\}$ is $(C,1)$-convergent in L_2-norm if and only if $g(x) = \sum_{n=1}^{\infty} c_n e^{2\pi inx}$ is a bounded function.*

Proof. Similar to the proof of Theorem 2.7, we have $\sum_{n=1}^{\infty} c_n f\{2^n x\}$ is $(C,1)$-convergent in L_2-norm if and only if there is a constant $M > 0$ such that

$$|\sigma_N(x)| \le M, \tag{2.39}$$

where

$$\sigma_N(x) = \frac{1}{N+1}\sum_{k=1}^{N}\sum_{n=1}^{k} c_n e^{2\pi inx} = \sum_{n=1}^{N}\left(1 - \frac{n}{N+1}\right)c_n e^{2\pi inx}. \tag{2.40}$$

If $g(x)$ is bounded, $|\sigma_N(x)| \le |g(x)| \le M$ for all integer N and real x. If $g(x)$ is unbounded, that is, $\|g\|_\infty = \infty$, it is not hard to prove that

$$\sup_{N,x}|\sigma_N(x)| = \infty. \tag{2.41}$$

□

Acknowledgments

This paper is written under guidance of Dr. Joseph Rosenblatt. I wish to express my sincere appreciation for his insight throughout the research.

References

[1] M. A. Akcoglu and A. del Junco, *Convergence of averages of point transformations*, Proceedings of the American Mathematical Society **49** (1975), no. 1, 265–266, English translation, Vol. I, II. (1964).
[2] A. del Junco and J. Rosenblatt, *Counterexamples in ergodic theory and number theory*, Mathematische Annalen **245** (1979), no. 3, 185–197.
[3] P. R. Halmos, *A nonhomogeneous ergodic theorem*, Transactions of the American Mathematical Society **66** (1949), 284–288.

[4] J. M. Marstrand, *On Khinchin's conjecture about strong uniform distribution*, Proceedings of the London Mathematical Society. Third Series **21** (1970), 540–556.
[5] J. Rosenblatt, *Convergence of series of translations*, Mathematische Annalen **230** (1977), no. 3, 245–272.
[6] W. Rudin, *Real and Complex Analysis*, 3rd ed., McGraw-Hill, New York, 1987.
[7] B. Sz.-Nagy and C. Foias, *Harmonic Analysis of Operators on Hilbert Space*, North-Holland, Amsterdam; American Elsevier, New York, 1970.
[8] A. Zygmund, *Trigonometric Series: Vols. I, II*, 2nd ed., Cambridge University Press, London, 1968.

Guodong Li: Buck Consultants, ACS Company, 231 S. Bemiston Avenue, St. Louis, MO 63017, USA
E-mail address: gli@maryville.edu

SMOOTH SOLUTIONS OF ELLIPTIC EQUATIONS IN NONSMOOTH DOMAINS

GARY M. LIEBERMAN

We discuss some situations in which the solution of an elliptic boundary value problem is smoother than the regularity of the boundary.

1. Introduction

In this lecture, we examine a special regularity result for solutions of second-order elliptic equations. We ask when the solution of a boundary value problem for such an equation is smoother than the boundary of the domain in which the problem is posed.

To see the significance of this question, we first recall that classical Schauder theory (see [6, Chapter 6]) says that if $\partial\Omega \in C^{k,\alpha}$ for some integer $k \geq 2$ and some $\alpha \in (0,1)$, then solutions of any of the standard boundary value problems (i.e., the Dirichlet problem, the Neumann problem, or the oblique derivative problem) with sufficiently smooth data are also in $C^{k,\alpha}$. Specifically, if the elliptic operator L has the form

$$Lu = a^{ij}D_{ij}u + b^iD_iu + cu \tag{1.1}$$

with a^{ij}, b^i, and c all in $C^{k-2,\alpha}(\overline{\Omega})$, then any solution of the Dirichlet problem

$$Lu = f \quad \text{in } \Omega, \qquad u = \varphi \quad \text{on } \partial\Omega \tag{1.2}$$

with $f \in C^{k-2,\alpha}(\overline{\Omega})$ and $\varphi \in C^{k,\alpha}(\partial\Omega)$ is in $C^{k,\alpha}(\overline{\Omega})$ with similar results for the Neumann and oblique derivative problems. In addition, if we only assume that $\partial\Omega \in C^{1,\alpha}$, then any solution of one of the boundary value problems (with appropriate smoothness on the other data) is also in $C^{1,\alpha}$ (see [5] for a precise statement of the result in the case of Dirichlet data and [9] in the case of Neumann or oblique derivative data). Moreover, this result is optimal in the following sense: given k and α, we can find a domain Ω with $\partial\Omega \in C^{k,\alpha}$ and Dirichlet data $\varphi \in C^{k,\alpha}$ such that the solution of

$$\Delta u = 0 \quad \text{in } \Omega, \qquad u = \varphi \quad \text{on } \partial\Omega, \tag{1.3}$$

Hindawi Publishing Corporation
Proceedings of the Conference on Differential & Difference Equations and Applications, pp. 677–682

is not in $C^{m,\beta}$ for $m+\beta > k+\alpha$ (where Δ denotes the Laplacian); similar results are true for the Neumann problem. Nonetheless, we will see that for some boundary value problems, the solutions are smoother than the boundary.

We first note that our concern is only with regularity measured in Hölder spaces. For information on regularity issues for nonsmooth domains in other spaces, especially Sobolev spaces, see [7] or [8]. We also point out that we are not going to consider trivial examples, such as noting that the solution of the boundary value problem $\Delta u = 0$ in Ω, $u = 0$ on $\partial\Omega$ always has the unique solution $u \equiv 0$, regardless of the smoothness of Ω. Finally, we state our results for two-dimensional domains. This restriction simplifies many of the regularity issues. In fact, all of our results in two-dimensional piecewise smooth domains are very close to the results in [7, Chapter 6]. There are two important distinctions to be made, however: first, Grisvard only considers two-dimensional problems while we present two-dimensional versions of results that are given in spaces with an arbitrary number of dimensions in the references cited, and second, we refer to results for problems in which the coefficients of the differential operators may be less smooth than the ones in [7].

2. Simple results in piecewise smooth domains

It is well known that regularity of solutions of elliptic equations is a purely local matter, so we only need to see how a solution behaves near a point on the boundary. For piecewise smooth two-dimensional domains, we only look in a neighborhood of a corner point, which we may take to be the origin.

The case of Dirichlet data is the most straightforward. In [1, 2], Azzam proved the following result: at a convex corner, the solution is in $C^{1,\alpha}$ for some α determined only by the angle at the corner and the behavior of the coefficient matrix $[a^{ij}(0)]$. Rather than writing the formula for α down directly, we first investigate a harmonic function that leads to many of the results (in [2], Azzam obtained a precise form for α while [1] only asserts that there is some such α).

To see how this estimate arises (and for future reference), we use (r,θ) to denote polar coordinates in the complex plane. Then, for any $\delta > 0$, the function $w = r^\delta \cos(\delta\theta)$ is harmonic in any simply connected subset of the plane which does not include the origin. In particular, if Ω is the sector $\{0 < r < \infty,\ |\theta| < \theta_0\}$ for some $\theta_0 > 0$ with $\delta\theta_0 < \pi/2$, then w is harmonic and positive in Ω, continuous in $\overline{\Omega}$, and it vanishes only at the origin (which is the only point at which $\partial\Omega$ is nonsmooth). If the corner at the origin is convex, then $\theta_0 < \pi/2$, so we can take $\delta > 1$. Using w as a comparison function, it can be shown that (for this choice of θ_0 and δ) $u \in C^{1,\alpha}$ for $\alpha = \delta - 1$. Note that decreasing θ_0 leads to better regularity. If $\theta_0 < \pi/4$, then $u \in C^{2,\alpha}$ for some $\alpha > 0$, and so on.

For a general operator, we first make a linear change of independent variable to convert $[a^{ij}(0)]$ into the identity matrix and compute the angle θ_0 at the nonsmooth point in this new coordinate system. (If the corner is originally convex, it remains convex.) A perturbation argument (spelled out in [1]) shows that the solution of the general problem is in $C^{1,\alpha}$ for any $\alpha \in (0, \pi/(2\theta_0))$.

When the angle θ_0 has the form $\pi/(2n)$ for some positive integer n, the situation is somewhat more complicated because the function w (with $\delta\theta_0 = \pi/2$) is now analytic even at the origin. As shown in [3], the regularity of solutions for the Dirichlet problem in this case is determined by some compatibility conditions on the data. The necessity of such conditions is easily seen for solutions of Laplace's equation in the first quadrant. Then $u_{xx}(0)$ and $u_{yy}(0)$ are determined only by the boundary data, but they must also satisfy the differential equation if the solution is to be C^2 at the origin.

A similar argument in [4] shows that if the boundary data are of mixed Dirichlet-Neumann type at the corner, then the solution is in $C^{1,\alpha}$ for some $\alpha > 0$ if the angle θ_0 at the corner (after the linear change of independent variable to convert $[a^{ij}(0)]$ into the identity matrix) is less than $\pi/4$. Here (although this point is not well explained in [4]), the Neumann condition has the form

$$a^{ij}\gamma_j D_i u = g, \tag{2.1}$$

where γ is the unit inner normal vector to $\partial\Omega$. In fact, a simple geometric interpretation of the condition which implies that solutions of the mixed Dirichlet-oblique derivative problem are $C^{1,\alpha}$ was given in [12]. To state this condition, we suppose that the domain Ω is given locally as the wedge $0 < \theta < \theta_1$ and that the boundary conditions are

$$\begin{aligned} u = \varphi \quad &\text{on } \{\theta = \theta_1\}, \\ \beta \cdot Du = \psi \quad &\text{on } \{\theta = 0\}, \end{aligned} \tag{2.2}$$

where $\beta = (\beta^1, \beta^2)$ is a smooth vector field with $\beta^2 > 0$. We also assume that $\beta_0 = \lim_{x\to 0}\beta(x, 0)$ exists. If the vector β_0 with initial point 0 points inside Ω, then the solution is C^α for some $\alpha > 0$ (but not C^1 in general) and if this vector points outside Ω, then the solution is $C^{1,\alpha}$ for some $\alpha > 0$. The proof of these facts (in [12]) is similar to the corresponding results for the Dirichlet-Neumann problem (from [4]), but more care is taken in matching the comparison function to the boundary condition.

3. The oblique derivative problem in Lipschitz and $C^{1,\alpha}$ domains with continuous directional derivative

It is possible to prescribe the boundary condition $\beta \cdot Du = \psi$ on the boundary of an arbitrary domain. If we want to prescribe this condition in a useful way, however, then we need some conditions on the vector β which match it in a suitable way with the domain Ω. The following definitions are taken from [14]. We say that a vector field β is *oblique on* $\partial\Omega$ if at every point $x_0 \in \partial\Omega$, there is an open finite cone with vertex at x_0 and axis parallel to $\beta(x_0)$ which is a subset of Ω. We say that a vector field β defined on $\partial\Omega$ has *modulus of obliqueness* δ near $x_0 \in \partial\Omega$ if for any $\varepsilon > 0$, there is a coordinate system $(x', x^n) = (x^1, \ldots, x^n)$ centered at x_0 such that $\beta^n(x_0)$ is parallel to the positive x^n-axis and if there is a Lipschitz function ω defined on some $(n-1)$-dimensional ball $B_{n-1}(x_0, R)$ such that

$$\Omega \cap B(x_0, R) = \{x \in \mathbb{R}^n : x^n > \omega(x'),\ |x| < R\}, \tag{3.1}$$

$$\sup|D\omega| \sup\left(\frac{|\beta'|}{\beta^n}\right) \le \delta + \varepsilon. \tag{3.2}$$

Here $\beta' = (\beta^1,\dots,\beta^{n-1})$. The theory developed in [14] shows that if β has modulus of obliqueness $\delta \in (0,1)$, then the Hölder norm of the solution of the oblique derivative can be estimated in terms of certain pointwise information on the coefficients without any assumptions of smoothness of the coefficients. Of course, in this case, the boundary condition $\beta \cdot Du = \psi$ must be interpreted to mean that an appropriate directional derivative is prescribed, that is,

$$|\beta(x_0)| \lim_{h\to 0^+} \frac{u(x+h\beta(x_0)/|\beta(x_0)|) - u(x_0)}{h} = \psi(x_0) \tag{3.3}$$

for each $x_0 \in \partial\Omega$. Unlike the Neumann problem for Laplace's equation, this problem requires that the boundary condition be satisfied at *every* point on the boundary (examples in [13] show what happens if the boundary condition fails to hold at just one point).

Amazingly, this definition of obliqueness allows a statement of the boundary value problem with solutions that are smoother than the boundary of the domain. Specifically, if Ω has Lipschitz boundary and if the vector field β is Hölder continuous on $\partial\Omega$, then solutions of the boundary value problem

$$Lu = f \quad \text{in } \Omega, \qquad \beta \cdot Du = \psi \quad \text{on } \partial\Omega, \tag{3.4}$$

have Hölder continuous gradient. This startling fact was proved almost simultaneously via two different methods by Lieberman [10] and Pipher [16]. The method in [10] was refined in [15], but the underlying principle in all three works is as follows. First, the regularity question is reduced to considering the operator $L = \Delta$ and the function f is zero and the vector field β is a unit vector field in the x_n direction with $\partial\Omega$ the graph of a Lipschitz function as in (3.1). In this situation, the boundary condition is considered as a Dirichlet condition for the new unknown function $v = \partial u/\partial x_n$. Then v is Hölder continuous by previously known results, and the proof is completed by showing that the other components of the gradient are also Hölder continuous. The main difference between [10, 15, 16] is in the details of the last step.

The methods of these papers also show that if $\partial\Omega$, β, and ψ are in $C^{1,\alpha}$ for some $\alpha \in (0,1)$ (and if the coefficients in the differential equation are all in C^α), then $u \in C^{2,\alpha}$. An alternative approach to this result, which also applies to a large class of nonlinear problems, is given in [17].

4. The oblique derivative problem with discontinuous directional derivative

When β is discontinuous, the situation becomes more complicated. The only case known to the author which gives $C^{1,\alpha}$ regularity is that in which β has only jump discontinuities on lower-dimensional subsets of $\partial\Omega$. In two dimensions, this will be the case if and only if the discontinuities are isolated. Moreover, at a discontinuity, the limits of β from two sides must be different. Thus, we need only to look in a neighborhood of a discontinuity of β, which we take as the origin. To illustrate the basic idea, we assume that there are numbers $R > 0$ and $\theta_1 \in (0,\pi]$ such that

$$\Omega \cap B(R) = \{0 < r < R,\ 0 < \theta < \theta_1\}. \tag{4.1}$$

(Note that $\theta_1 = \pi$ is allowed, so the domain need not have a singularity at the origin.) To see more clearly what is going on, we assume that β is constant on the two segments which meet at the origin. Specifically, there are constants ω_0 and ω_1 such that

$$\begin{aligned}\beta &= (\cos\omega_0, \sin\omega_0) \quad \text{on } \theta = 0,\\ \beta &= (\cos\omega_1, \sin\omega_1) \quad \text{on } \theta = \theta_1.\end{aligned} \tag{4.2}$$

For brevity, we write $\beta_i = (\cos\omega_i, \sin\omega_i)$ for $i = 0, 1$ and we assume that $\beta_0 \neq \beta_1$. To guarantee that β is oblique for $\theta = 0$ and $\theta = \theta_1$, we suppose first that

$$0 < \omega_0 < \pi, \qquad \theta_1 - \pi < \omega_1 < \theta_1. \tag{4.3}$$

Next, we need a condition which guarantees that β is oblique at the origin. Before giving the condition, we note that if u is C^1 at the origin, then the boundary conditions on $\theta = 0$ and $\theta = \theta_1$ give $\beta_0 \cdot Du(0)$ and $\beta_1 \cdot Du(0)$. Since these directional derivatives are given for linearly independent directions, it follows that we also are given $Du(0)$. A complete analysis of this problem takes advantage of the maximum principle, so we wish to choose $\beta(0)$ in such a way that inequalities on $\beta_0 \cdot Du(0)$ and $\beta_1 \cdot Du(0)$ imply a corresponding inequality for $\beta(0) \cdot Du(0)$. For this reason, we take $\beta(0)$ to be a (suitable) positive linear combination of β_0 and β_1.

Now suppose also that $\omega_1 < \omega_0$. (This inequality is true, for example, if β_0 and β_1 are the unit inner normals to Ω.) In this case, we take ω to be any number in

$$(\omega_1, \omega_0) \cap (0, \theta_1) \tag{4.4}$$

and set $\beta(0) = (\cos\omega, \sin\omega)$. The intersection is nonempty because $\omega_0 > 0$ and $\omega_1 < \theta_1$. It then follows that there is some $\alpha \in (0,1)$ such that $u \in C^{1,\alpha}$. A proof is given in [11]. Although that work claims that the proof also works for $\omega_0 < \omega_1$, a simple example shows that such a claim is false: suppose that $\omega_0 = \pi/2$, $\theta_1 = \pi$, and $\omega_1 = 3\pi/4$. If u has the form $u(x,y) = r^\delta \cos(\delta\theta)$ with $\delta = 3/4$, then u satisfies $\Delta u = 0$ for $r > 0$ and $0 < \theta < \pi$. Moreover, $\beta \cdot Du = 0$ on $\theta = 0$ or $\theta = \pi$. Since $u = 0$ for $\theta = 2\pi/3$, it follows that $\beta(0) \cdot Du(0) = 0$ for

$$\beta(0) = \left(\cos\frac{2\pi}{3}, \sin\frac{2\pi}{3}\right). \tag{4.5}$$

Therefore, there is a solution which is not C^1 if $\omega_0 < \omega_1$. Fortunately, the proof in [11] is valid for $\omega_1 < \omega_0$; the difficulty is that the argument there uses a homotopy between the normal derivative problem for Laplace's equation (assuming that $\theta_1 < \pi$) and the general problem. In brief, uniform estimates must be made for problems of the form

$$tLu + (1-t)\Delta u = f \quad \text{in } \Omega, \qquad t\beta \cdot Du + (1-t)\gamma \cdot Du = g \quad \text{on } \partial\Omega, \tag{4.6}$$

which are independent of the parameter $t \in [0,1]$. If $\omega_0 < \omega_1$, then for some choice of t, the direction of the two directional derivatives must be the same, and the regularity argument in [11] breaks down whenever the directions are the same.

Acknowledgment

Portions of this paper were written while the author was visiting the Mathematical Sciences Research Institute at the University of California, Berkeley.

References

[1] A. Azzam, *On Dirichlet's problem for elliptic equations in sectionally smooth n-dimensional domains*, SIAM Journal on Mathematical Analysis **11** (1980), no. 2, 248–253.

[2] ———, *On Dirichlet's problem for elliptic equations in sectionally smooth n-dimensional domains. II*, SIAM Journal on Mathematical Analysis **12** (1981), no. 2, 242.

[3] ———, *On the Dirichlet problem for linear elliptic equations in plane domains with corners*, Annales Polonici Mathematici **43** (1983), no. 1, 43–50.

[4] A. Azzam and E. Kreyszig, *On solutions of elliptic equations satisfying mixed boundary conditions*, SIAM Journal on Mathematical Analysis **13** (1982), no. 2, 254–262.

[5] D. Gilbarg and L. Hörmander, *Intermediate Schauder estimates*, Archive for Rational Mechanics and Analysis **74** (1980), no. 4, 297–318.

[6] D. Gilbarg and N. S. Trudinger, *Elliptic Partial Differential Equations of Second Order*, Classics in Mathematics, Springer, Berlin, 2001, reprint of 1998 edition.

[7] P. Grisvard, *Elliptic Problems in Nonsmooth Domains*, Monographs and Studies in Mathematics, vol. 24, Pitman, Massachusetts, 1985.

[8] V. A. Kondrat'ev and O. A. Oleĭnik, *Boundary value problems for partial differential equations in nonsmooth domains*, Uspekhi Matematicheskikh Nauk **38** (1983), no. 2(230), 3–76 (Russian), English translation in Russian Mathematical Surveys **38** (1983), no. 2, 1–86.

[9] G. M. Lieberman, *Intermediate Schauder estimates for oblique derivative problems*, Archive for Rational Mechanics and Analysis **93** (1986), no. 2, 129–134.

[10] ———, *Oblique derivative problems in Lipschitz domains. I. Continuous boundary data*, Unione Matematica Italiana. Bollettino. B. Serie VII **1** (1987), no. 4, 1185–1210.

[11] ———, *Oblique derivative problems in Lipschitz domains. II. Discontinuous boundary data*, Journal für die reine und angewandte Mathematik **389** (1988), 1–21.

[12] ———, *Optimal Hölder regularity for mixed boundary value problems*, Journal of Mathematical Analysis and Applications **143** (1989), no. 2, 572–586.

[13] ———, *Nonuniqueness for some linear oblique derivative problems for elliptic equations*, Commentationes Mathematicae Universitatis Carolinae **40** (1999), no. 3, 477–481.

[14] ———, *Pointwise estimates for oblique derivative problems in nonsmooth domains*, Journal of Differential Equations **173** (2001), no. 1, 178–211.

[15] ———, *Higher regularity for nonlinear oblique derivative problems in Lipschitz domains*, Annali della Scuola Normale Superiore di Pisa. Classe di Scienze. Serie V **1** (2002), no. 1, 111–151.

[16] J. Pipher, *Oblique derivative problems for the Laplacian in Lipschitz domains*, Revista Matemática Iberoamericana **3** (1987), no. 3-4, 455–472.

[17] M. V. Safonov, *On the oblique derivative problem for second order elliptic equations*, Communications in Partial Differential Equations **20** (1995), no. 7-8, 1349–1367.

Gary M. Lieberman: Department of Mathematics, Iowa State University, Ames, IA 50011, USA
E-mail address: lieb@iastate.edu

ON MINIMAL (MAXIMAL) COMMON FIXED POINTS OF A COMMUTING FAMILY OF DECREASING (INCREASING) MAPS

TECK-CHEONG LIM

We prove that in a complete partially ordered set, every commutative family of decreasing maps has a minimal common fixed point.

Let $(X,\leq)$ be a partially ordered set. We call X *complete* if every linearly ordered subset of X has a greatest lower bound in X.

A mapping $f: X \to X$ is called a *decreasing* (resp., *increasing*) if $f(x) \leq x$ (resp., $f(x) \geq x$) for every $x \in X$. A family $\mathcal{F}$ of mappings of X into X is called *commutative* if $f \circ g = g \circ f$ for every $f, g \in \mathcal{F}$, where $\circ$ denotes the composition of maps.

A subset S of $(X,\leq)$ is a directed set if every two, and hence finitely many, elements of S have a *lower* bound in S. For a set S, $|S|$ denotes the cardinality of S.

We will use the following known fact whose proof can be found in [2].

Proposition 1. *Let $(X,\leq)$ be a complete partially ordered set. Then every directed subset of X has a greatest lower bound in X.*

Now we prove the following theorem.

Theorem 2. *Let $(X,\leq)$ be a nonempty complete partially ordered set. Let $\mathcal{F}$ be a commutative family of decreasing maps of X into X. Then $\mathcal{F}$ has a minimal common fixed point.*

Proof. First we prove that $\mathcal{F}$ has a common fixed point. Let x_0 be an arbitrary element of X. Let $\mathcal{S}$ be the (commutative) semigroup generated by $\mathcal{F}$. It is clear that each member of $\mathcal{S}$ is also decreasing. Let

$$D = \mathcal{S}(x_0) = \{s(x_0) : s \in \mathcal{S}\}. \tag{1}$$

D is a directed subset of X, since $s(x_0) \leq x_0$ and $t(x_0) \leq x_0$ imply that $s \circ t(x_0) = t \circ s(x_0) \leq t(x_0), s(x_0)$ for any $s, t \in \mathcal{S}$. By completeness assumption and Proposition 1, $\mathcal{S}(x_0)$ has a greatest lower bound, which we denote by $\bigwedge \mathcal{S}(x_0)$.

Hindawi Publishing Corporation
Proceedings of the Conference on Differential & Difference Equations and Applications, pp. 683–684

Define $x_1 = \bigwedge \mathcal{S}(l)$. Suppose that x_α have been defined for $\alpha < \gamma$ such that $x_\alpha \leq x_\beta$ for $\alpha < \beta < \gamma$. If γ has a predecessor $\gamma - 1$, we define $x_\gamma = \bigwedge \mathcal{S}(x_{\gamma-1})$ (the greatest lower bound exists since $\mathcal{S}(x_{\gamma-1})$ is a directed set as in the case for $x_0 = l$). If γ is a limit ordinal, we define $x_\gamma = \bigwedge\{x_\alpha : \alpha < \gamma\}$. By transfinite induction, x_α is defined for all ordinal α and satisfies $x_\alpha \leq x_\beta$ for $\alpha < \beta$.

Let κ be an ordinal with $|\kappa| > |X|$. Then x_α, $\alpha < \kappa$, cannot be all distinct, so there exist α_1,β with $\alpha_1 < \beta$ such that $x_{\alpha_1} = x_\beta$. This implies that $x_{\alpha_1} = x_{\alpha_1+1}$. It follows from the definition of x_{α_1+1} and the decreasingness of members of $\mathcal{S}$ that

$$s(x_{\alpha_1}) = x_{\alpha_1} \tag{2}$$

for all $s \in \mathcal{S}$, that is, x_{α_1} is a common fixed point of $\mathcal{S}$ and hence of $\mathcal{F}$.

Now we let K be the set of common fixed points of $\mathcal{F}$, which is nonempty by the above proof. Let C be a chain in K. By completeness, C has a (greatest) lower bound c_0 in X which may not be a common fixed point of $\mathcal{S}$. The set $L = \{x \in X : x \leq c_0\}$ with the order induced by the order of X is complete and is S-invariant, that is, $s(x) \in L$ for all $x \in L$. So by the above proof, there is a common fixed point of S in L, which is smaller than or equal to every member of C. Hence by Zorn's lemma, the set C has a minimal element. This completes the proof. □

Corollary 3. *Let $(X,\leq)$ be a nonempty complete partially ordered set and let f be a decreasing map from X into X. Then f has a minimal fixed point.*

By considering the dual of X, we obtain the following theorem and its corollary.

Theorem 4. *Let $(X,\leq)$ be a nonempty partially ordered set such that every chain in X has a least upper bound. Let $\mathcal{F}$ be a commutative family of increasing maps of X into X. Then $\mathcal{F}$ has a maximal common fixed point.*

Corollary 5. *Let $(X,\leq)$ be a nonempty partially ordered set such that every chain in X has a least upper bound, and let f be an increasing map from X into X. Then f has a maximal fixed point.*

Remark 6. (1) Note that in the last corollary, f may not have a minimal fixed point as erroneously stated in [1, page 188, Theorem 8.23]. For example, let $X = \{-\infty,\ldots,-2,-1,0\}$ with the usual ordering, and let $f(-\infty) = 0$, $f(x) = x$ for all $x \neq -\infty$. Then f is clearly increasing and has no minimal fixed point.

(2) It is clear from the proofs that all results above remain valid if one uses well-ordered sets instead of chains in definitions of completeness.

References

[1] B. A. Davey and H. A. Priestley, *Introduction to Lattices and Order*, 2nd ed., Cambridge University Press, New York, 2002.

[2] T.-C. Lim, *On the largest common fixed point of a commuting family of isotone maps*, Discrete and Continuous Dynamical Systems. Series A **2005** (2005), suppl., 621–623.

Teck-Cheong Lim: Department of Mathematical Sciences, George Mason University, 4400 University Drive, Fairfax, VA 22030, USA
E-mail address: tlim@gmu.edu

INTEGRAL ESTIMATES FOR SOLUTIONS OF A-HARMONIC TENSORS

BING LIU

We first discuss some properties of a class of $A_{r,\lambda}$ weighted functions. Then we prove a new version of weak reverse Hölder inequality, local versions of the Poincaré inequality and Hardy-Littlewood inequality with $A_{r,\lambda}$ double weights, and Hardy-Littlewood inequality with $A_{r,\lambda}$ double weights on δ-John domain for solutions of the A-harmonic equation.

1. Introduction and notation

In his book *Bounded Analytic Functions* [5], John Garnett showed that the A_r condition is one of the necessary and sufficient conditions for both Hardy-Littlewood maximal operator and Hilbert transform to be bounded on $L^r(\mu)$ space. Then Neugebauer introduced $A_{r,\lambda}$ condition and discussed its properties, see [6]. Since then, there have been many studies on inequalities with weighted norms that are related to either A_r or $A_{r,\lambda}$ conditions, see [1–4]. In this paper we discuss some properties of $A_{r,\lambda}$ double weights. We prove a new version of weak reverse Hölder inequality, local versions of the Poincaré inequality and Hardy-Littlewood inequality with $A_{r,\lambda}$-double weights. As an application, we prove Hardy-Littlewood inequality on δ-John domain with the $A_{r,\lambda}$ double weights for solutions of the A-harmonic equation. First, we introduce some notations.

We denote Ω as a connected open subset of $\mathbb{R}^n$. The weighted L^p-norm of a measurable function f over E is defined by

$$\|f\|_{p,E,w} = \left(\int_E |f(x)|^p w(x)dx\right)^{1/p}. \tag{1.1}$$

The space of differential l-forms is denoted as $D'(\Omega,\wedge^l)$. We write $L^p(\Omega,\wedge^l)$ for the l-forms $\omega(x)=\sum_I \omega_I(x)dx_I=\sum \omega_{i_1i_2\ldots i_l}(x)dx_{i_1}\wedge dx_{i_2}\wedge\cdots\wedge dx_{i_l}$ with $\omega_I\in L^p(\Omega,\mathbb{R})$ for all ordered l-tuples I. Then $L^p(\Omega,\wedge^l)$ is a Banach space with norm

$$\|\omega\|_{p,\Omega} = \left(\int_\Omega |\omega(x)|^p dx\right)^{1/p} = \left(\int_\Omega \left(\sum_I |\omega_I(x)|^2\right)^{p/2} dx\right)^{1/p}. \tag{1.2}$$

Hindawi Publishing Corporation
Proceedings of the Conference on Differential & Difference Equations and Applications, pp. 685–697

Similarly, $W_p^1(\Omega, \wedge^l)$ is the space of differential l-forms on Ω whose coefficients are in the Sobolev space $W_p^1(\Omega, \mathbb{R})$. The A-harmonic equation for differential forms is

$$d^* A(x, d\omega) = 0, \tag{1.3}$$

where $A : \Omega \times \wedge^l(\mathbb{R}^n) \to \wedge^l(\mathbb{R}^n)$ satisfies the following conditions:

$$|A(x,\xi)| \le a|\xi|^{p-1}, \qquad \langle A(x,\xi), \xi\rangle \ge |\xi|^p \tag{1.4}$$

for almost every $x \in \Omega$ and all $\xi \in \wedge^l(\mathbb{R}^n)$. Here $a > 0$ is a constant and $1 < p < \infty$ is a fixed exponent associated with (1.3). A solution to (1.3) is an element of the Sobolev space $W^1_{p,\mathrm{loc}}(\Omega, \wedge^{l-1})$ such that

$$\int_\Omega \langle A(x, d\omega), d\varphi\rangle = 0 \tag{1.5}$$

for all $\varphi \in W_p^1(\Omega, \wedge^{l-1})$ with compact support. We call u an A-harmonic tensor in Ω if u satisfies the A-harmonic equation (1.3) in Ω. A differential l-form $u \in D'(\Omega, \wedge^l)$ is called a closed form if $du = 0$ in Ω.

2. A class of double weights

Definition 2.1. A pair of weights $(w_1(x), w_2(x))$ is said to satisfy the $A_{r,\lambda}(\Omega)$ condition in a set $\Omega \subset \mathbb{R}^n$, for some $\lambda \ge 1$ and $1 < r < \infty$ with $1/r + 1/r' = 1$, if

$$\sup_{B\subset\Omega}\left(\frac{1}{|B|}\int_B (w_1)^\lambda dx\right)^{1/\lambda r}\left(\frac{1}{|B|}\int_B \left(\frac{1}{w_2}\right)^{\lambda r'/r} dx\right)^{1/\lambda r'} < \infty. \tag{2.1}$$

The class of $A_{r,\lambda}$ weights appears in [6] and it is an extension of the usual A_r weights [5].

The following is the general Hölder inequality.

Lemma 2.2. *Let $0 < p < \infty$ and $0 < q < \infty$ with $r^{-1} = p^{-1} + q^{-1}$. If f and g are measurable functions on $\mathbb{R}^n$, then*

$$\|fg\|_{r,\Omega} \le \|f\|_{p,\Omega}\|g\|_{q,\Omega} \tag{2.2}$$

for any $\Omega \subset \mathbb{R}^n$.

Lemma 2.3. *If $1 \le \lambda_1 < \lambda_2 < \infty$, then $A_{r,\lambda_2} \subset A_{r,\lambda_1}$.*

Proof. Let $(w_1, w_2) \in A_{r,\lambda_2}$. By general Hölder's inequality,

$$\begin{aligned}\left(\int_B w_1^{\lambda_1} dx\right)^{1/\lambda_1} &\le \left(\int_B w_1^{\lambda_2} dx\right)^{1/\lambda_2}\left(\int_B dx\right)^{(\lambda_2-\lambda_1)/\lambda_1\lambda_2} \\ &= |B|^{(\lambda_2-\lambda_1)/\lambda_1\lambda_2}\left(\int_B w_1^{\lambda_2} dx\right)^{1/\lambda_2}.\end{aligned} \tag{2.3}$$

Thus,

$$\frac{1}{|B|}\left(\int_B w_1^{\lambda_1}\,dx\right)^{1/\lambda_1} \le \left(\frac{1}{|B|}\int_B w_1^{\lambda_2}\,dx\right)^{1/\lambda_2}. \tag{2.4}$$

Similarly,

$$\left(\int_B \left(\frac{1}{w_2}\right)^{\lambda_1/(r-1)} dx\right)^{(r-1)/\lambda_1} \le |B|^{(r-1)(\lambda_2-\lambda_1)/\lambda_1\lambda_2}\left(\int_B \left(\frac{1}{w_2}\right)^{\lambda_2/(r-1)} dx\right)^{(r-1)/\lambda_2} \tag{2.5}$$

gives

$$\left(\frac{1}{|B|}\int_B \left(\frac{1}{w_2}\right)^{\lambda_1/(r-1)} dx\right)^{(r-1)/\lambda_1} \le \left(\frac{1}{|B|}\int_B \left(\frac{1}{w_2}\right)^{\lambda_2/(r-1)} dx\right)^{(r-1)/\lambda_2}. \tag{2.6}$$

From (2.4) and (2.6) we get

$$\begin{aligned}&\left(\left(\frac{1}{|B|}\int_B w_1^{\lambda_1}\,dx\right)^{1/\lambda_1}\left(\frac{1}{|B|}\int_B \left(\frac{1}{w_2}\right)^{\lambda_1/(r-1)} dx\right)^{(r-1)/\lambda_1}\right)^{1/r}\\ &\quad\le \left(\left(\frac{1}{|B|}\int_B w_1^{\lambda_2}\,dx\right)^{1/\lambda_2}\left(\frac{1}{|B|}\int_B \left(\frac{1}{w_2}\right)^{\lambda_2/(r-1)} dx\right)^{(r-1)/\lambda_2}\right)^{1/r} < \infty.\end{aligned} \tag{2.7}$$

□

With a similar proof, we have the following lemma.

LEMMA 2.4. *If* $1 < s < r < \infty$, *then* $A^s_{s,\lambda} \subset A^r_{r,\lambda}$.

Combining Lemmas 2.3 and 2.4, we have the following theorem.

THEOREM 2.5. *If* $1 \le \lambda_1 < \lambda_2$, $1 < s < r < \infty$, *then*

$$A^s_{s,\lambda_2} \subset A^r_{r,\lambda_1}. \tag{2.8}$$

Proof. For $0 \le \lambda_1 < \lambda_2$ and $1 < s < r$, $(r-1)/\lambda_1 > (s-1)/\lambda_2$. Thus,

$$\left(\int_B \left(\frac{1}{w_2}\right)^{\lambda_1/(r-1)} dx\right)^{(r-1)/\lambda_1} \le |B|^{(r-1)/\lambda_1-(s-1)/\lambda_2}\left(\int_B \left(\frac{1}{w_2}\right)^{\lambda_2/(s-1)}\right)^{(s-1)/\lambda_2}. \tag{2.9}$$

□

Combining (2.4), we proved Theorem 2.5.

3. Some inequalities with double weights

The following reverse Hölder's inequality and Poincaré inequality are proved in [7].

THEOREM 3.1. *Let u be an A-harmonic tensor in Ω, let $\sigma > 1$, and let $0 < s,t < \infty$. Then there exists a constant C, independent of u, such that*

$$\|u\|_{s,B} \le C|B|^{(t-s)/st}\|u\|_{t,\sigma B} \tag{3.1}$$

for all balls or cubes B with $\sigma B \subset \Omega$.

THEOREM 3.2. *Let $u \in D'(Q,\wedge^l)$ and let $du \in L^p(Q,\wedge^{l+1})$. Then there exists a closed form u_Q, defined in Q, such that $u - u_Q$ is in $W^1_p(Q,\wedge^l)$ with $1 < p < \infty$ and*

$$\|u-u_Q\|_{p,Q} \le C(n,p)|Q|^{1/n}\|du\|_{p,Q} \tag{3.2}$$

for Q a cube or a ball in $\mathbb{R}^n$, $l = 0,1,\dots,n$.

We extend Theorems 3.1 and 3.2 to the double weighted versions.

THEOREM 3.3. *Let $u \in D'(\Omega,\wedge^l)$, $l = 0,1,\dots,n$, be an A-harmonic tensor in a domain $\Omega \subset \mathbb{R}^n$, $\sigma > 0$. Assume that $0 < s,t < \infty$ and $(w_1,w_2) \in A_{r,\lambda}(\Omega)$ for some $r > 1$ and $\lambda \ge 1$. Then there exists a constant C, independent of u, such that*

$$\left(\int_B |u|^s w_1^{\alpha}dx\right)^{1/s} \le C|B|^{(t-s)/st}\left(\int_{\sigma B}|u|^t w_2^{\alpha t/s}dx\right)^{1/t} \tag{3.3}$$

for all balls B with $\sigma B \subset \Omega$ and any α with $\lambda > \alpha > 0$.

Proof. For any given $s > 0$, $\lambda \ge 1$, and $\lambda > \alpha > 0$, choose $\delta = s\lambda/(\lambda-\alpha)$, then $\delta > s$ and by general Hölder inequality

$$\begin{aligned}\left(\int_B |u|^s w_1^{\alpha}dx\right)^{1/s} &= \left(\int_B \left(|u|w_1^{\alpha/s}\right)^s dx\right)^{1/s}\\ &\le \left(\int_B |u|^{\delta}dx\right)^{1/\delta}\left(\int_B w_1^{\alpha\delta/(\delta-s)}dx\right)^{(\delta-s)/s\delta}.\end{aligned} \tag{3.4}$$

By the weak reverse Hölder inequality (Theorem 3.1), there exists constant C_1, such that

$$\left(\int_B |u|^{\delta}dx\right)^{1/\delta} \le C_1|B|^{(\xi-\delta)/\delta\xi}\left(\int_{\sigma B}|u|^{\xi}dx\right)^{1/\xi}, \tag{3.5}$$

where $0 < \xi = \lambda st/(\alpha t(r-1)+\lambda)$. Here $\xi < t$ since $r > 1$. Thus

$$
\begin{aligned}
\left(\int_{\sigma B}|u|^{\xi}dx\right)^{1/\xi} &= \left(\int_{\sigma B}(|u|w_2^{\alpha/s}w_2^{-\alpha/s})^{\xi}dx\right)^{1/\xi}\\
&\le \left(\int_{\sigma B}(|u|w_2^{\alpha/s})^{t}dx\right)^{1/t}\left(\int_{\sigma B}\left(\frac{1}{w_2}\right)^{(\alpha/s)(\xi t/(t-\xi))}dx\right)^{(t-\xi)/\xi t} \qquad (3.6)\\
&= \left(\int_{\sigma B}|u|^{t}w_2^{\alpha t/s}dx\right)^{1/t}\left(\int_{\sigma B}\left(\frac{1}{w_2}\right)^{(\alpha/s)(\xi t/(t-\xi))}dx\right)^{(t-\xi)/\xi t}.
\end{aligned}
$$

Substitute (3.5) and (3.6) into (3.4), we have

$$
\begin{aligned}
\left(\int_{B}|u|^{s}w_1^{\alpha}dx\right)^{1/s} &\le C_2|B|^{(\xi-\delta)/\delta\xi+(\delta-s)/s\delta+(t-\xi)/\xi t}\left(\int_{\sigma B}|u|^{t}w_2^{\alpha t/s}dx\right)^{1/t}, \qquad (3.7)\\
&\left(\frac{1}{|B|}\int_{\sigma B}w_1^{\alpha\delta/(\delta-s)}dx\right)^{(\delta-s)/s\delta}\left(\frac{1}{|B|}\int_{\sigma B}\left(\frac{1}{w_2}\right)^{(\alpha/s)(\xi t/(t-\xi))}dx\right)^{(t-\xi)/\xi t}.
\end{aligned}
$$

Because of our choices of δ and ξ, we have

$$
\begin{aligned}
&\left(\frac{1}{|B|}\int_{\sigma B}w_1^{\alpha\delta/(\delta-s)}dx\right)^{(\delta-s)/s\delta}\left(\frac{1}{|B|}\int_{\sigma B}\left(\frac{1}{w_2}\right)^{(\alpha/s)(\xi t/(t-\xi))}dx\right)^{(t-\xi)/\xi t}\\
&= \left(\frac{1}{|B|}\int_{\sigma B}w_1^{\lambda}dx\right)^{\alpha/s\lambda}\left(\frac{1}{|B|}\int_{\sigma B}\left(\frac{1}{w_2}\right)^{\lambda/(r-1)}dx\right)^{\alpha(r-1)/s\lambda} \qquad (3.8)\\
&= \left[\left(\frac{1}{|B|}\int_{\sigma B}w_1^{\lambda}dx\right)^{1/r\lambda}\left(\frac{1}{|B|}\int_{\sigma B}\left(\frac{1}{w_2}\right)^{\lambda/(r-1)}dx\right)^{(r-1)/r\lambda}\right]^{\alpha r/s} < C_3.
\end{aligned}
$$

Note that $(\xi-\delta)/\delta\xi+(\delta-s)/s\delta+(t-\xi)/\xi t = (t-s)/ts$, (3.7) is reduced to

$$\left(\int_{B}|u|^{s}w_1^{\alpha}dx\right)^{1/s} \le C_4|B|^{(t-s)/ts}\left(\int_{\sigma B}|u|^{t}w_2^{\alpha t/s}dx\right)^{1/t}. \qquad (3.9)$$

Thus, Theorem 3.3 is proved. □

Next, we prove the double weighted version of Poincaré inequality for A-harmonic tensors.

THEOREM 3.4. *Let $u \in D'(\Omega,\wedge^{l})$ be an A-harmonic tensor in a domain $\Omega \subset \mathbb{R}^n$ and $du \in L^s(\Omega,\wedge^{l+1})$, $l = 0,1,\ldots,n$. Assume that $\sigma > 1$, $1 < s < \infty$, and $(w_1,w_2) \in A_{r,\lambda}$ for some $r > 1$ and $\lambda \ge 1$. Then there exists a constant C, independent of u, such that*

$$\left(\frac{1}{|B|}\int_{B}|u-u_B|^{s}w_1^{\alpha}dx\right)^{1/s} \le C(n,s)|B|^{1/n}\left(\frac{1}{|B|}\int_{\sigma B}|du|^{s}w_2^{\alpha}dx\right)^{1/s} \qquad (3.10)$$

for all balls B with $\sigma B \subset \Omega$ and any α with $0 < \alpha < \lambda$.

Proof. For any given $\lambda \geq 1$ and $s > 1$, choose $t = \lambda s/(\lambda - \alpha)$, then $1 < s < t$, and $1/s = 1/t + (t-s)/st$. By the general Hölder's inequality, we have

$$\begin{aligned} \|u - u_B\|_{s,B,w_1^\alpha} &= \left(\int_B \left(|u - u_B| w_1^{\alpha/s}\right)^s dx\right)^{1/s} \\ &\leq \left(\int_B |u - u_B|^t dx\right)^{1/t} \left(\int_B \left(w_1^{\alpha/s}\right)^{st/(t-s)} dx\right)^{(t-s)/st} \\ &= \|u - u_B\|_{t,B} \cdot \left(\int_B w_1^\lambda dx\right)^{\alpha/s\lambda}. \end{aligned} \tag{3.11}$$

Since u_B is a closed form, by Theorems 3.1 and 3.2, we obtain

$$\|u - u_B\|_{t,B} \leq C_1(n,t)|B|^{1/n}\|du\|_{t,B} \leq C_2|B|^{1/n+(m-t)/mt}\|du\|_{m,\sigma B}, \tag{3.12}$$

where $m = \lambda s/(\lambda + \alpha(r-1))$, and by the choice of m, $m < s$. Also notice that $t = \lambda s/(\lambda - \alpha)$, we have

$$\begin{aligned} \|du\|_{m,\sigma B} &= \left(\int_{\sigma B} \left(|du| w_2^{\alpha/s} w_2^{-\alpha/s}\right)^m dx\right)^{1/m} \\ &\leq C_3\left(\int_{\sigma B} |du|^s w_2^\alpha dx\right)^{1/s} \left(\int_{\sigma B} \left(\frac{1}{w_2}\right)^{\alpha m/(s-m)} dx\right)^{(s-m)/ms} \\ &= C_3\left(\int_{\sigma B} |du|^s w_2^\alpha dx\right)^{1/s} \left(\int_{\sigma B} \left(\frac{1}{w_2}\right)^{\lambda/(r-1)} dx\right)^{\alpha(r-1)/\lambda s} \end{aligned} \tag{3.13}$$

for all balls B with $\sigma B \subset \Omega$. Thus, from (3.11) and (3.13)

$$\begin{aligned} &\left(\int_{\sigma B} w_1^\lambda dx\right)^{\alpha/s\lambda} \left(\int_{\sigma B} \left(\frac{1}{w_2}\right)^{\lambda/(r-1)} dx\right)^{(r-1)\alpha/\lambda s} \\ &\quad \leq C_4|\sigma B|^{-r\alpha/\lambda s}\left(\frac{1}{|\sigma B|}\int_{\sigma B} w_1^\lambda dx\right)^{\alpha/s\lambda} \left(\frac{1}{|\sigma B|}\int_{\sigma B} \left(\frac{1}{w_2}\right)^{\lambda/(r-1)} dx\right)^{(r-1)\alpha/\lambda s} \\ &\quad \leq C_5|B|^{-r\alpha/\lambda s}. \end{aligned} \tag{3.14}$$

Substituting (3.12), (3.13), and (3.14) into (3.11) and noticing that $(m-t)/mt - r\alpha/\lambda s = 0$, we have

$$\|u - u_B\|_{s,B,w^\alpha} \leq C_5|B|^{1/n}\|du\|_{s,\sigma B,w_2^\alpha}. \tag{3.15}$$

Thus the proof of Theorem 3.4 is completed. □

The following local version of Hardy-Littlewood inequality was also proved in [7].

THEOREM 3.5. *Let u, v be conjugate A-harmonic tensors in $\Omega \subset \mathbb{R}^n$, let $\sigma > 1$, and let $0 < s,t < \infty$. There exists a constant C, independent of u and v, such that*

$$||u - u_Q||_{s,Q} \le C|Q|^{\beta}||v - c_1||_{t,\sigma Q}^{q/p},$$
$$||v - v_Q||_{t,Q} \le C|Q|^{-\beta p/q}||u - c_2||_{s,\sigma Q}^{p/q} \tag{3.16}$$

for all cubes Q with $\sigma Q \subset \Omega$. Here c_1 is any form in $W^1_{p,\mathrm{loc}}(\Omega,\wedge)$ with $d^* c_1 = 0$. c_2 is any form in $W^1_{q,\mathrm{loc}}(\Omega,\wedge)$ with $dc_2 = 0$ and

$$\beta = \frac{1}{n} + \frac{1}{s} - \frac{q}{p}\left(\frac{1}{t} + \frac{1}{n}\right). \tag{3.17}$$

We extend Theorem 3.5 to the double weighted version.

THEOREM 3.6. *Let u and v be conjugate A-harmonic tensors in a domain $\Omega \subset \mathbb{R}^n$ and let $(w_1, w_2) \in A_{r,\lambda}(\Omega)$. Let $s = \Phi(t)$ as in (3.19). Then there exists a constant C, independent of u and v, such that*

$$\left(\int_B |u - u_B|^s w_1^{\alpha} dx\right)^{1/s} \le C\left(\int_{\sigma B} |v - c|^t w_2^{\alpha pt/qs} dx\right)^{q/pt} \tag{3.18}$$

for all cubes B with $\rho B \subset \Omega \subset \mathbb{R}^n$ and $\sigma > 1$. Here c is any form in $W^1_{q,\mathrm{loc}}(\Omega,\wedge)$ with $d^* c = 0$, $0 < \alpha < t$, and $\alpha < \lambda$, where $\lambda \ge 1$ is defined in Definition 2.1, and

$$s = \Phi(t) = \frac{npt}{nq + t(q-p)}. \tag{3.19}$$

Proof. The proof is similar as the proof of the Poincaré inequality. Let $\delta = s\lambda/(\lambda - \alpha)$ then $\delta > s$, and

$$\begin{aligned}\left(\int_B |u - u_B|^s w_1^{\alpha} dx\right)^{1/s} &= \left(\int_B (|u - u_B| w_1^{\alpha/s})^s dx\right)^{1/s} \\ &\le \left(\int_B |u - u_B|^{\delta} dx\right)^{1/\delta}\left(\int_B w_1^{\alpha\delta/(\delta-s)} dx\right)^{(\delta-s)/s\delta} \\ &= ||u - u_B||_{\delta,B}\left(\int_B w_1^{\alpha\delta/(\delta-s)} dx\right)^{(\delta-s)/s\delta}.\end{aligned} \tag{3.20}$$

By Theorem 3.5, for $q \le p$ and $0 < \delta, \xi < \infty$,

$$||u - u_B||_{\delta,B} \le C_1|B|^{\beta}||v - c_1||_{\xi,\sigma B}^{q/p}, \tag{3.21}$$

where $\beta = 1/\delta + 1/n - (1/\xi + 1/n)q/p$ and where we have chosen $0 < \xi = st\lambda q/((sq - \alpha p)t + \lambda sq)$. Note that $\alpha < t$ leads to $qs > pt$, and it implies $qs > p\alpha$, so that condition

(3.19) gives $\xi < t$. Then by general Hölder inequality

$$\begin{aligned} \|v-c_1\|_{\xi,\sigma B}^{q/p} &= \left(\int_{\sigma B} \left(|v-c_1| w_2^{\alpha p/sq} w_2^{-\alpha p/sq}\right)^{\xi} dx\right)^{q/\xi p} \\ &\le C_2 \left[\left(\int_{\sigma B} \left(|v-c_1| w_2^{\alpha p/sq}\right)^t dx\right)^{1/t} \left(\int_{\sigma B} \left(\frac{1}{w_2}\right)^{(\alpha p/sq)(\xi t/(t-\xi))} dx\right)^{(t-\xi)/\xi t}\right]^{q/p}. \end{aligned} \tag{3.22}$$

Substitute (3.21) and (3.22) into (3.20), then

$$\begin{aligned} \left(\int_B |u-u_B|^s w_1^{\alpha} dx\right)^{1/s} &\le C_3 |B|^{\beta} \left(\int_{\sigma B} \left(|v-c_1| w_2^{\alpha p/sq}\right)^t dx\right)^{q/pt}, \\ \left(\int_{\sigma B} \left(\frac{1}{w_2}\right)^{(\alpha p/sq)(\xi t/(t-\xi))} dx\right)^{(t-\xi)q/\xi tp} &\left(\int_B w_1^{\alpha\delta/(\delta-s)} dx\right)^{(\delta-s)/s\delta}. \end{aligned} \tag{3.23}$$

By the choice of δ and ξ, and by $sq/\alpha p > 1$, after denoting $r = sq/\alpha p$ we have

$$\begin{aligned} &\left(\int_{\sigma B} \left(\frac{1}{w_2}\right)^{(\alpha p/sq)(\xi t/(t-\xi))} dx\right)^{(t-\xi)q/\xi tp} \left(\int_B w_1^{\alpha\delta/(\delta-s)} dx\right)^{(\delta-s)/s\delta} \\ &\quad\le C_4 |\sigma B|^{\beta_1} \left(\frac{1}{|\sigma B|}\int_{\sigma B} \left(\frac{1}{w_2}\right)^{\alpha p\lambda/(sq-\alpha p)} dx\right)^{(sq-\alpha p)/\lambda sp} \left(\frac{1}{|\sigma B|}\int_{\sigma B} w_1^{\lambda} dx\right)^{\alpha/s\lambda} \\ &\quad\le C_5 |B|^{\beta_1} \left[\left(\frac{1}{|\sigma B|}\int_{\sigma B} \left(\frac{1}{w_2}\right)^{\lambda/(r-1)} dx\right)^{(r-1)/r\lambda} \left(\frac{1}{|\sigma B|}\int_{\sigma B} w_1^{\lambda} dx\right)^{1/\lambda r}\right]^{q/p} \\ &\quad\le C_6 |B|^{\beta_1}, \end{aligned} \tag{3.24}$$

where $\beta_1 = (1/\xi - 1/t)q/p + (1/s - 1/\delta)$. Substitute (3.24) into (3.23) and notice that $\beta + \beta_1 = 1/\delta + 1/n - (1/\xi + 1/n)q/p + (1/\xi - 1/t)q/p + (1/s - 1/\delta) = 0$ if $s = \Phi(t)$ as in (3.19). We finally get

$$\left(\int_B |u-u_B|^s w_1^{\alpha} dx\right)^{1/s} \le C_6 \left(\int_{\sigma B} |v-c_1|^t w_2^{\alpha pt/sq} dx\right)^{q/pt}. \tag{3.25}$$

□

As an application of Theorem 3.6, we show a global result on δ-John domain.

Definition 3.7. Ω, a proper subdomain of $\mathbb{R}^n$, is called a δ-John domain, $\delta > 0$, if there exists a point $x_0 \in \Omega$ which can be joined with any other point $x \in \Omega$ by a continuous curve $\gamma \subset \Omega$ so that

$$d(\xi, \partial\Omega) \ge \delta |x - \xi| \tag{3.26}$$

for each $\xi \in \gamma$. Here $d(\xi, \partial\Omega)$ is the Euclidean distance between ξ and $\partial\Omega$.

A δ-John domain has the following properties; see [7].

Lemma 3.8. *Let $\Omega \subset \mathbb{R}^n$ be a δ-John domain. Then there exists a covering W of Ω consisting of open cubes such that*

(i) $\sum_{Q\in W} \chi_{\sigma Q}(x) \le N\chi_\Omega(x)$, $x \in \mathbb{R}^n$,

(ii) *there is a distinguished cube $Q_0 \in W$ (called the central cube) which can be connected with every cube $Q \in W$ by a chain of cubes $Q_0, Q_1, \ldots, Q_k = Q$ from W such that for each $i = 0, 1, \ldots, k-1$,*

$$Q \subset NQ_i. \tag{3.27}$$

There is a cube $R_i \subset \mathbb{R}^n$ (this cube does not need to be a member of W) such that $R_i \subset Q_i \cap Q_{i+1}$, and $Q_i \cup Q_{i+1} \subset NR_i$.

Lemma 3.9. *If $1 \le s < \infty$, $0 < \rho < \infty$, $\{Q\}$ is an arbitrary collection of cubes in $\mathbb{R}^n$ and $\{a_Q\}$ are nonnegative numbers, then there is a constant C, depending only on s, n, and ρ, such that*

$$\left(\int_{R^n}\left(\sum_{Q\in W} a_Q\chi_{\rho Q}\right)^s dx\right)^{1/s} \le C\left(\int_{R^n}\left(\sum_{Q\in W} a_Q\chi_{Q}\right)^s dx\right)^{1/s}. \tag{3.28}$$

The following theorem (Theorem 3.10) is proved by Nolder, see [7].

Theorem 3.10. *Let $u \in D'(\Omega, \wedge^0)$ and $v \in D'(\Omega, \wedge^2)$ be conjugate A-harmonic tensors. If Ω is δ-John, $q \le p$, $v - c \in L^t(\Omega, \wedge^2)$, and*

$$s = \Phi(t) = \frac{npt}{nq + t(q-p)}, \tag{3.29}$$

then $u - u_{Q_0} \in L^s(\Omega, \wedge^0)$ and moreover, there exists a constant C, independent of u and v, such that

$$\|u - u_{Q_0}\|_{s,\Omega} \le C\|v - c\|_{t,\Omega}^{q/p}. \tag{3.30}$$

Here c is any form in $W^1_{p,\mathrm{loc}}(\Omega, \wedge)$ with $d^*c = 0$ and Q_0 is the distinguished cube of Lemma 3.8.

We prove the following theorem.

Theorem 3.11. *Let $u \in D'(\Omega, \wedge^0)$ and $v \in D'(\Omega, \wedge^2)$ be conjugate A-harmonic tensors. If Ω is δ-John, $q \le p$, $v - c \in L^t(\Omega, \wedge^2)$, and $s = \Phi(t)$ as in (3.29), $\alpha > 0$, weight $(w_1, w_2) \in A_{r,\lambda}$ as in Definition 2.1, then*

$$\|u - u_{Q_0}\|_{s,\Omega,w_1^\alpha} \le C\|v - c\|_{t,\Omega,w_2^{\alpha pt/qs}}^{q/p}, \tag{3.31}$$

where c is any form in $W^1_{q,\mathrm{loc}}(\Omega, \wedge)$ with $d^*c = 0$ and Q_0 is the distinguished cube of Lemma 3.8.

Proof. The proof is similar to the proof of [2, Theorem 3.4]. There is a modified Whitney cover of cubes $W = \{Q_i\}$ for Ω with $\max(|Q_i|,|Q_{i+1}|) \le N|Q_i \cap Q_{i+1}|$ for $i=0,1,\dots,k-1$, see [7], described in (ii) of Lemma 3.8. Note that $|a+b|^s \le 2^s(|a|^s+|b|^s)$ for all $s>0$, we have

$$\begin{aligned}\int_\Omega |u-u_{Q_0}|^s w_1^\alpha dx &= \int_\Omega (|u-u_{Q_0}|w_1^{\alpha/s})^s dx\\ &\le 2^s\int_\Omega (|u-u_Q|w_1^{\alpha/s})^s dx + 2^s\int_\Omega (|u_Q-u_{Q_0}|w_1^{\alpha/s})^s dx\\ &\le 2^s\sum_{Q\in W}\int_Q (|u-u_Q|w_1^{\alpha/s})^s dx + 2^s\sum_{Q\in W}\int_Q (|u_Q-u_{Q_0}|w_1^{\alpha/s})^s dx.\end{aligned} \tag{3.32}$$

The first sum can be estimated by Theorem 3.6 and condition (i) of Lemma 3.8:

$$\begin{aligned}\sum_{Q\in W}\int_Q (|u-u_Q|w_1^{\alpha/s})^s dx &\le C_1\sum_{Q\in W}\left(\int_{\sigma Q}|v-c|^t w_2^{\alpha pt/qs} dx\right)^{qs/pt}\\ &= C_1\sum_{Q\in W}\left(\int_\Omega |v-c|^t w_2^{\alpha pt/qs}\chi_{\sigma Q} dx\right)^{qs/pt} \le C_2 N\left(\int_\Omega |v-c|^t w_2^{\alpha pt/qs} dx\right)^{qs/pt}.\end{aligned} \tag{3.33}$$

To estimate the second sum in (3.32), let $Q \in W$ be a fixed cube and let $Q_0, Q_1, \dots, Q_k = Q$ be the chain in (ii) of Lemma 3.8. Then

$$|u_Q - u_{Q_0}| \le \sum_{i=0}^{k-1} |u_{Q_i} - u_{Q_{i+1}}|. \tag{3.34}$$

Because of $\max(|Q_i|,|Q_{i+1}|) \le N|Q_i \cap Q_{i+1}|$ for $i=0,1,\dots,k-1$, and $|u_{Q_i}-u_{Q_{i+1}}|^s \le 2^s(|u_{Q_i}-u|^s+|u-u_{Q_{i+1}}|^s)$, also by Theorem 3.6, we have

$$\begin{aligned}|u_{Q_i}-u_{Q_{i+1}}|^s w_1^\alpha &= \frac{1}{|Q_i\cap Q_{i+1}|}\int_{Q_i\cap Q_{i+1}} |u_{Q_i}-u_{Q_{i+1}}|^s w_1^\alpha dx\\ &\le \frac{N}{\max(|Q_i|,|Q_{i+1}|)}\int_{Q_i\cap Q_{i+1}} |u_{Q_i}-u_{Q_{i+1}}|^s w_1^\alpha dx\\ &\le C_3\sum_{j=i}^{i+1}\frac{1}{|Q_j|}\int_{Q_j}|u-u_{Q_j}|^s w_1^\alpha dx\\ &\le C_4\sum_{j=i}^{i+1}\frac{1}{|Q_j|}\left(\int_{\sigma Q_j}|v-c|^t w_2^{\alpha pt/qs} dx\right)^{qs/pt}.\end{aligned} \tag{3.35}$$

Since $Q \subset NQ_j$ for $j = i, i+1$, $0 \le i \le k-1$, from (ii) of Lemma 3.8, we have

$$|u_{Q_i} - u_{Q_{i+1}}|^s w_1^\alpha \chi_Q(x) \le C_4 \sum_{j=i}^{i+1} \frac{\chi_{NQ_j}(x)}{|Q_j|} \left(\int_{\sigma Q_j} |v - c|^t w_2^{\alpha pt/qs} dx \right)^{qs/pt}, \tag{3.36}$$

and by (3.34)

$$|u_Q - u_{Q_0}|^s \le \left(\sum_{i=0}^{k-1} |u_{Q_i} - u_{i+1}| \right)^s \le 2^s \sum_{i=0}^{k-1} |u_{Q_i} - u_{Q_{i+1}}|^s. \tag{3.37}$$

Thus by (3.36),

$$\begin{aligned} |u_Q - u_{Q_0}|^s w_1^\alpha \chi_Q(x) &\le 2^s \sum_{i=0}^{k-1} |u_{Q_i} - u_{i+1}|^s w_1^\alpha \chi_Q(x) \\ &\le 2^s \sum_{i=0}^{k-1} C_4 \left[\sum_{j=i}^{i+1} \frac{\chi_{NQ_j}}{|Q_j|} \left(\int_{\sigma Q_j} |v - c|^t w_2^{\alpha pt/qs} dx \right)^{qs/pt} \right] \\ &\le C_5 \sum_{R \in W} \frac{1}{|R|} \left(\int_{\sigma R} |v - c|^t w_2^{\alpha pt/qs} dx \right)^{qs/pt} \cdot \chi_{NR}(x) \end{aligned} \tag{3.38}$$

for every $x \in \mathbb{R}^n$. Thus,

$$\begin{aligned} |u_Q - u_{Q_0}| w_1^{\alpha/s} \chi_Q(x) &\le C_6 \left[\sum_{R \in W} \frac{1}{|R|} \left(\int_{\sigma R} |v - c|^t w_2^{\alpha pt/qs} dx \right)^{qs/pt} \chi_{NR}(x) \right]^{1/s} \\ &\le C_7 \sum_{R \in W} \left[\frac{1}{|R|} \left(\int_{\sigma R} |v - c|^t w_2^{\alpha pt/qs} dx \right)^{qs/pt} \right]^{1/s} \cdot \chi_{NR}(x) \end{aligned} \tag{3.39}$$

for every $x \in \mathbb{R}^n$. Hence

$$\begin{aligned} &\sum_{Q \in W} \int_Q |u_Q - u_{Q_0}|^s w_1^\alpha dx \\ &\le C_8 \int_{\mathbb{R}^n} \left| \sum_{R \in W} \left[\frac{1}{|R|} \left(\int_{\sigma R} |v - c|^t w_2^{\alpha pt/qs} dx \right)^{qs/pt} \right]^{1/s} \cdot \chi_{NR}(x) \right|^s dx. \end{aligned} \tag{3.40}$$

If $0 \le s \le 1$, then by inequality $|\sum t_i|^s \le \sum |t_i|^s$, and by (i) of Lemma 3.8,

$$\begin{aligned}
\sum_{Q\in W}\int_Q |u_Q - u_{Q_0}|^s w_1^\alpha dx &\le C_9 \int_{\mathbb{R}^n} \sum_{R\in W} \frac{1}{|R|}\left(\int_{\sigma R} |v-c|^t w_2^{\alpha pt/qs} dx\right)^{qs/pt} \chi_{NR}(x)dx \\
&\le C_{10} \sum_{R\in W}\left(\int_{\sigma R} |v-c|^t w_2^{\alpha pt/qs} dx\right)^{qs/pt} = C_{10} \sum_{R\in W}\left(\int_{\Omega} |v-c|^t w_2^{\alpha pt/qs} \chi_{\sigma R} dx\right)^{qs/pt} \\
&\le C_{10}\left(\int_{\Omega} |v-c|^t w_2^{\alpha pt/qs} \sum_{R\in W}\chi_{\sigma R} dx\right)^{qs/pt} \le C_{11}\left(\int_{\Omega} |v-c|^t w_2^{\alpha pt/qs} dx\right)^{qs/pt}.
\end{aligned} \tag{3.41}$$

If $1 \le s < \infty$, by (3.40) and Lemma 3.9, we have

$$\begin{aligned}
&\sum_{Q\in W}\int_Q |u_Q - u_{Q_0}|^s w_1^\alpha dx \\
&\quad\le C_{12} \int_{\mathbb{R}^n} \left| \sum_{R\in W}\left[\frac{1}{|R|}\left(\int_{\sigma R} |v-c|^t w_2^{\alpha pt/qs} dx\right)^{qs/pt}\right]^{1/s} \cdot \chi_R(x)\right|^s dx.
\end{aligned} \tag{3.42}$$

Since $\sum_{R\in W}\chi_R(x) \le \sum_{R\in W}\chi_{\sigma R}(x) \le N\chi_\Omega(x)$ and $|\sum_{i=1}^N t_i|^s \le N^{s-1}\sum_{i=1}^N |t_i|^s$, we have

$$\begin{aligned}
\sum_{Q\in W}\int_Q |u_Q - u_{Q_0}|^s w_1^\alpha dx &\le C_{13} \int_{\mathbb{R}^n} \left[\sum_{R\in W} \frac{1}{|R|}\left(\int_{\sigma R} |v-c|^t w_2^{\alpha pt/qs} dx\right)^{qs/pt} \cdot \chi_R(x)\right] dx \\
&= C_{13} \sum_{R\in W}\left(\int_{\sigma R} |v-c|^t w_2^{\alpha pt/qs} dx\right)^{qs/pt} \le C14\left(\int_{\Omega} |v-c|^t w_2^{\alpha pt/qs} dx\right)^{qs/pt}.
\end{aligned} \tag{3.43}$$

By (3.32), (3.33), (3.41), and (3.43), we have the theorem proved for any $s = \Phi(t)$ with $0 \le s < \infty$. □

References

[1] D. Cruz-Uribe and C. Pérez, *Two-weight, weak-type norm inequalities for fractional integrals, Calderón-Zygmund operators and commutators*, Indiana University Mathematics Journal **49** (2000), no. 2, 697–721.

[2] S. Ding, *Weighted Hardy-Littlewood inequality for A-harmonic tensors*, Proceedings of the American Mathematical Society **125** (1997), no. 6, 1727–1735.

[3] ———, *Two-weight Caccioppoli inequalities for solutions of nonhomogeneous A-harmonic equations on Riemannian manifolds*, Proceedings of the American Mathematical Society **132** (2004), no. 8, 2367–2375.

[4] S. Ding and B. Liu, *Generalized Poincaré inequalities for solutions to the A-harmonic equation in certain domains*, Journal of Mathematical Analysis and Applications **252** (2000), no. 2, 538–548.

[5] J. B. Garnett, *Bounded Analytic Functions*, Academic Press, New York, 1970.

[6] C. J. Neugebauer, *Inserting A_p-weights*, Proceedings of the American Mathematical Society **87** (1983), no. 4, 644–648.
[7] C. A. Nolder, *Hardy-Littlewood theorems for A-harmonic tensors*, Illinois Journal of Mathematics **43** (1999), no. 4, 613–632.

Bing Liu: Saginaw Valley State University, University Center, MI 48710-0001, USA
E-mail address: bliu@svsu.edu

BOUNDEDNESS OF SOLUTIONS OF FUNCTIONAL DIFFERENTIAL EQUATIONS WITH STATE-DEPENDENT IMPULSES

XINZHI LIU AND QING WANG

This paper studies the boundedness of functional differential equations with state-dependent impulses. Razumikhin-type boundedness criteria are obtained by using Lyapunov functions and Lyapunov functionals. Some examples are also given to illustrate the effectiveness of our results.

1. Introduction

Impulsive differential equations have attracted lots of interest in recent years due to their important applications in many areas such as aircraft control, drug administration, and threshold theory in biology [2, 3, 5, 7]. There has been a significant development in the theory of impulsive differential equations in the past decade, especially in the area where impulses are fixed. However, the corresponding theory of impulsive functional differential has been less developed because of numerous theoretical and technical difficulties. Recently, the existence and continuability results of solutions for differential equations with delays and state-dependent impulses have been presented in [1, 4], while some stability results of nontrivial solutions of delay differential equations with state-dependent impulses have been stated in [6]. In this paper, we will establish some boundedness criteria for the functional differential equations with state-dependent impulses. Some examples are also discussed to illustrate the effectiveness of our results.

2. Preliminaries

Let $\mathbb{R}$ denote the set of real numbers, $\mathbb{R}_+$ the set of nonnegative real numbers, and $\mathbb{R}^n$ the n-dimensional Euclidean linear space equipped with the Euclidean norm $\|\cdot\|$.

For $a,b \in \mathbb{R}$ with $a < b$ and for $S \subset \mathbb{R}^n$, define

$$\begin{aligned}\mathrm{PC}([a,b],S) = \{\phi : [a,b] \longrightarrow S \mid \phi(t^+) = \phi(t),\ \forall t \in [a,b);\ \phi(t^-) \\ \text{exists in } S,\ \forall t \in (a,b] \text{ and } \phi(t^-) = \phi(t) \text{ for all} \\ \text{but at most a finite number of points } t \in (a,b]\};\end{aligned} \tag{2.1}$$

Hindawi Publishing Corporation
Proceedings of the Conference on Differential & Difference Equations and Applications, pp. 699–710

$$\begin{aligned} \mathrm{PC}([a,b),S) = \{\phi : [a,b) \longrightarrow S \mid \phi(t^+) = \phi(t),\ \forall t \in [a,b);\ \phi(t^-) \\ \text{exists in } S,\ \forall t \in (a,b) \text{ and } \phi(t^-) = \phi(t) \text{ for all} \\ \text{but at most a finite number of points } t \in (a,b)\}; \end{aligned} \tag{2.2}$$

$$\mathrm{PC}([a,\infty),S) = \{\phi : [a,\infty) \longrightarrow S \mid \forall c > a,\ \phi|_{[a,c]} \in \mathrm{PC}([a,c],S)\}. \tag{2.3}$$

Here we use the abbreviated notation $x(t^+) = \lim_{s\to t^+} x(s)$ and $x(t^-) = \lim_{s\to t^-} x(s)$ to refer to right-hand and left-hand limits, respectively.

Given a constant $r > 0$ representing an upper bound on the time delay of our system, we equip the linear space $\mathrm{PC}([-r,0],\mathbb{R}^n)$ with the norm $\|\cdot\|_r$ defined by $\|\psi\|_r = \sup_{-r\le s\le 0}\|\psi(s)\|$. If $x \in \mathrm{PC}([t_0 - r,\infty),\mathbb{R}^n)$, where $t_0 \in \mathbb{R}_+$, then for each $t \ge t_0$, we define $x_t \in \mathrm{PC}([-r,0),\mathbb{R}^n)$ by $x_t(s) = x(t+s)$ for $-r \le s \le 0$.

Let $J \subset \mathbb{R}_+$ be an interval of the form $[a,b)$ where $0 \le a < b \le \infty$ and let $D \subset \mathbb{R}^n$ be an open set. Given $f, I : J \times \mathrm{PC}([-r,0],D) \to \mathbb{R}^n$, and $\tau_k \in C(D,\mathbb{R}_+)$. Consider the delay differential system with state-dependent impulses

$$\begin{aligned} x'(t) &= f(t,x_t), \quad t \ne \tau_k(x(t^-)), \\ \Delta x(t) &= I(t,x_{t^-}), \quad t = \tau_k(x(t^-)),\ k = 0,1,\ldots. \end{aligned} \tag{2.4}$$

The initial condition for system (2.4) is given by

$$x_{t_0} = \phi, \tag{2.5}$$

where $t_0 \in \mathbb{R}_+$ and $\phi \in \mathrm{PC}([-r,0],\mathbb{R}^n)$.

Throughout this paper, we assume the following hypotheses hold.

(A1) $f(t,\psi)$ is composite-PC, that is, if for each $t_0 \in J$ and $0 < \alpha \le \infty$, where $[t_0,t_0+\alpha) \subset J$, if $x \in \mathrm{PC}([t_0 - r,t_0+\alpha),D)$, then the composite function g defined by $g(t) = f(t,x_t)$ is an element of the function class $\mathrm{PC}([t_0,t_0+\alpha),\mathbb{R}^n)$.

(A2) $f(t,\psi)$ is continuous in ψ, that is, if for each fixed $t \in J$, $f(t,\psi)$ is a continuous function of ψ on $\mathrm{PC}([-r,0],F)$.

(A3) $f(t,\psi)$ is quasibounded, that is, if for each $t_0 \in J$ and $\alpha > 0$ where $[t_0,t_0+\alpha] \subset J$, and for each compact set $F \subset D$, there exists some $M > 0$ such that $|f(t,\psi)| \le M$ for all $(t,\psi) \in [t_0,t_0+\alpha] \times \mathrm{PC}([-r,0],F)$.

(A4) $\tau_k \in C^1(D,\mathbb{R}_+)$ for $k = 0,1,\ldots$, and for each $t^* \in J$, there exists some $\delta > 0$, where $[t^*,t^*+\delta] \subset J$ such that

$$\nabla\tau_k(\psi(0)) \cdot f(t,\psi) \ne 1 \tag{2.6}$$

for all $(t,\psi) \in (t^*,t^*+\delta] \times \mathrm{PC}([-r,0],D)$ and $k = 0,1,\ldots$.

Remark 2.1. It is shown in [4, Corollary 3.1] that if conditions (A1)–(A4) hold, the initial value problem (2.4)-(2.5) has a solution $x(t,t_0,\phi)$ existing in a maximal interval I.

Definition 2.2. The solution $x(t)$ of system (2.4) is said to be

(B1) uniformly bounded if for every $B_1 > 0$, there exists some $B_2 = B_2(B_1) > 0$ such that if $t_0 \in \mathbb{R}_+$, $\phi \in \mathrm{PC}([-r,0],\mathbb{R}^n)$ with $\|\phi\|_r \le B_1$ and $x(t) = x(t,t_0,\phi)$ is any solution of system (2.4), then $x(t,t_0,\phi)$ is defined and $\|x(t,t_0,\phi)\| \le B_2$ for all $t \ge t_0$;

(B2) uniformly ultimately bounded with bound B if (B1) holds and for every $B_3 > 0$, there exists some $T = T(B_3) > 0$ such that if $\phi \in \mathrm{PC}([-r,0],\mathbb{R}^n)$ with $\|\phi\|_r \le B_3$, then for any $t_0 \in \mathbb{R}_+$, $\|x(t,t_0,\phi)\| \le B$ for $t \ge t_0 + T$.

Definition 2.3. Given a function $V : J \times D \to \mathbb{R}_+$, the upper right-hand derivative of V with respect to system (2.4) is defined by

$$D^+_{(2.4)}V(t,\psi(0)) = \limsup_{h\to 0^+} \frac{1}{h}\left[V(t+h,\psi(0)+hf(t,\psi)) - V(t,\psi(0))\right] \tag{2.7}$$

for $(t,\psi) \in \mathrm{PC}([-r,0],D)$.

We may drop the subscript and simply write $D^+V(t,\psi(0))$, where it is obvious which system the derivative of V is with respect to. Note that $D^+V(t,\psi(0))$ is a functional, whereas V is a function.

We remark that if $V(t,x)$ has continuous partial derivatives with respect to t and x, then (2.7) reduces to

$$D^+_{(2.4)}V(t,\psi(0)) = \frac{\partial V(t,\psi(0))}{\partial t} + \nabla_x V(t,\psi(0)) \cdot f(t,\psi). \tag{2.8}$$

Definition 2.4. A function $V(t,x) : J \times \mathbb{R}^n \to \mathbb{R}_+$ belongs to class ν_0 if

(H1) V is continuous on each of the sets $[t_{k-1},t_k) \times \mathbb{R}^n$, and for all $x \in \mathbb{R}^n$ and $k = 0,1,\ldots$, $\lim_{(t,y)\to(t_k^-,x)} V(t,y) = V(t_k^-,x)$ exists;

(H2) $V(t,x)$ is locally Lipschitz in $x \in \mathbb{R}^n$ and $V(t,0) \equiv 0$.

Definition 2.5. A functional $V(t,\psi) : J \times \mathrm{PC}([-r,0],\mathbb{R}^n) \to \mathbb{R}_+$ belongs to class $\nu_0(\cdot)$ (a set of Lyapunov-like functionals) if

(B1) V is continuous on $[t_{k-1},t_k) \times \mathbb{R}^n$ for each $k = 0,1,\ldots$, and for all $\psi,\varphi \in \mathrm{PC}([-r,0],\mathbb{R}^n)$ and $k = 0,1,\ldots$, the limit $\lim_{(t,\psi)\to(t_k^-,\varphi)} V(t,\psi) = V(t_k^-,\varphi)$ exists;

(B2) $V(t,\psi)$ is locally Lipschitz in ψ in each compact set in $\mathbb{R}^n$ and $V(t,0) \equiv 0$.

Definition 2.6. A functional $V(t,\psi) : J \times \mathrm{PC}([-r,0],\mathbb{R}^n) \to \mathbb{R}_+$ belongs to class $\nu_0^*(\cdot)$, if $V(t,\psi) \in \nu_0(\cdot)$ and for any $x \in \mathrm{PC}([t_0 - r,\infty),\mathbb{R}^n)$, $V(t,x_t)$ is continuous for $t \ge t_0$.

Let us define the following notations for later use:

$$\begin{aligned} K_0 &= \{g \in C(\mathbb{R}_+,\mathbb{R}_+) \mid g(0) = 0 \text{ and } g(s) > 0 \text{ for } s > 0\}, \\ K &= \{g \in K_0 \mid g \text{ is strictly increasing in } s\}, \\ K_1 &= \{g \in K \mid g(s) \longrightarrow \infty \text{ as } s \longrightarrow \infty\}. \end{aligned} \tag{2.9}$$

3. Boundedness criteria

Our first two results utilize the Lyapunov-Razumkhin technique and the last result employs the Lyapunov functional method.

THEOREM 3.1. *Assume that there exist $V(t,x) \in \nu_0$, $W_1, W_2 \in K_1$, $W_3 \in K_0$ such that*

(i)

$$W_1(\|x\|) \le V(t,x) \le W_2(\|x\|); \tag{3.1}$$

(ii) *for any* $x \in \mathbb{R}^n$ *and* $\tau_k \in C^1(\mathbb{R}^n, \mathbb{R}_+)$,

$$V(\tau_k(x), x + I(\tau_k(x), x)) \le (1 + b_k) V(\tau_k^-(x), x), \quad k = 0, 1, \ldots, \tag{3.2}$$

where $b_k \ge 0$ *with* $\sum_{k=1}^{\infty} b_k < \infty$;

(iii) *there exists some constant* $\rho > 0$ *such that for any solution* $x(t)$ *of system (2.4)*

$$D^+_{(2.4)} V(t, x(t)) \le -W_3(\|x(t)\|) \tag{3.3}$$

whenever $\|x(t)\| \ge \rho$ *and* $P(V(t, x(t))) > V(s, x(s))$ *for* $s \in [t - r, t]$ *and* $t \ge t_0$, *where* $P \in C(\mathbb{R}_+, \mathbb{R}_+)$ *and* $P(s) > Ms$ *for* $s > 0$, *where* $M = \prod_{k=1}^{\infty}(1 + b_k)$;

then the solutions of (2.4) are uniformly bounded and uniformly ultimate bounded.

Proof. We first show uniform boundedness.

Let $B_1 > 0$ and assume, without loss of generality, that $B_1 \ge \rho$. Choose $B_2 = W_2^{-1}((1/M)(B_1))$. For any $t_0 \in \mathbb{R}_+$ and $\|\varphi\|_r \le B_1$, let $x(t) = x(t, t_0, \varphi)$ be a solution of (2.4)-(2.5), which exists in a maximal interval $I = [t_0 - r, t_0 + \beta)$. If $\beta < \infty$, then there exists some $t \in (t_0, t_0 + \beta)$ for which $\|x(t)\| > B_2$. We will prove that $\|x(t)\| \le B_2$ which in turn will imply that $\beta = \infty$ and hence the solutions of (2.4)-(2.5) are uniformly bounded.

For simplicity, let $\tau_0 = t_0 \in \mathbb{R}_+$ be the initial time and denote impulsive moments $\tau_k(x(\tau_k^-))$ for $k = 1, 2, \ldots$ by τ_k in case of not causing confusion.

In order to prove uniform boundedness, we first show

$$\begin{aligned} V(t) &< \frac{1}{M}(1 + b_0) \cdots (1 + b_m) W_1(B_2), \quad \tau_m \le t < \tau_{m+1}, \\ V(\tau_{m+1}) &\le \frac{1}{M}(1 + b_0) \cdots (1 + b_m)(1 + b_{m+1}) W_1(B_2), \quad m = 0, 1, \ldots, \end{aligned} \tag{3.4}$$

where $V(t) = V(t, x(t))$ and $b_0 = 0$.

Now we will show (3.4) holds for $m = 0$, that is,

$$V(t) < \frac{1}{M} W_1(B_2), \quad \tau_0 \le t < \tau_1. \tag{3.5}$$

For $\tau_0 - r \le t \le \tau_0$, we have

$$W_1(||x(t)||) \le V(t) \le W_2(||x(t)||) < W_2(B_1) = \frac{1}{M} W_1(B_2). \tag{3.6}$$

If (3.5) does not hold, then there is some $\bar{t} \in (\tau_0, \tau_1)$ such that

$$V(\bar{t}) = \frac{1}{M} W_1(B_2), \quad V(t) \le \frac{1}{M} W_1(B_2), \quad \tau_0 - r \le t \le \bar{t}, \tag{3.7}$$

$$V'(\bar{t}) \ge 0. \tag{3.8}$$

Thus

$$P(V(\bar{t})) > MV(\bar{t}) \ge V(s), \quad \bar{t} - r \le s \le \bar{t}, \tag{3.9}$$

and from $W_2(\|x(\bar{t})\|) \geq V(\bar{t}) = (1/M)W_1(B_2) = W_2(B_1)$ we have

$$||x(\bar{t})|| \geq B_1 \geq \rho, \tag{3.10}$$

then by assumption (iii) we obtain

$$V'(\bar{t}) \leq -W_3(||x(\bar{t})||) < 0, \tag{3.11}$$

which contradicts with (3.8), and hence we have (3.5) holds. By (3.5) and assumption (ii) we have

$$\begin{aligned} V(\tau_1) &= V(\tau_1, x(\tau_1^-) + I_m(\tau_1, x(\tau_1^-))) \\ &\leq (1+b_1)V(\tau_1^-, x(\tau_1^-)) = (1+b_1)V(\tau_1^-) \\ &\leq \frac{1}{M}(1+b_1)W_1(B_2), \end{aligned} \tag{3.12}$$

which implies that (3.4) holds for $m = 0$.

Now suppose that (3.4) holds for $m \leq i-1$ for $i = 1,2,\ldots$, we prove that (3.4) holds for $m = i$, that is,

$$\begin{aligned} V(t) &< \frac{1}{M}(1+b_0)\cdots(1+b_i)W_1(B_2), \quad \tau_i \leq t < \tau_{i+1}, \\ V(\tau_{i+1}) &\leq \frac{1}{M}(1+b_0)\cdots(1+b_i)(1+b_{i+1})W_1(B_2), \quad i = 1,2,\ldots. \end{aligned} \tag{3.13}$$

First we prove that

$$V(t) \leq \frac{1}{M}(1+b_0)\cdots(1+b_i)W_1(B_2), \quad \tau_i \leq t < \tau_{i+1}. \tag{3.14}$$

If (3.14) does not hold, then there is some $\bar{t} \in (\tau_i, \tau_{i+1})$ such that

$$V(\bar{t}) > \frac{1}{M}(1+b_0)\cdots(1+b_i)W_1(B_2) \geq V(\tau_i), \tag{3.15}$$

and so there exists a $t^* \in (\tau_i, \bar{t}]$ such that

$$V(t^*) \geq \frac{1}{M}(1+b_0)\cdots(1+b_i)W_1(B_2), \quad V(t) \leq V(t^*), \quad t^*-r \leq t \leq t^*, \tag{3.16}$$

$$V'(t^*) \geq 0. \tag{3.17}$$

Then we get

$$\begin{aligned} P(V(t^*)) > MV(t^*) \geq V(s), \quad t^*-r \leq s \leq t^*, \\ ||x(t^*)|| \geq B_1 \geq \rho \end{aligned} \tag{3.18}$$

since $W_2(\|x(t^*)\|) \geq V(t^*) \geq M^{-1}(1+b_0)\cdots(1+b_i)W_1(B_2) \geq M^{-1}W_1(B_2) = W_2(B_1)$. By assumption (iii),

$$V'(t^*) \leq -W_3(\|x(t^*)\|) < 0, \tag{3.19}$$

which contradicts (3.17) and so (3.14) holds.

From (3.14) and assumption (ii), we have

$$V(\tau_{i+1}) \leq V(\tau_{i+1}^-)(1+b_{i+1}) \leq \frac{1}{M}(1+b_0)\cdots(1+b_{i+1})W_1(B_2), \tag{3.20}$$

which implies that (3.13) holds for $m = i$, and hence (3.4) holds for all $m = 0, 1, \ldots$.

Therefore, we have

$$W_1(\|x(t)\|) \leq V(t) \leq W_1(B_2), \quad t \geq \tau_0. \tag{3.21}$$

This proves uniform boundedness.

Now we will prove uniformly ultimate boundedness. Let

$$B = W_1^{-1}(MW_2(\rho)) \tag{3.22}$$

and then

$$W_1(B) = MW_2(\rho). \tag{3.23}$$

Let $B_3 \geq \rho$ be given. By the preceding arguments, we could find a $B_4 > B$ such that $\|\varphi\|_r \leq B_3$ implies

$$V(t) \leq W_1(B_4), \quad t \geq \tau_0. \tag{3.24}$$

Let

$$0 < d < \inf\left\{P(s) - Ms : \frac{1}{M}W_1(B) \leq s \leq W_1(B_4)\right\} \tag{3.25}$$

and N be the first positive integer such that

$$W_1(B) + Nd \geq MW_1(B_4). \tag{3.26}$$

Set $\gamma = \inf_{\rho \leq s \leq B_4} W_3(s)$. Then $\gamma > 0$. We first show that

$$V(t) \leq W_1(B) + (N-1)d, \quad t \geq \tau_0 + h, \tag{3.27}$$

where $\rho = \max\{(1+A)W_1(B_4)/\gamma, r\}$, $A = \sum_{k=1}^{\infty} b_k$.

Suppose, for all $t \in I_1 = [\tau_0, \tau_0 + h]$,

$$V(t) > \frac{1}{M}[W_1(B) + (N-1)d]. \tag{3.28}$$

Then $M^{-1}W_1(B) < V(t) \leq W_1(B_4)$ for $t \in I_1$. Thus, for $t \in I_1$, we have

$$\begin{aligned} P(V(t)) &> MV(t) + d > \frac{M}{M}[W_1(B) + (N-1)d] + d \\ &= W_1(B) + Nd \geq W_1(B_4) \geq V(s), \quad t - r \leq s \leq t, \\ &\quad \|x(t)\| \geq \rho \end{aligned} \tag{3.29}$$

since $W_2(\|x(t)\|) \geq V(t) > M^{-1}W_1(B) = W_2(\rho)$. By assumption (iii), we have, for $t \in I_1$,

$$V'(t) \leq -W_3(\|x(t)\|) \leq -\gamma, \tag{3.30}$$

and so

$$\begin{aligned} V(t) &\leq V(\tau_0) - \gamma(t - \tau_0) + \sum_{\tau_0 < \tau_j \leq t} [V(\tau_j) - V(\tau_j^-)] \\ &\leq W_1(B_4) - \gamma(t - \tau_0) + \sum_{\tau_0 < \tau_j \leq t} b_j V(\tau_j^-) \\ &\leq W_1(B_4) - \gamma(t - \tau_0) + AW_1(B_4). \end{aligned} \tag{3.31}$$

Let $t = \tau_0 + h$, we have

$$V(\tau_0 + h) \leq (1 + A)W_1(B_4) - \gamma \cdot \frac{(1 + A)W_1(B_4)}{\gamma} = 0. \tag{3.32}$$

It is a contradiction, thus there is a $t^* \in I_1$ such that

$$V(t^*) \leq \frac{1}{M}[W_1(B) + (N-1)d]. \tag{3.33}$$

Let $q = \inf\{k \in Z^+ : \tau_k > t^*\}$. We claim that

$$V(t) \leq \frac{1}{M}[W_1(B) + (N-1)d], \quad t^* \leq t < \tau_q. \tag{3.34}$$

Otherwise, there is a $\bar{t} \in (t^*, \tau_q)$ such that

$$V(\bar{t}) > \frac{1}{M}[W_1(B) + (N-1)d] \geq V(t^*). \tag{3.35}$$

This implies that there is a $\hat{t} \in (t^*, \bar{t}]$ such that

$$\begin{aligned} V(\hat{t}) &\geq \frac{1}{M}[W_1(B) + (N-1)d], \\ V'(\hat{t}) &\geq 0. \end{aligned} \tag{3.36}$$

Thus

$$\begin{aligned} P(V(\hat{t})) &> MV(\hat{t}) + d \geq W_1(B) + (N-1)d + d \\ &= W_1(B) + Nd \geq W_1(B_4) \geq V(s), \quad \hat{t} - r \leq s \leq \hat{t}, \\ &\quad \|x(\hat{t})\| \geq \rho \end{aligned} \tag{3.37}$$

since $W_2(\|x(\hat{t})\|) \geq V(\hat{t}) \geq M^{-1}W_1(B) = W_2(\rho)$. By assumption (iii),

$$V'(\hat{t}) \leq -W_3(\|x(\hat{t})\|) < 0. \tag{3.38}$$

This is a contradiction and so (3.34) holds. From (3.34) and assumption (ii), we have

$$V(\tau_q) \leq (1+b_q)V(\tau_q^-) \leq \frac{1}{M}(1+b_q)[W_1(B)+(N-1)d]. \tag{3.39}$$

Similarly, we could prove that

$$\begin{aligned} V(t) &\leq \frac{1}{M}(1+b_q)[W_1(B)+(N-1)d], \quad \tau_q \leq t < \tau_{q+1}, \\ V(\tau_{q+1}) &\leq \frac{1}{M}(1+b_q)(1+b_{q+1})[W_1(B)+(N-1)d]. \end{aligned} \tag{3.40}$$

By induction, we could prove in general that

$$\begin{aligned} V(t) &\leq \frac{1}{M}(1+b_q)\cdots(1+b_{q+i})[W_1(B)+(N-1)d], \quad \tau_{q+i} \leq t < \tau_{q+i+1}, \\ V(\tau_{q+i+1}) &\leq \frac{1}{M}(1+b_q)\cdots(1+b_{q+i+1})[W_1(B)+(N-1)d], \quad i = 0,1,2,\dots. \end{aligned} \tag{3.41}$$

Thus (3.27) holds. Similarly, we may prove that

$$V(t) \leq W_1(B)+(N-2)d, \quad t \geq \tau_0 + 3h, \tag{3.42}$$

and by the induction, we have

$$V(t) \leq W_1(B)+(N-j)d, \quad t \geq \tau_0 + (2j-1)h,\ j = 1,2,\dots,N. \tag{3.43}$$

Thus we obtain

$$W_1(\|x(t)\|) \leq V(t) \leq W_1(B), \quad t \geq \tau_0 + (2N-1)h. \tag{3.44}$$

Let $T = (2N-1)h$, then

$$\|x(t)\| \leq B, \quad t \geq \tau_0 + T. \tag{3.45}$$

This proves uniformly ultimate boundedness. The proof is now completed. □

Due to page limitation, the proofs of the following theorems are omitted.

THEOREM 3.2. *Assume that there exist* $V_1(t,x)\in\nu_0$, $V_2(t,\phi)\in\nu_0^*(\cdot)$, *and* $W_1,W_2,W_3\in K_1$ *such that*

(i) $W_1(\|\phi(0)\|)\le V(t,\phi)\le W_2(\|\phi\|_r)$, *where* $V(t,\phi)=V_1(t,\phi(0))+V_2(t,\phi)\in\nu_0(\cdot)$;

(ii) *for each* $x\in\mathbb{R}^n$ *and* $\tau_k\in C^1(\mathbb{R}^n,\mathbb{R}_+)$, $k\in Z^+$,

$$V_1(\tau_k(x),x+I(\tau_k(x),x))\le(1+b_k)V_1(\tau_k^-(x),x), \tag{3.46}$$

where $b_k\ge 0$ *with* $\sum_{k=1}^{\infty}b_k<\infty$;

(iii) *for any solution* $x(t)=x(t,t_0,\varphi)$ *with* $t_0\in\mathbb{R}_+$, $\varphi\in PC([-r,0],\mathbb{R}^n)$,

$$\begin{aligned} V'(t,x_t(t_0,\varphi)) &\le A \quad \text{if } V(t,x_t(t_0,\varphi))\ge W_2(\|\varphi\|_r) \quad \text{for } t_0\le t\le t_0+r;\\ V'(t,x_t(t_0,\varphi)) &\le A-W_3(V(t,x_t(t_0,\varphi))) \quad \text{if } P(V(t,x_t(t_0,\varphi)))>V(s,x_s(t_0,\varphi))\\ &\qquad \text{for } t\ge t_0+r,\ t-r\le s\le t, \end{aligned} \tag{3.47}$$

where $A>0$ *is a constant,* $P(s)$ *is defined the same as in Theorem 3.1;*

then the solutions of (2.4) are uniform bounded and ultimately uniform bounded.

THEOREM 3.3. *Assume that there exist* $V(t,\phi)\in\nu_0^*(\cdot)$, $W_1,W_2\in K_1$, $W_3\in C(\mathbb{R}_+,\mathbb{R}_+)$, *and constants* $d_k,e_k\ge 0$ *with* $\sum_{k=1}^{\infty}d_k<\infty$ *and* $e=\sum_{k=1}^{\infty}e_k<\infty$ *such that*

(i)

$$W_1(\|\phi(0)\|)\le V(t,\phi)\le W_2(\|\phi\|_r); \tag{3.48}$$

(ii) *for each* $x\in\mathbb{R}^n$ *and* $\tau_k\in C^1(\mathbb{R}^n,\mathbb{R}_+)$, $k\in Z^+$,

$$V(\tau_k(x),x+I(\tau_k(x),x))\le(1+d_k)V(\tau_k^-(x),x)+e_k \tag{3.49}$$

for all $\tau_k>t_0$;

(iii) *for any solution* $x(t)=x(t,t_0,\varphi)$ *with* $t_0\in\mathbb{R}_+$, $\varphi\in PC([-r,0],\mathbb{R}^n)$,

$$D^+_{(2.4)}V(t,x_t)\le -W_3(\|\phi(0)\|); \tag{3.50}$$

then the solutions of (2.4) are uniformly bounded. If, in addition, we have $W_3\in K$, *and* $\liminf_{s\to\infty}W_3(s)>0$; $\tau_k-\tau_{k-1}>L$ *for some* $L>0$ *and for all* $k=1,2,\dots$; *and* f *maps* $\mathbb{R}_+\times$ *(bounded subsets of* $PC([-r,0],\mathbb{R}^n)$*) into bounded subsets of* $\mathbb{R}^n$*, then solutions of (2.4) are uniformly ultimately bounded.*

4. Examples

To illustrate the application of the preceding theorems we discuss the following examples.

Example 4.1. Consider the scalar equation

$$\begin{aligned} x'(t)&=A(t)x(t)+\int_{t-\tau}^{t}C(t-s)x(s)ds+f(t), \quad t\ne x(t)+k,\\ x(t_k)-x(t_k^-)&=b_kx(t_k^-), \quad t=x(t)+k,\ k\in Z^+, \end{aligned} \tag{4.1}$$

where A, C, and f are continuous functions, $|f(t)| \leq L$ for some $L > 0$. For the impulsive perturbations, we assume that $b_k \geq 0$ and $\sum_{k=1}^{\infty} b_k < \infty$. Suppose $A(t) < 0$ and

$$A(t) + M\int_0^{\tau} |C(u)|\,du \leq -\alpha, \tag{4.2}$$

where $\alpha > 0$ and $M = \prod_{k=1}^{\infty}(1+b_k)$. Let $V(t,x) = |x|$ and $q > 1$ such that

$$A(t) + Mq\int_0^{\tau} |C(u)|\,du \leq -\frac{\alpha}{2}, \tag{4.3}$$

and let $P(s) = Mqs$. Then for any solution $x(t) = x(t, t_0, \varphi)$ such that

$$P(V(t,x(t))) > V(s,x(s)) \quad \text{for } t \geq \sigma,\ t-\tau \leq s \leq t, \tag{4.4}$$

we have

$$\begin{aligned} V'(t,x(t)) &\leq A(t)|x(t)| + q\int_0^{\tau} |C(u)|\,|x(t-u)|\,du + |f(t)| \\ &\leq L - \frac{\alpha}{2}|x(t)| \leq -\frac{\alpha}{4}|x(t)| \quad \text{if } |x(t)| \geq H = \frac{4L}{\alpha}, \\ V(\tau_k, x + I(\tau_k, x)) &= |x + b_k x| = (1+b_k)V(\tau_k^-, x). \end{aligned} \tag{4.5}$$

By Theorem 3.1, we obtain uniform boundedness and ultimately uniform boundedness for (4.1).

Example 4.2. Consider the scalar impulsive delay differential equation

$$\begin{aligned} x' &= -p(t)x(t) + q(t)x(t-r) + w(t), \quad t \neq x^3(t) + 2k, \\ \Delta x(t) &= h_k x(t), \quad t = x^3(t) + 2k, \end{aligned} \tag{4.6}$$

where $r > 0$, $p, q \in \mathrm{PC}(\mathbb{R}_+, \mathbb{R})$, w is a square integrable function on $\mathbb{R}_+$ (i.e., $\int_0^{\infty} w^2(t)dt < \infty$), $h_k > 0$ for $k = 1, 2, \ldots$ and $\sum_{k=1}^{\infty} h_k < \infty$. Assume that for some $M_1 > 1/2$ and $0 < M_2 < M_1 - 1/2$, $p(t) \geq M_1$ and $|q(t)| \leq M_2$ for all $t \in \Re_+$. We will show that the conditions of Theorem 3.3 are satisfied and thereby conclude that solutions of this impulsive delay differential equation are uniformly ultimately bounded.

To begin with we note that f clearly satisfies the conditions given in Theorem 3.3: f maps $\mathbb{R}_+ \times$ (bounded subsets of $\mathrm{PC}([-r,0], \mathbb{R}^n)$) into bounded subsets of $\mathbb{R}$.

Define the Lyapunov functional V by

$$V(t,\psi) = \psi^2(0) + M_2\int_{-r}^{0} \psi^2(s)ds + \int_t^{\infty} w^2(s)ds. \tag{4.7}$$

Clearly, V satisfies condition (i) of Theorem 3.3 with $W_1(s)=s^2$ and $W_2(s)=(1+M_2r)s^2+\int_0^\infty w^2(t)dt$. Differentiating V along solutions of (4.6) gives us

$$\begin{aligned}
D^+_{(4.6)}V(t,\psi) &= 2\psi(0)[-p(t)\psi(0)+q(t)\psi(-r)+w(t)] \\
&\quad + M_2[\psi^2(0)-\psi^2(-r)]-w^2(t) \\
&\le (-2M_1+M_2)\psi^2(0)+2M_2|\psi(0)\psi(-r)| \\
&\quad + 2\psi(0)w(t)-M_2\psi^2(-r)-w^2(t) \\
&\le (-2M_1+M_2+1)\psi^2(0)+2M_2|\psi(0)\psi(-r)| \\
&\quad - M_2\psi^2(-r) \\
&\le -K\psi^2(0),
\end{aligned} \tag{4.8}$$

where $K=2M_1-2M_2-1>0$. Thus condition (iii) of Theorem 3.3 is satisfied with $W_3(s)=Ls^2$.

Finally, let us check condition (ii). If $t_0\in\mathbb{R}_+$ and $x\in PC([t_0-r,\infty),\mathbb{R})$ with discontinuities occurring only at impulse times, then

$$V(t,x_t)=x^2(t)+M_2\int_{t-r}^t x^2(s)ds+\int_t^\infty w^2(s)ds \tag{4.9}$$

is also continuous at all points except possibly impulse times. Moreover,

$$\begin{aligned}
V(\tau_k,x_{\tau_t}) &= (1+h_k)^2x^2(\tau_k)+M_2\int_{\tau_k-r}^{\tau_k}x^2(s)ds+\int_{\tau_k}^\infty w^2(s)ds \\
&\le (1+h_k)^2V(\tau_k,x_{\tau_k})=(1+d_k)V(\tau_k,x_{\tau_k}),
\end{aligned} \tag{4.10}$$

where $d_k=2h_k+h_k^2>0$. Since $\sum_{k=1}^\infty h_k<\infty$, then $\sum_{k=1}^\infty d_k<\infty$ also.

We can therefore conclude in light of Theorem 3.3 that solutions of system (4.6) are uniformly ultimately bounded. Note that in this example, the boundedness conclusion is independent of the delay term r. Also, what is interesting is that solutions are uniformly ultimately bounded despite the fact that the state x increases in magnitude at each impulse time.

Acknowledgment

This research is supported by NSERC-Canada.

References

[1] G. Ballinger and X. Liu, *Existence and uniqueness results for impulsive delay differential equations*, Dynamics of Continuous, Discrete and Impulsive Systems **5** (1999), no. 1–4, 579–591.

[2] ———, *Practical stability of impulsive delay differential equations and applications to control problems*, Optimization Methods and Applications, Appl. Optim., vol. 52, Kluwer Academic, Dordrecht, 2001, pp. 3–21.

[3] S. V. Krishna, J. Vasundhara Devi, and K. Satyavani, *Boundedness and dichotomies for impulse equations*, Journal of Mathematical Analysis and Applications **158** (1991), no. 2, 352–375.

[4] X. Liu and G. Ballinger, *Existence and continuability of solutions for differential equations with delays and state-dependent impulses*, Nonlinear Analysis **51** (2002), no. 4, 633–647.
[5] ———, *Boundedness for impulsive delay differential equations and applications to population growth models*, Nonlinear Analysis **53** (2003), no. 7-8, 1041–1062.
[6] X. Liu and Q. Wang, *Stability of nontrivial solution of delay differential equations with state-dependent impulses*, Applied Mathematics and Computation **174** (2006), 271–288.
[7] I. M. Stamova and G. T. Stamov, *Lyapunov-Razumikhin method for impulsive functional differential equations and applications to the population dynamics*, Journal of Computational and Applied Mathematics **130** (2001), no. 1-2, 163–171.

Xinzhi Liu: Department of Applied Mathematics, University of Waterloo, Waterloo, ON, Canada N2L 3G1
E-mail address: xzliu@math.uwaterloo.ca

Qing Wang: Department of Applied Mathematics, University of Waterloo, Waterloo, ON, Canada N2L 3G1
E-mail address: q7wang@math.uwaterloo.ca

MIXED RATIONAL-SOLITON SOLUTIONS TO THE TODA LATTICE EQUATION

WEN-XIU MA

We present a way to solve the Toda lattice equation using the Casoratian technique, and construct its mixed rational-soliton solutions. Examples of the resulting exact solutions are computed and plotted.

1. Introduction

Differential and/or difference equations serve as mathematical models for various phenomena in the real world. The study of differential and/or difference equations enhances our understanding of the phenomena they describe. One of important fundamental questions in the subject is how to solve differential and/or difference equations.

There are mathematical theories on existence and representations of solutions of linear differential and/or difference equations, especially constant-coefficient ones. Soliton theory opens the way to studies of nonlinear differential and/or difference equations. There are different solution methods for different situations in soliton theory, for example, the inverse scattering transforms for the Cauchy problems, Bäcklund transformations for geometrical equations, Darboux transformations for compatibility equations of spectral problems, Hirota direct method for bilinear equations, and truncated series expansion methods (including Painlevé series, and sech and tanh function expansion methods) for Riccati-type equations.

Among the existing methods in soliton theory, Hirota bilinear forms are one of the most powerful tools for solving soliton equations, a kind of nonlinear differential and/or difference equations. In this paper, we would like to construct mixed rational-soliton solutions to the Toda lattice equation:

$$\dot{a}_n = a_n(b_{n-1} - b_n), \qquad \dot{b}_n = a_n - a_{n+1}, \tag{1.1}$$

where $\dot{a}_n = da_n/dt$ and $\dot{b}_n = db_n/dt$. The approach we will adopt to solve this equation is the Casoratian technique. Its key is to transform bilinear forms into linear systems

Hindawi Publishing Corporation
Proceedings of the Conference on Differential & Difference Equations and Applications, pp. 711–720

of solvable differential-difference equations. For the Toda lattice equation (1.1), we will present the general solutions to the corresponding linear systems and further generate mixed rational-soliton solutions.

2. Constructing solutions using the Casoratian technique

Let us start from the Toda bilinear form. Under the transformation

$$a_n = 1 + \frac{d^2}{dt^2}\log\tau_n = \frac{\tau_{n+1}\tau_{n-1}}{\tau_n^2}, \qquad b_n = \frac{d}{dt}\log\frac{\tau_n}{\tau_{n+1}} = \frac{\dot{\tau}_n\tau_{n+1} - \tau_n\dot{\tau}_{n+1}}{\tau_n\tau_{n+1}}, \tag{2.1}$$

the Toda lattice equation (1.1) becomes

$$\left[D_t^2 - 4\sinh^2\left(\frac{D_n}{2}\right)\right]\tau_n \cdot \tau_n = 0, \tag{2.2}$$

where D_t and D_n are Hirota's operators. That is,

$$\ddot{\tau}_n\tau_n - (\dot{\tau}_n)^2 - \tau_{n+1}\tau_{n-1} + \tau_n^2 = 0. \tag{2.3}$$

In the Casoratian formulation, we use the Casorati determinant

$$\tau_n = \operatorname{Cas}(\phi_1, \phi_2, \ldots, \phi_N) = \begin{vmatrix} \phi_1(n) & \phi_1(n+1) & \cdots & \phi_1(n+N-1) \\ \phi_2(n) & \phi_2(n+1) & \cdots & \phi_2(n+N-1) \\ \vdots & \vdots & \ddots & \vdots \\ \phi_N(n) & \phi_N(n+1) & \cdots & \phi_N(n+N-1) \end{vmatrix} \tag{2.4}$$

to construct exact solutions, and we call such solutions Casoratian solutions. It is known [7] that such a τ-function τ_n solves the bilinear Toda lattice equation (2.3) if

$$\phi_i(n+1) + \phi_i(n-1) = 2\varepsilon_i(\cosh\alpha_i)\phi_i(n), \qquad (\phi_i(n))_t = \phi_i(n+1), \tag{2.5}$$

where $\varepsilon_i = \pm 1$, α_i are nonzero constants and $(\phi_i(n))_t = \partial_t\phi_i(n) = \partial_t\phi_i(n,t)$. The resulting solutions are negatons, that is, a kind of solutions only involving exponential functions of the space variable n.

There are other type solutions such as rational solutions [3], positons [5, 8], and complexitons [2]. Similar to [2, 3], we can prove that τ_n is a solution to the bilinear Toda lattice equation (2.3) if

$$\phi_i(n+1) + \phi_i(n-1) = \sum_{j=1}^{N}\lambda_{ij}\phi_j(n), \qquad (\phi_i(n))_t = \zeta\phi_i(n+\delta), \tag{2.6}$$

where $\zeta = \pm 1$, $\delta = \pm 1$ (i.e., $|\zeta| = |\delta| = 1$, $\zeta, \delta \in \mathbb{R}$), and λ_{ij} are arbitrary constants. Under the transformation $t \to -t$, the bilinear Toda lattice equation (2.3) is invariant, and $(\phi_i(n))_t = \phi_i(n+\delta)$ becomes $(\phi_i(n))_t = -\phi_i(n+\delta)$. Therefore, we only need to consider one of the cases $\zeta = \pm 1$ while constructing solutions, since the replacement of t with $-t$ generates solutions from one case to the other. We will only consider the case of $\zeta = 1$ below.

Let us now begin to analyze the system of differential-difference equations (2.6) with $\zeta = 1$. The corresponding system can be compactly written as

$$\Phi_N(n+1,t) + \Phi_N(n-1,t) = \Lambda\Phi_N(n,t), \qquad (\Phi_N(n,t))_t = \Phi_N(n+\delta,t), \tag{2.7}$$

where $\Phi_N = \Phi_N(n,t) := (\phi_1(n,t),\ldots,\phi_N(n,t))^T$ and $\Lambda := (\lambda_{ij})_{N\times N}$. Note that a constant similar transformation for the coefficient matrix Λ does not change the resulting Casoratian solution. Actually, if we have $M = P^{-1}\Lambda P$ for an invertible constant matrix P, then $\widetilde{\Phi}_N = P\Phi_N$ satisfies

$$\widetilde{\Phi}_N(n+1,t) + \widetilde{\Phi}_N(n-1,t) = M\widetilde{\Phi}_N(n,t), \qquad (\widetilde{\Phi}_N(n,t))_t = \widetilde{\Phi}_N(n+\delta,t). \tag{2.8}$$

Obviously, the Casorati determinants generated from Φ_N and $\widetilde{\Phi}_N$ have just a constant-factor difference, and thus the transformation (2.1) leads to the same Casoratian solutions from Φ_N and $\widetilde{\Phi}_N$. Therefore, as in the KdV case [4], we can focus on the following two types of Jordan blocks of Λ:

$$\begin{bmatrix} \lambda_i & & & 0 \\ 1 & \lambda_i & & \\ \vdots & \ddots & \ddots & \\ 0 & \cdots & 1 & \lambda_i \end{bmatrix}_{k_i\times k_i}, \qquad \begin{bmatrix} A_i & & & 0 \\ I_2 & A_i & & \\ \vdots & \ddots & \ddots & \\ 0 & \cdots & I_2 & A_i \end{bmatrix}_{l_i\times l_i}, \qquad A_i = \begin{bmatrix} \alpha_i & -\beta_i \\ \beta_i & \alpha_i \end{bmatrix}, \tag{2.9}$$

where λ_i, α_i and $\beta_i > 0$ are all real constants, I_2 is the identity matrix of order 2, and k_i and l_i are positive integers. A Jordan block of the first type has the real eigenvalue λ_i with algebraic multiplicity k_i, and a Jordan block of the second type has the pair of complex eigenvalues $\lambda_{i,\pm} = \alpha_i \pm \beta_i\sqrt{-1}$ with algebraic multiplicity l_i.

Case $k_i = 1$ of type 1. The representative systems read as follows:

$$\phi_i(n+1) + \phi_i(n-1) = \lambda_i\phi_i(n), \qquad (\phi_i(n))_t = \phi_i(n+\delta), \tag{2.10}$$

where $\delta = \pm 1$ and $\lambda_i =$ consts. Their eigenfunctions are classified as

$$\begin{aligned} &\phi_i = C_{1i}\varepsilon_i^n e^{\varepsilon_i t} + C_{2i}(n+\varepsilon_i\delta t)\varepsilon_i^n e^{\varepsilon_i t}, \quad \lambda_i = 2\varepsilon_i, \quad \varepsilon_i = \pm 1, \\ &\phi_i = C_{1i}e^{t\cos\alpha_i}\cos(\alpha_i n + \delta t\sin\alpha_i) \\ &\quad + C_{2i}e^{t\cos\alpha_i}\sin(\alpha_i n + \delta t\sin\alpha_i), \quad \lambda_i = 2\cos\alpha_i, \quad \alpha_i \neq m\pi,\ m\in\mathbb{Z}, \\ &\phi_i = C_{1i}\varepsilon_i^n e^{\alpha_i n + \varepsilon_i t e^{\delta\alpha_i}} + C_{2i}\varepsilon_i^n e^{-\alpha_i n + \varepsilon_i t e^{-\delta\alpha_i}}, \quad \lambda_i = 2\varepsilon_i\cosh\alpha_i, \quad \alpha_i \neq 0, \end{aligned} \tag{2.11}$$

where C_{1i} and C_{2i} are arbitrary constants. The above three sets of eigenfunctions generate rational solutions, positon solutions, and negaton solutions, respectively.

Generally, the following two results provide ways to solve the linear system (2.6). The detailed proof will be published elsewhere.

THEOREM 2.1 ($\lambda_i = \pm 2$). *Let* $\varepsilon = \pm 1$ *and* $\delta = \pm 1$ *(i.e.,* $|\varepsilon| = |\delta| = 1$, $\varepsilon, \delta \in \mathbb{R}$*). If* $(f(n,t))_t = f(n+\delta, t)$*, then the nonhomogeneous system*

$$\phi(n+1,t)+\phi(n-1,t) = 2\varepsilon\phi(n,t)+f(n,t), \qquad (\phi(n,t))_t = \phi(n+\delta,t), \tag{2.12}$$

has the general solution

$$\phi(n,t) = \left[\alpha(n)t+\beta(n)+\int_0^t\int_0^s f(n+\delta,r)e^{-\varepsilon r}\,dr\,ds\right]e^{\varepsilon t}, \tag{2.13}$$

where $\alpha(n)$ *and* $\beta(n)$ *are determined by*

$$\alpha(n+\delta)-\varepsilon\alpha(n) = f(n+\delta,0), \qquad \beta(n+\delta)-\varepsilon\beta(n) = \alpha(n). \tag{2.14}$$

THEOREM 2.2 ($\lambda_i \neq \pm 2$). *Let* $\lambda \neq \pm 2$ *and* $\delta = \pm 1$.

(a) *The homogeneous system*

$$\phi(n+1,t)+\phi(n-1,t) = \lambda\phi(n,t), \qquad (\phi(n,t))_t = \phi(n+\delta,t), \tag{2.15}$$

has its general solution

$$\phi(\lambda;c,d)(n) = c\omega^n e^{t\omega^\delta}+d\omega^{-n}e^{t\omega^{-\delta}}, \tag{2.16}$$

where c and d are arbitrary constants, and

$$\lambda = \omega+\omega^{-1}, \tag{2.17}$$

that is,

$$\omega^2-\lambda\omega+1 = 0. \tag{2.18}$$

(b) *Define* $f_k = \phi(\lambda_i;c_k,d_k)$, $1 \leq k \leq k_i$, *where* c_k *and* d_k *are arbitrary constants. The nonhomogeneous system*

$$\phi_k(n+1,t)+\phi_k(n-1,t) = \lambda_i\phi_k(n,t)+\phi_{k-1}(n,t), \qquad (\phi_k(n,t))_t = \phi_k(n+\delta,t), \tag{2.19}$$

where $1 \leq k \leq k_i$ *and* $\phi_0 = 0$*, has its general solution*

$$\phi_k = \sum_{p=0}^{k-1}\frac{1}{p!}\frac{\partial^p f_{k-p}}{\partial\lambda_i^p} = \sum_{p=0}^{k-1}\frac{1}{p!}\frac{\partial^p\phi(\lambda_i;c_{k-p},d_{k-p})}{\partial\lambda_i^p}, \quad 1 \leq k \leq k_i. \tag{2.20}$$

Remark 2.3. The soliton case of $\lambda_i = 2\cosh\alpha_i$ ($\alpha_i \neq 0$) corresponds to $\omega_i = e^{\alpha_i}$ in (a). The nonhomogeneous system in (b) is associated with one Jordan block of type 1.

Begin with

$$\Lambda = \begin{bmatrix} 2\varepsilon & & & 0 \\ * & 2\varepsilon & & \\ \vdots & \ddots & \ddots & \\ * & \cdots & * & 2\varepsilon \end{bmatrix}_{k_i\times k_i}, \quad *\text{-arbitrary consts.}, \tag{2.21}$$

where $\varepsilon = \pm 1$. By the general solution formula in Theorem 2.1, we can have

$$\phi_i(n,t) = \varepsilon^n e^{\varepsilon t} \psi_i(n,t), \quad 1 \le i \le N, \tag{2.22}$$

where $\psi_i(n,t)$ are polynomials in n and t. Thus,

$$\tau_n = \mathrm{Cas}\,(\psi_1,\ldots,\psi_N) \tag{2.23}$$

presents polynomial solutions to the bilinear Toda lattice equation (2.3) and thus rational solutions to the Toda lattice equation (1.1) through (2.1).

THEOREM 2.4. *The Jordan block of type 1 with $\lambda_i = \pm 2$ leads to rational solutions to the Toda lattice equation (1.1).*

This adds one case of $\lambda = -2$ to the result in [3]. A few examples of rational solutions associated with one Jordan block case with $\lambda = 2$ were presented in [3].

3. Mixed rational-soliton solutions

Let us now show a way to construct mixed rational-soliton solutions. We use the following procedure.

Step 1. Solve the triangular systems whose coefficient matrices possess Jordan blocks of type 1 with $\lambda_i = \pm 2$ or $\lambda_i = 2\cosh\alpha_i$ ($\alpha_i \neq 0$) to form a set of eigenfunctions $(\phi_1,\ldots,\phi_N)$.

Step 2. Evaluate the τ-function $\tau_n = \mathrm{Cas}(\phi_1,\ldots,\phi_N)$.

Step 3. Evaluate a_n and b_n by the transformation (2.1), to obtain mixed rational-soliton solutions to the Toda lattice equation (1.1).

The τ-functions generated above are quite general. In what follows, we would like to present two sets of special eigenfunctions required in forming such τ-functions.

Special eigenfunctions yielding rational solutions. We take two specific Taylor expansions as in [9]:

$$\begin{aligned}\phi_+(n,t) &= e^{kn+te^k} + e^{-kn+te^{-k}} = \sum_{i=0}^{\infty} a_{i+1}(n,t)k^{2i},\\ \phi_-(n,t) &= e^{kn+te^k} - e^{-kn+te^{-k}} = \sum_{i=0}^{\infty} a_{i+1}(n,t)k^{2i+1},\end{aligned} \tag{3.1}$$

the coefficients of which satisfy

$$a_i(n+1,t) + a_i(n-1,t) = \sum_{j=0}^{i} \frac{2}{(2j)!} a_{i-j+1}(n,t), \qquad (a_i(n,t))_t = a_i(n+1,t), \tag{3.2}$$

where $i \ge 1$. These two sets of functions are given by

$$a_{i+1}(n,t) = e^t \sum_{j=0}^{2i} \frac{2n^{2i-j}}{(2i-j)!}\beta_j(t), \qquad a_{i+1}(n,t) = e^t \sum_{j=0}^{2i+1} \frac{2n^{2i+1-j}}{(2i+1-j)!}\beta_j(t), \tag{3.3}$$

respectively. The functions $\beta_j(t)$ above are defined by

$$\sum_{j=0}^{\infty}\beta_j(t)k^j=\sum_{p=0}^{\infty}\frac{t^p}{p!}\left(\sum_{q=1}^{\infty}\frac{1}{q!}k^q\right)^p. \tag{3.4}$$

This is a rational solution case, since $\lambda_{ii}=2$, $1\le i\le N$.

Special eigenfunctions yielding solitons. We start from the same eigenfunctions

$$\begin{aligned}\phi_+(n,t)&=\mathrm{e}^{kn+te^k}+\mathrm{e}^{-kn+te^{-k}}=2\mathrm{e}^{t\cosh k}\cosh(kn+t\sinh k),\\ \phi_-(n,t)&=\mathrm{e}^{kn+te^k}-\mathrm{e}^{-kn+te^{-k}}=2\mathrm{e}^{t\sinh k}\cosh(kn+t\sinh k),\end{aligned} \tag{3.5}$$

which solve

$$\phi(n+1,t)+\phi(n-1,t)=2(\cosh k)\phi(n,t),\qquad (\phi(n,t))_t=\phi(n+\delta,t). \tag{3.6}$$

Computing derivatives of the above system with the parameter k leads to a set of eigenfunctions as follows:

$$b_i(n,t)=\partial_k^{i-1}\phi(n,t),\quad 1\le i\le N, \tag{3.7}$$

which satisfies

$$b_i(n+1,t)+b_i(n-1,t)=\sum_{j=1}^{i}\lambda_{ij}b_j(n,t),\qquad (b_i(n,t))_t=b_i(n+\delta,t), \tag{3.8}$$

where $1\le i\le N$ and $\lambda_{ij}=2\binom{i-1}{j-1}(\partial_k^{i-j}\cosh k)$. This is a soliton case if $k\ne 0$, since $\lambda_{ii}=2\cosh k$, $1\le i\le N$.

Examples of mixed rational-soliton solutions. Mixed rational-soliton solutions can now be computed, for example, by

$$\tau_n=\mathrm{Cas}\,(\mathrm{e}^{\pm t}a_1,\dots,\mathrm{e}^{\pm t}a_p,b_1,\dots,b_{N-p}). \tag{3.9}$$

In particular (in the case of ϕ_+), we have

$$\begin{aligned}\tau_n&=\mathrm{Cas}\,(\mathrm{e}^{-t}a_1,b_1)=4\mathrm{e}^{t\cosh k}\{\cosh[k(n+1)+t\sinh k]-\cosh(kn+t\sinh k)\},\\ \tau_n&=\mathrm{Cas}\,(\mathrm{e}^{-t}a_1,\mathrm{e}^{-t}a_2,b_1)\\ &=4\mathrm{e}^{t\cosh k}\{2(n+t+1)\cosh[k(n+2)+t\sinh k]\\ &\qquad-4(2n+2t+1)\cosh[k(n+1)+t\sinh k]\\ &\qquad+(2n+2t+3)\cosh(kn+t\sinh k)\}.\end{aligned} \tag{3.10}$$

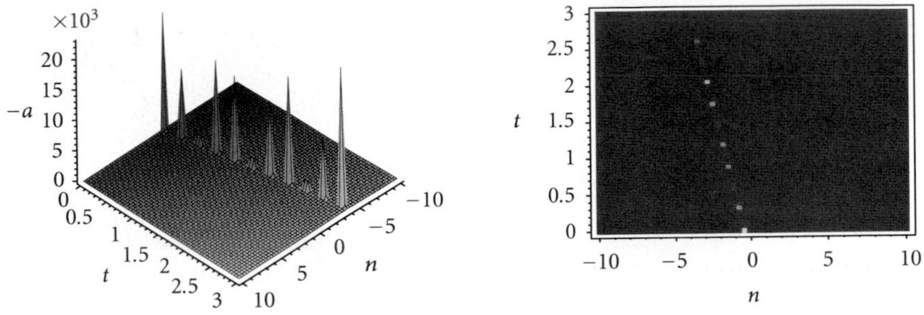

(a) (b)

Figure 3.1. 3D and density plots of a_n.

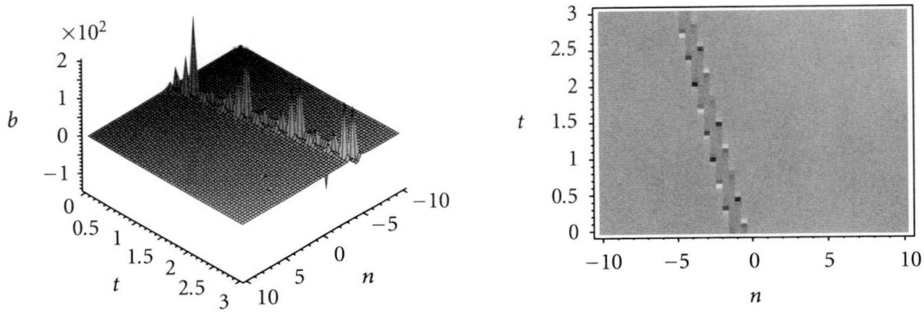

(a) (b)

Figure 3.2. 3D and density plots of b_n.

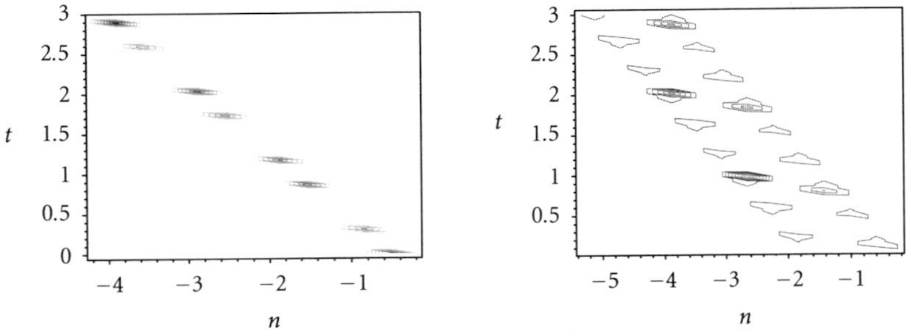

(a) (b)

Figure 3.3. Contour plots of (a) a_n and (b) b_n.

The solution from $\tau_n = \mathrm{Cas}(\mathrm{e}^{-t}a_1, b_1)$ with $k = 1$ is depicted in Figures 3.1, 3.2, and 3.3, and the solution from $\tau_n = \mathrm{Cas}(\mathrm{e}^{-t}a_1, \mathrm{e}^{-t}a_2, b_1)$ with $k = -1$ in Figures 3.4, 3.5, and 3.6.

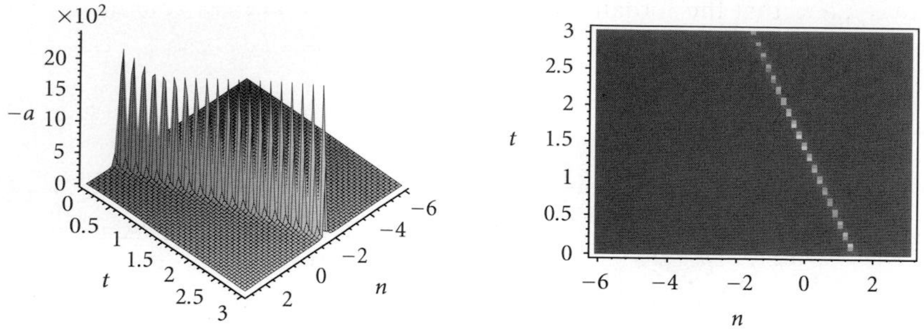

(a) (b)

Figure 3.4. 3D and density plots of a_n.

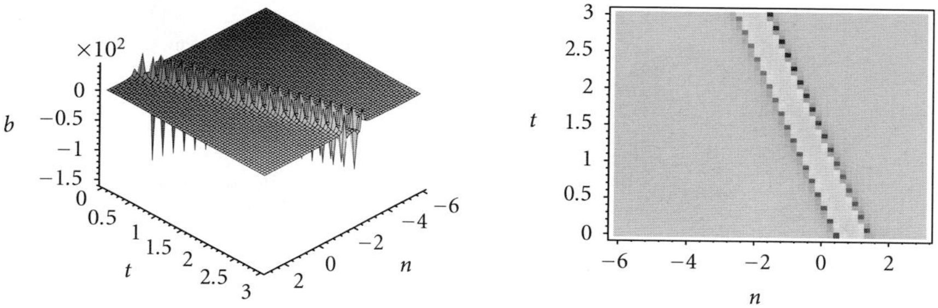

(a) (b)

Figure 3.5. 3D and density plots of b_n.

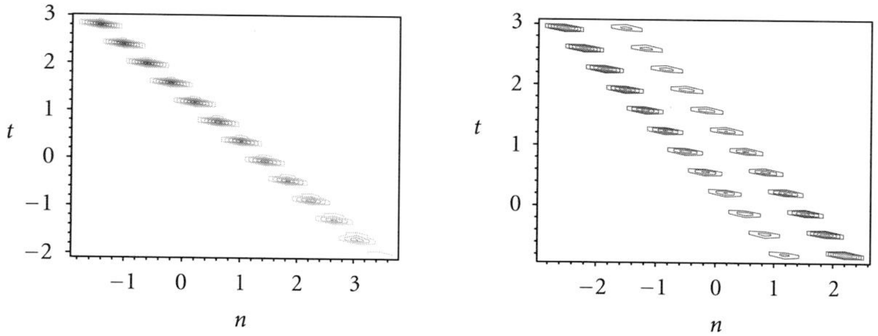

(a) (b)

Figure 3.6. Contour plots of (a) a_n and (b) b_n.

4. Discussions

A careful analysis based on Theorems 2.1 and 2.2 can prove that the Jordan blocks of type 1 with $\lambda_i = \pm 2$, $|\lambda_i| > 2$, and $|\lambda_i| < 2$ generate rational solutions, negatons, and positons, respectively; and that the Jordan blocks of type 2, which possess complex eigenvalues, generate complexitons. Moreover, we can have another case of conditions on eigenfunctions:

$$\begin{aligned} \phi_i(n+1)+\phi_i(n-1) &= \sum_{j=1}^{N} \lambda_{ij}\phi_j(n), \\ (\phi_i(n,t))_t &= \frac{1}{2}\zeta(\phi_i(n+1,t)-\phi_i(n-1,t)), \end{aligned} \tag{4.1}$$

where $\zeta = \pm 1$ and λ_{ij} are arbitrary constants. An analysis is left for future publication, on this case of conditions and its representative system

$$\begin{aligned} \phi(n+1,t)+\phi(n-1,t) &= \lambda\phi(n,t)+f(n,t), \\ (\phi(n,t))_t &= \frac{1}{2}\phi(n+1,t)-\frac{1}{2}\phi(n-1,t), \end{aligned} \tag{4.2}$$

where $(f(n,t))_t = 1/2f(n+1,t)-(1/2)f(n-1,t)$, which will lead to different mixed rational-soliton solutions to the Toda lattice equation (1.1).

The above construction of mixed rational-soliton solutions is direct and much easier than the existing approach by computing long-wave limits of soliton solutions [1, 6]. The basic idea can also be applied to other integrable lattice equations, for example, the Volterra lattice equation:

$$\dot{u}_n = u_n(u_{n+1}-u_{n-1}). \tag{4.3}$$

The transformation of $u_n = \tau_{n+2}\tau_{n-1}/\tau_{n+1}\tau_n$ puts the Volterra lattice equation into the following bilinear form:

$$\dot{\tau}_{n+1}\tau_n - \tau_{n+1}\dot{\tau}_n - \tau_{n+2}\tau_{n-1} + \tau_{n+1}\tau_n = 0. \tag{4.4}$$

The Casorati determinant $\tau_n = \mathrm{Cas}(\phi_1,\ldots,\phi_N)$ solves this equation if

$$\phi_i(n+1,t)+\phi_i(n-1,t) = \sum_{j=1}^{N} \lambda_{ij}\phi_j(n,t), \qquad (\phi_i(n,t))_t = \phi_i(n+2,t), \tag{4.5}$$

where $1 \le i \le N$ and λ_{ij} are arbitrary constants. Therefore, this allows us to construct Casoratian solutions to the Volterra lattice equation in a simple and direct way. The details of constructing Casoratian solutions will be published elsewhere.

Acknowledgment

The author would like to thank Professors K. Maruno and Y. You for stimulating discussions.

References

[1] A. S. Cârstea and D. Grecu, *On a class of rational and mixed soliton-rational solutions of the Toda lattice*, Progress of Theoretical Physics **96** (1996), no. 1, 29–36.

[2] W. X. Ma and K.-I. Maruno, *Complexiton solutions of the Toda lattice equation*, Physica A **343** (2004), no. 1–4, 219–237.

[3] W. X. Ma and Y. You, *Rational solutions of the Toda lattice equation in Casoratian form*, Chaos, Solitons & Fractals **22** (2004), no. 2, 395–406.

[4] ———, *Solving the Korteweg-de Vries equation by its bilinear form: Wronskian solutions*, Transactions of the American Mathematical Society **357** (2005), no. 5, 1753–1778.

[5] K. Maruno, W. X. Ma, and M. Oikawa, *Generalized Casorati determinant and positon-negaton-type solutions of the Toda lattice equation*, Journal of the Physical Society of Japan **73** (2004), 831–837.

[6] K. Narita, *Solutions for the Mikhailov-Shabat-Yamilov difference-differential equations and generalized solutions for the Volterra and the Toda lattice equations*, Progress of Theoretical Physics **99** (1998), no. 3, 337–348.

[7] J. J. C. Nimmo, *Soliton solution of three differential-difference equations in Wronskian form*, Physics Letters. A **99** (1983), no. 6-7, 281–286.

[8] A. A. Stahlhofen and V. B. Matveev, *Positons for the Toda lattice and related spectral problems*, Journal of Physics. A. Mathematical and General **28** (1995), no. 7, 1957–1965.

[9] H. Wu and D.-J. Zhang, *Mixed rational-soliton solutions of two differential-difference equations in Casorati determinant form*, Journal of Physics. A. Mathematical and General **36** (2003), no. 17, 4867–4873.

Wen-Xiu Ma: Department of Mathematics, University of South Florida, Tampa, FL 33620, USA
E-mail address: mawx@cas.usf.edu

MODELLING THE EFFECT OF SURGICAL STRESS AND BACTERIAL GROWTH IN HUMAN CORNEA

D. ROY MAHAPATRA AND R. V. N. MELNIK

This paper reports a mathematical model and finite-element simulation of the dynamic piezoelectricity in human cornea including the effect of dehydration and stress generated due to incision and bacterial growth. A constitutive model is proposed for the numerical characterization of cornea based on the available experimental data. The constitutive model is then employed to derive the conservation law for the dynamic piezoelectricity supplemented by the time-dependent equation for the electromagnetic field. The resulting system of partial differential equations is solved numerically with finite-element methodology. Numerical results presented here demonstrate promising applications of the developed model in aiding refractive surgery and a better understanding of regenerative processes in cornea.

1. Introduction

Cornea is one of the most delicate and active tissue systems in human and several other species. Any major change in the equilibrium stress in the sclera and cornea due to incision, excessive swelling, and bacterial growth can cause deterioration of the refractive performance of the cornea. Cornea consists of a complex architecture of the collagen fibrils dispersed in the matrix containing proteoglycans. The anisotropic structure of this composite system is distributed over the stromal layer. Computer models for surgical aid in the past had been developed, these models neglected the effect of complex tissue architecture and the resulting constitutive behavior in the long-term tissue remodelling. The role of these factors in context of surgical procedures has been brought into focus only recently and mathematical model has been proposed (see [6]).

Apart from the collagen orientation-dependent anisotropy in cornea, it may be noted that the dynamic nature of the refractive property, which is very little understood in the case of cornea as compared to the sclera, is dependent on the electrical permittivity,

Hindawi Publishing Corporation
Proceedings of the Conference on Differential & Difference Equations and Applications, pp. 721–731

magnetic permeability, and the piezoelectric constants of the cell-matrix composition. Complication arises because of the piezoelectricity of collagen tissue. Mechanics of collagen tissue in corneal fibroblast has been studied extensively by several researchers. Petroll et al. [5] studied the correlation between the movement of cell-matrix adhesion sites and the force generation in corneal fibroblasts. A detailed discussion of the mechanism of cell-regulated collagen tissue remodelling in stromal fibroblasts can be found in the work of Girard et al. [3]. The experimental studies indicate a strong influence of stress-induced charge transport on the site-specific remodelling of the collagen structure in cornea. The resulting piezoelectricity is due to anisotropy of the collagen lattice [2, 8]. In cornea, stroma is the basic collagen fibril structure over which the extrafibrilar matrix is found with significant anisotropy. The cell-matrix adhesion is mainly controlled by the cross-linking agent (proteoglycans) which are negatively charged. The complex structure transforms or breaks down due to change in the concentration of H_2O. Thus, the state of hydration and the anisotropy of collagen fibrils are two interlinked and important factors that affect the piezoelectric property and hence the long-term tissue remodelling in cornea under various environmental and surgical conditions. As a fundamental cause of piezoelectricity, the structural transformation in collagen during dehydration was reported by Pratzl and Daxer [7]. Although mathematical models for characterizing the collagen structure, as observed in the X-ray diffraction results, have been reported recently by Pinsky et al. [6], not many mathematical modelling studies are found in the literature which can be applied to characterize the influence of piezoelectricity on the delicate *dynamic* activity in cornea. Furthermore, it is highly desirable to incorporate the residual stress generation into new mathematical models when analyzing the bacterial growth-induced effects on the cornea.

Experimental studies of the influence of the directional effect of the collagen structure in human cornea have been carried out in the work of Jayasuriya et al. [4]. These studies show a significant influence of the orientation of the collagen fibers on the stiffness and the piezoelectric coefficients of the cell-matrix composition. Furthermore, the stiffness increases and the piezoelectric constants decrease as functions of the dehydration over time. Although the related experimental investigations involve specially prepared laboratory samples, in which the mechanical states of stress and deformation are already changed compared to that in living cornea, they essentially describe the long-term behavior of the mechanical and piezoelectric properties. Also, the anisotropic collagen structure in three dimensions is difficult to characterize experimentally and one can obtain only the correlated response using optical and X-ray measurements. Because of the above complexities, in order to provide a detailed characterization of the collagen structure and the resulting piezoelectricity, one requires comprehensive mathematical models that incorporate the important effects such as the anisotropy, the dehydration, and the small-scale dynamics of the cell-matrix adhesion.

In the present paper, we develop a mathematical model for the dynamic piezoelectricity of the corneal membrane and analyze the electric polarization of the composition due to circumferential stresses produced by bacterial growth or incision. The experimentally measured mechanical and piezoelectric properties reported in the work of Jayasuriya et al. [4] are used to construct the constitutive model. A mechanism of long-term

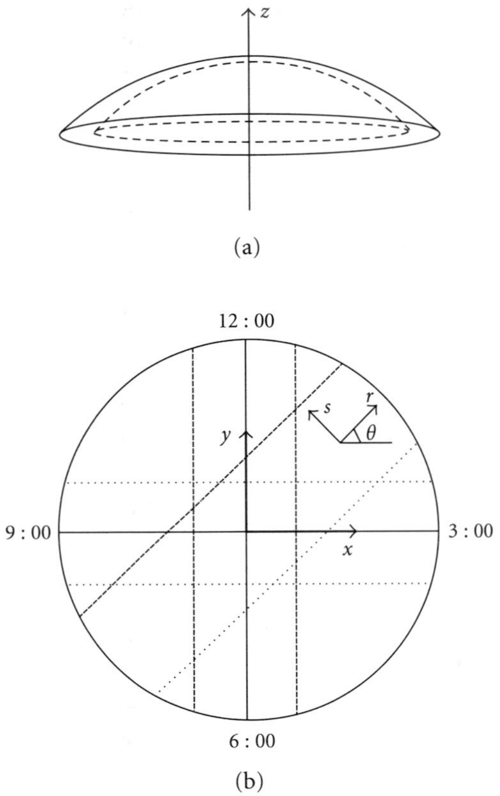

Figure 2.1. Schematic representation of (a) cornea model geometry and (b) angular orientation of the samples used in measuring the directional properties.

dehydration based on the experimental observations is included in the model. Coupling between the elastodynamics and the electromagnetics is dealt with in a systematic manner. A phenomenological approach to introduce the bacterial and antibiotic stress is discussed. Numerical results on the effect of circumferential stress is reported.

2. Constitutive model

Electromechanical characterization of the cornea tissue properties generally involves static and dynamic testing of samples with controlled state of dehydration and different cut angles (θ) from the cornea as schematically shown in Figure 2.1. In the published literature, some results on the corneal tissue invasive measurements are available, for example [4]. Such measurements are made by taking into consideration the effect of the cut angle θ on the anisotropic constitutive relation. They provide further insight into orthotropic properties (stiffness and piezoelectric constants) in the plane (x, y) assuming "no out-of-the-plane curvature." However, the collagen structure in various layers in the stroma and the type of anisotropy of the extrafibrilar structure are different. An experimental electromechanical characterization of these differences would involve multiaxially controlled measurements which are not available at present in the published literature. Also, the site-dependence of the piezoelectric properties is most likely influenced by the presence of fibroblasts and cell-regulated processes. This would make the constitutive model dependent on the high-angle X-ray data (see discussions in [6]) that reveals the structural details as some function of (x,y,z), $z \in [h_i, h_0]$, where h_i and h_0 stand for the inner and the outer surfaces, respectively. However, at present, due to the lack of experimental data, we have not included such details in the developed mathematical model. Another important aspect is the variation of the electromechanical properties as functions of dehydration over time. In our proposed constitutive model, we introduce these details at the extent available from experimental observations.

Here, we first introduce a general mathematical setting for our problem. First we define the Cartesian components of stress ($\boldsymbol{\sigma}$), strain ($\boldsymbol{\varepsilon}$), electric charge displacement ($\boldsymbol{D}$), electric field intensity ($\boldsymbol{E}$), magnetic flux ($\boldsymbol{B}$), and the magnetic field intensity ($\boldsymbol{H}$) in (x,y,z). The general objective is to construct a constitutive model

$$\boldsymbol{\sigma} = \boldsymbol{c}\boldsymbol{\varepsilon} - \boldsymbol{\sigma}_p(\boldsymbol{E}), \tag{2.1a}$$

$$\boldsymbol{D} = \boldsymbol{\epsilon}\boldsymbol{E} + \boldsymbol{P}(\boldsymbol{\varepsilon}), \tag{2.1b}$$

$$\boldsymbol{B} = \boldsymbol{\mu}\boldsymbol{H} + \mu_0\boldsymbol{M}(\boldsymbol{\varepsilon}), \tag{2.1c}$$

where $\boldsymbol{c}$ is the stiffness, $\boldsymbol{\sigma}_p$ is the electric polarization induced stress, $\boldsymbol{\epsilon}$ is the dielectric permittivity, $\boldsymbol{P}$ is the electrical polarization vector due to transformation and deformation of the macromolecular structure, $\boldsymbol{\mu}$ is the magnetic permeability, and $\boldsymbol{M}$ is the magnetic polarization vector due to molecular spin. Splitting the total charge density ρ_{total} and the total conduction current $\boldsymbol{J}_{\text{total}}$ as

$$\rho_{\text{total}} = \rho_c + \rho_p, \qquad \boldsymbol{J}_{\text{total}} = \boldsymbol{J} + \boldsymbol{J}_p + \boldsymbol{J}_m, \tag{2.2}$$

where ρ_c is the true charge density, ρ_p is the bound charge density, $\boldsymbol{J}$ is the true conduction current, $\boldsymbol{J}_p$ is the conduction current due to bound charge, $\boldsymbol{J}_m$ is the molecular current density, we have the local conservation laws:

$$\nabla \cdot \boldsymbol{P} = -\rho_p, \qquad \nabla \times \boldsymbol{M} = \boldsymbol{J}_m, \tag{2.3}$$

and the local continuity condition

$$\nabla \cdot \boldsymbol{J}_p = -\dot{\rho}_p. \tag{2.4}$$

In order to characterize the constitutive mechanism that is likely to influence the refractive property most significantly, we consider the horizontal ($\theta = 0$), the vertical ($\theta = 90°$), and the diagonal ($\theta = 45°$) cuts as discussed in [4]. Dynamics of the horizontal cut sample involves (σ_{xx}, E_z) so that the longitudinal stiffness is obtained as

$$c_{11} = c_{11}^0 e^{t/\tau_1}, \qquad \tau_1 > 0, \tag{2.5a}$$

and the piezoelectric coefficient under transverse electric polarization is obtained as

$$d_{31} = d_{31}^0 e^{t/\tau_1'}, \quad \tau_1' > 0, \tag{2.5b}$$

where the superscript 0 indicates the corresponding quantities at some initial state at time ($t = t_0$) and τ_n, τ_n' (with $n = 1,2,\ldots$) are the time constants that are estimated from the time-resolved measurements of the corresponding quantities. Similarly, for the vertical cut, which involves (σ_{yy}, E_z), one can write

$$c_{22} = c_{22}^0 e^{t/\tau_2}, \quad \tau_2 > 0, \tag{2.6a}$$

$$d_{32} = d_{32}^0 e^{t/\tau_2'}, \quad \tau_2' > 0. \tag{2.6b}$$

With simple assumptions of aligned collagen fibers undergoing transverse electric polarization in the diagonal cut, which involves measurements in the transformed coordinate system (r,s,z) (see Figure 2.1), it is reasonable to write

$$\sigma_{rr} = c_{rr}\varepsilon_{rr} - d_{3r}E_z, \tag{2.7a}$$

$$c_{rr} = c_{rr}^0 e^{-t/\tau_3}, \quad \tau_3 > 0, \tag{2.7b}$$

$$d_{3r} = d_{3r}^0 e^{-t/\tau_3'}, \quad \tau_3' > 0, \tag{2.7c}$$

where

$$\sigma_{rr} = \sigma_{xx}\cos^2\theta + \sigma_{yy}\sin^2\theta - 2\sigma_{xy}\sin\theta\cos\theta, \tag{2.7d}$$

$$\sigma_{tt} = 0 = \sigma_{xx}\sin^2\theta - \sigma_{yy}\cos^2\theta - 2\sigma_{xy}\sin\theta\cos\theta, \tag{2.7e}$$

so that the orientation-dependent properties are obtained from experiments as

$$c_{12} = (c_{rr} - c_{11})\cot^2\theta, \qquad c_{21} = (c_{rr} - c_{22})\tan^2\theta, \tag{2.7f}$$

$$d_{36} = \frac{d_{3r} - d_{31}\cos^2\theta - d_{32}\sin^2\theta}{2\sin\theta\cos\theta}. \tag{2.7g}$$

Note that the properties estimated in this method are the effective properties of the composition. The underlying mechanism of viscopiezoelasticity may be postulated as follows. Let us consider a representative volume element (RVE) of the cell-matrix composition and assume that the volume fraction (v_h) of the fluid phase is governed by a convection-diffusion process and can be expressed as

$$v_h = v_h^0 e^{-t/\tau_0} \tag{2.8}$$

and the piezoelectricity is only due to the structural transformation of the collagen fibers. Then the true charge density can be approximated as

$$\rho_c = v_h e_h, \tag{2.9}$$

where e_h is the specific electric dipole. Equation (2.1a) takes the form

$$\boldsymbol{\sigma} = [v_h \boldsymbol{c}_h + (1 - v_h)\boldsymbol{c}_f][1 - \alpha b(t)]\boldsymbol{\varepsilon} - (1 - v_h)\boldsymbol{e}_f \boldsymbol{E}, \tag{2.10}$$

where $\boldsymbol{c}_h$ is the stiffness of the fluid phase, $\boldsymbol{c}_f$ is the stiffness of the oriented collagen fiber, $\boldsymbol{e}_f = \boldsymbol{e}$ denotes the electromechanical coupling coefficient matrix due to piezoelectricity in the collagen fibers. Here we introduce the influence of the bacterial growth in the stress generation through the bacterial concentration $b(t)$, where α denotes the volume occupied by the bacterial cells within the RVE. Equation (2.1b) takes the form

$$\boldsymbol{D} = [v_h \boldsymbol{\epsilon}_h + (1 - v_h)\boldsymbol{\epsilon}_f]\boldsymbol{E} + (1 - v_h)\boldsymbol{e}^T \boldsymbol{\varepsilon} + \epsilon_0 \boldsymbol{\chi}(\omega_j)\boldsymbol{E}, \tag{2.11}$$

where ϵ_0 is the dielectric constant of air, $\boldsymbol{\epsilon}_h$ and $\boldsymbol{\epsilon}_f$ are, respectively, the electric permittivity for fluid phase and the collagen fibers, $\boldsymbol{\chi}(\omega_j)$ is the electric susceptibility due to the potentially active macromolecules if present in the RVE with resonant frequencies ω_j. Setting $\boldsymbol{M} = 0$ in (2.1c) leads to $\boldsymbol{B} = \boldsymbol{\mu H}$. In our numerical simulation, we drop the above molecular susceptibility term due to unavailability of experimental data. To this end, we further simplify the general anisotropic nature of the constitutive model by neglecting certain elastic constants and certain electromechanical coupling terms, which gives finally the constitutive equations in the following matrix-vector form:

$$\begin{Bmatrix} \sigma_{xx} \\ \sigma_{yy} \\ \sigma_{zz} \\ \sigma_{yz} \\ \sigma_{zx} \\ \sigma_{xy} \end{Bmatrix} = \begin{bmatrix} c_{11} & c_{12} & c_{13} & 0 & 0 & c_{16} \\ c_{21} & c_{22} & c_{23} & 0 & 0 & c_{26} \\ c_{31} & c_{32} & c_{33} & 0 & 0 & c_{36} \\ 0 & 0 & 0 & c_{44} & c_{45} & 0 \\ 0 & 0 & 0 & c_{54} & c_{55} & 0 \\ c_{16} & c_{26} & c_{36} & 0 & 0 & c_{66} \end{bmatrix} \begin{Bmatrix} \varepsilon_{xx} \\ \varepsilon_{yy} \\ \varepsilon_{zz} \\ \varepsilon_{yz} \\ \varepsilon_{zx} \\ \varepsilon_{xy} \end{Bmatrix} - \begin{bmatrix} 0 & 0 & 0 & 0 & 0 & 0 \\ 0 & 0 & 0 & 0 & 0 & 0 \\ e_{31} & e_{32} & e_{33} & 0 & 0 & e_{36} \end{bmatrix}^T \begin{Bmatrix} E_x \\ E_y \\ E_z \end{Bmatrix}, \tag{2.12}$$

where

$$e_{ij} = c_{jk} d_{ik} \tag{2.13}$$

with Einstein's summation in tensorial index k. Having obtained an explicit form of the constitutive model, the electromechanical conservation equations are derived in the next section.

In context of (2.10) and (2.11), note that we have introduced the effect of bacterial cells or antibiotic agents through the variable $b(t)$. For simplicity, it is assumed here that these external agents do not alter the electrical polarization properties of the macromolecules responsible for piezoelectricity. However, such an assumption may not hold in real situations and a more detailed model may need to be developed in such cases. On the other hand, introduction of the variable $b(t)$ can also be useful in analyzing the long-term remodelling of site-specific collagen structure. The associated evolution law can be written as

$$\frac{\partial b}{\partial t} = \nabla\left(\mathcal{D}(b)\nabla b\right) + \beta n_d b - \mu_d b, \tag{2.14}$$

where the first term in the right-hand side represents the remodelling mechanism of bacterial cell movement with $\mathcal{D}(b) = \mathcal{D}_0 b^k$, $k > 0$, and $\mathcal{D}_0$ constants. The second term represents the dosimetric effect, that is, consumption of nutrients with concentration $n_d(\boldsymbol{x}, t)$ and β a nutrient-cell conversion factor. The third term represents formation of stationary cell-tissue structure. A detailed experimental observation of bacterial growth in chemically inert environment based on the above evolution law can be found in [1]. Since not much detailed information related to corneal collagen growth or dosimetric parameters is available, in the present study we do not couple (2.14) in the computational model, but assume various spatiotemporal states of b in (2.10) with the following distribution:

$$b(r,\theta,t) = \alpha'(t)e^{-k'(R-r)}\left[1 - \alpha'' e^{-k''(\theta^2-\theta_0^2)}\right], \tag{2.15}$$

where (r,θ) are the polar coordinates in the projected plane, R is the radius of the corneal anterior on the projected plane, θ_0 is the angular orientation of the active site, $\alpha'(t)$ is prescribed at a given time assuming a different time scale for growth as compared to the dehydration, and k', α'', k'' are constants.

3. Dynamic piezoelectricity

The momentum conservation equation is derived in the usual manner, which is given by

$$\rho\frac{\partial^2 \boldsymbol{u}}{\partial t^2} - \nabla\cdot(\boldsymbol{c}\nabla\boldsymbol{u}) = \boldsymbol{f}(\nabla\boldsymbol{E}), \tag{3.1}$$

where the effective mass density is

$$\rho = \nu_h\rho_h + (1-\nu_h)\rho_f, \tag{3.2}$$

and the components of the right-hand electrical source term are written as

$$f_x = -e_{31}\frac{\partial E_z}{\partial x} - e_{36}\frac{\partial E_z}{\partial y}, \qquad f_y = -e_{36}\frac{\partial E_z}{\partial x} - e_{32}\frac{\partial E_z}{\partial y}, \qquad f_z = -e_{33}\frac{\partial E_z}{\partial y}. \tag{3.3a}$$

We note that $\boldsymbol{f}$ is a function of only the transverse electric field E_z. This is due to the particular form of electromechanical coupling assumed in (2.12). For practical applications, this is a reasonably simple type of electromechanical coupling, yet an important one to analyze the direct influence of piezoelectricity on the refraction of incident ray $E_z \rightarrow E_\perp$ at the outer surface $z = h_o$, with the constitutive model defined in (x, y, z) and transformed to $(x, y, z_\perp)$, where the subscript $\perp$ denotes the outer surface normal. In the finite-element computations that follow, the deformations at the surfaces and at the annular base (see Figure 2.1) have to satisfy the appropriate boundary conditions in a weak sense.

The transverse electric field in (3.3a) has to satisfy Maxwell's equations for the electromagnetic field:

$$\nabla \times \boldsymbol{E} = -\dot{\boldsymbol{B}}, \tag{3.4a}$$

$$\nabla \times \boldsymbol{H} = \dot{\boldsymbol{D}} + \sigma_c \boldsymbol{E} + \boldsymbol{J}, \tag{3.4b}$$

$$\nabla \cdot \boldsymbol{D} = \rho_c, \tag{3.4c}$$

$$\nabla \cdot \boldsymbol{B} = 0, \tag{3.4d}$$

where σ_c is the effective conductivity of the RVE. The associated general impedance boundary conditions (GIBCs) are

$$\boldsymbol{n} \times (\boldsymbol{E} - \boldsymbol{E}_\perp) = -\boldsymbol{J}_{sm}, \qquad \boldsymbol{n} \times (\boldsymbol{H} - \boldsymbol{H}_\parallel) = \boldsymbol{J}_s \tag{3.5a}$$

at surfaces $z_\perp = h_o, h_i$, and

$$\boldsymbol{n} \cdot \boldsymbol{D} = \rho_s, \qquad \boldsymbol{n} \cdot \boldsymbol{B} = 0 \tag{3.5b}$$

at the annular base near the corneal anterior and scleral interface with ρ_s as the surface charge, $\boldsymbol{n}$ is the unit outward surface normal.

By using the constitutive model derived in Section 2, Maxwell's equations in (3.4a)–(3.4d) are combined into the following system of coupled hyperbolic equations:

$$\boldsymbol{\mu\epsilon}\frac{\partial^2 \boldsymbol{E}}{\partial t^2} + \sigma_c \boldsymbol{\mu}\frac{\partial \boldsymbol{E}}{\partial t} - \boldsymbol{\nabla}^2 \boldsymbol{E} + \boldsymbol{\mu e}^T \frac{\partial^2 \boldsymbol{\varepsilon}}{\partial t^2} - \boldsymbol{\epsilon}^{-1}\boldsymbol{\nabla\nabla} \cdot (\boldsymbol{e}^T \boldsymbol{\varepsilon}) = \boldsymbol{\epsilon}^{-1}\boldsymbol{\nabla}\rho_c + \boldsymbol{\mu}\dot{\boldsymbol{J}}, \tag{3.6a}$$

$$\boldsymbol{\mu\epsilon}\frac{\partial^2 \boldsymbol{H}}{\partial t^2} + \sigma_c \boldsymbol{\mu}\frac{\partial \boldsymbol{H}}{\partial t} - \boldsymbol{\nabla}^2 \boldsymbol{H} - \boldsymbol{\nabla} \times \left(\boldsymbol{e}^T \frac{\partial \boldsymbol{\varepsilon}}{\partial t}\right) = -\boldsymbol{\nabla} \times \boldsymbol{J}, \tag{3.6b}$$

where the right-hand-side terms in (3.6a)-(3.6b) are governed by the equation of the conduction of true charge, that is,

$$\boldsymbol{\nabla} \cdot \boldsymbol{J} = -\rho_c. \tag{3.7}$$

In the finite-element simulations reported next, we have omitted the conduction part, for the sake of simplicity, while analyzing the direct piezoelectric effect. Due to this simplification, we finally have

$$\mu\epsilon \frac{\partial^2 \boldsymbol{E}}{\partial t^2} + \sigma_c \boldsymbol{\mu} \frac{\partial \boldsymbol{E}}{\partial t} - \boldsymbol{\nabla}^2 \boldsymbol{E} = \boldsymbol{g}^E(\partial_{tt}, \boldsymbol{\nabla}, \boldsymbol{\varepsilon}), \tag{3.8a}$$

$$\mu\epsilon \frac{\partial^2 \boldsymbol{H}}{\partial t^2} + \sigma_c \boldsymbol{\mu} \frac{\partial \boldsymbol{H}}{\partial t} - \boldsymbol{\nabla}^2 \boldsymbol{H} = \boldsymbol{g}^H(\partial_t, \boldsymbol{\nabla}, \boldsymbol{\varepsilon}), \tag{3.8b}$$

where the components of the right-hand-side source terms, which are coupled with (3.1), are given by

$$g_x^E = \epsilon_{11}^{-1} \frac{\partial^2 \bar{P}}{\partial x \partial z}, \qquad g_y^E = \epsilon_{22}^{-1} \frac{\partial^2 \bar{P}}{\partial y \partial z}, \qquad g_z^E = \epsilon_{33}^{-1} \frac{\partial^2 \bar{P}}{\partial^2 z} - \mu_{33} \frac{\partial^2 \bar{P}}{\partial t^2}, \tag{3.9a}$$

$$g_x^H = \frac{\partial^2 \bar{P}}{\partial y \partial t}, \qquad g_y^H = -\frac{\partial^2 \bar{P}}{\partial x \partial t}, \qquad g_z^H = 0, \tag{3.9b}$$

and $\bar{P}$ is the effective polarization (a scalar quantity) due to piezoelectricity, which is given by

$$\bar{P} = e_{31}\varepsilon_{xx} + e_{32}\varepsilon_{yy} + e_{33}\varepsilon_{zz} + e_{36}\varepsilon_{xy}. \tag{3.10}$$

We solve the coupled system of hyperbolic equations (3.1), (3.8a), and (3.8b), supplemented by associated boundary conditions in $\{\boldsymbol{u}, \boldsymbol{E}, \boldsymbol{H}\}$ by using a three-dimensional finite-element discretization of the domain shown in Figure 2.1(a). COMSOL has been used for the solution where the constitutive model and the coupled system of equations have been implemented with the boundary conditions as weak constraints. Tetrahedral Lagrangian finite-elements and the second-order accurate time-stepping scheme have been used for computation.

4. Results and discussions

For numerical simulations, we consider a model of (x, y) cut of the corneal section as shown in Figure 2.1(a). It contains most of the usual geometric features with inner radius 5.685 mm and outer radius 7.259 mm. The conic-angle at the focal point is assumed to be $2 \times 59.434^\circ$ with $h_i = 2.794$ mm, $h_0 - h_i = 0.449$ mm at $(x, y) = (0, 0)$. Thickness at the annular base is assumed to be 1.574 mm. A 100 Hz harmonic shear stress with amplitude of 10 MPa is applied at the base along x. A residual stress pattern over a circumferential arc segment can also be used to study the effect of incision. Figures 4.1(a) and 4.1(b), respectively, show the deformation contours without any circumferential activity and with bacterial growth, $\alpha\alpha' = 0.1$, $k' = 10/R$, $\alpha'' = 0$. The contour of transverse electric field in Figure 4.2 reveals the possible regions of refractive property modification as under the deformation pattern shown in Figure 4.1(b). Attention has been paid to avoid the spurious effect due to mesh discretization error. The results presented here have been obtained for a refined mesh with 11987 tetrahedral elements and nonuniform time-stepping set by the direct nonsymmetric sparse matrix solver used. It can be seen from Figure 4.1(b) that

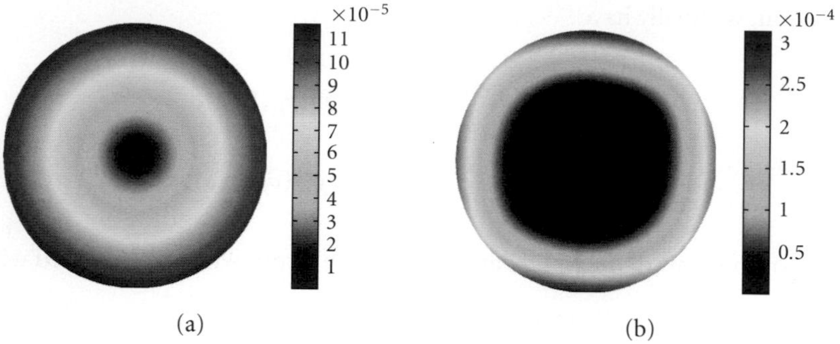

Figure 4.1. Deformation contours ($\sqrt{u_1^2 + u_2^2}$) for (a) symmetric circumferential stress distribution with $\alpha'' = 0$, (b) circumferential stress distribution with $\alpha'' = 0.9$.

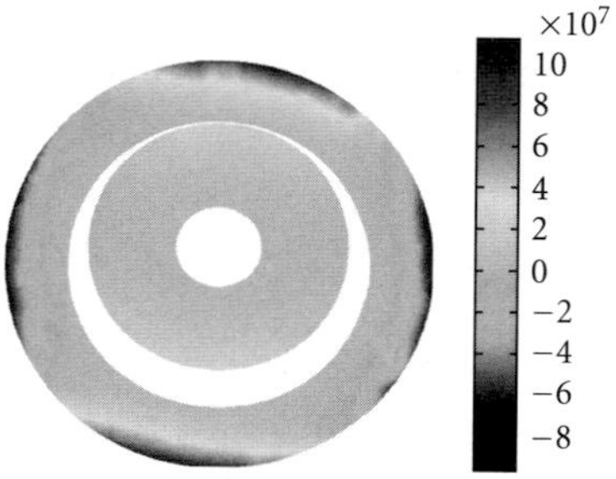

Figure 4.2. Sliced contour of transverse electric field E_3.

the residual stress at the circumferences due to bacterial growth (or incision) significantly alters the deformation profile and this observation is in close agreement with the studies reported in [6]. Further detailed analysis of the realistic situation of tunneling incision and astigmatism will be studied based on the present model in future research.

References

[1] E. Ben-Jacob, I. Cohen, I. Golding, D. L. Gutnick, M. Tcherpakov, D. Helbing, and I. G. Ron, *Bacterial cooperative organization under antibiotic stress*, Physica A **282** (2000), no. 1-2, 247–282.

[2] E. Fukuda and I. Yasuda, *Piezoelectric effect in collagen*, Journal of Applied Physics **3** (1964), no. 2, 117–121.

[3] M. T. Girard, M. Matsubara, C. Kublin, M. J. Tessler, C. Cintron, and M. E. Fini, *Stromal fibroblasts synthesize collagens and stromelysin during long-term tissue remodelling*, Journal of Cell Science **104** (1993), no. 4, 1001–1011.

[4] A. C. Jayasuriya, S. Ghosh, J. I. Scheinbeim, V. Lubkin, G. Bennett, and P. Kramer, *A study of piezoelectric and mechanical anisotropy of the human cornea*, Biosensors and Bioelectronics **18** (2003), 381–387.

[5] W. M. Petroll, L. Ma, and V. Jester, *Direct correlation of collagen matrix deformation with focal adhesion dynamics in living corneal fibroblasts*, Journal of Cell Science **116** (2003), 1489–1491.

[6] P. M. Pinsky, D. van der Heide, and D. Chernyak, *Computational modelling of mechanical anisotropy in the cornea and sclera*, Journal of Cataract & Refractive Surgery **31** (2005), no. 1, 136–145.

[7] P. Pratzl and A. Daxer, *Structural transformation of collagen fibrils in corneal stroma during drying*, Biophysical Journal **64** (1993), no. 4, 1210–1214.

[8] M. H. Shamos and L. S. Lavine, *Piezoelectricity as a fundamental property of biological tissues*, Nature **213** (1967), no. 73, 267–269.

D. Roy Mahapatra: Mathematical Modelling and Computational Sciences, Wilfrid Laurier University, Waterloo, ON, Canada N2L 3C5
E-mail address: droymahapatra@wlu.ca

R. V. N. Melnik: Mathematical Modelling and Computational Sciences, Wilfrid Laurier University, Waterloo, ON, Canada N2L 3C5
E-mail address: rmelnik@wlu.ca

PURELY VECTOR GROUND STATE FOR A NONLINEAR NONAUTONOMOUS SCHRÖDINGER SYSTEM

LILIANE DE ALMEIDA MAIA, EUGENIO MONTEFUSCO,
AND BENEDETTA PELLACCI

Existence of a positive purely vector ground state solution is established, via variational methods, for a nonautonomous system of weakly coupled nonlinear Schrödinger equations.

1. Introduction

This paper is concerned with the existence of nontrivial solutions and among them, ground state solutions for systems of coupled nonlinear Schrödinger equations. Such systems arise in several branches of mathematical physics, in particular in describing the interaction between waves of different frequencies and also the interaction between orthogonally polarized components in nonlinear optical fibers (see [6, 13]). After performing suitable simplifications and variable rescaling, such models are written as systems of partial differential equations of the form

$$\begin{aligned} i\phi_t + \phi_{xx} + (|\phi|^2 + b|\psi|^2)\phi = 0, \\ i\psi_t + \psi_{xx} + (|\psi|^2 + b|\phi|^2)\psi = 0, \end{aligned} \tag{1.1}$$

where ϕ and ψ represent the complex amplitudes of two-wave packets and b is a real-valued cross-phase modulation coefficient. Looking for standing wave solutions of (1.1), that is, solutions of the form

$$\phi(x,t) = e^{i\omega_1^2 t}u(x), \qquad \psi(x,t) = e^{i\omega_2^2 t}v(x), \tag{1.2}$$

and performing a rescaling of variables, one obtains that u and v satisfy the following system:

$$-u_{xx} + u = |u|^2u + b|v|^2u \quad \text{in } \mathbb{R}, \qquad -v_{xx} + \omega^2 v = |v|^2v + b|u|^2v \quad \text{in } \mathbb{R}, \tag{1.3}$$

where $\omega^2 = \omega_2^2/\omega_1^2$. The existence of vector solitary waves (1.2) as solutions to (1.1) has been investigated by theoretical and numerical means, as reviewed in [13]. If $b = 0$, in

Hindawi Publishing Corporation
Proceedings of the Conference on Differential & Difference Equations and Applications, pp. 733–742

(1.3) are two copies of a single nonlinear Schrödinger equations which is integrable; when $b=1$, (1.3) is known as the Manakov system (see [11]) which is also integrable. Our purpose here is to consider the following nonautonomous weakly coupled nonlinear elliptic system which generalizes (1.3):

$$\begin{aligned} -\Delta u+u &= |u|^{2q-2}u+b(x)|v|^{q}|u|^{q-2}u \quad \text{in } \mathbb{R}^N, \\ -\Delta v+\omega^2 v &= |v|^{2q-2}v+b(x)|u|^{q}|v|^{q-2}v \quad \text{in } \mathbb{R}^N. \end{aligned} \tag{1.4}$$

This nonlinear Schrödinger system has the same peculiarities of (1.3). Indeed, also for (1.4) there exist scalar solutions $(u_0,0)$ or $(0,v_0)$ where u_0 and v_0 are the unique positive radial solutions (see [3]), respectively, of the following equations:

$$-\Delta u+u=|u|^{2q-2}u, \qquad -\Delta v+\omega^2 v=|v|^{2q-2}v \quad \text{in } \mathbb{R}^N. \tag{1.5}$$

Brezis and Lieb in [4] proved the existence of a solution $(u,v)\neq(0,0)$ for a general class of autonomous systems which contains (1.4) as a particular case, when b is constant. Furthermore, they have shown that, among the nontrivial solutions, there is one that minimizes the associated action. A more general system of (1.4) with b constant has been also studied in [7], again by concentration compactness arguments, and the study proved the existence and the regularity of a ground state solution $(u,v)\neq(0,0)$.

In [10] we showed that for b constant and sufficiently large, the ground state solution of (1.4) is a vector solution (u,v) with both components u and v strictly positive. As far as we know ours is one of the first results on necessary and sufficient conditions that provides a vector minimal action solution for this problem (see also [1] for related results). Our main aim here is to search for a purely vector solitary wave for the nonautonomous system (1.4), that is, a solution (u,v) with both u, v nontrivial.

We consider the nonautonomous system (1.4) where b is a positive funcion of the variable x and we apply variational methods to obtain a nontrivial least action solution (see Theorem 3.1). A main difficulty in treating the nonautonomous problem in $\mathbb{R}^N$ is the possible lack of compactness. Working under appropriate restrictions on the function b at infinity, we are able to prove that the associated functional in fact satisfies Palais-Smale condition and to recover some compactness for the problem. We may again find solutions which are positive in both components and of minimal action, using some comparison argument with the autonomous problem at infinity.

The paper is organized as follows. In Section 2 we state the definitions and preliminary results and recall our main results for the autonomous system. In Section 3 we give the proofs of our existence results for the nonautonomous problem.

2. Preliminary results

In order to find a solution of problem (1.4) we will use variational methods. Therefore, we consider the following Hilbert space:

$$\begin{aligned} E &= H^1(\mathbb{R}^N)\times E_\omega, \qquad \|w\|_E^2=\|(u,v)\|_E^2=\|u\|^2+\|v\|_\omega^2, \\ E_\omega &= H^1(\mathbb{R}^N) \qquad \text{with } (v\mid v)_\omega=\|v\|_\omega^2=\|\nabla v\|_2^2+\omega^2\|v\|_2^2, \end{aligned} \tag{2.1}$$

where $\|\cdot\|$ stands for the norm in $H^1(\mathbb{R}^N)$, $\|\cdot\|_p$ denotes the standard norm in $L^p(\mathbb{R}^N)$ and $\|(\cdot,\cdot)\|_p = (\|\cdot\|_p^p + \|\cdot\|_p^p)^{1/p}$ is the norm of a vector in $L^p(\mathbb{R}^N)\times L^p(\mathbb{R}^N)$.

Let us consider a measurable function $b:\mathbb{R}^N \to \mathbb{R}$, such that the following hypothesis is satisfied:

$$b = b_1 + b_2 \in L^\infty(\mathbb{R}^N) + L^m(\mathbb{R}^N) \quad \text{with } m = \frac{N}{N-q(N-2)},\ b \geq 0,\ b \not\equiv 0, \tag{2.2}$$

and let us define the functional $I: E \to \mathbb{R}$ by

$$I(u,v) = \frac{1}{2}\|(u,v)\|_E^2 - \frac{1}{2q}\|(u,v)\|_{2q}^{2q} - \frac{1}{q}\int_{\mathbb{R}^N} b(x)|u|^q|v|^q, \tag{2.3}$$

where ω is a constant and q is such that

$$2 < 2q < 2^* = \begin{cases} +\infty & \text{if } N = 1,2, \\ \dfrac{2N}{N-2} & \text{if } N \geq 3. \end{cases} \tag{2.4}$$

First notice that hypotheses (2.4) and (2.2) imply that I is of class C^1, so that its differential is given by

$$\begin{aligned} \langle I'(u,v),(\varphi,\psi)\rangle = (u \mid \phi) + (v \mid \psi)_w &- \int_{\mathbb{R}^N} \left[|u|^{2q-2}u\varphi + |v|^{2q-2}v\psi\right] \\ &- \int_{\mathbb{R}^N} b(x)\left[|v|^q|u|^{q-2}u\varphi + |u|^q|v|^{q-2}v\psi\right]. \end{aligned} \tag{2.5}$$

Hence, the critical points of I in E are the weak solutions of (1.4) and by standard regularity theory are, in fact, classical solutions.

Moreover, we can define the Nehari manifold

$$\mathcal{N} := \{w \in E \setminus \{0\} : \langle I'(w), w\rangle = 0\}. \tag{2.6}$$

We have proved the following results in [10] for system (1.4) with $b > 0$ constant.

Theorem 2.1. *Assume (2.4). Then, for every constant $b > 0$ there exists a least energy solution (ground state) $w = (u,v) \neq (0,0)$ of problem (1.4), with $u \geq 0$, $v \geq 0$, and both u and v radial.*

Theorem 2.2. *Assume (2.4) and suppose that*

$$b \geq \begin{cases} \dfrac{1}{2}f(\omega) - 1 & \text{if } \omega \geq 1, \\ \dfrac{1}{2}f(1/\omega) - 1 & \text{if } \omega \leq 1, \end{cases} \tag{2.7}$$

where

$$f(\omega) = \left[1 + \frac{N}{2}\left(1 - \frac{1}{q}\right) + \frac{1}{\omega^2}\left(1 - \frac{N}{2}\left(1 - \frac{1}{q}\right)\right)\right]^q \omega^{2q-N(q-1)}. \tag{2.8}$$

Then there exists a least energy solution $w = (u,v)$ with $u > 0$ and $v > 0$.

In order to work out those results we have defined

$$c_{\mathcal{N}} := \inf_{\mathcal{N}} I(w), \tag{2.9}$$

$$c_1 := \inf_{w\in E\setminus\{0\}} \max_{t\geq 0} I(tw), \tag{2.10}$$

$$c := \inf_{\Gamma} \max_{[0,1]} I(\gamma(t)), \tag{2.11}$$

where

$$\Gamma = \{\gamma : [0,1] \longrightarrow E,\ \gamma \text{ is continuous and } \gamma(0) = 0,\ I(\gamma(1)) < 0\}. \tag{2.12}$$

Moreover, for any $w = (u,v) \in E \setminus \{0\}$ and $t > 0$, let

$$g(t) := I(tw) = I((tu,tv)), \tag{2.13}$$

then there exists $\bar{t} = \bar{t}(w) > 0$ such that

$$g(\bar{t}) = \max_{t>0} g(t), \tag{2.14}$$

and every positive critical point t of g satisfies the following equation:

$$\|(u,v)\|_E^2 - t^{2q-2}\left[\|(u,v)\|_{2q}^{2q} + 2\int_{\mathbb{R}^N} b(x)|u|^q|v|^q\right] = 0, \tag{2.15}$$

so that, as $q > 1$, the point $\bar{t} = \bar{t}(w)$ is the unique value of $t > 0$ at which $\bar{t}(w)w \in \mathcal{N}$.

The following result is proved in [12] for functionals associated to a single equation and in [10] for the system.

LEMMA 2.3. *One has* $c_{\mathcal{N}} = c_1 = c$.

In order to find a solution (u,v) with $u \geq 0$ and $v \geq 0$, the following result was used.

LEMMA 2.4. *Let $w \in \mathcal{N}$ and $I(w) = c$, where c is defined in (2.11). Then, w is a critical point of I.*

3. Nonautonomous systems

In this section the nonautonomous system will be studied.

$$\begin{gathered} -\Delta u + u = |u|^{2q-2}u + b(x)|v|^q|u|^{q-2}u \quad \text{in } \mathbb{R}^N, \\ -\Delta v + \omega^2 v = |v|^{2q-2}v + b(x)|u|^q|v|^{q-2}v \quad \text{in } \mathbb{R}^N, \\ u, v \in H^1(\mathbb{R}^N), \end{gathered} \tag{3.1}$$

where q satisfies (2.4). We will consider a general function $b(x)$, and we will prove the counterpart of Theorem 2.2 for the nonautonomous case. More precisely, we will show that there exists a least energy solution with both nontrivial components under suitable hypotheses on b (see Theorem 3.1).

Theorem 3.1. *Assume (2.4), (2.2). Moreover, suppose that the following conditions are satisfied.*

There exists

$$\lim_{|x|\to\infty} b_1(x) =: b_\infty > 0, \tag{3.2}$$

$$b(x) > b_\infty. \tag{3.3}$$

Then, the following conditions hold.

(i) *There exists a least energy solution $w = (u,v) \not\equiv (0,0)$ of (3.1), with $u \geq 0$, $v \geq 0$.*

(ii) *If b_∞ satisfies (2.7), then $u > 0$ and $v > 0$.*

In order to prove Theorem 3.1 we will show that Palais-Smale condition holds at some suitable level for the functional (2.3). Let us first give some notions we will use in the sequel. We define the functional $I_\infty : E \to \mathbb{R}$ by

$$I_\infty(u,v) = \frac{1}{2}||(u,v)||_E^2 - \frac{1}{2q}||(u,v)||_{2q}^{2q} - \frac{b_\infty}{q}\|uv\|_q^q. \tag{3.4}$$

Moreover, denoting by $\mathcal{N}_\infty$ the Nehari manifold associated to I_∞, we set

$$c_\infty = \inf_{\mathcal{N}_\infty} I_\infty(u,v). \tag{3.5}$$

We can now state a compactness result.

Lemma 3.2. *Assume (2.4), (2.2), and (3.2). Then, Palais-Smale condition holds at every level c such that*

$$c < c_\infty. \tag{3.6}$$

Proof. Let us take (u_n,v_n) a Palais-Smale sequence, that is, a sequence $w_n = (u_n,v_n)$ such that

$$I(w_n) \longrightarrow c, \tag{3.7}$$

$$I'(w_n) \longrightarrow 0 \quad \text{strongly in } E'. \tag{3.8}$$

By arguing as in the proof of Theorem 2.2 and taking into account (2.2) we get that there exists (u,v) such that

$$\begin{gathered}(u_n,v_n) \rightharpoonup (u,v) \quad \text{weakly in } E,\\ (u_n,v_n) \longrightarrow (u,v) \quad \text{strongly in } L^p_{\text{loc}}(\mathbb{R}^N)\times L^p_{\text{loc}}(\mathbb{R}^N)\ \forall\, p\in[1,2^*),\\ (u_n,v_n) \longrightarrow (u,v) \quad \text{almost everywhere in } \mathbb{R}^N\end{gathered} \tag{3.9}$$

are satisfied. Then (u,v) is a weak solution of problem (3.1).

In order to prove that $(u,v) \neq (0,0)$, we will show the strong convergence of (u_n, v_n) in E following the argument in [9]. There are only two possibilities for (u_n, v_n):

(a) for every $\delta > 0$, there exists $\overline{R} > 0$, such that for every $n > \overline{R}$, it holds

$$\int_{|x|\geq \overline{R}} |\nabla u_n|^2 + |u_n|^2 + |\nabla v_n|^2 + \omega^2 |v_n|^2 < \delta; \tag{3.10}$$

(b) there exists δ_0, such that for every $\overline{R} > 0$, there exists $n = n(\overline{R}) \geq \overline{R}$ with

$$\int_{|x|\geq \overline{R}} |\nabla u_n|^2 + |u_n|^2 + |\nabla v_n|^2 + \omega^2 |v_n|^2 \geq \delta_0. \tag{3.11}$$

Case (a) corresponds to the case in which we can recover some compactness. Indeed, if (a) holds, it results in

$$\lim_{n\to\infty} \int_{\mathbb{R}^N} |b(x)(|u_n v_n|^q - |uv|^q)| = 0. \tag{3.12}$$

Indeed, Young and Sobolev inequalities and (3.10) yield

$$\lim_{n\to\infty} \int_{\mathbb{R}^N} |b(x)(|u_n v_n|^q - |uv|^q)| \leq c\delta + \lim_{n\to\infty} \int_{\{|x|<\overline{R}\}} |b(x)(|u_n v_n|^q - |uv|^q)|, \tag{3.13}$$

so that (3.12) follows from (2.4), (2.2), and from the arbitrariness of δ. In an analogous way it is possible to prove that $(u_n, v_n) \to (u,v)$ strongly in $L^{2q}(\mathbb{R}^N) \times L^{2q}(\mathbb{R}^N)$. These facts and (3.8) imply that $(u_n, v_n) \to (u,v)$ in E.

Let us now rule out case (b). For every $\varepsilon > 0$, we can fix R_0 such that

$$\begin{gathered} \int_{|x|\geq R_0} |\nabla u|^2 + |u|^2 + |\nabla v|^2 + \omega^2 |v|^2 < \varepsilon, \\ \left[\int_{|x|\geq R_0} |b_2(x)|^m\right]^{1/m} < \varepsilon, \\ b_1(x) \leq b_\infty + \varepsilon \quad \text{for } |x| \geq R_0. \end{gathered} \tag{3.14}$$

If case (b) occurs, we can construct a subsequence (u_{n_k}, v_{n_k}) and we find $R > R_0$ such that (see [9] for more details)

$$\int_{|x|\geq R} |\nabla u_{n_k}|^2 + |u_{n_k}|^2 + |\nabla v_{n_k}|^2 + \omega^2 |v_{n_k}|^2 > \delta_0, \tag{3.15}$$

$$\int_{\{R\leq |x|<R+1\}} |\nabla u_{n_k}|^2 + |u_{n_k}|^2 + |\nabla v_{n_k}|^2 + \omega^2 |v_{n_k}|^2 < \varepsilon. \tag{3.16}$$

Next, we take a cutoff function $\rho \in C_c^{\infty}(\mathbb{R}^N)$ such that

$$\rho(x) = \begin{cases} 1, & |x| \le R, \\ 0, & |x| \ge R+1, \qquad |\nabla \rho| \le 2, \quad \forall x \in \mathbb{R}^N, \\ 0, \le \rho \le 1, & R \le |x| \le R+1, \end{cases} \tag{3.17}$$

and we set

$$\begin{aligned} \underline{u}_k &= \rho(x) u_{n_k}, & \underline{v}_k &= \rho(x) v_{n_k}, \\ \overline{u}_k &= (1-\rho(x)) u_{n_k}, & \overline{v}_k &= (1-\rho(x)) v_{n_k}. \end{aligned} \tag{3.18}$$

By applying (3.8), and by using (2.2), (3.16), and Sobolev inequality we obtain

$$\begin{aligned} o(1) &= \langle I'(u_{n_k}, v_{n_k}), (\overline{u}_k, \overline{v}_k) \rangle \\ &= \|(\overline{u}_k, \overline{v}_k)\|_E^2 - \|(\overline{u}_k, \overline{v}_k)\|_{2q}^{2q} - 2\int_{\mathbb{R}^N} b_1(x) |\overline{u}_k|^q |\overline{v}_k|^q \\ &\quad - 2\int_{\{|x|>R\}} b_2(x) \left(|u_{n_k}|^{q-2} u_{n_k} \overline{u}_k |v_{n_k}|^q + |v_{n_k}|^{q-2} v_{n_k} \overline{v}_k |u_{n_k}|^q \right) + O(\varepsilon), \end{aligned} \tag{3.19}$$

where $o(1)$ is a quantity that tends to zero as $k \to \infty$ and $O(\varepsilon)$ is a quantity that tends to zero as $\varepsilon \to 0$. Since $R > R_0$, from (3.14) one obtains

$$\|(\overline{u}_k, \overline{v}_k)\|^2 = \|(\overline{u}_k, \overline{v}_k)\|_{2q}^{2q} + 2\int_{\mathbb{R}^N} b_1(x) |\overline{u}_k|^q |\overline{v}_k|^q + O(\varepsilon) + o(1). \tag{3.20}$$

If we take $(\underline{u}_k, \underline{v}_k)$ as test function in (3.8) and argue in an analogous way, we deduce

$$\|(\underline{u}_k, \underline{v}_k)\|^2 = \|(\underline{u}_k, \underline{v}_k)\|_{2q}^{2q} + 2\int_{\mathbb{R}^N} b(x) |\underline{u}_k|^q |\underline{v}_k|^q + O(\varepsilon) + o(1) \tag{3.21}$$

which, together with (2.4), yields

$$I(\underline{u}_k, \underline{v}_k) = \frac{1}{2}\left(1 - \frac{1}{q}\right) \|(\underline{u}_k, \underline{v}_k)\|^2 + O(\varepsilon) + o(1) \ge O(\varepsilon) + o(1). \tag{3.22}$$

Moreover, we take into account (2.2), (3.16), and (3.18) in (3.7) we obtain

$$c + o(1) = I(u_{n_k}, v_{n_k}) = I(\underline{u}_k, \underline{v}_k) + I(\overline{u}_k, \overline{v}_k) + O(\varepsilon). \tag{3.23}$$

Let $\bar{t}(\bar{u}_k,\bar{v}_k)$ be the unique positive real number such that $I_\infty(\bar{t}(\bar{u}_k,\bar{v}_k)(\bar{u}_k,\bar{v}_k)) = \max I_\infty(t(\underline{u}_k,\underline{v}_k))$ then $\bar{t}(\bar{u}_k,\bar{v}_k)$ satisfies (2.15) for $b \equiv b_\infty$. From (2.15), (3.14), and (3.20) we deduce the following estimate:

$$(\bar{t}(\bar{u}_k,\bar{v}_k))^{2q-2} \le 1 + O(\varepsilon)\frac{1}{||\bar{u}_k||_{2q}^{2q} + ||\bar{v}_k||_{2q}^{2q} + 2b_\infty||\bar{u}_k\bar{v}_k||_q^q}. \tag{3.24}$$

On the other hand, (3.15) and (3.20) imply that for ε sufficiently small, the following inequality holds:

$$||\bar{u}_k||_{2q}^{2q} + ||\bar{v}_k||_{2q}^{2q} + 2b_\infty||\bar{u}_k\bar{v}_k||_q^q \ge \frac{\delta_0}{2}. \tag{3.25}$$

When we use this inequality in (3.24), we get

$$\bar{t}(\bar{u}_k,\bar{v}_k) \le 1 + C_3\varepsilon. \tag{3.26}$$

Since $\bar{t}(\bar{u}_k,\bar{v}_k)(\bar{u}_k,\bar{v}_k)$ belongs to $\mathcal{N}_\infty$, (2.15), (3.20), (3.23), and (3.26) yield

$$\begin{aligned} c_\infty &\le I_\infty(\bar{t}(\bar{u}_k,\bar{v}_k)(\bar{u}_k,\bar{v}_k)) \le \frac{1}{2}(1+C_4\varepsilon)\left(1-\frac{1}{q}\right)||(\bar{u}_k,\bar{v}_k)||_E^2 \\ &= I(\bar{u}_k,\bar{v}_k) + C_5\varepsilon = I(u_{n_k},v_{n_k}) - I(\underline{u}_k,\underline{v}_k) + O(\varepsilon). \end{aligned} \tag{3.27}$$

The last inequality together with (3.7) and (3.22) yields

$$c_\infty \le c - O(\varepsilon), \tag{3.28}$$

which contradicts (3.6). □

Remark 3.3. In order to prove Lemma 3.2, we can assume a weaker hypothesis. Indeed, take b_∞ a positive constant such that

$$b_\infty \ge \limsup_{|x|\to\infty} b_1(x). \tag{3.29}$$

Then, we can follow the same argument of the proof of Lemma 3.2 to deduce that Palais-Smale condition holds at every level $c < c_\infty$.

Proof of Theorem 3.1. In order to prove (i) we apply [2, Mountain-Pass theorem]. Consider the functional $I : E \to \mathbb{R}$ defined by (2.3). Let us first notice that we can follow a standard argument in order to show that $(0,0)$ is a strict local minimum of I, moreover, (2.2) and (3.3) imply that

$$I(u,v) < I_\infty(u,v). \tag{3.30}$$

Then we can prove that $I(Tw) < 0$ for every w in E and for T sufficiently large. We consider Γ and c defined in (2.11), (2.12), respectively. In order to get the conclusion we only have to show that c satisfies (3.6). Lemma 2.3 and (3.30) yield

$$c < \inf_{\Gamma}\max_{[0,1]} I_\infty(\gamma(t)) = \inf_{\mathcal{N}_\infty} I_\infty(w) = c_\infty, \tag{3.31}$$

so that (3.6) is satisfied, showing that there exists a solution $(u,v) \not\equiv (0,0)$, with $I(u,v) = c$. Moreover, we can apply Lemmas 2.3 and 2.4 in order to get that (u,v) is a least energy solution and $u,\ v \geq 0$.

Finally, if b_∞ satisfies (2.7) we have that c_∞ is strictly less than the energy level of the solution $(u_0,0)$ and $(0,v_0)$, so that (3.31) implies that $u \not\equiv 0$ and $v \not\equiv 0$. □

Remark 3.4. Consider the following system:

$$\begin{gathered} -\Delta u + u = |u|^{2q-2}u + b_R(x)|v|^q|u|^{q-2}u \quad \text{in } \mathbb{R}^N, \\ -\Delta v + \omega^2 v = |v|^{2q-2}v + b_R(x)|u|^q|v|^{q-2}v \quad \text{in } \mathbb{R}^N, \\ u,v \in H^1(\mathbb{R}^N), \end{gathered} \tag{3.32}$$

where q satisfies (2.4) and $b_R(x) = b\eta(R|x|)$, with $b > 0$ and η a smooth and radially decreasing function such that $\eta \equiv 1$ in $B(O,1)$, $\eta \equiv 1/2$ outside $B(O,2)$.

Theorem 3.1 states that (3.32) possesses a least energy solution $(u_R, v_R) \not\equiv (0,0)$ for any $R > 0$, since the assumptions (3.2), (3.3) easily hold. Moreover we can state that the solutions of the system are radial functions, because [5] implies that if u_R and v_R are positive functions, then they are radially symmetric with respect to $O \in \mathbb{R}^N$, otherwise if $u_R = 0$ (or $v_R = 0$), then v_R (u_R, resp.) is a positive radial function by the results in [8].

Now it is easy to show that we can give an alternative proof of Theorem 2.1. Choose a sequence R_n tending to $+\infty$ and let (u_n, v_n) be the corresponding least energy solution of (3.32). We have a bounded sequence in $H^1(\mathbb{R}^N)$, since, using the weak form of (3.32), it holds that

$$\frac{1}{4}||(u_n,v_n)||_E^2 = I(u_n,v_n) = c_n < c_\infty. \tag{3.33}$$

So we have a sequence of radial (and radially decreasing) functions in $H^1(\mathbb{R}^N)$, this kind of sequence is relatively compact in $L^p(\mathbb{R}^N) \times L^p(\mathbb{R}^N)$, for any $p \in (2, 2^*)$, so passing to the limit we obtain that its limit $(\overline{u}, \overline{v})$ is a critical point of I_∞ (with $b_\infty = b$), moreover the fact that

$$\frac{1}{4}||(\overline{u},\overline{v})||_E^2 \leq c_\infty \tag{3.34}$$

shows that the critical point is a least energy solution of (1.4).

Remark 3.5. Actually, we can prove a better result than Theorem 3.1. More precisely, (ii) holds if $b(x)$ is such that

$$\frac{1}{||u_0||^2}\int_{\mathbb{R}^N} b(x)\,|\,u_0\,|^{2q} > \frac{2^{q-1}}{\omega^{2q-N(q-1)}} - 1 \quad \text{if } \omega < 1,$$

$$\frac{1}{||v_0||_\omega^2}\int_{\mathbb{R}^N} b(x)\,|\,v_0\,|^{2q} > 2^{q-1}\omega^{2q-N(q-1)} - 1 \quad \text{if } \omega > 1,$$

where u_0 and v_0 are defined by (1.5), respectively. Thi[illegible] result is p[illegible] another argument.

Acknowledgments

This work was done while the first author was visiting the Università degli Studi di Roma *La Sapienza*. She thanks the members of the Department of Mathematics for their hospitality. The first author's research was partially supported by CAPES/Brazil, Pronex/MAT-UNB and FINATEC. The second and third authors' research was supported by MIUR project *Metodi Variazionali ed Equazioni Differenziali non lineari*.

References

[1] A. Ambrosetti and E. Colorado, *Bound and ground states of a coupled nonlinear Schrödinger equations*, Comptes Rendus Mathématique. Académie des Sciences. Paris **342** (2006), no. 7, 453–458.

[2] A. Ambrosetti and P. H. Rabinowitz, *Dual variational methods in critical point theory and applications*, Journal of Functional Analysis **14** (1973), 349–381.

[3] H. Berestycki and P.-L. Lions, *Nonlinear scalar field equations. I. Existence of a ground state*, Archive for Rational Mechanics and Analysis **82** (1983), no. 4, 313–345.

[4] H. Brezis and E. H. Lieb, *Minimum action solutions of some vector field equations*, Communications in Mathematical Physics **96** (1984), no. 1, 97–113.

[5] J. Busca and B. Sirakov, *Symmetry results for semilinear elliptic systems in the whole space*, Journal of Differential Equations **163** (2000), no. 1, 41–56.

[6] A. R. Champneys and J. Yang, *A scalar nonlocal bifurcation of solitary waves for coupled nonlinear Schrödinger systems*, Nonlinearity **15** (2002), no. 6, 2165–2192.

[7] R. Cipolatti and W. Zumpichiatti, *On the existence and regularity of ground state for a nonlinear system of coupled Schrödinger equations in* $\mathbb{R}^N$, Computational and Applied Mathematics **18** (1999), no. 1, 15–29.

[8] M. K. Kwong, *Uniqueness of positive solutions of* $\Delta u - u + u^p = 0$ *in* $\mathbb{R}^n$, Archive for Rational Mechanics and Analysis **105** (1989), no. 3, 243–266.

[9] Y. Y. Li, *Existence of multiple solutions of semilinear elliptic equations in* $\mathbb{R}^N$, Variational Methods (Paris, 1988), Progr. Nonlinear Differential Equations Appl., vol. 4, Birkhäuser Boston, Massachusetts, 1990, pp. 133–159.

[10] L. A. Maia, E. Montefusco, and B. Pellaci, *Positive solutions for a weakly coupled nonlinear Schrödinger system*, to appear in Journal of Differential Equations.

[11] S. V. Manakov, *On the theory of two-dimensional stationary self-focusing of electromagnetic waves*, Soviet Physics: JETP **38** (1974), 248–253.

[12] P. H. Rabinowitz, *On a class of nonlinear Schrödinger equations*, Zeitschrift für Angewandte Mathematik und Physik **43** (1992), no. 2, 270–291.

[13] J. Yang, *Classification of the solitary waves in coupled nonlinear Schrödinger equations*, Physica D **108** (1997), no. 1-2, 92–112.

Liliane de Almeida Maia: Departmento de Matemática, Universidade de Brasília, 70.910-900 Brasília, Brazil
E-mail address: lilimaia@unb.br

Eugenio Montefusco: Dipartimento di Matematica, Università degli Studi di Roma *La Sapienza*, Piazzale Aldo Moro 5, 00185 Roma, Italy
E-mail address: montefusco@mat.uniroma1.it

Benedetta Pellacci: Dipartimento di Scienze Applicate, Università degli Studi di Napoli, Parthenope, via A. De Gasperi, 80133 Napoli, Italy
E-mail address: benedetta.pellacci@uniparthenope.it

LIMIT CYCLES OF LIÉNARD SYSTEMS

M. AMAR AND Y. BOUATTIA

We calculate the amplitude and period of the limit cycle of the following classes of Liénard equations by using the method of Lopez and Lopez-Ruiz: $\ddot{x}+\varepsilon(x^2-1)\dot{x}+x^{2n-1}=0$; $\ddot{x}+\varepsilon(x^{2m}-1)\dot{x}+x^{2n-1}=0$; $\ddot{x}+\varepsilon(|x|^n-1)\dot{x}+\operatorname{sign}(x)\cdot|x|^m=0$; $\ddot{x}+\varepsilon(x^{2m}-1)\dot{x}+x^{1/(2n-1)}=0$, where $m,n\in\mathbb{N}$. We give numerical results.

1. Introduction

Limit-cycle behavior is observed in many physical and biological systems. The problem of determining when a nonlinear dynamical system exhibits limit cycle has been of great interest for more than a century. Limit cycles cannot occur in linear systems, conservative systems, and gradient systems. The limit cycles are caused by nonlinearities. It was found that many oscillatory circuits can be modeled by the Liénard equation

$$\ddot{x}+f(x)\dot{x}+g(x)=0, \tag{1.1}$$

where

$$\cdot=\frac{d}{dt}. \tag{1.2}$$

It can be interpreted mechanically as the equation of motion for a unit mass subject to a nonlinear damping force $-f(x)\dot{x}$ and a nonlinear restoring force $-g(x)$. Applications of Liénard's equation can be found in many important examples including chemical reactions, growth of a single species, predator-prey systems, and vibration analysis. In Section 2, we give the theorem of existence and uniqueness of the limit cycle for the Liénard equation. In Section 3, we give the method of calculation of the amplitude of the limit cycle of the perturbed centers (see [2]),

$$\begin{aligned}\dot{x}&=-y^{2l-1}+\varepsilon P(x,y),\\ \dot{y}&=x^{2k-1}+\varepsilon Q(x,y),\end{aligned} \tag{1.3}$$

Hindawi Publishing Corporation
Proceedings of the Conference on Differential & Difference Equations and Applications, pp. 743–755

with $0 < |\varepsilon| \ll 1$, $k, l \in \mathbb{N}$. In Section 4, we calculate the amplitude and the period of the limit cycle of five classes of Liénard equations. In Section 5, we give numerical results of the limit cycles of some equations.

2. Existence and uniquiness of the limit cycle

We consider the Liénard equation

$$\ddot{x} + f(x)\dot{x} + g(x) = 0, \tag{2.1}$$

where f and g are continuous functions, we put

$$F(x) = \int_0^x f(t)dt. \tag{2.2}$$

Theorem 2.1 (see [1]). *Equation (2.1) has one limit cycle if*

(i) *F is odd (f is even);*
(ii) *$F(x) = 0$ only for $x = 0, a, -a$ for $a > 0$;*
(iii) *$F(x) \underset{x\to+\infty}{\longrightarrow} +\infty$, $F(x)$ is increasing monotonically;*
(iv) *$g(x)$ is odd and $g(x) > 0$ for $x > 0$.*

3. Method

We consider the perturbed system

$$\begin{aligned} \dot{x} &= y + \varepsilon f(x,y), \\ \dot{y} &= -x + \varepsilon g(x,y), \end{aligned} \qquad 0 < |\varepsilon| \ll 1. \tag{3.1}$$

By putting $\dot{x}(t) = y(x)$, $y'(x) = dy/dx$, we obtain

$$yy' + x + \varepsilon[f(x,y)y' - g(x,y)] = 0. \tag{3.2}$$

We suppose that the origin is the only fixed point of (3.1). We put

$$\beta(a) \equiv \int_{-a}^{a} \left[\bar{g}(x, \sqrt{a^2 - x^2}) + \frac{x\bar{f}(x, \sqrt{a^2 - x^2})}{\sqrt{a^2 - x^2}}\right]dx = 0, \tag{3.3}$$

where

$$\begin{aligned} \bar{f}(x,y) &\equiv \frac{1}{2}[f(x,y) + f(x,-y) - f(-x,y) - f(-x,-y)], \\ \bar{g}(x,y) &\equiv \frac{1}{2}[g(x,y) - g(x,-y) + g(-x,y) - g(-x,-y)]. \end{aligned} \tag{3.4}$$

Each solution $a > 0$ for the equation $\beta(a) = 0$ is the amplitude of a limit cycle of the system (3.1) (see [2]).

We consider the perturbed centers

$$\begin{aligned} \dot{x} &= -y^{2l-1} + \varepsilon P(x,y), \\ \dot{y} &= x^{2k-1} + \varepsilon Q(x,y), \end{aligned} \tag{3.5}$$

with $0 < |\varepsilon| \ll 1$, $k, l \in \mathbb{N}$.

For $\varepsilon = 0$, we have a center

$$\begin{aligned} \dot{x} &= -y^{2l-1}, \\ \dot{y} &= x^{2k-1}, \end{aligned} \tag{3.6}$$

we have

$$\frac{x^{2k}}{2k} + \frac{y^{2l}}{2l} = c. \tag{3.7}$$

By putting $\dot{x}(t) = y(x)$, (3.5) becomes

$$y^{2l-1}\frac{dy}{dx} + x^{2k-1} + \varepsilon\left[Q(x,y) - P(x,y)\frac{dy}{dx}\right] = 0. \tag{3.8}$$

We consider the homeomorphism $\Gamma : (x,y) \to (X,Y)$:

$$\begin{aligned} X &= \operatorname{sign}(x)\frac{|x|^k}{\sqrt{k}}, \\ Y &= \operatorname{sign}(y)\frac{|y|^l}{\sqrt{l}}, \end{aligned} \tag{3.9}$$

which is equivalent to

$$\begin{aligned} x &= \operatorname{sign}(X)\left(\sqrt{k}|X|\right)^{1/k}, \\ y &= \operatorname{sign}(Y)\left(\sqrt{l}|Y|\right)^{1/l}. \end{aligned} \tag{3.10}$$

It transforms the closed curve

$$\frac{x^{2k}}{2k} + \frac{y^{2l}}{2l} = c \tag{3.11}$$

to the circle

$$\frac{X^2}{2} + \frac{Y^2}{2} = c. \tag{3.12}$$

Equation (3.8), in the new variables (X,Y), becomes

$$Y\frac{dY}{dX} + X + \varepsilon\left[\frac{|X|^{1/k-1}}{k^{1-1/2k}}Q(x,y) - \frac{|Y|^{1/l-1}}{l^{1-1/2l}}P(x,y)\frac{dY}{dX}\right] = 0 \tag{3.13}$$

or

$$Y\frac{dY}{dX}+X+\varepsilon\Big[-\frac{|Y|^{1/l-1}}{l^{1-1/2l}}P(x,y)\frac{dY}{dX}+\frac{|X|^{1/k-1}}{k^{1-1/2k}}Q(x,y)\Big]=0, \tag{3.14}$$

where x and y are given by (3.10).

We put

$$\begin{aligned} f(X,Y) &= -\frac{|Y|^{1/l-1}}{l^{1-1/2l}}P\Big(\operatorname{sign}(X)\big(\sqrt{k}|X|\big)^{1/k}, \operatorname{sign}(Y)\big(\sqrt{l}|Y|\big)^{1/l}\Big),\\ g(X,Y) &= -\frac{|X|^{1/k-1}}{k^{1-1/2k}}Q\Big(\operatorname{sign}(X)\big(\sqrt{k}|X|\big)^{1/k}, \operatorname{sign}(Y)\big(\sqrt{l}|Y|\big)^{1/l}\Big). \end{aligned} \tag{3.15}$$

Therefore, if A is the amplitude of a limit cycle of (3.14), when $\varepsilon \to 0$, it verifies the equation

$$\bar{\beta}(A)=\int_{-A}^{A}\Big\{\bar{f}(X,Y_A(X))\frac{X}{Y_A(X)}+\bar{g}(X,Y_A(X))\Big\}dX=0, \tag{3.16}$$

where $Y_A(X)=\sqrt{A^2-X^2}$ and $\bar{f}$, $\bar{g}$ are given by (3.4). The relation between the amplitudes A and a of the systems (3.14) and (3.5) is given by

$$a^{2k}=kA^2. \tag{3.17}$$

4. Applications

By applying Theorem 2.1, each of the following equations has one limit cycle:

(1) $\ddot{x}+\varepsilon(x^2-1)\dot{x}+x^3=0$;
(2) $\ddot{x}+\varepsilon(x^2-1)\dot{x}+x^{2n-1}=0$;
(3) $\ddot{x}+\varepsilon(x^{2m}-1)\dot{x}+x^{2n-1}=0$;
(4) $\ddot{x}+\varepsilon(\sum_{i=0}^{m}b_{2i}\cdot x^{2i})\dot{x}+x^{2n-1}=0$;
(5) $\ddot{x}+\varepsilon(|x|^n-1)\dot{x}+\operatorname{sign}(x)\cdot|x|^m=0$;
(6) $\ddot{x}+\varepsilon(x^{2m}-1)\dot{x}+x^{1/(2n-1)}=0$.

(1) $\ddot{x}+\varepsilon(x^2-1)\dot{x}+x^3=0$ or

$$\begin{aligned} \dot{x} &= -y,\\ \dot{y} &= x^3+\varepsilon(x^2-1)y. \end{aligned} \tag{4.1}$$

From (3.15), we have

$$\begin{aligned} f(X,Y) &= 0,\\ g(X,Y) &= -2^{-3/4}|X|^{-1/2}(\sqrt{2}|X|-1)Y,\\ \bar{g}(X,Y) &= -2^{1/4}|X|^{-1/2}(\sqrt{2}|X|-1)Y,\\ \bar{\beta}(A) &= -\int_{-A}^{A}2^{1/4}|X|^{-1/2}(\sqrt{2}|X|-1)(A^2-X^2)^{1/2}dX\\ &= -2^{3/4}\int_{0}^{A}(\sqrt{2}X^{1/2}-X^{-1/2})(A^2-X^2)^{1/2}dX. \end{aligned} \tag{4.2}$$

By putting $X = A\alpha^{1/2}$, we obtain

$$\begin{aligned}\bar{\beta}(A) &= -2^{1/4}A^{3/2}\int_0^1 [\sqrt{2}\alpha^{-1/4}(1-\alpha)^{1/2}A - \alpha^{-3/4}(1-\alpha)^{1/2}]d\alpha\\ &= -2^{1/4}A^{3/2}\left[\sqrt{2}\beta\left(\frac{3}{4},\frac{3}{2}\right)A - \beta\left(\frac{1}{4},\frac{3}{2}\right)\right],\\ \beta\left(\frac{3}{4},\frac{3}{2}\right) &= \frac{\Gamma(3/4)\Gamma(3/2)}{\Gamma(9/4)} = \frac{\Gamma(3/4)(\sqrt{\pi}/2)}{(5/4)(1/4)\Gamma(1/4)} = \frac{8}{5}\sqrt{\pi}\frac{\Gamma(3/4)}{\Gamma(1/4)} = \frac{2^{7/2}}{5}\pi^{3/2}\left(\frac{1}{\Gamma(1/4)}\right)^2,\\ \beta\left(\frac{1}{4},\frac{3}{2}\right) &= \frac{2}{3}\sqrt{\pi}\frac{\Gamma(1/4)}{\Gamma(3/4)} = \frac{\sqrt{2}}{3}\pi^{-1/2}\left(\Gamma\left(\frac{1}{4}\right)\right)^2.\end{aligned} \tag{4.3}$$

We have used the relations

$$\begin{aligned}\Gamma(x) &= \frac{2^{x-1}}{\sqrt{\pi}}\Gamma\left(\frac{x}{2}\right)\Gamma\left(\frac{x+1}{2}\right), \quad x = \frac{1}{2},\\ \Gamma(x+1) &= x\Gamma(x), \qquad \beta(x,y) = \frac{\Gamma(x)\Gamma(y)}{\Gamma(x+y)},\\ \bar{\beta}(A) &= -2^{1/4}A^{3/2}\left[\frac{2^4}{5}\pi^{3/2}\left(\frac{1}{\Gamma(1/4)}\right)^2 A - \frac{\sqrt{2}}{3}\pi^{-1/2}\left(\Gamma\left(\frac{1}{4}\right)\right)^2\right] = 0.\end{aligned} \tag{4.4}$$

We obtain

$$A = \frac{5}{3.2^{7/2}\pi^2}\left(\Gamma\left(\frac{1}{4}\right)\right)^4 \tag{4.5}$$

$a^2 = \sqrt{2}A \Rightarrow a = 2^{1/4}\sqrt{A} \Rightarrow$

$$a = \sqrt{\frac{5}{3}\frac{(\Gamma(1/4))^2}{2^{3/2}\pi}} \simeq 1.9098. \tag{4.6}$$

Calculation of the period T of the limit cycle. We have $y(x) = (1/\sqrt{2})\sqrt{a^4 - x^4}$ and $\dot{x} = -y \Rightarrow dt = -dx/y \Rightarrow$

$$T = 2\int_{-a}^{a}\frac{\sqrt{2}}{\sqrt{a^4 - x^4}}dx = 4\sqrt{2}\int_0^a (a^4 - x^4)^{-1/2}dx. \tag{4.7}$$

By putting $x = at^{1/4}$, we obtain

$$\begin{aligned}T &= \frac{\sqrt{2}}{a}\int_0^1 t^{-3/4}(1-t)^{-1/2}dt = \frac{\sqrt{2}}{a}\beta\left(\frac{1}{4},\frac{1}{2}\right),\\ T &= 2\sqrt{\frac{6\pi}{5}} \simeq 3.8833.\end{aligned} \tag{4.8}$$

(2) $\ddot{x} + \varepsilon(x^2 - 1)\dot{x} + x^{2n-1} = 0$ or

$$\begin{aligned}\dot{x} &= -y,\\ \dot{y} &= x^{2n-1} + \varepsilon(x^2 - 1)y.\end{aligned} \tag{4.9}$$

From (3.15) and (3.4), we have

$$\begin{aligned}
\bar{f}(X,Y) &= 0, \\
\bar{g}(X,Y) &= -2n^{1/2n-1}|X|^{1/n-1}(n^{1/n}|X|^{2/n}-1)Y, \\
\bar{\beta}(A) &= -4n^{1/2n-1}\int_0^A X^{1/n-1}(n^{1/n}X^{2/n}-1)\sqrt{A^2-X^2}dX.
\end{aligned} \tag{4.10}$$

By putting $X = A\alpha$, then $t = \alpha^2$, and we obtain

$$\bar{\beta}(A) = -4n^{1/2n-1}A^{1/n+1}(n^{1/n}A^{2/n}I_1 - I_2), \tag{4.11}$$

where

$$\begin{aligned}
I_1 &= \frac{1}{2}\int_0^1 t^{3/2n-1}(1-t)^{1/2}dt = \frac{1}{2}\beta\left(\frac{3}{2n},\frac{3}{2}\right) = \frac{n}{n+3}2^{3/n-2}\frac{(\Gamma(3/2n))^2}{\Gamma(3/n)}, \\
I_2 &= \frac{1}{2}\int_0^1 t^{1/2n-1}(1-t)^{1/2}dt = \frac{1}{2}\beta\left(\frac{1}{2n},\frac{3}{2}\right) = 2^{1/n-2}\frac{n}{n+1}\frac{(\Gamma(1/2n))^2}{\Gamma(1/n)}.
\end{aligned} \tag{4.12}$$

We find

$$\bar{\beta}(A) = -2^{1/n}n^{1/2n}A^{1/n+1}\left(\frac{n^{1/n}}{n+3}A^{2/n}2^{2/n}\frac{(\Gamma(3/2n))^2}{\Gamma(3/n)} - \frac{1}{n+1}\frac{(\Gamma(1/2n))^2}{\Gamma(1/n)}\right). \tag{4.13}$$

We find

$$a = n^{1/2n}A^{1/n} = 2^{-1/n}\sqrt{\frac{n+3}{n+1}\frac{\Gamma(1/2n)}{\Gamma(3/2n)}}\sqrt{\frac{\Gamma(3/n)}{\Gamma(1/n)}}. \tag{4.14}$$

If $n = 1$, we have

$$2^{-1}\sqrt{2}\frac{\Gamma(1/2)}{\Gamma(3/2)}\sqrt{\frac{\Gamma(3)}{\Gamma(1)}} = \frac{1}{2}\sqrt{2}\frac{\sqrt{\pi}}{\sqrt{\pi}/2}\sqrt{\frac{2}{1}} = 2, \tag{4.15}$$

which is the amplitude of the Van der Pol equation $\ddot{x} + \varepsilon(x^2-1)\dot{x} + x = 0$.

For $n = 2$, we find the first example

$$a = \frac{1}{\sqrt{2}}\sqrt{\frac{5}{3}\frac{\Gamma(1/4)}{\Gamma(3/4)}}\sqrt{\frac{\Gamma(3/2)}{\Gamma(1/2)}} = \sqrt{\frac{5}{3}\frac{(\Gamma(1/4))^2}{2^{3/2}\pi}}, \tag{4.16}$$

$n = 3$, we find

$$a = \frac{1}{2^{1/3}}\sqrt{\frac{3}{2\pi}\frac{\Gamma(1/6)}{\sqrt{\Gamma(1/3)}}}. \tag{4.17}$$

The period of the limit cycle. $y = (1/\sqrt{n})(a^{2n} - x^{2n})^{1/2}$, $dt = -dx/y$, so

$$T = 4\int_0^a \frac{\sqrt{n}}{\left(a^{2n} - x^{2n}\right)^{1/2}} dx. \tag{4.18}$$

We put $x = at^{1/2n}$, and we have

$$T = \frac{2\sqrt{n}}{na^{n-1}} \int_0^1 t^{1/2n-1}(1-t)^{-1/2}dt = \frac{2}{\sqrt{n}}\left(\frac{n+1}{n+3}\right)^{(n-1)/2} \frac{(\Gamma(3/2n))^{n-1}(\Gamma(1/n))^{(n-3)/2}}{(\Gamma(1/2n))^{n-3}(\Gamma(3/n))^{(n-1)/2}}. \tag{4.19}$$

(3) $\ddot{x} + \varepsilon(x^{2m} - 1)\dot{x} + x^{2n-1} = 0$ or

$$\begin{aligned} \dot{x} &= -y, \\ \dot{y} &= x^{2n-1} + \varepsilon(x^{2m} - 1)y. \end{aligned} \tag{4.20}$$

From (3.15) and (3.4), we have

$$\begin{aligned}
\bar{f}(X,Y) &= 0,\\
\bar{g}(X,Y) &= -2n^{1/2n-1}|X|^{1/n-1}(n^{m/n}|X|^{2m/n} - 1)Y,\\
\bar{\beta}(A) &= -4n^{1/2n-1}\int_0^A X^{1/n-1}(n^{m/n}X^{2m/n} - 1)\sqrt{A^2 - X^2}dX\\
&= -n^{1/2n-1}A^{1/n+1}\left(n^{m/n}A^{2m/n}\int_0^1 t^{(2m+1)/2n-1}(1-t)^{1/2}dt - \int_0^1 t^{1/2n-1}(1-t)^{1/2}dt\right)\\
&= -2n^{1/2n-1}A^{1/n+1}\left(n^{m/n}A^{2m/n}\beta\left(\frac{2m+1}{2n},\frac{3}{2}\right) - \beta\left(\frac{1}{2n},\frac{3}{2}\right)\right).
\end{aligned} \tag{4.21}$$

The relation between the amplitude is

$$\begin{aligned}
a^{2m} &= n^{m/n}A^{2m/n},\\
a &= \frac{1}{2^{1/n}}\left(\frac{2m+n+1}{n+1}\right)^{1/2m}\left(\frac{\Gamma(1/2n)}{\Gamma((2m+1)/2n)}\right)^{1/m}\left(\frac{\Gamma((2m+1)/n)}{\Gamma(1/n)}\right)^{1/2m}.
\end{aligned} \tag{4.22}$$

If $m = n = 1$,

$$a = 2. \tag{4.23}$$

If $n = 1$,

$$a = 2\sqrt[2m]{\frac{(m+1)!m!}{(2m)!}}. \tag{4.24}$$

The period of the limit cycle is

$$T = \frac{2}{\sqrt{n}}\left(\frac{n+1}{2m+n+1}\right)^{(n-1)/2m}\left(\frac{(\Gamma((2m+1)/2n))^2}{\Gamma((2m+1)/n)}\right)^{(n-1)/2m}\left(\frac{\Gamma(1/n)}{(\Gamma(1/2n))^2}\right)^{(n-2m-1)/2m}. \tag{4.25}$$

If $n = m = 1$,

$$T = 2\pi. \tag{4.26}$$

(4) $\ddot{x} + \varepsilon(\sum_{i=0}^{m} b_{2i} \cdot x^{2i})\dot{x} + x^{2n-1} = 0$ or

$$\begin{aligned} \dot{x} &= -y, \\ \dot{y} &= x^{2n-1} + \varepsilon\left(\sum_{i=0}^{m} b_{2i} \cdot x^{2i}\right) y. \end{aligned} \tag{4.27}$$

From (3.15) and (3.4), we have

$$\begin{aligned} \bar{f}(X,Y) &= 0, \\ \bar{g}(X,Y) &= -2n^{1/2n-1}|X|^{1/n-1}Y\sum_{i=0}^{m} b_{2i} \cdot n^{i/n}|X|^{2i/n}, \\ \bar{\beta}(A) &= -4n^{1/2n-1}\sum_{i=0}^{m} b_{2i} \cdot n^{i/n}\int_0^A X^{(2i+1)/n-1}\sqrt{A^2-X^2}\,dX \\ &= -2\sqrt{\pi}n^{1/2n}A^{(n+1)/n}\sum_{i=0}^{m} b_{2i} \cdot \frac{n^{i/n}}{2i+n+1}\frac{\Gamma((2i+1)/2n)}{\Gamma((n+2i+1)/2n)}A^{2i/n} \end{aligned} \tag{4.28}$$

or $A = (1/\sqrt{n})a^n$, therefore

$$\beta(a) = -2\sqrt{\frac{\pi}{n}}a^{n+1}\sum_{i=0}^{m}\frac{b_{2i}}{2i+n+1}\frac{\Gamma((2i+1)/2n)}{\Gamma((n+2i+1)/2n)} \cdot a^{2i}. \tag{4.29}$$

By putting $\alpha_{2i} = (b_{2i}/(2i+n+1))(\Gamma((2i+1)/2n)/\Gamma((n+2i+1)/2n))$, we obtain

$$\beta(a) = -2\sqrt{\frac{\pi}{n}}a^{n+1}\sum_{i=0}^{m}\alpha_{2i} \cdot a^{2i}. \tag{4.30}$$

The amplitudes are the roots of $\beta(a) = 0$.

Remark 4.1. In this case, we have at most m limit cycles.

(5) $\ddot{x} + \varepsilon(|x|^n - 1)\dot{x} + \text{sign}(x) \cdot |x|^m = 0$, with

$$\text{sign}(x) = \begin{cases} 1 & \text{if } x > 0, \\ -1 & \text{if } x < 0, \end{cases} \tag{4.31}$$

or

$$\begin{aligned} \dot{x} &= y, \\ \dot{y} &= -\text{sign}(x) \cdot |x|^m - \varepsilon(|x|^n - 1)\,y. \end{aligned} \tag{4.32}$$

From (3.15) and (3.4), we have

$$\begin{aligned}
\bar{f}(X,Y) &= 0,\\
\bar{g}(X,Y) &= -2\left(\frac{m+1}{2}\right)^{-m/(m+1)}\left(\left(\frac{m+1}{2}\right)^{n/(m+1)}|x|^{(2n-m+1)/(m+1)} - |x|^{(1-m)/(1+m)}\right)Y,\\
\bar{\beta}(A) &= -4\left(\frac{m+1}{2}\right)^{-m/(m+1)}\left(\left(\frac{m+1}{2}\right)^{n/(m+1)}\int_0^A x^{(2n-m+1)/(m+1)}\sqrt{A^2-X^2}\,dX\right.\\
&\qquad \left. - \int_0^A x^{(1-m)/(1+m)}\sqrt{A^2-X^2}\,dX\right)\\
&= -2A^{(3+m)/(1+m)}\left(\frac{m+1}{2}\right)^{-m/(m+1)}\left(\left(\frac{m+1}{2}\right)^{n/(m+1)}A^{2n/(1+m)}\beta\left(\frac{n+1}{m+1},\frac{3}{2}\right)\right.\\
&\qquad \left. - \beta\left(\frac{1}{m+1},\frac{3}{2}\right)\right) = 0,\\
A^{2n/(m+1)} &= \left(\frac{m+1}{2}\right)^{-n/(m+1)}\cdot\frac{\beta(1/(m+1),(3/2))}{\beta((n+1)/(m+1),(3/2))}.
\end{aligned} \tag{4.33}$$

We find

$$a = 2^{-2/(m+1)}\left(\frac{2n+m+3}{m+3}\right)^{1/n}\left(\frac{\Gamma(1/(m+1))}{\Gamma((n+1)/(m+1))}\right)^{2/n}\left(\frac{\Gamma(2(n+1)/(m+1))}{\Gamma(2/(m+1))}\right)^{1/n}. \tag{4.34}$$

If $n = m = 1$, we have

$$a = \frac{3}{4}\pi. \tag{4.35}$$

If $n = 1$, $m = 3$, we have

$$a = \frac{1}{3}\left(\frac{2}{\pi}\right)^{3/2}\left(\Gamma\left(\frac{1}{4}\right)\right)^2. \tag{4.36}$$

The period of the limit cycle is

$$\begin{aligned}
T &= 2\sqrt{\frac{2}{m+1}}\left(\frac{2n+m+3}{m+3}\right)^{(1-m)/2n}\left(\frac{(\Gamma(1/(m+1)))^2}{\Gamma(2/(m+1))}\right)^{(2n-m+1)/2n}\\
&\quad\times\left(\frac{\Gamma((2(n+1))/(m+1))}{(\Gamma((n+1)/(m+1)))^2}\right)^{(1-m)/2n}.
\end{aligned} \tag{4.37}$$

(6) $\ddot{x} + \varepsilon(x^{2m} - 1)\dot{x} + x^{1/(2n-1)} = 0$.
It is equivalent to the system

$$\begin{aligned}
\dot{x} &= -y,\\
\dot{y} &= x^{1/(2n-1)} + \varepsilon(x^{2m} - 1)y.
\end{aligned} \tag{4.38}$$

From (3.15) and (3.4), we have

$$\begin{aligned}
\bar{f}(X,Y) &= 0,\\
\bar{g}(X,Y) &= -\left(\frac{2n-1}{n}\right)^{1/2n}|X|^{(n-1)/n}\left(\left(\frac{n}{2n-1}\right)^{(m/n)(2n-1)}\cdot|X|^{(2m/n)(2n-1)}-1\right)Y,\\
\bar{\beta}(A) &= -2\left(\frac{2n-1}{n}\right)^{1/2n}\\
&\quad\times\int_{-A}^{A}|X|^{(n-1)/n}\left(\left(\frac{n}{2n-1}\right)^{(m/n)(2n-1)}\cdot|X|^{(2m/n)(2n-1)}-1\right)\sqrt{A^2-X^2}dX.
\end{aligned}\tag{4.39}$$

By putting $X = A\alpha$ and $t = \alpha^2$, we obtain

$$\begin{aligned}
\bar{\beta}(A) &= -2\left(\frac{2n-1}{n}\right)^{1/2n}A^{(3n-1)/n}\\
&\quad\times\int_{0}^{1}t^{-1/2n}\left(\left(\frac{n}{2n-1}\right)^{(m/n)(2n-1)}\cdot A^{(2m/n)(2n-1)}\cdot t^{(m/n)(2n-1)}-1\right)(1-t)^{1/2}dt.
\end{aligned}\tag{4.40}$$

Let $\lambda = -2((2n-1)/n)^{1/2n}A^{(3n-1)/n}$, and we obtain

$$\bar{\beta}(A) = \lambda\left(\left(\frac{n}{2n-1}\right)^{(m/n)(2n-1)}\cdot A^{(2m/n)(2n-1)}\cdot\beta\left(\frac{(2m+1)(2n-1)}{2n},\frac{3}{2}\right)-\beta\left(\frac{2n-1}{2n},\frac{3}{2}\right)\right).\tag{4.41}$$

We have

$$a^{2m} = \left(\frac{n}{2n-1}\right)^{(m/n)(2n-1)}\cdot A^{(2m/n)(2n-1)}.\tag{4.42}$$

We find from $\bar{\beta}(A) = 0$ that

$$a^{2m} = \frac{\beta((2n-1)/2n,(3/2))}{\beta((2m+1)(2n-1)/2n,(3/2))},\tag{4.43}$$

$$\begin{aligned}
a &= 2^{-(1/n)(2n-1)}\left(\frac{(2m+1)(2n-1)+n}{3n-1}\right)^{1/2m}\left(\frac{\Gamma((2n-1)/2n)}{\Gamma((2m+1)(2n-1)/2n)}\right)^{1/m}\\
&\quad\times\left(\frac{\Gamma((2m+1)(2n-1)/n)}{\Gamma((2n-1)/n)}\right)^{1/2m}.
\end{aligned}\tag{4.44}$$

For $n = 2, m = 1$, we have the equation

$$\begin{gathered}
\ddot{x}+\varepsilon(x^2-1)\dot{x}+x^{1/3} = 0,\\
a = \frac{2^{3/2}}{5}\pi\sqrt{231}\frac{1}{(\Gamma(1/4))^2}\simeq 2.0548.
\end{gathered}\tag{4.45}$$

This equation is studied by Mickens [3].

The period of the limit cycle. $dt = -dx/y$, $y = (\sqrt{(2n-1)/n})(a^{2n/(2n-1)} - x^{2n/(2n-1)})^{1/2}$,

$$T = 4\int_0^a \frac{dx}{y} = 4\sqrt{\frac{n}{2n-1}}\int_0^a \left(a^{2n/(2n-1)} - x^{2n/(2n-1)}\right)^{-1/2} dx. \tag{4.46}$$

By putting $t = (x/a)^{2n/(2n-1)}$, we obtain

$$\begin{aligned} T &= 4\sqrt{\frac{n}{2n-1}}\,\frac{2n-1}{2n}a^{(n-1)/(2n-1)}\int_0^1 t^{-1/2n}(1-t)^{-1/2}dt, \\ T &= 2\sqrt{\frac{2n-1}{n}}a^{(n-1)/(2n-1)}\beta\left(\frac{2n-1}{2n}, \frac{1}{2}\right), \\ T &= 2^{(2n+1)/n}\pi\frac{\sqrt{n(2n-1)}}{n-1}a^{(n-1)/(2n-1)}, \quad \text{where } a \text{ is defined as (4.44)}. \end{aligned} \tag{4.47}$$

5. Numerical results

(1) $\ddot{x} + \varepsilon(x^2 - 1)\dot{x} + x^3 = 0$,

$$\begin{aligned} a &= \sqrt{\frac{5}{3}\frac{(\Gamma(1/4))^2}{2^{3/2}\pi}} \simeq 1.9098, \\ T &= 2\sqrt{\frac{6\pi}{5}} \simeq 3.8833. \end{aligned} \tag{5.1}$$

(2) $\ddot{x} + \varepsilon(|x| - 1)\dot{x} + x^3 = 0$,

$$\begin{aligned} a &= \frac{1}{3}\left(\frac{2}{\pi}\right)^{3/2}\left(\Gamma\left(\frac{1}{4}\right)\right)^2 \simeq 2.2257, \\ T &= \frac{3}{4}\sqrt{2}\pi \simeq 3.3322. \end{aligned} \tag{5.2}$$

(3) $\ddot{x} + \varepsilon(|x| - 1)\dot{x} + x = 0$,

$$\begin{aligned} a &= \frac{3}{4}\pi \simeq 2.3562, \\ T &= 2\pi \simeq 6.2832. \end{aligned} \tag{5.3}$$

(4) $\ddot{x} + \varepsilon(x^2 - 1)\dot{x} + x^{1/3} = 0$,

$$\begin{aligned} a &= \frac{2^{3/2}}{5}\pi\sqrt{231}\frac{1}{(\Gamma(1/4))^2} \simeq 2.0548, \\ T &= 2^{5/2}\pi\sqrt{6}\left(\frac{2^{3/2}}{5}\pi\sqrt{231}\frac{1}{(\Gamma(1/4))^2}\right)^{1/3} \simeq 55.342. \end{aligned} \tag{5.4}$$

Conclusion. We remark that in every case, the amplitude is the same (see Figures 5.1, 5.2, 5.3, 5.4).

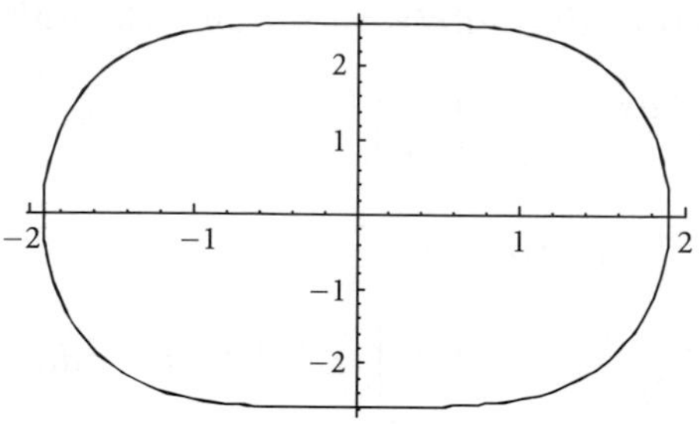

Figure 5.1. The limit cycle for $\varepsilon = 0.01$.

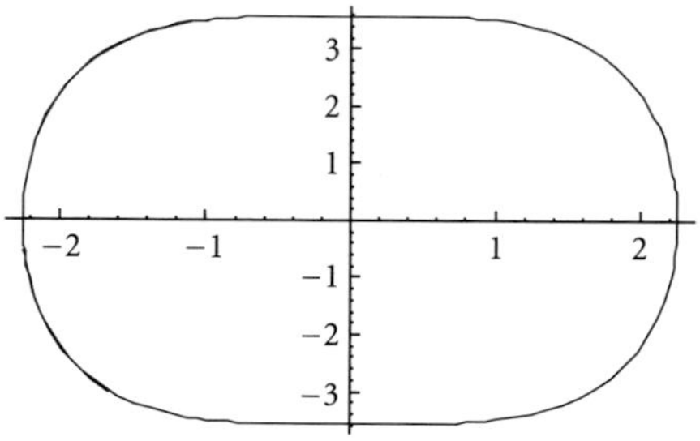

Figure 5.2. The limit cycle for $\varepsilon = 0.01$.

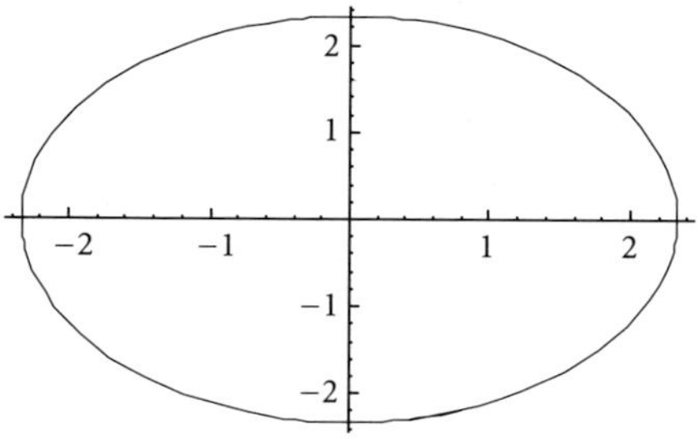

Figure 5.3. The limit cycle for $\varepsilon = 0.01$.

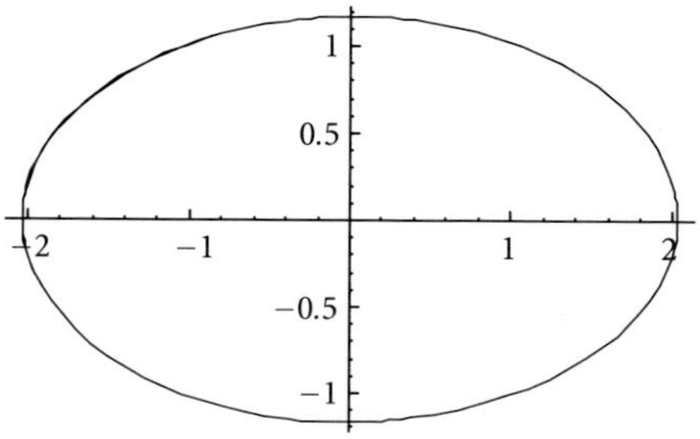

Figure 5.4. The limit cycle for $\varepsilon = 0.01$.

References

[1] D. W. Jordan and P. Smith, *Nonlinear Ordinary Differential Equations. An Introduction to Dynamical Systems*, 3rd ed., Oxford Texts in Applied and Engineering Mathematics, vol. 2, Oxford University Press, Oxford, 1999.
[2] J. L. Lopez and R. Lopez-Ruiz, *Number and amplitude of limit cycles emerging from topologically equivalent perturbed centers*, Chaos, Solitons and Fractals **17** (2003), no. 1, 135–143.
[3] R. E. Mickens, *A combined equivalent linearization and averaging perturbation method for nonlinear oscillator equations*, Journal of Sound and Vibration **264** (2003), no. 5, 1195–1200.

M. Amar: Department of Mathematics, University of Annaba, P.O. Box 12,
Annaba 23000, Algeria
E-mail address: makhloufamar@yahoo.fr

Y. Bouattia: Department of Mathematics, University of Annaba, P.O. Box 12,
Annaba 23000, Algeria
E-mail address: bouattiay@yahoo.fr

THEORY OF FUNCTIONAL DIFFERENTIAL EQUATIONS AND SOME PROBLEMS IN ECONOMIC DYNAMICS

V. P. MAKSIMOV

This paper focuses on boundary value problems and control problems for functional differential equations in the abstract form. Key questions of developing techniques for the computer-assisted study of such problems are discussed. Within the framework of the general approach, the problems of impulse and hybrid control are considered with regard to applications in economic mathematical modeling.

1. Introduction

Economic dynamics is one of the possible and very actively developing area in applications of the theory of functional differential equations (FDEs). The subject to study is an in time developing process as a sequence of the states of an economy system with possible structural breaks. An essential feature of any economic process is the presence of a lag which means a period of time between the moment of an external action and a reply of the system, for instance, between capital investments moment and a moment of an actual growth in output. Thus a model governing the dynamics of the economic system under consideration can be written in the form of FDE. First we give below some preliminaries from the theory of FDEs in an abstract form. Those are concerned around boundary value problems (BVPs) and control problems (CPs). Next some corollaries from the general theorems are formulated in a form that allows one to apply the results to some problems that arise in economic dynamics, also some questions of the computer-assisted study of BVPs and CPs are discussed. Finally, we present two problems from economic dynamics that are formulated in the form of impulse (hybrid) control problems.

2. Preliminaries

Let $\mathbf{D}$ and $\mathbf{B}$ be Banach spaces such that $\mathbf{D}$ is isomorphic to the direct product $\mathbf{B} \times \mathbb{R}^n$ (in what follows we write $\mathbf{D} \simeq \mathbf{B} \times \mathbb{R}^n$).

Hindawi Publishing Corporation
Proceedings of the Conference on Differential & Difference Equations and Applications, pp. 757–765

The equation

$$\mathcal{L}x = f \tag{2.1}$$

with a linear bounded operator $\mathcal{L} : \mathbf{D} \to \mathbf{B}$ is called the linear abstract functional differential equation (AFDE). The theory of (2.1) was thoroughly treated in [4, 5]. Let us fix an isomorphism $J = \{\Lambda, Y\} : \mathbf{B} \times \mathbb{R}^n \to \mathbf{D}$ and denote the inverse $J^{-1} = [\delta, r]$. Here $\Lambda : \mathbf{B} \to \mathbf{D}$, $Y : \mathbb{R}^n \to \mathbf{D}$ and $\delta : \mathbf{D} \to \mathbf{B}$, $r : \mathbf{D} \to \mathbb{R}^n$ are the corresponding components of J and J^{-1}:

$$\begin{aligned} J\{z,\alpha\} &= \Lambda z + Y\alpha \in \mathbf{D}, \quad z \in \mathbf{B},\ \alpha \in \mathbb{R}^n, \\ J^{-1}x &= \{\delta x, rx\} \in \mathbf{B} \times \mathbb{R}^n, \quad x \in \mathbf{D}. \end{aligned} \tag{2.2}$$

The system

$$\delta x = z, \qquad rx = \alpha \tag{2.3}$$

is called the principal boundary value problem (PBVP). Thus, for any $\{z,\alpha\} \in \mathbf{B} \times \mathbb{R}^n$,

$$x = \Lambda z + Y\alpha \tag{2.4}$$

is the solution of (2.3). The representation (2.4) gives the representation of $\mathcal{L}$: $\mathcal{L}x = \mathcal{L}(\Lambda z + Y\alpha) = \mathcal{L}\Lambda z + \mathcal{L}Y\alpha = Qz + A\alpha$, where the so-called principal part of $\mathcal{L}$, $Q : \mathbf{B} \to \mathbf{B}$ and the finite-dimensional $A : \mathbb{R}^n \to \mathbf{D}$ are defined by $Q = \mathcal{L}\Lambda$ and $A = \mathcal{L}Y$. The general theory of (2.1) assumes Q to be a Fredholm operator (i.e., a Noether one with the zero index).

Consider the general BVP

$$\mathcal{L}x = f, \qquad lx = \beta \tag{2.5}$$

with $l = [l^1, \dots, l^N] : \mathbf{D} \to \mathbb{R}^N$, linear bounded vector-functional. BVP (2.5) is the central subject in the theory of AFDE. In the case that $N = n$ and (2.5) is uniquely solvable for any $\{f, \beta\} \in \mathbf{B} \times \mathbb{R}^n$, we have the representation of the solution in the form

$$x = Gf + X\beta. \tag{2.6}$$

The operator $G : \mathbf{B} \to \mathbf{D}$ is called the Green operator, the operator $X : \mathbb{R}^n \to \mathbf{D}$ is called the fundamental vector. A way to study BVP (2.5) for the unique solvability is as follows. Suppose that the principal BVP for (2.1)

$$\mathcal{L}x = f, \qquad rx = \alpha \tag{2.7}$$

is uniquely solvable. In such a case, denoting the Green operator of the problem by G_r, we have the representation

$$x = G_r f + X\alpha \tag{2.8}$$

of the general solution to $\mathcal{L}x = f$ assuming α to be arbitrary element from $\mathbb{R}^n$. Representation (2.8) implies that the unique solvability of (2.5) is equivalent to the unique solvability of the algebraic system $lX\alpha = \beta - lG_r f$. Thus BVP (2.5) is uniquely solvable if and only if the matrix lX is invertible. This condition cannot be verified immediately because the fundamental vector X cannot be (as a rule) evaluated explicitly. In addition, even if X were known, then the elements of lX, generally speaking, could not be evaluated explicitly. By the theorem about inverse operators, the matrix lX is invertible if one can find an invertible matrix Γ such that $\|lX - \Gamma\| < 1/\|\Gamma^{-1}\|$. As it has been shown in [3], such a matrix Γ for the invertible matrix lX can always be found among the matrices $\Gamma = \bar{l}\bar{X}$, where $\bar{l} : \mathbf{D} \to \mathbb{R}^n$ is a vector-functional near to l, and $\bar{X}$ is an approximation of X. That is why the basis of the so-called constructive study of linear BVPs includes a special technique of constructing the approximate solutions to FDE with guaranteed explicit error bounds as well as the reliable computing experiment (RCE), whose theory has been worked out in [10] (see Section 4).

Consider the abstract control problem

$$\mathcal{L}x = Fu + f, \qquad rx = \alpha, \qquad lx = \beta, \tag{2.9}$$

where the control u belongs to a Hilbert space $\mathbf{H}$, $F : \mathbf{H} \to \mathbf{B}$ is the linear bounded operator, $l = [l_1, \dots, l_n]$ is the on target vector-functional that defines the aim of controlling: $lx = \beta$. Here we give a theorem that allows us to use the idea of constructive approach as applied to (2.9).

Let us define the linear bounded functional $\lambda_i : \mathbf{H} \to \mathbb{R}$, $i = 1, \dots, n$, by $\lambda_i u = l_i G_r F u$. It is clear that we can write $\lambda_i u$ in the form $\lambda_i u = \langle \mu_i, u \rangle$, where $\langle \cdot, \cdot \rangle$ stands for the inner product of $\mathbf{H}$ and μ_i means the element of $\mathbf{H}$ that generates $\lambda_i : \mathbf{H} \to \mathbb{R}$.

Theorem 2.1. *The control problem (2.9) is solvable for any $f \in \mathbf{B}$ and $\alpha, \beta \in \mathbb{R}^n$ if and only if the matrix $M \overset{\text{def}}{=} \{\langle \mu_i, \mu_j \rangle\}_{i,j=1,\dots,n}$ is invertible. The control $u_0 = \sum_{i=1}^n \mu_i c_i$ with* $\operatorname{col}(c_1, \dots, c_n) = M^{-1}[\beta - lG_r f - lX\alpha]$ *solves CP (2.9).*

Proof. For any $u \in \mathbf{H}$ we have the representation $u = \sum_{i=1}^n \mu_i c_i + v$, where $v \in \mathbf{H}$ is orthogonal to the linear span of $\mu_1, \dots, \mu_n$. Let us find a control u that solves CP (2.9) by searching for coefficients $c_1, \dots, c_n$. By (2.8) we have

$$x = G_r F u + G_r f + X\alpha \tag{2.10}$$

for solutions of (2.7). Applying l to both sides of (2.10) and taking into account the conditions $lx = \beta$, we obtain the system $Mc = \beta - lG_r f - lX\alpha$. □

Similarly to the study of BVP, we establish the solvability of (2.9) if we can construct a matrix $\widetilde{M}$ such that it has the inverse $\widetilde{M}^{-1}$ and the inequality $\|M - \widetilde{M}^{-1}\| < 1/\|\widetilde{M}^{-1}\|$ holds.

In what follows we restrict our attention to the following examples of the spaces $\mathbf{D} \simeq \mathbf{B} \times \mathbb{R}^n$ (see [4] for details).

(1) Let $\mathbf{D} = \mathbf{AC}$ be the space of absolutely continuous functions $x : [0,T] \to \mathbb{R}^n$. We have $x(t) = \int_0^t \dot{x}(s)ds + x(0)$, $\mathbf{B} = \mathbf{L}$, the space of Lebesgue summable functions $z : [0,T] \to \mathbb{R}^n$ with $\|z\|_L = \int_0^T \|z(s)\|_{\mathbb{R}^n} ds$. Thus

$$(\Lambda z)(t) = \int_0^t z(s)ds, \qquad Y = E, \qquad \delta x = \dot{x}, \qquad rx = x(0). \tag{2.11}$$

Here and in what follows, E is the identity matrix. The isomorphism between the space of absolutely continuous functions $x : [0,T] \to \mathbb{R}^n$ and the direct product $\mathbf{L} \times \mathbb{R}^n$ is fundamental to many assertions of the theory of FDE and makes it possible to reduce many problems in the space **AC** to ones in the space **L**. The theory of BVPs and CPs in the space **AC** is outlined in [3].

(2) Let us fix a collection of points $t_k \in (0,T)$, $0 < t_1 < \cdots < t_m < T$. Consider the space $\mathbf{D} = \mathbf{DS}(m)$ of functions $x : [0,T] \to \mathbb{R}^n$ that are representable in the form

$$x(t) = \int_0^t z(s)ds + x(0) + \sum_{k=1}^m \chi_{[t_k,T]}(t)\Delta x(t_k), \tag{2.12}$$

where $z \in \mathbf{L}$, $\Delta x(t_k) = x(t_k) - x(t_k - 0)$, $\chi_{[t_k,T]}(t)$ is the characteristic function of the segment $[t_k,T]$. In this case $\mathbf{D} \simeq \mathbf{L} \times \mathbb{R}^{n+mn}$ with

$$\begin{gathered} (\Lambda z)(t) = \int_0^t z(s)ds, \qquad (Y\alpha)(t) = \alpha^0 + \sum_{k=1}^m \chi_{[t_k,T]}(t)\alpha^k, \quad \alpha = \operatorname{col}(\alpha^0,\dots,\alpha^m), \\ \delta x = \dot{x}, \qquad rx = \{x(0), \Delta x(t_1),\dots,\Delta x(t_m)\}. \end{gathered} \tag{2.13}$$

3. Impulsive and hybrid controls

An approach to the study of differential equations with discontinuous solutions is associated with the so-called "generalized ordinary differential equations" whose theory was initiated by Kurzweil [7]. Nowadays this theory is highly developed (see, e.g., [2, 11]). According to the accepted approaches impulsive equations are considered within the class of functions of bounded variation. In this case the solution is understood as a function of bounded variation satisfying an integral equation with the Lebesgue-Stieltjes integral or Perron-Stieltjes one. Integral equations in the space of functions of bounded variation became the subject of its own interest and are studied in details in [12]. Recall that the function of bounded variation is representable in the form of the sum of an absolutely continuous function, a break function, and a singular component (a continuous function with the derivative being equal to zero almost everywhere). The solutions of equations with impulse impact, which are considered below, do not contain the singular component and may have discontinuity only at finite number of prescribed points. We consider these equations on a finite-dimensional extension $\mathbf{DS}(m)$ of the traditional space **AC** of absolutely continuous functions. This approach to the equations with impulsive impact was offered in [1]. It does not use the complicated theory of generalized functions, turned out to be rich in content and finds many applications in the cases where the question about the singular component does not arise, in particular, in certain economic dynamics problems that are considered in Section 5 (see [8] for details).

Consider the functional differential system

$$(\mathcal{L}x)(t) = f(t), \quad t \in [0,T], \tag{3.1}$$

where $\mathcal{L} : \mathbf{DS}(m) \to \mathbf{L}$ is linear bounded and has the principal part of the form

$$(Qz)(t) = z(t) - \int_0^t K(t,s)z(s)ds. \tag{3.2}$$

Here the elements $k^{ij}(t,s)$ of the kernel $K(t,s)$ are measurable on the set $0 \le s \le t \le T$ and such that $|k^{ij}(t,s)| \le \mu(t)$, $i,j = 1,\dots,n$, $\mu(\cdot)$ is summable on $[0,T]$. Notice that the form of (3.1) covers many classes of dynamic models including differential systems with distributed or/and concentrated delay and integrodifferential systems.

The space of all solutions to the homogeneous system $\mathcal{L}x = 0$ is finite dimensional, its dimension equals $n+nm$. Let $\{x_1,\dots,x_{n+nm}\}$ be a basis in this space. The matrix $X = \{x_1,\dots,x_{n+nm}\}$ is called a fundamental matrix. We deal with X such that $rX = E$. The principal BVP $\mathcal{L}x = f$, $rx = \sigma$ is uniquely solvable for any $f \in \mathbf{L}, \sigma \in \mathbb{R}^{n+nm}$, its solution is representable in the form

$$x(t) = X(t) \cdot \sigma + \int_0^t C(t,s)f(s)ds, \tag{3.3}$$

where $C(t,s)$ is the Cauchy matrix. Let $l : \mathbf{DS}(m) \to \mathbb{R}^N$ be a linear bounded vector-functional. There takes place the representation

$$lx = \int_0^T \Phi(s)\dot{x}(s)ds + \Psi_0 x(0) + \sum_{k=1}^m \Psi_k \Delta x(t_k), \tag{3.4}$$

where the elements of measurable $N \times n$-matrix Φ are essentially bounded and Ψ_k, $k = 0,\dots,m$, are $N \times n$-matrices with real elements.

Consider the control problem

$$\mathcal{L}x = Fu + f, \qquad x(0) = \alpha, \qquad lx = \beta. \tag{3.5}$$

Here $F : \mathbf{L}_2 \to \mathbf{L}$ is a given linear bounded operator, $\mathbf{L}_2$ is the space of square summable functions $u : [0,T] \to \mathbb{R}^r$ with the inner product $(u,v) = \int_0^T u^\top(s)v(s)ds$, $\cdot^\top$ is the symbol of transposition. In the problem (3.5), the target of controlling is defined by the vector-functional $l : \mathbf{DS}(m) \to \mathbb{R}^N$ whose value on a trajectory of $\mathcal{L}x = Fu + f$ must reach (under control) the vector $\beta \in \mathbb{R}^N$. The problem (3.5) includes in particular the control problem with L_2-control (the case that the condition $lx = \beta$ includes the equalities $\Delta x(t_k) = 0$, $k = 1,\dots,m$) and the control problem with only impulse control (the case $F = 0$, where the role of control actions is played only by the jumps $\Delta x^i(t_k)$). Here we give conditions of controllability through the hybrid control.

Let us denote

$$\Theta(s) = \Phi(s) + \int_s^T \Phi(\tau)C'_\tau(\tau,s)d\tau, \qquad \Xi = \int_0^T \Phi(s)\dot{X}(s)ds = (\Xi_1 \mid \Xi_2), \tag{3.6}$$

where Ξ_1 is the $N \times n$-matrix consisting of the first n columns of $N \times (n+nm)$-matrix Ξ;

$$M = \int_0^T [F^* \Theta](s)[F^* \Theta]^\top(s)ds, \tag{3.7}$$

where $F^* : \mathbf{L}^* \to \mathbf{L}_2^*$ is the adjoint operator to F.

THEOREM 3.1. *The control problem (3.5) is solvable if and only if the linear algebraic system*

$$[\Xi_2 + (\Psi_1,\dots,\Psi_m)] \cdot \delta + M \cdot \gamma = \beta - \int_0^T \Theta(s)f(s)ds - (\Xi_1 + \Psi_0) \cdot \alpha \tag{3.8}$$

is solvable in $(N+nm)$*-vector* $\operatorname{col}(\delta,\gamma)$. *Each solution* $\operatorname{col}(\delta_0,\gamma_0)$, $\delta_0 = \operatorname{col}(\delta_0^1,\dots,\delta_0^m)$, *of the system (3.8) defines the control that solves CP (3.5):* $\Delta x(t_k) = \delta_0^k$, $k = 1,\dots,m$, $u(t) = [F^*\Theta]^\top(t) \cdot \gamma_0$.

Some questions of computer-assisted studying CP (3.5) through system (3.8) are discussed in the next Section.

Notice that the main results and algorithms for CP (3.5) allow extending for the control problem

$$\mathcal{L}x = Fu + f, \qquad x(0) = \alpha, \qquad lx \leq \beta \tag{3.9}$$

with target constraints in the form of functional inequalities (see, e.g., [8]).

4. Reliable computing experiment

The effective study of the original problem (3.5) is based on the use of the corresponding problem (3.8). In doing so we have to understand that all the parameters of (3.8) can be only approximately calculated. Thus the study of (3.8) for solvability requests a special technique with the use of the so-called reliable computing experiment (RCE) [4, 10]. Both the theoretical background and practical implementation of RCE need the elaboration of some specific constructive methods of investigation based on the fundamental statements of the general theory with making use of contemporary software. It is relevant to notice that the main destination of such methods is reliable establishing the fact of the solvability of the problem. If it is done, the next task is to construct an approximate solution in common with an error bound of quite high quality. RCE as a tool for the study of differential and integral models is very actively developing during the last 20 years. There are some main directions in this field: the study of the Cauchy problem for ordinary differential equations (ODEs) as well as for certain classes of partial DEs (PDEs) (H. Bauch, M. Berz, G. Corliss, B. Dobronetz, E. Kaucher, and W. Miranker); the study of boundary value problems (BVPs) for ODEs and PDEs (S. Godunov, M. Plum, N. Ronto, and A. Samoilenko); the study of integral equations (E. Kaucher and W. Miranker, C. Kennedy, R. Wang); the study of nonlinear operator equations (S. Kalmykov, R. Moor, Yu. Shockin, Z. Yuldashev). A common idea in these studies is the interval calculus in finite-dimensional and functional spaces and, as a consequence, the special techniques of rounding off when calculations are produced by real computer. Our approach allows us to consider essentially more wide class of problems that are complicated by such properties as the property of not being a local operator, the presence of discontinuous solutions, the presence of the inner superposition operator, as well as the general form of boundary condition. In addition, we do not use interval calculations, which are characterized by high speed of the accumulation of rounding errors, but make use of the rational numbers arithmetics with a specific technique of definitely oriented rounding. The key idea of the constructive study is as follows: by the original problem there is being constructed an auxiliary problem with reliably computable parameters, which allows one to produce the efficient computer-assisted testing for the solvability. If such a problem is solvable, the final result depends on the closeness of the original problem and the auxiliary one. The theorems, which stand for a background of RCE, give efficiently testable (by means of computer) conditions of the solvability for the original problem. In the case where these conditions are failed one has to construct a new (and more close to the original problem) auxiliary problem and then to test the conditions again. The implementation of the constructive methods in the form of a computer program (of course, it must be oriented to quite definite class of problems) allows one to study a concrete problem by a many times repeated RCE. A theoretical background and some details of the practical implementation of RCE for the study of functional differential systems are presented in [10]. As to problem (3.5), the corresponding RCE includes the construction and the successive refinement of approximation to $C(t,s)$, $\Theta(s)$, M with reliable error bounds. The key point is the approximate construction of C with a high reliable accuracy. An efficient computer-aided technique of such a construction under the condition that the kernel $K(t,s)$ admits a piecewise constant approximation, being as accurate as we wish, is proposed in [9].

5. Some control problems in economic dynamics

First we present a problem of controlling multisectors economic models through bank loaning. Let the dynamics of a multisector production model under L_2-control be governed by the system (3.1):

$$(\mathcal{L}x)(t) = (Fu)(t), \quad t \in [0,T], \; x(0) = \alpha, \tag{5.1}$$

(see (3.5)), where $u(t)$ is defined as an intensity of constantly entering investments. Let $u : [0,T] \to \mathbf{L}_2$ be given. Thus there exists a unique trajectory $x_0 \in \mathbf{AC}$ as the solution to (5.1). Let us assess x_0 by the indicators $l_j : \mathbf{DS}(m) \to \mathbb{R}$, $j = 1,\dots,q : l_j x_0 = \beta_j$. The problem is to provide the increase of $l_j x$ on the trajectories x of (5.1) through bank loaning as follows: using solutions $x \in \mathbf{DS}(m)$ (with jumps $\Delta x_i(t_k)$), given $\rho_j \geq 0$, $j = 1,\dots,q$, find $\Delta x_i(t_k)$ such that the conditions of increasing $l_j x = (1+\rho_j)\beta_j$, $j = 1,\dots,q$, hold subject to the constraints $\Delta x_i(t_1) \geq 0$, $i = 1,\dots,n$, (getting banks loans at the moment t_1); $\Delta x_i(t_k) = -(1+r_i)^{k-1} \cdot \gamma_{i,k-1} \cdot \Delta x_i(t_1)$, $k = 2,\dots,m$, $i = 1,\dots,n$, (back payment taking into account the interest rates r_i and the weight coefficients $0 \leq \gamma_{i,k-1} \leq 1$, $\sum_{k=1}^{m-1} \gamma_{i,k-1} = 1$). Thus we have a problem of the form (3.5).

Next let us dwell on a problem of controlling the bank portfolio as it is set in [6]. Denote by $x(t)$ the vector of bank resources at the moment $t \in [0,T]$ (cash assets, liquid securities, interest-earning long-term assets, investment portfolio, interbank credits, deposits, and so on): $x = \text{col}\{x_1,\dots,x_n\}$, x_i is the ith kind of resources. Let us consider $x(\cdot) \in \mathbf{DS}(m)$ with t_k, $k = 1,\dots,m$, being the points in time, at which control is being brought into operation. In such points a jump-like change of bank resources is possible. The equation governing the resources dynamics can be written in the form

$$\dot{x}(t) = (Vx)(t) - (Wx)(t), \quad t \in [0,T], \tag{5.2}$$

where a given operator V describes an increase of the resources and W a decrease. In addition to the initial conditions, there are three groups of restrictions with respect to the desired trajectory: (a) the qualitative restrictions; (b) the restrictions imposed by the Central Bank; (c) the market restrictions. The restrictions (a) are generated primarily due to the bank risks. To bound the risk of loss in the liquidity, the restrictions to a minimal value of the liquid assets are entered. Due to similar reasoning with respect to the credit risk and the interest risk, certain restrictions are added too. The restrictions (b) include the balance equations taking into account obligatory reserves at prescribed points in time. The restrictions (c) are entered to take into account practical possibilities of the bank resources operation in financial markets. In particular, there are imposed requirements on a maximum value of investments securities under operation. All the above constraints can be written in the form of the inequalities $lx \leq \beta$ and we obtain a problem (3.9).

Acknowledgment

This work was supported by the RFBR Grant 04-06-96002 and Grant UR.03.01.238 from the Scientific Programme "Universities of Russia - Fundamental Research."

References

[1] A. V. Anokhin, *Linear impulsive systems for functional-differential equations*, Doklady Akademii Nauk SSSR **286** (1986), no. 5, 1037–1040 (Russian).

[2] M. Ashordia, *On the stability of solutions of the multipoint boundary value problem for the system of generalized ordinary differential equations*, Memoirs on Differential Equations and Mathematical Physics **6** (1995), 1–57, 134.

[3] N. V. Azbelev, V. P. Maksimov, and L. F. Rakhmatullina, *Introduction to the Theory of Functional-Differential Equations*, Nauka, Moscow, 1991.

[4] ———, *The Elements of the Contemporary Theory of Functional Differential Equations. Methods and Applications*, Institute of Computer-Assisted Studies, Moscow, 2002.

[5] N. V. Azbelev and L. F. Rakhmatullina, *Theory of linear abstract functional-differential equations and applications*, Memoirs on Differential Equations and Mathematical Physics **8** (1996), 1–102.

[6] E. M. Krasavina, A. P. Kolchanov, and A. N. Rumyantsev, *A mathematical model of controlling the portfolio of a commercial bank*, Mathematical Modelling. Problems, Methods, Applications, Kluwer Academic / Plenum, New York, 2002, pp. 129–134.

[7] Ja. Kurzweil, *Generalized ordinary differential equations and continuous dependence on a parameter*, Czechoslovak Mathematical Journal **7 (82)** (1957), 418–449.

[8] V. P. Maksimov and A. N. Rumyantsev, *Boundary value problems and problems of impulse control in economic dynamics. Constructive investigation*, Russian Mathematics (Izvestiya VUZ. Matematika) **37** (1993), no. 5, 48–62.

[9] ———, *Reliable computing experiment in the study of generalized controllability of linear functional differential systems*, Mathematical Modelling. Problems, Methods, Applications (L. Uvarova and A. Latyshev, eds.), Kluwer Academic / Plenum, New York, 2002, pp. 91–98.

[10] A. N. Rumyantsev, *Reliable Computing Experiment in the Study of Boundary Value Problems*, Perm State University, Perm, 1999.
[11] Š. Schwabik, *Generalized Ordinary Differential Equations*, Series in Real Analysis, vol. 5, World Scientific, New Jersey, 1992.
[12] Š. Schwabik, M. Tvrdý, and O. Vejvoda, *Differential and Integral Equations. Boundary Value Problems and Adjoints*, D. Reidel, Dordrecht, 1979.

V. P. Maksimov: Department of Economic Cybernetics, Perm State University, 15 Bukireva Street, Perm 614990, Russia
E-mail address: maksimov@econ.psu.ru

MAXIMUM PRINCIPLES AND DECAY ESTIMATES FOR PARABOLIC SYSTEMS UNDER ROBIN BOUNDARY CONDITIONS

M. MARRAS AND S. VERNIER PIRO

We investigate nonlinear parabolic systems when Robin conditions are prescribed on the boundary. Sufficient conditions on data are imposed to obtain decay estimates for the solution. In addition, a maximum principle is proved for an auxiliary function, from which we deduce an exponential decay estimate for the gradient.

1. Introduction

Reaction diffusion parabolic systems are studied with interest as they provide models for various chemical and biological problems. Recently some qualitative properties of their solutions like blow-up and time decay estimates have been studied in [7, 9] (for the applications, see also the references therein). The aim of this paper is to investigate these properties for the following system with Robin boundary conditions:

$$\begin{aligned}
\Delta u + f_1(v) &= \frac{\partial u}{\partial t} \quad \text{in } \Omega \times (t > 0),\\
\Delta v + f_2(u) &= \frac{\partial v}{\partial t} \quad \text{in } \Omega \times (t > 0),\\
\frac{\partial u}{\partial n} + \alpha u &= 0 \quad \text{on } \partial\Omega \times (t > 0),\\
\frac{\partial v}{\partial n} + \alpha v &= 0 \quad \text{on } \partial\Omega \times (t > 0),\\
u(x,0) &= h_1(x) \quad \text{in } \Omega,\\
v(x,0) &= h_2(x) \quad \text{in } \Omega,
\end{aligned} \tag{1.1}$$

where Ω is a bounded domain in $\mathbb{R}^2$, $\alpha > 0$, and for $i = 1,2$, $f_i(s)$ are C^1 functions which

Hindawi Publishing Corporation
Proceedings of the Conference on Differential & Difference Equations and Applications, pp. 767–773

satisfy

$$f_i(0) = 0, \quad f_i(s) \geq 0, \quad f_i'(s) \leq p_i(s), \quad s > 0, \tag{1.2}$$

with $p_i(s)$ nondecreasing functions with respect to $s > 0$.

The functions $h_i \in C^1(\Omega)$, $(h_i \neq 0)$, are positive in Ω with

$$\frac{\partial h_i}{\partial n} + \alpha h_i = 0, \quad x \in \partial\Omega. \tag{1.3}$$

Here $\partial/\partial n$ indicates the normal derivative directed outward from Ω.

As a consequence (u, v) will be nonnegative.

In Section 2, we first consider (1.1) in the domain $Q_T = \Omega \times (0, T)$, where T is any time prior to possible blow-up time. We introduce the function

$$U(x,t) := u^2 + v^2, \tag{1.4}$$

the squared norm of the solution (u, v), and for it we prove an exponential decay estimate in $(0, T)$. Then, with additional restrictions on data, we extend the estimate for all $t > 0$.

In Section 3, we introduce in $Q = \Omega \times (t > 0)$ the auxiliary function

$$\Psi(x,t) = \Phi(x,t) - Kt \tag{1.5}$$

with

$$\Phi(x,t) := \{|\nabla u|^2 + |\nabla v|^2 + 2\delta(u^2 + v^2)\}e^{2\delta t}, \tag{1.6}$$

where K and δ are two positive constants which will be specified later on.

We prove that Ψ satisfies a parabolic inequality, and by applying the maximum principle (see [2, 3]), we obtain a decay estimate also for the gradient of the solution.

We remark that in [7] the authors consider a nonlinear system similar to (1.1) with Dirichlet boundary conditions instead of Robin, and derive decay bounds both for solutions and their gradients in a bounded convex domain in $\mathbb{R}^N$, under different choices of the nonlinearities.

In [9], a different class of reaction diffusion systems is investigated, where the Laplacian operator is replaced by an operator in a divergence form and Ω, a bounded domain in $\mathbb{R}^N$, is not required to be convex, while on $\partial\Omega \times (t > 0)$, Dirichlet-type conditions are imposed as in [7]. There the author determines explicit restrictions on data which insure that the solution does not blow up in finite time; moreover sufficient conditions are established to obtain that the solution and its gradient decay exponentially in time.

For the case of only one equation with Dirichlet boundary conditions, decay bounds have been obtained in [4, 5], and in a series of papers of Payne and Philippin cited in [5]. When the conditions on the boundary are of Robin type or of mixed type, such bounds are obtained in [6] for the linear heat problem in two space dimensions, and for the nonlinear in one dimension only.

Throughout the paper, we will use the following notation:

$$u_{,i} = \frac{\partial u}{\partial x_i}, \quad u_{,ik} = \frac{\partial^2 u}{\partial x_i \partial x_k}, \quad i = 1, 2, \; k = 1, 2, \tag{1.7}$$

and the repeated index indicates summation over $i = 1,2$ as in

$$u_{,i}u_{,i} = \left(\frac{\partial u}{\partial x_1}\right)^2 + \left(\frac{\partial u}{\partial x_2}\right)^2 = |\nabla u|^2. \tag{1.8}$$

2. Exponential decay results for $u^2 + v^2$

It is well known that the solution (u,v) of (1.1) may blow up (see [1, 4]). Let T^* be the possible blow-up time, which may be finite or infinite. We know that the solution exists in (0,T), with $T < T^*$.

In order to derive decay estimate for the solution of (1.1), we first consider (1.1) in the interval $(0,T)$ and prove the following.

Theorem 2.1. *Let (u,v) be a classical solution of (1.1) with $t \in (0,T)$. Assume that the functions f_i satisfy (1.2), and let*

$$M := \{p_1(v_m) + p_2(u_m)\} \tag{2.1}$$

with

$$u_m := \max_{Q_T}\{u(x,t)\}, \qquad v_m := \max_{Q_T}\{v(x,t)\}. \tag{2.2}$$

Then $U(x,t)$ satisfies the parabolic inequality

$$\Delta U - U_{,t} + MU \geq 0, \quad (x,t) \in Q_T. \tag{2.3}$$

In fact, using (1.2), the monotonicity of the functions p_i, and (2.1), we have

$$\begin{aligned} \Delta U - U_{,t} &\geq -2uv\left\{\frac{f_1(v)}{v} + \frac{f_2(u)}{u}\right\} \\ &\geq -(u^2+v^2)\{p_1(\eta_1) + p_2(\eta_2)\} \geq -MU \end{aligned} \tag{2.4}$$

with η_1 and η_2 some intermediate value.

As a consequence of (2.3) and (1.1) in $(0,T)$, $U(x,t)$ satisfies the following initial boundary value problem:

$$\begin{aligned} \Delta U - U_{,t} + MU &\geq 0, \quad (x,t) \in Q_T, \\ \frac{\partial U}{\partial n} &= -2\alpha U, \quad (x,t) \in \Gamma_T, \\ U(x,0) &= h(x), \quad x \in \Omega, \end{aligned} \tag{2.5}$$

with $h(x) = h_1^2(x) + h_2^2(x)$.

In order to obtain a decay estimate for $U(x,t)$, we introduce the auxiliary function $w(x,t) = U(x,t)e^{-Mt}$, which satisfies

$$\begin{aligned} \Delta w - w_{,t} &\geq 0, \quad (x,t) \in Q_T, \\ \frac{\partial w}{\partial n} &= -2\alpha w, \quad (x,t) \in \Gamma_T, \\ w(x,0) &= h(x), \quad x \in \Omega. \end{aligned} \tag{2.6}$$

Now if $\tilde{w}(x,t)$ is a solution of the following problem:

$$\begin{aligned} \Delta\tilde{w} - \tilde{w}_{,t} &= 0, \quad (x,t) \in Q_T, \\ \frac{\partial \tilde{w}}{\partial n} &= -2\alpha\tilde{w}, \quad (x,t) \in \Gamma_T, \\ \tilde{w}(x,0) &= h(x), \quad x \in \Omega, \end{aligned} \tag{2.7}$$

from a classical comparison theorem [8], we know that

$$w(x,t) \le \tilde{w}(x,t). \tag{2.8}$$

From a result in [6], we can prove the following.

LEMMA 2.2. *Let $\tilde{w}$ be a classical solution of (2.7). If Ω is a convex domain in $\mathbb{R}^2$ and $\partial\Omega$ is a $C^{2+\epsilon}$ surface and h has bounded second derivatives, then*

$$\tilde{w}(x,t) \le \Gamma_\beta e^{-\beta t}, \quad (x,t) \in Q_T, \tag{2.9}$$

with

$$\Gamma_\beta = \frac{\Gamma}{\sqrt{\beta}} := \max_{\Omega} \sqrt{h^2 + \frac{|\nabla h|^2}{\beta}}, \tag{2.10}$$

where the positive constant β is restricted by the conditions

$$\sqrt{\beta}\,\mathrm{tg}\sqrt{\beta}d < 2\alpha, \quad \sqrt{\beta}d < \frac{\pi}{2}, \tag{2.11}$$

$$\Delta h + 2(2\alpha^2 + \beta)h \ge 0. \tag{2.12}$$

In (2.11), d is the radius of the largest disk inscribed in Ω.

To prove Lemma 2.2, we first observe that under the hypotheses introduced, Payne and Schaefer in [6] prove the more general result

$$|\nabla\tilde{w}|^2 + \beta\tilde{w}^2 \le \Gamma^2 e^{-2\beta t} \quad \text{in } \Omega \times (t > 0), \tag{2.13}$$

with

$$\Gamma^2 = \max_{\Omega} \{|\nabla h|^2 + \beta h^2\}. \tag{2.14}$$

From (2.13), we derive (2.9).

Finally for the function $U(x,t) = we^{Mt}$, we get from (2.8) and (2.9) the following estimate:

$$U(x,t) \le \Gamma_\beta e^{-(\beta - M)t}, \quad (x,t) \in Q_T. \tag{2.15}$$

We note that from (2.15), if $\beta - M \ge 0$, we obtain $U(x,t) \le \Gamma_\beta$, and in Q_T,

$$u \le \sqrt{\Gamma_\beta}, \quad v \le \sqrt{\Gamma_\beta}, \tag{2.16}$$

are valid only in the time interval $(0,T)$.

Now in order to prove that the solution does not blow up and exists for all $t > 0$, we restrict the initial data $h_1(x)$ e $h_2(x)$ which are present in Γ_β.

We start with the following.

LEMMA 2.3. *Let (u,v) be the solution of problem (1.1) in $(0,T)$. Assume that f_i and p_i satisfy (1.2), and the initial data $h_1(x)$ and $h_2(x)$ satisfy*

$$p_1(\sqrt{\Gamma_\beta}) + p_2(\sqrt{\Gamma_\beta}) < \beta, \tag{2.17}$$

where β satisfies (2.11), (2.12), and Γ_β is defined in (2.10). Then (u,v) exists for all time $t > 0$ and satisfies the inequality

$$p_1(v(x,t)) + p_2(u(x,t)) < \beta, \quad \forall x \in \Omega,\ t > 0. \tag{2.18}$$

To prove Lemma 2.3, we suppose that (2.18) does not hold. Lemma 5 in [5], in view of (2.15), (2.16), and (2.17), we reach a contradiction.

By using Lemma 2.3, (2.15), and (2.1) it is easy to prove the following.

LEMMA 2.4. *Assume Lemma 2.3 holds. If for some positive constant ξ, the initial data $h_1(x)$ and $h_2(x)$ are restricted by the following condition:*

$$p_1(\sqrt{\Gamma_\beta}) + p_2(\sqrt{\Gamma_\beta}) \leq \beta - \xi, \tag{2.19}$$

then,

$$U(x,t) \leq \Gamma_\beta e^{-\xi t}, \quad \forall x \in \Omega,\ t > 0. \tag{2.20}$$

Formula (2.20) is the wanted estimate, which decays exponentially in time.

3. Maximum principle and decay results for the gradient of the solution

The goal of this section is to establish a decay estimate also for the gradient of the solution. To this end, we introduce an auxiliary function, where both the solution and its gradient are involved. Then we prove for it a maximum principle, from which we deduce the wanted estimate.

Let us consider auxiliary function $\Psi(x,t)$ defined in (1.5), where we select $\delta = \xi/2$.

We prove that $\Psi(x,t)$ satisfies a decay estimate in the following.

THEOREM 3.1. *Let (u,v) be the solution of (1.1) under the hypotheses of Lemma 2.4 and Ψ defined in (1.5). If*

$$\overline{M} \leq 2\delta, \quad \overline{M} := p_1(\sqrt{\Gamma_\beta}) + p_2(\sqrt{\Gamma_\beta}), \tag{3.1}$$

then $\Psi(x,t)$ takes its maximum value either at a boundary point on Γ or at an initial point $(t = 0)$ on Ω, that is,

$$\Psi(x,t) \leq \mathcal{M}, \quad (x,t) \in Q, \tag{3.2}$$

where $\mathcal{M} = \max\{\mathcal{M}_0, \mathcal{M}_1\}$, *with*

$$\mathcal{M}_0 = \max_{x\in\Omega}\{|\nabla h_1|^2 + |\nabla h_2|^2 + 2\delta(h_1^2 + h_2^2)\}, \qquad \mathcal{M}_1 = \max_{(x,t)\in\Gamma}\Psi(x,t). \tag{3.3}$$

Proof. We initially compute $\Delta\Phi - \Phi_{,t}$, with Φ defined in (1.6). After some standard calculations, we obtain

$$\begin{aligned}\Delta\Phi - \Phi_{,t} = e^{2\delta t}\Big\{ &-2u_{,i}v_{,i}\left[f_1'(v) + f_2'(u)\right] + 2(u_{,ik}u_{,ik} + v_{,ik}v_{,ik}) \\ &- 4\delta uv\left[\frac{f_1(v)}{v} + \frac{f_2(u)}{u}\right] + 2\delta(|\nabla u|^2 + |\nabla v|^2) - 4\delta^2(u^2+v^2)\Big\},\end{aligned} \tag{3.4}$$

where we used the equations in (1.1).

By hypotheses (1.2) and using (2.1), from (3.4), we obtain

$$\Delta\Phi - \Phi_{,t} \geq e^{2\delta t}\{(2\delta - \overline{M})(|\nabla u|^2 + |\nabla v|^2) - 2\delta(\overline{M} + 2\delta)U\}. \tag{3.5}$$

By using (3.1), the first term on the right-hand side of (3.5) is nonnegative and can be neglected, then with $k = 2\delta(\overline{M} + 2\delta)$, we obtain

$$\Delta\Phi - \Phi_{,t} \geq -kUe^{2\delta t}. \tag{3.6}$$

If we replace in (3.6) the estimate of U proved in Lemma 2.4

$$U(x,t) \leq \Gamma_\beta e^{-\xi t}, \tag{3.7}$$

since we have assumed $\delta = \xi/2$, we obtain

$$\Delta\Phi - \Phi_{,t} \geq -k\Gamma_\beta e^{(2\delta-\xi)t} = -K \tag{3.8}$$

with $K = k\Gamma_\beta$. This implies that the function Ψ satisfies the inequality

$$\Delta\Psi - \Psi_{,t} = \Delta\Phi - (\Phi_{,t} - K) \geq 0, \tag{3.9}$$

and from the standard maximum principle [3, 8] Ψ attains its maximum value either at a point on $\delta\Omega$ for some $t > 0$, or at a point $x \in \Omega$ at $t = 0$. Then from the definition of Ψ we have

$$|\nabla u|^2 + |\nabla v|^2 + 2\delta(u^2 + v^2)e^{2\delta t} - Kt \leq \mathcal{M} \tag{3.10}$$

with $\mathcal{M}$ in (3.2) and (3.3). □

References

[1] J. M. Ball, *Remarks on blow-up and nonexistence theorems for nonlinear evolution equations*, The Quarterly Journal of Mathematics. Oxford **28** (1977), no. 112, 473–486.

[2] A. Friedman, *Remarks on the maximum principle for parabolic equations and its applications*, Pacific Journal of Mathematics **8** (1958), 201–211.

[3] L. Nirenberg, *A strong maximum principle for parabolic equations*, Communications on Pure and Applied Mathematics **6** (1953), 167–177.

[4] L. E. Payne and G. A. Philippin, *Decay bounds for solutions of second order parabolic problems and their derivatives*, Mathematical Models & Methods in Applied Sciences **5** (1995), no. 1, 95–110.

[5] L. E. Payne, G. A. Philippin, and S. Vernier Piro, *Decay bounds for solutions of second order parabolic problems and their derivatives IV*, Applicable Analysis **85** (2006), no. 1–3, 293–302.

[6] L. E. Payne and P. W. Schaefer, *Decay results for the heat equation under radiation boundary conditions*, Mathematical Inequalities & Applications **4** (2001), no. 4, 573–584.

[7] ———, *Decay bounds for initial-boundary value problems for nonlinear parabolic systems*, Nonlinear Analysis **50** (2002), no. 7, 899–912.

[8] M. H. Protter and H. F. Weinberger, *Maximum Principles in Differential Equations*, Prentice-Hall, New Jersey, 1967.

[9] S. Vernier Piro, *Qualitative properties for solutions of reaction diffusion systems and their gradients*, submitted to Nonlinear Analysis. Series A: Theory, Methods & Applications.

M. Marras: Dipartimento di Matematica e Informatica, Universitá di Cagliari, 09123 Cagliari, Italy
E-mail address: mmarras@unica.it

S. Vernier Piro: Dipartimento di Matematica e Informatica, Universitá di Cagliari,
09123 Cagliari, Italy
E-mail address: svernier@unica.it

STOCHASTIC SIS AND SIR MULTIHOST EPIDEMIC MODELS

ROBERT K. MCCORMACK AND LINDA J. S. ALLEN

Pathogens that infect multiple hosts are common. Zoonotic diseases, such as Lyme disease, hantavirus pulmonary syndrome, and rabies, by their very definition are animal diseases transmitted to humans. In this investigation, we develop stochastic epidemic models for a disease that can infect multiple hosts. Based on a system of deterministic epidemic models with multiple hosts, we formulate a system of Itô stochastic differential equations. Through numerical simulations, we compare the dynamics of the deterministic and the stochastic models. Even though the deterministic models predict disease emergence, this is not always the case for the stochastic models.

1. Introduction

Most pathogens are capable of infecting more than one host. Often these hosts, in turn, transmit the pathogen to other hosts. Approximately sixty percent of human pathogens are zoonotic including diseases such as Lyme disease, influenza, sleeping sickness, rabies, and hantavirus pulmonary syndrome [18]. Generally, there is only a few species (often only one species) considered reservoir species for a pathogen. Other species, infected by the pathogen, are secondary or spillover species, where the disease does not persist. For example, domestic dogs and jackals in Africa may both serve as reservoirs for the rabies virus [7, 12]. Humans and other wild carnivores are secondary hosts. Hantavirus, a zoonotic disease carried by wild rodents, is generally associated with a single reservoir host [2, 11, 13]. Spillover infection occurs in other rodent species. Human infection results in either hantavirus pulmonary syndrome or hemorrhagic fever with renal syndrome [13].

To study the role played by multiple reservoirs and secondary hosts, in previous research, we developed deterministic epidemic models with multiple hosts and showed that the disease is more likely to emerge with multiple hosts [10]. In this research, we

Hindawi Publishing Corporation
Proceedings of the Conference on Differential & Difference Equations and Applications, pp. 775–785

extend the deterministic models to stochastic models and compare the stochastic and the deterministic dynamics.

2. Deterministic models

We describe the deterministic multihost epidemic models developed in previous research and summarize their dynamics [10]. In the first model, known as an SIS epidemic model, individuals in the host population are either susceptible, S, or infected (and infectious), I. When individuals recover, they do not develop immunity but become susceptible again. In the multihost SIS epidemic model, let S_j and I_j denote the total number of susceptible and infected hosts of species j, respectively, $j = 1,2,\ldots,n$. Then the SIS model is given by the following system of equations:

$$\begin{aligned}\frac{dS_j}{dt} &= N_j b_j - S_j d_j(N_j) - S_j \sum_{k=1}^{n} \left(\beta_{jk}(N_k)\frac{I_k}{N_k}\right) + \gamma_j I_j,\\ \frac{dI_j}{dt} &= -I_j d_j(N_j) + S_j \sum_{k=1}^{n} \left(\beta_{jk}(N_k)\frac{I_k}{N_k}\right) - (\gamma_j + \alpha_j) I_j,\end{aligned} \tag{2.1}$$

where $S_j(0) > 0$, $I_j(0) \geq 0$, and $N_j = S_j + I_j$ for $j = 1,2,\ldots,n$. The parameter b_j is the birth rate, γ_j is the recovery rate, and α_j is the disease-related death rate. All parameters are positive. The contact rate between an infected individual of species j and a susceptible individual of species k is dependent on the population size of species k: $\beta_{jk}(N_k)$. We assume two forms for $\beta_{jk}(N_k)$: standard incidence, where $\beta_{jk}(N_k) \equiv \lambda_{jk}$, and mass action incidence, where $\beta_{jk}(N_k) \equiv \lambda_{jk} N_k$. The density-dependent natural death rate also depends on the population size N_j, and satisfies the following assumptions:

(i) $d_j \in C^1[0,\infty)$;
(ii) $0 < d_j(0) < b_j - \alpha_j$;
(iii) d_j is increasing for $N_j \geq 0$;
(iv) there exists $K_j > 0$ such that $d_j(K_j) = b_j$.

In the absence of infection, $\lim_{t\to\infty} N_j(t) = K_j$.

In the multihost SIR epidemic model, let S_j, I_j, and R_j denote the total number of susceptible, infected, and immune hosts of species j, respectively, $j = 1,2,\ldots,n$. The SIR epidemic model is given by the following differential equations:

$$\begin{aligned}\frac{dS_j}{dt} &= N_j b_j - S_j d_j(N_j) - S_j \sum_{k=1}^{n} \left(\beta_{jk}(N_k)\frac{I_k}{N_k}\right),\\ \frac{dI_j}{dt} &= -I_j d_j(N_j) + S_j \sum_{k=1}^{n} \left(\beta_{jk}(N_k)\frac{I_k}{N_k}\right) - (\gamma_j + \alpha_j) I_j,\\ \frac{dR_j}{dt} &= -R_j d_j(N_j) + \gamma_j I_j,\end{aligned} \tag{2.2}$$

where $S_j(0) > 0$, $I_j(0) \geq 0$, $R_j(0) \geq 0$, and $N_j = S_j + I_j + R_j$ for $j = 1,2,\ldots,n$. All parameters are interpreted as in the SIS model except that recovered individuals develop immunity. It should be noted that the only interaction between the hosts is through contact and spread of disease. Competition and predator-prey interactions are not considered [5, 6, 8, 15–17].

The basic reproduction number $\mathcal{R}_0$ for the multihost SIS and SIR epidemic models can be defined using the next generation approach of Diekmann et al. [3] and van den Driessche and Watmough [14]. The multihost SIS and SIR epidemic models have a unique disease-free equilibrium (DFE), where $I_j \equiv 0 \equiv R_j$ and $S_j = K_j$. The next generation matrix for a multihost SIS or SIR epidemic model with n hosts is an $n \times n$ matrix $M_n = (\mathcal{R}_{jk})_{j,k=1}^n$, where

$$\mathcal{R}_{jk} = \frac{K_j \beta_{jk}(K_k)}{K_k(\gamma_k + \alpha_k + b_k)} \tag{2.3}$$

is the jk entry in the matrix M_n, $j,k = 1,2,\dots,n$. Hence, the basic reproduction number for the epidemic models is the spectral radius of M_n,

$$\mathcal{R}_0 = \rho(M_n). \tag{2.4}$$

The DFE of the multihost SIS and SIR epidemic models is locally asymptotically stable if $\mathcal{R}_0 < 1$ and unstable if $\mathcal{R}_0 > 1$ [14]. In addition, it can be shown that as the number of hosts increases, so does the basic reproduction number. In particular, if one more host is added to the system and the original parameters do not change, then

$$\rho(M_n) \le \rho(M_{n+1}). \tag{2.5}$$

This result holds because M_n and M_{n+1} are nonnegative matrices and M_n is the leading principal submatrix of M_{n+1} of order n [10]. It also holds for more complex epidemic models such as a multihost SEIR epidemic model. As a result, multiple reservoirs and secondary species that become infected and transmit the disease can contribute to persistence of the disease in a multihost system by increasing $\mathcal{R}_0$.

3. Stochastic models

We formulate new stochastic differential equation (SDE) models for the multihost SIS and SIR epidemic models described in the previous section. Variability in the stochastic models is due to births, deaths, and infections. Let $\mathcal{S}_j$, $\mathcal{I}_j$, and $\mathcal{R}_j$ denote continuous random variables for the susceptible, infected, and immune states, respectively. Random variables are denoted by calligraphic letters.

The random variables for the SIS model satisfy $\mathcal{S}_j, \mathcal{I}_j \in [0,\infty)$, where $\mathcal{S}_j + \mathcal{I}_j = \mathcal{N}_j$ and $\mathcal{N}_j \in [0,\infty)$. Let the random vector

$$\mathcal{X}(t) = (\mathcal{S}_1(t),\mathcal{S}_2(t),\dots,\mathcal{S}_n(t),\mathcal{I}_1(t),\mathcal{I}_2(t),\dots,\mathcal{I}_n(t))^T. \tag{3.1}$$

The SDE formulation is based on a Markov chain model with a small time step Δt, where $\Delta\mathcal{X}(t) = \mathcal{X}(t+\Delta t) - \mathcal{X}(t)$ is approximately normally distributed [1, 9].

First, we make assumptions regarding the probability of a change in state during Δt. We assume there can be a change of at most one unit, ± 1, during Δt. Let $\Delta\mathcal{S}(t) = \Delta\mathcal{S}_j(t+\Delta t) - \mathcal{S}_j(t)$ and $\Delta\mathcal{I}(t) = \mathcal{I}(t+\Delta t) - \mathcal{I}(t)$. Then

$$\begin{gathered}
\operatorname{Prob}\{\Delta\mathcal{S}_j = 1 \mid \mathcal{X}(t)\} = b_j\mathcal{N}_j\Delta t + o(\Delta t),\\
\operatorname{Prob}\{\Delta\mathcal{S}_j = -1 \mid \mathcal{X}(t)\} = \mathcal{S}_j d_j(\mathcal{N}_j)\Delta t + o(\Delta t),\\
\operatorname{Prob}\{\Delta\mathcal{I}_j = -1 \mid \mathcal{X}(t)\} = (\mathcal{I}_j d_j(\mathcal{N}_j) + \alpha_j\mathcal{I}_j)\Delta t + o(\Delta t),\\
\operatorname{Prob}\{\Delta\mathcal{S}_j = 1,\ \Delta\mathcal{I}_j = -1 \mid \mathcal{X}(t)\} = \gamma_j I_j\Delta t + o(\Delta t),\\
\operatorname{Prob}\{\Delta\mathcal{S}_j = -1,\ \Delta\mathcal{I}_k = 1 \mid \mathcal{X}(t)\} = \mathcal{S}_j\beta_{jk}(\mathcal{N}_k)\frac{\mathcal{I}_k}{\mathcal{N}_k}\Delta t + o(\Delta t).
\end{gathered} \tag{3.2}$$

Applying these transition probabilities, the expected rate of change $E(\Delta\mathcal{X}(t))$ satisfies

$$\begin{pmatrix}
\mathcal{N}_1 b_1 - \mathcal{S}_1 d_1(\mathcal{N}_1) - \mathcal{S}_1\sum_{k=1}^{n}\beta_{1k}(\mathcal{N}_k)\frac{\mathcal{I}_k}{\mathcal{N}_k} + \gamma_1\mathcal{I}_1\\
\vdots\\
\mathcal{N}_n b_n - \mathcal{S}_n d_n(\mathcal{N}_n) - \mathcal{S}_n\sum_{k=1}^{n}\beta_{nk}(\mathcal{N}_k)\frac{\mathcal{I}_k}{\mathcal{N}_k} + \gamma_n\mathcal{I}_n\\
-\mathcal{I}_1 d_1(\mathcal{N}_1) + \mathcal{S}_1\sum_{k=1}^{n}\beta_{1k}(\mathcal{N}_k)\frac{\mathcal{I}_k}{\mathcal{N}_k} - (\gamma_1 + \alpha_1)\mathcal{I}_1\\
\vdots\\
-\mathcal{I}_n d_n(\mathcal{N}_n) + \mathcal{S}_n\sum_{k=1}^{n}\beta_{nk}(\mathcal{N}_k)\frac{\mathcal{I}_k}{\mathcal{N}_k} - (\gamma_n + \alpha_n)\mathcal{I}_n
\end{pmatrix} + \mathbf{o}(\Delta t). \tag{3.3}$$

Denote this $2n$ vector as $\mu(\mathcal{X}(t))\Delta t + \mathbf{o}(\Delta t)$. The stochastic variability for the system comes from the covariance for the rate of change in the state variables. The $2n \times 2n$ covariance matrix $C(\Delta\mathcal{X}(t))$ to order Δt is

$$C(\Delta\mathcal{X}(t)) = \begin{pmatrix} C_{11} & C_{12}\\ C_{21} & C_{22}\end{pmatrix}\Delta t, \tag{3.4}$$

where

$$C_{11} = \text{diag}\left(\mathcal{N}_j b_j + \mathcal{S}_j d_j(\mathcal{N}_j) + \mathcal{S}_j \sum_{k=1}^{n} \beta_{jk}(\mathcal{N}_k)\frac{\mathcal{I}_k}{\mathcal{N}_k} + \gamma_j \mathcal{I}_j\right),$$
$$C_{22} = \text{diag}\left(\mathcal{I}_j d_j(\mathcal{N}_j) + \mathcal{S}_j \sum_{k=1}^{n} \beta_{jk}(\mathcal{N}_k)\frac{\mathcal{I}_k}{\mathcal{N}_k} + (\gamma_j + \alpha_j)\mathcal{I}_j\right) \tag{3.5}$$

are $n \times n$ submatrices. Matrix $C(\mathcal{X}(t))$ is symmetric, so that the $n \times n$ submatrices C_{12} and C_{21} satisfy $C_{12} = C_{21}^T = (c_{jk})$, where

$$c_{jk} = \begin{cases} -\mathcal{S}_j \beta_{jk}(\mathcal{N}_k)\dfrac{\mathcal{I}_k}{\mathcal{N}_K} - \gamma_j \mathcal{I}_j & \text{if } j = k, \\ -\mathcal{S}_j \beta_{jk}(\mathcal{N}_k)\dfrac{\mathcal{I}_k}{\mathcal{N}_K} & \text{if } j \neq k. \end{cases} \tag{3.6}$$

To order Δt, it follows that

$$\Delta\mathcal{X}(t) = E(\Delta\mathcal{X}(t)) + \sqrt{C(\Delta\mathcal{X}(t))}. \tag{3.7}$$

Let

$$B(\mathcal{X}(t)) = \sqrt{\begin{pmatrix} C_{11} & C_{12} \\ C_{21} & C_{22} \end{pmatrix}}, \tag{3.8}$$

where the C_{ij} are defined by (3.5) and (3.6). Matrix B is the unique positive definite square root. Taking the limit as $\Delta t \to 0$ of (3.7), we obtain a system of Itô SDEs [1, 4, 9],

$$\frac{d\mathcal{X}(t)}{dt} = \mu(\mathcal{X}(t)) + B(\mathcal{X}(t))\frac{d\mathcal{W}(t)}{dt}, \tag{3.9}$$

where $\mathcal{W}(t) = (\mathcal{W}_1(t), \ldots, \mathcal{W}_{2n}(t))^T$, and each $\mathcal{W}_j(t)$, $j = 1, \ldots, 2n$, is an independent Wiener process.

A system of SDEs for the multihost SIR epidemic model can be formulated in a similar manner. Let $\mathcal{X}(t)$ denote the random vector

$$(\mathcal{S}_1(t), \mathcal{S}_2(t), \ldots, \mathcal{S}_n(t), \mathcal{I}_1(t), \mathcal{I}_2(t), \ldots, \mathcal{I}_n(t), \mathcal{R}_1(t), \mathcal{R}_2(t), \ldots, \mathcal{R}_n(t))^T. \tag{3.10}$$

The transition probabilities for the multihost SIR model are similar in form to the multihost SIS model given in (3.2). The expected rate of change $E(\Delta\mathcal{X}(t))$ for the SIR model satisfies

$$\begin{pmatrix} \mathcal{N}_1 b_1 - \mathcal{S}_1 d_1(\mathcal{N}_1) - \mathcal{S}_1 \sum_{k=1}^{n} \beta_{1k}(\mathcal{N}_k) \dfrac{\mathcal{I}_k}{\mathcal{N}_k} \\ \vdots \\ \mathcal{N}_n b_n - \mathcal{S}_n d_n(\mathcal{N}_n) - \mathcal{S}_n \sum_{k=1}^{n} \beta_{nk}(\mathcal{N}_k) \dfrac{\mathcal{I}_k}{\mathcal{N}_k} \\ -\mathcal{I}_1 d_1(\mathcal{N}_1) + \mathcal{S}_1 \sum_{k=1}^{n} \beta_{1k}(\mathcal{N}_k) \dfrac{\mathcal{I}_k}{\mathcal{N}_k} - (\gamma_1 + \alpha_1)\mathcal{I}_1 \\ \vdots \\ -\mathcal{I}_n d_n(\mathcal{N}_n) + \mathcal{S}_n \sum_{k=1}^{n} \beta_{nk}(\mathcal{N}_k) \dfrac{\mathcal{I}_k}{\mathcal{N}_k} - (\gamma_n + \alpha_n)\mathcal{I}_n \\ -\mathcal{R}_1 d_1(\mathcal{N}_1) + \gamma_1 \mathcal{I}_1 \\ \vdots \\ -\mathcal{R}_n d_n(\mathcal{N}_n) + \gamma_n \mathcal{I}_n \end{pmatrix} + \mathbf{o}(\Delta t). \tag{3.11}$$

Denote this $3n$ vector as $\mu(\mathcal{X}(t))\Delta t + \mathbf{o}(\Delta t)$. The covariance matrix for $\Delta\mathcal{X}(t)$ is a $3n \times 3n$ matrix satisfying, to order Δt,

$$C(\mathcal{X}(t)) = \begin{pmatrix} C_{11} & C_{12} & \mathbf{0} \\ C_{21} & C_{22} & C_{23} \\ \mathbf{0} & C_{32} & C_{33} \end{pmatrix} \Delta t, \tag{3.12}$$

where the $n \times n$ submatrices are

$$\begin{aligned} C_{11} &= \operatorname{diag}\left(\mathcal{N}_j b_j + \mathcal{S}_j d_j(\mathcal{N}_j) + \mathcal{S}_j \sum_{k=1}^{n} \beta_{jk}(\mathcal{N}_k) \frac{\mathcal{I}_k}{\mathcal{N}_k}\right), \\ C_{22} &= \operatorname{diag}\left(\mathcal{I}_j d_j(\mathcal{N}_j) + \mathcal{S}_j \sum_{k=1}^{n} \beta_{jk}(\mathcal{N}_k) \frac{\mathcal{I}_k}{\mathcal{N}_k} + (\gamma_j + \alpha_j)\mathcal{I}_j\right), \\ C_{33} &= \operatorname{diag}\left(\mathcal{R}_j d_j(\mathcal{N}_j) + \gamma_j \mathcal{I}_j\right), \\ C_{23} &= \operatorname{diag}\left(-\gamma_j \mathcal{I}_j\right) = C_{32}. \end{aligned} \tag{3.13}$$

Submatrices C_{12} and C_{21} satisfy $C_{12} = C_{21}^T = (c_{jk})$, where

$$c_{jk} = -\mathcal{S}_j \beta_{jk}(\mathcal{N}_k) \frac{\mathcal{I}_k}{\mathcal{N}_k}. \tag{3.14}$$

Let $B(\mathcal{X}(t)) = \sqrt{(C_{ij})}$. It follows that the system of Itô SDEs for the SIR model is given by (3.9).

4. Numerical examples

Two numerical examples illustrate the dynamics of the stochastic and deterministic models. For both examples, there are three hosts in an SIS epidemic model, one reservoir species and two spillover species. Standard incidence is used in the first example, $\beta_{jk}(N_k) = \lambda_{jk}$. Mass action incidence is used in the second example, $\beta_{jk}(N_k) = \lambda_{jk}N_k$. It is reasonable to assume that the reservoir species ($j = 1$) has a greater contact rate and longer period of infectivity than the spillover species. Therefore, we assume $\lambda_{11} > \lambda_{jk}$, $\lambda_{j1} > \lambda_{jk}$, for $j \neq 1$ and $k \neq 1$, and $\gamma_1 < \gamma_j$, $j = 2,3$ [10].

In the first example, we let $\lambda_{11} = 3.5$, $\lambda_{1k} = 0.3 = \lambda_{kk}$, $k = 2,3$, $\lambda_{21} = 0.6 = \lambda_{31}$, and $\lambda_{23} = 0 = \lambda_{32}$ [10]. The disease is not spread between the spillover species. Hantavirus in rodents results in very few, if any, disease-related deaths. Therefore, we let $\alpha_j = 0.01$, $j = 1,2,3$. All species have the same birth rate, $b_j = 3 = b$, $j = 1,2,3$, but different carrying capacities, K_j. The recovery rate for the reservoir species is $\gamma_1 = 0.55$, and for the spillover species $\gamma_j = 1$, $j = 2,3$. The natural death rate for each species is given by $d_j(N_j) = a + (b-a)N_j/K_j$, $j = 1,2,3$, where $a = 0.5$, $K_1 = 500$, and $K_j = 250$, $j = 2,3$.

The basic reproduction number corresponding to this first model is slightly greater than one, $\mathcal{R}_0 = 1.0101$. There exists a unique locally stable endemic equilibrium,

$$(\bar{S}_1,\bar{I}_1,\bar{S}_2,\bar{I}_2,\bar{S}_3,\bar{I}_3) \approx (495,5,249.6,0.4,249.6,0.4). \tag{4.1}$$

The simulation is initiated with a small number of infected individuals: $S_1(0) = 200$, $S_2(0) = 100 = S_3(0)$, $I_1(0) = 5$, $I_2(0) = 1$, and $I_3(0) = 0$.

The deterministic solution, one stochastic sample path, the mean of 1000 sample paths, and the frequency distribution at $t = 50$ for the first example are graphed in Figures 4.1(a), 4.1(b), 4.1(c), and 4.1(d), respectively. The deterministic solution approaches the endemic equilibrium given by (4.1). However, the sample paths and the frequency distribution show that this is not the case for the stochastic model. The means of the sample paths are close to the DFE: $\mu_{S_1} = 498.9$, $\mu_{S_2} = 248.4$, $\mu_{S_3} = 248.3$, $\mu_{I_1} = 0.0023$, $\mu_{I_2} = 0.0001$, and $\mu_{I_3} = 0.0004$ (at $t = 50$). The disease cannot persist even in the reservoir species. This is due to the variance inherent in the stochastic model and the relatively low endemic equilibrium values for the infected hosts. In addition, the basic reproduction number for the reservoir species is less than one (in the absence of the spillover species), $\mathcal{R}_0^1 = 0.983$.

In the second example, all of the parameter values and initial conditions are the same as in the first example, with the exception of the transmission rates and the carrying capacities. The carrying capacities are $K_1 = 1000$ and $K_2 = 500 = K_3$. The values of the transmission rates at the carrying capacities satisfy $\beta_{11}(K_1) = 3.5$, $\beta_{1k}(K_k) = 0.3 = \beta_{kk}(K_k)$, $k = 2,3$, $\beta_{j1}(K_1) = 2(\beta_{1j}(K_j))$, $j = 2,3$, and $\beta_{23}(K_3) = 0 = \beta_{32}(K_2)$, so that they agree with the preceding example [10]. The basic reproduction number is $\mathcal{R}_0 = 2.0202$. There exists a locally stable endemic equilibrium given by

$$(\bar{S}_1,\bar{I}_1,\bar{S}_2,\bar{I}_2,\bar{S}_3,\bar{I}_3) \approx (483.7,514.3,424.8,74.9,424.8,74.9). \tag{4.2}$$

The deterministic solution, one stochastic sample path, the mean of 1000 sample paths, and the frequency distribution at $t = 50$ for the second example are graphed in

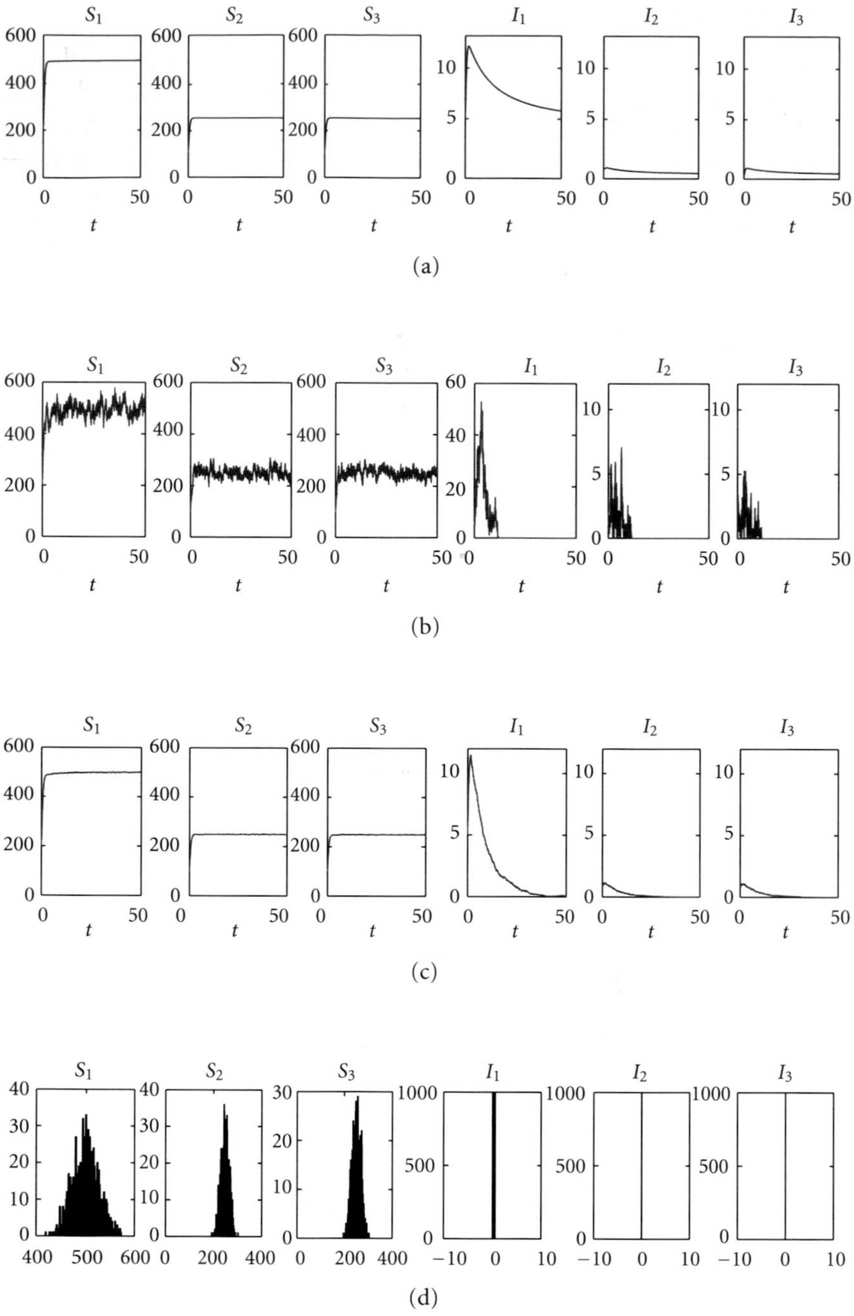

Figure 4.1. Solutions of the three-host deterministic and stochastic SIS epidemic model with standard incidence, $\mathcal{R}_0 = 1.0101$: (a) solution of the deterministic model; (b) one sample path of the stochastic model; (c) mean of 1000 sample paths of the stochastic model; (d) frequency distribution of the stochastic model at $t = 50$ based on 1000 sample paths.

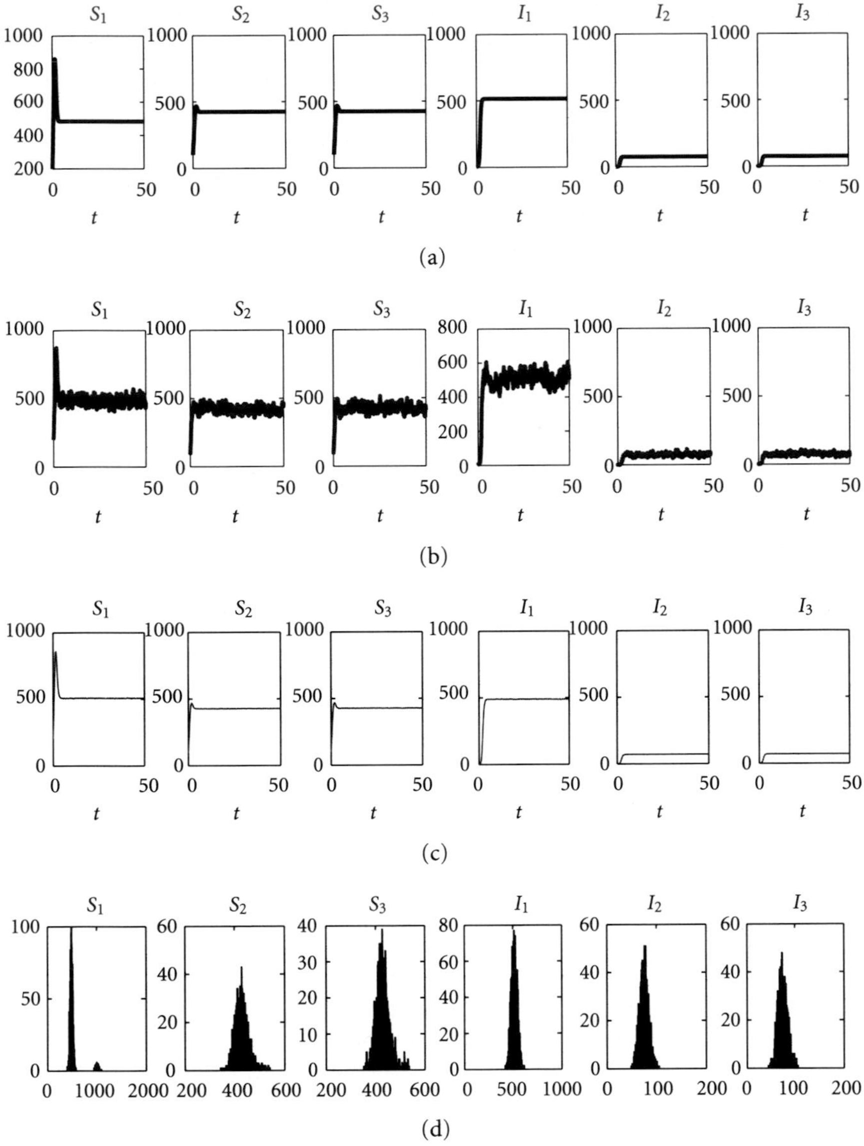

Figure 4.2. Solutions of the three-host deterministic and stochastic SIS epidemic model with mass action incidence, $\mathcal{R}_0 = 2.0202$: (a) solution of the deterministic model; (b) one sample path of the stochastic model; (c) mean of 1000 sample paths of the stochastic model; (d) frequency distribution of the stochastic model at $t = 50$ based on 1000 sample paths.

Figures 4.2(a), 4.2(b), 4.2(c), and 4.2(d), respectively. Because of the large reproduction number and high prevalence of disease, there is less chance for disease extinction than in the previous example. The means of the sample paths are close to the deterministic solution; $\mu_{S_1} = 508.0$, $\mu_{S_2} = 427.3$, $\mu_{S_3} = 428.0$, $\mu_{I_1} = 489.3$, $\mu_{I_2} = 71.2$, and $\mu_{I_3} = 71.2$ (at $t = 50$). Because in a few of the sample paths there is disease extinction, the frequency distribution is bimodal, with one mode at the DFE and another at the endemic equilibrium.

In summary, for multihost epidemic models, the deterministic models show that disease persistence can be enhanced by the presence of secondary or spillover species. However, if the level of prevalence in these spillover species is relatively low and the reproduction number in the reservoir host is less than one, the stochastic models show that the disease does not persist in the multihost system.

Acknowledgment

This research was supported by Grant R01TW006986-02 from the Fogarty International Center under the NIH NSF Ecology of Infectious Diseases Initiative.

References

[1] E. J. Allen, *Stochastic differential equations and persistence time for two interacting populations*, Dynamics of Continuous, Discrete and Impulsive Systems **5** (1999), no. 1–4, 271–281.

[2] Y.-K. Chu, R. D. Owen, L. M. Gonzalez, and C. B. Jonsson, *The complex ecology of hantavirus in Paraguay*, The American Journal of Tropical Medicine and Hygiene **69** (2003), no. 3, 263–268.

[3] O. Diekmann, J. A. P. Heesterbeek, and J. A. J. Metz, *On the definition and the computation of the basic reproduction ratio R_0 in models for infectious diseases in heterogeneous populations*, Journal of Mathematical Biology **28** (1990), no. 4, 365–382.

[4] T. C. Gard, *Introduction to Stochastic Differential Equations*, Monographs and Textbooks in Pure and Applied Mathematics, vol. 114, Marcel Dekker, New York, 1988.

[5] K. P. Hadeler and H. I. Freedman, *Predator-prey populations with parasitic infection*, Journal of Mathematical Biology **27** (1989), no. 6, 609–631.

[6] L. Han, Z. Ma, and H. W. Hethcote, *Four predator prey models with infectious diseases*, Mathematical and Computer Modelling **34** (2001), no. 7-8, 849–858.

[7] D. T. Haydon, S. Cleaveland, L. H. Taylor, and M. K. Laurenson, *Identifying reservoirs of infection: a conceptual and practical challenge*, Emerging Infectious Diseases **8** (2002), no. 12, 1468–1473.

[8] H. W. Hethcote, W. Wang, L. Han, and Z. Ma, *A predator-prey model with infected prey*, Theoretical Population Biology **66** (2004), no. 3, 259–268.

[9] N. Kirupaharan and L. J. S. Allen, *Coexistence of multiple pathogen strains in stochastic epidemic models with density-dependent mortality*, Bulletin of Mathematical Biology **66** (2004), no. 4, 841–864.

[10] R. K. McCormack, *Multi-host and multi-patch mathematical epidemic models for disease emergence with applications to hantavirus in wild rodents*, Ph.D. dissertation, Texas Tech University, Lubbock, TX, 2006.

[11] J. N. Mills, T. L. Yates, T. G. Ksiazek, C. J. Peters, and J. E. Childs, *Long-term studies of hantavirus reservoir populations in the southwestern United States: rationale, potential, and methods*, Emerging Infectious Diseases **5** (1999), no. 1, 95–101.

[12] C. J. Rhodes, R. P. D. Atkinson, R. M. Anderson, and D. W. Macdonald, *Rabies in Zimbabwe: reservoir dogs and the implications for disease control*, Philosophical Transactions of the Royal Society of London. Series B, Biological Sciences **353** (1998), no. 1371, 999–1010.

[13] C. Schmaljohn and B. Hjelle, *Hantaviruses: a global disease problem*, Emerging Infectious Diseases **3** (1997), no. 2, 95–104.

[14] P. van den Driessche and J. Watmough, *Reproduction numbers and sub-threshold endemic equilibria for compartmental models of disease transmission*, Mathematical Biosciences **180** (2002), no. 1-2, 29–48.

[15] E. Venturino, *Epidemics in predator-prey models: diseae in the prey*, Mathematical Population Dynamics: Analysis of Heterogenity, Vol. 1: Theory of Epidemics, Wuerz, California, 1995, pp. 381–393.

[16] ———, *The effects of diseases on competing species*, Mathematical Biosciences **174** (2001), no. 2, 111–131.

[17] ———, *Epidemics in predator-prey models: disease in the predators*, IMA Journal of Mathematics Applied in Medicine and Biology **19** (2002), no. 3, 185–205.

[18] M. E. J. Woolhouse, L. H. Taylor, and D. T. Haydon, *Population biology of multi-host pathogens*, Science **292** (2001), no. 5519, 1109–1112.

Robert K. McCormack: Department of Mathematics and Statistics, Texas Tech University, Lubbock, TX 79409-1042, USA
E-mail address: rmccormack16@hotmail.com

Linda J. S. Allen: Department of Mathematics and Statistics, Texas Tech University, Lubbock, TX 79409-1042, USA
E-mail address: linda.j.allen@ttu.edu

LIPSCHITZ REGULARITY OF VISCOSITY SOLUTIONS IN SOME NONLINEAR PARABOLIC-FREE BOUNDARY PROBLEMS

EMMANOUIL MILAKIS

We study the regularity of solutions in Stefan-type free boundary problems. We prove that viscosity solutions to a fully nonlinear free boundary problem are Lipschitz continuous across the free boundary, provided that the free boundary is a Lipschitz graph in some space direction.

1. Introduction

We present the author's result [4, 5] concerning the regularity of the solution to a class of free boundary problems. More precisely, we study a two-phase Stefan-like free boundary problem in which a fully nonlinear parabolic equation is verified by the solution in the positive and the negative domains. These problems arise when a state variable, v, (temperature, an enthalphy concentration) diffuses in any of two given states (solid-liquid, burnt-unburnt, etc.) but suffers a discontinuity in its behavior across some value (e.g., $v = 0$) that indicates state transition. The case of the heat equation was studied by Athanasopoulos et al. [1, 2].

We start our approach by giving some basic definitions and notations. Denote a point in $\mathbb{R}^{n+1}$ by $(x,t) = (x', x_n, t)$ and let $\mathcal{S}$ be the space of $n \times n$ symmetric matrices. Consider an operator $F : \mathcal{S} \subseteq \mathbb{R}^{n\times n} \to \mathbb{R}$ to be smooth, concave, fully nonlinear, homogeneous of degree 1, $F(0) = 0$, and uniformly elliptic. Denote by $x_n = f(x', t)$ a Lipschitz function with Lipschitz constant L. We give the definition of a viscosity solution.

Definition 1.1. Let v be a continuous function in $D_1 := B_1(0) \times (-1,1)$. Then v is called a subsolution (supersolution) to a free boundary problem if

(i) $F(D^2 v) - v_t \geq 0$ (≤ 0) in $\Omega^+ := D_1 \cap \{v > 0\}$;

(ii) $F(D^2 v^-) - (v^-)_t \leq 0$ (≥ 0) in $\Omega^- := D_1 \cap \{v \leq 0\}^o$;

(iii) $v \in C^1(\overline{\Omega}^+) \cap C^1(\overline{\Omega}^-)$;

(iv) for any $(x,t) \in \partial\Omega^+ \cap D_1$, $\nabla_x v^+(x,t) \neq 0$,

$$V_\nu \geq -G((x,t), \nu, v_\nu^+, v_\nu^-) \quad (\leq) \tag{1.1}$$

Hindawi Publishing Corporation
Proceedings of the Conference on Differential & Difference Equations and Applications, pp. 787–793

is the speed of the surface $\mathcal{F}_t := \partial\Omega^+ \cap \{t\}$ in the direction $\nu := \nabla_x v^+/|\nabla_x v^+|$. We say that v is a solution to a free boundary problem if it is both subsolution and supersolution. The basic requirements on G are continuity in all its arguments, increasing in v_ν^+, decreasing in v_ν^-, and that $G \to +\infty$ when $v_\nu^+ - v_\nu^- \to +\infty$.

Definition 1.2. Assume that u is a continuous function in D_1, then u is a viscosity subsolution (supersolution) to a free boundary problem if, for any subcylinder Q of D_1 and for every supersolution (subsolution) v in Q, $u \le v$ $(u \ge v)$ on $\partial_p Q$ implies that $u \le v$ $(u \ge v)$ in Q.

Let us introduce the following useful notations, for $(\xi,\tau) \in \{x_n = f(x',t)\}$, $r > 0$:

$$\begin{gathered} A_r(\xi,\tau) := (\xi',\xi_n + b_0 r,\tau), \qquad \overline{A}_r(\xi,\tau) := \left(\xi',\xi_n + b_0 r,\tau + \frac{3}{2}r^2\right), \\ \underline{A}_r(\xi,\tau) := \left(\xi',\xi_n + b_0 r,\tau - \frac{3}{2}r^2\right), \\ Q_r(\xi,\tau) := \{(x,t) \in \mathbb{R}^{n+1} : |x' - \xi'| < r,\ |x_n - \xi_n| < b_0 r,\ |t-\tau| < r^2\}, \\ K_r(\xi,\tau) := \{(x,t) \in \mathbb{R}^{n+1} : |x' - \xi'| < t,\ |x_n - \xi_n| < b_0 r,\ |t-\tau| < r\}. \end{gathered} \tag{1.2}$$

Finally we assume $d_{x,t} := \inf\{\operatorname{dist}((x,t),(y,t)) : y_n = f(y',t)\}$ and $(0,0) \in \{x_n = f(x',t)\}$.

We state our main regularity result in the following theorem.

Theorem 1.3. *Let u be a viscosity solution of a free boundary problem in $B_1(0) \times (-1,1)$ and $\partial\Omega^+$ is Lipschitz in some space direction ν with Lipschitz constant L. Assume that $u(\underline{A}_{3/4}(0,0)) = m > 0$ where $b_0 = \max(4L,1)$ and the free boundary contains the origin. Then u is Lipschitz continuous.*

The paper is organized as follows. Section 1 consists of introduction, preliminaries, and the statement of the main result. In Section 2 we develop some properties for the solutions of the problem and finally in Section 3 we sketch the proof of the main Theorem 1.3.

2. Properties of solutions

We start with the usual backward Harnack inequality which may lead us to the Hölder continuity of the quotient of two solutions as in [4, 5].

Theorem 2.1 (backward Harnack). *Let u be a solution in $Q_1 \cap \Omega$ for $\Omega := \{x_n > f(x',t)\}$ and $u(\underline{A}_{3/4}(0,0)) = m > 0$ which vanishes locally on $Q_1 \cap \partial\Omega$. Then there exists a constant $C = C(n,L,m/M,\lambda,\Lambda)$ such that*

$$u(x,t+\rho^2) \le Cu(x,t-\rho^2) \tag{2.1}$$

for all $(x,t) \in Q_{1/2} \cap \Omega$ and for all $\rho : 0 < \rho < d_{x,t}/b_0$.

Proof. Define

$$Lu \equiv \alpha_{ij}(x,t)u_{x_i x_j}(x,t) - u_t(x,t), \tag{2.2}$$

where

$$\alpha_{ij}(x,t) := \int_0^1 \frac{\partial F}{\partial R_{ij}}(sD^2u)\,ds. \tag{2.3}$$

Note that if u is a solution in $Q_1 \cap \Omega$, then $Lu = 0$ in $Q_1 \cap \Omega$ and L has the same ellipticity constants λ, Λ as F. Let $w^{(x,t)}$ be the L-caloric measure in $Q_1 \cap \Omega$ evaluated at (x,t).

For any $(x,t) \in Q_{1/2} \cap \Omega$, take $(\xi,\tau) \in Q_{1/2} \cap \partial\Omega$ and $r > 0$ such that $(x,t) = A_r(\xi,\tau) = A_r$ and define $B := \{t = -1\} \cap Q_1 \cap \Omega$. Then

$$u(\overline{A}_r) = \int_\Sigma u\,dw^{\overline{A}_r} + \int_B u\,dw^{\overline{A}_r} =: u_1(\overline{A}_r) + u_2(\overline{A}_r). \tag{2.4}$$

From [3] we have

$$u_2(\overline{A}_r) \le C u_2(\underline{A}_r). \tag{2.5}$$

On the other hand, if $\gamma := \Sigma \cap \{-1 < t < -9/16\}$ and the doubling property of L-caloric measure [6], we have

$$\begin{gathered} w^{(x,t)}(\Sigma) \le C w^{(x,t)}(\gamma), \\ u(\underline{A}_r) = \int_\Sigma u\,dw^{\underline{A}_r} + \int_B u\,dw^{\underline{A}_r} \ge \int_\gamma u\,dw^{\underline{A}_r} + \int_B u\,dw^{\underline{A}_r}. \end{gathered} \tag{2.6}$$

Since $w^{(x,t)}(\gamma)$ is zero on the lateral part of $Q_1 \cap \Omega$ except on γ, we get

$$w^{\overline{A}_r}(\gamma) \le C w^{\underline{A}_r}(\gamma). \tag{2.7}$$

□

In the following two lemmas we show that u is actually monotone in any direction entering the domain.

LEMMA 2.2. *Let u be as in Theorem 2.1.*

(a) *If $D_{e_n}u \ge 0$ in $Q_{1/2} \cap \Omega$, then there exists a constant $C = C(n,L,\lambda,\Lambda,m,M)$ such that*

$$\frac{1}{C}\frac{u(x,t)}{d_{x,t}} \le D_{e_n}u(x,t) \le C\frac{u(x,t)}{d_{x,t}} \tag{2.8}$$

for every $(x,t) \in Q_{1/2} \cap \Omega$.

(b) *In $Q_\delta \cap \Omega$ for some $\delta = \delta(n,L,\lambda,\Lambda,m/M)$, we have*

$$D_{e_n}u \ge 0. \tag{2.9}$$

Proof. In order to prove (a) note that since u is an F-solution,

$$\frac{u(x+he_n,t) - u(x,t)}{h} \in S \tag{2.10}$$

for all $h > 0$ and, in particular $D_{e_n}u \in S$, since S is closed under uniform limits in compact sets, Harnack principle is valid for $D_{e_n}u$. Take $(x,t) \in Q_{1/2} \cap \Omega$ and choose $r > 0$ and

$(\xi,\tau) \in Q_{1/2} \cap \partial\Omega$ such that $(x,t) = A_r(\xi,\tau)$. Now

$$u(\underline{A}_r(\xi,\tau)) - u\left(\xi + \delta e_n, \tau - \frac{3}{2}r^2\right) = \int_\delta^{br} D_{e_n} u\left(\xi + s e_n, \tau - \frac{3}{2}r^2\right) ds. \tag{2.11}$$

By the usual Carleson estimate and Harnack inequality for u, we have

$$u\left(\xi + \delta e_n, \tau - \frac{3}{2}r^2\right) \le C\left(\frac{\delta}{r}\right)^\alpha u(\overline{A}_r(\xi,\tau)). \tag{2.12}$$

Now

$$\begin{aligned}\int_\delta^{br} D_{e_n} u\left(\xi + s e_n, \tau - \frac{3}{2}r^2\right) ds &= (br - \delta) D_{e_n} u\left(\xi + \omega e_n, \tau - \frac{3}{2}r^2\right) \\ &\le br D_{e_n} u\left(\xi + \omega e_n, \tau - \frac{3}{2}r^2\right)\end{aligned} \tag{2.13}$$

for $\omega \in (\delta, br)$. Since $D_{e_n} u \in S$ and $D_{e_n} u \ge 0$ by Harnack, we get

$$D_{e_n} u\left(\xi + \omega e_n, \tau - \frac{3}{2}r^2\right) \le C D_{e_n} u(A_r(\xi,\tau)). \tag{2.14}$$

On the other hand, using backward Harnack

$$u\left(\xi + \delta e_n, \tau - \frac{3}{2}r^2\right) \le C\left(\frac{\delta}{r}\right)^\alpha u(\overline{A}_r(\xi,\tau)) \le C\left(\frac{\delta}{r}\right)^\alpha u(\underline{A}_r(\xi,\tau)) \le C\left(\frac{\delta}{r}\right)^\alpha u(A_r(\xi,\tau)), \tag{2.15}$$

thus

$$\begin{aligned}u(A_r(\xi,\tau)) - u\left(\xi + \delta e_n, \tau - \frac{3}{2}r^2\right) &\ge u(\underline{A}_r(\xi,\tau)) - \left(\frac{\delta}{r}\right)^\alpha u(A_r(\xi,\tau)) \\ &\ge u(\overline{A}_r(\xi,\tau)) - \left(\frac{\delta}{r}\right)^\alpha u(A_r(\xi,\tau)) \\ &\ge u(A_r(\xi,\tau)) - \left(\frac{\delta}{r}\right)^\alpha u(A_r(\xi,\tau)).\end{aligned} \tag{2.16}$$

Now choose δ small enough to get

$$\frac{1}{2} u(A_r(\xi,\tau)) \le C r D_{e_n} u(A_r(\xi,\tau)). \tag{2.17}$$

For the remaining part use Harnack for $\omega \in (br/2, br)$,

$$\begin{aligned}C r D_{e_n} u(A_r(\xi,\tau)) &\le r D_{e_n} u\left(\xi + \omega e_n, \tau + \frac{3}{2}r^2\right), \\ \int_{br/2}^{br} D_{e_n} u\left(\xi + s e_n, \tau + \frac{3}{2}r^2\right) ds &= \frac{br}{2} D_{e_n} u\left(\xi + \omega e_n, \tau + \frac{3}{2}r^2\right),\end{aligned} \tag{2.18}$$

thus from backward Harnack

$$\begin{aligned}\int_{br/2}^{br} D_{e_n}u\Big(\xi+se_n,\tau+\frac{3}{2}r^2\Big)ds &= u\Big(\xi+bre_n,\tau+\frac{3}{2}r^2\Big)-u\Big(\xi+\frac{br}{2}e_n,\tau+\frac{3}{2}r^2\Big)\\ &\le u\Big(\xi+bre_n,\tau+\frac{3}{2}r^2\Big)\le Cu\Big(\xi+bre_n,\tau-\frac{3}{2}r^2\Big)\\ &\le Cu(A_r(\xi,\tau)),\\ rD_{e_n}u(A_r(\xi,\tau)) &\le Cu(A_r(\xi,\tau)).\end{aligned} \tag{2.19}$$

Since $r \sim d_{x,t}$, the proof is complete. For (b) we refer the reader to [4]. □

LEMMA 2.3. *Let u as in Theorem 2.1. Then for any direction μ entering into Ω, that is, $\mu = \alpha e_n + \beta e_{n+1}$, $\alpha^2+\beta^2 = 1$, such that $0 < \tan^{-1}(\beta/\alpha) < (1/2)\cot^{-1}(L)$ for some $\delta = \delta(n,L,\lambda,\Lambda,m,M,\|\nabla u\|_{L^2})$ small enough*

$$D_\mu u(x,t) \ge 0 \tag{2.20}$$

for every $(x,t) \in Q_\delta \cap \Omega$.

A detailed proof of Lemma 2.3 can be found in [4]. Combining Lemmas 2.2 and 2.3 we have the following.

COROLLARY 2.4. *Let u be as in Theorem 2.1. Then there exist $\varepsilon > 0$ and $\delta > 0$ depending on n, L, λ, Λ such that the functions*

$$w_+ := u + u^{1+\varepsilon}, \qquad w_- := u - u^{1+\varepsilon} \tag{2.21}$$

are subsolution and supersolution, respectively, of equation $F(D^2v) = 0$ in the viscosity sense in $Q_\delta \cap \Omega \cap \{t = 0\}$.

In the next lemma we examine the behavior of an F-solution near the boundary where it vanishes.

LEMMA 2.5. *Let u be an F-solution in $K_1 \cap \Omega$ monotone for every $\mu \in \Gamma(e_n,\overline{\theta})$ with $\cot(2\overline{\theta}) > L$. If there is an n-dimensional ball $B \subset K_1 \cap \Omega \cap \{t = 0\}$ (resp., $B \subset K_1 \cap \Omega^c \cap \{t = 0\}$) such that $\overline{B} \cap \partial\Omega = \{(0,0)\}$, then*

$$u(x,0) = \alpha(x,\nu)^+ + o(|x|) \tag{2.22}$$

near $(0,0)$ in $K_1 \cap \Omega$, for some $\alpha \in (0,\infty]$ (resp., $\alpha \in [0,\infty)$) where ν denotes the inward (resp., outward) radial direction of B at $(0,0)$.

3. Proof of Theorem 1.3

The object of this section is to present a sketch of the proof of Theorem 1.3. We refer the reader to [4, 5] for the technical parts.

Proof of Theorem 1.3. Let $(x_0,t_0) \in \Omega^+$ be of distance d from $\partial\Omega^+$, where

$$d < \frac{1}{2}\operatorname{dist}\big((x_0,t_0),\ \partial_p D_1\big) \tag{3.1}$$

small enough such that all the previous estimates can be applied. Take $h := \text{dist}((x_0,0),(0,0))$ and set

$$u(x_0,0) = Mh. \tag{3.2}$$

Using Harnack we can prove

$$Mh \le C \inf_{B_{h/4}(x_0)} w_-(x) \tag{3.3}$$

for k large, small h.

Choose a coordinate system so that $x_0 = |x_0| e_n$ and set

$$R := \left\{ x \in \mathbb{R}^n : |x_i| \le \xi h,\ i = 1,\dots,n-1,\ |x_n| \le \frac{h}{8} \right\}, \tag{3.4}$$

where ξ is a constant chosen so that

$$\left(x_1,\dots,x_{n-1},\frac{h}{8} \right) \in B_h(x_0), \qquad \left(x_1,\dots,x_{n-1},-\frac{h}{8} \right) \in \{u < 0\} \tag{3.5}$$

when $|x_i| \le \xi h$, $i = 1,\dots,n-1$. Observe that $R \subset B_{h/2}(0)$ for ξ small.

Integrate w_+ along lines parallel to e_n from the free boundary to the side $(x_1,\dots,x_{n-1}, h/8)$ of R:

$$w_+ \left(x_1,\dots,x_{n-1},\frac{h}{8} \right) = \int_l (w_+)_{x_n} dx_n \tag{3.6}$$

and therefore

$$\int_l (w_+)_{x_n} dx_n = w_+ \left(x_1,\dots,x_{n-1},\frac{h}{8} \right) \ge w_- \left(x_1,\dots,x_{n-1},\frac{h}{8} \right) \ge CMh, \tag{3.7}$$

thus

$$C_1 M^2 \le \int_{B_{h/2}} |\nabla (w_+)^+|^2 dx. \tag{3.8}$$

On the other hand, using the asymptotic development of w_+, we have

$$w_+(x,0) = -\alpha x_n^+ + o(|x|) \tag{3.9}$$

for $x \in B_{h/2}(0)$ where $\alpha > 0$, thus

$$C_2 \alpha^2 \le \int_{B_{h/2}} |\nabla (w_+)^-|^2 dx. \tag{3.10}$$

Hence by the monotonicity formula (see [4, Remark 2.2]), we obtain

$$M^2 \alpha^2 \le C. \tag{3.11}$$

So if M is *large*, then α is *small*.

Let $B_\rho \subset \{u > 0\}$ be tangent to $B_h(x_0)$ at the origin. Take $\rho < h/8$ and $\delta > 0$ small such that $u > (1/2)Mx_n^+$ in $B_\delta(0) \cap B_\rho$ and $u > -(1/2)\alpha_- x_n^-$ in $B_\delta(0) \setminus B_\rho$, where $\alpha_- = \alpha$ if $\alpha > 0$ and α_- is a small positive constant otherwise. Consider functions

$$\begin{gathered}\psi(x,t) := \frac{1}{3}Mx_n^+ + \beta_+ t + \frac{1}{2\lambda}\beta_+ x_n^2 - c_1\left(t^2 + \frac{1}{\Lambda n}t|x|^2\right) - c_2\left(\frac{1}{4^n\Lambda}|x'|^2 - \frac{1}{\lambda}x_n^2\right),\\ \phi(x,t) := \psi^+(x,t) - \frac{9}{2M}\alpha_-\psi^-(x,t),\end{gathered} \tag{3.12}$$

where β_+ satisfies

$$\frac{M}{10}G\left((0,0),e_n,\frac{1}{3}M,\frac{3}{2}\alpha_-\right) < \beta_+ < \frac{M}{3}G\left((0,0),e_n,\frac{1}{3}M,\frac{3}{2}\alpha_-\right). \tag{3.13}$$

Choosing c_1, c_2, it is not hard to prove that ϕ is a subsolution to a free boundary problem in $B_\delta(0) \times (0,t_0)$ for t_0 small. Taking δ, t_0 even smaller we have that

$$u \geq \phi \tag{3.14}$$

on $\partial B_\delta(0) \times [0,t_0]$ and on $B_\delta(0) \times \{0\}$. Therefore $u > \phi$ in $B_\delta(0) \times (0,t_0)$ (u is a viscosity solution).

On the other hand, if M is very large (thus α_- is small), $\phi_t^+(0,0)/\phi_{x_n}^+(0,0)$ becomes very large and by assumption the free boundary of u is *Lipschitz* thus u and ϕ must cross each other in $B_\delta(0) \times (0,t_0)$, a contradiction. Therefore M is controlled by a constant. □

Acknowledgment

The author was supported by Operational Programme for Education and Initial Vocational Training "Herakleitos" 2002–2005.

References

[1] I. Athanasopoulos, L. A. Caffarelli, and S. Salsa, *Caloric functions in Lipschitz domains and the regularity of solutions to phase transition problems*, Annals of Mathematics **143** (1996), no. 3, 413–434.

[2] ———, *Regularity of the free boundary in parabolic phase-transition problems*, Acta Mathematica **176** (1996), no. 2, 245–282.

[3] E. B. Fabes, M. V. Safonov, and Y. Yuan, *Behavior near the boundary of positive solutions of second order parabolic equations. II*, Transactions of the American Mathematical Society **351** (1999), no. 12, 4947–4961.

[4] E. Milakis, *Two-phase transition problems for fully nonlinear parabolic equations of second order*, Indiana University Mathematics Journal **54** (2005), no. 6, 1751–1768.

[5] ———, *Free boundaries and phase transition problems*, Ph.D. thesis, Spring 2006.

[6] M. V. Safonov and Y. Yuan, *Doubling properties for second order parabolic equations*, Annals of Mathematics **150** (1999), no. 1, 313–327.

Emmanouil Milakis: Department of Mathematics, University of Crete, Knossos Avenue, 714 09 Heraklion, Greece
E-mail address: milakis@math.uoc.gr

A FOURTH-ORDER BVP OF STURM-LIOUVILLE TYPE WITH ASYMMETRIC UNBOUNDED NONLINEARITIES

F. MINHÓS, A. I. SANTOS, AND T. GYULOV

It is obtained an existence and location result for the fourth-order boundary value problem of Sturm-Liouville type $u^{(iv)}(t) = f(t,u(t),u'(t),u''(t),u'''(t))$ for $t \in [0,1]$; $u(0) = u(1) = A$; $k_1 u'''(0) - k_2 u''(0) = 0$; $k_3 u'''(1) + k_4 u''(1) = 0$, where $f : [0,1] \times R^4 \to R$ is a continuous function and $A, k_i \in R$, for $1 \leq i \leq 4$, are such that $k_1, k_3 > 0$, $k_2, k_4 \geq 0$. We assume that f verifies a one-sided Nagumo-type growth condition which allows an asymmetric unbounded behavior on the nonlinearity. The arguments make use of an a priori estimate on the third derivative of a class of solutions, the lower and upper solutions method and degree theory.

1. Introduction

In this paper it is considered the fourth-order fully nonlinear differential equation

$$u^{(iv)}(t) = f(t,u(t),u'(t),u''(t),u'''(t)) \quad \text{for } t \in I = [0,1], \tag{1.1}$$

with the Sturm-Liouville boundary conditions

$$\begin{gathered} u(0) = u(1) = A, \\ k_1 u'''(0) - k_2 u''(0) = 0, \qquad k_3 u'''(1) + k_4 u''(1) = 0, \end{gathered} \tag{1.2}$$

where $A, k_1, k_2, k_3, k_4 \in R$ are such that $k_1, k_3 > 0$, $k_2, k_4 \geq 0$, and $f : [a,b] \times R^4 \to R$ is a continuous function verifying one-sided Nagumo-type growth assumption.

This problem generalizes the classical beam equation and models the study of the bending of an elastic beam simply supported [8, 9, 11].

As far as we know it is the first time, in fourth-order problems, that the nonlinearity f is assumed to satisfy a growth condition from above but no restriction from below. This asymmetric type of unboundedness is allowed since f verifies one-sided Nagumo-type

Hindawi Publishing Corporation
Proceedings of the Conference on Differential & Difference Equations and Applications, pp. 795–804

condition, that is, there exists a positive continuous function φ such that

$$f(t,x_0,x_1,x_2,x_3) \le \varphi(|x_3|), \quad \forall (t,x_0,x_1,x_2,x_3) \in E, \tag{1.3}$$

on some given subset $E \subset I \times R^4$, and $\int_0^{+\infty}(s/\varphi(s))ds = +\infty$.

Some boundedness of Nagumo-type plays a key role in these results because, as it is known for second-order boundary value problems, the existence of well-ordered lower and upper solutions, by itself, is not sufficient to ensure the existence of solutions (see [10, 15]).

When a one-sided Nagumo-type condition is assumed, the situation becomes more delicate since this condition does not provide a priori estimates for the third-order derivative of all solutions of (1.1) which is usually the key point for studying this sort of problem, as it can be seen in [2, 3, 13, 14].

However, it is still possible to establish a priori bounds for classes S_η of solutions of (1.1) (see Lemma 2.2). More precisely, if we define for $\eta \ge 0$

$$S_\eta = \{u \text{ solution of } (1.1) : u'''(0) \le \eta,\ u'''(1) \ge -\eta\}, \tag{1.4}$$

we prove that there is $r > 0$ such that if $u \in S_\eta$, then it satisfies $\|u'''\|_\infty < r$.

The existence and location of a solution for problem (1.1)-(1.2) (see Theorem 3.1) are established by using the method of lower and upper solutions to obtain a priori estimations on a class of solution and some derivatives, which allow us to define an open set where the topological degree is well defined [12].

This kind of arguments was suggested by [1] for second-order boundary value problems and by [4–7] for higher-order separated boundary value problems.

2. Preliminaries

In this section we will introduce the main concepts that we will use throughout this paper. Given $y,z \in C(I)$ such that $y \le z$ in I, we denote

$$[y,z] := \{x \in C(I) : y(t) \le x(t) \le z(t),\ \forall t \in I\}. \tag{2.1}$$

In order to obtain an a priori bound for the third-order derivative $u'''(t)$ of a class of solutions of problem (1.1)-(1.2), we will introduce the concept of one-sided Nagumo-type growth condition.

Definition 2.1. Given a subset $E \subset I \times R^4$, a function $f : I \times R^4 \to R$ is said to satisfy a one-sided Nagumo-type condition in E if there exists, for some $a > 0$, $\varphi \in C(R_0^+, [a,+\infty))$ such that

$$f(t,x_0,x_1,x_2,x_3) \le \varphi(|x_3|), \quad \forall (t,x_0,x_1,x_2,x_3) \in E, \tag{2.2}$$

with

$$\int_0^{+\infty} \frac{s}{\varphi(s)} ds = +\infty. \tag{2.3}$$

This asymmetric growth condition will be an important tool in the proof of next lemma.

Lemma 2.2. *Consider, for $i = 0,1,2$, the functions $\gamma_i, \Gamma_i \in C(I,R)$ such that $\gamma_i(t) \leq \Gamma_i(t)$, for all $t \in I$, and define the set*

$$E = \{(t,x_0,x_1,x_2,x_3) \in I \times R^4 : \gamma_i(t) \leq x_i \leq \Gamma_i(t),\ i = 0,1,2\}. \tag{2.4}$$

Let $\varphi : R_0^+ \to [a,+\infty)$, for some $a > 0$, be a continuous function such that

$$\int_\eta^{+\infty} \frac{s}{\varphi(s)} ds > \max_{t\in I} \Gamma_2(t) - \min_{t\in I} \gamma_1(t), \tag{2.5}$$

where $\eta \geq 0$ is given by $\eta = \max\{\Gamma_2(0) - \gamma_2(1), \Gamma_2(1) - \gamma_2(0)\}$.

Then there is $r > 0$ (depending only on φ, γ_2, and Γ_2), such that, for every continuous function $f : I \times R^4 \to R$ satisfying one-sided Nagumo-type condition and every solution $u(t)$ of (1.1) verifying

$$u'''(0) \leq \eta, \quad u'''(1) \geq -\eta, \tag{2.6}$$

$$u^{(i)}(t) \in [\gamma_i, \Gamma_i] \quad \text{for } i = 0,1,2,\ \forall t \in I, \tag{2.7}$$

satisfies

$$\|u'''\|_\infty < r. \tag{2.8}$$

Proof. The proof follows the arguments used in [7] and the technique suggested in [13] for fourth-order boundary value problems. □

This lemma still holds if condition (2.2) is replaced by

$$f(t,x_0,x_1,x_2,x_3) \geq -\varphi(|x_3|), \quad \forall (t,x_0,x_1,x_2,x_3) \in E, \tag{2.9}$$

and (2.7) by $u'''(0) \geq -\eta$, $u'''(1) \leq \eta$.

Lower and upper solutions for problem (1.1)-(1.2) must be defined as a pair of functions, in the following way.

Definition 2.3. Consider $A, k_i \in R$, for $1 \leq i \leq 4$, such that $k_1, k_3 > 0$ and $k_2, k_4 \geq 0$. The functions $\alpha, \beta \in C^4(I)$ satisfying

$$\alpha(t) \leq \beta(t), \quad \alpha'(t) \geq \beta'(t), \quad \alpha''(t) \leq \beta''(t), \quad \forall t \in I, \tag{2.10}$$

define a pair of lower and upper solutions of problem (1.1)-(1.2) if the following conditions are verified:

(i) $\alpha^{(iv)}(t) \geq f(t,\alpha(t),\alpha'(t),\alpha''(t),\alpha'''(t))$,

$$\alpha(1) \leq A, \quad k_1\alpha'''(0) - k_2\alpha''(0) \geq 0, \quad k_3\alpha'''(1) + k_4\alpha''(1) \leq 0; \tag{2.11}$$

(ii) $\beta^{(iv)}(t) \leq f(t,\beta(t),\beta'(t),\beta''(t),\beta'''(t))$,

$$\beta(1) \geq A, \quad k_1\beta'''(0) - k_2\beta''(0) \leq 0, \quad k_3\beta'''(1) + k_4\beta''(1) \geq 0; \tag{2.12}$$

(iii) $\alpha'(1) - \beta'(1) \geq \max\{\beta(0) - \beta(1), \alpha(1) - \alpha(0)\}$.

Remark 2.4. (a) Condition (iii) is optimal and cannot be removed, as it will be proved forward (see counterexample).

(b) If the maximum refereed in (iii) is nonnegative, that is,

$$\alpha'(1) - \beta'(1) \geq \max\{\beta(0) - \beta(1), \alpha(1) - \alpha(0), 0\}, \tag{2.13}$$

then assumption (2.10) can be replaced by $\alpha''(t) \leq \beta''(t)$ in I, since the other inequalities can be deduced by integration.

3. Existence and location results

The main result of this work is the following existence and location theorem.

THEOREM 3.1. *Assume that there exists a pair of lower and upper solutions of problem (1.1)-(1.2), $\alpha(t)$ and $\beta(t)$, respectively. Consider the set*

$$E_1 = \left\{ \begin{matrix} (t,x_0,x_1,x_2,x_3) \in I \times R^4 : \alpha(t) \leq x_0 \leq \beta(t), \\ \alpha'(t) \geq x_1 \geq \beta'(t),\ \alpha''(t) \leq x_2 \leq \beta''(t) \end{matrix} \right\}, \tag{3.1}$$

and let $f : I \times R^4 \to R$ be a continuous function such that:

(a) *f satisfies the one-sided Nagumo-type condition in E_1;*

(b) *for $(t,x_2,x_3) \in I \times R^2$, $\alpha(t) \leq x_0 \leq \beta(t)$ and $\alpha'(t) \geq x_1 \geq \beta'(t)$*

$$f(t,\alpha,\alpha',x_2,x_3) \geq f(t,x_0,x_1,x_2,x_3) \geq f(t,\beta,\beta',x_2,x_3). \tag{3.2}$$

Then problem (1.1)-(1.2) has at least one solution $u(t) \in C^4(I)$ that satisfies

$$u \in [\alpha,\beta], \quad u' \in [\beta',\alpha'], \quad u'' \in [\alpha'',\beta''], \quad \forall t \in I. \tag{3.3}$$

Proof. For $\lambda \in [0,1]$, consider the homotopic equation

$$u^{(iv)}(t) = \lambda f(t,\xi_0(t,u(t)),\xi_1(t,u'(t)),\xi_2(t,u''(t)),u'''(t)) + u''(t) - \lambda\xi_2(t,u''(t)), \tag{3.4}$$

where $\xi_i : I \times R \to R$ are the auxiliary continuous functions defined by

$$\begin{aligned} \xi_i(t,x_i) &= \max\{\alpha^{(i)}(t), \min\{x_i,\beta^{(i)}(t)\}\} \quad \text{for } i = 0,2, \\ \xi_1(t,x_1) &= \max\{\beta'(t), \min\{x_1,\alpha'(t)\}\} \end{aligned} \tag{3.5}$$

with the boundary conditions

$$\begin{gathered} u(0) = u(1) = \lambda A, \\ u'''(0) = \lambda\left(\frac{k_2}{k_1}\right)u''(0), \qquad u'''(0) = -\lambda\left(\frac{k_4}{k_3}\right)u''(1). \end{gathered} \tag{3.6}$$

Take $r_1 > 0$ large enough such that, for every $t \in I$,

$$-r_1 < \alpha''(t) \le \beta''(t) < r_1,$$
$$f(t,\alpha(t),\alpha'(t),\alpha''(t),0) - r_1 - \alpha''(t) < 0, \tag{3.7}$$
$$f(t,\beta(t),\beta'(t),\beta''(t),0) + r_1 - \beta''(t) > 0. \tag{3.8}$$

The proof is deduced from the following four steps.

Step 1. Every solution $u(t)$ of problem (3.4)-(3.6) satisfies $|u^{(i)}(t)| < r_1$, for every $t \in I$ and $i = 0,1,2$, independently of $\lambda \in [0,1]$.

Assume, by contradiction, that the above estimate does not hold for $i = 2$. So, for $\lambda \in [0,1]$, there exist $t \in I$ and a solution u of (3.4)-(3.6) such that $|u''(t)| \ge r_1$. In the case $u''(t) \ge r_1$ define

$$u''(t_0) := \max_{t\in I} u''(t) \ge r_1. \tag{3.9}$$

If $t_0 \in (0,1)$, then $u'''(t_0) = 0$ and $u^{(iv)}(t_0) \le 0$. For $\lambda \in [0,1]$, by (3.2) and (3.8), the following contradiction is obtained:

$$\begin{aligned} 0 &\ge u^{(iv)}(t_0) \\ &\ge \lambda f(t_0,\beta(t_0),\beta'(t_0),\beta''(t_0),0) + u''(t_0) - \lambda\beta''(t_0) \\ &= \lambda[f(t_0,\beta(t_0),\beta'(t_0),\beta''(t_0),0) + r_1 - \beta''(t_0)] + u''(t_0) - \lambda r_1 > 0. \end{aligned} \tag{3.10}$$

So $t_0 \notin (0,1)$. If $t_0 = 0$, for $\lambda \in [0,1]$, we obtain, by (3.6),

$$0 \ge u'''(0) = \lambda\left(\frac{k_2}{k_1}\right)u''(0) \ge \lambda\left(\frac{k_2}{k_1}\right)r_1 \ge 0. \tag{3.11}$$

Thus $u'''(0) = 0$ and $u^{(iv)}(0) \le 0$. Replacing in the above computations t_0 by 0, it can be proved that $t_0 \ne 0$. For $t_0 = 1$ the technique is similar and so $u''(t) < r_1$, for every $t \in I$. The case $u''(t) \le -r_1$ follows analogous arguments and then $|u''(t)| < r_1$, for all $t \in I$.

By (3.4), there exists $\xi \in (0,1)$ such that $u'(\xi) = 0$. Then, integrating on $[\xi,t]$ first and then on $[0,t]$, we obtain

$$|u'(t)| = \left|\int_\xi^t u''(s)ds\right| < r_1|t-\xi| \le r_1, \qquad |u(t)| = \left|\int_0^t u'(s)ds\right| < r_1 t \le r_1. \tag{3.12}$$

Step 2. There is $r_2 > 0$ such that, for every solution $u(t)$ of problem (3.4)-(3.6), $|u'''(t)| < r_2$ in I, independently of $\lambda \in [0,1]$.

Consider the set

$$E_{r_1} = \{(t,x_0,x_1,x_2,x_3) \in I \times R^4 : -r_1 \le x_i \le r_1,\ i = 0,1,2\}, \tag{3.13}$$

and, for $\lambda \in [0,1]$, the function $F_\lambda : E_{r_1} \to R$ is given by

$$F_\lambda(t,x_0,x_1,x_2,x_3) = \lambda f(t,\xi_0(t,x_0),\xi_1(t,x_1),\xi_2(t,x_2),x_3) + x_2 - \lambda\xi_2(t,x_2). \tag{3.14}$$

As

$$F_\lambda(t,x_0,x_1,x_2,x_3) \le \lambda\varphi(|x_3|) + r_1 - \lambda\alpha''(t) \le \varphi(|x_3|) + 2r_1, \tag{3.15}$$

then F_λ satisfies one-sided Nagumo-type condition in E_{r_1} with φ replaced by $\overline{\varphi} := 2r_1 + \varphi(t)$, independently of $\lambda \in [0,1]$. By (3.6) and Step 1, we have

$$\begin{aligned} u'''(0) &= \lambda\left(\frac{k_2}{k_1}\right)u''(0) \le \lambda\left(\frac{k_2}{k_1}\right)r_1 \le \left(\frac{k_2}{k_1}\right)r_1 \le \rho, \\ u'''(1) &= -\lambda\left(\frac{k_4}{k_3}\right)u''(1) \ge -\lambda\left(\frac{k_4}{k_3}\right)r_1 \ge -\left(\frac{k_4}{k_3}\right)r_1 \ge -\rho. \end{aligned} \tag{3.16}$$

So, applying Lemma 2.2 with $\gamma_i(t) \equiv -r_1$, $\Gamma_i(t) \equiv r_1$, for $i = 0,1,2$, and

$$\rho := \max\left\{\left(\frac{k_2}{k_1}\right)r_1, \left(\frac{k_4}{k_3}\right)r_1\right\}, \tag{3.17}$$

there is $r_2 > 0$ such that $|u'''(t)| < r_2$, for all $t \in I$. As r_1 and φ do not depend on λ, then r_2 is independent of λ.

Step 3. For $\lambda = 1$, problem (3.4)-(3.6) has at least a solution $u_1(t)$.

Define the operators $\mathcal{L} : C^4(I) \subset C^3(I) \to C(I) \times R^4$ by

$$\mathcal{L}u = \left(u^{(iv)} - u''(t), u(0), u(1), u''(0), u''(1)\right) \tag{3.18}$$

and, for $\lambda \in [0,1]$, $\mathcal{N}_\lambda : C^3(I) \to C(I) \times R^4$ by

$$\begin{aligned} \mathcal{N}_\lambda u = \Big(&\lambda f(t,\xi_0(t,u(t)),\xi_1(t,u'(t)),\xi_2(t,u''(t)),u'''(t)) \\ &- \lambda\xi_2(t,u''(t)), \lambda A, \lambda A, \lambda\left(\frac{k_2}{k_1}\right)u''(0), -\lambda\left(\frac{k_4}{k_3}\right)u''(1)\Big). \end{aligned} \tag{3.19}$$

As $\mathcal{L}$ has a compact inverse, we can define the completely continuous operator $\mathcal{T}_\lambda : (C^3(I),R) \to (C^3(I),R)$ by

$$\mathcal{T}_\lambda(u) = \mathcal{L}^{-1}\mathcal{N}_\lambda(u). \tag{3.20}$$

For r_2 given by Step 2, consider the set

$$\Omega = \left\{x \in C^3(I) : \|x^{(i)}\|_\infty < r_1,\ i = 0,1,2,\ \|x'''\|_\infty < r_2\right\}. \tag{3.21}$$

By Steps 1 and 2, for every u solution of (3.4)–(3.6), $u \notin \partial\Omega$ and so the degree $d(I - \mathcal{T}_\lambda, \Omega, 0)$ is well defined, for every $\lambda \in [0,1]$. By the invariance under homotopy,

$$d(I - \mathcal{T}_0, \Omega, 0) = d(I - \mathcal{T}_1, \Omega, 0). \tag{3.22}$$

Since the equation $x = \mathcal{T}_0(x)$, equivalent to the problem

$$\begin{aligned} u^{(iv)}(t) - u''(t) &= 0, \\ u(0) = u(1) = u'''(0) = u'''(1) &= 0, \end{aligned} \tag{3.23}$$

has only the trivial solution, then $d(I-\mathcal{T}_0,\Omega,0)=\pm 1$. Therefore, by degree theory, the equation $x=\mathcal{T}_1(x)$ has at least one solution. That is, the problem

$$u^{(iv)}(t)=f(t,\xi_0(t,u),\xi_1(t,u'),\xi_2(t,u''),u'''(t))+u''(t)-\xi_2(t,u'') \tag{3.24}$$

with the boundary condition (1.2) has at least one solution $u_1(t)$ in Ω.

Step 4. The function $u_1(t)$ is a solution of problem (1.1)-(1.2).

We remark that this statement holds if $u_1(t)$ verifies (3.3). Assume, by contradiction, that there is $t\in I$ such that $u_1''(t)>\beta''(t)$ and define

$$(u_1-\beta)''(t_1):=\max_{t\in I}\{(u_1-\beta)''(t)\}>0. \tag{3.25}$$

If $t_1\in(0,1)$, then $u_1'''(t_1)=\beta'''(t_1)$ and $u_1^{(iv)}(t_1)\le\beta^{(iv)}(t_1)$. By (b) and (ii), the following contradiction is achieved:

$$\begin{aligned}u_1^{(iv)}(t_1)&\ge f(t_1,\beta(t_1),\beta'(t_1),\beta''(t_1),\beta'''(t_1))+u_1''(t_1)-\beta''(t_1)\\&>f(t_1,\beta(t_1),\beta'(t_1),\beta''(t_1),\beta'''(t_1))\ge\beta^{(iv)}(t_1).\end{aligned} \tag{3.26}$$

If $t_1=0$, then $(u_1-\beta)'''(0)\le 0$ so, by (3.6) and Definition 2.1,

$$0\ge u_1'''(0)-\beta'''(0)=\frac{[k_2u_1''(0)-k_1\beta'''(0)]}{k_1}\ge\left(\frac{k_2}{k_1}\right)[u_1''(0)-\beta''(0)]\ge 0. \tag{3.27}$$

Thus $u_1'''(0)=\beta'''(0)$ and $u_1^{(iv)}(0)\le\beta^{(iv)}(0)$. Therefore, replacing in the above inequality t_1 by 0 a contradiction is obtained. By similar arguments it can be proved that $t_1\neq 1$ and so $u_1''(t)\le\beta''(t)$, for every $t\in I$. Using an analogous technique, we prove that $\alpha''(t)\le u_1''(t)$, for all $t\in I$. So $u_1''\in[\alpha'',\beta'']$. Then, by integration and (iii), we have

$$\beta'(1)\le\alpha(0)-\alpha(1)+\alpha'(1)=\int_0^1\int_t^1\alpha''(s)\,ds\,dt\le\int_0^1\int_t^1u_1''(s)\,ds\,dt=u_1'(1). \tag{3.28}$$

As $(\beta-u_1)'(t)$ is nondecreasing, then $\beta'(t)-u_1'(t)\le\beta'(1)-u_1'(1)\le 0$, for every $t\in I$. By the monotony of $(\beta-u_1)(t)$ and (ii), we have $0\le\beta(1)-u_1(1)\le\beta(t)-u_1(t)$, for all $t\in I$. The inequalities $u_1'(t)\le\alpha'(t)$ and $u_1(t)\ge\alpha(t)$, for all $t\in I$, can be deduced in a similar way. □

If f satisfies the reversed one-sided Nagumo-type condition (2.2), then Theorem 3.1 still holds.

Moreover, if in Definition 2.3 we consider the following new assumptions:

$$\alpha(t)\le\beta(t),\quad\alpha'(t)\le\beta'(t),\quad\alpha''(t)\le\beta''(t),\quad\forall t\in I, \tag{3.29}$$

the initial value inequalities $\alpha(0)\le A$, $\beta(0)\ge A$, and

(iii′) $\alpha'(0) - \beta'(0) \le \min\{\beta(0) - \beta(1), \alpha(1) - \alpha(0)\}$,
then Theorem 3.1 remains true for

$$E_2 = \left\{ \begin{array}{c} (t, x_0, x_1, x_2, x_3) \in I \times R^4 : \alpha(t) \le x_0 \le \beta(t), \\ \alpha'(t) \le x_1 \le \beta'(t),\ \alpha''(t) \le x_2 \le \beta''(t) \end{array} \right\}, \tag{3.30}$$

and f verifying

$$f(t, \alpha(t), \alpha'(t), x_2, x_3) \ge f(t, x_0, x_1, x_2, x_3) \ge f(t, \beta(t), \beta'(t), x_2, x_3) \tag{3.31}$$

for $(t, x_2, x_3) \in I \times R^2$, $\alpha(t) \le x_0 \le \beta(t)$, $\alpha'(t) \le x_1 \le \beta'(t)$.

4. Example and counterexample

Next example shows the applicability and improvement given by Theorem 3.1, since the nonlinearity considered does not satisfy the usual two-sided Nagumo condition.

Example 4.1. Consider the fully fourth-order differential equation

$$u^{(iv)}(t) = 8 - e^{u(t)} + [u'(t) - 4][2 - u''(t)]^2 - |u'''(t)|^\theta, \quad t \in I, \tag{4.1}$$

where $\theta > 2$, with the boundary conditions of Sturm-Liouville type

$$u(0) = u(1) = 0, \qquad u'''(0) - 2u''(0) = 0, \qquad u'''(1) + u''(1) = 0. \tag{4.2}$$

It is easy to see that the continuous functions $\alpha, \beta : I \to R$ given by

$$\alpha(t) = -t^2 + 3t - 2, \qquad \beta(t) = t^2 - 3t + 2 \tag{4.3}$$

define a pair of lower and upper solutions for problem (4.1)-(4.2). On

$$E = \left\{ \begin{array}{c} (t, x_0, x_1, x_2, x_3) \in I \times R^4 : -t^2 + 3t - 2 \le x_0 \le t^2 - 3t + 2, \\ 3 - 2t \ge x_1 \ge 2t - 3,\ -2 \le x_2 \le 2 \end{array} \right\}, \tag{4.4}$$

the continuous function $f : E \to R$ given by

$$f(t, x_0, x_1, x_2, x_3) = 8 - e^{x_0} + (x_1 - 4)(2 - x_2)^2 - |x_3|^\theta, \tag{4.5}$$

verifies (3.2) and the one-sided Nagumo-type condition with $\varphi(x_3) \equiv 8 - e^{-2}$.

Therefore, by Theorem 3.1, there is at least a solution $u(t)$ of problem (4.1)-(4.2) such that, for every $t \in I$,

$$-t^2 + 3t - 2 \le u(t) \le t^2 - 3t + 2, \qquad 3 - 2t \ge u'(t) \ge 2t - 3, \qquad -2 \le u''(t) \le 2. \tag{4.6}$$

Notice that the nonlinearity f given by (4.5) does not verify the two-sided Nagumo-type condition. In fact, assume, by contradiction, that there is a positive continuous function φ verifying (2.3) and such that

$$|f(t, x_0, x_1, x_2, x_3)| \le \varphi(|x_3|), \quad \forall (t, x_0, x_1, x_2, x_3) \in E. \tag{4.7}$$

In particular, $-f(t,x_0,x_1,x_2,x_3) \le \varphi(|x_3|)$, for every $(t,x_0,x_1,x_2,x_3) \in E$, and so, for $t \in [0,1]$, $x_0 = 2$, $x_1 = 2$, $x_2 = 0$, and $x_3 \in R$, we have

$$-f(t,2,2,0,x_3) = e^2 + |x_3|^\theta \le \varphi(|x_3|). \tag{4.8}$$

As $\int_0^{+\infty}(s/(e^2+s^\theta))ds$, with $\theta > 2$, is finite, then we have the following contradiction:

$$+\infty > \int_0^{+\infty} \frac{s}{e^2+s^\theta} ds \ge \int_0^{+\infty} \frac{s}{\varphi(s)} ds = +\infty. \tag{4.9}$$

Counterexample 4.2. We will show that assumption (iii) in Definition 2.3 cannot be removed. In fact, considering the fourth-order boundary value problem

$$\begin{gathered} u^{(iv)}(t) = -2u'''(t) + 3u''(t), \\ u(0) = u(1) = 0, \\ u'''(0) - u''(0) = 0, \qquad u'''(1) + 3u''(1) = 0, \end{gathered} \tag{4.10}$$

the functions $\alpha(t) = -(t-1)(3t-1)/3$, $\beta(t) = (1-t)(4-t)/3$ are lower and upper solutions of problem (4.10) but condition (iii) does not hold. As (4.10) has only the trivial solution $u(t) \equiv 0$, then condition (3.3) is not satisfied. In fact, $0 \equiv u(t) < \alpha(t) < \beta(t)$, for $t \in]1/3,1[$, and $0 \equiv u'(t) > \alpha'(t) > \beta'(t)$, for $t \in]2/3,1[$.

References

[1] C. De Coster and P. Habets, *Upper and lower solutions in the theory of ODE boundary value problems: classical and recent results*, Non-Linear Analysis and Boundary Value Problems for Ordinary Differential Equations (Udine), CISM Courses and Lectures, vol. 371, Springer, Vienna, 1996, pp. 1–78.

[2] J. Ehme, P. W. Eloe, and J. Henderson, *Upper and lower solution methods for fully nonlinear boundary value problems*, Journal of Differential Equations **180** (2002), no. 1, 51–64.

[3] D. Franco, D. O'Regan, and J. Perán, *Fourth-order problems with nonlinear boundary conditions*, Journal of Computational and Applied Mathematics **174** (2005), no. 2, 315–327.

[4] M. R. Grossinho and F. Minhós, *Existence result for some third order separated boundary value problems*, Nonlinear Analysis **47** (2001), no. 4, 2407–2418.

[5] M. Grossinho and F. Minhós, *Solvability of some higher order two-point boundary value problems*, Equadiff 10, 2001, pp. 183–189, CD-ROM papers.

[6] M. R. Grossinho and F. Minhós, *Upper and lower solutions for higher order boundary value problems*, Nonlinear Studies **12** (2005), no. 2, 165–176.

[7] M. R. Grossinho, F. Minhós, and A. I. Santos, *Solvability of some third-order boundary value problems with asymmetric unbounded nonlinearities*, Nonlinear Analysis **62** (2005), no. 7, 1235–1250.

[8] C. P. Gupta, *Existence and uniqueness theorems for the bending of an elastic beam equation*, Applicable Analysis **26** (1988), no. 4, 289–304.

[9] ———, *Existence and uniqueness theorems for a fourth order boundary value problem of Sturm-Liouville type*, Differential and Integral Equations **4** (1991), no. 2, 397–410.

[10] P. Habets and R. L. Pouso, *Examples of the nonexistence of a solution in the presence of upper and lower solutions*, The Australian & New Zealand Industrial and Applied Mathematics Journal **44** (2003), no. 4, 591–594.

[11] T. F. Ma and J. da Silva, *Iterative solutions for a beam equation with nonlinear boundary conditions of third order*, Applied Mathematics and Computation **159** (2004), no. 1, 11–18.

[12] J. Mawhin, *Topological Degree Methods in Nonlinear Boundary Value Problems*, CBMS Regional Conference Series in Mathematics, vol. 40, American Mathematical Society, Rhode Island, 1979.

[13] F. Minhós, T. Gyulov, and A. I. Santos, *Existence and location result for a fourth order boundary value problem*, Proceedings of 5th International Conference on Dynamical Systems and Differential Equations, USA, 2004, to appear.

[14] ———, *Existence and location theorems for the bending of an elastic beam fully equation*, to appear.

[15] M. Nagumo, *On principally linear elliptic differential equations of the second order*, Osaka Journal of Mathematics **6** (1954), 207–229.

F. Minhós: Departamento de Matemática, Universidade de Évora, Centro de Investigação em Matemática e Aplicações da U.E. (CIMA-UE), Rua Romão Ramalho 59, 7000-671 Évora, Portugal
E-mail address: fminhos@uevora.pt

A. I. Santos: Departamento de Matemática, Universidade de Évora, Centro de Investigação em Matemática e Aplicações da U.E. (CIMA-UE), Rua Romão Ramalho 59, 7000-671 Évora, Portugal
E-mail address: aims@uevora.pt

T. Gyulov: Centre of Applied Mathematics and Informatics, University of Rousse, 8 Studenska Street, 7017 Rousse, Bulgaria
E-mail address: tgyulov_03@yahoo.com

ON AN ELASTIC BEAM FULLY EQUATION WITH NONLINEAR BOUNDARY CONDITIONS

F. MINHÓS, T. GYULOV, AND A. I. SANTOS

We study the fourth-order nonlinear boundary value problem $u^{(iv)}(t) = f(t,u(t),u'(t), u''(t),u'''(t))$ for $t \in]0,1[$, $u(0) = A$, $u'(0) = B$, $g(u''(0),u'''(0)) = 0, h(u''(1),u'''(1)) = 0$, with $f : [0,1] \times \mathbb{R}^4 \to \mathbb{R}$ is a continuous function verifying a Nagumo-type condition, $A, B \in \mathbb{R}$ and g, $h : \mathbb{R}^2 \to \mathbb{R}$ are continuous functions with adequate monotonicities. For this model of the bending of an elastic beam, clamped at the left endpoint, we obtained an existence and location result by lower- and upper-solution method and degree theory. Similar results are presented for the same beam fully equation with different types of boundary conditions.

1. Introduction

In this paper we considered the fourth-order fully nonlinear differential equation:

$$u^{(iv)}(t) = f(t,u(t),u'(t),u''(t),u'''(t)) \quad \text{for } t \in]0,1[, \tag{1.1}$$

where $f : [0,1] \times \mathbb{R}^4 \to \mathbb{R}$ is a continuous function verifying a Nagumo-type growth assumption and the nonlinear boundary conditions:

$$u(0) = A, \qquad u'(0) = B, \tag{1.2}$$

$$g(u''(0),u'''(0)) = 0, \qquad h(u''(1),u'''(1)) = 0, \tag{1.3}$$

with $A, B \in \mathbb{R}$ and g, $h : \mathbb{R}^2 \to \mathbb{R}$ continuous functions with some monotone assumptions.

This problem models the bending of a single elastic beam and improves [5, 6, 8, 12, 13, 17] where linear boundary conditions are considered, [10] since a more general equation and nonlinear boundary conditions are assumed, and [16] because weaker lower- and upper-solution definitions are used. Applications to suspension bridges can be considered, too (see [1] and the references therein).

Hindawi Publishing Corporation
Proceedings of the Conference on Differential & Difference Equations and Applications, pp. 805–814

A growth restriction of Nagumo type [14] plays a key role in these results not only to obtain an a priori bound on the third derivative, but also because, as it is known for second-order boundary-value problems, the existence of well-ordered lower and upper solutions, by itself, is not sufficient to ensure the existence of solutions (see [7, 15]).

The existence and location result for problem (1.1)–(1.3) (see Theorem 3.1) is established by using lower- and upper-solution method to obtain a priori estimations of the solution and some derivatives, which allow us to define an open set where the topological degree is well defined [11]. The arguments used were suggested by [2–4, 9] for higher-order separated boundary-value problems.

Replacing (1.2) by boundary conditions with data on the right endpoint, that is, by

$$u(1) = A, \qquad u'(1) = B \tag{1.4}$$

or on both endpoints

$$u(0) = A, \qquad u'(1) = B \tag{1.5}$$

or

$$u(1) = A, \qquad u'(0) = B, \tag{1.6}$$

similar existence and location results can be obtained (see Theorems 3.2, 3.4, 3.5). Remark that different definitions and assumptions on the nonlinear part must be considered in order to obtain well-ordered lower and upper solutions. Even so, in some cases, the corresponding first and/or second derivatives verify a reversed order.

An application to an elastic beam cantilevered and without bending at the left endpoint and with a nonlinear relation between the shear force and the bending at the right endpoint will be presented.

2. Definitions and a priori bound

The growth restriction on the nonlinear part of (1.1) is given by a Nagumo-type condition and it plays an important role in the arguments.

Definition 2.1. Given a subset $E \subset [0,1] \times \mathbb{R}^4$, a function $f : [0,1] \times \mathbb{R}^4 \to \mathbb{R}$ is said to satisfy a Nagumo-type condition in E if there exists a continuous function $\psi_E : [0,+\infty[\to \mathbb{R}^+$ such that

$$|f(t,x_0,x_1,x_2,x_3)| \leq \psi_E(|x_3|) \quad \text{in } E, \tag{2.1}$$

with

$$\int_0^{+\infty} \frac{s}{\psi_E(s)} ds = +\infty. \tag{2.2}$$

With the next lemma an a priori estimation for the third-order derivative $u'''(t)$ of solutions of problem (1.1)–(1.3) can be obtained.

Lemma 2.2 ([13, Lemma 2.2]). *Let $\gamma_i, \Gamma_i : [0,1] \to \mathbb{R}$, for $i = 0,1,2$, be continuous functions such that $\gamma_i(t) \le \Gamma_i(t)$, for all $t \in [0,1]$, and define the set*

$$E = \{(t, x_0, x_1, x_2, x_3) \in [0,1] \times \mathbb{R}^4 : \gamma_i(t) \le x_i \le \Gamma_i(t),\ i = 0,1,2\}. \tag{2.3}$$

Assume that there exist $\psi_E \in C([0,+\infty[, \mathbb{R}^+)$ such that

$$\int_\eta^{+\infty} \frac{s}{\psi_E(s)} ds > \max_{t \in [0,1]} \Gamma_2(t) - \min_{t \in [0,1]} \gamma_2(t), \tag{2.4}$$

where $\eta \ge 0$ is given by $\eta = \max\{\Gamma_2(0) - \gamma_2(1), \Gamma_2(1) - \gamma_2(0)\}$. Then, there is $r > 0$ such that, for every continuous function $f : [0,1] \times \mathbb{R}^4 \to \mathbb{R}$ satisfying (2.1) and every solution $u(t)$ of (1.1) such that

$$\gamma_i(t) \le u^{(i)}(t) \le \Gamma_i(t) \quad \text{for } i = 0,1,2,\ \forall t \in [0,1], \tag{2.5}$$

we have

$$\|u'''\|_\infty < r. \tag{2.6}$$

Remark 2.3. Notice that the a priori bound is independent of (1.2) and r depends only on ψ_E, γ_2, and Γ_2.

Lower and upper solutions for problem (1.1)–(1.3) can be defined in the following way.

Definition 2.4. Consider $A, B \in \mathbb{R}$ and $g, h : \mathbb{R}^2 \to \mathbb{R}$ continuous functions.

(i) A function $\beta(t) \in C^4(]0,1[) \cap C^3([0,1])$ is an upper solution of problem (1.1)–(1.3) if

$$\beta^{(iv)}(t) \le f(t, \beta(t), \beta'(t), \beta''(t), \beta'''(t)), \tag{2.7}$$

$$\beta(0) \ge A, \qquad \beta'(0) \ge B, \tag{2.8}$$

$$g(\beta''(0), \beta'''(0)) \le 0, \qquad h(\beta''(1), \beta'''(1)) \le 0. \tag{2.9}$$

(ii) A function $\alpha(t) \in C^4(]0,1[) \cap C^3([0,1])$ is a lower solution of problem (1.1)–(1.3) if the reversed inequalities are verified.

3. Existence and location results

In this section several existence and location results are obtained, that is, theorems that not only prove the existence of a solution but also give some information about its localization and some derivatives.

To assume well-ordered lower and upper solutions for problems with (1.1) and some different types of boundary conditions, the corresponding definitions must assume different inequalities and the nonlinear part f must have different variations as well.

THEOREM 3.1. *Assume that there exist $\alpha(t)$ and $\beta(t)$ lower and upper solutions of problem (1.1)–(1.3), respectively, such that $\alpha''(t) \le \beta''(t)$ for every $t \in [0,1]$. Consider the set*

$$E_1 = \{(t,x_0,x_1,x_2,x_3) \in [0,1] \times \mathbb{R}^4 : \alpha^{(i)}(t) \le x_i \le \beta^{(i)}(t),\ i = 0,1,2\}, \tag{3.1}$$

and let $f : [0,1] \times \mathbb{R}^4 \to \mathbb{R}$ be a continuous function satisfying Nagumo-type condition in E_1 and verifying, for $(t,x_2,x_3) \in [0,1] \times \mathbb{R}^2$, $\alpha(t) \le x_0 \le \beta(t)$, and $\alpha'(t) \le x_1 \le \beta'(t)$,

$$f(t,\alpha,\alpha',x_2,x_3) \ge f(t,x_0,x_1,x_2,x_3) \ge f(t,\beta,\beta',x_2,x_3). \tag{3.2}$$

If g, $h : \mathbb{R}^2 \to \mathbb{R}$ are continuous functions nondecreasing and nonincreasing on the second variable, respectively, then problem (1.1)–(1.3) has at least one solution $u(t) \in C^4([0,1])$ such that

$$\alpha(t) \le u(t) \le \beta(t), \qquad \alpha'(t) \le u'(t) \le \beta'(t), \qquad \alpha''(t) \le u''(t) \le \beta''(t), \tag{3.3}$$

for every $t \in [0,1]$.

Proof. For $i = 0,1,2$, consider the continuous truncations

$$\delta_i(t,x_i) = \begin{cases} \beta^{(i)}(t), & x_i > \beta^{(i)}(t), \\ x_i, & \alpha^{(i)}(t) \le x_i \le \beta^{(i)}(t), \\ \alpha^{(i)}(t), & x_i < \alpha^{(i)}(t), \end{cases} \tag{3.4}$$

and, for $\lambda \in [0,1]$, the homotopic problem composed by the differential equation

$$u^{(iv)}(t) = \lambda f(t,\delta_0(t,u),\delta_1(t,u'),\delta_2(t,u''),u'''(t)) + u''(t) - \lambda\delta_2(t,u''), \tag{3.5}$$

with the boundary conditions

$$\begin{gathered} u(0) = \lambda A, \qquad u'(0) = \lambda B, \\ u''(0) = \lambda[g(\delta_2(0,u''(0)),u'''(0)) + \delta_2(0,u''(0))], \\ u''(1) = \lambda[h(\delta_2(1,u''(1)),u'''(1)) + \delta_2(1,u''(1))]. \end{gathered} \tag{3.6}$$

Take $r_2 > 0$ large enough such that, for every $t \in [0,1]$,

$$\begin{gathered} -r_2 < \alpha''(t) \le \beta''(t) < r_2, \\ f(t,\alpha(t),\alpha'(t),\alpha''(t),0) - r_2 - \alpha''(t) < 0, \\ f(t,\beta(t),\beta'(t),\beta''(t),0) + r_2 - \beta''(t) > 0, \\ |g(\alpha''(0),0) + \alpha''(0)| < r_2; \qquad |g(\beta''(0),0) + \beta''(0)| < r_2, \\ |h(\alpha''(1),0) + \alpha''(1)| < r_2; \qquad |h(\beta''(1),0) + \beta''(1)| < r_2. \end{gathered} \tag{3.7}$$

Step 1. Every solution $u(t)$ of problem (3.5)-(3.6) verifies

$$|u''(t)| < r_2, \quad |u'(t)| < r_1, \quad |u(t)| < r_0, \tag{3.8}$$

with $r_1 := r_2 + |B|$ and $r_0 := r_1 + |A|$, for every $t \in [0,1]$, independently of $\lambda \in [0,1]$.

Assume, by contradiction, that the first inequality does not hold. So, for $\lambda \in [0,1]$, there exist $t \in [0,1]$ and a solution u of (3.5)-(3.6) such that $|u''(t)| \geq r_2$. In the case $u''(t) \geq r_2$ define $u''(t_0) := \max_{t\in[0,1]} u''(t) \geq r_2$. Applying the same technique as in [12] it can be proved that $t_0 \notin (0,1)$.

If $t_0 = 0$, then $u''(0) \geq r_2$ and $u'''(0^+) = u'''(0) \leq 0$. So, by (3.6), (3.7), and the monotonicity of g, we obtain, for $\lambda \in [0,1]$, the following contradiction:

$$\begin{aligned} r_2 \leq u''(0) &= \lambda[g(\delta_2(0,u''(0)),u'''(0)) + \delta_2(0,u''(0))] \\ &\leq \lambda[g(\beta''(0),0) + \beta''(0)] \leq |g(\beta''(0),0) + \beta''(0)| < r_2. \end{aligned} \tag{3.9}$$

Thus $t_0 \neq 0$ and for $t_0 = 1$, the same technique follows. Therefore $u''(t) < r_2$ for all $t \in [0,1]$. For the case $u''(t) \leq -r_2$, the arguments are similar and so $|u''(t)| < r_2$ for every $t \in [0,1]$.

Integrating on $[0,t]$, we obtain

$$\begin{aligned} |u'(t)| &= \left| \int_0^t u''(s)ds + u'(0) \right| < r_2 + |B| := r_1, \\ |u(t)| &= \left| \int_0^t u'(s)ds + u(0) \right| < r_2 + |B| + |A| := r_0. \end{aligned} \tag{3.10}$$

Step 2. There is $r_3 > 0$ such that every solution $u(t)$ of (3.5)-(3.6) verifies $\|u'''(t)\|_\infty < r_3$, independently of $\lambda \in [0,1]$.

Consider the set

$$E_* = \{(t,x_0,x_1,x_2,x_3) \in [0,1] \times \mathbb{R}^4 : -r_i \leq x_i \leq r_i,\ i = 0,1,2\}, \tag{3.11}$$

and, for $\lambda \in [0,1]$, the function $F_\lambda : E_* \to \mathbb{R}$ given by

$$F_\lambda(t,x_0,x_1,x_2,x_3) = \lambda f(t,\delta_0(t,x_0),\delta_1(t,x_1),\delta_2(t,x_2),x_3) + x_2 - \lambda\delta_2(t,x_2). \tag{3.12}$$

As

$$|F_\lambda(t,x_0,x_1,x_2,x_3)| \leq \psi_E(|x_3|) + |x_2| + |\delta_2(t,x_2)| \leq \psi_E(|x_3|) + 2r_2, \tag{3.13}$$

then F_λ satisfies Nagumo-type condition in E_* with ψ_E replaced by $\overline{\psi_E} := 2r_2 + \psi_E(t)$, independently of $\lambda \in [0,1]$.

So, applying Lemma 2.2 with $\gamma_i(t) \equiv -r_i$, $\Gamma_i(t) \equiv r_i$, for $i = 0,1,2$, there is $r_3 > 0$ such that $|u'''(t)| < r_3$ for all $t \in [0,1]$.

Since r_2 and ψ_E are independent of λ, we conclude that r_3 is independent of λ, too.

Step 3. For $\lambda = 1$, the problem (3.5)-(3.6) has at least a solution $u_1(t)$.

Define the operators $\mathcal{L} : C^4([0,1]) \subset C^3([0,1]) \to C([0,1]) \times \mathbb{R}^4$ by

$$\mathcal{L}u = (u^{(iv)}, u(0), u'(0), u''(0), u''(1)) \tag{3.14}$$

and, for $\lambda \in [0,1]$, $\mathcal{N}_\lambda : C^3([0,1]) \to C([0,1]) \times \mathbb{R}^4$ by

$$\begin{aligned}\mathcal{N}_\lambda u = (&\lambda f(t, \delta_0(t,u(t)), \delta_1(t,u'(t)), \delta_2(t,u''(t)), u'''(t)) + u''(t)\\ &- \lambda\delta_2(t,u''(t)), \lambda A, \lambda B, C_\lambda, D_\lambda)\end{aligned} \tag{3.15}$$

with

$$\begin{aligned}C_\lambda &= \lambda[g(\delta_2(0,u''(0)), u'''(0)) + \delta_2(0,u''(0))],\\ D_\lambda &= \lambda[h(\delta_2(1,u''(1)), u'''(1)) + \delta_2(1,u''(1))].\end{aligned} \tag{3.16}$$

As $\mathcal{L}^{-1}$ is compact, we can define the completely continuous operator

$$\mathcal{T}_\lambda : (C^3([0,1]), \mathbb{R}) \longrightarrow (C^3([0,1]), \mathbb{R}) \tag{3.17}$$

by $\mathcal{T}_\lambda(u) = \mathcal{L}^{-1}\mathcal{N}_\lambda(u)$. For r_i, $i = 0,1,2,3$ given by previous steps, consider the open set

$$\Omega = \{x \in C^3([0,1]) : \|x^{(i)}\|_\infty < r_i,\ i = 0,1,2,3\}. \tag{3.18}$$

By Steps 1 and 2, the degree $d(\mathcal{T}_\lambda, \Omega, 0)$ is well defined, for every $\lambda \in [0,1]$, and, by the invariance under homotopy, $d(\mathcal{T}_0, \Omega, 0) = d(\mathcal{T}_1, \Omega, 0)$. The equation $x = \mathcal{T}_0(x)$ is equivalent to the problem

$$\begin{aligned}u^{(iv)}(t) &= u''(t),\\ u(0) = u'(0) &= u''(0) = u''(1) = 0,\end{aligned} \tag{3.19}$$

and has only the trivial solution. Thus, by degree theory, $d(\mathcal{T}_0, \Omega, 0) = \pm 1$. Therefore, $x = \mathcal{T}_1(x)$ has at least one solution, that is,

$$u^{(iv)}(t) = f(t, \delta_0(t,u(t)), \delta_1(t,u'(t)), \delta_2(t,u''(t)), u'''(t)) + u''(t) - \delta_2(t,u''(t)), \tag{3.20}$$

with the boundary conditions

$$\begin{aligned}u(0) = A, \qquad u'(0) &= B,\\ u''(0) = g(\delta_2(0,u''(0)), u'''(0)) &+ \delta_2(0,u''(0)),\\ u''(1) = h(\delta_2(1,u''(1)), u'''(1)) &+ \delta_2(1,u''(1)),\end{aligned} \tag{3.21}$$

has at least one solution $u_1(t)$ in Ω.

Step 4. The function $u_1(t)$ is a solution of problem (1.1)–(1.3).

Notice that this statement holds if $u_1(t)$ verifies (3.3).

Assume, by contradiction, that there is $t \in [0,1]$ such that $u_1''(t) > \beta''(t)$ and define

$$(u_1-\beta)''(t_1) := \max_{t\in[0,1]}\{(u_1-\beta)''(t)\} > 0. \tag{3.22}$$

Following the arguments used in [12] it can be proved that $t_1 \notin (0,1)$.

If $t_1 = 0$ then $(u_1-\beta)'''(0) \le 0$. By the monotonicity of g and (2.9), the following contradiction is obtained:

$$\beta''(0) < u_1''(0) = g(\beta''(0), u_1'''(0)) + \beta''(0) \le g(\beta''(0), \beta'''(0)) + \beta''(0) \le \beta''(0). \tag{3.23}$$

By similar arguments it can be shown that $t_1 \neq 1$ and so $u_1''(t) \le \beta''(t)$ for every $t \in [0,1]$. Using an analogous technique, the inequality $\alpha''(t) \le u_1''(t)$ holds, for all $t \in [0,1]$, and so $\alpha''(t) \le u_1''(t) \le \beta''(t)$ for every $t \in [0,1]$.

As $(\beta - u_1)'(t)$ is nondecreasing, then, by (2.8),

$$0 \le \beta'(0) - u_1'(0) \le \beta'(t) - u_1'(t), \quad \forall t \in [0,1]. \tag{3.24}$$

By the monotony of $(\beta - u_1)(t)$ and (2.8) we have $0 \le \beta(0) - u_1(0) \le \beta(t) - u_1(t)$ for all $t \in I$.

The inequalities $\alpha'(t) \le u_1'(t)$ and $\alpha(t) \le u_1(t)$, for all $t \in [0,1]$, can be deduced in a similar way. □

For problem (1.1)-(1.4)-(1.3) upper solutions will be defined as in Definition 2.4 replacing (2.8) by

$$\beta(1) \ge A, \qquad \beta'(1) \le B, \tag{3.25}$$

and the corresponding reversed inequalities for lower solutions. Then the following existence and location result holds.

Theorem 3.2. *Assume that $\alpha(t)$ and $\beta(t)$ are lower and upper solutions of problem (1.1)-(1.4)-(1.3) such that $\alpha''(t) \le \beta''(t)$, for every $t \in [0,1]$, f verifies a Nagumo-type condition in*

$$E_2 = \{(t, x_0, x_1, x_2, x_3) : \alpha^{(i)}(t) \le x_i \le \beta^{(i)}(t),\ i = 0,2,\ \beta'(t) \le x_1 \le \alpha'(t)\}, \tag{3.26}$$

and, for $(t, x_2, x_3) \in [0,1] \times \mathbb{R}^2$, $\alpha(t) \le x_0 \le \beta(t)$, and $\beta'(t) \le x_1 \le \alpha'(t)$, condition (3.2) holds. If $g(x,y)$ and $h(x,y)$ are continuous functions, respectively, nondecreasing and nonincreasing on y, then there exists $u(t) \in C^4([0,1])$ solution of (1.1)-(1.4)-(1.3) such that

$$\alpha(t) \le u(t) \le \beta(t), \qquad \beta'(t) \le u'(t) \le \alpha'(t), \qquad \alpha''(t) \le u''(t) \le \beta''(t), \quad \forall t \in [0,1]. \tag{3.27}$$

Consider now the beam equation (1.1) with the boundary conditions on both endpoints, (1.5), then new definitions of lower and upper solutions must be considered.

Definition 3.3. For $A, B \in \mathbb{R}$ and $g, h : \mathbb{R}^2 \to \mathbb{R}$ continuous functions:

(i) $\beta(t) \in C^4(]0,1[) \cap C^3([0,1])$ is an upper solution of problem (1.1)-(1.5)-(1.3) if it verifies

$$\begin{aligned} \beta^{(iv)}(t) &\geq f(t,\beta(t),\beta'(t),\beta''(t),\beta'''(t)), \\ \beta(0) &\geq A, \qquad \beta'(1) \geq B, \\ g(\beta''(0),\beta'''(0)) &\geq 0, \qquad h(\beta''(1),\beta'''(1)) \geq 0; \end{aligned} \tag{3.28}$$

(ii) $\alpha(t) \in C^4(]0,1[) \cap C^3([0,1])$ is a lower solution of problem (1.1)-(1.5)-(1.3) if the reversed inequalities are verified.

The corresponding theorem is the following.

Theorem 3.4. *Suppose that $\alpha(t)$ and $\beta(t)$ are lower and upper solutions of (1.1)-(1.5)-(1.3) such that $\alpha''(t) \geq \beta''(t)$ for every $t \in [0,1]$.*

Let $f : [0,1] \times \mathbb{R}^4 \to \mathbb{R}$ be a continuous function satisfying Nagumo-type condition in

$$E_3 = \{(t,x_0,x_1,x_2,x_3) : \alpha^{(i)}(t) \leq x_i \leq \beta^{(i)}(t),\ i = 0,1,\ \beta''(t) \leq x_2 \leq \alpha''(t)\}, \tag{3.29}$$

and, for $(t,x_2,x_3) \in [0,1] \times \mathbb{R}^2$, $\alpha^{(i)}(t) \leq x_i \leq \beta^{(i)}(t)$, $i = 0,1$,

$$f(t,\alpha,\alpha',x_2,x_3) \leq f(t,x_0,x_1,x_2,x_3) \leq f(t,\beta,\beta',x_2,x_3). \tag{3.30}$$

If $g, h : \mathbb{R}^2 \to \mathbb{R}$ are continuous functions such that $g(x,y)$ is nondecreasing on y and $h(x,y)$ nonincreasing on y, then there is $u(t) \in C^4([0,1])$ solution of (1.1)-(1.5)-(1.3) such that

$$\alpha(t) \leq u(t) \leq \beta(t), \qquad \alpha'(t) \leq u'(t) \leq \beta'(t), \qquad \beta''(t) \leq u''(t) \leq \alpha''(t), \quad \forall t \in [0,1]. \tag{3.31}$$

A similar result can be obtained for problem (1.1)-(1.6)-(1.3) defining upper solutions as in Definition 3.3, replacing (3.28) by

$$\beta(1) \geq A, \qquad \beta'(0) \leq B, \tag{3.32}$$

and the related lower solutions verifying the reversed inequalities.

Theorem 3.5. *Suppose that $\alpha(t)$ and $\beta(t)$ are lower and upper solutions of (1.1)-(1.6)-(1.3) such that $\alpha''(t) \geq \beta''(t)$ for every $t \in [0,1]$. Let $f : [0,1] \times \mathbb{R}^4 \to \mathbb{R}$ be a continuous function satisfying Nagumo-type condition in*

$$E_4 = \{(t,x_0,x_1,x_2,x_3) : \alpha(t) \leq x_0 \leq \beta(t),\ \beta^{(i)}(t) \leq x_i \leq \alpha^{(i)}(t),\ i = 1,2\}, \tag{3.33}$$

and, for $(t,x_2,x_3) \in [0,1] \times \mathbb{R}^2$, $\alpha(t) \leq x_0 \leq \beta(t)$, and $\beta'(t) \leq x_1 \leq \alpha'(t)$,

$$f(t,\alpha,\alpha',x_2,x_3) \leq f(t,x_0,x_1,x_2,x_3) \leq f(t,\beta,\beta',x_2,x_3). \tag{3.34}$$

If $g, h : \mathbb{R}^2 \to \mathbb{R}$ are continuous functions such that $g(x,y)$ is nondecreasing on y and $h(x,y)$ nonincreasing on y, then there exists a solution $u(t) \in C^4([0,1])$ of (1.1)-(1.6)-(1.3) such that

$$\alpha(t) \leq u(t) \leq \beta(t), \qquad \beta'(t) \leq u'(t) \leq \alpha'(t), \qquad \beta''(t) \leq u''(t) \leq \alpha''(t), \quad \forall t \in [0,1]. \tag{3.35}$$

As an example to show the applicability of Theorem 3.1, consider the following fourth-order boundary-value problem:

$$\begin{gathered} u^{(iv)}(t) = f(t, u(t), u'(t), u''(t), u'''(t)), \\ u(0) = u'(0) = 0, \\ u''(0) = 0, \qquad u'''(1) = \varphi(u''(1)), \end{gathered} \tag{3.36}$$

where f, φ are continuous functions. Notice that (3.36) is a particular case of (1.1)-(1.2)-(1.3) for $g(x,y) = -x$ and $h(x,y) = \varphi(x) - y$. In fact, this problem models the deformation of an elastic beam cantilevered and without bending moment at the left endpoint and with an eventually nonlinear relation between the shear force (u''') and the bending moment at the right endpoint.

Continuous functions $\alpha, \beta : [0,1] \to \mathbb{R}$ given by $\alpha(t) = -\theta t^2$ and $\beta(t) = \theta t^2$, for some $\theta > 0$, are lower and upper solutions of (3.36) for θ and φ such that $\varphi(2\theta) \leq 0 \leq \varphi(-2\theta)$.

By Theorem 3.1, for every continuous function f that verifies Nagumo-type condition (e.g., f with a subquadratic growth on u''') and such that

$$f(t, -\theta t^2, -2\theta t, x_2, x_3) \geq f(t, x_0, x_1, x_2, x_3) \geq f(t, \theta t^2, 2\theta t, x_2, x_3) \tag{3.37}$$

(e.g., f nonincreasing on x_0 and x_1), there exists a solution $u(t)$ of problem (3.36) such that

$$-\theta t^2 \leq u(t) \leq \theta t^2, \quad -2\theta t \leq u'(t) \leq 2\theta t, \quad -2 \leq u''(t) \leq 2, \quad \forall t \in [0,1]. \tag{3.38}$$

References

[1] P. Drábek, G. Holubová, A. Matas, and P. Nečesal, *Nonlinear models of suspension bridges: discussion of the results*, Applications of Mathematics **48** (2003), no. 6, 497–514.

[2] M. R. Grossinho and F. Minhós, *Existence result for some third order separated boundary value problems*, Nonlinear Analysis. Series A. Theory, Methods & Applications **47** (2001), no. 4, 2407–2418.

[3] ———, *Upper and lower solutions for higher order boundary value problems*, Nonlinear Studies **12** (2005), no. 2, 165–176.

[4] ———, *Solvability of some higher order two-point boundary value problems*, in *Equadiff 10*, CD-ROM papers (2001), 183–189.

[5] C. P. Gupta, *Existence and uniqueness theorems for the bending of an elastic beam equation*, Applicable Analysis **26** (1988), no. 4, 289–304.

[6] ———, *Existence and uniqueness theorems for a fourth order boundary value problem of Sturm-Liouville type*, Differential and Integral Equations **4** (1991), no. 2, 397–410.

[7] P. Habets and R. L. Pouso, *Examples of the nonexistence of a solution in the presence of upper and lower solutions*, The ANZIAM Journal **44** (2003), no. 4, 591–594.

[8] A. C. Lazer and P. J. McKenna, *Large-amplitude periodic oscillations in suspension bridges: some new connections with nonlinear analysis*, SIAM Review **32** (1990), no. 4, 537–578.

[9] F. Li, Q. Zhang, and Z. Liang, *Existence and multiplicity of solutions of a kind of fourth-order boundary value problem*, Nonlinear Analysis **62** (2005), no. 5, 803–816.

[10] T. F. Ma and J. da Silva, *Iterative solutions for a beam equation with nonlinear boundary conditions of third order*, Applied Mathematics and Computation **159** (2004), no. 1, 11–18.

[11] J. Mawhin, *Topological Degree Methods in Nonlinear Boundary Value Problems*, CBMS Regional Conference Series in Mathematics, vol. 40, American Mathematical Society, Rhode Island, 1979.

[12] F. Minhós, T. Gyulov, and A. I. Santos, *Existence and location result for a fourth order boundary value problem*, Proceedings of 5th AIMS International Conference on Dynamical Systems and Differential Equations, Discrete and Continuous Dynamical Systems, 2005, pp. 662–671.

[13] ———, *Existence and location theorems for the bending of an elastic beam fully equation*, to appear.

[14] M. Nagumo, *Über die differentialgleichung $y'' = f(t, y, y')$*, Proceedings of the Physico-Mathematical Society of Japan **19** (1937), 861–866.

[15] ———, *On principally linear elliptic differential equations of the second order*, Osaka Journal of Mathematics **6** (1954), 207–229.

[16] F. Sadyrbaev, *Nonlinear fourth-order two-point boundary value problems*, The Rocky Mountain Journal of Mathematics **25** (1995), no. 2, 757–781.

[17] ———, *Ważewski method and upper and lower functions for higher order ordinary differential equations*, Universitatis Iagellonicae. Acta Mathematica (1998), no. 36, 165–170.

F. Minhós: Departamento de Matemática, Centro de Investigação em Matemática e Aplicações da U.E. (CIMA-UE), Universidade de Évora, Rua Romão Ramalho 59, 7000-671 Évora, Portugal
E-mail address: fminhos@uevora.pt

T. Gyulov: Centre of Applied Mathematics and Informatics, University of Rousse, 8 Studenska Street, 7017 Rousse, Bulgaria
E-mail address: tgyulov_03@yahoo.com

A. I. Santos: Departamento de Matemática, Centro de Investigação em Matemática e Aplicações da U.E. (CIMA-UE), Universidade de Évora, Rua Romão Ramalho 59, 7000-671 Évora, Portugal
E-mail address: aims@uevora.pt

REMARKS ON THE STABILITY CROSSING CURVES OF SOME DISTRIBUTED DELAY SYSTEMS

CONSTANTIN-IRINEL MORĂRESCU, SILVIU-IULIAN NICULESCU, AND KEQIN GU

This paper characterizes the stability crossing curves of a class of linear systems with gamma-distributed delays with a gap. First, we describe the crossing set, that is, the set of frequencies where the characteristic roots may cross the imaginary axis as the parameters change. Then, we describe the corresponding stability crossing curves, that is, the set of parameters such that there is at least one pair of characteristic roots on the imaginary axis. Such stability crossing curves divide the parameter space $\mathbb{R}_+^2$ into different regions. Within each such region, the number of characteristic roots on the right-hand complex plane is fixed. This naturally describes the regions of parameters where the system is stable.

1. Introduction

The stability of dynamical systems in the presence of time-delay is a problem of recurring interest (see, e.g., [5, 7, 8, 10], and the references therein). The presence of a time-delay may induce instabilities, and complex behaviors. The problem becomes even more difficult when the delays are *distributed*. Systems with distributed delays are present in many scientific disciplines such as physiology, population dynamics, and engineering.

Cushing [4] studied the population dynamics using a model with *gamma-distributed delay*. The linearization of this model is

$$\dot{x}(t) = -\alpha x(t) + \beta \int_{-\infty}^{t} g(t-\theta)x(\theta)d\theta, \tag{1.1}$$

where the integration kernel of the distributed delay is the *gamma distribution*

$$g(\xi) = \frac{a^{n+1}}{n!}\xi^n e^{-a\xi}. \tag{1.2}$$

Hindawi Publishing Corporation
Proceedings of the Conference on Differential & Difference Equations and Applications, pp. 815–823

A Laplace transform of (1.1) with $g(\xi)$ expression (1.2) yields a parameter-dependent polynomial characteristic equation

$$D(s,\bar{\tau},n) := (s+\alpha)\left(1+s\frac{\bar{\tau}}{n+1}\right)^{n+1} - \beta = 0, \tag{1.3}$$

where $\bar{\tau} = (n+1)/a$ is the *mean delay*. Cooke and Grossman [3] discussed the change of stability of (1.3) when one of the parameters, mean delay value $\bar{\tau}$, or the exponent n, varies while the other is fixed.

Nisbet and Gurney [11] modified the gamma distribution $g(\xi)$ expressed in (1.2) to the *gamma distribution with a gap*

$$\hat{g}(\xi) = \begin{cases} 0, & \xi < \tau, \\ \dfrac{a^{n+1}}{n!}(\xi-\tau)^n e^{-a(\xi-\tau)}, & \xi \geq \tau, \end{cases} \tag{1.4}$$

to more accurately reflect the reality. See [1, 9] for additional discussions. In this case, a simple computation shows that the *mean delay* is $\hat{\tau} = \tau + (n+1)/a$. The characteristic equation becomes a parameter-dependent quasipolynomial equation [1, 2]:

$$\hat{D}(s,\bar{\tau},\tau,n) := (s+\alpha)\left(1+s\frac{\bar{\tau}}{n+1}\right)^{n+1} - \beta e^{-s\tau} = 0. \tag{1.5}$$

It is interesting to note that some of the earlier results in [1, 3] on stability analysis contain mistakes as pointed out by Boese [2].

More recently, it was pointed out that such gamma-distributed delays with a gap can also be encountered in the problem of controlling objects over communication networks [12]. More explicitly, the overall communication delay in the network is modeled by a gamma-distributed delay with a gap, where the *gap* value corresponds to the minimal *propagation delay* in the network, which is always strictly positive. The stability problem of the closed-loop system in [12] reduces to a parameter-dependent characteristic quasipolynomial equation of the following form:

$$D(s,\bar{\tau},\tau,n) := P(s)\left(1+s\frac{\bar{\tau}}{n+1}\right)^{n+1} + Q(s)e^{-s\tau} = 0, \tag{1.6}$$

where $P(s)$, $Q(s)$ are polynomials. Obviously, (1.5) is a special case of (1.6).

In this paper, we will study the stability of (1.6) as the parameters $\bar{\tau}$ and τ vary. Specifically, we will describe the stability crossing curves, that is, the set of parameters such that there is at least one pair of characteristic roots on the imaginary axis. Such stability crossing curves divide the parameter space $\mathbb{R}_+^2$ into different regions. Within each such region, the number of characteristic roots on the right-hand complex plane is fixed. This naturally describes the regions of parameters where the system is stable.

It should be noted that there have been numerous works in the literature to describe the stability regions of parameter space, known as stability charts [13, 14]. These descriptions are typically valid for one specific system except that the parameters are allowed to vary. In a recent paper, Gu et al. [6] gave a characterization of the stability crossing curves for systems with two discrete delays as the parameters. One significant difference of [6] as compared to the stability charts is the fact that such characterization applies to any systems within the class, that is, any system with two delays. The current paper follows the line of [6] since our conclusion is valid for any system of the form (1.6).

Due to space constraint, the proofs are omitted.

2. Problem formulation

Consider a system with the following characteristic equation:

$$D(s,T,\tau) = P(s)(1+sT)^n + Q(s)\,\mathrm{e}^{-s\tau} = 0, \tag{2.1}$$

where the two parameters T and τ are nonnegative. We will try to describe the *stability crossing curves*, which is the set of (T,τ) such that (2.1) has imaginary solutions. We will denote the stability crossing curves as $\mathcal{T}$. As the parameters (T,τ) cross the stability crossing curves, some characteristic roots cross the imaginary axis. Therefore, the number of roots on the right-half complex plane are different on the two sides of the crossing curves, from which, we may describe the parameter regions of (T,τ) in $\mathbb{R}^2_+$ for the system to be stable.

Another related useful concept is the *crossing set* Ω, which is defined as the collection of all $\omega > 0$ such that there exists a parameter pair (T,τ) such that $D(j\omega,T,\tau) = 0$. In other words, as the parameters T and τ vary, the characteristic roots may cross the imaginary axis at $j\omega$ if and only if $\omega \in \Omega$.

We will restrict our discussions on the systems that satisfy the following assumptions.

(I) $\deg(Q) < \deg(P)$.

(II) $P(0) + Q(0) \neq 0$.

(III) $P(s)$ and $Q(s)$ do not have common zeros.

(IV) If $P(s) = p$, $Q(s) = q$, where p and q are constant real, then $|p| \neq |q|$.

(V) $P(0) \neq 0$, $|P(0)| \neq |Q(0)|$.

(VI) $P'(j\omega) \neq 0$ whenever $P(j\omega) = 0$.

Assumption (I) means that the system represented by (2.1) has retarded delays. While not discussed here, it is possible to extend the analysis to systems with neutral delays by relaxing this assumption to also allow $\deg(Q) = \deg(P)$, as long as $\lim_{s\to\infty} Q(s)/P(s) < 1$ is satisfied. Assumption (II) is made to exclude some trivial cases. If it is not satisfied, then $s = 0$ is a solution of (2.1) for arbitrary (T,τ), and therefore, the system can never be stable.

Regarding assumption (III), if it is violated, we may find a common factor of the highest order $c(s) \neq$ constant of $P(s)$ and $Q(s)$. This would indicate that $D(s,T,\tau) = c(s)\hat{D}(s,T,\tau)$, where $\hat{D}(s,T,\tau)$ satisfies assumption (III), and our analysis can still proceed on $\hat{D}(s,T,\tau)$.

Assumptions (IV) to (VI) are made to exclude some rare singular cases in order to simplify presentation.

Notice, we have restricted any element ω of the crossing set Ω to satisfy $\omega > 0$. Indeed, the discussion of $\omega < 0$ is redundant in view of the fact that $D(-j\omega,T,\tau)$ is the complex conjugate of $D(j\omega, T, \tau)$, and therefore, $D(-j\omega, T, \tau) = 0$ if and only if $D(j\omega, T, \tau)$. Also, $\omega = 0$ is never an element of Ω in view of assumption (II).

3. Main results

3.1. Crossing set and stability crossing curves. Consider a fixed $\omega > 0$, we first observe that as T and τ each varies within $[0, \infty)$, that is, (T, τ) vary in $\mathbb{R}_+^2$, $|1 + j\omega T|^n \in [1, \infty)$, and $|e^{j\omega\tau}| = 1$, and $\angle e^{j\omega\tau}$ may assume any nonnegative value. From this observation, it is not difficult to conclude the following proposition.

Proposition 3.1. *Given any $\omega > 0$, $\omega \in \Omega$ if and only if it satisfies*

$$0 < |P(j\omega)| \leq |Q(j\omega)|. \tag{3.1}$$

There are only a finite number of solutions to the equations

$$P(j\omega) = 0, \tag{3.2}$$

$$|P(j\omega)| = |Q(j\omega)|, \tag{3.3}$$

because P and Q are both polynomials satisfying assumptions (I) to (IV). Therefore, Ω consists of a finite number of intervals. Denote these intervals as $\Omega_1, \Omega_2, \ldots, \Omega_N$. Then

$$\Omega = \bigcup_{k=1}^{N} \Omega_k. \tag{3.4}$$

Without loss of generality, we may order these intervals from left to right, that is, for any $\omega_1 \in \Omega_{i_1}$, $\omega_2 \in \Omega_{i_2}$, $i_1 < i_2$, we have $\omega_1 < \omega_2$.

For any given point in the crossing set, $\omega \in \Omega$, we may calculate the corresponding points in the stability crossing curves as follows:

$$T = \frac{1}{\omega}\left(\left|\frac{Q(j\omega)}{P(j\omega)}\right|^{1/n} - 1\right)^{1/2}, \tag{3.5}$$

$$\tau = \frac{1}{\omega}\left(\angle Q(j\omega) - \angle P(j\omega) - n\arctan(\omega T) + \pi + m2\pi\right), \quad m = 0, \pm 1, \pm 2, \ldots. \tag{3.6}$$

We will not restrict $\angle Q(j\omega)$ and $\angle P(j\omega)$ to a 2π range. Rather, we allow them to vary continuously within each interval Ω_k. Thus, for each fixed m, (3.5) and (3.6) is a continuous curve. We denote such as a curve as $\mathcal{T}_m^k$. Therefore, corresponding to a given interval Ω_k, we have an infinite number of continuous stability crossing curves $\mathcal{T}_m^k$, $m = 0, \pm 1, \pm 2, \ldots$. It should be noted that, for some m, part or the entire curve may be outside of the range $\mathbb{R}_+^2$, and therefore, may not be physically meaningful. The collection of all the points in $\mathcal{T}$ corresponding to Ω_k may be expressed as

$$\mathcal{T}^k = \bigcup_{m=-\infty}^{+\infty} \left(\mathcal{T}_m^k \bigcap \mathbb{R}_+^2\right) \tag{3.7}$$

Obviously,

$$\mathcal{T} = \bigcup_{k=1}^{N} \mathcal{T}^k \tag{3.8}$$

3.2. Classification of stability crossing curves. Let the left and right end points of interval Ω_k be denoted as ω_k^l and ω_k^r, respectively. It is not difficult to see that each end point ω_k^l or ω_k^r must belong to one of the following three types.

Type 1. It satisfies (3.3).

Type 2. It satisfies (3.2).

Type 3. It equals 0.

Denote an end point as ω_0, which may be either a left end or a right end of an interval Ω_k. Then the corresponding points in $\mathcal{T}_k^m$ may be described as follows.

If ω_0 is of Type 1, then $T = 0$. In other words, $\mathcal{T}_k^m$ intersects the τ-axis at $\omega = \omega_0$.

If ω_0 is of Type 2, then as $\omega \to \omega_0$, $T \to \infty$, and

$$\tau \longrightarrow \frac{1}{\omega_0}\left(\angle Q(j\omega_0) \pm \angle\left(\frac{d}{d\omega}P(j\omega)\right)_{\omega=\omega_0} - \frac{n\pi}{2} + \pi + m2\pi\right), \tag{3.9}$$

where "+" applies when ω_0 is a right end, and "−" applies when it is a left end. In other words, $\mathcal{T}_k^m$ approaches a horizontal line.

Obviously, only ω_1^l may be of Type 3. Due to nonsingularity assumptions, if $\omega_1^l = 0$, we must have $0 < |P(0)| < |Q(0)|$. In this case, as $\omega \to 0$, both T and τ approach ∞. In fact, (T,τ) approaches a straight line with slope

$$\tau/T \longrightarrow \frac{(\angle Q(0) - \angle P(0) - n\arctan\alpha + \pi + m2\pi)}{\alpha}, \tag{3.10}$$

where

$$\alpha = \left(\left|\frac{Q(0)}{P(0)}\right|^{1/n} - 1\right)^{1/2}. \tag{3.11}$$

We say an interval Ω_k is of type lr if its left end is of type l and its right end is of type r. We may accordingly divide these intervals into the following six types.

Type 4. In this case, $\mathcal{T}_k^m$ starts at a point on the τ-axis, and ends at another point on the τ-axis.

Type 5. In this case, $\mathcal{T}_k^m$ starts at a point on the τ-axis, and the other end approaches ∞ along a horizontal line.

Type 6. This is the reverse of Type 5. $\mathcal{T}_k^m$ starts at ∞ along a horizontal line, and ends at the τ-axis.

Type 7. In this case, both ends of $\mathcal{T}_k^m$ approach horizontal lines.

Type 8. In this case, $\mathcal{T}_k^m$ begins at ∞ with an asymptote of slope expressed in (3.10). The other end is at the τ-axis.

Type 9. In this case, $\mathcal{T}_k^m$ again begins at ∞ with an asymptote of slope expressed in (3.10). The other end approaches ∞ along a horizontal line.

3.3. Tangents and smoothness. For a given k, we will discuss the smoothness of the curves in $\mathcal{T}_k^m$ and thus $\mathcal{T} = \bigcup_{k=1}^{N}\bigcup_{m=-\infty}^{+\infty}(\mathcal{T}_k^m \bigcap \mathbb{R}_+^2)$. In this part we use an approach based on the implicit function theorem. For this purpose we consider T and τ as implicit functions of $s = j\omega$ defined by (2.1). For a given m and k, as s moves along the imaginary axis within Ω_k, $(T,\tau) = (T(\omega),\tau(\omega))$ moves along $\mathcal{T}_k^m$. For a given $\omega \in \Omega_k$, let

$$\begin{aligned}
R_0 &= \operatorname{Re}\left(\frac{j}{s}\frac{\partial D(s,T,\tau)}{\partial s}\right)_{s=j\omega} \\
&= \frac{1}{\omega}\operatorname{Re}\Big\{\big[nTP(j\omega) + (1+j\omega T)P'(j\omega)\big] \\
&\qquad \cdot (1+j\omega T)^{n-1} + \big(Q'(j\omega) - \tau Q(j\omega)\big)\,\mathrm{e}^{-j\omega\tau}\Big\}, \\
I_0 &= \operatorname{Im}\left(\frac{j}{s}\frac{\partial D(s,T,\tau)}{\partial s}\right)_{s=j\omega} \\
&= \frac{1}{\omega}\operatorname{Im}\Big\{\big[nTP(j\omega) + (1+j\omega T)P'(j\omega)\big] \\
&\qquad \cdot (1+j\omega T)^{n-1} + \big(Q'(j\omega) - \tau Q(j\omega)\big)\,\mathrm{e}^{-j\omega\tau}\Big\}, \\
R_1 &= \operatorname{Re}\left(\frac{1}{s}\frac{\partial D(s,T,\tau)}{\partial T}\right)_{s=j\omega} = \operatorname{Re}\left(n(1+j\omega T)^{n-1}P(j\omega)\right), \\
I_1 &= \operatorname{Im}\left(\frac{1}{s}\frac{\partial D(s,T,\tau)}{\partial T}\right)_{s=j\omega} = \operatorname{Im}\left(n(1+j\omega T)^{n-1}P(j\omega)\right), \\
R_2 &= \operatorname{Re}\left(\frac{1}{s}\frac{\partial D(s,T,\tau)}{\partial \tau}\right)_{s=j\omega} = -\operatorname{Re}\left(Q(j\omega)\mathrm{e}^{-j\omega\tau}\right), \\
I_2 &= \operatorname{Im}\left(\frac{1}{s}\frac{\partial D(s,T,\tau)}{\partial \tau}\right)_{s=j\omega} = -\operatorname{Im}\left(Q(j\omega)\mathrm{e}^{-j\omega\tau}\right).
\end{aligned} \tag{3.12}$$

Then, since $D(s,T,\tau)$ is an analytic function of s, T, and τ, the implicit function theorem indicates that the tangent of $\mathcal{T}_k^m$ can be expressed as

$$\begin{pmatrix} \dfrac{dT}{d\omega} \\[2mm] \dfrac{d\tau}{d\omega} \end{pmatrix} = \frac{1}{R_1 I_2 - R_2 I_1}\begin{pmatrix} R_0 I_2 - I_0 R_2 \\ I_0 R_1 - R_0 I_1 \end{pmatrix}, \tag{3.13}$$

provided that

$$R_1I_2 - R_2I_1 \neq 0. \tag{3.14}$$

It follows that $\mathcal{T}_k$ is smooth everywhere except possibly at the points where either (3.14) is not satisfied, or when

$$\frac{dT}{d\omega} = \frac{d\tau}{d\omega} = 0. \tag{3.15}$$

From the above discussions, we can conclude the following proposition.

PROPOSITION 3.2. *The curve T_k^m is smooth everywhere except possibly at the point corresponding to $s = j\omega$ as a multiple solution of (2.1).*

3.4. Direction of crossing. Next we will discuss the direction in which the solutions of (2.1) cross the imaginary axis as (T,τ) deviates from the curve $\mathcal{T}_k^m$. We will call the direction of the curve that corresponds to increasing ω the *positive direction*. We will also call the region on the left-hand side as we head in the positive direction of the curve *the region on the left*.

To establish the direction of crossing, we need to consider T and τ as functions of $s = \sigma + j\omega$, that is, functions of two real variables σ and ω, and partial derivative notation needs to be adopted. Since the tangent of $\mathcal{T}_k^m$ along the positive direction is $(\partial T/\partial\omega, \partial\tau/\partial\omega)$, the normal to $\mathcal{T}_k^m$ pointing to the left-hand side of positive direction is $(-\partial\tau/\partial\omega, \partial T/\partial\omega)$. Corresponding to a pair of complex conjugate solutions of (2.1) crossing the imaginary axis along the horizontal direction, (T,τ) moves along the direction $(\partial T/\partial\sigma, \partial\tau/\partial\sigma)$. So, if a pair of complex conjugate solutions of (2.1) crosses the imaginary axis to the right-half plane, then,

$$\left(\frac{\partial T}{\partial\omega}\frac{\partial\tau}{\partial\sigma} - \frac{\partial\tau}{\partial\omega}\frac{\partial T}{\partial\sigma}\right)_{s=j\omega} > 0, \tag{3.16}$$

that is, the region on the left of $\mathcal{T}_k^m$ gains two solutions on the right-half plane. If inequality (3.16) is reversed, then the region on the left of $\mathcal{T}_k^m$ loses has two right-half plane solutions. Similar to (3.13) we can express

$$\begin{pmatrix} \dfrac{dT}{d\sigma} \\ \dfrac{d\tau}{d\sigma} \end{pmatrix}_{s=j\omega} = \frac{1}{R_1I_2 - R_2I_1}\begin{pmatrix} R_0R_2 + I_0I_2 \\ -R_0R_1 - I_0I_1 \end{pmatrix}. \tag{3.17}$$

Using this we arrive at the following proposition.

PROPOSITION 3.3. *Let $\omega \in (\omega_k^l, \omega_k^r)$ and $(T,\tau) \in T_k$ such that $j\omega$ is a simple solution of (2.1) and $D(j\omega', T, \tau) \neq 0$, for all $\omega' > 0$, $\omega' \neq \omega$ (i.e., (T,τ) is not an intersection point of two curves or different sections of a single curve of T). Then a pair of solutions of (2.1) crosses* *the imaginary axis to the right through* $s = \pm j\omega$ *if* $R_2 I_1 - R_1 I_2 > 0$. *The crossing is to the left if the inequality is reversed.*

4. Concluding remarks

This paper addressed the stability problem of a class of distributed delay systems. More specifically, we have characterized the geometry of the stability crossing curves in the parameter space.

Acknowledgments

The first author is also with the Department of Mathematics, University "Politehnica" of Bucharest, Romania. The work of C.-I. Morărescu was (partially) supported through a European Community Marie Curie Fellowship and in the framework of the CTS. The work of S.-I. Niculescu was partially funded by the CNRS-US grant: "*Delays in interconnected dynamical systems: Analysis, and applications*" (2005-2007). The work of K. Gu was partially funded by the CNRS-US grant: "*Delays in interconnected dynamical systems: Analysis, and applications*" (2005-2007).

References

[1] S. P. Blythe, R. M. Nisbet, W. S. C. Gurney, and N. MacDonald, *Stability switches in distributed delay models*, Journal of Mathematical Analysis and Applications **109** (1985), no. 2, 388–396.

[2] F. G. Boese, *The stability chart for the linearized Cushing equation with a discrete delay and with gamma-distributed delays*, Journal of Mathematical Analysis and Applications **140** (1989), no. 2, 510–536.

[3] K. L. Cooke and Z. Grossman, *Discrete delay, distributed delay and stability switches*, Journal of Mathematical Analysis and Applications **86** (1982), no. 2, 592–627.

[4] J. M. Cushing, *Volterra integrodifferential equations in population dynamics*, Mathematics of Biology (M. Iannalli, ed.), Ligouri Editore, Naples, 1981, pp. 81–148.

[5] K. Gu, V. L. Kharitnov, and J. Chen, *Stability and Robust Stability of Time-Delay Systems*, Birkhauser, Massachusetts, 2003.

[6] K. Gu, S.-I. Niculescu, and J. Chen, *On stability crossing curves for general systems with two delays*, Journal of Mathematical Analysis and Applications **311** (2005), no. 1, 231–253.

[7] J. K. Hale and S. M. Verduyn Lunel, *Introduction to Functional-Differential Equations*, Applied Mathematical Sciences, vol. 99, Springer, New York, 1993.

[8] Y. Kuang, *Delay Differential Equations with Applications in Population Dynamics*, Mathematics in Science and Engineering, vol. 191, Academic Press, Massachusetts, 1993.

[9] N. MacDonald, *Biological Delay Systems: Linear Stability Theory*, Cambridge Studies in Mathematical Biology, vol. 9, Cambridge University Press, Cambridge, 1989.

[10] S.-I. Niculescu, *Delay Effects on Stability. A Robust Control Approach*, Lecture Notes in Control and Information Sciences, vol. 269, Springer, London, 2001.

[11] R. M. Nisbet and W. S. C. Gurney, *The Formulation of Age-Structure Models*, edited by T. Hallam, Lectures Notes on Mathematical Ecology, vol. 17, Springer, New York, 1983.

[12] O. Roesch, H. Roth, and S.-I. Niculescu, *Remote control of mechatronic systems over communication networks*, Proceedings of IEEE International Conference on Mechatronics and Automation, Ontario, July 2005.

[13] G. Stépán, *Retarded Dynamical Systems: Stability and Characteristic Functions*, Pitman Research Notes in Mathematics Series, vol. 210, John Wiley & Sons, New York, 1989.

[14] ———, *Delay-differential equation models for machine tool chatter*, Dynamics and Chaos in Manufacturing Process (F. C. Moon, ed.), John Wiley & Sons, New York, 1998, pp. 165–192.

Constantin-Irinel Morărescu: HeuDiaSyC (UMR CNRS 6599), Centre de Recherche de Royallieu, Université de Technologie de Compiègne, BP 20529-60205, Compiègne, France
E-mail address: cmorares@hds.utc.fr

Silviu-Iulian Niculescu: HeuDiaSyC (UMR CNRS 6599), Centre de Recherche de Royallieu, Université de Technologie de Compiègne, BP 20529-60205, Compiègne, France
E-mail address: niculescu@hds.utc.fr

Keqin Gu: Department of Mechanical and Industrial Engineering, Southern Illinois University at Edwardsville, IL 62026-1805, USA
E-mail address: kgu@siue.edu

BOUNDARY VALUE PROBLEMS ON THE HALF-LINE WITHOUT DICHOTOMIES

JASON R. MORRIS AND PATRICK J. RABIER

Given a piecewise continuous function $A : \overline{\mathbb{R}}_+ \to \mathscr{L}(\mathbb{C}^N)$ and a projection P_1 onto a subspace X_1 of $\mathbb{C}^N$, we investigate the injectivity, surjectivity and, more generally, the Fredholmness of the differential operator with boundary condition $(\dot{u} + Au, P_1 u(0))$ acting on the "natural" space $W_A^{1,2} = \{u : \dot{u} \in L^2,\ Au \in L^2\}$. It is not assumed that A is bounded or that $\dot{u} + Au = 0$ has any dichotomy, except to discuss the impact of the results on this special case. All the functional properties of interest, including the Fredholm index, can be related to a selfadjoint solution H of the Riccati differential inequality $HA + A^*H - \dot{H} \geq \nu(A^*A + H^2)$.

1. Introduction

The problem of interest is the existence and possible uniqueness of solutions in Sobolev-like spaces of the linear boundary value problem on $\overline{\mathbb{R}}_+ = [0, \infty)$,

$$\begin{aligned} \dot{u} + Au &= f, \\ P_1 u(0) &= \xi, \end{aligned} \tag{1.1}$$

where $A : \overline{\mathbb{R}}_+ \to \mathscr{L}(\mathbb{C}^N)$ is locally bounded and P_1 and P_2 are the projections associated with a given splitting $\mathbb{C}^N = X_1 \oplus X_2$.

When $P_1 = I$, that is, $X_1 = \mathbb{C}^N$ and $X_2 = \{0\}$, the familiar Cauchy problem is recovered, but, even in this case, the existence question in spaces constraining the possible behavior of the solutions at infinity (such as $W^{1,2}(\mathbb{R}_+, \mathbb{C}^N)$) does not follow from local existence and uniqueness and is far from being fully resolved. Furthermore, many concrete problems arise in the form (1.1) with $P_1 \neq I$. For instance, second-order equations $\ddot{v} + B\dot{v} + Cv = g$ with Dirichlet condition $v(0) = \xi$ or Neumann condition $\dot{v}(0) = \xi$ correspond to first-order systems (1.1) with $N = 2M$, $\mathbb{C}^N = \mathbb{C}^M \times \mathbb{C}^M$, $u = (v, \dot{v})$, and P_1 the projection onto the first factor (Dirichlet) or the second one (Neumann). We will denote

Hindawi Publishing Corporation
Proceedings of the Conference on Differential & Difference Equations and Applications, pp. 825–833

by D_A the differential operator

$$D_A u := \dot{u} + Au \tag{1.2}$$

and by Λ_{A,P_1} the differential operator with boundary condition

$$\Lambda_{A,P_1} u := (D_A u, P_1 u(0)) = (\dot{u} + Au, P_1 u(0)), \tag{1.3}$$

whenever these expressions make sense. With this notation, the system (1.1) may be rewritten as

$$\Lambda_{A,P_1} u = (f, \xi), \tag{1.4}$$

so that the solvability of (1.1) is translated by functional properties of the operator Λ_{A,P_1} (surjectivity, injectivity, or Fredholmness).

When A is bounded, the relationship between exponential dichotomies and the Fredholmness of D_A was clarified by Palmer [10, 11]. In turn, a well-known differential inequality characterizes exponential dichotomies when A is bounded (Coppel [2]): D_A has an exponential dichotomy if and only if there is a bounded and locally Lipschitz continuous Hermitian family $H(t)$ such that

$$HA + A^*H - \dot{H} \geq \nu I, \tag{1.5}$$

where $\nu > 0$ is a constant.

Therefore, when A is bounded, there is a relationship between the differential inequality (1.5) and the Fredholm properties of D_A, the connection being made via exponential dichotomies. The purpose of this paper is to show that in a suitable functional setting, the "Riccati" variant of (1.5),

$$HA + A^*H - \dot{H} \geq \nu(A^*A + H^2), \tag{1.6}$$

still with H Hermitian (and weaker than (1.5) when A and H are bounded) controls the Fredholmness and even the injectivity or surjectivity of Λ_{A,P_1} for a much larger class of operators D_A than those having dichotomies.

The following sections discuss the functional setting, the Fredholmness and injectivity of Λ_{A,P_1}, an alternate characterization of the index, and the surjectivity of Λ_{A,P_1}, respectively. No proofs are given due to space limitation, but full details can be found in [9].

2. The function spaces

For brevity, we set $W^{1,2} := W^{1,2}(\mathbb{R}_+, \mathbb{C}^N)$ and $L^2 := L^2(\mathbb{R}_+, \mathbb{C}^N)$, with norms $\|\cdot\|_{1,2}$ and $\|\cdot\|_{0,2}$, respectively. Given $A : \overline{\mathbb{R}}_+ \to \mathcal{L}(\mathbb{C}^N)$ measurable, we define the space

$$W_A^{1,2} := \{u \in \mathcal{D}' : \dot{u} \in L^2,\ Au \in L^2\}, \tag{2.1}$$

where $\mathscr{D}'$ is the space of distributions on $\mathbb{R}_+$ with values in $\mathbb{C}^N$ and $\dot{u}$ denotes the derivative of u in the sense of distributions. Clearly, the operator D_A in (1.2) maps $W_A^{1,2}$ into L^2. This section discusses the properties of the space $W_A^{1,2}$.

For $u \in W_A^{1,2}$, we set

$$\|u\|_{1,2,A} := \left(\|\dot{u}\|_{0,2}^2 + \|Au\|_{0,2}^2\right)^{1/2}. \tag{2.2}$$

As is customary, we will say that $A : \overline{\mathbb{R}}_+ \to \mathscr{L}(\mathbb{C}^N)$ is piecewise continuous if there is a partition of $\overline{\mathbb{R}}_+$ into countably many consecutive nontrivial intervals I_n (open, semiopen, or closed) such that $A_{|I_n}$ is the restriction of a continuous function on $\bar{I}_n$. In particular, a piecewise continuous A is locally bounded on $\overline{\mathbb{R}}_+$. The subsequent results are obtained under the extra assumption that $\bigcap_{t\geq 0} \ker A(t) = \{0\}$, a mild restriction in practice.

Theorem 2.1. *Assume that A is piecewise continuous and that $\bigcap_{t\geq 0} \ker A(t) = \{0\}$. Then, $\|\cdot\|_{1,2,A}$ is a norm on $W_A^{1,2}$ for which $W_A^{1,2}$ is a Hilbert space and $W_A^{1,2} \hookrightarrow C^0(\overline{\mathbb{R}}_+)$ (continuous embedding), where $C^0(\overline{\mathbb{R}}_+)$ is equipped with the topology of uniform convergence on the compact subsets of $\overline{\mathbb{R}}_+$. Furthermore, there is a constant $C > 0$ such that $|u(0)| \leq C\|u\|_{1,2,A}$ for every $u \in W_A^{1,2}$ and C depends only upon the restriction of A to some large enough interval $[0,T]$.*

The denseness of smooth functions is behind a variety of crucial results in many function spaces. Such a denseness property is true with $W_A^{1,2}$.

Theorem 2.2. *Assume that A is piecewise continuous and that $\bigcap_{t\geq 0} \ker A(t) = \{0\}$. Then,*

(i) *$C_0^\infty(\overline{\mathbb{R}}_+)$ is dense in $W_A^{1,2}$,*

(ii) *the closure of $C_0^\infty(\mathbb{R}_+)$ in $W_A^{1,2}$ is the space $\overset{\circ}{W}{}_A^{1,2} := \{u \in W_A^{1,2} : u(0) = 0\}$.*

In addition to being a natural question, it is also useful to know what features of A ensure that $W_A^{1,2} \subset L^2$. Since nonzero constant functions are not in L^2, the condition $\bigcap_{t\geq 0} \ker A(t) = \{0\}$ is necessary. A sufficient condition is given in Theorem 2.3. We denote by r_A the function

$$r_A(t) := \begin{cases} 0 & \text{if } A(t) \text{ is not invertible,} \\ \dfrac{1}{|A^{-1}(t)|} & \text{if } A(t) \text{ is invertible.} \end{cases} \tag{2.3}$$

The following result is derived from a general embedding theorem between weighted Sobolev spaces (Maz'ja [8]).

Theorem 2.3. *Assume that A is piecewise continuous and that $\bigcap_{t\geq 0} \ker A(t) = \{0\}$. Assume also that there are constants $\ell > 0$ and $\delta > 0$ such that $\|r_A\|_{0,2,J} \geq \delta$ whenever $J \subset \mathbb{R}_+$ is an interval with $|J| \geq \ell$. Then, $W_A^{1,2} \subset L^2$ and the embedding is continuous (and then $W_A^{1,2} \subset W^{1,2}$, with continuous embedding).*

It is readily checked that Theorem 2.3 is applicable if there is some constant $\gamma > 0$ such that $|A^{-1}(t)| \leq \gamma$ for a.e. $t > 0$ large enough, or if A is periodic and $A(t_0)$ is invertible for some $t_0 > 0$.

3. Fredholmness and injectivity

To put things in perspective, recall that the problem

$$D_A u := \dot{u} + Au = 0 \tag{3.1}$$

is said to have an exponential dichotomy (on $\mathbb{R}_+$) if there are a projection Π and positive constants K, L, α, and β such that

$$|\Phi(t)\Pi\Phi^{-1}(s)| \leq Ke^{-\alpha(t-s)}, \quad \forall t \geq s \geq 0, \tag{3.2}$$

$$|\Phi(t)(I-\Pi)\Phi^{-1}(s)| \leq Ke^{-\beta(s-t)}, \quad \forall s \geq t \geq 0, \tag{3.3}$$

where $\Phi(t)$ denotes the fundamental matrix of the system (3.1) satisfying $\Phi(0) = I$.

It is well known that the range of Π (though not Π itself) is uniquely determined, that is, if D_A also has an exponential dichotomy with projection Π', then $\operatorname{rge}\Pi' = \operatorname{rge}\Pi$. For this and other standard properties of exponential dichotomies, see Coppel [2] or Massera and Schäffer [7].

As in the introduction, $A : \overline{\mathbb{R}}_+ \to \mathcal{L}(\mathbb{C}^N)$ is a given mapping and $\mathbb{C}^N = X_1 \oplus X_2$ is a splitting with corresponding projections P_1 and P_2. Recall also the definition of Λ_{A,P_1} in (1.3).

Part (i) of Lemma 3.1, with A continuous and $W^{1,2}$ and L^2 replaced by BC^1 and BC (bounded C^1 functions with bounded derivative and bounded continuous functions, respectively) was first proved by Palmer [10]. Part (ii) and its converse are essentially given in [1, Theorem 1.1].

Lemma 3.1. *Assume that $A \in L^\infty$ and that D_A has an exponential dichotomy with projection Π. Then, for every $p \in [1,\infty]$, the following properties hold.*

(i) *The operator $D_A : W^{1,2} \to L^2$ is surjective and* $\dim\ker D_A = \operatorname{rank}\Pi$.

(ii) *The operator $\Lambda_{A,P_1} : W^{1,2} \to L^2 \times X_1$ is Fredholm of index* $\operatorname{rank}\Pi - \dim X_1$. *Furthermore, Λ_{A,P_1} is one-to-one if and only if $X_2 \cap \operatorname{rge}\Pi = \{0\}$. In particular, Λ_{A,P_1} is an isomorphism of $W^{1,2}$ onto $L^2 \times X_1$ if and only if* $\dim X_1 = \operatorname{rank}\Pi$ *and* $X_2 \cap \operatorname{rge}\Pi = \{0\}$.

(iii) $W^{1,2} = W_A^{1,2}$.

Conversely, if $A \in L^\infty$ and there is $p \in [1,\infty]$ such that $\Lambda_{A,P_1} : W^{1,p} \to L^p \times X_1$ is semi-Fredholm, then D_A has an exponential dichotomy.

The main shortcoming of part (ii) of Lemma 3.1 is that even when D_A is known to have an exponential dichotomy, the range of the projection Π is not explicitly available, except in rather trivial cases. As a result, it is often impossible to check whether $X_2 \cap \operatorname{rge}\Pi = \{0\}$, and therefore whether Λ_{A,P_1} is one-to-one. Part (ii) of Theorem 3.4 gives a more readily verifiable criterion for injectivity, also valid in a much broader setting.

Remark 3.2. Of course, $X_2 \cap \operatorname{rge}\Pi = \{0\}$ if $X_2 = \{0\}$, that is, $X_1 = \mathbb{C}^N$. If so, $P_1 = I$ and $\Lambda_{A,I}$ accounts for the initial value problem

$$\begin{aligned} \dot{u} + Au &= f, \\ u(0) &= \xi. \end{aligned} \tag{3.4}$$

From Lemma 3.1, when $A \in L^\infty$ and D_A has an exponential dichotomy, the unique solution of this problem is in $W^{1,2}$ whenever $(f,\xi) \in L^2 \times \mathbb{C}^N$ satisfies $N - \operatorname{rank}\Pi$ linear compatibility conditions (no condition if $\Pi = I$).

We denote by $\mathcal{L}_{\mathcal{H}}(\mathbb{C}^N)$ the space of linear *Hermitian* operators on $\mathbb{C}^N$. The main ingredient is an a priori estimate (Lemma 3.3), obtained by a variational argument, integration by parts, and careful majorizations.

LEMMA 3.3. *Assume that A is piecewise continuous, that $\bigcap_{t\geq 0} \ker A(t) = \{0\}$, and that there are a constant $\nu > 0$ and a locally Lipschitz continuous function $H : \overline{\mathbb{R}}_+ \to \mathcal{L}_{\mathcal{H}}(\mathbb{C}^N)$ such that*

(i) $HA + A^*H - \dot{H} \geq \nu(A^*A + H^2)$ *a.e. on* $\mathbb{R}_+$,

(ii) $H(0)_{|X_2} \leq 0$.

Then, for every $u \in W_A^{1,2}$, the estimate

$$\|u\|_{1,2,A} \leq \sqrt{\left(\frac{15}{\nu^2} + 2\right)} \|D_A u\|_{0,2} + \left(\sqrt{+\frac{6|H(0)|}{\nu}} + \frac{12 e_A |H(0)|\,|P_2|}{\nu}\right) |P_1 u(0)| \tag{3.5}$$

holds, where $e_A > 0$ is the smallest constant such that $|v(0)| \leq e_A \|v\|_{1,2,A}$ for every $v \in W_A^{1,2}$ (norm of the evaluation map).

With Lemma 3.3 at hand, it is easy to obtain the following criterion for Fredholmness and injectivity.

THEOREM 3.4. *Assume that A is piecewise continuous, that $\bigcap_{t\geq 0} \ker A(t) = \{0\}$, and that there are a constant $\nu > 0$ and a locally Lipschitz continuous function $H : \overline{\mathbb{R}}_+ \to \mathcal{L}_{\mathcal{H}}(\mathbb{C}^N)$ such that*

(i) $HA + A^*H - \dot{H} \geq \nu(A^*A + H^2)$ *a.e. on $\mathbb{R}_+$; then, $D_A : W_A^{1,2} \to L^2$ is onto with* $\dim\ker D_A < \infty$ *and $\Lambda_{A,P_1} : W_A^{1,2} \to L^2 \times X_1$ is Fredholm with index* $\dim\ker D_A - \dim X_1$.

In addition, if

(ii) $H(0)_{|X_2} \leq 0$,

then $\Lambda_{A,P_1} : W_A^{1,2} \to L^2 \times X_1$ is one-to-one (hence an isomorphism when $\dim\ker D_A = \dim X_1$).

In contrast to the condition $X_2 \bigcap \operatorname{rge}\Pi = \{0\}$ of Lemma 3.1, condition (ii) of Theorem 3.4 is readily verifiable once a suitable H is known, a point to which we will return to later. On the other hand, the formula for the index of Λ_{A,P_1} given in part (i) of Theorem 3.4 requires knowing $\dim\ker D_A$ when D_A has domain $W_A^{1,2}$. In dimension $N > 1$, an explicit identification of $\ker D_A$ is often out of reach. In Theorem 4.3, we will obtain a more convenient characterization of $\dim\ker D_A$.

Condition (ii) of Theorem 3.4 is of course vacuous when $X_2 = \{0\}$ (standard initial value problem). Thus, Theorem 3.4 yields a generalization of Remark 3.2 for this example under condition (i) alone, without assuming that A is bounded or that D_A has an exponential dichotomy.

In Theorem 3.4, the case when $H = A + A^*$ yields an especially simple result.

COROLLARY 3.5. *Assume that A is locally Lipschitz continuous on $\overline{\mathbb{R}}_+$, that $\bigcap_{t\geq 0}\ker A(t) = \{0\}$, and that*

(i) $A^2 + A^*A - \dot{A} \geq \nu(A^*A + AA^*)$ *a.e. on* $\mathbb{R}_+$ *for some* $\nu > 0$.

Then, the operator $D_A : W_A^{1,2} \to L^2$ *is onto,* $\dim\ker D_A < \infty$, *and the operator* $\Lambda_{A,P_1}\colon W_A^{1,2} \to L^2 \times X_1$ *is Fredholm of index* $\dim\ker D_A - \dim X_1$. *If also*

(ii) $A(0)_{|X_2} \leq 0$, *then* $\Lambda_{A,P_1}\colon W_A^{1,2} \to L^2 \times X_1$ *is one-to-one (hence an isomorphism when* $\dim\ker D_A = \dim X_1$*).*

When $A = A^*$, condition (i) of Corollary 3.5 is simply that $\dot{A} \leq \beta A^2$ for some $\beta < 2$. Many variants of Corollary 3.5 can be obtained by making other choices for H (e.g., $AA^*, A^*A, -(A + A^*)$, or suitable functions of those). These variants implicitly put severe restrictions on A and will not be discussed further here.

This brings the question whether a more systematic procedure exists to find the desired Hermitian family H, especially since a suitable H may have no obvious relationship to A, even when $N = 1$ (see Example 3.8). To date, the answer to that question is essentially negative. In principle, it suffices of course that $\dot{H} - HA - A^*H + \nu H^2 = -\nu A^*A$ is solvable for Hermitian H and small enough $\nu > 0$ (and with $H(0)_{|X_2}$ specified or not). The applicable existence theorems are rather scarce, because the right-hand side has the "wrong" sign for classical results (Reid [12]).

When A is real, it follows from the existence theorem of Knobloch and Pohl [5, Theorem 3.1] that condition (i) of Corollary 3.5 may be replaced by $(1/2)A^2 + (3/4)A^*A - (1/4)AA^* - \dot{A} \geq \nu A^*A$ a.e. on $\mathbb{R}_+$ for some $\nu > 0$. This is only marginally different from, and not even more general than, condition (i) of Corollary 3.5 (derived from a mere educated guess). Other existence theorems for Riccati equations are given in the recent survey by Freiling [4], but they seem to be of limited use for the equation of interest here.

The following examples illustrate various aspects discussed in this section.

Example 3.6. With $N = 1$ and $A(t) = -t$, all the hypotheses of Corollary 3.5 hold with $X_1 = \{0\}$ (hence $P_1 = 0$) and $X_2 = \mathbb{C}$ as well as with $X_1 = \mathbb{C}$ (hence $P_1 = I$) and $X_2 = \{0\}$. Here, $D_A u = 0$ if and only if u is a scalar multiple of $e^{t^2/2}$, whence $\ker D_A = \{0\}$ when D_A has domain $W_A^{1,2}$. The operator $\Lambda_{A,0} = D_A$ is an isomorphism in the first case and $\Lambda_{A,I}$ has index -1 in the second. Here, D_A has an exponential dichotomy, but A is not bounded.

Example 3.7. With $N = 1$ and $A(t) = t$, all the hypotheses of Corollary 3.5, except condition (i), hold with $X_1 = \{0\}$ and $X_2 = \mathbb{C}$, so that $\Lambda_{A,0} = D_A$. Clearly, $\ker\Lambda_{A,0}$ is generated by $e^{-t^2/2} \in W_A^{1,2}$. Thus, the injectivity breaks down for this example, even though the missing condition (i) does hold for large enough t.

Example 3.8. With $N = 1$, $A(t) = \sin t/4(t+1)$ fails to satisfy condition (i) of Corollary 3.5. However, all the hypotheses of Theorem 3.4 hold with $X_1 = \mathbb{C}$, $X_2 = \{0\}$, and $H(t) = 1/t+1$. Since $e^{-\int \sin t dt/4(t+1)} \in W_A^{1,2}$, $\ker D_A \subset W_A^{1,2}$ is one-dimensional, so that $\Lambda_{A,I}$ is an isomorphism. Although A is bounded, D_A does not have an exponential dichotomy (indeed, $1 \in W_A^{1,2}$; see Lemma 3.1).

Example 3.9. With $N = 1$ and $A(t) = \sin t$, condition (i) of Corollary 3.5 does not hold. Note that $W_A^{1,2} = W^{1,2}$ since A is periodic (see the comments following Theorem 2.3).

Thus, if $D_A : W^{1,2}_A \to L^2$ were semi-Fredholm, D_A would have an exponential dichotomy by Lemma 3.1. This is not the case since $D_A u = 0$ if and only if u is a multiple of $e^{\cos t}$. As a result, no locally Lipschitz continuous function $H : \overline{\mathbb{R}}_+ \to \mathbb{R}$ exists such that condition (i) of Theorem 3.4 holds.

It is easy to find examples in higher dimension.

Example 3.10. With $N = 2$ and $A(t) = \begin{pmatrix} t & 1 \\ 1/t+1 & -t \end{pmatrix}$, all the hypotheses of Corollary 3.5 hold with $X_1 = \mathbb{C} \times \{0\}$ and $X_2 = \{0\} \times \mathbb{C}$ (a Maple plot shows that $\nu = 1/4$ works in (i); a much smaller value can also be proved to work). Thus, Λ_{A,P_1} is one-to-one. However, the calculation of $\ker D_A \subset W^{1,2}_A$, and hence of the index of Λ_{A,P_1}, is not as trivial as in the previous examples. This issue will be resolved in Example 4.4.

4. Characterization of the index

We now address the issue of finding a more convenient characterization of $\dim\ker D_A$ when D_A is viewed as an operator from $W^{1,2}_A$ to L^2. By Theorem 3.4, this also gives a characterization of the index of $\Lambda_{A,P_1} : W^{1,2}_A \to L^2 \times X_1$.

In what follows, we denote by $E_+(L)$, $E_-(L)$ the sum of the generalized eigenspaces of the operator $L \in \mathcal{L}(\mathbb{C}^N)$ corresponding to the eigenvalues of L with positive (negative) real part. The main step towards the desired characterization is contained in the following lemma.

LEMMA 4.1. *Assume that A is piecewise continuous, that $\bigcap_{t\geq 0} \ker A(t) = \{0\}$, and that there are a constant $\nu > 0$ and a locally Lipschitz continuous function $H : \overline{\mathbb{R}}_+ \to \mathcal{L}_{\mathcal{H}}(\mathbb{C}^N)$ such that*

(i) *$HA + A^*H - \dot{H} \geq \nu(A^*A + H^2)$ a.e. on $\mathbb{R}_+$.*

Assume also that

(ii) *$H(t)$ is invertible for all $t \geq 0$.*

Then, the null space of $D_A : W^{1,2}_A \to L^2$ has dimension $\dim E_+(H(0))$.

In fact, condition (ii) of Lemma 4.1 is essentially redundant. The general idea in the proof of the following lemma is taken from Coppel [3].

LEMMA 4.2. *Assume that A is piecewise continuous, that $\bigcap_{t\geq T} \ker A(t) = \{0\}$ for all $T \geq 0$, and that there are a constant $\nu > 0$ and a locally Lipschitz continuous function $H : \overline{\mathbb{R}}_+ \to \mathcal{L}_{\mathcal{H}}(\mathbb{C}^N)$ such that*

$$HA + A^*H - \dot{H} \geq \nu(A^*A + H^2) \text{ a.e. on } \mathbb{R}_+. \tag{4.1}$$

Then, $H(t)$ is invertible for all $t > 0$ large enough. In particular, $\dim E_\pm(H(t))$ is independent of t large enough.

By combining Lemmas 4.1 and 4.2, we get the following theorem.

THEOREM 4.3. *Assume that A is piecewise continuous, that $\bigcap_{t\geq T} \ker A(t) = \{0\}$ for all $T \geq 0$, and that there are a constant $\nu > 0$ and a locally Lipschitz continuous function $H : \overline{\mathbb{R}}_+ \to \mathcal{L}_{\mathcal{H}}(\mathbb{C}^N)$ such that*

$$HA + A^*H - \dot{H} \geq \nu(A^*A + H^2) \quad \text{a.e. on } \mathbb{R}_+. \tag{4.2}$$

Then,

(a) *if t is large enough, $d_+(H) = \dim E_+(H(t))$ is independent of t,*
(b) *the operator $D_A : W_A^{1,2} \to L^2$ is onto and* $\dim\ker D_A = d_+(H)$,
(c) *the operator $\Lambda_{A,P_1} : W_A^{1,2} \to L^2 \times X_1$ is Fredholm of index $d_+(H) - \dim X_1$.*

In practice, it is not difficult to calculate $d_+(H)$ since this can be done without finding the eigenvalues of $H(t)$ (see Jacobi's criterion [6, page 296]).

Example 4.4. Returning to Example 3.10 where $A(t) = \begin{pmatrix} t & 1 \\ 1/t+1 & -t \end{pmatrix}$ and condition (i) of Theorem 4.3 holds with $H(t) = A(t) + A^*(t) = \begin{pmatrix} 2t & (2+t)/1+t \\ (2+t)/1+t & -2t \end{pmatrix}$, we have $d_+(H) = 1$, so that $\dim\ker D_A = 1$ by Theorem 4.3, and hence that Λ_{A,P_1} in Example 3.10 is an isomorphism.

Example 4.5. Let $N = 3$ and $A(t) = \begin{pmatrix} 1 & t & 1 \\ t & -1 & t \\ 1 & t & 2 \end{pmatrix}$. Condition (i) of Theorem 4.3 holds with $H = A$ and the principal minors of $H(t)$ are $1, -1-t^2$, and $-1-t^2$. Thus, $d_+(H) = 2$ by Jacobi's criterion, and so $\dim\ker D_A = 2$.

5. Surjectivity

Lastly, we discuss the surjectivity of the operator $\Lambda_{A,P_1} : W_A^{1,2} \to L^2 \times X_1$ beyond the invertibility result obtained in Theorem 3.4. When Λ_{A,P_1} is (semi-) Fredholm, this amounts to the injectivity of $\Lambda_{A,P_1}^*: L^2 \times X_1 \to (W_A^{1,2})^*$. Under suitable assumptions, this is equivalent to the injectivity of $\Lambda_{-A^*,P_2^*} : W_{A^*}^{1,2} \to L^2 \times X_1^\perp$, for which the criterion given in Theorem 3.4 is available. With $r_A(t)$ given by (2.3), we set

$$\rho_A(t) := \int_0^t r_A(\tau)\,d\tau. \tag{5.1}$$

THEOREM 5.1. *Assume that A is piecewise continuous, that $\bigcap_{t\ge 0}\ker A(t) = \bigcap_{t\ge 0}\ker A^*(t) = \{0\}$, that $e^{-s\rho_A}A \in L^\infty$ for every $s > 0$, and that there are a constant $\nu > 0$ and locally Lipschitz continuous functions $H, K : \overline{\mathbb{R}}_+ \to \mathcal{L}_{\mathcal{H}}(\mathbb{C}^N)$ such that*

(i) $HA + A^*H - \dot{H} \ge \nu(A^*A + H^2)$ *a.e. on* $\mathbb{R}_+$,
(ii) $KA^* + AK + \dot{K} \ge \nu(AA^* + K^2)$ *a.e. on* $\mathbb{R}_+$,
(iii) $K(0)_{|X_2^\perp} \ge 0$.

Then, the operator $\Lambda_{A,P_1} : W_A^{1,2} \to L^2 \times X_1$ is surjective. If also

(iv) $H(0)_{|X_2} \le 0$, *then $\Lambda_{A,P_1} : W_A^{1,2} \to L^2 \times X_1$ is an isomorphism.*

Remark 5.2. It is well known that $|A^{-1}(t)| \le (2^N - 1)(|A(t)|^{N-1}/|\det A(t)|)$ whenever $A(t)$ is invertible, which shows that $r_A(t) \ge (1/(2^N - 1))(|\det A(t)|/|A(t)|^{N-1})$ when $A(t)$ is invertible. This is often useful to check the condition $e^{-s\rho_A}A \in L^\infty$ without calculating A^{-1}.

When $H = K = A + A^*$ in Theorem 5.1, we obtain the following corollary.

COROLLARY 5.3. *Assume that A is locally Lipschitz continuous, that $\bigcap_{t\ge 0}\ker A(t) = \bigcap_{t\ge 0}\ker A^*(t) = \{0\}$, that $e^{-s\rho_A}A \in L^\infty$ for every $s > 0$, and that there is a constant $\nu > 0$ such that*

(i) $A^2 + A^*A - \dot{A} \ge \nu(A^*A + AA^*)$ *a.e. on* $\mathbb{R}_+$,

(ii) $A^2 + AA^* + \dot{A} \geq \nu(A^*A + AA^*)$ *a.e. on* $\mathbb{R}_+$,

(iii) $A(0)_{|X_2^\perp} \geq 0$.

Then, the operator $\Lambda_{A,P_1} : W_A^{1,2} \to L^2 \times X_1$ *is surjective. If also*

(iv) $A(0)_{|X_2} \leq 0$, *then* $\Lambda_{A,P_1} : W_A^{1,2} \to L^2 \times X_1$ *is an isomorphism.*

Example 5.4. Let A be as in Example 4.5. If $X_2 = \{0\} \times \mathbb{C}^2$ and X_1 is any (one-dimensional) direct complement of X_2 in $\mathbb{C}^3$, conditions (i) to (iv) (and also (vi)) of Corollary 5.3 hold. Since $\det A(t) = -t^2 - 1$ and $|A(t)| \leq C(t+1)$ for some constant $C > 0$, it follows from Remark 5.2 that $r_A(t) \leq c$, where $c > 0$ is a constant. As a result, $e^{-s\rho_A(t)} \leq e^{-cst}$, so that $e^{-s\rho_A} A \in L^\infty$. This shows that $\Lambda_{A,P_1} : W_A^{1,2} \to L^2 \times X_1$ is surjective. Note that condition (v) fails since $A(0)$ is Hermitian with two positive eigenvalues. Actually, from Example 4.5 and Theorem 4.3, $\Lambda_{A,P_1} : W_A^{1,2} \to L^2 \times X_1$ has index 1, thus cannot be one-to-one.

References

[1] A. Ben-Artzi, I. Gohberg, and M. A. Kaashoek, *Invertibility and dichotomy of differential operators on a half-line*, Journal of Dynamics and Differential Equations **5** (1993), no. 1, 1–36.

[2] W. A. Coppel, *Dichotomies in Stability Theory*, Lecture Notes in Mathematics, vol. 629, Springer, Berlin, 1978.

[3] ———, *Dichotomies and Lyapunov functions*, Journal of Differential Equations **52** (1984), no. 1, 58–65.

[4] G. Freiling, *A survey of nonsymmetric Riccati equations*, Linear Algebra and Its Applications **351/352** (2002), 243–270.

[5] H. W. Knobloch and M. Pohl, *On Riccati matrix differential equations*, Results in Mathematics **31** (1997), no. 3-4, 337–364.

[6] P. Lancaster and M. Tismenetsky, *The Theory of Matrices*, 2nd ed., Computer Science and Applied Mathematics, Academic Press, Florida, 1985.

[7] J. L. Massera and J. J. Schäffer, *Linear Differential Equations and Function Spaces*, Pure and Applied Mathematics, vol. 21, Academic Press, New York, 1966.

[8] V. G. Maz'ja, *Sobolev Spaces*, Springer Series in Soviet Mathematics, Springer, Berlin, 1985.

[9] J. R. Morris and P. J. Rabier, *Riccati inequality and functional properties of differential operators on the half line*, Journal of Differential Equations **225** (2006), no. 2, 573–604.

[10] K. J. Palmer, *Exponential dichotomies and transversal homoclinic points*, Journal of Differential Equations **55** (1984), no. 2, 225–256.

[11] ———, *Exponential dichotomies and Fredholm operators*, Proceedings of the American Mathematical Society **104** (1988), no. 1, 149–156.

[12] W. T. Reid, *Riccati Differential Equations*, Academic Press, New York, 1972.

Jason R. Morris: Department of Mathematics, School of Natural Sciences and Mathematics, The University of Alabama at Birmingham, Birmingham, AL 35294-1170, USA
E-mail address: morris@math.uab.edu

Patrick J. Rabier: Department of Mathematics, University of Pittsburgh, Pittsburgh, PA 15260, USA
E-mail address: rabier@imap.pitt.edu

POSITIVE SOLUTIONS OF SECOND-ORDER DIFFERENTIAL EQUATIONS WITH PRESCRIBED BEHAVIOR OF THE FIRST DERIVATIVE

OCTAVIAN G. MUSTAFA AND YURI V. ROGOVCHENKO

Using Banach contraction principle, we establish global existence of solutions to the nonlinear differential equation $u'' + f(t,u,u') = 0$ that have asymptotic developments $u(t) = c + o(1)$ and $u(t) = ct + o(t^d)$ as $t \to +\infty$ for some $c > 0$ and $d \in (0,1)$. Our theorems complement and improve recent results reported in the literature. As a byproduct, we derive a multiplicity result for a large class of quasilinear elliptic equations in exterior domains in $\mathbb{R}^n$, $n \geq 3$.

1. Introduction

The quasilinear elliptic equation

$$\Delta u + f(x,u) + g(|x|)x \cdot \nabla u = 0, \quad |x| > A > 0, \tag{1.1}$$

describes several important phenomena arising in mathematical physics. Equation (1.1) has been investigated recently in [1, 2, 4, 15, 16], where existence of eventually positive and decaying-to-zero solutions was discussed by using approaches based on Banach contraction principle and exponentially weighted metrics, sub- and supersolutions, and variational techniques.

Let $G_A = \{x \in \mathbb{R}^n : |x| > A\}$, $n \geq 3$. Similarly to [14], we assume that the function $f : \overline{G_A} \times \mathbb{R} \to \mathbb{R}$ is locally Hölder continuous and $g : [A,+\infty) \to \mathbb{R}$ is continuously differentiable. Following [2, 4], we also suppose that f satisfies

$$0 \leq f(x,t) \leq a(|x|)w(t), \quad t \in [0,+\infty),\ x \in \overline{G_A}, \tag{1.2}$$

where $a : [A,+\infty) \to [0,+\infty)$, $w : [0,+\infty) \to [0,+\infty)$ are continuous functions,

$$w(t) \leq Mt, \quad t \in [0,\varepsilon], \tag{1.3}$$

for certain $M, \varepsilon > 0$, and g takes on only nonnegative values.

Hindawi Publishing Corporation
Proceedings of the Conference on Differential & Difference Equations and Applications, pp. 835–842

Existence of positive and decaying-to-zero solutions to (1.1) in G_B, for some $B \geq A$, has been established in [1, 2, 4, 16] under the assumption

$$\int_A^{+\infty} sa(s)ds < +\infty, \tag{1.4}$$

and in [15] under a stronger condition

$$\int_A^{+\infty} s^{n-1}a(s)ds < +\infty. \tag{1.5}$$

The arguments in [1, 2, 4, 16] make use of the *comparison equation*

$$h''(t) + k_1(t)h(t) + k_2(t)\left(h'(t) - \frac{h(t)}{t}\right) = 0, \quad t \geq A, \tag{1.6}$$

where the functions $k_i : [A, +\infty) \to [0, +\mathbb{R})$ are continuous and such that

$$\int_A^{+\infty} [s|k_1(s)| + |k_2(s)|]ds < +\infty. \tag{1.7}$$

The authors of the cited papers exploit the fact that (1.6) has bounded, eventually positive increasing solutions. Recently, Ehrnström [4] noticed that when assuming that g takes on only nonnegative values rather than requiring that g satisfies the standard hypothesis (1.4), one can take in (1.6) $k_2 \equiv 0$. This conclusion is based on the existence of a solution $h(t)$ of (1.6) satisfying

$$0 < h'(t) < \frac{h(t)}{t} < \varepsilon \tag{1.8}$$

for all $t \geq T_0$, where $T_0 \geq A$ is chosen appropriately, and

$$h(t) = O(1), \quad h'(t) = O(t^{-1}) \quad \text{as } t \longrightarrow +\infty. \tag{1.9}$$

Condition (1.8) suggests that the function

$$\Psi(t) \stackrel{\text{def}}{=} \frac{1}{t}W[t,h](t) = \frac{1}{t}\begin{vmatrix} t & h(t) \\ 1 & h'(t) \end{vmatrix} = h'(t) - \frac{h(t)}{t} \tag{1.10}$$

plays an important role in the in-depth analysis of asymptotically linear solutions to (1.6), that is, solutions satisfying, for some $a, b \in \mathbb{R}$,

$$h(t) = at + b + o(1) \quad \text{as } t \longrightarrow +\infty \tag{1.11}$$

(cf. [8, 9]). Properties of the function $\Psi(t)$ were studied by the authors in [12, 13]. Note that if $b < 0$, for a solution $h(t)$ satisfying (1.11), one has $\Psi(t) > 0$, for $t \geq T_0$, and (1.11) does not yield (1.8).

The paper is organized as follows. First, we present two theorems inspired by the work by Hale and Onuchic [5], thus enhancing recent results on asymptotic behavior of solutions of the celebrated Emden-Fowler equation that has many important applications in physics [3, 10, 16]. As a byproduct, we improve the standard asymptotic representation (1.9) (cf. [5–7]), and explore the properties of the function $\Psi(t)$ for solutions of (1.6) with the asymptotic development

$$h(t) = at + o(t^{\lambda}) \quad \text{as } t \longrightarrow +\infty, \tag{1.12}$$

where $\lambda \in (0,1)$ (cf. [9]). Finally, we establish existence of two positive solutions $u_1(x)$ and $u_2(x)$ to (1.1) satisfying, respectively,

$$\lim_{|x|\to+\infty} u_1(x) = 0, \qquad \liminf_{|x|\to+\infty} u_2(x) > 0. \tag{1.13}$$

2. Positive solutions to a nonlinear ODE

Consider the second-order nonlinear differential equation

$$u'' + f(t,u,u') = 0, \quad t \in I = [t_0, +\infty),\ t_0 \geq 1, \tag{2.1}$$

where the function f, though assumed continuous and locally Lipschitz continuous on subsets of $\mathbb{R}^3$, might have singularities. We will call a pair (α,β) of nonnegative, bounded, continuous on I functions satisfying $\alpha(t) \leq \beta(t)$ for $t \in I$ a *comparison pair.*

Fix a $c \in \mathbb{R}$ and let (α,β) be a comparison pair of integrable functions. Define the sets

$$\begin{aligned} C_c &= \left\{u \in C(I,\mathbb{R}) \mid c - \int_t^{+\infty} \beta(s)ds \leq u(t) \leq c - \int_t^{+\infty} \alpha(s)ds \text{ for all } t \in I\right\}, \\ D &= \{v \in C(I,\mathbb{R}) \mid \alpha(t) \leq v(t) \leq \beta(t) \text{ for all } t \in I\}. \end{aligned} \tag{2.2}$$

THEOREM 2.1. *Assume that, for all $t \in I$, $u, u_1, u_2 \in C_c$ and $v, v_1, v_2 \in D$, the function $t \mapsto f(t,u(t),v(t))$ is continuous,*

$$|f(t,u_1,v_1) - f(t,u_2,v_2)| \leq k(t)(|u_1 - u_2| + |v_1 - v_2|), \tag{2.3}$$

where $k \in C(I,\mathbb{R})$ is a nonnegative function satisfying (1.4). Suppose further that, for all $t \in I$, $u \in C_c$, and $v \in D$,

$$\alpha(t) \leq \int_t^{+\infty} f(s,u(s),v(s))ds \leq \beta(t). \tag{2.4}$$

Then there exists a unique solution $u(t)$ of (2.1), defined on I, such that

$$\lim_{t\to+\infty} u(t) = c, \quad \alpha(t) \leq u'(t) \leq \beta(t), \quad t \in I. \tag{2.5}$$

Furthermore, $u(t)$ is positive provided that

$$c - \int_{t_0}^{+\infty} \beta(s)ds > 0. \tag{2.6}$$

Proof. For a fixed $r > 1$, introduce the weighted distance between two functions $v_1, v_2 \in D$,

$$d_r(v_1,v_2) = \sup_{t\in I}\left[\left(\int_t^{+\infty} |v_1(s)-v_2(s)|\,ds + t_0|v_1(t)-v_2(t)|\right)\exp\left(-r\int_t^{+\infty} sk(s)ds\right)\right], \tag{2.7}$$

and define the operator $T : D \to D$ by

$$T(v)(t) = \int_t^{+\infty} f\left(s, c-\int_s^{+\infty} v(\tau)d\tau, v(s)\right)ds, \quad v \in D,\ t \in I. \tag{2.8}$$

Similarly to [10, 16], we deduce from Lebesgue's dominated convergence theorem that the operator T is a contraction in the complete metric space $E = (D, d_r)$ with the coefficient $1/r$ and, accordingly, T has a fixed point $v_0 \in D$. Then the function u defined by

$$u(t) = c - \int_t^{+\infty} v_0(s)ds, \quad t \in I, \tag{2.9}$$

is a sought for solution of (2.1). □

Remark 2.2. Assume that condition (2.6) in Theorem 2.1 is replaced with a stronger one,

$$c - \int_t^{+\infty} \beta(s)ds > t\beta(t) \geq 0, \quad t \in I. \tag{2.10}$$

Then $u(t)$ satisfies, for all $t \in I$,

$$u'(t) < \frac{u(t)}{t}. \tag{2.11}$$

Fix now $a, c \geq 0$, $b \in (0,1]$, and let (α,β) be a comparison pair. Define the set

$$\begin{aligned} C_{a,b} = \Big\{ u \in C(I,\mathbb{R}) \mid\ & at + c + t\int_t^{+\infty} \frac{\alpha(s)}{s^{1+b}}ds \leq u(t) \\ & \leq at + c + t\int_t^{+\infty} \frac{\beta(s)}{s^{1+b}}ds \text{ for all } t \in I \Big\}. \end{aligned} \tag{2.12}$$

Theorem 2.3. *Let $f(t,u,u') = f(t,u)$, and assume that, for all $t \in I$ and $u, u_1, u_2 \in C_{a,b}$, the function $t \mapsto f(t,u(t))$ is continuous,*

$$|f(t,u_1) - f(t,u_2)| \leq k(t)|u_1 - u_2|, \tag{2.13}$$

where $k \in C(I,\mathbb{R})$ is a nonnegative function satisfying

$$\int_{t_0}^{+\infty} sk(s)ds < b. \tag{2.14}$$

Suppose also that, for all $t \in I$ and $u \in C_{a,b}$,

$$\alpha(t) \leq \frac{1}{t^{1-b}}\int_{t_0}^{t} sf(s,u(s))ds \leq \beta(t). \tag{2.15}$$

Then there exists a unique solution $u(t)$ of (2.1) defined on I such that

$$u(t) = at + O(t^{1-b}) \quad \text{as } t \longrightarrow +\infty \tag{2.16}$$

and, for $t \in I$,

$$u(t) \geq c, \quad \alpha(t) \leq t^b\left[\frac{u(t)-c}{t} - u'(t)\right] \leq \beta(t). \tag{2.17}$$

Proof. Let

$$D = \{v \in C(I,\mathbb{R}) \mid -t^{-b}\beta(t) \leq v(t) \leq -t^{-b}\alpha(t) \text{ for all } t \in I\}. \tag{2.18}$$

Introduce the distance between two functions $v_1, v_2 \in D$ by

$$d(v_1,v_2) = \sup_{t\in I}\left[t^b \left| v_1(t) - v_2(t)\right|\right], \tag{2.19}$$

and the operator $T : D \to D$ by

$$t[T(v)(t)] = -\int_{t_0}^{t} sf\left(s, as + c - s\int_s^{+\infty}\frac{v(\tau)}{\tau}d\tau\right)ds. \tag{2.20}$$

One can easily check that T is a contraction in the complete metric space $E = (D,d)$ with the coefficient $(1/b)\int_{t_0}^{+\infty} sk(s)ds$ and, accordingly, T has a fixed point $v_0 \in D$. Then the function $u(t)$ defined by

$$u(t) = at + c - t\int_t^{+\infty}\frac{v_0(s)}{s}ds, \quad t \in I, \tag{2.21}$$

is a solution of (2.1) with the desired properties. □

3. Positive solutions to (1.1)

Existence of two positive solutions to (1.1) can be established similarly to [1, 2, 4, 14, 16] provided that one proves existence of two subsolutions h_1^-, h_2^- and two supersolutions h_1^+, h_2^+ of (1.1) such that

$$0 \leq h_1^-(t) \leq h_1^+(t) < h_2^-(t) \leq h_2^+(t), \quad t \geq T_0, \tag{3.1}$$

and $h_i^{\mp}(t) = O(t)$ as $t \to +\infty$.

Let $k_2 \equiv 0$ in (1.6),

$$h''(t) + k_1(t)h(t) = 0, \quad t \geq A, \tag{3.2}$$

and assume that

$$\int_A^{+\infty} s\left|k_1(s)\right| ds < +\infty. \tag{3.3}$$

Fix an $a \in (0,\varepsilon)$ and a $\lambda \in (0,1)$. Following [11], we deduce that there exist a $T_0 \geq A$ and a solution h_2^+ of (3.2) such that, for all $t \geq T_0$,

$$\lambda a < (h_2^+)'(t) < \frac{h_2^+(t)}{t} < a. \tag{3.4}$$

Let now $k_1 \equiv 0$ in (1.6),

$$h''(t) + k_2(t)\Big(h'(t) - \frac{h(t)}{t}\Big) = 0, \quad t \geq A, \tag{3.5}$$

and suppose that $k_2 \geq 0$. As noticed in [4], k_2 should not necessarily be integrable on $[A,+\infty)$. Furthermore, as opposed to [1], g is not assumed to be bounded. Adapting the technique from [12], one can show that (3.5) has a solution h_2^-,

$$h_2^-(t) = t\left[\frac{h_0}{T_0} + \int_{T_0}^{t} \frac{y(s)}{s^2}ds\right], \tag{3.6}$$

where

$$y(t) = -\exp\Big(-\int_{T_0}^{t} k_2(s)ds\Big), \quad t \geq T_0. \tag{3.7}$$

For a fixed $b \in (0,1]$ and T_0 large enough, pick an $h_0 = T_0^{1-b/2}$ to make certain that

$$\frac{1}{bT_0^b} < \frac{h_0 - 1}{T_0}, \qquad \frac{h_0}{T_0} = T_0^{-1} + T_0^{-b/2} < \lambda a. \tag{3.8}$$

Then (1.1) has a solution $u_2(x)$, defined in $\overline{G}_B$ for some $B > T_0$, such that

$$\frac{h_2^-(t)}{t} \leq u_2(x) \leq \frac{h_2^+(t)}{t}, \quad t \geq T_0, \tag{3.9}$$

where

$$|x| = \Big(\frac{t}{n-1}\Big)^{1/(n-2)} \geq B. \tag{3.10}$$

Furthermore,

$$\liminf_{|x|\to+\infty} u_2(x) \geq \frac{h_0 - 1}{T_0}. \tag{3.11}$$

Consider again (3.2), assuming that (3.3) holds. In Theorem 2.3, take $\alpha \equiv 0$ and $\beta \equiv 1$ as a comparison pair. Choose the numbers $b \in (0,1/2)$ and $T_0 \geq \max(e,A)$ to ensure that (3.8) is satisfied and to guarantee that

$$\int_{T_0}^{+\infty} sk_1(s)ds < \frac{b}{2}. \tag{3.12}$$

Consider the operator T, defined by (2.20), for $a = 0$ and for some $c \in (0, b^{-1}T_0^{1-b})$. Then one can prove that there exists a solution h_1^+ of (3.2) such that

$$h_1^+(t) \geq c, \quad (h_1^+)'(t) < \frac{h_1^+(t)}{t} \leq \frac{2}{bt^b} < \lambda a < \varepsilon. \tag{3.13}$$

Finally, let $h_1^- \equiv 0$. Then (1.1) has a solution $u_1(x)$, defined in $\overline{G}_B$ for some $B > T_0$, such that

$$\begin{gathered} 0 < u_1(x) < \frac{h_1^+(t)}{t}, \quad t \geq T_0, \\ \lim_{|x| \to +\infty} u_1(x) = 0. \end{gathered} \tag{3.14}$$

We conclude by mentioning that if (1.5) holds, a multiplicity theorem is presented in [15]; whereas no similar results are known for the case when (1.4) is satisfied. Furthermore, our investigation reveals that solutions $u_1(x)$ and $u_2(x)$ of (1.1) have different asymptotic behaviors, induced by the behavior of h_2^- as $|x| \to +\infty$. Although existence of such solutions has been already established in the literature, the arguments employed in [1, 2, 4, 16] and the choice of sub- and supersolutions in these papers do not allow for the detailed analysis of the asymptotic behavior of $u_1(x)$ and $u_2(x)$ undertaken in this paper.

Acknowledgments

This work has been completed during the visit of Mustafa to the Mathematics Department of Lund University, Sweden, in June 2005 and has been supported by SFI grant VR 621-2003-5287. Mustafa thanks the Mathematics Department for making his stay very agreeable. The research of Rogovchenko has been supported in part by the Abdus Salam International Centre of Theoretical Physics, Trieste, Italy, through the Associate Membership Program.

References

[1] A. Constantin, *Existence of positive solutions of quasilinear elliptic equations*, Bulletin of the Australian Mathematical Society **54** (1996), no. 1, 147–154.

[2] ———, *Positive solutions of quasilinear elliptic equations*, Journal of Mathematical Analysis and Applications **213** (1997), no. 1, 334–339.

[3] S. G. Dubé and A. B. Mingarelli, *Note on a non-oscillation theorem of Atkinson*, Electronic Journal of Differential Equations **2004** (2004), no. 22, 1–6.

[4] M. Ehrnström, *Positive solutions for second-order nonlinear differential equations*, Nonlinear Analysis **64** (2006), no. 7, 1608–1620.

[5] J. K. Hale and N. Onuchic, *On the asymptotic behavior of solutions of a class of differential equations*, Contributions to Differential Equations **2** (1963), 61–75.

[6] P. Hartman and A. Wintner, *On non-oscillatory linear differential equations*, American Journal of Mathematics **75** (1953), 717–730.

[7] T. Kusano and W. F. Trench, *Existence of global solutions with prescribed asymptotic behavior for nonlinear ordinary differential equations*, Annali di Matematica Pura ed Applicata. Serie Quarta **142** (1985), 381–392 (1986).

[8] O. Lipovan, *On the asymptotic behaviour of the solutions to a class of second order nonlinear differential equations*, Glasgow Mathematical Journal **45** (2003), no. 1, 179–187.

[9] O. G. Mustafa, *On the existence of solutions with prescribed asymptotic behavior for perturbed nonlinear differential equations of second order*, Glasgow Mathematical Journal **47** (2005), 177–185.

[10] ———, *Positive solutions of nonlinear differential equations with prescribed decay of the first derivative*, Nonlinear Analysis **60** (2005), no. 1, 179–185.

[11] O. G. Mustafa and Y. V. Rogovchenko, *Asymptotic behavior of nonoscillatory solutions of second-order nonlinear differential equations*, Proceedings of Dynamic Systems and Applications. Vol. 4, Dynamic, Georgia, 2004, pp. 312–319.

[12] ———, *Global existence and asymptotic behavior of solutions of nonlinear differential equations*, Funkcialaj Ekvacioj **47** (2004), no. 2, 167–186.

[13] ———, *On asymptotic integration of a nonlinear second-order differential equation*, Nonlinear Studies **13** (2006), no. 2, 155–166.

[14] E. S. Noussair and C. A. Swanson, *Positive solutions of quasilinear elliptic equations in exterior domains*, Journal of Mathematical Analysis and Applications **75** (1980), no. 1, 121–133.

[15] A. Orpel, *On the existence of positive radial solutions for a certain class of elliptic BVPs*, Journal of Mathematical Analysis and Applications **299** (2004), no. 2, 690–702.

[16] E. Wahlén, *Positive solutions of second-order differential equations*, Nonlinear Analysis **58** (2004), no. 3-4, 359–366.

Octavian G. Mustafa: Department of Mathematics, University of Craiova, Al. I. Cuza 13, RO-1100, Craiova, Romania
E-mail address: octavian@central.ucv.ro

Yuri V. Rogovchenko: Department of Mathematics, Eastern Mediterranean University, Famagusta, TRNC, Mersin 10, Turkey
E-mail address: yuri.rogovchenko@emu.edu.tr

EXISTENCE AND UNIQUENESS OF AN INTEGRAL SOLUTION TO SOME CAUCHY PROBLEM WITH NONLOCAL CONDITIONS

GASTON M. N'GUÉRÉKATA

Using the contraction mapping principle, we prove the existence and uniqueness of an integral solution to a semilinear differential equation in a Banach space with a nondensely defined operator and nonlocal conditions.

1. Preliminaries and notations

The aim of this short note is to prove the existence and uniqueness of an integral solution to the nonlocal evolution equation in a Banach space E,

$$\begin{aligned} \frac{du(t)}{dt} &= Au(t) + F(t, Bu(t)), \quad t \in [0,T], \\ u(0) + g(u) &= u_0, \end{aligned} \tag{1.1}$$

where $A : D(A) \subset E \to E$ and $B : D(B) \to E$ are closed linear operators.

We assume that the domain $D(A)$ of A is not dense in E and

(i) $F : [0,T] \times E \to E$ is continuous,

(ii) $g : C \to E$ is continuous, where $C := C([0,T];E)$ is the Banach space of all continuous functions $[0,T] \to E$ equipped with the uniform norm topology.

An example of such problem is the following.

Example 1.1. Consider the partial differential equation

$$\begin{aligned} \frac{\partial}{\partial t}u(t,x) &= \frac{\partial^2}{\partial x^2}u(t,x) + f(t, Bx), \quad (t,x) \in [0,T] \times (0,1), \\ u(t,0) &= u(t,1) = 0, \quad t \in [0,T], \\ u(0,x) + \sum_{i}^{n} \lambda_i u(t_i,x) &= \Phi(x), \quad x \in (0,1), \end{aligned} \tag{1.2}$$

Hindawi Publishing Corporation
Proceedings of the Conference on Differential & Difference Equations and Applications, pp. 843–849

where $u(t,x)$, $f(t,x)$ are scalar, λ_i, $i = 1,\dots,n$, are some constants, and $0 < t_1 \le t_2 \le \cdots \le T$. B is an operator defined by $Bv := q(x)v$ for each $v \in C$ with $q \in L^\infty(0,T)$. Here we write $v(t) = u(t,\cdot)$ regarded as a function of x. If we study (1.2) in $E := C[0,T]$ (the space of all continuous functions on $[0,T]$ with the sup-norm), and define

$$Av = v'', \qquad D(A) = \{v \in C^2[0,T] : v(0) = v(T) = 0\}, \tag{1.3}$$

then the closure of $D(A)$ is

$$\overline{D(A)} = \{v \in C[0,T] : v(0) = v(T) = 0\} \neq C[0,T]; \tag{1.4}$$

so, A is not densely defined on $C[0,T]$. Therefore, if we assume that $f(t,\cdot) \in C[0,T]$ depends continuously on t and bounded on $\mathbb{R}$, then we will be concerned with the evolution equation (1.2) with the nondensely defined operator A.

Many problems with nondensely defined operators and nonlocal conditions arise in physics (see, i.e., [7]). Indeed it appears, for instance, that the nonlocal condition $u(0) + g(u) = u_0$ produces better effects than the classical Cauchy problem with $u(o) = u_0$ for diffusion phenomenon of small amounts of gas in a transparent tube when

$$g(u) = \sum_{i=0}^{n} \lambda_i u(t_i), \tag{1.5}$$

where $0 < t_1 \le t_2 \le \cdots \le T$ and λ_i, $i = 1,\dots,n$, are some given constants.

Several papers investigate the existence and uniqueness of classical or mild solutions of Cauchy problems with nonlocal conditions; see, for instance, [1, 2, 5–9] and many references within. Most of these papers deal with a densely defined operator A. In [8], Liu and Ezzinbi studied the existence and uniqueness of integrated solutions of (1.1) above where A is nondensely defined on E. The main result (Theorem 2.1) is a generalization of Theorem 4 in their work [8].

Throughout the paper, $L(E)$ will denote the Banach space of all bounded linear operators $E \to E$.

In order to define an integral solution to (1.1), we first present a collection of some results on the so-called integrated semigroups, a notion introduced by Arendt [3] in the context of resolvent positive operators. Neubrander then studied n-times integrated semigroups, $n \ge 0$, (see also [4, 10]).

Definition 1.2 [4]. A family $(T_t)_{t\ge 0}$ of bounded linear operators on E is called an integrated semigroup if

(i) $T_0 = 0$,
(ii) $t \to T_t$ is strongly continuous,
(iii) $T_sT_t = \int_0^s (T_{t+\sigma} - T_\sigma)d\sigma$ for all $t,s \ge 0$.

Let us recall some examples from [11].

Example 1.3. (i) Let $(S_t)_{t\geq 0}$ be a C_0-semigroup on a Banach space E. Then $(T_t)_{t\geq 0}$, defined by $T_t := \int_0^t S(s)ds$ for each $t \geq 0$, is an integrated semigroup.

(ii) Let $(\cos(t))_{t\geq 0}$ be the cosine function on a Banach space E and define the sine function by $\sin(t) := \int_0^t \cos(s)ds$. Then the 2×2 matrix $T_t := (a(t))_{ij}$, where $(a(t))_{11} = (a(t))_{22} = \sin(t)$, $(a(t))_{12} = \int_0^t \sin(s)ds$, and $(a(t))_{21} = \cos(t) - I$, is an integrated semigroup on $E\times E$.

Remark 1.4. One can check also that

$$T_sT_t = \int_0^{s+t} T_\sigma d\sigma - \int_0^s T_\sigma d\sigma - \int_0^t T_\sigma d\sigma \quad \text{for } s,t \geq 0. \tag{1.6}$$

Therefore, $T_sT_t = T_tT_s$ for $s,t \geq 0$.

Definition 1.5. An integrated semigroup $(T_t)_{t\geq 0}$ is said to be

(i) locally Lipschitz continuous if for all $b > 0$, there exists a constant L such that

$$||T_t - T_s|| \leq L|t-s|, \quad t,s \in [0,b]; \tag{1.7}$$

(ii) nondegenerate if $T_tx = 0$ for all $t \geq 0$, implies $x = 0$.

As in the case of the classical semigroup theory, we can define the generator of an integrated semigroup as follows.

Definition 1.6. A linear operator A is said to be a generator of an integrated semigroup if there exists $\omega \in \mathbb{R}$ such that $(\omega,\infty) \subset \rho(A)$, the resolvent set of A, and there exists a strongly continuous exponentially bounded family of bounded linear operators $(T_t)_{t\geq 0}$ such that

(i) $T_0 = 0$;

(ii) $R(\lambda;A) = \int_0^\infty e^{-\lambda t}T_tdt$ exists for all $\lambda > \omega$.

PROPOSITION 1.7 [4, Proposition 3.3]. *Let A be the generator of an integrated semigroup $(T_t)_{t\geq 0}$. Then for all $x \in D(A)$ and $t \geq 0$, we have*

(i) $\int_0^t T_\sigma x d\sigma \in D(A)$,

(ii) $T_tx = A\int_0^t T_\sigma x d\sigma + tx$.

We now recall the well-known result.

The Hille-Yosida condition. A linear operator A is said to satisfy a Hille-Yosida condition if there exist real constant M and ω such that $(\omega,\infty) \in \rho(A)$ and

$$||(\lambda - A)^{-n}|| \leq \frac{M}{(\lambda-\omega)^n} \quad \text{for } n \in \mathbb{N},\ \lambda > \omega. \tag{1.8}$$

THEOREM 1.8 [4]. *A is the generator of a nondegenerate, locally Lipschitz continuous semigroup if and only if A satisfies the Hille-Yosida condition.*

THEOREM 1.9. *Assume A is the generator of an integrated semigroup $(T_t)_{t\geq 0}$ and let $f \in C([0,T],E)$. Then for each $u_0 \in D(A)$, there exists a unique function $u \in C([0,T],E)$ such* *that for each* $t \in [0,T]$, *there exist*

(i) $\int_0^t u(\sigma)d\sigma \in D(A)$,

(ii) $u(t) = u_0 + A\int_0^t u(\sigma)d\sigma + \int_0^t f(\sigma)d\sigma$,

(iii) $\|u(t)\| \le Me^{\omega t}(\|u_0\| + \int_0^t e^{-\omega\sigma}\|f(\sigma)\|d\sigma)$.

Moreover, u satisfies the variation of constant formula

$$u(t) = T_t' u_0 + \frac{d}{dt}\int_0^t T_{t-\sigma} f(\sigma)d\sigma, \quad t \ge 0. \tag{1.9}$$

If we define $B_\lambda := \lambda R(\lambda, A)$, then for all $u \in \overline{D(A)}$, $B_\lambda u \to u$ as $\lambda \to \infty$.

It is clear that

$$\frac{d}{dt}\int_0^t T_{t-\sigma} f(\sigma)d\sigma \in \overline{D(A)} \quad \text{for every } f \in L^1(0,T). \tag{1.10}$$

Therefore

$$B_\lambda \frac{d}{dt}\left(\int_0^t T_{t-\sigma} f(\sigma)d\sigma\right) \longrightarrow \frac{d}{dt}\int_0^t T_{t-\sigma} f(\sigma)d\sigma \quad \text{if } \lambda \longrightarrow \infty. \tag{1.11}$$

Now by continuity of B_λ, we have

$$B_\lambda \frac{d}{dt}\left(\int_0^t T_{t-\sigma} f(\sigma)d\sigma\right) = \frac{d}{dt}\left(\int_0^t T_{t-\sigma} B_\lambda f(\sigma)d\sigma\right). \tag{1.12}$$

Since T_t is differentiable on $D(A)$, then $t \to T_{t-\sigma} f(\sigma)$ is also differentiable in t for all $t \ge 0$.

Using now the fact that $T_0 = 0$, we obtain

$$\frac{d}{dt}\left(\int_0^t T_{t-\sigma} B_\lambda f(\sigma)d\sigma\right) = \int_0^t T_{t-\sigma}' B_\lambda f(\sigma)d\sigma. \tag{1.13}$$

Therefore

$$u(t) = T_t' u_0 + \lim_{\lambda\to\infty}\int_0^t T_{t-\sigma}' B_\lambda f(\sigma)d\sigma, \quad t \ge 0. \tag{1.14}$$

Finally we give the definition of an integral solution to (1.1).

Definition 1.10. A function $u \in C([0,T];E)$ is said to be an integral solution of (1.1) if the following hold:

(i) $\int_0^t u(\sigma)d\sigma \in D(A)$, $t \in [0,T]$;

(ii) $u(t) = u_0 - g(u) + A\int_0^t u(\sigma)d\sigma + \int_0^t F(\sigma, u(\sigma))d\sigma$, $t \in [0,T]$.

2. Main results

Now we state and prove the following (compare with [8, Theorem 4]). Unlike [8], $T > 0$ is an a priori fixed number and $\omega > 0$.

Theorem 2.1. *Assume A satisfies a Hille-Yosida condition with $\omega > 0$ and $B \in L(E)$ is a bounded linear operator. Assume further that*

(i) $\|F(t,x) - F(t,y)\| \le N(t)\|x - y\|$, $t \in [0,T]$, $x, y \in E$, *with* $N \in L^1_{\text{loc}}(\mathbb{R},(0,\infty))$ *and* $\|N\|_{L^1_{\text{loc}}(\mathbb{R})} \le (1/M\|B\|_{L(E)})\omega e^{-\omega T}$;

(ii) $g : C \to \overline{D(A)}$ *and* $\|g(u) - g(v)\| \le b\|u - v\|_C$, *with* $b < (1/M)e^{-2\omega T}$;

(iii) $r > 0$ *can be chosen such that*

$$Me^{\omega T}\left[||u_0|| + K + \frac{1}{\omega}\left(a + \frac{r\omega e^{-\omega T}}{M}\right)(1 - e^{-\omega T})\right] \le r, \tag{2.1}$$

where $K = \sup_{w \in B_r} \|g(w)\|$, $B_r = \{w \in C : \|w\| \le r\}$, *and* $a = \sup_{t \in [0,T]} \|F(t,0)\|$;

(iv) $u_0 \in \overline{D(A)}$.

Then (1.1) admits a unique integral solution on $[0,T]$.

Proof. Define an operator $\Gamma : C \to C$ by

$$\Gamma u(t) := T'_t[u_0 - g(u)] + \frac{d}{dt}\int_0^t T_{t-s}F(s,Bu(s))\,ds, \quad t \in [0,T]. \tag{2.2}$$

We like to show that Γ possesses a fixed point in C.

First, we note that Γ is well defined and we can show that $\Gamma B_r \subset B_r$.

Indeed, by Theorem 1.9, if $u \in B_r$, then

$$\begin{aligned}
||\Gamma u(t)|| &\le Me^{\omega t}\left[||u_0|| + K + \int_0^t e^{-\omega s}||F(s,Bu(s))||ds\right] \\
&= Me^{\omega t}\left[||u_0|| + K + \int_0^t e^{-\omega s}||F(s,Bu(s)) - F(s,0) + F(0,s)||ds\right] \\
&\le Me^{\omega t}\left[||u_0|| + K + \int_0^t e^{-\omega s}||F(s,Bu(s)) - F(s,0)||ds + \int_0^t e^{-\omega s}||F(s,0)||ds\right] \\
&\le Me^{\omega t}\left[||u_0|| + K + \int_0^t e^{-\omega s}N(s)\|B\|_{L(E)}||u(s)||ds + a\int_0^t e^{-\omega s}ds\right] \\
&\le Me^{\omega T}\left[||u_0|| + K + (r\|B\|_{L(E)}\|N\|_{L^1_{\text{loc}}\mathbb{R}} + a)\int_0^T e^{-\omega s}ds\right] \\
&\le Me^{\omega T}\left[||u_0|| + K + \frac{1}{\omega}(r\|B\|_{L(E)}\|N\|_{L^1_{\text{loc}}\mathbb{R}} + a)(1 - e^{-\omega T})\right] \\
&< Me^{\omega T}\left[||u_0|| + K + \frac{1}{\omega}\left(a + \frac{r\omega e^{-\omega T}}{M}\right)(1 - e^{-\omega T})\right] \le r.
\end{aligned} \tag{2.3}$$

Now if $u, v \in B_r$, then we get

$$\begin{aligned} \|\Gamma u(t) - \Gamma v(t)\| &\leq \left\| T_t' \left[g(u) - g(v) + \frac{d}{dt} \int_0^t T_{t-s}[F(s, Bu(s)) - F(s, Bv(s))] ds \right] \right\| \\ &\leq Me^{\omega t} \left[b\|u - v\|_C + \int_0^t e^{-\omega s} \|F(s, u(s)) - F(s, v(s))\| ds \right] \\ &\leq Me^{\omega T} \left[b + \|B\|_{L(E)} \|N\|_{L^1_{\text{loc}}(\mathbb{R})} (1 - e^{-\omega T}) \frac{1}{\omega} \right] \|u - v\|_C \\ &= \Theta_{\omega, M, T} \|u - v\|_C, \end{aligned} \tag{2.4}$$

where the constant

$$\Theta_{\omega, M, T} < 1. \tag{2.5}$$

Hence by the contraction mapping principle, Γ has a unique fixed point $\overline{u(t)}$, that is,

$$\overline{u(t)} = T_t' [u_0 - g(\overline{u})] + \frac{d}{dt} \int_0^t T_{t-s} F(s, \overline{u(s)}) ds, \quad t \in [0, T], \tag{2.6}$$

which is an integral solution to (1.1). □

We also have the following whose proof is straightforward.

Corollary 2.2. *Assume A satisfies a Hille-Yosida condition with $\omega > 0$. Assume further that*

(i) *$F(t, x)$ is Lipschitzian in x uniformly in t and the Lipschitz constant L satisfies the inequality $L < (1/M)\omega e^{-\omega T}$;*
(ii) *$g : C \to \overline{D(A)}$ with $g(u) = \sum_{i=0}^n \lambda_i u(t_i)$, where $0 < t_1 \leq t_2 \leq \cdots \leq T$ and λ_i, $i = 1, \ldots, n$, are some given constants and $\sum_i^n |\lambda_i| < (1/M)e^{-2\omega T}$;*
(iii) *$r > 0$ can be chosen such that*

$$Me^{\omega T} \left[\|u_0\| + K + \frac{1}{\omega} \left(a + \frac{r\omega e^{-\omega T}}{M} \right) (1 - e^{-\omega T}) \right] \leq r, \tag{2.7}$$

where $K = \sup_{w \in B_r} \|g(w)\|$, $B_r = \{ w \in C \mid \|w\| \leq r \}$, and $a = \sup_{t \in [0,T]} \|F(t, 0)\|$;
(iv) *$u_0 \in \overline{D(A)}$.*

Then (1.1) admits a unique integral solution on $[0, T]$.

Proof. It is straightforward from Theorem 2.1. □

Acknowledgment

We thank Professor Khalil Ezzinbi and Professor James Liu for their useful comments.

References

[1] S. Aizicovici, *Differential and Functional Differential Problems Together with Nonlocal Conditions*, Cracow University of Technology, Cracow, 1995.

[2] S. Aizicovici and M. McKibben, *Existence results for a class of abstract nonlocal Cauchy problems*, Nonlinear Analysis **39** (2000), no. 5, 649–668.

[3] W. Arendt, *Resolvent positive operators*, Proceedings of the London Mathematical Society. Third Series **54** (1987), no. 2, 321–349.

[4] ______, *Vector-valued Laplace transforms and Cauchy problems*, Israel Journal of Mathematics **59** (1987), no. 3, 327–352.

[5] L. Byszewski, *Theorems about the existence and uniqueness of solutions of a semilinear evolution nonlocal Cauchy problem*, Journal of Mathematical Analysis and Applications **162** (1991), no. 2, 494–505.

[6] ______, *Existence and uniqueness of solutions of semilinear evolution nonlocal Cauchy problem*, Zeszyty Naukowe Politechniki Rzeszowskiej. Matematyka i Fizyka (1993), no. 18, 109–112.

[7] K. Deng, *Exponential decay of solutions of semilinear parabolic equations with nonlocal initial conditions*, Journal of Mathematical Analysis and Applications **179** (1993), no. 2, 630–637.

[8] K. Ezzinbi and J. H. Liu, *Nondensely defined evolution equations with nonlocal conditions*, Mathematical and Computer Modelling **36** (2002), no. 9-10, 1027–1038.

[9] E. Hernández M., *Existence of solutions to a second order partial differential equation with nonlocal conditions*, Electronic Journal of Differential Equations **2003** (2003), no. 51, 1–10.

[10] S. Kalabušić and F. Vajzović, *Exponential formula for one-time integrated semigroups*, Novi Sad Journal of Mathematics **33** (2003), no. 2, 77–88.

[11] H. Kellerman and M. Hieber, *Integrated semigroups*, Journal of Functional Analysis **84** (1989), no. 1, 160–180.

Gaston M. N'Guérékata: Department of Mathematics, Morgan State University, 1700 E. Cold Spring Lane, Baltimore, MD 21251, USA

E-mail address: gnguerek@jewel.morgan.edu

AN H^1-GALERKIN MIXED FINITE ELEMENT METHOD FOR LINEAR AND NONLINEAR PARABOLIC PROBLEMS

NEELA NATARAJ AND AMBIT KUMAR PANY

An H^1-Galerkin mixed finite element method is proposed to approximate the solution as well as flux of one-dimensional linear and nonlinear parabolic initial boundary value problems. Error estimates have been given and the results of numerical experiments for two examples have been shown.

1. Introduction

In [9], an H^1-Galerkin mixed finite element method is proposed to solve linear parabolic problems. Contrary to the standard H^1-Galerkin finite element method [6, 10], the C^1-continuity condition in the definition of the finite element spaces for approximating the solution has been relaxed in this method.

The standard mixed finite element procedure demands the satisfaction of the LBB condition by the approximating finite element subspaces. This restricts the choice of the finite element spaces for approximating u and its flux. This bottle neck has been overcome in this method and the approximating finite element spaces V_h and W_h are allowed to be of different polynomial degrees. Also, the quasiuniformity condition on the finite element mesh need not be imposed in this method.

In this paper, first of all, an implementation of the H^1-Galerkin mixed finite element method [9] which gives a simultaneous approximation to the solution as well as its flux for linear parabolic problems has been done. Secondly, an interesting application of this mixed method for approximating the solution and flux of Burgers' equation has been described. The unknown and its derivative are approximated simultaneously using globally continuous piecewise linear elements in the discrete level. Error estimate results have been stated and results of some numerical experiments are presented.

Burgers' equation, being a simplified form of Navier-Stokes equation and also due to its immense physical applications, has attracted researcher's attention since the past few decades. Numerical methods like finite difference, finite element, as well as spectral

Hindawi Publishing Corporation
Proceedings of the Conference on Differential & Difference Equations and Applications, pp. 851–860

and mixed finite element methods (see [1, 2, 4, 7], and the references therein) have been developed in the past to solve this equation.

An outline of the paper is as follows. In Section 2, the H^1-Galerkin continuous mixed variational formulation, and finite element formulation has been discussed. A priori error estimates results for the mixed finite element scheme have been stated. In Section 3, a fully discrete scheme has been described. Results of the numerical experiments performed are discussed in Section 4. The numerical experiments confirm the theoretical rate of convergence obtained.

2. H^1-Galerkin mixed finite element method

2.1. A linear parabolic initial boundary value problem. We consider the following problem. Find u such that

$$u_t - (au_x)_x + bu_x + cu = f(x,t), \quad (x,t) \in (0,1)\times J, \tag{2.1}$$

with Dirichlet boundary conditions $u(0,t) = u(1,t) = 0$ for all $t \in \bar{J}$ and initial condition $u(x,0) = u_0(x)$ for all $x \in I$ where $I = (0,1)$, $J = (0,T]$ with $T < \infty$, $u_t = \partial u/\partial t$, $u_x = \partial u/\partial x$. The coefficients a, b, c are smooth functions of x, and a is bounded below by a positive constant, say a_0.

Introduce a new variable $v = au_x$ to reduce (2.1) to the following 1st order system:

$$\begin{aligned} u_x &= \alpha(x)v, \\ u_t - v_x + \beta v + cu &= f. \end{aligned} \tag{2.2}$$

Here $\alpha(x) = 1/a(x)$, $\beta(x) = \alpha(x)b(x)$. Denote the natural inner product in $L^2(I)$ as $(\cdot,\cdot)$ and the standard Sobolev spaces $H^1(I)$, $H_0^1(I)$ as H^1 and H_0^1, respectively. After multiplying the first equation in (2.2) by χ_x with $\chi \in H_0^1$ and the second equation in (2.2) by $-w_x$ with $w \in H^1$, we integrate the second equation by parts. Using the Dirichlet boundary conditions, we obtain the H^1-Galerkin mixed formulation as follows.

Find $\{u,v\} : (0,T] \to H_0^1 \times H^1$ such that

$$\begin{aligned} (u_x,\chi_x) &= (\alpha(x)v,\chi_x), \quad \forall \chi \in H_0^1, \\ (\alpha v_t, w) + (v_x, w_x) &= (\beta v, w_x) + (cu, w_x) - (f, w_x), \quad \forall w \in H^1. \end{aligned} \tag{2.3}$$

Let V_h and W_h be the finite-dimensional subspaces of H_0^1 and H^1, respectively, defined by

$$V_h = \{\chi_h : \chi_h \in C^0(\bar{I}),\ \chi_h|_{I_j} \in P_k(I_j)\ \forall I_j \in \mathcal{T}_h,\ \chi_h(0) = \chi_h(1) = 0\}, \tag{2.4}$$

$$W_h = \{w_h : w_h \in C^0(\bar{I}),\ w_h|_{I_j} \in P_r(I_j)\ \forall I_j \in \mathcal{T}_h\}, \tag{2.5}$$

where $\mathcal{T}_h$ is a partition of $\bar{I} = [0,1]$ into N_h subintervals $I_j = [x_j, x_{j+1}]$, $j = 0,1,2,\ldots,(N_h - 1)$, $h_j = x_{j+1} - x_j$, $h = \max_{0\le j\le N_h-1} h_j$, $V_h \subset H_0^1$, $W_h \subset H^1$, and $P_m(I_j)$ denotes the polynomials of degree less than or equal to m in I_j.

The semidiscrete H^1-Galerkin mixed finite element method for (2.2) is determined by a pair $(u_h, v_h) \in V_h \times W_h$ such that

$$(u_{hx}, \chi_{hx}) = (\alpha(x)v_h, \chi_{hx}), \quad \forall \chi \in V_h, \tag{2.6}$$

$$(\alpha v_{ht}, w_h) + (v_{hx}, w_{hx}) = (\beta v_h, w_{hx}) + (cu_h, w_{hx}) - (f, w_{hx}), \quad \forall w_h \in W_h, \tag{2.7}$$

with given $(u_h(0), v_h(0))$. The above system of equations yields a system of differential algebraic equations. This is of index one since the stiffness matrix associated with (u_{hx}, χ_{hx}) is positive definite. Therefore, the system (2.6)-(2.7) is uniquely solvable for a consistent initial condition [3].

2.2. A nonlinear parabolic initial boundary value problem. We consider Burgers' equation

$$\frac{\partial u}{\partial t} - \nu \frac{\partial^2 u}{\partial x^2} + u\frac{\partial u}{\partial x} = 0 \quad \text{in } I \times J \tag{2.8}$$

with Dirichlet boundary conditions $u(0,t) = u(1,t) = 0$ for all $t \in \bar{J}$ and initial condition $u(x,0) = u_0(x)$ for all $x \in I$ where $I = (0,1)$, $J = (0,T]$ with $T < \infty$, u is the unknown velocity, $\nu = 1/\mathrm{Re}$ is the viscosity of the fluid, Re being Reynolds' number, and $u_0(x)$ is a given function.

Proceeding as in the linear case, we introduce a new variable $v = u_x$, and obtain the H^1-Galerkin mixed method corresponding to (2.8) as follows.

Find $\{u, v\} : (0,T] \to H_0^1 \times H^1$ such that

$$\begin{aligned} (u_x, \chi_x) &= (v, \chi_x), \quad \forall \chi \in H_0^1, \\ (v_t, w) + \nu(v_x, w_x) &= (uv, w_x), \quad \forall w \in H^1. \end{aligned} \tag{2.9}$$

The semidiscrete H^1-mixed finite element scheme is defined as follows.

Find $\{u_h, v_h\} : [0,T] \to V_h \times W_h$ such that for $t \in (0,T]$,

$$(u_{hx}, \chi_{hx}) = (v_h, \chi_{hx}), \quad \forall \chi_h \in V_h, \tag{2.10}$$

$$(v_{ht}, w_h) + \nu(v_{hx}, w_{hx}) = (u_h v_h, w_{hx}), \quad \forall w_h \in W_h, \tag{2.11}$$

where $u_h(0)$ and $v_h(0)$ are approximations of u_0 and u_{0x}, respectively, and V_h and W_h are the finite-dimensional spaces defined in (2.4)-(2.5). The above system of equations yields a system of differential algebraic equations of index one. Therefore, this system is uniquely solvable for a consistent initial condition.

The error estimate results for the semidiscrete scheme for both linear and nonlinear cases are stated now. The proof for the linear case is given in [9], and that for the nonlinear case is given in [8].

THEOREM 2.1. *Let $v(0) = u_{0x}$. Then there exist positive constants $C > 0$, independent of h such that*

$$\begin{aligned} &||(u-u_h)(t)|| + ||(v-v_h)(t)|| + h||(u-u_h)(t)||_1 \\ &\quad \leq Ch^{\min(k+1,r+1)}\Big\{\|u\|_{L^\infty(H^{k+1})} + \|v\|_{L^\infty(H^{r+1})} + ||v_t||_{L^2(H^{r+1})}\Big\}, \\ &||(v-v_h)(t)||_1 \\ &\quad \leq Ch^{\min(k+1,r)}\Big\{\|u\|_{L^\infty(H^{k+1})} + ||u_t||_{L^2(H^{k+1})} + \|v\|_{L^\infty(H^{r+1})} + ||v_t||_{L^2(H^{r+1})}\Big\}, \end{aligned} \tag{2.12}$$

and for $2 \leq p \leq \infty$,

$$\begin{aligned} &||(u-u_h)(t)||_{L^p} + ||(v-v_h)(t)||_{L^p} \\ &\quad \leq Ch^{\min(k+1,r+1)}\Big\{\|u\|_{L^\infty(W^{k+1,p})} + ||u_t||_{L^2(H^{k+1})} + \|v\|_{L^\infty(W^{r+1,p})} + ||v_t||_{L^2(H^{r+1})}\Big\}. \end{aligned} \tag{2.13}$$

3. A fully discrete scheme

We first describe a fully discrete scheme corresponding to (2.6)-(2.7) (resp., (2.10)-(2.11)). We use the backward Euler method for approximating v_{ht}. Let $0 = t_0 < t_1 < \cdots < t_M = T$ be a given partition of the time interval $[0,T]$ with step length $\Delta t = T/M$ for some positive integer M. For a smooth function ϕ on $[0,T]$, define $\phi^n = \phi(t_n)$ and $\bar{\partial}\phi^n = (\phi^n - \phi^{n-1})/\Delta t$. Let U^n and V^n be the approximations of u_h and v_h at $t = t_n$.

The fully discrete schemes corresponding to (2.6)-(2.7), respectively, (2.10)-(2.11), can be defined as follows.

Given V^{n-1}, find $\{U^n, V^n\} \in V_h \times W_h$ such that

$$\begin{aligned} (U_x^n, \chi_{hx}) &= (\alpha V^{n-1}, \chi_{hx}), \quad \forall \chi_h \in V_h, \\ (\alpha V^n, w_h) + \Delta t(V_x^n, w_{hx}) &= \Delta t(\beta V^{n-1}, w_{hx}) + \Delta t(cU^n, w_{hx}) \\ &\quad + (\alpha V^{n-1}, w_h) - \Delta t(f, w_{hx}), \quad \forall w_h \in W_h. \end{aligned} \tag{3.1}$$

Respectively, given V^{n-1}, find $\{U^n, V^n\} \in V_h \times W_h$ such that

$$\begin{aligned} (U_x^n, \chi_{hx}) &= (V^{n-1}, \chi_{hx}), \quad \forall \chi_h \in V_h, \\ (V^n, w_h) + \nu\Delta t(V_x^n, w_{hx}) &= \Delta t(U^n V^{n-1}, w_{hx}) + (V^{n-1}, w_h), \quad \forall w_h \in W_h. \end{aligned} \tag{3.2}$$

The error estimate results for the fully discrete scheme for both linear [9] and nonlinear [8] cases are stated now.

THEOREM 3.1. *Under the assumptions* $V^0 = v_h(0)$ *with* $v(0) = u_{0x}$, *there exists a positive constant* $C > 0$, *independent of* h *and* Δt *such that for* $0 < \Delta t \le \Delta t_0$ *and* $J = 0,1,\ldots,M$,

$$\begin{aligned}||u(t_J) - U^J|| + ||v(t_J) - V^J|| + h||u(t_J) - U^J||_1 \\ \le Ch^{\min(k+1,r+1)}\Big\{||u||_{L^\infty(H^{k+1})} + ||v||_{L^\infty(H^{r+1})} + ||v_t||_{L^2(H^{r+1})}\Big\} + C\Delta t||v_{tt}||_{L^2(L^2)}.\end{aligned} \tag{3.3}$$

Moreover,

$$\begin{aligned}||v(t_J) - V^J||_1 \le Ch^{\min(k,r)}\Big\{||u||_{L^\infty(H^{k+1})} + ||u_t||_{L^2(H^{k+1})} + ||v||_{L^\infty(H^{r+1})} + ||v_t||_{L^2(H^{r+1})}\Big\} \\ + C\Delta t||v_{tt}||_{L^2(L^2)}.\end{aligned} \tag{3.4}$$

4. Numerical experiments

The mixed finite element approximation scheme is implemented for a linear and a nonlinear parabolic initial boundary value problem.

In our implementation scheme, we have assumed that continuous piecewise linear polynomials are used to approximate the finite-dimensional spaces V_h and W_h.

Example 4.1 (a linear parabolic initial boundary value problem). Consider

$$u_t - (u_x)_x + u_x + u = f(x,t) \tag{4.1}$$

with Dirichlet boundary conditions $u(0,t) = u(1,t) = 0$ for all $t \in (0,T]$, initial condition $u(x,0) = \sin(\pi x)$ for all $x \in [0,1]$, and $f(x,t) = e^{-\pi t}(\sin \pi x(1 - \pi - \pi^2) + \pi \cos \pi x)$. The exact solution to this problem can be expressed as $u(x,t) = e^{-\pi t} \sin \pi x$.

For applying the mixed finite element method, we divide $I = [0,1]$ into N uniform intervals with length $h = 1/N$. Continuous, piecewise, linear polynomials are used to approximate functions in V_h and W_h.

In Figure 4.1(a), the graph of the relative errors $E_1 = ||u - u_h||_\infty$ and $E_2 = ||v - v_h||_\infty$ is plotted as a function of the discretization step h in the log-log scale when $T = 1$. The slopes of the graphs give the computed order of convergence as approximately 2. This is in agreement with the theoretical order of convergence.

In Table 4.1, the computation of order of convergence of u and v is shown (when $T = 1$).

Example 4.2 (Burgers' equation). We consider (2.8) with Dirichlet boundary conditions $u(0,t) = u(1,t) = 0$ for all $t \in (0,T]$ and initial condition $u(x,0) = \sin(\pi x)$ for all

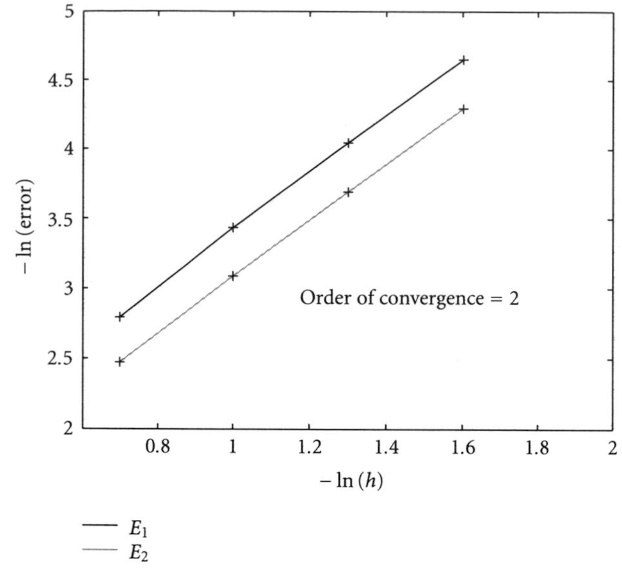

(a) Relative error versus discretization step h.

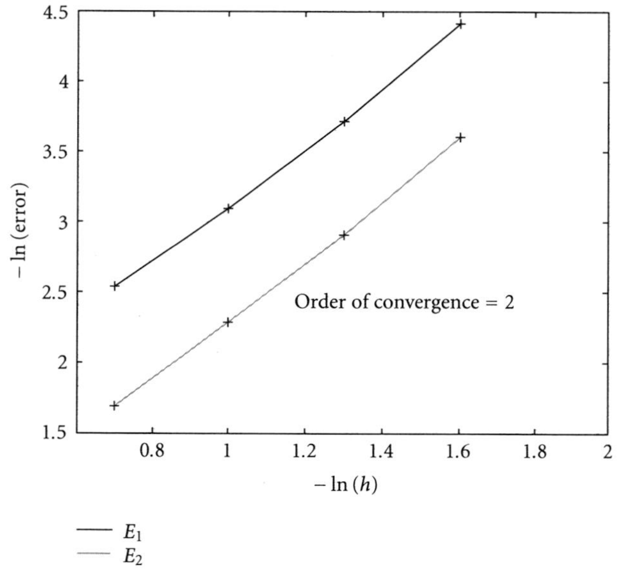

(b) Relative error versus discretization step h.

Figure 4.1

Table 4.1. The computation of order of convergence of u and v when $T = 1$.

h	$E_1 = \|u - u_h\|_\infty$	Order of convergence	$E_2 = \|v - v_h\|_\infty$	Order of convergence
1/5	0.00161062154939	—	0.00336297943347	—
1/10	3.67965936194203e-004	2.1300	8.18699280648954e-004	2.0383
1/20	8.99200357053417e-005	2.0329	2.03385937364936e-004	2.0091
1/40	2.235204441825012e-005	2.0082	5.076721598365475e-005	2.0023

Table 4.2. A comparison of numerical and exact solutions (u_h and v_h) for $\nu = 1$, $N = 8,16,32,64$, and $T = 0,0.05,0.1,0.2,0.25$ at different points in $(0,1)$.

x	T	$N = 8$	$N = 16$	$N = 32$	$N = 64$	Exact [5]
	0.0	0.6980	0.7048	0.7065	0.7070	0.7071
	0.05	0.4103	0.4124	0.4129	0.4130	0.4131
0.25	0.1	0.2536	0.2536	0.2536	0.2536	0.2536
	0.2	0.0987	0.09700	0.0966	0.0965	0.0964
	0.25	0.0617	0.0598	0.0594	0.0593	0.0592
	0.0	0.9871	0.9968	0.9992	0.9998	1.0000
	0.05	0.6034	0.6077	0.6087	0.6090	0.6091
0.5	0.1	0.3708	0.3714	0.3715	0.3716	0.3716
	0.2	0.1417	0.1393	0.1387	0.1385	0.1385
	0.25	0.0881	0.0854	0.0848	0.0846	0.0845
	0.0	0.6980	0.7048	0.7065	0.7070	0.7071
	0.05	0.4446	0.4488	0.4498	0.4501	0.4502
0.75	0.1	0.2713	0.2723	0.2725	0.2726	0.2726
	0.2	0.1017	0.1000	0.0996	0.0995	0.0994
	0.25	0.0629	0.0610	0.0605	0.0604	0.0603

$x \in [0,1]$. The exact solution to this problem can be expressed as an infinite series

$$u(x,t) = 2\pi\nu \frac{\sum_{n=1}^{\infty} a_n e^{-n^2\pi^2\nu t} n \sin(n\pi x)}{a_0 + \sum_{n=1}^{\infty} a_n e^{-n^2\pi^2\nu t} \cos(n\pi x)}, \tag{4.2}$$

where a_0, a_n, $n = 1,2,\ldots$, are the Fourier coefficients defined by $a_0 = \int_0^1 e^{-(2\pi\nu)^{-1}[1-\cos(\pi x)]}dx$ and $a_n = 2\int_0^1 e^{-(2\pi\nu)^{-1}[1-\cos(\pi x)]}\cos(n\pi x)dx$, $n = 1,2,\ldots$.

In Figure 4.1(b), the graph of the relative errors $E_1 = \|u - u_h\|_\infty$ and $E_2 = \|v - v_h\|_\infty$ is plotted as a function of the discretization step h in the log-log scale when $T = 0.1$ and $\nu = 1$. As in the linear case, the slopes of the graphs give the computed order of convergence as approximately 2. This is also in agreement with the theoretical order of convergence.

In Table 4.2, a comparison of numerical and exact solutions (u_h and v_h) (as given in [5]) for $\nu = 1$, $N = 8,16,32,64$, and $T = 0,0.05,0.1,0.2,0.25$ at different points in $(0,1)$ is shown.

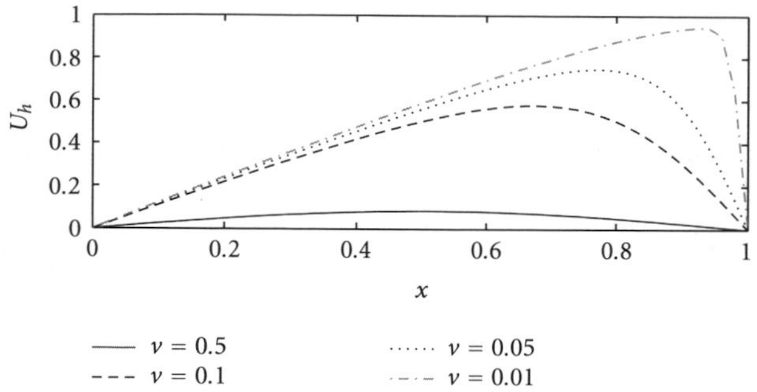

(a) Graph of U_h, $T = 0.5$.

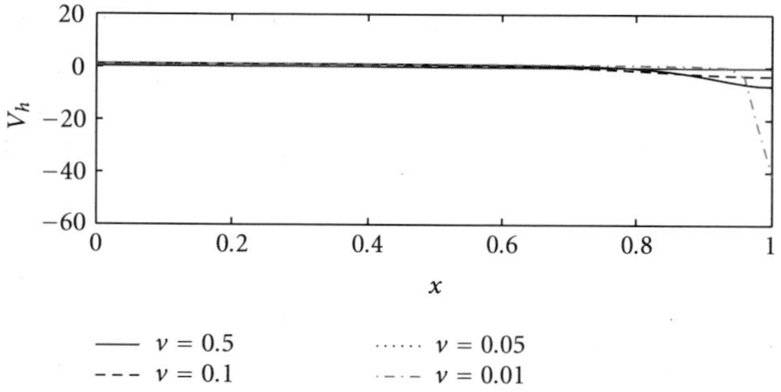

(b) Graph of V_h, $T = 0.5$.

Figure 4.2

Figures 4.2(a), 4.2(b) show the profiles of the approximate solutions and derivatives for a fixed value of $T = 0.5$ and different values of $\nu = 0.5, 0.1, 0.05, 0.01$. From Figure 4.2, we observe that for smaller value of viscosity, the propagation front is steeper. In Figures 4.3(a), 4.3(b), the profiles of approximate solutions and derivatives for a fixed value of $\nu = 0.02$ and for different values of T have been given. The graph shows that for the different values of $T = 0, 0.5, 1, 2$ the maximum point of the solution shifts towards the right.

5. Conclusions

An H^1-Galerkin mixed finite element method approximating velocity and flux simultaneously for linear and nonlinear parabolic problems has been described. A priori error estimates have been stated, and numerical experiments have been done. The mixed method allows us to use two different finite element spaces for approximating u and its flux ν. Another striking feature of this mixed method is that the LBB condition need not be satisfied. Although a higher regularity on the solution is assumed, better convergence

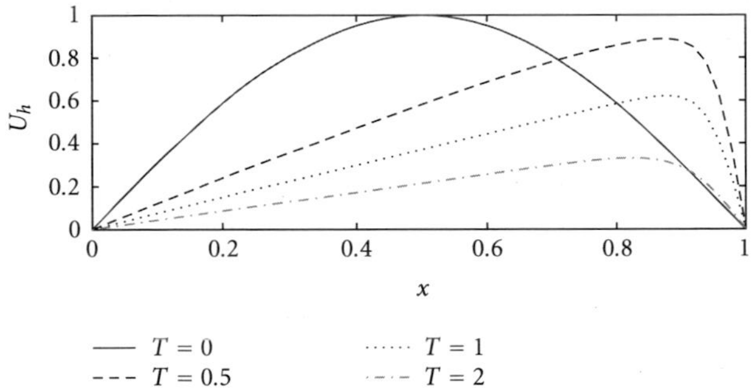

(a) Graph of U_h, $\nu = 0.02$.

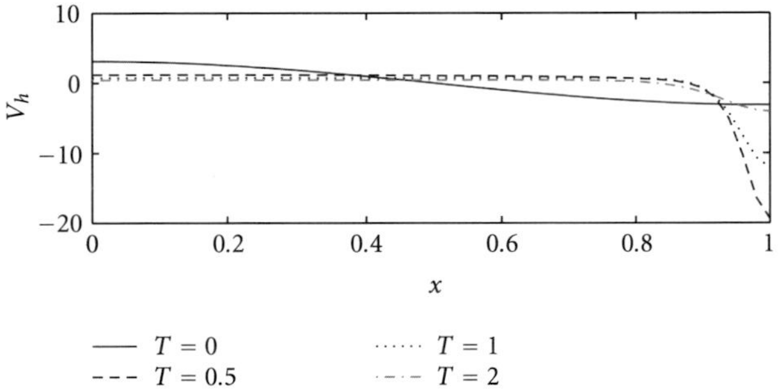

(b) Graph of V_h, $\nu = 0.02$.

Figure 4.3

results are proved for the flux. Note that if $r < k$, then standard mixed method fails, but the present method yields required error estimates.

References

[1] N. Bressan and A. Quarteroni, *An implicit/explicit spectral method for Burgers' equation*, Calcolo **23** (1986), no. 3, 265–284 (1987).

[2] J. Caldwell, P. Wanless, and A. E. Cook, *A finite element approach to Burgers' equation*, Applied Mathematical Modelling **5** (1981), no. 3, 189–193.

[3] S. L. Campbell, K. E. Brenan, and L. R. Petzold, *Numerical Solution of Initial Value Problems in Differential-Algebraic Equations*, American Elsevier Science, New York, 1989.

[4] H. Chen and Z. Jiang, *A characteristics-mixed finite element method for Burgers' equation*, Journal of Applied Mathematics & Computing **15** (2004), no. 1-2, 29–51.

[5] A. Dogan, *A Galerkin finite element approach to Burgers' equation*, Applied Mathematics and Computation **157** (2004), no. 2, 331–346.

[6] J. Douglas Jr., T. F. Dupont, and M. F. Wheeler, *H^1-Galerkin methods for the Laplace and heat equations*, Mathematical Aspect of Finite Elements in Partial Differential Equations (C. de Boor, ed.), Academic Press, New York, 1957, pp. 383–415.

[7] C. A. J. Fletcher, *A comparison of finite element and finite difference solutions of the one- and two-dimensional Burgers' equations*, Journal of Computational Physics **51** (1983), no. 1, 159–188.

[8] N. Nataraj, A. K. Pany, and S. Singh, *A new mixed finite element method for Burgers' equation*, paper communicated, 2005.

[9] A. K. Pany, *An H^1-Galerkin mixed finite element method for parabolic partial differential equations*, SIAM Journal on Numerical Analysis **35** (1998), no. 2, 712–727.
[10] V. Thomée and L. B. Wahlbin, *On Galerkin methods in semilinear parabolic problems*, SIAM Journal on Numerical Analysis **12** (1975), 378–389.

Neela Nataraj: Department of Mathematics, Indian Institute of Technology, Bombay, Powai, Mumbai 400076, India
E-mail address: neela@math.iitb.ac.in

Ambit Kumar Pany: Department of Mathematics, Indian Institute of Technology, Bombay, Powai, Mumbai 400076, India
E-mail address: ambit_math@yahoo.com

STABILITY OF SOME MODELS OF CIRCULATING FUEL NUCLEAR REACTORS—A LYAPUNOV APPROACH

SILVIU-IULIAN NICULESCU AND VLADIMIR RĂSVAN

The basic models in circulating fuel nuclear reactors are described by partial differential equations (PDE): the transients define mixed initial boundary value problems for these equations. According to a classical technique there are associated to such models some functional differential equations (FDE) which, generally speaking, are of neutral type. The paper considers these equations from the point of view of the stability of equilibria which is studied via a suitably chosen Lyapunov functional, the stability conditions being expressed through a frequency domain inequality.

1. Introduction (state of the art)

Dynamics and stability for nuclear reactors have a relatively short history—about 50 years. Various models were considered and analyzed in hundreds of papers and dozens of books. We cite here just one, the book of Goriačenko et al. [4] which is in fact the third stage in an evolution marked by two other books of Goriačenko [2, 3], because of the broad variety of models and long list of references going back to the very beginning of the problem.

The circulating fuel reactor is somehow different than the other models since the neutron kinetics is described by PDE hence the overall model displays distributed parameters regardless the structure of the external feedback block. Only a rough simplification replaces the PDE by FDE of delayed type [2, 3]. The case of this simplified model being already considered [2] and some errors corrected [11], we will consider here the model with distributed parameters. The paper is therefore organized as follows: starting from the basic model described by PDE, it is presented its analysis and transformation in order to obtain the stability analysis model. For this model, a Lyapunov-Krasovskii functional is proposed and some stability inequalities are described. Finally, a comparison is performed with other models and some open problems pointing to future research are discussed.

Hindawi Publishing Corporation
Proceedings of the Conference on Differential & Difference Equations and Applications, pp. 861–870

2. The model and its properties

We start from the model of [4] where some normalization of the state variables in the neutron/hydraulic kinetics is performed

$$\frac{dn}{dt} = \left(\varrho - \sum_1^m \beta_i\right)n + \sum_1^m \beta_i \bar{c}_i(t),$$
$$\bar{c}_i(t) = \int_0^h \varphi(\eta)c_i(\eta,t)d\eta, \tag{2.1}$$
$$\frac{\partial c_i}{\partial t} + \frac{\partial c_i}{\partial \eta} + \sigma_i c_i = \sigma_i \varphi(\eta)n(t), \quad 0 \le \eta \le h,\ t > 0,$$
$$c_i(0,t) = c_i(h,t), \quad \forall t, i = 1,\dots,m,$$

where n, c_i are the normalized state variables representing the neutron density and the delayed circulating neutrons density, respectively. The assumptions about the coefficients are the usual ones, based on their physical significance: $\beta_i > 0$, $\sigma_i > 0$. The function $\varphi : [0,h] \mapsto \mathbb{R}_+$ is supposed to be continuously differentiable almost everywhere and extended through h-periodicity to the entire real axis. The reactivity ϱ is supposed to depend linearly on the neutron density n and on the external variables (temperature, Xenon poisoning, control).

(A) The properties of (2.1) may be studied as usually in the case of hyperbolic PDE, by associating a system of FDE via integration along the characteristics (see, e.g., [10]). Here the only family of characteristics is defined by the differential equation

$$\frac{d\eta}{dt} = 1. \tag{2.2}$$

If $(n(t), c_i(\eta,t))$ is a solution of (2.1), then we may define

$$q_i(t) = c_i(h,t) \tag{2.3}$$

and find the following equation for $q_i(t)$:

$$q_i(t) = e^{-h\sigma_i}q_i(t-h) + \sigma_i \int_{-h}^0 e^{\lambda\sigma_i}\varphi(\lambda)n(t+\lambda)d\lambda, \quad t > h \tag{2.4}$$

with the initial condition

$$q_i^0(t) = e^{-t\sigma_i}c_i^0(h-t) + \sigma_i \int_{-t}^0 e^{\lambda\sigma_i}\varphi(\lambda)n(t+\lambda)d\lambda, \quad 0 \le t \le h, \tag{2.5}$$

where $c_i^0(\eta) = c_i(\eta,0)$ represent the initial conditions for (2.1).

The solution of (2.4) may be constructed by steps on $[kh,(k+1)h]$ for given $c_i^0(\eta)$ and $n(t)$, $t > 0$. Obviously, $q_i(t)$ has the degree of smoothness of its initial conditions and of $n(t)$ except the discontinuities at kh which represent the propagation of the discontinuity at h.

This last discontinuity is due to the "mismatch" of the initial and boundary conditions: in general *the initial conditions need not satisfy the boundary conditions* since they are, as usually, incorporating the effect of the unknown short-period disturbances.

Conversely, if we consider a solution of (2.4) defined via (2.5) by the differentiable initial condition $c_i^0(\eta)$, then

$$c_i(\eta,t) = e^{(h-\eta)\sigma_i}\left[q_i(t+h-\eta) - \sigma_i\int_{-h+\eta}^{0} e^{\lambda\sigma_i}\varphi(\lambda)n(t+h+\lambda-\eta)d\lambda\right] \tag{2.6}$$

verifies the PDE almost everywhere, that is, except the characteristics $t-\eta = kh$, $k = 0,1,2,\ldots$, the boundary conditions and the initial ones. Consequently, we may compute $\bar{c}_i(t)$ of (2.1) using the solution of (2.4) with the initial condition (2.5).

This expression may be substituted in the first equation of (2.1) to obtain a functional equation. Summarizing we may associate to (2.1) the following system of FDE:

$$\begin{aligned}\frac{dn}{dt} &= \left(\varrho - \sum_1^m \beta_i\right)n + \sum_1^m \beta_i\sigma_i \times \int_{-h}^{0} e^{\lambda\sigma_i}\left(\int_{-\lambda}^{h} \varphi(\theta)\varphi(\theta+\lambda)d\theta\right)n(t+\lambda)d\lambda \\ &\quad + \sum_1^m \beta_i \int_{-h}^{0} e^{\theta\sigma_i}\varphi(-\theta)q_i(t+\theta)d\theta,\end{aligned} \tag{2.7}$$

$$q_i(t) = e^{-h\sigma_i}q_i(t-h) + \sigma_i\int_{-h}^{0} e^{\lambda\sigma_i}\varphi(\lambda)n(t+\lambda)d\lambda, \quad t>h$$

with the initial conditions

$$\begin{aligned}\frac{dn}{dt} &= \left(\varrho - \sum_1^m \beta_i\right)n + \sum_1^m \beta_i\sigma_i \int_{0}^{t}\left(\int_{0}^{h} \varphi(\theta)\varphi(\theta+\lambda-t)d\theta\right)e^{-\sigma_i(t-\lambda)}n(t+\lambda)d\lambda \\ &\quad + \sum_1^m \beta_i e^{-\sigma_i t}\int_{0}^{h} \varphi(t+\theta)c_i^0(t+\theta)d\theta, \quad n(0) = n_0,\end{aligned} \tag{2.8}$$

$$q_i(t) = e^{-t\sigma_i}c_i^0(h-t) + \sigma_i\int_{-t}^{0} e^{\lambda\sigma_i}\varphi(\lambda)n(t+\lambda)d\lambda, \quad 0<t<h.$$

Observe that, given n_0, we may solve the integrodifferential equation to find $n(t)$ on $(0,h)$ and then using the difference equation to find $q_i(t)$ on $(0,h)$. Then we may proceed to the construction of the solution of (2.7) for $t>h$ we have proved in fact.

THEOREM 2.1. *Let $n(t)$, $c_i(\eta,t)$, $i = 1,\ldots,m$, $0\le\eta\le h$, $t>0$, be a solution of (2.1) defined by the initial conditions n_0, $c_i^0(\eta)$, $i = 1,\ldots,m$, $0\le\eta\le h$. Then $n(t)$, $q_i(t)$, $i = 1,\ldots,m$, $t>0$, where $q_i(t) = c_i(h,t)$ is a solution of (2.7) with the initial conditions (2.8). Conversely, let $n(t)$, $q_i(t)$, $i = 1,\ldots,m$, $t>0$, be a solution of (2.7) on $t>h$ and of (2.8) on $0<t<h$ with the initial conditions n_0, $c_i^0(\eta)$, $i = 1,\ldots,m$, $0\le\eta\le h$. Then $n(t)$, $c_i(\eta,t)$, $i = 1,\ldots,m$, $0\le\eta\le h$, $t>0$, with $c_i(\eta,t)$ defined by (2.6) is a solution of (2.1) defined by the initial conditions n_0, $c_i^0(\eta)$, $i = 1,\ldots,m$, $0\le\eta\le h$.*

This one-to-one correspondence of the solutions for the two mathematical objects (2.1) and (2.7)-(2.8) allows substituting analysis of one of them by the analysis of the other. System (2.7)-(2.8) appears as closer to control engineer's representations. Worth mentioning, nevertheless, that it belongs to the class of FDE of neutral type and this is due to various reasons (see [10, 12, 13]).

(B) We will not insist on the basic theory for (2.7)-(2.8), that is, existence, uniqueness, and data dependence since the standard tools of the theory of neutral FDE are available (e.g., [7]). A more interesting subject is concerned with physical significance of the state variables. They have to be positive and this property reads as existence of an invariant set of (2.7)-(2.8). More precisely, we have the following theorem.

THEOREM 2.2. *Consider systems (2.1) and (2.7)-(2.8) with the initial conditions* $n_0 \geq 0$, $c_i^0(\eta) \geq 0$, $i = 1,\dots,m$, $0 \leq \eta \leq h$. *Then* $n(t) > 0$, $q_i(t) > 0$, $c_i(\eta,t) > 0$, $i = 1,\dots,m$, $0 \leq \eta \leq h$.

Proof. This result is proved by straightforward computation, in the spirit of the proofs of this kind (see [1, 6]). Namely, we take first (2.8) and obtain the property on $[0,h]$. Since $\varphi(\lambda) \geq 0$ and $c_i^0(\lambda) \geq 0$, the last integral in the integro-differential equation of (2.8) is positive. Since $n_0 \geq 0$, we will have $n(t) \geq 0$ on some interval $[0,\hat{t})$ for continuity reasons hence the first integral is positive; therefore $dn/dt \geq 0$ on $[0,\hat{t})$ hence $n(t) \geq 0$ on $[0,h]$; this shows that $q_i(t) \geq 0$ on $[0,h]$ from the second equation of (2.8). We switch now to (2.7) constructing the solution by steps. On $[h,2h]$ the two integrals in the RHS of the first equation are positive hence $n(t) \geq 0$ on this interval; from the second equation we will have that $q_i(t) \geq 0$ on this interval hence $n(t) \geq 0$ on $[2h,3h]$ and so forth.

It remains to show that $c_i(\eta,t) \geq 0$, $i = 1,\dots,m$, $0 \leq \eta \leq h$. For this we use (2.6) and take into account (2.4) and (2.5), which ends the proof. □

3. Equilibria, deviations, and the external dynamics

(A) Let n_∞ be a given level of the neutron density (which is a measure of the available power of the reactor). The steady-state solution of (2.1) follows by taking 0 the time derivatives

$$
\begin{gathered}
0 = \left(\varrho - \sum_1^m \beta_i\right) n_\infty + \sum_1^m \beta_i \bar{\bar{c}}_i, \\
\bar{\bar{c}}_i = \int_0^h \varphi(\eta)\hat{c}_i(\eta)\,d\eta, \\
\frac{d\hat{c}_i}{d\eta} + \sigma_i \hat{c}_i = \sigma_i \varphi(\eta) n_\infty, \quad 0 \leq \eta \leq h, \\
\hat{c}_i(0) = \hat{c}_i(h), \quad i = 1,\dots,m,
\end{gathered}
\tag{3.1}
$$

where $\hat{c}_i(\eta)$ are the steady-state distributions of the delayed circulating neutrons. A straightforward computation will give

$$
\begin{gathered}
\hat{c}_i(\eta) = \left[\frac{e^{-h\sigma_i}}{1 - e^{-h\sigma_i}}\left(\int_0^h e^{\theta\sigma_i}\varphi(\theta)\,d\theta\right) + \int_0^\eta e^{\theta\sigma_i}\varphi(\theta)\,d\theta\right]\sigma_i e^{-\eta\sigma_i} n_\infty, \\
\bar{\bar{c}}_i = \sigma_i \int_0^h e^{-\eta\sigma_i}\hat{c}_i(\eta)\,d\eta = n_\infty \xi_i.
\end{gathered}
\tag{3.2}
$$

The introduction of ξ_i is just a notation *but it may be shown that* $0 < \xi_i < 1$*; these inequalities will turn useful in further development.* For instance, by substituting $\bar{\bar{c}}_i$ in the first equation of (3.1) we find an equation that has to be fulfilled for any $n_\infty \neq 0$, that is, the reactor has available power at any (reasonable) level and this level is controlled by the reactivity $\varrho > 0$ which holds provided $\varrho(n_\infty) = \sum_1^m \beta_i(1-\xi_i) > 0$ which at its turn requires $\xi_i < 1$.

The steady-state solution of (2.7) follows from (3.2) since $\bar{q}_i = \hat{c}_i(h)$ and is given by $(n_\infty, \hat{c}_i(h))$. By straightforward computation it is shown that $(n_\infty, \bar{q}_i)$ thus defined verifies (2.7) with $dn/dt = 0$.

(B) Following the standard line in control and stability studies, we introduce the deviations with respect to the steady state and the system in deviations (e.g., [6])

$$\zeta(t) = n(t) - 1, \qquad y_i(\eta,t) = c_i(\eta,t) - \hat{c}_i(\eta),$$
$$\bar{y}_i(t) = \left(\frac{1}{\xi_i}\right)(\bar{c}_i(t) - \xi_i), \qquad \nu = \varrho - \sum_1^m \beta_i(1-\xi_i), \tag{3.3}$$

(we took $n_\infty = 1$ without any loss of generality).

Using the steady-state equations we find the PDE system in deviations which are the same as in (2.1) due to linearity. Therefore we may associate the FDE

$$\frac{d\zeta}{dt} = \nu(1+\zeta) - \sum_1^m \beta_i\left[\xi_i\zeta(t) - \sigma_i\int_{-h}^0 e^{\lambda\sigma_i}\left(\int_{-\lambda}^h \varphi(\theta)\varphi(\theta+\lambda)d\theta\right)\zeta(t+\lambda)d\lambda\right]$$
$$+\sum_1^m \beta_i\int_{-h}^0 e^{\theta\sigma_i}\varphi(-\theta)y_i(t+\theta)d\theta, \tag{3.4}$$
$$y_i(t) = e^{-h\sigma_i}y_i(t-h) + \sigma_i\int_{-h}^0 e^{\lambda\sigma_i}\varphi(\lambda)\zeta(t+\lambda)d\lambda, \quad t>h,\ i=1,\dots,m$$

with an associated system of the initial conditions.

Note that (3.4) might have been obtained using (2.7) and (2.8). From Theorem 2.2 and from (3.3) it follows that system (3.4) has an invariant set defined by

$$n(t) = 1+\zeta(t) > 0, \quad q_i(t) = \bar{q}_i + y_i(t) > 0, \quad i = 1,\dots,m, \tag{3.5}$$

while the system of PDE in deviations has the invariant set

$$n(t) = 1+\zeta(t) > 0,$$
$$c_i(\eta,t) = \hat{c}_i(\eta) + y_i(\eta,t) > 0, \quad 0 \le \eta \le h,\ i = 1,\dots,m. \tag{3.6}$$

(C) We will consider now the dynamics of the external circuits: we assume them linear and written in deviations with respect to the corresponding steady state ensuring the steady state of the reactor; the deviation of the reactivity will be viewed as a linear output of the external block whose input is the neutron density

$$\frac{dx}{dt} = Ax + b\zeta(t),$$
$$\nu = -(c^*x + h_0\zeta(t)). \tag{3.7}$$

In this way the external block acts as a power level controller for the nuclear reactor. The overall equations of the feedback system in deviations are as follows:

$$\begin{aligned}
\frac{dx}{dt} &= Ax + b\zeta, \\
\frac{d\zeta}{dt} &= -(c^*x + h_0\zeta)(1+\zeta) \\
&\quad - \sum_1^m \beta_i \left[\xi_i\zeta(t) - \sigma_i \int_{-h}^0 e^{\lambda\sigma_i} \left(\int_{-\lambda}^h \varphi(\theta)\varphi(\theta+\lambda)d\theta \right) \zeta(t+\lambda)d\lambda \right] \\
&\quad + \sum_1^m \beta_i \int_{-h}^0 e^{\theta\sigma_i}\varphi(-\theta)y_i(t+\theta)d\theta, \\
y_i(t) &= e^{-h\sigma_i}y_i(t-h) + \sigma_i \int_{-h}^0 e^{\lambda\sigma_i}\varphi(\lambda)\zeta(t+\lambda)d\lambda, \quad t > h,\ i = 1,\dots,m.
\end{aligned} \tag{3.8}$$

We have here a *system of coupled delay differential and difference equations*, with lumped and distributed delays [12, 13]. For the stability of the zero steady state of this system, it is important to point out that the difference operator is stable, that is, the essential spectrum is located inside the unit disk $\mathbb{D}_1 \subset \mathbb{C}$: its eigenvalues are $e^{-h\sigma_i} < 1$.

4. Stability of the linearized system

The linearized system is obtained from (3.8) by neglecting the quadratic terms in the equation of ζ,

$$\begin{aligned}
\frac{dx}{dt} &= Ax + b\zeta, \\
\frac{d\zeta}{dt} &= -c^*x - \left(h_0 + \sum_1^m \beta_i\xi_i \right)\zeta(t) \\
&\quad + \sum_1^m \beta_i\sigma_i \int_{-h}^0 e^{\lambda\sigma_i} \left(\int_{-\lambda}^h \varphi(\theta)\varphi(\theta+\lambda)d\theta \right) \zeta(t+\lambda)d\lambda \\
&\quad + \sum_1^m \beta_i \int_{-h}^0 e^{\theta\sigma_i}\varphi(-\theta)y_i(t+\theta)d\theta, \\
y_i(t) &= e^{-h\sigma_i}y_i(t-h) + \sigma_i \int_{-h}^0 e^{\lambda\sigma_i}\varphi(\lambda)\zeta(t+\lambda)d\lambda, \quad t > h,\ i = 1,\dots,m.
\end{aligned} \tag{4.1}$$

This system is of the form considered in [8] but with a specific structure: some matrices are diagonal, some coefficients are positive, and so forth. We will associate to (4.1) a quadratic Lyapunov functional having the structure in [8] with some differences: some matrices are diagonal, some items under the integrals are varying thus giving more freedom aiming to fulfill the conditions required for a linear matrix inequality of negative sign.

More precisely, we take the following Lyapunov functional:

$$\begin{aligned} V&(x,\zeta(0),\zeta(\cdot),y_i(\cdot)) \\ &= x^*Px + \frac{1}{2}\zeta(0)^2 + \int_{-h}^{0} \psi_1(\lambda)\zeta^2(\lambda)d\lambda \\ &+ \sum_{1}^{m}\int_{-h}^{0} \psi_2^i(\lambda)y_i^2(\lambda)d\lambda, \end{aligned} \tag{4.2}$$

where $\psi_1 : [-h,0] \mapsto \mathbb{R}_+$ and $\psi_2^i : [-h,0] \mapsto \mathbb{R}_+$ have to be chosen, as well as the positive definite matrix P, in order to obtain a nonincreasing functional along system's trajectories. Making the following notations:

$$\begin{aligned} \kappa_1^i(\lambda) &= \beta_i e^{\lambda\sigma_i}\varphi(-\lambda), \qquad \kappa_2^i(\lambda) = \sigma_i e^{\lambda\sigma_i}\varphi(\lambda), \\ \bar{\kappa}_1(\theta) &= \sum_{1}^{m}\int_{-h}^{\theta} \kappa_1^i(\theta-\lambda)\kappa_2^i(\lambda)d\lambda, \end{aligned} \tag{4.3}$$

we obtain after simple but tedious manipulation based on standard inequalities the following estimate of the derivative function:

$$\begin{aligned} W(x,\zeta(0),\zeta(\cdot),y_i(\cdot)) &\le x^*P(Ax+b\zeta(0)) + (Ax+b\zeta(0))^*Px - \zeta(0)c^*x \\ &- \left(h_0 + \sum_{1}^{m}\beta_i\xi_i - \psi_1(0)\right)\zeta^2(0) - \psi_1(-h)\,|\,\zeta(-h)\,|^2 \\ &+ |\,\zeta(0)\,|\left(\sup_{-h\le\theta\le 0}\bar{\kappa}_1(\theta)\right)\int_{-h}^{0}|\,\zeta(\theta)\,|\,d\theta \\ &+ |\,\zeta(0)\,|\sum_{1}^{m}\left(\sup_{-h\le\theta\le 0}\kappa_1^i(\theta)\right)\int_{-h}^{0}|\,y_i(\theta)\,|\,d\theta \\ &- \sum_{1}^{m}\left(\inf_{-h\le\theta\le 0}\dot{\psi}_2^i(\theta)\right)\left(\int_{-h}^{0}|\,y_i(\theta)\,|\,d\theta\right)^2 \\ &- \left(\inf_{-h\le\theta\le 0}\sqrt{\dot{\psi}_1(\theta) - \int_{-h}^{0}\sum_{1}^{m}\psi_2^i(0)\kappa_2^i(\lambda)d\lambda}\right)\left(\int_{-h}^{0}|\,\zeta(\theta)\,|\,d\theta\right)^2 \end{aligned}$$

$$+2\sum_{1}^{m} |\gamma_i(-h)|\,\psi_2^i(0)e^{-h\sigma_i}\left(\sup_{-h\le\theta\le 0}\kappa_2^i(\theta)\right)\int_{-h}^{0}|\zeta(\theta)|\,d\theta$$
$$-\sum_{1}^{m}\left(\psi_2^i(-h)-\psi_2^i(0)e^{-2h\sigma_i}\right)|\gamma_i(-h)|^2. \tag{4.4}$$

The RHS of (4.4) is a quadratic form in the following arguments:

$$x,\qquad \zeta(0),\qquad \int_{-h}^{0}|\zeta(\theta)|\,d\theta,\qquad |\zeta(-h)|,$$
$$\int_{-h}^{0}|\gamma_i(\theta)|\,d\theta,\qquad |\gamma_i(-h)|, \tag{4.5}$$

where the quadratic term $|\zeta(-h)|^2$ is helpful but less significant. The quadratic form in x and $\zeta(0)$ suggests making use of the Yakubovich-Kalman-Popov lemma (e.g., [9]) which at its turn would send to a *Welton-type criterion* [3, 9] for stability; the result is as follows.

THEOREM 4.1. *Consider system (4.1) under the assumptions of Section 2 concerning the coefficients. If A is a Hurwitz matrix and the following frequency domain inequality holds*

$$h_0+\Re c^*(\imath\omega I-A)^{-1}b\ge 0, \tag{4.6}$$

then system (4.1) is exponentially stable.

Outline of proof. The proof of this *main result* of the paper is performed in several steps.

(A) We consider the Lyapunov functional (4.2) whose derivative along the solutions satisfies (4.4). The frequency domain inequality (4.6) ensures via Yakubovich-Kalman-Popov lemma existence of a matrix $P>0$ and of some $\delta_0>0$ such that

$$x^*P(Ax+b\zeta(0))+(Ax+b\zeta(0))^*Px-\zeta(0)c^*x$$
$$-\left(h_0+\sum_{1}^{m}\beta_i\xi_i-\psi_1(0)\right)\zeta^2(0)\le-\delta_0\left(|x|^2+\zeta^2(0)\right) \tag{4.7}$$

provided $\psi_1(0)<h_0+\sum_1^m\beta_i\xi_i$.

(B) The choice of $\psi_1(\cdot)>0$ and $\psi_2^i(\cdot)>0$ is possible in order that the RHS of (4.4) should be negative definite in its arguments enumerated above. From (4.4) it is also clear that this choice allows $\psi_1(0)>0$ small enough to fulfill the inequality at (A), and also that $\psi_1(\cdot)$ and $\psi_2^i(\cdot)>0$ are *well delimited from 0.* Therefore we obtain from the Lyapunov inequality

$$\delta_1\left(|x(t)|^2+|\zeta(t)|^2\right)+\delta_1\left(\int_{-h}^{0}|\zeta(t+\theta)|^2d\theta+\sum_{1}^{m}\int_{-h}^{0}|\gamma_i(t+\theta)|^2d\theta\right)$$
$$\le V(x(0),\zeta(0),\zeta_0(\cdot),\gamma_{i0}(\cdot)) \tag{4.8}$$

which gives Lyapunov stability.

For the asymptotic behavior we follow the approach of [9]: both $x(t)$ and $\zeta(t)$ are in $L^2(0,\infty)$ (see (4.8)) and uniformly continuous since their derivatives are bounded (see (4.1) and take again (4.8) into account). The Barbălat lemma [9] gives $\lim_{t\to\infty} x(t) = 0$, $\lim_{t\to\infty} \zeta(t) = 0$. For $y_i(t)$, we use the difference equation

$$y_i(t) = e^{-h\sigma_i} y_i(t-h) + \Omega_i(t), \tag{4.9}$$

where $\lim_{t\to\infty} \Omega_i(t) = 0$. Using the asymptoticity theorems of [9] we deduce $\lim_{t\to\infty} y_i(t) = 0$.

(C) Using a construction of Persidskii type [5] it is proved in the specific case that for a linear system the asymptotic stability is exponential. The proof ends. □

5. Conclusions and further research problems

The circulating fuel reactor is, technologically speaking, at least half of century old if we are to judge according to the very first published paper around 1954. This technology could be by now obsolete, however the mathematical models might be still interesting from a purely scientific point of view since a lot of problems are still challenging the mathematical researcher.

The model considered in this paper has been obtained in a rigorous way, without approximating assumptions, by applying the integration along the characteristics of the solutions of the PDE and taking into account the boundary conditions. Due to its structure, it is much alike to the quite popular system of lossless propagation [10, 12]. For this reason we have been tempted to apply our results concerning the use of a specific Lyapunov-Krasovskii quadratic functional [8]. Not only that a Welton-type criterion has been obtained but also a linear matrix inequality has been shown as feasible by elementary manipulation. The result is nevertheless valid for the linearized model since the basic results of [8] are such.

References

[1] R. E. Bellman, *Introduction to Matrix Analysis*, McGraw-Hill, New York, 1960.

[2] V. D. Goriačenko, *Methods of Stability Theory in the Dynamics of Nuclear Reactors*, Atomizdat, Moscow, 1971.

[3] ———, *Methods for Nuclear Reactor Stability Studies*, Atomizdat, Moscow, 1977.

[4] V. D. Goriačenko, S. L. Zolotarev, and V. A. Kolchin, *Qualitative Methods in Nuclear Reactor Dynamics*, Energoatomizdat, Moscow, 1988.

[5] A. Halanay, *Differential Equations: Stability, Oscillations, Time Lags*, Academic Press, New York, 1966.

[6] A. Halanay and Vl. Răsvan, *Applications of Lyapunov Methods to Stability*, Kluwer Academic, Dordrecht, 1993.

[7] J. K. Hale and S. M. Verduyn Lunel, *Introduction to Functional-Differential Equations*, Applied Mathematical Sciences, vol. 99, Springer, New York, 1993.

[8] S.-I. Niculescu, Vl. Răsvan, and K. Gu, *On delay-dependent stability in lossless propagation models: a Liapunov-Krasovskii analysis*, Proceedings of 6th Mediterranean Conference on Automation and Control (IEEE-MED ’03), Rhodes, June 2003.

[9] V.-M. Popov, *Hyperstability of Control Systems*, Springer, New York, 1973.

[10] Vl. Răsvan, *Absolute Stability of Time Lag Control Systems*, Editura Academiei, Bucharest, 1975, improved Russian version by Nauka, Moscow, 1983.

[11] ———, *A stability result for a system of differential equations with delay describing a controlled circulant fuel nuclear reactor*, Revue Roumaine de Mathématiques Pures et Appliquées **39** (1994), no. 4, 365–373.

[12] ———, *Dynamical systems with lossless propagation and neutral functional differential equations*, Proceedings of Mathematical Theory of Networks and Systems (MTNS '98), Il Poligrafo, Padova, 1998, pp. 527–531.

[13] ———, *Dynamical systems with lossless propagation and delay differential algebraic equations*, Proceedings of 6th SIAM Conference on Control and Its Applications, Louisiana, July 2005.

Silviu-Iulian Niculescu: HEUDIASYC (UMR CNRS 6599), Centre de Recherche de Royallieu, Université de Technologie de Compiègne, BP. 20529, 60205 Compiègne, France
E-mail address: niculescu@hds.utc.fr

Vladimir Răsvan: Department of Automatic Control, University of Craiova, A. I. Cuza 13, Craiova, RO-200585, Romania
E-mail address: vrasvan@automation.ucv.ro

INFINITESIMAL FOURIER TRANSFORMATION FOR THE SPACE OF FUNCTIONALS

TAKASHI NITTA AND TOMOKO OKADA

A functional is a function from the space of functions to a number field, for example, $f : \{a : (-\infty,\infty) \to (-\infty,\infty)\} \to (-\infty,\infty)$. These three ∞'s are written as the same notation, but these original meanings are quite different. The purpose of this proceeding is to formulate a Fourier transformation for the space of functionals, as an infinitesimal meaning. For it we divide three ∞'s to three types of infinities. We extend $\mathbb{R}$ to $^*({}^*\mathbb{R})$ under the base of nonstandard methods for the construction. The domain of a functional is the set of all internal functions from a $*$-finite lattice to a $*$-finite lattice with a double meaning. Considering a $*$-finite lattice with a double meaning, we find how to treat the domain for a functional in our theory of Fourier transformation, and calculate two typical examples.

1. Introduction

Recently, many kinds of geometric invariants are defined on manifolds and they are used for studying low-dimensional manifolds, for example, Donaldson's invariant, Chern-Simon's invariant, and so forth. They are originally defined as Feynman path integrals in physics. The Feynman path integral is in a sense an integral of a functional on an infinite-dimensional space of functions. We would like to study the Feynman path integral and the originally defined invariants. For the purpose, we would be sure that it is necessary to construct a theory of Fourier transformation on the space of functionals. For it, as the later argument, we would need many stages of infinitesimals and infinites, that is, we need to put a concept of stage on the field of real numbers. We use nonstandard methods to develop a theory of Fourier transformation on the space of functionals.

Feynman [3] used the concept of his path integral for physical quantizations. The word "physical quantizations" has two meanings: one is for quantum mechanics and the other is for quantum field theory. We usually use the same word "Feynman path integral." However, the meanings included in "Feynman path integral" have two sides, according to the above. One is of quantum mechanics and the other is of quantum field theory. To

Hindawi Publishing Corporation
Proceedings of the Conference on Differential & Difference Equations and Applications, pp. 871–883

understand the Feynman path integral of the first type, Fujiwara [4] studied it as a fundamental solution. In stochastic mathematics, Loeb [10] constructed Loeb measure theory and investigated Brownian motion that relates to Itô integral [6]. Anderson [2] developed it. Kamae [7] proved Ergodic theory using nonstandard analysis. From a nonstandard approach, Nelson [16], Nakamura [14, 15] studied Schrödinger equation, Dirac equation and Loo [11, 12] calculated rigidly the quantum mechanics of harmonic oscillator. It corresponds to functional analysis on the space of functions in standard mathematics.

On the other hand, we would like to construct a frame of a path integral of the second type, that is, a functional analysis on the space of functionals. Our idea is the following: in nonstandard analysis, model theory, especially non-well-founded set theory [18], we can extend $\mathbb{R}$ to $^*\mathbb{R}$, furthermore a double extension $^\star({}^*\mathbb{R})$, and so forth. For formulation of a path integral of the first type, it was necessary only one extension $^*\mathbb{R}$ of $\mathbb{R}$ in nonstandard analysis [1]. In fact, there exists an infinite in $^*\mathbb{R}$, however there are no elements in $^*\mathbb{R}$, that is greater than images of the infinite for any functions. The same situation occurs for infinitesimals. Hence we consider the need of a further extension of $\mathbb{R}$ to construct a formulation of a path integral of the second type. If the further extension satisfies some condition, the extension $^\star({}^*\mathbb{R})$ has a higher degree of infinite and also infinitesimal. We use these to formulate the space of functionals. We would like to try to construct a theory of Fourier transformation on the space of functionals and calculate two typical examples of it.

Historically, for the theories of Fourier transformations in nonstandard analysis, in 1972, Luxemburg [13] developed a theory of Fourier series with *-finite summation on the basis of nonstandard analysis. The basic idea of his approach is to replace the usual ∞ of the summation with an infinite natural number N. He approximated the Fourier transformation on the unit circle by the Fourier transformation on the group of Nth roots of unity.

Takeuti [19] introduced an infinitesimal delta function δ, and Kinoshita [8, 9] defined in 1988 a discrete Fourier transformation for each even *-finite number $H(\in {}^*\mathbb{R})$: $(F\varphi)(p) = \sum_{-H^2/2\le z<H^2/2}(1/H)\exp(-2\pi i p(1/H)z)\varphi((1/H)z)$, called "infinitesimal Fourier transformation." He developed a theory for the infinitesimal Fourier transformation and studied the distribution space deeply, and proved the same properties hold as usual Fourier transformation of $L^2(\mathbb{R})$. Especially saying, the delta function δ satisfies that $\delta^2,\delta^2,\ldots,\sqrt{\delta},\ldots$ are also hyperfunctions as their meaning, and $F\delta = 1$, $F\delta^2 = H$, $F\delta^3 = H^2,\ldots$, $F\sqrt{\delta} = 1/\sqrt{H},\ldots$.

In 1989, Gordon [5] independently defined a generic, discrete Fourier transformation for each infinitesimal Δ and *-finite number M, defined by

$$(F_{\Delta,M}\varphi)(p) = \sum_{-M\le z\le M} \Delta \exp(-2\pi i p\Delta z)\varphi(\Delta z). \tag{1.1}$$

He studied under that condition the discrete Fourier transformation $F_{\Delta,M}$ approximates the usual Fourier transformation $\mathcal{F}$ for $L^2(\mathbb{R})$. His proposed condition is (A') of his notation: let Δ be an infinitely small and M an infinitely large natural number such that $M\cdot\Delta$ is infinitely large. He showed that under the condition (A') the standard part of $F_{\Delta,M}\varphi$ approximates the usual $\mathcal{F}\varphi$ for $\varphi\in L^2(\mathbb{R})$. One of the different points between Kinoshita's and Gordon's is that whether or not there is the term $\Delta \exp(-2\pi ip\Delta M)\varphi(\Delta M)$ in the summation of their two definitions. We mention that both definitions are the same for the standard part of the dicrete Fourier transformation for $\varphi \in L^2(\mathbb{R})$ and Kinoshita's definition satisfies the condition (A') for an even infinite number H if $\Delta = 1/H$, $M = H^2/2$.

We will extend their theory of Fourier transformation for the space of functions to a theory of Fourier transformation for the space of functionals. For the purpose of this, we will represent a space of functions from $\mathbb{R}$ to $\mathbb{R}$ as a space of functions from a set of lattices in an infinite interval $[-H/2, H/2)$ to a set of lattices in an infinite interval $[-H'/2, H'/2)$. We consider what H' is to treat any function from $\mathbb{R}$ to $\mathbb{R}$. If we put a function $a(x) = x^n$ $(n \in \mathbb{Z}^+)$, we need that $H'/2$ is greater than $(H/2)^n$, and if we choose a function $a(x) = e^x$, we need that $H'/2$ is greater than $e^{H/2}$. If we choose any infinite number, there exists a function whose image is beyond the infinite number. Since we treat all functions from $\mathbb{R}$ to $\mathbb{R}$, we need to put $H'/2$ as an infinite number greater than any infinite number of ${}^*\mathbb{R}$. Hence we make $[-H'/2, H'/2)$ not in ${}^*\mathbb{R}$ but in ${}^\star({}^*\mathbb{R})$, where ${}^\star({}^*\mathbb{R})$ is a double extension of $\mathbb{R}$, that is, H' is an infinite number in ${}^\star({}^*\mathbb{R})$. First we will develop an infinitesimal Fourier transformation theory for the space of functionals, and second we calculate fundamental two examples for our infinitesimal Fourier transformation. In our case, we define an infinitesimal delta function δ satisfies $F\delta = 1$, $F\delta^2 = H'^{H^2}$, $F\delta^3 = H'^{2H^2}, \ldots, F\sqrt{\delta} = H'^{-(1/2)H^2}, \ldots$, that is, $F\delta^2, F\delta^3, \ldots$ are infinite and $F\sqrt{\delta}, \ldots$ are infinitesimal. These are a functional f and an infinite-dimensional Gaussian distribution g, where $\mathbf{st}(f(\alpha)) = \exp(\pi i \int_{-\infty}^{\infty} \alpha^2(t)dt)$, $\mathbf{st}(g(\alpha)) = \exp(-\pi \int_{-\infty}^{\infty} \alpha^2(t)dt)$ for $\alpha \in L^2(\mathbb{R})$. We obtain the following results of standard meanings: $(Ff)(b) = \overline{f(b)}$ or $-\overline{f(b)}$ and $(Fg)(b) = C_2(b)g(b)$, $\mathbf{st}(C_2(b)) = 1$ if b is finite-valued. Our infinitesimal Fourier transformation of g is also g when the domain of g is standard.

2. Preliminaries

To explain our infinitesimal Fourier transformation for the space of functionals, we introduce Kinoshita and Gordon's infinitesimal Fourier transformation for the space of functions. We fix an infinite set Λ and an ultrafilter F of Λ so that F includes the Fréchet filter $F_0(\Lambda)$. We remark that the set of natural numbers is naturally embedded in Λ. Let H be an even infinite number where the definition being even is the following: if H is written as $[(H_\lambda, \lambda \in \Lambda)]$, then $\{\lambda \in \Lambda \mid H_\lambda \text{ is even}\} \in F$, where $[\cdot]$ denotes the equivalence class with respect to the ultrafilter F. Let ε be $1/H$, that is, if ε is $[(\varepsilon_\lambda, \lambda \in \Lambda)]$, then ε_λ is $1/H_\lambda$. Then we will define a lattice space $\mathbf{L}$, a sublattice space L, and a space of functions $R(L)$ as follows:

$$\begin{aligned}
\mathbf{L} &:= \varepsilon^*\mathbb{Z} = \{\varepsilon z \mid z \in {}^*\mathbb{Z}\}, \\
L &:= \left\{\varepsilon z \mid z \in {}^*\mathbb{Z},\ -\frac{H}{2} \le \varepsilon z < \frac{H}{2}\right\} = \{[(\varepsilon_\lambda z_\lambda), \lambda \in \Lambda] \mid \varepsilon_\lambda z_\lambda \in L_\lambda\} (\subset \mathbf{L}), \\
R(L) &:= \{\varphi \mid \varphi \text{ is an internal function from } L \text{ to } {}^*\mathbb{C}\} \\
&= \{[(\varphi_\lambda, \lambda \in \Lambda)] \mid \varphi_\lambda \text{ is a function from } L_\lambda \text{ to } \mathbb{C}\},
\end{aligned} \tag{2.1}$$

where $L_\lambda := \{\varepsilon_\lambda z_\lambda \mid z_\lambda \in \mathbb{Z},\ -H_\lambda/2 \le \varepsilon_\lambda z_\lambda < H_\lambda/2\}$.

Takeuti [19] introduced an infinitesimal delta function $\delta(x)(\in R(L))$ and Kinoshita [8, 9], Gordon [5] defined an infinitesimal Fourier transformation on $R(L)$. From now on, functions in $R(L)$ are extended to periodic functions on $\mathbf{L}$ with the period H and we denote them by the same notations. For $\varphi(\in R(L))$, the infinitesimal Fourier transformation $F\varphi$, the inverse infinitesimal Fourier transformation $\overline{F}\varphi$, and the convolution of φ, $\psi(\in R(L))$ are defined as follows:

$$\begin{aligned}
\delta(x) &:= \begin{cases} H & (x=0), \\ 0 & (x \neq 0), \end{cases} \\
(F\varphi)(p) &:= \sum_{x\in L} \varepsilon \exp(-2\pi i p x)\varphi(x), \\
(\overline{F}\varphi)(p) &:= \sum_{x\in L} \varepsilon \exp(2\pi i p x)\varphi(x), \\
(\varphi * \psi)(x) &:= \sum_{y\in L} \varepsilon \varphi(x-y)\psi(y).
\end{aligned} \tag{2.2}$$

He obtained the following equalities as the same as the usual Fourier analysis:

$$\begin{gathered}
\delta = F1 = \overline{F}1, \quad F \text{ is unitary}, \quad F^4 = 1, \quad \overline{F}F = F\overline{F} = 1, \\
\varphi * \delta = \delta * \varphi = \varphi, \\
\varphi * \psi = \psi * \varphi, \\
F(\varphi * \psi) = (F\varphi)(F\psi), \\
F(\varphi\psi) = (F\varphi) * (F\psi), \\
\overline{F}(\varphi * \psi) = (\overline{F}\varphi)(\overline{F}\psi), \\
\overline{F}(\varphi\psi) = (\overline{F}\varphi) * (\overline{F}\psi).
\end{gathered} \tag{2.3}$$

The most different point is that $\delta^l (l \in \mathbb{R}^+)$ are also elements of $R(L)$ and the Fourier transformations are able to be calculated as $F\delta^l = H^{(l-1)}$, by the above definition.

On the other hand, we obtain the following theorem from his result and an elementary calculation.

Theorem 2.1. *For an internal function with two variables $f : L \times L \to^* \mathbb{C}$ and $g(\in R(L))$,*

$$F_x\left(\sum_{y\in L} \varepsilon f(x-y,y)g(y)\right)(p) = \{F_y(F_u(f(u,y))(p)) * F_y(g(y))\}(p), \tag{2.4}$$

where F_x, F_y, F_u are Fourier transformations for x, y, u, and $*$ is the convolution for the variable paired with y by the Fourier transformation.

Proof. By the above Kinoshita's result, $F(\varphi\psi) = (F\varphi) * (F\psi)$. We use it and obtain the following:

$$
\begin{aligned}
F_x&\left(\sum_{y\in L} \varepsilon f(x-y,y)g(y)\right)(p)\\
&= \sum_{x,y\in L} \varepsilon \exp(-2\pi ipx)\varepsilon f(x-y,y)g(y)\\
&= \sum_{y,u\in L} \varepsilon^2 \exp\left(-2\pi ip(y+u)\right) f(u,y)g(y)(u := x-y) \qquad (2.5)\\
&= \sum_{y\in L}\left(\varepsilon \exp(-2\pi ipy)\left(\sum_{u\in L} \varepsilon \exp(-2\pi pu) f(u,y)\right)g(y)\right)\\
&= F_y(F_u(f(u,y))(p)\cdot g(y))(p) = \{F_y(F_u(f(u,y))(p)) * F_y(g(y))\}(p).
\end{aligned}
$$

To treat a $*$-unbounded functional f in the nonstandard analysis, we need a second nonstandardization. Let $F_2 := F$ be a nonprincipal ultrafilter on an infinite set $\Lambda_2 := \Lambda$ as above. Denote the ultraproduct of a set S with respect to F_2 by $^*S$ as above. Let F_1 be another nonprincipal ultrafilter on an infinite set Λ_1. Take the $*$-ultrafilter $^*F_1$ on $^*\Lambda_1$. For an internal set S in the sense of $*$-nonstandardization, let $^\star S$ be the $*$-ultraproduct of S with respect to $^*F_1$. Thus, we define a double ultraproduct $^\star(^*\mathbb{R})$, $^\star(^*\mathbb{Z})$, and so forth for the set $\mathbb{R}$, $\mathbb{Z}$, and so forth. It is shown easily that

$$
^\star(^*\mathbf{S}) = \frac{S^{\Lambda_1\times\Lambda_2}}{F_1^{F_2}}, \qquad (2.6)
$$

where $F_1^{F_2}$ denotes the ultrafilter on $\Lambda_1 \times \Lambda_2$ such that for any $A \subset \Lambda_1 \times \Lambda_2$, $A \in F_1^{F_2}$ if and only if

$$
\{\lambda \in \Lambda_1 \mid \{\mu \in \Lambda_2 \mid (\lambda,\mu) \in A\} \in F_2\} \in F_1. \qquad (2.7)
$$

We always work with this double nonstandardization. The natural embedding $^\star S$ of an internal element S which is not considered as a set in $*$-nonstandardization is often denoted simply by S. □

Definition 2.2 (cf. [17]). Let $H(\in {}^*\mathbb{Z})$, $H'(\in {}^\star(^*\mathbb{Z}))$ be even positive numbers such that H' is larger than any element in $^*\mathbb{Z}$, and let $\varepsilon(\in {}^*\mathbb{R})$, $\varepsilon'(\in {}^\star(^*\mathbb{R}))$ be infinitesimals satifying $\varepsilon H = 1$, $\varepsilon' H' = 1$. We define as follows:

$$
\begin{aligned}
\mathbf{L} &:= \varepsilon^*\mathbb{Z} = \{\varepsilon z \mid z \in {}^*\mathbb{Z}\},\\
\mathbf{L}' &:= \varepsilon'^\star(^*\mathbb{Z}) = \{\varepsilon' z' \mid z' \in^\star (^*\mathbb{Z})\},
\end{aligned}
$$

$$L := \left\{ \varepsilon z \mid z \in {}^*\mathbb{Z}, -\frac{H}{2} \le \varepsilon z < \frac{H}{2} \right\} (\subset \mathbf{L}),$$
$$L' := \left\{ \varepsilon' z' \mid z' \in^\star ({}^*\mathbb{Z}), -\frac{H'}{2} \le \varepsilon' z' < \frac{H'}{2} \right\} (\subset \mathbf{L}'). \tag{2.8}$$

Here L is an ultraproduct of lattices

$$L_\mu := \left\{ \varepsilon_\mu z_\mu \mid z_\mu \in \mathbb{Z}, -\frac{H_\mu}{2} \le \varepsilon_\mu z_\mu < \frac{H_\mu}{2} \right\} (\mu \in \Lambda_2) \tag{2.9}$$

in $\mathbb{R}$, and L' is also an ultraproduct of lattices

$$L'_\lambda := \left\{ \varepsilon'_\lambda z'_\lambda \mid z'_\lambda \in {}^*\mathbb{Z}, -\frac{H'_\lambda}{2} \le \varepsilon'_\lambda z'_\lambda < \frac{H'_\lambda}{2} \right\} (\lambda \in \Lambda_1) \tag{2.10}$$

in ${}^*\mathbb{R}$ that is an ultraproduct of

$$L'_{\lambda\mu} := \left\{ \varepsilon'_{\lambda\mu} z'_{\lambda\mu} \mid z'_{\lambda\mu} \in \mathbb{Z}, -\frac{H'_{\lambda\mu}}{2} \le \varepsilon'_{\lambda\mu} z'_{\lambda\mu} < \frac{H'_{\lambda\mu}}{2} \right\} (\mu \in \Lambda_2). \tag{2.11}$$

We define a latticed space of functions X as follows:

$$X := \{a \mid a \text{ is an internal function with double meanings, from } \star(L) \text{ to } L'\}$$
$$= \{[(a_\lambda), \lambda \in \Lambda_1] \mid a_\lambda \text{ is an internal function from } L \text{ to } L'_\lambda\}, \tag{2.12}$$

where $a_\lambda : L \to L'_\lambda$ is $a_\lambda = [(a_{\lambda\mu}), \mu \in \Lambda_2]$, $a_{\lambda\mu} : L_\mu \to L'_{\lambda\mu}$. We define three equivarence relations $\sim_H$, $\sim_{\star(H)}$, and $\sim_{H'}$ on $\mathbf{L}$, $\star(\mathbf{L})$, and $\mathbf{L}'$:

$$x \sim_H y \Longleftrightarrow x - y \quad \in H^*\mathbb{Z},$$
$$x \sim_{\star(H)} y \Longleftrightarrow x - y \quad \in \star(H)^\star({}^*\mathbb{Z}), \tag{2.13}$$
$$x \sim_{H'} y \Longleftrightarrow x - y \quad \in H'^\star({}^*\mathbb{Z}).$$

Then we identify $\mathbf{L}/\sim_H$, ${}^\star\mathbf{L}/\sim_{\star(H)}$, and $\mathbf{L}'/\sim_{H'}$ as L, ${}^\star L$, and L'. Since ${}^\star L$ is identified with L, the set ${}^\star\mathbf{L}/\sim_{\star(H)}$ is identified with $\mathbf{L}/\sim_H$. Furthermore, we represent X as the following internal set:

$$\{a \mid a \text{ is an internal function with a double meaning, from } {}^\star\mathbf{L}/\sim_{\star(H)} \text{ to } \mathbf{L}'/\sim_{H'}\}. \tag{2.14}$$

We use the same notation as a function from ${}^\star L$ to L' to represent a function in the above internal set. We define the space A of functionals as follows.

Definition 2.3.

$$\delta(a) := \begin{cases} (H')^{(^*H)^2} & (a = 0), \\ 0 & (a \neq 0), \end{cases}$$

$$\varepsilon_0 := (H')^{-(^*H)^2} \in {}^\star(^*\mathbb{R}),$$

$$(Ff)(b) := \sum_{a\in X} \varepsilon_0 \exp\left(-2\pi i \sum_{k\in L} a(k)b(k) \right) f(a), \tag{2.15}$$

$$(\overline{F}f)(b) := \sum_{a\in X} \varepsilon_0 \exp\left(2\pi i \sum_{k\in L} a(k)b(k) \right) f(a),$$

$$(f * g)(a) := \sum_{a'\in X} \varepsilon_0 f(a - a')g(a').$$

We define an inner product on A : $(f,g) := \sum_{b\in X} \varepsilon_0 \overline{f(b)} g(b)$, where $\overline{f(b)}$ is the complex conjugate of $f(b)$. Then we obtain the following theorem.

Theorem 2.4. (1) $\delta = F1 = \overline{F}1$;
(2) *F is unitary,* $F^4 = 1$, $\overline{F}F = F\overline{F} = 1$;
(3) $f * \delta = \delta * f = f$;
(4) $f * g = g * f$;
(5) $F(f * g) = (Ff)(Fg)$;
(6) $\overline{F}(f * g) = (\overline{F}f)(\overline{F}g)$;
(7) $F(fg) = (Ff) * (Fg)$;
(8) $\overline{F}(fg) = (\overline{F}f) * (\overline{F}g)$.
The definition implies the following proposition.

Proposition 2.5. *If $l \in \mathbb{R}^+$, then* $F\delta^l = (H')^{(l-1)(^*H)^2}$.

We define two types of infinitesimal divided differences. Let f and a be elements of A and X, respectively, and let $b(\in X)$ be an internal function whose image is in ${}^\star(^*\mathbb{Z}) \cap L'$. We remark that $\varepsilon' b$ is an element of X.

Definition 2.6.

$$(D_{+,b}f)(a) := \frac{f(a + \varepsilon' b) - f(a)}{\varepsilon'},$$
$$(D_{-,b}f)(a) := \frac{f(a) - f(a - \varepsilon' b)}{\varepsilon'}. \tag{2.16}$$

Let $\lambda_b(a) := (\exp(2\pi i\varepsilon' ab) - 1)/\varepsilon'$, $\overline{\lambda}_b(a) := (\exp(-2\pi i\varepsilon' ab) - 1)/\varepsilon'$. Then we obtain the following theorem corresponding to Kinoshita's result for the relationship between the infinitesimal Fourier transformation and the infinitesimal divided differences.

THEOREM 2.7. (1) $(F(D_{+,b}f))(a) = \lambda_b(a)(Ff)(a)$;
(2) $(F(D_{-,b}f))(a) = -\overline{\lambda}_b(a)(Ff)(a)$;
(3) $(F(\lambda_b f))(a) = -(D_{-,b}(Ff))(a)$;
(4) $(F(\overline{\lambda_b} f))(a) = (D_{+,b}(Ff))(a)$;
(5) $(D_{+,b}(\overline{F}f))(a) = (\overline{F}(\lambda_b f))(a)$;
(6) $(D_{-,b}(\overline{F}f))(a) = -(\overline{F}(\overline{\lambda_b} f))(a)$;
(7) $\lambda_b(a) = 2\pi i(\sin(\pi\varepsilon' ab)/\pi\varepsilon')\exp(\pi i\varepsilon' ab)$.

Theorem 2.7 implies the following corollary.

COROLLARY 2.8. *If $\varepsilon' b$ is an element of X, then $(f, D_{+,b}g) = -(D_{+,b}f, g)$ for $f, g \in A$.*

Replacing the definitions of L', δ, ε_0, F, $\overline{F}$ in Definitions 2.2 and 2.3 by the following, we will define another type of infinitesimal Fourier transformation. The different point is only the definition of an inner product of the space of functions X. In Definition 2.3, the inner product of a, $b(\in X)$ is $\sum_{k\in L} a(k)b(k)$, and in the following definition, it is ${}^\star\varepsilon \sum_{k\in L} a(k)b(k)$.

Definition 2.9.

$$L' := \left\{\varepsilon' z' \mid z' \in {}^\star({}^*\mathbb{Z}), -{}^\star H\frac{H'}{2} \leq \varepsilon' z' <{}^\star H\frac{H'}{2}\right\},$$

$$\delta(a) := \begin{cases} ({}^\star H)^{({}^\star H)^2/2} H'^{({}^\star H)^2} & (a = 0), \\ 0 & (a \neq 0), \end{cases}$$

$$\varepsilon_0 := ({}^\star H)^{-({}^\star H)^2/2} H'^{-({}^\star H)^2}, \tag{2.17}$$

$$(Ff)(b) := \sum_{a\in X} \varepsilon_0 \exp\left(-2\pi i^\star \varepsilon \sum_{k\in L} a(k)b(k)\right) f(a),$$

$$(\overline{F}f)(b) := \sum_{a\in X} \varepsilon_0 \exp\left(2\pi i^\star \varepsilon \sum_{k\in L} a(k)b(k)\right) f(a).$$

In this case, we obtain the same theorems as Theorems 2.4 and 2.7, and the following theorem corresponding to Theorem 2.1.

THEOREM 2.10. *For an internal function with two variables $f : X \times X \to {}^\star({}^*\mathbb{C})$ and $g(\in A)$,*

$$F_a\left(\sum_{b\in X} \varepsilon_0 f(a-b,b)g(b)\right)(d) = \{F_b(F_c(f(c,b))(d)) * F_b(g(b))\}(d), \tag{2.18}$$

where F_a, F_b, F_c are Fourier transformations for a, b, c, and $*$ is the convolution for the variable pairing with b by the Fourier transformation.

3. Proofs of theorems

Proof of Theorem 2.4. (1) $(F1)(0) = \sum_{a\in X} \varepsilon_0 = \varepsilon_0 (H'^2)^{(^*H)^2} = (H')^{(^*H)^2}$. If $b \neq 0$, then

$$\begin{aligned}
(F1)(b) &= \sum_{a\in X} \varepsilon_0 \exp\left(-2\pi i \sum_{k\in L} a(k)b(k)\right) = \varepsilon_0 \prod_{k\in L} \sum_{a(k)\in L'} \exp(-2\pi i a(k)b(k)) \\
&= \varepsilon_0 \prod_{k\in L, b(k)\neq 0} \sum_{a(k)\in L'} \exp(-2\pi i a(k)b(k)) \cdot \prod_{k\in L, b(k)=0} \sum_{a(k)\in L'} \exp(-2\pi i a(k)b(k)) \\
&= \prod_{k\in L, b(k)\neq 0} \varepsilon_0 \frac{\exp(-2\pi i\varepsilon'(-H'^2/2)b(k))(1-\exp(-2\pi i\varepsilon' H'^2 b(k)))}{1-\exp(-2\pi i\varepsilon' b(k))} \\
&\quad \cdot \prod_{k\in L, b(k)=0} \sum_{a(k)\in L'} \exp(-2\pi i a(k)b(k)) = 0.
\end{aligned} \tag{3.1}$$

Hence $F1 = \delta$. The same argument implies that $\overline{F}1 = \delta$;

(2)

$$\begin{aligned}
(Ff, Fg) &= \sum_{b\in X} \varepsilon_0 \overline{(Ff)(b)}(Fg)(b) \\
&= \sum_{b\in X} \varepsilon_0 \overline{\sum_{a\in X} \varepsilon_0 \exp\left(-2\pi i \sum_{k\in L} a(k)b(k)\right) f(a)} \sum_{c\in X} \varepsilon_0 \exp\left(-2\pi i \sum_{k\in L} c(k)b(k)\right) g(c) \\
&= \sum_{a\in X}\sum_{c\in X} \varepsilon_0^2 \overline{f(a)} g(c) \sum_{b\in X} \varepsilon_0 \exp\left(-2\pi i \sum_{k\in L} (c(k)-a(k))b(k)\right) \\
&= \sum_{a\in X}\sum_{c\in X} \varepsilon_0^2 \overline{f(a)} g(c)\delta(c-a) = \sum_{a\in X} \varepsilon_0 \overline{f(a)} g(a) = (f,g).
\end{aligned} \tag{3.2}$$

Hence F is unitary. Since $(F^2 f)(c) = (F(Ff))(c) = f(-c)$, $F^4 = 1$. Thus the eigenvalues of F are $1, -1, -i, i$. Furthermore,

$$\begin{aligned}
(\overline{F}(Ff))(c) &= \sum_{b\in X} \varepsilon_0 \exp\left(2\pi i \sum_{k\in L} c(k)b(k)\right)\left(\sum_{a\in X} \varepsilon_0 \exp\left(-2\pi i \sum_{k\in L} a(k)b(k)\right) f(a)\right) \\
&= \sum_{a\in X}\left(\sum_{b\in X} \varepsilon_0^2 \exp\left(-2\pi i \sum_{k\in L} b(k)(a(k)-c(k))\right)\right) f(a) \\
&= \sum_{a\in X} \varepsilon_0 \delta(a-c) f(a) = f(c).
\end{aligned} \tag{3.3}$$

The same argument implies $(F(\overline{F}f))(c) = f(c)$;

(3) $(f * \delta)(a) = \sum_{b\in X} \varepsilon_0 f(a-b)\delta(b) = f(a)$, $(\delta * f)(a) = \sum_{b\in X} \varepsilon_0 \delta(a-b) f(b) = f(a)$;

(4) $(f*g)(a)=\sum_{b\in X}\varepsilon_0 f(a-b)g(b)=\sum_{(a-b)\in X}\varepsilon_0 f(a-b)g(a-(a-b))=(g*f)(a)$;
(5)

$$\begin{aligned}(F(f*g))(c)&=\sum_{a\in X}\varepsilon_0\exp\Big(-2\pi i\sum_{k\in L}c(k)a(k)\Big)\sum_{a\in X}\varepsilon_0 f(a-b)g(b)\\&=\sum_{a\in X}\varepsilon_0\exp\Big(-2\pi i\sum_{k\in L}c(k)\big(b(k)+d(k)\big)\Big)\sum_{b\in X}\varepsilon_0 f(a-b)g(b),\end{aligned}\tag{3.4}$$

where

$$d(k):=a(k)-b(k)$$

$$=\sum_{b\in X}\varepsilon_0\exp\Big(-2\pi i\sum_{k\in L}c(k)b(k)\Big)g(b)\sum_{d\in X-b}\varepsilon_0\exp\Big(-2\pi i\sum_{k\in L}c(k)d(k)\Big)f(d),\tag{3.5}$$

where

$$X-b:=\{x-b\mid x\in X\}$$

$$\begin{aligned}&=\sum_{b\in X}\varepsilon_0\exp\Big(-2\pi i\sum_{k\in L}c(k)b(k)\Big)g(b)\sum_{d\in X}\varepsilon_0\exp\Big(-2\pi i\sum_{k\in L}c(k)d(k)\Big)f(d)\qquad(3.6)\\&=(Fg)(c)(Ff)(c)=(Ff)(c)(Fg)(c);\end{aligned}$$

(6) similarly, $\overline{F}(f'*g')=(\overline{F}f')(\overline{F}g')$;

(7) the above (6) implies $f'*g'=F((\overline{F}f')(\overline{F}g'))$. We put $f'=Ff, g'=Fg$. Then we obtain $(Ff)*(Fg)=F(fg)$;

(8) similarly, $(\overline{F}f)*(\overline{F}g)=\overline{F}(fg)$. □

Proof of Theorem 2.7. (1)

$$\begin{aligned}(F(D_{+,b}f))(a)&=\sum_{c\in X}\varepsilon_0\exp(-2\pi iac)\frac{1}{\varepsilon'}\big(f(c+\varepsilon'b)-f(c)\big)\\&=\sum_{c\in X}\varepsilon_0\Big(\frac{1}{\varepsilon'}\big(\exp(-2\pi iac)f(c+\varepsilon'b)-\exp(-2\pi iac)f(c)\big)\Big)\\&=\sum_{c\in X}\varepsilon_0\Big(\frac{1}{\varepsilon'}\big(\exp(2\pi i\varepsilon'ab)\big(\exp\big(-2\pi ia(c+\varepsilon'b)\big)f(c+\varepsilon'b)\\&\qquad-\exp(-2\pi iac)f(c)\big)\big)\Big)\\&=\frac{1}{\varepsilon'}\big(\exp(2\pi i\varepsilon'ab)-1\big)(Ff)(a)=\lambda_b(a)Ff(a);\end{aligned}\tag{3.7}$$

(2)

$$
\begin{aligned}
(F(D_{-,b}f))(a) &= \sum_{c\in X} \varepsilon_0 \exp(-2\pi iac)\frac{1}{\varepsilon'}(f(c) - f(c-\varepsilon b')) \\
&= \sum_{c\in X} \varepsilon_0 \Big(\frac{1}{\varepsilon'}(\exp(-2\pi iac)f(c) \\
&\qquad - \exp(-2\pi i\varepsilon' ab)\exp(-2\pi ia(c-\varepsilon' b))f(c-\varepsilon' b))\Big) \\
&= \frac{1}{\varepsilon'}(1-\exp(-2\pi i\varepsilon' ab))(Ff)(a) = -\bar{\lambda}_b(a)Ff(a);
\end{aligned}
\tag{3.8}
$$

(3)

$$
\begin{aligned}
(F(\lambda_b f))(a) &= \sum_{c\in X} \varepsilon_0 \exp(-2\pi iac)(\lambda_b f)(c) \\
&= \sum_{c\in X} \varepsilon_0 \exp(-2\pi iac)\frac{1}{\varepsilon'}(\exp(2\pi ibc\varepsilon') - 1)f(c) \\
&= \sum_{c\in X} \varepsilon_0 \frac{\exp(-2\pi i(a-b\varepsilon')c) - \exp(-2\pi iac)}{\varepsilon'} f(c) = -D_{-,b}(Ff)(a);
\end{aligned}
\tag{3.9}
$$

(4)

$$
\begin{aligned}
(F(\bar{\lambda}_b f))(a) &= \sum_{c\in X} \varepsilon_0 \exp(-2\pi iac)(\bar{\lambda}_b f)(c) \\
&= \sum_{c\in X} \varepsilon_0 \exp(-2\pi iac)\frac{1}{\varepsilon'}(\exp(-2\pi ibc\varepsilon') - 1)f(c) \\
&= \sum_{c\in X} \varepsilon_0 \frac{\exp(-2\pi i(a+b\varepsilon')c) - \exp(-2\pi iac)}{\varepsilon'} f(c) = D_{+,b}(Ff)(a).
\end{aligned}
\tag{3.10}
$$

(1), (2) imply (5), (6). □

Proof of Corollary 2.8.

$$
\begin{aligned}
(f, D_{+,b}g) &= \sum_{a\in X} \varepsilon_0 \overline{f(a)} D_{+,b} g = \sum_{c\in X} \varepsilon_0 \overline{(Ff)(c)}(FD_{+,b})g(c) \\
&= \sum_{c\in X} \varepsilon_0 \overline{(Ff)(c)}\lambda_b(c)(Fg)(c) = \sum_{c\in X} \varepsilon_0 \overline{\bar{\lambda}_b(c)(Ff)(c)}(Fg)(c) \\
&= -\sum_{c\in X} \varepsilon_0 \overline{F(D_{-,b}f)(c)}(Fg)(c) = -\sum_{a\in X} \varepsilon_0 \overline{D_{-,b}f(a)}g(a) \\
&= -(D_{-,b}f, g).
\end{aligned}
\tag{3.11}
$$

□

4. Examples (see [17])

We obtain two examples of the infinitesimal Fourier transformation for the space A of functionals. Let $\star \circ * : \mathbb{R} \to {}^\star({}^*\mathbb{R})$ be the natural elementary embedding and let $\mathbf{st}(c)$ for $c \in {}^\star({}^*\mathbb{R})$ be the standard part of c with respect to the natural elementary embedding $\star \circ *$. The first is for $\exp(i\pi{}^\star\varepsilon\sum_{k\in L} a^2(k))$ and the second is for $\exp(-\pi{}^\star\varepsilon\sum_{k\in L} a^2(k))$. We denote the two functionals by $f(a)$, $g(a)$. If there is an L^2-function $\alpha(t)$ on $\mathbb{R}$ for $a(k)$ so that $a(k) = \star(({}^*\alpha)(k))$, then $\mathbf{st}(f(a)) = \exp(i\pi\int_{-\infty}^{\infty}\alpha^2(t)dt)$, and $\mathbf{st}(g(a)) = \exp(-\pi\int_{-\infty}^{\infty}\alpha^2(t)dt)$. Then we obtain the following results.

Example 4.1. $(Ff)(b) = C_1\overline{f(b)}$, where $C_1 = \sum_{a\in X}\varepsilon_0\exp(i\pi{}^\star\varepsilon\sum_{k\in L} a^2(k))$, it is just a standard number $(-1)^{H/2}$.

Example 4.2. $(Fg)(b) = C_2(b)g(b)$, where $C_2(b) = \sum_{a\in X}\varepsilon_0\exp(-\pi{}^\star\varepsilon\sum_{k\in L}(a(k)+ib(k))^2)$, and if b is a finite-valued function, then it satisfies that $\mathbf{st}(\mathbf{st}(C_2(b))) = 1$.

References

[1] S. Albeverio, R. Høegh-Krohn, J. E. Fenstad, and T. Lindstrøm, *Nonstandard Methods in Stochastic Analysis and Mathematical Physics*, Pure and Applied Mathematics, vol. 122, Academic Press, Florida, 1986, pp. xii+514.

[2] R. M. Anderson, *A non-standard representation for Brownian motion and Itô integration*, Israel Journal of Mathematics **25** (1976), 15–46.

[3] R. P. Feynman and A. R. Hibbs, *Quantum Mechanics and Path Integrals*, McGraw-Hill, New York, 1965.

[4] D. Fujiwara, *A construction of the fundamental solution for the Schrödinger equation*, Journal d'Analyse Mathématique **35** (1979), 41–96.

[5] E. I. Gordon, *Nonstandard Methods in Commutative Harmonic Analysis*, Translations of Mathematical Monographs, vol. 164, American Mathematical Society, Rhode Island, 1997.

[6] K. Itô, *Differential equations determinig a Markoff process (original Japanese: Zenkoku Sizyo Sugaku Danwakai-si)*, Journ. Pan-Japan Math. Coll. (1942), no. 1077.

[7] T. Kamae, *A simple proof of the ergodic theorem using nonstandard analysis*, Israel Journal of Mathematics **42** (1982), no. 4, 284–290.

[8] M. Kinoshita, *Nonstandard representations of distributions. I*, Osaka Journal of Mathematics **25** (1988), no. 4, 805–824.

[9] ———, *Nonstandard representations of distributions. II*, Osaka Journal of Mathematics **27** (1990), no. 4, 843–861.

[10] P. A. Loeb, *Conversion from nonstandard to standard measure spaces and applications in probability theory*, Transactions of the American Mathematical Society **211** (1975), 113–122.

[11] K. Loo, *Nonstandard Feynman path integral for the harmonic oscillator*, Journal of Mathematical Physics **40** (1999), no. 11, 5511–5521.

[12] ———, *A rigorous real-time Feynman path integral and propagator*, Journal of Physics. A **33** (2000), no. 50, 9215–9239.

[13] W. A. J. Luxemburg, *A nonstandard analysis approach to Fourier analysis*, Contributions to Non-Standard Analysis (Sympos., Oberwolfach, 1970), Studies in Logic and Foundations of Math., vol. 69, North-Holland, Amsterdam, 1972, pp. 15–39.

[14] T. Nakamura, *A nonstandard representation of Feynman's path integrals*, Journal of Mathematical Physics **32** (1991), no. 2, 457–463.

[15] ———, *Path space measure for the 3 + 1-dimensional Dirac equation in momentum space*, Journal of Mathematical Physics **41** (2000), no. 8, 5209–5222.

[16] E. Nelson, *Feynman integrals and the Schrödinger equation*, Journal of Mathematical Physics **5** (1964), no. 3, 332–343.
[17] T. Nitta and T. Okada, *Poisson summation formula for the space of functionals*, Nihonkai Mathematical Journal **16** (2005), no. 1, 1–21.
[18] T. Nitta, T. Okada, and A. Tzouvaras, *Classification of non-well-founded sets and an application*, Mathematical Logic Quarterly **49** (2003), no. 2, 187–200.
[19] G. Takeuti, *Dirac space*, Proceedings of the Japan Academy **38** (1962), 414–418.

Takashi Nitta: Department of Education, Mie University, Kamihama, Tsu 514-8507, Japan
E-mail address: nitta@edu.mie-u.ac.jp

Tomoko Okada: Division of General Education, Aichigakuin University, Iwasaki-cho Araike 12, Nisshin 470-0195, Japan
E-mail address: m98122c@math.nagoya-u.ac.jp

LIPSCHITZ CLASSES OF A-HARMONIC FUNCTIONS IN CARNOT GROUPS

CRAIG A. NOLDER

The Hölder continuity of a harmonic function is characterized by the growth of its gradient. We generalize these results to solutions of certain subelliptic equations in domains in Carnot groups.

1. Introduction

Theorem 1.1 follows from results in [7].

Theorem 1.1. *Let u be harmonic in the unit disk $\mathbb{D} \subset \mathbb{R}^2$ and $0 < \alpha \leq 1$. If there exists a constant C_1 such that*

$$|\nabla u(z)| \leq C_1(1-|z|)^{\alpha-1} \tag{1.1}$$

for all $z \in \mathbb{D}$, then there exists a constant C_2, depending only on α and C_1, such that

$$\sup\left[\frac{|u(x_1)-u(x_2)|}{|x_1-x_2|^{\alpha}} : x_1, x_2 \in \mathbb{D},\ x_1 \neq x_2\right] \leq C_2. \tag{1.2}$$

We give generalizations in Section 5. Theorem 5.1 characterizes local Lipschitz conditions for A-harmonic functions in domains in Carnot groups by the growth of a local average of the horizontal gradient. These functions are solutions to certain subelliptic equations. Theorem 5.2 gives global results in Lipschitz extension domains. In Section 2 we describe Carnot groups. Section 3 presents subelliptic equations and integral inequalities for their solutions. Section 4 contains Lipschitz conditions and extension domains.

2. Carnot groups

A Carnot group is a connected, simply connected, nilpotent Lie group G of topological $\dim G = N \geq 2$ equipped with a graded Lie algebra $\mathcal{G} = V_1 \oplus \cdots \oplus V_r$ so that $[V_1, V_i] = V_{i+1}$ for $i = 1, 2, \ldots, r-1$, and $[V_1, V_r] = 0$. As usual, elements of $\mathcal{G}$ will be identified with

Hindawi Publishing Corporation
Proceedings of the Conference on Differential & Difference Equations and Applications, pp. 885–894

left-invariant vectors fields on G. We fix a left-invariant Riemannian metric g on G with $g(X_i,X_j) = \delta_{ij}$. We denote the inner product with respect to this metric, as well as all other inner products, by $\langle\cdot\rangle$. We assume that $\dim V_1 = m \geq 2$ and fix an orthonormal basis of $V_1 : X_1, X_2, \ldots, X_m$. The horizontal tangent bundle of G, HT is the subbundle determined by V_1 with horizontal tangent space HT_x the fiber $\operatorname{span}[X_1(x),\ldots,X_m(x)]$. We use a fixed global coordinate system as $\exp : \mathcal{G} \to G$ is a diffeomorphism. We extend $X_1,\ldots,X_m$ to an orthonormal basis $X_1,\ldots,X_m, T_1,\ldots,T_{N-m}$ of $\mathcal{G}$. All integrals will be with respect to the binvariant Harr measure on G which arises as the push-forward of the Lebesgue measure in $\mathbb{R}^N$ under the exponential map. We denote by $|E|$ the measure of a measurable set E. We normalize the Harr measure so that the measure of the unit ball is one. We denote by Q the homogeneous dimension of the Carnot group G defined by $Q = \sum_{i=1}^{r} i \dim V_i$. We write $|v|^2 = \langle v, v\rangle$, d for the distributional exterior derivative and δ for the codifferential adjoint. We use the following spaces where U is an open set in G:

$C_0^\infty(U)$: infinitely differentiable compactly supported functions in U,

$HW^{1,q}(U)$: horizontal Sobolev space of functions $u \in L^q(U)$ such that the distributional derivatives $X_i u \in L^q(U)$ for $i = 1,\ldots,m$.

When u is in the local horizontal Sobolev space $HW^{1,q}_{\text{loc}}(U)$, we write the horizontal differential as $d_0 u = X_1 u dx_1 + \cdots + X_m u dx_m$. (The horizontal gradient $\nabla_0 u = X_1 u X_1 + \cdots + X_m u X_m$ appears in the literature. Notice that $|d_0 u| = |\nabla_0 u|$.)

The family of dilations on G, $[\delta_t : t > 0]$ is the lift to G of the automorphism δ_t of $\mathcal{G}$ which acts on each V_i by multiplication by t^i. A path in G is called horizontal if its tangents lie in V_1. The (left-invariant) Carnot-Carathéodory distance, $d_c(x,y)$, between x and y is the infimum of the lengths, measured in the Riemannian metric g, of all horizontal paths which join x to y. A homogeneous norm is given by $|x| = d_c(0,x)$. All homogeneous norms on G are equivalent as such $|\cdot|$ is equivalent to the homogeneous norms used below. We have $|\delta_t(x)| = t|x|$. We write $B(x,r) = [y \in G : |x^{-1}y| < r]$ for the ball centered at x of radius r. Since the Jacobian determinant of the dilation δ_r is r^Q and we have normalized the measure, $|B(x,r)| = r^Q$. For $\sigma \geq 1$, we write σB for the ball with the same center as B and σ times the radius.

We write Ω throughout for a connected open subset of G. We give some examples of Carnot groups.

Example 2.1. Euclidean space $\mathbb{R}^n$ with its usual Abelian group structure is a Carnot group. Here $Q = n$ and $X_i = \partial/\partial x_i$.

Example 2.2. Each Heisenberg group H_n, $n \geq 1$, is homeomorphic to $\mathbb{R}^{2n+1}$. They form a family of noncomutative Carnot groups which arise as the nilpotent part of the Iwasawa decomposition of $U(n,1)$, the isometry group of the complex n-dimensional hyperbolic space. Denoting points in H_n by (z,t) with $z = (z_1,\ldots,z_n) \in \mathbb{C}^n$ and $t \in \mathbb{R}$ we have the group law given as

$$(z,t) \circ (z',t') = \left(z + z', t + t' + 2\sum_{j=1}^{n} \operatorname{Im}(z_j \bar{z}_j')\right). \tag{2.1}$$

With the notation $z_j = x_j + iy_j$, the horizontal space V_1 is spanned by the basis

$$X_j = \frac{\partial}{\partial x_j} + 2y_j \frac{\partial}{\partial t}, \qquad Y_j = \frac{\partial}{\partial y_j} - 2x_j \frac{\partial}{\partial t}. \tag{2.2}$$

The one-dimensional center V_2 is spanned by the vector field $T = \partial/\partial t$ with commutator relations $[X_j, Y_j] = -4T$. All other brackets are zero. The homogeneous dimension of H_n is $Q = 2n+2$. A homogeneous norm is given by

$$N(z,t) = \left(|z|^4 + t^2\right)^{1/4}. \tag{2.3}$$

Example 2.3. A generalized Heisenberg group, or H-type group, is a Carnot group with a two-step Lie algebra $\mathcal{G} = V_1 \oplus V_2$ and an inner product $\langle \cdot \rangle$ in $\mathcal{G}$ such that the linear map $J : V_2 \to End V_1$ defined by the condition

$$\langle J_z(u), v\rangle = \langle z, [u,v]\rangle \tag{2.4}$$

satisfies

$$J_z^2 = -\langle z,z\rangle \mathbf{Id} \tag{2.5}$$

for all $z \in V_2$ and all $u,v \in V_1$. For each $g \in G$, let $v(g) \in V_1$ and let $z(g) \in V_2$ be such that $g = \exp(v(g) + z(g))$. Then

$$N(g) = \left(|v(g)|^4 + 16|z(g)|^2\right)^{1/4} \tag{2.6}$$

defines a homogeneous norm in G. For each $l \in \mathbb{N}$, there exist infinitely many generalized Heisenberg groups with $\dim V_2 = l$. These include the nilpotent groups in the Iwasawa decomposition of the simple rank-one groups $SO(n,1)$, $SU(n,1)$, $Sp(n,1)$, and F_4^{-20}.

See [1, 5, 14] for material about these groups.

3. Subelliptic equations

We consider solutions to equations of the form

$$\delta A(x,u,d_0u) = B(x,u,d_0u), \tag{3.1}$$

where $u \in HW^{1,p}(\Omega)$ and $A : \Omega \times \mathbb{R} \times \mathbb{R}^m \to \mathbb{R}^m$, $B : \Omega \times \mathbb{R} \times \mathbb{R}^m \to \mathbb{R}$ are measurable and for some $p > 1$ satisfy the structural equations

$$\begin{aligned} |A(x,u,\xi)| &\le a_0|\xi|^{p-1} + (a_1(x)|u|)^{p-1}, \\ \xi \cdot A(x,u,\xi) &\ge |\xi|^p - (a_2(x)|u|)^p, \\ |B(x,u,\xi)| &\le b_1(x)|\xi|^{p-1} + (b_2(x))^p|u|^{p-1} \end{aligned} \tag{3.2}$$

with $(x,u,\xi) \in \Omega \times \mathbb{R} \times \mathbb{R}^N$. Here $a_0 > 0$ and $a_i(x), b_i(x)$, $i = 1,2$, are measurable and non-negative and are assumed to belong to certain subspaces of $L^t(\Omega)$, where $t = \max(p,Q)$, see [11]. We refer to these quantities as the structure constants.

A weak solution to (3.1) means that

$$\int_{\Omega} \{\langle A(x,u,d_0u), d_0\phi\rangle - \phi B(x,u,d_0u)\}\,dx = 0 \tag{3.3}$$

for all $\phi \in C_0^\infty(\Omega)$.

We use the exponent $p > 1$ for this purpose throughout. We assume that u is a solution to (3.1) in Ω throughout. We may assume that u is a continuous representative [8]. We write u_B for the average of u over B.

We use the following results.

Theorem 3.1. *Here C is a constant independent of u.*

(a) *(Poincaré-Sobolev inequality) If $0 < s < \infty$,*

$$\int_B |u - u_B|^s \le C|B|^{s/Q} \int_B |d_0u|^s \tag{3.4}$$

for all balls $B \subset \Omega$.

(b) *If $s > p - 1$, then*

$$|u(x) - c| \le C\left(\frac{1}{|B|}\int_{\sigma B} |u - c|^s\right)^{1/s} \tag{3.5}$$

for all $x \in B$, $\sigma B \subset \Omega$, and any constant c.

(c) *If $0 < s, t < \infty$, then*

$$\left(\frac{1}{|B|}\int_B |u - u_B|^t\right)^{1/t} \le C\left(\frac{1}{|B|}\int_{\sigma B} |u - u_B|^s\right)^{1/s} \tag{3.6}$$

for any $\sigma B \subset \Omega$.

(d) *(A Caccioppoli inequality)*

$$\int_B |d_0u|^p \le C|B|^{-p/Q} \int_{\sigma B} |u - c|^p \tag{3.7}$$

for any constant c and $\sigma B \subset \Omega$.

See [2, 6, 8, 9, 11].

Theorem 3.2. *There exists an exponent $p' > p$, depending only on Q, p, s, and the structure constants, and there exists a constant C, depending only on Q, p, s, σ, and the structure constants, such that*

$$\left(\frac{1}{|B|}\int_B |d_0u|^{p'}\right)^{1/p'} \le C\left(\frac{1}{|B|}\int_{\sigma B} |d_0u|^s\right)^{1/s} \tag{3.8}$$

for $s > 0$ and all balls B with $\sigma B \subset \Omega$.

Proof. We combine the Caccioppoli estimate (3.7), inequality (3.6), and the Poincaré-Sobolev inequality (3.4),

$$\begin{aligned}\left(\frac{1}{|B|}\int_B |d_0u|^p\right)^{1/p} &\le C|B|^{-1/Q}\left(\frac{1}{|B|}\int_{\sqrt{\sigma}B}|u-u_{\sqrt{\sigma}B}|^p\right)^{1/p}\\ &\le C|B|^{-1/Q}\frac{1}{|B|}\int_{\sigma B}|u-u_{\sigma B}| \le C\frac{1}{|B|}\int_{\sigma B}|d_0u|.\end{aligned} \tag{3.9}$$

This is a reverse Hölder inequality. As such it improves to all positive exponents on the right-hand side and to some exponent $p' > p$ on the left, see [2, 8, 9]. □

For $E \subset G$, we write $\operatorname{osc}(u,E) = \sup_E u - \inf_E u$.

THEOREM 3.3. *Let $0 < s < \infty$. There is a constant C, depending only on s, p, Q, σ, and the structure constants such that*

$$\operatorname{osc}(u,B) \le C|B|^{(s-Q)/sQ}\left(\int_{\sigma B}|d_0u|^s\right)^{1/s} \tag{3.10}$$

for all balls B with $\sigma B \subset \Omega$.

Proof. Fix B with $\sigma B \subset \Omega$ and $x, y \in B$. Using (3.5) with $s = p$, the Poincaré inequality (3.4) and (3.8),

$$\begin{aligned}|u(x)-u(y)| &\le |u(x)-u_{\sqrt{\sigma}B}| + |u(y)-u_{\sqrt{\sigma}B}|\\ &\le C\left(\frac{1}{|B|}\int_{\sqrt{\sigma}B}|u-u_{\sqrt{\sigma}B}|^p\right)^{1/p}\\ &\le C|B|^{(p-Q)/pQ}\left(\int_{\sqrt{\sigma}B}|d_0u|^p\right)^{1/p}\\ &\le C|B|^{(s-Q)/sQ}\left(\int_{\sigma B}|d_0u|^s\right)^{1/s}.\end{aligned} \tag{3.11}$$

□

When $p > Q$, Theorem 3.3 holds for all $u \in HW^{1,p}(\sigma B)$, see [8].
The last result follows from Harnack's inequality and also appears in [8].

THEOREM 3.4. *There exist constants $\beta, 0 < \beta \le 1$, and C, depending only on p, Q, and the structure constants, such that*

$$\operatorname{osc}(u,B) \le C\sigma^{-\beta}\operatorname{osc}(u,\sigma B) \tag{3.12}$$

for all balls B with $\sigma B \subset \Omega$ with $\sigma \ge 1$.

4. Lipschitz classes and domains

We use the following notations for $f:\Omega\to\mathbb{R}^m$ and $0<\alpha\le 1$:

$$\|f\|^{\alpha}=\sup\left\{\frac{|f(x_1)-f(x_2)|}{d_c(x_1,x_2)^{\alpha}}:x_1,\,x_2\in\Omega,\,x_1\neq x_2\right\},$$

$$\|f\|^{\alpha}_{\partial}=\sup\left\{\frac{|f(x_1)-f(x_2)|}{(d_c(x_1,x_2)+d_c(x_1,\partial\Omega))^{\alpha}}:x_1,\,x_2\in\Omega,\,x_1\neq x_2\right\},$$

$$\|f\|^{\alpha}_{\mathrm{loc}}=\sup\left\{\frac{|f(x_1)-f(x_2)|}{d_c(x_1,x_2)^{\alpha}}:x_1,\,x_2\in\Omega,\,x_1\neq x_2,\,d_c(x_1,x_2)<d_c(x_1,\partial\Omega)\right\},$$

$$\|f\|^{\alpha}_{\mathrm{loc},\partial}=\sup\left\{\frac{|f(x_1)-f(x_2)|}{(d_c(x_1,x_2)+d_c(x_1,\partial\Omega))^{\alpha}}:x_1,x_2\in\Omega,\,x_1\neq x_2,\,d_c(x_1,x_2)<d_c(x_1,\partial\Omega)\right\}. \tag{4.1}$$

Notice

$$\|f\|^{\alpha}_{\mathrm{loc},\partial}\le\min\left(\|f\|^{\alpha}_{\mathrm{loc}},\|f\|^{\alpha}_{\partial}\right)\le\max\left(\|f\|^{\alpha}_{\mathrm{loc}},\|f\|^{\alpha}_{\partial}\right)\le\|f\|^{\alpha}. \tag{4.2}$$

Definition 4.1. A domain $\Omega\subset G$ is uniform if there exist constants $a,b>0$ such that each pair of points $x_1,x_2\in\Omega$ can be joined by a horizontal curve $\gamma\subset\Omega$ satisfying the following:

(a) $l(\gamma)\le ad_c(x_1,x_2)$;

(b) $\min_{i,j}l(\gamma(x_j,x))\le bd_c(x,\partial\Omega)$ for all $x\in\gamma$.

Here $l(\gamma)$ is the length of γ in the d_c-metric and $l(x_j,x)$ is this length between x_j and x.

We give some known examples.

(1) Metric balls in the Heisenberg groups are uniform.

(2) The Euclidean cube $\{(x_1,y_1,\dots,t)\in\mathbb{H}^n\,|\max(|x_i|,|y_i|,|t|)<1\}$ is a uniform domain in the Heisenberg groups $\mathbb{H}^n$ [4].

(3) The hyperspace $\{(x_1,y_1,\dots,t)\in\mathbb{H}^n\,|\,t>0\}$ is a uniform domain in the Heisenberg groups $\mathbb{H}^n$ [4].

(4) The hyperspace $\{x\in G\mid x_i>0,\ i=1,\dots,m\}$ is a uniform domain in a Carnot group G [4].

For domains in $\mathbb{R}^n$, the following definition appears in [10] and with $\alpha=\alpha'$ in [3].

Definition 4.2. A domain Ω is a $\mathrm{Lip}_{\alpha,\alpha'}$-extension domain, $0<\alpha'\le\alpha\le 1$, if there exists a constant M, independent of $f:\Omega\to\mathbb{R}^n$, such that

$$\|f\|^{\alpha'}\le M\|f\|^{\alpha}_{\mathrm{loc}}. \tag{4.3}$$

When $\alpha=\alpha'$, we write Lip_{α}-extension domain.

Theorem 4.3. *For $0 < \alpha' \le \alpha \le 1$, Ω is a $\mathrm{Lip}_{\alpha,\alpha'}$-extension domain if there exists a constant N such that each pair of points $x_1, x_2 \in \Omega$ can be joined by a horizontal path $\gamma \subset \Omega$ for which*

$$\int_\gamma d_c(\gamma(s), \partial\Omega)^{\alpha-1} ds \le N d_c(x_1, x_2)^{\alpha'}. \tag{4.4}$$

If metric balls are uniform domains, then the converse holds.

The proof is the same as the corresponding result in Euclidean space given in [3] with minor modification.

It follows that if Ω is a $\mathrm{Lip}_{\alpha,\alpha'}$-extension domain, then

$$\|f\|_\partial^{\alpha'} \le M \|f\|_{\mathrm{loc},\partial}^{\alpha}. \tag{4.5}$$

Theorem 4.4. *If Ω is a uniform domain, then it is a Lip_α-extension domain.*

The proof is similar to that in [3] in $\mathbb{R}^n$. We give the simple proof here to show the connection with uniform domains.

Proof. Let γ join x_1 to x_2 in Ω satisfy Definition 4.1. We have

$$\begin{aligned} \int_\gamma d_c(x, \partial\Omega)^{\alpha-1} ds &\le b^{\alpha-1} \int_0^{l(\gamma)} \min(s, l(\gamma) - s)^{\alpha-1} ds \\ &\le 2b^{\alpha-1} \int_0^{l(\gamma)/2} s^{\alpha-1} ds \\ &\le 2^{1-\alpha} \alpha^{-1} b^{\alpha-1} a^\alpha d_c(x_1, x_2)^\alpha. \end{aligned} \tag{4.6}$$

□

We also require the following results which characterize the local Lipschitz classes. We assume from here on that metric balls are uniform domains.

Theorem 4.5. *Assume that $f : \Omega \to \mathbb{R}$ and $0 < \eta < 1$.*
The following are equivalent:
(1) *there exists a constant C_1, independent of f, such that*

$$|f(x_1) - f(x_2)| \le C_1 |x_1 - x_2|^\alpha \tag{4.7}$$

for all $x_1, x_2 \in \Omega$ with $|x_1 - x_2| \le \eta d_c(x_1, \partial\Omega)$;
(2) *there exists a constant C_2, independent of f, such that*

$$\|f\|_{\mathrm{loc}}^\alpha \le C_2. \tag{4.8}$$

Theorem 4.6. *Assume that $f : \Omega \to \mathbb{R}$ and $0 < \eta < 1$.*
The following are equivalent:
(1) *there exists a constant C_1, independent of f, such that*

$$|f(x_1) - f(x_2)| \le C_1 |x_1 - x_2|^\alpha \tag{4.9}$$

for all $x_1, x_2 \in \Omega$ with $|x_1 - x_2| = \eta d_c(x_1, \partial\Omega)$;

(2) *there exists a constant C_2, independent of f, such that*

$$\|f\|^{\alpha}_{\text{loc},\partial} \leq C_2. \tag{4.10}$$

Again the proofs are similar to those given in [3, 10].

5. Lipschitz classes of solutions

Recall we are assuming that u is a solution to (3.1). In the Euclidean case Theorems 5.1 and 5.2 appear in [13].

THEOREM 5.1. *The following are equivalent:*
(1) *there exists a constant C_1, independent of u, such that*

$$D_u(x) \leq C_1 d_c(x,\partial\Omega)^{\alpha-1} \tag{5.1}$$

for all $x \in \Omega$;
(2) *there exists a constant C_2, independent of u, such that*

$$\|u\|^{\alpha}_{\text{loc},\partial} \leq C_2. \tag{5.2}$$

Proof. Assume 1. Fix $x_1, x_2 \in \Omega$ with $|x_1 - x_2| = d_c(x_1,\partial\Omega)/4$ and let $B = B(x_1, 2|x_1 - x_2|)$. We have, using (3.10),

$$|u(x_1) - u(x_2)| \leq C|B|^{(p-Q)/pQ}\left(\int_B |d_0u|^p\right)^{1/p} = C|B|^{1/Q}D_u(x_1) \leq C|x_1 - x_2|^{\alpha}. \tag{5.3}$$

Statement 2 then follows from Theorem 4.6.

Conversely, using the Caccioppoli inequality (3.7),

$$\begin{aligned} D_u(x_1) &= |B|^{-1/p}\left(\int_B |d_0u|^p\right)^{1/p} \\ &\leq C|B|^{-(p+Q)/pQ}\left(\int_{2B} |u - u(x_1)|^p\right)^{1/p} \\ &\leq d_c(x_1,\partial\Omega)^{\alpha-1}. \end{aligned} \tag{5.4}$$

□

THEOREM 5.2. *Suppose that Ω is a $\text{Lip}_{\alpha,\alpha'}$-extension domain, $0 < \alpha' \leq \alpha \leq 1$. If there exists a constant C_1, independent of u, such that*

$$D_u(x) \leq C_1 d(x,\partial\Omega)^{\alpha-1}, \tag{5.5}$$

then there is a constant C_2, independent of u, such that

$$\|u\|^{\alpha'}_{\partial} \leq C_2. \tag{5.6}$$

Moreover, there are constants β and C_3, independent of u, such that if in addition $\alpha' \leq \beta$, then

$$\|u\|^{\alpha'} \leq C_3. \tag{5.7}$$

Otherwise, (5.5) only implies that

$$\|u\|^{\beta} \leq C(\operatorname{diam}\Omega)^{\alpha'-\beta}. \tag{5.8}$$

The first implication follows from (4.5) and Theorem 5.1. The second part is a consequence of the next result.

THEOREM 5.3. *Assume along with u being a solution in Ω that it is also continuous in $\bar{\Omega}$. There exists a constant β, depending only on Q, p, and the structure constants, such that if $\alpha \leq \beta$ and if there exists a constant C_1 such that*

$$|u(x_1) - u(x_2)| \leq C_1 |x_1 - x_2|^{\alpha} \tag{5.9}$$

for all $x_1 \in \Omega$ and $x_2 \in \partial\Omega$, then

$$\|u\|^{\alpha} \leq C_2, \tag{5.10}$$

where C_2 depends only on Q, p, C_1, and the structure constants. If $\beta < \alpha$, (5.9) only implies that

$$\|u\|^{\beta} \leq C_2(\operatorname{diam}\Omega)^{\alpha-\beta}. \tag{5.11}$$

The proof is similar to the Euclidean case, see [12]. It requires here inequality (3.12) in the Carnot case with an appropriate choice of σ.

References

[1] J. Berndt, F. Tricerri, and L. Vanhecke, *Generalized Heisenberg Groups and Damek-Ricci Harmonic Spaces*, Lecture Notes in Mathematics, vol. 1598, Springer, Berlin, 1995.

[2] S. M. Buckley, P. Koskela, and G. Lu, *Subelliptic Poincaré inequalities: the case $p < 1$*, Publicacions Matemàtiques **39** (1995), no. 2, 313–334.

[3] F. W. Gehring and O. Martio, *Lipschitz classes and quasiconformal mappings*, Annales Academiae Scientiarum Fennicae. Series A I. Mathematica **10** (1985), 203–219.

[4] A. V. Greshnov, *On uniform and NTA-domains on Carnot groups*, Siberian Mathematical Journal **42** (2001), no. 5, 851–864 (Russian).

[5] M. Gromov, *Carnot-Carathéodory spaces seen from within*, Institut des Hautes Etudes Scientifiques, 6, 1994.

[6] P. Hajlasz and P. Koskela, *Sobolev met Poincaré*, Max-Plank-Institut für math, Leipzig, preprint 41, 1998.

[7] G. H. Hardy and J. E. Littlewood, *Some properties of conjugate functions*, Journal für die reine und angewandte Mathematik **167** (1932), 405–432.

[8] J. Heinonen and I. Holopainen, *Quasiregular maps on Carnot groups*, The Journal of Geometric Analysis **7** (1997), no. 1, 109–148.

[9] T. Iwaniec and C. A. Nolder, *Hardy-Littlewood inequality for quasiregular mappings in certain domains in $\mathbb{R}^n$*, Annales Academiae Scientiarum Fennicae. Series A I. Mathematica **10** (1985), 267–282.

[10] V. Lappapainen, *Lip_h-extension domains*, Annales Academiae Scientiarum Fennicae. Series A I. Mathematica Dissertationes **71** (1988).
[11] G. Lu, *Embedding theorems into the Orlicz and Lipschitz classes and applications to quasilinear subelliptic equations*, preprint, 1994.
[12] C. A. Nolder, *Hardy-Littlewood theorems for solutions of elliptic equations in divergence form*, Indiana University Mathematics Journal **40** (1991), no. 1, 149–160.
[13] ———, *Lipschitz classes of solutions to certain elliptic equations*, Annales Academiae Scientiarum Fennicae. Series A I. Mathematica **17** (1992), no. 2, 211–219.
[14] P. Pansu, *Métriques de Carnot-Carathéodory et quasiisométries des espaces symétriques de rang un*, Annals of Mathematics. Second Series **129** (1989), no. 1, 1–60.

Craig A. Nolder: Department of Mathematics, Florida State University, Tallahassee, FL 32306-4510, USA
E-mail address: nolder@math.fsu.edu

ASYMPTOTIC BEHAVIOR IN STOCHASTIC FUNCTIONAL DIFFERENTIAL EQUATIONS OF NEUTRAL TYPE

ZEPHYRINUS C. OKONKWO

This paper deals with asymptotic behavior of the solution process of a class of neutral stochastic functional differential equations of Itô-Volterra form. Criteria for the existence of the solution process are outlined. Using the results of Corduneanu, Mahdavi, and Okonkwo, asymptotic behaviors of such solution processes (at $+\infty$) are discussed.

1. Introduction

We study the asymptotic behavior of the solutions to stochastic functional differential equations of the form

$$d(Vx)(t,\omega) = (Ax)(t,\omega)dt + \phi(t,x(t,\omega))dz(t,\omega) \tag{1.1}$$

with the random initial condition

$$x(0,\omega) = x^0 \in R^n. \tag{1.2}$$

Here and in the sequel, V and A will denote causal operators on the function space $C(R_+ \times \Omega, R^n)$, which is the space of product measurable random functions $x : R_+ \times \Omega \to R^n$ with continuous sample paths on every compact subset of R_+. Ω is the sample space, with $\omega \in \Omega$. $\phi \in M_0(R_+ \times R^n, R^{n\times k})$, the space of $n \times k$ product measurable matrix-valued random functions with the property that

$$\mathcal{P}\left(\omega : \int_0^{T_1} \sup_{0\le t\le T_1} |\phi(t,x(t,\omega))|^2 dt < \infty\right) = 1, \quad T_1 < \infty. \tag{1.3}$$

The integral in (1.3) is assumed to be in the Lebesgue sense for each $\omega \in \Omega$. We will present a remark concerning the asymptotic behavior of (1.1), where the underlying space is $L^p_{\text{loc}}(R_+ \times \Omega, R^n)$, $1 \le p \le \infty$.

Hindawi Publishing Corporation
Proceedings of the Conference on Differential & Difference Equations and Applications, pp. 895–903

The following assumptions are in order; $(\Omega, \chi, \mathcal{P})$ Ω is the set of all elementary events, χ_t is a nondecreasing σ-algebra of subsets of Ω, and $\mathcal{P}$ is the probability measure which takes every event $\omega \in \Omega$ to the associated probability $\mathcal{P}(\omega)$. The random process $x(t, \cdot)$ is nonanticipating, and $z(t, \omega)$ is a normalized R^k-valued Wiener process. Furthermore, the random initial condition x^0 is a Gaussian random variable independent of the Wiener process z. Asymptotic behavior of solutions of various classes of functional differential equations has been a focus of study because of its importance in the study of stability of systems. Corduneanu [2] discussed the asymptotic behavior of functional differential equations of the form

$$\dot{x}(t) + (Lx)(t) + f(x(t)) = g(t), \tag{1.4}$$

where x, f, and g are vectors in R^n, and L is a linear abstract Volterra operator acting on prescribed function spaces. Two distinct methods of discussing asymptotic behavior of the solutions of equations of the form (1.4) appear in the literature. The first, based on monotonicity assumption, initiated by Moser [6], enables us to compare the behavior of the Volterra equations with that of convenient ordinary differential equations. Corduneau [2] extended this method to the case of nonconvolution integral operators. The second method, which uses admissibility techniques, was initiated by Massera and Schäffer [5]. Mahdavi [4] dealt with asymptotic behavior in some classes of functional differential equations of the form

$$\dot{x}(t) + (Lx)(t) = M(x(t)) \tag{1.5}$$

on the positive half-axes R_+, where L is a linear causal operator, and M is a nonlinear causal operator acting on the prescribed function spaces.

In this paper (see Corduneanu [3], Okonkwo [7]), $(Vx)(t, \omega)$ in (1.1) will be of the form

$$(Vx)(t, \omega) = x(t, \omega) + g(x(\mu(t), \omega)), \tag{1.6}$$

where $\mu : [0, T_1] \to [0, \infty)$ is continuous, with $\mu(0) = 0$, and $0 \leq \mu(t) \leq t$ for $t \in R_+$.

Other auxiliary conditions will be imposed on g and μ in the sequel. On integration of both sides of (1.1) and using V in the form of (1.6), and imposing the condition

$$g(x(\mu(0), \omega)) = g(x_0) = \theta \in R^n, \tag{1.7}$$

we have

$$x(t, \omega) + g(x(\mu(t), \omega)) = x_0 + \int_0^t (Ax)(s, \omega) ds + \int_0^t \phi(s, x(s, \omega)) dz(s, \omega). \tag{1.8}$$

We will also assume that the following conditions hold true for (1.1):

$$\int_0^{T_1} \sup_{0 \le t \le T_1} E[\phi(x(t,\omega),t)dz(t,\omega)] = 0,$$

$$\int_0^{T_1} \sup_{0 \le t \le T_1} E|\phi(x(t,\omega),t)dz(t,\omega)|^2 = \int_0^{T_1} \sup_{0 \le t \le T_1} E|\phi(x(t,\omega),t)|^2 dt < \infty, \quad T_1 < \infty. \tag{1.9}$$

The results obtained in Corduneanu [2, 3] and Mahdavi [4], based on monotonicity assumptions, will be used to obtain asymptotic behavior results for (1.1), (1.2). In Section 2, preliminary remarks and auxiliary results are presented. In particular, the ultimate behavior of the solution process of a stochastic functional differential equation not perturbed by a Weiner process is presented. The main results are discussed in Section 3.

2. Preliminary remarks and results

Let us consider the functional differential equation

$$dx(t,\omega) = (Lx)(t,\omega)dt \tag{2.1}$$

with the random initial condition

$$x(0,\omega) = x^0 \in R^n, \tag{2.2}$$

where L is a linear continuous operator of Volterra type defined on $C([0,T] \times \Omega, R^n)$. Integrating (2.1), we get

$$x(t,\omega) = x^0 + \int_0^t (Lx)(s,\omega)ds. \tag{2.3}$$

Since $dx(t,\omega) = (Lx)(t,\omega)dt$, one can write (2.3) in the form

$$x(t,\omega) = x^0 + \int_0^t dx(s,\omega)ds. \tag{2.4}$$

On application of the linear operator L to both sides of (2.4), we get

$$Lx(t,\omega) = L\left\{x^0 + \int_0^t dx(s,\omega)ds\right\} = L\{x^0\} + L\left\{\int_0^t dx(s,\omega)ds\right\} = \mathcal{F}x^0 + \mathcal{Q}x'. \tag{2.5}$$

Equation (2.5) implies that the linear operator L can be decomposed into two parts: the principal part; $\mathcal{Q}$: $C([0,T] \times \Omega, R^n) \to C([0,T) \times \Omega, R^n)$, and the finite-dimensional part $\mathcal{F}$: $R^n \to C([0,T) \times \Omega, R^n)$, see, for example, Azbelev [1].

Suppose

$$\dot{x} = (Lx)(t) + f(t), \tag{2.6}$$

where L is a linear continuous operator of Volterra type defined on $C([0,T) \times \Omega, R^n)$ and $f \in C([0,T) \times \Omega, R^n)$. Then, for each $x^0 \in R^n$, there exists a unique solution $x(t)$

in the space of absolutely continuous functions satisfying (2.6). Such a solution can be represented by the variation of parameters formula (Corduneanu [2])

$$x(t,\omega) = X(t,0)x^0 + \int_0^t X(t,s)f(s)ds, \tag{2.7}$$

where $X(t,s)$ is the Cauchy kernel uniquely associated with L. Indeed, the relation

$$\int_0^t (Lx)(t,s)ds = \int_0^t X(t,s)x(s)ds \tag{2.8}$$

is established by means of Riesz representation theorem. Suppose $\overline{X}(t,s)$ is the resolvent kernel associated with $X(t,s)$, then the Cauchy kernel is related to the reslovent kernel as follows:

$$X(t,s) = I_{n\times n} + \int_0^t \overline{X}(t,u)du. \tag{2.9}$$

Using the results discussed above therefore, it is easy to see that if, in (1.1), $(Ax)(t,\omega) = (Lx)(t,\omega) + (Dx)(t,\omega)$, the solution of (1.1), (1.2) can be put in the form

$$\begin{aligned} x(t,\omega) + g(x(\mu(t),\omega)) &= X(t,0)x_0 + \int_0^t X(t,s)(Dx)(s,\omega)ds \\ &\quad + \int_0^t X(t,s)\phi(s,x(s,\omega))dz(s,\omega). \end{aligned} \tag{2.10}$$

Here, (1.7) has been used. Existence and uniqueness of the solution process of (1.1), (1.2) given by (1.8) in various function spaces have been discussed in several recent papers. Let us assume that the following hypotheses hold true:

(A1) g is a contraction operator on $C([0,T)\times\Omega,R^n)$, that is,

$$E\left|g(x(\mu(t),\omega)) - g(y(\mu(t),\omega))\right| \le \lambda \sup_{0\le s\le t} E\left|x(s,\omega) - y(s,\omega)\right|, \quad 0 < \lambda < 1; \tag{2.11}$$

(A2) $A : C([0,T)\times\Omega,R^n) \to C([0,T)\times\Omega,R^n)$ is causal, and takes bounded sets into bounded sets. Furthermore,

$$E\left|(Ax)(t,\omega) - (Ay)(t,\omega)\right| \le \gamma(t) \sup_{0\le s\le t} E\left|x(s,\omega) - y(s,\omega)\right|; \tag{2.12}$$

(A3) $E|\phi(t,x(t,\omega)) - \phi(y,(t,\omega))| \le \zeta(t)\sup_{0\le s\le t} E|x(s,\omega) - y(s,\omega)|$.

Here, we will assume that $3\lambda < 1$, $\zeta(t)$, and $\gamma(t)$ are in L^1 for every $x \in C([0,T)\times\Omega,R^n)$ with $0 \le t \le T < \infty$.

Theorem 2.1 (Okonkwo [7]). *Consider the neutral stochastic functional differential equation (1.1), with V given by formula (1.6), under the initial condition (1.2). Suppose that assumptions (A1), (A2), and (A3) are satisfied, μ being a real-valued function with $\mu(0) = 0$, and $0 \le \mu(t) \le t$ for $t \in [0,T]$. Then, there exists a solution process $x = x(t,\omega)$ of the problem on $[0,T_1]\times\Omega \subset [0,T]\times\Omega$ such that $x(t,\omega) + g(x(\mu(t),\omega))$ is differentiable almost everywhere.*

Remark 2.2. The proof of the above Theorem has been presented in [7] and will not be repeated here. Note that the uniqueness of the solution process was also established. The deterministic version of the above theorem has been proven by Corduneanu in [3].

Let us present preliminary results concerning asymptotic behavior of a functional differential equation related to (1.1).

THEOREM 2.3. *Consider the functional differential equation*

$$d(x(t,\omega)+g(x(\mu(t),\omega))) = -((Lx)(t,\omega)+f(x(t,\omega)))dt+v(t,\omega)dt \tag{2.13}$$

with the initial condition (1.2), and assume that the following hypotheses hold true:

(i) $L : C(R_+ \times \Omega, R^n) \to C(R_+ \times \Omega, R^n)$ *is causal, and takes bounded sets into bounded sets, that is,*

$$E\int_t^{t+1} |(Lx)(s,\omega)|\, ds \longrightarrow 0 \quad as\ t \longrightarrow \infty,\ \forall x \in BC(R_+ \times \Omega, R^n); \tag{2.14}$$

(ii) $g : R^n \to R^n$ *is almost surely continuous contraction operator, with* $g(x(0,\omega)) = g(x_0) \equiv \theta$, *and*

$$E|g(x(\mu(t),\omega)) - g(y(\mu(t),\omega))| \le \alpha \sup_{0\le s\le t} E|x(t,\omega)-y(t,\omega)|, \quad 0<\alpha<1; \tag{2.15}$$

(iii) $f : R^n \to R^n$ *is continuous, and such that*

$$E\int_0^t \sup_{0\le s\le t} \langle (Lx)(s,\omega)+f(x(s,\omega)), x(s,\omega)\rangle ds \ge 0, \quad t\in R_+; \tag{2.16}$$

(iv) $v \in L^1(R_+\Omega, R^n)$, *that is*, $\int_0^\infty E|v(t,\omega)|\,ds < \infty$.

Furthermore, $v(t,\omega)$ *is uncorrelated with* $x(t,\omega)$, *that is,*

$$E[v(t,\omega)\cdot x(t,\omega)] = E[v(t,\omega)]E[x(t,\omega)]. \tag{2.17}$$

Then any solution process of (2.13) is defined on $R_+ \times \Omega$, *it is almost surely bounded there, and the limit sets of the sample paths will coincide with that of a convenient solution of an ordinary differential equation.*

Proof. Suppose $x = x(t,\omega)$ is a solution of (2.1) and such that $x(0,\omega) = x_0 \in R^n$, then such solution is defined on some interval $[0,T_1)$, $T_1 \le \infty$ (or possibly for very small T_1 only). On scalar multiplication of both sides of (2.13) by $x(t,\omega)$, we get

$$\begin{aligned}&\langle d(x(t,\omega)+g(x(\mu(t),\omega))), x(t,\omega)\rangle \\ &\quad= \langle -((Lx)(t,\omega)+f(x(t,\omega)))dt, x(t,\omega)\rangle \\ &\qquad+ \langle v(t,\omega)dt, x(t,\omega)\rangle.\end{aligned} \tag{2.18}$$

On integration of both sides of the above equation and rearranging, we get

$$\begin{aligned}\frac{1}{2}|x(t,\omega)|^2+\alpha|x(t,\omega)|^2+\int_0^t\langle (Lx)(s,\omega)+f(x(s,\omega)),x(s,\omega)\rangle ds\\ =\frac{1}{2}|x_0|^2+\int_0^t\langle v(s,\omega),x(s,\omega)\rangle ds.\end{aligned} \tag{2.19}$$

On taking inequality (2.16) into account, we get

$$\frac{1}{2}|x(t,\omega)|^2+\alpha|x(t,\omega)|^2\le\frac{1}{2}|x_0|^2+\int_0^t\langle v(s,\omega),x(s,\omega)\rangle ds. \tag{2.20}$$

Taking the mathematical expectation of both sides of (2.20), we have

$$(1+2\alpha)\sup_{0\le t\le T}E|x(t,\omega)|^2\le E|x_0|^2+2\sup_{0\le t\le T}E|x(t,\omega)|\int_0^t E|v(s,\omega)|ds. \tag{2.21}$$

Let $\xi(t)=\sup_{0\le t\le T}E|x(t,\omega)|$. Inequality (2.21) becomes

$$(1+2\alpha)\xi^2(t)\le E|x_0|^2+2\xi(t)\int_0^t E|v(s,\omega)|ds. \tag{2.22}$$

Inequality (2.22) implies that

$$(1+2\alpha)\xi^2(t)\le E|x_0|^2+2\xi(t)\int_0^\infty E|v(s,\omega)|ds. \tag{2.23}$$

Hence

$$\xi^2(t)\le E|x_0|^2+2\xi(t)\int_0^\infty E|v(s,\omega)|ds \tag{2.24}$$

From (2.24), we have

$$\xi(t)\le\int_0^\infty E|v(s,\omega)|ds+\left\{E|x_0|^2+\left(\int_0^\infty E|v(s,\omega)|ds\right)^2\right\}^{1/2}. \tag{2.25}$$

Inequality (2.25) means that

$$E|x(t,\omega)|\le\int_0^\infty E|v(s,\omega)|ds+\left\{E|x_0|^2+\left(\int_0^\infty E|v(s,\omega)|ds\right)^2\right\}^{1/2}. \tag{2.26}$$

Observe that the left-hand side of inequality (2.26) is a constant with respect to t. We therefore conclude that $x=x(t,\omega)$ remains bounded on its maximal interval of existence, which implies that $x(t,\omega)$ (for each $\omega\in\Omega$) can be extended on the positive half-axes $R_+=[0,\infty)$. That is, $x=x(t,\omega)$ is almost surely bounded on the positive half-axes $R_+=[0,\infty)$. One can easily show that the limit set of the solutions coincides with that of the convenient solution of an ordinary differential equation, see Corduneanu [2]. □

3. Main results

In this section, we will establish the criteria for boundedness and asymptotic behavior of the solution process of Itô-Volterra functional differential equations of the form (1.1), (1.2).

Suppose we assume that in (1.1),

$$(Ax)(t,\omega) = -((Lx)(t,\omega) + (Nx)(t,\omega)) + v(t,\omega), \tag{3.1}$$

then, (1.1) can be put in the form

$$\begin{aligned} d(x(t,\omega) + g(x(\mu(t),\omega))) &= -[(Lx)(t,\omega) - (Nx)(t,\omega) - v(t,\omega)]dt \\ &\quad + \phi(t,x(t,\omega))dz(t,\omega). \end{aligned} \tag{3.2}$$

In (3.2), we will assume that $N : C(R_+ \times \Omega, R^n) - > C(R_+ \times \Omega, R^n)$ is an operator of Niemytzki type, that is, $(Nx)(t,\omega) = f(t,x(t,\omega))$, $x \in R^n$. Furthermore, we will assume that $(N\theta)(t,\omega) \equiv \theta$, $E|(Nx)(t,\omega)| \le r(t)E|x(t,\omega)|^2$, with $r(t) \ge 0$, $t \in R_+$, and

$$\int_0^\infty r(t)dt \le \xi < \infty. \tag{3.3}$$

Theorem 3.1. *Consider the functional differential equation (3.2) with the initial condition (1.2), and assume that the following hypotheses are satisfied:*

(H1) *L is a linear operator of Volterra type on the function space $C(R_+ \times \Omega, R^n)$ and satisfies the condition*

$$E\int_0^t \sup_{0\le s\le t} \langle (Lx)(s,\omega), x(s,\omega)\rangle ds \ge \beta(t) \sup_{0\le s\le t} E\left|x(s,\omega)\right|^2 \tag{3.4}$$

for each $t \in R_+$, with $\beta(t)$ being a nondecreasing function of t on R_+;

(H2) *there exists a function $u \in L^2(R_+,R)$, such that*

$$E\left|(Nx)(t,\omega)\right| \le u(t), \tag{3.5}$$

almost everywhere on R_+ for all $x \in C(R_+ \times \Omega, R^n)$;

(H3) *$g : R^n \to R^n$ is almost surely continuous contraction operator, with $g(x(0,\omega)) = g(x_0) \equiv \theta$, and*

$$E\left|g(x(\mu(t),\omega)) - g(y(\mu(t),\omega))\right| \le \alpha \sup_{0\le s\le t} E\left|x(t,\omega) - y(t,\omega)\right|, \quad 0 < \alpha < 1. \tag{3.6}$$

Furthermore, $E|\langle g(x(\mu(t),\omega)), x(t,\omega)\rangle| \le \alpha E|x(t,\omega)|^2$ for $0 < \alpha < 1$;

(H4) *$v \in L^2(R_+ \times \Omega, R^n)$, that is, $\int_0^\infty E\left|v(t,\omega)\right|^2 ds < \infty$.*

Furthermore, $v(t,\omega)$ is uncorrelated with $x(t,\omega)$, that is, $E[v(t,\omega)\cdot x(t,\omega)] = E[v(t,\omega)]E[x(t,\omega)]$;

(H5) *there exists a function $l \in L^2(R_+,R)$, such that*

$$E|\phi(t,x(t,\omega))| \le l(t), \tag{3.7}$$

almost everywhere on R_+ for all $x \in C(R_+ \times \Omega, R^n)$.

Then any sample path of the solution process of (3.2) is defined and bounded on R_+.

Proof. Suppose $x = x(t,\omega)$ is a solution of (3.2) and such that $x(0,\omega) = x^0 \in R^n$, then such solution is defined on some interval $[0,T_2)$, $T_2 \leq \infty$ (or possibly for very small T_2 only). On scalar multiplication of both sides of (3.2) by $x(t,\omega)$, we get

$$\begin{aligned} &\langle d(x(t,\omega)+g(x(\mu(t),\omega))),x(t,\omega)\rangle \\ &\quad = \langle -[(Lx)(t,\omega)-(Nx)(t,\omega)-v(t,\omega)]dt,x(t,\omega)\rangle \\ &\quad\quad + \langle \phi(t,x(t,\omega))dz(t,\omega),x(t,\omega)\rangle. \end{aligned} \tag{3.8}$$

Integrating both sides of (3.8) and on rearranging we have

$$\begin{aligned} &\frac{1}{2}|x(t,\omega)|^2+\alpha|x(t,\omega)|^2+\int_0^t \langle (Lx)(x,\omega),x(s,\omega)\rangle ds \\ &\quad = \frac{1}{2}|x_0|^2+\int_0^t \langle (Nx)(s,\omega),x(s,\omega)\rangle ds \\ &\quad\quad + \int_0^t \langle v(s,\omega),x(s,\omega)\rangle ds+\int_0^t \langle (\phi(s,x(s,\omega)),x(s,\omega)\rangle dz(s,\omega). \end{aligned} \tag{3.9}$$

On application of hypotheses (H1)–(H5), we get

$$\begin{aligned} &\frac{1}{2}|x(t,\omega)|^2+\alpha|x(t,\omega)|^2+\beta(t)\int_0^t |(x,\omega)|^2 ds \\ &\quad \leq \frac{1}{2}|x_0|^2+\frac{1}{2}\epsilon\int_0^t \langle u^2(s)\rangle ds+\frac{\epsilon}{2}\int_0^t |x(s,\omega)|^2 ds \\ &\quad\quad + \frac{1}{2}\delta\int_0^t l^2(s)ds+\frac{\epsilon}{2}\int_0^t |x(s,\omega)|^2 dz \\ &\quad\quad + \frac{1}{2}\rho\int_0^t |v(s,\omega)|^2 ds+\frac{\rho}{2}\int_0^t |x(s,\omega)|^2 ds. \end{aligned} \tag{3.10}$$

In the above inequality, the following inequalities have been used:

$$\begin{aligned} \int_0^t \langle (Nx)(s,\omega),x(s,\omega)\rangle ds &\leq \frac{1}{2\epsilon}\int_0^t u^2(s)ds+\frac{\epsilon}{2}\int_0^t |x(s,\omega)|^2 ds, \\ \int_0^t \langle v(s,\omega),x(s,\omega)\rangle ds &\leq \frac{1}{2\rho}\int_0^t |v(s,\omega)|^2 ds+\frac{\rho}{2}\int_0^t |x(s,\omega)|^2 ds, \\ \int_0^t \langle \phi(s,x(s,\omega)),x(s,\omega)\rangle dz(s,\omega) &\leq \frac{1}{2\delta}\int_0^t l^2(s)ds+\frac{\rho}{2}\int_0^t |x(s,\omega)|^2 ds, \end{aligned} \tag{3.11}$$

where ϵ, δ, ρ are arbitrary positive numbers. On simplification of inequality (3.10), rearranging, and taking the mathematical expectations of both sides of (3.10), we get

$$\begin{aligned} &(1+2\alpha)\sup_{0\leq t\leq T} E|x(t,\omega)|^2+(2\beta(t)-\epsilon-\delta-\rho)\sup_{0\leq t\leq T} E\int_0^t |x(s,\omega)|^2 ds \\ &\quad \leq E|x_0|^2+\frac{1}{\epsilon}\int_0^t u^2(s)ds+\frac{1}{\delta}\int_0^t l^2(s)ds+\frac{1}{\rho}E\int_0^t |v(s,\omega)|^2 ds. \end{aligned} \tag{3.12}$$

Hence

$$\begin{aligned}(1+2\alpha)E|x(t,\omega)|^2 &+ (2\beta(t)-\epsilon-\delta-\rho)E\int_0^t |x(s,\omega)|^2 ds \\ &\le E|x_0|^2 + \frac{1}{\epsilon}\int_0^\infty u^2(s)ds + \frac{1}{\delta}\int_0^\infty l^2(s)ds + \frac{1}{\rho}E\int_0^\infty |v(s,\omega)|^2 ds.\end{aligned} \tag{3.13}$$

□

The right-hand side of inequality (3.12) is independent of t. Therefore the solution process of (3.2), (1.2) remains bounded on its interval of local existence. This implies that the solution process $x(t,\omega)$ (for each $\omega \in \omega$) can be extended on the whole on the positive half-axes $R_+ = [0,\infty)$. That is, $x = x(t,\omega)$ is almost surely bounded on the positive half-axes R_+.

Remark 3.2. Asymptotic behavior of second-order functional differential equations of the form

$$x''(t) + (Lx')(t) + \operatorname{grad} F(x(t)) = g(t), \tag{3.14}$$

where the underlying space is the $L^p_{\text{loc}}(R_+, R^n)$, has been discussed in Corduneanu [3].

Acknowledgments

This paper is dedicated to my mother, Mrs. Ezinne Anastasia Urichi Okonkwo, who departed this world the week I was preparing to attend this conference. I also thank Albany State University for supporting my research work.

References

[1] N. Azbelev, *Stability and asymptotic behavior of solutions of equations with aftereffect*, Volterra Equations and Applications (Arlington, Tex, 1996) (C. Corduneanu and I. W. Sandberg, eds.), Stability Control Theory Methods Appl., vol. 10, Gordon and Breach, Amsterdam, 2000, pp. 27–38.

[2] C. Corduneanu, *Integral Equations and Applications*, Cambridge University Press, Cambridge, 1991.

[3] ———, *Functional Equations with Causal Operators*, Stability and Control: Theory, Methods and Applications, vol. 16, Taylor & Francis, London, 2002.

[4] M. Mahdavi, *Asymptotic behavior in some classes of functional differential equations*, Nonlinear Dynamics and Systems Theory **4** (2004), no. 1, 51–57.

[5] J. L. Massera and J. J. Schäffer, *Linear Differential Equations and Function Spaces*, Pure and Applied Mathematics, vol. 21, Academic Press, New York, 1966.

[6] J. Moser, *On nonoscillating networks*, Quarterly of Applied Mathematics **25** (1967), 1–9.

[7] Z. C. Okonkwo, *Existence of neutral stochastic functional differential equations with abstract Volterra operators*, International Journal of Differential Equations and Applications **7** (2003), no. 1, 101–107.

Zephyrinus C. Okonkwo: Department of Mathematics and Computer Science, Albany State University, Albany, GA 31705, USA

E-mail address: zephyrinus.okonkwo@asurams.edu

A TWO-DEGREES-OF-FREEDOM HAMILTONIAN MODEL: AN ANALYTICAL AND NUMERICAL STUDY

RAFFAELLA PAVANI

A well-studied Hamiltonian model is revisited. It is shown that known numerical results are to be considered unreliable, because they were obtained by means of numerical methods unsuitable for Hamiltonian systems. Moreover, some analytical results are added.

1. Introduction

Our aim is to study a well-known structural engineering problem about anomalous elastic-plastic responses of a two-degrees-of-freedom model of a fixed ended beam with short pulse loading (e.g., [2] and references therein). In particular, the resulting elastic vibrations may be chaotic. We will tackle this problem mainly from the point of view of numerical analysis, but we provide even some new theoretical results.

This system was already extensively studied using Runge-Kutta methods with variable stepsize and many results can be found in [2] and references therein, but here we want to show that some other numerical methods can be more effective in order to understand the qualitative behavior of the orbits, in particular when chaotic behavior is detected. Moreover, some new analytical results support our conclusions.

In Section 2, the problem is described and equations of the used mathematical model are provided. In Section 3, we present some theoretical results about the behavior of solutions close to the equilibrium point. In Section 4, numerical results are reported and comparisons with already known results are shown. At last, Section 5 is devoted to a final discussion.

2. Beam mathematical model

The two-degrees-of-freedom model of a fixed ended beam is provided by Carini et al. [2]. This model was deeply studied in the field of structural engineering and enjoys a large literature, which we do not cite here for the sake of brevity (e.g., see references in [2]). In particular it is known that a beam, deformed into the plastic range by a short transverse

Hindawi Publishing Corporation
Proceedings of the Conference on Differential & Difference Equations and Applications, pp. 905–913

force pulse, can exhibit anomalous behavior when its fixed ends prohibit axial displacements. Indeed, the resulting elastic vibrations may be chaotic. Here we consider the "generalized" problem proposed in [2], where the plastic strains in the beam are regarded as given and the "loading" is taken as the imposition of initial conditions of displacement and velocity. Damping is neglected. So the system becomes a conservative Hamiltonian system.

The beam model is provided with two cells B and C with two flanges as in the sandwich beam, each exhibiting elastic-perfectly plastic behavior. Assuming symmetrical deflections with respect to the midsection, there are two unknown transverse displacements, that is, w_1 at the quarterpoint and w_2 at the midsection, and an axial displacement u at the quarterpoint. The axial force is assumed to be constant over the span, therefore the axial displacement can be found in terms of the transverse displacements. Consequently, the configuration is defined by two transverse displacements w_1 and w_2, which serve as generalized coordinates of the configuration.

The *nonlinear* system modeling the given beam is given by Carini et al. [2] as follows:

$$\begin{aligned} 4\ddot{w}_1 + \ddot{w}_2 &= -\beta[4w_1^3 - 6w_1^2w_2 + 4w_1w_2^2 - w_2^3] - 5kw_1 + 3kw_2, \\ \ddot{w}_1 + 2\ddot{w}_2 &= -\beta[w_2^3 - 3w_2^2w_1 + 4w_2w_1^2 - 2w_1^3] + 3kw_1 - 2kw_2, \end{aligned} \tag{2.1}$$

where $\beta = 3.5555556 \times 10^{12}$, $k = 2.61123556 \times 10^7$.

Here we neglect the four plastic strains and assume that the stress $\sigma_{\alpha i}$ ($\alpha = B, C$; $i = 1, 2$) are given by

$$\begin{aligned} \sigma_{B1} &= C\left[2\frac{w_1^2}{0.1} - 0.0271(w_2 - 2w_1) + \left(\frac{-w_1^2}{0.1} + \frac{(w_1 - w_2)^2}{0.1}\right)\right], \\ \sigma_{B2} &= C\left[2\frac{w_1^2}{0.1} + 0.0271(w_2 - 2w_1) + \left(\frac{-w_1^2}{0.1} + \frac{(w_1 - w_2)^2}{0.1}\right)\right], \\ \sigma_{C1} &= C\left[2\frac{(w_1 - w_2)^2}{0.1} + 0.0271(w_2 - w_1) - \left(\frac{-w_1^2}{0.1} + \frac{(w_1 - w_2)^2}{0.1}\right)\right], \\ \sigma_{C2} &= C\left[2\frac{(w_1 - w_2)^2}{0.1} - 0.0271(w_2 - w_1) - \left(\frac{-w_1^2}{0.1} + \frac{(w_1 - w_2)^2}{0.1}\right)\right], \end{aligned} \tag{2.2}$$

where $C = 4e + 9$.

Kinetic energy $T(\dot{w}_1, \dot{w}_2)$ and potential energy $V(w_1, w_2)$, relevant to half beam, have the following expressions:

$$\begin{aligned} T &= 1.8e - 3\left(2\dot{w}_1^{\,2} + \dot{w}_1\dot{w}_2 + \dot{w}_2^{\,2}\right), \\ V &= 2.5e - 17\left(\sigma_{B1}^2 + \sigma_{B2}^2 + \sigma_{C1}^2 + \sigma_{C2}^2\right), \end{aligned} \tag{2.3}$$

and the Hamiltonian function is given by $H = T + V$.

Alternatively, Hamiltonian function can be written as

$$H = 79.365(p_1^2 - p_1p_2 + 2p_2^2) + V(w_1, w_2). \tag{2.4}$$

The dynamical equations in canonical Hamiltonian form can be derived from the Hamiltonian function H; so the generalized momenta (p_1, p_2) are defined by

$$p_1 = \frac{\partial T}{\partial \dot{w}_1} = 0.0018(4\dot{w}_1 + \dot{w}_2), \qquad p_2 = \frac{\partial T}{\partial \dot{w}_2} = 0.0018(\dot{w}_1 + 2\dot{w}_2). \tag{2.5}$$

Therefore the nonlinear model of the given beam can be written as the following first-order system:

$$\begin{aligned}
\dot{q}_1 &= \dot{w}_1 = 79.365(2p_1 - p_2),\\
\dot{q}_2 &= \dot{w}_2 = 79.365(-p_1 + 4p_2),\\
\dot{p}_1 &= -3.2e+9[8w_1^3 - 12w_1^2w_2 + 8w_1w_2^2 - 2w_2^3 + 0.0073w_1 - 0.0044w_2),\\
\dot{p}_2 &= -3.2e+9[2w_2^3 - 6w_2^2w_1 + 8w_2w_1^2 - 4w_1^3 + 0.0029w_2 - 0.0044w_1).
\end{aligned} \tag{2.6}$$

The system is a *two-degrees-of-freedom conservative Hamiltonian system*, which turns out to be *nonintegrable*, but it can be considered nearly integrable for sufficiently small values of Hamiltonian H.

3. Analytical results

It is easy to check that the *origin* is the only equilibrium point of the nonlinear system (2.6); no saddles are present. Here we will show that, in spite of the fact that the given Hamiltonian system is nonintegrable, an analytical approximation of the solution can be found in a neighborhood of the equilibrium point and such approximation can be as good as we want. Our results are founded on [7, 8], where the basic theorems are established for one degree of freedom and n ($n \geq 2$) degrees of freedom.

At first we recall the following definition.

We call *semitrigonometric polynomial* (hereinafter STP) every function

$$f(t) = \sum a_{r,h,k} t^r (\sin ht + \cos kt) \tag{3.1}$$

with $h, k \in \mathbb{R}$, $r \geq 0$, r integer. The class of STPs is closed with respect to integration and derivation. We remark that a primitive of an STP can always be expressed in closed form through elementary integrations, giving rise to functions of the same kind. We consider these polynomials for $0 \leq t \leq 1$. This is *not a restriction*, because, if the considered integration time interval is longer, we can use a union of closed bounded time intervals with length equal to 1.

We notice that system (2.1) can be written in a more general form as follows:

$$\begin{aligned}
\ddot{x}_1 + \omega_1^2 x_1 &= P_1(x_1, x_2),\\
\ddot{x}_2 + \omega_2^2 x_2 &= P_2(x_1, x_2),
\end{aligned} \tag{3.2}$$

where $P_1(x_1, x_2)$, $P_2(x_1, x_2)$ are polynomials of degree 3. Then we can apply to this system our general results reported in [7], which can be summarized for two degrees of freedom in the following way.

If we assume that the following hypotheses are satisfied:

(1) $P_1(x_1,x_2)$ and $P_2(x_1,x_2)$ are polynomials in $x_1(t)$, $x_2(t)$ without terms of degree < 2, with coefficients such that the sum of their absolute values is less than or equal to 1;

(2) $\omega_i > 3\sqrt{2}$, $i = 1,2$;

(3) initial conditions are such that solution $x_0(t)$ of the homogeneous system satisfies the condition $|x_0(t)| \leq 0.25 - 0.25^r$, where r is the minimum degree of $P_i(x_1,x_2)$, $i = 1,2$,

then there exists a domain $D \subset \mathbb{R}^{2n}$ such that for each initial condition belonging to D, the solution $x(t) = (x_1,x_2)$ of (3.2) can be expressed in the following way:

$$x_i(t) = \sum_{j=1}^{\infty} s_{i,j}(t), \quad i = 1,2, \tag{3.3}$$

where the series converges uniformly in $[0,1]$, and $s_{i,j}(t)$ are semitrigonometric functions in $[0,1]$, which can be computed in closed form from the initial data.

Observe that, according to our previous definition of STP, every function $s_{i,j}$, $i = 1,2$, $j \geq 1$ can be explicitly written as

$$s_{i,j}(t) = \sum_{n=1}^{N_j} a_n t^{r_n} (\sin h_n t + \cos k_n t), \tag{3.4}$$

where the indices i, j are fixed and the summand exhibits N_j terms, $N_j \geq 0$, N_j integer, $h_n, k_n \in \mathbb{R}$, $r \geq 0$, r integer.

It is clear that system (2.1) does not satisfy the above assumptions. Therefore we have to *rearrange* it so that our results can be applied. To this end we write system (2.1) in matricial form

$$M\ddot{w} + \mathbf{N}w = -\beta Y, \tag{3.5}$$

where $w = \begin{bmatrix} w_1 \\ w_2 \end{bmatrix}$, $M = \begin{bmatrix} 4 & 1 \\ 1 & 2 \end{bmatrix}$, $\mathbf{N} = \begin{bmatrix} 5k & -3k \\ -3k & 2k \end{bmatrix}$, $Y = \begin{bmatrix} 4w_1^3 - 6w_1^2 w_2 + 4w_1 w_2^2 - w_2^3 \\ w_2^3 - 3w_2^2 w_1 + 4w_2 w_1^2 - 2w_1^3 \end{bmatrix}$.

We *change the time scale*, so that $s = \alpha t$, with $\alpha = 10^2$, and *the space scale*, setting $w = \varepsilon w^*$, with $\varepsilon = 10^{-5}$.

Then using simultaneous diagonalization by congruencies, we find a unique nonsingular matrix T such that $T^T M T = I$ and $T^T N T = D$, where I is the identity matrix and D is a diagonal matrix. At last using the change of variables $w^*(s) = Tq(s)$, $q = (q_1,q_2) \in \mathbb{R}^2$, from (3.5) we obtain

$$\frac{d^2 q}{ds^2} + Dq = -Z, \tag{3.6}$$

where $D = \begin{bmatrix} 110.16 & 0 \\ 0 & 8842.6 \end{bmatrix}$ and $Z = \begin{bmatrix} Z_1 \\ Z_2 \end{bmatrix}$ with

$$\begin{aligned} Z_1 &= -5.0572e - 4q_1^3 + 8.0311e - 3q_1^2 q_2 - 1.9344e - 2q_1 q_2^2 + 4.5443e - 2q_2^3, \\ Z_2 &= 1.0564e - 3q_1^3 - 6.1083e - 3q_1^2 q_2 + 2.6003e - 2q_1 q_2^2 - 1.6526e - 3q_2^3. \end{aligned} \tag{3.7}$$

Now hypotheses (1) and (2) are satisfied.

About the initial conditions, since they have to be close enough to the origin, we chose: $w_1(0) = w_2(0) = 0$, $\dot{w_1}(0) = 0.56343$, $\dot{w_2}(0) = -0.28172$, corresponding to the energy level $H = 1e-3$. Changing these initial conditions according to the previous transformation, we applied our method presented in [7] by the following steps.

(1) We solved the homogeneous form of system (3.6) and we obtained $q_{01}(s) = -53.749\sin 10.4959s$, $q_{02}(s) = -9.4692\sin 94.035s$. We notice that, as here $r = 3$, the condition $|q_0(s)| \leq 0.25 - 0.25^3$ *was fulfilled only for* $s \leq 4e-4$, that is, $t \leq 4e-6$.

(2) We computed the first iterate $q_1 = (q_{11}, q_{12})$, solving system (3.6), where in Z we replaced $q_1(s)$ with $q_{01}(s)$ and $q_2(s)$ with $q_{02}(s)$.

(3) We recovered the original variables (with the first approximated solutions denoted w_0 and w_1).

We observe that step 2 can be repeated as many times as it suffices, substituting the kth approximated solution in Z, in order to get the $(k+1)$th approximated solution.

For the sake of brevity we report just the second element in both vectors w_0 and w_1:

$$\begin{aligned} w_{02} &= 2.4417e-4\sin 1049.6t - 5.7212e-5\sin 9403.5t, \\ w_{12} &= -5.7269e-5\sin 9403.5t + 2.4226e-4\sin 1049.6t \\ &\quad - 6.9642e-8\sin 3148.7t + 5.8135e-10\sin 28210t \\ &\quad + 1.1712e-8\sin 17757t + 7.6531e-8\sin 11502t \\ &\quad - 2.4214e-8\sin 7304.4t - 8.8818e-9\sin 19856t. \end{aligned} \tag{3.8}$$

As we expected, this orbit is nearly quasiperiodic and the fundamental frequencies are given by the following (rounded) values:

$$\omega_1 = 1049.6, \qquad \omega_2 = 9403.5. \tag{3.9}$$

We remark that our proposed method belongs to the class of iterative methods; indeed it is *not* a series development method. So the accuracy of the approximation can be estimated in terms of the difference between two successive iterates $|x_{k+1}(t) - x_k(t)|$, $k = 0, 1, 2, \ldots$. In this case, $|w_1(t) - w_0(t)| < 2e-6$ for $t \leq 6e-3$, where $6e-3$ is about the length of the first cycle of the solution w_{12}. This enlightens the fact that convergence happens in a longer interval than expected. Actually, convergence is guaranteed for $t \leq 4e-6$ only, as pointed above, but this condition is just sufficient.

4. Numerical results

In order to carry out a reliable numerical study of our mathematical model (2.1), we compared results obtained by the following different numerical methods:

(1) an explicit Runge-Kutta method of order 4 (*RK*4 in public domain);

(2) an explicit Runge-Kutta method with variable stepsize of order 4 (MATLAB routine *ODE*45);

(3) an implicit symplectic Runge-Kutta method of order 12 (*gni_irk*2 in public domain by E. Hairer);

(4) a conservative method of order 10, which numerically preserves energy (*TOMG*).

Table 4.1

	*RK*4	*ODE*45	*gni_irk*2	*TOMG*
h	$1e-5$	$2.9e-5$	$1e-5$	$9e-6$
Δs	$9.032e-6$	$9.528e-6$	$9.035e-6$	$9.035e-6$
ΔH	$4.1e-9$	$1.7e-6$	$1e-18$	$1e-17$

The symplectic method is described in [5], whereas the conservative method will be available as soon as possible, since at the present it is just a preliminary version (by F. Mazzia and the author) of a new program inspired by both TOM methods for BVM problems and GAM methods for IVP problems [1].

In particular, we considered two types of orbits: a close-to-equilibrium orbit and a far-from-equilibrium orbit. As the considered system is nonintegrable, but nearly integrable for small values of Hamiltonian, we should obtain different qualitative behaviors of computed orbits.

4.1. A close-to-equilibrium orbit. We refer to the initial conditions chosen in Section 3. Within the first cycle of the considered orbit, that is, for $t \leq 6e-3$, we report for each method the maximum difference Δs between the computed solution and the analytical one, that is, w_{12} reported in Section 3; the corresponding integration step h; the maximum differences ΔH between the computed Hamiltonian and the analytical one (see Table 4.1).

Here the value of h for *ODE*45 has to be read as the maximum of the used integration steps. Moreover, we recall that here the used machine precision is $2.2e-16$.

It is clear that all the numerical methods are equivalent about the approximation of the solution, but they behave in a different way about the conservation of energy. Indeed, in this short interval of time, the symplectic and the conservative methods preserve exactly energy, but the Runge-Kutta methods do not. Now a fundamental question arises: what happens over long time, when the analytical solution is not easily feasible?

The conservation of energy exhibits a completely different behavior, as Figure 4.1 shows; here the maximum error in Hamiltonian is reported versus increasing intervals of time.

We observe that the conservative method *TOMG* goes on conserving the energy with high constant accuracy, as requested. Actually, the Hamiltonian error always retains the order 10^{-12}.

On the contrary, *gni_irk*2 loses an order of magnitude in Hamiltonian error within 420 seconds; this means that in a couple of hours the system stops, instead of oscillating indefinitely.

Even *ODE*45 exhibits the same linearly increasing behavior of Hamiltonian error (not reported in Figure 4.2). This means that again the considered system is numerically simulated as it were dissipative. This is in accordance with the fact that *Hamiltonian systems are not structurally stable against non Hamiltonian perturbations*, such as those introduced by classical explicit Runge-Kutta methods (with both fixed and variable stepsizes).

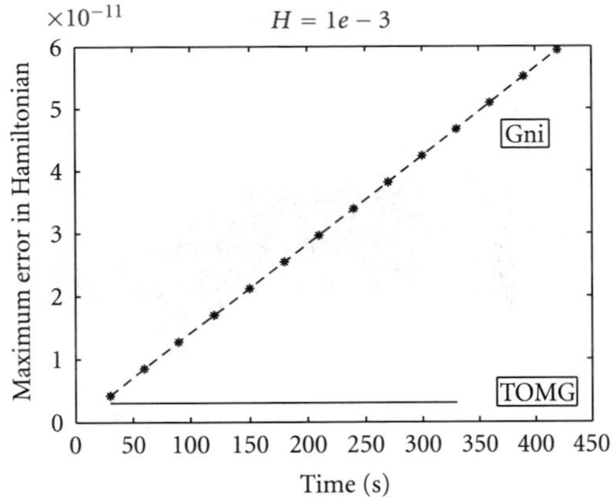

Figure 4.1

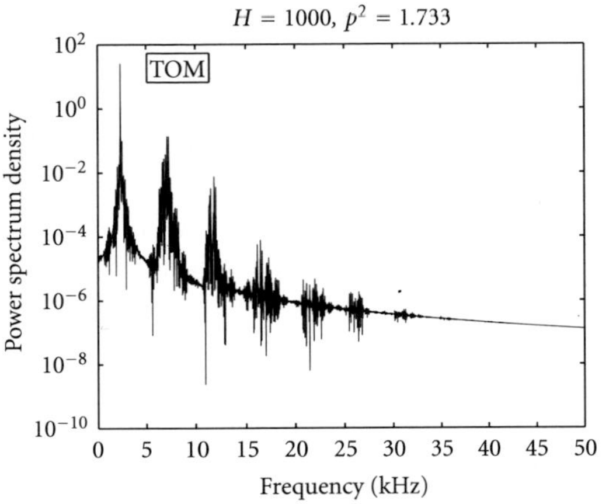

Figure 4.2

About *gni_irk*2, we carried out many other different tests and we concluded that the behavior of *gni_irk*2 does not change decreasing the stepsize, but it *does change* if we solve the scaled system (3.6) instead of system (2.1). In this case, the symplectic method preserves energy with a constant maximum error ΔH, which turns out to be $\mathcal{O}(10^{-12})$, exactly as *TOMG* does. It is clear that for the highly nonlinear Hamiltonian model (2.1), *gni_irk*2 experiences stability problems, which are well known indeed (e.g., [3]) for general symplectic methods.

Consequently, we suggest to choose the numerical method with great care, even for close-to-equilibrium orbits.

4.2. A far-from-equilibrium orbit. We chose a second set of initial conditions: $w_1(0) = w_2(0) = 0$, $\dot{w}_1(0) = 430.16$, $\dot{w}_2(0) = 266.31$, corresponding to the energy level $H = 1000$. Unfortunately, no analytical approximation of the solution is available for this case. Here the oscillation cycle is long about $4e-4$ seconds.

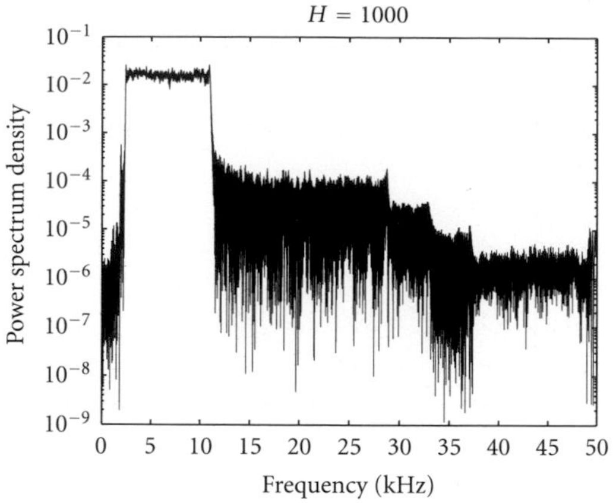

Figure 4.3

For $t \in [0, 10]$, we compare solutions computed by *TOMG* and *ODE*45, since all the results presented in literature are obtained by explicit Runge-Kutta methods of order 4 with variable stepsize, such as the method implemented by *ODE*45. There is no robust way to distinguish chaotic from quasiperiodic solutions on the basis of the computed waveform. So different tools (e.g., power spectra, Lyapunov exponents, Poincaré maps, phase diagrams, etc.) should be used to detect a chaotic behavior. Here we resort just to power spectrum, because it suffices to show how explicit Runge-Kutta methods can be misleading in the study of Hamiltonian systems.

In Figure 4.2, we report the power spectrum computed using the MATLAB *FFT* routine applied to the data provided by *TOMG*; the semilogarithmic scale is used. It is clear that the main frequencies are still two, as in the case of close-to-equilibrium orbit given in Section 4.1. However here the main frequencies are perturbed by others; this means that the nearly quasiperiodic orbit is going to become chaotic; indeed, the orbit exhibits the so-called "Nekhoroshev" regime (e.g., [4]). The same qualitative results are obtained by *gni_irk*2, but with larger perturbations of the main frequencies, as expected.

In Figure 4.3, we report the power spectrum computed using the MATLAB *FFT* routine applied to the data provided by *ODE*45 routine; again the semilogarithmic scale is used. Here the power spectrum suggests a *chaotic* behavior, which means a *completely different conclusion.* Actually, it does not present any dominant frequency, but a large band of frequencies very close one to another. It is obvious that any other tool, such as, for example, a Poincaré map should exhibit an analogous chaotic behavior, whenever it uses the same discrete set of numerical data, provided by *ODE*45.

5. Conclusions

Conservative dynamical systems *are not structurally stable* against nonconservative perturbations. Actually, the popular *explicit* Runge-Kutta methods (with both fixed and variable stepsizes) introduce such kind of perturbations. Indeed, mathematical models are often discretized according to algorithms that have little to do with the original problem, whereas computational methods should reflect known structural features of the problem under consideration, in particular they should preserve Hamiltonian for Hamiltonian problems (e.g., [6] and references therein).

As well known, the most basic structural property of Hamiltonian systems is that they are symplectic (i.e., they conserve phase-space volume); so symplectic numerical methods seem to be the first choice. However, according to the seminal paper by Ge Zhong and Marsed [9], if an integrator is both symplectic and conservative, it must be exact. Normally the luxury of an exact discretization is not available, therefore in general symplectic integration does not conserve Hamiltonian, in particular for highly nonlinear nonintegrable Hamiltonian systems. Here we suggest to use conservative methods, which guarantee the conservation of Hamiltonian. Then the drawback is that Hamiltonian phase-space structure will not be preserved. Indeed, the problem of the choice between symplectic and conservative methods remains open.

Actually, the integration method that is most suitable for a given Hamiltonian system ultimately depends on the nature of the physical problem, the integration time scale, and the kinds of questions addressed by the numerical simulation.

However, for systems which are to remain essentially nondissipative through numerical simulations (such as systems in structural engineering), conservative numerical methods seem to be the best choice.

References

[1] L. Brugnano and D. Trigiante, *Solving Differential Problems by Multistep Initial and Boundary Value Methods*, Stability and Control: Theory, Methods and Applications, vol. 6, Gordon and Breach Science, Amsterdam, 1998.

[2] A. Carini, L. Castiglioni, and P. S. Symonds, *Regular and chaotic responses of a Hamiltonian beam model*, European Journal of Mechanics. A Solids **16** (1997), no. 2, 341–368.

[3] O. Gonzalez and J. C. Simo, *On the stability of symplectic and energy-momentum algorithms for non-linear Hamiltonian systems with symmetry*, Computer Methods in Applied Mechanics and Engineering **134** (1996), no. 3-4, 197–222.

[4] M. Guzzo, *Long-term stability analysis of quasi integrable degenerate systems through the spectral formulation of the Nekhoroshev theorem*, Celestial Mechanics & Dynamical Astronomy **83** (2002), no. 1–4, 303–323.

[5] E. Hairer and M. Hairer, *GniCodes-Matlab Programs for Geometric Integration*, under the item "software", 2002, http://www.unige.ch/math/folks/hairer.

[6] R. Pavani, *Numerical Hamiltonian chaos*, Proceedings of 10th Jubilee National Congress on Theoretical and Applied Mathematics, Varna (Ya. Ivanov, E. Manoach, and R. Kazandjiev, eds.), Prof. Marin Drinov Academic Publishing House, Sofia, September 2005.

[7] ———, *On the representation of close-to-equilibrium solutions of n-dimensional conservative oscillators*, preprint in Quad. Dip. Mat. - Politecnico di Milano N. 644/P (2005).

[8] R. Pavani and R. Talamo, *On the representation of periodic solutions of Newtonian systems*, Mathematical and Computer Modelling **42** (2005), 1255–1262.

[9] G. Zhong and J. E. Marsden, *Lie-Poisson Hamilton-Jacobi theory and Lie-Poisson integrators*, Physics Letters. A **133** (1988), no. 3, 134–139.

Raffaella Pavani: Department of Mathematics, Politecnico di Milano, 20133 Milano, Italy
E-mail address: rafpav@mate.polimi.it

MULTIPLE POSITIVE SOLUTIONS OF SINGULAR p-LAPLACIAN PROBLEMS VIA VARIATIONAL METHODS

KANISHKA PERERA AND ELVES A. B. SILVA

We obtain multiple positive solutions of singular p-Laplacian problems using variational methods.

1. Introduction

Consider the boundary value problem

$$\begin{aligned} -\Delta_p u &= f(x,u) \quad \text{in } \Omega, \\ u &> 0 \quad \text{in } \Omega, \\ u &= 0 \quad \text{on } \partial\Omega, \end{aligned} \tag{1.1}$$

where Ω is a bounded domain in $\mathbb{R}^n$, $n \geq 1$ of class $C^{1,\alpha}$ for some $\alpha \in (0,1)$, $\Delta_p u = \operatorname{div}(|\nabla u|^{p-2}\nabla u)$ is the p-Laplacian of u, $1 < p < \infty$, and f is a Carathéodory function on $\Omega \times (0,\infty)$ satisfying

(f_1) $a_0(x) \leq f(x,t) \leq a_1(x)t^{-\gamma}$ for $0 < t < t_0$,

(f_2) $M_T := \sup_{(x,t)\in\Omega\times[t_0,T]} |f(x,t)| < \infty$ for all $T \geq t_0$

for some nontrivial measurable functions $a_0, a_1 \geq 0$ and constants $\gamma, t_0 > 0$, so that it may be singular at $t = 0$ and changes sign. We assume that

(f_3) there exists $\varphi \geq 0$ in $C_0^1(\overline{\Omega})$ such that $a_1\varphi^{-\gamma} \in L^q(\Omega)$, where $q = (p^*)'$ if $p \neq n$ (resp., $q > 1$ if $p = n$).

Here $(p^*)' = p^*/(p^* - 1)$ is the Hölder conjugate of the critical Sobolev exponent $p^* = np/(n-p)$ if $p < n$ (resp., $p^* = \infty$ if $p \geq n$).

The semilinear case $p = 2$ has been studied extensively in both bounded and unbounded domains (see, e.g., [2–4, 8–13, 15, 17–21, 24–26, 29, 30] and their references). The quasilinear ODE case $1 < p < \infty$, $n = 1$, was studied using fixed point theory by Agarwal et al. [1]. The general quasilinear case $1 < p < \infty$, $n \geq 1$, was studied using a simple cutoff argument and variational methods by Perera and Zhang [23] for $q > n$ and by Agarwal et al. [5], and Perera and Silva [22] for $q > n/p$. We remove these restrictions on q in this paper.

Hindawi Publishing Corporation
Proceedings of the Conference on Differential & Difference Equations and Applications, pp. 915–924

Note that (f_3) implies $a_1 \in L^q(\Omega)$. If $a_1 \in L^\infty(\Omega)$ and $\gamma < 1/(p^*)'$, (f_3) is satisfied with any φ whose interior normal derivative $\partial\varphi/\partial\nu > 0$ on $\partial\Omega$. A typical example is $f(x,t) = t^{-\gamma} + g(x,t)$, where g is a Carathéodory function on $\Omega \times [0,\infty)$ that is bounded on bounded t intervals. However, (f_3) does not necessarily require $\gamma < 1$ as usually assumed in the literature. For example, when Ω is the unit ball, $a_1(x) = (1-|x|^2)^\sigma$, $\sigma \ge 0$, and $\gamma < \sigma + 1/(p^*)'$, we can take $\varphi(x) = 1 - |x|^2$.

We may assume that $a_0 \in L^\infty(\Omega)$ by replacing it with $\min\{a_0, 1\}$ if necessary, so the problem

$$-\Delta_p u = a_0(x) \quad \text{in } \Omega, \qquad u = 0 \quad \text{on } \partial\Omega \tag{1.2}$$

has a unique weak solution $u \in C_0^1(\overline{\Omega})$ (see, e.g., Azizieh and Clément [7, Lemma 1.1]). Since $a_0 \ge 0$ and is nontrivial, so is u and hence

$$u > 0 \quad \text{in } \Omega, \qquad \frac{\partial u}{\partial \nu} > 0 \quad \text{on } \partial\Omega, \tag{1.3}$$

by the strong maximum principle of Vázquez [28]. Fix $0 < \varepsilon \le 1$ so small that $\underline{u} := \varepsilon^{1/(p-1)} u < t_0$. Then

$$-\Delta_p \underline{u} - f(x,\underline{u}) \le -(1-\varepsilon)a_0(x) \le 0 \tag{1.4}$$

by (f_1), so $\underline{u}$ is a subsolution of (1.1).

Let

$$f_{\underline{u}}(x,t) = \begin{cases} f(x,t), & t \ge \underline{u}(x), \\ f(x,\underline{u}(x)), & t < \underline{u}(x), \end{cases} \tag{1.5}$$

and consider the problem

$$-\Delta_p u = f_{\underline{u}}(x,u) \quad \text{in } \Omega, \qquad u = 0 \quad \text{on } \partial\Omega. \tag{1.6}$$

A standard argument shows that weak solutions of this problem are $\ge \underline{u}$ and hence also solutions of (1.1). We have

$$a_0(x) \le f_{\underline{u}}(x,t) \le a_1(x)\underline{u}(x)^{-\gamma}, \quad t < t_0, \tag{1.7}$$

by (f_1), $\inf_\Omega(\underline{u}/\varphi) > 0$ by (1.3) and hence $a_1 \underline{u}^{-\gamma} \in L^q(\Omega)$ by (f_3), and $f_{\underline{u}}(x,t) = f(x,t)$ for $t \ge t_0$. So the solutions of the modified problem (1.6) are the critical points of the C^1 functional:

$$\Phi(u) = \int_\Omega |\nabla u|^p - pF(x,u), \quad u \in W_0^{1,p}(\Omega), \tag{1.8}$$

where $F(x,t) = \int_0^t f_{\underline{u}}(x,s)\,ds$ if f grows at most critically:

(f_4) $|f(x,t)| \le Ct^{r-1}$ for $t \ge t_0$, where $r = p^*$ if $p < n$ (resp., $r > p$ if $p \ge n$).
As usual, C denotes a generic positive constant. We exploit this variational framework to seek $W_0^{1,p}(\Omega)$ solutions to the original problem.

2. Existence

LEMMA 2.1. *If (f_1) and (f_3) hold, and (1.1) has a supersolution $\overline{u} \ge \underline{u}$ in $W^{1,p}(\Omega)$, then it has a solution in the order interval $[\underline{u}, \overline{u}]$ in the cases:*
(i) $\overline{u} \in L^\infty(\Omega)$ *and (f_2) holds;*
(ii) (f_4) *holds.*

Proof. Let

$$\widetilde{f}_{\underline{u}}(x,t) = \begin{cases} f_{\underline{u}}(x,\overline{u}(x)), & t > \overline{u}(x), \\ f_{\underline{u}}(x,t), & t \le \overline{u}(x). \end{cases} \tag{2.1}$$

If $\overline{u} \in L^\infty(\Omega)$ and (f_2) holds,

$$|\widetilde{f}_{\underline{u}}| \le a_1 \underline{u}^{-\gamma} + M_{|\overline{u}|_\infty} \in L^q(\Omega) \tag{2.2}$$

by (1.7), where we set $M_T = 0$ for $T < t_0$ for convenience. If (f_4) holds,

$$|\widetilde{f}_{\underline{u}}| \le a_1 \underline{u}^{-\gamma} + C\overline{u}^{r-1} \in L^q(\Omega). \tag{2.3}$$

So the functional Φ with $F(x,t) = \int_0^t \widetilde{f}_{\underline{u}}(x,s)ds$ is bounded from below and coercive, and hence has a global minimizer by weak lower semicontinuity, in both cases. □

THEOREM 2.2. *If (f_1)–(f_3) hold and there is a $t_1 > t_0$ such that*

$$f(x,t_1) \le 0, \quad x \in \Omega, \tag{2.4}$$

then (1.1) has a solution $\le t_1$.

Proof. It follows from Lemma 2.1, taking $\overline{u} \equiv t_1$. □

Example 2.3. Problem (1.1) with $f(x,t) = t^{-\gamma} - e^t$ has a solution ≤ 1 for all $\gamma < 1/(p^*)'$.

Let $\lambda_1 > 0$ be the first eigenvalue of $-\Delta_p$, with the eigenfunction $\varphi_1 > 0$.

THEOREM 2.4. *If (f_1), (f_3), and (f_4) hold, and*

$$f(x,t) \le \lambda t^{p-1} + C, \quad t \ge t_0, \tag{2.5}$$

for some $0 \le \lambda < \lambda_1$, then (1.1) has a solution.

Proof. Let

$$\overline{f}(x,t) = \lambda (t^+)^{p-1} + C + a_1(x)\underline{u}(x)^{-\gamma}. \tag{2.6}$$

The functional Φ with $F(x,t) = \int_0^t \overline{f}(x,s)ds$ has a global minimizer $\overline{u}$ since $\lambda < \lambda_1$, and $\overline{u} \geq \underline{u}$ since

$$-\Delta_p \overline{u} = \overline{f}(x,\overline{u}) \geq a_1(x)\underline{u}(x)^{-\gamma} \geq a_0(x) \geq \varepsilon a_0(x) = -\Delta_p \underline{u} \tag{2.7}$$

by (f_1). Then

$$-\Delta_p \overline{u} \geq \lambda \overline{u}^{p-1} + C + a_1(x)\overline{u}^{-\gamma} \geq f(x,\overline{u}) \tag{2.8}$$

by (2.5) and (f_1), so $\overline{u}$ is a supersolution of (1.1), and the conclusion follows from Lemma 2.1. □

Example 2.5. Problem (1.1) with $f(x,t) = t^{-\gamma} + \lambda t^{p-1} + t^{s-1}$ has a solution for all $\gamma < 1/(p^*)'$, $\lambda < \lambda_1$, and $1 \leq s < p$.

THEOREM 2.6. *If (f_1), (f_3), and (f_4) hold, and*

$$f(x,t) \leq \lambda_1 t^{p-1} - g(x,t), \quad t \geq t_1, \tag{2.9}$$

for some $t_1 \geq t_0$ and a Carathéodory function g on $\Omega \times [t_1, \infty)$ satisfying

$$|g(x,t)| \leq Ct^{r-1}, \tag{2.10}$$

where r is as in (f_4),

$$G(x,t) := \int_{t_1}^t g(x,s)ds \geq -C, \tag{2.11}$$

$$\lim_{t\to\infty} G(x,t) = \infty \quad \text{on a set of positive measure}, \tag{2.12}$$

then (1.1) has a solution.

Proof. Take $h \in C(\mathbb{R}, [0,1])$ such that $h(t) = 1$ for $t \leq t_1$ and $h(t) = 0$ for $t \geq$ some $t_2 > t_1$, and let

$$\overline{f}(x,t) = (1 - h(t))\left[\lambda_1 t^{p-1} - g(x,t)\right] + h(t)a_1(x)\underline{u}(x)^{-\gamma}. \tag{2.13}$$

Following the proof of Theorem 2.4, it suffices to show that the functional Φ with $F(x,t) = \int_{t_2}^t \overline{f}(x,s)ds$ is bounded from below and coercive.

We have

$$F(x,t) \leq \begin{cases} \dfrac{\lambda_1}{p}t^p - G(x,t) + C, & t \geq t_2, \\ C, & t < t_2, \end{cases} \tag{2.14}$$

and hence

$$\Phi(u) \geq \int_\Omega |\nabla u|^p - \lambda_1 (u^+)^p + p\int_{u \geq t_2} G(x,u) - C, \tag{2.15}$$

so Φ is bounded from below by (2.11).

Suppose Φ is not coercive, say, $\rho_j := \|u_j\| \to \infty$ and $\Phi(u_j) \leq C$. Then for a subsequence, $\widetilde{u}_j := u_j/\rho_j$ converges to some $\widetilde{u}$ weakly in $W_0^{1,p}(\Omega)$, strongly in $L^p(\Omega)$, and a.e. in Ω. Since $\|\widetilde{u}_j\| \equiv 1$, $\|\widetilde{u}\| \leq 1$. By (2.11) and (2.15),

$$\lambda_1 \int_\Omega (u_j^+)^p \geq \rho_j^p - C, \tag{2.16}$$

and dividing by ρ_j^p and passing to the limit give

$$\lambda_1 |\widetilde{u}^+|_p^p \geq 1 \geq \|\widetilde{u}\|^p \geq \lambda_1 |\widetilde{u}|_p^p, \tag{2.17}$$

so $\widetilde{u} = \varphi_1$. Then $u_j(x) = \rho_j \widetilde{u}_j(x) \to \infty$ a.e., and hence

$$\Phi(u_j) \geq p \int_{u_j \geq t_2} G(x, u_j) - C \longrightarrow \infty \tag{2.18}$$

by (2.11), (2.12), (2.15), and Fatou's lemma, a contradiction. □

Example 2.7. Problem (1.1) with $f(x,t) = t^{-\gamma} + \lambda_1 t^{p-1} - t^{s-1}$ has a solution for all $\gamma < 1/(p^*)'$ and $1 \leq s < p$.

Remark 2.8. When $p > n$, the supersolutions $\overline{u}$ constructed in the proofs of Theorems 2.4 and 2.6 are in $L^\infty(\Omega)$ by the Sobolev embedding and hence the weaker condition (f_2) can be used in place of (f_4). The same is true when $p \leq n$ by the regularity results of Guedda and Véron [16] if $q > n/p$ in (f_3), in which case solutions $\geq \underline{u}$ of (1.1) are also in $L^\infty(\Omega)$ (see Agarwal et al. [5, proof of Proposition 2.1]).

3. Multiplicity

Throughout this section, we assume (f_1), (f_3), (f_4), and

(f_5) there exists $t_2 > t_1 > t_0$ and $\lambda < \lambda_1$ such that $\int_{t_1}^t f(x,s)ds \leq (\lambda/p)(t - t_1)^p$ for $t_1 \leq t \leq t_2$.

In particular, $f(x,t_1) \leq 0$ and hence (1.1) has a solution $u_0 \in [\underline{u}, t_1]$ by Theorem 2.2. Noting that u_0 is also a subsolution of (1.1), we seek a second solution $u_1 \geq u_0$ as another critical point of the functional Φ with

$$F(x,t) = \int_{t_1}^t f_{u_0}(x,s)ds, \qquad f_{u_0}(x,t) = \begin{cases} f(x,t), & t \geq u_0(x), \\ f(x,u_0(x)), & t < u_0(x). \end{cases} \tag{3.1}$$

By (f_1) and (f_2),

$$|f_{u_0}(x,t)| \leq a_1(x)\underline{u}(x)^{-\gamma} + M_{t_1} \in L^q(\Omega), \quad t < t_1, \tag{3.2}$$

since $u_0 \geq \underline{u}$.

The functional $\widetilde{\Phi}$ given by (1.8) with F replaced by

$$\widetilde{F}(x,t) = \int_{t_1}^{t} \widetilde{f}_{u_0}(x,s)\,ds, \qquad \widetilde{f}_{u_0}(x,t) = \begin{cases} f_{u_0}(x,t_1), & t > t_1, \\ f_{u_0}(x,t), & t \le t_1, \end{cases} \tag{3.3}$$

has a global minimizer in $[u_0,t_1]$ as in the proof of Lemma 2.1, which we assume is u_0 itself since otherwise we are done.

Lemma 3.1. *u_0 is a local minimizer of Φ.*

Proof. If $u_j \to u_0$, writing $u_j = v_j + w_j$, where

$$v_j = \min\{u_j,t_1\} \longrightarrow u_0, \qquad w_j = \max\{u_j,t_1\} - t_1 \longrightarrow 0, \tag{3.4}$$

we have

$$\Phi(u_j) = \Phi(v_j) + \|w_j\|^p - p\int_\Omega F(x,w_j+t_1). \tag{3.5}$$

Since $v_j, u_0 \le t_1$ and u_0 is a global minimizer of $\widetilde{\Phi}$,

$$\Phi(v_j) = \widetilde{\Phi}(v_j) \ge \widetilde{\Phi}(u_0) = \Phi(u_0). \tag{3.6}$$

By (f_4) and (f_5),

$$F(x,t) \le \frac{\lambda}{p}(t-t_1)^p + C(t-t_1)^r, \quad t \ge t_1, \tag{3.7}$$

and hence

$$p\int_\Omega F(x,w_j+t_1) \le \frac{\lambda}{\lambda_1}\|w_j\|^p + C\|w_j\|^r. \tag{3.8}$$

Since $\lambda < \lambda_1$ and $r > p$, it follows that $\Phi(u_j) \ge \Phi(u_0)$ for large j. □

We recall that Φ satisfies the Cerami compactness condition (C) if every sequence (u_j), such that

$$\Phi(u_j) \text{ is bounded}, \qquad (1+\|u_j\|)\|\Phi'(u_j)\| \longrightarrow 0, \tag{3.9}$$

has a convergent subsequence. For $t \ge t_1$, let

$$\begin{aligned} g(x,t) &= f(x,t) - \lambda_1 t^{p-1}, \\ G(x,t) &= \int_{t_1}^{t} g(x,s)\,ds = F(x,t) - \frac{\lambda_1}{p}(t^p - t_1^p). \end{aligned} \tag{3.10}$$

LEMMA 3.2. *If* (f_1) *and* (f_3)–(f_5) *hold,*

$$G(x,t) \geq -C, \quad t \geq t_1, \tag{3.11}$$

$$\lim_{t\to\infty} G(x,t) = \infty \quad \text{on a set of positive measure}, \tag{3.12}$$

and Φ *satisfies (C), then (1.1) has two solutions* $u_1 \geq u_0$.

Proof. We have

$$\Phi(t\varphi_1) \leq C - p\int_{t\varphi_1 \geq t_1} G(x,t\varphi_1) \longrightarrow -\infty \quad \text{as } t \longrightarrow \infty \tag{3.13}$$

by (3.2), (3.11), (3.12), and Fatou's lemma, and the conclusion follows from Lemma 3.1 and the mountain pass lemma. □

THEOREM 3.3. *If* (f_1) *and* (f_3)–(f_5) *hold,*

$$G(x,t) \leq Ct^p, \quad t \geq t_1, \tag{3.14}$$

$$\lim_{t\to\infty} \frac{G(x,t)}{t^p} = 0 \quad \text{a.e.}, \tag{3.15}$$

$$H(x,t) := pG(x,t) - tg(x,t) \geq -C, \quad t \geq t_1, \tag{3.16}$$

$$\lim_{t\to\infty} H(x,t) = \infty \quad \text{on a set of positive measure}, \tag{3.17}$$

then (1.1) has two solutions $u_1 \geq u_0$.

Proof. We apply Lemma 3.2. We have

$$\frac{\partial}{\partial t}\left[\frac{G(x,t)}{t^p}\right] = -\frac{H(x,t)}{t^{p+1}}, \tag{3.18}$$

and hence

$$G(x,t) = t^p \int_t^\infty \frac{H(x,s)}{s^{p+1}}\,ds \geq \frac{1}{p} \inf_{s\geq t} H(x,s) \quad \text{a.e.} \tag{3.19}$$

by (3.15), so (3.16) and (3.17) imply (3.11) and (3.12), respectively.

As usual, to verify (C) it suffices to show that every sequence (u_j) satisfying (3.9) is bounded. Suppose $\rho_j := \|u_j\| \to \infty$ along a subsequence. Then for a further subsequence, $\widetilde{u}_j := u_j/\rho_j$ converges to some $\widetilde{u}$ weakly in $W_0^{1,p}(\Omega)$, strongly in $L^p(\Omega)$, and a.e. in Ω. By (3.2),

$$\Phi(u_j) \geq \rho_j^p - \lambda_1 \int_\Omega (u_j^+)^p - p\int_{u_j\geq t_1} G(x,u_j) - C(\rho_j + 1). \tag{3.20}$$

Dividing by ρ_j^p and noting that

$$\int_{u_j\geq t_1} \frac{G(x,u_j)}{\rho_j^p} = \int_{u_j\geq t_1} \frac{G(x,u_j)}{u_j^p}\widetilde{u}_j^p \longrightarrow 0 \tag{3.21}$$

by (3.14), (3.15), and Lebesgue's dominated convergence theorem, $\tilde{u} = \varphi_1$ as in the proof of Theorem 2.6. Then $u_j(x) \to \infty$ a.e., and hence

$$\frac{1}{p}\Phi'(u_j)(u_j^+ + 2u_j^-) - \Phi(u_j) \geq \|u_j^-\|^p + \int_{u_j \geq t_1} H(x,u_j) - C(\|u_j^-\| + 1) \longrightarrow \infty \tag{3.22}$$

by (3.2), (3.16), (3.17), and Fatou's lemma, contradicting (3.9). □

Example 3.4. Problem (1.1) with $f(x,t) = t^{-\gamma} + \lambda_1 t^{p-1} + t^{s-1} - \mu$ has two-ordered solutions for all $\gamma < 1/(p^*)'$, $1 < s < p$, and large $\mu > 0$.

Theorem 3.5. *If (f_1)–(f_3) and (f_5) hold, and*

$$\lambda \leq \frac{f(x,t)}{t^{p-1}} \leq C, \quad t \geq t_3, \tag{3.23}$$

for some $t_3 > t_2$ and $\lambda > \lambda_1$, then (1.1) has two solutions $u_1 \geq u_0$.

Proof. Clearly, (3.23) implies (3.11) and (3.12). To verify (C), suppose (u_j) satisfies (3.9), $\rho_j := \|u_j\| \to \infty$, and $\tilde{u}_j := u_j/\rho_j \to \tilde{u}$ weakly in $W_0^{1,p}(\Omega)$, strongly in $L^p(\Omega)$, and a.e. in Ω as in the proof of Theorem 3.3. By (3.2) and (f_4),

$$\frac{\Phi'(u_j)v}{p\rho_j^{p-1}} = \int_\Omega |\nabla\tilde{u}_j|^{p-2}\nabla\tilde{u}_j \cdot \nabla v - \alpha_j(x)\tilde{u}_j^{p-1}v + o(\|v\|), \tag{3.24}$$

where

$$\alpha_j(x) = \begin{cases} \dfrac{f(x,u_j(x))}{u_j(x)^{p-1}}, & u_j(x) \geq t_3, \\ 0, & u_j(x) < t_3. \end{cases} \tag{3.25}$$

By (3.23), $0 \leq \alpha_j \leq C$, so taking $v = \tilde{u}^-$, $\tilde{u}_j$ and passing to the limit give $\tilde{u} \geq 0$, $\not\equiv 0$, respectively. Moreover, a subsequence of (α_j) converges to some $0 \leq \alpha \leq C$ weakly in $L^s(\Omega)$ for any $1 < s < \infty$, and passing to the limit in (3.24) shows that $\tilde{u}$ satisfies

$$\begin{aligned} -\Delta_p\tilde{u} &= \alpha(x)\tilde{u}^{p-1} \quad \text{in } \Omega, \\ \tilde{u} &= 0 \quad \text{on } \partial\Omega. \end{aligned} \tag{3.26}$$

So $\tilde{u} \in L^\infty(\Omega) \cap C^1(\Omega)$ by Anane [6] and DiBenedetto [14], and hence $\tilde{u} > 0$ by the Harnack inequality of Trudinger [27]. This implies that $\alpha \geq \lambda$ and that the first eigenvalue of $-\Delta_p$ with weight α given by

$$\inf_{u \in W_0^{1,p}(\Omega)\setminus\{0\}} \frac{\int_\Omega |\nabla u|^p}{\int_\Omega \alpha(x)|u|^p} = 1. \tag{3.27}$$

Then

$$1 \leq \frac{\int_\Omega |\nabla \varphi_1|^p}{\int_\Omega \alpha(x)\varphi_1^p} \leq \frac{\lambda_1}{\lambda} < 1, \tag{3.28}$$

a contradiction. □

Example 3.6. Problem (1.1) with $f(x,t) = t^{-\gamma} + \lambda t^{p-1} - t^{s-1} - \mu$ has two-ordered solutions for all $\gamma < 1/(p^*)'$, $\lambda > \lambda_1$, $1 \leq s < p$, and large $\mu > 0$.

THEOREM 3.7. *If* (f_1), (f_3), (f_4) *with* $r < p^*$, *and* (f_5) *hold, and*

$$0 < \theta F(x,t) \leq t f(x,t), \quad t \geq t_3, \tag{3.29}$$

for some $t_3 > t_2$ *and* $\theta > p$, *then (1.1) has two solutions* $u_1 \geq u_0$.

Proof. It follows from Lemma 3.2 since (3.29) implies that

$$F(x,t) \geq F(x,t_3)\left(\frac{t}{t_3}\right)^\theta, \quad t \geq t_3, \tag{3.30}$$

and that Φ satisfies (C). □

Example 3.8. Problem (1.1) with $f(x,t) = t^{-\gamma} + t^{\theta-1} - \mu$ has two-ordered solutions for all $\gamma < 1/(p^*)'$, $p < \theta < p^*$, and large $\mu > 0$.

References

[1] R. P. Agarwal, H. Lü, and D. O'Regan, *Existence theorems for the one-dimensional singular p-Laplacian equation with sign changing nonlinearities*, Applied Mathematics and Computation **143** (2003), no. 1, 15–38.

[2] R. P. Agarwal and D. O'Regan, *Singular boundary value problems for superlinear second order ordinary and delay differential equations*, Journal of Differential Equations **130** (1996), no. 2, 333–355.

[3] ———, *Singular initial and boundary value problems with sign changing nonlinearities*, IMA Journal of Applied Mathematics **65** (2000), no. 2, 173–198.

[4] R. P. Agarwal, K. Perera, and D. O'Regan, *Multiple positive solutions of singular problems by variational methods*, Proceedings of the American Mathematical Society **134** (2006), no. 3, 817–824.

[5] ———, *A variational approach to singular quasilinear elliptic problems with sign changing nonlinearities*, to appear in Applicable Analysis.

[6] A. Anane, *Simplicité et isolation de la première valeur propre du p-Laplacien avec poids*, Comptes Rendus de l'Académie des Sciences. Série I. Mathématique **305** (1987), no. 16, 725–728.

[7] C. Azizieh and Ph. Clément, *A priori estimates and continuation methods for positive solutions of p-Laplace equations*, Journal of Differential Equations **179** (2002), no. 1, 213–245.

[8] A. Canino, *Minimax methods for singular elliptic equations with an application to a jumping problem*, Journal of Differential Equations **221** (2006), no. 1, 210–223.

[9] A. Canino and M. Degiovanni, *A variational approach to a class of singular semilinear elliptic equations*, Journal of Convex Analysis **11** (2004), no. 1, 147–162.

[10] M. M. Coclite and G. Palmieri, *On a singular nonlinear Dirichlet problem*, Communications in Partial Differential Equations **14** (1989), no. 10, 1315–1327.

[11] M. G. Crandall, P. H. Rabinowitz, and L. Tartar, *On a Dirichlet problem with a singular nonlinearity*, Communications in Partial Differential Equations **2** (1977), no. 2, 193–222.
[12] M. A. del Pino, *A global estimate for the gradient in a singular elliptic boundary value problem*, Proceedings of the Royal Society of Edinburgh. Section A. Mathematics **122** (1992), no. 3-4, 341–352.
[13] J. I. Diaz, J.-M. Morel, and L. Oswald, *An elliptic equation with singular nonlinearity*, Communications in Partial Differential Equations **12** (1987), no. 12, 1333–1344.
[14] E. DiBenedetto, *$C^{1+\alpha}$ local regularity of weak solutions of degenerate elliptic equations*, Nonlinear Analysis. Theory, Methods & Applications **7** (1983), no. 8, 827–850.
[15] A. L. Edelson, *Entire solutions of singular elliptic equations*, Journal of Mathematical Analysis and Applications **139** (1989), no. 2, 523–532.
[16] M. Guedda and L. Véron, *Quasilinear elliptic equations involving critical Sobolev exponents*, Nonlinear Analysis. Theory, Methods & Applications **13** (1989), no. 8, 879–902.
[17] N. Hirano, C. Saccon, and N. Shioji, *Existence of multiple positive solutions for singular elliptic problems with concave and convex nonlinearities*, Advances in Differential Equations **9** (2004), no. 1-2, 197–220.
[18] ———, *Brezis-Nirenberg type theorems and multiplicity of positive solutions for a singular elliptic problem*, preprint, 2004.
[19] T. Kusano and C. A. Swanson, *Entire positive solutions of singular semilinear elliptic equations*, Japanese Journal of Mathematics. New Series **11** (1985), no. 1, 145–155.
[20] A. V. Lair and A. W. Shaker, *Classical and weak solutions of a singular semilinear elliptic problem*, Journal of Mathematical Analysis and Applications **211** (1997), no. 2, 371–385.
[21] A. C. Lazer and P. J. McKenna, *On a singular nonlinear elliptic boundary-value problem*, Proceedings of the American Mathematical Society **111** (1991), no. 3, 721–730.
[22] K. Perera and E. A. B. Silva, *Existence and multiplicity of positive solutions for singular quasilinear problems*, to appear in Journal of Mathematical Analysis and Applications.
[23] K. Perera and Z. Zhang, *Multiple positive solutions of singular p-Laplacian problems by variational methods*, Boundary Value Problems **2005** (2005), no. 3, 377–382.
[24] A. W. Shaker, *On singular semilinear elliptic equations*, Journal of Mathematical Analysis and Applications **173** (1993), no. 1, 222–228.
[25] J. Shi and M. Yao, *On a singular nonlinear semilinear elliptic problem*, Proceedings of the Royal Society of Edinburgh. Section A **128** (1998), no. 6, 1389–1401.
[26] Y. Sun, S. Wu, and Y. Long, *Combined effects of singular and superlinear nonlinearities in some singular boundary value problems*, Journal of Differential Equations **176** (2001), no. 2, 511–531.
[27] N. S. Trudinger, *On Harnack type inequalities and their application to quasilinear elliptic equations*, Communications on Pure and Applied Mathematics **20** (1967), 721–747.
[28] J. L. Vázquez, *A strong maximum principle for some quasilinear elliptic equations*, Applied Mathematics and Optimization **12** (1984), no. 3, 191–202.
[29] M. Wiegner, *A degenerate diffusion equation with a nonlinear source term*, Nonlinear Analysis. Theory, Methods & Applications **28** (1997), no. 12, 1977–1995.
[30] Z. Zhang, *Critical points and positive solutions of singular elliptic boundary value problems*, Journal of Mathematical Analysis and Applications **302** (2005), no. 2, 476–483.

Kanishka Perera: Department of Mathematical Sciences, College of Science, Florida Institute of Technology, Melbourne, FL 32901-6975, USA
E-mail address: kperera@fit.edu

Elves A. B. Silva: Departamento de Matemática, Instituto de Ciências Exatas, Universidade de Brasília, CEP 70910-900 Brazília, DF, Brazil
E-mail address: elves@unb.br

QUANTIZATION OF LIGHT FIELD IN PERIODIC DIELECTRICS WITH AND WITHOUT THE COUPLED MODE THEORY

VLASTA PEŘINOVÁ AND ANTONÍN LUKŠ

The known form (separated variables) of modal functions of a rectangular cavity may be more easily compared with the modal functions of a rectangular waveguide if a rectangular waveguide of a finite length is considered (the usual periodic boundary conditions). Perfect acquaintance with modal functions allows one to understand macroscopic quantization of the electromagnetic field in a homogeneous or inhomogeneous medium.

1. Introduction

Waveguides are useful optical devices. An optical circuit can be made using them and various optical couplers and switches. Classical theory of optical waveguides and couplers has been elaborated in the 1970s [2], performance and the quantum theory have been gaining importance. Recently, quantum entanglement has been pointed out as another resource. Quantum descriptions may be very simple, but essentially, they ought to be based on a perfect knowledge of quantization. By way of paradox, quantization is based on classical normal modes. Therefore, it is appropriate to concentrate ourselves on normal modes of rectangular mirror waveguide. It will be assumed that the waveguide is filled with homogeneous refractive medium.

2. Classical description of the electromagnetic field

Vast literature has been devoted to the solution of the Maxwell equations and their value for the wave and quantum optics cannot be denied. Depending on the system of physical units used, the Maxwell equations have several forms. Let us mention only two of them, appropriate to the SI units and the Gaussian units. The time-dependent vector fields, which enter these equations, are $\mathbf{E}(x,y,z,t)$, the electric strength vector field, and $\mathbf{B}(x,y,z,t)$, the magnetic induction vector field. In fact, other two fields are used, but they can also be eliminated through the so-called constitutive relations. The so-called

Hindawi Publishing Corporation
Proceedings of the Conference on Differential & Difference Equations and Applications, pp. 925–934

monochromaticity assumption

$$\begin{aligned} \mathbf{E}(x,y,z,t) &= \mathbf{E}(x,y,z;\omega)\exp(i\omega t), \\ \mathbf{B}(x,y,z,t) &= \mathbf{B}(x,y,z;\omega)\exp(i\omega t) \end{aligned} \tag{2.1}$$

allows one to treat the time-independent Maxwell equations.

As stated in the introduction, we restrict ourselves to a rectangular mirror waveguide. We assume that it has an infinite length, a width $2a_x$, and the heigth $2b_y$. The coordinate system is chosen so that the z-axis is the axis of the waveguide and the x-, y-axes are parallel with sides of the waveguide.

We deal with nonvanishing solutions of the time-independent Maxwell equations:

$$\begin{aligned} \nabla \times \frac{1}{\mu(x,y,z;\omega)}\mathbf{B}(x,y,z;\omega) - i\omega\epsilon(x,y,z;\omega)\mathbf{E}(x,y,z;\omega) &= \mathbf{0}, \\ \nabla \times \mathbf{E}(x,y,z;\omega) + i\omega\mathbf{B}(x,y,z;\omega) &= \mathbf{0}, \\ \nabla \cdot [\epsilon(x,y,z;\omega)\mathbf{E}(x,y,z;\omega)] &= 0, \\ \nabla \cdot \mathbf{B}(x,y,z;\omega) &= 0, \end{aligned} \tag{2.2}$$

where $\mathbf{E}(x,y,z;\omega)$, $\mathbf{B}(x,y,z;\omega)$ are vector-valued functions in a domain

$$G = \{(x,y,z) : -a_x < x < a_x, -a_y < y < a_y, -\infty < z < \infty\} \tag{2.3}$$

and $\omega > 0$ is a parameter. The desired solutions are to obey the boundary conditions

$$\mathbf{n}(x,y,z) \times \mathbf{E}(x,y,z;\omega) = \mathbf{0}, \qquad \mathbf{n}(x,y,z) \cdot \mathbf{B}(x,y,z;\omega) = 0, \tag{2.4}$$

where $\mathbf{n}(x,y,z)$ is any unit exterior normal vector at the point $(x,y,z) \in \partial G$. The boundary conditions (2.4) are a formal expression of the fact that the walls of the waveguide are perfect mirrors.

Here $\mu(x,y,z;\omega) = \mu_0$, $\epsilon(x,y,z;\omega)$ is a function defined up to a finite number of z-values such that

$$\epsilon(x,y,z;\omega) = \begin{cases} \epsilon_0\epsilon_{r0} & \text{for } z < 0,\ z > L, \\ \epsilon_0\epsilon_r(z) & \text{for } 0 < z < L, \end{cases} \tag{2.5}$$

with $\mu_0 > 0$, $\mu_0 = 4\pi \times 10^{-7}$ Hm^{-1} the free-space magnetic permeability, $\epsilon_0 > 0$ the free-space electric permittivity, $\epsilon_{r0} > 0$, $\epsilon_r(z)$ are relative electric permittivities of the medium. The medium electric permittivity $\epsilon(z) = \epsilon_0\epsilon_r(z)$ has a period Λ, $\Lambda \mid L$, or $\epsilon(z) = \epsilon(z+\Lambda)$ for $0 < z < L - \Lambda$, and is a positive function $\int_0^L \epsilon(z)dz = L\epsilon_0\epsilon_{r0}$.

We assume that the waveguide is filled with a homogeneous nonmagnetic refractive medium, which is also nondispersive and lossless for simplicity. This assumption holds on infinite intervals $(-\infty,0)$ and (L,∞) in the z-coordinate. On the finite interval $(0,L)$, the medium is not homogeneous, but it is periodic. On average, its electric permittivity equals to that of the homogeneous medium assumed.

3. Modal functions

For illustration, we will consider examples where solutions have finite norms in Section 4. Let us assume that $\epsilon(x,y,z;\omega) = \epsilon_0\epsilon_{r0}$ everywhere in G. We will express the solution in the form

$$\mathbf{E}(x,y,z;\omega) = \mathbf{E}(x,y)\exp(-ik_z z), \qquad \mathbf{B}(x,y,z;\omega) = \mathbf{B}(x,y)\exp(-ik_z z), \tag{3.1}$$

with $k_z \neq 0$. In analogy with the electromagnetic field theory, from (2.2) we derive the time-independent wave equation

$$\left(\Delta + \frac{\omega^2}{v^2}\right)\mathbf{C} = 0, \tag{3.2}$$

where

$$v = \frac{1}{\sqrt{\epsilon_0\epsilon_{r0}\mu_0}}, \tag{3.3}$$

and $\mathbf{C} \equiv \mathbf{C}(x,y,z;\omega)$ stands for $\mathbf{E}$ and $\mathbf{B}$ substitutionally. Respecting (3.1), we may rewrite (3.2) in the form

$$\left(\frac{\partial^2}{\partial x^2} + \frac{\partial^2}{\partial y^2}\right)\mathbf{C} + \left(\frac{\omega^2}{v^2} - k_z^2\right)\mathbf{C} = 0. \tag{3.4}$$

Introducing the notation $E_r(x,y)$, $B_r(x,y)$, $r = x,y,z$, for the components of the vectors $\mathbf{E}(x,y)$, $\mathbf{B}(x,y)$, respectively, we have [1]

$$\begin{aligned}
E_x(x,y) &= \alpha\cos\left(\frac{m\pi}{2a_x}(x+a_x)\right)\sin\left(\frac{n\pi}{2a_y}(y+a_y)\right),\\
E_y(x,y) &= \beta\sin\left(\frac{m\pi}{2a_x}(x+a_x)\right)\cos\left(\frac{n\pi}{2a_y}(y+a_y)\right),\\
E_z(x,y) &= -i\gamma\sin\left(\frac{m\pi}{2a_x}(x+a_x)\right)\sin\left(\frac{n\pi}{2a_y}(y+a_y)\right),\\
B_x(x,y) &= -i\alpha'\sin\left(\frac{m\pi}{2a_x}(x+a_x)\right)\cos\left(\frac{n\pi}{2a_y}(y+a_y)\right),\\
B_y(x,y) &= i\beta'\cos\left(\frac{m\pi}{2a_x}(x+a_x)\right)\sin\left(\frac{n\pi}{2a_y}(y+a_y)\right),\\
B_z(x,y) &= \gamma'\cos\left(\frac{m\pi}{2a_x}(x+a_x)\right)\cos\left(\frac{n\pi}{2a_y}(y+a_y)\right),
\end{aligned} \tag{3.5}$$

where $m,n = 0,1,\ldots,\infty$. Equation (3.4) yields the relation among m,n,k_z, and ω,

$$\left(\frac{m\pi}{2a_x}\right)^2 + \left(\frac{n\pi}{2a_y}\right)^2 + k_z^2 = \frac{\omega^2}{v^2}. \tag{3.6}$$

No solution of this kind exists if $\omega < \omega_g$, where

$$\omega_g = \omega_{mn} = v\sqrt{\left(\frac{m\pi}{2a_x}\right)^2 + \left(\frac{n\pi}{2a_y}\right)^2}. \tag{3.7}$$

We can specify one of two linear independent solutions for $m, n = 0, 1, \ldots, \infty$, $m+n \geq 1$,

$$\begin{aligned}
\alpha_{\mathrm{TE}} &= i\omega\frac{k_y}{k_x^2+k_y^2}\gamma'_{\mathrm{TE}}, & \alpha'_{\mathrm{TE}} &= \frac{k_x k_z}{k_x^2+k_y^2}\gamma'_{\mathrm{TE}},\\
\beta_{\mathrm{TE}} &= -i\omega\frac{k_x}{k_x^2+k_y^2}\gamma'_{\mathrm{TE}}, & \beta'_{\mathrm{TE}} &= \frac{k_y k_z}{k_x^2+k_y^2}\gamma'_{\mathrm{TE}},\\
\gamma_{\mathrm{TE}} &= 0, & \gamma'_{\mathrm{TE}} &= \gamma'_{\mathrm{TE}},
\end{aligned} \tag{3.8}$$

$$\begin{aligned}
\alpha_{\mathrm{TM}} &= \frac{k_x k_z}{k_x^2+k_y^2}\gamma_{\mathrm{TM}}, & \alpha'_{\mathrm{TM}} &= \frac{1}{v^2}\frac{i\omega k_y}{k_x^2+k_y^2}\gamma_{\mathrm{TM}},\\
\beta_{\mathrm{TM}} &= \frac{k_y k_z}{k_x^2+k_y^2}\gamma_{\mathrm{TM}}, & \beta'_{\mathrm{TM}} &= \frac{1}{v^2}\frac{-i\omega k_x}{k_x^2+k_y^2}\gamma_{\mathrm{TM}},\\
\gamma_{\mathrm{TM}} &= \gamma_{\mathrm{TM}}, & \gamma'_{\mathrm{TM}} &= 0.
\end{aligned} \tag{3.9}$$

Here TE means transverse electric and TM transverse magnetic. For $m = 0$, a TE solution exists, but no TM solutions exist, for $n = 0$, the same occurs and otherwise, both solutions exist. In (3.8) and (3.9), k_x, k_y are abbreviations, $k_x \equiv m\pi/2a_x$, $k_y \equiv n\pi/2a_y$. Let us remark that γ'_{TE} and γ_{TM} are complex parameters.

4. Normalized modes of the electromagnetic field

The normalization of modal functions of the electromagnetic field, which is made for the sake of quantization, can be based, in optics, on a simple connection of the vector potential with the electric field strength vector. This connection follows from the use of the so-called Coulomb gauge. We assume that the waveguide is filled with a refractive medium. To work with a finite volume, we will consider a subset $G = G_\perp \times \mathrm{S}^1(-a_z \leq z < a_z)$, with the boundary $\partial G = \partial G_\perp \times \mathrm{S}^1(-a_z \leq z < a_z)$, of a flat non-Euclidean space $\mathrm{R}^2 \times \mathrm{S}^1(-a_z \leq z < a_z)$, where $\mathrm{S}^1(-a_z \leq z < a_z)$ means a topological circle of the length $2a_z$.

In optics, the quantization is a definition of the vector potential operator $\hat{\mathbf{A}}^{(\mathrm{t})}(\mathbf{x},t)$ by the relation

$$\hat{\mathbf{A}}^{(\mathrm{t})}(\mathbf{x},t) = \sum_{j\in J}\left[\mathbf{A}_j^{(\mathrm{phot})}(\mathbf{x},t)\hat{a}_j + \mathbf{A}_j^{(\mathrm{phot})*}(\mathbf{x},t)\hat{a}_j^\dagger\right], \tag{4.1}$$

where J is an index set and the photon annihilation and creation operators $\hat{a}_j$ and $\hat{a}_j^\dagger$ in the jth mode fulfill the commutation relations

$$[\hat{a}_j, \hat{a}_{j'}^\dagger] = \delta_{jj'}\hat{1}, \qquad [\hat{a}_j, \hat{a}_{j'}] = [\hat{a}_j^\dagger, \hat{a}_{j'}^\dagger] = \hat{0}. \tag{4.2}$$

Further,

$$\mathbf{A}_j^{(\mathrm{phot})}(\mathbf{x},t) = \sqrt{\frac{\hbar}{2\epsilon_0\omega_j}}\mathbf{u}_j^{(\mathrm{t})}(\mathbf{x})\exp\left(-i\omega_j t\right), \tag{4.3}$$

with $\hbar$ the reduced Planck constant, ϵ_0 the vacuum (free-space) electric permittivity, ω_j and $\mathbf{u}_j^{(\mathrm{t})}(\mathbf{x})$ satisfying the Helmholtz equation

$$\nabla^2\mathbf{u}_j^{(\mathrm{t})}(\mathbf{x}) + \epsilon_{\mathrm{r}0}\frac{\omega_j^2}{c^2}\mathbf{u}_j^{(\mathrm{t})}(\mathbf{x}) = \mathbf{0}, \tag{4.4}$$

where $\epsilon_{\mathrm{r}0}$ is the relative electric permittivity of the medium, the transversality condition

$$\nabla \cdot \mathbf{u}_j^{(\mathrm{t})}(\mathbf{x}) = 0, \tag{4.5}$$

and boundary conditions

$$\begin{gathered}\mathbf{n}_{\mathbf{x}} \times \mathbf{u}_j^{(\mathrm{t})}(\mathbf{x})\,|_{\partial G} = \mathbf{0},\\ \mathbf{n}_{\mathbf{x}} \cdot \left(\nabla \times \mathbf{u}_j^{(\mathrm{t})}(\mathbf{x})\right)\Big|_{\partial G} = (\mathbf{n}_{\mathbf{x}} \times \nabla) \cdot \mathbf{u}_j^{(\mathrm{t})}(\mathbf{x})\Big|_{\partial G} = 0,\end{gathered} \tag{4.6}$$

where $\mathbf{n}_{\mathbf{x}}$ is the normal vector at the point $\mathbf{x}$. It is required that the modal functions $\mathbf{u}_j^{(\mathrm{t})}(\mathbf{x})$ be orthogonal and normalized as expressed by the relation

$$\epsilon_{\mathrm{r}0}\int_G \mathbf{u}_j^{(\mathrm{t})}(\mathbf{x}) \cdot \mathbf{u}_{j'}^{(\mathrm{t})}(\mathbf{x})d^3\mathbf{x} = \delta_{jj'}. \tag{4.7}$$

4.1. Rectangular waveguide filled with a refractive medium and located in a flat space. For illustration, we will assume that

$$G = \left\{\mathbf{x} : -a_x < x < a_x, -a_y < y < a_y, -a_z \le z < a_z\right\}, \tag{4.8}$$

where a_x, a_y, a_z are positive. It can be proved that the index set J is a collection of $j = (n_x, n_y, n_z, s)$, where $n_r \in \{0\} \cup \mathrm{N}$, $r = x, y, n_z \in \mathrm{Z}$, $s = \mathrm{TE}, \mathrm{TM}$, $n_x > 0$ or $s = \mathrm{TE}$, $n_y > 0$ or $s = \mathrm{TE}$, and $n_x + n_y \ge 1$.

The solutions ω_j have the form

$$\omega_j = v\sqrt{k_x^2 + k_y^2 + k_z^2} \tag{4.9}$$

with

$$v = \frac{1}{\sqrt{\epsilon_0\epsilon_{\mathrm{r}0}\mu_0}}, \qquad k_r = \frac{n_r\pi}{2a_r}, \qquad r = x, y, \qquad k_z = \frac{n_z\pi}{a_z}, \tag{4.10}$$

and the solutions $\mathbf{u}_j^{(\mathrm{t})}(\mathbf{x})$ are connected with the classical solutions

$$E_{jx}(\mathbf{x}) = \alpha_j \cos\left(\frac{n_x\pi}{2a_x}(x+a_x)\right)\sin\left(\frac{n_y\pi}{2a_y}(y+a_y)\right)\exp\left(i\frac{2n_z\pi}{2a_z}(z+a_z)\right),$$
$$E_{jy}(\mathbf{x}) = \beta_j \sin\left(\frac{n_x\pi}{2a_x}(x+a_x)\right)\cos\left(\frac{n_y\pi}{2a_y}(y+a_y)\right)\exp\left(i\frac{2n_z\pi}{2a_z}(z+a_z)\right), \tag{4.11}$$
$$E_{jz}(\mathbf{x}) = i\gamma_j \sin\left(\frac{n_x\pi}{2a_x}(x+a_x)\right)\sin\left(\frac{n_y\pi}{2a_y}(y+a_y)\right)\exp\left(i\frac{2n_z\pi}{2a_z}(z+a_z)\right)$$

to the equivalent boundary value problem of the form

$$\nabla\cdot\mathbf{E}_j^{(\mathrm{t})} = 0, \qquad \nabla\times\mathbf{B}_j^{(\mathrm{t})} + i\epsilon_{\mathrm{r}0}\frac{\omega_j}{c^2}\mathbf{E}_j^{(\mathrm{t})} = \mathbf{0},$$
$$\nabla\cdot\mathbf{B}_j^{(\mathrm{t})} = 0, \qquad \nabla\times\mathbf{E}_j^{(\mathrm{t})} - i\omega_j\mathbf{B}_j^{(\mathrm{t})} = \mathbf{0}, \tag{4.12}$$
$$\mathbf{n_x}\cdot\mathbf{B}_j^{(\mathrm{t})}(\mathbf{x},\omega_j)\Big|_{\partial G} = 0, \qquad \mathbf{n_x}\times\mathbf{E}_j^{(\mathrm{t})}(\mathbf{x},\omega_j)\Big|_{\partial G} = \mathbf{0}.$$

In (4.11),

(i) for $s = \mathrm{TE}$,

$$\alpha_j = -i\omega_j\frac{k_y}{k_x^2+k_y^2}\gamma_j', \quad \beta_j = i\omega_j\frac{k_x}{k_x^2+k_y^2}\gamma_j', \quad \gamma_j = 0; \tag{4.13}$$

(ii) for $s = \mathrm{TM}$,

$$\alpha_j = -\frac{k_xk_z}{k_x^2+k_y^2}\gamma_j, \qquad \beta_j = -\frac{k_yk_z}{k_x^2+k_y^2}\gamma_j; \tag{4.14}$$

with γ_j', γ_j complex parameters. The connecting relation is

$$\mathbf{u}_j^{(\mathrm{t})}(\mathbf{x}) = -i\sqrt{\frac{2\epsilon_0}{\hbar\omega_j}}\mathbf{E}_j^{(\mathrm{phot})}(\mathbf{x}) \tag{4.15}$$

with

$$\mathbf{E}_j^{(\mathrm{phot})}(\mathbf{x}) = \sum_{r=x,y,z} E_{jr}^{(\mathrm{phot})}(\mathbf{x})\mathbf{e}_r, \tag{4.16}$$

where $E_{jr}^{(\mathrm{phot})}(\mathbf{x})$ are given by the formulas (4.11), (4.13), (4.14), in which

$$\gamma_j' = \sqrt{\frac{\hbar\omega_j}{2\epsilon_0}}\sqrt{\frac{1}{\epsilon_{\mathrm{r}0}}}\sqrt{\frac{4}{(1+\delta_{k_x0})(1+\delta_{k_y0})V}}\frac{\sqrt{k_x^2+k_y^2}}{\omega_j}\zeta_j',$$
$$\gamma_j = c\sqrt{\frac{\hbar\omega_j}{2\epsilon_0}}\sqrt{\frac{1}{\epsilon_{\mathrm{r}0}}}\sqrt{\frac{4}{(1-\delta_{k_x0})(1-\delta_{k_y0})V}}\frac{\sqrt{k_x^2+k_y^2}}{\omega_j}\zeta_j \tag{4.17}$$

are substituted.

The modal functions are eigenfunctions of a selfadjoint operator. Hence, they are orthogonal. It can be verified that the vector-valued functions $\mathbf{u}_j^{(t)}(\mathbf{x})$, $j \in J$, are normalized too. It can be easily derived that the vector-valued functions $\mathbf{u}_j^{(t)}(\mathbf{x})$, $j \in J$, satisfy a completeness relation

$$\sum_{j\in J} \epsilon_{r0}\mathbf{u}_j^{(t)}(\mathbf{x})\mathbf{u}_j^{(t)*}(\mathbf{x}') = \delta(\mathbf{x}-\mathbf{x}')\mathbf{1} - \nabla_{\mathbf{x}}\nabla_{\mathbf{x}'}\mathcal{G}(\mathbf{x},\mathbf{x}'), \tag{4.18}$$

where $\mathcal{G}(\mathbf{x},\mathbf{x}')$ is a Green's function for (a Dirichlet problem for) the Laplace operator.

4.2. Rectangular waveguide filled with a refractive medium. We will consider a subset $G = G_\perp \times \mathrm{R}^1$, with the boundary $\partial G = \partial G_\perp \times \mathrm{R}^1$, of the usual Euclidean space R^3. In optics, the quantization may be a definition of the vector potential operator $\hat{\mathbf{A}}^{(t)}(\mathbf{x},t)$ by the relation

$$\hat{\mathbf{A}}^{(t)}(\mathbf{x},t) - \sum_{j_\perp\in J_\perp}\int_{-\infty}^{\infty}\left[\mathbf{A}_{j_\perp}^{(\mathrm{phot})}(\mathbf{x},k_z,t)\hat{a}_{j_\perp}(k_z) + \mathbf{A}_{j_\perp}^{(\mathrm{phot})*}(\mathbf{x},k_z,t)\hat{a}_{j_\perp}^\dagger(k_z)\right]dk_z, \tag{4.19}$$

where $J_\perp$ is an index set and the photon annihilation and creation operators $\hat{a}_{j_\perp}(k_z)$ and $\hat{a}_{j_\perp}^\dagger(k_z)$ in the mode $(j_\perp,k_z)$ fulfill the commutation relations

$$\begin{aligned}
[\hat{a}_{j_\perp}(k_z),\hat{a}_{j'_\perp}^\dagger(k'_z)] &= \delta_{j_\perp j'_\perp}\delta(k_z-k'_z)\hat{1},\\
[\hat{a}_{j_\perp}(k_z),\hat{a}_{j'_\perp}(k'_z)] &= [\hat{a}_{j_\perp}^\dagger(k_z),\hat{a}_{j'_\perp}^\dagger(k'_z)] = \hat{0}.
\end{aligned} \tag{4.20}$$

Further,

$$\mathbf{A}_{j_\perp}^{(\mathrm{phot})}(\mathbf{x},k_z,t) = \sqrt{\frac{\hbar}{2\epsilon_0\omega_{j_\perp}}}\mathbf{u}_{j_\perp}^{(t)}(\mathbf{x},k_z)\exp(-i\omega_{j_\perp}(k_z)t), \tag{4.21}$$

with ϵ_0 the vacuum (free-space) electric permittivity, $\omega_{j_\perp}(k_z)$ and $\mathbf{u}_{j_\perp}^{(t)}(\mathbf{x},k_z)$ satisfying the Helmholtz equation

$$\nabla^2\mathbf{u}_{j_\perp}^{(t)}(\mathbf{x},k_z) + \epsilon_{r0}\frac{\omega_{j_\perp}^2(k_z)}{c^2}\mathbf{u}_{j_\perp}^{(t)}(\mathbf{x},k_z) = \mathbf{0}, \tag{4.22}$$

the transversality condition

$$\nabla\cdot\mathbf{u}_{j_\perp}^{(t)}(\mathbf{x},k_z) = 0, \tag{4.23}$$

and boundary conditions

$$\begin{aligned}
\mathbf{n}_{\mathbf{x}}\times\mathbf{u}_{j_\perp}^{(t)}(\mathbf{x},k_z)\Big|_{\partial G} &= \mathbf{0},\\
\mathbf{n}_{\mathbf{x}}\cdot\left(\nabla\times\mathbf{u}_{j_\perp}^{(t)}(\mathbf{x},k_z)\right)\Big|_{\partial G} = (\mathbf{n}_{\mathbf{x}}\times\nabla)\cdot\mathbf{u}_{j_\perp}^{(t)}(\mathbf{x},k_z)\Big|_{\partial G} &= 0,
\end{aligned} \tag{4.24}$$

where $\mathbf{n_x}$ is the normal vector at the point $\mathbf{x}$. It is required that the modal functions $\mathbf{u}^{(t)}_{j_\perp}(\mathbf{x}, k_z)$ be orthogonal and normalized as expressed by the relation

$$\int_G \epsilon_{r0} \mathbf{u}^{(t)*}_{j_\perp}(\mathbf{x}, k_z) \cdot \mathbf{u}^{(t)}_{j'_\perp}(\mathbf{x}, k'_z) d^3\mathbf{x} = \delta_{j_\perp j'_\perp} \delta(k_z - k'_z). \tag{4.25}$$

For illustration, we will assume that

$$G = \{\mathbf{x} : -a_x < x < a_x, -a_y < y < a_y, -\infty < z < \infty\}, \tag{4.26}$$

where a_x, a_y are positive. It can be proved that the index set $J_\perp$ is a collection of $j_\perp = (n_x, n_y, s)$, where $n_r \in \{0\} \cup \mathrm{N}$, $r = x,\ y$, $s = \mathrm{TE}, \mathrm{TM}$, $n_x > 0$ or $s = \mathrm{TE}$, $n_y > 0$ or $s = \mathrm{TE}$, and $n_x + n_y \geq 1$.

The solutions $\omega_{j_\perp}(k_z)$ have the form

$$\omega_{j_\perp}(k_z) = v\sqrt{k_x^2 + k_y^2 + k_z^2} \tag{4.27}$$

with

$$v = \frac{1}{\sqrt{\epsilon_0 \epsilon_{r0} \mu_0}}, \quad k_r = \frac{n_r \pi}{2a_r}, \quad r = x, y, \tag{4.28}$$

and the solutions $\mathbf{u}^{(t)}_{j_\perp}(\mathbf{x}, k_z)$ are connected with the classical solutions

$$\begin{aligned}
E_{j_\perp x}(\mathbf{x}, k_z) &= \alpha_{j_\perp}(k_z) \cos\left(\frac{n_x \pi}{2a_x}(x + a_x)\right) \sin\left(\frac{n_y \pi}{2a_y}(y + a_y)\right) \exp(ik_z z), \\
E_{j_\perp y}(\mathbf{x}, k_z) &= \beta_{j_\perp}(k_z) \sin\left(\frac{n_x \pi}{2a_x}(x + a_x)\right) \cos\left(\frac{n_y \pi}{2a_y}(y + a_y)\right) \exp(ik_z z), \\
E_{j_\perp z}(\mathbf{x}, k_z) &= i\gamma_{j_\perp}(k_z) \sin\left(\frac{n_x \pi}{2a_x}(x + a_x)\right) \sin\left(\frac{n_y \pi}{2a_y}(y + a_y)\right) \exp(ik_z z)
\end{aligned} \tag{4.29}$$

to the equivalent boundary value problem

$$\begin{aligned}
\nabla \cdot \mathbf{E}^{(t)}_{j_\perp} &= 0, \qquad \nabla \times \mathbf{B}^{(t)}_{j_\perp} + i\epsilon_{r0} \frac{\omega_{j_\perp}(k_z)}{c^2} \mathbf{E}^{(t)}_{j_\perp} = \mathbf{0}, \\
\nabla \cdot \mathbf{B}^{(t)}_{j_\perp} &= 0, \qquad \nabla \times \mathbf{E}^{(t)}_{j_\perp} - i\omega_{j_\perp}(k_z) \mathbf{B}^{(t)}_{j_\perp} = \mathbf{0}, \\
\mathbf{n_x} \cdot \mathbf{B}^{(t)}_{j_\perp}\Big|_{\partial G} &= 0, \qquad \mathbf{n_x} \times \mathbf{E}^{(t)}_{j_\perp}\Big|_{\partial G} = \mathbf{0}.
\end{aligned} \tag{4.30}$$

Here $\mathbf{E}^{(t)}_{j_\perp} \equiv \mathbf{E}^{(t)}_{j_\perp}(\mathbf{x}, k_z, \omega_{j_\perp}(k_z))$, $\mathbf{B}^{(t)}_{j_\perp} \equiv \mathbf{B}^{(t)}_{j_\perp}(\mathbf{x}, k_z, \omega_{j_\perp}(k_z))$,

(i) for $s = \mathrm{TE}$,

$$\begin{aligned}
\alpha_{j_\perp}(k_z) &= -i\omega_{j_\perp}(k_z) \frac{k_y}{k_x^2 + k_y^2} \gamma'_{j_\perp}, \\
\beta_{j_\perp}(k_z) &= i\omega_{j_\perp}(k_z) \frac{k_x}{k_x^2 + k_y^2} \gamma'_{j_\perp}, \qquad \gamma_{j_\perp}(k_z) = 0;
\end{aligned} \tag{4.31}$$

(ii) for $s = \mathrm{TM}$,

$$\begin{aligned} \alpha_{j_\perp}(k_z) &= -\frac{k_x k_z}{k_x^2 + k_y^2}\gamma_{j_\perp}, \\ \beta_{j_\perp}(k_z) &= -\frac{k_y k_z}{k_x^2 + k_y^2}\gamma_{j_\perp} \end{aligned} \tag{4.32}$$

with $\gamma'_{j_\perp}$, $\gamma_{j_\perp}$ complex parameters.

The connecting relation is

$$\mathbf{u}_{j_\perp}^{(\mathrm{t})}(\mathbf{x}, k_z) = -i\sqrt{\frac{2\epsilon_0}{\hbar\omega_{j_\perp}}}\mathbf{E}_{j_\perp}^{(\mathrm{phot})}(\mathbf{x}, k_z), \tag{4.33}$$

where

$$\mathbf{E}_{j_\perp}^{(\mathrm{phot})}(\mathbf{x}, k_z) = \sum_{r=x,y,z}{}^{\cdot}\, E_{j_\perp r}^{(\mathrm{phot})}(\mathbf{x}, k_z)\mathbf{e}_r \tag{4.34}$$

with $E_{j_\perp r}^{(\mathrm{phot})}(\mathbf{x}, k_z)$ given by the formulas (4.29), (4.31), (4.32), in which

$$\begin{aligned} \gamma'_{j_\perp}(k_z) &= \sqrt{\frac{\hbar\omega_{j_\perp}(k_z)}{2\epsilon_0}}\sqrt{\frac{1}{\epsilon_{\mathrm{r}0}}}\sqrt{\frac{4}{(1+\delta_{k_x 0})(1+\delta_{k_y 0})2\pi V_\perp}}\frac{\sqrt{k_x^2+k_y^2}}{\omega_{j_\perp}(k_z)}\zeta'_{j_\perp}, \\ \gamma_{j_\perp}(k_z) &= c\sqrt{\frac{\hbar\omega_{j_\perp}(k_z)}{2\epsilon_0}}\sqrt{\frac{1}{\epsilon_{\mathrm{r}0}}}\sqrt{\frac{4}{(1-\delta_{k_x 0})(1-\delta_{k_y 0})2\pi V_\perp}}\frac{\sqrt{k_x^2+k_y^2}}{\omega_{j_\perp}(k_z)}\zeta_{j_\perp} \end{aligned} \tag{4.35}$$

are substituted, $V_\perp = a_x a_y$, $|\zeta'_{j_\perp}| = |\zeta_{j_\perp}| = 1$.

It can be easily derived that the vector-valued functions $\mathbf{u}_{j_\perp}^{(\mathrm{t})}(\mathbf{x}, k_z)$, $j_\perp \in J_\perp$, satisfy a completeness relation

$$\sum_{j_\perp \in J_\perp}\int_{-\infty}^{\infty}\epsilon_{\mathrm{r}0}\mathbf{u}_{j_\perp}^{(\mathrm{t})}(\mathbf{x}, k_z)\mathbf{u}_{j_\perp}^{(\mathrm{t})*}(\mathbf{x}', k_z)\,dk_z = \delta(\mathbf{x}-\mathbf{x}')\mathbf{1} - \nabla_{\mathbf{x}}\nabla_{\mathbf{x}'}\mathcal{G}(\mathbf{x}, \mathbf{x}'), \tag{4.36}$$

where $\mathcal{G}(\mathbf{x}, \mathbf{x}')$ is a Green's function for (a Dirichlet problem for) the Laplace operator.

5. Method of coupled modes

To any $\omega > \min\{\omega_{10}, \omega_{01}\}$, there exists only a finite number of modal functions. A solution of the problem formulated in Section 2 can be expressed in terms of these functions (see Section 4, where a different sign convention was adopted) for $z < 0$ or $z > L$.

The coupled mode method determines a form of the solution, even for $z \in [0, L]$. This method is approximate. Complex coefficients at the modal functions are obtained as solutions of ordinary differential equations whose number is equal to the number of these coefficients.

6. Conclusions

We have shown how known modal functions of a rectangular waveguide are those of a rectangular waveguide of a finite length (the usual periodic boundary conditions). Modal functions are related with macroscopic quantization of a field in such a medium and with the coupled mode theory as well which is an approximative method for seeking modal functions (e.g.) of a rectangular waveguide with a finite segment of periodic modulation of the electric permittivity along the optical axis of the waveguide. Our objective is to assess to what extent the explicit expression of the modal functions preserves its form with separated variables when modulation of the electric permittivity along the axis takes place.

Acknowledgment

This work is supported by the Ministry of Education of the Czech Republic, project no. MSM 6198959213.

References

[1] W. Greiner, *Classical Electrodynamics*, Classical Theoretical Physics, Springer, New York, 1998.
[2] A. Yariv and P. Yeh, *Optical Waves in Crystals*, John Wiley & Sons, New York, 1984.

Vlasta Peřinová: Laboratory of Quantum Optics, Faculty of Natural Sciences, Palacký University, Třída Svobody 26, 77146 Olomouc, Czech Republic
E-mail address: perinova@prfnw.upol.cz

Antonín Lukš: Laboratory of Quantum Optics, Faculty of Natural Sciences, Palacký University, Třída Svobody 26, 77146 Olomouc, Czech Republic
E-mail address: luks@prfnw.upol.cz

ON QUENCHING FOR SEMILINEAR PARABOLIC EQUATIONS WITH DYNAMIC BOUNDARY CONDITIONS

JOAKIM H. PETERSSON

We present a quenching result for semilinear parabolic equations with dynamic boundary conditions in bounded domains with a smooth boundary.

1. Introduction

For semilinear partial differential equations, a particular type of blow-up phenomenon may arise when the nonlinearity has a pole at a finite value of the solution. Namely, the solution itself remains bounded while some derivative of it blows up. This is referred to by saying that the solution "quenches." The study of quenching phenomena for parabolic differential equations with singular terms and classical boundary conditions (of Dirichlet- or Neumann-type) was initiated by Kawarada [7] in connection with the study of electric current transients in polarized ionic conductors, and has attracted much attention since then (see the survey [8]). Recently, parabolic differential equations with dynamic boundary conditions aroused the interest of several researchers (see [1, 3, 6]). The question of the occurrence of quenching phenomena in the case of dynamic boundary conditions comes up naturally. In this paper, we provide a simple example.

In Section 2, we present some recent results on parabolic equations with dynamic boundary conditions in bounded domains with a smooth boundary and we prove some needed facts about the behavior of the solutions. Section 3 is devoted to a simple criterion (positivity of the nonlinearities) for the appearance of quenching for certain semilinear equations of this type.

2. Preliminary considerations

We will consider the semilinear problem with dynamic boundary conditions

$$\begin{aligned} u_t - \Delta u &= f(x,u), \quad t > 0,\ x \in \Omega, \\ u_t + u_\nu &= g(x,u), \quad t > 0,\ x \in \partial\Omega, \\ u(0,x) &= u_0(x), \quad x \in \overline{\Omega}, \end{aligned} \tag{2.1}$$

Hindawi Publishing Corporation
Proceedings of the Conference on Differential & Difference Equations and Applications, pp. 935–941

where Ω is a bounded domain in $\mathbb{R}^n$ with a C^2 boundary $\partial\Omega$ and ν denotes the outer unit normal on $\partial\Omega$. If we further demand that $f \in C^1(\overline{\Omega} \times \mathbb{R})$ and $g \in C^2(\partial\Omega \times \mathbb{R})$, then a recent result in [3] implies the following existence and uniqueness result for (2.1).

THEOREM 2.1. *Let there be given an initial datum $u_0 \in C^2(\overline{\Omega})$. Then there exists a unique classical solution u of (2.1) in some maximal time interval $[0,T)$ depending on u_0 with*

$$u \in C^1\big((0,T),C(\overline{\Omega})\big) \cap C\big((0,T),C^2(\overline{\Omega})\big) \cap C\big([0,T),C^1(\overline{\Omega})\big). \tag{2.2}$$

Moreover, if $T < \infty$, then

$$\limsup_{t \to T^-} \Big[\max_{x \in \overline{\Omega}} |u(t,x)| \Big] = \infty. \tag{2.3}$$

These classical solutions may be studied by means of their maxima and minima over $\overline{\Omega}$. The special case $f(u) = g(u)$ is treated in [9]. We will use the following lemma ([2, Theorem 2.1]). Note that our classical solution is in the Sobolev space $W^{1,1}((a,b),C(\overline{\Omega}))$ whenever $0 < a < b < T$.

LEMMA 2.2. *Let $a < b$ and $u \in W^{1,1}((a,b),C(\overline{\Omega}))$. Let there be given for every $t \in (a,b)$ one pair of points $\xi(t),\zeta(t)$ in $\overline{\Omega}$ such that*

$$\begin{aligned} m(t) &:= \min_{x \in \overline{\Omega}} u(t,x) = u(t,\xi(t)), \\ M(t) &:= \max_{x \in \overline{\Omega}} u(t,x) = u(t,\zeta(t)). \end{aligned} \tag{2.4}$$

Then the functions $m(t)$, $M(t)$ are absolutely continuous on $[a,b]$ with

$$m'(t) = u_t(t,\xi(t)), \quad M'(t) = u_t(t,\zeta(t)) \quad \text{a.e. in } (a,b). \tag{2.5}$$

With regard to the existence of global solutions of (2.1) and their behavior, we offer the following result that will be used in Section 3.

THEOREM 2.3. *Assume that for all $s \in \mathbb{R}$,*

$$0 \le f(x,s) \le \omega(s), \quad x \in \Omega, \quad 0 \le g(x,s) \le \omega(s), \quad x \in \partial\Omega, \tag{2.6}$$

where ω is a continuous positive function with $\int_0^\infty ds/\omega(s) = \infty$. Then every classical solution u of (2.1) with nonnegative initial datum $u_0 \in C^2(\overline{\Omega})$ is global. Moreover, the minimum $m(t) = \min_{x \in \overline{\Omega}} u(t,x)$ is nondecreasing. In particular, u is nonnegative.

Proof. Let u be the classical solution of (2.1) under the given hypotheses, and let $T > 0$ be the maximal time of existence for u. Let (a,b) be a subinterval such that $0 < a < b < T$. For every $t \in (a,b)$, the minimum $m(t)$ is attained at some point $\xi(t) \in \overline{\Omega}$. If $\xi(t) \in \Omega$, then, in view of (2.5),

$$m'(t) = u_t(t,\xi(t)) = \Delta u(t,\xi(t)) + f(\xi(t),u(t,\xi(t))) \ge f(\xi(t),m(t)) \ge 0 \tag{2.7}$$

for almost all such t. Similarly, if $\xi(t) \in \partial\Omega$, then since clearly $u_\nu(t,\xi(t)) \le 0$ at a minimum point on the boundary, the dynamic boundary condition together with (2.5) lead to the inequality

$$m'(t) = u_t(t,\xi(t)) = -u_\nu(t,\xi(t)) + g(\xi(t),u(t,\xi(t))) \ge g(\xi(t),m(t)) \ge 0 \tag{2.8}$$

for almost all such t. Thus $m(t)$, which is continuous on $[0,T)$, is nondecreasing since $m'(t) \ge 0$ almost everywhere. Also, $m(0) \ge 0$ if the initial datum u_0 is nonnegative.

By reversing the inequalities, we get for the maximum $M(t)$ that

$$M'(t) \le \omega(M(t)) \quad \text{a.e. in } (0,T). \tag{2.9}$$

We compare (2.9) with the solution of

$$z'(t) = \omega(z(t)), \qquad z(t_0) = M(t_0) \tag{2.10}$$

for some $t_0 > 0$. Then clearly

$$t - t_0 = \int_{t_0}^{t} \frac{z'(s)}{\omega(z(s))} ds = \int_{z(t_0)}^{z(t)} \frac{ds}{\omega(s)}. \tag{2.11}$$

But by absolute continuity, we also have $M(t) \le z(t)$ (see, e.g., [4]), so

$$t - t_0 \ge \int_{M(t_0)}^{M(t)} \frac{ds}{\omega(s)}. \tag{2.12}$$

This shows that $M(t)$ stays bounded in finite time and the solution u exists globally in time in view of Theorem 2.1. □

3. Quenching

Using the results above, we may now give examples of the occurrence of quenching for parabolic equations with dynamic boundary conditions. We still consider the equation

$$\begin{aligned} u_t - \Delta u &= f(x,u), \quad t > 0,\ x \in \Omega, \\ u_t + u_\nu &= g(x,u), \quad t > 0,\ x \in \partial\Omega, \\ u(0,x) &= u_0(x), \quad x \in \overline{\Omega}, \end{aligned} \tag{3.1}$$

where $f \in C^1(\overline{\Omega} \times [0,b))$ and $g \in C^2(\partial\Omega \times [0,b))$. Defining

$$\begin{aligned} \underline{f}(s) &:= \min_{x\in\overline{\Omega}} f(x,s), \qquad \overline{f}(s) := \max_{x\in\overline{\Omega}} f(x,s), \\ \underline{g}(s) &:= \min_{x\in\partial\Omega} g(x,s), \qquad \overline{g}(s) := \max_{x\in\partial\Omega} g(x,s), \end{aligned} \tag{3.2}$$

we will require that

$$\begin{aligned} 0 < \underline{f}(s) \le f(x,s) \le \overline{f}(s), \quad x \in \overline{\Omega},\ 0 \le s < b, \\ 0 < \underline{g}(s) \le g(x,s) \le \overline{g}(s), \quad x \in \partial\Omega,\ 0 \le s < b, \end{aligned} \tag{3.3}$$

and also that either $\overline{f}(s) \to \infty$ or $\overline{g}(s) \to \infty$ as $s \to b^-$ (or possibly both). Incidentally, $\underline{f}, \overline{f}$, $\underline{g}$, and $\overline{g}$ are absolutely continuous by Lemma 2.2. The initial datum u_0 is supposed to be a nonnegative function in $C^2(\overline{\Omega})$ with $\max_{x\in\overline{\Omega}} u_0(x) = M(0) < b$. Under these conditions, the following holds.

Proposition 3.1. *The problem (3.1) has a unique classical solution u defined on the maximal interval $[0,T)$, where $T > 0$. Moreover, $0 \le u(t,x) < b$ for all $(t,x) \in [0,T) \times \overline{\Omega}$ and if $T < \infty$, then*

$$\limsup_{t\to T^-}\left[\max_{x\in\overline{\Omega}} u(t,x)\right] = b. \tag{3.4}$$

Proof. The proof consists of a standard approximation argument. By multiplying with a smooth cutoff function in the variable s, for every sufficiently small $\varepsilon > 0$ we can choose nonnegative bounded functions $f_\varepsilon \in C^1(\overline{\Omega}\times\mathbb{R})$ and $g_\varepsilon \in C^2(\partial\Omega\times\mathbb{R})$ such that

$$\begin{aligned} \forall x \in \overline{\Omega}: \ f_\varepsilon(x,s) &= f(x,s) \quad \text{for } 0 \le s \le b-\varepsilon, \\ \forall x \in \partial\Omega: \ g_\varepsilon(x,s) &= g(x,s) \quad \text{for } 0 \le s \le b-\varepsilon. \end{aligned} \tag{3.5}$$

Then, in view of Theorem 2.3, there is a unique nonnegative global classical solution u_ε of (3.1) with f,g replaced by $f_\varepsilon, g_\varepsilon$. The maximum $M_\varepsilon(t) = \max_{x\in\overline{\Omega}} u_\varepsilon(t,x)$ is continuous for $t \ge 0$ by uniform continuity since $\overline{\Omega}$ is compact. Since $M_\varepsilon(0) = M(0) < b$, there is for all sufficiently small $\varepsilon > 0$ a maximal interval $[0,T_\varepsilon)$, where $u_\varepsilon < b-\varepsilon$. Furthermore, if $0 < \varepsilon' < \varepsilon$, then $u_{\varepsilon'}$ is a solution of the problem with $f_\varepsilon, g_\varepsilon$ as long as it is less than $b-\varepsilon$, and so the uniqueness implies that $u_{\varepsilon'} = u_\varepsilon$ in $[0,T_\varepsilon)$. Now if $T_\varepsilon < \infty$, then the continuity of $M_{\varepsilon'}$ gives that $u_{\varepsilon'} < b-\varepsilon'$ in a neighborhood of T_ε. Hence $T_{\varepsilon'} > T_\varepsilon$ if $T_\varepsilon < \infty$, and we may define that $T = \lim_{\varepsilon\to 0^+} T_\varepsilon$. T can be either finite or infinite. On the other hand, if u is a classical solution of (3.1) in an interval $[0,t_0)$ and if $u < b-\varepsilon$ in $[0,t_0)$, then u is a solution of the problem with f,g replaced by $f_\varepsilon, g_\varepsilon$ in $[0,t_0)$, so the uniqueness once again implies that $u = u_\varepsilon$ in $[0,t_0)$. Therefore, the problem (3.1) has a unique classical solution u in $[0,T)$ and if $T < \infty$, then (3.4) holds, for otherwise u could be extended past T by way of some u_ε with sufficiently small $\varepsilon > 0$. □

We are now in a position to deal with possible quenching of solutions of our problem.

Definition 3.2. Let u be a nonnegative classical solution of (3.1), where at least one of f and g is singular for $u = b$. It is said to be quenching in finite time if for some finite $T > 0$ the maximal interval of existence is $[0,T)$ and (3.4) holds.

It is clear by Proposition 3.1 that in order to prove that quenching in finite time occurs, we only need to find an upper bound on T. As a matter of fact, under these assumptions we can deduce the following theorem on quenching in the case of dynamic boundary conditions.

Theorem 3.3. *Let $\Omega \subset \mathbb{R}^n$ be a bounded domain with a C^2 boundary and let u be the unique classical solution of the problem (3.1), where f and g satisfy the conditions stated at the beginning of the section. Suppose that u_0 is a nonnegative function in $C^2(\overline{\Omega})$ with*

$\max_{x\in\overline{\Omega}} u_0(x) = M(0) < b$. *Then u quenches at a finite time $T = T(f,g,u_0)$, and there exist the estimates*

$$\int_{M(0)}^{b} \frac{ds}{R(s)} \le T \le \int_{m(0)}^{b} \frac{ds}{r(s)}, \tag{3.6}$$

where

$$R = \max(\overline{f},\overline{g}), \qquad r = \min(\underline{f},\underline{g}). \tag{3.7}$$

Proof. Let $T > 0$ be the maximal existence time of the solution. Then from the proof of Theorem 2.3, we have

$$m'(t) \ge \min\left(\underline{f}(m(t)),\underline{g}(m(t))\right) = r(m(t)) \tag{3.8}$$

almost everywhere in $(0,T)$. Here r is continuous and positive. Comparing with the (unique) solution of the equation

$$z'(t) = r(z(t)), \qquad z(t_0) = m(t_0) \tag{3.9}$$

as in the proof of Theorem 2.3, we get

$$t - t_0 = \int_{z(t_0)}^{z(t)} \frac{ds}{r(s)} \le \int_{m(t_0)}^{m(t)} \frac{ds}{r(s)}. \tag{3.10}$$

Letting $t_0 \to 0^+$ and using that $m(t) < b$ in $[0,T)$, we conclude that

$$T \le \int_{m(0)}^{b} \frac{ds}{r(s)}. \tag{3.11}$$

The lower bound follows similarly from (2.12). There, we let $t_0 \to 0^+$ and let $t \to T$ over a sequence $\{t_n\}$ such that $M(t_n) \to b$. In the limit,

$$T \ge \int_{M(0)}^{b} \frac{ds}{R(s)}. \tag{3.12}$$

□

The following comparison lemma may be used in connection with suitable sub- and supersolutions.

Lemma 3.4. *Under the assumptions in Theorem 3.3, if u_0 develops into a classical solution u defined on $[0,T_{u_0})$ while v_0 develops into a classical solution v defined on $[0,T_{v_0})$, and if $u_0(x) < v_0(x)$ for every $x \in \overline{\Omega}$, then $T_{u_0} \ge T_{v_0}$ and $u < v$.*

Proof. Let $w = v - u$ and put $m_w(t) = \min_{x\in\overline{\Omega}} w(t,x)$ for $0 \le t < T_{\min} = \min(T_{u_0}, T_{v_0})$. Note that $m_w(0) > 0$ by assumption. But $m_w(t)$ is continuous on $[0, T_{\min})$ by uniform continuity, so if not $m_w(t) > 0$ for all $t \in [0, T_{\min})$, there is a $T \in (0, T_{\min})$ with $m_w(T) = 0$ and $m_w(t) > 0$ when $0 \le t < T$. Let $0 < t_0 < T$. By Lemma 2.2, $m_w(t)$ is absolutely continuous on $[t_0, T]$, and for any choice of $\xi(t) \in \overline{\Omega}$ with $m_w(t) = w(t,\xi(t))$, we have $m_w'(t) = w_t(t,\xi(t))$ almost everywhere in (t_0, T). But in view of (3.1) we get, in case $\xi(t) \in \Omega$,

$$\begin{aligned} m_w'(t) = w_t(t,\xi(t)) &= \Delta w(t,\xi(t)) + f(\xi(t), v(t,\xi(t))) - f(\xi(t), u(t,\xi(t))) \\ &\ge f(\xi(t), v(t,\xi(t))) - f(\xi(t), u(t,\xi(t))), \end{aligned} \tag{3.13}$$

and in case $\xi(t) \in \partial\Omega$,

$$\begin{aligned} m_w'(t) = w_t(t,\xi(t)) &= -w_\nu(t,\xi(t)) + g(\xi(t), v(t,\xi(t))) - g(\xi(t), u(t,\xi(t))) \\ &\ge g(\xi(t), v(t,\xi(t))) - g(\xi(t), u(t,\xi(t))). \end{aligned} \tag{3.14}$$

Dividing and multiplying with $v(t,\xi(t)) - u(t,\xi(t))$, we may write this as

$$m_w'(t) \ge D(t) m_w(t) \quad \text{a.e. in } (t_0, T). \tag{3.15}$$

Since $0 \le u(t,x), v(t,x) \le a < b$ for every $x \in \overline{\Omega}$ and $t \in [0,T]$, the mean value theorem and the fact that $f \in C^1(\overline{\Omega} \times [0,a])$ and $g \in C^2(\partial\Omega \times [0,a])$ imply that there is a constant $c > 0$ such that $|D(t)| \le c$ in $[0,T]$. Now the differential inequality $m_w'(t) \ge -c m_w(t)$ almost everywhere in (t_0, T) can be integrated (using the integrating factor e^{ct}, e.g.) to give

$$m_w(t) \ge m_w(t_0) e^{c(t_0 - t)}, \quad t \in [t_0, T], \tag{3.16}$$

which contradicts the definition of T. This shows that $u < v$, where they are both defined and therefore $T_{u_0} \ge T_{v_0}$ in view of Proposition 3.1. □

Sometimes a better upper bound on the quenching time can be found by simultaneously approximating f and g from below by lines or other convex functions as in the approach of [5]. In that case, one may consider the evolution of $\int_\Omega u\,dx + \int_{\partial\Omega} u\,d\sigma$ in addition to that of the minimum of u.

It is not known to us where quenching occurs and which derivative blows up (possibly more than one). For example, it would be interesting to know under what conditions quenching occurs on the boundary. Of course, an x-independent solution is possible if f and g only depend on u and are equal. Then if $u_0 \equiv M < b$, the quenching time T is precisely $\int_M^b ds/f(s)$.

References

[1] J. M. Arrieta, P. Quittner, and A. Rodríguez-Bernal, *Parabolic problems with nonlinear dynamical boundary conditions and singular initial data*, Differential and Integral Equations **14** (2001), no. 12, 1487–1510.

[2] A. Constantin and J. Escher, *Global solutions for quasilinear parabolic problems*, Journal of Evolution Equations **2** (2002), no. 1, 97–111.

[3] ———, *Global existence for fully parabolic boundary value problems*, NoDEA: Nonlinear Differential Equations and Applications **13** (2006), no. 1, 91–118.

[4] A. Constantin, J. Escher, and Z. Yin, *Global solutions for quasilinear parabolic systems*, Journal of Differential Equations **197** (2004), no. 1, 73–84.

[5] Q. Dai and Y. Gu, *A short note on quenching phenomena for semilinear parabolic equations*, Journal of Differential Equations **137** (1997), no. 2, 240–250.

[6] M. Fila and P. Quittner, *Large time behavior of solutions of a semilinear parabolic equation with a nonlinear dynamical boundary condition*, Topics in Nonlinear Analysis (J. Escher and G. Simonett, eds.), Progr. Nonlinear Differential Equations Appl., vol. 35, Birkhäuser, Basel, 1999, pp. 251–272.

[7] H. Kawarada, *On solutions of initial-boundary problem for* $u_t = u_{xx} + 1/(1 - u)$, Publications of Research Institute for Mathematical Sciences **10** (1975), no. 3, 729–736.

[8] H. A. Levine, *Advances in quenching*, Nonlinear Diffusion Equations and Their Equilibrium States, 3 (Gregynog, 1989) (N. G. Lloyd, W. M. Ni, L. A. Peletier, and J. Serrin, eds.), Progr. Nonlinear Differential Equations Appl., vol. 7, Birkhäuser Boston, Massachusetts, 1992, pp. 319–346.

[9] J. H. Petersson, *A note on quenching for parabolic equations with dynamic boundary conditions*, Nonlinear Analysis **58** (2004), no. 3-4, 417–423.

Joakim H. Petersson: Department of Mathematical Sciences, Norwegian University of Science and Technology, NO-7491 Trondheim, Norway
E-mail address: joakim.petersson@math.ntnu.no

CONSERVATION LAWS IN QUANTUM SUPER PDEs

A. PRÁSTARO

Conservation laws are considered for PDEs built in the category $\mathfrak{Q}_S$ of quantum supermanifolds. These are functions defined on the integral bordism groups of such equations and belonging to suitable Hopf algebras *(full quantum Hopf algebras)*. In particular, we specialize our calculations on the quantum super Yang-Mills equations and quantum black holes.

1. Introduction

In this section we will resume some of our fundamental definitions and results for PDEs in the *category of quantum supermanifolds*, $\mathfrak{Q}_S$, where the objects are just quantum supermanifolds, and the morphisms are maps of class Q^k_w, $k \in \{0,1,2,\dots,\infty,\omega\}$ [1–8]. A small subcategory is $\mathfrak{S}_M \subset \mathfrak{Q}_S$ of supermanifolds as defined in [3].

Example 1.1. Let $\pi : W \to M$ be a fiber bundle, in the category $\mathfrak{Q}_S$, such that $\dim W = (m|n,r|s)$, over the quantum superalgebra $B \equiv A \times E$ and $\dim M = (m|n)$ over A and such that E is a Z-module, with $Z \equiv Z(A) \subset A$, the center of A. The *quantum k-jet-derivative space* $J\hat{D}^k(W)$ of $\pi : W \to M$ is the k-jet-derivative space of sections of π, belonging to the class Q^k_w. The k-jet-derivative $J\hat{D}^k(W)$ is a quantum supermanifold modeled on the quantum superalgebra $B_k \equiv \prod_{0\le s\le k}(\prod_{i_1+\cdots+i_s\in\mathbb{Z}_2,\, i_r\in\mathbb{Z}_2} \widehat{A}^s_{i_1\cdots i_s}(E))$, with $\widehat{A}^s_{i_1\cdots i_s}(E) \equiv \mathrm{Hom}_Z(A_{i_1}\otimes_Z \cdots \otimes_Z A_{i_s};E)$, $\widehat{A}^0(E) \equiv A \times E$, $\widehat{A}^1_i(E) \equiv \widehat{A}_0(E) \times \widehat{A}_1(E) \equiv \mathrm{Hom}_Z(A_0;E) \times \mathrm{Hom}_Z(A_1;E)$. Each $\widehat{A}^s_{i_1\cdots i_s}(E)$ is a quantum superalgebra with $\mathbb{Z}_2$-gradiation induced by E. Hence, $\widehat{A}^s_{i_1\cdots i_s}(E)_q \equiv \mathrm{Hom}_Z(A_{i_1}\otimes_Z \cdots \otimes_Z A_{i_s};E_p)$, $i_r,p,q \in \mathbb{Z}_2$, $q \equiv i_1 + \cdots + i_s + p$. If $(x^A, y^B)_{1\le A\le m+n, 1\le B\le r+s}$ are fibered quantum coordinates on the quantum supermanifold W over M, then $(x^A, y^B, y^B_A, \dots, y^B_{A_1\cdots A_k})$ are fibered quantum coordinates on $J\hat{D}^k(W)$ over M, with the following gradiations: $|x^A| = |A|$, $|y^B| = |B|$, $|y^B_{A_1\cdots A_s}| = |B| + |A_1| + \cdots |A_s|$. Note, also, that there is not symmetry in the indexes A_i. $J\hat{D}^k(W)$ is an affine

Hindawi Publishing Corporation
Proceedings of the Conference on Differential & Difference Equations and Applications, pp. 943–952

bundle over $J\hat{D}^{k-1}(W)$ with an associated vector bundle $\pi_{k,0}^{*}\mathrm{Hom}_Z(\dot{S}_0^k M; vTW)$, where $\dot{S}_0^k M$ is the k-times symmetric tensor product of TM, considered as a bundle of Z-modules over M, and $\pi_{k,0}: J\hat{D}^k(W) \to W$ is the canonical surjection. Another important example is $\hat{J}^k_{m|n}(W)$, that is, the *k-jet space for quantum supermanifolds* of dimension $(m|n)$ (over A) contained in the quantum supermanifold W. This quantum supermanifold locally looks like $J\hat{D}^k(W)$. Set $J\hat{D}^\infty(W) \equiv \lim_{\leftarrow} J\hat{D}^k(W)$, $\hat{J}^\infty_{m|n}(W) \equiv \lim_{\leftarrow} \hat{J}^k_{m|n}(W)$. These are quantum supermanifolds modeled on $B \equiv \prod_k B_k$.

A *quantum super PDE* of order k on the fiber bundle $\pi: W \to M$, defined in the category of quantum supermanifolds, $\mathfrak{Q}_S$, is a subset $\hat{E}_k \subset J\hat{D}^k(W)$ or $\hat{E}_k \subset \hat{J}^k_{m|n}(W)$. A geometric theory of quantum (super) PDEs can be formulated introducing suitable hypotheses of regularity on $\hat{E}_k$. (See [1, 3, 5–7].)

2. Bordism groups and conservation laws

The characterization of global solutions of a PDE $\hat{E}_k \subseteq \hat{J}^k_{m|n}(W)$, in the category $\mathfrak{Q}_S$, can be made by means of its integral bordism groups $\Omega_{p|q}^{\hat{E}_k}$, $p \in \{0,1,\dots,m-1\}$, $q \in \{0,1,\dots,n-1\}$. Let us shortly recall some fundamental definitions and results about. Let $f_i : X_i \to \hat{E}_k$, $f_i(X_i) \equiv N_i \subset \hat{E}_k$, $i = 1,2$, be $(p|q)$-dimensional admissible compact closed smooth integral quantum supermanifolds of $\hat{E}_k$. The admissibility requires that N_i should be contained into some solution $V \subset \hat{E}_k$, identified with an (m,n)-chain, with coefficients in A [3, 5–7]. Then, we say that they are $\hat{E}_k$*-bordant* if there exist $(p+1|q+1)$-dimensional smooth quantum supermanifolds $f : Y \to \hat{E}_k$, such that $\partial Y = X_1 \dot{\bigcup} X_2$, $f|_{X_i} = f_i$, $i = 1,2$, and $V \equiv f(Y) \subset \hat{E}_k$ is an admissible integral quantum supermanifold of $\hat{E}_k$ of dimension $(p+1|q+1)$. We say that N_i, $i = 1,2$, are $\hat{E}_k$*-quantum-bordant* if there exist $(p+1|q+1)$-dimensional smooth quantum supermanifolds $f : Y \to \hat{J}^k_{m|n}(W)$, such that $\partial Y = X_1 \dot{\bigcup} X_2$, $f|_{X_i} = f_i$, $i = 1,2$, and $V \equiv f(Y) \subset \hat{J}^k_{m|n}(W)$ is an admissible integral manifold of $\hat{J}^k_{m|n}(W)$ of dimension $(p+1|q+1)$. Let us denote the corresponding bordism groups by $\Omega_{p|q}^{\hat{E}_k}$ and $\Omega_{p|q}(\hat{E}_k)$, $p \in \{0,1,\dots,m-1\}$, $q \in \{0,1,\dots,n-1\}$, called, respectively, $(p|q)$*-dimensional integral bordism group* of $\hat{E}_k$ and $(p|q)$*-dimensional quantum bordism group* of $\hat{E}_k$. Therefore these bordism groups work, for $(p,q) = (m-1,n-1)$, in the category of quantum supermanifolds that are solutions of $\hat{E}_k$. Let us emphasize that singular solutions of $\hat{E}_k$ are, in general, (piecewise) smooth quantum supermanifolds into some prolongation $(\hat{E}_k)_{+s} \subset \hat{J}^{k+s}_{m|n}(W)$, where the set, $\Sigma(V)$, of *singular points* of a solution V is a nowhere dense subset of V. Here we consider *Thom-Boardman singularities*, that is, $q \in \Sigma(V)$ if $(\pi_{k,0})_*(T_qV) \not\cong T_qV$. However, in the case where $\hat{E}_k$ is a differential equation of finite type, that is, the symbols $\hat{g}_{k+s} = 0$, $s \geq 0$, then it is useful to include also in $\Sigma(V)$, discontinuity points, $q, q' \in V$, with $\pi_{k,0}(q) = \pi_{k,0}(q') = a \in W$, or with $\pi_k(q) = \pi_k(q') = p \in M$, where $\pi_k = \pi \circ \pi_{(k,0)} : \hat{J}^k_{m|n}(W) \to M$. We denote such a set by $\Sigma(V)_S$, and in such cases we will talk more precisely of *singular boundary* of V, like $(\partial V)_S = \partial V \setminus \Sigma(V)_S$. Such singular solutions are also called *weak solutions*.

Let us define some notation to distinguish between some integral bordisms.

Definition 2.1. Let $\Omega^{\widehat{E}_k}_{m-1|n-1}$, (resp., $\Omega^{\widehat{E}_k}_{m-1|n-1,s}$, resp., $\Omega^{\widehat{E}_k}_{m-1|n-1,w}$), be the integral bordism group for $(m-1|n-1)$-dimensional smooth admissible regular integral quantum supermanifolds contained in $\widehat{E}_k$, borded by smooth regular integral quantum supermanifold-solutions, (resp., piecewise-smooth or singular solutions; resp., singular-weak solutions), of $\widehat{E}_k$.

Theorem 2.2. *One has the following exact commutative diagram:*

$$
\begin{array}{ccccccccc}
 & & 0 & & 0 & & 0 & & \\
 & & \downarrow & & \downarrow & & \downarrow & & \\
0 & \longrightarrow & K^{\widehat{E}_k}_{m-1|n-1,w/(s,w)} & \longrightarrow & K^{\widehat{E}_k}_{m-1|n-1,w} & \longrightarrow & K^{\widehat{E}_k}_{m-1|n-1,s,w} & \longrightarrow & 0 \\
 & & \downarrow & & \downarrow & & \downarrow & & \\
0 & \longrightarrow & K^{\widehat{E}_k}_{m-1|n-1,s} & \longrightarrow & \Omega^{\widehat{E}_k}_{m-1|n-1} & \longrightarrow & \Omega^{\widehat{E}_k}_{m-1|n-1,s} & \longrightarrow & 0 \\
 & & \downarrow & & \downarrow & & \downarrow & & \\
 & & 0 & \longrightarrow & \Omega^{\widehat{E}_k}_{m-1|n-1,w} & \longrightarrow & \Omega^{\widehat{E}_k}_{m-1|n-1,w} & \longrightarrow & 0 \\
 & & & & \downarrow & & \downarrow & & \\
 & & & & 0 & & 0 & &
\end{array}
\tag{2.1}
$$

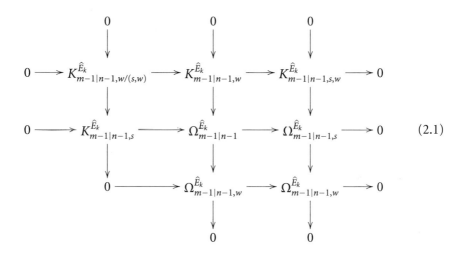

Therefore, one has the canonical isomorphisms: $K^{\widehat{E}_k}_{m-1|n-1,w/(s,w)} \cong K^{\widehat{E}_k}_{m-1|n-1,s}$; $\Omega^{\widehat{E}_k}_{m-1|n-1}/K^{\widehat{E}_k}_{m-1|n-1,s} \cong \Omega^{\widehat{E}_k}_{m-1|n-1,s}$; $\Omega^{\widehat{E}_k}_{m-1|n-1,s}/K^{\widehat{E}_k}_{m-1|n-1,s,w} \cong \Omega^{\widehat{E}_k}_{m-1|n-1,w}$; $\Omega^{\widehat{E}_k}_{m-1|n-1}/K^{\widehat{E}_k}_{m-1|n-1,w} \cong \Omega^{\widehat{E}_k}_{m-1|n-1,w}$. *If* $\widehat{E}_k$ *is formally quantum superintegrable [3, 5–7], then one has the following isomorphisms:* $\Omega^{\widehat{E}_k}_{m-1|n-1} \cong \Omega^{\widehat{E}_\infty}_{m-1|n-1} \cong \Omega^{\widehat{E}_\infty}_{m-1|n-1,s}$; $\Omega^{\widehat{E}_k}_{m-1|n-1,w} \cong \Omega^{\widehat{E}_\infty}_{m-1|n-1,w}$.

Proof. The proof follows directly from the definitions and standard results of algebra. Furthermore, for $k=\infty$, one has that all nonweak singular solutions are smooth solutions. □

Theorem 2.3. *Let* $\widehat{E}_k \subset \hat{J}^k_{m|n}(W)$ *be a quantum super PDE that is formally quantum superintegrable, and completely superintegrable. Assume that the symbols* $\hat{g}_{k+s} \neq 0$, $s=0,1$. *(This excludes the case* $k=\infty$*.) Then one has the following isomorphisms:* $\Omega^{\widehat{E}_k}_{p|q,s} \cong \Omega^{\widehat{E}_k}_{p|q,w} \cong \Omega_{p|q}(\widehat{E}_k)$, *with* $p \in \{0,\dots,m-1\}$ *and* $q \in \{0,\dots,n-1\}$.

Proof. In fact, in these cases any weak solution identifies a singular solution, by connecting its branches by means of suitable pieces of fibers. Furthermore, since $\widehat{E}_{k+1}$ is a strong retract of $\hat{J}^{k+1}_{m|n}(W)$, we can deform any quantum bording $V \subset \hat{J}^{k+1}_{m|n}(W)$, $\dim V = (m|n)$, with $\partial V \subset \widehat{E}_{k+1}$, into a (singular) solution of $\widehat{E}_{k+1}$, and hence into a solution of $\widehat{E}_k$. (For details see [1, 3, 8].) □

COROLLARY 2.4. *Let $\widehat{E}_k \subset \widehat{J}^k_{m|n}(W)$ be a quantum super PDE, that is formally superintegrable and completely superintegrable. One has the following isomorphisms: $\Omega^{\widehat{E}_k}_{m-1|n-1,w} \cong \Omega_{m-1|n-1}(\widehat{E}_k) \cong \Omega^{\widehat{E}_{k+h}}_{m-1|n-1,w} \cong \Omega^{\widehat{E}_\infty}_{m-1|n-1,w} \cong \Omega_{m-1|n-1,w}(\widehat{E}_{k+h}) \cong \Omega_{m-1|n-1}(\widehat{E}_\infty)$.*

In order to distinguish between quantum integral supermanifolds V representing singular solutions, where $\Sigma(V)$ has no discontinuities, and quantum integral supermanifolds where $\Sigma(V)$ contains discontinuities, we can also consider "'conservation laws" valued on quantum integral supermanifolds N representing the integral bordism classes $[N]_{\widehat{E}_k} \in \Omega^{\widehat{E}_k}_{p|q}$.

Definition 2.5. Set $\widehat{\mathfrak{I}}(\widehat{E}_k) \equiv \oplus_{p,q\geq 0}(\widehat{\Omega}^{p|q}(\widehat{E}_k) \cap d^{-1}C\widehat{\Omega}^{p+1|q+1}(\widehat{E}_k)/d\widehat{\Omega}^{p-1|q-1}(E_k) \oplus \{C\widehat{\Omega}^{p|q}(\widehat{E}_k) \cap d^{-1}(C\widehat{\Omega}^{p+1|q+1}(\widehat{E}_k))\} \equiv \oplus_{p,q\geq 0}\widehat{\mathfrak{I}}(\widehat{E}_k)^{p|q}$. Here $C\widehat{\Omega}^{p|q}(\widehat{E}_k)$ denotes the space of all quantum $(p|q)$-forms on $\widehat{E}_k$. Then, define *integral characteristic supernumbers* of N, with $[N]_{\widehat{E}_k} \in \widehat{\Omega}^{\widehat{E}_k}_{p|q}$, the numbers $\hat{i}[N] \equiv \langle [N]_{\widehat{E}_k}, [\alpha]\rangle \in B$ for all $[\alpha] \in \widehat{\mathfrak{I}}(\widehat{E}_k)^{p|q}$.

Then, one has the following theorems.

THEOREM 2.6. *Assume that $\widehat{\mathfrak{I}}(\widehat{E}_k)^{p|q} \neq 0$. One has a natural homomorphism: $\underline{j}_{p|q} : \Omega^{\widehat{E}_k}_{p|q} \to \mathrm{Hom}_A(\widehat{\mathfrak{I}}(\widehat{E}_k)^{p|q}; A)$, $[N]_{\widehat{E}_k} \mapsto \underline{j}_{p|q}([N]_{\widehat{E}_k})$, $\underline{j}_{p|q}([N]_{\widehat{E}_k})([\alpha]) = \int_N \alpha \equiv \langle [N]_{\widehat{E}_k}, [\alpha]\rangle$. Then, a necessary condition that $N' \in [N]_{\widehat{E}_k}$ is the following: $\hat{i}[N] = \hat{i}[N']$ for all $[\alpha] \in \widehat{\mathfrak{I}}(\widehat{E}_k)^{p|q}$. Furthermore, if the classic limit, N_C [3, 5–7], of N is orientable, then the above condition is sufficient also in order to say that $N' \in [N]_{\widehat{E}_k}$.*

Proof. The proof can be conduced by analogy to ones for PDEs and quantum PDEs. (For details see [1, 3, 5–7].) □

COROLLARY 2.7. *Let $\widehat{E}_k \subseteq \widehat{J}^k_{m|n}(W)$ be a quantum super PDE. Consider admissible $(p|q)$-dimensional, $0 \leq p \leq m-1$, $0 \leq q \leq n-1$, integral quantum supermanifolds, with orientable classic limits. Let $N_1 \in [N_2]_{E_k} \in \Omega^{\widehat{E}_k}_{p|q}$, then there exists a $(p+1|q+1)$-dimensional admissible integral quantum supermanifold $V \subset \widehat{E}_k$, such that $\partial V = N_1 \dot{\bigcup} N_2$, where V is without discontinuities if and only if the integral supernumbers of N_1 and N_2 coincide.*

The above considerations can be generalized to include more sophisticated quantum solutions of quantum super PDEs.

Definition 2.8. Let $\widehat{E}_k \subset \widehat{J}^k_{m|n}(W)$ be a quantum super PDE and let B be a quantum superalgebra. Let us consider the following chain complex *(bigraded bar quantum chain complex of $\widehat{E}_k$)*: $\{\bar{C}_{\bullet|\bullet}(\widehat{E}_k;B),\partial\}$, induced by the $\mathbb{Z}_2$-gradiation of B on the corresponding bar quantum chain complex of $\widehat{E}_k$, that is, $\{\bar{C}_{\bullet}(\widehat{E}_k;B),\partial\}$. (See [1, 3, 5–7].) More precisely, $\bar{C}_p(\widehat{E}_k;B)$ is the free two-sided B-module of formal linear combinations with coefficients in B, $\sum \lambda_i c_i$, where c_i is a singular p-chain $f : \triangle^p \to \widehat{E}_k$, that extends on a neighborhood $U \subset \mathbb{R}^{p+1}$, such that f on U is differentiable and $Tf(\triangle^p) \subset \widehat{\mathbf{E}}^k_{m|n}$, where $\widehat{\mathbf{E}}^k_{m|n}$ is the Cartan distribution of $\widehat{E}_k$.

THEOREM 2.9. *The homology $\bar{H}_{\bullet|\bullet}(\widehat{E}_k;B)$ of the bigraded bar quantum chain complex of $\widehat{E}_k$ is isomorphic to (closed) bar integral singular $(p|q)$-bordism groups, with coefficients* *in B, of* $\widehat{E}_k$: ${}^B\bar{\Omega}^{\widehat{E}_k}_{p|q,s} \cong \bar{H}_{q|q}(\widehat{E}_k;B) \cong (\bar{\Omega}^{\widehat{E}_k}_{p,s} \otimes_{\mathbb{K}} B_0)\bigoplus(\bar{\Omega}^{\widehat{E}_k}_{q,s} \otimes_{\mathbb{K}} B_1)$, $p \in \{0,1,\dots,m-1\}$, $q \in \{0,1,\dots,n-1\}$. *(If* $B = \mathbb{K}$*, omit the apex B.) If* $\widehat{E}_k \subset \hat{J}^k_{m|n}(W)$ *is formally quantum superintegrable and completely superintegrable, and the symbols* $\hat{g}_{k+s} \neq 0$*, then one has the following canonical isomorphisms:* ${}^A\bar{\Omega}^{\widehat{E}_k}_{p|q,s} \cong \Omega^{\widehat{E}_k}_{p|q,w} \cong \Omega^{\widehat{E}_k}_{p|q,s} \cong \Omega_{p|q}(\widehat{E}_k)$*. Furthermore, the quantum* $(p|q)$*-bordism groups* $\Omega_{p|q}(\widehat{E}_k)$ *is an extension of a subgroup of* ${}^A\underline{\Omega}_{p|q,s}(W) \cong H_{p|q}(W;A)$*, and the integral* $(p|q)$*-bordism group* $\Omega^{\widehat{E}_k}_{p|q}$ *is an extension of the quantum* $(p|q)$*-bordism group.*

Proof. It follows from an exact commutative diagram naturally associated to the bigraded bar quantum chain complex of $\widehat{E}_k$, and from the above results. (See analogous situation for quantum PDEs in [1, 3, 5–7]). □

Corollary 2.10. *Let* $\widehat{E}_k \subset \hat{J}^k_{m|n}(W)$ *be a quantum super PDE, that is formally superintegrable and completely superintegrable. One has the following isomorphisms:* $\Omega^{\widehat{E}_k}_{m-1|n-1,w} \cong \Omega_{m-1|n-1}(\widehat{E}_k) \cong \Omega^{\widehat{E}_{k+h}}_{m-1|n-1,w} \cong \Omega^{\widehat{E}_\infty}_{m-1|n-1,w} \cong \Omega_{m-1|n-1,w}(\widehat{E}_{k+h}) \cong \Omega_{m-1|n-1}(\widehat{E}_\infty) \cong {}^A\underline{\Omega}_{m-1|n-1,s}(W) \cong H_{m-1|n-1}(W;A)$.

The spaces of conservation laws of quantum super PDEs identify quantum Hopf algebras that now are $\mathbb{Z}_2$-graded with a natural structure of induced quantum superalgebra. Quantum Hopf algebras are generalizations of such algebras [1, 3, 5–7].

Definition 2.11. The *full space of* $(p|q)$*-conservation laws*, (or *full* $(p|q)$*-Hopf superalgebra*), of $\widehat{E}_k$ is the following one: $\mathbf{H}_{p|q}(E_k) \equiv B^{\Omega^{\widehat{E}_k}_{p|q}}$, where B is defined in Example 1.1. Call *full Hopf superalgebra*, of $\widehat{E}_k$, the following: $\mathbf{H}_{m-1|n-1}(\widehat{E}_\infty) \equiv B^{\Omega^{\widehat{E}_\infty}_{m-1|n-1}}$.

Definition 2.12. The *space of (differential) conservation laws* of $\widehat{E}_k \subset \hat{J}^k_{m|n}(W)$ is $\mathfrak{Cons}(\widehat{E}_k) = \widehat{\mathfrak{I}}(\widehat{E}_\infty)^{m-1|n-1}$.

Theorem 2.13. *The full* $(p|q)$*-Hopf superalgebra of a quantum super PDE* $\widehat{E}_k \subset \hat{J}^k_{m|n}(W)$ *has a natural structure of quantum Hopf superalgebra.*

Proof. The proof is similar to the one made for quantum PDEs [1]. □

Proposition 2.14. *The space of conservation laws of* $\widehat{E}_k$ *has a canonical representation in* $\mathbf{H}_{m-1|n-1}(\widehat{E}_\infty)$.

Proof. In fact, one has the following homomorphism: $j : \mathfrak{Cons}(E_k) \to \mathbf{H}_{m-1|n-1}(\widehat{E}_\infty)$, $j[\alpha]([N]_{\widehat{E}_\infty}) = \langle [\alpha], [N]_{\widehat{E}_\infty}\rangle = \int_{N_C} i^*\alpha \in B$, where $i : N_C \to N$ is the canonical injection. □

Theorem 2.15. *Set:* $\mathbf{K}^{\widehat{E}_k}_{m-1|n-1,w/(s,w)} \equiv B^{K^{\widehat{E}_k}_{n-1,w/(s,w)}}$, $\mathbf{K}^{\widehat{E}_k}_{m-1|n-1,w} \equiv B^{K^{\widehat{E}_k}_{m-1|n-1,w}}$, $\mathbf{K}^{\widehat{E}_k}_{m-1|n-1,s,w} \equiv B^{K^{\widehat{E}_k}_{m-1|n-1,(s,w)}}$, $\mathbf{K}^{\widehat{E}_k}_{m-1|n-1,s} \equiv B^{K^{\widehat{E}_k}_{m-1|n-1,s}}$, $\mathbf{H}_{m-1|n-1}(\widehat{E}_k) \equiv B^{\Omega^{\widehat{E}_k}_{m-1|n-1}}$, $\mathbf{H}_{m-1|n-1,s}(\widehat{E}_k) \equiv B^{\Omega^{\widehat{E}_k}_{m-1|n-1,s}}$, $\mathbf{H}_{m-1|n-1,w}(\widehat{E}_k) \equiv B^{\Omega^{\widehat{E}_k}_{m-1|n-1,w}}$. *One has the following canonical isomorphisms:*

$$\mathbf{K}^{\widehat{E}_k}_{m-1|n-1,w/(s,w)} \cong \mathbf{K}^{K^{\widehat{E}_k}_{m-1|n-1,s}};$$

$$\mathbf{K}^{\widehat{E}_k}_{m-1|n-1,w}/\mathbf{K}^{\widehat{E}_k}_{n-1,s,w} \cong \mathbf{K}^{K^{\widehat{E}_k}_{m-1|n-1,w/(s,w)}};$$

$$\begin{aligned}
\mathbf{H}_{m-1|n-1}(\widehat{E}_k)/\mathbf{H}_{m-1|n-1,s}(\widehat{E}_k) &\cong \mathbf{K}^{\widehat{E}_k}_{m-1|n-1,s};\\
\mathbf{H}_{m-1|n-1}(\widehat{E}_k)/\mathbf{H}_{m-1|n-1,w}(\widehat{E}_k) &\cong \mathbf{K}^{\widehat{E}_k}_{m-1|n-1,w}\\
&\cong \mathbf{H}_{m-1|n-1,s}(\widehat{E}_k)/\mathbf{H}_{m-1|n-1,w}(\widehat{E}_k)\\
&\cong \mathbf{K}^{\widehat{E}_k}_{m-1|n-1,s,w}.
\end{aligned} \tag{2.2}$$

Proof. The proof is obtained directly by duality of the exact commutative diagram (2.1). □

THEOREM 2.16. *Under the same hypotheses of Theorem 2.3, one has the following canonical isomorphism:* $\mathbf{H}_{m-1|n-1,s}(E_k) \cong \mathbf{H}_{m-1|n-1,w}(\widehat{E}_k)$. *Furthermore, it is possible to represent differential conservation laws of* E_k *in* $\mathbf{H}_{m-1|n-1,w}(\widehat{E}_k)$.

Proof. Let us note that $\widehat{\mathfrak{I}}(\widehat{E}_k)^{m-1|n-1} \subset \widehat{\mathfrak{I}}(\widehat{E}_\infty)^{m-1|n-1}$. If $j : \mathfrak{C}\mathrm{ons}(\widehat{E}_k) \to \mathbf{H}_{m-1|n-1}(\widehat{E}_\infty)$ is the canonical representation of the space of the differential conservation laws in the full Hopf superalgebra of $\widehat{E}_k$, (corresponding to the integral bordism groups for regular smooth solutions), it follows that one has also the following canonical representation $j|_{\widehat{\mathfrak{I}}(\widehat{E}_k)^{m-1|n-1}} : \widehat{\mathfrak{I}}(\widehat{E}_k)^{m-1|n-1} \to \mathbf{H}_{m-1|n-1,s}(\widehat{E}_k) \cong \mathbf{H}_{m-1|n-1,w}(\widehat{E}_k)$. In fact for any $N' \in [N]_{\widehat{E}_k,s} \in \Omega^{\widehat{E}_k}_{m-1|n-1,s} \cong \Omega^{\widehat{E}_k}_{m-1|n-1,w}$, one has $\int_{N'} \beta = \int_N \beta$ for any $[\beta] \in \widehat{\mathfrak{I}}(\widehat{E}_k)^{m-1|n-1}$. □

3. Conservation laws in quantum black holes

We will consider, now, the *quantum* $N = 2$ *super-Poincaré group* over a quantum superalgebra $A = A_0 \oplus A_1$, that is a quantum Lie supergroup G having as quantum Lie superalgebra $\widehat{\mathfrak{g}}$ one identified by the following infinitesimal generators: $\{Z_K\}_{1\le K\le 19} \equiv \{J_{\alpha\beta}, P_\alpha, \overline{Z}, Q_{\beta i}\}_{0\le\alpha,\beta\le 3;1\le a\le 2}$, such that $J_{\alpha\beta} = -J_{\beta\alpha}$, $P_\alpha, \overline{Z} \in \mathrm{Hom}_Z(A_0;\mathfrak{g})$, $Q_{\beta i} \in \mathrm{Hom}_Z(A_1;\mathfrak{g})$. The corresponding nonzero $\mathbb{Z}_2$-graded brackets are the following: $[J_{\alpha\beta}, J_{\gamma\delta}] = \eta_{\beta\gamma}J_{\alpha\delta} + \eta_{\alpha\delta}J_{\beta\gamma} - \eta_{\alpha\gamma}J_{\beta\delta} - \eta_{\beta\delta}J_{\alpha\gamma}$, $[P_\alpha, P_\beta] = -8e^2 J_{\alpha\beta}$, $[J_{\alpha\beta}, P_\gamma] = \eta_{\beta\gamma}P_\beta - \eta_{\alpha\gamma}P_\beta$, $[J_{\alpha\beta}, Q_{\gamma i}] = (\sigma_{\alpha\beta})^{\mu j}_{\gamma} Q_{\mu j}$, $[Q_{\beta i}, Q_{\mu j}] = (C\gamma^\alpha)_{\beta\mu}\delta_{ij}P_\alpha + C_{\beta\mu}\epsilon_{ij}\overline{Z}$. Here $C_{\alpha\beta}$ is the antisymmetric charge conjugation matrix, $\sigma_{\beta\mu} = (1/4)[\gamma_\beta, \gamma_\mu]$, with γ^μ the Dirac matrices. $\overline{Z}$ commutes with all the other ones. Then, with reference to the above notation, one has $\dim G = (d|N_2) = (11|8)$, and we will consider the following principal bundle in the category of quantum supermanifolds: P is a quantum supermanifold of dimension $(15|8)$; M is a quantum supermanifold of dimension $(4|N_1) = (4|0)$. Then a pseudoconnection can be written by means of the following full quantum differential 1-forms on P: ${}_1\mu^K = \mu^K_H dY^H$, $(\mu^K_H) = ((1/2)\omega^{\alpha\beta}_H, \theta^\mu_H, A_H, \psi^{aj}_H)$. With respect to a section $s : M \to P$, we get $(s^*{}_1\mu)^K = \bar{\mu}^K_\gamma dX^\gamma$, $(\bar{\mu}^K_\gamma) = ((1/2)\bar{\omega}^{\alpha\beta}_\gamma, \bar{\theta}^\mu_\gamma, \bar{A}_\gamma, \bar{\psi}^{aj}_\gamma)$, where $\bar{\omega}^{\alpha\beta}_\gamma$ is the usual Levi-Civita connection, $\bar{\theta}^\mu_\gamma$ is the vierbein, $\bar{A}_\gamma$ is the electromagnetic field, and $\bar{\psi}^{aj}_\gamma$ is the usual spin 3/2 field. The blow-up structure $\pi^*\widehat{C}(P) \hookrightarrow \mathrm{Hom}_Z(TP;\mathfrak{g})$ implies that we can identify our fields with sections ${}_1\mu$ of the fiber bundle $\bar{\pi} : \bar{C} \equiv \mathrm{Hom}_Z(TM;\mathfrak{g}) \to M$. ($\widehat{C}(P) \cong J\widehat{D}(P)/G$ is the fiber bundle, over M, of principal quantum connections on the G-principal fiber bundle $\pi : P \to M$.) The corresponding curvatures can be written in the form ${}_1R^K_{\beta\alpha} = (\partial x_\beta \mu^K_\alpha) + C^K_{IJ}[\mu^I_\beta, \mu^J_\alpha]_+$. The

Table 3.1. Dynamic equation on macroscopic shell: $\widehat{E}_2[i] \subset J\widehat{\mathcal{D}}^2(i^*\bar{C})$ and Bianchi identity.

Fields equations	$(\partial\omega^{\gamma}_{ab} \cdot L) - \partial_\mu(\partial\omega^{\gamma\mu}_{ab} \cdot L) = 0$ (*curvature equation*)
	$(\partial\theta^{\gamma}_{\alpha} \cdot L) - \partial_\mu(\partial\theta^{\gamma\mu}_{\alpha} \cdot L) = 0$ (*torsion equation*)
$(\widehat{E}_2[i])$	$(\partial\psi^{\gamma}_{\beta i} \cdot L) - \partial_\mu(\partial\psi^{\gamma\mu}_{\beta i} \cdot L) = 0$ (*gravitino equation*)
	$(\partial A^{\gamma} \cdot L) - \partial_\mu(\partial A^{\gamma\mu} \cdot L) = 0$ (*Maxwell's equation*)
Bianchi identity	$(\partial x_{[\gamma} \cdot R^{ab}_{\beta\alpha]}) + 2\omega^{a}_{e[\gamma}R^{eb}_{\beta\alpha]} = 0$
	$(\partial x_{[\gamma} \cdot R^{\alpha}_{\beta\omega]}) + \omega^{\alpha b}_{[\gamma}R_{\beta\omega]b} + \frac{1}{2}(C\gamma^{\alpha})_{\delta\mu}\psi^{\delta}_{j[\gamma}\rho^{\mu j}_{\beta\omega]} = 0$
$(B[i])$	$(\partial x_{[\gamma} \cdot \rho^{\beta i}_{\omega\alpha]}) + \frac{1}{2}(\sigma_{ab})^{\beta i}_{\delta j}\omega^{ab}_{[\gamma}\rho^{\delta j}_{\omega\alpha]} = 0$
	$(\partial x_{[\gamma}F_{\beta\alpha]}) + \frac{1}{2}C_{\delta\mu}\epsilon_{ij}\psi^{\delta i}_{[\gamma}\rho^{\mu j}_{\beta\alpha]} = 0$
Fields	$R^{ab}_{\mu\nu} = (\partial x_{[\mu} \cdot \omega^{ab}_{\nu]}) + 2\omega^{a}_{e[\mu}\omega^{eb}_{\nu]}$ (*curvature*)
	$R^{\alpha}_{\mu\nu} = (\partial x_{[\mu} \cdot \theta^{\alpha}_{\nu]}) + \omega^{\alpha}_{\beta[\mu},\theta^{\beta}_{\nu]} + \frac{1}{2}(C\gamma^{\alpha})_{\beta\delta}\psi^{\beta}_{j[\mu}\psi^{\delta j}_{\nu]}$ (*torsion*)
	$\rho^{\beta i}_{\mu\nu} = (\partial x_{[\mu} \cdot \psi^{\beta i}_{\nu]}) + \frac{1}{2}(\sigma_{ab})^{\beta i}_{\gamma j}\omega^{ab}_{[\mu}\psi^{\gamma j}_{\nu]}$ (*gravitino*)
	$F_{\mu\nu} = (\partial x_{[\mu} \cdot A_{\nu]}) + \frac{1}{2}C_{\beta\gamma}\epsilon_{ij}\psi^{\beta i}_{[\mu}\psi^{\gamma j}_{\nu]}$ (*electromagnetic field*)

local expression of the *dynamic equation*, $\widehat{E}_2[i] \subset J\widehat{\mathcal{D}}^2(i^*\bar{C})$, evaluated on a macroscopic shell, that is, an embedding $i : N \to M$, of a globally hyperbolic; p-connected manifold N, $0 \leq p \leq 3$, is given by the quantum super PDE reported in Table 3.1, where $L : J\widehat{\mathcal{D}}(\underline{E}) \to \widehat{A}$ is a quantum Lagrangian function. Possible Lagrangian densities are polynomial in the curvature, (see example below), and hence we can assume that they give formally quantum superintegrable, and completely quantum superintegrable, quantum super PDEs. Then, assuming that $\widehat{E}_2[i]$ is formally integrable and completely superintegrable, the integral bordism groups of $\widehat{E}_2[i]$ and its full quantum p-Hopf superalgebras can be calculated. More precisely, we use the fact that $\widehat{C}(P) \to M$ is a contractible fiber bundle of dimension $(4|0,44|32)$ over the quantum superalgebra $A \times \widehat{A} = (A_0 \times A_1) \times \widehat{A}^1_0(A) \times \widehat{A}^1_1(A)$, and that N is topologically trivial. In fact, we can apply Theorem 2.9 and Corollary 2.10 to obtain the quantum and integral bordism groups of $\widehat{E}_2[i]$: $\Omega^{\widehat{E}_2[i]}_{p,s} \cong \Omega^{\widehat{E}_2[i]_{+\infty}}_{p,w} \cong 0$ for $p = 1,2,3$ and $\Omega^{\widehat{E}_2[i]}_{0,s} \cong \Omega^{\widehat{E}_2[i]_{+\infty}}_{0,w} \cong A$. Therefore, we have that 1-dimensional admissible integral closed quantum submanifolds contained into $\widehat{E}_2[i]$, (*admissible quantum closed strings*), can propagate and interact between them by means of 2-dimensional admissible integral quantum manifolds contained into $\widehat{J}^2_4(i^*\bar{C})$, or by means of 2-dimensional admissible integral quantum manifolds contained into $\widehat{E}_2[i]$, in such a way to generate (quantum) tunnel effects. Finally, as a consequence of the triviality of the 3-dimensional integral bordism groups, we get the existence of global quantum solutions of such equations.

As a byproduct we get the following theorems.

THEOREM 3.1 (quantum tunnel effects). *The quantum supergravity equation $\widehat{E}_2 \subset J\widehat{D}^2(i^*\bar{C})$ admits global solutions having a change of sectional topology (quantum tunnel effects). In general these solutions are not globally representable as second derivative of sections of the fiber bundle $i^*\bar{C} \to N$ (Such solutions with nontrivial topology well interpret the meaning of "quantum geometrodynamics" as first conjectured by J. A. Wheeler. Compare also with the more recent approach on the "topological quantum field theory" by M. Atiayah and E. Witten, (see references quoted in [3]).)*

Proof. This statement can be proved by using surgery techniques and taking into account that for the 3-dimensional integral bordism group of $\widehat{E}_k$, one has $\Omega_{3,s}^{\widehat{E}_k} = 0 = \Omega_{3,w}^{(\widehat{E}_2)_{+\infty}}$. In fact, a boundary value problem for $\widehat{E}_k[i]$ can be directly implemented in the manifold $\widehat{E}_k[i] \subset J\widehat{D}^2(i^*\bar{C}) \subset \hat{J}_4^2(i^*\bar{C})$ by requiring that a 3-dimensional compact space-like (for some $t = t_0$), admissible integral manifold $B \subset \widehat{E}_k[i]$ propagates in $\widehat{E}_k[i]$ in such a way that the boundary ∂B describes a fixed 3-dimensional time-like integral manifold $Y \subset \widehat{E}_k[i]$. (We will require that the boundary ∂B of B is orientable.) Y is not, in general, a closed (smooth) manifold. However, we can solder Y with two other compact 3-dimensional integral manifolds X_i, $i = 1,2$, in such a way that the result is a closed 3-dimensional (smooth) integral manifold $Z \subset \widehat{E}_k[i]$. More precisely, we can take $X_1 = B$ so that $\widetilde{Z} \equiv X_1 \bigcup_{\partial B} Y$ is a 3-dimensional compact integral manifold, such that $\partial\widetilde{Z} \equiv C$ is a 2-dimensional space-like integral manifold. We can assume that C is an orientable manifold. Then, from the triviality of the integral bordism group, it follows that $\partial X_2 = C$, for some space-like compact 3-dimensional integral manifold $X_2 \subset \widehat{E}_k[i]$. Set $Z \equiv \widetilde{Z} \bigcup_C X_2$. Therefore, one has $Z = X_1 \bigcup_{\partial B} Y \bigcup_C X_2$. Then, again from the triviality of the integral bordism group, it follows also that there exists a 4-dimensional integral (smooth) manifold $V \subset \widehat{E}_k[i]$ such that $\partial V = Z$. Hence the integral manifold V is a solution of our boundary value problem between the times t_0 and t_1, where t_0 and t_1 are the times corresponding to the space-like boundaries where are soldered X_i, $i = 1,2$ to Y. Now, this process can be extended for any $t_2 > t_1$. So we are able to find (smooth) solutions for any $t > t_0$, and hence (smooth) solutions for any $t > t_0$, therefore, global (smooth) solutions. Remark that in order to assure the smoothness of the global solution so built it is enough to develop such construction in the infinity prolongation $\widehat{E}_k[i]_{+\infty}$ of $\widehat{E}_k[i]$. Finally, note that in the set of solutions of $\widehat{E}_k[i]$ there are ones that have change of sectional topology. In fact, the 3-dimensional integral bordism groups are trivial: $\Omega_{3,s}^{\widehat{E}_k[i]} = 0 = \Omega_{3,w}^{\widehat{E}_k[i]_{+\infty}}$. □

THEOREM 3.2 (quantum black holes). *If the 3-dimensional space-like compact domain B describes a region where a "quantum black hole" is present, (i.e., of physical dimension in the range of strong interactions [3]), a solution, like the one described in the proof of the previous theorem, represents an evaporating black hole. The point where there is the singularity of the characteristic flow of the solution is the explosive end [3] of the evaporation process with production of new particles and radiation described by the outgoing solution.*

Proof. In order to obtain such solutions we must have a Cauchy integral data with a geometric black hole B embedded in a compact 3-dimensional integral manifold N, $B \subset N$, such that its boundary ∂N propagates with a fixed flow. Then a solution, with quantum tunnel effect of such boundary problem, can describe a vaporization process of such black hole. The above results assure the existence of such solutions and a way to build them. □

Definition 3.3. Set $\widehat{\mathfrak{I}}(\widehat{E}_k[i]) \equiv \oplus_{q\geq 0}\widehat{\Omega}^q(\widehat{E}_k[i]) \cap d^{-1}(C\widehat{\Omega}^{q+1}(\widehat{E}_k[i]))/\widehat{\Omega}^{q-1}(\widehat{E}_k[i]) \oplus \{C\widehat{\Omega}^q(\widehat{E}_k[i]) \cap d^{-1}(C\widehat{\Omega}^{q+1}(\widehat{E}_k[i]))\} \equiv \oplus_{q\geq 0}\widehat{\mathfrak{I}}(\widehat{E}_k[i])^q$. Here $C\widehat{\Omega}^q(\widehat{E}_k[i])$ denotes the space of all Cartan quantum q-forms on $\widehat{E}_k[i]$. (See also [3, 5–7].) Then, define *integral characteristic supernumbers* of N with $[N] \in \widehat{\Omega}_q^{\widehat{E}_k[i]}$, the numbers $\hat{i}[N] \equiv \langle [N], [\alpha] \rangle \in B$ for all $[\alpha] \in \widehat{\mathfrak{I}}(\widehat{E}_k[i])^q$.

Theorem 3.4. *Assume that $\widehat{\mathfrak{I}}(\widehat{E}_k[i])^q \neq 0$. One has a natural homomorphism: $\underline{j}_q : \Omega_q^{\widehat{E}_k[i]} \to \mathrm{Hom}_A(\widehat{\mathfrak{I}}(\widehat{E}_k[i])^q; A)$, $[N] \mapsto \underline{j}_q([N])$, $\underline{j}_q([N])([\alpha]) = \int_N \alpha \equiv < [N], [\alpha] >$. Then, a necessary condition that $N' \in [N] \in \Omega_q^{\widehat{E}_k[i]}$ is the following: $\hat{i}[N] = \hat{i}[N']$ for all $[\alpha] \in \widehat{\mathfrak{I}}(\widehat{E}_k[i])^q$. Furthermore, if N is orientable, then the above condition is sufficient also in order to say that $N' \in [N]$.*

Proof. The proof follows directly from Definition 3.3 and the results given in [1, 3, 5–7]. See also [6, Theorem 3.18]. □

Remark 3.5. Theorem 3.2 proves that a quantum evaporation black hole process can be described by means of quantum smooth integral manifolds, and therefore for such a process "conservation laws" are not destroyed. By the way, as we can have also weak solutions around a quantum black hole, we can assume also that interactions with such objects could be described by means of weak solutions, like shock waves. Therefore we will more precisely talk of *weak quantum black holes* and *nonweak quantum black holes*, according to whether if they are described, respectively, by means of weak solutions or nonweak solutions.

Theorem 3.6 ("conservation laws" through nonweak quantum black holes). *All the integral characteristic supernumbers are conserved through a nonweak quantum evaporating black hole.*

Proof. This follows from Theorem 3.4 taking into account that solutions of $\widehat{E}_k[i]$, describing quantum black holes, are nonweak solutions. In particular, such a statement holds for any evaporation process of nonweak quantum black hole. □

References

[1] A. Prástaro, *(Co)bordism groups in quantum PDE's*, Acta Applicandae Mathematicae **64** (2000), no. 2-3, 111–217.

[2] ———, *Quantum manifolds and integral (co)bordism groups in quantum partial differential equations*, Nonlinear Analysis **47** (2001), no. 4, 2609–2620.

[3] ———, *Quantized Partial Differential Equations*, World Scientific, New Jersy, 2004.

[4] ———, *Quantum super Yang-Mills equations: global existence and mass-gap*, Dynamic Systems and Applications. Vol. 4, Dynamic, Georgia, 2004, pp. 227–232.

[5] ———, *(Co)bordism groups in quantum PDEs. I: quantum supermanifolds*, to appear in Nonlinear Analysis: Real World Applications.

[6] ———, *(Co)bordism groups in quantum PDEs. II: quantum super PDEs*, to appear in Nonlinear Analysis: Real World Applications.
[7] ———, *(Co)bordism groups in quantum PDEs. III: quantum super Yang-Mills equations*, to appear in Nonlinear Analysis: Real World Applications.
[8] A. Prástaro and Th. M. Rassias, *A geometric approach to a noncommutative generalized d'Alembert equation*, Comptes Rendus de l'Académie des Sciences. Série I. Mathématique **330** (2000), no. 7, 545–550.

A. Prástaro: Department of Methods and Mathematical Models for Applied Sciences, University of Rome "La Sapienza", Via A. Scarpa 16, 00161 Rome, Italy
E-mail address: prastaro@dmmm.uniroma1.it

SUPERLINEAR MIXED BVP WITH TIME AND SPACE SINGULARITIES

IRENA RACHŮNKOVÁ

Motivated by a problem arising in the theory of shallow membrane caps, we investigate the solvability of the singular boundary value problem $(p(t)u')' + p(t)f(t,u,p(t)u') = 0$, $\lim_{t\to 0+} p(t)u'(t) = 0$, $u(T) = 0$, where $[0,T] \subset \mathbb{R}$, $p \in C[0,T]$, and $f = f(t,x,y)$ can have time singularities at $t = 0$ and/or $t = T$ and space singularities at $x = 0$ and/or $y = 0$. A superlinear growth of f in its space variables x and y is possible. We present conditions for the existence of solutions positive and decreasing on $[0,T)$.

1. Introduction

Let $[0,T] \subset \mathbb{R} = (-\infty,\infty)$, $\mathcal{D} \subset \mathbb{R}^2$. We deal with the singular mixed boundary value problem

$$(p(t)u')' + p(t)f(t,u,p(t)u') = 0, \tag{1.1}$$

$$\lim_{t\to 0+} p(t)u'(t) = 0, \quad u(T) = 0, \tag{1.2}$$

where $p \in C[0,T]$ and f satisfies the Carathéodory conditions on $(0,T)\times\mathcal{D}$. Here, f can have time singularities at $t = 0$ and/or $t = T$ and space singularities at $x = 0$ and/or $y = 0$. We provide sufficient conditions for the existence of solutions of (1.1), (1.2) which are positive and decreasing on $[0,T)$.

Let $[a,b] \subset \mathbb{R}$, $\mathcal{M} \subset \mathbb{R}^2$. Recall that a real-valued function f satisfies the Carathéodory conditions on the set $[a,b]\times\mathcal{M}$ if

(i) $f(\cdot,x,y) : [a,b] \to \mathbb{R}$ is measurable for all $(x,y) \in \mathcal{M}$,

(ii) $f(t,\cdot,\cdot) : \mathcal{M} \to \mathbb{R}$ is continuous for a.e. $t \in [a,b]$,

(iii) for each compact set $K \subset \mathcal{M}$, there is a function $m_K \in L_1[0,T]$ such that $|f(t,x,y)| \le m_K(t)$ for a.e. $t \in [a,b]$ and all $(x,y) \in K$.

We write $f \in \text{Car}([a,b]\times\mathcal{M})$. By $f \in \text{Car}((0,T)\times\mathcal{D})$, we mean that $f \in \text{Car}([a,b]\times\mathcal{D})$ for each $[a,b] \subset (0,T)$ and $f \notin \text{Car}([0,T]\times\mathcal{D})$.

Hindawi Publishing Corporation
Proceedings of the Conference on Differential & Difference Equations and Applications, pp. 953–961

Definition 1.1. Let $f \in \text{Car}((0,T)\times\mathcal{D})$.

The function f has *a time singularity* at $t=0$ and/or at $t=T$ if there exists $(x,y)\in\mathcal{D}$ such that

$$\int_0^{\varepsilon} |f(t,x,y)|\,dt = \infty \qquad \text{and/or} \qquad \int_{T-\varepsilon}^{T} |f(t,x,y)|\,dt = \infty \tag{1.3}$$

for each sufficiently small $\varepsilon > 0$. The point $t=0$ and/or $t=T$ will be called *a singular point of* f.

The function f has *a space singularity* at $x=0$ and/or at $y=0$ if

$$\limsup_{x\to 0+} |f(t,x,y)| = \infty \quad \text{for a.e. } t\in[0,T] \text{ and for some } y\in(-\infty,0) \tag{1.4}$$

and/or

$$\limsup_{y\to 0-} |f(t,x,y)| = \infty \quad \text{for a.e. } t\in[0,T] \text{ and for some } x\in(0,\infty). \tag{1.5}$$

Definition 1.2. By *a solution* of problem (1.1), (1.2), we understand a function $u\in C[0,T]\cap C^1(0,T]$ with $pu'\in AC[0,T]$ satisfying conditions (1.2) and fulfilling

$$\big(p(t)u'(t)\big)' + p(t)f\big(t,u(t),p(t)u'(t)\big) = 0 \quad \text{for a.e. } t\in[0,T]. \tag{1.6}$$

The study of equations with the term $(pu')'$ was motivated by a problem arising in the theory of shallow membrane caps, namely,

$$(t^3u')' + \frac{t^3}{8u^2} - a_0\frac{t^3}{u} - b_0t^{2\gamma-1} = 0, \quad \lim_{t\to 0+} t^3u'(t) = 0, \quad u(1) = A, \tag{1.7}$$

where $a_0 \ge 0$, $b_0 > 0$, $A > 0$, $\gamma > 1$.

Singular mixed problem (1.1), (1.2) was studied, for example, in [1, 6], and special cases of (1.1), (1.2) were investigated in [3–5, 7]. In [2] we can find a mixed problem with ϕ-Laplacian and a real parameter. Here, we generalize the existence results of [7] and extend those of [1]. We offer new and rather simple conditions (in comparison with those in [1]) which guarantee the existence of positive solutions of the singular problem (1.1), (1.2), provided both time and space singularities are allowed.

2. Approximating regular problem

First, we will study the auxiliary regular mixed problem

$$\big(q(t)u'\big)' + h\big(t,u,q(t)u'\big) = 0, \quad u'(0) = 0,\ u(T) = 0, \tag{2.1}$$

where $q\in C[0,T]$ is positive on $[0,T]$ and $h\in \text{Car}([0,T]\times\mathbb{R}^2)$. In order to prove the solvability of problem (2.1), we will modify the classical lower- and upper-functions method (see, e.g., [5]).

Definition 2.1. A *solution* of the regular problem (2.1) is defined as a function $u\in C^1[0,T]$ with $qu'\in AC[0,T]$ satisfying $u'(0)=u(T)=0$ and fulfilling $(q(t)u'(t))' + h(t,u(t),q(t)u'(t)) = 0$ for a.e. $t\in[0,T]$.

Definition 2.2. A function $\sigma \in C[0,T]$ is called *a lower function of* (2.1) if there exists a finite set $\Sigma \subset (0,T)$ such that $q\sigma' \in AC_{\text{loc}}([0,T]\setminus\Sigma)$, $\sigma'(\tau+), \sigma'(\tau-) \in \mathbb{R}$ for each $\tau \in \Sigma$,

$$\begin{gathered}(q(t)\sigma'(t))' + h(t,\sigma(t),q(t)\sigma'(t)) \geq 0 \quad \text{for a.e. } t \in [0,T], \\ \sigma'(0) \geq 0, \qquad \sigma(T) \leq 0, \qquad \sigma'(\tau-) < \sigma'(\tau+) \quad \text{for each } \tau \in \Sigma.\end{gathered} \tag{2.2}$$

If the inequalities in (2.2) are reversed, then σ is called *an upper function of* (2.1).

THEOREM 2.3 (lower- and upper-functions method). *Let σ_1 and σ_2 be a lower function and an upper function for problem (2.1) such that $\sigma_1 \leq \sigma_2$ on $[0,T]$. Assume also that there is a function $\psi \in L_1[0,T]$ such that*

$$|h(t,x,y)| \leq \psi(t) \quad \textit{for a.e. } t \in [0,T], \textit{ all } x \in [\sigma_1(t),\sigma_2(t)],\ y \in \mathbb{R}. \tag{2.3}$$

Then problem (2.1) has a solution $u \in C^1[0,T]$ satisfying $qu' \in AC[0,T]$ and

$$\sigma_1(t) \leq u(t) \leq \sigma_2(t) \quad \textit{for } t \in [0,T]. \tag{2.4}$$

Proof

Step 1. For a.e. $t \in [0,T]$ and each $x, y \in \mathbb{R}$, $\varepsilon \in [0,1]$, $i = 1,2$, put

$$w_i(t,\varepsilon) = \sup\{|h(t,\sigma_i(t),q(t)\sigma_i'(t)) - h(t,\sigma_i(t),y)| : |q(t)\sigma_i'(t) - y| \leq \varepsilon\},$$

$$h^*(t,x,y) = \begin{cases} h(t,\sigma_2(t),y) - w_2\left(t,\dfrac{x-\sigma_2(t)}{x-\sigma_2(t)+1}\right) - \dfrac{x-\sigma_2(t)}{x-\sigma_2(t)+1} & \text{for } x > \sigma_2(t), \\ h(t,x,y) & \text{for } \sigma_1(t) \leq x \leq \sigma_2(t), \\ h(t,\sigma_1(t),y) + w_1\left(t,\dfrac{\sigma_1(t)-x}{\sigma_1(t)-x+1}\right) + \dfrac{\sigma_1(t)-x}{\sigma_1(t)-x+1} & \text{for } x < \sigma_1(t), \end{cases} \tag{2.5}$$

and consider the auxiliary problem

$$(q(t)u')' + h^*(t,u,q(t)u') = 0, \quad u'(0) = 0,\ u(T) = 0. \tag{2.6}$$

Define the operator $\mathcal{F} : C^1[0,T] \to C^1[0,T]$ by

$$(\mathcal{F}u)(t) = \int_t^T \frac{1}{q(\tau)} \int_0^\tau h^*(s,u(s),q(s)u'(s))\,ds\,d\tau. \tag{2.7}$$

Solving (2.6) is equivalent to finding a fixed point of the operator $\mathcal{F}$. Moreover, $h^* \in \text{Car}([0,T]\times\mathbb{R}^2)$ and there exists $\psi^* \in L_1[0,T]$ such that

$$|h^*(t,x,y)| \leq \psi^*(t) \quad \text{for a.e. } t \in [0,T] \text{ and each } x, y \in \mathbb{R}. \tag{2.8}$$

Therefore $\mathcal{F}$ is continuous and compact and the Schauder fixed point theorem yields a fixed point u of $\mathcal{F}$. By (2.7),

$$u(t) = \int_t^T \frac{1}{q(\tau)} \int_0^\tau h^*(s,u(s),q(s)u'(s))\,ds\,d\tau \quad \text{for } t \in [0,T], \tag{2.9}$$

which implies that u is a solution of (2.6).

Step 2. We prove that u satisfies the equation in (2.1). Put $v = u - \sigma_2$ on $[0,T]$ and assume that $\max\{v(t) : t \in [0,T]\} = v(t_0) > 0$. Since $\sigma_2(T) \geq 0$ and $u(T) = 0$, we can assume that $t_0 \in [0,T)$. Hence $v'(t_0) = 0$ and we can find $\delta > 0$ such that for $t \in (t_0, t_0 + \delta)$

$$v(t) > 0, \qquad |q(t)v'(t)| < \frac{v(t)}{v(t)+1} < 1. \tag{2.10}$$

Then for a.e. $t \in (t_0, t_0 + \delta)$, we get

$$\begin{aligned}(q(t)v'(t))' &= -h^*(t,u(t),q(t)u'(t)) - (q(t)\sigma_2'(t))' = -h(t,\sigma_2(t),q(t)u'(t)) \\ &\quad - (q(t)\sigma_2'(t))' + w_2\left(t, \frac{v(t)}{v(t)+1}\right) + \frac{v(t)}{v(t)+1} > 0.\end{aligned} \tag{2.11}$$

Therefore

$$0 < \int_{t_0}^{t} (q(s)v'(s))' ds = q(t)v'(t) \tag{2.12}$$

for each $t \in (t_0, t_0 + \delta)$, which contradicts the fact that $v(t_0)$ is the maximal value of v. So $u \leq \sigma_2$ on $[0,T]$. The inequality $\sigma_1 \leq u$ on $[0,T]$ can be proved analogously. Using the definition of h^*, we see that u is also a solution of (2.1). □

3. Main result

We are interested in positive and decreasing solutions of singular problem (1.1), (1.2), and hence the following existence result will be proved under the assumptions

$$p \in C[0,T], \quad p > 0 \text{ on } (0,T], \qquad \frac{1}{p} \in L_1[0,T], \tag{3.1}$$

$$\begin{gathered}\mathcal{D} = (0,\infty) \times (-\infty, 0), \quad f \in \operatorname{Car}((0,T) \times \mathcal{D}), \\ f \text{ can have time singularities at } t = 0,\ t = T, \\ \text{and space singularities at } x = 0,\ y = 0.\end{gathered} \tag{3.2}$$

Theorem 3.1 (existence result). *Let (3.1), (3.2) hold. Assume that there exist* $\varepsilon \in (0,1)$, $\nu \in (0,T)$, $c \in (\nu, \infty)$ *such that*

$$f(t,P(t),-c) = 0 \quad \text{for a.e. } t \in [0,T], \tag{3.3}$$

$$0 \leq f(t,x,y) \quad \text{for a.e. } t \in [0,T], \text{ all } x \in (0,P(t)],\ y \in [-c,0), \tag{3.4}$$

$$\varepsilon \leq f(t,x,y) \quad \text{for a.e. } t \in [0,\nu], \text{ all } x \in (0,P(t)],\ y \in [-\nu,0), \tag{3.5}$$

where

$$P(t) = c\int_t^T \frac{ds}{p(s)}. \tag{3.6}$$

Then problem (1.1), (1.2) has a positive decreasing solution $u \in C[0,T]$ with $pu' \in AC[0,T]$ satisfying

$$0 < u(t) \le P(t), \quad -c \le p(t)u'(t) < 0 \quad \textit{for } t \in (0,T). \tag{3.7}$$

Proof. Let $k \in \mathbb{N}$, where $\mathbb{N}$ is the set of all natural numbers and let $k \ge 3/T$.
Step 1. Approximate solutions. For $x, y \in \mathbb{R}$, put

$$\alpha_k(x) = \begin{cases} P(t) & \text{if } x > P(t), \\ x & \text{if } \dfrac{1}{k} \le x \le P(t), \\ \dfrac{1}{k} & \text{if } x < \dfrac{1}{k}, \end{cases}$$

$$\beta_k(y) = \begin{cases} -\dfrac{1}{k} & \text{if } y > -\dfrac{1}{k}, \\ y & \text{if } -c \le y \le -\dfrac{1}{k}, \\ -c & \text{if } y < -c, \end{cases} \tag{3.8}$$

$$\gamma(y) = \begin{cases} \varepsilon & \text{if } y \ge -\nu, \\ \varepsilon\dfrac{c+y}{c-\nu} & \text{if } -c < y < -\nu, \\ 0 & \text{if } y \le -c. \end{cases}$$

For a.e. $t \in [0,T]$ and $x, y \in \mathbb{R}$, define

$$f_k(t,x,y) = \begin{cases} \gamma(y) & \text{if } t \in \left[0, \dfrac{1}{k}\right), \\ f(t, \alpha_k(x), \beta_k(y)) & \text{if } t \in \left[\dfrac{1}{k}, T - \dfrac{1}{k}\right], \\ 0 & \text{if } t \in \left(T - \dfrac{1}{k}, T\right], \end{cases} \tag{3.9}$$

$$p_k(t) = \begin{cases} \max\left\{p(t), p\left(\dfrac{1}{k}\right)\right\} & \text{if } t \in \left[0, \dfrac{1}{k}\right), \\ p(t) & \text{if } t \in \left[\dfrac{1}{k}, T\right]. \end{cases}$$

Then $p_k f_k \in \mathrm{Car}([0,T] \times \mathbb{R}^2)$ and there is $\psi_k \in L_1[0,T]$ such that

$$|p_k(t) f_k(t,x,y)| \le \psi_k(t) \quad \text{for a.e. } t \in [0,T], \text{ all } x, y \in \mathbb{R}. \tag{3.10}$$

We have got a sequence of auxiliary regular problems:

$$(p_k(t)u')' + p_k(t) f_k(t,u,p_k(t)u') = 0, \quad u'(0) = 0,\ u(T) = 0, \tag{3.11}$$

for $k \in \mathbb{N}$, $k \geq 3/T$. Put

$$\sigma_1(t) = 0, \quad \sigma_{2k}(t) = c\int_t^T \frac{ds}{p_k(s)} \quad \text{for } t \in [0,T]. \tag{3.12}$$

Then $p_k(t)\sigma_{2k}'(t) = -c$ for $t \in [0,T]$, and conditions (3.3) and (3.4) yield

$$p_k(t)f_k(t,0,0) \geq 0, \quad p_k(t)f_k(t,\sigma_{2k}(t),-c) = 0 \quad \text{for a.e. } t \in [0,T]. \tag{3.13}$$

Hence σ_1 and σ_{2k} are lower and upper functions of (3.11). By Theorem 2.3, problem (3.11) has a solution $u_k \in C^1[0,T]$ satisfying

$$0 \leq u_k(t) \leq \sigma_{2k}(t) \quad \text{for } t \in [0,T]. \tag{3.14}$$

Note that since $p_k \in C[0,T]$ is positive on $[0,T]$, we have $\sigma_{2k} \in C^1[0,T]$.
Step 2. A priori estimates of approximate solutions. The conditions (3.14) and $u_k(T) = \sigma_{2k}(T) = 0$ give

$$p_k(t)\frac{u_k(T)-u_k(t)}{T-t} \geq p_k(t)\frac{\sigma_{2k}(T)-\sigma_{2k}(t)}{T-t}, \tag{3.15}$$

which yields $p_k(T)u_k'(T) \geq p_k(T)\sigma_{2k}'(T) = -c$. Further, by (3.11), $p_k(0)u_k'(0) = 0$. Since $p_k u_k'$ is nonincreasing on $[0,T]$, we have proved that

$$-c \leq p_k(t)u_k'(t) \leq 0 \quad \text{on } [0,T]. \tag{3.16}$$

Due to $p_k(0)u_k'(0) = 0$, there is $t_k \in (0,T]$ such that

$$-\nu \leq p_k(t)u_k'(t) \leq 0 \quad \text{for } t \in [0,t_k]. \tag{3.17}$$

If $t_k \geq \nu$, we get by (3.5)

$$p_k(t)u_k'(t) \leq -\varepsilon\int_0^t p(s)ds \quad \text{for } t \in [0,\nu]. \tag{3.18}$$

Assume that $t_k < \nu$ and $p_k(t)u_k'(t) < -\nu$ for $t \in (t_k,\nu]$. Then

$$p_k(t)u_k'(t) \leq -\varepsilon\int_0^t p(s)ds \quad \text{for } t \in [0,t_k] \tag{3.19}$$

and, since $-\nu < -\varepsilon t$ for $t \in (t_k,\nu]$, we get

$$p_k(t)u_k'(t) \leq -\varepsilon t \quad \text{for } t \in (t_k,\nu]. \tag{3.20}$$

Choose an arbitrary compact interval $[a,T] \subset (0,T]$ and denote

$$m = \min\{p(t) : t \in [a,T]\}, \qquad M = \max\{p(t) : t \in [a,T]\},$$
$$d = \min\left\{a,\nu,\int_0^a p(s)ds, \int_0^\nu p(s)ds\right\}. \tag{3.21}$$

Using the fact that $p_k u_k'$ is nonincreasing on $[0,T]$, we obtain by (3.16) and the above inequalities $-c \le p_k(t)u_k'(t) \le -\varepsilon d$ for $t \in [a,T]$, and hence, for each sufficiently large k, we get

$$-\frac{c}{m} \le u_k'(t) \le -\frac{\varepsilon d}{M} \quad \text{for } t \in [a,T], \tag{3.22}$$

$$(T-t)\frac{\varepsilon d}{M} \le u_k(t) \le (T-t)\frac{c}{m} \quad \text{for } t \in [a,T]. \tag{3.23}$$

Step 3. Convergence of a sequence of approximate solutions. Consider the sequence $\{u_k\}$. Choose an arbitrary compact interval $J \subset (0,T)$. By virtue of (3.22) and (3.23), there is $k_J \in \mathbb{N}$ such that for each $k \in \mathbb{N}$, $k \ge k_J$,

$$\begin{gathered} \frac{1}{k_J} \le u_k(t) \le k_J, \qquad -k_J \le u_k'(t) \le -\frac{1}{k_J}, \\ -c \le p_k(t)u_k'(t) \le -\frac{1}{k_J} \quad \text{for } t \in J, \end{gathered} \tag{3.24}$$

and hence there is $\psi \in L_1(J)$ such that

$$|\, p_k(t) f_k(t, u_k(t), p_k(t)u_k'(t)) \,| \le \psi(t) \quad \text{a.e. on } J. \tag{3.25}$$

Using conditions (3.24), (3.25), we see that the sequences $\{u_k\}$ and $\{p_k u_k'\}$ are equibounded and equicontinuous on J. Therefore by the Arzelà-Ascoli theorem and the diagonalization principle, we can choose $u \in C(0,T)$ and subsequences of $\{u_k\}$ and of $\{p_k u_k'\}$ which we denote for the simplicity in the same way such that

$$\lim_{k\to\infty} u_k = u, \qquad \lim_{k\to\infty} p_k u_k' = pu' \quad \text{locally uniformly on } (0,T). \tag{3.26}$$

Having in mind (3.14), (3.16), (3.24) and the fact that

$$\lim_{k\to\infty} p_k(t) = p(t), \qquad \lim_{k\to\infty} \sigma_{2k}(t) = P(t) \quad \text{for } t \in [0,T], \tag{3.27}$$

we get (3.7).

Step 4. Convergence of a sequence of approximate problems. Choose an arbitrary $\xi \in (0,T)$ such that

$$f(\xi,\cdot,\cdot) \quad \text{is continuous on } (0,\infty) \times (-\infty,0). \tag{3.28}$$

There exists a compact interval $J_\xi \subset (0,T)$ with $\xi \in J_\xi$, and, by (3.24), we can find $k_\xi \in \mathbb{N}$ such that and for each $k \ge k_\xi$,

$$u_k(\xi) \ge \frac{1}{k_\xi}, \qquad p_k(\xi)u_k'(\xi) \le -\frac{1}{k_\xi}, \qquad J_\xi \subset \left[\frac{1}{k}, T - \frac{1}{k}\right]. \tag{3.29}$$

Therefore

$$f_k(\xi, u_k(\xi), p_k(\xi)u_k'(\xi)) = f(\xi, u_k(\xi), p_k(\xi)u_k'(\xi)), \tag{3.30}$$

and, due to (3.26), (3.27), we have for a.e. $t \in (0,T)$,

$$\lim_{k\to\infty} p_k(t)f_k(t,u_k(t),p_k(t)u_k'(t)) = p(t)f(t,u(t),p(t)u'(t)). \tag{3.31}$$

Choose an arbitrary $s \in (0,T)$. Then there exists a compact interval $J_s \subset (0,T)$ containing s, and (3.25) holds for $J = J_s$ and for all sufficiently large k. By virtue of (3.11) we get

$$p_k\left(\frac{T}{2}\right)u_k'\left(\frac{T}{2}\right) - p_k(s)u_k'(s) = \int_{T/2}^{s} p_k(\tau)f_k(\tau,u_k(\tau),p_k(\tau)u_k'(\tau))\,d\tau. \tag{3.32}$$

Letting $k \to \infty$ and using (3.25)–(3.31) and the Lebesgue convergence theorem on J_s, we get for an arbitrary $s \in (0,T)$,

$$p\left(\frac{T}{2}\right)u'\left(\frac{T}{2}\right) - p(s)u'(s) = \int_{T/2}^{s} p(\tau)f(\tau,u(\tau),p(\tau)u'(\tau))\,d\tau. \tag{3.33}$$

Step 5. Properties of u and pu'. By virtue of (3.33) we have $pu' \in AC_{\text{loc}}(0,T)$ and

$$(p(t)u'(t))' + p(t)f(t,u(t),p(t)u'(t)) = 0 \quad \text{for a.e. } t \in (0,T). \tag{3.34}$$

According to (3.11) and (3.16) we have for each $k \ge 3/T$,

$$\int_0^T p_k(s)f_k(s,u_k(s),p_k(s)u_k'(s))\,ds = -p_k(T)u_k'(T) \le c, \tag{3.35}$$

which together with (3.4), (3.7), and (3.31) yield, by the Fatou lemma, that $p(t)f(t,u(t),p(t)u'(t)) \in L_1[0,T]$. Therefore, by (3.34), $pu' \in AC[0,T]$. Denote $v = pu'$. Since $v \in C[0,T]$, we have by (3.1) that $u' \in L_1[0,T]$ and consequently $u \in C[0,T] \cap C^1(0,T]$.

Further, for each $k \ge 3/T$ and $t \in (0,T)$,

$$\begin{aligned} |p_k(t)u_k'(t)| &\le \int_0^t |p_k(s)f_k(s,u_k(s),p_k(s)u_k'(s)) - p(s)f(s,u(s)p(s)u'(s))|\,ds \\ &\quad + \int_0^t |p(s)f(s,u(s),p(s)u'(s))|\,ds, \\ |u_k(t)| &\le \int_t^T |u_k'(s) - u'(s)|\,ds + \int_t^T |u'(s)|\,ds. \end{aligned} \tag{3.36}$$

Hence, by (3.26) and (3.31),

$$\begin{gathered} \forall \varepsilon > 0\ \exists \delta > 0, \quad \forall t \in (0,\delta)\ \exists k_1 = k_1(\varepsilon,t) \in \mathbb{N}: \\ |(pu')(t)| \le |(pu')(t) - (p_{k_1}u_{k_1}')(t)| + |(p_{k_1}u_{k_1}')(t)| < \varepsilon, \\ \forall \varepsilon > 0\ \exists \delta > 0, \quad \forall t \in (T-\delta,T)\ \exists k_2 = k_2(\varepsilon,t) \in \mathbb{N}: \\ |u(t)| \le |u(t) - u_{k_2}(t)| + |u_{k_2}(t)| < \varepsilon. \end{gathered} \tag{3.37}$$

This implies

$$u(T) = \lim_{t\to T-} u(t) = 0, \qquad (pu')(0) = \lim_{t\to 0+} (pu')(t) = 0. \tag{3.38}$$

□

Remark 3.2. By virtue of (3.38) there is a point $t_0 \in (0,T]$ such that

$$u(t) < P(t), \qquad -c < p(t)u'(t) \quad \text{for } t \in [0,t_0). \tag{3.39}$$

Example 3.3. Let $\alpha,\gamma \in (0,\infty)$, $\beta \in [0,\infty)$, $\theta \in (0,1)$. By Theorem 3.1, the problem

$$\begin{gathered}(t^\theta u')' + t^\theta(u^{-\alpha} + u^\beta + 1)\big(1 - (-t^\theta u')^\gamma\big) = 0,\\ \lim_{t\to 0+} t^\theta u'(t) = 0, \quad u(1) = 0,\end{gathered} \tag{3.40}$$

has a solution $u \in C[0,1]$ satisfying $t^\theta u' \in AC[0,1]$ and

$$0 < u(t) \le \frac{1 - t^{1-\theta}}{1-\theta}, \qquad -1 \le t^\theta u'(t) < 0 \quad \text{for } t \in (0,1). \tag{3.41}$$

To see this we put $p(t) = t^\theta$, $c = 1$, $\nu = 1/2$, $\varepsilon = 1 - (1/2)^\gamma$, and $f(t,x,y) = (x^{-\alpha} + x^\beta + 1)(1 - (-y)^\gamma)$.

Acknowledgment

This work is supported by the Council of Czech Government MSM 6198959214.

References

[1] R. P. Agarwal and D. O'Regan, *Nonlinear superlinear singular and nonsingular second order boundary value problems*, Journal of Differential Equations **143** (1998), no. 1, 60–95.

[2] R. P. Agarwal and S. Staněk, *Nonnegative solutions of singular boundary value problems with sign changing nonlinearities*, Computers & Mathematics with Applications **46** (2003), no. 12, 1827–1837.

[3] J. V. Baxley and G. S. Gersdorff, *Singular reaction-diffusion boundary value problems*, Journal of Differential Equations **115** (1995), no. 2, 441–457.

[4] R. Kannan and D. O'Regan, *Singular and nonsingular boundary value problems with sign changing nonlinearities*, Journal of Inequalities and Applications **5** (2000), no. 6, 621–637.

[5] I. T. Kiguradze and B. L. Shekhter, *Singular boundary value problems for second-order ordinary differential equations*, Current Problems in Mathematics. Newest Results, Vol. 30, Itogi Nauki i Tekhniki, Ser. Sovrm. Probl. Mat., Akad. Nauk SSSR Vsesoyuz. Inst. Nauchn. i Tekhn. Inform., Moscow, 1987, pp. 105–201, 204.

[6] D. O'Regan, *Theory of Singular Boundary Value Problems*, World Scientific, New Jersey, 1994.

[7] I. Rachůnková, *Singular mixed boundary value problem*, to appear in Journal of Mathematical Analysis and Applications.

Irena Rachůnková: Department of Mathematics, Palacký University, Tomkova 40, 77900 Olomouc, Czech Republic

E-mail address: rachunko@inf.upol.cz

ON SETS OF ZERO HAUSDORFF s-DIMENSIONAL MEASURE

MARIA ALESSANDRA RAGUSA

The goal of this paper is to investigate regularity properties of local minimizers u of some variational integrals and the Hausdorff measure of the set, where u is not Hölder continuous.

1. Introduction

We investigate some partial regularity results of local minimizers u of some quadratic functionals and the Hausdorff measure of the set, where u has not Hölder regularity.

We introduce the notion of Hausdorff s-dimensional measure. Let A be a metric space, F a subset of A, and s a nonnegative number. Let us call J_l an l cover of F, meaning that every point in F is covered by a set in J_l and that all sets $M \in J_l$ have diameter less than l. We say that

$$\mathcal{H}^s(F) = \lim_{l \to 0} \inf_{J_l} \sum_{M \in J_l} [\operatorname{diam}(M)]^s \tag{1.1}$$

is the s-dimensional Hausdorff measure (see, e.g., [4, 10]). We note that in general $\mathcal{H}^s$ may be infinite and that the notion involves the case that s is not an integer. From the above definition, we have that the Hausdorff 1-measure of a smooth rectificable curve is just the length of the curve.

Throughout the paper, we consider $\mathbb{R}^n$ as the environment and set Ω as an open bounded subset of $\mathbb{R}^n$, $n \geq 3$.

In the sequel, we need the following definition of Morrey class. We say that a function $f \in L^1_{\mathrm{loc}}(\Omega)$ belongs to the Morrey space $L^{p,\lambda}(\Omega)$ if it is finite

$$\|f\|^p_{L^{p,\lambda}(\Omega)} \equiv \sup_{x \in \Omega,\, \varrho > 0} \frac{1}{\varrho^\lambda} \int_{B_\varrho(x) \cap \Omega} |f(y)|^p dy, \tag{1.2}$$

where $B_\varrho(x)$ is a ball of radius ϱ centered at the point x.

Hindawi Publishing Corporation
Proceedings of the Conference on Differential & Difference Equations and Applications, pp. 963–968

Morrey's estimates have been considered in the study of partial regularity of minimizers of quadratic functionals with VMO coefficients in [9]. The authors investigate partial regularity of the minimizers of quadratic functionals, whose integrands have VMO coefficients, using some majorizations for the functionals, rather than the well-known Euler's equation associated with it. The functional is

$$\int_\Omega \{A_{ij}^{\alpha\beta}(x,u)D_\alpha u^i D_\beta u^j + g(x,u,Du)\}dx, \tag{1.3}$$

where $\Omega \subset \mathbb{R}^n$, $n \geq 3$, is a bounded open set, $u : \Omega \to \mathbb{R}^N$, $N > 1$, $u(x) = (u^1(x),\dots,u^N(x))$, $Du = (D_\alpha u^i)$, $D_\alpha = \partial/\partial x_\alpha$, $\alpha = 1,\dots,n$, $i = 1,\dots,N$.

We know that a function $u \in H^{1,2}(\Omega,\mathbb{R}^N)$ is a *minimizer* of the functional $\mathcal{A}(u,\Omega)$ if and only if

$$\mathcal{A}(u,\Omega) \leq \mathcal{A}(v,\Omega), \quad \forall v \in H^{1,2}(\Omega,\mathbb{R}^N), \tag{1.4}$$

with $u - v \in H_0^{1,2}(\Omega,\mathbb{R}^N)$.

We also recall that a function f belongs to the John-Nirenberg space BMO (see [8]) or that f has "bounded mean oscillation" if

$$\|f\|_* \equiv \sup_{B\subset\mathbb{R}^n} \frac{1}{|B|}\int_B |f(x) - f_B|\,dx < \infty, \tag{1.5}$$

where f_B is the integral average $(1/|B|)\int_B f(x)dx$ of the function $f(x)$ over the set B, considering B in the class of the balls of $\mathbb{R}^n$.

Let, for $f \in$ BMO,

$$\eta(r) = \sup_{x\in\mathbb{R}^n,\ \varrho\leq r} \frac{1}{|B_\varrho|}\int_{B_\varrho} |f(x) - f_{B_\varrho}|\,dx, \tag{1.6}$$

we say that f belongs to the class VMO (see [11]), or f has "vanishing mean oscillation" if

$$\lim_{r\to 0^+} \eta(r) = 0. \tag{1.7}$$

Let us suppose that $A_{ij}^{\alpha\beta}$ are bounded functions on $\Omega \times \mathbb{R}^N$ and satisfy the following conditions:

(1) $A_{ij}^{\alpha\beta} = A_{ji}^{\beta\alpha}$;

(2) for every $u \in \mathbb{R}^N$, $A_{ij}^{\alpha\beta}(\cdot,u) \in \mathrm{VMO}(\Omega)$;

(3) for every $x \in \Omega$ and $u,v \in \mathbb{R}^N$,

$$|A_{ij}^{\alpha\beta}(x,u) - A_{ij}^{\alpha\beta}(x,v)| \leq \omega(|u-v|^2) \tag{1.8}$$

for some monotone increasing concave function ω with $\omega(0) = 0$;

(4) there exists a positive constant ν such that

$$\nu|\xi|^2 \leq A_{ij}^{\alpha\beta}(x,u)\xi_\alpha^i\xi_\beta^j \tag{1.9}$$

for almost every $x \in \Omega$, all $u \in \mathbb{R}^N$, and $\xi \in \mathbb{R}^{nN}$.

We should mention that since C^0 is a proper subset of VMO, the continuity of $A_{ij}^{\alpha\beta}(x,u)$ with respect to x is not assumed.

Before we state the result contained in [9], we point out that g is a Carathéodory function and has growth less than quadratic.

Theorem 1.1. *Let $u \in W^{1,2}(\Omega,\mathbb{R}^N)$ be a minimum of the functional $\mathcal{A}(u,\Omega)$ above defined. Suppose that assumptions on $A_{ij}^{\alpha\beta}(x,u)$ and $g(x,u,Du)$ are satisfied.*

Then, for $\lambda = n(1-2/p)$,

$$Du \in L^{2,\lambda}_{\text{loc}}(\Omega_0,\mathbb{R}^{nN}), \tag{1.10}$$

where

$$\Omega_0 = \left\{x \in \Omega : \liminf_{R\to 0} \frac{1}{R^{n-2}}\int_{B(x,R)} |Du(y)|^2 dy = 0\right\}. \tag{1.11}$$

As a consequence, for $\alpha \in (0,1)$, there exists the following Hölder regularity:

$$u \in C^{0,\alpha}(\Omega_0,\mathbb{R}^N). \tag{1.12}$$

Also for some positive s,

$$\mathcal{H}^{n-2-s}(\Omega\setminus\Omega_0) = 0. \tag{1.13}$$

For linear systems regularity results assuming $A_{ij}^{\alpha\beta}$ constants or in $C^0(\Omega)$ have been obtained by Campanato in [2].

Without assuming continuity of coefficients, we mention the note [1] where the author refines Campanato's results considering that coefficients $A_{ij}^{\alpha\beta}$ belong to a class neither containing nor contained in $C^0(\Omega)$, hence in general discontinuous.

Moreover, we recall the study made by Huang in [7] where he shows regularity results of weak solutions of linear elliptic systems with coefficients in the class VMO. Therefore, it seems to be natural to expect partial regularity results under the condition that the coefficients of the principal terms $A_{ij}^{\alpha\beta} \in$ VMO, even for nonlinear cases.

Recently, Daněček and Viszus in [3] treated the regularity of minimizer for the functional

$$\int_\Omega \{A_{ij}^{\alpha\beta}(x)D_\alpha u^i D_\beta u^j + g(x,u,Du)\}dx, \tag{1.14}$$

where $g(x,u,Du)$ is a lower-order term which satisfies

$$|g(x,u,z)| \leq f(x) + L|z|^\gamma, \tag{1.15}$$

where $f \in L^p(\Omega)$, $2 < p \leq \infty$, $f \geq 0$, almost everywhere on Ω, L is a nonnegative constant, and $0 \leq \gamma < 2$. They obtain Hölder regularity of minimizer assuming that $A_{ij}^{\alpha\beta}(x) \in$ VMO.

In [9], the authors extend both the results by Huang and Daněček and Viszus because they study the functional whose integrand contains the term $g(x,u,Du)$ and has coefficients $A_{ij}^{\alpha\beta}$ dependent not only on x but also on u.

Let us now give an outline of the proof.

Basic tool is the following lemma for constant coefficients proved by Campanato (see [2]).

Lemma 1.2. *Let $u \in W^{1,2}(B(x_0,R),\mathbb{R}^N)$ be a weak solution of the system*

$$D_\alpha(g_{ij}^{\alpha\beta} D_\beta u^j) = 0 \quad \text{for } i = 1,\ldots,N, \tag{1.16}$$

where $g_{ij}^{\alpha\beta}$ are constant coefficients such that strong ellipticity holds. Then, for any $t \in [0,1]$,

$$\int_{B(x_0,tR)} |Du|^2 dx \leq ct^n \int_{B(x_0,R)} |Du|^2 dx. \tag{1.17}$$

Proof of Theorem 1.1. Let $R > 0$, $x_0 \in \Omega$, such that $B(x_0,R) \subset\subset \Omega$. To obtain the Morrey regularity result, let us consider $v \in W^{1,2}(B(x_0,R/2),\mathbb{R}^N)$ to be the minimum of the "freezing" functional $\mathcal{A}^0$:

$$\mathcal{A}^0\left(v, B\left(x_0, \frac{R}{2}\right)\right) = \int_{B\left(x_0,R/2\right)} A_{ij}^{\alpha\beta}(u_{R/2})_{R/2} D_\alpha v^i D_\beta v^j dx, \tag{1.18}$$

where $v - u \in H_0^{1,2}(B(x_0,R/2))$ and

$$A_{ij}^{\alpha\beta}(w)_{R/2} = \fint_{B(x_0,R/2)} A_{ij}^{\alpha\beta}(y,w) dy. \tag{1.19}$$

Having constant coefficients $A_{ij}^{\alpha\beta}(u_{R/2})_{R/2}$ from the above lemma by Campanato, we have

$$\int_{B(x_0,tR/2)} |Dv|^2 dx \leq c \cdot t^n \int_{B(x_0,R/2)} |Dv|^2 dx \tag{1.20}$$

for every $t \in [0,1]$. Let us define $w = u - v$.

Then,

$$\int_{B(x_0,tR/2)} |Du|^2 dx \leq c \cdot \left\{t^n \int_{B(x_0,R/2)} |Du|^2 dx + \int_{B(x_0,R/2)} |Dw|^2 dx\right\}. \tag{1.21}$$

We can write

$$\nu \int_{B(x_0,R/2)} |Dw|^2 dx \le c\left\{\mathscr{A}^0\left(u, B\left(x_0, \frac{R}{2}\right)\right) - \mathscr{A}^0\left(v, B\left(x_0, \frac{R}{2}\right)\right)\right\}. \tag{1.22}$$

Using the following majorizations:

$$\begin{aligned}
&\int_{B(x_0,R/2)} (A_{ij}^{\alpha\beta}(u_{R/2})_{R/2} - A_{ij}^{\alpha\beta}(x, u_{R/2})) \cdot D_\alpha u^i D_\beta u^j dx \\
&\quad \le c\left\{\eta\left(A(\cdot, u_{R/2}); \frac{R}{2}\right)\right\}^{1-2/p} \cdot \left\{\int_{B(x_0,R)} |Du|^2 dx + R^{(n-2/p)}\right\}, \\
&\int_{B(x_0,R/2)} (A_{ij}^{\alpha\beta}(x, u_{R/2}) - A_{ij}^{\alpha\beta}(x,u)) D_\alpha u^i D_\beta u^j dx \\
&\quad \le \left(\int_{B(x_0,R)} |Du|^2 dx\right) \omega\left(R^{2-n}\int_{B(x_0,R/2)} |Du|^2 dx\right),
\end{aligned} \tag{1.23}$$

the hypothesis on $A_{ij}^{\alpha\beta}$ and a lemma contained in the book [5] for R sufficiently small

$$\int_{B(x_0,\varrho)} |Du|^2 dx \le c \cdot \varrho^\lambda, \tag{1.24}$$

then we obtain the requested Morrey's estimate. Using Sobolev-Morrey embedding contained in [12], we get the Hölder regularity of the local minimizer u.

Following the lines of the proof of Giaquinta's [6, Theorem 6.2], we are able to prove that the Hausdorff measure of $\Omega \setminus \Omega_0$ is zero. □

References

[1] P. Acquistapace, *On BMO regularity for linear elliptic systems*, Annali di Matematica Pura ed Applicata. Serie Quarta **161** (1992), 231–269.

[2] S. Campanato, *Sistemi ellittici in forma divergenza. Regolarità all'interno*, Quaderni, Scuola Normale Superiore Pisa, Pisa, 1980.

[3] J. Daněček and E. Viszus, *$L^{2,\lambda}$-regularity for minima of variational integrals*, Bollettino della Unione Matematica Italiana. Serie VIII **6** (2003), no. 1, 39–48.

[4] H. Federer, *Geometric Measure Theory*, Die Grundlehren der mathematischen Wissenschaften, vol. 153, Springer, New York, 1969.

[5] M. Giaquinta, *Multiple Integrals in the Calculus of Variations and Nonlinear Elliptic Systems*, Annals of Mathematics Studies, vol. 105, Princeton University Press, New Jersey, 1983.

[6] ———, *Introduction to Regularity Theory for Nonlinear Elliptic Systems*, Lectures in Mathematics ETH Zürich, Birkhäuser, Basel, 1993.

[7] Q. Huang, *Estimates on the generalized Morrey spaces $L_\varphi^{p,\lambda}$ and BMO for linear elliptic systems*, Indiana University Mathematics Journal **45** (1996), no. 2, 397–439.

[8] F. John and L. Nirenberg, *On functions of bounded mean oscillation*, Communications on Pure and Applied Mathematics **14** (1961), 415–426.

[9] M. A. Ragusa and A. Tachikawa, *Partial regularity of the minimizers of quadratic functionals with VMO coefficients*, Journal of the London Mathematical Society. Second Series **72** (2005), no. 3, 609–620.

[10] C. A. Rogers, *Hausdorff Measure*, 2nd ed., Cambridge University Press, Cambridge, 1999.

[11] D. Sarason, *Functions of vanishing mean oscillation*, Transactions of the American Mathematical Society **207** (1975), 391–405.

[12] G. Stampacchia, *The spaces* $L^{p,\lambda}$, $N^{p,\lambda}$ *and interpolation*, Annali della Scuola Normale Superiore di Pisa **19** (1965), 443–462.

Maria Alessandra Ragusa: Dipartimento di Matematica e Informatica, Università di Catania, Viale Andrea Doria 6, 95125 Catania, Italy
E-mail address: maragusa@dmi.unict.it

FINITE-DIFFERENCES METHOD FOR SOLVING OF FIRST-ORDER HYPERBOLIC-TYPE EQUATIONS WITH NONCONVEX STATE FUNCTION IN A CLASS OF DISCONTINUOUS FUNCTIONS

MAHIR RASULOV AND BAHADDIN SINSOYSAL

A method for obtaining an exact and numerical solution of the Cauchy problem for a first-order partial differential equation with nonconvex state function is suggested. For this purpose, an auxiliary problem having some advantages over the main problem, but equivalent to it, is introduced. On the basis of the auxiliary problem, the higher-order numerical schemes with respect to time step can be written, such that the solution accurately expresses all the physical properties of the main problem. Some results of the comparison of the exact and numerical solutions have been illustrated.

1. Introduction

Many important problems of physics and engineering are reduced to finding the solution of equations of a first-order hyperbolic-type equations as

$$u_t + F_x(u) = 0 \tag{1.1}$$

with the following initial condition

$$u(x,0) = u_0(x). \tag{1.2}$$

In this study, we consider Cauchy problem for a 1-dimensional first-order nonlinear wave equation and propose a numerical method for obtaining the solution in a class of discontinuous functions when $F''(u)$ has alternative signs.

2. The Cauchy problem for the nonconvex state function

As usual, let $R^2(x,t)$ be the Euclidean space of points (x,t). We denote $Q_T = \{x \in R,\ 0 \leq t \leq T\} \subseteq R^2(x,t)$, here $R = (-\infty,\infty)$.

Suppose that the function $F(u)$ is known and satisfies the following conditions.

(i) $F(u)$ is twice continuously differentiable and a bounded function for bounded u.

(ii) $F'(u) \geq 0$ for $u \geq 0$.

Hindawi Publishing Corporation
Proceedings of the Conference on Differential & Difference Equations and Applications, pp. 969–977

(iii) $F''(u)$ is a function with alternating signs, that is, F has convex and concave parts.

Let us assume that $u_0(x)$ is given as a continuous function with compact support or piecewise function.

A solution of the problem (1.1)-(1.2) can easily be constructed by the method of characteristics [1–4] and has the form

$$u(x,t) = u_0(\xi), \quad \xi = x - F'(u)t, \tag{2.1}$$

where ξ is the spatial coordinate moving with speed $F'(u)$.

The relation (2.1) is an alternative form of the problem (1.1)-(1.2), and it is an implicit function for the solution.

It is known that if $u_0' < 0$ and $F'' > 0$, or ($u_0' > 0$ and $F'' < 0$), then for $t = -1/u_0'(\xi)F''(u)$, we have $u_x(x,t) = \infty$. At these points, $u_t(x,t)$ also becomes infinite. Therefore, the problem (1.1)-(1.2) has not a classical solution.

Definition 2.1. The function $u(x,t)$ is called the weak solution of the problem (1.1)-(1.2) if the integral relation

$$\iint_{Q_T} \{\varphi_t(x,t)u(x,t) + \varphi_x(x,t)F(u)\}\,dx\,dt + \int_{-\infty}^{\infty} u(x,0)\varphi(x,0)\,dx = 0 \tag{2.2}$$

holds for every function $\varphi(x,t)$ defined and twice differentiable in the upper half-plane, and which vanishes for sufficiently large $t+ \mid x \mid$.

2.1. Auxiliary problem. In order to determine the weak solution of the problem (1.1)-(1.2), in accordance with [3, 4], the auxiliary problem

$$v_t(x,t) + F(v_x(x,t)) = 0, \tag{2.3}$$

$$v(x,0) = v_0(x) \tag{2.4}$$

is introduced. Here, $v_0(x)$ is any absolutely continuous and differentiable function satisfying the equation $(v_0(x))_x = u_0(x)$.

Theorem 2.2. *If $v(x,t)$ is a soft solution of the auxiliary problem (2.3)-(2.4), then the function $u(x,t)$ defined by*

$$u(x,t) = v_x(x,t) \tag{2.5}$$

is the soft solution of the main problem (1.1)-(1.2).

The solution of the problem (2.3)-(2.4) can easily be obtained, and has the form

$$v(x,t) = [v_x F'(v_x) - F(v_x)]t + v_0(\xi), \quad \xi = x - F'((v_0)_x)t. \tag{2.6}$$

By calculation, it can be easily shown that $u(x,t) = v_x(x,t)$.

It can easily be shown that an integrable soft solution is a weak solution, that is, the following theorem holds.

Theorem 2.3. *If $v(x,t)$ is the solution of the auxiliary problem (2.3)-(2.4), then*

(1^0) *the function $u(x,t)$ defined by (2.5) is the weak solution of the main problem,*
(2^0) *$v(x,t)$ is an absolutely continuous function.*

The auxiliary solution has the following advantages:
(i) the function $v(x,t)$ is smoother than $u(x,t)$;
(ii) $u(x,t)$ can be determined without using the derivatives u_x and u_t which are not defined at the neighborhoods of the points of discontinuities.

2.1.1. Shock fitting. In order to obtain the location of the points of discontinuity which arise in the solution of the main problem, we will use the facts that $\int_{-\infty}^{\infty} u(x,t)dx = \text{const}$, and that this integral exists not only for multivalued and continuous functions but also for a single-valued piecewise continuous function as well. In addition, it is known that (1.1) expresses the conservation law of mass. Let $E_1(t)$ denote the integral $E_1(t) = \int_R u(x,t)dx$.

Definition 2.4. The number $E_1(0)$, defined by $E_1(0) = \int_R u(x,0)dx$, is called the critical value of the function $v(x,t)$.

Now we will investigate the problem of finding the locations of discontinuous points of $u(x,t)$ and the time evolution of these points. As it was expressed before, the solution of an auxiliary problem is not unique. In order to find a physically meaningful and unique solution, some additional conditions are required.

Definition 2.5. For every t, the geometrical location of the points, where $v(x,t)$ takes a critical value, is called the front curve.

Let $x_f = x_f(t)$ be the equation of discontinuity curve of $v(x,t)$. Considering Definition 2.5 and expression (2.5), we have $v(x_f(t),t) = \int_{-\infty}^{x_f} u(x,t)dx = E_1(0)$. From the last relation, we have

$$\frac{dx_f(t)}{dt} = \frac{[F(u)]}{[u]}\bigg|_{x=x_f(t)}. \tag{2.7}$$

Here $[f]$ shows the shock of the function f at a point $x = x_0$.

Definition 2.6. The function defined by

$$v_{ext}(x,t) = \begin{cases} v(x,t), & v < E_1(0), \\ E_1(0), & v \geq E_1(0), \end{cases} \tag{2.8}$$

is called the extended solution of the problem (2.3)-(2.4).

From Theorem 2.2, for the weak solution of the main problem (1.1)-(1.2), we have $u_{ext}(x,t) = (v_{ext}(x,t))_x$.

3. The Riemann problem for the nonconvex state function

In this section, we will study the Riemann problem for the case $F(u) = u^3$. In order to find the exact solution of this problem, according to [1, 2], we formulate the following

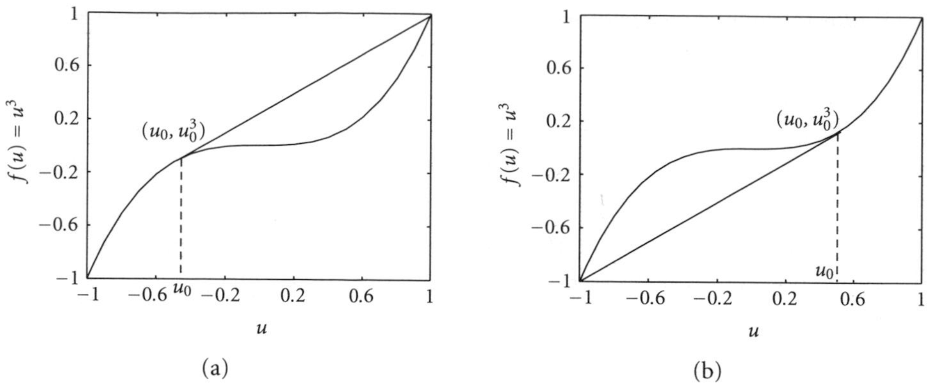

Figure 3.1. (a) The convex hull of the function $f(u) = u^3$; (b) the concave hull of the function $f(u) = u^3$.

definitions. By $\aleph$ we denote the set functions of $\widetilde{F}$ defined on $[\alpha,\beta]$ which satisfy the inequality $\widetilde{F} \geq F(u)$.

Definition 3.1. The function defined by the relation $\widehat{F} = \inf_{\widetilde{F}\in\aleph} \widetilde{F}(u)$ is called a convex hull on $[\alpha,\beta]$ of a function $F(u)$.

Definition 3.2. The function defined by the relation $\widehat{F} = \sup_{\widetilde{F}\in\aleph} \widetilde{F}(u)$ is called a concave hull on $[\alpha,\beta]$ of a function $F(u)$.

Case 1. In this case, we will obtain the solution of (1.1) with the following initial function:

$$u_0(x) = \begin{cases} u_1, & x < 0, \\ u_2, & x > 0, \end{cases} \tag{3.1}$$

here $u_1 = 1$, $u_2 = -1$. The exact solution of the problem (1.1), (3.1) was found in [1].

According to [1], at first, we will construct the convex hull of the function $F(u) = u^3$ on the interval $[-1,1]$. The graph of this convex hull is illustrated in Figure 3.1(a).

The exact solution of the problem (1.1), (3.1) is

$$u(x,t) = \begin{cases} u_1, & x < \dfrac{3}{4}t, \\ -\sqrt{\dfrac{x}{3t}}, & \dfrac{3}{4}t < \dfrac{x}{t} < 3t, \\ u_2, & x > 3t. \end{cases} \tag{3.2}$$

The graph of the weak solution of the problem (1.1), (3.1) is given in Figure 3.2(a).

For the cases $u_1 = -1$ and $u_2 = 1$, according to Definition 3.2, we will construct the concave hull of the function $f(u) = u^3$ on $[u_1,u_2]$. The graph of this concave hull is demonstrated in Figure 3.1(b). The graph of the problem (1.1), (3.1) for this case is demonstrated in Figure 3.2(b).

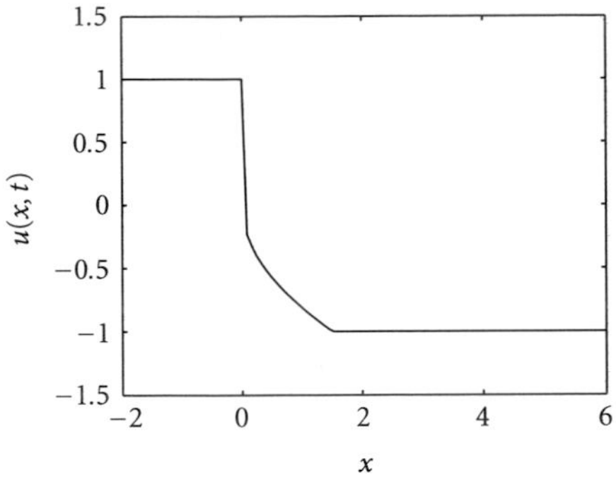

(a)

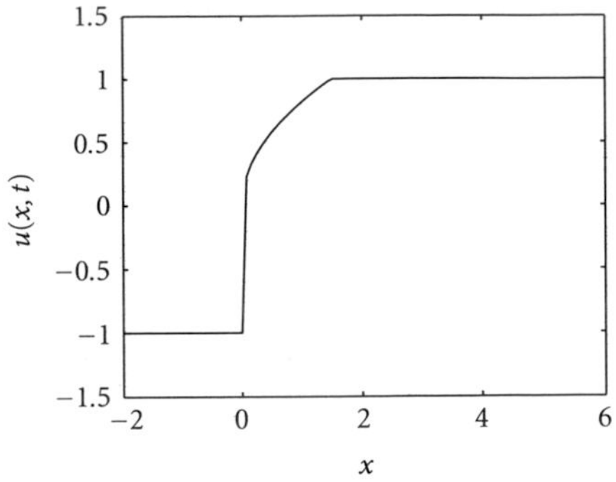

(b)

Figure 3.2. Time evaluation of exact solution $u(x,t)$ at $T = 0.5$: (a) $u_1 = 1$, $u_2 = -1$; (b) $u_1 = -1$, $u_2 = 1$.

Case 2. Now, we will investigate (1.1) when the function $F(u)$ is $-\cos 2u/2$ and $u_1 = 5\pi/4$, $u_2 = -5\pi/4$ (or $u_1 = -5\pi/4$, $u_2 = 5\pi/4$).

According to Definitions 3.1 and 3.2, we will construct the convex and concave hulls of the function $-\cos 2u/2$ on the interval $[-5\pi/4, 5\pi/4]$. The graphs of the convex and concave hulls of the function $-\cos 2u/2$ are shown in Figures 3.3(a) and 3.3(b), respectively.

The exact solution of the problem (1.1), (3.1) for the case $u_1 = 5\pi/4$, $u_2 = -5\pi/4$ is

$$u(x,t) = \begin{cases} \dfrac{5\pi}{4}, & x \le -kt, \\ -\dfrac{1}{2}\arcsin\dfrac{x}{t}, & -kt < x < 0, \\ \dfrac{1}{2}\arcsin\dfrac{x}{t}, & 0 < x < kt, \\ -\dfrac{5\pi}{4}, & x \ge kt, \end{cases} \tag{3.3}$$

and for the case $u_1 = -5\pi/4$, $u_2 = 5\pi/4$ is

$$u(x,t) = \begin{cases} -\dfrac{5\pi}{4}, & x \le -k_1t, \\ -\dfrac{1}{2}\arcsin\dfrac{x}{t} - \pi, & -k_1t < x < 0, \\ \dfrac{1}{2}\arcsin\dfrac{x}{t} + \pi, & 0 < x < k_1t, \\ \dfrac{5\pi}{4}, & x \ge k_1t. \end{cases} \tag{3.4}$$

The graphs of the solutions (3.3), (3.4) are illustrated in Figures 3.4(a) and 3.4(b), respectively.

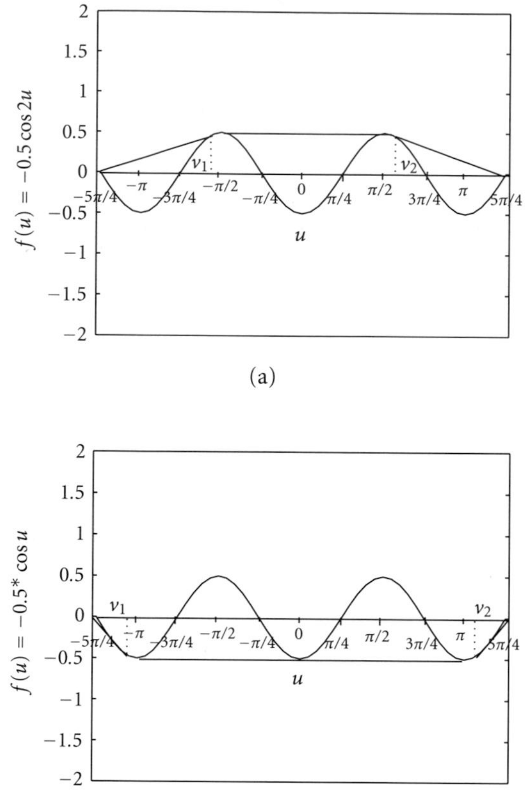

(a)

(b)

Figure 3.3. (a) The convex hull of the function $f(u) = -0.5\cos 2u$; (b) the concave hull of the function $f(u) = -0.5\cos 2u$.

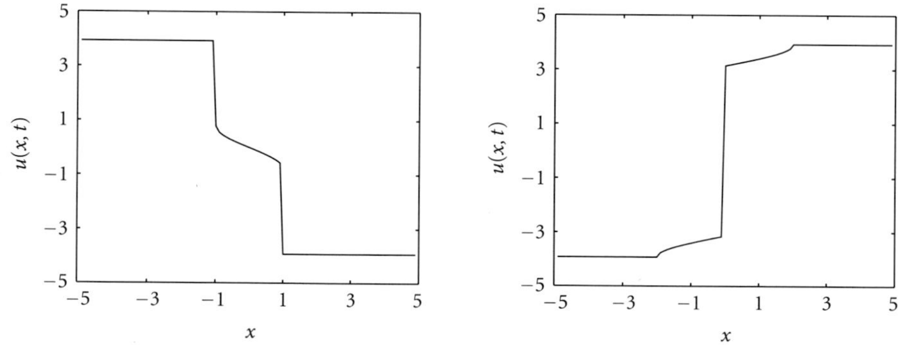

(a)

(b)

Figure 3.4. Time evaluation of exact solution $u(x,t)$: (a) $u_1 = 1$, $u_2 = -1$; (b) $u_1 = -1$, $u_2 = 1$.

4. Finite-differences schemes in a class of discontinuous functions

In order to construct the special finite-differences methods, at first the domain of definition of the problem is covered by the following grid:

$$\omega_{h,\tau} = \{(x_i, t_k) \mid x_i = ih,\ t_k = k\tau,\ i = 0, \pm 1, \pm 2, \ldots,\ k = 0, 1, 2, \ldots;\ h > 0,\ \tau > 0\}, \quad (4.1)$$

where h and τ are steps of the grid for x and t variables, respectively.

The problem (2.3)-(2.4) is approximated by the finite-difference scheme at any point (i,k) of the grid $\omega_{h,\tau}$ as follows:

$$V_{i,k+1} = V_{i,k} - \tau F\left(\frac{V_{i,k} - V_{i-1,k}}{h}\right), \quad (4.2)$$

$$V_{i,0} = v_0(x_i). \quad (4.3)$$

A function $v_0(x_i)$ is for any solution of the finite-difference equation $(V_0)_{\bar{x}} = u_0(x_i)$. It is easy to prove that

$$U_{i,k+1} = \frac{V_{i,k+1} - V_{i-1,k+1}}{h}. \quad (4.4)$$

Here, the grid functions $U_{i,k}$ and $V_{i,k}$ represent approximate values of the functions $u(x,t)$ and $v(x,t)$ at point (i,k), respectively.

In order to prove (4.4), it is sufficient first to write (4.2) at a point $(i-1,k)$, then subtract it from (1.1) and divide it by 2. By taking (4.4) into consideration, it is seen that $U_{i,k}$ satisfies the following nonlinear system of algebraic equations:

$$U_{i,k+1} = U_{i,k} - \frac{\tau}{h}\left(F(U_{i,k}) - F(U_{i-1,k})\right). \quad (4.5)$$

THEOREM 4.1. *The expression $E_1(t_k) = h\sum_i U_{i,k}$ is independent of time.*

Definition 4.2. The quantities $E_1(0)$ defined by $E_1(0) = h\sum_i U_{i,0}$ are called the critical values for the grid functions $V_{i,k}$.

Definition 4.3. The mesh function defined by

$$V_{i,k}^{ext} = \begin{cases} V_{i,k}, & V_{i,k} < E_1(0), \\ E_1(0), & V_{i,k} \geq E_1(0), \end{cases} \quad (4.6)$$

is called the extended solutions of the problem (4.2)-(4.3).

From Theorem 2.2, we have $U_{i,k}^{ext} = (V_{i,k}^{ext})_{\bar{x}}$, and this expression is called the extended numerical solution of the main problem.

By applying, for example, the Runge-Kutta method to (2.3), we can write a higher-order finite-difference scheme for the main problem with respect to τ.

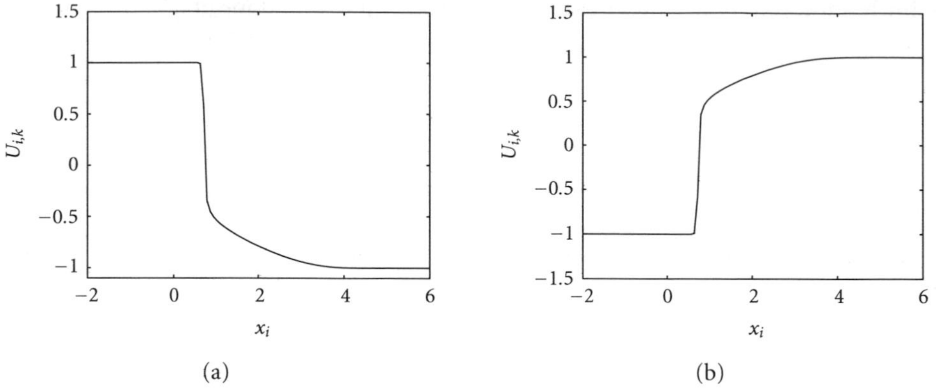

Figure 5.1. Numerical solutions for $f(u) = u^3$ at $T = 2$: (a) $u_1 = 1$, $u_2 = -1$; (b) $u_1 = -1$, $u_2 = 1$.

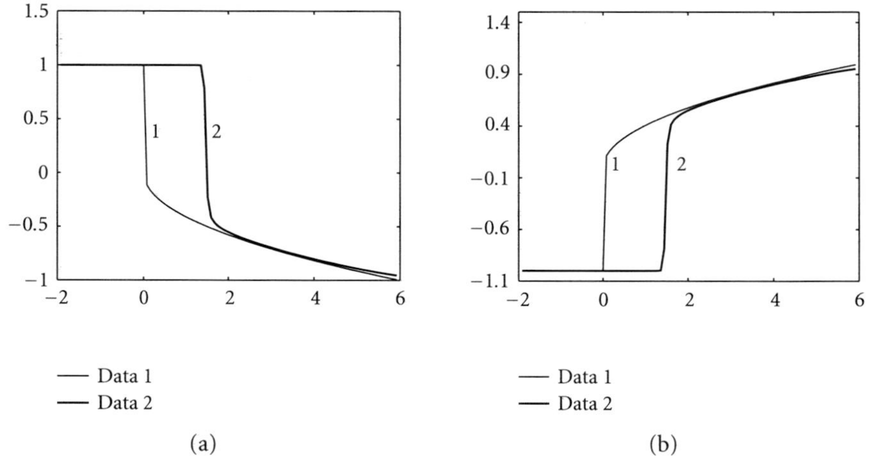

Figure 5.2. Comparison of the exact and numerical solutions at value $T = 2.0$: (a) $u_1 > u_2$; (b) $u_1 < u_2$.

5. Numerical experiments

In order to demonstrate the efficiency of the suggested numerical method, we adapt this algorithm for solving the following problem. We will investigate the numerical solution of (1.1) with the initial condition (3.1) when $F(u) = u^3$. The numerical solutions of the main problem (1.1), (3.1) obtained by the suggested method at the value $T = 1.0$ are given in Figures 5.1(a) and 5.1(b), respectively.

In Figures 5.2(a) and 5.2(b) with a view to compare, both the graphs of exact and numerical solutions of the problem (1.1), (3.1) with the same initial data are given. As seen from Figure 5.2 in the graph of the numerical solution, the jump appearing in the solution moves to the right with the increase of time, this is correct from the physical point of view. But, this phenomenon has not been observed in the graph of the exact solution. Certainly, it is related to the convex hull of the function $F(u)$ which is generated once, while the evaluation of solution u is not taken into account. Indeed, the state function changes from time to time. In general, the physical process described by nonlinear equations is not reversible.

Conclusion

A new numerical method for solving the Cauchy problem for the first-order nonlinear partial differential equation with nonconvex state function in a class of discontinuous functions is suggested. An auxiliary problem formed in a special way and having some advantages over the main problem is introduced.

References

[1] A. A. Goritskii, S. N. Krujkov, and G. A. Chechkin, *A First Order Quasi-Linear Equations with Partial Differential Derivaites*, Pub. Moskow University, Moskow, 1997.

[2] R. J. LeVeque, *Finite Volume Methods for Hyperbolic Problems*, Cambridge Texts in Applied Mathematics, Cambridge University Press, Cambridge, 2002.

[3] M. Rasulov, *On a method of solving the Cauchy problem for a first order nonlinear equation of hyperbolic type with a smooth initial condition*, Soviet Mathematics Doklady **43** (1991), no. 1, 150–153.

[4] M. Rasulov and T. A. Ragimova, *A numerical method of the solution of nonlinear equation of a hyperbolic type of the first order differential equations*, Minsk **28** (1992), no. 7, 2056–2063.

Mahir Rasulov: Department of Mathematics and Computing, Faculty of Science and Letters, Beykent University, Beykent 34500, Büyükçekmece, Istanbul, Turkey
E-mail address: mresulov@beykent.edu.tr

Bahaddin Sinsoysal: Department of Mathematics and Computing, Faculty of Science and Letters, Beykent University, Beykent 34500, Büyükçekmece, Istanbul, Turkey

ON THE GLOBAL ATTRACTOR IN A CLASS OF DYNAMIC SYSTEMS

R. RAUTMANN

We consider a class of dynamic systems $(*)$ $(d/dt)x = f(x)$ with a continuous function $f : \mathbb{R}^n_+ \to \mathbb{R}^n$ defined in the positive cone $\mathbb{R}^n_+$ of the Euclidean space $\mathbb{R}^n$, $n \geq 2$. In the stable case, from an observation concerning flow-invariant n-dimensional rectangles Q and contractivity of a flow in Q, we find that the unique stationary point E of $(*)$ is global attractor in $\mathbb{R}^n_+$. In the unstable case for more specialized systems, we get explicit conditions for blowing up and dying out by constructing lower and upper bounds for the solutions. By the well-known comparison methods, these results apply to solutions of weakly coupled quasimonotone parabolic systems with Dirichlet or Neumann boundary conditions. In addition, the systems $(*)$ in question could be used as models of cooperative societies in order to indicate future perspectives for such communities.

1. Introduction

1.1. Problems and results. In this contribution, we will consider dynamic systems,

$$\dot{x} = f(x), \quad \left(\dot{x} = \frac{d}{dt}x\right), \tag{1.1}$$

in the open positive cone $\mathbb{R}^n_+ = \{x = (x_i) \in \mathbb{R}^n \mid 0 < x_i \text{ for } i = 1,\dots,n\}$, $n \geq 2$. The right-hand sides $f = (f_i)$ taken into account are

$$f_i(x) = \psi_i\left(\prod_{j \neq i} |x_j|^{\alpha_{ij}} - |x_i|^{\gamma_i}\right) \cdot g_i(x), \tag{1.2}$$

the functions $\psi_i : \mathbb{R} \to \mathbb{R}$ being continuous, odd, and strictly monotone increasing, with $\psi_i(0) = 0$, g_i being continuous on a neighborhood of the closed cone $\overline{\mathbb{R}^n_+}$ in $\mathbb{R}^n$, $g_i(x) \in \mathbb{R}^1_+$, and the constants fulfilling $\alpha_{ii} = 0 < \alpha_{ij}$, $i \neq j$, $0 < \gamma_i$, and the matrix $\alpha = (\delta_{ij}\gamma_j - \alpha_{ij})$ being nonsingular. Thus the system (1.1) has the unique stationary point $E = (1,\dots,1)^T$ inside $\mathbb{R}^n_+$. Since each function g_i may depend on all components x_i of x, systems of sizes (1.1), (1.2) are slightly more general than quasimonotone systems.

Hindawi Publishing Corporation
Proceedings of the Conference on Differential & Difference Equations and Applications, pp. 979–987

We will see below that, if there are points $A = (A_i) \in \mathbb{R}^n_+$, $\delta = (\delta_i) \in \mathbb{R}^n_+$, fulfilling

$$\alpha \cdot A = \delta, \tag{1.3}$$

then the stationary point E is the global attractor of (1.1) in $\mathbb{R}^n_+$. Otherwise, if there are points $A, \delta \in \mathbb{R}^n_+$ satisfying

$$\alpha \cdot A = -\delta, \tag{1.4}$$

then all solutions of (1.1) starting (component-wise) above E will blow up, while all solutions of (1.1) starting (component-wise) below E will die out [5]. For the latter statement (which, in view of the page limitations, will be proved below only for systems (1.1) of a more specialized form), we will find lower and upper bounds of the solutions $x(t)$ to (1.1). Interfaces separating the domains of attraction of 0 or ∞, respectively, have been visualized in [5] for some systems of this type in $\mathbb{R}^3_+$. By the well-known comparison theorems [3, 8], these results extend to suitable solutions $u(t,z) \in \mathbb{R}^n_+$ (the vector function $u(t,z)$ having the additional spatial argument z varying in a smoothly bounded domain $\Omega \subset \mathbb{R}^m$, $m \geq 1$) to weakly coupled quasimonotone parabolic systems

$$\frac{\partial}{\partial t} u_i = F_i(u, u_{iz}, u_{izz}), \quad (t,z) \in \mathbb{R}^1_+ \times \Omega, \tag{1.5}$$

where

$$F_i(x,0,0) = f_i(x), \quad f_i \text{ from } (1.2),\ i = 1,\dots,n, \tag{1.6}$$

with Dirichlet or Neumann boundary conditions on $\mathbb{R}^1_+ \times \partial\Omega$ [3, 8].

1.2. Models for cooperative societies. The systems (1.1), (1.2) are modeling a cooperative society of n members, the ith one having the prosperity function $x_i(t) > 0$. The exponent α_{ij} measures the support given from member i to member j, the exponent γ_i expresses the self-restriction of member i, while the functions ψ_i, g_i specify the increase of $x_i(t)$.

The parabolic systems (1.5), (1.6) with Neumann boundary condition would describe some cooperative society with spatial prosperity diffusion in a domain Ω, where the flux of the prosperity functions $u_i(t,z)$ across the boundary $\mathbb{R}^1_+ \times \partial\Omega$ is given in a natural way.

On the other side, with Dirichlet boundary conditions to (1.5), we would model a cooperative society with spatial prosperity diffusion inside a domain Ω having a closed boundary on which the values of the prosperity functions are prescribed.

In the following for vectors $x = (x_i)$, $y = (y_i) \in \mathbb{R}^n$, we will sometimes use the component-wise ordering

$$\begin{gathered} x < y \quad \text{or} \quad x \leq y \text{ iff} \\ x_i < y_i \quad \text{or} \quad x_i \leq y_i, \quad \text{resp.}, \ \forall i = 1,\dots,n. \end{gathered} \tag{1.7}$$

As usual, a subset S of the domain of definition of the direction field f in (1.1) will be called flow invariant for this differential equation if each solution $x(t)$ of (1.1) starting at time t_0 at any point $x(t_0) \in S$ remains in S for all $t \geq t_0$ of its right maximal interval of existence. Since here we only suppose continuity of f, the initial value problem of (1.1) may have several solutions to the same initial value.

2. The stable case

The key to our results below is given by the following lemma on flow invariant rectangles Q in $\mathbb{R}^n$ and the contractivity of the flow on Q. We consider the n-dimensional axis-parallel rectangle

$$Q = [a^-, a^+] = \{x \in \mathbb{R}^n \mid a^- \leq x \leq a^+\}, \quad n \geq 2, \tag{2.1}$$

where $a^\pm = (a_i^\pm) \in \mathbb{R}^n$, $a^- < a^+$. The ith upper or lower $(n-1)$-dimensional faces are

$$Q_i^\pm = \{x \in Q \mid x_i = a_i^\pm\}. \tag{2.2}$$

For any $\epsilon = (\epsilon_i) \in \mathbb{R}_+^n$, the set

$$Q^\epsilon = \{x \in \mathbb{R}^n \mid a^- - \epsilon \leq x \leq a^+ + \epsilon\} \quad \text{or} \quad (Q_i^\pm)^\epsilon = \{x \in Q^\epsilon \mid a_i^\pm - \epsilon_i \leq x_i \leq a_i^\pm + \epsilon_i\} \tag{2.3}$$

represents some ϵ-neighborhood of Q or of $Q_i^\pm$ in $\mathbb{R}^n$, respectively. We will say that a continuous map $f = (f_i) : Q^\epsilon \to \mathbb{R}^n$ satisfies the direction condition on the boundary ∂Q if the restriction of f_i to $Q_i^\pm$ fulfills

$$\pm f_i \big|_{Q_i^\pm} < 0, \quad \forall i. \tag{2.4}$$

The notation "$\pm$" here and below means either the same sign "$+$" or "$-$", respectively, at all places of the relation in question.

Lemma 2.1. *Assume that the continuous map $f = (f_i) : Q^\epsilon \to \mathbb{R}^n$ fulfills the direction condition (2.4) on ∂Q. Then,*

(i) *the rectangle Q is flow invariant for the system*

$$\dot{x} = f(x), \qquad x(t_0) \in Q; \tag{2.5}$$

(ii) *each solution $x(t) \in Q$ of (2.5) exists for all $t \geq t_0$;*

(iii) *there exist $\delta = \delta_Q \in \mathbb{R}_+^n$, $\delta \leq \epsilon$, and $\tau > 0$, such that the subset (or "δ-retract of Q") $Q^{-\delta} =: \{x \in Q \mid a^- + \delta \leq x \leq a^+ - \delta\}$ is attractor for (2.5) in Q^δ, and each solution $x(t)$ of (2.5) with $x(t_0) \in Q^\delta$ satisfies $x(t_0 + \tau) \in Q^{-\delta}$.*

Remark 2.2. In case of locally Lipschitz-continuous f, (i) and (ii) result even from the weaker direction condition

$$\pm f_i \big|_{Q_i^\pm} \leq 0, \quad \forall i, \tag{2.6}$$

by Bony's theorem (cp. [1, 6]).

Proof of (i). By contradiction, if there exists some solution $x = \{x(t)\} \in C^1[t_0, t_1]$ with $x(t_0) \in Q$, $x(t_1) \notin Q$, taking $t^* = \sup\{t \in [t_0, t_1) \mid x(t) \in Q\}$, we find $x(t^*) \in \partial Q$ and there exist $(t_k) \downarrow t^*$, $x(t_k) \notin Q$.

Thus either

(a) $\exists i : x_i(t^*) = a_i^-$, $\exists (t_k) \downarrow t^*$, $x_i(t_k) < a_i^-$, or

(b) $\exists i : x_i(t^*) = a_i^+$, $\exists (t_k) \downarrow t^*$, $x_i(t_k) > a_i^+$.

In case (a), because of the continuity of $f_i(x(t))$, from (2.4) $f_i(x(t^*)) > 0$, we conclude that there exist $\gamma > 0$, $f_i(x(t)) > 0$ for all $t \in [t^*, t^* + \gamma]$. Choosing any $t_k \in (t^*, t^* + \gamma)$ and integrating (2.5), we get

$$x_i(t_k) - a_i^- = \int_{t^*}^{t_k} f_i(x(t'))\,dt' > 0 \tag{2.7}$$

in contradiction to the last inequality in (a). Similarly, we conclude in case (b). □

Note 2.3. In the proof of (i), we did not use the compactness of Q or ∂Q. Thus our conclusion holds, for example, if Q denotes the closed cone $\{x \in \mathbb{R}_+^n \mid a \le x\}$ for any point $a \in \mathbb{R}_+^n$.

Proof of (ii). By (i), the existence for all $t \ge t_0$ of each solution $x(t) \in Q$ starting at $t = t_0$ at some $x(t_0) \in Q$ follows immediately from the well-known fact that no solution of (2.5) can remain inside any compact subset of the time-space cylinder $[0, \infty) \times Q$, where f is continuous. □

Proof of (iii). To see (iii), for any rectangle $Q = [a^-, a^+]$ and $\xi = (\xi_i), \eta = (\eta_i) \in \mathbb{R}^n$, $|\xi_i|, |\eta_i| \le (a_i^+ - a_i^-)/2$ for all i, we introduce the (ξ, η)-near rectangle

$$\tilde{Q} = Q^{(\xi,\eta)} = \{x \in \mathbb{R}^n \mid a^- - \xi \le x \le a^+ + \eta\}. \tag{2.8}$$

Note 2.4. In case $\xi, \eta \in \mathbb{R}_+^n$ (or $-\xi, -\eta \in \mathbb{R}_+^n$), the rectangle $\tilde{Q}$ represents a neighborhood (or a retract, resp.) of Q.

Remark 2.5. Let the map $f : Q^\epsilon \to \mathbb{R}^n$ be continuous, f fulfilling the direction condition (2.4) on ∂Q. Then there exists some $\delta_Q \in \mathbb{R}_+^n$, such that (2.4) holds on the boundary of each rectangle $\tilde{Q} = Q^{(\xi,\eta)}$ for all $\xi, \eta \in \mathbb{R}^n$ with $(|\xi_i|) \le \delta_Q$, $(|\eta_i|) \le \delta_Q$, thus $\tilde{Q}$ being flow invariant for (2.5) by Lemma 2.1(i).

Namely, because of the continuity of f and the compactness of each $Q_i^\mp$, (2.4) holds even in the sharpened form $\pm f_i|_{Q_i^\mp} \le -2c_Q$ with some $c_Q > 0$, thus there exists some $\delta_Q \in \mathbb{R}_+^n$, $\delta_Q \le \epsilon$, such that we have

$$\pm f_i\big|_{(Q_i^\mp)^\delta} \le -c_Q, \quad \forall \delta \in \mathbb{R}_+^n,\ \delta \le \delta_Q, \tag{2.9}$$

since f is uniformly continuous on $(Q_i^\mp)^\epsilon$. From (2.9), we see the flow invariance of $\tilde{Q} = Q^{(\xi,\eta)}$ for all $(|\xi_i|), (|\eta_i|) \le \delta$ by Lemma 2.1(i).

Now with $\delta \equiv (\delta_i) =: \delta_Q$, let $x(t) \in Q^\delta$ denote some solution of (2.5) for $t \geq 0$. At any $t_0 \geq 0$, the ith coordinate $x_i = x_i(t_0)$, $i = 1,\dots,n$, fulfills either

(a) $a_i^- + \delta_i \leq x_i \leq a_i^+ - \delta_i$, or
(b) $a_i^- - \delta_i \leq x_i < a_i^- + \delta_i \leq a_i^+ - \delta_i$, or
(c) $a_i^- + \delta_i \leq a_i^+ - \delta_i < x_i \leq a_i^+ + \delta_i$.

By Remark 2.5, each one of the 3 rectangles $\{x \in Q^\delta \mid a_i^- + \delta_i \leq x_i \leq a_i^+ - \delta_i\}$, or $\{x \in Q^\delta \mid x_i \leq a_i^+ - \delta_i\}$, or $\{x \in Q^\delta \mid a_i^- + \delta_i \leq x_i\}$, respectively, is flow invariant for (2.5). In addition, on the ith lower layer $\{x \in Q^\delta \mid a_i^- - \delta_i \leq x_i \leq a_i^- + \delta_i\}$ of Q, we have $c_Q \leq f_i(x)$ by (2.9), therefore, if we choose $\tau > 0$ such that

$$0 < 2\delta_i \leq \tau \cdot c_Q \quad \text{holds } \forall i = 1,\dots,n, \tag{2.10}$$

in case (b), we find $a_i^- + \delta_i \leq x_i(t_0) + \tau \cdot c_Q \leq x_i(t_0 + \tau)$ from the differential equation (2.5). The analogous conclusion in case (c) with $f_i(x) \leq -c_Q$ gives $x_i(t_0 + \tau) \leq a_i^+ - \delta_i$. Since this holds true for all indices i for which (b) or (c) is valid, we find $x(t_0 + \tau) \in Q^{-\delta}$, $Q^{-\delta}$ being flow invariant by Remark 2.5. □

THEOREM 2.6 [4]. *For all $i = 1,\dots,n$, $n \geq 2$, assume*

$$f_i(x) = \psi_i\left(\prod_{j\neq i} |x_j|^{\alpha_{ij}} - |x_i|^{\gamma_i}\right) \cdot g_i(x), \tag{2.11}$$

where

(1) $\psi_i : \mathbb{R} \to \mathbb{R}$ *continuous, odd, strictly monotone increasing,* $\psi_i(0) = 0$,
(2) $g_i : \mathbb{R}_+^n \to \mathbb{R}_+^1$ *continuous,*
(3) $\alpha = (\delta_{ij} \cdot \gamma_j - \alpha_{ij})$, $\det \alpha \neq 0$,
(4) $\alpha_{ii} = 0 < \alpha_{ij}$, $i \neq j$, $0 < \gamma_i$,
(5) *there exist* $A = (A_i) \in \mathbb{R}_+^n$, $\alpha \cdot A = \delta \in \mathbb{R}_+^n$.

Then all solutions $x(t)$ of the differential equation

$$\dot{x} = f(x), \tag{2.12}$$

starting at $t = 0$ in any point $x(0) \in \mathbb{R}_+^n$, exist for all $t \geq 0$. Each such solution remains in the smallest rectangle

$$Q(s) =: \{f \in \mathbb{R}_+^n \mid a^-(s) \leq x \leq a^+(s),\ a^\pm(s) = (s^{\pm A_i})\}, \quad 1 < s, \tag{2.13}$$

containing $x(0)$, and has the limit set $\{E\}$, $E = (1,\dots,1)^T$.

Thus the unique stationary point E of (2.12) is the global attractor of (2.12) in $\mathbb{R}_+^n$.

Proof. (a) Firstly, we show that the direction condition (2.4) holds on the boundary $\partial Q(s)$ of each rectangle $Q(s)$, $s > 1$. For any x on the ith lower $(n-1)$-dimensional face $Q_i^-(s)$, we have $x_i = s^{-A_i}$, $s^{-A_j} \leq x_j \leq s^{A_j}$ for all $j \neq i$, thus recalling (5), we find

$$\prod_{j\neq i} |x_j|^{\alpha_{ij}} - |x_i|^{\gamma_i} \geq s^{-\gamma_i A_i} \cdot \{s^{\delta_i} - 1\} > 0 \quad \text{since } s > 1. \tag{2.14}$$

Therefore $0 < f_i|_{Q_i^-(s)}$ holds by our assumption on f_i from (2.11). Similarly, we get $f_i|_{Q_i^+(s)} < 0$ for all $i = 1,\dots,n$. Thus Lemma 2.1 gives the flow invariance of each $Q(s)$, $s > 1$, for (2.11), (2.12), as well as the global existence of each solution $x(t)$ for all positive t in the smallest $Q(s)$ containing $x(0)$.

(b) Evidently, we have $\{E\} = \bigcap_{1<s} Q(s)$. By contradiction, we will show $x(t) \to E$ with $t \to \infty$ for each solution $x(t)$ to (2.11), (2.12) starting at $t = 0$ inside of $\mathbb{R}_+^n$. Namely, in case

$$1 < s^* =: \inf\{s > 1 \mid \exists t > 0,\ x(t) \in Q(s)\} \tag{2.15}$$

from (a) we know that the direction condition (2.4) holds on $\partial Q(s^*)$. Therefore by Remark 2.5, we find some $\delta_{Q(s^*)} \in \mathbb{R}_+^n$ such that (2.4) even holds true on the boundary of each rectangle $Q^\delta(s^*)$ near $Q(s^*)$ with $(|\delta_i|) \le \delta_Q$. Now we will take $\delta = \delta_Q$.

By definition of s^*, there exist some sequences $(s_k) \downarrow s^*$ and (t_k) fulfilling $x(t_k) \in Q(s_k)$ for all $k = 1,2,\dots$. Since with $s_k \downarrow s^*$ the rectangles $Q(s_k)$ are contracting uniformly to $Q(s^*)$, we can find some k^*, such that $Q(s_k) \subset Q^\delta(s^*)$ for all $k \ge k^*$, but then by Lemma 2.1(iii), from $x(t_{k^*}) \in Q^\delta(s^*)$, we conclude $x(t_{k^*} + \tau) \in Q^{-\delta}(s^*)$ for some $\tau > 0$. Since with $s \uparrow s^*$ the rectangles $Q(s) \subset Q(s^*)$ are expanding uniformly to $Q(s^*)$, there exist some $s \in (1, s^*)$ such that $x(t_{k^*} + \tau) \in Q^{-\delta}(s^*) \subset Q(s)$ in contradiction to the definition of s^*. □

3. The unstable case

Up to elementary integrating, on $Q_1^\pm =: \{x \in \overline{\mathbb{R}_+^n} \mid \pm E < \pm x\}$, we will calculate lower and upper bounds $v(t)$ for solutions $x(t)$ to specialized systems (2.11), (2.12) which are cooperative (or quasimonotone increasing) in the sense of [2, 7, 8].

Theorem 3.1. *Let the vector function $x(t) \in \mathbb{R}_+^n$ denote a solution of*

$$\dot{x} = f(x), \quad x(0) = x_0 \in \mathbb{R}_+^n, \quad \text{where } f = (f_i), \tag{3.1}$$

$$f_i(x) = \left(\prod_{j \ne i} |x_j|^{\alpha_{ij}} - |x_i|^{\gamma_i}\right) \cdot |x_i|^{\zeta_i}, \tag{3.2}$$

on the right maximal interval $[0, T)$ of existence of $x(t)$ (with $0 < T \le \infty$).

The constants $\alpha_{ii} = 0 < \alpha_{ij}$, $i \ne j$, $0 < \gamma_i$, $0 \le \zeta_i$, $\alpha = (\delta_{ij} \cdot \gamma_j - \alpha_{ij})$, $\det\alpha \ne 0$, are given in such a way that there exist points

$$A = (A_i) \in \mathbb{R}_+^n, \quad \delta = (\delta_i) \in \mathbb{R}_+^n \quad \text{fulfilling } \alpha \cdot A = -\delta. \tag{3.3}$$

Define the vector functions $v^\pm(t) =: (\varphi^{\pm A_i}(t)) \in R_+^n$ with the help of the positive solution $\varphi(t)$ to the initial value problem

$$\dot{\varphi} = b \cdot \varphi^{1+c} \quad \text{for } t > 0,\ \varphi(0) = a. \tag{3.4}$$

(a) *In case $E < x(0)$ with the constants*

$$a_i = x_i(0)^{1/A_i}, \qquad b_i = \frac{1 - a_i^{-\delta_i}}{A_i}, \qquad c_i = \delta_i - A_i[1 - (\gamma_i + \zeta_i)], \tag{3.5}$$

the function $v^+(t) =: (\varphi^{A_i}(t))$ will represent

(a.1) *a lower bound of $x(t) \in Q_1^+$ if*

$$a = \min_i \{a_i\}, \qquad b = \min_i \{b_i\}, \qquad c = \min_i \{c_i\} \tag{3.6}$$

are taken, or

(a.2) *an upper bound of $x(t) \in Q_1^+$ (on the function's φ right maximal interval of existence) if*

$$a = \max_i \{a_i\}, \qquad b = \max_i \left\{\frac{1}{A_i}\right\}, \qquad c = \max_i \{c_i\} \tag{3.7}$$

are taken.

(b) *In case $x(0) < E$ with constants*

$$a_i = x_i(0)^{-1/A_i}, \qquad b_i = \frac{1 - a_i^{-\delta_i}}{A_i}, \qquad c_i = A_i \cdot [1 - (\gamma_i + \zeta_i)], \tag{3.8}$$

if additionally a local Lipschitz condition for f is required, the function $v^- =: (\varphi^{-A_i}(t))$ will represent

(b.1) *a lower bound of $x(t) \in Q_1^-$ if*

$$a = \max_i \{a_i\}, \qquad b = \max_i \left\{\frac{1}{A_i}\right\}, \qquad c = \max_i \{c_i\} \tag{3.9}$$

are taken, or

(b.2) *an upper bound of $x(t) \in Q_1^-$ if*

$$a = \min_i \{a_i\}, \qquad b = \min_i \{b_i\}, \qquad c = \min_i \{c_i\} \tag{3.10}$$

are taken.

(c) *If $c > 0$, the lower bounds defined in (a) blow up to ∞, and the upper bounds defined in (b) die out.*

An immediate consequence of the latter theorem is the following.

COROLLARY 3.2. *Under the requirements of Theorem 3.1 in case (a) with $c_i = \delta_i - A_i[1 - (\gamma_i + \zeta_i)] > 0$ for all $i = 1,\dots,n$, each solution $x(t)$ to (3.1), (3.2), $x(t)$ starting at $t = 0$ in any $x(0) > E$ will blow up in finite time, and in case (a) with $c_i = \delta_i - A_i \cdot [1 - (\gamma_i + \zeta_i)] \le 0$ for all $i = 1,\dots,n$, no solution $x(t)$ to (3.1), (3.2), $x(t)$ starting at $t = 0$ in any $x(0) > E$ will blow up in finite time (but, of course, each such one will blow up with $t \to \infty$).*

Proof of Corollary 3.2. The statement is evident because of Theorem 3.1 part (a) and the fact that the solution $\varphi(t)$ to (3.4) blows up in finite time if and only if $c > 0$ holds. □

Proof of Theorem 3.1. From the requirements of Theorem 3.1 in any point $a^+(s) =: (s^{A_i}) \in Q_1^+$, $s > 1$, we find

$$f_i(a^+(s)) = s^{[A_i(\gamma_i+\zeta_i)+\delta_i]} \cdot \{1 - s^{-\delta_i}\} > 0. \tag{3.11}$$

Using the Ansatz

$$v(t) =: a^+(\varphi(t)) \in \mathbb{R}_+^n \tag{3.12}$$

for a lower bound $v(t) \le x(t)$, where the function $\varphi(t) > 1$ has to be calculated, we get

$$\dot{v}_i = A_i \cdot \varphi^{A_i-1} \cdot \dot{\varphi}. \tag{3.13}$$

Since f from (3.2) is quasimonotone increasing, the function $v(t)$ will become the lower bound of $x(t)$ if

$$\dot{v}_i \le f_i(v), \qquad v_i(0) \le x_i(0), \quad \forall i = 1,\dots,n. \tag{3.14}$$

The equality signs are admissible since on Q_1^+ the functions f_i are locally Lipschitz continuous [8, pages 94, 96].

From (3.11) and (3.13) by a short calculation, we see that (3.14) results from the system

$$\dot{\varphi} \le b_i \cdot \varphi^{1+c_i}, \quad \varphi(0) \le a_i,\ i = 1,\dots,n, \tag{3.15}$$

of differential inequalities for the function φ, where the constants a_i, b_i, c_i are listed in (3.5).

Therefore we will get a lower bound $v(t) \le x(t)$ if we take for $\varphi > 1$ the maximal solution to all of the inequalities (3.15), thus φ from (3.4), (3.6). In order to similarly find an upper bound $v(t) =: a^+(\varphi(t)) \ge x(t)$, we only have to reverse the inequalities (3.14), (3.15), getting φ from (3.4), now with the constants from (3.7).

Below E we have to keep in mind that in $Q(s) = \{x \in \overline{\mathbb{R}_+^n} \mid 0 \le x \le a^-(s)\}$ with $a^-(s) = (s^{-A_i}) \in \mathbb{R}_+^n$, $1 < s$, on any lower $(n-1)$-dimensional face $Q_i^-(s) = \{x \in Q(s) \mid x_i = 0\}$, we only have

$$0 \le f_i(x)\big|_{Q_i^-(s)} \tag{3.16}$$

instead of (2.4). Therefore, roughly spoken, some solutions of (3.1), (3.2) could leave $Q(s)$ across any $Q_i^-(s)$.

On each upper face $Q_i^+(s)$ the direction condition (2.4) being valid, by inspection of the outer normals ν_x in any point x of the k-dimensional edges of $Q(s)$, $k = 0,\dots,n-1$, we see that the condition $\nu_x \cdot f(x) \le 0$ holds for the inner product of ν_x with $f(x)$ in all points $x \in \partial Q(s)$. Consequently, if additionally we require a local Lipschitz condition for f on a neighborhood of $\overline{\mathbb{R}_+^n}$ in $\mathbb{R}^n$, we can apply Bony's theorem [1, 6] which guarantees the flow invariance of $Q(s)$ for (3.1). Clearly, the function $f_i(x)$ in (3.2) will be Lipschitz continuous on $\overline{Q_1^-}$ if we require $1 \le \alpha_{ij}$ for $i \ne j$, $1 \le \gamma_i$, and $\zeta_i = 0$ or $1 \le \zeta_i$ for all $i, j = 1,\dots,n$.

Then the Ansatz $v(t) =: a^-(\varphi(t)) = (\varphi^{-A_i}(t)) \in \mathbb{R}^n_+$ with the requirements in part (b) leads to the lower and upper bounds (stated above in part (b)) for solutions $x(t) \in Q_1^-$ in a quite similar way as in the proof of part (a). Finally, the last statement (c) results immediately from the definition of the functions $v(t)$ and the convergence to ∞ of the solutions $\varphi(t)$ (3.4) with $t \to T \leq \infty$, $[0, T)$ denoting the right maximal interval of existence of φ. □

References

[1] J.-M. Bony, *Principe du maximum, inégalite de Harnack et unicité du problème de Cauchy pour les opérateurs elliptiques dégénérés*, Annales de l'Institut Fourier **19** (1969), no. fasc. 1, 277–304.

[2] M. W. Hirsch, *Systems of differential equations which are competitive or cooperative. I. Limit sets*, SIAM Journal on Mathematical Analysis **13** (1982), no. 2, 167–179.

[3] C. V. Pao, *Nonlinear Parabolic and Elliptic Equations*, Plenum Press, New York, 1992.

[4] R. Rautmann, *Geometric aspects of dynamical systems in* $\mathbb{R}^n$, Nonlinear Analysis **47** (2001), no. 6, 3617–3627.

[5] R. Rautmann and R. Breitrück, *On the global structure of a class of dynamic systems*, Proceedings of Dynamic Systems and Applications, vol. 4, Dynamic, to appear.

[6] R. M. Redheffer, *The theorems of Bony and Brezis on flow-invariant sets*, The American Mathematical Monthly **79** (1972), 740–747.

[7] H. L. Smith, *Monotone Dynamical Systems*, Mathematical Surveys and Monographs, vol. 41, American Mathematical Society, Rhode Island, 1995.

[8] W. Walter, *Differential and Integral Inequalities*, Springer, New York, 1970.

R. Rautmann: Mathematisches Institut, Universität Paderborn, 33098 Paderborn, Germany
E-mail address: rautmann@uni-paderborn.de

TYPES OF SOLUTIONS AND MULTIPLICITY RESULTS FOR FOURTH-ORDER NONLINEAR BOUNDARY VALUE PROBLEMS

F. SADYRBAEV AND I. YERMACHENKO

The multiplicity results for the problem $x^{(4)} = f(t,x,x'')$, (i) $x(0) = x'(0) = 0 = x(1) = x'(1)$, (ii) are presented, where the right side in (i) is monotone with respect to x and x'. Our considerations are based on the types of solutions, which are introduced using the notion of conjugate points by Leighton and Nehari. One of the main results is that the quasilinear equation $x^{(4)} - p(t)x'' - q(t)x = F(t,x,x'')$, (iii) along with the boundary conditions (ii), has a solution which possesses the oscillatory properties induced by the linear part in (iii). Results are applied to the Emden-Fowler-type equations.

1. Introduction

In this paper we consider the fourth-order nonlinear differential equations

$$x^{(4)} = f(t,x,x''), \quad t \in I := [0,1], \tag{1.1}$$

$$x^{(4)} - p(t)x'' - q(t)x = F(t,x,x'') \tag{1.2}$$

together with the boundary conditions

$$x(0) = x'(0) = 0 = x(1) = x'(1). \tag{1.3}$$

Function f is supposed to be continuous together with the partial derivatives f_x and $f_{x''}$. Functions F, F_x, $F_{x''}$ are continuous and F is bounded, that is, $|F(t,x,x'')| < M$, $p(t) \geq 0$, and $q(t) > 0$ are continuous functions. We prove first that quasilinear boundary value problem (1.2), (1.3) has a solution which hereditates oscillatory properties of the linear part $(L_4x)(t) := x^{(4)} - p(t)x'' - q(t)x$, provided that the linear part is nonresonant, that is, the homogeneous problem $(L_4x)(t) = 0$, (1.3) has only the trivial solution. We consider then (1.1) (together with the boundary conditions (1.3)) under some monotonicity-type

Hindawi Publishing Corporation
Proceedings of the Conference on Differential & Difference Equations and Applications, pp. 989–998

restrictions and show that there exist multiple solutions of the BVP (1.1), (1.3) if (1.1) can be represented in a quasilinear form (1.2) for various linear parts. Our results are applied then to the fourth-order Emden-Fowler equation

$$x^{(4)} = \alpha^2 \cdot |x|^\gamma \operatorname{sign} x, \quad \gamma > 0. \tag{1.4}$$

The boundary value problem ((1.3), (1.4)) is shown to have multiple solutions if γ is sufficiently close to unity.

Similar results were proven in [8] for the second-order boundary value problems of the form

$$\begin{gathered} x'' = f(t,x), \quad F \in C([0,1],R), \\ x'' + k^2 x = F(t,x), \quad F \in C([0,1],R), \\ x(0) = 0, \quad x(1) = 0. \end{gathered} \tag{1.5}$$

The results for the second-order BVPs, in turn, were inspired by the works of Jackson and Schrader [2], Knobloch [3, 4] and Erbe [1]. The interested reader may consult papers [8, 9] for details.

2. Fourth-order quasilinear problems

2.1. Linear theory by Leighton-Nehari-Pudei. We provide first basics of the oscillation theory for linear fourth-order differential equations of the form

$$y^{(4)} - p(t)y'' - q(t)y = 0, \tag{2.1}$$

where p and q are continuous functions and $q > 0$, $p \geq 0$. This theory was developed by Leighton and Nehari [5] for two-termed equation $y^{(4)} = q(t)y$ and generalized for equations of the form (2.1) by Pudei [6].

Theorem 2.1 [6, page 210]. *If there exists a solution $y(t)$ of (2.1) which vanishes for $t = a$ and has at least $n+3$ zeros (counting multiplicities) in $[a,+\infty)$, then there exist n points $\eta_1,\dots,\eta_n$ ($a < \eta_1 < \eta_2 < \cdots < \eta_n$) and n essentially unique (up to multiplication by a constant) solutions $y_1(t),\dots,y_n(t)$ of (2.1) with the following properties:*

(a) *$y_\nu(t)$ has double zeros at $t = a$ and $t = \eta_\nu$;*

(b) *$y_\nu(t)$ has exactly $\nu+3$ zeros in $[a,\eta_\nu]$ (double zeros are counted according to their multiplicities);*

(c) *any other solution $y(t)$ such that $y(a) = 0$ has fewer than $\nu+3$ zeros in $[a,\eta_\nu]$.*

Definition 2.2. The point η_n is called by *the* nth *conjugate point* of $t = a$ (with respect to (2.1)). The respective solution $y_n(t)$ is referred to as *the* nth *extremal function* since (a) and (c) imply that η_n is the minimum value of $(n+3)$th zeros of $y(t)$ as $y(t)$ ranges over all solutions of (2.1) for which $y(a) = 0$. Functions $y_n(t)$ are defined uniquely except for multiplicative constants.

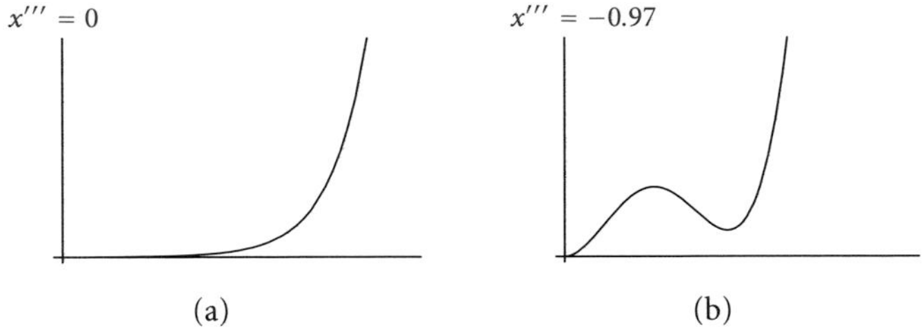

Figure 2.1

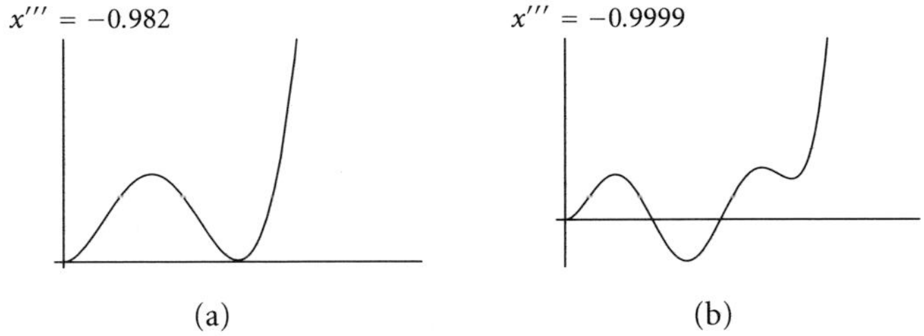

Figure 2.2

Corollary 2.3. *Equation* $y^{(4)} - Py'' - k^4 y = 0$, *where* $P \geq 0$ *and* $k \neq 0$ *are constants, has infinite sequence of conjugate (of the point* $t = 0$*) points* η_i.

Suppose that initial conditions are of the form

$$x(0) = x'(0) = 0,$$
$$x''(0) = r\cos\Theta, \qquad x'''(0) = r\sin\Theta. \tag{2.2}$$

It was shown in [6] that no extremal solutions are possible for $\Theta \in [0,\pi/2]$ and $\Theta \in [\pi,3\pi/2]$. Let Θ_i relate to an extremal solution $x_i(t)$. It was shown in [7] that Θ_i are ordered as follows for solutions with positive $x''(0)$ (and, resp., negative $x'''(0)$)

$$-\frac{\pi}{2} < \Theta_2 < \cdots < \Theta_{2n} < \cdots < \Theta_{2m+1} < \cdots < \Theta_1 < 0. \tag{2.3}$$

Some solutions of the Cauchy problem $x^{(4)} = x, x(0) = x'(0) = 0, x''(0) = 1, x'''(0) = r$ for various negative r are depicted in Figures 2.1, 2.2, 2.3, and 2.4.

Theorem 2.4 [7, Theorem 3]. *Conjugate points continuously depend on the coefficients* $p(t)$ *and* $q(t)$.

2.2. Quasilinear problems. Consider quasilinear equation (1.2) together with the boundary conditions (1.3). Suppose the following conditions are satisfied:

(A0) $p(t) \geq 0$, and $q(t) > 0$ are continuous functions;

(A1) F, F_x, and $F_{x''}$ are continuous functions;

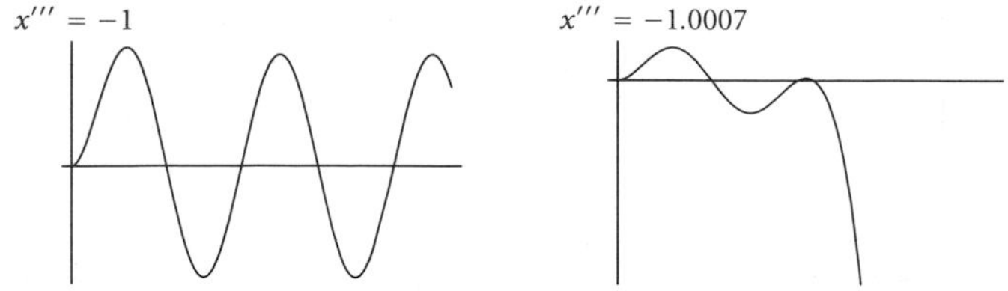

(a) (b)

Figure 2.3

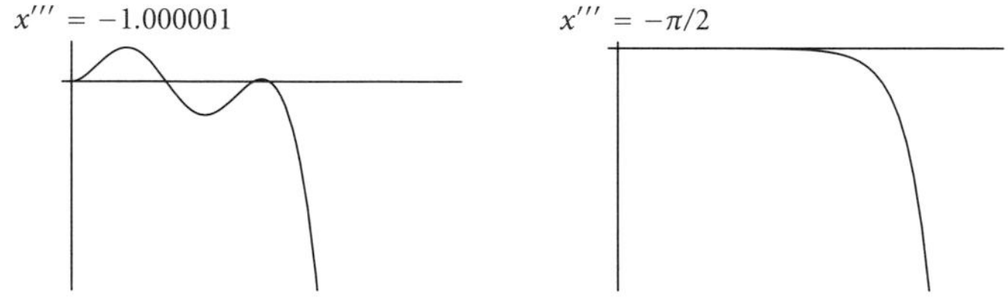

(a) (b)

Figure 2.4

(A2) $F(t,0,0) \equiv 0$;
(A3) $q(t) + F_x(t,x,x'') > 0$ for any $(t,x,x'') \in [0,1] \times R^2$;
(A4) $p(t) + F_{x''}(t,x,x'') \geq 0$ for any $(t,x,x'') \in [0,1] \times R^2$.

Definition 2.5. Say that the linear part $(L_4x)(t) := x^{(4)} - p(t)x'' - q(t)x$ is i-nonresonant with respect to the boundary conditions (1.3) if $(L_4x)(t) = 0$ has exactly i conjugate points (of the point $t = 0$) in the interval $(0,1)$ and $t = 1$ is not a conjugate point.

Definition 2.6. Say that $\xi(t)$ is an i-type solution of the problem (1.2), (1.3) if for small enough α, β the difference $u(t;\alpha,\beta) = x(t;\alpha,\beta) - \xi(t)$ has exactly $i+3$ zeros (counting multiplicities) in $(0,1)$ and $t = 1$ is not a zero, where $x(t;\alpha,\beta)$ is a solution of (1.2), which satisfies the initial conditions

$$\begin{aligned} x(0;\alpha,\beta) - \xi(0) &= 0, \\ x'(0;\alpha,\beta) - \xi'(0) &= 0, \\ x''(0;\alpha,\beta) - \xi''(0) &= \alpha, \\ x'''(0;\alpha,\beta) - \xi'''(0) &= \beta. \end{aligned} \tag{2.4}$$

Remark 2.7. Due to conditions (A3) and (A4) the linear theory above applies to the respective equation of variations

$$y^{(4)} = \big(p(t) + F_{x''}(t,\xi,\xi'')\big)y'' + \big(q(t) + F_x(t,\xi,\xi'')\big)y \tag{2.5}$$

and an i-type solution ξ of the problem (1.2), (1.3) has the following characteristics: (2.5) either has exactly i conjugate points in the interval $(0,1]$, or has exactly i conjugate points in the interval $(0,1)$ and $t=1$ is the $(i+1)$th conjugate point. The cases of the ith conjugate point being at $t=1$ or $(i+1)$th conjugate point being at $t=1$ are not excluded.

THEOREM 2.8. *Quasilinear problem (1.2), (1.3) with an i-nonresonant linear part* $(L_4x)(t)$ *has an i-type solution.*

We state several lemmas before proving the theorem.

LEMMA 2.9. *A set* S *of all solutions of the BVP (1.2), (1.3) is nonempty and compact in* $C^3([0,1])$.

Proof. Solvability can be proved by standard application of the Schauder principle to the operator $T: C^3(I) \to C^3(I)$, where T is defined by

$$(Tx)(t) = \int_0^1 G(t,s)F(s,x(s))\,ds \tag{2.6}$$

and $G(t,s)$ is the Green function for $(L_4x)(t)=0$, (1.3). Notice that F is bounded.

Compactness of S is obtained by routine application of the Arzela-Ascoli criterium. □

Remark 2.10. Solvability of quasilinear problems with nonresonant linear parts is well known.

Remark 2.11. Any solution $x(t)$ of the problem (1.2), (1.3) satisfies the estimate

$$\max_I |x(t)| \le \Gamma \cdot M, \tag{2.7}$$

where $\Gamma = \max_{0\le t,s\le 1}|G(t,s)|$, $M = \sup\{|F(t,x)| : (t,x) \in I \times R\}$.

LEMMA 2.12. *There is an element* $x^*(t)$ *in* S, *which possesses the property:* $x^{*\prime\prime 2}(0) + x^{*\prime\prime\prime 2}(0) = \max\{x''^2(0)+x'''^2(0) : x \in S\}$.

Proof. The set $S_1 = \{x''^2(0)+x'''^2(0) : x \in S\}$ is an image of a continuous map $M: C^3([0,1]) \to R$ defined by $M(x) = x''^2(0)+x'''^2(0)$. □

For some function $\xi(t)$, let $\xi(t)$ be given. Denote by $x(t;r,\Theta)$ a solution of the Cauchy problem (1.2)

$$\begin{gathered} x(0)=x'(0)=0, \qquad x''(0)-\xi''(0)=r\cos\Theta, \\ x'''(0)-\xi'''(0)=r\sin\Theta. \end{gathered} \tag{2.8}$$

LEMMA 2.13. *Assume that conditions* (A0) *to* (A4) *are satisfied. Let* ξ *be any element of* S *and* $x(t;r,\Theta)$ *as above. The function* $v(t;r,\Theta) = x(t;r,\Theta)-\xi(t)$ *satisfies then*

$$(L_4v)(t) = \Phi_1(t;r,\Theta)v + \Phi_2(t;r,\Theta)v'', \tag{2.9}$$

where

$$\Phi_1(t;r,\Theta) = \frac{F(t,x,x'') - F(t,\xi,x'')}{x-\xi} = F_x(t,\omega_1(t),x''),$$
$$\Phi_2(t;r,\Theta) = \frac{F(t,\xi,x'') - F(t,\xi,\xi'')}{x''-\xi''} = F_{x''}(t,\xi,\omega_2(t)) \tag{2.10}$$

(ω_1 and ω_2, by mean value theorem, stand for some intermediate points).

If (2.9) has a conjugate point at $t = 1$ for some r_* and Θ_* and $v(t;r_*,\Theta_*)$ is a respective extremal function, then $x(t;r_*,\Theta_*) = v(t;r_*,\Theta_*) + \xi(t)$ solves the BVP (1.2), (1.3). The opposite also is true, namely, if $x(t;r_*,\Theta_*)$ is a solution to the BVP, then $v(t) = x(t;r_*,\Theta_*) - \xi(t)$ is an extremal function for (2.9) with a conjugate point exactly at $t = 1$.

Proof. Essentially [7, Lemma 4]. □

LEMMA 2.14. *Assume that conditions* (A0) *to* (A4) *are satisfied. If $x(t)$ is a nontrivial solution of the BVP (1.2), (1.3), then $x''(0)x'''(0) < 0$.*

Proof. Let $\xi(t) \equiv 0$ in precedent lemma. Notice that $\Phi_1 > 0$ and $\Phi_2 \geq 0$ in (2.9). By results in [5, 6] any extremal function $v(t)$ satisfies $v''(0)v'''(0) < 0$. Since, by Lemma 2.13, $x(t) = v(t) + \xi(t) = v(t)$ for some extremal function $v(t)$, the assertion follows. □

LEMMA 2.15. *Let the conditions* (A1) *to* (A3) *be fulfilled. Suppose that the linear part $(L_4x)(t)$ in (1.2) is i-nonresonant. Let ξ be any element of S.*

Then the function $u(t;r,\Theta) = (x(t;r,\Theta) - \xi(t))/r$ for any $\Theta \in [0,2\pi)$ tends to a solution $y(t)$ of the Cauchy problem

$$y^{(4)} - p(t)y'' - q(t)y = 0, \qquad y(0) = y'(0) = 0,$$
$$y''(0) = \cos\Theta, \qquad y'''(0) = \sin\Theta \tag{2.11}$$

as $r \to +\infty$, where $x(t;r,\Theta)$ is a solution of the problem

$$x^{(4)} - p(t)x'' - q(t)x = F(t,x), \qquad x(0) = x'(0) = 0,$$
$$x''(0) - \xi''(0) = r\cos\Theta, \qquad x'''(0) - \xi'''(0) = r\sin\Theta. \tag{2.12}$$

Proof. The functions $u(t;r,\Theta)$ solve the initial value problems

$$(L_4u)(t) = \frac{1}{r}[F(t,x(t)) - F(t,\xi(t))],$$
$$u(0) = u'(0) = 0, \qquad u''(0) = \cos\Theta, \tag{2.13}$$
$$u'''(0) = \sin\Theta.$$

Let $r \to +\infty$. The right side in (2.13) then tends to zero uniformly in t for fixed Θ. By classical results, $u(t;r,\Theta)$ tends then to a solution $y(t)$ of the problem (2.11). □

Proof of Theorem 2.8. Identify $\xi(t)$ with a maximal solution $x^*(t)$ of Lemma 2.12. Consider solutions $x(t;r,\Theta)$ of the initial value problem (1.2), (2.8). The difference $u(t;r,\Theta) := x(t;r,\Theta) - \xi(t)$ satisfies the linear equation

$$(L_4u)(t) = \Phi_1(t;r,\Theta)u + \Phi_2(t;r,\Theta)u'', \tag{2.14}$$

where $\Phi_i(t;r,\Theta)$ are defined as above. Consider linear equation (2.14) for $r \sim 0$. Suppose that $\xi(t)$ is not an i-type solution. By Lemma 2.14, $\xi''(0)\xi'''(0) < 0$ if ξ is not trivial solution. Suppose that $\xi''(0) > 0$ and $\xi'''(0) < 0$. To be definite, consider the case of the difference $u(t;r,\Theta)$ to have more than i points of double zero in the interval $(0,1)$ for small values of r. Recall that $u'''(0) = r\sin\Theta < 0$ and $u''(0) = r\cos\Theta > 0$. Let $\Theta \in (-\pi/2,0)$ be fixed. For $r \sim +\infty$ the respective linear equation (2.14) has exactly i conjugate points. Thus there exists $r_1(\Theta)$ such that the respective linear equation (2.14) has $(i+1)$th conjugate point exactly at $t = 1$. This is true for any $\Theta \in (-\pi/2,0)$. The function $r_1(\Theta)$ is, possibly, multivalued. Define $R(\Theta) = \sup r_1(\Theta)$. This function is continuous in $(-\pi/2,0)$ since otherwise continuous dependence of conjugate points η_{i+1} on coefficients of (2.14) is violated.

Consider extremal solutions $v_{i+1}(t;R(\Theta),\Theta)$ of (2.14). Let $\omega(R(\Theta),\Theta)$ be the angle of initial data ($\omega = \arctan(v'''(0)/v''(0))$) for $v_{i+1}(t;R(\Theta),\Theta)$.

Consider the difference $\omega(R(\Theta),\Theta) - \Theta$ in the interval $(-\pi/2,0)$. It has different signs for $\Theta = 0$ and $\Theta = -\pi/2$. Therefore there exists Θ_0 such that $\omega(R(\Theta_0),\Theta_0) = \Theta_0$. Thus, by Lemma 2.13, a solution to the BVP exists which has $r^2 = x''^2(0) + x'''^2(0)$ greater than that for ξ. This contradicts the choice of $\xi = x^*$. Similarly, other cases can be considered.

Thus ξ is an i-type solution of the problem (1.2), (1.3). Other cases can be treated similarly. □

3. Application

3.1. Quasilinearization. Let us describe first the idea of quasilinearization which is used below to get the multiplicity results. Consider the BVP (1.1), (1.3). Let quasilinear equation be of the form (1.2). If the linear part in (1.2) is i-nonresonant with respect to the boundary conditions (1.3), then the problem (1.2), (1.3) has an i-type solution, by Theorem 2.8.

Suppose further that (1.1) and (1.2) are equivalent in a domain $D = \{(t,x,x'');0 \le t \le 1,\ |x| \le N,\ |x''| \le N_1\}$. If any solution $x(t)$ of the problem (1.2), (1.3) satisfies the estimates

$$|x(t)| \le N, \quad |x''(t)| \le N_1, \quad \forall t \in I, \tag{3.1}$$

then it solves also the problem (1.1), (1.3). We will say for brevity that the problem (1.1), (1.3) allows for quasilinearization with respect to the linear part $(L_4x)(t)$.

If the same procedure is possible for another, say, j-nonresonant linear part, then the problem (1.1), (1.3) has a j-type solution. Thus multiply solutions of the problem (1.1), (1.3).

3.2. Example. Consider the boundary value problem for

$$x^{(4)} = \alpha^2 \cdot |x|^\gamma \operatorname{sign} x, \tag{3.2}$$

$$x(0) = x'(0) = 0 = x(1) = x'(1), \tag{3.3}$$

where $\alpha \neq 0$, $\gamma > 0$, $\gamma \neq 1$.

After the appropriate smooth truncation ("cutoff") (cf. [9]) of the right-hand side in

$$x^{(4)} - k^4 x = \alpha^2 \cdot |x|^\gamma \operatorname{sign} x - k^4 x, \tag{3.4}$$

one gets multiple quasilinear problems for different values of k,

$$x^{(4)} - k^4 x = F_k(x), \tag{3.5}$$

where right sides in (3.4) and (3.5) coincide for $|x| < N_k$ and F_k is bounded in modulus by a constant M_k. Let $G_k(t,s)$ be the respective Green function which allows for estimate $|G_k| \le \Gamma_k$.

If the relation $\Gamma_k \cdot M_k < N_k$ is satisfied for some k, then quasilinearization in the above sense is possible with a linear part $x^{(4)} - k^4 x$.

After the laborious work on estimation of the respective Green function, the "key" relation $\Gamma_k \cdot M_k < N_k$ takes the form below.

In order to check either the quasilinearization with a given k is possible, one should verify the inequalities

$$k \cdot \frac{(1+\sqrt{2})e^k}{(e^k+1)} < \beta \cdot \frac{\gamma^{\gamma/(\gamma-1)}}{|\gamma-1|} \quad \text{for } k = (2n-1)\pi, \tag{3.6}$$

$$k \cdot \frac{(1+\sqrt{2})e^k}{(e^k-1)} < \beta \cdot \frac{\gamma^{\gamma/(\gamma-1)}}{|\gamma-1|} \quad \text{for } k = 2n\pi, \tag{3.7}$$

where $\beta > 1$ is a root of

$$\beta^\gamma = \beta + (\gamma - 1) \cdot \gamma^{\gamma/(1-\gamma)}. \tag{3.8}$$

In Table 3.1 the results of calculations are provided. It is shown for certain values of k in the form $k = \pi n$, $n = 1, 2\ldots$, which parameters are appropriate for the inequalities (3.6) and (3.7) to be satisfied.

This table may be interpreted as a set of multiplicity results for the boundary value problem (3.2), (3.3).

Table 3.1

$\gamma = \frac{4}{5}$	$\beta \approx 1.3632$	$k = \pi; k = 2\pi$
$\gamma = \frac{5}{6}$	$\beta \approx 1.3553$	$k = \pi; k = 2\pi$
$\gamma = \frac{6}{7}$	$\beta \approx 1.3499$	$k = \pi; k = 2\pi; k = 3\pi$
$\gamma = \frac{7}{8}$	$\beta \approx 1.3461$	$k = \pi; k = 2\pi; k = 3\pi$
$\gamma = \frac{8}{9}$	$\beta \approx 1.3431$	$k = \pi; k = 2\pi; k = 3\pi; k = 4\pi$
$\gamma = \frac{9}{10}$	$\beta \approx 1.3407$	$k = \pi; k = 2\pi; k = 3\pi; k = 4\pi$
$\gamma = \frac{10}{11}$	$\beta \approx 1.3388$	$k = \pi; k = 2\pi; k = 3\pi; k = 4\pi; k = 5\pi$
$\gamma = \frac{11}{12}$	$\beta \approx 1.3373$	$k = \pi; k = 2\pi; k = 3\pi; k = 4\pi; k = 5\pi$
$\gamma = \frac{12}{13}$	$\beta \approx 1.3359$	$k = \pi; k = 2\pi; k = 3\pi; k = 4\pi; k = 5\pi$
$\gamma = \frac{13}{14}$	$\beta \approx 1.3349$	$k = \pi; k = 2\pi; k = 3\pi; k = 4\pi; k = 5\pi; k = 6\pi$
...	...	...
$\gamma = \frac{14}{13}$	$\beta \approx 1.3076$	$k = \pi; k = 2\pi; k = 3\pi; k = 4\pi; k = 5\pi; k = 6\pi$
$\gamma = \frac{13}{12}$	$\beta \approx 1.3065$	$k = \pi; k = 2\pi; k = 3\pi; k = 4\pi; k = 5\pi$
$\gamma = \frac{12}{11}$	$\beta \approx 1.3053$	$k = \pi; k = 2\pi; k = 3\pi; k = 4\pi; k = 5\pi$
$\gamma = \frac{11}{10}$	$\beta \approx 1.3038$	$k = \pi; k = 2\pi; k = 3\pi; k = 4\pi$
$\gamma = \frac{10}{9}$	$\beta \approx 1.3019$	$k = \pi; k = 2\pi; k = 3\pi; k = 4\pi$
$\gamma = \frac{9}{8}$	$\beta \approx 1.2998$	$k = \pi; k = 2\pi; k = 3\pi$
$\gamma = \frac{8}{7}$	$\beta \approx 1.2969$	$k = \pi; k = 2\pi; k = 3\pi$
$\gamma = \frac{7}{6}$	$\beta \approx 1.2933$	$k = \pi; k = 2\pi; k = 3\pi$
$\gamma = \frac{6}{5}$	$\beta \approx 1.2884$	$k = \pi; k = 2\pi$
$\gamma = \frac{5}{4}$	$\beta \approx 1.2813$	$k = \pi; k = 2\pi$

References

[1] L. H. Erbe, *Nonlinear boundary value problems for second order differential equations*, Journal of Differential Equations **7** (1970), 459–472.

[2] L. K. Jackson and K. W. Schrader, *Comparison theorems for nonlinear differential equations*, Journal of Differential Equations **3** (1967), 248–255.

[3] H.-W. Knobloch, *Comparison theorems for nonlinear second order differential equations*, Journal of Differential Equations **1** (1965), 1–26.

[4] ———, *Second order differential equalities and a nonlinear boundary value problem*, Journal of Differential Equations **5** (1969), 55–71.

[5] W. Leighton and Z. Nehari, *On the oscillation of solutions of self-adjoint linear differential equations of the fourth order*, Transactions of the American Mathematical Society **89** (1958), 325–377.

[6] V. Pudei, *O vlastnostech řešeni diferencialni rovnice* $y^{(4)} + p(x)y'' + q(x)y = 0$, Československá Akademie Věd. Časopis Pro Pěstování Matematiky **93** (1968), 201–216.

[7] F. Sadyrbaev, *Multiplicity of solutions for fourth order boundary value problems*, Proceedings of the Latvian Academy of Sciences. Section B (1995), no. 5/6 (574/575), 115–121.

[8] F. Sadyrbaev and I. Yermachenko, *Types of solutions and multiplicity results for two-point nonlinear boundary value problems*, Nonlinear Analysis **63** (2005), no. 5–7, e1725–e1735, Proceedings of the 4th World Congress of Nonlinear Analysts (WCNA '04) Florida, July 2004.

[9] I. Yermachenko and F. Sadyrbaev, *Quasilinearization and multiple solutions of the Emden-Fowler type equation*, Mathematical Modelling and Analysis **10** (2005), no. 1, 41–50.

F. Sadyrbaev: Institute of Mathematics and Computer Science, University of Latvia, Riga, LV-1459, Latvia
E-mail address: felix@cclu.lv

I. Yermachenko: Department of Natural Sciences and Mathematics, Daugavpils University, Parades iela 1, Daugavpils, LV-5401, Latvia
E-mail address: inari@dau.lv

SANDWICH PAIRS

MARTIN SCHECHTER

Since the development of the calculus of variations, there has been interest in finding critical points of functionals. This was intensified by the fact that for many equations arising in practice the solutions are critical points of functionals. If a functional G is semibounded, one can find a Palais-Smale (PS) sequences: $G(u_k) \to a$, $G'(u_k) \to 0$. These sequences produce critical points if they have convergent subsequences (i.e., if G satisfies the PS condition). However, there is no clear method of finding critical points of functionals which are not semibounded. The concept of linking was developed to produce Palais-Smale (PS) sequences for C^1 functionals G that separate linking sets. In the present paper we discuss the situation in which one cannot find linking sets that separate the functional. We introduce a new class of subsets that accomplishes the same results under weaker conditions. We then provide criteria for determining such subsets. Examples and applications are given.

1. Introduction

Many problems arising in science and engineering call for the solving of the Euler equations of functionals, that is, equations of the form

$$G'(u) = 0, \tag{1.1}$$

where $G(u)$ is a C^1 functional (usually representing the energy) arising from the given data. As an illustration, the equation

$$-\Delta u(x) = f(x, u(x)) \tag{1.2}$$

is the Euler equation of the functional

$$G(u) = \frac{1}{2}\|\nabla u\|^2 - \int F(x, u(x))\,dx \tag{1.3}$$

Hindawi Publishing Corporation
Proceedings of the Conference on Differential & Difference Equations and Applications, pp. 999–1007

on an appropriate space, where

$$F(x,t) = \int_0^t f(x,s)ds, \tag{1.4}$$

and the norm is that of L^2. The solving of the Euler equations is tantamount to finding critical points of the corresponding functional. The classical approach was to look for maxima or minima. If one is looking for a minimum, it is not sufficient to know that the functional is bounded from below, as is easily checked. However, one can show that there is a sequence, called a *Palais-Smale (PS) sequence*, satisfying

$$G(u_k) \longrightarrow a, \qquad G'(u_k) \longrightarrow 0 \tag{1.5}$$

for $a = \inf G$. Such a sequence may not produce a critical point, but if it has a convergent subsequence, then it does. If every PS sequence for G has a convergent subsequence, then we say that G satisfies the PS condition. However, when extrema do not exist, there is no clear way of obtaining critical points. In particular, this happens when the functional is not bounded from either above or below. Until recently there was no organized procedure for producing critical points which are not extrema. What can be used to replace semiboundedness? We will describe an approach which is very useful in such cases. As a substitute for semiboundedness, one looks for suitable sets that separate the given functional. One looks for suitable subsets A, B of a Banach space E, which for a given C^1 functional G on E satisfy

$$a_0 := \sup_A G \le b_0 := \inf_B G. \tag{1.6}$$

Ideally, we would want (1.6) to imply that G has a critical point, that is, a point $u \in E$ such that

$$G(u) = a \ge b_0, \qquad G'(u) = 0. \tag{1.7}$$

Clearly, this is too much to ask, since even semiboundedness is not sufficient to imply the existence of a critical point. However, there are pairs of subsets such that (1.6) produces a PS sequence:

$$G(u_k) \longrightarrow a, \qquad G'(u_k) \longrightarrow 0, \tag{1.8}$$

where $a \ge b_0$. If A, B are such that (1.6) always implies (1.8), we say that A links B. Consequently, if A links B and G is a C^1 functional on E which satisfies (1.6) and the PS condition, then G has a critical point satisfying (1.7). Linking sets exist and are described in the literature.

In the present paper, we discuss the situation in which one cannot find linking sets that separate the functional, that is, satisfy (1.6). Are there weaker conditions that will imply (1.8)? Our answer is yes, and we find pairs of subsets such that a condition weaker than (1.6) produces a PS sequence. We have the following definition.

Definition 1.1. Say that a pair of subsets A, B of a Banach space E forms a sandwich, if for any $G \in C^1(E,\mathbb{R})$, inequality

$$-\infty < b_0 := \inf_B G \leq a_0 := \sup_A G < \infty \tag{1.9}$$

implies that there is a sequence satisfying

$$G(u_k) \longrightarrow c, \quad b_0 \leq c \leq a_0, \qquad G'(u_k) \longrightarrow 0. \tag{1.10}$$

Unlike linking, the order of a sandwich pair is immaterial, that is, if the pair A, B forms a sandwich, so B, A does. Moreover, we allow sets forming a sandwich pair to intersect. One sandwich pair has been studied in the past. We have (cf. [9–11]) the following theorem.

Theorem 1.2. *Let N be a closed subspace of a Hilbert space E, and let $M = N^\perp$. Assume that at least one of the subspaces M, N is finite-dimensional. Let G be a C^1-functional on E such that*

$$\begin{aligned} m_0 &:= \inf_{w\in M} G(w) \neq -\infty, \\ m_1 &:= \sup_{v\in N} G(v) \neq \infty. \end{aligned} \tag{1.11}$$

Then there are a constant $c \in \mathbb{R}$ and a sequence $\{u_k\} \subset E$ such that

$$G(u_k) \longrightarrow c, \quad m_0 \leq c \leq m_1, \qquad G'(u_k) \longrightarrow 0. \tag{1.12}$$

It follows from this that M, N form a sandwich pair if one of them is finite-dimensional. (Note that $m_0 \leq m_1$.)

Theorem 1.2 has been generalized as follows (cf. [8]).

Theorem 1.3. *Let N be a closed subspace of a Hilbert space E, and let $M = N^\perp$. Assume that at least one of the subspaces M, N is finite-dimensional. Let G be a C^1-functional on E such that*

$$\begin{aligned} m_0 &:= \sup_{v\in N} \inf_{w\in M} G(v+w) \neq -\infty, \\ m_1 &:= \inf_{w\in M} \sup_{v\in N} G(v+w) \neq \infty. \end{aligned} \tag{1.13}$$

Then there are a constant $c \in \mathbb{R}$ and a sequence $\{u_k\} \subset E$ such that

$$G(u_k) \longrightarrow c, \quad m_0 \leq c \leq m_1, \qquad G'(u_k) \longrightarrow 0. \tag{1.14}$$

This constitutes the sum total of results of this type. To date, only complementing subspaces have been considered with one of them being finite-dimensional. The purpose of the present paper is to show that other sets can qualify as well.

2. Criteria

In this section we present sufficient conditions for sets to qualify as sandwich pairs. We have the following proposition.

PROPOSITION 2.1. *If A, B is a sandwich pair, and J is a diffeomorphism on the entire space having a derivative J′ satisfying*

$$\|J'(u)^{-1}\| \le C, \quad u \in E, \tag{2.1}$$

then JA, JB is a sandwich pair.

THEOREM 2.2. *Let N be a finite-dimensional subspace of a Banach space E. Let F be a Lipschitz continuous map of E onto N such that F = I on N and*

$$\|F(g) - F(h)\| \le K\|g - h\|, \quad g,h \in E. \tag{2.2}$$

Then for each point p of N, A = N, B = $F^{-1}(p)$ forms a sandwich pair.

3. Applications

In the present section we assume that Ω is a bounded domain in $\mathbb{R}^n$ with boundary $\partial\Omega$ sufficiently regular so that the Sobolev inequalities hold and the embedding of $H^{m,2}(\Omega)$ in $L^2(\Omega)$ is compact (cf. [1]). Let A be a selfadjoint operator on $L^2(\Omega)$. We assume that $A \ge \lambda_0 > 0$ and that

$$C_0^\infty(\Omega) \subset D := D(A^{1/2}) \subset H^{m,2}(\Omega) \tag{3.1}$$

for some $m > 0$, where $C_0^\infty(\Omega)$ denotes the set of test functions in Ω (i.e., infinitely differentiable functions with compact supports in Ω), and $H^{m,2}(\Omega)$ denotes the Sobolev space. If m is an integer, the norm in $H^{m,2}(\Omega)$ is given by

$$\|u\|_{m,2} := \left(\sum_{|\mu| \le m} \|D^\mu u\|^2 \right)^{1/2}. \tag{3.2}$$

Here D^μ represents the generic derivative of order $|\mu|$, and the norm on the right-hand side of (3.2) is that of $L^2(\Omega)$. We will not assume that m is an integer.

Let q be any number satisfying

$$\begin{gathered} 2 \le q \le \frac{2n}{(n-2m)}, \quad 2m < n, \\ 2 \le q < \infty, \quad n \le 2m, \end{gathered} \tag{3.3}$$

and let $f(x,t)$ be a Carathéodory function on $\Omega \times \mathbb{R}$. This means that $f(x,t)$ is continuous in t for a.e. $x \in \Omega$ and measurable in x for every $t \in \mathbb{R}$. We make the following assumptions.

(A) The function $f(x,t)$ satisfies

$$|f(x,t)| \leq V(x)^q |t|^{q-1} + V(x)W(x),$$
$$\frac{f(x,t)}{V(x)^q} = o(|t|^{q-1}) \quad \text{as } |t| \longrightarrow \infty, \tag{3.4}$$

where $V(x) > 0$ is a function in $L^q(\Omega)$ such that

$$\|Vu\|_q \leq C\|u\|_D, \quad u \in D, \tag{3.5}$$

and W is a function in $L^{q'}(\Omega)$. Here

$$\|u\|_q := \left(\int_\Omega |u(x)|^q dx\right)^{1/q},$$
$$\|u\|_D := \|A^{1/2}u\|, \tag{3.6}$$

and $q' = q/(q-1)$. (If Ω and $V(x)$ are bounded, then (3.5) will hold automatically by the Sobolev inequality. However, there are functions $V(x)$ which are unbounded such that (3.5) holds even on unbounded regions Ω.) With the norm (3.6), D becomes a Hilbert space. Define

$$F(x,t) := \int_0^t f(x,s)ds,$$
$$G(u) := \|u\|_D^2 - 2\int_\Omega F(x,u)dx. \tag{3.7}$$

It is readily shown that G is a continuously differentiable functional on the whole of D (cf., e.g., [10]). Since the embedding of D in $L^2(\Omega)$ is a compact, the spectrum of A consists of isolated eigenvalues of finite multiplicity

$$0 < \lambda_0 < \lambda_1 < \cdots < \lambda_\ell < \cdots. \tag{3.8}$$

(We take λ_0 to be an eigenvalue.)

Let λ_ℓ, $\ell > 0$, be one of these eigenvalues. We assume that the eigenfunctions of λ_ℓ are in $L^\infty(\Omega)$ and that the following hold:

$$2F(x,t) \leq \lambda_\ell t^2 + W_1(x), \quad x \in \Omega,\ t \in \mathbb{R} \text{ for some } W_1(x) \in L^1(\mathbb{R}), \tag{3.9}$$

$$\lambda_\ell t^2 \leq 2F(x,t), \quad |t| \leq \delta \text{ for some } \delta > 0, \tag{3.10}$$

$$\nu t^2 \leq 2F(x,t), \quad x \in \Omega,\ t \in \mathbb{R} \text{ for some } \nu > \lambda_{\ell-1}, \tag{3.11}$$

$$H(x,t) := 2F(x,t) - tf(x,t) \leq C(|t|+1), \tag{3.12}$$

$$\sigma(x) := \limsup_{|t|\to\infty} \frac{H(x,t)}{|t|} < 0 \quad \text{a.e.} \tag{3.13}$$

We have the following theorem.

Theorem 3.1. *Under the above hypotheses,*

$$Au = f(x,u), \quad u \in D, \tag{3.14}$$

has at least one nontrivial solution.

The proof of Theorem 3.1 implies.

Corollary 3.2. *If λ_ℓ is a simple eigenvalue, then hypothesis (3.9) can be weakened to*

$$2F(x,t) \le \lambda_{\ell+1}t^2 + W_1(x), \quad x \in \Omega,\ t \in \mathbb{R} \text{ for some } W_1(x) \in L^1(\mathbb{R}) \tag{3.15}$$

in Theorem 3.1.

We can essentially reverse the inequalities (3.9)–(3.13) and obtain the same results. In fact we have the following theorem.

Theorem 3.3. *Equation (3.14) has at least one nontrivial solution if we assume $\ell > 0$ and*

$$\lambda_\ell t^2 \le 2F(x,t) + W_1(x), \quad x \in \Omega,\ t \in \mathbb{R} \text{ for some } W_1(x) \in L^1(\mathbb{R}), \tag{3.16}$$

$$\begin{gathered} 2F(x,t) \le \lambda_\ell t^2, \quad |t| \le \delta \text{ for some } \delta > 0, \\ 2F(x,t) \le \nu t^2, \quad x \in \Omega,\ t \in \mathbb{R} \text{ for some } \nu < \lambda_{\ell+1}, \\ H(x,t) \ge -C(|t|+1), \quad x \in \Omega,\ t \in \mathbb{R}, \\ \liminf_{|t|\to\infty} \frac{H(x,t)}{|t|} > 0 \quad \text{a.e.} \end{gathered} \tag{3.17}$$

The proof of Theorem 3.3 implies.

Corollary 3.4. *If λ_ℓ is a simple eigenvalue, then hypothesis (3.16) can be weakened to*

$$\lambda_{\ell-1}t^2 \le 2F(x,t) + W_1(x), \quad x \in \Omega,\ t \in \mathbb{R} \text{ for some } W_1(x) \in L^1(\mathbb{R}) \tag{3.18}$$

in Theorem 3.3.

4. Some generalizations

We now show that we can improve the results of the last section. For each fixed k, let N_k denote the subspace of $D := D(A^{1/2})$ spanned by the eigenfunctions corresponding to $\lambda_0,\dots,\lambda_k$, and let $M_k = N_k^\perp \cap D$. Then $D = M_k \oplus N_k$. We define

$$\alpha_k := \max\{(Av,v) : v \in N_k,\ v \ge 0,\ \|v\| = 1\}, \tag{4.1}$$

where $\|v\|$ denotes the $L^2(\Omega)$ norm of v. We assume that A has an eigenfunction φ_0 of constant sign a.e. on Ω corresponding to the eigenvalue λ_0.

Next we define for $a \in \mathbb{R}$,

$$\gamma_k(a) := \max\{(Av,v) - a\|v^-\|^2 : v \in N_k, \|v^+\| = 1\},$$
$$\Gamma_k(a) := \inf\{(Aw,w) - a\|w^-\|^2 : w \in M_k, \|w^+\| = 1\}, \tag{4.2}$$

where $u^{\pm} = \max\{\pm u, 0\}$.

We take any integer $\ell \geq 0$ and let N denote the subspace of $L^2(\Omega)$ spanned by the eigenspaces of A corresponding to the eigenvalues $\lambda_0, \lambda_1, \ldots, \lambda_\ell$. We take $M = N^\perp \cap D$, where $D = D(A^{1/2})$. We assume that $F(x,t)$ satisfies

$$a_1(t^-)^2 + \gamma_\ell(a_1)(t^+)^2 - W_1(x) \leq 2F(x,t) \leq a_2(t^-)^2 + \nu(t^+)^2, \quad x \in \Omega,\ t \in \mathbb{R}, \tag{4.3}$$

for numbers a_1, a_2 satisfying $\alpha_\ell < a_1 \leq a_2$, where W_1 is a function in $L^1(\Omega)$ and $\nu < \Gamma_\ell(a_2)$. We also assume that

$$2F(x,t) \leq \lambda_{\ell+1}t^2, \quad |t| \leq \delta \text{ for some } \delta > 0, \tag{4.4}$$

$$|f(x,t)| \leq C|t| + W(x), \quad W \in L^2(\Omega),$$
$$\frac{f(x,t)}{t} \longrightarrow \alpha_{\pm}(x) \quad \text{a.e. as } t \longrightarrow \pm\infty, \tag{4.5}$$

and the only solution of

$$Au = \alpha_+(x)u^+ - \alpha_-(x)u^- \tag{4.6}$$

is $u \equiv 0$. We have the following theorem.

THEOREM 4.1. *Under the above hypotheses, (3.14) has a nontrivial solution.*

5. Another application

We first show how Theorem 1.3 can be strengthened.

THEOREM 5.1. *Under the hypotheses of Theorem 1.3, the following is true. For any sequence $\{R_k\} \subset \mathbb{R}^+$ such that $R_k \to \infty$, there are a constant $c \in \mathbb{R}$ and a sequence $\{u_k\} \subset E$ such that*

$$G(u_k) \longrightarrow c, \quad m_0 \leq c \leq m_1, \qquad (R_k + \|u_k\|)\|G'(u_k)\| \leq \frac{m_1 - m_0}{\ln(4/3)}. \tag{5.1}$$

Note that the conclusion of this theorem produces a sequence stronger than a PS sequence. We apply it to the following situation.

THEOREM 5.2. *Let $g(x)$ be a function $\in L^2_{\text{loc}} = L^2_{\text{loc}}(\mathbb{R}^n)$ satisfying*

$$g(x) \geq c_0 > 0, \quad x \in \mathbb{R}^n, \tag{5.2}$$

for some positive constant c_0, and such that multiplication by g^{-1} is a compact operator from H^1 to L^2. Then there exists a sequence of eigenvalues for the equation

$$-\Delta u(x) + g(x)^2 u(x) = \lambda u(x), \quad x \in \mathbb{R}^n, \tag{5.3}$$

satisfying

$$0 < \lambda_0 < \lambda_1 < \cdots < \lambda_k < \cdots. \tag{5.4}$$

Let $f(x,t)$ be a Carathéodory function satisfying Hypothesis (A). Assume that

$$\begin{gathered} H(x,t) := 2F(x,t) - tf(x,t) \geq -W_1(x) \in L^1, \quad x \in \mathbb{R}^n,\ t \in \mathbb{R}, \\ H(x,t) \longrightarrow \infty \quad \text{a.e. as } |t| \longrightarrow \infty, \end{gathered} \tag{5.5}$$

where

$$F(x,t) := \int_0^t f(x,s)ds. \tag{5.6}$$

Assume also that for some $\ell > 0$ there are numbers a_1, a_2 such that $\alpha_\ell < a_1 \leq a_2$, and $F(x,t)$ satisfies (4.4). Then

$$-\Delta u(x) + g(x)^2 u(x) = f(x,u(x)), \quad x \in \mathbb{R}^n, \tag{5.7}$$

has at least one solution.

Remark 5.3. Sufficient conditions on $g(x)$ which guarantee that multiplication by g^{-1} is compact are given in [7]. The following is sufficient:

$$\mu\{x \in B_1(y) : g(x) < m\} \longrightarrow 0 \quad \text{as } |y| \longrightarrow \infty \tag{5.8}$$

for each $m > 0$. Here μ is the Lebesgue measure and $B_1(y)$ is the ball in $\mathbb{R}^n$ of radius 1 and center y.

This theorem generalizes results of several authors, including [2–6], with various conditions on the function $g(x)$ to insure that the spectrum of (5.3) is discrete. Most of the cited authors considered the superlinear problem.

References

[1] R. A. Adams, *Sobolev Spaces*, Academic Press, London, 1975.

[2] T. Bartsch and Z. Q. Wang, *Existence and multiplicity results for some superlinear elliptic problems on $\mathbb{R}^N$*, Communications in Partial Differential Equations **20** (1995), no. 9-10, 1725–1741.

[3] D. G. Costa, *On a class of elliptic systems in $\mathbb{R}^N$*, Electronic Journal of Differential Equations **1994** (1994), no. 7, 1–14.

[4] M. F. Furtado, L. A. Maia, and E. A. B. Silva, *On a double resonant problem in $\mathbb{R}^N$*, Differential and Integral Equations **15** (2002), no. 11, 1335–1344.

[5] W. Omana and M. Willem, *Homoclinic orbits for a class of Hamiltonian systems*, Differential and Integral Equations **5** (1992), no. 5, 1115–1120.

[6] P. H. Rabinowitz, *On a class of nonlinear Schrödinger equations*, Zeitschrift für Angewandte Mathematik und Physiks **43** (1992), no. 2, 270–291.

[7] M. Schechter, *Spectra of Partial Differential Operators*, 2nd ed., North-Holland Series in Applied Mathematics and Mechanics, vol. 14, North-Holland, Amsterdam, 1986.

[8] ———, *New saddle point theorems*, Generalized Functions and Their Applications (Varanasi, 1991), Plenum, New York, 1993, pp. 213–219.

[9] ———, *New linking theorems*, Rendiconti del Seminario Matematico della Università di Padova **99** (1998), 255–269.
[10] ———, *Linking Methods in Critical Point Theory*, Birkhäuser Boston, Massachusetts, 1999.
[11] E. A. B. Silva, *Linking theorems and applications to semilinear elliptic problems at resonance*, Nonlinear Analysis. Theary, Methods & Applications **16** (1991), no. 5, 455–477.

Martin Schechter: Department of Mathematics, University of California, Irvine, CA 92697-3875, USA
E-mail address: mschecht@math.uci.edu

REGULAR AND SINGULAR DEGENERATE BOUNDARY VALUE PROBLEMS IN BANACH-VALUED FUNCTION SPACES

VELI B. SHAKHMUROV

This study focuses on nonlocal boundary value problems (BVPs) for linear and nonlinear regular and singular degenerate differential operator equations (DOE) of second order, with varying coefficients and that contain Schrödinger-type equations. In regular degenerate case nonlocal BVPs, in singular case local BVPs are considered. Several conditions are obtained, which guarantee the maximal regularity, Fredholmness, and positivity of linear BVP in Banach-valued L_p-spaces. Then by using these results the maximal regularity of parabolic nonlocal initial boundary value problems (IBVP) and the existence and uniqueness of solution of nonlinear nonlocal BVPs are shown.

1. Statement of problems

Consider the following nonlocal BVPs for degenerate elliptic DOE:

$$\begin{gathered}\sum_{k=1}^{n} a_k(x)D_k^{[2]}u(x)+A_\lambda(x)u(x)+\sum_{k=1}^{n} A_k(x)D_k^{[1]}u(x)=f(x),\quad x\in G\subset R^n,\\ L_{kj}u=\left[\alpha_{kj}u^{[m_{kj}]}(G_{k0})+\beta_{kj}u^{(m_{kj})}(G_{kb})\right]+\sum_{i=1}^{N_{kj}}\delta_{kji}u^{[m_{kj}]}(G_{ki})=0,\\ j=1,2,\ k=1,2,\dots,n;\end{gathered}\tag{1.1}$$

nonlocal IBVP parabolic problem

$$\begin{gathered}\frac{\partial u(t,x)}{\partial t}+\sum_{k=1}^{n} a_k(x)D_k^{[2]}u(t,x)+A_\lambda(x)u(t,x)+\sum_{k=1}^{n} A_k(x)D_k^{[1]}u(x)=f(t,x),\\ L_{kj}u=\left[\alpha_{kj}u^{[m_{kj}]}(t,G_{k0})+\beta_{kj}u^{[m]_{kj}}(t,G_{kb})\right]+\sum_{i=1}^{N_{kj}}\delta_{kji}u^{[m_{kj}]}(t,G_{ki})\\ =0,\quad u(0,x)=0,\ j=1,2,\ k=1,2,\dots,n,\ t\in R_+,\ x\in G\subset R^n;\end{gathered}\tag{1.2}$$

Hindawi Publishing Corporation
Proceedings of the Conference on Differential & Difference Equations and Applications, pp. 1009–1018

and nonlinear nonlocal BVP

$$\sum_{k=1}^{n} a_k(x)D_k^{[2]}u(x) + A_\lambda(x)u(x) + \sum_{\sigma} A\left(x, D^{[\sigma]}u\right) = F\left(x, D^{[\sigma]}u\right), \quad x \in G \subset R^n,$$
$$L_{kj}u = \left[\alpha_{kj}u^{[m]_{kj}}(G_{k0}) + \beta_{kj}u^{[m_{kj}]}(G_{kb})\right] + \sum_{i=1}^{N_{kj}} \delta_{kji}u^{[m_{kj}]}(G_{ki}) = 0, \tag{1.3}$$
$$j = 1,2,\ k = 1,2,\ldots,n,$$

where

$$G = \{x = (x_1, x_2, \ldots, x_n),\ 0 < x_k < b_k\}, \qquad G_+ = R_+ \times G,$$
$$G_{k0} = (x_1, x_2, \ldots, x_{k-1}, 0, x_{k+1}, \ldots, x_n), \qquad \sigma = (\sigma_1, \sigma_2, \ldots, \sigma_n),$$
$$D^\sigma = D_k^{\sigma_k}, \quad \sigma_k = 0,1, \qquad G_{kb} = (x_1, x_2, \ldots, x_{k-1}, b_k, x_{k+1}, \ldots, x_n),$$
$$G_{ki} = (x_1, x_2, \ldots, x_{k-1}, x_{ki}, x_{k+1}, \ldots, x_n), \qquad \gamma_k(G_{k0}) = 0, \qquad \int_0^{b_k} \gamma_k^{-1}(z)dz < \infty, \tag{1.4}$$
$$m_k \in \{0,1\}, \qquad D_k^2 = \frac{\partial^2}{\partial x_k^2}, \quad k = 1,2,\ldots,n, \qquad A_\lambda(x) = A(x) + \lambda;$$

α_{jk}, β_{jk}, δ_{jki} are complex numbers, a_k are real-valued function on G and $A(x)$, $A_k(x)$ for $x, y \in G$ are possible unbounded operators in E, and $D_k^{[i]}u(x) = (\gamma_k(x_k)(d/dx))^i u(x)$, $0 \le \nu_k \le m - 1$.

In the singular degenerate case, that is, for $\int_0^{b_k} \gamma_k^{-1}(z)dz = \infty$ we consider BVPs of type (1.1) in which we do not contain degenerate lines G_{k0}. Let B denote a realization operator of BVP (1.1) in $L_p(G;E)$.

We say that the degenerate elliptic BVP (1.1) is a maximal L_p-regular, if for all $f \in L_p(G;E)$ there exists a unique solution $u \in W_{p,\gamma}^{[2]}(G;E(A),E)$ of the problem (1.1) satisfying this problem almost everywhere and there exists a positive constant C independent on f, such that has the following estimate:

$$\sum_{k=1}^{n} \left\|D_k^{[2]}u\right\|_{L_p(G;E)} + \|Au\|_{L_p(G;E)} \le C\|f\|_{L_p(G;E)}. \tag{1.5}$$

We say that the parabolic problem (1.2) is a maximal L_p-regular, if for all $f \in L_p(G_+;E)$ there exists a unique solution u satisfying the problem (1.2) almost everywhere and there exists a positive constant C independent on f, such that

$$\left\|\frac{\partial u(t,x)}{\partial t}\right\|_{L_p(G_+;E)} + \|Bu\|_{L_p(G_+;E)} \le C\|f\|_{L_p(G_+;E)}. \tag{1.6}$$

2. Maximal regularity for nonhomogeneous BVPs

In a Banach space E consider the following degenerate nonlocal boundary value problem with parameter:

$$Lu = -tu^{[2]}(x) + Au(x) + B_1(x)u^{[1]}(x) + B_2(x)u(x) = f(x), \quad x \in (0,1), \tag{2.1}$$

$$\begin{aligned} L_1 u &= \alpha_0 t^{\theta_1} u^{[m_1]}(0) + \sum_{j=1}^{M_1} t^{\eta_j} T_{1j} u(x_{1j}) = f_1, \\ L_2 u &= \beta_0 t^{\theta_2} u^{[m_2]}(1) + \sum_{j=1}^{M_2} t^{\eta_j} T_{2j} u(x_{2j}) = f_2, \end{aligned} \tag{2.2}$$

where $x_{kj} \in [0,1]$, $\eta_j = 1/2p(1-\nu)$ when $x_{kj} = 0$, and $\eta_j = 1/2p$ when $x_{kj} \neq 0$, moreover

$$\begin{gathered} \theta_1 = \frac{pm_1(1-\nu)+1}{2p(1-\nu)}, \quad \theta_2 = \frac{pm_2+1}{2p}, \quad u^{[i]} = \left(x^\nu \frac{d}{dx}\right)^i u(x), \\ \nu \geq 0, \ m_k \in \{0,1\}, \ k = 1,2; \end{gathered} \tag{2.3}$$

α_0, β_0 are complex numbers, t is a small parameter, and $f_k \in E_k = (E(A),E)_{\theta_k,p}$, $k = 1,2$, where A, $B_k(x)$ for $x \in [0,1]$, and T_{kj} are possible unbounded operators in E.

The function u that belongs to a space

$$\begin{aligned} W_{p,\nu}^{[2]}(0,1;E(A),E) &= \{u;\ u \in L_p(0,1;E(A)),\ u^{[2]} \in L_p(0,1;E)\}, \\ \|u\|_{W_{p,\nu}^{[2]}(0.1;E(A),E)} &= \{\|Au\|_{L_p(0,1);E} + \|u^{[2]}\|_{L_p(0,1;E)} < \infty\} \end{aligned} \tag{2.4}$$

and satisfies (2.1) a.e. on $(0,1)$ is said to be solution of (2.1).

Let

$$W_{p,\nu}^{[2]}(0,1;E(A),E,L_k) = \{u;\ u \in W_{p,\nu}^{[2]}(0,1;E(A),E),\ L_k u = 0,\ k = 1,2\}. \tag{2.5}$$

Consider the following BVP:

$$Lu = -tu^{[2]}(x) + Au(x) = f(x), \quad x \in (0,1), \tag{2.6}$$

$$\begin{aligned} L_1 u &= \alpha_0 t^{\theta_1} u^{[m_1]}(0) + \sum_{j=1}^{M_1} t^{\eta_j} T_{1j} u(x_{1j}) = f_1, \\ L_2 u &= \beta_0 t^{\theta_2} u^{[m_2]}(1) + \sum_{j=1}^{M_2} t^{\eta_j} T_{2j} u(x_{2j}) = f_2. \end{aligned} \tag{2.7}$$

The following results are obtained.

THEOREM 2.1. *Let E be a Banach space that satisfies the multiplier condition with respect to p and weighted function $\gamma = y^{\nu/(1-\nu)}$, $0 \leq \nu < 1 - 1/p$, let A be an R-positive operator in E for $\varphi \in (0,\pi]$, $0 < t \leq t_0 < \infty$ and $\alpha_0 \neq 0$, $\beta_0 \neq 0$.*

Then the operator $u \to D_0(\lambda,t)u = \{L_0(\lambda,t)u, L_{10}u, L_{20}u\}$ *for* $|\arg\lambda| \le \pi - \varphi$ *and for sufficiently large* $|\lambda|$ *is an isomorphism from* $W_{p,\nu}^{[2]}(0,1;E(A),E)$ *onto* $L_p(0,1;E) + E_1 + E_2$ *and the coercive uniform estimate for the solution of (2.6)-(2.7)*

$$|\lambda| \|u\|_{L_p(0,1;E)} + \left\| tu^{[2]} \right\|_{L_p(0,1:E)} + \|Au\|_{L_p(0,1:E)} \le C\Big[\|f\|_{L_p(0,1:E)} + \sum_{k=1}^{2} \left(\|f_k\|_{E_k} + |\lambda|^{1-\theta_k} \|f_k\|_E \right) \Big] \tag{2.8}$$

holds with respect to parameters λ *and* t.

3. Coerciveness on the space variable and Fredholmness

Theorem 3.1. *Let all conditions of Theorem 2.1 be satisfied and* $A^{-1} \in \sigma(E)$. *Moreover, suppose*

(1) *for any* $\varepsilon > 0$ *and for almost all* $x \in [0,1]$,

$$\begin{aligned} \|B_1(x)u\| &\le \varepsilon \|u\|_{(E(A),E)_{1/2,1}} + C(\varepsilon)\|u\|, \quad u \in (E(A),E)_{1/2,1}, \\ \|B_2(x)u\| &\le \varepsilon \|Au\| + C(\varepsilon)\|u\|, \quad u \in D(A), \end{aligned} \tag{3.1}$$

for $u \in (E(A),E)_{1/2,1}$ *the function* $B_1(x)u$ *and for* $u \in D(A)$ *the function* $B_2(x)u$ *are measurable on* $[0,1]$ *in E;*

(2) *if* $m_k = 0$, *then* $T_{kj} = 0$; *if* $m_k = 1$, *then for* $u \in (E(A),E)_{\sigma,p}$ *and* $\varepsilon > 0$,

$$\|T_{kj}u\|_{(E(A),E)_{1/2+\sigma,p}} \le \varepsilon \|u\|_{(E(A),E)_{\sigma,p}} + C(\varepsilon)\|u\|, \tag{3.2}$$

where $\sigma = 1/2p(1-\nu)$, *if* $x_{kj} = 0$, $\sigma = 1/2p$ *if* $x_{kj} \ne 0$.

Then

(a) *the coercive uniform estimate for the solution of (2.1)-(2.2)*

$$\left\| tu^{[2]} \right\|_{L_p(0,1:E)} + \|Au\|_{L_p(0,1:E)} \le C\Big[\|Lu\|_{L_p(0,1;E)} + \sum_{k=1}^{2} \|L_k u\|_{(E(A),E)\theta_k,p} + \|u\|_{L_p(0,1;E)} \Big] \tag{3.3}$$

holds with respect to the parameter t;

(b) *the operator* $u \to D(t)u = \{Lu, L_1u, L_2u\}$ *from* $W_{p,\nu}^{[2]}(0,1;E(A),E)$ *into* $L_p(0,1;E) + (E(A),E)_{\theta_1} + (E(A),E)_{\theta_2}$ *is bounded and Fredholm.*

4. Maximal regularity for regular degenerate nonlocal BVPs

Let us now consider a nonlocal BVP for ordinary DOE

$$(L+\lambda)u = au^{[2]}(x) + A_\lambda u(x) = f(x), \quad x \in (0,b), \tag{4.1}$$

$$L_k u = \alpha_k u^{[m_k]}(0) + \beta_k u^{[m_k]}(b) + \sum_{j=1}^{N_k} \delta_{kj} u^{[m_k]}(x_{kj}) = 0, \quad k = 1,2, \tag{4.2}$$

where $D^{[i]}u(x) = (\gamma(x)(d/dx))^i u(x)$, $m_k \in \{0,1\}$; a, α_k, β_k, δ_{kj} are complex numbers and $x_{kj} \in (0,b)$; A is a possible unbounded operator in E. Let ω_j, $j = 1,2$, be roots of an equation $a\omega^2 + 1 = 0$.

Condition 4.1. Let A be a positive operator in a Banach space E for $\varphi \in (0,\pi/2)$, $a \neq 0$, and $|\arg\omega_1 - \pi| \leq \pi/2 - \varphi$, $|\arg\omega_2| \leq \pi/2 - \varphi$, $\eta = (-1)^{m_1}\alpha_1\beta_2 - (-1)^{m_2}\alpha_2\beta_1 \neq 0$; and $\gamma \in C([0,1]) \cap C^2(0,1)$, $\int_0^1 \gamma^{-1}(z)dz < \infty$, for $0 < y_1 \leq y_2 \leq 1$, there exist the positive constants C_k, $k = 1,2,3$, such that

$$\gamma(y_1) \leq C_1\gamma(y_2),$$

$$\gamma^{1/p}(y_2)\gamma^{-1/p}(y_1) \leq C_2 \left| \left[\int_0^{y_2} \gamma^{-1}(z)dz\right]^\nu \left[\int_0^{y_1} \gamma^{-1}(z)dz\right]^{-\nu} \right|,$$

$$\left|\gamma^{1/p}(y_2)\gamma^{-1/p}(y_1) - 1\right| \leq C_3 \left| \left[\int_0^{y_2} \gamma^{-1}(z)dz\right]^\nu \left[\int_0^{y_1} \gamma^{-1}(z)dz\right]^{-\nu} - 1 \right|, \quad 0 \leq \nu < 1 - \frac{1}{p}. \tag{4.3}$$

THEOREM 4.2. *Let Condition 4.1 be satisfied for $\varphi \in (0,\pi/3)$. Let E be a Banach space satisfying the multiplier condition with respect to $p \in (1,\infty)$ and A is an R-positive operator in E. Then for all $f \in L_p(0,b;E)$ there exists a unique solution $u \in W_p^{[2]}(0,b;E(A),E)$ of the problem (4.1)-(4.2) and the coercive uniform estimate for the solution of (4.1)-(4.2)*

$$\sum_{j=0}^{2} |\lambda|^{1-j/2} \left\| u^{[j]} \right\|_{L_p} + \|Au\|_{L_p} \leq C\|f\|_{L_p} \tag{4.4}$$

holds with respect to parameter λ.

Remark 4.3. If a is a real negative number, then part (2) of Condition 4.1 is satisfied for $0 < \varphi \leq \pi$ and Theorems 2.1, 3.1 are valid for $0 < \varphi \leq \pi$.

5. Regular degenerate partial DOE

5.1. Regular degenerate partial DOE with constant coefficients

$$\sum_{k=1}^{n} a_k D_k^{[2]} u(x) + A_\lambda u(x) = f(x), \quad x \in G, \tag{5.1}$$

$$L_{kj}u = \left[\alpha_{kj}u^{[m_{kj}]}(G_{k0}) + \beta_{kj}u^{[m_{kj}]}(G_{kb})\right] + \sum_{i=1}^{N_{kj}} \delta_{kji}u^{[m_{kj}]}(G_{ki}) = 0, \quad j = 1,2, \tag{5.2}$$

$\alpha_k, \beta_k, \delta_{kj}$ are complex numbers, a_k are complex numbers, and A is a possible unbounded operator in E.

Let ω_{kj}, $j = 1,2$, $k = 1,2,\dots,n$, be roots of $a_k\omega^2 + 1 = 0$.

Condition 5.1. Let the following conditions be satisfied:

(1) E is a Banach space satisfying multiplier condition with respect to $p \in (1,\infty)$;

(2) $a_k \neq 0$, and $|\arg\omega_{k1} - \pi| \leq \pi/2 - \varphi$, $|\arg\omega_{k2}| \leq \pi/2 - \varphi$ for $\varphi \in (0,\pi/3)$;

(3) $\eta_k = (-1)^{m_1}\alpha_{k1}\beta_{k2} - (-1)^{m_2}\alpha_{k2}\beta_{k1} \neq 0$, $k = 1,2,\dots,n$;

(4) $\gamma_k \in C([0,b_k]) \cap C^2(0,b_k)$, $\int_0^{b_k}\gamma_k^{-1}(z)dz < \infty$, for $0 < y_1 \leq y_2 \leq b_k$, there exist the positive constants C_j, $j = 1,2,3$, such that

$$\gamma(y_{1k}) \leq C_1\gamma(y_{2k}),$$

$$\gamma_k^{1/p}(y_{2k})\gamma_k^{-1/p}(y_{1k}) \leq C_2\left|\left[\int_0^{y_{2k}}\gamma_k^{-1}(z)dz\right]^{\nu_k}\left[\int_0^{y_{1k}}\gamma^{-1}(z)dz\right]^{-\nu_k}\right|,$$

$$\left|\gamma_k^{1/p}(y_{2k})\gamma_k^{-1/p}(y_{1k}) - 1\right| \leq C_3\left|\left[\int_0^{y_{2k}}\gamma_k^{-1}(z)dz\right]^{\nu_k}\left[\int_0^{y_{1k}}\gamma_k^{-1}(z)dz\right]^{-\nu_k} - 1\right|, \tag{5.3}$$

$$0 \leq \nu_k < 1 - \frac{1}{p}.$$

Theorem 5.2. *Let Condition 5.1 be satisfied and A is an R-positive operator in E. Then*

(a) *the problem (5.1)-(5.2) for $f \in L_p(G;E)$, $\lambda \in S(\varphi)$, and for sufficiently large $|\lambda|$, has a unique solution that belongs to the space $W_{p,\gamma}^{[2]}(G;E(A),E)$ and the coercive uniform estimate for the solution of (5.1)-(5.2)*

$$\sum_{k=1}^{n}\sum_{i=0}^{2}(1+|\lambda|)^{1-i/2}\left\|D_k^{[i]}u\right\|_{L_p(G;E)} + \|Au\|_{L_p(G;E)} \leq M\|f\|_{L_p(G;E)} \tag{5.4}$$

holds with respect to parameter λ;

(b) *the realization operator L_0 that generated by BVP (5.1)-(5.2) is positive in $L_p(G;E)$.*

5.2. Regular degenerate partial DOE with variable coefficients. Consider the boundary value problem (1.1). By using localization arguments as in [2] and Theorem 5.2, we obtain the following.

Theorem 5.3. *Let Condition 5.1 be satisfied for all $x \in G$ and*

(1) *$A(x)$ is an R-positive in E uniformly with respect to x and $A(G_{0k}) = A(G_{bk})$, $a_k(x)$ are continuous functions on $\bar{G}$ such that $a_k(G_{j0}) = a_k(G_{jb})$, $k,j = 1,2,\dots,n$;*

(2) *$A(x)A^{-1}(x^0) \in C(G;B(E))$ and for any $\varepsilon > 0$, for a.e. $x \in G$ and for $u \in (E(A),E)_{1/2,\infty}$,*

$$\|A_k(x)u\| \leq \varepsilon\|u\|_{(E(A),E)_{1/2,\infty}} + C(\varepsilon)\|u\|. \tag{5.5}$$

Then

(a) *the problem (1.1) for $f \in L_p(G;E)$, $\lambda \in S(\varphi)$, and for sufficiently large $|\lambda|$, has a unique solution that belongs to the space $W^{[2]}_{p,\gamma}(G;E(A),E)$ and the coercive uniform estimate for the solution of (1.1)*

$$\sum_{k=1}^{n}\sum_{i=0}^{2}(1+|\lambda|)^{1-i/2}\left\|D_k^{[i]}u\right\|_{L_p(G;E)}+\|Au\|_{L_p(G;E)}\leq M\|f\|_{L_p(G;E)} \tag{5.6}$$

holds with respect to parameter λ;

(b) *the operator O generated by BVP (1.1) is positive in $L_p(G;E)$.*

Result 5.4. Theorem 5.3 implies that the differential operator O has a resolvent operator $(O+\lambda I)^{-1}$ for $\lambda \in S(\varphi)$, $\varphi \in (0,\pi/3)$, and the estimate holds

$$\sum_{k=1}^{n}\sum_{i=0}^{2}|\lambda|^{1-i/2}\left\|D_k^{[i]}(O+\lambda I)^{-1}\right\|_{B(L_p(G;E))}+\left\|A(O+\lambda I)^{-1}\right\|_{B(L_p(G;E))}\leq C. \tag{5.7}$$

Theorem 5.5. *Let all conditions of Theorem 5.3 hold and $A^{-1} \in \sigma_\infty(E)$. Then the operator O from $W^{[2]}_{p,\gamma}(G;E(A),E)$ into $L_p(G;E)$ is Fredholm.*

Proof. Theorem 5.3 implies that the operator $O+\lambda I$ sufficiently large $|\lambda|$ has a bounded inverse $(O+\lambda I)^{-1}$ from $L_p(G;E)$ to $W^{[2]}_{p,\gamma}(G;E(A),E)$, that is, the operator $O+\lambda I$ is Fredholm from $W^{[2]}_{p,\gamma}(G;E(A),E)$ into $L_p(G;E)$. Moreover, by virtue of Remark 1, Theorem A_2 and the perturbation theory [1] we obtain that the operator O is Fredholm from $W^{[2]}_{p,\gamma}(G;E(A),E)$ into $L_p(G;E)$. □

Remark 5.6. If a_k are negative-valued functions, then part (2) of Condition 5.1 is satisfied for $0<\varphi\leq\pi$ and Theorems 5.2–5.5 are valid for $0<\varphi\leq\pi$.

Remark 5.7. Conditions $a_k(G_{j0}) = a_k(G_{jb})$, $A(G_{k0}) = A(G_{kb})$ arise due to nonlocality of the boundary conditions (1.1). If boundary conditions are local, then conditions mentioned above are not required anymore.

6. IBVP for parabolic DOE

By applying Theorem 5.2 and using [3, Theorem 4.2] we obtain the following.

Theorem 6.1. *Let all conditions of Theorem 5.3 hold. Then the parabolic problem (1.2) for $\lambda \in S(\varphi_0)$, $\varphi < \varphi_0 \in (0,\pi/3)$, and sufficiently large $|\lambda|$ is maximal L_p-regular.*

Result 6.2. (a) If we put $a_k(x) = -1$, $A_k(x) = 0$, $k = 1,2,\ldots,n$, in (1.1), then we obtain from Theorem 5.2 the maximal regularity, R-positivity and Fredholmness of Schrödinger-type operator

$$S_1u = -\Delta u(x) + A(x)u(x) \tag{6.1}$$

with nonlocal boundary conditions in Banach-valued $L_p(G;E)$ space.

(b) If we put $a_k(x) = -i$, $A_k(x) = 0$, $k = 1,2,\ldots,n$, in (1.2), then we obtain from Theorem 5.5 the maximal regularity of Schrödinger-type operator

$$S_2 u = \frac{\partial u(x,t)}{\partial t} - i\Delta u(x,t) + A(x)u(x,t) \tag{6.2}$$

with nonlocal boundary conditions in $L_p(G_+;E)$ space.

7. BVP for nonlinear DOE

Let us consider the nonlinear BVP (1.3). We denote $L_p(G;E)$ and $W_{p,\gamma}^{[2]}(G;E(A),E)$ by X and Y, respectively. Moreover, we let

$$\begin{aligned} &A(x,u) = A_0(x), \quad G_k = (0,b_1)\times\cdots(0,b_{k-1})\times(0,b_{k+1})\times\cdots\times(0,b_n),\\ &B_{kj} = \left(W_{p,\gamma}^{[2]}(G_k,E(A),E),\quad L_p(G_k;E)\right)_{\eta_{kj}}, \quad \eta_{kj} = \frac{j+1/p}{2},\\ &Y_0 = \left\{u : u \in W_{p,\gamma}^{[2]}(G;E(A),E),\ L_{kj}u = 0\right\},\\ &\sigma = (\sigma_1,\sigma_2,\ldots,\sigma_n), \quad D^\sigma = \{D_k^{\sigma_k}\}, \quad \sigma_k = 0,1,\\ &B_0 = \prod B_{kj}, \quad j = 0,1, \quad k = 1,2,\ldots,n. \end{aligned} \tag{7.1}$$

Condition 7.1. Let the following conditions be satisfied:

(1) E is a Banach space satisfying the multiplier condition with respect to $p \in (1,\infty)$. Suppose there exist $h_{kj} \in B_{kj}$, such that the operator $A(x) = A(x,H)$ for $H = \{h_{kj}\}$ is R-positive in E uniformly with respect to $x \in G$;

(2) $a_k \neq 0$, $a_k(x)$ are continuous functions on $\bar{G}$ such that $a_k(G_{j0}) = a_k(G_{jb})$, $k,j = 1,2,\ldots,n$, and $|\arg\omega_{k1} - \pi| \le \pi/2 - \varphi$, $|\arg\omega_{k2}| \le \pi/2 - \varphi$ for $\varphi \in (0,\pi/3)$ for all $x \in G$;

(3) $\eta_k(x) \neq 0$, $k = 1,2,\ldots,n$, for all $x \in G$;

(4) $A(x)A^{-1}(x^0) \in C(G;B(E))$, $A(G_{0k}) = A(G_{bk})$, and for $u \in_{(E(A),E)_{1/2,1}}$,

$$||A_\alpha(x)u|| \le \varepsilon\|u\|_{(E(A),E)_{|\alpha:l|,1}} + C(\varepsilon)\|u\|; \tag{7.2}$$

(5) $A(x,U)$ for $x \in G$, $U = \{u_{kj}\} \in B_0$, $u_{kj} \in B_{kj}$ is a φ-positive operator in a Banach space E for $\varphi \in (0,\pi/2)$, where domain definition $D(A(x,U))$ does not depend on x,U and $A : G\times B_0 \to B(E(A),E)$ is continuous. Moreover, for each $R > 0$ there is a constant $L(R) > 0$ such that

$$||[A(x,U) - A(x,\bar{U})]v||_E \le L(R)||U-\bar{U}||_{B_0}\|Av\|_E \tag{7.3}$$

for $x \in G$, $U,\bar{U} \in B_0$, $\bar{U} = \{\bar{u}_{kj}\}$, $\bar{u}_{kj} \in B_{kj}$, $\|U\|_{B_0}$, $\|\bar{U}\|_{B_0} \le R$;

(6) $f(\cdot) = F(\cdot,0) \in L_p(G;E)$; the function $F : G\times B_0 \to E$ such that $F(\cdot,U)$ is measurable for each $U \in B_0$ and $F(x,\cdot)$ is continuous for a.a. $x \in G$. Moreover, $\|F(x,U) - F(x,\bar{U})\|_E \le \varphi_R(x)\|U-\bar{U}\|_{B_0}$ for a.a. $x \in G$, $U,\bar{U} \in B_0$ and $\|U\|_{B_0}$, $\|\bar{U}\|_{B_0} \le R$.

Theorem 7.2. *Let Condition 7.1 be held. Then the problem (1.3) has a unique solution that belongs to space $W_{p,\gamma}^{[2]}(G;E(A),E)$.*

8. BVP for singular degenerate partial DOE

Consider the BVP

$$\sum_{k=1}^{n} a_k D_k^{[2]} u(x) + A_\lambda(x)u(x) + \sum_{k=1}^{n} A_k(x) D_k^{[1]} u(x) = f(x), \quad x \in G \subset R^n,$$
$$L_{kj}u = \beta_{kj} u^{(m_{kj})}(G_{kb}) + \sum_{i=1}^{N_{kj}} \delta_{kji} u^{[m_{kj}]}(G_{ki}) = 0, \quad j \le 2,\ k = 1,2,\ldots,n, \tag{8.1}$$

where α_{jk}, β_{jk}, δ_{jki} are complex numbers, a_k are complex numbers, and $A(x)$, $A_k(x)$ for $x, y \in G$ are, generally speaking, unbounded operators in E and

$$D_k^{[i]} u(x) = \left(\gamma_k(x_k)\frac{d}{dx}\right)^i u(x), \quad \gamma_k(0) = 0,$$
$$\int_0^{b_k} \gamma_k^{-1}(z)\,dz = \infty, \quad 0 \le \nu_k \le m - 1. \tag{8.2}$$

Condition 8.1. Let the following conditions be satisfied:

(1) E is a Banach space satisfying multiplier condition with respect to $p \in (1,\infty)$;
(2) $a_k \neq 0$, and $|\arg\omega_{k1} - \pi| \le \pi/2 - \varphi$, $|\arg\omega_{k2}| \le \pi/2 - \varphi$ for $\varphi \in (0,\pi/3)$;
(3) $\eta_k = (-1)^{m_1}\alpha_{k1}\beta_{k2} - (-1)^{m_2}\alpha_{k2}\beta_{k1} \neq 0$, $k = 1,2,\ldots,n$;
(4) $\gamma_k \in C([0,b_k]) \cap C^2(0,b_k)$, for $0 < y_1 \le y_2 \le b_k$, there exist the positive constants C_j, $j = 1$, β_k, and δ_k such that

$$\gamma(y_{1k}) \le C_1 \gamma(y_{2k}),$$
$$\gamma_k(y_{2k})\gamma_k^{-1}(y_{1k}) \le C_2\left[\delta_k \int_{y_{1k}}^{y_{2k}} \gamma_k^{-1}(z)\,dz\right] \left|\gamma_k^{1/p}(y_{2k})\gamma_k^{-1/p}(y_{1k}) - 1\right| \le g_k\left(\int_{y_{1k}}^{y_{2k}} \gamma_k^{-1}(z)\,dz\right), \tag{8.3}$$

where g_k such nonnegative functions that

$$\int_{-\infty}^{\infty} \exp\left[-\beta_k |z|\right] g_k(z)|z|^{-1}\,dz < \infty. \tag{8.4}$$

THEOREM 8.2. *Let Condition 8.1 be satisfied and A is an R-positive operator in E. Then*

(a) *the BVPs (8.1) for $f \in L_p(G;E)$ and for sufficiently large $|\lambda|$ has a unique solution that belongs to the space $W_{p,\gamma}^{[2]}(G;E(A),E)$ and the coercive uniform estimate for the solution of (8.1)*

$$\sum_{k=1}^{n}\sum_{i=0}^{2}(1+|\lambda|)^{1-i/2}\left\|D_k^{[i]}u\right\|_{L_p(G;E)} + \|Au\|_{L_p(G;E)} \le M\|f\|_{L_p(G;E)} \tag{8.5}$$

holds with respect to parameter λ;

(b) *the realization operator L_0 that generated by BVP (8.1) is positive in $L_p(G;E)$.*

References

[1] V. B. Shakhmurov, *Imbedding theorems for abstract function- spaces and their applications*, Mathematics of the USSR Sbornik **134** (1987), no. 1-2, 261–276.
[2] ______, *Embedding theorems and their applications to degenerate equations*, Differential Equations **24** (1988), no. 4, 475–482.
[3] ______, *Coercive boundary value problems for regular degenerate differential-operator equations*, Journal of Mathematical Analysis and Applications **292** (2004), no. 2, 605–620.

Veli B. Shakhmurov: Department of Electrical-Electronics Engineering, Engineering Faculty, Istanbul University, Avcilar 34320, Istanbul, Turkey
E-mail address: sahmurov@istanbul.edu.tr

EXISTENCE RESULTS FOR EVOLUTION INCLUSIONS IN BANACH SPACES

VASILE STAICU

We survey some new results obtained recently in joint papers with S. Aizicovici and N. S. Papageorgiou, concerning the existence of integral solutions for nonlocal Cauchy problem and for the periodic problem to evolution inclusions in Banach spaces.

1. Introduction

In this paper we study the existence of integral solutions for the nonlocal Cauchy problem

$$u'(t) \in -Au(t) + F(t,u(t)), \quad t \in [0,b];\ u(0) = g(u), \tag{1.1}$$

and for the periodic problem

$$-u'(t) \in Au(t) + F(t,u(t)), \quad t \in [0,b];\ u(0) = u(b), \tag{1.2}$$

where $A : D(A) \subset X \to X$ is an m-accretive operator, $F : T \times X \to 2^X$ is a multivalued map, and $g : C(I;\overline{D(A)}) \to \overline{D(A)}$.

The study of nonlocal initial value problems in Banach spaces was initiated by Byszewski [14], who considered an equation of the form (1.1) with A linear, F single valued, and g of a special structure. Results on fully nonlinear abstract nonlocal Cauchy problem have been obtained in [2–4] and very recently in [24]. These papers are primarily concerned with equations governed by accretive operators and single-valued perturbations. To our knowledge, the only existing result for (1.1) with A nonlinear and F multivalued was obtained in [4], where F is supposed to be closed-valued and lower semicontinuous in its second variable. On the other hand, finite-dimensional versions of (1.1) (with $A = 0$) appear in [12, 18], while abstract semilinear evolution inclusions with nonlocal initial conditions have been considered in [1, 9–11]. In particular, in [1], the problem (1.1) is analyzed under the assumption that $-A$ is the infinitesimal generator

Hindawi Publishing Corporation
Proceedings of the Conference on Differential & Difference Equations and Applications, pp. 1019–1027

of a linear C_0-semigroup on X, F is closed, convex-valued, and upper semicontinuous in its second argument, and g is an integral operator. Our result for problem (1.1) complements [4] by allowing F to be upper semicontinuous in its second variable (as opposed to lower semicontinuous) and also generalizes the theory of [1] to the case when A is fully nonlinear.

The periodic problem (1.2) has been studied by many authors, mainly the case when the perturbation is a single-valued map. A common approach is to impose conditions on the perturbation term strong enough in order to guarantee the uniqueness of solutions of a related Cauchy problem and then to apply some of the classical fixed point theorems to the corresponding Poincaré map. The first result in this direction is due to Browder [13], who considered the case when A is a linear, time-dependent, monotone operator in a Hilbert space. The next major result on periodic solutions for semilinear evolution equations can be traced in the work of Pruss [22], who considered the case when the linear operator $-A$ generates a compact semigroup and $F: T \times D \to X$ is continuous and such that $A+F$ satisfies a Nagumo-type tangential condition. Subsequently, Becker [8] considered the case in which $-A$ generates a compact semigroup, and satisfies an extra condition (which amounts to saying that $A - \lambda I$ is m-accretive for some $\lambda > 0$). The first fully nonlinear existence results for the periodic problem (1.2) with F single-valued were obtained by Vrabie [23] and Hirano [19]. Vrabie's result can be viewed as an extension of Becker's result to general Banach spaces and to fully nonlinear operators A and F. Hirano, on the other hand, improved Vrabie's result to the specific case in which A is the subdifferential of a lower semicontinuous convex and proper function acting on a real Hilbert space. Cascaval and Vrabie [15] extended Hirano's result to the case when A is m-accretive and $-A$ generates a compact semigroup in a Hilbert space. A usual assumption to get existence of solutions for the periodic problem is a kind of coercivity condition relating A and F. Nonlinear periodic problems with a multivalued perturbation were studied by many authors within the framework of evolution triples. Bader's paper [5] considered semilinear problems and extended to evolution inclusions some of the results of Pruss, while the work of Hu and Papageorgiou [20] is related to the papers of Vrabie and Hirano. Recently, Bader and Papageorgiou [6] and Hu and Papageorgiou [21] studied the existence of strong solutions for the periodic problem for nonlinear evolution inclusions of subdifferential type in Hilbert spaces.

For the nonlinear periodic evolution inclusion (1.2), we proved three existence results in the broader framework of reflexive Banach spaces and m-accretive operators using the notion of integral solution. The first one deals with the case when the multivalued nonlinearity $F(t,u)$ is convex-valued, the second one with the case when $F(t,u)$ is nonconvex-valued, and finally the third existence result is for the case when $F(t,u)$ is replaced by $\operatorname{ext} F(t,u)$, the set of extreme points of $F(t,u)$. We emphasize that with the exception of the third theorem, we do not impose any strong accretivity restriction on A. Also, as compared to earlier works, we do not need any condition relating A and F. The plan of the paper is as follows. In Section 2 we review some background material on multifunctions, m-accretive operators, and evolution equations. The existence result for the problem (1.1) is presented in Section 3 and the existence results for the periodic problem (1.2) are given in Section 4.

2. Preliminaries

For easy reference, in this section we present some notations, basic definitions, and facts from nonlinear operator theory and multivalued analysis, which we will need in the sequel.

Throughout this paper, X is a reflexive, separable Banach space with norm $\|\cdot\|$ and 2^X denotes the collection of all subsets of X. For $\Omega \in 2^X$, we denote by $\overline{\Omega}$ the closure of a set Ω. Let X^* be the dual space of X, with norm $\|\cdot\|_*$, let $\sigma(X,X^*)$ be the weak topology on X, and denote by X_w the space X endowed with the topology $\sigma(X,X^*)$. The duality pairing between X and X^* will be denoted by $\langle\cdot,\cdot\rangle$. The duality mapping $J : X \to 2^{X^*}$ is given by $J(x) := \{x^* \in X^* : x^*(x) = \|x\|^2 = \|x^*\|_*^2\}$, for all $x \in X$. The so-called upper semi-inner product on X is then defined by $\langle y,x\rangle_+ := \sup\{x^*(y) : x^* \in J(x)\}$. Recall that if X^* is uniformly convex, then J is single-valued and uniformly continuous on bounded subsets of X.

Let $A : X \to 2^X$ be a multivalued operator in X. The *domain* and the *range* of A are defined by $D(A) := \{x \in X : Ax \neq \varnothing\}$ and $R(A) := \bigcup_{x\in D(A)} Ax$, respectively. The operator A is called *m-accretive* if the following conditions are satisfied:

(i) $\langle y' - y, x' - x\rangle_+ \geq 0$, for all $x, x' \in D(A)$, $y \in Ax$, and $y' \in Ax'$;

(ii) $R(I + \lambda A) = X$, for all $\lambda > 0$, where I is the identity on X.

By a celebrated result of Crandall and Liggett [16], if A is m-accretive, then $-A$ generates a semigroup of contractions $\{S(t) : t \geq 0\}$ on $\overline{D(A)}$. If $S(t)$ maps bounded subsets of $\overline{D(A)}$ into precompact subsets of $\overline{D(A)}$, for each $t > 0$, then the semigroup $\{S(t) : t \geq 0\}$ is called a *compact semigroup*.

Let $T = [0,b]$, with $0 < b < \infty$. We denote by $C(T,X)$ the Banach space of all continuous functions $u : I \to X$ with norm. $\|u\|_\infty = \sup_{t\in T}\|u(t)\|$ and for $1 \leq p < \infty$, we denote by $L^p(T,X)$ the Banach space of (equivalence classes of) measurable functions $u : I \to X$ such that $\|u\|^p$ is Lebesgue integrable, endowed with the norm $\|u\|_p = (\int_0^T \|u(t)\|^p dt)^{1/p}$.

Let A be m-accretive operator in X. For $f \in L^1(T,X)$ we consider the evolution equation

$$u'(t) \in -Au(t) + f(t), \quad t \in I;\ u(0) = u_0, \tag{2.1}$$

whose solutions are meant in the sense of the following definition that is due to Bénilan [7].

Definition 2.1. An *integral solution* to (2.1) is a continuous function $u : I \to \overline{D(A)}$ with $u(0) = u_0$, such that, for all $x \in D(A)$, $y \in Ax$, and all $0 \leq s \leq t \leq T$,

$$\|u(t) - x\|^2 \leq \|u(s) - x\|^2 + 2\int_s^t \langle f(\tau) - y, u(\tau) - x\rangle_+ d\tau. \tag{P_f}$$

It is well known that (2.1) has a unique solution $u \in C(I,\overline{D(A)})$. Moreover, if u and v are integral solutions of (2.1) that correspond to (u_0, f) and (v_0, g), respectively, (where $u_0, v_0 \in \overline{D(A)}$ and $f, g \in L^1(T,X)$), then

$$\|u(t) - v(t)\| \leq \|u_0 - v_0\| + \int_0^t \|f(s) - g(s)\| ds. \tag{2.2}$$

Definition 2.2. Let $F : T \times X \to 2^X$ be a multivalued map. A function $u \in C(I, \overline{D(A)})$ is called an integral solution of the problem

$$\dot{x} \in -Ax + F(t,x), \quad x(0) = x_0, \tag{2.3}$$

if there exists $f \in L^1(T,X)$ with $f(t) \in F(t,u(t))$, a.e. on I, such that u is an integral solution of the corresponding problem (P_f).

The remainder of this section is devoted to a brief review of multifunctions. We denote by $\mathcal{P}_f(X)$ (resp., $\mathcal{P}_{(w)k(c)}(X)$) the collection of all nonempty closed (resp., (weakly-) compact (convex)) subsets of X. We also denote by $\mathcal{B}(X)$ the Borel σ-algebra on X. Let (Ω,Σ) be a measurable space. We are particularly interested in the case when $(\Omega,\Sigma) = (T,\mathcal{L})$, with $T = [0,b]$, $\mathcal{L}$ the σ-algebra of Lebesgue measurable subsets, as well as in the case when $(\Omega,\Sigma) = (T \times X, \mathcal{L} \otimes \mathcal{B}(X))$, where $\mathcal{L} \otimes \mathcal{B}(X)$ is the product σ-algebra on $T \times X$ generated by sets of the form $A \times B$ with $A \in \mathcal{L}$ and $B \in \mathcal{B}(X)$.

We say that a multifunction $\Phi : \Omega \to \mathcal{P}_f(X)$ is measurable if for all $x \in X$, the function $\omega \to d(x,\Phi(\omega)) = \inf\{\|x - z\| : z \in \Phi(\omega)\}$ is measurable. Recall that Φ is measurable if and only if it is graph measurable, that is, $Gr\Phi := \{(\omega,x) \in \Omega \times X : x \in \Phi(\omega)\} \in \Sigma \otimes \mathcal{B}(X)$. By $\mathcal{S}^p_\Phi$ $(1 \le p < \infty)$ we denote the set of all measurable selections of Φ that belong to the Bochner-Lebesgue space $L^p(\Omega,X)$, that is, $\mathcal{S}^p_\Phi = \{\varphi \in L^p(\Omega,X) : \varphi(t) \in \Phi(t)$, a.e. on $\Omega\}$.

By the Kuratowski-Ryll-Nardzewski theorem one has that for a measurable multifunction $\Phi : \Omega \to \mathcal{P}_f(X)$, the set $\mathcal{S}^p_\Phi$ is nonempty if and only if the function $\omega \to \inf\{\|z\| : z \in \Phi(\omega)\}$ belongs to $L^p_+(\Omega) := L^p(\Omega,\mathbb{R}^+)$. Recall that a set $K \subseteq L^p(T,X)$ is said to be *decomposable* if for all $u,v \in K$ and all $A \in \Sigma$ we have $u\chi_A + v\chi_{T/A} \in K$, where χ_A denotes the characteristic function of A. Clearly $\mathcal{S}^p_\Phi$ is decomposable.

Let now Y be a Hausdorff topological space and let $\Psi : Y \to 2^X$. The multifunction Ψ is said to be *upper semicontinuous on X* (u.s.c., for short) if the set $\Psi^+(A) := \{y \in Y : \Psi(y) \subset A\}$ is open in Y for any open subset of A of Z. Equivalently, Ψ is u.s.c. if $\Psi^-(A) := \{y \in Y : \Psi(y) \cap A \neq \varnothing\}$ is closed in Y for each closed subset C of Z. If Ψ is an upper semicontinuous, closed-valued multifunction, then Ψ is closed, that is, its graph $Gr\Psi$ is closed in $Y \times X$. Conversely, if $\Psi : Y \to \mathcal{P}(Z)$ is closed and locally compact (i.e., for each $y \in Y$, there exists a neighborhood U of y such that $\Psi(U)$ is precompact), then Ψ is u.s.c. We say that $\Psi : Y \to 2^X$ is *lower semicontinuous* (l.s.c., for short) if $\Psi^+(C)$ is closed in Y for each closed subset C of Z.

We conclude this section by recalling the notion of Hausdorff continuity for multifunctions. Let $h(\cdot,\cdot)$ be the so-called Hausdorff-Pompeiu generalized metric on $\mathcal{P}_f(X)$, defined by

$$h(A,B) = \max\left\{\sup_{a\in A}\inf_{b\in B}\|a-b\|, \sup_{b\in B}\inf_{a\in A}\|a-b\|\right\}, \quad \forall A,B \in \mathcal{P}_f(X). \tag{2.4}$$

A multifunction $\Psi : Y \to \mathcal{P}_f(X)$ is said to be Hausdorff continuous if it is a continuous map from Y into the matric space $(\mathcal{P}_f(X),h)$, that is, for every $y_0 \in Y$ and every $\varepsilon > 0$ there exists a neighborhood U_0 of y_0 such that for every $y \in U_0$, we have $h(F(y),F(y_0)) < \varepsilon$.

3. Evolution inclusions with nonlocal initial conditions

This section is concerned with the existence of solutions to the nonlocal Cauchy problem

$$u'(t) \in -Au(t) + F(t,u(t)), \quad t \in T := [0,b];\ u(0) = g(u), \tag{3.1}$$

where $A : D(A) \subset X \to 2^X$ is a nonlinear operator on a Banach space X, $F : I \times X \to 2^X \setminus \{\varnothing\}$ is a multifunction with closed, convex, and nonempty values, and $g : C(I;\overline{D(A)}) \to \overline{D(A)}$. Our existence result is the following.

Theorem 3.1. *Assume X is a real separable Banach space with uniformly convex dual X^*, $T := [0,b]$, with $0 < b < \infty$, and $\mathbb{R}^+ := [0,\infty)$. Let A be an m-accretive operator in X, such that $-A$ generates a compact semigroup $\{S(t) : t \geq 0\}$ on $\overline{D(A)}$, $g : C(I,\overline{D(A)}) \to \overline{D(A)}$ is such that*

$$\|g(u) - g(v)\| \leq m\|u - v\|_\infty, \quad \forall u,v \in C(I,\overline{D(A)}), \tag{3.2}$$

for some m with $0 < m < 1$, and $F : I \times X \to \mathcal{P}_c(X)$ satisfies the following conditions:
(i) *$F(\cdot,x)$ is measurable for each $x \in X$;*
(ii) *$F(t,\cdot)$ is upper semicontinuous from X to X_w for a.a. $t \in I$;*
(iii) *there exists a function $\gamma : I \times \mathbb{R}^+ \to \mathbb{R}^+$ such that $\gamma(\cdot,r) \in L^1(I,\mathbb{R})$ for every $r \in \mathbb{R}^+$, $\gamma(t,\cdot)$ is continuous and nondecreasing for a.a. $t \in I$, and*

$$\limsup_{r\to\infty} \frac{1}{r}\int_0^T \gamma(t,r)dt < 1 - m, \tag{3.3}$$

where m is the same as in condition (H_g), with the additional property that

$$|F(t,x)| := \sup\{\|w\| : w \in F(t,x)\} \leq \gamma(t,\|x\|) \tag{3.4}$$

for a.a. $t \in I$, and all $x \in \overline{D(A)}$. Then the set of integral solutions of the problem (3.1) is a nonempty, compact subset of $C(T,X)$.

Sketch of the proof. We start with the initial value problem

$$u'(t) \in -Au(t) + f(t), \quad t \in I;\ u(0) = g(u), \tag{3.5}$$

where $f \in L^1(T,X)$, A is m-accretive in X, and prove that it has a unique integral solution that will be denoted by u_f. Indeed, for each $v \in C(I,\overline{D(A)})$, there exists a unique integral solution u_v of the initial value problem

$$u'(t) \in -Au(t) + f(t), \quad t \in I;\ u(0) = g(v), \tag{3.6}$$

and for all $v,w \in C(I,\overline{D(A)})$ we have

$$\|u_v(t) - u_w(t)\| \leq \|g(v) - g(w)\| \leq m\|v - w\|_\infty, \quad \forall t \in I, \tag{3.7}$$

hence $\|u_v - u_w\|_\infty \leq m\|v - w\|_\infty$. Since $0 < m < 1$, it follows that $v \to u_v$ is a strict contraction in $C(I,\overline{D(A)})$, therefore, by the contraction mapping principle, it has a unique fixed point in $C(I,\overline{D(A)})$, which is obviously the unique integral solution of (3.5). Next, we obtain an a priori bound for all possible solutions of (3.1): we prove that there exists a finite positive constant M such that for each integral solution u of (3.1) one has

$$\|u\|_\infty \le M. \tag{3.8}$$

For such constant M and for γ satisfying condition (iii) we set $\varphi(t) := \gamma(t,M)$ and remark that $\varphi \in L^1(I,\mathbb{R})$. Moreover, for each integral solution u of (3.1) we get

$$|F(t,u(t))| \le \varphi(t) \quad \text{a.e. on } I, \tag{3.9}$$

In view of (3.9), we may assume without loss of generality that

$$|F(t,x)| \le \varphi(t), \quad \forall x \in X, \text{ a.e. on } I. \tag{3.10}$$

Otherwise, we replace $F(t,x)$ by $\tilde{F}(t,x) = F(t,p_M(x))$, where $p_M : X \to X$ is given by

$$p_M(x) = \begin{cases} x & \text{if } \|x\| \le M, \\ M\dfrac{x}{\|x\|} & \text{if } \|x\| > M, \end{cases} \tag{3.11}$$

with M as in (3.8). We now introduce the set $K \subset L^1(T,X)$ by

$$K = \{f \in L^1(T,X) : \|f(t)\| \le \varphi(t) \text{ a.e. on } T\}. \tag{3.12}$$

Clearly, K is nonempty, closed, and convex. In addition, K is uniformly integrable, hence it is compact in $L^1(T,X)$ equipped with its weak topology. We also note (see [17, Theorem V.6.3]) that K endowed with the relative $L^1(T,X)_w$ topology is a metric space. Define the map $\mathcal{F} : K \to 2^{L^1(T,X)}$ by

$$\mathcal{F}(f) := S^1_{F(\cdot,u_f(\cdot))} = \{v \in L^1(T,X) : v(t) \in F(t,u_f(t)) \text{ a.e. on } T\}, \tag{3.13}$$

where, remember, $u_f(\cdot)$ denotes the integral solution of (3.5), for a given $f \in K$. One has that $\mathcal{F}(f)$ has nonempty, closed, and convex values. Moreover, $\mathcal{F}(K) \subset K$. We regard K as a compact convex subset, denoted as K_w, of $L^1(T,X)_w$ and show that $\mathcal{F}$ is u.s.c. from K_w into 2^{K_w} and for this we prove that $Gr(\mathcal{F})$ is sequentially closed in $K_w \times K_w$. We can now invoke the Kakutani-Ky Fan fixed point theorem to deduce that there exists $\hat{f} \in K$ such that $\hat{f} \in \mathcal{F}(\hat{f})$, hence the corresponding integral solution of the problem (3.5), denoted by $u_{\hat{f}}$, is an integral solution of the problem (3.1). This shows that the set of integral solutions of the problem (3.1) is a nonempty subset of $C(T,X)$, which will be denoted by $\mathcal{S}$.

In order to show that $\mathcal{S}$ is compact in $C(T,X)$, let $(u_n)_{n\in\mathbb{N}}$ be a sequence in $\mathcal{S}$. Then $u_n = u_{f_n}$ for some $f_n \in K$, with $f_n(t) \in F(t,u_n(t))$, a.e. on I. Recalling that K is compact in $L^1(T,X)_w$ and arguing as before, we may assume (without changing the notation for subsequences) that $u_n \to u$ in $C(T,X)$, $f_n \to f$ weakly in $L^1(T,X)$, as $n \to \infty$. We then conclude that $u = u_f$, with $f(t) \in F(t,u(t))$, a.e. on I. In other words, $u \in \mathcal{S}$, and $\mathcal{S}$ is compact in $C(T,X)$. □

4. Periodic solutions to nonlinear evolution inclusions

In this section we consider following periodic problem to evolution inclusions:

$$-u'(t) \in Au(t) + F(t,u(t)), \quad t \in T := [0,b];\ u(0) = u(b), \tag{4.1}$$

where $A : D(A) \subseteq X \to 2^X$ is an m-accretive operator in a reflexive Banach space X and $F : T \times X \to 2^X$ is a multivalued perturbation. For the first result concerning existence of solutions for the periodic problem (4.1) we will assume that X is a real separable Banach space with a uniformly convex dual X^* and the following conditions are satisfied:

(H_A) A is an m-accretive operator in X, with $0 \in A0$, such that $-A$ generates a compact semigroup on $\overline{D(A)}$;

(H_F) $F : T \times X \to \mathcal{P}_{wkc}(X)$ is a multifunction such that (i) $t \to F(t,u)$ is measurable, for each $x \in X$; (ii) the graph of $x \to F(t,x)$ is sequentially closed in $X \times X_w$, for a.a. $t \in T$; (iii) for each $\rho > 0$ there exists a function $a_\rho \in L^1_+(T)$ such that for all $x \in X$ with $\|x\| \leq \rho$,

$$|F(t,x)| := \sup\{\|w\| : w \in F(t,x)\} \leq a_\rho(t) \quad \text{a.e. on } T; \tag{4.2}$$

(iv) there exists $r > 0$ such that $\langle v, Jx\rangle \geq 0$ for all $v \in F(t,x)$, all $t \in T$, and all $x \in X$ with $\|x\| = r$:

$$|F(t,x)| := \sup\{\|w\| : w \in F(t,x)\} \leq a_\rho(t) \quad \text{a.e. on } T \tag{4.3}$$

Our result for the *convex problem* is the following.

THEOREM 4.1. *Let assumptions (H_A) and (H_F) be satisfied. Then the problem (4.1) has at least one integral solution.*

Our next result is concerned with the problem (4.1) where F is no longer convex-valued. We assume instead that F is closed-valued and lower semicontinuous in its second argument. More precisely, assumption (H_F) changes as follows:

(H_F^1) $F : T \times X \to \mathcal{P}_f(X)$ satisfies the following: (i) $(t,x) \to F(t,x)$ is $\mathcal{L} \otimes \mathcal{B}(X)$ measurable; (ii) $x \to F(t,x)$ is lower semicontinuous for a.a. $t \in T$; (iii) for each $\rho > 0$, there exists a function $a_\rho \in L^1_+(T)$ such that for all $x \in X$ with $\|x\| \leq \rho$,

$$|F(t,x)| := \sup\{\|w\| : w \in F(t,x)\} \leq a_\rho(t) \quad \text{a.e. on } T; \tag{4.4}$$

(iv) there exists $r > 0$ such that $\langle v, Jx\rangle \geq 0$ for all $v \in F(t,x)$, all $t \in T$, and all $x \in X$ with $\|x\| = r$.

THEOREM 4.2. *Let assumptions (H_A) and (H_F^1) be satisfied. Then there exists an integral solution to problem (4.1).*

We consider now the evolution inclusion

$$-x'(t) \in Ax(t) + \operatorname{ext} F(t,x(t)), \quad t \in T;\ x(0) = x(b), \tag{4.5}$$

where $\operatorname{ext} F(t,x(t))$ denotes the set of extreme points of $F(t,x(t))$. We assume that F has nonempty, weakly compact values which insures that $\operatorname{ext} F(t,x) \neq \varnothing$ for all $(t,x) \in T \times X$.

However, since in general the multivalued map $(t,x) \to \operatorname{ext} F(t,x)$ is neither convex- nor closed-valued, the previous theorems are not applicable to (4.5). We impose the following conditions on A and F:

(H_A^1) A satisfies (H_A) and in addition there exists $\omega > 0$ such that $A - \omega I$ is accretive,

(H_F) $F : T \times X \to \mathcal{P}_{wkc}(X)$ is such that: (i) $t \to F(t,x)$ is measurable, for each $x \in X$; (ii) $x \to F(t,x)$ is Hausdorff continuous for a.a. $t \in T$; (iii) for each $\rho > 0$, there exists a function $a_\rho \in L_+^p(T)$, $1 < p < \infty$, such that for all $x \in X$ with $\|x\| \le \rho$,

$$|F(t,x)| := \sup\{\|w\| : w \in F(t,x)\} \le a_\rho(t) \quad \text{a.e. on } T; \tag{4.6}$$

(iv) there exists $r > 0$ such that $\langle v, Jx\rangle \ge 0$ for all $v \in F(t,x)$, all $t \in T$, and all $x \in X$ with $\|x\| = r$.

Theorem 4.3. *If conditions (H_A^1) and (H_F^2) are satisfied, then the problem (4.1) has at least one integral solution.*

References

[1] N. U. Ahmed, *Differential inclusions on Banach spaces with nonlocal state constraints*, Nonlinear Functional Analysis and Applications **6** (2001), no. 3, 395–409.

[2] S. Aizicovici and Y. Gao, *Functional-differential equations with nonlocal initial conditions*, Journal of Applied Mathematics and Stochastic Analysis **10** (1997), no. 2, 145–156.

[3] S. Aizicovici and H. Lee, *Nonlinear nonlocal Cauchy problems in Banach spaces*, Applied Mathematics Letters **18** (2005), no. 4, 401–407.

[4] S. Aizicovici and M. McKibben, *Existence results for a class of abstract nonlocal Cauchy problems*, Nonlinear Analysis **39** (2000), no. 5, 649–668.

[5] R. Bader, *On the semilinear multi-valued flow under constraints and the periodic problem*, Commentationes Mathematicae Universitatis Carolinae **41** (2000), no. 4, 719–734.

[6] R. Bader and N. S. Papageorgiou, *On the problem of periodic evolution inclusions of the subdifferential type*, Zeitschrift für Analysis und ihre Anwendungen **21** (2002), no. 4, 963–984.

[7] P. Bénilan, *Solutions intégrales d'équations d'évolution dans un espace de Banach*, Comptes Rendus de l'Académie des Sciences **274** (1972), A47–A50.

[8] R. I. Becker, *Periodic solutions of semilinear equations of evolution of compact type*, Journal of Mathematical Analysis and Applications **82** (1981), no. 1, 33–48.

[9] M. Benchohra, E. P. Gatsori, and S. K. Ntouyas, *Existence results for semi-linear integro-differential inclusions with nonlocal conditions*, The Rocky Mountain Journal of Mathematics **34** (2004), no. 3, 833–848.

[10] ———, *Multivalued semilinear neutral functional differential equations with nonconvex-valued right-hand side*, Abstract and Applied Analysis **2004** (2004), no. 6, 525–541.

[11] M. Benchohra and S. K. Ntouyas, *Nonlocal Cauchy problems for neutral functional differential and integrodifferential inclusions in Banach spaces*, Journal of Mathematical Analysis and Applications **258** (2001), no. 2, 573–590.

[12] A. Boucherif, *Nonlocal Cauchy problems for first-order multivalued differential equations*, Electronic Journal of Differential Equations **2002** (2002), no. 47, 1–9.

[13] F. E. Browder, *Existence of periodic solutions for nonlinear equations of evolution*, Proceedings of the National Academy of Sciences of the United States of America **53** (1965), 1100–1103.

[14] L. Byszewski, *Theorems about the existence and uniqueness of solutions of a semilinear evolution nonlocal Cauchy problem*, Journal of Mathematical Analysis and Applications **162** (1991), no. 2, 494–505.

[15] R. Caşcaval and I. I. Vrabie, *Existence of periodic solutions for a class of nonlinear evolution equations*, Revista Matemática de la Universidad Complutense de Madrid **7** (1994), no. 2, 325–338.

[16] M. G. Crandall and T. M. Liggett, *Generation of semi-groups of nonlinear transformations on general Banach spaces*, American Journal of Mathematics **93** (1971), 265–298.

[17] N. Dunford and J. T. Schwartz, *Linear Operators. Part I*, John Wiley & Sons, New York, 1958.

[18] E. Gatsori, S. K. Ntouyas, and Y. G. Sficas, *On a nonlocal Cauchy problem for differential inclusions*, Abstract and Applied Analysis **2004** (2004), no. 5, 425–434.

[19] N. Hirano, *Existence of periodic solutions for nonlinear evolution equations in Hilbert spaces*, Proceedings of the American Mathematical Society **120** (1994), no. 1, 185–192.

[20] S. C. Hu and N. S. Papageorgiou, *On the existence of periodic solutions for a class of nonlinear evolution inclusions*, Bollettino dell'Unione Matematica Italiana **7B** (1993), no. 3, 591–605.

[21] S. Hu and N. S. Papageorgiou, *Extremal periodic solutions for subdifferential evolution inclusions*, Differential Equations and Dynamical Systems **10** (2002), no. 3-4, 277–304.

[22] J. Prüss, *Periodic solutions of semilinear evolution equations*, Nonlinear Analysis **3** (1979), no. 5, 601–612.

[23] I. I. Vrabie, *Periodic solutions for nonlinear evolution equations in a Banach space*, Proceedings of the American Mathematical Society **109** (1990), no. 3, 653–661.

[24] X. Xue, *Nonlinear differential equations with nonlocal conditions in Banach spaces*, submitted.

Vasile Staicu: Department of Mathematics, Aveiro University, 3810-193 Aveiro, Portugal
E-mail address: vasile@ua.pt

POSITIVE SOLUTIONS OF A CLASS OF SINGULAR FUNCTIONAL BOUNDARY VALUE PROBLEMS WITH ϕ-LAPLACIAN

SVATOSLAV STANĚK

The paper discusses the existence of positive solutions (in $C^1[0,T]$) to the functional differential equations of the form $(\phi(x'))' = F(t,x,x',x'(0),x'(T))$ satisfying the Dirichlet boundary conditions $x(0) = x(T) = 0$. The nonlinearity F may be singular at $x = 0$ and changes its sign.

1. Introduction

Let T be a positive number. Consider the functional-differential equation

$$(\phi(x'(t)))' = f(x(t))\omega(x'(t)) - p_1(t,x(t),x'(t))x'(0) + p_2(t,x(t),x'(t))x'(T) \tag{1.1}$$

together with the Dirichlet boundary conditions

$$x(0) = 0, \qquad x(T) = 0. \tag{1.2}$$

A function $x \in C^1[0,T]$ is said to be *a positive solution of the boundary value problem* (BVP) (1.1), (1.2) if $\phi(x') \in C^1(0,T)$, $x > 0$ on $(0,T)$, x satisfies the boundary conditions (1.2), and (1.1) holds for $t \in (0,T)$.

The aim of this paper is to give conditions for the existence of a positive solution of the BVP (1.1), (1.2). Our results generalize those in [1] where the equation $(\phi(x'(t)))' = f(x(t)) - q(t)h(x(t))x'(0) + r(t)p(x(t))x'(T)$ was discussed. The form of our equation (1.1) is motivated by a regular functional-differential equation considered in [2] together with (1.2). This problem is a mathematical model for a biological population.

Throughout this paper, we will use the following assumptions on the functions ϕ, f, ω, p_1, and p_2.

(H_1) $\phi \in C^0(\mathbb{R})$ is increasing and odd on $\mathbb{R}$ and $\lim_{u\to\infty}\phi(u) = \infty$.

(H_2) $f \in C^0(0,\infty)$, $\lim_{x\to 0^+} f(x) = -\infty$, there is a $\chi > 0$ such that $f < 0$ on $(0,\chi)$, $f > 0$ on (χ,∞), and $\int_0^\chi f(s)ds > -\infty$, $\int_\chi^\infty f(s)ds = \infty$.

Hindawi Publishing Corporation
Proceedings of the Conference on Differential & Difference Equations and Applications, pp. 1029–1039

(H_3) $\omega \in C^0(\mathbb{R})$ is positive and even and there exist $K > 0$ and $\gamma > 1$ such that

$$H(u) \geq Ku^{\gamma} \quad \text{for } u \in [0,\infty), \tag{1.3}$$

where

$$H(u) = \int_0^{\phi(u)} \frac{\phi^{-1}(s)}{\omega(\phi^{-1}(s))} ds, \quad u \in \mathbb{R}. \tag{1.4}$$

(H_4) $p_j \in C^0([0,T] \times (0,\infty) \times \mathbb{R})$

$$0 < p_j(t,x,y) \leq q_j(t) r_j(x) \omega(y) \tag{1.5}$$

for $(t,x,y) \in [0,T] \times (0,\infty) \times \mathbb{R}$ and $j = 1,2$, where $q_j \in C^0[0,T]$ and $r_j \in C^0(0,\infty)$ are positive, $\lim_{x\to 0^+} r_j(x) = \infty$, and $\int_0^1 r_j(s)ds < \infty$.

(H_5) There exists $\Delta > 0$ such that r_j $(j = 1,2)$ is decreasing and f is increasing on $(0,\Delta]$.

(H_6) $\lim_{x\to\infty} f(x)/(r_1(x) + r_2(x)) = \infty$ and

$$\liminf_{x\to\infty} \frac{\int_0^x f(s)ds}{\left(\|q_1\| \int_0^x r_1(s)ds + \|q_2\| \int_0^x r_2(s)ds\right)^{\gamma/(\gamma-1)}} > K^{-1/(\gamma-1)}. \tag{1.6}$$

Remark 1.1. If ϕ and ω satisfy (H_1) and (H_3), then the function H defined in (1.4) is continuous and even on $\mathbb{R}$, $H(0) = 0$, and $H(u) > 0$ for $u \in \mathbb{R} \setminus \{0\}$.

From now on, $\|x\| = \max\{|x(t)| : 0 \leq t \leq T\}$ stands for the norm in $C^0[0,T]$. The space of Lebesgue integrable functions on $[0,T]$ will be denoted by $L_1[0,T]$.

Our existence result for the BVP (1.1), (1.2) is proved by a regularization and sequential technique.

2. Auxiliary regular BVPs

Let assumptions (H_2)–(H_5) be satisfied. Let $N_* = \{n \in \mathbb{N} : 1/n < \min\{\chi, \Delta\}\}$, where χ and Δ are taken from (H_2) and (H_5). For $n \in \mathbb{N}_*$ and $j = 1,2$, define $f_n \in C^0(\mathbb{R})$ and $p_{j,n} \in C^0([0,T] \times \mathbb{R}^2)$ by the formulas

$$f_n(x) = \begin{cases} f(x) & \text{for } x \geq \dfrac{1}{n}, \\ f\left(\dfrac{1}{n}\right) & \text{for } 0 \leq x \leq \dfrac{1}{n}, \\ f\left(\dfrac{1}{n}\right) - \delta_n |x|^{1/(\gamma-1)} & \text{for } x < 0, \end{cases} \tag{2.1}$$

where

$$\delta_n = \frac{2\gamma}{\gamma - 1} K^{-1/(\gamma-1)} \left(\|q_1\| r_1 \left(\frac{1}{n} \right) \right)^{\gamma/(\gamma-1)}, \tag{2.2}$$

$$p_{j,n}(t,x,y) = \begin{cases} p_j(t,x,y) & \text{for } (t,x,y) \in [0,T] \times \left[\frac{1}{n}, \infty \right) \times \mathbb{R}, \\ p_j\left(t, \frac{1}{n}, y\right) & \text{for } (t,x,y) \in [0,T] \times \left(-\infty, \frac{1}{n} \right) \times \mathbb{R}. \end{cases} \tag{2.3}$$

Then

$$0 < p_{j,n}(t,x,y) \le q_j(t) r_{j,n}(x) \omega(y), \quad (t,x,y) \in [0,T] \times \mathbb{R}^2, \tag{2.4}$$

where

$$r_{j,n}(x) = \begin{cases} r_j(x) & \text{for } x \ge \frac{1}{n}, \\ r_j\left(\frac{1}{n}\right) & \text{for } x < \frac{1}{n}. \end{cases} \tag{2.5}$$

Also, $0 < p_{j,n}(t,x,y) \le q_j(t) r_j(x) \omega(y)$ for $(t,x,y) \in [0,T] \times (0,\infty) \times \mathbb{R}$ and

$$\begin{gathered} f(x) \le f_{n+1}(x) \le f_n(x), \qquad |f(x)| \ge |f_n(x)|, \\ r_j(x) \ge r_{j,n+1}(x) \ge r_{j,n}(x) \end{gathered} \tag{2.6}$$

for $x \in (0,\infty)$, $n \in \mathbb{N}_*$, and $j = 1,2$.

Consider the family of regular functional-differential equations

$$\begin{aligned} (\phi(x'(t)))' = \lambda \big(& f_n(x(t)) \omega(x'(t)) - p_{1,n}(t,x(t),x'(t)) x'(0) \\ & + p_{2,n}(t,x(t),x'(t)) \min\{0, x'(T)\} \big) . \end{aligned} \tag*{$(2.6)_n^\lambda$}$$

depending on the parameters $\lambda \in [0,1]$ and $n \in \mathbb{N}_*$.

One can easily check the following result which is used in the proofs of Lemmas 2.2 and 2.4.

Lemma 2.1. *Let assumptions* (H_1) *and* (H_3) *be satisfied. Let* $H(u) \le A + B|u|$ *for some* $u \in \mathbb{R}$*, where* $A \ge 0$ *and* $B > 0$*. Then*

$$|u| < \left(\frac{A+B}{K} \right)^{1/(\gamma-1)} + 1, \tag{2.7}$$

and if $A = 0$*, then*

$$|u| < \left(\frac{B}{K} \right)^{1/(\gamma-1)}. \tag{2.8}$$

LEMMA 2.2. *Let assumptions* (H_1)–(H_5) *be satisfied and let* $x(t)$ *be a solution of the BVP* $(2.6)_n^\lambda$, *(1.2). Then*

$$x(t) \geq 0, \quad t \in [0,T]. \tag{2.9}$$

Proof. If $\lambda = 0$, then $x = 0$ and (2.9) is true. Let $\lambda \in (0,1]$. Suppose $\min\{x(t) : 0 \leq t \leq T\} = x(\xi) < 0$. Then $\xi \in (0,T)$ and $x'(\xi) = 0$. If $x'(0) \geq 0$, then (see (2.1) and (2.2)) $(\phi(x'(t)))'|_{t=\xi} \leq \lambda f_n(x(\xi))\omega(0) = \lambda(f(1/n) - \delta_n|x(\xi)|^{1/(\gamma-1)})\omega(0) < 0$. Therefore x' is decreasing on a neighborhood of $t = \xi$, which contradicts the minimal value of x at $t = \xi$. Hence $x'(0) < 0$ and there exists $\nu \in (0,\xi]$ such that $x' < 0$ on $[0,\nu)$ and $x'(\nu) = 0$. Since $p_{2,n}(t,x(t),x'(t))\min\{0,x'(T)\}x'(t) \geq 0$ for $t \in [0,\nu]$, we have $(\phi(x'(t)))'x'(t) \geq \lambda(f_n(x(t)) - q_1(t)r_{1,n}(x(t))x'(0))\omega(x'(t))x'(t)$ and (see (2.5)) $(\phi(x'(t)))'x'(t)/\omega(x'(t)) \geq \lambda(f_n(x(t)) - q_1(t)r_1(1/n)x'(0))x'(t)$ for $t \in [0,\nu]$. Integrating the last inequality over $[0,\nu]$ yields

$$-H(x'(0)) \geq \lambda\left(\int_0^{x(\nu)} f_n(s)ds - x'(0)r_1\left(\frac{1}{n}\right)\int_0^\nu q_1(t)x'(t)dt\right) \tag{2.10}$$

and using $\int_0^{x(\nu)} f_n(s)ds > 0$, we obtain

$$H(x'(0)) < \lambda x'(0)r_1\left(\frac{1}{n}\right)\int_0^\nu q_1(t)x'(t)dt \leq |x'(0)|\,r_1\left(\frac{1}{n}\right)\left|\int_0^\nu q_1(t)x'(t)dt\right|. \tag{2.11}$$

Now Lemma 2.1 gives $|x'(0)| < (r_1(1/n)/K|\int_0^\nu q_1(t)x'(t)dt|)^{1/(\gamma-1)}$. From (2.10) and $H(x'(0)) > 0$, we also have $\int_0^{x(\nu)} f_n(s)ds < x'(0)r_1(1/n)\int_0^\nu q_1(t)x'(t)dt$, and so

$$\int_0^{x(\nu)} f_n(s)ds < K^{-1/(\gamma-1)}\left(r_1\left(\frac{1}{n}\right)\|q_1\|\,|x(\nu)|\right)^{\gamma/(\gamma-1)}. \tag{2.12}$$

Since (see (2.1))

$$\begin{aligned}\int_0^{x(\nu)} f_n(s)ds &= \int_0^{x(\nu)}\left(f\left(\frac{1}{n}\right) - \delta_n|s|^{1/(\gamma-1)}\right)ds\\ &= f\left(\frac{1}{n}\right)x(\nu) + \left(1 - \frac{1}{\gamma}\right)\delta_n|x(\nu)|^{\gamma/(\gamma-1)},\end{aligned} \tag{2.13}$$

we have (see (2.12)) $f(1/n)x(\nu) + (1 - 1/\gamma)\delta_n|x(\nu)|^{\gamma/(\gamma-1)} < K^{-1/(\gamma-1)}(r_1(1/n)\|q_1\|\,|x(\nu)|)^{\gamma/(\gamma-1)}$ and $|f(1/n)| < [K^{-1/(\gamma-1)}(r_1(1/n)\|q_1\|)^{\gamma/(\gamma-1)} - (1 - 1/\gamma)\delta_n]|x(\nu)|^{1/(\gamma-1)}$, contrary to (see (2.2))

$$\begin{aligned}&K^{-1/(\gamma-1)}\left(r_1\left(\frac{1}{n}\right)\|q_1\|\right)^{\gamma/(\gamma-1)} - \left(1 - \frac{1}{\gamma}\right)\delta_n\\ &\quad = -K^{-1/(\gamma-1)}\left(r_1\left(\frac{1}{n}\right)\|q_1\|\right)^{\gamma/(\gamma-1)} < 0.\end{aligned} \tag{2.14}$$

We have proved that (2.9) is true. □

Remark 2.3. Lemma 2.2 shows that any solution x of the BVP $(2.6)_n^\lambda$, (1.2) satisfies (2.9). Therefore $x'(0) \geq 0$ and $x'(T) \leq 0$. Hence

$$(\phi(x'(t)))' = \lambda\big(f_n(x(t))\omega(x'(t)) - p_{1,n}(t,x(t),x'(t))x'(0) \\ + p_{2,n}(t,x(t),x'(t))x'(T)\big), \quad t \in [0,T]. \tag{2.15}$$

LEMMA 2.4. *Let assumptions* (H_1)–(H_6) *be satisfied. Then there exist positive constants* S_0 *and* S_1 *such that*

$$0 < x(t) < S_0, \quad \|x'\| < S_1, \quad t \in (0,T), \tag{2.16}$$

for any solution x of the BVP $(2.6)_n^\lambda$*, (1.2) with* $\lambda \in (0,1]$ *and* $n \in \mathbb{N}_*$.

Proof. Let x be a solution of the BVP $(2.6)_n^\lambda$, (1.2) for some $\lambda \in (0,1]$ and $n \in \mathbb{N}_*$. By Lemma 2.2, $x \geq 0$ on $[0,T]$ and therefore (2.15) is satisfied for $t \in [0,T]$. Set $V = |\int_0^\chi f(s)ds|$, where $\chi > 0$ appears in (H_2). The conditions (1.6) and $\int_\chi^\infty f(s)ds = \infty$ in (H_2) guarantee the existence of an $L > 0$ such that

$$\int_0^u f(s)ds > \left[1 + K^{-1/(\gamma-1)}\left(V + \|q_1\|\int_0^u r_1(s)ds + \|q_2\|\int_0^u r_2(s)ds\right)^{1/(\gamma-1)}\right] \\ \times \left(\|q_1\|\int_0^u r_1(s)ds + \|q_2\|\int_0^u r_2(s)ds\right) \tag{2.17}$$

for any $u \geq L$. Let $\bar{t} = 0, T$. Then $(\phi(x'(t)))'|_{t=\bar{t}} \leq \lambda f(1/n)\omega(x'(\bar{t})) < 0$, and therefore x' is decreasing on a right neighborhood of $t = 0$ and on a left neighborhood of $t = T$. Hence $x(0) = x(T) = 0$ implies that $x'(0) > 0$, $x'(T) < 0$, and x' vanishes on $(0,T)$. Let $\nu_1 = \min\{t : x'(t) = 0\}$, $\nu_2 = \max\{t : x'(t) = 0\}$. Then $0 < \nu_1 \leq \nu_2 < T$. We now show that

$$x(t) > 0, \quad t \in (0,T), \tag{2.18}$$

$$\max\{x(t) : t \in [0,\nu_1] \cup [\nu_2,T]\} < L, \tag{2.19}$$

$$\max\{x'(0), |x'(T)|\} < W, \tag{2.20}$$

where $W = K^{-1/(\gamma-1)}(V + \|q_1\|\int_0^L r_1(s)ds + \|q_2\|\int_0^L r_2(s)ds)^{1/(\gamma-1)} + 1$. To see (2.18), assume $x(\tau) = 0$ for $\tau \in (0,T)$. Then $\nu_1 < \tau < \nu_2$ and $x'(\tau) = 0$. Since $(\phi(x'(t)))'|_{t=\tau} < \lambda f(1/n)\omega(0) < 0$, x' is decreasing on a neighborhood of $t = \tau$, which is impossible. Hence (2.18) is true and also

$$\frac{(\phi(x'(t)))'}{\omega(x'(t))} \geq \lambda\big(f(x(t)) - q_1(t)r_1(x(t))x'(0) + q_2(t)r_2(x(t))x'(T)\big) \tag{2.21}$$

for $t \in (0,T)$. Integrating

$$\frac{(\phi(x'(t)))'x'(t)}{\omega(x'(t))} \geq \lambda\big(f(x(t)) - q_1(t)r_1(x(t))x'(0) + q_2(t)r_2(x(t))x'(T)\big)x'(t) \tag{2.22}$$

over $[0,\nu_1]$ and

$$\frac{(\phi(x'(t)))'x'(t)}{\omega(x'(t))} \le \lambda(f(x(t)) - q_1(t)r_1(x(t))x'(0) + q_2(t)r_2(x(t))x'(T))x'(t) \tag{2.23}$$

over $[\nu_2,T]$, we get

$$\begin{aligned} 0 > -H(x'(0)) \ge \int_0^{x(\nu_1)} f(s)ds - x'(0)\int_0^{\nu_1} q_1(t)r_1(x(t))x'(t)dt \\ - |x'(T)|\int_0^{\nu_1} q_2(t)r_2(x(t))x'(t)dt, \end{aligned} \tag{2.24}$$

$$\begin{aligned} 0 < H(x'(T)) \le -\int_0^{x(\nu_2)} f(s)ds + x'(0)\left|\int_{\nu_2}^{T} q_1(t)r_1(x(t))x'(t)dt\right| \\ + |x'(T)|\left|\int_{\nu_2}^{T} q_2(t)r_2(x(t))x'(t)dt\right|. \end{aligned} \tag{2.25}$$

In addition, we have

$$\int_0^u f(s)ds \ge -V \quad \text{for } u \in [0,\infty), \tag{2.26}$$

$$\int_0^{\nu_1} q_j(t)r_j(x(t))x'(t)dt \le \|q_j\|\int_0^{\nu_1} r_j(x(t))x'(t)dt = \|q_j\|\int_0^{x(\nu_1)} r_j(s)ds, \tag{2.27}$$

$$\left|\int_{\nu_2}^{T} q_j(t)r_j(x(t))x'(t)dt\right| \le \|q_j\|\left|\int_{\nu_2}^{T} r_j(x(t))x'(t)dt\right| = \|q_j\|\int_0^{x(\nu_2)} r_j(s)ds \tag{2.28}$$

for $j = 1,2$. Let $x(\nu_i) = \max\{x(\nu_1), x(\nu_2)\} = \max\{x(t) : t \in [0,\nu_1] \cup [\nu_2,T]\}$ for $i \in \{1,2\}$ and set $A_j = \|q_j\| \int_0^{x(\nu_i)} r_j(s)ds$, $j = 1,2$. Then (2.24)–(2.28) give

$$\begin{aligned} H(x'(0)) \le V + A_1x'(0) + A_2|x'(T)|, \\ H(x'(T)) \le V + A_1x'(0) + A_2|x'(T)|. \end{aligned} \tag{2.29}$$

Consequently, $(\max\{x'(0),|x'(T)|\}) \le V + (A_1 + A_2)\max\{x'(0),|x'(T)|\}$ and therefore

$$\max\{x'(0),|x'(T)|\} < \left(\frac{V + A_1 + A_2}{K}\right)^{1/(\gamma-1)} + 1, \tag{2.30}$$

by Lemma 2.1. Returning to (2.24) and (2.25), if $i = 1$, then

$$\int_0^{x(\nu_i)} f(s)ds < x'(0)\int_0^{\nu_i} q_1(t)r_1(x(t))x'(t)dt - x'(T)\int_0^{\nu_i} q_2(t)r_2(x(t))x'(t)dt \tag{2.31}$$

and if $i = 2$, then

$$\int_0^{x(\nu_i)} f(s)ds < -x'(0)\int_{\nu_i}^{T} q_1(t)r_1(x(t))x'(t)dt + x'(T)\int_{\nu_i}^{T} q_2(t)r_2(x(t))x'(t)dt. \tag{2.32}$$

Now using (2.27)–(2.30), we have

$$\int_0^{x(\nu_i)} f(s)ds < \left[1+\left(\frac{V+A_1+A_2}{K}\right)^{1/(\gamma-1)}\right](A_1+A_2)$$
$$= \left[1+K^{-1/(\gamma-1)}\left(V+\|q_1\|\int_0^{x(\nu_i)} r_1(s)ds+\|q_2\|\int_0^{x(\nu_i)} r_2(s)ds\right)^{1/(\gamma-1)}\right] \tag{2.33}$$
$$\times \left(\|q_1\|\int_0^{x(\nu_i)} r_1(s)ds+\|q_2\|\int_0^{x(\nu_i)} r_2(s)ds\right),$$

and consequently (see (2.17)) $x(\nu_i) < L$, which proves (2.19). The validity of (2.20) follows immediately from (2.30) and $A_j < \|q_j\| \int_0^L r_j(s)ds$, $j = 1,2$. The rest part of the proof is divided into two cases.

Case 1. Suppose $\nu_1 = \nu_2$. Then the first inequality in (2.16) holds with $S_0 = L$. Let $\max\{|x'(t)| : 0 \le t \le T\} = |x'(\eta)|$. Assume that $x'(\eta) > 0$ (when $x'(\eta) < 0$ we proceed similarly). Then $0 \le \eta < \nu_1$. Integrating (2.22) from η to ν_1 and using (2.20) and (2.26), we obtain by a simple calculation that

$$-H(x'(\eta)) > -V - W\left(\|q_1\|\int_0^L r_1(s)ds+\|q_2\|\int_0^L r_2(s)ds\right). \tag{2.34}$$

Hence

$$x'(\eta) < H^{-1}\left(V+W\left(\|q_1\|\int_0^L r_1(s)ds+\|q_2\|\int_0^L r_2(s)ds\right)\right) =: Z \tag{2.35}$$

and the second inequality in (2.16) is satisfied with $S_1 = Z$. Here H^{-1} denotes the inverse function to the restriction of H on $[0,\infty)$.

Case 2. Suppose $\nu_1 < \nu_2$. Let $\max\{x(t) : \nu_1 \le t \le \nu_2\} = x(\delta)$. Since the assumption $\lim_{u\to\infty} f(u)/(r_1(u)+r_2(u)) = \infty$ implies $\lim_{u\to\infty}(\|q_1\|r_1(u)+\|q_2\|r_2(u))/f(u) = 0$, from

$$f(u)\left(1-W\frac{\|q_1\|r_1(u)+\|q_2\|r_2(u)}{f(u)}\right) = f(u)-W(\|q_1\|r_1(u)+\|q_2\|r_2(u)), \tag{2.36}$$

we see that a constant $C > 0$ exists such that $f(u) - W(\|q_1\|r_1(u)+\|q_2\|r_2(u)) > 0$ whenever $u > C$. We now claim that $x(\delta) \le C$. If not, there exists $\varepsilon > 0$ such that $x > C$ on $[\delta-\varepsilon,\delta+\varepsilon]$. Then (see (2.20) and (2.21))

$$\frac{(\phi(x'(t)))'}{\omega(x'(t))} \ge \lambda(f(x(t)) - W[\|q_1\|r_1(x(t))+\|q_2\|r_2(x(t))]) > 0 \tag{2.37}$$

for $t \in [\delta-\varepsilon,\delta+\varepsilon]$. Hence $\phi(x')$ is increasing on $[\delta-\varepsilon,\delta+\varepsilon]$, which contradicts the maximality of x at $t = \delta$. Therefore $x \le C$ on $[\nu_1,\nu_2]$ and the first inequality in (2.16) is satisfied with $S_0 = \max\{L, C+1\}$. Finally, we give an upper bound of $|x'|$ on $[0,T]$. Let $\max\{|x'(t)| : 0 \le t \le T\} = |x'(\kappa)|$. Assume that $x'(\kappa) < 0$ (when $x'(\kappa) > 0$ we proceed similarly). Then there exists $\tau_* \in [\nu_1,\nu_2]$ such that $x'(\tau_*) = 0$ and $x' < 0$ on the open interval with the end points τ_* and κ. Assuming, for example, $\tau_* < \kappa$ and integrating (2.23) over $[\tau_*, \kappa]$, we get

$$H(|x'(\kappa)|) \leq \int_0^{S_0} |f(s)|\,ds + W\left(||q_1|| \int_0^{S_0} r_1(s)ds + ||q_2|| \int_0^{S_0} r_2(s)ds\right) =: Q. \tag{2.38}$$

Consequently, the second inequality in (2.16) holds with $S_1 = H^{-1}(Q)$.

Summarizing, we have proved the validity of (2.16) with $S_0 = \max\{L, C+1\}$ and $S_1 = \max\{Z, H^{-1}(Q)\}$. □

Lemma 2.5. *Let assumptions* (H_1)–(H_6) *be satisfied. Then for each* $n \in \mathbb{N}_*$, *there exists a solution* x_n *of the BVP* $(2.6)_n^\lambda$, *(1.2) and*

$$0 < x_n(t) < S_0, \quad ||x_n'|| < S_1, \; t \in (0,T), \; n \in \mathbb{N}_*, \tag{2.39}$$

where S_0 *and* S_1 *are positive constants independent of* n.

Proof. Fix $n \in \mathbb{N}_*$. First observe that, by Lemma 2.4, any solution of the BVP $(2.6)_n^\lambda$, (1.2) with $\lambda \in (0,1]$ satisfies (2.16), where S_0 and S_1 are positive constants independent of n and λ. Let $F_n : C^1[0,T] \to C^0[0,T]$ be defined by

$$\begin{aligned}(F_n x)(t) = f_n(x(t))\omega(x'(t)) - p_{1,n}(t, x(t), x'(t))x'(0) \\ + p_{2,n}(t, x(t), x'(t)) \min\{0, x'(T)\}.\end{aligned} \tag{2.40}$$

Then F_n is a continuous operator and for each $r > 0$,

$$\sup\{||F_n x|| : x \in C^1[0,T], \; ||x|| + ||x'|| \leq r\} < \infty. \tag{2.41}$$

Since $(2.6)_n^\lambda$ can be written in the form $(\phi(x'))' = \lambda F_n x$, the assertion of our lemma follows from [1, Theorem 2.1]. □

Lemma 2.6. *Let assumptions* (H_1)–(H_6) *be satisfied. Then there exists* $c > 0$ *independent of* n *such that*

$$x(t) \geq \begin{cases} ct & \text{for } t \in \left[0, \dfrac{T}{2}\right], \\ c(T-t) & \text{for } t \in \left[\dfrac{T}{2}, T\right] \end{cases} \tag{2.42}$$

for any solution x *of the BVP* $(2.6)_n^\lambda$, *(1.2) with* $n \in \mathbb{N}_*$.

Proof. Let x be a solution of the BVP $(2.6)_n^\lambda$, (1.2) for some $n \in \mathbb{N}_*$. Then $x \geq 0$ on $[0,T]$ by Lemma 2.2 and $(\phi(x'(t)))'|_{t=t_*} \leq f(1/n)\omega(x'(t_*)) < 0$ for $t_* = 0, T$. Hence $x'(0) > 0$ and $x'(T) < 0$. Also (2.16) holds where S_0, S_1 are positive constants independent of n. Since $(\phi(x'(t)))' < 0$ whenever $x(t) \leq \chi$, where χ appears in (H_2), x' is decreasing and x is concave on any subinterval of $[0,T]$, where $x \leq \chi$. Next part of the proof is divided into two cases.

Case 1. Suppose $\max\{x(t) : 0 \le t \le T\} \le \chi$. Then x' is decreasing on $[0,T]$, $x'(\xi) = 0$ for a unique $\xi \in (0,T)$, x is concave on $[0,T]$, and

$$(\phi(x'(t)))'\big|_{t=\tau} = \max\{(\phi(x'(t)))' : 0 \le t \le T\} =: \alpha < 0, \tag{2.43}$$

where $\tau \in [0,T]$. Therefore $x'(t) \ge \phi^{-1}(|\alpha|(\tau - t))$ on $[0,\tau]$, $x'(t) \le \phi^{-1}(|\alpha|(\tau - t))$ on $[\tau,T]$, and consequently $x(\tau) \ge \int_0^\tau \phi^{-1}(|\alpha|t)dt$, $-x(\tau) \le -\int_0^{T-\tau} \phi^{-1}(|\alpha|t)dt$. Hence

$$x(\tau) \ge \max\left\{\int_0^\tau \phi^{-1}(|\alpha|t)dt, \int_0^{T-\tau} \phi^{-1}(|\alpha|t)dt\right\} \ge \int_0^{T/2} \phi^{-1}(|\alpha|t)dt. \tag{2.44}$$

If $|\alpha| \ge 1$, then $x(\tau) \ge \int_0^{T/2} \phi^{-1}(t)dt$ and x being concave on $[0,T]$ gives $x(T/2) \ge (1/2)\int_0^{T/2} \phi^{-1}(t)dt$. To give a lower bound for $x(T/2)$ if $\alpha > -1$, notice that the assumption $\lim_{x\to 0^+} f(x) = -\infty$ guarantees $f(x) \le -1/\Lambda$ for $x \in (0,d]$ with some $d \in (0,T]$, where $\Lambda = \min\{\omega(u) : 0 \le u \le S_1\}$. Now $\alpha = (\phi(x'(t)))'|_{t=\tau} < f_n(x(\tau))\omega(x'(\tau))$ implies $f_n(x(\tau)) > \alpha/\omega(x'(\tau)) > \alpha/\Lambda$. Hence $x(\tau) > d$ if $\alpha > -1$ and using u being concave on $[0,T]$, we get $x(T/2) > d/2$. Set $c_1 = \min\{\int_0^{T/2} \phi^{-1}(t)dt,\ d\}$. Then c_1 is independent of n, $x(T/2) \ge c_1/2$ and

$$x(t) \ge \begin{cases} \dfrac{c_1 t}{T} & \text{for } t \in \left[0, \dfrac{T}{2}\right], \\[2mm] \dfrac{c_1(T-t)}{T} & \text{for } t \in \left[\dfrac{T}{2}, T\right]. \end{cases} \tag{2.45}$$

Case 2. Suppose $\max\{x(t) : 0 \le t \le T\} > \chi$. Set $a = \min\{t : x'(t) = 0\}$ and $b = \max\{t : x'(t) = 0\}$. Then $0 < a \le b < T$. We claim that

$$\min\{x(t) :\ a \le t \le b\} > \chi. \tag{2.46}$$

To see this, let $x(\eta) = \min\{x(t) : a \le t \le b\} \le \chi$, where $\eta \in [a,b]$. Then $x'(\eta) = 0$ which contradicts $(\phi(x'(t)))'|_{t=\eta} < 0$. Hence (see (2.46)) $x(a) > \chi$ and $x(b) > \chi$. Let $c = \min\{t : x(t) = \chi\}$ and $d = \max\{t : x(t) = \chi\}$. Then $0 < c < a \le b < d < T$ and, since x is concave on $[0,c]$ and $[d,T]$, we have

$$x(t) \ge \begin{cases} \dfrac{\chi t}{c} & \text{for } t \in [0,c], \\[2mm] \dfrac{\chi(T-t)}{(T-d)} & \text{for } t \in [d,T]. \end{cases} \tag{2.47}$$

Now using (2.46) and the fact that x is increasing on $[0,a]$ and decreasing on $[b,T]$, we deduce that $x(T/2) > \chi/2$, and consequently

$$x(t) \ge \begin{cases} \dfrac{\chi t}{T} & \text{for } t \in \left[0, \dfrac{T}{2}\right], \\[2mm] \dfrac{\chi(T-t)}{T} & \text{for } t \in \left[\dfrac{T}{2}, T\right]. \end{cases} \tag{2.48}$$

Summarizing, from (2.45) and (2.48), we see that (2.42) is true with $c = (1/T)\min\{c_1,\chi\}$. Clearly, c is independent on n. □

3. Existence result

Theorem 3.1. *Suppose assumptions* (H_1)–(H_6) *are satisfied. Then the BVP (1.1), (1.2) has a positive solution.*

Proof. Let $\Omega = \{x : x \in C^1[0,T],\ \|x\| < S_0,\ \|x'\| < S_1\}$, where S_0 and S_1 are positive constants in Lemma 2.5. By Lemmas 2.5 and 2.6, for each $n \in \mathbb{N}_*$, there exists a solution $x_n \in \Omega$ of the BVP $(2.6)_n^\lambda$, (1.2) and

$$x_n(t) \geq \begin{cases} ct & \text{for } t \in \left[0, \dfrac{T}{2}\right], \\ c(T-t) & \text{for } t \in \left[\dfrac{T}{2}, T\right], \end{cases} \tag{3.1}$$

where c is a positive constant. Set $t_* = \min\{\Delta/S_1, T/2\}$. Then $ct \leq x_n(t) = \int_0^t x_n'(t)dt \leq S_1 t \leq \Delta$ for $t \in [0,t_*]$ and $c(T-t) \leq x_n(t) = -\int_t^T x_n'(t)dt \leq S_1(T-t) \leq \Delta$ for $t \in [T-t_*, T]$. Without loss of generality we can assume that $\Delta \leq \chi$, that is, $f(u) \leq 0$ for $u \in (0,\Delta]$. Then (see (2.6))

$$\begin{gathered} |f_n(x_n(t))| \leq |f(x_n(t))| \leq |f(ct)|, \\ r_{j,n}(x_n(t)) \leq r_j(x_n(t)) \leq r_j(ct) \end{gathered} \tag{3.2}$$

for $t \in (0,t_*]$ and similarly

$$|f_n(x_n(t))| \leq |f(c(T-t))|, \quad r_{j,n}(x_n(t)) \leq r_j(c(T-t)), \quad t \in [T-t_*, T). \tag{3.3}$$

Set $P = \max\{\omega(u) : 0 \leq u \leq S_1\}$ and

$$\begin{aligned} Q_n(t) = {} & f_n(x_n(t))\omega(x_n'(t)) - p_{1,n}(t, x_n(t), x_n'(t))x_n'(0) \\ & + p_{2,n}(t, x_n(t), x_n'(t))x_n'(T) \end{aligned} \tag{3.4}$$

for $t \in [0,T]$ and $n \in \mathbb{N}_*$. Then (see (2.4), (3.2), and (3.3))

$$|Q_n(t)| \leq P|f(ct)| + \|q_1\|S_1 P r_1(ct) + \|q_2\|S_1 P r_2(ct), \quad t \in (0,t_*], \tag{3.5}$$

$$\begin{aligned} |Q_n(t)| \leq {} & P|f(c(T-t))| + \|q_1\|S_1 P r_1(c(T-t)) \\ & + \|q_2\|S_1 P r_2(c(T-t)), \quad t \in [T-t_*, T), \end{aligned} \tag{3.6}$$

$$\begin{aligned} |Q_n(t)| \leq {} & P\max\{|f(u)| : ct_* \leq u \leq S_0\} + \|q_1\|S_1 P\max\{r_1(u) : ct_* \leq u \leq S_0\} \\ & + \|q_2\|S_1 P\max\{r_2(u) : ct_* \leq u \leq S_0\}, \quad t \in [t_*, T-t_*]. \end{aligned} \tag{3.7}$$

From (H_2), (H_4), and (3.5)–(3.7), we get $|Q_n(t)| \leq \varrho(t)$ for $t \in (0,T)$ and $n \in \mathbb{N}_*$, where $\varrho \in L_1[0,T]$. Therefore $\{\phi(x_n)\}_{n\in\mathbb{N}_*}$ is equicontinuous on $[0,T]$, and using the fact that ϕ is continuous and increasing on $\mathbb{R}$, we see that $\{x_n\}_{n\in\mathbb{N}_*}$ is equicontinuous on $[0,T]$ as well. It follows that there exists a subsequence $\{x_{k_n}\}$ of $\{x_n\}_{n\in\mathbb{N}_*}$ converging to some x in

$C^1[0,T]$. Then $x \in C^1[0,T]$, x satisfies (1.2), and (see (3.1))

$$x(t) \geq \begin{cases} ct & \text{for } t \in \left[0, \dfrac{T}{2}\right], \\ c(T-t) & \text{for } t \in \left[\dfrac{T}{2}, T\right]. \end{cases} \tag{3.8}$$

Hence $x > 0$ on $(0,T)$ and

$$\lim_{n\to\infty} Q_{k_n}(t) = f(x(t))\omega(x'(t)) - p_1(t,x(t),x'(t))x'(0) + p_2(t,x(t),x'(t))x'(T) \tag{3.9}$$

for $t \in (0,T)$. Then x is a solution of the BVP (1.1), (1.2) by [1, Theorem 2.3]. □

Acknowledgment

This work is supported by Grant no. 201/04/1077 of the Grant Agency of Czech Republic and by the Council of Czech Government MSM 6198959214.

References

[1] R. P. Agarwal, D. O'Regan, and S. Staněk, *General existence principles for nonlocal boundary value problems with ϕ-Laplacian and their applications*, Abstract and Applied Analysis **2006** (2006), Article ID 96826, 1–30.

[2] L. E. Bobisud, T. S. Do, and Y. S. Lee, *Existence for a diffusing population with returns from the boundary to the interior*, Applicable Analysis **72** (1999), no. 1-2, 1–16.

Svatoslav Staněk: Department of Mathematical Analysis, Faculty of Science, Palacký University, Tomkova 40, 779 00 Olomouc, Czech Republic
E-mail address: stanek@inf.upol.cz

Definition 2.1. A domain $D \subset \mathbb{R}^n$ is called an $L^p(\mu)$-averaging domain, $p \geq 1$, if $\mu(D) < \infty$, and there exists a constant C such that

$$\left(\frac{1}{\mu(D)}\int_D |u(x) - u_{B_0}|^p d\mu\right)^{1/p} \leq C\left(\sup_{4B\subset D}\frac{1}{\mu(B)}\int_B |u(x) - u_B|^p d\mu\right)^{1/p} \tag{2.1}$$

for some ball $B_0 \subset D$ and all $u \in L^p_{\text{loc}}(D,\mu)$.

Various weight conditions on $w(x)$ produced analogues of the results in [21]. We focus here only on the three main classes of weights examined in [12]: doubling measures, weak reverse Hölder weights, and Muckenhoupt weights.

Definition 2.2. A weight w is called a doubling weight if there exists a constant C such that $\mu(B) \leq C\mu(B/2)$ for all balls $B \subset D$.

Definition 2.3. Let $\sigma > 1$. It is said that w satisfies a weak reverse Hölder inequality, $w \in \text{WRH}(D)$, if there exist constants $\beta > 1$ and $C > 0$ such that

$$\left(\frac{1}{|B|}\int_B w^\beta dx\right)^{(1/\beta)} \leq C\frac{1}{|B|}\int_{\sigma B} w\,dx \tag{2.2}$$

for all balls B with $\sigma B \subset D$.

Definition 2.4. A weight w is said to satisfy the Muckenhoupt A_r-condition, $r > 1$, and is written $w \in A_r(D)$ when

$$\sup_{B\subset D}\left(\frac{1}{|B|}\int_B w\,dx\right)\left(\frac{1}{|B|}\int_B w^{1/(r-1)}dx\right)^{r-1} < \infty. \tag{2.3}$$

In the case where $w(x) \in \text{WRH}(D)$, Ding and Nolder proved that if D is an $L^p(\mu)$-averaging domain, then the quasihyperbolic metric is L^p integrable over D with respect to the measure μ. For the converse they only needed to assume that $w(x)$ was a doubling weight.

When the weight $w(x)$ was further assumed to satisfy the A_r-condition, the authors established that John domains are $L^p(\mu)$-averaging domains. Moreover, they proved certain norm inequalities for conjugate A-harmonic tensors in $L^p(\mu)$-averaging domains. These inequalities serve as generalizations of the Hardy-Littlewood theorem for conjugate harmonic functions. In a subsequent work, Agarwal et al. [1] studied the integrability of the solutions to the conjugate A-harmonic equation in $L^p(\mu)$-averaging domains.

In a series of papers Ding and Liu [10, 11, 19] examined a number of properties of $L^p(\mu)$-averaging domains in the Muckenhoupt A_r-weight case. They showed quasiisometries preserve $L^p(\mu)$-averaging domains, described the Whitney cube decomposition of these domains, and established the monotonic property of this class of domains. They proved versions of the Poincaré inequality for solutions to the A-harmonic equation on $L^p(\mu)$-averaging domains as well.

Ding and Shi [13] studied other weighted analogues. They generalized the Poincaré inequality of Theorem 1.3 to the case of differential forms on $L^p(\mu)$-averaging domains. The weights $w(x)$ they considered satisfied a condition denoted by $A_r(\lambda)$ which for $\lambda = 1$ coincides with the class of A_r-weights.

Later Ding [9] extended averaging domains to the case of $L^\varphi(\mu)$-averaging domains.

Definition 2.5. Let $\varphi : [0,\infty) \to \mathbb{R}$ be a continuous, increasing, and convex function with $\varphi(0) = 0$. A domain $D \subset \mathbb{R}^n$ is called an $L^\varphi(\mu)$-averaging domain if there exists a constant C such that

$$\begin{aligned} &\frac{1}{\mu(D)} \int_D \varphi(\tau \,|\, u(x) - u_{B_0,\mu} \,|\,) d\mu \\ &\qquad \le C \sup_{4B \subset D} \frac{1}{\mu(B)} \int_B \varphi(\sigma \,|\, u - u_{B,\mu} \,|\,) d\mu \end{aligned} \tag{2.4}$$

for some ball $B_0 \subset D$ and all u such that $\varphi(|u|) \in L^1_{\text{loc}}(D,\mu)$. Here τ and σ are constants such that $0 < \tau, \sigma < 1$. Note that for the special case $\varphi(t) = t^p$, the class of $L^p(\mu)$-averaging domains is recovered.

Ding proved that if $\varphi(t) \le e^{bt}$ and if $w(x)$ satisfies a weak reverse Hölder inequality, then D is an $L^\varphi(\mu)$-averaging domain if and only if $\int_D \varphi(\alpha k(x,x_0))d\mu < \infty$ for each $x_0 \in D$ and some $\alpha > 0$.

Bao and Ding [2] proved that if $w(x)$ actually satisfies the A_r-condition, then John domains are $L^\varphi(\mu)$-averaging domains. In this same paper they also showed that $L^\varphi(\mu)$-averaging domains are invariant with respect to quasi-isometries.

3. Averaging domains in homogeneous spaces

A most recent work [22] extends the notion of averaging domains to spaces of homogeneous type possessing an intrinsic metric. The space (X,d,μ) under study is a complete locally compact metric space equipped with a metric d and a doubling measure μ. In particular, this metric condition guarantees that any pair of points x and y in X can be joined by a curve of finite length and that there exists a path joining x to y of length $d(x,y)$.

The measure μ is doubling means that for all metric balls, $B(x,r) \subset X$, $\mu(B(x,r)) \le C_\mu \mu(B(x,r/2))$, where C_μ is independent of x and r.

Examples of these spaces include (i) $\mathbb{R}^n$ with a measure $\omega(x)dx$, where the weight ω satisfies a Muckenhoupt A_∞-condition, (ii) stratified homogeneous groups with the Carnot-Carathéodory metric and a measure $\omega(x)dx \in A_\infty$, and (iii) compact Riemannian manifolds with a Riemannian metric and measure. The text by Heinonen [15] provides an excellent reference for such metric spaces.

Various concepts of Euclidean spaces can be extended to these generalized metric spaces. For example, such spaces were utilized by Vodop'yanov and Greshnov [23] in their work examining extensions of bounded mean oscillation functions. In this setting, they generalized the notion of the quasihyperbolic metric and developed an analogue of Jones' [17] result on $\mathbb{R}^n$ establishing uniform domains as precisely the class of BMO extension domains.

The definition for the quasihyperbolic metric basically replaces Euclidean distance with the intrinsic metric d and Euclidean arc length with arc length in the metric. That is, given any pair of points x and y,

$$k_D(x,y) = \inf_{\gamma} \int_{\gamma} \frac{dl}{d(z,\partial D)}, \tag{3.1}$$

where the infimum is calculated over all rectifiable curves in D joining x to y. When the domain in question is clearly understood we will abbreviate $k_D(x,y)$ to $k(x,y)$.

In this setting, we say the following.

Definition 3.1. D is an L^p-averaging domain if for some $\tau > 1$ the following holds:

$$\left(\frac{1}{\mu(D)} \int_D |u(x) - u_D|^p d\mu\right)^{1/p} \le C_{\text{ave}} \left(\sup_{\tau B \subset D} \frac{1}{\mu(B)} \int_B |u(x) - u_B|^p d\mu\right)^{1/p}, \tag{3.2}$$

where the constant C_{ave} is independent of u and B is any metric ball in D, such that $\tau B \subset D$.

The main theorem in [22] characterizes averaging domains in these homogeneous spaces.

THEOREM 3.2. *Let D be a domain in the metric space (X,d,μ) with $\mu(D) < \infty$. Then D is an L^p-averaging domain if and only if the quasihyperbolic metric is L^p integrable over D with respect to the measure μ.*

The crucial features of homogeneous spaces (see [6, 8, 18]) that allow the generalization of the results to this case include the weak Vitali-type covering property of these spaces and homogeneous space versions of the John-Nirenberg theorem.

The critical notion linking the definition of averaging domains remains as in all of the previous cases. Namely, the quasihyperbolic distance between two points plays a natural role in estimating the average amount of change of the function between these two points, when the function under consideration is of bounded mean L^p-oscillation. More precisely, a central lemma needed to prove Theorem 3.2 is the following.

LEMMA 3.3. *Suppose that*

$$\left(\sup_{\tau B \subset D} \frac{1}{\mu(B)} \int_B |u(x) - u_B|^p d\mu\right)^{1/p} \le C_0, \tag{3.3}$$

then there exist constants s and q such that

$$|u_{B(x)} - u_{B(y)}| \le C_0(s(k(x,y)) + q) \tag{3.4}$$

for all $x, y \in D$. Here $B(x)$ and $B(y)$ denote the balls $B(x, d(x,\partial D)/\tau)$ and $B(y, d(y,\partial D)/\tau)$, respectively, and the constants s and q depend only on τ and C_μ.

Staples [22] also proved that the domains satisfying a Boman chain condition are L^p-averaging domains.

Definition 3.4. A domain E in X is said to satisfy the *Boman chain condition* if there exist constants M, $\lambda > 1$, $C_2 > C_1 > 1$, $C_3 > 1$, and a family $\mathfrak{F}$ of disjoint metric balls B such that

(i) $E = \bigcup_{B\in\mathfrak{F}} C_1 B$,
(ii) $\sum_{B\in\mathfrak{F}} \chi_{C_2 B} \le M\chi_E(x)$ for all $x \in X$,
(iii) there is a so-called central ball $B_* \in \mathfrak{F}$ such that for each ball $B \in \mathfrak{F}$, there is a positive integer $k = k(B)$ and a chain of balls $\{B_j\}_{j=0}^{k}$ such that $B_0 = B$, $B_k = B_*$, and $C_1 B_j \cap C_1 B_{j+1}$ contains a metric ball D_j for which $\mu(D_j) \ge C_3 \max(\mu(B_j), \mu(B_{j+1}))$,
(iv) $B \subset \lambda B_j$ for all $j = 0,\dots,k(B)$.

THEOREM 3.5. *If D satisfies a Boman chain condition, then D is an L^p-averaging domain.*

Buckley et al. [5] pioneered the study of such chain domains in homogeneous spaces. Their paper included the result that all John domains are Boman chain domains.

In the standard hierarchy of domains, it is well known that the class of NTA domains is a proper subset of uniform domains which are in turn a proper subclass of John domains. The pathologies of metrics in Carnot-Carathéodory spaces make it difficult to produce examples of NTA, uniform and John domains. In fact, even metric balls in a Carnot-Carathéodory space are not necessarily NTA [7], although they are always uniform [23]. The integrability criterion characterizing L^p-averaging domains provides another means to check if a domain is John.

John domains support the Sobolev-Poincaré inequalities and provide a standard setting for much of the study of inequalities in homogeneous spaces. Buckley and Koskela, [3, 4], proved that John domains are nearly the largest class of domains that support the Sobolev-Poincaré embedding theorem. Semmes [20] proved a version of the Poincaré inequality for Q-regular homogeneous metric spaces which are locally linearly contractible. Staples [22] extends this result to averaging domains. To understand the statement of this theorem, we provide the requisite definitions.

First we recall how upper gradients are defined on abstract homogeneous spaces and state the Poincaré inequality. Here we use the terminology of [14].

Definition 3.6. It is said that a Borel function $g : X \to [0,\infty]$ is an upper gradient of another Borel function $u : X \to \mathbb{R}$, if for every 1-Lipschitz curve $\gamma : [a,b] \to X$, the following holds $|u(\gamma(b)) - u(\gamma(a))| \le \int_a^b g(\gamma(t))dt$.

Definition 3.7. It is said that the space X supports a p-Poincaré inequality, $1 \le p < \infty$, if for every pair u,g of a continuous function $u \in L^1_{\mathrm{loc}}(X)$ and its upper gradient g on X,

$$\frac{1}{\mu(B)} \int_B |u - u_B| \, d\mu \le C_p r \left(\frac{1}{\mu(\tau B)} \int_{\tau B} g^p \, d\mu \right)^{1/p}, \tag{3.5}$$

on each ball B with $\tau B \subset X$, where r is the radius of B and $\tau \ge 1$, $C_p > 0$ are fixed constants.

The metric space conditions considered in [20] are as follows.

Definition 3.8. The metric space (X,d,μ) as defined in Section 3 is called Q-regular if there exist constants $a_1,a_2>0$ such that μ also satisfies

$$a_1 r^Q \le \mu(B(x,r)) \le a_2 r^Q \tag{3.6}$$

whenever $x\in X$ and $r\le \operatorname{diam} X$.

Definition 3.9. The metric space X satisfies a local linear contractibility condition if there exists $a_3\ge 1$ such that, for each $x\in X$ and radius $r\le a_3^{-1}\operatorname{diam} X$, the ball $B(x,r)$ can be contracted to a point inside $B(x,a_3r)$.

The Poincaré inequality on averaging domains in homogeneous spaces is the following.

THEOREM 3.10. *Let X be a connected linearly locally contractible Q regular metric space that is also an orientable topological Q-dimensional manifold, $Q\ge 2$ an integer. Let D be an L^p-averaging domain in X. Then the following Poincaré inequality holds on D,*

$$\left(\frac{1}{\mu(D)}\int_D |u-u_D|\,d\mu\right) \le C(p,\tau,a_1,a_2,a_3,C_{\text{ave}})\mu(D)^{1/Q}\left(\frac{1}{\mu(D)}\int_D g^p\,d\mu\right)^{1/p} \tag{3.7}$$

when $p\ge Q$.

The study of various types of domains in homogeneous spaces is still in its early stages. Concrete examples in even the simplest cases [7] remain elusive. The characterization of averaging domains generates one more geometric technique to utilize in assessing example domains.

References

[1] R. P. Agarwal, S. Ding, and P. Shi, *Integrability of the solutions to conjugate A-harmonic equations in $L^s(\mu)$-averaging domains*, Archives of Inequalities and Applications **2** (2004), no. 4, 517–526.

[2] G. Bao and S. Ding, *Invariance properties of $L^\varphi(\mu)$-averaging domains under some mappings*, Journal of Mathematical Analysis and Applications **259** (2001), no. 1, 241–252.

[3] S. Buckley and P. Koskela, *Sobolev-Poincaré implies John*, Mathematical Research Letters **2** (1995), no. 5, 577–593.

[4] ———, *Criteria for imbeddings of Sobolev-Poincaré type*, International Mathematics Research Notices **1996** (1996), no. 18, 881–901.

[5] S. Buckley, P. Koskela, and G. Lu, *Boman equals John*, XVIth Rolf Nevanlinna Colloquium (Joensuu, 1995), de Gruyter, Berlin, 1996, pp. 91–99.

[6] N. Burger, *Espace des fonctions à variation moyenne bornée sur un espace de nature homogène*, Comptes Rendus de l'Académie des Sciences, Paris **286** (1978), no. 3, A139–A142.

[7] L. Capogna, N. Garofalo, and D.-M. Nhieu, *Examples of uniform and NTA domains in Carnot groups*, Proceedings on Analysis and Geometry (Russian) (Novosibirsk Akademgorodok, 1999), Izdat. Ross. Akad. Nauk Sib. Otd. Inst. Mat., Novosibirsk, 2000, pp. 103–121.

[8] R. R. Coifman and G. Weiss, *Analyse Harmonique Non-Commutative sur certains Espaces Homogènes*, Springer, Berlin, 1971.

[9] S. Ding, *$L^\varphi(\mu)$-averaging domains and the quasi-hyperbolic metric*, Computers & Mathematics with Applications **47** (2004), no. 10-11, 1611–1618.

[10] S. Ding and B. Liu, *Generalized Poincaré inequalities for solutions to the A-harmonic equation in certain domains*, Journal of Mathematical Analysis and Applications **252** (2000), no. 2, 538–548.

[11] ———, *Whitney covers and quasi-isometry of $L^s(\mu)$-averaging domains*, Journal of Inequalities and Applications **6** (2001), no. 4, 435–449.

[12] S. Ding and C. A. Nolder, *$L^s(\mu)$-averaging domains*, Journal of Mathematical Analysis and Applications **283** (2003), no. 1, 85–99.

[13] S. Ding and P. Shi, *Weighted Poincaré-type inequalities for differential forms in $L^s(\mu)$-averaging domains*, Journal of Mathematical Analysis and Applications **227** (1998), no. 1, 200–215.

[14] P. Hajłasz and P. Koskela, *Sobolev met Poincaré*, Memoirs of the American Mathematical Society **145** (2000), no. 688, x+101.

[15] J. Heinonen, *Lectures on Analysis on Metric Spaces*, Universitext, Springer, New York, 2001.

[16] F. John, *Rotation and strain*, Communications on Pure and Applied Mathematics **14** (1961), 391–413.

[17] P. W. Jones, *Extension theorems for BMO*, Indiana University Mathematics Journal **29** (1980), no. 1, 41–66.

[18] M. Kronz, *Some function spaces on spaces of homogeneous type*, Manuscripta Mathematica **106** (2001), no. 2, 219–248.

[19] B. Liu and S. Ding, *The monotonic property of $L^s(\mu)$-averaging domains and weighted weak reverse Hölder inequality*, Journal of Mathematical Analysis and Applications **237** (1999), no. 2, 730–739.

[20] S. Semmes, *Finding curves on general spaces through quantitative topology, with applications to Sobolev and Poincaré inequalities*, Selecta Mathematica. New Series **2** (1996), no. 2, 155–295.

[21] S. G. Staples, *L^p-averaging domains and the Poincaré inequality*, Annales Academiae Scientiarum Fennicae. Series A I. Mathematica **14** (1989), no. 1, 103–127.

[22] ———, *L^p-averaging domains in homogeneous spaces*, Journal of Mathematical Analysis and Applications **317** (2006), no. 2, 550–564.

[23] S. K. Vodop'yanov and A. V. Greshnov, *On the continuation of functions of bounded mean oscillation on spaces of homogeneous type with intrinsic metric*, Siberian Mathematical Journal **36** (1995), no. 5, 873–901.

Susan G. Staples: Department of Mathematics, Texas Christian University, P. O. Box 298900, Fort Worth, TX 76129, USA
E-mail address: s.staples@tcu.edu

ON A BIFURCATION DELAY IN DIFFERENTIAL EQUATIONS WITH A DELAYED TIME $2n\pi$

K. TCHIZAWA AND R. MIYAZAKI

In the dynamic Hopf bifurcation it is known that the bifurcation delay occurs. In this paper we will show that the bifurcation delay is persistent under adding a delayed feedback control term with a delayed time $2n\pi$ (n is any positive integer) if the period of the Hopf bifurcating solution is 2π. We will also give some numerical simulation results which suggest that the length of the bifurcation delay is shorter as n increases.

1. Introduction

Neishtadt [4] shows the existence of a delay for the general Hopf bifurcation. Lobry [2] gives an introductory explanation of the "delay" phenomenon as follows. Consider the planar system

$$\begin{aligned} x_1' &= \mu x_1 + x_2 - x_1(x_1^2 + x_2^2), \\ x_2' &= -x_1 + \mu x_2 - x_2(x_1^2 + x_2^2) \end{aligned} \tag{1.1}$$

which exhibits a supercritical Hopf bifurcation for $\mu = 0$. More precisely, if $\mu < 0$, the origin is stable, and if $\mu > 0$, the origin becomes unstable and a stable closed orbit surrounding the origin with a radius $\rho = \sqrt{\mu}$ appears (see Figure 1.1). Then the closed orbit has a period $2n\pi$. By contrast, consider the parameter μ growing slowly with time in system (1.1),

$$\begin{aligned} x_1' &= \mu x_1 + x_2 - x_1(x_1^2 + x_2^2), \\ x_2' &= -x_1 + \mu x_2 - x_2(x_1^2 + x_2^2), \\ \mu' &= \varepsilon, \end{aligned} \tag{1.2}$$

where ε is small, and consider the solution which starts from (x_0, y_0, μ_0), where $x_0^2 + y_0^2$ is very small and $\mu_0 < 0$. Lobry shows that $x^2 + y^2$ remains close to 0 until μ is positive, and from the value $\mu = 0$ to $\mu = -\mu_0$ the solution remains infinitesimal and then departs very

Hindawi Publishing Corporation
Proceedings of the Conference on Differential & Difference Equations and Applications, pp. 1049–1054

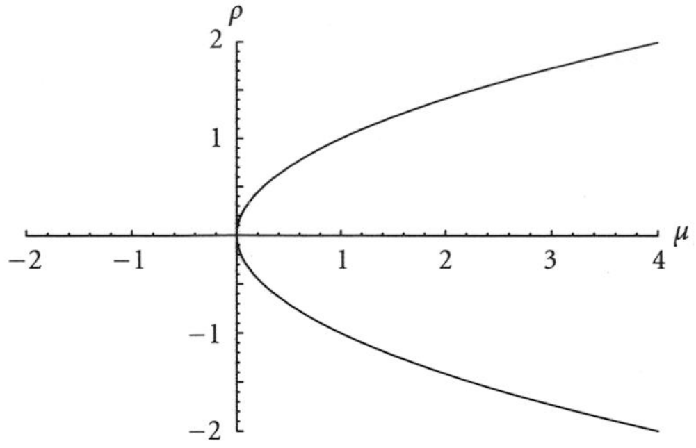

Figure 1.1. The amplitude of the stable closed orbit of (1.1).

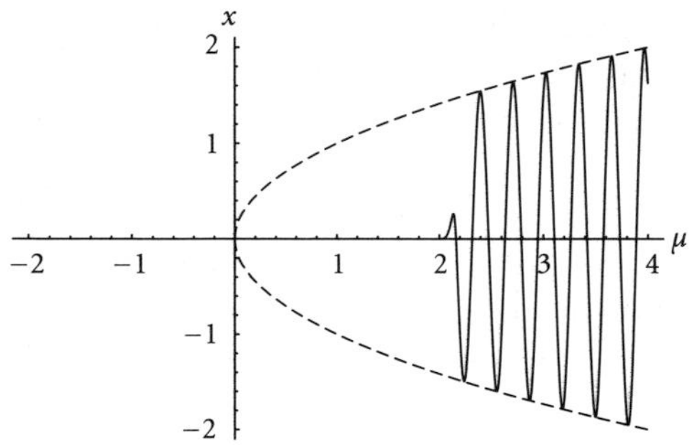

Figure 1.2. The phase portrait of (1.2) for $\varepsilon = 0.05$, $\mu(0) = -2$.

suddenly to an oscillation of large amplitude (see Figure 1.2). The phenomenon is called a "delay" in the bifurcation.

Let us consider the effects of a delayed feedback control term on the "delay" phenomenon in the bifurcation.

$$\begin{gathered} x_1' = \mu x_1 + x_2 - x_1(x_1^2 + x_2^2) + b_1 u(t), \\ x_2' = -x_1 + \mu x_2 - x_2(x_1^2 + x_2^2) + b_2 u(t), \\ \mu' = \varepsilon; \\ u(t) = -k_1(x(t) - x(t-\tau)) - k_2(y(t) - y(t-\tau)), \end{gathered} \tag{1.3}$$

where k_1, k_2, b_1, b_2 are real constants, and $u(t)$ is called a delayed feedback control term with a delayed time τ. In [3] the authors consider the case when $n = 1$ and obtain the following results.

THEOREM 1.1. *Assume $\tau = 2\pi$ and $|k_1|$, $|k_2|$, $|b_1|$, $|b_2|$ are sufficiently small. Then bifurcation delay is persistent under the time delayed feedback for system (1.2).*

In this paper we consider the case when $\tau = 2n\pi$ $(n = 1, 2, \dots)$ and we obtain the similar results as Theorem 1.1. Moreover, we give some numerical simulation results which suggest that the length of the bifurcation delay is shorter as n increases.

2. Analysis of the first system

Consider planar ordinary differential equations with a scalar parameter μ:

$$\frac{dx}{dt} = F(x;\mu). \tag{2.1}$$

Assume that the Hopf bifurcation occurs at $\mu = 0$. In this paper we consider only the normalized case when

$$F(x;\mu) = A(\mu)x + f(|x|)x, \quad A(\mu) = \begin{pmatrix} \mu & 1 \\ -1 & \mu \end{pmatrix}, \tag{2.2}$$

where $x = \mathrm{col}(x_1, x_2)$, $|x| = \sqrt{x_1^2 + x_2^2}$, and $f : [0,\infty) \to \mathbb{R}$ is a C^k $(k \geq 3)$ function satisfying $f(0) = 0$. Note that we refer to [1, Theorem 11.15] as the Hopf bifurcation theorem reformulated to be more directly applicable to this system.

Adding a time delayed feedback control term $bu(t)$ to system (2.1), we have

$$\begin{aligned} \frac{dx}{dt} &= A(\mu)x + f(|x|)x + bu(t), \qquad A(\mu) = \begin{pmatrix} \mu & 1 \\ -1 & \mu \end{pmatrix}, \\ u(t) &= -k^T(x(t) - x(t-\tau)), \end{aligned} \tag{2.3}$$

where b and k are in $\mathbb{R}^2$, and k^T represents a transpose of k.

The linearized equation of (2.3) at $x = 0$ becomes

$$\frac{dx(t)}{dt} = A(\mu)x(t) - bk^T(x(t) - x(t-\tau)). \tag{2.4}$$

The characteristic equation of (2.4) is

$$p(z) := \det[zI - A(\mu) + (1 - e^{-\tau z})bk^T] = 0. \tag{2.5}$$

Define two sets of the characteristic roots of (2.4) as

$$\Lambda := \{z : p(z) = 0 \text{ and } \Re z > 0\}, \qquad \Lambda_0 := \{z : p(z) = 0 \text{ and } \Re z = 0\}. \tag{2.6}$$

Here $\Re z$ represents the real part of a complex number z.

To avoid complication in calculating, throughout this paper we assume

$$k^T b = 0. \tag{H1}$$

Then it is convenient to write b and k as follows:

$$b = \hat{b}\begin{pmatrix} \cos\delta \\ -\sin\delta \end{pmatrix}, \qquad k = \hat{k}\begin{pmatrix} \sin\delta \\ \cos\delta \end{pmatrix}, \tag{2.7}$$

where $\hat{b} \leq 0$, $\hat{k} \in \mathbb{R}$ and $0 \leq \delta < 2\pi$.

Lemma 2.1. *Suppose that (H1) holds and $|\hat{b}\hat{k}|$ is sufficiently small. If $\tau = 2n\pi$, then for any small $|\mu|$,*

(i) $\mu < 0$ *implies* $\Lambda \cup \Lambda_0 = \emptyset$,

(ii) $\mu = 0$ *implies* $\Lambda = \emptyset$, $\Lambda_0 = \{\pm i\}$. *Moreover the multiplicity of* $\pm i$ *is 1 and*

$$\Re \frac{dz}{d\mu}\bigg|_{\substack{\mu=0\\ z=\pm i}} > 0, \tag{2.8}$$

(iii) $\mu > 0$ *implies* $\Lambda_0 = \emptyset$ *and* Λ *has two elements.*

Proof. The proof is given by using Rouché's theorem. □

By the similar calculation in [3], we can show that the dynamics of the center manifold at the equilibrium are given by the following system:

$$\frac{dy}{dt} = A(0)y + \Psi_0\{\mu + f(|y|)\}y, \tag{2.9}$$

where

$$\Psi_0 = (\Psi, \Phi)^{-1} = \frac{1}{1 + (\hat{b}\hat{k}n\pi)^2}\left\{I + \hat{b}\hat{k}n\pi R\left(\frac{\pi}{2}\right)\right\}. \tag{2.10}$$

3. Bifurcation delay and delayed feedback term

Consider the effects of a time delayed feedback term on the "delay" phenomenon in system (1.2):

$$\begin{aligned} x_1' &= \mu x_2 + x_1 - x_1(x_1^2 + x_2^2) + b_1 u(t), \\ x_2' &= -x_1 + \mu x_2 - x_2(x_1^2 + x_2^2) + b_2 u(t), \\ \mu' &= \varepsilon; \\ u(t) &= -k_1(x(t) - x(t-\tau)) - k_2(y(t) - y(t - 2n\pi)). \end{aligned} \tag{3.1}$$

This is the case when $f(\rho) = -\rho^2$, $b = \text{col}(b_1, b_2) = \hat{b}\,\text{col}(\cos\delta, -\sin\delta)$, $k = (k_1, k_2) = \hat{k}\,\text{col}(\sin\delta, \cos\delta)$, and $\tau = 2n\pi$ in (2.3), so that we can use the results calculated in the previous section. Moreover, the same argument given by Lobry [2, pages 1–4] can be applicable and we can expect the "delay" phenomenon in the bifurcation. Translating to polar coordinates (ρ, θ) for (2.9) given by $y_1 = \rho\cos\theta$, $y_2 = -\rho\sin\theta$, we have

$$\begin{aligned} \frac{d\rho}{dt} &= \frac{1}{1 + (\hat{b}\hat{k}n\pi)^2}(\mu + f(\rho))\rho, \\ \frac{d\theta}{dt} &= 1 - \frac{\hat{b}\hat{k}n\pi}{1 + (\hat{b}\hat{k}\pi)^2}(\mu + f(\rho)). \end{aligned} \tag{3.2}$$

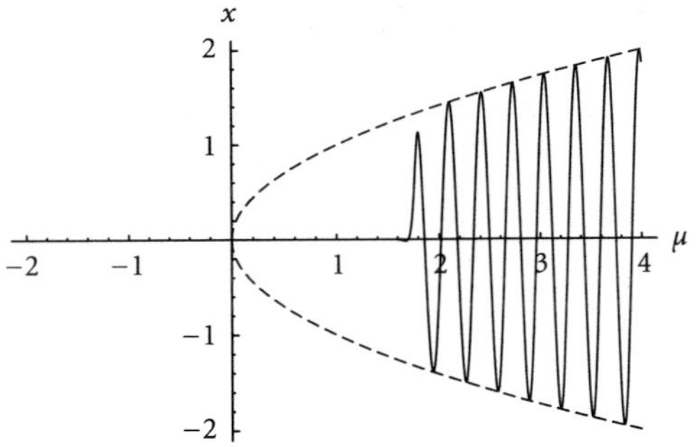

Figure 3.1. The phase portrait of (3.1) for $n = 1$.

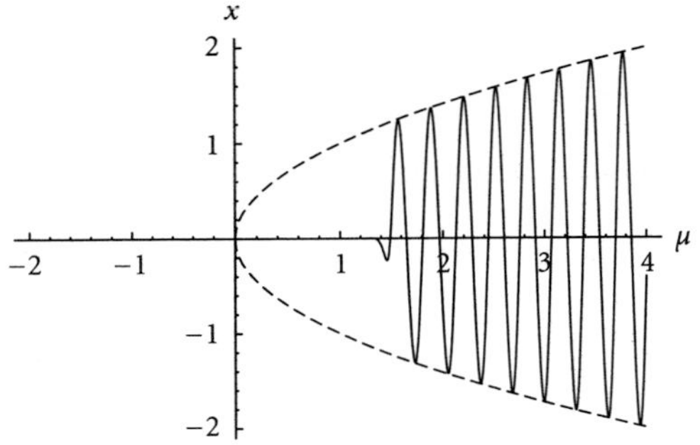

Figure 3.2. The phase portrait of (3.1) for $n = 2$.

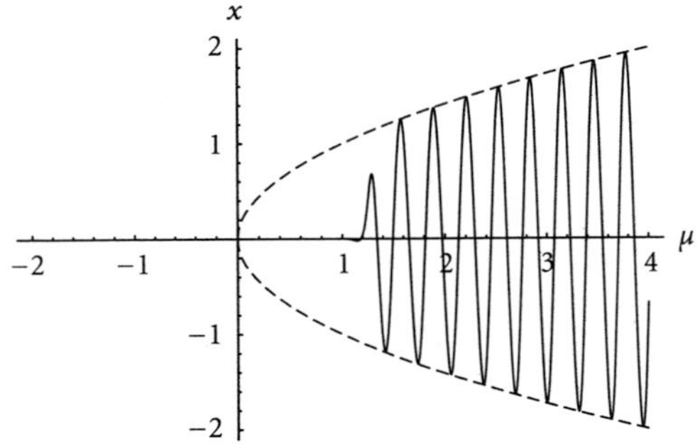

Figure 3.3. The phase portrait of (3.1) for $n = 3$.

THEOREM 3.1. *Assume $|k_1|$, $|k_2|$, $|b_1|$, $|b_2|$ are sufficiently small. For any positive integer n, the bifurcation delay is persistent under the time delayed feedback with a delayed time $2n\pi$ for system (1.2).*

Figures 3.1, 3.2, 3.3, and 3.4 illustrate the phase portraits of (3.1) for $n = 1,2,3,4$, where $\varepsilon = 0.05$, $\mu(0) = -2$, $b = (0.1/\sqrt{2})\binom{1}{-1}$, $k = (0.1/\sqrt{2})\binom{1}{1}$. It seems that the length of the bifurcation delay is shorter as n increases.

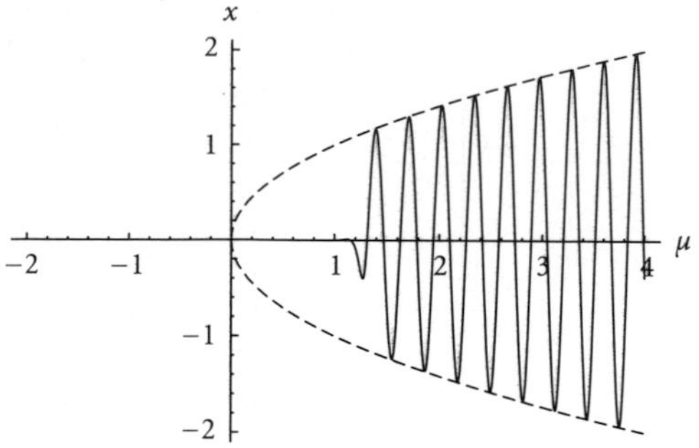

Figure 3.4. The phase portrait of (3.1) for $n = 4$.

References

[1] J. K. Hale and H. Koçak, *Dynamics and Bifurcations*, Texts in Applied Mathematics, vol. 3, Springer, New York, 1991.

[2] C. Lobry, *Dynamic bifurcations*, Dynamic Bifurcations (Luminy, 1990), Lecture Notes in Math., vol. 1493, Springer, Berlin, 1991, pp. 1–13.

[3] R. Miyazaki and K. Tchizawa, *Bifurcation delay in a delay differential equation*, Nonlinear Analysis **63** (2005), no. 5–7, e2189–e2195.

[4] A. I. Neĭshtadt, *Prolongation of the loss of stability in the case of dynamic bifurcations. I*, Differentsial'nye Uravneniya **23** (1987), no. 12, 2060–2067, 2204, translation in Differential Equations **23** (1987), no. 12, 1385–1391.

K. Tchizawa: Department of Mathematics, Musashi Institute of Technology, 1-28-1 Tamazutsumi, Setagaya-ku, Tokyo 158-8557, Japan
E-mail address: tchizawa@aol.com

R. Miyazaki: Department of Systems Engineering, Shizuoka University, 3-5-1 Johoku, Hamamatsu, Shizuoka 432-8561, Japan
E-mail address: rinko@sys.eng.shizuoka.ac.jp

CONCENTRATION-COMPACTNESS PRINCIPLE FOR MOUNTAIN PASS PROBLEMS

KYRIL TINTAREV

We show that critical sequences associated with the mountain pass level for semilinear elliptic problems on $\mathbb{R}^N$ converge when the nonlinearity is subcritical, superlinear, and satisfies the penalty condition $F_\infty(s) < F(x,s)$. The proof suggests a concentration-compactness framework for minimax problems, similar to that of P.-L. Lions for constrained minima.

1. Introduction

In this paper we prove an existence result for the classical semilinear elliptic problem on $\mathbb{R}^N$:

$$-\Delta u + u = f(x,u), \quad u \in H^1(\mathbb{R}^N). \tag{1.1}$$

The classical existence proof for the analogous Dirichlet problem on bounded domain, based on the mountain pass lemma of [1], fails in the case of $\mathbb{R}^N$, since the Palais-Smale condition does not anymore follow from compactness of Sobolev embeddings and a concentration-compactness argument is needed. There are numerous publications where the concentration compactness is used in minimax problems, including the problem considered here (a representative bibliography on the subject can be found in the books of Chabrowski [4] and Willem [13]), but given that in problems on $\mathbb{R}^N$ the $(PS)_c$ condition fails, typically, for every c that is a linear combination, with positive integer coefficients, of critical values, the Palais-Smale condition has been proved only with severe restrictions on the nonlinearity $f(x,s)$.

We consider here a set of conditions on the functional, similar to the concentration-compactness framework as set by Lions (see [6–9]), where conditions for existence of minima can be formulated as the following prototype assumptions: (a) the functionals are continuous; (b) critical sequences are bounded in norm (achieved by regarding constrained minima); (c) constrained minimal values are subadditive with respect to the parameter of constraint level; and (d) the functionals are invariant relative to

Hindawi Publishing Corporation
Proceedings of the Conference on Differential & Difference Equations and Applications, pp. 1055–1060

transformations causing the loss of compactness or their asymptotic values (with respect to the unbounded sequences of the transformations) satisfy a penalty condition.

In the present paper we consider a functional G on a Hilbert space H with an asymptotic (with respect to unbounded sequence of transformations responsible for loss of compactness) value G_∞. Let Φ be an appropriate set of mappings from a metric space X into H with fixed values on a subset X_0 of X, and let

$$\rho := \sup G(\varphi(X_0)) < c =: \inf_{\varphi\in\Phi} \sup G(\varphi(X)). \tag{1.2}$$

We regard the following heuristic conditions, whose formal counterparts for the functional associated with (1.1) will be given in Section 2:

(a′) $G \in C^1(H)$ (in the semilinear elliptic case, subcritical growth of f);

(b′) critical sequences at the level c are bounded (in the semilinear elliptic case it follows from an assumption of superlinearity for f);

(c′) a condition of convexity type for G_∞—in the semilinear elliptic case with a mountain pass, the sufficient condition is $s \mapsto f_\infty(s)/|s|$ monotone increasing;

(d′) invariance or penalty condition (resp., $f(x,s) = f(s)$ or $F(x,s) > F_\infty(s)$, where $F(x,t) = \int_0^t f(x,s)ds$).

A weaker version of (c′) may be given as follows:

(c″) for every critical point w of G_∞ such that $\rho < G_\infty(w) \le c$, there is a sequence of paths φ_k such that $d(w,\varphi_k(X)) \to 0$ and $\sup_{x\in X} G_\infty(\varphi_k(x)) \to G(w)$.

Existence of critical points is proved by verifying $(PS)_c$ for a single value c, namely, the one given by the mountain pass statement. Sharp estimates of c are based on the global compactness theorem by Schindler and the author [11], which is a functional-analytic generalization of earlier "multibump" weak convergence lemmas (Struwe [12], Lions [10], Cao and Peng [3]).

2. Existence theorem

We consider the Hilbert space $H^1(\mathbb{R}^N)$, $N \in \mathbb{N}$, defined as the completion of $C_c^\infty(\mathbb{R}^N)$ with respect to the norm

$$\|u\|^2 = \int_{\mathbb{R}^N} |\nabla u|^2 + u^2. \tag{2.1}$$

In what follows the notation of norm without other specification will refer to this H^1-norm. The space $H^1(\mathbb{R}^N)$ is continuously embedded into $L^p(\mathbb{R}^N)$ for $2 \le p \le 2N/(N-2)$ when $N > 2$ and for $p \ge 2$ for $N = 1,2$. For convenience we set $2^* = 2N/(N-2)$ for $N > 2$ and $2^* = \infty$ for $N = 1,2$. Let $f : \mathbb{R}^N \times \mathbb{R}$ be continuous function and let

$$F(x,t) = \int_0^t f(x,s)ds, \tag{2.2}$$

$$g(u) = \int_{\mathbb{R}^N} F(x,u(x))dx, \tag{2.3}$$

$$G(u) = \frac{1}{2}\|u\|^2 - g(u). \tag{2.4}$$

We assume that $f(x,s) \to f_\infty(s)$ as $|x| \to \infty$ and follow the definitions above to define F_∞, g_∞, and G_∞.

Let

$$\Phi = \Big\{\varphi \in C([0,\infty);H^1(\mathbb{R}^N)) : \varphi(0) = 0,\ \lim_{t\to\infty} G_\infty(\varphi(t)) = -\infty\Big\}. \tag{2.5}$$

Theorem 2.1. *Assume that for every $\epsilon > 0$ there exist $p_\epsilon \in (2,2^*)$ and $C_\epsilon > 0$ such that*
(A) $|f(x,s)| \le \epsilon(|s| + |s|^{2^*-1}) + C_\epsilon |s|^{p_\epsilon - 1}$, $s \in \mathbb{R}$, $x \in \mathbb{R}^N$, *there exists* $\mu > 2$, *such that*
(B) $f(x,s)s \ge \mu F(x,s)$, $s \in \mathbb{R}$, $x \in \mathbb{R}^N$,
(C) $s \mapsto f_\infty(s)/|s|$, $s \in \mathbb{R}$, *is increasing,*
(D) $F(x,s) > F_\infty(s)$, $s \in \mathbb{R}\setminus\{0\}$, $x \in \mathbb{R}^N$.
Then $\Phi \neq \emptyset$;

$$c := \inf_{\varphi\in\Phi}\max_{t\in[0,\infty)} G(\varphi(t)) > 0; \tag{2.6}$$

there is a sequence $u_k \in H^1(\mathbb{R}^N)$ such that $G'(u_k) \to 0$, $G(u_k) \to c$; every such sequence has a subsequence convergent in $H^1(\mathbb{R}^N)$. Consequently, $u = \lim u_k$ satisfies $G(u) = c$ and $G'(u) = 0$ (and therefore, u is a solution of (1.1)).

Condition (A) is a well-known sufficient condition for $G \in C^1(H^1(\mathbb{R}^N))$.

Lemma 2.2. *Let G be as in (2.4). Assume conditions* (A) *and* (C) *of Theorem 2.1. Then for every $w \in H^1(\mathbb{R}^N)\setminus\{0\}$, the path $\varphi(t) = tw$, $t \in (0,\infty)$, is in Φ and the constant (2.6) is positive. If, in addition, $G'_\infty(w) = 0$, then $\max_t G_\infty(\varphi(t))$ is attained at $\varphi(1) = w$.*

Proof. The first assertion of the lemma follows easily from (C) and the second is a consequence of (A) (the proof is a trivial modification of the one in [1]).

Let $w \neq 0$ satisfy $G'_{-\infty}(w) = 0$. From (C) follow that the function $s \mapsto s^{-1}(d/ds)G_\infty(sw^{(n)})$ is decreasing on $(0,\infty)$. Then, since

$$\begin{aligned}\frac{d}{ds}G_\infty(sw) &= s\|w\|^2 - \int f_\infty(sw)w \\ &= s\left(\|w\|^2 - \int \frac{f_\infty(sw)}{sw}w^2\,dx\right),\end{aligned} \tag{2.7}$$

the function $s \mapsto \gamma(s) := G_\infty(sw)$ has at most one critical point. Since $\gamma(0) = 0$, $\gamma(s) < 0$ for s large and has positive values (because $c > 0$), the critical point of γ is a point of maximum. Since $G'_{-\infty}(w) = 0$, $(G'_{-\infty}(w),w) = 0$, which is equivalent to $\gamma'(1) = 0$. Since $\gamma(s)$ has a unique critical point, which is a point of maximum, $s \mapsto G_{-\infty}(sw)$ attains its maximum at $s = 1$. □

3. Global compactness

In this section we present statements from [11] concerning weak convergence that will be used in the proof. In what follows D denotes the group of lattice shifts on $H^1(\mathbb{R}^N)$, namely,

$$D = \{u \mapsto u(\cdot + y),\ y \in \mathbb{Z}^N\}. \tag{3.1}$$

We will say that $u_k \overset{D}{\rightharpoonup} u$ if for every sequence $g_k \in D$, $g_k(u_k - u) \rightharpoonup 0$.

Theorem 3.1. *Let $u_k \in H^1(\mathbb{R}^N)$ be a bounded sequence. Then there exists $w^{(n)} \in H$, $g_k^{(n)} \in D$, $k,n \in \mathbb{N}$ such that for a renumbered subsequence*

$$g_k^{(1)} = id, \qquad g_k^{(n)^{-1}} g_k^{(m)} \rightharpoonup 0 \quad \text{for } n \neq m, \tag{3.2}$$

$$w^{(n)} = w - \lim g_k^{(n)^{-1}} u_k, \tag{3.3}$$

$$\sum_{n\in\mathbb{N}} \|w^{(n)}\|^2 \leq \limsup \|u_k\|^2, \tag{3.4}$$

$$u_k - \sum_{n\in\mathbb{N}} g_k^{(n)} w^{(n)} \overset{D}{\rightharpoonup} 0. \tag{3.5}$$

In particular, $u \mapsto u(\cdot - y)$, $y \in \mathbb{Z}^N$, form a dislocation group in $H_0^1(\mathbb{R}^N)$, and $u_k \overset{D}{\rightharpoonup} 0$ is equivalent to $u_k \to 0$ in $L^p(\mathbb{R}^N)$, $p \in (2, 2^*)$ (an equivalent statement is found in [5]).

The following lemma is similar to the Brézis-Lieb lemma from [2] and is a trivial modification of analogous lemma from [11].

Lemma 3.2. *Assume that F satisfies (A) and that u_k and $(w^{(n)})$ are as in Theorem 3.1. Then*

$$\int F(x,u_k) \longrightarrow \int F(x,w^{(1)}) + \sum_{n\geq 2} \int F_\infty(w^{(n)}). \tag{3.6}$$

4. Proof of Theorem 2.1

Step 1. By Lemma 2.2, $\Phi \neq \emptyset$ and $c > 0$. By (A), (2.6), and the mountain pass lemma [1], there is a sequence u_k such that $G'(u_k) \to 0$ and $G(u_k) \to c$. By (B), u_k is bounded in H^1 (see, again, the argument of [1]) and we can apply Theorem 3.1, referring in what follows to the renamed subsequence. By (3.6) and (3.4),

$$c \geq \frac{1}{2} \sum_{n\in\mathbb{N}} \|w^{(n)}\|^2 - \int F(x,w^{(1)}) - \sum_{n\geq 2} \int F_\infty(w^{(n)}). \tag{4.1}$$

From $G'(u_k) \to 0$ (since (A), by compactness of local embeddings of H^1 into L^p, implies weak convergence of $g'(u_k)$ for weakly convergent u_k) follow

$$\|w^{(1)}\|^2 = \int f(x,w^{(1)})w^{(1)}, \quad \|w^{(n)}\|^2 = \int f_\infty(w^{(n)})w^{(n)} \quad \text{for } n \geq 2. \tag{4.2}$$

Substituting (4.2) into (4.1) we get

$$c \geq \int \left(\frac{1}{2} f(x,w^{(1)})w^{(1)} - F(x,w^{(1)})\right) + \sum_{n\geq 2} \int \left(\frac{1}{2} f_\infty(w^{(n)})w^{(n)} - F_\infty(w^{(n)})\right). \tag{4.3}$$

Step 2. Note that

$$\frac{1}{2}f(x,s)s - F(x,s) > 0, \quad \frac{1}{2}f_\infty(s)s - F_\infty(s) > 0, \quad s \neq 0. \tag{4.4}$$

The first relation follows from (B):

$$\frac{1}{2}f(x,s)s - F(x,s) \geq \left(\frac{\mu}{2} - 1\right)F(x,s), \tag{4.5}$$

$F(x,s) > F_\infty(s)$ by (D) and $F_\infty(s) > 0$ for $s \neq 0$ due to (A). The second relation follows from going to the limit in (4.5) as $|x| \to \infty$ and using positivity of $F_\infty(s)$.
Step 3. Assume that

$$w^{(n)} \neq 0 \quad \text{for some } n \neq 1. \tag{4.6}$$

Let us estimate c from above by choosing paths $s \mapsto sw^{(n)}(\cdot - y_k) \in H^1(\mathbb{R}^N)$ with $y_k \in \mathbb{Z}^N$, $|y_k| \to \infty$. Then

$$c \leq \sup_{s\in(0,\infty)} G(sw^{(n)}(\cdot - y_k)). \tag{4.7}$$

By taking $k \to \infty$, we have

$$c \leq \sup_{s\in(0,\infty)} G_\infty(sw^{(n)}). \tag{4.8}$$

By Lemma 2.2, $\sup_{s\in(0,\infty)} G_\infty(sw^{(n)}) = G_\infty(w^{(n)})$, and therefore

$$c \leq G_\infty(w^{(n)}). \tag{4.9}$$

Comparing this with (4.3), we see, due to (4.4), that for $m \neq n$, $w^{(m)} = 0$ with necessity and therefore

$$c = G_\infty(w^{(n)}). \tag{4.10}$$

This is clearly false: consider a path $s \mapsto sw^{(n)}$. Then by (D),

$$\sup_s G(sw^{(n)}) < \sup_s G_\infty(sw^{(n)}) = G_\infty(w^{(n)}) = c, \tag{4.11}$$

which contradicts the definition of c.

We conclude that the assumption (4.6) is false and $w^{(n)} = 0$ for all $n \neq 1$.
Step 4. We conclude from Step 3 and (3.5) that $u_k \to w^{(1)}$ in L^r for any $r \in (2, 2^*)$. Then from (A) follows $g'(u_k) \to g'(w^{(1)})$, and, since $u_k - g'(u_k) \to 0$, u_k is a convergent sequence in $H^1(\mathbb{R}^N)$. We conclude that $u_k \to w^{(1)}$ in $H^1(\mathbb{R}^N)$. By continuity, $G'(w^{(1)}) = 0$ and $G(w^{(1)}) = c$.

Acknowledgment

This research is done while visiting Technion–Israel Institute of Technology and supported in part by a grant from Swedish Research Council.

References

[1] A. Ambrosetti and P. H. Rabinowitz, *Dual variational methods in critical point theory and applications*, Journal of Functional Analysis **14** (1973), 349–381.

[2] H. Brézis and E. Lieb, *A relation between pointwise convergence of functions and convergence of functionals*, Proceedings of the American Mathematical Society **88** (1983), no. 3, 486–490.

[3] D. Cao and S. Peng, *A global compactness result for singular elliptic problems involving critical Sobolev exponent*, Proceedings of the American Mathematical Society **131** (2003), no. 6, 1857–1866.

[4] J. Chabrowski, *Weak Convergence Methods for Semilinear Elliptic Equations*, World Scientific, New Jersey, 1999.

[5] E. Lieb, *On the lowest eigenvalue of the Laplacian for the intersection of two domains*, Inventiones Mathematicae **74** (1983), no. 3, 441–448.

[6] P.-L. Lions, *The concentration-compactness principle in the calculus of variations. The locally compact case. I*, Annales de l'Institut Henri Poincaré. Analyse Non Linéaire **1** (1984), no. 2, 109–145.

[7] ———, *The concentration-compactness principle in the calculus of variations. The locally compact case. II*, Annales de l'Institut Henri Poincaré. Analyse Non Linéaire **1** (1984), no. 4, 223–283.

[8] ———, *The concentration-compactness principle in the calculus of variations. The limit case. I*, Revista Matemática Iberoamericana **1** (1985), no. 1, 145–201.

[9] ———, *The concentration-compactness principle in the calculus of variations. The limit case. II*, Revista Matemática Iberoamericana **1** (1985), no. 2, 45–121.

[10] ———, *Solutions of Hartree-Fock equations for Coulomb systems*, Communications in Mathematical Physics **109** (1987), no. 1, 33–97.

[11] I. Schindler and K. Tintarev, *An abstract version of the concentration compactness principle*, Revista Matemática Complutense **15** (2002), no. 2, 417–436.

[12] M. Struwe, *A global compactness result for elliptic boundary value problems involving limiting nonlinearities*, Mathematische Zeitschrift **187** (1984), no. 4, 511–517.

[13] M. Willem, *Minimax Theorems*, Progress in Nonlinear Differential Equations and Their Applications, vol. 24, Birkhäuser Boston, Massachusetts, 1996.

Kyril Tintarev: Department of Mathematics, Uppsala University, SE-751 06 Uppsala, Sweden
E-mail address: kyril.tintarev@math.uu.se

SCATTERING THEORY FOR A WAVE EQUATION OF HARTREE TYPE

KIMITOSHI TSUTAYA

We consider a scattering problem for a wave equation with a cubic convolution together with a potential in three space dimensions. We show the sharp conditions on the decay rates at infinity of the potentials and initial data for the existence of scattering operators.

1. Introduction

This paper is intended to present an extension of the result in the paper [9], which treats the Cauchy problem.

We consider a scattering problem for the nonlinear wave equation

$$\partial_t^2 u - \Delta u = V_1(x)u + (V_2 * u^2)u \quad \text{in } \mathbb{R}\times\mathbb{R}^3, \tag{NW}$$

where $V_1(x) = O(|x|^{-\gamma_1})$ as $|x| \to \infty$, $V_2(x) = \nu_2|x|^{-\gamma_2}$, $\nu_2 \in \mathbb{R}$, $\gamma_1,\gamma_2 > 0$, and $*$ denotes spatial convolution. The potential V_1 is assumed to be a smooth function.

The Schrödinger equation with the interaction term $V_1(x)u + (V_2 * u^2)u$ was studied by Hayashi and Ozawa [3]. See also Coclite and Georgiev [2].

We study the scattering problem for (NW) with small initial data. Moreover, in this paper the potential V_1 is assumed to be small since the solution may blow up in a finite time unless V_1 is small. See Strauss and Tsutaya [8].

In case $V_1(x) \equiv 0$, the initial data have small amplitude, and $V_2(x)$ satisfies some conditions, it is known by [4–7] that the scattering operator exists for small initial data. In particular, Mochizuki and Motai [7] proved the existence of scattering operators for (NW) in n-dimensional space if

$$2 + \frac{2}{3(n-1)} < \gamma_2 < n. \tag{1.1}$$

Hidano [4] showed the existence of scattering operators for (NW) in three dimensions if $2 < \gamma_2 < 5/2$ using the Lorentz invariance method. He also proved blow up in a finite time for $0 < \gamma_2 < 2$.

Hindawi Publishing Corporation
Proceedings of the Conference on Differential & Difference Equations and Applications, pp. 1061–1065

For the Klein-Gordon equation with a cubic convolution, we refer to [5–7].

One aim of this paper is to permit $V_1(x)$ which is small and decays like $|x|^{-\gamma_1}$. We show that if $\gamma_1 > 2$, $2 \le \gamma_2 < 3$, and the small initial data decay like $|x|^{-1-k}$ with $k > 1 + (3 - \gamma_2)/2$, then there exist scattering operators for (NW), which improves on the requirement $2 < \gamma_2 < 5/2$ in Hidano [4].

On the other hand, we show that if any of these three conditions are relaxed, then there exist arbitrarily small initial data such that the corresponding solutions blow up in a finite time.

2. Main result

In this section we state the main theorem. Consider the scattering problem for (NW) with $V_2(x) = \nu_2 |x|^{-\gamma_2}$, $\nu_2 \in \mathbb{R}$, $\gamma_2 > 0$. We also assume the following condition: the potential $V_1(x)$ satisfies

$$\sum_{|\alpha| \le 2} |\partial_x^\alpha V_1(x)| \le \frac{\nu_1}{(1+|x|)^{\gamma_1}} \tag{H1}$$

with $\gamma_1 > 0$, where $\nu_1 > 0$ is a small parameter.

Let $u_-(t,x)$ be a C^2-solution of

$$\begin{gathered} \partial_t^2 u - \Delta u = 0 \quad \text{in } \mathbb{R} \times \mathbb{R}^3, \\ (u(0,x), \partial_t u(0,x)) = (\varphi(x), \psi(x)), \quad x \in \mathbb{R}^3. \end{gathered} \tag{W}$$

We assume that the initial data $\varphi \in C^3(\mathbb{R}^3)$ and $\psi \in C^2(\mathbb{R}^3)$ satisfy

$$\sum_{|\alpha| \le 3} |\partial_x^\alpha \varphi(x)| + \sum_{|\beta| \le 2} |\partial_x^\beta \psi(x)| \le \frac{\varepsilon}{(1+|x|)^{1+k}} \tag{H2}$$

with $k > 0$, where $\varepsilon > 0$ is a small parameter.

THEOREM 2.1. (i) *Assume (H1) and (H2). Let $\gamma_1 > 2$, $2 \le \gamma_2 < 3$, and $k > 1 + (3 - \gamma_2)/2$. If ν_1 and ε are sufficiently small, depending on k, γ_1, γ_2, and ν_2, then there exists a unique C^2-solution $u(t,x)$ of (NW) such that*

$$\|u(t) - u_-(t)\|_e \longrightarrow 0 \quad (t \longrightarrow -\infty), \tag{2.1}$$

where

$$\|u(t)\|_e = \left\{ \|\nabla u(t)\|_{L^2(\mathbb{R}^3)}^2 + \|\partial_t u(t)\|_{L^2(\mathbb{R}^3)}^2 \right\}^{1/2}. \tag{2.2}$$

(ii) *Moreover, there exists a unique C^2-solution $u_+(t,x)$ of $\partial_t^2 u - \Delta u = 0$ such that for the solution u given by* (i),

$$\|u(t) - u_+(t)\|_e \longrightarrow 0 \quad (t \longrightarrow +\infty). \tag{2.3}$$

Therefore, the scattering operator for (NW) can be defined:

$$S : (u_-(0), \partial_t u_-(0)) \longmapsto (u_+(0), \partial_t u_+(0)). \tag{2.4}$$

Proof of Theorem 2.1. Part (i). To prove Theorem 2.1(i) we use the pointwise estimate method developed by F. John.

Let $F(u) = V_1(x)u + (V_2 * u^2)u$ and let $u_-(t,x)$ be a solution of (W). We consider to solve the integral equation:

$$u(t,x) = u_-(t,x) + \frac{1}{4\pi}\int_{-\infty}^{t}(t-s)\int_{|\omega|=1} F(u(s,x+(t-s)\omega))\,d\omega\,ds \quad \text{for } t \in \mathbb{R} \tag{2.5}$$

in the space X, where

$$\begin{gathered} X = \{u(x,t) : \partial_x^\alpha u(t,x) \in C(\mathbb{R}^3 \times \mathbb{R}) \text{ for } |\alpha| \le 2,\ \|u\|_X < \infty\}, \\ \|u\|_X = \sum_{|\alpha|\le 2} \|\partial_x^\alpha u\|, \\ \|u\| = \sup_{\substack{t\in\mathbb{R}\\ x\in\mathbb{R}^3}} w(t,x)\,|u(t,x)|, \\ w(t,x) = (1+|t|+|x|)(1+\big||t|-|x|\big|)^m, \end{gathered} \tag{2.6}$$

where $m = \min\{1, k-1\}$. We use the following lemma.

LEMMA 2.2 (Asakura [1]). *Suppose that $\varphi(x)$, $\psi(x)$ satisfy (H2). Let $k > 1$. Then the solution u_- of (W) satisfies*

$$\sum_{|\alpha|\le 2} |\partial_x^\alpha u_-(t,x)| \le \frac{C_k\varepsilon}{(1+|t|+|x|)(1+\big||t|-|x|\big|)^{k-1}}, \tag{2.7}$$

where the constant C_k depends only on k.

We next define

$$LF(t,x) = \frac{1}{4\pi}\int_{-\infty}^{t}(t-s)\int_{|\omega|=1} F(s,x+(t-s)\omega)\,d\omega\,ds. \tag{2.8}$$

The following lemma is the basic estimate for the existence proof.

LEMMA 2.3. *Let $V_1(x)$ satisfy (H1). If $\gamma_1 > 2$, $2 \le \gamma_2 < 3$, and $k > 1 + (3-\gamma_2)/2$, then there exists a constant $C > 0$ depending only on k, γ_1, γ_2, and ν_2 such that*

$$\|LF(u)\| \le C(\nu_1\|u\| + \|u\|^3). \tag{2.9}$$

Using Lemmas 2.2 and 2.3, we can prove the existence of the solution in Theorem 2.1(i) by the contraction mapping principle. It also follows that

$$\int_{-\infty}^{t} \|F(u(s))\|_{L^2(\mathbb{R}^3)}\,ds \longrightarrow 0 \quad (t \longrightarrow -\infty), \tag{2.10}$$

which yields (2.1).

Part (ii) *of Theorem 2.1.* We define

$$u_+(t,x) = u(t,x) + \frac{1}{4\pi}\int_{-\infty}^{t}(t-s)\int_{|\omega|=1}F(u(s,x+(t-s)\omega))\,d\omega\,ds. \tag{2.11}$$

Then, clearly u_+ is a C^2-solution of (W) and as before, we can show that

$$\|u(t)-u_+(t)\|_e \longrightarrow 0 \quad (t \longrightarrow +\infty). \tag{2.12}$$

□

3. Blow up

In this section we state a blow-up result. We consider (NW) for $t > 0$. We can verify local existence and uniqueness for the problem, and existence of nonnegative solutions, provided that

$$V_1 \in L^\infty, \qquad V_1 \geq 0, \qquad \nu_2 > 0, \qquad 0 < \gamma_2 < 3, \qquad \varphi \equiv 0, \qquad \psi \geq 0. \tag{3.1}$$

Let T be the existence time. The following theorem is proved in [9].

THEOREM 3.1. *Assume condition (3.1). Let one of the following conditions be satisfied:*
(i) $0 < \gamma_1 < 2$ *and* $V_1(x) \geq C(1+|x|)^{-\gamma_1}$ *for* $C > 0$;
(ii) $0 < \gamma_2 < 2$;
(iii) $1/2 < k < 1+(3-\gamma_2)/2$ *and* $\psi(x) \geq \varepsilon(1+|x|)^{-1-k}$ *for* $\varepsilon > 0$.
Then $T < \infty$.

Acknowledgment

This work is supported by a JSPS research grant.

References

[1] F. Asakura, *Existence of a global solution to a semilinear wave equation with slowly decreasing initial data in three space dimensions*, Communications in Partial Differential Equations **11** (1986), no. 13, 1459–1487.
[2] G. M. Coclite and V. Georgiev, *Solitary waves for Maxwell-Schrödinger equations*, Electronic Journal of Differential Equations **2004** (2004), no. 94, 1–31.
[3] N. Hayashi and T. Ozawa, *Smoothing effect for some Schrödinger equations*, Journal of Functional Analysis **85** (1989), no. 2, 307–348.
[4] K. Hidano, *Small data scattering and blow-up for a wave equation with a cubic convolution*, Funkcialaj Ekvacioj **43** (2000), no. 3, 559–588.
[5] G. Perla Menzala and W. A. Strauss, *On a wave equation with a cubic convolution*, Journal of Differential Equations **43** (1982), no. 1, 93–105.
[6] K. Mochizuki, *On small data scattering with cubic convolution nonlinearity*, Journal of the Mathematical Society of Japan **41** (1989), no. 1, 143–160.
[7] K. Mochizuki and T. Motai, *On small data scattering for some nonlinear wave equations*, Patterns and Waves—Qualitative Analysis of Nonlinear Differential Equations, Stud. Math. Appl., vol. 18, North-Holland, Amsterdam, 1986, pp. 543–560.
[8] W. A. Strauss and K. Tsutaya, *Existence and blow up of small amplitude nonlinear waves with a negative potential*, Discrete and Continuous Dynamical Systems **3** (1997), no. 2, 175–188.

[9] K. Tsutaya, *Global existence and blow up for a wave equation with a potential and a cubic convolution*, Nonlinear Analysis and Applications: to V. Lakshmikantham on His 80th Birthday. Vol. 2, Kluwer Academic, Dordrecht, 2003, pp. 913–937.

Kimitoshi Tsutaya: Department of Mathematics, Hokkaido University, Sapporo 060-0810, Japan
E-mail address: tsutaya@math.sci.hokudai.ac.jp

NONLINEAR VARIATIONAL INCLUSION PROBLEMS INVOLVING A-MONOTONE MAPPINGS

RAM U. VERMA

Based on the notion of A-*monotonicity*, a new class of nonlinear variational inclusion problems is introduced. Since A-*monotonicity* generalizes H-*monotonicity* (and in turn generalizes maximal monotonicity), results thus obtained are general in nature.

1. Introduction

Resolvent operator techniques have been in literature for a while for solving problems from several fields, including complementarity, optimization, mathematical programming, equilibria in economics, and variational inclusions, but the generalized resolvent operator technique (referred to as A-*resolvent* operator technique) based on A-*monotonicity* [13, 14] is a new development. This gave rise to several generalized resolvent operator-like techniques that can be applied to several variational inclusion problems from sensitivity analysis, model equilibria problems in economics, and optimization and control theory. Just recently, the author [13, 14] generalized the notion of the maximal monotonicity to A-*monotonicity*, and applied A-*resolvent* operator technique, thus developed, to establishing existence and uniqueness of the solution as well as algorithmic convergence analysis for the solution of nonlinear variational inclusions.

We explore in this paper the role of A-*monotonicity* in constructing a general framework for A-*resolvent* operator technique, and then we consider the existence and uniqueness of the solution and convergence analysis for approximate solution of a new class of nonlinear variational inclusion problems involving relaxed cocoercive mappings using A-*resolvent* operator technique. As there is a vast literature on variational inequalities and their applications to several fields of research, the obtained nonlinear variational inclusion results generalize the recent research works of Fang and Huang [3, 4], Liu et al. [9], and Jin [7] to the case of A-*monotone* mappings. For more details, we refer to [1–14].

Hindawi Publishing Corporation
Proceedings of the Conference on Differential & Difference Equations and Applications, pp. 1067–1076

2. General A-monotonicity

In this section we recall the notion of *A-monotonicity* [13, 14] that generalizes the well-known class of maximal monotone mappings, as well as the notion of *H-monotonicity* [3]. It seems that *A-monotone* mappings have a wide range of applications to several fields. We also recall the notion of relaxed cocoercive mappings along with examples.

Let $M : X \to 2^X$ be a multivalued mapping from a Hilbert space X to 2^X, the power set of X. We recall the following.

(i) The set $D(M)$ defined by

$$D(M) = \{u \in X : M(u) \neq \emptyset\} \tag{2.1}$$

is called the effective domain of M.

(ii) The set $R(M)$ defined by

$$R(M) = \bigcup_{u \in X} M(u) \tag{2.2}$$

is called the range of M.

(iii) The set $G(M)$ defined by

$$G(M) = \{(u,v) \in X \times X : \ u \in D(M), \ v \in M(u)\} \tag{2.3}$$

is the graph of M.

Definition 2.1. A mapping $M : X \to 2^X$ is said to be

(i) monotone if and only if

$$\langle u^* - v^*, u - v\rangle \geq 0, \quad \forall u,v \in D(M), \ u^* \in M(u), \ v^* \in M(v), \tag{2.4}$$

(ii) pseudomonotone if and only if

$$\langle v^*, u - v\rangle \geq 0 \quad \text{implies } \langle u^*, u - v\rangle \geq 0 \tag{2.5}$$

for all $u,v \in D(M)$, $u^* \in M(u)$, $v^* \in M(v)$,

(iii) (r)-*strongly* monotone if and only if there exists a positive constant r such that

$$\langle u^* - v^*, u - v\rangle \geq r\|u - v\|^2, \quad \forall u,v \in D(M), \ u^* \in M(u), \ v^* \in M(v), \tag{2.6}$$

(iv) (m)-*relaxed* monotone if and only if there exists a positive constant m such that

$$\langle u^* - v^*, u - v\rangle \geq -m\|u - v\|^2, \quad \forall u,v \in D(M), \ u^* \in M(u), \ v^* \in M(v), \tag{2.7}$$

(v) maximal monotone

(a) if and only if M is monotone,

(b) for every $u \in D(M)$ and $u^* \in X$ such that

$$\langle u^* - v^*, u - v\rangle \geq 0, \quad \forall v \in D(M), \ v^* \in M(v), \tag{2.8}$$

implies $u^* \in M(u)$.

Definition 2.2 [13]. Let $A : X \to X$ be a nonlinear mapping on a Hilbert space X and let $M : X \to 2^X$ be a multivalued mapping on X. The map M is said to be *A-monotone* if

(i) M is (m)-*relaxed* monotone,

(ii) $A + \rho M$ is maximal monotone for $\rho > 0$.

Next, we recall some results that reflect general properties of *A-monotonicity* and its connections to the maximal monotonicity.

Proposition 2.3. *Let $A : X \to X$ be an (r)-strongly monotone single-valued mapping and let $M : X \to 2^X$ be an A-monotone mapping. Then M is maximal monotone.*

Next we state some general properties on *A-monotone* mappings regarding the generalized resolvent operator technique.

Proposition 2.4. *Let $A : X \to X$ be an r-strongly monotone mapping and let $M : X \to 2^X$ be an A-monotone mapping. Then the operator $(A + \rho M)^{-1}$ is single-valued.*

Definition 2.5 [13]. Let $A : X \to X$ be an (r)-*strongly* monotone mapping and let $M : X \to 2^X$ be an *A-monotone* mapping. Then the generalized resolvent operator $J^M_{\rho,A} : X \to X$ is defined by

$$J^M_{\rho,A}(u) = (A + \rho M)^{-1}(u). \tag{2.9}$$

Definition 2.6. Let $T, A : X \to X$ be any two mappings on X. The map T is called

(i) monotone with respect to A if

$$\langle T(x) - T(y), A(x) - A(y)\rangle \geq 0, \quad \forall x, y \in X, \tag{2.10}$$

(ii) strictly monotone with respect to A if

$$\langle T(x) - T(y), A(x) - A(y)\rangle > 0, \quad \forall x, y \in X \text{ with } x \neq y, \tag{2.11}$$

(iii) (r)-*strongly* monotone with respect to A if there exists a constant $r > 0$ such that

$$\langle T(x) - T(y), A(x) - A(y)\rangle \geq r\|x - y\|^2, \quad \forall x, y \in X, \tag{2.12}$$

(iv) (m)-*cocoercive* with respect to A if there exists a constant $m > 0$ such that

$$\langle T(x) - T(y), A(x) - A(y)\rangle \geq m\|T(x) - T(y)\|^2, \quad \forall x, y \in X, \tag{2.13}$$

(v) (m)-*relaxed* cocoercive with respect to A if there exists a constant $m > 0$ such that

$$\langle T(x) - T(y), A(x) - A(y)\rangle \geq -m\|T(x) - T(y)\|^2, \quad \forall x, y \in X, \tag{2.14}$$

(vi) (γ, r)-*relaxed* cocoercive with respect to A if there exist constants $\gamma, r > 0$ such that

$$\langle T(x) - T(y), A(x) - A(y)\rangle \geq -\gamma\|T(x) - T(y)\|^2 + r\|x - y\|^2, \quad \forall x, y \in X, \tag{2.15}$$

(vii) (s)-*Lipschitz* continuous if there exists a constant $s > 0$ such that

$$\|T(x) - T(y)\| \leq s\|x - y\|, \quad \forall x, y \in X. \tag{2.16}$$

3. Nonlinear quasivariational inclusions

Let X be a real Hilbert space with the norm $\|\cdot\|$ and inner product $\langle\cdot,\cdot\rangle$, and let $N : X \times X \to X$ be a nonlinear mapping. Let $A : X \to X$ and $M : X \times X \to 2^X$ be any nonlinear mappings. Then we have the nonlinear variational inclusion (NVI) problem: determine an element $u \in X$ for a given element $f \in X$ such that

$$f \in N(u,u) + M(u,u). \tag{3.1}$$

The solvability of the NVI problem (3.1) depends on the equivalence between (3.1) and the problem of finding the fixed point of the associated A-*resolvent* operator.

We note that if $A : X \to X$ is (r)-*strongly* monotone and $M : X \times X \to 2^X$ is A-*monotone* in the first variable, then A-*resolvent* operator $J_{\rho,A}^{M(\cdot,u)}$ is defined by

$$J_{\rho,A}^{M(\cdot,u)}(u) = (A + \rho M(\cdot,u))^{-1}(u), \quad \forall u \in X, \tag{3.2}$$

where $\rho > 0$.

Lemma 3.1 [14]. *Let X be a real Hilbert space, let $A : X \to X$ be (r)-strongly monotone, and let $M : X \times X \to 2^X$ be A-monotone in the first variable. Then A-resolvent operator associated with M and defined by*

$$J_{\rho,A}^{M(\cdot,u)}(u) = (A + \rho M(\cdot,u))^{-1}(u), \quad \forall u \in X, \tag{3.3}$$

is $(1/(r-\rho m))$-Lipschitz continuous; that is,

$$\left\|J_{\rho,A}^{M(\cdot,u)}(u) - J_{\rho,A}^{M(\cdot,u)}(v)\right\| \le \frac{1}{r-\rho m}\|u-v\|, \quad \forall u,v \in X. \tag{3.4}$$

Lemma 3.2. *Let X be a real Hilbert space, let $A : X \to X$ be (r)-strongly monotone, and let $M : X \times X \to 2^X$ be A-monotone. Then the following statements are mutually equivalent.*

(i) *An element $u \in X$ is a solution to (3.1).*

(ii) *There is $u \in X$ such that*

$$u = J_{\rho,A}^{M(\cdot,u)}(A(u) - \rho N(u,u) + \rho f). \tag{3.5}$$

(iii) *The map $G : X \to X$ defined by*

$$G(u) = (1-t)u + tJ_{\rho,A}^{M(\cdot,u)}(A(u) - \rho N(u,u) + \rho f), \quad \forall u \in X, \tag{3.6}$$

has a fixed point $u \in X$ for $0 < t \le 1$.

Theorem 3.3. *Let $A : X \to X$ be (r)-strongly monotone and (s)-Lipschitz continuous, and let $M : X \times X \to 2^X$ be A-monotone in the first variable. Let $N : X \times X \to X$ be (γ,α)-relaxed cocoercive with respect to A and (β)-Lipschitz continuous in the first variable, and let N be (μ)-Lipschitz continuous in the second variable. Let*

$$\left\|J_{\rho,A}^{M(\cdot,u)}(x) - J_{\rho,A}^{M(\cdot,v)}(x)\right\| \le \eta\|u-v\|, \quad \forall x,u,v \in X. \tag{3.7}$$

Then

$$\|G(u) - G(v)\| \leq (1 - t(1 - \theta))\|u - v\|, \quad \forall (u,v) \in X \times X, \tag{3.8}$$

where

$$\begin{aligned} \theta &= \frac{1}{r - \rho m}\left[\sqrt{s^2 - 2\rho\alpha + 2\rho\gamma\beta^2 + \rho^2\beta^2} + \rho\mu\right] + \eta < 1, \\ \left\|\rho - \frac{\alpha - r(1-\eta)(m(1-\eta)+\mu) - \gamma\beta^2}{\beta^2 - (m(1-\eta)+\mu)^2}\right\| &< \frac{\sqrt{A - B}}{\beta^2 - (m(1-\eta)+\mu)^2}, \end{aligned} \tag{3.9}$$

where

$$A = (\alpha - r(1-\eta)(m(1-\eta)+\mu) - \gamma\beta^2)^2,$$

$$B = \left(\beta^2 - (m(1-\eta)+\mu)^2\right)(s^2 - r^2(1-\eta)^2),$$

$$\alpha > r(1-\eta)(m(1-\eta)+\mu) + \gamma\beta^2 + \sqrt{\left(\beta^2 - (m(1-\eta)+\mu)^2\right)(s^2 - r^2(1-\eta)^2)}, \tag{3.10}$$

$$\beta > (m(1-\eta)+\mu)\sqrt{(s^2 - r^2(1-\eta)^2)}, \quad \eta < 1,$$

$$\rho < \frac{r(1-\eta)}{m(1-\eta)+\mu}, \quad s > r(1-\eta),\ 0 < t \leq 1.$$

Furthermore, NVI problem (3.1) has a unique solution.

Proof. For any element $(u,v) \in X \times X$, we have

$$\begin{aligned} G(u) &= (1-t)u + tJ_{\rho,A}^{M(\cdot,u)}(A(u) - \rho N(u,u) + \rho f), \\ G(v) &= (1-t)v + tJ_{\rho,A}^{M(\cdot,v)}(A(v) - \rho N(v,v) + \rho f). \end{aligned} \tag{3.11}$$

It follows that

$$\begin{aligned} &\|G(u) - G(v)\| \\ &\quad = \left\|(1-t)(u-v) + t\left[J_{\rho,A}^{M(\cdot,u)}(A(u) - \rho N(u,u) + \rho f) - J_{\rho,A}^{M(\cdot,v)}(A(v) - \rho N(v,v) + \rho f)\right]\right\| \\ &\quad \leq (1-t)\|u-v\| + t\left\|\left[J_{\rho,A}^{M(\cdot,u)}(A(u) - \rho N(u,u) + \rho f) - J_{\rho,A}^{M(\cdot,u)}(A(v) - \rho N(v,v) + \rho f)\right]\right\| \\ &\qquad + t\left\|\left[J_{\rho,A}^{M(\cdot,u)}(A(v) - \rho N(v,v) + \rho f) - J_{\rho,A}^{M(\cdot,v)}(A(v) - \rho N(v,v) + \rho f)\right]\right\| \\ &\quad \leq (1-t)\|u-v\| + \frac{t}{r - \rho m}\|A(u) - A(v) - \rho(N(u,u) - N(v,v))\| + \eta\|u-v\| \\ &\quad = (1-t)\|u-v\| + \frac{t}{r - \rho m}[\|A(u) - A(v) - \rho(N(u,u) - N(v,u) + N(v,u) - N(v,v))\|] \\ &\qquad + \eta\|u-v\| \\ &\quad \leq (1-t)\|u-v\| + \frac{t}{r - \rho m}[\|A(u) - A(v) - \rho(N(u,u) - N(v,u))\| \\ &\qquad + \|\rho(N(v,u) - N(v,v))\|] + \eta\|u-v\|. \end{aligned} \tag{3.12}$$

The (γ,α)-*relaxed* cocoercivity with respect to A and (β)-*Lipschitz* continuity of N in the first argument imply that

$$\begin{aligned}
&\|A(u)-A(v)-\rho(N(u,u)-N(v,u))\|^2\\
&\quad=\|A(u)-A(v)\|^2-2\rho\langle N(u,u)-N(v,u),A(u)-A(v)\rangle\\
&\qquad+\rho^2\|N(u,u)-N(v,u)\|^2\\
&\quad\le(s^2-2\rho\alpha+\rho^2\beta^2+2\rho\gamma\beta^2)\|u-v\|^2,
\end{aligned}\tag{3.13}$$

while the (μ)-*Lipschitz* continuity where of N in the second argument results in

$$\|N(v,u)-N(v,v)\|\le\mu\|u-v\|.\tag{3.14}$$

In light of the above arguments, we infer

$$\|G(u)-G(v)\|\le(1-t)\|u-v\|+t\theta\|u-v\|=(1-t(1-\theta))\|u-v\|,\tag{3.15}$$

where

$$\theta=\frac{1}{r-\rho m}\left[\sqrt{s^2-2\rho\alpha+\rho^2\beta^2+2\rho\gamma\beta^2}+\rho\mu\right]+\eta,\tag{3.16}$$

for $0<t\le1$.

Since $\theta<1$, it implies that G is a contraction, and hence, there exists a unique element $z\in X$ such that

$$G(z)=z\tag{3.17}$$

which is equivalent to

$$z=(1-t)z+J_{\rho,A}^{M}(A(z)-\rho N(z,z)+\rho f).\tag{3.18}$$

Consequently, the mapping $G(u)$ in light of Lemma 3.2(ii) has a unique fixed point $z\in X$ such that

$$G(z)=z.\tag{3.19}$$

It follows from Lemma 3.2 that z is a unique solution to NVI problem (3.1). This completes the proof. □

4. Algorithmic convergence analysis

This section deals with convergence analysis for the iterative procedure, while the existence and uniqueness of the solution of the nonlinear variational inclusion problem (3.1) are dealt with Section 3.

Algorithm 4.1. Let X be a real Hilbert space, and let $A : X \to X$ and $M : X \times X \to 2^X$ be any mappings. Let $N : X \times X \to X$ be a suitable mapping. For a given element $f \in X$ and an arbitrarily chosen initial point $x^0 \in X$, compute sequences $\{x^k\}_{k\geq 0}$ and $\{y^k\}_{k\geq 0}$ such that

$$\begin{aligned} x^{k+1} &= (1-a^k)x^k + a^k J_{\rho,A}^{M(\cdot,y^k)}\big(A(y^k) - \rho N(y^k,y^k) + \rho f\big) + a^k e^k, \\ y^k &= (1-b^k)x^k + b^k J_{\rho,A}^{M(\cdot,x^k)}\big(A(x^k) - \rho N(x^k,x^k) + \rho f\big) + b^k f^k, \end{aligned} \tag{4.1}$$

where ρ is a positive constant, and sequences $\{a^k\}_{k\geq 0}$ and $\{b^k\}_{k\geq 0}$ satisfy

$$\begin{aligned} 0 \leq a^k, \qquad b^k \leq 1, \qquad a^k + b^k \leq 1, \\ b^k \leq a^k, \qquad \Sigma_{k=0}^{\infty} a^k = \infty. \end{aligned} \tag{4.2}$$

Furthermore, let $\{z^k\}_{k\geq 0}$ be a sequence in X such that sequences $\{\epsilon^k\}_{k\geq 0}$ and $\{t^k\}_{k\geq 0}$ satisfy

$$\begin{aligned} \epsilon^k &= \Big\| z^{k+1} - \big[(1-a^k)z^k + a^k J_{\rho,A}^{M(\cdot,y^k)}\big(A(y^k) - \rho N(y^k,y^k) + \rho f\big) + a^k e^k\big]\Big\|, \\ t^k &= (1-b^k)z^k + b^k J_{\rho,A}^{M(\cdot,z^k)}\big(A(z^k) - \rho N(z^k,z^k) + \rho f\big) + b^k f^k. \end{aligned} \tag{4.3}$$

THEOREM 4.2. *Let X be a real Hilbert space, let $A : X \to X$ be (r)-strongly monotone and (s)-Lipschitz continuous, and let $M : X \times X \to 2^X$ be A-monotone. Let $N : X \times X \to X$ be (γ,α)-relaxed cocoercive with respect to A and (β)-Lipschitz continuous in the first variable, and let N be (μ)-Lipschitz continuous in the second variable. Let*

$$\begin{aligned} &\Big\| J_{\rho,A}^{M(\cdot,u)}(x) - J_{\rho,A}^{M(\cdot,v)}(x)\Big\| \leq \eta \|u-v\|, \quad \forall x,u,v \in X, \\ &\theta = \frac{1}{r-\rho m}\Big[\sqrt{s^2 - 2\rho\alpha + 2\rho\gamma\beta^2 + \rho^2\beta^2} + \rho\mu\Big] + \eta < 1, \\ &\left|\rho - \frac{\alpha - r(1-\eta)(m(1-\eta)+\mu) - \gamma\beta^2}{\beta^2 - (m(1-\eta)+\mu)^2}\right| < \frac{\sqrt{A-B}}{\beta^2 - (m(1-\eta)+\mu)^2}, \end{aligned} \tag{4.4}$$

where

$$\begin{aligned} A &= \big(\alpha - r(1-\eta)(m(1-\eta)+\mu) - \gamma\beta^2\big)^2, \\ B &= \big(\beta^2 - (m(1-\eta)+\mu)^2\big)\big(s^2 - r^2(1-\eta)^2\big), \end{aligned}$$

$$\alpha > r(1-\eta)(m(1-\eta)+\mu) + \gamma\beta^2 + \sqrt{\big(\beta^2 - (m(1-\eta)+\mu)^2\big)\big(s^2 - r^2(1-\eta)^2\big)}, \tag{4.5}$$

$$\beta > \sqrt{(m(1-\eta)+\mu)^2\big(s^2 - r^2(1-\eta)^2\big)}, \quad \eta < 1, \ \rho < \frac{r(1-\eta)}{m(1-\eta)+\mu},$$

$$s > r(1-\eta), \quad 0 < t \leq 1.$$

If, for an arbitrarily chosen initial point $x^0 \in X$, sequences $\{x^k\}_{k\geq 0}$ and $\{y^k\}_{k\geq 0}$ are generated by Algorithm 4.1, then the sequence $\{x^k\}_{k\geq 0}$ converges to the unique solution z of NVI problem (3.1), where

$$\lim_{k\to\infty} ||e^k|| = \lim_{k\to\infty} ||f^k|| = 0. \tag{4.6}$$

If, in addition, $0 < \delta \leq a^k$, then

$$\lim_{k\to\infty} z^k = z \quad \text{if and only if } \lim_{k\to\infty} \epsilon^k = 0, \tag{4.7}$$

where ϵ^k is defined in Algorithm 4.1.

Proof. Since Theorem 3.3 ensures the existence and uniqueness of the solution $z \in X$ to NVI problem (3.1), it follows from Algorithm 4.1 that

$$\begin{aligned}
&||x^{k+1} - z||\\
&\quad = ||(1-a^k)x^k + a^k J_{\rho,A}^{M(\cdot,y^k)}(A(y^k) - \rho N(y^k,y^k) + \rho f) + a^k e^k\\
&\qquad - (1-a^k)z + a^k J_{\rho,A}^{M(\cdot,z)}(A(z) - \rho N(z,z) + \rho f)||\\
&\quad \leq (1-a^k)||x^k - z||\\
&\qquad + a^k\left|\left|J_{\rho,A}^{M(\cdot,y^k)}(A(y^k) - \rho N(y^k,y^k) + \rho f) - J_{\rho,A}^{M(\cdot,z)}(A(z) - \rho N(z,z) + \rho f)\right|\right| + a^k||e^k||\\
&\quad \leq (1-a^k)||x^k - z|| + \frac{a^k}{r - \rho m}||A(y^k) - A(z) - \rho(N(y^k,y^k) - N(z,z))||\\
&\qquad + a^k\eta||y^k - z|| + a^k||e^k|| \leq (1-a^k)||x^k - z||\\
&\qquad + \frac{a^k}{r - \rho m}[||A(y^k) - A(z) - \rho(N(y^k,y^k) - N(z,x^k))|| + \rho(N(z,y^k) - N(z,z))||]\\
&\qquad + a^k\eta||y^k - z|| + a^k||e^k||.
\end{aligned} \tag{4.8}$$

Since

$$\begin{aligned}
&||A(y^k) - A(z) - \rho(N(y^k,y^k) - N(z,y^k))||^2\\
&\quad = ||A(y^k) - A(z)||^2\\
&\qquad - 2\rho\langle A(y^k) - A(z), N(y^k,y^k) - N(z,y^k)\rangle\\
&\qquad + \rho^2||N(y^k,y^k) - N(z,y^k)||^2\\
&\quad \leq (s^2 - 2\rho\alpha + 2\rho\gamma\beta^2 + \rho^2\beta^2)||y^k - z||^2,
\end{aligned} \tag{4.9}$$

we have, using (4.12), that

$$\begin{aligned}||x^{k+1}-z|| &\le (1-a^k)||x^k-z|| + a^k\frac{1}{r-\rho m}[\theta||y^k-z||+\rho\mu||y^k-z||]\\ &\quad + a^k\eta||y^k-z|| + a^k||e^k|| \\ &= (1-a^k)||x^k-z|| + a^k\theta||y^k-z|| + a^k||e^k||,\end{aligned} \tag{4.10}$$

where

$$\theta = \frac{1}{r-\rho m}\Big[\sqrt{s^2-2\rho\alpha+2\rho\gamma\beta^2}+\rho\mu\Big]+\eta. \tag{4.11}$$

Similarly, we have

$$||y^k-z|| \le (1-b^k)||x^k-z|| + b^k\theta||x^k-z|| + b^k||f^k||. \tag{4.12}$$

It follows that

$$\begin{aligned}||x^{k+1}-z|| &\le (1-a^k)||x^k-z|| + a^k\theta(1-b^k)||x^k-z|| \\ &\quad + a^kb^k\theta^2||x^*-z|| + a^k(\theta b^k||f^k||+||e^k||) \\ &= (1-a^k(1-\theta))||x^k-z|| - a^kb^k\theta(1-\theta)||x^k-z|| \\ &\quad + a^k(\theta b^k||f^k||+||e^k||) \\ &\le (1-a^k(1-\theta))||x^k-z|| + a^k(\theta b^k||f^k||+||e^k||).\end{aligned} \tag{4.13}$$

Hence, the sequence $\{x^k\}$ converges to z, and by Lemma 3.2, the unique solution to NVI problem (3.1). □

References

[1] R. P. Agarwal, Y. J. Cho, and N. J. Huang, *Sensitivity analysis for strongly nonlinear quasi-variational inclusions*, Applied Mathematics Letters **13** (2000), no. 6, 19–24.

[2] X. P. Ding and C. L. Luo, *On parametric generalized quasi-variational inequalities*, Journal of Optimization Theory and Applications **100** (1999), no. 1, 195–205.

[3] Y. P. Fang and N. J. Huang, *H-monotone operator and resolvent operator technique for variational inclusions*, Applied Mathematics and Computation **145** (2003), no. 2-3, 795–803.

[4] ———, *H-monotone operators and system of variational inclusions*, Communications on Applied Nonlinear Analysis **11** (2004), no. 1, 93–101.

[5] N. J. Huang and Y. P. Fang, *Auxiliary principle technique for solving generalized set-valued nonlinear quasi-variational-like inequalities*, to appear in Mathematical Inequalities & Applications.

[6] H. Iiduka and W. Takahashi, *Strong convergence theorem by a hybrid method for nonlinear mappings of nonexpansive and monotone type and applications*, Advances in Nonlinear Variational Inequalities **9** (2006), 1–9.

[7] M. M. Jin, *Perturbed algorithm and stability for strongly nonlinear quasivariational inclusion involving H-monotone operators*, to appear in Mathematical Inequalities & Applications.

[8] J. Kyparisis, *Sensitivity analysis framework for variational inequalities*, Mathematical Programming **38** (1987), no. 2, 203–213.

[9] Z. Liu, J. S. Ume, and S. M. Kang, *H-monotone operator and resolvent operator technique for nonlinear variational inclusions*, to appear in Mathematical Inequalities & Applications.

[10] A. Moudafi, *Mixed equilibrium problems: sensitivity analysis and algorithmic aspect*, Computers & Mathematics with Applications **44** (2002), no. 8-9, 1099–1108.

[11] R. L. Tobin, *Sensitivity analysis for variational inequalities*, Journal of Optimization Theory and Applications **48** (1986), no. 1, 191–209.

[12] R. U. Verma, *Nonlinear variational and constrained hemivariational inequalities involving relaxed operators*, ZAMM: Zeitschrift für Angewandte Mathematik und Mechanik **77** (1997), no. 5, 387–391.

[13] ———, *A-monotonicity and applications to nonlinear variational inclusion problems*, Journal of Applied Mathematics & Stochastic Analysis **2004** (2004), no. 2, 193–195.

[14] ———, *Approximation-solvability of a class of a-monotone variational inclusion problems*, Journal of the Korea Society for Industrial and Applied Mathematics **8** (2004), 55–66.

Ram U. Verma: Division of Applied Mathematics, Department of Theoretical and Applied Mathematics, The University of Akron, Akron, OH 44325, USA
E-mail address: rverma@internationalpubls.com

WEIGHTED EXPONENTIAL TRICHOTOMY OF LINEAR DIFFERENCE EQUATIONS

CLAUDIO VIDAL AND CLAUDIO CUEVAS

We introduce the weighted exponential trichotomy notion to difference equation and we study the behavior in the future and the past of the solutions for linear system.

1. Introduction

The notion of dichotomy for a linear system of differential equations has gained prominence since the appearance of two fundamental books: Dalietzkii and Krein [2], and Massera and Schäffer [6]. These were followed by the important book of Coppel [1] who synthesized and improved the results that existed in the literature up to 1978.

Two generalizations of dichotomy in differential equations have been introduced: the first by Sacker and Sell [10] called (S-S) trichotomy and the second by Elaydi and Hájek [3] called (E-H)-trichotomy. But it was not until 1990 that the notions of dichotomy and trichotomy were extended to nonlinear difference equations by Papaschinopoulos in [8] and by Elaydi and Janglajew in [4]. Pinto in [9] introduced a generalized notion of dichotomies, called (h,k)-dichotomies, which contains the usual notion of ordinary or exponential dichotomies.

In this paper we introduce a new notion of trichotomy, which is very useful in order to study the asymptotic behavior for linear system of difference equations

$$x(n+1) = A(n)x(n), \quad n \in \mathbb{Z}, \tag{1.1}$$

in the nonhomogeneous linear case. It consists essentially in taking into account the above concepts of (E-H)-trichotomies and (h,k)-dichotomies; that is, we introduce both concepts in only one, such trichotomies will be called weighted exponential trichotomy. Our main purpose in this work is to extend the study of dichotomy and trichotomy in linear ordinary difference equations and to study the asymptotic behavior of the solutions of both the future and the past under the existence of weighted exponential trichotomy.

Hindawi Publishing Corporation
Proceedings of the Conference on Differential & Difference Equations and Applications, pp. 1077–1086

The results given in this paper are essentially motivated by the corresponding ones in [1, 4, 5, 7]. As will be evident in the next sections, by our approach we get to generalize several results presented in the previous papers as qualitatively as extending to a more general class of equations.

The paper is organized as follows. In Section 2, we introduce the concept of weighted exponential trichotomy for linear ordinary difference equations (1.1), and from a more calculational point of view in Section 3 the authors present genuine examples of this new class of trichotomy. In Section 4, we make a complete study of the linear difference systems (1.1) possessing weighted exponential trichotomy; in particular, in Theorem 4.5 we characterize the space S of all the solutions, and the asymptotic behavior is given. Here we point out that the results obtained in this section generalize substantially some of the results in [4, 8] valid only for (E-H)-trichotomy. In fact, with our approach we can characterize the asymptotic behavior of a great variety of important linear systems, which are not included when the notion of (h,k)-trichotomy is considered only.

At present we are working in the nonhomogeneous linear case and in the nonlinear case with strong perturbations.

2. Weighted exponential trichotomy for linear ordinary difference equations

Consider the linear difference equation (1.1), where $A(n)$ is an $m\times m$ invertible matrix defined on $\mathbb{Z}$.

Now we are going to introduce the new notion of trichotomy.

Definition 2.1. Let $X(n)$ denote the fundamental matrix of (1.1) with $X(0)=I$. Suppose that there are h and k two positive sequences $\{h(t)\}_{t\in\mathbb{Z}}$, $\{k(t)\}_{t\in\mathbb{Z}}$; three mutually orthogonal $m\times m$ matrix projections P_1, P_2, P_3, with $P_1+P_2+P_3=I$ (with ranks n_1, n_2, and n_3, resp., with $n_1+n_2+n_3=m$); positive constants γ_1, γ_2, γ_3, and q such that

(a) $|X(n)P_1X^{-1}(j+1)|\leq \gamma_1\, q^{n-j}h(n)h^{-1}(j+1)$ for $n\geq j+1$;

(b) $|X(n)P_2X^{-1}(j+1)|\leq \gamma_2\, q^{j-n}k(n)k^{-1}(j+1)$ for $n\leq j+1$;

(c) $|X(n)P_3X^{-1}(j+1)|\leq \gamma_3\, q^{|n-j|}$ for $n\geq j+1\geq 1$ or $n\leq j+1\leq 1$.

If $q\in(0,1)$, it will be said that the linear system (1.1) in $\mathbb{R}^m$ has a weighted exponential trichotomy.

It is worth to remark that the weighted exponential trichotomy is a property that does not depend on the fixed fundamental matrix. Indeed, if $Y(n)$ is another fundamental matrix of system (1.1), then there exists a nonsingular matrix C such that $X(n)=Y(n)C$ and $|X(n)P_iX^{-1}(j+1)|=|Y(n)CP_iC^{-1}Y^{-1}(j+1)|$.

This new concept combines the notion of trichotomy and (h,k)-dichotomy, and it is general enough to include interesting particular situations, namely, the following remarks.

Remarks 2.2. (1) If in the above definition $h=$ constant and $k=$ constant following the notation in [10], the system (1.1) is said to have an exponential trichotomy on $\mathbb{Z}$, or considering [4], the system (1.1) has an (E-H)-trichotomy on $\mathbb{Z}$. This kind of trichotomy was introduced first by Elaydi and Hájek in [3] in the case of ordinary differential equations;

Papaschinopoulos in [8] adapted this concept in the case of ordinary difference equations, he gave necessary and sufficient conditions in order a linear difference equation to have trichotomy, he also had studied roughness of trichotomy and studied the existence of bounded solutions for nonlinear systems. Elaydi and Janglajew in [4] extended the notion of dichotomy and trichotomy to nonlinear ordinary difference equations.

(2) If in (a) and (b) we set $q = 1$ and $P_3 \equiv 0$, we have an (h,k)-dichotomy (see [8]). If in this situation $h =$ constant, $k =$ constant, in (b) $q = 1$, and in (a) $q \in (0,1)$, Pinto in [9] called this kind of dichotomy expo-ordinary dichotomy.

(3) If in the above definition $h =$ constant and $k =$ constant and we assume $q = 1$, then according to the notation in [4], the system (1.1) is said to have an (S-S) trichotomy. If in (c) in the above definition we put $q = 1$, then we will say that system (1.1) has a weighted expo-ordinary trichotomy on $\mathbb{Z}$.

(4) If in (a), (b), and (c) we put $q = 1$, then according to [8], (1.1) has an (h,k)-trichotomy on $\mathbb{Z}$.

(5) If $P_3 = 0$, $h =$ constant, and $k =$ constant, then the system (1.1) has an exponential dichotomy on $\mathbb{Z}$.

(6) Since $0 < q \leq 1$, defining $\widetilde{h}(n) = h(n)q^n$ and $\widetilde{k}(n) = k(n)q^{-n}$, then using again the definition in [8], we have that system (1.1) has an $(\widetilde{h},\widetilde{k})$-trichotomy. Therefore, every weighted exponential trichotomy is an (h,k)-trichotomy. But, clearly not all (h,k)-trichotomy is a weighted exponential trichotomy.

Although the concept of (h,k)-trichotomy is more general than weighted exponential trichotomy, we will see in the next sections that the behavior of system that possesses a weighted exponential trichotomy is too different than that system that only possesses an (h,k)-trichotomy. For example, we obtain results about the behavior at the infinity $(n \to \pm\infty)$ which cannot be obtained under the hypothesis that system (1.1) possesses only an (h,k)-trichotomy. On the other hand, in [5] the authors did not study the asymptotic behavior of the solution of (1.1) and its perturbations. In fact, they studied the case of solutions moving inside and in a neighborhood of an invariant manifold called (h,k)-hyperbolic.

We emphasize that weighted exponential trichotomy is more useful than (h,k)-trichotomy when we are interested in specializing the study of asymptotic behavior at the infinity, and it is useful when compared with (E-H)-trichotomy because we have the possibility of including the unbounded solutions in the asymptotic relation of system (1.1) and its perturbations. Also, it is useful for applications, since the results include a large class of systems. This will be evident in the next sections.

Another important definition that we will use in the next sections is the following definition.

Definition 2.3. Say that a pair of sequences h and k is compensated if there exists a positive constant $C \geq 1$ such that

$$h(n)h^{-1}(m) \leq Ck(n)k^{-1}(m), \quad \forall n \geq m,\ n,m \in \mathbb{Z}. \tag{2.1}$$

We remark that if the system (1.1) has an (h,k)-dichotomy which is compensated, then one can reduce it in a system with ordinary dichotomy. In fact, it suffices making the following change of variables $x(n) = h(n)y(n)$, thus we can infer that the system $y(n+1) = B(n)y(n)$ has an ordinary dichotomy, where $B(n) = (h(n)/h(n+1))A(n)$. However, it makes sense to study a system that admits a weighted exponential trichotomy compensated, because it is not possible to make this reduction.

To end this section we point out the following remarks.

Remarks 2.4. Equation (1.1) has a weighted exponential trichotomy on $\mathbb{Z}$ with projections P_i $(i = 1,2,3)$ and positive constants γ_i $(i = 1,2,3)$ and $q \in (0,1)$ if and only if there are positive constants $\tilde{\gamma}_i$ $(i = 1,2,3)$ and $\tilde{q} \in (0,1)$, and three families of projections $P_i(n)$, $n \in \mathbb{Z}$ $(i = 1,2,3)$ such that

(i) for each $n \in \mathbb{Z}$, $P_i(n)P_j(n) = 0$, if $i \neq j$ and $P_1(n) + P_2(n) + P_3(n) = I$,

(ii) $P_i(n+1)A(n) = A(n)P_i(n)$ for all $n \in \mathbb{Z}$, $i = 1,2,3$,

(iii) (a) $|X(n)X^{-1}(j+1)P_1(j+1)| \leq \tilde{\gamma}_1\tilde{q}^{n-j}h(n)h^{-1}(j+1)$ for $n \geq j+1$,

(b) $|X(n)X^{-1}(j+1)P_2(j+1)| \leq \tilde{\gamma}_2\tilde{q}^{j-n}k(n)k^{-1}(j+1)$ for $n \leq j+1$,

(c) $|X(n)X^{-1}(j+1)P_3(j+1)| \leq \tilde{\gamma}_3\tilde{q}^{|n-j|}$ for $n \geq j+1 \geq 1$ or $n \leq j+1 \leq 1$.

In fact, let us assume that (1.1) has a weighted exponential trichotomy as in Definition 2.1. Taking $\tilde{\gamma}_i = \gamma_i$, $\tilde{q} = q$, $P_i(n) = X(n)P_iX^{-1}(n)$, then it follows immediately that (i), (ii), and (iii) are satisfied (observe that $X^{-1}(n) = X^{-1}(n+1)A(n)$). Reciprocally, let the positive constants $\tilde{\gamma}_i$, $\tilde{q}$, and a family of projections $P_i(n)$, $n \in \mathbb{Z}$ such that the previous conditions are satisfied. We take $\gamma_i = \tilde{\gamma}_i$, $q = \tilde{q}$, $P_i = P_i(0)$, then it follows from (i) that $P_i(j+1) = A(j)A(j-1)\cdots A(0)P_i(0)A^{-1}(0)\cdots A^{-1}(j-2)A^{-1}(j) = X(j+1)P_iX^{-1}(j+1)P_i$.

Hence,

$$\left|X(n)P_iX^{-1}(j+1)\right| = \left|X(n)X^{-1}(j+1)P_i(j+1)\right| \tag{2.2}$$

and by (iii) follows the affirmation.

3. Examples

At this stage some examples and their associated projections are given. We will see that the projections play a distinguished role in the trichotomies. We will concentrate on (1.1) when

$$A(n) = \operatorname{diag}\left(\lambda_1(n),\lambda_2(n),\dots,\lambda_m(n)\right) \tag{3.1}$$

with $\lambda_j(n) \in \mathbb{R}$. Here we have that the fundamental matrix is given by

$$X(n) = \begin{cases} \operatorname{diag}\left(\prod_{j=0}^{n-1}\lambda_1(j),\dots,\prod_{j=0}^{n-1}\lambda_m(j)\right) & \text{if } n > 0, \\ I & \text{if } n = 0, \\ \operatorname{diag}\left(\prod_{j=n}^{-1}\lambda_1^{-1}(j),\dots,\prod_{j=n}^{-1}\lambda_m^{-1}(j)\right) & \text{if } n < 0. \end{cases} \tag{3.2}$$

Now, we will analyze the case $m = 3$. It is necessary to choose adequate projections in order to get an (h,k)-trichotomy, in our case we can assume that $P_1 = \operatorname{diag}(1,0,0)$, $P_2 = \operatorname{diag}(0,1,0)$, $P_3 = \operatorname{diag}(0,0,1)$. In this situation we obtain

$$X(n)P_iX^{-1}(j+1) = \begin{cases} \operatorname{diag}\left[\prod_{l=j+1}^{n-1} \lambda_i(l)\right]\mathbf{e}_i & \text{if } n \geq j+1, \\ \operatorname{diag}\left[\prod_{l=n}^{j} \lambda_i^{-1}(l)\right]\mathbf{e}_i & \text{if } n \leq j+1, \end{cases} \tag{3.3}$$

where $\mathbf{e}_i$ $(i = 1,2,3)$ is the canonical basis of $\mathbb{R}^3$.

Example 3.1. We consider

$$\lambda_1(l) = a\frac{|l|+1}{|l+1|+1}, \qquad \lambda_2(l) = b\frac{|l+1|+1}{|l|+1}, \qquad \lambda_3(l) = c^{2l+1}\frac{|l \bmod N|+1}{|(l+1) \bmod N|+1}, \tag{3.4}$$

where N is arbitrary > 1. Taking $h(n) = 1/[|n|+1]$ and $k(n) = |n|+1$, we obtain the estimates

$$\begin{aligned} |X(n)P_1X^{-1}(j+1)| &\leq |a|^{n-j}h(n)h(j+1)^{-1}, \quad n \geq j+1, \\ |X(n)P_2X^{-1}(j+1)| &\leq \left(\frac{1}{|b|}\right)^{j-n} k(n)k(j+1)^{-1}, \quad n \leq j+1. \end{aligned} \tag{3.5}$$

Since

$$X(n)P_3X^{-1}(j+1) = \begin{cases} c^{n^2-(j+1)^2}\dfrac{[(j+1) \bmod N+1]}{[n \bmod N+1]}, & n \geq j+1 \geq 1, \\ c^{-n^2+(j+1)^2}\dfrac{[|(j+1) \bmod N|+1]}{[|n \bmod N|+1]}, & n \leq j+1 \leq 1, \end{cases} \tag{3.6}$$

it follows that

$$|X(n)P_3X^{-1}(j+1)| \leq \begin{cases} \dfrac{N}{|c|}|c|^{n-j}, & n \geq j+1 \geq 1, \\ N|c|\,|c|^{j-n}, & n \leq j+1 \leq 1. \end{cases} \tag{3.7}$$

Therefore, taking $q = \max\{|a|, |b|^{-1}, |c|, N\}$ with $|a| < 1$, $|b|^{-1} < 1$, $|c| < 1$, $h(n) = 1/(|n|+1)$, and $k(n) = |n|+1$, we obtain system (1.1) with a weighted exponential trichotomy. Note that this example is a "genuine" case of weighted exponential trichotomy;

in the sense that is impossible to have $h(n)h^{-1}(j+1)$ bounded or $k(n)k^{-1}(j+1)$ bounded for all $n \geq j+1$, that is, this example cannot be reduced to one with (E-H)-trichotomy.

Example 3.2. In order to generalize Example 3.1, we will consider any function γ, for instance, such that $\gamma : \mathbb{Z} \to \mathbb{R}^+ \setminus \{0\}$. If

$$\alpha(l) = \frac{\gamma(l)}{\gamma(l+1)}, \quad l \in \mathbb{Z}, \tag{3.8}$$

we get

$$\begin{aligned} \prod_{l=j+1}^{n-1} |\alpha(l)| &= \frac{|\gamma(j+1)|}{|\gamma(n)|} \quad \text{if } n \geq j+1, \\ \prod_{l=n}^{j} |\alpha(l)|^{-1} &= \frac{|\gamma(j+1)|}{|\gamma(n)|} \quad \text{if } n \leq j+1. \end{aligned} \tag{3.9}$$

Analogously, defining $\beta(l) = \gamma(l+1)/\gamma(l)$, $l \in \mathbb{Z}$, we get

$$\begin{aligned} \prod_{l=j+1}^{n-1} |\beta(l)| &= \frac{|\gamma(n)|}{|\gamma(j+1)|} \quad \text{if } n \geq j+1, \\ \prod_{l=n}^{j} |\beta(l)|^{-1} &= \frac{|\gamma(n)|}{|\gamma(j+1)|} \quad \text{if } n \leq j+1. \end{aligned} \tag{3.10}$$

Now considering

$$\lambda(l) = \frac{\gamma(l) \bmod N + 1}{\gamma(l+1) \bmod N + 1}, \tag{3.11}$$

we obtain the following expression:

$$\begin{aligned} \prod_{l=j+1}^{n-1} |\lambda(l)| &= \frac{[|\gamma(j+1) \bmod N| + 1]}{[|\gamma(n) \bmod N| + 1]} \quad \text{if } n \geq j+1, \\ \prod_{l=n}^{j} |\lambda(l)|^{-1} &= \frac{[|\gamma(j+1) \bmod N| + 1]}{[|\gamma(n) \bmod N| + 1]} \quad \text{if } n \leq j+1. \end{aligned} \tag{3.12}$$

Therefore, with this kind of arguments we can construct a great variety of examples of weighted exponential trichotomy, we only need to choose the function γ associated with the eigenvalue function λ_3 such that $(|\gamma(j+1) \bmod N| + 1)/(|\gamma(n) \bmod N| + 1)$ is bounded for all $n, j \in \mathbb{Z}$. Observe that the weight is defined through the function γ associated and this function can have several behaviors depending on the function γ.

4. Asymptotic behavior for linear systems with weighted exponential trichotomy

The results obtained in this section for homogeneous extend those of [5, 10].

From the definition immediately follows the lemma.

LEMMA 4.1. *Equation (1.1) has a weighted exponential trichotomy if and only if there are h and k two positive sequences* $\{h(t)\}_{t\in\mathbb{Z}}$, $\{k(t)\}_{t\in\mathbb{Z}}$; *three mutually orthogonal* $m\times m$ *matrix projections* P_1, P_2, P_3, *with* $P_1+P_2+P_3=I$ *(with ranks* n_1, n_2, *and* n_3, *resp., with* $n_1+n_2+n_3=m$*); positive constants* γ_1, γ_2, γ_3, *and* $q\in(0,1)$ *such that*

(a) $|X(n)P_1\xi|\le\gamma_1\, q^{n-j}h(n)h^{-1}(j+1)|X(j+1)\xi|$ *for* $n\ge j+1$,
(b) $|X(n)P_2\xi|\le\gamma_2\, q^{j-n}k(n)k^{-1}(j+1)|X(j+1)\xi|$ *for* $n\le j+1$,
(c) $|X(n)P_3\xi|\le\gamma_3\, q^{|n-j|}|X(j+1)\xi|$ *for* $n\ge j+1\ge 1$ *or* $n\le j+1\le 1$,

for all vector $\xi\in\mathbb{R}^k$.

The following proposition gives us the asymptotic behavior of the solutions of a linear system with weighted exponential trichotomy.

PROPOSITION 4.2. *Assume that system (1.1) has a weighted exponential trichotomy. Then every solution* $x(n)$ *of (1.1) has a decomposition into solutions of (1.1)*

$$x(n)\equiv x_1(n)+x_2(n)+x_3(n) \tag{4.1}$$

such that

(1) $x_1(n)=o(h(n))$ *and* $x_3(n)=o(1)$ *as* $n\to+\infty$,
(2) $x_2(n)=o(k(n))$ *and* $x_3(n)=o(1)$ *as* $n\to-\infty$,
(3) *either* $|x_1(n)|=o(h(n))$ *as* $n\to-\infty$ *or* $x_1\equiv 0$,
(4) *either* $|x_2(n)|=o(k(n))$ *as* $n\to+\infty$ *or* $x_2\equiv 0$.

Remark 4.3. If we put $q=1$ in Definition 2.1(c), then the same properties from the above proposition are true except that in this particular situation where $x_3(n)$ is only bounded for all $n\in\mathbb{Z}$.

Proof. By definition we have that any solution $x(n)$ of (1.1) with initial condition $a\in\mathbb{R}^m$ is given by

$$\begin{aligned} x(n)&=X(n)a\\ &=X(n)P_1a+X(n)P_2a+X(n)P_3a\\ &\equiv x_1(n)+x_2(n)+x_3(n). \end{aligned} \tag{4.2}$$

By case (a) from Lemma 4.1 we have

(a-1) $|x_1(n)|/h(n)\le\gamma_1\, q^{n-j}(|X(j+1)a|/h(j+1))$, for $n\ge j+1$, which implies that $x_1(n)/h(n)\to 0$ as $n\to+\infty$,

(a-2) and on the other hand, $(1/\gamma_1)q^{j-n}(|X(n)P_1a|/h(n))\le|X(j+1)P_1a|/h(j+1)=|x_1(j+1)|/h(j+1)$, for $n\ge j+1$, which implies that $|x_1(j+1)|/h(j+1)\to+\infty$ as $j\to-\infty$.

From (b) of Lemma 4.1 we have

(b-1) $|x_2(n)|/k(n)\le\gamma_2\, q^{j-n}(|X(j+1)P_2a|/k(j+1))$, for $n\le j+1$, which implies that $x_2(n)/k(n)\to 0$ as $n\to-\infty$,

(b-2) also it is valid $(1/\gamma_2)q^{n-j}(|X(n)P_2a|/k(n))\le|X(j+1)P_2a|/k(j+1)=|x_2(j+1)|/k(j+1)$, for $n\le j+1$, which implies that $|x_2(j+1)|/k(j+1)\to+\infty$ as $j\to+\infty$.

From the case (c) of Lemma 4.1 follows that

(c-1) $|x_3(n)| \le \gamma_3 q^{|n-j|}|X(j+1)P_3a|$, for $n \ge j+1 \ge 1$ or $n \le j+1 \le 1$, which implies that $x_3(n) \to 0$ as $n \to \pm\infty$.

This concludes the proof of the proposition. □

Remark 4.4. If we assume that $q = 1$ in Definition 2.1, that is, the system (1.1) has an (h,k)-trichotomy, then we do not obtain the same results about the asymptotic behavior of the solutions of the linear system with a weighted exponential trichotomy as in Proposition 4.2. In fact, using the same arguments as in the above proposition, we have that

(a′-1) $x(n) = O(h(n))$ as $n \to +\infty$,

(a′-2) $(1/\gamma_1)(|X(n)P_1a|/h(n)) \le |X(j+1)P_1a|/h(j+1) = |x_1(j+1)|/h(j+1)$ for $n \ge j+1$.

In case (b) we have

(b′-1) $x(n) = O(k(n))$ as $n \to -\infty$,

(b′-2) $(1/\gamma_2)(|X(n)P_2a|/k(n)) \le |X(j+1)P_2a|/k(j+1) = |x_2(j+1)|/k(j+1)$ for $n \le j+1$.

For case (c) follows that

(c′-1) $x(n) = O(1)$ as $n \to \pm\infty$.

The results obtained in the above proposition permit us to give a complete description of the asymptotic behavior of the solutions of (1.1), both in future and in past. More precisely, we have the following theorem.

Theorem 4.5. *If the system (1.1) has a weighted exponential trichotomy, with projections P_1, P_2, P_3 corresponding to the fundamental matrix $X(n)$ such that $X(0) = I$. Then the m-dimensional space S of all the solutions of (1.1) can be written as direct sum $S = B_1 \oplus B_2 \oplus B_3$, where*

(i) *B_1 is the n_1-dimensional subspace of solutions $\mathbf{x}$ such that $\mathbf{x}(0) = \xi \in \mathrm{Range}(P_1)$, where $n_1 = \mathrm{Rank}(P_1)$. If $\mathbf{x} \in B_1$, then $x(n) = o(h(n))$ as $n \to +\infty$ and $\mathbf{x}$ is h-unbounded for $n \to -\infty$.*

(ii) *B_2 is the n_2-dimensional subspace of solutions $\mathbf{x}$ such that $\mathbf{x}(0) = \eta \in \mathrm{Range}(P_2)$, where $n_2 = \mathrm{Rank}(P_2)$. If $\mathbf{x} \in B_2$, then $x(n) = o(k(n))$ as $n \to -\infty$ and $\mathbf{x}$ is k-unbounded for $n \to +\infty$.*

(iii) *B_3 is the n_3-dimensional subspace of solutions $\mathbf{x}$ such that $\mathbf{x}(0) = \zeta \in \mathrm{Range}(P_3)$, where $n_3 = \mathrm{Rank}(P_3)$. If $\mathbf{x} \in B_3$, then $x(n) = o(1)$ as $n \to \pm\infty$.*

Proof. Let $\mathbf{x}$ be a solution of (1.1). Then it can be written in the unique form

$$\mathbf{x}(n) = X(n)P_1\mathbf{x}(0) + X(n)P_2\mathbf{x}(0) + X(n)P_3\mathbf{x}(0) \equiv x_1(n) + x_2(n) + x_3(n); \tag{4.3}$$

thus the first part of the theorem is proved. Now considering the previous notation, we obtain that $\lim_{n\to+\infty}|x_1(n)|/h(n) = 0$, by the first part in (1) of Proposition 4.2. Also, $\lim_{n\to-\infty}|x_1(n)|/h(n) = +\infty$ if $P_1\mathbf{x}(0) \ne 0$, by (3) of Proposition 4.2.

It is clear that $\lim_{n\to+\infty}|x_2(n)|/k(n) = +\infty$ if $P_2\mathbf{x}(0) \ne 0$, by (4) from Proposition 4.2. On the other hand, $\lim_{n\to-\infty}|x_2(n)|/k(n) = 0$, by the first part in (2) of Proposition 4.2.

By the second part in (1) of Proposition 4.2 follows that $\lim_{n\to+\infty} x_3(n) = 0$. It is clear that $\lim_{n\to-\infty}|x_3(n)| = 0$ by the second part in (2) of Proposition 4.2. □

Remark 4.6. This theorem extends [7, Theorem 1] proved here in the case of l^p trichotomy for difference systems. We observe that this is another point of view different of us. Our result can be applied to the case (E-H)-trichotomy of difference equations considered in [4]. We note that the authors in this last paper did not consider this kind of approach.

COROLLARY 4.7. *Let $x(n) \equiv x_1(n) + x_2(n) + x_3(n)$ be a solution of (1.1). The solutions of (1.1) that satisfy that $x_1(n)$ is h-bounded, for all n, $x_2(n)$ is k-bounded, for all n, $x_3(n)$ is bounded, for all n are the solutions with initial conditions on B_3.*

Proof. To prove the corollary it is sufficient to observe that necessarily by Theorem 4.5 $P_1\mathbf{x}(0) = P_2\mathbf{x}(0) = 0$ in order to have solution of (1.1) that satisfies the above conditions. □

Remark 4.8. If we choose $x(0) \in B_3$, then the solution of (1.1) with this initial conditions satisfies $x_1 \equiv 0$ and $x_2 \equiv 0$, and we obtain the reciprocal of the above corollary.

COROLLARY 4.9. *Assume that (1.1) has a weighted exponential trichotomy which is compensated and satisfies the condition $q^{|n|}/k(n) \to 0$ as $n \to \pm\infty$. Let $x(n)$ be any solution of (1.1), then*

(i) *if $x(0) \in B_1$, then $x(n) = o(k(n))$ as $n \to +\infty$, and $|x(n)|/k(n) \to +\infty$ as $n \to -\infty$;*
(ii) *if $x(0) \in B_2$, then $x(n) = o(k(n))$ as $n \to -\infty$, and $|x(n)|/k(n) \to +\infty$ as $n \to +\infty$;*
(iii) *if $x(0) \in B_3$, then $x(n) = o(k(n))$ as $n \to \pm\infty$.*

COROLLARY 4.10. *Assume that system (1.1) has a weighted exponential trichotomy which is compensated and satisfies the condition $q^{|n|}/k(n)$ bounded for all $n \in \mathbb{Z}$. Let $x(n)$ be any solution of (1.1), then*

(i) *if $x(0) \in B_1$, then $x(n) = o(k(n))$ as $n \to +\infty$, and $|x(n)|/k(n) \to +\infty$ as $n \to -\infty$;*
(ii) *if $x(0) \in B_2$, then $x(n) = o(k(n))$ as $n \to -\infty$, and $|x(n)|/k(n) \to +\infty$ as $n \to +\infty$;*
(iii) *if $x(0) \in B_3$, then $x(n)$ is k-bounded in $\mathbb{Z}$.*

Remarks 4.11. If the compensated trichotomy is an (h,k)-trichotomy, that is, $q = 1$, the condition $q^{|n|}/k(n) \to 0$ as $n \to \pm\infty$ is equivalent to impose that $k(n) \to +\infty$ as $n \to \pm\infty$.

On the other hand, if the compensated trichotomy is (E-H)-trichotomy, that is, $h =$ constant and $k =$ constant, then the condition $q^{|n|}/k(n) \to 0$ as $n \to \pm\infty$ is trivially verified, since $q \in (0,1)$.

If $P_3 = 0$, that is, the system (1.1) has an exponential dichotomy, then the unique solution that is bounded for all $n \in \mathbb{Z}$ is the trivial solution, that is, $x \equiv 0$.

Example 4.12. We have seen in Section 3 that there is a great variety of examples, for instance, taking $k(n) = |n| + 1$ (resp., $k(n) = 1/[|n| + 1]$) for $n \in \mathbb{Z}$, we have that $q^{|n|}/k(n) \to 0$ as $n \to \pm\infty$ for all $q \in (0,1)$.

Now considering $k(n) = p^n$ with $p > 0$ fixed, we have

$$\frac{q^{|n|}}{k(n)} = \begin{cases} \left(\dfrac{q}{p}\right)^n & \text{if } n \geq 0, \\ (qp)^{-n} & \text{if } n \leq 0. \end{cases} \tag{4.4}$$

Therefore if we take p satisfying $q < p < 1/q$, the desired condition is satisfied.

References

[1] W. A. Coppel, *Dichotomies in Stability Theory*, Lecture Notes in Mathematics, vol. 629, Springer, Berlin, 1978.

[2] Yu. L. Dalietzkii and M. G. Krein, *Stability of Solutions of Differential Equations in Banach Spaces*, American Mathematical Society, Rhode Island, 1978.

[3] S. Elaydi and O. Hájek, *Exponential dichotomy and trichotomy of nonlinear differential equations*, Differential and Integral Equations **3** (1990), no. 6, 1201–1224.

[4] S. Elaydi and K. Janglajew, *Dichotomy and trichotomy of difference equations*, Journal of Difference Equations and Applications **3** (1998), no. 5-6, 417–448.

[5] J. López-Fenner and M. Pinto, *(h,k)-trichotomies and asymptotics of nonautonomous difference systems*, Computers & Mathematics with Applications **33** (1997), no. 10, 105–124.

[6] J. L. Massera and J. J. Schäffer, *Linear Differential Equations and Function Spaces*, Pure and Applied Mathematics, vol. 21, Academic Press, New York, 1966.

[7] S. Matucci, *The l^p trichotomy for difference systems and applications*, Archivum Mathematicum (Brno) **36** (2000), 519–529.

[8] G. Papaschinopoulos, *On exponential trichotomy of linear difference equations*, Applicable Analysis **40** (1991), no. 2-3, 89–109.

[9] M. Pinto, *Discrete dichotomies*, Computers & Mathematics with Applications **28** (1994), no. 1–3, 259–270.

[10] R. J. Sacker and G. R. Sell, *Existence of dichotomies and invariant splittings for linear differential systems. III*, Journal of Differential Equations **22** (1976), no. 2, 497–522.

Claudio Vidal: Departamento de Matemática, Univêrsidade Federal de Pernambuco. Recife-PE, CEP 50740-540, Brazil
E-mail address: claudio@dmat.ufpe.br

Claudio Cuevas: Departamento de Matemática, Univêrsidade Federal de Pernambuco. Recife-PE, CEP 50740-540, Brazil
E-mail address: cch@dmat.ufpe.br

MAXIMUM PRINCIPLES FOR ELLIPTIC EQUATIONS IN UNBOUNDED DOMAINS

ANTONIO VITOLO

We investigate geometric conditions to have the maximum principle for linear second-order elliptic equations in unbounded domains. Next we show structure conditions for nonlinear operators to get the maximum principle in the same domains, then we consider viscosity solutions, for which we can establish at once a comparison principle when one of the solutions is regular enough. We also note that the methods underlying the present results can be used to obtain related Phragmén-Lindelöf principles.

1. Introduction

Let us consider the linear second-order elliptic operator

$$Lw = a_{ij}(x)D_{ij}w + b_i(x)Dw + c(x)w, \tag{1.1}$$

acting on a function space of twice differentiable functions $D(\Omega) \subset C^2(\Omega)$, where Ω is a domain (open connected set) of $\mathbb{R}^n$. Here the matrix of principal coefficients $a_{ij}(x)$ will be taken definite positive and bounded (uniformly with respect to x), satisfying the uniform ellipticity condition

$$\lambda|X|^2 \le a_{ij}(x)X_iX_j \le \Lambda|X|^2, \quad X \in \mathbb{R}^n, \tag{1.2}$$

with ellipticity constants $0 < \lambda \le \Lambda$, the first-order coefficients $b_i(x)$ in $L^\infty(\Omega)$, and the zero-order coefficient $c(x) \le 0$.

We are interested in the *weak maximum principle* (weak MP) for solutions w of the equation $Lw \ge 0$ (see [3, 14]), which is extensively applied to linear and nonlinear problems.

Definition 1.1 (weak MP). The weak MP holds for L in $D(\Omega)$ if

$$Lw \ge 0 \quad \text{in } \Omega, \qquad \limsup_{x\to\partial\Omega} w(x) \le 0 \quad \text{on } \partial\Omega \Longrightarrow w \le 0 \text{ in } \Omega \tag{1.3}$$

whenever $w \in D(\Omega)$.

Hindawi Publishing Corporation
Proceedings of the Conference on Differential & Difference Equations and Applications, pp. 1087–1097

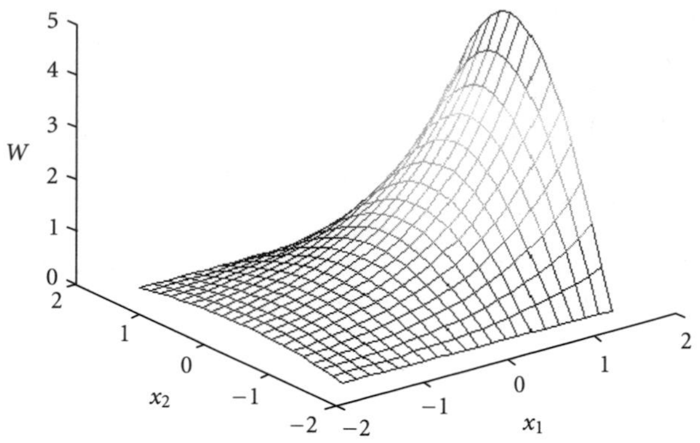

$$\Delta w = 0 \ \text{ in } \Omega =]-\infty, +\infty[\times] - \pi/2, \pi/2[$$
$$w = 0 \ \text{ on } \partial\Omega$$
$$w > 0 \ \text{ in } \Omega$$

Figure 1.1

(Note that the function w is not necessarily defined up to the boundary.)

In a bounded domain Ω, the weak MP is implied by the *strong maximum principle* (strong MP), which means that the subsolutions $w \in W^{2,n}_{\text{loc}}(\Omega)$ of the equation $Lw = 0$ cannot achieve a nonnegative maximum inside Ω unless $w =$ constant (see [10]). In fact, if the strong MP holds in a bounded domain Ω, then a maximizing sequence for a non-constant function w should approach $\partial\Omega$. This is no more true in general in the case that Ω is an unbounded domain, in which a maximizing sequence could go to infinity. On the other side, the weak MP can be viewed as a particular case of the Alexandroff-Bakelman-Pucci estimate (ABP estimate):

$$w \le \limsup_{x \to \partial\Omega} w^+ + C \operatorname{diam}(\Omega) \|f\|_{L^n(\Omega)} \tag{1.4}$$

with a positive constant $C = C(n, \lambda, \Lambda, \|b_i\|_{L^\infty(\Omega)})$. This again holds for bounded domains, but can be improved and rearranged to cover a large class of unbounded domains, as we will see below.

We also note that if $C(\Omega) \subset D(\Omega)$, then the assumptions of the weak MP imply that the subsolution w is bounded above in a bounded domain. This is not true in unbounded domains. Moreover, the weak MP may fail when w is not bounded above as shown by the following counterexample: in the strip $\Omega =]-\infty, +\infty[\times] - \pi/2, +\pi/2[$ of $\mathbb{R}^2$, the Laplace equation $\Delta w = 0$ has the solution $w(x_1, x_2) = \exp(x_1)\cos(x_2)$ such that w is null on the boundary lines $x_2 = -\pi/2$ and $x_2 = +\pi/2$, while tends to infinity on the middle axis of the strip $x_2 = 0$ as $x_1 \to +\infty$ (see Figure 1.1).

This suggests to require the functions of $D(\Omega)$ to be bounded above as a reasonable assumption to get the weak MP. But, even assuming this, the weak MP may equally fail.

Indeed, for $n \geq 3$, the fundamental solution $u(x) = 1/|x|^{n-2}$ provides a counterexample: in the exterior domain $\Omega = \mathbb{R}^n \setminus \bar{B}(0;1)$ of $\mathbb{R}^n$, the Laplace equation has the radial solution $w(x) = 1 - 1/|x|^{n-2}$, such that $w = 0$ on the boundary $|x| = 1$ while $w(x) \to 1$ as $|x| \to +\infty$. This is since $u(x)$ is bounded above. Differently, for $n = 2$, the fundamental solution $u(x) = \log|x|$, going to infinity as $|x| \to \infty$, can be used to show the weak MP in any domain, as shown by the following result.

THEOREM 1.2. *The weak MP holds for the Laplace operator Δ in the space $D(\Omega) = \{w \in C^2(\Omega)/w^+(x) = O(1)\}$, where Ω is the punctured plane $\mathbb{R}^2 \setminus \{0\}$ and $w^+(x) = \max(w(x),0)$.*

Proof. Let us fix $\delta > 0$. Considering a subsolution $w(x)$, bounded above, of the equation $\Delta w = 0$ in Ω, we set $v(x) = w(x) - \varepsilon \log|x|$ for any fixed $\varepsilon > 0$. Since $v(x) \to -\infty$ as $|x| \to +\infty$, then by the strong MP we get

$$w(x) - \varepsilon \log|x| = v(x) \leq \max_{|x|=\delta} w^+(x) - \varepsilon \log\delta, \quad |x| > \delta, \tag{1.5}$$

and therefore, letting $\varepsilon \to 0$, we get

$$w \leq \max_{|x|=\delta} w^+(x), \quad |x| > \delta, \tag{1.6}$$

which yields the weak MP in the exterior domain $\mathbb{R}^2 \setminus \bar{B}(0;\delta)$. As limit case, letting $\delta \to 0$, we obtain $w \leq \limsup_{|x|\to 0} w^+(x)$, $x \in \Omega$, as claimed. □

However, the above result does not hold for all linear second-order elliptic operators in $\mathbb{R}^2$. Indeed, in the exterior domain $\Omega = \mathbb{R}^2 \setminus \bar{B}(0;e^2)$ of $\mathbb{R}^2$, the equation

$$\Delta w - \frac{2}{2+\log|x|} \frac{x_i x_j}{|x|^2} D_{ij} w = 0 \tag{1.7}$$

has the radial solution $w(x) = 1 - 2/\log|x|$, such that $w = 0$ on the boundary $|x| = e^2$ while $w(x) \to 1$ as $|x| \to +\infty$.

The above discussion shows that some condition is needed on the domain, in order that the weak MP holds for all the linear second-order elliptic operators.

2. Geometric conditions

We start with a local geometric condition for the points of a domain Ω of $\mathbb{R}^n$, where $|\cdot|$ denotes the n-dimensional Lebesgue measure.

Definition 2.1 (condition $\mathbf{G}_\sigma$). A point $x \in \Omega$ satisfies condition $\mathbf{G}_\sigma$, for $0 < \sigma < 1$, if there exists a ball $B_{\mathbb{R}_x}$ such that

$$x \in B_{\mathbb{R}_x}, \quad |B_{\mathbb{R}_x} \setminus \Omega_{\mathbb{R}_x}| \geq |B_{\mathbb{R}_x}|, \tag{2.1}$$

where $\Omega_{\mathbb{R}_x}$ is the component of $B_{\mathbb{R}_x} \cap \Omega$ containing x (see Figure 2.1).

Here below different global conditions will be described.

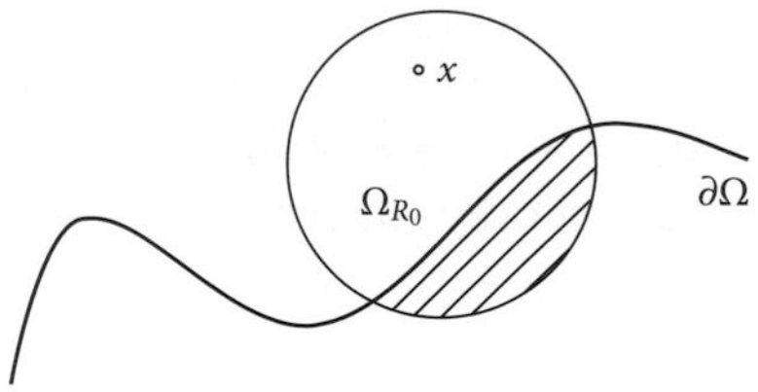

Figure 2.1

Definition 2.2 (condition **G**). A domain Ω satisfies condition **G** if each point $x \in \Omega$ satisfies condition $\mathbf{G}_\sigma$ with $\mathbb{R}_x \leq \mathbb{R}_0$ for a fixed positive number $\sigma < 1$ and a positive constant $\mathbb{R}_0$.

Example 2.3. Condition **G** is satisfied by bounded domains, cylinders, and in general slabs in $\mathbb{R}^n$ as $B \times \mathbb{R}^{n-k}$, where B is a bounded subset of $\mathbb{R}^k$. In all previous examples the complement of the domain is large enough. Nonetheless, since only the complement of the connected components has to be considered, there are domains Ω satisfying condition **G**, but with complement of null measure. For instance, considering in $\mathbb{R}^2$ the half-lines H_i^+ and H_i^- defined, respectively, by $x_1 \geq 0$, $x_2 = 2i$ and $x_1 \leq 0$, $x_2 = 2i+1$, setting $H^\pm = \bigcup_{i \in Z} H_i^\pm$ and $K = H^+ \cup H^-$, we construct a domain $\Omega = \mathbb{R}^2 \backslash K$ satisfying condition **G**, but $|K| = |\mathbb{R}^2 \backslash \Omega| = 0$.

Remark 2.4. In all the examples considered above, the domain Ω satisfies the condition that

$$\sup \{r > 0/B(x;r) \subset \Omega,\ x \in \Omega\} < +\infty. \tag{2.2}$$

This is true in general for a domain satisfying condition **G**. But the converse does not hold in general. For instance, complements of infinite regular lattices of balls $\bar{B}(\mathbf{i};\rho)$ of radius ρ, centered at points with integer coordinates $\mathbf{i} \in Z^n$, also satisfy condition **G** and hence (2.2). But in the limit case, as $\rho \to 0$, we obtain $\Omega = \mathbb{R}^n \backslash \bigcup_{\mathbf{i} \in \mathbf{Z}^n}$, which satisfies condition (2.2) but not condition **G**.

Remark 2.5. A stronger two-parameter local geometric condition for the domain Ω, which originates from Berestycki-Nirenberg-Varadhan [3], has been used by Cabré [5] to show, for the subsolutions $w \in W^{2,n}_{\text{loc}}(\Omega)$ bounded above of the equation $Lw = f$, the improved ABP estimate

$$w \leq \limsup_{x \to \partial\Omega} w^+ + CR_0 \|f\|_{L^n(\Omega_{\mathbb{R}_0})}, \tag{2.3}$$

where C depends only on the structure parameters λ, Λ, $\|b_i\|_{L^\infty(\Omega)}$ of the operator and the geometric constants of the domain. We observe that here the diameter of Ω of the classical ABP estimate (1.4) is replaced by the new geometric constant $\mathbb{R}_0$, and, as it can be deduced from the proof of Theorem 3.2, condition **G** of Definition 2.2 is actually sufficient to have (2.3).

Next, we weaken condition **G**, removing the uniformly boundedness of the radii $\mathbb{R}_x$.

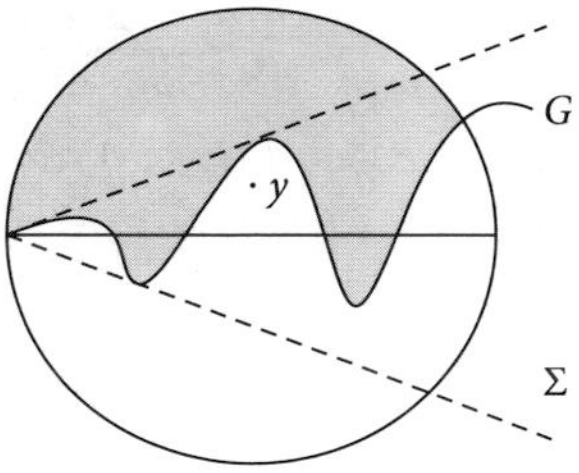

Figure 2.2

Definition 2.6 (condition **wG**). A domain Ω satisfies condition **G** if for each point of Ω condition $\mathbf{G}_\sigma$ holds for a positive constant $\sigma < 1$ (see [6] for a two-parameter local condition and the proof of Theorem 3.2 to be convinced that condition **wG**, as given here, is sufficient for our purposes).

Next, let Ω^σ be the set of the points $x \in \Omega$ for which condition $\mathbf{G}_\sigma$ holds. A domain Ω satisfies condition **wG** a.e. if there is a covering of Ω with balls $B_{\mathbb{R}}$ of radius $\mathbb{R}$ such that

$$|\Omega^\sigma \cup (B_{\mathbb{R}} \backslash \Omega)| \geq \eta |B_{\mathbb{R}}| \tag{2.4}$$

for a positive constant η.

We can also weaken this assumption. We say that Ω satisfies condition **wG** *a.e. by components* if there exists $H \subset \Omega^\sigma$ such that in each component of $\Omega \backslash H$ condition **wG** a.e. holds for positive constants $\sigma < 1$ and η.

Example 2.7. Condition **wG** is satisfied by infinite open connected cones Σ of $\mathbb{R}^n$ with closure $\bar{\Sigma} \neq \mathbb{R}^n$ for which condition **G** does not hold.

The complements in $\mathbb{R}^n$ of hypersurfaces G, which are graphs of a continuous function with sublinear growth g, for example, $x_n = g(x_1, \ldots, x_{n-1})$, $x_i \geq 0$, $i = 1, \ldots, n-1$, provide examples of condition **wG** a.e.

In particular, for $n = 2$ and $g = 0$, we get the cut plane and $\Omega^{1/2} \supset \mathbb{R}^2_+ \backslash G$, where $\mathbb{R}^2_+$ is the half-plane $x_1 > 0$. Instead, in the case of an arbitrary g with sublinear growth, we can always find a positive constant $\sigma < 1$ such that $\Omega^\sigma \supset \Sigma \backslash G$, where Σ is any convex cone, which contains G (see Figure 2.2).

If we consider the sequence of balls with the same radius centered on a half-line, for example, $B(\mathbf{i}; \rho)$, and put $K = \bigcup_{\mathbf{i} \in N \times \{0\}} \bar{B}(\mathbf{i}; \rho)$, choosing $H = \Omega \cap [0, +\infty[\times \{0\}$, we can see that the domain $\Omega = \mathbb{R}^2 \backslash K$ satisfies condition **wG** a.e. by components.

We will search for conditions on the coefficients of the linear second-order operator L in order that the weak MP holds in this kind of domains.

3. The method

The basic tool will be the Krylov-Safonov boundary weak Harnack inequality due to Trudinger (see [10]), as formulated by Cabré [5], which holds with functions in $W^{2,n}_{\text{loc}}$. This will justify the choice of the function space $D(\Omega)$ for the weak MP.

LEMMA 3.1 (boundary weak Harnack inequality). *Let $u \in W^{2,n}_{\text{loc}}(A)$ be a nonnegative solution of the equation $Lu = f$ in a domain $A \in \mathbb{R}^n$. Denote by u_s^- the extension of the function $\min(u,s)$, setting $u_s^- = s$ outside A. Let $B_{\mathbb{R}}$ and $B_{\mathbb{R}/\tau}$, $0 < \tau < 1$, be two concentric balls such that $B_{\mathbb{R}} \cap \Omega$, $B_{\mathbb{R}/\tau} \backslash \Omega$ are nonempty. Choosing $s = \liminf_{x \to B_{\mathbb{R}/\tau} \cap A}$, then*

$$\left(\frac{1}{|B_{\mathbb{R}}|} \int_{B_{\mathbb{R}}} (u_s^-)^p \right)^{1/p} \le C \left(\inf_{B_{\mathbb{R}} \cap A} u + \mathbb{R} \| f \|_{L^n(B_{\mathbb{R}/\tau} \cap A)} \right) \tag{3.1}$$

with p and $C > 1$ positive constants depending only on n, λ, Λ, τ, $\mathbb{R}\|b_i\|_{L^\infty(B_{\mathbb{R}/\tau} \cap A)}$, and $\mathbb{R}^2 \|c\|_{L^\infty(B_{\mathbb{R}/\tau} \cap A)}$.

In order to exemplify the method let us begin considering a linear elliptic operator with the only second-order term

$$Lw = a_{ij}(x) D_{ij} w. \tag{3.2}$$

THEOREM 3.2. *Let Ω be a domain of $\mathbb{R}^n$ satisfying condition **wG** a.e. by components. Then the weak MP holds for the operator L as (3.1) in $D(\Omega) = \{w \in W^{2,n}_{\text{loc}}(\Omega)/w^+(x) = O(1)\}$.*

Sketch of the proof. To be short we limit ourselves to show the case of condition **wG**. Letting w be a subsolution of the equation $Lw = 0$ and putting $M = \sup_\Omega w^+$, by means of condition $\mathbf{G}_\sigma$, in spite of the Krylov-Safonov growth lemma, we search, in the case $\limsup_{x \to \partial\Omega} w \le 0$, for a pointwise estimate

$$w(y) \le \kappa M, \tag{3.3}$$

where $\kappa < 1$ is a positive constant independent of $y \in \Omega$.

In fact, from (3.3), passing to the sup over $y \in \Omega$, we get $w \le 0$ in Ω, as we have to show. To obtain (3.3), firstly we pass to a supersolution setting $u = M - w$, where $M = \sup_\Omega w^+$. Next, using condition $\mathbf{G}_\sigma$ in y, we apply Lemma 3.1 in $A = \Omega_{\mathbb{R}_y}$, with $B_{\mathbb{R}} = B_{\tau\mathbb{R}_y}$ and $\tau = \tau(\sigma)$ sufficiently close to 1, to get

$$\begin{aligned} (\sigma/2)^{1/p} M \le (\sigma/2)^{1/p} s &\le \left(\frac{|B_{\tau\mathbb{R}_y} \backslash \Omega_{\mathbb{R}_y}|}{|B_{\tau\mathbb{R}_y}|} \right)^{1/p} \le \left(\frac{1}{|B_{\tau\mathbb{R}_y}|} \int_{B_{\tau\mathbb{R}_y}} (u_s^-)^p \right)^{1/p} \\ &\le C \inf_{B_{\tau\mathbb{R}_y} \cap \Omega_{\mathbb{R}_y}} u \le C \left(M - \sup_{B_{\tau\mathbb{R}_y} \cap \Omega_{\mathbb{R}_y}} w \right), \end{aligned} \tag{3.4}$$

whence for a positive $\kappa < 1$ we have

$$\sup_{B_{\tau\mathbb{R}_y} \cap \Omega_{\mathbb{R}_y}} w \le \kappa M + (1 - \kappa) \limsup_{x \to \partial\Omega} w^+. \tag{3.5}$$

If $y \in B_{\tau\mathbb{R}_y}$, from (3.5) we have at once (3.3). This motivated the earlier two-parameter local geometric condition of [5, 6] (see Remark 2.5 before).

Otherwise, by a continuity argument we reduce to a ball B_{r_y} such that both $|B_{r_y} \backslash \Omega_{r_y}| = \sigma |B_{r_y}|$ and $|\Omega_{r_y}| = (1 - \sigma)|B_{r_y}|$, in order that (3.2) holds for a set of appreciable measure, for example, $(1 - \sigma/2)|B_{r_y}|$.

Then, applying Lemma 3.1 in $A = \{x \in \Omega / w(x) > \kappa M\}$, with $B_{\mathbb{R}} = B_{r_y}$ and $\tau = \tau(\sigma)$ sufficiently close to 1, and arguing as before as in (3.4) for (3.5), we get the estimate (3.2) in all Ω_{r_y} with a slightly larger $\kappa < 1$, as we needed.

To consider an operator with the first-order term (see [16, 17]) we have to look at the dependence of the constants C and p occurring in the boundary weak Harnack inequality, which influences the dependence of the constant κ of the proof of Theorem 3.2. Indeed, using the same argument for the elliptic operator

$$Lw = a_{ij}(x)D_{ij}w + b_i(x)D_iw, \tag{3.6}$$

the existence of a positive constant $\kappa < 1$ to have the Krylov-Safonov growth lemma will depend on the cross condition

$$\sup_{y\in\Omega} \mathbb{R}_y ||b_i||_{L^\infty(B_{\mathbb{R}_y/\tau}\cap\Omega)} < +\infty \tag{3.7}$$

for some positive constant $\tau < 1$. Therefore, when $\mathbb{R}_y \to \infty$, we should assume a suitable decay rate for the b_i's, but, to take advantage from this assumption to get (3.7), we should also be able to choose balls $B_{\mathbb{R}_y/\tau}$ which are not too much close to the origin.

4. The weak MP in the linear case

Using the arguments of the previous section, we get, for linear second-order elliptic operators, the following results.

THEOREM 4.1. *Let Ω be a domain of $\mathbb{R}^n$ satisfying condition* **wG** *and let L be a linear second-order operator as (3.2) such that the cross condition (3.7) holds for the covering $B_{\mathbb{R}_y}$ which realizes condition* **wG**. *Then the weak MP holds for L in $D(\Omega) = \{w \in W^{2,n}_{\text{loc}}(\Omega)/w^+(x) = O(1)\}$.*

In the case of a domain Ω satisfying condition **G**, *the ABP estimate of Remark 2.5 yields at once the weak MP under the only assumption that $b_i(x) = O(1)$, since also $\mathbb{R}_y = O(1)$. For a parabolic-shaped domain, defined by $x_2^{1/p} > |x_1|$, the covering $B_{\mathbb{R}_y}$ to realize* **wG** *can be chosen in order that the cross condition (3.7) is satisfied with $b_i(x) = O(1/|x|^{1/p})$ as $|x| \to \infty$. As limit cases (see Figure 4.1), for $p = +\infty$ (half-strip, condition* **wG**), *we need $b_i(x) = O(1)$ for $p = 1$ (cone) $b_i(x) = O(1/|x|)$.*

Using a boundary weak Harnack inequality for annuli instead that for balls, as stated by Cabré [5], we can avoid to check the cross condition (3.7) case by case.

THEOREM 4.2. *Let Ω be a domain of $\mathbb{R}^n$ satisfying condition* **wG** *a.e by components as in Definition 2.6 and let L be a linear second-order operator as (3.2) such that*

$$b_i(x) = O\left(\frac{1}{|x|}\right), \quad |x| \longrightarrow \infty, \tag{4.1}$$

then the weak MP holds for L in $D(\Omega) = \{w \in W^{2,n}_{\text{loc}}(\Omega)/w^+(x) = O(1)\}$.

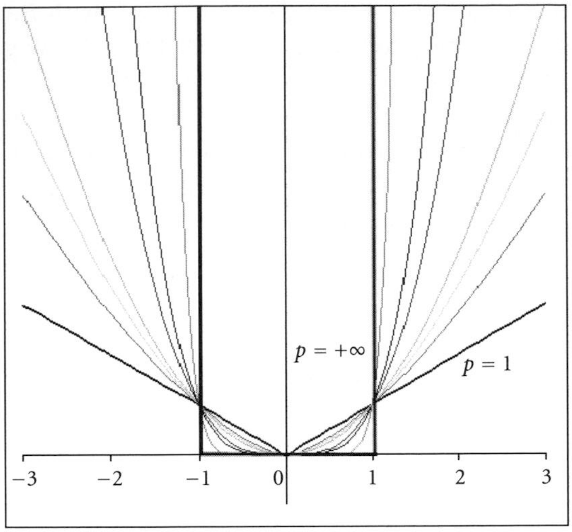

Figure 4.1

Remark 4.3. The admissible decay (4.1) is almost optimal, as shown in the quarter-plane $x_1 > 1, x_2 > 1$ by the equation

$$\Delta w + \left(\frac{\alpha}{x_1^{1-\alpha}} + \frac{1-\alpha}{x_1}\right) D_1 w + \left(\frac{\alpha}{x_2^{1-\alpha}} + \frac{1-\alpha}{x_2}\right) D_2 w \geq 0, \tag{4.2}$$

solved by the function $w(x_1,x_2) = (1 - e^{1-x_1^\alpha})(1 - e^{1-x_2^\alpha})$, which is null on the boundary lines $x_1 \geq 0$, $x_2 = 1$ and $x_1 = 1$, $x_2 \geq 0$, but goes to 1^- as $x_1 = x_2 \to \infty$.

However, it is not true in general that a first-order coefficient $b_i(x) = O(1/|x|)$ yields an admissible perturbation of an operator for which the weak MP holds. Indeed, as we saw in the proof of Theorem 1.2, the weak MP holds for the Laplace operator Δ in the exterior domain $\mathbb{R}^2 \backslash \bar{B}(0;1)$. But the equation

$$\Delta w + \frac{x_1}{|x|^2} D_1 w + \frac{x_2}{|x|^2} D_2 w = 0 \tag{4.3}$$

has the solution $w(x) = 1 - 1/|x|$, which violates the weak MP.

Remark 4.4. The condition on the zero-order coefficient (see [5, 17]) can also be relaxed to allow a slightly positive sign. In the case of condition **G**, we may assume that $c(x) \leq c_0$, where c_0 is a positive constant depending on the structure and geometric parameters. In the case of condition **wG**, we need to strengthen the assumption on the covering $B_{\mathbb{R}_y}$, which realizes **wG**, supposing that $\mathbb{R}_y \leq \chi|y|$ for some positive constant χ, and at the same time assuming $c(x) \leq c_0/|x|^2$ as $|x| \to \infty$.

The weak MP with zero-order coefficient can be used to relax the condition of the above boundedness of the subsolutions to get Phragmèn-Lindelöf theorems, namely, the weak MP holds for subsolution with exponential growth in domains with condition **G** (see [1, 4, 9, 11, 17]), with polynomial growth in the case of condition **wG** (see [2, 9, 11–14, 17]). For the details we refer to [17], where the geometric conditions were still given as two-parameter local condition (see the proof of Theorem 3.2).

5. The weak MP in the fully nonlinear case

Let us consider a fully nonlinear operator (see [7, 10])

$$F[w] = F(x,w,Dw,D^2w) \tag{5.1}$$

acting on $W^{2,n}_{\mathrm{loc}}(\Omega)$. Here F is a real function on the set $\Omega \times \mathbb{R} \times \mathbb{R}^n \times S[n]$, where $S[n]$ denotes the space of real symmetric $n \times n$ matrices.

F will be said uniformly elliptic if

$$\lambda \|T\| \le F(x,t,X,S+T) - F(x,t,X,S) \le \Lambda \|T\|, \quad T \ge 0, \tag{5.2}$$

for positive (ellipticity) constants $\lambda \le \Lambda$, where $\|T\| = \sup_{|x|=1} |Tx|$.

Meaningful examples of fully nonlinear uniformly elliptic operators are the extremal Pucci operators (see [7, 15]), defined by

$$P^{\pm}_{\lambda,\Lambda}(S) = \pm\Lambda \sum_{i=1}^{n} \mu_i^{\pm} \mp \lambda \sum_{i=1}^{n} \mu_i^{\mp}, \tag{5.3}$$

where the μ_i's are the eigenvalues of the matrix S, which are uniformly elliptic with ellipticity constants λ and $n\Lambda$. If we consider a fully nonlinear uniformly elliptic operator with ellipticity constants λ and Λ, the difference for a matrix-variable increment T is controlled by means of the maximal Pucci operator with constants λ/n and Λ, namely,

$$F(x,t,X,S+T) - F(x,t,X,S) \le P^{+}_{\lambda/n,\Lambda}(T), \quad S,T \in S[n]. \tag{5.4}$$

Suppose that $F(x,t,X,0) \le b(x)|X|$ for a positive function $b(x)$. Then, using (5.4) with $S = 0$, we deduce that a subsolution v of the equation $F[v] = 0$ is in turn a subsolution of the equation

$$P^{+}_{\lambda/n,\Lambda}(D^2v) + b(x)|Dv| = 0, \tag{5.5}$$

but for this it is sufficient to assume

$$F(x,t,X,T) \le P^{+}_{\lambda/n,\Lambda}(T) + b(x)|X|, \tag{5.6}$$

which is not equivalent to the uniform ellipticity on any account unless F is linear in the matrix-variable. In fact, in the linear case, (5.6) implies (5.4), which in turn yields the uniform ellipticity for the operator $F_0[w] = F(x,w,0,D^2w)$.

At this stage, we note that there is a linear elliptic operator L with the only second-order term as (3.2) such that $P^{+}_{\lambda/n,\Lambda}(D^2v) = Lv$, which can be dealt with as the linear equations of the previous sections. This implies that the weak MP continues to hold for a fully nonlinear second-order elliptic operator as (3.2), under the structure assumption

(5.6), with strong subsolutions in $W^{2,n}_{\text{loc}}(\Omega)$, bounded above, provided that $b(x) = O(1)$ in the case of condition **G** and $b(x) = O(1/|x|)$ as $|x| \to \infty$ in the case of condition **wG**.

In the case of linear operators, the weak MP for subsolutions v bounded above yields at once a weak minimum principle (weak mP) for supersolutions u bounded from below. As well as we obtain a weak comparison principle (weak CP), namely, $v \leq u$ on $\partial\Omega \Rightarrow v \leq u$ in Ω, considering the difference $w = v - u$. In the case of nonlinear operators we need dual assumptions for the weak mP and additional assumptions for the weak CP.

In the case of fully nonlinear operators, we can state a minimum principle for supersolutions bounded from below, under the dual structure assumption

$$F(x,t,X,T) \geq P^{-}_{\lambda/n,\Lambda}(T) - b(x)|X|. \tag{5.7}$$

For what concerns comparison principles, we could linearize the equation under suitable assumptions on the differentiability of the operator F with respect on the matrix-variable.

An alternative approach is to consider the so-called viscosity solutions (see [7]).

Definition 5.1. An upper (lower) semicontinuous w is said to be a viscosity subsolution (supersolution) of the equation $F[w] = f$ in Ω if, for each point $x \in \Omega$, the following inequality

$$F(x,\phi(x),D\phi(x),D^2\phi(x) \geq f(x)(\leq f(x))) \tag{5.8}$$

holds for any $\phi \in C^2(\Omega)$ such that the difference $w - \phi$ has a local maximum (minimum) in x. A solution is a continuous functions which is both subsolution and supersolution.

In [8] a weak MP has been obtained, in the case of fully nonlinear second-order elliptic operator F as (5.1), under the the structure assumption (5.6), and a weak mP, under the dual structure assumption (5.7), with $b(x)$ as above in the case of strong solutions. Furthermore, a weak CP, when at least one between the subsolution and the supersolution is regular, has been obtained under the assumption of uniform ellipticity.

We notice that while in the case of strong solutions we can directly use the results of the linear case, apart the nonlinearity on the first-order term (which does not invalidate the argument); in this case we only take the method from the linear setting, using the fact that a weak Harnack inequality continues to hold for viscosity solutions (see [7]).

6. Conclusions

We have seen that some useful linear techniques can be extended to nonlinear problems, and this provides a wide range of applications. For instance, remaining in the topic discussed here, we have in mind to extend the Phragmén-Lindelöf results to fully nonlinear operators in the viscosity sense, eventually considering a superlinear growth in the gradient variable. It would be also interesting to obtain weak CP in unbounded domains for viscosity subsolutions and supersolutions, without the regularity assumption used in the previous section.

Acknowledgment

I feel to thank Professors Robert Finn and Mikhail Safonov for suggesting helpful readings on the subject and related topics in view of future developments.

References

[1] H. Berestycki, L. A. Caffarelli, and L. Nirenberg, *Inequalities for second-order elliptic equations with applications to unbounded domains. I*, Duke Mathematical Journal **81** (1996), no. 2, 467–494.

[2] ———, *Monotonicity for elliptic equations in unbounded Lipschitz domains*, Communications on Pure and Applied Mathematics **50** (1997), no. 11, 1089–1111.

[3] H. Berestycki, L. Nirenberg, and S. R. S. Varadhan, *The principal eigenvalue and maximum principle for second-order elliptic operators in general domains*, Communications on Pure and Applied Mathematics **47** (1994), no. 1, 47–92.

[4] J. Busca, *Existence results for Bellman equations and maximum principles in unbounded domains*, Communications in Partial Differential Equations **24** (1999), no. 11-12, 2023–2042.

[5] X. Cabré, *On the Alexandroff-Bakel'man-Pucci estimate and the reversed Hölder inequality for solutions of elliptic and parabolic equations*, Communications on Pure and Applied Mathematics **48** (1995), no. 5, 539–570.

[6] V. Cafagna and A. Vitolo, *On the maximum principle for second-order elliptic operators in unbounded domains*, Comptes Rendus de l'Academie des Sciences. Serie I. Mathematique **334** (2002), 1–5.

[7] L. A. Caffarelli and X. Cabré, *Fully Nonlinear Elliptic Equations*, American Mathematical Society Colloquium Publications, vol. 43, American Mathematical Society, Rhode Island, 1995.

[8] I. Capuzzo Dolcetta, F. Leoni, and A. Vitolo, *The Alexandrov-Bakelman-Pucci weak Maximum Principle for fully nonlinear equations in unbounded domains*, Communications in Partial Differential Equations **30** (2005), 1863–1881.

[9] L. E. Fraenkel, *An Introduction to Maximum Principles and Symmetry in Elliptic Problems*, Cambridge Tracts in Mathematics, vol. 128, Cambridge University Press, Cambridge, 2000.

[10] D. Gilbarg and N. S. Trudinger, *Elliptic Partial Differential Equations of Second Order*, 2nd ed., Grundlehren der Mathematischen Wissenschaften, vol. 224, Springer, Berlin, 1983.

[11] E. M. Landis, *On the behaviour of solutions of elliptic equations in unbounded domains*, Transactions of the Moscow Mathematical Society **31** (1976), 30–54.

[12] K. Miller, *Extremal barriers on cones with Phragmèn-Lindelöf theorems and other applications*, Annali di Matematica Pura ed Applicata. Serie Quarta **90** (1971), 297–329.

[13] J. K. Oddson, *Phragmèn-Lindelöf theorems for elliptic equations in the plane*, Transactions of the American Mathematical Society **145** (1969), 347–356.

[14] M. H. Protter and H. F. Weinberger, *Maximum Principles in Differential Equations*, Springer, New York, 1997.

[15] C. Pucci, *Operatori ellittici estremanti*, Annali di Matematica Pura ed Applicata. Series IV **74** (1966), 141–170.

[16] A. Vitolo, *On the maximum principle for complete second-order elliptic operators in general domains*, Journal of Differential Equations **194** (2003), no. 1, 166–184.

[17] ———, *On the Phragmèn-Lindelöf principle for second-order elliptic equations*, Journal of Mathematical Analysis and Applications **300** (2004), no. 1, 244–259.

Antonio Vitolo: Dipartimento di Matematica e Informatica, Universitá di Salerno,
Piazza Grahamstown, 84084 Fisciano (SA), Italy
E-mail address: vitolo@unisa.it

BAYESIAN FORECASTING IN UNIVARIATE AUTOREGRESSIVE MODELS WITH NORMAL-GAMMA PRIOR DISTRIBUTION OF UNKNOWN PARAMETERS

IGOR VLADIMIROV AND BEVAN THOMPSON

We consider the problem of computing the mean-square optimal Bayesian predictor in univariate autoregressive models with Gaussian innovations. The unknown coefficients of the model are ascribed a normal-gamma prior distribution providing a family of conjugate priors. The problem is reduced to calculating the state-space realization matrices of an iterated linear discrete time-invariant system. The system theoretic solution employs a scalarization technique for computing the power moments of Gaussian random matrices developed recently by the authors.

1. Introduction

We consider the problem of computing the mean-square optimal Bayesian predictor for a univariate time series whose dynamics is described by an autoregressive model with Gaussian innovations [3]. The coefficients of the model are assumed unknown and ascribed a normal-gamma prior distribution [1, page 140] providing a family of conjugate priors.

The problem reduces to computing the power moments of a square random matrix which is expressed affinely in terms of a random vector with multivariate Student distribution [1, page 139]. The latter is a randomized mixture of Gaussian distributions, thereby allowing us to employ a matrix product scalarization technique developed in [7] for computing the power moments $\mathbf{E}X^s$ of Gaussian random matrices $X = A + B\zeta C$, where ζ is a standard normal random vector and A, B, C are appropriately dimensioned constant matrices.

Note that developing an exact algorithm for the power moment problem, alternative to an approximate solution via Monte Carlo simulation, is complicated by the noncommutativity of the matrix algebra that is only surmountable in special classes of random matrices, of which a more general one is treated by sophisticated graph theoretic methods in [8].

Hindawi Publishing Corporation
Proceedings of the Conference on Differential & Difference Equations and Applications, pp. 1099–1108

In the context of the problem considered in the present paper, application of the scalarization technique yields a system theoretic algorithm which reduces the computation of the Bayesian forecast to recursively calculating the state-space realization matrices of an iterated linear discrete time-invariant system.

The results of the paper are applicable to the forecasting problems in econometrics and adaptive control where predicting a time series must be accompanied by model identification, including parameter estimation, in the framework of the Bayesian theory [1]. A related circle of questions for diffusion processes is studied in [6].

The paper is organized as follows. Section 2 provides the necessary background material on multivariate normal-gamma distributions. Section 3 specifies the class of autoregressive time series. Section 4 shows that the normal-gamma family supplies conjugate priors. Section 5 reduces the Bayesian forecast to a power moment of a Student distributed random matrix. Section 6 describes the state-space system theoretic solution to the problem. Proofs are relegated to the appendix.

2. Multivariate normal-gamma distributions

Let $\mathbb{P}_n$ denote the set of positive definite real symmetric matrices of order n, and let $S \in \mathbb{P}_{p+1}$ be partitioned into four blocks as

$$S = \begin{bmatrix} P & q \\ q^\top & r \end{bmatrix}, \quad P \in \mathbb{P}_p,\ q \in \mathbb{R}^p,\ r > \|q\|_{P^{-1}}^2. \tag{2.1}$$

Here, $(\cdot)^\top$ is the matrix transpose, and $\|a\|_U = \sqrt{a^\top U a}$ is the Euclidean (semi-)norm of a vector a induced by a positive (semi-)definite real symmetric matrix U. Unless otherwise indicated, vectors are organized as columns. With S, we associate a map $V_S : \mathbb{R}^p \to \mathbb{R}_+$ by

$$V_S(a) = \left\| \begin{bmatrix} a \\ -1 \end{bmatrix} \right\|_S^2 = \|a\|_P^2 - 2q^\top a + r = M(S) + \|a - P^{-1}q\|_P^2, \tag{2.2}$$

where

$$M(S) = r - \|q\|_{P^{-1}}^2 = \min_{a \in \mathbb{R}^p} V_S(a) \tag{2.3}$$

is the Schur complement of the diagonal block P in (2.1). Since (2.2) is linear in S, the function M is concave on $\mathbb{P}_{p+1}$ as the lower envelope of linear functions.

For S in (2.1) and for $\lambda > 0$, we denote by $D_p(\lambda, S)$ a probability measure on $\mathbb{R}^p \times \mathbb{R}_+$ with density

$$\begin{aligned} d_{p,\lambda,S}(a,b) &= \left(\frac{b}{2\pi}\right)^{p/2} \sqrt{\det P} \exp\left(-\frac{1}{2}\|a - P^{-1}q\|_{bP}^2\right) \\ &\quad \times \frac{(M(S)/2)^\lambda}{\Gamma(\lambda)} b^{\lambda-1} \exp\left(-M(S)\frac{b}{2}\right) \\ &= (2\pi)^{-p/2}\sqrt{\det P}\frac{(M(S)/2)^\lambda}{\Gamma(\lambda)} b^{\lambda+(p/2)-1} \exp\left(-V_S(a)\frac{b}{2}\right), \end{aligned} \tag{2.4}$$

where Γ is the Euler gamma function. In terminology of [1, page 140], $D_p(\lambda,S)$ is the multivariate normal-gamma distribution $\mathbf{Ng}_p(P^{-1}q,P,\lambda,M(S)/2)$. We will write $(\alpha,\beta) \sim D_p(\lambda,S)$ for an $\mathbb{R}^p$-valued random vector α and for an $\mathbb{R}_+$-valued random variable β whose joint pdf is given by (2.4). The conditional distribution of α with respect to β is Gaussian with mean $P^{-1}q$ and precision matrix βP:

$$\operatorname{Law}(\alpha \mid \beta) = \mathbf{N}_p\left(P^{-1}q, (\beta P)^{-1}\right). \tag{2.5}$$

Furthermore, β is gamma-distributed and α has the multivariate Student distribution [1, pages 118–139]:

$$\alpha \sim \mathbf{St}_p\left(P^{-1}q, \frac{2\lambda P}{M(S)}, 2\lambda\right), \qquad \beta \sim \mathbf{Ga}\left(\lambda, \frac{M(S)}{2}\right). \tag{2.6}$$

Remark 2.1. If the last diagonal entry in (2.1) is rescaled so that

$$S_\lambda = \begin{bmatrix} P & q \\ q^\top & 2\lambda r \end{bmatrix}, \tag{2.7}$$

then the distribution $D_p(\lambda,S_\lambda)$ is weakly convergent [2], as $\lambda \to +\infty$, to the direct product of $\mathbf{N}_p(P^{-1}q,rP^{-1})$ and of the atomic probability measure concentrated on $1/r$. Indeed, from (2.3), $\lim_{\lambda\to+\infty}(M(S_\lambda)/(2\lambda)) = r$ and hence, β in (2.6) converges in probability to $1/r$. It now remains to combine the last convergence with the conditional law (2.5) and to apply the well-known result on the preservation of weak convergence under continuous maps [2, Theorem 5.5 on page 34].

3. Autoregressive model

Let $X = (X_k)_{k>-p}$ be an $\mathbb{R}$-valued random sequence governed by an autoregressive (AR) equation of order $p \in \mathbb{N}$,

$$X_k = \sum_{j=1}^{p} \alpha_j X_{k-j} + \sqrt{c}\,W_k, \quad k \in \mathbb{N}. \tag{3.1}$$

Here, $W = (W_k)_{k\in\mathbb{N}}$ is an innovation sequence, and $\alpha_1,\ldots,\alpha_p \in \mathbb{R}$ and $c > 0$ are unknown parameters. Let $\alpha \in \mathbb{R}^p$, $\beta > 0$, and an $\mathbb{R}^p$-valued sequence $Y = (Y_k)_{k\in\mathbb{Z}_+}$ be given by

$$\alpha = \begin{bmatrix} \alpha_1 \\ \vdots \\ \alpha_p \end{bmatrix}, \qquad \beta = \frac{1}{c}, \qquad Y_k = \begin{bmatrix} X_k \\ \vdots \\ X_{k-p+1} \end{bmatrix}. \tag{3.2}$$

Denote by $\mathcal{F}_0$ the σ-algebra of random events describing the prior information on the AR(p)-model (3.1) at time 0, so that $X_0,\ldots,X_{1-p}$ are $\mathcal{F}_0$-measurable. Let Π_0 be the prior probability distribution of the unknown parameter $\theta = (\alpha,\beta)$ on the set

$$\Theta = \mathbb{R}^p \times \mathbb{R}_+. \tag{3.3}$$

We assume that the innovation sequence W is constituted by independent standard normal random variables which are independent of $\mathcal{F}_0$ and θ. Furthermore, the unknown parameter is assumed to have a normal-gamma prior,

$$\Pi_0 = D_p(\lambda_0, S_0), \tag{3.4}$$

as defined in Section 2, where $\lambda_0 > 1$ and, similarly to (2.1), $S_0 \in \mathbb{P}_{p+1}$ is partitioned into four blocks as

$$S_0 = \begin{bmatrix} P_0 & q_0 \\ q_0^\top & r_0 \end{bmatrix}, \quad P_0 \in \mathbb{P}_p,\ q_0 \in \mathbb{R}^p,\ r_0 > \|q_0\|^2_{P_0^{-1}}. \tag{3.5}$$

Since, by the second relation in (2.6), $\mathrm{Law}(\beta \mid \mathcal{F}_0) = \mathbf{Ga}(\lambda_0, M(S_0)/2)$, where M is given by (2.3), the random variable c is integrable with respect to Π_0, with

$$\mathbf{E}(c \mid \mathcal{F}_0) = \frac{M(S_0)}{2(\lambda_0 - 1)}. \tag{3.6}$$

By Remark 2.1, the situation, where c is known precisely while the prior distribution of α is Gaussian, is a limiting case of (3.4).

4. The posterior parameter distribution

For any $k \in \mathbb{N}$, let $\mathcal{F}_k$ denote the σ-algebra generated by $\mathcal{F}_0$ and by the observations $X_1, \ldots, X_k$ available at time k, and let

$$\Pi_k = \mathrm{Law}(\theta \mid \mathcal{F}_k) \tag{4.1}$$

be the corresponding posterior distribution of the unknown parameter θ. The resultant filtration is denoted by $\mathbb{F} = (\mathcal{F}_k)_{k \in \mathbb{Z}_+}$. Define an $\mathbb{R}^{p+1}$-valued $\mathbb{F}$-adapted sequence $Z = (Z_k)_{k \in \mathbb{N}}$ by

$$Z_k = \begin{bmatrix} Y_{k-1} \\ X_k \end{bmatrix}. \tag{4.2}$$

Proposition 4.1. *Under the assumptions of Section 3, for any $k \in \mathbb{Z}_+$, the posterior distribution (4.1) is given by*

$$\Pi_k = D_p(\lambda_k, S_k), \tag{4.3}$$

where

$$\lambda_k = \lambda_0 + \frac{k}{2}, \qquad S_k = \begin{bmatrix} P_k & q_k \\ q_k^\top & r_k \end{bmatrix} = S_0 + \sum_{j=1}^{k} Z_j Z_j^\top. \tag{4.4}$$

The proposition shows that the family of normal-gamma distributions D_p provides conjugate priors for the parameters α and β of the AR(p)-model (3.1)-(3.2). Its proof is given in Appendix A to make the exposition self-contained.

5. Bayesian prediction

By (3.1), the $\mathbb{F}$-adapted sequence Y given by (3.2) follows the multivariate AR(1)-equation

$$Y_k = \Phi Y_{k-1} + \sqrt{c}\Psi W_k. \tag{5.1}$$

Here,

$$\Phi = \Psi\alpha^{\top} + \Upsilon, \qquad \Psi = \begin{bmatrix} 1 \\ 0_{(p-1)\times 1} \end{bmatrix}, \qquad \Upsilon = \left[\frac{0_{1\times p}}{I_{p-1} \mid 0_{(p-1)\times 1}}\right], \tag{5.2}$$

where $0_{m\times n}$ is the $(m \times n)$-matrix of zeros, and I_n is the identity matrix of order n. From (5.1) and (5.2), for any $k \in \mathbb{Z}_+$ and $s \in \mathbb{N}$,

$$X_{k+s} = (\Phi^s Y_k)_1 + \sqrt{c}\sum_{j=0}^{s-1} (\Phi^j)_{11} W_{k+s-j}, \tag{5.3}$$

where $(\cdot)_1$ is the first entry of a vector, and $(\cdot)_{11}$ is the $(1,1)$st entry of a matrix. Note that $(W_j)_{j>k}$ consists of independent standard normal random variables which are independent of $\mathcal{F}_k$ and θ. Hence, by (5.3), the s steps ahead mean-square optimal Bayesian predictor of X based on $\mathcal{F}_k$ is

$$\mathbf{E}(X_{k+s} \mid \mathcal{F}_k) = (\mathbf{E}(\Phi^s \mid \mathcal{F}_k) Y_k)_1. \tag{5.4}$$

Its mean-square accuracy is quantified by the conditional variance

$$\mathbf{var}(X_{k+s} \mid \mathcal{F}_k) = \mathbf{var}((\Phi^s Y_k)_1 \mid \mathcal{F}_k) + \sum_{j=0}^{s-1} \mathbf{E}(c(\Phi^j)_{11}^2 \mid \mathcal{F}_k). \tag{5.5}$$

In particular, for the one step ahead predictor with $s = 1$, the relations (5.4) and (5.5) give

$$\begin{aligned} \mathbf{E}(X_{k+1} \mid \mathcal{F}_k) &= \widehat{\alpha}_k^{\top} Y_k, \\ \mathbf{var}(X_{k+1} \mid \mathcal{F}_k) &= \|Y_k\|^2_{\mathbf{cov}(\alpha\mid\mathcal{F}_k)} + \mathbf{E}(\beta^{-1} \mid \mathcal{F}_k) = \left(\|Y_k\|^2_{P_k^{-1}} + 1\right)\frac{M(S_k)}{2(\lambda_k - 1)}. \end{aligned} \tag{5.6}$$

Here, $\mathbf{cov}(\alpha \mid \mathcal{F}_k) = \mathbf{E}(\beta^{-1} \mid \mathcal{F}_k)P_k^{-1}$ is the conditional covariance matrix of α with respect to $\mathcal{F}_k$;

$$\widehat{\alpha}_k = \mathbf{E}(\alpha \mid \mathcal{F}_k) = P_k^{-1} q_k, \tag{5.7}$$

and the relation $\mathbf{E}(\beta^{-1} \mid \mathcal{F}_k) = M(S_k)/(2(\lambda_k - 1))$, similar to (3.6), is used.

The problems of computing the Bayesian predictor (5.4) and evaluating its mean-square accuracy (5.5) for arbitrary $s > 1$ are more difficult, and we will restrict ourselves to the first of these. Clearly, (5.4) reduces to the sth power moment of the random matrix

Φ in (5.2) which is affinely expressed in terms of α. By Proposition 4.1 and by (2.5)-(2.6), $\mathrm{Law}(\alpha \mid \mathcal{F}_k)$ is the multivariate Student distribution, with

$$\alpha = \widehat{\alpha}_k + (\beta P_k)^{-1/2} \gamma_k. \tag{5.8}$$

Here, γ_k is an $\mathbb{R}^p$-valued standard normal random vector, independent of β and of $\mathcal{F}_k$,

$$\mathrm{Law}(\gamma_k \mid \beta, \mathcal{F}_k) = \mathbf{N}_p(0_{p\times 1}, I_p), \tag{5.9}$$

and $\sqrt{U} \in \mathbb{P}_p$ is the matrix square root of $U \in \mathbb{P}_p$. Therefore, substituting (5.8) into (5.2) yields

$$\Phi = \widehat{\Phi}_k + \Psi \gamma_k^\top (\beta P_k)^{-1/2}, \qquad \widehat{\Phi}_k = \mathbf{E}(\Phi \mid \mathcal{F}_k) = \Psi \widehat{\alpha}_k^\top + \Upsilon. \tag{5.10}$$

6. A system theoretic solution

A triplet $(A, B, C) \in \mathbb{R}^{n\times n} \times \mathbb{R}^{n\times m} \times \mathbb{R}^{\ell\times n}$ can be interpreted as a state-space realization of a linear discrete time-invariant (LDTI) system with appropriately dimensioned input $i = (i_t)_{t\in\mathbb{Z}_+}$, internal state $\sigma = (\sigma_t)_{t\in\mathbb{Z}_+}$, and output $o = (o_t)_{t\in\mathbb{Z}_+}$ governed by the equations

$$\sigma_t = A\sigma_{t-1} + Bi_t, \qquad o_t = C\sigma_t, \tag{6.1}$$

with $\sigma_{-1} = 0_{n\times 1}$; see, for example, [4, pages 90–93] or [5, page 35]. The linear operator $(\mathbb{R}^m)^{\mathbb{Z}_+} \ni i \mapsto o \in (\mathbb{R}^\ell)^{\mathbb{Z}_+}$ is described by $\sigma_t = \sum_{u=0}^{t} CA^{t-u}Bi_u$, where the sequence $(CA^uB)_{u\in\mathbb{Z}_+}$ is the impulse response of the system. The input-output operator is denoted by (A, B, C) or, interchangeably, by

$$\left[\begin{array}{c||c} A & B \\ \hline\hline C & 0_{\ell\times m} \end{array}\right]. \tag{6.2}$$

Since we only deal with LDTI systems in the sequel, the qualifier LDTI will be omitted. The class of such systems is closed under composition, and the state-space representation of the operation is well known in linear control; see also [7, Lemma 2 and Appendix B].

Proposition 6.1. *Let the output of $\Sigma_1 = (A_1, B_1, C_1)$ be the input to $\Sigma_2 = (A_2, B_2, C_2)$. Then the composition of the systems is given by*

$$\Sigma_2 \circ \Sigma_1 = \left[\begin{array}{c|c||c} A_1 & 0 & B_1 \\ B_2C_1A_1 & A_2 & B_2C_1B_1 \\ \hline\hline 0 & C_2 & 0 \end{array}\right]. \tag{6.3}$$

The dimensions of the zero blocks in (6.3) are omitted for the sake of brevity. Note that (6.3) is an equality between linear operators, not between their state-space realization matrices.

The theorem below provides a system theoretic solution to the problem of computing the Bayesian forecast (5.4). In order to facilitate its formulation, we introduce subsidiary systems

$$E = F \circ G = (\mathbf{A}, \mathbf{B}, \mathbf{C}), \tag{6.4}$$

$$F = (\widehat{\Phi}_k^{\top}, I_p, I_p), \tag{6.5}$$

$$G = (\widehat{\Phi}_k, \Omega, P_k^{-1}), \tag{6.6}$$

where

$$\Omega = \Psi\Psi^{\top} = \left[\begin{array}{c|c} 1 & 0_{1\times(p-1)} \\ \hline 0_{(p-1)\times 1} & 0_{(p-1)\times(p-1)} \end{array}\right], \tag{6.7}$$

and (4.4), (5.2), and (5.10) are used. The state-space realization matrices $\mathbf{A} \in \mathbb{R}^{2p\times 2p}$, $\mathbf{B} \in \mathbb{R}^{2p\times p}$, and $\mathbf{C} \in \mathbb{R}^{p\times 2p}$ in (6.4) are computed using Proposition 6.1 which yields

$$\mathbf{A} = \left[\begin{array}{c|c} \widehat{\Phi}_k & 0_{p\times p} \\ \hline P_k^{-1}\widehat{\Phi}_k & \widehat{\Phi}_k^{\top} \end{array}\right], \qquad \mathbf{B} = \begin{bmatrix} I_p \\ P_k^{-1} \end{bmatrix} \Omega, \qquad \mathbf{C} = [0_{p\times p} \mid I_p]. \tag{6.8}$$

For any $t \in \mathbb{N}$, let $E^t = \underbrace{E \circ \cdots \circ E}_{t \text{ times}}$ denote the t-fold iterate of the system E, and let H_t be the system associated with (6.4) and (6.5) as

$$H_t = E^t \circ F = (\mathbf{A}_t, \mathbf{B}_t, \mathbf{C}_t). \tag{6.9}$$

Remark 6.2. The state-space realization of (6.9) is completely determined by $\widehat{\Phi}_k$ and P_k. The system F in (6.5) does not depend on the matrix P_k, while (6.6) is positively homogeneous in P_k of degree -1 in the sense that for any $\rho > 0$, the rescaling $P_k \mapsto \rho P_k$ implies $G \mapsto \rho^{-1} G$. Hence, the dependence of the linear operator H_t on P_k is positively homogeneous of degree $-t$. That is, in terms of the impulse response, $P_k \mapsto \rho P_k$ induces $\mathbf{C}_t \mathbf{A}_t^u \mathbf{B}_t \mapsto \rho^{-t} \mathbf{C}_t \mathbf{A}_t^u \mathbf{B}_t$ for all $u \in \mathbb{Z}_+$.

In the sequel, $\lfloor \cdot \rfloor$ and $\lceil \cdot \rceil$ denote the floor and ceiling integer parts of a real number, respectively.

Theorem 6.3. *For any $s \in \mathbb{N}$ satisfying $s < 2\lceil \lambda_k \rceil$, the sth posterior power moment of the random matrix Φ in (5.4) is expressed in terms of the state-space realization matrices of the system (6.9) as*

$$\mathbf{E}(\Phi^s \mid \mathcal{F}_k) = \widehat{\Phi}_k^s + \sum_{t=1}^{\lfloor s/2 \rfloor} (2t-1)!! \frac{(M(S_k)/2)^t}{\prod_{u=1}^{t} (\lambda_k - u)} (\mathbf{C}_t \mathbf{A}_t^{s-2t} \mathbf{B}_t)^{\top}. \tag{6.10}$$

Here, λ_k and S_k are the hyperparameters (4.4) of the posterior distribution (4.3), and the function M is given by (2.3).

We prove Theorem 6.3 in Appendix B. The theorem encapsulates a system theoretic algorithm which reduces the computation of the posterior power moments of Φ in (5.4) to calculating the state-space realization matrices $\mathbf{A}_t \in \mathbb{R}^{(2t+1)p\times(2t+1)p}$, $\mathbf{B}_t \in \mathbb{R}^{(2t+1)p\times p}$, and $\mathbf{C}_t \in \mathbb{R}^{p\times(2t+1)p}$ recursively in t. More precisely, applying Proposition 6.1 to the recurrence relation $H_{t+1} = E\circ H_t$ and using (6.8) yield

$$\mathbf{A}_{t+1} = \left[\begin{array}{c|c} \mathbf{A}_t & 0_{(2t+1)p\times 2p} \\ \hline \mathbf{BC}_t\mathbf{A}_t & \mathbf{A} \end{array}\right], \qquad \mathbf{B}_{t+1} = \left[\begin{array}{c} \mathbf{B}_t \\ \hline \mathbf{BC}_t\mathbf{B}_t \end{array}\right], \qquad \mathbf{C}_t = \left[0_{p\times 2tp} \mid I_p\right], \tag{6.11}$$

with

$$\mathbf{A}_0 = \widehat{\Phi}_k^\top, \qquad \mathbf{B}_0 = \mathbf{C}_0 = I_p. \tag{6.12}$$

Both $\mathbf{A}_t$ and $\mathbf{B}_t$ in (6.11) are submatrices of $\mathbf{A}_{t+1}$ and $\mathbf{B}_{t+1}$, respectively, with $\mathbf{A}_t$ being block lower triangular. From (6.8) and from the special structure of the matrices $\mathbf{C}_t$, it follows that

$$\mathbf{C}_{t+1}\mathbf{A}_{t+1} = \left[P_k^{-1}\Omega\mathbf{C}_t\mathbf{A}_t \mid \mathbf{CA}\right], \qquad \mathbf{C}_{t+1}\mathbf{B}_{t+1} = P_k^{-1}\Omega\mathbf{C}_t\mathbf{B}_t, \tag{6.13}$$

where $\mathbf{CA} = [P_k^{-1}\widehat{\Phi}_k \mid \widehat{\Phi}_k^\top]$. Moreover, by the special structure of the matrix Ω in (6.7), the rightmost relations in (6.12) and in (6.13) imply that for any $t \in \mathbb{N}$,

$$\mathbf{C}_t\mathbf{B}_t = \left(P_k^{-1}\Omega\right)^t = \left[\left(P_k^{-1}\right)_{11}^{t-1}\left(P_k^{-1}\right)_{\bullet 1} \mid 0_{p\times(p-1)}\right], \tag{6.14}$$

where $(\cdot)_{\bullet 1}$ is the first column of a matrix.

The proposed system theoretic algorithm (6.8)–(6.14) for computing $\mathbf{E}(\Phi^s \mid \mathcal{F}_k)$ is expensive for large s, since the order of $\mathbf{A}_t$ grows linearly in t. The burden, however, is partially alleviated by the sparsity of the state-space realization matrices due to the special structure of Ω. Also recall that, in order to assure the integrability of Φ^s with respect to the posterior distribution Π_k given by (4.3)-(4.4), s is limited by the number of observations k on which the forecast (5.4) is based.

Although this last restriction originates from the particular family of conjugate priors used, it conforms with the qualitative principle that a meaningful long term forecast of a time series, whose dynamics incorporates unknown parameters, requires an appropriately long past history in order to estimate them accurately enough to attenuate the dynamic propagation of the remaining posterior uncertainty in the knowledge of the parameters.

Appendices

A. Proof of Proposition 4.1

The assertion of the proposition for $k = 0$ replicates the assumption (3.4). In order to establish its validity for any $k \in \mathbb{N}$, we rewrite (3.1) in notation (3.2) as

$$X_k = \alpha^\top Y_{k-1} + \frac{W_k}{\sqrt{\beta}}. \tag{A.1}$$

Recall that W is a discrete time Gaussian white noise, independent of $\mathcal{F}_0$ and of θ. Hence, by (A.1), the conditional likelihood function of $X_1,\ldots,X_k$, that is, their joint pdf, conditioned on $\mathcal{F}_0$ and on $\theta = (a,b) \in \Theta$, and considered as a function of the latter, is

$$\Lambda_k(\theta) = \left(\frac{b}{2\pi}\right)^{k/2} \exp\left(-\frac{b}{2}\sum_{j=1}^{k}(X_j - a^\top Y_{j-1})^2\right), \tag{A.2}$$

where (3.3) is used. Hence, applying the Bayes theorem, it follows that the density π_k of Π_k is given by

$$\pi_k(\tau) = \frac{\pi_0(\tau)\Lambda_k(\tau)}{\int_\Theta \pi_0(\tau')\Lambda_k(\tau')d\tau'}, \qquad \tau = (a,b) \in \Theta, \tag{A.3}$$

where $\pi_0 = d_{p,\lambda_0,S_0}$ is the prior pdf of θ defined by (2.4). As always with posterior pdf's, omitting all those multipliers in the numerator of (A.3) which do not depend on τ, we obtain

$$\pi_k(\tau) \propto b^{\lambda_0+(p/2)-1+k/2} \exp\left(-\frac{b}{2}\left(V_{S_0}(a) + \sum_{j=1}^{k}(a^\top Y_{j-1} - X_j)^2\right)\right). \tag{A.4}$$

Now combining (4.2) with (2.2), one verifies that

$$V_{S_0}(a) + \sum_{j=1}^{k}(a^\top Y_{j-1} - X_j)^2 = V_{S_0}(a) + \sum_{j=1}^{k}\left\|\begin{bmatrix} a \\ -1 \end{bmatrix}\right\|^2_{Z_jZ_j^\top} = V_{S_k}(a), \tag{A.5}$$

where $S_k = S_0 + \sum_{j=1}^{k} Z_jZ_j^\top$. Substituting (A.5) into (A.4), and comparing the resultant expression with (2.4), it follows that $\pi_k = d_{p,\lambda_k,S_k}$, where $\lambda_k = \lambda_0 + k/2$. Therefore, the posterior distribution of θ with respect to $\mathcal{F}_k$ is indeed given by (4.3)-(4.4), completing the proof of the proposition.

B. Proof of Theorem 6.3

To simplify notation throughout the proof, we will omit the subscript k which specifies the current moment of time in (5.4). With this convention, (5.9) and (5.10) give

$$\Phi^\top = \widehat{\Phi}^\top + (\beta P)^{-1/2}\gamma\Psi^\top, \tag{B.1}$$

where $\gamma \sim \mathbf{N}_p(0_{p\times 1}, I_p)$ is independent of β and of $\mathcal{F}$. Since the matrices $\widehat{\Phi}$ and P are $\mathcal{F}$-measurable and the vector Ψ is constant, $\mathbf{E}(\Phi^s \mid \beta,\mathcal{F})$ can be found using the scalarization technique developed in [7] for computing the power moments of Gaussian random matrices $A + B\zeta C$, where ζ is a standard normal random vector, and A, B, C are appropriately dimensioned constant matrices. More precisely, setting $A = \widehat{\Phi}^\top$, $B = (\beta P)^{-1/2}$, and $C = \Psi^\top$, and applying [7, Theorem 1 and Proposition 1], one verifies that

$$(\mathbf{E}(\Phi^s \mid \beta,\mathcal{F}))^\top = (\widehat{\Phi}^\top)^s + \sum_{t=1}^{\lfloor s/2 \rfloor}(2t-1)!!\beta^{-t}\mathbf{C}_t\mathbf{A}_t^{s-2t}\mathbf{B}_t, \tag{B.2}$$

where $\mathbf{A}_t$, $\mathbf{B}_t$, $\mathbf{C}_t$ are the state-space realization matrices of the system H_t defined by (6.4)–(6.9). Here, we have also used the positive homogeneity of H_t in the matrix P of degree $-t$; see Remark 6.2. Now by Proposition 4.1 and by (2.6), $\mathrm{Law}(\beta \mid \mathcal{F}) = \mathbf{Ga}(\lambda, M(S)/2)$, where λ and S are the hyperparameters of the posterior distribution Π. Consequently, for any $t \in \mathbb{N}$ satisfying $t < \lambda$, the random variable β^{-t} is integrable with respect to Π, with

$$\mathbf{E}(\beta^{-t} \mid \mathcal{F}) = \frac{(M(S)/2)^t \Gamma(\lambda - t)}{\Gamma(\lambda)} = \frac{(M(S)/2)^t}{\prod_{u=1}^{t}(\lambda - u)}. \tag{B.3}$$

Using (B.2) and the $\mathcal{F}$-measurability of the matrices $\mathbf{A}_t$, $\mathbf{B}_t$, $\mathbf{C}_t$, we arrive at

$$\mathbf{E}(\Phi^s \mid \mathcal{F}) = \widehat{\Phi}^s + \sum_{t=1}^{\lfloor s/2 \rfloor} (2t-1)!!\,\mathbf{E}(\beta^{-t} \mid \mathcal{F}) \left(\mathbf{C}_t \mathbf{A}_t^{s-2t} \mathbf{B}_t\right)^{\top}. \tag{B.4}$$

Since the assumption $s < 2\lceil \lambda \rceil$ is equivalent to $\lfloor s/2 \rfloor < \lambda$, substituting (B.3) into (B.4) yields (6.10) that completes the proof of the theorem.

Acknowledgment

The work is supported by the Australian Research Council SPIRT Grant C 0010 6980 and Tarong Energy Ltd.

References

[1] J.-M. Bernardo and A. F. M. Smith, *Bayesian Theory*, Wiley Series in Probability and Mathematical Statistics: Probability and Mathematical Statistics, John Wiley & Sons, Chichester, 1994.
[2] P. Billingsley, *Convergence of Probability Measures*, John Wiley & Sons, New York, 1968.
[3] J. D. Hamilton, *Time Series Analysis*, Princeton University Press, New Jersey, 1994.
[4] T. Kailath, *Linear Systems*, Prentice-Hall, New Jersey, 1980.
[5] R. E. Skelton, T. Iwasaki, and K. M. Grigoriadis, *A Unified Approach to Linear Control Design*, Taylor & Francis, London, 1998.
[6] B. Thompson and I. Vladimirov, *Bayesian parameter estimation and prediction in mean reverting stochastic diffusion model*, Nonlinear Analysis, Theory, Methods and Application **63** (2005), no. 5-7, 2367–2375.
[7] I. Vladimirov and B. Thompson, *A scalarization technique for computing the power and exponential moments of Gaussian random matrices*, Journal of Applied Mathematics and Stochastic Analysis **2006** (2006), Article ID 42542, 20 pages.
[8] ———, *Algebraic moments of Gaussian random matrices via graphs generated by translated bipartitions*, submitted.

Igor Vladimirov: Department of Mathematics, The University of Queensland, Brisbane, QLD 4072, Australia
E-mail address: igv@maths.uq.edu.au

Bevan Thompson: Department of Mathematics, The University of Queensland, Brisbane, QLD 4072, Australia
E-mail address: hbt@maths.uq.edu.au

GLOBAL CONVERGENT ALGORITHM FOR PARABOLIC COEFFICIENT INVERSE PROBLEMS

QUAN-FANG WANG

The globally convergent algorithm, that is, convexification approach will be applied to coefficient inverse problems of parabolic differential equations when spatial dimensions are two. Based on the unified framework of convexification approach, a developed global iteration scheme for solving numerical solution will be implemented to verify the effectiveness of convexification approach for 2D parabolic case.

1. Introduction

Global convergent algorithm is to solve the multidimensional coefficient inverse problems both in theoretical and computation issues using a unified framework (cf. [6]). Its application to a class of inverse problems has been reported in literatures (cf. [1–7]). The main thoughts of convexification approach focus on several aspects. Comparing the local convergent iteration to exact solution, convexification approach is a global convergent algorithm, which avoids leading to false solution under incomplete boundary data and inconsistency of a mathematical model with the reality. A couple of points clearly show its advantages. The sequential minimization algorithm (i) provides stable approximate solution via minimization of a finite sequence of strictly convex objective functions, which is constructed by applying the nonlinear weighted least-squares method with Carleman's weight function; (ii) provides the convergence to the "exact" solution independent of starting vector, which is directly determined from the data eliminating for the descent methods.

The purpose is to use convexification approach for solving the coefficient inverse problem arising in parabolic partial differential equations. Numerical study will be implemented for two dimensions to show the effectiveness.

The contents of this paper are as follows. In Section 2, the formulation is given in the unified framework of convexification approach. In Section 3, the global convergent algorithm is applied to parabolic coefficient inverse problems. In Section 4, experiments

Hindawi Publishing Corporation
Proceedings of the Conference on Differential & Difference Equations and Applications, pp. 1109–1119

demonstration verifies the effectiveness of global convergent algorithm. Section 5 contains the conclusions.

2. Notations and formulations

Consider the Cauchy problems described by parabolic partial differential equations in $\mathbb{R}^3 \times (0,\infty)$:

$$\begin{aligned} \partial_t u + a(\mathbf{x})u - \nabla^2 u &= -s(\mathbf{x},t), \\ \partial_\eta u(\mathbf{x},0) + ku(\mathbf{x},0) &= u_0(\mathbf{x}), \end{aligned} \tag{2.1}$$

where $a(\mathbf{x}) \geq 0$ is unknown coefficient, and k is constant. Consider $\mathbb{R}_+ = \{\mathbf{x} \in \mathbb{R}^3 \mid x_2 > 0,\ x_3 > 0\}$, $\mathbf{x} = (x_1,x_2,x_3)$ with the plane $S = \{x_2 = 0,\ x_3 = 0\}$. Assume that the source function $s(\mathbf{x},t) \geq 0$ with compactly support in $\mathbb{R}^3$. Let $\Omega \in \mathbb{R}^3_+$ be a prism,

$$\Omega = \{\mathbf{x} \in \mathbb{R}_+ : -\mathbb{R} < x_1 < \mathbb{R},\ x_2 \in (0,L),\ x_3 \in (0,L)\}. \tag{2.2}$$

A support of the source function $s(\mathbf{x},t)$ belongs to the set $\mathbb{R}_+ \backslash \bar{\Omega}$ (taking $s(\mathbf{x},t) = 0$, $u_0(\mathbf{x}) = 0$ in experiments).

2.1. Inverse problems

Definition 2.1. Given the lateral data $\partial_\eta u(\mathbf{x},t) + ku(\mathbf{x},t) = u_0(\mathbf{x}), (\mathbf{x},t) \in S \times (0,T)$ for a fixed source position and sufficiently large T, find approximately coefficient $a(\mathbf{x})$ in Ω.

Let Laplace transform of $u(\mathbf{x},t)$ be denoted as

$$w(\mathbf{x},t) = \int_0^\infty e^{-st} u(\mathbf{x},t)\,dt, \tag{2.3}$$

where the parameter $s > 0$. By applying Laplace transform to Cauchy problem (2.1) to obtain that

$$\begin{aligned} [s + a(\mathbf{x})]w - \nabla^2 w &= S(\mathbf{x},s), \\ \lim_{|\mathbf{x}|\to\infty} w &= 0, \\ \partial_\eta w(\mathbf{x},s) + kw(\mathbf{x},s) &= \tilde{u}_0(\mathbf{x},s), \quad x \in S, \end{aligned} \tag{2.4}$$

where $\tilde{u}_0(\mathbf{x},s)$ is the Laplace transform of u_0, $\partial_\eta(w)$ is the normal derivative of the function w at the boundary. For simplicity, assume that $S(\mathbf{x},s) = \delta(\mathbf{x} - \mathbf{x}_0)$, where $\mathbf{x}_0 = (x_2, 1-a) \in \mathbb{R}^3_+ \backslash \bar{\Omega}$ is a fixed source position, and a is a small positive number. It is obvious that the function is the Laplace transform of $s(\mathbf{x},t) = \delta(\mathbf{x} - \mathbf{x}_0)\delta(t)$. Assume that the observation $w(x_2,0,s) = \tilde{u}_0(\mathbf{x},s)$ is known, $s > 0$ in the computation experiments. For the positivity of function $w(\mathbf{x},s)$, [6, Lemmas 1 and 2] can be used.

3. Sequential minimization algorithm

3.1. Transformations. Assume that coefficient $a(\mathbf{x})$ is unknown, our aim is to deduce an equation without this coefficient. From [6, Lemma 1] that $w > 0$ in Ω, let new function $v = \ln w$ and transform (2.4) to

$$\nabla^2 v + (\nabla v)^2 + S(\mathbf{x},s)e^v = s + a(\mathbf{x}), \quad \mathbf{x} \in \Omega. \tag{3.1}$$

Introduce $f(\mathbf{x},s) = v + s \cdot l(\mathbf{x},\mathbf{x}_0)$, $q(\mathbf{x},s) = \partial f/\partial s$. Lemma 2 in [6] implies that $f(\mathbf{x},s) = O(s^{-1})$, $q(\mathbf{x},s) = O(s^{-2})$ as $s \to \infty$. Hence, it can be approximated by

$$f(\mathbf{x},s) \approx -\int_s^{\bar{s}} q(\mathbf{x},v)dv, \tag{3.2}$$

where $\bar{s}$ is a sufficiently large number. For $\mathbf{x} \in \Omega$, $s \in (s_0,\bar{s})$, the boundary problems (2.4) are approximated by

$$\begin{gathered}\int_s^{\bar{s}} \nabla^2 q(\mathbf{x},v)dv - 2s\left(\int_s^{\bar{s}} \nabla q(\mathbf{x},v)dv\right) + \left(\int_s^{\bar{s}} \nabla q(\mathbf{x},v)dv\right)^2 \\ + S(\mathbf{x},s)e^{-\int_s^{\bar{s}} q(\mathbf{x},v)dv - s|\mathbf{x}-\mathbf{x}_0|} + s^2 - s = 0, \\ \partial_\eta q(\mathbf{x},v) + kq(\mathbf{x},v) = q_0(\mathbf{x},v), \quad \mathbf{x} \in \Gamma,\end{gathered} \tag{3.3}$$

where q_0 corresponds to $\bar{u}_0$. Especially, q_0 is computed by some regularizing algorithm of numerical differential with respect to s. Obviously, (3.3) does not contain unknown coefficient $a(\mathbf{x})$. Consider a set of functions

$$H(m) = \left\{q(\mathbf{x},s) \mid \partial_\eta q + kq = q_0,\ \mathbf{x} \in \Gamma,\ \max_{s\in(s_0,\bar{s})} ||q(\mathbf{x},s)||_{C^3(\bar{\Omega})} \le m\right\}, \tag{3.4}$$

where $m > 0$ is a given number, which is not necessarily small.

THEOREM 3.1. *There exists at most one solution $q(\mathbf{x},s)$ to problems (3.3) such that*

$$\max_{s\in(s_0,\bar{s})} ||q(\mathbf{x},s)||_{C^3(\bar{\Omega})} < \infty. \tag{3.5}$$

3.2. Approximations. Recall that $\Omega = \Omega_1 \times [0,L] \times [0,L]$, $L > 0$, where $\Omega_1 = \{x_1 | -\mathbb{R} \le x_1 \le \mathbb{R}\}$. Also assume that q_0 are observed on $\Gamma = \Omega_1 = \bar{\Omega} \cap S \subset \{x_2 = 0,\ x_3 = 0\}$. Let $\{\phi_k(x_1)\}|_{k=1}^K \subset C^2(\bar{\Omega}_1)$ be a set of linearly independent functions that approximate $q(\mathbf{x},s)$ and its $\mathbf{x}$-derivatives up to second order, that is,

$$D_{\mathbf{x}}^\alpha q(\mathbf{x},s) \approx D_{\mathbf{x}}^\alpha \sum_{k=1}^K \eta_k(x_2,x_3,s)\phi_k(x_1), \quad (\mathbf{x},s) \in \bar{\Omega} \times [s_0,\bar{s}],\ |\alpha| \le 2. \tag{3.6}$$

Therefore, for $q \in H(m)$, a number $J(\varepsilon,m)$ can be chosen for sufficiently small $\varepsilon > 0$ and $\eta_k(x_2,x_3,s)$, such that

$$\max_{s\in(s_0,\bar{s})} \left\| q - \sum_{k=1}^K \eta_k(x_2,x_3,s)\phi_k(x_1)\right\|_{C^2(\bar{\Omega})} < \varepsilon. \tag{3.7}$$

Denote $\mathbf{p}(x_2,x_3,s)=(\eta_1(x_2,x_3,s),\ldots,\eta_k(x_2,x_3,s),\ldots,\eta_K(x_2,x_3,s))^T$ and substitute the right-hand side of (3.6) in (3.3). $\mathbf{p}_0$ response to the initial value $\mathbf{q}_0$ in (3.3). The results are quoted as in [6] to parabolic coefficient inverse problems. Let

$$q(\mathbf{x},s) \approx \sum_{k=1}^{K} \eta_k(x_2,x_3,s)\phi_k(x_1), \quad (\mathbf{x},s) \in \bar{\Omega} \times [s_0,\bar{s}]. \tag{3.8}$$

Then one can deduce that

$$\nabla q(\mathbf{x},s) = \begin{pmatrix} \dfrac{\partial q(\mathbf{x},s)}{\partial x_1} \\ \dfrac{\partial q(\mathbf{x},s)}{\partial x_2} \\ \dfrac{\partial q(\mathbf{x},s)}{\partial x_3} \end{pmatrix} = \begin{pmatrix} \sum_{k=1}^{K} \eta_k(x_2,x_3,s)\dfrac{\partial \phi_k(x_1)}{\partial x_1} \\ \sum_{k=1}^{K} \dfrac{\partial \eta_k(x_2,x_3,s)}{\partial x_2}\phi_k(x_1) \\ \sum_{k=1}^{K} \dfrac{\partial \eta_k(x_2,x_3,s)}{\partial x_3}\phi_k(x_1) \end{pmatrix},$$

$$\nabla^2 q(\mathbf{x},s) = \sum_{k=1}^{K} \eta_k(x_2,x_3,s)\frac{\partial \phi_k^2(x_1)}{\partial x_1^2} + \sum_{k=1}^{K} \frac{\partial^2 \eta_k(x_2,x_3,s)}{\partial x_2^2}\phi_k(x_1) + \sum_{k=1}^{K} \frac{\partial^2 \eta_k(x_2,x_3,s)}{\partial x_3^2}\phi_k(x_1). \tag{3.9}$$

Therefore, (3.3) implies that

$$\begin{aligned} &\sum_{k=1}^{K} \eta_k(x_2,x_3,s)\frac{\partial \phi_k^2(x_1)}{\partial x_1^2} + \sum_{k=1}^{K} \frac{\partial^2 \eta_k(x_2,x_3,s)}{\partial x_2^2}\phi_k(x_1) + \sum_{k=1}^{K} \frac{\partial^2 \eta_k(x_2,x_3,s)}{\partial x_3^2}\phi_k(x_1) \\ &- 2s^2 \begin{pmatrix} \sum_{k=1}^{K} \eta_k(x_2,x_3,s)\dfrac{\partial \phi_k(x_1)}{\partial x_1} \\ \sum_{k=1}^{K} \dfrac{\partial \eta_k(x_2,x_3,s)}{\partial x_2}\phi_k(x_1) \\ \sum_{k=1}^{K} \dfrac{\partial \eta_k(x_2,x_3,s)}{\partial x_3}\phi_k(x_1) \end{pmatrix} \cdot \begin{pmatrix} \int_s^{\bar{s}} \sum_{k=1}^{K} \eta_k(x_2,x_3,\nu)\dfrac{\partial \phi_k(x_1)}{\partial x_1}d\nu \\ \int_s^{\bar{s}} \sum_{k=1}^{K} \dfrac{\partial \eta_k(x_2,x_3,\nu)}{\partial x_2}\phi_k(x_1)d\nu \\ \int_s^{\bar{s}} \sum_{k=1}^{K} \dfrac{\partial \eta_k(x_2,x_3,\nu)}{\partial x_3}\phi_k(x_1)d\nu \end{pmatrix} \\ &+ 2s \begin{pmatrix} \int_s^{\bar{s}} \sum_{k=1}^{K} \eta_k(x_2,x_3,\nu)\dfrac{\partial \phi_k(x_1)}{\partial x_1}d\nu \\ \int_s^{\bar{s}} \sum_{k=1}^{K} \dfrac{\partial \eta_k(x_2,x_3,\nu)}{\partial x_2}\phi_k(x_1)d\nu \\ \int_s^{\bar{s}} \sum_{k=1}^{K} \dfrac{\partial \eta_k(x_2,x_3,\nu)}{\partial x_3}\phi_k(x_1)d\nu \end{pmatrix}^2 + s^{-2} + 2s^{-3}a(x_2,x_3) \\ &+ \delta(\mathbf{x}-\mathbf{x}_0)e^{-\int_s^{\bar{s}}\sum_{k=1}^{K}\eta_k(x_2,x_3,\nu)\phi_k(x_1)d\nu - s|\mathbf{x}-\mathbf{x}_0|} = 0. \end{aligned} \tag{3.10}$$

Considering $\mathbf{p}(x_2,x_3,s) = (\eta_1(x_2,x_3,s),\dots,\eta_k(x_2,x_3,s),\dots,\eta_K(x_2,x_3,s))^T$, then

$$\begin{aligned}
\mathbf{p}_1' &= \frac{\partial \mathbf{p}}{\partial x_2} = \left(\frac{\partial \eta_1}{\partial x_2}(x_2,x_3,s),\dots,\frac{\partial \eta_k}{\partial x_2}(x_2,x_3,s),\dots,\frac{\partial \eta_K}{\partial x_2}(x_2,x_3,s)\right)^T;\\
\mathbf{p}_2' &= \frac{\partial \mathbf{p}}{\partial x_3} = \left(\frac{\partial \eta_1}{\partial x_3}(x_2,x_3,s),\dots,\frac{\partial \eta_k}{\partial x_3}(x_2,x_3,s),\dots,\frac{\partial \eta_K}{\partial x_3}(x_2,x_3,s)\right)^T;\\
\mathbf{p}_1'' &= \frac{\partial^2 \mathbf{p}}{\partial x_2^2} = \left(\frac{\partial^2 \eta_1}{\partial x_2^2}(x_2,x_3,s),\dots,\frac{\partial^2 \eta_k}{\partial x_2^2}(x_2,x_3,s),\dots,\frac{\partial^2 \eta_K}{\partial x_2^2}(x_2,x_3,s)\right)^T;\\
\mathbf{p}_2'' &= \frac{\partial^2 \mathbf{p}}{\partial x_3^2} = \left(\frac{\partial^2 \eta_1}{\partial x_3^2}(x_2,x_3,s),\dots,\frac{\partial^2 \eta_k}{\partial x_3^2}(x_2,x_3,s),\dots,\frac{\partial^2 \eta_K}{\partial x_3^2}(x_2,x_3,s)\right)^T.
\end{aligned} \tag{3.11}$$

Hence,

$$\begin{aligned}
\mathcal{L}(\mathbf{p}) &= \mathbf{p}_1'' + \mathbf{p}_2''\\
&\quad + F\left(\mathbf{p}_1',\mathbf{p}_2',\mathbf{p},\int_s^{\bar{s}}\mathbf{p}_1'(x_2,x_3,\nu)\,d\nu,\int_s^{\bar{s}}\mathbf{p}_2'(x_2,x_3,\nu)\,d\nu,\int_s^{\bar{s}}\mathbf{p}(x_2,x_3,\nu)\,d\nu,x_2,x_3\right).
\end{aligned} \tag{3.12}$$

Then one can obtain that

$$\begin{gathered}
\mathcal{L}(\mathbf{p}) = 0, \quad x_2 \in (0,L),\ x_3 \in (0,L),\ s \in (s_0,\bar{s}),\\
\partial_t \mathbf{p}(0,0,s) + k\mathbf{p}(0,0,s) = \mathbf{p}_0(s).
\end{gathered} \tag{3.13}$$

3.3. Numerical solution. For taking of boundary condition, the extrapolated boundary condition is commonly used. Namely, let $\Omega_0 = [0,L] \times [0,L]$, $c_0 = \text{const} > 0$, $G \subset \mathbb{R}^2$ be a square larger than Ω, $\Omega \subset G$, and let 0 be the center of G. Choose G such that for any point $\mathbf{x} \in G$ (not near a corner), there exists a unique point $\mathbf{x}' \in \partial\Omega$ such that the outward distance in the normal direction is given by $|\mathbf{x} - \mathbf{x}'| = c_0 l_t$. Then ∂G is an extrapolated boundary of the domain Ω. The constant c_0 depends on the mismatch of the speed of light in two media. A simple explanation is quoted to get the flux $\psi(x,t)$ using the extrapolated boundary. For $\mathbf{x} \in \partial\Omega$, let $\eta = \eta(\mathbf{x})$ be the outward unit normal vector on $\partial\Omega$. Then

$$\frac{\partial u}{\partial \eta}(\mathbf{x},t) = \lim_{s\to 0}\frac{u(\mathbf{x}+s\eta,t) - u(\mathbf{x},t)}{s}. \tag{3.14}$$

Since $(\mathbf{x} + c_0 l_t \eta) \in \partial G$, it implies that $u(\mathbf{x}, c_0 l_t \eta, t) = 0$. Hence, if the number $c_0 l_t$ is sufficiently small, then $(\partial u/\partial\eta)(\mathbf{x},t) \approx -(1/c_0 l_t)u(\mathbf{x},t)$ for $\mathbf{x} \in \partial\Omega, t \in (T_0,T)$. Thus, assume that

$$\frac{\partial u}{\partial \eta}(\mathbf{x},t) = \psi(\mathbf{x},t) = -\frac{1}{c_0 l_t}\phi(\mathbf{x},t), \quad \mathbf{x} \in \partial\Omega,\ t \in (T_0,T). \tag{3.15}$$

Equation (3.15) really implies that in the case of the extrapolated boundary condition, $(\partial p/\partial\eta)|_{\partial\Omega} \equiv 0$. The condition (3.15) is equivalent to the boundary condition of the third kind on $\partial\Omega$, $\partial u/\partial\eta + S_0 u = 0$, for $\mathbf{x} \in \partial\Omega$, $t \in (T_0,T)$, where $S_0 = 1/(c_0 l_t)$. Hence, in principle, original parabolic boundary value problem with third-kind boundary condition can be converted to Dirichlet boundary condition.

Discrete the parabolic coefficient inverse problems (3.13) on the rectangle $[0,L] \times [0,L]$, denote $y = x_2$, $z = x_3$, and consider the grid

$$0 = y_0 < y_1 < \cdots < y_{n-1} < y_n = L, \quad h^i = y_i - y_{i-1},$$
$$0 = z_0 < z_1 < \cdots < z_{n-1} < z_n = L, \quad h^j = z_i - z_{i-1}. \tag{3.16}$$

We approximate the vector function $\mathbf{p}(x_2,x_3,s)$ by a quadratic polynomial in each subrectangle, that is,

$$\begin{aligned}\mathbf{p}(y,z,s) &\approx p_{ij}(y,z,s)\\ &= a_i(s)\frac{(y-y_{i-1})^2}{2} + b_j(s)\frac{(z-z_{j-1})^2}{2} + c_{ij}(s)(y-y_{i-1})(z-z_{j-1})\\ &\quad + p'(y_{i-1},z_{j-1},s)(y-y_{i-1}) + p'(y_{j-1},z_{j-1},s)(z-z_{j-1}) + p_{ij}(y_{i-1},z_{i-1},s).\end{aligned} \tag{3.17}$$

By considering the boundary condition at each element, let $S_0 = (1/zl_t + k)$ by $\mathbf{p}(y,z,s) = (1/S_0)\mathbf{p}_0$ at boundary, then one can get

$$\begin{aligned}p_{11}(y,z,s) &= a_1(s)\frac{(y-y_0)^2}{2} + b_1(s)\frac{(z-z_0)^2}{2} + c_{11}(s)(y-y_0)(z-z_0)\\ &\quad + (S_0 y + S_0 z + 1)p_{11}(y_0,z_0,s),\\ p_{1j}(y,z,s) &= a_1(s)\frac{(y-y_0)^2}{2} + b_j(s)\frac{(z-z_{j-1})^2}{2} + c_{1j}(s)(y-y_0)(z-z_{j-1})\\ &\quad + p'(y_0,z_{j-1},s)(y-y_0) + p'(y_0,z_{j-1},s)(z-z_{j-1})\\ &\quad + (S_0(z-z_{j-1})+1)p_{ij}(y_0,z_{i-1},s),\\ p_{i1}(y,z,s) &= a_i(s)\frac{(y-y_{i-1})^2}{2} + b_1(s)\frac{(z-z_0)^2}{2} + c_{i1}(s)(y-y_{i-1})(z-z_0)\\ &\quad + p'(y_{i-1},z_0,s)(y-y_{i-1}) + p'(y_{i-1},z_0,s)(z-z_0)\\ &\quad + (S_0(y-y_{i-1})+1)p_{i1}(y_{i-1},z_{i-1},s),\\ p_{in}(y,z,s) &= a_i(s)\frac{(y-y_{i-1})^2}{2} + b_n(s)\frac{(z-z_{n-1})^2}{2} + c_{in}(s)(y-y_{i-1})(z-z_{n-1})\\ &\quad + p'(y_{i-1},z_{n-1},s)(y-y_{i-1}) + p'(y_{i-1},z_{n-1},s)(z-z_{n-1})\\ &\quad + (S_0(y-y_{i-1})+1)p_{in}(y_{i-1},z_{n-1},s),\\ p_{nj}(y,z,s) &= a_n(s)\frac{(y-y_{n-1})^2}{2} + b_j(s)\frac{(z-z_{j-1})^2}{2} + c_{nj}(s)(y-y_{n-1})(z-z_{j-1})\\ &\quad + p'(y_{n-1},z_{j-1},s)(y-y_{n-1}) + p'(y_{n-1},z_{j-1},s)(z-z_{j-1})\\ &\quad + (S_0(z-z_{n-1})+1)p_{in}(y_{n-1},z_{j-1},s),\end{aligned}$$

$$\begin{aligned} p_{nn}(y,z,s) &= a_n(s)\frac{(y-y_{n-1})^2}{2} + b_n(s)\frac{(z-z_{n-1})^2}{2} + c_{nn}(s)(y-y_{n-1})(z-z_{n-1}) \\ &+ p'(y_{n-1},z_{n-1},s)(y-y_{n-1}) + p'(y_{n-1},z_{n-1},s)(z-z_{n-1}) \\ &+ (S_0(y-y_{n-1}) + S_0(z-z_{n-1}) + 1)p_{nn}(y_{n-1},z_{n-1},s). \end{aligned} \tag{3.18}$$

For 2-dimensional case, the $a_i(s), b_j(s), c_{ij}(s)$ will be determined by calculating at each element:

$$a_i(s) = \alpha_i s^2 + s, \qquad b_j(s) = \beta_j s^2 + s, \qquad c_{ij}(s) = \gamma_{ij} s^2 + s, \qquad \alpha_i, \beta_j, \gamma_{ij} \in \mathbb{R}^1. \tag{3.19}$$

The resulting functionals with respect to the (i,j)th leading coefficients α_i, β_i, γ_{ij} of the quadratic polynomial are

$$J_{\lambda,i,j}(\mathbf{p}) = \int_{s_0}^{\bar{s}} \int_{z_{i-1}}^{z_i} \int_{y_{j-1}}^{y_j} \left| \mathcal{L}(p_{ij}(y,z,v)) \right|^2 C_{\lambda,i,j}^2(y,z)\,dy\,dz\,dv, \tag{3.20}$$

where $C_{\lambda,i,j}(z) = \exp[-\lambda(y - y_{i-1}) - \lambda(z - z_{j-1})]$, $\lambda = 1$ in experiments, are Carleman's weight functions, which appear in Carleman estimates for the operators d^2/dy^2, d^2/dz^2. The calculation of $J_{\lambda,i,j}$ uses Gauss-Legendre quadrature to find the approximate

$$\widehat{J}_{\lambda,i,j} = \sum_{tt=1}^{TT} w_{tt} \sum_{ii=1}^{II} w_{ii} \sum_{jj=1}^{JJ} w_{jj} \left| \mathcal{L}(p_{ij}(y_{ii}, z_{jj}, tt)) \right|^2 C_{\lambda,ii,jj}(y_{ii}, z_{jj}), \tag{3.21}$$

where w_{ii}, w_{jj}, w_{tt} are Gauss weights, and y_{ii}, z_{jj}, tt are Gauss points at y, z, and t directions, respectively. Sequentially minimizers of $J_{\lambda,i}(p_i)$ will be searched on the set

$$G(m) = \left\{ \mathbf{p}(s) : \|\mathbf{p}(s)\| = \max_{s\in[s_0,\bar{s}]} |\mathbf{p}(s)| \le m \right\}. \tag{3.22}$$

As in [6], the convexity of $J_{\lambda,i,j}(\mathbf{p})$, the uniqueness of minimizers of these functionals, and the convergence result can be proved. If assuming that there exists a vector function $\mathbf{p}^*(y,z,s)$, such that

$$\begin{aligned} \widehat{\mathcal{L}}(\mathbf{p}^*) = 0, \quad y \in (0,L),\ z \in (0,L),\ s \in (s_0, \bar{s}), \\ \partial_t \mathbf{p}^*(0,0,s) + k\mathbf{p}^*(0,0,s) = \mathbf{p}_0^*(s), \end{aligned} \tag{3.23}$$

where

$$\widehat{\mathcal{L}}(\mathbf{p}^*) \equiv \mathbf{p}^{*\prime\prime} + \mathbf{p}^{*\prime} + F^*\left(\mathbf{p}^{*\prime}, \mathbf{p}^*, \int_s^{\bar{s}} \mathbf{p}^{*\prime}(y,z,v)dv, \int_s^{\bar{s}} \mathbf{p}^*(y,z,v)dv, y, z\right), \tag{3.24}$$

the $\mathbf{p}^*(y,z,s)$ will be called the exact solution to (3.13). Assume that

$$\mathbf{p}^* \in C^3[0,L], \qquad \max_{s\in(s_0,\bar{s})} \|\mathbf{p}^*(y,z,s)\|_{C^3[0,L]} \le \frac{m}{2}, \tag{3.25}$$

and the function F and data are known approximately. Assume that

$$\max_{s\in[s_0,\bar{s}]} ||\hat{\varepsilon}(z,s)||_{C[0,L]} \leq \varepsilon, \qquad \max_{s\in[s_0,\bar{s}]} |\mathbf{p}_0(s) - \mathbf{p}_0^*(s)| \leq \varepsilon. \tag{3.26}$$

THEOREM 3.2. *Let $\lambda = 1$, let the above assumption be satisfied, and let $\mathbf{p}_0 \in G(m/2)$. Then there exist sufficiently small positive numbers $\varepsilon_0(m)$, $h_{10}(m)$, $h_{20}(m)$ such that for all $\varepsilon \in (0,\varepsilon_0)$, $h_1 \in (0,h_{10})$, $h_2 \in (0,h_{20})$,*

$$\mathbf{p}_i(y_{i-1},z_{i-1},s) \in G(m) \quad (i = 1,2,\dots,n) \tag{3.27}$$

all functionals $J_{\lambda,i,j}(\mathbf{p})$ are strictly convex on $G(m)$, the unique minimizer $\bar{\mathbf{p}}_{\lambda,i,j}$ of $J_{\lambda,i,j}(\mathbf{p})$ is an interior point of $G(m)$.

Proof. Refer to [6, 8], it is easy to obtain the proof for 2D case of parabolic equations. The theorem implies the global convergence of sequential minimization algorithm. □

3.4. Inversion. Once the approximating field $\tilde{f}(\mathbf{x},\nu)$ is found, the unknown coefficient $a(\mathbf{x})$ can be approximately determined from (3.1). By taking $S(\mathbf{x},0) = 0$, the inversion formula for $\tilde{a}(\mathbf{x})$ is deduced that

$$\tilde{a}(\mathbf{x}) = \nabla^2\tilde{f} + (\nabla\tilde{f})^2 - s, \quad \forall s \in [\underline{s},\bar{s}]. \tag{3.28}$$

It is no need to compute quantities $\nabla\tilde{f}$ and $\nabla^2\tilde{f}$ for getting $\tilde{a}(\mathbf{x})$.

4. Numerical experiments

The experiments aim is to find the continuous coefficients $a(\mathbf{x})$, and recover it from parabolic equation (2.1) without solving the exactly solution of (2.1). Take the $\phi_k(x_1)$ in (3.6) as follows:

$$\phi_k(x_1) = \begin{cases} \dfrac{x_1-(k-1)h}{h}, & (k-1)h \leq x_1 \leq kh, \\ -\dfrac{x_1-(k+1)h}{h}, & kh \leq x_1 \leq (k+1)h. \end{cases} \tag{4.1}$$

Set $n = 8$, $h_i = h_j = 1/8$, then 64 elements of $[y_{i-1},z_{j-1}] \times [y_i,z_j]$ are used in sequential minimization algorithm. Taking $\bar{s} = 10^8$ in (3.2) and $s_0 = 0$, $\underline{s} = 0$, $c_0 = 1.1$, $l_t = 0.5$ during all calculations. Approximate unknown coefficients $a(\mathbf{x}) = a(y,z)$ in 2-dimensional spaces (assume $x_1 = 1.0$) in Figures 4.1 and 4.2. Taking $x_1 = 5.0$, unknown coefficients $a(\mathbf{x}) = a(y,z)$, see Figures 4.3 and 4.4. Let $x_1 = 10.0$, unknown coefficients $a(\mathbf{x}) = a(y,z)$ are in Figures 4.5 and 4.6.

5. Conclusions

This work solved the coefficient inverse problems of nonlinear parabolic differential equations for 2-dimensional spaces using globally convergent algorithm (i.e., convexification approach). The sequential minimization algorithm is used to optimize the cost function given by Carleman's weight functions.

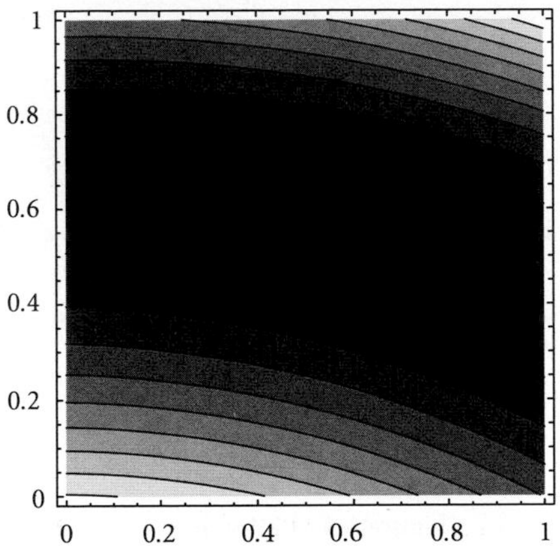

Figure 4.1. Contour plot of $a(y,z)$.

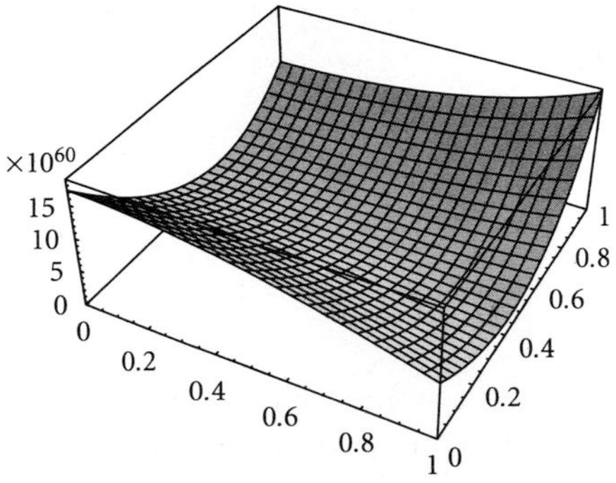

Figure 4.2. Plot of $a(y,z)$.

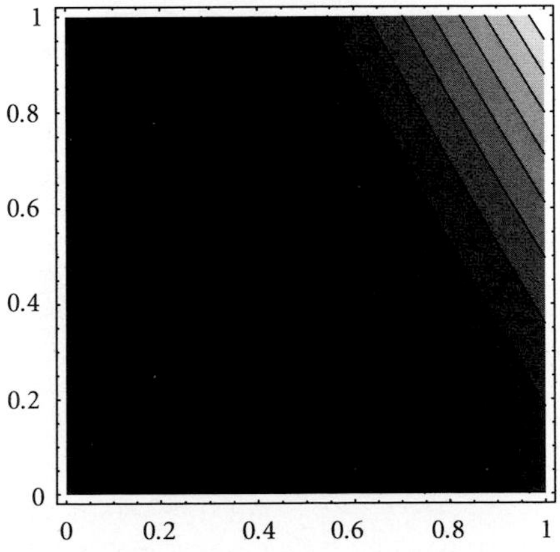

Figure 4.3. Contour plot of $a(y,z)$.

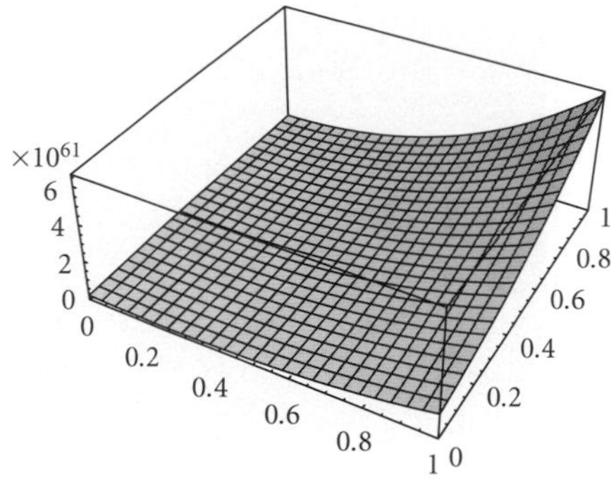

Figure 4.4. Plot of $a(y,z)$.

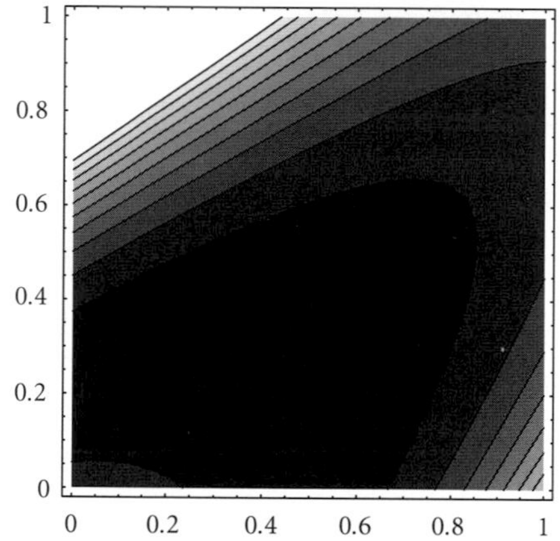

Figure 4.5. Contour plot of $a(y,z)$.

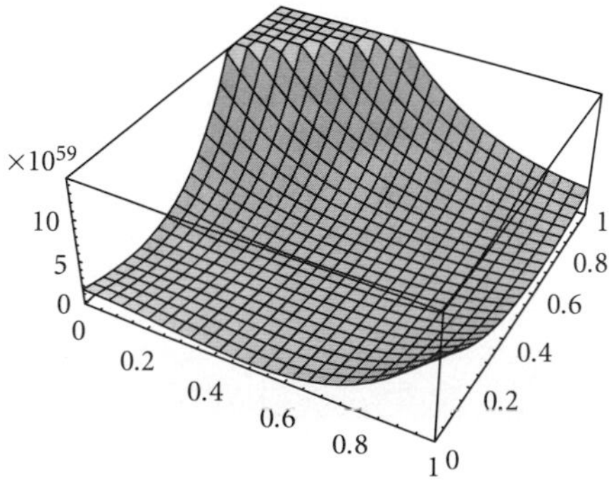

Figure 4.6. Plot of $a(y,z)$.

Acknowledgment

The author wishes to thank Professor M. Klibanov, The University of North Carolina at Charlotte, for useful comments.

References

[1] Y. A. Gryazin, M. V. Klibanov, and T. R. Lucas, *Imaging the diffusion coefficient in a parabolic inverse problem in optical tomography*, Inverse Problems **15** (1999), no. 2, 373–397.
[2] M. V. Klibanov and T. R. Lucas, *Numerical solution of a parabolic inverse problem in optical tomography using experimental data*, SIAM Journal on Applied Mathematics **59** (1999), no. 5, 1763–1789.
[3] M. V. Klibanov and A. Timonov, *A new slant on the inverse problems of electromagnetic frequency sounding: "convexification" of a multiextremal objective function via the Carleman weight functions*, Inverse Problems **17** (2001), no. 6, 1865–1887.
[4] ———, *A globally convergent convexification algorithm for the inverse problem of electromagnetic frequency sounding in one dimension*, Numerical Methods and Programming **4** (2003), 52–81.
[5] ———, *A sequential minimization algorithm based on the convexification approach*, Inverse Problems **19** (2003), no. 2, 331–354.
[6] ———, *A unified framework for constructing globally convergent algorithms for multidimensional coefficient inverse problems*, Applicable Analysis **83** (2004), no. 9, 933–955.
[7] A. I. Nachman, *Global uniqueness for a two-dimensional inverse boundary value problem*, Annals of Mathematics **143** (1996), no. 1, 71–96.
[8] Q.-F. Wang, *Convergent algorithm for parabolic coefficient inverse problems*, Conference on Differential and Difference Equations and Applications, Presentation, 2005.

Quan-Fang Wang: Department of Automation and Computer-Aided Engineering, Faculty of Engineering, The Chinese University of Hong Kong, Shatin, New Territories, Hong Kong
E-mail address: qfwang@acae.cuhk.edu.hk

MULTIPLE POSITIVE RADIAL SOLUTIONS FOR QUASILINEAR EQUATIONS IN ANNULAR DOMAINS

HAIYAN WANG

We study the number of positive radial solutions of elliptic equations when nonlinearity has zeros. We show that the problem has k positive solutions if the nonlinearity has k zeros. Similar results are also true for elliptic systems.

1. Introduction

In this paper we consider the multiplicity of positive radial solutions for the quasilinear equations

$$\begin{gathered} \operatorname{div}(A(|\nabla u|)\nabla u)+\lambda b(|x|)f(u)=0 \quad \text{in } D, \\ u=0 \quad \text{for } x\in\partial D, \end{gathered} \tag{1.1}$$

$$\begin{gathered} \operatorname{div}(A(|\nabla u|)\nabla u)+\lambda b_1(|x|)g_1(u,v)=0 \quad \text{in } D, \\ \operatorname{div}(A(|\nabla v|)\nabla v)+\lambda b_2(|x|)g_2(u,v)=0 \quad \text{in } D, \\ u=v=0 \quad \text{for } x\in\partial D, \end{gathered} \tag{1.2}$$

where $D=\{x : x\in\mathbb{R}^n,\ n\geq 2,\ 0<R_1<|x|<R_2<\infty\}$.

The function A originates from a variety of practical applications, for instance, the degenerate m-Laplace operator, namely, $A(|p|)=|p|^{m-2}$, $m>1$. When $A\equiv 1$, we recall that (1.1) reduces to the classical semilinear elliptic equation

$$\begin{gathered} \Delta u+\lambda b(|x|)f(u)=0 \quad \text{in } D, \\ u=0 \quad \text{for } x\in\partial D. \end{gathered} \tag{1.3}$$

In the recent paper [5], the author discussed the problem under assumption (H1) on the function A, which covers the two important cases $A\equiv 1$ and $A(|p|)=|p|^{m-2}$, $m>1$,

Hindawi Publishing Corporation
Proceedings of the Conference on Differential & Difference Equations and Applications, pp. 1121–1130

that is, the degenerate m-Laplace operator. It was proved that appropriate combinations of superlinearity and sublinearity of the quotient $f(u)/A(u)$ at zero and infinity guarantee the existence, multiplicity, and nonexistence of positive radial solutions of (1.1) and (1.2).

The purpose of this paper is to study the number of positive radial solutions of (1.1) if f has zeros. We will show that (1.1) has at least k positive radial solutions if f has k zeros. A similar result is also true for (1.2). For the scalar equation (1.1) and the case $A \equiv 1$, previous work on this problem has been done by Hess [2]. We also obtain a similar multiplicity result for elliptic systems. Our arguments are based on a fixed point theorem in a cone due to Krasnoselskii.

2. Multiplicity results

Let $\mathbb{R} = (-\infty,\infty)$, $\varphi(t) = A(|t|)t$. We make the following assumptions.

(H1) φ is an odd increasing homeomorphism of $\mathbb{R}$ onto $\mathbb{R}$ and there exist two increasing homeomorphisms ψ_1 and ψ_2 of $(0,\infty)$ onto $(0,\infty)$ such that

$$\psi_1(\sigma)\varphi(t) \le \varphi(\sigma t) \le \psi_2(\sigma)\varphi(t), \quad \forall \sigma, t > 0. \tag{2.1}$$

(H2) $b : [R_1,R_2] \to [0,\infty)$ is continuous and $b \not\equiv 0$ on any subinterval of $[R_1,R_2]$.

(H3) $f : [0,\infty) \to [0,\infty)$ is continuous.

(H4) There exist k numbers $a_k > a_{k-1} > \cdots > a_1 > 0$ such that $a_i > 4a_{i-1}$, $f(a_i) = 0$ for $i = 1,\dots,k$ and $f(u) > 0$ for $a_{i-1} < u < a_i$, $i = 1,\dots,k$, where $a_0 = 0$.

Our multiplicity result for (1.1) is as follows.

Theorem 2.1. *Assume* (H1)–(H4) *hold. Then there exists λ_0 such that for $\lambda > \lambda_0$ (1.1) has k positive solutions, $u_1,u_2,\dots,u_k$, such that*

$$a_{i-1} < \sup_{t\in[0,1]} u_i(t) \le a_i, \quad i = 1,\dots,k. \tag{2.2}$$

We assume the following additional conditions for (1.2).

(H5) $b_i : [R_1,R_2] \to [0,\infty)$ is continuous and $b_i \not\equiv 0$ on any subinterval of $[R_1,R_2]$, $i = 1,2$.

(H6) $g_i : [0,\infty) \to [0,\infty)$ is continuous, $i = 1,2$.

(H7) There exist k numbers $a_k > a_{k-1} > \cdots > a_1 > 0$ such that $a_i > 4a_{i-1}$, $g_1(u,v) = 0$, and $g_2(u,v) = 0$ for $u+v = a_i$, $i = 1,\dots,k$, and $g_1(u,v) > 0$ and $g_2(u,v) > 0$ for $a_{i-1} < u+v < a_i$, $i = 1,\dots,k$, where $a_0 = 0$.

Our multiplicity result for (1.2) is as follows.

Theorem 2.2. *Assume* (H1) *and* (H5)–(H7) *hold. Then there exists λ_0 such that for $\lambda > \lambda_0$ (1.2) has k positive solutions, $(u_1v_1),(u_2,v_2),\dots,(u_k,v_k)$, such that*

$$a_{i-1} < \sup_{t\in[0,1]} \big(u_i(t)+v_i(t)\big) \le a_i, \quad i = 1,\dots,k. \tag{2.3}$$

3. Preliminaries

A radial solution of (1.1) can be considered as a solution of the equation

$$(r^{n-1}\varphi(u'(r)))' + \lambda r^{n-1}b(r)f(u(r)) = 0 \quad \text{in } R_1 < r < R_2,$$
$$u(R_1) = u(R_2) = 0. \tag{3.1}$$

We will treat classical solutions of (3.1), namely, functions u of class C^1 on $[R_1,R_2]$ with $\varphi(u') \in C^1(R_1,R_2)$, which satisfies (3.1). A solution u is positive if $u(r) > 0$ for all $r \in (R_1,R_2)$.

Applying the change of variables, $r = (R_2 - R_1)t + R_1$, we can transform (3.1) into the form

$$(q(t)\varphi(pu'))' + \lambda h(t)f(u) = 0, \quad 0 < t < 1,$$
$$u(0) = u(1) = 0, \tag{3.2}$$

where

$$q(t) = ((R_2 - R_1)t + R_1)^{n-1}, \qquad p = \frac{1}{R_2 - R_1},$$
$$h(t) = (R_2 - R_1)((R_2 - R_1)t + R_1)^{n-1}b((R_2 - R_1)t + R_1). \tag{3.3}$$

We will prove there are k positive solutions for (3.2), which immediately implies that Theorem 2.1 is true.

The following well-known result of the fixed point index is crucial in our arguments.

LEMMA 3.1 [1, 3]. *Let E be a Banach space and K a cone in E. For $r > 0$, define $K_r = \{u \in K : \|x\| < r\}$. Assume that $T : \bar{K}_r \to K$ is completely continuous such that $Tx \neq x$ for $x \in \partial K_r = \{u \in K : \|x\| = r\}$.*

(i) *If $\|Tx\| \geq \|x\|$ for $x \in \partial K_r$, then*

$$i(T,K_r,K) = 0. \tag{3.4}$$

(ii) *If $\|Tx\| \leq \|x\|$ for $x \in \partial K_r$, then*

$$i(T,K_r,K) = 1. \tag{3.5}$$

In order to apply Lemma 3.1 to (3.2), let X be the Banach space $C[0,1]$ with $\|u\| = \sup_{t\in[0,1]} |u(t)|$, $u \in X$.

Define K to be a cone in X by

$$K = \left\{u \in X : u(t) \geq 0, \min_{1/4\leq t\leq 3/4} u(t) \geq \frac{1}{4}\|u\|\right\}. \tag{3.6}$$

Also, define, for r a positive number, Ω_r by

$$\Omega_r = \{u \in K : \|u\| < r\}. \tag{3.7}$$

Note that $\partial\Omega_r = \{u \in K : \|u\| = r\}$.

For $i = 1,\dots,k$, let f_i satisfy

$$f_i(u) = \begin{cases} f(u), & 0 \le u \le a_i, \\ 0, & a_i \le u, \end{cases} \tag{3.8}$$

and let the map $T_\lambda^i : K \to X$ be defined by

$$T_\lambda^i u(t) = \begin{cases} \displaystyle\int_0^t p^{-1}\varphi^{-1}\left(\frac{1}{q(s)}\int_s^\sigma \lambda h(\tau) f_i(u(\tau))\,d\tau\right) ds, & 0 \le t \le \sigma, \\ \displaystyle\int_t^1 p^{-1}\varphi^{-1}\left(\frac{1}{q(s)}\int_\sigma^s \lambda h(\tau) f_i(u(\tau))\,d\tau\right) ds, & \sigma \le t \le 1, \end{cases} \tag{3.9}$$

where $\sigma \in (0,1)$ is a solution of the equation

$$\Theta_i u(t) = 0, \quad 0 \le t \le 1, \tag{3.10}$$

where the map $\Theta_i : K \to C[0,1]$ is defined by

$$\begin{aligned} \Theta_i u(t) = {} & \int_0^t \varphi^{-1}\left(\frac{1}{q(s)}\int_s^t \lambda h(\tau) f_i(u(\tau))\,d\tau\right) ds \\ & - \int_t^1 \varphi^{-1}\left(\frac{1}{q(s)}\int_t^s \lambda h(\tau) f_i(u(\tau))\,d\tau\right) ds, \quad 0 \le t \le 1. \end{aligned} \tag{3.11}$$

By virtue of Lemma 3.2, the operator T_λ^i is well defined.

Lemma 3.2 [4, 5]. *Assume* (H1)–(H3) *hold. Then, for any* $u \in K$, $\Theta_i u(t) = 0$, $i = 1,\dots,k$, *has at least one solution in* $(0,1)$. *In addition, if* $\sigma^1 < \sigma^2 \in (0,1)$ *are two solutions of* $\Theta_i u(t) = 0$, *then* $h(t) f_i(u(t)) \equiv 0$ *for* $t \in [\sigma^1,\sigma^2]$ *and any* $\sigma \in [\sigma^1,\sigma^2]$ *is also a solution of* $\Theta_i u(t) = 0$. *Furthermore,* $T_\lambda^i u(t)$ *is independent of the choice of* $\sigma \in [\sigma^1,\sigma^2]$.

Lemma 3.3 follows from the concavity of u.

Lemma 3.3 [4, 5]. *Assume* (H1)-(H2) *hold. Let* u *and* $v \in X$ *with* $u(t) \ge 0$ *and* $v(t) \le 0$ *for* $t \in [0,1]$. *If* $(q(t)\varphi(pu'))' = v$, *then*

$$u(t) \ge \min\{t, 1-t\}\|u\|, \quad t \in [0,1]. \tag{3.12}$$

In particular,

$$\min_{1/4 \le t \le 3/4} u(t) \ge \frac{1}{4}\|u\|. \tag{3.13}$$

We remark that, according to Lemma 3.3, any nonnegative solution of (3.2) is positive unless it is identical to zero.

LEMMA 3.4. *Assume* (H1)–(H3) *hold. If* $u \in K$ *such that* $T_\lambda^i u = u$ *in* K, *then* u *is a solution of (3.2) such that*

$$\sup_{t\in[0,1]} u(t) \le a_i. \tag{3.14}$$

Proof. It is easy to see that u satisfies the following problem:

$$\begin{gathered}(q(t)\varphi(pu'))' + \lambda h(t) f_i(u) = 0, \quad 0 < t < 1, \\ u(0) = u(1) = 0.\end{gathered} \tag{3.15}$$

Let $t_0 \in (0,1)$ such that $u(t_0) = \sup_{t\in[0,1]} u(t)$. It follows that $u'(t_0) = 0$. If $u(t_0) > a_i$, then there exist two numbers $0 \le t_1 < t_0 < t_2 \le 1$ such that $u(t) > a_i$ for $t \in (t_1,t_2)$ and $u(t_1) = u(t_2) = a_i$. Since $f_i(u) = 0$ for $u \ge a_i$, we have

$$(q(t)\varphi(pu'(t)))' = 0 \quad \text{for } t \in [t_1,t_2]. \tag{3.16}$$

Thus, $\varphi(pu'(t))$ is constant on $[t_1,t_2]$. Since $u'(t_0) = 0$, it follows that $u'(t) = 0$ for $t \in [t_1,t_2]$. Consequently, $u(t)$ is constant on $[t_1,t_2]$. This is a contradiction. Therefore, $\sup_{t\in[0,1]} u(t) \le a_i$. On the other hand, since $f(u) \equiv f_i(u)$ for $0 \le u \le a_i$, u is a solution of (3.2). □

LEMMA 3.5 [4, 5]. *Assume* (H1)–(H3) *hold. Then* $\Theta_i : K \to C[0,1]$, $i = 1,\dots,k$, *is compact and continuous.*

LEMMA 3.6 [4, 5]. *Assume* (H1)–(H3) *hold. Then* $T_\lambda(K) \subset K$ *and* $T_\lambda^i : K \to K$, $i = 1,\dots,k$, *are compact and continuous.*

LEMMA 3.7 [4, 5]. *Assume* (H1) *holds. Then for all* $\sigma, t \in (0,\infty)$,

$$\psi_2^{-1}(\sigma)t \le \varphi^{-1}(\sigma\varphi(t)) \le \psi_1^{-1}(\sigma)t. \tag{3.17}$$

Set

$$\gamma(t) = \frac{1}{2}\left[\int_{1/4}^{t} p^{-1}\psi_2^{-1}\left(\frac{1}{q(s)}\int_s^t h(\tau)d\tau\right)ds + \int_t^{3/4} p^{-1}\psi_2^{-1}\left(\frac{1}{q(s)}\int_t^s h(\tau)d\tau\right)ds\right], \tag{3.18}$$

where $t \in [1/4,3/4]$. It follows from (H1)-(H2) that

$$\Gamma = \inf\left\{\gamma(t) : \frac{1}{4} \le t \le \frac{3}{4}\right\} > 0. \tag{3.19}$$

LEMMA 3.8. *Assume* (H1)–(H4) *hold. For* $i = 1,\dots,k$, *let* $r > 0$ *such that* $[r/4,r] \subset (a_{j-1},a_j)$ *for some* $1 \le j \le i$. *Then*

$$\|T_\lambda^i u\| \ge \Gamma\psi_2^{-1}(\lambda)\varphi^{-1}(\omega_r^i) \quad \text{for } u \in \partial\Omega_r, \tag{3.20}$$

where $\omega_r^i = \min_{1/4r\le t\le r}\{f_i(t)\} > 0$.

Proof. Note, from the definition of $T_\lambda^i u$, that $T_\lambda^i u(\sigma)$ is the maximum value of $T_\lambda^i u$ on $[0,1]$. If $\sigma \in [1/4,3/4]$, we have

$$\begin{aligned}\|T_\lambda^i u\| \geq \frac{1}{2}\bigg[&\int_{1/4}^{\sigma} p^{-1}\varphi^{-1}\bigg(\frac{1}{q(s)}\int_s^{\sigma}\lambda h(\tau)f_i(u(\tau))\,d\tau\bigg)ds \\ &+\int_{\sigma}^{3/4} p^{-1}\varphi^{-1}\bigg(\frac{1}{q(s)}\int_{\sigma}^{s}\lambda h(\tau)f_i(u(\tau))\,d\tau\bigg)ds\bigg].\end{aligned} \tag{3.21}$$

Since $f_i(u(t)) \geq \omega_r^i = \varphi(\varphi^{-1}(\omega_r^i))$ for $t \in [1/4,3/4]$, we find, by condition (H1),

$$\begin{aligned}\|T_\lambda^i u\| &\geq \frac{1}{2}\bigg[\int_{1/4}^{\sigma} p^{-1}\varphi^{-1}\bigg(\frac{1}{q(s)}\int_s^{\sigma} h(\tau)\,d\tau\,\psi_2(\psi_2^{-1}(\lambda))\varphi(\varphi^{-1}(\omega_r^i))\bigg)ds \\ &\qquad+\int_{\sigma}^{3/4} p^{-1}\varphi^{-1}\bigg(\frac{1}{q(s)}\int_{\sigma}^{s} h(\tau)\,d\tau\,\psi_2(\psi_2^{-1}(\lambda))\varphi(\varphi^{-1}(\omega_r^i))\bigg)ds\bigg] \\ &\geq \frac{1}{2}\bigg[\int_{1/4}^{\sigma} p^{-1}\varphi^{-1}\bigg(\frac{1}{q(s)}\int_s^{\sigma} h(\tau)\,d\tau\,\varphi(\psi_2^{-1}(\lambda)\varphi^{-1}(\omega_r^i))\bigg)ds \\ &\qquad+\int_{\sigma}^{3/4} p^{-1}\varphi^{-1}\bigg(\frac{1}{q(s)}\int_{\sigma}^{s} h(\tau)\,d\tau\,\varphi(\psi_2^{-1}(\lambda)\varphi^{-1}(\omega_r^i))\bigg)ds\bigg].\end{aligned} \tag{3.22}$$

Now, because of Lemma 3.7, we have

$$\begin{aligned}\|T_\lambda^i u\| &\geq \frac{\psi_2^{-1}(\lambda)\varphi^{-1}(\omega_r^i)}{2}\bigg[\int_{1/4}^{\sigma} p^{-1}\psi_2^{-1}\bigg(\frac{1}{q(s)}\int_s^{\sigma} h(\tau)\,d\tau\bigg)ds \\ &\qquad+\int_{\sigma}^{3/4} p^{-1}\psi_2^{-1}\bigg(\frac{1}{q(s)}\int_{\sigma}^{s} h(\tau)\,d\tau\bigg)ds\bigg] \\ &\geq \Gamma\psi_2^{-1}(\lambda)\varphi^{-1}(\omega_r^i).\end{aligned} \tag{3.23}$$

For $\sigma > 3/4$, it is easy to see

$$\|T_\lambda^i u\| \geq \int_{1/4}^{3/4} p^{-1}\varphi^{-1}\bigg(\frac{1}{q(s)}\lambda\int_s^{3/4} h(\tau)f_i(u(\tau))\,d\tau\bigg)ds. \tag{3.24}$$

On the other hand, we have

$$\|T_\lambda^i u\| \geq \int_{1/4}^{3/4} p^{-1}\varphi^{-1}\bigg(\frac{1}{q(s)}\lambda\int_{1/4}^{s} h(\tau)f_i(u(\tau))\,d\tau\bigg)ds \quad \text{for } \sigma < \frac{1}{4}. \tag{3.25}$$

Therefore, the same arguments show that

$$\|T_\lambda^i u\| \geq \Gamma\psi_2^{-1}(\lambda)\varphi^{-1}(\omega_r^i) \quad \text{if } \sigma > \frac{3}{4} \text{ or } \sigma < \frac{1}{4}. \tag{3.26}$$

□

4. Proof of Theorem 2.1

For each $i = 1,\dots,k$, in view of condition (H4), there is an $r_i < a_i$ such that $r_i > 4a_{i-1}$. It follows that $[r_i/4, r_i] \subset (a_{i-1}, a_i)$. By Lemma 3.8, we infer that there exists a $\lambda_i > 0$ such that

$$||T_\lambda^i u|| > \|u\| \quad \text{for } u \in \partial\Omega_{r_i},\ \lambda > \lambda_i. \tag{4.1}$$

On the other hand, since $f_i(u)$ is bounded, there is an $R_i > r_i$ such that

$$||T_\lambda^i u|| < \|u\| \quad \text{for } u \in \partial\Omega_{R_i},\ \lambda > \lambda_i. \tag{4.2}$$

It follows from Lemma 3.1 that

$$i(T_\lambda^i, \Omega_{r_i}, K) = 0, \qquad i(T_\lambda^i, \Omega_{R_i}, K) = 1, \tag{4.3}$$

and hence $i(T_\lambda^i, \Omega_{R_i} \setminus \bar{\Omega}_{r_i}, K) = 1$. Thus, T_λ^i has a fixed point u_i in $\Omega_{R_i} \setminus \bar{\Omega}_{r_i}$. Lemma 3.4 implies that the fixed point u_i is a solution of (3.2) such that $a_i < \|u_i\| \le a_i$. Consequently, (3.2) has k positive solutions, $u_1, u_2, \dots, u_k$, such that

$$0 = a_0 < ||u_1|| \le a_1 < ||u_2|| \le a_2 < \cdots \le a_{k-1} < ||u_k|| \le a_k \quad \text{for } \lambda > \lambda_0, \tag{4.4}$$

where $\lambda_0 = \max_{i=1,\dots,n}\{\lambda_i\}$.

5. Elliptic systems

With the same transformation for (1.1), we can transform (1.2) to the following system:

$$\begin{gathered}
(q(t)\varphi(pu'))' + \lambda h_1(t) g_1(u,v) = 0, \quad 0 < t < 1, \\
(q(t)\varphi(pv'))' + \lambda h_2(t) g_2(u,v) = 0, \quad 0 < t < 1, \\
u(0) = u(1) = v(0) = v(1) = 0,
\end{gathered} \tag{5.1}$$

where

$$h_i(t) = (R_2 - R_1)((R_2 - R_1)t + R_1)^{n-1} b_i((R_2 - R_1)t + R_1), \quad i = 1,2, \tag{5.2}$$

$q(t)$ and p are the same as in (3.2).

In this section, let $\mathbb{X}$ be the Banach space $C[0,1] \times C[0,1]$ with

$$||(u,v)|| = \sup_{t\in[0,1]} |u(t)| + \sup_{t\in[0,1]} |u(t)|, \quad (u,v) \in \mathbb{X}. \tag{5.3}$$

Define $\mathbb{K}$ to be a cone in $\mathbb{X}$ by

$$\mathbb{K} = \left\{(u,v) \in \mathbb{X} : u(t), v(t) \ge 0, \min_{1/4 \le t \le 3/4} (u(t) + v(t)) \ge \frac{1}{4}(\|u\| + \|v\|)\right\}, \tag{5.4}$$

where $\|u\| = \sup_{t\in[0,1]} u(t)$, $u \in C[0,1]$.

Also, define, for r a positive number, $\mathbb{U}_r$ by

$$\mathbb{U}_r = \{(u,v) \in \mathbb{K} : \|(u,v)\| < r\}. \tag{5.5}$$

Note that $\partial\mathbb{U}_r = \{(u,v) \in \mathbb{K} : \|(u,v)\| = r\}$.

For $i = 1,\dots,k$, $j = 1,2$, let g_j^i satisfy

$$g_j^i(u,v) = \begin{cases} g_j(u,v), & 0 \le u+v \le a_i, \\ 0, & a_i \le u+v, \end{cases} \tag{5.6}$$

and let the map $T^i = (T_1^i, T_2^i) : \mathbb{K} \to \mathbb{X}$ be defined by

$$T_j^i(u,v)(t) = \begin{cases} \displaystyle\int_0^t p^{-1}\varphi^{-1}\left(\frac{1}{q(s)}\int_s^{\sigma_j} \lambda h_j(\tau) g_j^i(u(\tau),v(\tau))\,d\tau\right)ds, & 0 \le t \le \sigma_j, \\ \displaystyle\int_t^1 p^{-1}\varphi^{-1}\left(\frac{1}{q(s)}\int_{\sigma_j}^{s} \lambda h_j(\tau) g_j^i(u(\tau),v(\tau))\,d\tau\right)ds, & \sigma_j \le t \le 1, \end{cases} \tag{5.7}$$

where $\sigma_j \in (0,1)$ is a solution of the equation

$$\Theta_j^i(u,v)(t) = 0, \quad 0 \le t \le 1, \tag{5.8}$$

and the map $\Theta_j^i : \mathbb{K} \to C[0,1]$ is defined by

$$\begin{aligned} \Theta_j^i(u,v)(t) = &\int_0^t \varphi^{-1}\left(\frac{1}{q(s)}\int_s^t \lambda h_j(\tau) g_j^i(u(\tau),v(\tau))\,d\tau\right)ds \\ &- \int_t^1 \varphi^{-1}\left(\frac{1}{q(s)}\int_t^s \lambda h_j(\tau) g_j^i(u(\tau),v(\tau))\,d\tau\right)ds, \quad 0 \le t \le 1. \end{aligned} \tag{5.9}$$

Lemma 5.1 can be proved in a similar manner as in [4, 5].

Lemma 5.1. *Assume* (H1), (H5), *and* (H6) *hold. Then for* $i = 1,\dots,k$, T^i *is well defined,* $T^i(\mathbb{K}) \subset \mathbb{K}$ *and* $T^i : \mathbb{K} \to \mathbb{K}$ *are compact and continuous.*

Lemma 5.2. *Assume* (H1) *and* (H5)–(H7) *hold. If* $(u,v) \in \mathbb{K}$ *such that* $T^i(u,v) = (u,v)$ *in* $\mathbb{K}$, *then* (u,v) *is a solution of (5.1) such that*

$$\sup_{t\in[0,1]} (u(t)+v(t)) \le a_i. \tag{5.10}$$

Proof. It is easy to see that (u,v) satisfies the following problem:

$$\begin{gathered} (q(t)\varphi(pu'))' + \lambda h_1(t) g_1^i(u,v) = 0, \quad 0 < t < 1, \\ (q(t)\varphi(pv'))' + \lambda h_2(t) g_2^i(u,v) = 0, \quad 0 < t < 1, \\ u(0) = u(1) = v(0) = v(1) = 0. \end{gathered} \tag{5.11}$$

Let $t_0 \in (0,1)$ such that $u(t_0)+v(t_0)=\sup_{t\in[0,1]}(u(t)+v(t))$. It follows that $u'(t_0)+v'(t_0)=0$. If $u(t_0)+v(t_0) > a_i$, then there exist two numbers $0 \le t_1 < t_0 < t_2 \le 1$ such that $u(t)+v(t) > a_i$ for $t \in (t_1,t_2)$ and

$$u(t_1)+v(t_1) = u(t_2)+v(t_2) = a_i. \tag{5.12}$$

Since $g_j^i(u,v) = 0$, $j = 1,2$, for $u+v \ge a_i$, we have

$$\begin{aligned} (q(t)\varphi(pu'(t)))' &= 0 \quad \text{for } t \in [t_1,t_2], \\ (q(t)\varphi(pv'(t)))' &= 0 \quad \text{for } t \in [t_1,t_2]. \end{aligned} \tag{5.13}$$

Thus, $\varphi(pu'(t))$ and $\varphi(pu'(t))$ are constant on $[t_1,t_2]$, and so are $u'(t)$ and $v'(t)$. Since $u'(t_0)+v'(t_0) = 0$, it follows that $(u(t)+v(t))' = 0$ for $t \in [t_1,t_2]$. Consequently, $u(t)+v(t)$ is constant on $[t_1,t_2]$. This is a contradiction. Therefore, $\sup_{t\in[0,1]}(u(t)+v(t)) \le a_i$. On the other hand, since $g_j^i(u,v) \equiv g_j(u,v)$ for $0 \le u+v < a_i$, $j = 1,2$, (u,v) is a solution of (1.2). □

Set

$$\gamma_j(t) = \frac{1}{2}\left[\int_{1/4}^{t} p^{-1}\psi_2^{-1}\left(\frac{1}{q(s)}\int_s^t h_j(\tau)d\tau\right)ds + \int_t^{3/4} p^{-1}\psi_2^{-1}\left(\frac{1}{q(s)}\int_t^s h_j(\tau)d\tau\right)ds\right], \tag{5.14}$$

where $t \in [1/4,3/4]$, $j = 1,2$. It follows from (H1) and (H5) that

$$\widehat{\Gamma} = \inf\left\{\gamma_j(t) : \frac{1}{4} \le t \le \frac{3}{4},\ j = 1,2\right\} > 0. \tag{5.15}$$

The following lemma can be proved in the same manner as in Lemma 3.8.

Lemma 5.3. *Assume* (H1) *and* (H5)–(H7) *hold. For* $i = 1,\dots,k$, *let* $r > 0$ *such that* $[r/4,r] \subset (a_{m-1},a_m)$ *for some* $1 \le m \le i$. *Then*

$$\|T^i(u,v)\| \ge \widehat{\Gamma}\psi_2^{-1}(\lambda)\varphi^{-1}(\omega_r^i) \quad \text{for } (u,v) \in \partial\mathbb{U}_r, \tag{5.16}$$

where $\omega_r^i = \min_{1/4r \le t+s \le r}\{g_j(t,s),\ j = 1,2\} > 0$.

6. Proof of Theorem 2.2

For each $i = 1,\dots,k$, in view of condition (H7), there is an $r_i < a_i$ such that $r_i > 4a_{i-1}$. It follows that $[r_i/4,r_i] \subset (a_{i-1},a_i)$. By Lemma 5.3, we infer that there exists a $\lambda_i > 0$ such that

$$\|T^i(u,v)\| > \|(u,v)\| \quad \text{for } (u,v) \in \partial\mathbb{U}_{r_i},\ \lambda > \lambda_i. \tag{6.1}$$

On the other hand, since $f_j^i(u,v)$, $j = 1,2$, are bounded, there is an $R_i > r_i$ such that

$$\|T^i(u,v)\| < \|(u,v)\| \quad \text{for } (u,v) \in \partial\mathbb{U}_{R_i},\ \lambda > \lambda_i. \tag{6.2}$$

It follows from Lemma 3.1 that

$$i(T^i, \mathbb{U}_{r_i}, \mathbb{K}) = 0, \qquad i(T^i, \mathbb{U}_{R_i}, \mathbb{K}) = 1, \tag{6.3}$$

and hence, $i(T^i, \mathbb{U}_{R_i} \setminus \bar{\mathbb{U}}_{r_i}, \mathbb{K}) = 1$. Thus, T^i has a fixed point (u_i, v_i) in $\mathbb{U}_{R_i} \setminus \bar{\mathbb{U}}_{r_i}$. Lemma 5.2 implies that the fixed point (u_i, v_i) is a solution of (1.2) such that $a_{i-1} < \sup_{t\in[0,1]}(u_i(t) + v_i(t)) \leq a_i$. Consequently, (1.2) has k positive solutions, $(u_1, v_1), (u_2, v_2), \ldots, (u_k, v_k)$, such that

$$a_{i-1} < \sup_{t\in[0,1]} (u_i(t) + v_i(t)) \leq a_i, \quad i = 1, \ldots, k, \text{ for } \lambda > \lambda_0, \tag{6.4}$$

where $\lambda_0 = \max_{i=1,\ldots,n}\{\lambda_i\}$.

References

[1] D. J. Guo and V. Lakshmikantham, *Nonlinear Problems in Abstract Cones*, Notes and Reports in Mathematics in Science and Engineering, vol. 5, Academic Press, Massachusetts, 1988.
[2] P. Hess, *On multiple positive solutions of nonlinear elliptic eigenvalue problems*, Communications in Partial Differential Equations **6** (1981), no. 8, 951–961.
[3] M. A. Krasnosel'skiĭ, *Positive Solutions of Operator Equations*, P. Noordhoff, Groningen, 1964.
[4] H. Wang, *On the number of positive solutions of nonlinear systems*, Journal of Mathematical Analysis and Applications **281** (2003), no. 1, 287–306.
[5] ———, *On the structure of positive radial solutions for quasilinear equations in annular domains*, Advances in Differential Equations **8** (2003), no. 1, 111–128.

Haiyan Wang: Department of Mathematical Sciences and Applied Computing, Arizona State University, Phoenix, AZ 85069-7100, USA
E-mail address: wangh@asu.edu

SECOND-ORDER NONLINEAR OSCILLATIONS: A CASE HISTORY

JAMES S. W. WONG

This paper gives an updated account on a nonlinear oscillation problem originated from the earlier works of F. V. Atkinson and Z. Nehari.

1. Introduction

We are here concerned with the study of oscillatory behavior of solutions of second-order Emden-Fowler equations:

$$y''(x) + a(x) \mid y(x) \mid^{\gamma - 1} y(x) = 0, \quad \gamma > 0, \tag{1.1}$$

where $a(x)$ is nonnegative and absolutely continuous on $(0, \infty)$. Under these conditions, it is well known that every solution of (1.1) is uniquely continuable to the right throughout $(0, \infty)$; see Hastings [17], Heidel [18], Coffman and Wong [10]. A solution $y(x)$ of (1.1) is said to be oscillatory if it has arbitrarily large zeros, that is, for any $x_0 \in (0, \infty)$, there exists $x_1 > x_0$ such that $y(x_1) = 0$. Otherwise, the solution $y(x)$ is said to be nonoscillatory and it has only finitely many zeros on $(0, \infty)$, that is, there exists a last zero $\hat{x}$ depending on $y(x)$ so that $|y(x)| > 0$ for all $x > \hat{x}$.

Equation (1.1) is said to be superlinear if $\gamma > 1$ and sublinear if $0 < \gamma < 1$. Furthermore, (1.1) is said to be oscillatory if every solution is oscillatory. Likewise, it is said to be nonoscillatory if all its solutions are nonoscillatory. In the nonlinear case, that is, $\gamma \neq 1$, (1.1) can possess both oscillatory and nonoscillatory solutions.

The title of this paper is borrowed from a well-known paper of Atkinson [2] which was published over fifty years ago. The same title was used by a second author in a survey paper [46] for more general second-order equations with coefficient $a(x)$ which may assume negative values for arbitrarily large values of x. What we describe here may also be considered to be an expanded and updated version of one section of another survey paper by the author in [48].

Hindawi Publishing Corporation
Proceedings of the Conference on Differential & Difference Equations and Applications, pp. 1131–1138

2. Oscillation and existence of oscillatory solutions

The first result in this area of research is the following oscillation theorem due to F. V. Atkinson.

THEOREM 2.1 (Atkinson [2]). *Let $\gamma > 1$. Equation (1.1) is oscillatory if and only if*

$$\int^{\infty} xa(x)dx = +\infty. \tag{2.1}$$

When $\gamma = 1$, it was known that $\int^{\infty} a(x)dx = +\infty$ implied the oscillation of the linear equation $y'' + a(x)y = 0$, a result due to Fite [14]. The sufficiency part of (2.1) was not so unexpected because in general superlinearity enhanced oscillation. It was somewhat surprising that condition (2.1) was in fact also necessary. Following Atkinson [2], the sublinear analogue was given by the following.

THEOREM 2.2 (Belohorec [4]). *Let $0 < \gamma < 1$. Equation (1.1) is oscillatory if and only if*

$$\int^{\infty} x^{\gamma} a(x)dx = +\infty. \tag{2.2}$$

When $\gamma \neq 1$, (1.1) can possess both oscillatory and nonoscillatory solutions, a situation ruled out by Sturm's separation theorem for the linear equation. The first result on the existence of oscillatory solutions of (1.1), which does not also guarantee oscillation of all solutions, was given by the following.

THEOREM 2.3 (Jasný [21], Kurzweil [28]). *Let $\gamma > 1$. If the function $\phi(x) = x^{(\gamma+3)/2}a(x)$ is nondecreasing in x for all large values of x, then (1.1) has oscillatory solutions.*

Theorem 2.3 was improved to conclude that every solution of (1.1) with a zero within the range of x for which $\phi(x)$ is nondecreasing must be oscillatory, an observation made by Heidel and Hinton [19]. The sublinear analogue of Theorem 2.3 was given in the following.

THEOREM 2.4 (Heidel and Hinton [19], Chiou [8]). *Let $0 < \gamma < 1$. If $\phi(x) = x^{(\gamma+3)/2}a(x)$ is nondecreasing for all large values of x, then (1.1) has oscillatory solutions.*

Both Theorems 2.3 and 2.4 were improved in a single result by Ou and Wong [41] who proved the following.

THEOREM 2.5 (Ou and Wong [41]). *Let $\gamma \neq 1$ and $\phi(x) = x^{(\gamma+3)/2}a(x)$. Suppose that $\phi'_-(x) \in L^1(0,\infty)$, where $\phi'_-(x) = \min(-\phi'(x),0)$, and there exists a positive constant k such that $\phi(x) \geq k > 0$ for all large values of x, then (1.1) has oscillatory solutions.*

Theorem 2.5 implies the following corollary.

COROLLARY 2.6. *Let $\gamma \neq 1$. If $\phi(x) \geq k > 0$ for all large values of x and $\phi'_+(x) \in L^1(0,\infty)$, where $\phi'_+(x) = \max(\phi'(x),0)$, then (1.1) has oscillatory solutions.*

The condition that $\phi(x)$ is bounded away from zero by a positive constant plays an important role in Theorems 2.3, 2.4, and 2.5, and similarly for nonoscillation theorems which we will discuss in the next section. Indeed, we have as a consequence of Corollary 2.6 the following result.

Theorem 2.7 (Belohorec [5], Erbe and Muldowney [12], Wong [51]). *Let* $\gamma \neq 1$. *If* $\phi(x)$ *is monotone and bounded either below or above by a positive constant for all large values of* x, *then (1.1) has oscillatory solutions.*

3. Nonoscillation theorems

In this section, we discuss criteria which imply that all solutions of (1.1) are nonoscillatory. We begin with the following theorem.

Theorem 3.1 (Kiguradze [23]). *Let* $\gamma > 1$. *If for some* $\delta > 0$, $\psi(x) = x^{\delta}\phi(x) = x^{(\gamma+3)/2+\delta}a(x)$ *is nonincreasing for all large values of* x, *then (1.1) is nonoscillatory.*

Nehari showed that Kiguardze's result could also be improved to the following.

Theorem 3.2 (Nehari [38]). *Let* $\gamma > 1$. *If for* $\sigma \geq (\gamma+3)/2$, *the function* $(\log x)^{\sigma}\phi(x)$ *is nonincreasing for all large values of* x, *(1.1) is nonoscillatory.*

Nehari indicated through a private communication that Theorem 3.2 would remain valid for any $\sigma > 0$. Indeed, Chiou [6] proved that Theorem 3.2 remained valid for $\sigma \geq (\gamma+5)/4$. In a subsequent paper, Chiou [7] claimed that Theorem 3.2 remained valid for any $\sigma > 0$. Unfortunately, in a mathematical review, Nehari [40] pointed out an error in Chiou's proof but his new proof did improve the lower bound to $\sigma \geq (\gamma+1)/4 - 1/(\gamma+1)$; see also Erbe and Muldowney [13]. Finally, in a substantive paper, Nehari's conjecture was settled by Kaper and Kwong in the following.

Theorem 3.3 (Kaper and Kwong [22]). *Let* $\gamma > 1$. *If the function* $(\log x)^{\sigma}x^{(\gamma+3)/2}a(x)$ *is nonincreasing for any* $\sigma > 0$, *then (1.1) is nonoscillatory.*

Again, we seek for similar results in the sublinear case. Kiguradze [25] conjectured that his Theorem 3.1 remained valid when $0 < \gamma < 1$. This conjecture was settled only recently in the following.

Theorem 3.4 (Wong [54]). *Let* $0 < \gamma < 1$. *If for some* $\delta > 0$, $x^{\delta}\phi(x)$ *is nonincreasing for all large values of* x, *then (1.1) is nonoscillatory.*

The natural question arises whether the Nehari type of improvement, namely; Theorems 3.2, and 3.3, are also valid for sublinear equations. Coffman and Wong [11] advocated a general principle that results on the existence of oscillatory solutions and nonoscillation, which are in certain sense sharp, are always valid for both superlinear and sublinear equations. This observation was given credence by Theorems 2.4, 2.5, 2.7, and 3.4, and others, for example, Hinton [20] and Wong [50], and also Gollwitzer [16], Kwong and Wong [30], and Wong [49]. Recently, using the technique developed in [54], Kwong and Wong succeeded in proving the following improvement of Theorem 3.4.

Theorem 3.5 (Kwong and Wong [33]). *Let* $0 < \gamma < 1$. *If* $\phi(x) = x^{(\gamma+3)/2}a(x)$ *is nonincreasing in* x *for all large values of* x *and in addition* $\lim_{x\to\infty}\phi(x) = 0$, *then (1.1) is nonoscillatory.*

Thus as a consequence of Theorem 3.5, we have the sublinear analogue of Theorem 3.3, namely, the following.

Corollary 3.6. *Let* $0 < \gamma < 1$. *If* $\phi(x)(\log x)^\sigma$, $\sigma > 0$, *is nonincreasing in* x, *then (1.1) is nonoscillatory.*

Using Theorem 3.5, we can state an improved version of Corollary 3.6 by requiring that $\phi(x)(\log\log x)^\sigma$, $\sigma > 0$, is nonincreasing. Indeed, for any positive integer n, denote $\log^{[n]} x = \log(\log^{[n-1]} x)$, $n = 1, 2, 3\ldots$, and $\log^{[0]} x = x$ by definition, we have the following.

Corollary 3.7. *Let* $0 < \gamma < 1$. *If* $\phi(x)(\log^{[n]} x)^\sigma$, $\sigma > 0$, *is nonincreasing in* x, *then (1.1) is oscillatory.*

As for Theorem 3.5, it is unfortunate that its analogue for the superlinear equation is not ture, because Nehari [39] gave an example which shows for every $\gamma > 1$, a function $a(x)$ could be constructed with the property that $\phi(x) = x^{(\gamma+3)/2}a(x)$ is nonincreasing in x and $\lim_{x\to\infty} \phi(x) = 0$ but (1.1) has oscillatory solutions. This example together with Theorem 3.5 showed that the "duality principle" advocated by Coffman and Wong [9] was false after all.

In light of Nehari's ingenious counterexample, it is natural to ask whether Corollary 3.7 remains valid for the superlinear equation. This would generalize Theorem 3.3 of Kaper and Kwong [22]. We have recently also succeeded in proving this, which is stated as a separate theorem.

Theorem 3.8 (Kwong and Wong [34]). *Let* $\gamma > 1$. *If* $\phi(x)(\log^{[n]} x)^\sigma$, $\sigma > 0$, *is nonincreasing in* x, *then (1.1) is nonoscillatory.*

Finally, we mention that we may relax the monotonicity condition in Kiguradze's Theorem 3.1 on nonoscillation in a similar manner as Theorem 2.5 with regard to the existence of oscillatory solutions as the following result shows.

Theorem 3.9 (Wong [53]). *Let* $\gamma \neq 1$ *and* $\psi(x) = \phi(x)x^\delta$, *when* $\delta > 0$. *If* $\psi(x)$ *is bounded below by a positive constant and* $\psi'_+(x) \in L^1(0,\infty)$, *where* $\psi'_+(x) = \max(\psi'(x), 0)$, *then (1.1) is nonoscillatory.*

Note that the condition $\psi(x)$ bounded away from zero cannot be removed entirely. An example was given in another recent paper by Kwong and Wong [32], where a function $a(x)$ was exhibited with the property that $\liminf_{x\to\infty} \psi(x) = 0$ but (1.1) has oscillatory solutions for every $\gamma > 0$. Thus Theorem 3.9 does not imply Theorems 3.1 and 3.4.

4. Remarks and open problems

In this final section, we give a few remarks and indicate how some of the results cited above may be extended to more general equations. At the same time, we also pose some open problems.

(i) Equation (1.1) is related to the radial symmetric equation of semilinear elliptic partial differential equations under suitable transformations, where the behavior of the solution $y(x)$ near infinity has the same meaning for the solution of the partial differential equation near zero. Pohožaev [44] studied the existence of a positive solution to the Dirichlet boundary value problem of the semilinear elliptic equation in a bounded star-shaped domain Ω in $\mathbb{R}^n$ with $n \geq 3$, namely,

$$\Delta u + u^{\gamma} = 0, \quad u = 0 \text{ on } \partial\Omega, \tag{4.1}$$

where $\partial\Omega$ is the boundary of Ω. When $\Omega = \{\xi \in \mathbb{R}^n : |\xi| \leq M, \ M > 0\}$, solutions of (4.1) are radially symmetric; see Gidas et al. [15]. Equation (4.1) can be reduced to the Emden-Fowler equation (1.1) after a suitable change of independent variables. Pohožaev proved that (4.1) always possesses a positive solution, called the ground-state solution, if and only if $\gamma < (n+2)/(n-2) = \gamma^*$, where γ^* is the well-known Sobolev critical constant. It turns out the transformed equation corresponding to (4.1) is the Emden-Fowler equation: $y''(x) + x^a|y|^{\gamma-1}y = 0$ with $a = -(2n-2)/(n-2)$, which is nonoscillatory if $a < -(\gamma+3)/2$. This translates to $\gamma < (n+2)/(n-1) = \gamma^*$. This is not at all surprising since in case Ω is a ball, the existence and uniqueness of the ground-state solution are indeed equivalent to the nonoscillation of the transformed Emden-Fowler equation; see Atkinson and Peletier [3], Kaper and Kwong [22], and also Wong [53, Remark 3, pages 752–753].

(ii) It is natural to seek further extensions of results described in Sections 2 and 3. The possibility of relaxing the assumption that the coefficient $a(x)$ is nonnegative is the first question one would ask. Indeed, for oscillation theorems of Atkinson [2] in the superlinear case and of Belohorec [4] in the sublinear case, this superfluous assumption can be dropped as shown by Kiguradze [26], Kwong and Wong [29, 31], and Wong [47]. In other words, conditions (2.1) and (2.2) are valid oscillation criteria for (1.1) in cases $\gamma > 1$ and $0 < \gamma < 1$, respectively, without assuming that $a(x)$ is nonnegative. Unfortunately, for results similar to Theorems 2.3 and 2.4 on the existence of oscillatory solutions and Theorems 3.1 and 3.4 on nonoscillation, there has been little progress in this direction.

(iii) It will be of great interest to obtain similar results for the more general second-order nonlinear equation

$$y' + f(x, y) = 0, \tag{4.2}$$

where $f(x, y)$ is suitably restricted, for example, nondecreasing in y for every x. Even in the simpler case of

$$y'' + a(x)f(y) = 0, \tag{4.3}$$

where $a(x) \geq 0$ and $f(-y) = -f(y), f(y) > 0$, whenever $y > 0$, there are few results other than oscillation theorems. When $f(y)$ satisfies $f'(y) \geq 0$ for all y and the superlinear condition

$$0 < \int_y^{\infty} \frac{du}{f(u)} < \infty, \quad y > 0, \tag{4.4}$$

then the oscillation theorem of Atkinson [2] was extended to (4.3), and also more generally to (4.2) by Macki and Wong [36]. See also Nehari [37], and the recent monograph by Agarwal et al. [1]. With regard to results on nonoscillation and existence of oscillatory solutions, see Coffman and Wong [9, 10], and Wong [52].

Equation (4.2) contains the interesting case when $f(x,y)$ has mixed nonlinearities, namely,

$$y'' + a(x)|y|^{\gamma-1}y + b(x)|y|^{\beta-1}y = 0, \tag{4.5}$$

where $\gamma > 1$ and $0 < \beta < 1$. When $a(x)$ and $b(x)$ are both nonnegative, then condition (2.1) in Theorem 2.1 or condition (2.2) in Theorem 2.2, if valid for either $a(x)$ or $b(x)$, would imply oscillation of all solutions of (4.5). Little is known if we relax the nonnegativeness on $a(x)$, $b(x)$, or both. We refer the reader to Sun and Wong [45] for a more detailed discussion and related open problems.

(iv) Finally, we should also mention higher-order Emden-Fowler equations which are thoroughly discussed in the seminar book by Kiguradze and Chanturia [27]. Both Theorems 2.1 and 2.2 were generalized to even-order equations by Kiguradze [24] and independently by Ličko and Švec [35]. For some recent results on the existence of oscillatory solutions for higher-order equations, see Ou and Wong [42, 43]. It seems difficult to develop a theory for higher-order equations similar to that described in this paper for the second-order equations. We believe new analytical and geometric techniques need to be devised. It suffices to say that this subject is wide open.

References

[1] R. P. Agarwal, S. R. Grace, and D. O'Regan, *Oscillation Theory for Second Order Linear, Half-Linear, Superlinear and Sublinear Dynamic Equations*, Kluwer Academic, Dordrecht, 2002.

[2] F. V. Atkinson, *On second-order non-linear oscillations*, Pacific Journal of Mathematics **5** (1955), 643–647.

[3] F. V. Atkinson and L. A. Peletier, *Emden-Fowler equations involving critical exponents*, Nonlinear Analysis **10** (1986), no. 8, 755–776.

[4] S. Belohorec, *Oscillatory solutions of certain nonlinear differential equations of second order*, Matematicky Časopis Slovenskej Akadémie Vied **11** (1961), 250–255 (Czech).

[5] ———, *On some properties of the equation $y''(x) + f(x)y^{\alpha}(x) = 0$, $0 < \alpha < 1$*, Matematicky Časopis Slovenskej Akadémie Vied **17** (1967), 10–19.

[6] K. L. Chiou, *A second order nonlinear oscillation theorem*, SIAM Journal on Applied Mathematics **21** (1971), no. 2, 221–224.

[7] ———, *A nonoscillation theorem for the superlinear case of second order differential equations $y'' + yF(y^2,x) = 0$*, SIAM Journal on Applied Mathematics **23** (1972), no. 4, 456–459.

[8] ———, *The existence of oscillatory solutions for the equation $d^2y/dt^2 + q(t)y^r = 0$, $0 < r < 1$*, Proceedings of the American Mathematical Society **35** (1972), no. 1, 120–122.

[9] C. V. Coffman and J. S. W. Wong, *On a second order nonlinear oscillation problem*, Transactions of the American Mathematical Society **147** (1970), no. 2, 357–366.

[10] ———, *Oscillation and nonoscillation of solutions of generalized Emden-Fowler equations*, Transactions of the American Mathematical Society **167** (1972), 399–434.

[11] ———, *Oscillation and nonoscillation theorems for second order ordinary differential equations*, Funkcialaj Ekvacioj **15** (1972), 119–130.

[12] L. H. Erbe and J. S. Muldowney, *On the existence of oscillatory solutions to nonlinear differential equations*, Annali di Matematica Pura ed Applicata **109** (1976), no. 1, 23–38.

[13] ———, *Nonoscillation results for second order nonlinear differential equations*, The Rocky Mountain Journal of Mathematics **12** (1982), no. 4, 635–642.

[14] W. B. Fite, *Concerning the zeros of the solutions of certain differential equations*, Transactions of the American Mathematical Society **19** (1918), no. 4, 341–352.

[15] B. Gidas, W.-M. Ni, and L. Nirenberg, *Symmetry and related properties via the maximum principle*, Communications in Mathematical Physics **68** (1979), no. 3, 209–243.

[16] H. E. Gollwitzer, *Nonoscillation theorems for a nonlinear differential equation*, Proceedings of the American Mathematical Society **26** (1970), no. 1, 78–84.

[17] S. P. Hastings, *Boundary value problems in one differential equation with a discontinuity*, Journal of Differential Equations **1** (1965), no. 3, 346–369.

[18] J. W. Heidel, *Uniqueness, continuation, and nonoscillation for a second order nonlinear differential equation*, Pacific Journal of Mathematics **32** (1970), 715–721.

[19] J. W. Heidel and D. B. Hinton, *The existence of oscillatory solutions for a nonlinear differential equation*, SIAM Journal on Mathematical Analysis **3** (1972), no. 2, 344–351.

[20] D. B. Hinton, *An oscillation criterion for solutions of* $(ry')' + qy^{\gamma} = 0$, The Michigan Mathematical Journal **16** (1969), no. 4, 349–352.

[21] M. Jasný, *On the existence of an oscillating solution of the nonlinear differential equation of the second order* $y'' + f(x)y^{2n-1} = 0$, $f(x) > 0$, Časopis Pro Pěstování Matematiky **85** (1960), 78–83 (Russian).

[22] H. G. Kaper and M. K. Kwong, *A nonoscillation theorem for the Emden-Fowler equation: ground states for semilinear elliptic equations with critical exponents*, Journal of Differential Equations **75** (1988), no. 1, 158–185.

[23] I. T. Kiguradze, *On the conditions for oscillation of solutions of the differential equation* $u'' + a(t)|u|^n \operatorname{sgn} u = 0$, Časopis Pro Pěstování Matematiky **87** (1962), 492–495 (Russian).

[24] ———, *The capability of certain solutions of ordinary differential equations to oscillate*, Doklady Akademii Nauk SSSR **144** (1962), 33–36 (Russian).

[25] ———, *A note on the oscillation of solutions of the equation* $u'' + a(t)|u|^n \operatorname{sgn} u = 0$, Časopis Pro Pěstování Matematiky **92** (1967), 343–350 (Russian).

[26] ———, *On the oscillatory and monotone solutions of ordinary differential equations*, Archivum Mathematicum: Scripta Facultatis Scientiarum Naturalium **14** (1978), no. 1, 21–44.

[27] I. T. Kiguradze and T. A. Chanturia, *Asymptotic Properties of Solutions of Nonautonomous Ordinary Differential Equations*, Mathematics and Its Applications (Soviet Series), vol. 89, Kluwer Academic, Dordrecht, 1993.

[28] J. Kurzweil, *A note on oscillatory solution of equation* $y'' + f(x)y^{2n-1} = 0$, Časopis Pro Pěstování Matematiky **85** (1960), 357–358 (Russian).

[29] M. K. Kwong and J. S. W. Wong, *Linearization of second-order nonlinear oscillation theorems*, Transactions of the American Mathematical Society **279** (1983), no. 2, 705–722.

[30] ———, *Nonoscillation theorems for a second order sublinear ordinary differential equation*, Proceedings of the American Mathematical Society **87** (1983), no. 3, 467–474.

[31] ———, *On an oscillation theorem of Belohorec*, SIAM Journal on Mathematical Analysis **14** (1983), no. 3, 474–476.

[32] ———, *On nonoscillation of sublinear Emden-Fowler equations*, Dynamics of Continuous, Discrete and Impulsive Systems, Series A, for the International Workshop on Differential Equations and Dynamical Systems, Guelph, July 2005, (to appear).

[33] ———, *A nonoscillation theorem for sublinear Emden-Fowler equations*, Nonlinear Analysis. Theory, Methods & Applications **64** (2006), no. 7, 1641–1646.

[34] ———, *A non-oscillation Theorem for superlinear Emden-Fowler equations with near-critical coefficients*, submitted for publication.

[35] I. Ličko and M. Švec, *Le caractère oscillatoire des solutions de l'équation* $y^{(n)} + f(x)y^{\alpha} = 0, n > 1$, Czechoslovak Mathematical Journal **13 (88)** (1963), 481–491.

[36] J. W. Macki and J. S. W. Wong, *Oscillation of solutions to second-order nonlinear differential equations*, Pacific Journal of Mathematics **24** (1968), 111–117.

[37] Z. Nehari, *On a class of nonlinear second-order differential equations*, Transactions of the American Mathematical Society **95** (1960), no. 1, 101–123.
[38] ______, *A nonlinear oscillation problem*, Journal of Differential Equations **5** (1969), no. 3, 452–460.
[39] ______, *A nonlinear oscillation theorem*, Duke Mathematical Journal **42** (1975), no. 1, 183–189.
[40] ______, Mathematical Review No. 11661 **48** (1974).
[41] C. H. Ou and J. S. W. Wong, *On existence of oscillatory solutions of second order Emden-Fowler equations*, Journal of Mathematical Analysis and Applications **277** (2003), no. 2, 670–680.
[42] ______, *Oscillation and non-oscillation theorems for superlinear Emden-Fowler equations of the fourth order*, Annali di Matematica Pura ed Applicata **183** (2004), no. 1, 25–43.
[43] ______, *Oscillation and nonosocillation theorems for superlinear Emden-Fowler equations of even order*, Georgian Mathematical Journal **12** (2005), 769–802.
[44] S. I. Pohožaev, *On the eigenfunctions of the equation* $\Delta u + \lambda f(u) = 0$, Doklady Akademii Nauk SSSR **165** (1965), 36–39 (Russian).
[45] Y.-G. Sun and J. S. W. Wong, *Oscillation criteria for second order forced ordinary differential equations with mixed nonlinearities*, to appear in Applied Mathematics and Computation.
[46] J. S. W. Wong, *On second order nonlinear oscillation*, Funkcialaj Ekvacioj **11** (1968), 207–234 (1969).
[47] ______, *A second order nonlinear oscillation theorem*, Proceedings of the American Mathematical Society **40** (1973), no. 2, 487–491.
[48] ______, *On the generalized Emden-Fowler equation*, SIAM Review **17** (1975), no. 2, 339–360.
[49] ______, *Remarks on nonoscillation theorems for a second order nonlinear differential equation*, Proceedings of the American Mathematical Society **83** (1981), no. 3, 541–546.
[50] ______, *On existence of oscillatory solutions for a second order sublinear differential equation*, Proceedings of the American Mathematical Society **92** (1984), no. 3, 367–371.
[51] ______, *Nonoscillation theorems for second order nonlinear differential equations*, Proceedings of the American Mathematical Society **127** (1999), no. 5, 1387–1395.
[52] ______, *On existence of nonoscillatory solutions of sublinear Emden-Fowler equations*, Communications on Applied Nonlinear Analysis **8** (2001), no. 3, 19–25.
[53] ______, *A nonoscillation theorem for Emden-Fowler equations*, Journal of Mathematical Analysis and Applications **274** (2002), no. 2, 746–754.
[54] ______, *A nonoscillation theorem for sublinear Emden-Fowler equations*, Analysis and Applications **1** (2003), no. 1, 71–79.

James S. W. Wong: Institute of Mathematical Research, Department of Mathematics, The University of Hong Kong, Pokfulam Road, Hong Kong
E-mail address: jsww@chinneyhonkwok.com

TRIPLE FIXED-SIGN SOLUTIONS FOR A SYSTEM OF THIRD-ORDER GENERALIZED RIGHT FOCAL BOUNDARY VALUE PROBLEMS

PATRICIA J. Y. WONG

We consider the following system of third-order differential equations $u_i'''(t) = f_i(t,u_1(t), u_2(t),\dots,u_n(t))$, $t \in [a,b]$, $1 \le i \le n$, together with generalized right focal boundary conditions $u_i(a) = u_i'(t^*) = 0$, $\xi u_i(b) + \delta u_i''(b) = 0$, $1 \le i \le n$, where $(1/2)(a+b) < t^* < b$, $\xi > 0$, and $\delta > 0$. By using Leggett-Williams' fixed point theorem, we establish the existence of three solutions of the system which are of fixed signs on the interval $[a,b]$.

1. Introduction

In this paper we will consider a *system* of third-order differential equations subject to generalized right focal boundary conditions. To be precise, our system is

$$\begin{gathered} u_i'''(t) = f_i(t,u_1(t),u_2(t),\dots,u_n(t)), \quad t \in [a,b], \\ u_i(a) = u_i'(t^*) = 0, \qquad \xi u_i(b) + \delta u_i''(b) = 0, \\ i = 1,2,\dots,n, \end{gathered} \tag{F}$$

where t^*, ξ, δ are fixed with

$$\begin{gathered} \frac{1}{2}(a+b) < t^* < b, \qquad \xi \ge 0, \qquad \delta > 0, \\ \eta \equiv 2\delta + \xi(b-a)(b+a-2t^*) > 0. \end{gathered} \tag{1.1}$$

A solution $u = (u_1,u_2,\dots,u_n)$ of (F) will be sought in $(C[a,b])^n = C[a,b] \times C[a,b] \times \cdots \times C[a,b]$ (n times). We say that u is a solution of *fixed sign* if for each $1 \le i \le n$, we have $\theta_i u_i(t) \ge 0$ for $t \in [a,b]$, where $\theta_i \in \{1,-1\}$ is fixed. In particular, our definition of *fixed-sign* solution includes *positive* solutions, the usual consideration in the literature.

Hindawi Publishing Corporation
Proceedings of the Conference on Differential & Difference Equations and Applications, pp. 1139–1148

Existence of positive solutions to the two-point right focal boundary value problem

$$(-1)^{3-k}y'''(t) = f(t,y(t)), \quad t \in [0,1];$$
$$y^{(j)}(0) = 0, \quad 0 \le j \le k-1; \qquad y^{(j)}(1) = 0, \quad k \le j \le 2, \tag{1.2}$$

where $k \in \{1,2\}$, has been well discussed in the literature [1, 2]. The related discrete problem can be found in [7, 8, 11]. Work on a three-point right focal problem, a special case of (F) when $n = 1$, $\delta = 1$, $\xi = 0$, is available in [3, 5]. Recently, Anderson [4] considered (F) when $n = 1$ and developed Green's function for the boundary value problem. In our present work, we generalize the problem considered in [4] to a *system* of boundary value problems, with very *general* nonlinear terms f_i; this yields a much more appropriate and robust model for many nonlinear phenomena. We will establish the existence of *three fixed-sign* solutions using Leggett-Williams' fixed point theorem. Estimates on the norms of these solutions will also be provided. Related work concerning (F) can be found in [9, 10].

2. Preliminaries

In this section we will state some necessary definitions and the relevant fixed point theorem. Let B be a Banach space equipped with norm $\|\cdot\|$.

Definition 2.1. Let C ($\subset B$) be a nonempty closed convex set. It is said that C is a *cone*, provided that the following conditions are satisfied:
(a) if $u \in C$ and $\alpha \ge 0$, then $\alpha u \in C$;
(b) if $u \in C$ and $-u \in C$, then $u = 0$.

Definition 2.2. Let C ($\subset B$) be a cone. A map ψ is a *nonnegative continuous concave functional* on C if the following conditions are satisfied:
(a) $\psi : C \to [0,\infty)$ is continuous;
(b) $\psi(ty + (1-t)z) \ge t\psi(y) + (1-t)\psi(z)$ for all $y,z \in C$ and $0 \le t \le 1$.

Let ψ be a nonnegative continuous concave functional on C. For nonnegative numbers w_1, w_2, the following notations are introduced:

$$C(w_1) = \{u \in C \mid \|u\| < w_1\},$$
$$C(\psi,w_1,w_2) = \{u \in C \mid \psi(u) \ge w_1, \ \|u\| \le w_2\}. \tag{2.1}$$

Theorem 2.3 (Leggett-Williams' fixed point theorem) [6]. *Let C ($\subset B$) be a cone, and let $w_4 > 0$ be given. Assume that ψ is a nonnegative continuous concave functional on C such that $\psi(u) \le \|u\|$ for all $u \in \overline{C}(w_4)$, and let $S : \overline{C}(w_4) \to \overline{C}(w_4)$ be a continuous and completely continuous operator. Suppose that there exist numbers w_1, w_2, w_3, where $0 < w_1 < w_2 < w_3 \le w_4$ such that*
(a) *$\{u \in C(\psi,w_2,w_3) \mid \psi(u) > w_2\} \neq \emptyset$, and $\psi(Su) > w_2$ for all $u \in C(\psi,w_2,w_3)$,*
(b) *$\|Su\| < w_1$ for all $u \in \overline{C}(w_1)$,*
(c) *$\psi(Su) > w_2$ for all $u \in C(\psi,w_2,w_4)$ with $\|Su\| > w_3$.*

Then, S has (at least) three fixed points u^1, u^2, and u^3 in $\overline{C}(w_4)$. Furthermore,

$$\begin{gathered} u^1 \in C(w_1), \qquad u^2 \in \{u \in C(\psi, w_2, w_4) \mid \psi(u) > w_2\}, \\ u^3 \in \overline{C}(w_4) \backslash (C(\psi, w_2, w_4) \cup \overline{C}(w_1)). \end{gathered} \tag{2.2}$$

We also require the definition of an L^q-*Carathéodory function.*

Definition 2.4. A function $P : [a,b] \times \mathbb{R}^n \to \mathbb{R}$ is an L^q-*Carathéodory function* if the following conditions hold.

(a) The map $t \to P(t,u)$ is measurable for all $u \in \mathbb{R}^n$.

(b) The map $u \to P(t,u)$ is continuous for almost all $t \in [a,b]$.

(c) For any $r > 0$, there exists $\mu_r \in L^q[a,b]$ such that $|u| \le r$ implies that $|P(t,u)| \le \mu_r(t)$ for almost all $t \in [a,b]$.

3. Main results

Throughout we will denote $u = (u_1, u_2, \ldots, u_n)$. Let the Banach space $B = (C[a,b])^n$ be equipped with norm

$$\|u\| = \max_{1 \le i \le n} \sup_{t \in [a,b]} |u_i(t)| = \max_{1 \le i \le n} |u_i|_0, \tag{3.1}$$

where we denote $|u_i|_0 = \sup_{t \in [a,b]} |u_i(t)|$, $1 \le i \le n$.

Let $g(t,s)$ be Green's function of the boundary value problem

$$\begin{gathered} y'''(t) = 0, \quad t \in [a,b], \\ y(a) = y'(t^*) = 0, \qquad \xi y(b) + \delta y''(b) = 0. \end{gathered} \tag{3.2}$$

Define the operator $S : B \to B$ by

$$Su(t) = (S_1u(t), S_2u(t), \ldots, S_nu(t)), \quad t \in [a,b], \tag{3.3}$$

where

$$S_iu(t) = \int_a^b g(t,s) f_i(s, u(s)) ds, \quad t \in [a,b],\ 1 \le i \le n. \tag{3.4}$$

Clearly, a fixed point of the operator S is a solution of the system (F).

Our first lemma gives the properties of Green's function $g(t,s)$ which will be used later.

Lemma 3.1 [4]. *It is known that for $t,s \in [a,b]$,*

$$g(t,s) \geq 0, \quad t,s \in [a,b]; \qquad g(t,s) > 0, \quad t,s \in (a,b], \tag{3.5}$$

$$g(t,s) \leq g(t^*,s), \quad t,s \in [a,b], \tag{3.6}$$

$$\text{for fixed } h \in (0,b-t^*),$$

$$\begin{gathered} g(t,s) \geq Mg(t^*,s), \quad t \in [t^*-h,t^*+h],\ s \in [a,b], \\ \text{where } M = \frac{(t^*-a+h)(t^*-a-h)}{(t^*-a)^2} \in (0,1). \end{gathered} \tag{3.7}$$

For clarity, we will list the conditions that are needed later. Note that in these conditions $\theta_i \in \{1,-1\}$, $1 \leq i \leq n$, are fixed,

$$\begin{gathered} [0,\infty)_i = \begin{cases} [0,\infty) & \text{if } \theta_i = 1, \\ (-\infty,0] & \text{if } \theta_i = -1, \end{cases} \\ \widetilde{K} = \{u \in B \mid \text{for each } 1 \leq i \leq n,\ \theta_i u_i(t) \geq 0 \text{ for } t \in [a,b]\}, \\ K = \{u \in \widetilde{K} \mid \text{for some } j \in \{1,2,\ldots,n\},\ \theta_j u_j(t) > 0 \text{ for some } t \in [a,b]\}. \end{gathered} \tag{3.8}$$

(C1) For each $1 \leq i \leq n$, $f_i : [a,b] \times \mathbb{R}^n \to \mathbb{R}$ is an L^1-Carathéodory function.
(C2) For each $1 \leq i \leq n$ and a.e. $t \in (a,b)$,

$$\begin{gathered} \theta_i f_i(t,u) \geq 0, \quad u \in \widetilde{K}, \\ \theta_i f_i(t,u) > 0, \quad u \in K. \end{gathered} \tag{3.9}$$

(C3) There exist continuous functions p, ν, μ_i, $1 \leq i \leq n$, with $p : \prod_{j=1}^{n} [0,\infty)_j \to [0,\infty)$ and $\nu, \mu_i : (a,b) \to [0,\infty)$ such that for each $1 \leq i \leq n$,

$$\mu_i(t)p(u) \leq \theta_i f_i(t,u) \leq \nu(t)p(u), \quad u \in \widetilde{K},\ \text{a.e. } t \in (a,b). \tag{3.10}$$

(C4) For each $1 \leq i \leq n$, there exists a number $0 < \rho_i \leq 1$ such that

$$\mu_i(t) \geq \rho_i \nu(t) \quad \text{a.e. } t \in (a,b). \tag{3.11}$$

Using a standard argument, we have the following lemma.

Lemma 3.2. *Let (C1) hold. Then, the operator S defined in (3.3), (3.4) is continuous and completely continuous.*

Let $h \in (0,b-t^*)$ be fixed. Define a cone C in B as

$$\begin{gathered} C = \Big\{u \in B \mid \text{for each } 1 \leq i \leq n,\ \theta_i u_i(t) \geq 0 \text{ for } t \in [a,b], \\ \min_{t \in [t^*-h,t^*+h]} \theta_i u_i(t) \geq M\rho_i |u_i|_0\Big\}, \end{gathered} \tag{3.12}$$

where M and ρ_i are defined in (3.7) and (C4), respectively. Clearly, $C \subseteq \widetilde{K}$.

Remark 3.3. If (C2) and (C3) hold, then it follows from (3.4) and (3.5) that for $u \in \widetilde{K}$, $t \in [a,b]$ and $1 \le i \le n$,

$$0 \le \int_a^b g(t,s)\mu_i(s)p(u(s))ds \le \theta_i S_i u(t) \le \int_a^b g(t,s)\nu(s)p(u(s))ds. \tag{3.13}$$

LEMMA 3.4. *Let (C1)–(C4) hold. Then, the operator S maps C into C.*

Proof. Let $u \in C$. From (3.13) we have $\theta_i S_i u(t) \ge 0$ for $t \in [a,b]$ and $1 \le i \le n$. Next, using (3.13) and (3.6) gives for $t \in [a,b]$ and $1 \le i \le n$,

$$|S_i u(t)| \le \int_a^b g(t,s)\nu(s)p(u(s))ds \le \int_a^b g(t^*,s)\nu(s)p(u(s))ds. \tag{3.14}$$

Hence, we have

$$|S_i u|_0 \le \int_a^b g(t^*,s)\nu(s)p(u(s))ds, \quad 1 \le i \le n, \tag{3.15}$$

and therefore

$$\|Su\| = \max_{1 \le i \le n} |S_i u|_0 \le \int_a^b g(t^*,s)\nu(s)p(u(s))ds. \tag{3.16}$$

Now, employing (3.13), (3.7), (C4), and (3.15), we find for $t \in [t^* - h, t^* + h]$ and $1 \le i \le n$,

$$\begin{aligned} \theta_i S_i u(t) &\ge \int_a^b M g(t^*,s)\mu_i(s)p(u(s))ds \\ &\ge \int_a^b M g(t^*,s)\rho_i \nu(s)p(u(s))ds \\ &\ge M\rho_i |S_i u|_0. \end{aligned} \tag{3.17}$$

This leads to

$$\min_{t \in [t^* - h, t^* + h]} \theta_i S_i u(t) \ge M\rho_i |S_i u|_0, \quad 1 \le i \le n. \tag{3.18}$$

We have shown that $Su \in C$. □

For subsequent results, we define the following constants for each $1 \le i \le n$ and fixed $h \in (0, b - t^*)$:

$$\begin{aligned} q &= \int_a^b g(t^*,s)\nu(s)ds, \\ r_i &= \min_{t \in [t^* - h, t^* + h]} \int_{t^* - h}^{t^* + h} g(t^*,s)\mu_i(s)ds. \end{aligned} \tag{3.19}$$

Lemma 3.5. *Let (C1)–(C4) hold, and assume that*

(C5) *the function* $g(t^*,s)\nu(s)$ *is nonzero on a subset of* $[a,b]$ *of positive measure.*

Suppose that there exists a number $d>0$ *such that for* $|u_j|\in[0,d]$, $1\le j\le n$,

$$p(u_1,u_2,\dots,u_n)<\frac{d}{q}. \tag{3.20}$$

Then,

$$S(\overline{C}(d))\subseteq C(d)\subset\overline{C}(d). \tag{3.21}$$

Proof. Let $u\in\overline{C}(d)$. Then, $|u_j|\in[0,d]$, $1\le j\le n$. Applying (3.14), (C5), and (3.20), we find for $1\le i\le n$ and $t\in[a,b]$,

$$\begin{aligned}|S_iu(t)| &\le \int_a^b g(t^*,s)\nu(s)p(u(s))\,ds\\ &<\int_a^b g(t^*,s)\nu(s)\frac{d}{q}\,ds\\ &=q\frac{d}{q}=d.\end{aligned} \tag{3.22}$$

This implies $|S_iu|_0<d$, $1\le i\le n$, and so $\|Su\|<d$. Coupling with the fact that $Su\in C$ (Lemma 3.4), we have $Su\in C(d)$. The conclusion (3.21) is now immediate. □

The next lemma is similar to Lemma 3.5 and hence we will omit the proof.

Lemma 3.6. *Let (C1)–(C4) hold. Suppose that there exists a number* $d>0$ *such that for* $|u_j|\in[0,d]$, $1\le j\le n$,

$$p(u_1,u_2,\dots,u_n)\le\frac{d}{q}. \tag{3.23}$$

Then,

$$S(\overline{C}(d))\subseteq\overline{C}(d). \tag{3.24}$$

We are now ready to establish existence criteria for three fixed-sign solutions.

Theorem 3.7. *Let* $h\in(0,b-t^*)$ *be fixed. Let (C1)–(C5) hold, and assume*

(C6) *for each* $1\le i\le n$ *and each* $t\in[t^*-h,t^*+h]$, *the function* $g(t,s)\mu_i(s)$ *is nonzero on a subset of* $[t^*-h,t^*+h]$ *of positive measure.*

Suppose that there exist numbers w_1, w_2, w_3 *with*

$$0<w_1<w_2<\frac{w_2}{M\min_{1\le i\le n}\rho_i}\le w_3 \tag{3.25}$$

such that the following hold:

(P) $p(u_1,u_2,\ldots,u_n) < w_1/q$ *for* $|u_j| \in [0,w_1]$, $1 \le j \le n$;

(Q) *one of the following holds:*

(Q1) $\limsup_{|u_1|,|u_2|,\ldots,|u_n|\to\infty} p(u_1,u_2,\ldots,u_n)/|u_j| < 1/q$ *for some* $j \in \{1,2,\ldots,n\}$;

(Q2) *there exists a number* d $(\ge w_3)$ *such that* $p(u_1,u_2,\ldots,u_n) \le d/q$ *for* $|u_j| \in [0,d]$, $1 \le j \le n$;

(R) *for each* $1 \le i \le n$, $p(u_1,u_2,\ldots,u_n) > w_2/r_i$ *for* $|u_j| \in [w_2,w_3]$, $1 \le j \le n$.

Then, the system (F) has (at least) three fixed-sign solutions $u^1,u^2,u^3 \in C$ *such that*

$$\begin{gathered} \|u^1\| < w_1; \quad \theta_i u_i^2(t) > w_2, \quad t \in [t^*-h,t^*+h],\ 1 \le i \le n; \\ \|u^3\| > w_1, \qquad \min_{1\le i\le n}\ \min_{t\in[t^*-h,t^*+h]} \theta_i u_i^3(t) < w_2. \end{gathered} \tag{3.26}$$

Proof. We will employ Theorem 2.3. First, we will prove that condition (Q) implies the existence of a number w_4, where $w_4 \ge w_3$ such that

$$S(\overline{C}(w_4)) \subseteq \overline{C}(w_4). \tag{3.27}$$

Suppose that (Q2) holds. Then, by Lemma 3.6 we immediately have (3.27) where we pick $w_4 = d$. Suppose now that (Q1) is satisfied. Then, there exist $N > 0$ and $\epsilon < 1/q$ such that

$$\frac{p(u_1,u_2,\ldots,u_n)}{|u_j|} < \epsilon, \quad |u_1|,|u_2|,\ldots,|u_n| > N. \tag{3.28}$$

Define

$$L = \max_{|u_m|\in[0,N],1\le m\le n} p(u_1,u_2,\ldots,u_n). \tag{3.29}$$

In view of (3.28), it is clear that for some $j \in \{1,2,\ldots,n\}$, the following holds for all $(u_1,u_2,\ldots,u_n) \in \mathbb{R}^n$,

$$p(u_1,u_2,\ldots,u_n) \le L + \epsilon|u_j|. \tag{3.30}$$

Now, pick the number w_4 so that

$$w_4 > \max\left\{w_3, L\left(\frac{1}{q} - \epsilon\right)^{-1}\right\}. \tag{3.31}$$

Let $u \in \overline{C}(w_4)$. For $t \in [a,b]$ and $1 \le i \le n$, using (3.14), (3.30), and (3.31) gives

$$\begin{aligned} |S_i u(t)| &\le \int_a^b g(t^*,s)\nu(s)p(u(s))\,ds \\ &\le \int_a^b g(t^*,s)\nu(s)(L+\epsilon|u_j(s)|)\,ds \\ &\le \int_a^b g(t^*,s)\nu(s)(L+\epsilon w_4)\,ds \\ &= q(L+\epsilon w_4) \\ &< q\left[w_4\left(\frac{1}{q}-\epsilon\right)+\epsilon w_4\right] = w_4. \end{aligned} \tag{3.32}$$

This leads to $|Su_i|_0 < w_4$, $1 \le i \le n$. Hence, $\|Su\| < w_4$ and so $Su \in C(w_4) \subset \overline{C}(w_4)$. Thus, (3.27) follows immediately.

Let $\psi : C \to [0,\infty)$ be defined by

$$\psi(u) = \min_{1\le i\le n}\ \min_{t\in[t^*-h,t^*+h]} \theta_i u_i(t). \tag{3.33}$$

Clearly, ψ is a nonnegative continuous concave functional on C and $\psi(u) \le \|u\|$ for all $u \in C$.

We will verify that condition (a) of Theorem 2.3 is satisfied. In fact, it is obvious that

$$u(t) = \left(\frac{\theta_1}{2}(w_2+w_3),\dots,\frac{\theta_n}{2}(w_2+w_3)\right) \in \{u \in C(\psi,w_2,w_3) \mid \psi(u) > w_2\} \tag{3.34}$$

and so $\{u \in C(\psi,w_2,w_3) \mid \psi(u) > w_2\} \ne \varnothing$. Next, let $u \in C(\psi,w_2,w_3)$. Then, $w_2 \le \psi(u) \le \|u\| \le w_3$ and hence we have

$$\theta_j u_j(s) = |u_j(s)| \in [w_2,w_3], \quad s \in [t^*-h,t^*+h],\ 1 \le j \le n. \tag{3.35}$$

In view of (3.13), (3.35), (C6), (R), (3.7), and (3.19), it follows that

$$\begin{aligned} \psi(Su) &= \min_{1\le i\le n}\ \min_{t\in[t^*-h,t^*+h]} \theta_i(S_i u)(t) \\ &\ge \min_{1\le i\le n}\ \min_{t\in[t^*-h,t^*+h]} \int_{t^*-h}^{t^*+h} g(t,s)\mu_i(s)p(u(s))\,ds \\ &> \min_{1\le i\le n}\ \min_{t\in[t^*-h,t^*+h]} \int_{t^*-h}^{t^*+h} g(t,s)\mu_i(s)\frac{w_2}{r_i}\,ds \\ &= \min_{1\le i\le n} \frac{r_i}{r_i} w_2 = w_2. \end{aligned} \tag{3.36}$$

Therefore, we have shown that $\psi(Su) > w_2$ for all $u \in C(\psi,w_2,w_3)$.

Next, by Lemma 3.5 and condition (P), we have $S(\overline{C}(w_1)) \subseteq C(w_1)$. Hence, condition (b) of Theorem 2.3 is fulfilled.

Finally, we will show that condition (c) of Theorem 2.3 holds. Let $u \in C(\psi, w_2, w_4)$ with $\|Su\| > w_3$. Using (3.13), (3.7), (C4), and (3.16), we find

$$\begin{aligned}
\psi(Su) &= \min_{1\le i\le n} \min_{t\in[t^*-h,t^*+h]} \theta_i(S_iu)(t) \\
&\ge \min_{1\le i\le n} \min_{t\in[t^*-h,t^*+h]} \int_a^b g(t,s)\mu_i(s)p(u(s))\,ds \\
&\ge \min_{1\le i\le n} \int_a^b Mg(t^*,s)\mu_i(s)p(u(s))\,ds \\
&\ge \min_{1\le i\le n} \int_a^b Mg(t^*,s)\rho_i\nu(s)p(u(s))\,ds \\
&\ge \min_{1\le i\le n} M\rho_i\|Su\| \\
&> \min_{1\le i\le n} M\rho_i w_3 \ge w_2.
\end{aligned} \tag{3.37}$$

Hence, we have proved that $\psi(Su) > w_2$ for all $u \in C(\psi, w_2, w_4)$ with $\|Su\| > w_3$.

It now follows from Theorem 2.3 that the system (F) has (at least) three *fixed-sign* solutions $u^1, u^2, u^3 \in \overline{C}(w_4)$ satisfying (2.2). It is easy to see that here (2.2) reduces to (3.26). □

References

[1] R. P. Agarwal, *Focal Boundary Value Problems for Differential and Difference Equations*, Mathematics and Its Applications, vol. 436, Kluwer Academic, Dordrecht, 1998.

[2] R. P. Agarwal, D. O'Regan, and P. J. Y. Wong, *Positive Solutions of Differential, Difference and Integral Equations*, Kluwer Academic, Dordrecht, 1999.

[3] D. Anderson, *Multiple positive solutions for a three-point boundary value problem*, Mathematical and Computer Modelling **27** (1998), no. 6, 49–57.

[4] ———, *Green's function for a third-order generalized right focal problem*, Journal of Mathematical Analysis and Applications **288** (2003), no. 1, 1–14.

[5] D. Anderson and J. M. Davis, *Multiple solutions and eigenvalues for third-order right focal boundary value problems*, Journal of Mathematical Analysis and Applications **267** (2002), no. 1, 135–157.

[6] R. W. Leggett and L. R. Williams, *Multiple positive fixed points of nonlinear operators on ordered Banach spaces*, Indiana University Mathematics Journal **28** (1979), no. 4, 673–688.

[7] P. J. Y. Wong, *Positive solutions of difference equations with two-point right focal boundary conditions*, Journal of Mathematical Analysis and Applications **224** (1998), no. 1, 34–58.

[8] ———, *Two-point right focal eigenvalue problems for difference equations*, Dynamic Systems and Applications **7** (1998), no. 3, 345–364.

[9] ———, *Contant-sign solutions for a system of generalized right focal problems*, Nonlinear Analysis. Theory, Methods and Applications **63** (2005), 2153–2163.

[10] ———, *Eigenvalue characterization for a system of generalized right focal problems*, Dynamic Systems and Applications **15** (2006), no. 1, 173–191.

[11] P. J. Y. Wong and R. P. Agarwal, *Existence of multiple positive solutions of discrete two-point right focal boundary value problems*, Journal of Difference Equations and Applications **5** (1999), no. 6, 517–540.

Patricia J. Y. Wong: School of Electrical and Electronic Engineering, Nanyang Technological University, 50 Nanyang Avenue, Singapore 639798
E-mail address: ejywong@ntu.edu.sg

ANALYTIC SOLUTIONS OF UNSTEADY CRYSTALS AND RAYLEIGH-TAYLOR BUBBLES

XUMING XIE

We study the initial value problem for 2-dimensional dendritic crystal growth with zero surface tension and classical Rayleigh-Taylor problems. If the initial data is analytic, it is proved that unique analytic solution exists locally in time. The analysis is based on a Nirenberg theorem on abstract Cauchy-Kovalevsky problem in properly chosen Banach spaces.

1. Introduction

The phenomenon of dendritic crystal growth is one of the earliest scientific problems, tackled first by Kepler [4] in 1661 in his work on six-sided snowflake crystals. It has long been a subject of continued interest to physicists, metallurgists as well as mathematicians. Dendrite constitutes a good example of pattern selection and stability in nonequilibrium systems. From mathematical point of view, dendrite formation is a free boundary problem like the Stefan problem. Many review papers on this subject have appeared in the literature, for example, Langer [8], Kessler et al. [5], Pelce [13], Levine [9]. For unsteady dendritical crystal growth, Kunka et al. [6, 7] studied the linear theory of localized disturbances and a class exact zero-surface-tension solutions if the initial conditions include only poles. They also studied the singular behavior of unsteady dendritical crystal with surface tension. In those situations, a zero of the conformal map that describes the crystal gives birth to a daughter singularity that moves away from the zero and approaches the interface.

The motion of the interface of a heavy fluid resting above a lighter fluid in the presence of gravity (Rayleigh-Taylor flow) is very basic but important problem. When the fluids are immiscible, the sharp interface deforms into a pattern containing rising bubbles of lighter fluid and falling spikes of heavier fluid. Model equations for the location of the interface have been derived (see Baker et al. [2], Moore [10], Sharp [16], and references therein). These studies are numerical and asymptotic, but important to furthering physical understanding of the flow dynamics. Numerical calculation ran into the traditional

Hindawi Publishing Corporation
Proceedings of the Conference on Differential & Difference Equations and Applications, pp. 1149–1157

difficulties associated with singularity formation.There have been a lot of literature with regard to singularity formation of Rayleigh-Taylor instabilities. Numerical evidence for singularity was performed by Pugh [14] for Boussinesq limit and by Siegel [17]. Inspired by studies of the evolution of vortex sheets in homogeneous fluid, Baker et al. [1] developed a simple approximation for Rayleigh-Taylor flow as a generalization of Moore's approximation for Kevin-Helmholtz instability. Tanveer [19] explored the dynamics of singularity formation in the classical Rayleigh-Taylor problem without resort to any localized approximation. Under some assumptions, Tanveer showed that the only possible singularity is of a "fold" type, that is, one-half, one-third, or one-fourth singularity, and so.

In this paper, we are going to establish existence results of analytical solution to the dendrite crystal growing problem with no surface tension and Rayleigh-Taylor problem. Our approach is to apply the following Nirenberg's theorem [11] on an abstract evolutionary equation in certain appropriately chosen Banach spaces.

Theorem 1.1 (Nirenberg). *Let $\{\mathbf{B_s}\}_{0<s\leq 1}$ be a scale of Banach spaces satisfying that $\mathbf{B}_s \subset \mathbf{B}_{s'}$, $\|\cdot\|_{s'} \leq \|\cdot\|_s$ for any $0 < s' < s$. Consider the abstract Cauchy-Kovalevsky problem*

$$\frac{du}{dt} = \mathcal{L}(u(t),t), \quad u(0) = 0. \tag{1.1}$$

Assume the following conditions on $\mathcal{L}$:

(i) *for some constants $M > 0$, $\delta > 0$ and every pair of numbers s, s' such that $0 \leq s' < s < 1$, $(u,t) \to \mathcal{L}(u,t)$ is a continuous mapping of*

$$\{u \in \mathbf{B}_s : \|u\|_s < M\} \times \{t;\ |t| < \delta\} \quad \textit{into } \mathbf{B}_{s'}; \tag{1.2}$$

(ii) *for any $s' < s < 1$ and all $u, v \in \mathbf{B}_s$ with $\|u\|_s < M$, $\|v\|_s < M$ and for any t, $|t| < \delta$, $\mathcal{L}$ satisfies*

$$\|\mathcal{L}(u,t) - \mathcal{L}(v,t)\|_{s'} \leq C\frac{\|u-v\|_s}{s-s'}, \tag{1.3}$$

where C is some positive constant independent of t, u, v, s, s';

(iii) *$\mathcal{L}(0,t)$ is a continuous function of t, $|t| < \delta$ with values in $\mathbf{B}_s$ for every $s < 1$ and satisfies, with some positive constant K,*

$$\|\mathcal{L}(0,t)\|_s \leq \frac{K}{(1-s)}. \tag{1.4}$$

Under the preceding assumptions there is a positive constant a_0 such that there exists a unique function $u(t)$ which, for every $0 < s < 1$ and $|t| < a_0(1-s)$, is a continuously differentiable function of t with values in $\mathbf{B}_s$, $\|u\|_s < M$, and satisfies (1.1).

It is to be noted that Nirenberg's theorem has been successfully applied to other problems such as Hele-Shaw flow [15] and vortex sheet problem [3].

2. Unsteady crystal with zero surface tension

Following [6], the unsteady crystal problem with zero surface tension is to find function $F(\xi,t)$ analytic in the upper-half plane $\mathrm{Im}\,\xi > 0$ such that $F(\xi,t)$ satisfies (2.1) and (2.4):

$$F_t + i = (-i\xi + 1 + F_\xi)\big[H[F](\xi,t) + R[F](\xi,t)\big] \quad \text{for real } \xi, \tag{2.1}$$

where

$$H[F](\xi,t) = \frac{1}{\pi}(P)\int_{-\infty}^{\infty} \frac{R[F](\xi',t)}{(\xi'-\xi)}\,d\xi', \tag{2.2}$$

$$R[F](\xi,t) = \frac{1}{\big|-i\xi + 1 + F_\xi(\xi,t)\big|^2}. \tag{2.3}$$

The initial condition is

$$F(\xi,0) - F_0(\xi), \tag{2.4}$$

where the initial data $F_0(\xi)$ is a function which is analytic in the upper-half plane $\mathrm{Im}\,\xi > 0$.

Definition 2.1. Let $\mathcal{R}_s$ be the open region on complex ξ plane above line r_l defined as follows:

$$r_l = \left\{\xi : \xi = -\frac{1+s}{4}i + re^{-i(\varphi_0+s)/4}\right\} \cup \left\{\xi : \xi = -\frac{1+s}{4}i + re^{i[\pi+(\varphi_0+s)/4]}\right\}, \tag{2.5}$$

where $0 < s \le 1$, $0 < \varphi_0 < \pi/8$.

Remark 2.2. In the above definition, ϕ_0 is fixed, and s can vary. For $s > 0$, the upper-half plane $\mathrm{Im}\,\xi > 0$ is a proper angular subset of $\mathcal{R}_s$. For $0 \le s' < s \le 1$, $\mathcal{R}_{s'}$ is a proper angular subset of $\mathcal{R}_s$ and $\mathrm{dist}(\partial\mathcal{R}_{s'}, \partial\mathcal{R}_s) \ge C(s-s')$.

We introduce spaces of functions.

Definition 2.3. For $k = 0,1,2$, define

$$\mathbf{B}_{s,k} = \left\{F : F(\xi) \text{ analytic in } \mathcal{R}_s \text{ and continuous in } \overline{\mathcal{R}_s}, \text{with } \sup_{\xi\in\overline{\mathcal{R}}} \big|(\xi+2i)^{-k}F(\xi)\big| < \infty\right\},$$

$$\|F\|_{s,k} := \sup_{\xi\in\overline{\mathcal{R}_s}} \big|(\xi+2i)^{-k}F(\xi)\big|. \tag{2.6}$$

Remark 2.4. $\mathbf{B}_{s,k}$ are Banach spaces and $\mathbf{B}_{s,k} \subset \mathbf{B}_{s',k}$ for $0 < s' \le s \le 1$. Furthermore, the norm of the canonical embedding operator $I_{s\to s'} \le 1$.

Remark 2.5. If $F \in \mathbf{B}_{s,k}$, then F satisfies the property

$$F(\xi) \sim O(\xi^k) \quad \text{as } |\xi| \longrightarrow \infty,\ \xi \in \mathcal{R}_s. \tag{2.7}$$

Definition 2.6. Let $\mathcal{D}$ be any connected set in the complex ξ plane; introduce norms: $\|F\|_{k,\mathcal{D}} := \sup_{\xi\in\mathcal{D}} |(\xi+2i)^{-k}F(\xi)|$, $k = 0,1,2$.

Definition 2.7. Define

$$\bar{F}(\xi) = [F(\xi^*)]^*, \tag{2.8}$$

where $*$ denotes the complex conjugate.

Remark 2.8. If F is analytic in domain $\mathcal{D}$ containing real axis, then $\bar{F}$ is analytic in $\mathcal{D}^*$ and $\bar{F}(\xi) = F^*(\xi)$ for ξ real, and $\mathcal{D}^*$ denotes the conjugate domain obtained by reflecting $\mathcal{D}$ about the real axis. Furthermore, $\|\bar{F}\|_{k,\mathcal{D}^*} \leq \|F\|_{k,\mathcal{D}}$.

Definition 2.9. Let $\mathcal{D}_0$ be the open region on complex ξ plane above line r_0 defined as follows:

$$r_0 = \left\{\xi : \xi = -\frac{1}{8}i + re^{-i(\varphi_0/8)}\right\} \cup \left\{\xi : \xi = -\frac{1}{8}i + re^{i[\pi+(\varphi_0/8)]}\right\}, \tag{2.9}$$

where $0 < \varphi_0 < \pi/8$ is the same as in Definition 2.1.

Remark 2.10. The upper-half plane $\operatorname{Im}\xi > 0$ is a proper angular subset of $\mathcal{D}_0$ and $\mathcal{D}_0$ is a proper angular subset of $\mathcal{R}_s$ for any $s > 0$.

Some properties of the Banach space $\mathbf{B}_{s,k}$ are given in the following lemma.

Lemma 2.11. *If $F \in \mathbf{B}_{s,k}$, $s > 0$, then $\|F_\xi\|_{k-1,\mathcal{D}_0} \leq K_1\|F\|_{0,k}$, where $K_1 > 0$ is a constant independent of s and F.*

Let $K_2 = \min_{\mathcal{R}_1} |-i\xi+1||(\xi+2i)^{-(k-1)}|$, $K_3 = \min_{\mathcal{R}_1} |i\xi+1||(\xi+2i)^{-(k-1)}|$, define

$$M = \min\left\{\frac{K_3}{2K_1}, \frac{K_3}{2K_1}\right\}. \tag{2.10}$$

The following lemma is essential to application of Nirenberg's theorem.

Lemma 2.12. *If $F \in \mathbf{B}_{s,k}$, $0 < s' < s \leq 1$, then $F_\xi \in \mathbf{B}_{s',k-1}$ and*

$$||F_\xi||_{s',k-1} \leq \frac{K_4}{s-s'}\|F\|_{s,k}, \tag{2.11}$$

where K_4 is independent of s, s', and F.

We are going to prove the following theorem.

Theorem 2.13. *If the initial data $F_0(\xi) \in \mathbf{B}_{1,2}$ and $\|F_0\|_{1,2} \leq M/2$, then there exists one and only one solution: $F(\xi,t) \in C^1([0,T],\mathbf{B}_{s,k})$, $\|F\|_{s,k} \leq M$, to the unsteady crystal problem, where T is a suitable positive constant.*

The proof of the above theorem will be based on Nirenberg's theorem [11, 12]. Equation (2.1) can be written as

$$F_t = L(F,t) \equiv (-i\xi+1+F_\xi)[H[F](\xi,t)+R[F](\xi,t)] - i \quad \text{for real } \xi. \tag{2.12}$$

Using Plemej formula, we analytically extend (2.12) to region $\mathcal{R}_s$. We can extend $L(F,t)$ in upper-half plane as

$$L(F,t) \equiv (-i\xi + 1 + F_\xi)H^+[F](\xi,t) - i, \quad \text{Im}\,\xi > 0, \tag{2.13}$$

and $L(F,t)$ in lower-half plane is

$$\begin{aligned} L(F,t) &\equiv (-i\xi + 1 + F_\xi)[H^-[F](\xi,t) + 2R(\xi,t)] - i \\ &= (-i\xi + 1 + F_\xi)H^-(\xi,t) + 2R_1[F](\xi,t) - i, \quad \xi \in \mathcal{R}_s \cap \{\text{Im}\,\xi < 0\}, \end{aligned} \tag{2.14}$$

where

$$R_1[F](\xi,t) = \frac{1}{i\xi + 1 + \bar{F}_\xi}. \tag{2.15}$$

The following lemma can be proved.

LEMMA 2.14. *Let* $u \in \mathbf{B}_{s,2}, v \in \mathbf{B}_{s,2}$, *then for* $0 < s' < s \le 1$, $\|L(u,t) - L(v,t)\|_{s',2} \le C\|u - v\|_{s,2}/(s - s')$, *where* C *is a positive constant independent of* s, s'.

Proof of Theorem 2.13. For $F_0(\xi) \in B_{1,2}$, $\|F_0\|_{1,2} \le M/2$, $0 < s' < 1$, applying Lemma 2.14 with $u = F_0$, $s = 1$, $v = 0$, we have

$$\|L(F_0,t)\|_{s',2} \le \frac{C\|F_0\|_{1,2}}{1 - s'}. \tag{2.16}$$

Let $f(\xi,t) = F(\xi,t) - F_0(\xi)$, then $f(\xi,t)$ satisfies the initial value problem

$$\begin{aligned} f_t &= \mathcal{L}(f,t) \equiv L(f + F_0, t), \\ f(\xi,0) &= 0. \end{aligned} \tag{2.17}$$

Since $\mathcal{L}(0,t) = L(F_0,t)$, (1.4) holds due to (2.16). For $u \in \mathbf{B}_{s,2}$, $\|u\|_{s,2} \le M/2, 0 < s' < s \le 1$, using Lemma 2.14 with $v = 0$, we have $\mathcal{L}(u,t) \equiv L(u + F_0, t) \in \mathbf{B}_{s',2}$; hence assumption (i) of Nirenberg's theorem holds. Equation (1.3) follows from Lemma 2.14. Therefore the main theorem follows from Nirenberg's theorem. □

3. The classical Rayleigh-Taylor flow

We are going to use the same formulation of the classical Rayleigh-Taylor flow as in [18, 19]. The unsteady classical Rayleigh-Taylor problem is equivalent to finding (g,h) which is analytic in $|\xi| < 1$ and satisfies in $|\xi| < 1$:

$$h_t = \xi h_\xi I_1^-[f,g] - \xi h(I_1^-[g,h])_\xi, \tag{3.1}$$

$$g_t = \xi g_\xi I_1^-[g,h] + 1 - h - \xi h(I_2^-[g])_\xi, \tag{3.2}$$

where I_1^- and I_2^- defined in $|\xi| < 1$ can be written as

$$I_1^-[g,h](\xi,t) = \frac{1}{4\pi i}\int_{|\xi'|=1}\frac{d\xi'}{\xi'}\left[\frac{\xi+\xi'}{\xi'-\xi}\right][\bar{g}(\xi',t)h(\xi',t)+g(\xi',t)\bar{h}(\xi',t)], \tag{3.3}$$

$$I_2^-[g](\xi,t) = \frac{1}{4\pi i}\int_{|\xi'|=1}\frac{d\xi'}{\xi'}\left[\frac{\xi+\xi'}{\xi'-\xi}\right][g(\xi',t)\bar{g}(\xi',t)], \tag{3.4}$$

and the initial conditions are

$$h|_{t=0} = h_0(\xi), \qquad g|_{t=0} = g_0(\xi). \tag{3.5}$$

The analytic continuation of (3.1) and (3.2) to $|\xi| > 1$ is

$$g_t = (R_3[g,h]+R_2[h]g)g_\xi + \xi gh(R_1[g])_\xi - (1+\xi(I_2^+)_\xi)h + 1, \tag{3.6}$$

$$\begin{aligned} h_t = {} & (R_3[g,h]+R_2[h]g)h_\xi - R_2[h]hg_\xi + \frac{R_3[g,h]}{\xi}h - \frac{R_3[g,h]}{\xi}h^2 \\ & - \xi R_4[g,h]h^2 - \xi\left(\frac{R_2[h]}{\xi}\right)_\xi gh - (R_3[g,h])_\xi h + (R_3[g,h])_\xi h^2, \end{aligned} \tag{3.7}$$

where

$$R_1[g](\xi,t) = -\bar{g}(\xi,t), \tag{3.8}$$

$$R_2[h](\xi,t) = \xi\bar{h}(\xi,t), \tag{3.9}$$

$$R_3[g,h](\xi,t) = \xi I_1^+[g,h](\xi,t), \tag{3.10}$$

$$R_4[g,h] = I_1^+[g,h] + \bar{g}(\xi,t). \tag{3.11}$$

I_1^+ and I_2^+ defined in $|\xi| > 1$ can be written as

$$I_1^+[g,h](\xi,t) = \frac{1}{4\pi i}\int_{|\xi'|=1}\frac{d\xi'}{\xi'}\left[\frac{\xi+\xi'}{\xi'-\xi}\right][\bar{g}(\xi',t)h(\xi',t)+g(\xi',t)\bar{h}(\xi',t)], \tag{3.12}$$

$$I_2^+[g](\xi,t) = \frac{1}{4\pi i}\int_{|\xi'|=1}\frac{d\xi'}{\xi'}\left[\frac{\xi+\xi'}{\xi'-\xi}\right][g(\xi',t)\bar{g}(\xi',t)]. \tag{3.13}$$

Let $r > 1$ be a fixed number.

Definition 3.1. Let $\mathcal{R}_s$ be the disk in complex ξ plane with radius s, that is, $\mathcal{R}_s = \{\xi, |\xi| < s\}$. Define function space $\mathbf{B}_s$ so that

$$\mathbf{B}_s = \{f(\xi) : f(\xi) \text{ is analytic in } \mathcal{R}_s \text{ and continuous on } \overline{\mathcal{R}_s}\} \tag{3.14}$$

with norm $\|f\|_s = \sup_{\mathcal{R}_s}|f(\xi)|$.

Remark 3.2. Let r_1 be a number such that $1 < r_1 < r$. $\mathbf{B}_s$ are Banach spaces and $\mathbf{B}_s \subset \mathbf{B}_{s'}$ for $r_1 < s' \leq s \leq r$. Furthermore, the norm of the canonical embedding operator $I_{s \to s'} \leq 1$.

We define $\mathcal{B}_s$ as

$$\mathcal{B}_s = \mathbf{B}_s \times \mathbf{B}_s \tag{3.15}$$

with norm $\|(g,h)\|_s = \|g\|_s + \|h\|_s$. $\mathcal{B}_s$ is a Banach space. We assume $h_0 \in \mathbf{B}_r$, $g_0 \in \mathbf{B}_r$. Let M be a positive number defined by

$$M = ||g_0||_r + ||h_0||_r. \tag{3.16}$$

We are going to prove the following theorem.

THEOREM 3.3. *If $g_0 \in \mathbf{B}_r$, $h_0 \in \mathbf{B}_r$, M is defined as in (3.16), then there exists one and only one solution $(g,h) \in C^1([0,T],\mathcal{B}_s)$, $r_1 < s < r$, $\|(g,h)\|_s \leq 2M$ to the problem (3.1), (3.2), and (3.5), where T is a suitable positive constant.*

Definition 3.4. Let $(g,h) \in \mathcal{B}_s$. The following operators: for $|\xi| < 1$, $L_1[g,h]$ and $L_2[g,h]$ are defined by

$$L_1[g,h](\xi,t) = \xi g_\xi I_1^-[g,h](\xi,t) + 1 - h - \xi h(I_2^-[g](\xi,t))_\xi, \tag{3.17}$$

$$L_2[g,h](\xi,t) = \xi h_\xi I_1^-[f,g](\xi,t) - \xi h(I_1^-[g,h](\xi,t))_\xi. \tag{3.18}$$

Analytic continuation of $L_1[g,h]$ and $L_2[g,h]$ to $|\xi| > 1$ is

$$L_1[g,h] = (R_3 + R_2 g)g_\xi + \xi gh(R_1)_\xi - \left(1 + \xi(I_2^+)_\xi\right)h + 1, \tag{3.19}$$

$$\begin{aligned} L_2[g,h] &= (R_3 + R_2 g)h_\xi - R_2 h g_\xi + \frac{R_3}{\xi}h - \frac{R_3}{\xi}h^2 - \xi R_4 h^2 \\ &\quad - \xi\left(\frac{R_2}{\xi}\right)_\xi gh - (R_3)_\xi h + (R_3)_\xi h^2. \end{aligned} \tag{3.20}$$

Let $p = g - g_0$, $q = h - h_0$, then (g,h) is a solution of initial problem (3.1), (3.2), and (3.5) if and only if (p,q) solves the following initial problem:

$$(p_t, q_t) = \mathcal{L}(p,q), \quad (p,q)|_{t=0} = (0,0), \tag{3.21}$$

where the operator $\mathcal{L}$ is defined by

$$\mathcal{L}(p,q) = (L_1[p+g_0, q+h_0], L_2[p+g_0, q+h_0]). \tag{3.22}$$

We can prove the following two lemmas.

LEMMA 3.5. *If $(p,q) \in \mathcal{B}_s$, $(u,v) \in \mathcal{B}_s$, $\|(p,q)\|_s \leq M$, and $\|(u,v)\|_s \leq M$, $r_1 < s' < s < r$, then*

$$||\mathcal{L}(p,q) - \mathcal{L}(u,v)||_{s'} \leq \frac{C}{s-s'}||(p,q) - (u,v)||_{s'}. \tag{3.23}$$

LEMMA 3.6. *If* $r_1 < s' < r$, *then* $\|\mathcal{L}(0,0)\|_{s'} \leq K/(r-s')$.

Proof of Theorem 3.3. We first apply Nirenberg's theorem to system (3.21). For $(p,q) \in \mathcal{B}_s$, by Lemma 3.5 with $(u,v) = (0,0)$, we have $(L_1[p,q], L_2[p,q]) \in \mathcal{B}_{s'}$; hence $\mathcal{L}(p,q) \in \mathcal{B}_{s'}$ from (3.22). Since the system (3.21) is autonomous, the continuity of the operator $\mathcal{L}$ is implied by Lemma 3.5; hence (1.2) holds. Equations (1.3) and (1.4) are given by Lemmas 3.5 and 3.6, respectively. Therefore, there exists unique solution $(p,q) \in \mathcal{B}_s$, $\|(p,q)\|_s \leq M$, so $g = p + g_0$, $h = q + h_0$ is the unique solution of Rayleigh-Taylor problem (3.1), (3.2), and (3.5). □

Acknowledgment

This work is supported by NSF grant DMS-0500642.

References

[1] G. R. Baker, R. E. Caflisch, and M. Siegel, *Singularity formation during Rayleigh-Taylor instability*, Journal of Fluid Mechanics **252** (1993), 51–78.

[2] G. R. Baker, D. I. Meiron, and S. A. Orszag, *Generalized vortex methods for free-surface flow problems*, Journal of Fluid Mechanics **123** (1982), 477–501.

[3] T. Y. Hou and G. Hu, *A nearly optimal existence result for slightly perturbed 3-D vortex sheets*, Communications in Partial Differential Equations **28** (2003), no. 1-2, 155–198.

[4] J. Kepler, *De Nive Sexangula*, published in Frankfurt am Main (1611).

[5] D. Kessler, J. Koplik, and H. Levine, *Patterned selection in fingered growth phenomena*, Advances in Physics **37** (1988), no. 3, 255–399.

[6] M. D. Kunka, M. R. Foster, and S. Tanveer, *Dendritic crystal growth for weak undercooling*, Physical Review E **56** (1997), no. 3, part B, 3068–3100.

[7] ______, *Dendritic crystal growth for weak undercooling. II. Surface energy effects on nonlinear evolution*, Physical Review E **59** (1999), no. 1, part B, 673–710.

[8] J. S. Langer, *Chance and Matter*, edited by J. Souletie, North-Holland, Amsterdam, 1987.

[9] H. Levine, *Dendritic crystal growth: overview*, Asymptotics Beyond All Orders (H. Segur, ed.), Plenum Press, New York, 1991, pp. 67–73.

[10] D. W. Moore, *A vortex method applied to interfacial waves*, Vortex Motion (H. G. Hornung and E. A. Muller, eds.), Vieweg & Sons, Braunschweig, 1982.

[11] L. Nirenberg, *An abstract form of the nonlinear Cauchy-Kowalewski theorem*, Journal of Differential Geometry **6** (1972), 561–576.

[12] T. Nishida, *A note on a theorem of Nirenberg*, Journal of Differential Geometry **12** (1977), no. 4, 629–633 (1978).

[13] P. Pelce, *Dynamics of Curved Fronts*, Perspectives in Physics, Academic Press, Massachusetts, 1988.

[14] D. A. Pugh, *Development of vortex sheets in Boussinesq flows-formation of singularities*, Ph.D. thesis, Imperial College, London, 1989.

[15] M. Reissig, *The existence and uniqueness of analytic solutions for a moving boundary problem for Hele-Shaw flows in the plane*, Nonlinear Analysis. Theory, Methods & Applications **23** (1994), no. 5, 565–576.

[16] D. H. Sharp, *An overview of Rayleigh-Taylor instability*, Physica D **12** (1984), 3–18.

[17] M. Siegel, *An analytical and numerical study of singularity formation in the Rayleigh-Taylor problem*, Ph.D. thesis, New York University, New York, 1989.

[18] S. Tanveer, *Singularities in water waves and Rayleigh-Taylor instability*, Proceedings of the Royal Society. London. Series A **435** (1991), no. 1893, 137–158.

[19] ———, *Singularities in the classical Rayleigh-Taylor flow: formation and subsequent motion*, Proceedings of the Royal Society. London. Series A **441** (1993), no. 1913, 501–525.

Xuming Xie: Department of Mathematics, Morgan State University, Baltimore, MD 21251, USA
E-mail address: xxie@morgan.edu

TWO-WEIGHT INEQUALITIES FOR SOME OPERATORS APPLIED TO HARMONIC FORMS

YUMING XING

We obtain two-weight integral inequalities for the composition $T \circ G$, where T is the homotopy operator and G is Green's operator applied to A-harmonic forms.

1. Introduction and statement of results

The aim of this paper is to prove different versions of two-weight embedding inequalities for the composition of homotopy operator T and Green's operator G applied to the A-harmonic forms on manifolds and establish two-weight norm estimates for the composition $T \circ G$. Our main results are presented in the following Theorems 1.1 and 1.2, respectively.

Theorem 1.1. *Let $u \in L^p_{\mathrm{loc}}(\Lambda^l M, w^\alpha)$, $l = 1,\dots,n$, $1 < p < \infty$, be an A-harmonic form on a manifold M. If $\rho > 1$ and $(w_1(x), w_2(x)) \in A_{r,\lambda}(M)$ for some $\lambda \geq 1$ and $1 < r < \infty$, then there exists a constant C, independent of u, such that*

$$||T(G(u))||_{p,B,w_1^\alpha} \leq C|B|\operatorname{diam}(B)\|u\|_{p,\rho B,w_2^\alpha}, \tag{1.1}$$

$$||T(G(u))||_{W^{1,p}(B),w_1^\alpha} \leq C|B|\|u\|_{p,\rho B,w_2^\alpha} \tag{1.2}$$

for all balls B with $\rho B \subset M$ and any real number α with $0 < \alpha < \lambda$.

Theorem 1.2. *Let M be a compact, oriented, C^∞ smooth, Riemannian manifold without boundary and let $u \in L^p(\Lambda^l M, w^\alpha)$, $l = 1,2,\dots,n$, $1 < p < \infty$, be an A-harmonic form on M. Assume that $(w_1(x), w_2(x)) \in A_{r,\lambda}(M)$ for some $\lambda \geq 1$ and $1 < r < \infty$. Then there exists a constant C, independent of u, such that*

$$||T(G(u))||_{p,M,w_1^\alpha} \leq C|M|\operatorname{diam}(M)\|u\|_{p,M,w_2^\alpha}, \tag{1.3}$$

$$||T(G(u))||_{W^{1,p}(M),w_1^\alpha} \leq C|M|\|u\|_{p,M,w_2^\alpha} \tag{1.4}$$

for any real number α with $0 < \alpha < \lambda$.

Hindawi Publishing Corporation
Proceedings of the Conference on Differential & Difference Equations and Applications, pp. 1159–1165

2. Some preliminary results

We always assume that M is a Riemannian, compact, oriented, and C^∞ smooth manifold without boundary on $\mathbb{R}^n$ and B is a ball or a cube. σB, $\sigma > 0$, is the ball with the same center as B and with $\operatorname{diam}(\sigma B) = \sigma \operatorname{diam}(B)$. The Hodge star operator $\star: \Lambda \to \Lambda$ is defined by the rule $\star 1 = e_1 \wedge e_2 \wedge \cdots \wedge e_n$ and $\alpha \wedge \star\beta = \beta \wedge \star\alpha = \langle \alpha, \beta \rangle (\star 1)$ for all $\alpha, \beta \in \Lambda$. We denote the exterior derivative by $d : D'(M, \Lambda^l) \to D'(M, \Lambda^{l+1})$ for $l = 0, 1, \ldots, n-1$. The Hodge codifferential operator $d^\star : D'(M, \Lambda^{l+1}) \to D'(M, \Lambda^l)$ is defined by $d^\star = (-1)^{nl+1} \star d \star$, $l = 0, 1, \ldots, n-1$. We always use G to denote Green's operator and T to denote homotopy operator in this paper, and see definitions and more properties of them in [1, 7]. Let $\Lambda^l M$ be the lth exterior power of the cotangent bundle and let $C^\infty(\Lambda^l M)$ be the space of smooth l-forms on M. We use $D'(M, \Lambda^l)$ to denote the space of all differential l-forms and $L^p(\Lambda^l M, w^\alpha)$ to denote the l-forms $\omega(x) = \sum_I \omega_I(x) dx_I = \sum \omega_{i_1 i_2 \cdots i_l}(x) dx_{i_1} \wedge dx_{i_2} \wedge \cdots \wedge dx_{i_l}$ on M satisfying $\int_M |\omega_I|^p w^\alpha < \infty$ for all ordered l-tuples I, where w is a weight. In this way, $L^p(\Lambda^l M, w^\alpha)$ becomes a Banach space with norm $\|\omega\|_{p,M,w^\alpha} = (\int_M |\omega(x)|^p w^\alpha dx)^{1/p} = (\int_M (\sum_I |\omega_I(x)|^2)^{p/2} w^\alpha dx)^{1/p}$, where α is a real number. $W^{1,p}(M, \Lambda^l)$ is used to denote the space of all differential l-forms on M whose coefficients are in $W^{1,p}(M, \mathbb{R})$. The notations $W^{1,p}_{\text{loc}}(M, \mathbb{R})$ and $W^{1,p}_{\text{loc}}(M, \Lambda^l)$ are self-explanatory. For $0 < p < \infty$ and a weight $w(x)$, the weighted norm of $\omega \in W^{1,p}(M, \Lambda^l, w^\alpha)$ over M is denoted by

$$\|\omega\|_{W^{1,p}(M), w^\alpha} = \operatorname{diam}(M)^{-1} \|\omega\|_{p,M,w^\alpha} + \|\nabla \omega\|_{p,M,w^\alpha}, \tag{2.1}$$

where α is a real number. Also, for $\omega \in D'(M, \Lambda^l)$, the vector-valued differential form $\nabla \omega = (\partial \omega / \partial x_1, \ldots, \partial \omega / \partial x_n)$ consists of differential forms $\partial \omega / \partial x_i \in D'(M, \Lambda^l)$, where the partial differentiation is applied to the coefficients of ω. Some new results about harmonic forms have been established in the study of the A-harmonic equation

$$d^\star A(x, d\omega) = 0 \tag{2.2}$$

for differential forms, where $A : M \times \Lambda^l(\mathbb{R}^n) \to \Lambda^l(\mathbb{R}^n)$ satisfies the following conditions:

$$\begin{gathered} |A(x, \xi)| \le a |\xi|^{p-1}, \\ \langle A(x, \xi), \xi \rangle \ge |\xi|^p \end{gathered} \tag{2.3}$$

for almost every $x \in M$ and all $\xi \in \Lambda^l(\mathbb{R}^n)$. Here $a > 0$ is a constant and $1 < p < \infty$ is a fixed exponent associated with (2.2). The solutions of the A-harmonic equation are called A-harmonic tensors. The following definition of $A_{r,\lambda}(E)$-weights appears in [5], and see [2] for more applications of the two-weight.

Definition 2.1. A pair of weights $(w_1(x), w_2(x))$ satisfies the $A_{r,\lambda}(E)$-condition in a set $E \subset \mathbb{R}^n$, write $(w_1(x), w_2(x)) \in A_{r,\lambda}(E)$, for some $\lambda \ge 1$ and $1 < r < \infty$ with $1/r + 1/r' = 1$ if

$$\sup_{B \subset E} \left(\frac{1}{|B|} \int_B (w_1)^\lambda dx \right)^{1/\lambda r} \left(\frac{1}{|B|} \int_B \left(\frac{1}{w_2} \right)^{\lambda r'/r} dx \right)^{1/\lambda r'} < \infty. \tag{2.4}$$

Lemma 2.2. *Let $0 < \alpha < \infty$, $0 < \beta < \infty$, and $s^{-1} = \alpha^{-1} + \beta^{-1}$. If f and g are measurable functions on $\mathbb{R}^n$, then for any $E \subset \mathbb{R}^n$,*

$$\|fg\|_{s,E} \le \|f\|_{\alpha,E} \cdot \|g\|_{\beta,E}. \tag{2.5}$$

The following weak reverse Hölder inequality appears in [6].

Lemma 2.3. *Let u be an A-harmonic tensor in M, $\rho > 1$, and $0 < s,t < \infty$. Then for all balls or cubes B with $\rho B \subset M$, there exists a constant C, independent of u, such that*

$$\|u\|_{s,B} \le C|B|^{(t-s)/st}\|u\|_{t,\rho B}. \tag{2.6}$$

From [8], we have the following L^p-estimates for the composition $T \circ G$ acted on differential forms.

Lemma 2.4. *Let $u \in L^p_{\text{loc}}(\Lambda^l M)$, $l = 1,2,\dots,n$, $1 < p < \infty$, be a smooth differential form on a manifold M. Then for all balls $B \subset \mathbb{R}^n$, there exists a constant C, independent of u, such that*

$$||T(G(u))||_{p,B} \le C|B|\operatorname{diam}(B)\|u\|_{p,B}, \tag{2.7}$$

$$||\nabla(T(G(u)))||_{p,B} \le C|B|\|u\|_{p,B}, \tag{2.8}$$

$$||T(G(u))||_{W^{1,p}(B)} \le C|B|\|u\|_{p,B}. \tag{2.9}$$

3. Proofs of the main results

In this section, we prove both the local and global two-weight embedding inequalities for the composition $T \circ G$.

Proof of Theorem 1.1. Firstly, we prove inequality (1.1). Let $t = \lambda p/(\lambda - \alpha)$, then $p < t$. Using Lemma 2.2 and inequality (2.7), we obtain

$$\begin{aligned}
\left(\int_B |T(G(u))|^p w_1^\alpha dx\right)^{1/p} &\le \left(\int_B |T(G(u))|^t dx\right)^{1/t}\left(\int_B (w_1^{\alpha/p})^{pt/(t-p)} dx\right)^{(t-p)/(pt)} \\
&\le ||T(G(u))||_{t,B} \cdot \left(\int_B w_1^\lambda dx\right)^{\alpha/(\lambda p)} \\
&\le C_1|B|\operatorname{diam}(B)\|u\|_{t,B}\left(\int_B w_1^\lambda dx\right)^{\alpha/(\lambda p)}.
\end{aligned} \tag{3.1}$$

Choosing $m = \lambda p/(\lambda + \alpha(r-1))$, then $m < p < t$. From Lemma 2.3 and inequality (3.1), we have

$$\begin{aligned}
||T(G(u))||_{p,B,w_1^\alpha} &\le C_1|B|\operatorname{diam}(B)\|u\|_{t,B}\left(\int_B w_1^\lambda dx\right)^{\alpha/(\lambda p)} \\
&\le C_2|B|\operatorname{diam}(B)|B|^{(m-t)/mt}\|u\|_{m,\rho_1 B}\left(\int_B w_1^\lambda dx\right)^{\alpha/(\lambda p)},
\end{aligned} \tag{3.2}$$

where $\rho_1 > 1$. Applying Lemma 2.2 with $1/m = 1/p + (p-m)/pm$ yields

$$\begin{aligned} \|u\|_{m,\rho_1 B} &\leq \left(\int_{\rho_1 B} |u|^p w_2^\alpha dx\right)^{1/p} \left(\int_{\rho_1 B} \left(\frac{1}{w_2}\right)^{\alpha m/(p-m)} dx\right)^{(p-m)/(pm)} \\ &= \|u\|_{p,\rho_1 B, w_2^\alpha} \left(\int_{\rho_1 B} \left(\frac{1}{w_2}\right)^{\lambda/(r-1)} dx\right)^{\alpha(r-1)/(\lambda p)} \end{aligned} \tag{3.3}$$

for all balls B with $\rho_1 B \subset M$. Combining (3.3) and (3.2), we find that

$$\begin{aligned} \|T(G(u))\|_{p,B,w_1^\alpha} &\leq C_2 |B| \operatorname{diam}(B) |B|^{(m-t)/mt} \|u\|_{p,\rho_1 B, w_2^\alpha} \\ &\quad \times \left(\int_B w_1^\lambda dx\right)^{\alpha/(\lambda p)} \left(\int_{\rho_1 B} \left(\frac{1}{w_2}\right)^{\lambda/(r-1)} dx\right)^{\alpha(r-1)/(\lambda p)}. \end{aligned} \tag{3.4}$$

Since $(w_1(x), w_2(x)) \in A_{r,\lambda}(M)$, it follows that

$$\begin{aligned} &\|w_1^\lambda\|_{1,B}^{\alpha/(p\lambda)} \left\| \left(\frac{1}{w_2}\right)^\lambda \right\|_{1/(r-1),\rho_1 B}^{\alpha/(p\lambda)} \\ &\quad \leq \left(\left(\int_{\rho_1 B} w_1^\lambda dx\right) \left(\int_{\rho_1 B} \left(\frac{1}{w_2}\right)^{\lambda/(r-1)} dx\right)^{r-1} \right)^{\alpha/(\lambda p)} \\ &\quad = \left(|\rho_1 B|^r \left(\frac{1}{|\rho_1 B|} \int_{\rho_1 B} w_1^\lambda dx\right) \left(\frac{1}{|\rho_1 B|} \int_{\rho_1 B} \left(\frac{1}{w_2}\right)^{\lambda/(r-1)} dx\right)^{r-1} \right)^{\alpha/(\lambda p)} \\ &\quad \leq C_3 |B|^{\alpha r/(\lambda p)}. \end{aligned} \tag{3.5}$$

Substituting (3.5) into (3.4) with $(m-t)/mt = -\alpha r/\lambda p$, we arrive at the estimate

$$\|T(G(u))\|_{p,B,w_1^\alpha} \leq C_4 |B| \operatorname{diam}(B) \|u\|_{p,\rho_1 B, w_2^\alpha} \tag{3.6}$$

for all balls B with $\rho_1 B \subset M$ and any real number α with $0 < \alpha < \lambda$.

Secondly, based on inequality (2.8), we can get the following inequality (3.7) by the method similar to the proof of inequality (1.1):

$$\|\nabla(T(G(u)))\|_{p,B,w_1^\alpha} \leq C_5 |B| \|u\|_{p,\rho_2 B, w_2^\alpha}. \tag{3.7}$$

Now, let us show inequality (1.2). Combining inequalities (2.1), (1.1), and (3.7) yields

$$\begin{aligned} \|T(G(u))\|_{W^{1,p}(B),w_1^\alpha} &= \operatorname{diam}(B)^{-1} \|T(G(u))\|_{p,B,w_1^\alpha} + \|\nabla(T(G(u)))\|_{p,B,w_1^\alpha} \\ &\leq \operatorname{diam}(B)^{-1} C_4 \operatorname{diam}(B) |B| \|u\|_{p,\rho_1 B, w_2^\alpha} + C_5 |B| \|u\|_{p,\rho_2 B, w_2^\alpha} \\ &\leq C_6 |B| \|u\|_{p,\rho B, w_2^\alpha} \end{aligned} \tag{3.8}$$

with $\rho = \max\{\rho_1, \rho_2\}$. This ends the proof of Theorem 1.1. □

Based on the above results, we can prove the global cases now.

Proof of Theorem 1.2. Since the manifold M is compact, then M is bounded and has a finite open cover $\mathcal{U} = \{B_1, B_2, \dots, B_n\}$. Let $d_i = \operatorname{diam}(B_i)$, $i = 1, 2, \dots, n$, and $d = \min\{d_1, d_2, \dots, d_n\}$. Thus there exists a constant C_1 satisfies

$$\frac{1}{d} \le \frac{C_1}{\operatorname{diam}(M)}. \tag{3.9}$$

Applying inequality (1.1) and (3.9), we conclude that

$$\begin{aligned}
\left(\int_M |T(G(u))|^p w_1^\alpha dx\right)^{1/p} &\le \sum_{B\in\mathcal{U}} \left(\int_B |T(G(u))|^p w_1^\alpha dx\right)^{1/p} \\
&\le \sum_{B\in\mathcal{U}} C_2 |B| \operatorname{diam}(B) \left(\int_{\rho B} |u|^p w_2^\alpha dx\right)^{1/p} \\
&\le \sum_{B\in\mathcal{U}} C_2 |M| \operatorname{diam}(M) \left(\int_M |u|^p w_2^\alpha dx\right)^{1/p} \\
&\le C_3 |M| \operatorname{diam}(M) \left(\int_M |u|^p w_2^\alpha dx\right)^{1/p}.
\end{aligned} \tag{3.10}$$

Hence (1.3) follows. We can prove inequality (1.4) by the similar method used in the proof of inequality (1.2), and we do not list the details here. The proof of Theorem 1.2 is complete. □

4. Some other two-weight inequalities

From [4, 3], we have the following definitions and properties of these two weights.

Definition 4.1. A pair of weights $(w_1(x), w_2(x))$ satisfies $A_r(\lambda, E)$-condition in a set $E \subset \mathbb{R}^n$ for some $r > 1$ and $\lambda > 0$, write $(w_1(x), w_2(x)) \in A_r(\lambda, E)$, if $w_1(x), w_2(x) > 0$ a.e., and satisfies

$$\sup_{B\subset E}\left(\frac{1}{|B|}\int_B w_1^\lambda dx\right)\left(\frac{1}{|B|}\int_B \left(\frac{1}{w_2}\right)^{1/(r-1)} dx\right)^{r-1} < \infty. \tag{4.1}$$

Definition 4.2. A pair of weights $(w_1(x), w_2(x))$ satisfies $A_r^\lambda(E)$-condition in a set $E \subset \mathbb{R}^n$ for some $r > 1$ and $\lambda > 0$, write $(w_1(x), w_2(x)) \in A_r^\lambda(E)$, if $w_1(x), w_2(x) > 0$ a.e., and satisfies

$$\sup_{B\subset E}\left(\frac{1}{|B|}\int_B w_1 dx\right)\left(\frac{1}{|B|}\int_B \left(\frac{1}{w_2}\right)^{1/(r-1)} dx\right)^{\lambda(r-1)} < \infty. \tag{4.2}$$

Note that if we set $w_1(x) = w_2(x) = w(x)$ and $\lambda = 1$ in the above definitions, they become the famous Muckenhoupt weights. Then, we can obtain the following local two-weight embedding inequalities by the method used in the proof of Theorem 1.1.

Theorem 4.3. *Let $u \in L^p_{\text{loc}}(\Lambda^l M, w^\alpha)$, $l = 1,\dots,n$, $1 < p < \infty$, be an A-harmonic tensor on a manifold M. If $\rho > 1$ and $(w_1(x), w_2(x)) \in A_r(\lambda, M)$ for some $\lambda > 0$ and $1 < r$, then there exists a constant C, independent of u, such that*

$$\begin{gathered} \|T(G(u))\|_{p,B,w_1^\alpha} \le C|B|\operatorname{diam}(B)\|u\|_{p,\rho B,w_2^{\alpha/\lambda}}, \\ \|T(G(u))\|_{W^{1,p}(B),w_1^\alpha} \le C|B|\|u\|_{p,\rho B,w_2^{\alpha/\lambda}} \end{gathered} \tag{4.3}$$

for all balls B with $\rho B \subset M$ and any real number α with $0 < \alpha < \lambda$.

Theorem 4.4. *Let $u \in L^p_{\text{loc}}(\Lambda^l M, w^\alpha)$, $l = 1,\dots,n$, be an A-harmonic tensor on a manifold M. Assume that $(w_1(x), w_2(x)) \in A_r^\lambda(M)$ for some $r > 1$ and $\lambda > 0$. If $0 < \alpha < 1$, $\rho > 1$, and $p > \alpha\lambda(r-1)+1$, then there exists a constant C, independent of u, such that*

$$\begin{gathered} \|T(G(u))\|_{p,B,w_1^\alpha} \le C|B|\operatorname{diam}(B)\|u\|_{p,\rho B,w_2^{\alpha\lambda}}, \\ \|T(G(u))\|_{W^{1,p}(B),w_1^\alpha} \le C|B|\|u\|_{p,\rho B,w_2^{\alpha\lambda}} \end{gathered} \tag{4.4}$$

for all balls B with $\rho B \subset M$.

We also can extend the above local L^p-estimates to the global cases, and the proofs are similar to the proof of Theorem 1.2. Considering the length of this paper, we just list the global results according to the two weights here.

Theorem 4.5. *Let $u \in L^p(\Lambda^l M, w^\alpha)$, $l = 1,2,\dots,n$, $1 < p < \infty$, be an A-harmonic form on M. Assume that $(w_1(x), w_2(x)) \in A_r(\lambda, M)$ for some $\lambda > 0$ and $1 < r$. Then there exists a constant C, independent of u, such that*

$$\begin{gathered} \|T(G(u))\|_{p,M,w_1^\alpha} \le C|M|\operatorname{diam}(M)\|u\|_{p,M,w_2^{\alpha/\lambda}}, \\ \|T(G(u))\|_{W^{1,p}(M),w_1^\alpha} \le C|M|\|u\|_{p,M,w_2^{\alpha/\lambda}} \end{gathered} \tag{4.5}$$

for any real number α with $0 < \alpha < \lambda$.

Theorem 4.6. *Let $u \in L^p(\Lambda^l M, w^\alpha)$, $l = 1,2,\dots,n$, be an A-harmonic form on M. Assume that $(w_1(x), w_2(x)) \in A_r^\lambda(M)$ for some $\lambda > 0$, $r > 1$, and $p > \alpha\lambda(r-1)+1$. Then there exists a constant C, independent of u, such that*

$$\begin{gathered} \|T(G(u))\|_{p,M,w_1^\alpha} \le C|M|\operatorname{diam}(M)\|u\|_{p,M,w_2^{\alpha\lambda}}, \\ \|T(G(u))\|_{W^{1,p}(M),w_1^\alpha} \le C|M|\|u\|_{p,M,w_2^{\alpha\lambda}} \end{gathered} \tag{4.6}$$

for any real number α with $0 < \alpha < 1$.

Remark 4.7. (1) We can obtain many interesting versions of local and global L^p-estimates from different choices of weights and parameters α and λ. (2) These results can be used to study the integral properties of the compositions of the operators.

References

[1] R. P. Agarwal and S. Ding, *Advances in differential forms and the A-harmonic equation*, Mathematical and Computer Modelling **37** (2003), no. 12-13, 1393–1426.

[2] D. Cruz-Uribe and C. Pérez, *Two-weight, weak-type norm inequalities for fractional integrals, Calderón-Zygmund operators and commutators*, Indiana University Mathematics Journal **49** (2000), no. 2, 697–721.

[3] S. Ding, *New weighted integral inequalities for differential forms in some domains*, Pacific Journal of Mathematics **194** (2000), no. 1, 43–56.

[4] S. Ding and P. Shi, *Weighted Poincaré-type inequalities for differential forms in $L^S(\mu)$-averaging domains*, Journal of Mathematical Analysis and Applications **227** (1998), no. 1, 200–215.

[5] C. J. Neugebauer, *Inserting A_p-weights*, Proceedings of the American Mathematical Society **87** (1983), no. 4, 644–648.

[6] C. A. Nolder, *Hardy-Littlewood theorems for A-harmonic tensors*, Illinois Journal of Mathematics **43** (1999), no. 4, 613–632.

[7] C. Scott, *L^p theory of differential forms on manifolds*, Transactions of the American Mathematical Society **347** (1995), no. 6, 2075–2096.

[8] Y. Xing and C. Wu, *Global weighted inequalities for operators and harmonic forms on manifolds*, Journal of Mathematical Analysis and Applications **294** (2004), no. 1, 294–309.

Yuming Xing: Department of Mathematics, Harbin Institute of Technology, Harbin 150001, China
E-mail address: xyuming@hit.edu.cn

UNBOUNDEDNESS OF SOLUTIONS OF PLANAR HAMILTONIAN SYSTEMS

XIAOJING YANG

The unboundedness of solutions for the following planar Hamiltonian system: $Ju' = \nabla H(u) + h(t)$ is discussed, where the function $H(u) \in C^3(\mathbb{R}^2, \mathbb{R})$ a.e. in $\mathbb{R}^2$, is positive for $u \neq 0$ and positively homogeneous of degree 2, $h \in L^1[0,2\pi] \times L^1[0,2\pi]$ is 2π-periodic, and J is the standard symplectic matrix.

1. Introduction

We are interested in this paper in the unboundedness of solutions of the planar Hamiltonian system

$$Ju' = \nabla H(u) + h(t), \quad \left({}' = \frac{d}{dt}\right), \tag{1.1}$$

where $H(u) \in C^3(\mathbb{R}^2, \mathbb{R})$ a.e. in $\mathbb{R}^2$ is positive for $u \neq 0$, and positively homogeneous of degree 2, that is, for every $u \in \mathbb{R}^2$, $\lambda > 0$,

$$\begin{gathered} H(\lambda u) = \lambda^2 H(u), \\ \min_{\|u\|=1} H(u) > 0, \end{gathered} \tag{1.2}$$

$h \in L^1[0,2\pi] \times L^1[0,2\pi]$ is 2π-periodic, and $J = \left(\begin{smallmatrix} 0 & -1 \\ 1 & 0 \end{smallmatrix}\right)$ is the standard symplectic matrix.

Under the above conditions, it is easy to see that the origin is an isochronous center for the autonomous system

$$Ju' = \nabla H(u), \tag{1.3}$$

that is, all solutions of (1.3) are periodic with the same minimal period, which will be denoted as τ.

Hindawi Publishing Corporation
Proceedings of the Conference on Differential & Difference Equations and Applications, pp. 1167–1176

Throughout this paper, we denote by $\langle a,b\rangle$ the scale product of the vectors a, b. The boundedness problem of solutions of second-order differential equations has been discussed by many authors, for example, the linear equation

$$x'' + n^2x = \cos nt, \quad n \in \mathbb{N}, \tag{1.4}$$

has no bounded solution. The next example is due to Ding [3], he showed that the equation

$$x'' + n^2x + \arctan x = 4\cos nt, \quad n \in \mathbb{N}, \tag{1.5}$$

has no 2π-periodic solution. Therefore, by Massera's theorem [12], we know that all the solutions of the above equation are unbounded.

In 1996, Ortega [15] considered the equation

$$x'' + \alpha x^+ - \beta x^- = 1 + \varepsilon h(t), \quad \alpha \neq \beta, \tag{1.6}$$

where α, β are positive constants and h is a smooth 2π-periodic function. He proved that if $|\varepsilon|$ is sufficiently small, then all the solutions of (1.6) are bounded. This result is in contrast with the well-known fact of linear resonance that occurs in the case $\alpha = \beta = n^2$ for some $n \in \mathbb{N}$. For example, all the solutions of

$$x'' + n^2x = 1 + \varepsilon\cos nt \tag{1.7}$$

are unbounded if $\varepsilon \neq 0$.

Let $C(t)$ be the solution of the following initial value problem:

$$x'' + ax^+ - bx^- = 0, \quad x(0) = 0, \quad x'(0) = 1, \tag{1.8}$$

where

$$\frac{1}{\sqrt{a}} + \frac{1}{\sqrt{b}} = \frac{2m}{n}, \quad m,n \in \mathbb{N}. \tag{1.9}$$

In [10], Liu proved the boundedness of all the solutions of

$$x'' + ax^+ - bx^- = h(t) \tag{1.10}$$

under the condition that $h \in C^6(S^1)$, ($S^1 =: R/2\pi\mathbb{Z}$) and the $2\pi/n$-periodic function

$$\Phi_h(\theta) = \int_0^{2\pi} h(mt)C(\theta + mt)dt \tag{1.11}$$

has no zero for all $\theta \in S^1$.

In contrast to Liu's result, Alonso and Ortega [2] proved that if $\Phi_h(\theta)$ has only finite zeros $\{\theta_i\}$ and every zero of it is simple, that is, $\Phi_h'(\theta_i) \neq 0$ if $\Phi_h(\theta_i) = 0$, then all the solutions of (1.10) with large initial values, that is, $|x(t_0)| + |x'(t_0)| \gg 1$, are unbounded.

Fabry and Mawhin [5] consider the behavior of the solutions of the following more general equation:

$$x'' + ax^+ - bx^- = f(x) + g(x) + h(t), \tag{1.12}$$

where $a > 0$, $b > 0$, $a^{-1/2} + b^{-1/2} = 2/n$, $n \in \mathbb{N}$, f is bounded, and the limits

$$\lim_{x \to +\infty} f(x) = f(+\infty), \qquad \lim_{x \to -\infty} f(x) = f(-\infty) \tag{1.13}$$

exist, g is bounded and satisfies

$$\lim_{|x| \to \infty} \int_0^x \frac{g(s)ds}{x} = 0. \tag{1.14}$$

Let

$$\phi_h(\theta) = \frac{n}{\pi}\left(\frac{f(+\infty)}{a} - \frac{f(-\infty)}{b}\right) + \frac{1}{2\pi\sqrt{a}} \int_0^{2\pi} h(t)C(\theta + t)dt, \tag{1.15}$$

they showed that any solution $x(t)$ of (1.12) is unbounded if $|x(0)| + |x'(0)| \gg 1$ and $\phi_h(\theta)$ has finite zeros and all of them are simple. But one would ask the following question: what will happen if the function $\phi_h(\theta)$ has multiple zeros or is a zero function? In this paper, we will consider the unboundedness of the solutions of (1.1) and give some sufficient conditions for the unboundedness of all the solutions of (1.1) with large initial value, that is, those solutions $u(t)$ of (1.1) satisfying $u(0) = u_0$ and $\|u_0\| \gg 1$. For more recent results on boundedness and unboundedness of solutions of the form $x'' + g(x) = f(t)$ or more general quasilinear differential equations, we refer to [1, 4, 6–11, 13, 14, 16–21] and the references therein.

Let $\phi(t)$ be the solution of (1.3) satisfying

$$H(\phi(t)) = \frac{1}{2}, \quad \forall t \in \mathbb{R}. \tag{1.16}$$

The main results of this paper are the following.

THEOREM 1.1. *Suppose that $\omega = 2\pi/\tau = n/m \in \mathbb{Q}^+$ for some $n, m \in \mathbb{N}$. Define 2π-periodic functions λ_1, μ_1, λ_3 as*

$$\lambda_1(\theta) = \frac{n}{m} \int_0^{2m\pi} \left\langle h(t), \phi\left(\frac{m\theta}{n} + t\right)\right\rangle dt,$$

$$\mu_1(\theta) = -\int_0^{2m\pi} \left\langle h(t), \phi''\left(\frac{m\theta}{n} + t\right)\right\rangle \int_0^t \left\langle h(s), \phi\left(\frac{m\theta}{n} + s\right)\right\rangle ds\,dt, \tag{1.17}$$

$$\lambda_3(\theta) = \alpha(\theta) - \frac{n}{2m} \int_0^{2m\pi} \left\langle h(t), \phi''\left(\frac{m\theta}{n} + t\right)\right\rangle \left(\int_0^t \left\langle h(s), \phi\left(\frac{m\theta}{n} + s\right)\right\rangle ds\right)^2 dt,$$

where

$$\alpha(\theta) = \lambda_1(\theta)[(\lambda_1'(\theta))^2 - \mu_1(\theta)]. \tag{1.18}$$

Then any solution of (1.1) with large initial value goes to infinity either in the future or in the past, provided that one of the following conditions holds.

(I) *The function* $\lambda_1(\theta)$ *has only finite zeros in* $S^1 =: \mathbb{R}/2\pi\mathbb{Z}$. *Let*

$$\Omega = \Omega_1 \cup \Omega_2 \subset S^1 \tag{1.19}$$

be the set of zeros of $\lambda_1(\theta)$, *where*

$$\begin{aligned} \Omega_1 &= \{\theta_i : \lambda_1(\theta_i) = 0,\ \lambda_1'(\theta_i) \neq 0\}, \\ \Omega_2 &= \{\theta_j : \lambda_1(\theta_j) = 0,\ \lambda_1'(\theta_j) = 0\}, \end{aligned} \tag{1.20}$$

and for each $\theta_j \in \Omega_2$, *one has* $\mu_1(\theta_j) \neq 0$ *and* $\lambda_1'(\theta)\mu_1(\theta) \leq 0$ *holds in a neighborhood of* θ_j.

(II) $\lambda_1(\theta) \equiv 0$ *and* $\lambda_3(\theta)$ *has only finite zeros* $\{\theta_i\}_{i=1}^k \in S^1$. *For each zero* θ_i *of* λ_3, *one has* $\mu_1(\theta_i) \neq 0$ *and*

$$\mu_1(\theta_i)\lambda_3(\theta)(\theta - \theta_i) < 0 \quad \text{for } 0 < \|\theta - \theta_i\| \ll 1. \tag{1.21}$$

(III) $\lambda_1(\theta) = \mu_1(\theta) \equiv 0$ *and* $\lambda_3(\theta)$ *has only finite zeros in* S^1 *and all of them are simple.*

(IV) $\lambda_1'(\theta) \equiv 0$, $\mu_1(\theta)$ *has no zero in* S^1.

Theorem 1.2. *Assume that* $H \in C^2$, $\omega \in \mathbb{R}^+ \setminus \mathbb{Q}$. *Define* 2π*-periodic functions* $\overline{\lambda}_1(\theta)$, $\overline{\mu}_1(\theta)$ *as*

$$\begin{aligned} \overline{\lambda}_1(\theta) &= \omega \int_0^{2\pi} \left\langle h(t), \phi\left(\frac{\theta}{\omega} + t\right)\right\rangle dt, \\ \overline{\mu}_1(\theta) &= -\int_0^{2\pi} \left\langle h(t), \phi''\left(\frac{\theta}{\omega} + t\right)\right\rangle \int_0^t \left\langle h(s), \phi\left(\frac{\theta}{\omega} + s\right)\right\rangle ds\, dt. \end{aligned} \tag{1.22}$$

If

$$\overline{\lambda}_1'(\theta) \equiv 0, \qquad \int_0^{2\pi} \overline{\mu}_1(\theta)d\theta \neq 0, \tag{1.23}$$

then any solution of (1.1) with large initial value goes to infinity either in the future or in the past.

Remark 1.3. We say that $u(t)$ goes to infinity in the future if $\lim_{t\to\infty} \|u(t)\| = \infty$, and $u(t)$ goes to infinity in the past if $\lim_{t\to-\infty} \|u(t)\| = \infty$.

2. Generalized polar coordinates transformation

Since H is positively homogeneous of degree 2, by Euler's identity, for every $u \in \mathbb{R}^2$,

$$\langle \nabla H(u), u\rangle = 2H(u). \tag{2.1}$$

Let $\phi(t)$ be a solution of (1.3) satisfying (1.16) with the minimal period τ.

For $r > 0$, $\theta(\mathrm{mod}\, 2\pi) \in \mathbb{R}$, we define the generalized polar coordinates transformation $T:(r,\theta) \to u$ as

$$u = r\phi\left(\frac{\theta}{\omega}\right), \tag{2.2}$$

where $\omega = 2\pi/\tau$. Then the map T is a diffeomorphism from the half plane $\{r > 0\}$ to $\mathbb{R}^2 \backslash \{(0,0)\}$, the functions r, θ are of C^3 almost everywhere in $(0,\infty) \times \mathbb{R}$ as far as $u(t)$ does not cross the origin. Substituting (2.6) in to (1.1) yields

$$r' J\phi + \frac{r\theta'}{\omega} J\phi' = r\nabla H(\phi) + h. \tag{2.3}$$

Since for any $u \in \mathbb{R}^2$, $\langle Ju, u\rangle = 0$. By Euler's identity (1.3), (1.16), and (2.1), a scalar product in (2.3) with ϕ yields

$$\frac{r\theta'}{\omega} = r + \langle h, \phi\rangle, \tag{2.4}$$

while a scalar product with ϕ' yields

$$-r' = \langle h, \phi'\rangle. \tag{2.5}$$

Therefore for $u(t) \neq 0$, we get

$$\begin{aligned} \theta' &= \omega(1 + r^{-1}\langle h, \phi\rangle), \\ r' &= -\langle h, \phi'\rangle, \end{aligned} \tag{2.6}$$

where

$$h = h(t), \qquad \phi = \phi\left(\frac{\theta}{\omega}\right), \qquad \phi' = \phi'\left(\frac{\theta}{\omega}\right). \tag{2.7}$$

Let $(\theta(t;\theta_0,r_0), r(t;\theta_0,r_0))$ be the solution of (2.6) with initial value (θ_0,r_0). Then for $r_0 \gg 1$, by the assumption that $h \in L^1(0,2\pi) \times L^1(0,2\pi)$, we get for $t \in [0,T]$, where $T > 0$ is any fixed number,

$$r(t) = r_0 + O(1), \qquad r^{-1}(t) = r_0^{-1} + O(r_0^{-2}), \qquad \theta(t) = \theta_0 + \omega t + O(r_0^{-1}). \tag{2.8}$$

For the proof of theorems, we need the following lemmas (the proofs are omitted).

Lemma 2.1. *Let $\omega = n/m \in \mathbb{Q}$ for some $n, m \in \mathbb{N}$. Then, for $r_0 \gg 1$, the Poincaré map*

$$P:(\theta_0,r_0) \longrightarrow (\theta_1,r_1) = (\theta(2m\pi;\theta_0,r_0),\ r(2m\pi;\theta_0,r_0)) \tag{2.9}$$

of the solution of (2.6) with initial value (θ_0,r_0) has the following asymptotic expression:

$$\begin{aligned} \theta_1 &= \theta_0 + 2n\pi + \lambda_1(\theta_0)r_0^{-1} + \lambda_1(\theta_0)\lambda_1'(\theta_0)r_0^{-2} + \lambda_3(\theta_0)r_0^{-3} + O(r_0^{-4}), \\ r_1 &= r_0 - \lambda_1'(\theta_0) + \mu_1(\theta_0)r_0^{-1} + (\lambda_3'(\theta_0) - \alpha'(\theta_0))r_0^{-2} + O(r_0^{-3}), \end{aligned} \tag{2.10}$$

where λ_1, μ_1, λ_3, and α are given by Theorem 1.1.

LEMMA 2.2. *Let $\omega \in \mathbb{R}^+\backslash\mathbb{Q}$. Then, for $r_0 \gg 1$, the Poincaré map*

$$P : (\theta_0, r_0) \longrightarrow (\theta_1, r_1) = (\theta(2\pi;\theta_0,r_0),\, r(2\pi;\theta_0,r_0)) \tag{2.11}$$

of the solution of (2.6) with initial value (θ_0, r_0) has the following asymptotic expression:

$$\begin{aligned}\theta_1 &= \theta_0 + 2\omega\pi + \overline{\lambda}_1(\theta_0)r_0^{-1} + O(r_0^{-2}),\\ r_1 &= r_0 - \overline{\lambda}_1'(\theta_0) + \overline{\mu}_1(\theta_0)r_0^{-1} + O(r_0^{-2}),\end{aligned} \tag{2.12}$$

where $\overline{\lambda}_1(\theta)$, $\overline{\mu}_1(\theta)$ are given in (1.22).

3. Planar mappings and unbounded motions

In this section, we adopt the notations used in [2]. Given $\sigma > 0$, let the set E_σ be the exterior of the open ball B_σ centered at the origin and of radius σ, that is,

$$E_\sigma = R^2 - B_\sigma, \tag{3.1}$$

then $E_\sigma = \{(\theta, r) \mid r \geq \sigma\}$. Define $S^1 = R/2\pi Z$, then the points in S^1 are defined by

$$\bar{\theta} = \theta + 2k\pi, \quad k \in Z,\, \theta \in R, \tag{3.2}$$

and the group distance in S^1 is defined by

$$\|\theta\| = \|\bar{\theta}\| = \min\{|\theta + 2k\pi| \mid k \in Z\}. \tag{3.3}$$

Let $\bar{P} : E_\sigma \to R^2$ be a mapping that is one to one and continuous. We assume that its lift, denoted by P, can be expressed in the following form:

$$\begin{aligned}\theta_1 &= \theta_0 + 2m\pi + \lambda_i(\theta_0)r_0^{-i} + F_i(\theta_0, r_0),\\ r_1 &= r_0 + \mu_j(\theta_0)r_0^{-j} + G_j(\theta_0, r_0)\end{aligned} \tag{3.4}$$

for $r_0 \gg 1$, $\theta_0 \in S^1$, and $\lambda_i, \mu_j \in C(S^1)$, $m, i \in \mathbb{N}$, $j \geq 0$, $F_i = o(r_0^{-i})$, $G_j = o(r_0^{-j})$ uniformly in θ_0, are continuous and 2π-periodic in θ_0. Given a point $(\theta_0, r_0) \in E_\sigma$, let $\{(\theta_k, r_k)\}_{k\in I}$ be the unique solution of the initial value problem for the difference equation

$$(\theta_{k+1}, r_{k+1}) = P(\theta_k, r_k). \tag{3.5}$$

This solution is defined in a maximal interval

$$I = \{k \in Z \mid k_a < k < k_b\}, \tag{3.6}$$

where k_a, k_b are certain numbers in the set $Z \cup \{+\infty, -\infty\}$ satisfying

$$-\infty \leq k_a < 0 < k_b \leq +\infty. \tag{3.7}$$

The solution $\{(\theta_k, r_k)\}$ is said to be defined in the future if $k_b = +\infty$, and is said to be defined in the past if $k_a = -\infty$.

LEMMA 3.1. *Consider the mapping (3.4). Assume the function $\lambda_i(\theta)$ has an isolated zero $\theta^* \in S^1$. If*

$$\mu_j(\theta^*) > 0, \quad \lambda_i(\theta)(\theta - \theta^*) < 0 \quad \text{for } 0 < \|\theta - \theta^*\| \ll 1. \tag{3.8}$$

Then there exist $\varepsilon > 0$ and $R_0 \geq \sigma$ such that if $\|\theta_0 - \theta^*\| < \varepsilon$ and $r_0 \geq R_0$, the solution $\{(\theta_k, r_k)\}$ is defined in the future and satisfies

$$\lim_{n \to +\infty} r_n = +\infty. \tag{3.9}$$

LEMMA 3.2. *Consider the mapping (3.4). Assume the function $\lambda_i(\theta)$ has an isolated zero $\theta^* \in S^1$. If*

$$\mu_j(\theta^*) < 0, \quad \lambda_i(\theta)(\theta - \theta^*) > 0 \quad \text{for } 0 < \|\theta - \theta^*\| \ll 1. \tag{3.10}$$

Then there exist $\varepsilon > 0$ and $R_0 \geq \sigma$ such that if $\|\theta_0 - \theta^*\| < \varepsilon$ and $r_0 \geq R_0$, the solution $\{(\theta_k, r_k)\}$ is defined in the past and satisfies

$$\lim_{n \to -\infty} r_n = +\infty. \tag{3.11}$$

LEMMA 3.3. *Consider the following mapping:*

$$\begin{aligned} \theta_1 &= \theta_0 + 2m\pi + \lambda_i(\theta_0) r_0^{-i} + F_i(\theta_0, r_0), \\ r_1 &= r_0 - \lambda_i'(\theta_0) r_0^{-(i-1)} + \mu_j(\theta_0) r_0^{-j} + G_j(\theta_0, r_0), \end{aligned} \tag{3.12}$$

where $m, i, j \in \mathbb{N}$, $0 \leq i \leq j$, $\lambda_i \in C^1(S^1)$, $\mu_j \in C(S^1)$, $F_i = o(r_0^{-i})$, $G_j = o(r_0^{-j})$ uniformly in θ_0, are 2π-periodic in θ_0 and continuous. If the function $\lambda_i(\theta)$ has only finitely zeros, $\{\theta_i\}_{i=1}^{n_0} =: \Omega \in S^1$ and $\Omega = \Omega_1 \cup \Omega_2$ with

$$\begin{aligned} \lambda_i'(\theta_i) &\neq 0, \quad \forall \theta_i \in \Omega_1, \\ \lambda_i'(\theta_j) &= 0, \quad \forall \theta_j \in \Omega_2. \end{aligned} \tag{3.13}$$

If for each $\theta_j \in \Omega_2$, $\mu_j(\theta_j) \neq 0$ and $\lambda_i'(\theta)\mu_j(\theta) \leq 0$ holds in a neighborhood of θ_j, then there exists $R_0 \geq \sigma$ such that if $r_0 \geq R_0$, then for any $\theta_0 \in S^1$ such that $\|\theta_0 - \theta_j\| \ll 1$, the orbit $\{(\theta_k, r_k)\}$ is either defined in the future and satisfies

$$r_k \longrightarrow +\infty \quad \text{as } k \longrightarrow +\infty, \tag{3.14}$$

or is defined in the past and satisfies

$$r_k \longrightarrow +\infty \quad \text{as } k \longrightarrow -\infty. \tag{3.15}$$

LEMMA 3.4. *Consider the following mapping:*

$$\begin{aligned} \theta_1 &= \theta_0 + 2m\pi + \lambda_i(\theta_0) r_0^{-i} + F_i(\theta_0, r_0), \\ r_1 &= r_0 + \mu_j(\theta_0) r_0^{-j} + G_j(\theta_0, r_0), \end{aligned} \tag{3.16}$$

where $m,i,j \in \mathbb{N}$, $j < i$, $\theta_0 \in S^1$, $\lambda_i,\mu_j \in C(S^1)$ with $F_i = o(r_0^{-i})$, $G_j = o(r_0^{-j})$ uniformly in θ_0 are continuous and 2π-periodic in θ_0. If the function $\lambda_i(\theta)$ has only finite zeros $\{\theta_k\}_{k=1}^{M} =: \Omega \in S^1$ and for each $\theta_k \in \Omega$, $\mu_j(\theta_k) \neq 0$ and

$$\mu_j(\theta_k)\lambda_i(\theta)(\theta - \theta_k) < 0 \quad \text{for } 0 < \|\theta - \theta_k\| \ll 1. \tag{3.17}$$

Then there exists $R_0 \geq \sigma$ such that if $r_0 \geq R_0$, then for any $\theta_0 \in S^1$ with $\|\theta_0 - \theta_k\| \ll 1$, the orbit $\{(\theta_n, r_n)\}_{n=1}^{\infty}$ is either defined in the future and satisfies

$$r_n \longrightarrow +\infty \quad \text{as } n \longrightarrow +\infty, \tag{3.18}$$

or is defined in the past and satisfies

$$r_n \longrightarrow +\infty \quad \text{as } n \longrightarrow -\infty. \tag{3.19}$$

Lemma 3.5. *Let $r_0 \gg 1$, consider the following mapping:*

$$\begin{aligned} \theta_1 &= \theta_0 + 2\omega\pi + \lambda_i(\theta_0)r_0^{-i} + F_i(\theta_0, r_0), \\ r_1 &= r_0 + \mu_j(\theta_0)r_0^{-j} + G_j(\theta_0, r_0), \end{aligned} \tag{3.20}$$

where $\omega \in \mathbb{R}^+\backslash\mathbb{Q}$, $i > 0$, $j \geq 0$, $\theta_0 \in S^1$, and $\lambda_i,\mu_j \in C(S^1)$, $F_i = o(r_0^{-i})$, $G_j = o(r_0^{-j})$ uniformly in θ_0, are continuous and 2π-periodic in θ_0. If

$$\int_0^{2\pi} \mu_j(\theta)d\theta > 0, \tag{3.21}$$

then there exists $R_0 \geq \sigma$ such that if $r_0 \geq R_0$, the orbit $\{(\theta_n, r_n)\}$ of (3.20) with initial value (θ_0, r_0) is defined in the future and satisfies

$$\lim_{n \to +\infty} r_n = +\infty. \tag{3.22}$$

If

$$\int_0^{2\pi} \mu_j(\theta)d\theta < 0, \tag{3.23}$$

then there exists $R_0 > \sigma$ such that if $r_0 \geq R_0$, $\theta_0 \in S^1$, the orbit $\{(\theta_n, r_n)\}$ of (3.20) is defined in the past and satisfies

$$\lim_{n \to -\infty} r_n = +\infty. \tag{3.24}$$

4. Proof of the theorems

Proof of Theorem 1.1. It follows from Lemma 2.1 that the Poincaré map $P : (\theta_0, r_0) \to (\theta_1, r_1)$ of the solutions of (2.6) has the form of (2.10).

In case (I), (2.10) has the form of (3.4) with $i = 1$, $j = 0$, $\mu_j(\theta) = -\lambda_1'(\theta)$. If $\theta_i \in \Omega_1$, then Lemmas 3.1 and 3.2 apply, if $\theta_j \in \Omega_2$, then (2.10) has the form of (3.12) with $i = 1$, $j = 1$, and Lemma 3.3 applies.

In case (II), (2.10) has the following form:

$$\begin{aligned}\theta_1 &= \theta_0 + 2n\pi + \lambda_3(\theta_0)r_0^{-3} + O(r_0^{-4}),\\ r_1 &= r_0 + \mu_1(\theta_0)r_0^{-1} + \lambda_3'(\theta_0)r_0^{-2} + O(r_0^{-3}).\end{aligned} \tag{4.1}$$

Now, Lemma 3.4 with $i = 3$, $j = 1$ applies in this situation.

In case (III), (2.10) has the form of

$$\begin{aligned}\theta_1 &= \theta_0 + 2n\pi + \lambda_3(\theta_0)r_0^{-3} + O(r_0^{-4}),\\ r_1 &= r_0 + \lambda_3'(\theta_0)r_0^{-2} + O(r_0^{-3}).\end{aligned} \tag{4.2}$$

Lemmas 3.1 and 3.2 with $i = 3$, $j = 2$, $\mu_2(\theta) \equiv \lambda_3'(\theta)$ are applicable.

Finally, in case (IV), since $\mu_1(\theta)$ has no zero, we have either

$$0 < 2c_0 =: \min_{\theta\in S^1}\mu_1(\theta) \le \max_{\theta\in S^1}\mu_1(\theta) =: c_1 < \infty \tag{4.3}$$

or

$$-2d_0 =: \min_{\theta\in S^1}\mu_1(\theta) \le \max_{\theta\in S^1}\mu_1(\theta) =: -d_1 < 0. \tag{4.4}$$

In the former case, for $r_0 \gg 1$, we have

$$r_1 = r_0 + \mu_1(\theta_0)r_0^{-1} + O(r_0^{-2}) \ge r_0 + c_0 r_0^{-1} > r_0, \tag{4.5}$$

$$r_1 \le r_0 + 2c_1 r_0^{-1}. \tag{4.6}$$

By induction, we can show for each $n \in \mathbb{N}$,

$$r_n \le r_0 + 2nc_1 r_0^{-1} \tag{4.7}$$

which implies that r_n is defined in the future. Replacing r_0 by r_n and r_1 by r_{n+1} in (4.5), we get

$$r_{n+1} \ge r_n + c_0 r_n^{-1} \tag{4.8}$$

which implies that

$$\lim_{n\to\infty} r_n = \infty. \tag{4.9}$$

(Otherwise, if $r^* = \lim_{n\to\infty} r_n < \infty$ by taking limits on both sides of (4.8), we get $r^* > r^*$, a contraction.)

Similarly, we can prove that in the later case, r_n is defined in the past and satisfies

$$\lim_{n\to-\infty} r_n = \infty. \tag{4.10}$$

□

Proof of Theorem 1.2. Theorem 1.2 is a direct consequence of Lemma 3.5 with $i = 3$, $j = 1$, and λ_3, μ_1 are replaced by $\overline{\lambda}_3$, $\overline{\mu}_1$, respectively. □

References

[1] J. M. Alonso and R. Ortega, *Unbounded solutions of semilinear equations at resonance*, Nonlinearity **9** (1996), no. 5, 1099–1111.

[2] ______, *Roots of unity and unbounded motions of an asymmetric oscillator*, Journal of Differential Equations **143** (1998), no. 1, 201–220.

[3] T. R. Ding, *Nonlinear oscillations at a point of resonance*, Scientia Sinica. Series A **25** (1982), no. 9, 918–931.

[4] C. Fabry and A. Fonda, *Nonlinear resonance in asymmetric oscillators*, Journal of Differential Equations **147** (1998), no. 1, 58–78.

[5] C. Fabry and J. Mawhin, *Oscillations of a forced asymmetric oscillator at resonance*, Nonlinearity **13** (2000), no. 3, 493–505.

[6] A. Fonda, *Positively homogeneous Hamiltonian systems in the plane*, Journal of Differential Equations **200** (2004), no. 1, 162–184.

[7] M. Kunze, T. Küpper, and B. Liu, *Boundedness and unboundedness of solutions for reversible oscillators at resonance*, Nonlinearity **14** (2001), no. 5, 1105–1122.

[8] M. Levi, *Quasiperiodic motions in superquadratic time-periodic potentials*, Communications in Mathematical Physics **143** (1991), no. 1, 43–83.

[9] J. E. Littlewood, *Some Problems in Real and Complex Analysis*, D. C. Heath, Massachusetts, 1968.

[10] B. Liu, *Boundedness in asymmetric oscillations*, Journal of Mathematical Analysis and Applications **231** (1999), no. 2, 355–373.

[11] ______, *Boundedness in nonlinear oscillations at resonance*, Journal of Differential Equations **153** (1999), no. 1, 142–174.

[12] J. L. Massera, *The existence of periodic solutions of systems of differential equations*, Duke Mathematical Journal **17** (1950), 457–475.

[13] G. R. Morris, *A case of boundedness in Littlewood's problem on oscillatory differential equations*, Bulletin of the Australian Mathematical Society **14** (1976), no. 1, 71–93.

[14] J. W. Norris, *Boundedness in periodically forced second order conservative systems*, Journal of the London Mathematical Society. Second Series **45** (1992), no. 1, 97–112.

[15] R. Ortega, *Asymmetric oscillators and twist mappings*, Journal of the London Mathematical Society. Second Series **53** (1996), no. 2, 325–342.

[16] ______, *Boundedness in a piecewise linear oscillator and a variant of the small twist theorem*, Proceedings of the London Mathematical Society. Third Series **79** (1999), no. 2, 381–413.

[17] P. Walters, *An Introduction to Ergodic Theory*, Graduate Texts in Mathematics, vol. 79, Springer, New York, 1982.

[18] Z. Wang, *Irrational rotation numbers and unboundedness of solutions of the second order differential equations with asymmetric nonlinearities*, Proceedings of the American Mathematical Society **131** (2003), no. 2, 523–531.

[19] X. Yang, *Boundedness in nonlinear asymmetric oscillations*, Journal of Differential Equations **183** (2002), no. 1, 108–131.

[20] ______, *Boundedness of solutions of a class of nonlinear systems*, Mathematical Proceedings of the Cambridge Philosophical Society **136** (2004), no. 1, 185–193.

[21] ______, *Unboundedness of the large solutions of an asymmetric oscillator*, Journal of Mathematical Analysis and Applications **303** (2005), no. 1, 304–314.

Xiaojing Yang: Department of Mathematics, Tsinghua University, Beijing 100084, China
E-mail address: yangxj@mail.tsinghua.edu.cn

PICONE-TYPE INEQUALITIES FOR A CLASS OF QUASILINEAR ELLIPTIC EQUATIONS AND THEIR APPLICATIONS

NORIO YOSHIDA

Picone-type inequalities are established for quasilinear elliptic equations with first-order terms, and oscillation results are obtained for forced superlinear elliptic equations and superlinear-sublinear elliptic equations.

1. Introduction

There is an increasing interest in oscillation problems for half-linear differential equations. There are many papers dealing with half-linear partial differential equations (see, e.g., Bognár and Došlý [1], Došlý and Mařík [2], Dunninger [3], Kusano et al. [6], Mařík [7], Yoshida [8], and the references cited therein). Superlinear elliptic equations with p-Laplacian principal part and superlinear-sublinear elliptic equations were studied by Jaroš et al. [4, 5]. Picone identity or inequality plays an important role in establishing Sturmian comparison and oscillation theorems for partial differential equations.

The objective of this paper is to establish Picone-type inequalities for quasilinear partial differential operators P and $\widetilde{P}$ defined by

$$\begin{aligned} P[v] &\equiv \nabla \cdot (A(x)|\nabla v|^{\alpha-1}\nabla v) + (\alpha+1)|\nabla v|^{\alpha-1}B(x) \cdot \nabla v + C(x)|v|^{\beta-1}v, \\ \widetilde{P}[v] &\equiv \nabla \cdot (A(x)|\nabla v|^{\alpha-1}\nabla v) + (\alpha+1)|\nabla v|^{\alpha-1}B(x) \cdot \nabla v \\ &\quad + C(x)|v|^{\beta-1}v + D(x)|v|^{\gamma-1}v, \end{aligned} \tag{1.1}$$

where α, β, and γ are constants satisfying $\alpha > 0$, $\beta > \alpha$, $0 < \gamma < \alpha$, and to employ the inequalities thus obtained to derive oscillation theorems for the forced quasilinear elliptic equation

$$P[v] = f(x) \tag{1.2}$$

Hindawi Publishing Corporation
Proceedings of the Conference on Differential & Difference Equations and Applications, pp. 1177–1185

and the quasilinear elliptic equation

$$\widetilde{P}[v] = 0. \tag{1.3}$$

In Section 2 we establish Picone-type inequality for (1.2), and in Section 3 we derive oscillation results for (1.2) in an unbounded domain $\Omega \subset \mathbb{R}^n$. Sections 4 and 5 concern Picone-type inequality and oscillation results for (1.3).

2. Picone-type inequality for (1.2)

Let G be a bounded domain in $\mathbb{R}^n$ with piecewise smooth boundary ∂G. It is assumed that

(A_1) $A(x) \in C(\overline{G};(0,\infty))$, $B(x) \in C(\overline{G};\mathbb{R})$, and $C(x) \in C(\overline{G};[0,\infty))$;

(A_2) $f(x) \in C(\overline{G};\mathbb{R})$.

The domain $\mathcal{D}_P(G)$ of P is defined to be the set of all functions v of class $C^1(\overline{G};\mathbb{R})$ with the property that $A(x)|\nabla v|^{\alpha-1}\nabla v \in C^1(G;\mathbb{R}) \cap C(\overline{G};\mathbb{R})$.

Theorem 2.1. *If $v \in \mathcal{D}_P(G)$, $v \neq 0$ in G, and $v \cdot f(x) \leq 0$ in G, then the following Picone-type inequality holds for any $u \in C^1(G;\mathbb{R})$:*

$$\begin{aligned}
&-\nabla\cdot\left(u\varphi(u)\frac{A(x)\Phi(\nabla v)}{\varphi(v)}\right)\\
&\quad\geq -A(x)\left|\nabla u - \frac{u}{A(x)}B(x)\right|^{\alpha+1} + \frac{\beta}{\alpha}\left(\frac{\beta-\alpha}{\alpha}\right)^{(\alpha-\beta)/\beta} C(x)^{\alpha/\beta}|f(x)|^{(\beta-\alpha)/\beta}|u|^{\alpha+1}\\
&\qquad + A(x)\bigg[\left(\nabla u - \frac{u}{A(x)}B(x)\right)\cdot\Phi\left(\nabla u - \frac{u}{A(x)}B(x)\right) + \alpha\left(\frac{u}{v}\nabla v\right)\cdot\Phi\left(\frac{u}{v}\nabla v\right)\\
&\qquad\quad - (\alpha+1)\left(\nabla u - \frac{u}{A(x)}B(x)\right)\cdot\Phi\left(\frac{u}{v}\nabla v\right)\bigg] - \frac{u\varphi(u)}{\varphi(v)}(P[v]-f(x)),
\end{aligned} \tag{2.1}$$

where $\varphi(s) = |s|^{\alpha-1}s$ ($s \in \mathbb{R}$) and $\Phi(\xi) = |\xi|^{\alpha-1}\xi$ ($\xi \in \mathbb{R}^n$).

Proof. The following identity holds:

$$\begin{aligned}
&-\nabla\cdot\left(u\varphi(u)\frac{A(x)\Phi(\nabla v)}{\varphi(v)}\right)\\
&\quad= -A(x)\left|\nabla u - \frac{u}{A(x)}B(x)\right|^{\alpha+1}\\
&\qquad + A(x)\bigg[\left(\nabla u - \frac{u}{A(x)}B(x)\right)\cdot\Phi\left(\nabla u - \frac{u}{A(x)}B(x)\right)\\
&\qquad\quad + \alpha\left(\frac{u}{v}\nabla v\right)\cdot\Phi\left(\frac{u}{v}\nabla v\right) - (\alpha+1)\left(\nabla u - \frac{u}{A(x)}B(x)\right)\cdot\Phi\left(\frac{u}{v}\nabla v\right)\bigg]\\
&\qquad - \frac{u\varphi(u)}{\varphi(v)}\left(\nabla\cdot\left(A(x)|\nabla v|^{\alpha-1}\nabla v\right) + (\alpha+1)|\nabla v|^{\alpha-1}B(x)\cdot\nabla v\right)
\end{aligned} \tag{2.2}$$

(see Yoshida [8, Theorem 1.1]). It is easy to check that

$$\begin{aligned}&\nabla\cdot(A(x)|\nabla v|^{\alpha-1}\nabla v)+(\alpha+1)|\nabla v|^{\alpha-1}B(x)\cdot\nabla v\\&\quad=P[v]-f(x)+f(x)-C(x)|v|^{\beta-1}v\end{aligned}\tag{2.3}$$

and therefore

$$\begin{aligned}&\frac{u\varphi(u)}{\varphi(v)}(\nabla\cdot(A(x)|\nabla v|^{\alpha-1}\nabla v)+(\alpha+1)|\nabla v|^{\alpha-1}B(x)\cdot\nabla v)\\&\quad=\frac{u\varphi(u)}{\varphi(v)}(P[v]-f(x)+f(x)-C(x)|v|^{\beta-1}v)\\&\quad=\frac{u\varphi(u)}{\varphi(v)}(P[v]-f(x))-u\varphi(u)\left(C(x)\frac{|v|^{\beta-1}v}{\varphi(v)}-\frac{f(x)}{\varphi(v)}\right)\\&\quad=\frac{u\varphi(u)}{\varphi(v)}(P[v]-f(x))-|u|^{\alpha+1}\left(C(x)|v|^{\beta-\alpha}-\frac{f(x)}{|v|^{\alpha-1}v}\right).\end{aligned}\tag{2.4}$$

The following inequality holds:

$$\begin{aligned}C(x)|v|^{\beta-\alpha}-\frac{f(x)}{|v|^{\alpha-1}v}&=C(x)|v|^{\beta-\alpha}+\frac{|f(x)|}{|v|^{\alpha}}\\&\geq\frac{\beta}{\alpha}\left(\frac{\beta-\alpha}{\alpha}\right)^{(\alpha-\beta)/\beta}C(x)^{\alpha/\beta}|f(x)|^{(\beta-\alpha)/\beta}\end{aligned}\tag{2.5}$$

(see, e.g., Jaroš et al. [4, page 712]). Combining (2.2)–(2.5) yields the desired inequality (2.1). The proof is complete. □

Theorem 2.2. *If there exists a nontrivial function $u\in C^1(\overline{G};\mathbb{R})$ such that $u=0$ on ∂G and*

$$\begin{aligned}M_G[u]\equiv\int_G\Bigg[&A(x)\left|\nabla u-\frac{u}{A(x)}B(x)\right|^{\alpha+1}\\&-\frac{\beta}{\alpha}\left(\frac{\beta-\alpha}{\alpha}\right)^{(\alpha-\beta)/\beta}C(x)^{\alpha/\beta}|f(x)|^{(\beta-\alpha)/\beta}|u|^{\alpha+1}\Bigg]dx\leq 0,\end{aligned}\tag{2.6}$$

then every solution $v\in\mathcal{D}_P(G)$ of (1.2) satisfying $v\cdot f(x)\leq 0$ must vanish at some point of $\overline{G}$.

Proof. Suppose to the contrary that there exists a solution $v\in\mathcal{D}_P(G)$ of (1.2) satisfying $v\cdot f(x)\leq 0$ and $v\neq 0$ on $\overline{G}$. Theorem 2.1 implies that the Picone-type inequality (2.1) holds for the nontrivial function u. Integrating (2.1) over G and proceeding as in the proof of [8, Theorem 1.1], we are led to a contradiction. □

Corollary 2.3. *Assume that $f(x)\geq 0$ (or $f(x)\leq 0$) in G. If there exists a nontrivial function $u\in C^1(\overline{G};\mathbb{R})$ such that $u=0$ on ∂G and $M_G[u]\leq 0$, then (1.2) has no negative (or positive) solution on $\overline{G}$.*

Proof. Suppose that (1.2) has a negative (or positive) solution v on $\overline{G}$. It is easily seen that $v \cdot f(x) \le 0$ in G. Therefore it follows from Theorem 2.2 that v must vanish at some point of $\overline{G}$. This is a contradiction, and the proof is complete. □

THEOREM 2.4. *Assume that G is divided into two subdomains G_1 and G_2 by an $(n-1)$-dimensional piecewise smooth hypersurface in such a way that*

$$f(x) \ge 0 \quad \text{in } G_1, \qquad f(x) \le 0 \quad \text{in } G_2. \tag{2.7}$$

If there are nontrivial functions $u_k \in C^1(\overline{G_k};\mathbb{R})$ $(k=1,2)$ such that $u_k = 0$ on ∂G_k and

$$\begin{aligned} M_{G_k}[u_k] \equiv \int_{G_k} \Bigg[& A(x) \left| \nabla u_k - \frac{u_k}{A(x)} B(x) \right|^{\alpha+1} \\ & - \frac{\beta}{\alpha}\left(\frac{\beta-\alpha}{\alpha}\right)^{(\alpha-\beta)/\beta} C(x)^{\alpha/\beta} |f(x)|^{(\beta-\alpha)/\beta} |u_k|^{\alpha+1} \Bigg] dx \le 0, \end{aligned} \tag{2.8}$$

then every solution $v \in \mathcal{D}_P(G)$ of (1.2) has a zero on $\overline{G}$.

Proof. Suppose that there is a solution $v \in \mathcal{D}_P(G)$ of (1.2) which has no zero on $\overline{G}$. Then, either $v > 0$ on $\overline{G}$ or $v < 0$ on $\overline{G}$. If $v > 0$ on $\overline{G}$, then $v > 0$ on $\overline{G_2}$, and therefore $v \cdot f(x) \le 0$ in G_2. It follows from corollary that (1.2) has no positive solution $\overline{G_2}$. This is a contradiction. In the case where $v < 0$ on $\overline{G}$, a similar argument leads us to a contradiction. The proof is complete. □

3. Oscillation results for (1.2)

Let Ω be an unbounded domain in $\mathbb{R}^n$. It is assumed that

(H_1) $A(x) \in C(\Omega;(0,\infty))$, $B(x) \in C(\Omega;\mathbb{R})$, and $C(x) \in C(\Omega;\mathbb{R})$,

(H_2) $f(x) \in C(\Omega;\mathbb{R})$,

(H_3) β is a constant satisfying $\beta > \alpha (> 0)$.

The domain $\mathcal{D}_P(\Omega)$ of P is defined to be the set of all functions $v \in C^1(\Omega;\mathbb{R})$ with the property that $A(x)|\nabla v|^{\alpha-1}\nabla v \in C^1(\Omega;\mathbb{R})$.

Definition 3.1. A function $v : \Omega \to \mathbb{R}$ is said to be *oscillatory* in Ω if v has a zero in Ω_r for any $r > 0$, where

$$\Omega_r = \Omega \cap \{x \in \mathbb{R}^n;\ |x| > r\}. \tag{3.1}$$

THEOREM 3.2. *Assume that for any $r > 0$, there is a bounded and piecewise smooth domain G with $\overline{G} \subset \Omega_r$, which can be divided into two subdomains G_1 and G_2 by an $(n-1)$-dimensional hypersurface in such a way that $f(x) \ge 0$ in G_1 and $f(x) \le 0$ in G_2. Furthermore, assume that $C(x) \ge 0$ in G and that there are nontrivial functions $u_k \in C^1(\overline{G_k};\mathbb{R})$ such that $u_k = 0$ on ∂G_k and $M_{G_k}[u_k] \le 0$ $(k=1,2)$, where M_{G_k} are defined by (2.8). Then every solution $v \in \mathcal{D}_P(\Omega)$ of (1.2) is oscillatory in Ω.*

Proof. For any $r > 0$, there is a bounded domain G as mentioned in the hypotheses of Theorem 3.2. Theorem 2.4 implies that every solution v of (1.2) has a zero on $\overline{G} \subset \Omega_r$, that is, v is oscillatory in Ω. □

Example 3.3. Let us consider the forced quasilinear elliptic equation

$$\begin{aligned} &\nabla\cdot(|\nabla v|^2\nabla v)+4|\nabla v|^2\left(\frac{\partial v}{\partial x_1}+\frac{\partial v}{\partial x_2}\right)+K(\sin x_1\cdot\sin x_2)|v|^{\beta-1}v \\ &\quad=\cos x_1\cdot\sin x_2,\qquad (x_1,x_2)\in\Omega, \end{aligned} \tag{3.2}$$

where β and K are the constants satisfying $\beta>3$, $K>0$, and Ω is an unbounded domain in $\mathbb{R}^2$ containing a horizontal strip such that

$$[2\pi,\infty)\times[0,\pi]\subset\Omega. \tag{3.3}$$

Here, $n=2$, $\alpha=3$, $A(x)=1$, $B(x)=(1,1)$, $C(x)=K(\sin x_1\cdot\sin x_2)$, and $f(x)=\cos x_1\cdot\sin x_2$. For any fixed $j\in\mathbb{N}$, we consider the rectangle

$$G^{(j)}=(2j\pi,(2j+1)\pi)\times(0,\pi), \tag{3.4}$$

which is divided into two subdomains

$$\begin{aligned} G_1^{(j)}&=\left(2j\pi,\left(2j+\frac{1}{2}\right)\pi\right)\times(0,\pi), \\ G_2^{(j)}&=\left(\left(2j+\frac{1}{2}\right)\pi,(2j+1)\pi\right)\times(0,\pi) \end{aligned} \tag{3.5}$$

by the vertical line $x_1=(2j+(1/2))\pi$. It is easily seen that $f(x)\geq 0$ in $G_1^{(j)}$, $f(x)\leq 0$ in $G_2^{(j)}$, and $C(x)\geq 0$ in $G^{(j)}$. Letting $u_k=\sin 2x_1\cdot\sin x_2$ $(k=1,2)$, we find that $u_k=0$ on $\partial G_k^{(j)}$ $(k=1,2)$. A simple computation shows that

$$M_{G_k^{(j)}}[u_k]=\frac{261}{128}\pi^2-\frac{128}{15}K^{3/\beta}\frac{\beta}{3}\left(\frac{\beta-3}{3}\right)^{(3-\beta)/\beta}B\left(\frac{5}{2}+\frac{3}{2\beta},3-\frac{3}{2\beta}\right), \tag{3.6}$$

where $B(s,t)$ is the beta function. If $K>0$ is chosen sufficiently large, then $M_{G_k^{(j)}}[u_k]\leq 0$ hold for $k=1,2$. It follows from Theorem 2.4 that every solution v of (3.2) is oscillatory in Ω for all sufficiently large $K>0$.

4. Picone-type inequality for (1.3)

In addition to the hypothesis (A_1) of Section 2 we assume that

(A_3) $D(x)\in C(\overline{G};[0,\infty))$.

The domain $\mathcal{D}_{\widetilde{P}}(G)$ of $\widetilde{P}$ is defined to be the same as that of P, that is, $\mathcal{D}_{\widetilde{P}}(G)=\mathcal{D}_P(G)$.

THEOREM 4.1. *If $v \in \mathfrak{D}_{\widetilde{P}}(G)$, $v \neq 0$ in G, then the following Picone-type inequality holds for any $u \in C^1(G;\mathbb{R})$:*

$$\begin{aligned}
&-\nabla\cdot\left(u\varphi(u)\frac{A(x)\Phi(\nabla v)}{\varphi(v)}\right)\\
&\quad\geq -A(x)\left|\nabla u-\frac{u}{A(x)}B(x)\right|^{\alpha+1}\\
&\quad\quad+\frac{\beta-\gamma}{\alpha-\gamma}\left(\frac{\beta-\alpha}{\alpha-\gamma}\right)^{(\alpha-\beta)/(\beta-\gamma)}C(x)^{(\alpha-\gamma)/(\beta-\gamma)}D(x)^{(\beta-\alpha)/(\beta-\gamma)}|u|^{\alpha+1}\\
&\quad\quad+A(x)\left[\left(\nabla u-\frac{u}{A(x)}B(x)\right)\cdot\Phi\left(\nabla u-\frac{u}{A(x)}B(x)\right)+\alpha\left(\frac{u}{v}\nabla v\right)\cdot\Phi\left(\frac{u}{v}\nabla v\right)\right.\\
&\quad\quad\left.-(\alpha+1)\left(\nabla u-\frac{u}{A(x)}B(x)\right)\cdot\Phi\left(\frac{u}{v}\nabla v\right)\right]-\frac{u\varphi(u)}{\varphi(v)}\widetilde{P}[v].
\end{aligned}\tag{4.1}$$

Proof. We note that the identity (2.2) holds for any $v \in \mathfrak{D}_{\widetilde{P}}(G)$ and $u \in C^1(G;\mathbb{R})$. It is easy to see that

$$\begin{aligned}
&\nabla\cdot\left(A(x)|\nabla v|^{\alpha-1}\nabla v\right)+(\alpha+1)|\nabla v|^{\alpha-1}B(x)\cdot\nabla v\\
&\quad=\widetilde{P}[v]-C(x)|v|^{\beta-1}v-D(x)|v|^{\gamma-1}v
\end{aligned}\tag{4.2}$$

and hence

$$\begin{aligned}
&\frac{u\varphi(u)}{\varphi(v)}\left(\nabla\cdot\left(A(x)|\nabla v|^{\alpha-1}\nabla v\right)+(\alpha+1)|\nabla v|^{\alpha-1}B(x)\cdot\nabla v\right)\\
&\quad=\frac{u\varphi(u)}{\varphi(v)}\left(\widetilde{P}[v]-C(x)|v|^{\beta-1}v-D(x)|v|^{\gamma-1}v\right)\\
&\quad=\frac{u\varphi(u)}{\varphi(v)}\widetilde{P}[v]-|u|^{\alpha+1}\left(C(x)|v|^{\beta-\alpha}+\frac{D(x)}{|v|^{\alpha-\gamma}}\right).
\end{aligned}\tag{4.3}$$

The following inequality was obtained by Jaroš et al. [4, page 717]:

$$C(x)|v|^{\beta-\alpha}+\frac{D(x)}{|v|^{\alpha-\gamma}}\geq\left(\frac{\beta-\gamma}{\alpha-\gamma}\right)\left(\frac{\beta-\alpha}{\alpha-\gamma}\right)^{(\alpha-\beta)/(\beta-\gamma)}C(x)^{(\alpha-\gamma)/(\beta-\gamma)}D(x)^{(\beta-\alpha)/(\beta-\gamma)}.\tag{4.4}$$

Combining (2.2), (4.3), and (4.4) yields the desired inequality (4.1). □

THEOREM 4.2. *If there exists a nontrivial function $u \in C^1(\overline{G};\mathbb{R})$ such that $u = 0$ on ∂G and*

$$\begin{aligned}
\widetilde{M}_G[u]\equiv\int_G\Bigg[&A(x)\left|\nabla u-\frac{u}{A(x)}B(x)\right|^{\alpha+1}\\
&-\frac{\beta-\gamma}{\alpha-\gamma}\left(\frac{\beta-\alpha}{\alpha-\gamma}\right)^{(\alpha-\beta)/(\beta-\gamma)}C(x)^{(\alpha-\gamma)/(\beta-\gamma)}D(x)^{(\beta-\alpha)/(\beta-\gamma)}|u|^{\alpha+1}\Bigg]dx\leq 0,
\end{aligned}\tag{4.5}$$

then every solution $v \in \mathfrak{D}_{\widetilde{P}}(G)$ of (1.3) vanishes at some point of $\overline{G}$.

Proof. Suppose to the contrary that there exists a solution $v \in \mathcal{D}_{\tilde{P}}(G)$ of (1.3) such that $v \neq 0$ on $\overline{G}$. It follows from Theorem 4.1 that the Picone-type inequality (4.1) holds for the nontrivial function u. Integrating (4.1) over G and proceeding as in the proof of Theorem 2.2, we observe that we are led to a contradiction. The proof is complete. □

5. Oscillation results for (1.3)

Let Ω be an unbounded domain in $\mathbb{R}^n$. In this section we assume that the following hypotheses hold:

(H_4) $A(x) \in C(\Omega;(0,\infty))$, $B(x) \in C(\Omega;\mathbb{R})$, $C(x) \in C(\Omega;[0,\infty))$, and $D(x) \in C(\Omega;[0,\infty))$;

(H_5) γ is a constant such that $0 < \gamma < \alpha$.

The domain $\mathcal{D}_{\tilde{P}}(\Omega)$ of $\tilde{P}$ is defined to be the same as that of P, that is, $\mathcal{D}_{\tilde{P}}(\Omega) = \mathcal{D}_P(\Omega)$.

Theorem 5.1. *Assume that for any $r > 0$, there exists a bounded and piecewise smooth domain G with $\overline{G} \subset \Omega_r$. If there is a nontrivial function $u \in C^1(\overline{G};\mathbb{R})$ such that $u = 0$ on ∂G and $\widetilde{M}_G[u] \leq 0$, where $\widetilde{M}_G$ is defined in Theorem 4.2, then every solution $v \in \mathcal{D}_{\tilde{P}}(\Omega)$ of (1.3) is oscillatory in Ω.*

Proof. Let $r > 0$ be an arbitrary number. Theorem 4.2 implies that every solution $v \in \mathcal{D}_{\tilde{P}}(\Omega)$ of (1.3) has a zero on $\overline{G} \subset \Omega_r$, that is, every solution v of (1.3) is oscillatory in Ω. □

The following Theorems 5.2 and 5.3 follow by using the same arguments as those of [8, Theorems 2.2 and 2.3].

Theorem 5.2. *Let $0 < \alpha < 1$. Assume that for any $r > 0$, there exist a bounded and piecewise smooth domain G with $\overline{G} \subset \Omega_r$ and a nontrivial function $u \in C^1(\overline{G};\mathbb{R})$ such that $u = 0$ on ∂G and*

$$\int_G \left[\frac{A(x)}{1-\alpha} |\nabla u|^{\alpha+1} - \left\{ H(x) - \frac{|B(x)|^{\alpha+1}}{(1-\alpha)|A(x)|^{\alpha}} \right\} |u|^{\alpha+1} \right] dx \leq 0, \tag{5.1}$$

where

$$H(x) = \frac{\beta-\gamma}{\alpha-\gamma} \left(\frac{\beta-\alpha}{\alpha-\gamma} \right)^{(\alpha-\beta)/(\beta-\gamma)} C(x)^{(\alpha-\gamma)/(\beta-\gamma)} D(x)^{(\beta-\alpha)/(\beta-\gamma)}. \tag{5.2}$$

Then every solution $v \in \mathcal{D}_{\tilde{P}}(\Omega)$ of (1.3) is oscillatory in Ω.

Theorem 5.3. *Let $A(x) > \alpha$ in Ω. Assume that for any $r > 0$, there exist a bounded and piecewise smooth domain G with $\overline{G} \subset \Omega_r$ and a nontrivial function $u \in C^1(\overline{G};\mathbb{R})$ such that $u = 0$ on ∂G and*

$$\int_G \left[\frac{A^2(x)}{A(x)-\alpha} |\nabla u|^{\alpha+1} - \left\{ H(x) - \frac{A(x)}{A(x)-\alpha} |B(x)|^{\alpha+1} \right\} |u|^{\alpha+1} \right] dx \leq 0. \tag{5.3}$$

Then every solution $v \in \mathcal{D}_{\tilde{P}}(\Omega)$ of (1.3) is oscillatory in Ω.

Let $\{Q(x)\}_S(r)$ *denote the spherical mean of* $Q(x)$ *over the sphere* $S_r = \{x \in \mathbb{R}^n : |x| = r\}$, *that is,*

$$\{Q(x)\}_S(r) = \frac{1}{\omega_n r^{n-1}} \int_{S_r} Q(x)d\sigma = \frac{1}{\omega_n} \int_{S_1} Q(r,\theta)d\omega, \tag{5.4}$$

where ω_n *is the surface area of the unit sphere* S_1 *and* (r,θ) *is the hyperspherical coordinates on* S_1.

THEOREM 5.4. *Let* $0 < \alpha < 1$. *If the half-linear differential equation*

$$\left(r^{n-1}\left\{\frac{A(x)}{1-\alpha}\right\}_S(r)|y'|^{\alpha-1}y'\right)' + r^{n-1}\left\{H(x) - \frac{|B(x)|^{\alpha+1}}{(1-\alpha)|A(x)|^{\alpha}}\right\}_S(r)|y|^{\alpha-1}y = 0 \tag{5.5}$$

is oscillatory, then every solution $v \in \mathcal{D}_{\tilde{P}}(\mathbb{R}^n)$ *of (1.3) is oscillatory in* $\mathbb{R}^n$.

Proof. Let $\{r_k\}$ be the zeros of a nontrivial solution $y(r)$ of (5.5) such that $r_1 < r_2 < \cdots$, $\lim_{k\to\infty} r_k = \infty$. Letting

$$G_k = \{x \in \mathbb{R}^n;\ r_k < |x| < r_{k+1}\} \quad (k = 1,2,\ldots) \tag{5.6}$$

and $u_k(x) = y(|x|)$, we find that

$$\begin{aligned}
&\int_{G_k}\left[\frac{A(x)}{1-\alpha}|\nabla u_k|^{\alpha+1} - \left\{H(x) - \frac{|B(x)|^{\alpha+1}}{(1-\alpha)|A(x)|^{\alpha}}\right\}|u_k|^{\alpha+1}\right]dx \\
&\quad = \omega_n \int_{r_k}^{r_{k+1}}\left[\left\{\frac{A(x)}{1-\alpha}\right\}_S(r)|y'(r)|^{\alpha+1}\right. \\
&\qquad\qquad \left. - \left\{H(x) - \frac{|B(x)|^{\alpha+1}}{(1-\alpha)|A(x)|^{\alpha}}\right\}_S(r)|y(r)|^{\alpha+1}\right]r^{n-1}dr \\
&\quad = -\omega_n \int_{r_k}^{r_{k+1}}\left[\left(r^{n-1}\left\{\frac{A(x)}{1-\alpha}\right\}_S(r)|y'(r)|^{\alpha-1}y'(r)\right)'\right. \\
&\qquad\qquad \left. + r^{n-1}\left\{H(x) - \frac{|B(x)|^{\alpha+1}}{(1-\alpha)|A(x)|^{\alpha}}\right\}_S(r)|y(r)|^{\alpha-1}y(r)\right]y(r)dr = 0.
\end{aligned} \tag{5.7}$$

Hence, the conclusion follows from Theorem 5.2. □

THEOREM 5.5. *Let* $A(x) > \alpha$ *in* $\mathbb{R}^n$. *If the half-linear differential equation*

$$\left(r^{n-1}\left\{\frac{A^2(x)}{A(x)-\alpha}\right\}_S(r)|y'|^{\alpha-1}y'\right)' + r^{n-1}\left\{H(x) - \frac{A(x)}{A(x)-\alpha}|B(x)|^{\alpha+1}\right\}_S(r)|y|^{\alpha-1}y = 0 \tag{5.8}$$

is oscillatory, then every solution $v \in \mathcal{D}_{\tilde{P}}(\mathbb{R}^n)$ *of (1.3) is oscillatory in* $\mathbb{R}^n$.

Example 5.6. We consider the quasilinear elliptic equation

$$\nabla \cdot (3|\nabla v|\nabla v) + 3|\nabla v|\left(\frac{\partial v}{\partial x_1} + \frac{\partial v}{\partial x_2}\right) + 32|v|^3 v + 32|v|^{-1/2} v = 0 \qquad (5.9)$$

for $x = (x_1, x_2) \in \mathbb{R}^2$. Here, $n = 2$, $\alpha = 2$, $\beta = 4$, $\gamma = 1/2$, $A(x) = 3$, $B(x) = (1,1)$, and $C(x) = D(x) = 32$. A simple calculation yields

$$\frac{A^2(x)}{A(x) - \alpha} = 9,$$
$$H(x) - \frac{A(x)}{A(x) - \alpha}|B(x)|^{\alpha+1} = 16 - 6\sqrt{2} > 0. \qquad (5.10)$$

It follows from Theorem 5.5 that every solution v of (5.9) is oscillatory in $\mathbb{R}^2$.

References

[1] G. Bognár and O. Došlý, *The application of Picone-type identity for some nonlinear elliptic differential equations*, Acta Mathematica Universitatis Comenianae. New Series **72** (2003), no. 1, 45–57.

[2] O. Došlý and R. Mařík, *Nonexistence of positive solutions of PDE's with p-Laplacian*, Acta Mathematica Hungarica **90** (2001), no. 1-2, 89–107.

[3] D. R. Dunninger, *A Sturm comparison theorem for some degenerate quasilinear elliptic operators*, Unione Matematica Italiana. Bollettino. A. Serie VII **9** (1995), no. 1, 117–121.

[4] J. Jaroš, T. Kusano, and N. Yoshida, *Picone-type inequalities for half-linear elliptic equations and their applications*, Advances in Mathematical Sciences and Applications **12** (2002), no. 2, 709–724.

[5] J. Jaroš, K. Takaŝi, and N. Yoshida, *Picone-type inequalities for nonlinear elliptic equations with first-order terms and their applications*, Journal of Inequalities and Applications **2006** (2006), Article ID 52378, 17 pages.

[6] T. Kusano, J. Jaroš, and N. Yoshida, *A Picone-type identity and Sturmian comparison and oscillation theorems for a class of half-linear partial differential equations of second order*, Nonlinear Analysis **40** (2000), no. 1–8, 381–395.

[7] R. Mařík, *Oscillation criteria for PDE with p-Laplacian via the Riccati technique*, Journal of Mathematical Analysis and Applications **248** (2000), no. 1, 290–308.

[8] N. Yoshida, *Oscillation of half-linear partial differential equations with first order terms*, Studies of the University of Žilina. Mathematical Series **17** (2003), no. 1, 177–184.

Norio Yoshida: Department of Mathematics, University of Toyama, Toyama 930-8555, Japan
E-mail address: nori@sci.u-toyama.ac.jp

QUENCHING OF SOLUTIONS OF NONLINEAR HYPERBOLIC EQUATIONS WITH DAMPING

JIANMIN ZHU

A hyperbolic initial-boundary value problem with nonlinear damping and singular source terms is studied. A criterion for a solution to reach the value 1 in a finite time is established.

1. Introduction

The concept of quenching was introduced in 1975 by Kawarada [6] through a first initial-boundary value problem for a semilinear heat equation. Chang and Levine [4] extended the concept to a first initial-boundary value problem for a semilinear wave equation in 1981. Over more than twenty years, there has been an extensive study on quenching of solution to various partial differential equations, particularly for parabolic equations. Because of the lack of a maximum principle for hyperbolic equations as useful as that for parabolic equations, quenching phenomena for hyperbolic equations have not been studied as extensively as for parabolic equations. The study of quenching phenomena for hyperbolic initial-boundary value problems has been focused on two types of problems: one with singular nonlinearities in the differential equations, and the other with singular nonlinearities in the boundary conditions. Chang and Levine [4] considered the quenching problem to a first initial-boundary value problem for a semilinear wave equation with singular nonlinearities in the differential equations in 1981. Later, Smith [12] and Levine and Smiley [9] generalized the results to the multidimensional case. The effect of nonlinear boundary conditions on the homogeneous wave equation was investigated by Levine [7] in 1-dimensional space while Rammaha [10] in the multidimensional space. For other related works, we refer the reader to [2, 8, 11] and the references therein.

For the initial-boundary value problem with nonlinear damping and source terms, Georgiev and Todorova [5] studied the existence and the blow-up of solutions in 1994, Chan and Zhu [3] studied the corresponding quenching problem, and Agre and Rammaha [1] studied the existence and the quenching of solutions for a wave equation in one space dimension. Here, we would like to study the quenching phenomena for the

Hindawi Publishing Corporation
Proceedings of the Conference on Differential & Difference Equations and Applications, pp. 1187–1194

following hyperbolic initial-boundary value problem with nonlinear damping and source terms.

Let Ω be an open, bounded, connected domain in $\mathbb{R}^n$ with a sufficiently smooth boundary $\partial\Omega$, we consider the following initial-boundary value problem:

$$\begin{gathered} u_{tt} - \Delta u + a(t)u_t\,|\,u_t\,|^{q-1} = b\left(\frac{1}{1-u}\right)^p, \quad (x,t) \in \Omega \times [0,T], \\ u(x,t) = 0, \quad (x,t) \in \partial\Omega \times [0,T], \\ u(x,t) = u_0(x), \quad u_t(x,t) = u_1(x), \quad x \in \Omega, \end{gathered} \tag{1.1}$$

where Δ denotes the n-dimensional Laplace operator, $0 < a(t) \leqslant a$, and $p,q > 1$, $a,b > 0$.

2. Quenching results

Let $\int_\Omega dx = |\Omega|$, $\beta = p/(p-1)$, and α be any positive constant less than $[p/(p+1)]^{1/\beta}$.

Let

$$\begin{gathered} E(t) = \frac{b}{p-1}\left\|\frac{1}{1-u}\right\|_{p-1}^{p-1} - \frac{1}{2}||u_t||_2^2 - \frac{1}{2}||\nabla u||_2^2, \\ h(t) = \int_\Omega u u_t dx, \qquad G(t) = cE(t) + \varepsilon h(t), \end{gathered} \tag{2.1}$$

where c, ε, and γ are some constants.

Theorem 2.1. *For the problem (1.1), assume that*
(i) $G^\beta(0) > \gamma 2^\beta + 2a|\Omega|\varepsilon/(\beta-1)$,
(ii) $E(0) > \max\{0, -(\varepsilon/c)\int_\Omega u_0 u_1 dx\}$,
(iii) $p > (q+1)/q$.
Then a solution of (1.1) quenches in finite time.

Proof. By multiplying u_t on both sides of the equation in (1.1), we have

$$u_t u_{tt} - u_t \Delta u + a(t)\,|\,u_t\,|^{q+1} = b u_t \left(\frac{1}{1-u}\right)^p. \tag{2.2}$$

Integrating (2.2) over the domain Ω, we have

$$\int_\Omega \left(u_t u_{tt} - u_t \Delta u + a(t)\,|\,u_t\,|^{q+1}\right) dx = b\int_\Omega u_t \left(\frac{1}{1-u}\right)^p dx. \tag{2.3}$$

It follows Green's identity and the boundary condition that

$$\frac{d}{dt}\left[\frac{1}{2}||u_t||_2^2 + \frac{1}{2}||\nabla u||_2^2 - \frac{b}{p-1}\left\|\frac{1}{1-u}\right\|_{p-1}^{p-1}\right] = -a(t)||u_t||_{q+1}^{q+1}. \tag{2.4}$$

Define

$$E(t) = -\frac{1}{2}||u_t||_2^2 - \frac{1}{2}||\nabla u||_2^2 + \frac{b}{p-1}\left\|\frac{1}{1-u}\right\|_{p-1}^{p-1}. \tag{2.5}$$

By (2.4), we have

$$\frac{dE(t)}{dt} = a(t)||u_t||_{q+1}^{q+1} > 0. \tag{2.6}$$

Define

$$h(t) = \int_\Omega uu_t dx. \tag{2.7}$$

Then,

$$\begin{aligned} h'(t) &= \left(\int_\Omega uu_t dx\right)_t' \\ &= 2\int_\Omega u_t^2 dx + 2E(t) - \frac{b(p+1)}{p-1}\int_\Omega \left(\frac{1}{1-u}\right)^{p-1} dx \\ &\quad + b\int_\Omega \left(\frac{1}{1-u}\right)^p dx - a(t)\int_\Omega uu_t\,|\,u_t\,|^{q-1} dx. \end{aligned} \tag{2.8}$$

It follows $E(t) \geqslant 0$ and $\int_\Omega u_t^2 dx \geqslant 0$ that

$$\begin{aligned} h'(t) \geqslant &-\frac{b(p+1)}{p-1}\int_\Omega \left(\frac{1}{1-u}\right)^{p-1} dx + b\int_\Omega \left(\frac{1}{1-u}\right)^p dx \\ &- a(t)\int_\Omega uu_t\,|\,u_t\,|^{q-1} dx. \end{aligned} \tag{2.9}$$

Since

$$a(t)\int_\Omega uu_t\,|\,u_t\,|^{q-1} dx \leqslant a(t)|\Omega| + a(t)||u_t||_{q+1}^{q+1}, \tag{2.10}$$

$$\frac{b(p+1)}{p-1}\int_\Omega \left(\frac{1}{1-u}\right)^{p-1} dx \leqslant \frac{b(p+1)|\Omega|}{p-1}\left(\frac{1}{\alpha}\right)^p + \frac{b(p+1)\alpha^{p/(p-1)}}{p}\int_\Omega \left(\frac{1}{1-u}\right)^p dx. \tag{2.11}$$

From (2.9), (2.10), and (2.11), we have

$$\begin{aligned} h'(t) \geqslant &\, b\left(1 - \frac{(p+1)\alpha^{p/(p-1)}}{p}\right)\left|\left|\frac{1}{1-u}\right|\right|_p^p - a(t)|\Omega| \\ &- \frac{b(p+1)|\Omega|}{p-1}\left(\frac{1}{\alpha}\right)^p - a(t)||u_t||_{q+1}^{q+1}. \end{aligned} \tag{2.12}$$

Denote $c_1 = a|\Omega|$, $c_2 = a$, and $c_3 = 1 - (p+1)\alpha^{p/(p-1)}/p$, then (2.12) becomes

$$h'(t) \geqslant bc_3\left|\left|\frac{1}{1-u}\right|\right|_p^p - c_1 - c_2||u_t||_{q+1}^{q+1}. \tag{2.13}$$

Define

$$G(t) = cE(t) + \varepsilon h(t). \tag{2.14}$$

Then, from (2.13) and (2.14), we have

$$G'(t) = cE'(t) + \varepsilon h'(t) \geqslant (c - c_2\varepsilon)E'(t) - c_1\varepsilon + \varepsilon bc_3\left\|\frac{1}{1-u}\right\|_p^p. \tag{2.15}$$

Let

$$\alpha_1 = c - \varepsilon c_2, \qquad \alpha_2 = -c_1\varepsilon. \tag{2.16}$$

Then

$$G'(t) \geqslant \alpha_1 E'(t) + \varepsilon bc_3\left\|\frac{1}{1-u}\right\|_p^p + \alpha_2. \tag{2.17}$$

It follows the definitions of c, c_2, and (2.17) that

$$G'(t) \geqslant \alpha_2. \tag{2.18}$$

Therefore,

$$G(t) \geqslant G(0) + \alpha_2 t. \tag{2.19}$$

Let

$$t^* = \frac{G(0)}{-\alpha_2}. \tag{2.20}$$

It follows $G(0) > 0$ and $\alpha_2 < 0$ that $t^* > 0$. Therefore,

$$G(t) > 0, \quad t \in [0, t^*). \tag{2.21}$$

It follows (2.19) and (2.21) that

$$G^\beta(t) \geqslant (G(0) + \alpha_2 t)^\beta, \quad t \in [0, t^*). \tag{2.22}$$

From (2.22) and $\alpha_2 < 0$, we have

$$G^\beta(t) \geqslant \left(G(0) + \frac{\alpha_2 t^*}{2}\right)^\beta, \quad t \in \left[0, \frac{t^*}{2}\right). \tag{2.23}$$

It follows (2.23) that

$$G^\beta(t) \geqslant \frac{G^\beta(0)}{2^\beta}, \quad t \in \left[0, \frac{t^*}{2}\right). \tag{2.24}$$

We want to prove that

$$\frac{dG(t)}{dt} \geqslant G^\beta(t) - \gamma. \tag{2.25}$$

Since

$$G'(t) \geqslant G^{\beta}(t) + \alpha_1 E'(t) + \varepsilon b c_3 \left\| \frac{1}{1-u} \right\|_p^p + \alpha_2 - G^{\beta}(t), \tag{2.26}$$

we consider the following two cases.

Case 1. $\int_\Omega u u_t dx \leqslant 0$. It follows (2.21) and $\int_\Omega u u_t dx \leqslant 0$ that

$$\begin{aligned} &\alpha_1 E'(t) + \varepsilon b c_3 \left\| \frac{1}{1-u} \right\|_p^p - G^{\beta}(t) \\ &\geqslant \alpha_1 E'(t) + \varepsilon b c_3 \left\| \frac{1}{1-u} \right\|_p^p - \frac{b^{\beta} c^{\beta}}{(p-1)^{\beta}} \left\| \frac{1}{1-u} \right\|_{p-1}^{(p-1)\beta}, \quad t \in [0, t^*). \end{aligned} \tag{2.27}$$

Define

$$c = \frac{a\varepsilon + 2^{\beta-1} q \varepsilon^{\beta}}{q}. \tag{2.28}$$

It follows the definitions of c, c_2, α_1, and ε that $\alpha_1 = c - c_2\varepsilon = 2^{\beta-1}\varepsilon^{\beta} > 0$, since $E'(t) \geqslant 0$, therefore,

$$\begin{aligned} &\alpha_1 E'(t) + \varepsilon b c_3 \left\| \frac{1}{1-u} \right\|_p^p - \frac{b^{\beta} c^{\beta}}{(p-1)^{\beta}} \left\| \frac{1}{1-u} \right\|_{p-1}^{(p-1)\beta} \\ &\geqslant \int_\Omega \frac{\varepsilon b c_3}{(1-u)^p} - \frac{b^{\beta} c^{\beta}}{(p-1)^{\beta}} \left(\int_\Omega \frac{1}{(1-u)^{p-1}} dx \right)^{\beta}, \quad t \in [0, t^*). \end{aligned} \tag{2.29}$$

Define

$$\varepsilon = \frac{p(2b|\Omega|)^{\beta-1} c^{\beta}}{(p-1)^{\beta}[p-(p+1)\alpha^{\beta}]}. \tag{2.30}$$

Let $\beta = p/(p-1) > 1$, it follows Jensen's inequality, and the definition of ε, and $2^{\beta-1} > 1$ that

$$\alpha_1 E'(t) + \varepsilon b c_3 \left\| \frac{1}{1-u} \right\|_p^p - \frac{b^{\beta} c^{\beta}}{(p-1)^{\beta}} \left\| \frac{1}{1-u} \right\|_{p-1}^{(p-1)\beta} \geqslant 0. \tag{2.31}$$

Therefore,

$$\alpha_1 E'(t) + \varepsilon b \left\| \frac{1}{1-u} \right\|_p^p - G^{\beta}(t) \geqslant 0, \quad t \in [0, t^*). \tag{2.32}$$

From (2.26) and (2.32), we have

$$\frac{dG(t)}{dt} \geqslant G^{\beta}(t) + \alpha_2, \quad t \in [0, t^*). \tag{2.33}$$

Case 2. $\int_\Omega uu_t dx > 0$. It follows $(x+y)^\beta \leqslant 2^{\beta-1}(x^\beta + y^\beta)$ for $\beta > 1, x \geqslant 0, y \geqslant 0$ that

$$\begin{aligned}
&\alpha_1 E'(t) + \varepsilon b c_3 \left\| \frac{1}{1-u} \right\|_p^p - G^\beta(t) \\
&\quad \geqslant \alpha_1 \int_\Omega |u_t|^{q+1} dx - 2^{\beta-1}\varepsilon^\beta |\Omega|^{\beta-1}\left(\int_\Omega |u_t|^\beta dx\right) + \varepsilon b c_3 \left\| \frac{1}{1-u} \right\|_p^p \\
&\qquad - 2^{\beta-1}\left(\frac{bc}{p-1}\right)^\beta \left\| \frac{1}{1-u} \right\|_{p-1}^{(p-1)\beta}.
\end{aligned} \tag{2.34}$$

Applying Jensen's inequality and $\beta = p/(p-1)$, we have

$$\varepsilon b c_3 \left\| \frac{1}{1-u} \right\|_p^p \geqslant \frac{\varepsilon b c_3}{|\Omega|^{\beta-1}} \left\| \frac{1}{1-u} \right\|_{p-1}^p. \tag{2.35}$$

It follows (2.35) and the definition of ε that

$$\varepsilon b c_3 \left\| \frac{1}{1-u} \right\|_p^p - 2^{\beta-1}\left(\frac{bc}{p-1}\right)^\beta \left\| \frac{1}{1-u} \right\|_{p-1}^{(p-1)\beta} \geqslant 0. \tag{2.36}$$

Therefore, (2.34) becomes

$$\begin{aligned}
&\alpha_1 E'(t) + \varepsilon b \left\| \frac{1}{1-u} \right\|_p^p - G^\beta(t) \\
&\quad \geqslant \alpha_1 \int_\Omega |u_t|^{q+1} dx - 2^{\beta-1}\varepsilon^\beta |\Omega|^{\beta-1}\left(\int_\Omega |u_t|^\beta dx\right).
\end{aligned} \tag{2.37}$$

It follows $q+1 > \beta$, $\alpha_1 - 2^{\beta-1}\varepsilon^\beta = 0$, $a(t) > 0$, and (2.37) that

$$\alpha_1 E'(t) + \varepsilon b c_3 \left\| \frac{1}{1-u} \right\|_p^p - G^\beta(t) \geqslant -2^{\beta-1}\varepsilon^\beta |\Omega|. \tag{2.38}$$

Let

$$\bar{\alpha}_2 = -2^{\beta-1}\varepsilon^\beta |\Omega| - \alpha_2 < 0. \tag{2.39}$$

Then, from (2.26), (2.34), and (2.38), we have

$$G'(t) \geqslant G^\beta(t) - |\bar{\alpha}_2|. \tag{2.40}$$

Define

$$\gamma = \max\{|\alpha_2|, |\bar{\alpha}_2|\} = a\varepsilon|\Omega| + 2^{\beta-1}\varepsilon^\beta |\Omega|, \tag{2.41}$$

then, from (2.33) and (2.40), we have

$$G'(t) \geqslant G^\beta(t) - \gamma, \quad t \in [0, t^*). \tag{2.42}$$

It follows (2.21), (2.24), (2.42), and $\gamma > 0$ that

$$\frac{G'(t)}{G^{\beta}(t)} \geqslant 1 - \frac{\gamma 2^{\beta}}{G^{\beta}(0)}, \quad t \in \left[0, \frac{t^*}{2}\right). \tag{2.43}$$

From (2.43), we have

$$G^{1-\beta}(t) \leqslant G^{1-\beta}(0) - (\beta - 1)\left(1 - \frac{\gamma 2^{\beta}}{G^{\beta}(0)}\right)t, \quad t \in \left[0, \frac{t^*}{2}\right). \tag{2.44}$$

It follows (2.44) and $1 - \gamma 2^{\beta}/G^{\beta}(0) > 0$ that

$$G^{\beta-1}(t) \geqslant \left[G^{1-\beta}(0) - (\beta - 1)\left(1 - \frac{\gamma 2^{\beta}}{G^{\beta}(0)}\right)t\right]^{-1}. \tag{2.45}$$

From (2.45), and condition (i) in Theorem 2.1, we have

$$G(t) \longrightarrow \infty \quad \text{as } t \longrightarrow T < \infty, \tag{2.46}$$

where

$$T = \frac{G^{1-\beta}(0)}{(\beta - 1)(1 - \gamma 2^{\beta}/G^{\beta}(0))} < \frac{t^*}{2}. \tag{2.47}$$

By the definition of $G(t)$ in (2.14), we have

$$u(x,t) \longrightarrow 1 \quad \text{as } t \longrightarrow T < \infty. \tag{2.48}$$

Therefore, u quenches in finite time. □

References

[1] K. Agre and M. A. Rammaha, *Quenching and non-quenching for nonlinear wave equations with damping*, The Canadian Applied Mathematics Quarterly **9** (2001), no. 3, 203–223 (2002).

[2] C. Y. Chan and K. K. Nip, *Quenching for semilinear Euler-Poisson-Darboux equations*, Partial Differential Equations, Longman Scientific and Technical, Harlow, 1992, pp. 39–43.

[3] C. Y. Chan and J. Zhu, *Hyperbolic quenching with nonlinear damping and source terms*, Dynamic Systems and Applications, Vol. 3 (Atlanta, GA, 1999), Dynamic, Georgia, 2001, pp. 135–138.

[4] P. H. Chang and H. A. Levine, *The quenching of solutions of semilinear hyperbolic equations*, SIAM Journal on Mathematical Analysis **12** (1981), no. 6, 893–903.

[5] V. Georgiev and G. Todorova, *Existence of a solution of the wave equation with nonlinear damping and source terms*, Journal of Differential Equations **109** (1994), no. 2, 295–308.

[6] H. Kawarada, *On solutions of initial-boundary problem for $u_t = u_{xx} + 1/(1-u)$*, Publications of Research Institute for Mathematical Sciences **10** (1975), no. 3, 729–736.

[7] H. A. Levine, *The quenching of solutions of linear parabolic and hyperbolic equations with nonlinear boundary conditions*, SIAM Journal on Mathematical Analysis **14** (1983), no. 6, 1139–1153.

[8] ———, *The phenomenon of quenching: a survey*, Trends in the Theory and Practice of Nonlinear Analysis (Arlington, Tex, 1984), North-Holland Math. Stud., vol. 110, North-Holland, Amsterdam, 1985, pp. 275–286.

[9] H. A. Levine and M. W. Smiley, *Abstract wave equations with a singular nonlinear forcing term*, Journal of Mathematical Analysis and Applications **103** (1984), no. 2, 409–427.

[10] M. A. Rammaha, *On the quenching of solutions of the wave equation with a nonlinear boundary condition*, Journal für die reine und angewandte Mathematik **407** (1990), 1–18.
[11] M. A. Rammaha and T. A. Strei, *Nonlinear wave equations on the two-dimensional sphere*, Journal of Mathematical Analysis and Applications **267** (2002), no. 2, 405–417.
[12] R. A. Smith, *On a hyperbolic quenching problem in several dimensions*, SIAM Journal on Mathematical Analysis **20** (1989), no. 5, 1081–1094.

Jianmin Zhu: Department of Mathematics and Computer Science, Fort Valley State University, Fort Valley, GA 31030-4313, USA
E-mail address: zhuj@fvsu.edu

NECESSARY AND SUFFICIENT CONDITIONS FOR THE EXISTENCE OF NONCONSTANT TWICE CONTINUOUSLY DIFFERENTIABLE SOLUTIONS OF $x'' = f(x)$

RODRIGO LÓPEZ POUSO

We deduce necessary and sufficient conditions for having nonconstant classical solutions of the scalar equation $x'' = f(x)$.

1. Introduction

In this note, we complement the results obtained in [1] concerning necessary and sufficient conditions for the existence of nontrivial Carathéodory solutions of the initial value problem

$$x'' = f(x), \qquad x(0) = x_0, \qquad x'(0) = x_1, \tag{1.1}$$

where $f : \mathrm{Dom}(f) \subset \mathbb{R} \to \mathbb{R} \cup \{-\infty, +\infty\}$ and $x_0, x_1 \in \mathbb{R}$.

In order to present the main result in [1] we need some preliminaries. First, a Carathéodory solution of (1.1) is any mapping $x : I \subset \mathbb{R} \to \mathbb{R}$, where I is a nontrivial interval that contains 0, such that x' exists and is locally absolutely continuous on I, $x(0) = x_0$, $x'(0) = x_1$, and x satisfies the differential equation almost everywhere on I (in Lebesgue's measure sense). Let us remark that classical (twice continuously differentiable) solutions of (1.1) are Carathéodory solutions but the converse is not true in general.

Let $J \subset \mathrm{Dom}(f)$ be a nontrivial interval that contains x_0 (if no such interval exists, then (1.1) would have no nonconstant solution). Without further assumptions over f, we formally define the time map

$$\tau : y \in J \longmapsto \tau(y) := \int_{x_0}^{y} \frac{dr}{\sqrt{x_1^2 + 2\int_{x_0}^{r} f(s)ds}}, \tag{1.2}$$

and now we are in a position to state the main result in [1], which gives a characterization of the nontrivial solvability of (1.1).

Hindawi Publishing Corporation
Proceedings of the Conference on Differential & Difference Equations and Applications, pp. 1195–1199

THEOREM 1.1. *The problem (1.1) has the constant solution if and only if* $f(x_0) = 0 = x_1$.
Moreover, the following statements are pairwise equivalent for a nontrivial interval J that contains x_0:

(i) *the problem (1.1) has a (nonconstant) Carathéodory solution with range J;*
(ii) $f \in L^1_{\text{loc}}(J)$, $x_1^2 + \int_{x_0}^{y} f(s)ds > 0$ *for a.a.* $y \in J$, *and*

$$\frac{\max\{1,|f|\}}{\sqrt{x_1^2 + 2\int_{x_0}^{\cdot} f(s)ds}} \in L^1_{\text{loc}}(J); \tag{1.3}$$

(iii) *the problem (1.1) has a strictly monotone Carathéodory solution x implicitly given by*

$$\int_{x_0}^{x(t)} \frac{dr}{\sqrt{x_1^2 + 2\int_{x_0}^{r} f(s)ds}} = \operatorname{sgn}(x_1)t, \quad \forall t \in \operatorname{sgn}(x_1)\tau(J), \tag{1.4}$$

where $\operatorname{sgn}(z) = z/|z|$ *for* $z \neq 0$, *and* $\operatorname{sgn}(0) = \pm 1$.

In Section 2, we include some remarks to Theorem 1.1 that may be helpful when reading the work in [1]. In Section 3, we prove an analogous result for nonconstant classical solutions of (1.1).

2. Some remarks to Theorem 1.1

Note that the equivalence between conditions (i), (ii), and (iii) in Theorem 1.1 concerns nonconstant solutions. Obviously, nonconstant solutions are the unique ones we can expect to exist when $x_1 \neq 0$, therefore it is not a surprise that existence of nonconstant solutions when $x_1 \neq 0$ requires less restrictive hypotheses compared to the case $x_1 = 0$.

We have the following corollary of Theorem 1.1 for the case $x_1 \neq 0$.

COROLLARY 2.1. *If $x_1 \neq 0$, then the following statements are pairwise equivalent:*

(a) *the problem (1.1) has a Carathéodory solution;*
(b) *f is integrable on some nontrivial interval that contains x_0;*
(c) *the problem (1.1) has a strictly monotone Carathéodory solution x implicitly given by*

$$\int_{x_0}^{x(t)} \frac{dr}{\sqrt{x_1^2 + 2\int_{x_0}^{r} f(s)ds}} = \operatorname{sgn}(x_1)t \tag{2.1}$$

for all t in a nontrivial interval that contains 0.

Proof. Condition (c) implies condition (a).

Moreover, (a) implies (ii) in Theorem 1.1, therefore we can ensure that f is integrable on a compact nontrivial interval that contains x_0.

Finally, to show that (b) implies (c), let K be the nontrivial interval that contains x_0 such that $f \in L^1(K)$. It suffices to show that f satisfies condition (ii) in Theorem 1.1 for some interval $J \subset K$ and then use the equivalence between (ii) and (iii) in Theorem 1.1.

Since f is integrable in K and $x_1 \neq 0$, we can choose a nontrivial subinterval $J \subset K$ that contains x_0 such that

$$x_1^2 + 2\int_{x_0}^{y} f(s)ds > 0, \quad \forall y \in J. \tag{2.2}$$

Hence the mapping

$$y \in J \longmapsto \frac{1}{\sqrt{x_1^2 + 2\int_{x_0}^{y} f(s)ds}} \tag{2.3}$$

is continuous and then (1.3) holds true. □

Remark 2.2. Integrability of f around x_0 is not sufficient for the existence of nonconstant solutions when $x_0 = 0$. As an example, consider the case $x'' = x$ with conditions $x(0) = 0 = x'(0)$, whose unique solution is constant.

3. Nonconstant classical solutions

In this section we will prove the following result on nonconstant classical solutions of (1.1).

THEOREM 3.1. *The following statements are pairwise equivalent for a nontrivial interval J that contains x_0:*

(i*) *the problem (1.1) has a (nonconstant)* classical *solution with range J;*

(ii*) $f_{|J}$ *is* finite-valued and continuous *on J, $x_1^2 + \int_{x_0}^{y} f(s)ds > 0$ for a.a. $y \in J$, and*

$$\frac{1}{\sqrt{x_1^2 + 2\int_{x_0}^{\cdot} f(s)ds}} \in L^1_{\text{loc}}(J); \tag{3.1}$$

(iii*) *the problem (1.1) has a* strictly monotone *classical* solution x implicitly given by

$$\int_{x_0}^{x(t)} \frac{dr}{\sqrt{x_1^2 + 2\int_{x_0}^{r} f(s)ds}} = \operatorname{sgn}(x_1)t, \quad \forall t \in \operatorname{sgn}(x_1)\tau(J), \tag{3.2}$$

where $\operatorname{sgn}(z) = z/|z|$ *for* $z \neq 0$, *and* $\operatorname{sgn}(0) = \pm 1$.

Proof. Clearly, (iii*) implies (i*).

To show that (i*) implies (ii*) note first that (i*) implies (i) in Theorem 1.1 and then conditions (ii) in Theorem 1.1 immediately hold true, thus it suffices to prove that $f_{|J}$ is finite-valued and continuous on J. Suppose then that $x : I \to \mathbb{R}$ is a classical solution of (1.1) with $x(I) = J$.

Claim 1. f is finite-valued on J. To each $y \in J$, there corresponds some $t \in I$ such that $x(t) = y$, hence $f(y) = f(x(t)) = x''(t) \in \mathbb{R}$.

Claim 2. $f_{|J}$ is continuous on J. Let $\{y_n\}_n$ be a sequence of elements of J that converges to some $y_0 \in J$; we have to show that $\{f(y_n)\}_n$ converges to $f(y_0)$.

In order to use compactness arguments we fix $R > 0$ such that $y_n \in [y_0 - R, y_0 + R] \cap J =: [a,b]$, for all $n \in \mathbb{N}$, we take $t_a, t_b \in I$ such that $x(t_a) = a$ and $x(t_b) = b$, and we define $\tilde{I}$ as the compact interval with extreme points t_a and t_b. Since x is continuous, we have that $[a,b] \subset x(\tilde{I})$ and thus for each $n \in \mathbb{N}$ there exists $t_n \in \tilde{I}$ such that $y_n = x(t_n)$.

Now the proof of Claim 2 follows two steps.

Step 1. $\{f(y_n)\}_n$ is a bounded sequence. Indeed, the relations

$$f(y_n) = f(x(t_n)) = x''(t_n) \in x''(\tilde{I}), \quad \forall n \in \mathbb{N}, \tag{3.3}$$

imply that $\{f(y_n)\}_n$ is bounded because $x''(\tilde{I})$ is compact.

Step 2. Every convergent subsequence of $\{f(y_n)\}_n$ tends to $f(y_0)$. To prove this fact, let $\{f(y_{n_k})\}_k$ be a subsequence of $\{f(y_n)\}_n$ that tends to some limit $l \in \mathbb{R}$. We have that $y_{n_k} = x(t_{n_k})$ with $t_{n_k} \in \tilde{I}$, for all $n \in \mathbb{N}$. Since $\tilde{I}$ is compact, we have a subsequence of $\{t_{n_k}\}_k$, that we denote again as $\{t_{n_k}\}_k$, which tends to some $t_0 \in \tilde{I}$. Now the continuity of x implies that $x(t_0) = y_0$ and then

$$\lim_{k\to\infty} f(y_{n_k}) = \lim_{k\to\infty} f(x(t_{n_k})) = \lim_{k\to\infty} x''(t_{n_k}) = x''(t_0) = f(x(t_0)) = f(y_0), \tag{3.4}$$

which implies that $l = f(y_0)$.

Finally, we have to prove that (ii*) implies (iii*). Since (ii*) implies (ii) in Theorem 1.1, we have that (1.4) is a Carathéodory solution of (1.1), so we have

$$x''(t) = f(x(t)) \quad \text{for a.a. } t \in I. \tag{3.5}$$

Moreover, we know that $x(I) = J$ and $f_{|J}$ is continuous, so x'' is equal to a continuous function almost everywhere on I which implies that $x \in \mathscr{C}^2(I)$ and satisfies the differential equation everywhere on I. □

Remark 3.2. When $x_0 \in \operatorname{Int}(J)$ in condition (ii*) then we have that f is continuous on a neighborhood of x_0 and thus Peano's theorem ensures that (1.1) has at least one classical solution, but not necessarily a nonconstant solution.

Remark 3.3. Note that (1.1) may have a nonconstant classical solution and f may be discontinuous at x_0 (according to Theorem 3.1 we only know that the restriction of f to the solution's range is continuous). As an example, note that $x(t) = \cos t$, $t \in \mathbb{R}$, is a classical solution of the problem

$$x'' = \begin{cases} -x & \text{if } x \le 1, \\ -2 & \text{if } x > 1, \end{cases} \qquad x(0) = 1, \qquad x'(0) = 0, \tag{3.6}$$

and clearly the right-hand side of the differential equation is discontinuous precisely at the initial position $x_0 = 1$.

However, in this case the range of the solution is the interval $[-1,1]$, and the restriction of the right-hand side to that interval is a continuous function.

References

[1] R. L. Pouso, *Necessary and sufficient conditions for existence and uniqueness of solutions of second-order autonomous differential equations*, Journal of the London Mathematical Society **71** (2005), no. 2, 397–414.

Rodrigo López Pouso: Departamento de Análise Matemática, Facultade de Matemáticas, Universidade de Santiago de Compostela, 15782 Santiago de Compostela, Spain
E-mail address: rodrigolp@usc.es

VARIATION-OF-PARAMETERS FORMULAE AND LIPSCHITZ STABILITY CRITERIA FOR NONLINEAR MATRIX DIFFERENTIAL EQUATIONS WITH INITIAL TIME DIFFERENCE

COSKUN YAKAR

This paper investigates the relationship between an unperturbed matrix differential equation and a perturbed matrix differential system which both have different initial positions and an initial time difference. Variation-of-parameter techniques are employed to obtain integral formulae and to establish Lipschitz stability criteria for nonlinear matrix differential systems and make use of the variational system associated with the unperturbed differential system.

1. Introduction

The method of variation-of-parameters formulae (VPF) has been a very useful technique in the qualitative theory of system of differential equations and nonlinear matrix differential equations since it is a practical tool in the investigation of the properties of solutions. Recently in [1–3], the study of nonlinear matrix initial value problems with an initial time difference (ITD) has been initiated and the corresponding theory of differential inequalities has been investigated. Below, we will derive VPF showing the relationship between unperturbed matrix differential systems with different initial conditions and unperturbed and perturbed systems with different initial conditions.

The qualitative behavior of matrix differential equations has been explored extensively and the investigation of initial value problems with a perturbation in the space variable is well known when the perturbation is restricted to the space variable with the initial time unchanged [1–4, 6, 7]. Recently, several investigations have been initiated to explore the qualitative behavior of matrix differential systems that have a different initial position and a different initial time. We call this type of stability analysis ITD stability analysis. In Section 3, variation-of-parameter formulae were used to investigate the relationship between (1) unperturbed matrix equations with different initial conditions and (2) unperturbed and perturbed matrix equations with ITD. ITD Lipschitz stability criteria for matrix differential systems are established by employing the variational system associated with the unperturbed matrix differential system.

Hindawi Publishing Corporation
Proceedings of the Conference on Differential & Difference Equations and Applications, pp. 1201–1216

A significant difference between ITD Lipschitz stability and the classical notions of stability is that the classical notions of Lipschitz stability are with respect to the null solution, but ITD stability is with respect to the unperturbed matrix differential equations where the unperturbed matrix differential equation and the perturbed matrix differential system have a change in initial position and in initial time. We show in Section 4 that the transformation that allows the classical notions of Lipschitz stability to be studied with respect to the null solution gives a different result for ITD Lipschitz stability which is not equivalent to the classical approach.

We utilize the variational system associated with the unperturbed matrix differential system to establish Lipschitz stability (LS) criteria for initial time difference Lipschitz stability (ITDLS) in variation and ITD exponential asymptotic LS in variation. In Section 2, we introduce the variational system and give the definitions necessary for the various types of ITDLS and of LS with a time difference only. We compare classical stability of the null solution with ITD stability and show that the two are different and that we cannot limit our study of stability just to that of the null solution. Moreover, we compare ITDLS with ITD stability and show that ITDLS is sufficient for ITD stability, but ITD stability is necessary for ITDLS. Also, we present theorems for ITDLS in variation, ITD exponential asymptotic LS in variation, ITD (uniform) stability, and ITD (uniform) (LS) of the perturbed differential system with respect to the unperturbed differential system.

2. Preliminaries

Let us consider the nonlinear matrix differential systems

$$X' = F(t,X), \quad X(t_0) = X_0 \quad \text{for } t \geq t_0,\ t_0 \in \mathbb{R}_+, \tag{2.1}$$

$$X' = F(t,X), \quad X(\tau_0) = Y_0 \quad \text{for } t \geq \tau_0,\ \tau_0 \in \mathbb{R}_+, \tag{2.2}$$

and the perturbed nonlinear matrix differential system of (2.1):

$$Y' = F(t,Y) + R(t,Y), \quad Y(\tau_0) = Y_0 \quad \text{for } t \geq \tau_0, \tag{2.3}$$

where $F, R \in C[\mathbb{R}_+ \times \mathbb{R}^{n\times n}, \mathbb{R}^{n\times n}]$, $F(t,X)$, $R(t,Y)$ are $n \times n$ continuous matrices for $t \in \mathbb{R}_+$, (t,X), $(t,Y) \in \mathbb{R}_+ \times \mathbb{R}^{n\times n}$, and $R(t,Y)$ is a perturbation matrix term.

The operator $\text{Vec}(\cdot)$ is defined in [5] which maps an $m \times n$ matrix $A = (a_{ij})$ onto the vector composed of columns of A:

$$\text{Vec}(A) = \left(a_{11}, a_{21}, \ldots, a_{m1}, a_{12}, a_{22}, \ldots, a_{m2}, \ldots, a_{1n}, a_{2n}, \ldots, a_{mn}\right)^T. \tag{2.4}$$

Then the corresponding vector differential systems can be written as

$$x' = f(t,x), \quad x(t_0) = x_0 \quad \text{for } t \geq t_0,\ t_0 \in \mathbb{R}_+, \tag{2.5}$$

$$x' = f(t,x), \quad x(\tau_0) = y_0 \quad \text{for } t \geq \tau_0,\ \tau_0 \in \mathbb{R}_+, \tag{2.6}$$

and the perturbed nonlinear vector differential system of (2.3) as

$$y' = f(t,y) + R^*(t,y), \quad y(\tau_0) = y_0 \quad \text{for } t \geq \tau_0, \tag{2.7}$$

where $f, R^* \in C[\mathbb{R}_+ \times \mathbb{R}^{n^2}, \mathbb{R}^{n^2}]$ and $x = \text{Vec}(X)^T$, $y = \text{Vec}(Y)^T$, $f = \text{Vec}(F)^T$, $R^* = \text{Vec}(R)^T$.

Definition 2.1. The solution $Y(t,\tau_0,Y_0)$ of the nonlinear matrix differential system (2.3) through (τ_0, Y_0) is said to be initial time difference stable with respect to the solution $X(t-\eta,t_0,X_0)$ for $t \geq \tau_0$ and $t_0 \in \mathbb{R}_+$, where $X(t,t_0,X_0)$ is any solution of the nonlinear matrix differential system (2.1) for $t \geq \tau_0 \geq 0$ and $\eta = \tau_0 - t_0 \geq 0$. If given any $\varepsilon > 0$, there exist $\delta_1 = \delta_1(\tau_0,\varepsilon) > 0$ and $\delta_2 = \delta_2(\tau_0,\varepsilon) > 0$ such that

$$\begin{gathered} \|Y(t,\tau_0,Y_0) - X(t-\eta,t_0,X_0)\| < \varepsilon \quad \text{whenever } \|Y_0 - X_0\| < \delta_1, \\ |\tau_0 - t_0| < \delta_2 \quad \text{for } t \geq \tau_0. \end{gathered} \tag{2.8}$$

If δ_1 and δ_2 are independent of τ_0, then the solution $Y(t,\tau_0,Y_0)$ of the nonlinear matrix differential system (2.3) is initial time difference uniformly stable with respect to the solution $X(t-\eta,t_0,X_0)$ for $t \geq \tau_0$.

Definition 2.2. The solution $Y(t,\tau_0,Y_0)$ of the nonlinear matrix differential system (2.3) through (τ_0, Y_0) is said to be initial time difference Lipschitz stable with respect to the solution $X(t-\eta,t_0,X_0)$ for $t \geq \tau_0$, where $X(t,t_0,X_0)$ is any solution of the nonlinear matrix differential system (2.1) and $\eta = \tau_0 - t_0 \geq 0$ if and only if there exists an $L = L(\tau_0) > 0$ such that

$$\|Y(t,\tau_0,Y_0) - X(t-\eta,t_0,X_0)\| \leq L(\tau_0)[\|Y_0 - X_0\| + |\tau_0 - t_0|], \quad t \geq \tau_0. \tag{2.9}$$

If L is independent of τ_0, then the solution $Y(t,\tau_0,Y_0)$ of the nonlinear matrix differential system (2.3) is initial time difference uniformly Lipschitz stable with respect to the solution $X(t-\eta,t_0,X_0)$ for $t \geq \tau_0$, related to the solution of nonlinear matrix differential system (2.1).

Definition 2.3. The solution $Y(t,\tau_0,Y_0)$ of the nonlinear matrix differential system (2.3) through (τ_0, Y_0) is said to be initial time difference asymptotically Lipschitz stable with respect to the solution $X(t-\eta,t_0,X_0)$ for $t \geq \tau_0$, where $X(t,t_0,X_0)$ is any solution of the nonlinear matrix differential system (2.1) and $\eta = \tau_0 - t_0 \geq 0$ if and only if there exists an $L = L(\tau_0) > 0$ such that

$$\|Y(t,\tau_0,Y_0) - X(t-\eta,t_0,X_0)\| \leq L(\tau_0)[\|Y_0 - X_0\| + |\tau_0 - t_0|]\sigma(t-\tau_0), \quad t \geq \tau_0, \tag{2.10}$$

where $\sigma \to 0$ as $t \to \infty$.

If L is independent of τ_0, then the solution $Y(t,\tau_0,Y_0)$ of the nonlinear matrix differential system (2.3) is initial time difference uniformly asymptotically Lipschitz stable with respect to the solution $X(t-\eta,t_0,X_0)$ for $t \geq \tau_0$, related to the solution of nonlinear matrix differential system (2.1).

Definition 2.4. The solution $Y(t,\tau_0,Y_0)$ of the nonlinear matrix differential system (2.3) through (τ_0,Y_0) is said to be initial time difference asymptotically Lipschitz stable in variation with respect to the solution $X(t-\eta,t_0,X_0)$ for $t\geq\tau_0$, where $X(t,t_0,X_0)$ is any solution of the nonlinear matrix differential system (2.1) and $\eta=\tau_0-t_0\geq 0$ if and only if

(i) there exists an $L=L(\tau_0)>0$ such that

$$\|Y(t,\tau_0,Y_0)-X(t-\eta,t_0,X_0)\|\leq L(\tau_0)[\|Y_0-X_0\|+|\tau_0-t_0|]\sigma(t-\tau_0),\quad t\geq\tau_0, \tag{2.11}$$

where $\sigma\to 0$ as $t\to\infty$,

(ii) for each $\alpha>0$, there exists an $N>0$ such that the fundamental matrix $\varphi(t,\tau_0,Y_0)$ solution of the variational equation (i) in Theorem 3.1 satisfies

$$\|\varphi(t,\tau_0,Y_0)\|\leq N,\quad \forall t\geq\tau_0,\ \|Y_0\|\leq\alpha. \tag{2.12}$$

If L is independent of τ_0, then the solution $Y(t,\tau_0,Y_0)$ of the nonlinear matrix differential system (2.3) is initial time difference uniformly asymptotically Lipschitz stable in variation with respect to the solution $X(t-\eta,t_0,X_0)$ for $t\geq\tau_0$, related to the solution of nonlinear matrix differential system (2.1).

Definition 2.5. The solution $Y(t,\tau_0,Y_0)$ of the nonlinear matrix differential system (2.3) through (τ_0,Y_0) is said to be initial time difference generalized exponentially asymptotically Lipschitz stable with respect to the solution $X(t-\eta,t_0,X_0)$ for $t\geq\tau_0$, where $X(t,t_0,X_0)$ is any solution of the nonlinear matrix differential system (2.1) and $\eta=\tau_0-t_0\geq 0$ if and only if there exists an $L=L(\tau_0)>0$ such that

$$\|Y(t,\tau_0,Y_0)-X(t-\eta,t_0,X_0)\|\leq L(\tau_0)[\|Y_0-X_0\|+|\tau_0-t_0|]\exp[P(\tau_0)-P(t)],\quad t\geq\tau_0, \tag{2.13}$$

where $P\in\mathcal{K}=\{P\in C[\mathbb{R}_+,\mathbb{R}_+]:P(t)$ is strictly increasing in t and $P(0)=0\}$, $P(t)\to\infty$ as $t\to\infty$.

If L is independent of τ_0, then the solution $Y(t,\tau_0,Y_0)$ of the nonlinear matrix differential system (2.3) is initial time difference uniformly generalized exponentially asymptotically Lipschitz stable with respect to the solution $X(t-\eta,t_0,X_0)$ for $t\geq\tau_0$, related to the solution of nonlinear matrix differential system (2.1).

In particular, if $P(t)=\alpha t$ for $\alpha>0$, we have initial time difference exponentially asymptotically Lipschitz stable for matrix differential equations.

3. Variation-of-parameters formulae for perturbed and unperturbed nonlinear matrix differential equations with initial time difference

Now we have the following results for the systems (2.1), (2.2), and (2.3).

THEOREM 3.1. *Assume that f is continuous and has continuous partial derivatives $\partial f/\partial x$ on $\mathbb{R}_+\times\mathbb{R}^{n\times n}$. Let $x(t,\tau_0,y_0)$ be the unique solution of (2.6) existing for $t\geq\tau_0$, $\tau_0\in\mathbb{R}_+$, and* *let* $H(t,\tau_0,y_0) = (\partial f/\partial x)(t,x(t,\tau_0,y_0))$. *Then*

(i) $\varphi(t,\tau_0,y_0) = \partial x(t,\tau_0,y_0)/\partial y_0$ *exists and is the solution of*

$$z' = H(t,\tau_0,y_0)z \tag{3.1}$$

such that $\varphi(\tau_0,\tau_0,y_0) = I_{n\times n}$ *is the* $n\times n$ *identity matrix,*

(ii) $\partial x(t,\tau_0,y_0)/\partial\tau_0$ *exists and is the solution of (3.1) with* $\partial x(t,\tau_0,y_0)/\partial\tau_0 = -f(t_0,x_0)$ *and satisfies the relation*

$$\frac{\partial x(t,\tau_0,y_0)}{\partial\tau_0} + \varphi(t,\tau_0,y_0)f(\tau_0,y_0) = 0 \tag{3.2}$$

for $t \geq \tau_0$, $\tau_0 \in \mathbb{R}_+$,

(iii) *any solution* $y(t,\tau_0,y_0)$ *of (2.7) satisfies the integral equation, well-known Alekseev's formula,*

$$y(t,\tau_0,y_0) = x(t,\tau_0,y_0) + \int_{\tau_0}^{t} \varphi(t,s,y(s,\tau_0,y_0))R^*(s,y(s,\tau_0,y_0))ds, \tag{3.3}$$

where $\varphi(t,\tau_0,y_0) = \partial x(t,\tau_0,y_0)/\partial y_0$ *for* $t \geq \tau_0$.

THEOREM 3.2. *Assume that* $W(t,\tau_0,X_0)$ *and* $Z(t,\tau_0,X_0)$ *are the solutions of matrix differential systems of (3.4), (3.5), respectively, for* $t \geq \tau_0$. *Consider the matrix differential systems*

$$W' = A(t,\tau_0,X_0)W, \qquad Y(\tau_0) = I,\ t \geq \tau_0, \tag{3.4}$$

$$Z' = ZB(t,\tau_0,X_0), \qquad Z(\tau_0) = I,\ t \geq \tau_0, \tag{3.5}$$

and the perturbed matrix differential system of (3.4)

$$X' = A(t,\tau_0,X_0)X + XB(t,\tau_0,X_0), \quad X(\tau_0) = C,\ t \geq \tau_0, \tag{3.6}$$

where I *is* $n\times n$ *identity matrix,* $A(t,\tau_0,y_0)$ *and* $B(t,\tau_0,y_0)$ *are* $n\times n$ *continuous matrices for* $t \geq \tau_0$, *and* C *is* $n\times n$ *constant matrix.*

Then the solution of the matrix differential system of (3.6) satisfies the relation

$$X(t,\tau_0,X_0) = W(t,\tau_0,X_0)CZ(t,\tau_0,X_0), \quad t \geq \tau_0. \tag{3.7}$$

THEOREM 3.3. *Assume that* $f(t,x)$ *in (2.6) has continuous partial derivatives on* $\mathbb{R}_+ \times \mathbb{R}^{n\times n}$ *and let*

$$G(t,\tau_0,y_0) = \frac{\partial f}{\partial x}(t,x(t,\tau_0,y_0)). \tag{3.8}$$

If there exist $n\times n$ *matrices* $A(t,\tau_0,y_0)$ *and* $B(t,\tau_0,y_0)$ *as in Theorem 3.2 such that*

$$G = (A\otimes I) + (I\otimes B^T), \tag{3.9}$$

then

(i) $\varphi(t,\tau_0,y_0) = \partial x(t,\tau_0,y_0)/\partial y_0$ *exists, and is the fundamental matrix solution of*

$$\varphi' = G(t,\tau_0,y_0)\varphi \tag{3.10}$$

such that $\varphi(\tau_0,\tau_0,y_0) = I$, *and therefore*

$$\varphi(t,\tau_0,y_0) = W(t,\tau_0,y_0) \otimes Z^T(t,\tau_0,y_0), \tag{3.11}$$

where W and Z are the solutions of (3.4) and (3.5), respectively,

(ii) *any solution of (2.3) satisfies the integral equation*

$$\begin{aligned} Y(t,\tau_0,Y_0) &= X(t,\tau_0,Y_0) \\ &\quad + \int_{\tau_0}^{t} W(t,s,Y(s,\tau_0,Y_0))R(s,Y(s,\tau_0,Y_0))Z(t,s,Y(s,\tau_0,Y_0))ds, \quad t \geq \tau_0. \end{aligned} \tag{3.12}$$

The detailed proof of the theorem is in [4].

In this section, we will introduce the relation among the systems of perturbed and unperturbed matrix differential equations.

Theorem 3.4. *Assume that the solutions of (2.1) and (2.2) of the nonlinear matrix differential equations* $X(t-\eta,t_0,X_0)$ *through* (t_0,X_0) *and* $X(t,\tau_0,Y_0)$ *through* (τ_0,Y_0) *admit unique solutions for* $t \geq \tau_0$, *respectively. Then* $X(t,\tau_0,Y_0)$ *and* $X(t-\eta,t_0,X_0)$ *satisfy the integral equation*

$$\begin{aligned} X(t,\tau_0,Y_0) &= X(t-\eta,t_0,X_0) + \int_0^1 \varphi(t,\tau_0,\Omega(s))ds[Y_0 - X_0] \\ &\quad - \int_{\tau_0}^{t} \left[\frac{\partial X}{\partial \tau_0}(t,s,X(s-\eta)) + \varphi(t,s,X(s-\eta))F(s-\eta,X(s-\eta))\right]ds \end{aligned} \tag{3.13}$$

for $t \geq \tau_0 \geq 0$, *where* $\Omega(s) = Y_0 s + (1-s)X_0$ *for* $0 \leq s \leq 1$.

Proof. Let the systems (2.1) and (2.2) admit unique solutions $X(t-\eta,t_0,X_0)$, where $X(t,t_0,X_0)$ is any solution of the system (2.1) for $t \geq t_0 \geq 0$, through (t_0,X_0) and $X(t,\tau_0,Y_0)$ through (τ_0,Y_0) for $t \geq \tau_0 \geq 0$, $\tau_0 \in \mathbb{R}_+$.

Let us set $Q(s) = X(t,s,X(s-\eta))$ for $\tau_0 \leq s \leq t$, where $X(\tau_0-\eta,t_0,X_0) = X_0$, then we have

$$\frac{d}{ds}[Q(s)] = \frac{\partial X}{\partial \tau_0}(t,s,X(s-\eta)) + \frac{\partial X}{\partial Y_0}(t,s,X(s-\eta))X'(s-\eta). \tag{3.14}$$

Integrating (3.14) with respect to s between τ_0 and t, we get

$$\begin{aligned} X(t-\eta,t_0,X_0) &= X(t,\tau_0,X_0) \\ &\quad + \int_{\tau_0}^{t} \left[\frac{\partial X}{\partial \tau_0}(t,s,X(s-\eta)) + \varphi(t,s,X(s-\eta))F(s-\eta,X(s-\eta))\right]ds. \end{aligned} \tag{3.15}$$

Now, let

$$P(s) = X(t,\tau_0,\Omega(s)), \quad \Omega(s) = Y_0 s + (1-s)X_0, \quad 0 \le s \le 1, \tag{3.16}$$

then we have

$$\frac{d}{ds}[P(s)] = \frac{\partial X}{\partial Y_0}(t,\tau_0,\Omega(s))[Y_0 - X_0]. \tag{3.17}$$

Integrating (3.17) with respect to s between 0 and 1, we get

$$X(t,\tau_0,Y_0) = X(t,\tau_0,X_0) + \int_0^1 \varphi(t,\tau_0,\Omega(s))\,ds[Y_0 - X_0], \quad t \ge \tau_0. \tag{3.18}$$

Combining (3.15) and (3.18) yields (3.13). This completes the proof. □

Remark 3.5. Assume that the solutions of (2.2) of the nonlinear matrix differential equations $X(t,\tau_0,X_0)$ through (t_0,X_0) and $X(t,\tau_0,Y_0)$ through (τ_0,Y_0) admit unique solutions for $t \ge \tau_0$, respectively. If $\eta = 0$, then $X(t,\tau_0,Y_0)$ and $X(t,\tau_0,X_0)$ satisfy the integral equation

$$X(t,\tau_0,Y_0) = X(t,\tau_0,X_0) + \int_0^1 \varphi(t,\tau_0,\Omega(s))\,ds[Y_0 - X_0], \quad t \ge \tau_0, \tag{3.19}$$

where $\Omega(s) = Y_0 s + (1-s)X_0$ for $0 \le s \le 1$.

Hence, (3.19) gives us the relation between the solution of the nonlinear unperturbed matrix differential equations of (2.2) starting at different initial positions.

Theorem 3.6. *Assume that the solution of nonlinear perturbed matrix differential equation (2.3) $Y(t,\tau_0,Y_0)$ has continuous partial derivatives $\partial Y/\partial \tau_0$ and $\partial Y/\partial Y_0$ on $\mathbb{R}_+ \times \mathbb{R}_+ \times \mathbb{R}^{n\times n}$ and the solution of nonlinear unperturbed and perturbed matrix differential systems (2.1), (2.2), and (2.3) admit unique solutions $X(t,t_0,X_0)$ through (t_0,X_0) for $t \ge t_0$, $X(t,\tau_0,Y_0)$ through (τ_0,Y_0) for $t \ge \tau_0$, and $Y(t,\tau_0,Y_0)$ through (τ_0,Y_0) for $t \ge \tau_0$, respectively. Then $Y(t,\tau_0,Y_0)$ and $X(t-\eta,t_0,X_0)$ satisfy the integral equation*

$$\begin{aligned} Y(t,\tau_0,Y_0) - X(t-\eta,t_0,X_0) = &-\int_{\tau_0}^t \left[\frac{\partial Y}{\partial \tau_0}(t,\sigma,X(\sigma-\eta))\right] d\sigma \\ &- \int_{\tau_0}^t \left[\frac{\partial Y}{\partial Y_0}(t,\sigma,X(\sigma-\eta))F(\sigma-\eta,X(\sigma-\eta))\right] d\sigma \\ &+ \int_0^1 \frac{\partial Y}{\partial Y_0}(t,\tau_0,\Omega(s))\,ds[Y_0 - X_0], \end{aligned} \tag{3.20}$$

where $\Omega(s) = Y_0 s + (1-s)X_0$ for $0 \le s \le 1$ and $t \ge \tau_0$.

Proof. Let us consider the unique solution $X(t,\tau_0,Y_0)$ through (τ_0,Y_0) for $t \ge \tau_0$ of the system (2.2) $X(t-\eta,t_0,X_0)$ for $t \ge \tau_0$, where $X(t,t_0,X_0)$ is the unique solution through (t_0,X_0) of the differential system (2.1) for $t \ge t_0$, $t_0 \in \mathbb{R}_+$, and let the differential system (2.3) admit the unique solution $Y(t,\tau_0,Y_0)$ through (τ_0,Y_0) for $t \ge \tau_0$.

Let $\tilde{Q}(\sigma) = Y(t,\sigma,X(\sigma-\eta))$ for $\tau_0 \le \sigma \le t$, where $X(\tau_0-\eta,t_0,X_0) = X_0$; differentiating $\tilde{Q}$ with respect to σ and integrating between τ_0 and t, we get

$$\begin{aligned} X(t-\eta,t_0,X_0) = Y(t,\tau_0,X_0) &+ \int_{\tau_0}^{t} \frac{\partial Y}{\partial \tau_0}(t,\sigma,x(\sigma-\eta))\,d\sigma \\ &+ \int_{\tau_0}^{t} \frac{\partial Y}{\partial Y_0}(t,\sigma,x(\sigma-\eta))F(\sigma-\eta,x(\sigma-\eta))\,d\sigma. \end{aligned} \tag{3.21}$$

Now, let

$$\tilde{P}(s) = Y(t,\tau_0,\Omega(s)), \quad \Omega(s) = Y_0 s + (1-s)X_0 \quad \text{for } 0 \le s \le 1, \tag{3.22}$$

then we have

$$\frac{d}{ds}[\tilde{P}(s)] = \frac{\partial Y}{\partial Y_0}(t,\tau_0,\Omega(s))[Y_0 - X_0]. \tag{3.23}$$

Integrating with respect to s from 0 to 1, we get

$$Y(t,\tau_0,Y_0) = Y(t,\tau_0,X_0) + \int_0^1 \frac{\partial Y}{\partial Y_0}(t,\tau_0,\Omega(s))\,ds[Y_0 - X_0], \quad t \ge \tau_0 \ge 0. \tag{3.24}$$

Combining (3.21) and (3.24) yields (3.20) which is equivalent to (3.12). Here (3.20) gives us the relation between the solutions of the nonlinear unperturbed matrix differential equation (2.1) and nonlinear perturbed matrix differential equation (2.3) starting at different initial data in time and space. □

Remark 3.7. Assume that the solution of nonlinear perturbed matrix differential equation (2.3) $Y(t,\tau_0,Y_0)$ has continuous partial derivatives $\partial Y/\partial \tau_0$ and $\partial Y/\partial Y_0$ on $\mathbb{R}_+ \times \mathbb{R}_+ \times \mathbb{R}^{n\times n}$ and the solution of nonlinear unperturbed and perturbed matrix differential systems (2.2) and (2.3) admit unique solutions $X(t,\tau_0,Y_0)$ through (τ_0,Y_0) for $t \ge \tau_0$ and $Y(t,\tau_0,Y_0)$ through (τ_0,Y_0) for $t \ge \tau_0$, respectively. If $\eta = 0$, then $Y(t,\tau_0,Y_0)$ and $X(t,\tau_0,X_0)$ satisfy the integral equation

$$\begin{aligned} Y(t,\tau_0,Y_0) - X(t,\tau_0,X_0) = &-\int_{\tau_0}^{t} \left[\frac{\partial Y}{\partial \tau_0}(t,\sigma,X(\sigma)) + \frac{\partial Y}{\partial Y_0}(t,\sigma,X(\sigma))F(\sigma,X(\sigma))\right] d\sigma \\ &+ \int_0^1 \frac{\partial Y}{\partial Y_0}(t,\tau_0,\Omega(s))\,ds[Y_0 - X_0], \end{aligned} \tag{3.25}$$

where $\Omega(s) = Y_0 s + (1-s)X_0$ for $0 \le s \le 1$ and $t \ge \tau_0$.

Here (3.25) gives us the relation between the solutions of the nonlinear unperturbed matrix differential equation (2.1) and nonlinear perturbed matrix differential equation (2.3) starting at the same in time and at different initial positions in space.

Recently, the qualitative behavior of nonlinear differential systems with an initial time difference has been investigated for systems with a different initial position and a different initial time [8–11]. The definitions of the notions of Lipschitz stability are not with respect to the null solution but with respect to the unperturbed differential system that also has a difference in initial time and in initial position. We use these definitions of initial time difference Lipschitz stability to obtain results in Section 4.

4. Lipschitz stability criteria for nonlinear matrix differential systems with initial time difference

Next, we will show that in the nonlinear case, initial time difference Lipschitz stability for matrix system of equations is stronger than stability with initial time difference in uniform or not in uniform.

THEOREM 4.1. *Lipschitz stability for the nonlinear matrix differential system with initial time difference does imply stability for the nonlinear matrix differential system with initial time difference.*

Proof. By using the definition of Lipschitz stability with initial time difference in Definition 2.1, assume that the solution $Y(t,\tau_0,Y_0)$ of the nonlinear matrix differential system (2.3) through (τ_0,Y_0) is initial time difference Lipschitz stable with respect to the solution $X(t-\eta,t_0,X_0)$ for $t \geq \tau_0$, where $X(t,t_0,X_0)$ is any solution of the nonlinear matrix differential system (2.1) and $\eta = \tau_0 - t_0 \geq 0$. Then there exists an $L = L(\tau_0) > 0$ such that

$$||Y(t,\tau_0,Y_0) - X(t-\eta,t_0,X_0)|| \leq L(\tau_0)[||Y_0 - X_0|| + |\tau_0 - t_0|], \quad t \geq \tau_0. \tag{4.1}$$

Given any $\varepsilon > 0$, we can choose

$$||Y_0 - X_0|| < \frac{\varepsilon}{2L} = \delta_1(\varepsilon,\tau_0), \qquad |\tau_0 - t_0| < \frac{\varepsilon}{2L} = \delta_2(\varepsilon,\tau_0), \tag{4.2}$$

then we get

$$||Y(t,\tau_0,Y_0) - X(t-\eta,t_0,X_0)|| < \varepsilon, \quad t \geq \tau_0, \tag{4.3}$$

and so $Y(t,\tau_0,Y_0)$ the solution of the nonlinear matrix differential system (2.3) through (τ_0,Y_0) is initial time difference Lipschitz stable with respect to the solution $X(t-\eta,t_0,X_0)$ for $t \geq \tau_0$, where $X(t,t_0,X_0)$ is any solution of the nonlinear matrix differential system (2.1) and $\eta = \tau_0 - t_0 \geq 0$.

If L is independent of τ_0, then so are δ_1 and δ_2 and the result holds uniformly. □

THEOREM 4.2. *Initial time difference stability for nonlinear matrix differential system does not imply Lipschitz stability for nonlinear matrix differential system with initial time difference.*

For the proof, see [7].

For the special case of $Y_0 = X_0$ and $\tau_0 = t_0$, there is a counterexample previously constructed in [2, Example 1.4].

THEOREM 4.3. *Let the nonlinear matrix differential systems (2.2) and (2.1) admit unique solutions $X(t,\tau_0,Y_0)$ through (τ_0,Y_0) for $t \geq \tau_0$ and $X(t,t_0,X_0)$ through (t_0,X_0) for $t \geq t_0$,* *respectively. Let $X(t-\eta,t_0,X_0)$ be defined for $t \geq \tau_0$ and $\eta = \tau_0 - t_0 \geq 0$. Assume that*

(i) *there exist finite, nonnegative constants $K(\tau_0)$ and $\ln(M(\tau_0))$ such that $\int_{\tau_0}^{\infty} N(s)ds = K(\tau_0)$ and $\int_{\tau_0}^{\infty} \lambda(s)ds = \ln(M(\tau_0))$, where $N(s),\lambda(s) \in C[[0,\infty),\mathbb{R}_+]$,*

(ii) *F is Lipschitzian in time and space such that*

$$\begin{aligned}&||F(t,V(t,\tau_0,V_0)+X(t-\eta,t_0,X_0)) - F(t-\eta,X(t-\eta,t_0,X_0))||\\&\quad\leq \lambda(t)||V(t)|| + \frac{|\eta|}{K(\tau_0)}N(t),\end{aligned} \tag{4.4}$$

where $V(t,\tau_0,V_0) = X(t,\tau_0,Y_0) - X(t-\eta,t_0,X_0)$, $V_0 = Y_0 - X_0$ for $t \geq \tau_0$.

Then the solution $X(t,\tau_0,Y_0)$ of nonlinear matrix differential equation of (2.2) is initial time difference Lipschitz stable with respect to the solution $X(t-\eta,t_0,X_0)$.

Proof. Let us consider the unique solutions $X(t,\tau_0,Y_0)$ through (τ_0,Y_0) and $X(t-\eta,t_0,X_0)$ through (t_0,X_0) for $t \geq \tau_0$ of (2.1) and (2.2), respectively. Let us set

$$V(t,\tau_0,V_0) = X(t,\tau_0,Y_0) - X(t-\eta,t_0,X_0), \quad V_0 = Y_0 - X_0,\ t \geq \tau_0. \tag{4.5}$$

By using assumptions (i) and (ii), we obtain

$$\begin{aligned}||V(t,\tau_0,V_0)|| &\leq ||Y_0 - X_0|| + \int_{\tau_0}^{t}\left[\lambda(s)||V(s)|| + \frac{|\eta|}{K(\tau_0)}N(s)\right]ds,\\ Z(t) &\leq Z(t_0) + |\eta| + \int_{\tau_0}^{t}[\lambda(s)Z(s)]ds,\end{aligned} \tag{4.6}$$

where $Z(t) = ||X(t,\tau_0,Y_0) - X(t-\eta,t_0,X_0)||$, $Z_0 = ||Y_0 - X_0||$ for $t \geq \tau_0$. By using Gronwall's inequality for $Z(t)$ and $\lambda(s)$ in (4.6),

$$||X(t,\tau_0,Y_0) - X(t-\eta,t_0,X_0)|| \leq L[||Y_0 - X_0|| + |\tau_0 - t_0|] \tag{4.7}$$

for $M(\tau_0) \leq L$. Definition 2.2 leads to the desired conclusion.

If $\ln(M(\tau_0))$ is independent of τ_0, then the solution $X(t,\tau_0,Y_0)$ of nonlinear matrix differential equation of (2.2) is initial time difference uniformly Lipschitz stable with respect to the solution $X(t-\eta,t_0,X_0)$. □

Theorem 4.4. *Let the nonlinear matrix differential systems of (2.1), (2.2), and (2.3) admit unique solutions $X(t,t_0,X_0)$ through (t_0,X_0) for $t \geq t_0$, $X(t,\tau_0,Y_0)$ through (τ_0,Y_0), and $Y(t,\tau_0,Y_0)$ through (τ_0,Y_0) for $t \geq \tau_0$, respectively. Let $X(t-\eta,t_0,X_0)$ be defined for $t \geq \tau_0$ and $\eta = \tau_0 - t_0 \geq 0$. Assume that the hypotheses of Theorem 4.3 are satisfied, and*

(i) *the solution $X(t,\tau_0,Y_0)$ of nonlinear matrix differential equation of (2.2) is initial time difference uniformly Lipschitz stable with respect to the solution $X(t-\eta,t_0,X_0)$,*

(ii) *there exist an M_1 and $\lambda_1 \in C[[0,\infty),\mathbb{R}_+]$, and the matrices W and Z as in Theorem 3.2*

$$||W(t,s,Y(s))||||Z(t,s,Y(s))|| \leq M_1, \qquad ||R(s,Y(s))|| \leq \lambda_1(s)||Y(s)||, \tag{4.8}$$

where $||Y(s)|| \leq \alpha$ for $\alpha > 0$.

Then the solution $Y(t,\tau_0,Y_0)$ of nonlinear matrix differential equation of (2.2) is initial time difference uniformly Lipschitz stable in variation with respect to the solution $X(t-\eta,t_0,X_0)$.

Proof. By using Theorem 3.3, formula (3.12), and $V(t)$, $V_0 = Y_0 - X_0$, $t \geq \tau_0$, as in Theorem 4.3(ii), we have

$$\begin{aligned} &Y(t,\tau_0,Y_0) - X(t-\eta,t_0,X_0) \\ &\quad = V(t,\tau_0,V_0) + \int_{\tau_0}^{t} W(t,s,Y(s,\tau_0,Y_0))R(s,Y(s,\tau_0,Y_0))Z(t,s,Y(s,\tau_0,Y_0))ds, \end{aligned} \tag{4.9}$$

the integral equation with different initial time and position for perturbed and unperturbed nonlinear matrix differential systems. Then,

$$\begin{aligned} &||Y(t,\tau_0,Y_0) - X(t-\eta,t_0,X_0)|| \\ &\quad \leq [||Y_0 - X_0|| + |\tau_0 - t_0|]L(\tau_0) \\ &\quad + \int_{\tau_0}^{t} ||W(t,s,Y(s,\tau_0,Y_0))||\,||R(s,Y(s,\tau_0,Y_0))||\,||Z(t,s,Y(s,\tau_0,Y_0))||ds, \quad t \geq \tau_0. \end{aligned} \tag{4.10}$$

Setting $T(t) = \|Y(t,\tau_0,Y_0) - X(t-\eta,t_0,X_0)\|$, $\int_{\tau_0}^{t} \lambda_1(s)ds = \Omega(\tau_0)$, $M_1\lambda_1(t) = \lambda(t)$ for $t \geq \tau_0$, we obtain

$$T(t) \leq C + \int_{\tau_0}^{t} \lambda(s)T(s)ds, \tag{4.11}$$

where $C = [(\|Y_0 - X_0\| + |\tau_0 - t_0|)L(\tau_0) + \alpha M_1^2\Omega(\tau_0)]$. Applying Gronwall's inequality,

$$||Y(t,\tau_0,Y_0) - X(t-\eta,t_0,X_0)|| \leq M[||Y_0 - X_0|| + |\tau_0 - t_0|], \quad t \geq \tau_0, \tag{4.12}$$

where

$$\begin{aligned} M = [||Y_0 - X_0|| + |\tau_0 - t_0|]^{-1}[[(||Y_0 - X_0|| + |\tau_0 - t_0|)L(\tau_0) \\ + \alpha M_1^2\Omega(\tau_0)]]\exp[M_1N_1(\tau_0)]. \end{aligned} \tag{4.13}$$

By using Definition 2.2, the solution $Y(t,\tau_0,Y_0)$ of the nonlinear matrix differential system (2.3) through (τ_0,Y_0) is initial time difference uniformly Lipschitz stable in variation with respect to the solution $X(t-\eta,t_0,X_0)$ for $t \geq \tau_0$. This completes the proof. □

THEOREM 4.5. *Let the nonlinear matrix differential systems of (2.2) admit the unique solution $X(t,\tau_0,Y_0)$ through (τ_0,Y_0) for $t \geq \tau_0$ and let the nonlinear matrix differential systems of (2.1) admit the unique solution $X(t-\eta,t_0,X_0)$ through (t_0,X_0) for $t \geq \tau_0$ and $\eta = \tau_0 - t_0 \geq 0$. Assume that*

(i) *for $P, p \in \mathcal{K}$, p is antiderivative of P and $V(t,\tau_0,V_0) = X(t,\tau_0,Y_0) - X(t-\eta,t_0,X_0)$ for $t \geq \tau_0$,*

$$\lim_{h\to 0^-} \frac{\|V(t,\tau_0,V_0)+[F(t,X(t-\eta,t_0,X_0)+V(t,\tau_0,V_0))-F(t,X(t-\eta,t_0,X_0))]h\|-\|V(t,\tau_0,V_0)\|}{h} \leq -p(t)\|V(t,\tau_0,V_0)\|, \tag{4.14}$$

(ii) *nonlinear Matrix F is Lipschitz in time such that*

$$\|F(t,X(t-\eta,t_0,X_0)) - F(t-\eta,X(t-\eta,t_0,X_0))\| \leq L_1(t)\frac{|\eta|}{L_2(\tau_0)}, \tag{4.15}$$

where $L_2 \in C[\mathbb{R}_+,\mathbb{R}_+]$ and $\int_{\tau_0}^{\infty} \exp[P(u)-P(\tau_0)]L_1(u)du = L_2(\tau_0)$.

Then the solution $X(t,\tau_0,Y_0)$ of nonlinear unperturbed matrix differential equation of (2.2) is initial time difference generalized exponentially asymptotically Lipschitz stable with respect to the solution $X(t-\eta,t_0,X_0)$.

Proof. Let us consider the unique solution $X(t,\tau_0,Y_0)$ through (τ_0,Y_0) of the system (2.2) for $t \geq \tau_0$ and let the nonlinear matrix differential systems of (2.1) admit the unique solution $X(t-\eta,t_0,X_0)$ through (t_0,X_0) for $t \geq \tau_0$ and $\eta = \tau_0 - t_0 \geq 0$, where $X(t,t_0,X_0)$ is the solution of the system (2.1) through (t_0,X_0) for $t \geq t_0$. Setting $T(t) = \|V(t,\tau_0,V_0)\|$, by differentiating and using a Taylor approximation for V, we have

$$T'(t) \leq -p(t)T(t) + \frac{|\eta|}{L_2(\tau_0)}L_1(t), \qquad T(\tau_0) = \|Y_0 - X_0\| \tag{4.16}$$

differential inequality which leads to the inequality

$$T(t) \leq \exp\left[-\int_{\tau_0}^{t} p(s)ds\right]\left[T(\tau_0) + \frac{|\eta|}{L_2(\tau_0)}\int_{\tau_0}^{t} \exp\left[\int_{\tau_0}^{u} p(s)ds\right]L_1(u)du\right]. \tag{4.17}$$

By using assumption (ii), we obtain

$$\begin{gathered} T(t) \leq \exp[P(\tau_0)-P(t)]\left[T(\tau_0) + \frac{|\eta|}{L_2(\tau_0)}\int_{\tau_0}^{\infty} \exp\left[\int_{\tau_0}^{u} p(s)ds\right]L_1(u)du\right], \\ T(t) \leq \exp[P(\tau_0)-P(t)][T(\tau_0)+|\eta|], \quad T(\tau_0) = \|Y_0 - X_0\|, \end{gathered} \tag{4.18}$$

which is

$$\|X(t,\tau_0,Y_0) - X(t-\eta,t_0,X_0)\| \leq \exp[P(\tau_0)-P(t)][\|Y_0 - X_0\| + |\tau_0 - t_0|]. \tag{4.19}$$

By using Definition 2.5 with $L = 1$, the solution $X(t,\tau_0,Y_0)$ of nonlinear unperturbed matrix differential equation of (2.2) is initial time difference generalized exponentially asymptotically Lipschitz stable with respect to the solution $X(t-\eta,t_0,X_0)$. This completes the proof. □

Remark 4.6. Let the nonlinear matrix differential systems of (2.2) admit the unique solution $X(t,\tau_0,Y_0)$ through (τ_0,Y_0) for $t\geq\tau_0$ and let the nonlinear matrix differential systems of (2.1) admit the unique solution $X(t-\eta,t_0,X_0)$ through (t_0,X_0) for $t\geq\tau_0$ and $\eta=\tau_0-t_0\geq 0$. Assume that

(i) for $\vartheta>0$ and $V(t,\tau_0,V_0)=X(t,\tau_0,Y_0)-X(t-\eta,t_0,X_0)$ for $t\geq\tau_0$,

$$\lim_{h\to 0^-}\frac{\|V(t,\tau_0,V_0)+[F(t,X(t-\eta,t_0,X_0)+V(t,\tau_0,V_0))-F(t,X(t-\eta,t_0,X_0))]h\|-\|V(t,\tau_0,V_0)\|}{h}$$
$$\leq -\vartheta\|V(t,\tau_0,V_0)\|, \tag{4.20}$$

(ii) nonlinear Matrix F is Lipschitz in time such that

$$\|F(t,X(t-\eta,t_0,X_0))-F(t-\eta,X(t-\eta,t_0,X_0))\|\leq L_1(t)\frac{|\eta|}{L_2(\tau_0)}, \tag{4.21}$$

where $L_2\in C[\mathbb{R}_+,\mathbb{R}_+]$ and $\int_{\tau_0}^{\infty}\exp[\vartheta(s-\tau_0)]L_1(s)ds=L_2(\tau_0)$.

Then the solution $X(t,\tau_0,Y_0)$ of nonlinear unperturbed matrix differential equation of (2.2) is initial time difference exponentially asymptotically Lipschitz stable with respect to the solution $X(t-\eta,t_0,X_0)$.

Proof. Let us consider the unique solution $X(t,\tau_0,Y_0)$ through (τ_0,Y_0) of the system (2.2) for $t\geq\tau_0$ and let the nonlinear matrix differential systems of (2.1) admit the unique solution $X(t-\eta,t_0,X_0)$ through (t_0,X_0) for $t\geq\tau_0$ and $\eta=\tau_0-t_0\geq 0$, where $X(t,t_0,X_0)$ is the solution of the system (2.1) through (t_0,X_0) for $t\geq t_0$. Setting $T(t)=\|V(t,\tau_0,V_0)\|$, by differentiating and using a Taylor approximation for V, we have

$$T'(t)\leq -\vartheta T(t)+\frac{|\eta|}{L_2(\tau_0)}L_1(t),\qquad T(\tau_0)=\|Y_0-X_0\| \tag{4.22}$$

differential inequality which leads to the inequality

$$T(t)\leq \exp[-\vartheta(t-\tau_0)]\left[T(\tau_0)+\frac{|\eta|}{L_2(\tau_0)}\int_{\tau_0}^{\infty}\exp[\vartheta(s-\tau_0)]L_1(s)ds\right]. \tag{4.23}$$

By using assumption (ii), we obtain

$$T(t)\leq \exp[-\vartheta(t-\tau_0)][T(\tau_0)+|\eta|],\qquad T(\tau_0)=\|Y_0-X_0\|, \tag{4.24}$$

which is

$$\|X(t,\tau_0,Y_0)-X(t-\eta,t_0,X_0)\|\leq \exp[-\vartheta(t-\tau_0)][\|Y_0-X_0\|+|\tau_0-t_0|]. \tag{4.25}$$

By using Definition 2.5 with $L=1$ and $P(t)=\vartheta t$, $\vartheta>0$, the solution $X(t,\tau_0,Y_0)$ of nonlinear unperturbed matrix differential equation of (2.2) is initial time difference exponentially asymptotically Lipschitz stable with respect to the solution $X(t-\eta,t_0,X_0)$. This completes the proof. □

Theorem 4.7. *Let the nonlinear matrix differential systems of (2.1), (2.2), and (2.3) admit unique solutions* $X(t,t_0,X_0)$ *through* (t_0,X_0) *for* $t \geq t_0$, $X(t,\tau_0,Y_0)$ *through* (τ_0,Y_0), *and* $Y(t,\tau_0,Y_0)$ *through* (τ_0,Y_0) *for* $t \geq \tau_0$, *respectively. Let* $X(t-\eta,t_0,X_0)$ *be defined for* $t \geq \tau_0$ *and* $\eta = \tau_0 - t_0 \geq 0$. *In addition to the hypotheses of Theorem 4.3 being satisfied, assume that*

(i) *the solution* $X(t,\tau_0,Y_0)$ *of nonlinear matrix differential equation of (2.2) is initial time difference exponentially asymptotically Lipschitz stable with respect to the solution* $X(t-\eta,t_0,X_0)$,

(ii) *there exist an* N *and* $\lambda \in C[[0,\infty),\mathbb{R}_+]$, *the matrices* W *and* Z *as in Theorem 3.2, and*

$$\begin{aligned} ||W(t,s,Y(s))||\,||Z(t,s,Y(s))|| &\leq N\exp[-\alpha(t-s)], \\ ||R(s,Y(s))|| &\leq \lambda(s)||Y(s)||, \end{aligned} \tag{4.26}$$

where $\|Y(s)\| \leq \alpha$ *for* $\alpha > 0$.

Then the solution $Y(t,\tau_0,Y_0)$ *of nonlinear perturbed matrix differential equation of (2.3) is initial time difference exponentially asymptotically Lipschitz stable in variation with respect to the solution* $X(t-\eta,t_0,X_0)$.

Proof. By Theorem 4.3 and the assumptions (i) and (ii), we have

$$\begin{aligned} &||Y(t,\tau_0,Y_0) - X(t-\eta,t_0,X_0)|| \\ &\quad \leq ||V(t,\tau_0,V_0)|| \\ &\qquad + \int_{\tau_0}^{t} ||W(t,s,Y(s,\tau_0,Y_0))||\,||R(s,Y(s,\tau_0,Y_0))||\,||Z(t,s,Y(s,\tau_0,Y_0))||ds \\ &\quad \leq M[||Y_0 - X_0|| + |\tau_0 - t_0|\exp -\alpha(t-\tau_0)] + \int_{\tau_0}^{t} N\lambda(s)\exp[-\alpha(t-s)]||Y(s)||ds. \end{aligned} \tag{4.27}$$

Setting $T(t) = \exp[-\alpha(t-\tau_0)]\|Y(t,\tau_0,Y_0) - X(t-\eta,t_0,X_0)\|$, we obtain

$$T(t)[M[||Y_0 - X_0|| + |\tau_0 - t_0|] + N^2\alpha N_1(\tau_0)] + \int_{\tau_0}^{t} N\lambda(s)T(s)ds, \quad t \geq \tau_0, \tag{4.28}$$

where $N_1(\tau_0) = \int_{\tau_0}^{t} \lambda(s)ds$. By using Gronwall's inequality, we have

$$\begin{aligned} &T(t) \leq [M[||Y_0 - X_0|| + |\tau_0 - t_0|] + N^2\alpha N_1(\tau_0)]\exp\left[\int_{\tau_0}^{t} N\lambda(s)ds\right], \quad t \geq \tau_0, \\ &||Y(t,\tau_0,Y_0) - X(t-\eta,t_0,X_0)|| \\ &\quad \leq [M[||Y_0 - X_0|| + |\tau_0 - t_0|] + N^2\alpha N_1(\tau_0)]\exp[NN_1(\tau_0)]\exp[-\alpha(t-\tau_0)]. \end{aligned} \tag{4.29}$$

If we choose

$$L(\alpha,\tau_0) = [||Y_0 - X_0|| + |\tau_0 - t_0|]^{-1}[M[||Y_0 - X_0|| + |\tau_0 - t_0|] + N^2\alpha N_1(\tau_0)]\exp[NN_1(\tau_0)], \tag{4.30}$$

then we get the desired conclusion. Hence,

$$||Y(t,\tau_0,Y_0) - X(t-\eta,t_0,X_0)|| \le L[||Y_0 - X_0|| + |\tau_0 - t_0|]\exp[-\alpha(t-\tau_0)], \tag{4.31}$$

where $L = L(\alpha,\tau_0)$. The solution $Y(t,\tau_0,Y_0)$ of nonlinear perturbed matrix differential equation of (2.2) is initial time difference exponentially asymptotically Lipschitz stable in variation with respect to the solution $X(t-\eta,t_0,X_0)$. This completes the proof of the theorem. □

THEOREM 4.8. *Exponentially asymptotically (uniform) Lipschitz stability with initial time difference for the nonlinear matrix differential system does imply asymptotically (uniform) Lipschitz stability with initial time difference for the nonlinear matrix differential system.*
Proof. One can prove this theorem very easily by using Definition 2.3 of asymptotically (uniform) Lipschitz stability with initial time difference. The details are omitted. □

THEOREM 4.9. *Exponentially asymptotically (uniform) Lipschitz stability in variation with initial time difference for the nonlinear matrix differential system does imply asymptotically (uniform) Lipschitz stability in variation with initial time difference for the nonlinear matrix differential system.*

Proof. One also can prove this theorem very easily by using Definition 2.4 of asymptotically Lipschitz stability in variation with initial time difference. The details are omitted. □

References

[1] F. Brauer and A. Strauss, *Perturbations of nonlinear systems of differential equations. III*, Journal of Mathematical Analysis and Applications **31** (1970), no. 1, 37–48.

[2] F. M. Dannan and S. Elaydi, *Lipschitz stability of nonlinear systems of differential equations*, Journal of Mathematical Analysis and Applications **113** (1986), no. 2, 562–577.

[3] ______, *Lipschitz stability of nonlinear systems of differential equations. II. Lyapunov functions*, Journal of Mathematical Analysis and Applications **143** (1989), no. 2, 517–529.

[4] D. W. Fausett and S. Köksal, *Variation of parameters formula and Lipschitz stability of nonlinear matrix differential equations*, World Congress of Nonlinear Analysts '92, Vol. I–IV (Tampa, FL, 1992), de Gruyter, Berlin, 1996, pp. 1415–1426.

[5] R. A. Horn and C. R. Johnson, *Topics in Matrix Analysis*, Cambridge University Press, Cambridge, 1991.

[6] V. Lakshmikantham and S. G. Deo, *Method of Variation of Parameters for Dynamic Systems*, Series in Mathematical Analysis and Applications, vol. 1, Gordon and Breach Science, Amsterdam, 1998.

[7] V. Lakshmikantham, S. Leela, and A. A. Martynyuk, *Stability Analysis of Nonlinear Systems*, Monographs and Textbooks in Pure and Applied Mathematics, vol. 125, Marcel Dekker, New York, 1989.

[8] V. Lakshmikantham and A. S. Vatsala, *Differential inequalities with initial time difference and applications*, Journal of Inequalities and Applications **3** (1999), no. 3, 233–244.

[9] M. D. Shaw and C. Yakar, *Generalized variation of parameters with initial time difference and a comparison result in terms of Lyapunov-like functions*, International Journal of Nonlinear Differential Equations Theory-Methods and Applications **5** (1999), no. 1-2, 86–108.

[10] ______, *Stability criteria and slowly growing motions with initial time difference*, Problems of Nonlinear Analysis in Engineering Systems **1** (2000).

[11] C. Yakar, *Stability analysis of nonlinear differential systems with initial time difference*, Ph.D dissertation, Florida Institute of Technology, Melbourne, Florida, December 2000.

Coskun Yakar: Department of Mathematics, Faculty of Sciences, Gebze Institute of Technology, Gebze, Kocaeli 141-41400, Turkey
E-mail address: cyakar@gyte.edu.tr

MONOTONE TECHNIQUE FOR NONLINEAR SECOND-ORDER PERIODIC BOUNDARY VALUE PROBLEM IN TERMS OF TWO MONOTONE FUNCTIONS

COSKUN YAKAR AND ALI SIRMA

This paper investigates the fundamental theorem concerning the existence of coupled minimal and maximal solutions of the second-order nonlinear periodic boundary value problems involving the sum of two different functions. We have such a problem in applied mathematics, which has several applications to the theory of monotone iterative techniques for periodic problems, as has been pointed in the several results and theorems made in the paper.

1. Introduction

The method of upper and lower solutions has been effectively used, an interesting and fruitful technique, for proving the existence results for a wide variety of nonlinear periodic boundary value problems. When coupled with monotone iterative technique, it manifests itself as an effective and flexible mechanism that offers theoretical as well as constructive existence results in a closed set, generated by lower and upper solutions. One obtains a constructive procedure for obtaining the solutions of the nonlinear problems besides enabling the study of the qualitative properties of the solutions of periodic boundary value problems. The concept embedded in these techniques has proved to be of enormous value and has played an important role consolidating a wide variety of nonlinear problems [1–4]. Moreover, iteration schemes are also useful for the investigation of qualitative properties of the solutions, particularly, in unifying a variety of periodic nonlinear boundary value problems.

We have to refer [1, 2] for an excellent and comprehensive introduction to the monotone iterative techniques for nonlinear periodic boundary value problems.

This method has further been exploited in combination with the method of quasilinearization to obtain concurrently the lower and upper bounding monotone sequences, whose elements are solutions of linear boundary value problems which converge unifomly and monotonically to the unique solution of (2.1) and the convergence is quadratic.

Hindawi Publishing Corporation
Proceedings of the Conference on Differential & Difference Equations and Applications, pp. 1217–1229

This extemporization, known as generalized quasilinearization, has also been effectively used to study the second-order nonlinear periodic boundary problems [1, 2].

In many cases, we can find a minimal solution and a maximal solution for (2.1) between the lower and upper solutions using the monotone iterative technique. The following fundamental theorems are of importance in this context.

2. Basic definitions and theorems

Consider the second-order periodic boundary value problem

$$-u'' = f(t,u), \qquad u(0) = u(2\pi), \qquad u'(0) = u'(2\pi), \tag{2.1}$$

where $f \in C[Jx\mathbb{R},\mathbb{R}]$ and $J = [0,2\pi]$.

Before the main theorems, let us give the definition of lower and upper solutions of (2.1) and the comparison lemma.

Definition 2.1. Given $\alpha,\beta \in C^{2,0}[J,\mathbb{R}]$ and α,β satisfy

(i) $-\alpha'' \leq f(t,\alpha)$, $t \in J$, $\alpha(0) = \alpha(2\pi)$, and $\alpha'(0) \geqslant \alpha'(2\pi)$,

(ii) $-\beta'' \geqslant f(t,\beta)$, $t \in J$, $\beta(0) = \beta(2\pi)$, and $\beta'(0) \leq \beta'(2\pi)$,

then α and β are called lower and upper solutions of second-order PBVP, respectively.

Now we have the comparison lemma.

Lemma 2.2. *Let $m \in C^{2,0}[J,\mathbb{R}]$ and let m satisfy*

$$-m''(t) \leq -M^2 m(t), \quad m(0) = m(2\pi), \quad m'(0) \geq m'(2\pi), \quad t \in J, \tag{2.2}$$

then $m(t) \leq 0$ on J. If equality holds in the above formula, then it becomes $m(t) = 0$ on J.

Proof. Assume by contradiction that there exists $t_0 \in [0,2\pi]$ and there exists $\varepsilon > 0$ such that $m(t_0) = \varepsilon$ for all $t \in J$ $m(t) \leq \varepsilon$. Assume that $t_0 \in (0,2\pi)$. In this case since m has local maximum at $t = t_0$ on J, then it becomes $m'(t_0) = 0$ and $m''(t_0) \leq 0$ so that

$$0 \leq -m''(t_0) \leq -M^2 m(t_0) = -M^2\varepsilon < 0, \tag{2.3}$$

which is a contradiction. Let $t_0 = 0$ or 2π, then $m(0) = m(2\pi) = \varepsilon$ and $m(t) \leq \varepsilon$ on J. This implies that $m'(0) \leq 0$ and $m'(2\pi) \geq 0$. Using the boundary conditions, we arrive at $0 \geq m'(0) \geq m'(2\pi) \geq 0$, that is, $m'(0) = m'(2\pi) = 0$. Hence for $i = 1$ or 2π, and

$$-m''(i) \leq -M^2 m(i) = -M^2\varepsilon < 0, \tag{2.4}$$

this contradicts with $m(0) = m(2\pi) = \varepsilon$. □

Theorem 2.3. *Assume that α and β are lower and upper solutions of second-order PBVP (2.1), respectively. Assume also that for $\alpha(t) \leq u_2 \leq u_1 \leq \beta(t)$, f satisfying*

$$f(t,u_1) - f(t,u_2) \geq -M^2(u_1 - u_2), \tag{2.5}$$

then there exist monotone sequences $\{\alpha_n(t)\}$ *and* $\{\beta_n(t)\}$ *with* $\alpha_0 = \alpha$ *and* $\beta_0 = \beta$, *and*

$$\alpha = \alpha_0 \leq \alpha_1 \leq \cdots \leq \alpha_n \leq \beta_n \leq \cdots \leq \beta_1 \leq \beta_0 = \beta \tag{2.6}$$

such that they converge uniformly to minimal and maximal solutions of (2.5), respectively, on $[\alpha,\beta] = \{u \in C[J,\mathbb{R}] : \alpha \leq u \leq \beta\}$.

Proof. For any

$$\eta \in [\alpha,\beta] = \{\eta \in C[J,\mathbb{R}] : \alpha(t) \leq \eta(t) \leq \beta(t),\ t \in J\}, \tag{2.7}$$

consider the second-order linear PBVP

$$-u''(t) + M^2 u(t) = \sigma(t,\eta), \qquad u(0) = u(2\pi), \qquad u'(0) = u'(2\pi), \tag{2.8}$$

where

$$\sigma(t,\eta) \equiv f(t,\eta) + M^2\eta. \tag{2.9}$$

We can find solution $u(t)$ of (2.1) in the following way.

First solve homogeneous equation

$$u''(t) - M^2 u(t) = 0. \tag{2.10}$$

It has solution in the form of

$$u(t) = c_1 e^{Mt} + c_2 e^{-Mt}, \tag{2.11}$$

where c_1 and c_2 are real constants. Using the method of undetermined coefficients, solution of (2.8) becomes in the form of

$$u(t) = c_1(t)e^{Mt} + c_2(t)e^{-Mt}. \tag{2.12}$$

Now we need to find the functions $c_1(t)$ and $c_2(t)$. Therefore

$$w(t) = \begin{vmatrix} e^{Mt} & e^{-Mt} \\ Me^{Mt} & -Me^{-Mt} \end{vmatrix} = -2M \neq 0,$$

$$\begin{gathered} w_1(t) = \begin{vmatrix} 0 & e^{-Mt} \\ 1 & -Me^{-Mt} \end{vmatrix} = -e^{-Mt}, \qquad w_2(t) = \begin{vmatrix} e^{Mt} & 0 \\ Me^{Mt} & 1 \end{vmatrix} = e^{Mt}, \\ c_1(t) = \int_0^t \frac{w_1(s)h(s)}{w(s)}\,ds = -\int_0^t \frac{e^{-Ms}\sigma(s,\eta)}{2M}\,ds, \\ c_2(t) = \int_0^t \frac{w_2(s)h(s)}{w(s)}\,ds = \int_0^t \frac{e^{-Ms}\sigma(s,\eta)}{2M}\,ds. \end{gathered} \tag{2.13}$$

So that the general solution

$$u(t) = \left[c_1 - \int_0^t \frac{e^{-Ms}\sigma(s,\eta)}{2M}ds\right]e^{Mt} + \left[c_2 + \int_0^t \frac{e^{Ms}\sigma(s,\eta)}{2M}ds\right]e^{-Mt}. \tag{2.14}$$

If we substitute the boundary condition on (2.14), then we can find constants c_1 and c_2 such that

$$u(0) = c_1 + c_2 = u(2\pi),$$

$$u(2\pi) = -\frac{e^{2M\pi}}{2M}\int_0^{2\pi} e^{-Ms}\sigma(s)ds + \frac{e^{-2M\pi}}{2M}\int_0^{2\pi} e^{Ms}\sigma(s)ds + c_1e^{2M\pi} + c_2e^{-2M\pi}, \tag{2.15}$$

therefore

$$(1-e^{2M\pi})c_1 + (1-e^{-2M\pi})c_2 = -\frac{e^{2M\pi}}{2M}\int_0^{2\pi} e^{-Ms}\sigma(s,\eta)ds + \frac{e^{-2M\pi}}{2M}\int_0^{2\pi} e^{Ms}\sigma(s,\eta)ds,$$

$$u'(t) = -\frac{e^{Mt}}{2}\int_0^t e^{-Ms}\sigma(s,\eta)ds - \frac{e^{-Mt}}{2}\int_0^t e^{Ms}\sigma(s,\eta)ds + c_1M\cdot e^{Mt} - c_2M\cdot e^{-Mt} \tag{2.16}$$

so that

$$u'(0) = c_1M - c_2M = u'(2\pi)$$

$$= -\frac{e^{2M\pi}}{2}\int_0^{2\pi} e^{-Ms}\sigma(s)ds - \frac{e^{-2M\pi}}{2}\int_0^{2\pi} e^{Ms}\sigma(s)ds + c_1M\cdot e^{2M\pi} - c_2M\cdot e^{-2M\pi}, \tag{2.17}$$

and hence

$$(1-e^{2M\pi})c_1 - (1-e^{-2M\pi})c_2 = -\frac{e^{2M\pi}}{2M}\int_0^{2\pi} e^{-Ms}\sigma(s,\eta)ds - \frac{e^{-2M\pi}}{2M}\int_0^{2\pi} e^{Ms}\sigma(s,\eta)ds. \tag{2.18}$$

Combining (2.16) and (2.18), we have

$$c_1 = \frac{e^{2M\pi}}{2M(e^{2M\pi}-1)}\int_0^{2\pi} e^{-Ms}\sigma(s,\eta)ds. \tag{2.19}$$

If we subtract (2.17) from (2.18), we get

$$c_2 = \frac{1}{2M(e^{2M\pi}-1)}\int_0^{2\pi} e^{Ms}\sigma(s,\eta)ds. \tag{2.20}$$

Now we claim that the solution $u(t)$ is unique. Using proof by contradiction, assume that $v(t)$ is another solution of the problem (2.1). Define $p(t) = v(t) - u(t)$ on J,

$$\begin{aligned} -p'' &= -v''(t) + u''(t) = \sigma(t,\eta) - M^2v(t) - [\sigma(t,\eta) - M^2u(t)], \\ -p'' &= -M^2p, \qquad p(0) = p(2\pi), \qquad p'(0) = p'(2\pi). \end{aligned} \tag{2.21}$$

Using Lemma 2.2, we get

$$p(t) \equiv 0, \tag{2.22}$$

that is,

$$v(t) \equiv u(t). \tag{2.23}$$

Linear second-order PBVP (2.8) has a unique solution.

Now for any $\eta \in [\alpha,\beta]$, we can define an operator A by $A\eta = u$, where u is the unique solution of the PBVP (2.1). We show that

(i) $\alpha \le A\alpha$, $\beta \ge A\beta$,

(ii) A is monotone and nondecreasing on $[\alpha,\beta]$.

To prove (i), define $p = \alpha - \alpha_1$, where $\alpha_1 = A\alpha$. Then

$$\begin{gathered} -p'' = -\alpha'' - (-\alpha_1'') \le f(t,\alpha) - [f(t,\alpha) + M^2\alpha - M^2\alpha_1], \\ -p'' \le -M^2 p, \\ p(0) = p(2\pi), \qquad p'(0) \ge p'(2\pi). \end{gathered} \tag{2.24}$$

Hence by Lemma 2.2, we get

$$p(t) \le 0, \tag{2.25}$$

implying that

$$\alpha \le A\alpha. \tag{2.26}$$

Similar arguments hold for $\beta \ge A\beta$.

To prove (ii), take $\eta_1, \eta_2 \in [\alpha,\beta]$ such that $\eta_1 \le \eta_2$. Let $A\ \eta_1 = u_1$ and let $A\ \eta_2 = u_2$. Setting $p = u_1 - u_2$, then

$$\begin{aligned} -p'' &= -u_1'' - (-u_2'') \\ &= -[f(t,\eta_2) - f(t,\eta_1)] + M^2[\eta_1 - \eta_2] - M^2[u_1(t) - u_2(t)]. \end{aligned} \tag{2.27}$$

Since $\alpha \le \eta_1 \le \eta_2 \le \beta$ using inequality (2.5), we get

$$\begin{gathered} -p'' \le M^2[\eta_2 - \eta_1] + M^2[\eta_1 - \eta_2] - M^2[u_1(t) - u_2(t)] = -M^2 p, \\ p(0) = p(2\pi), \qquad p'(0) = p'(2\pi), \end{gathered} \tag{2.28}$$

hence by Lemma 2.2, on J,

$$p(t) \le 0, \tag{2.29}$$

this implies that A is monotone and nondecreasing on $[\alpha,\beta]$. It therefore follows that we can define sequences $\{\alpha_n\}$ and $\{\beta_n\}$ in such a way that

$$\begin{gathered} \alpha_n = A\alpha_{n-1}, \\ \beta_n = A\beta_{n-1} \end{gathered} \tag{2.30}$$

with $\alpha_0 = \alpha$ and $\beta_0 = \beta$ on J. By (i) and (ii), we can obtain

$$\begin{aligned} \alpha = \alpha_0 \le \alpha_1 \le \alpha_2 \le \cdots \le \alpha_n, \\ \beta = \beta_0 \ge \beta_1 \ge \beta_2 \ge \cdots \ge \beta_n. \end{aligned} \tag{2.31}$$

By using (ii) and mathematical induction, we have

$$\alpha_0 \le \beta_0,\ \alpha_1 \le \beta_1,\ \alpha_2 \le \beta_2, \ldots,\ \alpha_n \le \beta_n, \tag{2.32}$$

so that we get the result

$$\alpha = \alpha_0 \le \alpha_1 \le \alpha_2 \le \cdots \le \alpha_n \le \beta_n \le \cdots \le \beta_2 \le \beta_1 \le \beta_0 = \beta. \tag{2.33}$$

Now we will show that the monotone sequences $\{\alpha_n(t)\}$ and $\{\beta_n(t)\}$ converge uniformly to continuous functions $\rho(t)$ and $r(t)$ on J, respectively, by using standard argument. According to Arzela-Ascoli theorem, if a sequence is uniformly bounded and equicontinuous, then it has a uniformly convergent subsequence. Namely, since for all $n \in N$, $\alpha_0 \le \alpha_n \le \beta_0$ on J, then the sequence $\{\alpha_n(t)\}$ is pointwise bounded on J. Since J is compact, and α_0 and β_0 are continuous on J, then α_0 and β_0 have minimum and maximum values on J. This shows that $\{\alpha_n\}$ is a uniform bounded sequence of functions on J. Then

$$\alpha_n'(t) = -\frac{e^{Mt}}{2}\int_0^t e^{-Ms}\sigma(s,\alpha_{n-1})\,ds - \frac{e^{-Mt}}{2}\int_0^t e^{Ms}\sigma(s,\alpha_{n-1})\,ds + c_{n_1}Me^{Mt} - c_{n_2}Me^{-Mt} \tag{2.34}$$

so that

$$\begin{aligned} |\alpha_n'(t)| \le \frac{e^{Mt}}{2}\int_0^t e^{-Ms}|\sigma(s,\alpha_{n-1})|\,ds + \frac{e^{-Mt}}{2}\int_0^t e^{Ms}|\sigma(s,\alpha_{n-1})|\,ds \\ + |c_{n_1}|Me^{Mt} + |c_{n_2}|Me^{-Mt}. \end{aligned} \tag{2.35}$$

Since f is continuous on J and $\{\alpha_n\}$ is uniformly bounded, and there exists an $N > 0$ such that $|\sigma(s,\alpha_n)| \le N$ for each n, therefore

$$\begin{aligned} |\alpha_n'(t)| &\le \frac{e^{2\pi M}}{2}\int_0^{2\pi} |\sigma(s,\alpha_{n-1})|\,ds + \frac{e^{2\pi M}}{2}\int_0^{2\pi} |\sigma(s,\alpha_{n-1})|\,ds + |c_{n_1}|Me^{2\pi M} + |c_{n_2}|M \\ &\le \frac{e^{2\pi M}}{2}2\pi N + \frac{e^{2\pi M}}{2}2\pi N + 2\pi N M e^{2\pi M} + 2\pi N M = K. \end{aligned} \tag{2.36}$$

This shows that the sequence $\{\alpha_n'\}$ is uniformly bounded on J.

Using mean value theorem, for all $x, y \in J$, there exists $\xi \in (x,y)$ such that

$$\alpha_n(y) - \alpha_n(x) = (y-x)\alpha_n'(\xi), \qquad |\alpha_n(y) - \alpha_n(x)| \le |(y-x)|K. \tag{2.37}$$

As it is seen, K is independent of x and y. Taking $\delta = \varepsilon/K$, we see that $\{\alpha_n\}$ is equicontinuous on J. Since $\{\alpha_n\}$ is uniformly bounded and equicontinuous on J, then by Arzela-Ascoli theorem $\{\alpha_n\}$ has uniform convergent subsequence $\{\alpha_{n_k}\}$. Since $\{\alpha_n\}$ is a monotone sequence, then

$$\lim_{n\to\infty} \alpha_n(t) = \vartheta(t) \tag{2.38}$$

uniformly. And because of the uniform convergence on J, for all $t^* \in J$,

$$\lim_{t\to t^*} \vartheta(t) = \lim_{t\to t^*}\left(\lim_{n\to\infty}\alpha_n(t)\right) = \lim_{n\to\infty}\left(\lim_{t\to t^*}\alpha_n(t)\right) = \lim_{n\to\infty}\alpha_n(t^*) = \vartheta(t^*). \tag{2.39}$$

That is, ϑ is continuous on J. Now let us show that $\vartheta(t)$ is a minimal solution of second-order PBVP (2.1). Since for all $n \geq 1$, α_n is the solution of the periodic boundary value problem

$$\begin{aligned} -\alpha_n''(t) + M^2\alpha_n(t) = f(t,\alpha_n) + M^2\alpha_n, \qquad \alpha_n(0) = \alpha_n(2\pi),\\ \alpha_n'(0) = \alpha_n'(2\pi), \end{aligned} \tag{2.40}$$

then if we take limit of both sides for $n \to \infty$ using the continuity of f,

$$-\vartheta''(t) + M^2\vartheta(t) = f(t,\vartheta) + M^2\vartheta, \qquad \vartheta(0) = \vartheta(2\pi), \qquad \vartheta'(0) = \vartheta'(2\pi), \tag{2.41}$$

that is, we get

$$-\vartheta''(t) = f(t,\vartheta), \qquad \vartheta(0) = \vartheta(2\pi), \qquad \vartheta'(0) = \vartheta'(2\pi). \tag{2.42}$$

This shows that $\vartheta(t)$ is a solution of PBVP (2.1).

Now assume that $u(t)$ is a solution of (2.1) with $\alpha(t) \leq u(t) \leq \beta(t)$ on J. Using mathematical induction, let us show that for all $n \geq 1$, $\alpha_n(t) \leq u(t)$ on J. For this, let us set $p_1(t) = \alpha_1(t) - u(t)$. Then

$$\begin{aligned} -p_1''(t) &= -\alpha_1''(t) + u''(t)\\ &= f(t,\alpha_0) + M^2\alpha_0 - M^2\alpha_1(t) - f(t,u)\\ &\leq -M^2(\alpha_0 - u) + M^2\alpha_0 - M^2\alpha_1 = -M^2 p_1(t). \end{aligned} \tag{2.43}$$

Using $p_1(0) = p_1(2\pi)$ and $p_1'(0) = p_1'(2\pi)$ by comparison lemma, we get $\alpha_1(t) \leq u(t)$ so that we obtain that all $n > 1$, $\alpha_n(t) \leq u(t)$. $p_{n+1}(t) = \alpha_{n+1}(t) - u(t)$,

$$\begin{aligned} -p_{n+1}''(t) &= -\alpha_{n+1}''(t) + u''(t)\\ &= f(t,\alpha_n) + M^2\alpha_n - M^2\alpha_{n+1}(t) - f(t,u)\\ &\leq -M^2(\alpha_n - u) + M^2\alpha_n - M^2\alpha_{n+1},\\ -p_{n+1}''(t) &\leq -M^2 p_{n+1}(t). \end{aligned} \tag{2.44}$$

Using $p_{n+1}(0) = p_{n+1}(2\pi)$ and $p'_{n+1}(0) = p'_{n+1}(2\pi)$ then by comparison lemma, we get $\alpha_{n+1}(t) \le u(t)$ so that we obtain that for all $n \ge 1$, $\alpha_n(t) \le u(t)$. If we take the limit for $n \to \infty$, we get the result $\vartheta(t) \le u(t)$. This shows that $\vartheta(t)$ is the minimum solution of second-order PBVP (2.1) on $[\alpha,\beta]$. With the same way, we can show that the sequence

$$\beta = \beta_0 \ge \beta_1 \ge \beta_2 \ge \cdots \ge \beta_n \tag{2.45}$$

converges uniformly to the maximal solution of PBVP (2.1) on $[\alpha,\beta]$. □

3. Main results

In this section we will consider the case when the right-hand side of (2.1) is the sum of the two functions with some special properties. Consider second-order nonlinear periodic boundary value problem involving two functions,

$$-u'' = f(t,u) + g(t,u), \qquad u(0) = u(2\pi), \qquad u'(0) = u'(2\pi), \tag{3.1}$$

where $f,g \in C[Jx\mathbb{R},\mathbb{R}]$.

Definition 3.1. Let $\alpha,\beta \in C^{2,0}[J,\mathbb{R}]$ and if
(i) $-\alpha'' \le f(t,\alpha) + g(t,\beta)$, $t \in J$, $\alpha(0) = \alpha(2\pi)$, and $\alpha'(0) \geqslant \alpha'(2\pi)$,
(ii) $-\beta'' \geqslant f(t,\beta) + g(t,\alpha)$, $t \in J$, $\beta(0) = \beta(2\pi)$, and $\beta'(0) \le \beta'(2\pi)$
are satisfied, then α and β are called coupled lower and upper solutions of the PBVP (3.1).

Theorem 3.2. *Assume that α and β are coupled lower and upper solutions of second-order PBVP (3.1), respectively, with $\alpha(t) \le \beta(t)$ on J. Furthermore, the function*

$$F(t,x,y) = f(t,x) + g(t,y) \tag{3.2}$$

satisfies the inequality

$$F(t,\hat{x},\hat{y}) - F(t,x,y) \le -M^2[(\hat{x} - x) + (\hat{y} - y)] \tag{3.3}$$

with $\hat{x} \le x$ and $\hat{y} \ge y$. Then there exist monotone sequences $\{\alpha_n(t)\}$ and $\{\beta_n(t)\}$ with $\alpha_0 = \alpha$ and $\beta_0 = \beta$ and they satisfy

$$\alpha = \alpha_0 \le \alpha_1 \le \alpha_2 \le \cdots \le \alpha_n \le \beta_n \le \cdots \le \beta_2 \le \beta_1 \le \beta_0 = \beta \tag{3.4}$$

such that they converge uniformly to coupled minimal and maximal solutions of (3.1), respectively, on $[\alpha,\beta] = \{u \in C[J,\mathbb{R}] : \alpha \le u \le \beta\}$.

Proof. Take $\alpha_0 = \alpha$ and $\beta_0 = \beta$. We can construct elements of monotone sequences using the following linear periodic boundary value recursive equations of second order:

$$\begin{gathered} -\alpha''_{n+1} + M^2\alpha_{n+1} = f(t,\alpha_n) + g(t,\beta_n) + M^2\alpha_n = H(t,\alpha_n,\beta_n), \\ \alpha_{n+1}(0) = \alpha_{n+1}(2\pi), \qquad \alpha'_{n+1}(0) = \alpha'_{n+1}(2\pi), \end{gathered} \tag{3.5}$$

$$\begin{gathered} -\beta''_{n+1} + M^2\beta_{n+1} = f(t,\beta_n) + g(t,\alpha_n) + M^2\beta_n = H(t,\beta_n,\alpha_n), \\ \beta_{n+1}(0) = \beta_{n+1}(2\pi), \qquad \beta'_{n+1}(0) = \beta'_{n+1}(2\pi). \end{gathered} \tag{3.6}$$

By a similar manner as in Theorem 2.3, it can be shown that (3.5) and (3.6) have unique solutions, and these solutions are

$$\alpha_{n+1}(t) = -\int_0^t \frac{e^{-Ms}H(t,\alpha_n,\beta_n)}{2M}ds\,e^{Mt} + \int_0^t \frac{e^{Ms}H(t,\alpha_n,\beta_n)}{2M}ds\,e^{-Mt} + c_1e^{Mt} + c_2e^{-Mt}, \tag{3.7}$$

where

$$\begin{aligned} c_1 &= \frac{e^{2M\pi}}{2M(e^{2M\pi}-1)}\int_0^{2\pi} e^{-Ms}H(t,\alpha_n,\beta_n)ds,\\ c_2 &= \frac{1}{2M(e^{2M\pi}-1)}\int_0^{2\pi} e^{Ms}H(t,\alpha_n,\beta_n)ds,\\ \beta_{n+1}(t) &= -\int_0^t \frac{e^{-Ms}H(t,\beta_n,\alpha_n)}{2M}ds\,e^{Mt} + \int_0^t \frac{e^{Ms}H(t,\beta_n,\alpha_n)}{2M}ds\,e^{-Mt} + c_3e^{Mt} + c_4e^{-Mt}, \end{aligned} \tag{3.8}$$

where

$$\begin{aligned} c_3 &= \frac{e^{2M\pi}}{2M(e^{2M\pi}-1)}\int_0^{2\pi} e^{-Ms}H(t,\beta_n,\alpha_n)ds,\\ c_4 &= \frac{1}{2M(e^{2M\pi}-1)}\int_0^{2\pi} e^{Ms}H(t,\beta_n,\alpha_n)ds. \end{aligned} \tag{3.9}$$

Now let us show that $\{\alpha_n\}$ is a monotone nondecreasing sequence and $\{\beta_n\}$ is a monotone nonincreasing sequence. For this, it is enough to show that

(i) $\alpha_1 \geq \alpha_0$ and $\beta_1 \leq \beta_0$,

(ii) if $\alpha_n \geq \alpha_{n-1}$ and $\beta_n \leq \beta_{n-1}$, then $\alpha_{n+1} \geq \alpha_n$ and $\beta_{n+1} \leq \beta_n$. First, for $t \in J$, let us show that $\alpha_1 \geq \alpha_0$. For this, set $p_1(t) = \alpha_0 - \alpha_1$. Then

$$\begin{aligned} -p_1''(t) &= -\alpha_0'' + \alpha_1'' \leq f(t,\alpha_0) + g(t,\beta_0) + \alpha_1''\\ &= f(t,\alpha_0) + g(t,\beta_0) - [f(t,\alpha_0) + g(t,\beta_0) + M^2(\alpha_0 - \alpha_1)], \end{aligned} \tag{3.10}$$

therefore

$$\begin{gathered} -p_1''(t) \leq -M^2 p_1(t),\\ p_1(0) = \alpha_0(0) - \alpha_1(0) = \alpha_0(2\pi) - \alpha_1(2\pi) = p_1(2\pi),\\ p_1'(0) = \alpha_0'(0) - \alpha_1'(0) \geq \alpha_0(2\pi) - \alpha_1(2\pi) = p_1'(2\pi). \end{gathered} \tag{3.11}$$

By using Lemma 2.2, $p_1(0) \leq 0$, that is, $\alpha_0 \leq \alpha_1$. With the same way, it can be shown that $\beta_1 \leq \beta_0$.

Now assume that for all $n \geq 1$, $\alpha_n \geq \alpha_{n-1}$ and $\beta_n \leq \beta_{n-1}$. Define

$$p_{n+1}(t) = \alpha_n - \alpha_{n+1}. \tag{3.12}$$

Then

$$\begin{aligned} -p''_{n+1}(t) + M^2 p_{n+1}(t) &= -\alpha''_n + M^2\alpha_n - [-\alpha''_{n+1} + M^2\alpha_{n+1}] \\ &= [f(t,\alpha_{n-1}) - f(t,\alpha_n)] + [g(t,\beta_{n-1}) - g(t,\beta_n)] \\ &\quad + M^2(\alpha_{n-1} - \alpha_n). \end{aligned} \tag{3.13}$$

Since $\alpha_{n-1} \leq \alpha_n$ and $\beta_{n-1} \geq \beta_n$ using inequality (3.3), we get

$$-p''_{n+1}(t) + M^2 p_{n+1}(t) \leq -M^2[\alpha_{n-1} - \alpha_n + \beta_{n-1} - \beta_n] + M^2(\alpha_{n-1} - \alpha_{n+1}), \tag{3.14}$$

and then

$$-p''_{n+1}(t) \leq -M^2[\beta_{n-1} - \beta_n] \leq 0. \tag{3.15}$$

$p(0) = p(2\pi)$ and $p'(0) = p'(2\pi)$ imply again by comparison lemma that $p_{n+1}(t) \leq 0$, that is, $\alpha_n \leq \alpha_{n+1}$ on J. With the same way, it can be shown that $\beta_n \leq \beta_{n-1}$ so that we get the results

$$\begin{aligned} \alpha = \alpha_0 \leq \alpha_1 \leq \alpha_2 \leq \cdots \leq \alpha_n, \\ \beta = \beta_0 \geq \beta_1 \geq \beta_2 \geq \cdots \geq \beta_n. \end{aligned} \tag{3.16}$$

Now let us show that

$$\alpha = \alpha_0 \leq \alpha_1 \leq \alpha_2 \leq \cdots \leq \alpha_n \leq \beta_n \leq \cdots \leq \beta_2 \leq \beta_1 \leq \beta_0 = \beta. \tag{3.17}$$

We know that $\alpha_0 \leq \beta_0$. Let $p_1(t) = \alpha_1 - \beta_1$ on J. Then

$$\begin{aligned} -p''_1(t) + M^2 p_1(t) &= -\alpha''_1 + M^2\alpha_1 - (-\beta''_1 + M^2\beta_1) \\ &= [f(t,\alpha_0) - f(t,\beta_0)] + [g(t,\beta_0) - g(t,\alpha_0)] + M^2(\alpha_0 - \beta_0), \end{aligned} \tag{3.18}$$

since $\alpha_0 \leq \beta_0$ using (3.3), we get

$$\begin{aligned} -p''_1(t) + M^2 p_1(t) &\leq -M^2[(\alpha_0 - \beta_0) + (\beta_0 - \alpha_0)] + M^2(\alpha_0 - \beta_0) \\ &= M^2(\alpha_0 - \beta_0) \leq 0. \end{aligned} \tag{3.19}$$

By $p_1(0) = p_1(2\pi)$ and $p'_1(0) = p'_1(2\pi)$ using comparison lemma (Lemma 2.2), we obtain $\alpha_1 \leq \beta_1$. Now assume that $\alpha_n \leq \beta_n$. To show that

$$\alpha_{n+1} \leq \beta_{n+1}, \tag{3.20}$$

define

$$p_{n+1}(t) = \alpha_{n+1} - \beta_{n+1}. \tag{3.21}$$

Then

$$\begin{aligned}-p_{n+1}''(t)+M^2p_{n+1}(t)&=-\alpha_{n+1}''+M^2\alpha_{n+1}-(-\beta_{n+1}''+M^2\beta_{n+1})\\&=[f(t,\alpha_n)-f(t,\beta_n)]+[g(t,\beta_n)-g(t,\alpha_n)]\\&\quad+M^2(\alpha_n-\beta_n).\end{aligned}\tag{3.22}$$

Since $\alpha_n\le\beta_n$ using (3.3),

$$\begin{gathered}-p_{n+1}''(t)+M^2p_{n+1}(t)\le -M^2(\alpha_n-\beta_n+\beta_n-\alpha_n)+M^2(\alpha_n-\beta_n)\le 0,\\ p_{n+1}(0)=p_{n+1}(2\pi),\qquad p_{n+1}'(0)=p_{n+1}'(2\pi).\end{gathered}\tag{3.23}$$

Again using comparison lemma, we get the result

$$\alpha_{n+1}\le\beta_{n+1}\tag{3.24}$$

so that

$$\alpha=\alpha_0\le\alpha_1\le\alpha_2\le\cdots\le\alpha_n\le\beta_n\le\cdots\le\beta_2\le\beta_1\le\beta_0=\beta\tag{3.25}$$

is satisfied. The fact that the monotone sequences $\{\alpha_n(t)\}$ and $\{\beta_n(t)\}$ converge to continuous functions $\rho(t)$ and $r(t)$, which are the coupled solutions of (3.1), can be shown as in Theorem 2.3 by using standard argument. Now let us show that the functions $\rho(t)$ and $r(t)$ are coupled minimal and maximal solutions of PBVP (3.1). For this, let u be a solution of (3.1) with $\alpha_0\le u\le\beta_0$ on J. Now let us show that

(i) $\alpha_1\le u$ and $u\le\beta_1$,

(ii) $\alpha_{n+1}\le u$ and $u\le\beta_{n+1}$ whenever $\alpha_n\le u$ and $u\le\beta_n$.

To prove (i), define $p_1(t)=\alpha_1(t)-u(t)$. Then

$$\begin{aligned}-p_1''(t)+M^2p_1(t)&=-\alpha_1''(t)+u''(t)+M^2[\alpha_1(t)-u(t)]\\&=[f(t,\alpha_0)-f(t,u)]+[g(t,\beta_0)-g(t,u)]+M^2[\alpha_0-u(t)].\end{aligned}\tag{3.26}$$

Since $\alpha_0\le u\le\beta_0$ using (3.3),

$$\begin{aligned}-p_1''(t)+M^2p_1(t)&\le -M^2[(\alpha_0-u)+(\beta_0-u)]+M^2[\alpha_0-u(t)]\\&=-M^2(\beta_0-u)\le 0,\end{aligned}\tag{3.27}$$

and by $p_1(0)=p_1(2\pi)$, $p_1'(0)\ge p_1'(2\pi)$ using comparison lemma, we get $\alpha_1(t)\le u(t)$. In the same way, it can be shown that $\beta_1(t)\ge u(t)$. Now assume that $\alpha_n\le u$ and $u\le\beta_n$ and define $p_{n+1}(t)=\alpha_{n+1}(t)-u(t)$,

$$\begin{aligned}-p_{n+1}''(t)+M^2p_{n+1}(t)&=-\alpha_{n+1}''(t)+u''(t)+M^2[\alpha_{n+1}(t)-u(t)]\\&=[f(t,\alpha_n)-f(t,u)]+[g(t,\beta_n)-g(t,u)]\\&\quad+M^2[\alpha_n-u(t)].\end{aligned}\tag{3.28}$$

Since $\alpha_n \le u$ and $u \le \beta_n$ using inequality (3.3),

$$\begin{aligned} -p''_{n+1}(t)+M^2p_{n+1}(t) &\le -M^2[(\alpha_n-u)+(\beta_n-u)]+M^2[\alpha_n-u(t)] \\ &= -M^2(\beta_n-u)\le 0. \end{aligned} \tag{3.29}$$

By $p_{n+1}(0)=p_{n+1}(2\pi)$, $p'_{n+1}(0)\ge p'_{n+1}(2\pi)$ using comparison lemma again, $\alpha_{n+1}(t)\le u(t)$. With the same way, one can show that $\beta_{n+1}(t)\ge u(t)$ so that for all $n\ge 1$, we obtain $\alpha_n(t)\le u(t)$ and $\beta_n(t)\ge u(t)$. If we take the limit for $n\to\infty$, we get the results $\rho(t)\le u(t)$ and $r(t)\le u(t)$ so that we show that $\rho(t)$ and $r(t)$ are coupled extremal solutions of second-order PBVP (3.1). This completes the proof. □

THEOREM 3.3. *If the condition in Theorem 3.2 is substituted by inequality (3.3) that f is nondecreasing and g is nonincreasing with respect to the second variable, then the conclusion of Theorem 3.2 remains the same.*

Proof. The proof is similar to Theorem 3.2 with small differences such that whenever we use inequality (3.3) in previous proof, we use the fact that f is nondecreasing and g is nonincreasing with respect to second variable. For example, let us show that for all $n\ge 1$, $\alpha_{n+1}\ge\alpha_n$ whenever $\alpha_n\ge\alpha_{n-1}$ and $\beta_n\le\beta_{n-1}$ using this new condition. For this again, let us define

$$p_{n+1}(t)=\alpha_n-\alpha_{n+1}. \tag{3.30}$$

Then

$$\begin{aligned} -p''_{n+1}(t)+M^2p_{n+1}(t) &= -\alpha''_n+M^2\alpha_n-[-\alpha''_{n+1}+M^2\alpha_{n+1}] \\ &= [f(t,\alpha_{n-1})-f(t,\alpha_n)]+[g(t,\beta_{n-1})-g(t,\beta_n)] \\ &\quad +M^2(\alpha_{n-1}-\alpha_n). \end{aligned} \tag{3.31}$$

Since $\alpha_{n-1}\le\alpha_n$ and $\beta_{n-1}\ge\beta_n$, f is nondecreasing, and g is nonincreasing with respect to second variable, we obtain $f(t,\alpha_{n-1})-f(t,\alpha_n)\le 0$ and $g(t,\beta_{n-1})-g(t,\beta_n)\le 0$ so that

$$-p''_{n+1}(t)+M^2p_{n+1}(t)\le M^2(\alpha_{n-1}-\alpha_n)\le 0. \tag{3.32}$$

By $p(0)=p(2\pi)$ and $p'(0)=p'(2\pi)$ using comparison lemma, we obtain $p_{n+1}(t)\le 0$ which implies that $\alpha_n\le\alpha_{n+1}$.

Other inequalities can be shown similarly. This completes the proof. □

THEOREM 3.4. *If the condition in Theorem 2.3 is substituted by inequality (3.3) that f is nonincreasing and g is nondecreasing with respect to second variable, we get the same result in Theorem 3.2.*

Remark 3.5. In PBVP (3.1), if we take $g(t)=0$, then we obtain PBVP (2.1) and inequality (3.3) turns into (2.5).

References

[1] S. Koksal and C. Yakar, *Generalized quasilinearization method with initial time difference*, Simulation, an International Journal of Electrical, Electronic and other Physical Systems **24** (2002), no. 5.

[2] G. S. Ladde, V. Lakshmikantham, and A. S. Vatsala, *Monotone Iterative Techniques for Nonlinear Differential Equations*, Monographs, Advanced Texts and Surveys in Pure and Applied Mathematics, vol. 27, Pitman, Massachusetts, 1985.

[3] V. Lakshmikantham and S. Leela, *Differential and Integral Inequalities: Theory and Applications Vol. I: Ordinary Differential Equations*, Mathematics in Science and Engineering, vol. 55-I, Academic Press, New York, 1969.

[4] V. Lakshmikantham and A. S. Vatsala, *Generalized Quasilinearization for Nonlinear Problems*, Mathematics and Its Applications, vol. 440, Kluwer Academic, Dordrecht, 1998.

Coskun Yakar: Department of Mathematics, Faculty of Sciences, Gebze Institute of Technology, Gebze, Kocaeli 141-41400, Turkey
E-mail address: cyakar@gyte.edu.tr

Ali Sırma: Department of Mathematics, Faculty of Sciences, Gebze Institute of Technology, Gebze, Kocaeli 141-41400, Turkey
E-mail address: asirma@gyte.edu.tr

DIFFERENCE EQUATIONS AND THE ELABORATION OF COMPUTER SYSTEMS FOR MONITORING AND FORECASTING SOCIOECONOMIC DEVELOPMENT OF THE COUNTRY AND TERRITORIES

D. L. ANDRIANOV

A review of the author's results concerning boundary value problems and control problems for difference systems is given in context of economic mathematical modeling. The role of difference models in the elaboration of computer systems for monitoring and forecasting socioeconomic development of the country and territories is discussed.

1. Introduction

An actual problem in the improvement of economy management methods is increasing the scientifically grounded validity of the decisions made on all levels of economy. One of the most important trends in its studying is connected with an on-target approach to forecasting and controlling socioeconomic systems. This approach gives an opportunity to discover methods of reaching strategic targets, balance aims, and their means of achieving on the level of macroeconomic indexes, and to define attainable target values.

The basic principle of program-target planning is a principle of planning from terminal targets to means (resources and tools of influence), which provides aims reaching. This principle has been embodied in the decision-making support system (in what follows - the System) elaborated under the supervision of the author [3]. In the System, on-target control problem is considered and solved as a task of defining operating parameters of economic policy (tax load, distribution of government investments between regions, etc.); these parameters provide given dynamics of indexes of the socioeconomic development (production in economic branches, ecology standards maintain, etc.). As economic problems are so hard to solve, one can develop a solution only as a result of joint work of specialists experienced in synthesizing particular, productive, and industry-sectoral decisions and are aware of the real content of key processes and relationships, which take place on micro-, meso-, and macrolevels in modern economy of the Russian Federation [1, 2, 5, 6]. The key points of the System are based on the dynamic models of economy in the form of difference equations with some constraints (boundary conditions, target conditions, etc.).

Hindawi Publishing Corporation
Proceedings of the Conference on Differential & Difference Equations and Applications, pp. 1231–1237

In this paper we give a very brief review of some results concerning boundary value problems (BVPs) and control problems (CPs) for difference systems (see, e.g., [1, 4]), which are used in the construction of the System. Then a description of the System elaborated is presented.

2. Boundary value problems and control problems for difference equations

Consider the system

$$x(t+1)=\sum_{i=0}^{t}A(t,i)x(t)+f(t), \quad t=0,\dots,T-1, \tag{2.1}$$

where $x(t)\in\mathbb{R}^n$ for any $t=0,\dots,T$.

Let us denote by x the $T\times(T+1)$-matrix with the columns $x(0),x(1),\dots,x(T)$. The set of all such matrices is denoted by M^n_{T+1}. Thus we can write (2.1) in the form

$$\mathcal{L}x=f, \tag{2.2}$$

where $\mathcal{L}:M^n_{T+1}\to M^n_T$ is the linear operator defined by $(\mathcal{L}x)(t)=x(t+1)-\sum_{i=0}^{t}A(t,i)x(i)$, $f\in M^n_T$.

The Cauchy problem

$$\mathcal{L}x=f, \qquad x(0)=\alpha, \tag{2.3}$$

is uniquely solvable for any $f\in M^n_T$, $\alpha\in\mathbb{R}^n$, and its solution $x\in M^n_{T+1}$ has the representation

$$x(t)=X(t)\alpha+(Cf)(t), \quad t=0,\dots,T. \tag{2.4}$$

Here, $X(\cdot)$ is the fundamental matrix of the homogeneous equation $\mathcal{L}x=0$, $C:M^n_T\to M^n_{T+1}$ is the Cauchy operator of (2.1). The Cauchy operator has the representation

$$(Cf)(t)=\sum_{i=1}^{t}C(t,i)f(i), \quad t=0,\dots,T. \tag{2.5}$$

The matrices $X(t)$ and $C(t,i)$ are defined by the recurrent equalities

$$\begin{gathered}X(t+1)=\sum_{i=0}^{t}A(t+1,i)X(i), \quad t=0,\dots,T-1,\ X(0)=E;\\ C(t,i)=\sum_{j=1}^{t-1}A(t,j)C(j,i), \quad 1\le i<t\le T;\\ C(t,i)=0, \quad 1\le t<i\le T, \qquad C(t,t)=E, \quad t=0,\dots,T.\end{gathered} \tag{2.6}$$

Here and in what follows E stands for the identity matrix. The linear BVP for (2.1) is the system

$$\mathcal{L}x = f, \qquad lx = \alpha, \tag{2.7}$$

where $l: M^n_{T+1} \to \mathbb{R}^n$ is a given linear vector-functional,

$$lx = B_0x(0) + \cdots + B_Tx(T). \tag{2.8}$$

BVP (2.7) is uniquely solvable if and only if $\det lX \neq 0$. In the case $\det lX \neq 0$, the solution of (2.7) can be written in the form

$$x(t) = X(t)[lX]^{-1}\alpha + (Gf)(t), \quad t = 0,\dots,T, \tag{2.9}$$

where $G: M^n_T \to M^n_{T+1}$ is the Green operator of BVP (2.7).

Consider the quasilinear BVP

$$\mathcal{L}x = Fx, \qquad lx = \psi x, \tag{2.10}$$

where $F: M^n_{T+1} \to M^n_T$ and $\psi: M^n_{T+1} \to \mathbb{R}^n$ are in general nonlinear continuous operators.

Theorem 2.1. *Assume that (a)* $\det lX \neq 0$ *and (b) for all solutions of the problems*

$$\mathcal{L}x = \lambda Fx, \quad lx = \lambda\psi x, \quad \lambda \in [0,1], \tag{2.11}$$

the total a priori estimate $\|x_\lambda\|_{M^n_{T+1}} \leq d < \infty$ *holds.*

Then BVP (2.10) has at least one solution $x \in M^n_{T+1}$.

The proof is based on the representation (2.9). The cases when condition (b) of the theorem is fulfilled are studied in [1, 4].

The linear control problem (CP) for system (2.1) is the problem

$$\mathcal{L}x = Hu + f, \quad x(0) = \alpha,\ x(T) = \beta, \tag{2.12}$$

where $u = \{u(0),\dots,u(T-1)\} \in M^r_T$ is the control, $H: M^r_T \to M^n_T$ is a given linear operator, and $(Hu)(t) = \sum_{i=0}^{T-1} H(t,i)u(i)$, $t = 0,\dots,T-1$, with $n \times r$-matrices $H(t,i)$. The system $\mathcal{L}x = Hu + f$ is called controllable if, for any $f \in M^n_T$ and $\alpha,\beta \in \mathbb{R}^n$, there exists a control $u \in M^r_T$ such that BVP (2.12) is solvable. Let us denote $B(j) = \sum_{i=1}^T C(T,i)H(i,j-1)$, $j = 1,\dots,T$, where $C(t,i)$, $i = 1,\dots,T$, are $n \times n$-matrices generating the Cauchy operator C, and let the $n \times n$ matrix W be defined by $W = B \cdot B^*$, where $B = (B(1),\dots,B(T))$, $\cdot^*$ is the symbol of transposition.

Theorem 2.2. *CP (2.12) is solvable for any* $f \in M^n_T$ *and* $\alpha,\beta \in \mathbb{R}^n$ *if and only if* $\det W \neq 0$. *In the case* $\det W \neq 0$, *CP (2.12) is solved by the control u such that* $\operatorname{col}(u(0),\dots,u(T-1)) = B^*W^{-1}(\beta - X(T)\alpha - (Cf)(T))$.

Conditions of the solvability of the nonlinear CP

$$\mathcal{L}x = Hu + F(x,u), \quad x(0) = \alpha,\ x(T) = \beta, \tag{2.13}$$

where $F : M^n_{T+1} \times M^r_T \to M^n_T$ is a nonlinear continuous operator, are given by the following.

THEOREM 2.3. *Assume that (a)* $\det W \neq 0$ *and (b) for all solutions of the problems*

$$\begin{aligned} x &= \lambda[CHu + CF(x,u)] + X\alpha, \\ u &= -\lambda B^* W^{-1}(CF(x,u))(T) + B^* W^{-1}(\beta - X(T)\alpha), \end{aligned} \tag{2.14}$$

where $\lambda \in [0,1]$, *the total a priori estimate*

$$\|(x_\lambda, u_\lambda)\|_{M^n_{T+1} \times M^r_T} \le d < \infty \tag{2.15}$$

holds.

Then CP (2.13) has at least one solution $(x,u) \in M^n_{T+1} \times M^r_T$.

Among the problems that arise in economic modeling, a special place is occupied by the problems of the form

$$\mathcal{L}x = F(\hat{x}, u), \tag{2.16}$$

$$lx = \psi(\hat{x}, u), \tag{2.17}$$

$$\eta(x,u) \le 0. \tag{2.18}$$

Here, $F : \mathbb{R}^\nu \times M^r_T \to M^n_T$, $\psi : \mathbb{R}^\nu \times M^r_T \to \mathbb{R}^n$, and $\eta : M^n_{T+1} \times M^r_T \to \mathbb{R}^m$ are nonlinear continuous operators; the components of $\hat{x} \in \mathbb{R}^\nu$, $\nu < n$, belong to a fixed collection of components of $x \in M^n_{T+1}$ (thus the mapping $x \to \hat{x}$ is a projector). Assuming $\mathcal{L}$ and l to be such that $\det lX \neq 0$ and using the representation (2.9), we can reduce problem (2.16)–(2.18) to the system of inequalities

$$\eta(X\psi(\hat{x},u) + GF(\hat{x},u), u) \le 0. \tag{2.19}$$

This system is to be solved if we are going to find a control u under which the trajectories of the dynamic model (2.16) satisfy the constraints (2.17) and (2.18). The main feature of (2.19) as compared to (2.16)–(2.18) is that in practice it has a much smaller dimension and allows one to apply the effective algorithms for solving. The techniques of the study of the problems (2.7), (2.10), (2.12), (2.13), (2.16)–(2.18) are translated into the System whose description is given in the next section.

3. Econometric modeling, difference systems, and decision-making support systems

The main source of economy-wide models in the form of difference systems is the econometric modeling. As it was outlined in [7, page 10], "the value of adopting an econometric model-building approach to economics increases, and is indeed necessitated, because of the fact that both governments and industry are involved in some kind of planning and target-setting. Furthermore, there is no serious alternative to economy-wide model-building in carrying out such functions. Even in academic research a large model is sometimes the only vehicle by which the implications and dynamic effects of a theoretical argument can be evaluated."

Building, continuously updating, and developing an economy-wide model is a multifaceted process. Among the features of the process, the following are to be marked off: it uses a large amount of historical data, covering many aspects of economic activity; in modeling practice, measurement problems, lag responses, and stability questions are recurrent issues which have to be faced and to be fully specified.

The estimated model can then be used for the following different but related purposes: to make conditional forecasts of the future—the conditions being the alternative assumptions on future values of exogenous variables or policy strategies, to simulate the consequences of alternative economic policies, and to search for an optimal way of controlling certain targets through manipulation of certain instruments.

The targets and constraints are set by the so-called decision maker. The defining of operating parameters and resources is made step by step [5, 6]. Let us discuss the main steps.

(1) Defining basic variant of economic development.

Compilation of the program (complex of arrangements) begins by analyzing current socioeconomic states of regions to estimate tendencies and mark problems out.

To forecast regional development, recursive imitation model is used; it is described by difference equations (linear and nonlinear ones). The model is based on integrated economic and mathematical methods and models (multiple regression models, models of static and dynamic balances, etc.). With the help of an imitation model, the tool can detect possible negative changes in socioeconomic development of the regions and thus include problem solving into the program today, in case they appear in future.

(2) Searching for operating parameters needed to achieve the target.

Operating parameter here is a means of achieving the aim and element of resources. Most aims of socioeconomic development have alternative ways to be achieved. For instance, one can raise government investments on the territory of the region, or cut taxes and meet a lack of budgetary profits by grants and transfers. That is why when searching for operating parameters (by solving a control problem) one can consider interchangeable variants or take an appropriate proportion and correlation in operating parameters usage [3].

(3) Choosing the best combination of operating parameters according to the criteria stated.

As soon as all variants of possible operating parameters are found, we select the most effective parameter using the prescribed criteria.

The necessity to solve complicated tasks of analysis, forecasting, and controlling (conducting many model calculations and working with data) caused the creation of program complex which contains database constructor; reporting form constructor; and constructor of dynamic models of socioeconomic processes.

Database is aimed at store housing and processing of reporting and perspective information on the major indexes of socioeconomic development in the Russian Federation and its regions.

Reports are formed by report constructor, which conducts information proceeding (putting in order, clasterization, arithmetic transformations, etc.) and displays data on the electronic map of the territory.

Constructor of dynamic models of socioeconomic processes makes it possible to form new models using fitted macro language and apply existing multilinked "chains" of local models of economic dynamics, financial planning, which are based on different mathematical methods of analysis and forecasting.

As for the models, the complex contains the following:

(i) econometric macroeconomic model of Russia allows forecasting most aggregated indexes: GDP, inflation, production volumes of the most important branches, investments, export, import, currency volumes, gold currency reserves, and national currency rate, which are transferred into models that describe separate economic sectors in detail. This model contains about 250 econometric and balance equations;

(ii) model of the payment balance of Russia is aimed at modeling external economic activity of Russia. It includes indexes of current operations with capital and financial ones by balance correlation and considers the dynamics of economic and political relationships between Russia and the rest of the world, including future. This model consists of about 80 econometric differences and balance equations;

(iii) model of the federal budget of Russia allows forecasting the main parameters of the state budget in a period given considering the perspective economic situation. The model's calculation algorithms of forming and the assessment of the federal budget are equal to calculations on articles of profit and expenses classifications, which were used by forming the 2004 federal budget. The model has about 200 econometric and balance equations;

(iv) interbranch model of Russia provides an opportunity to receive variant balanced forecasts of socioeconomic development of Russia, which consider structural shifts of the economy;

(v) complex of imitation models of the RF regions reflects the dynamics of the regional economy functioning on the basis of the integrated system of interconnected macroeconomic indexes which are included into national accounts system. The model includes about 300 econometric and balance equations.

Information provision includes aggregated indexes of socioeconomic development, indexes of income and expenses balance of the population, external trade, branch structure of production and distribution of goods, products and services, indexes of budgetary process and inter-budgetary relations, financial markets indexes, as well as classificatory and reference books used to describe index sections. Sources of information are official data from ministries, departments, state and international organizations, and information agencies: Federal Service of the State Statistics, Ministry of Finance of Russia, Bank of Russia, International Monetary Fund, Reuters, Bloomberg, and so forth; structure, format, methods, and conditions of data transmitting are determined by applied tasks to be solved.

Acknowledgment

This work was supported by the RFBR Grants 04-06-96002 and UR.03.01.238 from the Scientific Programme "Universities of Russia, Fundamental Research."

References

[1] D. L. Andrianov, *Boundary value problems and control problems for linear difference systems with aftereffect*, Russian Mathematics **37** (1993), no. 5, 1–12 (Russian).

[2] D. L. Andrianov, M. Yu. Kulakov, et al., *Imitation modeling and scenario approach in Decision Making Support Systems*, Theory and practice problems of management (2002), no. 5, (Russian).

[3] D. L. Andrianov, M. Yu. Kulakov, A. O. Selyanin, et al., *Information-analytical support of managerial decisions in the regions and federal center*, http://cnews.ru/reviews/free/gov/part3/prognoz.html.

[4] D. L. Andrianov and V. P. Maksimov, *Objective control and boundary value problems for macroeconomic models with aftereffect*, Bulletin of the Perm State University, Economics (1995), no. 2, 102–123 (Russian).

[5] D. L. Andrianov, G. K. Polushkina, and T. A. Puchkina, *Objective Approach in Managing of the Social Sphere Resource Potential in the Region, Interregional System of Coordinating Macro Proportions of Socio-Economic Development*, Central Economic Mathematical Institute, Moscow, 1990.

[6] D. L. Andrianov, G. K. Polushkina, and E. D. Raspopova, *Objective Forecasting of the Regional Economy in Limited Labor Conditions*, Institute of Economics, Ekaterinburg, 1998.

[7] P. Arestis and G. Hadjimatheou, *Introducing Macroeconomic Modelling. An Econometric Study of the United Kingdom*, Macmillan, London, 1982.

D. L. Andrianov: Department of Economic Cybernetics, Perm State University, Bukirev Street 15, Perm 614990, Russia
E-mail address: adl@prognoz.ru